Introduction to Data Processing

Introduction to Data Processing

Third Edition

Carl Feingold
BSBA, MSBA, CPA, CDP

Department of Data Processing
West Los Angeles College
Culver City, California

wcb WM. C. BROWN
COMPANY PUBLISHERS
2460 Kerper Boulevard, Dubuque, Iowa 52001

wcb

Wm. C. Brown
Chairman of the Board

Larry W. Brown
President, WCB Group

Book Team

Bill Cox
Editor
William J. Evans
Designer
Julie A. Kennedy
Production Editor
Barbara Grantham
Design Layout Assistant
Mary Heller
Visual Research
Mavis M. Oeth
Permissions Editor

Wm. C. Brown Company Publishers, College Division

Lawrence E. Cremer
President
Raymond C. Deveaux
Vice President/Product Development
David Wm. Smith
Assistant Vice President/National Sales Manager
Matt Coghlan
National Marketing Manager
David A. Corona
Director of Production Development and Design
Marilyn A. Phelps
Manager of Design
William A. Moss
Production Editorial Manager
Mary M. Heller
Visual Research Manager

Cover photo courtesy of Bob Coyle

Chapter opening photos courtesy of the following:

Gregory Head	Chapters 1, 2, 4, 6, 8, 9, 11, 12, 14, 15, 18
Jim Schaffer	Chapters 3, 7, 19
Ken Firestone	Chapters 5, 13, 16, 17
Bob Coyle	Chapter 10

Library of Congress Catalog
Card Number: 79-53827

ISBN 0-697-08136-2

Printed in the United States of America

To Sylvia

contents

preface

The field of data processing continues its phenomenal growth with new devices and innovations being announced each day. Data processing is evolving to meet the ever-increasing demands of a technological society and in turn is contributing to even greater technical advancement. Those who work with data processing or have close contact with it must be prepared for a constant learning situation. Regulatory agencies are demanding that those who work with data-processing equipment possess some working knowledge of the operations. These agencies no longer hire people who do not understand the intricacies of data-processing equipment. It is toward this objective that the text was written—to provide a basic understanding of data processing to all concerned with its operations. This book is intended for today's student of data processing or computer science who must work from here toward the future. The student's role is not that of a historian but of a pioneer in computer technology.

This revised edition preserves the same basic concepts of its predecessor with the addition of new developments in the field. Many current topics are included, such as structured programming, microcomputers, data base management systems, distributed processing, networks, and EDP auditors. All of these vital subjects are covered in an understandable form with many illustrations. The material is accurate and up-to-date. Much of the outdated material has been deleted or condensed substantially, such as punched-card data processing, data-processing history, and some programming languages. Many new illustrations have been added.

Introduction to Data Processing serves as an introductory text in data processing or computer science and, as such, presumes that the student has no prior knowledge of data processing. It deals with the nature and matter of computer data processing and how these concepts relate to specific problems of today. The material is presented in simple nontechnical language with many illustrations. These topics include all of the areas of data processing that are important for any beginning student of data processing or computer science. I have attempted to arrange the subject matter in a logical sequence to provide "in-depth" coverage of the important areas giving the student an appreciation for the field while furnishing a solid background for further courses in data processing or computer science.

Part 1 serves as an introduction to the study of data processing. This introduction presents the importance of data, its source, and the future of data processing. Many new applications are presented in which the computer is used, in areas never before dreamed of.

The history of data processing is combined with punched-card data processing. A brief history of data processing shows the natural progression of data processing through the ages so the student does not get the impression that data processing just "happened." Only the important events and devices that have contributed significantly to the present state of data processing are discussed.

Punched-card data processing is discussed briefly, highlighting the important aspects of unit record processing. Although punched-card data processing does not enjoy the popularity it once had, it still is an integral part of many data-processing applications.

Computer components and computer arithmetic are discussed in Part 2. Computer components and arithmetic are important to any student of data processing or computer science to provide an insight to the operation of a computer. The hardware and storage features are presented, including all the latest data entry devices, so the student can have a complete understanding of the physical operations of a computer. Through simple explanations and illustrations, the student learns the basic calculation functions of the computer and the different number systems employed.

Computer programming is the most important segment of data processing. In Parts 3 and 4, the student is made aware of the numerous problems encountered in the study, planning, and preparation of computer programs. The student is introduced to the various tools, such as flowcharts and decision tables, available to the programmer to make the task of programming easier and more logical. Such programming elements as structured programming, subroutines, and job control language are discussed so the student becomes aware of the many problems of writing and processing computer programs.

Commonly used programming languages, such as COBOL, RPG II, and FORTRAN, are explained in Part 4 so the student will understand the capabilities and features of each language.

Real-time processing and time sharing, the fastest growing segment of the data-processing field, are explained in Part 5. New hardware features, including the latest innovations in data base management systems, distributed data processing, conversational time sharing, and remote batch time sharing, are explained in easy-to-read language. Data communications, a vital link in any real-time system, is discussed, including its new techniques and equipment. BASIC, the most popular conversational time-sharing language, which is gaining popularity in personal computers, is discussed and explained so the student has a thorough knowledge of the writing and operation of BASIC programs.

Finally, Part 6, computer systems and management, discusses the wide range of computers available, from the microcomputer to super computers. The introduction of the personal computer has brought an entirely new dimension in data processing.

The problems of operating a data-processing unit, including staffing and organization, are discussed. The current problems in data management, including computer security, data security, telecommunications protection, data-processing responsibility, and feasibility studies, are discussed in this section. The emergence of the EDP auditor has created a new dimension in computer auditing.

A detailed explanation of the operation of the card-punch machine is included in the appendix. Also added to the appendix are descriptions of data-processing positions and other aids to the data processor. A new glossary includes many of the definitions of the American National Dictionary for Information Processing.

New Features in This Edition

1. A new chapter on data entry devices, including the latest innovations in data entry.
2. A new chapter on programming elements, including structured programming, the latest innovation in computer programming.
3. The chapter on COBOL programming has been revised to reflect the latest techniques of structured programming.
4. The chapter on real-time processing now includes data base management systems and distributed data processing.
5. The chapter on BASIC programming has been completely revised and expanded.
6. The role of the EDP auditor has been added as an important segment of computer management.
7. The personal computer, the new small business computers, and the changing role of the minicomputers, as well as the rise of the microcomputers, are thoroughly explained.
8. Data base management systems are illustrated in a case study about the Screen Actors Guild.

Summaries at the end of each chapter serve as an outline of the chapter for review. Identification questions can serve as a review of the many terms that appear in each chapter.

A student workbook accompanies this edition, which can provide the proper feedback for the material covered in each chapter. The instructor's manual includes a brief commentary of each chapter. The commentary states each chapter's intent, useful teaching suggestions, and a summary of the important points. The instructor's manual also provides answers for the discussion questions and identification questions found in the text and the answers for all of the questions in the student workbook.

Introduction to Data Processing is comprehensive in all aspects of data processing. It is ideally suited as a basic text for introductory data-processing or computer science courses, for first and second year students in the junior college, university, or technological institution. It may be used as a semester, quarter, or a full year course depending upon the instructional program of the particular institution. This text will provide the beginning student with the basic principles of data processing.

The following guides are recommended for particular objectives of data processing courses.

Beginning Data-Processing or Computer Science Course

Business student
No emphasis on programming languages

Part 1 Introduction and History
- Chapter 1 Introduction to Data Processing
- 2 History of Data Processing and Punched-Card Data Processing

Part 2 Computer Components and Arithmetic
- Chapter 3 Computer Components—Input/Output Devices
- 4 Computer Components—Data Entry Devices
- 5 Computer Components—Processing and Storage Devices
- 6 Computer Data Representation and Arithmetic

Part 3 Introduction to Programming
- Chapter 7 Data-Processing Systems and Procedures
- 8 Preparation for a Computer Program
- 9 Introduction to Computer Programming
- 10 Programming Elements

Part 5 Real-Time Processing and Time Sharing
- Chapter 14 Introduction to Real-Time Processing and Time Sharing

Part 6 Computer Systems and Management
- Chapter 16 Computer Systems—Micro, Mini, Small, and Super Computers
- 17 Operation of a Data-Processing Installation
- 18 Data Management
- 19 Management of Data Processing

Beginning Data-Processing or Computer Science Course

Business programming student
Emphasis on programming languages

Part 1 Introduction and History
- Chapter 1 Introduction to Data Processing
- 2 History of Data Processing and Punched-Card Data Processing

Part 2 Computer Components and Arithmetic
- Chapter 3 Computer Components—Input/Output Devices
- 4 Computer Components—Data Entry Devices
- 5 Computer Components—Processing and Storage Devices
- 6 Computer Data Representation and Arithmetic

Part 3 Introduction to Programming
- Chapter 7 Data-Processing Systems and Procedures
- 8 Preparation for a Computer Program
- 9 Introduction to Computer Programming
- 10 Programming Elements

Part 4 Programming Languages
- Chapter 11 COBOL
- 12 Report Program Generator (RPG) II
- 13 FORTRAN

Part 6 Computer Systems and Management
- Chapter 16 Computer Systems—Micro, Mini, Small, and Super Computers
- 17 Operation of a Data-Processing Installation
- 18 Data Management
- 19 Management of Data Processing

One Semester Course

Business student
Emphasis on terminal devices

Part 1 Introduction and History
- Chapter 1 Introduction to Data Processing
- 2 History of Data Processing and Punched-Card Data Processing

Part 2 Computer Components and Arithmetic
- Chapter 3 Computer Components—Input/Output Devices
- 4 Computer Components—Data Entry Devices
- 5 Computer Components—Processing and Storage Devices
- 6 Computer Data Representation and Arithmetic

Part 3 Introduction to Programming
- Chapter 7 Data-Processing Systems and Procedures
- 8 Preparation for a Computer Program
- 9 Introduction to Computer Programming
- 10 Programming Elements

Part 5 Real-Time Processing and Time Sharing
- Chapter 14 Introduction to Real-Time Processing and Time Sharing
- 15 Time-Sharing Programming—BASIC Programming Language

Part 6 Computer Systems and Management
- Chapter 16 Computer Systems—Micro, Mini, Small, and Super Computers
- 17 Operation of a Data-Processing Installation
- 18 Data Management
- 19 Management of Data Processing

Full Year Course

Business student
Emphasis on all topics

Part 1 Introduction and History
- Chapter 1 Introduction to Data Processing
- 2 History of Data Processing and Punched-Card Data Processing

Part 2 Computer Components and Arithmetic
- Chapter 3 Computer Components—Input/Output Devices
- 4 Computer Components—Data Entry Devices
- 5 Computer Components—Processing and Storage Devices
- 6 Computer Data Representation and Arithmetic

Part 3 Introduction to Programming
- Chapter 7 Data-Processing Systems and Procedures
- 8 Preparation for a Computer Program
- 9 Introduction to Computer Programming
- 10 Programming Elements

Part 4 Programming Languages
- Chapter 11 COBOL
- 12 Report Program Generator (RPG) II
- 13 FORTRAN

Part 5 Real-Time Processing and Time Sharing
- Chapter 14 Introduction to Real-Time Processing and Time Sharing
- 15 Time-Sharing Programming—BASIC Programming Language

Part 6 Computer Systems and Management
Chapter 16 Computer Systems—Micro, Mini, Small, and Super Computers
17 Operation of a Data-Processing Installation
18 Data Management
19 Management of Data Processing

A Short Intensified Course

Executive type student

Part 1 Introduction and History
Chapter 1 Introduction to Data Processing
2 History of Data Processing and Punched-Card Data Processing
Part 2 Computer Components and Arithmetic
Chapter 3 Computer Components—Input/Output Devices
4 Computer Components—Data Entry Devices
5 Computer Components—Processing and Storage Devices
6 Computer Data Representation and Arithmetic
Part 5 Real-Time Processing and Time Sharing
Chapter 14 Introduction to Real-Time Processing and Time Sharing
Part 6 Computer Systems and Management
Chapter 16 Computer Systems—Micro, Mini, Small, and Super Computers
17 Operation of a Data-Processing Installation
18 Data Management
19 Management of Data Processing

acknowledgments

No text is solely the effort of an individual. Rather, it is the collective work of many individuals and organizations that make valuable contributions to the final product. I would be remiss if I did not acknowledge the assistance that I have received from numerous people and organizations.

My personal thanks to Ms. Paulyne Golden for giving so much of her time and for allowing me to use excellent examples of the data base management system of the Screen Actors Guild.

I wish to thank the following for their technical assistance, critical reviews, excellent suggestions, and constructive criticism that contributed so much to the development of the third edition: Dennis R. Rebhuhn, Black Hawk Community College; Alfred C. St. Onge, Springfield Technical College; Joan M. Roberts, Community College of Denver; and Jacquelyn Zehring, San Jose College.

I owe a special thanks to Ms. Julie Kennedy for her excellent editing of the text including the correction of numerous grammatical errors and the integration of the illustrations and the narrative into a meaningful book.

My special thanks to the numerous computer vendors and publications for graciously granting permission to use the illustrations, charts, diagrams, and photos that make the text more meaningful.

A deep expression of gratitude is due my wife Sylvia for her forebearance during the preparation of the manuscript, her expertise in the typing of the manuscript, and her effort, patience, and encouragement, without which this text never would have been written.

part 1

introduction and history

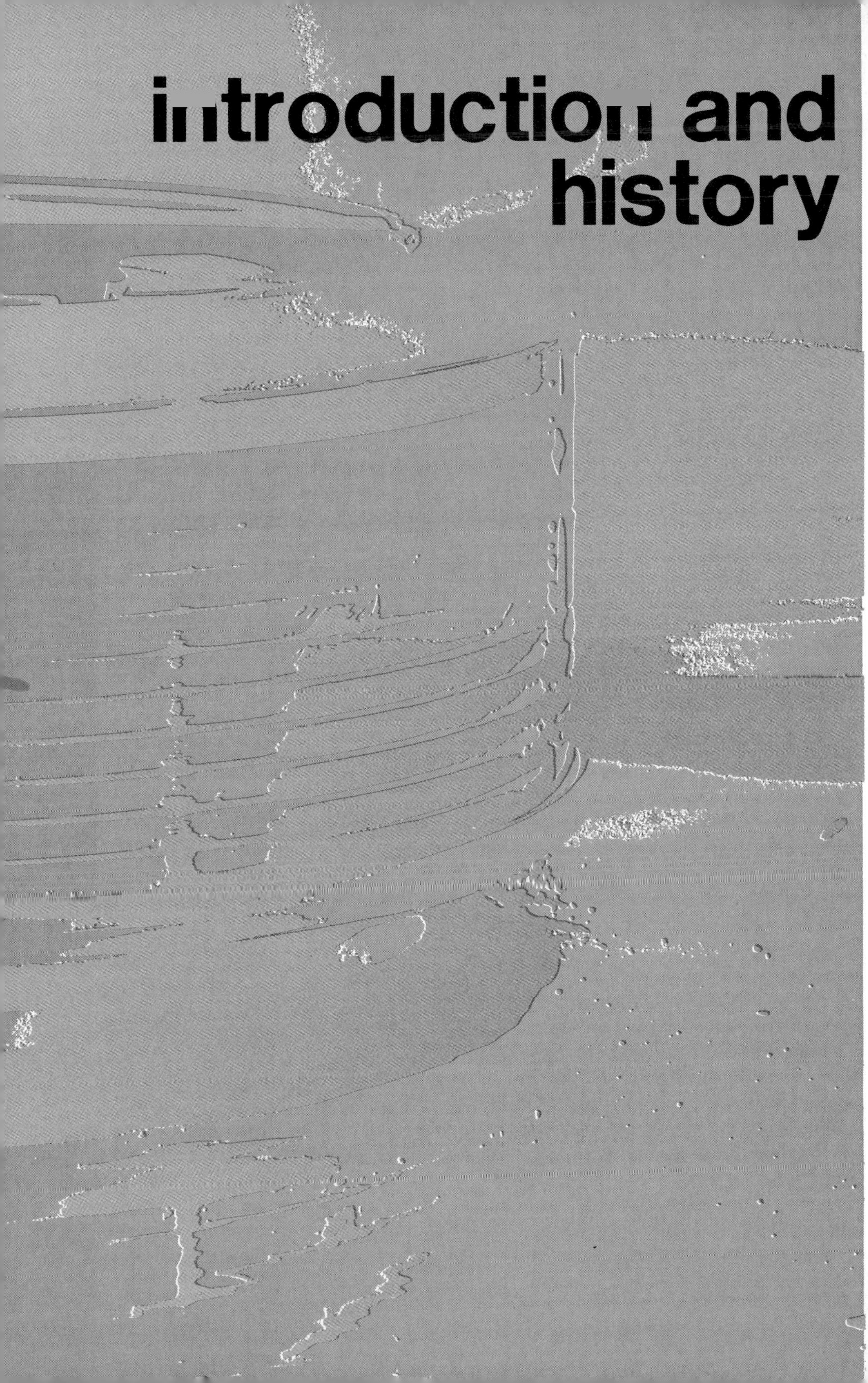

introduction to data processing 1

Chapter Outline

Importance of Data Processing

Demands for Data

Sources of Data

Types of Data Processing

Data-Processing Applications
- Computers in Business
- Computers in Science
- Computers in Medical Care
- Computers in Law
- Computers in Congress
- Computers in the Home

The Future

Chapter Objectives

The learning objectives of this chapter are

1. to introduce the data-processing concepts and to show how data processing affects our daily lives.
2. to explore the vital role played by the computer in our everchanging world.
3. to explain the different informational needs and how these are met by the computer.
4. to demonstrate the various application areas of the computer in our society.
5. to project what the future has in store for the further exploitation of the computer.

The dynamic introduction of the computer in the last quarter century has changed our information needs entirely. Since the resources of society are limited, we have developed methods of compiling and analyzing large quantities of data with a minimum amount of human intervention. With each new application, data-processing systems have demonstrated still newer ways in which they can be used to help us increase our productivity and advance civilization a little further. Data processing is not just another new industry or innovation but a giant step forward in the utilization of science and knowledge as a means of progress.

Computers are perhaps the most useful tools ever invented. In this, the era of computers, they count our votes, figure our bank accounts, help plan new buildings and bridges, guide our astronauts through space, and assist management in its everyday decisions. Beyond problem-solving applications, computers have a broad range of uses in business accounting and bookkeeping, including inventory control, payroll, income taxes, accounts receivable and accounts payable, pension and profit-sharing fund calculations, rate-of-return calculations, new acquisition appraisals, sales performance, and critical path estimates.

Business dilemmas can be solved by hand, but that would involve long and tedious procedures. Deadlines may be missed. Errors may slip by unnoticed. Alternative courses may be ignored or not fully developed. Valuable workhours could be tied up doing what the machines can do in minutes. And when the procedure has to be repeated for the next new bid, or new acquisition, you'll have to start from scratch with all of the calculations.

The computer, whether giant-sized or desktop, is much more than a machine that can do very rapid mathematical calculations. It has the capacity for storing and instantly recalling vast amounts of information.

Our lives are affected each day in some manner by computers. Life as we know it would not be possible without them. Patterns of consumer spending have changed. Credit cards have become a way of life. Almost all of our needs can be satisfied with a credit card.

Daily interest computation on bank savings would be an impossibility without the present methods of processing data. Service industries have greatly increased, providing numerous services to make life more convenient and pleasant. A car is waiting for you as you embark from your plane. To make reservations for some distant hotel or to plan a trip to another part of the world all that is required is to reach for the telephone. Sporting events and other entertainment tickets are now available to us at our favorite stores, conveniently located. No longer is it necessary to make a special trip to the sports complex or theatre or to stand in lines. Every individual is touched by the computer in some manner—some, unhappily, by the Internal Revenue Service.

One of the driving forces behind the development of computers was the need to find faster and more efficient methods of handling paperwork. Paper handling alone would probably have overwhelmed all of our enormous productive capabilities if clerical mechanization had not kept pace with the technological advances in the field. To see how well this purpose has been fulfilled you need only to look at the ways computers serve you in your everyday life.

In this morning's mail there is perhaps a magazine that came days earlier than it used to because it was addressed automatically by the computer. There are probably the usual charge and credit account bills, end products of a valuable service that depends almost entirely on the ability of the computers to collect, process, and record vast amounts of credit and billing information.

Computers have gone beyond merely taking over the jobs accomplished by paperwork and doing them faster and better. Computers are doing things for business and industry that could never have been done before.

A company may test the design of a new processing plant by simulating every detail of its operation with a computer. Computer simulation frequently provides more information in a week than an expensive pilot plant could provide in a year of actual operation.

Another pressure hastening the spread of the computer is the need for better resource management. Decision-making controllers and processors are needed in many organizations at every stage of the production or administrative process. Although computers offer a solution to these pressures, they must also be cost-effective. Computers are a bargain and they will remain a bargain.

More and more management decisions now are based on information supplied by computers—information about inventories, production schedules, market forecasts, and sales analyses (fig. 1.1). Although management could always get this information, it was not always obtainable in time to take effective action. In some cases today, advanced mathematical techniques, worked out on computers, are used to find answers

Figure 1.1 Management often makes decisions using information supplied by computers.

quickly to complex marketing and production problems that a few years ago would have been solved only with extreme difficulty and a considerable consumption of time.

Computers of the future will go even further toward freeing us from the drudgery of paperwork and repetitive manual tasks. The net effect will place the computer's unique abilities in the hands of more people doing work that to date has remained largely outside the computer's sphere. Examples of the future are here today:

> The supermarket employee, with less than two hours of training, presides over a sophisticated computerized scanning system which automatically checks out shoppers' purchases with unprecedented speed and accuracy.
>
> The 24-hour unattended self-service banking machine accepts payments for utility bills, handles saving deposits, and dispenses cash.
>
> A nurse, perhaps unaware she is operating a computer, uses a scanning device to order medication for a patient. The order is automatically added to the patient's account by a computer, is sent to the hospital's pharmacy for action, and is relayed to other hospital departments as needed.

These examples are only part of a worldwide trend which is taking the computer to places it has never been, to be used by people who have never used it, to do things it has never done. The surprise may well be the speed with which the processing capability of the computer will permeate these previously untouched areas.

All of the aforementioned activities illustrate ways that data has become a part of life and indicate the part that the computer has played in its development. Great opportunities lie ahead in the data-processing field with the addition of the computer. Expanded markets, greater productivity, corporate growth, and increased governmental activity provide the data processor with new challenges each day.

Figure 1.2 An example of a data-processing system.

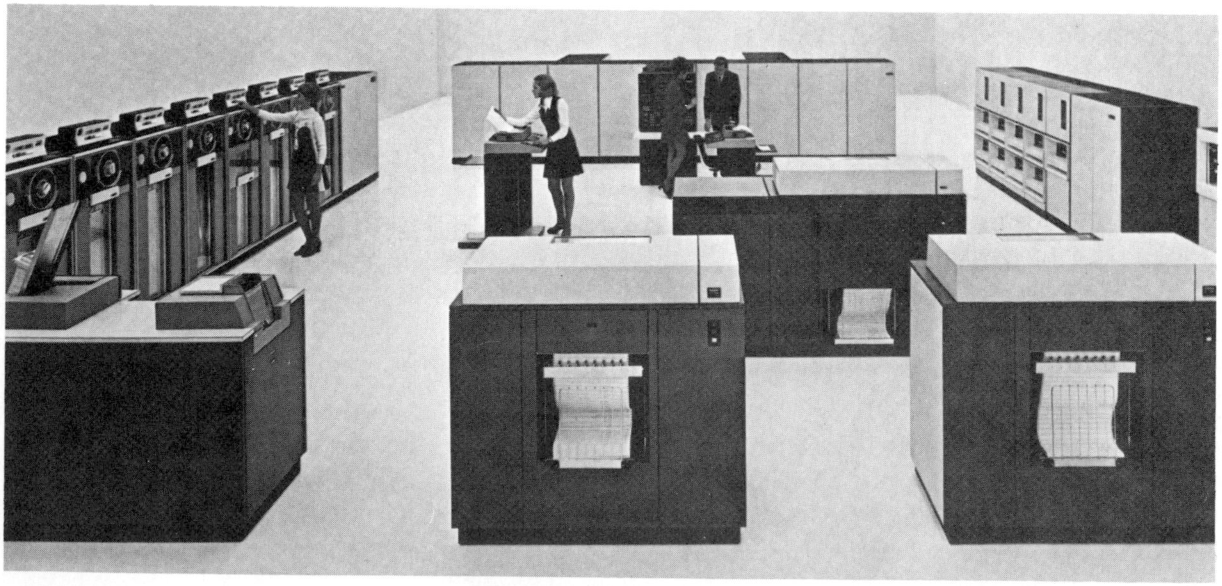

Importance of Data Processing

Data processing is a planned series of actions and operations upon information, using various forms of data-processing equipment, to achieve a desired result. The data-processing equipment came into being primarily to satisfy needs for information under increasingly complex conditions. Computer programs and physical equipment are combined into data-processing systems to handle business and scientific data at high rates of speed with self-checking accuracy features. The physical data-processing equipment consists of various units, such as input and output devices, storage devices, and processing devices, to handle information at electronic speed (fig. 1.2).

An estimated 35 billion checks circulate annually in the United States. Each check must be handled at least six times before it is finally cancelled and returned (fig. 1.3). Without the efforts of the computer manufacturers and the American Banking Association, the processing of these checks in a reasonable amount of time would be impossible. Through their efforts, the magnetic character-sensing mechanism was developed, making possible the high-speed sorting and processing of checks.

Some of the more spectacular examples of the remarkable advances in data processing are *image processing* and *audio response.* The processing of pictures transmitted from the planet Mars was an example of image processing. Rapid microfilm scanning was combined with automatic interpretation of light and dark spots into 0s and 1s for computer storage. These pictures were then displayed on the viewer's screen. The same techniques were used to send pictures to earth from the planet Jupiter by the various space missions.

Computers are used in business for a variety of reasons. When properly applied, they can save time or money (or both) in producing reports for management and government (fig. 1.4), in preparing checks and earnings statements (fig. 1.5), in writing invoices to customers (fig. 1.6), in keeping records of accounts payable to suppliers, and in numerous other ways. In many situations they make it possible to obtain

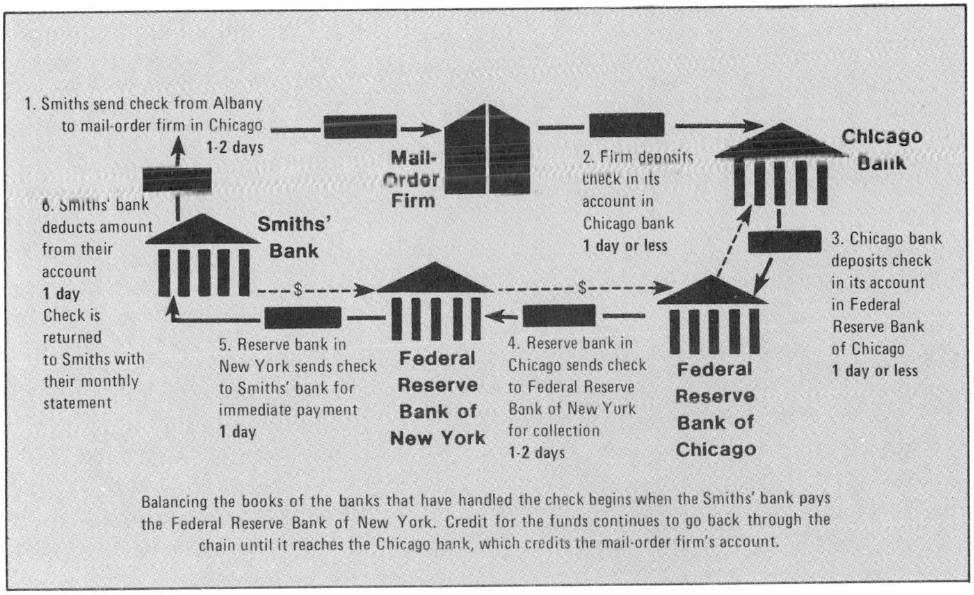

Figure 1.3 How a check goes through a Federal Reserve System.

Figure 1.4
Examples of management reports.

PAGE 2 — ON HAND STATUS REPORT — 12-06-8-

ITEM NO	BIN NO	QTY	CODE	ITEM NO	BIN NO	QTY	CODE	ITEM NO	BIN NO	QTY	CODE	ITEM NO	BIN NO	QTY	CODE
1002000121	229	188	1	1002000122	148	7		1013000134	262	235		1127000179	54	16	
1130002681	468	20		1141029736	29	0	2	1142029746	30	132		1156217368	68	5	
1156321762	19	86		1157316299	336	8		1157332068	561	36		1158260177	1620	261	
1160223466	9067	56		1160223588	10689	29		1160246899	1690	177		1161462133	447	33	
1163281971	887	16		1163281981	893	40		1163281990	78	22		1163282766	79	12	
1164009883	1993	101		1164009944	1110	61		1164009948	1122	70		1164009966	1233	80	
1165002344	10628	17		1165002355	10629	129		1165004141	1988	35		1165012687	474	12	
1168017936	12	48		1173201631	7680	22		1174062812	53	206		1181326819	2216	78	

LOAD REPORT

DATE 9-13-8- PAGE 1

DEPT WK/CTR	BEHIND SCH HRS	1ST PERIOD AVAIL	1ST PERIOD LOADED	%	2ND PERIOD AVAIL	2ND PERIOD LOADED	%	3RD PERIOD AVAIL	3RD PERIOD LOADED	%	4TH PERIOD AVAIL	4TH PERIOD LOADED	%	FUTURE LOAD
029-001	18.5	40	44.6	111	40	82.1	205	40	66.3	166	80	64.3	80	181.0
049-015		160	64.8	40	160	178.4	111	160	12.4	8	160	2.8	2	
049-020		240	184.3	77	240	200.6	84	240	124.3	52	240	81.5	34	168.0
049-021		40	32.6	81	40	24.2	60	40	17.6	44	40	9.8	25	
049-032	32.6	120	182.4	152	120	105.4	88	120	42.3	35	120	38.7	32	121.2

SALES AND PROFIT, BY SALESMAN, BY CUSTOMER

SALESMAN 5 PAGE 7 12-06-8-

THIS PERIOD

CUSTOMER	CUST NO	NET SALES	GROSS PROFIT	CUST % PROFIT	% TOTAL PROFIT	NO INVOICES	TOTAL LINES	AVG $ LINE
ALLIED GROCERY	1006	10000	1500	150	10	15	1900	666
LAST YEAR		9000	1080	120	8	14	1400	643
PCT INC OR DEC		11.1	38.9	30	2	7.1	35.7	3.6
AL'S SUPER MARKET	1086	8238	1224	149	8	12	1812	545
LAST YEAR		7927	1120	141	8	11	1579	512
PCT INC OR DEC		3.6	9.3	8	0	9.1	14.8	6.4
RALPH'S SUPER THRIFT	7263	42681	6492	152	44	16	7919	539
LAST YEAR		44800	6787	151	48	16	8517	526
PCT INC OR DEC		4.7-	4.3-	1	4-	.0	7.0-	2.5
SALES TOTAL THIS YEAR		186534	28017	150	190	190	35395	527
LAST YEAR		170436	25599	150	180	192	32903	518
PCT INC OR DEC		8.6	9.4	0	10	1.0-	7.6	1.7
GRAND TOTALS THIS YEAR		977438	147398	151	1000	997	185824	526
LAST YEAR		950637	142405	150	1000	978	183167	519
PCT INC OR DEC		2.8	3.5	1	0	1.9	1.5	1.3

YEAR-TO-DATE

CUSTOMER	NET SALES	GROSS PROFIT	CUST % PROFIT	% TOTAL PROFIT	NO INVOICES	TOTAL LINES	AVG $ LINE
ALLIED GROCERY	110000	15000	136	9	165	20000	555
LAST YEAR	100000	13000	130	9	159	19500	513
PCT INC OR DEC	10.0	15.4	6	0	3.8	2.6	7.2
AL'S SUPER MARKET	90268	12872	143	8	131	16120	560
LAST YEAR	87197	12242	140	8	126	17063	511
PCT INC OR DEC	3.5	5.1	3	0	4.0	5.5-	9.6
RALPH'S SUPER THRIFT	460821	69952	152	43	175	86860	531
LAST YEAR	492600	74481	151	51	178	93650	526
PCT INC OR DEC	6.5-	6.1-	1	8-	1.7-	7.3-	1.0
SALES TOTAL THIS YEAR	2051874	308602	150	190	2068	385265	533
LAST YEAR	1864329	278158	149	190	2116	361304	516
PCT INC OR DEC	10.1	10.9	1	0	2.3-	6.6	3.3
GRAND TOTALS THIS YEAR	10747621	1627190	151	1000	9425		531
LAST YEAR	9780351	1464119	150	1000	8593		515
PCT INC OR DEC	9.9	11.1	1	0	9.7		3.1

information that would otherwise not be economically justifiable. In some cases, they provide a basis for improved management of a business that would not, for time or money reasons, be feasible without computers.

Engineering and scientific computations require the extensive use of computers. Scientific research has itself grown into a multibillion-dollar-a-year undertaking, and the new computer technology has provided most of the impetus for this remarkable growth. Information needs in both of these areas have, obviously, greatly increased, thus giving data, extractable from computers, a vast new importance.

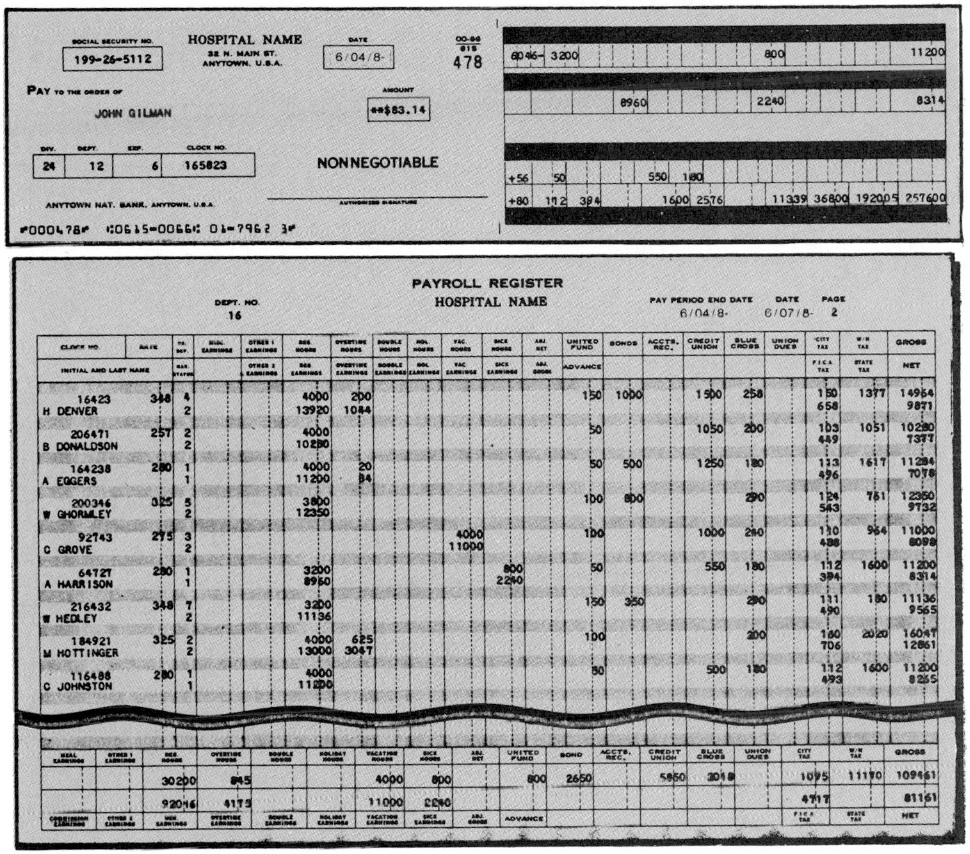

Figure 1.5 An example of a payroll check and a register.

Demands for Data

The demands for data stem basically from two sources: *internal* and *external* demands.

Internal demands are requests from management for accurate, classified, and summarized data used in the analysis that is necessary for daily, weekly, or cyclical decision making. Transactions that occur in the everyday operations of an enterprise provide the necessary historical records. From this group of data, information is extracted and accumulated to provide reports used in business decisions and in facilitating other managerial functions. Unless this information is furnished on a current and accurate basis, the company's competitive position may be weakened. A decision to buy, sell, or produce a commodity should be based on information supplied by the data-processing system after all significant factors have been evaluated. The computer can present possible alternative actions, thus providing the user with the information necessary to make an intelligent decision.

External demands for data originate outside the organization. These demands are created by customers, unions, governmental agencies, and other parties who have an interest in the operations of the enterprise.

Customers need statements or invoices in order to pay obligations on time and to record the transactions properly. The union has the responsibility of looking after the interests of its members and, in order to accomplish this objective, it needs reports

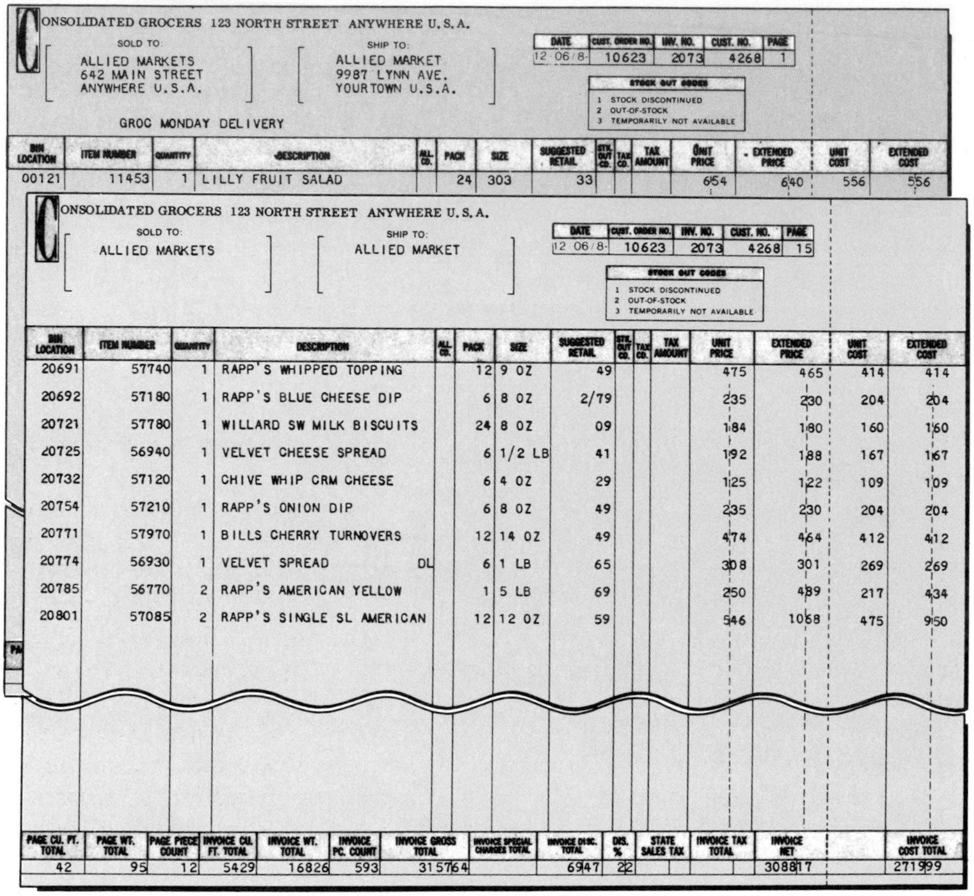

CONSOLIDATED GROCERS 123 NORTH STREET ANYWHERE U. S. A.

SOLD TO: ALLIED MARKETS, 642 MAIN STREET, ANYWHERE U.S.A.

SHIP TO: ALLIED MARKET, 9987 LYNN AVE., YOURTOWN U.S.A.

GROC MONDAY DELIVERY

DATE	CUST. ORDER NO.	INV. NO.	CUST. NO.	PAGE
12 06 8-	10623	2073	4268	1

STOCK OUT CODES
1 STOCK DISCONTINUED
2 OUT-OF-STOCK
3 TEMPORARILY NOT AVAILABLE

BIN LOCATION	ITEM NUMBER	QUANTITY	DESCRIPTION	ALL. CD.	PACK	SIZE	SUGGESTED RETAIL	STK. OUT CD.	TAX CD.	TAX AMOUNT	UNIT PRICE	EXTENDED PRICE	UNIT COST	EXTENDED COST
00121	11453	1	LILLY FRUIT SALAD		24	303	33				654	640	556	556

CONSOLIDATED GROCERS 123 NORTH STREET ANYWHERE U. S. A.

SOLD TO: ALLIED MARKETS

SHIP TO: ALLIED MARKET

DATE	CUST. ORDER NO.	INV. NO.	CUST. NO.	PAGE
12 06 8-	10623	2073	4268	15

STOCK OUT CODES
1 STOCK DISCONTINUED
2 OUT-OF-STOCK
3 TEMPORARILY NOT AVAILABLE

BIN LOCATION	ITEM NUMBER	QUANTITY	DESCRIPTION	ALL. CD.	PACK	SIZE	SUGGESTED RETAIL	STK. OUT CD.	TAX CD.	TAX AMOUNT	UNIT PRICE	EXTENDED PRICE	UNIT COST	EXTENDED COST
20691	57740	1	RAPP'S WHIPPED TOPPING		12	9 OZ	49				475	465	414	414
20692	57180	1	RAPP'S BLUE CHEESE DIP		6	8 OZ	2/79				235	230	204	204
20721	57780	1	WILLARD SW MILK BISCUITS		24	8 OZ	09				184	180	160	160
20725	56940	1	VELVET CHEESE SPREAD		6	1/2 LB	41				192	188	167	167
20732	57120	1	CHIVE WHIP CRM CHEESE		6	4 OZ	29				125	122	109	109
20754	57210	1	RAPP'S ONION DIP		6	8 OZ	49				235	230	204	204
20771	57970	1	BILLS CHERRY TURNOVERS		12	14 OZ	49				474	464	412	412
20774	56930	1	VELVET SPREAD DL		6	1 LB	65				308	301	269	269
20785	56770	2	RAPP'S AMERICAN YELLOW		1	5 LB	69				250	489	217	434
20801	57085	2	RAPP'S SINGLE SL AMERICAN		12	12 OZ	59				546	1068	475	950

PAGE CU. FT. TOTAL	PAGE WT. TOTAL	PAGE PIECE COUNT	INVOICE CU. FT. TOTAL	INVOICE WT. TOTAL	INVOICE PC. COUNT	INVOICE GROSS TOTAL	INVOICE SPECIAL CHARGES TOTAL	INVOICE DISC. TOTAL	DIS. %	STATE SALES TAX	INVOICE TAX TOTAL	INVOICE NET	INVOICE COST TOTAL
42	95	12	5429	16826	593	315764		6947	22			308817	271999

Figure 1.6 An example of a customer invoice.

relative to the status of the employees. The government, with its enormous need for data in the form of tax returns and other reports, requires that each report be filed on time and reported accurately.

All of these demands must be integrated into a common purpose which makes an organic whole of the entire organization; all functions must balance. A successful data-processing system must combine these demands into an integrated data-processing system satisfying the needs of all users without duplicating the effort of processing.

Sources of Data

Data can originate as *internal* or *external data*.

Internal data is the medium on which the data is recorded at the time the transaction occurs: a bank check, voucher, sales slip, purchase requisition, etc. The design of these forms can be controlled to make the recording of the data as simple and accurate as possible. The layout of the form should provide the data in the sequence in which it will be later transcribed into a data-processing media, for example, a punched card. Transcriptions of the data should be kept at a minimum as this will increase the costs of processing and the possibilities for errors.

Internal data can be controlled much more accurately as to the form used, the information to be collected, and the care exercised in the collection of the information. This control is not possible with data originating outside of the organization (external data) as each individual organization prepares forms that will accommodate its own needs.

External data is created outside of the organization; therefore, it is designed to satisfy the needs of the supplier. The data may be in the form of a vendor invoice, government tax form, or a utility bill. Transcription of this form to one suitable to the needs of the recipient is usually required. This may necessitate the creation of a new form, such as an accounts payable voucher document, that contains all the necessary coded information for transcription into a machine-processible media.

Types of Data Processing

Data processing is divided into two main categories: *business data processing* and *scientific data processing.*

In *business data processing,* all necessary activities, such as payroll preparation, inventory control, sales analysis, and general accounting files, are processed, and the required outputs of statements and reports are prepared. *Business data processing is characterized by the processing of many files, used repeatedly, requiring few calculations and many output reports.* For example, a payroll application would require such outputs as updated personnel files, payroll checks, payroll registers, deduction reports, and various internal and external reports. All of these reports would be prepared with the same inputs. The reports prepared may be *mandatory* or *operational.*

Mandatory reports are those reports required by governmental agencies, stockholders, customers, etc. These reports must be prepared in a fixed format according to the needs of the user. There isn't a great deal of flexibility in the printed output (fig. 1.7).

Operational reports are the reports that aid management in making the many necessary decisions in everyday business operations. In these reports, data processing can provide valuable aids to management. The analysis, ratios, trends, and comparisons, heretofore impossible, are now being prepared on a current basis with self-checking accuracy (fig. 1.8).

Management must make decisions daily relative to the operations of a business. How much to produce, where to sell, budgets, and pricing are just a few of the problems confronting administrative executives each day. High-speed computers provide the analysis and reports stipulating any alternative actions that are available to the decision maker. Computers also provide the necessary paperwork in accordance with these decisions. The *management-by-exception* technique is used by many companies to reduce the amount of detail that the decision maker is faced with. In this concept, only the exceptional facts are drawn to the attention of these executives. For example, a complete accounts receivable report listing all account balances would not be presented to the credit manager, but only those accounts that are delinquent. Thus, the manager concentrates only on those accounts that require attention and is relieved of the tedious task of reviewing all accounts.

The measuring of the actual progress of an organization and the feedback for management control is another important function that data-processing equipment is

Figure 1.7
Examples of mandatory reports.

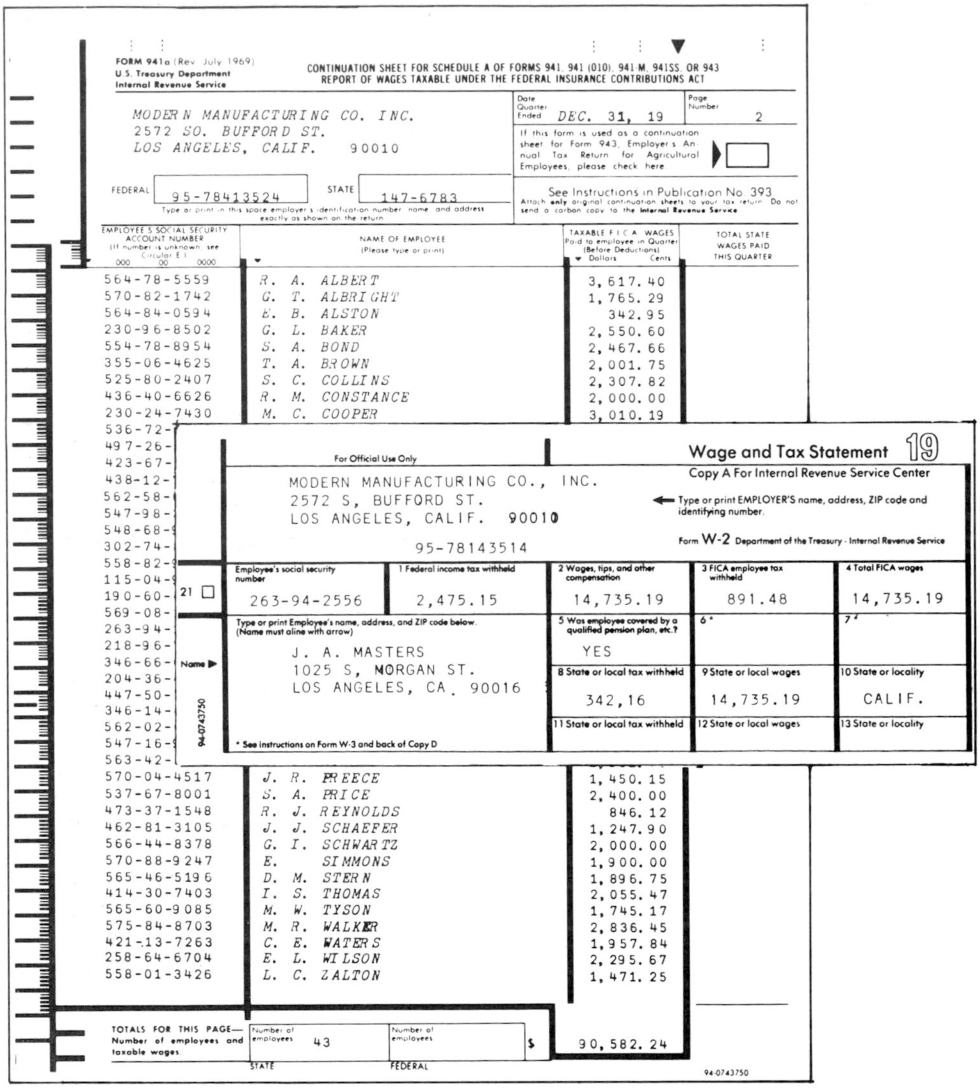

FORM 941a (Rev. July 1969)
U.S. Treasury Department
Internal Revenue Service

CONTINUATION SHEET FOR SCHEDULE A OF FORMS 941, 941 (010), 941-M, 941SS, OR 943
REPORT OF WAGES TAXABLE UNDER THE FEDERAL INSURANCE CONTRIBUTIONS ACT

MODERN MANUFACTURING CO. INC.
2572 SO. BUFFORD ST.
LOS ANGELES, CALIF. 90010

Date Quarter Ended DEC. 31, 19 — Page Number 2

If this form is used as a continuation sheet for Form 943, Employer's Annual Tax Return for Agricultural Employees, please check here

FEDERAL 95-78413524 — STATE 147-6783

Type or print in this space employer's identification number, name, and address exactly as shown on the return

See Instructions in Publication No. 393
Attach only original continuation sheets to your tax return. Do not send a carbon copy to the Internal Revenue Service

EMPLOYEE'S SOCIAL SECURITY ACCOUNT NUMBER (If number is unknown, see Circular E) 000 00 0000	NAME OF EMPLOYEE (Please type or print)	TAXABLE F.I.C.A. WAGES Paid to employee in Quarter (Before Deductions) Dollars Cents	TOTAL STATE WAGES PAID THIS QUARTER
564-78-5559	R. A. ALBERT	3,617.40	
570-82-1742	G. T. ALBRIGHT	1,765.29	
564-84-0594	E. B. ALSTON	342.95	
230-96-8502	G. L. BAKER	2,550.60	
554-78-8954	S. A. BOND	2,467.66	
355-06-4625	T. A. BROWN	2,001.75	
525-80-2407	S. C. COLLINS	2,307.82	
436-40-6626	R. M. CONSTANCE	2,000.00	
230-24-7430	M. C. COOPER	3,010.19	
536-72-			
497-26-			
423-67-			
438-12-			
562-58-			
547-98-			
548-68-			
302-74-			
558-82-			
115-04-			
190-60-			
569-08-			
263-94-			
218-96-			
346-66-			
204-36-			
447-50-			
346-14-			
562-02-			
547-16-			
563-42-			
570-04-4517	J. R. PREECE	1,450.15	
537-67-8001	S. A. PRICE	2,400.00	
473-37-1548	R. J. REYNOLDS	846.12	
462-81-3105	J. J. SCHAEFER	1,247.90	
566-44-8378	G. I. SCHWARTZ	2,000.00	
570-88-9247	E. SIMMONS	1,900.00	
565-46-5196	D. M. STERN	1,896.75	
414-30-7403	I. S. THOMAS	2,055.47	
565-60-9085	M. W. TYSON	1,745.17	
575-84-8703	M. R. WALKER	2,836.45	
421-13-7263	C. E. WATERS	1,957.84	
258-64-6704	E. L. WILSON	2,295.67	
558-01-3426	L. C. ZALTON	1,471.25	

TOTALS FOR THIS PAGE— Number of employees and taxable wages. STATE: Number of employees 43 — FEDERAL: Number of employees — $ 90,582.24

94-0743750

For Official Use Only

Wage and Tax Statement 19
Copy A For Internal Revenue Service Center

MODERN MANUFACTURING CO., INC.
2572 S, BUFFORD ST.
LOS ANGELES, CALIF. 90010
95-78143514

← Type or print EMPLOYER'S name, address, ZIP code and identifying number.

Form W-2 Department of the Treasury - Internal Revenue Service

21 ☐

Employee's social security number	1 Federal income tax withheld	2 Wages, tips, and other compensation	3 FICA employee tax withheld	4 Total FICA wages
263-94-2556	2,475.15	14,735.19	891.48	14,735.19

Type or print Employee's name, address, and ZIP code below. (Name must aline with arrow)

Name ▶ J. A. MASTERS
1025 S, MORGAN ST.
LOS ANGELES, CA. 90016

5 Was employee covered by a qualified pension plan, etc.?	6 *	7 *
YES		

8 State or local tax withheld	9 State or local wages	10 State or locality
342,16	14,735.19	CALIF.

11 State or local tax withheld	12 State or local wages	13 State or locality

* See instructions on Form W-3 and back of Copy D

94-0743750

performing for management each day. Reports are prepared periodically that management can compare with predicted results. The feedback can indicate what corrective action, if any, must be taken to achieve management goals.

Scientific data processing includes the analysis of the data required and used for engineering and research purposes. It is *mathematically oriented, usually nonrepetitive in nature, or file oriented, requiring small amounts of input and output data with many calculations.* For example, a mathematical formula is programmed into a computer, a small amount of data is entered into the machine, and one line of output is produced on the printer, although the machine was required to go through many computing cycles.

DATE 9-20-8- QUANTITY DEVIATION REPORT PAGE 1

DEPT WK/CTR	PRODUCTION ORDER NBR	PART NUMBER	OPN SEQ NUMBER	QNTY ORDERED	PREVIOUS OPN QNTY	QNTY COMPL	%	QNTY SCRAP	%	QNTY SHRINKAGE	%
029-001	5200029	5A13982	0200	10000	10000	9000	90	1000	10		
029-001	5200029	5A13982	0300	10000	9000	7000	78			2000	22

SCHOOL NAME U N S C H E D U A B L E S T U D E N T S R E P O R T 9/08/8- PAGE 2

ST.NO.	NAME		COMMENTS
121376	MEADE JOHN D	002 171 192 322 533 724 737 806 808	UNSCHEDUARLE CONFLICT
121564	SMITH JANIS	002 123 313 428 523 723	NO ROOM IN SOME CLASS
121584	SPURSEL DEBORAH	002 121 426 523 635 720 807 809	UNSCHEDUABLE CUTOFF
121616	THOMPSON NANCY	002 133 426 523 635 727 806 808	NO ROOM IN SOME CLASS
121642	TURNER PAUL J	002 171 193 428 533 635 710 807 809	UNSCHEDUABLE CONFLICT
121674	WEAVER ROSALIE W	002 123 533 635 727 806 808 811	NO ROOM IN SOME CLASS
121683	WEAVER WILLIAM R	002 123 533 635 727 735 806 808	NO ROOM IN SOME CLASS
121688	WIEDMAN JOSEPH C	001 113 413 711 726 802 804	UNSCHEDUABLF CONFLICT
121706	YOUNG CLARENCE	001 113 312 413 711 802 804	NO ROOM IN SOME CLASS
121782	ZINDORF ALBERT C	001 123 352 451 496 726 727 806 808	NO ROOM IN SOME CLASS

TOTAL CONFLICTS 039

AGED ACCOUNT BALANCE REPORT

DATE: 05/31/--

	CYCLE: 10	REGULAR	COMBINATION	REVOLVING	CONTRACT	TOTAL
	CURRENT	$5,560.09	$ 863,891.66	.00	$138,065.07	$1,007,516.82
	30 DAYS		454,096.98	.00	19,591.47	473,688.45
	60 DAYS		268,233.97	.00	8,668.90	276,902.87
TOTAL OF	90 DAYS		198,438.51	.00	16,243.91	214,682.42
ACCOUNT BALANCES	120 DAYS		89,439.95	.00	6,724.54	96,164.49
	150 DAYS		54,022.67	.00	4,525.62	58,540.29
	180 DAYS		44,985.18	.00	3,104.90	48,090.08
	OVER 180		.00	.00	.00	.00
	TOTAL	$5,560.09	$1,973,108.92	.00	$196,924.41	$2,175,593.42
	WRITE OFF					.00
	CURRENT		$ 70,633.12	.00	$ 8,563.01	$ 79,196.13
	30 DAYS		20,438.21	.00	1,956.89	22,395.10
TOTAL OF AMOUNT	60 DAYS		11,326.92	.00	1,201.43	12,528.35
NOW DUE ON	90 DAYS		5,115.63	.00	865.63	5,981.26
ABOVE BALANCE	120 DAYS		3,265.88	.00	406.46	3,672.34
	150 DAYS		1,985.25	.00	350.00	2,335.25
	180 DAYS		1,190.01	.00	275.50	1,465.51
	OVER 180		.00	.00	.00	.00
	TOTAL		$ 113,955.02	.00	[illegible]	[illegible]
	REGULAR					5,560.09
	TOTAL					$ 133,134.03

Figure 1.8 Examples of operational reports.

Data-Processing Applications

Computers in Business

No one took to the computer more eagerly or saw its usefulness more quickly than businesses. Now twenty-six years after General Electric became the first company to acquire a computer, these versatile machines have become the galley slaves of capitalism. In the airline industry, computers make it possible to reserve a seat on a jumbo jet, pay for it by credit card, and enable the plane to fly. In many industries, computers design the products the company sells. Automakers, for example, use computers to view a prospective car from any angle; then the computers analyze the market to see if the design will sell (fig. 1.9).

Figure 1.9
Technicians use computer graphics-display systems. (Photo by Ken Firestone)

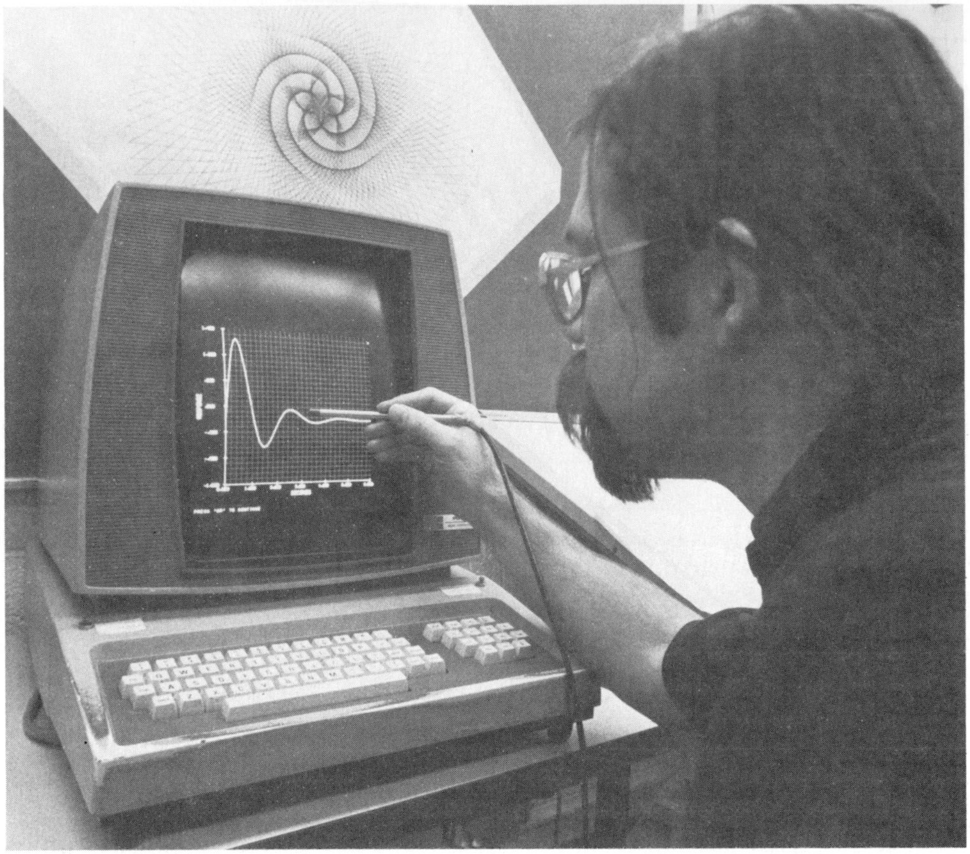

In fact, the ravenous appetite of United States companies for data-processing machines and control devices accounts for a major portion of the $41 billion computer business. Only seventeen years ago, IBM was, for all practical purposes, *the* computer industry, but the explosive rise in demand has surpassed even IBM's ability to gobble up the new orders. The clamoring demand has created markets for smaller, younger companies that make minicomputers and peripheral equipment, such as data storage facilities and keyboard terminals, to be used with the big "main frames."

Inventory control offers a practical application of the power of the computer. The retailer can feed an entire inventory into the computer, including style, size, price, profit margin, supplier, quantity, and reorder time. The inventory can be updated daily by feeding in sales for that day. And the computer can be programmed to signal when a reorder is needed. By direct tie-in with major suppliers, orders can actually be placed by the machine, with order verification and delivery time quoted back into the machine.

If the computer operator wants to know how many items of a given size or color are in stock, a series of electronic impulses is punched, which, in effect, asks that question of the computer. Those impulses cause the computer to scan its memory banks, virtually at the speed of light, seeking the stored information. When it's found, it can be displayed on a TV-like tube, printed on paper, or just held in the machine waiting for further instructions.

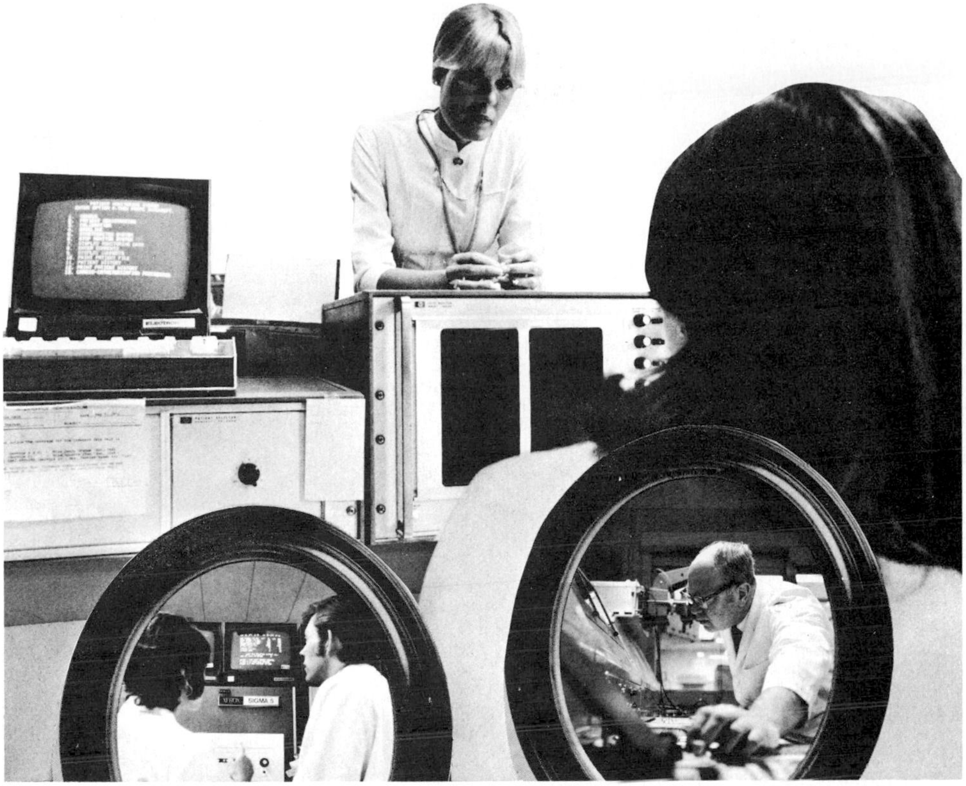

Figure 1.10 Computers are often used in medicine.

Computers in Science

Space technology would be almost unthinkable without the power of the computer. This is an area of science that requires the combined knowledge of almost all the other sciences—physics, chemistry, thermodynamics, electronics, mathematics, even psychology. Only computers can bring this incredibly large amount of information under control to make it serve rather than impede our efforts.

For almost a century weather scientists have had mathematical formulas for predicting weather changes. Now they are able to work out the astronomical number of calculations the formulas require. They are even working on a mathematical model of the world's weather that may some day enable us to make reasonably accurate weather forecasts a year or more ahead of time.

In medicine, computers are helping researchers test drugs by extrapolating the information gained in limited trials, so that large-scale tests will not only be safer, but will yield far more useful information. Computers are helping doctors make diagnoses by winnowing down the information a doctor has to go through to arrive at a valid conclusion (fig. 1.10).

Biochemists are using computers as a sort of mathematical microscope. By delving into the secret of the living cell, they have found a physical limit to the information they can obtain with their instruments. By using computers to comb through and extend the data they have already obtained, they are beginning to construct an accurate picture of the giant molecules that are the building blocks of all living things (fig. 1.11).

Figure 1.11 An example of a biomedical report.

UTAH BIOMEDICAL TEST LABORATORY — 8 JAN 1973, PAGE 3

PRESSURE PROGRAM - 7203
PATIENT CLASS - 0 PROJECT - 2
PATIENT I.D. - 88 UNIT NO. - 32
FROM 1 73 0: 0 TO 365 73 23:59

DATE	TIME	PRES. TYPE	MAX. PRES. MM-HG	MIN. PRES. MM-HG	MEAN PRES. MM-HG	HEART RATE
8 JAN 73	5 :53:21	13	0.	0.	0.	73.
8 JAN 73	6 :9 :21	13	0.	0.	0.	70.
8 JAN 73	6 :25:21	13	0.	0.	0.	95.
8 JAN 73	6 :41:21	13	0.	0.	0.	78.
8 JAN 73	6 :57:21	13	0.	0.	0.	75.
8 JAN 73	7 :13:21	13	0.	0.	0.	61.
8 JAN 73	7 :29:21	13	0.	0.	0.	24.*
8 JAN 73	8 :17:21	13	0.	0.	0.	82.
8 JAN 73	8 :18:4	13	0.	0.	0.	74.
8 JAN 73	8 :33:21	13	0.	0.	0.	89.
8 JAN 73	8 :49:21	13	0.	0.	0.	0.*
8 JAN 73	9 :5 :21	13	0.	0.	0.	81.
8 JAN 73	9 :21:21	13	0.	0.	0.	98.
8 JAN 73	9 :53:21	13	32.	12.	20.*	81.
8 JAN 73	10:25:21	13	23.	-25.	0.	18.*
8 JAN 73	10:57:21	13	31.	-8.	10.	71.

*NOTE-ASTERISK INDICATES AN ALARMED VALUE.

In astronomy, computers serve as computational workhorses, figuring out the exact positions and orbits of planets, stars, and other heavenly bodies. With the growing importance of radio telescopy, computers have been especially valuable in analyzing the patterns of signals received from outer space, separating the meaningful signals from the electronic roar of background "noise" that accompanies them.

The achievements of computers in the fields of space exploration, weather reporting, medical research, and other areas of scientific study have been fantastic. The tremendous storage capabilities and rapid processing of data have produced the valuable information necessary for research in the unknown areas of science. Scientific research has advanced as a human activity. In both the pure and applied sciences, computers are being used to multiply our thinking power and to multiply the time we can spend thinking.

Computers in Medical Care

In no area of American life is personal service so precious as in medical care. Here, the computer has become the humanizing factor; patients tend to give more candid accounts of symptoms, regimen and medical history to a machine programmed to ask the proper preliminary questions than to a doctor who is harassed and possibly intimidating.

At an Eastern hospital, for example, some patients sit down at a computer terminal before meeting a physician to provide their medical history and to receive information about the hospital. The computer interviews can be done in French and Spanish, as well as English, with a physician receiving an instantaneous translation. At these hospitals, much of the literature on some major ailments, such as stroke and blood pressure disease, has been computerized for doctors' consultations. Computers are already capable of detecting and monitoring ocular and cerebral ailments, such as glaucoma and brain tumors.

In some hospitals, computers are programmed not only to remind the pharmacy department to prepare prescriptions but also to alert nurses to give the proper dosage at the right time. After a physician examines a patient, a report, including lab test results, is logged in a data bank. One of the hospital's more than one hundred terminals will then handle the patient's history in an intelligible language.

More broadly, computers enable patients to receive health profiles at a far lower cost than previously possible; analyze vast amounts of blood; and, by systematizing information, cut down on the patient's hospital stay and pare both institutional and patient costs.

Computers in Law

More and more, lawyers are counting on computers for assistance not only in research but in the courtroom itself. An estimated 30,000 lawyers are already using *Lexis,* an electronic law library containing four million pages of federal and state court decisions, administrative rulings, and statutory laws. Terminals for *Lexis* are installed in law firms and law schools where, for a fee, users are able to get the information they want on a video screen.

Computers are also helping lawyers manage cases by storing a massive electronic index called a *litigation support system.* Prior to a trial, attorneys, aided by software companies, store in a computer's memory information about thousands or even millions of documents that may be needed during the trial. The actual documents are stored in file cabinets. Later, to locate a document filed months before, a lawyer punches in a few key words and the computer will report the paper's location.

For some lawyers, automated litigation support has proved a lifesaver. One New York lawyer, who used it in a lengthy litigation, was able to locate every paper on file that contained a witness's name by giving the name to the computer. The alternative would have been to go through thousands of documents manually and file them in witness folders, but sometimes that will not help as witnesses are not always known before the time of the trial.

Computers in Congress

No one could contend that Congress has rushed pell-mell into the computer age. The executive branch hums along on 10,000 big computers, the care and feeding of which costs as much as $10 billion a year; whereas, the legislative branch limps along with six medium-sized computers (and several smaller special-duty machines), costing as much as $29 million a year. Increasing pressure from taxpayers for reduced costs of operations and demands for more detailed and accurate reporting of transactions have caused the conversion of large heretofore manual operations to high-speed data-processing applications.

Computers have provided some obvious benefits that aren't always related to voter communication. With a system called *Scorpio,* members of Congress, using terminals in their offices, can look into files in the Library of Congress, including briefs on major issues. With *Legis,* members can track bills and resolutions. With *Sopad,* they can

Figure 1.12 A computer can be used in the home. (Photo by Ken Firestone)

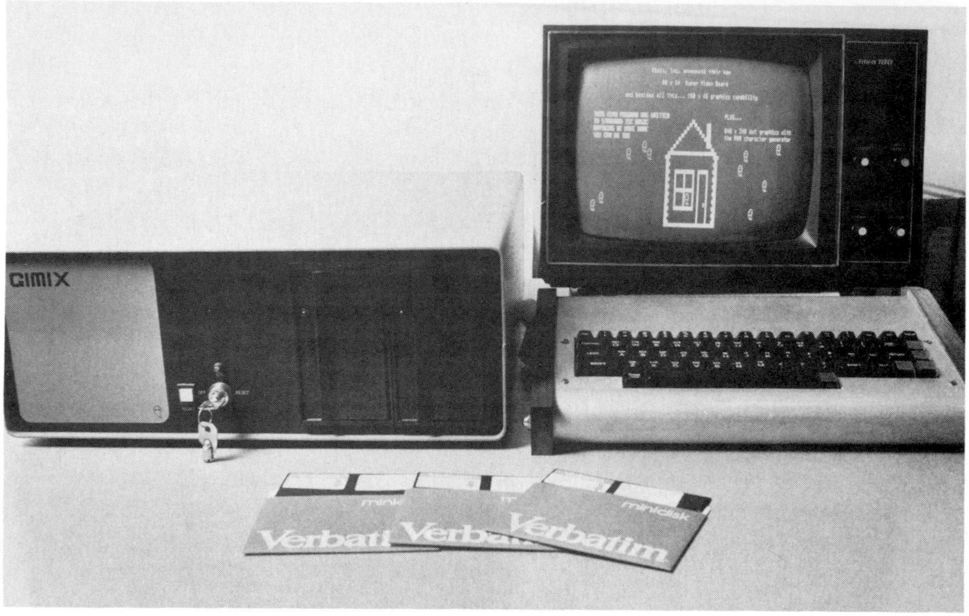

find out what's going on down on the floor. With *Faprs,* they can discover what federal loans and grants might be useful for their constituents. And in the House, there is even an electronic voting system that saves time and energy.

With a computer, members can group their constituents in hundreds, even in thousands or they can single out specific voters by where they live, right down to specific neighborhoods.

Computers provide a personal touch for the representatives. When planning a trip to a certain area, they can ask the computer to display on the screen all the letters received in the past month from that area and when visiting the town they can mention the nice letters from Mr. Jones and Ms. Smith.

Another congressman stores paragraphs on hundreds of subjects that can be easily mixed and matched. Thus, if someone writes to him about the minimum wage, labor reform, pregnancy-disability payments, and social security, people in his office can fire off a personal four-page, single-spaced letter responding to all of those questions in a matter of minutes.

Computers in the Home

A wonderful thing has happened to computers—they have been *personalized.* You can now buy one for your very own, and quite reasonably, too (figs. 1.12 and 1.13). For under $1,000 (some models sell for less than $600 or the cost of a color TV set or refrigerator) you can possess the kind of electronic circuitry that puts astronauts into space and forecasts tomorrow's weather.

Tens of thousands of home computers are already operating in this country. The initial wave of buyers consisted largely of hobbyists ("bit-bangers" as they call themselves) with some knowledge of electronics. But novices are now beginning to frequent the nation's 300-plus computer stores. From the standpoint of both price and function,

Figure 1.13 An example of a personal computer. (Photo courtesy of Radio Shack, a division of Tandy Corporation)

it is realistic to say that the "Age of Personal Computers" has arrived and its possibilities are almost endless.

Within a year or two, home computers should be available in the nation's department stores like any other appliance. By 1981, sales are expected to top the million mark, creating a new $200 million market. But, while the home computer will be marketed like a TV set or a microwave oven, it is another kind of beast entirely; it is *programmable,* within reason, and it can do what it is told. With just a little training, the owner of a computer can write his or her own programs.

The person with a computer can do things that would be difficult or impossible without the help of all that electronic gadgetry. Thousands of home computer owners delight in sitting down before the blinking lights of their control consoles and waging intergalactic warfare. Popular games range from *Hammurabi* (in which you attempt to govern ancient Sumerica for ten years), *Wari* (a game similar to chess), and *Lunar Landing* (in which you plot the fuel usage rate for a spacecraft landing on the moon) to such old standbys as chess, craps, blackjack, and backgammon.

As educational tools, home computers are excellent; children can find them great fun. One simple program directs the computer to ask such questions as what is your name, who do you love, what are you afraid of, what is your favorite color, and who is your best friend. In a matter of seconds, the computer takes the answers and prints out a personalized story for the enraptured onlooker.

A Chicago dentist uses his home computer to analyze his fee structure; a Massachusetts math teacher keeps up with student's grades by computer; and a judge depends on her computer's memory to store legal data during trials. For the small businesses, the home computer is the great equalizer, affording the advantages of computer-based accounting, inventory, and information-retrieval controls.

In the future many domestic devices that use electric power will become increasingly computerized. Eventually, the household computer will be as much a part of the home as the kitchen sink. It will program washing machines, burglar and fire alarms, sewing machines, a robot vacuum cleaner, and a machine that rinses and stacks dirty dishes. When something goes wrong with an appliance, a question to the computer will elicit repair instructions; in future generations, repairs will be made automatically. Energy costs will be cut by a computerized device that will direct heat only to areas where it is needed; the device's ubiquitous eye, sensing where people are at all times, will similarly turn the lights on and off as needed.

Paper clutter will disappear as home information management systems take over from memo pads, notebooks, files, bills, and the kitchen bulletin board. The home computer will store all financial data, income tax records, things-to-do lists, appointments, phone numbers, and the equivalent of a desk calendar.

The Future

What the future will bring for data processing, no one can predict. Obviously, the rate of growth will accelerate with new equipment and devices, with new methods of data processing being introduced each day.

According to a report issued by the American Processing Societies, Inc. (AFIPS), entitled "Information in the United States; A Quantitative Summary," the following conclusions were drawn:

The data-processing industry will continue to double in dollar volume every five years worldwide from 1970 to 1990.

Total user spending on data processing in the United States will rise from 2.1% of the Gross National Product (GNP) in 1970 to 13% in 1990 and from $101 per capita to $1,253.

By 1990, as many as one in five of the United States labor force will require some knowledge of data processing. In addition, by that year, more than six out of ten in the United States labor force will depend in some way on data processing. Finally by 1990, more than 90% of the cost of data processing will be attributable to personnel costs, perhaps making data processing the nation's most labor-intensive field.

The wildest benefits of the electronic revolution will accrue to the young. It is estimated that there will be 5 million private computers in homes and available to students within two years; by year 1982, it is predicted that 80% of upper middle-class families will have computers "capable of playing important roles in the intellectual development of their children." In schools, computers will be more common than carousel slide projectors, movie projectors, and tape recorders. They'll be used from the moment the school opens, through recess, through lunch periods, and so on until the school closes.

The computers provide an intensely visual, multisensory learning experience that can take children in a matter of few months to a level they might never reach without it, and certainly would not reach by conventional methods after many years of study.

Isaac Asimov, in his article "The New Teachers," commented on new teaching methods that he foresees.

Suppose that over the next century, communications satellites become numerous and more sophisticated than those we've placed in space so far. Suppose that in place of radio waves, it is the more capacious laser beam of visible light that becomes the chief communications medium.

Under these circumstances, there would be room for many millions of separate channels for voice and picture, and it can be easily imagined that every human being on earth might have a particular television wavelength assigned to him.

Each person (child, adult or elderly) can have his own private outlet which could be attached to his own personal teaching machine. It would be a far more versatile and interactive machine than anything we could put together today, for computer technology will have advanced to permit interactive teaching between student and machine. Teachers may become inanimate objects. The machine will be sufficiently intricate and flexible to be capable of modifying its own program (that is "learning") as a result of the input of the student. In other words, the student will ask questions, answer questions, make statements, state opinions, and from all of this, the machine will be able to gauge the student well enough to adjust the speed and intensity of its course of instruction, and what's more, shift it in whatever direction student interest displays itself.

The machine might resemble a television set in size and appearance. Can so small an object contain enough information to teach the student as much as he wants to know in any direction intellectual curiosity may lead him? No, if the teaching machine is self-contained. But need it be?

In any civilization with its computer science so advanced as to make teaching machines possible, there will surely be computerized libraries. Such libraries may be even interconnected into a single library. All teaching machines will be plugged into this central library and each could have at its disposal any book, periodical, document, recording or video cassette that is encoded there. If the machine has it, the student would have it, too. Either it would be placed directly on a viewing screen or reproduced in print-on-paper for more leisurely study.

Of course, humans will not be totally eliminated as teachers. In some subjects, human interaction is essential—athletics, drama, public speaking, and so on. There is also value and interest in groups of students working in a particular field getting together to discuss and speculate with each other and with human experts, sparking each other to new insights. Yet after this they may return, with some relief, to the endlessly knowledgeable, endlessly flexible, and most of all, endlessly patient machines.

But who will teach the teaching machines? Surely the students who learn will also teach. The student who learns freely in those fields and activities that interest him is bound to think, speculate, observe, experiment and now and then, come up with something of his own that may not have been previously known. He would transmit that knowledge back to the machine which will in turn, record it (with due credit, presumably) in the central library—thus making it available to other teaching machines. All will thus be put back into the central hopper to serve as a new and higher starting point for those that come after. The teaching machines will thus make it possible for the human species to race forward to heights and in directions that is impossible now to foresee.*

*Isaac Asimov, "The New Teachers." Copyright © 1977 by American Way. Reprinted by permission of the author.

If we are to survive and enjoy the benefits of this new era, we must learn the principles and operations of modern data-processing systems. We must constantly update ourselves in the new methods of handling data. Technological developments will limit the employment growth for certain types of work. On the other hand, labor-saving innovations will affect, to some extent, the growing requirements for various personnel.

Based on the latest available data, employment in data processing currently totals more than one million people distributed among all occupations in other industries. More than 850,000 individuals are in computer-related occupations. By 1985, computer manufacturers predict a 74% increase in personnel employed in all occupations and an 86% increase in personnel employed by the computer service organizations, for a 78% increase overall.

These figures do not reflect the increasing use of computers by nonprogrammers. There are 1.2 million general- and special-purpose terminals employed in the United States. Many of these terminals are operated by airline and hotel reservation clerks, department store clerks, bank tellers, and consumers. This reflects an increasing use of computers by people who have primary occupations in other fields but interact with computers in their work.

Computer systems are destined to take on practically all the tasks of rote and drudgery which nature and society now imposes upon us. This was predicted long ago by Norbert Wiener, who observed that "it is degradation to a human being to chain him to an oar and use him as a source of power; but it is an equal degradation to assign him a purely repetitive task in a factory (or office) which demands less than a millionth of his brain capacity."

In the end, computer systems will benefit not only our managers but all of society by allowing us to achieve our ultimate goal—make human use of human beings.

Summary

This chapter introduces the concepts of data processing, demonstrates the importance of data processing in our economy, and explores the vital role played by the computer in this ever-changing area.

1. The growth of data processing has been dynamic and extensive. New services, made possible by computers, has made our everyday life more convenient and pleasant.
2. Data processing is defined as a planned series of actions and operations upon information using various forms of physical equipment to achieve a desired result. Data-processing systems consist of programs and physical equipment. The physical equipment consists of various units such as input and output, storage, and processing devices to handle information at electronic speeds.
3. Information demands are made by an organization both internally and externally. There is a growing need for rapid methods of processing data to satisfy these demands. All demands must be combined into an integrated data-processing system to satisfy the needs of all users without duplicating the effort of processing.

4. The sources of information emphasize the media upon which they are initially recorded. The problems of controlling the format of the input data can be controlled more accurately with internal data; whereas, external data is controlled by the individual organizations that create it. Both types of data are designed to accommodate the needs of the supplier.
5. The two types of data processing are business and scientific.

   Business data processing is characterized by the processing of many files, used repeatedly, requiring relatively few calculations and many output reports. The various management reports prepared by the computer help administrators make their everyday decisions and reduce the amount of paperwork.

   Mandatory reports are those reports that are required by governmental agencies, stockholders, customers, etc., that are usually prepared in a fixed format.

   Operational reports are those reports that aid management in their everyday decisions. They help to reduce the cost of operations and make the organization more competitive.

   Management-by-exception technique is a concept in which only the exceptional facts are noted for the decision maker to reduce the tedious task of reviewing the entire report.

   Scientific data processing is mathematically oriented, usually nonrepetitive, or file oriented, requiring small amounts of input and output with many calculations. The remarkable advances in space technology, weather forecasting, medicine, etc., are just a few of the spectacular achievements made possible by the tremendous calculating speed and storage of the computer.
6. There are many different uses for computers today. In business, computers are used for banking, airline reservations, inventory control, and designing new products. In the field of science, computers are used in space technology, weather predictions, biochemistry, and astronomy. In medicine, diagnosis, preparing prescriptions, and preparing health profiles are done through the computer. Computers help to simplify research, and courtroom and document reference storage. In the Congress, computers can brief representatives on major issues, and can track bills and resolutions. The uses for computers in the home range from personal computer games to household systems running all of the appliances.
7. The future of data processing will depend to a large extent upon the ingenuity of its users. The data-processing industry will continue to double in dollar volume every five years worldwide from 1970 to 1990.

   Computers will change conventional methods of teaching. They will provide an intensely visual, multisensory learning experience for youngsters.

   Computers will take on practically all the tasks of rote and drudgery which nature imposes upon us. A 78 percent increase overall in personnel employed in all computer-related occupations and associated industries is predicted by 1985. Computer systems of the future will be easier to use for nontechnical as well as technical personnel. The systems of the future will be larger, faster, and more reliable.

Identification Questions

Match the following terms with the statements below.

A. Business Data Processing
B. Data Processing
C. External Data
D. External Demands
E. Internal Data
F. Internal Demands
G. *Lexis*
H. Management by Exception
I. Mandatory Reports
J. Operational Reports
K. Personal Computer
L. Scientific Data Processing

1. The medium in which data is recorded at the time the transaction occurs.
2. Reports that aid management in making the many necessary decisions in every-day operations of a business.
3. Requests from management for information.
4. An electronic law library.
5. Characterized by the processing of many files, used repeatedly, requiring few calculations and many output reports.
6. A planned series of actions and operations upon information, using various forms of data-processing equipment, to achieve a desired result.
7. Data created outside of an organization.
8. Reports that are required by governmental agencies, stockholders, customers, etc.
9. Home or business computers that are programmable.
10. Characterized by being mathematically oriented, usually nonrepetitive in nature, or file oriented, requiring small amounts of input and output data with many calculations.
11. Requests for data originating outside of the organization.
12. Reduces the amount of detail that a decision maker is faced with.

Questions for Review

1. How does the computer affect our lives?
2. What is data processing and what units constitute a physical data-processing system?
3. What are the demands for data and how do they differ?
4. What constitutes a successful data-processing system?
5. What are the sources of information and how may the format of each be controlled? Give examples of each form.
6. What are the characteristics of business data processing? Give examples.
7. What are mandatory reports and how do they differ from operational reports?
8. What is management by exception and how does it aid the executive in making decisions?
9. What is scientific data processing and how does it differ from business data processing?
10. Briefly describe how computers are used in business, science, medical care, law, congress, and the home.
11. How will the computer affect our future?
12. Why is it important for all personnel directly or indirectly connected with data-processing equipment to possess some knowledge of its operations and functions?

Key Terms

- Business Data Processing
- Data Processing
- External Data
- External Demands
- Internal Data
- Internal Demands
- *Lexis*
- Management by Exception
- Mandatory Reports
- Operational Reports
- Personal Computers
- Scientific Data Processing

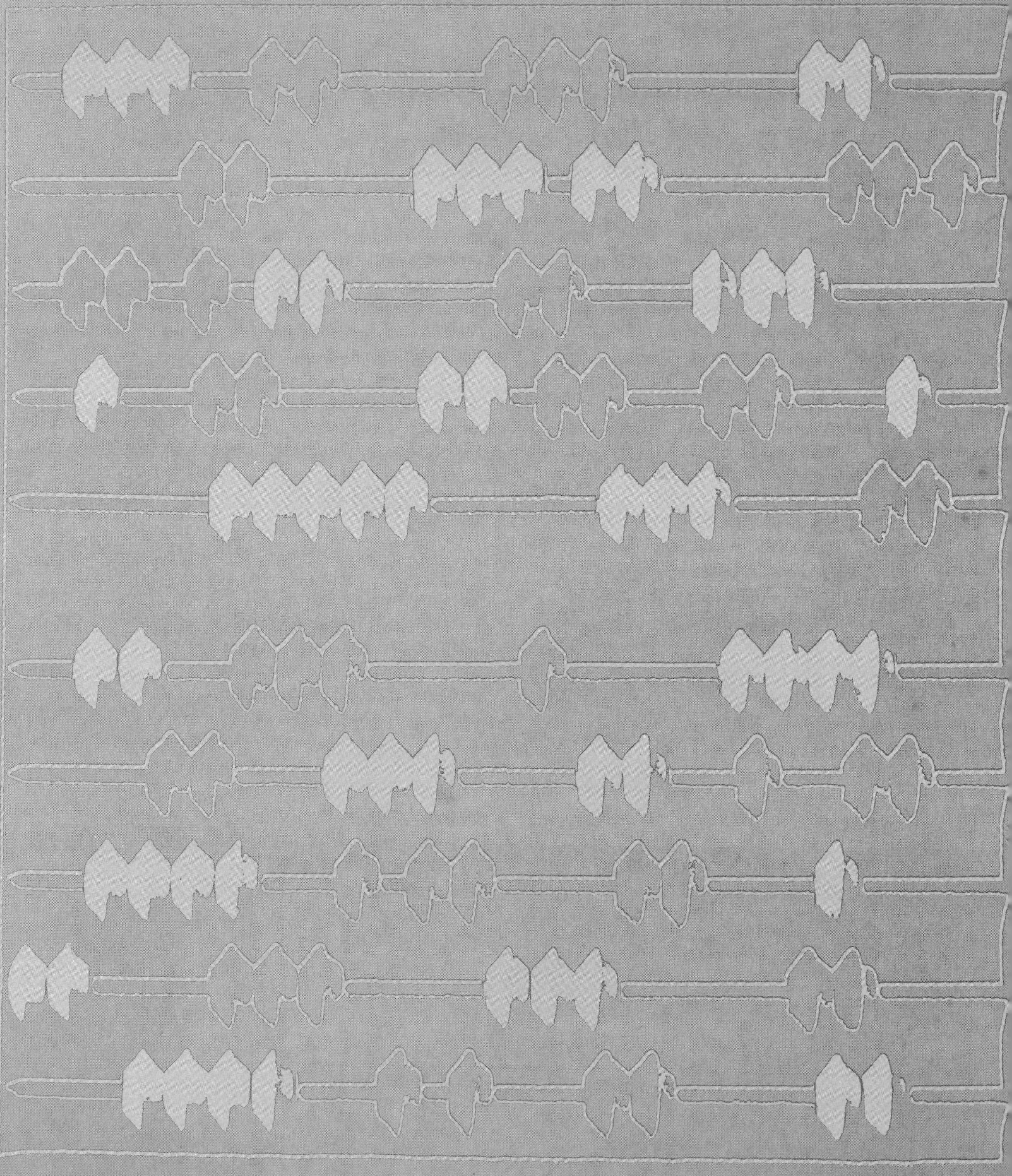

2 history of data processing and punched-card data processing

Chapter Outline

Chapter Objectives

The learning objectives of this chapter are

1. to realize that the computer did not just "happen" in the last twenty-five years but is an outgrowth of thousands of years of research and development.
2. to trace only the most significant events in data-processing history and show how each contributed to the development of the computer.
3. to show the major role that punched-card data processing played and still plays in the computer world.

4. to introduce punched-card data-processing concepts and to briefly explain operations and functions of the various punched-card machines.

5. to project what tomorrow's computer may look like and what role it will play in our future.

Although the most dramatic advances in processing information have occurred during the last quarter century, computing can be traced back to the primitive tribes. Ancient calculating involved the manipulation of the fingers to represent various numbers. The first data-processing tools were used to facilitate counting. Variations and refinements of counting led to fairly elaborate calculators involving addition, subtraction, multiplication, and division. As the work with numbers continued and the demand for information increased, more complex devices were developed (fig. 2.1).

To obtain thorough knowledge of data processing, we will study its history and background. Only then can we begin to realize that the computer is the outgrowth of thousands of years of research and development. This chapter traces the most significant events and shows how each contributed to the development of the computer. The history is brief, highlighting only those individuals and equipment that made vital contributions to modern data processing.

The Early Period

Abacus (3000 B.C.)

Today's computer is a direct descendant of a device that has been in existence for over four thousand years. The abacus, earliest known calculating device, has been used for so many years it is impossible to ascertain when it was first used (fig. 2.2). The design of the abacus is so simple that it has remained relatively unchanged from civilization to civilization. Movable beads are strung on a wire frame. These beads are divided into two groups to stipulate the various values of digits. Calculating or counting is performed by the manipulation of these beads.

The abacus was one of the first devices to designate the position of a number to represent a value. Usually in a decimal scale separate wires represent units, tens, hundreds, etc.

The abacus is used in the Far East by over half of the world's population. Many abacus operators have become so adept to the manipulation of the beads that they rival the speed of clerks using modern adding machines.

Jacquard Loom (1801)

Joseph Marie Jacquard developed an automatic loom which revolutionized the textile industry. Intricate designs were woven into the cloth using this loom. His machine was able to follow the instructions on a punched card. The punched-card principle was later used by Babbage in his "analytical machine" and by Hollerith in his punched-card machines.

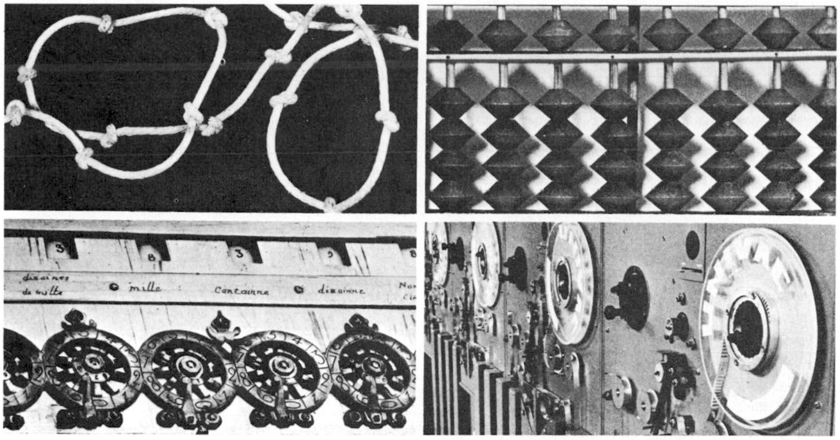

Figure 2.1 These examples show how calculating machines have evolved.

Figure 2.2 An abacus.

Babbage (1850)

Charles Babbage, an English mathematician and inventor, worked on desk calculators that revealed to him the feasibility of a machine that would greatly simplify the preparation of mathematical tables. While these simpler machines were still in their early development, he proposed the construction of two additional machines, the first of which he called a "difference engine"(fig. 2.3). This machine, designed for the construction and printing of mathematical tables, failed because the necessary parts could not be manufactured precisely. His second machine, the "analytical engine," was designed for general scientific calculation and stored data that could be manipulated.

Although Babbage's basic designs were good, he was never able to complete either of these machines. Babbage's work is, however, received as an important contribution to the later engineering of the computer.

Punched-Card Data-Processing History

Punched-card history began with Dr. Herman Hollerith, a statistician employed by the United States Census Bureau, who in 1880 was experimenting with a punched-card mechanism. He developed a working model that utilized the unit record principle, which coded and represented data by holes in a card.

Figure 2.3 Babbage's "difference engine."

Figure 2.4 The first census tabulator.

Realizing the potential of punched-card data processing, Dr. Hollerith organized the Tabulating Machine Company in 1896 to enter the commercial sales market. By the year 1900, Dr. Hollerith had developed an automatic sorting machine, which could sort at the rate of 300 cards per minute; a card-punch machine; and a semiautomatic tabulating machine (fig. 2.4). In 1924, the Tabulating Machine Company merged with the Time Recording Company and the Dayton Scale Company to form a new company, known as the International Business Machines Corporation.

Following Dr. Hollerith to the Census Bureau was a little-known statistical engineer, James Powers, who displayed some original ideas for punched cards. Powers developed a sorting machine, card-punch machines, and tabulators, which were used in the 1910 census. In 1925, he sold his patent rights to the Remington Rand Corporation.

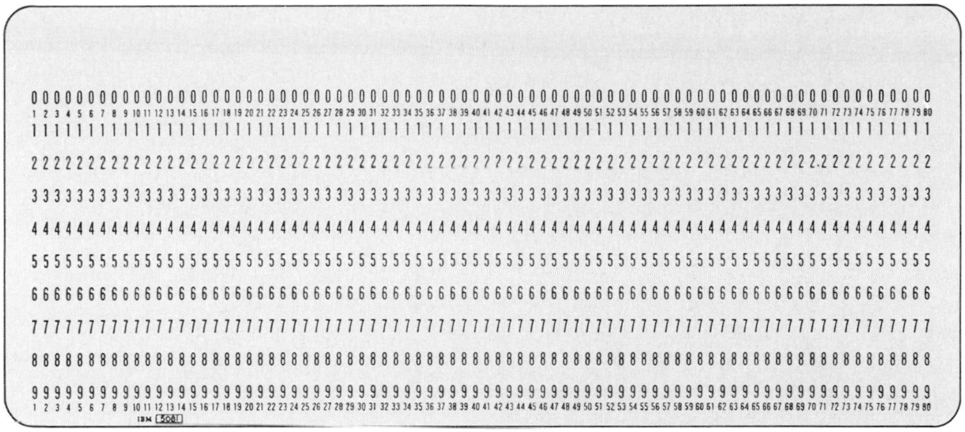

Figure 2.5 The Hollerith 80-column card.

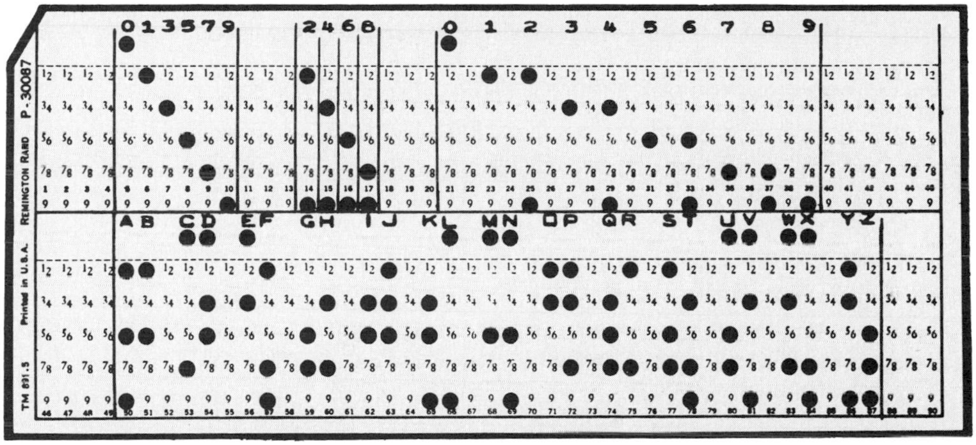

Figure 2.6 The Powers 90-column card.

Before World War II, there were just these two companies engaged in the punched-card data-processing field in the United States—the IBM Corporation with the "Hollerith" 80-column card (fig. 2.5) and the Remington Rand Corporation with the "Powers" 90-column card (fig. 2.6). Little progress was made in the data-processing field during the war.

Card Data-Recording Media and Equipment

Punched-card data processing is the procedure of recording, manipulating, and reporting information through the use of holes punched in a card (fig. 2.7). These holes in the card actuate machines to perform certain operations automatically.

Punched cards represent a versatile and important technique in data processing. They are commonly used in the preparation of computer programs. Instructions for the computer are punched into predefined fields of a card (fig. 2.8). Besides serving as an input media, the punched cards are used as original documents, such as checks,

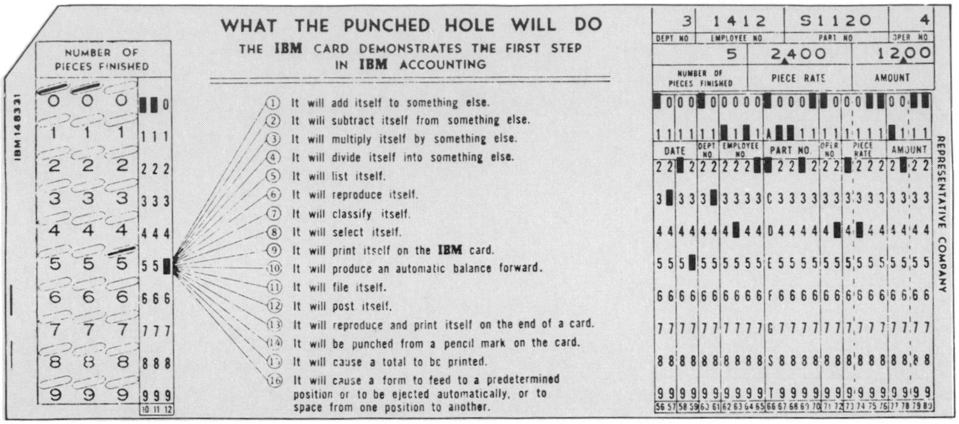

Figure 2.7 What a punched hole will do.

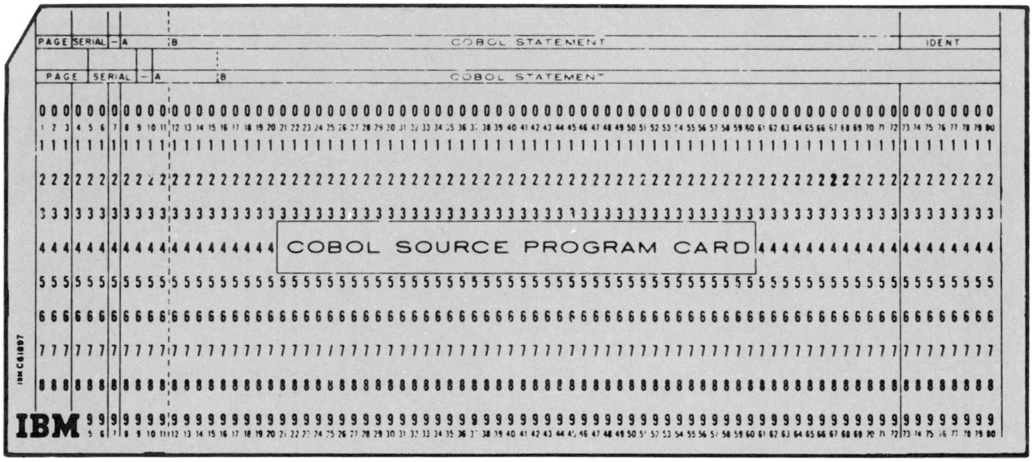

Figure 2.8 The COBOL program card.

time cards, invoices, and many other forms. Since the reliability of the output of data-processing equipment depends to a large extent upon the accuracy of the input data, it is essential that the information be recorded with great care.

There are a variety of uses for punched-card data processing. Primarily, it provides an input media that enters information into a machine. In addition, the card provides an output media for the equipment. The machine language of the card establishes the communication between human beings and equipment. The punched card also stores information in the form of machine processible files so that this information can be available for use when needed.

Unit Record Principle

The unit record principle of punched cards implies that the information concerning a single transaction is usually recorded in one card. This permits each card to be processed with other cards or other input media on a single record basis (fig. 2.9).

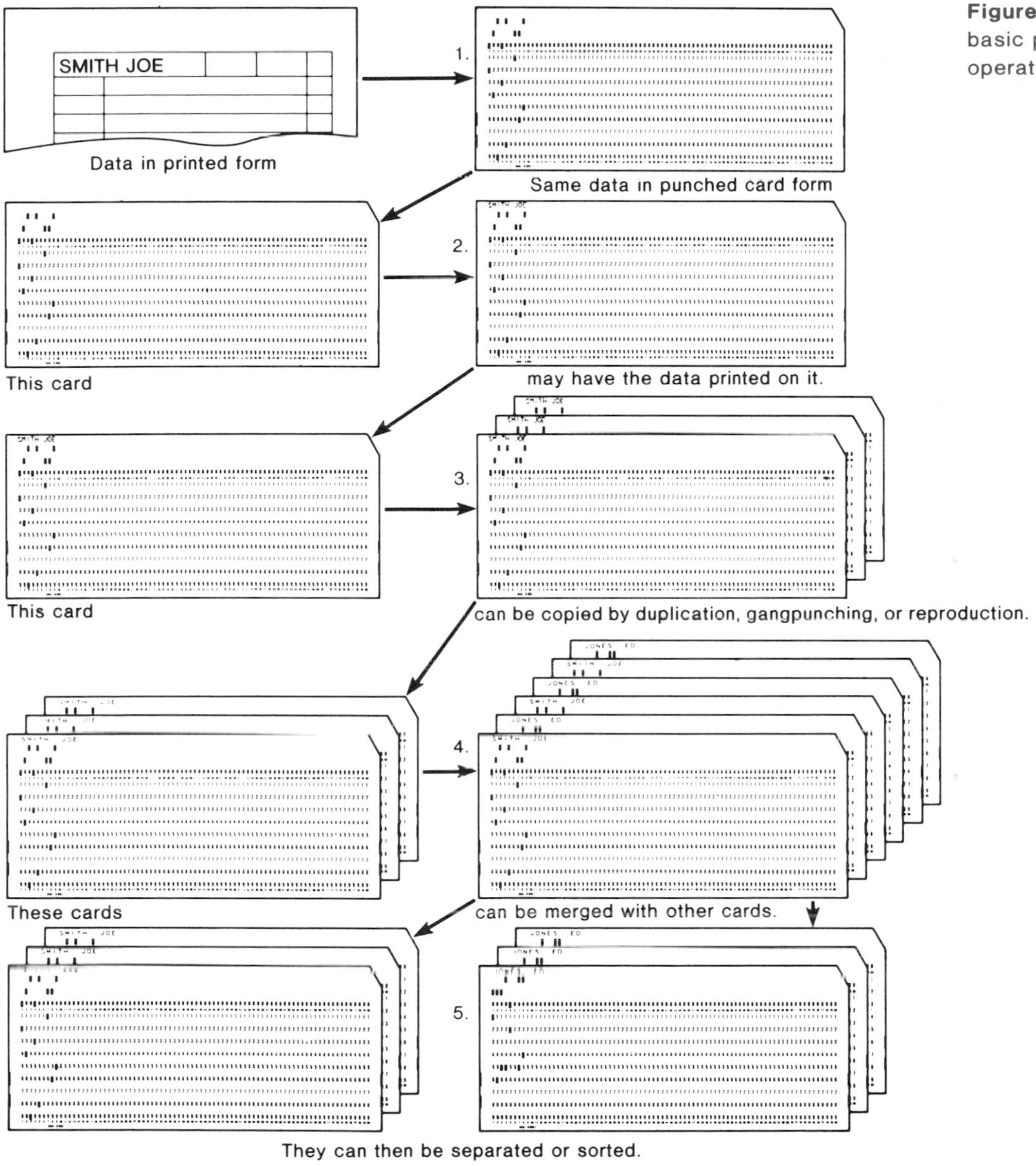

Figure 2.9 The basic punched-card operations.

Because of the unit record principle, each card can be processed by each of the specialized punched-card machines. However, cards must be physically taken from one machine to another for processing (fig. 2.10).

Types of Cards

The initial step in any punched-card procedure is the conversion of source information from printed or handwritten documents to punched cards. Original data is transcribed

Figure 2.10 The various pieces of unit record equipment that cards can be processed through.

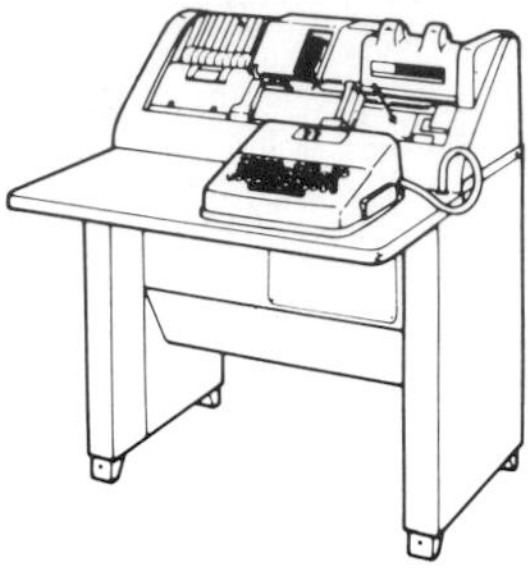

Card Punch

An operator can select data from printed records and, using a keyboard, can *record* it in cards, in the form of punched holes.

By pressing one key, the operator can cause data that has been recorded in one card to be *duplicated* (punched in the *same* places) in one or more cards that follow it.

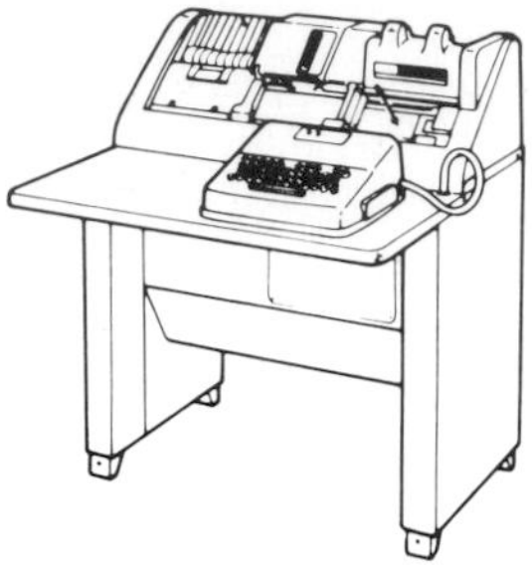

Card Verifier

An operator reads (from printed records) the data that has been recorded in the cards and, using a keyboard, *checks the holes* punched in those cards to ensure that the data has been recorded correctly.

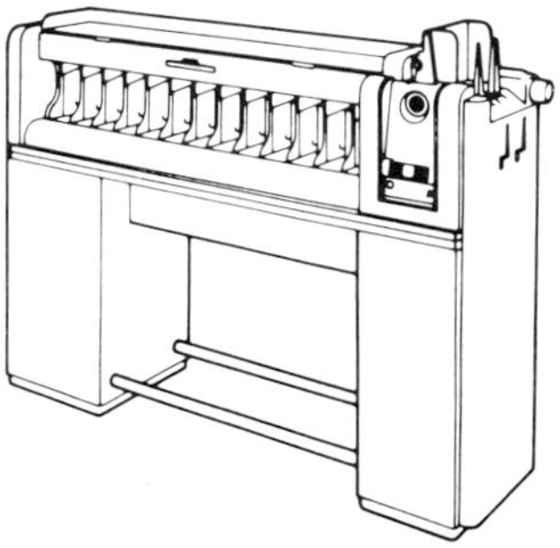

Sorter

The cards can be sorted (arranged in numerical or alphabetical order) for further machine operations or for filing.

Two files of cards can be *merged* (sorted together) to form one file, in numerical or alphabetical order.

Particular cards can be automatically *separated* from others in a file without disturbing the order of the rest of the cards.

Collator

Different types of cards, from two or more files, can be *collated* (combined so that each type of card is followed by another type, in a particular order).

Cards of the same type, arranged in numerical order in separate files, can be *merged* (combined to form one file, still in numerical order).

The collator can automatically *check the sequence of* the cards, to ensure that they are arranged in numerical order. Particular cards can be separated from others in a file, without changing the order of the rest of the cards.

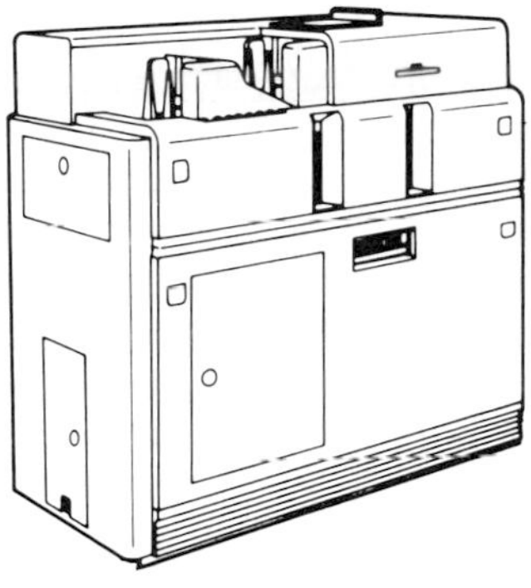

514 Reproducing Punch or
519 Document-Originating Machine

Data recorded in each card, as punched holes, can be *reproduced* (punched in another card) in order to produce a new file of punched cards.

Data that has been recorded (punched) in one card can be *gangpunched* (copied) in the same or *different* columns in one or more of the cards that follows.

Data recorded on each card by marking in pencil can be read by the machine (*mark sensing*) and recorded (punched) in that card.

If the 519 is used, some data punched in each card can be *end-printed* (printed across the end of the card). (The drawing shows the 514 Reproducing Punch.)

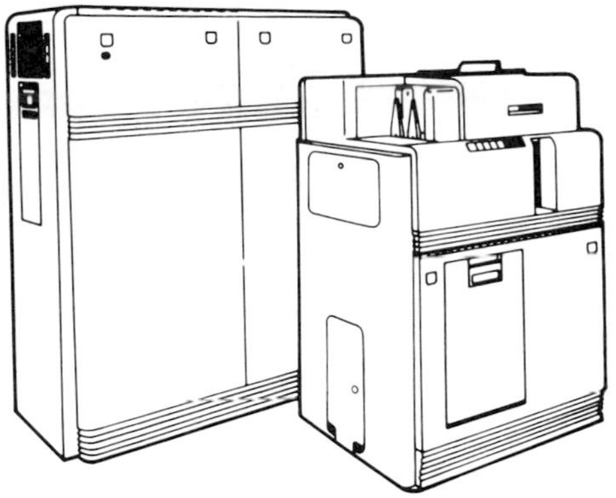

604 Electronic Calculating Punch and
521 Card Read Punch

The 521 can read data recorded in the form of punched holes; the 604 can perform *calculations* (adding, subtracting, multiplying, and dividing) with the data, and the 521 can then record (punch) the result in the same card.

Calculations can be performed on data from one or more cards, and results can be recorded (punched) in a following card.

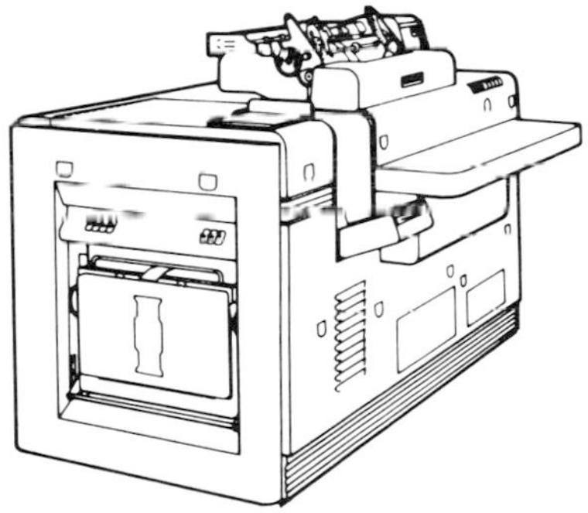

402 or 407 Accounting Machine

Data recorded in each card, as punched holes, can be listed (printed in a single line) on a report.

Simple calculations (adding and subtracting) can be performed with data recorded in the cards, and the results can be printed on a report.
(The drawing shows the 402 Accounting Machine.)

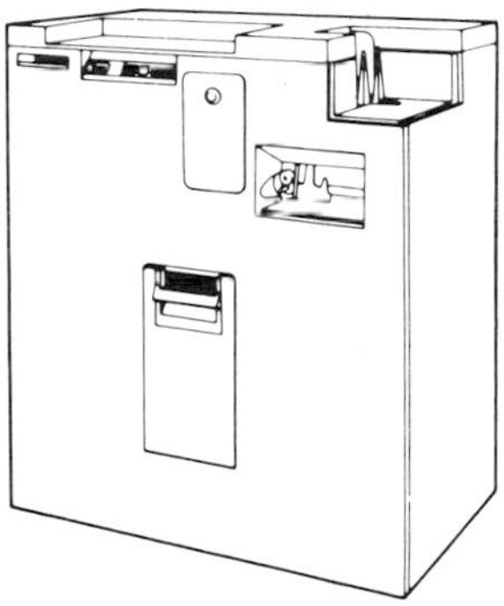

548 or 557 Interpreter

Data recorded in each card, in the form of punched holes, can be *printed* on that card, on either of two lines.

If the 557 is used for this operation, the data can be printed on any one of 25 lines.
In another 557 operation, data punched in *one* card can be printed on one or more cards that follow it.
(The drawing shows the 548 Interpreter.)

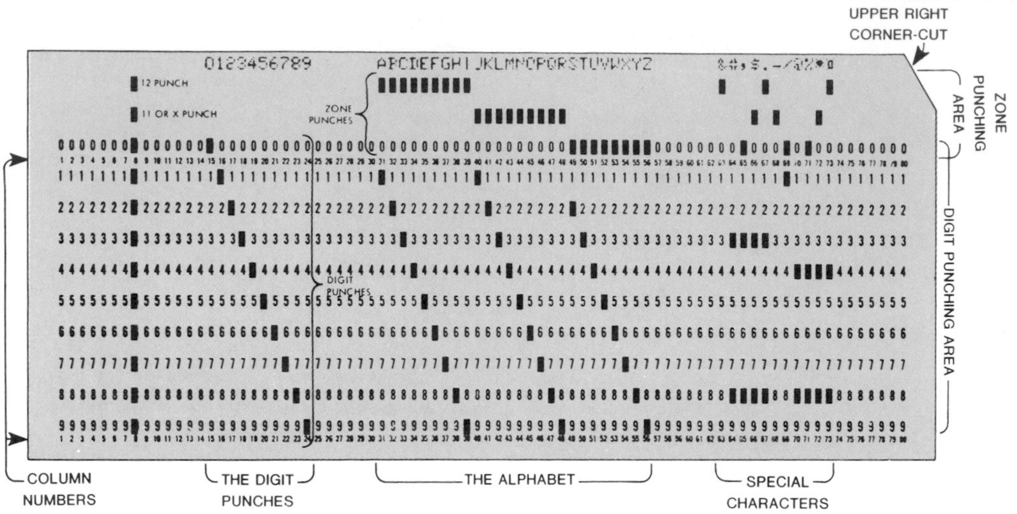

Figure 2.11 The various parts of the Hollerith card.

to punched cards by any of several types of card punches. Once the information is punched (recorded) in a card, the card is a permanent record. Its information can be used repeatedly and will be the same for each use. Since each card contains all the necessary information about a single transaction, all similar transactions can be easily grouped for further processing. There are two types of cards in use today—the "Hollerith" 80-column card and the 96-column card designed primarily for the IBM System/3 computers.

Hollerith 80-Column Card

The Hollerith card is divided into eighty vertical columns. In each of these columns, there are twelve possible punching positions (fig. 2.11). The top edge of the card is known as the *twelve* edge, and the bottom of the card is referred to as the *nine* edge. Each machine has a designation in the feed mechanism specifying how the card is to enter the machine. For example, *nine edge facedown* means the printed side of the card down and the nine edge facing the feeding mechanism of the machine.

The card is divided into two major sections. The upper three positions are known as the *zone* punches and contain holes in the 0, 11, and 12 position. The numeric section of the cards contains the digits 0 through 9. (The 0 punch may be either zone or numeric depending upon its use.) In order to accommodate any of the twenty-six letters of the alphabet in one column, a combination of zone and numeric punches are used. The zone and numeric punches are combined in the following manner to represent alphabetic characters.

A through I—represented by a 12 punch plus the numeric punches 1 through 9.

J through R—represented by an 11 punch plus the numeric punches 1 through 9.

S through Z—represented by a 0 punch plus the numeric punches 2 through 9.

Numeric information is represented by a single punch 0 through 9. Special characters, such as $,#,%,&, etc., may have 1, 2, or 3 punches in a single column.

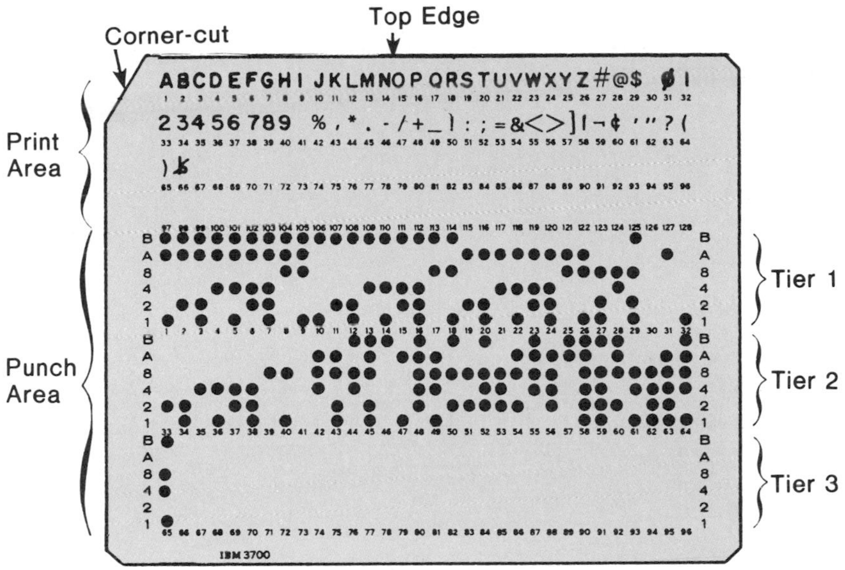

Figure 2.12 The IBM System/3 96-column card.

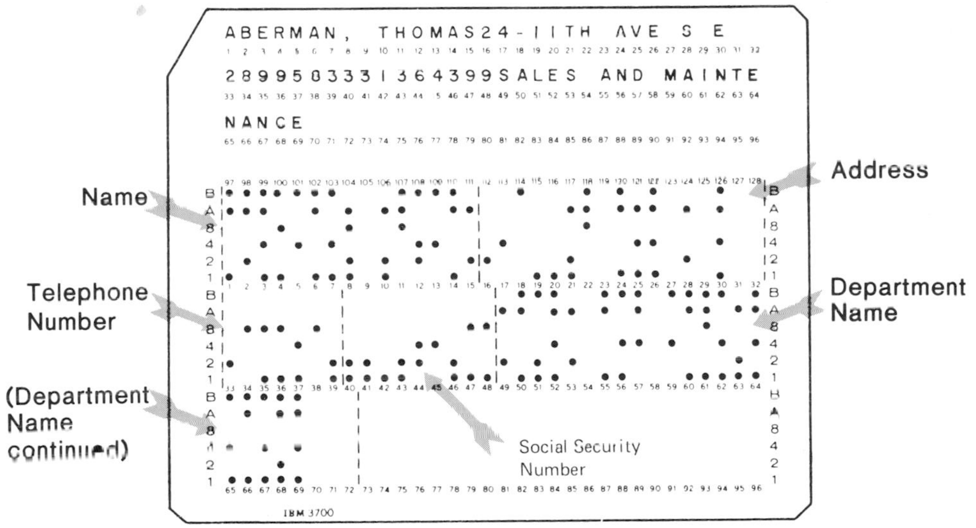

Figure 2.13 The IBM System/3 96-column card fields.

96-Column Card

The IBM Corporation designed a 96-column card for use in their System/3 series. The lower section of the card is the punch area, while the upper section of the card is the print area.

The lower section, or punch area, is divided into three equal, horizontal sections, called tiers. Each tier contains six vertical groups of six punch positions. There are thirty-two columns of punching positions in each tier (fig. 2.12, 2.13).

Figure 2.14 Card fields.

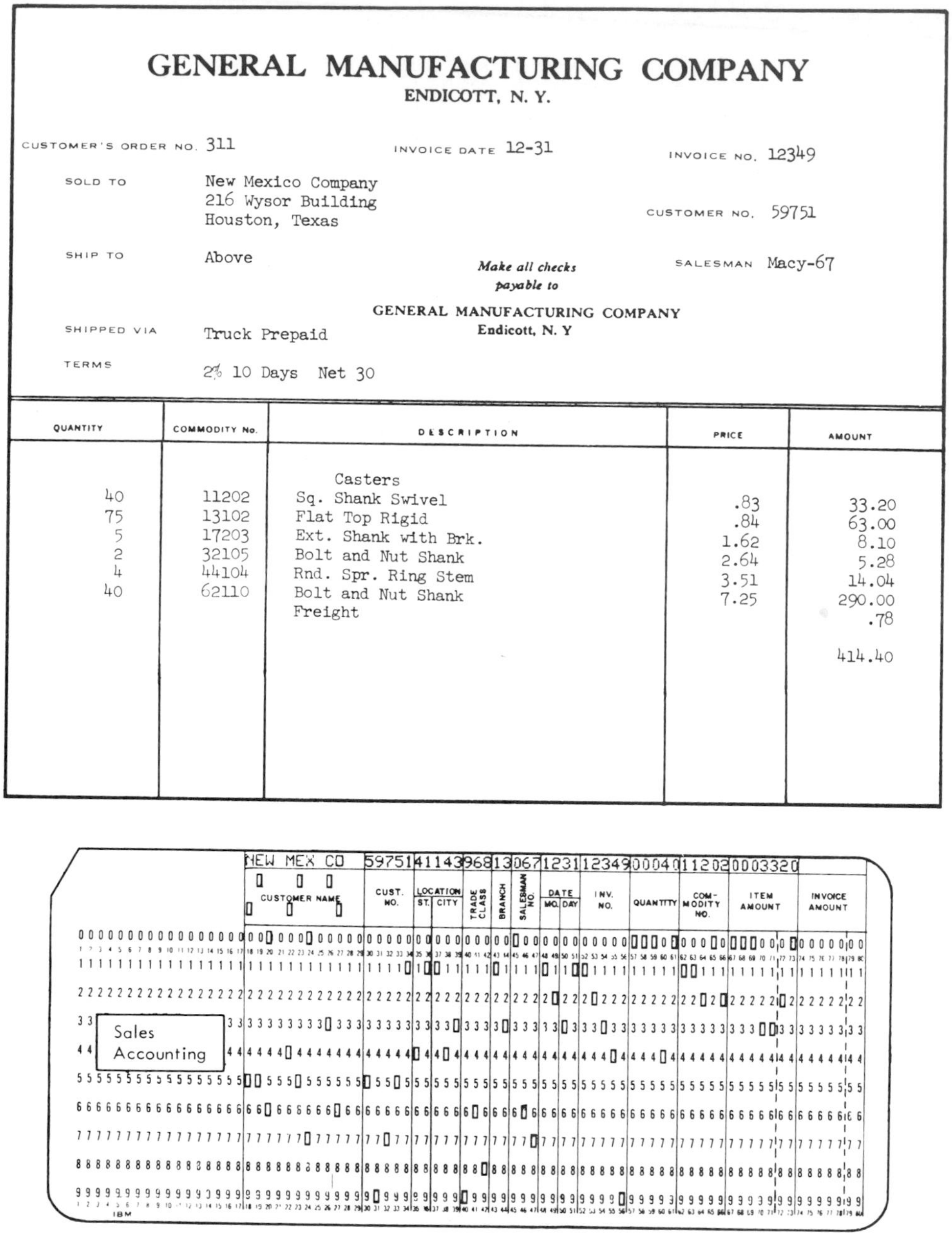

GENERAL MANUFACTURING COMPANY

ENDICOTT, N. Y.

CUSTOMER'S ORDER NO. 311 INVOICE DATE 12-31 INVOICE NO. 12349

SOLD TO New Mexico Company
216 Wysor Building
Houston, Texas

CUSTOMER NO. 59751

SHIP TO Above

Make all checks payable to
GENERAL MANUFACTURING COMPANY
Endicott, N. Y

SALESMAN Macy-67

SHIPPED VIA Truck Prepaid

TERMS 2% 10 Days Net 30

QUANTITY	COMMODITY No.	DESCRIPTION	PRICE	AMOUNT
		Casters		
40	11202	Sq. Shank Swivel	.83	33.20
75	13102	Flat Top Rigid	.84	63.00
5	17203	Ext. Shank with Brk.	1.62	8.10
2	32105	Bolt and Nut Shank	2.64	5.28
4	44104	Rnd. Spr. Ring Stem	3.51	14.04
40	62110	Bolt and Nut Shank	7.25	290.00
		Freight		.78
				414.40

Physical Characteristics of Cards

Data is usually recorded in a card in a group of consecutive columns called fields. A *field* is composed of a group of related characters that are treated as one unit of information (fig. 2.14). The information to be included in the card is determined by the requirements of the reports and documents which will be prepared from it. A field can consist of one to eighty columns depending upon the particular requirements for information to be recorded in it. There are three basic types of fields, *numeric, alphabetic,* and *alphameric.* Numeric fields consist only of the digits 0 through 9. Alphabetic fields may contain any of the letters of the alphabet plus blanks. Alphameric fields may contain any character, such as numerals, alphabetic, or special characters. Field lengths are determined by the maximum length of information entered in the field. For example, a company may have 80,000 employees with no prospect of having more than 99,999 employees; therefore, a five-column field would be assigned to the recording of the employee numbers. However, if the company is expanding its operations and an increase in the labor force to 100,000 or more is anticipated, a six-digit field should be assigned to accommodate numbers up to 999,999. The left-hand column of a field is known as the *high-order* position, while the right-hand column is known as the *low-order* position.

A *record* consists of a field or a series of fields normally grouped together for input and output operations. A card reader reads an entire card, while a card punch punches an entire card. A record can be reused and can become a permanent record; therefore, it should contain all the necessary information about a single transaction.

Corner cuts, upper left or upper right, are used to identify a card type and insure that all cards are facing the same direction. Corner cuts are also used to separate groups of cards; master from detail cards.

Cards may be in various colors and with different colored stripes across the front of the card. These colors and stripes are further identification for particular card groups. For example, a yellow card may represent an inventory balance card, while the same card format in green may signal a price card.

Card-Punch Machine Operations

The initial operation in punched-card data processing is the transcribing of written records into punched cards. This is one of the most expensive operations in data processing as it involves one operator to one machine. For many years, numerous efforts have been made to reduce the cost of card punching through various methods of converting source documents into a machine-language processible format. Numerous innovations in input processing, such as punching source document information directly onto disk or magnetic tape and the increasing use of source documents as direct input to data-processing systems without transcription, have lessened the role that punched cards play in a data-processing installation. However, the amount of card punching required is substantial, and there is still a big demand for trained card-punch operators.

The primary function of a card-punch machine is to convert a source document into a punched card. The card punch has numerous other uses.

Replaces cards that have been damaged in processing.

Corrects cards that have incorrect punches.

Prepares computer program cards.

Prepares test cards for the various machines.

Figure 2.15 The IBM numeric and combination keyboards and a drawing of the characters on a keyboard.

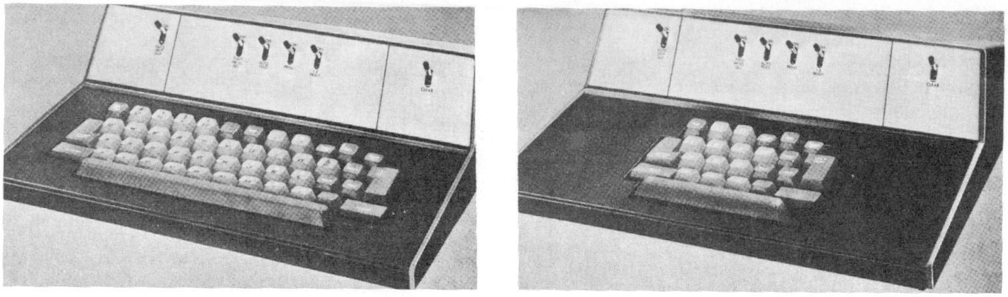

IBM 29 Numeric and Combination Keyboards

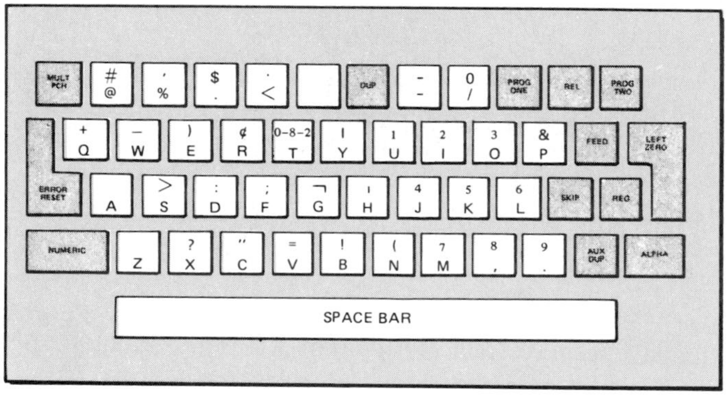

The operation of a card punch is similar to the operation of a typewriter. When a typist depresses a key, a character is printed on a piece of paper. When a card-punch operator depresses a key, a hole or combination of holes will be punched into the card. On the typewriter, numeric keys are located at the top of the keyboard. Since most card punching is composed of numeric information, the numeric keys are closely grouped for one-hand ten-key operation (fig. 2.15). This close grouping eliminates the back-and-forth motion that would be required if the numeric keys were arranged in the same manner as they are on a typewriter. (Numeric punching with one hand frees the left hand for document handling, thus expediting the punching operation.) The operations of the latest card-punch machine, the IBM model 129, are described in the appendix (fig. 2.16).

Reproducing Machines

Optimum efficiency in data processing is the recording of data once, as close to the beginning of the process as possible, and then using this recorded information repeatedly without duplication of the original effort. All or portions of the recorded information, which might be needed at various stages of a program, can be reused without requiring duplication of the recording. In some instances, however, partial changes must be made to update the original record. Common information, such as dates, batch numbers, etc., must be punched in a file of cards.

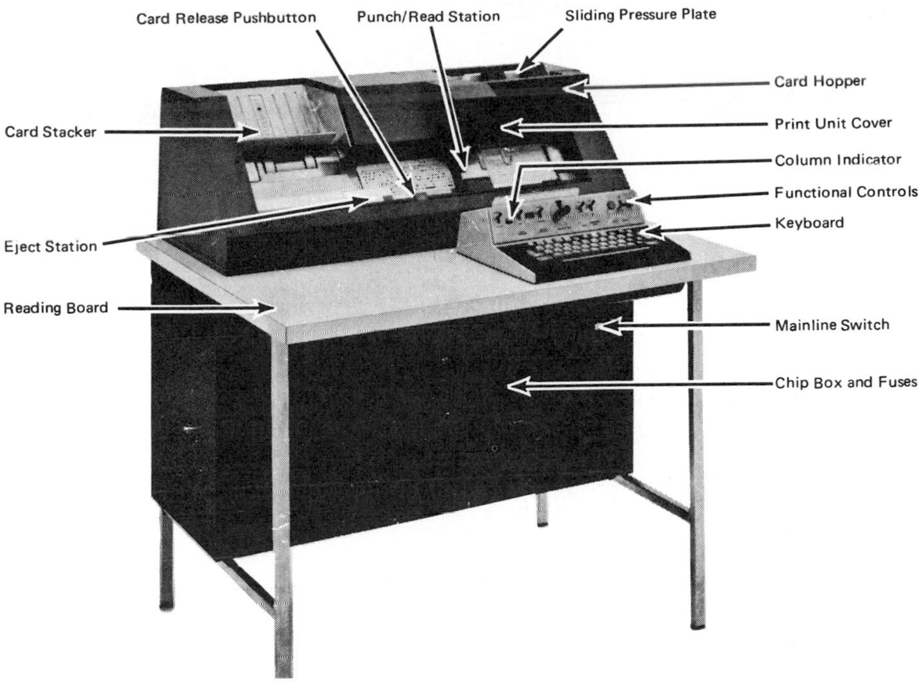

Figure 2.16 The IBM 129 card data recorder.

When the records are maintained in punched-card format, the repetitious operations can be performed automatically. *Automatic punches* were designed to transfer information from one card to another rapidly with a high degree of duplication accuracy (fig. 2.17).

The principal operations performed by the automatic punches are reproducing, gangpunching, and comparing. All of these operations can be performed simultaneously while the card is being processed.

Reproducing is the transferring of information from one card to another either in the same field or in different fields (fig. 2.18)

Gangpunching is the punching of common information from a master card into detail cards, usually in the same field (fig. 2.19).

Comparing is the checking of the source and the duplicated card for agreement of punches (fig. 2.20).

Interpreters

One of the basic concepts of data processing is the conversion of source data into machine language. The machine can sense the holes in the cards and translate them into processible data. However, if the cards are to be used as documents as well as for automatic production of reports, it is desirable that the punched information be translated into a printed form on the card itself. Machines designed to print information

Figure 2.17 An automatic punch device.

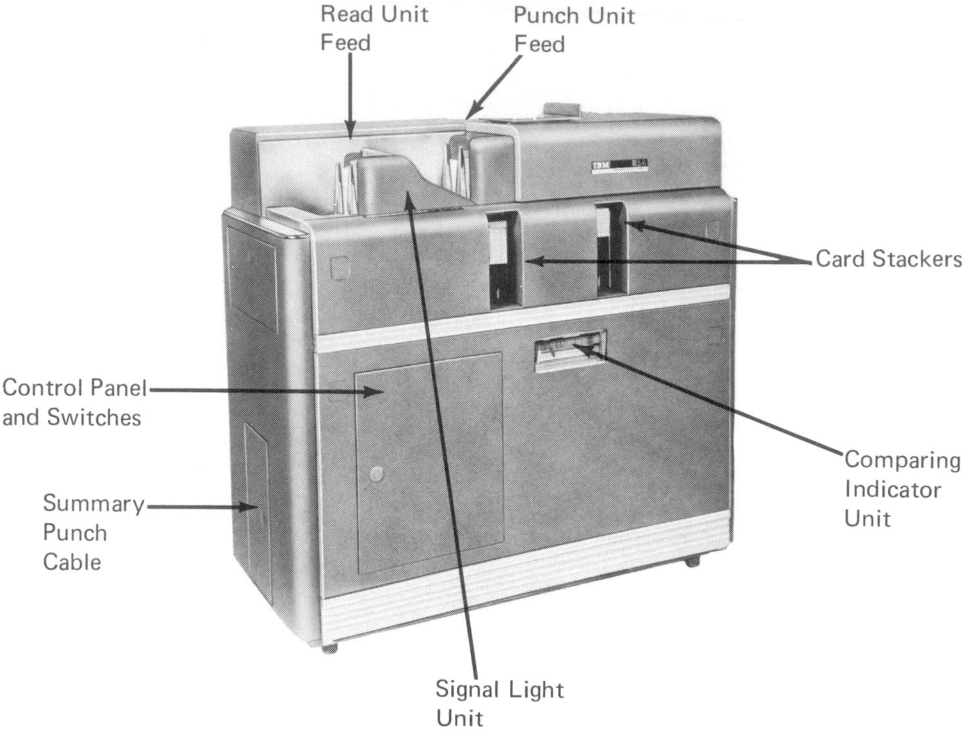

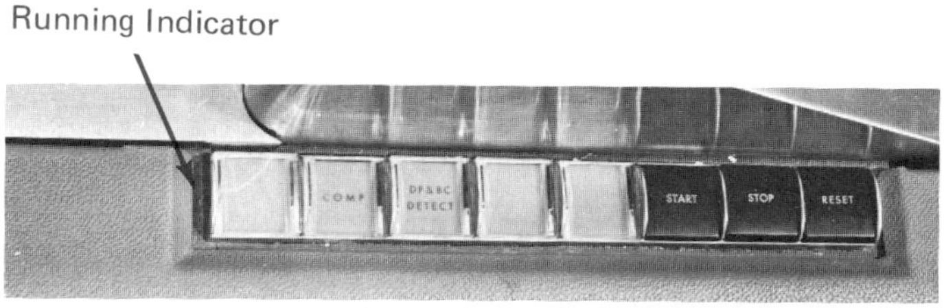

Figure 2.18 Reproducing.

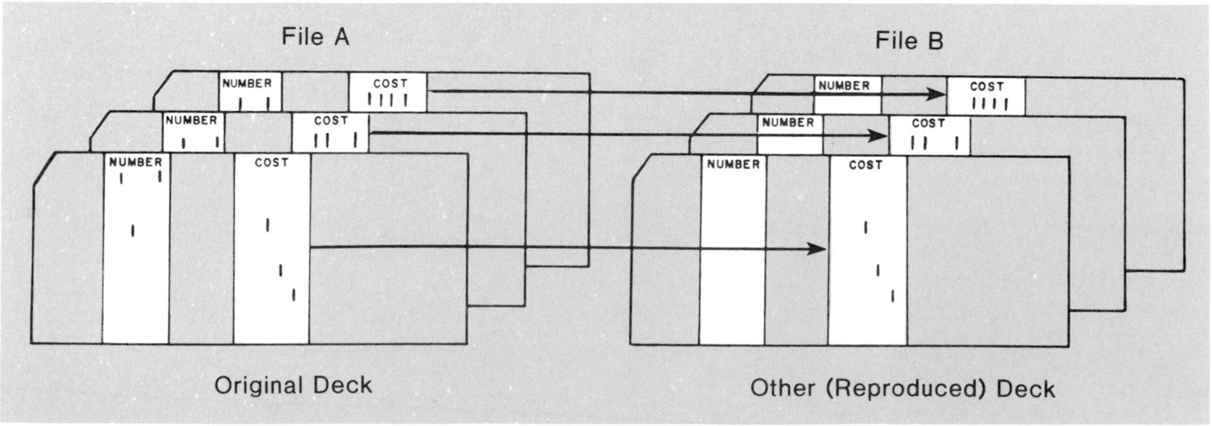

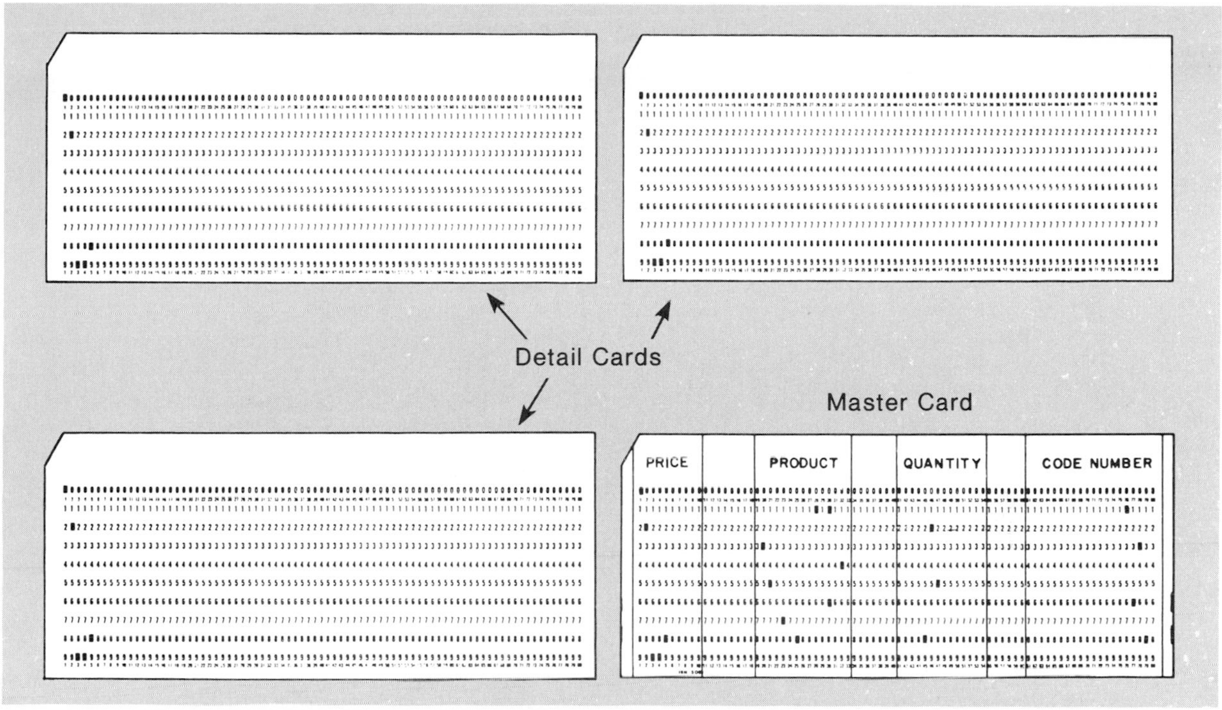

Figure 2.19
Gangpunching.

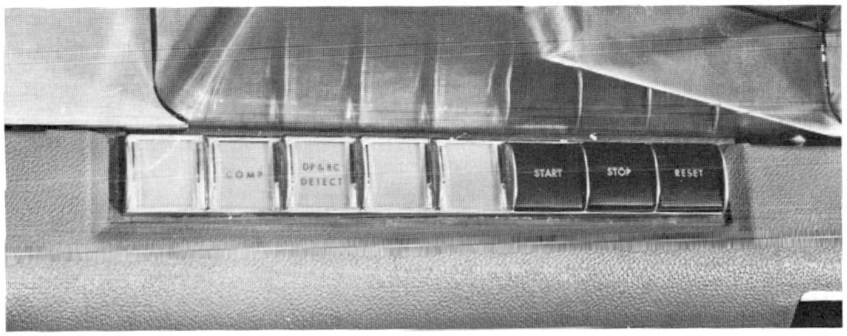

Figure 2.20
Comparing light and indicator.

that has been punched into cards are called *interpreters* (fig. 2.21). Thus the information in the cards can be read with the same ease as one reads a typewritten document.

Sorters

An important part of any data-processing system is the sorting and classifying of records. Using punched cards gives the advantage of being able to arrange record cards in sequence with the aid of high-speed sorters. *The main function of the sorter is to arrange cards in a predetermined sequence.* The sorter may also be used to select cards with a specific punch from a group of cards (fig. 2.22). Several models of sorters are available with various speeds and features. The selection of a particular model depends on the nature and volume of data to be sorted.

Figure 2.21 An example of an interpreter.

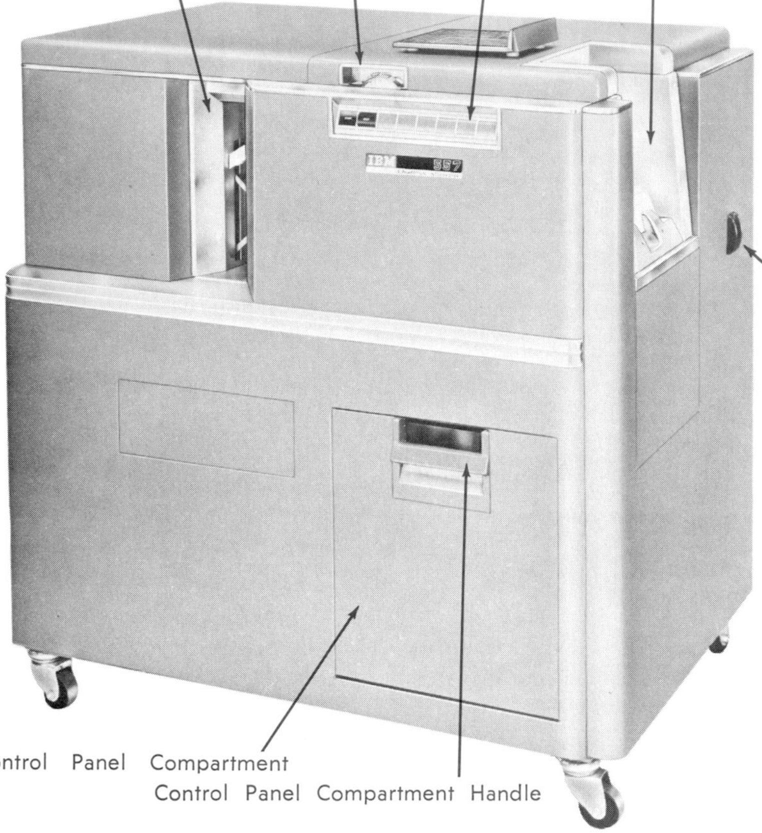

IBM Model 82 Sorter-Operating Principles And Features

1. The card-feed hopper has a capacity of 1,200 cards and is located at the right end of the machine.
2. Cards are placed in the feed hopper facedown with the nine edge facing the throat of the machine.
3. The column to be sorted is selected by turning the handle to the desired column. Each turn of the handle moves the reading brush one column. In a sorting operation, the machine sorts from the low-order position (rightmost position of field) to the high-order position (leftmost position of field) of a particular field. The sorter can sort only one column at a time.
4. There are thirteen possible pockets for the cards to fall into; one pocket for each possible punch position plus a reject pocket to hold cards without any punch in that particular column.
5. Sorting is automatic. All cards are fed from the bottom of the deck. Automatic shutoff occurs as soon as the last card is fed or as soon as any pocket is filled.

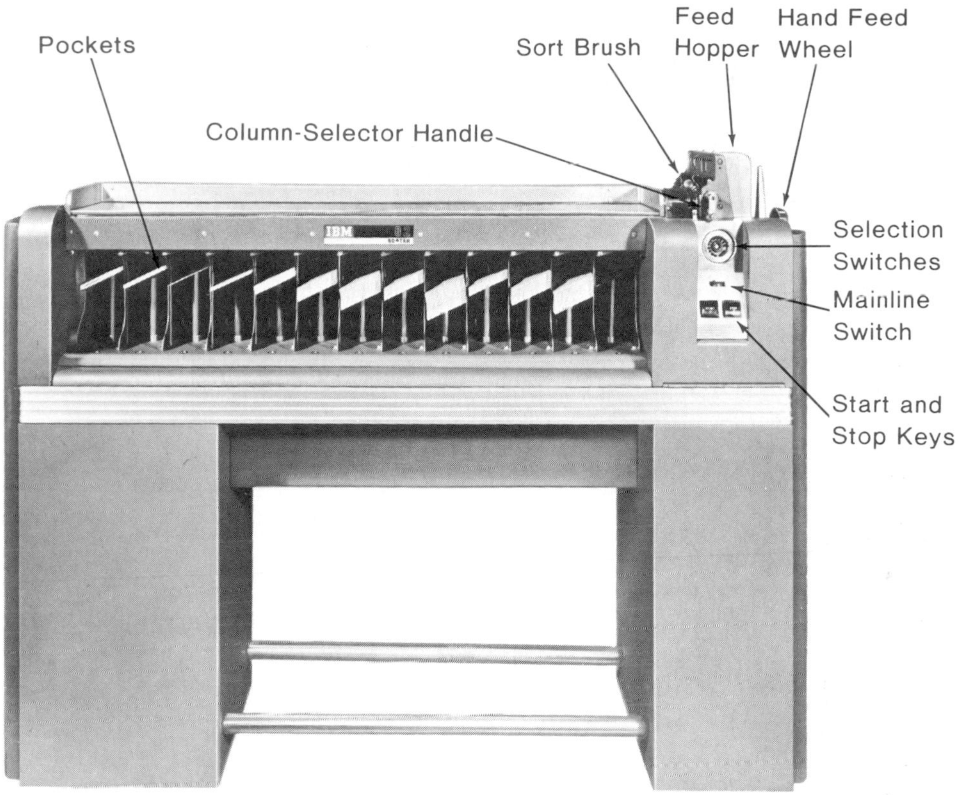

Figure 2.22 An example of a sorter.

6. Selection switches make it possible to separate certain types of cards without disturbing the basic sequence of the cards. An alphabetic sorting switch is used in sorting cards alphabetically.

Numerical Sorting

To arrange cards in a numerical sequence, each column in a field requires one sort. The first sort should be on the low-order position of a field (rightmost column). After the sort is completed, the cards are removed from the pockets right to left—the zero pocket, the one pocket on top of the zero, the two pocket on top of the previous combined group, and so forth, until all ten pockets are emptied. Cards are now ready for the next column to be sorted. The process is continued until the entire field is sorted, with the last sort being the high-order position (leftmost column).

Note—All selection switches must be in the outer position before the sorting operation is started.

In certain sorting operations, it is necessary to sort more than one field. The sequence of sorting is inverse to the importance of each field. The least important (minor) is sorted first. Next the more important field (intermediate), and finally the most important field (major) is sorted (assuming that three fields are to be sorted). For example, to arrange cards in sequence by area (major), territory (intermediate), and customer number (minor), the cards should be sorted to customer number sequence first, then territory, and finally area number to complete the sort.

Alphabetic Sorting

Alphabetic sorting requires two sorts per column, since each letter is represented by two holes, punched in a single column. The letters A through I combine a 12 punch with the numeric punches 1 through 9; J through R combines an 11 punch with the numeric punches 1 through 9; and S through Z combines a 0 punch with the numeric punches 2 through 9.

Each column is sorted on the numerical portion of the letters first. The cards should fall into pockets 1 through 9. When the alphabetic switch (red) on an 82 sorter is pushed towards the center of the dial, the cards will re-sort on the same column. This time the cards will fall into pockets 0, 11, and 12. Alphabetic items may contain blanks; therefore, if any cards fall into the reject pocket on the first sort of a particular column, it is not necessary to sort rejected cards a second time on the same column. However, at the completion of the sort, these rejected cards should be placed in front of the file when proceeding to the next column.

Collators

One of the major problems in data processing is updating and maintaining files. Records must be kept current and accessible. Filing and extracting cards from a file are necessary to keep the files up to date.

The principal function of the collator is to compare two or more fields in the same or different cards, and based on this comparison, to separate, segregate, or combine the cards (fig. 2.23). Separation of a file divides one group of cards into two groups. Segregation of a file arranges cards into specific groups. Combining files merges two groups into one.

Basic Operations

The basic operations that can be performed on the collator are:

1. *Checking the sequence of a file of cards (in either ascending or descending sequence).* For example, each card in an ascending file should have a control number equal to or greater than the preceding number—1245, 1247, 1247, 1251, etc.
2. *Selecting specific cards from a file of cards.* For example, it may be necessary to select card(s) from a file without disturbing the sequence of the file. Numbers 10,000 to 19,999 (or any numbers desired) can be extracted from the file in one pocket without altering the sequence of the other group of cards in another pocket of the machine.
3. *Merging.* Two files of cards are combined into one file (fig. 2.24).
4. *Match-Merging.* Only matched (equal) cards are merged with a selection of the unmatched cards from both files. For example, in a payroll application it may be necessary to merge only the cards of employees who have worked during the current pay period. The master employee name cards are placed in one card feed, while the detail current earning cards are placed in the other card feed. The merged cards represent the matched cards (employees that worked the current period). One pocket contains unmatched master employee cards (employees that

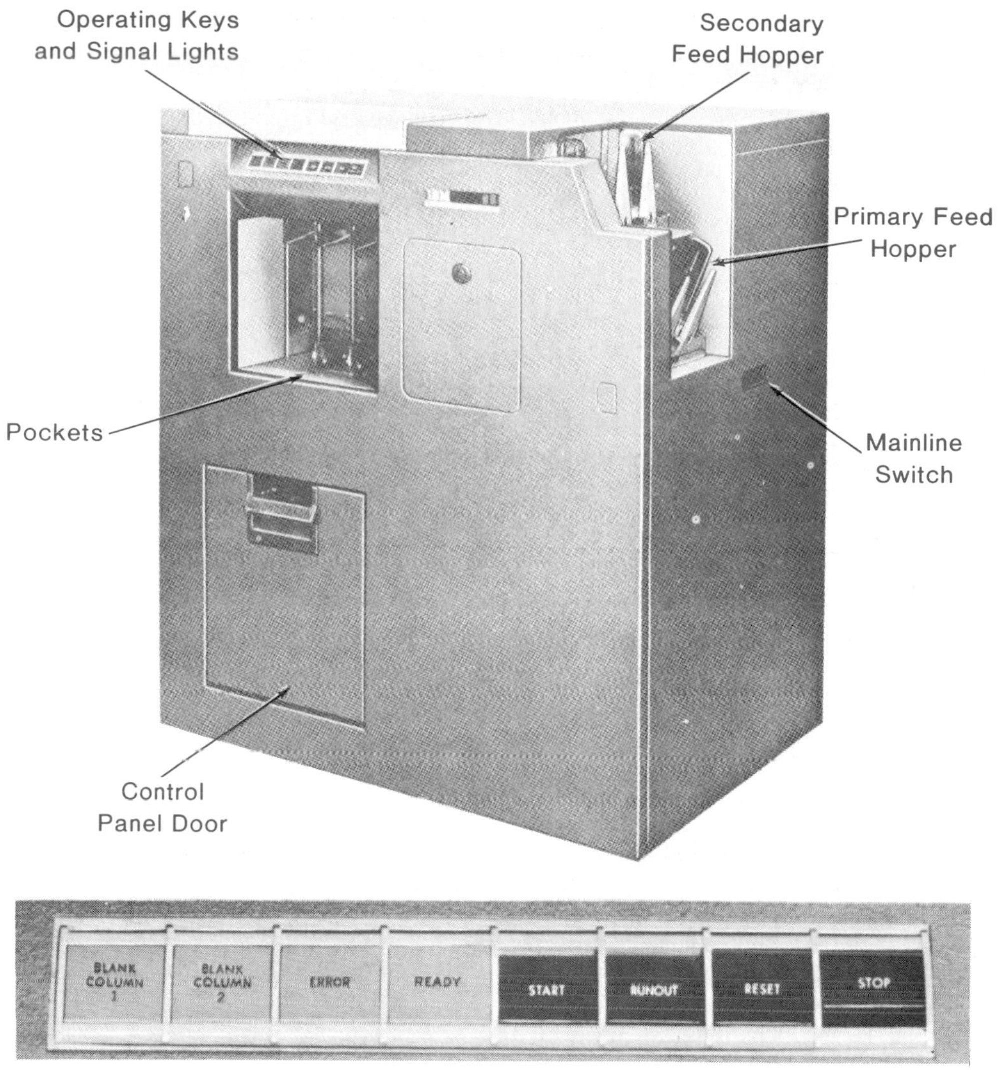

Figure 2.23 An example of a collator.

did not work); the other pocket contains unmatched detail current earning cards (new employees or incorrect employee numbers) (fig. 2.25).

5. *Match-Selecting.* Two files are matched with a selection of matched cards (not merged) and a selection of unmatched cards from both files. Using the same example as the match-merge example, instead of merging the matched master employee name and detail current earning cards, the cards could be selected in adjoining pockets (fig. 2.26).

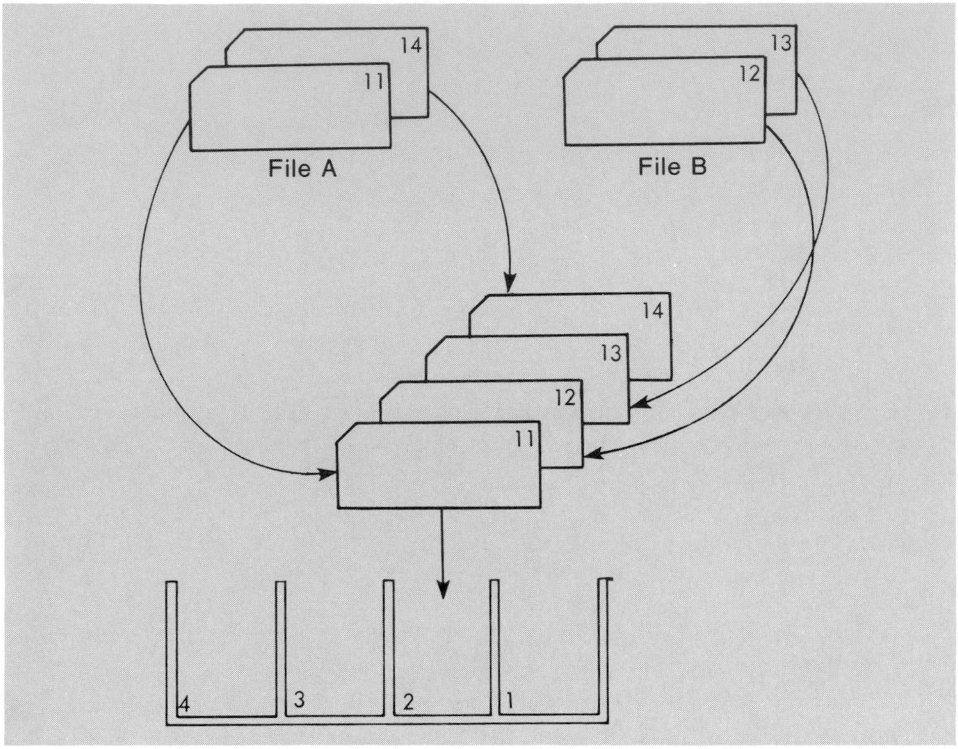

Figure 2.24 An example of merging.

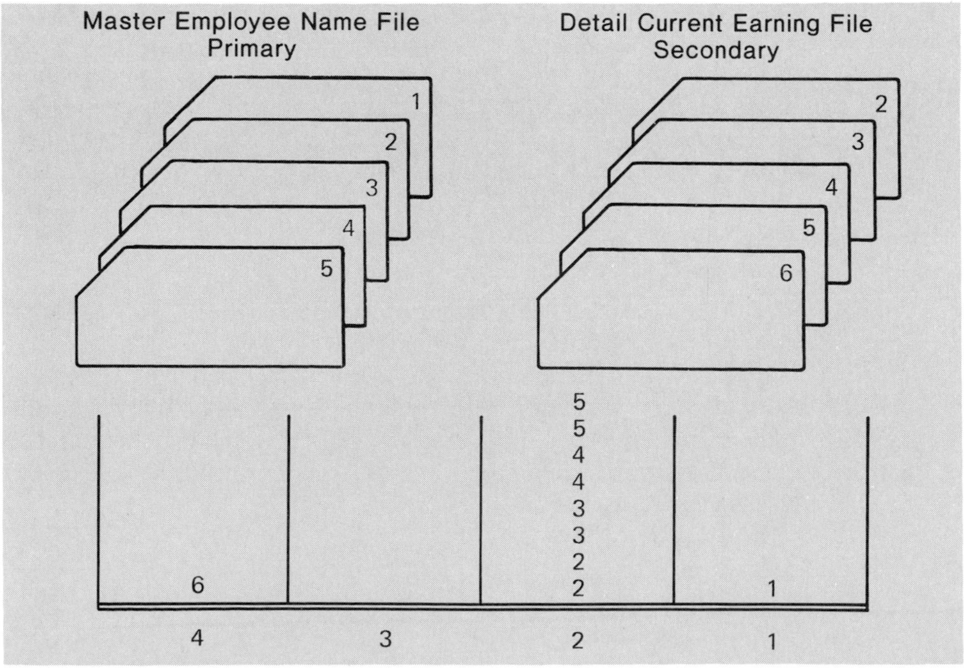

Figure 2.25 An example of match-merging.

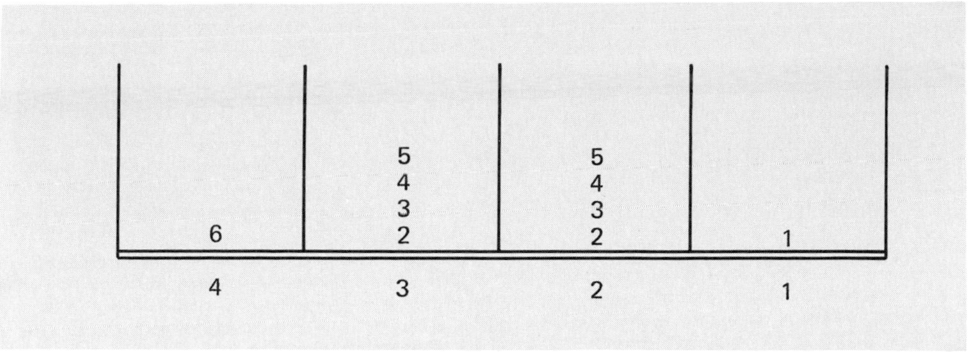

Figure 2.26 An example of match-selecting.

Additional Operations

Although most of the collator time is spent on the basic operations, there are still many other operations that can be performed on the collator.

1. The selection of certain types of cards from a file, such as the first card of a group, the last card of a group, single cards, cards within a given number group, cards with numbers between two levels, etc.
2. The selection of zero balances in certain fields.
3. The selection of duplicate cards.
4. The selection of cards out of sequence.
5. The detection of blank columns on a card.
6. The insertion of a predetermined number of cards behind or in front of each group.
7. Consecutive number checking.

Accounting Machines

Accounting machines automatically feed cards and print reports (fig. 2.27). The information read from the card is added, subtracted, selected, or compared according to the requirements of individual reports. Information can be read from any of the eighty columns of the card with complete flexibility provided in the arrangement of the printed output. Summary cards may be punched simultaneously with the preparation of the report.

The basic functions of the accounting machine are:

1. Summarizing in counters the information punched in cards through addition and subtraction.
2. Printing the summarized information in the forms of totals and subtotals.
3. Punching the summarized information into cards when the accounting machine is connected to the punch by cable.
4. Printing reports.
5. Positioning continuous form paper automatically through tape-controlled carriage.

All these functions can be performed simultaneously as the card is being read by the machine.

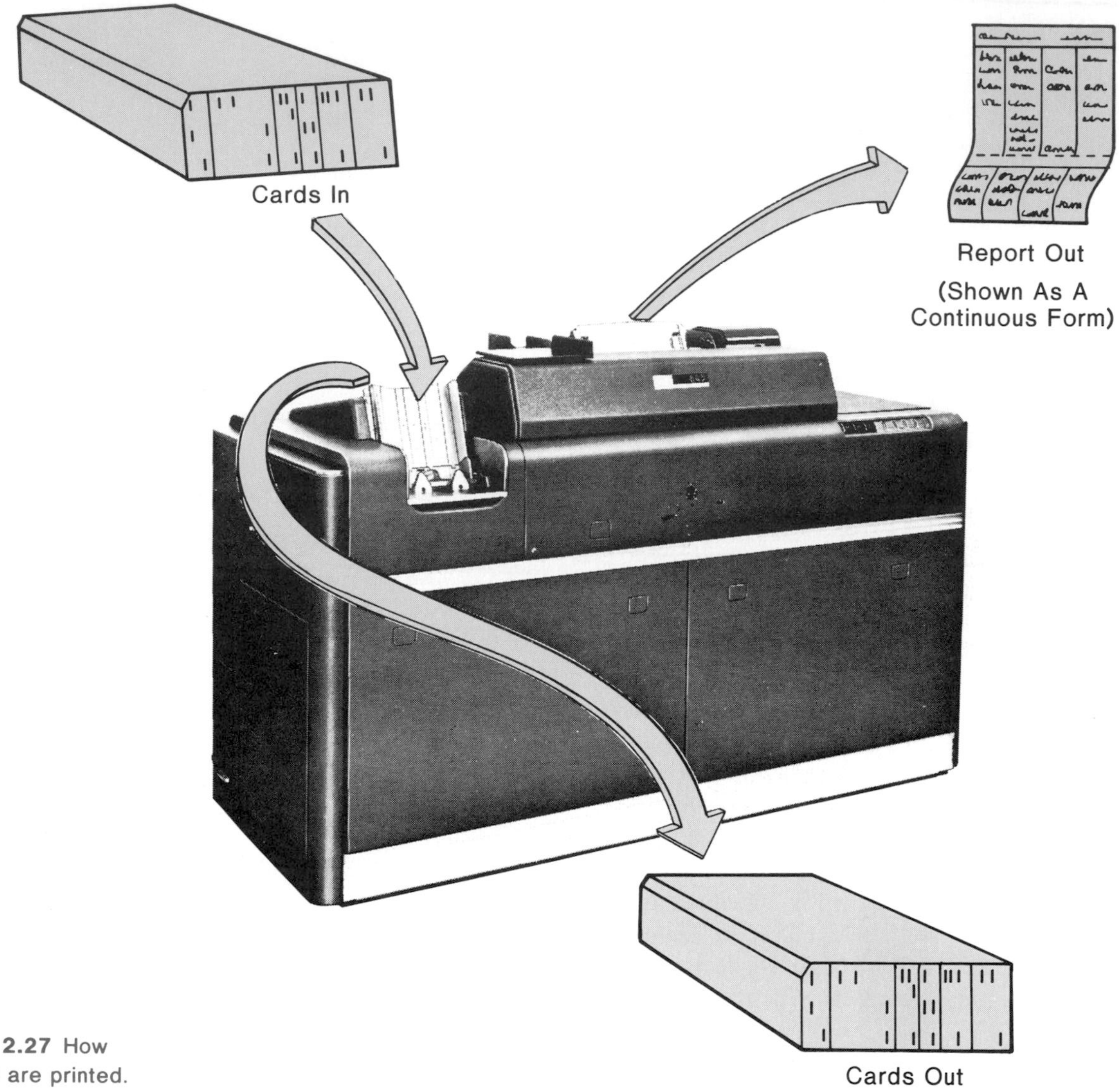

Figure 2.27 How reports are printed.

Tape-Controlled Carriage

The tape-controlled carriage controls the feeding and spacing of forms (fig. 2.28). A punched-hole tape, which corresponds to the form, controls all the spacing operations. The following are possible with the tape-controlled carriage:

1. Single, double, or triple spacing can be varied on the report form by control panel wiring.
2. Overflow skipping from form to form is accomplished by the sensing of a specified punch in the tape which starts the advancing of the form to the first printing line of the following form.
3. Page totals are possible before ejecting the form.

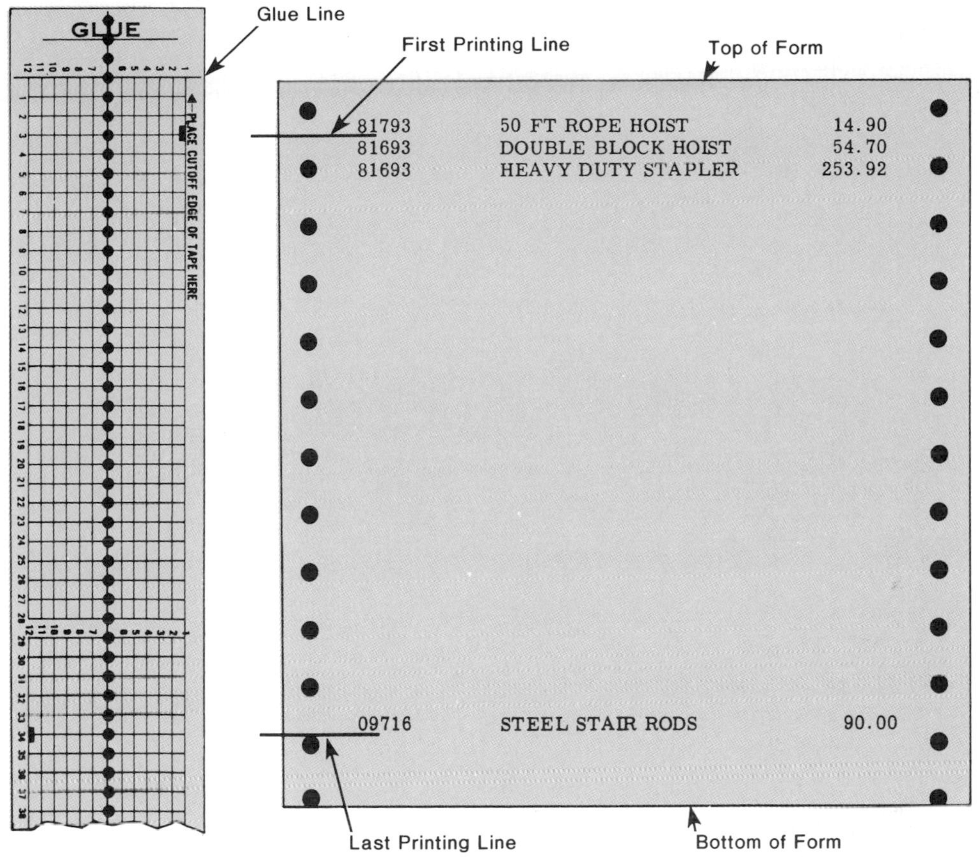

Figure 2.28 An example of tape-controlled carriage.

4. Any class of total can be printed on a predetermined line.
5. Channel 12 is the last printing line on the form. When a hole is detected by the carriage in channel 12, the form skips to the next sheet to channel 1.

Carriage Tape

Channel 1—This channel is always punched for the first printing line of a form. This is known as the "home" position.

Channel 2—This channel is always punched for the first body line of a conventional two-part form using heading cards.

Channel 3–11—These channels can be used in any sequence to control form skipping and ejecting to a controlled punch in the carriage tape.

Channel 12—This channel is used as the last printing line of a form. When this channel is sensed by the brushes of the carriage, the form is "overflowed" to channel 1 of the next form (fig. 2.29).

Figure 2.29 An example of invoice carriage control tape.

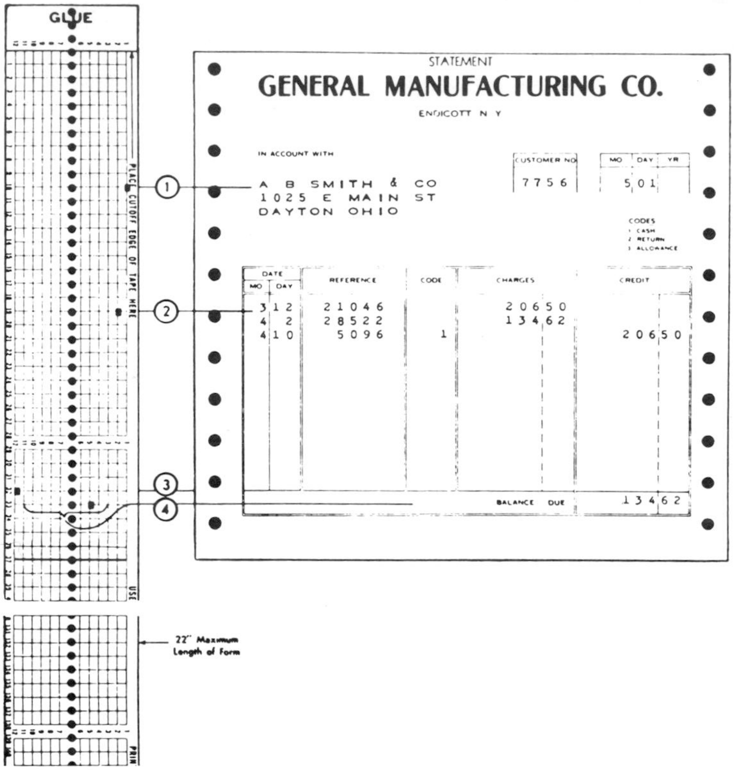

The Modern Period

World War II caused a swift change in data-processing needs. Urgent demands in science supplied the momentum for high-speed data processing. New requirements for data were encountered in aircraft design. The atomic bomb created a new dimension in calculating.

Mark I

After five years of effort, the Mark I emerged from the Harvard laboratories in 1944 (fig. 2.30). This was the world's first automatic computer, which had an automatic sequence-controlled calculator operated entirely by mechanical switches. It was an electromechanical machine built by the IBM Corporation and financed by the Navy Department. Punched cards were used for both input and output operations. A typewriter was used as a printing device. The sequencing of instructions was mainly through paper tape input. Limited program branching (the ability to change the sequence of instruction execution) was incorporated into the system later.

The Mark I, a milestone in computer history, virtually transformed Babbage's analytical engine into a reality. It was the first machine to do a long series of arithmetic and logical operations. A series of the machines were built for the Navy Department and they made a vital contribution to the war effort.

Figure 2.30 Work started on the Automatic Sequence Controlled Calculator, Mark I, in 1939 by Howard Aiken of Harvard University. It was unveiled in 1944 and contained 760,000 parts with switches, components, tubes, wheels, and 500 miles of wire.

ENIAC

The next important machine to appear in the computer field was ENIAC (Electronic Numerical Integrator and Calculator) in 1946 (fig. 2.31). This machine was originally designed to produce mathematical tables required in the firing of projectiles. In this machine, the switching and controlling functions once trusted to relays were now handled by vacuum tubes. With the replacement of the slow electromechanical relays by electronic tubes, the speed of calculation increased one thousand times.

The ENIAC was the first electronic computer and also the first to use *stored program techniques* (programs stored internally in the machine). Problems of greater complexity could now be handled by computers. The amount of human effort was greatly reduced by the centralization of control through the stored program. The ENIAC is regarded as the prototype of all later computer equipment.

UNIVAC I

The first commercial computer, UNIVAC I (Universal Automatic Computer), was delivered in 1951 to the Census Bureau and was immediately used in the 1952 biennial census statistics (fig.2.32). Several types of input and output, as well as automatic programming, were used by the equipment. UNIVAC I was one of the first computers to use magnetic tape for input and output operations.

First-Generation Computers

During the years 1954–1959, approximately three dozen different engineering groups in the United States and abroad completed the construction of modern, large-scale data-processing systems. It seemed that there was a new computer being announced

Figure 2.31 The first large-scale electronic computer was Electron-Numerical Integrator and Calculator (ENIAC) built by John W. Mauchly, J. Presper Eckert, and their coworkers at the University of Pennsylvania for the Ballistic Research Laboratories of the U.S. Army Ordinance Corps. It weighed more than 30 tons and occupied more than 15,000 square feet. With its 19,000 vacuum tubes, it performed 5,000 calculations each second. (Photo courtesy of Sperry Univac, a division of Sperry Corporation)

Figure 2.32 UNIVAC I was the world's first commercial Electronic Computer. The first user was the United States Government Bureau of the Census, which received the first model in June 1951. Work on the UNIVAC I was begun in 1948 by the Eckert-Mauchly Computer Corporation and completed in 1951. During this period, Eckert-Mauchly was acquired by Remington Rand, Inc. (subsequently merged with The Sperry Corporation in 1955 to form the Sperry Rand Corporation) The first nongovernment user of the UNIVAC I was the General Electric Co., which took delivery in 1954 at its Louisville, Kentucky, manufacturing facility. (Photo courtesy of Sperry Univac, a division of Sperry Corporation)

Figure 2.33 The IBM 650 computer, an example of a first-generation computer.

each day by some company. These *first-generation computers* were characterized as being rather bulky in size, requiring great amounts of air conditioning to dissipate the heat their many vacuum tubes created, and demanding a high rate of maintenance and repair. However, these computers had many advantages over their earlier electromechanical counterparts—speed of calculation, the use of stored and internal programs, an ability to apply logical decisions to calculated results, and the introduction of different types of input and output media, such as magnetic tape, paper tape, etc. These new techniques provided speeds up to fifty to seventy-five times greater than that of cards and brought improvements in input, output, and storage capabilities (fig. 2.33).

The computer now had immediate access to instructions given as rapidly as it called for them, inasmuch as the program was stored in a high-speed internal memory or storage unit. With this internal storage, the computer was able to process instructions in the same manner as data. It modified its own instructions in making simple decisions thus relieving the programmer of vast amounts of costly and repetitive programming. Later computers extended this principle until it became possible for computers to generate a considerable part of their own instructions.

Second-Generation Computers

During the late 1950s, *second-generation computers* were developed as a result of the replacement of the vacuum tube by the tiny transistor, requiring less power and offering greater reliability (fig. 2.34). Thanks to this change, the size of the computers was drastically reduced and the need for air conditioning was lessened. High-speed card readers and printers were introduced. Access to data and instructions was now thought of in terms of microseconds (millionths of a second). High-speed data processing became a reality. Sophisticated programs and compilers began to appear. The "natural" or mnemonic language replaced the machine language in programming. Maintenance costs were reduced by the reliability of the transistor and the use of new and better components resulting from continuing developments in the electronics and solid-state physics field.

Figure 2.34 The IBM 1401 computer, an example of a second-generation computer.

Random (direct) access devices appeared during this period, offering the user random accessing of data in addition to the sequential processing of data. Inline processing was now possible inasmuch as data could be recorded as received instead of having to wait to be batched for subsequent sequential processing. Information could be recorded on or retrieved from the data tracks without regard to the sequential order of the recorded data.

Third-Generation Computers

In the mid-1960s, the *third-generation computers* appeared. This era is characterized by the advanced miniaturization and the refined components that came with second-generation computers (figs. 2.35 and 2.36). The nanosecond (one billionth of a second) appeared as a method of measuring access and processing time. Newer and faster methods of input and output were introduced—optical scanning, magnetic-ink recognition, data-transmission displays, etc. Multiprogramming permitted the simultaneous processing of more than one program at a time. Tremendous storage capabilities permitted immediate access to millions of characters. All operational and functional data could be stored in a computer and be accessed from any location. Remote terminals located in the same building or across the nation could have access to the data stored in the computer, thus facilitating the transmission of data over great distances. Inquiries could be made through these terminals and the answers displayed on a video tube.

Fourth-Generation Computers

The 1970s marked the beginning of a new generation of computers (fig. 2.37). Although the changes were subtle, there were dramatic announcements in all sectors of the computer field. No previous period saw so many major data-processing concepts simultaneously undergoing such intensive study, experimentation, and development. The technology of operating systems, multiprogramming, multiprocessing, high-level user-oriented programming languages, time sharing, data communications, hardware miniaturization, and operating speeds were all subject to intensive research in both private and public sectors of the economy.

Figure 2.35 The IBM 360 computer, an example of a third-generation computer.

Figure 2.36 A comparison of second- and third-generation computer components.

Figure 2.37 The IBM 370 computer, an example of a fourth-generation computer.

The IBM System/370 appeared during this period. This system used many of the functions already provided in the third-generation System/360 but added an extensive array of enhancements:

Faster internal performance

Greater channel capabilities providing more efficient input and output processing of data

Integrated emulation of other systems

Added reliability, availability, and serviceability

Enhanced functional capabilities

Especially important to users of System/360 was the relative ease with which the transition could be made from the System/360 to System/370. Most System/360 input/output equipment, users programs, and programming systems can be used on the System/370 without change.

Minicomputers

The minicomputer has made spectacular advances in the field of data processing. Like a sports car, a minicomputer is easy to recognize, but hard to define. *A minicomputer is defined as a small, desktop computer with a central processing unit and at least 4K bytes of core storage* (fig. 2.38). Some people call a computer that is small enough to be carried a minicomputer, but many minicomputers grow into systems that almost fill a room. Sometimes a minicomputer is defined as almost any machine that costs under $25,000, but prices on a bona fide minicomputer system can vary from $3,000 to $200,000.

Low cost and small size make the minicomputer desirable and easier to use for applications that would be difficult to schedule or put on large centralized computing systems. Such applications range from simple operations, such as keeping track of library books, to running a warehouse. Minicomputers do not really compete with, nor will they replace, the large computers, but there are many jobs that they can do more

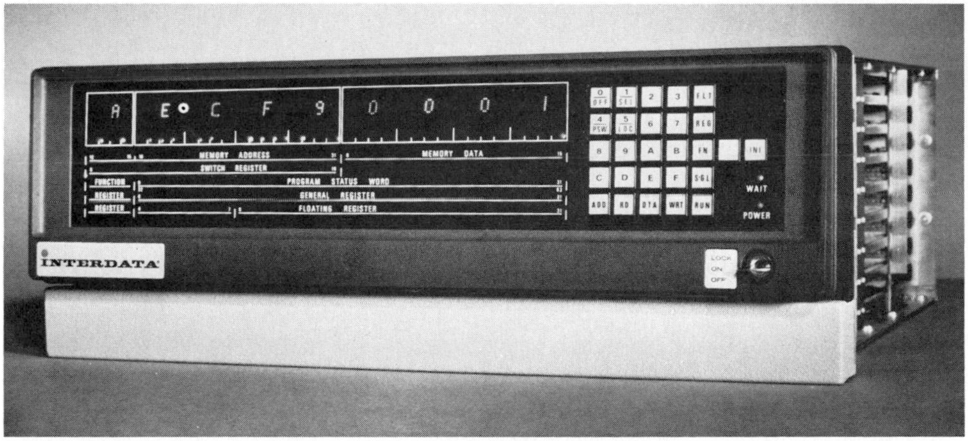

Figure 2.38 An example of a minicomputer.

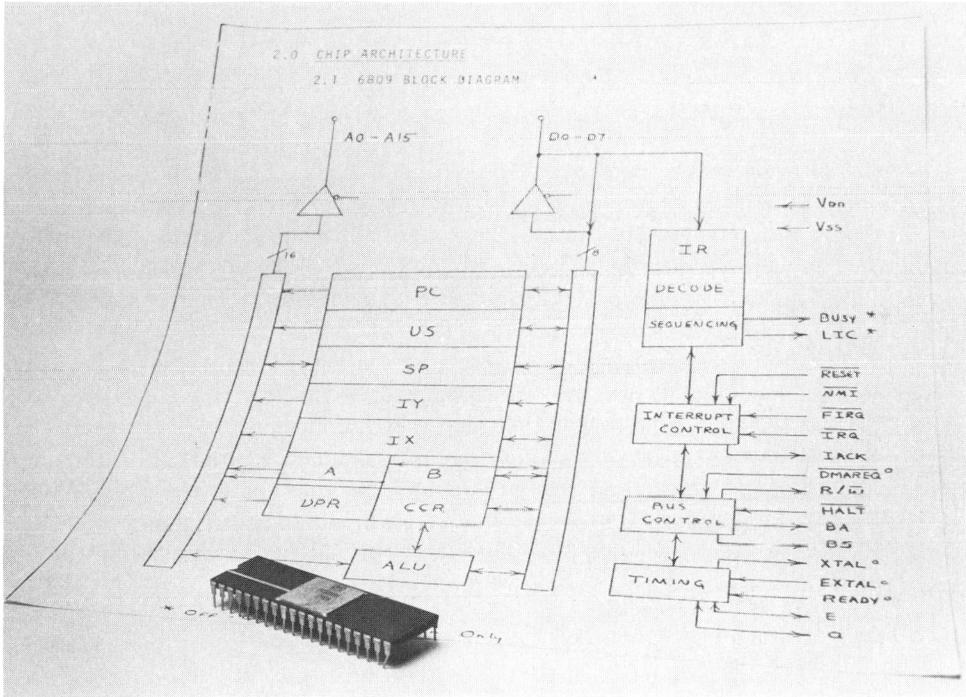

Figure 2.39 An example of a microprocessor and its functional block. (Photo by Ken Firestone)

inexpensively and easily. Sometimes they can easily do a payroll and will even preprocess data before it is sent to a large computer.

Microprocessors

The emerging microprocessor technology is having, and will continue to have, a strong impact on the electronic design that is carried out on existing electronic products and countless new products. *A microprocessor is defined as a miniature computer, manufactured on a small chip using solid-state integrated circuitry, that possesses characteristics of larger systems* (fig. 2.39).

Figure 2.40 An example of a terminal. (Photo by Ken Firestone)

The chip is about a quarter of an inch square and quite flat. This chip has the calculating capability equal to a room-size computer of only 25 years ago. Mass production of the chip has already made possible home computer systems that sell for less than $800, and prices will continue to fall.

The arrival of the chip has given a boost to an already vital industry. Far from rendering the big computers obsolete, the chip has opened ways for design of custom-made super computers more powerful than anything dreamed possible a few years ago. At the same time, the chips are lowering the cost of minicomputers. In turn, these small computers are being used increasingly for the routine functions that, until recently, had to be handled by main frames at a considerable cost to the user. Although still in its infancy, the chip has already given rise to one of the most astonishingly competitive and fastest growing industries the nation has ever seen.

Terminals and Software

Strong growth patterns in the terminal field continue at the rate of 18 to 20 percent per year. Computer terminals will keep pace with the rapid growth pattern as more of these devices for gaining access to the power of large-scale computers are made available to the user (fig. 2.40).

There is also evidence of strong increases in the number and kinds of software. With the industry moving swiftly toward total unbundling of hardware and software, there is a surge of new application programming and programming houses competing for this rapidly opening market. To serve the end-user or the average consumer, who is consuming more, computers and software will turn to direct applicability on what might be termed "the average person's problems," such as energy resources, transportation, health care, and education.

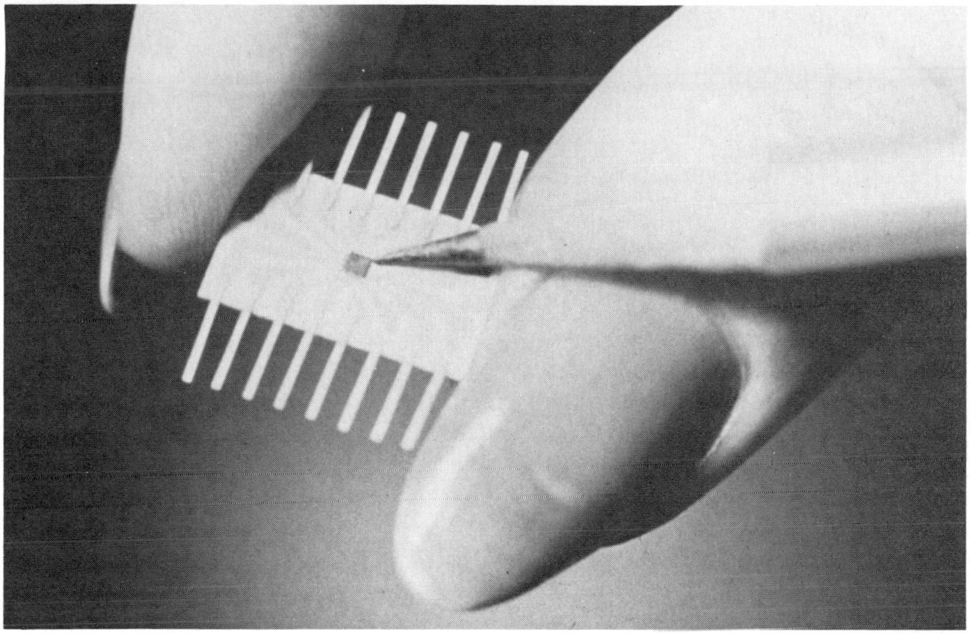

Figure 2.41 An example of miniaturization. (Photo courtesy of Western Electric)

Industry figures indicate that the average growth rate over the past two to three years in software devoted to data services availability is 87 percent. The software market, according to some industry observers, will pass $1 billion well before the end of the decade.

Future Computers

The computer industry of the future will place greater emphasis on the special needs of computer users. The trend toward miniaturization and high-speed processing will accelerate, opening new areas for the use of computers at a lower cost (fig. 2.41).

The storage capabilities of tomorrow's computers will increase tremendously, making them even more valuable as a management tool. This will increase the demand for advanced equipment, such as scanning devices, that will put large amounts of information into computers at high speeds.

Although it is easy, historically, to forecast dramatic changes in hardware, it is likely that the computer will change gradually. It is obvious that the fourth generation is not a dramatically different system, but one which was remade gradually with new and faster components. Better and more diverse peripherals, with emphasis on remote hard-copy and CRT devices, will team up with photo-optic memories, nonimpact electronic beam printers, and voice output systems to provide a more flexible, responsive system, capable of congeniality with the human user. Particularly significant will be price reductions and improvements in terminals and minicomputers, and the rapid convergence of mini- and microcomputers and intelligent terminals.

Further enhancements will also come from interconnecting several computers into an information network in which individual computers will perform increasingly specialized functions, such as data base management and telecommunications monitoring, as well as applications support for systems needed in management decision making.

The marriage of communication and computer technology will lower the cost of sending the processing information. As a result, transmission of data across national boundaries will become more common, perhaps encouraging the idea that worldwide problems require worldwide solutions.The energy crisis has made us painfully aware that our resources are limited. Computers are already important tools in programs to conserve energy and discover new resources. In the future, computers will play an even larger role.

The future of minicomputers seems clear; minicomputers will continue to be smaller, cheaper, and more powerful as new technology and new software continue to be developed. With each lowering of cost, additional applications of minicomputers become practical; as more people learn about computers, additional applications are discovered and developed.

The development of microelectronics is causing the computer to go public at an accelerated pace. Microelectronics has reduced development and manufacturing costs and brought greatly enhanced, more reliable products to the market more quickly. In the future, consumer products, such as the following, will be available. An alarm clock with a built-in hundred-year personal calendar could be preprogrammed to awaken its owner at an appointed time on each day of the year, excluding weekends and holidays. The same device could be used as an appointment calendar built into a wristwatch. A credit card with an individual's entire credit history stored in an imbedded microcomputer would eliminate the need for credit reports at time of sale; and the same card used to activate the lock on its owner's automobile, home, or office, in addition to activating a bank's memory money dispenser, a pay telephone, etc. The list of possibilities is endless. Most of these products exist today.

Computer technology is playing an ever-increasing role in the education of our youth and the reeducation of our adults. Consider the impact of the small electronic calculator. A pocket calculator is as common and as essential as a pencil and workbook. There is no need to teach the mechanics of arithmetic, no drills on times tables. Classroom time is spent teaching the thought processes required to solve problems with the calculator doing the mechanics of arithmetic and recording. Today the classroom is a learning laboratory centered around computer-assisted learning techniques. It is conceivable that a greater portion of our future citizens will be better informed and better able to cope with the powers of the computer, which can become a tool to enrich our lives.

In the future, programming as we know it may cease to exist. Instead, user languages will be developed and programmed into language interpreter chips, which may be built into the user's terminal, enabling the terminal to call a central system. Every home will have a built-in communications system, similar to cable television, which will allow the user to have the world's information available immediately without having to leave home. If we allow our imagination to work on all potential uses of computers, there will be no end.

From these speculations, we can see the character of jobs in data processing changing dramatically within the next ten years. The emphasis will be on system analysis, with the definition of *system* expanded to include psychological and sociological aspects of computer use. Preoccupation with jargon, programming problems, and hardware technology must give way to preoccupation with service. Popular acceptance of the computer will depend on our ability to adapt to an environment that emphasizes the importance of computer service to the user.

Scientific discovery cannot be predicted. It creates new technologies that were only dimly perceived a few years ago. Whatever future technology brings, it is the uses of the computer that counts. The potential of computers will continue to be harnessed for our benefit and the improvement of our quality of life.

Summary

Even though the most significant events in data processing have happened in the last twenty-five years, it is important to realize that the computer is the result of thousands of years of research and development. This chapter traces only the most significant events and shows how each has contributed to the development of the computer and modern data processing.

Punched cards play a major role in data-processing installation. Besides its role as chief input media, the punched card is used for original documents as well as for computer programming. Although punched-card data processing is not as important as it was thirty years ago, it is still a valuable part of data processing and knowledge of the operation and uses of the equipment is useful to all students of data processing.

1. The first important calculating machine was the abacus (3000 B.C.), which is still used by over half of the world's population, chiefly in the Far East. Jacquard (1801) developed the punched-card principle used in the textile industry for weaving. His punched-card principle was later used by Babbage and Hollerith. Babbage (1850) constructed large-scale calculating machines. His machines failed because the necessary parts could not be manufactured precisely. Despite failures, his work is a valuable contribution to the later engineering of calculating machines.
2. Hollerith (1880) used Jacquard's punched-card principle to develop his unit record principle by which data was coded and represented by holes in cards. Hollerith developed an automatic sorting machine, a card-punch machine, and a semiautomatic tabulating machine. In 1896, he organized the Tabulating Machine Company, which subsequentially merged with other companies to form the International Business Machines Corporation in 1924. The 80-column IBM punched card became known as the Hollerith card. Powers (1900) employed punched-card principles in developing his sorting machines, card-punch machines, and tabulators. His equipment was used in the 1910 census. He later sold his patent rights to the Remington Rand Corporation in 1925. The Powers punched card contained 90 columns. At the outbreak of World War II, there were just these two companies engaged in punched-card data processing, the IBM Corporation and the Remington Rand Corporation. Little progress was made in data processing during the war.
3. Punched-card data processing is defined as the recording, manipulating, and reporting of information through the use of holes punched in a card. Punched cards are used as input/output media because of their machine-language capa-

bilities. As facilities for storing information in a machine, they also provide a processible format for future use. The unit record principle implies that information concerning a single transaction is contained in one card, permitting each card to be processed with other cards or input media on a single record basis.

4. The two types of cards are the Hollerith 80-column card and the 96-column card for the IBM System/3.
5. Data is represented in cards in two major sections by zone punches (12, 11, and 0 upper positions) and the numeric punches (digits 0 through 9). Numbers are represented by a single punch 0 through 9. Alphabetic characters are represented by combinations of zone and numeric punches.

   A-I—12 punch plus 1 through 9 punches

   J-R—11 punch plus 1 through 9 punches

   S-Z—0 punch plus 2 through 9 punches

   Special characters may have 1, 2, or 3 punches in one column.

   A field is composed of related characters that are treated as one unit of information. The high-order position of a field is the left-hand column and low-order position is the right-hand column. A record is a series of fields (may be one field) grouped together for input and output operations.
6. The primary function of a card-punch operation is to convert a source document into a punched card. Other uses are replacing damaged cards, correcting cards, preparing computer program cards, and preparing test cards for data-processing machines. Reproducers and automatic punches were designed for reproducing, gangpunching, comparing, mark sensing, summary punching, and end printing. Interpreters translate holes into a printed form on the face of the card itself.
7. Sorters arrange cards in a predetermined sequence, either numerically or alphabetically. The sorter may also be used to select cards with a specific punch from a group of cards. Numerical sorting sorts each column in a field from low-order position (rightmost column) to high-order position (leftmost column). Alphabetical sorting requires two sorts per column, zone and numeric.
8. A collator compares two or more fields in the same or different cards and, based on the comparison, separates, segregates, or combines files of cards.

   a. The sequence of a file of cards is checked in either ascending or descending order.
   b. Specific cards are selected from a file of cards.
   c. Merging combines two files into one.
   d. Match-merging merges only matched (equal) cards with a selection of unmatched cards from both files.
   e. Match-selecting matches two files with a selection of matched cards (not merged) and a selection of unmatched cards from both files.
   f. Additional collating operations are the selection of zero balances, the selection of duplicate cards, etc.

9. Accounting machines print the reports, summarize and print data, and position continuous form paper. A tape-controlled carriage is used in both accounting machines and computer printers. It controls the automatic feeding and spacing of forms. The carriage tape is punched in channels.

   Channel 1—First printing line of a form.

   Channel 2—First printing line of the body of a form using heading cards.

   Channels 3–11—May be used in any sequence for automatic control of skipping and spacing.

   Channel 12—The last line printing of a form.

10. Mark I was the world's first automatic computer in that it had an automatic sequence-controlled calculator operated by mechanical switches. Developed by IBM and the Navy Department, it was the first machine to do a long series of arithmetic and logical operations. ENIAC (1946) was the first electronic (vacuum tube) computer and was the first to use stored programs (stored internally in the machine). It was the prototype of all later computer equipment. UNIVAC I (1951) was the first commercial computer. It was first used in the 1952 biennial census. Automatic programming and several types of input and output equipment were some of the features of this machine.
11. First-generation computers (1954–1959) were rather bulky in size, requiring large amounts of air conditioning to dissipate the heat created by the many vacuum tubes. They had a high ratio of maintenance and repair also. The important advantages over earlier machines were speed of calculation, use of the stored program, the ability to apply logical decisions to calculated results, various types of input and output equipment, magnetic tape, paper tape, ability to modify its own program, etc.

    Second-generation computers (1959–1964) replaced the vacuum tubes with the tiny transistor, requiring less power and offering greater reliability. The size of the computer was greatly reduced and the need for large amounts of air conditioning was eliminated. High-speed card readers and printers were introduced. Sophisticated programs and compilers began to appear. Symbolic programming replaced machine-language programming during this period. Random access devices were introduced. Repair and maintenance time was greatly reduced.

    Third-generation computers (1964–1970) were characterized by advanced miniaturization and refinement of computer components. Greater compilers, newer and faster methods of input and output, optical scanners, magnetic-ink character readers, data transmission over long distances, displays on video tubes, multiprogramming, tremendous storage capacities, and remote terminals with access to central computers are just a few of the innovations introduced during this period.

    Fourth-generation computers (1970-) featured many changes in all sectors of the computer field. The technology of operating systems, multiprogramming, multiprocessing, time sharing, data communications, hardware miniaturization, and operating speeds were all subject to intensive research and undergoing changes.

12. Minicomputers have made spectacular advances in the field of data processing. A minicomputer is defined as a small, desktop computer with a central processing unit and at least 4K bytes of core storage. Microprocessors are defined as miniature computers manufactured on a small chip, using solid-state circuitry, and possess the characteristics of larger systems.
13. The computer industry of the future will place great emphasis on the special needs of the computer users. The trend toward miniaturization and high-speed processing will accelerate. Storage capabilities will increase tremendously. Comnunication and computer technology will lower the cost of transmission of data and will improve our quality of life.

Identification Questions

Match the following terms with the statements below.

A. Abacus
B. Accounting Machine
C. Card-Punch Machine
D. Collators
E. ENIAC
F. Field
G. First-Generation Computers
H. Fourth-Generation Computers
I. High Order
J. Hollerith
K. Interpreters
L. Jacquard
M. Low Order
N. Mark I
O. Microprocessors
P. Minicomputers
Q. Punched-Card Data Processing
R. Record
S. Reproducers
T. Sorters
U. Third-Generation Computers
V. Unit Record Principle

1. A group of related characters treated as one unit of information.
2. Transfers information from one card to another at relatively high rates of speed with a high degree of duplication accuracy.
3. Compare information and separate, segregate, or combine cards based on the comparison.
4. Bulky in size, require large amounts of air conditioning, and have a high maintenance rate.
5. 80-column card.
6. Right column of a field.
7. Convert a source document into a punched card.
8. Arrange cards in a predetermined sequence.
9. World's first automatic computer.
10. Advanced miniaturization and refined computer components.
11. A miniature computer manufactured on a small chip using solid-state circuitry.
12. Earliest known calculating device.
13. Information concerning a single transaction usually recorded in one card.
14. A field or a series of fields normally grouped together for input and output operations.

15. Automatic feeding of cards and printing of reports.
16. IBM 370.
17. Punched-card principle used in an automatic loom.
18. Left column of a field.
19. First electronic computer to use stored program.
20. Procedure of recording, manipulating, and reporting information through the use of punched holes in cards.
21. Print information on the face of card that has been punched into the card.
22. Small, desktop computer with central processing unit.

Questions for Review

1. What were the early data-processing devices used for?
2. What important contributions did the abacus make to the data-processing field?
3. What important contributions did Babbage make in the field of data processing?
4. Describe Hollerith's and Powers's main contributions to the field of punched-card data processing.
5. What is punched-card data processing and why has it played such an important role in the development of data processing?
6. What are the principal uses for punched-card data processing?
7. What is the unit record principle?
8. How is data represented in the Hollerith code for alphabetic, numeric, and special characters?
9. What is the difference between a field and a record?
10. Differentiate between the high-order position and the low-order position of a punched card. Give an example.
11. What are the main operations of a card-punch machine?
12. What are the principal operations performed by automatic punches? Briefly explain the functions of each.
13. What is the principal function of the interpreter?
14. What are the functions of the sorter?
15. How does numerical sorting differ from alphabetical sorting?
16. What is the principal function of the collator? Briefly explain the basic operations performed on a collator.
17. Explain the basic functions of the accounting machine.
18. Explain the functions of the tape-controlled carriage and the functions of the carriage tape channels.
19. In the era of modern computers, the Mark I, ENIAC, and UNIVAC I made important contributions. What are they?
20. What characterized second-generation computers and how did they differ from the first- and third-generation computers?
21. What was the significance of the fourth-generation computers?
22. What is a minicomputer and how is it used in data-processing applications?
23. What is a microprocessor and what important role does it play in data processing?
24. What does the future hold for data processing?

Key Terms

Abacus
Accounting Machine
Card-Punch Machine
Collators
ENIAC
Field
First-Generation Computers
Fourth-Generation Computers
High Order
Hollerith
Interpreters
Jacquard
Low Order
Mark I
Microprocessors
Minicomputers
Punched-Card Data Processing
Record
Reproducers
Sorters
Third-Generation Computers
Unit Record Principle

part 2

computer components and arithmetic

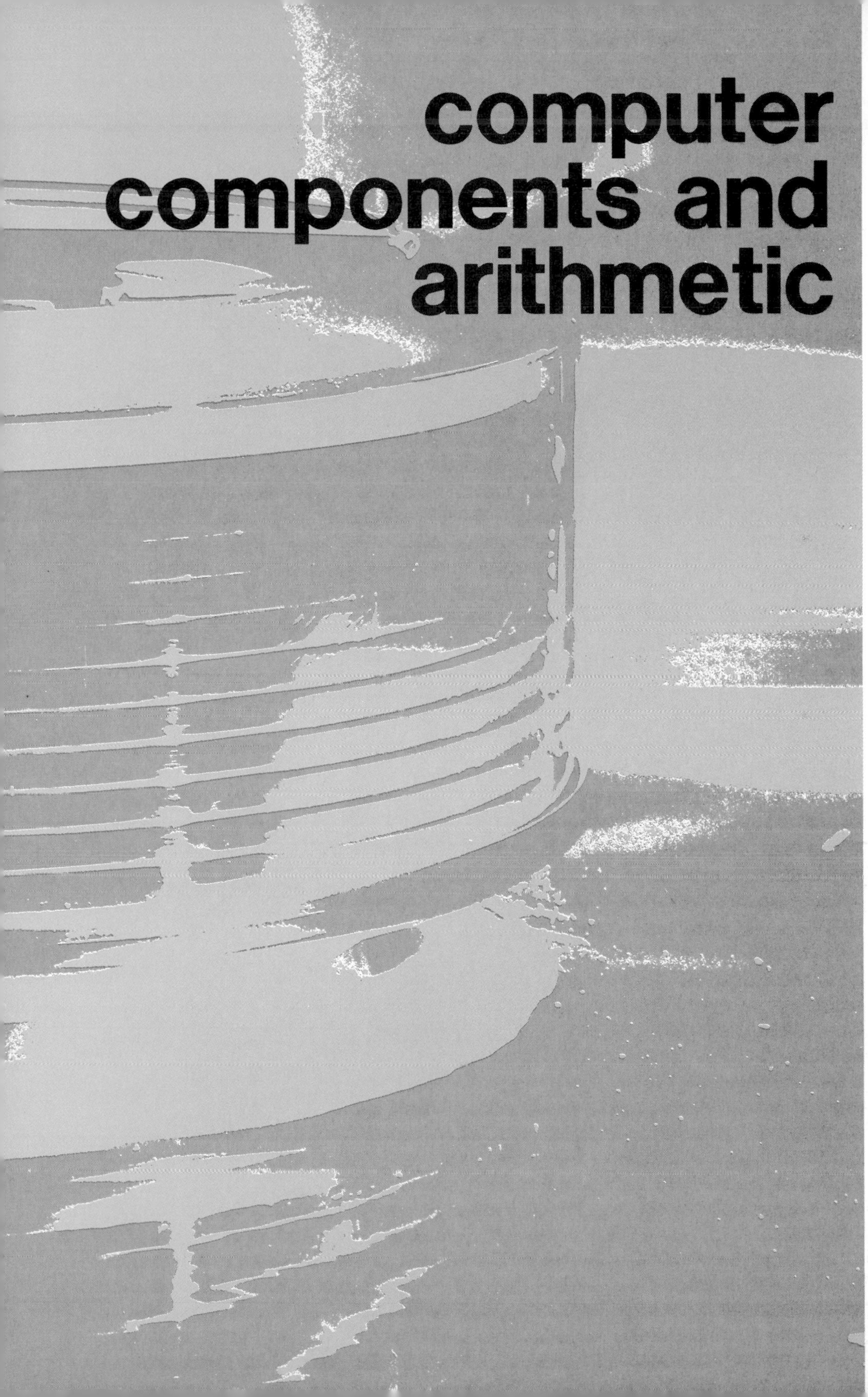

AUTO
MANUAL
ON
OFF
48
64
CHARACTER
MODE
ON
READ
ON
CLEAR
0-8-2
T
E
R
Y
U
I
O
P
&
S
D
F
G
H
J
K
L
X
C
V
B
N
M
?
=
%
$
*

computer components 3
input/output devices

Chapter Outline

Introduction to Computer Data Processing

Basic Considerations in Data Processing

Basic Elements of a Computer Data-Processing System
- Hardware Elements of the Computer

Input/Output Devices
- Control Unit
- Channel
- Buffers
- Card Reading and Punching Devices
  - Advantages
  - Disadvantages
  - Card Readers
  - Card Punches
- Magnetic Tape Devices
  - Advantages
  - Disadvantages
  - Reading/Writing on Magnetic Tape
  - Magnetic Tape Records
- Paper Tape Devices
  - Advantages
  - Disadvantages

Output
- Printers

Consoles

Computer Output Microfilm (COM)
- Advantages
- Disadvantages

Chapter Objectives

The learning objectives of this chapter are

1. to understand the operation of input/output devices because it is essential to the understanding of data-processing procedures.
2. to describe the physical characteristics of the input/output devices.
3. to explain the operating features and capabilities of the numerous input/output devices so you can properly evaluate each device and ascertain which is best suited for a particular application.
4. to serve as an introduction to computer data processing.

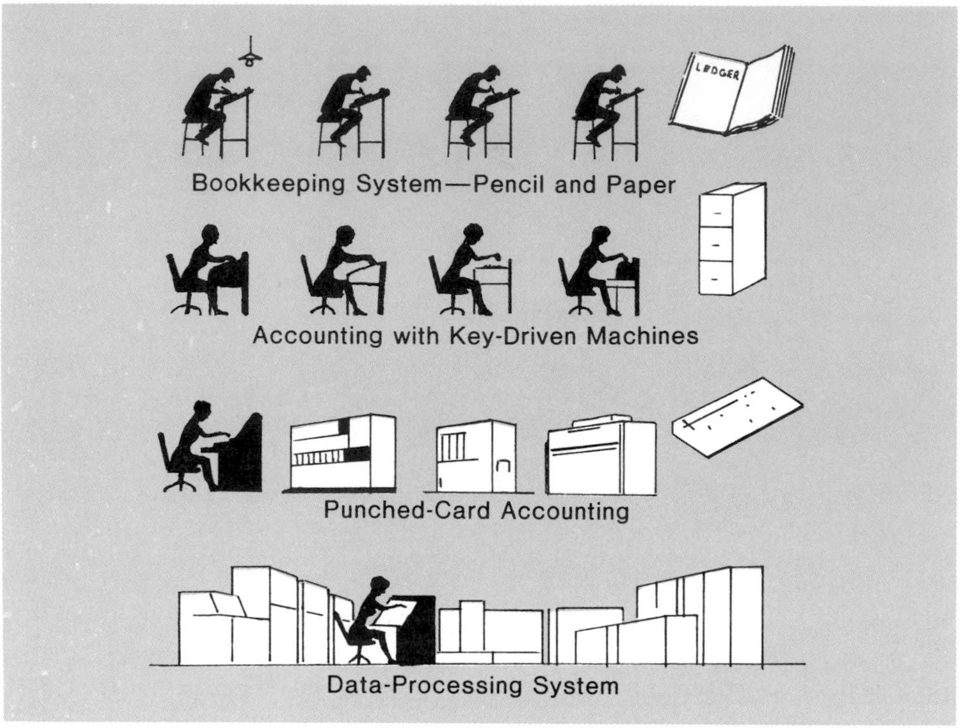

Figure 3.1 The progression of data-processing systems.

Introduction to Computer Data Processing

What is this thing called a computer? I don't know how it works. I'm not even sure what it does exactly; I know it's having a tremendous impact on business and science, and it seems to have a great deal to do with automation, but how does it relate to me? Can it outthink me? Where will it end—for me—for my children?

These are some thoughts and questions going through many people's minds today about computers. Start a conversation about computers and within a few moments someone will respond with "fantastic" or some expression like "it is too complicated for me to understand." Many people visualize a computer as a giant electronic monster possessing some mysterious power and wisdom. In reality, nothing could be further from the truth. Computers are not fantastic, marvelous, or awesome. They are the logical development of something that's been going on since the invention of the first tool (fig. 3.1). Their greatest assets are speed and accuracy. For all the talk about "giant brains" and for all the astonishing feats that modern computers perform, a computer is a remarkably simple machine. Almost every part in a computer has only one job to do; when the time comes for it to act, it must answer either "yes" or "no."

Basic Considerations in Data Processing

Data processing is a planned series of actions and operations upon information to achieve a desired result. All the necessary devices and procedures used in the operation constitute a data-processing system. The computer is a major tool used for implementing the solution to data-processing problems. In brief, a computer accepts data, processes data, and puts out results (fig. 3.2).

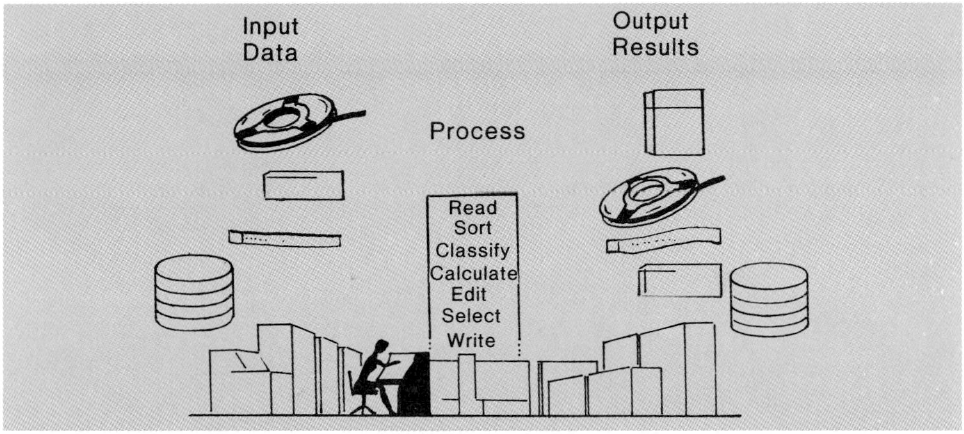

Figure 3.2 Data processing by a computer.

There are many computer systems. They vary in size, complexity, cost, and levels of programming systems and applications. Regardless of the nature of the information to be processed, all data processing involves the following basic considerations:

1. *Input*—the source data entering the system. Input relates to the information that goes into a computer. All data, such as numbers, letters, or symbols, must be recorded on punched cards, magnetic tape, punched paper tape, or other input media (fig. 3.3). The computer "reads" the information from these devices. Sometimes information is keyed directly into the computer through the use of a console.
2. *Processing*—the planned steps necessary to change the data into the desired result. The processing operation is carried out in a preestablished system of sequenced instructions that are followed automatically by a program. The computer without instructions from the programmer is worthless. Planning the process originates from the programmer and involves calculations, sorting, analysis, and other operations necessary to arrive at the desired solution. A series of instructions, called a *program,* is devised to accomplish a particular job and is fed into the computer. Assembling the instructions into a logical sequence that the computer will understand is called *programming.* The person who writes the program (the programmer) must know how to communicate with the computer, and must also understand the computer language.

   The *central processing unit* (CPU) consists of two sections, the control section and the arithmetic and logical section. The control section manipulates the data between core storage and the arithmetic and logical section according to the program. The arithmetic and logical section adds, subtracts, multiplies, divides, and compares data and directs the processing unit in making decisions when several alternate courses occur in the middle of a program.

   The core storage unit is the computer memory and stores original information, intermediate results, records, reference tables, and programmed instructions. Each storage location has an *address* so the computer knows where to find the information it wants. The speed of the computer is determined largely by how fast the computer can get this information out of storage and deliver it to another part of the computer.

Figure 3.3 Various data-recording media.

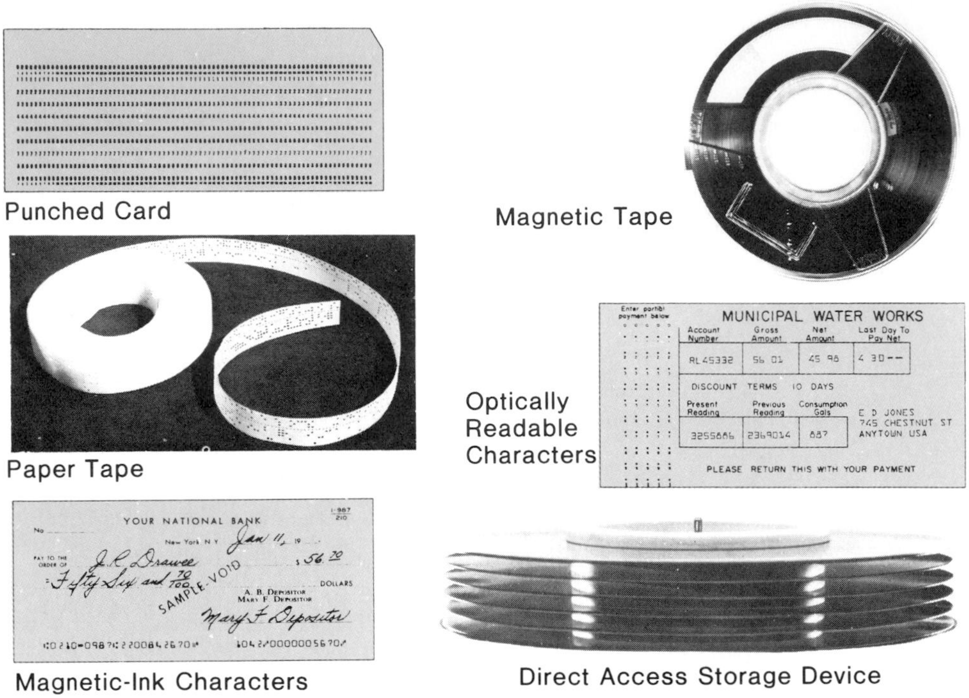

3. *Output*—the finished result or the end product of the system. Output is the end of the line. The computer delivers its processed information in pretty much the same way it was received—on punched cards, paper tape, or magnetic tape. In any of these forms, the information is always available for further processing when necessary. Computers can also print out results, often at speeds too fast for the eye to follow.

Basic Elements of a Computer Data-Processing System

The basic elements of a computer data-processing system consist of its *hardware* and *software* features. *Hardware consists of the physical equipment or devices of a system forming a computer and its peripheral equipment.* It includes all equipment necessary for the input, processing, and output functions of the system. The equipment may be directly connected to the system (online) or it may be used separately, not connected to the system (offline). A card reader is an example of an online unit and a card-punch machine is considered an offline unit.

Software is a set of programs, procedures, and possibly associated documentation concerned with the operation of a data-processing system. Computers without software are merely a collection of nuts, bolts, wires, electronic devices, and inanimate hardware. The software programs and routines are used to extend the capabilities of the computer. The term may also apply to an application program written for a particular installation, as well as various utility programs that are written to maintain files and records. COBOL and FORTRAN compilers and Sort/Merge programs are examples of soft-

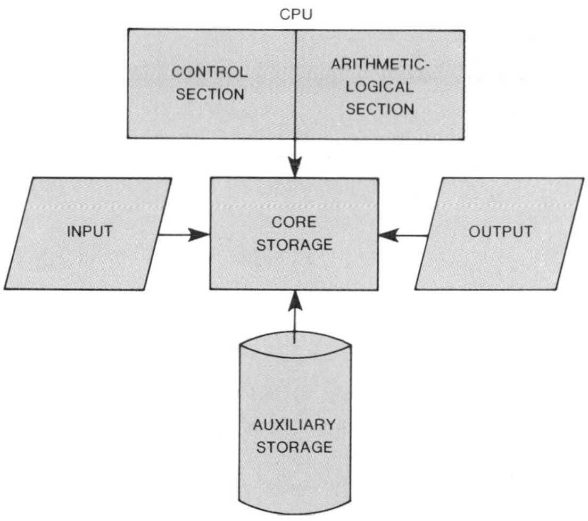

Figure 3.4 Major hardware elements.

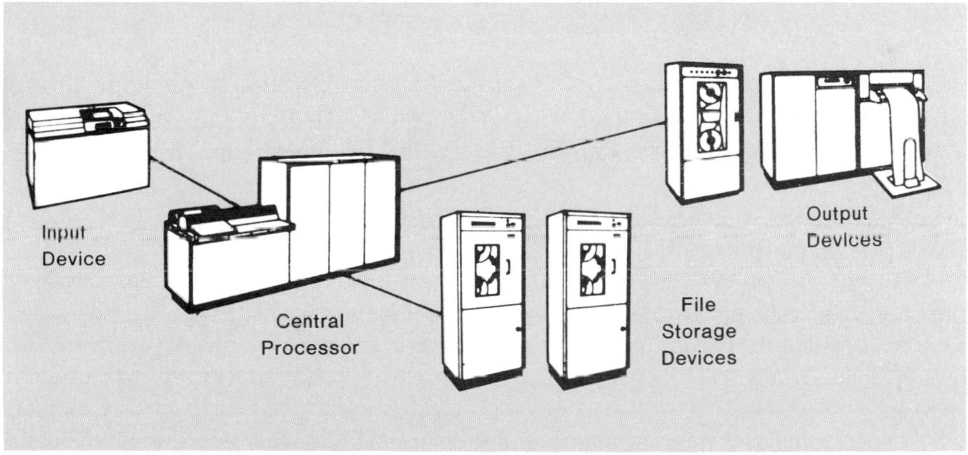

Figure 3.5 Major components of a computer system.

ware. Software is perhaps more important than the hardware since it extends the capabilities of the computer. Each year, as the demand for more software programs grows, the need for more programmers skilled in writing software programs increases.

Hardware Elements of the Computer

The major hardware elements of the computer are (fig. 3.4):

1. *Input devices*—used to enter data into the data-processing system.
2. *Output devices*—accept data from the system and record it.
3. *Central processing unit*—accepts the data for processing and makes results available for output devices.
4. *Storage devices*—used for temporary or permanent storage of data (fig. 3.5).

The presentation of information to a computer system requires that the data be reduced to a set of symbols that can be read, interpreted, and processed by various data-processing machines. Each medium requires its own specific arrangement of symbols to represent data. The choice of the particular symbols and their meanings is a matter of convention on the part of the system designers. These symbols differ from those commonly used by people in daily communication in that the information presented must conform to the design and operation of the data-processing equipment. A definite pattern of symbols, or *machine language,* is interpreted by the machines and becomes the important communication link between people and data-processing machines.

Information communicated to computer systems can be in the form of punched cards, paper tape, magnetic tape, magnetic-ink characters, optically recognizable characters, microfilm, display screen images, magnetic disks, communication network signals, etc. It seems that a new information communication medium is announced every day.

Data-processing systems are divided into three functional units—input/output units, a central processing unit, and storage.

Input / Output Devices

The data-processing system requires, as part of its information handling ability, input/output devices that are linked directly to the system. These devices can enter data into and record data from the data-processing system. These devices can read or sense coded data and make this information available to the computer. The data for input may be recorded in cards, in paper tape, in magnetic tape, on magnetic disks, as characters on paper documents, or as line images created with a light pen.

Output devices record and write information from the computer into cards as punches, as holes in paper tape, or as magnetized spots on magnetic tape. These devices may also print information in the form of reports, generate signals for transmission over telephone lines, produce graphic displays on cathode tubes, and produce microfilm images.

The number and types of input/output devices will depend upon the design of a particular system and the type of computer used. All computer systems have conversion systems that will transcribe information from one medium to another. For example, information initially entered as punched holes in cards can be transcribed automatically to magnetized spots along the length of the magnetic tape.

An input/output device is a unit for putting or getting data out of the storage unit. The device operation is usually initiated by a program instruction that generates a command to a particular input or output device. A control unit acts as intermediary between the command and the input and output device. The control unit decodes the command and synchronizes the device with the data-processing system.

The information is read by the input medium as the record moves through the input device. The data is then converted to a computer code and transmitted to the main storage area.

The output transfers the data from the main storage area to the particular output device. The computer code must be transcribed into the individual output medium.

The input/output devices function automatically and continue to operate as directed by the program until the entire file is processed. Program instructions select the required device, direct it to read or write, and indicate the storage locations into which the data will be entered or from which the data will be taken.

Data may be also entered directly into storage using a keyboard or switches. In this case, these input/output devices are used for manual entry directly into a computer without any medium for recording the data. The devices used are console keyboards, transmission terminals, and graphic display terminals. Terminals may be used at remote locations and the information transmitted over teleprocessing lines (fig. 3.6). No medium for recording the data is involved. Instead these terminals require some amount of internal storage for holding analyzing signals until the short message is completed or until the terminal is requested to transmit data.

Control Unit

Because many different types of input/output devices can be attached to a data-processing system, a unit is needed to coordinate input/output operations with the central processing unit. The control unit acts as a traffic police officer, directing information to the various input/output devices as they are read into the system or outputted by the system. The control unit also determines the priority of servicing and signaling the device identification when requesting service for the input device.

Figure 3.6 Terminal operation.

Figure 3.7 Channel organization.

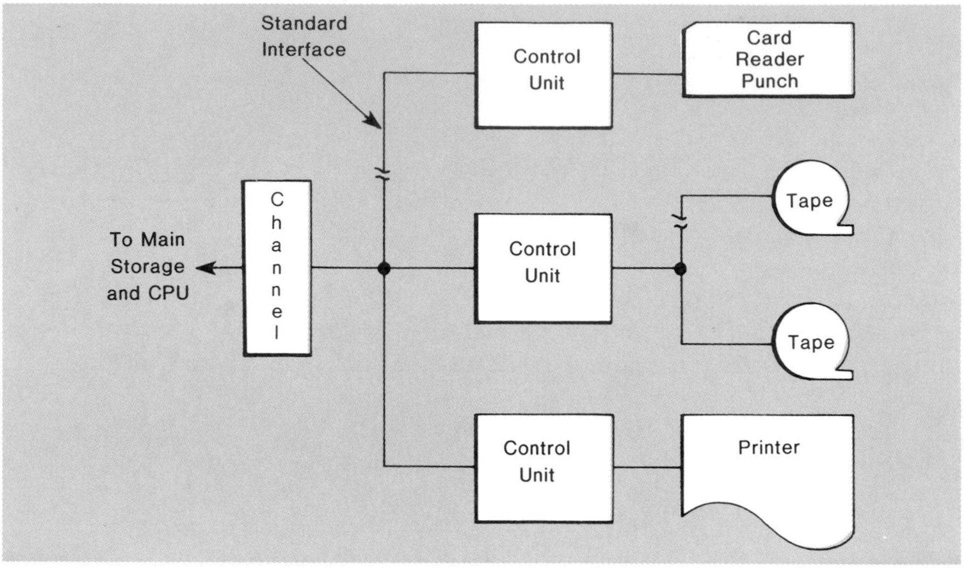

Channel

A channel is a separate piece of equipment devoted exclusively to managing the input/output devices and control units assigned to it. Once the channel has been activated, it carries out its own program, independent of the central processing unit. This permits the overlapping of input/output operations and computer processing. Sometimes this is performed in an interweaving pattern working with several input/output control units at one time and maintaining the proper destinations for storage allocation (input) or the control unit and device (output) (fig. 3.7).

Like the central processing unit, the channel is free to step through its commands (starting and terminating input/output operations). The channel serves as an intermediary input/output device, constantly switching the various input/output operations to make the most efficient use of the time, not only by overlapping operations of input/output units, but by doing so without tying up the central processing unit.

The channel performs the important function of permitting the simultaneous operation processing of input/output devices with the computer processing of data (fig. 3.8).

Buffers

The efficiency of any data-processing system can be increased so the input, output, and internal data handling operations can be overlapped and allowed to occur simultaneously (fig. 3.9). The usefulness of a computer is directly related to the speed at which it can complete a given procedure. To accomplish this, the central processing unit must be used to its full capacity. The speed of input/output units should be so arranged that the CPU (central processing unit) is always kept busy.

Input is divided into specific units or logical combinations of data, which enter storage under the control of the program. A number of output results can be developed from a single input, or conversely several input units can be combined to form one output unit. Inefficiency can result if processing is suspended during the reading and writing operations.

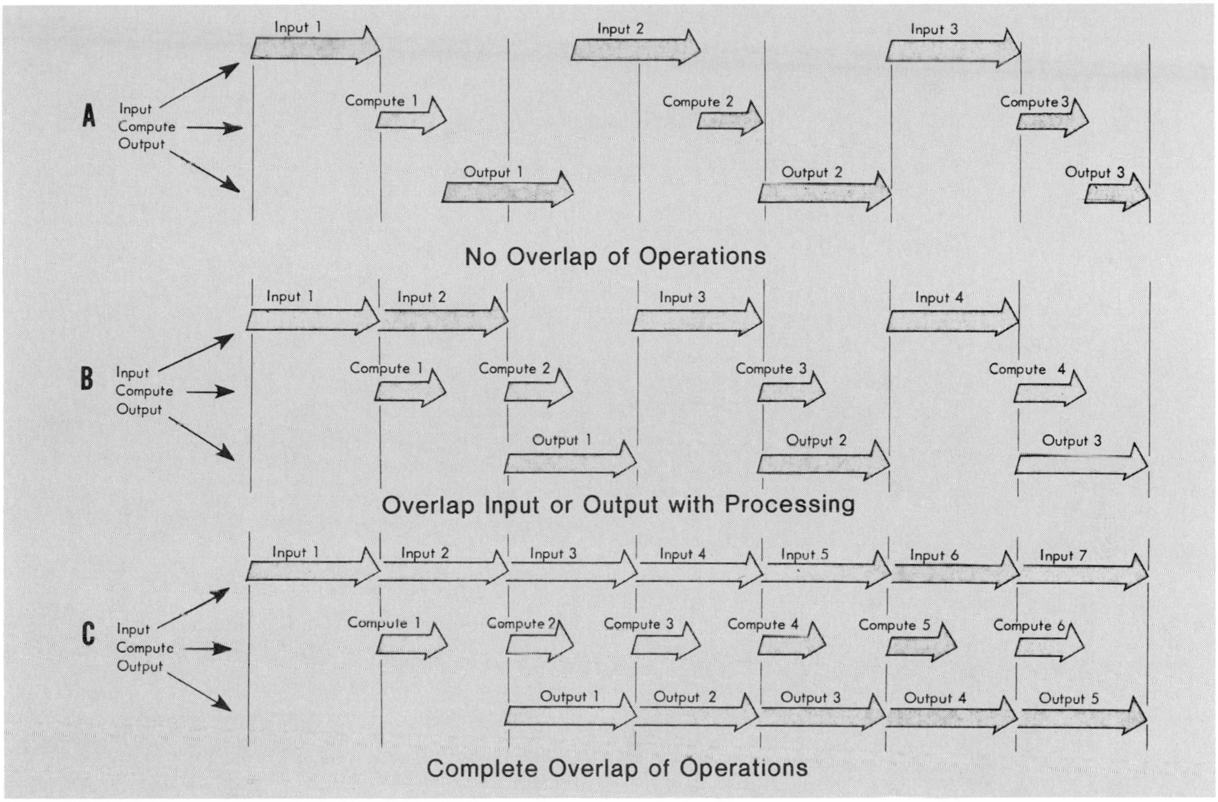

Figure 3.8 Channel processing.

To synchronize the processing of input/output operations and to provide an overlap of operations, a buffering system is used. Data is entered first into an external unit known as a *buffer*. When information is requested by the program, it is transferred to main storage in a fraction of the time necessary to read the information from the unit directly. Likewise output information is assembled in the buffer unit while the central processing unit is computing or manipulating the data. Processed data can be placed in these buffers at high speed. The output device proceeds to write the data while the CPU is free to continue its processing.

Spooling is another method that speeds up processing without waiting for slow input/output devices. The reading and writing of streams of input and output data is recorded on an auxiliary storage device (such as magnetic disk) concurrently with job execution and in a format convenient for later processing or output operations. As in a buffer, when information is requested by the program, it is transferred in a fraction of the time necessary to read directly from the input/output device. Spooling is also employed in conjunction with buffering methods.

Large computer systems have many buffers and spooling techniques to overlap the processing operations with the many input/output devices attached to the system.

Figure 3.9 How a buffer operation works.

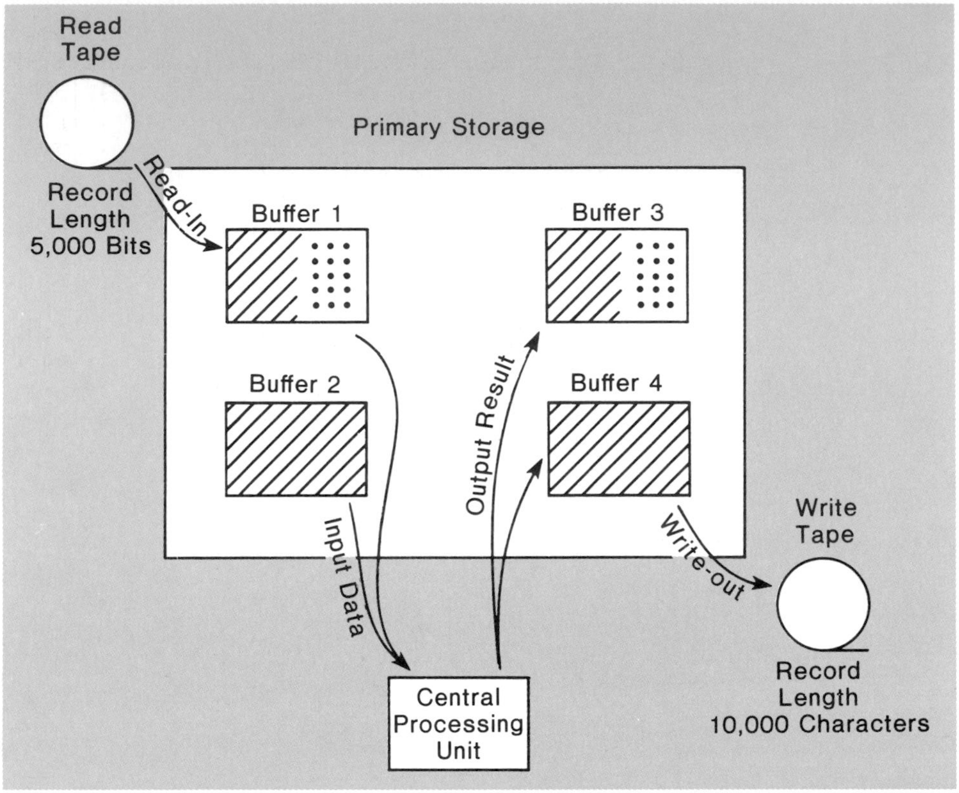

Card Reading and Punching Devices

The punched card is the most common medium for communication with data-processing machines. Data is recorded in a pattern of small rectangular holes punched in specified locations to represent numerals, alphabetic characters, and special characters. The special characters may be $, ., %, #, or other symbols commonly used in data-processing applications (fig. 3.10). A card reader (input) interprets the pattern of holes in the card and automatically converts the data into electronic impulses, thereby entering the information into the machine. The information can also be punched into a card (output) by an automatic card punch. This card can be used as original data and as a common medium of exchange of information between the machines.

Advantages

1. The standardized card format can be combined with other media in efficient data-processing operations.
2. The cards may be stored in an external file for future processing or for visual reference.
3. The cards may be processed through unit record as well as other data-processing equipment.
4. The necessary information concerning a single transaction is usually recorded in a single card.
5. The punched card can be used as an original document, such as checks, time cards, and invoices.

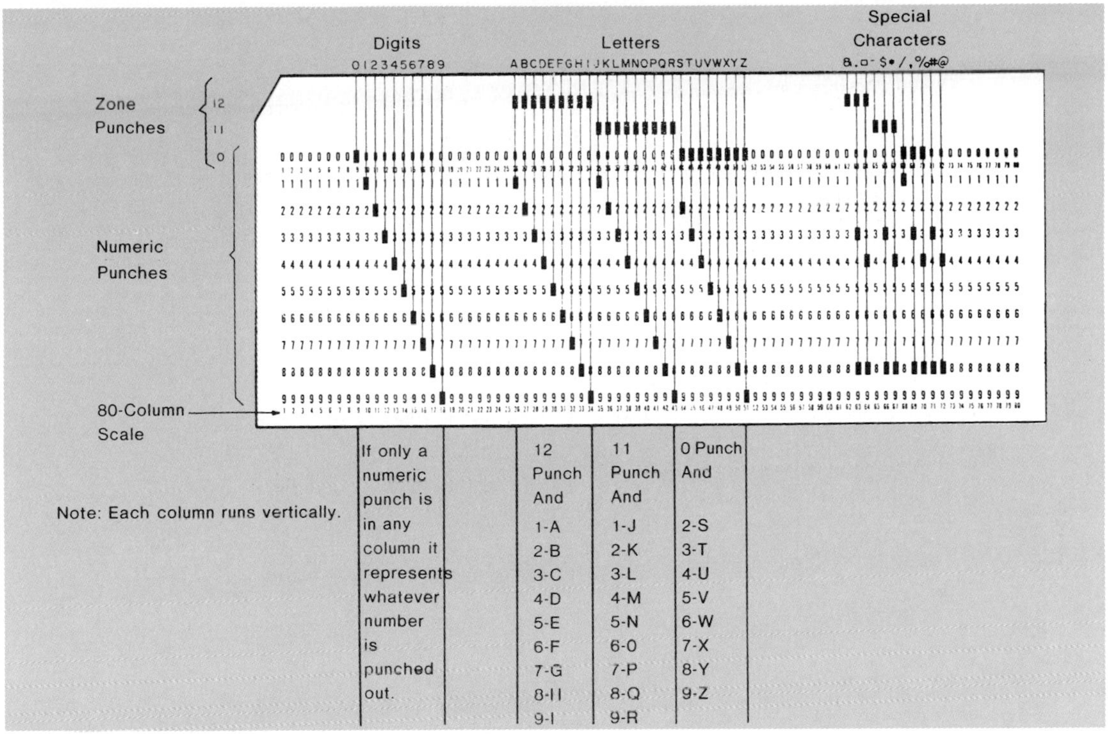

Figure 3.10 An example of a Hollerith coded punched card.

6. The punched card can serve as a communication link between the computer and the user programs in the form of job control cards and also as test media for the various computer programs.

Disadvantages

1. The limitation of eighty columns for information.
2. The relatively slow input and output access time to computer systems.
3. Cards may not be bent, mutilated, or damaged in any manner.
4. Large storage areas are required to store cards. Card file cabinets, racks, and trays can represent a sizable investment in equipment.
5. Because of the bulkiness of cards, transporting them from one location to another can be a problem.
6. Standardized card fields limit the flexibility of operations.

Card Readers

Card-reading devices introduce punched-card records into a data-processing system (fig. 3.11). The cards move past a reading unit that converts the data into a machine-processible electronic format. The speed of card-reading devices will vary.

Card Punches

The output from a data-processing system can be punched into a card by a card-punching device. This is the slowest manner of getting information out of a computer except for typewriter output, but the card punch is often used when the information is to be stored in cards for subsequent processing. The speed of the card punch also will vary.

Figure 3.11 An example of a card-reading device.

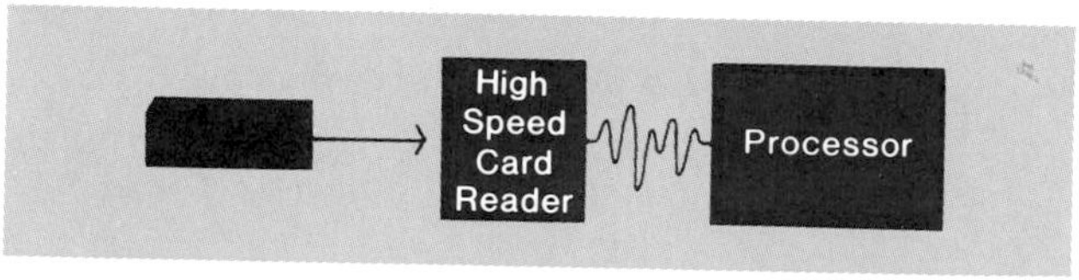

Magnetic Tape Devices

Magnetic tape is one of the fastest methods of entering data into a computer system. Its primary uses are for storing intermediate results of calculations and for compact storage of large files of data. In addition to its high-speed entry, magnetic tape offers efficient, extremely fast recording of processed data. Up to 640,000 numerical characters per second can be read from or written onto a tape.

The magnetic tape operates in the same manner as a home tape recorder. A read/write head accomplishes the actual reading and writing of the information on the tape. The symbols are recorded as a series of magnetized areas, called bits, arranged in a specific pattern along the length of the tape (fig. 3.12). The recordings can be retained indefinitely and reused many times with continued high reliability. The information on the tape is automatically erased by a new recording superimposed in the area. This is known as destructive read in.

The tape, a half-inch wide, is supplied in lengths up to 2400 feet per reel (fig. 3.13). It can be easily handled and stored. Simplified automatic threading and high-speed rewind decreases the processing time of magnetic tape. One inch of tape can store the contents of many cards (fig. 3.14).

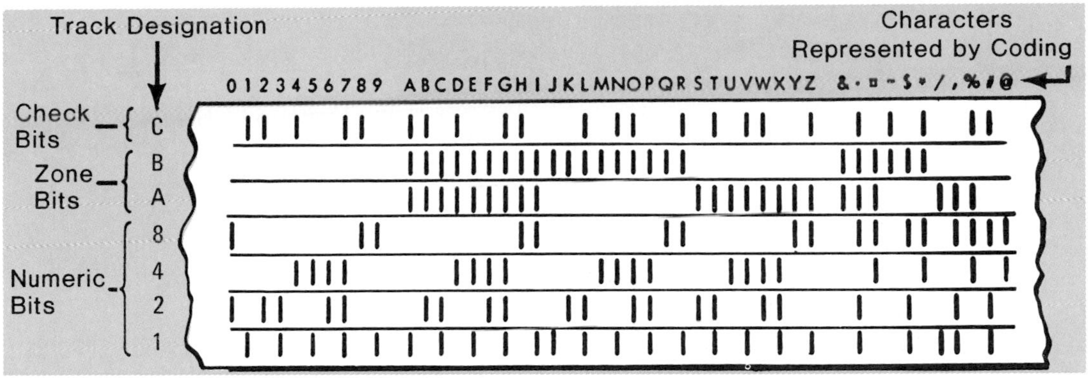

Figure 3.12 The magnetic tape character code.

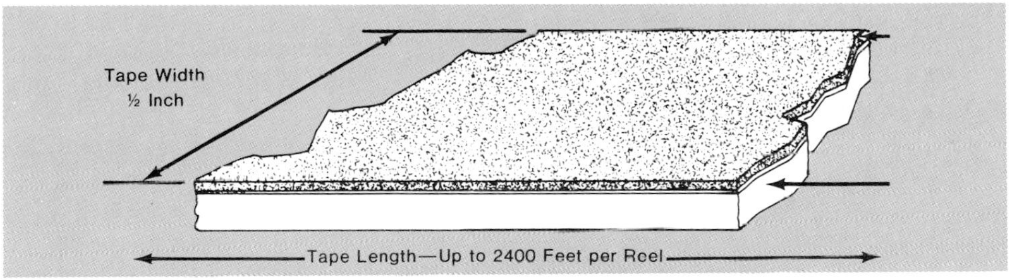

Figure 3.13 The composition of magnetic tape.

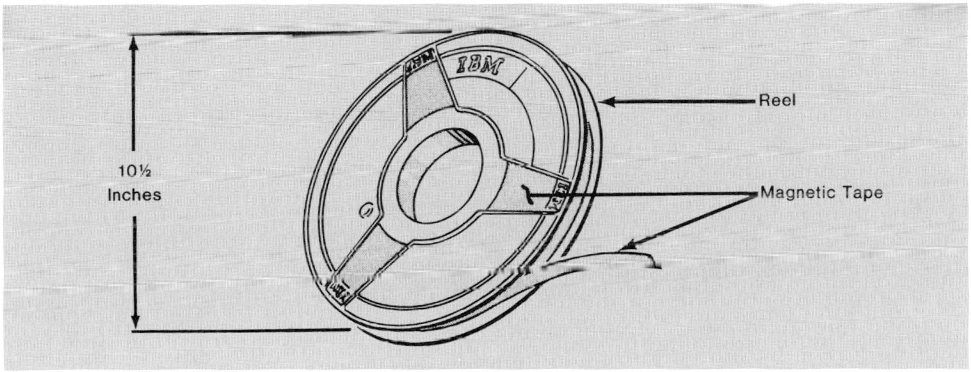

Figure 3.14 The parts of a reel of magnetic tape.

The tape is recorded in character densities of up to 1600 characters per inch. The spacing between the vertical rows is automatically generated during the writing operation. Records are recorded in blocks separated by a space called the interblock gap.

Advantages

1. High-speed input and output recording media.
2. Records are not limited in size and can be as long or as short as needed.
3. Intermediate results can be stored on tape for subsequent processing.
4. Compact storage for large files of information.
5. Reliability of reading and recording due to many self-checking accuracy features.

6. Compact size assures ease of transport.
7. Many tape units can be used simultaneously with the computer.
8. Errors can be corrected merely by writing corrected information over areas containing errors.
9. Available in different densities and lengths to serve individual processing needs.
10. Relative low cost of information storage.

Disadvantages

1. Sequential reading makes it necessary for each record to be examined in order to locate the desired record. This type of processing can be wasteful as the tape will have frequent stops, starts, and rewinds.
2. Magnetic tape is affected by physical elements, such as dust, humidity, and heat, which can affect the recording of the magnetized data on the tape.
3. Information can be lost if the tape is broken, despite the splicing done. The greater the density of the tape, the more information that can be destroyed.
4. A tape that is wound too tight may cause a *bleed-through* on another part of the tape. Some of the information of one section could thus be printed on another portion of the tape within the reel. Frequent rewinding of the tape could prevent some of the bleeding problems.

High-speed data processing demands high-speed input and output devices so the system operations are not slowed by waiting for data or by an inability to get processed data out of a computer. Magnetic tape units, with their dual capacity of input/output and storage, have provided the increased speed necessary to transmit the data to and from the computer and at the same time have provided increased storage capacity for data.

All magnetic tape units are basically the same, but design improvements have increased the tape applications and provided easier operating methods. The tape unit moves past a recording head in a continuous movement at a constant rate of speed. During the reading and writing operations, the tape is constantly in motion. A full tape reel holding 2400 feet of half-inch wide tape weighs about four pounds and contains the equivalent of information contained in approximately 400,000 fully punched cards.

Before tape units can read or write, they must be prepared for operation (fig. 3.15). Two tape reels are mounted on the unit and the tape is threaded through the tape transport mechanism. The head assembly can be separated for ease of threading and it is then closed to make contact with the read/write heads for the reading and writing of the tape.

Tape may be rewound or backspaced to the beginning of the reel. Rewind speeds are as high as 500 inches per second. The loading of the tape reel cartridge is accomplished automatically after the cartridge is placed on the drive by the operator. The time-consuming manual threading involved in the original loading of the tape has been eliminated (fig. 3.16).

Reading/Writing on Magnetic Tape

The magnetic tape unit reads or writes the data as the tape moves past the read/write head (fig. 3.17). The writing on magnetic tape is destructive in that the new information erases the old (destructible) information on the tape. A tape may be read repeatedly with the information on the tape remaining unaltered. Reading is nondestructive.

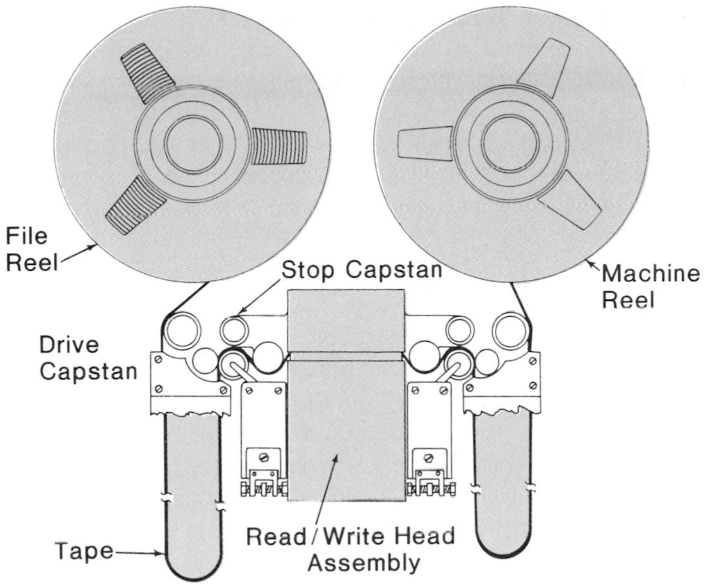

Figure 3.15
Threading of magnetic tape.

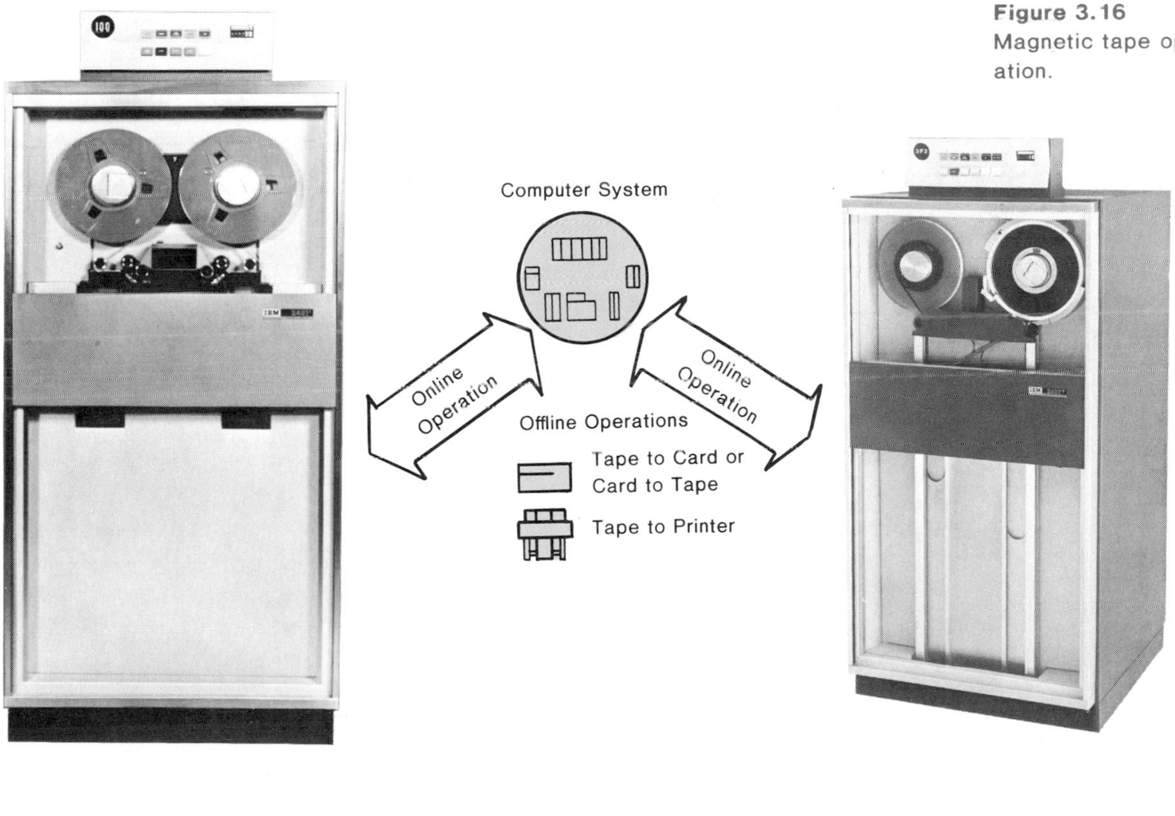

Figure 3.16
Magnetic tape operation.

Information is written in tape by magnetizing areas in parallel tracks along the length of the tape. Data recorded in tape must be checked for accuracy so no information errors are transmitted through the system. The data is checked to insure that only valid characters are recorded and also to verify that the recorded bits are of effective magnetic strength. A *parity check* is made as the information is read from a magnetic tape. A character code check (vertical) is made on each column of information to ensure that an even number of bits is detected for each character read. If an odd number of bits is detected for any character, an error is indicated unless the computer operates in odd parity; then the reverse would be true.

Magnetic Tape Records

Records on tape are not restricted to any fixed record size of characters, words, or blocks. They may be any size within the limits of the particular computer.

Blocks of records, which may be a single record or several records, are separated on the tape by an interblock gap, a length of blank tape averaging about .6 inch to .75 inch. This gap is automatically produced at the end of each block of records during

Figure 3.17 Magnetic tape read/write heads.

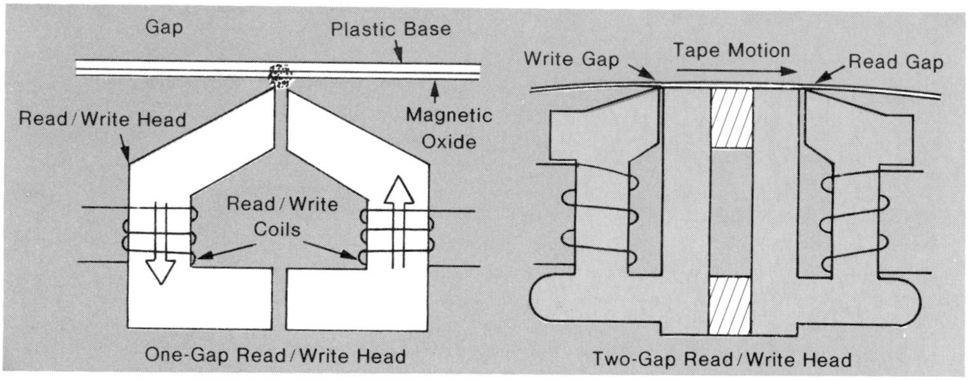

Figure 3.18 Magnetic tape records.

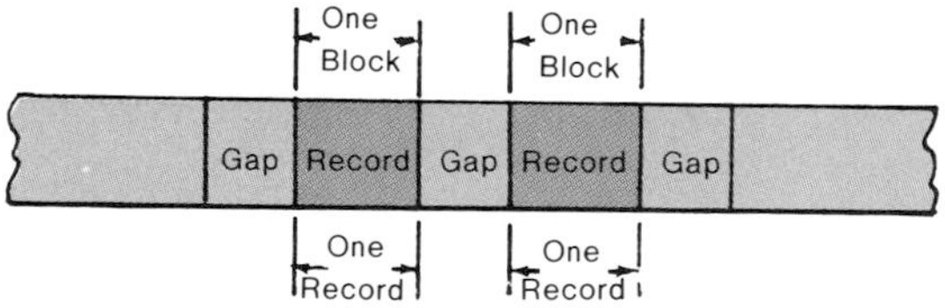

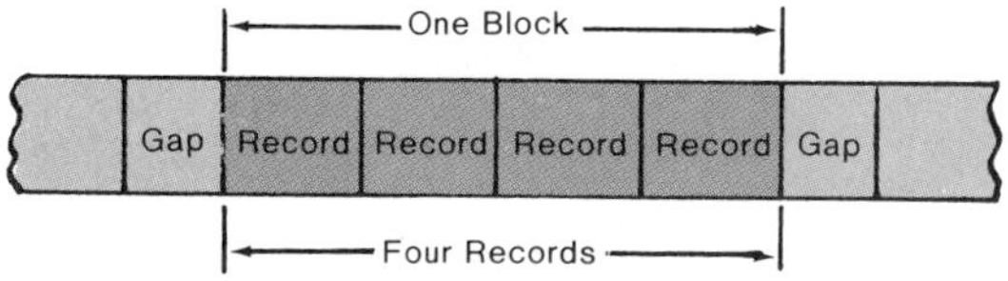

On magnetic tape, a single unit or block of information is marked by an interblock gap before and after the data. A record block may contain one record or several.

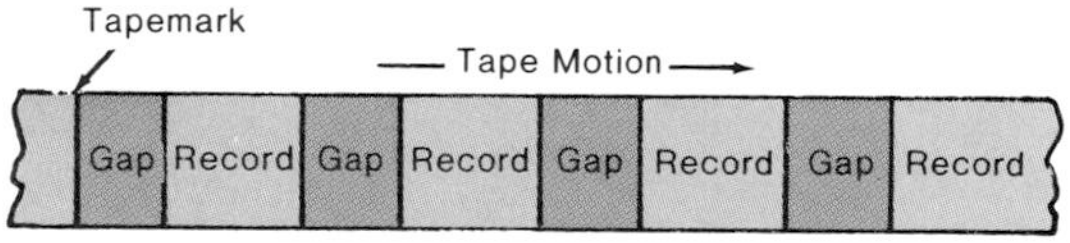

The interblock gap followed by a unique character record is used to mark the end of a file of information. The unique character, a tapemark, is generated in response to an instruction and is written on the tape following the last record of the file.

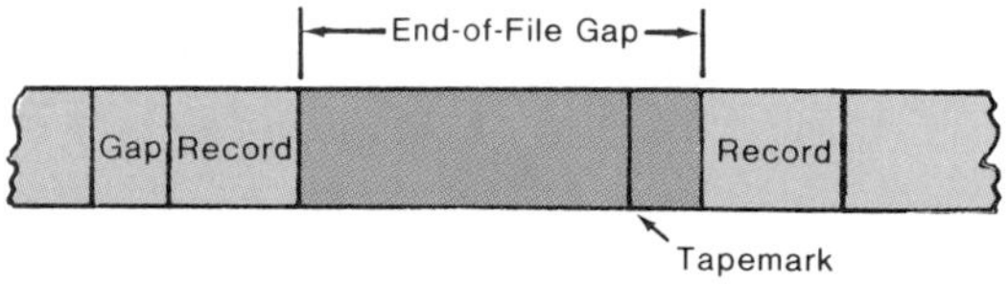

the writing of a tape. During the reading, the block begins with the first character sensed after the gap and continues the reading without interruption until the next gap is reached. The interblock gap provides the necessary time for starting and stopping the tape between blocks of records. The end of a file of records is indicated by a tapemark, which is written and read by most computers (fig. 3.18).

Blank space must be provided at the beginning and ending of a reel to allow threading through the feed mechanism. A reflective strip, called a marker, is usually placed at the beginning and end of the tape to enable the photoelectric cells in the tape unit to sense the loadpoint, where the reading or writing is to begin (see fig. 3.19), or the end-of-reel marker, where the writing is to stop.

Because of the destructive read-in feature of the write operation, it is wise to use a file protection device ring to prevent the accidental erasure of information that is to be saved for future reference. This device is a plastic ring that fits into a round groove molded in the tape reel. When the ring is in place, either reading or writing can occur. When the ring is removed, writing is suppressed and only reading can take place, protecting the file from accidental erasure (fig. 3.20).

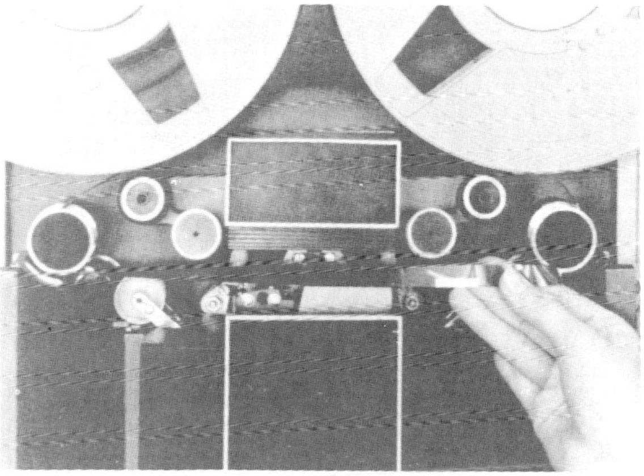

Figure 3.19 The loadpoint marker.

Figure 3.20 Examples of file protection devices. On noncartridge tape, the file protection device is a plastic ring that fits into a round groove molded in the tape reel. When the ring is in place, either reading or writing can occur. When the ring is removed, writing is suppressed and only reading can take place; thus, the file is protected from accidental erasure.

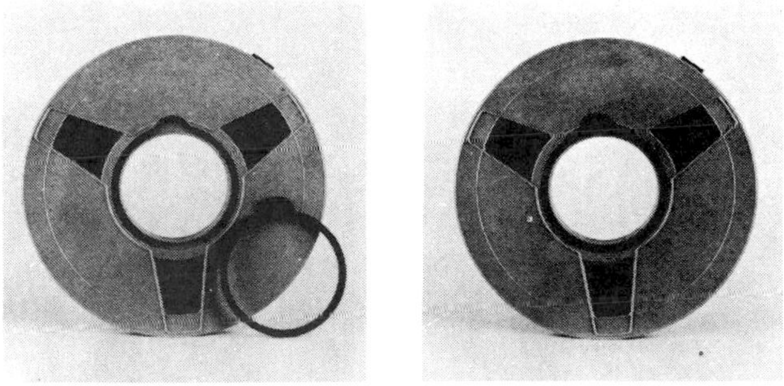

Paper Tape Devices

Paper tape serves the same purpose as punched cards. It is a continuous recording medium compared to the 80-character limit of punched cards. The tape can be used to record data in records of any length, limited only by the storage media into which the data is to be placed or from which the data is received. The data is recorded as a special arrangement of punched holes along the length of the tape.

A paper tape reader interprets the data (input) and a paper tape punch (output) punches holes in the paper tape. The data is recorded (punched) and read as holes in channels along the length of the tape. One column, similar to punched cards, is used to represent characters either alphabetic, numeric, or special. The eight-channel tape is the most commonly used. The lower four channels, excluding feed holes, are labeled 8, 4, 2, and 1 and are used to represent numeric values of characters. The sum of the values indicates the number value; for example, a combination of 1 and 4 is used to represent a numeric five.

The X and O channels are similar to zone punches of punched cards. These punches, combined with the numeric values, are used to form alphabetic and special characters. A check hole must be present for any channel whose basic code consists of an even number of holes. This technique is used to check that each character is recorded correctly in the tape with an odd number of holes (fig. 3.21).

Advantages

1. Paper tape can be used to transport data long distances over telephone or telegraph wires to produce a duplicate tape at the other end.
2. Punched cards can be converted to punched tape at the other end of the wire and later reconverted to punched cards or magnetic tape for processing.
3. Paper tape, not as heavy or as bulky as punched cards, is easy to transport and mail.
4. Paper tape is cheaper to produce (twenty-five cents per 100 feet).
5. Paper tape can be produced as a by-product of another operation; for example, a summary of cash register receipts can be punched in a paper tape and submitted to the data-processing unit for processing.
6. The paper tape is not limited in record size as punched cards.
7. The paper tape can be read into and out of a computer at a greater rate of speed than punched cards.

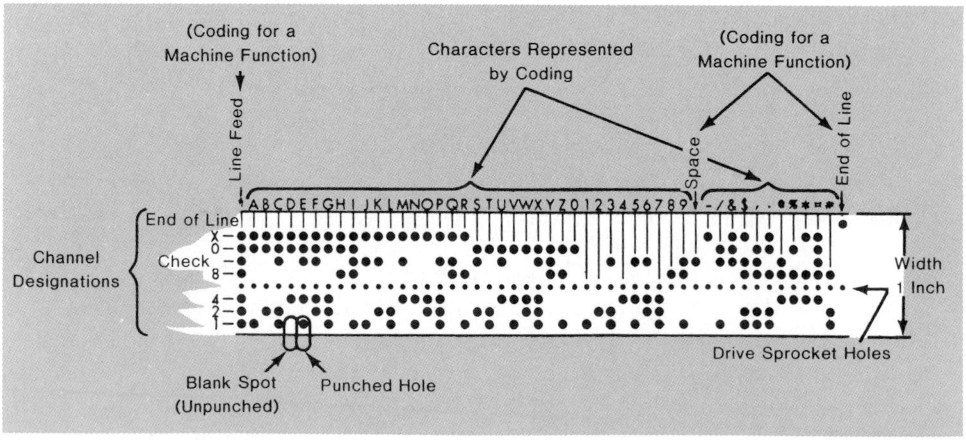

Figure 3.21 The coding of paper tape.

Disadvantages

1. Compared to other input media (magnetic tape), paper tape is rather slow.
2. Paper tape is not as durable as punched cards.
3. The data in paper tape must be converted to another form before the information can be manipulated.
4. The data in paper tape cannot be altered without punching another tape.

A telephone company uses paper tape extensively in recording long-distance telephone calls. As the user dials the long-distance number, such information as the calling number, receiving station, date, time of day, and amount of time is punched into the tape automatically and later transcribed into magnetic tape for high-speed processing. This use of paper tape has been a vital factor in the lowering of long-distance call charges.

The data punched in the paper tape is read or interpreted by a paper tape reader and recorded by a paper tape punch.

Output

A wide variety of output devices for data processing is available. Their capabilities keep changing with technologies. The selection criteria for output should be based on how it can improve productivity. The system implementation selected should be capable of change so that as technology changes occur, the system can be improved for better and wider use.

In the past, the predominant output medium was hard copy printed paper produced by computer output printers. Today, other choices are available for specific applications. Teletypewriters are used for communicating messages over telephone lines. Microfilm is used as a volume-saving technique for document storage. Display terminals started as a means for retrieval of information from systems with rapid change, such as reservation systems. Changes in the devices themselves and other system changes have affected the application areas for these different output approaches.

The factors that affect computer output selection are the cost per line of copy, the timeliness of the information, the convenience and availability of output, the necessary capital expenditures, and the effect on the present system's computing capability. Applications for communicating messages and interactive keyboard terminals use fairly low-quality printout, whereas word processing applications use higher quality.

Printers

The printers provide the permanent visual record (hard copy) from a data-processing system. As an output device, the printer receives data from the computer and prints the reports. A paper transport automatically spaces the form as the report is being prepared (fig. 3.22).

A printer is a read-only device, driven directly by a computer, that prints discrete symbols on paper. A teleprinter is usually understood to be a unit that interfaces over a communications link, such as a teletype or telephone network (fig. 3.23).

The output of a printer is printed information on paper. It is convenient to handle, readable by humans, and may be filed, retrieved, or modified by writing and erasing. It is possible to have personal control over the paper output. It is available when you want it and may be sent from place to place by means of the mail. Colored paper may

Figure 3.22 An example of a printer. (Photo by Ken Firestone)

Figure 3.23 Examples of printers and teleprinters.

be used to highlight certain aspects of information and control maintained by special paper with watermarks, such as currency or signatures that determine authenticity. Methods of distribution are available in every civilized country. With the information explosion, the demand could exceed the resource. Fortunately, there are alternatives for output that reduce this demand.

Printers are available on the marketplace, ranging in speed from 10 characters per second to 18,000 characters per second, from $1000 to $300,000 in price, and from barely readable print quality to quality obtainable from printing processes. The printing techniques range from impact to nonimpact serial character to parallel line printers, shaped character output to dot matrix character images, and plotters which use movable pens, or dot matrix imaging, with nonimpact printing technologies.

The application for different speed classes of output printers depends on the volume of output required, the price of the printer, and the quality of output.

A user can buy a printer from a distributor, systems house, a computer manufacturer, or directly from a printer manufacturer, but whatever the choice, the user should know what printer types are on the market, how they differ in performance and cost, and how to select equipment to meet specific needs.

A user can choose between an *impact* and a *nonimpact* printer. *Impact* printers transfer ink to paper in two ways (fig. 3.24). The front-striking mechanism operates like a typewriter—a character strikes a ribbon against the paper to form an image. In hammer devices, the ribbon and paper are struck against a character to form an image. *Nonimpact* printers generally use specially coated or sensitized papers that respond to thermal or electrostatic stimuli to form an image. Some use ink jets or xerography to form an image on plain paper.

Printers either employ *shaped* characters or use *dot matrix* image formation. *Shaped* characters are preformed alphanumeric symbols, which strike or are struck by the ribbon and paper via a hammer mechanism. The characters can be carried on such devices as drums, chains, belt bands, daisy wheels, or typeballs. *Dot matrix* print heads use a number of print needs or ink jets to form alphanumeric symbols on the paper, with the pattern generated according to the character being formed. Some newer matrix printers employ a very fine matrix of dots—as many as 300 to the inch—producing characters that look like shaped characters.

A user can also choose between *serial* printers and *line* printers. The *serial* printer produces one character at a time, usually printing from left to right across a page, although units now on the market can print in both directions. A *line* printer prints a group of characters simultaneously on the same line. The groups constituting a line are printed so quickly that the entire line appears to be printed at once. Line printers are generally faster than serial printers, but they are also more expensive.

When choosing a printer, the major selection criteria should include the printer's speed and cost; but the primary concern should be the nature of the application. For example, a 30 cps (characters per second) printer would be fast enough to be used as an interactive terminal, but too slow to handle the volume of invoices and reports produced by the average small business.

An application should also dictate print quality. Clean legible copy is a must in invoices, statements, or letters to customers. Poor print quality may be acceptable only if the printouts are to be used internally. Such consideration boils the choice down to either a dot matrix printer or a shaped character unit (fig. 3.25).

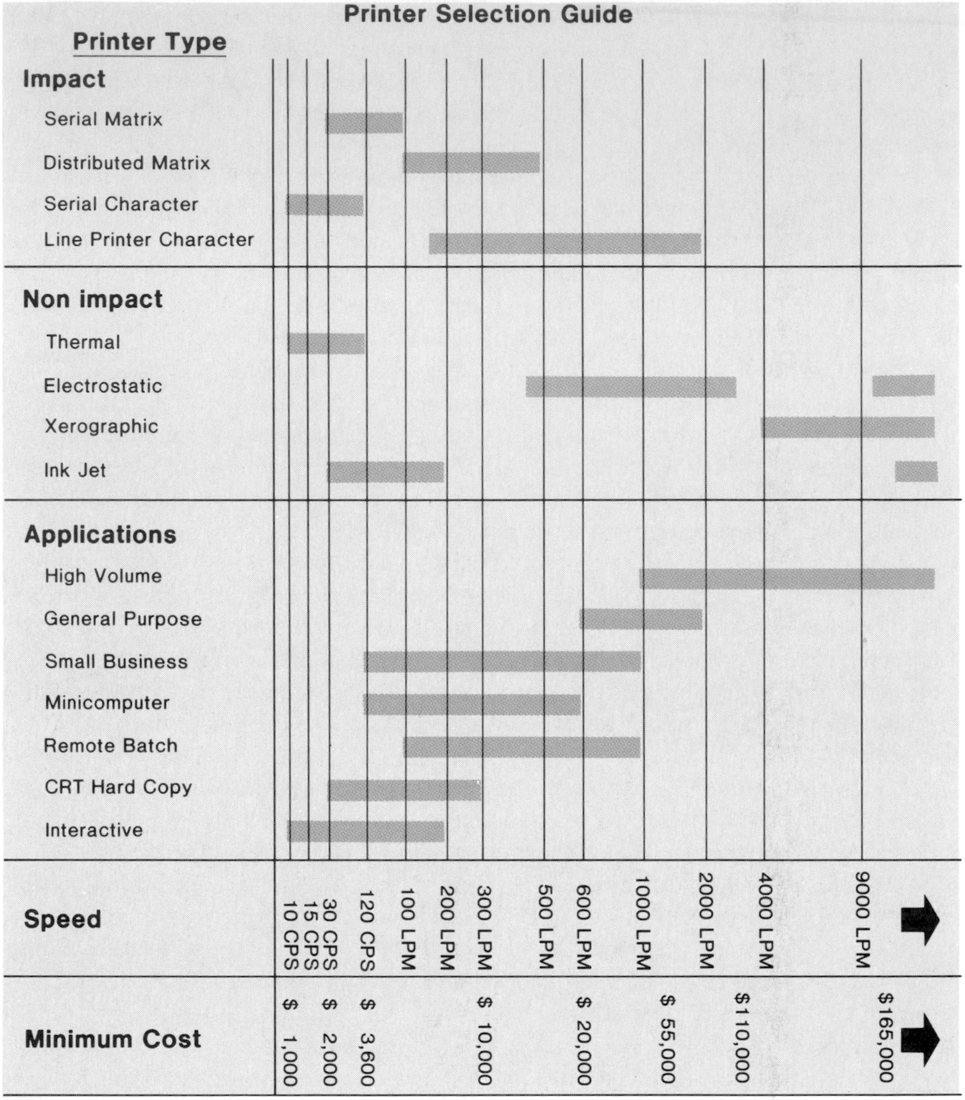

Figure 3.24 A printer selection guide. (Copyright 1978 by Cahners Publishing Company, Division of Reed Publishing Corporation. Reprinted with permission from *Mini-Micro Systems*, January 1978.)

Consoles

The console of a data-processing system is used by the operator to control the system and monitor its operations. Keys, switches, audible tone signals, and display lights are some of the manual controls available to the operator for manipulation and checking of the program (fig. 3.26).

Although the console of a data-processing system is not ordinarily used as a data-recording medium (except in small computer systems), small quantities of information can be entered at a relatively slow speed to keep the system operational. In many data-processing systems used for engineering applications, console typewriters are used to insert data needed to complete the computations. If the system is bottled up by an

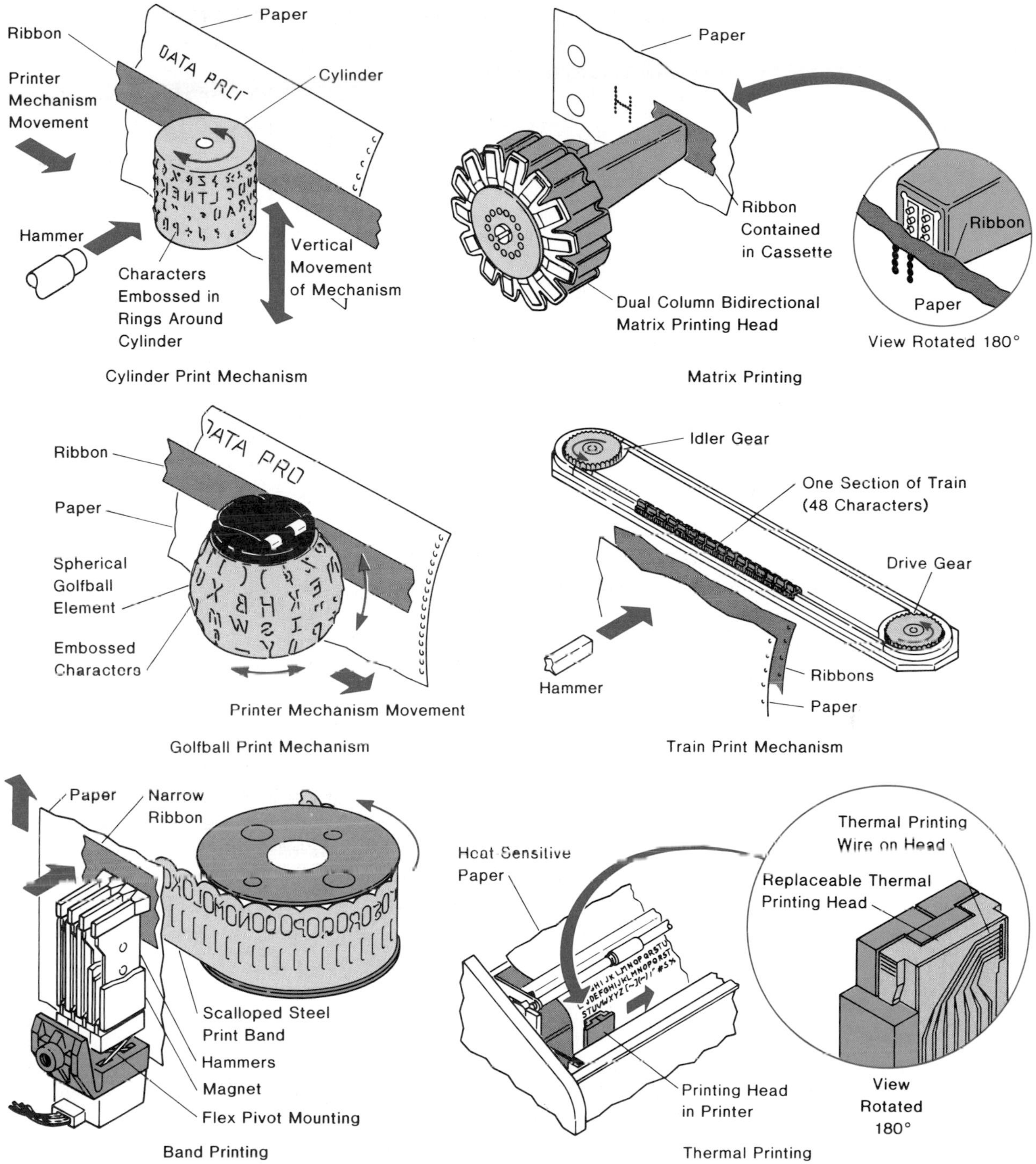

Figure 3.25 Examples of printers. (Copyright 1978 by Cahners Publishing Company, Division of Reed Publishing Corporation. Reprinted with permission from *Mini-Micro Systems*, January 1978.)

Figure 3.25
Continued.

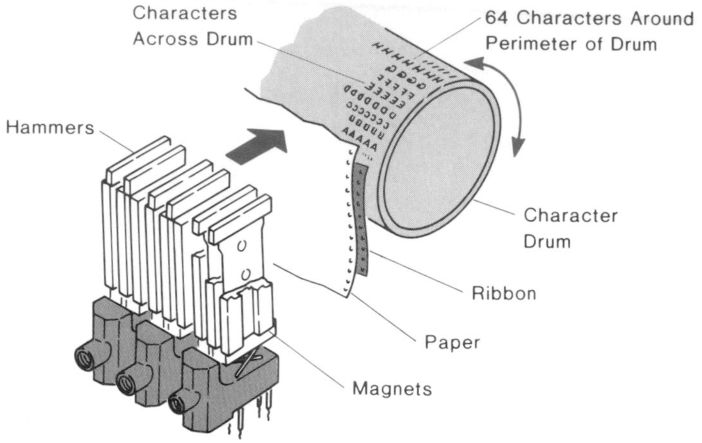

Drum Print Mechanism

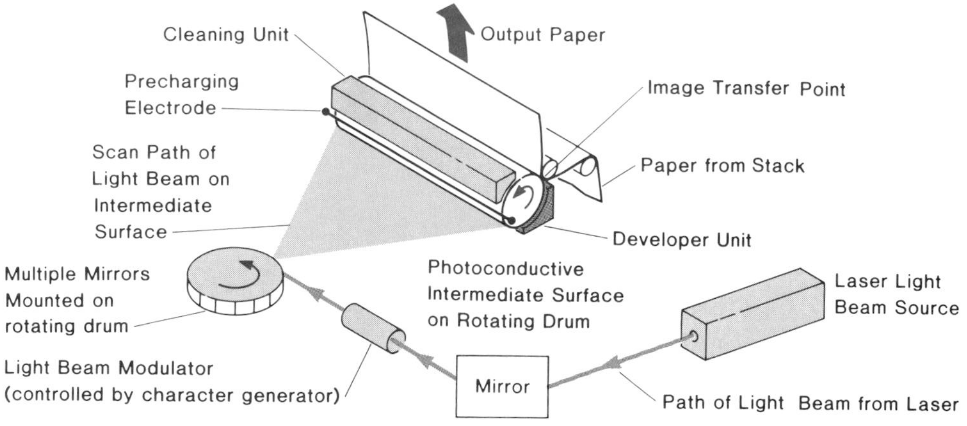

Laser Xerographic

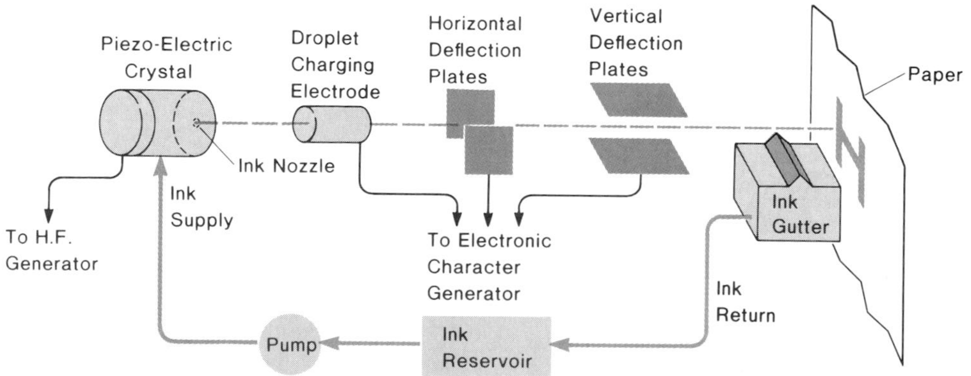

Ink Jet Mechanism

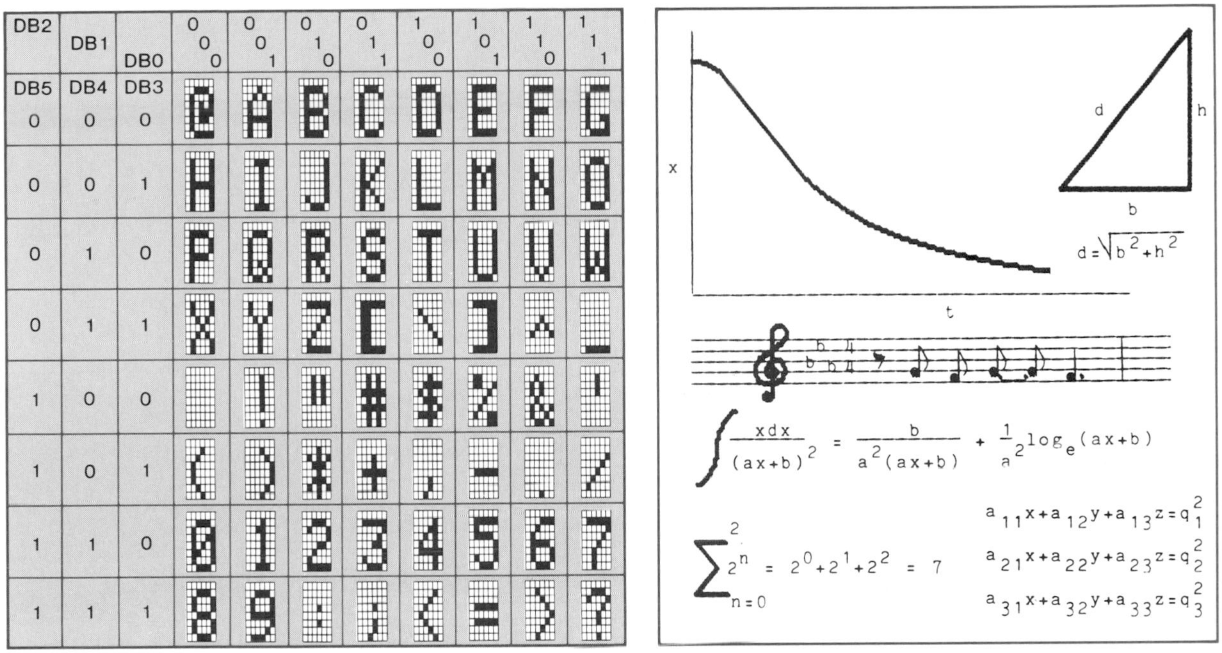

Figure 3.25
Continued.

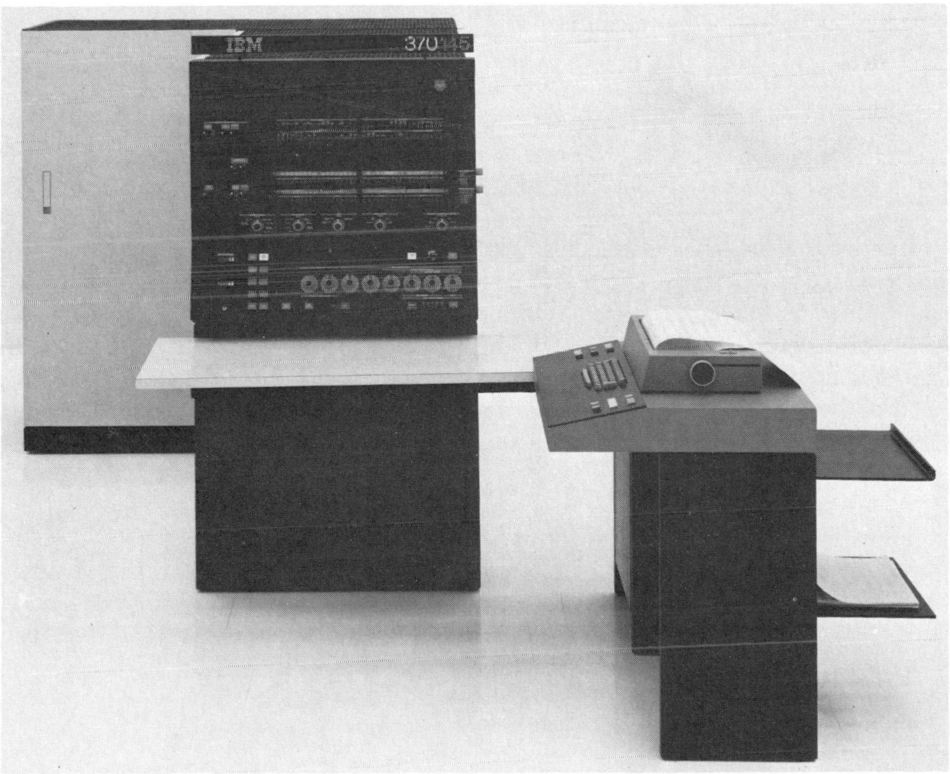

Figure 3.26 The IBM 370 console.

Figure 3.27
Console operation.

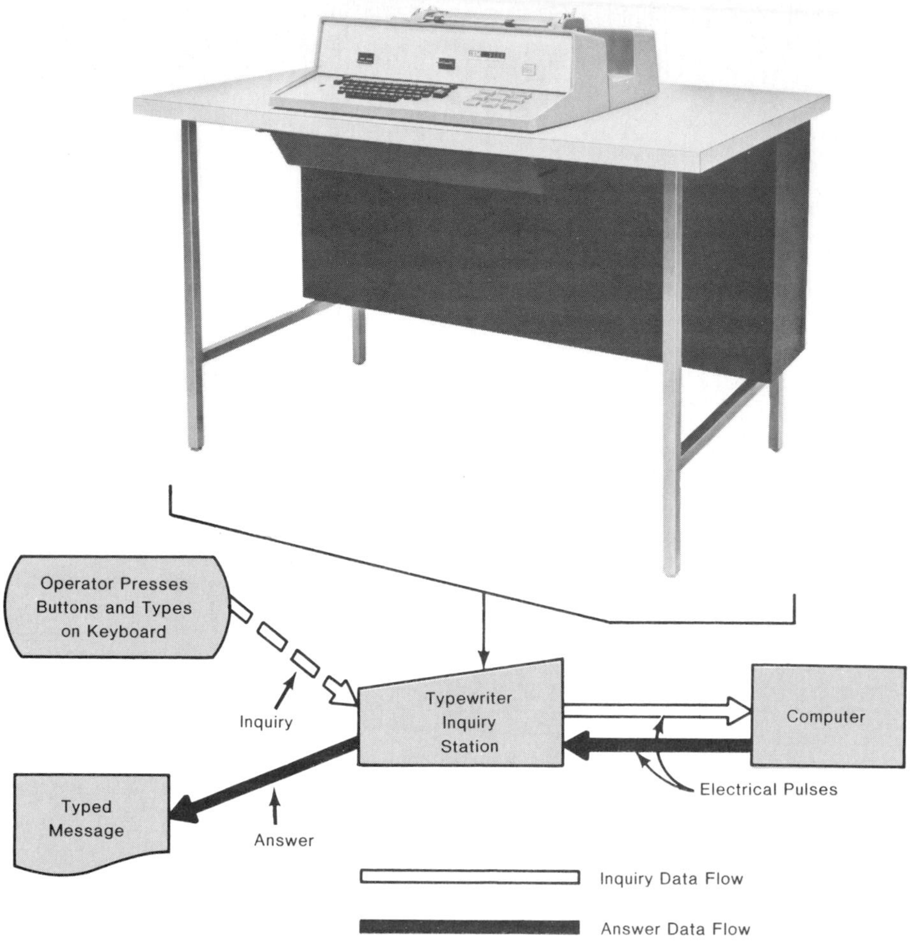

error condition or a condition requiring the entry of data into the system, such as code or reference numbers, the console operator can cause the operation of the system to be resumed by typing the correct information on the console (fig. 3.27).

Communication network signals, microfilm, and audio tones are just a few of the methods used to communicate with the computer. Due to the moon exploration, it is even conceivable that, in the future, data will be entered into and extracted from computers on the moon via the various satellites. The list of data-recording media grows larger each year.

Computer Output Microfilm (COM)

Since the paper shortage and the corresponding increase in cost of paper, computer output to microfilm has become very popular. Output from microfilm recorders can be stored in less space than any other computer output, therefore saving storage space

Figure 3.28 An example of microfilm.

(fig. 3.28). The user may look at the 35mm or 16mm file and decide if and when to print. Resolution is quite adequate for enlargements of thirty magnifications so that 24-by-36 inch or 30-by-42 inch drawings may be plotted.

In the *microfiche* process, many documents can be placed and photographed on a single sheet of film, typically 4 by 6 inches. New documents can be added to unused portions at any time, and the film can be accessed randomly.

A more conventional *microfilm* system, on the other hand, maintains data on a spool of film. Data is recorded, updated, and retrieved sequentially, as on computer magnetic tape.

The microfilm recorder is a peripheral system which processes a specially coded magnetic tape obtained as output from a computer program to produce alphanumeric, pictorial, or graphic output (fig. 3.29). As the tape is read, the desired lines and characters are displayed on a specialized display terminal. Sensitized paper and/or film is exposed to the display and the results are developed.

COM output is readable, but a film reader is necessary to allow the operator to read information stored on the film. Some COM equipment provides the capability of adding indexing data to and retrieving simplified data from the basic stored information.

Figure 3.29 The COM process; directing the computer output to microfilm. (Copyright 1976, *Data Management* magazine, Data Processing Management Association.)

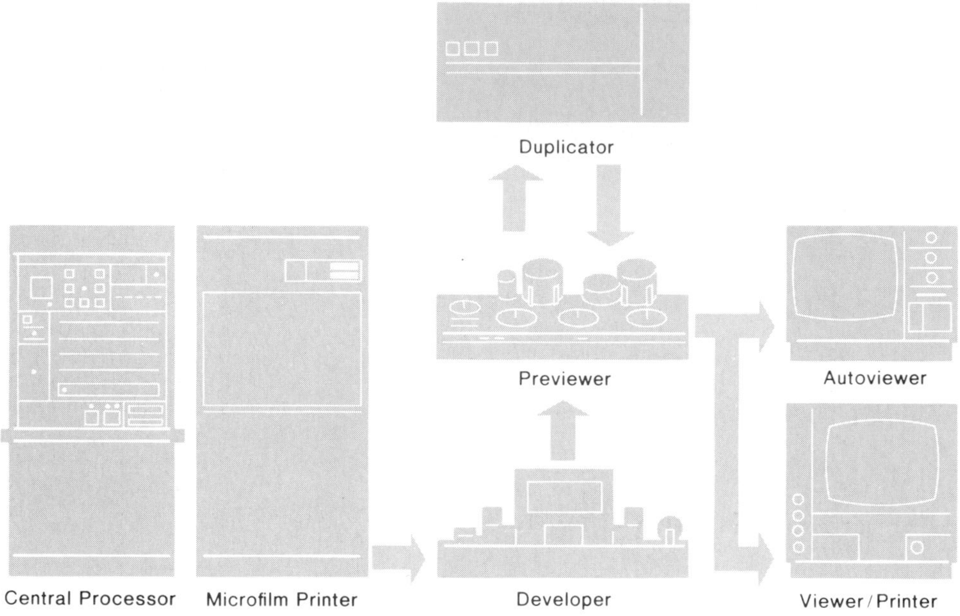

Advantages

The advantages of COM are the low-volume storage requirements, the low storage cost, and high output speed. A microfilm cassette occupies approximately 1 percent as much space as a comparable stack, whereas a microfiche occupies less than .05 percent as much space as equivalent paper (fig. 3.30). The storage costs are approximately one-tenth that of paper, and the speeds vary between 5000 and 30,000 lines per minute.

These speeds are comparable to the very high-speed nonimpact printers available today, but the price of the COM printer is 20 to 50 percent of the nonimpact printers. The distribution of reports on microfiche (rectangular sheet of film) is much simpler and less costly than comparable paper reports.

COM applications include output for archival storage and for inquiry situation reports (fig. 3.31). These include catalogs, lists, and status statements that are updated no more than once a day, but require significant retrieval. COM is being used where fairly large volumes of reports are produced each month. The telephone company uses the microfiche to answer inquiries relative to customers' telephone bills.

Disadvantages

COM's principal disadvantage is the psychological factor associated with having to read reports using a microfilm reader. It is strange and uncomfortable to operate a microfilm reader. The output is also not available for writing notes. Initial investment for COM equipment is relatively high, and many systems also require film-developing equipment. Finally, the cost for using COM equipment, which includes data preparation, a microfilm reader, and supplies, must be considered.

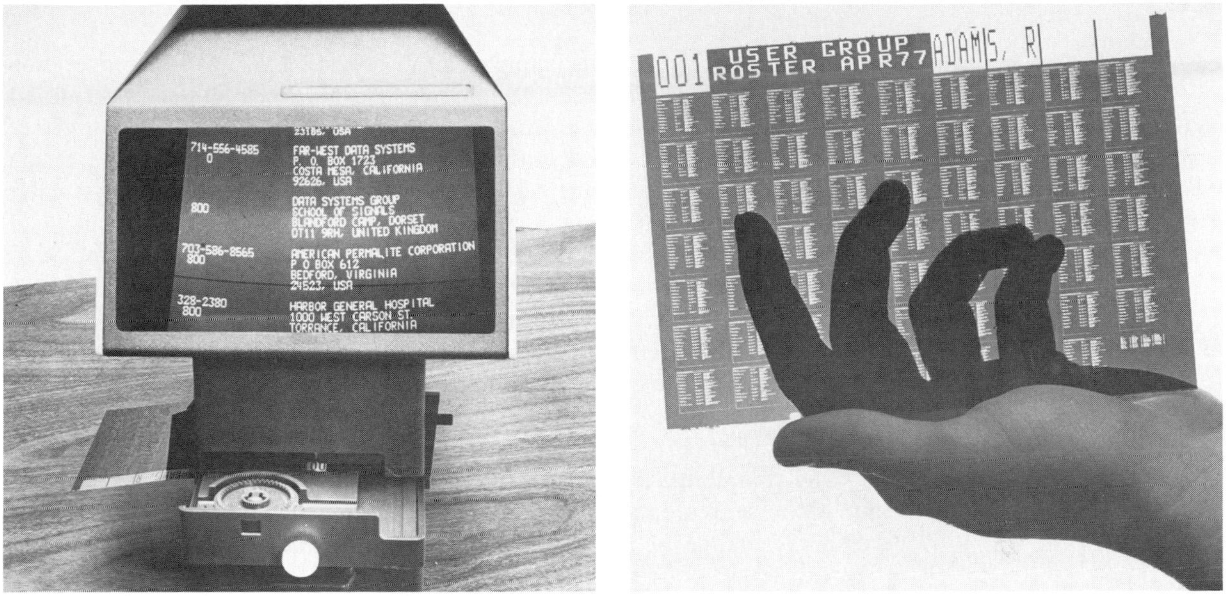

Figure 3.30 Examples of microfiche. (Photos by Ken Firestone)

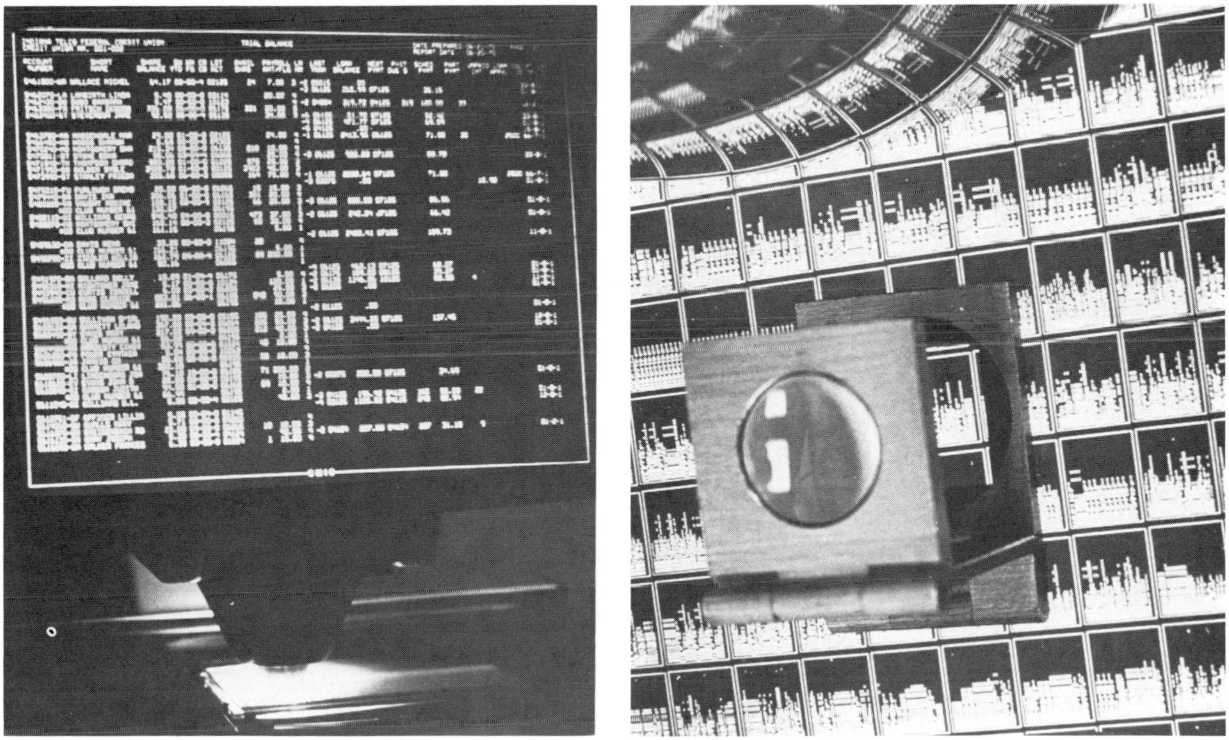

Figure 3.31 Examples of microfilm applications. (Courtesy of ANACOMP, Inc.)

Summary

The study of computer components is important in providing insight to the operation of the computer. This chapter describes the physical characteristics of the input/output devices and introduces computer processing. The advantages and disadvantages of each input/output device are listed so the user can become familiar with the media used to record data and can evaluate and determine the one best suited for a particular application.

The operation of input/output devices is essential to the understanding of data-processing procedures. The input/output devices are one of the most important segments of computer processing. An efficient data-processing installation must have a balanced input/output system. Because of the variety of input/output devices, it is important to understand the operations, the features, and the capabilities of each type of device.

1. The basic considerations in data processing are input, processing, and output. Input is the source data entering the system. Processing is the planned steps necessary to change the data into the desired result. Output is the finished result, or the end result of the system.
2. The basic elements of a computer system are the hardware and the software. The hardware is the physical equipment of a data-processing system, such as input/output devices, central processing unit, and storage. Software is a set of programs, procedures, and possible associated documentation concerned with the operation of a data-processing system. COBOL and FORTRAN compilers and Sort/Merge programs are examples of software.

   The hardware elements of a computer are input devices, output devices, a central processing unit, and storage devices. The input devices are used to enter data into a data-processing system. Output devices accept data from the system and record it. The central processing unit accepts data for processing and makes results available for output devices. Storage devices are used for temporary and permanent storage of data.
3. Input and output devices are units for putting data into and getting data out of a storage unit of a computer. The control unit coordinates input and output units with the central processing unit. The channel manages input/output devices and control units. The buffer is an external device used to store data prior to entry into storage or prior to output.
4. Card reading and punching devices are the most common data-processing media. Data is recorded in a pattern of small rectangular holes in specified locations to represent all characters. The advantages of this device are standardized card format, storage capability, unit record principle, and use as original documents. The disadvantages are the limitation of eighty columns, slow input and output, and bulkiness. The card readers introduce punched-card records into a data-processing system. Card punches punch information into cards.
5. Magnetic tape devices are the fastest method of entry into a computer. Data is recorded as a series of magnetized areas along the tape. The advantages of this device are high-speed input and output media, unlimited size of records, compact size, errors can be corrected in the same area of tape, and high reliability of

reading and recording. The disadvantages are sequential reading of records, is affected by physical elements, and information can be lost if the tape is broken. The parity check is used to insure correct number of bits in each character. The interrecord gap separates blocks of records. The file protection ring prevents accidental erasure of data on tape.

6. Paper tape devices are a continuous recording media. Data is recorded as special arrangement of punched holes in tape. The advantages of this device are electronic transportation over long distances, is not heavy or bulky, may be a by-product of another system, and records are not limited in size. The disadvantages are slow input and output as compared to other media, not durable, must be converted to another form before processing, and cannot be altered without repunching a new tape. The paper tape reader reads the punched holes in tape. The paper tape punch punches holes into blank tape as data is received from main storage.
7. As output devices, printers provide the permanent visual record (hard copy) from a data-processing system. Printers are available in a variety of types and speeds. Consoles are used to enter small amounts of data into a system. The console operator can control and monitor the system's operation.
8. Computer output microfilm (COM) is a specially coded magnetic tape obtained from a computer program. It can serve as output for archival storage and inquiry reports. The advantages of COM are low-volume storage requirements, low storage costs, and high output speed. The disadvantages are that the output is not available for notes, that it requires a large initial investment, and that it requires film development equipment, data preparation, microfilm readers, and supplies.

Identification Questions

Match the following terms with the statements below.

A. Arithmetic and Logical Section
B. Buffer
C. Card Punch
D. Card Reader
E. Central Processing Unit
F. Channel
G. Console
H. Control Section
I. Control Unit
J. Data Processing
K. Destructive Read In
L. Hardware
M. Input
N. Interblock Gap
O. Machine Language
P. Magnetic Tape
Q. Microfiche
R. Microfilm
S. Offline
T. Online
U. Output
V. Paper Tape
W. Parity Check
X. Printer
Y. Processing
Z. Program
AA. Software
BB. Spooling

1. Coordinates input/output operations with the central processing unit.
2. Equipment directly connected to the system.
3. Synchronizes the processing of input/output operations with the processing of the data.
4. Insures that only valid characters are recorded in a data-processing system.
5. Controls the system and monitors its operations.
6. A series in a logical sequence that accomplishes a particular job.

7. Physical equipment of a system forming a computer and its peripheral devices.
8. Manipulates data between core storage and the arithmetic and logical section.
9. An output device that prints discrete symbols on paper.
10. A planned series of actions and operations upon information using various forms of data-processing equipment to achieve a desired result.
11. A definite pattern of symbols interpreted by the machine.
12. Introduces punched cards into a data-processing system.
13. Many documents photographed on a single sheet of film.
14. Source data entering the system.
15. A set of programs, procedures, and possibly associated documentation concerned with the operation of a data-processing system.
16. Equipment not directly connected to the system.
17. One of the fastest methods of entering data into a data-processing system.
18. A space that separates records recorded in blocks.
19. Planned processing steps necessary to change the data into the desired result.
20. Data recorded on a spool of film.
21. Accepts data for processing and makes results available for output.
22. The reading and writing of input and output streams of data recorded on an auxiliary storage device.
23. The finished result.
24. Punches output from a data-processing system into cards.
25. Performs all functions of arithmetic and directs the processing unit in decision making.
26. A separate piece of equipment devoted exclusively to managing input/output devices and control units assigned to it.
27. Each new recording erases previous data.
28. Data recorded as holes in channels along length of tape.

Questions for Review

1. A computer accepts data, processes data, and puts out results. List the basic considerations in computer data processing.
2. Differentiate between hardware and software features of a computer system.
3. What is the difference between online and offline equipment? Give examples of each.
4. What are the major hardware elements used in a computer? Explain the function of each of these elements.
5. What is the primary function of the input/output devices?
6. What function does a control unit perform in an input/output device?
7. Explain the main function of a channel.
8. What part does the buffering system play in the processing of input/output operations?
9. What is spooling?
10. What are the main advantages and disadvantages of punched cards?
11. Explain the operation of a magnetic tape device.
12. How is data recorded on magnetic tape?
13. What are the important advantages and disadvantages of magnetic tape?

14. Explain the purpose of a parity check.
15. How are magnetic tape records recorded? What is the purpose of the interblock gap?
16. What are the main uses of paper tape?
17. What are the important advantages and disadvantages of paper tape?
18. What is a printer? Briefly describe the different types of printers.
19. What is the primary function of a console?
20. What are the advantages of microfilm?
21. How is data recorded on microfilm and how is it output?
22. What is the main difference between the microfiche process and the more conventional microfilm system?

Key Terms

Arithmetic and Logical Section
Buffer
Card Punch
Card Reader
Central Processing Unit
Channel
Console
Control Section
Control Unit
Data Processing
Destructive Read In
Hardware
Input
Interblock Gap
Machine Language
Magnetic Tape
Microfiche
Microfilm
Offline
Online
Output
Paper Tape
Parity Check
Printer
Processing
Program
Software
Spooling

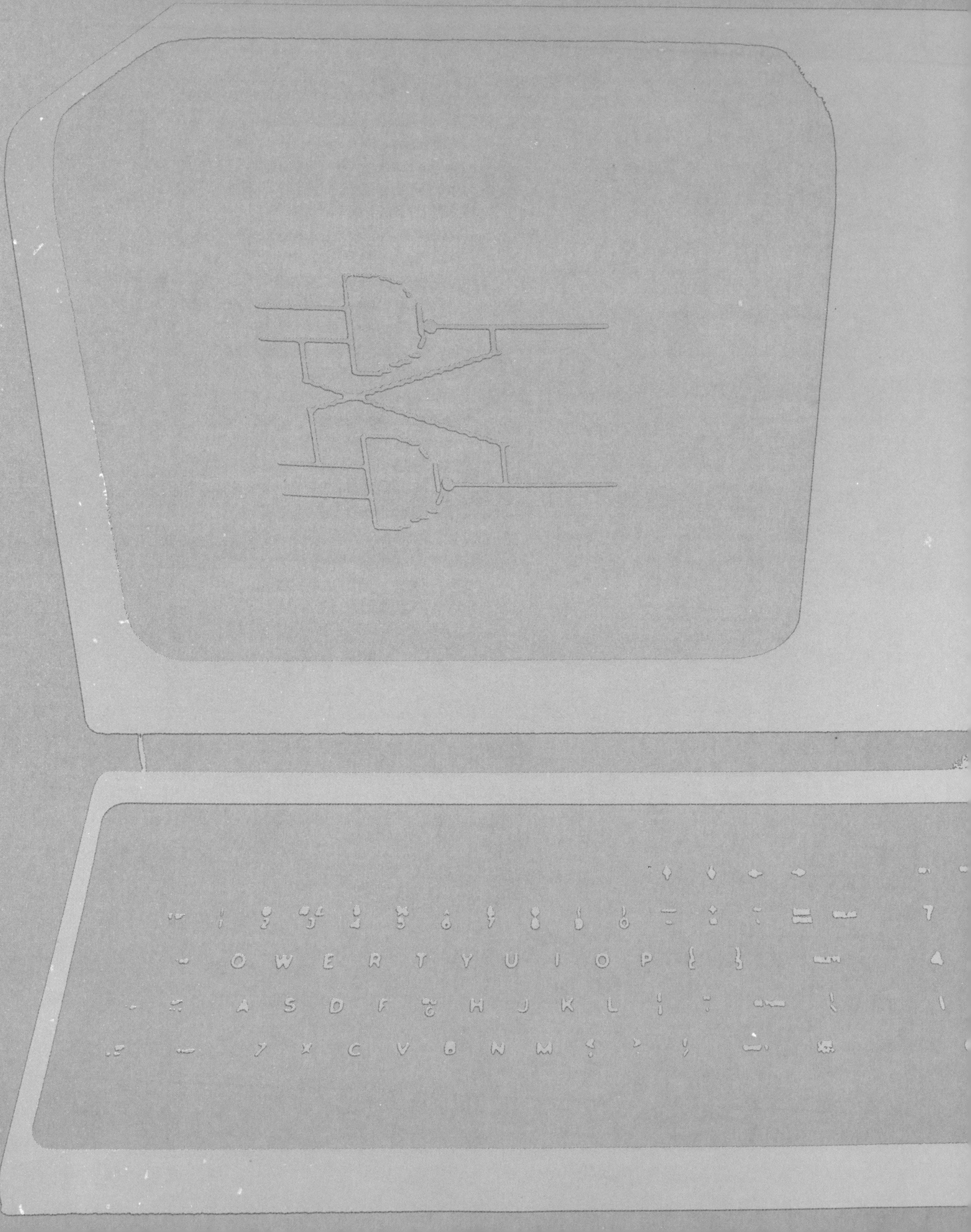
Q W E R T Y U I O P
A S D F G H J K L
C V N M

computer components 4
data entry devices

Chapter Outline

A Brief Overview of Data Entry Devices

Data Entry Devices

Keypunch and Keypunch Replacement
- Floppy Disks
  - Advantages
  - Disadvantages
- Bubble Storage
- Voice Recognition

Online Display Terminals
- Interactive Display Terminals (CRT)
  - Operation
  - Advantages
  - Disadvantages
- Intelligent Terminals
- Remote-Batch Terminals
- Graphics
  - Plotters

Character Recognition Devices
- Magnetic-Ink Character Readers (MICR)
  - Advantages
  - Disadvantages
- Optical Character Readers (OCR)
  - Uses
  - Advantages
  - Disadvantages

Shared Processor Data Terminal Systems
- Point of Sale (POS)
- Universal Product Code (UPC)
- Electronic Funds Transfer System (EFTS)
  - Types of EFTS Systems

Chapter Objectives

The learning objectives of this chapter are

1. to introduce conventional data entry devices as well as the latest advances in automatic data entry.
2. to present the strengths and weaknesses of each device so a proper evaluation can be made of a particular data entry device.
3. to present operational uses and techniques of data entry and their proper place in data-processing operations.
4. to present the different methods of data entry so a proper cost justification can be ascertained, since data entry costs constitute a large portion of the data-processing budget.

The data-processing industry has spent many years and many dollars translating marks on paper into digitized information. Data entry accounts for 40 to 50 percent of the data-handling dollar. Data entry now takes a disproportionate amount of corporate resources in increased personnel requirements, extensive responsive time, and the consequence of erroneous output. With the data entry costs exceeding one third of the total data-processing budget, more managers are turning their attention to the data entry process to maximize efficiency and minimize costs. As a result of recent technological advances, almost any organization can make effective use of data entry systems in its operations.

There are a number of methods for processing data into machine readable form that are economical in one or more situations. Examining the alternatives shows the wide variety of devices currently available.

Scanners can be divided into three classes—the magnetic-ink character readers (MICR), the bar encoding scanners used mainly in the point-of-sale (POS) terminals, and the optical character readers (OCR) used for high-volume applications.

Although the MICR solution is very effective in the banking community, it has not caught on elsewhere, since no other industry has the high degree of internal self-regulation and enforceable standards. The bankers have performed a notable service by creating and enforcing the use of MICR; without it, the body of financial data would have drowned in a sea of paper.

Widespread installation of POS devices is just beginning, but already a wide variety of terminals exists, many built for recording data on tape cassettes. Scanning simple encoded symbols allows a clerk or register operator to keep an accurate up-to-date inventory of goods sold and transaction volumes. Symbol printing is comparatively simple. The logic in the scanning device is elementary and the scanner is easy to operate. Simple cassette-to-magnetic tape converters already exist.

The big, expensive scanners that have been in use for years are limited by cost and complexity to applications with rigid formats and very high volumes, such as processing credit card charges and airline tickets. More recent installations include retail inventory ticket processing and a certain amount of well-defined sales data.

The problem with all scanners is the excessive document rejection. The quality of the input document is critical to a paper-handling machine; if the paper has been crunched, dampened, or otherwise mishandled, the rejection rate is apt to be enormous. With the new developments in scanners, these problems have been greatly reduced.

A Brief Overview of Data Entry Devices

Computer data entry has come a long way in the last thirteen years. Starting as a centralized keypunching operation, it has gone through numerous changes in equipment, medium, and methodology. In today's computer world, the modus operandi is "source data entry," which captures computer-bound data at its point of origin, the exact opposite of the original centralization concept.

This complete about-face is not surprising. A data entry system can be more complex than the computer systems it supports, not so much in software as in system design. A data entry system is a combination of hardware, software, and "peopleware." The people who operate the data entry machine are more critical to the data entry system than their counterparts. In a successful data entry system, all three elements must complement one another and operate in perfect synchronization. Changes in any one of these elements will inevitably have an impact on the other two.

Until 1964, keypunching and data entry were synonymous. Then came the key-to-tape unit, which offered the user a fast method of entering data because it bypassed the punched card. What followed has been a seemingly unlimited variety of data entry systems designed to replace keypunching in the centralized site and, more importantly, to collect data at remote locations.

The key-to-tape unit started as a stand-alone device, but soon evolved into the multiple-terminal key-to-disk system. The key-to-disk system was intended to replace the keypunch. However, with technical innovations in the minicomputer and micro-computer areas and with the maturity of data entry software, the key-to-disk system permitted the influence of data entry to extend beyond simple data conversion. Key-to-disk software permits validation of original source data as well as operator entry checks, data reformatting, separate data files for storage of constant data, validation tables, information retrieval, and execution of applications programs.

With all this inherent data entry and processing power in a rather small mini-computer system, it did not take long to realize the advantage of placing terminals in departments where the original data was generated. Because the system software enables validation of the data, errors can be corrected effectively within the depart-ments. Under this condition, it is only natural that operators take a personal interest in the accuracy of the data more so than in the centralized system.

Extending this concept, data entry at remote locations has been made possible by the use of remote online terminals and key-to-disk systems with data communications capability.

Today, with the implementation of business-oriented programming languages, the user is given the opportunity to not only enter data but also preprocess data at the source.

At the same time the key-to-tape system was introduced, the compact magnetic tape cassette also made its appearance as an alternative to the much bulkier computer-compatible magnetic tape. Unlike the centralized key-to-computer-compatible tape, the key-to-cassette was designed to provide low-cost data collection at the source and to transmit the data in batches to a central computer. The systems were composed of terminals or CRT (cathode-ray tube) keyboard displays.

The OCR was designed to read printed and typewritten data and to replace the keyboard entry. Today, the OCR serves as part of the multimedia data entry system.

The portable data recorder represents yet another means of capturing source data. Quite similar to keyboard-to-storage terminals, its main features are low weight and portability, allowing data to be captured in the field. Once such data is captured, the recorder can be used to transmit the data to a minicomputer over the telephone.

An exciting new data entry device is voice data entry. The ability to capture information by voice recognition permits people to simply speak into the system (qual-ity control, material movement, or the cashier). While it is presently limited to a small vocabulary, its future expansion is obvious.

Another data entry possibility is the small business computer, which was intro-duced after the minicomputer. It can provide a large company with a means of entering and processing data remotely.

While many of these data entry options seem diverse, they tend to converge into the concept of a multimedia, multiterminal system in which data, generated via various media, can be captured by the system with minimal human intervention. Major components of such a system might include a typewriter keyboard, optical reader, voice recognition unit, minicomputer, business programming language, magnetic disk, tape, printer, and data communications interface.

Data Entry Devices

There are many different data entry devices available in today's market, each with its own particular strengths and weaknesses (fig. 4.1). The basic categories include keypunch and keypunch replacement equipment, online display terminals, optical character recognition devices, and shared processor data terminal systems.

Included in the *keypunch and keypunch replacement* category are keypunches and verifiers, key-to-tape/cassette/diskette devices, and key-driven paper tapes. With this type of equipment, data is transcribed from source documents to the input media, retaining the original sequence in which it was captured (fig. 4.2). Format capability is severely limited. Key-to-tape/cassette/diskette and key-driven paper tape devices expand the 80-character record length of keypunches; but, with all three types of equipment, error detection cannot be performed prior to computer processing.

Online display terminals have the distinct advantage of direct communication with the computer. Online data entry permits the entry of a query to start a chain of events that results in work being done, files created, statistics formulated, and records updated, within certain preset time constraints. Disadvantages of online data input include waste of storage processing time, low keying productivity due to long response time, and the necessity for re-keying duplicate data rather than using automatic functions as is possible with offline data entry.

Optical character recognition devices are specialized data entry equipment designed to solve major information bottlenecks and quickly convert data to a computer-processible medium. The use of OCR devices requires close controls. Forms must meet rigid specification standards, and recorded data must obey restrictions concerning character fonts and character positioning. Expensive fixed equipment, complexity of error handling, and expensive clerical OCR mail processing and input forms are some of the constraints associated with OCR use. On the other hand, when the OCR device is used in a multimedia data entry environment, the rewards can be high. For example, the character input cost with keypunch equipment is about six to ten cents per 100 characters, while OCR can reduce this cost to little more than one cent per 1000 characters.

With *shared processor data terminal systems,* a number of data entry stations share a minicomputer. The stations display either single characters (panel display) or a full record (CRT). Input data is stored on intermediate storage devices, such as disks or drums. Edits during data capture, at logical record, and/or at batch end insure the validity of keyed data elements within the context of a logical record and the acceptability of a variety of records keyed under different formats. Many different peripherals can be added to these systems to create a true multimedia data entry environment.

Figure 4.1 Examples of data entry devices. (Photos by Ken Firestone)

Figure 4.2 A key-to-disk example. (Courtesy of Mohawk Data Sciences Corporation)

Keypunch and Keypunch Replacement

The keypunch category includes the keypunch and verifier. The following devices, which can replace the keypunch in the data-processing system, are used primarily for data entry, but also have other uses in the system.

Floppy Disks

The floppy disk is a compact, flexible computer storage device resembling a 45-RPM phonograph record. It is having a major impact on the design of many computer-based systems (fig. 4.3). A floppy disk drive, interchangeably called flexible disk drive and diskette drive, is a small, low-cost memory device used primarily for storage and retrieval of data in low-cost data-handling systems. Floppy disks, also known as diskettes, are replacing cards, punched paper tape, cassettes, and cartridges for use in remote terminals, minicomputer systems, small-scale business systems, data entry systems, calculators, and word-processing systems because of their speed, reliability, and low cost.

The floppy disk is a combination of tape and disk technology. Basically, it is a disk with tracks for data storage and a moving read/write head, resulting in random access capability and faster access than tape cassettes or cartridges. The diskette itself is made of coated mylar as a cassette tape approximately .025 inch thick, hence its low cost. It is round, 7.5 inches in diameter, with a large hole in the center, similar to a phonograph record. The diskette is enclosed in a jacket for protection, with a slot for access by the drive's read/write head. The diskette itself, in its protective jacket, is

Figure 4.3 An example of a floppy disk system. (Courtesy IBM Corporation)

easily inserted and removed from the drive. Once inserted, the diskette is automatically clamped and positioned for operation (fig. 4.4). The diskette has a storage capacity of 250,000 characters.

Recent innovations in the floppy disk field include new disk drives that double storage capacity by recording on both sides of the diskette. Floppy disk manufacturers have doubled floppy disk storage capacity on a single drive in five ways. A floppy disk can employ combinations of these techniques to multiply storage by four, eight, and N-fold times.

1. *Dual density*—Data is recorded on each track at twice the standard density.
2. *Dual disk*—Two drives are packaged in a single cabinet and have a common controller and computer interface.

Figure 4.4
Operation of a floppy disk. (Photo courtesy Ball Products)

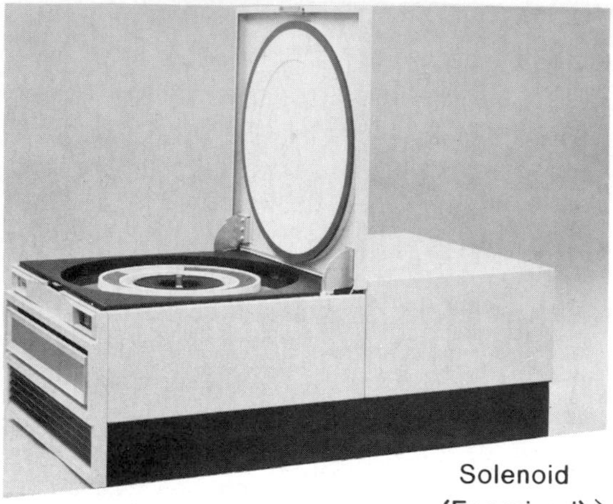

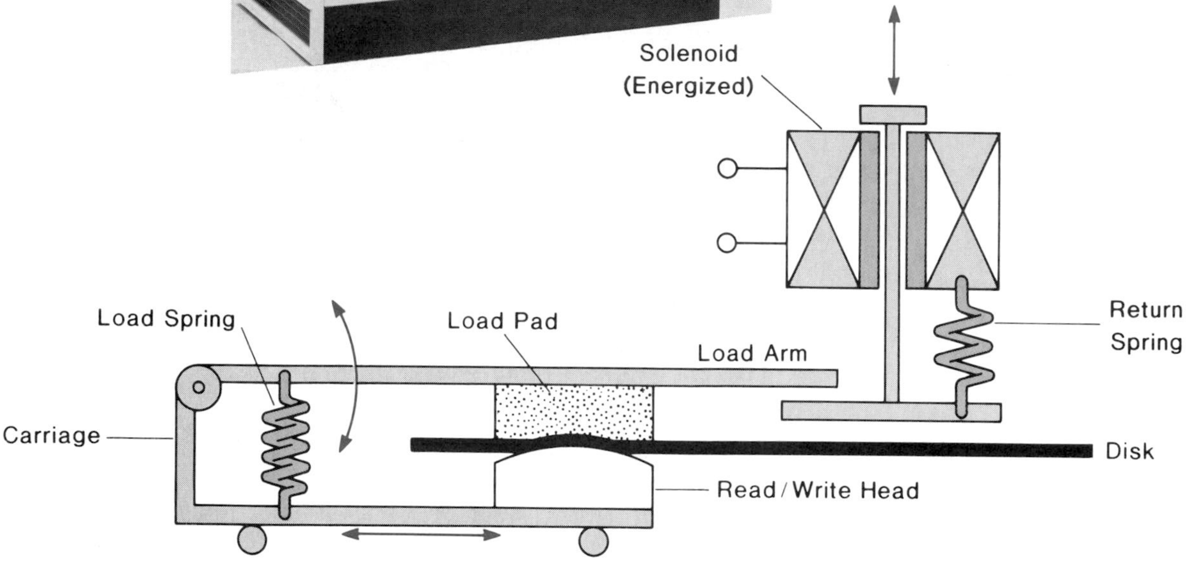

Head Load Assembly

3. *Double-sided*—Data is recorded on the two sides of the diskette.
4. *Double-sided and dual density*—A combination of the above.
5. *Double track*—This technique doubles the storage capacity by doubling the number of tracks on each disk surface.

Advantages

1. Floppy disks are excellent load devices for remote terminals, replacing card readers. They are inexpensive, easy to store offline, and load into the system.
2. Floppy disks are excellent for keyboard data entry applications, such as source data entry and word processing.
3. The low price of the floppy disk makes it attractive for data storage in minicomputers.
4. Low-cost limited-function business systems with limited data base requirements are ideal applications for floppy disks.

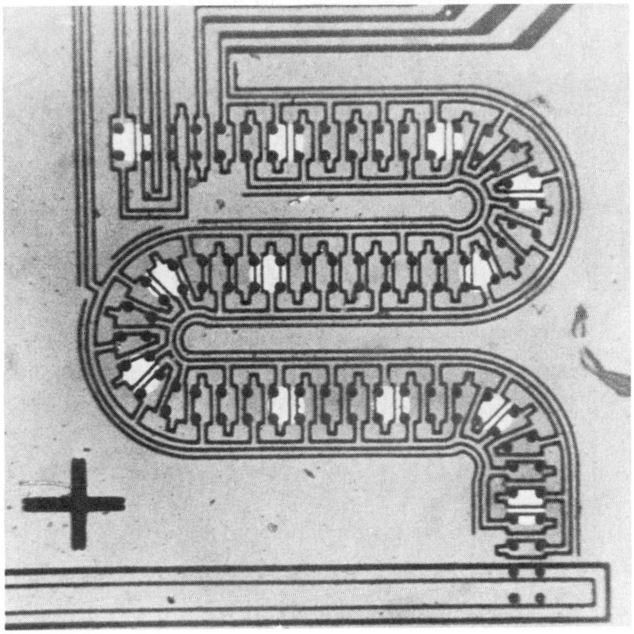

Figure 4.5 An example of bubble storage. (Photo by Ken Firestone)

5. Random access makes information retrieval with the floppy disk between 300 and 400 times faster than cassettes and cartridges. The error rate is much lower than cassettes and cartridges.

Disadvantages

1. Capacity is much smaller, sometimes too small, for online program and data file requirements of minicomputer systems.
2. Access time is much slower than most users would find acceptable for interactive applications.
3. Reliability is somewhat poorer than larger disks, although far superior to cassettes.
4. Because the floppy disk head is always in contact with the media, it is subject to wear.

Today's primary application for floppy disks, data entry, will continue to grow. Applications will grow even more rapidly for floppy disks in intelligent terminals and drives in point-of-sales (POS) and small business systems.

The most successful users of floppy disks will be those who carefully insure that this is the appropriate storage media for their application; those who actively seek methods and programs in which they can take advantage of the capabilities offered by diskettes over cards and other less flexible media; and those who employ sophisticated electronics necessary to insure reliable data when replacing the cartridge drive.

Bubble Storage

Data-recording technology is obviously dynamic (fig. 4.5). Floppy disks have hurt cassette sales and preempted the tape cartridge market. A new technology has come along to upset the market preeminence of the floppy disk as a low-cost storage device.

Magnetic bubble technology was developed at Bell Laboratories about eleven years ago. A group of engineers found that tiny magnetized bubblelike areas in thin films of magnetic material could be controlled and ordered in a "digital" format similar to that used by computers to process information. This finding and the others that followed have brought the technology to a point where magnetic bubble devices are able to store and transport quantities of digital information.

Since their invention, magnetic bubbles have shown great promise as reliable, low-cost alternatives to other memory devices. For example, the storage capacity of a magnetic bubble memory, which is the same physical size as other memory devices that store 16,000 bits of information, is about 70,000 bits.

Bubbles, tiny magnetized areas that can be generated, moved, and detected in a specialized crystalline material, offer moderately fast data retrieval. Bubbles are being promoted by computer manufacturers as the most likely threat to floppy disks for low-cost storage.

The advantages of bubble storage include low-power consumption and nonvolatility. Bubble memories do not lose stored information in the event of a power failure, are more reliable since they have no moving parts, have a long life, are less expensive than diskettes that have to be replaced frequently, and are also suited to applications in hostile environments, in which heat, vibration, and dust preclude the use of the more sensitive floppy disks.

Bubble technology is a feasible alternative to a floppy disk where peripheral storage will be used in close conjunction with the main memory of the computer. As an online storage device, the bubble can be expected to inhibit floppy growth, especially in the mini/micro markets.

Large-scale production of bubble memories still needs to be proven feasible to bring prices down to levels that are competitive with the floppy disk. The floppy disk is a safer form than other technologies, at least through the early 1980s, wherever an application requires a permanent or semipermanent library.

Voice Recognition

A large midwestern company contends with 25,000 pieces of mail each day and needs to find the correct mail zones for each. To make the job easier, letter-sized mail is handled by an electronic mail sorter—anything larger has to be handled manually. They streamlined this sorting task by using voice input. An operator wearing a microphone headset reads aloud the initial of the first name of the addressee and the first four letters of the surname. On a small CRT, the addressee's name and mail zone will appear. If these five alpha characters can apply to a number of addressees, they are listed for the operator to select. According to the company representative, the system has doubled the speed of mail processing at the facility.

The advantages of voice recognition are evident. The ability to speak data into a computer bypasses the writing and keying of data into machine-readable form. The time saved can often justify going to voice input, not to mention the cost associated with the writing, keypunching, and error-correcting activities.

The system uses "discrete" or "isolated" word recognition systems; that is, the speaker must pause briefly between each word. The length of silence surrounding each word must be at least a tenth of a second, a quarter of a second for some devices.

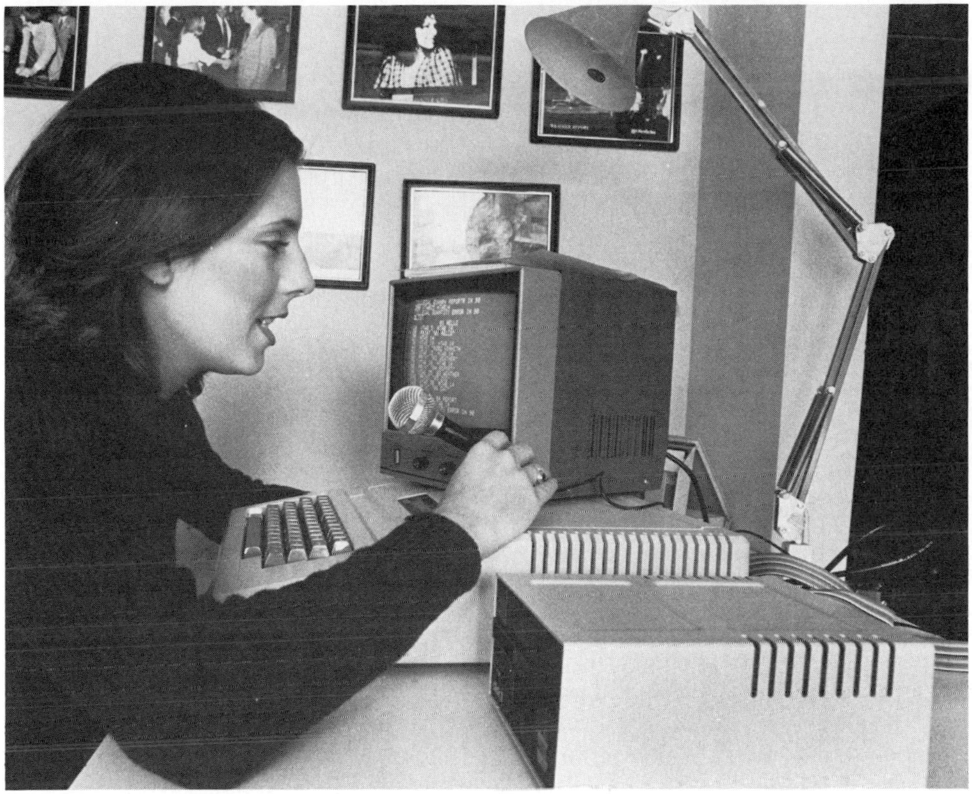

Figure 4.6
Examples of voice recognition. (Photo by Ken Firestone)

Initially, the user must "train" the system to recognize his/her enunciation of the words in the vocabulary. This is done through repetitive utterances of those words to produce a reference pattern that can be stored in main memory or on a disk or cassette. After this training, the system will respond to the user's spoken command with an appropriate action. This action might be as simple, in effect, as depressing a key; it could be as complex as executing an entire computer program.

One system, designed for programmers who are severely disabled, will store fifty COBOL statements so the user doesn't have to spell out each word. For example, the user will say *dimension,* and the system will output the ASCII characters for *dimension,* plus probably a space at the end, since one is always there. In a similar system for the blind, the action also includes a voice response for verification (fig. 4.6).

Today, basic systems seem to handle a vocabulary of twenty to forty words, expandable by adding memory size. These figures depend on the actions to be taken by the system for each spoken command.

One system uses a seventeen-word vocabulary that includes ten digits, plus such commands as *code, height, clear, erase,* and *enter.* Words were spoken into the system by men and women in German, Polish, Tagalog, Russian, Armenian, French, Czechoslovakian, Japanese, and Swahili. This shows that the system doesn't care whether the user chooses *one, uno,* or *ein.* So the system is really vocabulary and language independent.

There are many uses for voice recognition.

At one firm, the programmer voices the programming functions to the system, thereby freeing hands to handle blueprints or to perform calculations.

On the floor of a commodities exchange, voice input is used by floor reporters who speak into wireless microphones reporting the latest transactions and prices. Getting visual confirmation, the reporter then says *go.* The data is captured.

At a large department store distribution center, cartons are sorted in this manner. A warehouse worker reads the label on a carton, says *number four go,* and thereby sets up the designated conveyor routing for that package. This method keeps unauthorized personnel from moving goods and also records each employee's work volume, an important consideration where piece-count affects compensation.

No longer experimental, voice recognition systems are asked to do real work in data entry and control applications. The results, especially for data collection, are increased productivity and decreased error rates.

Online Display Terminals

Modern computer terminals span a wide range of types, uses, and features, from simple remote-batch transfer units to highly intelligent network "nodes," capable of running multiple programs interactively, maintaining and manipulating local data bases, and acting as "subhosts" to clusters of subservient, less-intelligent terminals (figs. 4.7, 4.8).

Generally, the market consists of interactive and remote-batch systems applications. As a rule, the interactive terminals are used online for central data base inquiry/response, data entry, and time-sharing applications via the common carrier data networks. The remote-batch systems are used for remote processing of data batched into the central site either via the common carrier network or manually.

The remote-batch terminal is the simplest terminal acting as an extension to the main computer by direct interaction through remote-batch transfer operations. The terminal acts as a "store-and-forward" mechanism to gather data, transmit the batched data to the main computer for processing, and await the results.

Intelligent terminals go beyond the store-and-forward function. They are capable of acting locally to edit, refine, and consolidate information before it enters the main computer, thus saving costly processing time by the main computer.

Interactive Display Terminals (CRT)

Display terminals (cathode-ray tubes) have replaced hard-copy computer output with a display station on which users may obtain desired information by requesting it from the system (fig. 4.9).

The simplest use of the display terminal is for inquiry and update of a data base, as in a reservation system. In interactive keyboard applications, they allow for high-speed transmission and provide editing and formatting capabilities not generally available with printer terminals. They are used as data entry and acquisition devices replacing conventional keypunches. Information is stored on a disk or magnetic tape for later entry in the computer system.

Figure 4.7 An example of a data terminal. (Courtesy of Hewlitt Packard)

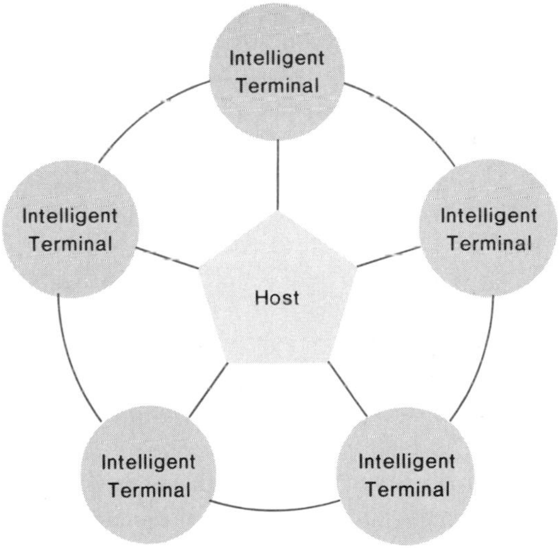

Figure 4.8 A diagram of an intelligent terminal.

The display units permit the user of a data-processing system to see reports that would take much longer to produce on any other output device. The display units present tables, charts, graphs, and various other configurations of alphameric letters and figures on a cathode-ray tube screen. An operator console is used in conjunction with the display unit. There are many applications for CRTs (fig. 4.9).

Figure 4.9 Examples of terminal applications. (Copyright 1976 *Data Management* magazine, Data Processing Management Corporation)

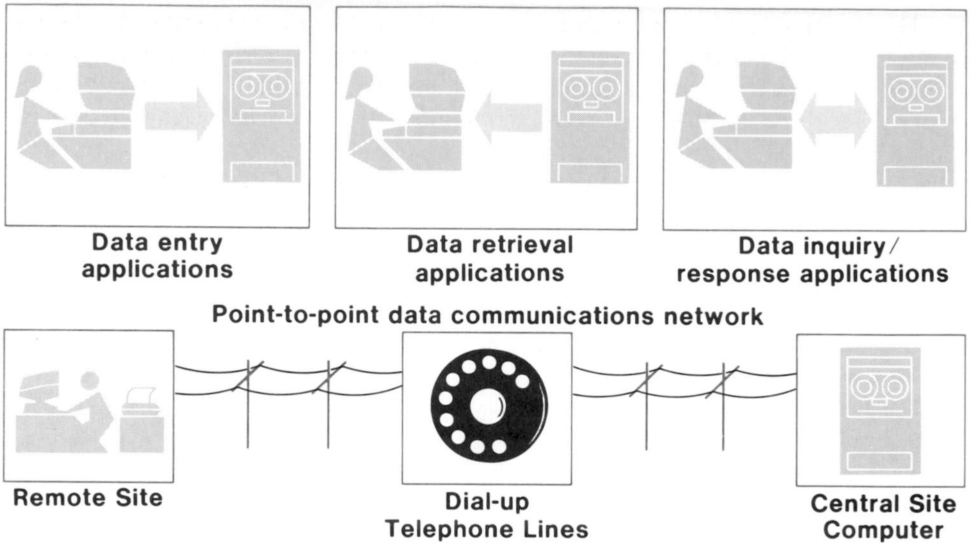

1. *An inquiry for vital information can be made from a computer.* This can be made by an executive at a terminal located near or in the office. The information can be displayed on the unit and the necessary decision can be made.

   This is the most powerful aid for business provided by the computer. The executive can make quicker, more accurate decision analysis by using a display device. Using this resource, an executive or manager creates and analyzes data relating to business decisions by direct interaction with a computer which has been programmed to produce this information on a visual display screen. With this equipment in the office, the executive can portray on the CRT screen the information that is desired. The proper terminal in an executive's office produces an interaction between people and computers which overcomes the traditional obstacles to effective decision making. The first is the deteriorating effect of time on data. The freshness of carefully compiled business data deteriorates rapidly with time. Often current decisions are not really derived from current data. Raw data becomes usable only after feedback has been received and analyzed.

   The second obstacle is the lack of opportunity for private reflections by the decision maker. The executive needs a quiet place to anticipate, develop, and test the consequences of following various courses of action before making a commitment public.
2. *An inquiry for information about the status of a client's account can be received by telephone.* The account can be retrieved and presented on the display unit. The record can be updated immediately by using the entry keyboard, and the corrected record placed in storage.
3. *Inquiries for payroll information relative to an employee's record can be made.*
4. *Inventory information inquiries can be made relative to the status of stock items.*

They are also used as order entry devices, eliminating the conventional order on paper with later data entry. They are also available as part of word-processing systems in which text is edited and formatted using the display terminal rather than a typewritten page. Generally, display terminals have the option of providing a printed hard-copy output of the information stored on the display tube. The majority of display terminals utilize cathode-ray tube displays but solid-state displays are now being introduced into the marketplace as well.

Operation

Terminals are commonly used to produce a visual display of the records in storage. An operator initiates the request for information and the data is transferred to and from the computer at high speeds. The displayed information can be retained as long as needed.

The display station has a 4-by-9-inch receiving area. As many as six to twelve rows of 40 or 80 characters can be displayed depending upon the model used. Thirty-six alphameric plus 25 special characters are displayed on a matrix with an appearance similar to a printer.

All input to be displayed is entered through an alphameric or numeric keyboard. The keyed information is displayed immediately on the tube for a visual accuracy check. The operator can correct, erase, backspace, reenter, or clear an entire input message before the information is released to the computer.

Output information is written on the tube face under operator or program control. The information can be written in a cleared display unit or added to an existing display on the tube face. The display may also be directed to an output printer.

Advantages

The most important advantage of display devices is the reduction of the time gap between the actual occurrence of the transaction and its subsequent entry into the data-processing system. Real-time processing has become an actuality because it is possible to process the actual transaction almost the moment it occurs. Remote terminals can be strategically located throughout an organization with inquiries possible from any station in the building or throughout the United States. The distance gap between the location of the transaction and the computer has been bridged.

The use of display terminals has been strongly influenced by technological changes in the computer and in communications. The decreasing cost of storage using high-speed disk files has lowered the cost of display utilization. High-speed circuitry and multi-port access to the files also has decreased the impact of the display terminal on the overall capability of the computer system. In addition, communication costs are being reduced continually.

Disadvantages

The chief disadvantage in the extensive use of display units is the cost factor. Data transmission of large quantities of data over telephone and by other communication devices is still rather expensive. While display terminals often eliminate the need for hard-copy reports, significant costs are associated with the convenience. These include costs involved with the terminal rental, communication lines for remote terminals, and the computer system involved in serving the terminal. This latter cost is not trivial, since relatively simple computer systems can generate other forms of output reports. The system support expense should be examined when display terminals are being considered as an alternative to hard-copy output reports.

Intelligent Terminals

According to the dictionary, intelligence implies an ability to cope with novel situations and new problems, and to apply what is learned from experience. It is an amorphous, ambiguous term that can be applied to atomic scientists, ballplayers, and dolphins. In brief, the term is sufficiently vague to serve as a dream-marketing slogan describing a class of computer terminals.

Intelligent terminals derive their programmability from the use of integrated processors (built-in minicomputers). The processor permits the communications protocol, CRT functions, and keyboard and peripheral control functions to be fully programmed in response to specific assignments, as well as changes in assignments. The CRT provides a window of its computing systems. It is rapidly becoming the human to machine interface in the computer systems networks. As the programming becomes easier and more software is available, transitions from application to application can often be accomplished at the touch of a button, and the system expansion becomes a matter of nearly routine simplicity (fig. 4.10).

The *heartland* of intelligent terminals consists of a mini-cluster made up of as many as four display terminals and peripherals, usually disk and printers but sometimes tape and card readers. These easily identifiable units are large enough to be programmable, yet too small and too slow to handle very large tasks or very many tasks.

The distinction between a "dumb" terminal and an "intelligent" terminal is the level at which a data entry device works. At a "dumb" terminal, an operator strikes a key and the corresponding coded signals are sent to a remote computer. If an error has occurred in the transmission, the terminal shows a special character and the cursor (indicator) does not move; this tips the operator to any bad data transmissions.

Upon completing a job, the operator causes a special character sequence to be sent to the computer to signal that the terminal has relinquished line control. The computer will transmit a message to the terminal or, if it has nothing to send, return control to the terminal.

The "intelligent" terminals can interface with communications networks, employing such protocols as store, retrieve, and edit text locally, without depending on the remote processor, processing data locally, beyond simple edit checks, and defining display formats locally.

Recent market predictions show the growth of the terminal market to be greater than 50 percent annually. The computing power of the intelligent CRT terminal systems has grown as rapidly as the use of the basic CRT terminal. Intelligent CRT terminal systems allow greater flexibility, reduce the line time, and eliminate much of the data-processing load to the central computer.

Remote-Batch Terminals

Remote-batch terminals are similar to other remote computer terminals because both extend the processing capability of a large central computer via communication lines to a distant site. Remote-batch terminals differ from other terminals because they

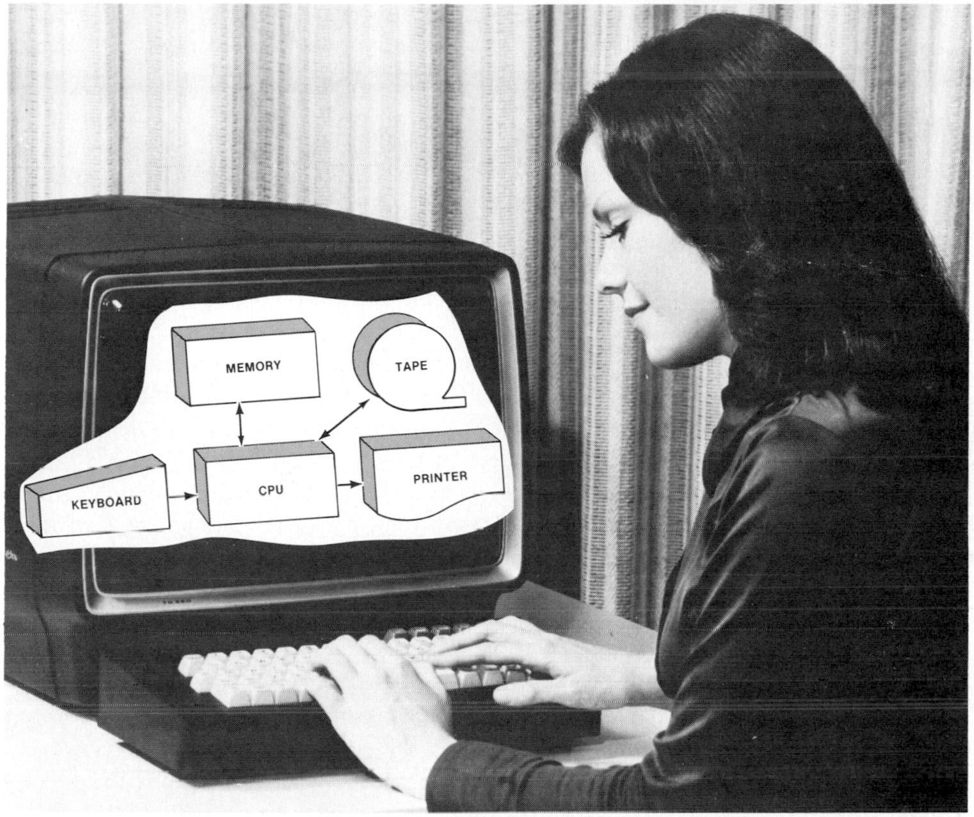

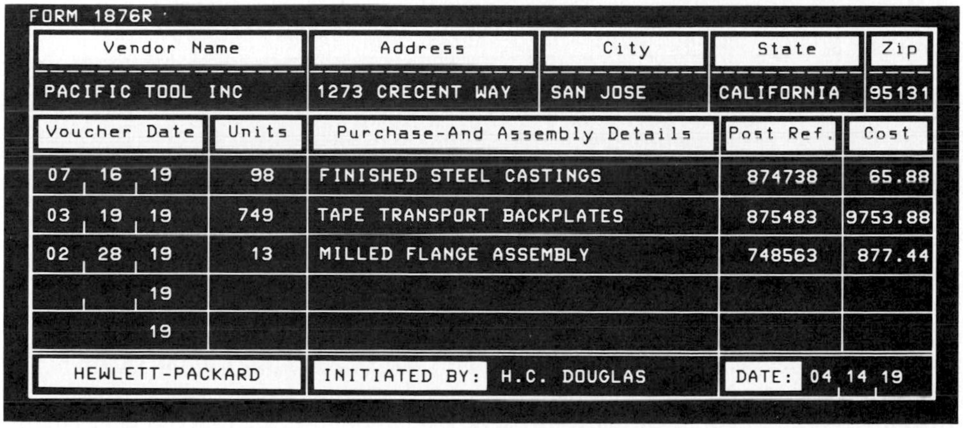
FORM 1876R

Vendor Name	Address	City	State	Zip
PACIFIC TOOL INC	1273 CRECENT WAY	SAN JOSE	CALIFORNIA	95131

Voucher Date	Units	Purchase-And Assembly Details	Post Ref.	Cost
07 16 19	98	FINISHED STEEL CASTINGS	874738	65.88
03 19 19	749	TAPE TRANSPORT BACKPLATES	875483	9753.88
02 28 19	13	MILLED FLANGE ASSEMBLY	748563	877.44
19				
19				

HEWLETT-PACKARD	INITIATED BY: H.C. DOUGLAS	DATE: 04 14 19

Figure 4.10
Intelligent terminal operations. (Photo courtesy of Burroughs Corporation. Display screen—Copyright 1977 by Modern Data Services, Inc. Reprinted with permission from *Mini-Micro Systems,* March 1977.)

Figure 4.11 The IBM 3780 data communications terminal.

handle large amounts (batches) of important day-to-day operational data at high speeds and produce output comparable to that attained at the computer site.

Remote-batch terminals offer fast printers (which can use the entire range of business forms), card readers, and high-speed data transmission facilities, and can contain processors that enable them to do things that most small terminals can't do by themselves. Among the options are keyboard-to-magnetic medium facilities, data checking and reformation software, optical input, and automatic dial-out or line-answering gear (figs. 4.11, 4.12).

The remote processing concept was initially restricted to transmitting virtually raw, unedited data through fixed logic terminals. Things have changed. These changes are a result of adding intelligence to the terminal end of the communications line through the inclusion of the minicomputer. This has enabled users to distribute more and more of their processing to remote sites, while providing increased transmission capability. For example, with the addition of the data entry capability at the remote site, intelligent remote-batch terminals are now able to pre-edit large quantities of information prior to transmission for central processing. This is the direction in which information technology is moving. The installation of intelligent terminals provides significant flexibility in future applications of data processing.

Figure 4.12 An example of remote-batch processing. (Photo by Ken Firestone)

Graphics

Picture the possibilities! A terminal that's so smart that it can draw. Computer graphics, built into terminals, provide business with unique solutions to numerous problems (fig. 4.13). A graphic display can say in an instant what takes hundreds of numbers and hours of translation to explain. Virtually all statistical and forecast calculations can be more readily understood and acted upon when computer graphics eliminates printout and handplotting.

There is a tremendous market for computer graphics in the business community. Modern computers and their associated peripheral devices are capable of producing a great variety of information in the form of graphs, bar charts, Gantt charts, Program Evaluation and Review Technique (PERT) charts, pie charts, histograms, maps, pictures, and other powerful aids to business.

Plotters

One device that produces computer graphics is the plotter. Currently there are many types of plotters on the market (fig. 4.14). Plotters can

Produce a recording of the pen movement relative to the surface of the paper. The pictorial representation may include any desired combination of letters, symbols, lines, and axes with unlimited choice of scale factors.

Produce software that enables many plotters to produce three-dimensional drawings.

Figure 4.13 An example of computer graphics. (Photo by Ken Firestone)

Be programmed to plot in three or four colors.

Plot at high speeds and record on microfilm for computer output data. The plot is generated electronically on an 8-by-10-inch CRT screen and recorded automatically on microfilm or paper.

Uses

Architects use plotters to help design buildings, bridges, aircraft, helicopters, hydrofoils, and ships.

Plotters have contributed to decision making even in the placement of computer equipment, when a layout of computer main frame with its component hardware was programmed.

A government agency produces more readable flip charts for presentations by producing them on plotters. Automated flip charts can be made more uniform and cleaner than those written by hand.

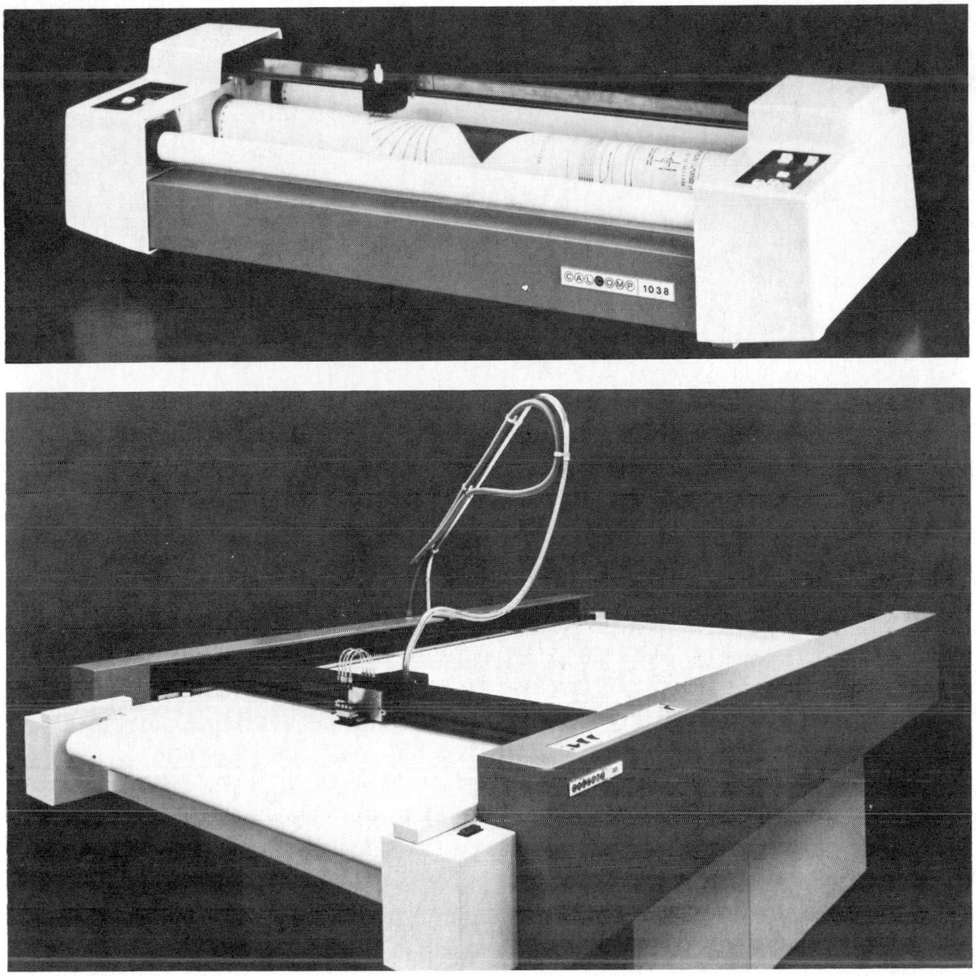

Figure 4.14
Examples of plotters. (Photos by California Computer Products, Inc.)

Many industries produce parts swiftly, accurately, and with a minimum of tool tries. They use the automatic programmed tools (APT) program to produce a sequence of operations on paper tape, which in turn is used to direct a specific machine tool.

Other areas in business in which the use of plotters helps are studies of inventory and budget control, advertising and market research, and profit-and-loss trends as well as financial analysis. Gantt charts and critical path method (CPM) charts can be produced accurately and easily using plotters.

Computer graphics as a tool for business decision making is a relatively new technique growing out of the computer age. It is the vehicle that carries an improved method for examining, handling, and communicating data of all kinds, and increasing the speed and reliability of the manager's decision-making ability. The manager is not required to know how to manipulate complex mathematics or to learn a computer language.

Figure 4.15 A magnetic document sorter and reader.

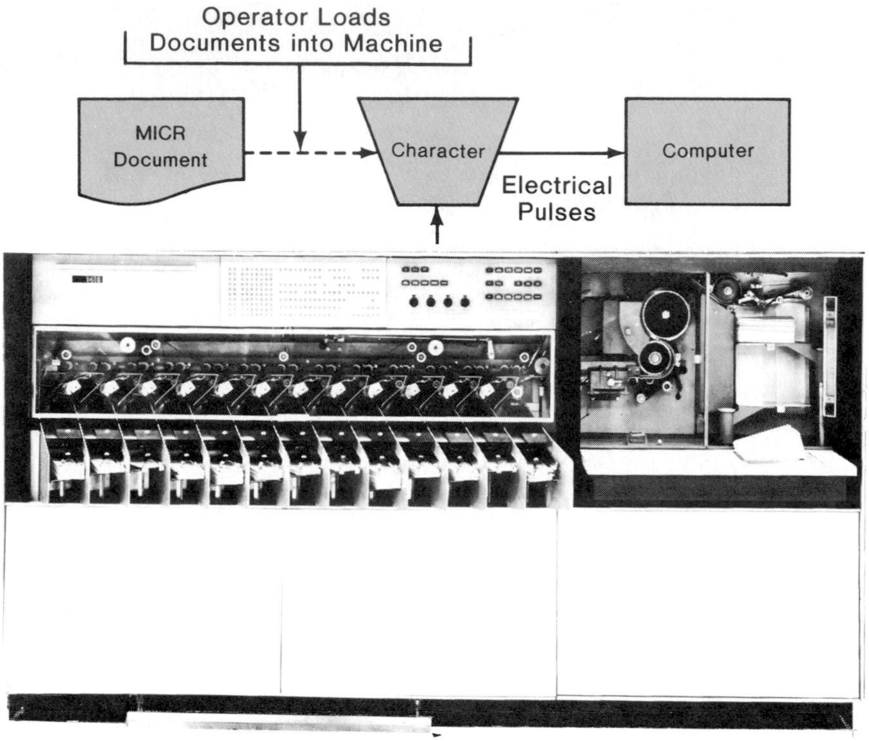

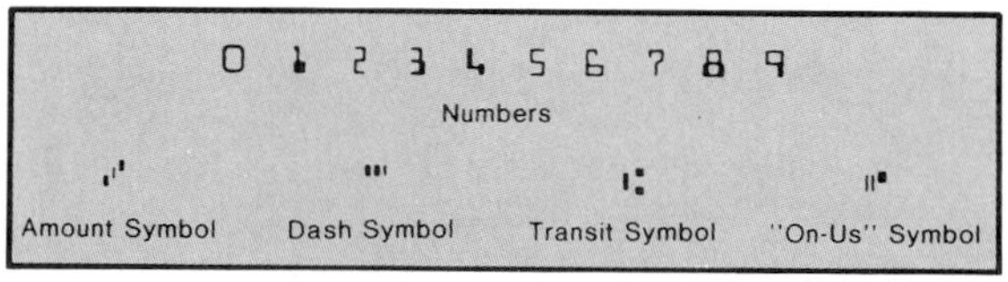

Character Recognition Devices

Magnetic-Ink Character Readers (MICR)

These machines read card and paper documents inscribed with magnetic-ink characters. The shape of a character permits easy recognition, visualization, and interpretation. The special magnetic ink is read by the reader and interpreted for the system (fig. 4.15).

Machine-recognizable characters are printed on a paper document or card by a machine. This creates language that is readable by both people and machines. The shape of the characters permits the easy visualization by people and the special magnetic ink permits the same interpretation by the machine. This information can be

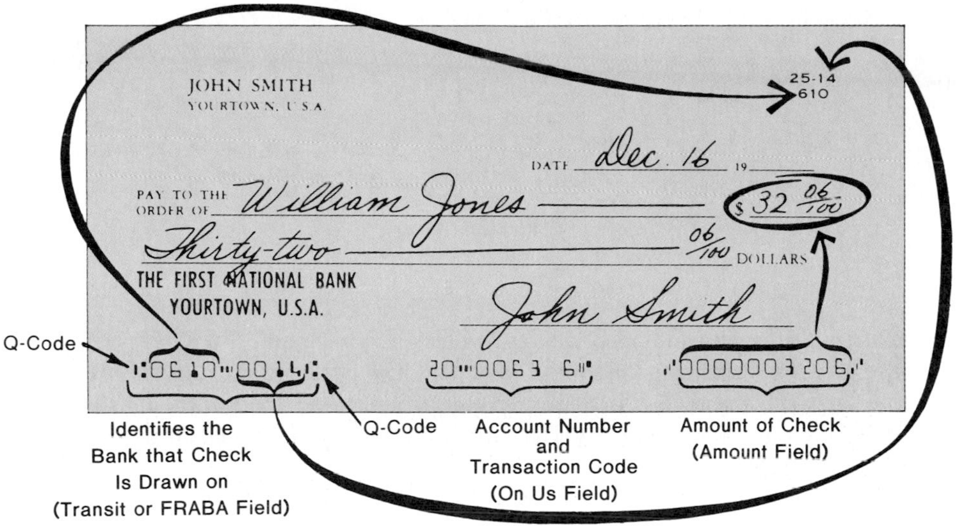

Figure 4.16 A sample check with MICR coding.

entered directly into a data-processing system without any further transcribing. MICRs are used extensively in banking operations and are directly responsible for the wide use of checks in the consumer world (fig. 4.16). These machines have the capability of reading card and paper documents at a relatively high rate of speed. Another important feature of the MICR is its ability to sort magnetically inscribed documents in offline operations. As many as 1200 documents can be sorted in one minute. There are also many built-in validity checking devices to assure the accuracy of the readings.

These time-saving methods of recording and processing large volumes of data have greatly reduced the cost of checking operations for banks, thereby vastly increasing the use of checks in all phases of business operations.

Advantages

1. MICRs have the ability to read paper documents directly and enter the information into a data-processing system.
2. They save time in processing large quantities of paper documents.
3. They are able to sort documents at a high rate of speed.
4. Characters are readable by both people and machines.

Disadvantages

1. Magnetic ink must be inscribed properly, otherwise data will be read incorrectly.
2. Torn or otherwise mutilated paper documents cannot be read by the reader. The documents must be entered manually into the system.
3. Information read cannot be transferred over communication lines.

Optical Character Readers (OCR)

Over the years, as computer technology has advanced, OCR manufacturers have concentrated on providing system solutions that reduce and control data entry costs while simultaneously improving information quality.

Optical character readers can read uppercase letters, numbers, and certain special characters from printed paper documents and can enter the data into a computer

ABCDEFGHIJKLMNOPQRSTU
VWXYZ,.$/*-1234567890

Figure 4.17 The OCR character set.

system (fig. 4.17). Printed reports can also be read by the OCR. Printed paper tape from cash registers and adding machines can also be read by the OCR. This eliminates the necessity of transcribing the source document into cards or tape and greatly reduces the time between the receipt of the source documents and their entry into the data-processing system (fig. 4.18). OCRs can also read mark-sensed information (the recording of ordinary pen and pencil markings in specified locations in the source document).

By addressing data entry at its source, scanners can read real-word field-prepared source documents and bypass the highly labor-intensive key entry function (fig. 4.19).

The significant categories of OCR development are the following:

1. *Optical character recognition.* This includes the capability of scanners to read even badly degraded real-word characters at high speeds.
2. *Capability to reliably handle paper.* The scanning equipment must handle a wide variety of document sizes and weights (ranging from flimsy carbon-backed airline tickets to very heavy letter mail) on an intermixed basis. These documents may even be folded, spindled, or bent.
3. *System and software integration.* Equipment must be able to integrate complex, multiple processors into efficient systems that include large-scale computers communicating with mini- and micro-processors.
4. *Nonimpact printing.* In this process, the equipment prints characters or bars on documents by projecting droplets of ink directly on the paper in a predetermined pattern under program control.

Uses

OCR is used extensively in the following areas:

In retail department stores, an OCR wand is a hand-held OCR character reader that reads typed or printed data typically found on merchandise tags and tickets at the cash register (fig. 4.20).

Most airline tickets are processed on OCR systems.

Verification of credit is done on OCR systems.

Payments for insurance premiums, charge sales invoices, utility bills, and credit card transactions and partial payments can be processed directly to a customer's account and immediate processing of the payment can be made.

Traveling and entertainment companies use OCR for remittance processing.

Post offices, the government, health departments, and banks use OCR for various functions.

Figure 4.18 The optical character operation.

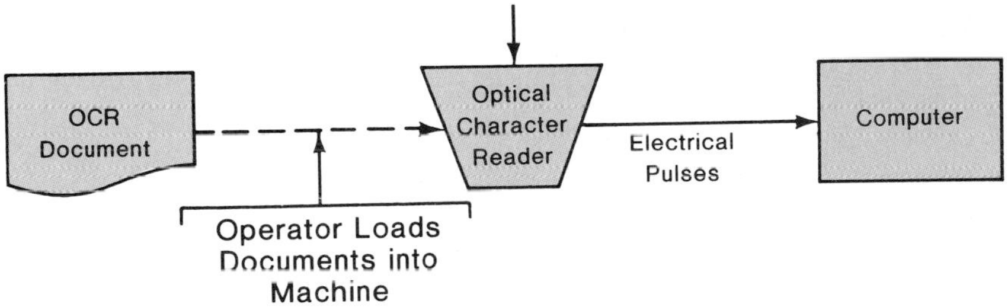

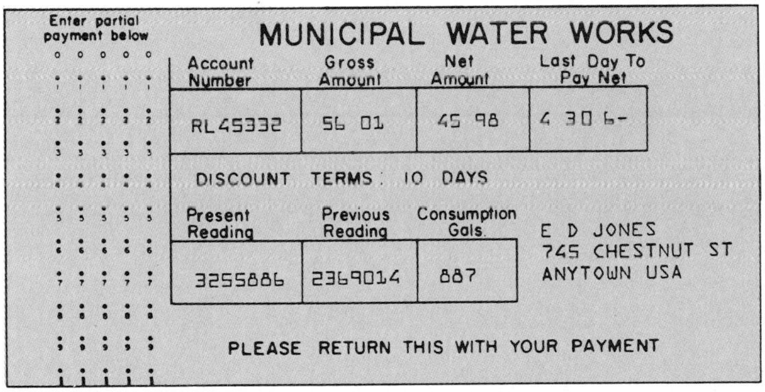

Enter partial payment below

MUNICIPAL WATER WORKS

Account Number	Gross Amount	Net Amount	Last Day To Pay Net
RL45332	56 01	45 98	4 30 6-

DISCOUNT TERMS : 10 DAYS

Present Reading	Previous Reading	Consumption Gals.
3255886	2369014	887

E D JONES
745 CHESTNUT ST
ANYTOWN USA

PLEASE RETURN THIS WITH YOUR PAYMENT

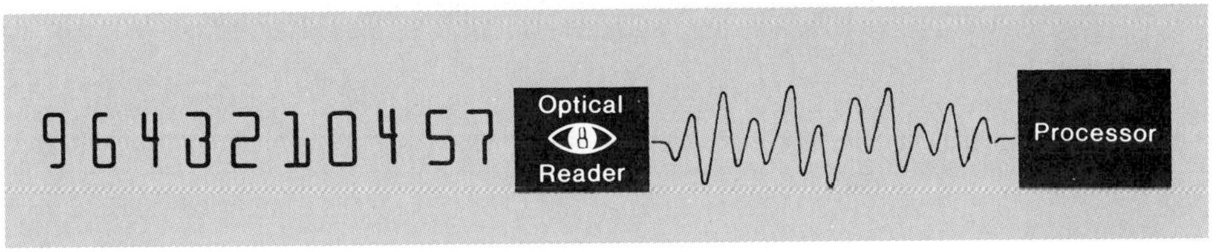

Figure 4.19
Examples of OCR. (Reprinted with permission of *Datamation* © magazine, © Copyright by Technical Publishing Company, A Division of Dun-Donnelley Publishing Corporation, A Dun & Bradstreet Company, 1978—all rights reserved.)

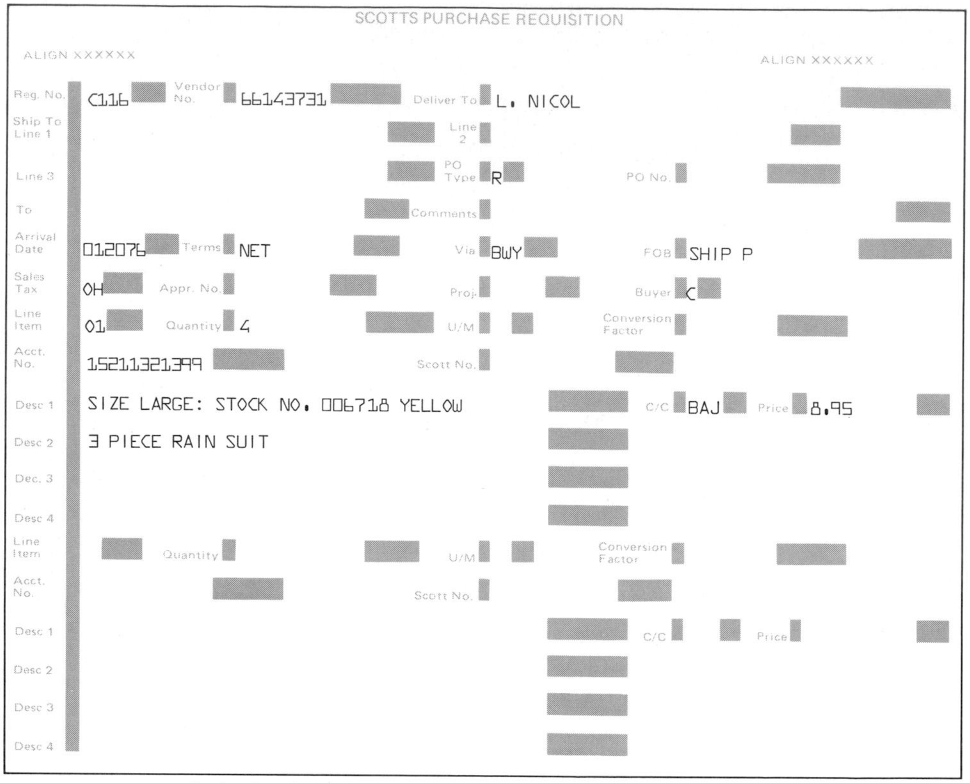

By having the user department, in this case purchasing, enter data directly onto this specially designed OCR form, no transcription is necessary—and transcription errors are accordingly reduced.

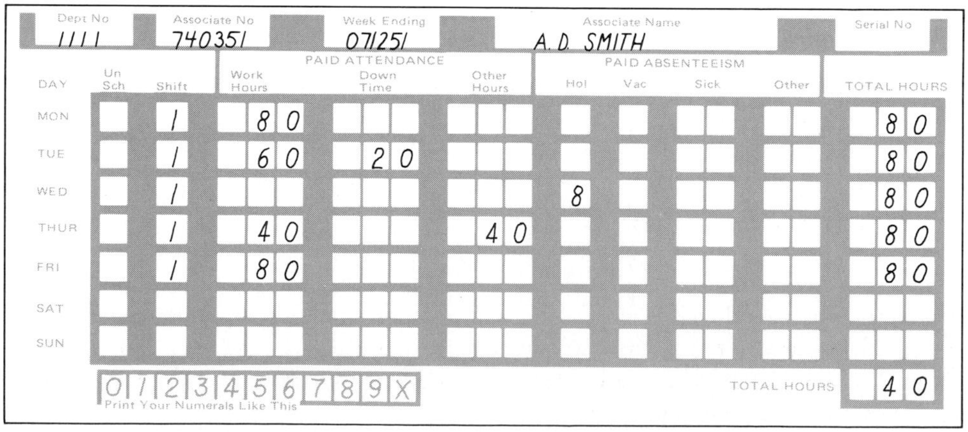

Handprinted timecards represent a novel application for OCR, and will soon become part of standard procedures.

Figure 4.20 An example of OCR wand application. (Courtesy of MSI Data Corporation)

Advantages

1. The greatest advantage is the direct reading of the paper document into the system, which reduces the processing time between the receipt of the document and processing into the system.
2. Ordinary hand-written, typed, computer-printed, and other source documents can be read into the system.
3. Mark-sensed information can be read by the reader.

Disadvantages

The one big disadvantage is still the degree of reliability (or unreliability) of the reading of these printed symbols. Although the readers are being improved each day, there still are quite a few printed characters that cannot be read for various reasons and must be processed manually.

Total data entry consists of mixing the media of readable data. When coupled with reliable OCR capability, this integrated key-to-disk system enables a user to handle virtually all data entry requirements on one powerful integrated data entry system.

Shared Processor Data Terminal Systems

Point of Sale (POS)

Years ago, manufacturers of retail marketing equipment recognized the need for automated systems of merchandise marketing. Because there was no alternative at the time, each manufacturer was forced to develop a standard for automated data input. A need for accuracy, a need for more information, and a need for speed are all problems to be solved at the point of sale. The electronic control of credit and the electronic capture of merchandising information are the functions of the POS equipment (fig. 4.21).

The retail minicomputer provides control totals, operating statistics, data-processing flexibility, and an economical approach for even smaller retailers to install electronic POS terminals to replace their conventional cash registers (fig. 4.22). The electronic POS unit was developed to operate in a number of areas within the retail environment.

1. The customer POS—records transactions.
2. The point-of-receipt of merchandise.
3. The shipping dock—records the transfer of merchandise between locations, or records the return of merchandise to a vendor.
4. The warehouse—records the inventory.
5. The back office of a store—reads merchandise tags, captures payroll information for subsequent processing, or reads information from accounting documents, such as purchase orders or invoices (fig. 4.23).

The advantages created by implementation of POS in all areas are as follows:

1. POS terminals reduce the workload of buyers through valid data reporting.
2. POS terminals improve merchandise information, which improves inventory mix.

Figure 4.21 A schematic example of POS checkout stand. (Copyright 1976 by Modern Data Services, Inc. Reprinted with permission from *Mini-Micro Systems*, June 1976.)

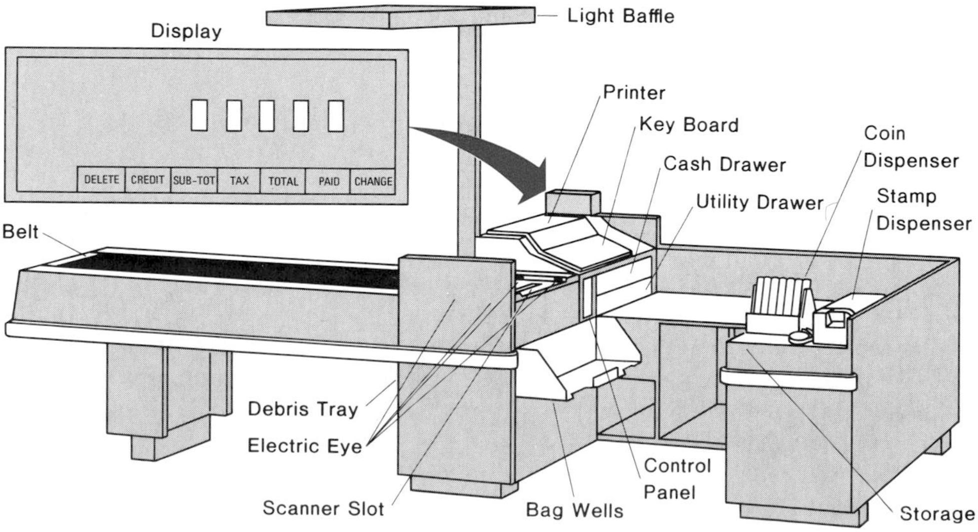

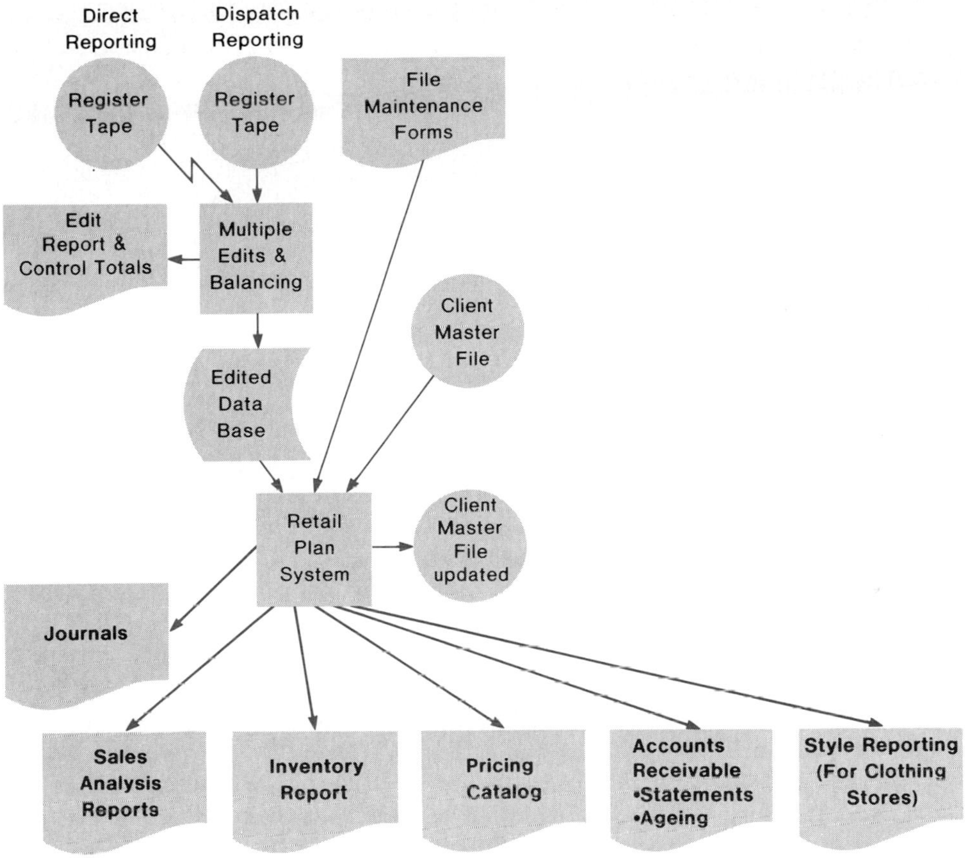

Figure 4.22 A schematic example of POS. (Copyright *Data Management* magazine, Data Processing Management Association)

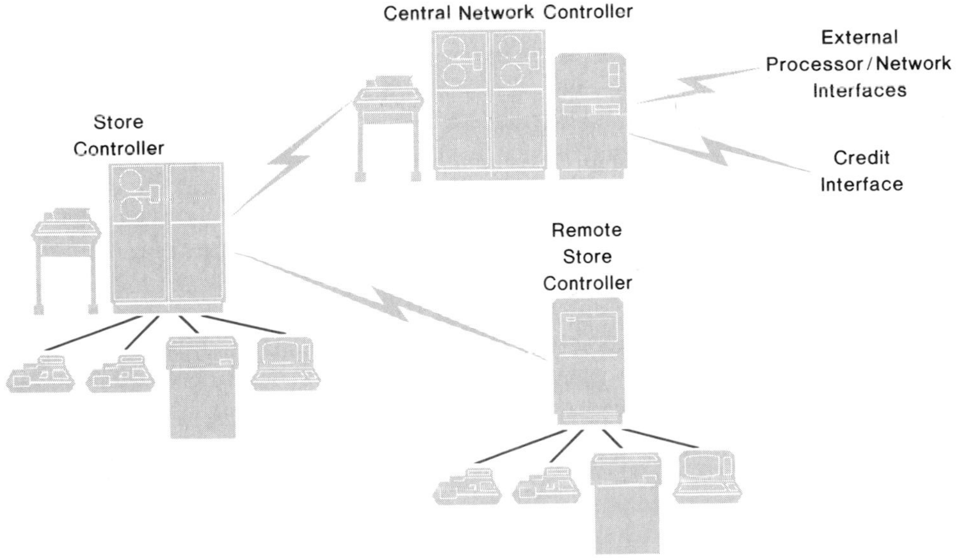

Figure 4.23 An integrated POS network. (Copyright *Data Management* magazine, Data Processing Management Association)

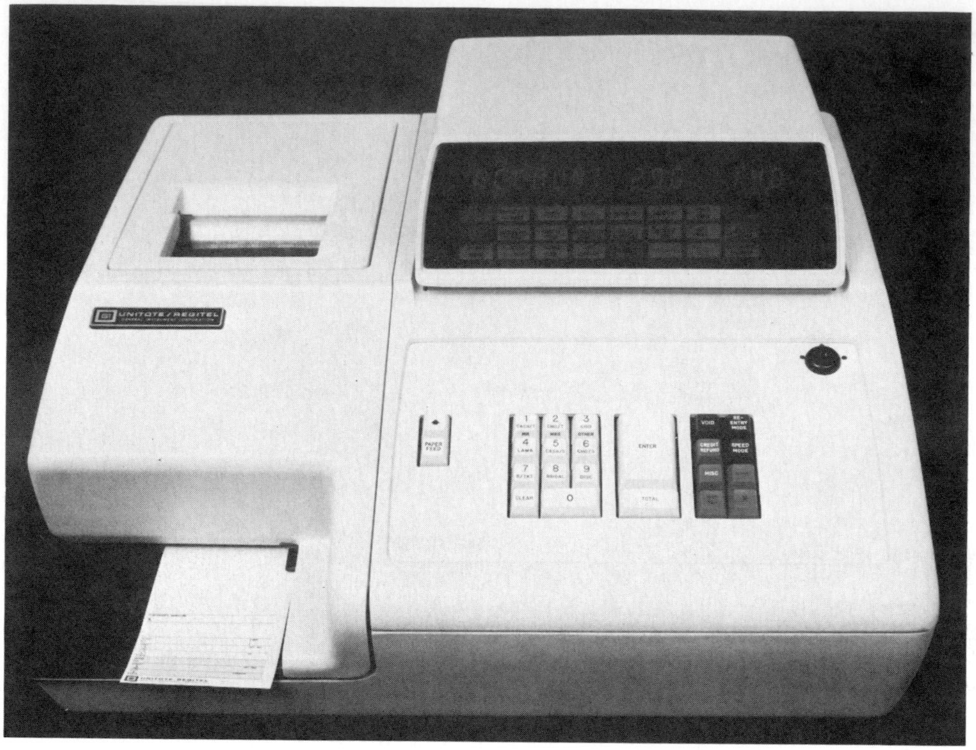

Figure 4.24 This POS terminal provides full alphanumeric display to guide the salesperson through various transaction sequences. (Copyright *Data Management* magazine, Data Processing Management Association)

3. More accurate identification of merchandise price-ticketing can be made through POS; therefore, the data captured by POS registers is more reliable.
4. The use of POS terminals reduces the cost of receiving, order checking, and accounts payable operations.
5. Inventory carrying charges are lowered and there are greater sales because of the POS system's ability to maximize inventory turnover and to minimize stock-outs and to maximize customer service and minimize stock on hand.

A miniprocessor provides the communications facilities for control of messages to and from hundreds of terminals. The miniprocessor will allow a mixture of terminal types to share a common communications line and provide access to common files.

Features of this nature allow integrated techniques to be employed to bring together the related business functions of the back office and the sales floor (fig. 4.24). For example, consider credit authorization. Credit is automatically checked by the terminal as a by-product of recording the sale. If the account status is in a doubtful condition, this status is flashed to a large positive file, which is automatically retrieved and printed or displayed at an appropriate referral location. All of this takes place, of course, without any conscious effort on either the part of the salesperson or the referral clerk.

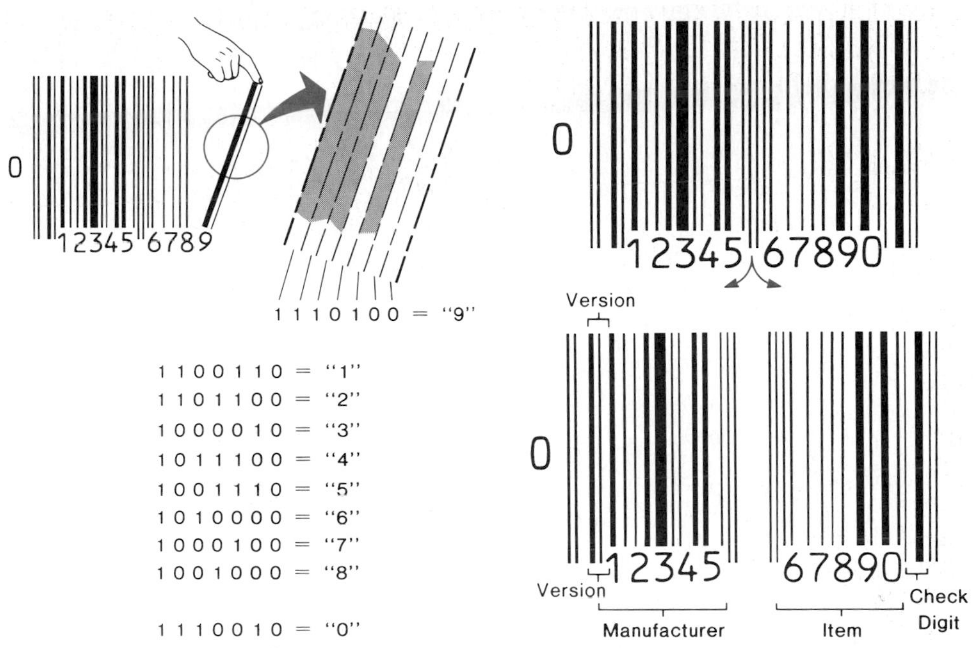

(a) Binary and bar-coded representation of even-parity characters

(b) Decomposition into two symbol blocks

Figure 4.25 The universal product code (UPC) structure. (Copyright *Data Management* magazine, Data Processing Management Association)

Universal Product Code (UPC)

You may have noticed a block of little lines and numbers on cereal boxes, bread bags, and other food packages (fig. 4.25). These are part of a new marking system, called the universal product code (UPC), being tried in some stores. Eventually it's expected that almost everything in the supermarket, even wrapped fresh produce and meat, will be marked with this type of code.

Every checkout counter will have an automatic scanner. As the printed UPC symbol passes over the scanner, these little blank lines will tell a computer who made the product and will describe it—size, flavor, date of manufacture, and so forth. The computer records this information, which helps the supermarket plan what products to reorder. At the same time, it produces, for the customer, a printed tape listing the name of the item as well as the price.

UPC is supposed to help customers both directly, by avoiding mistakes at the checkout counter and speeding up waiting lines, and indirectly, by eliminating waste and errors that inflate retail prices.

POS is another revolution in retailing. The introduction of electronic point of sale is to the retail industry what the landing on the moon was to the world in general.

Electronic Funds Transfer System (EFTS)

The key to any economy's success is the proper functioning of one or more payment systems to provide the means for conducting exchanges of value. The electronic funds transfer system (EFTS) provides a new and complex means of computer-based exchanges of value. This system was designed to facilitate the exchange of monetary value through electronic means.

Figure 4.26 An example of EFTS. (Photo by Ken Firestone)

Money transmission, or electronic funds transfer (EFT) as the financial community prefers to call it, has long been heralded as the solution to banking's increasing problems in processing a constantly growing check volume and in coping with check fraud. Eventually, systems for transferring funds electronically instead of via paper will undoubtedly provide all of these as they grow and probably merge into regional and national systems. Branches of the Federal Reserve Bank already transfer hundreds of millions of dollars daily via their computers and a variety of terminals, often in member banks.

Because of the new terminal devices, EFTS is proliferating at a different level, not just for the benefit of financial institutions, but also for the retail merchant and the average person.

Perhaps, the most straightforward examples of money terminals are the new self-serve teller terminals (fig. 4.26). Depositors with the bank's machine-readable identification card or "cash" card utilize this terminal for cash deposit and withdrawals, loan payments, and the transfer of funds from one account to another. The terminal is often on the outer wall of the bank building for after-hours use or in a shopping center for the convenience of the depositor. This terminal is usually linked to the bank's computer system, which verifies the customer's account balance, in the case of a cash withdrawal. To issue the cash wanted, the depositor keys in the amount, and the terminal automatically updates the depositor's account records accordingly.

Types of EFT Systems

The types of EFT systems can be grouped into four major functional areas—remote banking services, pay-by-phone systems, retail point-of-sale services, and direct deposit and preauthorized payment services.

Remote banking services are provided through the use of *automated teller machines* (ATM) and through the use of touch-tone telephones. The functions normally performed by remote banking EFT systems are divided into five categories—deposits, withdrawals, transfers between accounts, bill paying, and inquiry on account status.

In the ATM system, the customer inserts a plastic *debit card,* similar to a credit card, and enters data for a specific transaction, such as identification number, amount, and type.

Customer reluctance to let an impersonal machine do their banking has led to personalizing the ATM. To encourage confidence, one bank decided to seek out an ATM called "Aunt Bea." When customers insert their cards into the slot, they are greeted by Aunt Bea's soothing down-home voice with a friendly "howdy." The video instruction continues Aunt Bea's conversational approach with, "Thank you. Wasn't that fun? I enjoy doing business with you." Another personalizing feature of the ATM is greeting the customer by name.

Pay-by-phone systems provide for the telephonic transfer of funds between a customer and a merchant through a financial institution. The central computer communicates with the customer by means of a voice response system. This system groups prerecorded words into meaningful phrases to confirm to the customer that the data has been entered into the system.

Retail point-of-sales services are provided through the use of *point-of-sales (POS)* terminals. The simplest terminals can be used to verify and/or guarantee checks or perform credit card authorizations. The more sophisticated systems use units not only to capture sales and inventory data but also to directly transfer funds from the customer's account to the merchant's account.

Direct deposit and preauthorized payment systems are used to send regular payments electronically to and from customers without manual intervention. For direct deposits, the customer notifies either an employer or other payer (such as the Social Security Administration) with a standing authorization to directly deposit funds due to a specific account.

The move toward EFTS is receiving its greatest stimulus from new electronic terminals that read cash cards, capture sales data, and bring the consumer, the merchant, and the local financial service institution into the electronic transfer process.

Summary

Data entry costs constitute a large portion of the total data-processing budget. With recent technological advances in data entry devices, it is important that one become familiar with the methods for processing data into machine-readable form. This chapter introduces conventional data entry devices as well as the latest advances in automated data entry so you will be aware of all alternatives available in this dynamic field.

There are many different types of data entry devices available, each with its particular strengths and weaknesses. Each technique has its value, its place in the data-processing operation, and its cost justification in a particular application. The basic categories include keypunch and keypunch replacement, online display terminals, character recognition devices, and shared processor data terminal systems.

1. The keypunch and keypunch replacement category includes keypunches and verifiers, key-to-tape/cassette/diskette devices, and key-driven paper tape. With this type of equipment, data is transcribed from source documents to input media, retaining the original sequence in which it was captured.
2. Online display terminals provide direct communication with the computer which permits direct data entry and queries to start a chain of events.
3. The character recognition device is a specialized data entry system designed to solve major information bottlenecks and get data quickly converted to machine-processible media.
4. With shared processor data terminal systems, a number of data entry stations share a minicomputer. The stations display either single characters (panel display) or a full record (CRT), and input data is stored on intermediate storage devices, such as disks or drums.
5. Floppy disks are small sized, low-cost memory devices used primarily for storage and retrieval of data in a low-cost data-handling system. It replaces cards, paper tape, cassettes, and cartridges and resembles a 45-RPM phonograph record. It has a moving read/write head capable of random access processing that is faster than tape cassettes or cartridges. Recent innovations include dual density disks, dual disks, double-sided disks, double-sided dual density disks, and double track disks.
6. Bubble storage of data is done in tiny magnetized areas that can be generated, moved, and detected in a specialized crystalline material. Bubble storage uses very little power, which makes it less expensive to use. Since it has no movable parts, it is more reliable. It also does not lose information in case of power failure.
7. Voice recognition is the ability to speak directly into the computer. This bypasses the writing and keying of data.
8. Interactive terminals are used online to replace hard-copy computer output with display stations, which display information that the user requests. Display units can present tables, graphs, charts, and various other configurations of characters. These units also have editing and formatting capabilities and can transmit data at high speeds.
9. Intelligent terminals possess program capabilities. They can store, retrieve, and edit data locally. They are usually interfaced with a communications network.
10. Remote-batch terminals transmit large amounts of data at high speeds to a central computer. Data can be edited before transmission.
11. Graphics can be produced on computers in a variety of forms—graphs, charts, tables, pictures, and maps. Plotters produce a recording of the pen movement on the surface of paper, three-dimensional drawings, color plotting, and microfilm recording.

12. Magnetic-ink character readers (MICR) print data that is readable by both people and machines. These devices are used extensively in banking.
13. Optical character readers (OCR) print data that can be read by both people and machines. These devices have the capability of reading paper documents directly into the system without transcription, including hand-written, typed, or printed documents.
14. Point-of-sale (POS) devices electronically control credit and electronically capture merchandise information. POS devices can be located at various sites in a business and integrate their related business functions.
15. The universal product code (UPC) provides information such as product price, name, and date of manufacture. It also produces a printed tape together with name and price for the customer automatically.
16. The electronic funds transfer system (EFTS) facilitates the exchange of monetary values through electronic means. This may be done by remote banking services, pay-by-phone services, retail point-of-sale services, and direct deposit and preauthorized payment systems.

Identification Questions

Match the following terms with the statements below.

A. Bubble Storage
B. Electronic Funds Transfer System (EFTS)
C. Floppy Disk
D. Graphics
E. Intelligent Terminals
F. Interactive Terminals (CRT)
G. Magnetic-Ink Character Reader (MICR)
H. Online Display Terminal
I. Optical Character Reader (OCR)
J. Plotters
K. Point of Sale (POS)
L. Remote-Batch Terminals
M. Shared Processor Data Terminal System
N. Universal Product Code (UPC)
O. Voice Recognition

1. Tiny magnetized areas that can be generated, moved, and detected in specialized crystalline material.
2. Ability to produce a great variety of information in the form of graphics, charts, pictures, and maps.
3. Facilitates the exchange of monetary values through electronic means.
4. Provide direct communication with computers.
5. Used online with display stations where user obtains information.
6. Reads paper documents directly into system without transcription.
7. Electronic control of credit and the electronic capture of merchandise information.
8. Number of data entry stations sharing a minicomputer.
9. Possess program capability through integrated processors or built-in microprocessors.
10. Produces a recording of the pen movement on surface of paper.
11. Provides merchandise information on printed tape for customer.

12. Compact, flexible computer storage device resembling 45 RPM phonograph record.
13. A "discrete" or "isolated" word recognition system.
14. Transmits large amounts of data at high speeds to a central computer.
15. Reads cards and paper documents inscribed with magnetic ink.

Questions for Review

1. What are the three classes of scanners available and what is each used for primarily?
2. What are the major developments in data entry devices?
3. Explain the different types of data entry devices available in today's market.
4. What is a floppy disk and what is its main purpose?
5. What are the advantages and disadvantages of floppy disks?
6. What is bubble storage and what is its main advantage over floppy disks?
7. Briefly explain the main advantage and operation of a voice recognition system.
8. Briefly describe the purposes of the different types of terminals.
9. What are some possible applications for interactive terminals?
10. What are the main advantages and disadvantages of interactive terminals?
11. What is an intelligent terminal and how does it differ from a "dumb" terminal?
12. What are remote-batch terminals and how do they differ from other terminals?
13. How does computer graphics aid business?
14. What are plotters and what are their principal uses?
15. Explain the uses of two major character recognition devices.
16. What is the importance of magnetic-ink character readers in the banking field?
17. What are the principal uses of optical character readers?
18. What is meant by point-of-sale processing and what are its main advantages?
19. What is meant by universal product code and how is it used in the retail industry?
20. What is an electronic funds transfer system and how is the system used?

Key Terms

Bubble Storage
Electronic Funds Transfer System (EFTS)
Floppy Disks
Graphics
Intelligent Terminals
Interactive Terminals (CRT)
Magnetic-Ink Character Readers (MICR)
Online Display Terminals
Optical Character Readers (OCR)
Plotters
Point of Sale (POS)
Shared Processor Data Terminal Systems
Universal Product Code (UPC)
Voice Recognition

computer components 5

processing and storage devices

Chapter Outline

Chapter Objectives

The learning objectives of this chapter are

1. to describe the various components of the central processing unit.
2. to describe the physical characteristics of storage devices that are available because the data-processing system must have the capacity to store large amounts of data to be effective.
3. to explain direct access processing concepts because the effectiveness of a data-processing system depends upon its ability to process data as soon as it becomes available.
4. to explain the operations of direct access units because the methods of processing and the functions of each unit are essential to understanding the data-processing function.

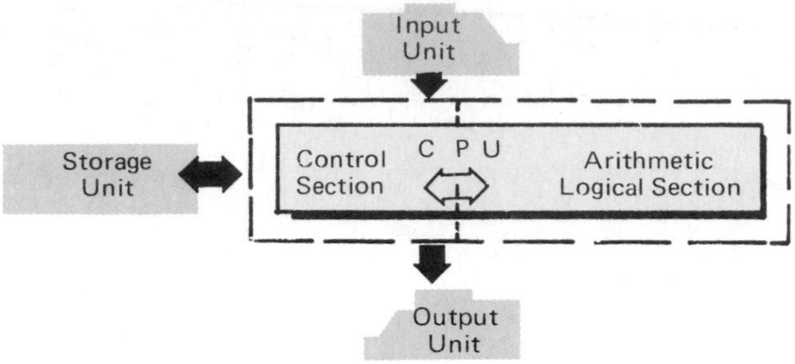

Figure 5.1 The central processing unit.

Central Processing Unit (CPU)

The central processing unit (CPU) is the heart of the entire data-processing system. It supervises and controls the data-processing components, performs the actual arithmetic, and makes the logical decisions. Processing includes the data movement, the computations, and the logical decisions necessary to edit the data into meaningful information in the desired format of the output.

The CPU is not limited by speeds of peripheral units. Since the CPU is the unit that performs all the internal processing, it is permitted to do most of its arithmetic and logical functions while the other units in the system are performing their assigned tasks.

The central processing unit is divided into two sections—the arithmetic and logical section and the control section plus main storage (fig. 5.1).

Arithmetic and Logical Section

The arithmetic and logical section contains the circuitry that makes the necessary arithmetic computations and logical decisions called for by the computer commands (fig. 5.2). A computer can execute thousands of arithmetic operations per second compared to the several problems per minute performed by an experienced desk-calculator operator. The arithmetic portion performs such operations as addition, subtraction, multiplication, division, shifting, moving, and storing under control of the stored program. The logical portion of the section is capable of decision making to test various conditions encountered during the processing and to alter the sequence of the instruction execution. Logical decisions determine the relationship between two items, such as equal to, less than, or greater than. Once the relationship is established, the computer follows the instructions programmed for that condition.

Certain logical decisions, such as a compare instruction, can be made and acted upon as the situation requires. Based on whether or not a stated condition exists, the processing unit can be directed to go to one series of instructions or another. For example, in an inventory application, when a disbursement quantity is subtracted from the stock balance, a negative balance may occur. Noting this condition, the processing unit can be directed to another series of instructions that will call the attention of the user of the report to this condition in the form of a printed output.

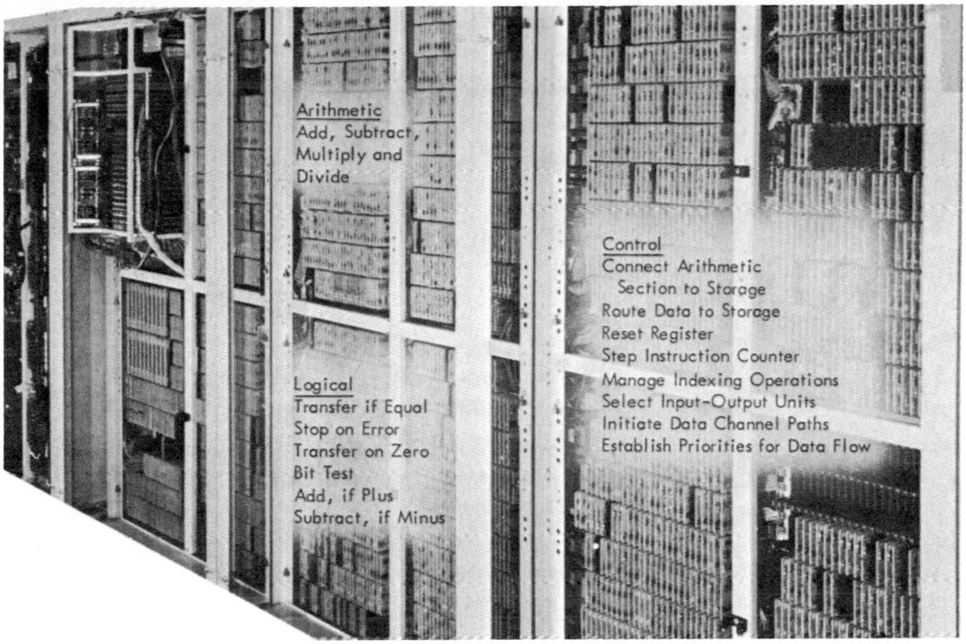

Figure 5.2 The control and the arithmetic and logical sections.

Control Section

The control section acts as a traffic manager directing and coordinating all operations called for by the instructions of the computer system. This involves control of input/output devices, entry and removal of information from storage, and routing of information between storage and the arithmetic and logical section. The control section automatically integrates the operation of the entire computer system.

The control aspect of the processing unit comes from the individual commands contained in the program. These commands are instructions to the various devices to perform a function as specified. Each time a card is read or punched, or a line is printed on the output printer, or two amounts are added together, it is because an instruction in the processing unit caused it to happen. An instruction tells the computer what operation is to be done (add, subtract, multiply, move, read a card) and where the data is that will be affected by this operation.

This section directs the system according to the procedure and instructions received from its human operators and programmers.

Operational Units

Registers

A register is a device capable of storing information temporarily, receiving information from other areas, and transferring information as directed by the control section.

Registers are named according to the function they perform (fig. 5.3). For example, an accumulator accumulates results, a storage register contains information that is taken from or being sent to storage, an address register contains the address of a storage location or device, and an instruction register contains the instruction being executed. The IBM System/370 has sixteen general-purpose registers that can be used as index registers, relocation registers, and accumulators for fixed-point arithmetic and logical operations.

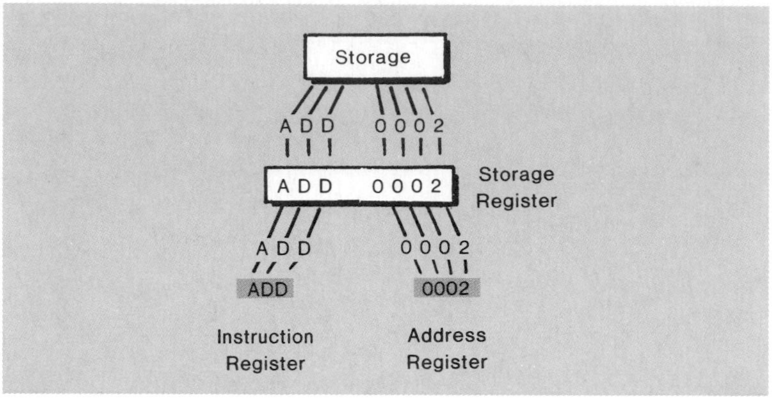

Figure 5.3 The register nomenclature and function.

Counter

A counter is closely related to a register and performs the same functions. It can function as an accumulator in that its contents may be increased or decreased. Counter functions will vary depending upon the computer. Usually their contents may be displayed upon the console.

Adder

The adder performs arithmetic functions by accumulating the value of two data items and sending the results to an accumulator or register. Automatic carries to the next higher order position are performed on the data. When a command is given, the addition, subtraction, multiplication, or division will be performed in the adder, and then the answer will be stored in a counter or register (fig. 5.4).

Machine Cycles

In computer usage, time is stated in terms of milliseconds, microseconds, and nanoseconds. How short is a period of time? The blink of an eye takes one tenth of a second or 100 milliseconds. The following are some abbreviations for time intervals.

.1	=	1/10 second	=	100 milliseconds
.001	=	1/1,000 second	=	1 millisecond (MS)
.000001	=	1/1,000,000 second	=	1 microsecond (m sec)
.000000001	=	1/1,000,000,000 second	=	1 nanosecond (NS)

During a machine cycle, the computer can perform a specific machine operation. The number of operations required to execute a single instruction will depend on the instruction. Many machine operations are combined to execute each program instruction.

Instructions

There are at least two parts to each instruction—an operation and operand. The *operation* denotes the function that the machine is to perform, such as add, subtract, multiply, write, move, or read. The *operand* can be the address of the data or instruction in main storage; the address of a program in secondary storage; or the address of an input/output device.

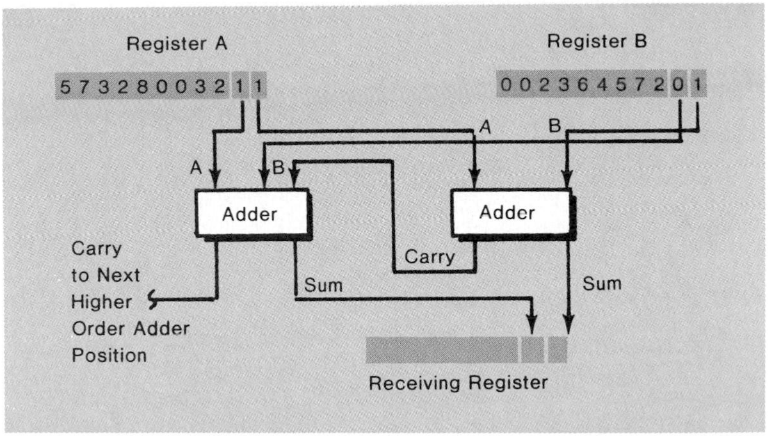

Figure 5.4 Adders in a computer system.

During an instruction cycle, an instruction is selected from storage and analyzed by the central processing unit. The operation portion of the instruction indicates the operation to be performed. This is coded information that has a particular meaning to the computer. For example, in an IBM System/370 computer, the letter *A* is interpreted as *add* and the letter *C* as *compare.* Each computer has its own unique coding techniques.

The operand further defines or augments the function of the operation. For example, to perform an arithmetic operation, the storage location of one or both of the factors involved would be indicated. For reading or writing operations, the area of storage needed for the input and output is indicated or fixed by machine design.

In most data-processing units, no particular area of storage is reserved for instructions. They are usually grouped together in ascending sequential locations, according to the sequence in which the instructions are to be executed normally. Unless altered by a branch-type instruction (the changing of the sequence of instruction execution due to a condition detected during the processing), the process is as follows.

1. The computer locates the first instruction either in a predetermined location of storage assigned for this purpose or by the manual resetting of the switches on the console.
2. After each instruction is executed, the next sequential instruction is fetched unless the program directs it to another location.
3. The process continues automatically, instruction by instruction, until the program is complete or the computer is instructed to stop.

To receive, interpret, and execute the various instructions, the central processing unit must operate in a prescribed sequence.

Instruction Cycle

The following operations occur during the instruction cycle (fig. 5.5).

1. The instruction is brought to the CPU from main storage.
2. The operation code is decoded.

Figure 5.5 The instruction cycle.

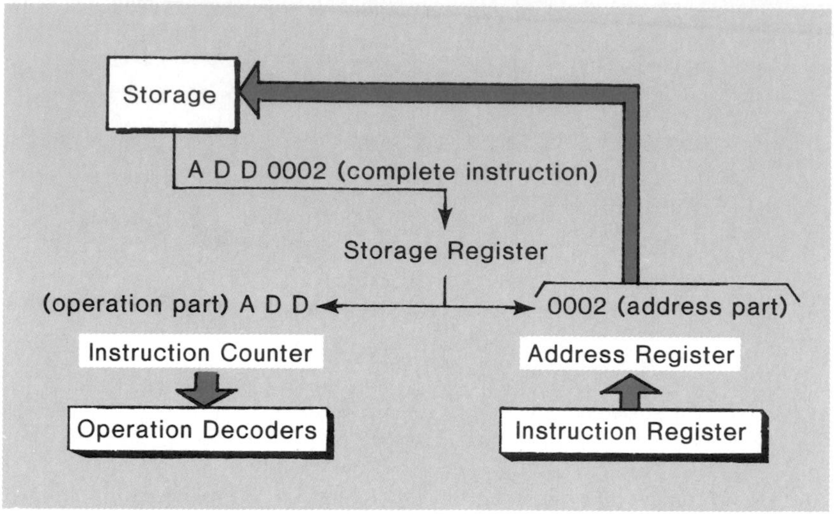

3. The operand is placed in an address register, indicating the location of the factors involved in the operation.
4. The location of the next instruction to be executed is indicated.

Execution Cycle

The execution cycle follows the instruction cycle (fig. 5.6). The number of execution cycles to be performed will depend on the instruction to be executed.

The address register may contain information other than the location of the data. The address of the input/output device or a control function to be performed can be indicated. The operating portion of the instruction informs the computer how to interpret the information (fig. 5.7).

Storage

Since the completion of the ENIAC computer over thirty years ago, there has been a continuous search for one type of memory that could serve all of a computer's storage requirements. Memories have come a long way since then; so far, that the fastest forms are limited by the speed of light. Still no single form of memory has been found to do all of a computer's work. There are fast, expensive internal memories for calculations and slower, less expensive ones for peripheral storage; but there is a gap between them in terms of speed and cost.

All data entering a computer to be processed must be placed in storage first. Storage can be compared to a giant electronic file cabinet, completely indexed and available for instant accessing. Information is entered into storage by an input device and is then available for internal processing. Storage is arranged so that each position has a specific location called an *address*, just as your house has its own street address. This unique address enables the programmer to have access to data stored in storage as well as to place new data into storage. For example, consider a group of numbered mailboxes in a post office. Each of these boxes is identified and located by its unique number. Storage is also divided into locations, each with its assigned address. Each location holds a special character of information. However, unlike the mailbox, a

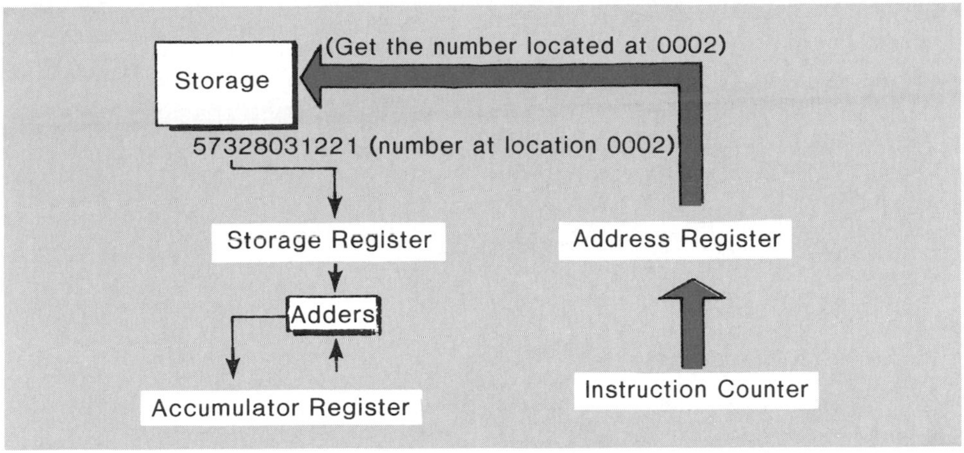

Figure 5.6 The execution cycle.

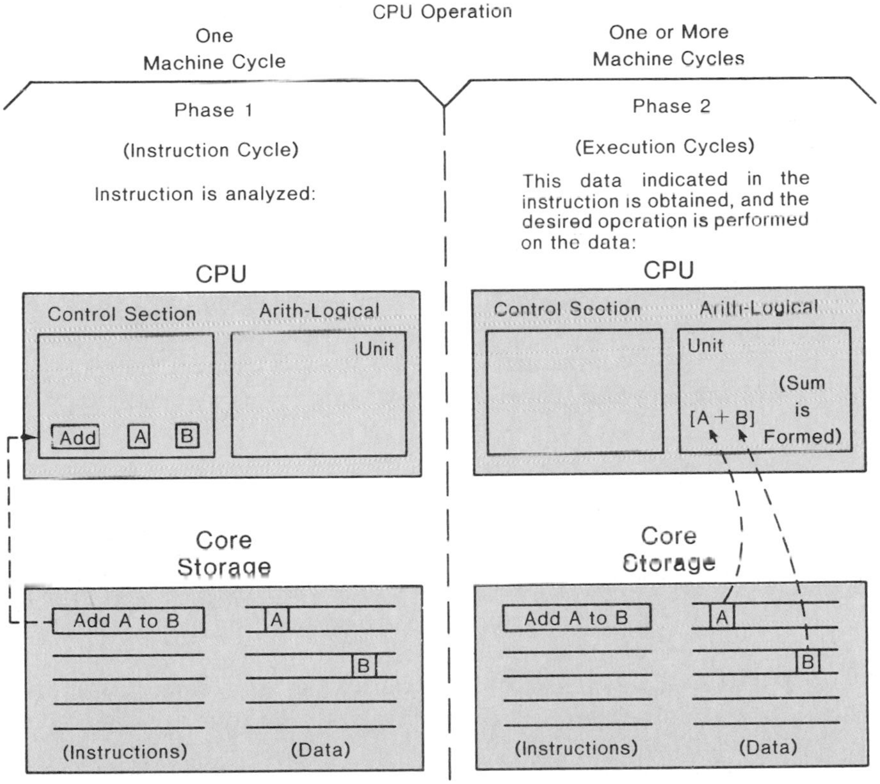

Figure 5.7 A schematic diagram of the instruction and the execution cycles.

computer storage location holds only one piece of information at a time; the placing of another piece of information into this same location automatically erases its previous contents.

Data may be rearranged by sorting and collating different types of information received from the various input units. Data may also be taken from storage, processed, and the result placed back in storage. The size and capacity of storage determines the

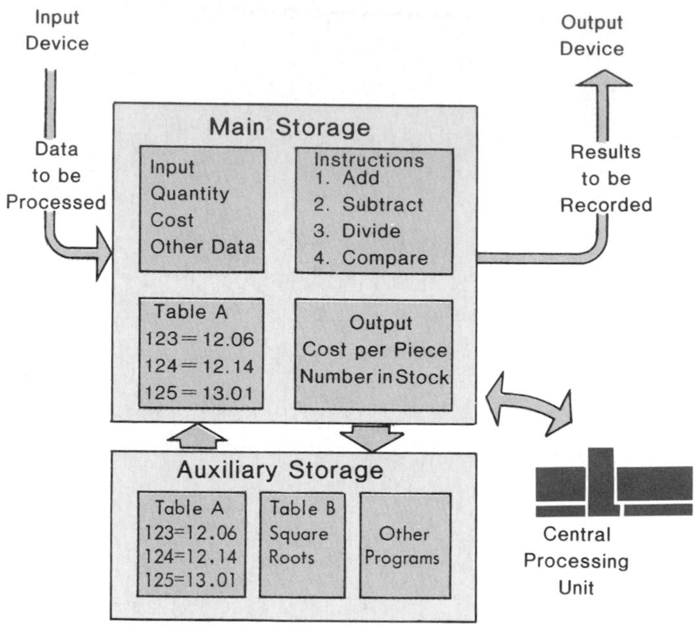

Figure 5.8 A schematic diagram of the main and auxiliary storage.

amount of information that can be held within a system at one time. The larger the capacity, the more powerful and expensive the computer. A computer containing 256,000 storage locations is commonly referred to as 256K system. (K stands for 1,000. 256K = 256 × 1000, or 256,000.) In some computers, the storage capacity is measured in millions of characters while other systems have smaller storage facilities. The capacity and design of the storage unit has an effect upon the method of processing data through the computer. Storage may be classified as main or auxiliary storage (fig. 5.8).

Main Storage

Main storage is usually referred to as core storage. *All data to be processed must pass through main storage.* Main storage accepts the data from the input unit, holds processed data, and can furnish data to an output unit. Since all data passes through main storage, the unit must therefore have the capacity to retain a usable amount of data and all necessary instructions for processing.

If additional storage is required, the capacity of main storage is augmented by auxiliary storage units; however, all information to and from auxiliary storage must be routed through main storage.

Auxiliary Storage

There are two types of auxiliary storage—random (direct) access units and sequential access units.

Random access units, such as drum, disk, and data cell devices, can process data randomly; that is, records can be accessed without reading from the beginning of a file to find them.

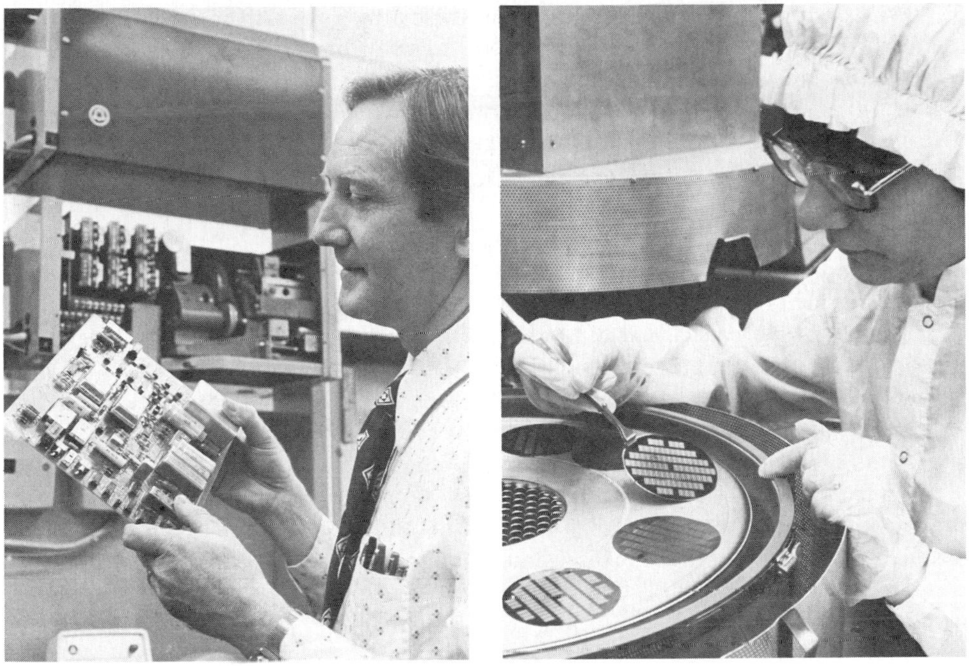

Figure 5.9 Various storage technologies. (Courtesy of Bell Laboratories)

The magnetic tape unit is the chief type of sequential access unit. This type of processing indicates that the tape reels must be read from the beginning of the tape to find the desired record.

To date, random access memory (RAM) dominates the secondary (auxiliary) storage area. This secondary storage area includes magnetic drum, magnetic disks, and data cells. Semiconductor, integrated circuit (IC), charged coupled devices (CCDs), and bubble memory devices are competing to fill the memory "gap" between internal memory (core storage) and auxiliary storage (direct access devices).

Storage Devices

Storage devices are essentially information storehouses. Storage capacity in a memory device, and the rate at which information can be channeled into or out of it, largely determines what tasks it can perform.

Today, there is a large variety of storage devices from which to choose. Some devices offer large storage capacities and fast data retrieval, but at a relatively high per-unit cost. Others offer cost savings and huge storage capacity, but at the expense of speed. Each has its place in the wide range of applications (fig. 5.9).

Core

The majority of computer storage devices today are ferrite cores, which are essentially tiny "doughnuts" of magnetic material. Wires threaded through the center of each doughnut serve as electrical pathways to and from the magnetic storage medium. Binary information can be stored in this medium by electronically manipulating magnetism of the core material.

For example, current traveling in a clockwise direction inscribes a "one." Reversing the flow of the current results in a "zero." This information can be electronically sensed and retrieved in millionths of a second and will remain in the storage device, even if the power fails. To get at that information, however, a computer with a ferrite core memory has to use a host of peripheral electronic circuits. All this circuitry contributes to the core and complexity of ferrite core memories.

Magnetic

These devices contain a magnetic element (disk, drum, or reel of magnetic tape) that is moved past recording heads, similar to those found on a small cassette tape recorder. Data is recorded in various "tracks" on the magnetic element.

Magnetic tape is usually cut into thin strips, which are wound on reels. (Magnetic tape is discussed in chapter 3.) Drums are rotatable metal cylinders. Disks are metal platters, resembling phonograph records. All three can store large quantities of information at a low cost and are available in many forms. Each device has the advantage of retaining information, even when the power source fails.

Their primary disadvantage is slow speed. For example, magnetic tape storage can take anywhere from one tenth of a second to 100 seconds to retrieve just one piece of stored information. Magnetic disks and drums are faster, from 8 to 200 thousandths of a second, but they are still slower than core storage.

Semiconductor, Integrated Circuit

Integrated circuit (IC) storage devices store information in the form of simple electronic charges in small functional components on silicon chips. A typical memory chip is less than a quarter-inch square and can contain as many as 16,000 bits of information. Information stored in the individual components is accessed by accompanying circuitry also located on the same silicon chip.

Integrated circuits do have the inherent problem of losing stored information if power is disconnected from the circuit.

Charged Coupled Devices

Charged coupled devices (CCDs), invented at Bell Laboratories about eight years ago, are the semiconductors analogous to magnetic bubbles. CCDs store information as packets of charges within a semiconductor chip. These charge packets are manipulated by applying voltages to a routing pattern inscribed on the chip's surface. The attendant circuitry required to store, move, and access the packets is also contained on the same chip.

Like magnetic bubbles, CCDs can be manufactured with a large number of bits per chip. They perform many functions of highly complex integrated circuits; yet they are simple, three-layered structures. CCDs are also used as imaging devices in solid-state cameras and other applications.

Although CCDs lose stored information when power supplies are removed, they are almost ten times faster than magnetic bubbles in accessing information. (Bubble storage is discussed in chapter 4.)

Storage Processing

All data in storage is arranged so that it can be accessed by its individual address. Each location holds a specific unit of data, be it a character, a digit, a word, or an entire record, depending upon the particular computer. To insert or remove data at a location, the address must be known either to the programmer or to a control program.

When information is placed in a location, it replaces the previous contents of that location. Once stored, the same data may be used repeatedly. The original contents remain unaltered when information is moved from one location to another.

Access time is the time required to locate and transfer information to and from storage. Access time is measured in billionths of a second. To fully appreciate such a minute interval of time, imagine a spaceship traveling at 100,000 miles per hour. In one microsecond (millionth of a second) the spaceship travels about 1¾ inches, while in a nanosecond (billionth of a second) it travels one thousandth of 1¾ inches.

In all data-processing systems, the access time has a direct bearing on the efficiency of the entire system.

Main Storage

Core Storage

A magnetic core is a doughnut-shaped ferromagnetic-coated material, vertically aligned. The tiny ring measures a few hundredths of an inch in diameter. Aside from its compact size, the core is easily magnetized in a few millionths of a second and, unless changed, retains its magnetism indefinitely.

Cores are placed on a wire in a series similar to a string of beads. An electric current is sent through, magnetizing the individual cores. The direction of the current determines the polarity of the magnetic state of the core. By reversing the current, the magnetic state of the core can be reversed. In a binary system of information, only one of two conditions need to be tested. Core storage lends itself perfectly to binary in that each position will have a reading of 1 or 0 depending upon the state of the magnetism (fig. 5.10). Any single core can be selected for reading without affecting the others. Any combination of 1s (ones) or 0s (zeros) representing a character can be written magnetically or read back when needed.

To select certain cores to be magnetized, two wires are run through each core at right angles to each other. When half of the current needed to magnetize is sent through each wire, only the core at the intersection is magnetized. No other core in

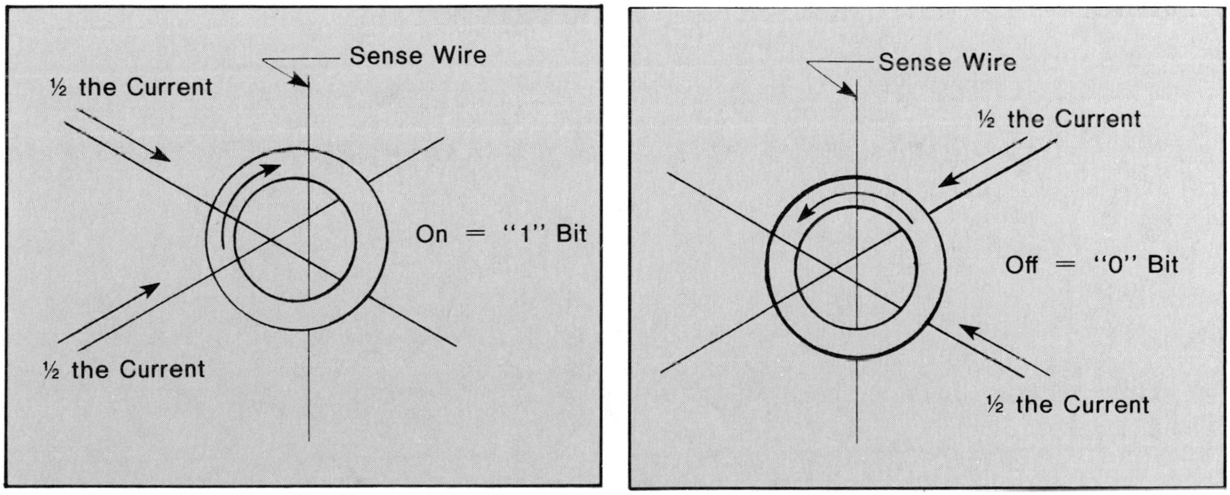

Figure 5.10 A schematic diagram of a magnetic core.

the string is affected. Employing these principles, any single core in a screen may be selected for storage or reading without affecting any other.

If the magnetic state of the core is reversed, the abrupt change induces current in a third wire. This signal is sent by the sense wire and can be used to determine whether the core contained a 1 or *on* status. Since only one core at any one time in any plane is tested for its magnetic state, only one sense wire is needed for an entire plane.

The core storage is the "workhorse" of a computer system. All processing takes place in the magnetic core. Core storage is the most expensive storage device in cost per storage location, but it provides the fastest access time and may be the least expensive per machine calculation.

Auxiliary Storage

Magnetic Drum

Auxiliary storage devices (fig. 5.11) are usually used in larger computer systems. A drum is vertically mounted in a shaft and the data is recorded on its outer surface. Data is recorded around the drum in a series of tracks. The drum has a fixed read/write head for each track. Data is transferred to and from the drum as the single recording surface rotates past the fixed head. A drum storage device (fig. 5.12) has a maximum capacity of over 4 million characters.

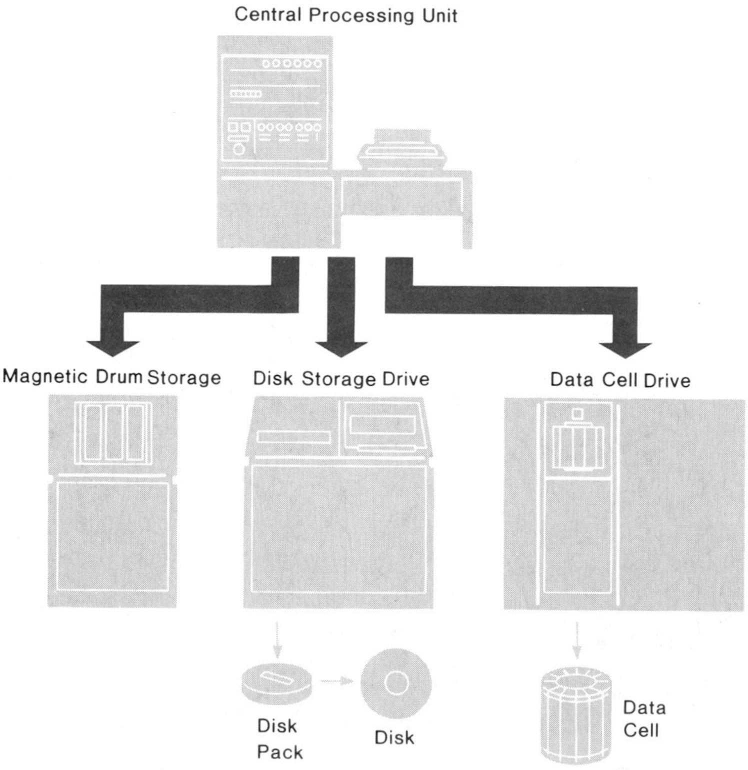

Figure 5.11 A schematic diagram of auxiliary storage. (Courtesy IBM Corporation)

A *magnetic drum* is a constant-speed rotating cylinder with an outer surface coated with magnetic material. The chief function of the drum is to serve as a low capacity, intermediate access storage device, storing results temporarily for future processing (fig. 5.13). The primary uses of a magnetic drum are storage for data that is repetitively referenced during processing (tables, rates, codes) and supplementary storage for core storage. Another important use is to serve as a random access device providing program storage and program modification of data, and as temporary storage for high-activity random access operations involving limited amounts of data.

Magnetic drum storage offers the advantage of lower direct cost to offset the faster speed of the core storage units.

Magnetic Disk

Disk storage is the most popular type of auxiliary storage. Magnetic disk, like drum storage, provides data-processing systems with the ability to read or retrieve records sequentially or randomly (direct access). The *magnetic disk* is a thin disk of metal coated on both sides with magnetic recording material (fig. 5.14).

The recording surface of each device is divided into many tracks. *A track is defined as a circumference of the recording surface.* The tracks are concentric, not a spiral like a phonograph record.

Figure 5.12 An example of drum storage.

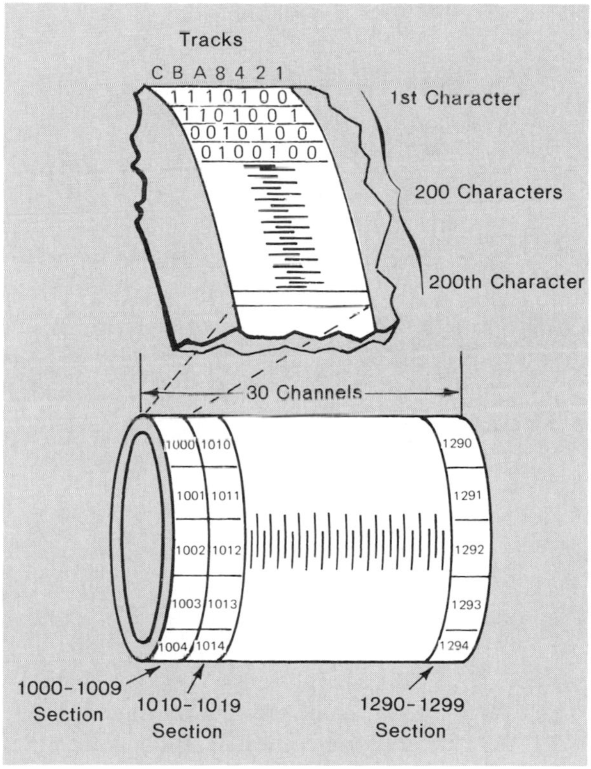

Figure 5.13 Magnetic drum storage.

Figure 5.14
Magnetic disk layout.

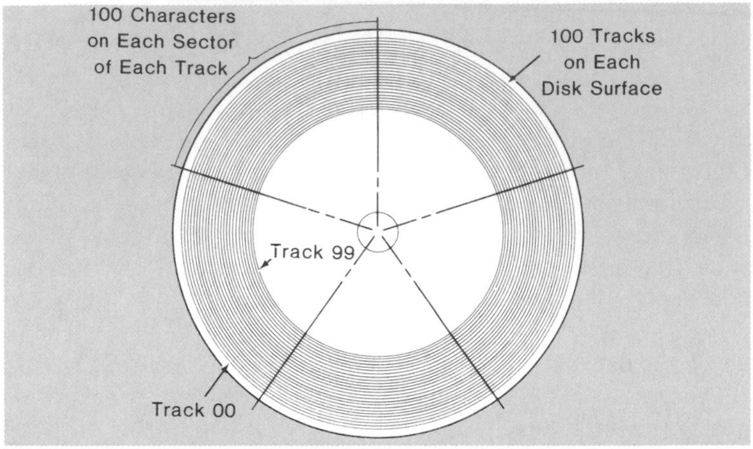

Figure 5.15
Magnetic disk recording.

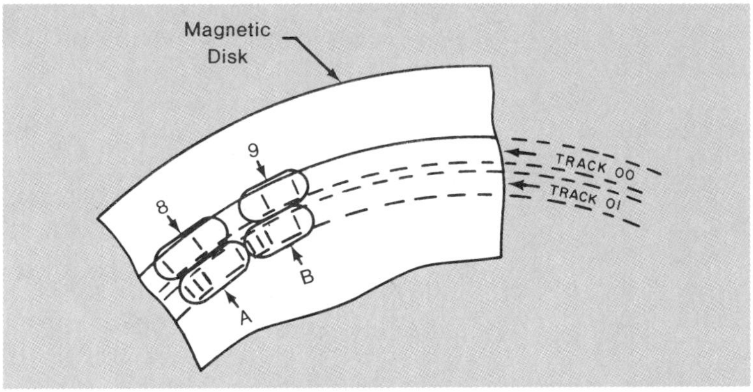

Data is stored as magnetic spots on the tracks on each surface of the disk. Data is recorded serially bit by bit, eight bits per byte (one character), along a track (fig. 5.15). The number of tracks per recording surface and the capacity of track for each device will vary according to a particular model. These tracks are accessible for reading or writing by positioning the read/write heads between the spinning disks.

Independent portable disks can be used with interchangeable disk packs. Disk packs are mounted as a single unit, which can be easily removed from the disk drive and stored in a library of disks (fig. 5.16). Read/write heads are mounted on an access arm arranged like teeth in a comb that moves horizontally between the disks, thus providing access to all tracks. Each arm has two read/write heads with one head servicing the bottom surface of the top disk and the other head servicing the top surface of the lower disk. It is possible to read and write on either side of the disk (fig. 5.17).

The concept of removable disk packs means that only those disk records needed for a particular application need be in use. Data records for other applications can be removed and stored.

The types of disk drives presently available are devices with removable disk packs, devices with nonremovable disk packs, and direct access storage facility.

Figure 5.16 Disk operations. (Courtesy IBM Corporation)

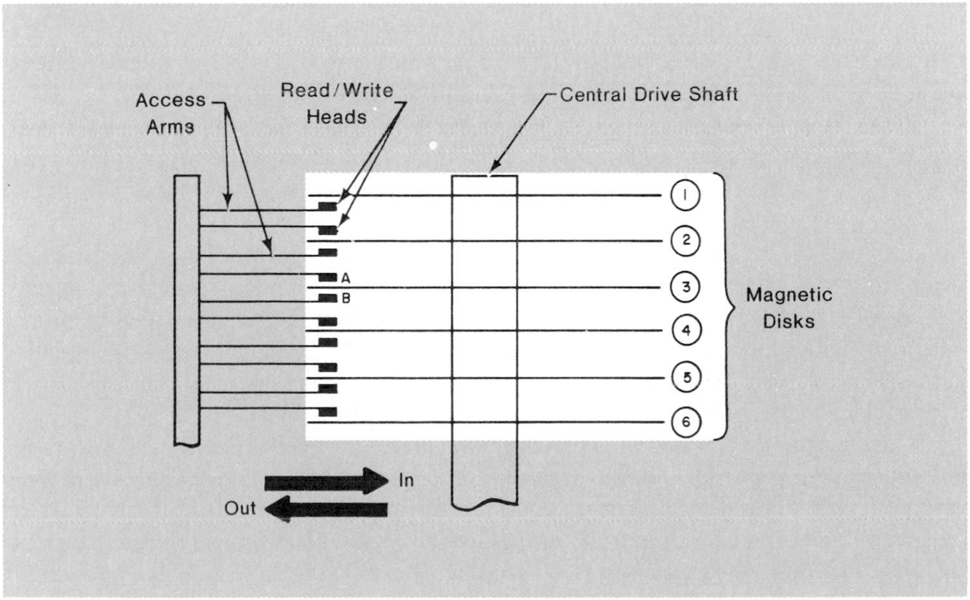

Figure 5.17 A schematic drawing of a magnetic disk.

Figure 5.18 Direct access storage facilities. (Courtesy IBM)

The *removable disk pack* are disks mounted on a vertical shaft that may be removed from the drive and enclosed in a protective cover.

The *nonremovable disk pack* has a nonremovable access mechanism, positioned around the disk, that reads the data on the tracks.

The *direct access storage facility* contains a number of drives, depending upon the particular model, that may be removed for offline storage. One device is used for backup if one of the other drives requires service (fig. 5.18).

Each pack is divided into cylinders. *A cylinder of data is the amount of information that is accessible with one position of the access mechanism* (fig. 5.19). Since the movement of the access mechanism requires a significant portion of the time needed to access and transfer data, the storing of a large amount of data in a single cylinder can save processing time by minimizing the amount of access time.

Disks provide the data-processing systems with the ability to read and retrieve records randomly and sequentially. They permit the immediate access to specific areas of information without the need to examine each record as in magnetic tape operations.

Data Cells

The data cell drive (fig. 5.20) economically extends the online random access storage capabilities to a volume of data beyond that of other storage devices. A data cell device consists of ten cells. Each cell is divided into twenty subcells. Each subcell contains ten strips, which are the recording medium for the device. Each strip is 2¼ inches wide, 13 inches long, and about three times as thick as magnetic tape. The strips are held in place at the bottom of the cell and by the adjacent strips.

The strips are processed by being wrapped around a drum. The data is recorded on concentric tracks, not a spiral track as on a phonograph record. The strips are selected for processing. As the drum continues to rotate, the strip is withdrawn from the subcell and wrapped around the drum. As the rotation continues, the strip moves

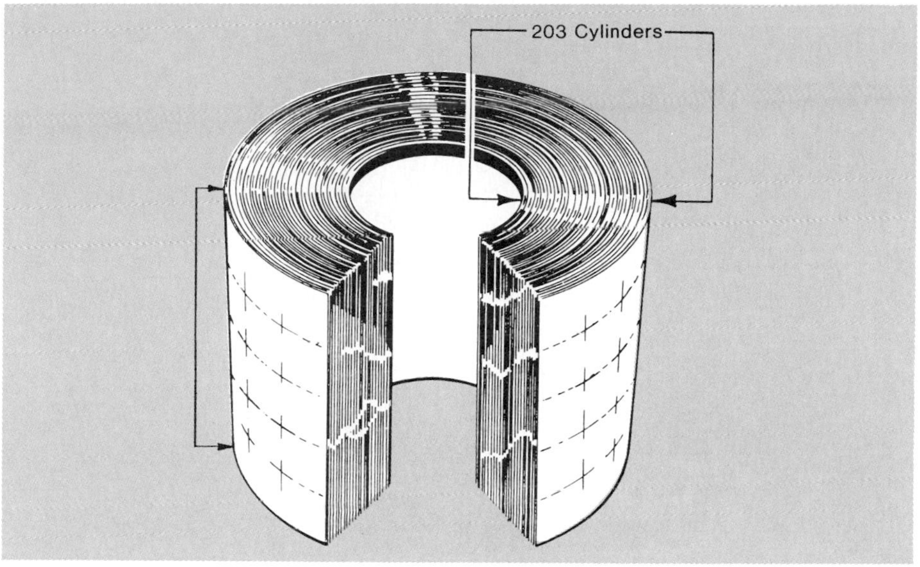

Figure 5.19 A cylinder.

past a bar of twenty read/write heads. There is no actual physical contact between the head and the strip since there is an air cushion between them. The strip remains attached to the drum until another strip is selected.

The maximum capacity of a data cell drive is 400 million characters.

Direct Access

Inline processing denotes the ability of the data-processing system to process the data as soon as it becomes available. This implies that the input data does not have to be sorted in any manner, manipulated, or edited, before it is entered into the system, whether the input consists of transactions of a single application or of many applications.

Direct access mass storage devices have made inline processing feasible for many applications. While sorting transactions are still advantageous before certain processing runs, in most instances the necessity for presorting has been eliminated. The ability to process data inline provides solutions to problems, once thought impractical. A typical application of inline processing is inventory control where direct access processing is now being used extensively. For example, a large school district established a central warehouse for distributing supplies to its many schools. The records for the 20,000 items of inventory are maintained using a nine-digit stock number for identification purposes. Minimum balances, which allow the storekeeper ample time to reorder each item, are established for all items of inventory. The storekeeper wishes to be notified immediately when this minimum balance has been reached to avoid an out-of-stock condition. Under the previous system, all transactions were batched and processed together. All transactions affecting inventory were accumulated and sorted into stock number sequence and processed against the master file. This type of processing would result in a delay of days from the time the transaction occurred until it was processed. Sufficient time was not provided for the necessary reordering pro-

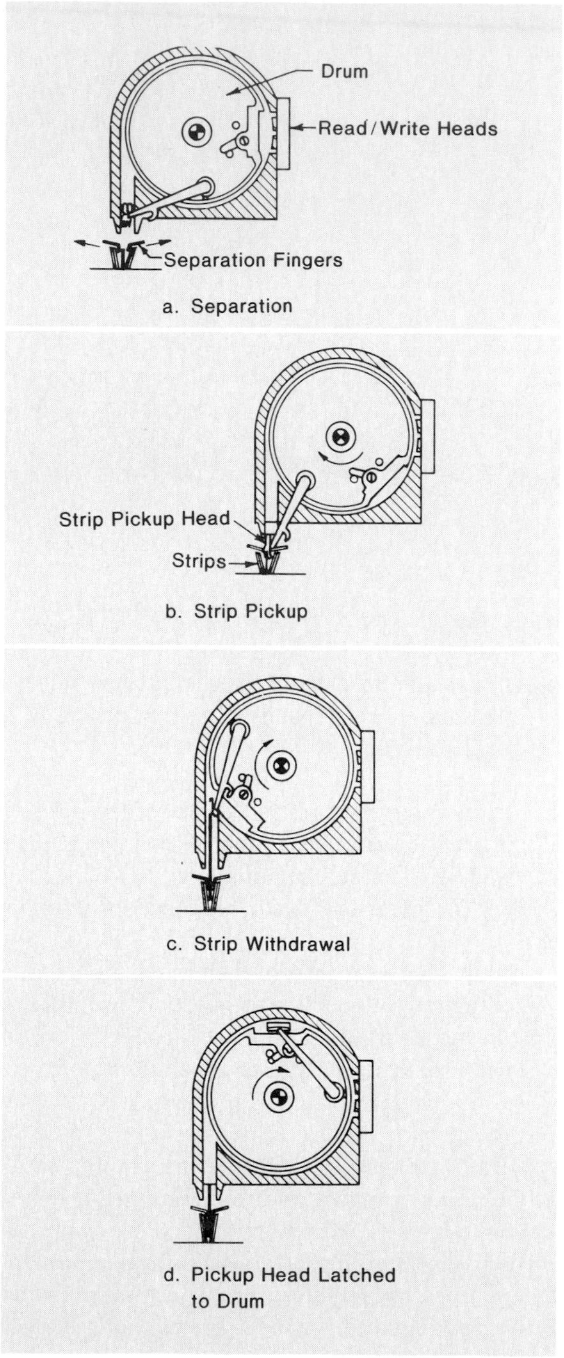

Figure 5.20 The data cell drive operation.

cedures. The problem was solved with the installation of direct access devices in which the transactions were processed inline, as they occurred, and the required notifications of stock status were provided almost immediately to the storekeeper.

Direct access storage enables the user to maintain current records of diversified applications and to process nonsequential and intermixed data for multiple application areas.

Applications

Inquiries

Prior to the development of direct access devices, the ability to request information directly from a storage device was limited. It involved the preparation of a complex time-consuming interruption procedure, which did not always provide current information. The ability of direct access storage systems to process input data of various types inline for multiple applications and in addition to immediately update all the affected records makes it possible to interrogate the system and receive current information directly in readable form. There is no longer a need to disrupt the normal processing of the data, nor is there a delay between the request for information and the response. For example, a bank teller may need information immediately about the status of a depositor's account. When the teller inserts the depositor's account number in an input device, the information will be displayed in readable format.

This ability to request information directly from the computer and receive an immediate response may in itself be a justification for the use of direct acccss storage devices.

Modification of Records

In most data-processing applications, there is an interrelationship between records. Various applications may require the same input records, or, for processing, require reference to the same master file records used in other applications. Modification of existing records to change the sequence of file referencing and/or to accommodate additional references is more easily accomplished with direct access storage systems. For example, if the company manufactured a new product and several procedures had to be altered, all necessary activities could be changed at the same time. Direct access units, containing the records of production control, inventory maintenance, and budgeting, could be changed with a minimum of effort to accommodate the new product.

Another example is a payroll activity which requires a change for ratc, number of exemptions, and so forth. The payroll change could be entered into the system once and the necessary records of personnel and payroll updated at the same time.

This provides solutions to data-processing problems which require multiple interdependent activities and multiple references to interrelated records.

Low-Activity Data Processing

Many applications involve a limited number of input transactions with a large master file of records. Although a small portion of the master file is referenced by the input data for a particular run, the entire master file, which is maintained in sequence, must be searched. For example, in an inventory application of 20,000 items where only 2,000 items may be active each day, the 2,000 items must be collected and sorted in a predetermined sequence and processed against the file.

Direct access devices permit the retrieval of a single record without the extensive searching of an entire file.

Online Processing

Online processing permits the operation of input and output devices under the control of the central processing unit at the same time the processing function is being performed. The online devices are physically connected to the CPU, a printer for example. A data communication unit such as a teletypewriter is considered online even though it is not "physically" connected to the central processing unit, because a communication device provides the linkage between the two. In the previously mentioned example of inventory control, an inquiry about the status of a particular item of stock can be made from any location. With a direct access storage system, the inventory items are kept current all the time and the information is available to all users. Without these online activities of teleprocessing, the ability to change records or to inquire regarding information relative to these records would be difficult.

Direct Access Storage Devices

The term *direct access* implies access at random by multiple users of data (files, programs, subroutines, programming aids) involving mass storage devices. These storage devices differ in physical appearance, capability, and speed but functionally they are similar in terms of data recording, checking, and programming. The direct access devices used for mass memory storage are drums, disks, and data cells.

Add-on Memories

Whenever a user has exhausted present computing resources and a system upgrade is required, add-on memory is one alternative that is considered. Adding memory will nearly always make the CPU more efficient, and therefore, more work can be completed per shift. The whole system is much more cost effective.

Adding memory made by an independent source has several advantages over memory acquired from the manufacturer of the CPU. First, it is common for independent memory manufacturers to allow the user to attach a larger amount of memory than those attainable from the manufacturer of the CPU. This added memory increases the power of the CPU, which increases the life expectancy of the total computing system. Second, the independent memory manufacturer normally has more and better features on the add-on memory. These features make the memory and the complete system more flexible. Third, one of the most important advantages when purchasing memory from an independent manufacturer is price. It is common knowledge that memory from an independent manufacturer is less expensive than memory obtained from the manufacturer of the CPU (fig. 5.21).

The advent of the independently manufactured memory has helped to lower the price of memory supplied with the CPU, but its price is even lower. The new lower price allows the user to have more memory and still stay within the budget. More memory on a CPU makes the whole system more efficient.

Figure 5.21 An example of add-on memory. (Photo by Ken Firestone)

Summary

The effectiveness of a data-processing system is measured by its ability to process data as soon as it becomes available. In order to accomplish this all-important objective, the data-processing system must have the capacity to store large amounts of data. Direct access storage devices have made real-time processing a reality. The ability to process data as soon as it becomes available implies that the input does not have to be sorted or manipulated in any manner before it is introduced into the system. Direct access mass storage devices have made inline processing feasible for many applications because it enables the user to maintain current records of diversified applications and to process nonsequential and intermixed records of multiple application areas. This chapter describes the various components of a central processing unit, the physical characteristics of storage devices available to the users of the equipment, and direct access processing concepts together with the operation of the direct access devices.

The methods of processing data and the function of each of the units involved is essential to a clear understanding of the data-processing function. You should be aware that the computer processing unit is composed of a series of devices that act together in processing the data to produce the desired output, and that each of these individual units has a particular function to perform.

The potential processing capabilities of any computer system is determined by its storage capacity. Computer storage is an important factor in determining the number of operations and the extent of processing to be performed by the computer. Direct access storage devices are used more extensively in data-processing applications each day. Large storage capacities have reduced the price of storage and have made possible heretofore impractical applications. You should possess knowledge of all types of storage available and how each operates within a data-processing system.

1. The central processing unit (CPU) supervises and controls data-processing components. The arithmetic and logical section performs the necessary arithmetic and logical operations. The control section automatically integrates operations of the entire system.
2. There is a variety of operational units. Registers are capable of storing information temporarily and are classified according to function performed. Counters act as accumulators. Adders perform the actual accumulating process. Machine cycles are the amount of time to perform a specific operation. These time intervals are usually recorded in milliseconds, microseconds, and nanoseconds.
3. The instruction is a command to the system to perform an operation. The operation is the function the machine is to perform, such as add, move, shift, and so forth. The operand is the address of the data in storage, a program in storage, or an input/output device.
4. Processing is the sequential execution of instructions, except for branch-type instructions. In the instruction cycle, instructions are brought from the main storage and decoded. In the execution cycle, the data is actually processed.
5. Storage receives information from input/output devices and makes the information available for processing. All data to be processed must pass through core (main) storage. Auxiliary storage is additional storage that augments core storage. All data must be transferred to main storage for processing. In random access units, records may be accessed randomly. In sequential access units, each record must be examined before the desired record is reached.
6. There are many types of storage devices. In core storage, information is stored on tiny doughnuts of magnetic material. In magnetic devices (disks, drums, or reels of magnetic tape), data is recorded on tracks on the magnetic unit. Integrated circuits store information in the form of simple electronic charges in small functional components on chips of silicon. Charged-coupled devices store information as packets of charge within a semiconductor chip. These charge packets are manipulated by applying voltages to a routing pattern inscribed on the chip's surface.
7. Access time is the time required to locate and transfer data to and from storage.
8. In direct access processing, information can be requested directly from the computer and an immediate response received. Direct access processing also makes possible the changing of many interrelated records in a data-processing system at the same time. It also becomes possible to retrieve a single record without the extensive search through an entire file. In online processing, input/output operations can be performed at the same time the processing function is performed.
9. Add-on memories are used when a user has exhausted present computing resources and a system upgrade is required. They make the CPU more effective and the whole system more cost efficient.

Identification Questions

Match the following terms with the statements below.

A. Access Time	J. Cylinder	V. Operation
B. Adder	K. Data Cell	W. Random Access Unit
C. Address	L. Direct Access	X. Register
D. Arithmetic and Logical Section	M. Execution Cycle	Y. Sequential Access Units
E. Central Processing Unit	N. Instruction Cycle	Z. Track
F. Charged-Coupled Device	O. Integrated Circuit	
G. Control Section	P. Machine Cycle	
H. Cores	Q. Magnetic	
I. Counter	R. Magnetic Disk	
	S. Magnetic Drum	
	T. Online Processing	
	U. Operand	

1. Acts as a traffic manager directing and coordinating all operations called for by the instructions.
2. Acts as an accumulator.
3. The time it takes a computer to perform a specific machine operation.
4. Denotes the function that the machine is to perform.
5. Instructions brought from main storage and decoded.
6. Data recorded on tracks on the element.
7. Stores information as packets of charges within a semiconductor chip.
8. Thin metal disk coated on both sides with magnetic material.
9. Supervises and controls the data-processing components.
10. A device capable of storing information temporarily.
11. Accumulates values of two data items and sends results to accumulator.
12. A specific location in storage.
13. Data must be read from the beginning of file to find desired record.
14. Metallic recording medium strip.
15. Makes the necessary arithmetic computation and logical decisions called for by the computer commands.
16. The address of data, instructions, program, or input/output devices.
17. The actual performance of an instruction.
18. Tiny "doughnuts" of magnetic material.
19. Stores data in the form of simple electronic charges in small functional components on chips of silicon.
20. Circumference of the recording surface of a magnetic disk.
21. Records can be read without reading from beginning of a file.
22. A constant-speed rotating cylinder with an outer surface coated with magnetic material.
23. Amount of information accessible with one position of access mechanism.
24. Ability of data-processing system to process data as soon as it is available.
25. The operation of input/output devices under control of the central processing unit at the same time the processing function is being performed.
26. The time required to locate and transfer data from storage.

Questions for Review

1. What is the chief function of the central processing unit?
2. What two sections compose the central processing unit and what is the main function of each section?
3. How is a register used in data processing?
4. What is a machine cycle?
5. What are the two parts of each instruction?
6. What steps are involved in an instruction process?
7. What is storage?
8. What is main storage? Auxiliary storage?
9. Briefly describe the major storage technologies available today.
10. What is meant by access time?
11. Describe the different types of storage available and ennumerate the important aspects of each type.
12. What is inline processing?
13. What is the basic purpose of direct access storage devices in inline processing?
14. Describe some of the principal uses for direct access processing.
15. What are direct access storage devices?
16. What are the important advantages of adding memory from an independent source?

Key Terms

Access Time
Adder
Address
Arithmetic and Logical Section
Central Processing Unit
Charged Coupled Device
Control Section
Cores
Counter
Cylinder
Data Cell
Direct Access
Execution Cycle
Instruction Cycle
Integrated Circuit
Machine Cycle
Magnetic
Magnetic Disk
Magnetic Drum
Online Processing
Operand
Operation
Random Access Unit
Register
Sequential Access Units
Track

computer data representation and arithmetic 6

Chapter Outline

Chapter Objectives

The learning objectives of this chapter are

1. to explain the meaning and operation of the various number systems used in data processing.
2. to demonstrate how to convert from one number system to another.
3. to explain the coding systems used by computers.
4. to explain the arithmetic functions of the number system so you will be able to read computer storage dumps and debug computer programs.

Figure 6.1 This example shows the number 1,264 broken into the decimal counting system.

1,	2	6	4
Thousands	**Hundreds**	**Tens**	**Units**

This is just one other way of representing one thousand two hundred and sixty four units . . . each carrying a value of one (1).

Numeric symbols or numbers were invented to facilitate counting. Over the years, many symbols were used to represent and communicate information. Early number systems frequently employed cumbersome symbols and inconvenient rules that hindered the advance of systematic mathematical solutions. These early computers were designed to manipulate the data in decimal and alphabetic formats (fig. 6.1). The use of these early symbolic codes in a modern computer would make the solution of the complex mathematical problems of today extremely complicated—if even possible. As a result, simpler and faster methods of representing data had to be found.

The number system with which we are most familiar is the decimal system, which is the base 10 system. Each position in a number is worth ten times as much as the position on its right. For example, in the number 222, the leftmost 2 stands for 2 "hundreds," the second 2 stands for 2 "tens," and the rightmost 2 stands for 2 "ones."

There is nothing sacred about the decimal system, particularly when you are faced with the problem of designing the most efficient computing machines. In the decimal system, ten different digits (0 through 9) are needed; whereas, in the binary system, base 2, only two different symbols (0 and 1) are needed.

Computer Number Systems

The Arabs invented the numerical symbols and system of positional notation on which our present decimal and other number systems are based. Each numeric symbol has a fixed value one higher than that of the symbol immediately preceding it in the progression from the smallest to the largest number—0,1,2,3,4,5,6,7,8,9. When several positions are used, the value is dependent upon the relative position of the digits as well as the digit values. In any system of numbers, the digit position on the extreme right has the smallest value and is known as the low-order position (least significant digit). The increase in value of each digit position depends upon the *base* or *radix* of the number system. Each numbering system is identifiable by its base or radix, which indicates the number of digits used in the system. The decimal system with a base of 10 uses the digits 0 through 9. *The highest number to be represented by a single digit is one less than the base.*

Characteristic of all numbering systems is the positional numbering system. In the decimal numbering system, each digital position is assigned a value equal to a power of 10. These positions of the decimal system are commonly called units, tens, hundreds, thousands, etc. The following contains some values of powers of 10.

$10^0 = 1$	$10^4 = 10{,}000$
$10^1 = 10$	$10^5 = 100{,}000$
$10^2 = 100$	$10^6 = 1{,}000{,}000$
$10^3 = 1{,}000$	$10^7 = 10{,}000{,}000$

The values positioned to the left of the least significant digit increases by powers of 10. For example, the decimal number 8,952 actually implies

8 thousands + 9 hundreds + 5 tens + 2 units or = 8,952
8,000 + 900 + 50 + 2

These positional values can be expressed more simply using the powers of 10 for each position. Positional notation is not possible without the zero. Its presence within a number means that the power of the base is not used by that digit position.

Thousands 10^3 or 1,000	Hundreds 10^2 or 100	Tens 10^1 or 10	Units 10^0 or 1
8	9	5	2
4	0	0	8

The decimal number in each digital position is multiplied by its respective digital position value. The products added together form the total.

The first number

$$
\begin{aligned}
8 \times 1{,}000 &= 8{,}000 \\
9 \times 100 &= 900 \\
5 \times 10 &= 50 \\
2 \times 1 &= \underline{2} \\
& 8{,}952
\end{aligned}
$$

The second number

$$
\begin{aligned}
4 \times 1{,}000 &= 4{,}000 \\
8 \times 1 &= \underline{8} \\
& 4{,}008
\end{aligned}
$$

In the decimal number 8,952, the rightmost digit (2) has the smallest value and is considered the least significant digit, while the leftmost digit (8) has the highest value and is considered the most significant digit.

Remember, in any positional numbering system, any base (or radix) to the zero power equals (1).

$$2^0 = 1,\ 8^0 = 1,\ 10^0 = 1,\ 16^0 = 1$$

Binary Number System

Today, most computers employ the binary system, which uses a combination of ones and zeros in various configurations, by which a computer can represent all numerals, letters, and special characters. (Binary digits are called *bits*, a contraction of the words *BI*nary digi*T*.)

Working with long strings of 1s and 0s would be cumbersome for humans, but it is a snap for computers. Composed mostly of parts that are essentially on-off switches, the machines are perfectly suited for binary computation. When a switch is open, it corresponds to the binary digit 0; when it is closed, it stands for the digit 1. Vacuum tubes and transistors are used as switching devices and can be turned at a rapid pace.

How does the computer translate the binary numbers represented by its open and closed switches? The language the computer uses was developed by two gifted Englishmen. One of them was the nineteenth-century mathematician, George Boole, who devised a system of algebra, or mathematical logic, that can reliably determine if a statement is true or false. The other was Alan Turing, who stated in the 1930s that, with Boolean algebra, only three logical functions, greater than, less than, and equal to, are needed to process these "true" and "false" statements—or, in computer terms, 1s and 0s.

The binary form indicates the presence of only two conditions, the presence of a bit (on) or the absence of a bit (off). This principle can be compared to an electric light bulb that functions in the binary mode; either it is in the on or the off position. The position of a particular bit establishes its value (fig. 6.2). The bit values start at the right with one value and then proceed upward by 2, 4, 8, 16, etc. The decimal values 0 through 15 can be expressed with these four bits, 8, 4, 2, and 1 (fig. 6.3). It is the binary method of data representation and computation that permits the computer to process data at fantastic speeds since it is necessary for the machine to test for only one of two possible conditions.

The data is encoded in binary form by the presence or absence of an electrical impulse or by the direction of magnetization. Tiny magnetic cores are used to store individual binary bits and the direction of polarity indicates a 1 (one) or 0 (zero) bit.

There are various binary coding systems used by different computers. In the computer, the code relates to a fixed number of binary indicators. By the proper arrangement of these indicators, it is possible to represent numeric, alphabetic, and special characters.

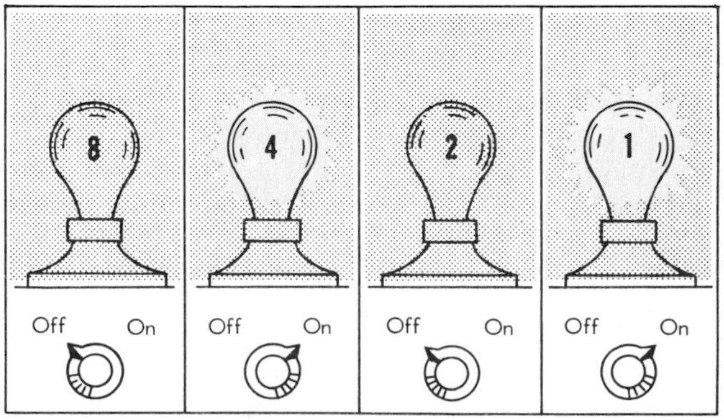

Figure 6.2 An example of representing data with binary components.

Decimal Number	Binary Number
0	0 0 0 0 0
1	0 0 0 0 1
2	0 0 0 1 0
3	0 0 0 1 1
4	0 0 1 0 0
5	0 0 1 0 1
6	0 0 1 1 0
7	0 0 1 1 1
8	0 1 0 0 0
9	0 1 0 0 1
10	0 1 0 1 0
11	0 1 0 1 1
12	0 1 1 0 0
13	0 1 1 0 1
14	0 1 1 1 0
15	0 1 1 1 1
16	1 0 0 0 0

Bit Values → 16 8 4 2 1

Figure 6.3 Binary and decimal numbers.

In contrast to the decimal system, the place values of binary digits to the left of the least significant digit increase by powers of 2 compared to the decimal increments of 10. For example, the decimal number 435 is merely the sum of 4 × 100 plus 3 × 10 plus 5 × 1 or 435. In the binary system, we multiply by 2 as we go left. Thus the binary number 111 is really 1 × 4 plus 1 × 2 plus 1 × 1 or 7.

The binary system lends itself to computer circuitry, as only one of the two conditions need be tested to determine the value of the bit position. In the binary system, each digital position is assigned an ascending power of 2, beginning with the right digital position and progressing to the left (fig. 6.4). The following contains some of the decimal values of the powers of two (fig. 6.5).

$2^0 = 1$	$2^4 = 16$	$2^8 = 256$
$2^1 = 2$	$2^5 = 32$	$2^9 = 512$
$2^2 = 4$	$2^6 = 64$	$2^{10} = 1024$
$2^3 = 8$	$2^7 = 128$	$2^{11} = 2048$

Figure 6.4 Binary and decimal counting.

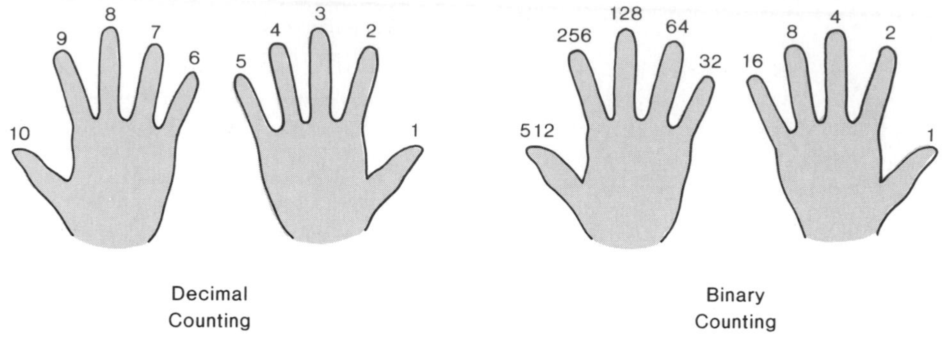

Figure 6.5 Place values of binary numbers.

8192	4096	2048	1024	512	256	128	64	32	16	8	4	2	1

To represent a quantity, each bit (either 0 or 1) is multiplied by its respective bit (digital) position. The products are then added together giving the decimal equivalent of the binary number. Since the multiplier is either 1 or 0, it is only necessary to add the value of the binary digital positions where the 1s appear. For example, the binary number 101101 signifies

Decimal Value	32	16	8	4	2	1
Power	2^5	2^4	2^3	2^2	2^1	2^0
Binary Number	1	0	1	1	0	1

$$32 + 0 + 8 + 4 + 0 + 1 = 45$$ Decimal Equivalent Number

To avoid confusion when several different numbering systems are used, it is customary to enclose each number in parentheses and to write the base as a subscript. For instance, the numbers in the previous example would be expressed as

$$(101101)_2 = (45)_{10}$$

Binary to Decimal Conversion

Two methods may be used to convert binary numbers to their decimal equivalent—the expansion method and the double-dabble method.

Expansion Method

Binary numbers may be easily converted to decimal numbers by direct expansion in powers of 2. The literal method of expansion of the numbers of its base readily yields the *decimal* equivalent of the number provided all arithmetic is carried out in the decimal system. Each position has its own assigned value. Simply write down the power of 2 of the binary number in column format beginning with the least significant digit. The values are then added together to obtain the decimal equivalent. For example, convert 111011 to a decimal number.

	32	16	8	4	2	1
	1	1	1	0	1	1
Add values	32	16	8		2	1 = 59

Double-Dabble Method

The double-dabble method (double and add) is a shortcut method of binary to decimal conversion. The procedure is as follows:

1. Double the highest-order (leftmost) binary digit and add it to the digit at its right.
2. Double the sum and add 1 or 0 depending upon whether the next digit to the right is 1 or 0.
3. Repeat the process until the sum contains the lowest-order digit at the right.

Using the previous example, convert 111011 to a decimal number using a double-dabble system.

```
           Binary Digits        1    1    1    0    1    1
-----------------------------------------------------------------
Decimal Numbers
  2 + 1 = 3 × 2 + 1 = 7 × 2 + 0 = 14 × 2 + 1 = 29 × 2 + 1 = 59
  d   a       d   a     d   a        d   a        d   a
  o   d       o   d     o   d        o   d        o   d
  u   d       u   d     u   d        u   d        u   d
  b           b         b            b            b
  l           l         l            l            l
  e           e         e            e            e
```

This double-dabble technique has a decided advantage over the expansion method in large binary numbers. The technique can be applied quickly with simple practice by properly remembering to double each time if the next digit is 0 and to double and add 1 if the next digit is 1. In most cases, the partial sums can be retained mentally.

Decimal to Binary Conversion

Two methods of converting decimal numbers to binary are the remainder and the binary expansion method.

The Remainder Method

The most common method of decimal to binary conversion is the *remainder* method. The decimal is divided by two and that quotient and all succeeding quotients are in turn divided by two. The division is repeated until a quotient of 0 is obtained. The equivalent binary number is composed of the remainders, the first remainder being the rightmost or least significant digit, while the final remainder is the leftmost, most significant digit. For example, convert decimal number 27 to a binary number. Divide the decimal number by the base.

```
                    13 quotient
Binary base    2)27
                 26
                  1 remainder
```

The conversion is not complete. The binary base is now divided into the quotient of the previous division. The remainder from the previous division is retained.

$$
\begin{array}{rl}
 & \;6 \\
\text{Binary base} \quad 2 & \overline{)\,13} \text{ quotient from previous division} \\
 & \,\underline{12} \\
 & \;\;1 \text{ remainder}
\end{array}
$$

The process is repeated until the quotient of a division is zero. The remaining divisions for the problem are shown below.

$$
\begin{array}{rl}
 & 3 \\
2 & \overline{)\,6} \\
 & \underline{6} \\
 & 0 \text{ remainder}
\end{array}
$$

$$
\begin{array}{rl}
 & 1 \\
2 & \overline{)\,3} \\
 & \underline{2} \\
 & 1 \text{ remainder}
\end{array}
$$

$$
\begin{array}{rl}
 & 0 \text{ (quotient } = 0\text{; division portion of conversion now complete)} \\
2 & \overline{)\,1} \\
 & \underline{0} \\
 & 1 \text{ remainder}
\end{array}
$$

All the divisions are now complete and the remainders are either 0 or 1. These remainders become the bits of the binary number. In order to determine the positional notation of each bit, the order of the divisions must be carefully noted. The first division yields the remainder that becomes the least significant or rightmost bit, while the last division performed yields the remainder that is the most significant or leftmost bit of the binary number.

$$
\begin{array}{rl}
 & 13 \\
2 & \overline{)\,27} \\
 & \underline{26} \\
 & \;\;1 \text{ rem.}
\end{array}
\quad
\begin{array}{rl}
 & \;6 \\
2 & \overline{)\,13} \\
 & \underline{12} \\
 & \;\;1 \text{ rem.}
\end{array}
\quad
\begin{array}{rl}
 & 3 \\
2 & \overline{)\,6} \\
 & \underline{6} \\
 & 0 \text{ rem.}
\end{array}
\quad
\begin{array}{rl}
 & 1 \\
2 & \overline{)\,3} \\
 & \underline{2} \\
 & 1 \text{ rem.}
\end{array}
\quad
\begin{array}{rl}
 & 0 \\
2 & \overline{)\,1} \\
 & \underline{0} \\
 & 1 \text{ rem.}
\end{array}
$$

1 1 0 1 1

Multiply each bit position by the decimal value of its bit position and add the products together to verify the accuracy of the conversion.

Decimal Value	16	8	4	2	1
Binary Number	1	1	0	1	1

$16 + 8 + 2 + 1 = 27$

Convert the decimal number 51 to a binary number.

25	12	6	3	1	0
2)51	2)25	2)12	2)6	2)3	2)1
50	24	12	6	2	0
1 rem.	1 rem.	0 rem.	0 rem.	1 rem.	1 rem.

1 1 0 0 1 1

Check the results

Decimal Value	32	16	8	4	2	1
Binary Number	1	1	0	0	1	1

32 + 16 + 2 + 1 = 51

This division method can convert any decimal number to a binary number. It can also be used to convert decimal numbers to other numbering systems by substituting the base of those numbering systems as the divisor.

The Binary Expansion Method

Although the remainder method is the conventional method of decimal to binary converting, another method employing the *binary expansion* table may be used, especially with the use of a hand calculator, and may be shorter in many instances. The steps involved are

1. Using a binary expansion table, find the highest decimal expansion number that will fit into the decimal number being converted.
2. Note the position in the table by placing a 1 in that position.
3. Subtract the decimal expansion number from the decimal number being converted and proceed to the next decimal expansion number at the right.
4. If the difference from step 3 can fit into the next decimal expansion number, repeat steps 2 and 3, otherwise place a 0 in that position and proceed to the next decimal expansion number at the right.
5. Continue process until the last decimal position number at right is reached.

For example, using the same number 51 from the preceding example,

32	16	8	4	2	1	Binary Expansion Table
1	1	0	0	1	1	Binary Equivalent Number

51	
− 32	The highest number 32 is subtracted from 51.
19	Remainder
− 16	The number 16 is subtracted from 19.
3	Remainder
− 2	The number 2 is subtracted from 3.
1	Remainder
− 1	The number 1 is subtracted from 1.
0	Remainder

Binary Addition

Binary arithmetic follows the same general rules as decimal arithmetic with one exception—a base 2 table is used instead of base 10 tables. Addition is essentially a shortcut to counting. Whenever the sum of two digits exceeds the available number symbols of the system (limit of any digit position), a one is carried to the next higher-order digit position. Thus, in the decimal system, $4 + 3 = 7$, while $9 + 1 = 0$ with a carry of 1 (that is, 10).

In binary addition only two symbols, 0 and 1, are used. Hence adding 1 to 1 in binary arithmetic exceeds the limit of counting and the result is 0 with a one carried to the next higher-order digit position. The rules for binary addition are

Binary		Addition
0 + 0	=	0
0 + 1	=	1
1 + 0	=	1
1 + 1	=	0 with a carry of 1

In the following examples, we will perform the addition calculations just as they would be performed in decimal arithmetic, starting with the rightmost bit position and proceeding to the leftmost bit position generating any necessary carries.

Binary	Decimal
1 0 1 0	10
+ 0 1 0 1	+ 5
1 1 1 1	15

Bit Position	Computation	Result	Carries
1	0 + 1	1	0
2	1 + 0	1	0
3	0 + 1	1	0
4	1 + 0	1	0

When adding several binary numbers, more than one carry may be developed to a single column. Decimal-binary tables are very helpful when adding a list of binary numbers. Below is a partial decimal-binary table.

Decimal	Binary	Decimal	Binary
0	0	5	1 0 1
1	1	6	1 1 0
2	1 0	7	1 1 1
3	1 1	8	1 0 0 0
4	1 0 0	9	1 0 0 1

	Binary						Decimal
Carries 1			1	1			2
			1	0	1	1	11
			1	1	0	1	13
			1	0	0	1	9
			0	0	0	1	1
+			1	0	0	1	9
	1	0	1	0	1	1	43

Bit Position	Computation	Result	Carries
1	1 + 1 + 1 + 1 + 1	1	1 carry to 3 bit position
2	1 + 0 + 0 + 0 + 0	1	0
3	Carry (1) + 0 + 1 + 0 + 0 + 0	0	1
4	Carry (1) + 1 + 1 + 1 + 0 + 1	1	1 carry to 6 bit position
5		0	
6	Carry (1)	1	

In the problem above, the first bit position addition equals 5. By referencing the decimal-binary table, we find the binary number for 5 is 101. We only carry the 1 to the third bit position as zeros are not carried. The same procedure is followed when adding the fourth bit position.

Using only addition, the other three functions, subtraction, multiplication, and division, can be performed by the computer. Subtraction is performed with the two's complement of the positive number—1s changed to 0s and 0s changed to 1s—through the addition of the complements. Multiplication is performed by repeated additions and division by repeated subtractions.

To verify the accuracy of binary addition, binary numbers should be converted to decimal and the results checked.

Binary Subtraction

In checking programs, it is necessary to be familiar with the conventional direct method of subtraction, "borrowing" when necessary. One of the basic rules taught in elementary school is that subtraction is the reverse of addition. We also learned that when a digit being subtracted is larger than the digit from which it is being subtracted, you must borrow a quantity from one of the next higher positions. The rules for direct binary subtraction are

$0 - 0 = 0$
$1 - 0 = 1$
$1 - 1 = 0$
$0 - 1 = 1$ with a borrow of "1" from a next high order position

By incorporating the borrow concept, the last rule is interpreted as $10 - 1 = 1$ or the decimal equivalent of $2 - 1 = 1$.

In the following examples, we will perform the subtraction calculations just as they would be performed in decimal arithmetic starting with the rightmost bit position and proceeding to the leftmost bit position employing any necessary borrowing procedures.

Decimal Problem

					Borrows	0	9	9	10
1,	0	0	0			~~1~~	Ø	Ø	Ø
−			1			−			1
	9	9	9		or		9	9	9

In this decimal problem, it is necessary to borrow 1 in the thousands position. To mentally short-cut this process, we can write the quantity (after borrowing) as zero 1000s, nine 100s, nine 10s, and ten 1s. Then when we perform the subtraction, we obtain the answer 999.

Binary Problem

	Binary				Decimal
Borrows		0	1	10	
	0	~~1~~	Ø	Ø	4
	−0	0	0	1	−1
	0	0	1	1	3

Subtraction in binary arithmetic follows the same rules of "take-away and borrow" used in decimal arithmetic. In the binary subtraction example, we could not subtract 1 from 0 in the first bit position, so we move to the left searching for something to borrow from. The first quantity we could borrow is the 1 in the third bit position. Since we are borrowing the quantity 4, we distribute the quantity over the remaining low-order positions. To do this, we change the third bit position from 1 to 0 to reflect the borrow, change the second bit position from 0 to 1, and change the first bit position from 0 to 10 (2). If you add the distribution across, you will find that the binary number still represents the quantity 4. Now, however, we have a condition where we can perform the subtraction.

We will use the same technique of "borrowing" in the following example.

	Binary				Decimal
Borrows	0	1	1	10	
	~~1~~	Ø	Ø	Ø	8
	−0	0	0	1	−1
	0	1	1	1	7

In this problem, it is necessary to borrow from the fourth bit position and distribute the remaining quantity among the remaining low-order positions.

Octal Number System

Binary to Octal Conversion

Binary numbers are rather bulky and become unwieldy and extremely difficult to communicate other than in a computer. A binary number requires several times as many positions for display as does the equivalent decimal number. A long string of ones and zeros can be extremely difficult to transmit from one individual to another. Since the internal circuitry of the computer understands only binary 1s (ones) and 0s (zeros), some shorthand method becomes necessary. The octal number system is a shorthand method of displaying binary numbers. Because of their simple relationship to binary, octal numbers can be converted from one system to another by inspection. The base or radix of the octal system is eight, which means that the largest possible single digit is 7 (0, 1, 2, 3, 4, 5, 6, 7). There are no 8s or 9s in an octal number system. The conversion from binary to octal is rather simple, because *one octal position is equivalent to three binary positions* (fig. 6.6).

Any binary number can be converted to octal by grouping the bits in 3s, starting at the rightmost bit and then reconverting each group into its octal equivalent (fig. 6.7). For example, to convert the binary number 1 1 0 0 1 0 1 0 to octal

$$\frac{011}{3}\ \frac{001}{1}\ \frac{010}{2} = 312 \text{ Octal Equivalent}$$

Necessary zeros are added to left if less than 3. Convert the following octal number 431 to binary.

$$\frac{4}{100}\ \frac{3}{011}\ \frac{1}{001} = 1\,0\,0\,0\,1\,1\,0\,0\,1 \text{ Binary Equivalent}$$

Binary	Octal	Decimal
000	0	0
001	1	1
010	2	2
011	3	3
100	4	4
101	5	5
110	6	6
111	7	7

At this point, a carry to the next-higher position of the number is necessary, since all eight symbols have been used.

Binary	Octal	Decimal
001 000	10	8
001 001	11	9
001 010	12	10
001 011	13	11
001 100	14	12
•	•	•
•	•	•

Figure 6.6 A binary-octal-decimal conversion chart.

Octal Number	Bit Equivalents		
0	0	0	0
1	0	0	1
2	0	1	0
3	0	1	1
4	1	0	0
5	1	0	1
6	1	1	0
7	1	1	1
Bit Values →	4	2	1

Figure 6.7 Octal bit equivalents.

Octal to Decimal Conversion

By remembering what a number represents in octal (or binary), the number can be easily converted to decimal using the following table.

Octal Values

$8^0 = 1$	$8^4 = 4{,}096$
$8^1 = 8$	$8^5 = 32{,}768$
$8^2 = 64$	$8^6 = 262{,}144$
$8^3 = 512$	

To represent a quantity, each octal digit is multiplied by its digital position value (power of 8) and the products are added together. The total, then, is the decimal equivalent of the octal value. For example, the value of an octal number 765 is determined below.

Decimal Value	64	8	1
Power	8^2	8^1	8^0
Octal Number	7	6	5

Digit		Digit Position Value	Value
5	×	1	5
6	×	8	48
7	×	64	448
			501 Decimal Value of octal number 765

Convert the binary number 1 0 0 1 1 1 to its octal equivalent and prove your answers in decimal.

Binary Number	1 0 0	1 1 1
Octal Number	4	7

$$(1\ 0\ 0\ 1\ 1\ 1)_2 = (47)_8$$

Check the result.

Binary

32	16	8	4	2	1
1	0	0	1	1	1

1
2
4
32
———
39

$(1\ 0\ 0\ 1\ 1\ 1)_2 = (39)_{10}$

Octal

8	1
4	7

7
32 (4 × 8)
———
39

$(47)_8 = (39)_{10}$

Another method that converts an octal number to its decimal equivalent (similar to the double-dabble method of converting binary numbers to decimal) is to continuously multiply by eight and add the next octal digit. For example, convert the octal number 312 to its decimal equivalent.

```
3 1 2    Octal Equivalent Number

     3
    ×8
   ---
    24
  +  1
   ---
    25
  ×  8
   ---
   200
  +  2
   ---
   202   Decimal Equivalent
```

Decimal to Octal Conversion

Conversion from a decimal to its octal equivalent can be accomplished by using the division discussed earlier in the binary system. The divisor must be the base of the numbering system; in this case it is 8. To convert a decimal number to octal, divide the number continuously by 8 until the quotient is zero and develop the actual number from the remainders of each division. For example, convert the decimal number 202 to its octal equivalent.

```
    25               3              0
8)202            8)25           8)3
  200              24             0
    2 remainder     1 remainder    3 remainder

               3  1  2
      Decimal 202 equals Octal 312
```

All actual arithmetic operations in octal are performed in a method similar to binary except that the base is 8 instead of 2. The last remainder is the most important with the first remainder being the least important.

Octal Addition

	Octal	Decimal
Carries	1 1	11
	2 3 6	158
	7 7	+ 63
	3 3 5	221

The addition is performed as follows:

Digit Position	Computation	Result	Carry
1	6 + 7 = 13	5	1
	The base 8 is subtracted from sum (13) leaving a remainder of 5 and a carry of 1.		
2	Carry (1) + 3 + 7 = 11	3	1
	The base 8 is subtracted from the sum (11) leaving a remainder of 3 and a carry of 1.		
3	Carry (1) + 2	3	0

To check sum convert octal number 335 to its decimal equivalent.

64	8	1			
3	3	5	5 × 1	5	
			3 × 8	24	
			3 × 64	192	
				221	Decimal Equivalent

Octal Subtraction

	Octal			Decimal
Borrows		4	12	
	7	5	4	492
	−3	4	5	−229
	4	0	7	263

A borrow of the base 8 was made from the second digit position (5 − 1 = 4) and added to the value appearing in the first position (4 + 8 = 12). Now the subtraction can be performed. Rules are the same as for decimal and binary arithmetic with one exception; the base is now 8.

To check the result, convert the octal number 407 to its decimal equivalent.

64	8	1			
4	0	7	7 × 1	7	
			0 × 8	0	
			4 × 64	256	
				263	Decimal Equivalent

Hexadecimal Number System

The hexadecimal number system, like the octal number system, is simply a shorthand method of expressing the binary bit patterns within a computer. *Each hexadecimal digit stands for four binary bits.* Hexadecimal means 16 and the system requires 16 symbols to represent the possible values. It does not count to 16 but uses the 10 decimal digits (0 through 9) plus the letters, A, B, C, D, E, F, to represent these values. The entire list of hexadecimal symbols consists of 0,1,2,3,4,5,6,7,8,9,A,B,C,D,E,F (fig. 6.8).

The hexadecimal number system uses the decimal value of 16 as its base. The decimal system can count as high as 9 before a carry occurs.

Decimal	Hexadecimal	Binary	Decimal	Hexadecimal	Binary
0	0	0000	16	10	10000
1	1	0001	17	11	10001
2	2	0010	18	12	10010
3	3	0011	19	13	10011
4	4	0100	20	14	10100
5	5	0101	21	15	10101
6	6	0110	22	16	10110
7	7	0111	23	17	10111
8	8	1000	24	18	11000
9	9	1001	25	19	11001
10	A	1010	26	1A	11010
11	B	1011	27	1B	11011
12	C	1100	28	1C	11100
13	D	1101	29	1D	11101
14	E	1110	30	1E	11110
15	F	1111	31	1F	11111

Figure 6.8 Decimal, hexadecimal, and binary notation.

1. 8 + 1 = 9
2. 9 + 1 = 0 with a carry

The binary system can only count as high as 1 before a carry occurs.

1. 0 + 1 = 1
2. 1 + 1 = 0 with a carry

The octal system can only count as high as 7 before a carry occurs.

1. 6 + 1 = 7
2. 7 + 1 = 0 with a carry

In the hexadecimal numbering system, you can count as high as 15 or F before a carry occurs.

1. E + 1 = F
2. F + 1 = 0 with a carry

To express the value *10 to 15,* the symbols *a to f* are used. This will probably be the hardest thing to get used to, seeing alphabetic characters in a number.

Figure 6.9 Hexadecimal bit equivalents.

Decimal Value	Hexadecimal Notation	Group of Four Bits
0	0	0 0 0 0
1	1	0 0 0 1
2	2	0 0 1 0
3	3	0 0 1 1
4	4	0 1 0 0
5	5	0 1 0 1
6	6	0 1 1 0
7	7	0 1 1 1
8	8	1 0 0 0
9	9	1 0 0 1
10	A	1 0 1 0
11	B	1 0 1 1
12	C	1 1 0 0
13	D	1 1 0 1
14	E	1 1 1 0
15	F	1 1 1 1

Bit Values ⟶ 8 4 2 1

Binary to Hexadecimal Conversion

To convert a binary number to a hexadecimal equivalent, it is only necessary to divide the number into groups of four binary digits starting from the right and replacing each group of four by the hexadecimal equivalent (fig. 6.9). For example, to convert the following binary number to its hexadecimal equivalent.

$$(1\;1\;1\;1\;1\;0\;0\;1\;1\;0\;1\;1\;0\;1\;0\;0\;1\;1)_2 = \frac{0011/}{(3}\;\frac{1110/}{E}\;\frac{0110/}{6}\;\frac{1101/}{D}\;\frac{0011}{3)_{16}}$$

3E6D3 = Hexadecimal Equivalent

Note: If lefthand group is incomplete (less than four bits), fill in excess positions at left with zeros.

Hexadecimal to Binary Conversion

Similarly, to convert hexadecimal numbers into binary, substitute the corresponding group of four binary digits for each hexadecimal number. For example, convert the following hexadecimal number to its binary equivalent.

$(6C4F2E7B8)_{16}$

6	C	4	F	2	E	7	B	8
0110	1100	0100	1111	0010	1110	0111	1011	1000

$(110110001001111001011100111101111000)_2$
= Equivalent Binary Number

Hexadecimal to Decimal Conversion

Although division can be used for conversion of hexadecimal integers into decimal, the following three methods will be found to give results more rapidly. The *direct method* consists of expanding hexadecimal numbers into powers of 16, using the decimal for the calculations.

Multiply the decimal equivalent of each hexadecimal digit by the place value of the digit expressed in decimal (that is, by the power of 16).

Hexadecimal Values			
16^0	1	16^3	4,096
16^1	16	16^4	65,536
16^2	256	16^5	1,048,576

For example, the value of hexadecimal number 6AE is determined below.

Decimal Value	256	16	1
Power	16^2	16^1	16^0
Hexadecimal Number	6	A	E

Digit		Digit Position Value	Value	
14 (E)	×	1	14	
10 (A)	×	16	160	
6	×	256	1,536	
			1,710	Decimal value of hexadecimal number 6AE

The direct method requires memorization of the powers of 16 and becomes unwieldy for large hexadecimal numbers. Another technique (similar to double-dabble method used in binary), which is a *combination of multiplication and addition*, is frequently easier than the direct expansion method.

1. Multiply the decimal equivalent of the high-order (leftmost) hexadecimal digit by 16.
2. Add to the product, the decimal equivalent of the next lower hexadecimal digit to the right and multiply sum by 16.
3. Continue the process until the last (rightmost) hexadecimal is added to the product.
4. The last sum is the decimal equivalent. *Do not multiply it by 16.*

For example, use the previous example $(6AE)_{16}$ to convert to decimal.

		6	← 6 A E
Multiply	×	16	
		96	
Add A	+	10	← A
		106	
Multiply	×	16	
		1696	
Add E	+	14	← E
		1710	Decimal Equivalent

$$(1710)_{10} = (6AE)_{16}$$

The conversion of large hexadecimal numbers by either the direct expansion or the multiplication and addition method is quite tedious and difficult. Reference conversion tables should be used whenever available for conversion from hexadecimal to decimal or from decimal to hexadecimal.

For example, to convert the hexadecimal number of the previous example to its decimal equivalent:

$(6AE)_{16}$	E in hexadecimal position 1 equals	14
	A in hexadecimal position 2 equals (10 × 16)	160
	6 in hexadecimal position 3 equals (6 × 256)	1536
	$(6AE)_{16} = (1710)_{10}$	1710

Decimal to Hexadecimal Conversion

Two methods may be used to convert a decimal number into its hexadecimal equivalent. The first, *division method,* is similar to the ones discussed earlier in the binary and octal systems. The divisor must be the base of the numbering system, which is 16 in this case.

1. Divide the decimal number repeatedly by 16 until a zero quotient is obtained.
2. Convert remainders of 10 to 15 into hexadecimal symbols A to F.
3. The first remainder is the least significant hexadecimal digit, with the last remainder the most significant.

For example, convert the decimal number 1710 to its hexadecimal equivalent.

16) 1710 = 106	16) 106 = 6	16) 6 = 0
1696	96	0
14 remainder (E)	10 remainder (A)	6

6 A E

Decimal 1710 = Hexadecimal 6AE

	HEX	DEC	HEX	DEC	HEX		HEX	DEC	HEX	DEC	HEX	DEC	HEX	DEC	HEX	DEC
	0	0	0	0	0	0	0	0	0	0	0	0	0	0	0	0
	1	268,435,456	1	16,777,216	1	1,048,576	1	65,536	1	4,096	1	256	1	16	1	1
	2	536,870,912	2	33,554,432	2	2,097,152	2	131,072	2	8,192	2	512	2	32	2	2
	3	805,306,368	3	50,331,648	3	3,145,728	3	196,608	3	12,288	3	768	3	48	3	3
	4	1,073,741,824	4	67,108,864	4	4,194,304	4	262,144	4	16,384	4	1,024	4	64	4	4
	5	1,342,177,280	5	83,886,080	5	5,242,880	5	327,680	5	20,480	5	1,280	5	80	5	5
	6	1,610,612,736	6	100,663,296	6	6,291,456	6	393,216	6	24,576	6	1,536	6	96	6	6
	7	1,879,048,192	7	117,440,512	7	7,340,032	7	458,752	7	28,672	7	1,792	7	112	7	7
	8	2,147,483,648	8	134,217,728	8	8,388,608	8	524,288	8	32,768	8	2,048	8	128	8	8
	9	2,415,919,104	9	150,994,944	9	9,437,184	9	589,824	9	36,864	9	2,304	9	144	9	9
	A	2,684,354,560	A	167,772,160	A	10,485,760	A	655,360	A	40,960	A	2,560	A	160	A	10
	B	2,952,790,016	B	184,549,376	B	11,534,336	B	720,896	B	45,056	B	2,816	B	176	B	11
	C	3,221,225,472	C	201,326,592	C	12,582,912	C	786,432	C	49,152	C	3,072	C	192	C	12
	D	3,489,660,928	D	218,103,808	D	13,631,488	D	851,968	D	53,248	D	3,328	D	208	D	13
	E	3,758,096,384	E	234,881,024	E	14,680,064	E	917,504	E	57,344	E	3,584	E	224	E	14
	F	4,026,531,840	F	251,658,240	F	15,728,640	F	983,040	F	61,440	F	3,840	F	240	F	15
Hexadecimal Positions	8		7		6		5		4		3		2		1	

Figure 6.10 Hexadecimal-decimal integer conversion table.

Another method for converting numbers into hexadecimal digits is using the *hexadecimal-decimal integer conversion tables* (fig. 6.10) whenever available.

1. Look up the next smaller number in the table. Note the hexadecimal equivalent position.
2. Subtract the decimal value of the hexadecimal digit in the table from the hexadecimal number.
3. Look up the remainder in the table and repeat the process until all hexadecimal digits are converted.

For example, using the previous example $(1710)_{10}$, convert to a hexadecimal number.

	1710
6 in hexadecimal position 3 equals	−1536
	174
A in hexadecimal 2 equals	− 160
	14
E in hexadecimal position 1 equals	− 14
$(1710)_{10} = (6AE)_{16}$	0

Hexadecimal Addition

Addition in hexadecimal follows the same rules as those in decimal, binary, and octal addition. Working with alphameric characters (numbers and letters) will appear strange at first since the results long familiar under the decimal system have a different value in hexadecimal arithmetic. For instance, $5 + 4 = 9$ in both decimal and hexadecimal arithmetic, while $8 + 6 = E$ (not 14) in hexadecimal. Whenever the sum of two hexadecimal digits exceeds F (15), the highest single digit value in the system, a carry of one is developed and is added to the next high-order hexadecimal position. Thus, 8 + 8 = 10 (0 with a 1 carry), 9 + 9 = 12 (2 with a carry of 1), and D + 8 = 15 (5 with a carry of 1), etc. Having a table of the values of decimal and hexadecimal numbers above 9 handy will greatly simplify hexadecimal calculations. Digits up to 9 are the same in both systems.

Decimal	Hexadecimal
10	A
11	B
12	C
13	D
14	E
15	F

	Hexadecimal	Decimal
Carries	1 1	
	6 A E	1710
	+1 F A	+506
	8 A 8	2216

Digit Position	Computation	Result	Carry
1	14(E) + 10(A) = 24	8	1
	The base of 16 is subtracted from the sum (24) leaving a remainder of 8 and a carry of 1.		
2	Carry (1) + 10(A) + 15(F) = 26	A	1
	The base of 16 is subtracted from the sum (26) leaving a remainder of A(10) and a carry of 1.		
3	Carry (1) + 6 + 1 = 8	8	0

Convert hexadecimal number 8A8 to its decimal equivalent.

256	16	1
8	A	8

8	× 1	8	
10(A)	× 16	160	
8	×256	2,048	Decimal
		2,216	Equivalent

The hexadecimal addition table in the appendix can greatly simplify hexadecimal addition. Whenever feasible, decimal conversion addition should be used to verify the results of a hexadecimal addition.

Hexadecimal Subtraction

Hexadecimal subtraction follows the same rules as decimal, binary, and octal subtraction, except that a carry or borrow of 1 in hexadecimal represents 16.

	Hexadecimal					Decimal
(Borrows)				19		
			7	~~9~~	18	
			~~8~~	~~A~~	~~8~~	2216
			−1	F	A	− 506
			6	A	E	1710
(Borrows)	0	15	13	D	13	
	~~1~~	~~6~~	~~3~~	~~E~~	~~3~~	91107
	−	D	4	4	C	−54348
		8	F	9	7	36759

In the first example, starting with the lowest-order digit at the right, A cannot be subtracted from 8 since it exceeds 8. Hence, hexadecimal 10 is borrowed from the next high-order digit at the left, reducing the digit to 9 (A − 1) and increasing the minuend digit to 18. Using the addition table in the appendix under the A column (subtrahend), the minuend digits 18 appear in the E row; therefore, 18 − A = E. Proceeding to the next high-order digit position, F cannot be subtracted from 9; hence, a 1 is borrowed from the 8 at the left, reducing it to 7 and increasing the minuend to 19. In the table in the appendix going down in the F column (subtrahend), the A is put down. Finally the difference between the 7 and 1 is 6. The 6 is put down to complete the result. A method for performing hexadecimal addition and subtraction using a hand calculator can be found in the appendix.

Computer Codes

The method used to represent (symbolize) data in a data-processing system is known as a code or system. In the computer, the code relates to a fixed number of symbols (binary numbers). For example, a code used to represent numeric and alphabetic characters may use eight positions of binary numbers. By the proper arrangement of these binary numbers (0 bit and 1 bit), all characters can be represented by a different combination of bits. Parity checking is used to check the computer code to assure that no bits are lost in the transmission of the data throughout the system.

Binary-Coded Decimal (BCD)

This number system simply uses four bits to represent any of the decimal digits 0–9 (fig. 6.11). The four numeric positions are assigned the decimal values 8, 4, 2, and 1 and represent in binary-coded form the digits 0 through 9. For example, the decimal number 47 is represented by 0100 0111 in the 8–4–2–1 type of binary-coded decimal notation.

Figure 6.11 The binary-coded decimal representation of decimal numbers.

Decimal Digits	2	6	5	4	9	8
Binary Value	0 0 1 0	0 1 1 0	0 1 0 1	0 1 0 0	1 0 0 1	1 0 0 0
Place Value	8 4 2 1	8 4 2 1	8 4 2 1	8 4 2 1	8 4 2 1	8 4 2 1

The decimal number 13 is represented in BCD as:

1	3
0001	0011

The decimal number 256 is represented in BCD as:

2	5	6
0010	0101	0110

The decimal number 9740 is represented in BCD as:

9	7	4	0
1001	0111	0100	0000

Figure 6.12 An example of a 7-bit alphameric character.

Check Bit	Zone Bits		Numeric Bits			
C	B	A	8	4	2	1

7 Bit Alphameric Code (Binary-Coded Decimal System)

In this particular number system, seven bits are used to represent all characters (fig. 6.12). In this method of coding, all characters are coded using one check bit (parity bit), two zone position bits, and four numeric bits.

The four numeric bit positions (8,4,2,1) represent the binary-coded decimal and form the digits 0–9. The zone bits (B and A) are not used in numeric coding and are coded with zeros.

Combinations of zone and numeric bits are used to represent alphabetic and special characters. Four possible bit combinations (10, 01, 11, and 00) provide the needed zone configuration (fig. 6.13).

The check bit is used as a check code. An even parity code indicates that the total number of bits used represent an even total. A check bit is added if the total number is odd. In an odd parity check, a check bit is added to an even number of bits.

8 Bit Extended Binary-Coded Decimal Interchange Code (EBCDIC)

This code uses eight binary positions for each character format. By using eight bit positions, 256 different characters can be coded (fig. 6.14). This code permits the coding of uppercase and lowercase alphabetic letters, which allows a wider range of special characters and many control characters that are meaningful to certain input/output devices. At present, many bit patterns have no assigned function and are reserved for future assignments.

Collating Sequence	Character: Report	Character: Program	Card Code	BCD Code (Core Storage)						
Low→	b̸		No Punches	C						
	.		12-3-8		B	A	8		2	1
	□	)	12-4-8	C	B	A	8	4		
	[		12-5-8		B	A	8	4		1
	<		12-6-8		B	A	8	4	2	
	⧧		12-7-8	C	B	A	8	4	2	1
	&	+	12	C	B	A				
	$		11-3-8	C	B		8		2	1
	*		11-4-8		B		8	4		
	]		11-5-8	C	B		8	4		1
	;		11-6-8	C	B		8	4	2	
	△		11-7-8		B		8	4	2	1
	—		11		B					
	/		0-1	C		A				1
	,		0-3-8	C		A	8		2	1
	%	(	0-4-8			A	8	4		
	⌒		0-5-8	C		A	8	4		1
	\		0-6-8	C		A	8	4	2	
	⫳		0-7-8			A	8	4	2	1
	ƀ		2-8			A				
	#	=	3-8				8		2	1
	@	'	4-8	C			8	4		
	:		5-8				8	4		1
	>		6-8				8	4	2	
	√		7-8	C			8	4	2	1
	?		12-0	C	B	A	8		2	
	A		12 1		B	A				1
	B		12-2		B	A			2	
	C		12-3	C	B	A			2	1
	D		12-4		B	A		4		
	E		12-5	C	B	A		4		1
	F		12-6	C	B	A		4	2	
	G		12-7		B	A		4	2	1
	H		12-8		B	A	8			
	I		12-9	C	B	A	8			1
	!		11-0		B		8		2	
	J		11-1	C	B					1
	K		11-2	C	B				2	
	L		11-3		B				2	1
	M		11-4	C	B			4		
	N		11-5		B			4		1
	O		11-6		B			4	2	
	P		11-7	C	B			4	2	1
	Q		11-8	C	B		8			
	R		11-9		B		8			1
	ǂ		0-2-8			A	8		2	
	S		0-2	C		A			2	
	T		0-3			A			2	1
	U		0-4	C		A		4		
	V		0-5			A		4		1
	W		0-6			A		4	2	
	X		0-7	C		A		4	2	1
	Y		0-8	C		A	8			
	Ƶ		0-9			A	8			1
	Ø		0	C			8		2	
	1		1							1
	2		2						2	
	3		3	C					2	1
	4		4					4		
	5		5	C				4		1
	6		6	C				4	2	
	7		7					4	2	1
	8		8				8			
High→	9		9	C			8			1

Note: Tape may use even parity.

Figure 6.13 The 7-bit alphameric code.

EBCDIC	Bit Configuration
NUL	0000 0000
SOH	0000 0001
STX	0000 0010
ETX	0000 0011
PF	0000 0100
HT	0000 0101
LC	0000 0110
DEL	0000 0111
	0000 1000
RLF	0000 1001
SMM	0000 1010
VT	0000 1011
FF	0000 1100
CR	0000 1101
SO	0000 1110
SI	0000 1111
DLE	0001 0000
DC1	0001 0001
DC2	0001 0010
TM	0001 0011
RES	0001 0100
NL	0001 0101
BS	0001 0110
IL	0001 0111
CAN	0001 1000
EM	0001 1001
CC	0001 1010
CU1	0001 1011
IFS	0001 1100
IGS	0001 1101
IRS	0001 1110
IUS	0001 1111
DS	0010 0000
SOS	0010 0001
FS	0010 0010
	0010 0011
BYP	0010 0100
LF	0010 0101
ETB	0010 0110
ESC	0010 0111
	0010 1000
	0010 1001
SM	0010 1010
CU2	0010 1011
	0010 1100
ENQ	0010 1101
ACK	0010 1110
BEL	0010 1111
	0011 0000
	0011 0001
SYN	0011 0010
	0011 0011
PN	0011 0100
RS	0011 0101
UC	0011 0110
EOT	0011 0111
	0011 1000
	0011 1001
	0011 1010
CU3	0011 1011
DC4	0011 1100
NAK	0011 1101
	0011 1110
SUB	0011 1111
SP	0100 0000
	0100 0001
	0100 0010
	0100 0011
	0100 0100

EBCDIC	Bit Configuration
	0100 0101
	0100 0110
	0100 0111
	0100 1000
	0100 1001
¢ [	0100 1010
.	0100 1011
<	0100 1100
(	0100 1101
+	0100 1110
|	0100 1111
&	0101 0000
	0101 0001
	0101 0010
	0101 0011
	0101 0100
	0101 0101
	0101 0110
	0101 0111
	0101 1000
	0101 1001
!]	0101 1010
$	0101 1011
*	0101 1100
)	0101 1101
;	0101 1110
¬	0101 1111
–	0110 0000
/	0110 0001
	0110 0010
	0110 0011
	0110 0100
	0110 0101
	0110 0110
	0110 0111
	0110 1000
	0110 1001
7/12	0110 1010
,	0110 1011
%	0110 1100
_	0110 1101
>	0110 1110
?	0110 1111
	0111 0000
	0111 0001
	0111 0010
	0111 0011
	0111 0100
	0111 0101
	0111 0110
	0111 0111
	0111 1000
6/0	0111 1001
:	0111 1010
#	0111 1011
@	0111 1100
'	0111 1101
=	0111 1110
"	0111 1111
	1000 0000
a	1000 0001
b	1000 0010
c	1000 0011
d	1000 0100
e	1000 0101
f	1000 0110
g	1000 0111
h	1000 1000
i	1000 1001

EBCDIC	Bit Configuration
	1000 1010
	1000 1011
	1000 1100
	1000 1101
	1000 1110
	1000 1111
	1001 0000
j	1001 0001
k	1001 0010
l	1001 0011
m	1001 0100
n	1001 0101
o	1001 0110
p	1001 0111
q	1001 1000
r	1001 1001
	1001 1010
	1001 1011
	1001 1100
	1001 1101
	1001 1110
	1001 1111
	1010 0000
—	1010 0001
s	1010 0010
t	1010 0011
u	1010 0100
v	1010 0101
w	1010 0110
x	1010 0111
y	1010 1000
z	1010 1001
	1010 1010
	1010 1011
	1010 1100
	1010 1101
	1010 1110
	1010 1111
	1011 0000
	1011 0001
	1011 0010
	1011 0011
	1011 0100
	1011 0101
	1011 0110
	1011 0111
	1011 1000
	1011 1001
	1011 1010
	1011 1011
	1011 1100
	1011 1101
	1011 1110
	1011 1111
PZ 7/11	1100 0000
A	1100 0001
B	1100 0010
C	1100 0011
D	1100 0100
E	1100 0101
F	1100 0110
G	1100 0111
H	1100 1000
I	1100 1001
	1100 1010
	1100 1011
⑁	1100 1100
	1100 1101
⑂	1100 1110

EBCDIC	Bit Configuration	ASCII-8
	1100 1111	
<	1101 0000	
J	1101 0001	
K	1101 0010	
L	1101 0011	
M	1101 0100	
N	1101 0101	
O	1101 0110	
P	1101 0111	
Q	1101 1000	
R	1101 1001	
	1101 1010	
	1101 1011	
	1101 1100	
	1101 1101	
	1101 1110	
	1101 1111	
‡	1110 0000	
	1110 0001	a
S	1110 0010	b
T	1110 0011	c
U	1110 0100	d
V	1110 0101	e
W	1110 0110	f
X	1110 0111	g
Y	1110 1000	h
Z	1110 1001	i
	1110 1010	j
	1110 1011	k
	1110 1100	l
	1110 1101	m
	1110 1110	n
	1110 1111	o
	1111 0000	p
1	1111 0001	q
2	1111 0010	r
3	1111 0011	s
4	1111 0100	t
5	1111 0101	u
6	1111 0110	v
7	1111 0111	w
8	1111 1000	x
9	1111 1001	y
	1111 1010	z
	1111 1011	
	1111 1100	
	1111 1101	
	1111 1110	ESC
	1111 1111	DEL

Figure 6.14 The 8-bit hexadecimal number code.

Decimal System	Hexadecimal System	Binary System 8 4 2 1 Bit Values
0	0	0 0 0 0
1	1	0 0 0 1
2	2	0 0 1 0
3	3	0 0 1 1
4	4	0 1 0 0
5	5	0 1 0 1
6	6	0 1 1 0
7	7	0 1 1 1
8	8	1 0 0 0
9	9	1 0 0 1
10	A	1 0 1 0
11	B	1 0 1 1
12	C	1 1 0 0
13	D	1 1 0 1
14	E	1 1 1 0
15	F	1 1 1 1

Figure 6.15 The relationship among decimal, hexadecimal, and binary systems.

EBCDIC uses each byte as though it were two hexadecimal number systems. For example,

Decimal	248	
Binary	1111	1000
Hexadecimal	F	8

The output representation in hexadecimal is just the division of the binary numbers into groups of four binary digits starting from right to left. The hexadecimal number system employs four zone bits plus four numeric bits to represent each character.

This is the principal data representation system used by many computer manufacturers. This hexadecimal number system is simply a shorthand method used to express the binary bit patterns within a computer, such as the IBM System/370 (fig. 6.15).

American National Standard Code for Information Exchange (ASCII)

This code uses a seven-bit configuration (eight bits including parity check) developed through the cooperation of the users of equipment communication and data-processing industries, in an attempt to simplify and standardize machine-to-machine and system-to-system communication. The ASCII set consists of control characters and graphic characters.

Data Processing

In the past, commercial computers were usually variable word length (character-oriented) machines that used binary-coded representation of decimal information. On the other hand, scientific computers were usually fixed word. The term fixed word assumed that each data item was of the same length and had an assumed decimal point at the right-hand end of the field; thus, the fixed-point number is treated as an integer. Today's computers use both BCD as well as binary and have both variable and fixed-length fields.

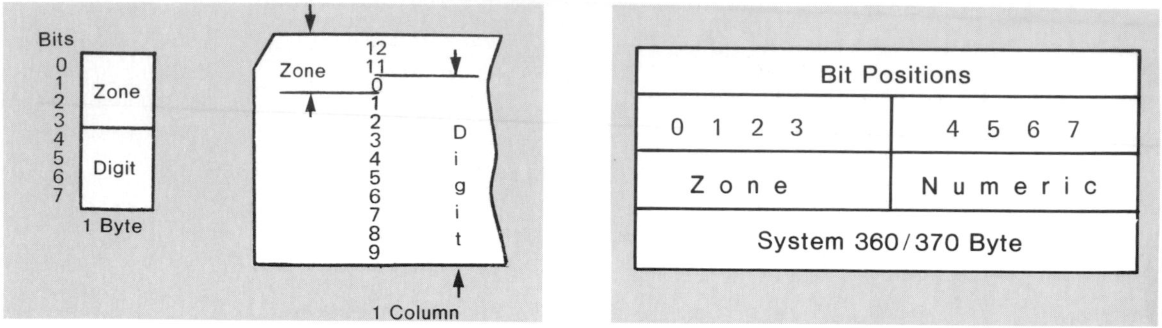

Figure 6.16 An example of a byte.

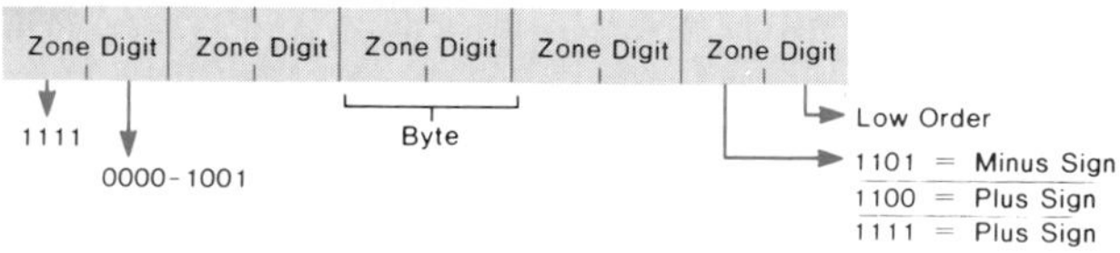

Figure 6.17 An example of a zoned format.

Instructions are provided by the computer manufacturer for the automatic conversion of data into the proper format for processing either as decimal or fixed point.

Since most computers use EBCDIC, data entering a computer from a source input device (such as a card reader) or going to an output device (such as a printer) is in units of eight bits (byte) with a specified length code. Each byte, in this sense, is made up of four zone bits and four numeric bits (EBCDIC) (fig. 6.16). When each data character occupies a byte of internal storage, the data format is called *zoned* (unpacked) *format* (fig. 6.17). Data fields that are alphabetic or alphanumeric must always be in zoned format; that is, a full eight-bit byte must be used to express each character. Likewise, data fields that include special characters, such as punctuation and mathematical symbols, must be in zoned format. Zoned format is used for all input/output operations.

Decimal Processing

Since all numeric characters have the same zone bits, packing two digits into one byte (except the rightmost byte, which contains the sign of the number) results in more efficient use of storage, increased arithmetic performance, and improved data transmission (fig. 6.18).

Instructions are provided by the computer manufacturer for the automatic packing data for internal processing and the later unpacking of the data for subsequent output.

Fixed-Point Processing

Whereas the length of decimal data is specified by a length code in the instruction, the length of fixed-point data is implied by the instruction type. In the IBM System 360/370, a fixed length of 16 bits (halfword), 32 bits (word), and 64 bits (doubleword) are used in fixed-point operations (fig. 6.19). The sign of each number is expressed in the first bit position of the fixed data. The sign bit of a fixed-point number is a zero bit for positive values and a one bit for negative values (fig. 6.20).

Zoned Format

Packed Format

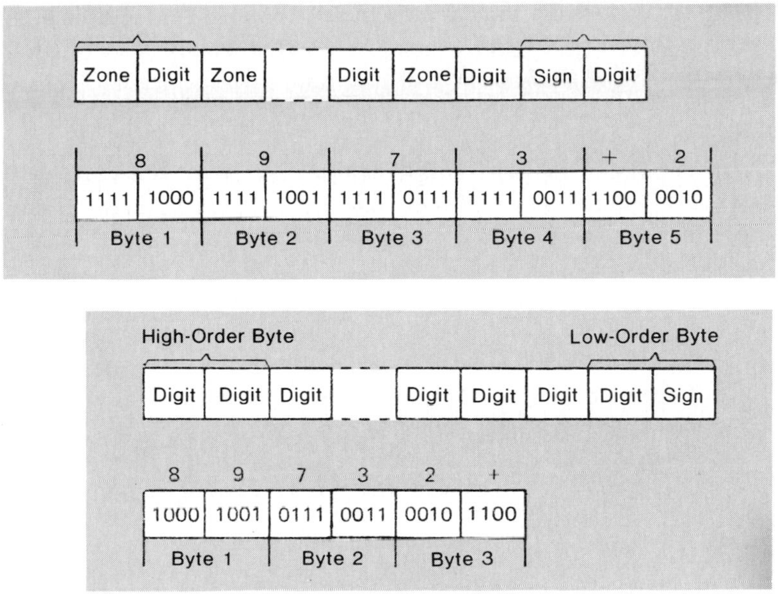

Figure 6.18 Zoned and packed decimal number formats.

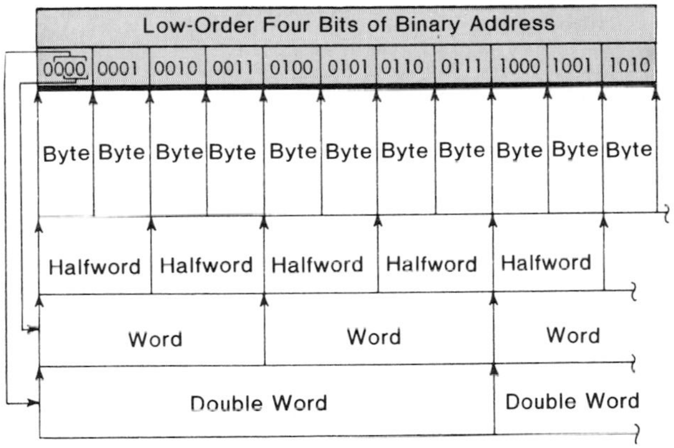

Figure 6.19 Halfwords, words, and doublewords.

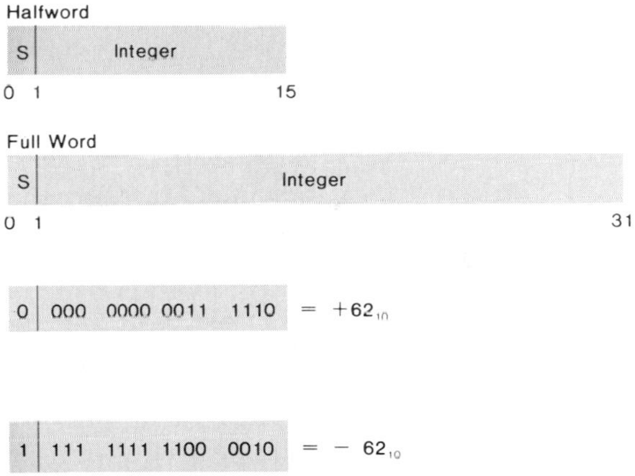

Figure 6.20 Fixed-point number formats. In this example, the negative number is in two's complement notation.

Instructions are provided by the computer manufacturer for the automatic conversion from EBCDIC to binary for processing and back to EBCDIC for subsequent output.

Negative Numbers

In fixed-point arithmetic representation, positive numbers appear in true binary form with a "0" bit in their leftmost position. For example, the positive value 25 would appear in binary as follows.

0 0 0 0 0 0 0 1 9 (Hexadecimal notation—each hex character represents 4 binary digits.)

A negative number appears in *two's complement* form. Thus the negative value of 25 would appear as follows.

F F F F F F E 7 (Hex notation)

Method for Interpreting Negative Numbers

When interpreting the number, it is necessary to convert negative complement value to true format. For example, *to convert a negative value of 25 to its two's complement form,* the following steps should be taken.

1. Bit positions of rightmost 8 positions	0 0 0 1 1 0 0 1 = 25 decimal
2. Reverse bit positions	1 1 1 0 0 1 1 0
3. Add 1	+ 1
4. Binary representation of number	1 1 1 0 0 1 1 1 Last 8 bits.
5. Hex notation of entire number	F F F F F F E 7

To convert a two's complement number to its true negative value, the following steps should be taken.

1. Reverse the bits of two's complement (last 8 bit positions)	1 1 1 0 0 1 1 1
Reverse bits	0 0 0 1 1 0 0 0
2. Add 1 to the result	+ 1
3. True negative value	0 0 0 1 1 0 0 1 = − 25

Summary

In the study of computer processing, you should understand the meaning and operation of various number systems used in data processing. Most of us are familiar with the decimal number system. This chapter presents the operations of various computer number systems and the coding systems used in computers.

Knowledge of binary numbers and its related number systems is mandatory to the understanding of computer operations regardless how deep you will ultimately go in data processing. Binary arithmetic is basic for octal and hexadecimal number systems. A thorough knowledge of the operations of octal and hexadecimal number systems is important because they are used extensively in data-processing operations. You should be able to convert numbers from one system to the symbols of any other system.

1. The value of each digit position is dependent upon the relative position of the digits as well as the digit value itself. The least significant digit (extreme right) is the low-order position with the smallest value. The most significant digit (extreme left) is the high-order position with the largest value.
2. The base or radix indicates the number of digits used in the number system. The highest number that can be represented by a single digit is one less than its base.
3. The binary number system is a simple two digit system used by computers. The symbol 0 represents no bits and the symbol 1 represents the presence of a bit. A bit is the contraction of *BI*nary digi*T*.
4. Converting binary numbers to decimal equivalents is done by either the expansion method or the double-dabble method. The expansion method used direct expansions in powers of 2 of each digit, beginning with the least significant and proceeding to the most significant digit. The decimal equivalent is the sum of these values. The double-dabble method doubles the most significant digit and adds to it the digit at the right. Then double the sum and add to the next digit. Repeat until the sum contains the lowest digit at the right.
5. Converting decimals to binary equivalents is done by either the remainder method or the binary expansion method. In the remainder method, the decimal is divided by two and that quotient and all succeeding quotients are in turn divided by two until the quotient is zero. The equivalent binary number is composed of the remainders of each division in reverse sequence as the division. The last division remainder produces the most significant digit and the first division remainder produces the least significant digit. The binary expansion method uses the binary expansion table through successive subtractions of the expansion number from the number to be converted and using differences for successive searches through the table.

6. Binary addition and subtraction follow basically the same general rules as decimal, except that a base of 2 is used rather than 10.
7. The octal number system (0,1,2,3,4,5,6,7) is a shorthand method of displaying binary numbers. Each octal position is equivalent to three binary digits. Any binary number can be converted to octal by grouping the bits in 3s, starting at the rightmost bit and reconverting each group into its octal equivalent. Converting octal to decimal numbers is done by multiplying each octal digit by its digital position value (power of 8) and the products added together to produce the decimal number. Converting decimal to octal numbers can be accomplished by using the remainder method except using a divisor of 8 instead of 2, as in decimal to binary conversion. Octal addition and subtraction follow the same rules as decimal except that a base of 8 is used instead of 10.
8. The hexadecimal number system (0,1,2,3,4,5,6,7,8,9,A,B,C,D,E,F) is a shorthand method of displaying binary numbers. Each hexadecimal position is equivalent to four binary positions. Any binary number can be converted to hexadecimal by grouping the bits into groups of 4, starting at the rightmost bit and reconverting each group into its hexadecimal equivalent. To convert hexadecimal numbers to their decimal equivalents, each hexadecimal digit is multiplied by its digital position value (power of 16) and the products are added together to produce the decimal equivalent. Decimal to hexadecimal conversion can be made by the division method. The number is continually divided by 16 and the remainder from each division produces the hexadecimal equivalent. Decimal to hexadecimal conversion can also be made by using the hexadecimal-decimal integer conversion tables. Hexadecimal addition and subtraction follow the same general rules as decimal except that a base of 16 is used instead of 10.
9. Computer codes are used to symbolize data in a data-processing system. The code relates to the fixed number of symbols (binary numbers). The binary-coded decimal (BCD) uses four bits to represent any decimal number. The 7 bit alphameric code (binary-coded decimal system) uses seven bits to represent all characters, one check bit, two zone bits, and four numeric bits. The check bit is used as a parity check to insure the correct number of bits for each character. The 8 bit extended binary-coded decimal interchange code (EBCDIC) uses eight bits to represent all characters—four zone bits and four numeric bits. The American National Standard Code for Information Exchange (ASCII) is used for information exchange among data-processing systems, communication systems, and associated equipment.
10. Decimal processing uses packed and unpacked (zone) formats with variable length records. Fixed-word processing uses a fixed number of bits for fixed length data, such as halfwords (16 bits), words (32 bits), and doublewords (64 bits). All numbers appear as integers with a fixed decimal point in the rightmost position. Negative numbers appear in two's complement form that must be converted for interpretation.

Identification Questions

Match the following terms with the statements below.

A. 7 Bit Alphameric Code
B. 8 Bit Extended Binary-Coded Decimal Interchange Code
C. Base (Radix)
D. Binary-Coded Decimal
E. Binary Number System
F. Bit
G. Byte
H. Double-Dabble Method
I. Doubleword
J. Fixed Word
K. Halfword
L. Hexadecimal Number System
M. Least Significant Digit
N. Most Significant Digit
O. Negative Numbers
P. Octal Number System
Q. Packed Format
R. Remainder Method
S. Variable Word
T. Word
U. Zoned Format

1. The number of digits in a number system.
2. Conventional method of converting decimal numbers to their binary equivalent.
3. A number system consisting of sixteen digits where each digit represents four binary digits.
4. The use of sixteen different numbers consisting of four zone bits and four numeric bits to represent characters.
5. A number system consisting of two digits.
6. The digit position at the extreme left with the highest value.
7. Numbers appear in two's complement form.
8. The use of four bits to represent any of the decimal digits 0–9.
9. Consists of four zone bits and four numeric bits.
10. The length of the data is specified in the instruction.
11. Consists of sixty-four bits.
12. Each data item occupies one byte of storage.
13. The digit position at the extreme right with the lowest value.
14. A short-cut method of performing the binary to decimal conversion.
15. A code consisting of one check bit, two zone bits, and four numeric bits to represent sixty-four characters.
16. Consists of thirty-two bits.
17. Putting two digits in each byte except the rightmost byte.
18. Contraction of the words binary and digit.
19. A number system consisting of eight digits where each digit represents three binary digits.
20. Consists of sixteen bits.
21. Assumed that each data item has the same length and an assumed decimal point at the right.

Questions for Review

1. Why is the binary form of arithmetic used in most computers today?
2. Describe the basic principles of a number system.
3. Explain the binary number system.
4. What are the two methods used to convert binary numbers into their decimal equivalent?
5. What is the remainder method?
6. What are the main advantages of using an octal number system?
7. How do you convert a decimal number to its octal equivalent?
8. Describe the hexadecimal number system and its importance in computer arithmetic.
9. Describe the direct method of converting hexadecimal numbers to their decimal equivalents.
10. What is the importance of conversion tables?
11. What is a computer code?
12. Describe the 7 bit alphameric code.
13. Describe the 8 bit extended binary-coded decimal interchange code.
14. What was the main purpose of the American National Standard Code for Information Exchange?
15. What is the difference between variable word length machines and fixed-point machines?
16. What is meant by zoned format and what is its main use? How does it differ from packed format?

Key Terms

7 Bit Alphameric Code
8 Bit Extended Binary-Coded Decimal Interchange Code
Base (Radix)
Binary-Coded Decimal
Binary Number System
Bit
Byte
Double-Dabble Method
Doubleword
Fixed Word
Halfword
Hexadecimal Number System
Least Significant Digit
Most Significant Digit
Negative Numbers
Octal Number System
Packed Format
Remainder Method
Variable Word
Word
Zoned Format

introduction to programming

part 3

data-processing systems and procedures 7

Chapter Outline

Systems Analysis
- Problem Definition
- Analysis and Design
- Procedure, Programs, and Conversion

The Systems Analyst
- Roles
  - Persuader
  - Catalyst
  - Confronter
  - Imposer

Systems and Procedures Approach
- Systems Elements
- Systems Design Concepts
- Advantages
- Selling the System

Chapter Objectives

The learning objectives of this chapter are

1. to present the numerous procedures and problems involved in a systems study.
2. to demonstrate the importance of a good systems study upon the eventual success of the data-processing application.
3. to point out that the programming effort is begun only after the entire problem has been defined, and flowcharts, analysis sheets, and other documents that resulted from the systems study have been prepared.
4. to show that the entire study is centered around management objectives and what management expects from data processing.
5. to become aware of the complexity of systems analysis, conversion problems, and the meaning of the terms used in systems study.

Industry is becoming aware of its paperwork burden—the size of its clerical force, the amount and kinds of records that it must keep of its products, purchases, and other transactions, and the reports that it must make periodically on its operations. Companies are attempting to expand their use of computers to reduce both their data-processing costs and the time lag between the source document information availability and the distribution of the ultimate report on that specific.

Management is conscious of the enormous number of problems involved in making data processing an effective management decision-making tool. Growing awareness of these problems on the part of management defines the realistic limits of what should be expected of a computer and how to expand its capabilities. A constant challenge to management lies in extracting more from this potent management tool.

The computer is in a period of transition from initial acceptance to massive exploitation by business. The computer must be applied to the increasing number of variables and the accelerating rate of changes with which every business has to deal. It is difficult to find a company that does not lease or own a computer.

The transition in data processing is from the single self-contained computer to complex electronic systems in which the computer plays only a part. Data processing has changed from accounting and record keeping to a far broader range of management information systems that are necessary for effective decision making. Also there has been a great increase in the breadth of expectations held by management for data processing. Initially, most computers were installed on the strength of anticipated savings in clerical activities. Now the shift is toward the infinitely broader concept of profit improvement.

A firm leases or purchases computer equipment with the intent of performing applications faster, more economically, and more efficiently than previous methods of processing data. Unlike some machines whose new design may assure speed, economy, and efficiency simply through their installation; computer hardware requires extensive preparation in planning, documenting, and preparing programs for the jobs to be performed. Computer use involves more than simply buying and "plugging-in" new machines.

Four major steps precede the use of a computer.

1. An application must be studied in relation to the present or intended operations and also in terms of computer requirements.
2. The application is divided into a series of procedures that satisfy both operation and computer requirements.
3. The flow of information between procedures must be determined to coordinate operations between each procedure.
4. Finally, each procedure can be treated as a system part that requires incorporation of programs and documentation.

For many years, data processing has been primarily used for automating administrative applications, resulting in the reduction of required clerical operations. It was felt that the data-processing functions could only be justified by having machines do repetitive work and perform one-to-one replacement of routine manual steps. With increased technology of hardware, software, and integrated systems, the emphasis is now rapidly moving towards making the computer an integral part of daily operations and management organizations.

Instead of designing and implementing systems to perform one part of a functional area, systems are designed to perform an entire function, crossing organization lines. Remember, data processing's ultimate reason for existence is to satisfy the informational requirements of its users, both for operational and managerial purposes. In doing so, the facilities must capture, store, and present data in a meaningful, timely, and efficient manner. The justification to computerize has now shifted from clerical reduction to an expanded range of benefits including economic, informational, integrity, response, and security improvements.

Systems Analysis

Systems analysis, the commonly advocated method used for evaluating information systems, is a set of steps required to examine an existing system in order to identify the problems causing inefficiency or inadequacy. This approach begins with the determination of the firm's objectives. From these objectives certain strategies and organizational structures are developed.

A good data-processing system is designed to solve a particular problem and, if well done, it in itself will never become a problem. *A system reflects a cohesive collection of items or a representation of connected parts that are related by a "network of relationships." This includes the required information that makes possible the exercise of effective controls* (fig. 7.1).

When it is decided to use the data-processing system to solve a problem, it is seldom clear what results are expected. Many data-processing applications have proved a disappointment due to an inadequate systems study.

The best results in a data-processing systems design are achieved if a fully defined sequence of steps is followed. Systems analysts are familiar with these steps from training and experience. They believe in them and will try to follow them. To anticipate the thoughts of systems analysts and understand what they are trying to accomplish, top management should be familiar with all phases of systems design and the operations peculiar to each phase. This familiarity on the part of management will prove helpful to systems analysts in the preparation of the best system possible. Analysts must be free to cut across departmental lines to learn all aspects of the problem so they can make worthwhile recommendations (fig. 7.2).

The inital step in a systems analysis study is the survey. *A survey is a preliminary study undertaken by company personnel to determine whether or not a proposed computer system is feasible and whether or not it will give improved operation at a lower cost.* Initially, someone gets the idea that there may be benefits to computerizing some data-processing operation. A survey of the area determines the feasibility of such a step. If the computerization is feasible as defined, responsibility for the construction of the new data-processing operation is detailed. If the proposed application is extensive, the result of the study determines whether a more expensive feasibility study is to be authorized. The creation of an information processing system for an application can be divided into three phases—*problem definition, analysis and design,* and *procedure programs and conversion.*

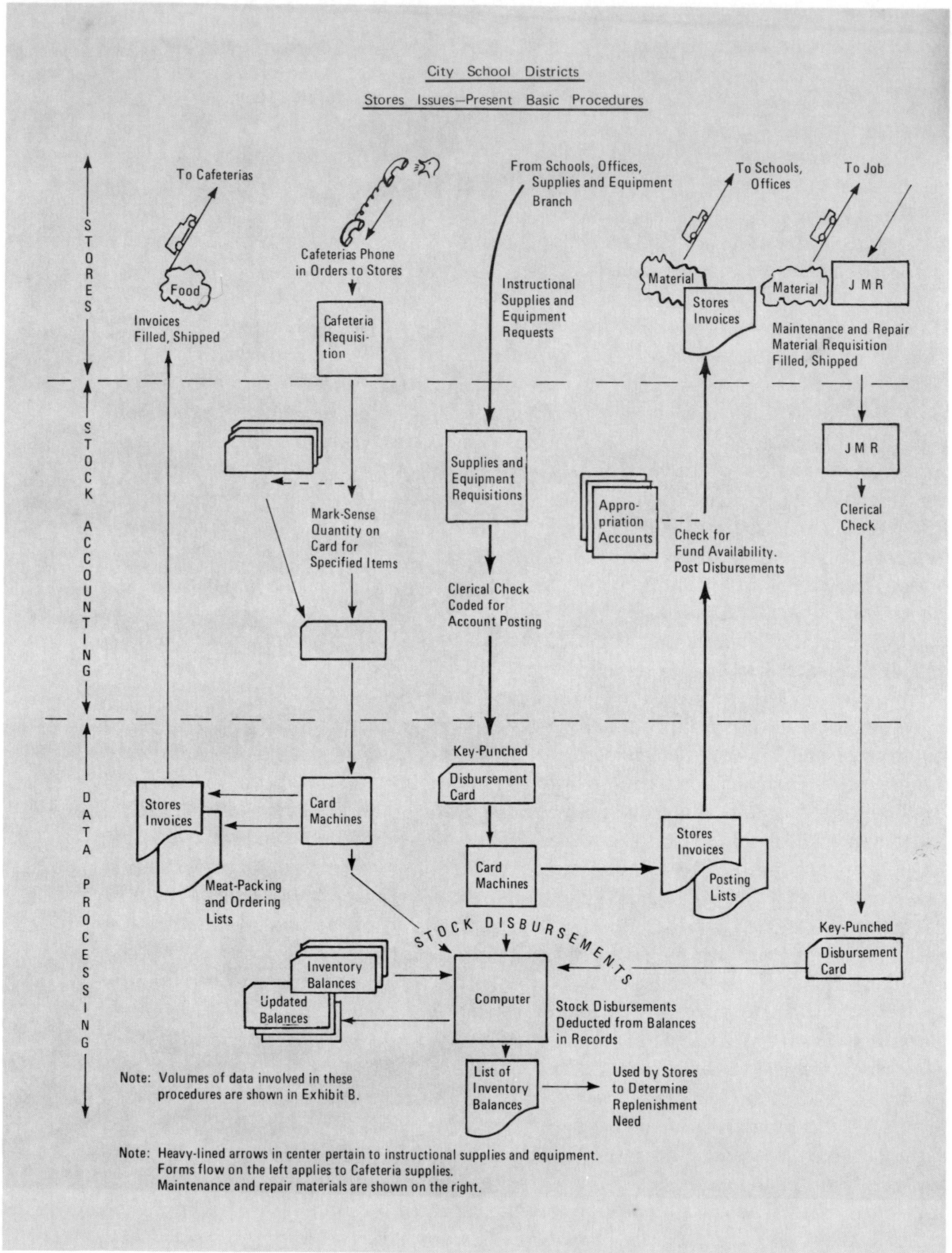

Figure 7.1 An example of a procedural flowchart; a city school district's basic storage procedures.

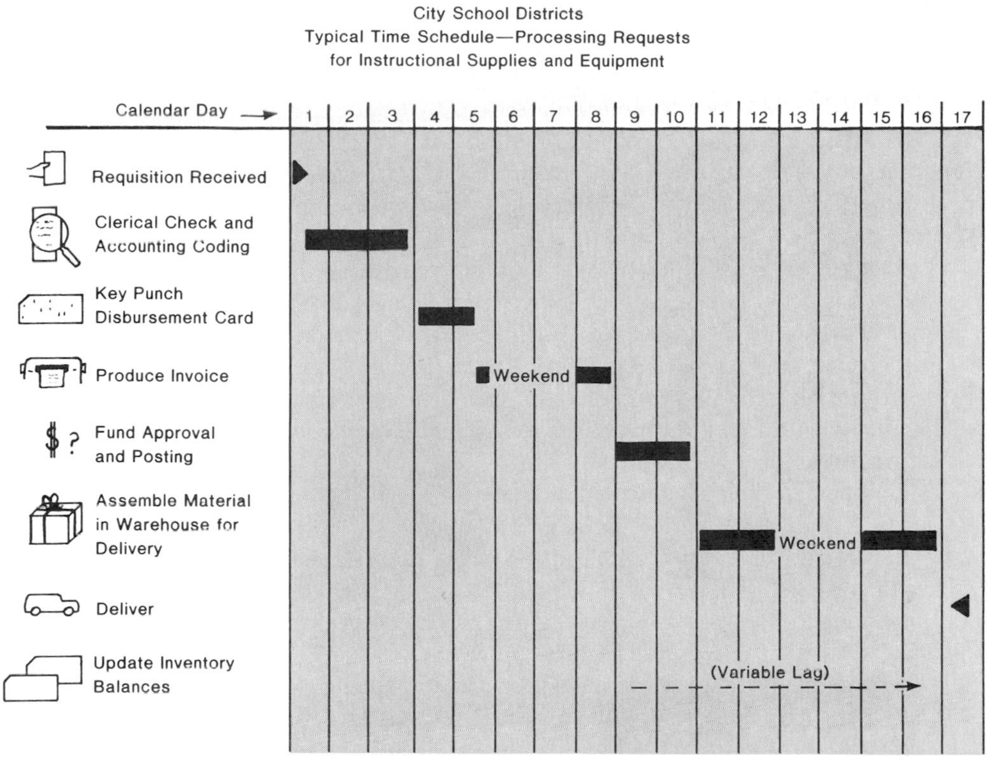

Figure 7.2 An example of a procedural flowchart; a city school district's typical time schedule for processing requests.

Problem Definition

A computer is the *heart* of an electronic data-processing system, but the heart is only part of a whole. The whole, the entire data-processing system, is a means to an end, and that end is the *solving of a problem.* Problems of one kind or another are solved everyday, usually without our awareness of the steps involved. But solving problems by computer processing is a more complex procedure that requires a thorough study. We cannot depend on intuition alone to carry us through successfully.

The key to a good information system involves a total understanding of the entire problem. *Proper problem definition will help insure the achievement of the objectives—the creation of an efficient and effective data-processing system to solve the specific problem.*

1. A complete record of the present operations should be obtained for analysis.
2. Key personnel should be interviewed to determine the flow of data.
3. Sample source documents should be collected for analysis.

Upon completion of the analysis, a flowchart of the existing procedures in a sequence of operations should be prepared.

Analysis and Design

Analysis consists of two phases—defining area objectives and reviewing existing procedures. In defining area objectives, the scope of the area to be covered is analyzed, the overall objectives are determined, and the functions required to meet these objectives are evaluated. Also, an appraisal is made of how this area relates to other data-processing operations and to the company as a whole.

In reviewing existing procedures, a study is made of the operation with emphasis on exceptional as well as routine characteristics. All basic documents are reviewed as to origin, distribution, material and format, and master record reference. All outputs are studied to reveal distribution, content, and format of finished reports, vouchers, checks, etc. Another phase of this study determines operating restrictions for the new system.

Design begins with a study of the documentation prepared during systems analysis. This study determines the relationships between all parts of the system. Next, a layout is prepared depicting the major relationships in the proposed system and giving consideration to what reference records must be created. Following this, an analysis of the report to be generated is made with emphasis on the fulfillment of legal and management control requirements. The source and reference data required to produce the desired reports are then defined.

The important points to remember are:

1. The main objective is to design a system that will meet all the established requirements.
2. The method is one of basic problem definition concerning the organization of the data files and the required reports.
3. Key documents must be examined for content, frequency, and purpose.
4. Key personnel must review the proposed procedures to insure an understanding of the methods and end products. At this stage, output specifications must become firm and complete.
5. The analysis and preliminary design are completed when the present revisions are acceptable and the final flowcharts and documents prove satisfactory to all personnel concerned.

Procedures, Programs, and Conversion

During this phase, the procedures are converted to flowcharts and the programming function begins. During *programming,* the run descriptions are parceled out to programmers. The programmer's first step is to analyze the run description and prepare a flowchart which pictures in detail how this run is to be executed on the computer. The flowchart is used for coding the run in computer language. After the coding has been completed, the run is tested for accuracy by processing specific transaction material on the computer (this is the "debugging" process). On completion of the testing, a run book and computer center procedures are prepared.

Filemaking constitutes a major part of the work in the initial application of a computer system. It involves construction of the records used for reference to obtain information or to accumulate data. For example, in a payroll system, a file is maintained on a disk of each employee's record, including such data as earnings, deductions, and accumulated data for the year.

Defining the files required and their format is an important phase of the job. In addition, arrangements must be made to enable the clerical organization to gather the necessary data and establish the file. The data is then converted to disk and an audit of the file is made. Finally, after establishing the file, but before going into production, the file is updated.

The installation of a new computer system will involve changes in clerical routings and will require documentation of these manual procedures. After documentation has been completed, training must be provided for all personnel involved in the new system. Following the completion of the training phase, the new system is tried with test data before it is installed on a production basis.

Testing and installation of the computer system is the last step, one that involves testing the system prior to installation and making the necessary changes to produce the required data. The system is then turned over to operations personnel.

The important features to remember are:

1. The objective is to write detailed procedures for the overall system.
2. The method is to analyze the flowcharts, documentation, and narrative from the analysis and design phase. These will show that the final system was agreed upon by all.
3. The technique of systems design should include:
   a. A detailed outline of the new system.
   b. Samples of source documents with scaled images of reports.
   c. Detailed procedures.
4. The entire system should be submitted to management for approval.
5. Upon written authorization, the installation of the new system should begin.
6. The system should be released to operating personnel.
7. A follow-up should be made after the release of the new system to operating personnel to confirm the results and the adequacy of the procedures. Any evidence of "backsliding" to the old system should be stopped. A ninety-day follow-up is an adequate trial period to make a realistic cost analysis of the system.

Before the installation of a computer is undertaken, management must be convinced of the practicability as well as the cost justification of the application (fig. 7.3).

The Systems Analyst

A system is a process of reaching an objective. An objective is a goal to accomplish. A systems analyst must be able to understand and motivate people (fig. 7.4).

The analyst must understand the capabilities of the people who will perform the functions within the system. First, the analyst must be able to evaluate their current abilities and then their capabilities for learning and upgrading their own abilities. If the input data needed cannot be accurately or intelligently obtained, it is obvious that the system is doomed to failure. The time period of the learning process also must be understood. Too often, systems are designed with outputs too sophisticated for the user to actually use.

The understanding of the individuals in the systems process is the key. Once this is done, a plan can be devised to implement the system.

Systems mean change. People will only change if they are motivated to do so. Therefore, if the training is to be effective, there must be a reason for an individual to change an old way of doing things. Often "for the good of the company" is not enough; there must be a personal benefit.

Figure 7.3 An example of a system flowchart; a city school district's proposed computer programs.

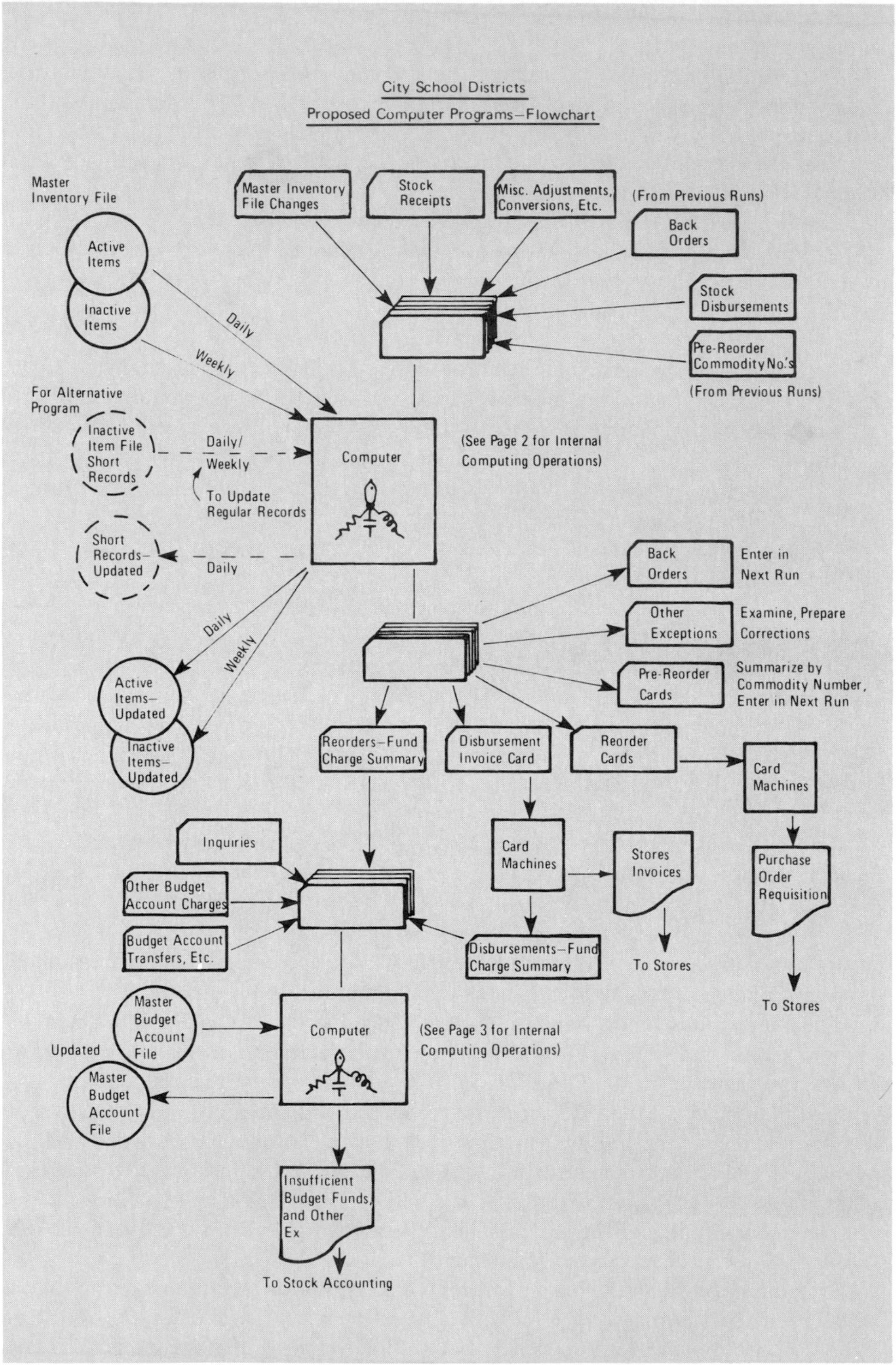

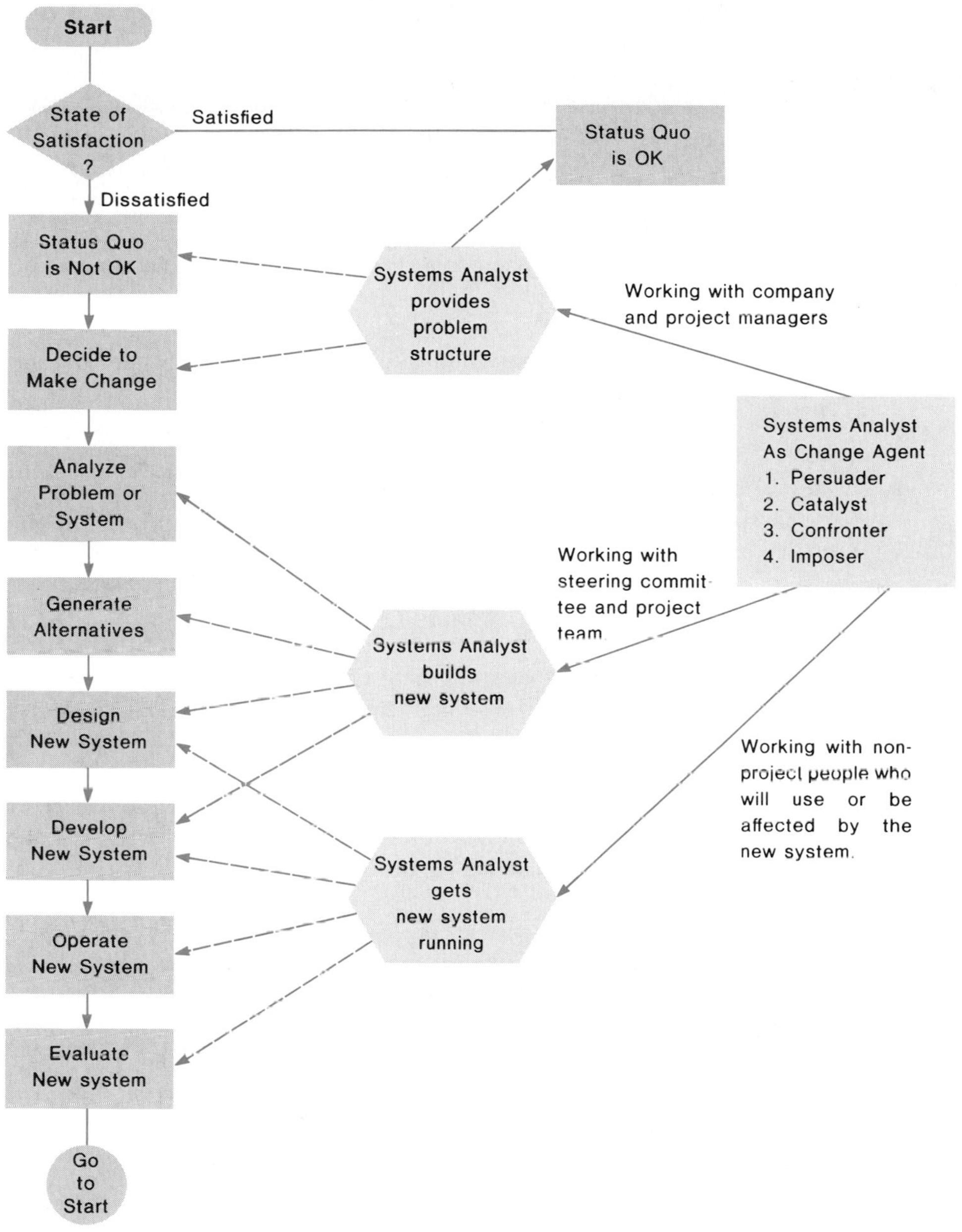

Figure 7.4 The activities and roles of the systems analyst. (Reprinted with permission of *Datamation* © magazine, © Copyright by Technical Publishing Company, a division of Dun-Donnelley Publishing Corporation, a Dun & Bradstreet Company, 1978—all rights reserved.)

The systems analyst may work with many people at various stages in the development of a system, including managers, programmers, operators, and users. He may have to play a different kind of role—persuader, catalyst, confronter, or imposer—at each stage.

People can be motivated to record and report new information as part of revised input systems by letting them know how that information is to be used by other people. A little knowledge of their personal roles in the total information process results in their desire to create accurate data for the system.

Today, few systems work without the full participation and cooperation of the people involved. If the analyst wants to be successful, then he/she must make the people who will "run the system" successful. This is done only through understanding and motivating people. Success of the systems analyst is usually measured by the success of others, not how fancy the system is or how many reports it produces.

Roles

The systems analyst plans and gains acceptance for organizational change. Organizations are complex systems with interacting parts. Each part influences all the other parts. For example, a new system in the accounting department may impact marketing and, ultimately, the company's suppliers and buyers. Furthermore, organizations are made of people, and it is with people that the change agent deals.

By being sensitive to the organizational setting, the systems analyst will have a better idea of the extent and force of a change and how to accomplish project goals. Specifically, the analyst may assume the role of persuader, catalyst, confronter, or imposer (fig. 7.5).

Persuader

The systems analyst persuades employees to accept change dictated by the company and management. This is the mildest form of intervention for a systems analyst, merely helping people to change their attitudes and to adjust.

Catalyst

The systems analyst introduces new ideas to the change process, but lets the user determine the changes. The amount of intervention as a catalyst is greater than in the persuader role, but still the analyst is acting as a helper.

Confronter

As a confronter, the systems analyst opposes the user because, in the analyst's best judgment, the user will not achieve satisfactory change unless jolted into a completely different approach. This role frequently generates conflict and should be used with care.

Imposer

The system analyst, with authority given by company management, imposes the plan for change on the users. Severe conflict and even job reassignments are common when this role is assumed.

Over the life of the project, the analyst may take on any of these roles. However, the goal is always to gain short- and long-term acceptance for the systems effort with a minimum of organizational agony.

Systems and Procedures Approach

1. The objective of systems and procedures is to reduce everyday activities to simple routines, thereby minimizing the task of decision making and relieving the employees of many details of execution.
2. The system will be a network of procedures that are integrated and designed to carry out a major activity.

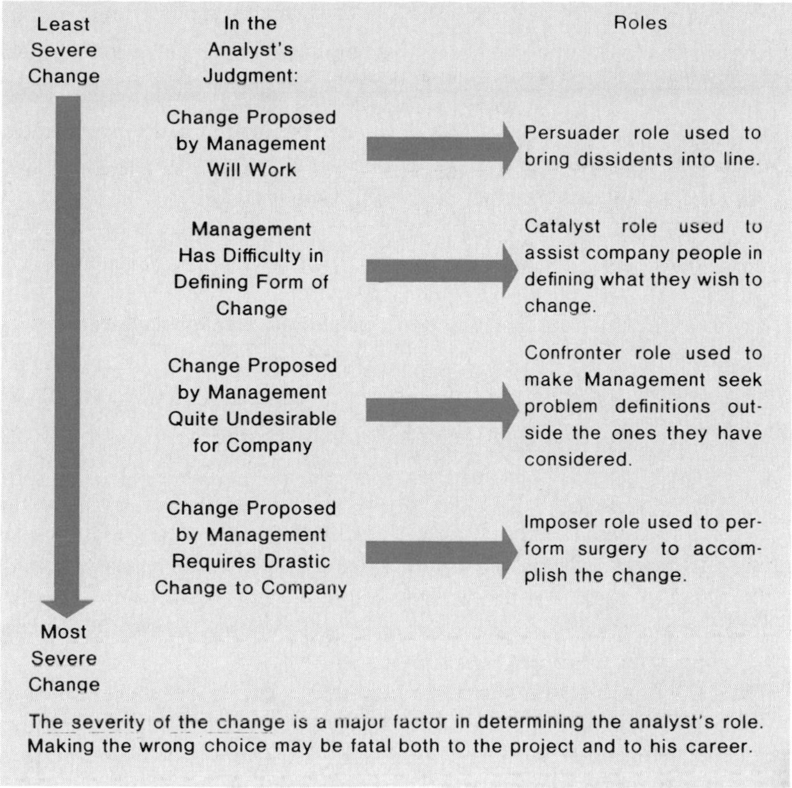

Figure 7.5 The role selection strategy for the systems analyst. (Reprinted with permission of *Datamation* © magazine, © Copyright by Technical Publishing Company, a division of Dun-Donnelley Publishing Corporation, a Dun & Bradstreet Company, 1978—all rights reserved.)

3. The size and number of work specialities make it difficult and time-consuming for managers to inspect each operation personally. The manager should secure pertinent information regarding operations via the system and procedure methods.
4. The use of systems expedites comprehension, forces the identification of activities, and prescribes the sequence of operations to achieve the stated goal. The *problem* is to design a system that will bring together all forces to accomplish an effective pattern.

	Systems Elements
The basic goals of the organization.	Objectives
Selections that must be made between alternative actions.	Decisions
Written guidelines of management for guiding administrative action.	Policies
Activities to carry out the management policies. A series of related steps to carry out an activity.	Procedures

System A network of procedures that is large in scope.

Subsystem Subordinate to the system that is an integral part of the larger system usually consisting of two or more procedures.

Integrated Information System A network of related subsystems developed according to an integrated scheme. A single transcription of the source data will be used and combined with all interrelated activities without the necessity of recopying the original data.

System Flowchart An overall visual of the system showing the flow of information from the input to the output media.

Program Flowchart The breakdown, step-by-step, in sequence, of each procedure of the operation to be performed.

Block Diagram A further breakdown of the program flowchart. Both the program flowchart and the block diagram are used in the coding of the program.

Systems Design Concepts

1. A good system should permit reasonably rapid changes to be made as the necessity arises, without completely disrupting the entire operation.
2. Data should be captured in machine-acceptable format as close to the source as is economically possible, for example, punched cards, OCR, and magnetic tape. This prevents repetitive copying.
3. Adequate controls should be maintained over all parts of the system. Costs should be ascertained at the different degrees of control to assure the most economical cost consistent with adequate controls. There is a tendency to "over control" a system. Too many checkpoints intend to increase costs without compensatory benefits.
4. There should be a straight flow of the operating procedures. Backtracking should be avoided.
5. Exception procedures should be eliminated, if possible, or at least minimized.
6. Authority should be defined so that decisions can be made as close to the point of operation as possible.
7. The system must be sold to all levels of management to gain acceptance (fig. 7.6).

Advantages The important advantages of an effective systems and procedures program are:

1. It supplies an overall look at the enterprise. The overall objectives are defined.
2. It increases the appreciation of the total problem. The limited departmentalized and outmoded notions are cut through by the system.
3. The input and output ingredients are identified. Source documents are standardized and output formats are formalized.
4. The system brings order and a desirable mode of operations to office work. The work patterns are reduced to simple routines.
5. It provides uniformity of action and formalized work. Procedures and other types of manuals guarantee uniform operating procedures.
6. The emphasis is on accurate and reliable controls. With an effective system, management has tighter control of the operations.

	Yes	Comment
I. Test Preparation.		
1. Test team members given assignments.		
2. Final operating environment defined.		
3. All conditions to be tested, identified, and documented.		
4. Test files created for execution of all system functions.		
a. file sequences correct		
b. meaningful starting values established		
c. all record types included		
d. file volume large enough to demonstrate control groups, totals, page breaks on reports		
e. meaningful time period established		
5. Test transactions developed to demonstrate all test cases.		
a. unit testing criteria satisfied		
b. system testing criteria satisfied		
c. transactions created for at least two cycles of system execution		
d. end-of-period (month, year) system options demonstrated		
6. Test results predicted and documented for later comparison with computer output.		
7. Parallel system output identified for standard of correctness.		
8. Acceptability and accuracy standards established and documented for later assessment of results.		
a. core availability in production mode		
b. timing constraints in production mode		
c. if 100% accuracy not required—justify		

	Yes	Comment
II. Test Operations.		
1. Test transactions entered by data entry department using standard procedures.		
2. Tests executed by operations personnel without programmer supervision.		
3. Transaction listing obtained before test execution.		
4. File dumps obtained prior to program execution.		
5. System executed to demonstrate all test cases. (May require multiple executions of the system or of individual modules.)		
6. All hardcopy (reports, control totals) obtained.		
7. Transcription of console messages (and timing information) obtained.		
8. File dumps taken after test execution.		
9. Output from parallel run available.		

Figure 7.6 A system testing checklist. (Reprinted with permission of *Datamation* © magazine, © Copyright by Technical Publishing Company, a division of Dun-Donnelley Publishing Corporation, a Dun & Bradstreet Company, 1978—all rights reserved.)

Figure 7.6
Continued.

	Yes	Comment
III. Unit-Test Evaluation.		
1. JCL executes program without errors or unnecessary operator intervention, and file labels are correct.		
2. JCL-defined file capacities adequate, assuming moderate expansion.		
3. Execute time acceptable according to preestablished standards.		
4. Sufficient core available for execution and moderate expansion of program size.		
5. Input data accepted as formatted without data exception.		
6. All logical paths executed correctly.		
a. all invalid data trapped		
• troublesome transaction combinations discovered		
• edit messages all forced		
• no-match or invalid-key conditions forced		
b. program-controlled terminations before normal EOJ tested		
c. no-file case executing		
d. empty-file case (file exists, but has no member records) executing		
e. file updating accurate, complete, according to specifications		
• first-record processing accurate		
• addition of a record prior to the first record executes correctly		
• multiple-file match logic working		
• last-record EOF processing accurate		
• addition of a record after the last record executes correctly		
• fields updated as specified: quantity replacement, quantity addition, etc.		
• record deletion, addition executes correctly		
• multiple transactions per master record all execute correctly		
• changes to keys handled accurately		
f. all report breaks demonstrated		
• page overflow		
• detail, minor and major control breaks, final control break		
7. Created files conform to design specifications.		
8. Field sizes in files adequate: no unexpected truncation, loss of significant digits.		
9. Mathematical accuracy, rounding		

Figure 7.6
Continued.

10. Reports conform to designed layout.
11. Report information contents agrees with titles, headers.
12. Report page numbering accurate.
13. Spelling correct on report titles, headers.
14. Field sizes on reports adequate.
15. Audit trails (control totals) accurate.

IV. System Test Evaluation.

1. JCL executes system without errors or unnecessary operator intervention, and file labels are correct.
2. JCL-defined file capacities adequate, assuming moderate expansion.
3. Execute time acceptable according to preestablished standards.
4. File sequences (sort specs) accurate throughout system execution.
5. No-file case executing throughout all system steps.
6. Empty-file case executing throughout all system steps.
7. Available means for cross-checking system results exhausted.
   a. different reports with same or derivative information
   b. file contents vs. report values
   c. control break totals vs. final totals
8. Interfaces working accurately.
   a. between programs
   b. between subsystems
   c. between other computer systems
   d. with existing manual systems
9. Files closed at EOJ (normal or due to error).
10. Execution sequence (system flow) accurate and workable.
11. Audit trails (control totals) accurate.
12. Error-correction procedure loops work.
13. System restart procedures satisfactory.
14. File recovery procedures satisfactory.
15. Files and reports conform to output from parallel test, if applicable.
16. Output accurate after more than one execution cycle.
17. End-of-period output accurate, and period-totals reset to zero.

V. Acceptability Test

1. User review of output.
2. Judgment of acceptability according to predetermined standards.
3. Services provided by the system conform to originally stated user requirements
4. Changes in user requirements since original statement.
5. System testing judged complete.
6. User sign-off on output.

7. Problems that arise are more readily identified and isolated.
8. Uniform management policies are encouraged through a standardized system of operation.
9. It facilitates automatic data processing. The installation of a data-processing system is simplified, if there is an effective system in operation.
10. Personnel training is simplified. New personnel are easily trained because the duties of each job are properly defined.
11. Service to the operating departments is improved with a more effective system reducing the amount of confusion.
12. Savings in operating costs usually accrue as the result of the elimination of duplicated activities and simplified methods of operation.

Selling the System

The job of the systems person is 10 percent technique and 90 percent sales, because there is often a wide divergence between the objectives of the individual employee, the functional area, and the business enterprise as a whole.

Even if this situation does not exist in fact, it is imagined by many employees. Therefore an extraordinary sales effort is required of the systems person. The selling starts with the receipt of the assignment and does not end until full implementation of the new system has been accomplished.

Selling should not be limited to top management. If the system is not sold to all personnel involved, it is destined to fail. It will be sabotaged in a myriad of subtle ways by the operations personnel, who can make the most unlikely system operable or the best system fail.

The success of the system depends on the acceptance by operating personnel. All people need to "belong" and all want status; the systems person must be sure to fulfill these needs. If properly approached, most operating personnel will be anxious to join a systems staff effort. The operating staff must gain confidence in the new system to remove all the mystery.

People fear what they don't understand. The rank and file fear for their security when confronted with system change and improvement. Operations personnel should be assigned to the systems staff for the duration of the project to orient them in the techniques that are applicable to each domain.

The proposed new system should be presented formally after the preliminary work of selling has been accomplished. The purpose of the presentation is:

1. To gain management commitment.
2. To gain political support for a proposed system (approval is not sought in this presentation).
3. To orient indirectly concerned members of management about the direction and goals of the new system.

The presentation should include the history of the systems study, who requested the study, participants, and the development status. It is not necessary to depict the existing system in terms of computer logic, matching flow, or multiple card formats. It is only necessary to simply provide a basic understanding of the existing system.

Several organizations will benefit from the new system and these benefits, both corporate and by individual department, should be pointed out. All points should be covered in the presentation, inviting questions and comments from all personnel. All questions should be answered honestly.

The presentation should end with a summary of decisions made and the future correspondence necessary to confirm decisions. A successful presentation can be made only if the listener fully understands the value of the system.

Summary

A good data-processing system is designed to solve a particular problem, and, if well done, it will never become a problem. A data-processing application doesn't just happen. It is the culmination of the work of many people who contribute their knowledge toward the conversion of manual procedures to a *computer application.* Systems and procedures are an important part of the data-processing area. The success of a computer system will depend to a large extent upon the ability of the systems analyst to understand and motivate people.

Before the programming phase can begin, a thorough systems analysis must be completed. This chapter presents the numerous procedures and problems involved in a systems study. You should be aware of the complexity of systems analysis, conversion problems, and many of the terms used in a systems study.

The eventual success of the entire data-processing effort is dependent upon a good systems study. Many people have the impression that programming is the most important phase of computer processing. It should be pointed out that the programming effort is begun only after the entire problem has been properly defined—the flowcharts, analysis sheets, and other documents prepared that have resulted from the systems study. The entire study is centered around management objectives and what management expects from data processing.

1. A system is a cohesive collection of items or a representation of connected parts that are related through a network of relationships.
2. A survey is a preliminary study undertaken to determine whether or not a proposed system is feasible and whether or not it will give improved operation at a lower cost.
3. Problem definition will insure the setting up of objectives for creating an efficient and effective data-processing system to solve a particular problem.
4. Analysis defines area objectives and reviews existing procedures. Design determines the relationship between all parts of a system and designs the system with the emphasis on the fulfillment of legal and management control requirements.
5. During the procedures, programs, and conversion phase, procedures are converted to flowcharts and the programming begins. Filemaking constructs records to be used for reference to obtain information or to accumulate data. Installation of a new system necessitates changes in personnel, training new personnel, documentation, and testing the new system. The follow-up confirms the results of the systems installation and the adequacy of the procedures.

6. A systems analyst must understand and motivate the people, who will perform the functions within a system, and must plan and gain acceptance for organizational change.
7. The objective of systems and procedures is to reduce everyday activities to simple routines, thereby minimizing the task of decision making and relieving the employees of many details of execution. The system is made up of many elements, such as objectives, decisions, policies, subsystems, etc. In order to be effective the system must be sold to all of the people in the organization.

Identification Questions

Match the following terms with the statements below.

A.	Block Diagram	E.	Objectives	J.	Survey
B.	Decisions	F.	Policies	K.	System
C.	Filemaking	G.	Procedures	L.	Systems Analysis
D.	Integrated Information System	H.	Program Flowchart	M.	Systems Design
		I.	Subsystem	N.	System Flowchart

1. A preliminary study undertaken by company personnel to determine whether a proposed computer system is feasible.
2. Selections that must be made between alternative actions.
3. A network of related subsystems developed according to an integrated scheme.
4. The breakdown, step-by-step, in sequence of each procedure to be performed.
5. A network of procedures that is large in scope.
6. A study made for the purpose of determining the relationship between parts of a system.
7. The basic goals of an organization.
8. Written guidelines of management for guiding administrative action.
9. A further breakdown of the program flowchart.
10. A set of steps required to examine an existing system to determine its adequacy.
11. The construction of records used for reference to obtain information or to accommodate data.
12. The necessary activities to carry out management policies.
13. An integral part of a large system consisting of two or more procedures.
14. An overall visual of the system showing the flow of information from input to output.

Questions for Review

1. Why is management involved with data-processing problems?
2. What important changes have been made in data processing?
3. What is the criteria for designing systems?
4. What is the purpose of systems analysis?
5. What is a survey?
6. What requirements are necessary to correctly define the problem?
7. What qualities should a systems analyst have? What roles does a systems analyst play in a systems study?

8. What are the objectives of the analysis and design phase of the study?
9. What are the important aspects of the procedures, programs, and conversion phase of the study?
10. Describe the important points in the systems and procedures approach.
11. What are the important design concepts?
12. List the important advantages of systems and procedures.
13. Why is it important that the system be sold to all personnel involved? What are the important points to be reiterated in the selling of the system?

Key Terms

Block Diagram
Decisions
Filemaking
Integrated Information System
Objectives
Policies
Procedures
Program Flowchart
Subsystem
Survey
System
Systems Analysis
Systems Design
System Flowchart

preparation for a computer program 8

Chapter Outline

Introduction to Computer Programming
- Instructions

Methods of Processing Data
- Sequential (Batch) Processing
- Random Processing (Inline)

Flowcharts
- System Flowcharts
- Program Flowcharts
- The Comparison Process
  - A Word Flowchart
  - A Symbolic Flowchart

Decision Tables

Programming
- Analysis
- Preparation
- Operation
- Planning a Program
- Input
- Arithmetic
- Logic

Chapter Objectives

The learning objectives of this chapter are

1. to prepare you for the programming phase of data processing.
2. to represent logical solutions to complex data-processing problems in the form of flowcharts and decision tables.
3. to learn the facets of programming, such as instructions, methods of processing data, planning the program, and the program itself.
4. to prepare you to analyze the problem properly, prepare the program to solve a particular problem, and to operate the program.

A computer really is a simple machine, made up of simple components that operate on simple physical principles. What makes a computer complicated, what gives it its wonderful capabilities, is the ingenious logic with which its parts are organized. That logic, that organization, is something its human designers are responsible for.

Introduction to Computer Programming

Running an automatic machine is such an easy job that it is easy to overlook the many hours that have to be spent in designing, testing, and adjusting all of the automatic features until the operation becomes effortless. The same meticulous care and preparation is necessary before the computer can function automatically. It must be instructed on how to perform every task. This job of writing detailed instructions for the computer and making them work correctly is called *programming.*

A data-processing problem is born from the needs of company management; for example, a report about monthly sales, a payroll plan for employees, or an inventory control system. This results in a precise problem statement which has been developed by the systems analyst. It should contain a job description, special processing information, a description of the kind of data desired, and the layout specifications for input and output of that data. The information contained in the problem statement will be further translated into the necessary tools that enable the programmer to both solve and program the problem (fig. 8.1). In the absence of such information, the programmer must develop such specifications as are necessary for solving the problem.

In order to process data with a computer, the machine must be provided with a set of instructions (program). *The instruction is a command to the machine, expressed in a coded combination of characters, to carry out some operation.* With the preliminary data-processing tasks of analysis and definition of the problem accomplished, the job of coding is put together in a set of elementary instructions to carry out the prescribed task. When these instructions are loaded into the predetermined storage area of the computer, the data is entered and the instructions are ready to be executed by the machine and the desired data-processing project is accomplished. The ability of the machine to store internally its own program allows the computer to alter its own instructions at electronic speeds to conditions encountered during the processing of the data. This ability to manipulate instructions during processing provides the almost unlimited flexibility and the so-called logical capability of the stored program system.

Instructions

After a programmer has developed the necessary tools, he must next develop a program (fig. 8.2). *A program is a series of instructions that, when properly translated, will direct the computer in how it will receive, process, and output data* (fig. 8.3).

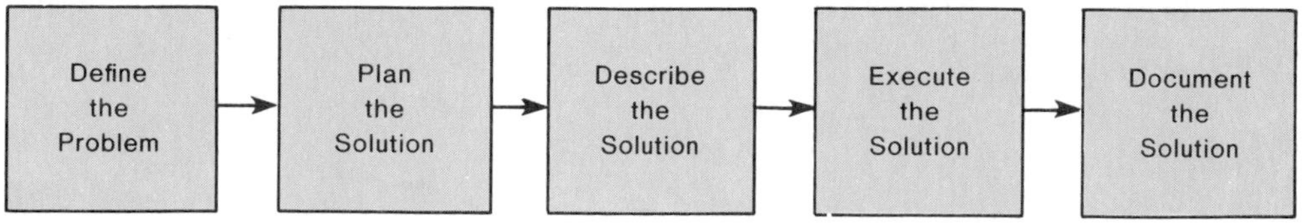

Figure 8.1 The problem-solving procedure.

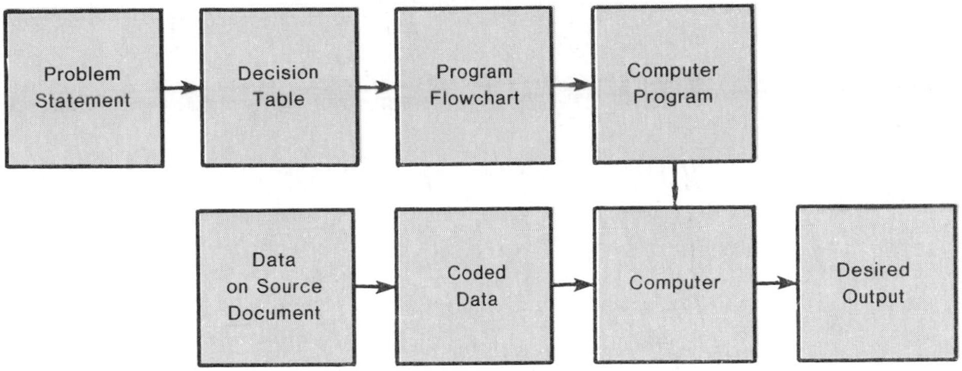

IBM COBOL Program Sheet

System | Punching Instructions | Sheet of
Program | Graphic | Card Form # | Identification
Programmer | Date | Punch

```
Sequence  A   B
01        PROCEDURE DIVISION.
02
03        START-RUN.
04            OPEN INPUT FILE-IN, OUTPUT FILE-OUT.
05
06        READ-RECORD.
07            READ FILE-IN AT END CLOSE FILE-IN, FILE-OUT STOP RUN.
08            MOVE RECORD-IN TO RECORD-OUT.
09            WRITE RECORD-OUT AFTER ADVANCING 2 LINES.
10            GO TO READ-RECORD.
11
12
13
```

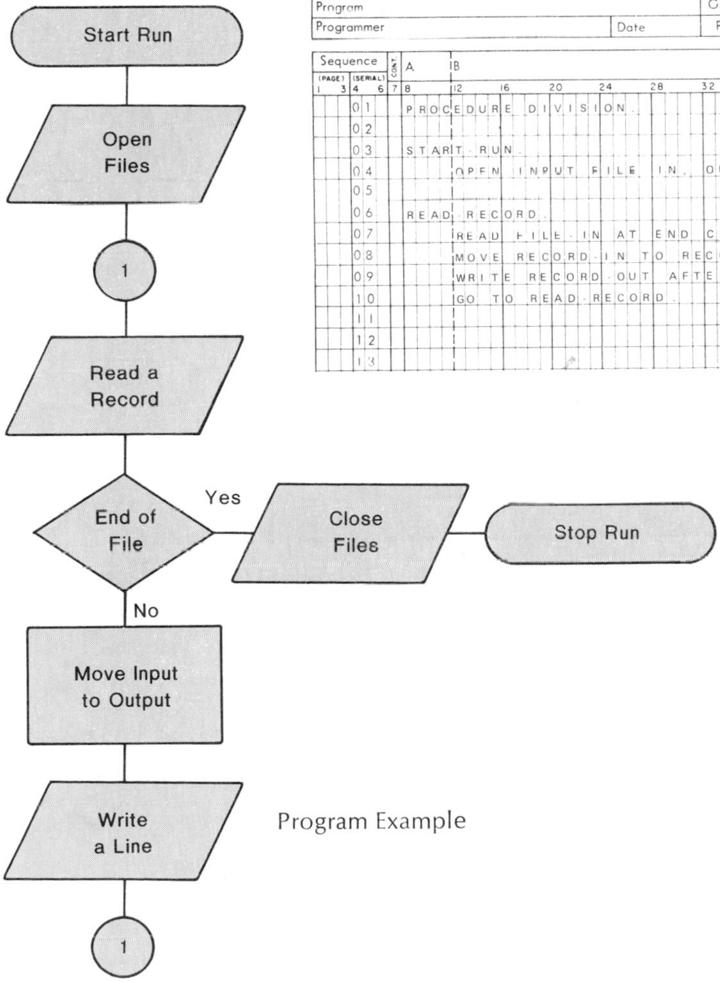

Program Example

Figure 8.2 Problem solving using a computer.

Figure 8.3 An example of a computer program.

```
                                    IDENTIFICATION DIVISION.
                                    PROGRAM-ID.
                                        ADDRESS-LISTING.
                                    ENVIRONMENT DIVISION.
                                    CONFIGURATION SECTION.
                                    SOURCE-COMPUTER.            IBM-370-I155
                                    OBJECT-COMPUTER.            IBM-370-I155.
                                    INPUT-OUTPUT SECTION.
                                    FILE-CONTROL.
Links file name to equipment            SELECT INPUT-FILE       ASSIGN TO UR-2540R-S-INFILE.
to be used for the file                 SELECT ADDRESS-FILE     ASSIGN TO UR-1403-S-OUTFILE.
                                    DATA DIVISION.
                                    FILE SECTION.
Specifies whether file contains     FD INPUT-FILE
records used to label the file          LABEL RECORDS ARE OMITTED.
                                    01  INPUT-RECORD.
                                        02 NAME.
                                          03  SUR               PICTURE X(12).
Defines an input area and                 03  GIVEN             PICTURE X(8).
associates it with a file name          02 HOME-ADDRESS         PICTURE X(40).
                                        02 FILLER               PICTURE X(20).
                                    FD ADDRESS-LIST
                                        LABEL RECORDS ARE OMITTED.
                                    01  OUTPUT-RECORD.
                                        02  LAST-NAME           PICTURE X(12).
                                        02  ADDRESS-O           PICTURE X(40).
                                    PROCEDURE DIVISION.
Prepares file for processing        MAIN-ROUTINE.
and specifies its use as input          OPEN  INPUT  INPUT-FILE
                                          OUTPUT ADDRESS-LIST.
Reads a record from the file            READ INPUT-FILE
into the input area associated            AT END MOVE 'NO' TO MORE-DATA-FLAG.
with the file in the File Section   PERFORM MAIN-SEQUENCE
                                        UNTIL NO-MORE-DATA.
Terminates processing                   CLOSE INPUT-FILE
of the file                               ADDRESS-LIST.
                                        STOP RUN.
                                    MAIN SEQUENCE.
                                        MOVE SUR TO LAST-NAME.
                                        MOVE HOME-ADDRESS TO ADDRESS-O,
                                        WRITE OUTPUT-RECORD.
                                        READ INPUT-FILE
Reads a record from the file              AT END MOVE 'NO' TO MORE-DATA-FLAG.
into the input area associated
with the file in the File Section
```

The repertory of instructions allows the programmer to specify all operations quickly and easily (fig. 8.4). Each instruction has a standard format and may range in complexity from a simple element operation code to an operation code with many elements. All instructions have an *operation code, which uniquely identifies the operation to be performed.* Some instructions may include variant characters which further define an operation or specify a piece of data to be used in the operation (fig. 8.5).

Some instructions call for information to be read into internal storage from an input device, such as a card reader, or to be written out on an output device, such as a printer. Other instructions perform arithmetic operations. Still other instructions move and rearrange data within a computer and make various decisions based on data

```
  SOURCE STATEMENT
PROB1     START 0                                                                        001
          PRINT NOGEN                 DON'T PRINT MACROS                                 002
BEGIN     SAVE (14,12)                SAVE CONTENTS OF REGS.14-16 & 0-12                 003
          BALR 3,0                    STORE BASE ADDRESS IN REG.3                        004
          USING *,3                   DEFINE BASE AS REG.3                               005
          ST   13,SAVE+4              STORE CONTENTS OF REG.13                           006
          LA   13,SAVE                LOAD ADDRESS OF 'SAVE' IN REG.13                   007
          OPEN  (RDR,INPUT,PRTR,OUTPUT)  OPEN FILES                                      008
*                                                                                        009
* PRINT   HEADING LINES                                                                  010
*                                                                                        011
START     XC   PRTOUT,PRTOUT          CLEAR PRINTOUT AREA                                016
          MVC  PRTOUT,TITLE           MOVE TITLE TO PRINTOUT AREA                        021
          CNTRL  PRTR,SK,1            SKIP TO NEXT PAGE OF PRINTOUT                      026
          BAL  10,WRITE               BRANCH TO WRITE-SUBROUTINE, RECORD AD-             031
*                                     DRESS OF NEXT INSTRUCTION IN REG.10                032
```

Figure 8.4 An example of instructions.

Operation	Operand
Select	Tape Unit 200
Read	One Record into Storage Positions 1000-1050
Clear & Add	Quantity in Storage Location 1004 in Accumulator
Subtract	Quantity in Storage Location 1005 from Contents of Accumulator
Store	Result in Storage Location 1051
Branch	To Instruction in Storage Location 5004

Figure 8.5 The standard format of an instruction.

or results of processing. Some instructions can specify the location of the next instruction and, in this way, may be used to alter the sequence in which any instruction or block of instructions are executed.

An important thing to realize is that the program of instructions must be prepared before the processing can be done, and the program must be in storage before it is executed. Since it is frequently necessary to repeat the execution of groups of instructions or to skip around in the program, there has to be a way to identify an instruction by where it is located in storage.

The instructions must be storable in the same location that is used for storing data. The instructions must be set up to handle data of a general type. If a condition occurs in a program that was not anticipated, the program will do what the instructions say to do even though the result may be meaningless. The fundamental thing to remember is that by the time the instructions are executed by the machine, the human factor is no longer part of the picture.

The instruction address is not part of the instruction; it merely tells where the instruction is located (or, rather where it will be located after the program is put into storage).

The only distinction between instructions and data is when they are brought into the central processing unit. A program may be stored in any location that does not conflict with the storage of data. Since the program is stored in the same manner as data, there must be no overlapping. If the information is brought in during an instruction cycle, it is interpreted as an instruction; at any other time, it is interpreted as data. The computer can operate upon its own instructions if the instructions are supplied as data. A storage location can store one character of an instruction or one character of data.

Methods of Processing Data

The two methods of processing data through a computer are sequential (batch) processing and random (inline) processing. The type of method used depends upon the application requirements.

Sequential (Batch) Processing

In sequential processing, data is recorded in files outside of the computer, on magnetic tape, for example, and is arranged in a predetermined sequence. Each record has to be examined for possible processing. Before the transaction record can be applied against the main or master file, it must be arranged in the same sequence as the master file. It is feasible, therefore, to accumulate these records in convenient groups or batches for subsequent processing.

Sequential processing is feasible in operations that have a high rate of activity—payroll, for instance, where a large percentage of the records are active each time the payroll is processed. Transactions are batched for processing at one time.

One of the principal disadvantages of sequential processing is the fact that each record has to be examined and processing cannot occur as the transaction appears. For economical operations, data is accumulated in batches for subsequent processing at one time. It does, however, have the advantage of rather fast processing time for reading and processing compared to random processing.

Random Processing (Inline)

In random processing, the data is usually stored in large-capacity storage units, such as magnetic disks, and is fed into the computer as the need for processing occurs. All records need not be examined, only those that need updating. Transactions are not batched and there is no need for sorting as in sequential processing. A low-activity operation such as inventory updating, in which a small percentage of the records are active at any one time, is a typical example of a random processing. Random processing does have the advantage of processing the transaction as the activity occurs without having to wait to batch the items.

Flowcharts

The increased use of data processing has focused attention upon the need for the logical representation of data flows. Once the problem has been defined and the objectives established, the next step is the orderly presentation of procedures so that the objectives can be realized sequentially (fig. 8.6). Any successful program depends upon well-defined steps prior to the actual program. The steps involve the processes to be performed and the sequence of these processes. The processes must be precisely stated before any programming can begin.

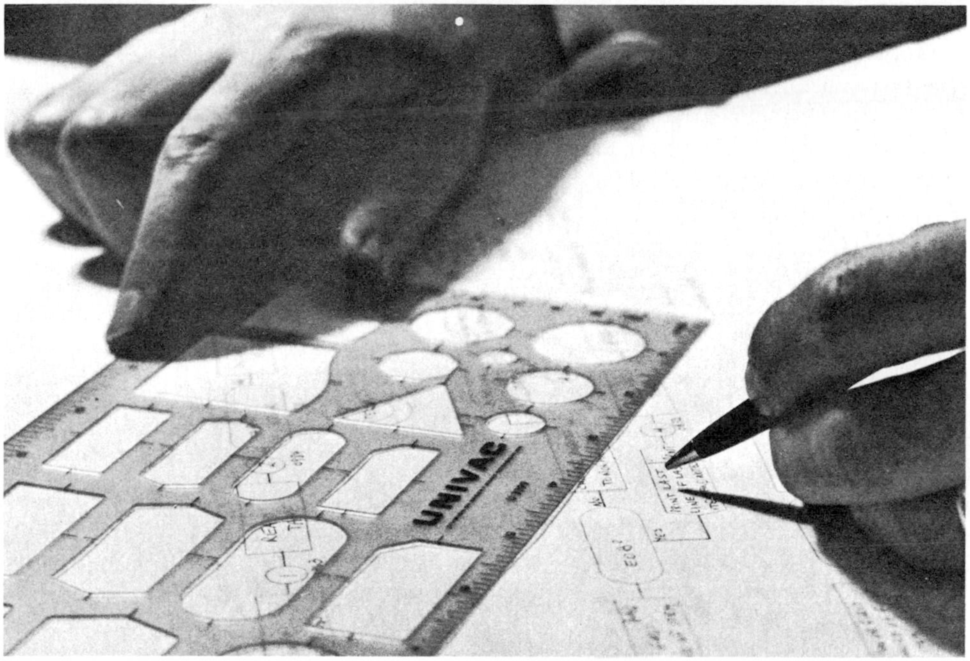

Figure 8.6 Flowcharting.

The programmer must know all the different operations to be performed. A complete analysis of the procedures, both existing and proposed, must be made to ascertain the ultimate goals to be accomplished. Many times, data-processing applications fail or fall short of expectations due to inadequate planning or analysis.

The analysis is normally accomplished by developing flowcharts. *The flowchart is a graphic representation of the flow of information through a system in the course of which the information is converted from the source document to the final reports.* Because most data-processing applications involve a large number of alternatives, variations, decisions, and exceptions, it would be impractical to state these possibilities verbally. The value of a flowchart is that it can show graphically, at a glance, the organized procedures and data flows so their apparent interrelationships can be readily understood. Such relationships would be difficult to abstract from a detailed narrative text. Meaningful symbols are used in place of narrative statements. The flowchart is the "roadmap" by which the data travels through the entire system.

Flowcharting systematizes the thinking of the systems analyst and clarifies intricate procedures for the programmer. When properly prepared by a systems analyst or programmer, a flowchart opens the way to communication among the individuals who work on or are affected by the data-processing system. For this reason, standardization of flowcharts are a necessity. Often the coding and flowcharting functions are done by different programmers or the entire program-writing assignment is transferred from one programmer to another. If flowcharts have been properly prepared, communication will be accurate and smooth. The drawing of the flowchart is often more difficult than the translation of the flowchart into computer instructions.

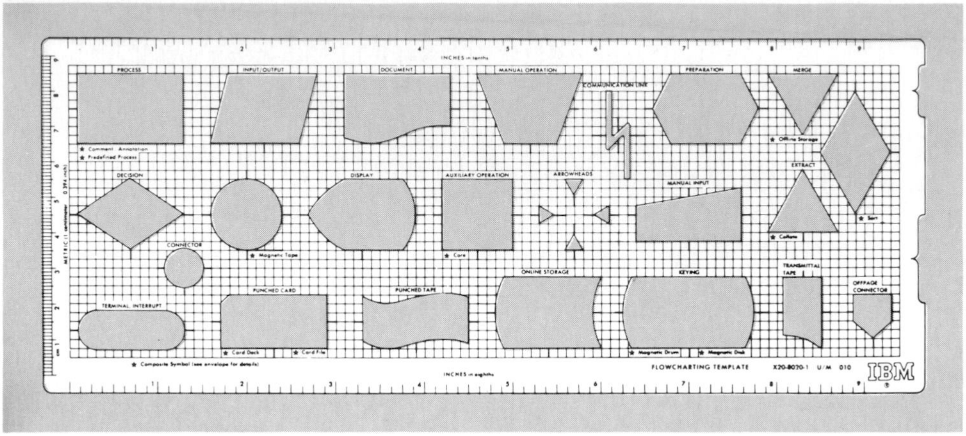

Figure 8.7 A flowchart template.

While flowcharts are widely used in the field of data processing, they have occasionally been misinterpreted, due primarily to the lack of uniformity in the meanings assigned to and the use of the symbols. As a result, a uniform set of flowcharting symbols was prepared by a subcommittee of the United States of America Standards Institute (fig. 8.7).

There are two types of flowcharts widely used in data-processing operations—a system flowchart and a program flowchart.

System Flowcharts

Before the system of programs is flowcharted, a systems analyst researches the problem, analyzes and summarizes existing methods of doing the job, and proposes a computer solution. The systems analyst determines the input and output requirements, surveys the existing computer system, determines the necessary programs and hardware to perform the overall job, and usually prepares the system flowcharts.

The system flowchart is a diagram that illustrates the flow of data into, through, and out of a system of programs. This flowchart establishes relationships between system inputs and outputs by means of intermediate files and establishes relationships concerning individual programs that compose the system.

A system flowchart is normally used to illustrate the overall objectives for the benefit of data-processing as well as non-data-processing personnel. The flowchart provides a picture indicating what is to be accomplished. Emphasis is on the documents and the work stations they must pass through. The flowchart also provides an application where source media is converted to a final report or stored in files. A brief mention is made of the actual operations to be performed.

Many symbols depicting documents and operations are used throughout the system flowchart. The symbols are designed so they are meaningful without further comment or text. Card symbols are used to indicate when the input or output may be a card. Document symbols are used to represent the prepared reports. The system flowchart is usually prepared on one sheet of paper, facilitating the presentation of the overall picture of the system to administrative personnel and executives (fig. 8.8).

A system flowchart indicates the job to be done without detailing the steps involved (figs. 8.9, 8.10).

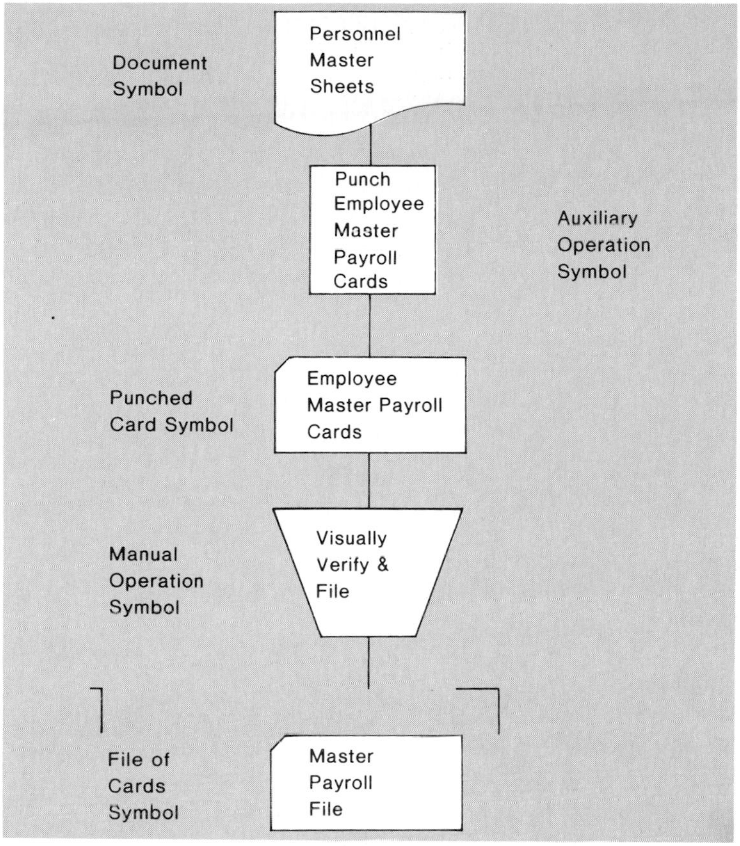

Figure 8.8 An example of system flowchart symbols.

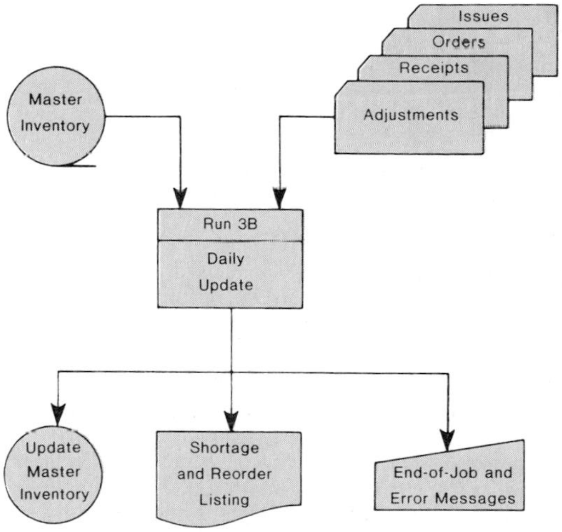

Figure 8.9 An example of a system flowchart.

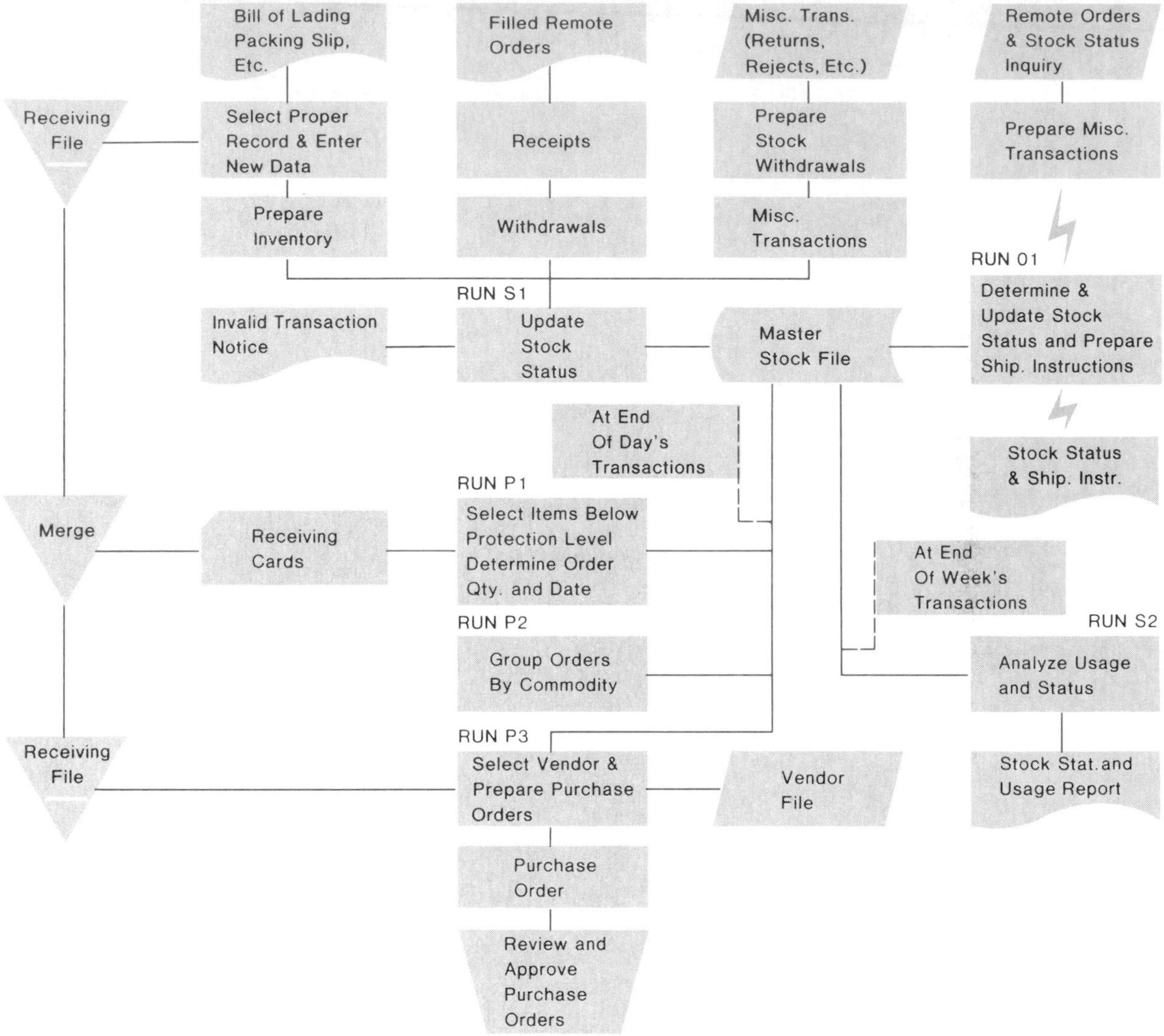

A typical system-flowchart description of an inventory-control application, this chart uses specific symbols for certain processing functions and input/output. The application involves a multiple-warehouse system: items are stocked in a central warehouse for distribution to remote warehouses; all customer orders are received by remotely-located warehouses and transmitted by teletype (communication-link symbol) to the central data-processing installation. The system provides four major groups of operations:

(1) updating stock status [run S1], based on actual transactions; (2) response to inquiries [run 01] from auxiliary warehouses and central warehouse; (3) reorder analysis [runs P1, P2, P3], including purchase-order preparation; (4) weekly analysis reports [run S2] to show slow-moving items, major changes in usage rates, behind-schedule deliveries, economic lot sizes, etc.

Figure 8.10 A system flowchart for an inventory control system. (Courtesy of IBM)

The following is a brief description of some of the most frequently used system flowchart symbols.

The process symbol represents any kind of processing function.

The punched-card symbol represents an input/output function in which the medium is punched cards, including mark-sense cards, partial cards, stub cards, and so forth.

The online storage symbol represents an input/output function utilizing any type of online storage, such as magnetic tape, magnetic drum, or magnetic disk.

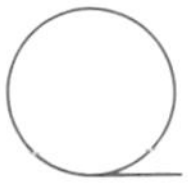

The magnetic tape symbol represents an input/output function in which the medium is magnetic tape.

The punched tape symbol represents an input/output function in which the medium is punched tape.

The magnetic drum symbol represents an input/output function in which the medium is magnetic drum.

The magnetic disk symbol represents an input/output function in which the medium is magnetic disk.

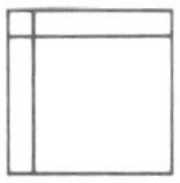

The core symbol represents an input/output function in which the medium is magnetic core.

The document symbol represents an input/output function in which the medium is a document.

The manual input symbol represents an input function in which the information is entered manually at the time of processing by means of online keyboards, switch settings, push buttons, and so forth.

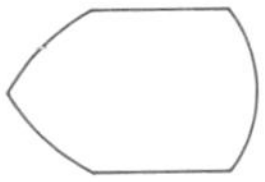

The display symbol represents an input/output function in which the information is displayed for human use at the time of processing by means of online indicators, video devices, console printers, plotters, and so forth.

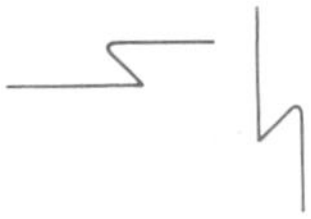

The communications link symbol represents a function in which information is transmitted by a telecommunications link.

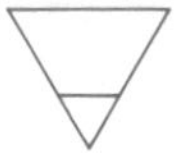

The offline storage symbol represents the function of storing information offline, regardless of the medium on which the information is recorded.

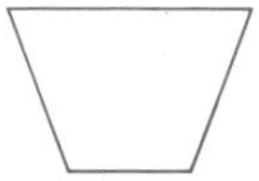

The manual operation symbol represents any offline process geared to the speed of a human being, without using mechanical aid.

The auxiliary operation symbol represents an offline operation performed on equipment not under direct control of the central processing unit.

Program Flowcharts

A program flowchart is a graphic representation of the procedures by which data is to be processed. The chart provides a picture of the problem solution, the program solution, the program logic used for coding, and the processing sequences. Specifically, it is a diagram of the operations and decisions to be made and the sequence in which they are to be performed by the machine. The major functions and sequences are shown and if any detail is required, a *block diagram* is prepared (fig. 8.11).

The program flowchart shows the relationship of one part of the program to another. The flowchart can be used to experiment or verify the accuracy of different approaches to coding the application. Where large segments of the program are indicated, a single processing symbol may be used and the detail for the segment shown on a separate block diagram which would be used for the machine coding. Once the flowchart has been proven sound and the procedures developed, it may be used for coding the program.

Figure 8.11 A program flowchart with a block diagram.

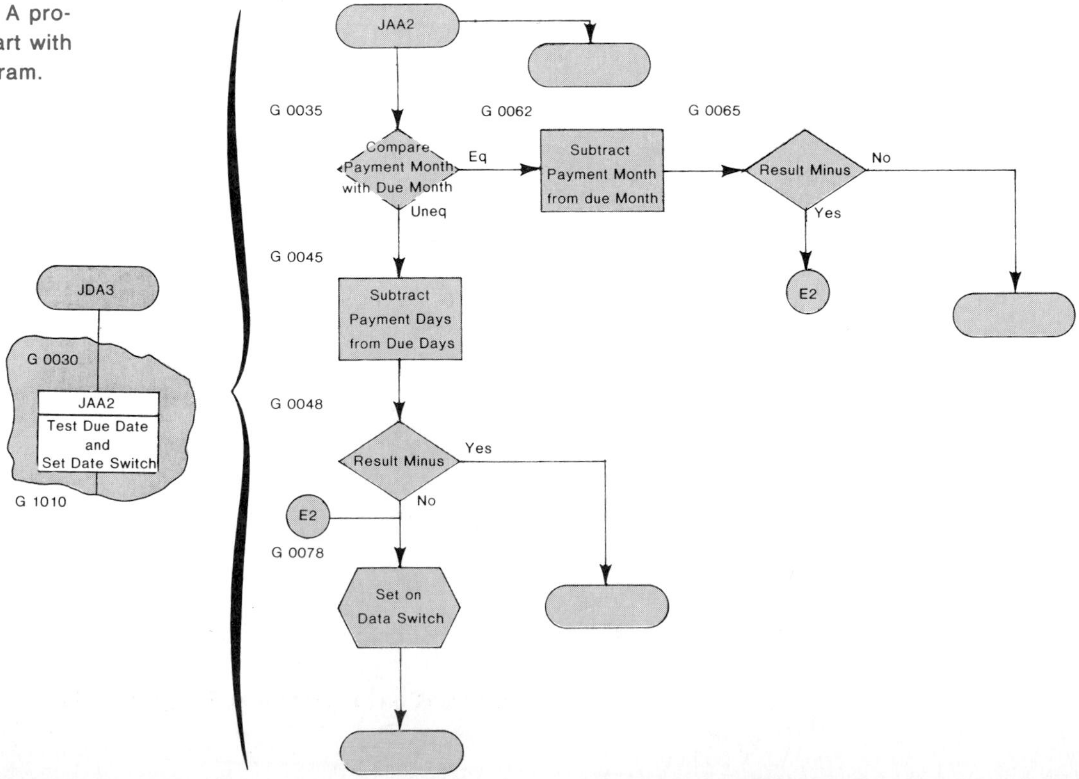

The Comparison Process

Suppose, as you walk to your car, you take a bunch of keys out of your pocket. There are three keys on the key ring—your house key, garage key, and car key. The keys are indistinguishable except for size. You know that your car key is the smallest. However, rather than try each key in the lock, you decide to compare them.

Naturally, the decision to compare the keys and the actual comparison process can be done at a glance. However, if it is put in slow motion, the comparison process actually involves comparing two things at a time, eliminating one, and comparing the remaining two.

Suppose the three keys are labeled A, B, and C. You compare key A and key B, choose the smaller, and compare it with key C. The smaller of these two is your car key.

Since the computer cannot look at the keys, it will have to work with information about the keys. For the purposes of comparison, key sizes will be used.

Three numbers, representing the three key sizes, are the information that the computing system operates on. These numbers can also be called A, B, and C to correspond to the keys. It is the computer's task to compare the numbers, choose the smallest, and print out the correct letter—A, B, or C.

Let's assume that this information—the data about the key sizes and the instructions telling the system what to do—is already contained within the main processing unit of the computer.

The symbol indicating that the operation begins here is shown in figure 8.12.

The computer operates by comparing two numbers at a time, symbolized by a diamond with two exit points (fig. 8.13).

If A is larger than B, the process continues from the exit point where the "greater than" sign (>) is indicated. If A is smaller than B, the process follows the path from the "less than" sign (<).

The next symbol, a rectangle, is used to indicate an addition, subtraction, or other arithmetic operation (absent in this problem) or a transfer of information to some other area in the computer (fig. 8.14).

Figure 8.12 A start symbol indicates the beginning of an operation.

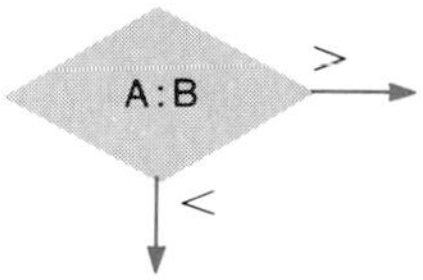

Figure 8.13 The symbol for comparing.

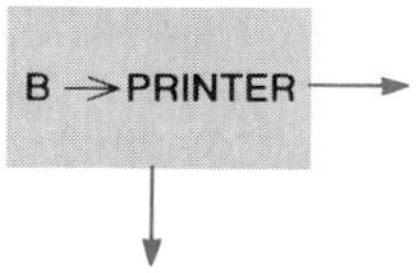

Figure 8.14 The symbol that indicates arithmetic operations or transfers of information.

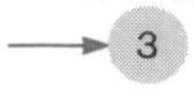

Figure 8.15 A connector symbol.

Figure 8.16 The stop symbol indicates the end of an operation.

At this point in the process, it is likely that two different comparisons will lead to a single common path. A small circle containing a number, called a connector, indicates entrance into a common operation (fig. 8.15).

When processing is completed, the end of the operation is indicated by the symbol shown in figure 8.16.

The reasoning of the problem, indicating four possibilities, is as follows:

1. If A is smaller than B, and A is smaller than C, then A is smallest.
2. If A is smaller than B, and C is smaller than A, then C is smallest.
3. If B is smaller than A, and C is smaller than B, then C is smallest.
4. If B is smaller than A, and B is smaller than C, then B is smallest.

A Word Flowchart

When the comparisons are represented in flowchart form, using the symbols shown in figures 8.12 through 8.16, the line of reasoning and the four possible paths to solution become clearer. The word picture in figure 8.17 shows the stages of the whole comparison process joined in logical sequence. If the computer could think through the process as a human being can, it might ask the questions illustrated in figure 8.17.

A Symbolic Flowchart

A word picture is a realistic description of the problem. However, a large flowchart would become cluttered with too many words. Therefore, symbols are substituted. The same operations are shown in figure 8.18.

Once the instructions for solving a certain problem are worked out, they can be recorded on tape or punched cards and used again and again, whenever the need arises. These "canned problems" enable computer users to take advantage of programming work that has already been done on problems that may be similar throughout an industry, or throughout business generally.

Now let's see how an ordinary business problem might be programmed and charted. A simplified payroll operation, for example, might be stated like this:

(Hours worked × pay rate per hour) + (overtime pay rate × overtime hours worked) − deductions = total pay.

You might chart the problem as shown in figure 8.19.

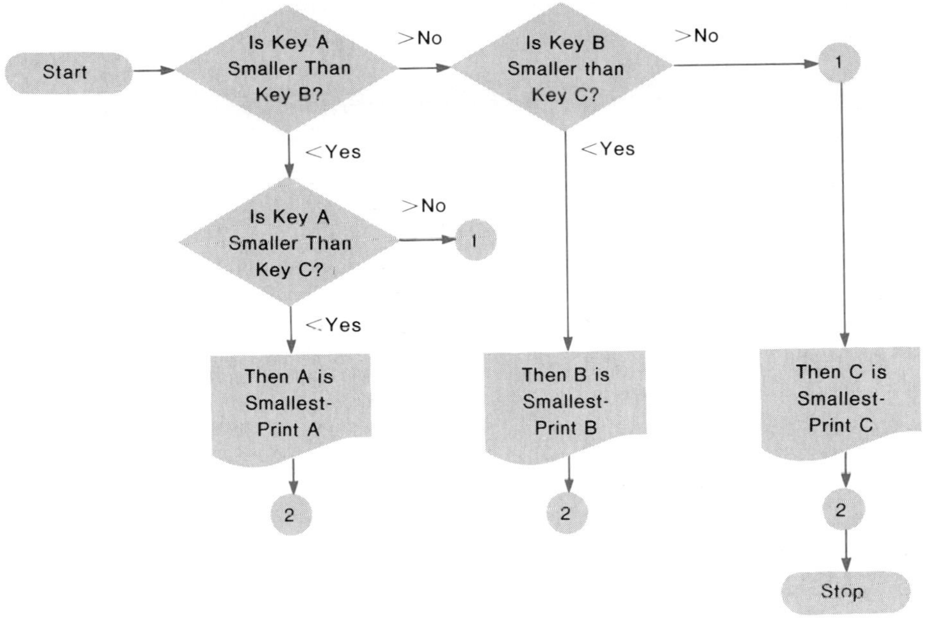

Figure 8.17 An example of a word flowchart.

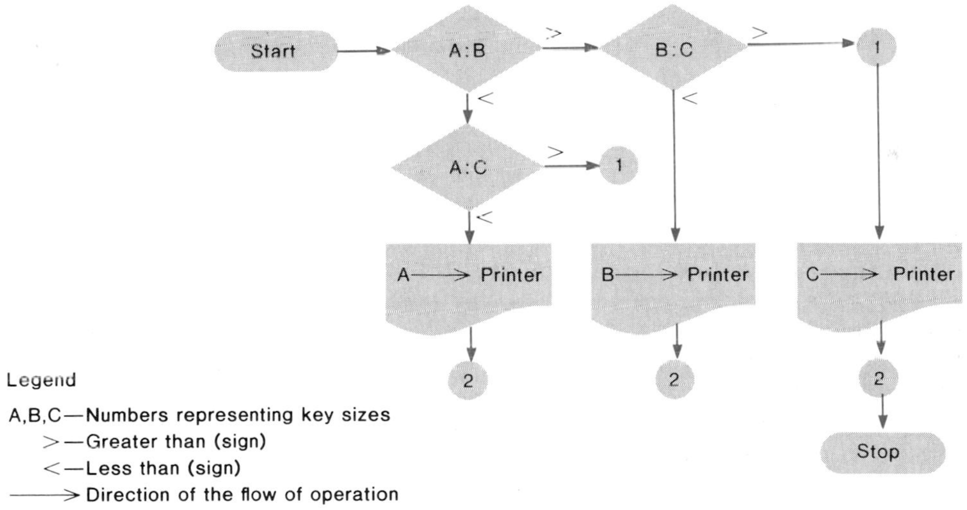

Figure 8.18 An example of a symbolic flowchart.

Once you've programmed this into the computer with all the appropriate names and figures, the computer will figure out your payroll month after month for as long as your company's money holds out.

A program flowchart (figs. 8.20, 8.21, 8.22) should provide:

Figure 8.19 A flowchart for a payroll operation.

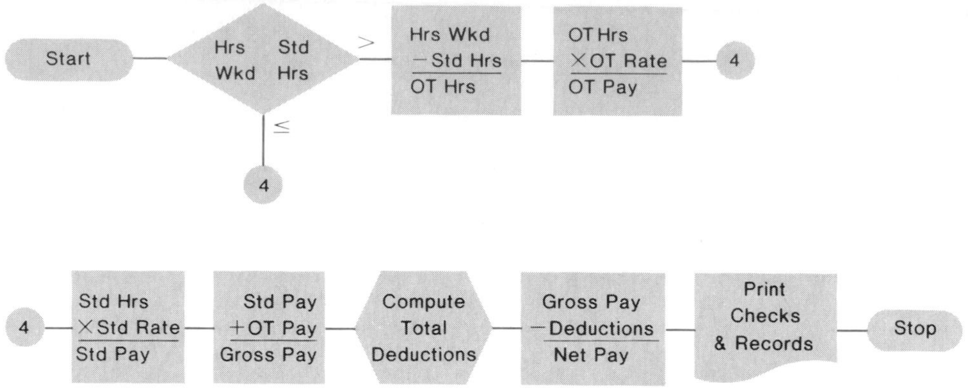

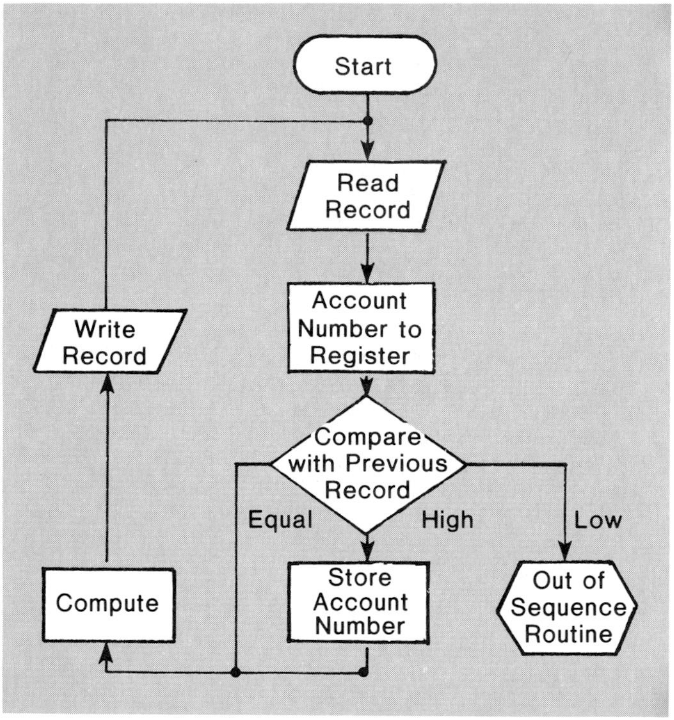

Figure 8.20 Sequence checking in a program flowchart.

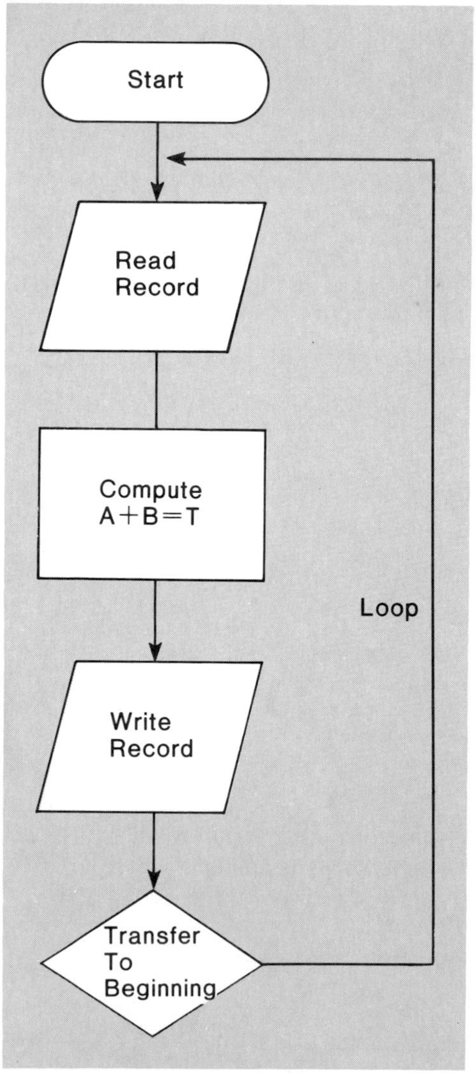

Figure 8.21 An example of a loop in a program flowchart.

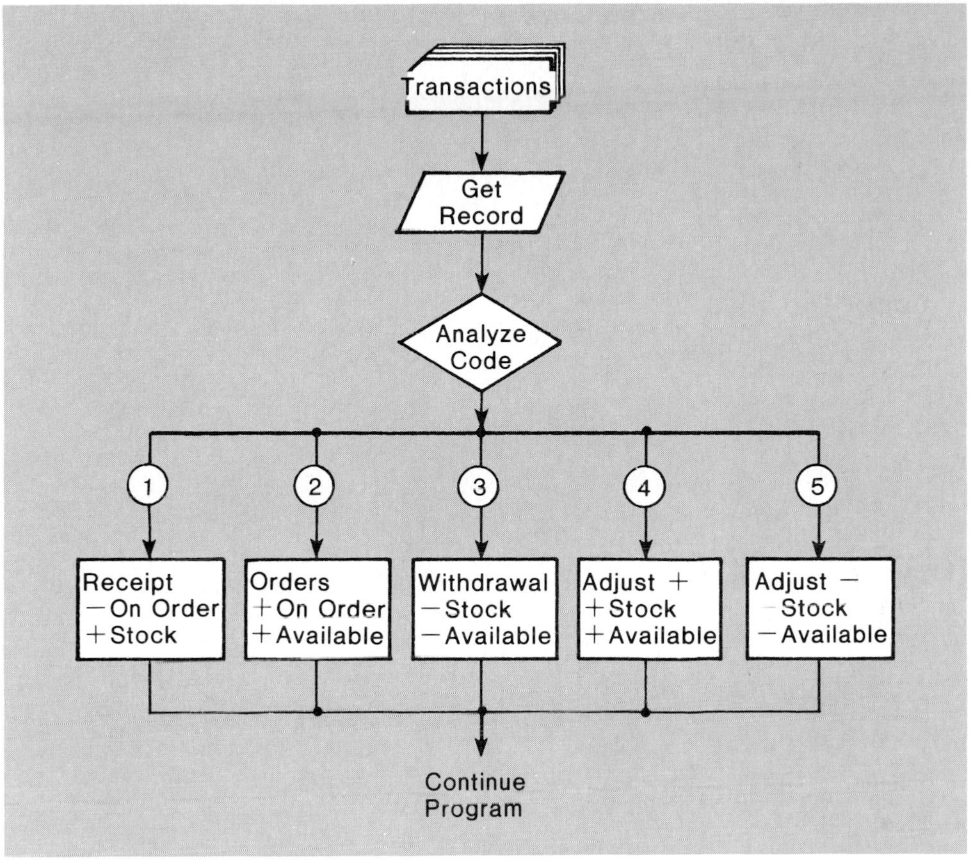

Figure 8.22 An example of branching in a program flowchart.

1. A pictorial diagram of the problem solution to act as a map of the program.
2. A symbolic representation of the program logic used for coding, desk checking, and debugging while testing all aspects of the program.
3. Verification that all possible conditions have been considered and have been taken care of (figs. 8.23, 8.24).
4. Documentation of the program, necessary to give an unquestionable historical reference record.
5. Aid in the development of programming and coding.

These are the important features and phases of program flowcharting:

1. It provides the programmer with a means of visualizing the entire program during its development. The sequence, the arithmetic and logical operations, the inputs and outputs of the system, and the relationship of one part of the program to another are indicated.
2. The system flowchart provides the various inputs and outputs, the general objective of the program, and the general nature of the operation. A program flowchart, however, will be prepared for each run and will serve as a means of experimenting with the program specifically, in order to achieve the most efficient program.

Figure 8.23 Examples of decision techniques.

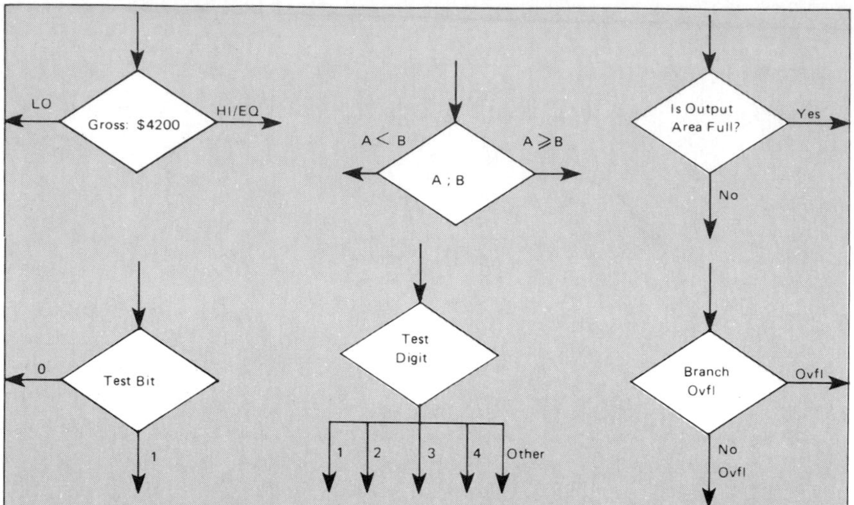

English Statement	Shorthand Statement
Compare A with B (where B is the common factor or constant value)	A:B
A is greater than B	A>B
A is less than B	A<B
A is equal to B	A=B
A is not greater than B (A is less than or equal to B)	A≤B
A is not less than B (A is greater than or equal to B)	A≥B
A is not equal to B	A≠B
Compare indicator settings	HI LO EQ
Check indicator settings	ON OFF

Figure 8.24 An example of a logical decision in a program flowchart.

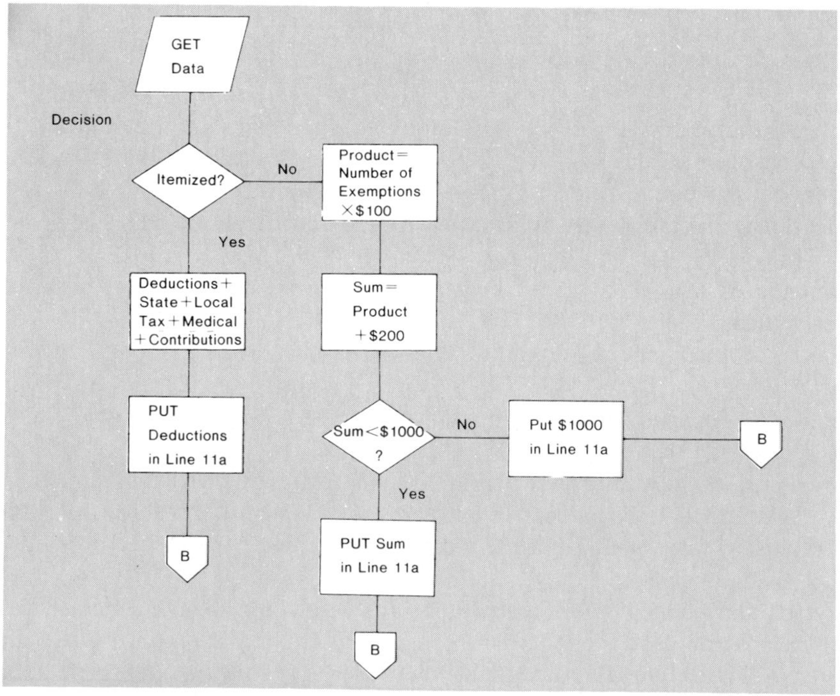

3. Starting with the symbol representing the major functions, the programmer must develop the overall logic by depicting blocks for input and output, identification, decisions, etc.
4. After the overall logic has been developed by the programmer, the programmer will extract the larger segments of the program and break them down into smaller detailed block diagrams.
5. After the flowchart has been proven sound, the coding for the program will commence.
6. Upon completion of the coding, the program will be documented for further modification that will always occur after the testing, installation, and operational stages.
7. Final documentation should encompass the overall main logic, the system flowcharts, and the program flowcharts right down to the detailed block diagrams. The general system flowcharts help in the understanding of the more detailed program flowcharts.

The use of standard techniques for the preparation of flowcharts for data-processing systems will greatly enhance the effectiveness of the programmer's conversion of the problem into a meaningful program. It will reduce the time necessary to program the application and, if properly done, will provide a proper communication between the analyst and the various groups.

Flowcharts are used extensively in the field and are the fundamental basis for all operations in data processing. A clear understanding of flowcharting techniques is a must for everyone who becomes involved with data processing at any level.

The following is a brief description of some of the most often used program flowchart symbols.

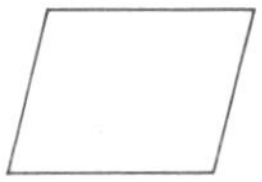

The input/output symbol represents an input/output (I/O) function; that is, the making available of information for processing (input) or the recording of processed information (output).

The process symbol represents any kind of processing function; for example, the process of executing a defined operation or group of operations results in a change in value, form, or location of information or determines which of several flow directions are to be followed.

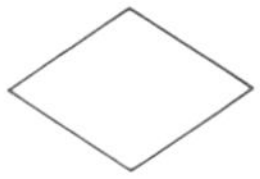

The decision symbol represents a decision or switching-type operation that determines which of a number of alternative paths should be followed.

The predefined process symbol represents a named procedure consisting of one or more operations, or program steps, that are specified elsewhere, such as a subroutine or logical unit. Elsewhere means not this set of flowcharts.

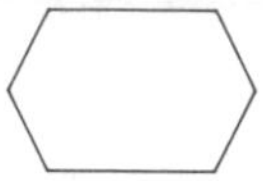

The preparation symbol represents modification of an instruction or group of instructions which change the program itself, such as set a switch, modify an index register, and initialize a routine.

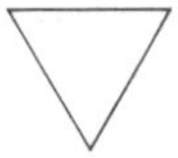

The merge symbol represents the combining of two or more sets of items into one set.

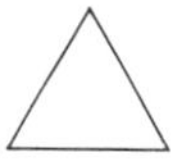

The extract symbol represents the removal of one or more specific sets of items from a single set of items.

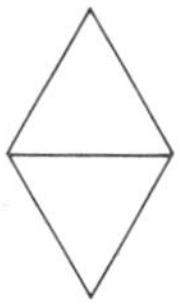

The sort symbol represents the arranging of a set of items into a particular sequence.

The collate symbol represents merging with extracting; that is, the formation of two or more sets of items from two or more other sets.

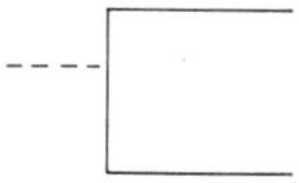

The comment, annotation symbol represents the annotation function; that is, the addition of descriptive comments or explanatory notes as clarification. The broken line is connected to any symbol at a point where the annotation is meaningful by extending the broken line in whatever fashion is appropriate.

The connector symbol represents an exit to or an entry from another part of the flowchart. It is a junction in a line of flow. A set of two connectors is used to represent a continued flow direction when the flow is broken by any limitation of the flowchart. A set of two or more connectors is used to represent the junction of several flowlines, or the junction of one flowline with one of several alternate flowlines.

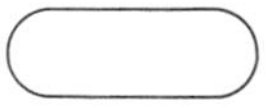

The terminal, interrupt symbol represents a terminal point in a flowchart; for example, start, stop, halt, delay, or interrupt.

Decision Tables

Another technique for presenting the conditions of a problem and the choices of action available is the *decision table.* Though not as widely used throughout the data-processing industry as the flowchart, many programmers feel that decision tables are easier to understand and follow. Decision tables show conditions and actions in a more orderly manner than flowcharts and facilitate complete development during the problem specification and programming phases of data processing. In a system of runs, both decision tables and flowcharts may be used. The mode of programming is the programmers' option. The decision table is very useful in reducing the problem state-

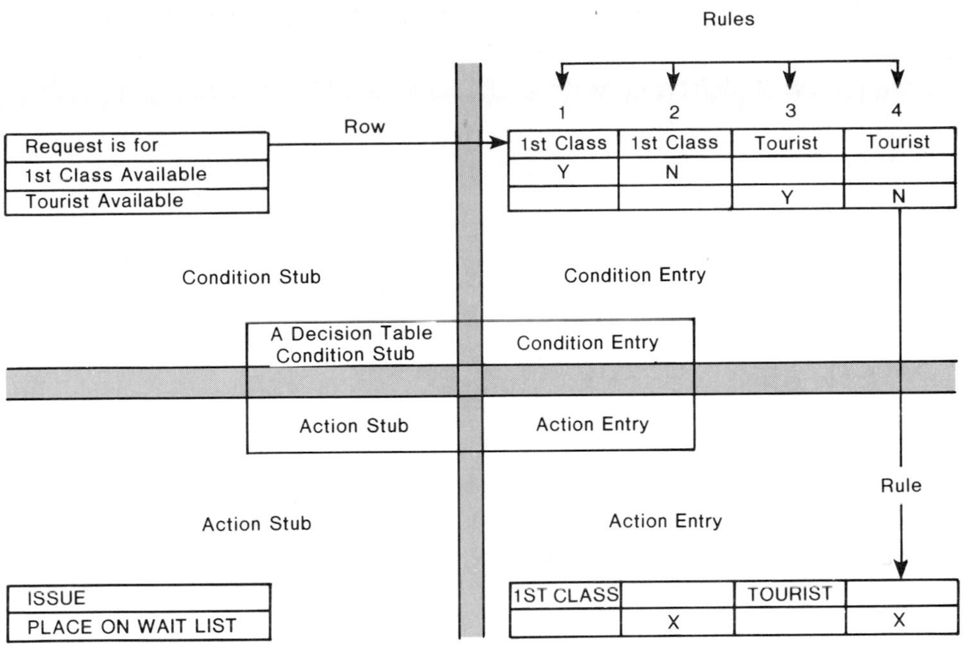

Rule No.	1	2	3	4
Request is 1st Class	Y	Y		
Request is Tourist			Y	Y
1st Class Available	Y	N		
Tourist Available			Y	N
Issue 1st Class	X			
Issue Tourist			X	
Place on Wait List		X		X

Figure 8.25 An airline reservation decision table.

ment to a table of condition/action statements. In addition, it will clarify the relationships between the various operations to be performed and the decisions to be made, which are expressed as condition/action statements in the table (fig. 8.25).

A decision table is a tool of convenience for the programmer and should be used as a supplement to the program flowchart. The complexity of the problem determines the extent to which the table is necessary. There are many times when the problem statement is so concise that the construction of a decision table would be time-consuming and of little value. However, when the problem statement requires close discriminations involving many complex logic decisions, the decision table provides a form for recording them (fig. 8.26). A programmer should know the elements of a decision table.

Decision tables are divided into four sections. Each section is marked off by a set of double vertical and horizontal lines.

1. The first section contains the *conditions* listed in the problem statement.
2. A second section contains the *actions* listed in the problem statement.
3. A third section contains a pattern of *yes* (Y) and *no* (N) answers to the *conditions*.

Figure 8.26 An example of a decision table.

PROBLEM STATEMENT:

If customer's credit is OK, and quantity ordered is equal to or less than order limit, and quantity ordered is equal to or less than quantity on hand, ship item. If customer's credit is not OK, or quantity ordered is greater than order limit, reject order. If quantity ordered is greater than quantity on hand, back order.

Decision Table

Customer's credit is OK	Y	N		
Quantity ordered is less than or equal to order limit	Y		N	
Quantity ordered is less than or equal to quantity on hand	Y			N
Ship item	X			
Reject order		X	X	
Back order				X

If . . . (Condition Statement)	**Condition Stub**	**Condition Entry**
Then . . . (Action Statement)	**Action Stub**	**Action Entry**

4. The fourth section indicates by an "X" what action should be taken based on the answers found in the third section. Each "X" indicates that a *decision* should be made to take the *action* listed in the same row in the second section (fig. 8.27).

Every possible combination of yes and no answers does not have to be shown. A decision table will only contain the basic pattern of answers necessary to determine which action is to be taken.

A decision table shows the major aspects of a problem and the major decisions and processing routines that must be established so that the data can be processed. As such, the decision table is oriented toward the problem.

Before a computer program can be written, the processing steps to be taken by the computer must be described in greater detail. This can be done by a succession of decision tables each showing more detail of a particular routine. To plan a computer program, the *program flowchart* is constructed like a decision table. The program flowchart is a way to represent visually a logical sequence of procedure steps which a computer must take in processing data. As such, the program flowchart is oriented toward the computer.

1. Decision tables are divided into FOUR sections.

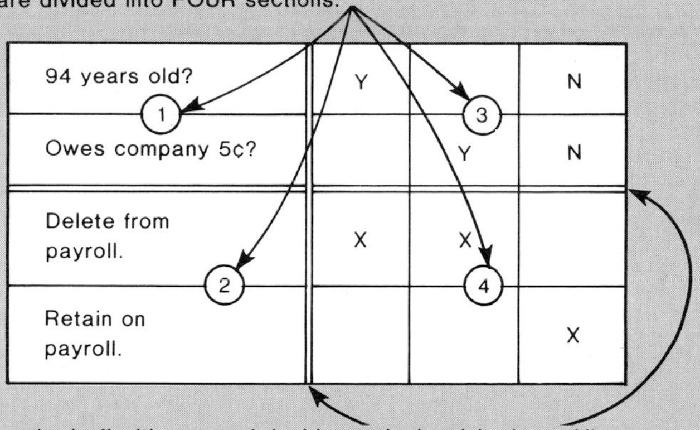

2. Each section is marked off with a set of double *vertical* and *horizontal* lines.
3. The section labeled (1) contains the *conditions* listed in the problem statement.
4. The section labeled (2) contains the *actions* listed in the problem statement.
5. The section labeled (3) contains a pattern of *yes* (Y) and *no* (N) answers to the *conditions.*
6. The section labeled (4) indicates by an "X" what action should be taken based on the answers found in section (3) Each X indicates that a *decision* should be made to take the *action* listed on the same row in section (2)

Figure 8.27 Decision table sections.

Programming

The success of a computer program depends upon the ability of the programmer to (1) analyze a problem, (2) prepare a program to solve a particular problem (fig. 8.28), and (3) operate the program (fig. 8.29).

Analysis

A problem must be thoroughly analyzed before any attempt is made at a solution. This requires that boundary conditions be established so the solution does not exceed the objectives of management or become too narrow to encompass all the necessary procedures. Output needs should be clearly stated and the essential input to produce the desired results should be carefully studied. If necessary, the source documents (input) should be revised so they can be more readily converted into machine language for data-processing operations. The relationship between the inputs and outputs must be clearly shown. The flowcharts will show the orderly logical steps that are necessary to arrive at the computer solution to the problem.

Preparation

After a careful analysis of the problem and flowcharting, the computer program should be written. Instructions are coded in the particular computer language using the program flowchart as a guide. The sequence of instructions will determine the computer program.

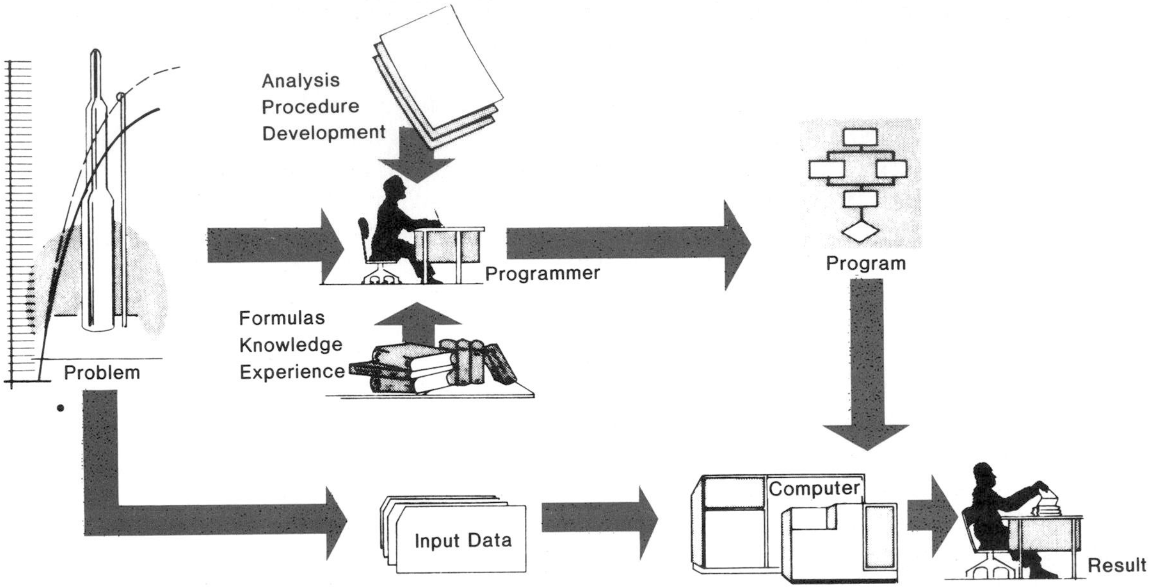

Figure 8.28 The direct conversion of a problem to a computer program.

Figure 8.29 The steps in problem solving.

Step	General Terms	Programming Terms
1	Defining the problem	Preparing job specifications
2	Planning the problem solution	Flowcharting (the program)
3	Describing the problem solution	Coding (the program)
4	Executing the problem solution	Program 'Translation' Program Testing Production Run
5	Documenting the problem solution	Documentation

Operation

The next step is usually to place the program and data into the storage unit of the computer. The program must be prepared on punched cards or other media for entry into the machine. The data must also be made available to the computer through some input unit. The program must be thoroughly checked with the test data and all necessary "debugging" accomplished before the program is ready for operation on actual data.

The following items should be checked to insure that the proper analysis and coding was made and that the computer will operate properly.

1. *Precise statement of the problem.* The statement must be exact, specifying what the program is to accomplish.
2. *List of inputs.* All sample copies of inputs to be used, together with the size of the fields, the type (alphabetic or numeric), and control fields, should be included.
3. *Outputs desired.* Samples of all outputs should be included with all headings indicated. The number of copies desired, type and size of paper to be used, tape density (if used) are some of the items of information to be included in this section.
4. *Flowcharts.* Include all necessary system flowcharts, program flowcharts, and block diagrams.
5. *Decision tables.* These tables will show relationships of conditions and actions pertaining to a particular problem.
6. *Program.* A printed copy of the computer program should be included with all necessary comments.
7. *Test data.* Include sample data to be used to test programs.
8. *Job control cards.* All job control cards necessary to load the program and the data into the computer should be included.
9. *Test results.* Include output listings and/or cards used to test the accuracy of the program.

Planning a Program

A computer program is the outcome of a programmer's applied knowledge of the problem and the operation of a particular computer. Problem definition, analysis, documentation, and flowcharting are just the initial steps in the preparation of a program. The following must be considered even in the simplest of programs (fig. 8.30).

1. The allocation of storage locations for the storing of data, instructions, work areas, constants, etc.
2. The necessary input procedures to convert the source data into machine-processible media.
3. The various reference tables and files that are essential to the program.
4. The checking of the accuracy of the data and the calculations.
5. The ability to restart the system in case of unscheduled interruptions, machine failures, or error conditions.
6. The necessary housekeeping procedures to clear storage areas, registers, and indicators prior to the execution of the program.
7. A thorough knowledge of the arithmetic and logical procedures to be used in the program.
8. The output formats of cards, printed reports, displayed reports, magnetic tapes, etc.
9. The subroutines available from other procedures to be used in the program.

Figure 8.30 The documentation of a program.

STEP 1. Preparation of Job Specifications consisting of:

A. Job Description
   1. Job title
   2. Summary of what is to be accomplished in run
   3. System flowchart for the run

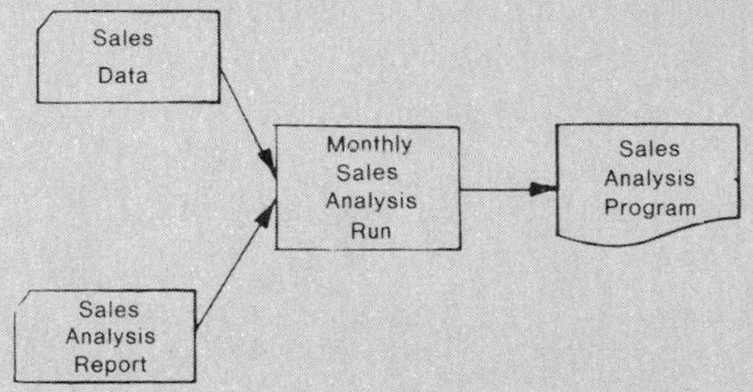

B. Input Files Description
C. Processing Requirements
D. Output Files Description

STEP 2. Flowcharting the Problem

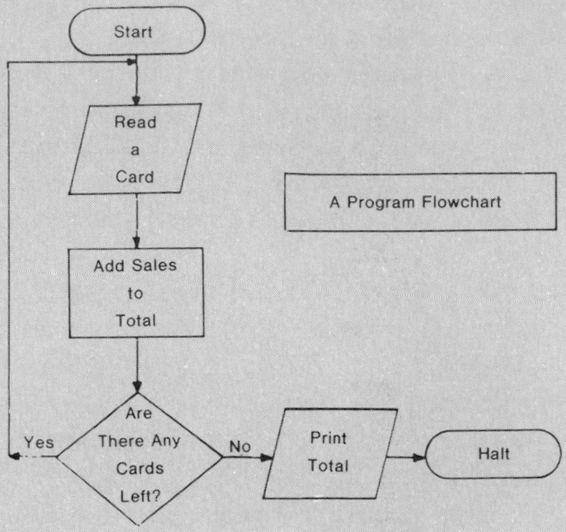

STEP 3.

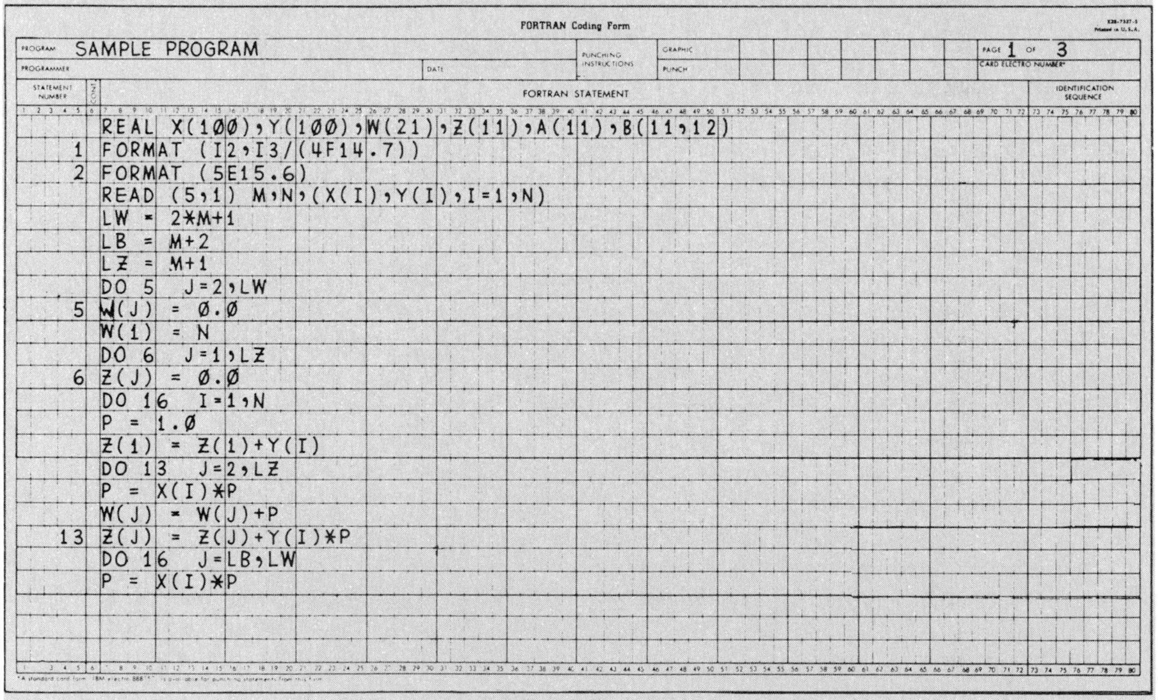


```
      REAL X(1ØØ),Y(1ØØ),W(21),Z(11),A(11),B(11,12)
    1 FORMAT (I2,I3/(4F14.7))
    2 FORMAT (5E15.6)
      READ (5,1) M,N,(X(I),Y(I),I=1,N)
      LW = 2*M+1
      LB = M+2
      LZ = M+1
      DO 5  J=2,LW
    5 W(J) = Ø.Ø
      W(1) = N
      DO 6  J=1,LZ
    6 Z(J) = Ø.Ø
      DO 16  I=1,N
      P = 1.Ø
      Z(1) = Z(1)+Y(I)
      DO 13  J=2,LZ
      P = X(I)*P
      W(J) = W(J)+P
   13 Z(J) = Z(J)+Y(I)*P
      DO 16  J=LB,LW
      P = X(I)*P
```

Programming Form

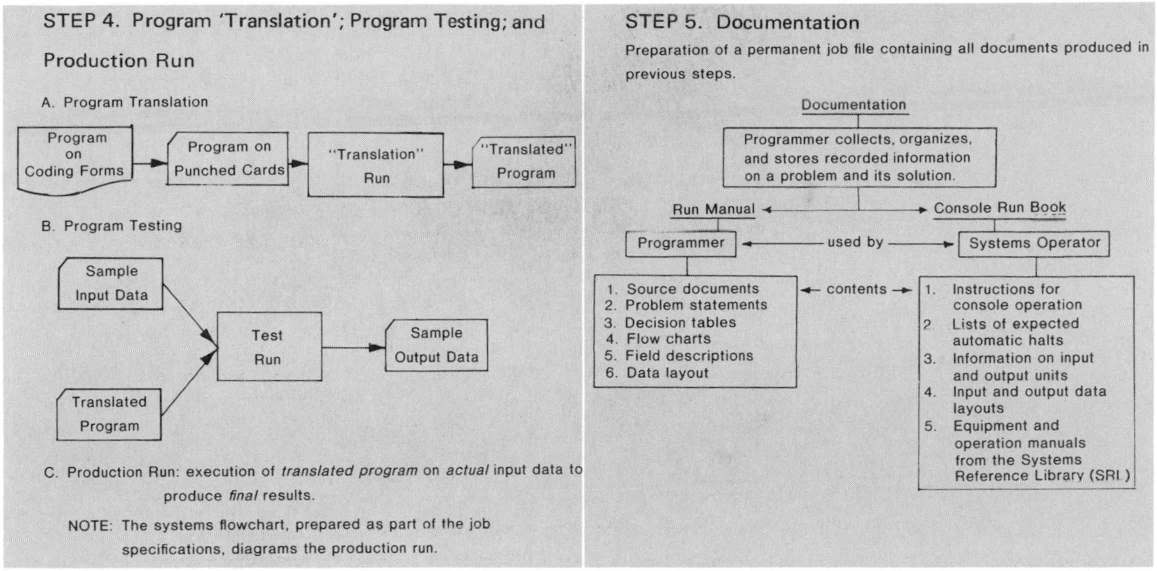

Figure 8.30 Continued.

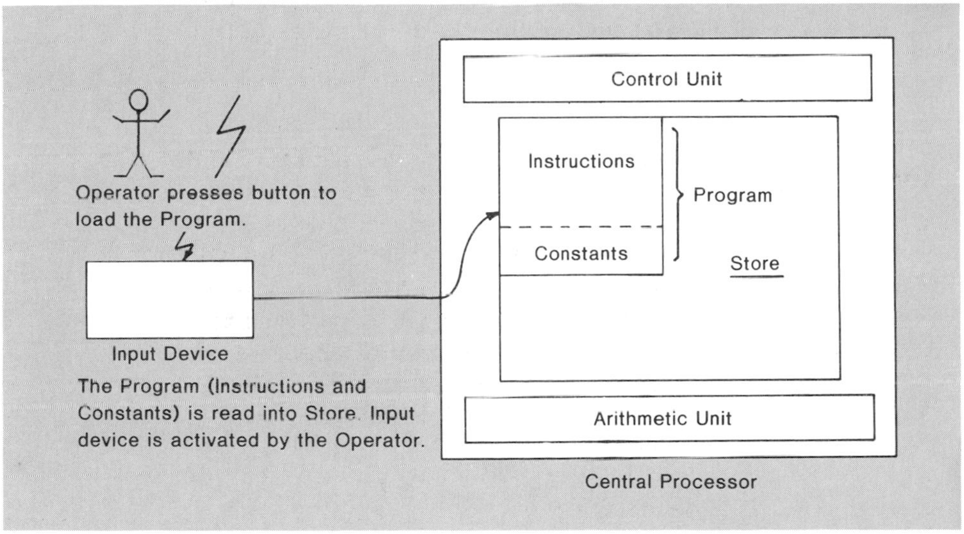

Figure 8.31 Loading the problem.

Input

All data entering a computer system must be read by an input device and stored at a preassigned location so the information is available to the programmer (fig. 8.31). The storage should be located in a logical manner so the instructions can have access to these files as the data is being manipulated. It is necessary to know at all times where to find the information in the successive stages of processing. The instructions of the program can later specify the location where these records may be found. The

Figure 8.32 Processing the data.

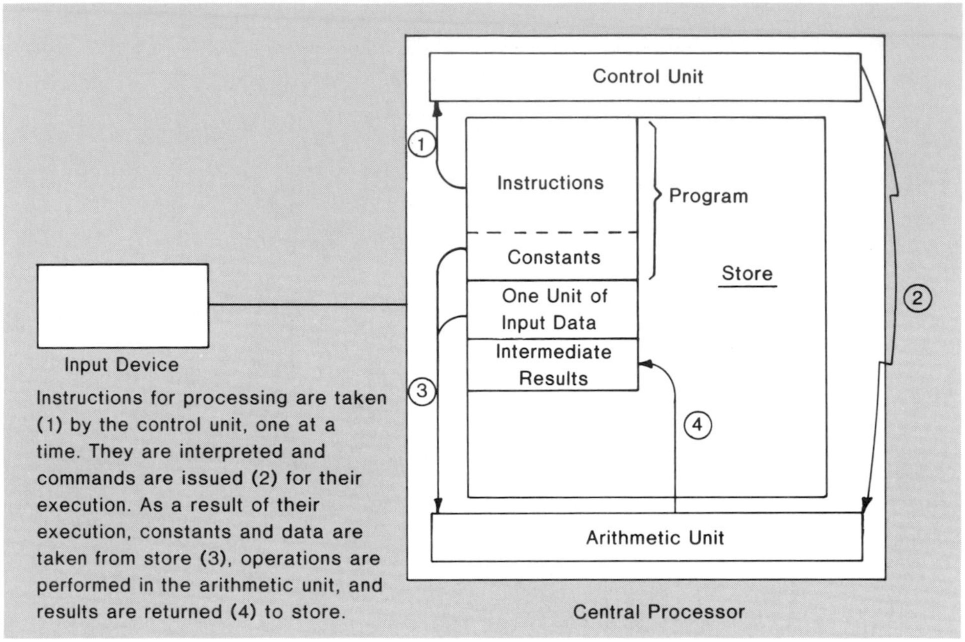

Instructions for processing are taken (1) by the control unit, one at a time. They are interpreted and commands are issued (2) for their execution. As a result of their execution, constants and data are taken from store (3), operations are performed in the arithmetic unit, and results are returned (4) to store.

input device is selected by the programmer before the actual reading begins. The reference is made to the particular device number known to the programmer. These device numbers are assigned by the system programmer to be used in all programs. The programmer determines the sequence of read instructions in which the files are to be read. The storage need is determined by the length and type of the records and by the construction of the files.

The read instruction causes the actual transfer of data to the particular area of storage assigned for input records. A number of areas may be assigned to handle several related records. These records are now available to the programmer for processing (fig. 8.32).

In most data-processing installations, certain areas of storage are assigned for individual programs and the programmer is confined to these storage boundaries. These restraints prevent the programmer from wandering into different areas reserved for other programs. This also eliminates the possibility of essential information being erased by the erroneous imposition of another program (fig. 8.33).

Arithmetic

Once the data has been read into the system by an input device, calculation can begin. Calculation in computer systems is carried out at much higher rates of speed than the reading of input or the writing of output. The input and output devices are mechanical and as such operate at a relatively slow speed while the calculating operations are performed at electronic speeds. Programs are written to overlap the operations of input and output with the processing function so the efficiency of the system is increased. In most business operations, calculations are rather simple and the overall speed of the

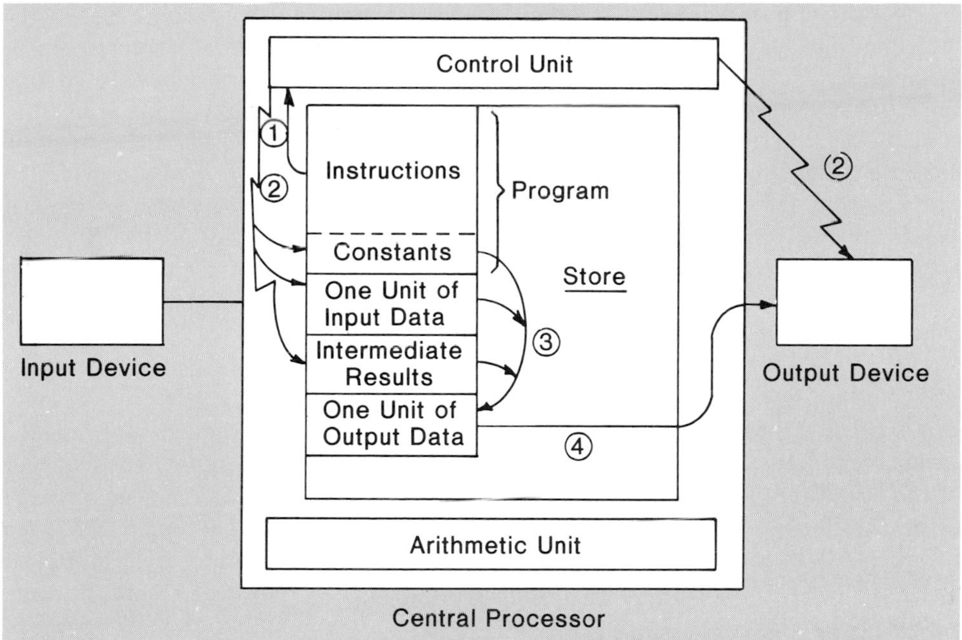

Instructions for this step are taken (1) by the control unit for interpretation. Commands (2) are issued to store, resulting in the assembly of a unit of output data (3), and to the output device (2), resulting in the writing (4) of a unit of output data.

Figure 8.33 Assembling and writing the output.

system is governed by the input and output units. In scientific operations, the calculations are more involved and complex, and high-speed calculating is essential. A successful system will have a balance between input and output devices and processing operation.

Each computer has the capacity for performing addition, subtraction, multiplication, and division as built-in operations or under the control of the program. In the simplest calculation, at least two factors are involved in all arithmetic operations, such as a dividend and divisor, or multiplier and multiplicand. All these factors must be available in storage and accessible to the arithmetic unit of the machine so the results can be calculated. The address portion of the instruction will specify the storage location of each factor involved in the calculation. The operation code of the instruction specifies the particular arithmetic operation to be performed on these factors. Any practical number of calculations can take place on many factors in a single series of instructions.

Arithmetic factors may be computed on a storage-to-storage basis in which the calculation is performed in storage with the results being placed in storage or in which the calculation can be performed in a register with one factor in a register and the other factor in storage or another register. The final result appears in a register and may be later moved to a storage location. The method of calculation employed will depend upon the program and the computer involved.

All calculations take into account the algebraic values of the factors; that is, the individual signs of the numbers. The computer follows the rules of algebra in all basic arithmetic calculations. The programmer must assign an area large enough to contain the result of the calculation. If the storage area assigned for the result is too small to contain the entire answer, truncation of the result will occur and the answer will be unpredictable. Other operations of shifting and rounding results are also provided to shorten, lenghten, or otherwise adjust the result. With these capabilities, decimal values may be handled by the computer and directions for placing the decimal point may be given to the system.

The design of a particular system must achieve a realistic balance between the calculating ability and the record-handling ability.

Logic

The logic of the computer is determined by its ability to make comparisons, test the various conditions, and take the appropriate action required by the result. The sequence of the computer instructions may be altered by the condition tested. The comparison of an identifying field in one record with that of another enables the computer to make these tests. The results of the comparison are registered as *low,* where the test number in one record is lower than the corresponding number of the other record; or *high,* where the test number exceeds the other; or *equal,* where both numbers are equal to each other. Each condition tested can be used to set an indicator, which may be interrogated later in the program.

Both fields of a record are placed in predetermined locations in storage and a *compare*-type instruction compares the first record with the second and sets the appropriate indicator based on the resulting condition. A *branch*-type instruction specifies the location of the next instruction to be executed if a certain condition exists. This permits the program to handle alternative actions due to exceptions in the procedure without writing a complete program for each different record in a file. A program may be arranged so the machine can recognize one or more types of records in a single file and process each according to its individual requirements. This method of computation can be revised according to the particular type of record in a storage unit. For example, in an inventory application containing many different records, such as receipts, disbursements, back orders, and adjustments, each different type of record could be identified by a particular code. The program could be written to test for each of these codes and, based on the type, the program will branch to the appropriate procedure, which will process the particular record.

The sequence checking of files is another application of the logical ability of the computer. If a file is in ascending sequence, each incoming record should be equal to or higher than the previous record, otherwise the record is out of sequence. Duplicate records can also be selected, if the second record equals the first. The same principle can be used to sort records into a predetermined sequence by testing the code number of each succeeding record. For example, in a payroll application it is known that each employee should have a single master record. If by error the old record was not removed when a change was made, duplicate records result. The computer through its logic ability could be so programmed to test for this condition by comparing each record with the preceding record. If an equal condition is detected, the program could branch to an error routine.

Another possible application is *conditional transfer,* in which the program is repeated if some predetermined condition has occurred. The conditional transfer may be used to execute a special purpose subroutine out of the normal portion of the program. This routine will be executed only if the predetermined condition exists. For example, when computing the social security taxes in a payroll procedure, it is necessary to test the accumulated earnings of each employee to see if they have reached the maximum for social security taxes. If this limit has been reached, the program would branch to a subroutine that bypasses the calculations for social security taxes and continues with the payroll procedure.

A logical operation may be used to vary the program by changing the operation part or the address of the instruction. The operation portion of an instruction can be altered as a result of a previous comparison or test of indicators. A *switch*-type instruction can be inserted in the program at a predetermined location. This switch will be turned on as a result of a certain condition and the operation code of the next instruction changed. If the test condition does not exist, the switch will be skipped and the next instruction executed in the normal manner. For example, in an inventory-updating application, it is known that each record is in ascending sequence, otherwise the processing should be terminated. Each succeeding record is compared with the previous one, and a switch is set if an out-of-sequence condition is detected. The switch will cause the program to be aborted.

The address part of an instruction may be treated as data which can be modified by arithmetic. An index register can add or subtract variable quantities contained in one or more special-purpose registers to the address portion of an instruction. This index feature permits repetitious calculations and other operations to be performed using the same program, thus reducing the sequential number of instructions. For example, in an inventory application, it is necessary to total all the on-hand values of each item. There are 20,000 items of inventory, each with a stock number separated by 10 digits. Twenty thousand or more program steps could be written to add these amounts from each inventory record or an index register could be initialized with a value of 10, and this could be added to the address in each instruction (modify the address), thus reducing the program to a few instructions. The program could be *looped* (repeated processing) until all of the 20,000 items have been accumulated.

The logical ability greatly expands the use of the computer. It permits the computer to alter its program to accommodate changed conditions without the intervention of the programmer. This ability increases the potential applications of computer operations.

Summary

The ability to solve computer problems logically hinges on the proper preparation of flowcharts, decision tables, and other tools available to the programmer. A majority of people entering the data-processing field will spend a considerable amount of time programming. The progress of potential programmers will depend on their ability to solve problems logically. To accomplish this objective, learn how to prepare for the programming effort. This chapter introduces the programming phase of data processing. The construction of flowcharts is important in solving complex problems. The use of decision tables is becoming increasingly popular with programmers.

It is equally important to learn the other facets of programming, such as instructions, methods of processing data, planning the programming, and the program itself. The computer program will be the result of the programmer's knowledge as applied to the problem and to the operation of the specific computer. The success of the computer program depends upon the ability of the programmer to analyze the problem properly, prepare the program to solve the particular problem, and operate the program.

1. An instruction is a coded statement used to write a program and when combined with other instructions is used by the computer to solve a specific problem. The operation code uniquely identifies the operation to be performed. The instruction address is the address of the instruction in storage. The program is a series of instructions that tell the computer how to receive, process, and return the data.
2. There are two methods of processing data. In sequential (batch) processing, the data is arranged in predetermined sequence and each record must be examined prior to processing. In random (inline) processing, transactions are not batched. All records need not be examined, only those requiring updating.
3. A flowchart is a graphic representation of the flow of information through a system in which the information is converted from the source document to the final report. There are two types of flowcharts. The system flowchart illustrates the overall flow of data through a system. The program flowchart is a graphic representation of the procedures by which data is processed. It is used to write the program.
4. Decision tables are sometimes used instead of flowcharts. Decision tables reduce the problem statement to a table or to a condition and action statement.
5. The program must analyze the problem, prepare a program to solve a particular problem, and operate the program. Hardware, output needs, source document must be analyzed. Then computer programs can be written using program flowcharts as a guide. The programs and data can be placed into storage of the computer. Now the program can be planned, as well as the allocation of storage, input and output procedures, arithmetic and logical procedures, the output format, and subroutines. The data is read by the input device and stored at a preassigned address. The arithmetic is the calculations made on the data whether it is in register or in storage. Logic is the ability of the computer to make comparisons, test various conditions, and then take the appropriate action called for by the results.

Identification Questions

Match the following terms with the statements below.

A. Block Diagram
B. Branch-Type Instruction
C. Compare-Type Instruction
D. Conditional Transfer
E. Decision Table
F. Flowchart
G. Instruction
H. Looped
I. Operation Code
J. Program
K. Program Flowchart
L. Random Processing
M. Sequential Processing
N. System Flowchart

1. A graphic representation of the flow of data through a data-processing system.
2. Each record has to be examined for possible processing.
3. The major functions and sequences are shown in detail.
4. A code that uniquely specifies the operations to be performed.
5. Specifies the location of the next instruction to be executed if a certain condition exists.
6. A command to the machine, expressed in a coded combination of characters, to carry out some operation.
7. All records need not be examined, only those that require updating.
8. A graphic representation of the procedures by which data is to be processed.
9. Reduces the problem to a table of condition/action statements.
10. The repeated processing of data.
11. A series of instructions which will direct the computer on how to read, process, and output the data.
12. A diagram that illustrates the flow of data into, through, and out of a series of programs.
13. Sets appropriate indicators based on a resulting condition.
14. Program is repeated if some predetermined condition exists.

Questions for Review

1. What is the job of the programmer? Where does the programmer get the basic facts?
2. How is the data processed within a computer?
3. What is an instruction and what is its chief function?
4. What is the difference between instructions and data in storage?
5. What is the difference between sequential and random processing?
6. What are the important advantages and disadvantages of sequential and random processing? Give examples of each.
7. What is the importance of flowcharting in data processing?
8. Explain the use and purposes of the two main types of flowcharts used in data processing.
9. List the important points in program flowcharts.
10. How are decision tables used in defining data-processing problems?
11. Describe the steps in programming.
12. List the necessary steps to insure that a proper analysis and coding was made.
13. What are the important considerations in planning a program?
14. Why is it important to arrange input data properly in computer storage?
15. Describe the operation of the arithmetic unit in a computer.
16. Describe the logic operation of the computer.

Key Terms

Block Diagram
Branch-Type Instruction
Compare-Type Instruction
Conditional Transfer
Decision Table
Flowchart
Instruction
Looped
Operation Code
Program
Program Flowchart
Random Processing
Sequential Processing
System Flowchart

introduction to computer programming 9

Chapter Outline

Chapter Objectives

The learning objectives of this chapter are

1. to furnish the transition between the expression of the problem in flowchart form and the technical methods for the processing of the data in the form of a complete program.
2. to learn the meanings of machine and symbolic programming languages and the problems inherent in translating the latter into machine language.
3. to study the compiler and what its importance is in the translation process.
4. to explain the characteristics of the computer-programming languages available today and their principal uses and features so you can choose a programming language that is best suited for a particular problem.

Computer capability is expanding at a fantastic rate, as is the technology of utilization and control. The improvements in programming techniques are as vitally important as the design of the data-processing system itself. To a large extent, the future of computers is dependent not only on increases in speed, logical ability, and storage capacity, but on the efficient use of these facilities as they become available.

A computer program is much more than a set of detailed instructions. It is the outcome of the programmer's applied knowledge of the problem and the operation of the computer system. The programmer receives a problem statement that contains a job description, a description of the different types of the data involved, and layout specifications for input and output of the data. After a complete analysis of the problem statement, the completed problem statement must be translated into flowcharts and decision tables. The flowcharts and any necessary decision tables must be translated into a program, which is a series of instructions that will instruct the computer on how the data will be received, how the data will be processed, and what output should be developed (fig. 9.1).

The problem is first analyzed in terms of operations that the computer can perform. The program is then written by the programmer who supplies the necessary tables, formulas, codes, and other reference material specified by the application. The problem then becomes the input data, and the computer, with its calculating and manipulating functions, produces the desired output.

Before the physical components of an electronic data-processing system can solve any problem, the programmer must be able to communicate to the hardware the instructions that have evolved from the flowchart and/or decision table. Both the data and the instructions are stored in the computer in configurations of 1-bits and 0-bits. The characters these bits represent make up the language of the computer called *machine language*. Though programmers can, and sometimes do, communicate with the computer in machine language, the process of writing computer instructions in binary representation is a cumbersome and time-consuming task.

Computer programs may be expressed in either machine language, which is a common language of a particular computer that does not require further modification before execution by the computer, or symbolic language, which is more meaningful to the programmer. The symbolic language must be later translated into machine language before the program can be executed by the computer.

Machine Language

A computer is a willing servant. It will invariably and reliably do exactly what it is told, as long as it is told in its own language. This is true of any computer.

Many years ago, when all programs were written in machine language, the most valuable tool programmers had was an eraser. They were concerned with an enormous amount of clerical detail and had to remember dozens of numerical codes for the computer operations and had to try to not make a mistake using them. Programmers had to keep track of the storage space used for instructions, data, and work areas and actually calculate any addresses of data needed in a program. Revising a program (a very frequent occurrence then, as it is now) often meant changing every address that followed the revisions. All this detail meant many errors and much time spent on checking, calculating, keeping tables, and other clerical tasks.

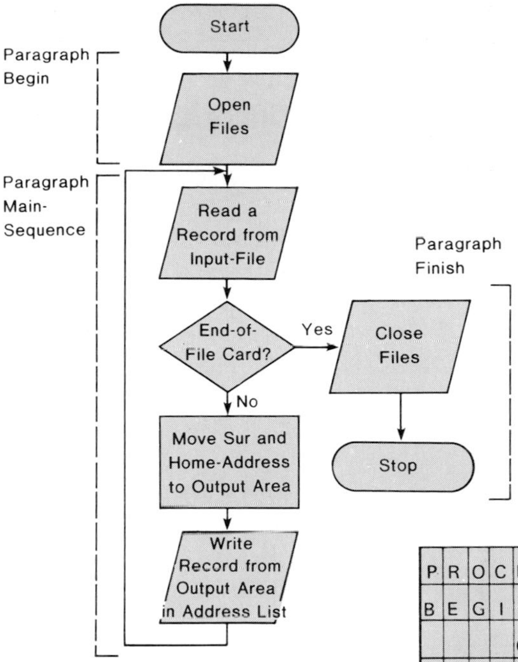

Figure 9.1
Flowchart coding.

```
PROCEDURE DIVISION.
BEGIN.
    OPEN INPUT INPUT-FILE,
        OUTPUT ADDRESS-LIST.
MAIN-SEQUENCE.
    READ INPUT-FILE
        AT END GO TO FINISH.
    MOVE SUR TO LAST-NAME.
    MOVE HOME-ADDRESS TO ADDRESS-O.
    WRITE OUTPUT-RECORD.
    GO TO MAIN-SEQUENCE.
FINISH.
    CLOSE INPUT-FILE ADDRESS-LIST.
    STOP RUN.
```

The realization that the computer was better suited than the programmer for doing this type of clerical work led to the development of symbolic programming languages.

Since the computer cannot understand any language except its own machine language, a program that translates the symbolic program into the machine language of the particular computer was developed by computer manufacturers. These translator programs, beside translating the symbolic program into a machine-language program, calculates storage locations for instructions and data, keeps track of symbols that are used in the program, and performs a number of other necessary functions.

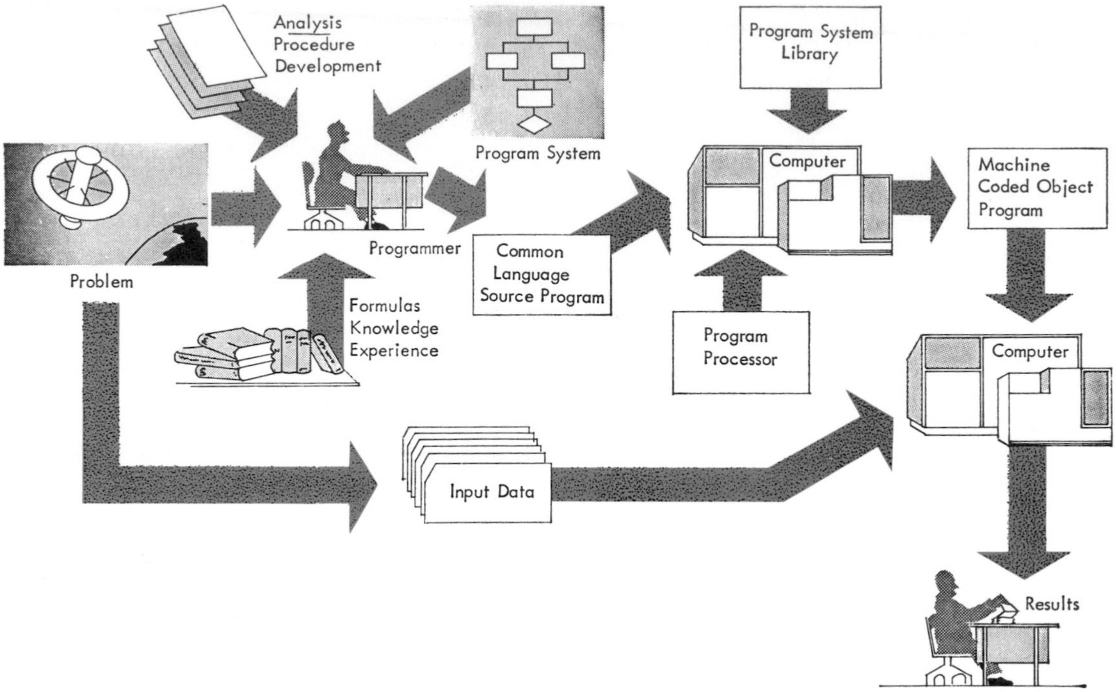

Figure 9.2 The conversion of a problem to machine program using programming symbols.

Symbolic Language

Many of the difficulties and inconveniences of machine-language coding can be eliminated or simplified by the more advanced systems of program writing (fig. 9.2). Programs can be made compatible by the computer, thus eliminating the need for direct machine coding. A computer can be programmed to recognize instructions written in a symbolic language and to translate these statements into the machine language of that particular computer (fig. 9.3). A number of programming languages have been developed that are easier to use and understand than machine language.

Symbolic programming, the use of mnemonic characters to write a program, has been developed to facilitate computer programming. Mnemonic symbols, such as MPY for multiply and MVC for move character instructions, assist the programmer's memory. The program written in the symbolic language is known as the source program.

The use of symbolic names (labels) makes a program independent of actual machine locations. Programs and routines written in symbolic language can be relocated and combined as desired. Routines within a program can be written independently without any loss of efficiency in the final program. Symbolic instructions may be added or deleted without reassigning storage addresses. The instructions can be inserted into the exact point in the program where they are needed.

The source program requires translation into an actual machine-language program (object program) before the computer can execute it. To bridge the gap between the source program and the machine language, a special type of conversion program must tell the computer how to change the operations from the symbolic language (source program) to actual machine instructions (object program). Several types of

Machine language   Symbolic language

```
   LOC  OBJECT CODE     ADDR1 ADDR2 STMT    SOURCE STATEMENT

                                       1          PRINT NOGEN
000000                                 2 ACCTNO   START 0
000000 05B0                            3 BEGIN    BALR  11,0
000002                                 4          USING *,11
000002 4130 0001              00001    5          LA    3,1             REG 3 WILL HAVE SIGN REVERSED IN LOOP
000006 4140 0009              00009    6          LA    4,9             COUNTER FOR 9 DIGITS IN NUMBER
00000A D201 B064 B066 00066 00068      7          MVC   SUM,ZERO        SUM OF DIGITS KEPT IN SUM
000010 1B55                            8          SR    5,5             CLEAR REG 5
000012 4354 B059              0005B    9 LOOP     IC    5,ACCT-1(4)     PICK UP 1 DIGIT OF INDEXED NUMBER
000016 8950 0004              00004   10          SLL   5,4             SHIFT LEFT 4 BITS
00001A 5650 B06A              0006C   11          O     5,PLUS          ATTACH A PACKED PLUS SIGN
00001E 4250 B068              0006A   12          STC   5,DIGIT         STORE IN TEMPORARY LOCATION
000022 FA10 B064 B068 00066 0006A     13          AP    SUM,DIGIT       ADD TO SUM OF DIGITS
000028 1333                           14          LCR   3,3             REVERSE SIGN OF REG 3
00002A 4720 B038              0003A   15          BC    2,EVEN          SKIP NEXT 2 INSTR ON PLUS ODD TIMES THRU
00002E FA10 B064 B068 00066 0006A     16          AP    SUM,DIGIT       IF NOT SKIPPED ADD DIGIT TO SUM
000034 FA10 B064 B068 00066 0006a     17          AP    SUM,DIGIT       SAME. HAS EFFECT OF MULTIPLYING BY 3
00003A 4640 B010              00012   18 EVFN     BCT   4,LOOP          BRANCH BACK IF NOT ALL DIGITS PROCESSED
00003E 4350 B063              00065   19          IC    5,ACCT+9        PUT CHECK DIGIT IN REG 5
000042 8950 0004              00004   20          SLL   5,4             SHIFT LEFT 4 BITS
000046 5650 B06A              0006C   21          O     5,PLUS          ATTACH SIGN TO PUT IN SAME FORMAT AS SUM
00004A 4250 B064              00066   22          STC   5,SUM           PUT ONE BYTE IN LEFT BYTE OF SUM
00004E D500 B064 B065 00066 00067     23          CLC   SUM(1),SUM+1    IS THIS BYTE SAME AS CHECK DIGIT
000054 4770 B058              0005A   24          BNE   ERROR           BRANCH TO ERROR ROUTINE IF NOT EQUAL
                                      25 OUT      EOJ                   PROGRAM WOULD NORMALLY CONTINUE HERE
                                      28 ERROR    EOJ
00005C                                31 ACCT     DS    CL9
000065                                32 CHECK    DS    CL1
000066                                33 SUM      DS    CL2
000068 000C                           34 ZERO     DC    PL2'0'
00006A                                35 DIGIT    DS    CL1
00006C                                36          DS    0F
00006C 0000000C                       37 PLUS     DC    XL4'0C'
000000                                38          END   BEGIN
```

Figure 9.3 Machine language and symbolic language.

conversion programs, especially written for the programmer are supplied by the computer manufacturer in its software package, to convert a symbolic language program to a machine-language program.

Initially these translations were performed on a one-for-one basis; that is, each instruction was translated into a single machine-language instruction. The processor program was called an *assembler*. An assembler translates item for item; that is, it produces an object program with the same number of instructions and constants as the source program. All symbolic entries are analyzed by the assembler and the conversion is made to actual machine-operating data and instructions establishing specified relationships between them (fig. 9.4).

A compiling program (called a *compiler*) converts a symbolic program into a machine-language program (fig. 9.5). A compiler differs from an assembler in that the compiler may generate a series of machine-language instructions from one instruction written in the compiler program language. When using the compiler language, the programmer gives just one symbolic language instruction; the compiler program generates the many absolute or machine-language instructions that are needed to perform the task.

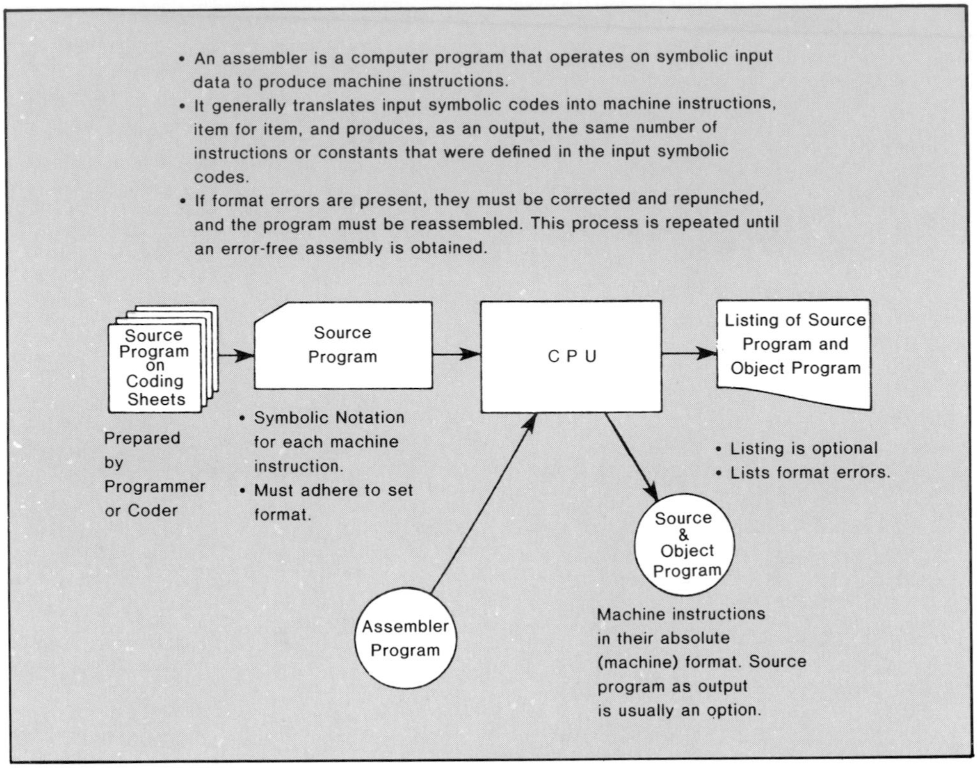

Figure 9.4 The assembler process.

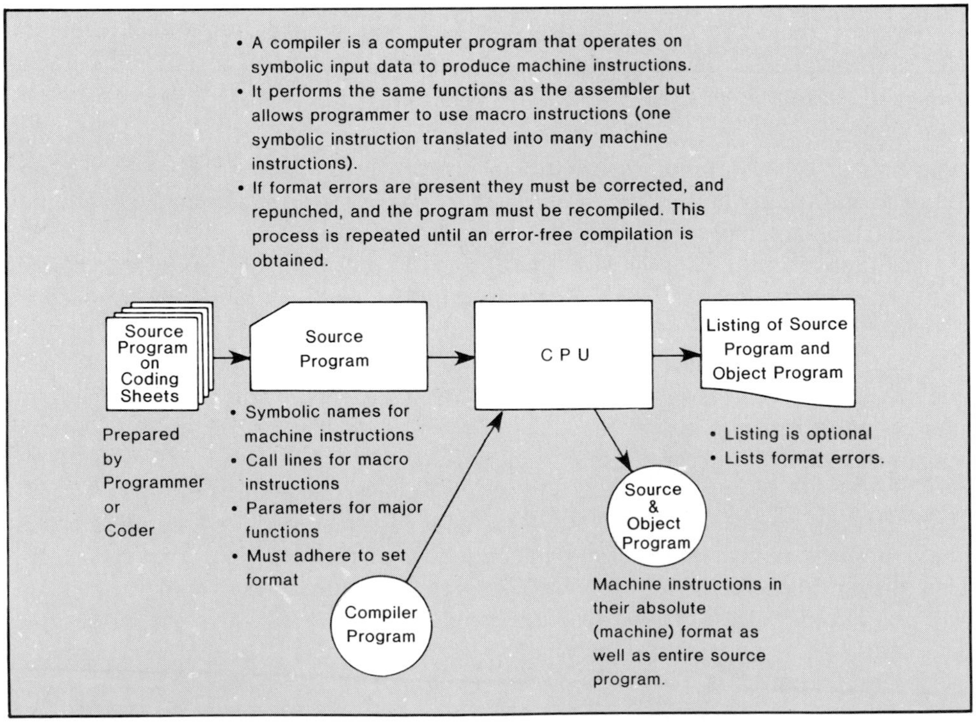

Figure 9.5 The compiler process.

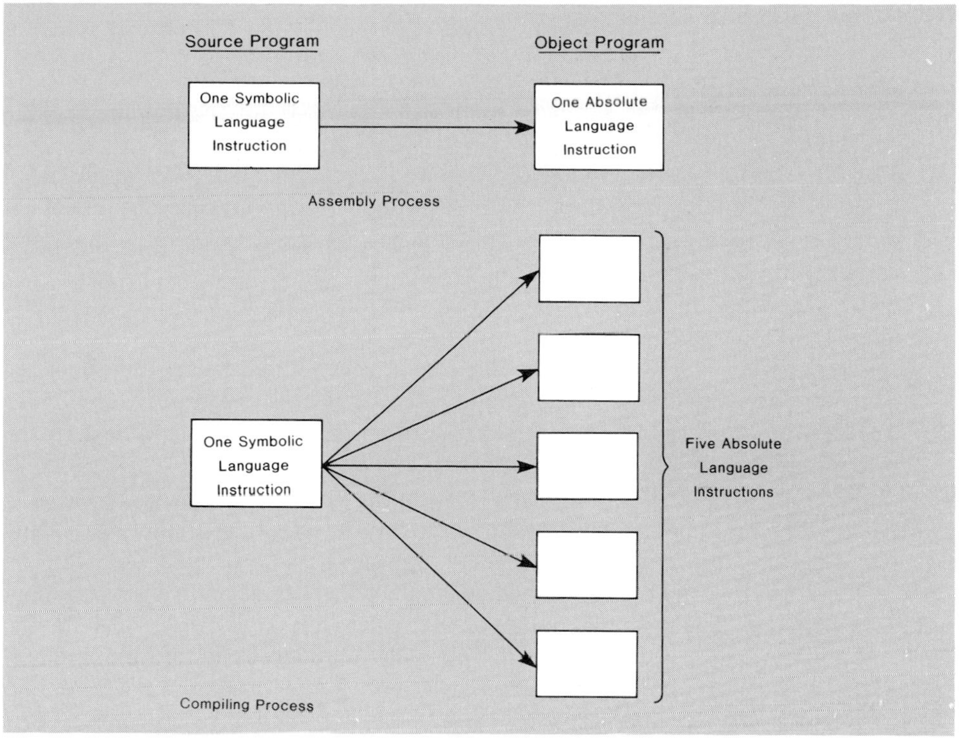

Figure 9.6 The assembler and compiler processes.

A macro instruction is equivalent to a specified sequence of machine instructions. Because of the macro capability, the compiler language is more powerful than the assembler language (fig. 9.6). The compiler performs the same functions as the assembler plus the use of macros. This development greatly increases the power of symbolic languages. The art of programming has advanced so much that it is possible to write instructions in an English-like format or mathematical format and have the compiler understand these statements and convert them into machine-language instructions.

As an additional feature, compiled programs also indicate various types of errors, such as coding or out-of-sequence cards. Symbolic programming saves time and simplifies coding because the actual machine addresses of the data and instructions are assigned automatically by the processor. The programmer does not need to be concerned with detail and can refer to these addresses symbolically.

Once there is an agreement on label terminology, subroutines (short programs or routines common to a number of programs) may be easily incorporated into any program, and a major program may be written in independent parts without any loss of efficiency in the final program. Corrections and modifications of program instructions will not require reassignment of addresses by the programmer. Finally, the automatic assignment of addresses makes programs and subroutines readily relocatable; they can be placed in varying machine locations as desired.

The advantages of symbolic programming are:

1. *Simplifies program writing and organization.* It is easier to write and refer to an instruction using the symbolic names than to look up the actual machine address.
2. *Provides continuity for group programming efforts.* Once the label terminology has been agreed upon, program routines can be written efficiently and independently, and can be combined for compilation because addresses are automatically assigned by the processor.
3. *Simplifies program adjustment.* If programs require partial revision, only the affected routines need to be rewritten.
4. *Detects coding errors.* Illegal operation codes, invalid addressing, and sequence errors are detected by the compiler and listed before the program is compiled.
5. *Facilitates program testing.* Explanatory comments may be listed next to the program instructions.

Symbolic programming permits the programmer to code in a symbolic language that is more meaningful and easier to handle than numerical machine language. As a result, the difficulties of coding in machine language, a tedious and time-consuming task, are eliminated. The compiler automatically assigns and keeps a record of storage locations, and checks for coding errors. By relieving the programmer of these burdensome tasks, symbolic programming reduces the amount of programming time and effort required.

Operation of Compilers

A compiler is a processor program supplied by the computer manufacturer that translates the program created by the programmer (source program) into a machine-language program (object program) for the particular computer. The compiler is loaded into the storage area of the computer. A source program is written by the programmer on a coding form that will be used as a guide for the punching of the program into cards. These cards will be entered into the machine and will be subsequently translated into an object program with the help of the computer. After the entire program has been written in the symbolic language, the source program is entered into the computer with the use of job control cards. The computer translates the symbols into the operation codes and absolute addresses in machine-language coding, according to the sequence and logic set up by the programmer. The object program may then be run to produce the problem results (fig. 9.7).

It is worth emphasizing that the compiler itself is a program, not a machine. It translates the source program into the object program; it does not cause the object program to be executed. In some systems, the object program may be executed; while in other systems, the object program is not in an executable format but must be processed by another program called the *linkage editor,* which produces the executable program.

Some examples of compilers (language processors) are COBOL and FORTRAN. These programming languages are written either in English-like statements or with mathematical formulas. Each of the individual statements is translated into one or more object program instructions.

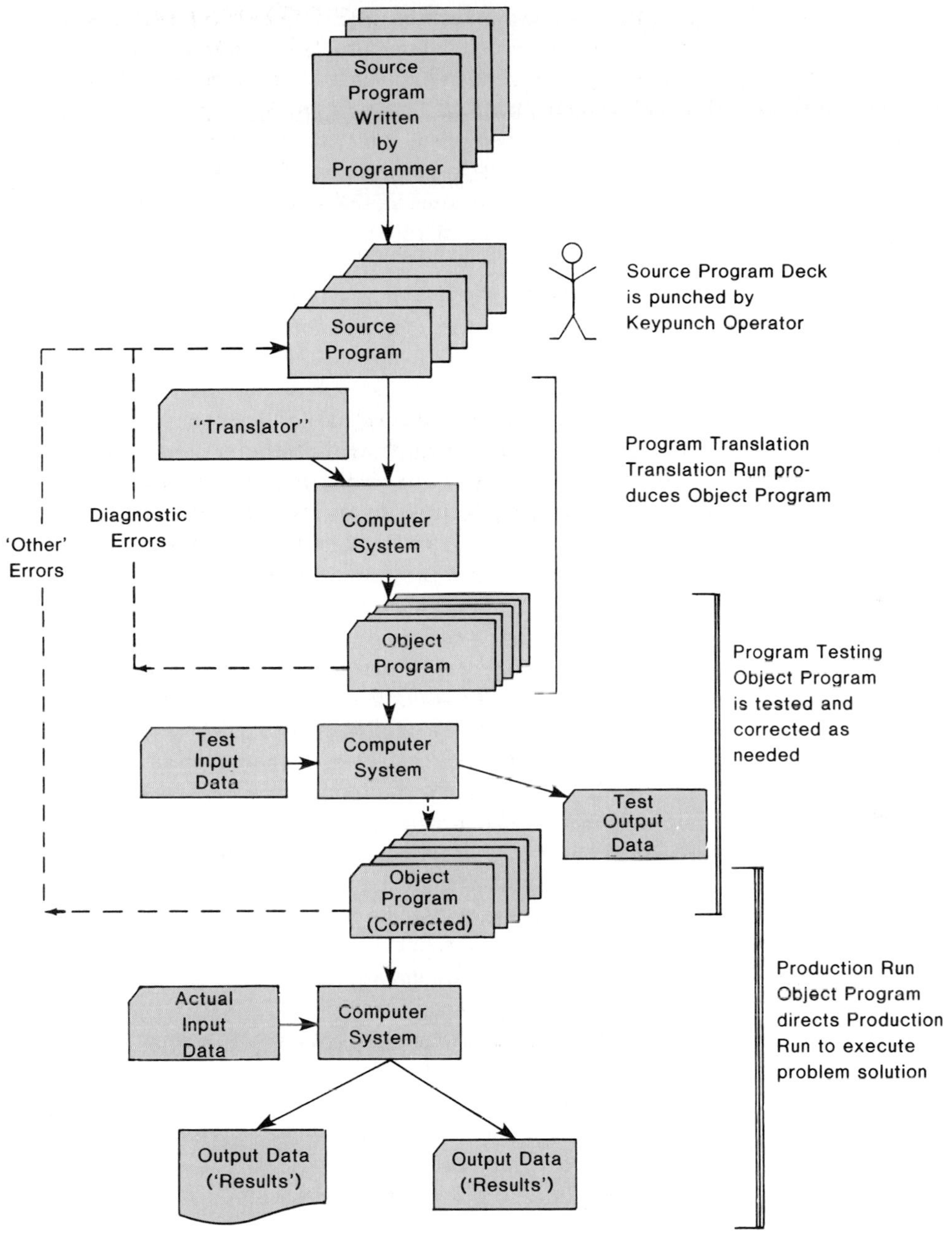

Figure 9.7
Execution—program translation and testing and the production run.

After the object program has been executed, the output may be recorded on magnetic tape or disk or in punched cards for later processing on offline equipment. The output results may be printed in the form of a report directly from the computer at the same time as the processing of the data.

Once an object program has been compiled, it can be used over and over again each time the particular job is run. Data-processing applications of the production type, such as payroll, inventory control and sales analysis, may use a previously prepared object program each time it is needed merely by requesting it from storage.

Machine-Oriented Programming Languages

In a machine-oriented programming language, the symbolic program is written by the programmer for a particular computer. The language was designed by the computer manufacturer to allow the programmer to take full advantage of the features and capabilities of the computer. For this reason, the most efficient program next to machine language that can be prepared for an individual computer is usually written using a machine-oriented language. The machine-oriented language is meant to be processed on a particular computer, while a problem-oriented or procedure-oriented language is written to solve a problem and may be processed on many different types of computers.

The programmer uses names and symbolic codes to designate the operations that the computer is to perform and the storage locations of the data to be used in the data-processing operation. The assembler processor then proceeds to translate the instruction into machine-language instructions with actual machine storage locations.

An example of machine-oriented language is the IBM System/360/370 assembler language. Coding sheets are used to write each instruction the machine is to perform (fig. 9.8). Each line of the coding sheet is punched into a card. The form corresponds to the eighty columns of a punched card. Instructions for punching and program identification are provided on the form.

The coding form permits a maximum of four fields in each line. These fields are called name, operation, operand, and comment. The *name,* which is created by the programmer, provides a reference identification (label) in case other parts of a program need to refer to it. An *operation* is a mnemonic operation code specifying the machine operation or assembler function desired. The content and the format of the entries in the *operand* field are governed by the requirements of the entry in the operation field. Operand entries indicate the storage location of the data to be processed. The *comment* entries may begin following the operand field as long as there is at least one space following the operand field entry. Comments are descriptive entries regarding the program. They usually provide the reader with the purpose of each instruction. A comment may also be indicated by an asterisk (*) in the first column, followed by the statement.

Despite the many advantages in using machine-oriented programming languages (such as program efficiency), there are some serious disadvantages.

1. The great number of instructions and variations of instructions in a machine-oriented language make it difficult for the average programmer to write a program and debug it in a short period of time.

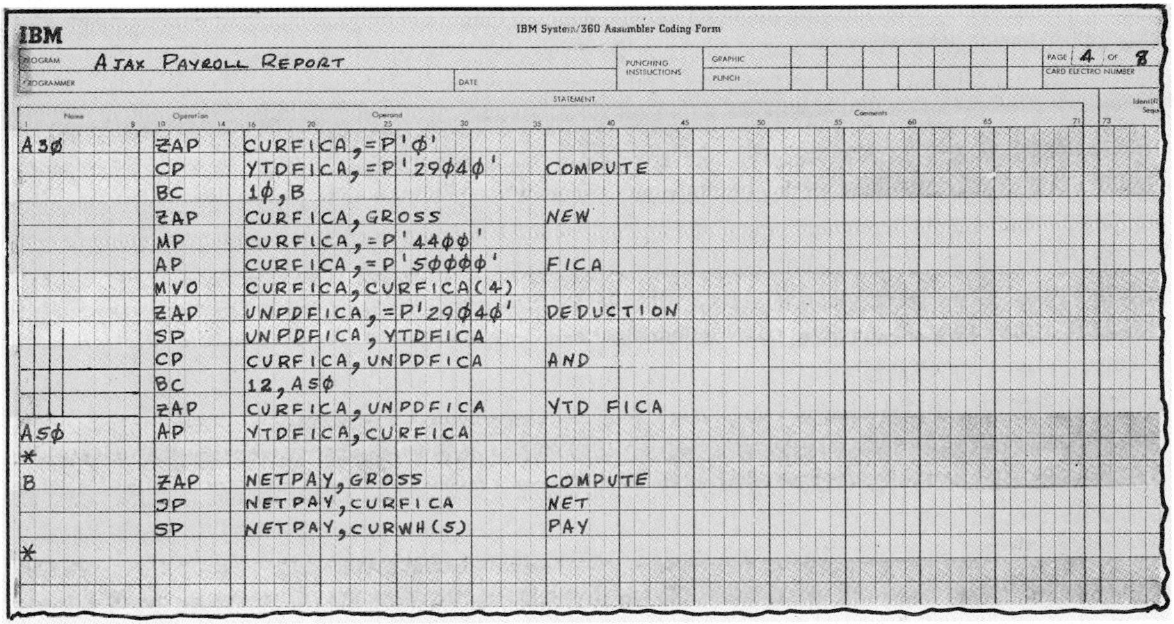

IBM System/360 Assembler Coding Form

PROGRAM: AJAX PAYROLL REPORT — PAGE 4 OF 8

```
A3Ø      ZAP   CURFICA,=P'Ø'
         CP    YTDFICA,=P'29Ø4Ø'        COMPUTE
         BC    1Ø,B
         ZAP   CURFICA,GROSS            NEW
         MP    CURFICA,=P'44ØØ'
         AP    CURFICA,=P'5ØØØØ'        FICA
         MVO   CURFICA,CURFICA(4)
         ZAP   UNPDFICA,=P'29Ø4Ø'       DEDUCTION
         SP    UNPDFICA,YTDFICA
         CP    CURFICA,UNPDFICA         AND
         BC    12,A5Ø
         ZAP   CURFICA,UNPDFICA         YTD FICA
A5Ø      AP    YTDFICA,CURFICA
*
B        ZAP   NETPAY,GROSS             COMPUTE
         SP    NETPAY,CURFICA           NET
         SP    NETPAY,CURWH(5)          PAY
*
```

Figure 9.8 An example of a machine-oriented programming language.

2. Any extensive revision or modification of a program can cause major changes in the program, at which point the possibility of reprogramming the entire problem exists. Most machine-oriented language instructions are compatible only within the same system for a particular computer. They are not compatible upwards as most computer manufacturers claim. A large system of the same computer family usually requires reprogramming when upgraded from a small system.
3. Programmers have difficulty learning the program because of the detail involved in each instruction format.

For these and other reasons, machine-oriented language programs are written mainly for system and supervisory programs. Problem-oriented and procedure-oriented programming languages have become very popular for the writing of application programs.

Problem-Oriented and Procedure-Oriented Programming Languages

The use of problem- and procedure-oriented programming languages in data-processing applications is increasing daily. Both of these programming languages are tailored to the solution of a particular problem rather than to a particular machine. *A problem-oriented programming language describes the problem to the computer; the compiler generates the necessary procedures for the solution of the problem; and the procedure-oriented programming language describes the procedures to the computer* (fig. 9.9).

A program written in this type of language can be compiled and executed on many different computers with only minor changes in the program for each computer.

Figure 9.9
Generating a program.

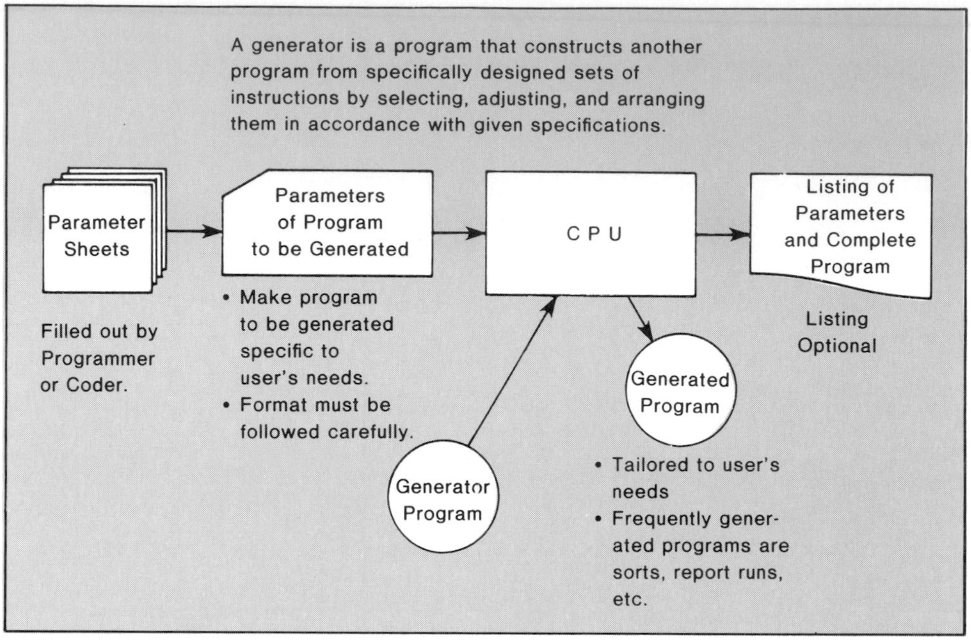

These programs are written in a more flexible form than the machine-oriented language. English-like statements and mathematical expressions are used in the writing of these programs. The fact is that the programs written bear little resemblance to the machine-language instruction, and the programmer does not need to be concerned with the method of translation.

One important advantage of these programming languages is that learning time is greatly reduced, especially for new programmers because they are writing in a form that is familiar to them. Non-data-processing personnel, as well as experienced programmers, can read these languages. Debugging time is reduced because of the ease of reading and writing them.

These languages are easier to change and modify without any drastic reprogramming. Programs can be changed by personnel other than the original programmer.

The report program generator (RPG) language is a problem-oriented language. RPG is a symbolic language designed specifically to ease the programmer's task in writing programs that produce reports. It is a very simple way of adapting an application to a computer. The file definition and input/output control considerations, normally required of the programmer by other programming languages, are reduced to filling out simplified control forms. The file description form details the file names for the program and the type of device that will handle each; the input specification form tells the machine what kind of information it is to receive; and the output-format specification describes how the desired output should appear. The calculations form is the heart of the logic of the program and describes the operations to be performed on the data (fig. 9.10).

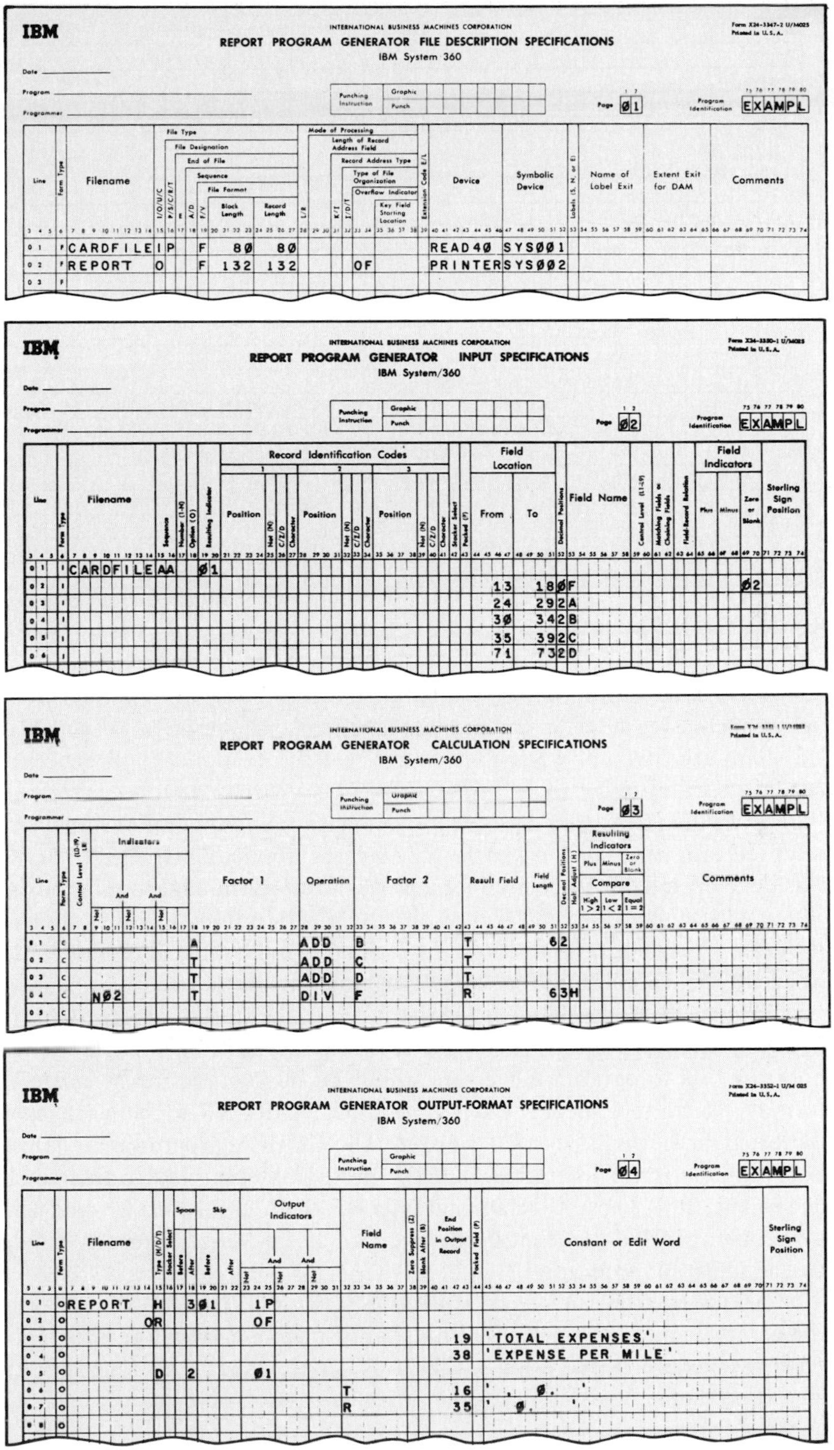

IBM INTERNATIONAL BUSINESS MACHINES CORPORATION
REPORT PROGRAM GENERATOR FILE DESCRIPTION SPECIFICATIONS
IBM System 360
Page Ø1 Program Identification EXAMPL

Line	Form Type	Filename	File Type	File Designation	File Format	Block Length	Record Length	Overflow Indicator	Device	Symbolic Device
01	F	CARDFILE	I	P	F	8Ø	8Ø		READ4Ø	SYSØØ1
02	F	REPORT	O		F	132	132	OF	PRINTER	SYSØØ2
03	F									

IBM INTERNATIONAL BUSINESS MACHINES CORPORATION
REPORT PROGRAM GENERATOR INPUT SPECIFICATIONS
IBM System/360
Page Ø2 Program Identification EXAMPL

Line	Form Type	Filename	Sequence	Resulting Indicator	From	To	Decimal Positions	Field Name	Zero or Blank
01	I	CARDFILE	AA	Ø1					
02	I				13	18	Ø	F	Ø2
03	I				24	29	2	A	
04	I				3Ø	34	2	B	
05	I				35	39	2	C	
06	I				71	73	2	D	

IBM INTERNATIONAL BUSINESS MACHINES CORPORATION
REPORT PROGRAM GENERATOR CALCULATION SPECIFICATIONS
IBM System/360
Page Ø3 Program Identification EXAMPL

Line	Form Type	Indicators	Factor 1	Operation	Factor 2	Result Field	Field Length	Decimal Positions	Half Adjust
01	C		A	ADD	B	T	6	2	
02	C		T	ADD	C	T			
03	C		T	ADD	D	T			
04	C	NØ2	T	DIV	F	R	6	3	H
05	C								

IBM INTERNATIONAL BUSINESS MACHINES CORPORATION
REPORT PROGRAM GENERATOR OUTPUT-FORMAT SPECIFICATIONS
IBM System/360
Page Ø4 Program Identification EXAMPL

Line	Form Type	Filename	Type (H/D/T)	Space After	Skip Before	Output Indicators	Field Name	End Position in Output Record	Constant or Edit Word
01	O	REPORT	H	3	Ø1	1P			
02	O		OR			OF			
03	O							19	'TOTAL EXPENSES'
04	O							38	'EXPENSE PER MILE'
05	O		D	2		Ø1			
06	O						T	16	' , Ø. '
07	O						R	35	' Ø. '
08	O								

Figure 9.10 Examples of RPG forms.

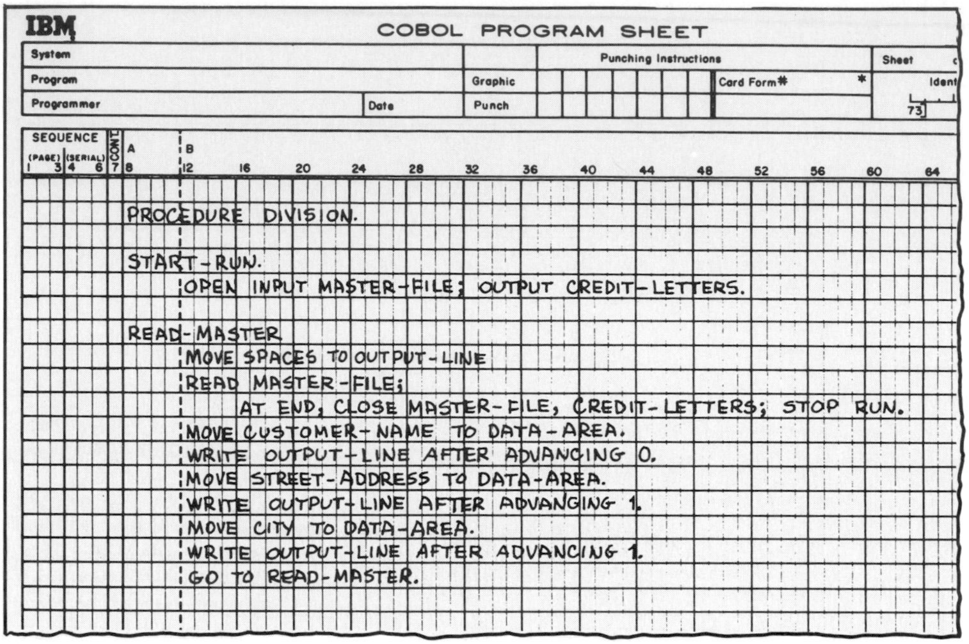

Figure 9.11 An example of a COBOL program sheet.

RPG language simplifies the programmer's job by eliminating the task of developing processing steps. Cards are punched from the specification sheets and read into the computer, which, when used with the RPG compiler, will generate the desired report.

COBOL (*CO*mmon *B*usiness *O*riented *L*anguage) is an example of a procedure-oriented language used primarily in business applications (fig. 9.11). The language was developed to meet the need for a programming language to solve business problems that could be processed on various computers with minimal modification of the original program. The program is written in readable English-like statements that are translated by the compiler into machine-language instructions.

The COBOL compiler writes the instructions for the object program. Therefore, not as many clerical errors are made as in the assembler language. In a COBOL program, the programmer's errors would be in logic or in the use of the COBOL format. (Refer to Checking the Program, page 278.) Thus, there are fewer places that the programmer must check for errors. The COBOL programming language has two advantages—it makes testing COBOL programs easy, and it assures clear program documentation. These COBOL statements, which can be easily read and understood by people, provide excellent documentation of the program being defined and solved by the COBOL program.

An instruction, such as ADD GROSS TO Y-T-D-GROSS, can be translated by the compiler into the appropriate number of machine-language instructions to accomplish the necessary operation. COBOL is widely used in all types of data-processing operations for processing business data-processing problems.

IBM FORTRAN CODING FORM

Form X28-7327-4 Printed in U.S.A.

Program: SAMPLE PROGRAM 1 | Programmer | Date | Punching Instructions: Graphic, Punch | Card Form # | Page 1 of 1 | Identification 73–80

C FOR COMMENT — STATEMENT NUMBER (1–5) | Cont. (6) | FORTRAN STATEMENT (7–72)

```
C PRIME NUMBER GENERATOR
      WRITE (3,1)
    1 FORMAT ('1FOLLOWING IS A LIST OF PRIME NUMBERS FROM 2 TO 1ØØØ'/
     *19X,'2'/19X,'3')
      DO 4 I=5,1ØØØ,2
      K=SQRT(FLOAT(I))
      DO 2 J=3,K,2
      IF (MOD(I,J)) 2,4,2
    2 CONTINUE
      WRITE (3,3) I
    3 FORMAT (I2Ø)
    4 CONTINUE
      WRITE (3,5)
    5 FORMAT (' THIS IS THE END OF THE PROGRAM')
      STOP
      END
```

Figure 9.12 An example of a FORTRAN coding form.

Another popular procedure-oriented language is FORTRAN (*FOR*mula *TRAN*slator). The FORTRAN language is similar to COBOL in concept. Whereas COBOL uses English-like statements, FORTRAN, a scientific-oriented language, uses mathematical formulas to state the problem (fig. 9.12). The COBOL instruction ADD GROSS TO Y-T-D-GROSS would have to be rewritten in a mathematical expression and abbreviated YTDGR = YTDGR + GROSS to accommodate the FORTRAN compiler.

The FORTRAN language is characterized by mathematical statements that indicate actions to be taken. These FORTRAN statements are input to the FORTRAN compiler program. The program generates machine-language instructions which perform the actions indicated in the original FORTRAN statements.

FORTRAN permits the programmer to use familiar arithmetic conventions to formulate a program. The symbols + − * / ** denote addition, subtraction, multiplication, division, and exponentiation. FORTRAN gives mathematicians or scientists a language to use to communicate with the computer, allowing them to concentrate on problems rather than on the computer's machine language. (RPG, COBOL, and FORTRAN are discussed in greater detail later in the text.)

It is important to recognize the role that procedure- and problem-oriented languages are playing in modern data processing. More application programs are being written in these languages. With the continued improvements in software, compilers are becoming more powerful, permitting the programmer to write more complex programs with a minimum number of instructions. With the built-in facility for program testing, capabilities of parallel program execution, self-monitoring systems, and procedure- and problem-oriented languages, the programming task has been simplified to the point where the definition of the problem and the subsequent analysis and solution are the most important aspects of computer programming, with the actual program coding being reduced to the writing of a series of statements in a language familiar to the programmer.

Checking the Program

The programmer's job does not end with coding. The computer program goes through many steps before the desired results are produced, and the programmer is very involved with most of them.

After the successful coding and compilation of the source program has been completed, the next phase in the program checkout procedure is to check the resultant machine-language program with the data (fig. 9.13). *Program testing or debugging determines whether the program will accomplish the desired results.* Few programs are written that work correctly the first time they are tried with actual data. Usually several runs are necessary before all mistakes are found and corrected. The most

Figure 9.13 An assembly listing with errors.

```
  LOC   OBJECT CODE     ADDR1 ADDR2  STMT    SOURCE STATEMENT

000100                                  1 PROGC      START 256
000100 05B0                             2 BEGIN      BALR  11,0
000102                                  3            USING *,11
000102 5820 B01E              0012^     4            L     2,DATA
000106 5A20 B026              00128     5            A     2,CON
                                        6            SLS   2,1
        *** ERROR ***
00010A 0000 0000              00000     7            S     2,DATA4
        *** ERROR ***
00010E 5020 B02A              0012C     8            ST    2,RESULT
000112 0000 0000              00000     9            L     6BIN1
        *** ERROR ***
000116 5A60 B02E              00130    10            A     6,BIN2
00011A 0000 0000              00000    11            CVD   6,BIN1
        *** ERRCR ***
                                       12            EOJ
                                       13+* 360N-CL-453 EOJ        CHANGE LEVEL 3-0
00011E 0A0E                            14+           SVC   14
000120 00000019                        15 DATA       DC    F'25'
000124 4CB016EA                        16            DC    F'9876543210'
        *** ERROR ***
000128 0000000A                        17 CON        DC    F'10'
00012C                                 18 RESULT     DS
        *** ERROR ***
00012C 0000 0000              00000    19 IN1        C     '12'
        *** ERROR ***
000130 0000004F                        20 BIN2       DC    F'78'
000138                                 21 DEC        DS    D
000140 00000019                        22 DATA       DC    F'25'
        *** ERROR ***
000100                                 23            END   BEGIN
```

```
                              DIAGNOSTICS

STMT  ERROR CODE   MESSAGE

  6   IJQ088       UNDEFINED OPERATION CODE
  7   IJQ024       UNDEFINED SYMBOL
  9   IJQ039       INVALID DELIMITER
  9   IJQ039       INVALID DELIMITER
 11   IJQ024       UNDEFINED SYMBOL
 16   IJQ017       DATA ITEM TOO LARGE
 18   IJQ031       UNKNOWN TYPE
 18   IJQ009       MISSING OPERAND
 19   IJQ039       INVALID DELIMITER
 19   IJQ018       INVALID SYMBOL
 22   IJQ023       PREVIOUSLY DEFINED NAME

  8 STATEMENTS FLAGGED IN THIS ASSEMBLY
```

frequent cause of errors in the source program is that the problem has been improperly or incompletely stated. Most of the obvious errors, such as unnamed storage areas called for by the program, card-punching errors, or arithmetic format errors, will be detected by the compiler. Computers rarely make mistakes, although at times during the debugging stage, it appears that some errors have been made by the computer. Built-in detection circuits will normally reflect the type of mistake the computer has made by turning on an indicator and stopping the computer. The matter of detecting and classifying programmer errors is more complex and difficult.

The two major types of errors that cause difficulty in programs are the logical errors and the clerical errors. *Logical errors result from poor analysis.* For example, the failure to anticipate the possibility of an employee having a negative amount of pay due to excessive payroll deductions will result in an error. The omission of a test for this possible condition could result in a paycheck being written for this negative amount. Errors of this type can result from a lack of understanding by the programmer of all the possibilities of this data-processing application. A more comprehensive analysis of the problem can eliminate many errors like these.

Clerical errors usually occur during the coding stage. A programmer, in error, may assign two different symbolic names for the same parameter, or may use the wrong operation code symbol, or may omit one or more instructions.

As the size and complexity of programs increase, the debugging phase will consume more time. Many techniques exist to aid the programmer in this checkout stage. The use of a particular technique will depend on the programmer's estimate of the extent and nature of the errors. Techniques that involve the testing of the program by the use of switches on the operator's console of the computer are very wasteful of valuable computer time and should be prohibited.

A successful technique of debugging is the printing out of storage contents relating to the particular problem. The contents of storage, registers, and indicators are presented in printed form. This printout (dump) routine will locate many errors on the listing, which the programmer may correct at this time (fig. 9.14).

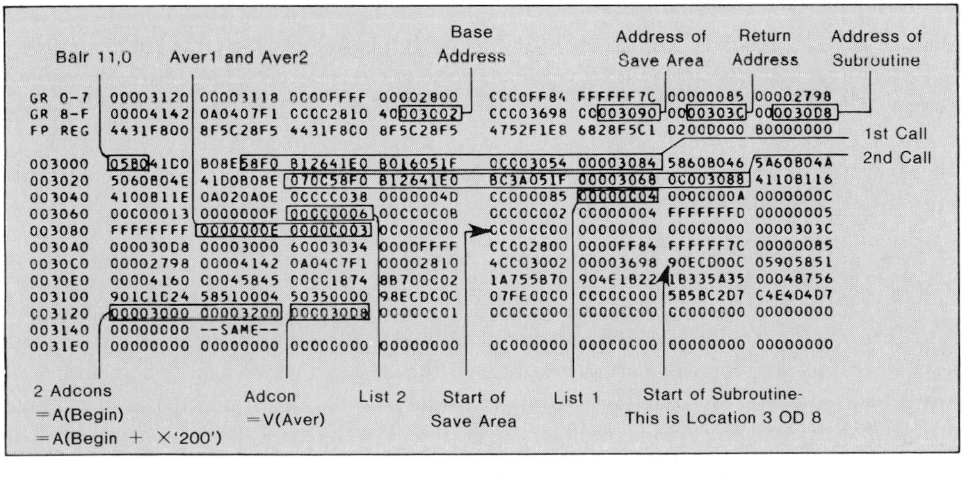

Figure 9.14 Dump of storage.

If the visually checked procedures do not reveal all the errors of a particular program, a tracing routine may be used. This method involves a routine program that executes a number of instructions for each program being traced. The printout received while tracing normally involves the location of the instruction being executed and the contents of the registers after execution of the instruction. This technique involves a great amount of computer time and should be used only after all other techniques have failed to locate the error.

The tracing technique can be modified to print only the contents of selected storage locations when the program reaches the specified point in the program.

When all bugs have been eliminated from the source program, it should be run with test data. The test data should include all possible conditions, particularly exception routines. The data should force the program through most of the exception routines. The test data should be checked with predetermined results to assure that the program is free from error.

Debugging will find most of the errors in a program and reduce the possibility of others, but it will not eliminate the possibility that some errors still exist that may be detected with actual data. The time consumed by the necessary debugging processes can be reduced if certain rules are followed.

1. Be aware of all debugging techniques available, and do not hesitate to use them. Do not be satisfied with concentrating on one basic technique.
2. A successful debugging does not assure that the program will run to completion with the actual data. The actual data may be too large for the storage area assigned, too slow for the processing procedure, or not in the planned format.
3. Ascertain that the program does all that is expected of it.
4. Document each program thoroughly, wherever possible, to enable the reader to understand what each program step should accomplish.
5. Leave room in the program for the possible insertion of testing or printing routines that may be used to test the program.
6. Check all source cards with documentation before compilation and test runs.

After all the expense and complexity of the debugging process, it is still impossible to determine that a complex program is completely error-free. This frustrating phase of programming may be lessened if the six rules above are followed. Debugging procedures are relatively ineffective with synthetic data as the program is not aware of all errors. In a complex program, it is difficult, if not virtually impossible, to write branches to test all possible clerical errors.

Summary

The future of computers is dependent not only on increases in speed of processing, logical ability, and storage capacities, but on the constant improvement in programming techniques as well. After a complete analysis of the problem, the completed problem statement must then be translated into flowcharts and decision tables. The flowchart and necessary decision tables are then translated into a program, a series of instructions. This chapter furnishes the transition between the expression of the problem in flowchart form and the technical methods for the processing of the data in the form of a complete program. You must learn to understand computer-programming languages in order to communicate with the computer.

You must learn the meanings of machine language, symbolic language, compilers, macro instructions, machine-, problem-, and procedure-oriented programming languages.

1. Machine language is a common language of a particular computer that does not require further modification before execution by computer. However, problems, such as writing programs with actual addresses and revision of programs, result from the machine language.
2. Symbolic language uses mnemonic characters to write programs (source programs) that must be later translated (compiler or assembler) into the machine language (object program) of a particular computer. This simplifies program writing and organization, simplifies program adjustments, facilitates program testing, and eliminates the need for direct machine coding.
3. Assemblers are processor programs supplied by the computer manufacturer that translates a program written in symbolic form into a machine language on a one-for-one basis.
4. Compilers are processor programs supplied by computer manufacturers that translate the source program into the object program.
5. Machine-oriented programming language is a symbolic programming language written by a programmer for a particular computer. It allows the programmer to take full advantage of the features and capabilities of the particular computer. The coding form provides the name, operation code, operand, and comments.
6. Problem-oriented and procedure-oriented programming languages are symbolic languages tailored to the solution of the problem rather than to the particular machine. Problem-oriented languages, such as RPG, describe the problem to the computer and the computer generates the necessary procedures for the solution of the problem. The procedure-oriented programming language, such as COBOL and FORTRAN, describe the procedures to the computer and the compiler translates the source program into the necessary machine language instructions to solve the program.
7. Programs are checked for logical and clerical errors. Logical errors result from poor analysis of a problem. Clerical errors result from poor coding of a program. A dump routine prints the contents of storage, registers, and indicators.

Identification Questions

Match the following terms with the statements below.

A. Assembler
B. Clerical Errors
C. COBOL
D. Compilers
E. Debugging
F. Dump
G. FORTRAN
H. Linkage Editor
I. Logical Errors
J. Machine Language
K. Machine-Oriented Programming Language
L. Macro Instruction
M. Mnemonic Symbols

N. Object Program
O. Problem-Oriented Programming Language
P. Procedure-Oriented Programming Language
Q. RPG
R. Source Program
S. Subroutines
T. Symbolic Language

1. Report Program Generator that is a problem-oriented programming language.
2. A program written in a symbolic language.
3. A processor program that translates a source program into a machine language on a one-for-one basis.
4. An instruction that is equivalent to a specified sequence of machine instructions.
5. It produces the executable program.
6. A symbolic language that describes the problem to the computer and the compiler generates the necessary procedures.
7. Errors that result from poor analysis.
8. Printing out of storage contents relating to a particular problem.
9. The common language of a particular computer.
10. A program written in machine language.
11. Short routines or programs common to a number of programs.
12. A symbolic programming language written for a particular computer.
13. Formula Translator that is a procedure-oriented programming language.
14. Errors that result from poor coding.
15. Symbols chosen to assist human memory.
16. The use of mnemonic characters to write a program.
17. A processor program that translates a source program into machine-language instructions to solve the program.
18. A symbolic language that describes procedures to the computer.
19. Common Business Oriented Language that is a procedure-oriented programming language.
20. The determination that the program will accomplish the desired result.

Questions for Review

1. What does the future of computers depend on?
2. List the steps involved in programming.
3. How is the program written by the programmer?
4. What is the difference between a machine-language and symbolic language programs?
5. How does symbolic programming overcome some of the disadvantages of machine-language coding?
6. What are the important advantages of symbolic programming?
7. What is a compiler? What is its main function? Give examples.
8. What is a machine-oriented programming language? Give an example.
9. Explain the functions of the four fields—name, operation, operand, comments—of the IBM System 360/370 coding form.

10. What are the serious disadvantages in using machine-oriented programming languages?
11. Describe problem-oriented and procedure-oriented programming languages and tell how they differ from machine-oriented programming languages. Give examples of problem- and procedure-oriented programming languages.
12. What are two main types of programming errors? Give examples of each.
13. What is a dump routine? How can it help programmers to debug their program?
14. What are some rules for successful debugging?

Key Terms

Assembler
Clerical Errors
COBOL
Compiler
Debugging
Dump
FORTRAN
Linkage Editor
Logical Errors
Machine Language
Machine-Oriented Programming Language
Macro Instructions
Mnemonic Symbols
Object Program
Problem-Oriented Programming Language
Procedure-Oriented Programming Language
RPG
Source Program
Subroutines
Symbolic Language

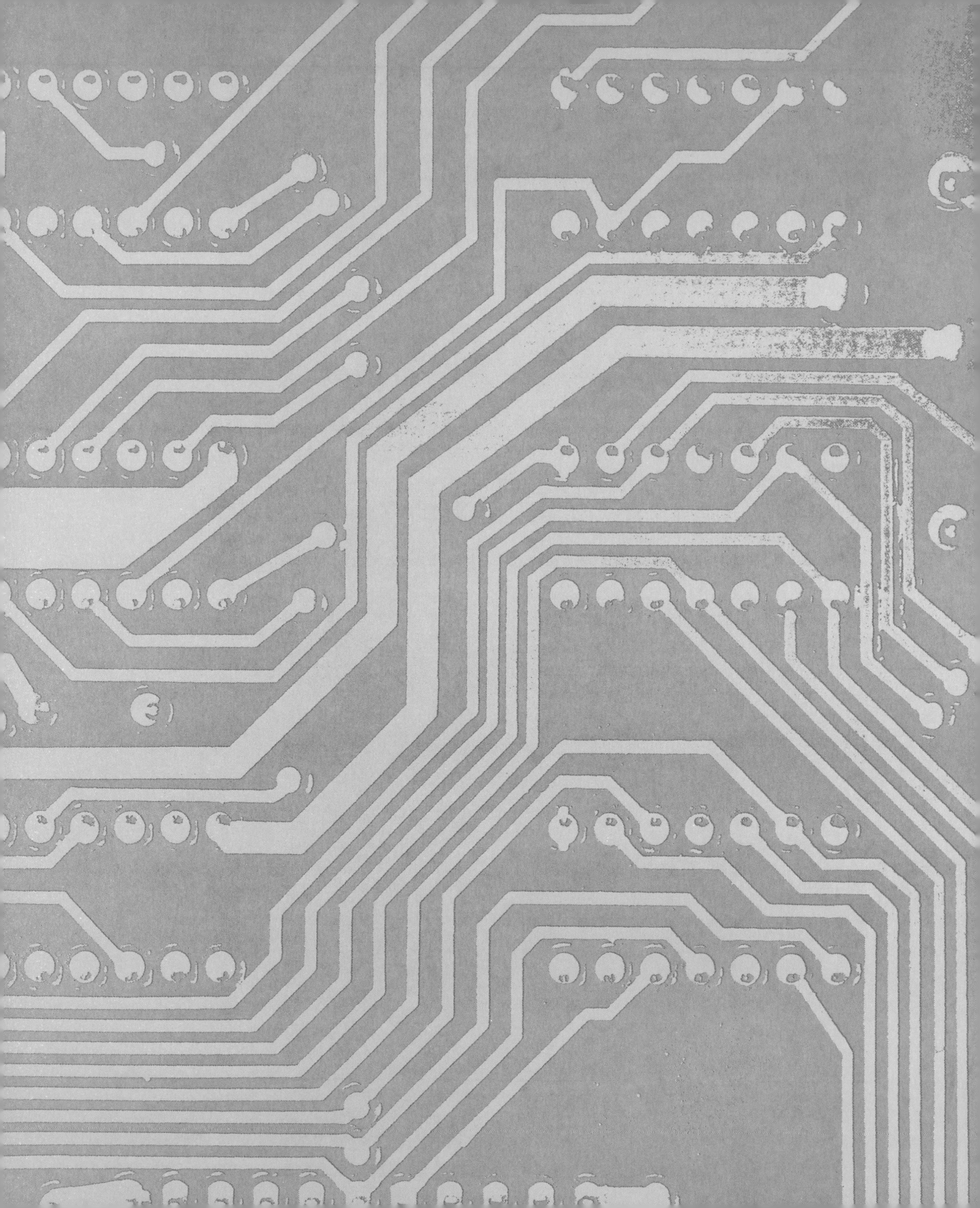

programming elements 10

Chapter Outline

Chapter Objectives

The learning objectives of this chapter are

1. to describe the various programming elements, such as structured programming, subroutines, and macro instructions, and the important role they play in the efficient operation of a computer system.
2. to explain the operation of the job control language that establishes the communication link between the programmer and the control system of the computer.
3. to describe the operation of an operating system that improves the total effectiveness of the computer system by eliminating manual intervention.
4. to explain how virtual storage can significantly speed and simplify the development of many computer applications by freeing the programmer from time-consuming routine tasks.

Effective programmers are faced with huge complex systems of many interacting components. After deciding upon a programming language, the next step is the orderly coding, testing, and documenting the computer program. Programmers use certain specialized data-processing techniques that help to make complex jobs easier to program and more readily understandable to those with whom they communicate. These data-processing techniques may vary according to the computer and the requirements of the program and programming language. Most programmers recognize them and use them when the job demands.

Aside from flowcharting and decision table techniques, the programmer may use structured programming, subroutines, and macro instructions to increase the efficiency of the program.

Structured Programming

Structured programming attempts to reduce the complexity of programs and make programs more readable and understandable. Less complex programs are more likely to reduce development time, if operated properly, and are certainly easier to change.

Structured programming applies a theoretical concept to the coding of computer programs. The main element of the concept is the use of very basic structures to create complex programs. To apply structured programming in a data-processing environment requires a change in program design methods and rigid application of standards to insure the best results.

A structured program tends to be much easier to understand than programs written in other styles. This capability of being more easily understood facilitates code checking, which in turn may reduce program testing and debugging time. This is true partly because structured programming concentrates on one of the most error-prone factors in programming, the logic.

Structured programming offers many benefits, but it should not be thought of as a panacea. Program development is still a demanding task requiring skill, effort, and creativity (fig. 10.1).

Figure 10.1 The benefits of structured programming.

BENEFITS

- **Encourages programming discipline**
- **Fewer errors**
- **More easily modified and maintained**
- **More nearly self-documenting**
- **Programmer can control larger amount of code**

The main objective of structured programming is to provide a single generalized method of program design to provide the following:

Objectives

1. Program development by segment.
2. Ease of coding.
3. Speed of coding.
4. Ease of debugging.
5. Ease of maintenance.

Structure

Structured programming is a style of programming in which the structure of a program (that is, the interrelationship of its parts) is made as clear as possible by restricting control logic to just three structures (fig. 10.2).

1. *Sequence*—In the absence of instructions to the contrary, statements are executed in the order in which they are written (fig. 10.3). This is true of all commonly used programming languages.
2. *Selection* (IF-THEN-ELSE) is the choice between two actions based on a condition (fig. 10.4).
3. *Iteration* (Loop Control or DO-WHILE) is used for the repeated execution of a code while a condition is true (fig. 10.5).

In a structured program, any program function can be performed using any of the three basic control logic structures, sequence, selection, or iteration. Any kind of processing, any combination of decisions, and any sort of logic can be accommodated with any one of these control structures or a combination of them. Each structure is

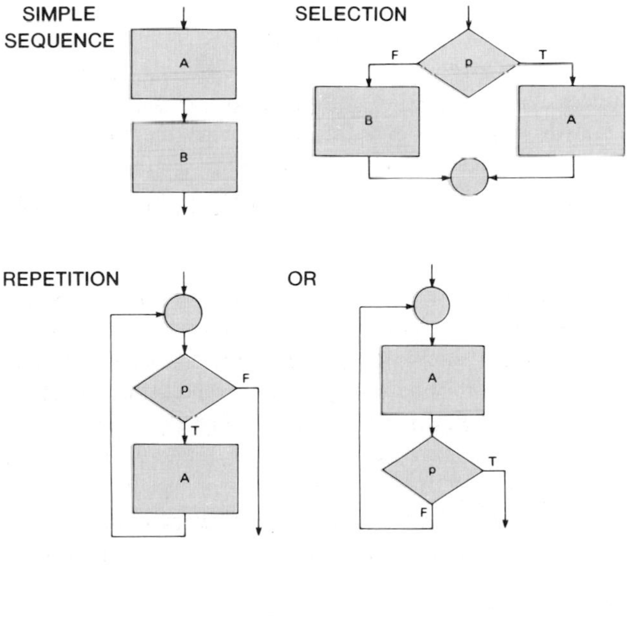

Figure 10.2 Examples of control structures.

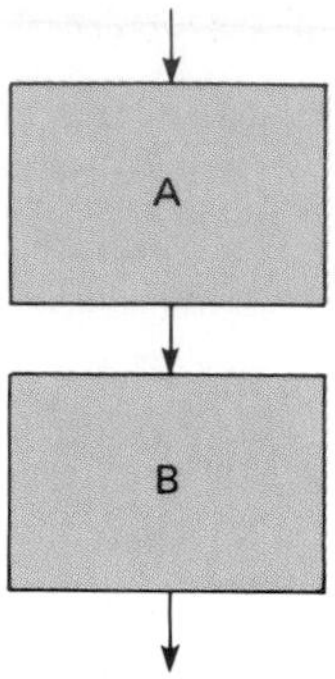

Figure 10.3 A flowchart for sequence program structure.

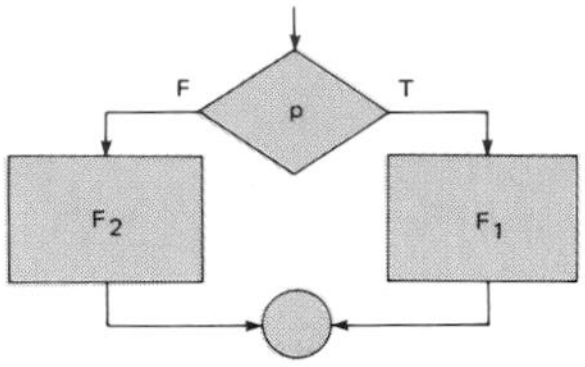

Figure 10.4 A flowchart for selection program structure.

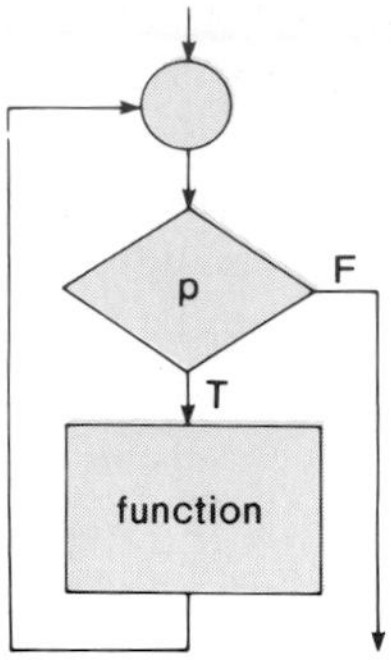

Figure 10.5 A flowchart for iteration program structure.

characterized by a simple and single point of transfer of control into the structure and a single point of transfer of control out of the structure. These structures can be combined to form a program that is simple, in sequence from top to bottom or from beginning to end. There is no backtracking. Simply stated, structured programming is programming with a limited set of well-defined control structures.

Segments

A structured program is composed of *segments,* which may range from a few statements to almost a page of code. Each segment is allowed to have just one entry and one exit point. These functional segments should ideally perform a single major function or a group of related functions. An entire program can be implemented as an integrated set of program segments.

Top-Down Design

Top-down design follows the adage of "divide and conquer." A difficult problem is successively reduced to component subproblems.

An important characteristic of a structured program is that it can be read in sequence, from top to bottom, without a great deal of the "skipping around" through the program. This is important because it is much easier to comprehend what a function does if all the statements that influence its action are physically close. Top-down readability is one consequence of using only three control logic structures and of avoiding the branch-type statements (switching sequence to other parts of the program), except in very special circumstances.

For example, assume that a program is to be written to retrieve information from a file. A file may be considered a collection of records with each record residing on some section of the disk. Each record is, in turn, composed of words, each word is composed of bytes, and each byte is composed of bits. The hierarchy of resources needed to retrieve a single bit from the file is as follows:

Lowest Level	bit
↑	byte
	word
↓	record
Highest Level	file

A set of instructions would be written to manipulate files, in this case, to locate and extract particular records. The next level of instructions would operate solely on records, extracting words from records, retrieved by manipulating the program. In turn, the next level would be represented by a set of instructions to extract bytes from words; at the top would be the program to extract bits from bytes.

Structured programming and top-down program development both emphasize the importance of segments that interact in precisely understood ways. Both involve looking at a program as a hierarchy of segments that are related to each other in a tree-like fashion.

Hierarchy plus Input-Process-Output (HIPO)

A precise definition of user requirements is essential to the development of a correct data-processing system. Hierarchy plus input-process-output (HIPO) is an approach to functional specification and documentation of programs. It is a method of graphically describing a program entity as an arrangement of functions to be performed. Each function is designed using a HIPO diagram, in which inputs and outputs are listed and the processing that will be carried out is specified (fig. 10.6). A table of contents diagram points to the HIPO diagrams in the package and, therefore, shows the functions and subfunctions to be carried out by the various parts of the program and the relationship between them. At the detailed design level, it also shows the hierarchy of segments (fig. 10.7). HIPO has successfully fulfilled two of the greatest needs in the data-processing industry—providing a means of precisely defining user requirements and expanding the essential lines of communication between the user and data processing, since the user is involved in the development of the HIPO diagram. HIPO is a good way to approach the design task, and is complementary to structured programming.

Conclusion

The development of these new techniques has been motivated by a desire to reduce the cost of developing and maintaining programs. Structured programming is simpler to write, easier to read and understand, and easier to modify. Furthermore, it will have fewer bugs when written.

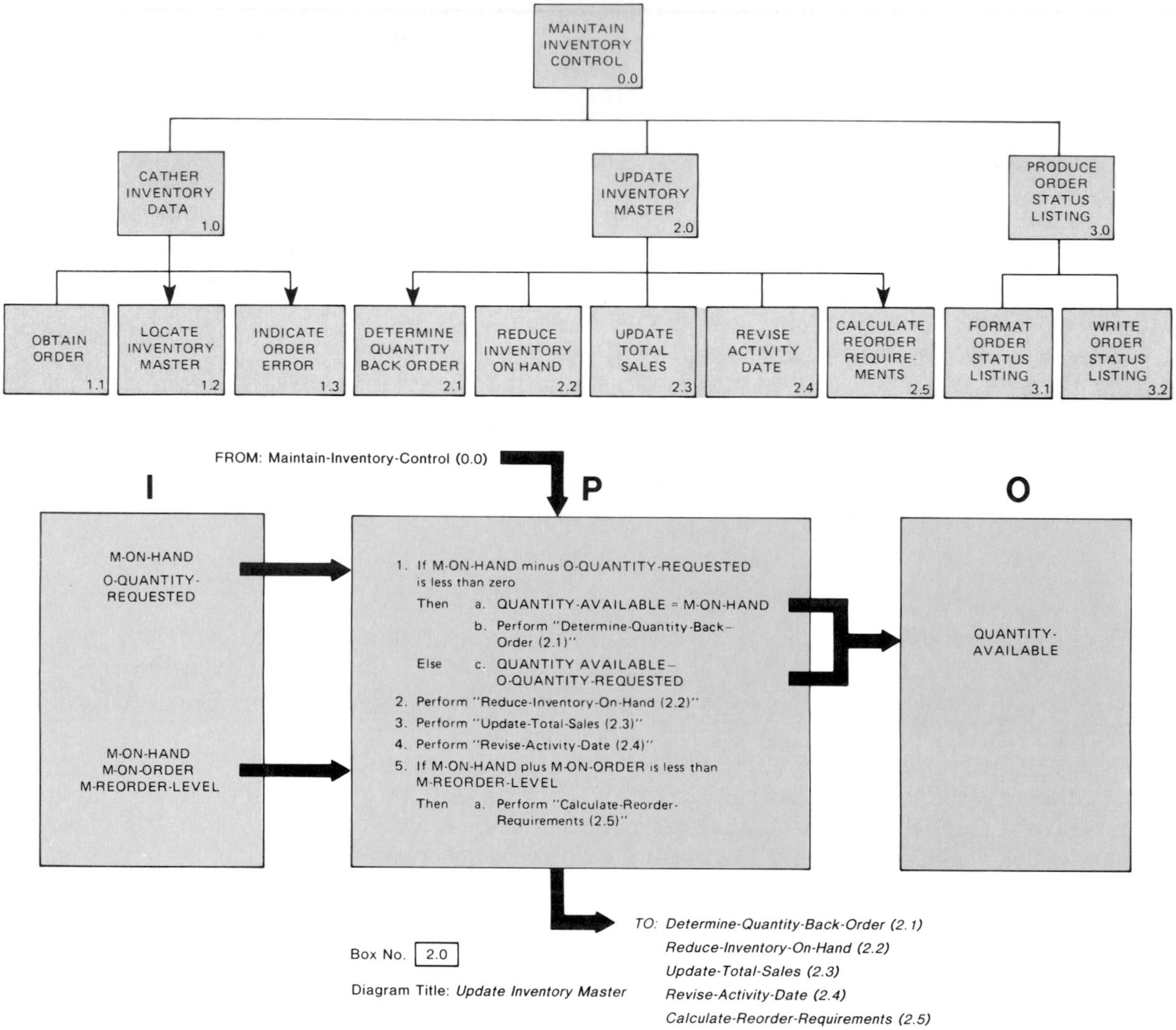

Figure 10.6 A detailed design level HIPO diagram.

Subroutines

Often a single routine within a program is performed several times for a given record or for a number of different records. This routine might be entered from several different points in the program. There are also times when a programmer might wish to jump to a routine not found in the immediate sequence of logic on the flowchart. After completion of this routine, the logic would return to the original flowchart exit point. The jump to the same routine might occur from several different points in the program. An out-of-mainline routine is classified as a subroutine (fig. 10.8).

A subroutine is a subprogram consisting of a set of instructions that performs some subordinate function within the program. There are two methods to include the subroutine in a program. The best method is to insert the subroutine directly into the

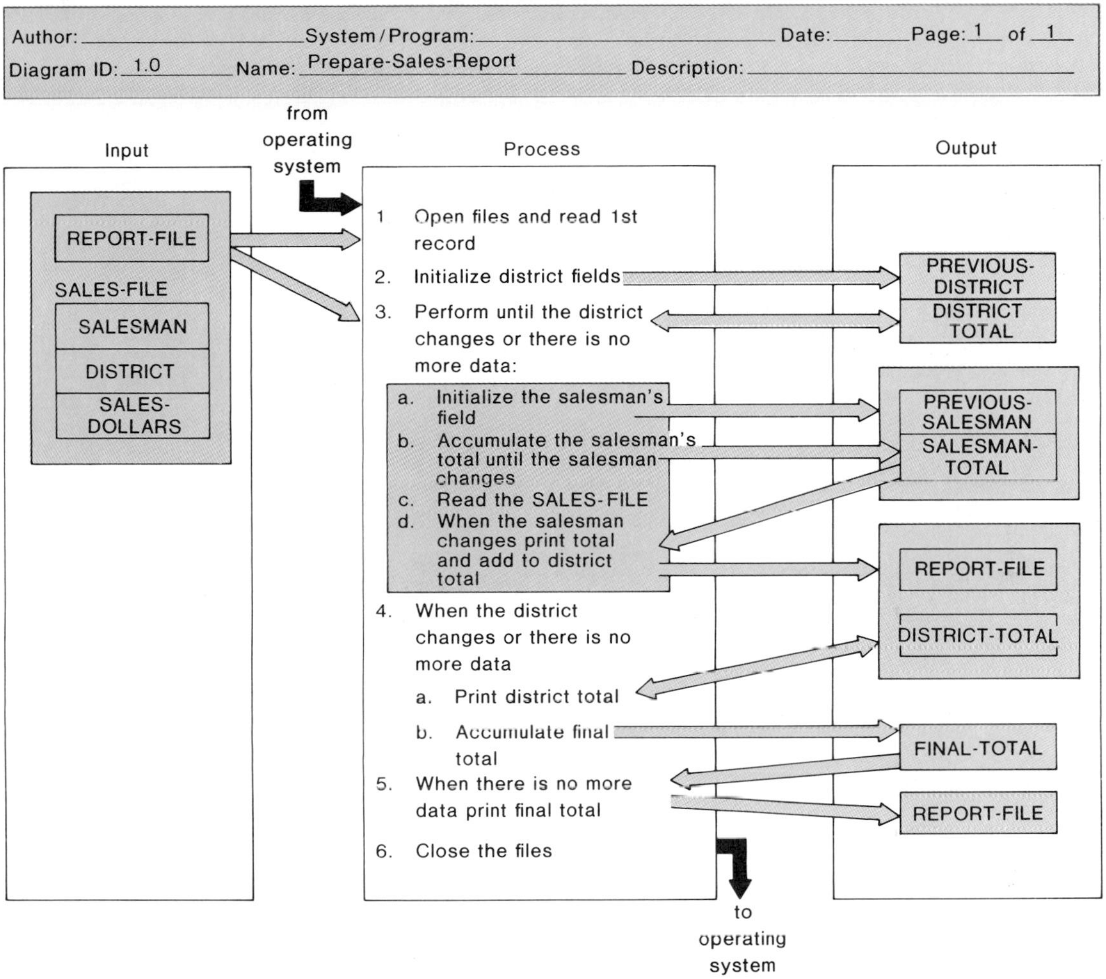

Figure 10.7 A detailed design level HIPO diagram.

main program where it is needed. A subroutine used in this manner is known as an *open* subroutine (fig. 10.9).

If the program requires the execution of the subroutine several times during the operation of the main program, the use of an open subroutine is not practical because of the storage limitations and the apparent waste of time and storage that would result from repeating the same set of instructions many times. A *closed* subroutine is included in the program only once but is referred to whenever the desired function is needed (fig. 10.10). This avoids the repetition of instructions. The closed subroutine presents the problem of returning to the main program at the proper place.

A closed subroutine is one that is entered by a jump or branch and one that provides return to the main routine by coding at the end of the subroutine's operations. The instructions necessary to effect the entry and reentry functions are known as *linkage*. Closed subroutines, which add versatility to a program, conserve memory space and programming time. The key to a successful closed subroutine is the subrou-

Figure 10.8 An example of a subroutine, a read error loop.

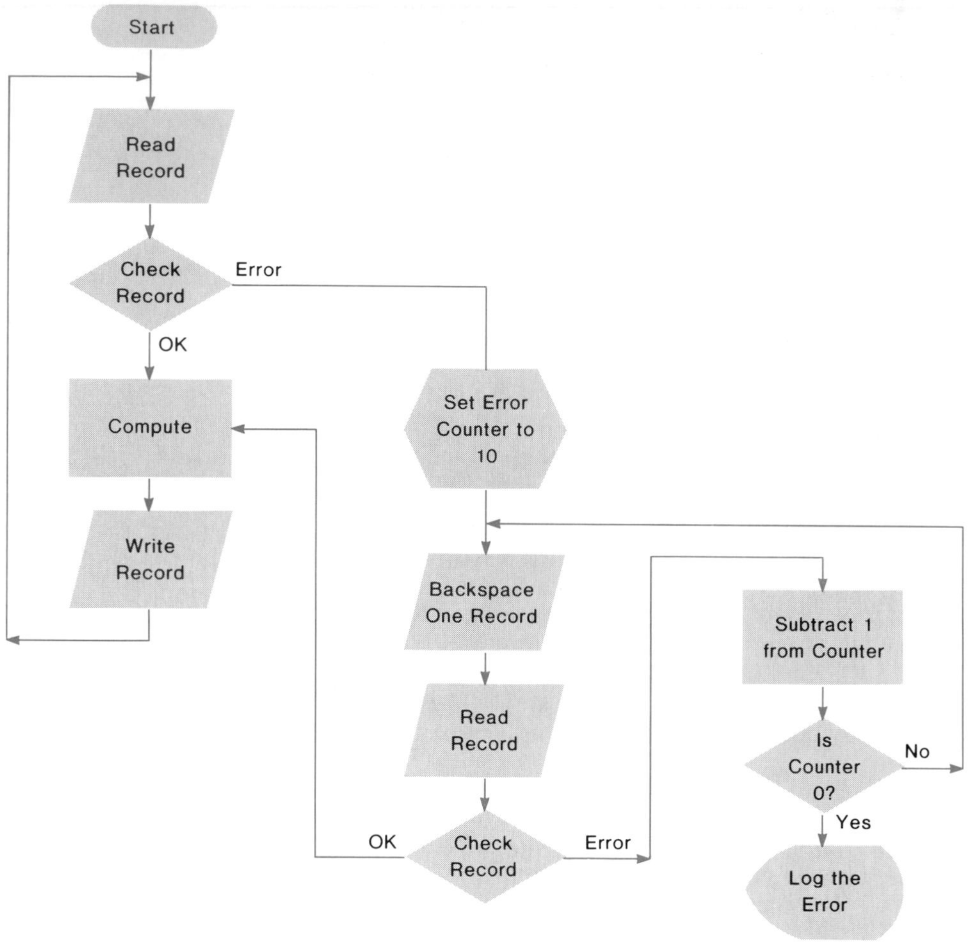

tine's logic. Linkage is the logic that enters the subroutine and, after the subroutine's operations have been performed, reenters the main line of coding at the point where the jump to the subroutine was originally made.

Subroutines ease the task of the programmer by reducing the number of instructions to be written and include pretested routines in the program. These subroutines can be written as a separate job by a programmer not acquainted with the main program. Routines that are reused in a large variety of programs can be kept in a library, where they can be made available to all users.

Macro Instructions

When a programmer writes a series of instructions for a routine that will be needed repeatedly during the program, he does not have to code the entire sequence each time. The programmer can make up a code word in a single statement whenever it is needed, which causes the sequence of instructions to be assembled and inserted (fig. 10.11). Incorporated into the system library, the sequence can also be used in entirely separate programs and by all programmers associated with the computer installation simply by writing one statement in a source program.

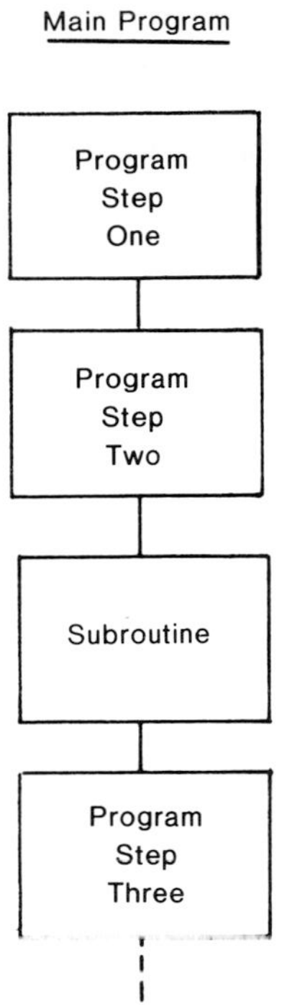

Figure 10.9 An example of an open subroutine.

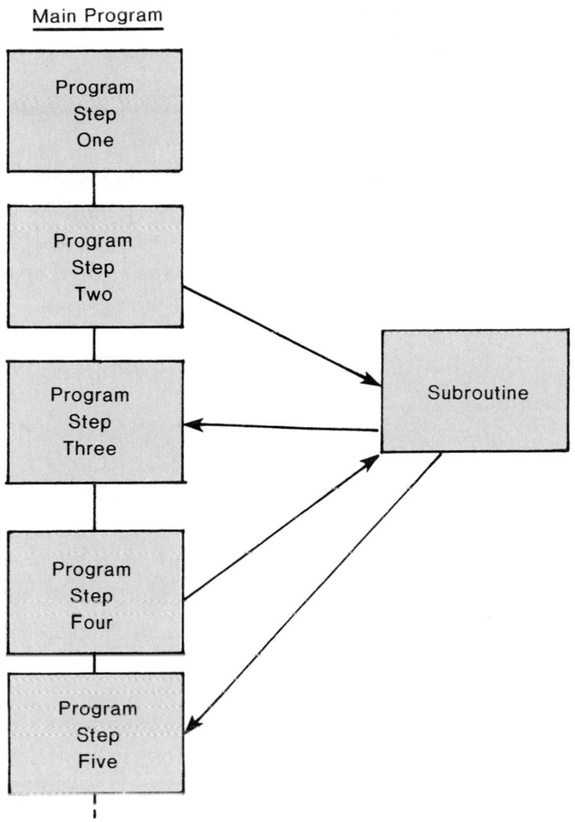

Figure 10.10 An example of a closed subroutine.

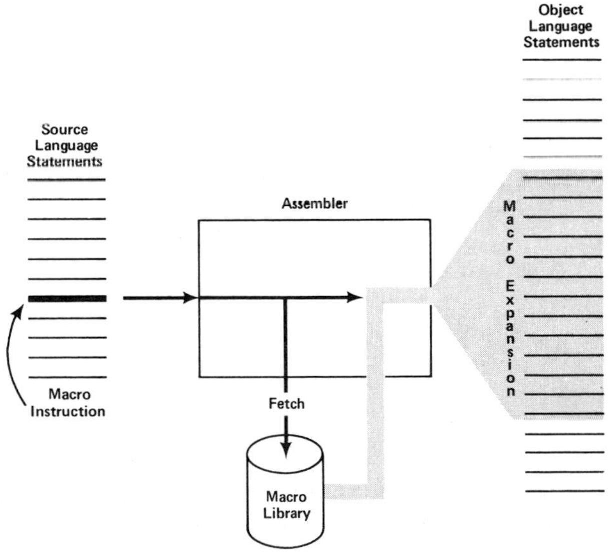

Figure 10.11 Macro instruction expansion.

The macro instructions supplied by the computer manufacturers are used mainly for procedures that affect other components of the operating system. Because most input/output routines are long and complicated, most of these macros are supplied by the computer manufacturer. Macro instructions can ensure accuracy and standardization of frequently repeated procedures.

A macro instruction is a symbolic statement that combines several operations into one. It provides a convenient way to generate a desired sequence of source program instructions many times in one or more source programs. The macro definition is written only once in a single statement. A macro instruction is written each time a programmer wants to generate the desired sequence of statements. This facility greatly simplifies the coding of programs, reduces chances of programming errors, and insures that standard sequences of source program statements are used to accomplish desired functions.

Most macro instructions are supplied by the computer manufacturer but programmers may develop their own to satisfy their particular needs. The macro instruction statement is a source program statement. It can produce a variable number of machine instructions for each occurrence of the same macro instruction. These generated statements are processed in the same way as any other source statement.

The use of macro instructions increases the effectiveness of a programming language by enlarging the functions of the translator.

Job Control Language

The operating system was designed to meet the many diverse needs of the computer user. Data-processing needs differ greatly from one installation to another and between individual users within an installation. The operating system aids computer users to get their work done. It achieves its purpose by managing all available resources, including the central processing unit, main storage, input/output devices, and any programs that are part of the system. To use the operating system, the programmer must describe to the system what work is to be done and what resources will be needed. This information is provided to the operating system through the use of job control language (fig. 10.12).

Job control language (JCL) cards establish the communication link between the programmer and the control system of the computer. The control system consists of a number of processing programs and a control program. The processing programs will include compilers, service programs, as well as user-written programs. The control program supervises the execution and loading of the processing programs; controls the location, storage, and retrieval of data; and schedules the jobs for continuous processing of problem programs.

Executing a Problem Program

The basic operations that are performed to execute a problem program are (fig. 10.13):

1. *Compilation* is the process of translating a source program into a series of instructions that are comprehensible to the computer. In computer terminology, the input (source program) to the compiler is called the *source module.* The output (compiled source program) from the compiler is called the *object module.*

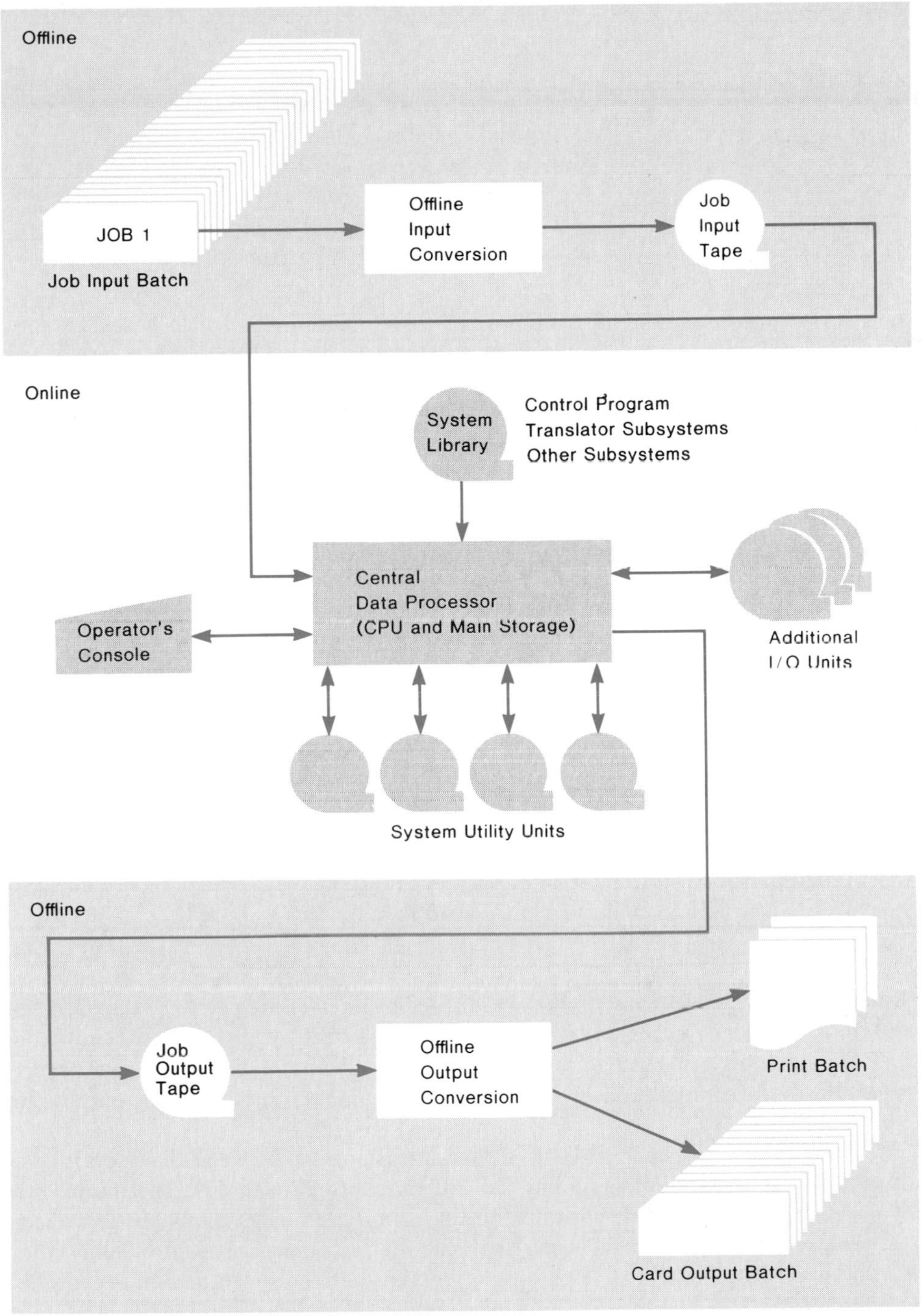

Figure 10.12 Job processing at a typical operating system installation. (Courtesy of IBM)

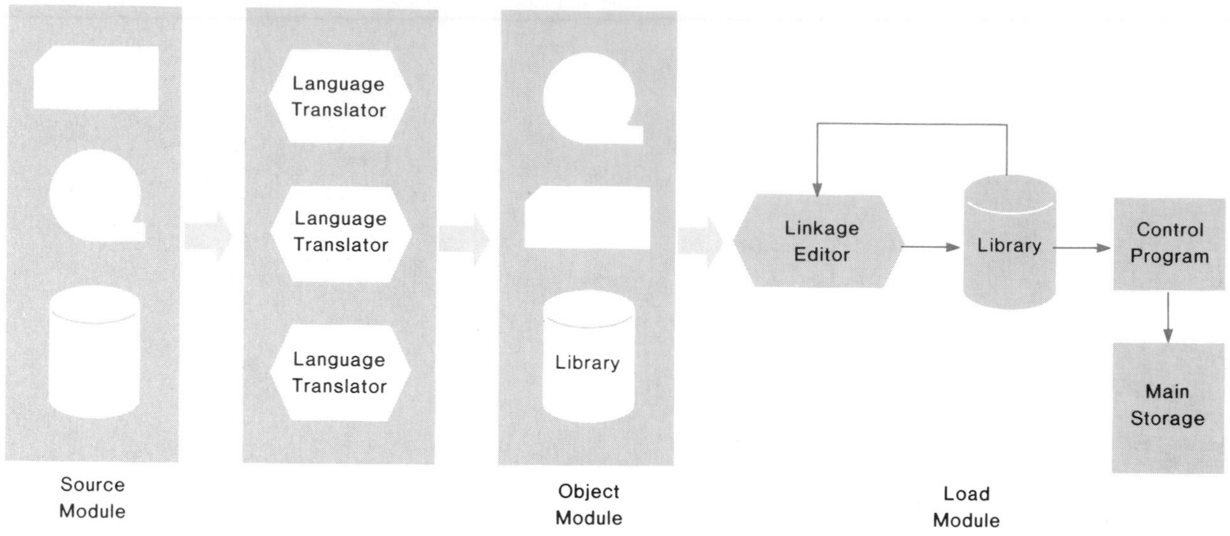

Figure 10.13 Program preparation. (Courtesy of IBM)

2. *Linkage editing* is a service program that prepares object modules for execution. It can also be used to combine two or more separately compiled object modules into a format suitable for execution as a single program. The executed output of linkage editing is called a *load module.* Linkage editing may also combine previously edited load modules with or without one or more object modules to form one load module.
3. *Loading* is a service program that processes object and load modules, resolves any references to subprograms, and executes the load module. All these functions are specified in one step.
4. *Execution* is under the supervision of the control program, which obtains a load module, loads it into main storage, and initiates execution of the machine-language instructions contained in the load module.

Job

A *job* is the independent unit of work performed by an operating system (the operating system is discussed in greater detail later in this chapter). A job can be a compilation or a problem program, such as payroll or inventory file maintenance and a sort-merge program. In short, any complete operation involving input, processing, and output may be a job.

The job control program is the communication link between the operator and other parts of the operating system. To call for a program to do a specific job, the operator must communicate with the job control program (figs. 10.14, 10.15).

Job scheduling within the operating system of a computer is controlled by information placed in the input stream by the programmer. This information is expressed in job control language for each type of computer. The job control language for the IBM System 360/370 operating system consists of the following types:

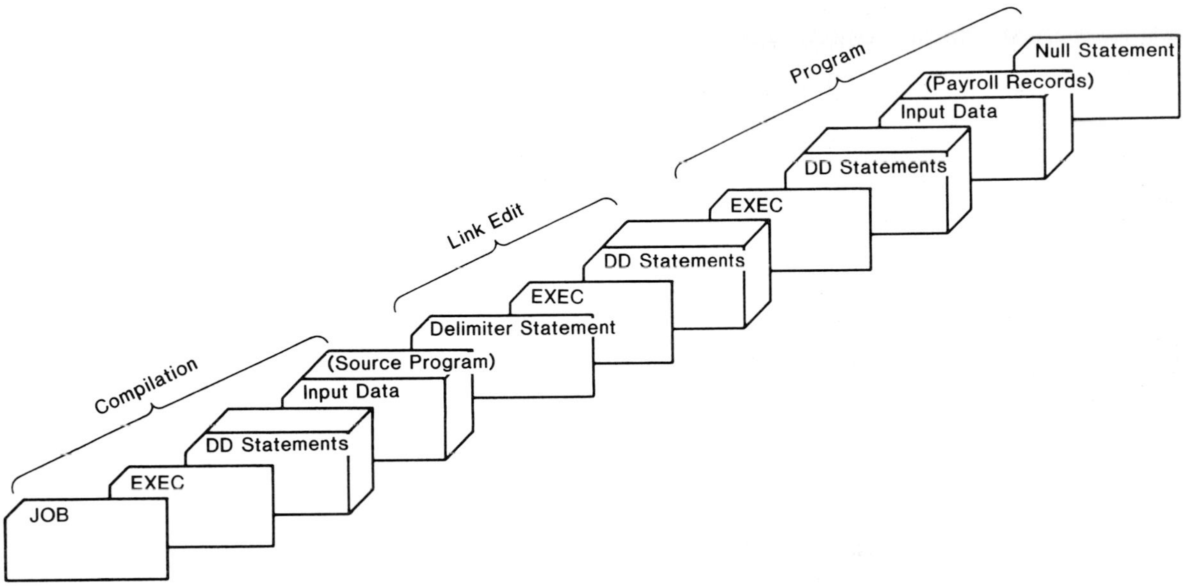

Figure 10.14 Compilation of a program.

Columns:

1 2 3

Name	Operation	Operand	Comments
/ /JOB8	JOB	MSGLEVEL=(1,1)	THE FIRST STATEMENT IN JOB
/ /STP1	EXEC	PGM=PROG4,REGION=80K	EXECUTES PROGRAM NAMED PROG4
/ /WORK	DD	UNIT=2400	DEFINES A TEMPORARY DATA SET

Figure 10.15 An example of the control statement fields.

Statement	**Function**
JOB	Indicates the beginning of a new job and describes that job.
EXEC	Indicates a job step and describes that job step; indicates a load module or catalogued procedure to be executed.
DD	Describes data sets and controls device and volume assignment.
Delimiter	Separates data sets in the input stream from control statements. It must follow each data set that appears in the input stream.
Comment	Contains miscellaneous remarks and notes written by the programmer. It may appear anywhere in the job stream.

The job control language statements used to describe a job to the system are:

1. Job (JOB) statement.
2. Execute (EXEC) statement.
3. Data definition (DD) statement.
4. Delimiter statement.
5. Null statement.
6. Procedure (PROC) statement.
7. Procedure end (PEND) statement.
8. Comment statement.
9. Command statement.

The *JOB statement* tells the system where a job begins. The name of the job is coded and used to identify messages to the operator and to identify the program output. Additional information, such as accounting information, conditions for early termination of a job, job priority, and maximum amount of time, can be specified in the card (fig. 10.16).

The *EXEC statement* marks the beginning of a job step and the end of the preceding step. The program to be executed is identified or the catalogued procedure or in-stream procedure is called. A catalogued procedure is a set of job control statements that has been assigned a name and placed in a partitioned data set, known as the procedure library (fig. 10.17). The EXEC statement may also be used to provide job step accounting information and to give conditions for bypassing or executing a job step.

A *DD statement* identifies a data set and describes its attributes. There must be a DD statement for each data set used or created in a job step. The DD statements are placed after the EXEC statement for the step. The DD statement provides such information as the name of the data set, the name of the volume on which it resides, the type of I/O device that holds the data set, the format of the records in the data set, whether the data set is old or new, the size of newly created data sets, and the method that will be used to create or access a data set. The name of the DD statement provides a symbolic link between the data set (or data file) named in the program and the actual name and location of the corresponding data set. This symbolic link allows the computer user to relate the data set in the program to different data sets on different occasions (fig. 10.18).

Figure 10.16
Examples of JOB statements.

```
//ALPHA    JOB   843,LINEE,CLASS=F,MSGLEVEL=(1,1)
//LOS      JOB   BROWNLY,REGION=90K,TIME=(4,30),
                 MSGLEVEL=(2,0)
//MART     JOB   1863,RESTART=STEP 4
//TRY8     JOB
```

```
// STEP 1 EXEC PGM=TABULATE
```

Specifies that the program named TABULATE is a member of SYS1.LINKLIB.

```
//JOB8      JOB    MSGLEVEL=(2,0)
//JOBLIB    DD     DDSNAME=DEPT12.LIB4,DISP=OLD,PASS)
//STEP1     EXEC   PGM=USCAN
```

Specifies that the system is to look for a program named USCAN in a private library named DEPT12.LIB4, and, if not found there, the system is to look in the system library.

```
//SP3  EXEC PROC=PAYWKRS
```

Specifies that the catalogued or in-stream procedure named PAYWKRS is to be called.

```
//BK3  EXEC OPERATE
```

Specifies that the cataloged or in-stream procedure named OPERATE is to be called. This specification has the same effect as coding PROC=OPERATE.

Figure 10.17 Examples of EXEC statements.

```
//DDA       DD     DSNAME=&&TEMP,UNIT=2400,DISP=(NEW,PASS)

//PRINT     DD     SYSOUT=F

//IN        DD     DSNAME=ALLOC,DISP=(,KEEP,DELETE),UNIT=2311,          X
//                 VOLUME=SER=541382,SPACE=(CYL,(12,1))

//DWN       DD     *
```

Figure 10.18 Examples of DD statements.

The *delimiter statement* (or /* statement) (fig. 10.19) and the *null statement* (or / /) (fig. 10.20) are markers in the input stream. The delimiter statement is used to separate data placed in the input stream from any JCL statement that may follow the data. The null statement can be used to mark the end of the JCL statements and data for a job.

The *PROC statement* may appear as the first JCL statement in a catalogued or in-stream procedure (fig. 10.21). For catalogued or in-stream procedures, the PROC statement is used to assign default values to parameters defined in a procedure. An in-stream procedure is a set of job control language statements that appear in the input stream. The PROC statement is used to mark the beginning of an in-stream procedure. The *PEND statement* is used to mark the end of an in-stream procedure (fig. 10.22).

The *comment statement* can be inserted either before or after any JCL statement that follows the JOB statement and can contain any information that would be helpful to anyone interested in the program (fig. 10.23).

Figure 10.19 An example of a delimiter statement.

```
//JOB54    JOB,'C BROWN',MSGLEVEL=(2,0)
//STEPA    EXEC PGM=SERS
//DD1      DD *
                .
                .
                .
           data
                .
                .
                .
/* END OF DATA FOR THIS STEP
```

Figure 10.20 An example of a null statement.

```
//MYJB     JOB ,'CDAVIS',MSGLEVEL=(1,1)
//STEP1    EXEC PROC=FIELD
//STEP2    EXEC PGM=XTRA
//DD1      DD   UNIT=2400
//DD2      DD   *
                .
                .
                .
           data
                .
                .
                .
/*
//
```

```
//DEF      PROC  STATUS=OLD,LIBRARY=SYSLIB,NUMBER=777777
//NOTIFY   EXEC  PGM=ACCUM
//DD1      DD    DSNAME=MGMT,DISP=(&STATUS,KEEP),UNIT=2400,       X
//               VOLUME=SER=888888
//DD2      DD    DSNAME=&LIBRARY,DISP=(OLD,KEEP),UNIT=2311,       X
//               VOLUME=SER=&NUMBER
```

Three symbolic parameters are defined in this cataloged procedure: &STATUS, &LIBRARY, and &NUMBER. Values are assigned to the symbolic parameters on the PROC statement. These values are used when the procedure is called and values are not assigned to the symbolic parameters by the programmer.

```
//CARDS  PROC
```

This PROC statement can be used to mark the beginning of an in-stream procedure named CARDS.

Figure 10.21 An example of a PROC statement.

```
//PROCEND1 PEND THIS STATEMENT IS REQUIRED FOR INSTREAM
```

This PEND statement contains a comment.

```
// PEND
```

A PEND statement can contain only the coded operation field preceded by // and one or more blanks and followed by blanks.

Figure 10.22 Examples of PEND statements.

```
//*THE COMMENT STATEMENT CANNOT BE CONTINUED,
//*BUT IF YOU HAVE A LOT TO SAY, YOU CAN FOLLOW A
//*COMMENT STATEMENT WITH ONE OR MORE COMMENT
//*STATEMENTS
```

Figure 10.23 An example of a COMMENT statement.

```
//  START INIT,,,AB START AN INITIATOR FOR MFT
```

This command tells the system to start an initiator. The characters A and B indicate that the initiator is to select for execution only jobs of job classes A and B.

Figure 10.24 An example of a COMMAND statement.

The *command statement* is used to enter commands through the input stream (fig. 10.24). Commands can activate and deactivate system input and output units, request printouts and displays, and perform a number of other operator functions.

Every job submitted for execution by the operating system must include JCL statements. Job control language is a very flexible language; with this flexibility come many optional features. You should become familiar with the language so you can decide what information the operating system will need to process the job and what features of the language will get the job done most efficiently.

Operating Systems

An operating system is an integrated set of processing programs and a control program designed to improve the total operating effectiveness of a computer. The operating system is directed by user-prepared control cards to pass automatically from job to job with a minimum of delay and operator intervention. Communication with the computer is via the operating system rather than directly, as was the case with most early computers.

With today's more powerful machines, setup time is becoming proportionately larger for each job. As a result, large, expensive computers sit idle at times while new work is being loaded. Even during the execution of a program, many components of the system may remain idle. Of all the resources available on a system, only parts of the total system may be required for a job. The operating system enables the user to stack jobs for continuous processing, thus reducing setup time between jobs. The

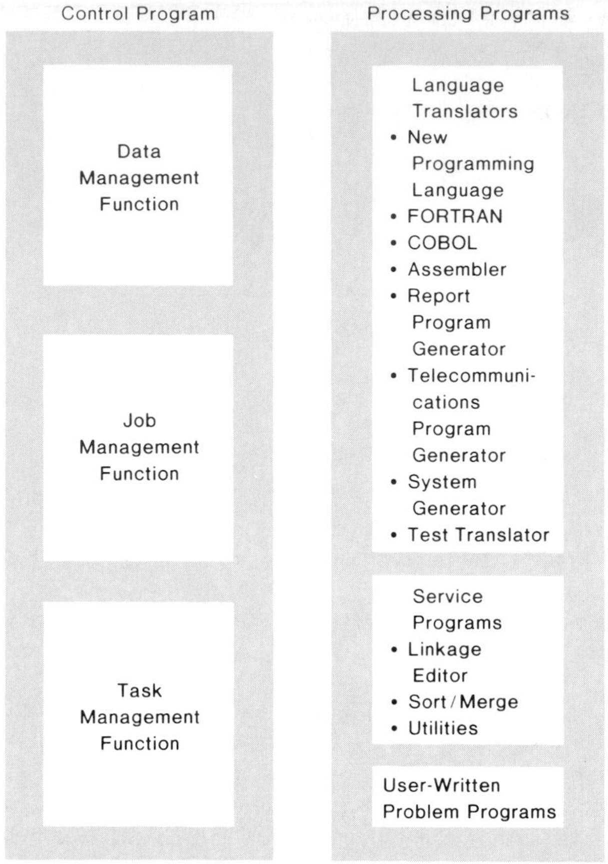

Figure 10.25 Control and processing programs. (Courtesy of IBM)

operating system has the ability to call in any required programs, routines, or data. Some operating systems have the ability to schedule jobs and allocate resources more efficiently by concurrently processing two or more independent programs (multiprogramming). They can compile symbolic languages (COBOL, FORTRAN, RPG II), organize files, and act as a supervisor for the entire system. In short, the operating system makes possible the maximum use of a computer.

Types of Operating Systems

There are two different systems operating with the IBM System 370—the DOS (disk operating system) and OS (operating system). Determining which system is best depends on the size of the system, the physical devices supported, and whether certain expanded functions are required, since features of one operating system may not be available in another.

Both systems are composed of two major sets of programs, which are known as control programs and processing programs (fig. 10.25). *Control programs* supervise the execution of the processing programs; control the location, storage, and retrieval of data; and schedule jobs for continuous processing. *Processing programs* consist of

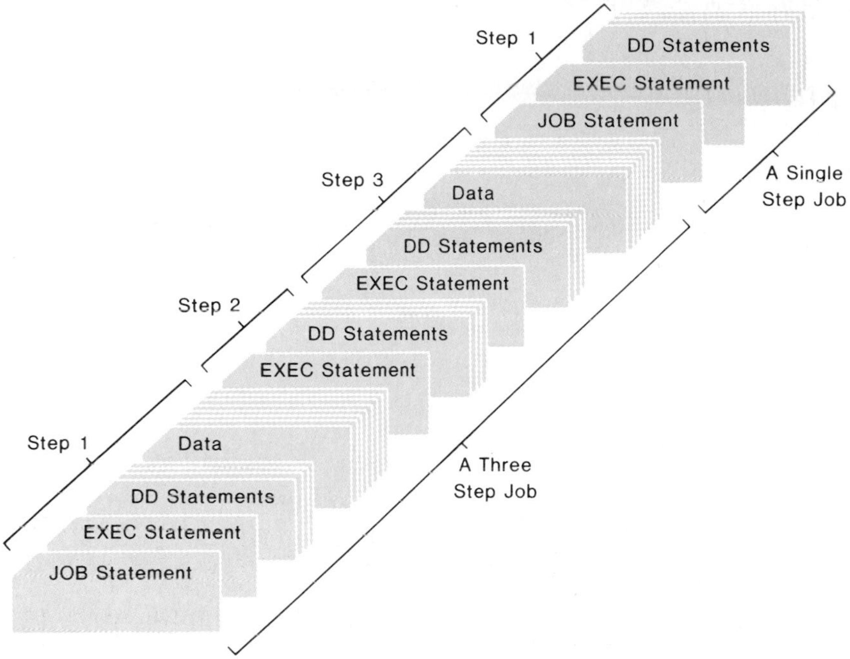

Figure 10.26 Job processing. (Courtesy of IBM)

language translators, service programs, and user-written problem programs, all of which the programmer uses to define the work that the computing system is to perform and to simplify program preparation.

System users may include their own service programs or language translators, which the programmer can then use in the same way as the manufacturer-supplied programs.

In both operating systems, the work to be done is regarded as a stack of jobs to be executed under the management of the control program. A job may contain one or more job steps and may be thought of as a series of logically related programs that must be executed in a given sequence. Job steps within a job are always executed in sequence and never operate concurrently.

Necessary information about each job is punched into job control cards by the user. These cards are read by a portion of the control program to instruct it as to which programs are to be executed, and in what sequence; they also contain information about the input/output device requirements for each job step. The control cards provide the information necessary to operate in a stacked job environment (fig. 10.26).

Control Programs

The control program is sectioned into functional components to carry out its controlling role for the operating system. The following are some of the functions of control programs.

1. The control program must analyze the signal (interrupt) that causes a transfer to the operating system (fig. 10.27). The interrupt control component performs this function for the control program and transfers to another appropriate component of the control program based on the signal received.

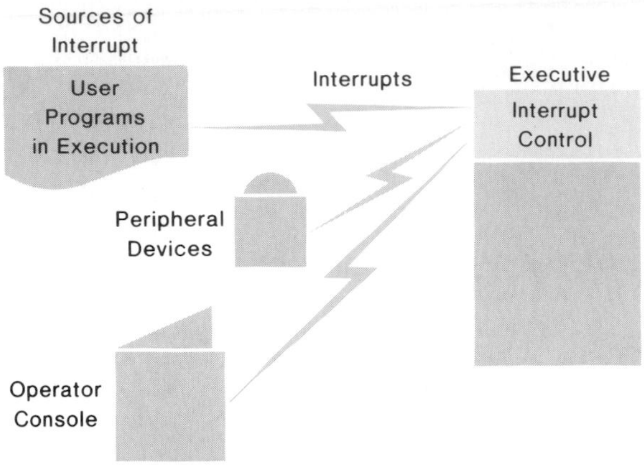

Figure 10.27 An example of the interrupt control function.

Figure 10.28 An example of the program control function.

Figure 10.29 An example of the console control function.

2. **If the signal originates because a program is completed,** the control program deallocates the resources assigned to the terminated program (fig. 10.28). It then initiates the next program to be executed and allocates such resources as memory, input/output devices, and processing time to the new program.
3. If the signal is generated by the operator at the console, the operator is given the opportunity to type in a coded message to which the operating system responds either by furnishing the desired information or by performing the function requested by the operator (fig. 10.29).
4. The input/output control component receives control if there is an input/output function to be performed, such as initiating or handling the termination of an input/output command (fig. 10.30).

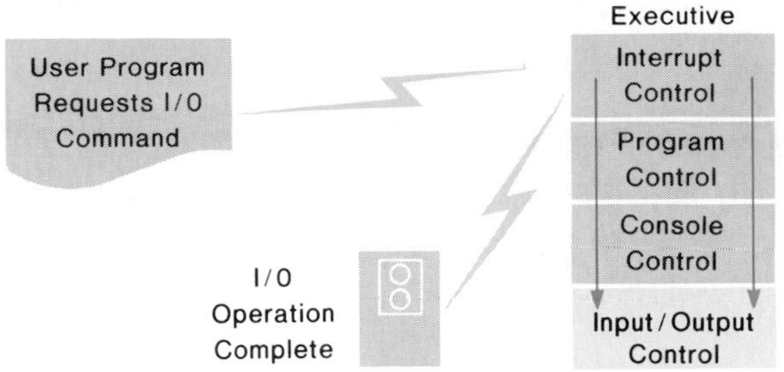

Figure 10.30 An example of the input/output control function.

Processing Programs

A processing program is sometimes defined as any program that is not a control program. Processing programs are kept on tape or direct access devices as a collection of data sets known as libraries and fall into three general categories.

1. *Language translators* range from the assembly of languages in machine format to compilation of the business-oriented COBOL language and the scientific-oriented FORTRAN language. A sequence of compilations for various languages can be performed as a total session.

   The purpose of the language translators is to enable the programmer to concentrate more on the definition of a problem and the best method for its solution and less on the details of coding.
2. *Service programs* can perform many common standardized functions, using prewritten programs which are selected and modified according to instructions supplied in the form of control cards or equivalent data developed as part of the user's processing routine. These programs include generalized sort/merge programs and utility programs.

   Generalized sort/merge programs are designed to satisfy the sorting and merging requirements of all tape or direct access systems. This generalized program can produce many different sorting/merging programs in accordance with control information supplied by the user.

   Utility programs provide the user with a means of standard, efficient handling of data transfer operations between input and output devices. These utility programs perform such jobs as transferring data from one input/output unit to another, interrelated dump and restore direct access unit program, a clear direct access unit program, and an output processor program that transfers data from the system output file for printing or punching.
3. *User-written problem programs* become part of the operating system library and are retrievable by name only.

Operating Systems (OS)

An operating system is a collection of programs that provides for the preparation and execution of the user's problem programs (jobs). OS is the most sophisticated and most powerful operating system. The control program is the framework of an operating system; it has three distinct functions.

Figure 10.31 An example of job management. (Courtesy of IBM)

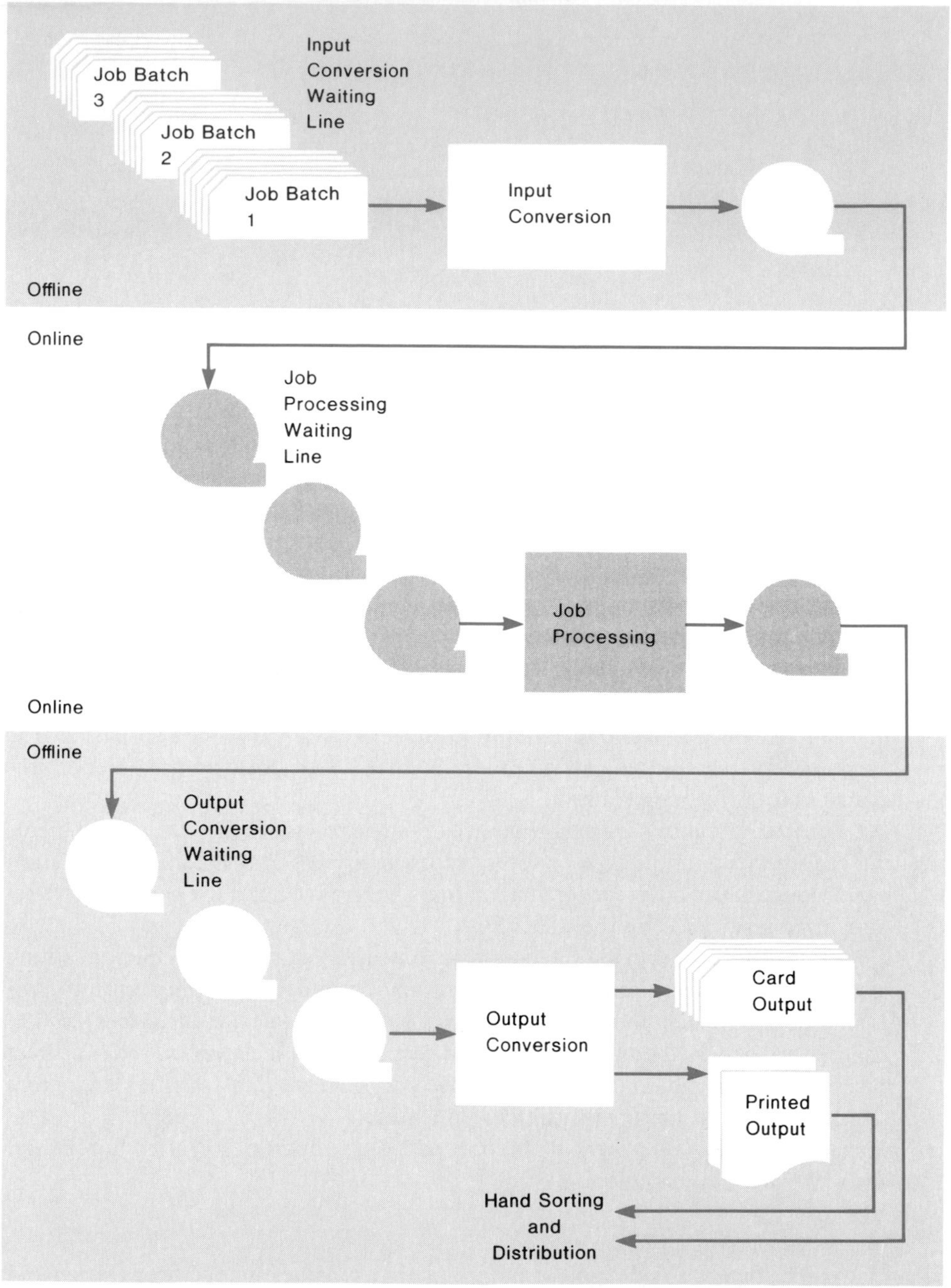

1. *Job management* provides the facilities to read, interpret, initiate, and terminate jobs submitted for processing (fig. 10.31). It also provides the facilities for the operator to communicate with the system.
2. *Task management* is the core of an operating system. Because it performs the

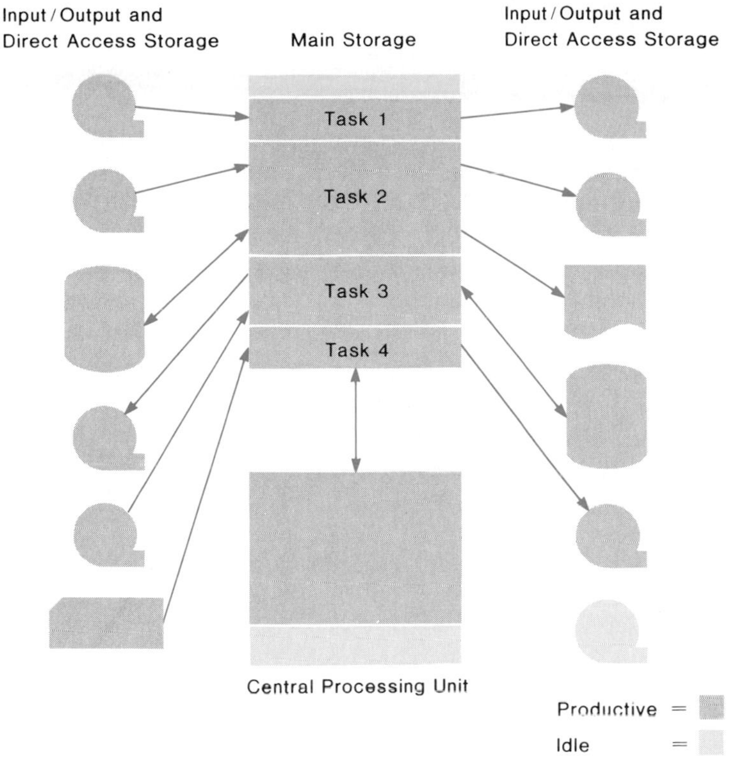

Figure 10.32 An example of task management. (Courtesy of IBM)

supervisory functions associated with the execution of a task, it is often called the *supervisor*. The functions provided generally include interruption handling, resource allocation, fetching of nonresident routines, time supervision, and transient-error recovery (fig. 10.32).

3. *Data management* provides the function of record blocking and deblocking, space allocation on direct access devices, processing of labels, and the transfer of data between main storage and external devices, all by means of various access methods. These functions free data sets and their processing from the input/output environment. The access methods, which are well-defined and consistent, handle data sets according to their basic organization, such as sequential, indexed sequential, direct, and partitioned (fig. 10.33). (Data organization methods will be discussed in chapter 19.)

Current Trends

Significant trends in data-processing systems are the following.

Growth toward more multiprogramming. Multiprogramming permits the user to install new applications, such as teleprocessing and inquiry or graphics applications that otherwise could not be justified (fig. 10.34). Multiprogramming support also has encouraged the growth of new computer environments.

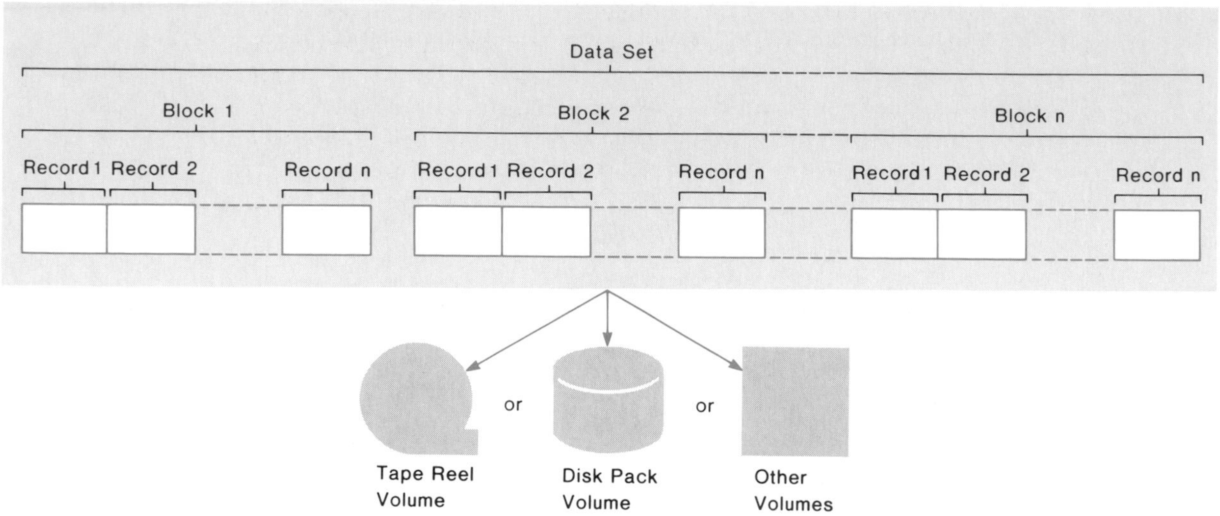

Figure 10.33 An example of data management. (Courtesy of IBM)

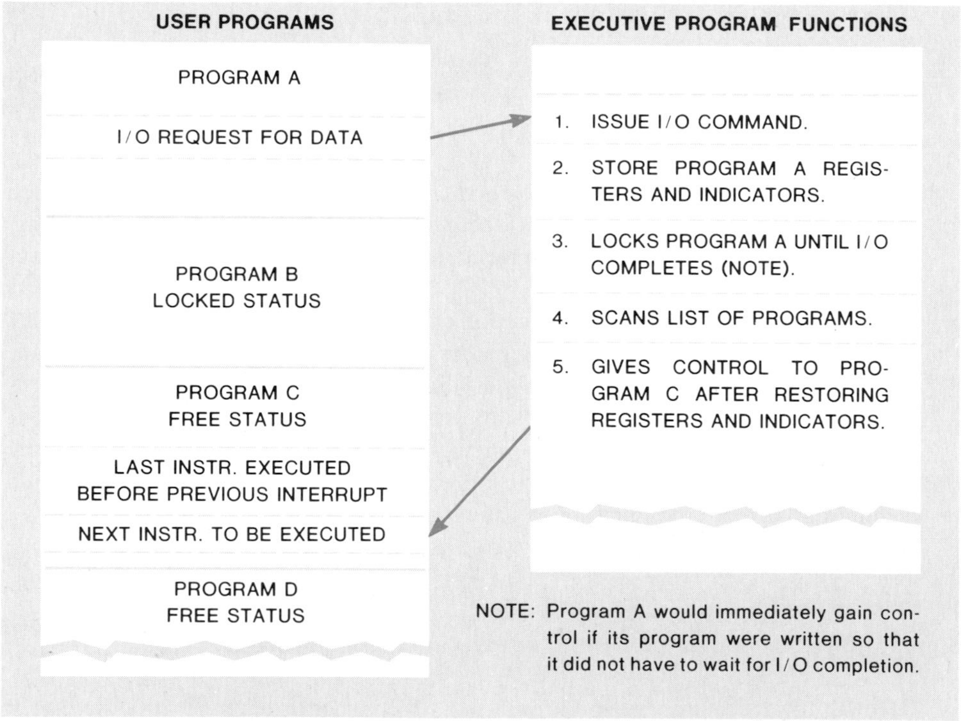

Figure 10.34 An example of multiprogramming.

Greater use of high-level languages, such as COBOL and FORTRAN, for applications programming. The cost of programming has been increasing, while the cost of computing hardware has been decreasing. More productive use of programmers can be achieved by the use of high-level languages. Improvements in compilation and the size and execution speed of codes produced by high-level language translators have been made and continue to be made. The support of many more functions within high-level languages has also increased their use, and the growth of interactive computing has stimulated the addition of even more facilities.

Growth of teleprocessing applications, such as remote inquiry, message switching, data collection, and management information systems. The ability of computing systems to handle teleprocessing and batch processing in one system eliminates the necessity of dedicated, special-purpose systems.

Growth of remote computing activities, such as remote job entry and interactive computing (or time sharing), in computing systems. Remote computing offers (1) fast turnaround for batch work submitted from remote locations, (2) remote user access to the large computing facilities and data base available at the central installation, and (3) interactive problem solving on a regular or nonscheduled basis for personnel in locations remote from the central computer. In-house interactive computing is also growing as users attempt to use programming time more efficiently.

Growth toward large, online data base systems. The growth in the marketplace of remote-computing, time-sharing, and real-time applications necessitates the instant availability of more data. High-capacity, fast, low-cost, reliable direct access devices supported by appropriate data organization, access techniques, and security measures will be required for this type of computing environment.

All of the above show the need for more sophisticated operating systems in the near future.

Virtual Storage

Pioneered by computer manufacturers during the 1960s, virtual storage is generally a software technique that continually swaps program data between a small, fast, expensive CPU main storage and an external, relatively large, slower, cheaper mass storage device. The external storage, controlled by a virtual storage operating system, appears to the program and programmer as merely more main storage.

In operation, only a portion of a large program on a virtual storage system is actually executing in the main storage at any one time; the remainder of the program and its variables resides on an external disk storage. As each part of a program is called for execution, it is swapped with another part already in main storage. *Virtual storage, simply stated, is the apparent extension of memory size beyond the available real memory* (*core or main storage*) (fig. 10.35). Therefore, though the main storage in the CPU may be only 10K to 20K bytes in size, the logical or virtual storage of the machine can be as large as the disk, usually 4 to 5 million bytes (fig. 10.36).

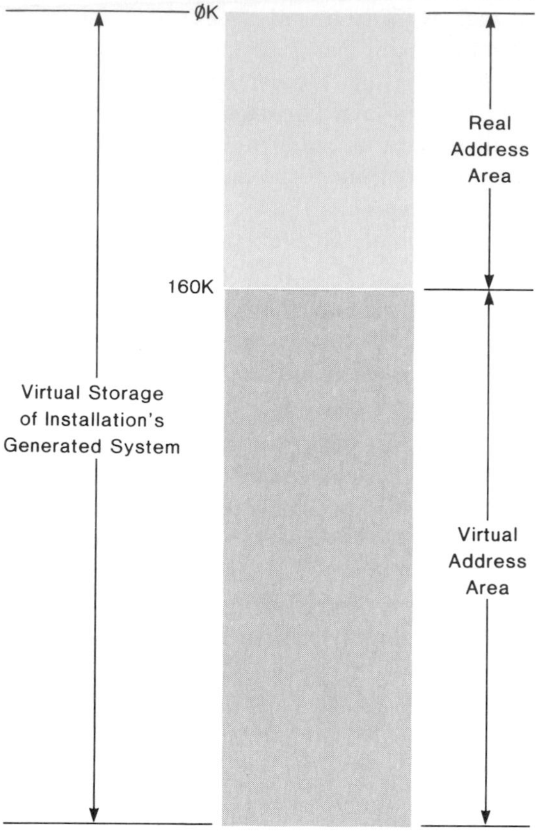

Figure 10.35
Virtual storage.

Virtual storage provides a vehicle for extending the powers of the computer in the user's department through the implementation of advanced data bases and data communication systems. It enables applications to be designed to solve the user department need instead of the machine need. It is an aid to the programmer in the following areas:

1. Greater accessibility of packages eases the programming burden.
2. More users can take advantage of interactive computing.
3. Better turnaround time is provided for programming testing.
4. Storage becomes a much smaller consideration with the implementation of the system.

Virtual storage can increase the productivity of programmers by freeing them from time-consuming, routine work. In addition, it enables a computer to process more jobs concurrently, adding new flexibility for user operations.

To provide virtual storage for computer systems, a new system control programming and circuitry had to be developed. The most compact storage circuits ever used in computer systems have been introduced. Present computer users can purchase the

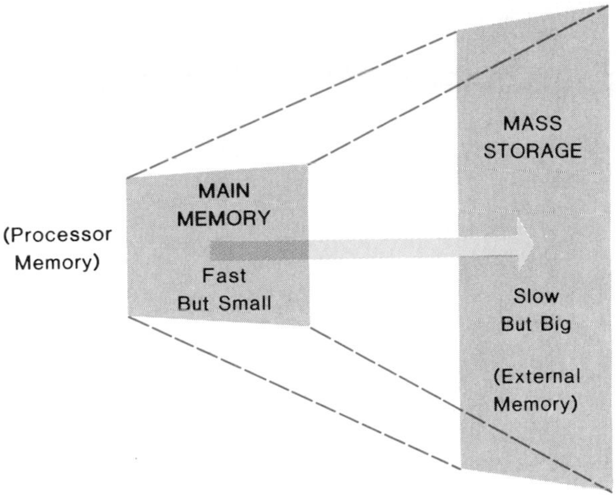

The virtual memory concept.

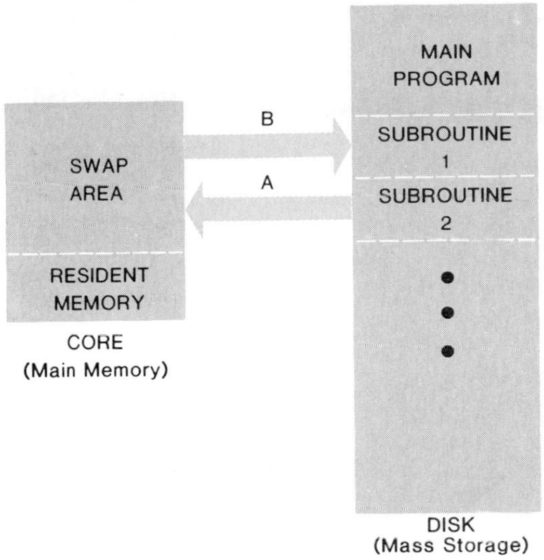

A block swap: subroutine 2 is originally in core and calls subroutine 1. Subroutine 2 is written on the disk (A) and subroutine 1 is read from the disk into core (B).

Figure 10.36 Virtual storage operation. (Copyright by Modern Data Services, Inc. Reprinted with permission from *Mini-Micro Systems*.)

dynamic translation facility (DAT) which permits their computer models to operate with virtual storage control programming.

The vast majority of existing applications programmed for present computer systems require little or no reprogramming to take advantage of virtual storage. In addition, compatibility between all computer virtual storage models makes it easier to move up to the larger and more powerful models as the processing requirements grow.

Virtual storage is a storage management technique. It makes a computer system appear to the user as if it had many times the number of characters it actually has in its main storage. This makes possible concurrent processing of computer programs that, in total size, exceed main storage capacity.

The computer's virtual storage is created by circuitry and advanced control programming, which links slower but less costly disk storage to main storage. During processing, only the active sections of each program need to occupy space in main storage; the rest are stored in the disk and are automatically moved into main storage for processing when needed.

With virtual storage, new large-scale applications, such as online order entry programs, can be tested immediately, without stopping regularly scheduled processing or waiting for time on the computer.

Benefits

The benefits that result from these hardware and software requirements are numerous (fig. 10.37). In fact, they make the virtual storage concept a profitable investment in almost any application environment.

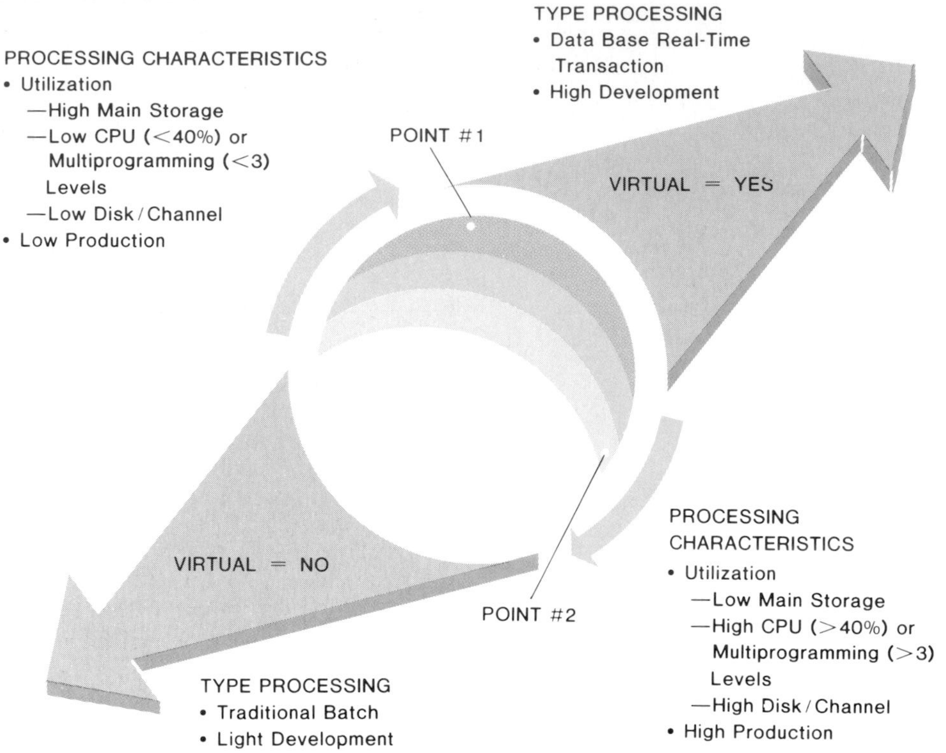

Figure 10.37 The benefit spectrum of virtual storage operation. (Reprinted with permission of *Datamation*© magazine, © Copyright by Technical Publishing Company, a division of Dun-Donnelley Publishing Corporation, a Dun & Bradstreet Company, 1978—all rights reserved.)

A virtual storage system's real storage is used only on demand, when referenced. This results in the following benefits.

1. Programs only require their working set for effective execution. This may enable the system to initiate and execute more jobs.
2. Real storage fragmentation is almost eliminated.
3. It is possible to design and implement an application the size of which greatly exceeds real storage size. This would be impossible in a conventional system without the use of overlays or a multitape job.
4. Long-run applications will use only the amount of real storage required at any point in time. Thus, a dedicated teleprocessing network will use very little real storage when idle.
5. Virtual storage systems might be unstable as backup for systems that have a larger real storage size.

From the programmer's point of view, virtual storage systems eliminate limitations that exist in static relocation systems. Because virtual storage is much larger than real storage, the programmer has more space to design problem solutions. This greatly reduces, if not completely eliminates, the need to overlay programs. In overlayed programs, the programmer must plan for storage requirements, storage content,

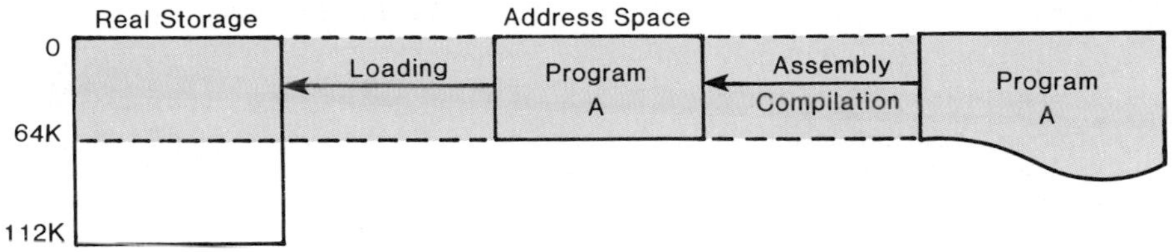

Figure 10.38 An example of static relocation.

and branching conventions. Revising a program or application that uses overlays can be a complicated job. In virtual storage systems, the system manages real storage. In effect, it automatically overlays programs too large for the available real storage. The programmer develops a program for execution in a large contiguous space in virtual storage. This saves time and eliminates complicated procedures. It lets the programmer concentrate on the solution (fig. 10.38).

Summary

The programmer has certain specialized techniques in processing data that will make coding easier. In addition to flowcharting and decision tables, the programmer may use structured programming, subroutines, and macro instructions to insure the efficiency of the program. This chapter describes the various programming elements and the important role that they play in the efficient operation of a computing system.

1. Structured programming applies a theoretical concept to the coding of computer programs. The main element of the concept is the use of very basic structures to create complex programs. A structured program is easier to understand than programs written in other styles, thus facilitating code checking, which in turn may reduce testing and debugging time.
2. A subroutine is an out-of-mainline routine that is performed several times for a given record or for a number of different records. A subroutine eases the task of the programmer by reducing the number of instructions to be written, and by enabling the programmer to include pretested routines in the program.
3. A macro instruction is a symbolic statement that combines several operations into one. It provides a convenient way to generate a desired sequence of source program instructions into one or more source programs. Macro instructions can increase accuracy and standardization of frequently repeated procedures.
4. Job control language (JCL) establishes the communication link between the programmer and the control system of the computer. Every job submitted for execution by the operating system of the computer must include JCL statements. It is important that one should be familiar enough with the job control language to be able to decide what information the operating system will need to process the job effectively.
5. An operating system is an integrated set of processing programs and a control program designed to improve the total operating effectiveness of a computer. Communication with the computer is via the operating system rather than directly, as was the case with most previous computers.

6. Virtual storage is the apparent extension of memory size beyond the available real memory (main or core storage). It extends the power of the computer system through the implementation of advanced data base and data communications. It enables the application to be designed to serve the user's needs instead of the machine's needs.

Identification Questions

Match the following terms with the statements below.

A. Closed Subroutine
B. Compilation
C. Control Program
D. Data Management
E. Delimiters
F. Dynamic Translation Facility (DAT)
G. Hierarchy plus Input-Process-Output (HIPO)
H. Iteration Structure
I. Job
J. Job Control Language
K. Job Management
L. Linkage Editing
M. Linkage Instructions
N. Load Module
O. Loader
P. Macro Instruction
Q. Object Module
R. Open Subroutine
S. Operating System
T. Processing Programs
U. Selection Structure
V. Sequence Structure
W. Service Programs
X. Source Module
Y. Structured Programming
Z. Subroutine
AA. Task Management
BB. Utility Programs
CC. Virtual Storage

1. A style of programming in which the structure of a program is made as clear as possible by restricting control logic to just three structures.
2. The choice of two actions based on a condition.
3. A subroutine that is included in the program only once but is referred to whenever the desired function is needed.
4. A symbolic statement that combines several operations into one.
5. Supervises the execution and loading of processing programs.
6. The input source program to the compiler.
7. The executed output of the linkage editor.
8. The independent unit of work performed by an operating system.
9. Performs the supervisory functions associated with an execution of a task.
10. An integrated set of processing programs and a control program to improve the total operating effectiveness of a computer.
11. In the absence of instructions to the contrary, statements are executed in the order they are written.
12. A subprogram consisting of a set of instructions that perform some subordinate function within a program.
13. Compilers, service programs, and user-written programs.
14. A service program that prepares object modules for execution.
15. Programs that provide the user with a means of standard, efficient handling of data transfer operations between input/output devices.

16. The apparent extension of memory size beyond the available real memory.
17. The repeated execution of a code while a condition is true.
18. A subroutine that is inserted directly into the main program at the point which it is needed.
19. Established communication between the programmer and the central system of the computer.
20. The process of translating a source program into a series of instructions comprehensible to the computer.
21. Provides the function of record blocking and deblocking, space allocation on direct access devices, processing labels, and the transfer of data between main storage and external devices, all by means of various access methods.
22. A method of graphically describing a program entity as an arrangement of functions to be performed.
23. Instructions necessary to affect the entry and reentry functions of a subroutine.
24. The output (compiled source program) from the compiler.
25. Marks used to separate data on an input stream.
26. Provides the facility to read, interpret, initiate, and terminate jobs submitted for processing.
27. Programs that perform many common standardized functions, using prewritten programs that are selected and modified according to the instructions from the user.
28. Permits the computer user to operate with virtual storage control programming.
29. A service program that processes object and load modules, resolves any references to subprograms, and executes the load module.

Questions for Review

1. What is a structured program and what is its chief purpose?
2. What are the main objectives of structured programming?
3. Briefly, what are the three basic structures of structured programming?
4. How are the basic structures combined into a program?
5. What is a segment and how is it used in structured programming?
6. What is the importance of top-down design?
7. What is meant by hierarchy plus input-process-output (HIPO) and how does it satisfy two of the greatest needs in the data-processing industry?
8. What is a subroutine and what is the difference between an open and closed subroutine?
9. What is meant by linkage?
10. How do subroutines ease the task of the programmer?
11. What is a macro instruction and how is it used in writing programs?
12. What is the chief purpose of job control cards?
13. What is the difference between the control program and processing programs?
14. What is meant by the source module, object module, and load module?
15. Briefly describe the steps involved in executing a problem program.
16. What is meant by a job?
17. Briefly describe the types of job control cards used for the IBM 360/370 operating system.

18. What is an operating system and what is its main purpose?
19. What are the chief functions of the control program?
20. What are the distinct functions of the control program of an operating system?
21. What are service programs? Utility programs?
22. What are the current trends in data-processing and programming systems?
23. What is the importance of virtual storage?
24. What are the important benefits of virtual storage?

Key Terms

Closed Subroutine
Compilation
Control Program
Data Management
Delimiters
Dynamic Translation Facility (DAT)
Hierarchy plus Input-Process-Output (HIPO)
Iteration Structure
Job
Job Control Language
Job Management
Linkage Editing
Linkage Instructions
Load Module
Loader
Macro Instruction
Object Module
Open Subroutine
Operating System
Processing Programs
Selection Structure
Sequence Structure
Service Programs
Source Module
Structured Programming
Subroutine
Task Management
Utility Programs
Virtual Storage

part 4

programming languages

0 0 0 0 0 0 0 0 0 0 0 0 0 0 0 0
12 13 14 15 16 17 18 19 20 21 22 23 24 25 26 27 28 29 30 31
1 1 1 1 1 1 1 1 1 1 1 1 1 1 1 1 1 1
2 2 2 2 2 2 2 2 2 2 2 2 2 2 2 2 2 2
3 3 3 3 3 3 3 3 3 3 3 3 3 3 3
4 4 4 4 4 4 4 4 4 4 4 4 4 4 4 4 4 4 4 4
5 5 5 5 5 5 5 5 5 5 5 5 5 5 5 5 5 5
6 6 6 6 6 6 6 6 6 6 6 6 6 6 6 6 6
7 7 7 7 7 7 7 7 7 7 7 7 7 7 7 7 7 7 7 7
8 8 8 8 8 8 8 8 8 8 8 8 8 8

COBOL 11

Chapter Outline

Chapter Objectives

The learning objectives of this chapter are

1. to describe the features of the most widely used programming language used in business.
2. to illustrate the relative ease of COBOL programming with its self-documenting features.
3. to write simple COBOL programs so you become familiar with the principal features of the language.
4. to introduce the latest techniques of structured programming in COBOL.

The *CO*mmon *B*usiness *O*riented *L*anguage (COBOL) is a near-English programming language designed primarily for programming business applications on computers. It is described as near-English because its free form enables the programmer to write in an easily readable form and because its general flow of logic can be understood by people who are unfamiliar with the program's details.

COBOL is the result of the efforts of computer users, both in industry and government, to establish a standard language for programming business data-processing applications. The COBOL language does not resemble machine language and the problem programmer does not have to be concerned with how the COBOL language program is translated into machine language.

COBOL is a high-level language that is procedure oriented and relatively machine independent. Designed for programmers, COBOL frees them from the many machine-oriented instructions of other languages and allows them to concentrate on the logical aspect of the program. The program is written in an English-like syntax that looks and reads like ordinary business English (fig. 11.1). Organization of the language is simple in comparison to machine-oriented languages; as such, it is much easier to teach to new programmers, thus reducing training time (fig. 11.2).

Advantages

1. The principal advantage of the COBOL system is the ability to use English-like statements. This solves language difficulties that have often existed between the advanced programmer and decision-making management.
2. The program is written in the English language, thus removing the programmer from the individual symbolic machine or language instructions required in the program. Although a knowledge of the individual instructions (symbolic and machine) are not required in COBOL programming, it is very useful to writing an efficient program, if the programmer possesses some knowledge of the hardware and coding of the particular computer.
3. Pretested modules of input and output, included in the COBOL processor, relieve the programmer of the tedious task of writing and testing input and output specifications.
4. The programmer is writing in a familiar language, which reduces the documentation required because the chance for clerical error is diminished. Generally, the quality and the quantity of documentation provided by the COBOL compiler is far superior to that of other language processors. The printed output, resulting from the compilation, improves the communication between people and the machine.
5. While COBOL is not completely machine independent, a program written for one type of machine can be easily converted for use on another with minimum modification. The standardization of a COBOL program provides this benefit.
6. Because COBOL is broken into separate divisions, a large program can be broken into various segments, and each programmer may write one division. The format definition can be made available to all programmers engaged in the problem.
7. Nonprogrammers and managers can read the COBOL program in English, which allows them to judge the program's logic.

```
SUBTRACT DEDUCTIONS FROM GROSS
    GIVING NET-AMOUNT.

MULTIPLY UNITS BY LIST-PRICE
    GIVING BILLING-AMT.

IF ON-HAND IS LESS THAN MINIMUM-BALANCE
    PERFORM REORDER-ROUTINE
ELSE
    NEXT SENTENCE.
```

Figure 11.1 Examples of typical COBOL statements.

COMPATIBILITY—COBOL makes it possible for the first time to use the same program on different computers with a minimum of change. Reprogramming can be reduced to making minor modifications in the COBOL source program, and re-compiling for the new computer.

STANDARDIZATION—The standardization of a computer-programming language overcomes the communication barrier which exists among programming language systems which are oriented to a single computer or a single family of computers.

COMMUNICATION—Easier communication between decision-making management, the systems analyst, the programmer, the coding technician, and the operator is established.

AUTOMATIC UNIFORM DOCUMENTATION—Easily understandable English documentation, provided automatically by the compiler, facilitates program analysis and thus simplifies any future modifications in the program.

COMPLETELY DEBUGGED PROGRAMS—Programs produced by the COBOL compiler are free from clerical errors.

CORRECTIONS AT ENGLISH LEVEL—Corrections and modifications in program logic may be made at the English level.

EASE OF TRAINING—New programming personnel can be trained to write productive programs with COBOL in substantially less time than it takes to train them in machine coding.

FASTER AND MORE ACCURATE PROGRAMMING—The English language notation expressed by the user and the computer-acceptable language produced by the COBOL computer ensure greater programming accuracy and a reduction in programming time.

REDUCTION IN PROGRAMMING COSTS—The ability to program a problem faster reduces the cost of programming. Also, reprogramming costs are greatly reduced since a program run on one system may be easily modified to run on another without being entirely recoded.

Figure 11.2 The benefits derived from using COBOL.

8. During compilation, the COBOL language processor generates a list of diagnostics. *A diagnostic is a statement provided by the compiler indicating all errors in a source program, excluding errors in logic.* Because diagnostics affect the measurement of compiling efficiency, as well as compiling speed, COBOL can greatly reduce the "debugging" time.

Disadvantages

Most of the disadvantages of using COBOL are due to the failure of personnel to fully understand the language and its use.

1. Most personnel expect that a single COBOL program will provide a permanent solution without ever reprogramming.
2. They assume that the programmer only needs to be taught the COBOL language without any knowledge of the hardware or the operation of the computer.
3. COBOL will not generate a sophisticated program similar to one written in the actual language of the particular computer.
4. COBOL processors will operate only with a computer that has a certain storage capacity. The newer COBOL compilers have drastically reduced the storage requirements. With the introduction of larger storage units, this problem has been greatly reduced.

Components of COBOL

COBOL is similar to the English language in the use of words, sentences, and paragraphs. The programmer can use English words and conventional arithmetic symbols to direct and control the operations of a computer.

```
ADD QUANTITY TO ON-HAND.
MULTIPLY GROSS-EARN BY SS-RATE
    GIVING SS-TAX.
IF Y-T-D-EARN IS LESS THAN SS-LIMIT,
THEN
    PERFORM SS-PROC
ELSE
    PERFORM OVER-SS-PROC.
```

Each of the above sentences can be understood by the computer, but all must be first translated into the particular machine language of the computer before the program can be executed. During compilation, a special system program known as a compiler is first entered into the computer.

The COBOL system consists of two basic elements, the source program and the compiler. The *source program* is a set of instructions that carry out the logic of a particular data-processing application. The *compiler* is the intermediate routine that converts the English-like statements of COBOL (source program) into computer-acceptable instructions. Since the COBOL language is directed primarily at those unfamiliar with machine coding, terms common to business applications rather than to computing systems are used in the language.

In order to write a COBOL program, the programmer should be familiar with the basic components of COBOL programming. There are many terms, rules, entry formats, and program structures to be learned before attempting COBOL programming.

Terms

The *source program* is the problem-solving program written in the COBOL language. It will be later compiled and translated into the machine language of the particular computer.

The *object program* is the machine language that resulted from the compilation of the COBOL source program. It is the program that will be used to process the data.

The *compiler* is the program supplied by a computer manufacturer. It will translate a COBOL source program into the object program.

The *source computer* is used to compile the source program. Usually the same computer is used for the object computer.

The *object computer* is the computer upon which the machine-language program will be processed.

The complete COBOL *character set* consists of fifty-one characters. These are the characters (alphabetic, numeric, and special characters or symbols) the computer manufacturer has included in the COBOL programming package (fig. 11.3).

Names are a means of establishing words to identify certain data within a program. A symbolic name is attached to an item that is being used in the program. All

Digits 0 through 9
Letters A through Z
Special characters:
Blank or space
+ Plus sign
— Minus sign or hyphen
* Check protection symbol, asterisk
/ Slash
= Equal sign
> Inequality sign (greater than)
< Inequality sign (less than)
$ Dollar sign
, Comma
. Period or decimal point
' Quotation mark
(Left parenthesis
) Right parenthesis
; Semicolon
The following characters are used for words:
0 through 9
A through Z
- (hyphen)
The following characters are used for punctuation:
' Quotation mark
(Left parenthesis
) Right parenthesis
, Comma
. Period
; Semicolon
The following characters are used in arithmetic expressions:
+ Addition
— Subtraction
* Multiplication
/ Division
** Exponentiation
The following characters are used in relation tests:
> Greater than
< Less than
= Equal to

Figure 11.3 The COBOL character set.

references to the item will be through this name, although the value may change many times throughout the execution of the program. The name must be unique or identified with a file in which it is found.

Types of Names

Data names are words assigned by the programmer to identify data items in the COBOL program. All items used in the Data Division must be identified by a unique or qualified name (fig. 11.4).

Figure 11.4 An example of data names.

```
ADD REGULAR-WAGES,
    OVERTIME,              } Data names
    GIVING GROSS-EARNINGS.
```

Procedure names are symbolic names attached to the various segments of the Procedure Division (fig. 11.5) and used for reference by the program in a decision-making operation. The basic concept of computer programming is the ability of the program to leave the sequential order to another part of the program for further processing.

Figure 11.5 An example of procedure names.

Procedure name

```
INSERT-NEW-RECORD.
    MOVE CARD-RECORD TO OUTPUT-RECORD.
    WRITE OUTPUT-RECORD.
    READ CARD-FILE,
        AT END, PERFORM FINISH-RUN.
    PERFORM TEST-RECORD-CODE.
```

Condition names are assigned to an item that may have various values. The data item itself is called a condition variable and may assume a specific value, a set of values, or a range of values (fig. 11.6). Condition names are often used in the Procedure Division to specify certain conditions for branching to another part of the program.

Figure 11.6 An example of condition names.

Condition names

```
02  MARITAL-STATUS, PICTURE 9.
    88  SINGLE, VALUE 0.
    88  MARRIED, VALUE 1.
    88  DIVORCED, VALUE 2.
    88  WIDOWED, VALUE 3.
```

Special names are the mnemonic names that are assigned to various components of the Environment Division. The term special names refers to the mnemonic name that is associated with a function name. Function names are fixed for each different type of computer (fig. 11.7).

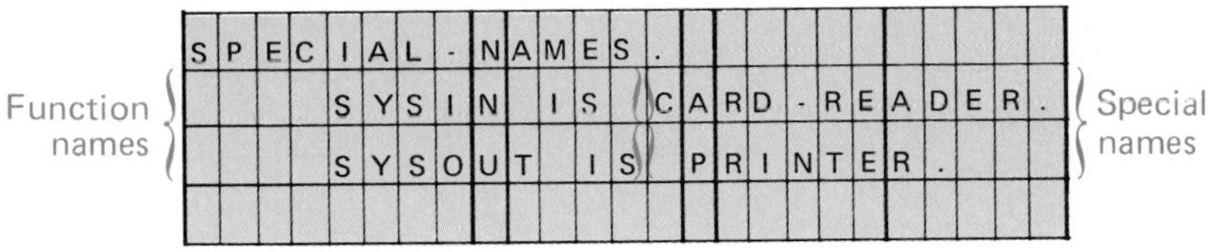

Figure 11.7 An example of special names.

Rules for the Assignment of Names

1. Names may range from one to thirty characters in length.
2. No spaces (blanks) may appear within a name.
3. Names may be formed from the alphabet, numerals, and the hyphen. No special characters may appear in a name except the hyphen.
4. Although a hyphen may appear in a name, no name may begin or end with a hyphen.
5. The procedure name may consist entirely of numerals, but all other names must have at least one alphabetic character.
6. Names that are identical must be qualified with a higher level name.

Words

A COBOL word consists of one or more COBOL characters chosen from the character set. A word is followed by a space, a period, a right parenthesis, a comma, or a semicolon (fig. 11.8).

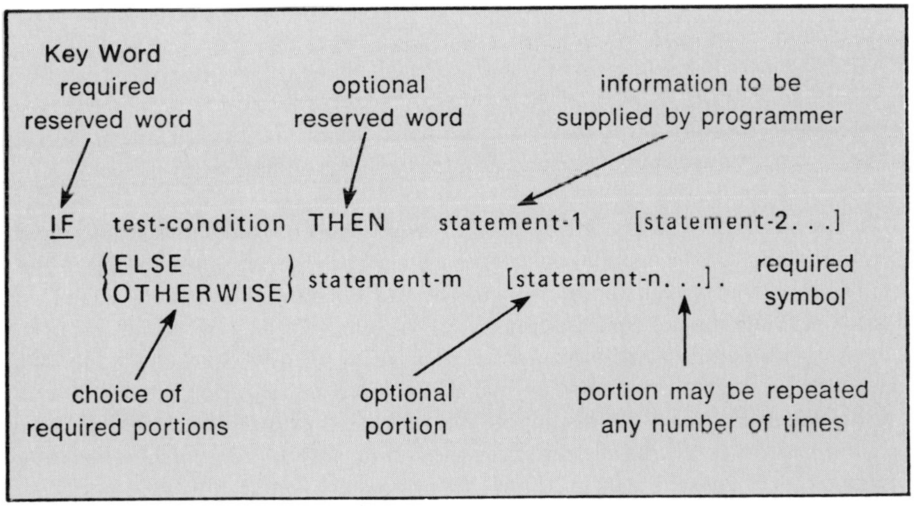

Figure 11.8 COBOL words.

Reserved words have preassigned meanings and must not be altered, misspelled, or changed in any way from the specific purpose of the word (fig. 11.9). Each of these COBOL reserved words has a special meaning to the compiler; hence, it should not be used out of context. A list of reserved words is available for all computers and must be checked before attempting to program, since there are slight differences in the lists among the different computers.

Figure 11.9 An example of reserved words and the programmer-supplied names.

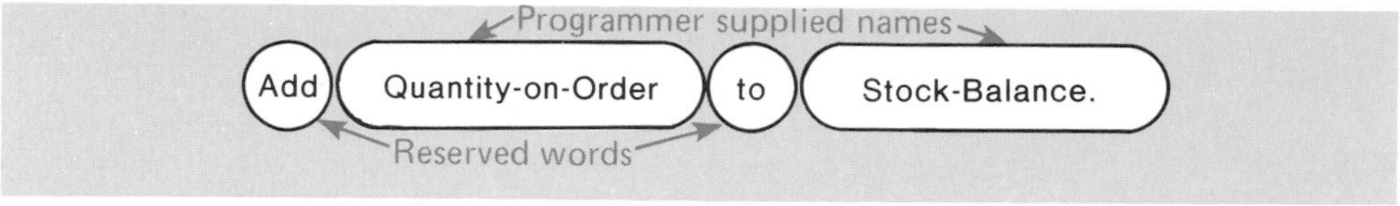

Constants

A constant is an actual value of data that remains unchanged during the execution of the program. The value for the constant is supplied by the programmer at the time the program is loaded into storage. There are two types of constants used in COBOL programming, literals and figurative constants.

Literals are composed of a string of characters where the value is determined by the set of characters of which the literal is a part. There are two types of literals, numeric and nonnumeric (fig. 11.10).

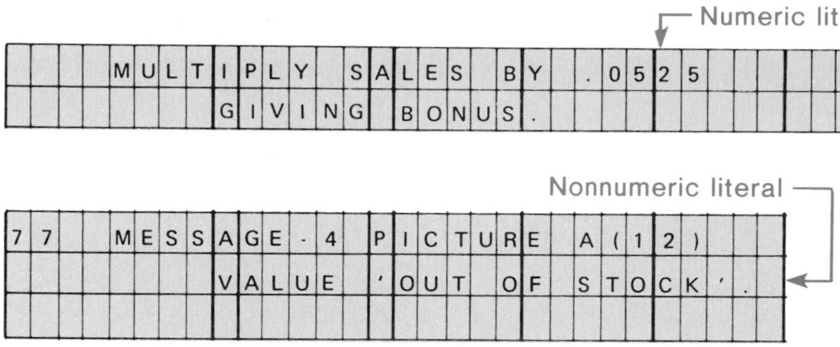

Figure 11.10 An example of numeric and nonnumeric literals.

A *numeric literal* is a string of characters chosen from the digits 0–9, the plus or minus sign, and the decimal point. The value of the literal is implicit in the character itself. Thus, 842 is both the literal and the value itself. The primary use of numeric literals is in arithmetic computations.

A *nonnumeric literal* is composed of a string of any character in the COBOL character set except the quotation marks, enclosed in quotation marks. Nonnumeric literals are used mainly for displaying messages and printing headings for reports.

Figurative constants are reserved words that have a predefined value recognized by the COBOL compiler (fig. 11.11). These words are frequently used in programming so the programmer is relieved of the responsibility of assigning names for commonly used constants. The use of the figurative constant ZEROS in the statement MOVE ZEROS TO WORK will fill the entire area WORK with zeros. Similarly, the use of the figurative constant SPACES in the statement MOVE SPACES TO OUT will blank out the entire area OUT.

High-value(s)	are assigned the highest value in the computer collating sequence
Low-value(s)	are assigned the lowest value in the computer collating sequence
Zero Zeros Zeroes	are assigned the value 0
Space Spaces	are assigned to one or more spaces (blanks)
Quote Quotes	are assigned to one or more quotation mark characters (apostrophes)

All "any literal" will represent a continuous sequence of "any literal."

The singular and plural forms of figurative constants are interchangeable.

Figure 11.11 Figurative constants.

Operators

Operators are used in the COBOL language to specify some action or relationship between two items in a program. Symbols are special characters that have a specific meaning to the compiler.

Arithmetic expression operators are used in the COMPUTE statement and in relational conditions (fig. 11.12). The characters used in arithmetic expressions are as follows.

Symbol	Name	Meaning
+	Addition	Plus
-	Subtraction	Minus
*	Multiplication	Asterisk (times)
/	Division	Slash (divided by)
**	Exponentiation	Double asterisk (raise to the power of)
=	Equal	Make equivalent to
( )	Parenthesis	To control sequence of calculations

```
COMPUTE CAPACITY = (UTILITY * SPAN)/
  (RANGE + CONSUMPTION * EFFICIENCY)
```

Figure 11.12 An example of arithmetic expression operators.

Relational expression operators. The logical flow of a program frequently depends on the ability to make comparisons of the current value of a data name and/or to compare this value with another or predetermined value. The expression can be reduced to a true or false statement. If the statement is true, the remainder of the statement is executed. If the statement is false, the program is directed to the next sentence unless an alternative action is specified (fig. 11.13). The following are the symbols used in relational expressions together with their meanings.

Symbol	Name	Meaning
=	Equal	IS EQUAL TO
>	Greater than	IS GREATER THAN
<	Less than	IS LESS THAN
( )	Parenthesis	To control the sequence of statements to be evaluated

Figure 11.13 An example of relational operators.

```
IF PAYMENT < PREVIOUS-BAL
    PERFORM PART-PAYMENT
ELSE
    IF PAYMENT > PREVIOUS-BAL
        PERFORM OVER-PAYMENT
    ELSE
        PERFORM PROCESS.
```

Logical expression operators are used to combine simple statements in the same expression for the purpose of testing the condition of the expression (fig. 11.14). The following are the operators used in logical operations together with their meanings.

Operator	Meaning
AND	Used to evaluate both statements
OR	Used to evaluate either or both statements
NOT	Used to negate a positive condition
( )	Used to control the sequence of enclosed statements

Punctuation symbols are important to the successful execution of a COBOL program (fig. 11.15). Unless symbols are used correctly, many diagnostic errors can be generated during the compilation phase. The following are the symbols and their meanings as used to punctuate entries.

Symbol	Name	Meaning
.	Period	Used to terminate entries
,	Comma	Used to separate operands, clauses in a series of entries
;	Semicolon	Used to separate clauses and statements
'	Quotation Mark	Used to enclose nonnumeric literals
( )	Parentheses	Used to enclose subscripts

```
IF A > B
    OR A = C
    AND D IS POSITIVE
        PERFORM PROC-1
ELSE
    NEXT SENTENCE.
```

Figure 11.14 An example of logical operators.

```
READ BILL-FILE;
    AT END, PERFORM FINISH.
```

Figure 11.15 An example of punctuation symbols.

Statements

A statement is a syntactically valid combination of words and symbols written in the Procedure Division and used to express a thought in COBOL. The statement combines COBOL reserved words with programmer-defined operands.

A COBOL statement may be either a simple or compound expression. A *simple* statement would specify one action, while a *compound* statement, usually joined by a logical operator, would specify more than one form of action.

The statement may be either imperative or conditional. An *imperative* statement directs the program to perform a particular operation under all conditions (fig. 11.16), while a *conditional* statement specifies that the operation be performed only if the condition is satisfied (true) or not (false) (fig. 11.17).

```
PERFORM READ-RECORD.
```

Figure 11.16 An example of a simple imperative statement.

```
IF CONTRIBUTION = 100.00
    OR CONTRIBUTION > 100.00
        DISPLAY 'GOOD SHOW'
            UPON CONSOLE
ELSE
    NEXT SENTENCE
```

Figure 11.17 An example of a compound conditional statement.

Writing COBOL Programs

COBOL Program Sheet Format

The source program is written by the programmer on a COBOL Program Sheet Coding Form. The form provides the programmer with a standard method of writing COBOL source programs and the subsequent punching of the program into cards. Despite the necessary restrictions, the program is written in rather free form. However, there are precise rules for using this form. Unless these rules are followed, especially with respect to spacing, many diagnostic errors will be generated unnecessarily (figs. 11.18, 11.19).

Sequence Numbers (1-6)

The sequence numbers are written in columns 1 through 6 of the form. The sequence number consisting of six digits is used to identify each card numerically to the COBOL compiler. The use of these sequence numbers has no effect on the object program. It is a good practice to use sequence numbers since they will provide a control on the sequence of the cards if the cards are scattered or if an insertion is to be made in the program. If sequence numbers are used, they must be in ascending order as the compiler will check the sequence and indicate any sequence errors. No sequence check is made if the columns are left blank.

Figure 11.18 COBOL program sheet rules.

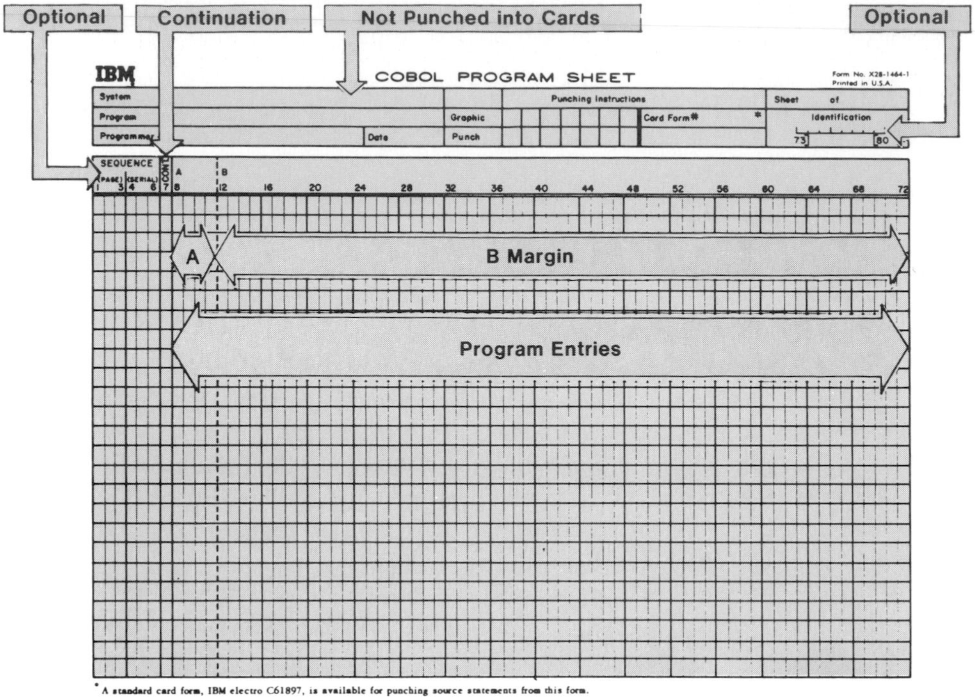

Figure 11.19 A COBOL program card.

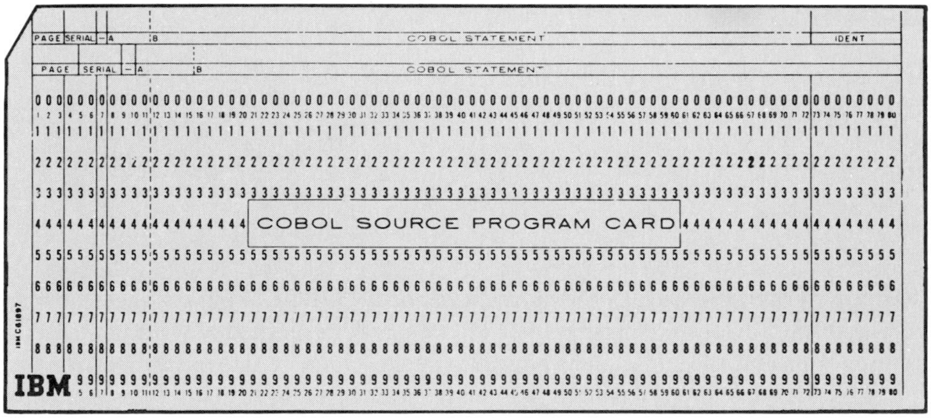

Continuation Indicator (7)

A coded statement may not extend beyond column 72 of the coding form. To continue a statement on a succeeding line, it is not necessary to use all the spaces up to column 72 on the first line. Any excess spaces are disregarded by the compiler. If a statement must be continued on a succeeding line (split words or literals), the continuing word must begin at the B margin (column 12 or any column to the right of column 12) and a hyphen placed in column 7 (fig. 11.20).

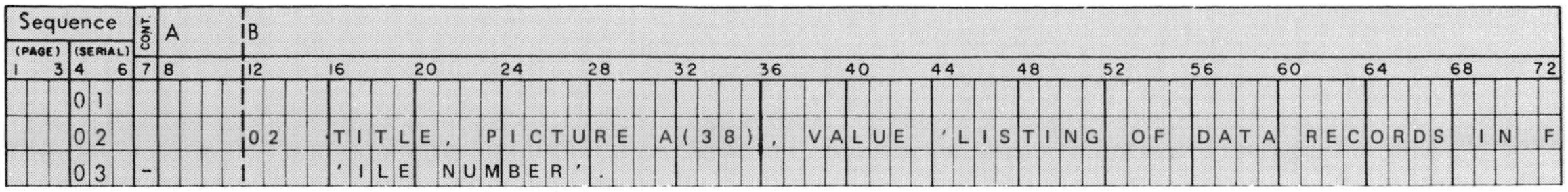

Figure 11.20 Continuation of a nonnumeric literal.

Program Statements (8-72)

These columns are used to write source program entries. These columns are grouped in margins. A margin begins at column 8 and continues through column 11. Any information between these two columns is considered to be written at the A margin. The B margin begins at column 12 and continues through column 72. Any information written between these two columns is considered to be written at the B margin. There are important rules for entries that are to begin at the A or B margins.

Identification Code (73-80)

These columns are used for the names of the program for identification purpose. The code has no effect on the object deck or compilation and may be left blank.

Program Structure

COBOL programs are arranged in a series of entries that comprise divisions, sections, and paragraphs. A division is composed of a series of sections, while a section is made up of paragraphs. Paragraphs are composed of a series of sentences containing statements (figs. 11.21, 11.22).

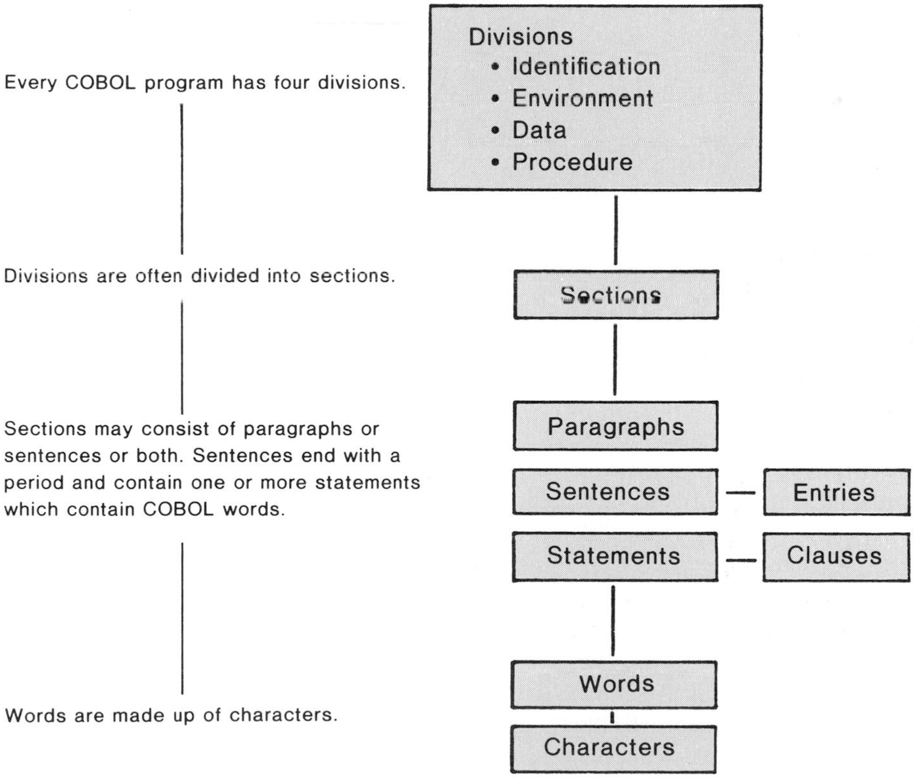

Figure 11.21 A schematic example of a COBOL program structure.

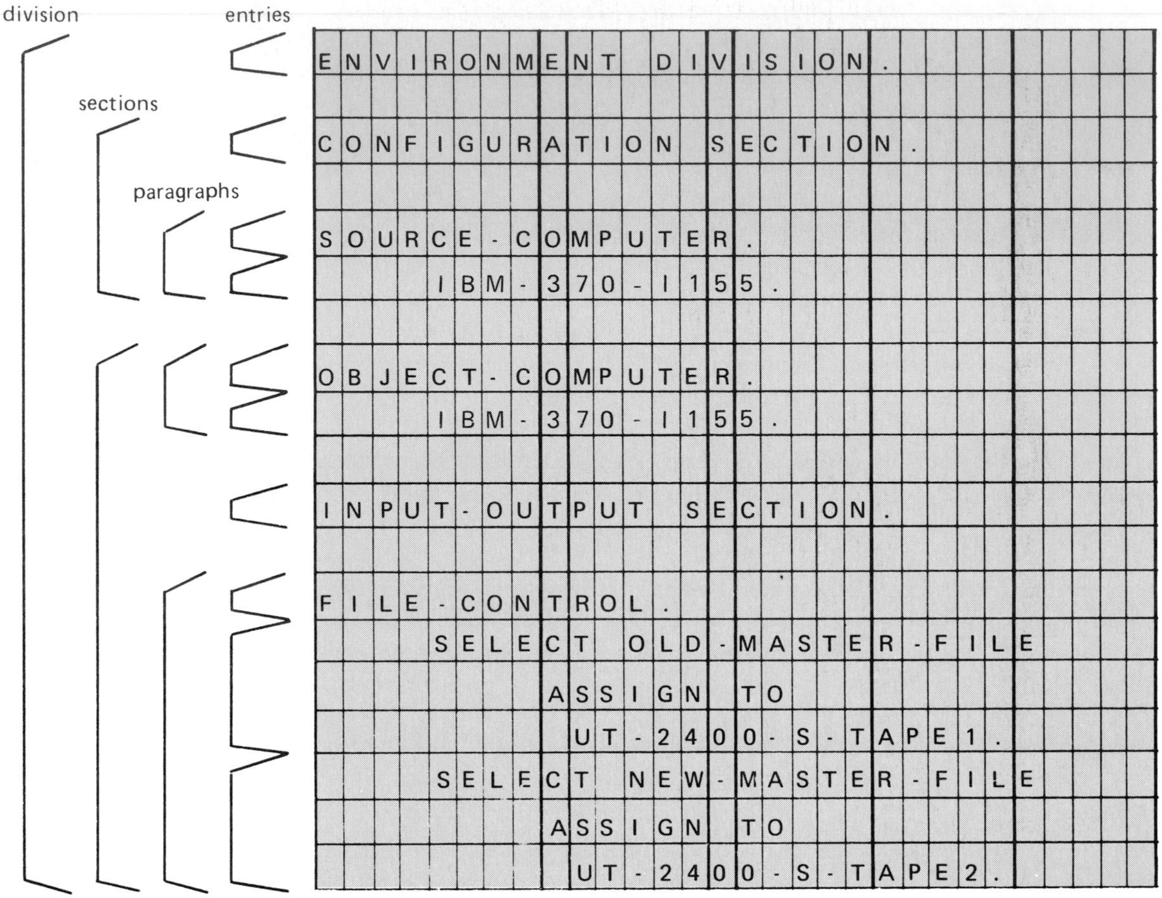

Figure 11.22 An example of a COBOL program structure.

Divisions

Four divisions are required in every COBOL program. They are Identification, Environment, Data, and Procedure. These divisions must always be written in this sequence. A fixed name header consists of the division name followed by a space, the word DIVISION, and a period on a line by itself.

Sections

The next group in the hierarchy is sections. All divisions do not necessarily contain sections. The Environment and Data Division always contain sections with fixed names. Sections are never found in the Identification Division, while the Procedure Division sections are optional and are created by the programmer if needed. The beginning of each section is preceded by the name of the section followed by a space, the word SECTION and a period on a line by itself.

Paragraphs

All divisions, except the Data Division, contain paragraphs. In the Identification and Environment Divisions, the paragraphs have fixed names. The paragraph names in the Procedure Division are supplied by the programmer.

Each paragraph is identified by a paragraph name followed by a period and space. Paragraph headers *do not* contain the word PARAGRAPH. The paragraph header need not appear on a line by itself; however, it must be the first entry and can be followed on the same line by a series of entries. A paragraph header entry consists of either a reserved word or a data name and a period.

Entries

Entries (sentences) consist of a series of statements terminated by a period and a space. These statements must follow precise format rules about sequence.

Divisions of COBOL

The source program is used to specify the method of obtaining a solution to a particular data-processing problem. There are four elements that must be provided in the source program.

1. The identification of the program.
2. The description of the equipment being used to process the data.
3. The description of the data to be processed.
4. The set of procedures that determines how the data is to be processed.

The COBOL system has a separate division within the source program for each of these elements (fig. 11.23). Each division must be placed in its proper sequence, beginning with a division header, and all the format rules must be followed for the particular division. The four divisions listed in sequence with their main functions are:

Identification Division	Identifies the program to the computer.
Environment Division	Describes the computer to be used and the hardware features to be used in the program.
Data Division	Defines the characteristics of the data to be used, including the files, record layouts, and storage areas.
Procedure Division	Consists of a series of statements directing the processing of the data according to the program logic as expressed in the detailed program flowchart.

Identification Division

The Identification Division contains the necessary information to identify the program that is written and compiled. A unique data name is assigned to the source program (fig. 11.24).

The Identification Division must first appear at compilation. The intended use of this division is to supply information to the reader. Usually it contains information about when the program was written, by whom, and any security information relative to the program. The REMARKS paragraph usually contains the purpose of the program, a brief description of the processing to be performed, and the outputs produced. This information will serve as documentation for the program (fig. 11.25).

Figure 11.23 The four divisions of a COBOL program.

Identification Division

Provides all of the necessary documentation for the program such as:

- the program name and number,
- the programmer's name,
- the system or application to which the program belongs,
- the security restrictions on the use of the program,
- a brief description of the processing performed and the output produced,
- the dates on which the program was written and compiled.

Environment Division

Configuration Section

Source-Computer — What computer will be used for compilation?

Object-Computer — What computer will be used for running the compiled object program?

Special Names — What names have you assigned to the sense (alteration) switches and the channels of the paper tape loop on the printer?

Input/Output Section

File Control — What name and hardware device have you assigned to each file used by the object program?

Data Division

File Section — For each file named in the FILE CONTROL paragraph above:

- the file name,
- the record name,
- the layout of the record—the name, location, size, and format of each field.

Working Storage Section — The size, format, and content of every counter, storage area, or constant value used by the program.

Procedure Division

The individual processing steps, written as COBOL-language statements. This division is divided into programmer-created paragraphs, each containing all of the procedure statements which constitute one particular routine.

```
Identification Division.

Program-ID. program-name.
[Author. [comment-entry] . . .]
[Installation. [comment-entry] . . .]
[Date-Written. [comment-entry] . . .]
[Date-Compiled. [comment-entry] . . .]
[Security. [comment-entry] . . .]
[Remarks. [comment-entry] . . .]
```

Figure 11.24 The Identification Division format.

```
IDENTIFICATION DIVISION.
PROGRAM-ID.
    EXPENSES.
AUTHOR.
    CHARLES BROWN.
INSTALLATION.
    DYNAMIC DATA DEVICES, INC.
DATE-WRITTEN.
    NOVEMBER 9, 1979.
DATE-COMPILED.
    NOVEMBER 10, 1979.
SECURITY.
    COMPANY-CONFIDENTIAL; AVAILABLE TO
    AUTHORIZED PERSONNEL ONLY.
REMARKS.
    PRODUCES A WEEKLY LISTING OF ALL
    OPERATING EXPENSES, BY DEPARTMENT.
```

Figure 11.25 An example of Identification Division.

Environment Division

Although COBOL is to a large degree machine independent, there are some aspects of programming that depend upon the particular computer to be used and the associated input/output devices. The Environment Division is the one division that is machine dependent, since it contains the necessary information about the equipment that will be used to compile and execute the source program. To exchange a COBOL program from one computer to another, the Environment Division would have to be modified or even replaced to make the source program compatible to the new computer.

The Environment Division describes the hardware features of the source as well as the object computer (fig. 11.26). Each data file to be used in the program must be

Figure 11.26 The Environment Division format.

Environment Division.
Configuration Section.
Source-Computer. paragraph
Object-Computer. paragraph
[Special-Names. paragraph]
[Input/Output Section.
File-Control paragraph.
[I-O-Control. paragraph]]

Figure 11.27 An example of Environment Division.

```
ENVIRONMENT DIVISION.

CONFIGURATION SECTION.


SOURCE-COMPUTER.
    IBM-370-I155.

OBJECT-COMPUTER.
    IBM-370-I155.

INPUT-OUTPUT SECTION.

FILE-CONTROL.
    SELECT PURCHASING-FILE
        ASSIGN TO SYS10Z-UR-2540R-S.
    SELECT PURCHASE-REPORT-FILE
        ASSIGN TO SYS109-UR-1403-S.
```

assigned to an input or output device. If special input or output techniques are to be used in the program, they have to be specified in this division. Any special names assigned to hardware devices must be stipulated here (fig. 11.27).

Data Division

The Data Division describes the formats and the detailed characteristics of the input and output data to be processed by the object program. The programmer attaches unique names to the files, the records within the files, and the items within the records (fig. 11.28). All files that are named in the Environment Division must be described in this division.

Data Division.
File Section.
file description entry
record description entry } . . . } . . .
Working-Storage Section.
[data item description entry] . . .
[record description entry] . . .

Figure 11.28 The Data Division format.

In addition to the file and record descriptions of data, work areas and constants to be used in the program must be described in the Working-Storage Section of this division (fig. 11.29).

Entries in this division will describe how the items are grouped and organized into records to be used in the processing. Information, such as the type of data and usage of the data, will be found in this division (fig. 11.30).

The Environment Division describes the computer that will be used to compile the source program and the computer that will be used to execute the object program; the Data Division describes the characteristics of the data; and the Procedure Division will describe the logical steps necessary to process the data.

Procedure Division

The Procedure Division specifies the actions expected of the object program to process the data to achieve the desired outputs. The division indicates the sequential order of the processing steps and also any alternate paths of actions where necessitated by decisions encountered during the processing (fig. 11.31).

This division is usually written from the program flowchart. The names of the data described in the Data Division are used to write sentences, employing program verbs to direct the computer to perform some action. The main types of action that may be specified are input and output, arithmetic, data transmission, and sequence control. All sentences are imperative even though they may be preceded by IF, since they direct the computer to perform some action. Some examples of program verbs are:

Input and Output	OPEN, READ, WRITE, CLOSE, ACCEPT, DISPLAY
Arithmetic	ADD, SUBTRACT, MULTIPLY, DIVIDE, COMPUTE
Data Transmission	MOVE, EXAMINE
Sequence Control	GO TO, PERFORM, ALTER, STOP

```
DATA DIVISION.

FILE SECTION.

FD  STOCK-TRANSACTION-FILE
    RECORDING MODE IS F
    BLOCK CONTAINS 40 RECORDS
    LABEL RECORDS ARE STANDARD
    DATA RECORD IS STOCK-TRANSACTION.

01  STOCK-TRANSACTION.
    02  STOCK-NUMBER.
        03  DISTRIBUTION-CENTER, PICTURE 99.
        03  CATALOG-NUMBER.
            04  CONTROLLING-PARTY, PICTURE 999.
            04  ACCOUNT-NUMBER, PICTURE 9(6).
            04  SHIPPING-CODE, PICTURE 99.
    02  DATE.
        03  YEAR, PICTURE 99.
        03  DAY, PICTURE 999.
    02  TRANSACTION-CODE, PICTURE X.
    02  QUANTITY, PICTURE 9(6).
    02  UNIT-VALUE, PICTURE 9(4)V9(3).

WORKING-STORAGE SECTION.

77  PRIORITY-LEVEL, PICTURE 999, VALUE 401.

77  SUM-OF-UNITS, PICTURE 9(7), VALUE ZERO.

77  TOTAL-VALUE, PICTURE 9(6)V9(3), VALUE ZERO.

77  PREVIOUS-STOCK-NUMBER, PICTURE 9(13).

01  SUMMARY.
    02  STOCK-NUMBER, PICTURE 99B999B9(6)B99.
    02  FILLER, PICTURE XXXX, VALUE SPACES.
    02  TRANSACTION-TYPE, PICTURE A(20).
    02  FILLER, PICTURE XXXX, VALUE SPACES.
    02  TOTAL-QUANTITY, PICTURE Z,ZZZ,ZZZ.
    02  FILLER, PICTURE XXXX, VALUE SPACES.
    02  TRANSACTION-VALUE, PICTURE $ZZZ,ZZZ.99.
```

File Description Entry

Record Description

Descriptions of Independent Items

Record Description

Item Description Entries

Figure 11.29 An example of Data Division entries.

COBOL Implementation of Structured Programming

The COBOL programming language provides and constructs sufficient control structures to allow implementation of structured program design principles. Since COBOL's native habitat is a business environment with recurring processing cycles and evolving system requirements, it demands, perhaps more than other languages, orderly structure and rigid standards for readability, maintainability, and flexibility.

```
01  ACCOUNTS-RECEIVABLE-RECORD.
    02  CUSTOMER.
        03  NUMBER              PICTURE X(6).
        03  NAME                PICTURE X(30).
    02  SALESMAN.
        03  BRANCH-OFFICE       PICTURE 999.
        03  SERIAL-NUMBER       PICTURE 9(5).
    02  INVOICE.
        03  NUMBER              PICTURE 9(5).
        03  DATE.
            04  MONTH           PICTURE 99.
            04  DAY             PICTURE 99.
            04  YEAR            PICTURE 99.
        03  AMOUNT              PICTURE 9(4)V99.
    02  PAYMENT.
        03  DATE.
            04  MONTH           PICTURE 99.
            04  DAY             PICTURE 99.
            04  YEAR            PICTURE 99.
        03  DISCOUNT            PICTURE 9(4)V99.
        03  NET-AMOUNT          PICTURE 9(4)V99.
    02  RECORD-CODE             PICTURE X.
```

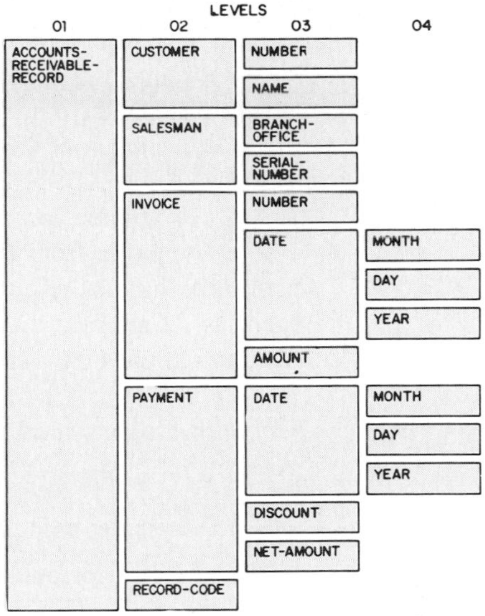

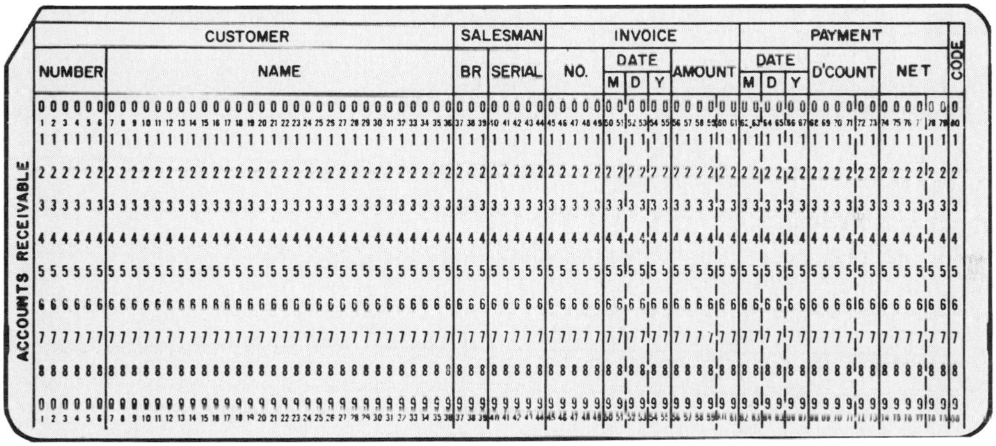

Figure 11.30 Examples of record description entries and levels.

<u>Procedure Division.</u>
procedure-name .
    sentence . . .
[procedure-name .
    sentence . . .] . . .

Figure 11.31 The Procedure Division format.

Once the principles of structured programming are understood, writing structured programs in COBOL is a matter of habitually following a few simple rules. The structure theorem states that any *proper program* can be written using only the control logic structures of *sequence, selection,* and *iteration* (loop mechanism). A proper program is defined as one that meets the following requirements.

1. It has exactly one entry point and one exit point for program control.
2. There are paths from the entry to the exit that lead through every part of the program; that is, there are no infinite loops and no unreachable code. This requirement is, of course, not a restriction but simply a statement that the structure theorem applies only to meaningful programs.

All control logic structures can be processed in COBOL, although in some cases not directly.

Basic Control Logic Structures

Sequence is simply a formularization of the idea that, unless otherwise stated, program statements are executed in the order in which they appear in the program (fig. 11.32). This is true of all commonly used programming languages; it is not always realized that sequence is in fact a control structure. Sequence is implemented in the COBOL language by simply writing statements in succession (fig. 11.33).

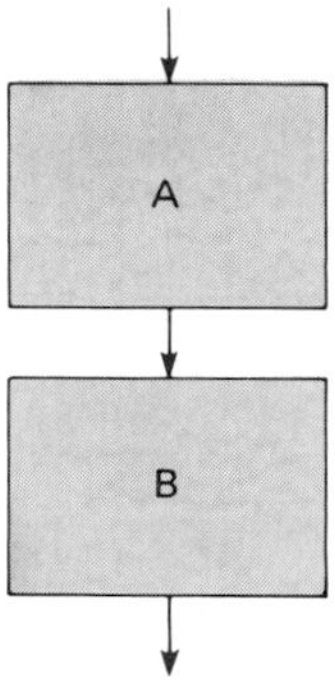

Figure 11.32 A flowchart for the sequence program structure.

```
IDENTIFICATION DIVISION
PROGRAM-ID
   ONE-CARD-LISTING
ENVIRONMENT DIVISION.
CONFIGURATION SECTION
SOURCE-COMPUTER              IBM-370-I155.
OBJECT-COMPUTER              IBM-370-I155.
INPUT-OUTPUT SECTION
FILE-CONTROL
   SELECT FILE-IN            ASSIGN TO UR-2540R-S-INFILE.
   SELECT FILE-OUT           ASSIGN TO UR-1403-S-OUTFILE.
DATA DIVISION
FILE SECTION
FD FILE-IN
   RECORDING MODE F
   LABEL RECORDS ARE OMITTED
   DATA RECORD IS RECORD-IN

01    RECORD-IN-                    PICTURE X(80).
FD    FILE-OUT
      RECORDING MODE F
      LABEL RECORDS ARE OMITTED
      DATA RECORD IS PRINTOUT.
01    PRINTOUT                      PICTURE X(133).

PROCEDURE DIVISION.
MAIN-PROGRAM.
      OPEN    INPUT     FILE-IN
              OUTPUT    FILE-OUT.
      READ FILE-IN
           AT END   CLOSE FILE-IN, FILE-OUT, STOP RUN.
      WRITE PRINTOUT FROM RECORD-IN
           AFTER ADVANCING 2 LINES.
```

The above is an example of an unlikely program written in simple sequence control logic structure where one record is read and printed and the program terminates.

Figure 11.33 An example of a simple sequence control logic structure program.

Selection is the choice between two actions based on a condition; this is called the IFTHENELSE structure (fig. 11.34). In the COBOL language, selection is implemented with the IF statement and the condition clauses (fig. 11.35).

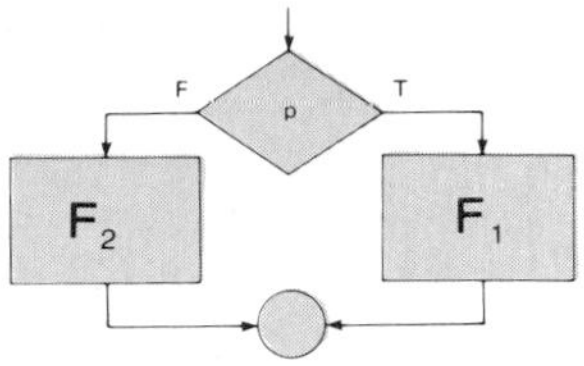

Figure 11.34 A flowchart for the IFTHENELSE program structure.

```
IF (condition)
THEN
        code for F1
ELSE
        code for F2.
```

Figure 11.35 An example of a IFTHENELSE program structure.

```
IF STOCK-ON-HAND = ZERO
THEN
   PERFORM STOCK-BAL-ZERO
ELSE
   MOVE STOCK-ON-HAND TO QUANTITY-OUT.
```

The *iteration* is the repeated execution of code while the condition is true (or false) (fig. 11.36). It is also referred to as the loop control. This is called the DOWHILE structure. In the COBOL language, it is implemented with the PERFORM verb and with UNTIL option (fig. 11.37).

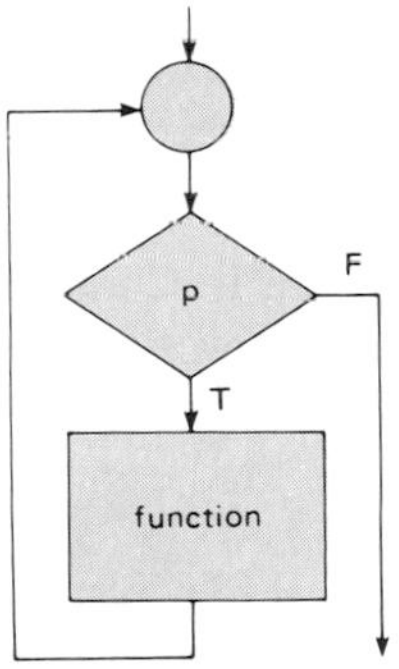

Figure 11.36 A flowchart for the DOWHILE program structure.

```
PERFORM paragraph name
        UNTIL (NOT condition).
```

Figure 11.37 An example of a DOWHILE program structure.

```
PERFORM MAIN PROCESS ROUTINE
    UNTIL MASTER-FILE-EOF.
```

The basic iteration structure is DOWHILE, but there is a closely related structure called DOUNTIL, which is sometimes used, depending on the procedure to be expressed and on the availability of appropriate language features (fig. 11.38).

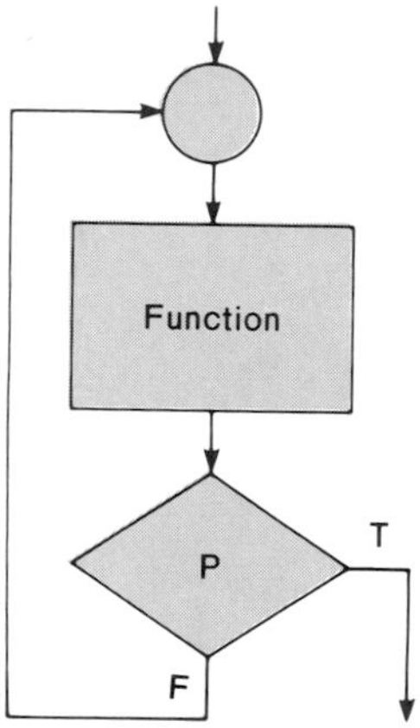

Figure 11.38 A flowchart for the DOUNTIL program structure.

The difference between the DOWHILE and the DOUNTIL structures is that with the DOWHILE, the condition is tested *before* executing the function; if the condition is false, the function is not executed at all. With the DOUNTIL, the condition is tested *after* executing the function; the function is always executed at least once, regardless of whether the condition is true or false (fig. 11.39).

Figure 11.39 An example of a DOUNTIL program structure.

```
PERFORM paragraph name.
PERFORM paragraph name
      UNTIL (condition).
```

```
PERFORM PROCEDURE-1.
PERFORM PROCEDURE-1
   UNTIL END-OF-TRANS.
```

It is sometimes helpful for readability and efficiency to have some way to express a multiway branch commonly referred to as the CASE structure (fig. 11.40). For example, it is necessary to execute appropriate routines based on a two-digit decimal code. It is certainly possible to write 100 IF statements or a compound statement with 99 ELSE IF statements, but common sense suggests that there is no reason to adhere so rigidly to the three basic structures.

The CASE structure uses the value of the variable to determine which of several routines is to be executed (fig. 11.41). Efficiency and convenience dictate reasonable use of language elements that may carry out logic functions in ways slightly different from those of the three basic structures.

```
        GO TO case-1-name, case-2-name,. . . .case-m-name
            DEPENDING ON integer-identifier.
case-1-name.
        code for F1
        GO TO case-end-name.
case-2-name.
        code for F2
        GO TO case-end-name.
case-m-name.
        code for Fm
        GO TO case-end-name.
case-end-name.
        EXIT.
```

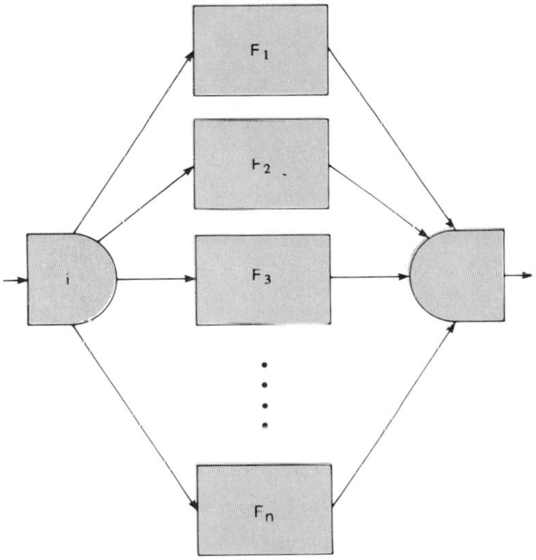

Figure 11.40 A flowchart for the CASE program structure.

Two of the standard programming structures, IFTHENELSE and DOWHILE, are implemented directly through COBOL statements. The DOUNTIL and CASE structures are simulated by conventional COBOL statements in particular structural forms.

Conclusion

The first few programs using structured programming techniques may be somewhat difficult. However, once the learning phase is over, the coding should be faster using structured programming and associated techniques (top-down design) than with previous programming methods.

Figure 11.41 An example of a CASE program structure.

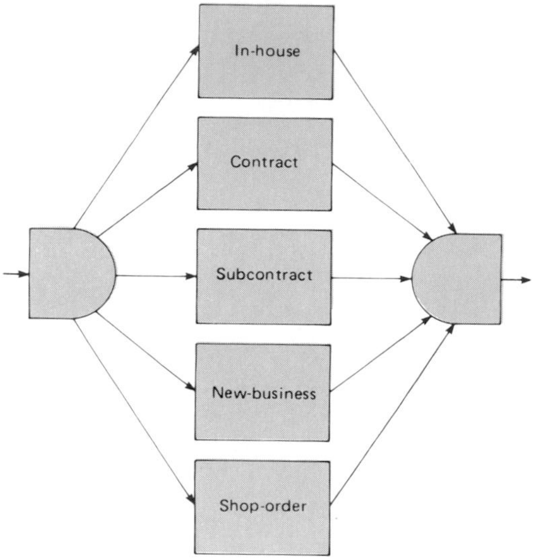


```
    PERFORM ACCOUNT-PROCESSING
        THRU ACCOUNT-PROCESSING- EXIT.
    .
    .
    .
ACCOUNT-PROCESSING.
    GO TO
        IN-HOUSE
        CONTRACT
        SUB-CONTRACT
        NEW-BUSINESS
        SHOP-ORDER
            DEPENDING ON ACCOUNT-CODE.
    error case processing statements.
    GO TO ACCOUNT-PROCESSING-EXIT.

IN-HOUSE.
    processing statements.
    GO TO ACCOUNT-PROCESSING-EXIT.

CONTRACT.
    processing statements.
    GO TO ACCOUNT-PROCESSING-EXIT.
.
.
.

SHOP-ORDER.
    processing statements.
    GO TO ACCOUNT-PROCESSING-EXIT.

ACCOUNT-PROCESSING-EXIT.
    EXIT.
```

Writing the First COBOL Program

To illustrate how a COBOL program is written, we will create a simplified procedure whereby we will pose a question and receive a response from the operator console. The program will *not* use files for input or output.

Identification Division

A name must be assigned to the program, presenting the information as follows:

```
IDENTIFICATION DIVISION.
PROGRAM-ID. DISPLAY-ACCEPT-EXAMPLE.
```

PROGRAM-ID has informed the compiler that the unique name DISPLAY-ACCEPT-EXAMPLE was chosen for the program. In addition to the name of the program, optionally, the name of the programmer, the date the program was written, and other information that would serve to document the program could have been written in the Identification Division.

Environment Division

Although COBOL is to a large degree machine independent, there are some aspects of any program that depend on a particular computer being used and on its associated input and output devices. In the Environment Division, the characteristics of the computer used may be identified.

In the Configuration Section, the source computer (the one that the compiler uses) and the object computer (the one that the object program uses) are described as follows:

```
ENVIRONMENT DIVISION.
CONFIGURATION SECTION.
SOURCE-COMPUTER. XEROX-530.
OBJECT-COMPUTER. XEROX-530.
```

These statements inform us that both computers will be the Xerox-530. If files were being used in the program, the location of each file referenced and how each would be used would have to be described. The identity of the files to be used in the program and the assignment of them to specific hardware devices would be specified in the Input-Output Section.

Data Division

The Data Division of the COBOL program gives a detailed description of all the data to be used in the program—whether to be read into the machine, used in intermediate processing, or written as output. Since no files will be used in the program, the File Section entry is not necessary. The Working-Storage Section must be constructed. This section describes the records and data items that are not part of files, but are used during the processing of the object program.

For our simplified program, only one entry will be necessary. The Data Division would appear as follows:

```
DATA DIVISION.
WORKING-STORAGE SECTION.
77 RESPONSE PICTURE X(40).
```

The level number 77 informs the compiler that RESPONSE is a noncontiguous data item, that this item has no relationship to any other data item described in the Working-Storage Section. RESPONSE is the unique data name, and PICTURE X(40) specifies that there are forty alphameric characters written for the item. X represents any character in the COBOL character set, and forty represents the number of characters within the data item.

Procedure Division The Procedure Division contains the instructions needed to solve the problem. To accomplish this, several types of COBOL statements are used. Since the program will be using only the operator console, the ACCEPT and DISPLAY statements will be the only ones used.

The ACCEPT statement with the FROM CONSOLE option enables the program to obtain information from the console operator during the running of the program. It allows the entry of low-volume data, up to one line of information, such as information needed to initialize program switches, balance totals, or serial numbers. It is not used to read files of data.

The DISPLAY statement with the UPON CONSOLE option enables low-volume data, up to one line of information, to be written on the console. It is used to write such information as exception records, control totals, or messages. It is not used to write files of data. The Procedure Division would appear as follows:

```
PROCEDURE DIVISION.
INIT.
    DISPLAY 'WHAT DOES COBOL STAND FOR'
      UPON CONSOLE.
    ACCEPT RESPONSE FROM CONSOLE.
    DISPLAY 'THE CORRECT RESPONSE IS . . .'
      UPON CONSOLE.
    DISPLAY 'CO-MMON B-USINESS O-RIENTED L-ANGUAGE'
      UPON CONSOLE.
    STOP RUN.
```

The first DISPLAY statement is used to type a one-line message to the operator in the form of an inquiry. Everything between the apostrophes (') will be printed.

The ACCEPT statement allows the entry of up to forty columns of data from the operator as defined by the RESPONSE statement in the Working-Storage Section of the Data Division.

The last two DISPLAY statements will display two lines of messages on the console. There is an automatic space with each DISPLAY statement.

The last statement STOP RUN is used to end the job and turn control of the system back to the operating system (figs. 11.42, 11.43).

Figure 11.42 Illustrative COBOL structured program 1.

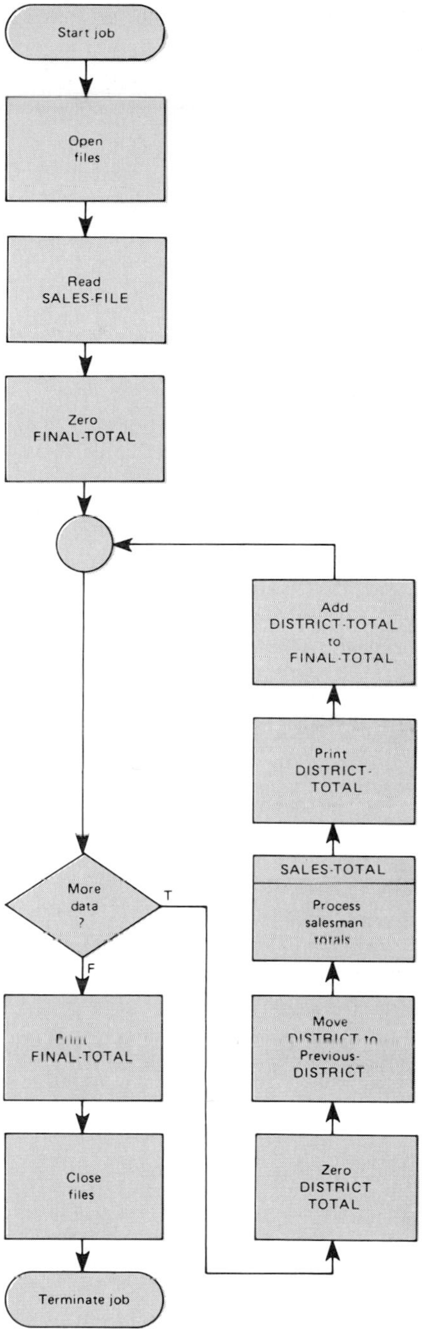

Flowchart for the mainline processing portion of a two-level control total processing application

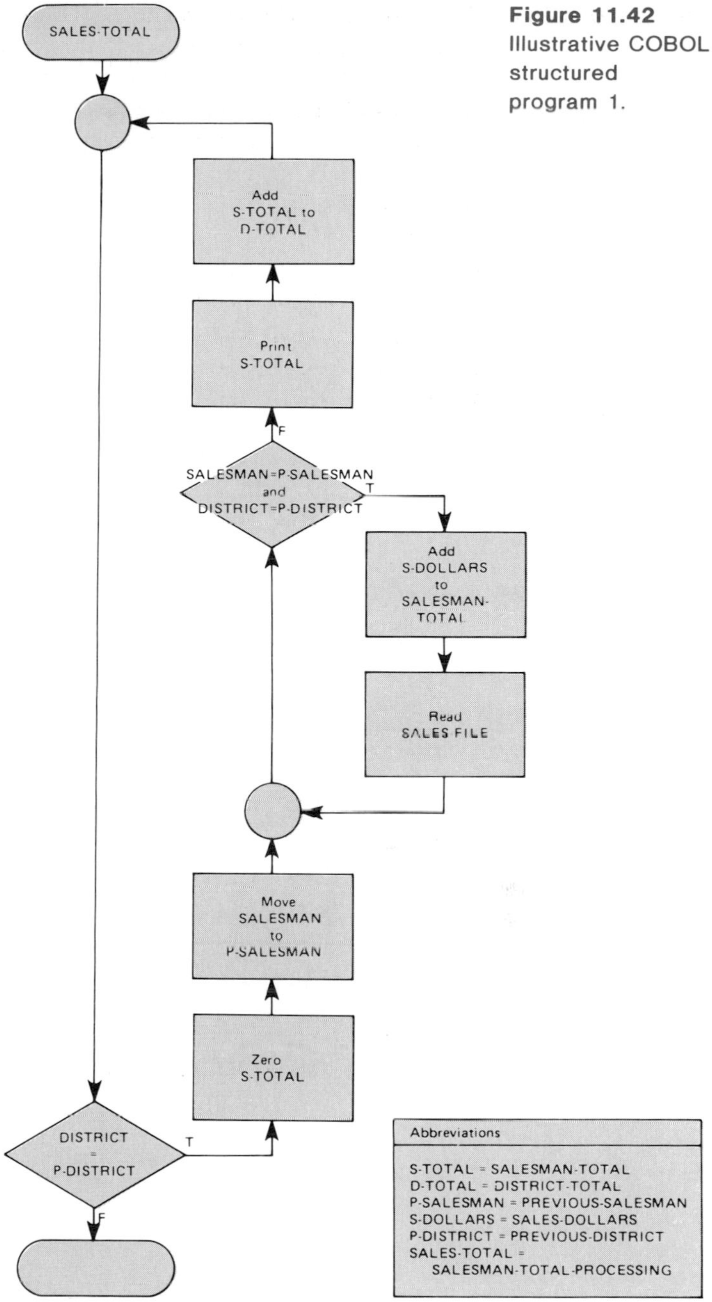

Flowchart for the record processing portion of a two-level control total processing application

Figure 11.42 Continued.

```
IDENTIFICATION DIVISION.
PROGRAM-ID.
    TWOLEVEL.

ENVIRONMENT DIVISION.
INPUT-OUTPUT SECTION.
FILE-CONTROL.
    SELECT SALES-FILE ASSIGN TO SYS012-UR-2540R-S.
    SELECT REPORT-FILE ASSIGN TO SYS009-UR-1403-S.

DATA DIVISION.
FILE SECTION.

FD SALES-FILE
    RECORD CONTAINS 80 CHARACTERS
    RECORDING MODE IS F
    LABEL RECORDS ARE OMITTED
    DATA RECORD IS SALES-RECORD.
01  SALES-RECORD.
    05  SALESMAN                PICTURE X(5).
    05  DISTRICT                PICTURE XXX.
    05  SALES-DOLLARS           PICTURE 9(5)V99.

FD REPORT-FILE
    RECORD CONTAINS 133 CHARACTERS
    RECORDING MODE IS F
    LABEL RECORDS ARE OMITTED
    DATA RECORD IS REPORT-RECORD.
01  REPORT-RECORD.
    05  CARRIAGE-CONTROL        PICTURE X.
    05  SALESMAN-OUT            PICTURE ZZZZ9.
    05  FILLER                  PICTURE XXX.
    05  SALESMAN-TOTAL-OUT      PICTURE $$$,$$$,$$9.99.
    05  FILLER                  PICTURE X(8).
    05  DISTRICT-OUT            PICTURE ZZ9.
    05  FILLER                  PICTURE XXX.
    05  DISTRICT-TOTAL-OUT      PICTURE $$$,$$$,$$9.99.
    05  FILLER                  PICTURE X(8).
    05  FINAL-TOTAL-OUT         PICTURE $$$,$$$,$$9.99.

WORKING-STORAGE SECTION.

01  FLAGS.
    05  MORE-DATA-FLAG          PICTURE XXX     VALUE 'YES'.
        88  MORE-DATA                           VALUE 'YES'.
        88  NO-MORE-DATA                        VALUE 'NO'.

01  SAVE-ITEMS.
    05  PREVIOUS-SALESMAN       PICTURE X(5).
    05  PREVIOUS-DISTRICT       PICTURE XXX.
01  TOTALS COMPUTATIONAL-3.
    05  SALESMAN-TOTAL          PICTURE S9(8)V99 VALUE ZERO.
    05  DISTRICT-TOTAL          PICTURE S9(8)V99 VALUE ZERO.
    05  FINAL-TOTAL             PICTURE S9(8)V99 VALUE ZERO.

PROCEDURE DIVISION.
PREPARE-SALES-REPORT.
    OPEN INPUT    SALES-FILE
         OUTPUT   REPORT-FILE.
    READ SALES-FILE
         AT END MOVE 'NO' TO MORE-DATA-FLAG.
    MOVE ZERO TO FINAL-TOTAL.
    PERFORM DISTRICT-TOTAL-PROCESSING
         UNTIL NO-MORE-DATA.
    MOVE SPACES TO REPORT-RECORD.
    MOVE FINAL-TOTAL TO FINAL-TOTAL-OUT.
    WRITE REPORT-RECORD.
    CLOSE   SALES-FILE
            REPORT-FILE.
    STOP RUN.

DISTRICT-TOTAL-PROCESSING.
    MOVE ZERO TO DISTRICT-TOTAL.
    MOVE DISTRICT TO PREVIOUS-DISTRICT.
    PERFORM SALESMAN-TOTAL-PROCESSING
         UNTIL DISTRICT IS NOT EQUAL TO PREVIOUS-DISTRICT
         OR NO-MORE-DATA.
    MOVE SPACES TO REPORT-RECORD.
    MOVE PREVIOUS-DISTRICT TO DISTRICT-OUT.
    MOVE DISTRICT-TOTAL TO DISTRICT-TOTAL-OUT.
    WRITE REPORT-RECORD.
    ADD DISTRICT-TOTAL TO FINAL-TOTAL.

SALESMAN-TOTAL-PROCESSING.
    MOVE ZERO TO SALESMAN-TOTAL.
    MOVE SALESMAN TO PREVIOUS-SALESMAN.
    PERFORM PROCESS-AND-READ
         UNTIL DISTRICT IS NOT EQUAL TO PREVIOUS- DISTRICT
         OR SALESMAN IS NOT EQUAL TO PREVIOUS- SALESMAN
         OR NO-MORE-DATA.
    MOVE SPACES TO REPORT-RECORD.
    MOVE PREVIOUS-SALESMAN TO SALESMAN-OUT.
    MOVE SALESMAN-TOTAL TO SALESMAN-TOTAL-OUT.
    WRITE REPORT-RECORD.
    ADD SALESMAN-TOTAL TO DISTRICT-TOTAL.

PROCESS-AND-READ.
    ADD SALES-DOLLARS TO SALESMAN-TOTAL.
    READ SALES-FILE
         AT END MOVE 'NO' TO MORE-DATA-FLAG.
```

Structured program for a two-level control total processing application

```
  41    $203.37
  52    $110.00
  69    $134.65
                     1     $448.02
  18    $207.69
  32    $185.60
                     2     $393.29
  36    $194.15
  39    $121.40
  50     $51.80
                     3     $367.35     $1,208.66
```

Illustrative output from the two-level control total program

Figure 11.43 Illustrative COBOL structured program 2.

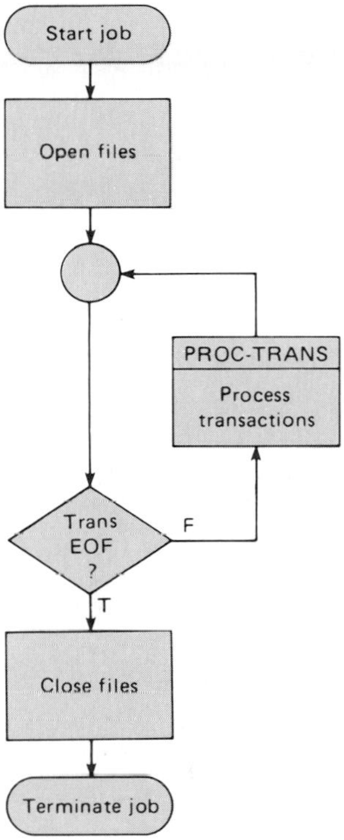

Flowchart of the mainline processing for an inquiry response application

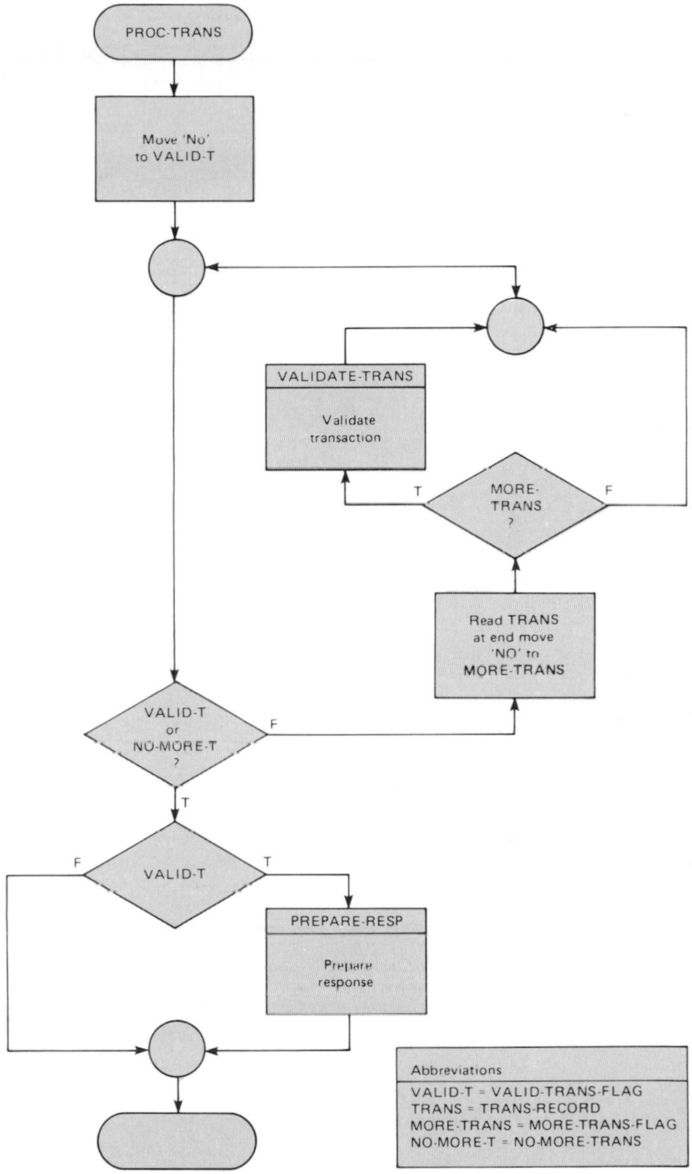

Flowchart of the transaction processing logic for an inquiry response application

Figure 11.43 Continued.

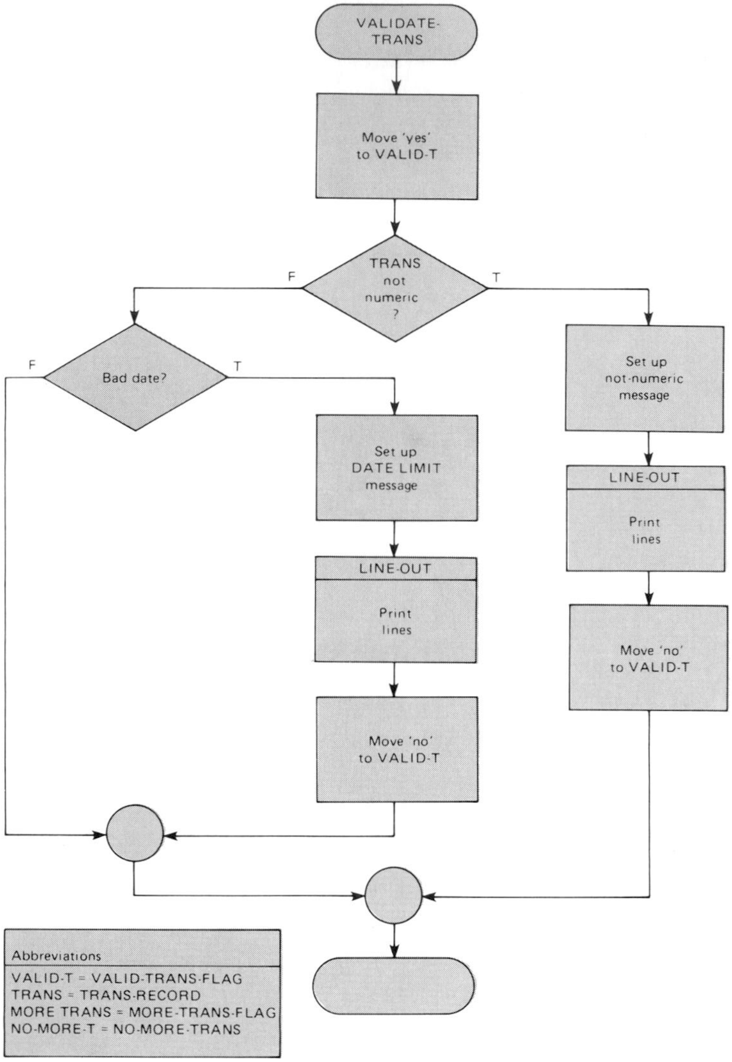

Flowchart for the validation portion of an inquiry response application

Figure 11.43 Continued.

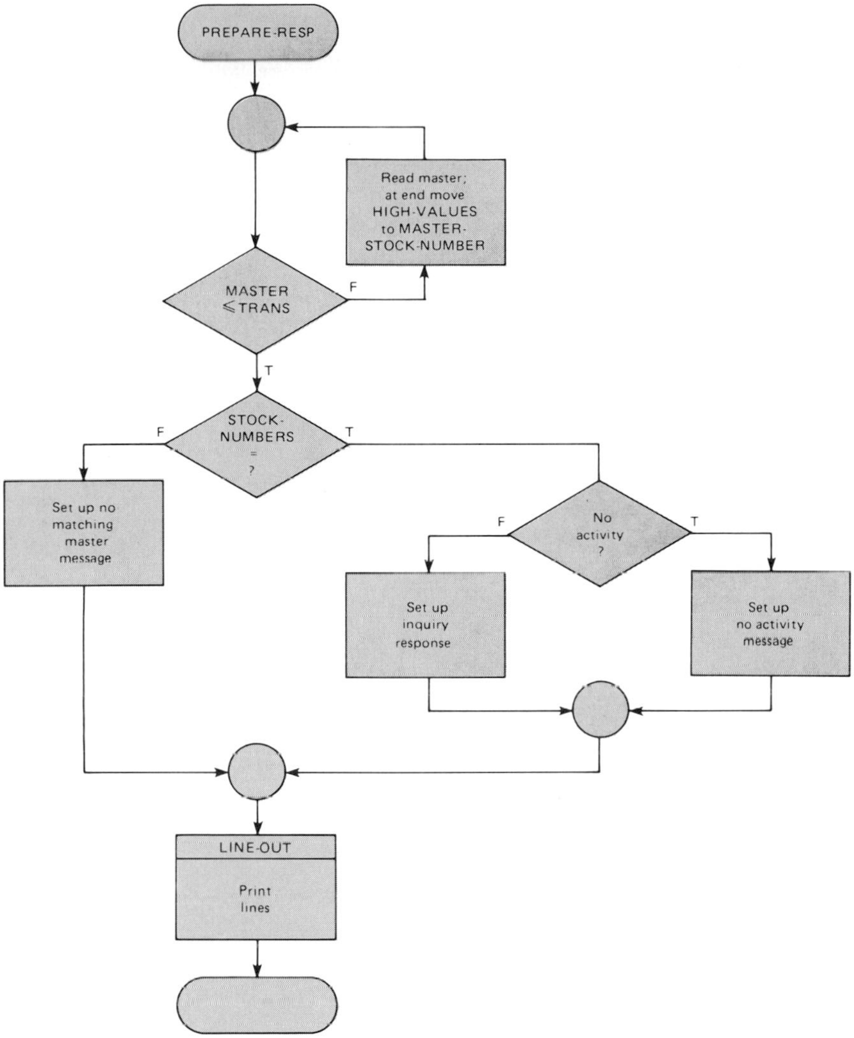

Flowchart of the logic for preparing a response in an inquiry response application

Figure 11.43 Continued.

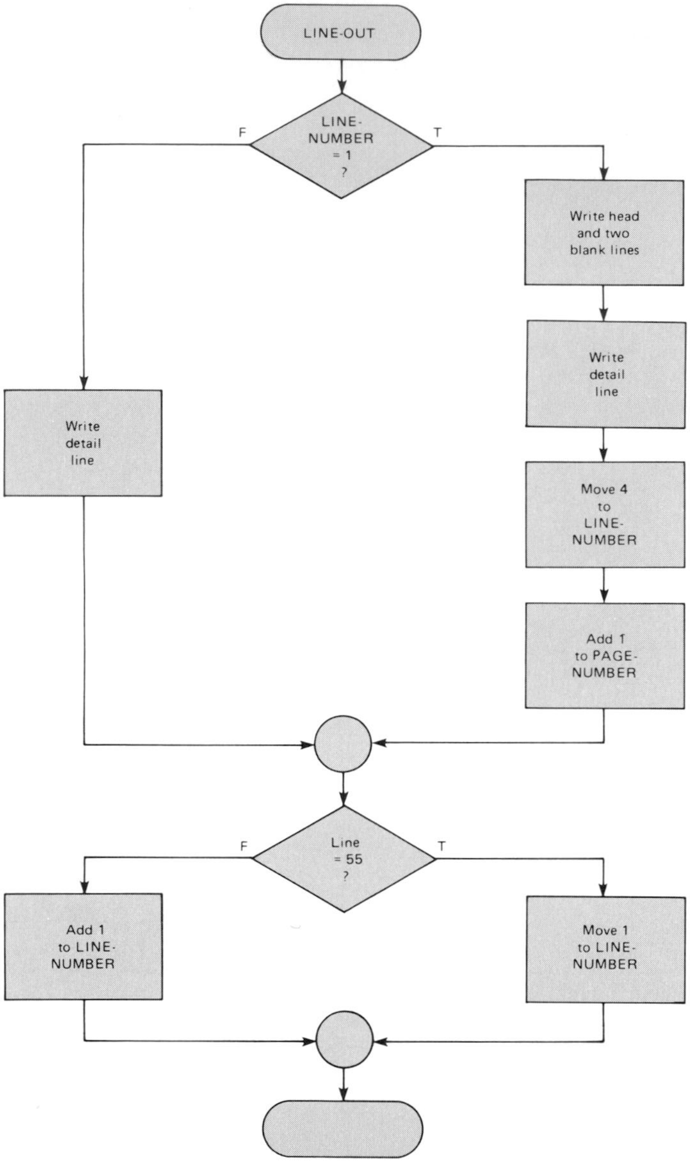

Flowchart of the logic for printing heading and detail lines in an inquiry response application

Figure 11.43 Continued.

```
IDENTIFICATION DIVISION.
PROGRAM-ID.
       STRUCTURED PROGRAMMING EXAMPLE.

ENVIRONMENT DIVISION.
INPUT-OUTPUT SECTION.
FILE-CONTROL.
       SELECT MASTER-FILE ASSIGN TO SYS011-UT-2400-S.
       SELECT TRANS-FILE   ASSIGN TO SYS012-UR-2540R-S.
       SELECT REPORT-FILE ASSIGN TO SYS009-UR-1403-S.

DATA DIVISION.

FILE SECTION.

FD    MASTER-FILE
       RECORD CONTAINS 80 CHARACTERS
       RECORDING MODE IS F
       LABEL RECORDS ARE OMITTED
       DATA RECORD IS MASTER-RECORD-BUFFER.
01     MASTER-RECORD-BUFFER            PICTURE X(80).

FD    TRANS-FILE
       RECORD CONTAINS 80 CHARACTERS
       RECORDING MODE IS F
       LABEL RECORDS ARE OMITTED
       DATA RECORD IS TRANS-RECORD.
01     TRANS-RECORD.
       05    STOCK-NUMBER              PICTURE X(6).
       05    DATE-LIMIT.
             10    YEAR                PICTURE XX.
             10    DAY-OF-YEAR         PICTURE XXX.
       05    FILLER                    PICTURE X(69).
FD    REPORT-FILE
       RECORDING MODE IS F
       LABEL RECORDS ARE OMITTED
       DATA RECORD IS REPORT-RECORD.
01     REPORT-RECORD.
       05  FORMS-CONTROL               PICTURE X.
       05  FILLER                      PICTURE X (132).

WORKING-STORAGE SECTION.

01     MASTER-RECORD.
       05    STOCK-NUMBER              PICTURE X(6) VALUE LOW-VALUES.
       05    DESCRIPTION               PICTURE X(20).
       05    UNIT-PRICE                PICTURE 9(5)V99.
       05    QUANTITY-ON-HAND          PICTURE 9(5)V99.
       05    LAST-ACTIVITY-DATE.
             10    YEAR                PICTURE XX.
             10    DAY-OF-YEAR         PICTURE XXX.
       05    FILLER                    PICTURE X(35).

01    FLAGS.
      05    MORE-TRANS-FLAG           PICTURE XXX    VALUE 'YES'.
            88    MORE-TRANS                         VALUE 'YES'.
            88    NO-MORE-TRANS                      VALUE 'NO'.
      05    VALID-TRANS-FLAG          PICTURE XXX.
            88    VALID-TRANS                        VALUE 'YES'.

01    MESSAGES.
      05    NO-ACTIVITY-MSG
            VALUE 'NO ACTIVITY FOR THIS ITEM SINCE DATE IN INQUIRY'.
      05    NO-MATCHING-MASTER-MGS   PICTURE X(50)
            VALUE 'NO MASTER FOR THIS STOCK NUMBER'.
      05    NOT-NUMERIC-MSG          PICTURE X(50)
            VALUE 'ALL ITEMS IN INQUIRY MUST BE NUMERIC'.
      05    DATE-LIMIT-MSG           PICTURE X(50)
            VALUE 'DATE-LIMIT MUST NOT BE LESS THAN 70001'.

01    LINE-AND-PAGE-COUNTERS.
      05    LINE-NUMBER               PICTURE 99     VALUE 1.
      05    PAGE-NUMBER               PICTURE 999    VALUE 1.
01    OUTPUT-LINE.
      05    FORMS-CONTROL             PICTURE X.
      05    FILLER                    PICTURE X(132).

01    INQUIRY-RESPONSE.
      05    FORMS-CONTROL             PICTURE X.
      05    STOCK-NUMBER              PICTURE X(6).
      05    FILLER                    PICTURE XXX    VALUE SPACES.
      05    DATE-LIMIT                PICTURE X(5).
      05    FILLER                    PICTURE X(5)   VALUE SPACES.
      05    DESCRIPTION               PICTURE X(20).
      05    FILLER                    PICTURE XXX    VALUE SPACES.
      05    UNIT-PRICE                PICTURE $$$,$$9.99.
      05    FILLER                    PICTURE XXX    VALUE SPACES.
      05    QUANTITY-ON-HAND          PICTURE Z(4)9.99.
      05    FILLER                    PICTURE XXX    VALUE SPACES.
      05    COST-OF-STOCK             PICTURE $$,$$$,$$9.99.
      05    FILLER                    PICTURE XXX    VALUE SPACES.
      05    LAST-ACTIVITY-DATE.
            10    CENTURY             PICTURE XX     VALUE '19'.
            10    YEAR                PICTURE XX.
            10    FILLER              PICTURE XX     VALUE SPACES.
            10    DAY-OF-YEAR         PICTURE XXX.
      05    FILLER                    PICTURE X(9)   VALUE SPACES.

01    MESSAGE-RECORD.
      05    FORMS-CONTROL             PICTURE X.
      05    STOCK-NUMBER              PICTURE X(6).
      05    FILLER                    PICTURE XXX    VALUE SPACES.
      05    DATE-LIMIT                PICTURE X(5).
      05    FILLER                    PICTURE X(5)   VALUE SPACES.
      05    MESSAGE-FIELD             PICTURE X(82).

01    HEADING-LINE.
      05    FORMS-CONTROL             PICTURE X.
      05    FILLER                    PICTURE X(46)
            VALUE ' TRANSACTION               DESCRIPTION        UNIT'.
      05    FILLER                    PICTURE X(44)
            VALUE ' PRICE     QOH       TOTAL COST    LAST ACTIVITY'.
      05    PAGE-NUMBER-OUT           PICTURE Z(6)9.

PROCEDURE DIVISION.
ANSWER-INQUIRIES.
      OPEN INPUT MASTER-FILE
                 TRANS-FILE
           OUTPUT REPORT-FILE.
      PERFORM PROCESS-TRANSACTIONS
           UNTIL NO-MORE-TRANS.
      CLOSE MASTER-FILE
           TRANS-FILE
           REPORT-FILE.
      STOP RUN.

PROCESS-TRANSACTIONS.
      MOVE 'NO' TO VALID-TRANS-FLAG.
      PERFORM GET-VALID-TRANSACTION
           UNTIL VALID-TRANS
           OR NO-MORE-TRANS.
      IF VALID-TRANS
      THEN
           PERFORM PREPARE-RESPONSE.

GET-VALID-TRANSACTION.
      READ TRANS-FILE
           AT END MOVE 'NO' TO MORE-TRANS-FLAG.
      IF MORE-TRANS
      THEN
           PERFORM VALIDATE-TRANSACTION.

VALIDATE-TRANSACTION.
      MOVE 'YES' TO VALID-TRANS-FLAG.
      IF STOCK-NUMBER OF TRANS-RECORD IS NOT NUMERIC
           OR DATE-LIMIT OF TRANS-RECORD IS NOT NUMERIC
      THEN
           MOVE CORRESPONDING TRANS-RECORD TO MESSAGE-RECORD
           MOVE NOT-NUMERIC-MSG TO MESSAGE-FIELD
           MOVE MESSAGE-RECORD TO OUTPUT-LINE
           PERFORM LINE-OUT
           MOVE 'NO' TO VALID-TRANS-FLAG
      ELSE
           IF DATE-LIMIT OF TRANS-RECORD IS LESS THAN '70001'
           THEN
                MOVE CORRESPONDING TRANS-RECORD TO
                     MESSAGE-RECORD
                MOVE DATE-LIMIT-MSG TO MESSAGE-FIELD
                MOVE MESSAGE-RECORD TO OUTPUT-LINE
                PERFORM LINE-OUT
                MOVE 'NO' TO VALID-TRANS-FLAG.

 PREPARE-RESPONSE.
      PERFORM READ-MASTER
           UNTIL STOCK-NUMBER OF MASTER-RECORD
                IS EQUAL TO STOCK-NUMBER OF TRANS-RECORD
             OR STOCK-NUMBER OF MASTER-RECORD
                IS GREATER THAN STOCK-NUMBER OF TRANS-RECORD.
```

Structured program for an inquiry response application

Figure 11.43 Continued.

```
IF STOCK-NUMBER OF TRANS-RECORD
    IS EQUAL TO STOCK-NUMBER OF MASTER-RECORD
THEN
    IF DATE-LIMIT OF TRANS-RECORD IS NOT LESS THAN
        LAST-ACTIVITY-DATE OF MASTER-RECORD
    THEN
        MOVE CORRESPONDING TRANS-RECORD TO
            MESSAGE-RECORD
        MOVE NO-ACTIVITY-MSG TO MESSAGE-FIELD
        MOVE MESSAGE-RECORD TO OUTPUT-LINE
    ELSE
        MOVE CORRESPONDING MASTER-RECORD TO
            INQUIRY-RESPONSE
        MOVE DATE-LIMIT OF TRANS-RECORD TO
            DATE-LIMIT OF INQUIRY-RESPONSE
        MULTIPLY UNIT-PRICE OF MASTER-RECORD
            BY QUANTITY-ON-HAND OF MASTER- RECORD
            GIVING COST-OF-STOCK
        MOVE INQUIRY-RESPONSE TO OUTPUT-LINE
ELSE
    MOVE CORRESPONDING TRANS-RECORD TO MESSAGE-RECORD
    MOVE NO-MATCHING-MASTER-MSG TO MESSAGE- FIELD
    MOVE MESSAGE-RECORD TO OUTPUT-LINE.
PERFORM LINE-OUT.

READ-MASTER.
    READ MASTER-FILE INTO MASTER-RECORD
        AT END MOVE HIGH-VALUES TO STOCK-NUMBER
            OF MASTER-RECORD.

LINE-OUT.
    IF LINE-NUMBER = 1
    THEN
        MOVE PAGE-NUMBER TO PAGE-NUMBER-OUT
        WRITE REPORT-RECORD FROM HEADING-LINE
            AFTER POSITIONING 0
        WRITE REPORT-RECORD FROM OUTPUT-LINE
            AFTER POSITIONING 2
        MOVE 4 TO LINE-NUMBER
        ADD 1 TO PAGE-NUMBER
    ELSE
        WRITE REPORT-RECORD FROM OUTPUT-LINE
            AFTER POSITIONING 1.
    IF LINE-NUMBER = 55
    THEN
        MOVE 1 TO LINE-NUMBER
    ELSE
        ADD 1 TO LINE-NUMBER.
```

Structured program for an inquiry response application

```
000108DESK                  0018500000160075010
000115CHAIR, FOLDING        0001810001270075100
000180LAMP, FLOOR           0003750000120075180
000181LAMP, DESK            0002200001170075093
000200TYPEWRITER STAND      0002490000400074350
000309BOOKCASE, 5 SHELF     0004125000200075105
000310BOOKCASE, 4 SHELF     0003650000310075090
000311BOOKCASE, 3 SHELF     0002800000170075110
000480FILE CABINET, 4 DWR   0006180001000075130
000481FILE CABINET, 2 DWR   0003990000500075150
010684WASTEBASKET, GREEN    0000417000120075190
010686WASTEBASKET, GRAY     0000417001900075120
010687WASTEBASKET, BLUE     0000417000570075182
021732SOFA, LEATHER, BROWN0035620000290075070
021739SOFA, LEATHER, RED    0035620000370075040
```

Illustrative master file for the inquiry response program

```
00010875001
00018075001
00020075001
00025075001
000310 75001
00031075001
00048075140
00048175140
010.68575140
01069075150
02173975030
03194075150
```

Illustrative transaction file for the inquiry response program

```
TRANSACTION     DESCRIPTION                        UNIT PRICE  QOH    TOTAL COST   LAST ACTIVITY

000108  75001   DESK                               $185.00     16.00  $2,960.00    1975   010
000180  75001   LAMP, FLOOR                        $37.50      12.00  $450.00      1975   180
000200  75001   NO ACTIVITY FOR THIS ITEM SINCE DATE IN INQUIRY
000250  75001   NO MASTER FOR THIS STOCK NUMBER
000310   7500   ALL ITEMS IN INQUIRY MUST BE NUMERIC
000310  75001   BOOKCASE, 4 SHELF                  $36.50      31.00  $1,131.50    1975   090
000480  75140   NO ACTIVITY FOR THIS ITEM SINCE DATE IN INQUIRY
000481  75140   FILE CABINET, 2 DWR                $39.90      50.00  $1,995.00    1975   150
010.68  57514   ALL ITEMS IN INQUIRY MUST BE NUMERIC
010690  75150   NO MASTER FOR THIS STOCK NUMBER
021739  75030   SOFA, LEATHER, RED                 $356.20     37.00  $13,179.40   1975   040
031940  75150   NO MASTER FOR THIS STOCK NUMBER
```

Output of the program

Summary

COBOL is a near-English programming language designed primarily for programming business applications on computers. COBOL is the most popular programming language used in business. The program is written in an English-like syntax using words, sentences, and paragraphs that look and read like ordinary business English. This chapter describes the features of the most widely used business programming language, including the latest techniques of structured programming.

1. COBOL establishes a standard language for programming business data-processing applications. Its English-like statements solve many language difficulties between the programmers and management. It also removes the programmer from individual machine or symbolic instructions. Separate divisions of a COBOL program permit a large program to be broken down into segments. Although there are many advantages of using COBOL, some problems can result because personnel does not fully understand the language and its uses.
2. The COBOL system consists of the source program and the compiler. The source program is the problem-solving COBOL program, which will be later compiled and translated into the machine language of the particular computer. The compiler converts the source program into computer-acceptable object program. The source computer is the computer that is used to compile the COBOL source program. The object computer is the computer that is used to process the machine-language program. The character set consists of fifty-one characters, composed of alphabetic, numeric, and special characters.
3. Within a COBOL system, names establish words that identify certain data within a program. Data names are assigned to identify data items in a program. Procedure names are symbolic names attached to various segments of the Procedure Division for reference. Condition names are assigned to items that may have various values. Special names are mnemonic names given to various components of the environment division.
4. Words consist of one or more characters chosen from the character set. Reserved words have preassigned meanings and must not be altered, misspelled, or changed in any way.
5. A constant is an actual value of data that remains unchanged during the execution of the program. There are two types of constants, literals and figurative constants. Literals are a string of characters whose value is determined by a set of characters of which the literal is a part. The numeric literal is a string of characters chosen from the digits 0–9, the plus or minus sign, and the decimal point. The nonnumeric literal is a string of any characters in the COBOL character set, enclosed in quotation marks. Figurative constants are reserved words that have predefined value recognized by the COBOL compiler.
6. Operators specify some sort of action or relationship between two items in a program. They might be an arithmetic expression, such as addition (+) or equal (=); a logical expression, such as AND or NOT; or punctuating symbols, such as (.) or (;).
7. Statements are syntactically valid combinations of words and symbols written in the Procedure Division that are used to express a thought in COBOL.

8. Coding forms provide programs with a standard method of writing COBOL source programs. The sequence number (columns 1–6) identify numerically each card to the COBOL compiler. The continuation indicator (column 7) will contain a hyphen if the statement continues on a second line. The program statement (columns 8–72) is used to write the source program. The identification code (columns 73–80) is used for names of programs for identification purposes.
9. The structure of a COBOL program is arranged in a series of entries that comprise divisions, sections, and paragraphs. Divisions are composed of a series of sections in the following sequence—Identification, Environment, Data, and Procedure. Each section is composed of a series of paragraphs. Paragraphs are composed of a series of sentences containing statements and ending with a period.
10. The Identification Division appears first at compile time and contains the necessary information to identify the program that is written and compiled. The Environment Division is a machine-dependent division that describes the computer to be used and the hardware features to be used in the program. The Data Division defines the characteristics of the data to be processed, including files, record layouts, and storage areas. The Procedure Division consists of a series of statements directing the processing of the data according to the program logic as expressed in the detailed program flowchart.
11. In structured programming, the program statements are written using only the control logic structures of sequence, selection, and iteration. Sequence statements are executed in sequence unless otherwise stated. Selection (IFTHENELSE) will occur when there are two actions based on a condition. Iteration (DOWHILE) is the repeated execution of a code while a condition is true or false.

Identification Questions

Match the following terms with the statements below.

A. Case Structure
B. Character Set
C. Compiler
D. Constant
E. COBOL
F. Data Division
G. Diagnostic
H. Division
I. Entries
J. Environment Division
K. Figurative Constant
L. Identification Division
M. Iteration Structure
N. Literals
O. Names
P. Object Computer
Q. Object Program
R. Operators
S. Paragraphs
T. Procedure Division
U. Proper Program
V. Reserved Words
W. Sections
X. Sequence Structure
Y. Selection Structure
Z. Source Computer
AA. Source Program
BB. Statements
CC. Word

1. The actual value of data that remains unchanged during the execution of the program.
2. The machine language used to process the data.
3. The complete set of COBOL characters consisting of fifty-one characters.

4. Composed of a series of sections.
5. Identifies the program to the computer.
6. Repeated execution of code while a condition is true (or false).
7. Has one entry point and one exit point for program control.
8. Uses the value of a variable to determine which of several routines is to be executed.
9. A means of establishing words to identify certain data within a program.
10. Composed of a series of statements terminated by a period and space.
11. Defines the characteristics of the data to be processed.
12. Common Business Oriented Language.
13. A program supplied by the computer manufacturer that is used to translate a source program.
14. A string of characters where the value is determined by the set of characters in which it is a part.
15. Program statements are executed in the order in which they appear in the program.
16. A statement provided by the compiler indicating all errors in a source program, excluding errors in logic.
17. The computer used to compile the source program.
18. Consists of one or more COBOL characters chosen from the character set.
19. Words that specify some sort of action or relationship between two items in a program.
20. Composed of a series of paragraphs.
21. A set of statements that direct the computer to perform the necessary processing.
22. Reserved words that have a predefined value recognized by the COBOL compiler.
23. A problem-solving program, which will be later compiled into the machine language of the particular computer.
24. The computer upon which the machine-language program will be processed.
25. Words that have a preassigned meaning that cannot be altered in any manner.
26. Composed of a series of sentences.
27. Describes the computer to be used and the hardware features to be used in the program.
28. Choice of two actions based on a condition.
29. A syntactically valid combination of words and symbols used to express a thought.

Questions for Review

1. What is COBOL and what is its main purpose?
2. What are the important advantages of COBOL as a programming language?
3. COBOL has some serious disadvantages. What are they?
4. What is the difference between the source computer and the object computer in a COBOL program?
5. What is the significance of the following COBOL terms—name, reserved word, figurative constant, operator, statement, literals.
6. Describe the program structure of a COBOL program.
7. What are the divisions of COBOL and what are their main purposes?

8. What are the two requirements for a proper program?
9. What is the sequence control structure and how is it implemented in COBOL?
10. What is the selection control structure and how is it implemented in COBOL?
11. What is the iteration control structure and how is it implemented in COBOL?
12. What is the basic difference between the DOWHILE and DOUNTIL structures?
13. What is the CASE structure?

Key Terms

Case Structure
Character Set
Compiler
Constant
COBOL
Data Division
Diagnostic
Division
Entries
Environment Division
Figurative Constants
Identification Division
Iteration Structure
Literals
Names
Object Computer
Object Program
Operators
Paragraphs
Procedure Division
Proper Program
Reserved Words
Sections
Sequence Structure
Selection Structure
Statements
Source Computer
Source Program
Word

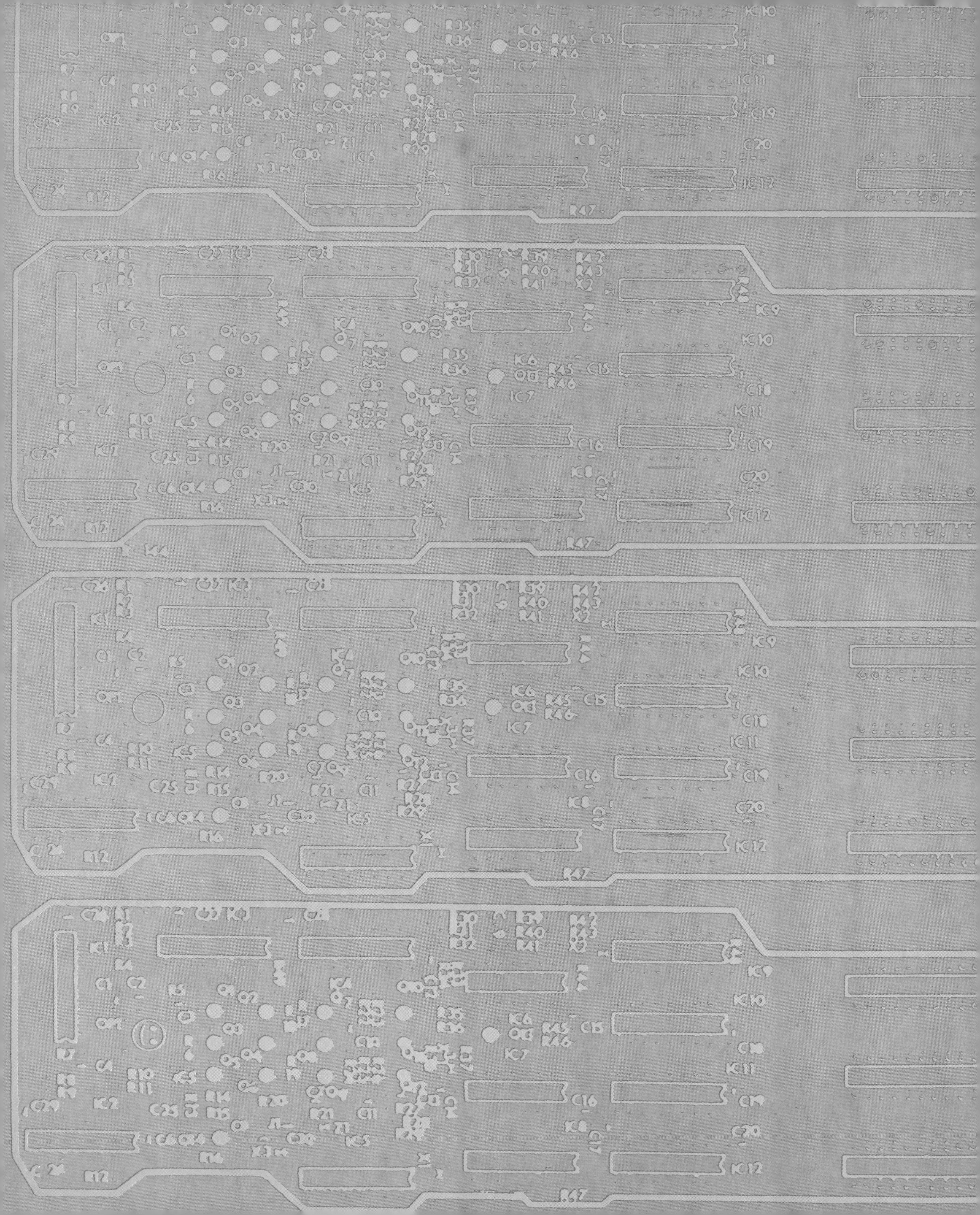

IC1
IC2
IC5
IC6
IC7
IC8
IC9
IC10
IC11
IC12
C1
C2
C4
C11
C15
C16
C17
C18
C19
C20
C24
C25
C29
R4
R5
R7
R10
R11
R12
R14
R15
R16
R20
R21
R35
R36
R40
R41
R42
R43
R45
R46
R47
Q1
Q2
Q3
Q14
Z1
X3

Report Program Generator II 12

Chapter Outline

Features

Advantages

RPG and RPG II

Specification Sheets—Functions

Principles of RPG II Programming
- Printer Spacing Chart
- Specification Forms
  - Common Entries
  - File Description Specifications
  - File Extension and Line Counter Specifications
  - Input Specifications
  - Calculation Specifications
  - Output-Format Specifications
- Editing

Chapter Objectives

The learning objectives of this chapter are

1. to describe the features of the most widely used problem-oriented programming language, the Report Program Generator II.
2. to enable you to define the problem, prepare a printer spacing chart, and fill out the necessary specification forms.
3. to provide you with the self-satisfying feeling of having a program run on the computer in spite of the numerous errors that may exist in the program.
4. to provide the impetus for debugging programs in RPG II, which will aid you in the better understanding of the RPG II programming language.

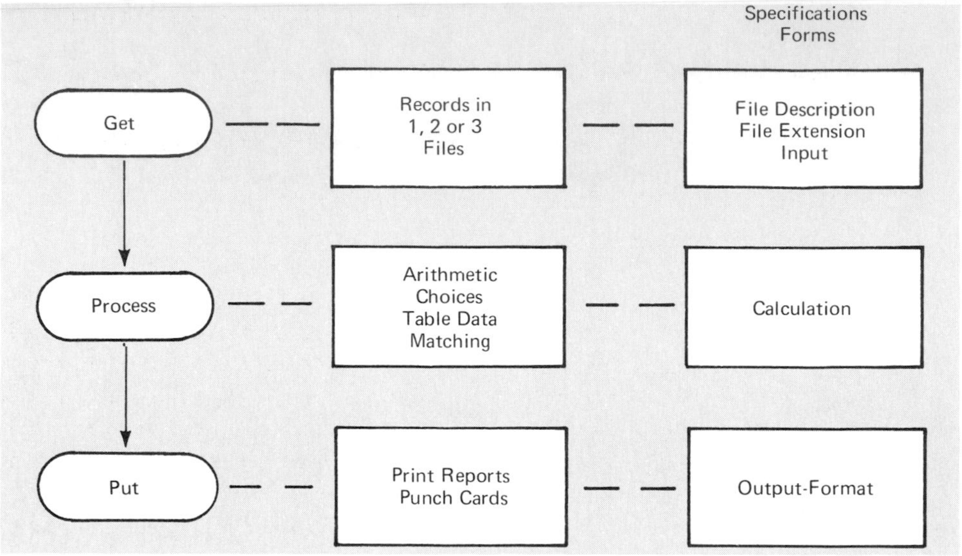

Figure 12.1 Uses of RPG II specification forms.

*R*eport *P*rogram *G*enerator (RPG) II is a problem-oriented language designed to solve a particular problem. A problem-oriented language describes the problem without detailing the procedures involved.

The Report Program Generator (RPG II) source language was designed to provide the programmer with an easy and efficient method of generating programs. It is a simple way of adapting an application to a computer (fig. 12.1). The file definitions and the input/output control considerations required normally of other programming languages are reduced to the filling out of simplified forms. Output reports are described on specification sheets to the compiler. Specification sheets are also written for the input source document formats. The calculation form, which is the heart of the program logic, will perform the necessary calculations of the two addresses and store the result in the third. All operands are described on the forms. All that need to be specified for the calculation forms are the sequence in which the calculations are to be performed, the types of calculations to be performed on the data, and any tests to be made on the results.

Features

RPG II provides its capabilities through generation (compilation) of object programs, each of which is tailored to produce a different set of report results and/or information file processing as desired by the user. The RPG II object programs are capable of

1. Accepting input data.
2. Retrieving data from existing files.
3. Performing calculations.
4. Changing formats of data.
5. Updating existing files.
6. Creating new files.

7. Comparing data values, one to another, to specify constants for the determination of appropriate handling.
8. Using processing subroutines internal to the object program as defined by the user.
9. Using library subroutines defined for other purposes by applying them to the user's problem.
10. Printing reports derived from input and file data.

Advantages

RPG II has several advantages over the more traditional method of writing source programs in a symbolic form. The RPG II specification language is oriented toward the problem, rather than toward the machines and the manipulation of the computer usage. This permits the describing of report requirements. Specification sheets can be written for input, calculation, and output formats. RPG II makes it easier to describe jobs to the computer than to write a program for doing them. Many different reports may be prepared from the same input specifications. The specification sheets with their self-explanatory headings makes it possible for nonprogrammers to write programs (fig. 12.2).

The language and specific techniques are easily learned. An extensive programming background is not required. A user can become proficient in RPG II after writing only a few programs, whereas equal ability in other symbolic programming languages would require considerable experience. The simpler report- and file-updating jobs can be specified and completed very quickly. A few hours from inception to the finished report is not an unreasonable time.

The RPG II language is compatible on all models of computers. It can support the minimum configuration of a system as well as the largest operating system.

RPG and RPG II

RPG II has several features not included in RPG. By far the most important of these is the ability to create arrays. In RPG II, arrays are lists that can be called by their relative record number or position in the list (that is, the first item, the second item, etc.). Other important features of RPG II are:

1. Exception time (operation EXCPT) allows output during calculation time. This is particularly helpful when several copies of a record are required.
2. RPG II can utilize the console printer-keyboard for input/output operations by the operation display (operation DSPLY).
3. Fields not yet in the processing area of storage (operation LOOK AHEAD) can be read. It can alter the normal RPG II process (often after comparing look ahead fields) for selecting the next record to be input or output (operation FORCE).
4. The Debug operation (operation DEBUG) is useful in finding errors in a program.
5. *PLACE is a special RPG II word that allows one data field to be output several times on the same line.

Figure 12.2
Examples of RPG II specification forms.

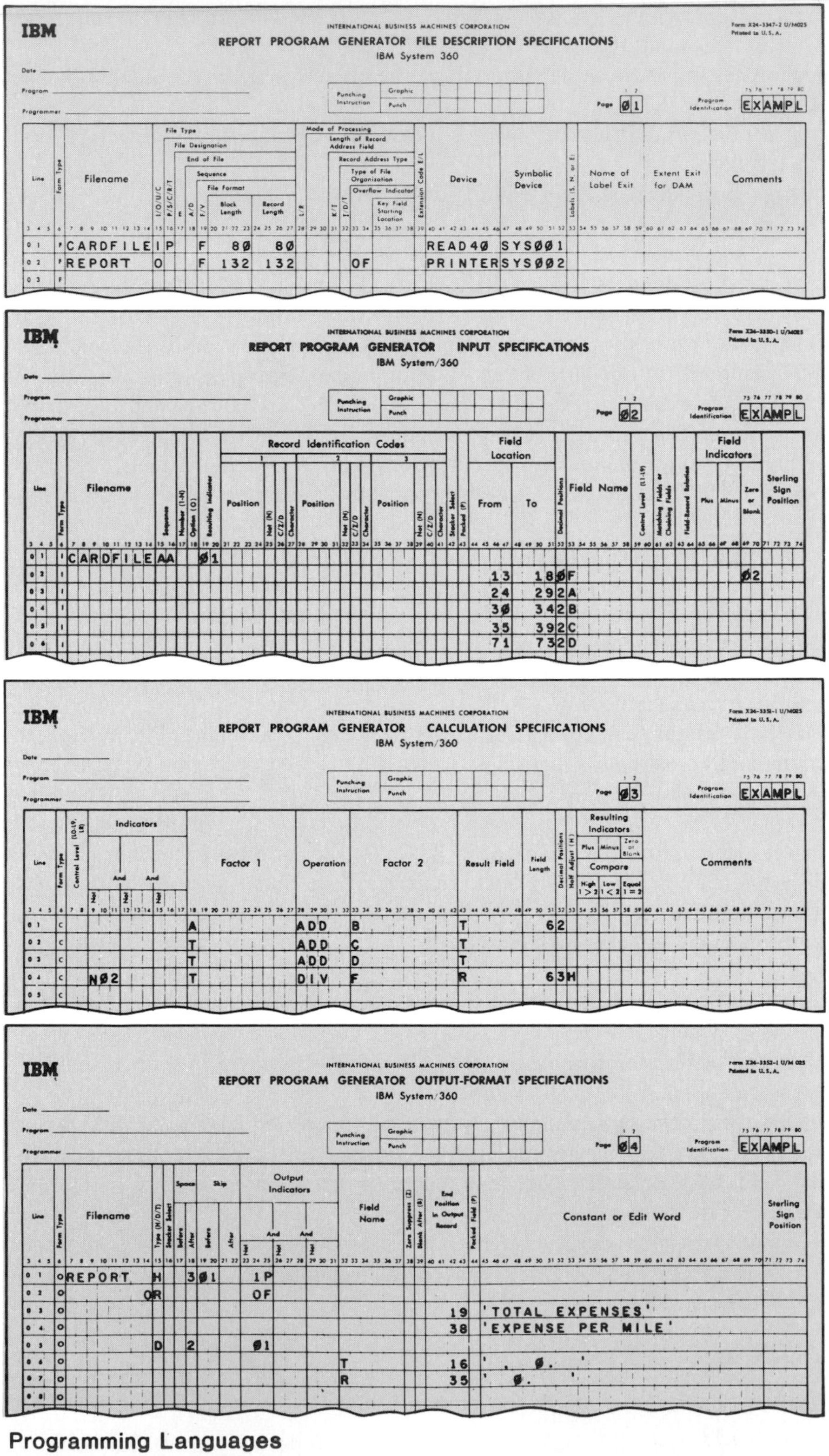

IBM — INTERNATIONAL BUSINESS MACHINES CORPORATION
REPORT PROGRAM GENERATOR FILE DESCRIPTION SPECIFICATIONS
IBM System 360
Page Ø1 — Program Identification EXAMPL

Line	Form Type	Filename	File Type	File Designation	File Format	Block Length	Record Length	Overflow Indicator	Device	Symbolic Device
01	F	CARDFILE	I	P	F	8Ø	8Ø		READ4Ø	SYSØØ1
02	F	REPORT	O		F	132	132	OF	PRINTER	SYSØØ2
03	F									

IBM — INTERNATIONAL BUSINESS MACHINES CORPORATION
REPORT PROGRAM GENERATOR INPUT SPECIFICATIONS
IBM System/360
Page Ø2 — Program Identification EXAMPL

Line	Form Type	Filename	Sequence	Resulting Indicator	Field Location From	Field Location To	Decimal Positions	Field Name	Field Indicators Zero or Blank
01	I	CARDFILE	AA	Ø1					
02	I				13	18	Ø	F	Ø2
03	I				24	29	2	A	
04	I				3Ø	34	2	B	
05	I				35	39	2	C	
06	I				71	73	2	D	

IBM — INTERNATIONAL BUSINESS MACHINES CORPORATION
REPORT PROGRAM GENERATOR CALCULATION SPECIFICATIONS
IBM System/360
Page Ø3 — Program Identification EXAMPL

Line	Form Type	Indicators	Factor 1	Operation	Factor 2	Result Field	Field Length	Decimal Positions	Half Adjust (H)
01	C		A	ADD	B	T	6	2	
02	C		T	ADD	C	T			
03	C		T	ADD	D	T			
04	C	NØ2	T	DIV	F	R	6	3	H
05	C								

IBM — INTERNATIONAL BUSINESS MACHINES CORPORATION
REPORT PROGRAM GENERATOR OUTPUT-FORMAT SPECIFICATIONS
IBM System/360
Page Ø4 — Program Identification EXAMPL

Line	Form Type	Filename	Type (H/D/T)	Space / Skip	Output Indicators	Field Name	End Position in Output Record	Constant or Edit Word
01	O	REPORT	H	3Ø1	1P			
02	O	OR			OF			
03	O						19	'TOTAL EXPENSES'
04	O						38	'EXPENSE PER MILE'
05	O		D	2	Ø1			
06	O					T	16	' . Ø. '
07	O					R	35	' Ø. '
08	O							

Report Program Generator Specifications Forms	
Form	**Use**
File Description	1. Describes each file as either input, output, or combined.
Input	1. Identifies each record type that is in each input or combined file. 2. Locates the data to be used from each record.
Calculation	1. Specifies the operations to be performed with the located data.
Output-Format	1. Specifies the arrangement of output data in printed lines or punched cards.

Figure 12.3 Functions of RPG II specification forms.

Specification Sheets—Functions

The specification sheets will generate machine-language program instructions together with automatically assigned storage areas for data input and output, work areas, and constants (fig. 12.3). The created machine language will be combined with the input data files to produce finished output reports and files.

Principles of RPG II Programming

In planning a job using RPG II, there are four points to be considered.

1. Find out what is wanted.
2. Find out about the records used to produce what is wanted.
3. Note the kinds of operations to be done in order to get what is wanted from the records used.
4. Note any additional requirements of job.

Before any attempt is made to fill out the specification forms, a thorough analysis must be made of the procedures to determine the descriptions of the source data and its formats, how the data is to be processed to develop the finished report, and all other information relative to the processing of the data. System and program flowcharts should be drawn to show the flow of data through the system.

The preparation of a report by means of RPG II consists of the following steps (fig. 12.4).

Figure 12.4 RPG II job steps.

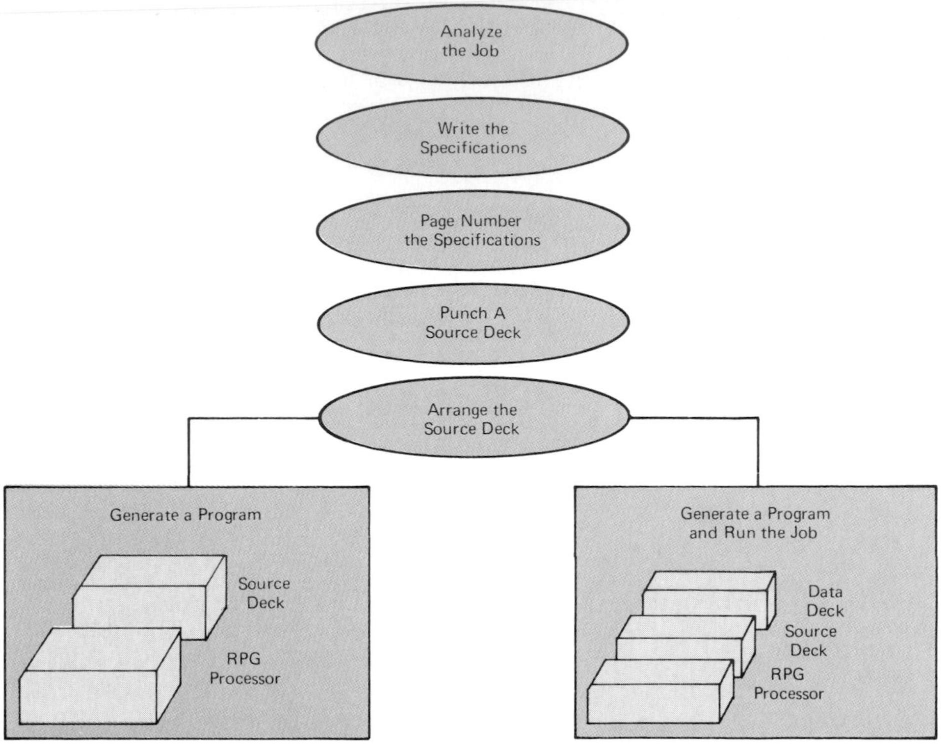

1. The programmer must evaluate the program through the preparation of flowcharts, analysis sheets, input and output requirements, and processing requirements. For example, the programmer determines what fields in the input records are to be used, what calculations are to take place, where the data is to be located in the output record, and how many and what kinds of totals must be accumulated.
2. After the programmer has evaluated the requirements of the report, the programmer must carefully define the output requirements by preparing a Printer Spacing Chart.
3. The programmer must provide the information to the RPG II compiler in the form of specification sheets. The programmer

   a. Describes all files used by the object program (such as input files, output files, and table files) by making entries on the file description specification sheets.
   b. When using record address files, tables, or arrays in the object program, furnishes information about them through entries on the extension specification sheets.
   c. Describes the input (record layout fields used). This is done by making entries on the input specification sheets.

d. States what processing is to be done (such as add, subtract, multiply, and divide) by means of entries on calculation specification sheets.
e. Defines the layout of the report (such as print positions and carriage control). This is accomplished by making entries on the output-format specification sheets.

4. After the specifications have been written on the appropriate forms, the data on the forms is recorded in punched cards (disks or diskettes). Each line on the form is punched in one card.
5. These punched cards (called a source deck) are preceded by the RPG II job control cards. The source deck and the control cards are placed in the computer and processed by the RPG II compiler. The program contains all the machine instructions required to prepare the desired report.
6. The input files are read for the preparation of the desired output reports and files (fig. 12.5).

Printer Spacing Chart

Prior to the writing of the specification sheets, the programmer should create a worksheet for the printer to use as a form for coding the particular operations (fig. 12.6). The Printer Spacing Chart provides the programmer with the following information.

1. The format of the desired headings.
2. The number of printing positions necessary for output including such editing symbols as commas, periods, and dollar signs.
3. The number of characters in each field and whether they are alphabetic, numeric, or alphanumeric characters.
4. The total lines and different levels of totals desired.
5. Any special skipping or vertical spacing.
6. Any zero suppression desired.
7. Any constant data needed.

Each field that is used must be given a name so it can be referred to in the program. This is usually done at the same time the spacing chart is prepared, since the names should be close to the fields for easy identification. The names are assigned by the programmer and should be similar to the actual field names for referral (fig. 12.7).

Specification Forms

After the problem has been evaluated to the requirements of the desired report, the programmer must make the information available to the RPG II processor program. This is accomplished through the preparation of the following specification sheets.

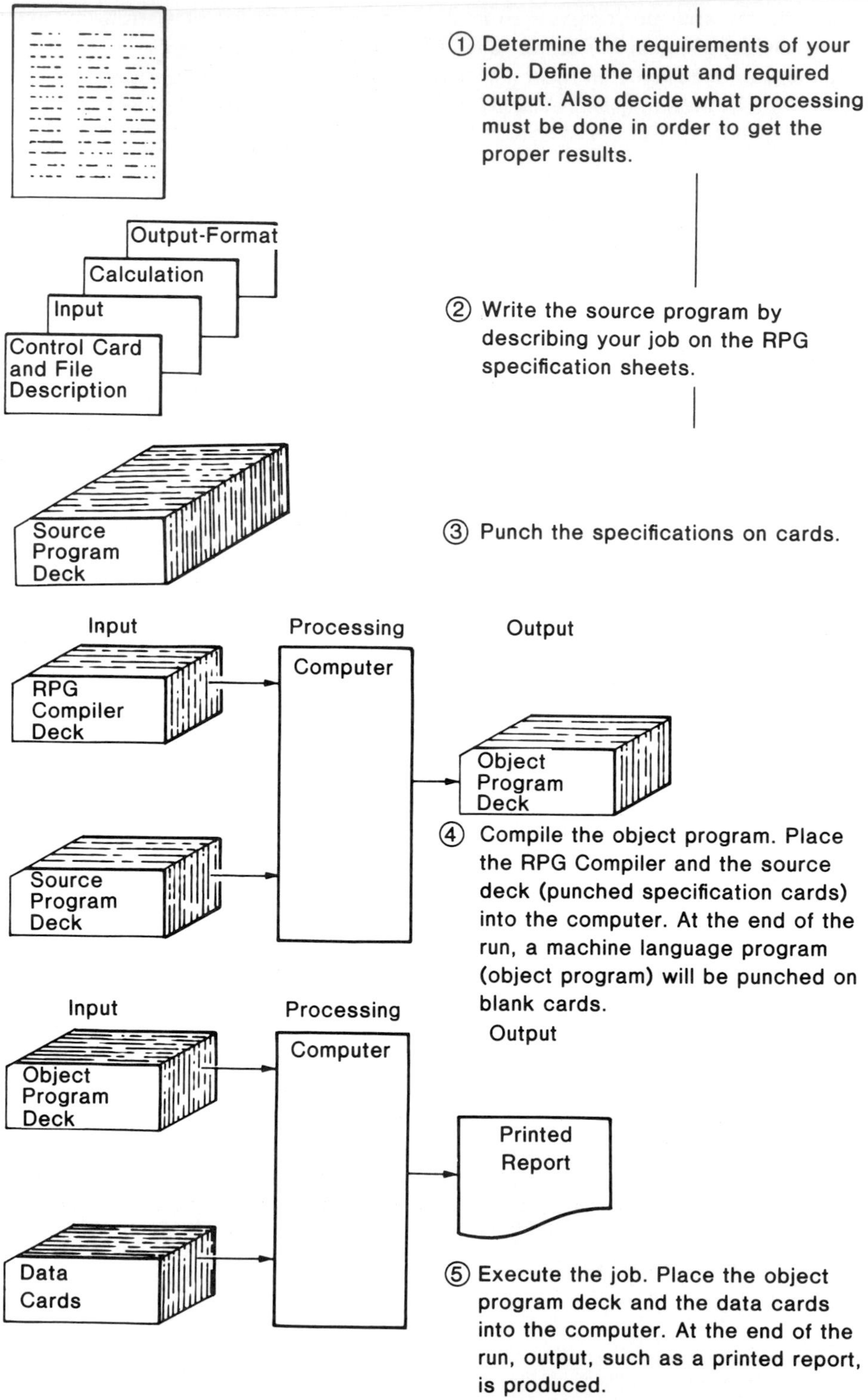

Figure 12.5 The RPG II processing cycle.

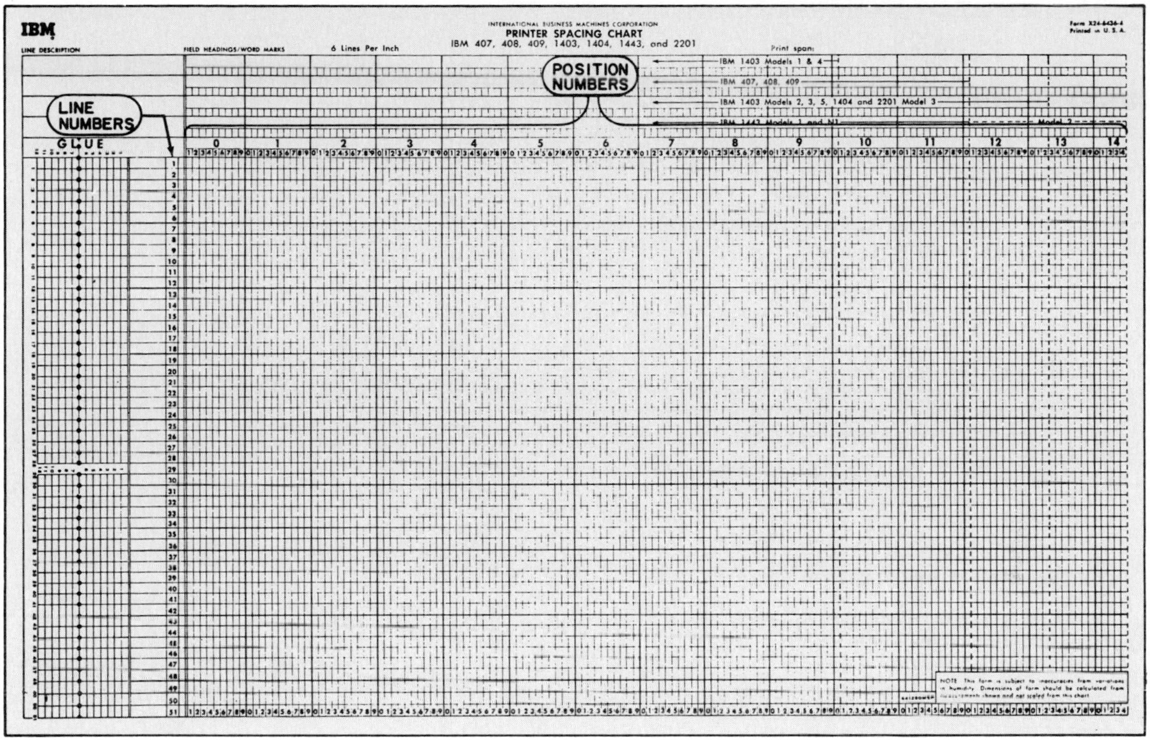

Figure 12.6 A Printer Spacing Chart.

Common Entries

The following entries on a RPG II coding sheet are common to all specification forms.

1. Columns 1–2	PAGE
2. Columns 3–5	LINE
3. Column 6	FORM TYPE
4. Column 7	COMMENTS
5. Columns 75–80	PROGRAM IDENTIFICATION

PAGE

Columns 1–2 in the upper right corner of each sheet are used to number the specification sheets for each job. More than one type of sheet may be used if needed, but all specification sheets of the same type must be kept together. When all the specification sheets are filled out, they are arranged in the following order.

1. *Control Card and File Description.* The control card is required for every program. The control card may provide special information about the program. An *H* must be entered in column 6 of the control card even if all the other control card columns are left blank.
2. *Extension and Line Counter.*
3. *Input.*
4. *Calculation.*
5. *Output-Format.*

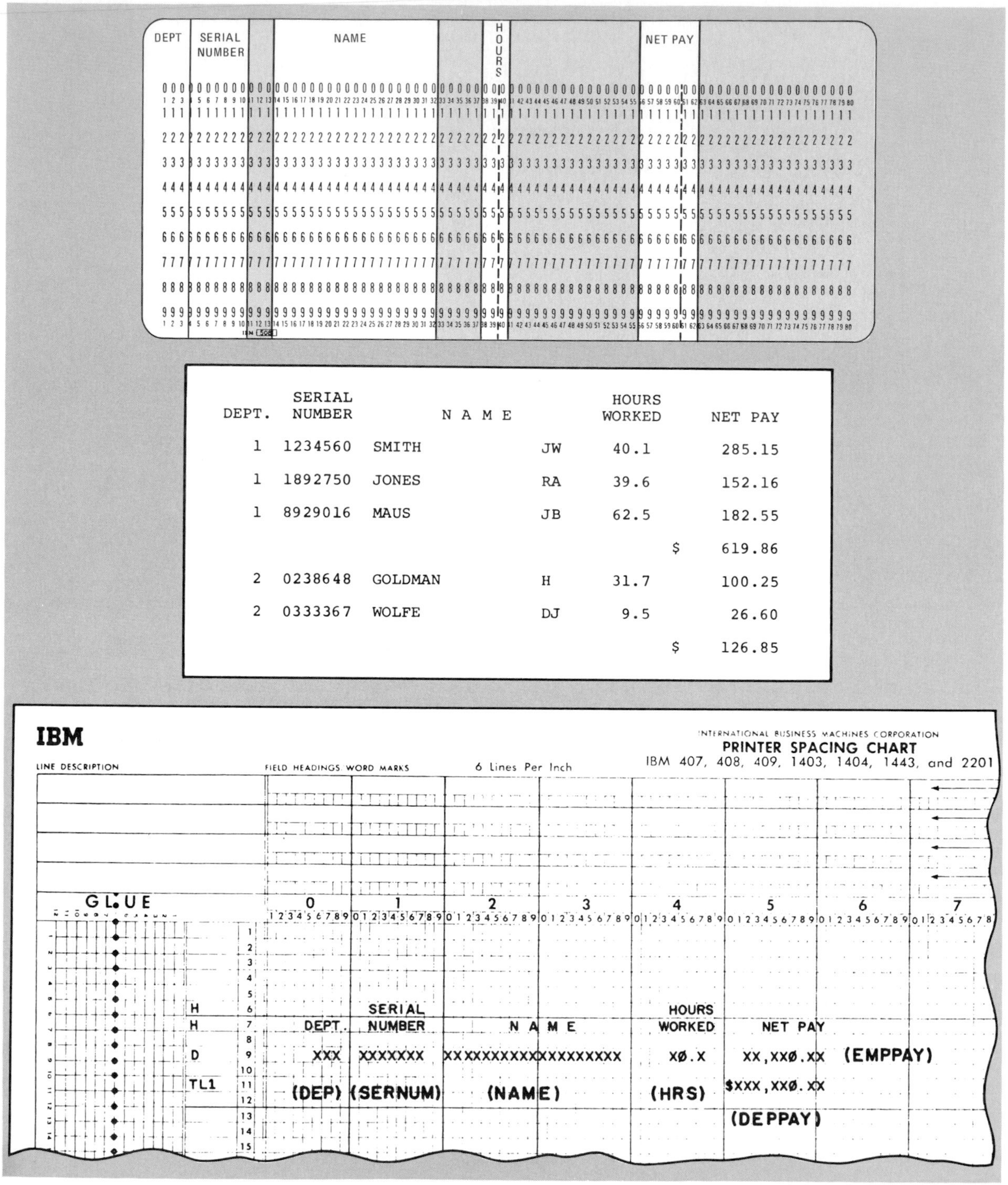

Figure 12.7 The RPG II layout of a Printer Spacing Chart.

The sheets should be numbered in ascending order.

LINE

Columns 3–5 are used to number the lines on each page. Columns 3–4 are preprinted on each sheet so, in most cases, line numbering is already done. A zero may be added to column 5.

FORM TYPE

Column 6 contains a preprinted letter on all sheets. The letter identifies the type of specifications for each line of coding. The control card containing *H* in column 6 must always be the first card in the RPG II source program deck.

Entry	**Explanation**
H	Header card (control card specification)
F	File description specifications
E	Extension specifications
L	Line counter specifications
I	Input specifications
C	Calculation specifications
O	Output-format specifications

COMMENTS

Comments are often written to help you understand or remember what you are doing in a certain section of coding. RPG II allows you to use an entire line for these comments. The comment line is identified by placing an asterisk in column 7. Any characters in the character set may be used in a comment line. A card is punched from this line and the comments appear in the source program listing. Comments are *not* instructions to the RPG II program. They serve only as a means of documenting your program.

PROGRAM IDENTIFICATION

Columns 75–80 may contain any characters. These columns are used to identify the program. These entries are ignored by the compiler but will appear in the source program listing.

File Description Specifications

These forms are used to describe all files to be used by the object program. Each line of the form describes one file. The forms are also used to identify input and output devices associated with the files (fig. 12.8).

File Extension and Line Counter Specifications

These forms contain two types of specifications (figs. 12.9, 12.10):

1. File extension specifications provide information about tables, arrays, and record address files.
2. Line counter specifications provide information about the number of lines to be printed on the forms that are used.

Figure 12.8 An example of a file description form.

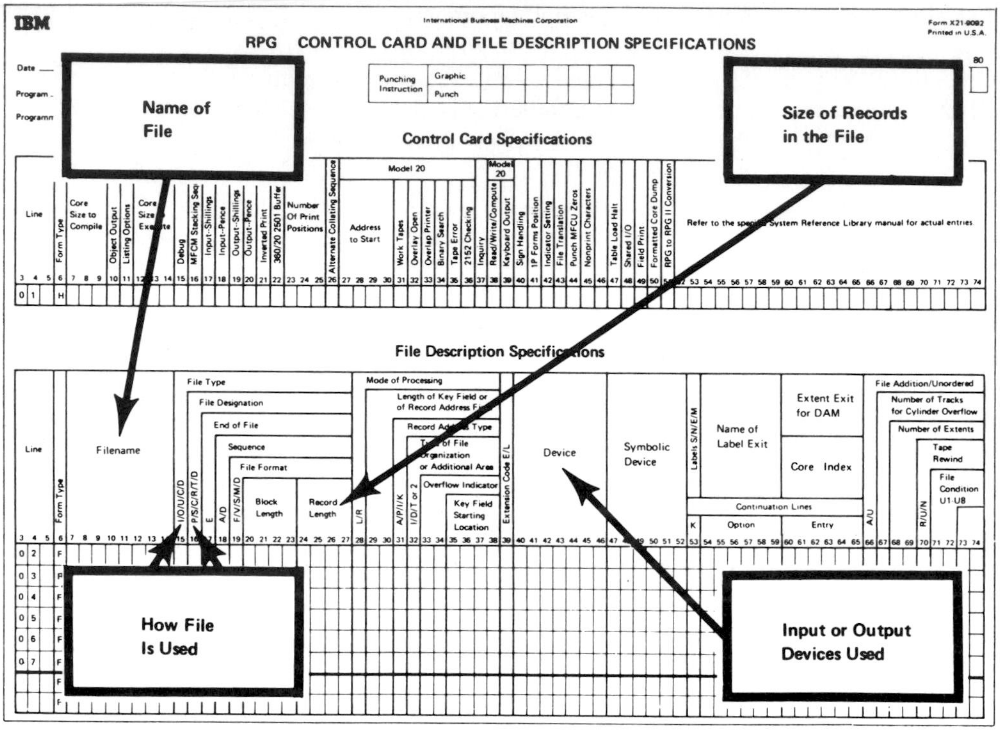

PURPOSE

1. To name each file.
2. To indicate whether a file is Input, Output, or Combined (both input and output).
3. To designate input files as Primary or Secondary.
4. To indicate the record and block length of each file.
5. To tell the computer on which device the particular file will be read or written at execution time.

File Description Specification

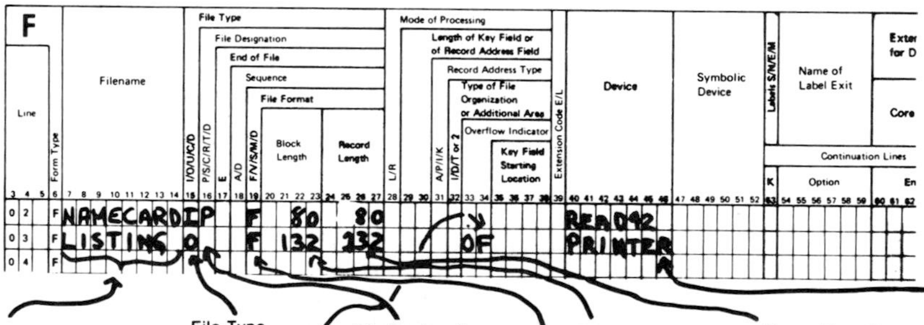

Filename
Each file must have unique name constructed to rules for file names.

File Type
I = Input
O = Output
C = Combined

Overflow Indicator
OF—Overflow indicator for printer.

File Designation
P—Primary File. If only one input file, it must be primary.
S—Secondary file. All input files other than primary.
Blank for output files.
Block Length

Block Length
Card files: 80
Printed files: 132

File Format
F—Format for card files and printers.

Record Length
For cards and printers same as block length.

Device
Input = Card Reader
Output = Printer

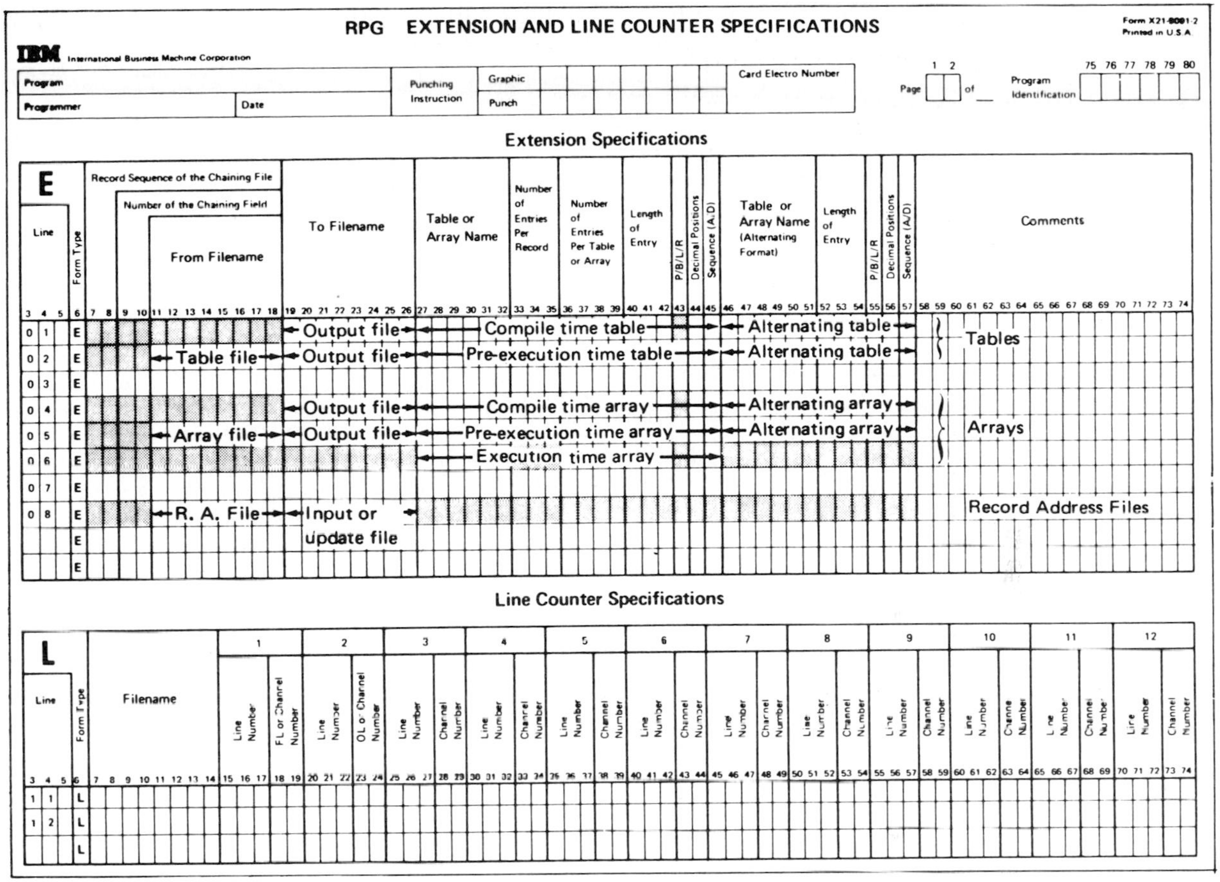

- The shaded columns must be blank for the file named.
- For tables and arrays except execution time arrays, columns 19-26 and columns 46-57 are optional.
- Execution arrays are loaded via input and/or calculation specifications.
- For record address files, columns 11-26 must have entries.

Figure 12.9 Possible file entries for extension specifications.

Input Specifications

These forms are used to describe the input files, such as record layouts and fields within the record. The records within each input or combined file are described. The relationship of one record to another is also specified in these forms. The first half of the form is used for record identification while the remaining columns are used to describe each field within a record. One line is used for each record and a separate line is used for each field. The specific input units used do not need to be identified on these forms if they have been specified in the file description sheets (fig. 12.11).

Calculation Specifications

These forms are used to specify all the operations to be performed on the data. The nature of the processing, such as add, subtract, multiply, and divide, are described in

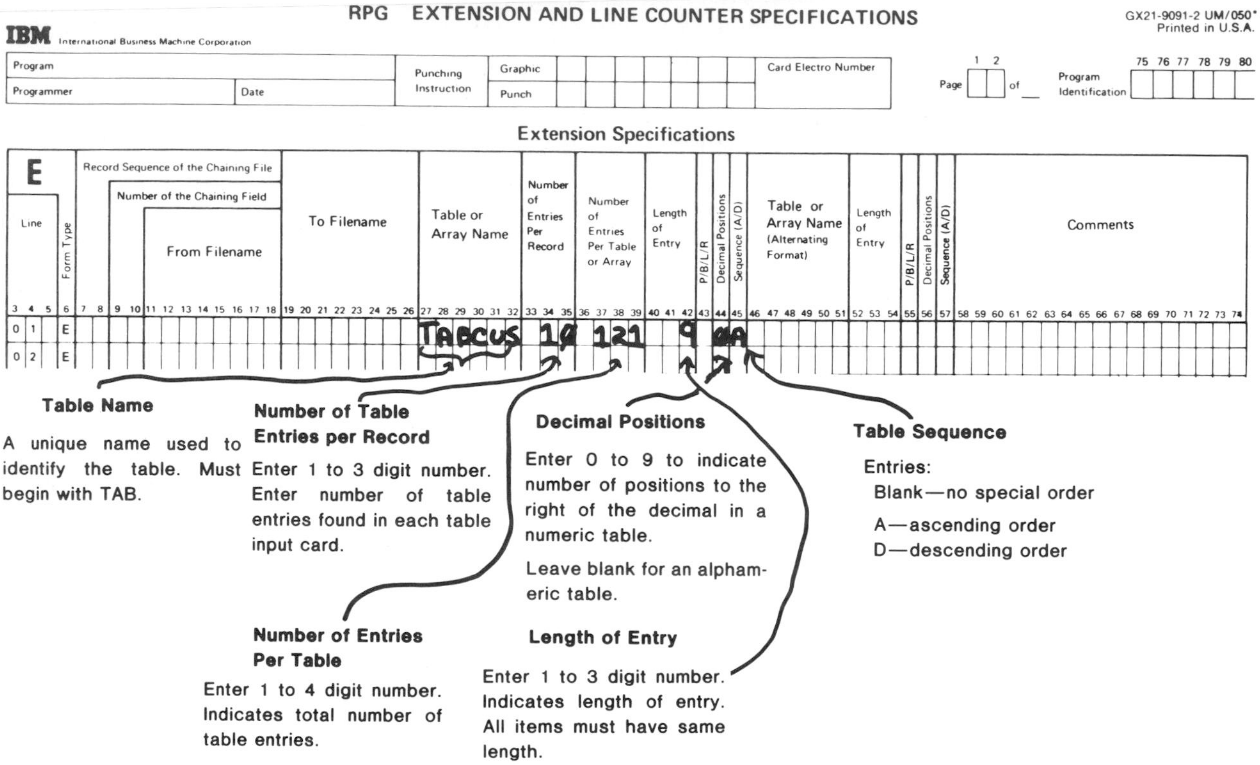

Figure 12.10 Extension specifications for simple tables.

these forms. Each operation is specified on a separate line of the form in the sequence in which it is to be processed (fig. 12.12). All detail calculations are performed before the total calculations.

Output-Format Specifications

These forms describe how the finished report should look. The types of output files to be produced as well as the location of the data in output records and reports are also described. The specification of these forms will identify the output records of which the files are comprised. The selection of the appropriate stacker for the cards, the spacing in the printed reports, and under what conditions the report is to be produced will also be described in these sheets.

All field descriptions will be written in entries immediately following the file in which they appear. These specifications will tell when and where the fields are to be placed in the output record. The specific output device does not need to be specified in these forms since the file description forms indicate the device to be used for each file. All that is required for identification with the file is the writing of the record on the output form (figs. 12.13, 12.14).

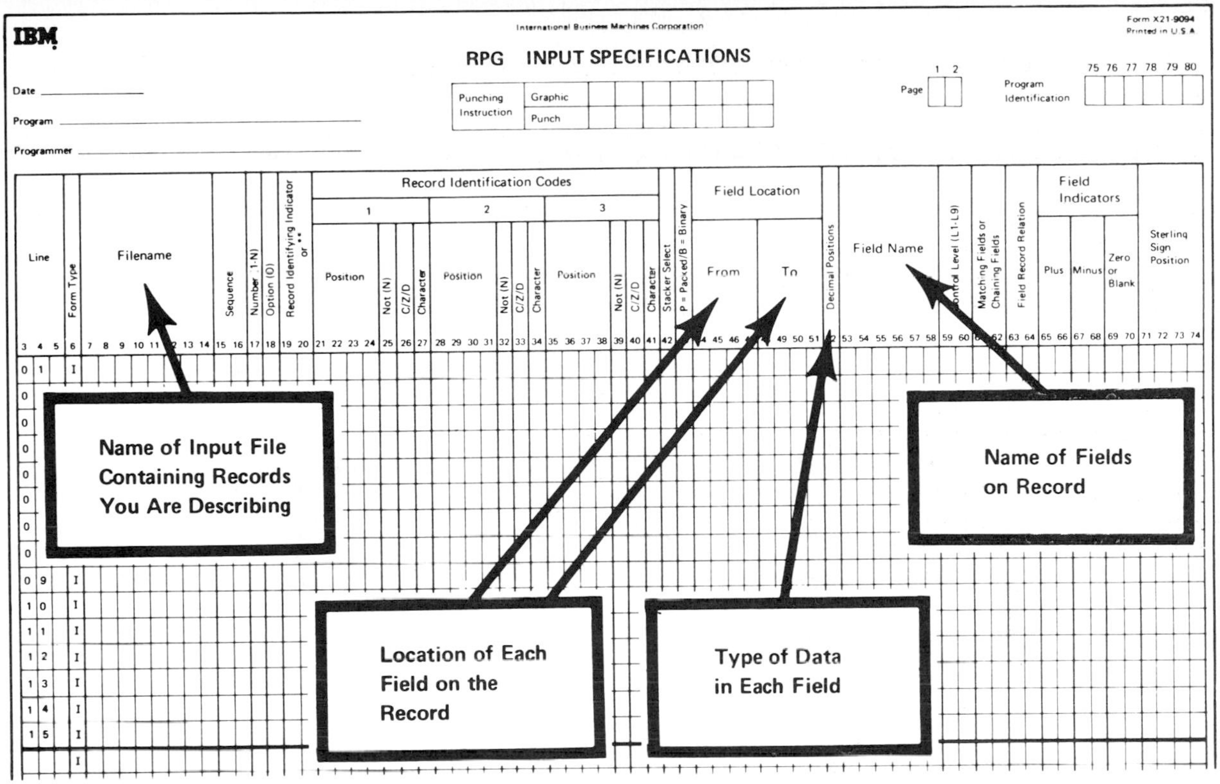

PURPOSE

1. To identify the input files.
2. To describe each type of record within each file.
3. To specify the sequence of records within each file.
4. To define fields of data in each record type.
5. To locate fields of data in each record type.

Record Identification

Field Description

Figure 12.11 An example of an input specifications form.

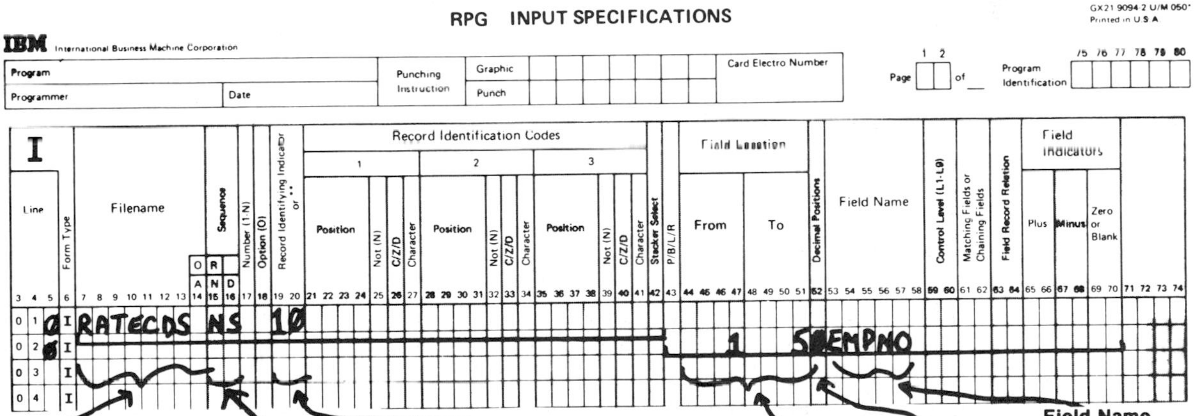

Filename
Must have been assigned on File Description Specifications sheet. Must be on first line of information about that file.

Sequence
If sequence of record types to checked, enter two-digit number 01-99 otherwise enter NS.

Record Identifying Indicator
Assign any two-digit number 01-99 for each record type.

Field Location
Identifies position of field in record.

Decimal Positions
Describes number of places to right of decimal point. Enter 0-9. *Must* be an entry for numeric fields.

Field Name
Alphameric 1-6 characters must start in column 53. Each field in record must have unique name and be described on separate line.

Record Identification

Record identification entries begin in column 7. There may be no entries to the right of column 42.

Field Description

Field description entries begin column 43. There may be no entries to the left of column 43.

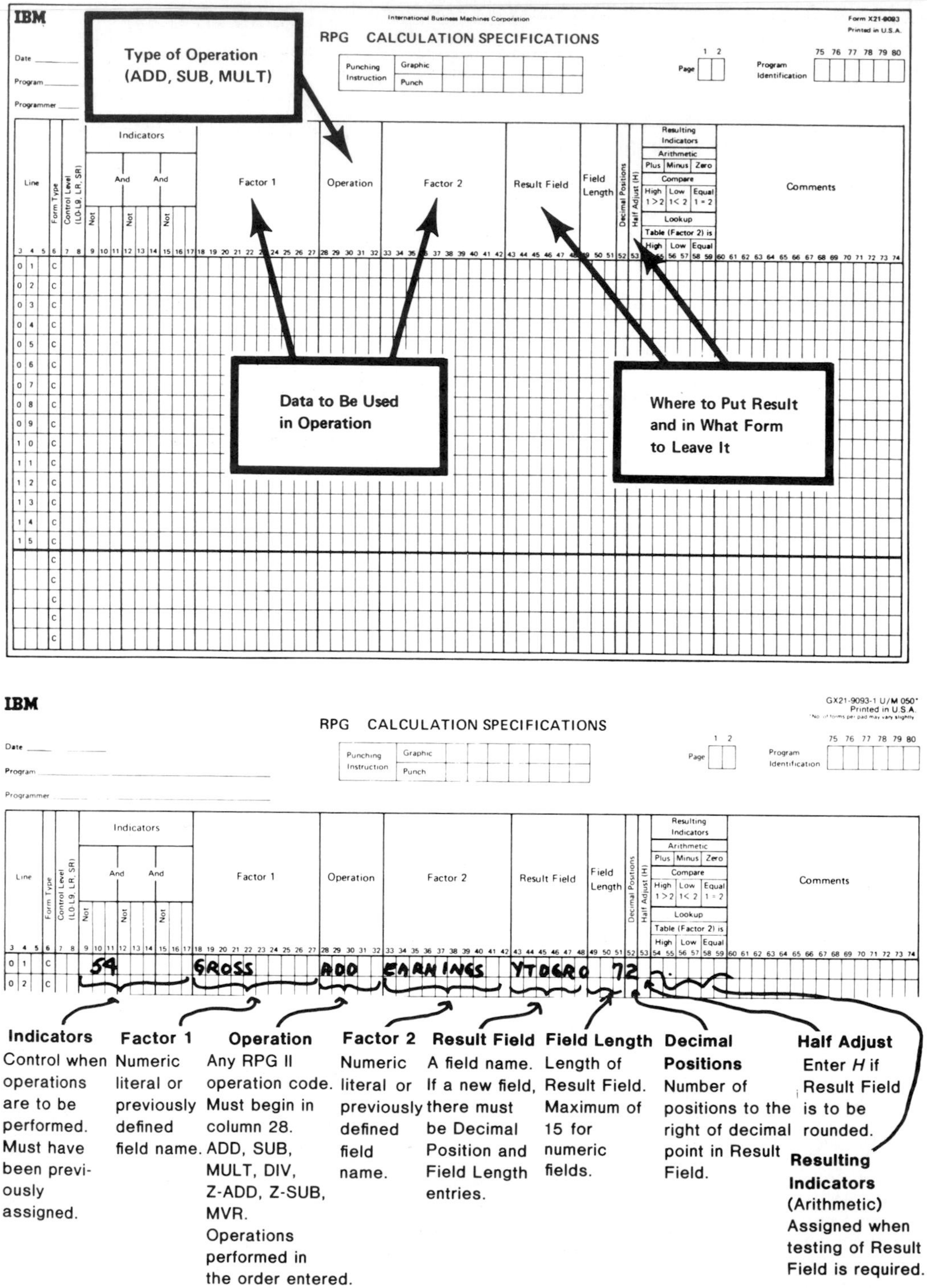

Figure 12.12 An example of a calculation specifications form.

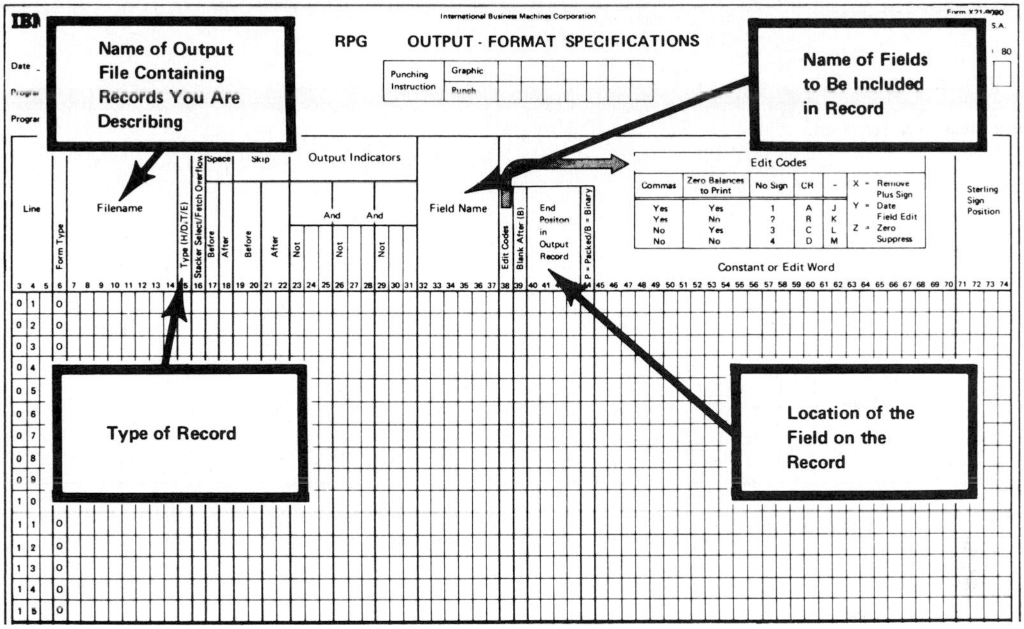

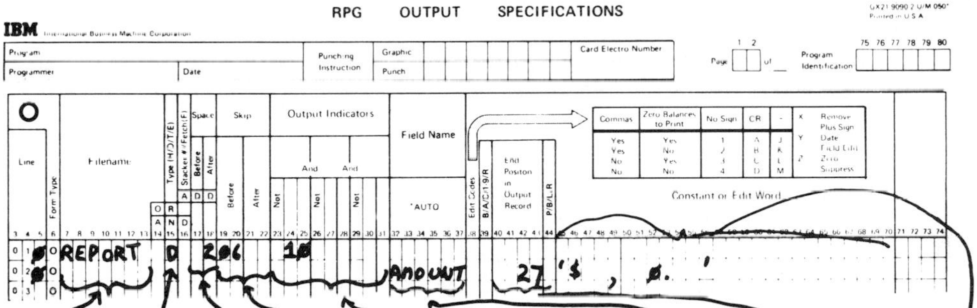

Filename
Must have been assigned to output on File Description Specifications sheet. Must be in first line of output description.

Type H/D/T
Type of line to be written. Must be in the order:
H = Heading
D = Detail
T = Total
E = Exception

Space
Number of lines paper moves *before* or *after* line is printed.
Blank = No space
0 = No space
1 = Single space
2 = Double space
3 = Triple space

Skip
Line of paper to which paper moves *before* or *after* printing. Any two-digit number.

Output Indicators
Must be previously defined.

Field Name
Name of data field to become output; must have been previously defined. Each field name must be entered on a new line.

End Position in Output Record
Specifies position of last character in output field; right justify.

Constant or Edit Word
Constant—Any unchanging information.
Edit Word—Supplies punctuation in numeric fields other than edit code. Each line must begin and end with an apostrophe ('CONSTANT'). Each line must have an end position entry and must begin in column 45. No field name may be specified on line containing constants.

Figure 12.13 An example of an output specifications form.

Figure 12.14 Types of records.

Heading Records / Detail Records / Total Record

ACCOUNTS RECEIVABLE TRANSACTION REGISTER

07/11/7 PAGE 01

DATE	CUST NO	CUSTOMER NAME	JOURNAL NO	INVOICE NO	CASH AMOUNT	INVOICE AMOUNT	JOURNAL AMOUNT
07/11/--	759820	SOUND OF THE SEVENTIE		063420		$ 46.23	
07/11/--	633870	OLDE VILLAGE SHOPPE		063421		89.70	
07/11/--	642990	PARAGON TV SALES		063422		20.30	
07/11/--	122620	CANNIZONI STUDIOS		063422		129.76	
07/11/--	682030	RAYMONDS RAPID REPAIR			$ 63.80		
07/11/--	742950	SARATOGA VARIETY			29.72		
07/11/--	014280	BAKER BRADLEY & CO			43.50		
07/11/--	872060	UNIVERSITY ELECTRIC			97.75		
07/11/--	883290	VILLAGE MUSIC & TV	07-036				$18.23CR
07/11/--	006280	ALLSTONS	07-037				10.70CR
		TOTALS			$234.77*	$285.99*	$28.93CR*

Heading records are printed at the top of a page. They include report titles, column headings, or any other information needed to identify the kinds of information found in the report.

Detail records contain information about an individual item. Information in a detail record is often taken directly from an input record.

Total records are written after a group of detail records. They usually contain data that is the result of calculations on information in a group of detail records.

Editing

Editing is the method by which data is made more readable and understandable. Editing a field means punctuating it by adding commas, decimal points, minus signs, dollar signs, or any other constant information. Nonsignificant zeros to the left of a number may be suppressed in editing.

A field may be edited in two ways—edit codes (fig. 12.15) and edit words (fig. 12.16). Several different codes are available. Each code edits in a slightly different manner according to a predefined pattern.

Edit words provide a pattern for punctuation. The edit word facility is provided where more unusual or complex editing may be needed (figs. 12.17, 12.18).

Field Length and Digits		1769532	02	00	000	041345
Field Characteristics		Positive Number—Two Decimal Positions	Negative Number—Two Decimal Positions	Zero—Two Decimal Positions	Zero—No Decimal Positions	Positive Number—Three Decimal Positions
Edit Codes	1	17,695.32	.02	.00	0	41.345
	2	17,695.32	.02			41.345
	3	17695.32	.02	.00	0	41.345
	4	17695.32	.02			41.345
	A	17,695.32	.02CR	.00	0	41.345
	B	17,695.32	.02CR			41.345
	C	17695.32	.02CR	.00	0	41.345
	D	17695.32	.02CR			41.345
	J	17,695.32	.02–	.00	0	41.345
	K	17,695.32	.02–			41.345
	L	17695.32	.02–	.00	0	41.345
	M	17695.32	.02–			41.345
	X	1769532	0K	00	000	041345
	Y	Must be used with a 3 to 6-digit field.			0/0	4/13/45
	Z	1769532	2			41345

The table above shows the effect of editing on five different fields. It illustrates what will be printed out by using each edit code on the fields.

Figure 12.15
Examples of the edit code usage.

Codes in the first category are:

Code	Meaning
X	Causes a plus sign to be shown for a nonnegative field.
Y	Causes a date field to be edited as follows: Three-digit dates—(n)n/n Four-digit dates—(n)n/nn Five-digit dates—(n)n/nn/n Six-digit dates—(n)n/nn/nn

The significance of (n) is that the first digit of the date is suppressed if zero.

Z	Causes suppression of leading zeros in the output field and the removal of the sign.

Codes in the second category are:

Code	Meaning
1	Print with commas. Print zero balances. Suppress sign.
2	Print with commas. Suppress zero balances. Suppress sign.
3	Print without commas. Print zero balances. Suppress sign.
4	Print without commas. Suppress zero balances. Suppress sign.
A	Print with commas. Print zero balances. Print sign as CR.
B	Print with commas. Suppress zero balances. Print sign as CR.
C	Print without commas. Print zero balances. Print sign as CR.

Figure 12.15 Continued	**D**	Print without commas. Suppress zero balances. Print sign as CR.
	J	Print with commas. Print zero balances. Print sign as —.
	K	Print with commas. Suppress zero balances. Print sign as —.
	L	Print without commas. Print zero balances. Print sign as —.
	M	Print without commas. Suppress zero balances. Print sign as —.

If the field is positive, no sign is printed.

EDIT WORD																										EXAMPLE NUMBER	SOURCE DATA	APPEARS IN OUTPUT RECORD AS:
45	46	47	48	49	50	51	52	53	54	55	56	57	58	59	60	61	62	63	64	65	66	67	68	69	70			
'			,				,			Ø	.			&	C	R	'									A	0000000005 –	ƀƀƀƀƀƀƀƀƀƀ.05 ƀCR
'			,				,		Ø		—	&	O	N	&	H	A	N	D	'						B	00000000	ƀƀƀƀƀƀƀƀƀ0 ƀ ƀONƀHAND
'				,				,	$	Ø		.			—	*	'									C	0000000005 +	ƀƀƀƀƀƀƀƀƀ$0.05 ƀ *
'				,				,		$	Ø	.			C	R	*	*	'							D	0034567890 –	ƀƀƀ$345,678.90 CR **
'	$			,				,			Ø	.			'											E	0000000000	$ƀƀƀƀƀƀƀƀƀƀ.00
'	$	&			,				,		Ø		.			&	—	&	G	R	O	S	S	'		F	1234567890 –	$ƀ12,345,678,90 ƀ – ƀGROSS
'				,				,				.			—	'										G	00000000123 –	ƀƀƀƀƀƀƀƀƀƀ1.23 –
'			,				,		*		.			&	—	'										H	0000135792	*****1,357.92 ƀƀ
																										1	0000135678	0000135678
																										2	0000135678 +	0000135678
																										3	0000135678 –	0000135670
'											'															4	0000000000	ƀƀƀƀƀƀƀƀƀƀ
'											'															5	0000135678 +	ƀƀƀƀ135678
'											'															6	0000135678 –	ƀƀƀƀ135678
'										Ø	'															7	0000135678 –	ƀƀƀƀ135678
'	Ø										'															8	0000135678 +	ƀ000135678
'											&	C	R	&	N	E	T	'								9	0000135678 +	ƀƀƀƀ135678 ƀƀƀ ƀNET
'											&	C	R	&	N	E	T	'								10	0000135678 –	ƀƀƀƀ135678 ƀCR ƀNET
'											&	—	&	&	N	E	T	'								11	0000135678 –	ƀƀƀƀ135678 ƀ – ƀƀNET
'											&	N	E	T	&	C	R	'								12	0000135678	ƀƀƀƀ135678 ƀƀƀƀƀƀƀ
'											&	N	E	T	&	C	R	'								13	0000135678 –	ƀƀƀƀ135678 ƀNETƀCR
'											&	&	P	R	O	F	I	T	'							14	0000135678	ƀƀƀƀ135678 ƀƀPROFIT
'	$											&	—	&	N	E	T	'								15	0000135678 +	$ƀƀƀƀ135678 ƀƀ ƀNET
'	$											&	—	&	N	E	T	'								16	0000135678 –	$ƀƀƀƀ135678 ƀ – ƀNET
'	$	Ø										—	&	N	E	T	'									17	0000135678	$0000135678 ƀ ƀNET
'								$	Ø			&	C	R	'											18	0000135678 –	ƀƀƀƀ$135678 ƀCR
'								$	Ø			&	C	R	'											19	1234567809 –	$1234567809 ƀCR
'	$								Ø			&	C	R	&	G	R	O	S	S	'					20	0000000000	$ƀƀƀƀƀƀƀƀ00 ƀƀƀ ƀGROSS
'	*										'															21	0000135678 –	*000135678
'	*										'															22	1234567890 +	1234567890
'										*	'															23	0000135678 –	****135678
'			,				,				.			&	C	R	&	&	N	E	T	'				24	0000135678 –	ƀƀƀƀƀ1,356,78 ƀCR ƀƀNET
'			,				,				.			&	C	R	&	—	N	E	T	'				25	0000135678	ƀƀƀƀƀ1,356,78 ƀƀƀ ƀ–NET
'				,				,	$	Ø		.			&	N	E	T	'							26	0000000005	ƀƀƀƀƀƀƀƀƀ$0,05 ƀNET
'				,				,		$	Ø	.			'											27	0000000005	ƀƀƀƀƀƀƀƀƀƀ$.05
'				,				,		$	Ø	.			—	'										28	1234567890 –	$12,345,678.90 –
'				,				,		$	Ø	.			C	R	'									29	0001356789 –	ƀƀƀƀ$13,567.89 CR
'			,				,			*	.			*	C	R	*	*	'							30	0000135678 +	*****1,356.78 ƀƀƀ **
'				,		$	Ø	,				.			—	S	A	L	E	S	'					31	0000001234	ƀƀƀƀƀƀ$,012.34 ƀ SALES
'	$	&			,				,			Ø	.			C	R	'								32	1234567890 –	$ƀ12,345,678.90 CR
'		,				,				,				—	O	L	D	&	B	A	L	N	C	E	'	33	1234567890 –	1,234,567,890 – OLDƀBALNCE
'		,				,				,		Ø		—	O	L	D	&	B	A	L	N	C	E	'	34	0000000000	ƀƀƀƀƀƀƀƀƀƀƀƀ0 ƀ OLDƀBALNCE
'			,				,				D	O	L	L	A	R	S			C	E	N	T	S	'	35	0000135678	ƀƀƀƀƀ1,356DOLLARS78 CENTS
'		,				D	O	L	L	A	R	S			C	E	N	T	S	'						36	000000	ƀƀƀƀƀƀƀƀƀƀƀƀƀƀ CENTS
'		,		Ø		D	O	L	L	A	R	S			C	E	N	T	S	&	C	R	'			37	000000	ƀƀƀƀ0DOLLARS00 ƀƀƀƀƀƀƀ
'			Ø			L	B	S	.	&			O	Z	.	T	A	R	E	&	—	'				38	000002 +	ƀƀƀ0LBS.ƀ02 ƀƀƀƀƀƀƀƀ
'				Ø	L	B	S	.				O	Z	.	T	A	R	E	&	—	'					39	000002 –	ƀƀƀƀLBS.02 OZ.TAREƀ–
'	Ø			—			—					'														40	095140036	ƀ95–14–0036
'	Ø		H	R	S	.			M	I	N	S	.	&	O	'	'	C	L	O	C	K	'			41	0042	ƀ0HRS.42 MINS.ƀO'CLOCK
'		,			Ø	.			'																	42	000000	ƀƀƀƀƀ.00
'		,				.	Ø		'																	43	000000	ƀƀƀƀƀƀƀ0
'		,			$	,	Ø			.			'													44	00123456	ƀƀƀ1$,234.56
'			,				,		Ø		*			'												45	0000000000	ƀƀƀƀƀƀƀƀƀ0*00
'	Ø	,				,	Ø			'																46	001234	ƀ,012,034
'			,			*	,				*			'												47	0000001234	******,012*34
'	&		,	*		Ø	,				'															48	013579	***130,579
'			—			—			&	L	A	T	E	R	'											49	093066	ƀ9–30–66 ƀLATER
'			&			&			&	L	A	T	E	R	'											50	093066	ƀ9ƀ30ƀ66 ƀLATER
'			/			/			'																	51	100166	10/01/66
'		,				,				.			—	'												52	000000015 –	ƀƀƀƀƀƀƀƀƀƀ15 –
'		,				,		Ø		.			—	'												53	000000005	ƀƀƀƀƀƀƀƀ0.05 ƀ

Figure 12.16 Examples of edit words.

Figure 12.17 Illustrative problem 1.

JOB DEFINITION:

Create an Aged-Trial Balance Report that lists:

1. Name and customer number of all charge customers who have payments due.
2. Amount due.
3. Overdue balances.

The customer master file, which contains records for all customers regardless of their balance, is used as the input file. The report is to show only those customers with payments due. Thus, information from customer records that contain a zero or credit balance should not be printed.

JOB REQUIREMENTS:

INPUT:

A customer master file consisting of one record type:

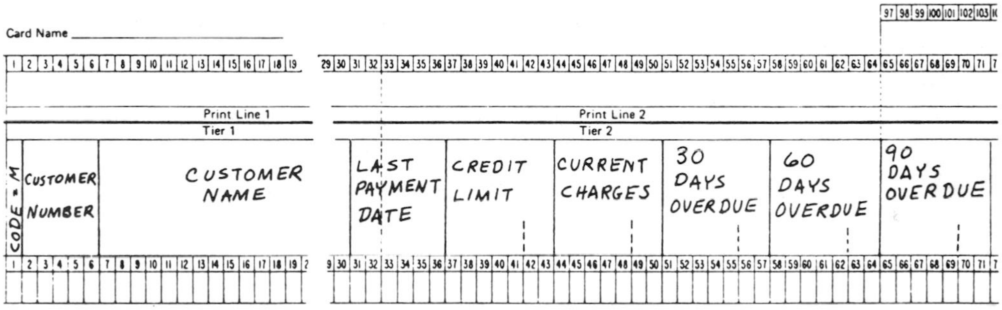

PROCESSING:

Check input balance due field for zero or credit balance (use field indicators).

OUTPUT:

An aged-trial balance report printed on a 132-position printer.

AGED TRIAL BALANCE

CUSTOMER NUMBER	CUSTOMER NAME	LAST PAY DATE	CREDIT LIMIT	CURRENT CHARGES	OVERDUE ACCOUNTS 30 DAYS	60 DAYS	90 DAYS
10867	ALLEN & CO.	2/16/70	15,000.00	6,919.77	376.58		
16535	ANDERSON AUTO SUPPLY	1/28/70	2,500.00	1,665.49			
17849	ANDREWS AND SONS INC	2/05/70	750.00			146.64	
18978	ARGONAUT ENGINEERING	12/27/69	2,000.00	2,111.30	611.54	312.13	90.44
24743	BERKLEY PAPER CO	2/21/70	6,300.00	1,185.50	2,652.45	1,400.05	51.00
25271	BEST DISTRIBUTION CO	10/06/69	1,000.00	3.25			762.19

Figure 12.17
Continued.

This Printer Spacing Chart shows how the report is formatted:

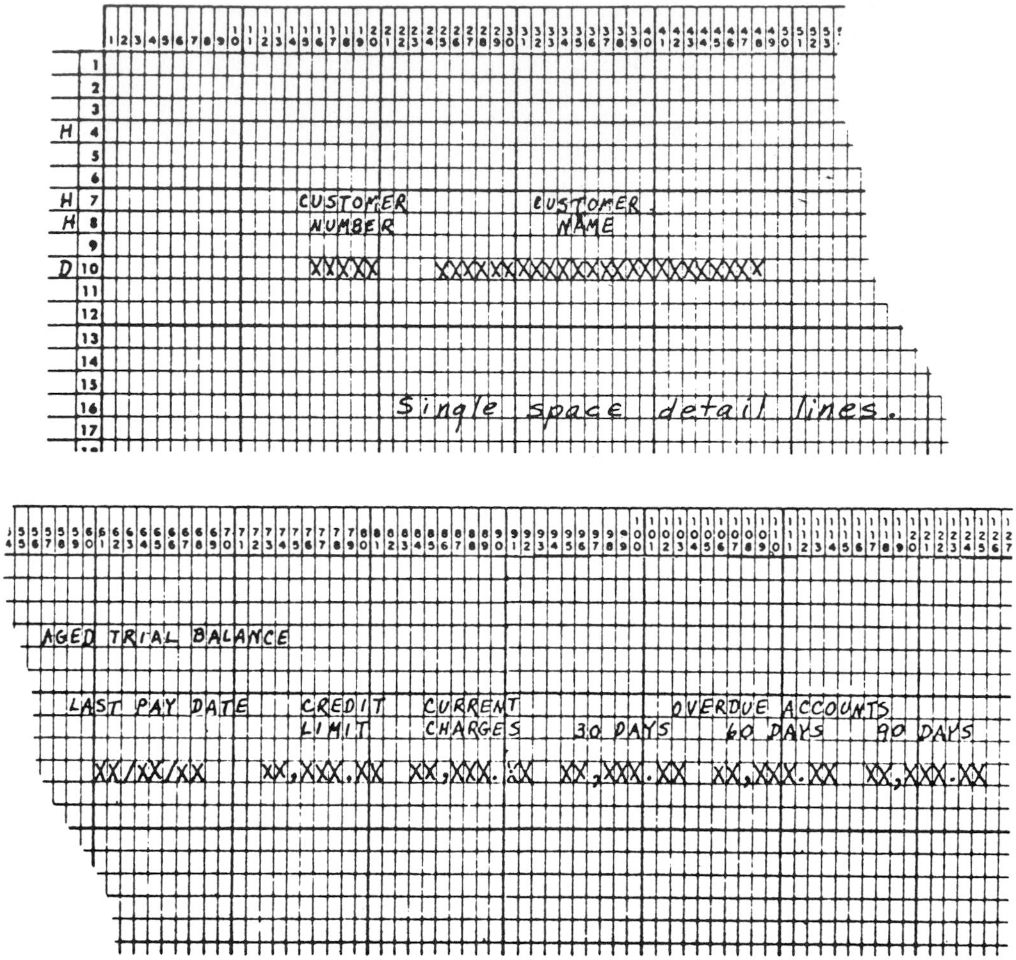

```
                                                                 RPG II C03       01/12/7   11:33  PAGE    1

        01010H
        01020FFILEIN  IPE F  80  80            READER
        01030FFILEØUT Ø   F 132 132      ØF    LPRINTER
        02010IFILEIN  JN  01   1 CM
        02020I                                        2   60CUSNØ
        02030I                                        7   30 NAME
        02040I                                       31   360DATE
        02050I                                       37   432LIMIT
        02060I                                       44   502CHARGE
        02070I                                       51   572THIRTY          20
        02080I                                       58   642SIXTY           30
        02090I                                       65   712NINETY          40
        04010ØFILEØUT H  3      1P
        04020Ø                                   74 'AGED TRIAL BALANCE'
        04030Ø        H  1      1P
        04040Ø                                   22 'CUSTØMER'
        04050Ø                                   39 'CUSTØMER'
        04060Ø                                   70 'LAST PAY DATE'
        04070Ø                                   81 'CREDIT'
        04080Ø                                   91 'CURRENT'
        04090Ø                                  118 'ØVERDUE ACCØUNTS'
        04100Ø        H  2      1P
        04110Ø                                   21 'NUMBER'
        04120Ø                                   37 'NAME'
        04130Ø                                   80 'LIMIT'
        04140Ø                                   91 CHARGES'

        04150Ø                                  102 '30 DAYS'
        04160Ø                                  113 '60 DATE'
        04170Ø                                  124 '90 DAYS'
        04180Ø        D  1      01
        04185Ø        ØR        20
        04186Ø        ØR        30
        04187Ø        ØR        40
        04190Ø                         CUSNØ Z   20
        04200Ø                         NAME      48
        05010Ø                         DATE  Y   68
        05020Ø                         LIMIT 1   81
        05030Ø                         CHARGE2   92
        05040Ø                         THIRTY2  103
        05050Ø                         SIXTY 2  114

                                                          RPG II C03       01/12/7   11:33  PAGE    2

        05060Ø                         NINETY2  125
```

AGED TRIAL BALANCE

CUSTØMER NUMBER	CUSTØMER NAME	LAST PAY DATE	CREDIT LIMIT	CURRENT	ØVERDUE ACCØUNTS 30 DAYS	60 DATE	90 DAYS
10867	ALLEN&CØ.	2/16/74	15,000.00	6,919.77	37,658.00		
16535	ANDERSØN AUTØ SUPPLY	1/28/74	2,500.00	1,665.49			
17849	ANDREWS &SØN INC	2/05/74	750.00			146.64	
18978	ARGØNAUT ENGINEERING	12/27/73	2,000.00	2,111.30	611.54	312.13	90.44
24743	BERKEY PAPER CØ	2/21/74	6,300.00	1,185.50	2,652.45	1,400.05	51.00
25271	BEST DISTRIBUTIØN CØ	10/06/73	1,000.00	3.25			762.19

Figure 12.17 Continued.

Figure 12.18 Illustrative problem 2.

DETERMINE THE JOB REQUIREMENTS

Assume that you are told the following things about a job:

1. An invoice is to be prepared like that shown in the Sample Invoice.
2. The input file contains two types of records: name/address records for all customers who made purchases on credit during the month and transaction records for each item purchased by the customers during the month. The name/address and transaction records look like this:

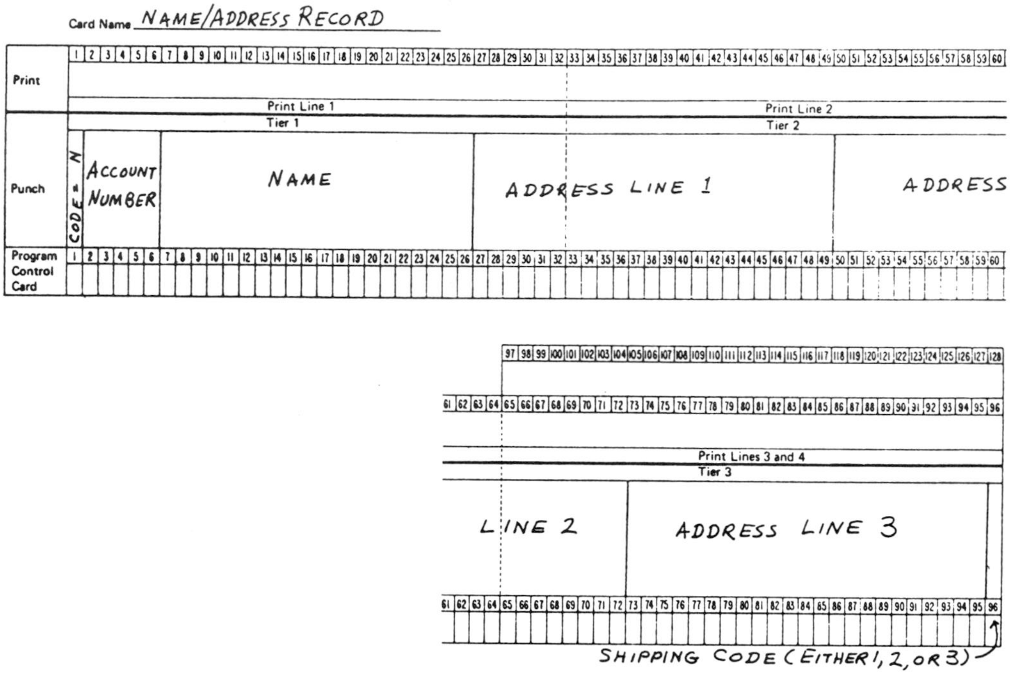

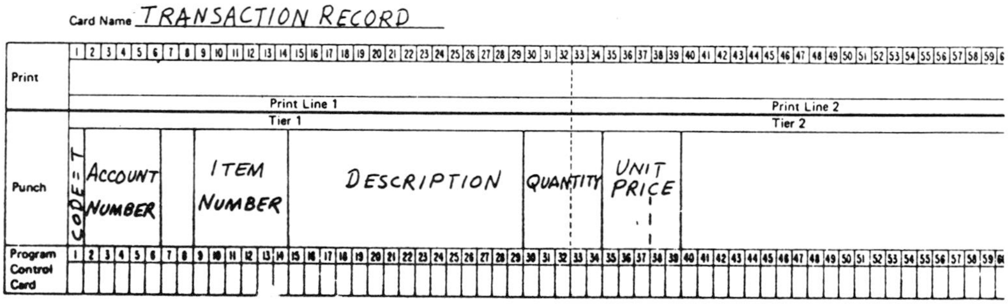

3. The input file is organized so that all transaction records for a customer follow the customer's name/address record.

Figure 12.18
Continued.

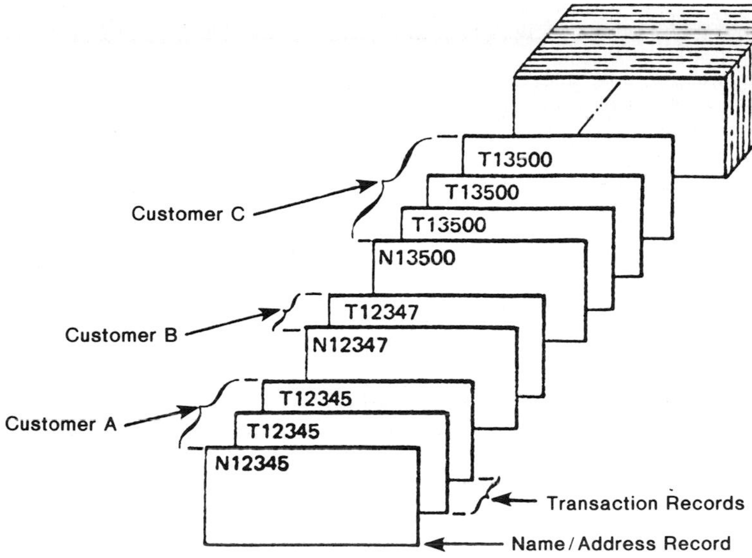

4. There will always be one name/address record for each customer, but there may be one or more transaction records per customer.

INVOICE

ACCOUNT NUMBER 09621

NAME SMITH MANUFACTURING

ADDRESS 13620 9TH ST NE
BERNALILLO
NEW MEXICO 56120

SHIPPING INSTRUCTIONS BY AIR

ITEM NUMBER	DESCRIPTION	QUANTITY	UNIT PRICE	AMOUNT
439167	SHEARS	100	27.56	2,756.00
629408	GASKET CORK	3000	1.15	3,450.00
102139	SPRIDGET WHITE	50	750.00	37,500.00

INVOICE TOTAL 212,157.92

Sample Invoice

5. Standard computer paper is to be used. Invoices should look like this:

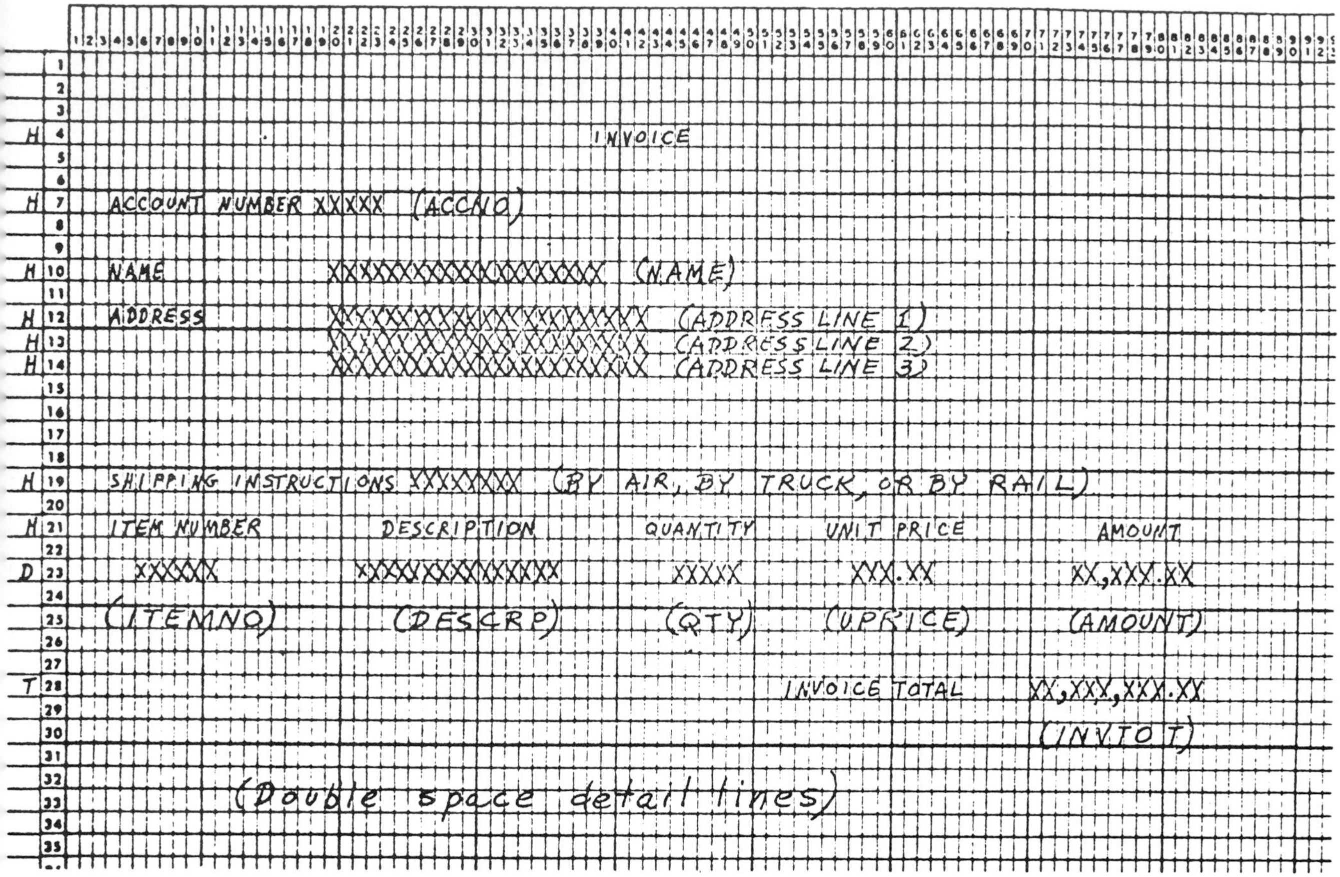

Figure 12.18 Continued.

Figure 12.18
Continued.

```
                                                   RPG II C03      01/13/7   11:26  PAGE    1

     01010H
     01020FFILEIN  IPE F  80  80             READER
     01030FFILEOUT O   F 132 132      OF     LPRINTER
     02010IFILEIN   11 01  .1 CN
     02020I                                          2   60ACCTNOL1
     02030I                                          7  26 NAME
     02040I                                         27  45 ADDNO1
     02050I                                         46  60 ADDNO2
     02055I                                         61  79 ADDNO3
     02060I                                         80  800CODE
     02070I             2N 02   1 CT
     02080I                                          2   60ACCTNOL1
     02090I                                          9  140ITEMNO
     02100I                                         15  29 DESCR
     02110I                                         30  340QUANTI
     02120I                                         35  392PRICE
     03030C                          SETOF                    30
     03040C                          SETOF                    20
     03050C                          SETOF                    10
     03070C    01       CODE         COMP 2                 301020
    S03010C    02       QUANTI       MULT PRICE     AMOUNT  72H
     03020C    02       AMOUNT       ADD  INVTOT    INVTOT 102
     04010OFILEOUT H  3      1P
     04030O                                   45 'INVOICE'
     04040O         H  3     01
     04060O                                   17 'ACCOUNT NUMBER'
     04070O                           ACCTNO4   23
     04080O         H  2     01
     04100O                                    7 'NAME'
     04110O                           NAME      39
     04120O         H  1     01
     04140O                                   10 'ADDRESS'
     04150O                           ADDNO1    38
     04160O         H  1     01
     04180O                           ADDNO2    34
     04184O         H  5     01
     04185O                           ADDNO3    38
     04190O         H  2     01
     05010O                                   24 'SHIPPING INSTRUCTIONS'
     05020O                  10               33 'BY AIR  '
     05060O                  20               33 'BY TRUCK'
     05100O                  30               33 'BY RAIL '

                                                   RPG II C03      01/13/7   11:26  PAGE    2

     05110O         H  2     01
     05130O                                   14 'ITEM NUMBER'
     05140O                                   34 'DESCRIPTION'
     05150O                                   50 'QUANTITY'
     05160O                                   65 'UNIT PRICE'
     05170O                                   81 'AMOUNT'
     05180O         D  1     02
     05190O                           ITEMNO    11
     05200O                           DESCR     36
     06010O                           QUANTIZ   49
     06020O                           PRICE 1   63
     06030O                           AMOUNT1   82
     06040O         T 25     L1
     06050O                                   65 'INVOICE TOTAL'
     06060O                           INVTOT1   82
```

```
                                INVOICE


ACCOUNT NUMBER  9621


NAME            SMITH MANUFACTURING

ADDRESS         13620 9TH ST NE
                BERNALILLO
                NEW MEXICO  56120



SHIPPING INSTRUCTIONS BY AIR

ITEM NUMBER         DESCRIPTION          QUANTITY    UNIT PRICE        AMOUNT

  439167            SHEARS                    100         27.56      2,756.00
  439167            GASKET CORK              3000          1.15      3,450.00
  102139            SPRIDGET WHITE             50        750.00     37,500.00

                                               INVOICE TOTAL        43,706.00
```

Summary

Report Program Generator (RPG II) is a problem-oriented programming language designed to solve a particular problem. A problem-oriented programming language describes the problem to the computer without detailing the procedures involved. This chapter describes the features of the most widely used problem-oriented programming language—Report Program Generator (RPG II).

1. RPG II provides the programmer with an easy and efficient method of generating a computer program. It accepts data input; retrieves data from existing files; performs calculations; changes formats of data; updates existing files; creates new files; compares data values, one to another; specifies constants for the determination of appropriate handling; uses library subroutines defined for other purposes by applying them to the user's problem; and prints reports derived from the input and file data.
2. RPG II is oriented toward the problem rather than the machine that will process it. This makes it easier to describe the job to the computer than to write a program for it. Many different reports may be prepared from the same input specifications. Self-explanatory headings make it possible for nonprogrammers to write programs. Language and specific techniques can be easily learned. It is compatible for all models of computers.
3. Specification sheets generate machine-language program instructions together with assigned storage areas for data input and output, work areas, and constants.
4. The printer spacing chart is a worksheet for the printer to use for coding the particular operations. The programmer then prepares the specification sheets. The file description describes each file to be used by the program. The input specification sheet describes input records, including record layouts and file fields within records. The calculation specification sheet specifies all operations to be performed on the data. The output-format specification sheet describes how the finished report should look.
5. Cards (disks or diskettes) are punched from the specification sheets. The punched cards with the necessary job control cards are entered into the machine for compilation. If compilation is successful, input cards are read from preparation of the desired output.

Identification Questions

Match the following terms with the statements below.

A. Calculation Specifications	E. File Description Specification	H. Output-Format Specifications
B. Comments	F. File Extension & Line Counter Specifications	I. Printer Spacing Chart
C. Edit Words	G. Input Specifications	J. RPG II
D. Editing		K. Specification Forms

1. These forms define the output format and serve as a coding form for the particular application.
2. These forms describe fields and record layouts of input files.
3. These forms are used to describe the finished report.
4. Problem-oriented programming language designed to solve a particular problem.
5. A means of documenting a program.
6. These forms provide information about tables and arrays and also specify the number of lines to be printed.
7. The method by which data is made more readable and understandable.
8. These forms specify all operations to be performed on the data.
9. These forms automatically generate machine-language instructions together with automatically assigned storage areas.
10. These forms are used to describe all files to be used by the object program.
11. Provide a pattern for punctuation.

Questions for Review

1. What are the features of RPG II?
2. What are the main advantages of RPG II?
3. What are the main functions of RPG II?
4. What is the difference between RPG and RPG II?
5. What steps are necessary to prepare a RPG II program?
6. What information must appear on a printer spacing chart?
7. What are the principal types of specification forms used in RPG and what are the principal purposes of each?
8. What are the main functions of each type of RPG II specification form?
9. What is meant by editing and how is editing accomplished in RPG II?

Key Terms

- Calculation Specifications
- Comments
- Edit Words
- Editing
- File Extension and Line Counter Specifications
- File Description Specifications
- Input Specifications
- Output-Format Specifications
- Printer Spacing Chart
- RPG II
- Specification Forms

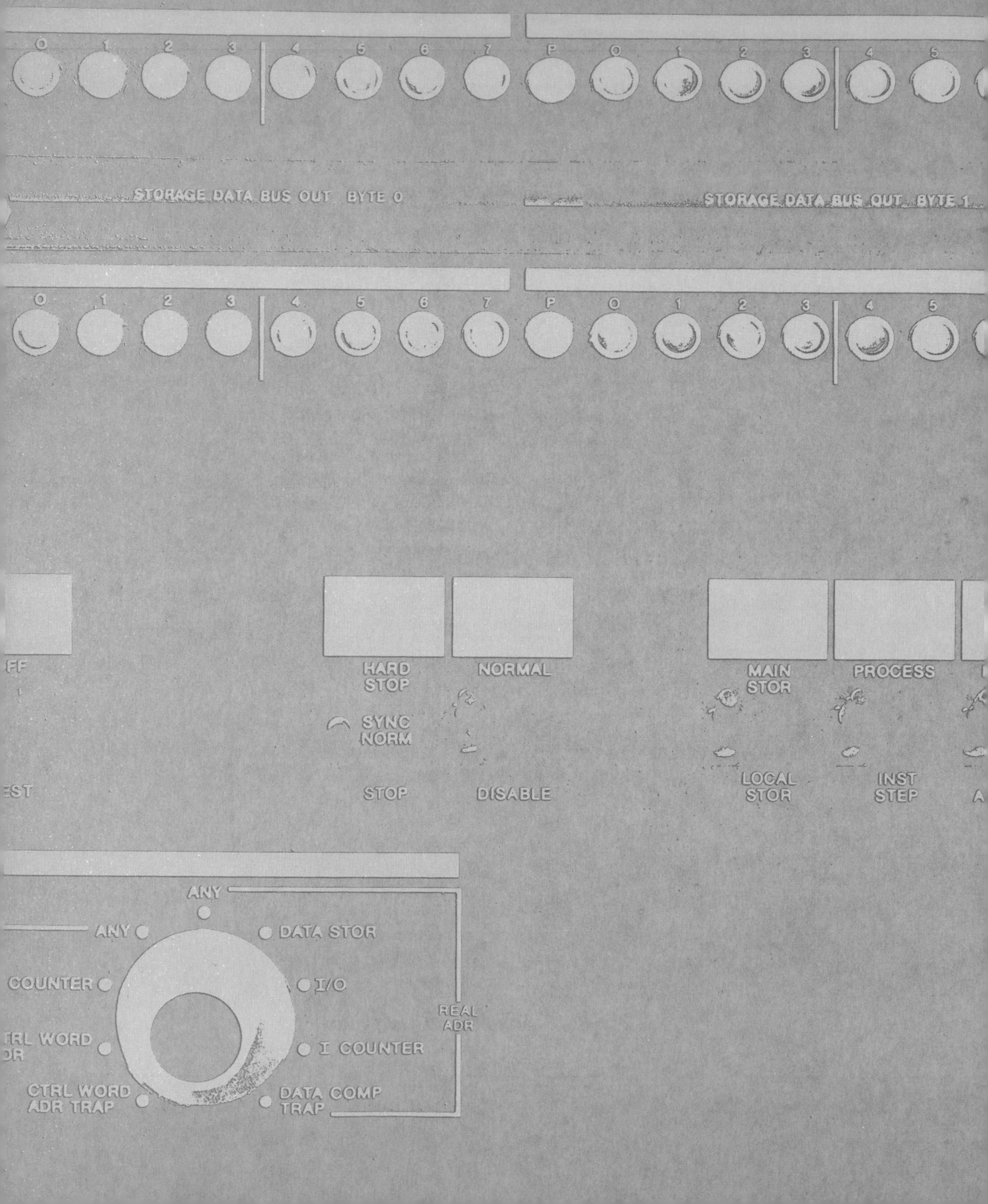

STORAGE DATA BUS OUT BYTE 0
STORAGE DATA BUS OUT BYTE 1
HARD STOP
NORMAL
MAIN STOR
PROCESS
SYNC NORM
STOP
DISABLE
LOCAL STOR
INST STEP
ANY
ANY
DATA STOR
COUNTER
I/O
REAL ADR
I COUNTER
CTRL WORD ADR TRAP
DATA COMP TRAP

FORTRAN 13

Chapter Outline

Chapter Objectives

The learning objectives of this chapter are

1. to describe the features of FORTRAN.
2. to enable you to define the problem, construct a flowchart, and write a program in FORTRAN.
3. to provide you with the self-satisfying feeling of having your program run on the computer in spite of the numerous errors that may exist in the program.
4. to provide the impetus for debugging programs, which will aid in the better understanding of the FORTRAN programming language.

The FORTRAN (*FOR*mula *TRAN*slation) language is a procedure-oriented programming language, designed primarily for writing programs to solve scientific and engineering problems involving mathematical computations. FORTRAN is a compromise between the language of the computer and the language of the engineer and scientist. To satisfy the computer, symbols are used that the computer can understand. This requires that the rules for their use be followed closely. To satisfy the engineer and scientist, as many of the detailed computer control operations as possible are eliminated from the writing of programs, and a problem statement format close to that of the mathematical notation is used.

The FORTRAN language is especially useful in writing programs for applications that involve mathematical computations and other manipulation of numeric data. With the increased use of mathematics in business, more FORTRAN programs are being written for commercial applications.

Source programs are written in the FORTRAN language. They consist of a set of statements constructed from the language elements described. In the compilation process, the source statements are translated into machine language (object program). In addition, when the FORTRAN compiler detects errors in the source program, it produces appropriate diagnostic messages (fig. 13.1).

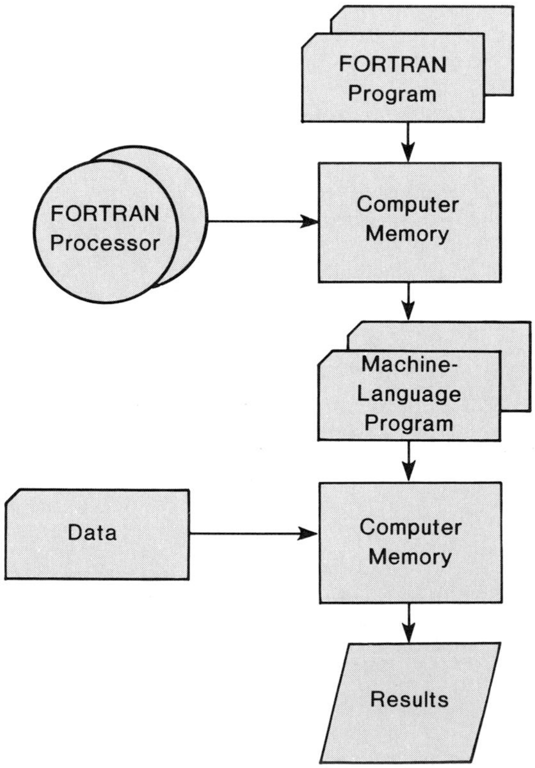

Figure 13.1 The general FORTRAN translation procedure.

Elements of FORTRAN

Statements

Source programs consist of a set of statements from which the compiler generates machine instructions, constants, and storage areas. The FORTRAN language is composed of statements (individual commands) of a program consisting of operation symbols (+, −, *, /, **) and expressions (A + B − C).

Statements are the sentences of FORTRAN, which may perform the following:

1. Define the arithmetic steps to be accomplished by the computer.
2. Provide information for control of the computer during the execution of the program.
3. Describe the input and output operations that are necessary to bring in data and punch or write the results.
4. Specify certain additional facts, such as the size of the input data that is read by the program.

FORTRAN statements consist of certain keywords that are used in conjunction with certain basic elements of the language—constants and variables. They may be divided into categories according to their function (fig. 13.2).

Figure 13.2 Types of FORTRAN statements.

TYPE	*PURPOSE*	*EXAMPLES*
Arithmetic	Specifies a numerical computation	A = C + D − G
Control	Governs the flow of control in the program	GO TO 20 GO TO (25, 31, 9), ITEM IF (X) 6, 8, 12 DO 6 I = 1, 10 CONTINUE PAUSE STOP END
Input or Output	Provides the means of getting information into or out of the computer	READ (5, 6) A, B, C WRITE (6, 76) N, A, B
Specification	Describes the arrangement of data on input or printed line, and also supplies information to the processor	DIMENSION B(25, 50), TABLE (5, 8, 4) INTEGER DEV, SMALL REAL ITA, JOB COMMON A, B, C, R (100) FORMAT (I3, F6.2/I5, F6.2) EQUIVALENCE (B, D(1))
Subprogram	Enables the programmer to define and use subprograms	CALL MATMPY (X, 5, 40, Y, 7, 2) FUNCTION DAV (D, E, F) SUBROUTINE COPY (A, B, N) RETURN

1. *Arithmetic statements* specify the mathematical calculations to be performed.
2. *Control statements* determine the sequence in which the statements will follow. These statements enable the user to govern the flow and terminate the execution of the program.
3. *Input/output statements* read data into the computer for printing or punching the results of the program. In addition to controlling the input and output devices, these statements enable the user to transfer data between internal storage and an input/output media.
4. *Specification statements* tell the FORTRAN program the amount and kind of input and output data it will process. In addition, these statements specify the amount of storage to be used by variables and the placement of alphabetic and numerical information on the printed page.
5. *Subprogram statements* enable the user to name and define functions and subroutines, which can be compiled separately or with the main program.

Character Set

The FORTRAN character set is composed of the following characters:

1. Twenty-six letters of the alphabet, A to Z.
2. Ten numerical digits, 0 to 9.
3. Punctuation characters.

period	.	apostrophe	'
comma	,	dollar sign	$
left parenthesis	(	space (indicated	
right parenthesis	)	by a small b)	b

4. Six algebraic symbols.

add	+	divide	/
subtract	−	exponentiation	**
multiply	*	equal	=

FORTRAN Coding Forms

A FORTRAN coding form should be used as a guide when preparing a source program. Besides providing a written record of the program, the form facilitates the subsequent transfer of the source statements to cards.

The statements of a FORTRAN source program can be written on a standard FORTRAN Coding Form (fig. 13.3). Each line of the form represents one 80-column card, and the FORTRAN statements are written one to a line on these forms. If a statement is too long to be completed on one line of the form, it may be continued on as many as nineteen successive lines by placing a continuation indicator in column 6 (any character other than blank or zero). The first card of a statement must always be blank (or contain a zero) in column 6. Blanks may be inserted anywhere in FORTRAN statements (except literals) to improve the readability of the statement.

The different fields of a FORTRAN Coding Form are (fig. 13.4):

1. *Comment (Column 1).* A *C* in the first column indicates that a comment is written in that statement. Comments are used as notes and help to clarify some of the

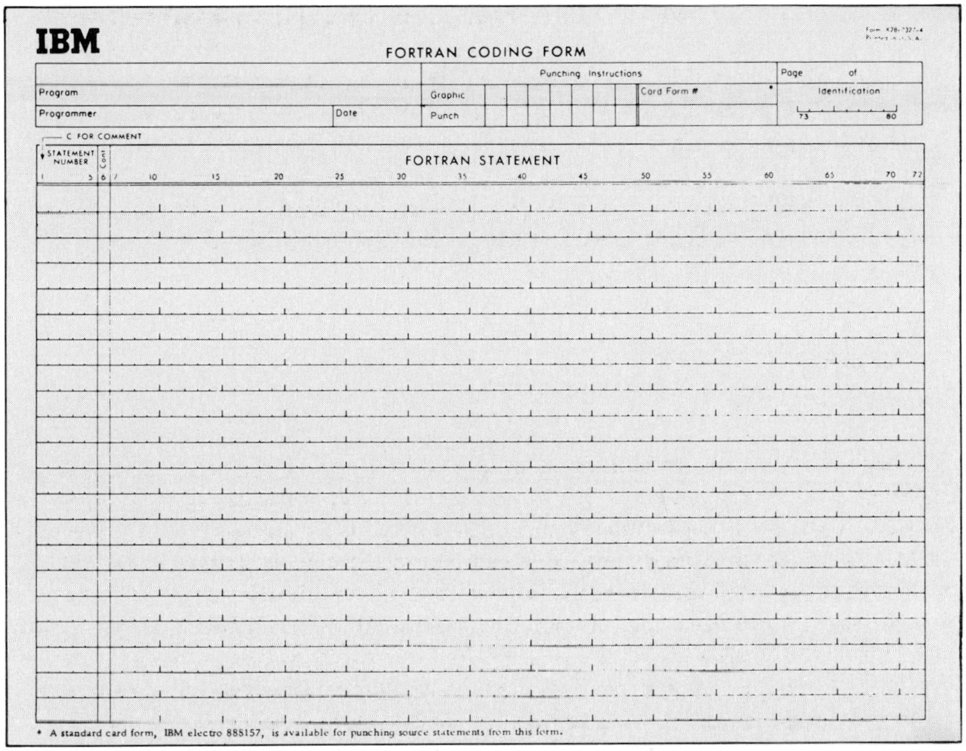

Figure 13.3 An example of a FORTRAN coding sheet.

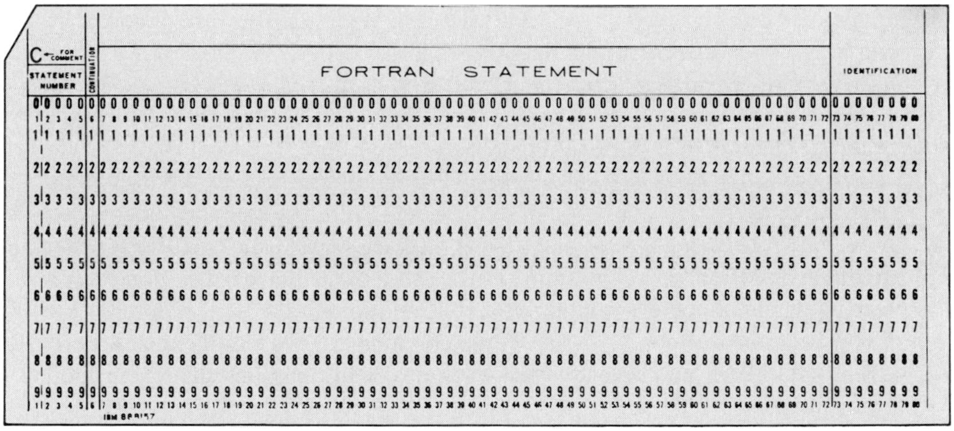

Figure 13.4 An example of a FORTRAN card.

statements and improve the readability of the statement. Comments may be written from column 2 through 72 of the form. The comments will be listed with the program; however, they are not processed by the FORTRAN compiler and no part of the comment is translated into machine language. A comment may appear between FORTRAN statements but must not precede a continuation card (fig. 13.5).

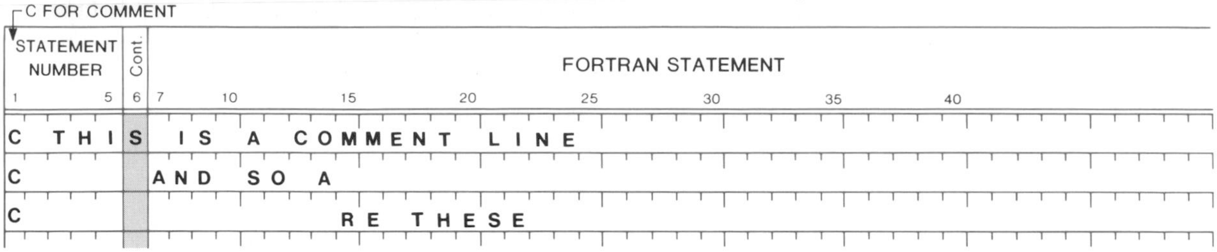

Figure 13.5 Examples of comment lines.

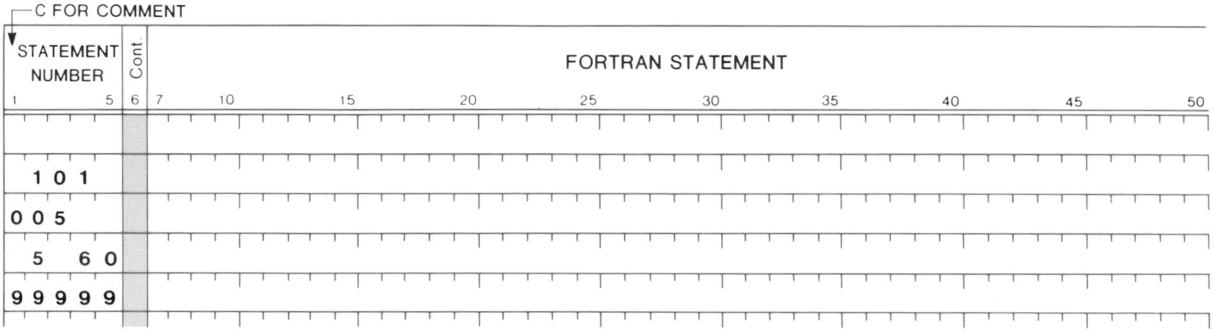

Figure 13.6 Examples of statement numbers.

2. *Statement Number (Columns 1–5).* These columns are used to write the statement number. A statement number may consist of one to five decimal digits. Blanks or zeros that may precede the statement number are ignored by the compiler. These numbers may be assigned in any order; *the value of the statement number does not affect the sequence in which the statements are executed in a FORTRAN program.* These numbers will be used as labels to be referred to by other statements in program (fig. 13.6).
3. *Continuation Indicator (Column 6).* A nonblank or nonzero character in this field indicates the continuation of a statement from the previous line.
4. *FORTRAN Statement (Columns 7–72).* Starting in column 7, FORTRAN statements are written up to column 72. One statement per card is punched into a card with the possible exception of a continuation.
5. *Identification (Columns 73–80).* These columns are not significant to the FORTRAN compiler and are used for program identification, sequencing, or any other purpose.

Mathematical problems usually contain some data that does not change throughout the entire problem and other data that may change many times during calculation. These two kinds of data are referred to as *constants* and *variables* respectively. Both constants and variables can be used in FORTRAN programs, if they are written so that the processor can distinguish one from the other.

Constants

A constant is a fixed, unvarying quantity that is used without change from one execution of the program to the next. It appears in its actual numeric form in the source statement. For example, to calculate employee social security tax, the FORTRAN formula would be:

```
SSTAX = GROSS * .0613
```

The current social security tax rate, .0613, will remain unchanged for the execution of the program for each employee. Numerical constants may be *integer* or *real*.

An *integer constant* is a whole number without a decimal point. It may be positive, negative, or zero. It may contain a sign. If unsigned, it is assumed to be positive. The constant may not contain embedded commas.

Valid Integer Constants	Invalid Integer Constants	
0	452.	Contains a decimal point.
152	5,396	Contains a comma.
-7452438		
+64217		

A *real constant* is a string of decimal digits with a decimal point. The constant may be positive, negative, or zero. If unsigned, it is assumed to be positive.

Valid Real Constants	Invalid Real Constants	
+456.78	456,678.91	Contains a comma.
-0.	589	Contains no decimal point.

Another type of constant is a literal constant. A *literal constant* is a string of alphameric and/or special characters that may be enclosed in apostrophes or the string can be preceded by *w*H, where *w* is the number of characters in the string. For example, if it is necessary to print a heading at the top of a report, one might write the FORTRAN instruction in either of the following ways:

```
  WRITE (3,3)
3 FORMAT ('SALES ANALYSIS REPORT')
```

or

```
  WRITE (3,3)
3 FORMAT (21HSALES ANALYSIS REPORT)
```

In both cases, when the WRITE statement is executed, the literal constant SALES ANALYSIS REPORT will be printed.

Variables

When a quantity in a FORTRAN problem varies for different executions of a program, it is known as a variable quantity. Variable names are symbols used to distinguish one variable from another. When reading the descriptions of variables, it is important to distinguish between the *value* of a variable and the *name* of a variable. For example, VOLT could be the variable name assigned to a series of values used in a calculation of current in a circuit.

The use of meaningful variable names can aid in documenting a program so that someone other than the programmer may look at the program and understand its function. It will be easier to follow the flow if meaningful symbols are used whenever possible. For example, to compute the distance a car traveled in a certain amount of time at a given rate of speed, you could use the following statement $X = Y * Z$. However, this statement would be more meaningful if the programmer had written DIST = RATE * TIME.

A variable name is a symbolic name that may consist of one to six alphameric characters (alphabet A to Z, numeric 0 to 9, and $). The first character must be a letter or $.

Valid Variable Names	Invalid Variable	
C4578	B789456	Contains more than six characters.
UNIT	5NUMB	First character is not alphabetic.
$VAR	BJ.7	Contains a special character.

An *integer* variable name begins with the letters I through N.

Data	Variable Name	
3467	JOB	
2145.76	NUMBER	Invalid variable name as data is in real mode.
-2467	INCR	

A variable name corresponds to the type of data the variable represents. A *real* variable name begins with the letters A through H and/or O through Z. The data must be in the real mode as explained in real constants.

Data	Variable Name	
1234	UNIT	Invalid variable name as data is in integer mode.
1234.56	AMOUNT	
-64.78	RATE	

Expressions

Expressions in their simplest form consist of a single constant or variable. They may also designate a computation between two or more constants and/or variables. Expressions may appear in arithmetic statements and in certain control statements (fig. 13.7).

FORTRAN Expression	Meaning
(C – D)/E	$\frac{C-D}{E}$
C –D/E	$C-\frac{D}{E}$
E/(C – D)	$\frac{E}{C-D}$
A/B *D	$\frac{A}{B}\times D$
A/(B*D)	$\frac{A}{B\times D}$
A/B/D	$\frac{A}{B}\div D$
A + C*B**D	$A+C\times B^{D}$

Figure 13.7 Examples of FORTRAN expressions and their mathematical meanings.

An expression in FORTRAN consists of a series of constants, variables, and their functions, separated by parentheses, commas, and/or operation symbols so a mathematical expression is formed.

Arithmetic Statements

The numerical computations that are to be performed in an object program are defined by arithmetic statements that closely resemble conventional arithmetic formulas. The simplest arithmetic expression consists of a single constant and/or a variable. The variable to be computed is followed by an equal (=) sign, which is followed by an arithmetic expression. For example, the arithmetic statement Z = A – JOE means to replace the value of the variable on the left side of the equal sign with the value of the expression on the right side of the equal sign. The meaning of the equal (=) sign is important in writing FORTRAN programs. The equal sign means "to be replaced by" rather than "is equivalent to" (fig. 13.8).

Five basic arithmetic operations may be performed in FORTRAN—addition, subtraction, multiplication, division, and exponentiation. The arithmetic operators used in FORTRAN are as follows:

Arithmetic Operator	Function
+	Addition
-	Subtraction
*	Multiplication
/	Division
**	Exponentiation

```
      READ (5,10) A,B,C,D
10    FORMAT (4F5.2)
      G =A +B
      H =C +D
      WRITE (6,11) G,H
11    FORMAT (F8.2,2X,F7.3)
      STOP
      END
```

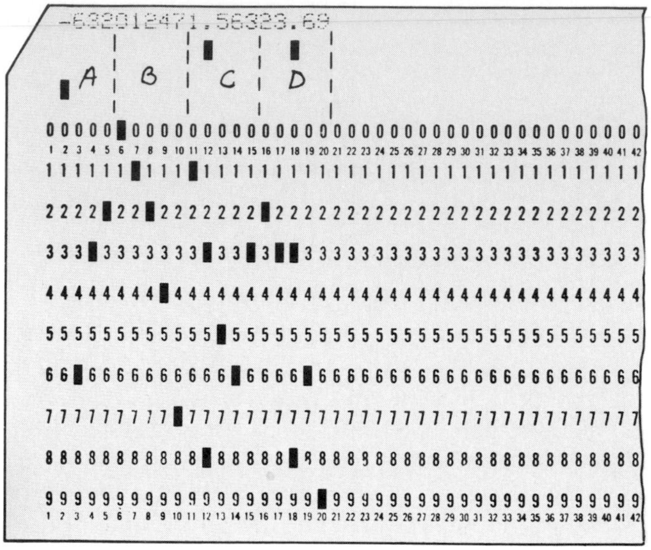

Figure 13.8 An example of a FORTRAN arithmetic operation problem.

Examples of Arithmetic Statements

Statement	Description
(Variable Arithmetic Expression)	
`AMT = UNITS*RATE`	The product of UNITS and RATE replaces the value of the variable AMT.
(Arithmetic Statement)	
`SSTAX = EARN * .0613`	The product replaces the value of SSTAX.
`SUM = PRINC`	The value of SUM is replaced by the current value of PRINC.

Computations are performed from left to right according to the hierarchy of operations as follows:

1. Parenthetical expressions from innermost to outermost pairs.
2. Exponentiation.
3. Multiplication and division from left to right.
4. Addition and subtraction from left to right.

Consider the following examples:

Example 1

The mathematical statement $E = \frac{AB}{CD}$ can be correctly written in FORTRAN as E = A * B / (C * D) and will be effectively evaluated in the following order:

1. (C * D)	Call the result X	A * B / X
2. A * B	Call the result Y	Y / X
3. Y / X	Final operation	

Example 2

The arithmetic statement D = B + ((A + B) * C) + A ** 2 will be effectively evaluated in the following order:

1. (A + B)	Call the result X	B +(X * C) + A ** 2
2. (X * C)	Call the result Y	B + Y + A ** 2
3. A ** 2	Call the result Z	B + Y + Z
4. B + Y	Call the result W	W + Z
5. W + Z	Final operation	

Control Statements

Normally FORTRAN statements in a program are executed sequentially as they are written on a coding sheet *unless a different sequence is specified.*

Control statements provide flexibility to program development. If statements could only be followed sequentially in a fixed pattern, a program would have to follow a single path of operation without any possibility of dealing with predefined exceptions to the procedure, and without any ability to choose alternatives based upon conditions encountered during the processing of the program.

Some of the statements that are commonly used to alter and control the normal execution of statements in a program are GO TO, IF, DO, CONTINUE, PAUSE, STOP, and END statements.

GO TO Statements

GO TO statements permit the transfer of control to an executable statement specified by the number in the GO TO statement. Control may be transferred unconditionally or conditionally. The GO TO statements are unconditional GO TO statements, and computed GO TO statements.

Unconditional GO TO Statement

The unconditional GO TO statement causes transfer of control to the statement number specified every time the GO TO statement is executed (fig. 13.9). In the following example, every time statement 50 is executed, control is transferred to statement 25.

```
50 GO TO 25
10 A = B + 6
      .
      .
25 C = E ** 2
```

Computed GO TO Statement

The computed GO TO statement causes transfer of control to the statement number specified depending upon the current value of the item in the statement (fig. 13.10). For example:

```
   GO TO (35,25,17), ITEM
        .
        .
```

```
C FOR COMMENT
STATEMENT NUMBER | Cont. | FORTRAN STATEMENT

                    .
                    .
                GØ TØ 362
    710         V(9) = TØP-V(7)**K+TEST+.25
                    .
                    .
    362         V(7)=Z1
                    .
                    .
                GØ TØ 710
                    .
                    .
```

In these statements, statement 362 precedes statement 710 in the logical flow of the program of which they are a part, because of the function of the GO TO statements.

Figure 13.9 An example of an unconditional GOTO statement.

```
C FOR COMMENT
STATEMENT NUMBER | Cont. | FORTRAN STATEMENT

                    .
                    .
                J = 3
                    .
                    .
     23          GØ TØ (115,306,700,819,73),J
                    .
                    .
                J = 5
                GØ TØ 23
                    .
                    .
```

When J = 3, statement 23 transfers control to statement 700. Changing J to 5 changes any subsequent execution of statement 23 to a transfer to statement 73. Making J = 0 or 6 would be an error because these values are outside the range $1 \leq j \leq n$.

Figure 13.10 An example of a computed GOTO statement.

```
17 AMT = UNITS * .15
        .
        .
35 AMT = UNITS * .10
        .
        .
25 AMT = UNITS * .05
```

If the value of integer variable ITEM is 1, statement 35 will be executed next. If the value of ITEM is 2, statement 25 is executed, and if the value of ITEM is 3, statement 17 is executed. If any other value is present in ITEM, the next statement after GO TO is executed.

```
15 IF (I - 1000) 10, 30, 30
30 A = B + C
   .
   .
```

The three statements (5, 10, and 25) required to control the previously shown loop can be replaced by a single DO statement as follows:

```
   .
   .
   DO 25 I = 1, 1000
25 STOCK(I) = STOCK(I) - OUT(I)
30 A = B + C
   .
   .
```

In example 1, the *DO variable,* I, is set to the *initial value* of 1. Before the second execution of the statement 25, I is increased by the *increment,* 1, and statement 25 is again executed. After 1,000 executions of the DO loop, I equals 1,000. Since I is now equal to the highest value that does not exceed the *test value,* 1000, control passes out of the DO loop and statement 30 is executed next. *Note* that variable I is now undefined; its value is not necessarily 1000 or 1001. If the increment value is not specified, the value of 1 is assumed.

xample 2

```
   .
   .
   DO 25 I = 1, 10, 2
15 J = I + K
25 ARRAY(J) = BRAY(J)
30 A = B + C
   .
   .
```

In example 2, statement 25 is the *end of the range* of the DO loop. The *DO variable,* I, is set to the *initial value* of 1. Before the second execution of the DO loop, I is increased by the increment, 2, and the statements 15 and 25 are executed a second time. After the fifth execution of the DO loop, I equals 9. Since I is now equal to the highest value that does not exceed the *test value,* 10, control passes out of the DO loop and statement 30 is executed next. *Note* that the DO variable I is now undefined; and its value is not necessarily 9 or 11.

CONTINUE is a dummy statement which may be placed anywhere in the source program without affecting the sequence of execution. It is frequently used as the terminal statement in a DO range when the statement that would normally be the

Statement	Expression Value	Transfer to
IF (ZAP) 3,4,5	376.	5
IF (Z-1.)50,73,9	0.	73
IF (AMTX(3,2))7,2,1	−576.	7

Figure 13.11 Examples of arithmetic IF statements.

IF Statements

The IF statement is used to test variables and to cause control to be transferred to the statement related to the value of the variable tested. There are two types of IF statements. They are arithmetic IF statements and logical IF statements.

Arithmetic IF Statement

The arithmetic IF statement causes control to be transferred to a particular statement number when the value of the arithmetic expression is negative, zero, or positive (fig. 13.11). Consider the following examples.

Example 1

```
   IF (YTDEAR - 22900.00) 10,20,20
      .
      .
10 SSTAX = EARN * .0613
      .
      .
20 SSTAX = 0
      .
      .
```

In this example, if the year-to-date carnings are equal to or greater than 22900, control is transferred to statement 20 where no social security tax is calculated. If the earnings are less than 22900, control is transferred to statement 10 where the appropriate social security taxes are calculated.

Example 2

```
   IF (A - B) 10,20,30
      .
      .
10 C = E + F
      .
      .
20 G = H ** 2
      .
      .
30 D = (F * B)/D - 1
```

In this example, if the value of the expression A − B is negative, the statement 10 is executed next. If the value of the expression is zero, the statement 20 is executed next. If the value of the expression is positive, the statement 30 is executed next.

Logical IF Statement

The logical IF statement is used to evaluate a logical expression and to execute or skip the statement depending on whether the value of the expression is .TRUE. or .FALSE.

Relational Operators

The six relational operators, each of which must be preceded and followed by a period, are:

Relational Operators	Meaning
.GT.	Greater than (>)
.GE.	Greater than or equal to (≥)
.LT.	Less than (<)
.LE.	Less than or equal to (≤)
.EQ.	Equal to (=)
.NE.	Not equal to (≠)

The relational operators express an arithmetic condition which can be true or false. For example:

```
   IF (A.LE.0.0) GO TO 25
    C = D - E
   IF (A.EQ.B) ANSWER = 2.0 * A/C
    F = G/H
      .
      .
25 W = X ** 2
```

In the first statement, if the value of the expression is .TRUE. (A is less than or equal to 0.0), the statement GO TO 25 is executed next and control is passed to the statement 25. If the statement is .FALSE. (A is greater than 0.0), the statement GO TO 25 is ignored and the next statement is executed.

In the third statement, if the value of the expression is .TRUE. (A is equal to B), the value of ANSWER is replaced by the value of the expression (2.0*A/C) and then the fourth statement is executed. If the value of the expression is .FALSE. (A is not equal to B), the value of ANSWER remains unchanged and the fourth statement is executed next.

Logical Operators

The three logical operators, each of which must be preceded and followed by a period, are as follows (where A and B represent logical constants or variables or expressions containing relational operators).

Logical Operator	Use	Meaning
.NOT.	.NOT.A	If A is .TRUE., then .NOT.A has the value .FALSE.; if A is .FALSE., then .NOT.A has the value .TRUE.
.AND.	A.AND.B	If A and B are both .TRUE., then A.AND.B has the value .TRUE.; if either A or B or both are .FALSE.; then A.AND.B has the value .FALSE.
.OR.	A.OR.B	If either A or B or both are .TRUE., then A.OR.B has the value .TRUE.; if neither A nor B is .TRUE., then A.OR.B has the value .FALSE.

Two logical operators may appear in sequence only if the second one is the logical operator. For example, assume that P and Q are logical variables.

```
      .
      .
IF (P.OR..NOT.Q) A = B
C = B ** 2
```

In the first statement if the value of the expression is .TRUE., the value of A is replaced by the value of B and the second statement is executed. If the value of the expression is .FALSE., the statement A = B is skipped and the second statement is executed.

DO Statem

The DO statement provides a method for controlled, repetitive execution of a series of statements. The DO statement is a command to execute repeatedly the statements that follow, up to and including the last statement, numbered *x*. In the execution of a DO statement, all statements in the range of DO are executed in sequence, with the counter or control variable *i* assuming a new value from its range, until the control variable attains a value exceeding the test value *m*2. Then the statement following the terminal statement *x* is executed. If the increment *m*3 is not specified, it is assumed to be 1. *In the DO statement,* m*1 equals the initial value;* m*2 equals the test value;* m*3 equals the increment; and* x *equals the last statement of the DO range.*

There are several ways in which looping (repetitively executing the same statements) may be accomplished when using the FORTRAN language. For exampl assume that a manufacturer carries 1,000 different machine parts in stock. Perio cally, the manufacturer may find it necessary to compute the amount of each diff part presently available. This amount may be calculated by subtracting the n of each item, OUT(I), from the previous stock on hand, STOCK (I). I repres item number starting with the first item.

CONTINUE Statement

```
   .
   .
 5 I = 0
10 I = I + 1
25 STOCK(I) = STOCK(I) - OUT(I)
```

terminal statement is one that is not allowed (GO TO, PAUSE, STOP, RETURN, arithmetic IF, or another DO statement). For example:

```
     .
     .
     DO 30 I = 1, 20
   7 IF (A(I) - B(I)) 5, 30,
   5 A(I) = A(I) + 1.0
     B(I) = B(I) - 2.0
     .
     .
     GO TO 7
  30 CONTINUE
  40 C = A(3) + B(7)
     .
     .
```

In the preceding example, the CONTINUE statement is used as the last statement in the range of the DO in order to avoid ending the DO loop with the statement GO TO 7 (fig. 13.12).

```
22   DO 54 I = 1, 15                       36   DO 70 I = 12,3,-2
25   SUM = SUM + Q(I)                      39   CHECKS = PIN-OUT
     IF (SUM. LT. 0.0) SUM = 0.0                IF (CHECKS .LT. 0.0) ERROR = CHECKS
     SIGMA = SUM + R(I)                         PASS(I) = CHECKS
     IF (SIGMA - H **3/T) 54,54,12         70   IF (TOTAL.GT. 100.0) GO TO 95
54   CONTINUE                              75   TEST(I) = DONE
12   L = Y(I)                                   .
                                                .
                                                .
                                           95   FLAG = ACNT(I)
```

In the example that begins with statement 22, the range of statements 25 through 54 is executed 15 times, unless the arithmetic IF statement causes a transfer to statement 12. If all 15 iterations are completed, control is passed to statement 12 at the end of the 15th iteration. In this case I will equal 16 at the end of the loop.

In the example that begins with statement 36, the range of statements 39 through 70 is executed 5 times (with I = 12, 10,8,6, and 4), unless the logical IF statement causes a transfer to statement 95. If all five iterations are completed, control is passed to statement 75 at the end of the fifth iteration. In this case I will equal 2 at the end of the loop.

Figure 13.12 Examples of DO statements.

PAUSE Statement

A PAUSE statement causes temporary cessation of program execution and displays PAUSE or, if '*message*' is specified, PAUSE 'message' is displayed. When the information is displayed, the program waits until the operator intervention causes it to resume execution. The PAUSE statement permits the operator to intervene in the program execution for setup and control functions, such as changing data tapes. The operator can signal the program to continue execution, beginning with the statement immediately after the pause. If no changes are made to the status of the program or the computer during PAUSE, resuming program execution causes the normal execution sequence to be continued.

STOP Statement

The STOP statement causes program execution to be terminated (logically the last statement of a program) and displays *n* if specified.

END Statement

The END statement is a nonexecutable statement that defines the end of a source program. Each FORTRAN program must have an END statement as its last line to inform the processor that it is at the physical end of the program. An END statement may follow any other type of statement and may not be continued.

Input/Output Statements

The input/output statements enable the user to transfer data belonging to a named collection of data, between input/output devices (such as card readers, disk units, and magnetic tape units) and internal storage (fig. 13.13). The named collection of data is called a *data set* and is a continuous string of data that may be divided into FORTRAN records.

```
      READ (5,8)DEDUCT,HOURS,YRDATE,WEARN
   8  FORMAT (F2.0,F4.1,F7.2,F6.2)
      WRITE (6,9) DEDUCT,HOURS
      WRITE (6,10) YRDATE,WEARN
   9  FORMAT (F4.0,F6.1)
  10  FORMAT (F9.2,F8.2)
      STOP
      END
```

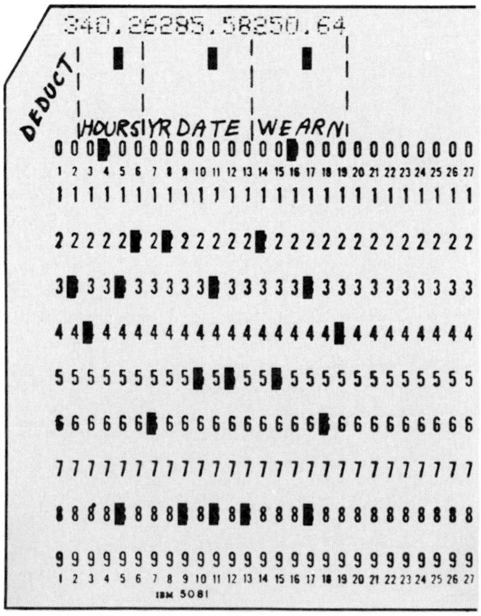

Figure 13.13 An example of a FORTRAN input/output operation problem.

Input/output statements in FORTRAN are primarily concerned with the transfer of data between storage locations in a FORTRAN program and records which are external to the program. On input, data is taken from a record and placed into storage locations that are not necessarily contiguous. On output, data is gathered from diverse storage locations and placed into a record. An input/output list containing variable names is used to specify which storage locations are used.

Input statements are used to read data into storage and output statements are used to print, punch, or otherwise output the results. There are three principal types of FORTRAN statements that are used for input/output operations—READ, WRITE, and FORMAT (which is actually a specification statement).

The general format of a READ statement is READ (A, B) list

A—symbolic number of an input device.

B—statement number of the FORMAT statement describing the records being read.

list—input/output list of variable names, separated by commas.

The input and output statements, each with its corresponding FORMAT statement, specify the number and sequence of the data input and output fields, the length of the data fields, and what mode they are in. For example:

```
  READ (1,4)K,M,A
4 FORMAT (I5,I4,F7.3)
```

The READ statement causes data to be read from the card reader (1) at object time and causes the quantities to become the values of the variables named in the list (K,M,A).

According to the FORMAT statement (4), the first variable in the card, K, has been assigned the format I5, which tells the processor that the first field in the card contains five columns and that the number is in the fixed-point mode.

The next variable M has been assigned the format of I4, which tells the processor that the next field is in the fixed-point mode and consists of four columns.

The floating-point variable A is read next according to F7.3. This format tells the processor that the value is to be a floating-point number and that the field contains seven digits and there will be three digits to the right of the decimal point.

The general format of a WRITE statement is WRITE (A,B) list

A—symbolic number of the output device.

B—statement number of the FORMAT statement describing the records being written.

list—optional, and is the input/output list of variable names, separated by commas.

For example:

```
   WRITE (3,15) A,B,J
15 FORMAT (F8.2,F8.3,I5)
```

This WRITE statement causes the printer (3) to print the information as follows.

1. The value of A as eight digits with two decimal positions.
2. The value of B as eight digits with three decimal positions.
3. The value of J as five digits with no decimal positions.

A WRITE statement may also be used without the list option. For example, to print the heading JOB ORDER LIST with three blank spaces on the left, the following FORTRAN statement may be written.

```
   WRITE (3,10)
10 FORMAT (3X,'JOB ORDER LIST')
```

Specification Statements

The specification statements provide the compiler with information about the nature of the data uses in the source program. In addition, they supply the information required to allocate locations in storage for this data. Specifications statements may appear anywhere in the program but must precede any statement that refers to them.

The FORMAT statement tells the FORTRAN processor the length of each input and output data field and whether the field is (or will be) in fixed-point or floating-point mode. The DIMENSION statement provides the processor with information necessary to allocate storage in the object program for arrays of quantities.

A DIMENSION or FORMAT statement is a nonexecutable statement inasmuch as neither one creates instructions in the object program but merely supplies information to the processor.

FORMAT

I FORMAT Code

The I FORMAT code is used in transmitting integer data. For example:

```
  READ (1,4) J
4 FORMAT (I5)
```

In this statement, for the variable J, an integer of five digits will be read (fig. 13.14).

Figure 13.14 Examples of the I FORMAT code.

Format Descriptor	Internal Value	Output (b indicates blanks)
I6	+281	bbb281
I6	−17631	−17631
I3	126	126
I3	−126	126
I3	46931	931

Format Descriptor	Input (b indicates blanks)	Internal Value
I4	b124	+124
I4	−124	−124
I7	bbb7631	7631
I6	−b1024	−1024
I5	−31024	−3102

Format Descriptor	Internal Value	Output (b indicates blanks)
F10.4	368.42	bb368.4200
F7.1	−4786.361	−4786.4
F8.4	.0375	bbb.0375
F6.4	4739.76	9.7600
F7.3	15.0	b15.000

Figure 13.15 Examples of the F FORMAT code.

Descriptor	Output (b = blanks)
1HR	R
8HbSTRINGb	bSTRINGb
12HXb(1,3) = 12.0	Xb(1,3) = 12.0

Format Descriptor	Input Characters	Resultant Descriptor
5H12345	ABCDE	5HABCDE
8HbFALSEbb	hFALSEbb	8HbFALSEbb
9Hbbbbbbbbb	bMATRIXbb	9HbMATRIXbb

(b = blanks)

Figure 13.16 Examples of the H FORMAT code.

F FORMAT Code

The F FORMAT code is used in transmitting floating-point (real) data. For example:

```
  READ (1,4) A
4 FORMAT (F5.3)
```

In this statement, for the variable A, a floating-point number of five digits with three decimal positions will be read (fig. 13.15).

H FORMAT Code

If thc H FORMAT code is used, the literal data following the H is printed according to the number specified before the H. For example:

```
   WRITE (3,25)
25 FORMAT (20H THIS IS MY REPORT)
```

In this statement, twenty characters will be printed including the three blanks preceding the word THIS (fig. 13.16).

T FORMAT Code

The T FORMAT code specifies the position in the FORTRAN record where the transfer of data is to begin. For example:

```
   WRITE (3,25)
25 FORMAT (T4, 'THIS IS MY REPORT')
```

Figure 13.17
Examples of the T FORMAT code.

Output Example:

14 FORMAT (T21, 'STRESS ANALYSIS',T1, 'REPORT 1', T45 'SEPT. '78)

This FORMAT statement would produce the following printed line:

REPORT 1	STRESS ANALYSIS	SEPT. '78
Print Position 1	Print Position 21	Print Position 45

Input Example:

The statement

9 FORMAT (T18,I6)

when used for input, would cause the first 17 characters of input data to be skipped and the next 10 characters to be read according to the format specification I6.

In this statement, the heading THIS IS MY REPORT will print starting in the third printing position as the first print position is reserved for carriage control (fig. 13.17).

X FORMAT Code

The X FORMAT code specifies a field of characters to be skipped on input or filled with blanks on output. For example:

```
  READ (1,5) I,J,K,L,M
5 FORMAT (I10,10X,4I10)
```

This causes the first ten characters of the input record to be read into variable I, the next ten characters are to be skipped without transmission and the next four fields (the 4 before I indicates the number of repetitions of the field in the same form) to be read into variables, J,K,L, and M (fig. 13.18).

DIMENSION

The DIMENSION statement is used to set aside arrays of data into storage locations. For example:

```
DIMENSION JOBS (12)
```

In this statement, the compiler will set aside four contiguous storage locations for the variable JOBS (fig. 13.19).

Subprograms

It is sometimes desirable to write a program which, at various points, requires the same computations to be performed with different data for each calculation. It would simplify the writing of that program if the statements required to perform the desired

Output Example:

If the variable ZAP contains 5.3 and the variable ZIP contains 7.6328, the statements

```
      WRITE (1,14) ZAP,ZIP
   14 FORMAT (F4.2,3X,F6.4)
```

would output the record

5.30bbb7.6328

Input Example:

If an external record contained

12.5ABC120

and the following statements are executed

```
      READ (1,23) ZIP,ZAP
   23 FORMAT(F4.1,3X,F3.0)
```

the variable ZAP will contain 12.5 and ZIP will contain 120. ABC is skipped.

Figure 13.18 Examples of the X FORMAT code.

computations could be written only once and then could be referred to freely, with each subsequent reference having the same effect as an instruction written at the point in the program where the reference was made.

```
C FOR COMMENT
STATEMENT NUMBER | Cont. | FORTRAN STATEMENT
      DIMENSION ABAR(20), ZAP(3,3)
```

This statement declares two arrays:

a. The 1-dimensional array of 20 elements named ABAR. The array elements are thus named as ABAR(1), ABAR(2), . . ., ABAR(20).
b. The 2-dimensional array of 9 elements named ZAP. The array elements are ZAP(1,1), ZAP(2,1), ZAP(3,1), ZAP(1,2), ZAP(2,2), ZAP(3,2), ZAP(1,3), ZAP(2,3), ZAP(3,3).

Figure 13.19 An example of a DIMENSION table.

```
C FOR COMMENT
STATEMENT NUMBER | Cont. | FORTRAN STATEMENT
C ROUTINE TO CALCULATE FACTORIALS
C                                           *****
      INTEGER FACTOR, K
      K =1
      READ (1,5), FACTOR
 10   IF (FACTOR) 12,13,11
   11 K = K * FACTOR
      FACTOR =
     C                 FACTOR - 1
       GO TO 10
   12    K = 0
13    WRITE (108,6), K
      STOP
    5 FORMAT (I6)
  6   FORMAT (1X,I6)
      END
```

Figure 13.20 A sample program.

For example, if a general program were written to take the cube root of any number, it would be desirable to be able to combine that program (or subprogram) with other programs in which cube root calculations are required.

The FORTRAN language provides for this situation through the use of subprograms. The discussion of subprograms in FORTRAN is beyond the scope of this book. If you desire more information relative to the use and writing of FORTRAN subprograms, refer to your computer manufacturer's reference manuals for more information (figs. 13.20, 13.21, 13.22, 13.23).

Figure 13.20
Continued.

Line	Meaning
1,2	The character C in column 1 defines these lines as comments. (An asterisk in column 1 would also denote a comment line.)
3	A nonexecutable statement that defines to the compiler the variables FACTOR and K as integers.
4	An assignment statement that sets K equal to 1.
5	An input command that causes the value of FACTOR to be read into storage. The value is read from unit 1. The form in which the value of FACTOR appears external to the computer is specified by FORMAT 5 (line 14).
6	Statement 10 tests the value of FACTOR and transfers control to statement 11, 12, or 13 as follows: If FACTOR <0, control is transferred to statement 12. If FACTOR >0, control is transferred to statement 11. If FACTOR $=0$, control is transferred to statement 13.
7	Statement 11 is another assignment statement that assigns to K the value of the expression K times factor. In other words, the current value of K is replaced by the current value of K multiplied by the value of FACTOR.
8	The statement appearing on lines 8 and 9 is an assignment statement, written as an initial line and one continuation line.
9	The C in column 6 causes line 9 to be a continuation of line 8. This statement assigns to FACTOR the value of the current value of FACTOR minus 1.
10	When the GO TO statement is executed, an unconditional transfer of control to statement 10 (line 6) occurs.
11	Statement 12, an assignment statement, assigns the value zero to the variable K.
12	The WRITE output statement, 13, causes the name of the variable K and its value to be written out on unit 108, which is normally assigned to the printer (see statement 6, line 15 for designated FORMAT statement).
13	The control statement STOP causes execution of the program to be terminated.
14	FORMAT statement corresponding to READ statement on line 5.
15	FORMAT statement corresponding to WRITE statement on line 12.
16	The END line informs the processor during compilation that it has reached the physical end of the source program.
	In this program, if the value of FACTOR is initially 3 as read by line 5, statement 10 will be executed four times, the statements on line 7 through 10 will be executed three times, and the statements on lines 4, 5, 12, and 13 will be executed once each.

```
C       STOCK-TURNOVER RATE
      1 FORMAT (I2,F8.2)
      2 FORMAT (F8.2)
      3 FORMAT (22HTOTAL RETAIL SALES FOR I3,10H PERIODS =F9.2)
      4 FORMAT (30HAVERAGE RETAIL STOCK VALUE FORI3,10H PERIODS =F9.2/)
      5 FORMAT (26HRATE OF STOCK-TURNOVER FOR I3,10H PERIODS -F5.1)
        TVAL = 0.0
        READ (5,1) N,S
        DO 10 J=1,N
        READ (5,2) VALUE
        TVAL = TVAL +VALUE
     10 CONTINUE
        FN =N
        A= TVAL/FN
        R= S/A
        WRITE (6,3) N,S
        WRITE (6,4) N,A
        WRITE (6,5) N,R
        STOP
        END
```

Input Data Listing

```
1372462.00
10000.00
12000.00
14000.00
14000.00
13000.00
09000.00
08000.00
10000.00
13000.00
16000.00
16000.00
13000.00
11000.00
```

Computer Output

```
TOTAL RETAIL SALES FOR 13 PERIODS = 72462.00
AVERAGE RETAIL STOCK VALUE FOR 13 PERIODS = 12230.76

RATE OF STOCK=TURNOVER FOR 13 PERIODS = 5.9
STOP
```

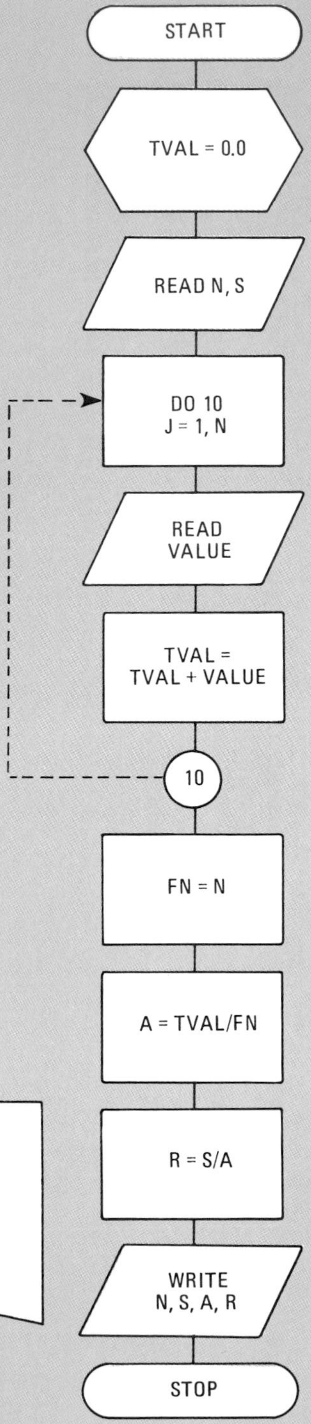

Figure 13.21 Illustrative problem 1.

C   DAILY CASH REPORT

```
C       DAILY CASH REPORT
     10 FORMAT (5F8.2)
        FUND = 40000.00
        READ (5,10) RMORT,RSAV,COUT,CHAND,CHECK
        RTOT =FUND +RMORT +RSAV
        OTOT =CHAND +CHECK +COUT
        RECON =OTOT - RTOT
        IF (CHAND-FUND) 11,12,12
     11 REIMB =FUND - CHAND
        DEPOS =CHECK
        GO TO 13
     12 REIMB =0.0
        DEPOS =CHECK +(CHAND - FUND)
     13 WRITE (6,14) RECON
     14 FORMAT (F10.2,26H OVERAGE(+) OR SHORTAGE(-))
        WRITE (6,15) CHAND,CHECK
     15 FORMAT (F10.2,13H CASH ON HAND,F10.2,15H CHECKS ON HAND)
        WRITE (6,16) REIMB,DEPOS
     16 FORMAT (F10.2,19H TO REIMBURSE FUND,F10.2,12H FOR DEPOSIT)
        STOP
        END
```

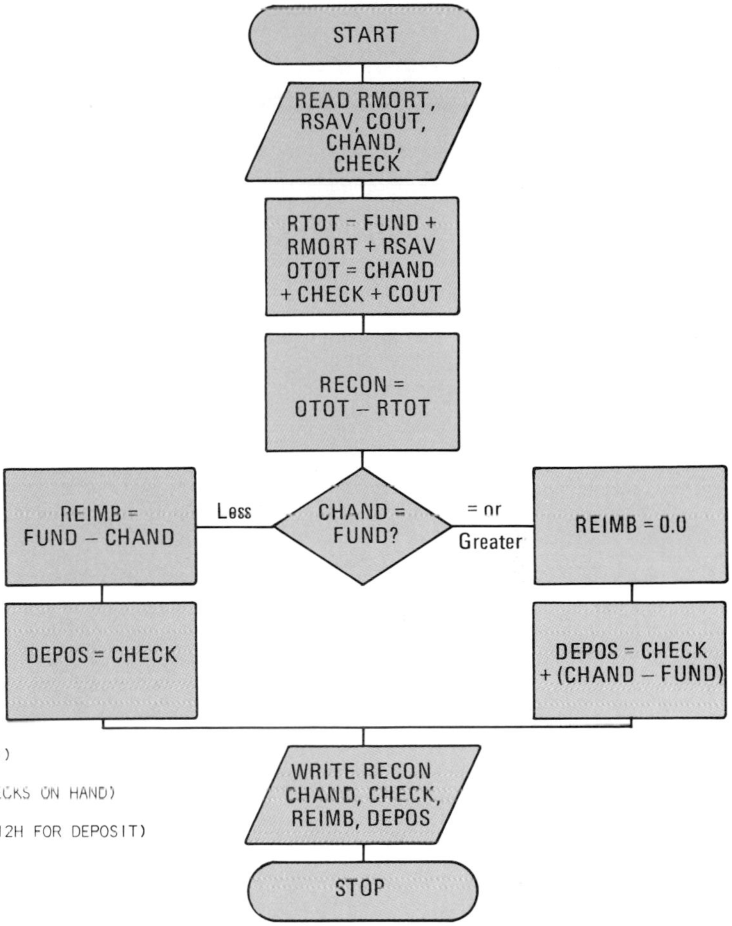

Input Data Listing

```
15000.0008050.0005000.0035000.0023000.00
```

Computer Output

```
      -50.00 OVERAGE (+) OR SHORTAGE (-)
    35000.00 CASH ON HAND,    23000.00 CHECKS ON HAND
     5000.00 TO REIMBURSE FUND,    23000.00 FOR DEPOSIT
STOP
```

Figure 13.22 Illustrative problem 2.

```
C                 ----COMPOUND INTEREST WITH
C      VARYING INITIAL PERIODS AND PERIOD INCREMENTS
       DIMENSION A(25,8),RATE(8)
       READ (5,100) NI,NL,NINC,CON,RINC,NRATE,P
       DO 50 KRATE=1,NRATE
       ZRATE=KRATE
       RATE(KRATE) =CON +ZRATE*RINC
       DO 50 N =NI,NL,NINC
       J =(N-NI)/NINC +1
       A(J,KRATE) =P*(1. +RATE(KRATE))**N
   50  CONTINUE
       WRITE (6,200) P
       WRITE (6,201)
       WRITE (6,202) (RATE(KRATE),KRATE=1,NRATE)
       DO 75 N=NI,NL,NINC
       J =(N-NI)/NINC +1
   75  WRITE (6,203) N, (A(J,KRATE),KRATE=1,NRATE)
       STOP
  100  FORMAT (3I2,2F4.2,I2,F8.2)
  200  FORMAT (13X,34HCOMPOUND INTEREST TABLE PAYMENT -F8.2/)
  201  FORMAT (25X,13HINTEREST RATE)
  202  FORMAT (6HPERIOD,8X,8(F4.2,5X)/)
  203  FORMAT (2X,I2,6X,8F9.2)
       END
```

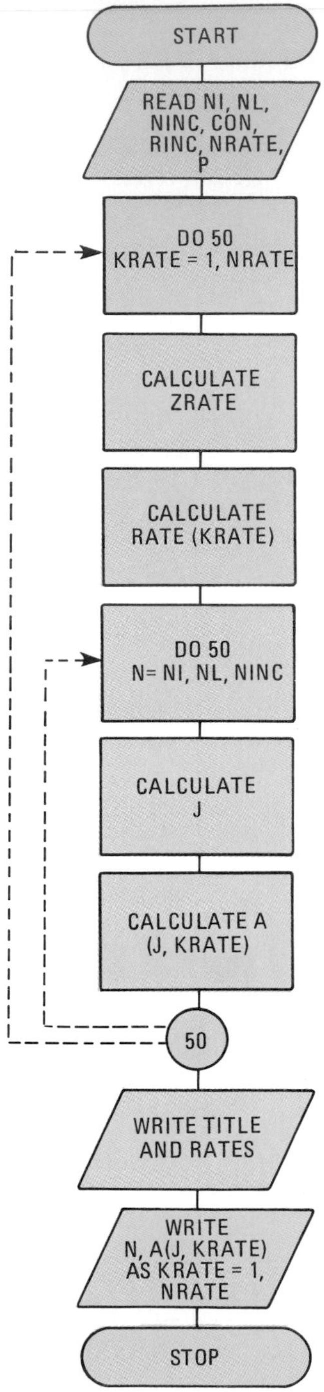

Input Data Listing

```
1050050.000.010600100.00
```

Computer Output

```
              COMPOUND INTEREST TABLE  PAYMENT =  100.00

                          INTEREST RATE
PERIOD        .01      .02      .03      .04      .05      .06
  10       110.46   121.89   134.39   148.02   162.88   179.08
  15       116.09   134.58   155.79   180.09   207.89   239.65
  20       122.01   148.59   180.61   219.11   265.32   320.71
  25       128.24   164.06   209.37   266.58   338.63   429.18
  30       134.78   181.13   242.72   324.33   432.19   574.34
  35       141.66   199.98   281.38   394.60   551.60   768.60
  40       148.88   220.80   326.20   480.10   703.99  1028.57
  45       156.48   243.78   378.15   584.11   898.50  1376.46
  50       164.46   269.15   438.39   710.66  1146.73  1842.01
STOP
```

Figure 13.23 Illustrative problem 3.

Summary

FORTRAN (*FOR*mula *TRAN*slator) is a procedure-oriented programming language designed primarily for writing programs to solve scientific and engineering problems involving mathematical computations. It uses English-like statements plus operators in a formula type method of instructions. This chapter introduces the most widely used scientific programming language, FORTRAN.

1. Statements are sentences of FORTRAN consisting of keywords that are used in conjunction with certain basic elements of the language that define the operations to be performed. The types of statements are arithmetic, control, specification, and character set statements.
2. Coding forms are used as a guide when preparing a source program. Each line of the form represents an 80-column card. A *C* in the first column indicates that a comment is to be written. Comments are notes that help to clarify some of the meanings of statements and improve the readability. Columns 1–5 display the statement number, which may consist of one to five digits and serve as labels to be referred to by other statements. Column 6 is the continuation indicator, which indicates the continuation of a statement from the previous line. The FORTRAN statement is written in columns 7–72. Columns 73–80 are used for identification or sequence control of cards.
3. Constants are the fixed value that is used without change from one execution of the program to another. An integer constant is a whole number without a decimal point. A real constant is a string of decimal digits with a decimal point. A literal constant is a string of alphameric and/or special characters enclosed in apostrophes used to denote headings or messages.
4. Variables are the quantity that may change many times during the execution of a program. Variable names consist of 1–6 alphameric characters assigned to the type of data that the variable represents. A real variable begins with the letters A through H and/or O through Z. The data must be in the real mode. An integer variable begins with the letters I through N. The data must be in the integer mode.
5. An expression is a series of constants and/or variables separated by operators and as a whole forms a mathematical expression.
6. Arithmetic statements specify mathematical calculations to be performed on the data. The equal sign means "to be replaced by" rather than "is equivalent to."
7. Control statements control the sequence of program instruction execution. The types of control statements are GO TO, IF, DO, CONTINUE, PAUSE, STOP, and END.
8. Input and output statements are used to read in data and output results. The READ statement causes data to be read into the computer. The WRITE statement causes data to become output from the computer.
9. Specification statements provide information to the computer regarding the nature of the data. The two types of specification statements are FORMAT and DIMENSION.
10. Subprograms enable the user to name and define functions and subroutines, which can be compiled separately or with the main program.

Identification Questions

Match the following terms with the statements below.

A. Arithmetic Statements
B. Constant
C. CONTINUE Statement
D. Control Statements
E. DIMENSION Statement
F. DO Statement
G. END Statement
H. Expression
I. FORMAT Statement
J. FORTRAN
K. GO TO Statement
L. IF Statement
M. Input/Output Statements
N. Integer Constant
O. Integer Variable Name
P. Literal Constant
Q. Logical Operators
R. PAUSE Statement
S. READ Statement
T. Real Constant
U. Real Variable Name
V. Relational Operators
W. Specification Statements
X. Statements
Y. STOP Statement
Z. Subprogram Statements
AA. Subprograms
BB. Variable
CC. WRITE Statement

1. A fixed unvarying quantity that is used without change from one execution of the program to another.
2. Statements that specify the mathematical calculations to be performed.
3. A variable name that begins with the letter I through N.
4. This statement permits transfer of control if certain conditions are satisfied.
5. These operators are used to determine whether the expression is true or false.
6. A statement that causes temporary cessation of a program execution and displays a message.
7. This statement causes data to be transferred from the record to internal storage.
8. Specific routines and programs that perform a function in the main program.
9. A procedure-oriented programming language designed primarily for writing programs to solve scientific and engineering problems.
10. A whole number constant without a decimal point.
11. A dummy statement which may be placed anywhere in a source program without affecting the sequence execution.
12. Statements that read data into the computer and put out results.
13. This statement causes data to be transferred from internal storage to output.
14. A constant string of alphameric characters enclosed in apostrophes.
15. A variable name that begins with the letters A through H and/or O through Z.
16. A statement that consists of constants and variables and forms a mathematical expression.
17. A statement that specifies the kind of input or output data.
18. Individual commands of the programmer.
19. Statements that specify to the processor the length and mode of input/output data.
20. A quantity that varies in value for different executions of the program.
21. These operators are used in compare operations.

22. This statement provides a method for controlled, repetitive execution of a series of statements.
23. This statement causes program execution to be terminated.
24. Statements that determine the sequence in which the statements will follow.
25. A constant string of decimal digits with a decimal point.
26. A statement that provides the processor with information to allocate storage areas for arrays.
27. Statements that enable the user to name and define functions and subroutines, which can be compiled separately or with the main program.
28. A statement that permits transfer of control conditionally or unconditionally to another statement.
29. A nonexecutable statement that defines the end of a source program.

Questions for Review

1. What is the importance of FORTRAN as a programming language?
2. Describe the different types of FORTRAN statements with their main functions.
3. What is the FORTRAN character set composed of?
4. What is the main purpose of a FORTRAN coding form?
5. What are the different fields of a FORTRAN coding form used for?
6. Briefly explain the following FORTRAN terms and give examples of each: Constant, Variable, Expression.
7. Explain how mathematical calculations are performed in FORTRAN. Give an example.
8. What is the purpose of control statements?
9. Differentiate between the GO TO and IF statement. Give examples of each.
10. What functions do relational and logical operators perform?
11. What function does a DO statement perform and how does it perform this function?
12. Briefly describe the following statements: CONTINUE, PAUSE, STOP, END.
13. What is the main function of input/output statements?
14. What are the primary functions of the READ and WRITE statements? Give examples.
15. Differentiate between the FORMAT and DIMENSION statements.
16. What is the purpose of subprograms?

Key Terms

Arithmetic Statements
Constant
CONTINUE Statement
Control Statements
DIMENSION Statement
DO Statement
END Statement
Expression
FORMAT Statements
FORTRAN
GO TO Statements
IF Statements
Input/Output Statements
Integer Constant
Integer Variable Name
Literal Constant
Logical Operators
PAUSE Statement
READ Statement
Real Constant
Real Variable Name
Relational Operators
Specification Statements
Statements
STOP Statement
Subprogram Statements
Subprograms
Variable
WRITE Statement

part 5

real-time processing and time sharing

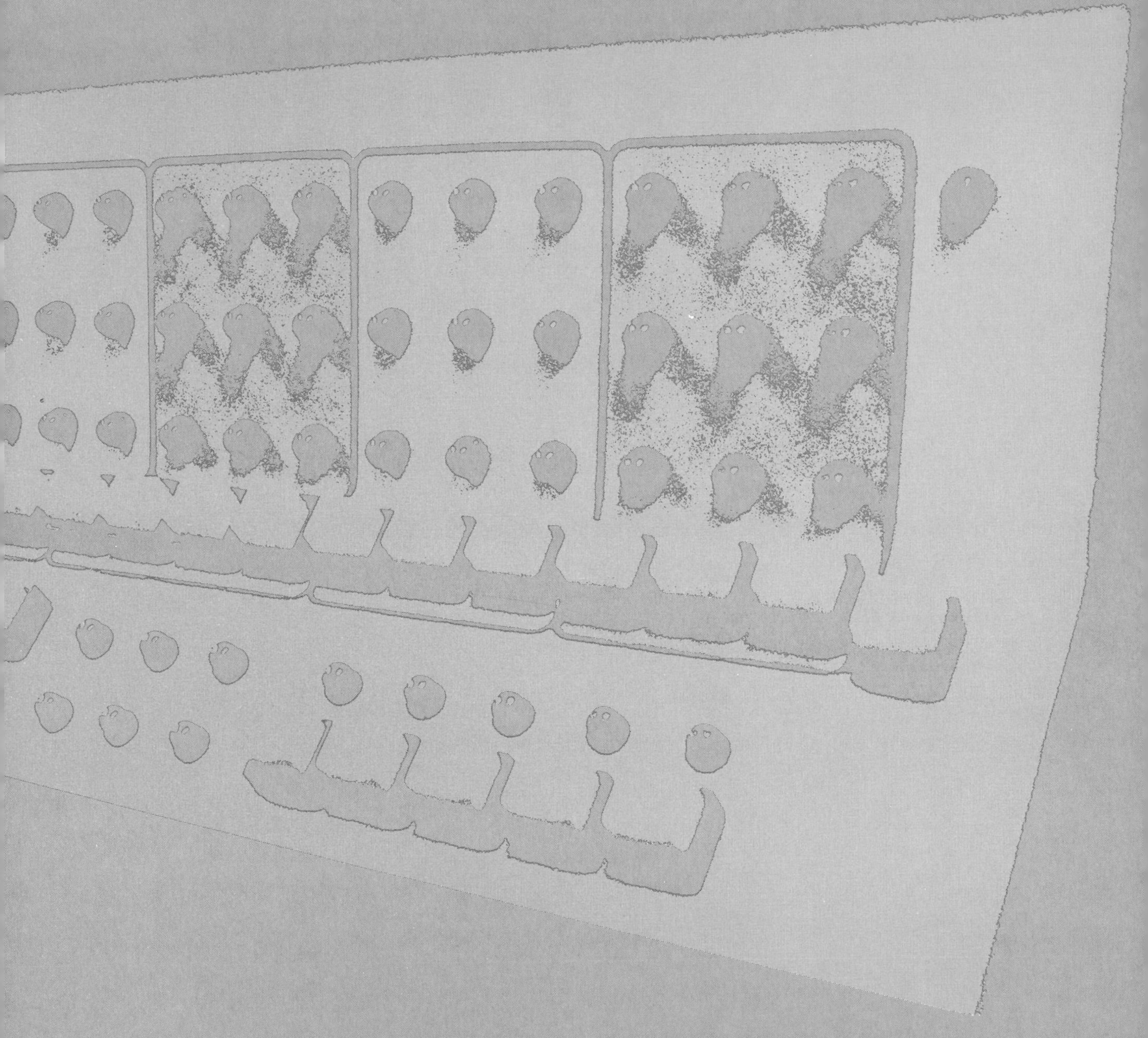

introduction to real-time processing and time sharing 14

Chapter Outline

Chapter Objectives

The learning objectives of this chapter are

1. to introduce and explain the ever-changing features of time sharing with online real-time processing, which is the fastest growing segment of data processing.

2. to present the important features of data communications, data base management, and distributed data processing, which are vital parts of online systems.
3. to present the segments of time sharing that allows many people at remote locations to share the facilities of a computer, thus eliminating many delays in processing information to and from a data-processing system.
4. to draw attention to the protection of personal privacy of individuals due to increased use of computerized data files or personal record files.

One of the most inconvenient restrictions to the user of a computer system is having to wait for critical reports while the computer is busy. Many users want facilities that are available for the execution of critical programs at any time. They are particularly interested in putting urgent inquiries to the information stored in the computer without being forced to abort the job on hand. In many companies, these requests for information originate at remote inquiring locations, a great distance from the central data-processing system. This means that the information must be transmitted back and forth over various communication networks. In order to accommodate these needs, data has to be collected at widely dispersed points and transmitted to the central computer with ever-increasing speed. In addition, these remote inquiry stations must have access to the files sorted in the central system.

Real-Time Processing

Real-time processing has developed into an activity that eliminates many delays in processing information to and from a data-processing system. *Real time is the ability of the system to provide the necessary data for a decision at such a time and in such a manner as is optimum for the needs of management.* This does not infer the instantaneous delivery of all information within a company, which would be neither economical or practical.

The remote terminal unit can accept and transmit data to the system, thus providing *online* operation for the system. This online function allows more than one unit to share the communication line to the computer (fig. 14.1).

Online real-time computer systems provide instant communication between a central computer and thousands of remote points. An airline reservation clerk, for example, can press a few buttons to request a reservation on a certain flight for a certain day. In seconds, a central computer thousands of miles away can check reservations for that flight made by all the airline's ticket offices around the country, establish the availability of the space requested, and flash back an answer. The reservations clerk then keys in the information needed to make the reservation and the central computer updates the records instantly.

Online real-time systems are adaptable to a wide variety of business applications. Steel companies are now processing orders, inventories, and other time-critical information with real-time computers. Tellers at savings banks now can give depositors their up-to-minute balance and accrued interest without hand-searching a file, seconds after they approach the window. A manufacturer of appliances links 300 remote

Car-Pooling Example:

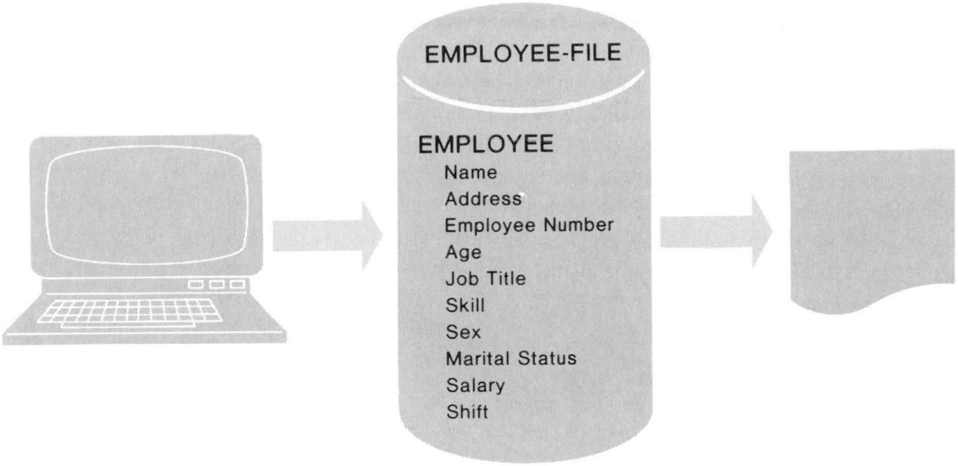

Figure 14.1 An example of an online operation.

terminals to a real-time system to speed order handling and reduce costly inventory levels. A large insurance company connects all agents and branches throughout the country to the home office. In effect, this makes the company's huge central policy file directly available to the most remote locations.

With fast, flexible data communications systems like these, we are beginning to eliminate the problems of time and distance which, until now, have limited many computer applications (figs. 14.2, 14.3).

Data Communications

Introduction

Management of today's complex and diversified businesses must have up-to-date knowledge of their geographically scattered operations in order to serve their customers and to maintain close surveillance over critical activities. This calls for rapid collection, processing, and subsequent use of business information.

Information is valueless unless you get it to where it's needed, and where it's needed is probably far from where it originates. A production schedule in Detroit may depend on inventory data in Denver; a bookkeeping balance in New York is based on figures collected daily from dozens of widely scattered plant locations.

In order to move data around the country at speeds that bear some relation to the speed with which it can be processed, computers are learning to use the telephone (fig. 14.4). Computer information can now be transmitted over regular telephone lines almost as easily as it can be transferred from one computer to another in the same room.

Data communications is designed to fulfill the requirements for the rapid transmission of information. Almost any transmission of data may be thought of as data communications. The term is usually limited to one particular area of technology. In this sense, a data communication system must have two characteristics—the information is transferred into a special code for transmission and the translated code is

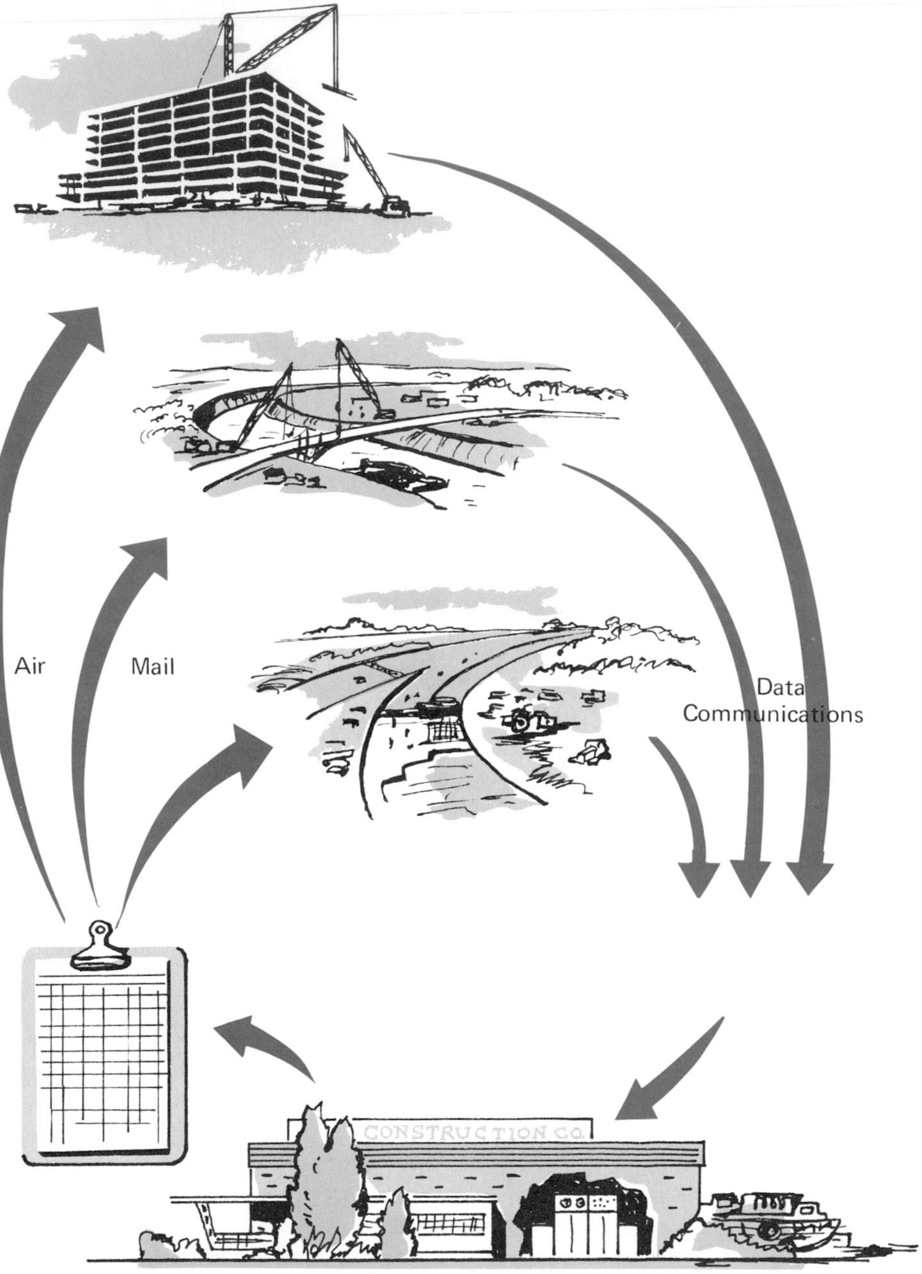

Figure 14.2 An example of real-time processing.

transmitted by electronic means. *Data communications may be defined as the movement of information by means of electronic transmission.* The transmission system includes input and output devices, the electronic and electrical transmission links, and the related circuit switching systems. A data communication system is used to transmit information almost instantaneously over considerable distances for various purposes.

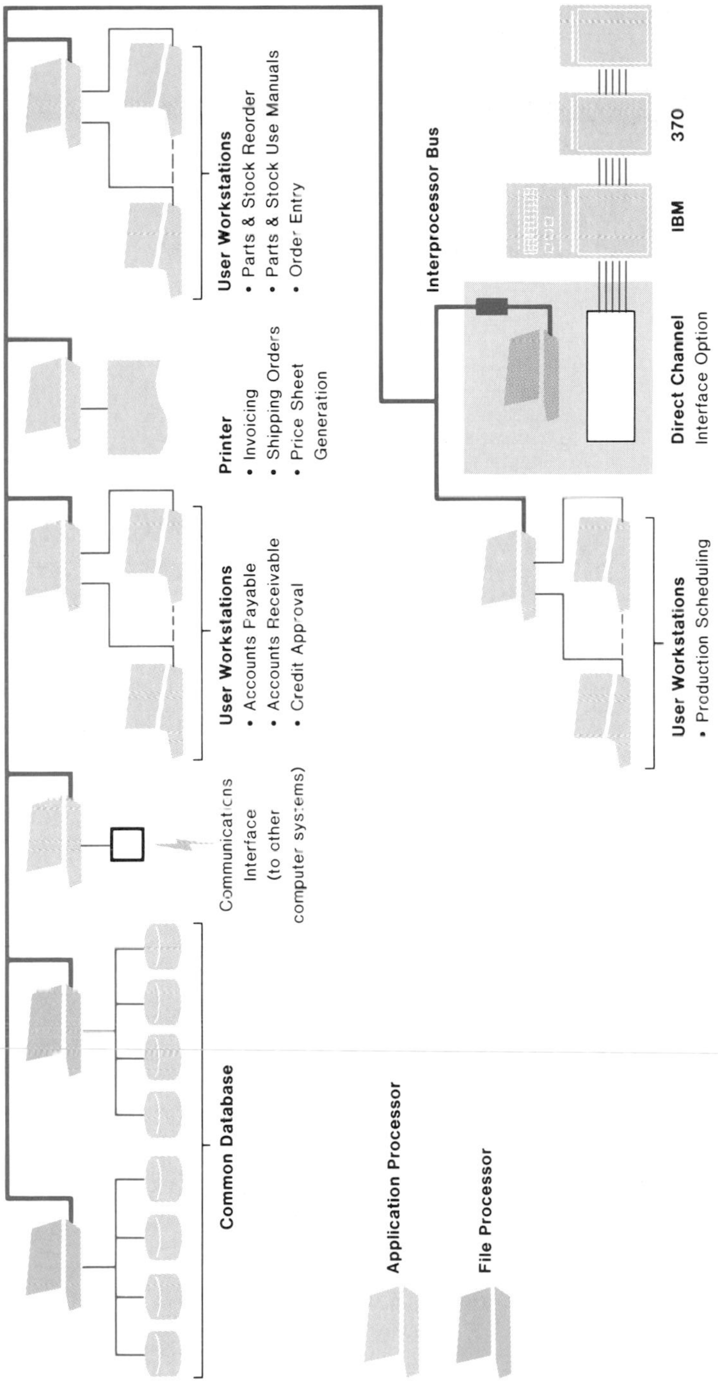

Figure 14.3 An example of a large-scale real-time system. (Copyright *Data Management* magazine, Data Processing Management Association.)

Figure 14.4 An example of a multidrop data communications network. (Copyright *Data Management* magazine, Data Processing Management Association.)

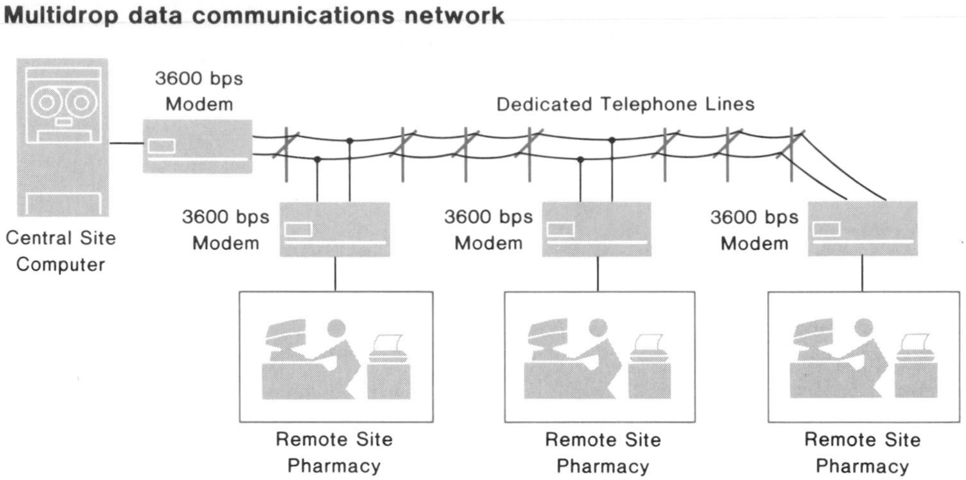

Telecommunications

An important segment of data communications is telecommunications. The developing relationship between the computer and telecommunications technology is possibly the most important event of our times. By themselves, the telecommunications or the computer industry were capable of bringing about major changes in business, government, and our whole way of life. But the two technologies complement each other; in combination their power is increased tremendously. Computers will control the immense communication switching centers and assist in managing the enormous capacity of the new linkages into usable channels; telecommunications in return will make available the power of computers and the information in the data bases to millions of users at remote locations (fig. 14.5).

Nearly all people in the computer field need to have a broad understanding of telecommunications or we will face the specter of creating poorly designed, inefficient systems.

Communication Networks

Telecommunications is grouped in clusters to form communication networks. A computer network is a very cost-effective way to distribute high-speed computing services to a large number of users. Networks are logical extensions of regional computer centers.

Teleprocessing networks comprise a vast and growing array of machines, in addition to computers, which can be attached to telecommunication lines for transmitting and receiving data.

Global networks provide electronic message and circuit switching services to an exponentially expanding cycle of users and yet, this is only the beginning; the real impact of electronic systems upon society and its structure will make itself felt for decades. International information and data bases, for example, will make computer power available to the public in the same way that electronic or other utilities service

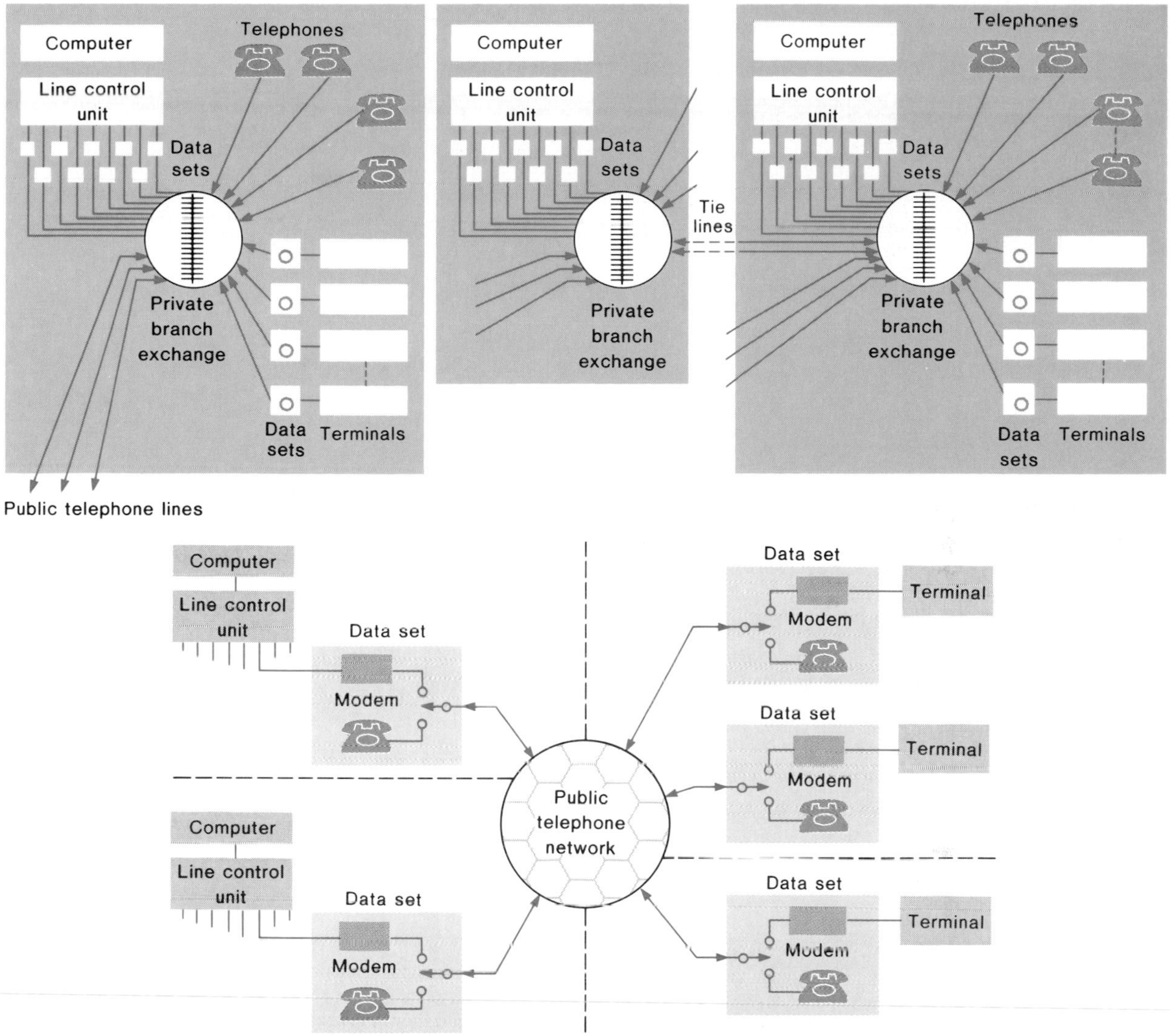

Figure 14.5 An example of telecommunications. (Copyright *Data Management* magazine, Data Processing Management Association.)

our homes and offices. High-speed communication systems, on a global basis, will transmit data and messages almost instantaneously between any two points on earth or of colonized space.

Specialized networks, such as airline reservation systems, are designed optimally around central applications. Many computer manufacturers provide communication network systems that can be adapted to the user's particular needs.

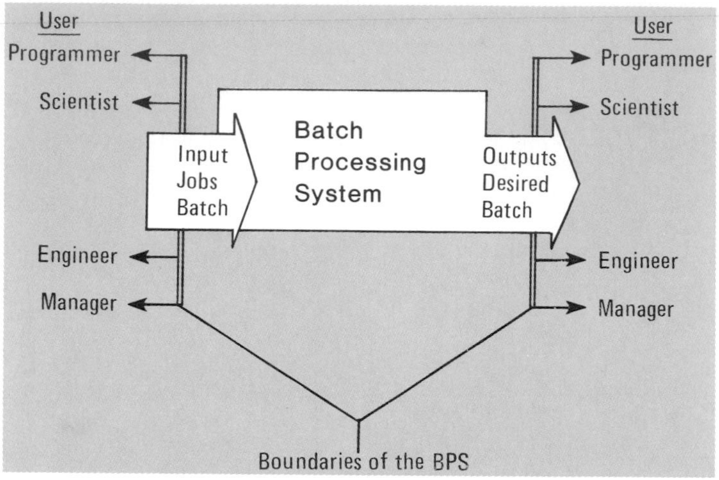

Figure 14.6 The batch processing system.

Conclusion

The cost of communications will be reduced significantly. We are moving from an era when Ma Bell's voice-oriented telephone system was adapted for transmission of digital data to a situation in which there are specialized carriers whose equipment and rates are designed specifically for digital data communications with its inherent requirements for availability, speed, and accuracy. There are new concepts of sending packets of information. The advent of competition among carriers of information for this attractive business is bound to reduce communication costs.

Huge networks are being undertaken by many leading computer manufacturers. These network control systems will reduce communication line costs significantly and provide for greater flexibility in routing traffic from the user to the proper computer which has the capability to meet the user's application needs. In addition, network control will significantly reduce the number of terminals needed to obtain access to the various processors.

Terms Used in Modes of Processing

Batch Processing (1) Pertaining to the technique of executing a set of computer programs so that each is completed before the next program of the set is started. (2) Pertaining to the sequential input of computer programs or data. (3) Loosely, the execution of computer programs serially (fig. 14.6).

Data Base A collection of data fundamental to an enterprise (fig. 14.7).

Data Communication The transmission and reception of data, often including such operations as coding, decoding, and validation.

Online (1) Pertaining to equipment or devices under control of the central processing unit. (2) Pertaining to a user's ability to interact with a computer.

Online System A system in which the input data enters the computer directly from the point of origin or in which output data is transmitted directly to where it is used (fig. 14.8).

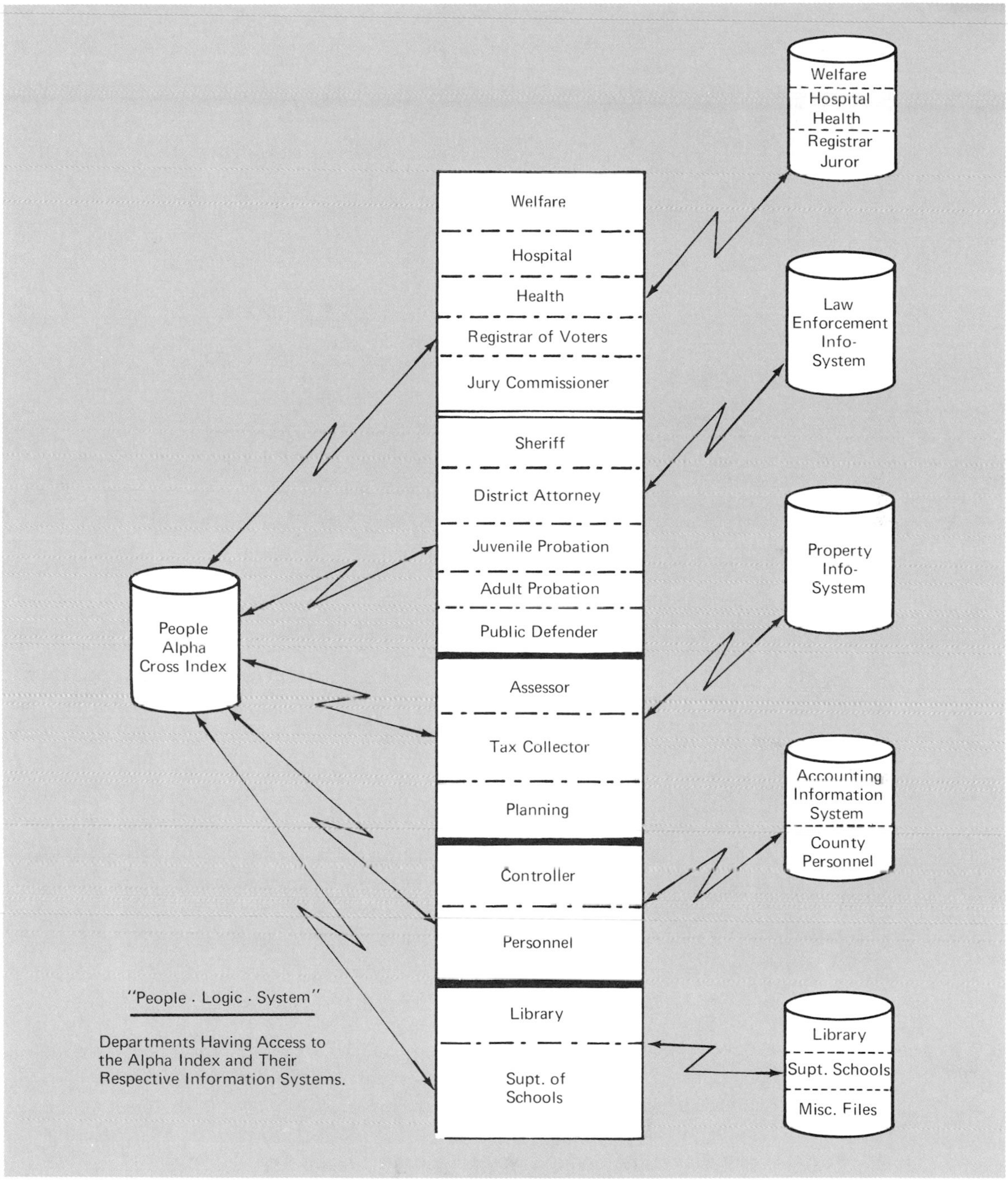

Figure 14.7 A data bank for cities and counties.

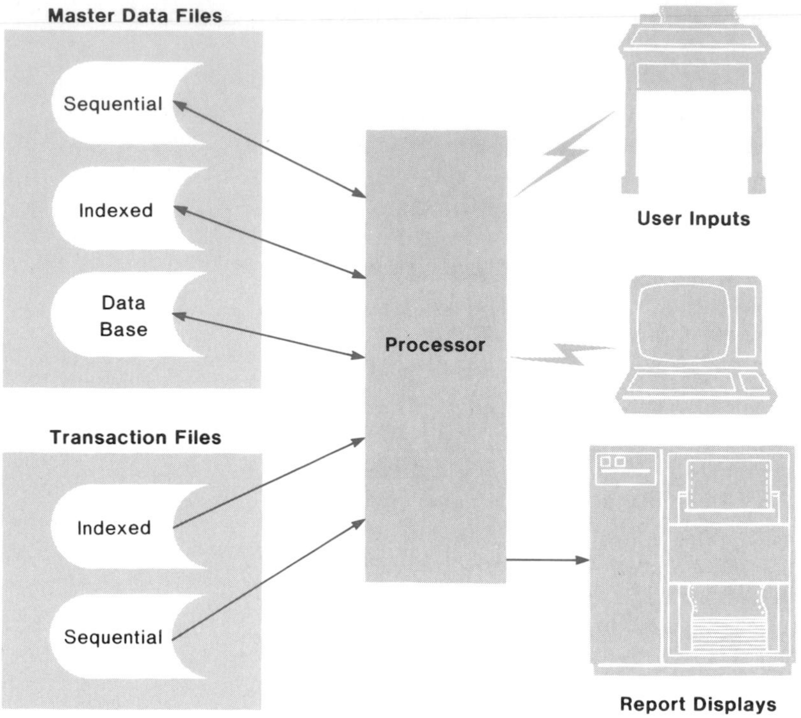

Figure 14.8 An example of an online system.

Real Time (1) Pertaining to the actual time during which a physical process transpires. (2) Pertaining to the performance of a computation during the actual time that the related physical process transpires so that results of the computation can be used in guiding the physical process. (3) Pertaining to an application in which response to input is fast enough to affect subsequent input, such as a process control system or a computer-assisted instruction system. It provides an almost immediate response.

Time Sharing (1) Pertaining to the interleaved use of the time of a device. (2) A method of using a computing system that allows a number of users to execute programs concurrently and to interact with the programs during execution. It gives the illusion that you are the only person using the system, when in reality several people are using the system simultaneously.

Online Processing

A major development in the computer field in the 1970s is the movement from offline to online systems. It is estimated that 70 percent of all data-processing installations will be connected to some type of communication facility by the 1980s. The technology to build online processing systems has been available for many years. Many companies have built and have used online systems for quite some time.

On the surface, online processing does not appear complicated. All that has to be done is to input some information or message from a terminal, get it to the right application program, and process it. Any desired response should be returned to the terminal. However, there is good deal more to most online systems than this simplistic notion presents.

Problems

Perhaps the most critical aspect of an online system is the response time. Most online systems interact directly with people. It is no longer acceptable to wait minutes or hours for turnaround.

Another problem is that the input to an online system is unfiltered. This means that any message could be erroneous. Since an online system serving many terminals simultaneously must not be susceptible to termination by such unfiltered input, much more programming must be done to examine the incoming data.

The element of surprise is another problem. All messages are a surprise to the system. The online system must be able to handle any mix of requests in whatever form.

Rescheduling peak loads is another problem. Since the online system programs are servicing many people who need the information quickly, it is not in a position to reschedule these requests.

Varying conditions can also be a problem. In an online system, if a resource becomes unavailable or a programming problem is detected, these varying conditions cannot be allowed to halt operation. Online systems become the mechanism by which the daily work of the organization is processed; if the online system does not run, the business does not function.

The final general problem is error detection and re-creation. The initial reaction is often why re-create an error? If you are going to diagnose and correct a problem to insure that the situation will not occur again as the environment changes, you must be able to re-create any error as quickly and precisely as possible. In any online system, the occurrences (in a given time frame) that cause the error may be transient (such as line errors) or time dependent (such as current updates). As a consequence, virtually all online systems fail to achieve the "bug-free" reliability. Since online systems are so susceptible to these types of problems, an integral part of the system must be recovery, which will allow the system to continue the execution of the program.

Online Real-Time Systems

An online real-time system is composed of one or more computers and other devices that control or monitor the environment by receiving and processing data and outputting the results in sufficient time to affect the function of the environment at that time. A short response time from the computer is necessary for the system to be effective. The speed of the response may vary according to the type of system and the needs of the user.

Online real-time systems range from very small computers with relatively simple programs to the largest and most expensive multi-computer systems (fig. 14.9). Regardless of the system involved, the major components are:

1. The *computer*—accepts the data, applies the prescribed processes to the data, and furnishes the results in the desired format to its user.
2. The *data base*—the random access files containing large quantities of information that provide the necessary information for processing (fig. 14.10).
3. The *terminals*—are attached to the communications network and provide the necessary input and output facilities.

Figure 14.9 Real-time data gathering and processing.

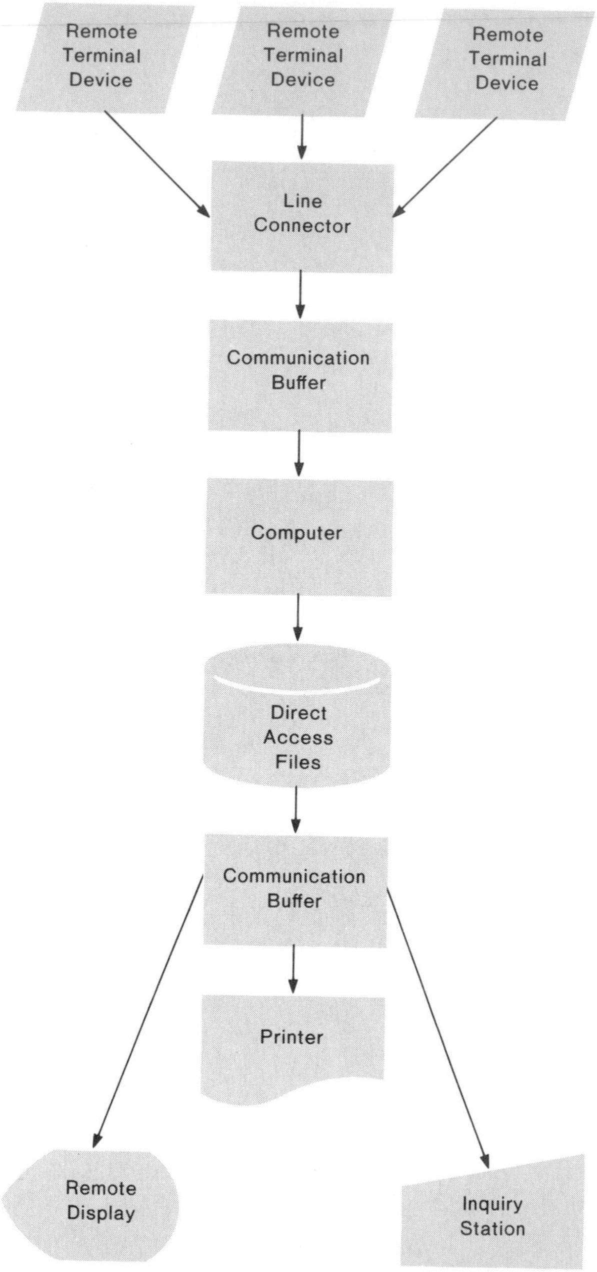

4. The *communication network*—links the remote terminals with the central processing unit.
5. The *software*—the necessary collection of the programs and routines to operate the system.

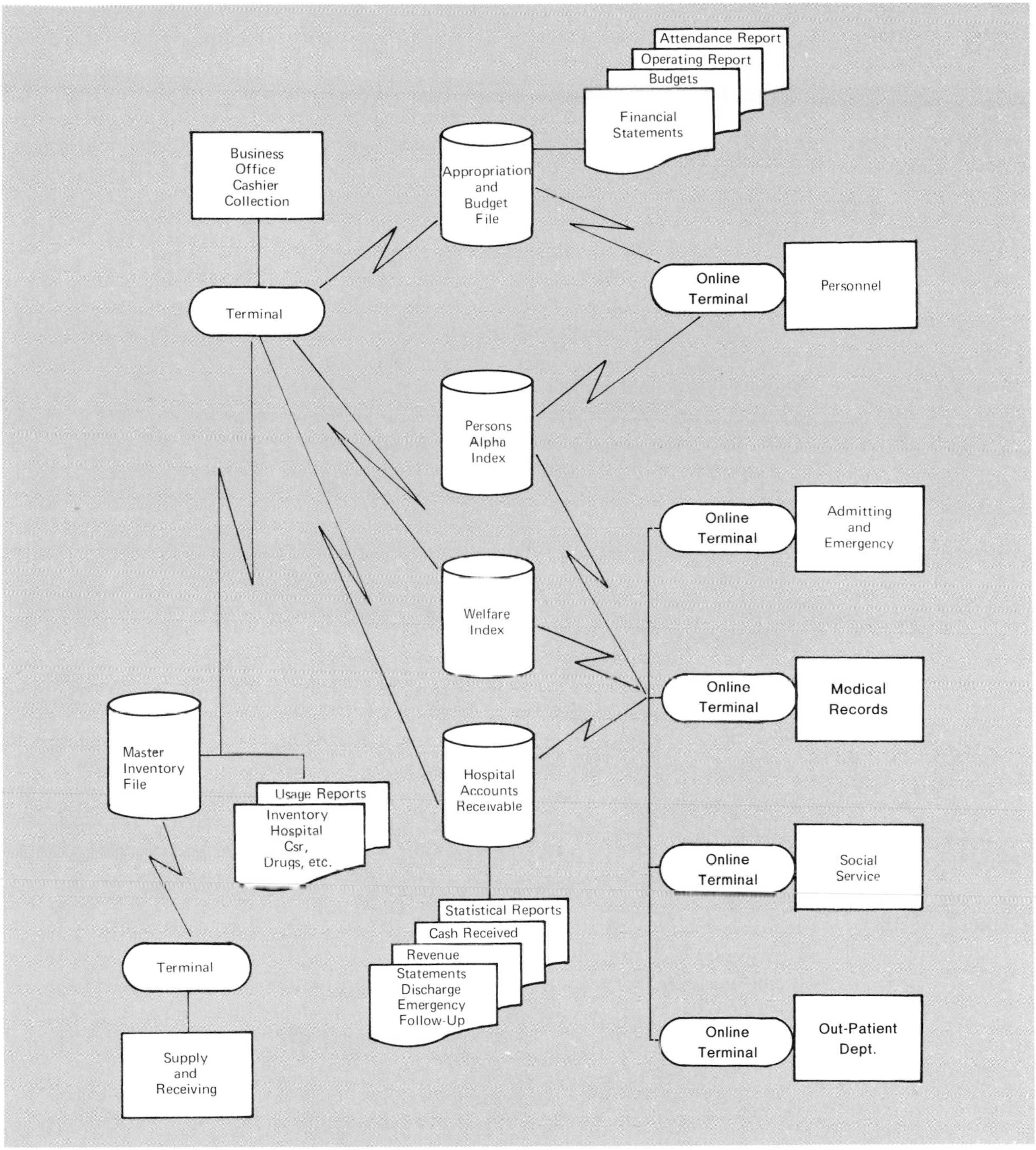

Figure 14.10 Hospital sections requiring access to information systems.

Advantages

Simplification of Input Preparation

An online real-time system eliminates the need for converting the data into a machine processible format. Each piece of data is transmitted directly from the terminal to the computer.

Reduction in the Number of Programs Needed

Each user of a system becomes an expert in transmission of data to the system. The terminals in a real-time system are designed to perform the specialized input/output functions, thus eliminating the need for transmitting data in prescribed output formats. The input itself may be the by-product of another process.

Elimination of Duplicate Records

Data is entered into an online real-time system only once, thus reducing the number of times a document is handled. This elimination of effort duplication in the clerical aspect of record keeping, by reducing the probability of clerical errors in the transcription of data, results in cost savings and greater efficiency in clerical operation.

Improvement of Editing, Accuracy, and Controls

By entering the data into an online real-time system at the source as the transaction occurs, many errors for control are eliminated. The errors of conflicting reports, caused by varied coding or interpretation, are reduced. Moreover, as each user receives faster and more economical data-processing service many of the intermediate steps are eliminated.

The economy of using equipment in this manner provides a more efficient method of operation. An online real-time system makes the most efficient use of both hardware and software. Two or more peripheral devices can be operating while the computer is working on a number of programs.

Timeliness of the Information Provided

An online real-time system is a reservoir of centrally updated information, which is immediately accessible to all users. Management may interrogate the computer and receive special reports vital to the successful operation of the business. All management reports can be generated automatically in a prescribed format or on a demand basis when so required by management.

Disadvantages

The expenses involved in online real-time systems constitute their main disadvantage. These costs are generally higher than those of batch processing systems.

Hardware Costs

Terminals, channels, scanning mechanisms, large core storage units, and vast random access processing storage memories are necessary to a successful online real-time system, but increase the costs of operation. The computers and files required in online real-time systems are usually more expensive than those used in batch processing systems.

Software Costs

Because of the difficulties in programming online real-time systems, software costs are increased. Some of the factors involved in programming for an online real-time system are:

1. The organization and addressing of direct access devices.
2. The control of the communication network and the various remote terminals.

3. Multiprogramming, which is the processing of two or more transactions simultaneously.
4. Integrating a complex system with programs written by many different programmers.
5. New difficulties in program management.

As the online real-time systems come into more general use, programming patterns will emerge and segments of earlier programs will prove reusable in later systems. Therefore, reductions can be expected in the programming effort.

As management recognizes the practical advantages and benefits of online real-time systems in business applications, such systems will become more widespread. Continued improvements in computer hardware technology will provide more efficient random access devices, larger storage capacities at reduced costs, and improved communication equipment and facilities permitting reliable and economically feasible remote processing.

Time Sharing

Time sharing is simply a technique for allocating computer time and services to multiple users at different locations so that the computer, in effect, processes a number of programs concurrently. It means sharing computer time and services among a number of users (fig. 14.11). This utility represents sharing on a broader scale so that more users can have shared access to a wider range of services.

Advances

Although early time-sharing systems were initially successful and popular with users, the systems could not cope efficiently with many users running large programs simultaneously. To solve this problem, designers are eliminating the early time-sharing systems, which were basically general-purpose computers with communication processors tacked on, replacing them with integrated hardware and software systems built exclusively to ensure efficient time sharing.

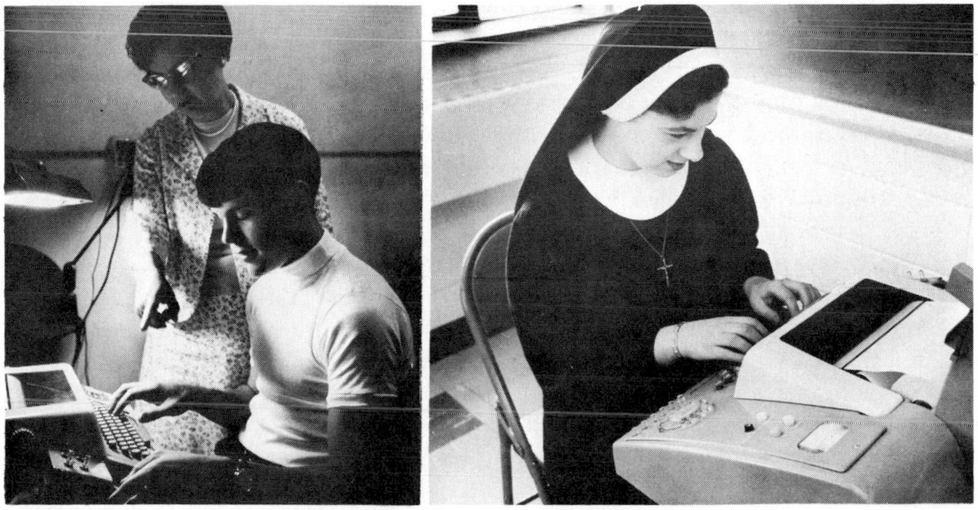

Figure 14.11 Time sharing.

In addition to system improvements, changes are being made to aid problem solvers directly. New, more efficient compilers are being designed to expand the capabilities and simplify the use of problem-solving languages.

Many programming languages have been modified so they can be used in an interactive mode. COBOL, FORTRAN, PL1, APL, and BASIC are just some of the programming languages being used in a conversational type of processing. BASIC (one of the more popular types of interactive languages) is discussed in detail in the next chapter.

The popularity of time sharing is due primarily to the fact that it allows many people at remote locations to use a central computer. Decision-making management personnel are given access to a system on a conversational basis—able to interrogate the computer from the office and have the system respond in the form of displays on a cathode tube or in a printed report of the various alternatives available to management.

Although time sharing is still rather new to most users, much has already been accomplished in this field. As users become more familiar with the capabilities of a system, they progress into more difficult problems. Time-sharing computers range from the simplest arithmetic calculations to complex mathematical formulas. Data bases, containing the records of many files, can be tapped by time-sharing terminals for information retrieval.

The development of special programs in the Question/Response mode has greatly simplified computer programming and minimized the need to learn sophisticated computer language. These programs instruct the user how to input the data and obtain the desired results.

Perhaps the single most important use of time sharing is the development of data bases for management information systems. Until recently one of the largest obstacles to the development of management information systems has been the difficulty of gathering from many remote locales the timely data needed as a data base. A time-sharing computer system is ideally suited for this task. Information can be entered from any number of terminals into one central location. It can then be used by the remote locations as well as by the central location.

With present applications of time sharing rising steadily, data bases are required to contain huge masses of data. With the many alternatives and variables available to management, executives may predict the consequences of an action before they input it. They may construct corporate models to test alternative courses and select the most desirable. Capital investment analysis will become a science, minimizing the number of risks involved and enabling companies to fully exploit their markets. Budgeting will be performed quickly and precisely.

Many valuable work hours could be saved if scientists could input a few keywords of a project into a terminal and have the data bank reply with all relevant information concerning the project. If all human ailments were placed in a data bank catalogued in some manner, a physician could input a patient's symptoms through a terminal at the office. The central computer would return a diagnosis of the ailment and suggest methods for its treatment.

Data bases are being established for entire industries and are available to business executives, scientists, engineers, and statisticians. When accessed by remote terminals, time-sharing computers will retrieve the data instantly from these bases, perform the necessary computations, and produce the desired output.

Computers will be kept busy around the clock offering additional associated data-processing services. Data entering a computer for processing can be accessed through the remote terminal on a current basis. The retrieval of such information from these batch files can be combined with computations to yield dynamic statistics that will enhance the decision-making function in all areas of management, production, sales, etc. For example, a salesperson will be able to access the data base in the central computer and bid firmly and realistically on an order. The same terminals may be used to transmit data from field offices to the central computer to update such files as inventory, payroll, and sales.

Data Base

A new dimension in data processing is receiving increased attention in the emerging era of information processing. This dimension recognizes that data, as the third resource, together with hardware and personnel resources, is required to develop information.

As data processing has developed over the past twenty-five years, emphasis has been placed on management of personnel and hardware. Personnel development and hardware selection and performance have been the major management problems.

An important change in approach has become evident. The hallmark of the change is *information.* Systems have become "management *information* systems (MIS)" and data processing has become "*information* processing." The emphasis on information reflects that the computer-oriented system is to be replaced by an information-oriented system.

Definitions

This revised concept of information processing requires specific definitions of data, information, and subsequently data base. *Data* is the representation of a fact or event. *Information* is the result of the collection, analysis, and summarization of data. A *data base* is the entire accumulation of data which is needed to meet the information requirements of the organization.

The era of information brought recognition to the data base as an existing resource requiring management control. With the growth and acceptance of data base management systems (DBMS), the computer industry has at long last given itself "information systems" potential (fig. 14.12). Information differs from data in that information "participates" in the organization—answers questions, solves problems. True information has an interesting characteristic. The value of information (a real measurable commodity) decreases across time. It loses "currency." The longer it takes data processing to get the information to the person who requires it, the less value it is to the organization. This is where data communication comes in. It is via online data base systems that the dissemination of information can be executed when it has reached its peak value. Maximum profitability of an organization can be achieved when questions can be answered to solve problems, and information can be provided on an immediate basis.

Figure 14.12 An example of a DBMS and a data base. (Reprinted with permission of *Datamation*© magazine, © Copyright by Technical Publishing Company, a division of Dun-Donnelley Publishing Corporation, a Dun & Bradstreet Company, 1978—all rights reserved.)

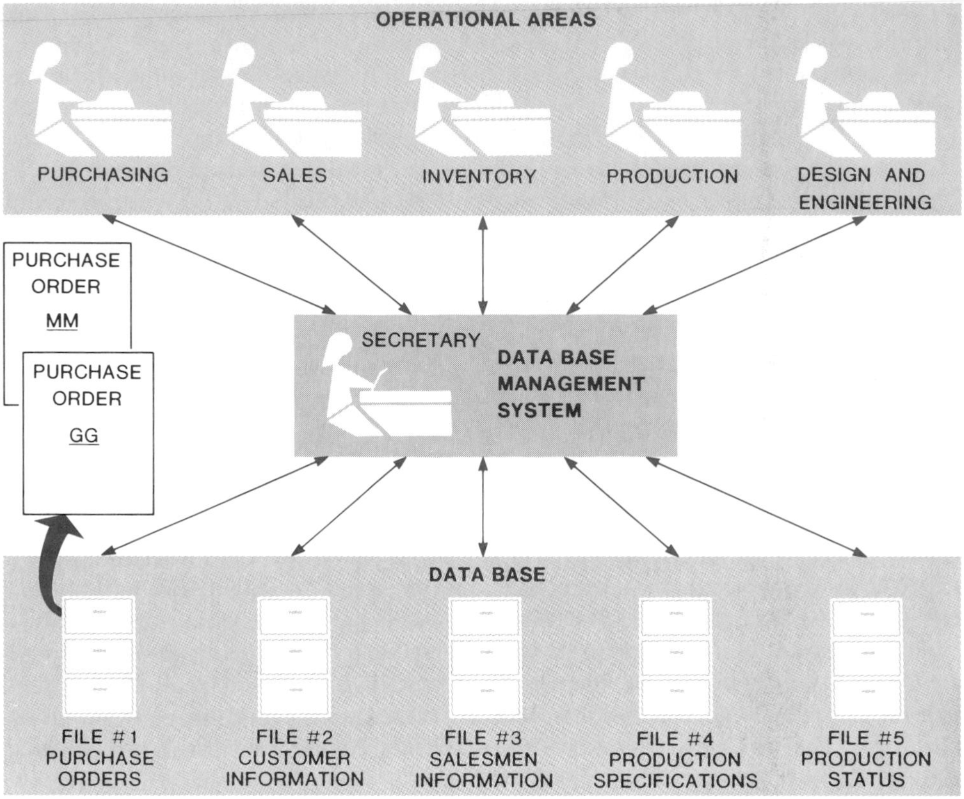

Data base management generates information by creating a framework of data within which data is turned into information. Online data base systems allow the bringing of information system into the mainline stream of the business, thus reducing the amount of time for its dissemination and making full use of its value and reducing cost.

Design

A data base design approach is a way of optimally organizing information stored in the data base so it can support processing demands imposed by a firm's operational areas (figs. 14.13, 14.14). Some of the important benefits are:

1. *Reduced data storage costs.* Data is stored once and is reorganized to support major application areas. Other applications requiring the same data gain access to it through a series of linkages maintained by the data base management system (DBMS).
2. *More current data.* A single update of common data provides all applications with new information simultaneously. So, the total integrated system is now able

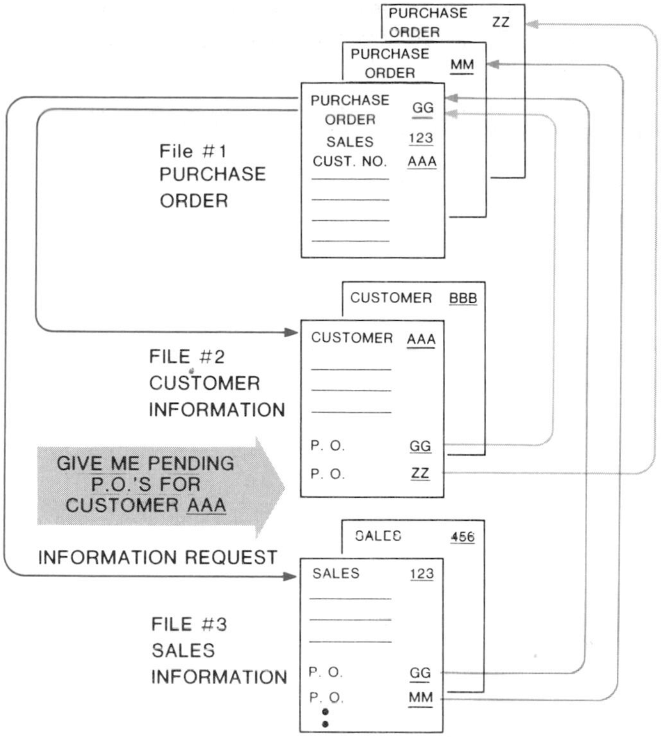

Figure 14.13 An example of a data base design approach. (Reprinted with permission of *Datamation*© magazine, © Copyright by Technical Publishing Company, a division of Dun-Donnelley Publishing Corporation, a Dun & Bradstreet Company, 1978—all rights reserved.)

to process this new data immediately after updating. For example, when a bank customer with multiple accounts submits an address change, her address is altered in one physical location. Thereafter, when access is made through any of her accounts, the new address is displayed properly.

3. *Reduced data entry costs.* Processing time can be cut because only one update is required to change data for all applications rather than one update per application file.
4. *Secure access to privileged data.* Data requests can be examined and, if desired, be granted or denied. Data security is more cumbersome to provide when not using DBMS.
5. *Eliminate concurrent data update conflicts.* Data requests are "scheduled" to avoid dangerous uncoordinated update and retrieval of the same physical data.
6. *Optimize performance and offer greater access flexibility.* Sophisticated routines are sometimes provided to manage data buffers, rescue channel conflicts and disk unit arm movements, and overlap I/O calls. Complex routines of automatically traversing data linkages can be included more economically in a DBMS because they serve many applications.
7. *Unify data recovery and backup functions.* A single internal recovery system works for all data processed through DBMS.

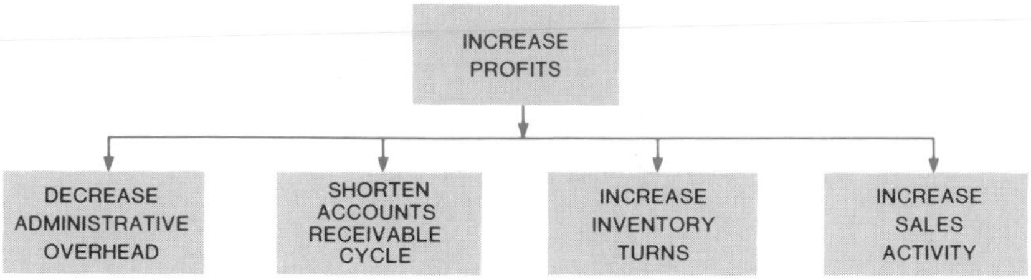

The general format of the functional analysis tree calls for a top-down ordering of business functions, subfunctions, or goals, each of which is identified by a box with an action verb and object.

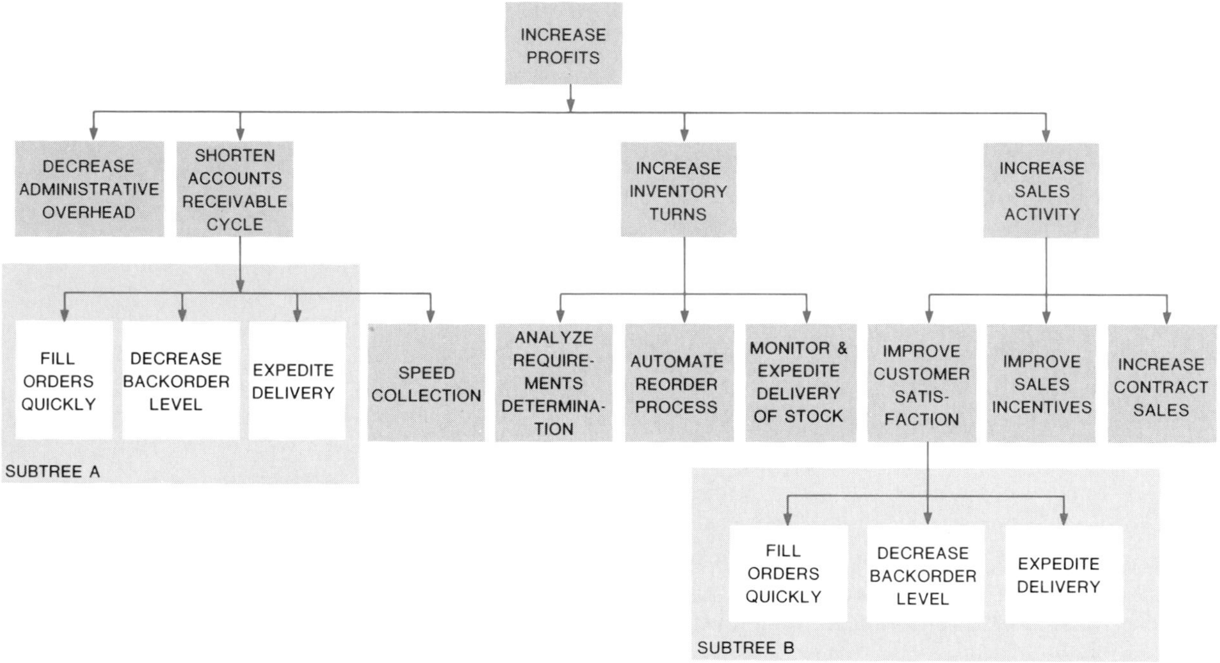

As the tree branches out, the interrelations of functions and sub-functions quickly become apparent, as illustrated by Subtrees A and B. Performing those operations will shorten the AR cycle and improve customer satisfaction.

Figure 14.14 An example of a data base design. (Reprinted with permission of *Datamation*© magazine, © Copyright by Technical Publishing Company, a division of Dun-Donnelley Publishing Corporation, a Dun & Bradstreet Company, 1978—all rights reserved.)

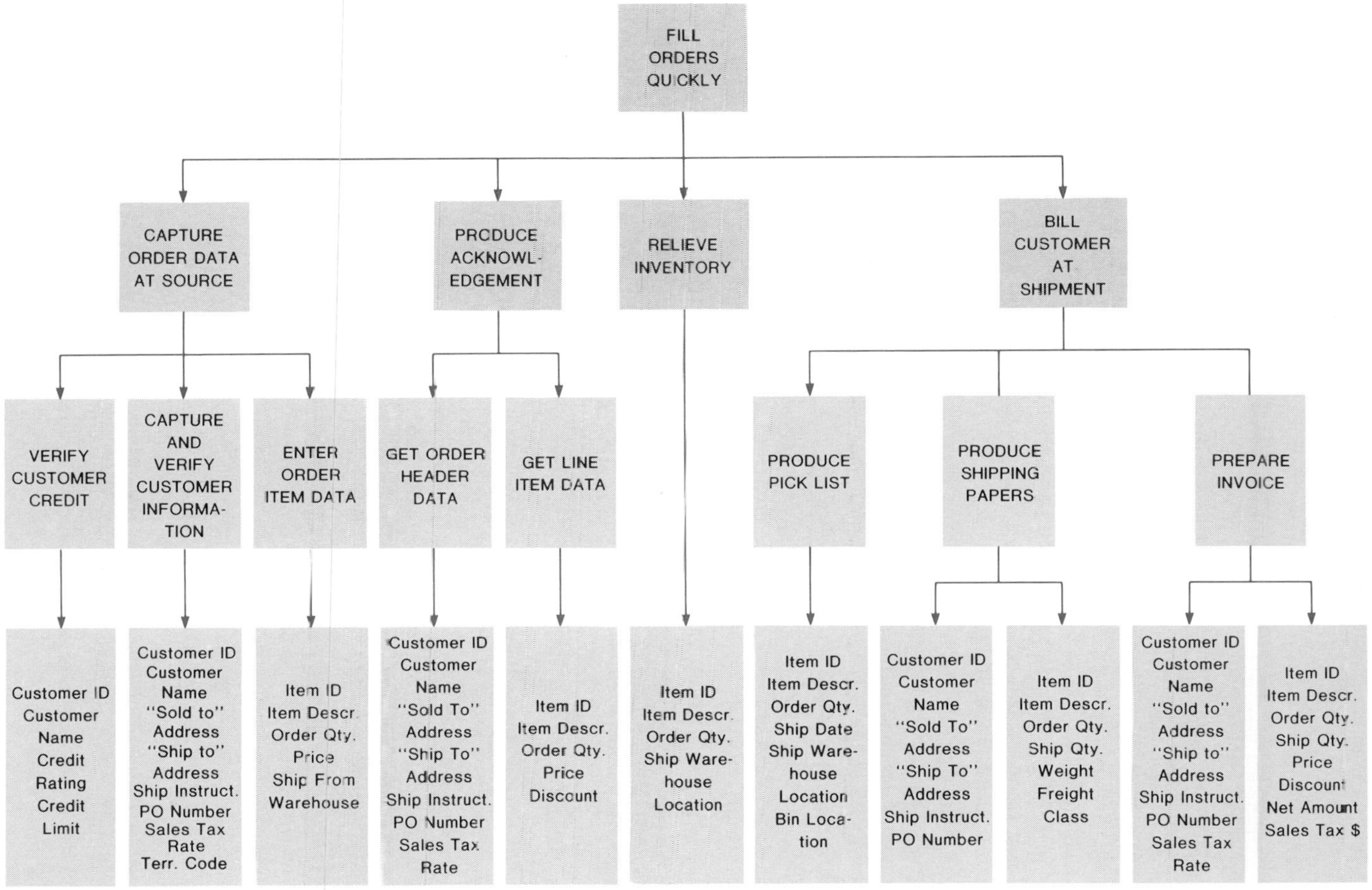

Once the elementary functions are defined (those which are completely handled by one person or group), the information elements necessary for performing those functions should be collected and listed. These lists will define the elements of the data base.

Figure 14.14 Continued.

Data Base Management Systems (DBMS)

Data base management systems (DBMS) have been part of the data-processing scene for the past decade and users have been turning to DBMS in growing numbers since the early 1970s.

The systems gained a reputation, probably deserved, as the way of the future, the way to overcome the frustrations and weaknesses of the conventional file-oriented ways of data processing. They seem to coincide with the awareness that information management is more than data processing.

The benefits of data base systems have been stated many times in the literature and ads of the growing number of vendors. They focus on three particular concepts:

1. *Data independence.* Application programmers, working with DBMS, no longer need to be concerned with where or how their data is stored or if the data base itself is modified or extended.
2. *Reduction of data redundancy.* A central depository of data generally means there is a need to maintain only one copy of any particular element. This hopefully leads to easier maintenance and more assurance that all applications working with the element have current and consistent value for the element.
3. *Making data available for other uses.* "A growing base of data for a growing ease of users" has long been a phrase that held the greatest hope for the installations of these new-fangled systems.

These benefits had to become realities if the installations and their managers were to cost-justify their acquisition of data base systems. Data base systems cost substantial amounts of time, money, and effort to obtain and use. The overhead they impose on the whole data-processing operation is also substantial and has to be offset by real gains.

System

Data base management system (DBMS) is a computerized system consisting of numerous components that have as their collective purposes the implementation, management, and protection of large-scale data bases.

The main feature of these systems is the physical linkage for data structuring (fig. 14.15). Physical linkage implies that addresses of related records are stored within records themselves so that linkage "paths" exist within and among files. The DBMS follows these paths in order to access data. Many computer manufacturers and software shops provide the software packages to implement simple and sophisticated data management systems.

The data base approach to information processing has gained considerable acceptance within the data-processing community. The concept of controlling data as an organizational resource, while easing many of the problems of traditional data management, has made the data base appealing to managers and technicians alike. Further, existing data base management systems allow previously unmanaged volumes of related data to be maintained and accessed under control of standardized software.

A data base management system (DBMS) is a software package designed to operate interactively upon a collection of computer-stored files, called a data base. Its primary operations are to count data base records that have in common whatever characteristics that may be specified by a user and to retrieve those records for further processing and display.

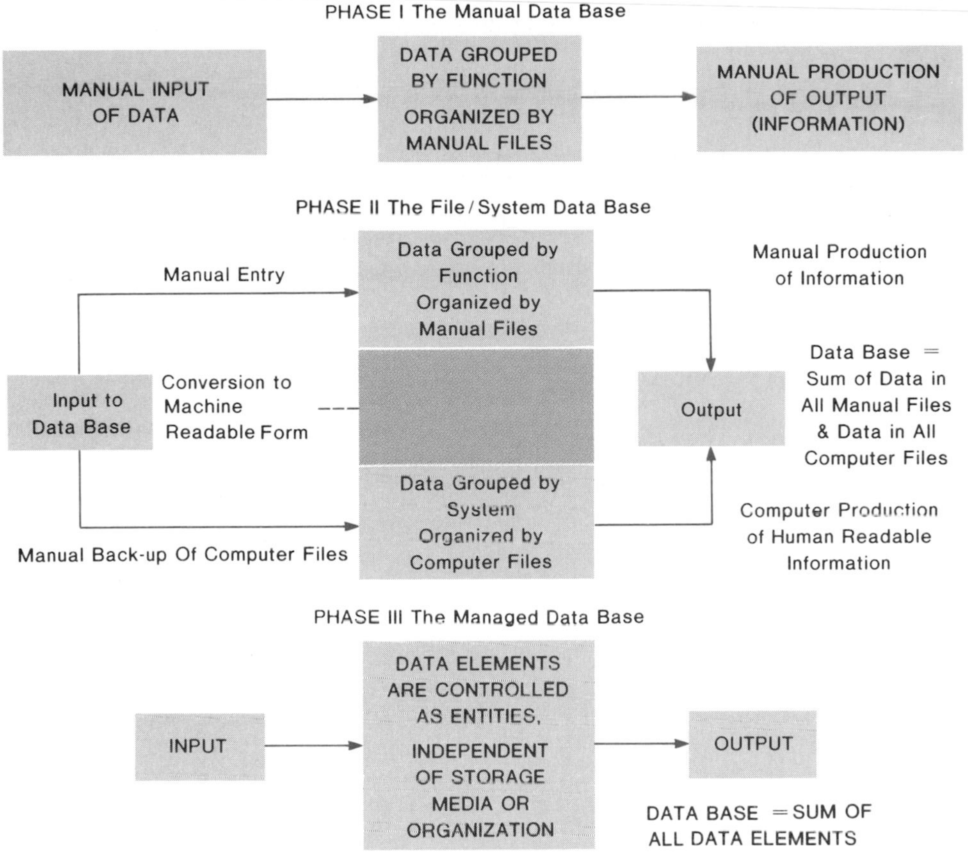

Figure 14.15 Creating a data base management system. (Copyright *Data Management* magazine, Data Processing Management Association.)

A data base management system is especially useful when a file is likely to be manipulated in many ways that cannot be anticipated when a data base is created. It enables the user to take a mass of data at a later date and to retrieve elements in an organized fashion and arranged in a structured format. A word of caution—a computer applier must take great care and spend lots of time on what should go into the data base and how it should be organized to get such benefits (fig. 14.16).

Data Base Administrator (DBA)

Data base is a concept. It embodies the management of all data for the production and control of business information. The burden of managing data base management systems is on the shoulders of the data base administrator. The primary function of data base administration is to manage that data resource and see that it is efficiently stored in such a way that it can be retrieved in the form of meaningful information. Depending on whose definition, the data base administrator (DBA) function and responsibility vary from organization to organization. According to one definition, the DBA's responsibilities include:

1. Designing the overall logical records.
2. Designing the logical records for each application system.
3. Defining the data relationship.
4. Managing physical data generation, reorganization, and security-related regulations.

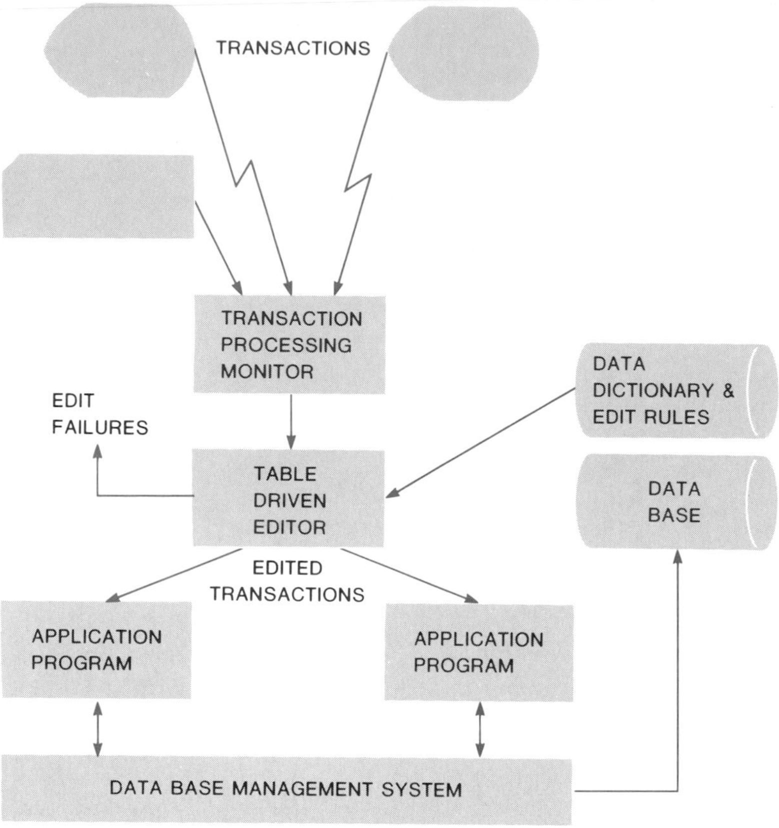

Figure 14.16 The operation of a data base management system. (Reprinted with permission of *Datamation*© magazine, © Copyright by Technical Publishing Company, a division of Dun-Donnelley Publishing Corporation, a Dun & Bradstreet Company, 1978—all rights reserved.)

The DBA is a sort of referee who controls the contents of the data base, enforces the standards, and steers potential intraorganizational conflicts over data base to the proper authorities for resolution. The DBA is involved in the design, development, and implementation and maintenance of a system. The DBA provides consultation, education, and assistance to the application analysts throughout the life of a system.

Modern data base structures are complex and sophisticated. More than a casual attention must be given to the storage and retrieval of data. The DBA provides the required coordination between the users of shared data and assures that the overall corporate interest will dominate in the development and operation of data base systems.

Proper administration requires a broad knowledge of the use of the data throughout the installation. The requirements for effective and efficient data base management call for a combination of technician and generalist, a synthesis of skills not previously needed in data processing.

Data Dictionary

The data dictionary is a recently developed tool that has found considerable success in data base development efforts. It aids in the important tasks of identifying, documenting, organizing, and even manipulating information about the data to be stored in the data base.

dic′tion·ā·ry, dā′ta, *n.; pl.* dā′ta dic′tion·ā·ries (there are many). [From L., *data dictionarium,* a tool for order.] **1.** a data and system documentation tool for the requirements, design, programming, implementation and post-implementation phase of system development; **2.** a data management control tool to answer questions about where a data element exists and which programs or systems use it; **3.** a program development tool.
Synonym – asset (properly selected and implemented).

Figure 14.17 A definition of a data dictionary. (Reprinted with permission of the *ICP Interface—Data Processing Management,* a publication of International Computer Programs, Inc., Indianapolis, Indiana.)

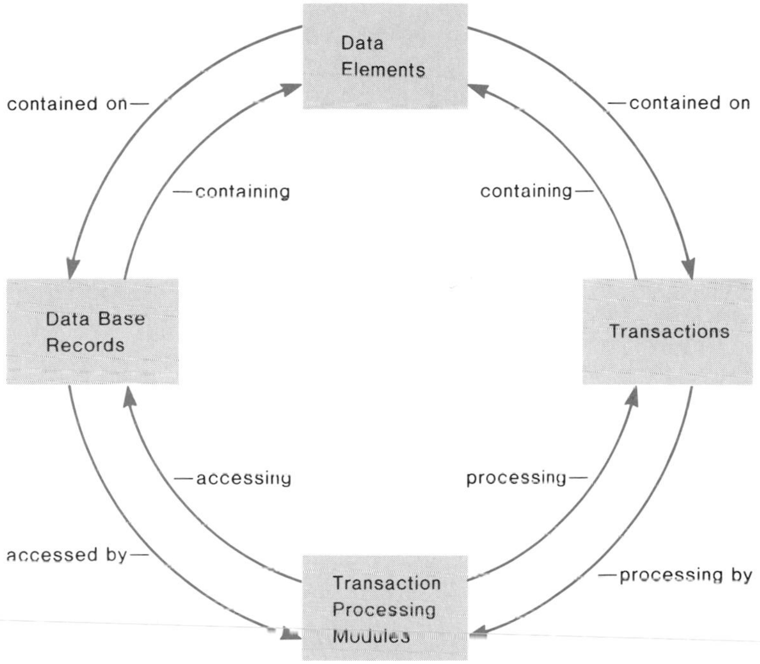

Figure 14.18 The functions of a data dictionary. (Reprinted with permission of *Datamation*© magazine, © Copyright by Technical Publishing Company, a division of Dun-Donnelley Publishing Corporation, a Dun & Bradstreet Company, 1978—all rights reserved.)

In its simplest form, a data dictionary is a well-organized, up-to-date notebook containing basic information about data elements (fig. 14.17). The data dictionary becomes the central authority source for all information about the data itself. The users will tailor the dictionary to meet their particular requirements (fig. 14.18).

Figure 14.19 An example of distributed data processing. (Reprinted with permission of *Datamation*© magazine, © Copyright by Technical Publishing Company, a division of Dun-Donnelley Publishing Corporation, a Dun & Bradstreet Company, 1978—all rights reserved.)

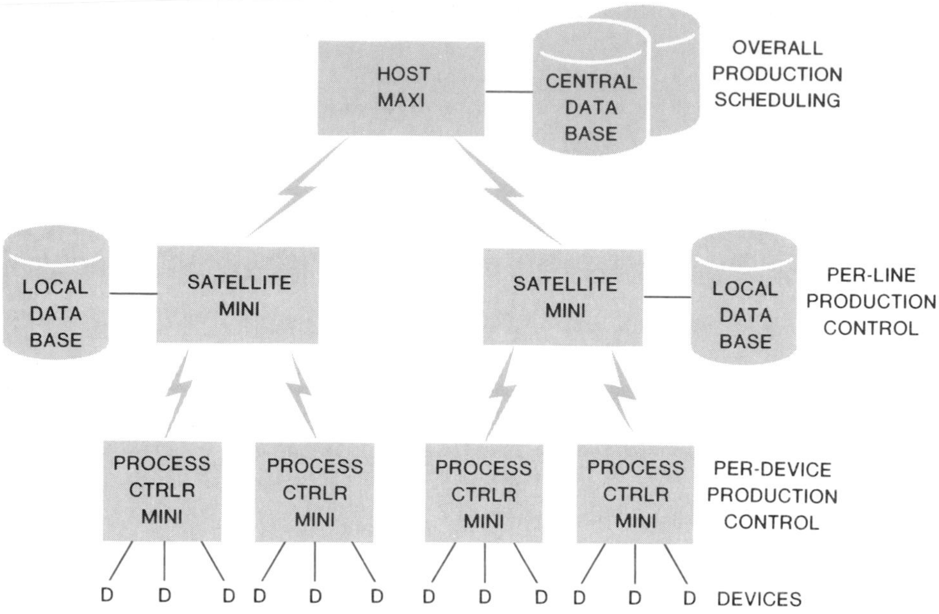

PRODUCTION control system with central data base and, at lower level, satellite minis with a copy of part of host data base. At next level minis and microcomputers control production devices.

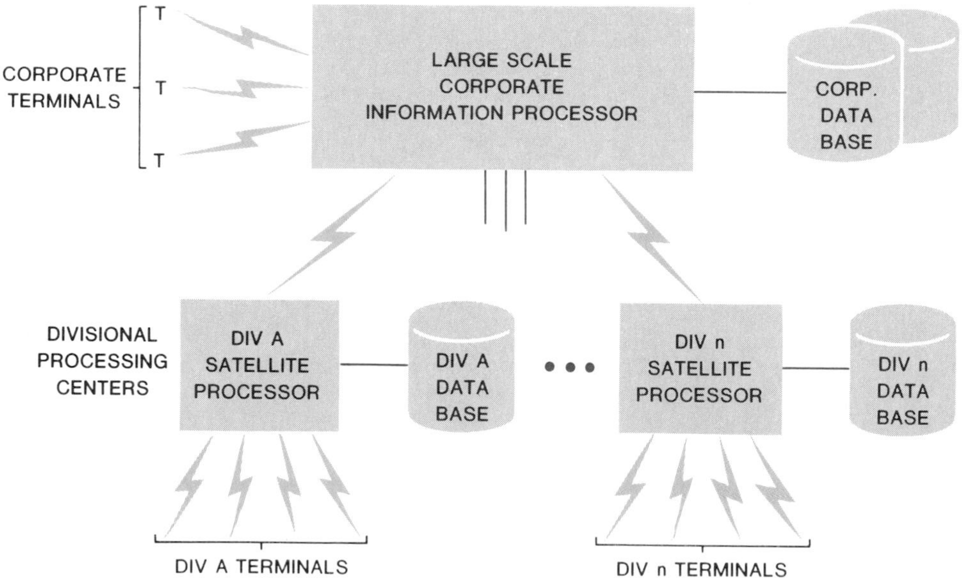

HIERARCHICAL partitioning: At corporate level, summaries of data from lower levels of a business are maintained and at divisional level there only are summaries from even lower levels.

Conclusion

Data base management systems are tools that are used to build a framework of data, which, when properly related, can generate information. In any organization, information has a value. In fact, information is the single most important asset of any organization. Without that information, an organization cannot exist, function, or reach profitability.

Distributed Data Processing

The concept of distributed data processing is to place the processing power at points where the data is generated or where the data is needed for supervision or management. The primary requirement for distributed data-processing function is to be more responsive to the end user and to bring the data-processing function closer to the user.

The two types of processors are the host and satellite computers. A host computer provides supporting services, the types of supporting services that a time-sharing user gets; whereas a satellite is dependent on the host for guidance.

For example, in a hierarchical arrangement, a company might have a maxi host in a production control system that has a central data base at which production in a factory is scheduled. At lower levels are the satellite minis, each maintaining a local data base; that is, a working copy of part of the host's data base. At the next lower level, communicating with the satellite minis, are minis and/or micros that control production devices on the factory floor. In the hierarchy, the specialization of the functions becomes greater as you go lower in the hierarchy (fig. 14.19).

In a banking operation, the host maxi maintains central customer accounts while satellite minis hold branch accounts and also control the teller terminals.

Networks

Some minicomputers are optimized to perform message switching, others do input/output functions, and still others carry out arithmetic calculations. In a complex computer application, the designer configures a system to utilize the unique strengths of each minicomputer type. A network results whenever two or more of these processors are linked together by communication lines, as opposed to being internally connected. A minicomputer network, in essence, distributes computer functions among its elements according to the most cost-effective arrangement in a specific application.

A computer system may also contain terminals and other input/output devices, but these can be considered network elements only if they possess integrated processors, the so-called intelligent terminals. Otherwise the definition of a network would have to include a simple time-sharing system. Network software, of course, is the key to linking all of these elements, and it makes the differences between a cluster of computers that act independently and the same cluster integrated into a smooth-working, cost-effective distributed data-processing operation (fig. 14.20).

Purposes

Distributed data processing:

1. Takes the computer to the job rather than the job to the computer. Powerful low-cost processors are connected to increasingly larger electronic corporate files.
2. Is able to access larger computation centers if required and to communicate with larger corporate files.
3. Has terminal interaction to end users at low costs. Terminals are able to talk to minicomputers.

Figure 14.20 Examples of network structures. (Reprinted with permission of *Datamation*© magazine, © Copyright by Technical Publishing Company, a division of Dun-Donnelley Publishing Corporation, a Dun & Bradstreet Company, 1978—all rights reserved.)

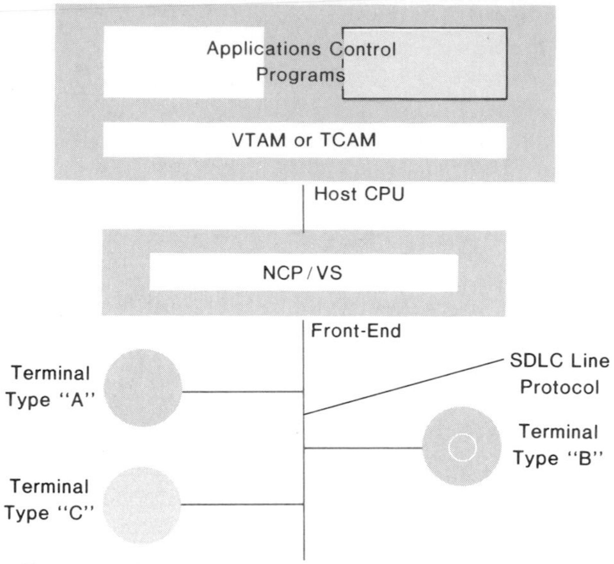

From a product standpoint, IBM's SNA incorporates four major components: the Telecommunications Access Method, the Network Control Program in the front end, the SDLC line protocol, and SDLC-compatible terminals.

NETWORKING MULTIPLE HOSTS IN IBM'S SNA

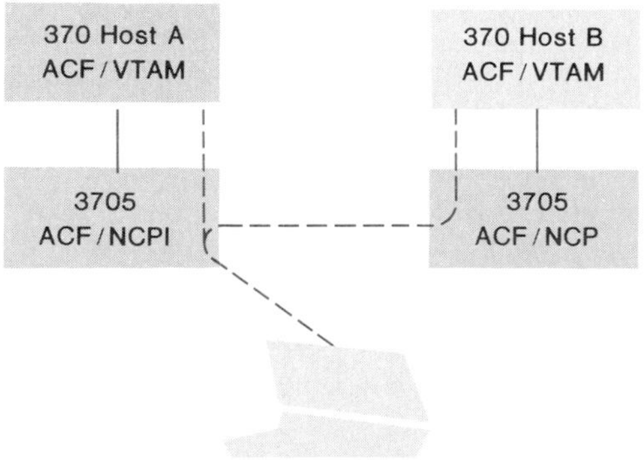

SNA was widely criticized for being dependent on a host computer, but facilities are now provided for multi-host networking and for taking over the domain of a processor that's down.

Conversational Time Sharing

4. Enables users to use data-processing power, to use computers, and to support their own particular business style in their own way, on their own terms, and at low costs.

Distributed data processing is one in which the data processing, data communications, and data base management functions are fully distributed.

Univac's Transport Network Structure

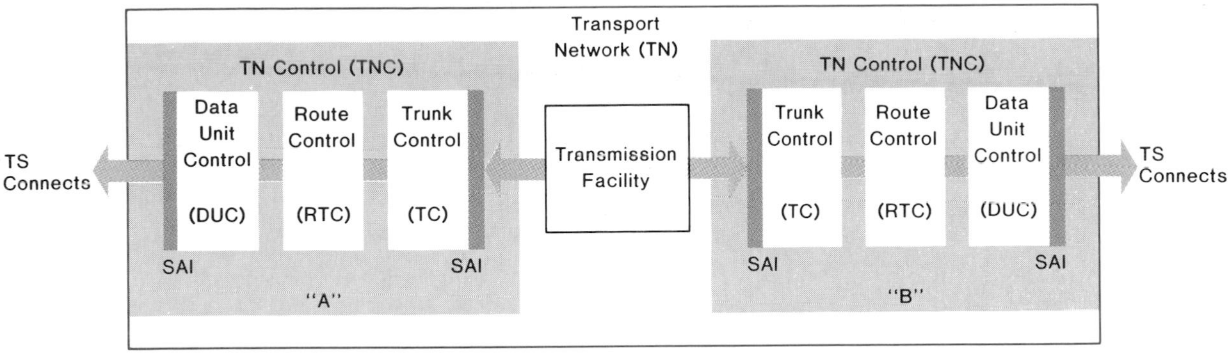

Univac's conception of the Transport Network includes the communications facility, plus Transport Network Control functions in communications processors at each end. Each Data Communications Processor performs three functions: Data Unit Control to interface the end user to the rest of the system, Route Control to manage the path level connection from the entry node to the exit node, and Trunk Control to manage the use of the links between any two nodes.

NCR's Distributed Network Architecture

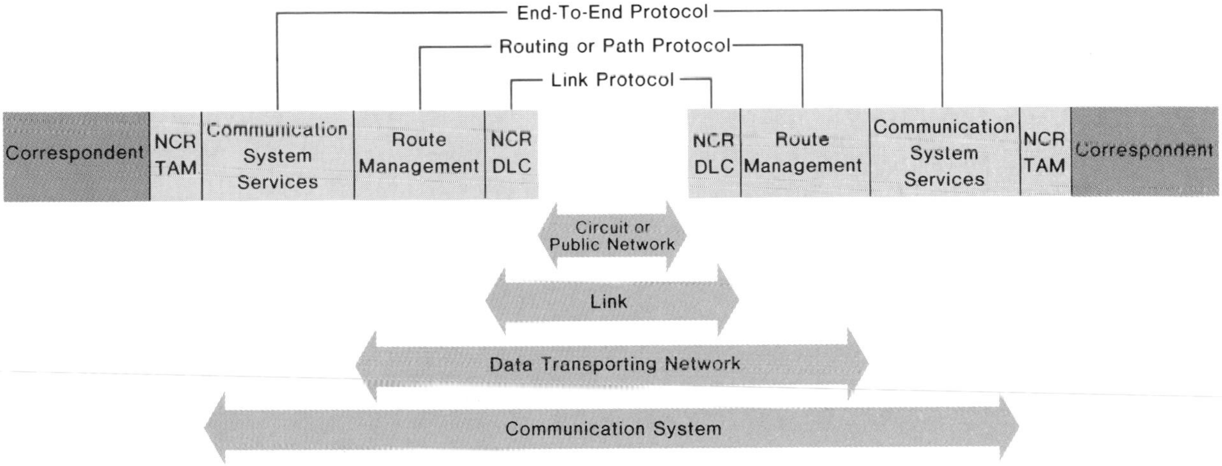

In NCR's parlance, "end users" are called "Correspondents" and are linked by NCR/TAM access method software to Communications System Services which handle the making and breaking up of packets. Route Management handles the steering of packets and the data link control NCR/DLC handles the links.

Figure 14.20 Continued.

Examples

Few companies operate entirely out of one location. Even small firms are likely to have regional sales offices, while larger businesses may have dozens of operating units scattered across the country. For such organizations, a distributed data-processing system may help to bring about some notable operating efficiencies.

The Wilson Sporting Goods Company of Chicago, a manufacturer and distributor of sporting goods, installed a distributed data-processing system that links all twenty-five locations to a central computer.

In the distributed data-processing system, the workload is shared between the central computer and smaller satellite units, which act as small processors. In the Wilson network, each location has a satellite online to a cluster of terminals and a printer, creating twenty-five small computer centers with local data-processing capability.

Typically, after an order is entered at the sales office, it is transmitted to the central computer, which forwards it to the appropriate regional center or centers. As the order is being processed, the company-wide data base, including open orders, shipped orders, and inventory, is updated. Customer inquiries concerning order status can be answered quickly through any terminal in the network. This system enables much closer coordination between manufacturing and sales.

In the banking industry, the Bank of America has developed an approach to distributed data processing for making current information on more than eleven million accounts accessible through terminals in all of its California branches. Their approach entails segmenting its data bases and distributing its application processing among minicomputer-based modules with several computers. Video teller terminals are connected through programmable control units in the offices to the data-processing centers over multidrop communication lines.

The two basic forms of time sharing are conversational and remote-batch processing. Today, most users of time sharing employ the conversational mode of computer usage. In this particular mode, a user sits at a standard terminal, dials the computer on a standard telephone, and puts the receiver into an accoustical receptacle interfaced with the terminal and is on the computer in the conversational or immediate response mode (fig. 14.21). The user may write a program in a simple language developed for this particular method of processing called BASIC. The user may also call out programs that have been written previously and stored in the computer. These programs can be returned and combined with the input that the user has inserted to receive an immediate solution. Numerous "canned" programs supplied by the various vendors are stored in the computer and are available to the user instantly to solve a problem. This method of processing has several important advantages:

1. Programs may be written simply and quickly.
2. An immediate response will be available to the inquiry.
3. Easy to use terminals, most employing simple keyboards and typewriter configurations that are usually small and easy to service.
4. The remote terminals may be installed wherever there is a telephone and electricity available.
5. The cost of the operation is relatively low. Most remote terminals rent for about $100 per month. The actual compute-time charges (for the actual time the terminals are connected to the central computer) range from $200 to $800 per month with the average at about $500 per month.

Figure 14.21 Visual terminal time sharing. (Photo by Ken Firestone)

Some typical business applications for conversational time-sharing processing are:

Banking—Savings and checking deposits, cash flow projections, scheduling loan payments, pro forma balance sheets (bank clients).

Management consulting—Cash budgets, enrollment projections for schools, lease or buy decisions, acquisition and merger analysis.

Investment—Corporate earnings projections, rate of return analysis, economic forecasting.

Manufacturing—Cost analysis, production scheduling, sales forecasting, sales analysis, inventory control.

Remote-Batch Time Sharing

Although the smallest portion of time-sharing operations, it is expected that remote-batch time sharing will eventually become the largest segment of data processing. Remote batching is not time sharing in the conversational mode, but fits the original definition because it is a time-sharing function—the shared use of a central computer by numerous remote users. There is no immediate response in remote-batch processing. On the contrary, there may be a time lag factor of hours, days, or even weeks.

Remote-batch processing uses terminals of entirely different types from those in the conversational time sharing. Terminals are usually small, simple input/output devices, such as a small card reader and printer connected to another small computer used as the remote terminal (fig. 14.22). This type of capability has great potential for business data processing.

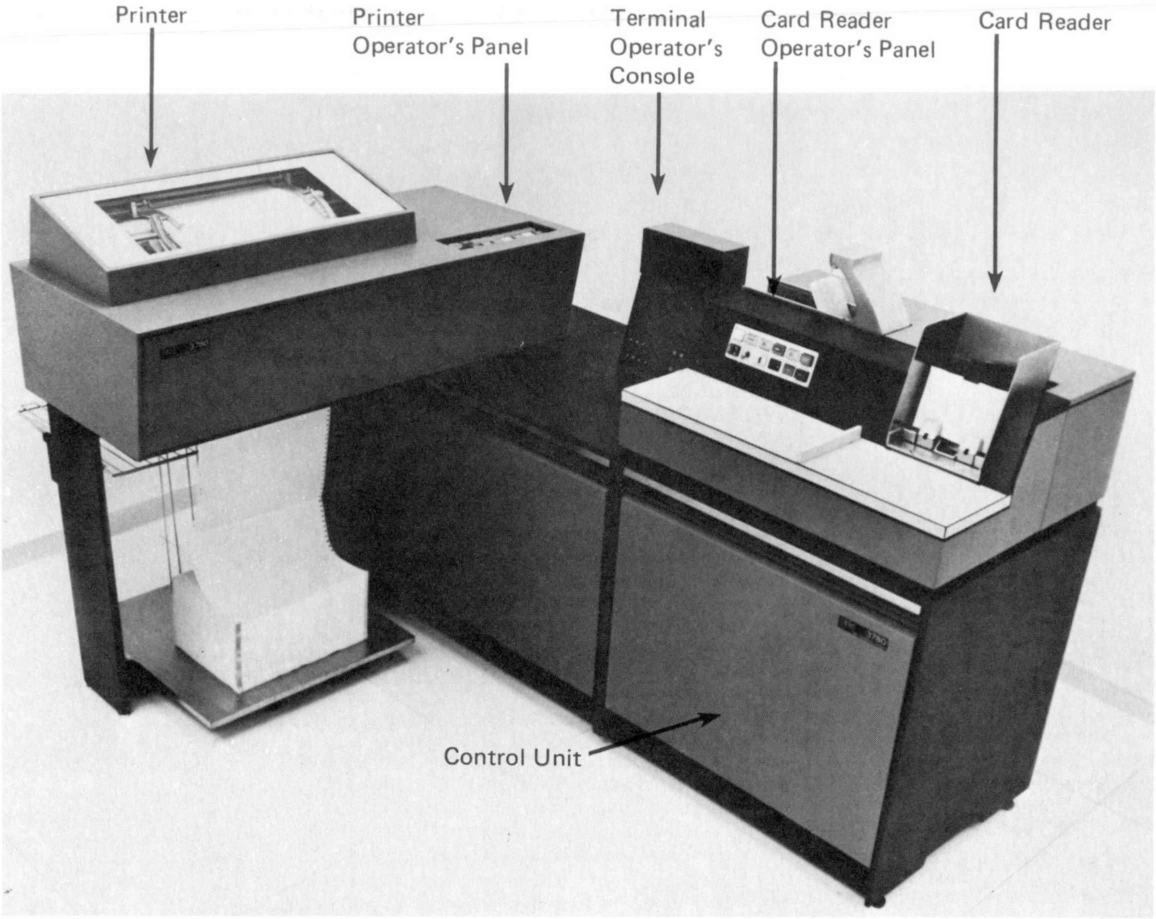

Figure 14.22 The IBM 3780 data communications terminal.

At the present time, telephone lines are the only practical source of communication. In spite of the numerous advances made by the telephone company in improving the communication media, there are still some serious problems. The major problem lies in the fact that the telephone is a voice-oriented system and cannot be easily changed to a data-oriented system. The principal difference between these two systems is that voice communications does not need to be error-free, while data communications must be at least error-predictable. The telephone company has built in safeguards to prevent many of the previous errors in data transmission generated by the malfunctioning of the equipment.

Additional communication sources, such as microwave transmission, satellite communicators, and laser transmission, are available, but they are either too expensive or too theoretical to be considered as alternatives to the telephone lines.

The Growing Threat to Personal Privacy

Immense data bases and the case with which they are used has created the problem of the invasion of personal privacy. Today's technology is so advanced that it is currently possible to carry within a single system, information in computerized data files equivalent to twenty single-spaced pages of personal facts on every man, woman, and child in the United States.

Personal Privacy

Privacy is an important, fragile element of personal freedom. One definition of *privacy is the right of an individual to be free in private affairs from surveillance and intrusion; to be free to keep private affairs private; and to be free from compulsion in action, thought, and experience.*

It is interesting to note that our constitution never mentions privacy. And, until recently our courts haven't addressed the issue of personal privacy. There appear to be many paradoxes in personal privacy. Though it is essential to freedom, it is compromised in almost every social, government, and commercial interchange. Most every American family lists (for all to see) their private home address and telephone number. We have permitted the government to assume many of our personal responsibilities; it educates us, houses us, and provides for our retirement. To fulfill these responsibilities, government must obtain and maintain significant amounts of personal information, such as where we live, how much we make, educational information, banking data, and even criminal records. Business must also invade personal privacy. Each family purchasing a home on credit surrenders countless amounts of personal information to the holder of their mortgage before the lender will even grant the loan.

The Social Security number, a relatively harmless piece of paper used to identify the individual as a participant in the Social Security Administration's insurance program, is used by government agencies, private industry, hospitals, education institutions, and other record keepers to identify individuals, to structure files, to indicate eligibility for benefits, and to link records.

Using a Social Security number as a link, information pertaining to school records, earnings and tax payments, driving history, credit rating, medical treatment, and arrest records can be easily obtained.

The issue of privacy arises, then, from the fact that information is power. All of us desire some degree of control over information about ourselves. Once information has been supplied and recorded, however, we have relinquished control and laid ourselves open to invasion of privacy.

There is a lack of controls on the accuracy of data now entered into data bases. Once recorded, users tend to assume accuracy; then, for all practical purposes, fiction becomes fact. Important decisions may be based on rumor, lies, or mistaken identity. The potential for anonymous character assassination is staggering.

Recent Developments

The Supreme Court has taken the "balancing approach," which is the right to privacy balanced against the legitimate right to know. In a lower court decision the court ruled that a small town police department, which had, during the Christmas shopping season, distributed a list of "active shoplifters" to local merchants, was within the legitimate need to know area, even though one person whose name appeared on the list was never convicted.

The first piece of major privacy legislation is the Privacy Act of 1974. This act covers many areas of privacy with a major emphasis on data processing and its impact on the right to privacy. The act, however, extends only to the federal government and

Figure 14.23 The AB 150 California Computer Privacy Act. (Copyright *Data Management* magazine, Data Processing Management Association.)

AB 150 California Computer Privacy Act

This bill would statutorily implement the right of privacy as guaranteed to individuals by the California Constitution, with regard to systems of records maintained by private business entities and state and local governmental agencies.

1. Specify principles of information practice for automated information management systems.
2. Require every business entity or agency to file notice . . . as to existence and character of (systems).
3. Disclose and/or display to data subject the purpose of information being requested, statutes or regulations requiring disclosure, and any adverse action which may be taken as result of subject's refusal to provide information.
4. Make available in a reasonable comprehensible form to data subject a record containing personal information, and permit subject to file written notice of dispute. Specific measures must be taken concerning such notice of dispute.
5. Set damages for noncompliance with act.
6. Specify it a misdemeanor to attempt to obtain, obtain or use personal information from a file where such person is knowingly not authorized to obtain or use the information.
7. Allow certain exemptions to act under specified circumstances.

not the private sector. In addition, it exempted agencies of the government dealing with law enforcement and national security.

Three basic principles underlying the Privacy Act of 1974 extend to data-processing systems as well as manual and mechanical (microfilm) records.

1. Individuals have the right to know what information has been collected regarding their affairs.
2. Individuals have the right to review all personal information maintained regarding them.
3. Individuals have the right to demand that erroneous information be removed and/or corrected.

State legislatures have taken a cue from the federal government and many have patterned laws after the Privacy Act of 1974 (fig. 14.23).

Summary

Time sharing with online real-time processing is the fastest-growing segment of data processing. The principal advantage of time sharing is that it allows many people at remote locations to share the facilities of the computer, thus eliminating many of the delays in processing information to and from a data-processing system.

Communication networks have been developed that move data at speeds similar to the speed at which it can be processed. The major shift from offline to online systems has focused attention on data base management systems as well as communication networks. DBMS have overcome the frustration of processing data in file-oriented systems and have paved the way for optimally storing data so that it can support a firm's processing demands. Distributed data processing has provided methods of distributing the data processing, data communications, and data base management functions so they can be more responsive to their users wherever they may be.

This chapter introduces and explains the ever-changing features of online real-time processing systems, including the important segments of data communications, data base management, and distributed data processing. With the increased use of computerized data files, data processing has an obligation to protect the personal privacy of the individual records contained in the files. It is important that one realizes the potential of online real-time processing and time sharing and what an important role it is playing in the data-processing field today.

1. Real-time processing enables the system to provide the necessary data for a decision at an optimal way and time for all the needs of management. Data communications is the movement of information by means of electronic transmission. Telecommunications transmit information over communication lines. Networks are an array of machines attached to telecommunication lines used for transmitting and receiving data.
2. Batch processing is the execution of programs serially. A data base is a collection of data fundamental to an enterprise. Online is the equipment and devices under the control of the central processing unit. Real time is the actual time during

which a physical process transpires. Time sharing is the interleaved use of the time of a device by a number of users.

3. Online real-time systems are composed of the computer, the data base, terminals, a communication network, and software. It simplifies input preparation, reduces the number of programs needed, eliminates duplicate records, improves editing accuracy and controls, and provides timely information. However, online real-time systems result in higher costs for processing, hardware, and software.
4. Time sharing allocates computer time and services to multiple users at different locations. Input/output processor is given direct access to the computer's main memory. Space is automatically allocated in the main memory for user's programs. Time sharing schedules the computing tasks performed by the central processor. It performs nearly all of the systems housekeeping tasks including keeping track of the usage of the system to facilitate task scheduling and to allow correct billing to be performed. The data base is the accumulation of the data necessary to meet the information requirements of the organization. The data base management system (DBMS) implements, manages, and protects large-scale data bases. The data base administrator has the responsibility for the data base design and development. The data dictionary is a well-organized, up-to-date notebook containing basic information about data elements. Distributed data processing places processing power at points where the data is generated or where the data is needed for supervision or management. Networks consist of two or more processors linked together by communication lines.
5. There are two types of time sharing. Conversational time sharing communicates with the computer through some computer language in an immediate response mode. Remote-batch time sharing gives no immediate response as data is entered into central computer at a convenient time.
6. The information explosion has resulted in the building of large data bases of personal records. This has raised the question of the right to personal privacy versus the right to know. The Privacy Act of 1974 states that a person has the right to know what information is collected, and can review all personal information, and has the right to demand corrections and/or removal of erroneous data.

Identification Questions

Match the following terms with the statements below.

A. Batch Processing
B. Conversational Time Sharing
C. Data
D. Data Base
E. Data Base Administrator (DBA)
F. Data Base Management Systems (DBMS)
G. Data Communications
H. Data Dictionary
I. Distributed Data Processing
J. Host Computer
K. Information
L. Networks
M. Online
N. Online Real-Time Systems
O. Online System
P. Privacy
Q. Real Time
R. Remote-Batch Time Sharing
S. Satellite Computer
T. Time Sharing

1. A collection of data fundamental to an enterprise.
2. Pertaining to an application in which the response to input is fast enough to affect subsequent processing.
3. One or more computers and other devices which control or monitor the environment by receiving and processing data and outputting results in sufficient time to affect the environment.
4. A computerized system consisting of numerous components, which has as a collective purpose, the implementation, management, and protection of large-scale data bases.
5. The user and computer are in an immediate response mode.
6. A computer that provides supporting service in a distributed data-processing system.
7. The movement of information by means of electronic transmission.
8. Equipment or devices under control of the central processing unit.
9. The use of the computer facility by various independent users.
10. The representation of a fact or event.
11. A well-organized, up-to-date notebook containing basic information about data elements.
12. Place the processing power at points where the data is generated or where the data is needed for supervision or management.
13. The user accesses a computer from remote locations and there is no immediate response.
14. The right of an individual to be free in private affairs from surveillance and intrusion.
15. The execution of computer programs serially.
16. A system in which input data enters the computer directly from the point of origin or in which output data is transmitted directly to where it is used.
17. The result of the collection, analysis, and summarization of data.
18. Management of data resources to see that it is efficiently stored so that it can be retrieved in the form of meaningful information.
19. Two or more processors linked together by communication lines to distribute complex computing services to a large number of users.
20. A computer that depends upon a host computer for guidance in a distributed data-processing system.

Questions for Review

1. What is the importance of online real-time processing in eliminating many of the delays in transmitting data?
2. What is meant by data communications and what are its main characteristics?
3. What is a communication network and what is its main purpose?
4. What is meant by an online real-time system?
5. Describe the major components of an online real-time system.
6. What are some of the problems of online processing?
7. What are the main advantages and serious disadvantages of an online processing system?
8. What is time sharing?

9. What are some of the important advances in time sharing?
10. In the revised concept of information processors, what is the relationship between data, information, and data base?
11. What is the importance of a data base to an organization?
12. What are the important benefits of an efficient data base design approach?
13. What are the important benefits of a data base management system (DBMS)?
14. What is a data base management system and what is its main features?
15. What are data base administrators and what are their primary functions?
16. What is a data dictionary and what purpose does it serve in a data base management system?
17. What is the concept and primary function of distributed data processing?
18. What are the roles of the host and satellite computers in distributed data processing?
19. What is a network and what is its main purpose in distributed data processing?
20. What is meant by conversational time sharing?
21. List the important advantages of conversational time sharing.
22. What is remote-batch time-sharing processing?
23. Discuss the problem of the growing threat to personal privacy. What is your opinion on this controversial subject?

Key Terms

Batch Processing
Conversational Time Sharing
Data
Data Base
Data Base Administrator (DBA)
Data Base Management Systems (DBMS)
Data Communications
Data Dictionary
Distributed Data Processing
Host Computer
Information
Networks
Online
Online Real-Time Systems
Online System
Privacy
Real Time
Remote-Batch Time Sharing
Satellite Computer
Time Sharing

SCREEN ACTORS GUILD
ON-LINE MEMBERSHIP SYSTEM

MASTER MENU

```
          KEY IN MODE YOU DESIRE:

          01 = INQUIRY                          13 = NEW AGENT
          02 = ALPHA LIST                       14 = NEW CLIENT OR CONTRACT
          03 = STATION 12 STATUS REQUEST        15 = AGENT CHANGES
          04 = NEW MEMBER                       16 = CLIENT CHANGES
          05 = MASTER FILE CHANGES              17 - CLIENT INQUIRY
          06 = WALK-UP RECEIPTS                 18 = TAFT HARTLEY ALPHA
          07 = MAIL RECEIPTS                    19 = SAG COMMUNICATIONS
          08 = MAILING CHANGES                  20 = MAILING INQUIRY
          09 = NEW MAILINGS                     21 = CLIENT ALPHA LIST
          10 = NEW TAFT HARTLEY                 22 = AGENT ALPHA LIST
          11 = TAFT HARTLEY CHANGES             23 = AGENT INQUIRY
          12 = TAFT HARTLEY INQUIRY
```

INQUIRY

```
MEMBER NO:   NY-080363
SOCIAL NO:   558-64-8631             BRANCH:        LA          TRANS FLAG:    0
L NAME:      OHARA                   STATUS:                    TRANS FROM:    NY
F NAME:      ADORE    M N:           SAG J/DATE:    05-04-73    TRNS FRM DT:   19-01-76
ADDR 1:      1349 CHEROKEE #124      PARENT:        01          MISC CD:       0000
ADDR 2:      LOS ANGELES CA          PD W/PAR CD:   C           L/YR EARN:     000548
ADDR 3:                              PD W/PAR DT:   05-77       CLASS:
ZIP CD:      90028 SEX: M N G ADDR:  WITHDR DATE:   00-00-00    PRM PAY DTE:   00-00-00
             1                       SPC DATE:                  INIT FEE:      0125.00
PHONE 1:     999-464-0101            REINSTMT DT:   01-11-75    INIT PD:       0125.00
PHONE 2:     999-464-0101            STATION 12:    00000-000   PAST DUES:     0000.00
L/MF CHG:    22-07-77                                           ADV PAY:       0000.00
BILL         PR   BR   DU   OWED     RECPT NO       RECPT NO    RECPT NO       RECPT NO
DATE    CL   CD   CD   DU   PAID     RECPT DT       RECPT DT    RECPT DT       REINST DT
05-77   09   C              25.00    051714         000000      000000         000000
                            25.00    27-05-77       00-00-00    00-00-00       00-00-00
11-76   09   Y              15.00    020882         000000      000000         000000
                            15.00    20-12-76       00-00-00    00-00-00       00-00-00
05-76   09   Y              12.50    026325         032086      000000         000000
                            12.50    19-07-76       01-10-76    00-00-00       00-00-00
11-75   09   C              20.00    002201         000000      000000         000000
                            20.00    11-11-75       00-00-00    00-00-00       00-00-00
05-75   09   C              20.00    000000         000000      000000         000000
                            20.00    00-00-00       00-00-00    00-00-00       00-00-00
XMIT TO CONTINUE.
```

ALPHA LIST

ALPH LIST . . . . KEY IN STARTING POINT . . *****

ALPHA LIST

```
MORE    NAMES?   (Y/N).  ENTER    SOCIAL    NO. IF    INQUIRY   DESIRED
. . . . _ . . . _ . . . .
                               000-00-0000  AARON         JOSHUA        550-98-3871
                               000-00-0000  AARON         NICHOLAS      544-52-6730
                               000-00-0000  AARON         RICHARD       017-34-3978
                               000-00-0000  AARON         WILLIAM     H 347-01-3872
                               000-00-0000  ABAD          JEAN          559-24-9990
                               000-00-0000  ABAGNALO      GEORGE        127-42-6448
                               000-00-0000  ABARCA        LYDIA         121-40-7158
                               000-00-0000  ABASCAL       NATY          103-40-2140
                               000-00-0000  ABBASSI       ELIZABETH     357-05-9995
TOLLEFSON   LISA               572-21-4680  ABBEY         CLAIRE        100-14-8734
$CHOTT      PROF             B 359-38-9579  ABBOTT        ANNIE         069-34-2432
(DANGELO)   CHARLENE         D 558-88-6580  ABBOTT JR     BUD           570-52-7664
AAKER       BILLY              556-25-5262  ABBOTT        CHARLES       334-32-9403
AAKER       GINA-MARI          560-98-2609  ABBOTT        CHRIS         074-38-2628
AAMES       WILLIE             572-96-3663  ABBOTT        DIAHNNE       103-34-5961
AANNING     ASTRID             087-32-8779  ABBOTT        JERRY         055-16-2466
AARIN       JAN                542-48-8495  ABBOTT        JOHN          102-14-9559
AARON       DAVID              522-60-3824  ABBOTT        LAWRENCE      572-46-8372
AARON       GEORGE             563-28-2009  ABBOTT        LORETTA       083-30-5493
AARON       HENRY            L 087-28-0671  ABBOTT        MICHELE     C 562-44-7059
AARON       JACK               121-26-0276  ABBOTT        PETER         187-20-2793
```

```
CALL NO=075
DATE 29-07-77 TIME 06:38
CALLER=MACKIE MANN                    PHONE-714-752-8692 EXT. 103
PROD CO=ADVERTISING MGMT INC          PROD NO-CENTURY 21
ADDRESS=18872 MACARTHUR BLVD
        IRVINE CA 92507
                                      MESSAGE: OK TO CLEAR PER FRANK
```

LAST NAME	FIRST NAME	M/NAME	SOC/MEM. NO.	START	STATUS
VALENTINE	RICHARD		005-30-4530	07-29-77	
VALENTINE	DICK		005-30-4530	07-29-77	NAME-OK
BONIWELL	NANCY		550-54-1248	07-29-77	
BONNIWELL	NANCY		550-54-1248	07-29-77	NAME-OK
WILEY	DAVE		234-42-0513	07-29-77	
WILEY	DAVID		234-42-0513	07-29-77	NAME-OK
BECK	MARY	ANN	556-52-0031	07-29-77	
BECK	MARY	ANN	556-52-0031	07-29-77	OK
YOTHERS	COREY	BUMPER	572-27-3771	08-01-77	
BUMPER			572-27-3771	08-01-77	NAME-OK
LOVELL	ROSEMARY		374-38-0592	08-01-77	
LOVELL	ROSEMARY		374-38-0592	08-01-77	OK
PARNELL	BERNARD		362-20-2838	08-01-77	
PARNELL	BERNARD		362-20-2388	08-01-77	-OK

N E W   M E M B E R

```
   MEMBER NO: NY-100974          SOC. SEC. NO:  376-52-0295          SEX:  F
   LAST NAME: BRYANT ............. FIRST NAME:  DEIRDRE. . .
                                  MIDDLE NAME:  D. . . . . .
      ADDR 1: 105 W 55TH ST, PH-2 .    ADDR 2:  NEW YORK     NY. . .
      ADDR 3: ....................     ZIP CD:  . . . .          PHONE 1: 212-582-0923
     PHONE 2: 999-753-2310             BRANCH:  NY                PARENT: 01
 PD/W PAR DT: 11/77               PD/W PAR CD:  Y               MISC CD: . . . . .
   BILL DATE: 05/77                 INIT OWED:  0250.00        DUES OWED: 0015.00
  BIRTH DATE: 06/07/48           HOW JOINED: 3  EDUCATION:   Y TALENT CD:
```

WALK-UP RECEIPTS

```
    MEMBER NO:  -074009 AMT PAID:  0025.00                 SAG RECEIPT NO:XX-XXXXX
     ADJ DUES:  XXXX.XX ADJ CODE:    REINST CHG: XXXX.XX         INIT CHG:XXXX.XX

      L/NAME:  BALES               F/NAME: WILLIAM          M/NAME:
  SOC. SC. NO:  509-56-5277

           INIT FEE  REST FEE  PST DUE   CURR DUE  ADV PAY   AMT OWED
    OWED:      .        .        .        25.00      .        25.00
 APPLIED:      .        .        .        25.00      .          .

 PAID W/PARENT DATE:  /  PWP CODE:  PARENT: 06
```

SCREEN ACTORS GUILD, INC.

074009
07/22

For Six Month Period Beginning
05-77

If Paid Currently with your Parent Actors Union, the Amount Due S.A.G. is:

This is a Temporary Receipt.
If no "Total Due," then this is a temporary Paid-up card until regular card is mailed to you.

Payment Received 07/22/77

Owed	Description	Applied
	Initiation	
25.00	Current Dues	25.00
	Arrears Due	
	Credit	
	*See Reverse	
25.00	Total Due	

Important: See Other Side

Branch of Associated Actors and Artistes of America
Affiliated with AFL-CIO

-074009 — Member's No.
509-56-5277 — Social Security No.
07/22/77 CK00000 — Receipt No.
10/31/77 — Expiration Date

Member Name
WILLIAM BALES

... = 05
...NGTH
THEN ;

003 000003

00 000000

00 000000

25 005101

37 040231

14 114632

00 120020

00 000000

time-sharing programming 15
BASIC programming language

Chapter Outline

Chapter Objectives

The learning objectives of this chapter are

1. to describe the features of BASIC, the most widely used programming language for conversational time sharing and personal computers.
2. to enable you to compose and debug your program right at the terminal keyboard.
3. to provide the necessary motivation for writing programs in BASIC and by seeing your own program compiled and executed.
4. to provide a sound basis for future programming efforts in more complex programming languages.

Figure 15.1 An example of a time-sharing system. (Photo by Ken Firestone)

Time sharing is working directly with a computer; whether you are in the same room with the computer or hundreds of miles away, essentially you are alone with the machine. To achieve this almost instantaneous usage by several people at the same time requires that computer equipment effectively share its time among various remote input terminals permitting a continuous flow of data between the central computer and its users.

The computer can be located anywhere and access to the central computer system is through a telephone connector and a terminal (fig. 15.1). To gain access to the central computer, the user must know how to operate the keyboard terminal and must know the language that the computer understands.

Using the system is rather simple, since the computer and its user talk back and forth via the printed page or visual display and the keyboard terminal. The user calls the computer center on the telephone, is identified with a user number, and proceeds to teletype a new problem or retrieve an old program. The only contact between the user and the central computer is the terminal. This "conversation" with the computer should produce the end result—the answer to a particular problem (fig. 15.2).

The other requirement for conversational time sharing is a language that the computer understands. If you have used a computer before, you probably had to wait a day or more for answers to your problem. You programmed your problem (usually requiring assistance from an experienced programmer) and had it keypunched. Then you took the deck of punched cards to the computer room where your program was

USER NUMBER-X15006	The computer asks you to identify yourself. You type in your number, **X15006**.
SYSTEM-BASIC	The computer asks what computing system you want to use. You reply with **BASIC**.
NEW OR OLD-NEW	The computer asks whether the program is already stored in the system **(OLD)** or is to this time **(NEW)**. You answer **NEW**.
NEW PROBLEM NAME- SOLU	The computer requests an identifying name so the program can be saved for future use. Y name, **SOLU**.
READY	The computer informs you that it is ready for the input of the new program named **SOLU**, be run in the **BASIC** programming system.
10 INPUT Y	In Statement **10**, the value of **Y** will be inputted at execution time when the computer request typing a question mark (?).
20 LET X=Y↑2	Statement **20** causes the value in Statement **10** to be squared and the results to be stored in a loca referred to as **X**.
30 INPUT Z	A value for **Z** is entered . . .
40 LET R=Z↑2	. . . and raised to the second power, with the results being stored in **R**.
50 LET S=X+R	This sums the values of the two squared quantities and stores this value in **S**.
60 LET T=SQR (S)	A function is requested to calculate the square root of the value of **S**, and this result is stored in **T**. A function is a series of instructions which can be called by a symbolic name to accomplish a complex task such as extracting a square root. **T** is your answer.
70 PRINT	You print a blank line for spacing.
80 PRINT "ANSWER IS" T	You print a legend "**Answer is**" with the value of **T**, the answer, following.
90 PRINT	Again, you cause a blank line to be inserted for appearance.
100 GO TO 10	Statement **100** cycles the program back to Statement **10**, so you can input another set of data and get another answer.
110 END	The **END** statement informs the computer that all the statements comprising the program have been entered.
	Now, you have the option of having your program **RUN** or **SAVED**.
RUN	Typing **RUN** causes the program to be executed.
SOLU 9:16 THURS 03-07-68	Before actual execution, the computer types out the symbolic name of the program, the time of day, the day of the week, and the date. Then it begins execution.
? 4	The computer executes the request for the first item of information by typing a question mark. This is the signal for you to input your first value, which in this case is **4**.
? 4	The computer asks for the second required item of information, and you respond with another **4**.
ANSWER IS 5.65685	The computer calculates the square of each inputted quantity, sums these squares, and extracts the square root of this sum, printing the legend and the answer.
?6	Since this problem was programmed to do multiple combinations, a question mark indicates the computer is now ready for the first of the next set of data to be entered. In this case, you input a **6**.
?9	The second question mark asks for the second item of data, and you input a **9**.
ANSWER IS 10.8167	The computer again makes its calculation and prints its answer.
?STOP	Another question mark awaits the next set. If you choose to stop, type in **STOP**.
RAN 6 SEC	The computer informs you that **6 seconds** of computer time were required to run your program.
STOP READY	Then it reminds you that you stopped execution and it is ready for your next desire.
SAVE	You type in **SAVE**, so the program will remain on the disc file.
LIST 10 INPUT Y 20 LET X=Y↑2 30 INPUT Z 40 LET R=Z↑2 50 LET S=X+R 60 LET T=SQR(S) 70 PRINT 80 PRINT "ANSWER IS" T 90 PRINT 100 GO TO 10 110 END	If you are interested in a final copy of what has been stored, type **LIST** and the program will be typed for you by the computer.
BYE	You type **BYE** to tell the computer you have terminated your work at this time.
OFF AT 9:35 RAN 30 SEC	The computer tells you the time you are off the machine and the total time you consumed using it for this specific operation.

Figure 15.2 Conversation with a computer.

scheduled to run along with others. Finally, the program was processed through the computer and returned to you with the finished results. More often than not, changes had to be made and the deck of punched cards had to be returned to the computer room with the corrections and rerun on the computer. This entire process can take from one to three days, depending upon the schedule and work load in the central computer center. Time sharing has eliminated many of these delays. Now you can check your program in a few minutes right at the machine.

ng

A program is a set of directions that is used to tell a computer how to provide an answer to some problem. It usually starts with the given data, contains a set of instructions to be performed or carried out in a certain order, and results in a set of answers.

Any program must fulfill two requirements before it can be carried out. First, it must be presented in a language that is understood by the computer. If the program is a set of instructions for solving a system of linear equations and the computer is an "English-speaking" machine, the program will be presented in some combination of mathematical notation and English.

Second, all programs must be completely and precisely stated. This requirement is crucial when dealing with a computer that has no ability to infer what is meant; it does what the user tells it to do, not what the user meant to tell it. This applies to programs that provide numerical answers to numerical problems. It is easy for a programmer to present a program in the English language, but such a program poses many difficulties for the computer because English is rich in ambiguities and redundancies, those qualities which make poetry possible, but computing impossible. Instead the program must be presented to the computer in a language, which resembles ordinary mathematical notation, has a simple vocabulary and grammar, and permits a complete and precise specification of the program. BASIC is precise, simple, and easy to understand.

Too often the teaching of computer programming and processing is complicated unnecessarily by the use of complex and hard-to-remember computer languages. The use of BASIC permits the user to concentrate on development of programming skills common to all programming rather than rules and formats peculiar to a particular language. This computer language foundation is applicable to any future computer experience, regardless of the languages that are available.

With time-shared BASIC, the user can get simultaneous "hands on" experience, in contrast to the inherent delays and lack of interaction common to most batch processing systems.

BASIC is so simple and natural that the user will spend only a minimum amount of time mastering it and can therefore concentrate on learning programming techniques. BASIC is a user's language that minimizes the clerical tasks of "set-up." It can be used at a terminal in rather free form for input and output, thus eliminating many of the problems in formulating data required by other computer languages.

The language and logic of BASIC was developed by faculty members and undergraduates at Dartmouth College. It is not unusual for beginners to start composing their own BASIC programs within a half hour after they have been introduced to the system. Debugging, updating, or composing programs can be done right at the remote terminal keyboard. BASIC makes every person a programmer. This person does not need to be concerned with the fact that the computer uses binary arithmetic, rather than decimal, or that the program (as the computer sees it) is complicated by being written in binary "words."

Operation of BASIC Programs

BASIC is a simple and efficient problem-solving language. It provides its users with efficient, rapid, flexible, and precise problem-solving activities. Users create, execute, debug, and save BASIC programs from typewriter-like terminals, conveniently located

Figure 15.3 The BASIC keyboard.

in classrooms, offices, or laboratories, which may be far from the central computer (fig. 15.3). At the terminal keyboard, the user types problem-solving statements and input data, one line at a time, transmitting them to the computer. Messages and output data are (at the user's request) printed at the terminal.

As the term *time sharing* implies, many users are sharing the same facilities of the computer. Because of the speed of computer processing, each user is unaware of any activity at any other terminal. All users have immediate access to the computer, the same priority and the same share of the computer resources. The programs are executed dynamically and results are available immediately. The computer and user are in constant conversation; programs are checked as they are entered, line by line, and errors can be corrected at once (fig. 15.4).

Features of BASIC Programs

Besides the ability to *build* and *execute* BASIC programs, each user can do the following at the terminal.

1. Test and debug programs dynamically.
2. Modify a program freely through a single or multiple line insertion, deletions, or replacements.
3. Build and modify text. *Text is a collection line that is typed at the terminal.* This can be useful for preparing reports, program documentation, and saving any kind of data. Unlike BASIC programming, text entries do not follow any programming rules.
4. Have the system store programs and text for later use. (Each user has programs, text, and files; the contents of a user's private library cannot be touched by any other user.)
5. Every terminal user has a password (user-identifier code) that is used to identify the user to the system every time the user signs on at the terminal. This password protects the user's programs and text from use or destruction by other users.
6. BASIC is designed to detect a wide variety of program errors and to inform the user of an error as soon as it is detected. In some cases (such as misspelling and other syntactical errors), an error will be found right after a BASIC statement has been typed. In other cases (such as missing statements and semantic errors),

Let's examine the following BASIC program which causes computer to square and cube each of the numbers 1 to 10, and provide a printout of these values.

Explanation	Statement
In the first statement, we assign the variable "I" a value of 1. (The teleprinter types a "Ø", for zero, to distinguish it from the letter O.)	1Ø LET I = 1
This statement specifies that if "I" is larger than 10, the computer will jump to statement 6Ø for the next instruction.	2Ø IF I > 1Ø THEN 6Ø
Now, since we want the computer to list the value I, the square of I, and the cube of I, we write statement 30 as shown. The ↑ is used to indicate raising to a power (the teleprinter cannot type subscripts and superscripts).	3Ø PRINT I, I↑2, I↑3
The computer is instructed to increment the value of "I" by one in this statement.	4Ø LET I = I + 1
Here the computer is instructed to jump back to statement 2Ø, creating a program loop. The computer will cycle around and around this loop until "I" is greater than 1Ø, at which time statement 2Ø instructs it to jump to statement 6Ø.	5Ø GO TO 2Ø
The computer is instructed to print the phrase "Program Complete."	6Ø PRINT "PROGRAM COMPLETE"
This statement identifies the end of the program.	7Ø END
If we want to print a heading, we add statement 5 to provide column headings. (The computer automatically places this statement in proper sequence, ahead of 1Ø.)	5 PRINT "VALUE", "SQUARE", "CUBE"

PROGRAM OUTPUT:

```
VALUE    SQUARE    CUBE
  1        1        1
  2        4        8
  3        9        27
  4        16       64
  5        25       125
  6        36       216
  7        49       343
  8        64       512
  9        81       729
  10       100      1000
  PROGRAM COMPLETE
```

Figure 17–6. BASIC Program Operation.

Figure 15.4 BASIC program operation.

errors can be detected only after the user has requested that the program be executed. Whenever an error is detected, a message will be printed to help the user to locate the error and correct it.

7. BASIC provides a common library into which an installation can place any programs, files, and text collections that it wants to make available to *all* users. The user uses the contents of the common library in the same manner as the contents of a private library. However, the user cannot in any way change the contents of the common library; only installation-authorized personnel can do that.

Terminal Operating Procedures

Before entering the program, the user must be identified to the system. The exact procedure to be followed will depend upon the particular time-sharing system being used. The following steps will help to get *online* with the system.

1. *Call the computer.* Telephone lines are used with computers in two ways, either dial-up or direct-line.

   Using the *dial-up* method, turn *on* the mainline switch on the terminal keyboard. Dial the telephone number of the computer. The computer should respond with a high-pitch tone or an indicator light. Place the telephone in the acoustical receptacle. Now log on in a prescribed manner.

   Using the *direct-line* method, merely turn on the mainline switch on the terminal keyboard and depress the RETURN key. This will connect you with the computer. *Note:* Each message to the computer must be completed by depressing the RETURN key on the terminal keyboard.

2. *Logging-on* is the process of identifying yourself to the computer. The method of logging on is dependent on the particular type of time-sharing system being used.

   For example, pressing the RETURN key will cause an inquiry message to be outputted asking which interactive programming language you want to use. The language is indicated together with a password. The password is a unique identification number for each user.

   Our time-sharing system asks you whether the program is new or old. This means that the computer wants to know whether you are going to work on an old program already stored in the computer's memory or whether you are going to write a new one.

   After you have successfully logged on, the computer will type a response message (such as date) and usually follow this with the word READY, which means that the computer is now ready to accept instructions written in BASIC. (Some time-sharing systems require further instructions including the word BASIC during the log-on procedure.)

   Note: Since each time-sharing system may be a little different, it is a good practice to review a sample of an actual log-on session for your system.

Figure 15.5 A sample of a LIST command.

To see what your program actually looks like after many insertions, deletions, replacements and typing corrections, just type LIST and the computer will print a clean copy of your program with statement numbers included and insertions appearing where they belong. Our previous example, including a LIST command, would look like this:

As you can see, the computer lists the program in statement number sequence immediately after the LIST command. All lowercase letters are converted to uppercase by the computer and hence appear as uppercase in the listing.

```
READY    edit abc basic
EDIT     10 rem this is just a sample program.
EDIT     20 input a
EDIT     30 let b = a
EDIT     40 let c = 2*b
EDIT     50 print b,c
EDIT     60 let z = sqr(b+c)
EDIT     70 print 'z is',z
EDIT     44 let d = 3*c
EDIT     47 let e = 4*d
EDIT     50 print b,c,d,e
EDIT     80 let x = sqr (d+e)
EDIT     90 print 'x is',x
EDIT     100 end
EDIT     list
00010    REM THIS IS JUST A SAMPLE PROGRAM.
00020    INPUT A
00030    LET B = A
00040    LET C = 2*B
00044    LET D = 3*C
00047    LET E = 4*D
00050    PRINT B,C,D,E
00060    LET Z = SQR(B+C)
00070    PRINT 'Z IS',Z
00080    LET X = SQR(D+E)
00090    PRINT 'X IS',X
00100    END
```

Commands

Commands are orders issued to the computer, such as LIST and LOGOFF. Commands do not cause the computer to perform any logical or mathematical operations (for example, they do not have any problem-solving capability); they control the function of the computer. *Commands do not need line numbers.* Some of the more common commands with their function are:

```
logon w0004
THANK YOU.             DATE 05/25/7      TIME 12.40.02
READY edit avg basic
EDIT  10 rem this finds the average of any 4 values
EDIT  20 input a,b,c,d
EDIT  30 let x = a+b+c+d
EDIT  40 let y = x/4
EDIT  50 print 'the average is:',y
EDIT  60 end
EDIT  run
?     95,78,93,79
THE AVERAGE IS:   86.25
EDIT  save
EDIT  end
READY logoff
LOGGED OFF AT 12.43.12
TIME USED 00.03.10
```

Figure 15.6 An example of creating, executing, and saving a program.

Command	Function
LIST	Causes the system to display all or part of a program or text collection at the terminal (fig. 15.5).
LISTCAT	Provides a list of the name of every program, text collection, and file that the user has in a private library.
LOGOFF	Ends a terminal session.
LOGON	Identifies the user to the system and initiates a session at the terminal.
RUN	Causes a program to be executed.
SAVE	Causes a program or text collection to be saved in the user's private library (fig. 15.6).
SCRATCH	Causes the erasure of the current program.

Writing a BASIC Program

Instructions

Each instruction must be entered on a separate line and followed by a carriage return. Each line of the program begins with a *line number* that identifies the lines, each of which is called a *statement*. A program is made up of a series of statements, which serve as instructions to the computer. The line number also serves to specify the sequence in which the statements are to be executed by the computer. This allows the programmer to type a program in any sequence and to specify the order of execution (fig. 15.7). Before the program is run, the computer sorts and edits the program according to its line numbers. This editing process facilitates the correcting and changing of programs.

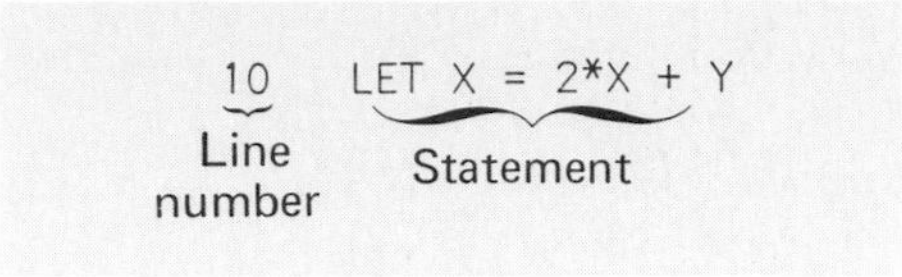

Figure 15.7 The BASIC statement format.

Every program must have an END statement so that the computer will know when it has performed all of the program. The END statement must be the highest numbered instruction in the program.

Elements of BASIC Instructions

Character Set

Numerals, 0 through 9.
Letters, A through Z.
Special characters, b. : ' < = > & + ,) (; ? − ! " / * ↑ $ (Small "b" denotes a blank character. The ↑ symbol is not used in IBM BASIC.)

Note: Sôme computers use single quotes (parentheses or apostrophes) while others use double quotes. Both designations have the same function.

Statement Number

One to four digits may be used, from 1 to 9999.

Label

Any group of characters enclosed in quotation marks, for example, "THIS IS BASIC PROGRAM 1." or "10/24/79."

Constant

A value, either signed or unsigned, that remains unchanged during the execution of the program, such as 515, 276.45, and −521.49645.

Variable

A variable is any letter or any letter followed by a number. It is a value that is not known by the programmer at the time the program is written. Variables are assigned values by LET, READ, or INPUT statements (fig. 15.8). Once these values are assigned, they will not change until the next time a LET, READ, or INPUT statement is encountered with a value for that variable. For example in the statement 140 LET X = T + 1, X is considered to be the variable.

Figure 15.8 Assigning values to variables.

```
10  let x = 40
20  let y = 172
30  let t = x + y
40  z = t + 120
```

Numbers

A number may be positive or negative and may contain up to nine digits. The number must be expressed in a decimal format, such as 5, 2.641, and −.0051.

Formulas

In the BASIC language, the computer performs its calculations by evaluating formulas that are supplied by the program. The formulas are similar to those used in ordinary mathematical calculations, except that each BASIC formula must be completed on one line.

Arithmetic

The operators used to write the formulas necessary for computations are:

Symbol	Function	Example	Meaning
+	Addition	A+B	Add B to A
-	Subtraction	A-B	Subtract B from A
*	Multiplication	A*B	Multiply B by A
/	Division	A/B	Divide A by B
↑	Exponentiation	A↑2	Raise to the power of A^2
**	(IBM "BASIC")	A**2	Raise to the power of A^2

The rules for the sequence of calculation of arithmetic expressions containing a combination of operators are:

1. Parenthetical arithmetic expressions are calculated first.
2. All exponentiations are performed next.
3. Multiplication and division are calculated next from left to right.
4. Addition and subtraction are performed last from left to right.

For example, in the arithmetic expression A + B * C ** D, the computer will first raise C to the power of D, then multiply the result by B, and lastly add A to the resulting product. If we want to alter the sequence of operations, we could write the arithmetic expression as A + (B*C)**D. The execution would then be, first B would be multiplied by C, the product would then be raised to the power D, and finally A would be added to the result.

The comparison operators are:

Symbol	Function	Example	Meaning
=	Is equal to	A=B	A is equal to B
<	Is less than	A<B	A is less than B
<=	Is less than or equal to	A<=B	A is less than or equal to B
>	Is greater than	A>B	A is greater than B
>=	Is greater than or equal to	A>=B	A is greater than or equal to B
<>	Is not equal to	A<>B	A is not equal to B

Loops

The computer is used most advantageously for repetitive work. Repetitive may mean doing a simple thing over and over for many different numbers, perhaps with slight changes each time. In order to write a simple program where a portion is written once and the program is continually repeated, a programming device known as a loop is used. For example, to repeat the same operation with fewer instructions, the following program is written:

```
10 LET X = 1
20 PRINT X, SQR (X)
30 LET X = X + 1
40 IF X < = 100 THEN 20
50 END
```

1. In the first instruction, the variable X is assigned the value of 1.
2. In the second instruction, the computer is instructed to print the values of the variable X and square root of X.
3. In the third instruction, the computer is instructed to increment the value of X by one.
4. In the fourth instruction, if X is less than or equal to 100, the computer is instructed to jump back to statement 20, creating a program loop. The computer will cycle around and around this loop until X is greater than 100, at which time the next statement will be executed.
5. In the fifth instruction, this statement identifies the end of the program. In the above program, five instructions were used instead of 101.

Statements

Statements may be either *executable* or *nonexecutable. Executable* statements are those that specify program actions, such as assigning a value to a variable (the LET statement), printing a value at the terminal (the PRINT statement), or directing the order of program flow (the GO TO statement). *Nonexecutable* statements are those that specify information necessary for program execution. The DATA statement, which provides values to be used, and the DIM statement, which specifies the size of the data arrays, are typical nonexecutable statements.

Executable and nonexecutable statements may be intermixed when a BASIC program is entered at the terminal. The statements will be presented and arranged according to the functions they perform. The functional groupings have been chosen for purposes of presentation only; they have no fundamental significance in the language. The groupings are:

1. The *assignment statement* assigns data from an expression to a variable within a program.
2. *Input/output statements* transmit data to a program for processing and from a program after processing.
3. *Control statements* direct the flow of program execution, including loops, unconditional and conditional branches, subroutines, and interruption and termination of programs.
4. The *array* is used to create lists and tables to be used in the program.

Assignment Statement

The assignment statement assigns the value of an expression to one or more variables. The LET statement is the only statement in this group.

LET

The LET statement evaluates an expression and assigns it to one or more variables. It is not a statement of algebraic equality but is rather an instruction to the computer to perform certain computations and to assign the answer to the particular variable (fig. 15.9).

```
10  LET Z$ = "CAT"
20  LET X = 9
30  LET Y(X) =2
```

After execution of statement 10, the character variable z$ will contain the word CAT followed by fifteen blank characters.

After execution of statement 20, the arithmetic variable X will have the integer value 9.

After execution of statement 30, the ninth member of the one-dimensional arithmetic array Y will have the integer value 2.

Figure 15.9 An example of a LET statement.

The format of the LET statement is

```
LET variable [, variable] = formula
```

Note: In some time-sharing systems, the word LET is optional.

Examples

`20 LET B = 6`	The constant 6 is assigned to the variable B.
`30 LET A,B,C = 5`	The constant 5 is assigned to the variable A, then to B, and finally to C.
`40 LET A1 = 62.416*Y`	The variable A1 is assigned the value of the evaluation of the expression.

Input / Output Statements

The input/output statements are used for transmitting data to a program for processing and from a program after processing. They are subdivided into two subgroups.

1. *Statements controlling the creation and use of internal files.*
   a. The READ statement assigns values to variables from the internal data file.
   b. The DATA statement creates an internal data file.
   c. The RESTORE statement causes the internal data file to be positioned at its beginning.
2. *Statements controlling data transmission to and from interactive terminals.*
   a. The PRINT statement causes data values to be printed at the terminal.
   b. The INPUT statement allows the user to assign values to variables from the terminal at execution time.
   c. The PRINT USING statement and image statements together allow the BASIC user to have data values printed at the terminal in a specified format.
   d. The PRINT TAB statement permits the computed placement of output.

READ and DATA

The LET statement is one method that is used to assign values to variables. An alternate method is through the combined use of READ and DATA statements.

A READ statement is used to assign to the listed variables values determined from a DATA statement. A READ statement causes the values listed in it to be given the next available numbers in the collection of DATA statements. Before the program is run, all of the DATA statements are collected by the computer in the order in which they are written and formed into a large data block. Each time a READ statement is encountered anywhere in the program, the data block will supply the next available number. When the data block runs out of data, the program will be assumed to be over (figs. 15.10, 15.11).

Figure 15.10
Examples of READ and DATA statements.

```
10  DATA 'JONES', 15.00, 'SMITH', 20.50
20  READ A$,A1,B$,B1
30  DATA 1,2,3,4,5,6
40  READ A,B,C,X(A),X(B),X(C)
```

After execution of the above statements, the character variables A$ and B$ will contain the characters strings JONES and SMITH respectively, each padded on the right with blanks to a length of eighteen. The arithmetic variables A1 and B1 will contain the decimal values 15.00 and 20.50, respectively. The arithmetic variables A, B, and C will contain the integer values 1, 2, and 3 respectively, and the first three members of the one-dimensional array named X will contain the integer values 4, 5, and 6, respectively.

Figure 15.11
Examples of READ and DATA statements.

```
10  read a,b$,x,#$
20  data  2507,"john doe",33,"new york"
```

The values would be assigned as follows:

```
A  = 2507
B$ = JOHN DOE
X  = 33
#$ = NEW YORK
```

You can actually have more than one DATA statement in a program; the effect is cumulative. For example:

```
10  read a,b,c,d,e,f,g
20  data 10012, -73621, 4308.973, 7.2, 15.0, -3.7
30  data 10
```

The values would be assigned like this:

```
A = 10012
B = -73621
C = 4308.973
D = 7.2
E = 15.0
F = -3.7
G = 10
```

Since data must be read in before it can be processed, READ statements normally occur near the beginning of a program. The location of DATA statements is arbitrary as long as they occur in the correct order.

The format of the READ statement is

```
READ [sequence of variables]
```

The format of the DATA statement is

```
DATA [sequence of numbers]
```

Example

```
10 LET X = 46.215*Y
20 READ Y
30 DATA 3,7,23,17
```

Whenever the computer encounters the READ statement in the program, it will read the next value of Y. The first time it will read 3, the next time 7, and so on, until there is no more data left to be read. At that time, the program will terminate. If the program had been written as 10 LET X = A * B, we would have to change the READ statement to READ A, B. The computer will then take two numbers from the DATA statement regarding the first number as A and the second as B, the third as A and the fourth as B, and so on.

RESTORE

The RESTORE statement causes the subsequent READ statement to begin assigning values from the first item in the first DATA statement of the program. The RESTORE statement returns the data table pointer from its current position to the beginning of the table. A RESTORE statement allows the data in the data table to be stepped through more than once (fig. 15.12). It restores the data table in such a way that the very next READ will start reading the data all over again. For example:

```
 10 DATA 5,29,31.2,"ABC"
 20 READ X,Y
     .
     .
     .
 80 READ Z,A$
 90 RESTORE
100 READ C1,D1
```

The DATA statement sets the values 5, 29, 31.2, and "ABC" into the data table. The first READ statement causes the first value in the data table (5) to be assigned to X and the second value (29) to be assigned to Y. At statement 80, the third value (31.2) is read into Z and the character constant (ABC) is read into A$. When the

Figure 15.12 An example of a RESTORE statement.

```
10 READ a,b,c,d
20 DATA 10012,-73621,4308.973,7.2,15.0,-3.7,10
30 RESTORE
40 READ e,f,g,h
50 READ x,y,z
```

The values would be assigned like this:

A = 10012
B = −73621
C = 4308.973
D = 7.2
E = 10012
F = −73621
G = 4308.973
H = 7.2
X = 15.0
Y = −3.7
Z = 10

data table is used up, another READ would result in the termination of execution; therefore, a RESTORE statement is used to reset the data table back to the first value. This restoring of the data table causes the READ statement in 100 to assign 5 to C1 and 29 to D1.

PRINT

The PRINT statement is used to get information out of the computer in the form of a printed report. The PRINT statement causes the value of given numerical expressions, variables, and constants to be printed at the terminal. The format of a print line is to a large extent controlled by the computer; the user can control the density of a line (such as number of items and spacing) to a certain degree, but the format of the value is standard (fig. 15.13). For example, if X has the value 472.15, B2 has the value NOTHING, and Y the value 27, this PRINT statement

```
PRINT ``X = ''; X,B2,Y
```

will result in the following printed output

```
X = 472.15000          NOTHING          27
```

Note the difference in spacing. The use of semicolons and commas between expressions in the PRINT statement controls the spacing.

STATEMENT	PRINTED OUTPUT
10 PRINT 'A','B'	A -14 blanks- B
20 PRINT 'A';'B'	AB
30 LET A$="B"	
40 PRINT 'A' A$	AB
50 PRINT A$ 'A',A$;A$	BA -13 blanks- BB
60 PRINT A$;'A'	BA
70 LET A$ = ''	
80 PRINT 'A';A$;'A'	AA

Figure 15.13 An example of a PRINT statement.

The PRINT statement may also be used to skip lines in the output form.

By using quotation marks, we can have the computer print out exactly what we specify for column headings, line titles, and so on. By omitting the quote marks, the computer will print out the value of an item. For example:

`175 PRINT ''G''`	will be outputted as G.
`185 PRINT G`	will be outputted as 475.25 (the value of G).

The format of the PRINT statement is:

```
PRINT   [label or     ] [label or          label or   ]
        [expression   ] [expression. .  .expression   ]
```

The output form in BASIC is 75 columns wide, divided into five print zones of fifteen columns each. Anything appearing in quotation marks will be printed just as it appears. When information does not appear in quotes, the comma is the signal to skip to the next print zone. As many as five printouts are possible across the page beginning at columns 0, 15, 30, 45, and 60. If more than five items are listed, the sixth would be printed in the first print zone on the next line. For example:

```
170 PRINT X,Y,Z
```

The output values would be:

```
3000  4  .09
```

```
190 PRINT U,V,W,X,Y,Z
```

The output values would be:

```
 7  1051  6.415  3000  4
.09
```

If more than five columns are required in a report, the printout can be packed by separating the variables with a semicolon instead of a comma. The spacing between the printouts will depend upon the number of characters in each variable. When each value is printed, one space appears before the number of the sign, the sign is printed only if it is minus, and as many as four spaces appear after the number. The following table shows the field widths for the different numbers of characters.

Number of Characters	Field Width
1	3
2,3,4	6
5,6,7	9
8,9,10	12
11,12,13	15

The rules for printing out numbers are:

1. No more than six significant digits are printed except for integers. If the number is an integer (in other words a whole number), the decimal point will not be printed and up to nine digits will be printed in full.
2. Any trailing zeros after the decimal point are not printed.
3. For numbers less than 0.1, the form X.XXXXXE−Y is used unless the significant part of the number can be printed as a six-digit number. For example, .0000478 is the same as 4.78×10^{-5} and will be printed as 4.78E−5.

Some of the common uses for the PRINT statement are:

1. *To print out a message in the program.* Anything included between the quote marks following the PRINT command word will be printed as is. For example, 150 PRINT "T" would cause the letter T to be printed, perhaps as a column heading.
2. *To print out the result of a computation.* For example, 150 PRINT T (without the quote marks) would cause the computer to print the value of T.
3. *To perform the combinations of the above.* For example, 150 PRINT "THE VALUE OF T IS" T will print out the message plus the value of T.
4. *To skip a line.* For example, 190 PRINT will cause the printer to advance a line each time this statement is encountered. This is a handy technique for improving the format.

INPUT

Often it is desirable to have data entered during the running of the program. This is particularly true if different people write programs. One person writes the program and other people doing the program are asked to supply the data. The INPUT statement is very similar to the READ statement but does not draw numbers from the DATA statement. The format for the INPUT statement is

```
INPUT [sequence of variables]
```

The INPUT statement allows the user to assign values dynamically during execution. When INPUT is executed, execution is interrupted and the user is asked to type values for the variables specified in the INPUT statement (fig. 15.14). For exam-

```
        10   INPUT   X,Y(X),Z(R+3),CI
        .
        .
        .
        90 RUN
     ?  25, 15.5, 4,
     TOO FEW 25, 15.5,4,.35

        10   INPUT   A$,R
        .
        .
        .
        90   RUN
     ?   'YES, 20
     MSNG QUOTE 'YES', 20
```

Figure 15.14 An example of a INPUT statement.

ple, if you wish the user to supply the values of L and M in a program, you would write the statement as 150 INPUT L, M before the first statement that is to use these values. When it encounters this statement, the computer types a question mark on the printout and waits for the input. The user types two numbers, separated by commas, and presses the RETURN key, and the computer goes on with the rest of the program. The two numbers will be used as the value of L and M in all subsequent computations. For example, if it is necessary to insert the values of X, Y, and Z into the program each time the program is executed, the following two instructions can be used.

```
150 PRINT "ENTER X, Y, Z"
160 INPUT X, Y, Z
```

The computer will now ask for the values of X, Y, and Z by typing ENTER X, Y, Z? Then you can enter such values as 8,15, and −35 by typing them in and depressing the RETURN key. The computer will then proceed to perform the necessary calculations using the values that you have furnished and print out the results. If you have programmed a *loop*, the computer will ask you each time it encounters the INPUT statement to insert the values for the variables.

Data entered by the INPUT statement is not saved with the program. It may also take a long time to enter a large amount of data using INPUT. INPUT statements should only be used when small amounts are to be entered, or when it is necessary to enter data during the program run.

PRINT USING

The PRINT USING statement is used in conjunction with an image statement to print values according to the format specified in the image statement. PRINT USING includes the values to be printed and the statement number of the image statement to be used; the image statement specifies the format of the print line (fig. 15.15). Assuming that A and B have the values 5 and −372.561, respectively, consider the result of this example.

Figure 15.15 An example of a PRINT USING statement.

```
          10 input p,i,n
          20 let a = p*(1+i/100)**n
          30 print using 40, n,a
          40 :in ## yrs amt = $####.##
          50 end
EDIT      run
?         1000.00, 5, 10
IN 10 YRS AMT = $1628.88
```

Statement 30 directs the computer to print the values of N and A using statement 40 as the image. The colon beginning statement 40 identifies it as the Image statement. The alphabetic characters are printed as they appear in the statement, the value of N replaces the first set of #'s, and the value of A replaces the final set of symbols. Note that the decimal point in the value of A is aligned on the decimal point in the image specification.

```
 50 PRINT USING 120,A,B
     .
     .
     .
120 :THE ANSWER TO QUESTION # IS + ###.###
```

The colon beginning statement 120 identifies it as an image statement. This statement causes the printed line to look like this:

```
THE ANSWER TO QUESTION 5 IS — 372.561
```

The alphabetic characters in the image statement are printed as they appear in the statement; the value of A replaces the first #, and the value of B replaces the final set of symbols. Note that the decimal point in the value of B is aligned on the decimal point in the image statement. Also note that the plus sign is overridden by the minus sign so that the negative value is accurately represented.

Another example:

```
30 PRINT USING 40, A,B
40 :RATE OF LOSS ###  EQUALS ###.## POUNDS
    RATE OF LOSS 342  EQUALS  42.04 POUNDS
                  ↑             ↑
                Value         Value
                 of A          of B
```

PRINT TAB

The TAB function is used in the PRINT statement to move the print mechanism to a position determined by the argument of the TAB. For example:

```
150 PRINT X; TAB(10); Y; TAB(2*N); Z
```

The argument of TAB refers to a print position. In the example, if the value of N is 10, the print head will move to the tenth print position after printing the value of X, and to the twentieth print position after printing the value of Y.

When using the TAB function, a semicolon should be used in the PRINT statement in order to minimize field width.

The TAB function helps to make graphs, draw designs, and plot curves. For example:

```
50 PRINT TAB(20);'*****'
```

This statement would print five asterisks starting in column 20. The TAB function overcomes some of the problems of the comma and semicolon, due to their predefined numeric fields.

Control Statements

The control statements are used to direct the flow of the program execution.

1. The GO TO (it doesn't matter if a space is left between GO and TO) causes control to be transferred either unconditionally (simple form) or conditionally (computed form).
2. The IF THEN statements are conditional branch statements that cause control to be transferred according to the result of the evaluation of a relational expression.
3. The FOR and NEXT statements define a loop which may be executed a number of times.
4. The GOSUB and RETURN statements define a subroutine.
5. The STOP statement causes the termination of program execution.
6. The END statement causes the termination of program compilation and execution.
7. The REM statement allows the user to insert comments in a BASIC program.

GO TO

There are times when it is necessary to change the sequence of commands to be executed. *The GO TO statement causes control to be unconditionally transferred to a specific statement number (simple GO TO), see figure 15.16, or to be transferred to one of a set of statement numbers, depending on the value of an expression (computed GO TO).*

```
READY  edit rtb basic
       10 let x = 1
       20 print x,x**2
       30 let x = x + 1
       40 go to 20
       50 end
```

In RTB we have created a loop in statements 20 through 40 so that when the program is run the PRINT statement will be executed once each time the value of X increases by 1. The statement that makes the loop possible is the GOTO statement. It alters the normal sequence of execution by actually specifying the next statement to be executed. It does this by referring to the number of that statement.

Figure 15.16 An example of a GOTO statement.

The format for the simple GO TO is:

```
GO TO statement number
```

Example

```
40 READ T,X,M
   .
   .
70 GO TO 40
```

The program will branch to line number 40 when it reaches the number 70. The computer will *loop* through the instruction 40–70.

The format for the computed GO TO is

GO TO S_1 (S_2. . . .S_n) ON arithmetic expression

This statement causes control to be transferred to the first, second . . . , nth statement number if the truncated integer value of the expression is 1,2, . . . *n* (respectively) at the time of execution. If the truncated integer value is less than 1 or greater than *n*, control passes to the next logically executable statement. For example:

```
50 GO TO 10,45,60 ON X/Y
```

Control is transferred to either the first, second, third, or fourth statement number depending on whether the value of X/Y is 1,2, or 3; if it is none of these, control falls through to the next sequential statement.

IF THEN

The IF THEN instructions are used when it is desirable to skip the normal sequence of commands if a certain condition exists (fig. 15.17). These statements are usually used with comparison operators.

Figure 15.17 An example of a IFTHEN statement.

```
10      let x = 1
20      print x,x**2
30      let x = x + 1
40      if x < = 50 then 20
50      end
```

As long as x satisfies the condition "x less than or equal to 50," execution will loop back to the PRINT statement. However, when x no longer satisfies the condition, then the loop will end automatically and the execution will "fall through" the IF statement to the statement on the next line, which in this case is an END statement signifying the end of the program.

The format of the IF THEN statements is

```
IF [formula] [relation] [formula] THEN [line number]
```

```
40 IF K <= L THEN 50
```

Example

If K is less than or equal to L, the program will branch to line number 50 otherwise the next line of the program will be executed.

IF THEN statements test relational expressions. If the relation is true, it transfers control to a specified line number; if the relation is false, control moves to the next sequential statement. For example:

```
 30 IF A + B = C THEN 80
120 IF X < 25.5 THEN 60
```

In statement 30, if the sum of A and B equals C, control is transferred to statement 80; otherwise, it goes to the statement sequentially following 30. In statement 120, if the value of X is less than 25.5, control is transferred to statement 60; otherwise, it goes to the statement sequentially following 120.

FOR NEXT

Sometimes it is necessary to have the same portion of a program repeated several times, possibly with some slight modification each time that portion is executed. This repetitive process in a program is called a *loop* (or program loop). Loops are a very important factor when writing programs. Because of this fact, two statements are provided in BASIC to make the task of writing loops much easier.

FOR initiates a FOR/NEXT loop, which causes the repeated execution of the statements that physically follow FOR, up to and including a matching NEXT statement (fig. 15.18).

```
10      for i = 1 to 50
20      print i,i**2
30      next i
40      end
```

In our example, the FOR statement specifies that the statement in the loop (the PRINT statement) will be executed repeatedly for successive values of I from 1 through 50 (an increment of 1 is added to I for each execution of the PRINT statement). When the value of I exceeds 50, execution of the loop is ended, and control is passed to the next logically executable statement following the NEXT statement. In this case, the following statement is an END statement denoting the end of the program. However, other instructions could precede it, or the NEXT could be the last statement in the program (in which case, the system would supply an END statement).

Figure 15.18 An example of a FOR NEXT statement.

Every FOR statement has the format:

```
FOR [variable] = [formula TO formula STEP formula]
```

The FOR and NEXT statements operate in this manner.

1. The *variable* is initialized with first formula found in the loop.
2. The *terminal value* is the second formula following TO.
3. The third formula contains the *increment value* (STEP).
4. The NEXT statement is at the bottom of the loop and must contain the same variable name as the FOR statement.

Example

```
30 FOR X = 0 to 100 STEP 5
   .
   .
80 NEXT X
```

The first time through the FOR/NEXT loop, the statements between FOR and NEXT are executed with the value of X set to 0. When NEXT is reached, X is incremented by 5 (as specified by STEP), and execution of the statements between FOR and NEXT is repeated for this new value of X. This process continues until X exceeds 100; then the loop is terminated. Note that STEP is optional; if it is omitted, an increment of 1 is assumed. Also note that at the normal termination of the loop, X is equal to 100 (figs. 15.19 and 15.20).

GOSUB and RETURN

When a particular part of a program is to be used more than once, or possibly at several different places in the overall program, it is most efficiently programmed as a subroutine. The subroutine is entered with a GOSUB statement. For example:

```
190 GOSUB 310
```

The line number, 310, is the line number of the first statement in the subroutine. The last line of the subroutine should be a RETURN statement, directing the computer to return to the earlier part of the program. For example:

```
450 RETURN
```

This statement, if it is the last line in the subroutine entered in the previous example, tells the computer to go back to the first line numbered *greater* than 190 and continue the program there.

The GOSUB statement causes control to be transferred to a specified statement, which heads a GOSUB subroutine. A GOSUB subroutine is ended by a RETURN statement, which automatically returns control to the statement sequentially following the associated GOSUB statement (fig. 15.21). Consider this example:

The following example shows the correct technique for nesting FOR loops. The inner loop is executed 100 times for each execution of the outer loop.

```
10  FOR J= A TO B STEP C(1) **3
        .
        .
        .
 (BASIC statements)
        .
        .
        .
150 FOR K = 1 TO 100
        .
        .
        .
 (BASIC statements)
        .
        .
        .
280  NEXT K
        .
        .
        .
 (BASIC statements)
        .
        .
        .
620  NEXT J
```

Figure 15.19 An example of a FOR NEXT statement.

```
10    FOR I = 1 TO 3
20        READ P(I)
30    NEXT I
40    FOR I = 1 TO 3
50        FOR J = 1 TO 5
60            READ S(I, J)
70        NEXT J
80    NEXT I
90    FOR J = 1 TO 5
100       LET S = 0
110       FOR I = 1 TO 3
120           LET S = S + P(I) * S(I, J)
130       NEXT I
140       PRINT "TOTAL SALES FOR SALESMAN "J, "$" S
150   NEXT J
900   DATA 1.25, 4.30, 2.50
910   DATA 40, 20, 37, 29, 42
920   DATA 10, 16, 3, 21, 8
930   DATA 35, 47, 29, 16, 33
999   END

RUN

SALES1        10:50

TOTAL SALES FOR SALESMAN 1                        $180.5
TOTAL SALES FOR SALESMAN 2                        $211.3
TOTAL SALES FOR SALESMAN 3                        $131.65
TOTAL SALES FOR SALESMAN 4                        $166.55
TOTAL SALES FOR SALESMAN 5                        $169.4

TIME:   0 SECS.
```

Figure 15.20 An example of a FOR NEXT statement.

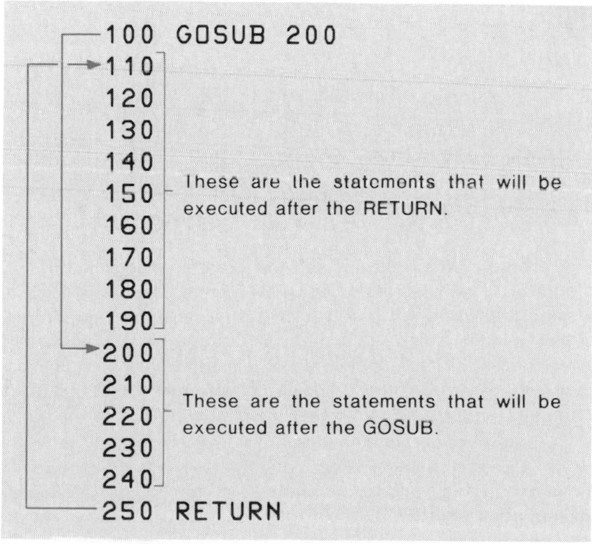

Figure 15.21 An example of the GOSUB and RETURN statements.

Figure 15.22 An example of a subroutine.

```
 10   print 'a', 'b', 'c', 'cd'
 20   read a,b,c
 30   let x = a
 40   let y = b
 50   gosub 200
 60   let x = g
 70   let y = c
 80   gosub 200
 90   print a,b,c,g
100   goto 20
110   data 60,90,120
120   data 38456,64872,98765
130   data 32,384,72
200   let q = int(x/y)
210   let r = x-q*y
220   if r = 0 then 300
230   let x = y
240   let y = r
250   goto 200
300   let g = y
310   return
320   end

EDIT save
EDIT run
A                     B              C              CD
 60                    90             120            30
 38456                 64872          98765          1
 32                    384            72             8
00020       0668        MSNG DATA
EDIT end
READY logoff
LOGGED OFF AT 12.00.42
TIME USED 00.04.12
```

A program which determines the greatest common divisor of three integers using the Euclidean algorithm, illustrates the use of a subroutine. The first two numbers are selected in statements 30 and 40 and their greatest common divisor (CD) is determined in the subroutine, statements 200-310. The CD just found is called X in statement 60, the third number is called Y in statement 70, and the subroutine is entered again from statment 80 to find the greatest common divisor (CD) of these two numbers. The result is, of course, the greatest common divisor of the three given numbers. It is printed out with them in statement 90. Note that execution ends when no more data remains to be read.

The system prints a message at the terminal giving the line at which execution was interrupted, the error message's numeric code, and the text of the message (in this case, indicating that the data has been exhausted), and then it prints "EDIT" on the next line to indicate that you are still in the edit mode. At this point you can do any of the following:

1. Edit your program (adding or deleting statements, or making changes to existing statements)
2. Type "END"—ending the edit mode, and then in response to the system cue "READY":
   a. type "LOGOFF"—ending the terminal sessions
   b. or enter "EDIT" and any program or text collection name and continue your session

```
 50 GOSUB 100
 60 . . .
 70 . . .
 80 . . .
 90 . . .
100 . . .
110 . . .
120 . . .
130 RETURN
```

The GOSUB statement causes control to be transferred to statement 100. After statements 100, 110, and 120 have been executed, the RETURN statement in 130 is executed and control is transferred back to the statement sequentially following the GOSUB associated with that RETURN (statement 60).

The GOSUB statement transfers control to a specified statement. The RETURN statement transfers control to the first executable statement following the GOSUB statement executed. Together GOSUB and RETURN statements are used in the creation of a subroutine. Execution of a subroutine begins with the GOSUB statement where the number specifies the number of the first statement in the subroutine (fig. 15.22).

STOP

The STOP statement causes execution of a BASIC program to be terminated. It can appear anywhere in the program. For example:

```
30 STOP
```

Unlike the END statement, which functions identically at execution time, the STOP statement has no effect on the compilation of the program.

The STOP statement is useful in programs having more than one natural finishing point. For example, the following two parts of a program are exactly equivalent.

```
250   GO TO 999              250   STOP
       .                            .
       .                            .
340   GO TO 999              340   STOP
       .                            .
       .                            .
999   END                    999   END
```

The STOP statement is equivalent to GO TO XXXXX, where XXXXX is the number of the END statement in the program (fig. 15.23).

```
80 STOP THIS IS THE END OF THE PROGRAM
```

Figure 15.23 An example of a STOP statement.

END

Every program must have an END statement so that the computer will know when it has performed all of the program. The END statement must be the highest numbered instruction in the program. Most programmers use a sufficiently large number to ensure that all other instructions will have lower line numbers.

The END statement indicates the logical end of a program. Any statements numerically following END are ignored in compilation and execution. Its form is simple; a line number with END. For example:

```
999 END
```

REM

An important part of any program is the description of what it does and what data should be supplied. One of the ways a program can be "documented" is by supplying remarks along with the program itself. The REM (remarks) statement provides this capability.

For example, the following REM statements could have been included in a program to calculate each student's final grade.

```
 10 REM FINAL MARK CALCULATION PROGRAM
 20 REM W IS THE WEIGHT OF EACH EXAM
 30 REM M IS THE STUDENT'S GRADE
 40 REM BEGIN TO READ DATA
850 REM CALCULATE FINAL GRADE
```

The REM statement allows the BASIC user to insert comments in the program listing. The statement is nonexecutable and has no effect on program execution. It may appear anywhere in the BASIC program. The REM statement is used to document a program and is ignored during execution (fig. 15.24).

Figure 15.24 An example of a REM statement.

```
10 REM THIS PROGRAM DETERMINES THE COST PER UNIT
```

Another example of REM:

```
10 REM THIS IS A REMARK
20 REM SO IS THIS
```

Arrays

An array is a named list or table of data items, all of which are the same type. If the array contains ten or fewer data items, no special indication of its size (dimension) is necessary. By referring to an individual data item (member) of the array in any program statement, the computer will recognize that you are working with an array and will automatically allow space for as many as ten members. An individual item (member) is referred to by giving its location in the array. For example, B (1) refers to the first member of the array named B; B (2) refers to the second member, B (3)

An array can be used quite successfully when working with programmed loops. For example, the following tabulates the marks that four different students received on five different examinations.

Figure 15.25 An example of a two-dimensional array.

	EXAMINATIONS				
	1	2	3	4	5
Student 1	75	82	85	79	91
Student 2	100	76	88	92	98
Student 3	63	60	75	72	83
Student 4	94	87	90	91	95

The weight given to each examination is as follows:

Examination	Weight
1	.10
2	.15
3	.20
4	.25
5	.30

In the following, the examination marks are represented by a two-dimensional array named M(S,E), where S is the student number (row) and E is the examination number (column). Examination weights are treated as a one-dimensional array named W(E), E being the examination number.

The following mark for each student is calculated by the following program.

```
10   FOR E=1 TO 5
20   READ W(E)
30   NEXT E
40   FOR S=1 TO 4
50   FOR E=1 TO %
60   READ M(S,E)
70   NEXT E
80   NEXT S
90   FOR S-1 TO 4
100  LET F=0
110  FOR E=1 TO 5
120  LET F=F+W(E)*M(S,E)
130  NEXT E
140  PRINT ``STUDENT'' S, ``FINAL MARK'' F
150  NEXT S
160  DATA .10,.15,.20,.25,.30
170  DATA 75,82,85,79,91
180  DATA 100,76,88,92,98
190  DATA 63,60,75,72,83
200  DATA 94,87,90,91,95
210  END
```

Steps 10 through 80 read the data into the arrays. The nested loops (loops within loops) cause the program to read the weight of each examination and the grades that each student received on the tests. Steps 90 through 150 determines the final mark received by each student, printing each grade as it is calculated.

refers to the third member; and so on. Each member giving the location of a particular member (such as 1, 2, and 3) is called a *subscript.* If the following statement was typed:

```
40 LET B(9) = 44
```

only the ninth member of B would be assigned the value 44; all other members would remain unchanged (fig. 15.25).

If more than ten members are needed in an array, the array dimension (size) must be stated so the computer will allow enough space. For example, to make T an array of 12 items, the following statement would have to be given:

```
10 DIM T(12)
```

The number appearing in parentheses is known as the bound of the dimension of the array. It specifies that the array T represents 12 different items.

DIM

The DIM statement is used to create lists and tables to be used in the program. The DIM statement informs the computer to set aside sufficient storage for the list or table. For example:

```
20 DIM H(35)
```

This statement will allow the user to enter a list of 35 items.

No special instruction is needed if no subscript greater than 10 occurs (figs. 15.26, 15.27).

Figure 15.26 An example of a DIM statement.

```
10      dim a(15)
20      for i = 1 to 15
30      read a(i)
40      next i
50      data
        2,3,5,7,11,13,17,19,23,29,31,37,41,43,47
```

A way of assigning input values is through the use of a FOR/NEXT group in conjunction with the READ and DATA statements.

Figure 15.27 An example of a DIM statement.

```
10 dim x(5), y(12)
20 input x(1), x(2), x(3), x(4), x(5), y(4)
```

The DIM statement says that X is an array representing five arithmetic values and Y is an array representing twelve arithmetic values. The INPUT statement says that you will assign values to all five members of X and to the fourth member of Y. Execution of the INPUT statement causes the computer to print a question mark (?) at the terminal. A valid response would be:

```
? 25, 33, 17, 62, 95, 43
```

The first five values of the input line are assigned to X(1) through X(5), respectively. The last value is assigned to Y(4).

Error Detection

The dialogue between the programmer and the computer is a powerful learning tool for the user. All diagnostic messages are in English and they are given to the programmer as early as possible.

With this technique, format mistakes are identified and brought to the programmer's attention when they are made. There is no waiting for a program to cycle through a batch computer queue to learn that a simple format error has prevented the execution of the program.

Diagnostics

Programming is simple when everything is done correctly. The real test of a language is what happens when there are bugs in the program. The computer can be taught to recognize errors of format and syntax and also recognize certain problems that can develop during the execution of the program, such as an attempted division by zero or a result that is too large. The computer, of course, cannot judge whether the program is going to compute what is intended. If the statements furnished to it are logical and meaningful, the computer must assume that the programmer knows how to build a program.

The system checks *each statement* for format and syntax as *it is entered.* If an error is found, a diagnostic message is typed at once. *A diagnostic message is a concise, compact, and abbreviated statement indicating what type of error it is and at what point in the program it appeared.* The system makes added checks when it is commanded to RUN and provides additional diagnostics as required.

BASIC is designed to detect a wide variety of program errors and to inform the user of an error as soon as it is detected. In some cases (such as misspelling and other syntactical errors), an error will be found right after a BASIC statement has been typed. In other cases (such as missing statements and semantic errors), errors can be detected only after the user has requested that the program be executed (run time). Whenever an error is detected, a message will be printed to help the user locate and correct the error.

Generally, the system provides three types of diagnostic errors to assist in building and executing a program. The three types of messages indicate the following:

1. *Syntax errors* are errors in the use of BASIC statements (such as invalid operators) or system commands.
2. *Semantic errors* are errors in the structure of the program (such as invalid loops and invalid GO TO) discovered after a RUN command is given but before execution actually begins.
3. *Execution errors* are logical errors discovered during the execution of a BASIC program (such as dividing by zero).

Any error causes the system to print a message at the terminal as soon as the error is detected. This message is very concise and compact (fig. 15.28). A list of error messages (both abbreviated and long form) is given in the computer manufacturer's reference manual for the language.

Figure 15.28
Examples of diagnostic messages.

Any error causes the system to print a message at the terminal as soon as the error is detected. This message is very concise and compact. For example, if the name of your program exceeds three characters, the system will respond with the following abbreviated message:

```
0172 COLL NM TOO LONG
```

If you are familiar with the system, you will probably understand (from the abbreviated message) the mistake you have made. If, however, you are unfamiliar with the system, or if the abbreviated message makes no sense to you, you can request a more explicit explanation by entering a question mark at the terminal. The system responds with a more detailed message explaining the error. For example:

```
READY edit number basic
0172 COLL NM TOO LONG
READY ?
0172 COLLECTION NAME MUST BE 3 CHARACTERS OR LESS
```

The message indicates at what point in the program the system cannot proceed. The system never attempts to second-guess you. If a statement is not syntactically correct, the message points to the item of the statement which makes it invalid but the system does not attempt to correct it. For example, the statement LET A = 7 * I/100) would cause the following:

```
0617 MSNG (
EDIT ?
0617 LEFT PARENTHESIS MISSING FROM STATEMENT
```

Corrections to a BASIC Program

Corrections can be made to a BASIC program as it is being inputted through the teletypewriter.

1. *To correct an entire line,* retype the line correctly using the original line number and end it with a carriage return.
2. *To delete a line*, retype the *line number only* and follow it with a carriage return.
3. *To correct a character in a line,* depress the backspace key. Then type the correct character. The character will not be erased from the page, but it will be deleted from the computer storage. For example, LEZ ← TZ = 4. If several incorrect characters have been typed, backspace once for each incorrect character (including spaces) and then retype the correct characters.
4. If an *instruction has been omitted* several lines back, just type it in with the correct line number. The computer will automatically arrange it in the proper sequence.

If you have made numerous corrections, just type LIST followed by a carriage return and the computer will type out a list of the corrected program. Once you are convinced that the program is correct, type RUN followed by a carriage return.

If you want to save your program, type SAVE *before* you type the END statement, depress the RETURN key, and wait for the computer to answer. Unless you save your program before you log off, the computer will "forget" it as soon as you sign off. To recall the saved program, all that is needed after the READY statement when you sign on is the name of the program that you have saved (figs. 15.29, 15.30, 15.31, 15.32).

```
                              DETERMINING GROSS PAY
**********************************************************************************
EMP.        NAME          HOURS BY DAYS    HOURS WORKED   REG.               EARNINGS
NO.                       S M T W T F S   REG. OT. TOTAL  HRLY.   REGULAR    OVERTIME   TOTAL
                                                          RATE
   345 LUGSCH J.            3 2 3 1 0       9    0    9   $0.98   $  8.82    $ 0.00    $  8.82
 95681 CHESTER J.           8 8 8 8 8      40    0   40   $2.85   $114.00    $ 0.00    $114.00
323456 DEVITA B.            8 4 6 8 8      34    0   34   $2.10   $ 71.40    $ 0.00    $ 71.40
231000 FOX J.               8 8 8 8 0      32    0   32   $2.50   $ 80.00    $ 0.00    $ 80.00
999990 ALLEN D.             9 8 9 9 9      40    4   44   $3.00   $120.00    $18.00    $138.00
908900 GRIER C.             8 8 5 8 5      34    0   34   $2.40   $ 81.60    $ 0.00    $ 81.60
123654 HEPP A.              8 8 8 8 8      40    0   40   $2.40   $ 96.00    $ 0.00    $ 96.00
987678 KAHN H.              8 8 0 8 8      32    0   32   $2.75   $ 88.00    $ 0.00    $ 88.00
389501 LILLY W.             8 8 4 8 8      36    0   36   $2.25   $ 81.00    $ 0.00    $ 81.00
110893 MORRIS D.            8 4 4 8 8      32    0   32   $2.60   $ 83.20    $ 0.00    $ 83.20

READY edit pii basic
EDIT  list
00010 PRINT''                                        DETERMINING GROSS PAY''
00015 PRINT00020 PRINT'' *********************************************************************************
''
00021 PRINT
00022 PRINT
00025 PRINT''  EMP.    NAME          HOURS BY DAYS    HOURS WORKED   REG.               EARNINGS''   TOTAL''
               NO.                   S M T W T F S    REG. OT. TOTAL HRLY.   REGULAR   OVERTIME
                                                                     RATE
00027 PRINT''
00028 PRINT
00029 PRINT
00030 READ E,N$,M,T1,W,T2,F,R
00031 X = 0
00034 H = M + T1 + W + T2 + F
00037 IF H <=40 GO TO 59
00040 X = H - 40
00042 LET H = 40
00045 LET O = H + X
00050 GO TO 60
00055 H = 40
00059 LET O = H
00060 E1 = H * R
00070 E2 = X * (1.5 * R)
00075 T = E1 + E2
00080 FRINT USING 85,E,N$,M,T1,W,T2,F,H,X,O,R,E1,E2,T
00085 :        ######   ############    # # # # #        ##    ##   ##    $#.##    $###.##    $###.##       $###.##
00086 PRINT
00087 PRINT
00088 GO TO 30
00089 DATA 000345,'LUGSCH J.',3,2,3,1,0,0.98
00090 DATA 095681,''CHESTER J.'',8,8,8,8,8,2.85, 323456,''DEVITA B.'',8,4,6,8,8,2.10, 231000,''FOX J.'',8,8,8,8,0,2.50
00091 DATA 999990,''ALLEN D.'',9,8,9,9,9,3.00
00100 DATA 908900,''GRIER C.'',8,8,5,8,5,2.40, 123654,''HEPP A.'',8,8,8,8,8,2.40, 987678,''KAHN H.'',8,8,0,8,8,2.75
00110 DATA 389501,''LILLY W.'',8,8,4,8,8,2.25, 110893,''MORRIS D.'',8,4,4,8,8,2.60, 908769,''ORLOW E.'',8,4,8,4,8,2.70
00120 DATA 780001,''ZINK N.'',8,8,4,4,0,2.95, 567000,''FEIN C.'',9,9,8,9,9,4.50, 300100,''JOI I.'',4,0,0,1,3,1.15
00121 END
EDIT  run
```

Figure 15.29 Illustrative BASIC program 1.

Figure 15.30 Illustrative BASIC program 2.

```
00120  END
EDIT run
  THIS IS A PROGRAM WHICH COMPUTES MARKON AND SELLING PRICE. THE COMPUTER HAS ALREADY DIGESTED
SEVERAL SETS OF DATA WHICH IT WILL COMPUTE THEN DISPLAY THE ANSWERS FOR YOU. YOU MAY ALSO
ENTER YOUR OWN DATA BY ACCURATELY FOLLOWING THE EXAMPLE BELOW:
      EXAMPLE:
                EDIT 100 DATA 40.80,30, 9.45,10
     P.S. PLEASE NOTE COMMAS ARE USED BETWEEN VALUES ONLY.
                                            PRICING MERCHANDISE
__________________________________________________________________________________________
            PERCENT OF    MARKON BASED                    MARKON BASED
MARKON       MARKON    ON SELLING PRICE  SELLING PRICE  ON COST PRICE  SELLING PRICE
$ 40.80      30.0%        $136.00          $176.80        $136.00        $ 95.20
$  9.45      10.0%        $ 94.50          $103.95        $ 94.50        $ 85.05
$ 33.60      40.0%        $ 84.00          $117.60        $ 84.00        $ 50.40
$ 16.40      15.0%        $109.33          $125.73        $109.33        $ 92.93
$  8.10      18.0%        $ 45.00          $ 53.10        $ 45.00        $ 36.90
$ 68.40      36.0%        $190.00          $258.40        $190.00        $121.60
$ 12.90      25.0%        $ 51.60          $ 64.50        $ 51.60        $ 38.70
$  8.55      20.0%        $ 42.75          $ 51.30        $ 42.75        $ 34.20
$ 33.75      12.5%        $270.00          $303.75        $270.00        $236.25
$ 46.92       8.3%        $563.27          $610.19        $563.27        $516.34
$  9.83      16.7%        $ 59.00          $ 68.83        $ 59.00        $ 49.17
$ 16.20      18.8%        $ 86.40          $102.60        $ 86.40        $ 70.20
EDIT
READY edit mer basic
EDIT list
00010 PRINT''   THIS IS A PROGRAM WHICH COMPUTES MARKON AND SELLING PRICE. THE COMPUTER HAS ALREADY DIGESTED''
00030 PRINT''   SEVERAL SETS OF DATA WHICH IT WILL COMPUTE THEN DISPLAY THE ANSWERS FOR YOU. YOU MAY ALSO ENTER''
00040 PRINT''   YOUR OWN DATA BY ACCURATELY FOLLOWING THE EXAMPLE BELOW:''
00045 PRINT''      EXAMPLE:''
00050 PRINT''         EDIT 100 DATA 40.80,30, 9.45,10''
00051 PRINT
00052 PRINT''    P.S. PLEASE NOTE COMMAS ARE USED BETWEEN VALUES ONLY.''
00055 PRINT
00057 PRINT
00058 PRINT''                                             PRICING MERCHANDISE
00060 PRINT
00062 PRINT'' ______________________________________________________________________________________________''
00063 PRINT
00064 PRINT
00065 PRINT''               PERCENT OF     MARKON BASED                        MARKON BASED''
00066 PRINT''    MARKON       MARKON     ON SELLING PRICE    SELLING PRICE   ON COST PRICE    SELLING PRICE''
00067 PRINT''
             ________  __________  _________________  _______________  _______________  _______________''
00068 PRINT
00069 PRINT
00070 READ A,B
00071 LET C = 100 * (A/B)
00072 LET S = C + A
00073 LET S2 = C - A
00074 PRINT USING 90, A, B, C, S, C, S2
00090 :           $###.##      ##.#%          $###.##           $###.##        $###.##       $###.##
00091 GO TO 70
00095 PRINT
00096 PRINT
00100 DATA 40.80,30, 9.45,10, 33.60,40, 16.40,15, 8.10,18, 68.40,36
00110 DATA 12.90,25, 8.55,20, 33.75,12.5, 46.92,8.33, 9.83,16.66, 16.20,18.75
```

```
THIS PROGRAM PRINTS OUT A DEPRECIATION SCHEDULE BASED ON STRAIGHT-LINE METHOD,
DECLINING-BALANCE METHOD, AND SUM-OF-DIGITS METHOD.  YOU WILL BE ABLE TO COMPUTE
YOUR PROBLEMS BY ENTERING THE DATA YOU WISH TO COMPUTE.  THE DATA SHOULD BE ENTERED
AS LISTED COST, SCRAP VALUE, NUMBER OF YEARS AND LIMIT. . . . ..USING COMMAS TO SEPARATE
EACH VALUE ONLY.  FOR EXAMPLE:
                          COST?    SCRAP?    YEARS?    LIMIT?
                          7000.00,    400.00,    6,    6,


    COST?    SCRAP?    YEARS?     LIMIT?

  ?   6000,1680,8,5



                                        DEPRECIATION SCHEDULE


     COST  6000                    SCRAP  1680                    YEARS  8                    LIMIT 5
*****************************************************************************************************

                    DEPRECIATION                                          BOOK VALUE


     YEAR     ST-LINE       DEC-BAL       SUM-DIGITS        ST-LINE      DEC-BAL       SUM-DIGITS

       1     $ 540.00      $1500.00       $ 960.00      $ 5460.00    $ 4500.00       $ 5040.00
       2     $ 540.00      $1125.00       $ 840.00      $ 4920.00    $ 3375.00       $ 4200.00
       3     $ 540.00      $ 843.75       $ 720.00      $ 4380.00    $ 2531.25       $ 3480.00
       4     $ 540.00      $ 632.81       $ 600.00      $ 3840.00    $ 1898.44       $ 2880.00
       5     $ 540.00      $ 474.61       $ 480.00      $ 3300.00    $ 1423.83       $ 2400.00
EDIT  end
```

```
00001  PRINT'THIS PROGRAM PRINTS OUT A DEPRECIATION SCHEDULE BASED ON STRAIGHT-LINE METHOD,'
00002  PRINT'DECLINING-BALANCE METHOD, AND SUM-OF-DIGITS METHOD.  YOU WILL BE ABLE TO COMPUTE'
00003  PRINT'YOUR PROBLEMS BY ENTERING THE DATA YOU WISH TO COMPUTE.  THE DATA SHOULD BE ENTERED'
00004  PRINT'AS LISTED COST, SCRAP VALUE, NUMBER OF YEARS AND LIMIT. . . . ..USING COMMAS TO SEPARATE'
00005  PRINT'EACH VALUE ONLY.  FOR EXAMPLE:'
00006  PRINT'                          COST?    SCRAP?    YEARS?    LIMIT?'
00007  PRINT'                          7000.00,    400.00,    6,    6,'
00008  PRINT
00009  PRINT
00010 PRINT'     COST?    SCRAP?    YEARS?     LIMIT?'
00011 PRINT
00012 INPUT C, S, Y, L
00013 PRINT
00014 PRINT
00015 PRINT
00016 PRINT
00017 PRINT'                                        DEPRECIATION SCHEDULE'
00018 PRINT
00019 PRINT
00022 PRINT'     COST ';C,'      SCRAP ';S,'      YEARS ';Y,'      LIMIT ';L
00023 PRINT'*****************************************************************************************************'
00024 PRINT
00025 PRINT'                    DEPRECIATION                                          BOOK VALUE'
00026 PRINT
00027 PRINT
00030 PRINT'     YEAR     ST-LINE       DEC-BAL       SUM-DIGITS        ST-LINE      DEC-BAL       SUM-DIGITS'
00031 PRINT
00035 T1 = 0
00036 D1 = 0
00037 M1 = 0
00040 V = 0
00042 B = 0
00044 X1 = 0
00046 I =0
00048 R =1.00 /Y
00050 IF X1 = Y THEN 60
00052 X1 =X1 +1
00054 I =I +X1
00055 GO TO 50
00060 V=V+1
00070 T= (C-S) *R
00080 D=(C-B) *2*R
00090 B=B+D
00100 M=(C-S)*(Y/I)
00101 T1 =T1+T
00102 A1 =C - T1
00103 D1 = D1 + D
00104 A2 = C - D1
00105 M1 =M1 +M
00106 A3 = C - M1
00110 PRINT USING 120, V,T,D,M,A1,A2,A3
00120 :      ##     $####.##     $####.##          $####.##        $#####.##    $#####.##       $#####.##
00130 Y=Y-1
00140 IF V=L THEN 160
00150 GO TO 60
00160 END
EDIT  save
EDIT  end
READY
```

Figure 15.31 Illustrative BASIC program 3.

Figure 15.32 Illustrative BASIC program 4.

```
                  ******CARRYING CHARGES ON INSTALLMENT PURCHASES******

                       DOWN    NUMBER OF  AMOUNT OF EACH   INSTALLMENT    CASH    CARRYING
      ARTICLE        PAYMENT    PAYMENT      PAYMENT          PRICE       PRICE     CHARGE
 SLIDE PROJECTOR     $ 32.00       6          $16.00         $128.00     $120.00    $ 8.00
 VACUUM CLEANER      $ 11.25       7          $ 9.00         $ 74.25     $ 70.50    $ 3.75
 RECORD PLAYER       $ 32.50       8          $ 9.25         $106.50     $ 96.50    $10.00
 TELEVISION SET      $ 72.00      12          $27.60         $403.20     $360.00    $43.20
 OUTBOARD MOTOR      $ 28.50      15          $13.50         $231.00     $210.00    $21.00
 ELECTRIC HEATER     $  8.00       8          $ 4.48         $ 43.84     $ 39.60    $ 4.24
 TAPE RECORDER       $ 35.40      15          $10.20         $188.40     $179.40    $ 9.00
 POWER SAW           $  9.50      11          $ 7.09         $ 87.49     $ 79.50    $ 7.99
 LIV-ROOM SUITE      $ 34.95      30          $11.65         $384.45     $349.50    $34.95
 TYPEWRITER          $135.00      18          $35.00         $765.00     $675.00    $90.00


READY edit ccp basic
EDIT list

00010 PRINT''*********CARRYING CHARGES ON INSTALLMENT PURCHASES*********''
00012 PRINT
00015 PRINT''                 DOWN     NUMBER OF    AMOUNT OF     INSTALLMENT    CASH     CARRYING''   CHARGE''
00020 PRINT''   ARTICLE     PAYMENT    PAYMENT   EACH PAYMENT      PRICE        PRICE
00022 PRINT''
              _______    _______    ________   ___________    __________   _________   ________''
00025 PRINT
00030 PRINT
00040 READ A$,D,N,A,P
00050 LET I = D + (N*A)
00060 LET C = I - P
00070 PRINT USING 80, A$, D, N, A, I, P, C
00080 :#################
             $###.##      ##       $##.##        $###.##       $###.##       $##.##
00085 PRINT
00090 GO TO 40
00100 DATA ``SLIDE PROJECTOR'',32.00,6,16.00,120.00, ``VACUUM CLEANER'',11.25,7,9.00,70.50
00110 DATA ``RECORD PLAYER'',32.50,8,9.25,96.50, ``TELEVISION SET'',72.00,12,27.60,360.00
00120 DATA ``OUTBOARD MOTOR'',28.50,15,13.50,210.00, ``ELECTRIC HEATER'',8.00,8,4.48,39.60
00130 DATA ``TAPE RECORDER'',35.40,15,10.20,179.40, ``POWER SAW'',9.50,11,7.09,79.50
00140 DATA ``LIV-ROOM SUITE'',34.95,30,11.65,349.50, ``TYPEWRITER'',135.00,18,35.00,675.00
00150 END
EDIT  run
```

Summary

One of the major requirements for conversational time sharing is a programming language that the computer understands. BASIC is a precise, simple, easy-to-understand user's language that minimizes the clerical task of "set-up." It provides the user with efficient, rapid, flexible, and precise problem-solving activities combined with ease of use and learning. Users can create, execute, debug, and save BASIC programs from terminals, conveniently located in classrooms, offices, or laboratories, which may be far from the central computer. BASIC programming not only provides a sound basis for future programming efforts in the more complex programming languages, but eliminates many of the problems in formulating data required by other programming languages as well. This chapter introduces the basic concepts of the BASIC programming language.

1. At the beginning of the BASIC programming operation, the user types problem-solving statements at the terminal keyboard. The user programs and data are transmitted to the central computer. Messages and output data are printed at the terminal upon the user's request. During the operation the user and the computer are in constant conversation.
2. BASIC programming allows many users to share the same computer facilities with each user unaware of other users. The user is able to build and execute programs; test and debug programs; build and modify texts; and save programs and/or texts for future use. Each user has a unique identifier code. BASIC is designed to detect a large variety of errors. It can also provide a common library for all users.
3. The user may gain access to the computer in two ways. The user can dial-up the computer by telephone. Or the user can use the direct-line method, which involves turning on a mainline switch on the terminal keyboard. The user logs on by entering the identifier code to the computer.
4. Commands are orders issued to computer to control functions. LIST displays the contents of current programs. LISTCAT lists the name of each member of the users library. LOGOFF ends a terminal session. LOGON initiates a terminal session. RUN executes the current program. SAVE saves the current program. SCRATCH erases the current program.
5. When writing a BASIC program, the user types a set of instructions used to tell a computer how to provide an answer to some problem. Each line is a statement beginning with a line number that specifies the order of execution in a program. Statements are either executable (specify program action) or nonexecutable (specify information necessary for program execution).
6. The assignment statement assigns data from an expression to a variable within the program. LET evaluates an expression and assigns it to one or more variables.
7. Input/output statements are used for transmitting data to a program for processing and from a program after processing. READ assigns values to variables from internal data files. DATA creates an internal file. RESTORE causes the internal data files to be positioned at its beginning. PRINT causes data to be printed at the terminal. INPUT allows the user to assign values to variables from

the terminal at execution time. PRINT USING allows the user to have data values printed in a specific format. PRINT TAB prints the computer placement of output.

8. Control statements are used to direct the flow of the program execution. GO TO causes control to be transferred either conditionally or unconditionally. IF THEN causes control to be transferred according to the result of the evaluation of a relational expression. FOR NEXT is used to define a loop which may be executed a number of times. GOSUB RETURN is used to define a subroutine. STOP causes termination of a program execution. END causes termination of program compilation and execution. REM allows users to insert comments in a BASIC program.
9. An array is used to create lists and tables of data to be used in the program. DIM is used to create lists and tables, but no DIM is required if the table or list contains ten or less items.
10. There are three types of errors in the BASIC program. The syntax errors are errors in the use of the BASIC statements. The semantic errors are errors in the structure of a program. The execution errors are logical errors discovered during the execution of the program.
11. Corrections may be made in the following ways. To correct an entire line, use the original line number and retype the entire line. To delete a line, type the line number only. To correct a character in a line, depress the backspace key and type the corrected character. To save a program, type the word SAVE before END. If numerous corrections have been made, type the word LIST and the computer will type out a list of the corrected program. Each corrected line should be followed by a carriage return.

Identification Questions

Match the following terms with the statements below.

Statements

A. Array
B. Array Statement
C. Assignment Statement
D. BASIC
E. Commands
F. Constants
G. Control Statements
H. Diagnostic
I. Executable Statements
J. Input/Output Statements
K. Label
L. Line Number
M. List
N. Listcat
O. Logging On
P. Logoff
Q. Logon
R. Nonexecutable Statements
S. Numbers
T. Password
U. Run
V. Save
W. Scratch
X. Statement
Y. Text
Z. Variable

1. Provides a list of the name of every program in a user's private library.
2. Specifies information necessary for program execution.
3. A user identifier code.
4. Ends a terminal session.
5. Causes the erasure of the current program.

6. Any group of characters enclosed in quotation marks.
7. A letter or any letter followed by a number whose value may change many times during the execution of a program.
8. A statement used to create lists and tables to be used in the program.
9. A concise, compact, and abbreviated statement indicating what type of error occurred.
10. The most widely used programming language for conversational time sharing.
11. Orders issued to the computer.
12. A statement that assigns data from an expression to a variable in the program.
13. Causes program to be executed.
14. Identifies the line.
15. May be positive or negative and may contain up to nine digits.
16. Every line of the program.
17. A collection line that is typed at the terminal.
18. The statement used to print some or all of a "current" collection.
19. A value that remains unchanged during the execution of a program.
20. Statements for directing the flow of program execution.
21. A named list or table of data items, all of which are of the same type.
22. The process of identifying the user to the computer.
23. Identifies a user to a system and initiates a terminal session.
24. Causes program or text collection to be saved in the user's private library.
25. Statements that specify program action.
26. Statements that transmit data to a program for processing and from a program after processing.

Instructions

Match the following terms with the statements below.

A. DATA	G. IF THEN	M. READ
B. DIM	H. INPUT	N. REM
C. END	I. LET	O. RESTORE
D. FOR NEXT	J. PRINT	P. RETURN
E. GOSUB	K. PRINT TAB	Q. STOP
F. GO TO	L. PRINT USING	

1. Creates an internal data file.
2. Permits the computer placement of output.
3. Allows the user to assign values to variables from the terminal at execution time.
4. Causes control to be transferred either conditionally or unconditionally.
5. Causes termination of program execution.
6. Used to create lists and tables to be used in the program.
7. Causes control to be transferred to a specified statement, which heads a subroutine.
8. Allows the user to insert comments in a BASIC program.
9. Assigns the value of an expression to one or more variables.
10. Allows the user to have data values printed at the terminal in a specific format.

11. Causes control to be transferred according to the result of the evaluation of a relational expression.
12. Causes internal data file to be positioned at its beginning.
13. Assigns values to variables from internal data file.
14. Automatically ends a subroutine and causes control to be transferred to a statement sequentially following the associated GOSUB statement.
15. Causes data values to be printed at the terminal.
16. Defines a loop which may be executed a number of times.
17. Causes termination of program compilation and execution.

Questions for Review

1. What two things are necessary to know before you can access a central computer from a time-sharing terminal?
2. What are the two basic requirements necessary before a program can be successfully executed?
3. How does BASIC fulfill all requirements of a time-sharing programming language?
4. What are some important features of BASIC programming?
5. What general steps are necessary to get online with the system?
6. What are commands? Briefly list each command with its function.
7. How is a BASIC program written and how does it operate?
8. Name some of the basic elements of a BASIC program.
9. What are statements and what is the difference between an executable and a nonexecutable statement?
10. What are the functional groupings of statements?
11. What are the main functions of the LET, READ, PRINT, and INPUT statements? Give examples of each.
12. What is the main purpose of the RESTORE statement?
13. What are the main uses of the PRINT statement?
14. What are the principal uses of the PRINT USING and PRINT TAB statements?
15. Differentiate the uses of GO TO, IF THEN, and FOR NEXT statements. Give examples of each.
16. What are the main purposes of GOSUB and RETURN statements? Give an example of their uses.
17. What is the difference between the STOP and END statements?
18. What purposes do the DIM and REM statements serve?
19. What is an array?
20. What is a diagnostic and what is its main purpose in BASIC programming? What are three types of diagnostic messages?
21. What types of corrections can be made to a BASIC program before it is executed?

Key Terms

Array
Array Statement
Assignment Statement
BASIC
Commands
Constant
Control Statements
DATA
Diagnostic
DIM
END
Executable Statements
FOR NEXT
GOSUB
GO TO
IF THEN
INPUT
Input/Output Statements
Label
LET
Line Number
LIST
LISTCAT
Logging-On
LOGOFF
LOGON
Nonexecutable Statements
Numbers
Password
PRINT
PRINT TAB
PRINT USING
READ
REM
RESTORE
RETURN
RUN
SAVE
SCRATCH
Statement
STOP
Text
Variable

part 6

computer systems and management

32
12
GND
GND
+12M

computer systems micro, mini, small, and super computers 16

Chapter Outline

Chapter Objectives

The learning objectives of this chapter are

1. to describe the main features and operations of the microcomputer.
2. to describe the main features and operations of minicomputers.
3. to describe the main features and operations of the remote job entry terminals.
4. to describe the main features and operations of small business computers.
5. to describe the main features and operations of super computers.

Computers, in their early stages, were classified on the basis of their monthly rentals—small, medium, or large. Now, with new types of computers being introduced almost daily, we have micro, mini, small, larger, and super computers on the market. Computer technology has advanced so far and so fast that as yet there are no generally accepted definitions for these new groups of computers.

Microcomputers

The prospect of $25 computers captures the imagination of clever system designers. The potential uses for microcomputers are so far reaching that new applications are being announced more quickly than most designers ever thought possible. Following the trend of the decades, technology continues its downward spiral in computer cost from the multimillion dollar monsters to $10,000 tabletop minicomputers to $1,000 computers on-a-card microcomputers. The result makes the computer an even more important element in our daily lives. Already, specialized computers may cost under $20 in certain uses. Just an on-chip computer rivals the power of the digital computers of the 1940s. The future may reduce today's large-scale data-processing systems to mere hand-held devices; such devices may cost a mere $20. Today's microcomputer is continuing this trend.

The potential for microcomputer applications has already outstripped even the most inventive minds. System designers have found more new uses for micros than any analyst ever dreamed possible. Each of these new ideas stimulates another inventive design. The end of the computer era is not in sight.

What large-scale computers used to do, minicomputers now handle. Similarly, microcomputers have begun to supplant the minicomputers in many applications.

When the central processing unit (CPU) of a computer is implemented in a single or very small number of integrated circuits, it is called a *microprocessor* (fig. 16.1). When a computer incorporates a microprocessor as its major component, the result is a *microcomputer*.

History

Since the microcomputer is the apparent successor to the minicomputer as the latest and most advanced evolutionary system in data processing, its lineage will be discussed briefly.

Figure 16.1 An example of a microprocessor. (Photo by Ken Firestone)

At their commercial introduction in 1965, minicomputers constituted a revolution in data processing. Their compact size and low cost permitted the development of systems that meet the specialized needs in communications control, data acquisition, and small business data processing.

At first, the potential of minicomputers was not recognized or appreciated by the system engineers weaned on large computers, who viewed the minis in terms, features, and programming languages offered by the larger machines. The program loading was awkward and the limited instruction sets made minicomputer programming tedious. Today, systems designers are more familiar with the advantages and disadvantages of minis and are implementing minis in a myriad of applications.

Microprocessor and microcomputers followed a similar course. In many existing minicomputer applications, micros offer improved price-performance, compactness, and reliability over the minis (fig. 16.2). Moreover, the characteristics of the microprocessor lend themselves to new applications and system concepts that are impractical with minis.

A prime difference between a minicomputer and a microcomputer is the physical size and complexity of components. The development of *microprogramming* (fig. 16.3), has contributed to the evolution of the microprocessor and the microcomputers. (*Microprogramming is the process where each machine instruction initiates a sequence of more elementary instructions (micro instructions).* A microprogramming approach allows replacing fixed conventional CPU control logic with control memory, which contains the basic micro instructions for the fundamental operations of the microcomputer (fig. 16.4).

Microcomputer Components

The microcomputer is the latest link in an evolutionary chain of computer technology, which has stressed faster speeds and micro-miniaturized electronics. Initially, early computers of the 1940s used miles of wiring and thousands of vacuum tubes (not to mention extremely expensive air-conditioning systems). In the 1950s, a first major breakthrough was made in miniaturization with the advent of the transistor. During

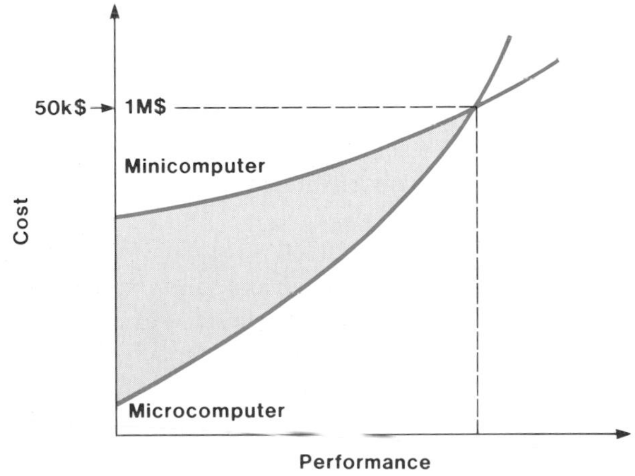

Figure 16.2 Cost performance curves for mini and micro computers. (Copyright 1977 by Modern Data Services, Inc. Reprinted with permission from *Mini-Micro Systems,* February, 1977.)

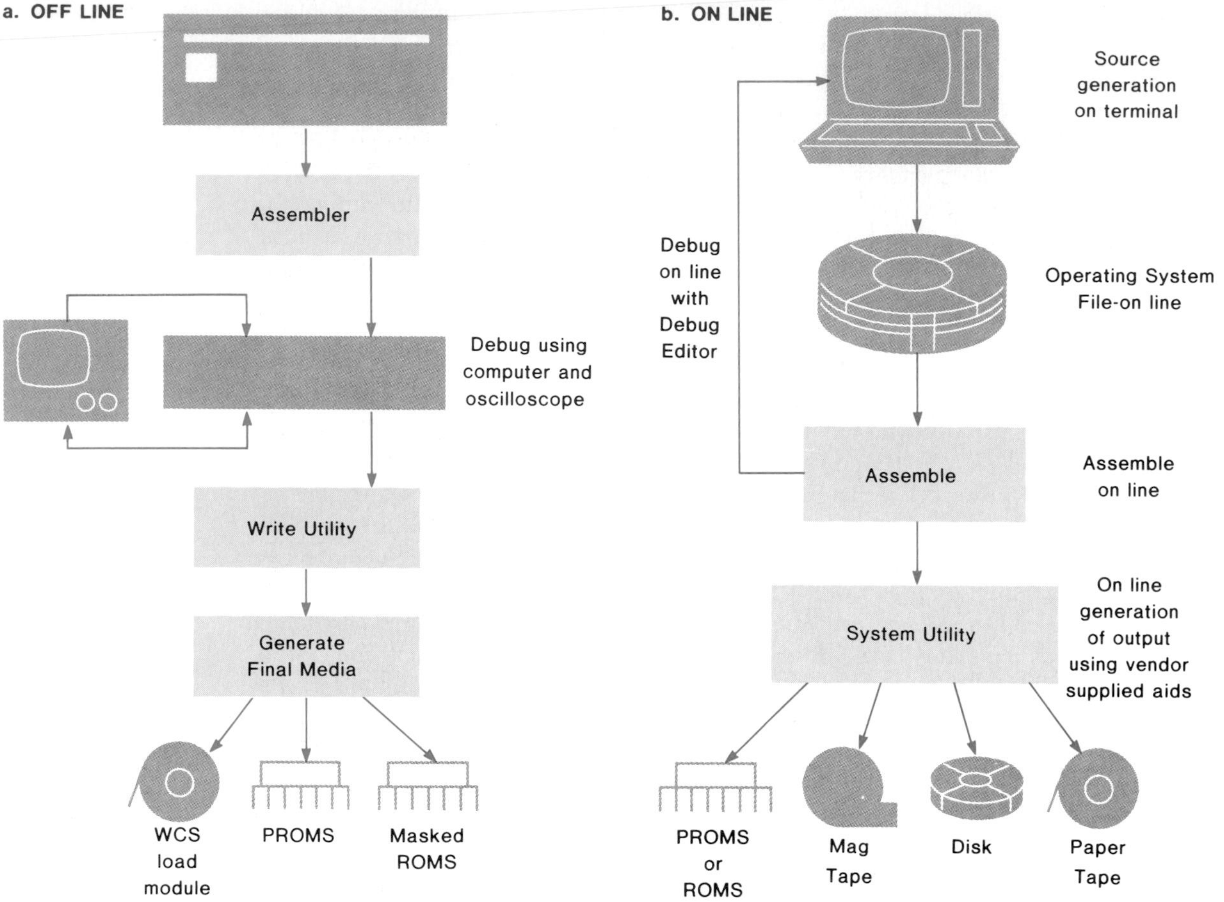

Figure 16.3 Batch and online microprogram development. (Copyright 1977 by Modern Data Services, Inc. Reprinted with permission from *Mini-Micro Systems*, September, 1977.)

Memory Chips

the 1960s, the electronics continued to shrink with transistorized circuits being incorporated into tiny, thin wafers of semiconducting material. These components were called "chips." Finally, in the 1970s, these microcircuits had been reduced in size to a point where the actual processing unit (the driving impulse of the computer) could be packed into a quarter-inch square. Some have called it *a computer on a chip* (fig. 16.5).

Memory on a chip comes in many forms, several of which are direct replacements for subunits commonly used in computer processors. Random access memory (RAM) is the direct functional equivalent of the core memories, which have been the mainstay of computer storage for two decades. Semiconductor RAM is now common, not only as the memory on a chip for microprocessor systems, but as a direct replacement of core memories for even the largest computer processors.

Figure 16.4 User microprogramming. (Photo courtesy of Radio Shack, a division of Tandy Corporation)

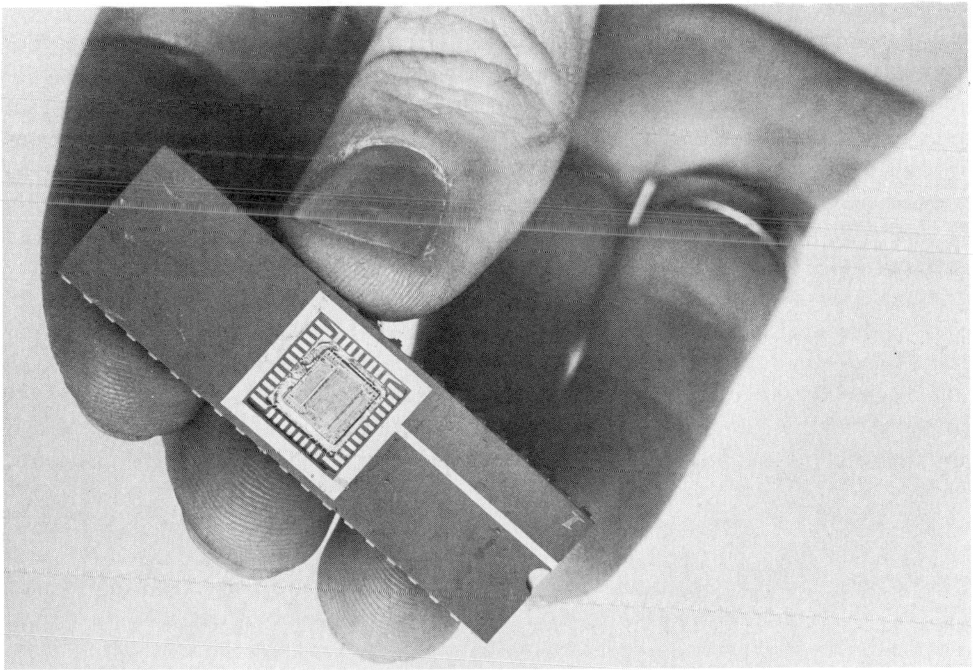

Figure 16.5 A microcomputer chip. (Photo by Ken Firestone)

A portion of the core memory for a conventional computer has always been devoted to the storage of the program. In the early 1960s, another form of storage, the read-only memory was introduced. The read-only memory (ROM) is the system on a chip that is used in a microcomputer for controlling the functions of the machine, such as defining the instructions that will be executed. Therefore, the characteristics of a machine can be appreciably altered by inserting a different ROM. There are, in fact, computers that can emulate any of several other computers, by changing the content of the ROM memory.

Components

The microcomputer is essentially a blending of five principal components (fig. 16.6)—a processor, a clock, preprogrammed read-only memory, random access memory, and input/output peripheral devices.

The heart of the microcomputer is the *microprocessor*. This system component performs all data manipulations, program and decision-making logic, and arithmetic functions.

The *electronic clock* provides the microcomputer system with the timing impulses that permit the synchronization of internal and external operations. Many processors are designed to split individual problems into several component parts. The timer provides the coordination functions that bring the results of each of these separate processing functions together again at the proper time.

Two types of memory are typically utilized within a microcomputer. The most common (and often least expensive) memory is called RAM (random access memory). This type of memory is fast and economical and usually provides the bulk of the microcomputer's internal storage. It is important to note, however, that RAM does have one significant limitation. When the power to the system is turned off, the RAM memory loses whatever data it was maintaining.

A second form of memory called PROM (programmable read-only memory) is typically used to provide *permanent* instruction capability to the microprocessor on the functions it performs each time it is used. PROM memory also solves the limitation problem that RAM memory has; that is, it does not lose the data and/or instructions it has stored when power is removed from the system. Unlike RAM memory, PROM memory can only be read and not used for any recording by the system.

Finally, the system must have some capability to allow the user to input data and receive results. Thus, the microcomputer typically has some form of keyboard for entry and some display mode for output. Keyboards can range from simple 10-key numeric pads to full typewriter-like alphabetic and numeric keyboard units. Visual output from the system can range from the simple precoded lights to full TV-type screens. In addition to the keyboard and visual display input/output mediums, many systems provide for other forms of input and output. These peripherals significantly expand the capability of the system and often its cost. Such units include cassette tape units, paper tape units, and even floppy disks.

Applications

The potential applications of microcomputers extend over a broad spectrum of products (fig. 16.7). Their principal use to date has been in electronic calculators. Terminals are the major market for microprocessors. Low-cost data terminals use microprocessor

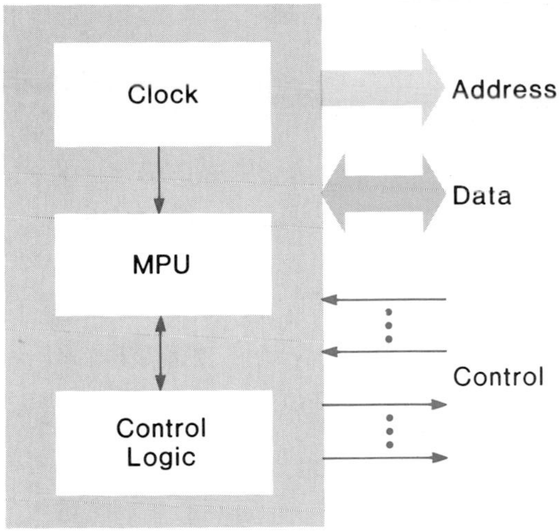

These are the main components of the central processor in a microcomputer. The clock steps the logic from one state to another and synchronizes data transfers. Control logic manages data transfers. In some cases, interrupt logic is also included.

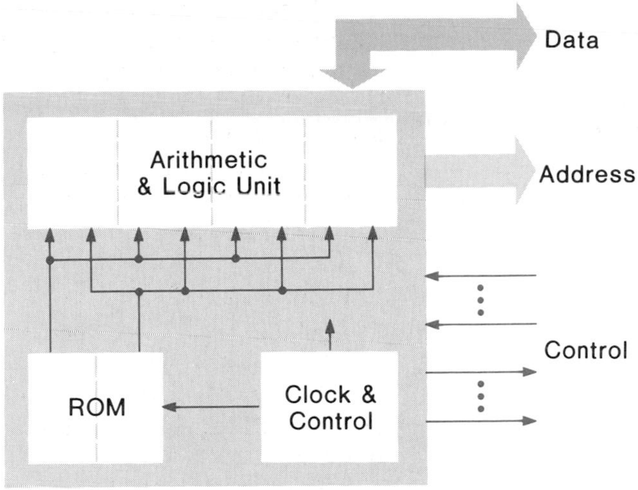

The microprocessor in a bit-slice microcomputer, as with any other central processor, must have arithmetic and holding registers, the program counter, instruction decoding logic, and sequencing logic. But it also must have a ROM associated with it to store the microprograms used for executing its instructions.

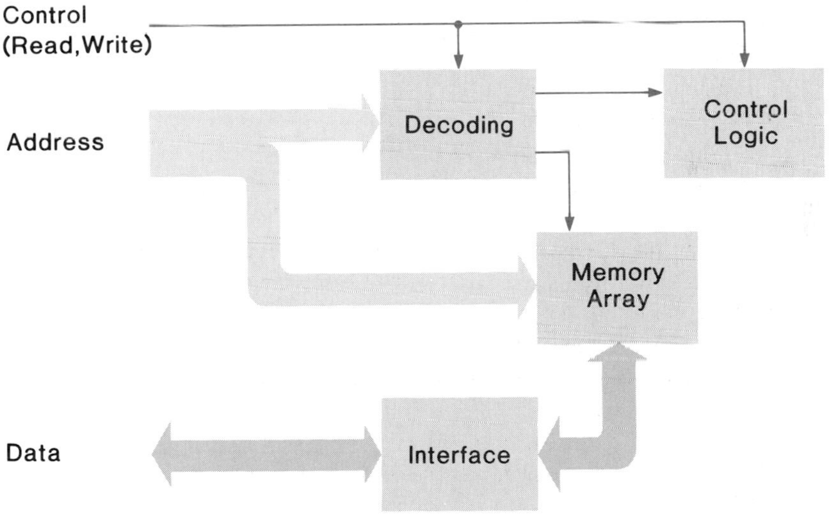

This illustrates how a typical microcomputer memory system might be organized. Certain bits of the address field are decoded to select elements of the memory array while lower-order bits select words within those elements. Data is read out to or written into those places from the data bus. The control logic might include latches for holding input or output data, refresh circuitry if the memory is dynamic, and so on.

Figure 16.6 An example of microcomputer operation. (Reprinted with permission of *Datamation*© magazine, ©Copyright by Technical Publishing Company, a division of Dun-Donnelley Publishing Corporation, a Dun & Bradstreet Company, 1978—all rights reserved.)

Figure 16.6
Continued.

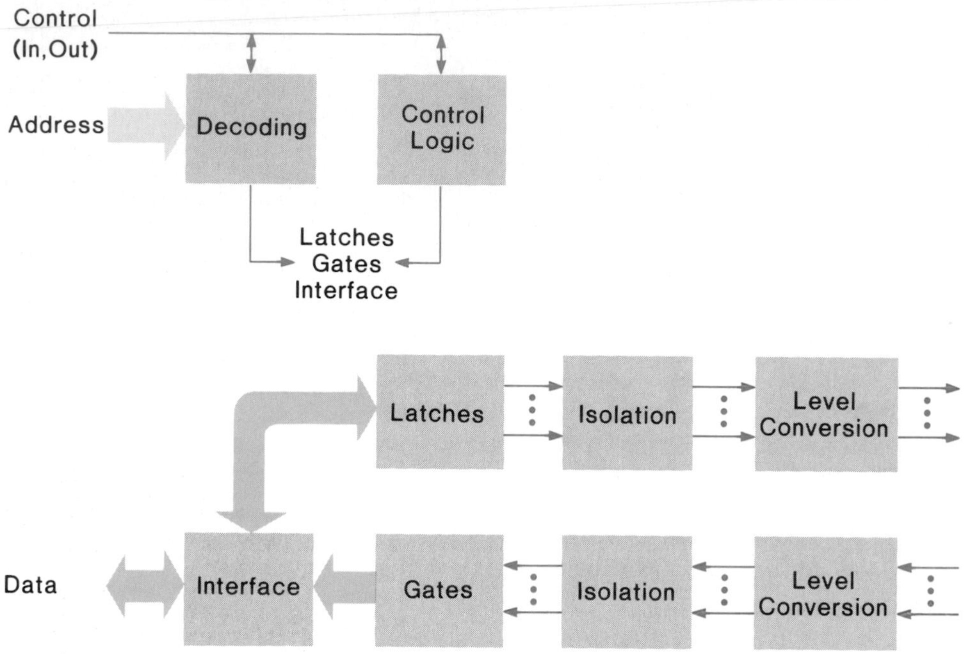

This illustrates how an I/O subsystem might be organized. Addresses are decoded to select specific ports—which will be sets of logic gates for outputs to the data bus or sets of latches for inputs to the memory.

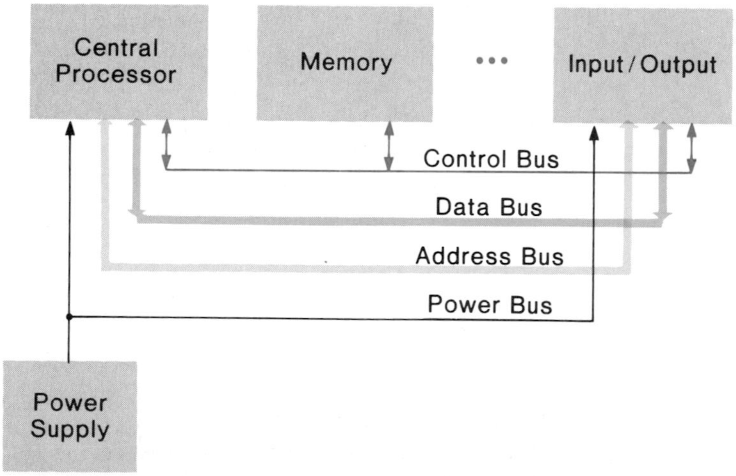

In modern microcomputers, the cpu, memory, and I/O subsystems are connected by busses for control signals, data, addresses, and power.

Figure 16.7 An example of a microcomputer system. (Photo courtesy of Texas Instruments)

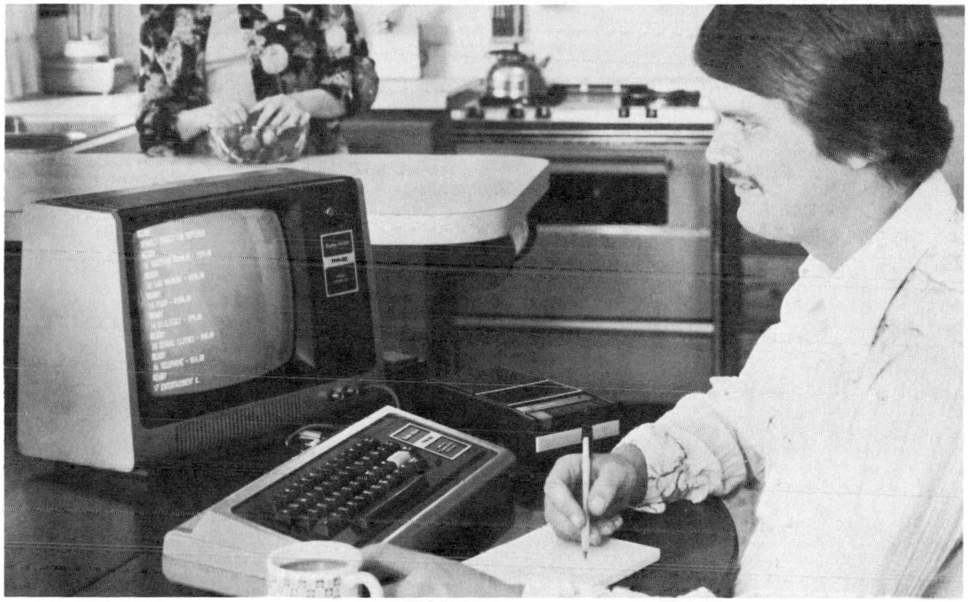

Figure 16.8 Microcomputer uses. (Photo courtesy of Apple Computer, Inc.)

for simple data-handling tasks. Remote terminals, by the addition of the microprocessor, become "intelligent" and perform offline editing, compiling, and processing. Point-of-sale (POS) terminals perform calculations on data storage and inventory control functions.

Today, entire computers are being installed in microwave ovens, telephones, and gas pumps; whole new markets are opening up for microbase products, such as the microcomputer. At the same time, traditional applications can be handled less expensively and more reliably (fig. 16.8). As a result, micros are found in transaction terminals, process control devices, and controllers in large computers (fig. 16.9). The concept of distributed processing is spurred by the inexpensive availability of minis and micros; indeed, many of the less expensive minis take advantage of micro technology internally.

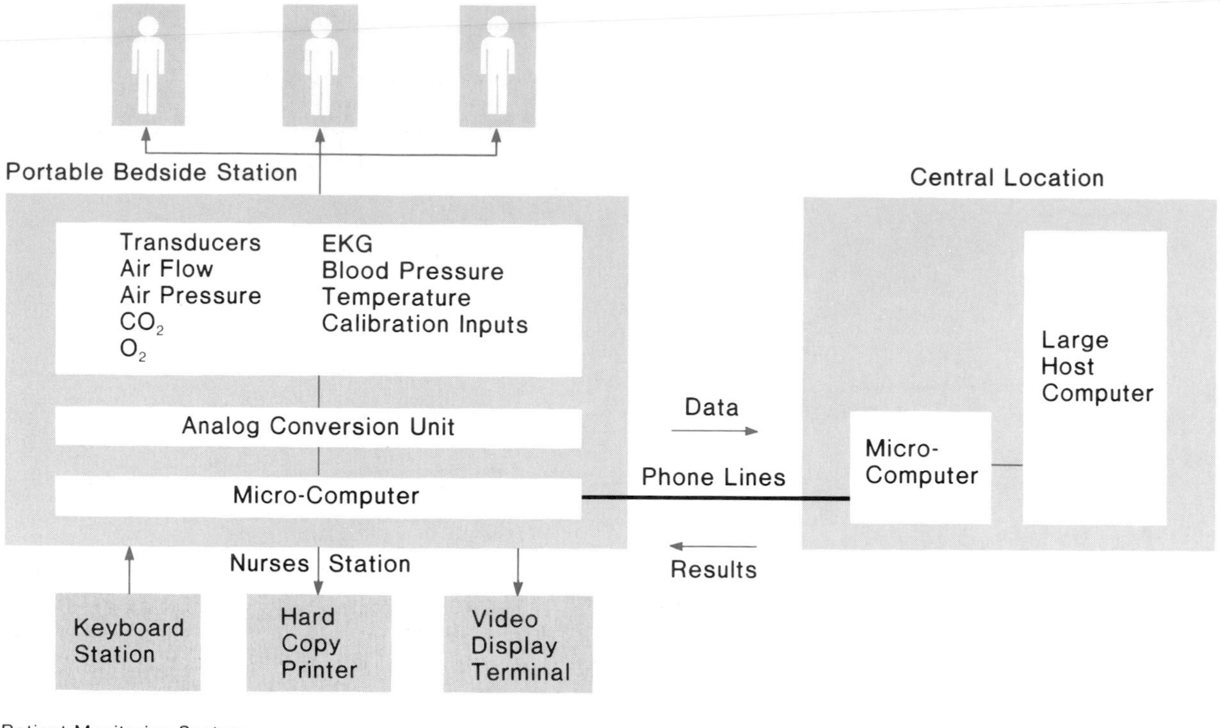

Figure 16.9 A patient monitoring system. (Copyright 1978 by Cahers Publishing Company, Division of Reed Publishing Corporation. Reprinted with permission from *Mini-Micro Systems,* August, 1978.)

Figure 16.10 An example of a micro-computer kit. (Photo by Ken Firestone)

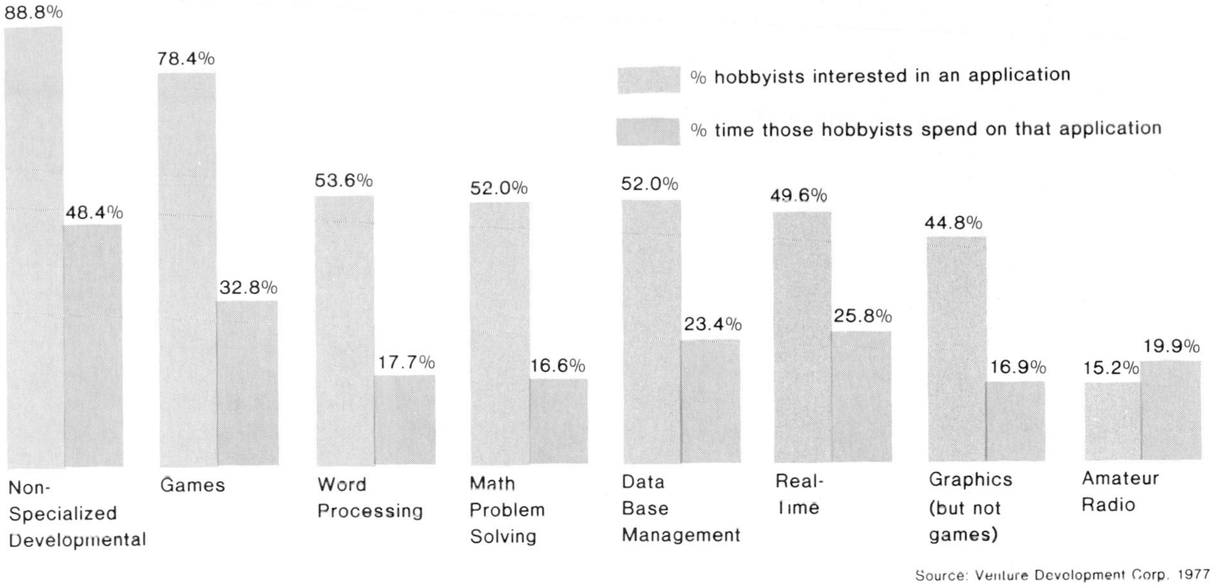

Hobbyists claim already to be involved in, or plan to be involved in, a variety of interesting applications. How they spend their machine time, however, may reflect very different interests. For example, the 49.6% of the group who claim to be interested in real-time applications spent only 25.8% of their time on them—the remainder may have been spent on games.

Figure 16.11 How hobbyist computers are used. (Reprinted with permission of *Datamation*© magazine, ©Copyright by Technical Publishing Company, a division of Dun-Donnelley Publishing Corporation, a Dun & Bradstreet Company, 1978—all rights reserved.)

Personal Computer

The microprocessor-based computers are showing up increasingly in homes and even more in schools. Home hobbyists, in fact, are buying kits and fully assembled machines faster, in some cases, than the manufacturers can supply them (fig. 16.10). As early as 1974, personal computing and home computers appeared on the market for computer hobbyists interested more in the design and construction of the machine than its use. Machine "kits" or combinations of various manufacturers' peripherals were available for the unique breed of hobbyist to whom the smell of molten solder was thrilling. It was not until 1976 that the microcomputer in a finished ready-to-use state was marketed to the public (fig. 16.11).

Currently there are in excess of 300 retail computer stores catering specifically to the personal computing market. In addition, several major retailers now offer a home computer available in many retail outlets (fig. 16.12).

Advantages

Microcomputing is destined to play a large part in our lives. Conventional computing technology, already quite influential, is embarking on an important new direction based on a radical revolution in size and cost of primary computer components. Large-scale integration (LSI) of circuits has made possible powerful computing devices that can be purchased by virtually everyone for home or personal use. Though not widespread yet, the future general use of these "microcomputing" devices seems probable and should have a considerable impact on our society.

Figure 16.12 An example of personal computers. (Photos courtesy of Radio Shack, a division of Tandy Corporation, and Apple Computer, Inc.)

People tend to get overwhelmed when they have to deal with machines that are much larger than themselves. It is clear that the physical size of microcomputers is small. They can be put on a desk, carried around, or taken to a friend's house; the whole system can be seen and grasped at one time.

This is an important departure from the conventional view of computers as large, complicated, and somewhat fearsome devices, demanding large buildings, special air conditioning, phalanxes of experts to care for them, and layers of bureaucrats to protect them.

Not necessarily related to size, simplicity promotes autonomous control and self-reliance. If a technology or tool is simple, then it is much easier for people to understand it, to use it, to modify it for their purposes, to fix it when it goes wrong, and in short to control it rather than be controlled by it. Unfortunately, microcomputers are simple only in a few, restricted aspects, but most people do not have a great deal of trouble using computer equipment.

Perhaps the most dramatic and publicized feature of the "microcomputer revolution" is the dramatic drop in price of hardware components. This drastic reduction in cost is probably the most important factor contributing to the rise of popular computing and this trend shows every sign of continuing.

It is important that a technology that is to find widespread use not harm people or damage the natural environment. In a direct sense, this is certainly true of microcomputer technology. The greatest physical danger to an average user is getting an electrical shock or having a computer drop on the user's toe. Environmentally, no

Figure 16.13
Microcomputers are fun. (Photo courtesy of Radio Shack, a division of Tandy Corporation)

aspect of computer technology, even with universal application, consumes much in the way of natural resources, demands large amounts of energy, or produces appreciable pollution.

Computers are not just serious business. Many people, children of all ages, enjoy playing with them (fig. 16.13). They have the potential to become great mind toys, since they are so flexible and can be adapted to represent such a wide variety of situations.

The widespread use of microcomputing will hopefully help people to gain a much better understanding of computers. This will tend to lessen the fear of computers based on ignorance and will provide a firm basis for real, justified fears, thus enabling people to deal more effectively with the technology.

The ability to process information quickly and cheaply is an important component in the exercise of power in our present society. Microcomputing is much more accessible to average people than conventional computing, but it still has, in some ways, the same exclusive cult feeling about it.

Future

There will be a widespread use of the microprocessor and microcomputer as the potential of the micro is realized. In business applications, the microprocessors and microcomputers will soon replace conventional minicomputers in many applications where a mini is overpriced or overpowered. Microprocessors will carry out tasks normally associated with large computers.

However, it is probable that more microprocessors will be buried in computer peripherals than will be used in computing devices. The computer industry has never really understood the potential of personal computing.

The revolutionary marketing and social aspects of the personal computer will exceed the recent interest in CB radios, digital watches, and electronic calculators. Applications for personal computers in the near future will most likely fall into three categories.

1. *Numerical uses,* such as personal figuring, bookkeeping, tax preparation, and financial planning.
2. *Informational retrieval and record keeping,* including home inventory, mailing lists, and family historical information.
3. *Text and word processing,* including correspondence, recipes, diaries, and potential "guest books."

In addition to those fairly obvious application areas, many in the field believe that the home will become a "front line" educational vehicle for both children and adults. In addition, many of the bolder futurists indicate that many professional and service-oriented business organizations will decentralize their operations to the home, in which the individual will work from a home computer into a central business computer network.

The popularity of micros has spawned the development of a number of small, low-cost peripherals. Newly configured business data-processing systems are already talked about for use as remote processors in distributed computing systems. Faster micros are appearing with multi-user, multi-task, time-shared operating systems.

Minicomputers

Among the factors that caused the development of the minicomputer were the need for an inexpensive programmable device to perform specific functions and the realization that the full resources of a larger computer were not needed for all tasks. As the minicomputer has evolved, it has started to acquire characteristics that previously were exclusive to larger computers. In many cases, using a full minicomputer for a simple control function becomes a case of overkill.

Minicomputers of both yesteryear and today are devices of power equaling that of their "maxi" compatriots. In essence, a minicomputer is first of all a computer, and then a computer with particular characteristics. Being a true computer, and not an accounting machine or a desktop calculator, it is an exceptionally powerful machine capable of supporting a full family of peripheral devices, such as huge disks, magnetic tapes, and high-speed printers. The characteristics of minis do not impact their power, but rather serve to differentiate them from maxis, the same way that sports cars are differentiated from standard-sized vehicles (fig. 16.14).

An important feature of minicomputers, important in every area of potential applications, is their low price. The areas in which minis were initially accepted in large numbers, process control and telecommunications, needed only computer logic and virtually no peripheral device support. They were able to buy this logic and processing speed in minicomputers at a small fraction of what they would have had to pay for a large machine.

Figure 16.14 Examples of minicomputers. (Photos copyright *Data Management* magazine, Data Processing Management Association)

Clearly, the simple minicomputer world has now changed. The minicomputer was titled originally because its physical size was small. The name had nothing to do with performance limitations. During the decade that followed the mini's introduction, both the machine's capabilities and price have climbed to approach that of the larger machines. Simultaneously, they have moved in opposite directions, toward the levels now occupied by the microcomputer. Today, the small machines can solve virtually

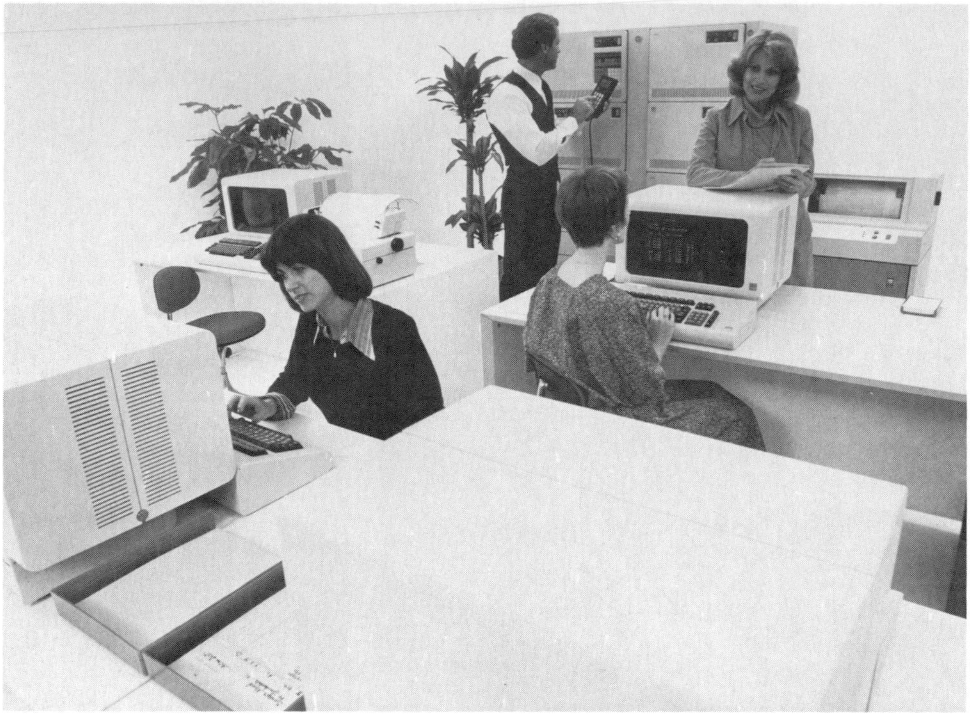

Figure 16.15 The IBM Series/1 minicomputer. (Courtesy IBM Corporation)

any kind of computation or control application. Because the large computers are also being extended in multiple directions, they and minicomputers borrow architectural innovations from each other.

So-called minicomputers are now available with more power than a typical IBM System/360 introduced over fifteen years ago. They are available in dual processor configurations and as time-sharing systems. Minicomputer networks can be adapted to disperse data-processing problems. In addition, minicomputers can be hooked up to any peripheral device. In fact, most minicomputers are linked to a conglomeration of disks, tapes, and terminals, whose combined cost can greatly outweigh that of the large computer.

Since minicomputers now reach into the market to compete with conventional computers, they also come with massive amounts of software, complete field service, and after-sales application support. All of this is a far cry from the original minicomputers that arrived in a box containing a manual and were programmed in machine language. Most large minicomputer systems are supplied on a "turnkey" basis by the manufacturer. Virtually all computing applications, such as business, control, instrumentation, and data collection, can be done by a minicomputer (fig. 16.15).

Applications

The many applications today may be described as either stand-alone or network configurations. Some typical application areas are,

Figure 16.16 Minicomputers used in process control. (Photo by Jim Shaffer)

1. *Process control, computer-aided manufacturing, and instrumentation,* the original dedicated functions of the first minis, are still their strongest and most diverse areas of application (fig. 16.16).
2. *Stand-alone minicomputers* are also being used as the central computer facility for smaller companies as well as the processor in multiple-station real-time, timesharing, and remote job entry systems. A single minicomputer can control large numbers of machines or instructions in a real-time mode; it can accept batch inputs from widely separated remote job entry stations, perform the necessary data-processing operations, and deliver the output to the stations.

Computer Network

A computer network consists of two or more computing elements (whatever their functions, sizes, and locations), working together to optimize the system's service to its users. There are four types of networks in which minicomputers may perform one or more functions.

1. *Hierarchical network.* Computers of different capacities and levels of data-processing responsibility are related, just as people are in successively higher levels within a business organization. For instance, machine tools may be individually controlled by a microcomputer, each group of machines supervised by a minicomputer, and the production department monitored by a medium-scale computer, which, in turn, communicates with a large central computer.

2. *Distributed processing network.* The total data-processing load is shared functionally among the computers in the network. In an airline reservation system, for example, groups of terminals at remote ticket offices feed data to mini-based terminal concentrators, which transmit blocks of messages over high-speed lines to the main office. Depending on what has to be done, the messages are then switched to one of several minicomputers with special jobs, such as keeping track of planes and fares, accounting and fare computation, and ticket and seat assignments.
3. *Resource sharing network.* A number of remote minis with limited local capacity can draw on the greater power of a larger minicomputer or large-scale host computer to handle the services available to a local user. In a laboratory system, for example, processors located at test instruments may perform data acquisition but the experimenter can call on a more powerful computer for program development and data base management. On the other hand, if the central computer shuts down, the local processor not only continues its functions but can also store information for updating the central data base when operation is begun again.
4. *Communications network.* The computers are usually separated by long distances and are connected by dedicated or common-carrier telephone lines. They vary in size and in the scope of their computing tasks. In any case, messages (such as transactions and data programs) must be transmitted between computers in the network in both real-time and batch modes. In addition to being remotely linked into the network as computers, minis perform special network management functions, such as message switching and data concentrating, in which they are not the actual users of the data.

Minicomputer-Data Base Management Systems

Data base management systems (DBMS), once applicable to only $1 million computers, can now be employed on a minicomputer to reduce the cost of developing computer programs and manipulating data files and to simplify the computers used by nondata-processing experts.

As a result of emerging interest, minicomputer manufacturers are beginning to make available DBMS software packages, either by developing their own or acquiring packages supplied by independent software houses.

Data Entry

Data entry is not ordinarily thought of as part of data communications, but minis are causing some big changes in this function as well. Minicomputers, and to a certain extent microcomputers, are making a long-held dream come true—source data entry. With the mini decreasing in cost, it is now possible to design a low-cost, small-scale data entry system that is a mini-communications network in its own right. Such systems have a controller or master key station to receive data entered at several remotely located key stations over telephone lines. Collected data is then edited, reformatted, and stored on disks for subsequent batch delivery to the host computer.

Future

In computing systems of the future, the mini will be even more important. The trend is away from the concept of one massive central computer to handle everything. This outdated approach uses multi-partitions, multi-programs, multi-processors, operating

Figure 16.17 Minicomputers used in map making. (Photo courtesy of Aero Services Division of Western Geophysical Company)

systems, supervisors, file management, and other unessential operations in a waste of storage space and time. This concept is one whose time is past. The future of the computer business is in distributed processing, which is the decentralization of computing power via small processors that are strategically placed from an application point of view (fig. 16.17).

Remote Job Entry (RJE) Terminals

Faced with rising costs and aided by advances in data base management systems, managers are turning to terminal systems as a means of coordinating dispersed operations. For some applications, such as airline reservations and credit authorizations, interactive usage, typified by the CRT or printing terminal operations, provides an optimal work environment. For many businesses, the volume of data that must be moved into and out of the central system and the flow of work in remote offices dictate the use of remote batch terminals.

Remote batch terminals are similar to all other remote computer terminals in that they extend the processing capability of a large central computer, via communication lines, to a distant site. They differ from other terminals in that they handle large amounts (batches) of important day-to-day operational data at high speeds with outputs comparable to those attainable at the computer site itself.

Remote batch terminals offer fast printers (that can use the entire range of business forms), card readers, card punches, and high-speed data transmission facilities. They can contain processors that enable them to do things that most small terminals can't do alone. Among the operations are keyboard-to-magnetic medium facilities, data checking and reformatting software, optical input, and automatic dial-out or line-answering gear.

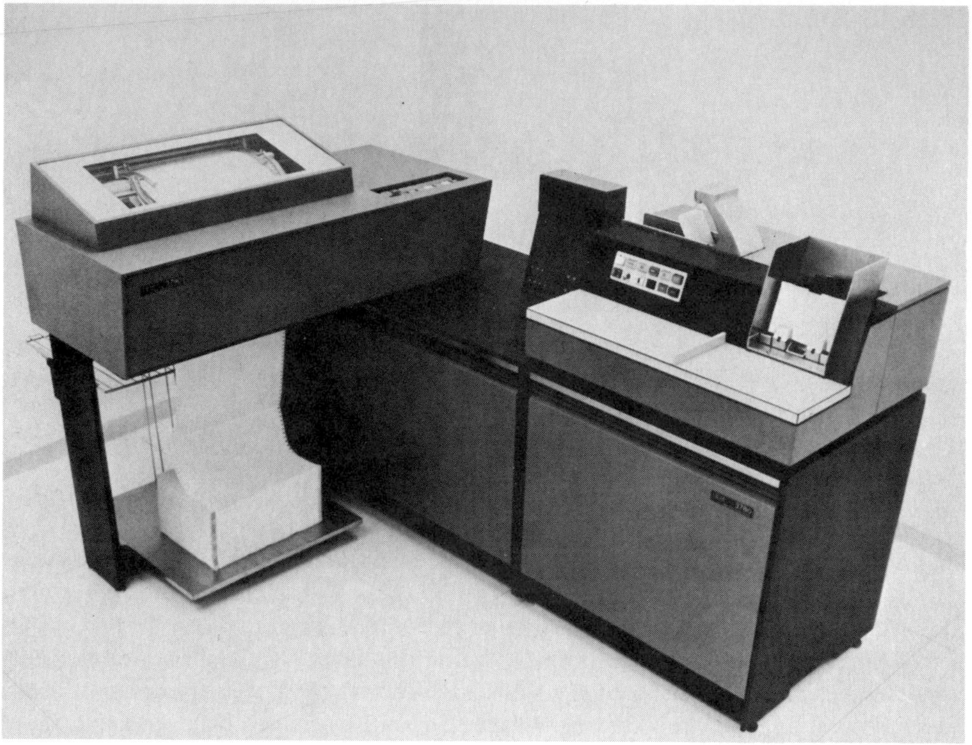

Figure 16.18 The IBM 3780 data communications terminal.

Terminal-oriented computing is a fact of data-processing life. Remote locations transmit data over communication lines to their control computing facility for processing and return. It is a swift, economical way to move large volumes of data at high speeds; the terminal can read all the data for a job or a series of jobs at one time, send it out for processing, and, upon its return, display the results in a printed or other form of output (fig. 16.18).

In the world of data processing, remote locations are remote in name only. Data communications has moved branch offices, plants, warehouses, and other remotely located sites into the data-processing mainstream of the decentralized organization. Through the use of a data communication system, these locations have full use of the centralized computing facilities. Data moves from the remote location to the computer and back again. Everyone benefits from this system. Central management receives timely operating information from all its sources for effective decision making; the specific locations have their processing work load handled without incurring attendant costs for staff or equipment.

Remote job entry is rapidly becoming one of the most active areas of minicomputer applications. Remote job entry techniques and applications have been firmly established for several years; however, recent advances in awareness and understanding of the capability of minicomputers is leading to an explosion in applications involving the marriage of conventional RJE processing with the flexibility of the minicomputer.

Typical examples demonstrating the versatility of RJE terminals utilization are:

1. Large organizations with operations widely spread over large geographic areas utilize RJE terminals to enable the various corporate branches to access and update centralized data bases with large computer-processing capability to achieve coordinated operation.
2. Warehouses and production areas use RJE terminals, which enable inventory and production levels to be maintained in a central data file accessible to management. In many cases, the RJE terminal prints customer invoices and shipping labels right at the remote facility under the direction of the large central computer.
3. Many universities and college campuses use RJE terminals in their instruction program. RJE terminals perform administrative jobs as well, through the use of the central computer. A single RJE terminal may be typically shared by the administrative office, engineering department, data processing, and computer science departments in order to utilize the substantial software application and processing power of the remote central-processing unit.

In these, and many other, established RJE terminal applications, the RJE terminal may be used strictly as a data communications terminal or in conjunction with the minicomputer, which provides the conventional operations of RJE entry/retrieval and provides flexibility and efficiency not possible with conventional "fixed logic" or hardware RJE terminals.

Components of RJE Terminals

RJE terminals are low-cost, general-purpose terminals useable in computer communications systems. The terminal was designed to move data to and from a central computer with speed and efficiency. It is a high-speed, high-volume terminal that can read batched data, transmit it swiftly, assure rapid response, and provide the ensuing punching or printing facility at the remote location. As a combination control unit, card reader, card punch, and printer, the terminal concentrates on the vital areas of reading, transmitting, printing, and punching.

Batch Processing

Batch-processing systems support multiple jobs by queuing them to be processed into one or more input "job streams," in which jobs are brought into storage by the operating system, processed to completion, and placed in an output "job stream" for delivery by the operating system to the designated output device.

Card readers typically provide job input, with printers and card punches receiving the results. The major aspects of batch processing are:

1. Jobs are "queued" or stacked in an input stream, brought into computer storage, processed to completion, and placed in an output stack or stream for printing or punching of results.
2. Job control information is provided with the input job stream itself. This setup makes it possible to proceed on job processing with a minimum of operator intervention.

Remote Job Entry

Remote job entry enters job and control information going into the job stream and retrieves the processed results from a remote terminal site.

The conventional RJE terminal provides the remote user with the ability to input a job into the central computer's input job stream and retrieve the processed job results at the remote output device. Conventional remote job entry terminals utilize input/output devices typical of the equivalent functions performed at the central facility. For example, a card reader can read punched cards and transmit the data to the remote computer facility; a line printer can print the processed results.

Communications between the RJE terminal and the central computer is performed via a data-link, consisting of modems and point-to-point or switched phone lines.

The minicomputer enables the data collection procedure to be customized for the application, not vice versa. In many cases, additional bulk storage (such as disk) can be introduced to facilitate accumulation of a local data base for immediate inventory update and order information.

The way the mini can be programmed to accommodate more than one central computer transmission convention, thus allowing a single RJE terminal to access application programs and data bases residing in diverse central facilities, is a further demonstration of the flexibility of the minicomputer for RJE terminal applications.

Changing Concepts

The merging of the technologies of computer-communications and minicomputer application programming has resulted in a coordinated "intelligent" mini-based RJE terminal, which provides data checking, reformatting, and other functions.

The remote processing concept was initially restricted to transmitting virtually raw, unedited data through fixed-logic terminals. Things have changed at the terminal end of the communications line by the inclusion of the minicomputer. This has enabled users to distribute more processing at remote sites while providing increased transmission capability. For example, with the addition of data entry capabilities at the remote site, intelligent remote batch terminals are now able to pre-edit large quantities of information prior to transmission for central processing. This is the direction in which information technology is moving. The installation of intelligent terminals provides significant flexibility for the data-processing manager for future applications.

Typical remote batch stations consist of a card reader for input, a printer, a keyboard for special input, and the communications interface. Operator display could be via a CRT or through hard copy. Larger stations can incorporate multiple displays, and input can be collected and transmitted from tape.

The intelligent mini-based RJE terminal has attained a predominant place in corporate, educational, and utility operations.

Small Business Computers

A small business computer system can be defined as a *stand-alone data-processing system, built around a general-purpose computer, dedicated to the processing of standard business applications (such as payroll, accounts receivable and payable, order entry, inventory, and general ledger). The small business system can handle input from mass storage devices (such as disk, magnetic tape, paper tape, and drum) and costs less than $100,000 complete, including all hardware and software* (fig. 16.19).

Figure 16.19 The Sperry Univac BC/7 business computer system. (Photo courtesy of Sperry Univac, a division of Sperry Corporation)

This definition deliberately excludes two major systems, the so-called accounting computer or office computer, which can't handle the mass storage devices and relies instead on unit-record data storage (magnetic ledger cards, punched cards), and the data entry system, whose primary mission is to capture data on disk or tape for subsequent entry to a central computer. The definition obviously leaves out systems that sell for more than $100,000 (figs. 16.20, 16.21, 16.22).

Classes of Small Business Computer Systems

The two major classes of small business computer systems are *batch systems,* which tend to dominate the upper end of the price range, and *online systems,* which seem to abound at the low end but may end up costing more when extras are added.

The online system, in which all files are available for inquiry and updating at one time, is probably most desirable in a small business environment. The management can readily keep up with sales, accounts payable, inventory, shipments, and so on. Unfortunately, the online system (the software that assigns devices and monitors terminal activity) tends to be more complex and therefore more expensive than the batch system. By the same token, the online system needs enough disk space to accommodate all files at one time. These two requirements tend to escalate system costs rapidly, as the file size increases to handle a large-scale processing application. As a result, manufacturers would rather scale down software and peripheral costs. So they turn to batch systems, which can handle more work on a given hardware configuration and accept larger files (only some of which are used in a given program) for a given price.

Figure 16.20 The IBM System/34 business computer system. (Courtesy IBM Corporation)

Figure 16.21 The IBM 5110 computer system. (Courtesy IBM Corporation)

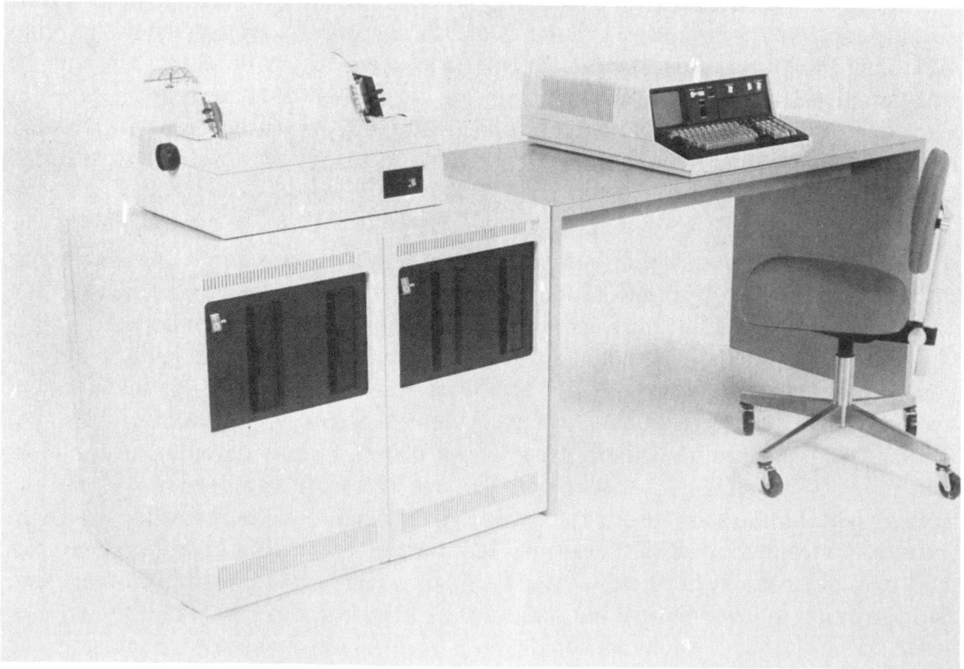

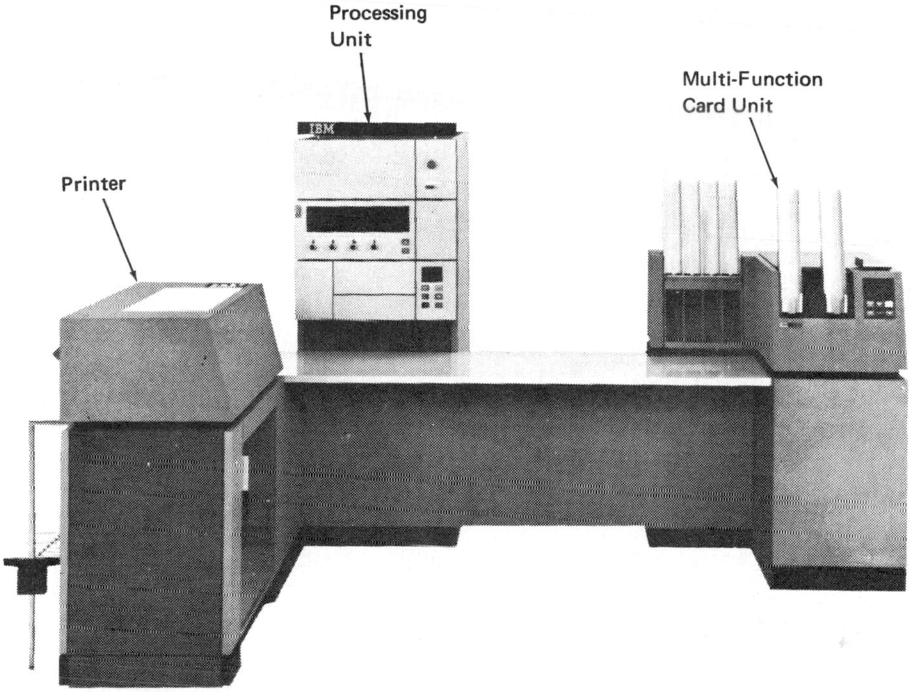

Figure 16.22 The IBM System/3. (Courtesy IBM Corporation)

The offsetting disadvantage of batch files, of course, lies in the relatively long turnaround times and the relatively long delays (days, rather than minutes) that occur in a decision-making loop as a result.

The batch system can be recognized by its card punch and reader, while the online system uses a video display terminal. Of course, as in every other segment of the data-processing business, there are systems that offer both the concurrent batch and online operations in multiple-partitions. The multiple-partition online system can be considered as a subclass of the online group, rather than a separate entity. Similarly, the multiple-partition batch system, commonly known as multi-programming system, is a special kind of batch system.

Hardware, Software, and Maintenance Services

The small business computer buyer, in many instances, will deal with one company for equipment, another for the programs, and a third for the maintenance. Sometimes this is a fine arrangement. But if any member of such a triumvirate doesn't have an intimate relationship with the others or if they don't share information freely, the customer is bound to suffer. In this respect, the small business computer doesn't measure up to larger systems where all the services are normally supplied by a single company.

There are some large manufacturers, like IBM and Digital Equipment Corporation, who provide the user with a full spectrum of services. But users shouldn't always go with a given system simply because it provides all the services. Perhaps the system won't satisfy their functional requirements or they can get a price break from a small vendor to justify a small risk.

The practice of separate hardware and software procurement (and separate maintenance agreements) is actually a viable, widespread arrangement. Despite the potential problems, it works and works well every day for thousands of small businesses. More small systems are being sold on the basis of separate suppliers all the time to experienced companies as well as first-time users.

Software—The Critical Element

Software, not hardware, is the critical element in system selection. Hardware is important, but the most elegant hardware in the world will be judged a hunk of junk by the small businessperson who finds that the staff gets twisted in knots trying to keep files intact and accurate because the software is poorly conceived.

Software is the key, partly because the hardware manufacturers understand so well how to match a CPU and a set of peripherals to do a given job. Computation speed isn't a problem; every application is input/output bound. Pick the right peripherals and you've got it made. This is an easy task for the salesperson. Find out how large the customer's inventory is, how many accounts the customer wants to maintain, how large the payroll is. Look up the configuration needed to do the job in the "cookbook."

In small business system software, the application programs (as opposed to operating systems, compilers, utilities, and the rest) are most important in an environment where the user has little, if any, inhouse programming expertise. Most vendors have relied upon turnkey application packages produced by software houses, who are specialists in a given industry to meet this challenge. Such an approach is an obvious choice for programless users, as long as they can live with it.

Recent Trends

The ever-increasing popularity of CRT terminals and disks has taken root among first-time users of small business systems, who have not been biased by years of unit record and magnetic tape experience. As a result, these second-generation peripherals are gradually disappearing from the small business computer marketplace.

Card readers and punches, for example, are still offered as *options* on many small business systems for customers who depend on cards; almost no one offers a card reader and punch as standard items. Instead virtually every small business system has at least one video display terminal having a keyboard for data entry. Such terminals are quieter than a keypunch and easier to use. Data is stored offline on disks or diskettes, a more compact medium than cards.

Similarly, the floppy disk and the hard disk are supplanting the old familiar magnetic tape or cassette drive as the standard online mass storage device. Again a twenty-year-old product is gradually making way for a less expensive replacement.

Magnetic tape will not disappear entirely, of course. Many systems include one optional tape drive to be used for archival storage, because tapes are still easier to handle and store than bulky disk packs. This, too, may change if the capacity of floppies increase dramatically in the next few years, as some observers predict.

Punched paper tape equipment is also disappearing, thankfully, from small business systems. It is comforting to know that at least some of the mistakes made by the last generation will not be made by the current and future generations.

Another encouraging development is the growth in main memory sizes. Some industry observers argue that the increase in memory size was inevitable because users were turning to structured programming techniques that "chew up core like crazy." More likely, manufacturers have recognized that users, even rookie users, will not buy a system having too little memory to fill their needs.

Software Trends

It is now a principle that a small business system should operate interactively. As a result, batch operations have all but vanished from small business systems. Instead, program development, utility runs, and application work now take place online. Accordingly, control software supports a number of concurrent tasks, all running independently.

Language development continues to creep at a snail's pace. RPG II, COBOL, and FORTRAN have emerged in addition to BASIC.

Turnkey Black Box

A most interesting phenomenon on the small business computer scene is the emergence of the turnkey black box—a system whose inputs and outputs are specified in detail, but whose innards remains a mystery to the purchaser. Some vendors promise to tailor the system to the user's needs; how the job gets done is none of the customer's affair.

The turnkey vendor does not have complete responsibility, outside of the equipment maintenance contract, once a system has been installed. If the user requires software changes, the vendor will supply them for a price.

For protection, the small business system user must make an effort to understand small systems or else to hire a consultant. Otherwise the customer is at the mercy of the vendor.

It is estimated that there are 500,000 small businesses in the United States that could use small business computers. Only ten percent of that market (if that much) has been sold to date. Obviously, the small business computer systems have a golden future.

Super Computers

These ultra high-performance data-processing systems were designed for high-speed large-scale scientific and commercial applications. Their scientific applications range from nuclear physics to weather forecasting and theoretical astronomy. In commercial applications, these computers can be used as control centers of the most complex airline reservation systems, coast-to-coast time-sharing networks, or process control systems (fig. 16.23).

Figure 16.23 The IBM System/370 Model 195. (Courtesy IBM Corporation)

The power and speed of this advanced system are primarily the result of:

1. Improved circuit technology.
2. High performance of buffer storage for main storage accesses.
3. Buffering within the processor.
4. Ultra fast execution time.
5. A high degree of concurrency in operation.
6. Highly efficient algorithms, particularly in floating-point operations.

Processing proceeds concurrently in five separate highly autonomous units; main storage; the storage control unit and buffer storage; the instruction processor; the fixed-point/variable-field-length/decimal processor; and the floating-point processor. Furthermore, each unit may be performing several functions at one time. The floating-point processor, for example, can execute as many as three floating-point operations concurrently (fig. 16.24).

Contributing significantly to the speed and power of these super computers are the main storage capabilities ranging from 1 million to 4 million bytes and a high-speed buffer unit, which can sharply reduce the time required for fetching currently used sections of main storage. The storage control unit is an intermediary between main storage and the other system units. As such, it controls the accesses to the high-speed buffer and to main storage. As many as thirteen channels may be attached to the central processing unit.

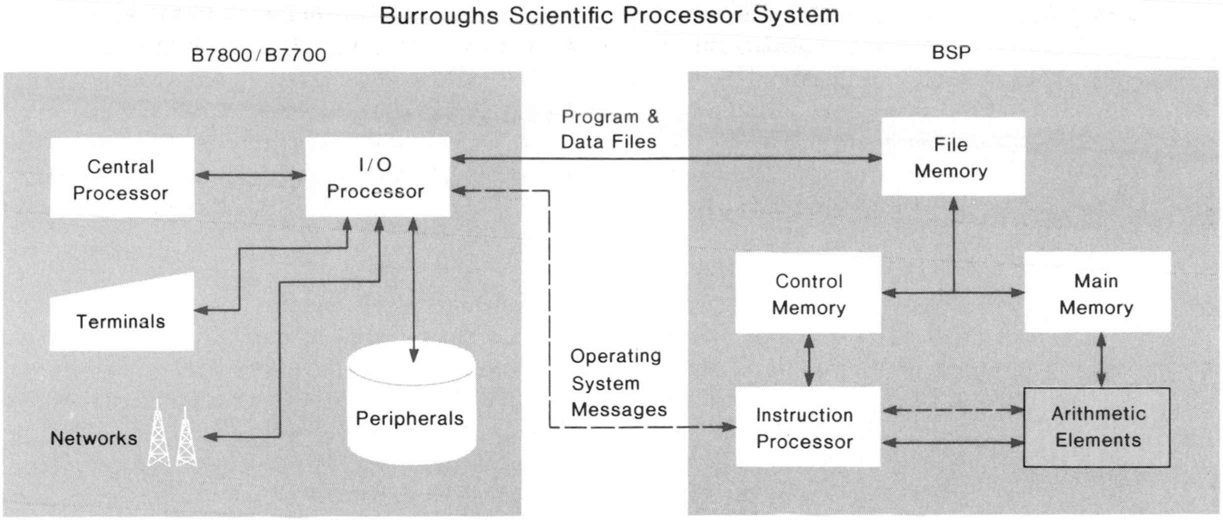

Unlike other array processing or pipeline processing computers, the Burroughs Scientific Processor was designed to be operated as a peripheral to another large-scale system.

Figure 16.24 A schematic diagram of a large-scale computer system. (Reprinted with permission of *Datamation*© magazine ©Copyright by Technical Publishing Company, a division of Dun-Donnelley Publishing Corporation, a Dun & Bradstreet Company, 1978—all rights reserved.)

Recent Trends

The number-crunching computers of current vintage will be replaced by quite different machines. Today's computers are wonderfully efficient at performing complex mathematical calculations, but they are woefully deficient at all the storing, sorting, and fetching operations that are necessary in data base management. Such mundane tasks constitute ninety percent of what computers are now called upon to do; the computer industry, in essence, has optimized machines to handle only ten percent of the work load.

Early computers were principally required to handle complex arithmetic calculations. True, they had to do simpler data manipulations as well, but designers naturally structured the machines to do the more difficult tasks. As a result, the computer architecture became optimized to do double precision arithmetic and other esoterica leading to the creation of enormously complex adding machines.

As the country moves toward a paperless society, the demands for efficient storage and retrieval grow more and more acute. If we are truly becoming a paperless society, still other applications will cry out for more efficient data base management. Banks are adopting electronic funds transfer; businesses are linking manufacturing plants to sales offices via phone lines and common data bases; and incipient word-processing explosion may double electronic storage requirements in the next few years.

Such growing demands cannot be met simply by making the number-crunching computers bigger and faster. The brute force approach is nearing the end of the line for both technical and economic reasons. Data base management calls for a radically different approach to computers, which will force the transformation. Because of all this, an entirely new type of processor will be developed over the next five to ten years to be optimized for data base functions. The machines may still be called computers, but they will be very different and will be built around a brand new architecture that will eliminate overhead and cataloging functions that today account for too much CPU time. Moreover, the new architecture will use mass storage more effectively.

Current file systems do not use substantial disk areas. The programmer may allot a contiguous file space that is larger than is needed for most batches. This approach suffers from the excessive amount of time required to record the data in that batch and subsequently to address this data.

Storage

Today's computer systems store huge amounts of redundant data, including blank spaces. The computer architecture cannot recover data in useable form unless it is recorded in a preset file format. Files containing common data are maintained on separate disks for each application because the CPU cannot be used efficiently to do the multiple fetching and reformatting necessary on different applications.

System access must also be simplified to implement a responsive data base system. Even in the "simplest" time-sharing system, a trained programmer cannot now enter and retrieve data efficiently. Such languages as BASIC have helped somewhat, but operators still must be trained, and generally the programs they write are extremely inefficient in terms of fetches, mass memory allocation, and the like. The new systems architecture must allow tomorrow's systems to be used by clerks not programmers.

As for the storage medium itself, electromechanical devices, such as disks and magnetic tapes, cannot be relied on much longer. Storage requirements will grow tremendously and fail-safe operations will be the key. Therefore, electromechanical devices, which are inherently subject to break down must be replaced by cost-effective, solid-state memories, unless the users wish to pay the price for completely redundant storage. Fortunately, work on electronic beam, laser, and super-cooled memories is extremely promising. In addition, the computer industry is starting to explore video tape as a storage medium.

The computer of the future will be able to store and process a bibliography of all literature that exists today in the United States and will be no larger than a conventional office desk. Today, such a gargantuan project would fill a room with computers.

Scientific Computers

The design for super computers in scientific operations differs substantially from business data-processing applications. In scientific computation, the dominant input/output patterns are quite different from those in business data processing, in which a small number of operations affect a very large data base. So, for business data processing, a computer's limiting factor may be input/output capacity, because any single job may not demand much memory to execute with adequate efficiency. This is an ideal environment for multiprogramming. Many programs may reside in main memory at once. Only a few will be active, the rest will be waiting for input/output.

In scientific data processing, a given job usually requires a large amount of memory before it can be executed efficiently. With present processor speeds and memory sizes, the larger jobs execute best if each one has main memory to itself.

It is obvious that the super computer problems are quite different for business applications as compared to scientific applications. A super computer that is a hundred times faster than any computer on the market today is being sought by scientists at NASA's research laboratory. Computers are needed to perform a million operations per second. The computer should have the capability to simulate the entire range of speeds for the space shuttle.

Summary

The past decade has produced many spectacular advances in computer systems. Besides the many new innovations introduced in general-purpose computers, new categories of computers have appeared.

The microcomputer, which stresses faster speeds and micro-miniaturized electronics, is the latest link in the evolutionary chain of computer technology. The actual processing unit of the micro could be packed into a quarter-inch square chip. The potential applications extend over a broad spectrum of products, such as electronic calculators, terminals, and the numerous uses as a personal computer.

Minicomputers were used originally as part of larger sophisticated computer systems. Today, they are used as stand-alone computers, each capable of operating independently, having a large number of peripheral devices and supported by large numbers of software packages. They compete with conventional computers. They are also used in remote job entry terminals. In addition, they perform important functions in computer networks.

Remote job entry terminals transmit data swiftly and economically over communication lines of central computing facilities for processing and return. It has become one of the most active areas of minicomputer applications.

Small business computer systems were designed to provide high-speed data-processing operations to standard business applications. They provide both batch and online system capabilities.

Super computers were designed for high-speed large-scale scientific and commercial applications. They offer fast processing speeds, greater storage capacities, and many forms of high-speed input/output devices.

This chapter describes the main features and operations of these new computer systems.

1. The microcomputer is a computer that incorporates a microprocessor as its principal component. A microprocessor is the CPU of a computer and consists of a single or very small number of integrated circuits. During microprogramming, each instruction initiates a sequence of more elementary instructions (micro instructions). A microcomputer system is made up of chips, random access memory or read-only memory, a microprocessor, an electronic clock, a keyboard, and visual display units.
2. The minicomputer is an exceptionally powerful machine capable of supporting a full line of peripheral devices. Minicomputers are used for process control, computer-aided manufacturing, and instrumentation, as well as stand-alone computers, computer networks, in data base management systems, and data entry.

3. Remote job entry terminals transmit data over communication lines to the central computer facility for processing and return. It is a swift and economical way to move large volumes of data at high speeds. Remote job entry terminals consist of a control unit, a card reader, a card punch, and printers. They perform batch processing, in which jobs are queued or stacked in an input stream, brought into computer storage, processed to completion, and placed in output stacks or streams for printing or punching of results. Job control information is provided with the input job stream which makes it possible to proceed on the job processing with a minimum of operator intervention.
4. Small business computer system, a stand-alone data-processing system, is built around a general-purpose computer, dedicated to the processing of standard business applications that can handle inputs from mass storage devices, and costs less than $100,000 complete, including all hardware and software. There are either batch systems or online systems. The hardware, software, and maintenance services may be purchased from separate vendors for each service or from a single company. Software is the critical element in the system because of the decreased importance of the programmer.
5. Super computers are large systems designed for high-speed, large-scale scientific and commercial applications. They feature large main storage capacities, high-speed buffer units, many channels for input/output devices, a high degree of concurrency in operation, and improved circuit technology.

Identification Questions

Match the following terms with the statements below.

A. Communications Network
B. Computer Network
C. Distributed Processing Network
D. Hierarchical Network
E. Microcomputer
F. Microprocessor
G. Microprogramming
H. Minicomputers
I. Personal Computer
J. Programmable Read-Only Memory (PROM)
K. Random Access Memory (RAM)
L. Read-Only Memory (ROM)
M. Remote Batch Terminals
N. Resource Sharing Network
O. Small Business Computers
P. Super Computers
Q. Turnkey Black Box

1. Each machine instruction initiates a sequence of more elementary instructions.
2. Provides permanent instruction capability on the functions it performs each time it is used.
3. Computers of different capacities and levels of data-processing responsibility that are related.
4. Stand-alone system, capable of operating and having a large number of physical devices, competing with conventional computers.

5. A number of remote minis with limited local capability can draw in the greater power of a large minicomputer or large-scale host computer to handle the service available to a local user.
6. The central processing unit is implemented in a single or very small number of integrated circuits.
7. Extend the processing capability of a large central computer via communication lines to a distant site.
8. The direct functional equivalent of core memory.
9. Based on concepts that are increasingly showing up in homes and schools.
10. Total data-processing load is shared functionally among the computers in this network.
11. Computers are usually long distances apart and are connected by dedicated common-carrier telephone lines.
12. Ultra high-performance data-processing systems designed for high-speed large-scale scientific and commercial applications.
13. Incorporates a microprocessor as its major component.
14. System on a chip that is used in a microcomputer for controlling the functions of a machine.
15. Two or more computing elements working together to optimize the systems service to the user.
16. A standard data-processing system, built around a general-purpose computer, dedicated to the processing of standard business applications.
17. A system whose inputs and outputs are specified in detail, but whose innards remains a mystery to the purchaser.

Questions for Review

1. What has been the trend in computers?
2. What is a microprocessor? A minicomputer?
3. How is the microcomputer replacing the minicomputer in many applications?
4. What is meant by microprogramming?
5. What is meant by "a computer on a chip"?
6. What is random access memory and how is it currently used in computers?
7. What is read-only memory and how is it used by microcomputers?
8. Briefly describe the components of a microcomputer.
9. What are typical applications of microcomputers?
10. What is a personal computer and what is it used for mainly?
11. What is the criteria of microcomputers?
12. What are the applications for personal computers in the near future?
13. How has the form and role of the minicomputer changed?
14. Briefly describe some typical minicomputer applications.
15. What part will the minicomputer play in future computer applications?
16. What are remote job entry terminals and what is their main purpose?
17. Explain batch processing and how the remote job entry terminal relates to it.
18. How has the RJE terminal changed?
19. What is a small business computer?

20. What are the two major classes of small business computers and what are the chief advantages and disadvantages?
21. What is the major problem for the small business computer user relative to hardware, software, and maintenance services?
22. Why is software such a problem to small business users?
23. What are the recent trends in small business computers?
24. What is a turnkey black box and what is the responsibility of the vendors?
25. What were super computers designed for?
26. What are the recent trends relative to super computers?

Key Terms

Communications Network
Computer Network
Distributed Processing Network
Hierarchical Network
Microcomputer
Microprocessor
Minicomputers
Personal Computer
Programmable Read-Only Memory (PROM)
Random Access Memory (RAM)
Read-Only Memory (ROM)
Remote Batch Terminals
Resource Sharing Network
Small Business Computers
Super Computers
Turnkey Black Box

1
2
3
4
STORAGE DATA BUS OUT
1
2
3
4

operation of a data-processing installation 17

Chapter Outline

Chapter Objectives

The learning objectives of this chapter are

1. to define the many problems of managing a data-processing installation and how it follows concepts and methods not ordinarily found in other units of the enterprise.
2. to examine the data-processing manager's skill and understanding as a technician and specialist and ability to manage data-processing people and relate to other people in other departments for the efficient operation of the data-processing department.
3. to show the relative position of the data-processing installation in an organization and the many positions that exist requiring specialized skills.
4. to show alternate approaches that may be utilized to represent the data-processing operations.
5. to show all problems inherent in installing a data-processing system.

Concepts of Organization

The organization of a data-processing installation requires an unusual blending of technical and managerial skills. The data-processing effort follows concepts and methods not ordinarily encountered in other functions. Data processing is a technical operation requiring highly trained, technically competent, and in many cases creative, personnel. Standards for control of data-processing operations and planning are necessarily distinct from those of other managerial functions (fig. 17.1).

Although data processing performs a service, the services it furnishes are frequently fundamentally important to the success of the operational departments involved. Good data-processing system design aims at integrating data-processing operations, which cut across organizational lines, thus creating unique problems in the relationship between the data-processing unit and other parts of the company.

The Data-Processing Manager's Role

Management control is defined as the ability to direct the achievement of management objectives. Data-processing management objectives exist in terms of services to be provided to users of data processing. *The principal objective of a data-processing organization is the production of user satisfactory information from raw data within a specific schedule and a specified budget.* Any data-processing manager, who satisfies users and management by providing services that meet this criteria, is clearly performing in an optimal manner.

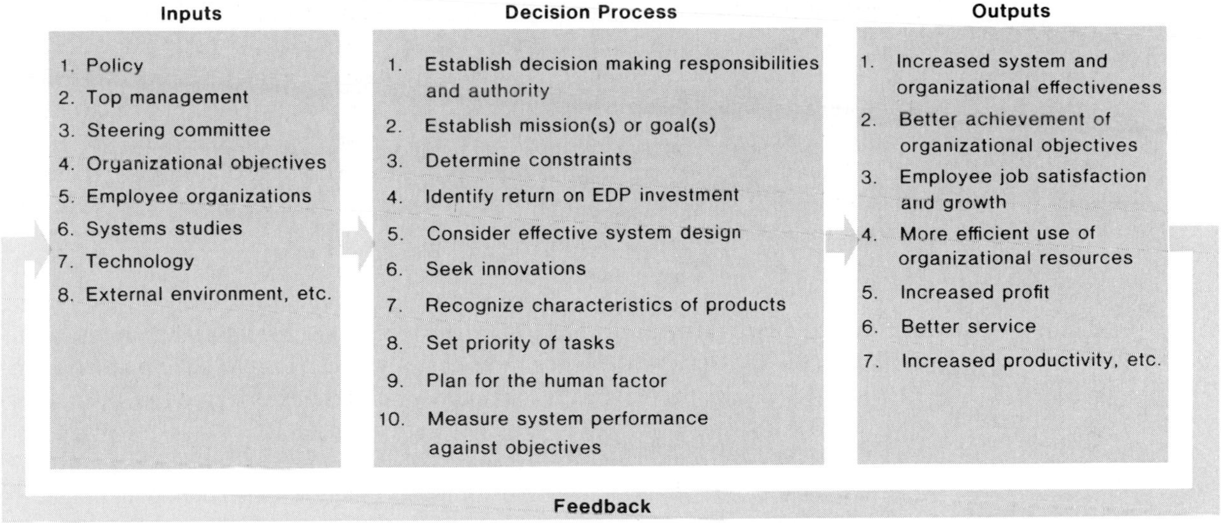

Figure 17.1 The framework for the management of EDP efforts. (Copyright *Data Management* magazine, Data Processing Management)

Data-processing managers must also know how to measure the utilization of their resources so they can effectively correlate them to performance requirements and maintain management control. Therefore, data-processing managers must insure that proper performance standards are applied to allow measurement and allocation of resources.

The job of a data manager has two main aspects—first, skill and technical knowledge; second, the ability to manage people in the data-processing department and relate to people in other departments. Data managers, therefore, need to be both technical specialists and have some competence in human relations.

Because the data-processing field is constantly evolving new technology, data-processing managers must be sufficiently flexible to avoid managerial obsolescence. They must have the capacity to deal logically with difficult problems and must have the ability to plan and implement new applications.

Larger data-processing installations might not require technically trained individuals heading the data-processing function. As administrators, they direct the activities of those who are qualified technicians. Smaller installations usually are not able to afford that luxury. All personnel must participate in the activities of conversion, production, and system development. A limited staff requires the manager of a small installation to function in many capacities and stand ready to fill in where needed.

An important managerial trait that is necessary when resources are limited is the ability to fully utilize available resources that can mean the difference between soaring costs or a balanced budget. Technical ability and budget awareness of managers will pay dividends. Being aware of this possible situation, data managers will maintain a balance between hardware and software to maximize storage and throughput without disproportionate budget increases.

The discipline of data processing is rapidly evolving toward the status and responsibility of a true profession. This process is vividly changing the nature and demands of the data manager's role. Required, in successively greater amounts, is the knowledge and ability to apply conventional techniques, previously felt dispensable, because data-processing managers were thought to hold a unique managerial position.

Data-processing managers must be concerned with coordinating their department's goals with those of the organization's overall goals. This synchronization is necessary for optimal goal congruence.

Data-Processing Objectives

The most important influence on the structure of the data-processing activity is exerted by its objectives and the ways in which these objectives relate to the large organizational units served. Defining these objectives requires a careful examination of the internal and external requirements of the organization (fig. 17.2).

Management Purposes

What important contributions can the data-processing unit make to management planning and control flow? Some management functions to which the data processing may be of great importance include planning and research, control and exceptional reporting, and the maintenance of the organization's basic information files.

Operational Purposes

How does data processing participate? Data processing controls inventory orders and production, maintains personnel and payroll records, maintains customer accounts, and so on.

Scope of Service

What are the number and different types of departments to be served? What services are to be provided? Accounting and record keeping and scientific, mathematical, real-time, and data transmission services are types of service to be furnished to users.

Means of Service

Will the data-processing department operate an "open" or "closed" shop activity? In open shop operations users have access to the equipment and provide their own personnel for programming and operations. In a closed shop users are not permitted to program or operate the equipment; they provide the data-processing department with the problem. This department performs the necessary programming and operations.

Another important factor to be considered is the establishment of deadlines and turn-around schedules that must be fulfilled by the data-processing activity.

Future Plans

Careful consideration should be given to the organization plans for growth, product expansion, and competitive position. Any major changes planned will have a direct bearing on the data-processing procedures to be adopted.

Data Center Functions

Data Control

Data control is responsible for seeing that data is prepared as the user submits it and for accuracy of processing through the data center. Data control should be measured by its ability to catch and correct errors through either manual or automated procedures before the errors end up in reports or data bases.

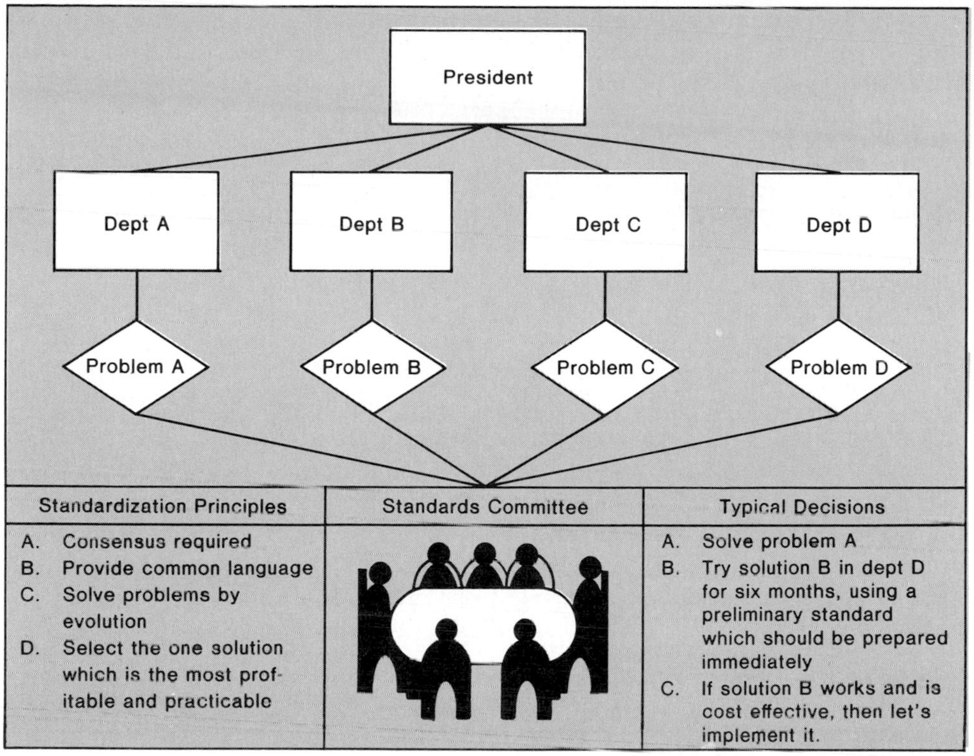

Figure 17.2 Problem-solving management objectives.

Scheduling

Scheduling is required to assure that optimum use of all resources is obtained and that the products are delivered on time. Scheduling can be measured by its ability to meet deadlines.

Data Preparation

All production data should be prepared using data preparation instructions as a guide. Data preparation should be measured by individual performance and as an aggregate against a prepared standard.

Computer Operations

The job is to get the programs run through the computer. Computer operations should be measured by its minimization of the operator wait time and operator errors, such as mounting the wrong tapes, using the wrong forms in the printer or card punch, or accidentally erasing a master file due to the improper use of the file protection feature.

Systems Programming

Systems programming has the responsibility for generating and maintaining the operating system; optimizing the performance of the computer through software and hardware monitoring; identifying inefficient programs in terms of usage made of the computer resources; and creating operating standards for the allocation of files, the number of devices that can be used, and the operating practices.

Systems programming should be measured by increasing throughput of the computer system. This may be an increased number of jobs processed in a fixed unit of time or the ability to handle more online transactions without an increase in the hardware configuration.

Planning

The data center manager must participate in long-range systems planning so as to be able to convert them into work load forecasts for the data center. The data center manager must develop a plan or tactic for meeting increased work loads.

Organizational Position—Data-Processing Unit

The important and unusual nature of the service provided by the data-processing unit makes its position within an organization of prime importance (fig. 17.3). This unit can serve the needs of the organization either in a centralized or decentralized position. In a centralized position, the data-processing unit is independent but at the same level with the departments it is servicing. In a decentralized operation, the data-processing unit is within the larger organizational unit that is its major customer. There are advantages and disadvantages to each position. Each has merits, which depend on the different environments and the objectives to be served within them. Recently, there has been a tendency toward the centralized use of data-processing units.

Figure 17.3 The organization of a data-processing unit.

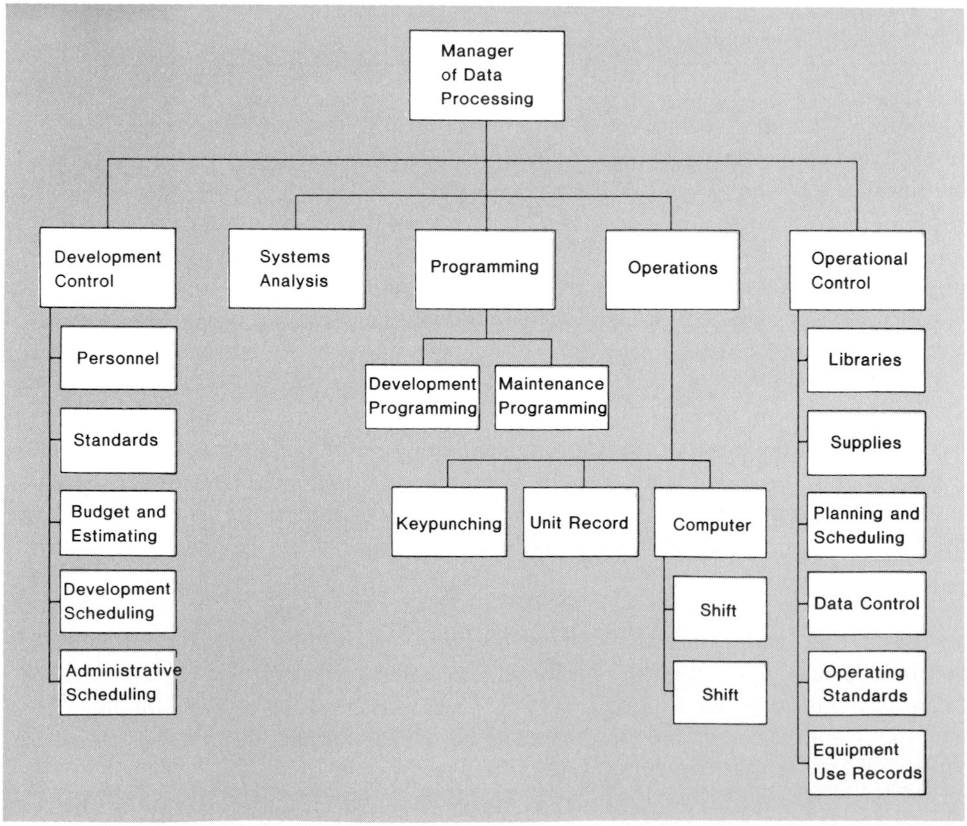

Centralized Data-Processing Unit

Through the centralization of computer facilities, the following primary goals are expected to be achieved (fig. 17.4):

1. Significant cost reduction because of improvement in the cost/efficiency ratio of the large-scale systems.
2. Improved overall work load performance with better service to users.
3. Broader range of computing services offered to the user.

By centralizing its data-processing operations, an organization can put itself in the position to realize the full potential of very large-scale computer systems.

Advantages

1. All departments receive equal consideration from the data-processing unit.
2. Program planning and systems research and development can be more efficiently integrated for the entire organization.
3. Disputes that may arise with reference to the use of data-processing service can be settled by managers of comparable status.
4. The centralization of data-processing personnel and equipment will reduce costs of any future expansion since additional volume can be more easily absorbed by a centralized unit.

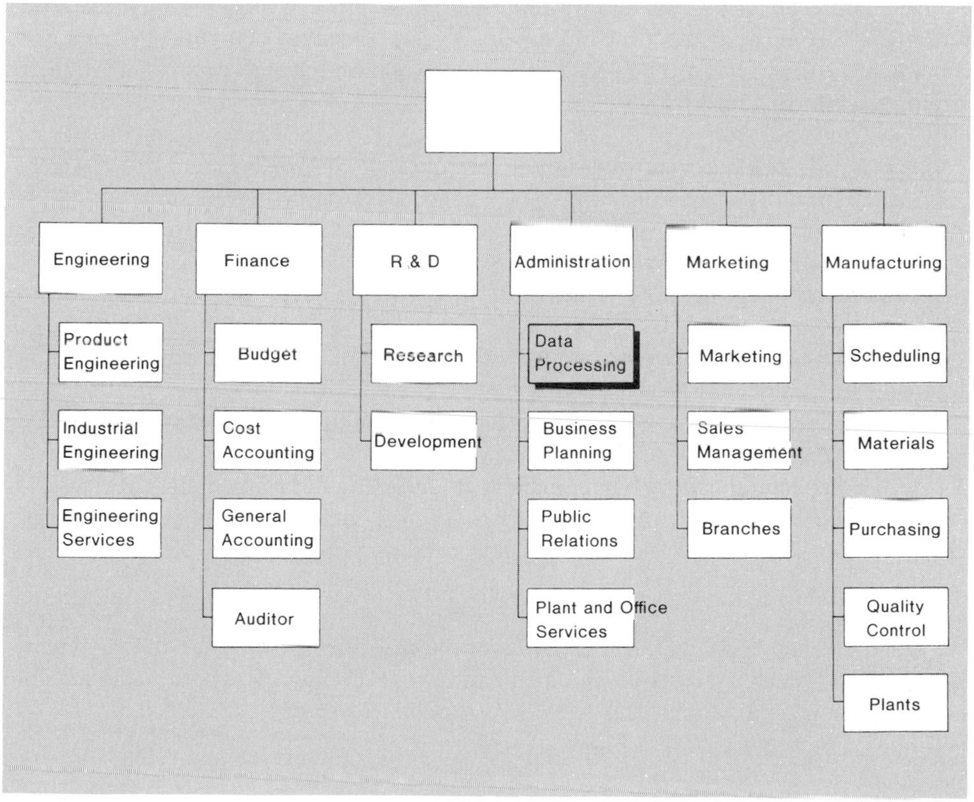

Figure 17.4 The organizational chart for a centralized data-processing unit.

Disadvantages

1. The largest user of the data-processing services may receive the same priority as the other users, thus reducing the effectiveness of the largest user's operations.
2. If each department has an equal right to use the data-processing facility without a chargeback through allotment or allocation, unprofitable use of the data-processing facility may result. This is due to the tendency of each department to reduce its operating budget at the expense of the data-processing department.
3. The physical distance between the data-processing facility and the user may create communication and deadline problems.

Decentralized Data-Processing Unit

Is the system "responsive" to the user's real needs? Many systems developed today are capable of producing more data than the user can possibly digest. The user ends up spending a great amount of time making corrections on several hundred sheets of output and little time for information analysis, which is why computer assistance was requested in the first place. A new approach in the organization of information systems development is needed. User-oriented systems can be defined as those in which the user and information systems professionals clearly delineate the thought process of the user, as opposed to the architectural approach of the technically trained systems professional.

Although many large organizations have obtained greater efficiency by centralizing their data-processing operations, the question is asked whether management has become an unresponsive bureaucracy. Communication between the user and the central system has become a serious problem in recent years. One way computer systems can be made more sensitive to the needs of the user would be through decentralization of computer facilities (fig. 17.5).

Advantages

1. Within a large decentralized organization, direct control by users may be necessary for daily operations.
2. Within each unit only the minimum equipment for the purpose served need be acquired.
3. Major users may be more sensitive to the economic use of the equipment.

Disadvantages

1. Establishing a formal corporate policy on the use of data-processing facilities is difficult in a decentralized activity.
2. The integration of data-processing functions and long-range planning will be more difficult.
3. Other departments may have difficulty in obtaining data-processing services.
4. The total cost of multiple data-processing units, each having its own personnel, may cost more than a centralized data-processing organization.

Centralization vs. Decentralization

The trend recently has certainly been toward centralizing computer management, planning, operations, systems development, and programming. But, with today's technology and new applications, this trend may possibly reverse.

After the perfect approach to computer utilization had been apparently reached, certain developments began to nibble at the philosophy of centralized computer management—to name a few, minicomputers, software overhead, and cheaper hardware.

The minicomputer, though it has been around for many years, attained a significant popularity in the seventies. The inexpensive price, the simplicity of operation, and the dedication of the mini for specific user requirements have helped in this growth, as has the utilization of the computer in increasingly smaller organizations and increasingly wider applications.

In many cases, the organization or the organizational segment could have utilized a time-sharing service or the central computer facility in the organization, but they chose not to.

Contributing Factors Toward Decentralized Computer Systems

The economy of scale argument, which contributed to large centralized computers, has been weakened today as the *hardware costs* have decreased. New technologies have caused prices of computers to drop and at the same time the capabilities have increased. Small users can obtain minicomputers as stand-alone systems to meet most of their computing needs. The concept of a mini talking to a large computer can be a worthwhile advantage when it is necessary, but in most applications the user only needs to use the minicomputer.

A more significant cost to the user is the development of *software* for the required application. The combination of a large, faster, centrally located computer with the ultimate in multi-programmable virtual machine operating systems is the trend today. Each additional enhancement not only costs more money, but it increases the software overhead. The core requirements of sophisticated operating systems have increased fifty percent from that of many systems. Obviously the computational speed of the larger computers is diminished by the amount of time the operating system facilities require for executing.

The application programs, which for the most part can be developed for a mini or central computer at the same cost, indicate no real advantage to the central facility, provided the decentralized mini has the capacity to handle the application.

The primary benefit of centralized computer management is the apparent improvement in efficiency when a central body can monitor the kinds of applications desired by the prospective users in the organization, insure that common procedures are followed by all users, and insure that no overlap or duplicate effort occurs among the users. The problems with this form of management are the same problems that occur in any bureaucracy. Often the rules, procedures, controls, and standards stifle the users and the computer's organization. The employees of the organization spend more time determining the procedures and trying to follow procedures than in actual systems analysis, design, and programming.

On the other hand, decentralization allows each functional area to determine how to meet its own computing needs. Given a certain amount of computing need, the decision would be made whether to utilize the central facility or whether to acquire n effective (and less expensive) tailor made mini system, which could be planned, anaged, programmed, and operated by the functional area.

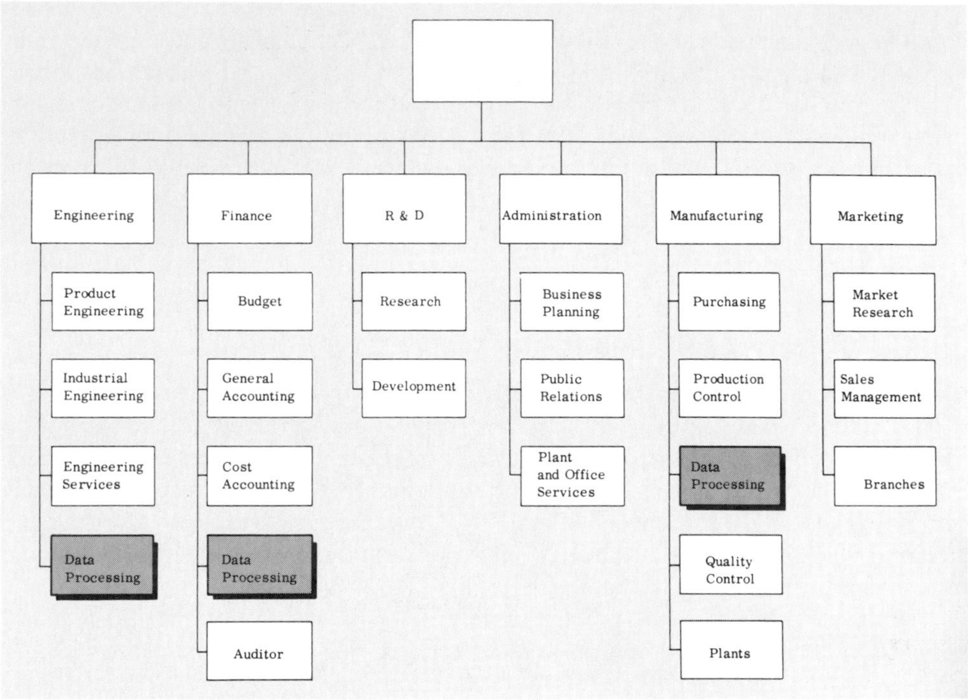

Figure 17.5 The organizational chart for a decentralized data-processing unit.

Contributi
Factor
Cer

Some say that economy of scale explains why this country was, and maybe still is, the greatest industrial nation the world has ever seen. As applied to the organization's computer requirements and costs, it also explains why organizations tend to go toward centralization.

With large, fast computers centrally located that can solve the engineer's problems, the controller's problems, and marketing problems, the organization could c tainly cut hardware and software costs by not having smaller computers loca each department of the organization.

With the centralized management approach, top management coul needs of the organization with the centralized (large) staff of specia dispatch systems analysts and programmers to any user in need. good scheduling, the peaks and valleys normally found in the personnel needed in the systems development cycle could approach also allows budgeting for systems programmers indispensable in a data-processing installation.

In the computer software area, the growth of for all sorts of users contributes further to the growth of data base management systems (D central computer that all users in the organiz are expensive and normally require larger comp space.

560 Compu

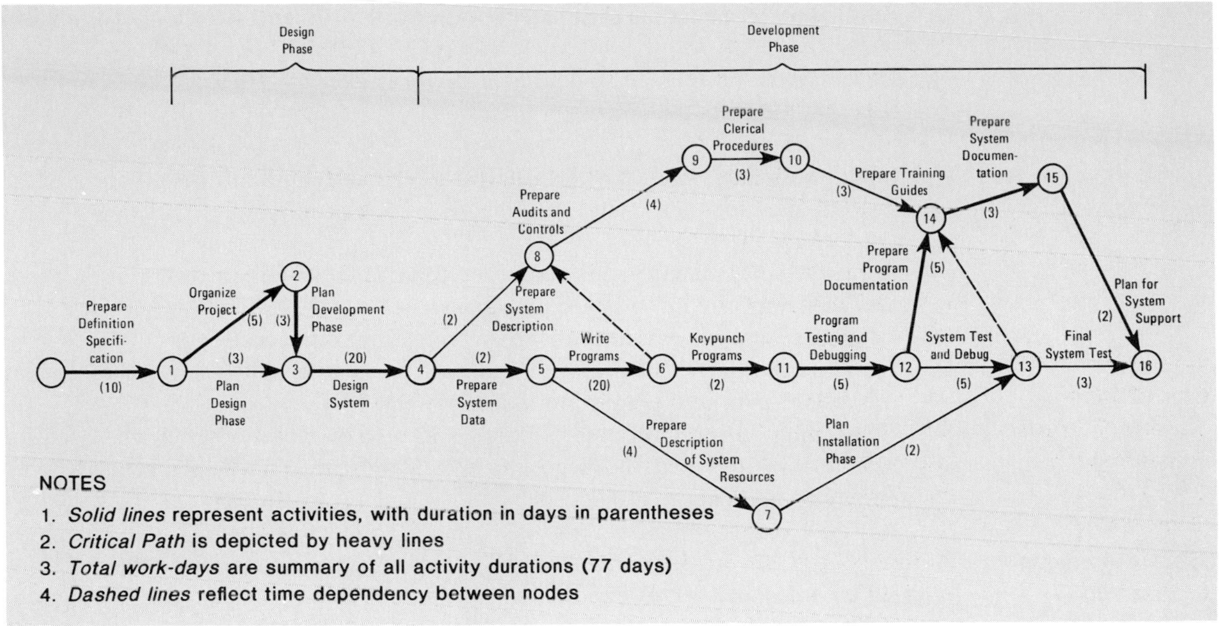

Figure 17.6 The critical path network for the design and development phase of a data-processing project.

Conclusion

The organization of the computer resource in the organization must obviously be dynamic. At each stage of growth, the approach once thought to be the best should be reevaluated. The debate on centralization versus decentralization should be revisited; for as history shows, whatever is being done now will not be the ultimate next year.

Data-Processing Functions

An organizational structure is a logical grouping of functions and the people who perform them. Basically, data-processing functions are divided into planning, operation, and management.

Planning Functions

Planning is the major activity that encompasses those functions concerned with establishing a data-processing installation and with selecting, designing, and preparing programs for new data-processing applications.

Installation Planning

This type of planning involves organization and scheduling of human and mechanical resources into an effective plan for establishing or changing a data-processing activity (fig. 17.6). This includes the following operations.

1. Schedule development for all tasks involved in installing the organization, applications, and equipment.
2. Budget development.

3. Staffing plans, including assignment of tasks, recruitment, selection, and training plans.
4. Development of detailed standards of performance.
5. Site and facilities planning.

Application Selection

This function includes the activities relative to the selection and definition of data-processing applications that fulfill the objectives of the company.

1. A review with management and other departments of their information needs and the translation into stated objectives.
2. Economic analysis to determine the justification of the costs.
3. A thorough analysis of proposed applications to ascertain whether they fit into the overall plan of the data-processing system.
4. Continuing liaison with other sections and management to review the need for new applications and the degree to which present applications are satisfying management goals.

System Analysis and Design

The analysis of the present methods, applications, objectives, and all pertinent data is followed by a design of improved systems using data-processing equipment and techniques. The primary aim of this function is to produce the optimum solution to application needs and the most economic solution consistent with management and operating objectives, equipment capabilities, and personnel resources (fig. 17.7). The analytical tasks of the function include:

1. Gathering data about present methods.
2. Recording data in suitable form for analysis, flowcharts, tables, graphs, and so forth.
3. Analyzing the data to define the desired results of the application, the restraints upon system design, time, cost, volume, the relationship of the application to other systems, and controls to be placed on the system's operations.

The tasks included in system design are:

1. Matching equipment requirements to the system's needs.
2. Finding the best way to meet the system's needs.
3. Calculating the economic and administrative effects of the new system.
4. Defining and documenting all clerical, control, and equipment procedures of the new system.
5. Getting agreement of all organizations affected by the new procedures and new systems.

Programming

Defined system requirements and procedures are translated into a logical process and a set of instructions for its operation on data-processing equipment (fig. 17.8). The major tasks in programming are:

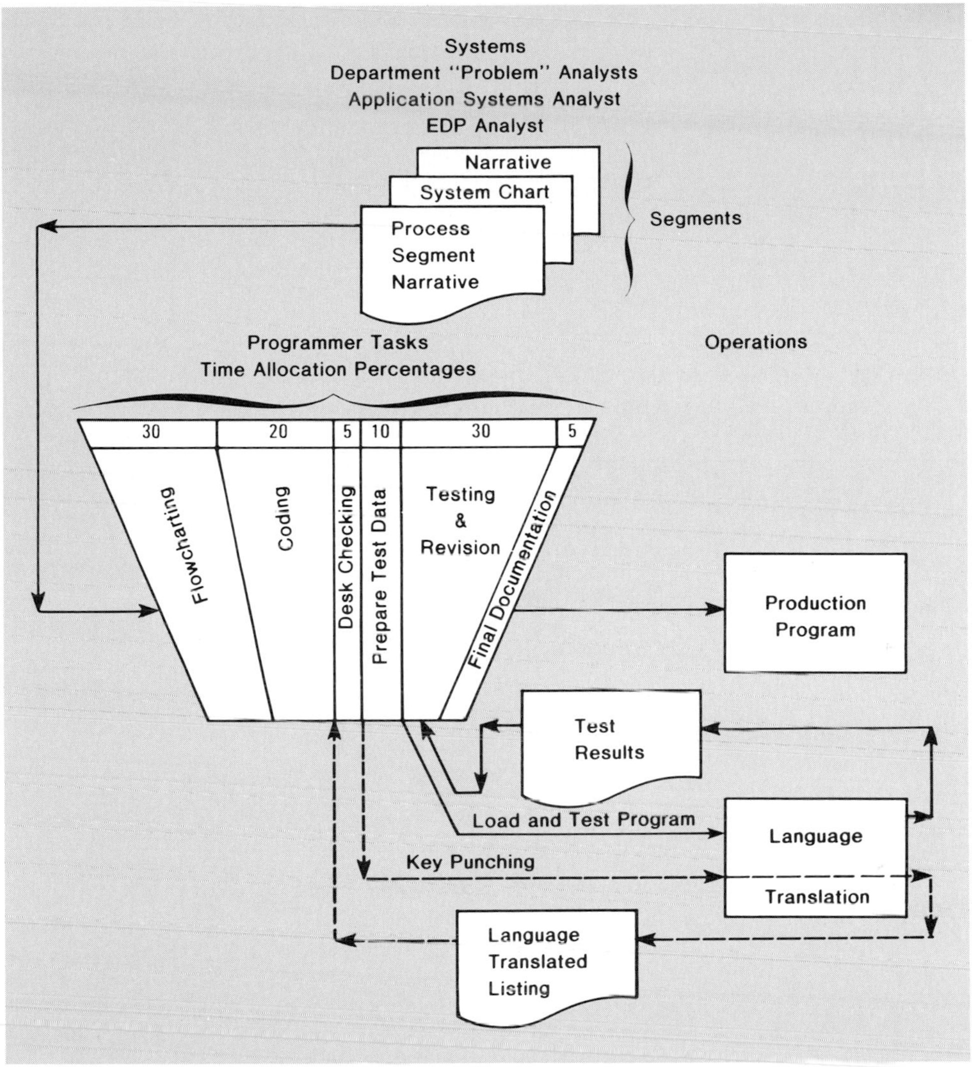

Figure 17.7 Data-processing operations.

1. Finding the best way to use the equipment efficiently to meet the needs of the system.
2. Designing the logical flow of the program (fig. 17.9).
3. Selecting standard program routines and available programming systems for incorporation into the program.
4. Preparing and coding the necessary instructions to carry out the program logic, incorporating program routines and systems as desired.

RULE No.	1	2	3	4	5	6	7	8
1st Class Request	Y	Y	Y	Y				
Tourist Request					Y	Y	Y	Y
1st Class Open	Y	N	N	N		Y	N	
Tourist Open		Y	N		Y	N	N	N
Alternate Class Acceptable		Y	Y	N		Y	Y	N
Issue 1st Class Ticket	X					X		
Issue Tourist Ticket		X			X			
Subtract 1 from 1st Class Avail	X					X		
Subtract 1 from Tourist Avail		X			X			
Place on Tourist Wait List			X				X	X
Place on 1st Class Wait List			X	X			X	

Decision table, airline reservations example

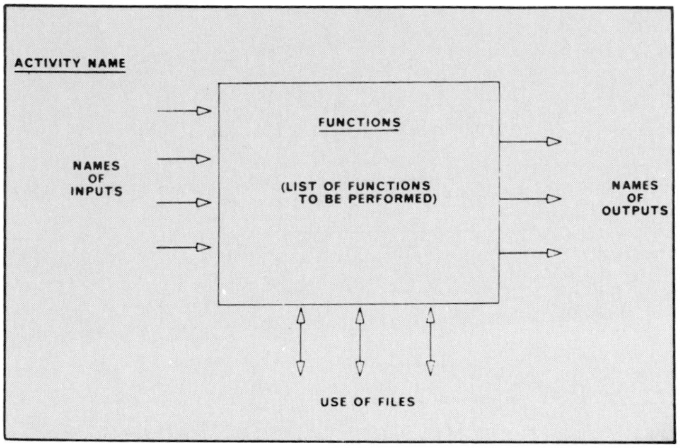

Activity requirements model

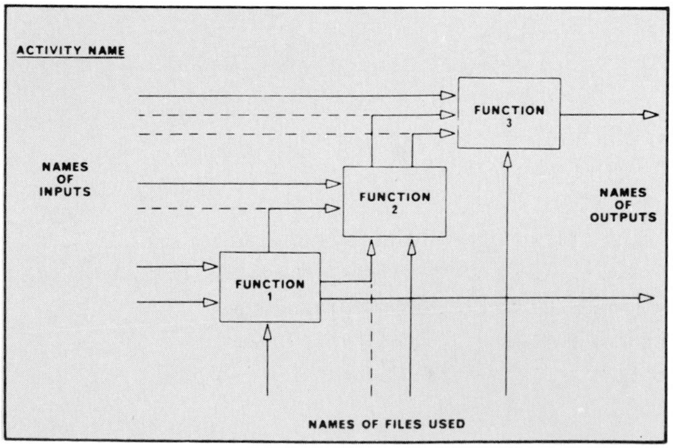

Function sequence chart

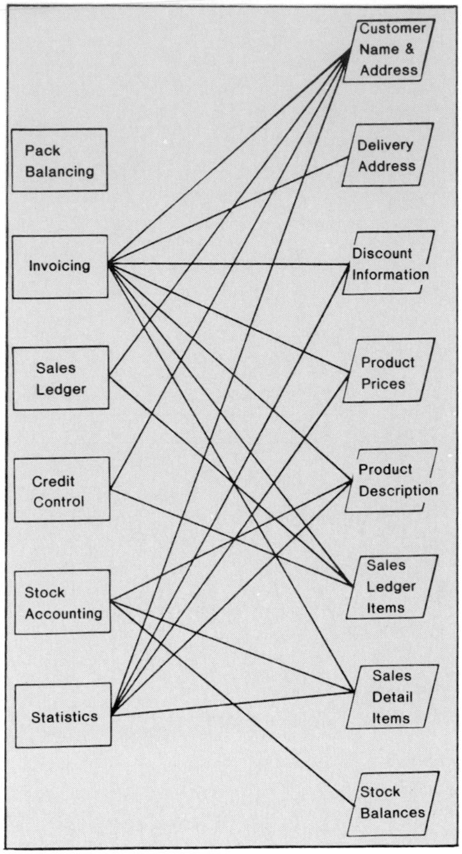

Interaction of files

Figure 17.8 An example of a decision table, an activity requirements model, a function sequence chart, and the interaction of files.

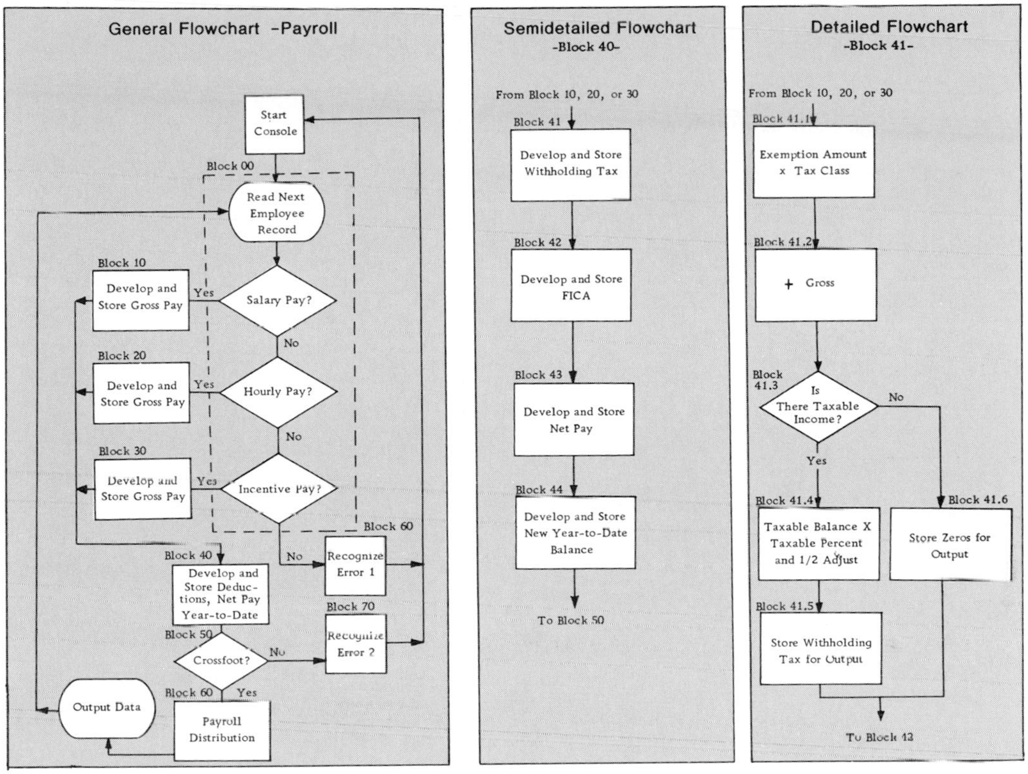

Figure 17.9 Examples of program flowcharts.

Testing

Testing determines the success of the program in meeting the defined system requirements and procedures of the total system in meeting the objectives of the application. The following tasks are important to successful testing.

1. Design of testing methods that will give a thorough trial to the new system and program.
2. Selection of appropriate source data for tests.
3. Isolation and correction of programming errors with a run using test cards and computer software.
4. Testing the manner of the program as it fits into the system.
5. Final testing of the computer system using "live" actual data.

Documentation

The documentation function requires reduction of the system and programs to a standardized written form for use in system and program modification, training, and machine operation. Documentation is usually in great detail, in rigid format, and absolutely up-to-date. Three common forms of documentation are:

Figure 17.10 An example of a table of contents for an applications manual.

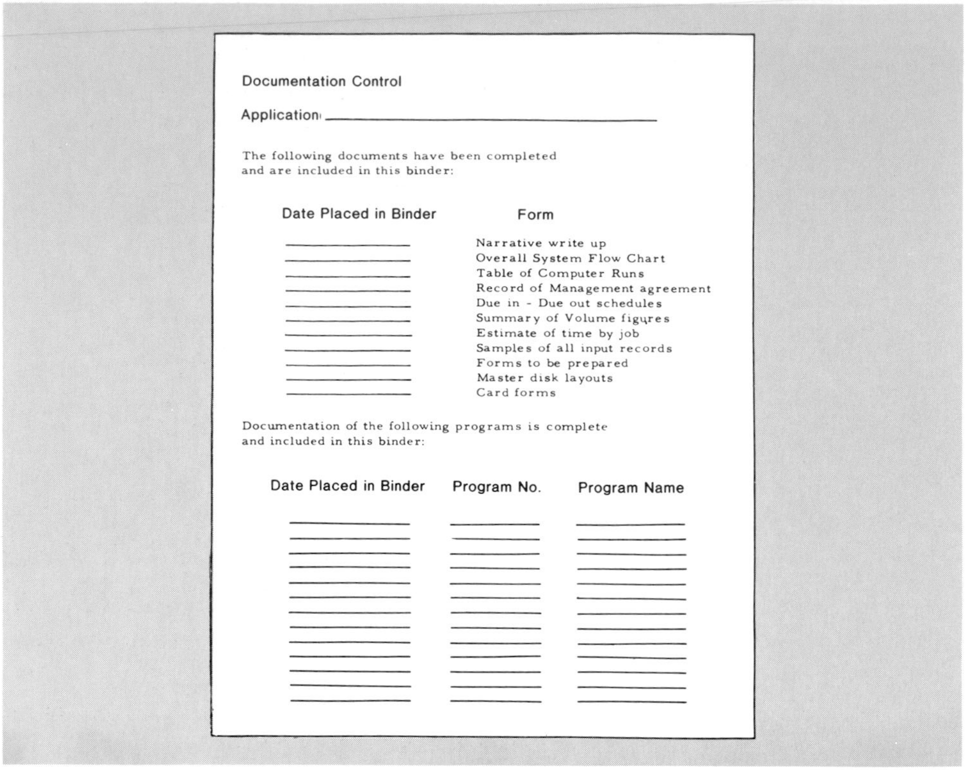

Documentation Control

Application: ______________________

The following documents have been completed
and are included in this binder:

Date Placed in Binder	Form
________	Narrative write up
________	Overall System Flow Chart
________	Table of Computer Runs
________	Record of Management agreement
________	Due in - Due out schedules
________	Summary of Volume figures
________	Estimate of time by job
________	Samples of all input records
________	Forms to be prepared
________	Master disk layouts
________	Card forms

Documentation of the following programs is complete
and included in this binder:

Date Placed in Binder	Program No.	Program Name

Figure 17.11 A data-processing operations manual.

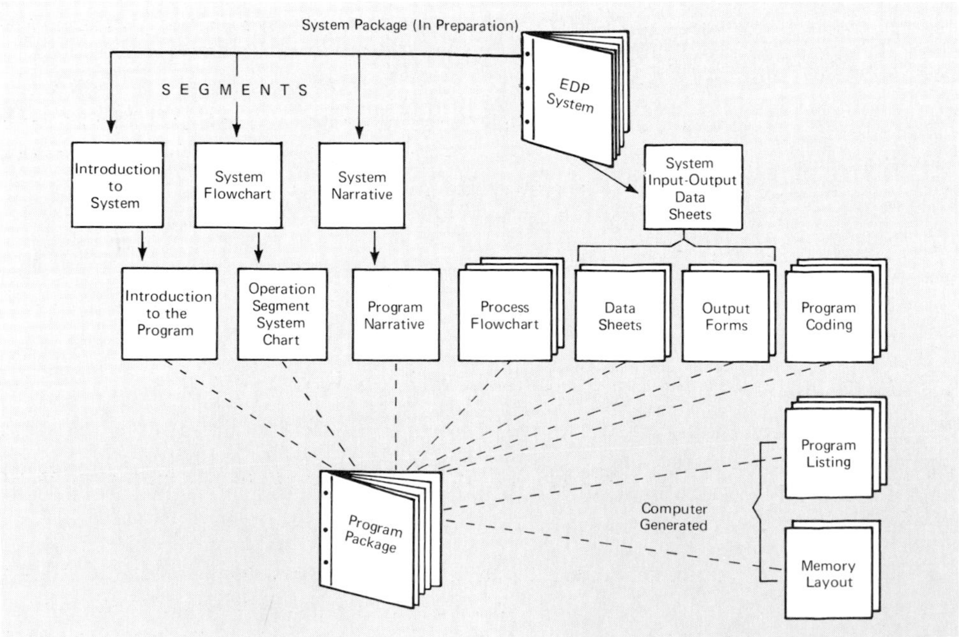

Field Characteristics:

A = Alphabetic or Alphanumeric
AS = Alphabetic or Alphanumeric (Units Pos. is Non-Numeric)
N = Numeric (Unsigned)
NX = Numeric (Minus only is Signed, Designate Position)
NS = Numeric (Signed + and - , Designate Position)

File RECORD DESCRIPTION

Record Name	Record Number
Customer Master	CM 123

Record Source	Size	Record Medium
UD-124	150	Tape

File Sequence	Date Submitted
Account within Cycle	7/1/6-

Prepared by		Revwd. by	Date	Superceded
J.R.		J.L	7/10	N.A.

Item No.	From To	Size	No. of Dec. Pos.	Field Char.	Label	Item Name	Page of
1	1	1		N	TYPE	Type of account	
2	2-10	9		N	NUM	Customer account number	
3	11-70	60		A	NAME	Customer name and address	
4	71	1		N	LIMIT	Credit limit	
5	72	1		N	STATUS	Status code	
6	73-74	2		N	TRANS	Number of transactions this month	
7	75-80	6	2	N	CHARGE	Current month charges	
8	81-86	6	2	N	PAY	Current month payments	
9	87-92	6	2	N	CREDIT	Current month credits	
10	93-98	6	2	N	BAL	Balance	
11	99-104	6	2	N	BAL 30	Aged balance over 30 days	
12	105-110	6	2	N	BAL 60	Aged balance over 60 days	
13	111-116	6	2	N	BAL 90	Aged balance over 90 days	
14	117-120	6	2	N	BAL 120	Aged balance over 120 days	
15	123-124	2		N	OPENED	Year account opened	
16	125-126	2		N	ACTIVE	Year last active	
17	127-131	5		N	PURCHY	Total purchases this year to date	
18	132-135	4		N	RETY	Total returns this year to date	
19	136-137	2		N	ACTIVE	Number of months active	
20	138-139	2		N	90 DAY	Number of months in over-90-day category	
21	140-144	5		N	PURCAL	Total purchases last year	
22	145-147	4		N	RETLY	Total returns last year	
23	148-149	2		N	MOACT	Number of months active last year	
24	150	1		N	MO 90	Number of months in over-90-day category last year	

Figure 17.12 An example of a record layout form.

1. *System's application* manuals, showing the input, output, and procedures for the total system and all programs within it (figs. 17.10, 17.11).
2. *Program* manuals, showing the detailed logic, instructions, and machine utilization for each program (fig. 17.12).
3. *Operation* manuals, providing precise instructions for running the programs and for dealing with unusual and emergency situations.

Conversion

A controlled transition is needed from the current system to the new one. The function requires the careful planning of the conversion steps and equally careful supervision of their execution. The conversion plan covers such items as:

1. Purging and cleaning of data files.
2. Training in the use of new procedures and formats.
3. Preparing special computer programs for the conversion of records.
4. Parallel operation of old and new systems.
5. Preparing and publishing training aids and procedure guides.

Operating Functions

These functions include the activities that make up the day-to-day operation of established procedures.

Machine Operation

The actual loading, unloading, setup, and control of the equipment that a data-processing installation is comprised of is included in machine operation. Data-processing equipment operation requires meticulous control of schedules and the maintenance of accurate records of equipment and program performance.

Figure 17.13 A system log.

DAILY LOG																				
		Time									Errors		Components Used							
Run Number	Dept.	On	Off	Min. Elapsed	Production	Preparation	Idle	Rerun	Maintenance	Other	Machine	User	CPU	RDR	PCH	PRT	MFCM	RDR-PCH	Other	Remarks

<u>Production</u>

01 Actual Run - Complete
02 Actual Run - Incomplete - Machine Error
03 Actual Run - Incomplete - Operator Error
04 Actual Run - Incomplete - Program Error
05 Actual Run - Incomplete - Material Failure
06 Other*

<u>Preparation</u>

07 Assembly
08 Testing
09 Check Out
10 Parallel Run
11 Demonstration
12 Machine Setup
13 Other*

<u>Idle</u>

14 Available - Not Used
15 Power
16 Other*

<u>Rerun</u>

17 Machine Error
18 Operator Error
19 Program Error
20 Material Failure
21 Other*

<u>Maintenance</u>

22 Scheduled
23 Unscheduled
24 Special*

<u>Machine</u>

25 CPU
26 RDR
27 PCH
28 PRT
29 MFCM
30 RDR-PCH
31 Other*

<u>User</u>

32 Operator Error
33 Program Error
34 Material Failure
35 Other*

* Indicate on Reverse Side

Input Preparation

Input data must be translated into codes and formats suitable for data processing. The goal of this activity is to prepare accurate, properly coded input data in the manner prescribed by the system and according to the schedules.

Input/Output Control

The control over data-processing input and output requires receiving, logging, controlling, and coordinating documents and input/output devices (fig. 17.13).

Maintenance of Record Libraries

The control and storage of all data files, programs, documentation, and operating records and reports is maintained in a library. Physically, the records are found in magnetic tapes, magnetic disks, data cells, punched paper tapes, punched cards, and a variety of forms and records. These records must be controlled on an item basis and detailed control records maintained throughout their existence.

Program Maintenance

Program maintenance includes the making of relatively minor changes in operating programs to update them, solve program-operating problems, adapt to scheduling changes, and correct errors found in programs after they have gone into an operating status. Efficient program maintenance depends to a great extent on the adequacy of the documentation prepared when the programs were developed. A significant aspect of program maintenance is a continuing liaison with system users and program operators.

Management Functions

Data processing shares with other activities the many functions of administering and supervising an operating unit (fig. 17.14).

Characteristics of Information	Operational Control	Management Control	Strategic Planning
Source	Internal	Internal/External	External
Scope	Deterministic	Det./Prob.	Probabilistic
Level of Detail Data	Detailed	Intermediate	Aggregate
Time Horizon	Historical	Current	Future
Currency of Data Base	Current	Intermediate	Old
Units of Measurement	Quantity	Dollars & Others	Dollars
Accuracy of Data Base	High	Average	Low
Frequency of Occurrence of Information Change	High	Average	Low
Frequency of Use of Information	Very Frequent	Frequent	Infrequent
End Result	Action within Procedures	Procedures	Policies
Mental Activity	Implementation	Persuasive	Creative & Analytical
Nature of Information	Functional Departmental	Divisional Inter-Departmental	Integrated
Level of Management Involvement	Supervisors; Workers	Middle Management	Senior Management

Figure 17.14 Information characteristics by decision category.

Supervision and Administration

Special aspects of data-processing administration and supervision are:

1. Good utilization of the equipment is a constant concern since meeting schedules is very important.
2. Rigid, detailed operations and creative development work must often be supervised simultaneously and as a combination.
3. Supervision of data-processing work is very difficult without a thorough knowledge of the technical details and technical skills capabilities of the equipment.

Reporting

The reporting function is an important part of any manager's job. Data-processing management faces two problems.

1. The translation of technical measures of progress and performance into commonly understood standards.
2. Continual reporting on planning and project performance.

Long-Range Planning and Project Control

Long-term plans occupy a very important part of the manager's time. Long-range plans are typically subject to periodic and often major revisions. Projects may be scheduled and developed within the long-range plan, available budgets, and personnel availability, often in the face of conflicting pressures from the other departments served. Data-processing management must keep abreast of the new developments in equipment and techniques to see how they may alter future planning.

Maintenance of Standards

Keeping the standards of performance and product high is extremely important in this as in any other function. But in the relatively new and constantly growing field of data processing, the establishment of standards and the maintenance of a high-quality level demands constant attention for:

1. Recruitment of qualified personnel.
2. Continual training of new employees and updating the training of old employees.
3. Development of a quantity and quality evaluation system based on meaningful standards.
4. Definition and publication of job descriptions.
5. Constant review of individual and group performance.

Liaison

The usual position of the data-processing activity within an organization greatly heightens the importance of its liaison function at the management level. Data-processing managers are faced with particularly difficult relationships; they often share in making decisions that do not relate directly to their own department and act as intermediaries with other departments. It is their problem to translate technical information into management terms. Finally, in day-to-day operations, they must act to assure a smooth, timely flow of data.

Alternate Approaches for Additional Computer Time

Service bureaus can be utilized in several ways. Perhaps a specific job, such as the company's payroll, can be very effectively processed outside, thereby freeing the company's computer for other work. In other cases, the computer might be print-bound on certain operations and by using spooling can either get printed reports or microfiche. (*Microfiche* consists of microfilm images on a single sheet of film. *Spooling* is the reading and writing of input and output streams on auxiliary storage devices, concurrently with job execution, in a format convenient for later processing or output operations.) In either case, some of the load is removed from an already overburdened computer. Finally, in a number of industries, an industry specialist is available to handle specific portions of the company's data-processing requirements, often the specialist's packages and programs will be superior to those of the company.

Time-sharing companies can offer a data-processing manager additional machine capabilities on a purely variable cost basis, based on actual equipment and time needed on these devices, particularly if requirements are for additional core, disk, or tape. Time-sharing companies also offer certain industry packages that may be utilized efficiently by the company, while microfiche and spooling techniques are also available through certain time-sharing companies in an online mode.

Add-on equipment can be used to provide additional computing time. The addition of input/output devices and core storage can help to alleviate critical computer time shortages. However, the user must be very careful to avoid expanding the programs that cannot be removed later if the volume should decline. This is not always possible to achieve because of certain manufacturers' marketing policies regarding the combining of owned and rented equipment. But where possible, it might provide a good solution to the problem and enable the company to maintain reasonable costs due to increased volume.

As the computer makes its transition from mysterious toy to a basic business tool, the data manager changes from a "witch doctor" into a responsible executive. The channeled end is not merely to get the work done but to do it at the lowest, most realistic cost.

Data-Processing Positions

Exact job titles and content are closely related to the size of the data-processing activity, the type of installation, the kind of organization, and other factors in the environment (fig. 17.15). The following are the major types of data-processing positions. (A detailed description of positions in each category can be found in Appendix C.)

Management—responsible for the overall operation of the functional units of a data-processing installation.

Systems Analysis and Programming—responsible for planning and programming new and revised applications (figs. 17.16, 17.17).

Systems Analysis—responsible for studies and system design for new applications.

Applications Programming—plan, organize, and control the preparation of applications programs.

Systems Programming—plan and direct the activities of software programming and determine hardware requirements, including data base management, auditing, telecommunications, and documentation.

Operations—concerned with the operations of the data center (fig. 17.18).

Data Control—plan, schedule, supervise, and direct preparation of records for data entry and distribution of reports.

Introduction of a System

Installation

A decision to establish a new data-processing system is usually reached as the result of a favorable feasibility study. Beneficial results of a good system are rarely maximized because the installation tasks were not properly met. The following are some of the important steps in a proper installation of a system (fig. 17.19).

1. All procedures must be converted to the new system and properly documented.
2. The new system must be sold to all levels of management to overcome resistance.
3. During the installation period, tight controls should be maintained over every phase of the new system. This will include the following controls.
    a. *Checkpoint controls*—a point in the program through which every document flows.
    b. *Data flow controls*—the recording of input and output through log sheets, registers, documents, etc.
    c. *Accounting controls*—dollar and unit controls on all volume quantities.
4. A calendar should be agreed upon. This includes the scheduling of personnel requirements (including training), necessary forms, and equipment for the proper installation at the appropriate time.
5. The necessary manuals and job instructions must be prepared for use during and after the installation period.
6. Necessary personnel must be educated and trained. This training may be at the computer manufacturer's school, at colleges or universities, or at the plant.
7. A method of installation must be decided upon.
    a. *All-at-once method*—recommended when the system is relatively simple and does not involve too many organizational units or the volume of data to be processed is relatively light.

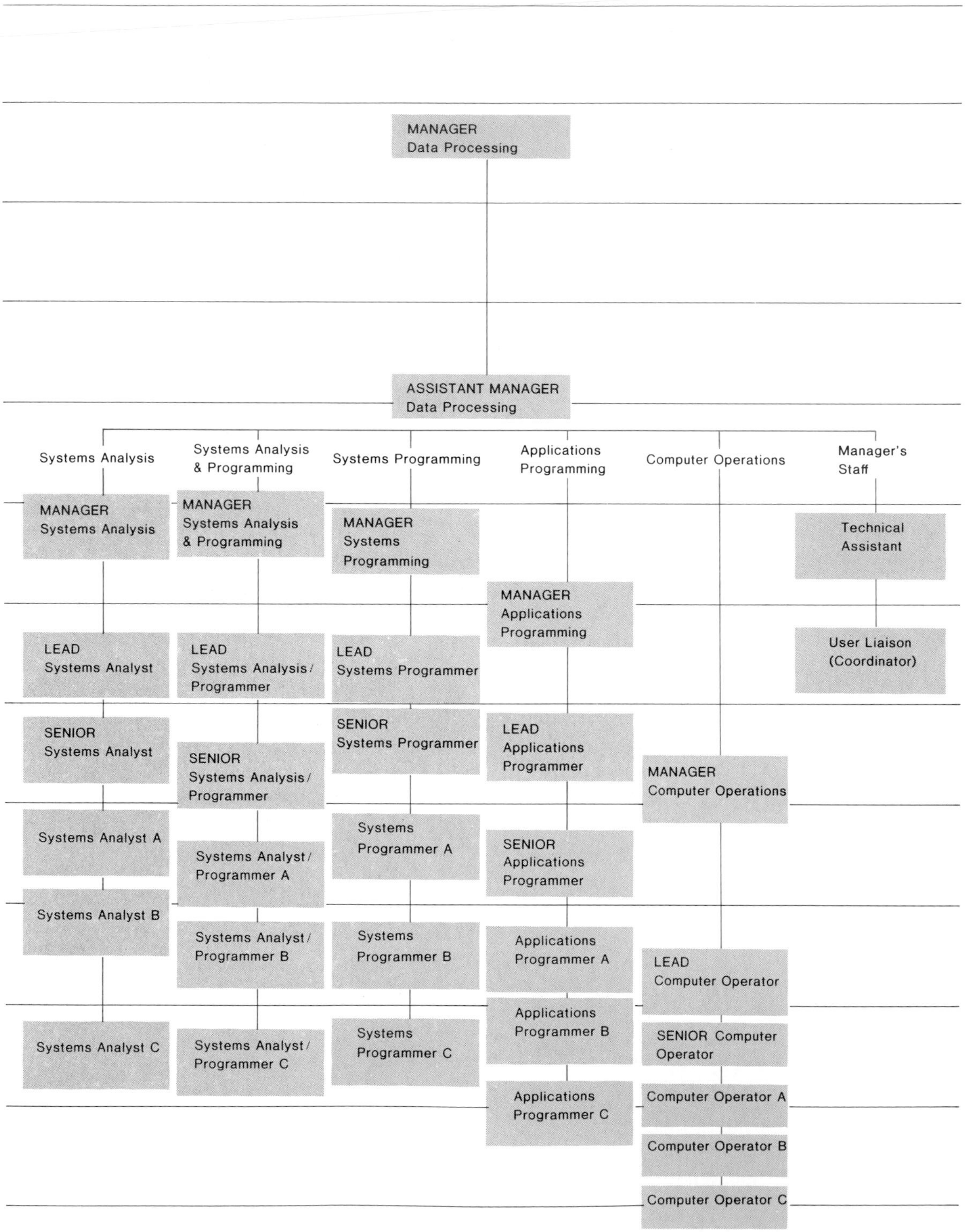

Figure 17.15 Data-processing positions.

1. TECHNICAL KNOWLEDGE. Keeping abreast of and retaining familiarity with software and hardware, learning new languages, application, utility routines, and/or executives, learning about central processors, peripherals, and other input/output media.
2. PLANNING, ORGANIZING, AND SCHEDULING. Effective utilization of time, planning, and scheduling of current and future work, reacting to potential problems, making schedules, etc.
3. MAINTAINING CUSTOMER RELATIONS. Trying to please the customer, answering customer questions in an understandable manner, "holding up" under customer demands and abuse, presenting new techniques on "selling" the customer whenever appropriate, providing continuing customer service, providing advice, assistance, and updating to the customer.
4. PROVIDING SUPERVISION AND LEADERSHIP. Giving technical work direction, directing and delegating assignments, motivating and utilizing personnel, calling meetings, coordinating activities, preparing cost estimates, and project schedules, etc.
5. TRAINING OTHERS. Providing instruction and guidance to customer personnel, coworkers, and/or subordinates, etc.
6. DOCUMENTATION. Providing formal narratives describing a program and/or system in sufficient detail so that others can understand and use the program and/or system.
7. MAINTAINING COMMUNICATIONS. Providing information through the use of written or verbal channels, such as letters to colleagues, established procedures, using the telephone, etc.
8. ASSESSING CUSTOMER NEEDS AND PROVIDING RECOMMENDATIONS. Studying and determining customer and/or internal management problems and requirements, including the isolation, definition, and analysis of problem and need areas. Recommending software and hardware to solve these problems and/or meet their requirements.
9. JOB COMMITMENT AND EFFORT. Putting in long hours and extra time, working on own time to acquire knowledge, putting in a full week's work, performing tasks that might be considered beyond the "call of duty," being committed to doing a good job.
10. DEBUGGING. Using various techniques (CRAM analysis, tracing of logic, etc.) in connecting the logic and associated problems in order to make a program or system operational.
11. PROGRAM AND/OR SYSTEMS MODIFICATION AND/OR DEVELOPMENT. Modifying and/or developing programs and/or systems that reflect unique solutions and/or a certain degree of "creativity."
12. CONDUCTING PRESENTATIONS. Formally providing information and/or materials to interested personnel, illustrating how a system works, developing seminars, etc.

Figure 17.16 Major dimensions of job behavior for systems analysts and programmer analysts. (Reprinted with permission of *Datamation*© magazine, ©Copyright by Technical Publishing Company, a division of Dun-Donnelley Publishing Corporation, a Dun & Bradstreet Company, 1978—all rights reserved.)

Figure 17.17 Average importance ratings for twelve dimensions of job behavior for systems analysts and programmer analysts. (Reprinted with permission of *Datamation*© magazine, ©Copyright by Technical Publishing Company, a division of Dun-Donnelley Publishing Corporation, a Dun & Bradstreet Company, 1978—all rights reserved.)

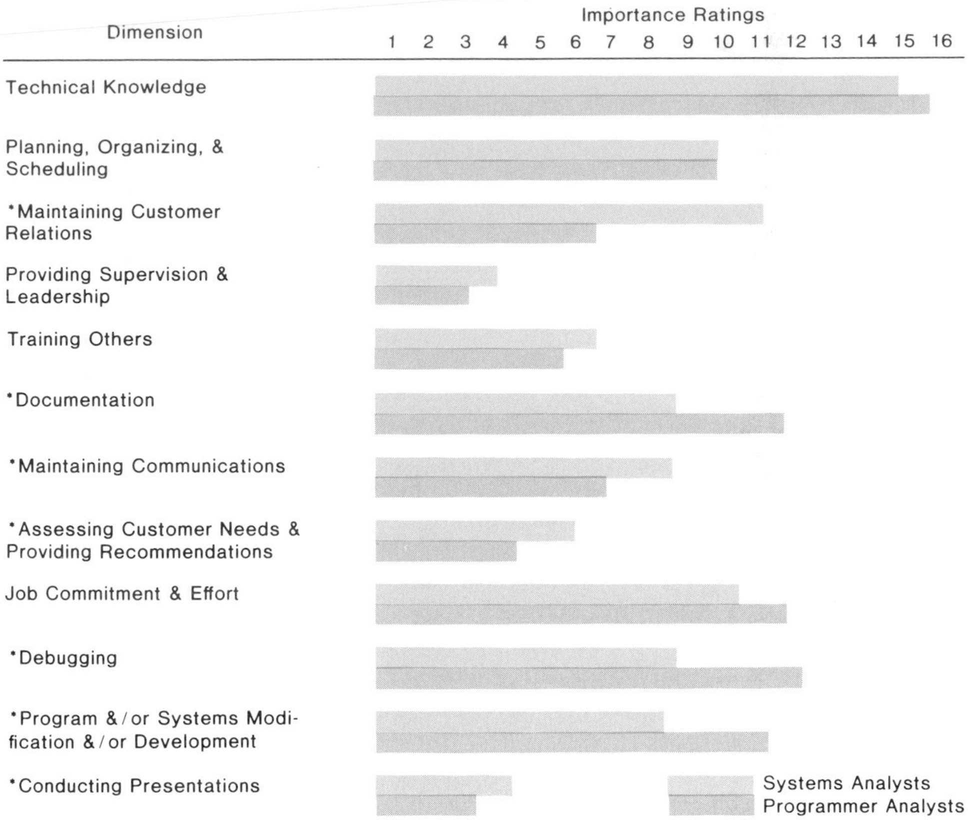

*The difference between the systems analysts and programmer analysts on this dimension is statistically significant such that a difference this large would only occur less than 1 time out of 20.

b. *Piecemeal installation*—usually recommended when there is a large volume job to be converted and it is simpler to convert a segment at a time.

c. *Parallel operations*—usually recommended for large-scale jobs involving intricate processing. A payroll application is usually converted using a parallel operation method, which is the old and new systems operating simultaneously. When the new system satisfies all the needs, the old system may be abandoned.

Duration of the Installation Period

Strict control of the system should continue until the system personnel are satisfied that the new system is functioning properly, that all problems are solved, that everyone is fully trained, and that the new system will operate without the supervision of the systems personnel. At this time, the system should be turned over in its entirety to the operating personnel.

Remedial Action

The control devices will point out whether the concepts and results are deviating from established standards. When this happens, swift and accurate changes must be made to the system.

1. TIME UTILIZATION. Planning and scheduling current and future work in order to effectively utilize the computer and associated equipment.
2. LOGGING. Recording pertinent information associated with computer runs and/or the labeling of output reports or measures and associated magnetic media (tapes, disks, data cells, etc.).
3. WORK AREA MAINTENANCE. Keeping the computer, peripherals, and surrounding work area in a clean and orderly condition.
4. SOFTWARE AND HARDWARE KNOWLEDGE. Maintaining general familiarity with, and showing the ability to learn and use utility routines, executive systems, general programming principles, central processor, associated peripherals and all input/output media.
5. COMPLIANCE WITH WRITTEN AND VERBAL INSTRUCTIONS. Taking and following instructions submitted with a job in accordance with established computer operator procedures.
6. JOB EFFORT AND ATTITUDE. Making self available to help out in critical and emergency situations. Doing more than just "carrying his load," coming in on time, spending own time learning to program, showing commitment to doing the job well, etc.
7. ERROR RESPONSE. Detecting and recording pertinent information upon encountering an error condition, taking corrective action when appropriate, and/or reporting the error to appropriate individual(s).
8. MAINTAINING PERSONAL RELATIONS. Interacting effectively with co-workers and/or supervisors on a personal or work-oriented basis.
9. PROVIDING SUPERVISION, LEADERSHIP, AND TRAINING. Giving work direction, providing instruction and guidance, planning and scheduling tasks, assigning responsibilities to coworkers and/or subordinates, etc.

Figure 17.18 Major dimensions of job behavior for computer operations.

Cost Considerations

Although the primary design of the system is to save money and time, during the installation period, costs may exceed those of the old system. This may be due to the following factors.

1. Duplication of effort. Two systems are operating at the same time.
2. More stringent controls. Excess controls during this period will require additional clerical efforts.
3. Learning curves. It will take employees longer to do a new job than it took to do the old job, using the old system (after months and years of practice).
4. One time costs. Such costs as site preparation, transportation costs, and additional employees, occur only once.
5. Resistance to changes. Old employees may be hesitant about learning new systems.

Figure 17.19 The critical path for computer installation.

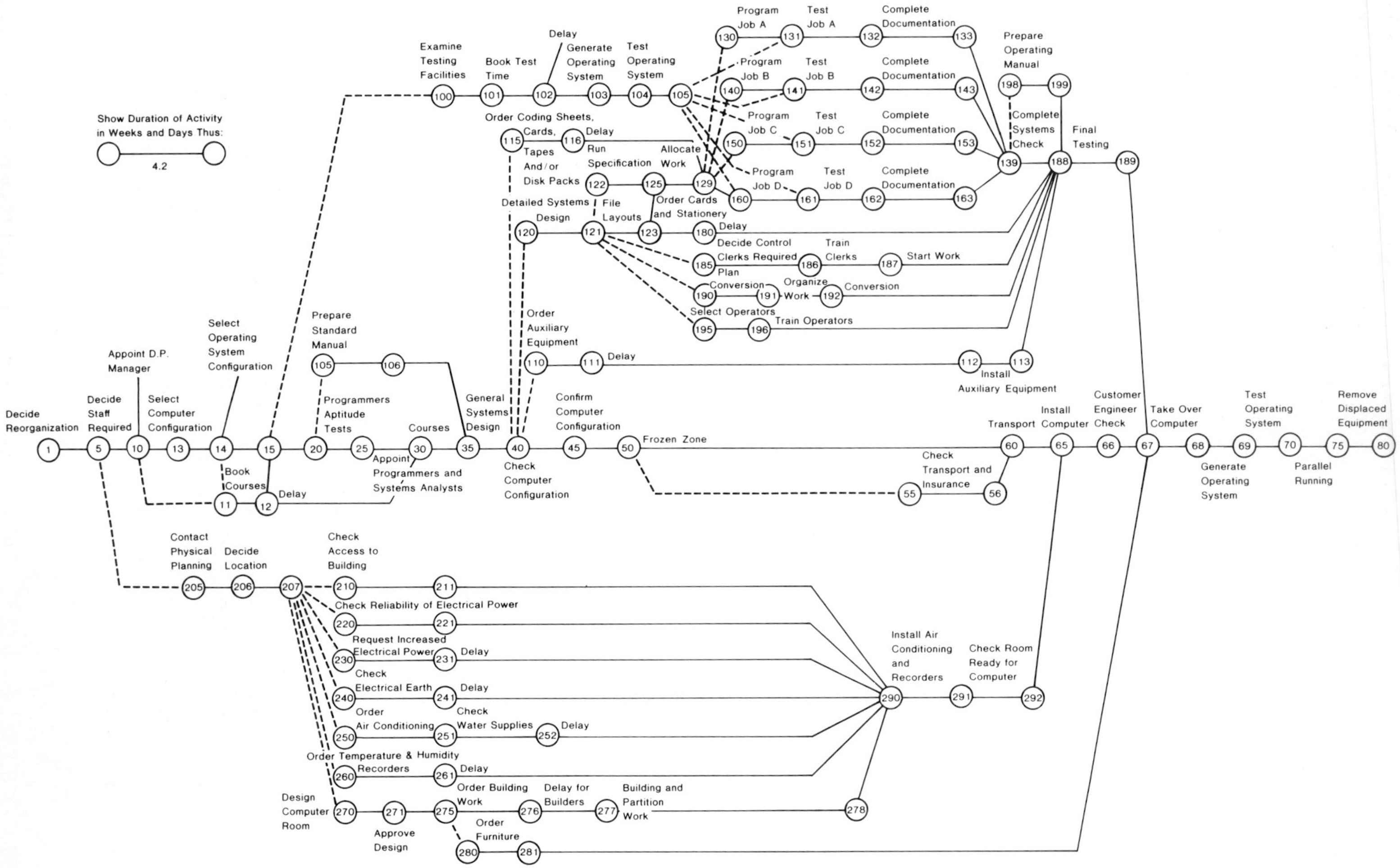

Personnel Problems

The new system must be properly communicated to the employees. They must be allowed the opportunity to participate in the planning of the new system and the conversion. This will satisfy their personal goals and make them more anxious to participate in the new system.

Follow-Up

The prime purpose of follow-up is to consolidate all new gains made by the new system and to eliminate any losses. When to follow up depends upon the complexity of the new system. Various methods may be used.

Continuous Theory

Every area in the system is visited and checked each time it is visited.

Spot Check

Check the system at specific time intervals. Check after the installation has been in operation for thirty days. The frequency thereafter will depend on the complexity of the system.

The systems analyst should check the following.

1. The costs are in line.
2. The facilities are adequate.
3. The employees' performances are acceptable.
4. The employees are accepting the new system.
5. There is no evidence of falling back to the old system.

In addition to consolidating gains and correcting misunderstandings, there are several other reasons for follow-up.

1. A feedback on the operation of the system.
2. Possible revisions of the system.
3. To prevent and discourage backsliding to the old system by participants.
4. Discovery of new ideas and improvements during this period.
5. The preparation of justification reports to management.

Summary

The problems encountered in managing data-processing installation are quite different from those found in managing other units of the enterprise. Data-processing organization requires the careful blending of technical and managerial skills to achieve a well-balanced data-processing unit. The data-processing effort follows concepts and methods not ordinarily followed in other units of an organization. Highly trained, technically competent, and in many cases creative, personnel are required in a data-processing unit. Data processing has created many new positions quite different from those found in other areas of the company. Data processing performs a service function and its primary obligation is to satisfy the needs of all units of an organization.

This chapter discusses the many problems that arise in the management function of the data-processing installation.

1. The principal objective of a data-processing organization is the production of user satisfactory information from raw data within a specified schedule and a specified budget. The data-processing manager measures the utilization of resources in order to effectively correlate them to performance requirements. The data manager must be both a technical specialist and must be competent in personal relations. The data manager must be concerned with the coordination of data-processing department goals with those of the overall organization's goals.
2. Data processing serves management through planning and research, control and exceptional reporting, and the maintenance of the organization's basic information files. Data processing serves many operational purposes, such as inventory orders and production controls, personnel and payroll records, and customer accounts. Accounting, record keeping, scientific, mathematical, real-time, and data transmission services are types of services to be furnished to users. A data-processing department may operate as an open shop, which provides personnel and equipment for programming and operations, or as a closed shop, which provides only the problem and the data-processing department provides personnel and equipment for analysis and programming. Other important considerations are deadlines and turn-around schedules, as well as plans for growth, product expansion, and competitive position.
3. The data center has various functions. Data control is responsible for seeing that data is prepared as the user submits it. Scheduling assures that optimum use of all resources is obtained and products are delivered on time. All production data should be prepared using data preparation instructions. The job of the computer operations is to get the programs run through as quickly and accurately as possible. Systems programming generates and maintains the operating system, optimizes the performance of the software and the hardware, identifies inefficient programs, and creates operating standards for efficient operation. The computer center also participates in long-range planning.
4. The advantage of a centralized data-processing unit are that all departments receive equal consideration; that there is more efficient program planning and systems research and development; that disputes between departments can be more easily settled; and that there are lower costs for expansion. The disadvantages are that large users have the same priority as others; that possible unprofitable use of data-processing facilities may result; and that physical distance between the data-processing facility and users may create problems.
5. The advantages of a decentralized data-processing unit are that users have direct control; that only equipment for the purpose served is required for each unit; and that the major users are more sensitive to economic use of equipment. The disadvantages are that formal corporate policy on use of equipment may be difficult; that integration of data-processing functions and long-range planning is difficult; that other departments may have difficulty in obtaining data-processing services; and that the total costs of multiple units is usually higher.
6. Large-scale computer operations have cut operating costs, because smaller computers located in each department are not needed. New technologies have caused lower prices of computer components, while their capacities have increased.

Developments in software have increased the cost due to large multi-programmable systems. A central operation is more efficient because it can monitor its operations. However, the alternative allows each functional area to determine its own computing needs.

7. Planning is the major activity that encompasses installation planning, application selection, system analysis and design, programming, testing, documentation, and conversion. Operating functions include machine operation, input preparation, input/output control, maintenance of record libraries, and program maintenance. Management functions include supervision and administration, long-range planning and project control, reporting, maintenance of standards, and acting as a liaison between departments. Additional approaches for additional computing time are service bureaus, time-sharing equipment, and add-on equipment.
8. The various categories in data processing are management, systems analysis and programming, systems analysis, applications programming, operations, and data control.
9. During the installation of a new system, tight controls should be maintained. These are checkpoint controls, data flow controls, and accounting controls. After scheduling has been agreed upon, preparation of the necessary manuals must be done. Personnel must be trained. There are three methods of installation, all at once, piecemeal, and parallel. Strict control of the installation should continue until the system personnel are satisfied that the new system is functioning properly. Control devices will point out any deviations from the standards. The various factors affecting cost are duplication of effort, more stringent controls, learning curves, and one-time costs. In order for a new system to be effective, it must be properly communicated to the employees. A follow-up must be made to insure that all new gains are consolidated and that backsliding to the old system is prevented. The continuous theory is followed—every area is visited and checked. Spot checking of the system is done at specific time intervals.

Identification Questions

Match the following terms with the statements below.

A. Application Selection
B. Centralized Data-Processing Unit
C. Checkpoint Controls
D. Computer Operations
E. Conversion
F. Data Control
G. Data Flow Controls
H. Data Preparation
I. Decentralized Data-Processing Unit
J. Documentation
K. Input Preparation
L. Input/Output Control
M. Installation Planning
N. Learning Curves
O. Machine Operation
P. Microfiche
Q. Operating Functions
R. Planning
S. Program Maintenance
T. Programming
U. Scheduling
V. Spooling
W. Systems Analysis and Design
X. Systems Programming
Y. Testing

1. The recording of input/output through log sheets, registers, and documents.
2. Production data prepared using data preparation instructions as a guide.
3. The data-processing department that is independent but at the same level with the department it services.
4. Major activity that encompasses those functions concerned with establishing a data-processing installation.
5. Defined system requirements and procedures are translated into a logical set of instructions.
6. The actual loading, setup, and control of the equipment that a data-processing installation is composed of.
7. Microfilm image on a single sheet of film.
8. Responsible for seeing that data is prepared as the user submits it and accuracy for the processing of data through the data center.
9. To get programs run through the computer by a minimization of operator wait time and operator errors.
10. Activities relative to the selection and definition of data-processing applications.
11. Determine the success of the program in meeting the defined systems requirements.
12. Controlled transition from current system to the new one.
13. The receiving, logging, controlling, and coordinating of documents and input/output devices.
14. The reading and writing of input/output streams on auxiliary storage devices.
15. Assures that optimum use of all resources is obtained and the products delivered on time.
16. Responsibility for generating and maintaining the operating system.
17. Organization and scheduling human and mechanical resources into an effective plan for establishing or changing a data-processing activity.
18. The data-processing department is within a larger organization unit that is its major user.
19. Analysis of present methods, applications, objectives, and all pertinent data is followed by design of improved system.
20. The reduction of the systems and programs into a standardized written form for use of system and program modification.
21. The activities that make up the day-to-day operation of established procedures.
22. The translation of input data into codes and formats suitable for data processing.
23. The making of relatively minor changes in operating programs to update them.
24. A point in the program through which every document flows.
25. It takes employees longer to do a new job than it took to do the old job.

Questions for Review

1. What are some of the problems encountered in data-processing installations?
2. Briefly itemize the important aspects of the job of the data-processing manager.
3. List the important factors to be considered in establishing the managerial objectives of a data-processing installation.
4. Describe the important data center functions.

5. What is the important difference between a centralized and decentralized data-processing unit?
6. What are the important advantages and disadvantages of a centralized data-processing unit?
7. What are the important advantages and disadvantages of a decentralized data-processing unit?
8. Briefly describe the contributing factors toward centralized computer systems.
9. What is the necessary planning function of the data-processing unit?
10. Describe the different types of planning activities involved with the planning function itself.
11. Describe the major operating functions of a data-processing unit.
12. What are some of the important management functions in the operation of a data-processing installation?
13. What are some alternate approaches available to data-processing managers for additional computer time?
14. Briefly describe the major types of data-processing positions.
15. List the important steps in the proper installation of a system.
16. Why are costs unusually higher during the installation period?
17. What is the prime purpose of follow-up?
18. What must the system analyst check before completely releasing the system to operating personnel?
19. What are the other reasons for follow-up in addition to the consolidation of gains and the correction of misunderstandings?

Key Terms

Application Selection
Centralized Data-Processing Unit
Checkpoint Controls
Computer Operations
Conversion
Data Control
Data Flow Controls
Decentralized Data-Processing Unit
Documentation
Input Preparation
Input/Output Control
Installation Planning
Learning Curves
Machine Operation
Microfiche
Operating Functions
Planning
Program Maintenance
Programming
Scheduling
Spooling
System Analysis and Design
System Programming

data management 18

Chapter Outline

Computer Security
- Computer Fraud—A Growing Problem
- The EDP Auditor
  - Responsibilities
  - EDP Auditor's Role
  - Disaster-Recovery Program
  - Experience and Education
  - Position in the Organization
- Role of Consultants
  - The Computer as an Audit Tool
    - Audit Uses of the Computer
    - Software—The Right Tool
  - Computer Audit Packages

Data Security
- Computer Room Security
  - Sources of Potential Damage and Danger
- Preventive Measures
  - Location
  - Site Construction
  - Operating Procedures
  - Data Protection
  - Legal Protection
  - Additional Measures

Telecommunications Protection
- Classification of Information
- System Design Factors
  - Control Audits
  - Detailed Logs
  - Lockward
  - Monte Carlo
  - Validation

Data-Processing Responsibility
- Usefulness of Reports
- Systems Design
- Communication
- Accuracy
- Timeliness
- Personnel
- Economy
- Technological Study
- Progress Reports

Chapter Objectives

The learning objectives of this chapter are

1. to become aware of the growing problem of computer fraud and to present some practical safeguards that can be used to assure the accuracy and protection of important programs, files, and data.

2. to examine the responsibilities of the EDP auditor.
3. to present the computer as an audit tool.
4. to become aware of the potential damage and danger that can cause undue harm to the computer investment and disrupt the day-to-day business of an enterprise.

The rapid expansion of computer usage and the vast increase in the variety of uses for computers during the past decade has created many problems for management. Today, both top management and data-processing executives recognize their responsibilities to the public and to company shareholders for protecting the company's investment in computer facilities, programs, and data. The survival of most companies and organizations rests on the information stored in data-processing media. Hence, practical safeguards must be installed to assure the accuracy and protection of important programs, files, and data.

Computer Security

Computer Fraud—A Growing Problem

A teller in a large bank shuffles hundreds of accounts in the bank's computerized system, stealing more than $1.5 million from the bank's deposits. A brilliant electronics expert taps into a large telephone company's computerized inventory system and steals almost a million dollars in equipment.

Incidents similar to these are occurring more frequently. They are examples of computer abuse and embezzlement. As the number of computers continues to grow, such frauds almost certainly will increase. *Computer abuse is defined as those incidents caused by intentional acts, negligent acts, or accidental occurrences in which a perpetrator realized or could have realized a gain and/or in which a victim suffered or could have suffered a loss.*

As pointed out in a recent magazine cover story on computers, "though electronic pilfering currently amounts to less than 1% of the $41 billion in annual thefts by employees and company executives, it is far more serious than stealing petty cash, and much harder to uncover."

The words "computer fraud" leapt into print on newspaper front pages after the Equity Funding scandal (fig. 18.1). The Equity Funding scandal, now approaching a $2 billion loss, blew apart because of the complaints of a former employee. This scandal is an example of a major computer abuse as the computers played a significant role in the fraud. The company is said to have been keeping two sets of books for several years and selling bogus life insurance policies. If the conspirators would have had to manually create some 64,000 bogus insurance policies, the fraud would have been impossible. The class action suit filed against Equity stated:

> That defendants, and each of them, so carelessly, negligently and wantonly designed, constructed and manufactured said data processing equipment that said equipment could be used for any business for the purpose of defrauding the public, of which plaintiffs are members; that there is no method available to prevent the insertion of false and fraudulent material in the computer printouts and no method to discover the insertion of false and fraudulent materials in a program otherwise legitimate.

Figure 18.1 Headlines about computer fraud.

What is the scope of computer crime? What can management, especially internal auditors, do about this threat? What kind of defenses are being established to prevent computer embezzlement? What kind of techniques are being developed to detect it?

Most data-processing experts have concluded that computer-assisted fraud is a major problem, but no one knows the extent of the problem. The problem is expected to grow even greater with the incredible proliferation of the computer systems, including the fast-growing minicomputer and microcomputer industry. Gradually, management is becoming aware of its vulnerability as far as data processing is concerned. However, there still are many organizations that are unaware of how defenseless they are in the face of potential, clever embezzlers.

A new field is developing in the control and security of data-processing systems, as well as the auditing of computerized systems. But it is in a catch-up mode with the auditors and security experts still struggling behind the technology and the increasing opportunities for theft of large sums of money. Auditors are in the process of upgrading their skills to adapt to a new, more difficult mode of operation, auditing through complex data-processing systems.

Most crimes go unreported; this is particularly true of computer-assisted crimes, according to experts in computer security. Most businesses do not report computer-assisted crimes because they feel that the unfavorable publicity will damage their company and because they often do not know how to prevent it from happening again and, therefore, do not want people to be aware of how it was managed.

The significance of computer-assisted fraud is that criminals can steal large amounts of money, and, in many cases, run little risk of being caught and punished. The typical computer malefactor is a white-collar individual who only gets involved in situations where there's little chance of getting caught.

The problem may get worse since minicomputers are giving many more people an opportunity to perpetrate frauds. Distributed processing, micros and minis, remote terminals, and integrated file structures all place new complex security demands on

Figure 18.2
Suggestions on how to prevent computer frauds.

1. Let as few people as possible use your computer.
2. Make them give the proper password—or better yet, a series of two or three—before the computer will do anything.
3. Limit the number of miscues. For example, the computer should holler for help on the third attempt in a row to use the wrong password.
4. Change passwords often.
5. Make everyone log in and out when using the computer.
6. Check the log frequently. If a program takes longer to run than it should, maybe it has been tampered with.
7. Give no one blanket access to computer data. Restrict users to what they have a right to know. Then, for example, production personnel can't tamper with financial records.
8. Keep tight security over the computer center itself.
9. Use a random monitoring system to spot-check what your computer's doing.

data-processing organizations, which can barely secure traditional "batch" operations. Nobody can guarantee systems that are foolproof and wholly adequate in the prevention and detection of fraud. The best line of defense against either error or fraud is a combination of properly supervised operations, systems that incorporate good management controls, and the proper kind of computer auditing (fig. 18.2).

The EDP Auditor

The role of the internal auditor has broadened tremendously. Not long ago the auditor was pretty much restricted to verifying the accuracy of accounting department computations. Now, at least in the more progressive firms, the functions of the auditor are as broad as the total operations of the business. The auditor's new job, which has been defined as operational or management auditing, is gradually gaining recognition.

Many companies are trying to do today's work with yesterday's auditors. Systems of the future will operate on a fast-response, online, real-time basis and will employ input and inquiry devices unheard of previously. Unless auditors become intimately acquainted with new developments, they will not even know what they are facing, let alone be able to cope with it.

In a very real sense, the auditor now must work through the machine, which means that the auditor must understand what the program is doing and how the machine does it. The auditor must be able to use the machine itself as a tool to audit its own operations. The auditor no longer has piles of paper to paw through. The classical "paper trail" or "audit trail" is vanishing and is being replaced by invisible arrangements of molecules in an iron oxide coating on magnetic tape or disks (fig. 18.3).

Today's EDP auditor is a rare individual whose special mix of skills can result in a good position in the organization. The auditor's job is to provide an independent review of computer-related activities as a direct service to management (fig. 18.4).

CONTROL SECTION A—Controls Overview

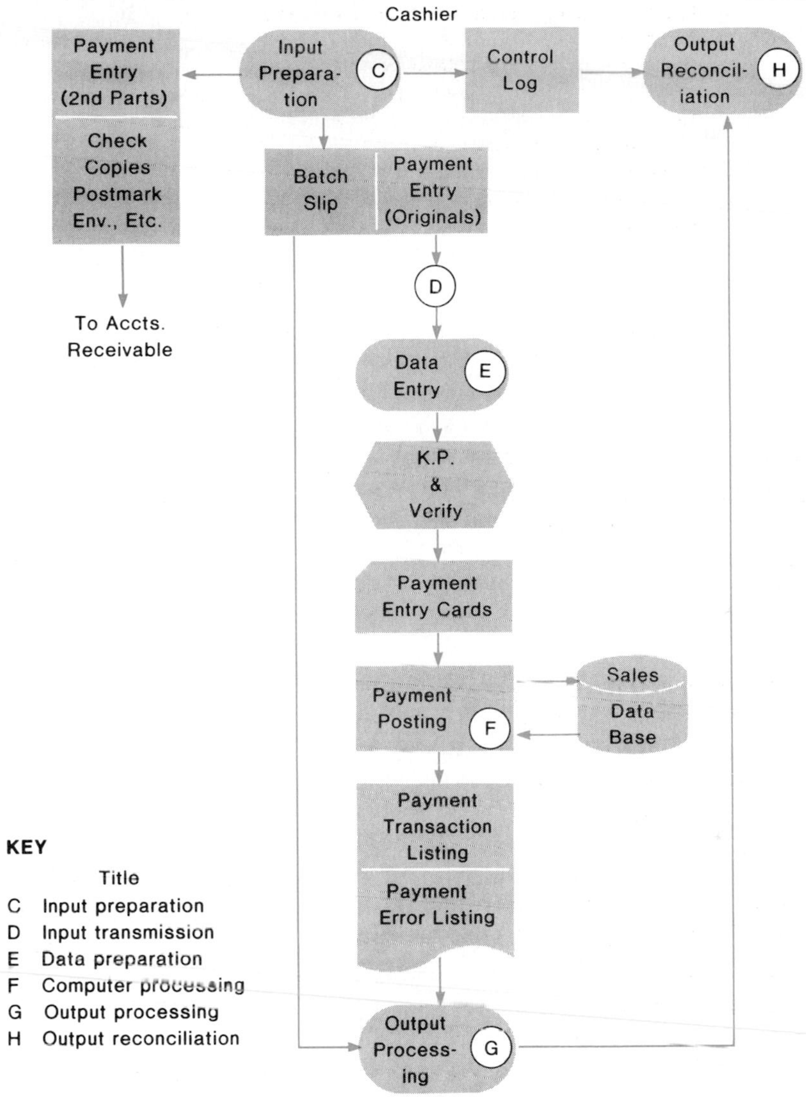

Figure 18.3 Audit procedures. (Copyright *Data Management* magazine, Data Processing Management Association)

CONTROL SECTION B—General Narrative

Payment entry is the process by which payment for finished goods that are shipped and invoiced are registered on the database. This posting reduces the customer's total indebtedness figure and creates a payment record for use in later reconciliation to accounts receivable detail records.

It is essential that this function be performed rapidly and with extreme accuracy.

Figure 18.3
Continued.

CONTROL SECTION C—Input Preparation

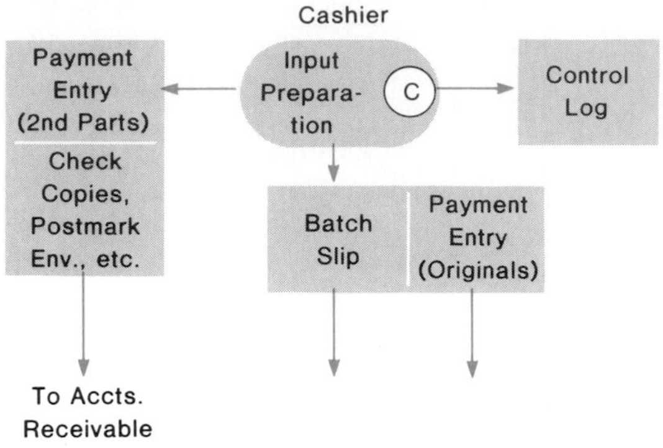

Control features
1. Pre-numbered forms
2. Batch slip
3. Control log

1. Pre-numbered forms: The forms to which the payment data is posted are pre-numbered and are used sequentially.
2. Batch Slip: This form contains two controls in addition to batch no.; a count of the forms attached and the range or pre-numbered forms numbers. The batch slip accompanies the input to data entry area where confirmation of the batch information takes place.
3. Control Log: This log provides a place where the cashier summarizes and keeps track of all the payment entry transactions. Totals by bank by date are posted here. The date that each deposit was received from the bank, date sent to Data Entry and date returned from Data Entry are also noted. When the payment entry processing by the computer has been accomplished, the totals by bank by date from the transaction listings are checked against the control log to insure that all input has been correctly and completely processed. The log also provides a ready reference of batches in process, last batch number assigned, and a basis for analyzing the timeliness of paperflow.

CONTROL SECTION D—Input Transmission

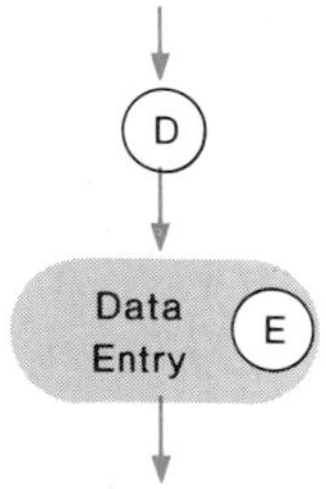

CONTROL SECTION E—Data Preparation

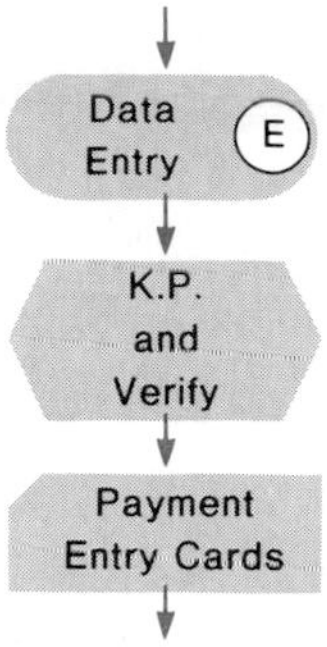

Control features
1. Batch checking
2. Key verification
3. Inclusion of batch number on each input record.

1. Batch Checking: Data entry personnel confirms number of forms on Batch Slips and range of pre-numbered forms in batch. If Batch Slip isn't completely and correctly filled out, the cashier is contacted and the discrepancy is reconciled.
2. Key Verification: The data from each P/E form is keypunched and key verified.
3. Inclusion of batch number on each input record: Batch number from batch slip is keyed into input record. The batch numbers then are carried through the program processing and appear on the transaction listings.

CONTROL SECTION F—Computer Processing

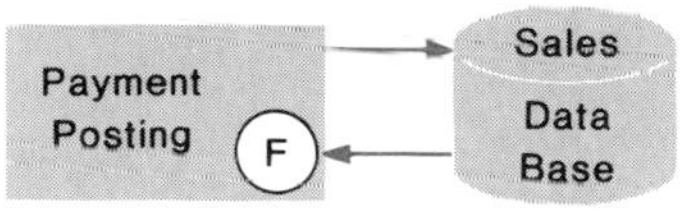

Control features
1. Input validity tests
2. Error log output
3. Transaction listing with control totals
4. Input-output total control.

1. Input validity tests:
   a. On card code, source code and bank code.
   b. Customer number tested by calc to Acct-Record in data base.
   c. Payment reference number must not be on data base—tested by calc to record in data base.
   d. Deposit and remittance dates are checked for reasonableness.
   e. Payment amount must be numeric and positive.
2. Error log output:
   a. Complete input record shown.
   b. All fields which failed edit checks are indicated by an asterisk to right of field and headings name the field.
3. Transaction listing with control totals:
   a. All valid input is listed in detail.
   b. Totals are produced by bank by deposit date.
   c. Total net change to accounts receivable balances is printed at end of report.
4. Input-output total control:
   Within the program total, all input amounts are accumulated. At end of program this total is compared to total net change to A/R balance. If they do not agree, a message is produced on the output report warning that an out-of-balance condition exists and instructing the cashier to notify the responsible analyst immediately.

Figure 18.3
Continued.

Figure 18.3
Continued.

CONTROL SECTION G—Output Processing

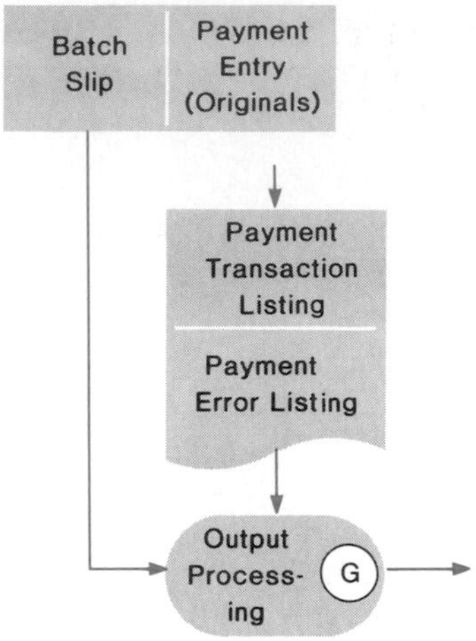

1. Batch numbers on output: The printing of batch numbers on the transaction listing insures a positive link to the input documents. Input and output documents are matched up by data clerk and forwarded to cashier for reconciliation.

CONTROL SECTION H—Output Reconciliation

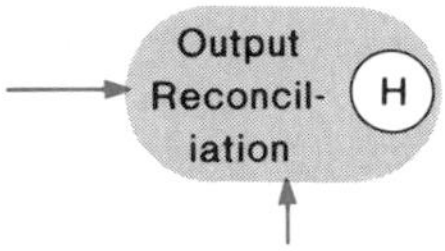

Control features

1. Comparison of control log to output reports.
2. Comparison of returned input batches to control log.

1. Comparison of control log to output report: The totals by bank by deposit date on the report are compared to the same totals which were developed manually by the cashier during input preparation. This procedure assures the cashier that all input was processed and returned.
2. Comparison of returned input batches to control log: This comparison assures the cashier that all input is being returned after processing.

At one level, it can be compared with traditional auditing, where a snapshot look at financial records is taken, enabling the auditors to say what a company's finances looked like as of the last day of the year. But in data processing, it's more of a motion picture than a snapshot as there are ongoing efforts in data-processing auditing that start on January 1 and end on December 31, being picked up the following day.

In auditing during the systems development, the auditor is not saying what did or did not happen, as traditional auditors say in their report card to management, but what *might* happen. So this approach to auditing is from an entirely different viewpoint and tone than management has seen before. While auditors are out to stop fraud in

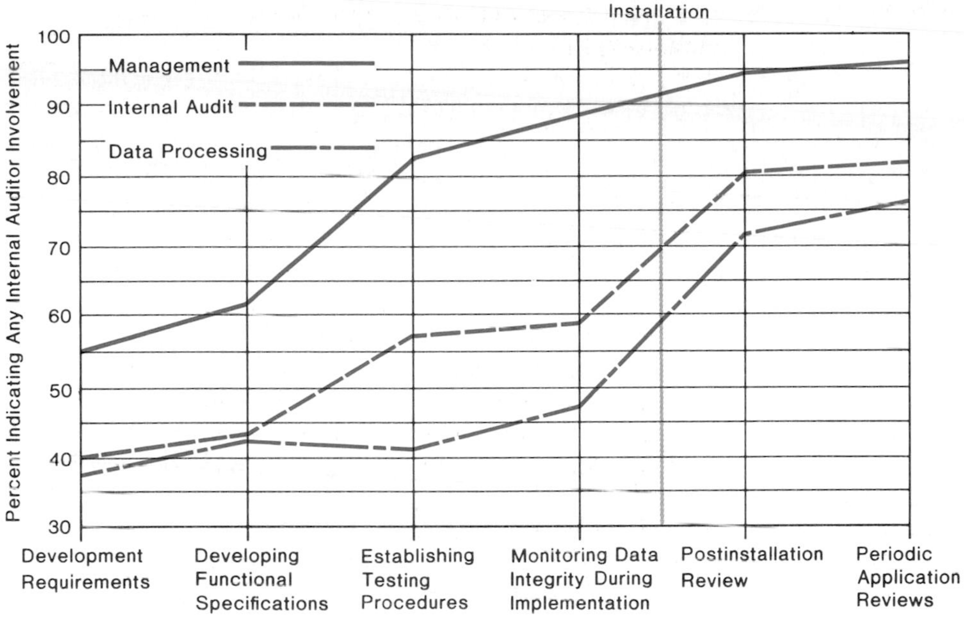

Figure 18.4 EDP auditor involvement. (Reprinted with permission of *Datamation*© magazine, ©Copyright by Technical Publishing Company, a division of Dun-Donnelley Publishing Corporation, a Dun & Bradstreet Company, 1978—all rights reserved.)

Above are Stanford Research Institute's best estimates for what the present involvement of internal audit staff in dp system development and operation is perceived to be. The figures are based on a response of 283 sets of three questionnaires (one each for the chief executive officer, auditor, and dp manager).

Two conclusions can be readily drawn. First, internal auditors think they are more deeply involved than dp managers think auditors are, but less than management wants them to be. Second, the internal audit staff is probably little involved in early stages of system design in any case.

data processing, they work to implement controls upstream to reduce errors at the output end. They work with data processing to spot the causes of errors and to implement the kinds of controls that would avoid those errors.

Responsibilities

The EDP auditor's primary responsibility is to those who use and depend on the data center's output in practical business operations. Thus, the auditor needs to determine, evaluate, and keep abreast of specific effects that would occur if the data center's capability is lost or diminished.

The EDP auditor's second responsibility is to the data processor. The EDP audit approach should be consistent with the state-of-art in computer technology. Recommendations for audit and control functions should be cost-effective and consistent with the needs of the user and data center procedures. For example, if an application is missing a key audit trail component, the auditor should determine the feasibility of appending an audit module in-line with the programs rather than recommending rerunning of the master and/or transaction files.

The EDP auditor's third responsibility is to the organization as a whole. The auditor should keep informed of changes in Generally Accepted Accounting Principles and Auditing Standards. Knowledge of legal requirements, that are consistent with

Figure 18.5 The auditor's role. (Reprinted with permission of *Datamation©* magazine, ©Copyright by Technical Publishing Company, a division of Dun-Donnelley Publishing Corporation, a Dun & Bradstreet Company, 1978—all rights reserved.)

Use of EDP Tools and Techniques

EDP Audit Tool/Technique	**Use in Auditing Development Systems and Modifications**	**Use in Auditing Production Systems**
Generalized audit software	12.5%	32.6%
Manual tracing and mapping routines	22.9	31.2
Test data method (e.g., test-decking)	27.1	26.6
Parallel operation	32.2	23.1
Tagged transactions (flagging transactions in "live" operation for later review)	12.0	20.9
Snapshot (picture-taking of selected transactions through the flow of transactions)	10.0	18.4
Systems performance monitoring and analysis (e.g., SMF, SCERT)	8.2	15.8
Program source code comparison	9.6	14.5
Control flowcharting	8.3	9.0
Program object code comparison	4.7	8.9
Integrated test facility (mini- or dummy-company)	4.2	5.0
Modeling (simulation)	9.5	7.6
Automatic tracing and mapping routines (analysis of source language and logic to determine if any program segments are not being utilized)	3.6	3.9
Other	6.5	10.5

Stanford Research Institute's best estimates for the present use of tools and techniques in auditing are based on 221 questionnaire responses.

the business design of the organization, will provide audit reviews that meet the needs of the user, can be integrated in application planning, and reduce the problems of application modification and technological upgrade.

EDP Auditor's Role

Obviously, the EDP auditor must evaluate controls to assure the accurate input and processing of financial data. While this includes income statement and balance sheet items, it should also include other financial data, such as forecasts, budgets and similar data (fig. 18.5).

In addition to concentrating on the financial data base, the auditor should evaluate nonfinancial data. To shore up operational security, the auditor should evaluate the effectiveness and, if necessary, recommend how to strengthen the organization's data and physical security and disaster-recovery program.

To achieve this goal, the auditor should be aware of the computer security systems that meet the needs of the organization. There are numerous devices on the market designed to restrict unauthorized entry and to protect information stored on disk and tape libraries.

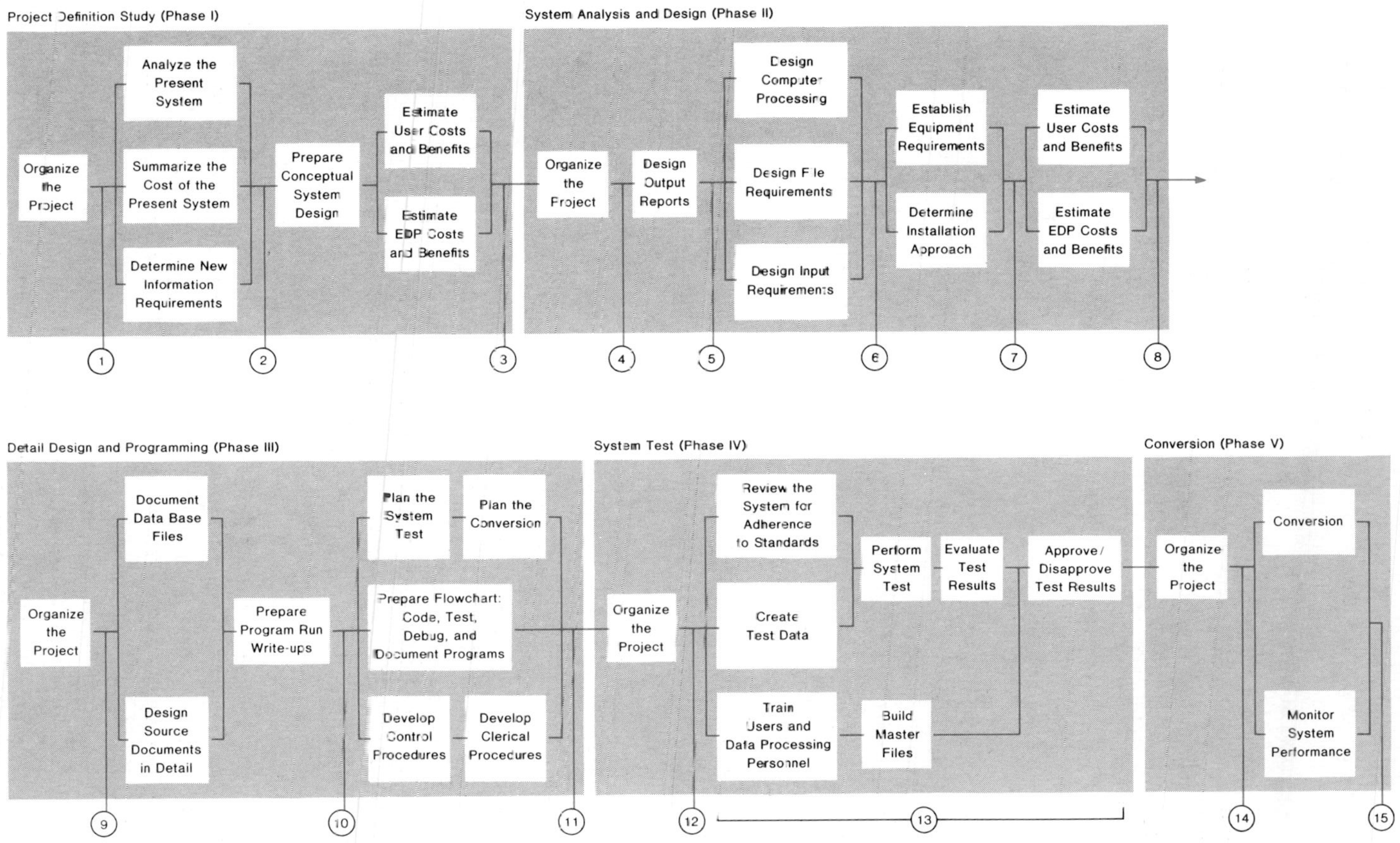

DP Audit will work continuously with System Development and Operations throughout this phase.
Source: Stanford Research Institute, 1977

In one large government organization's dp system development cycle—here illustrated serially—there are 15 control points where the dp auditor can apply some leverage to the design and operation of the resulting product. Quality control points are primarily point 1 and points 4 through 13. Points 1, 2, 3, 4, 14, and 15 are user or management interfaces.

Figure 18.5 Continued.

Other organizations often include two other phases in the life cycle: an "operational" phase concerned with ongoing use of the system, program changes, and maintenance; and a "post-implementation" phase concerned with user evaluation and focusing on ways to improve the development process.

Disaster-Recovery Program

The auditor should make sure that the organization has a well-prepared disaster-recovery program. Vital elements include emergency onsite procedures, back-up of essential systems and documentation at offsite locations, and personnel trained in what to do in case of disaster.

Experience and Education

Fraud and embezzlement as well as honest mistakes can go undetected not only because of lax auditing procedures but also if internal auditors lack the necessary skills required to audit the data-processing function.

The auditor should have five to seven years experience in positions of increasing responsibility in programming and systems development. Further, the auditor should be trained in accounting and auditing procedures and should be capable of clearly and concisely communicating ideas to all levels of management.

Position in the Organization

Generally the audit function assumes one of four positions in the organizational and communication structure.

1. As a member on the internal auditor's staff
2. As a member of management information systems (MIS)
3. As an independent department
4. As a control function of each user of the data center

Regardless of where the audit function is positioned in an organization, the auditor must have a direct line of communication to the chief executive officer.

Role of Consultants

By retaining a consultant, an organization can receive an unbiased opinion and an excellent cross check on its existing auditing procedures. As part of an assignment, the consultant can provide guidelines for auditing and emergency recovery planning and should assist in the preparation of detailed checklists that are specifically designed to meet the organization's needs.

Without question, auditing plays a major role in an organization's computer security program. Although it is impossible to develop security systems that are completely perfect, an EDP auditor with senior-level management support can do the best possible job.

The Computer as an Audit Tool

The consulting auditor can turn to the computer as a viable audit tool whether or not a client actually utilizes the computer as a part of the accounting system. In those client situations where the computer performs accounting functions, several audit functions may take place in addition to the actual use of the computer as an audit tool. Obviously, as in any audit situation, the auditor will evaluate the system of internal controls. When a computer is introduced as an integral part of the client's financial information systems, the auditor should document and understand the role that the computer plays in those systems prior to its potential use as an audit tool. Once the auditor has gained this basis of understanding and has evaluated internal controls, the auditor then may elect to use the computer as an advantage.

Audit Uses of the Computer

The computer can be used to assist the auditor to perform routine clerical functions, apply more effective auditing techniques that sometimes are not practical manually, and reduce the overall cost of performing certain audit procedures. Its use should be seriously considered for any auditing procedure that involves large volumes of data (such as testing extensions of sales invoices for the year) and for any auditing procedure that requires many repetitive clerical operations of calculations, regardless of the volume of such data (such as the preparation of mortgage amortization schedules). In addition, the computer can be used by the auditor in identifying internal control weaknesses and investigating their possible impact on the financial statements.

Software—The Right Tool

Software is the interface between the user's processing needs and the computer. In auditing, software is used to translate the auditor's instructions, prepared in accordance with certain rules of content and grammar, into instructions that the computer can perform.

The selection of software suitable for computer-assisted auditing is, at best, a difficult decision. The software can take the form of programming languages or generalized pre-programmed packages. While programming languages may satisfy all requirements for potential computer-assisted applications, they require, by their very nature, a higher level of technical knowledge. Generalized packages, on the other hand, require less data-processing expertise but quite often can solve only a subset of the potential audit applications.

Proper evaluation of software can only be made after a careful evaluation of all factors. Their relative importance will vary depending upon the specific auditing environment.

Computer Audit Packages

A new powerful tool is available to the computer auditor. It takes the form of computer programs known as Computer Audit Packages, which are designed to keep the auditor independent of the data-processing personnel. Using this package, the accountant is able to select, summarize, and study categories of records from magnetic tape or disk, even without a programming background. The auditor can select certain records for examination without the necessity of requiring programming assistance.

Computer Audit Packages are just another form of generalized computer programs designed to satisfy the particular needs of the auditor. During the past several years, many of these generalized audit programs have come on the market. All of them have different features and capabilities suitable for auditing a company computer system.

The auditor should realize that a generalized audit program is potentially a very powerful audit tool. If the auditor uses the program only to prepare confirmation letters and test extensions and footings, the program will not be properly utilized. With the universe of data to be audited now available in magnetic form, the auditor has the opportunity to select data that may indicate a real or potential problem area. In short, the auditor can perform an analysis electronically, ultimately providing management with a more meaningful and more effective audit report.

Some of the auditing functions that should be considered in evaluating a generalized audit program can be found in Appendix H.

Although audit packages will help to prevent human errors and frauds, there are still many areas of computer-processing audits that need investigation. Public accounting audit teams should include data-processing professionals. Certain audit files (such as usage statistics) should be generated automatically, stored online, and accessible only to the audit team. State insurance commissioners and other government regulatory agencies could greatly improve auditing abilities and procedures by establishing standards for master audit files, thus making it easier to maintain programs for reading them.

What has happened in the Equity insurance scandal will generate new interest in controls and audits. In light of this scandal, the American Institute of Certified Public Accountants has formed a special committee to investigate and to determine where there is a need for a change in auditing computer systems. Many companies will be looking carefully into their data-processing controls and a good many CPAs will be signing up for data-processing courses.

Data Security

In many organizations, computer security primarily includes the physical security of the computer or data-processing installation and the security of vital data, files, records, and programs as well. Recently, it has also come to mean human access and interaction with these vital data files, records, programs, and computer and data-processing equipment. This expanded definition of security does not undermine the importance of physical hardware, but merely places these in proper perspective with the people who interact in the larger, manufactured system.

Computer Room Security

Every company that relies on its computer to conduct day-to-day business without adequate computer room protection is risking extinction. In jeopardy is multimillion dollar equipment and irreplaceable data, such as accounts receivable, reorder and maintenance scheduling information, personnel payroll records, and valuable research data.

Sources of Potential Damage and Danger

A data-processing installation is subject to potential damage and danger from two primary sources.

1. The environment of the installation.
2. People within the installation or organization and people outside.

Environmental damages involve threats of fire, flood, and other natural disasters, as well as destruction caused by magnetic radiation. Most of the damage done to computer installations by people appears to be due to carelessness, errors in judgment, and incompetence.

Management has paid little attention to this problem. A catastrophe in the computer room can be just as devastating as lightning striking the plant. Without any countermeasures, there may be no company left to suffer another catastrophe. Managers can no longer ignore the risk involved in using computers. It is too vital a problem. The hazards in using computers should be analyzed and treated as any other business risk. Various risks associated with the use of computers are fire, explosion, natural disasters, sabotage as social protests, loss of programs and/or data, mechanical or electronic breakdown, data theft, fraud, and law suits.

Preventive Measures

Few, if any, data-processing installations have the funds needed to take all of the following precautions, which are enumerated and discussed as reference points for deciding which measures to employ. These possibilities are segregated into five categories—location, site construction, operating procedures, data protection, and legal protection.

Location

If choice of a building location is possible, consider the possible catastrophes. Select or build a strong fireproof building in a safe location. Location within the building should also be considered. Select a location away from the regular stream of pedestrians, out of sight, and not contiguous to danger.

Site Construction

Fireproof computer sites constructed in fireproof buildings provide the best protection against fire. Locked maximum-security doors provide the best protection against undesired intrusion. A plain lock, which can be opened easily from the inside, is preferable.

To protect against theft, unauthorized use of the computer, and sabotage during off-hours, closed circuit television provides comparatively inexpensive protection. A continuous picture of the computer installation can be relayed to the guard's station. If the danger is great enough, an ultrasonic detector system with alarm to the guard and to a central point will supply added protection.

Operating Procedures

There should be, if possible, only one entrance used to get into the building with a guard stationed there at all times. All windows and doors should have alarm devices. The guard should inspect all packages to insure against explosives or firearms being carried into the building.

Access to the computer facility should be limited to those whose presence is needed (fig. 18.6). The day of the computer as a showpiece is gone. Visitors should be limited in number and always accompanied by a supervisor. A log of all visitors should be kept. Any visitor permitted to take anything from the computer room or tape vault should be required to sign a receipt.

The tape room should be locked and under the control of a tape librarian. A tape log should be maintained with a complete record of tape withdrawals, returns, times, purposes, and persons involved. Access to this room should be severely limited (fig. 18.7).

Tapes are comparatively small and easily damaged. At a minimum, all tapes should have identification data, date of creation, and disposal date. Backup tapes for necessary programs and data should be maintained in a safe room, preferably in another building. As programs are changed and files updated, the current program or file should be substituted for the outdated one. This is a comparatively inexpensive means of insuring safety of programs and data.

Figure 18.6
Computer room access control methods. (Photos courtesy of Sperry Univac, a division of Sperry Corporation, and Sargent & Greenleaf, Inc.)

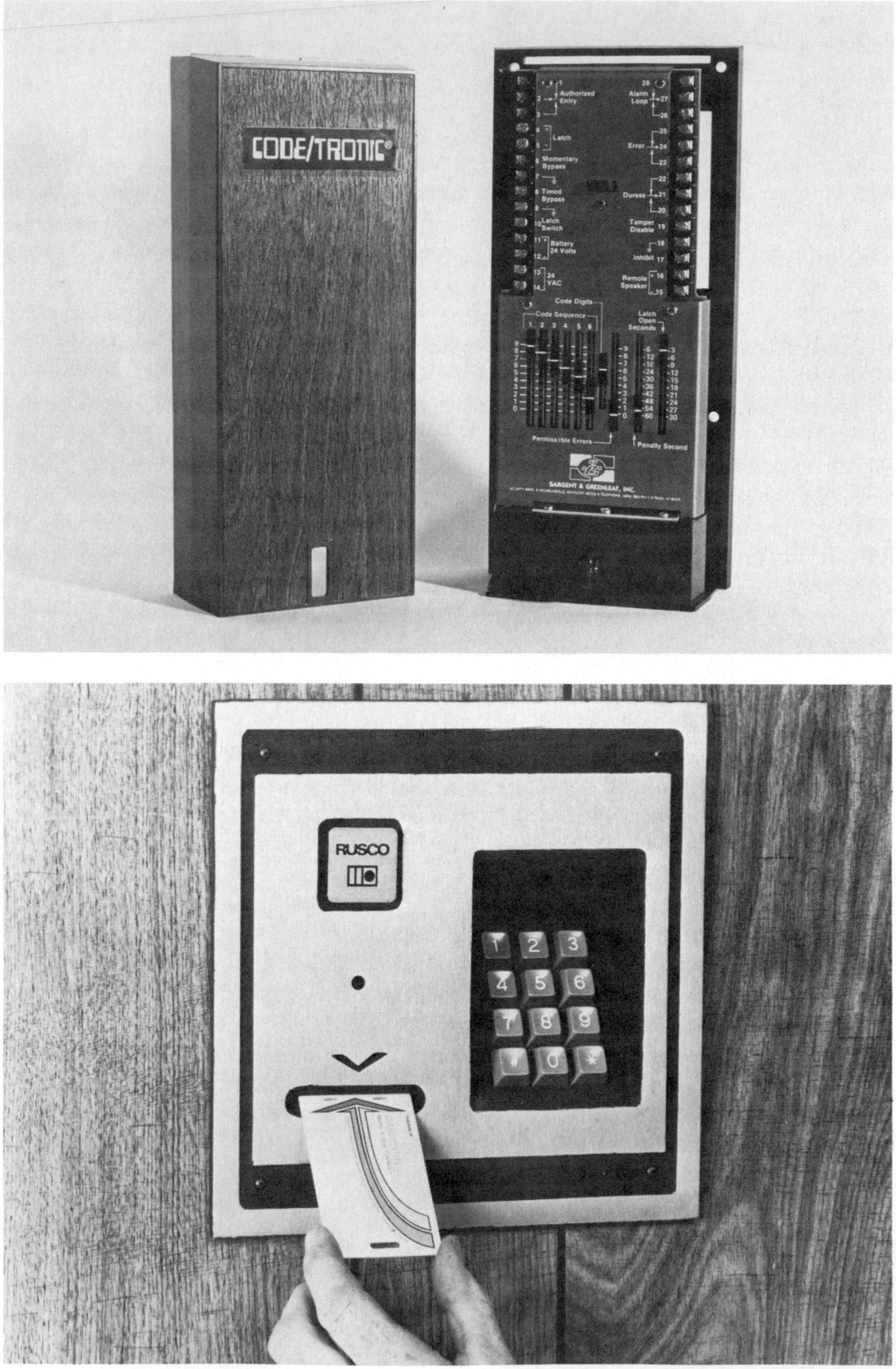

Figure 18.7 A magnetic tape room. (Photo by Ken Firestone)

Regardless of how good a security system is, undependable employees can negate it. Computer room employees should be checked carefully before employment.

Operating procedures, no matter how carefully supervised, quickly become ineffective without good supervision. Good procedures should be established and employees should be trained to follow them. Even this is not enough. Continual inspections and audits should be carried out to ensure that these procedures are followed faithfully.

Data Protection

The degree of protection depends upon the amount of secrecy needed. Overprotection of computer records can be a very costly matter. The data-processing manager normally cannot make the determination, but should state the risks, the possibilities of the data being stolen, an estimate of the possible consequences, and the costs of protection. The manager should give this information, together with any recommendations, to management, who makes the final decision concerning the precautions to be taken.

Unless proper precautions are taken, almost all input to or output from a computer can be read from outside the computer room without the knowledge or consent of those inside. Also data transmitted over wire or by radio can be tapped. Input/output gear should be located as close to the center of the computer room as possible. This will make reading them from outside more difficult.

Growth in the use of telecommunications, online systems, time sharing, and companies using remote terminals for access to the computer has raised an entire new crop of security problems. The ability of the computer to distinguish between different users of remote terminals and to limit their access to files accordingly is extremely important in today's online and time-sharing systems. Most systems depend upon keywords, special numbers, and person-terminal coordination for recognition. These methods require programs and the ability to make unreadable the typewritten record of the keyword or special number made by an authorized person. Furthermore, these keywords or numbers can be changed as often as necessary. The computer can contain a table listing of the files the user is permitted to use. This will help protect the files of other users.

No security system is completely safe. Assuming that all the methods discussed have been employed, a log of all users, their queries, and the files accessed should be kept where the user cannot control what goes into the log, and can neither read or change what is there. Regular and continual auditing of this file should reveal any attempted access of sensitive files before the person has gained access to the computer.

Legal Protection

With the growth of suits by users against manufacturers, software houses, and service bureaus, the data-processing manager must pay attention to the matter of legal protection. In dealing with a computer manufacturer, thousands, perhaps millions, of dollars are at stake. A standard contract must pertain to legal obligations. Let the legal department of the company handle all matters relative to computer leases, computer purchases, software rentals and purchases, and data-processing supplies. Particularly important are service and maintenance contracts with the computer manufacturer.

In order to be protected against derivative suits by stockholders or other interested parties, files should be kept. These files should give the details and cost of possible alternatives that were considered in making decisions. Escape routes, in case things go wrong, should be included. With such documentation, charges would be reduced to considering the merits of the decision, instead of charges to the effect that no consideration was given to alternatives.

Additional Measures

The computers of a multicomputer company can be decentralized. Then, if anything should put a computer installation out of operation, the complete data-processing capability of the company would not be wiped out. Another possibility would be to have an unused but duplicate installation in a remote location. Few companies, however, could afford this expense.

Almost as much protection, but with far less cost is the use of a backup facility. The agreement with the furnisher of the backup facility should be in writing.

Although installation of fire or heat-proof safes will not prevent fire, they will lessen damage if a fire occurs.

If you are using a time-sharing system, send one of your tapes to the central location. Have your files dumped on your tape, ensuring that it is clearly marked as your property. If the time-sharing company goes bankrupt or suffers any catastrophe, you will be able to recover your tape and data from the central location.

Business insurance is another preventive measure. Employees should be bonded if they are in a position to seize any assets of the company fraudulently. Fire insurance should be taken out, not only for hardware and the premises, but also for the software and the additional expenses involved in continuing operations in a backup site until the computer facility is restored. Insurance covering errors or omissions is available also. For almost any of the risks detailed previously, some form of insurance can be obtained.

What can and must the data-processing manager do? The manager must first recognize the potential dangers. After recognizing these dangers the manager should prepare a cost/value analysis by considering hazard, degree of damage, probability of occurrence, consequences, possible dollar damages, measures recommended, comparison of cost of probable damages with costs of measures recommended, and alternative measures considered. A data-processing manager completing this analysis will have qualified the major elements of hazards and countermeasures considered. The manager is now ready to make specific recommendations to top management.

There are many potential hazards to a computer installation. For each hazard, there is a preventive measure. It is extremely risky to fail to take appropriate preventive measures. The cost of taking all preventive measures is very high. The major problem is to determine what measures are appropriate. The data-processing manager's primary responsibility is to recognize all of the hazards that exist. Using a cost/value analysis, the manager should make recommendations to top management detailing those measures believed to be appropriate for that particular installation. Top management then has the tools with which to make the best decision for the company.

Telecommunications Protection

The increasing use of remote terminals for file maintenance, online testing, data inquiry and information retrieval, and management information reporting requires new types of protection and controls.

Telecommunications permit access to information from distant locations, via terminal or telephone. Thus, online files must be protected at the source, since potential access can occur from anywhere.

Classification of Information

The needs for data security must be related directly to the type of program or information that can be accessed through a terminal. Certain files probably should be restricted to only a few people, due to the proprietary value of those files to the company or due to their confidential nature. This category would include payroll information, lists of major customers and activities, unique engineering design solutions, and employee personnel files.

A second level of classification might be assigned to files, access to which is required by a large group of employees, but which, by modification, is available to a few people only. In this group are such files as demand deposit accounts, loan accounts, accounts receivable, employee personnel files (excluding payroll), and bills of material files.

A third level might permit broad access and interaction with minimal security. This might include the use of program instructions, general routines for financial or engineering problem solving, stock market information, product catalog information, or stolen car reports.

System Design Factors

Systems analysts designing online systems have a continuing responsibility to build in security controls to assure that only authorized personnel can have access or modify information. Sections of a particular file can be classified with different levels of access; individual *passwords* are required to enter these sections of the file. Multiple tests can include passwords, employee numbers, and the specific terminal location that is entered automatically on a hardware device. If all three tests are not met, access may be refused. Identification and passwords should be changed frequently and those of terminating or transferred employees deleted immediately.

Control Audits

Many different controls can be instituted to assure appropriate checks and balances and to permit early detection of accidental or intentional security breaches.

Detailed Logs

Records of all inquiries and access to critical data files should be maintained and computer-analyzed periodically to search for excessive usage, unauthorized terminal locations, extra long spans of communication, and unusual times of access.

Lockword

In addition to a required password permitting access to the file, a special *lockword* may be required to permit access to portions of a file or to accept modification. Normally, the lockword is changed frequently and limited to a very few authorized people.

Monte Carlo Validation

The internal audit group may periodically take samples from the online file and assure that no "dummy" records exist. Such techniques are frequently used to verify payroll files, banking files, and insurance files.

Data-Processing Responsibility

Data processing's foremost responsibility lies with answering management's requirements insofar as operational and statistical reports are concerned. The major areas of responsibility are usefulness of reports, systems design, communication, accuracy, timeliness, personnel, economy, technological study, and progress reports.

Usefulness of Reports

It should be the responsibility of all operational as well as management people connected with data processing to continually audit all output reports leaving the department and to inform management of any cases of duplication in the material being distributed to the various user departments.

Care must be taken to consider the potential usefulness of all new requests for data. If the expected result does not warrant the time required for programming, testing, and debugging, this information should be made known to people initiating such a request.

Data processing cannot allow itself the luxury of preparing reports for the sake of additional hours on the computer meter or for the sake of adding to the paper work within an organization.

Systems Design

The major systems design generally falls within the data-processing managers' realm of responsibility. It is up to the data-processing manager to understand and communicate management goals before setting out in any direction in the systems effort. Large sums of money are spent in an effort to obtain a long-range systems design that will enhance the competitive position of a company. However, only by bringing needed information that will, through efficient and timely operation, direct a company toward a better profit picture, can computer costs be justified.

Every effort should be made to avoid the mistake of overemphasizing the data-processing function so it would include poorly-thought-out sections, which should actually be done manually. Care must be taken to exclude any function from the automated system that could be accomplished more efficiently and/or more economically by a manual method. In areas of doubtful performance, great care should be taken before the decision is made to include such tasks in the data-processing function. Once a job has been erroneously included, it is very difficult to back it out.

Communication

It is the responsibility of data processing to recognize the necessity for breaking through the so-called communication gap between data processing and the rest of the organization and to inform management, as well as all users, of situations in which it would be more expedient and feasible to not run certain data through a data-processing routine.

Computers are expensive and should not become high-speed, high-priced typewriters. A majority of computer installations are overtaxed to maintain their schedules from a timeliness standpoint; when "out-of-system" jobs are entered into the priority system, a simple request for data can create a real scheduling nightmare. Management has a right to expect that it will be kept informed of the true status of any data-processing problems resulting from a conflict between scheduling and the time factor.

High sounding phrases of computerese jargon have become, in many cases, a way of life rather than a communication link for data-processing specialists. Use of such phrases as "management information system" has been so overextended as to distort the original concept. *Management information system defines an operation consisting of a series of steps designed to furnish all the data required by management, in a concise form, which will enable them to make the necessary decisions, on a timely basis, to result in a successful and profitable business operation.* It is supported by a single all-encompassing data base from which all information can be obtained.

The data-processing facility must accept the fact that it, like every other facility, must justify its existence with facts and results, not with an obscure vocabulary. Management should insist that systems and reports are created and explained in language that can be understood clearly by everyone.

The responsibility for sound communication rests on the information interchanged understandably between all people in data processing, those in nondata-processing management, and user departments personnel.

Accuracy

Data-processing departments are well known for being prone to user department criticism concerning accuracy. The first thought of the user is keypunch errors, programmer errors, or compute errors.

It is the responsibility of the data-processing department to keep as tight a rein as possible on quality control of output within the organization. By the use of checkpoint accounting, both internal and external crossfooting, and balancing data, data-processing output should be controlled to an error content of near zero.

Results can be expected to be only as good as the input. Therefore, it is important that accuracy of input be made emphatic to the other departments originating the data. The work must be continuous toward the goal of a full audit trail to be absolutely certain of as near-perfect accuracy as possible, in all data emanating from the department.

Timeliness

With the ever-changing and ever-increasing work load to schedule through today's data-processing departments, a continuous effort is required to keep schedules updated. Constant review is required to note priority changes and other happenings that may affect the timeliness of output reports.

Personnel

Due to the extreme diversity of material that is processed, data-processing personnel must be highly versatile. The point often missed by nondata-processing personnel is that data-processing people must be capable of switching their thinking through all phases of the operation. This thinking process requires a unique, alert mentality. Acceptance of one less-effective person within a department causes problems with accuracy and timeliness affecting the entire department.

Economy

An addiction fairly common with data-processing managers appears to be the constant and everlasting desire for acquiring the latest sophisticated equipment. Study and review for all such equipment is certainly a necessity. If there is a new piece of hardware or software that will truly improve the operation, management should be made aware of it. The responsibility still remains with the data-processing manager to be absolutely certain that there is an advantage and not just a desire to upgrade for the sake of prestige.

A great responsibility exists for the economic operation of the data-processing function; it becomes more critical as uses for computer-based data increase. Under the heading of such economy falls the prolific issuance of reports and copies without a periodic review for the purpose of deleting unnecessary material. The review of such reports and copies for deletion purposes is becoming an increasingly important economy measure.

Technological Study

The heavy outflow of new technology inherent in the data-processing profession continues unceasingly. It is the grave responsibility of the data-processing manager to keep up with the available information concerning this mass of advances and changes. It is also the manager's responsibility to apprise management of anything that is significant and might actually apply to the particular organization. The manager's greatest responsibility in this area is dissecting the mass of information and putting it into summary form for presentation to management in a way that will keep them up-to-date and knowledgeable, but only on subjects of significance to them.

Progress Reports

A formal method of reporting progress, or failure to progress, should be an integral part of the data-processing responsibility. The tendency often exists to ignore this procedure if management is not interested enough to ask for it.

Much will be learned about an operation if a data-processing manager institutes such a form of reporting (even if the results are used solely for personal study and consideration). All data-processing managers should be eager to make a report, on a regular basis, that compares present operations and cost factors with past performance. Also of interest to top management would be the inclusion, in each report of this kind, of a brief summary of plans for future systems and for improvements to be considered or accomplished on existing systems.

If data processing is to fulfill everyone's hopes and dreams of a true, real-time, optimized management information system or similar system of management information reporting that will lessen the chance of untimely decision making and heighten the profit expectancy of business, all of these reponsibilities must be acknowledged and accepted by the people involved in the control and operation of the sophisticated data-processing centers of the future.

Summary

The widespread use of computers during the last twenty-five years has created many problems for management. With tremendous investments in computer facilities, management is concerned with the accuracy of the data being processed and the protection of sensitive files and programs. Among the causes of alarm to computer users is the thievery and fraudulent use of the computer, which has seriously undermined the public's faith in computer processing. The success of most organizations depends on its ability to efficiently use the information stored in data-processing media. The files that accommodate the records necessary for any data-processing problem must be readily accessible to the computer. Computer systems are needed to expedite procedures in our complex society and to monitor its operations. To perform these important functions, new auditing procedures must be used. The design and installation of computer systems require extensive studies.

This chapter describes some practical safeguards that can be used to assure accuracy and protection of important programs, files, and data.

1. The responsibilities of an EDP auditor are to determine, evaluate, and keep abreast of specific effects that would occur if the data center's capability were lost or diminished. The auditor should make recommendations for audit and control functions that should be cost-effective and consistent with the needs of user and data center procedures. The auditor should also provide audit reviews that meet the needs of the user. It is the auditor's job to evaluate controls to assure the accuracy of input and output of financial data, to evaluate nonfinancial data, to shore up internal security, and to prepare a disaster-recovery plan. The EDP auditor should have experience in programming, systems, accounting, and auditing procedures. The EDP auditor should maintain direct communication with management.
2. Consultants can provide unbiased opinions and can cross-check existing auditing procedures. The computer can be used as an auditing tool by independent auditors to perform routine clerical operations, to apply more effective auditing techniques, to reduce overall costs of performing certain audit procedures, and to identify internal control weaknesses. Software translates auditor's instructions that a computer can perform. Audit packages are generalized computer programs designed to satisfy the particular need of the auditor.
3. Computer room security is subject to potential damage and danger from the environment of the installation and the people inside and outside of the installation. Preventive measures should include location, site construction, operating procedures, data protection, and legal protection. Additional measures, such as decentralization, backup facilities, time-sharing facilities, and business insurance can be taken.
4. Protection of telecommunications include classification of information and other system design features, such as passwords, detailed logs, lockwords, and Monte Carlo Validation.
5. It is data processing's responsibility to provide useful reports, to provide system designs that meet management's requirements, to provide good communication between data-processing and nondata-processing departments, accuracy of input and output, timeliness of data, qualified and highly skilled personnel, and to provide the latest advances and progress of data-processing operations.

Identification Questions

Match the following terms with the statements below.

A. Computer Abuse
B. Computer Audit Packages
C. Computer Security
D. Consultant
E. EDP Auditor
F. Lockword
G. Management Information Systems
H. Monte Carlo Validation
I. Software

1. The interface between the user's processing needs and the computer.
2. The physical security of the computer, vital data, files, records, and programs.
3. This technique allows the taking of samples periodically from online files to assure that there are no "dummy" records in the file.
4. Evaluates controls to assure the accurate input and processing of financial data.
5. Generalized computer programs designed to satisfy the particular needs of the auditors.
6. Provides an unbiased opinion and excellent cross check on its existing auditing procedures.
7. It permits access to a portion of a file or to accept modification of that file.
8. A series of steps designed to find all data requested by management in a concise form, which will enable them to make the necessary decisions on a timely basis, resulting in a successful and profitable business operation.
9. Those incidents caused by intentional acts, negligent acts, or accidental occurrences in which a person realized a gain and/or a victim suffered or could have suffered a loss.

Questions for Review

1. Why is computer fraud such a growing problem?
2. Briefly, what are the experts' conclusions about computer-assisted fraud?
3. Why is it important for the auditor to understand the operations of a computer?
4. What is the EDP auditor's job and principal responsibilities?
5. What is the EDP auditor's principal role in an organization?
6. What are the vital elements of a disaster-recovery program?
7. What are the experience and education requirements of an EDP auditor? What is the EDP auditor's position in an organization?
8. What is the role of consultants in an organization?
9. How may a computer be used as an auditing tool and how may the auditor use it to examine the records of an organization?
10. What is the importance of audit packages?
11. What is meant by computer security and what are the sources of potential damage and danger?
12. Enumerate the preventative measures that may be used to assure data security.
13. Why is it important to take measures to protect telecommunications? List some of the preventative measures that may be taken.
14. List and discuss the major areas of data-processing responsibility.

Key Terms

Computer Abuse
Computer Audit Packages
Computer Security
Consultant
EDP Auditor
Lockword
Management Information Systems
Monte Carlo Validation
Software

management of data processing 19

Chapter Outline

Chapter Objectives

The learning objectives of this chapter are

1. to present the problems inherent in a feasibility study and the reasons why an extensive study is necessary.
2. to present the problems inherent in the design of management information systems.
3. to explain how data is stored and how the information can be retrieved in a minimum of time.
4. to describe the most common methods of data organization employed by direct access processing systems.

Computer systems to be truly effective must be thoroughly studied and designed to achieve the most economical use of data-processing equipment. Extensive studies are required to assure the most efficient use of the work force and equipment. Modern computer-based information systems should provide enough information needed for all levels of management for decision making.

Studies provide management with enough information about proposed computer systems so an objective decision can be made by management relative to its value to the organization. Management information systems provide the information in a form that can be used by all that need it. A basic requirement of management information systems is that the data is organized so it can be stored and easily accessed by all those who require it.

Feasibility Study

A feasibility study is intended to provide management with enough information about the proposed systems project so an objective decision can be made regarding its value.

The feasibility study must provide answers to four basic questions. Can it be done? Is it practical? Is it economical? How should it be done?

In order to answer those questions, the existing system should be investigated, alternative solutions to the problem defined, alternatives compared with the existing method, and an alternative chosen and supported with economic justification.

The preliminary analysis and requirements determination must be carried out in sufficient detail to allow a technical and economic evaluation of a proposed system. Attention must be paid to:

1. Possible existence of problem areas in the present system.
2. User organization's level of experience in the use of computers.
3. Type of improvements that user management will expect from a new system.
4. Future organizational changes that will be required by the implementation of a new system.

The results of the feasibility study should be presented in a formal report. This is the master plan for the new system and will provide the basis for further systems effort. The master plan and its presentation should be regarded as the basis for a

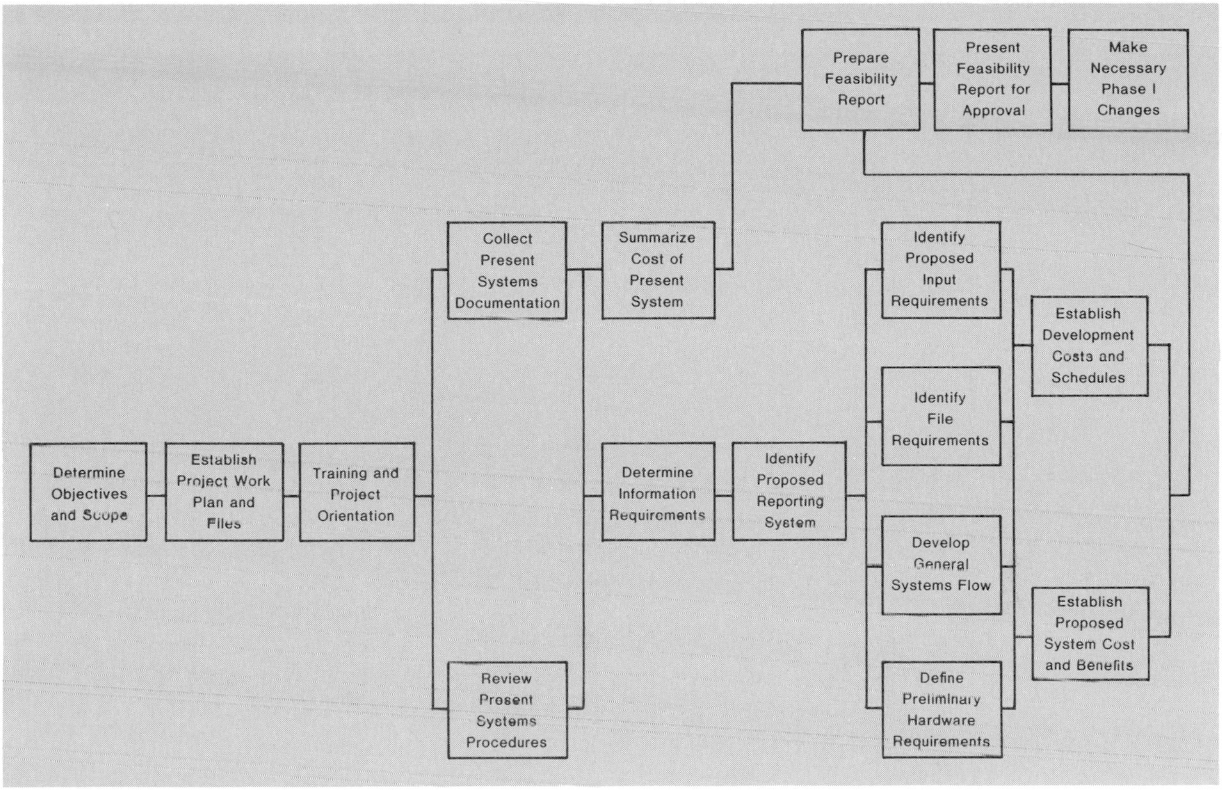

Figure 19.1 A feasibility study.

management decision. The presentation should therefore be designed to emphasize those aspects of the plan that most clearly assist the making of that decision. Figure 19.1 shows the specific tasks to be performed during the feasibility study and the order in which they are generally performed.

The Study

Before a detailed study is undertaken, a preliminary survey should be made of the proposed data-processing applications. Based on the conclusions and recommendations of this survey, it can be determined whether a more detailed study should be made. The primary reason for the recent interest of management in data-processing feasibility studies is that the investment in an "in-depth" systems study and evaluation involves a substantial expenditure regardless of whether the results support recommendation of a change of the present systems (figs. 19.2, 19.3). Other areas of concern to management are:

1. A systems study will cross established organizational lines.
2. The integration of the new system often results in the activities of some departments being altered or even eliminated.
3. Some of the basic, time-honored, traditional company policies may have to be changed.
4. Methods of management control of operations may be affected.

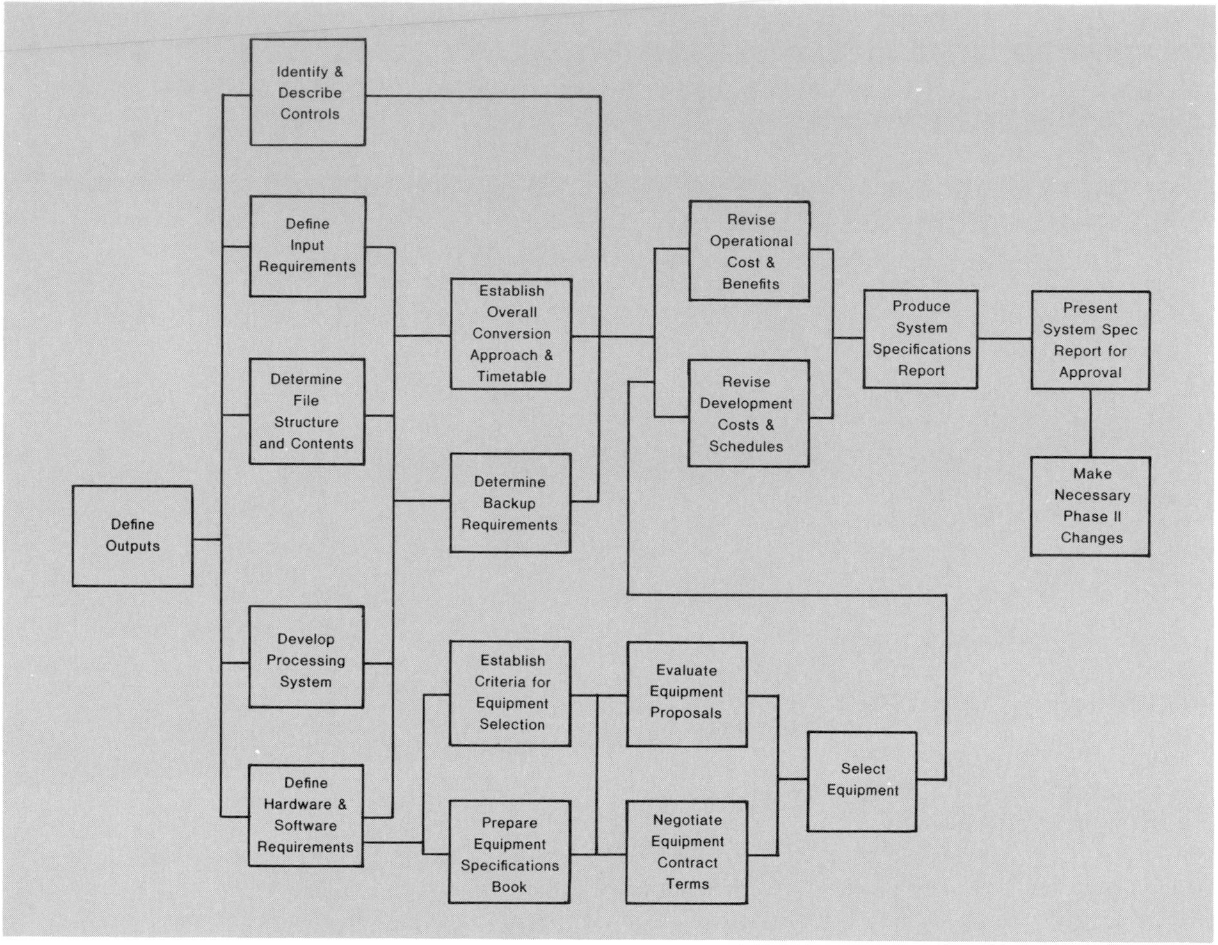

Figure 19.2 System specifications.

Management will be wise to issue a statement of the objectives of the study and to outline the broad general methods by which they are to be attained.

Areas to Be Specifically Delineated in the Study

1. Definition of the problem.
2. Scope of the study to be made.
3. Ultimate objectives that management hopes to achieve.
4. Authority to be delegated to the team carrying out its assignment.
5. Organization, selection, and training of the study team.
6. Timetable in skeleton form to indicate to study team members and management the amount of time allotted to the study.

Problem Definition

The problem itself and the scope of the study to be made should be stated so there is little doubt about the extent of the investigation and the areas within the firm to be covered. The problem may be as limited as one involving a delineation of the feasibility

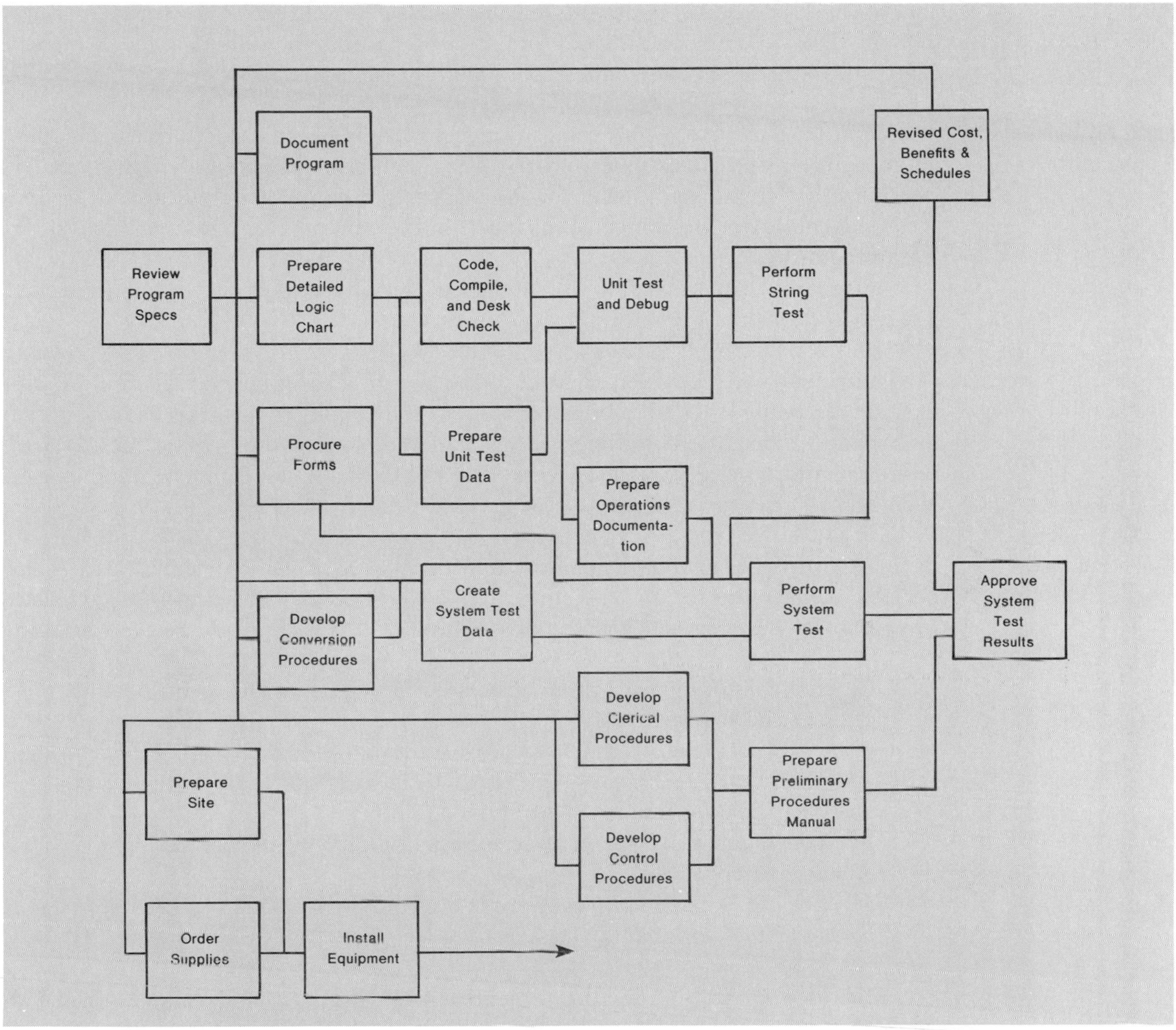

Figure 19.3 Programming and procedures.

of acquiring a computer to do current record-keeping procedures. It may also be so broad in scope as to include the possibility of a complete integrated data control system involving operations research techniques and other mathematical tools of scientific management.

Objectives Desired

A formal set of objectives forces management to give the whole subject matter serious thought. In the process of arriving at a set of objectives, the problems involved in attaining these objectives will be clearly defined.

A framework is developed within which the study team can operate, so it will know what is expected of it, the limitations under which it must work, and the time allowed for conclusions.

Authority Delegation The authority delegated to the group should be clearly outlined. This is necessary since not only those conducting the study, but those with whom they will have contact, must fully understand the powers and responsibilities assigned to the group.

Committee Considerations A committee may involve only company personnel or may represent some combination of consultants and company employees. The amount of training required to qualify the members of the study team for the work expected of them will depend on the knowledgeability of the individual members in the general area of system analysis in data processing.

A tentative time schedule will have to be developed to guide the committee on the progress of the assignment.

Organization of the Group An individual must be selected to head the group. This group leader's duties will include reviewing the work of members of the study team, policy decisions within the framework management provides, seeing that the work is progressing according to schedule, and generally directing the systems study activities. The actual number of members will depend upon the size of the study.

Selection of the Team If the company does not have qualified individuals or has them but cannot spare them for the period required for the study, it may be necessary to turn over complete responsibility to professional consultants. Normally, this is not recommended because:

1. Outside consultants will rarely have any knowledge of the firm's detailed procedures and requirements.
2. Company personnel will fail to receive the training in system work, programming, and operational techniques required of them at a later date in the installation and operational stages.
3. The consultant will have little or no responsibility for the continuing operation of a computer system.
4. Most of the "know how" developed in the study will be lost to the company and belong to the consultants.

Representatives from the departments involved in the study should be included because:

1. They will bring authoritative "know how."
2. They will be more cooperative if they feel that they have a voice in the decision.
3. There will be some individuals from top management in the group who will acquire at first-hand the necessary understanding of the problems involved.

Training Group Since most members of the group will not possess the special knowledge required of them as the study progresses, they should undergo a period of training. This will include visits to operating data-processing installations and instruction in data-processing courses taken at colleges and universities and at the computer manufacturers' schools.

Timetable for the Study

This will vary with the objectives and definition of the problem. Definite deadlines should be set for periodic progress reports.

General Considerations

The committee's basic obligation involves the major question about whether data-processing equipment will improve the overall company efficiency in terms of financial savings, customer relations, and operating efficiencies. To accomplish these ends, the committee will have to determine the company's requirements for data processing and place particular emphasis on the areas in which the greatest improvements can be made. These requirements should not only include those of a record-keeping system but, perhaps of even greater importance, those involving new management techniques that include important new areas, such as inventory control, purchasing, and production controls. The committee will need a broad view of the organization when charting the flow of information throughout the firm.

Areas of Vital Concern to Management in a Computer Feasibility Study

1. *The computer feasibility study should be the work of company-oriented personnel with supplementary help from outside sources.* Many computer manufacturers offer free feasibility studies. These companies are primarily interested in selling or leasing their own equipment. For this reason, it is highly unlikely that they will properly evaluate their competitor's equipment. Moreover it is probable that they will recommend equipment that will be *more* than adequate for the job.

   Outside consultants, on the other hand, can definitely play an important part in the study. They can supply the necessary technical knowledge in evaluating the proposals of various equipment manufacturers. However, consultants should be used to support the company personnel, not to supplant them. After all, the company personnel will have the ultimate responsibility of installing and operating without the benefit of the preparatory background available at the feasibility study stage.

   If the management is to obtain an accurate view of the computer adoption, the entire study should be directed, conducted, and the results presented by company personnel.
2. *The feasibility study should indicate the procedures and operations to be computerized and demonstrate the physical feasibility of so doing.* It should take the form of a narrative summary, backed up by solid documentary evidence in the form of system flowcharts, source document formats, and sample reports, describing each of the operations that will be computerized and how the computer auxiliary systems will go about handling them. Sufficient factual proof of the proposed application should be presented to remove management doubts about the ability to achieve the defined goals.
3. *The physical capability of the equipment selected to do the job should be thoroughly demonstrated.* A short narrative should describe the capabilities of the proposed equipment, including speeds. Also volumes, output requirements, and data transmission facilities must be directly linked with the timing demands of the proposed system for output report generation. In addition to this, a full

analysis of other equipment considered should be presented. An explanation of the factors that caused the proposed equipment to be selected instead of the other equipment examined should also be given.

4. *The physical facilities required to house the computer should be properly detailed.* Many businesspeople in their first dealings with the computer are under the illusion that the computer can be housed in the back of the warehouse or some other obscure location. Computers, they later learn, are delicate instruments that must be treated with extreme care. Among the other considerations, management should be made aware of the following facts.

    a. The computer must be located in an air-conditioned room that is properly humidified.
    b. Special elevated floors are required to cover the heavy wiring required for computer operation.
    c. Excess amounts of dust will disrupt the computer circuitry.
    d. Proper noise abatement facilities must be provided for people working close to the computer room.

    These physical facilities will increase the expense of computer operations and should be presented to management as part of the proposal.

5. *The proper cost of acquiring a computer should be presented in the proposal.* In the past, many computers have been acquired on the basis of savings. Many times these savings have not materialized, resulting in skepticism by management of the computer's ability to achieve savings. To combat this disillusionment, the following guidelines should be followed.

    a. The accounting personnel should certify all cost figures presented in the feasibility proposal.
    b. Equipment costs should include all costs associated with the operations, such as rental fees, transportation costs, and programmer's and analyst's salaries.
    c. The cost of housing the equipment, mentioned earlier, should be included.
    d. Itemize start-up costs, such as parallel operations and dual systems in operation, before the computer operation begins to function effectively.
    e. Intangible benefits, such as better management reports and improved employee morale, often ascribed to the computer, should be discarded since they may never materialize.

6. *The personnel problems of designing, implementing, and operating a computer should be properly presented in the report.* Many computer manufacturers tend to oversimplify the operation of a computer. To operate a computer effectively, many trained people are required—systems analysts, programmers, computer operators, data entry operators, auxiliary equipment operators, and a data-processing manager and/or a systems manager.

Many of these people are professionals and have received considerable training. Management should be told that, in most cases, most of the necessary professional help required to install and operate the computer must be hired from outside the company. It must also be pointed out that the hiring of outside personnel will be quite costly and possibly disruptive in terms of personnel relations within the company.

Many employees will be unhappy about the new routines to learn, new forms to fill in, and new reports to be read and understood.

Management should also be made aware of the steps that should be taken to assign, retrain, terminate the service of, or in some other way deal with the displaced person.

7. *The proposal must demonstrate that the system and computer selected are capable of expansion and change.* The corporate structure is ever changing. The computer selected must have at least the capability of absorbing the changes occurring in the various corporate structures without costly reprogramming and system redesign.

   Evidence must be demonstrated in the feasibility study that allowance has been made for future expansion in the proposed system, thus insuring that new, increased, or changing information requirements can be satisfied without serious reprogramming.

8. *The proposal should indicate that problems will occur during the installation and tell what these problems might be.* There must be indications that the existing information system, which has probably operated for many years and is presently operating without any difficulties, will have to be completely dismantled and rebuilt. Late reports, inaccuracies in reports, progress slower than actually planned, difficulty in getting competent help, and program "bugs" are some of the expected problem areas that should be outlined in the proposal. It must be realized that the installation of a computer is "no bed of roses."

9. *The proposal must give evidence of solid planning for the computer installation.* The solid planning is usually best expressed through a detailed critical path analysis of the steps to be completed in the implementation schedule. All activities necessary to complete the installation of the computer should be detailed and time-phased. This should be an all-inclusive schedule, including everything from the recruiting, selection, and training of the programming staff to the connecting of the air-conditioning system in the computer room.

10. *The proposal must give evidence of support from other functional areas within the company.* This point is especially important if applications are projected in several areas. If the accounting department is proposing the acquisition of a computer for such operations as cost distribution, payroll, billing, production scheduling, and marketing statistics, it is essential that manufacturing and marketing personnel strongly support the computer in their areas. The most direct way to insure this is to include personnel from these departments in the investigating team.

11. *All benefits to be derived from the computer installation should be effectively presented in the report.* While cost reduction is usually the most important consideration, there are often other important benefits to be derived. All benefits, including cost reductions, should be spelled out in the report. Some of these other benefits are better scheduling in production departments, better utilization of equipment, an ability to sell more, better cost control through budgetary reports, more accurate and up-to-date reports, new reports not previously possible, and advanced scientific analysis.

If a computer installation in the company is to be successful, it must have the unqualified support of management. The inclusion of this section in the feasibility report will gain the solid support of top management. Unfortunately, even if all of the eleven points (above) are covered in the feasibility study presentation, it still can fail in its main task of convincing management to go ahead with the proposal.

Finally, the reports to management, especially in the areas of computers and computer feasibility, must be written in an understandable format. Many management persons have been excessively burdened with computer feasibility reports written in "computereze." Top management does not understand the weird numeric codes that various computer manufacturers assign to their equipment or the jargon that programmers and systems personnel use when describing equipment and its applications. The final requirement is to present the case for or against the installation of a computer as simply as possible in plain everyday English. This will enable management to make a more intelligent assessment of the advisability of the proposed system.

Management Information Systems

The concept of management information systems (MIS) was originated by academicians and information systems personnel working with computers. It started with computer technology, emphasized the glories of rapid data processing, and envisioned every key executive having a desktop terminal linked to the most remote segment of the company.

MIS incorporates decision making on the following assumptions—that the quality of decisions is limited by the quantity of available information; that through advances in automatic programming, the manager can pose problems to the computer; and that with the aid of management science models, the manager should be able to make the best management decision for every aspect of the organization (fig. 19.4).

MIS is made up of subsystems, including marketing, distribution, manufacturing, and finance. The overall design is created by a separate MIS group reporting to a high-level official. The MIS concept implies that the subsystems must be a part of a total system with systems integration playing an important role. Each subsystem has equal priority.

Management information systems must provide information in a form that supports the business system that is followed. For example, centralized versus decentralized management philosophy must be clearly understood.

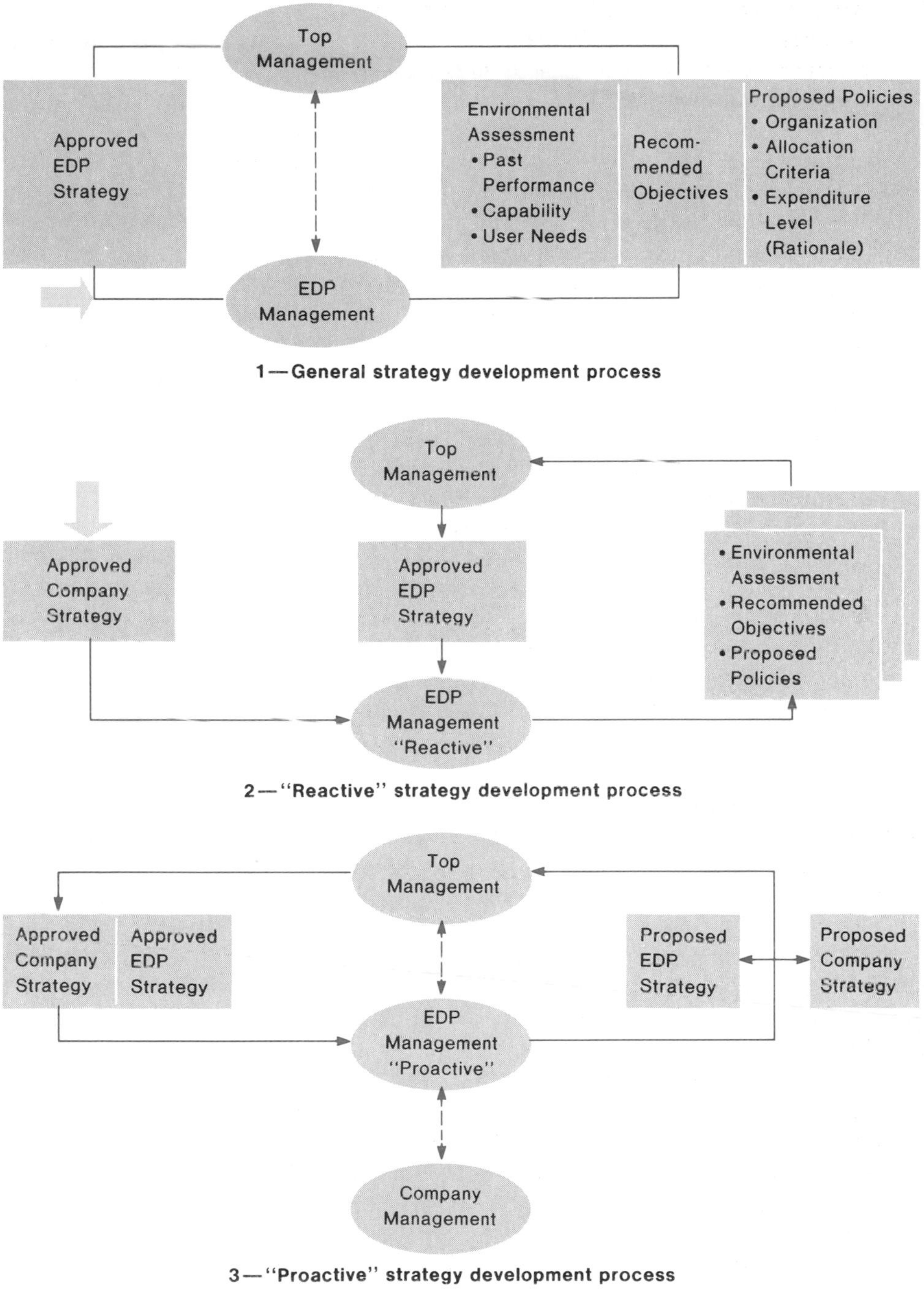

Figure 19.4 Development of a management information system. (Copyright *Data Management* magazine, Data Processing Management Association)

Figure 19.4
Continued.

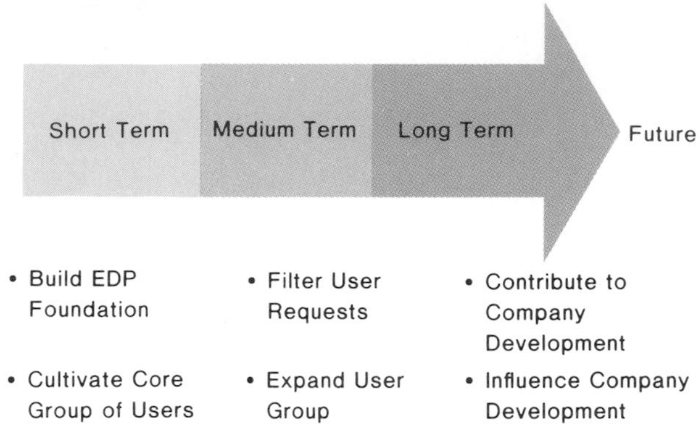

4—Strategic objectives

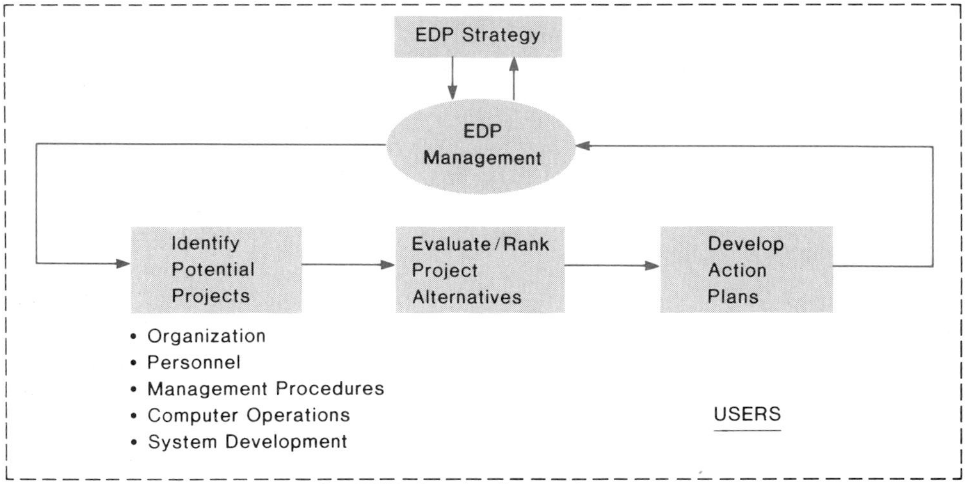

5—EDP plan development process

During the last quarter century, management information systems have been hailed as an appropriate approach to the harnessing of computer power. Hardware concepts during this period were developed along the lines of large-scale computer systems housing centralized data bases to which any senior manager could gain access through his/her own terminal. Software in support of MIS involved sophisticated operating systems and telecommunications monitors at the systems level. Emphasis on management decision making and control, facilitated by a structured data base and simulations and applied to specific managerial situations, have pervaded the MIS era.

The key to good information systems planning involves a total understanding of not only the major decisions and their causes that are made at each management level, but also the environment (external and/or internal influence) in which these decisions are made (fig. 19.5). It is these management decisions that should govern the planning and design of all new information systems (fig. 19.6).

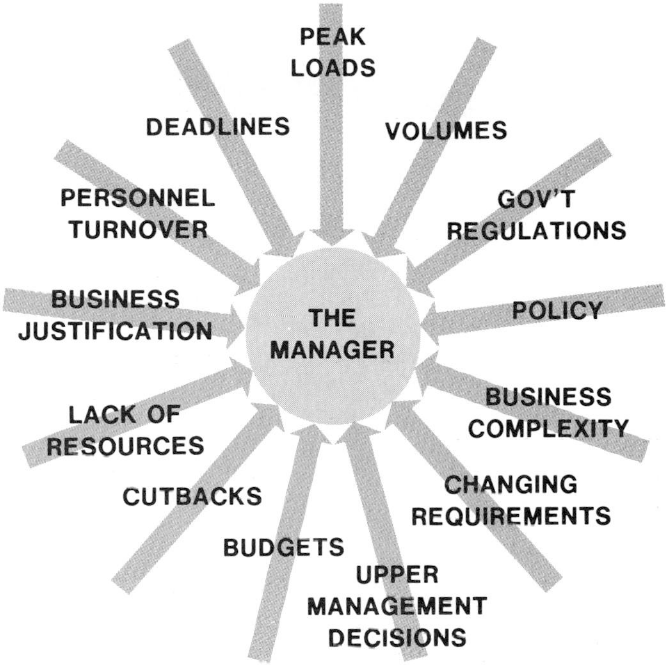

Figure 19.5 The constrained management environment. (Courtesy *Data Management* magazine, Data Processing Management Association)

The typical business-oriented data-processing system user knows very little about computers. Rather than being impressed by a complex and sophisticated computer system, the user may be hopelessly confused. The user must see clearly how using the computer will help. The better the user understands the information system, the more confidence the user will have in the computer. The user must understand the basic plan by which the user's needs will be met, so that the user can derive full benefit from the system (figs. 19.7, 19.8).

The user typically believes that the computer can produce results from a request instantaneously. The user should know that the computer does process large volumes of data very quickly, but that the entry of large volumes of data and manual intervention by the production management group are time-consuming and important for data-processing accuracy and record keeping. The user will surely realize that the time involved is a great deal less than that required by using an equivalent manual system.

Defining the System

When beginning to work on the information system, a systems analyst studies the entire area as it is done manually, or could be done manually, and decides which portions could possibly be performed by the computer. The analyst may interview the user at this point in an effort to discover how receptive the user is to an automated data-processing system and to estimate the user's ability or potential for grasping data-processing concepts. A cost analysis is performed on the parts of the system that may

Figure 19.6
Management information systems diagram.

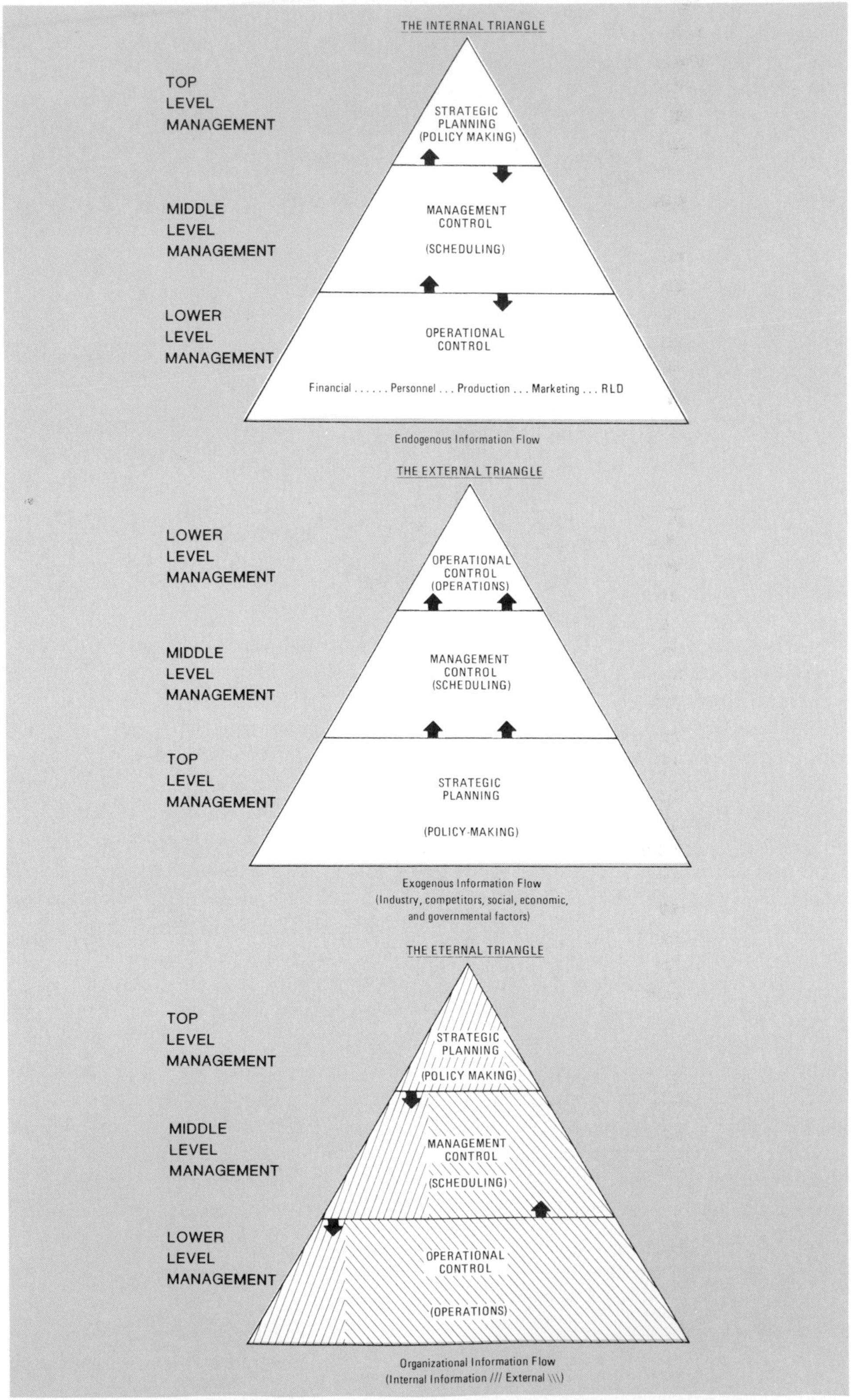

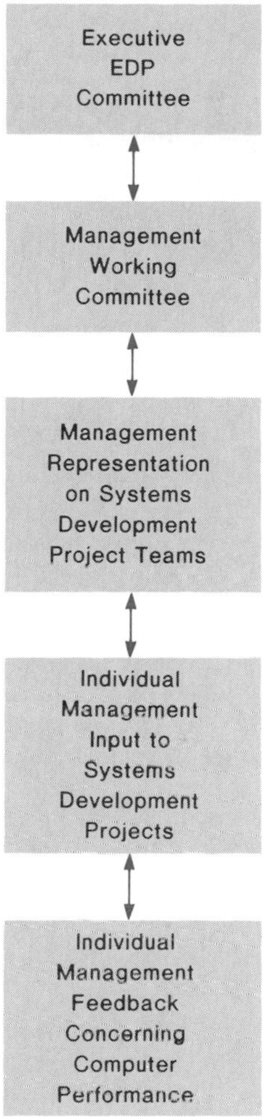

Figure 19.7 Levels of management involvement. (Copyright *Data Management* magazine, Data Processing Management Association)

be automated. The analysis performed and the facts learned in the study must be documented since the outcome of the study dictates whether or not further effort will be expended in that area.

If the outcome of the feasibility study permits, a broad plan can be developed to specify the manual portions of the system and the automated portions of the system. The plan may be further divided into subsystem definitions. The user should be involved so the user can perform the manual operations of the system and can furnish the input data needed and so the output documents will satisfy the user's needs.

Designing the System

The system designer studies the broad system plan and defines, within the plan, modules called *subsystems*. Each subsystem is then broken down into modules called runs, which are in turn broken down into modules called programs, which may be divided

Figure 19.8 Criteria for humanizing management information systems. (Reprinted with permission of *Datamation*© magazine, ©Copyright by Technical Publishing Company, a division of Dun-Donnelley Publishing Corporation, a Dun & Bradstreet Company, 1978—all rights reserved.)

A. Procedures for dealing with users
   1. The language of a system should be easy to understand.
   2. Transactions with a system should be courteous.
   3. A system should be quick to react.
   4. A system should respond quickly to users (if it is unable to resolve its intended procedure).
   5. A system should relieve the users of unnecessary chores.
   6. A system should provide for human information interface.
   7. A system should include provisions for corrections.
   8. Management should be held responsible for mismanagement.

B. Procedures for dealing with exceptions
   1. A system should recognize as much as possible that it deals with different classes of individuals.
   2. A system should recognize that special conditions might occur that could require special actions by it.
   3. A system must allow for alternatives in input and processing.
   4. A system should give individuals choices on how to deal with it.
   5. A procedure must exist to override the system.

C. Action of the system with respect to information
   1. There should be provisions to permit individuals to inspect information about themselves.
   2. There should be provisions to correct errors.
   3. There should be provisions for evaluating information stored in the system.
   4. There should be provisions for individuals to add information that they consider important.
   5. It should be made known in general what information is stored in systems and what use will be made of that information.

D. The problem of privacy
   1. In the design of a system, all procedures should be evaluated with respect to both privacy and humanization requirements.
   2. The decision to merge information from different files and systems should never occur automatically. Whenever information from one file is made available to another file, it should be examined first for its implications for privacy and humanization.

E. Guidelines for system design having a bearing on ethics
   1. A system should not trick or deceive.
   2. A system should assist participants and users and not manipulate them.
   3. A system should not eliminate opportunities for employment without a careful examination of consequences to other available jobs.
   4. System designers should not participate in the creation or maintenance of secret data banks.
   5. A system should treat with consideration all individuals who come in contact with it.

into program modules. The modular concept of system design is desirable for many reasons; a major advantage is that many separate modules can be assigned to many different people who can all supply development effort simultaneously.

Data Preparation Form Design

A very important and sometimes neglected part of system design is input data form design. All forms from which data will be input should be approved by the production data center where the data entry will be done. Input forms are designed so each form is logical for the user to fill out and is simple to input.

User Participation and Support

Output forms have to be designed with user participation. System function output reports typically must be designed within a list of requirements supplied by the user. A number of additional reports are usually generated for the purpose of data control;

the user may have preferences for the content and format of these reports also. Participation in output form design can help the user become function oriented during the design stage of the system.

Implementation of the System

The system test, which takes place after development personnel have determined that all programs will run together compatibly as a system, should mark the start of an earnest effort to educate the user, the data entry operator, the computer operator, and the production systems management groups in the proper use of the system.

Since the system test represents the initial education for all people who will be concerned with the production system, it should be well documented. It is particularly important that documentation include technical information about the computer runs and the maintenance of the data base.

Production Systems Management

The production systems management group should receive maximum consideration in the design of the information system. These people have the responsibility of giving support for the lifetime of the production system and the responsibility of continually meeting the user's needs.

The outcome of the system design should be a simple and easy-to-follow procedure by which an information system can fulfill the data-processing needs of a user group. The procedure must be flexible so it can fit any change that may occur in computer hardware configuration, computer software, or personnel available to support the production system. The production systems management group is responsible for updating the procedure so that the information system can be used to its fullest design intent as long as it is required.

Documentation

The system planning documentation available to the production systems management group should include a broad plan describing the intent and purpose of the system, a design document describing the detailed manual and data-processing procedure, and a system test documentation (fig. 19.9).

The Microcomputer's Effects on MIS

Recognition of the failure of management information systems to meet the objectives defined by their designers has created an atmosphere of uncertainty regarding appropriate applications of computer technology.

Modern computer-based information systems are supposed to provide information needed by *all* levels of management for decision making. The successful development of remote computing through remote job entry (RJE) devices and, to a lesser extent, the appearance of effective data base management systems have produced some efforts to return control to the local level. They have not diminished the role of the MIS specialist. The centralized computer center has become dangerously isolated into "information specialists" within the company's organizational structure. The decline of middle management may be on the horizon.

Figure 19.9 An information systems perspective on corporate general management. (Copyright *Data Management* magazine, Data Processing Management Association)

	Examples of managerial activities	Examples of inputs	Examples of outputs
Corporate general management	• Developing corporate long-range strategic plans. • Choosing overall corporate objectives. • Developing intermediate-range financial plans to implement the long range plans. • Continual evaluation and interpretation of how environment influences corporate policies, plans, performance, and products. • Acquire new divisions/merger. • In charge of interdivisional resource allocations and analysis of divisional plans for consistency and credibility. • Measuring the performance of divisional general management against established business plans.	• Economic Data: National macroeconomic data; Specific relevant sectors; Supplementary series of regional, national, and international data. • Market Analyses Data: Product class (market share, market segmentation, sales, trend, and volume); Customer's preferences and requirements; Industry data. • Government policies/taxation. • Competitive information and plans. • Foreign nation's investment policies. • Historical series on the firm's activities: Contain annual, quarterly, and monthly data on firm's sales, costs, profit, cash flow, etc.; Cross-sectional summary of divisional gross income, gross profit, net before and net after tax, for the entire corporation. • Corporate Financial Inputs: Income statement data; Debt maturities; Interest rates. • Project management information: Projection of the future stream of income and costs.	• Written statement of objectives and goals. • Written statement of policies. • Written approval of programs for projects. • Written approval of operational plans and capital expenditures. • Financial Statements; Balance sheets; Income statements; cash flow statements; Critical ratios.
Divisional general management	• Infusing corporate policies into the functional and production world by translating strategic long-range plans into short-term (annual) operating plans and programs, as well as allocating resources to achieve the goals. • Establishing control systems to measure the performance of functional operating managements within the division.	• Planning guides from corporate headquarters. • Economic forecasts. • Marketing information: Sales history; Advertising and promotion; field sales forecasts; Seasonal factors. • Manufacturing information: product inventories. • Purchasing and distribution information. • Forecasted production volume and price per unit. • Inflation rates for operating supplies and labor costs.	• Divisional level financial statements. • Functional operating programs and associated budgets. • Cash budgets.

The appearance of the microcomputer has created options for the computer user. The next ten years can produce clear and dramatic alternatives to present structures and practices of management information systems. One of these alternate structures is almost surrealistic.

1. The economy of the centralized facility has vanished. Cheap, micro-based, desk-top computers using cartridge-loaded application programs provide complete, free-standing, department-level processing and storage power.
2. The in-house technical specialities of MIS have disappeared. In the more complex units which require them, microprogrammed operating systems have removed the software programmer from the payroll. Application segments are ordered out of catalogs, tested prior to purchase, and installed without special skills by the operating department staff under direction of the designer of production methods.
3. The central data base has become an unwarranted administrative luxury for most companies. Departmental data bases remain in the operating department. Standardized data management *hardware* permits interdepartmental data passing by cartridge or by data-bus where more expensive communications hardware is justified.
4. Information flows in operating departments are engineered closely into work flows and decision making. The keyboard for data entry has at least partially yielded to a variety of more adaptable methods, such as voice data entry and recording styluses.

   Most administrative functions, consolidated and almost completely absorbed into operating departments, are performed as plug-in applications dedicated to departmental computers. Only contractual, statutory, and security requirements justify the maintenance of administrative staffs below the executive level.

   The organization itself is hierarchially flat. The long predicted thinning of middle management has taken place, and the work organization has taken on one of the new forms, which go under such names as "self-management" and "industrial democracy."

The Future of MIS

Strategic planning to provide the information services of the future will require more time than it does now. This is true in any situation where complexity is increasing. When computers could only cope with sequential files stored on magnetic tape, the complexity of the systems that could be built was limited and the systems development time rarely took more than a year. With the advent of disk storage, it became possible to store multifunctional data bases online and the complexity of systems development stretched such projects out to between three to five years. Now with the possibility of linking computers through networks and of sharing tasks between personal computers and centralized computer facilities, the planning to make the proper trade-offs among competing goals will stretch the development time to about ten years.

Some of the long-range issues that have to be faced today are:

1. Should we continue to maintain an integrated multifunctional data base or evolve to a system of local data bases, which are only loosely coupled?

2. When we replace our current computers, should we do it with larger computers or with a cluster of specialized minicomputers performing such functions as data base management and generalized inquiry processing?
3. Should we develop the next generation of systems to support the office, or should we move directly to the microcomputer or to minicomputers as an interim step, recognizing that we would have to solve a formidable security problem?
4. Should we place only general-purpose software in our dispersed minicomputers and microcomputers, or should we make compilers available so users can write their own programs?
5. How do we guarantee the sanctity of our information when so much of it is stored in our computers?

Data Organization

A basic requirement of a unified information management system is that the data should be organized in a consistent manner. Otherwise, the data cannot be easily shared by a community of users, nor can the activities of processing programs be coordinated with those of the control programs. In many respects the control program uses traditional methods of organizing data.

The operating system can store and retrieve records that are all the same length or different lengths. If the records are different lengths, a field at the beginning of each record must indicate how long the record is and a field preceding the first record of each block must indicate the length of the complete block. These two fields, indicating the record and block lengths, are used by the access method routines in extracting records from a block.

One or several related blocks of data separated by gaps form a *data set* or, as it is often called, a *data file*. Each set of data represents an organized body of related information, such as all of the information concerning a series or group of sales transactions. Data sets are usually independent of one another, both logically and physically. They may, for example, be stored in different auxiliary storage volumes.

A *volume* is a section or unit of auxiliary storage space that is serviced by a single read/write mechanism, whose operation is entirely independent of any other read/write mechanism. In any operating system installation, a volume may be a reel of tape, a disk pack, a drum, or a section of disk storage serviced by a single read/write head.

They are called volumes because, like collections of books, they store related sets of information (data sets). Sometimes, like books, they can be moved from place to place (disk pack and tape reel volumes, for example). Often the volume containing a particular set of data is located by searching through a series of indexes, in much the same way as a book in a library is found. Also each direct access volume contains a table of contents defining the sets of data contained in the volume and telling where they are located.

Since the organization of data has a profound effect upon the effectiveness of a computer system, it is important to become familiar with the most common methods of data organization.

Information is recorded on all devices in a format prescribed by the control unit and identical for each device. Each track contains certain nondata information, such as the address of the track, the address of each record, the length of each record and a gap between areas, as well as data information (figs. 19.10, 19.11).

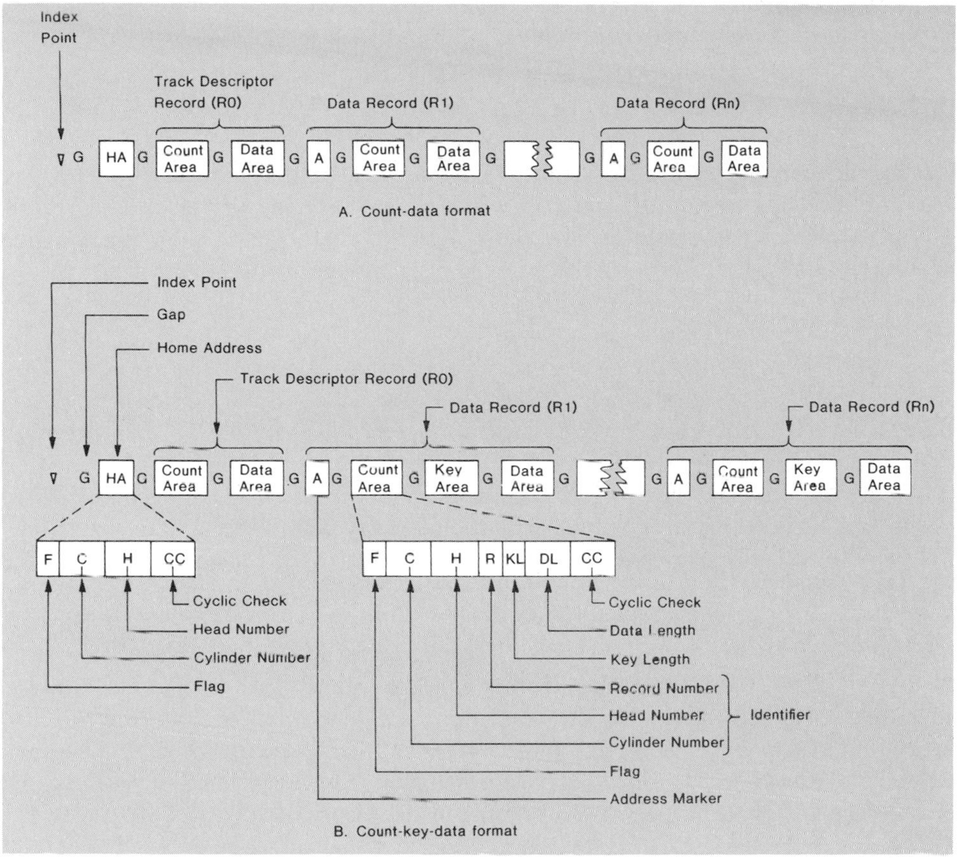

Figure 19.10 Track format.

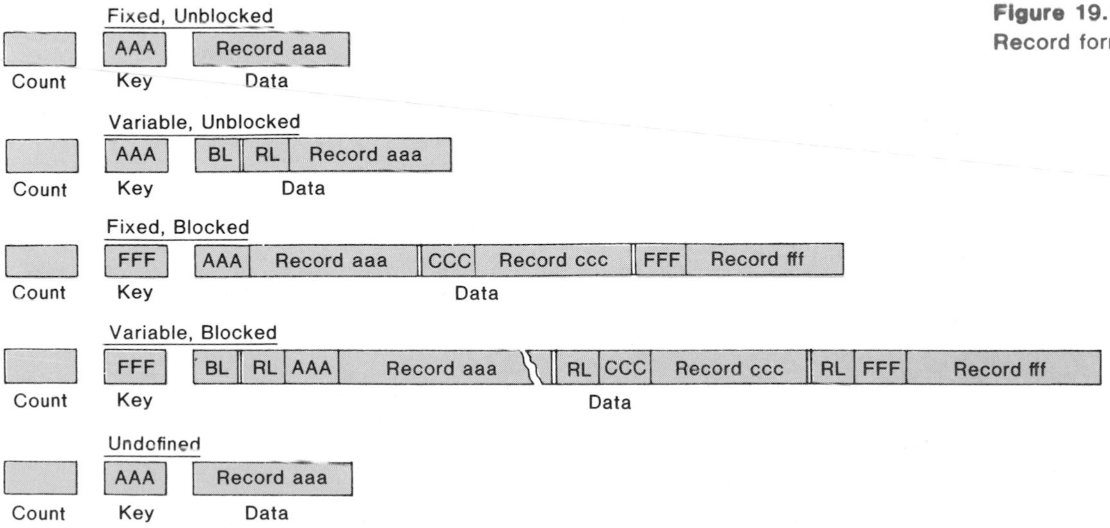

Figure 19.11 Record format.

Unblocked Records

Fixed Unblocked Records

All records in the file are of the same length. Each data area contains one logical record. If keys are used, they are usually not repeated in each of the data areas.

Variable Unblocked Records

The logical records contained in a file are of various lengths. Individual data areas contain one logical record. Special fields are added to define the block and record lengths. A block length (BL) indicates the number of characters in each block, and a record length field (RL) indicates the number of characters in each logical record.

Blocked Records

The primary reason for blocking is to pack more information in a storage area. This method uses direct access storage more efficiently because it is only necessary to have address marker, count areas, key areas, and interrecord gaps for each block of records rather than for each logical record.

If the records are to be processed consecutively, there is an advantage in blocking records because there will be only one rotational delay before the reading or writing of a block of records. However, if records are not processed consecutively, blocking may be a disadvantage because it will take longer to transfer an entire block than a single record.

Fixed Blocked Records

All the records in the file are of the same length, and each data area contains more than one logical record. All blocks are of the same length, except possibly the last block, which may be shorter. The key appears in each logical record in the same location and is used for identification purposes during processing. The *key area* usually contains the key of the highest logical record in the block.

Variable Blocked Records

The logical records in these files are of varying lengths. Each data area contains a block of logical records. A block length field and record length field are used to indicate the sizes of blocks and records.

Undefined Records

This particular format is used to permit the handling of records that do not fit any of the aforementioned formats. One record per block is used. An example would be a variable length record without a block length or record length field.

In order to retrieve records efficiently for data-processing operations, the records within the file must be properly organized. There are several important considerations in selecting an efficient method for file organization.

File Organizations—Considerations

Volatility

The time it takes to add or delete records from a file must be considered. A *static file* is one that has a low percentage of additions and deletions, while a *volatile file* is active at all times, requiring many additions and deletions. The file must be organized so that these additions and deletions are handled with ease. Some methods of organization are more suited to these types of transactions than others.

Activity

The percentage of activity is an important factor in file organization. If a small percentage of the records stored in a file are active at any one time, the file should be organized so that these active records can be quickly located without the necessity for searching the entire file. The records that are processed frequently should be located so they can be retrieved quickly.

Size

A file should be planned to anticipate growth over a period of time. In the process of this planning the possibility that the growth may exceed the present size of storage facilities should also be considered.

A file that is so large that it is not available to the system at one time (online) must be organized and processed in certain ways. On the other hand, a file may be so small that its organization will make little difference in processing time no matter how it is organized.

Processing Techniques

Sequential Processing

In sequential processing, input transactions are grouped together and sorted into a predetermined sequence and processed against the master file. When information is recorded in magnetic tape or punched cards, the most efficient method of processing is sequential. Direct access storage devices are also efficient sequential processors, especially when the percentage of activity against the master file is high.

Random Processing

The processing of detail transactions against a master file, regardless of the sequence of the input documents, is called random processing. With direct access devices, it can be very efficient, especially if the files are organized in such a way that each record can be located quickly. It is possible to process input transactions against more than one file in a single run. This saves time in both setup and sorting and minimizes the control problems, since the transactions are handled less frequently. It is feasible to handle transactions without the necessity of accumulating them. The transactions may be processed inline as soon as they are available. Inquiries to master files need not be scheduled. This is particularly significant in teleprocessing systems in which many inquiries can be made regarding the status of records within a file.

The use of direct access storage devices makes it possible to select the processing techniques that will suit the application best. Some applications may be processed sequentially, while those that require time to sort or that have delays associated with batching processes can be processed randomly. Real savings in overall processing time for a job can be made by combining runs in which the same input data affects several files, the detail items can be processed sequentially against a primary file, and randomly against the secondary file, all in one run. This is the basis of inline processing.

Data File Organizations

The files that accommodate the records necessary for any data-processing problem must be readily accessible to the computer. These records are organized within a file so they can be retrieved in the most expedient way for processing. The intended use of a file and the medium available for storage of the file determines its organization. If the records within a file are to be accessed on demand, as they are in an online

Figure 19.12 A sequentially organized data set.

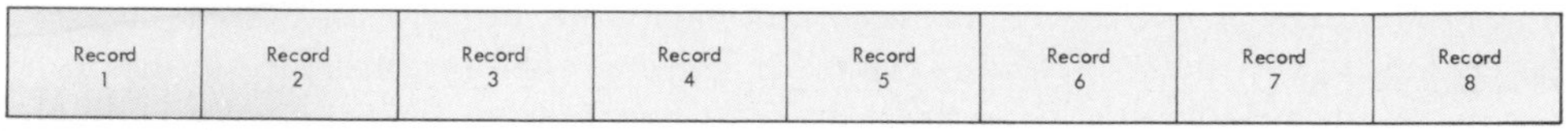

Figure 19.13 An example of a sequential organization file. (Copyright *Data Management* magazine, Data Processing Management Association)

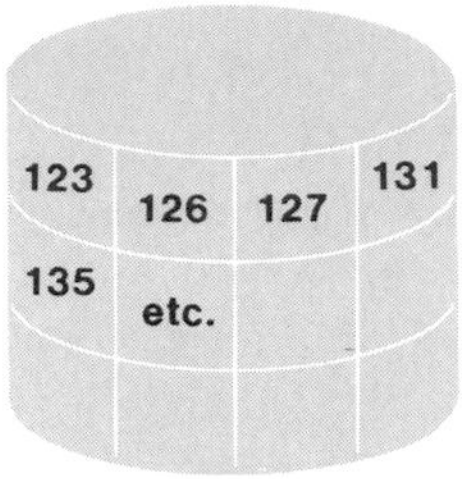

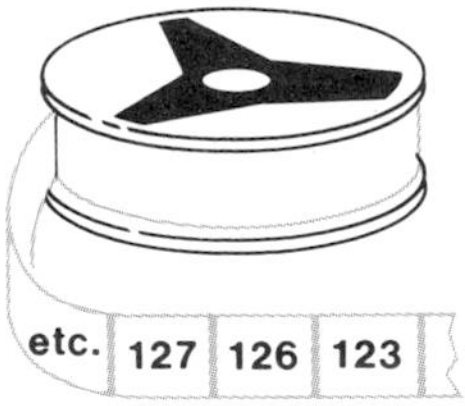

banking situation, the file is organized to access records quickly and accurately. If magnetic tape is the file storage medium and the user is batch processing (processing a large group of records at one time), then the files must be organized to accommodate both the medium and the operation.

Records are either organized within a file that is sorted sequentially by some key or organized in some way that does not require a sequential or serial arrangement (random).

To give the programmer maximum flexibility and efficiency in reading and writing data sets, the following methods of data file organizations are used—sequential, indexed sequential, direct (random), and partitioned.

Sequential Organization

In a sequential file, records are organized solely on the basis of their successive physical locations in the file (fig. 19.12). The records are written one after the other, track by track, cylinder by cylinder, at successively higher locations. The records are usually, but not necessarily, in sequence according to their keys (control numbers). The records are usually read or updated in the same sequence as they appear. For example, record 6 will be read only after the first five records have been read (fig. 19.13).

Random processing of a sequential file is very inefficient. Individual records cannot be located rapidly. Records cannot be inserted or deleted unless the entire file is rewritten. This method of organization is generally used where most of the records of a file are processed each time the file is used.

Sequential organization of a file is used in direct access storage devices primarily for tables and intermediate storage rather than master files. Its use is recommended for master files only if there is a high percentage of activity of a file each time the file is processed or if virtually all processing of the file is sequential.

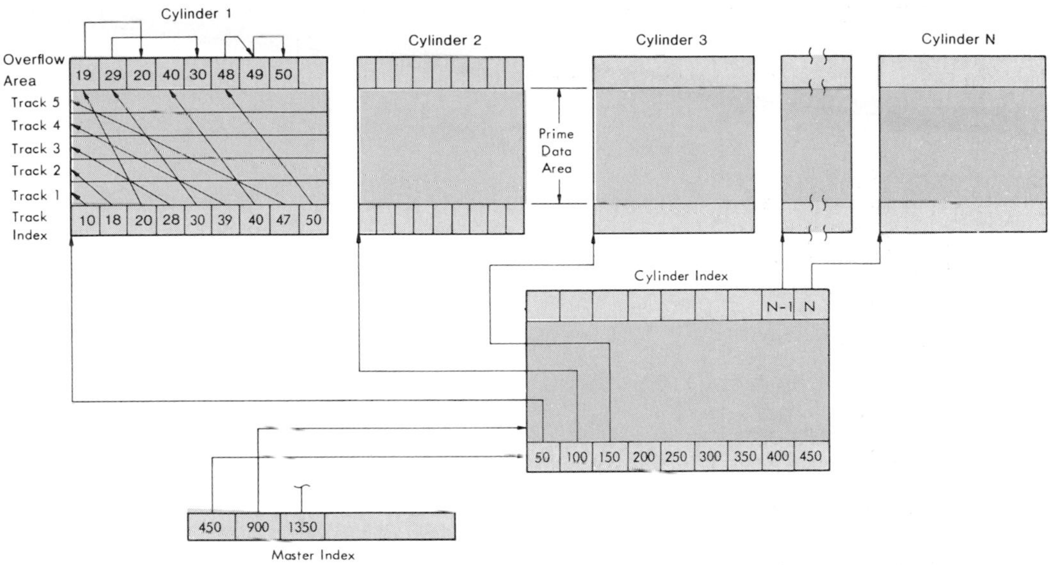

Figure 19.14 An example of an index structure for an indexed sequential data set.

The sequential file is, of course, the most familiar of all types. Like every construction it has advantages. They are familiarity to the user, rapid retrieval of record in sequence, and the ability to batch process for larger volumes of updating. Its disadvantages are that the records are difficult to update, that it is necessary to create a new record, and that retrieval of records in an alternate sequence is not possible without utility sorting.

Indexed Sequential Organization

With certain file processing applications, transactions have to be processed at the same time, or immediately after, the transaction occurs. Such an application might be an online banking situation where transactions are processed while the customer waits at the teller's window. If the master file is sequential, the best way to gain access to it is with the *indexed sequential accessing method.*

An indexed sequential organization file is a sequential file with indexes that permit rapid access to individual records as well as rapid sequential processing (fig. 19.14). The indexes are created and written by the system as the file is created or reorganized. A key precedes each block of data. An indexed sequential file is similar to a sequential file; however, by referring to the indexes maintained within the file, it is possible to quickly locate individual records for random processing. Moreover a separate area can be set aside for additions, which makes it unnecessary to rewrite the entire file, a process that would be required for sequential processing. Although the records are not maintained in key sequence, the indexes are referred to in order to retrieve the added records in key sequences, thus making rapid sequential processing possible (figs. 19.15, 19.16).

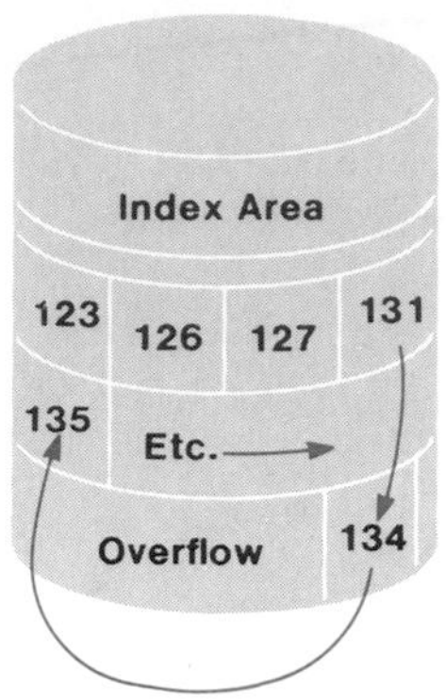

Figure 19.15 An example of an indexed sequential data set. (Courtesy of *Data Management* magazine, Data Processing Management Association)

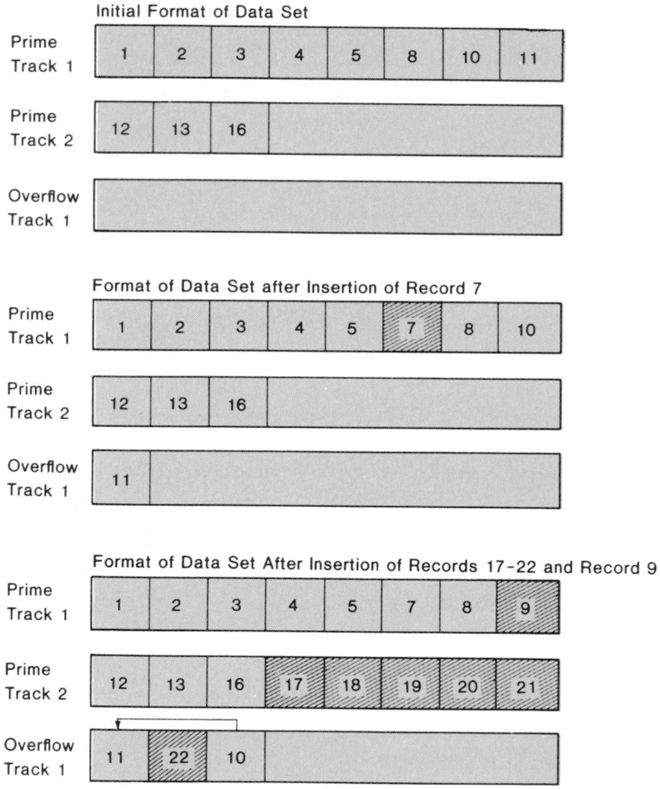

Figure 19.16 Addition of records to an indexed sequential data set.

The programming system has control over the location of the individual record in this method of organization. The user does very little input and output programming; the programming system does most of it inasmuch as the characteristics of the file are known.

Indexed sequential organization gives the programmer greater flexibility in the operations to perform on the data file. The programmer has the ability to read or write records in a manner similar to that for sequential organization. The programmer can also read or write individual records, whose keys may be in any order and add logical records with new keys. The system locates the proper position in the data file for the new record and makes all the necessary adjustments to the indexes.

As with sequential file methods, indexed sequential organization has both advantages and disadvantages.

Advantages

1. Logical sequence of a file is maintained on a key of the user's choice.
2. Sequential processing is possible in the batch environment.
3. Records can be updated in place. A new file does not need to be created to accommodate altered records.
4. Addition of new records into the sequence is possible.
5. Processing out of order records is possible.
6. It is easy to employ for random processing.

Disadvantages

1. The depth of the indexes determine the speed of processing, either in sequence or out of sequence.
2. Periodic file reorganization is necessary to accommodate data within overflow areas.
3. Extension of key ranges in the indexes is not normally possible.
4. Multiple physical searches and reads are necessary for random retrieval of records.
5. It requires relatively large memory consumption.
6. Large memory cycle overhead in calculations.

The indexed sequential file processing method continues to increase in use. It is particularly appropriate in an online real-time situation where files have to be updated as the transaction occurs. It is a convenient method because indexed files can be processed in both sequential and random sequence.

Direct (Random) Organization

A file organized in a direct (random) manner is characterized by some predictable relationship between the key of a record and the address of that record in a direct access storage device. The relationship is established by the user and permits the rapid access to any record of the file, if the file is carefully organized. The records will probably be distributed nonsequentially throughout the file (fig. 19.17). If so, processing the records in key sequence requires a preliminary sort or the use of a finder file.

When a request to store or retrieve a record is made, an address relative to the beginning of the file or an actual address (such as device, cylinder, track, and record

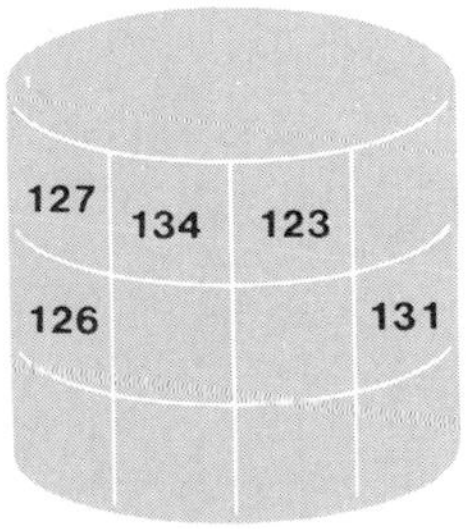

Figure 19.17 An example of direct organization. (Courtesy *Data Management* magazine, Data Processing Management Association)

Figure 19.18
Addition of records to a direct data set.

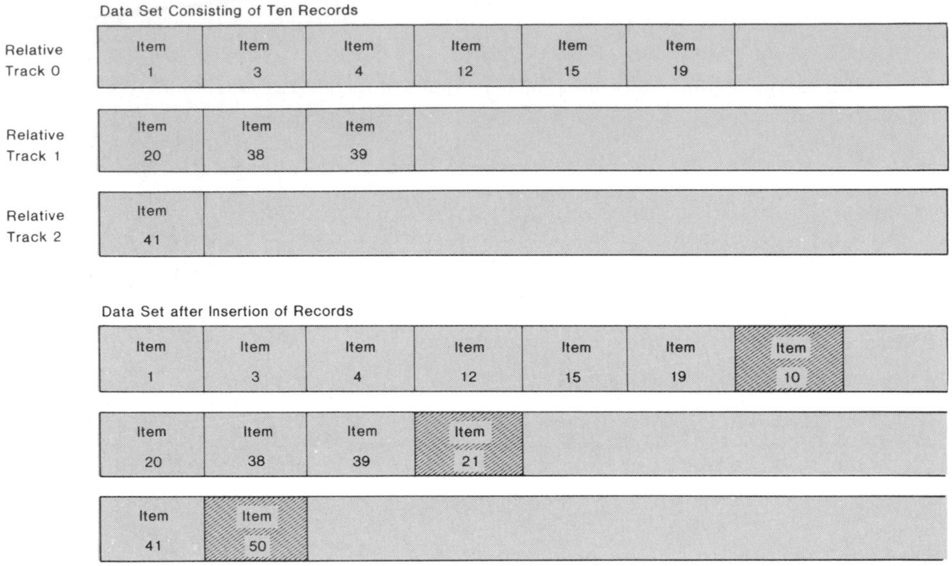

position) must be furnished. This address can be specified as being the address of the desired record or as a starting point within the file where the search for the record begins. When a record search is specified, the programmer must also furnish the key (such as a part number or a customer number) that is associated with the desired record. With direct addressing, every possible key in the file converts to a unique address, thus making it possible to locate any record in the file with one search and one read (fig. 19.18).

The user has complete freedom to decide where records are to be located in a direct organized file. When creating or making additions to the file, the user may specify the location for a record key by supplying the track address and identifier or just simply the track address, letting the system find a location for the record. The record is written in the first available location on the track specified. If the specified track is full, the system continues to search successive tracks until a location is found.

Direct organization is generally used for files whose characteristics do not permit the use of sequential or indexed sequential organizations, or for files where the time required to locate individual records must be kept at a minimum. This method has considerable flexibility but has a serious disadvantage in that the programming system provides the routines to read a file of this type. The user is largely responsible for the logic and programming requirements to locate records since the user establishes the relationship between the key of the record and the address in the direct access storage device.

The direct organization method is far superior to the sequential or indexed sequential techniques. Its chief advantage is the ability to retrieve a specific record without costly table searching or sequential search of an entire file. Also noteworthy is its ability to have additional records stored and existing records retrieved and updated in place without affecting other records on the storage media or, in the sequential case, without recreating an entire file.

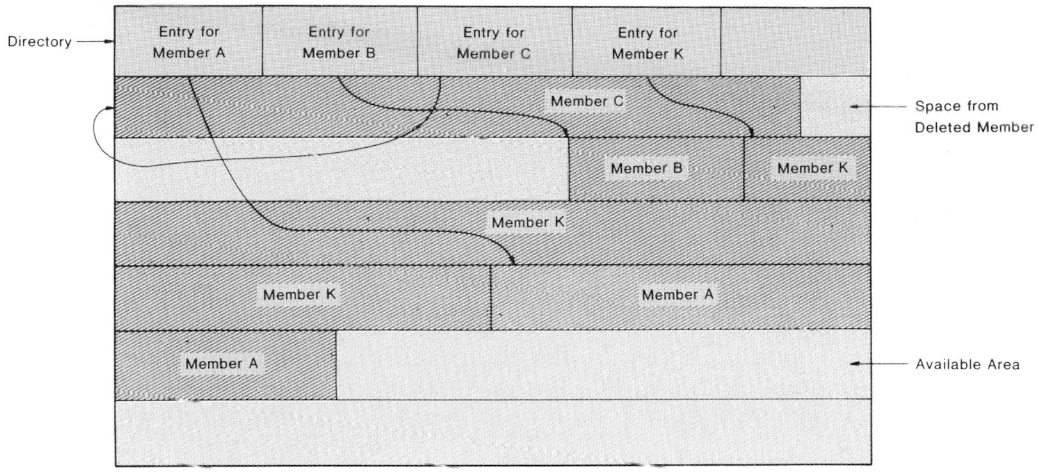

Figure 19.19 A partitioned data set.

Advantages

1. It does not require costly index searching.
2. No physical file degradation occurs.
3. It is the fastest method to retrieve records out of sequence.

Disadvantages

1. It is unable to have sequential order of data. Sort utility is necessary to do this.
2. Randomizing calculation is a user responsibility.
3. Calculation for file space utilization rarely achieves 70 percent physical record density.

These file organizations take both logical and physical constraints into consideration. In data base structures, however, it is desirable to divorce the two functions. By concentrating on the adaptability of these file types to logical construction of the files above, it is easy to understand why these are the three most popular techniques of file structuring today.

Partitioned Organization

A partitioned file is one that is divided into sequentially organized members made up of one or more records. Each member has a unique name (fig. 19.19). The file also includes a directory containing the names and beginning address of each member. Enough storage space is required to hold the sequentially organized members and the directory. As new members are added, the system allocates additional areas of assigned storage, if the assigned areas are filled. If the directory is filled, no new members may be added without reorganizing the file.

Members may be added or deleted as required. The records within the members are organized sequentially and are retrieved or stored successively according to their physical sequence.

Partitioned organization is used mainly for the storage of sequential data, such as programs, subroutines, compilers, and tables. The main advantage of a partitioned file is that it is possible for the programmer to retrieve specific members. For example, a library of subroutines might be a partitioned file whose members are subroutines. Within each subroutine, the records are sequentially organized.

Summary

The design of a computer system is an important element of successful operation of data-processing installations. Extensive studies are required to assure the efficient use of data-processing equipment. Studies provide management with enough information about system projects so an objective decision can be made regarding its value.

Management information systems provide information in a form that supports the system that is followed. Modern computer-based information systems should provide information needed by all levels of management for decision making.

Management information system requires data to be organized in a consistent manner so the data can be shared by a community of users. Since the organization of data has a profound effect upon the design and effectiveness of the system, it is important to become familiar with the most common methods of data organization.

This chapter presents the problems inherent in the study and design of management information systems.

1. The feasibility study provides management with enough information about the proposed system's project so an objective decision can be made regarding its value. By using this study management should be able to improve the efficiency of the company. The areas delineated in the study are the problem definition, the scope of the study, the proposed system's objectives, the authority of the various groups affected by the proposed system, the organization of the new system, and the timetables or schedules for the proposed system.
2. Management systems personnel study the entire system to determine whether or not further effort should be expended in a particular area. In designing a new system, subsystems are modules of a system. Input/output forms are designed, with participation by all users of the forms and the system. To implement the new system, the user, the data entry operator, the computer operator, and the production systems management must be educated in the proper use of the system. The production systems management is responsible for continually meeting the user's needs. Documentation of the new system include the broad plan describing intent and purpose of the system and the detailed manuals of data-processing procedures.
3. Data is organized into either unblocked records or blocked records. Volatility, activity, and size of the file determine how the records are organized. The two types of processing techniques are sequential and random. In sequential processing, input records are grouped together, sorted in a predetermined sequence, and processed against a master file. In random processing, detail transactions are not sorted and processed against the file regardless of the sequence. Data can be organized into sequential file organization in which all records are organized solely on their successive physical locations in a file; indexed sequential file organization, which is a sequential organized file with indexes that permit rapid access to individual records as well as sequential processing; direct (random) file organization in which there is some predictable relationship between the key of the records and the address of the record in the file; or a partitioned organization file, which is divided into sequentially organized members made up of one or more records with each member having a unique name.

Identification Questions

Match the following terms with the statements below.

A. Blocked Records
B. Data File (Set)
C. Data Organization
D. Direct (Random) File Organization
E. Feasibility Study
F. Fixed Records
G. Indexed Sequential File Organization
H. Management Information Systems (MIS)
I. Partitioned File Organization
J. Random Processing
K. Sequential File Organization
L. Sequential Processing
M. Static File
N. Variable Records
O. Volatile File
P. Volume

1. Physical arrangement of data records within a file.
2. A section or unit of auxiliary storage space that is serviced by a single read/write mechanism, whose operations are entirely independent of any other read/write medium.
3. A file that has a low percentage of additions and deletions.
4. Records are organized solely on the basis of their successive physical location in the file.
5. Records are grouped together.
6. Some predictable relationship between the key of a record and the address of that record in a direct access storage device.
7. A report to management with enough information about the proposed system project so a proper decision can be made about its value.
8. One or several related blocks of data separated by gaps.
9. All records in the file are of the same length.
10. A sequential file with indexes that permit access to individual items.
11. A file that is active at all times, requiring many additions and deletions.
12. Input transactions are grouped together and sorted into a predetermined sequence and processed against the master file.
13. A series of steps designed to find all data requested by management, in a concise form, which will enable them to make the necessary decisions on a timely basis, to result in a successful and profitable business operation.
14. All records in the file are of varying lengths.
15. The processing of detail transactions against a master file regardless of sequence of input documents.
16. A file that is divided into sequentially organized members made up of one or more records.

Questions for Review

1. Why are studies necessary?
2. What interest does management have in a feasibility study?
3. What are the specific areas to be delineated in the study?
4. What are the areas of vital concern to management in a computer feasibility study?
5. What important contributions can outside consultants make in the feasibility study?

6. How should the feasibility study be written?
7. Who originated the concept of management information systems? What assumptions are made for decision making?
8. Why is it important that management have a clear understanding of computer operations?
9. What are the important phases of management information systems? List the important points in defining the system, designing the system, implementation of the system, production system management, and documentation.
10. What effect will the microcomputer have on management information systems?
11. What are some of the long-range issues that will have to be faced regarding management information systems?
12. What is a basic requirement of a unified information management system?
13. What is a data set (file)?
14. What is a volume?
15. What is a format?
16. Describe briefly the five record formats available.
17. What are the reasons for blocking records?
18. List the important considerations in selecting an efficient method for file organization.
19. What is the important difference between sequential processing and random processing?
20. Describe sequential organization and state why it is inefficient in random processing.
21. What are the main advantages and disadvantages of sequential file organization?
22. Describe an indexed sequential file organization.
23. List the advantages and disadvantages of indexed sequential file organization.
24. What is a direct organization file? What is its main use?
25. List the advantages and disadvantages of direct organization.
26. What is a partitioned file and what is its principal use?

Key Terms

Blocked Records
Data File (Set)
Data Organization
Direct (Random) File Organization
Feasibility Study
Fixed Records
Indexed Sequential File Organization
Management Information Systems (MIS)
Partitioned File Organization
Random Processing
Sequential File Organization
Sequential Processing
Static File
Variable Records
Volatile File
Volume

appendix A

IBM model 129 card data recorder

General Features

The IBM 129 Card Data Recorder (fig. A.1) is a preprogrammed, data-storage, key-entry, card-punch, verifying machine used to punch a 80-column card for data processing. Similar in operation and appearance to the IBM 29 Card Punch and IBM 59 Card Verifier, the IBM 129 offers the following advantages:

1. Keyed input data simultaneous with automatic functions.
2. Keyed input error correction before punching.
3. Card read-in for verification at speeds of 80 columns per second.
4. Immediate error correction during verification, including repunching to provide a correct card.
5. Six program levels plus a "no-format" program.
6. An improved column indicator on the keyboard panel.
7. New special features for greater function and flexibility, such as the production statistics and accumulations and the direct punch control and verify read control.
8. Left-zero or left-blank insertion.
9. A 48/64-character keyboard mode switch.
10. An IBM 29-type interlocked keyboard.

Operation

Blank cards, placed in the card hopper, are fed (one at a time) into the card bed, which transports each card to the punch station. The operator keys in each character, and the information is saved in input storage until the 80-column (maximum) record is completed. When keying is completed, the data in storage is automatically punched into the card at the punch/read station. Storage is immediately available for keying the next record, while the previous record is being punched.

The punching process continues, independent of operator keying. At the next punching, all cards move up; thus, they are transported through the recorder and out into the card stacker. The punched cards can be removed from the card stacker for further processing.

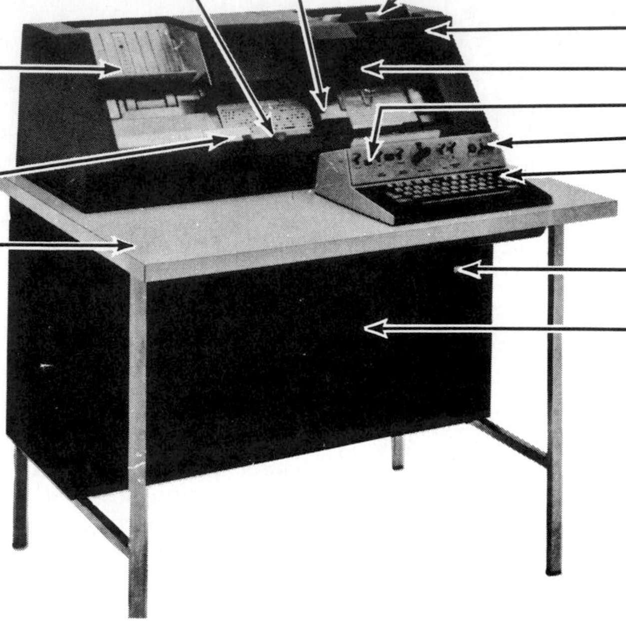

Figure A.1 IBM 129 card data recorder. (Courtesy IBM Corporation)

Keyed data is stored in electronic form before it is punched into a card. This allows an operator the capability to easily rekey data before it is punched into the card. The column indicator, provided with the data recorder, is a visual display device that shows the operator the next column to be keyed.

Automatic control of such functions as data formatting, duplicating, inserting left-zeros, and skipping is accomplished by a stored program with program cards for the six program levels. Before the card-punching operation begins, individual program cards for the six program levels are punched and may be read into program control storage, one at a time. Any of these programs may be selected to control the keying format (fig. A.2).

Keyed corrections may be made via *input storage* before the record is completed. The completed record is stored in *output storage,* ready to be punched and available for duplication of data into the next record fed into input storage.

Combination Keyboard

The combination keyboard contains character keys, function keys, and control keys for punching and verifying (fig. A.3). The keyboard permits keying of data into storage for card punching or verifying and provides operator control of the necessary accompanying functions. The keyboard can be switched to either a 48- or 64-character set. The alphabetic keys allow use of the standard typewriter touch system, while the numeric keys are placed so a rapid three-finger touch system can be used. A group of dual-purpose keys at the right serves for numeric keying. (These keys also serve for some alphabetic characters.) This permits numeric keying with the right hand from the normal "home" position used in alphabetic keying.

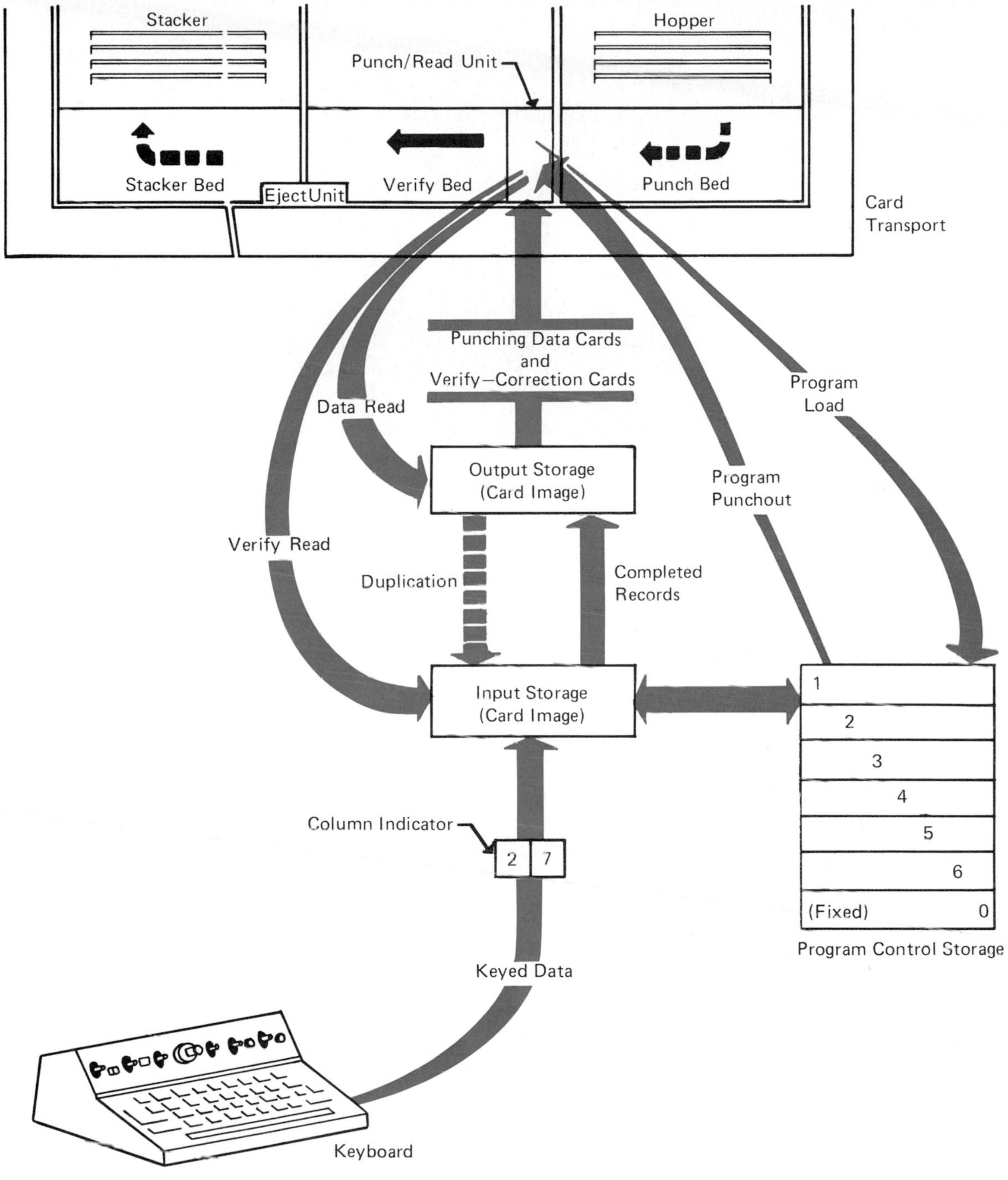

Figure A.2 IBM 129 storage and data flow.

Figure A.3 Keyboard.

The keying of a digit or a letter with any of the combination keys depends on the shift of the keyboard. For example, the pressing of the 4-J key while the card data recorder is in the numeric shift keys in a 4; pressing the key while the machine is in alphabetic shift keys in a J. This shifting is similar to uppercase and lowercase shifting on a standard typewriter, and may be controlled automatically by the program, or manually by pressing either key. When either shift key is manually operated, care should be taken to ensure that the shift key is fully pressed before data keying starts.

Keyboard Console Controls and Indicators

Function Controls — The function controls are located on the panel above the keyboard (fig. A.4).

Punch Verify — This mode switch makes the machine operate either in punch mode or verify mode.

Column Indicator — The column indicator shows the position of input storage that receives the next character.

Auto Skip/Dup — When this switch is ON, any field in the input storage unit programmed for automatic skip or automatic duplicate (automatic verify) is performed at electronic speeds. When this switch is OFF, these functions are not operative and information from the keyboard can be recorded or verified in these fields.

Verify — This light indicates errors during verify and self-check operations.

Rec Adv/Card Feed — This switch provides automatic program selection and automatic card feed with these positions.

Auto — As soon as column 80 is keyed, the machine proceeds to column 01 of the next record under control of the program card.

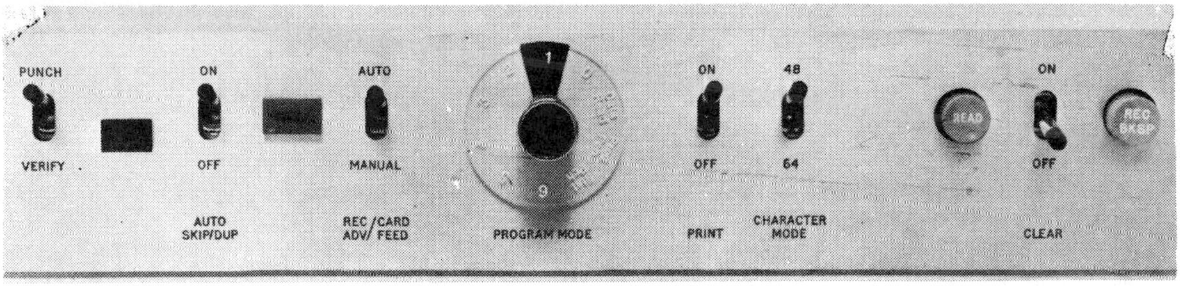

Figure A.4 Console controls.

Manual

After column 80 is keyed, the machine stops at column 00; the operator must either set Rec/Adv/Card Feed to Auto or press Prog Sel key, then press a valid program number (0–6) to advance the column indicator to 01 for the next record.

Program Mode

This mode switch selects the program level of the 129; it also has positions for reading data into storage, for punching out program cards, and for punching out production statistics if the feature is present. This switch sets a program level (1–6) during program load operation.

Print

This switch is effective during keying of the record into storage; that is, if the switch is OFF during keying, no printing occurs when the record is punched into the card. If it is ON during keying, all characters (those manually entered from the keyboard and those duplicated within the standard 64-character set) are printed at the top edge of the card.

Character Mode

This switch determines whether the keyboard is active for a 48- or 64-character set.

Read

This pushbutton is used to read a program card into program control storage or a data card into output storage.

Clear

When this spring-loaded switch is raised, the multiple cycles necessary to move all cards out of the card transport into the stacker are initiated and the column indicator returns to 01. No additional cards are fed from the card hopper. Duplication is suspended following a clear operation until one card is keyed or read into output storage.

Rec Bksp

Pressing the Rec Bksp pushbutton returns the column indicator to 01 of input storage without changing the current program level, erases the record in storage, and suspends any automatic skip or duplicate function that is programmed in column 01. All other programmed functions remain active.

Keyboard Keys

In addition to the usual alphabetic (letter) and numeric (digit) keys and symbols, the keyboard contains detailed function keys.

Space Bar

The space bar can be pressed at any time in a manual field to cause punching or verifying of a single space in the record.

Char Bksp

Pressing the Char Bksp causes unlocking of the keyboard, if it is locked due to an invalid keystroke, or causes a backspace of one column.

Alpha — Pressing this key converts the keyboard to the alpha mode for the duration of time that the key is held pressed. When the key is released, the card punch returns to the shift indicated by the program.

Skip — Pressing this key initiates a skip to the end-of-field definition in the punch mode, or verifies that the column in which it was pressed is blank and initiates a skip in verify mode at electronic speeds.

Reg — If a card is preregistered or manually inserted, the Reg key registers the card at the punch/read station.

Feed — Pressing the Feed key feeds a card from the hopper to the card bed.

Blank Columns/Left Zero Ctrl (LZ bar) — Pressing this bar (key) causes shifting of keyed data to the right (limited by a field definition) and inserts zeros to the left for the remaining positions in the field. To obtain leading blanks (such as in a name field), place the machine in alphabetic shift by program or manual operation and press the left zero (LZ) bar.

Prog Sel — During keying, press Prog Sel and select an associated data key (0–6); this causes a shift to the program level selected.

Rel — This key may be pressed at any column of the card. Operation of this key generally releases the card being punched.

Numeric — This key must be held pressed when operating in program level 0 and numeric keying is required. It can also be used to override alphabetic programming when under program control.

Mult Pch — When this key is held pressed, the column indicator does not advance, so more than one punch can be entered in a single column. This key can be used to prepare program cards or to enter special codes.

Dup — Pressing this key duplicates common information from any card into the following card.

Field/Word Bksp — Pressing this key returns the column indicator to the first column of the field being keyed under program control.

Ver Res and Ver Corr — These keys are used with verifying operations.

Program Control Card Punching

The program controls the field size, the automatic functions of skipping, duplicating, and shifting from numeric to alphabetic mode, and the operation of special features. Each of the operations performed under control of the program is defined by a specific code recorded in a *program card*. The program card is punched with the program card codes to fit the application desired. The program card is then stored (read) into the program control storage. Six program levels (1–6), plus a 0 (no-program) level provides exceptional flexibility to the program operation. Any of these stored programs may be selected by the operator (fig. A.5).

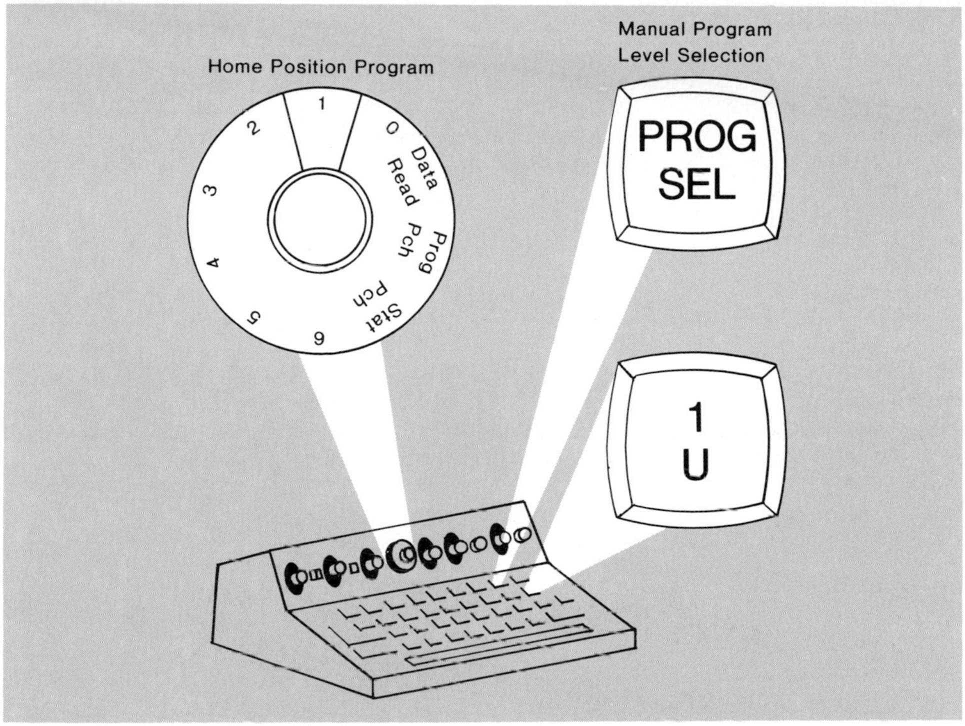

Figure A.5
Selecting the stored program.

The program is read into program control storage at the start of a particular application by inserting the prepunched program card at the read (or punch/read) station and by pressing Read. The Program Mode dial must be in the desired program level setting for proper program load operation.

Common Program Card Codes

Code	Function to be Performed
blank	Initiates beginning of a field to be punched manually with numeric information.
1	Initiates beginning of a field to be punched manually with alphabetic information.
0	Initiates automatic duplication.
11 (-)	Initiates automatic skipping.
12 (&)	Defines length of a numeric field.
A	Defines length of an alphabetic field.

One of the four codes (blank, 0, 1, or -) is punched in the first column of each field to indicate the operation desired for that field. The rest of the field is punched with 12 (&) for numeric fields or with an A for alphabetic fields. A complete list of program codes is found in figure A.6. Examples of fields on program cards are found in figure A.7.

Figure A.6 Program codes.

Function	Punch Code	Field Location
Standard Codes		
Field Definition (FD)	12	All columns, except first column
Auto Skip Field	11	First column
Auto Dup/Auto Ver Field	0	First column
Alpha Shift (Programmed)	1	Each column for alpha shift
Left-zero Control Field (Verify Only)	3	First and last columns*
Special Feature Codes		
Self-check Field	2	First and last columns*
Add Accumulator A	5	First column
Add Accumulator B	6	First column
Add Accumulator C	7	First column
Punch Accumulator A, B, or C	4 + (5 or 6 or 7)	First column
Punch and Reset Accumulator A, B, or C	4 + 8 + (5 or 6 or 7)	First column
Direct Punch Control for "Buffered" Field	3	First column for direct punch mode only
Verify Read Control to Stop Verify Read Operation	11-0	Column desired to stop card
Auto Auxiliary Storage Dup	11-0	First column
12 and 11-Punch Elimination (Interpret only)	0	Each column elimination required
Print Left-zeros (Interpret only)	1	First column

*Last column must also contain a 12-punch.

Notes:

1. Program codes apply in program levels 1-6. Program level 0 is 80 single-position fields, alpha shift.
2. LZ control (3-punch in units position) should be used so that punch and verify procedures are similar (that is, key the digits and press the LZ bar) and to ensure correct verification of adjacent LZ fields, or fields containing all zeros.
3. Only field definition is required for LZ punching. Program cards coded for LZ in verify mode (3-punches) may be used in punch mode without alteration because machine ignores 3-codes in punch mode, unless direct punch control feature is used (see chart).
4. Minimum field size is two columns for accumulate, self-check, and LZ.
5. Maximum field size is 79 columns for self-check and LZ.
6. Maximum input field size for accumulate is 14 columns; maximum punchout field size is 19 columns.
7. A field may be programmed to add into any or all accumulators; punchout is limited to one accumulator per field.
8. Self-check fields may be adjacent. Self-check and accumulate operate in both punch and verify mode. However, self-check cannot be programmed in the same field as accumulate or left zero.
9. Verify read control (11-0 code) must not be programmed in same column as auto skip (11) or auto dup (0) codes, nor in any self-check programmed field.
10. Programs remain in storage until another program is read in to replace the original program, or until mainline switch is turned off. This resets program 1-6 to blanks (equivalent to 80 single-position fields, numeric shift).

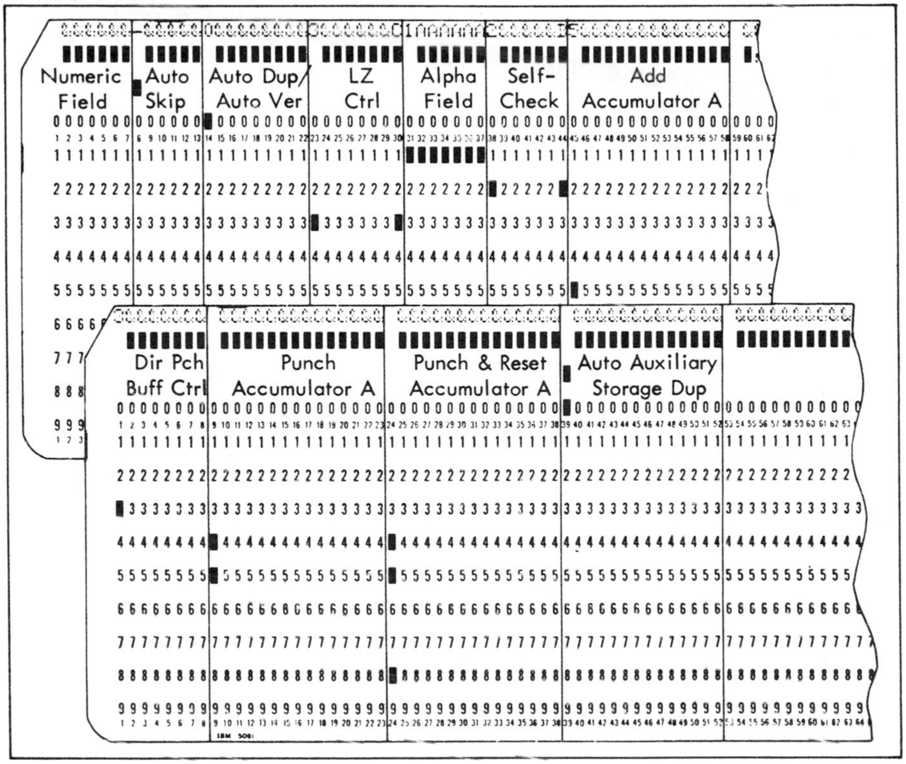

Figure A.7 Program card, field examples.

Inserting Cards Manually

In certain circumstances, it is desirable to insert cards manually, one at a time, to make over a damaged card, or to correct an error. Also, when an individual card accompanies each original document, manual insertion may be necessary. A single card may be inserted in the hopper or may be manually inserted directly in the card bed (through the upper and lower card guides) at the punch station or read station.

For more detailed information relative to the IBM 129 Data Recorder, refer to the operator's reference manual for the IBM 129 Data Recorder.

appendix B

binary representation for EBCDIC and ASCII-8

Character	EBCDIC	Hex.	ASCII–8	Hex.
0	1111 0000	F0	0101 0000	50
1	1111 0001	F1	0101 0001	51
2	1111 0010	F2	0101 0010	52
3	1111 0011	F3	0101 0011	53
4	1111 0100	F4	0101 0100	54
5	1111 0101	F5	0101 0101	55
6	1111 0110	F6	0101 0110	56
7	1111 0111	F7	0101 0111	57
8	1111 1000	F8	0101 1000	58
9	1111 1001	F9	0101 1001	59
A	1100 0001	C1	1010 0001	A1
B	1100 0010	C2	1010 0010	A2
C	1100 0011	C3	1010 0011	A3
D	1100 0100	C4	1010 0100	A4
E	1100 0101	C5	1010 0101	A5
F	1100 0110	C6	1010 0110	A6
G	1100 0111	C7	1010 0111	A7
H	1100 1000	C8	1010 1000	A8
I	1100 1001	C9	1010 1001	A9
J	1101 0001	D1	1010 1010	AA
K	1101 0010	D2	1010 1011	AB
L	1101 0011	D3	1010 1100	AC
M	1101 0100	D4	1010 1101	AD
N	1101 0101	D5	1010 1110	AE
O	1101 0110	D6	1010 1111	AF
P	1101 0111	D7	1011 0000	B0
Q	1101 1000	D8	1011 0001	B1
R	1101 1001	D9	1011 0010	B2
S	1110 0010	E2	1011 0011	B3
T	1110 0011	E3	1011 0100	B4
U	1110 0100	E4	1011 0101	B5
V	1110 0101	E5	1011 0110	B6
W	1110 0110	E6	1011 0111	B7
X	1110 0111	E7	1011 1000	B8
Y	1110 1000	E8	1011 1001	B9
Z	1110 1001	E9	1011 1010	BA

Unlisted bit representations are used to represent special characters, such as $, %, ., *, (, and). A full listing of these codes may be found in most reference manuals.

appendix C
data-processing job descriptions

Job Families

The data-processing job descriptions have been grouped into a number of families, ranging from manager to trainee. These classifications have the general qualifying characteristics listed below. Please note that *for a one-person department, neither the manager category nor lead applies.*

Manager

Usually in full charge of all activities of a section or department. May personally supervise the operations of a staff or direct the operation through subordinates.

Lead

May be a shift leader, section head, or a group head. Often a line supervisor with full technical knowledge with added duties of assigning, instructing, and checking other members.

Senior

A person fully qualified to work at the highest technical level of all phases of the activity. Works without supervision most of the time. May give some direction to lower classifications.

Member

Usually the most populous of the categories, whether a programmer, analyst, or operator. Works under general supervision, but is competent to work alone on some or many phases of the operation. Requires only general direction or instruction for the other phases.

Trainee

An employee who has no previous experience in doing these tasks.

Management

Director of Data Processing or MIS

Titles abound for this person. *The top executive over all computer processing.* May also have responsibility for such functions as office automation, information resources, and telecommunications. Is responsible for long-range planning, budgeting, and operations.

Administrative Assistant

A member of the director's staff. Directs the preparation and review of budgets and business plans. May negotiate contracts with vendors. Primarily concerned with money matters and sometimes with personnel administration. *Basically a business manager.*

A member of the director's staff. Usually the head of advanced planning for the data-processing function. Assists in analyzing proposed and ongoing projects, and in conducting feasibility studies. *The top technical staff member in the data-processing function,* charged with keeping abreast of technical developments and determining how those developments apply to the company. Also is involved in major hardware and software acquisitions or conversions, in network design, and in such considerations as choosing between centralized and distributed configurations. — Technical Assistant

Coordinates data-processing activities with those of other functions or departments, acts as the user's contact with data processing, and assists in establishing standards and priorities. — Services Coordinator

Systems Analysis and Programming

Responsible for the analysis of how data processing can be applied to specific users problems *and* for the *design* of effective and efficient data-processing solutions. Manages feasibility studies. Assigns personnel to projects and directs their activities. — Manager of Systems Analysis/Manager of Systems Analysis and Programming

This section is expected to produce designs or specifications for programs for use by other sections of the department, including especially applications programming, but may be involved in workflow and other analysis that do not lead to the production of programs.

Assists in planning, organizing, and controlling the activities of the section. May also assist in scheduling and assigning personnel, or may act as a project leader. *Usually is in semipermanent charge of a group* of analysts, and spends a significant amount of time directing their activities. May instruct lower classifications or design especially difficult or critical portions of systems. — Lead Systems Analyst/Lead Systems Analyst and Programmer

Broadly qualified to work on a variety of projects and fully competent to work alone. Confers with users to define data-processing projects. Formulates statements of problems or objectives and designs solutions. May produce block diagrams or pseudo-code descriptions or applications systems. May give some direction to lower classifications. — Senior Systems Analyst/Senior Systems Analyst and Programmer

Fully qualified to work alone; requires only some general direction and instruction. Works with users to define projects or project segments or to iron out details in specifications. *Usually works on only several types of projects; is not as broadly qualified as the senior systems analyst.* — Systems Analyst/Systems Analyst and Programmer

Usually works on one item at a time under direct supervision. May attend formal classes and is expected to spend a good deal of time learning rather than producing. Usually has some data-processing experience. — Systems Analyst Trainee/Systems Analyst and Programmer Trainee

Applications Programming

Responsible for the development of effective, efficient, well-documented programs. Assigns personnel to projects and directs their activities. This section may work from program specifications and designs prepared by systems analysis for new projects. Is responsible for the ongoing maintenance of existing programs. — Manager of Applications Programming

Lead Applications Programmer — Assists in planning, organizing, and controlling the activities of the section. May also assist in scheduling and assigning personnel. May act as a chief programmer on a programming team. *Usually is in semipermanent charge of a group* of programmers and spends a significant amount of time directing their activities. May instruct lower classifications; may program especially difficult code.

Senior Applications Programmer — *Broadly qualified to work on a variety of applications and is fully competent to work alone.* Works with program designs or specifications, which may be in block diagram or pseudo-code form, to produce working, debugged, and documented code; works with specifications or descriptions of program changes to maintain existing programs. May give some direction to lower classifications.

Applications Programmer — Fully qualified to work alone; *requires only some general direction and instruction.* Usually works on only one or a few types of applications; is not as broadly qualified as the senior applications programmer.

Applications Programmer Trainee — Usually works on one item under direct supervision. *Is learning to program.* Any work produced is carefully checked.

Programming Team Librarian — Supports the activities of a *programming team* by keeping track of program revisions, by enforcing documentation standards, and by maintaining program listings. May track the testing of individual software modules; may edit or produce program documentation and user manuals.

Operating Systems Programming

Manager of Systems Programming — Plans and directs the activities of the section; assigns personnel to projects. Is *responsible* for supporting the operations staff, as well as the programming and analysis staffs, by *maintaining the operating system software environment* in which the others work. Within boundaries established by management, is responsible for selection, evaluation, installation, and maintenance of operating systems and utilities (often called teleprocessing monitors and access methods). Participates in projecting hardware and software requirements.

The staff also usually provides consulting services, recommends standards, monitors computer performance, performs hardware troubleshooting, and may coordinate the installation of new equipment.

Lead Systems Programmer — May function as an assistant manager. Assists in planning, organizing, and controlling the activities of the section. *May be in semipermanent charge of a small group* of systems programmers, and may spend some time directing their activities. May act as a project leader in implementing or converting major systems, as in converting to a new operation system.

Senior Systems Programmer — *Competent to work at the highest levels of programming.* Depending on the size of the staff, may specialize in the support, maintenance, and use of one or more major operating systems components or subsystems, such as time-sharing monitors or several access methods. May also design and program specialized utilities or be in charge of such functions as maintaining online system logs and defining cost allocation algorithms. May specialize in computer performance monitoring.

Fully competent to work alone. May specialize in the support of one or a few operating system components or subsystems, such as compiler. Is capable of developing or modifying utilities or installing changes to the operating system. — Systems Programmer

Not a trainee in the usual sense. Has a good background in data processing and knows or is learning assembler language. May have had operations or programming experience. — Systems Programmer "Trainee"

Responsible for maintaining the online and offline libraries of production programs in source and object form. The libraries may include math, scientific, statistical, or other programs, depending on the nature of the work performed by the organization. Also responsible for the production of documentation for those library programs, although the writing, editing, printing, and filing of that documentation may be done by others with this person's concurrence. — Program Librarian

Data Base Administration

Since the data base administration function is still relatively new, and often performed by one person, *the manager position is uncommon.* When it does appear, the manager has all the usual functions of planning, organizing, and scheduling the activities of this section, including assigning personnel to projects or functions. — Manager of Data Base Administration

Analyzes the company's computerized information requirements; *coordinates the data collection and storage* needs of all users; organizes the data; chooses file organizations for shared data; creates data dictionaries; establishes standards for the use of data; and ensures data integrity and security. May provide guidance in the use of data base management systems. — Data Base Administrator

Data Communications / Telecommunications

Responsible for the design of data communications networks and for the installation and *operation of data links.* This section usually works in conjunction with others to evaluate and select communications processors, data transmission protocols, and standards for network operation, including encryption. This section may also be responsible for nondata links, including those for facsimile, message store and forward, voice lines, and office automation. — Data Communications / Telecommunications Manager

Specializes in network design, traffic analysis, and data communications software. Performs simulation and modeling tasks; defines standard block sizes and message formats; and works with persons in other departments on the evaluation and selection of communications processors, telecommunications access methods and protocols, and on specifying data communication links and network operating standards. — Data Communications Analyst

Primarily concerned with hardware selection, operation, and maintenance. Arranges for the installation of modems, multiplexors, and switches; often works directly with the communications carrier in diagnosing problems with the communications facility. Performs diagnostics on inhouse equipment and lines and arranges for service as required. — Technical Control Specialist

Computer Operations

Manager of Computer Operations

Responsible for the operation of the computers, including the scheduling of their operation, assignment of operators, and the monitoring of operations efficiency. Also responsible for scheduling preventive maintenance, calling for emergency maintenance, balancing the work load between available machines or facilities, training the operators, and responding to changes in priority. May also be responsible for the operation of remote sites.

Manager of Data-Processing Operations

This is a *less common position.* This manager is in charge of computer operations, data entry, production control, and post processing; but is *not* in charge of systems analysis or applications programming. May also be in charge of (operating) systems programming.

Lead Computer Operator

May be responsible for the operation of large-scale computers for the duration of *an eight-hour shift,* for the operation of a remote computer site, or for the operation of one computer system at a multisystem site. Assists in scheduling the operations, assigning personnel, and coordinating the activities of the operations group.

Senior Computer Operator

May be responsible for all operations on a medium-scale computer or for console operation of a large machine. In the latter case, will direct the activities of other operators working on the system. May maintain performance and production logs, call for reruns, log problems, and inform management of system failures.

Computer Operator

Assists in running the computers and may operate the central console of a large-scale machine in the absence of the senior operator. Functions usually include mounting and dismounting magnetic media, adding or removing paper from the printers, working with production controls and scheduling staff, and assisting in monitoring and logging functions. Is also capable of running a remote job entry terminal or a small-scale computer.

Computer Operator Trainee

Not qualified to work alone in operation of a computer. Usually assigned to mounting magnetic media, loading printers, or working on a peripheral subsystem, always under direct supervision.

Magnetic Media Librarian

Maintains the library of magnetic tapes, disks, and/or cartridges. Catalogs them, racks them, pulls them on request for operations use, maintains charge-out records, and schedules and performs media cleaning and inspection.

Post-Processing Clerk

Operates forms bursting, decollating, and binding equipment. May deal with microfilm and microfiche output as well as with printed output.

Production Control

Production Control Supervisor

Responsible for setting up and scheduling jobs for processing, including making certain that the correct generation of a file is used, that the correct job control commands are used, that jobs are processed in the correct sequence, and that the processing was performed without error. Usually this function is performed for all jobs in batch environments and for regularly scheduled production jobs in online environments. The supervisor is responsible for assigning personnel to tasks and for scheduling and instructing them.

Lead Production Control Clerk

This person may be responsible for the data control function for the duration of one eight-hour shift, or for the data control function of a single site in a multisite organization. *Usually is in semipermanent charge of a group* of *clerks and spends some time in directing their activities.*

Production Control Clerk

Prepares jobs for processing; attaches or enters the appropriate job commands; and *gathers the output for routing* to the appropriate department. May also log the receipt, processing, and delivery of output from the job.

Production Control Trainee

Is learning the production control function, and works under direct supervision. The work is carefully checked by a higher-level data control staff member.

Data Entry

Data Entry Supervisor

Is responsible for a staff that performs data entry and verification functions. The data entry may be centralized or performed at multiple sites; may employ keypunch, terminal, OCR, or other hardware. The supervisor is responsible for scheduling work, assigning work to operators, maintaining logs, training operators, and ensuring efficient accurate operation.

Lead Data Entry Operator

May be responsible for data entry during an eight-hour shift or may be responsible for data entry at one site in a multisite environment. Assists in assigning work to operators, in maintaining logs, and in training.

Data Entry Operator

Is qualified to operate one or more data entry devices; *requires only general supervision,* and may assist in training new operators.

Data Entry Trainee

Has not yet become fully qualified to operate one type of data entry device.

Other Positions

Staff Consultant/Trainee

Is sometimes found in the (operating) systems programming group; may report to the director instead. Thoroughly knowledgeable in broad aspects of data processing. *Provides guidance to users.* Helps in debugging and in understanding systems messages. Acts as technical liaison for individual users outside the data-processing department. Also teaches the use of languages and systems, and provides aid in conversions. May specialize in scientific processing, commercial processing, or narrower fields, depending on the organization site.

Librarian

Is responsible for the library of technical documentation, including manuals used by programmers, operators, and equipment specifiers. Maintains manuals; usually releases updates to holders of manuals; and acquires documentation from equipment and software suppliers on request.

Word-Processing Supervisor

Responsible for the staff that operates word-processing equipment. This equipment may consist of intelligent typewriters, multistation word-processing systems, or terminals connected to a general-purpose computer. The supervisor is responsible for the efficient and accurate operation of this equipment, for scheduling jobs, for assigning work to operators, for operator training, and for maintaining logs. Usually will understand the programming of this equipment; may be involved in the evaluation and selection of the hardware and software.

Word-Processing Operator

Qualified to operate either intelligent typewriters, word-processing system work stations, or terminals for text-editing/word processing. Is familiar with the command language of the equipment and *works under only general supervision.*

appendix D

using a hand calculator to perform hexadecimal addition and subtraction

To perform hexadecimal addition and subtraction on a hand calculator, you only need to remember the number 84. Always allow two decimal positions for each hexadecimal character and assign values as follows: 0=00, 1=01, . . ., 9=09, A=10, B=11, C=12, D=13, E=14, F=15.

During *addition,* when the sum of two decimal representations of hexadecimal numbers exceeds 15 (F), add 84 to it to perform the carry to the next place. For example, add 1B4D to 1C85.

Place	4	3	2	1	
Enter 1B4D as	1	11	04	13	
Add 1C85	1	12	08	05	
The result is	2	23	12	18	
To cause carry from 1st place			+	84	(since 18 is more than 15)
The result is	2	23	13	02	
To cause carry from 3rd place	+	84	00	00	(since 23 is more than 15)
Which equals	3	07	13	02	
Which translates to	3	7	D	2	Thus 1B4D + 1C85 = 37D2.

For *subtraction,* when a borrow is made from the next higher place, the result is in the range of 85 to 99. This result is corrected by subtracting 84 from that place. Using the preceding example, subtract 1C85 from 37D2.

Place	4	3	2	1	
Enter 37D2 as	3	07	13	02	
Subtract 1C85	1	12	08	05	
The difference is	1	95	04	97	Borrows made in 1st and 3rd places.
To correct the first			−	84	
Which equals	1	95	04	13	
To correct the 3rd place	−	84	00	00	
Which equals	1	11	04	13	
Which translates to	1	B	4	D	Thus 37D2 − 1C85 = 1B4D.

Rules for Negative Results

1. In addition, subtract 84 to perform carry.
2. In subtraction, add 84 in the borrowing place.

appendix E
tables of powers

Table of Powers of Two

Plus	n	Minus
1	0	1.0
2	1	0.5
4	2	0.25
8	3	0.125
16	4	0.0625
32	5	0.03125
64	6	0.01562 5
128	7	0.00781 25
256	8	0.00390 625
512	9	0.00195 3125
1,024	10	0.00097 65625
2,048	11	0.00048 82812 5
4,096	12	0.00024 41406 25
8,192	13	0.00012 20703 125
16,384	14	0.00006 10351 5625
32,768	15	0.00003 05175 78125
65,536	16	0.00001 52587 89062 5
131,072	17	0.00000 76293 94531 25
262,144	18	0.00000 38146 97265 625
524,288	19	0.00000 19073 48632 8125
1,048,576	20	0.00000 09536 74316 40625
2,097,152	21	0.00000 04768 37158 20312 5
4,194,304	22	0.00000 02384 18579 10156 25
8,388,608	23	0.00000 01192 09289 55078 125
16,777,216	24	0.00000 00596 04644 77539 0625
33,554,432	25	0.00000 00298 02322 38769 53125
67,108,864	26	0.00000 00149 01161 19384 76562 5
134,217,728	27	0.00000 00074 50580 59692 38281 25
268,435,456	28	0.00000 00037 25290 29846 19140 625
536,870,912	29	0.00000 00018 62645 14923 09570 3125
1,073,741,824	30	0.00000 00009 31322 57461 54785 15625
2,147,483,648	31	0.00000 00004 65661 28730 77392 57812 5
4,294,967,296	32	0.00000 00002 32830 64365 38696 28906 25
8,589,934,592	33	0.00000 00001 16415 32182 69348 14453 125
17,179,869,184	34	0.00000 00000 58207 66091 34674 07226 5625
34,359,738,368	35	0.00000 00000 29103 83045 67337 03613 28125
68,719,476,736	36	0.00000 00000 14551 91522 83668 51806 64062 5
137,438,953,472	37	0.00000 00000 07275 95761 41834 25903 32031 25
274,877,906,944	38	0.00000 00000 03637 97880 70917 12951 66015 625
549,755,813,888	39	0.00000 00000 01818 98940 35458 56475 83007 8125
1,099,511,627,776	40	0.00000 00000 00909 49470 17729 28237 91503 90625
2,199,023,255,552	41	0.00000 00000 00454 74735 08864 64118 95751 95312 5
4,398,046,511,104	42	0.00000 00000 00227 37367 54432 32059 47875 97656 25
8,796,093,022,208	43	0.00000 00000 00113 68683 77216 16029 73937 98828 125

Table of Powers of Sixteen

16^n	n	16^{-n}
1	0	0.10000 00000 00000 00000 × 10
16	1	0.62500 00000 00000 00000 × 10^{-1}
256	2	0.39062 50000 00000 00000 × 10^{-2}
4 096	3	0.24414 06250 00000 00000 × 10^{-3}
65 536	4	0.15258 78906 25000 00000 × 10^{-4}
1 048 576	5	0.95367 43164 06250 00000 × 10^{-6}
16 777 216	6	0.59604 64477 53906 25000 × 10^{-7}
268 435 456	7	0.37252 90298 46191 40625 × 10^{-8}
4 294 967 296	8	0.23283 06436 53869 62891 × 10^{-9}
68 719 476 736	9	0.14551 91522 83668 51807 × 10^{-10}
1 099 511 627 776	10	0.90949 47017 72928 23792 × 10^{-12}
17 592 186 044 416	11	0.56843 41886 08080 14870 × 10^{-13}
281 474 976 710 656	12	0.35527 13678 80050 09294 × 10^{-14}
4 503 599 627 370 496	13	0.22204 46049 25031 30808 × 10^{-15}
72 057 594 037 927 936	14	0.13877 78780 78144 56755 × 10^{-16}
1 152 921 504 606 846 976	15	0.86736 17379 88403 54721 × 10^{-18}

appendix F hexadecimal tables

The following tables aid in converting hexadecimal values to decimal values, or the reverse.

Direct Conversion Table

This table provides direct conversion of decimal and hexadecimal numbers in these ranges:

Hexadecimal	*Decimal*
000 to FFF	0000 to 4095

To convert numbers outside these ranges, use the hexadecimal and decimal conversion tables that follow the Direct Conversion Table in this Appendix.

	0	1	2	3	4	5	6	7	8	9	A	B	C	D	E	F
00_	0000	0001	0002	0003	0004	0005	0006	0007	0008	0009	0010	0011	0012	0013	0014	0015
01_	0016	0017	0018	0019	0020	0021	0022	0023	0024	0025	0026	0027	0028	0029	0030	0031
02_	0032	0033	0034	0035	0036	0037	0038	0039	0040	0041	0042	0043	0044	0045	0046	0047
03_	0048	0049	0050	0051	0052	0053	0054	0055	0056	0057	0058	0059	0060	0061	0062	0063
04_	0064	0065	0066	0067	0068	0069	0070	0071	0072	0073	0074	0075	0076	0077	0078	0079
05_	0080	0081	0082	0083	0084	0085	0086	0087	0088	0089	0090	0091	0092	0093	0094	0095
06_	0096	0097	0098	0099	0100	0101	0102	0103	0104	0105	0106	0107	0108	0109	0110	0111
07_	0112	0113	0114	0115	0116	0117	0118	0119	0120	0121	0122	0123	0124	0125	0126	0127
08_	0128	0129	0130	0131	0132	0133	0134	0135	0136	0137	0138	0139	0140	0141	0142	0143
09_	0144	0145	0146	0147	0148	0149	0150	0151	0152	0153	0154	0155	0156	0157	0158	0159
0A_	0160	0161	0162	0163	0164	0165	0166	0167	0168	0169	0170	0171	0172	0173	0174	0175
0B_	0176	0177	0178	0179	0180	0181	0182	0183	0184	0185	0186	0187	0188	0189	0190	0191
0C_	0192	0193	0194	0195	0196	0197	0198	0199	0200	0201	0202	0203	0204	0205	0206	0207
0D_	0208	0209	0210	0211	0212	0213	0214	0215	0216	0217	0218	0219	0220	0221	0222	0223
0E_	0224	0225	0226	0227	0228	0229	0230	0231	0232	0233	0234	0235	0236	0237	0238	0239
0F_	0240	0241	0242	0243	0244	0245	0246	0247	0248	0249	0250	0251	0252	0253	0254	0255
10_	0256	0257	0258	0259	0260	0261	0262	0263	0264	0265	0266	0267	0268	0269	0270	0271
11_	0272	0273	0274	0275	0276	0277	0278	0279	0280	0281	0282	0283	0284	0285	0286	0287
12_	0288	0289	0290	0291	0292	0293	0294	0295	0296	0297	0298	0299	0300	0301	0302	0303
13_	0304	0305	0306	0307	0308	0309	0310	0311	0312	0313	0314	0315	0316	0317	0318	0319
14_	0320	0321	0322	0323	0324	0325	0326	0327	0328	0329	0330	0331	0332	0333	0334	0335
15_	0336	0337	0338	0339	0340	0341	0342	0343	0344	0345	0346	0347	0348	0349	0350	0351
16_	0352	0353	0354	0355	0356	0357	0358	0359	0360	0361	0362	0363	0364	0365	0366	0367
17_	0368	0369	0370	0371	0372	0373	0374	0375	0376	0377	0378	0379	0380	0381	0382	0383
18_	0384	0385	0386	0387	0388	0389	0390	0391	0392	0393	0394	0395	0396	0397	0398	0399
19_	0400	0401	0402	0403	0404	0405	0406	0407	0408	0409	0410	0411	0412	0413	0414	0415
1A_	0416	0417	0418	0419	0420	0421	0422	0423	0424	0425	0426	0427	0428	0429	0430	0431
1B_	0432	0433	0434	0435	0436	0437	0438	0439	0440	0441	0442	0443	0444	0445	0446	0447
1C_	0448	0449	0450	0451	0452	0453	0454	0455	0456	0457	0458	0459	0460	0461	0462	0463
1D_	0464	0465	0466	0467	0468	0469	0470	0471	0472	0473	0474	0475	0476	0477	0478	0479
1E_	0480	0481	0482	0483	0484	0485	0486	0487	0488	0489	0490	0491	0492	0493	0494	0495
1F_	0496	0497	0498	0499	0500	0501	0502	0503	0504	0505	0506	0507	0508	0509	0510	0511

	0	1	2	3	4	5	6	7	8	9	A	B	C	D	E	F
20_	0512	0513	0514	0515	0516	0517	0518	0519	0520	0521	0522	0523	0524	0525	0526	0527
21_	0528	0529	0530	0531	0532	0533	0534	0535	0536	0537	0538	0539	0540	0541	0542	0543
22_	0544	0545	0546	0547	0548	0549	0550	0551	0552	0553	0554	0555	0556	0557	0558	0559
23_	0560	0561	0562	0563	0564	0565	0566	0567	0568	0569	0570	0571	0572	0573	0574	0575
24_	0576	0577	0578	0579	0580	0581	0582	0583	0584	0585	0586	0587	0588	0589	0590	0591
25_	0592	0593	0594	0595	0596	0597	0598	0599	0600	0601	0602	0603	0604	0605	0606	0607
26_	0608	0609	0610	0611	0612	0613	0614	0615	0616	0617	0618	0619	0620	0621	0622	0623
27_	0624	0625	0626	0627	0628	0629	0630	0631	0632	0633	0634	0635	0636	0637	0638	0639
28_	0640	0641	0642	0643	0644	0645	0646	0647	0648	0649	0650	0651	0652	0653	0654	0655
29_	0656	0657	0658	0659	0660	0661	0662	0663	0664	0665	0666	0667	0668	0669	0670	0671
2A_	0672	0673	0674	0675	0676	0677	0678	0679	0680	0681	0682	0683	0684	0685	0686	0687
2B_	0688	0689	0690	0691	0692	0693	0694	0695	0696	0697	0698	0699	0700	0701	0702	0703
2C_	0704	0705	0706	0707	0708	0709	0710	0711	0712	0713	0714	0715	0716	0717	0718	0719
2D_	0720	0721	0722	0723	0724	0725	0726	0727	0728	0729	0730	0731	0732	0733	0734	0735
2E_	0736	0737	0738	0739	0740	0741	0742	0743	0744	0745	0746	0747	0748	0749	0750	0751
2F_	0752	0753	0754	0755	0756	0757	0758	0759	0760	0761	0762	0763	0764	0765	0766	0767
30_	0768	0769	0770	0771	0772	0773	0774	0775	0776	0777	0778	0779	0780	0781	0782	0783
31_	0784	0785	0786	0787	0788	0789	0790	0791	0792	0793	0794	0795	0796	0797	0798	0799
32_	0800	0801	0802	0803	0804	0805	0806	0807	0808	0809	0810	0811	0812	0813	0814	0815
33_	0816	0817	0818	0819	0820	0821	0822	0823	0824	0825	0826	0827	0828	0829	0830	0831
34_	0832	0833	0834	0835	0836	0837	0838	0839	0840	0841	0842	0843	0844	0845	0846	0847
35_	0848	0849	0850	0851	0852	0853	0854	0855	0856	0857	0858	0859	0860	0861	0862	0863
36_	0864	0865	0866	0867	0868	0869	0870	0871	0872	0873	0874	0875	0876	0877	0878	0879
37_	0880	0881	0882	0883	0884	0885	0886	0887	0888	0889	0890	0891	0892	0893	0894	0895
38_	0896	0897	0898	0899	0900	0901	0902	0903	0904	0905	0906	0907	0908	0909	0910	0911
39_	0912	0913	0914	0915	0916	0917	0918	0919	0920	0921	0922	0923	0924	0925	0926	0927
3A_	0928	0929	0930	0931	0932	0933	0934	0935	0936	0937	0938	0939	0940	0941	0942	0943
3B_	0944	0945	0946	0947	0948	0949	0950	0951	0952	0953	0954	0955	0956	0957	0958	0959
3C_	0960	0961	0962	0963	0964	0965	0966	0967	0968	0969	0970	0971	0972	0973	0974	0975
3D_	0976	0977	0978	0979	0980	0981	0982	0983	0984	0985	0986	0987	0988	0989	0990	0991
3E_	0992	0993	0994	0995	0996	0997	0998	0999	1000	1001	1002	1003	1004	1005	1006	1007
3F_	1008	1009	1010	1011	1012	1013	1014	1015	1016	1017	1018	1019	1020	1021	1022	1023

	0	1	2	3	4	5	6	7	8	9	A	B	C	D	E	F
40_	1024	1025	1026	1027	1028	1029	1030	1031	1032	1033	1034	1035	1036	1037	1038	1039
41_	1040	1041	1042	1043	1044	1045	1046	1047	1048	1049	1050	1051	1052	1053	1054	1055
42_	1056	1057	1058	1059	1060	1061	1062	1063	1064	1065	1066	1067	1068	1069	1070	1071
43_	1072	1073	1074	1075	1076	1077	1078	1079	1080	1081	1082	1083	1084	1085	1086	1087
44_	1088	1089	1090	1091	1092	1093	1094	1095	1096	1097	1098	1099	1100	1101	1102	1103
45_	1104	1105	1106	1107	1108	1109	1110	1111	1112	1113	1114	1115	1116	1117	1118	1119
46_	1120	1121	1122	1123	1124	1125	1126	1127	1128	1129	1130	1131	1132	1133	1134	1135
47_	1136	1137	1138	1139	1140	1141	1142	1143	1144	1145	1146	1147	1148	1149	1150	1151
48_	1152	1153	1154	1155	1156	1157	1158	1159	1160	1161	1162	1163	1164	1165	1166	1167
49_	1168	1169	1170	1171	1172	1173	1174	1175	1176	1177	1178	1179	1180	1181	1182	1183
4A_	1184	1185	1186	1187	1188	1189	1190	1191	1192	1193	1194	1195	1196	1197	1198	1199
4B_	1200	1201	1202	1203	1204	1205	1206	1207	1208	1209	1210	1211	1212	1213	1214	1215
4C_	1216	1217	1218	1219	1220	1221	1222	1223	1224	1225	1226	1227	1228	1229	1230	1231
4D_	1232	1233	1234	1235	1236	1237	1238	1239	1240	1241	1242	1243	1244	1245	1246	1247
4E_	1248	1249	1250	1251	1252	1253	1254	1255	1256	1257	1258	1259	1260	1261	1262	1263
4F_	1264	1265	1266	1267	1268	1269	1270	1271	1272	1273	1274	1275	1276	1277	1278	1279
50_	1280	1281	1282	1283	1284	1285	1286	1287	1288	1289	1290	1291	1292	1293	1294	1295
51_	1296	1297	1298	1299	1300	1301	1302	1303	1304	1305	1306	1307	1308	1309	1310	1311
52_	1312	1313	1314	1315	1316	1317	1318	1319	1320	1321	1322	1323	1324	1325	1326	1327
53_	1328	1329	1330	1331	1332	1333	1334	1335	1336	1337	1338	1339	1340	1341	1342	1343
54_	1344	1345	1346	1347	1348	1349	1350	1351	1352	1353	1354	1355	1356	1357	1358	1359
55_	1360	1361	1362	1363	1364	1365	1366	1367	1368	1369	1370	1371	1372	1373	1374	1375
56_	1376	1377	1378	1379	1380	1381	1382	1383	1384	1385	1386	1387	1388	1389	1390	1391
57_	1392	1393	1394	1395	1396	1397	1398	1399	1400	1401	1402	1403	1404	1405	1406	1407
58_	1408	1409	1410	1411	1412	1413	1414	1415	1416	1417	1418	1419	1420	1421	1422	1423
59_	1424	1425	1426	1427	1428	1429	1430	1431	1432	1433	1434	1435	1436	1437	1438	1439
5A_	1440	1441	1442	1443	1444	1445	1446	1447	1448	1449	1450	1451	1452	1453	1454	1455
5B_	1456	1457	1458	1459	1460	1461	1462	1463	1464	1465	1466	1467	1468	1469	1470	1471
5C_	1472	1473	1474	1475	1476	1477	1478	1479	1480	1481	1482	1483	1484	1485	1486	1487
5D_	1488	1489	1490	1491	1492	1493	1494	1495	1496	1497	1498	1499	1500	1501	1502	1503
5E_	1504	1505	1506	1507	1508	1509	1510	1511	1512	1513	1514	1515	1516	1517	1518	1519
5F_	1520	1521	1522	1523	1524	1525	1526	1527	1528	1529	1530	1531	1532	1533	1534	1535

	0	1	2	3	4	5	6	7	8	9	A	B	C	D	E	F
60_	1536	1537	1538	1539	1540	1541	1542	1543	1544	1545	1546	1547	1548	1549	1550	1551
61_	1552	1553	1554	1555	1556	1557	1558	1559	1560	1561	1562	1563	1564	1565	1566	1567
62_	1568	1569	1570	1571	1572	1573	1574	1575	1576	1577	1578	1579	1580	1581	1582	1583
63_	1584	1585	1586	1587	1588	1589	1590	1591	1592	1593	1594	1595	1596	1597	1598	1599
64_	1600	1601	1602	1603	1604	1605	1606	1607	1608	1609	1610	1611	1612	1613	1614	1615
65	1616	1617	1618	1619	1620	1621	1622	1623	1624	1625	1626	1627	1628	1629	1630	1631
66_	1632	1033	1634	1635	1636	1637	1638	1639	1640	1641	1642	1643	1644	1645	1646	1647
67_	1648	1649	1650	1651	1652	1653	1654	1655	1656	1657	1658	1659	1660	1661	1662	1663
68_	1664	1665	1666	1667	1668	1669	1670	1671	1672	1673	1674	1675	1676	1677	1678	1679
69_	1680	1681	1682	1683	1684	1685	1686	1687	1688	1689	1090	1691	1692	1693	1694	1695
6A_	1696	1697	1698	1699	1700	1701	1702	1703	1704	1705	1706	1707	1708	1700	1710	1711
6B_	1712	1713	1714	1715	1716	1717	1718	1719	1720	1721	1722	1723	1724	1725	1726	1727
6C_	1728	1729	1730	1731	1732	1733	1734	1735	1736	1737	1738	1739	1740	1741	1742	1743
6D_	1744	1745	1746	1747	1748	1749	1750	1751	1752	1753	1754	1755	1756	1757	1758	1759
6E_	1760	1761	1762	1763	1764	1765	1766	1767	1768	1769	1770	1771	1772	1773	1774	1775
6F_	1776	1777	1778	1779	1780	1781	1782	1783	1784	1785	1786	1787	1788	1789	1790	1791
70_	1792	1793	1794	1795	1796	1797	1798	1799	1800	1801	1802	1803	1804	1805	1806	1807
71_	1808	1809	1810	1811	1812	1813	1814	1815	1816	1817	1818	1819	1820	1821	1822	1823
72_	1824	1825	1826	1827	1828	1829	1830	1831	1832	1833	1834	1835	1836	1837	1838	1839
73_	1840	1841	1842	1843	1844	1845	1846	1847	1848	1849	1850	1851	1852	1853	1854	1855
74_	1856	1857	1858	1859	1860	1861	1862	1863	1864	1865	1866	1867	1868	1869	1870	1871
75_	1872	1873	1874	1875	1876	1877	1878	1879	1880	1881	1882	1883	1884	1885	1886	1887
76_	1888	1889	1890	1891	1892	1893	1894	1895	1896	1897	1898	1899	1900	1901	1902	1903
77_	1904	1905	1906	1907	1908	1909	1910	1911	1912	1913	1914	1915	1916	1917	1918	1919
78_	1920	1921	1922	1923	1924	1925	1926	1927	1928	1929	1930	1931	1932	1933	1934	1935
79_	1936	1937	1938	1939	1940	1941	1942	1943	1944	1945	1946	1947	1948	1949	1950	1951
7A_	1952	1953	1954	1955	1956	1957	1958	1959	1960	1961	1962	1963	1964	1965	1966	1967
7B_	1968	1969	1970	1971	1072	1973	1974	1975	1976	1977	1978	1979	1980	1981	1982	1983
7C_	1984	1985	1986	1987	1988	1989	1990	1991	1992	1993	1994	1995	1996	1997	1998	1999
7D_	2000	2001	2002	2003	2004	2005	2006	2007	2008	2009	2010	2011	2012	2013	2014	2015
7E_	2016	2017	2018	2019	2020	2021	2022	2023	2024	2025	2026	2027	2028	2020	2030	2031
7F_	2032	2033	2034	2035	2036	2037	2038	2039	2040	2041	2042	2043	2044	2045	2046	2047

	0	1	2	3	4	5	6	7	8	9	A	B	C	D	E	F
80_	2048	2049	2050	2051	2052	2053	2054	2055	2056	2057	2058	2059	2060	2061	2062	2063
81_	2064	2065	2066	2067	2068	2069	2070	2071	2072	2073	2074	2075	2076	2077	2078	2079
82_	2080	2081	2082	2083	2084	2085	2086	2087	2088	2089	2090	2091	2092	2093	2094	2095
83_	2096	2097	2098	2099	2100	2101	2102	2103	2104	2105	2106	2107	2108	2109	2110	2111
84_	2112	2113	2114	2115	2116	2117	2118	2119	2120	2121	2122	2123	2124	2125	2126	2127
85_	2128	2129	2130	2131	2132	2133	2134	2135	2136	2137	2138	2139	2140	2141	2142	2143
86_	2144	2145	2146	2147	2148	2149	2150	2151	2152	2153	2154	2155	2156	2157	2158	2159
87_	2160	2161	2162	2163	2164	2165	2166	2167	2168	2169	2170	2171	2172	2173	2174	2175
88_	2176	2177	2178	2179	2180	2181	2182	2183	2184	2185	2186	2187	2188	2189	2190	2191
89_	2192	2193	2194	2195	2196	2197	2198	2199	2200	2201	2202	2203	2204	2205	2206	2207
8A_	2208	2209	2210	2211	2212	2213	2214	2215	2216	2217	2218	2219	2220	2221	2222	2223
8B_	2224	2225	2226	2227	2228	2229	2230	2231	2232	2233	2234	2235	2236	2237	2238	2239
8C_	2240	2241	2242	2243	2244	2245	2246	2247	2248	2249	2250	2251	2252	2253	2254	2255
8D_	2256	2257	2258	2259	2260	2261	2262	2263	2264	2265	2266	2267	2268	2269	2270	2271
8E_	2272	2273	2274	2275	2276	2277	2278	2279	2280	2281	2282	2283	2284	2285	2286	2287
8F_	2288	2289	2290	2291	2292	2293	2294	2295	2296	2297	2298	2299	2300	2301	2302	2303
90_	2304	2305	2306	2307	2308	2309	2310	2311	2312	2313	2314	2315	2316	2317	2318	2319
91_	2320	2321	2322	2323	2324	2325	2326	2327	2328	2329	2330	2331	2332	2333	2334	2335
92_	2336	2337	2338	2339	2340	2341	2342	2343	2344	2345	2346	2347	2348	2349	2350	2351
93_	2352	2353	2354	2355	2356	2357	2358	2359	2360	2361	2362	2363	2364	2365	2366	2367
94_	2368	2369	2370	2371	2372	2373	2374	2375	2376	2377	2378	2379	2380	2381	2382	2383
95_	2384	2385	2386	2387	2388	2389	2390	2391	2392	2393	2394	2395	2396	2397	2398	2399
96_	2400	2401	2402	2403	2404	2405	2406	2407	2408	2409	2410	2411	2412	2413	2414	2415
97_	2416	2417	2418	2419	2420	2421	2422	2423	2424	2425	2426	2427	2428	2429	2430	2431
98_	2432	2433	2434	2435	2436	2437	2438	2439	2440	2441	2442	2443	2444	2445	2446	2447
99_	2448	2449	2450	2451	2452	2453	2454	2455	2456	2457	2458	2459	2460	2461	2462	2463
9A_	2464	2465	2466	2467	2468	2469	2470	2471	2472	2473	2474	2475	2476	2477	2478	2479
9B_	2480	2481	2482	2483	2484	2485	2486	2487	2488	2489	2490	2491	2492	2493	2494	2495
9C_	2496	2497	2498	2499	2500	2501	2502	2503	2504	2505	2506	2507	2508	2509	2510	2511
9D_	2512	2513	2514	2515	2516	2517	2518	2519	2520	2521	2522	2523	2524	2525	2526	2527
9E_	2528	2529	2530	2531	2532	2533	2534	2535	2536	2537	2538	2539	2540	2541	2542	2543
9F_	2544	2545	2546	2547	2548	2549	2550	2551	2552	2553	2554	2555	2556	2557	2558	2559

	0	1	2	3	4	5	6	7	8	9	A	B	C	D	E	F
A0_	2560	2561	2562	2563	2564	2565	2566	2567	2568	2569	2570	2571	2572	2573	2574	2575
A1_	2576	2577	2578	2579	2580	2581	2582	2583	2584	2585	2586	2587	2588	2589	2590	2591
A2_	2592	2593	2594	2595	2596	2597	2598	2599	2600	2601	2602	2603	2604	2605	2606	2607
A3_	2608	2609	2610	2611	2612	2613	2614	2615	2616	2617	2618	2619	2620	2621	2622	2623
A4_	2624	2625	2626	2627	2628	2629	2630	2631	2632	2633	2634	2635	2636	2637	2638	2639
A5_	2640	2641	2642	2643	2644	2645	2646	2647	2648	2649	2650	2651	2652	2653	2654	2655
A6_	2656	2657	2658	2659	2660	2661	2662	2663	2664	2665	2666	2667	2668	2669	2670	2671
A7_	2672	2673	2674	2675	2676	2677	2678	2679	2680	2681	2682	2683	2684	2685	2686	2687
A8_	2688	2689	2690	2691	2692	2693	2694	2695	2696	2697	2698	2699	2700	2701	2702	2703
A9_	2704	2705	2706	2707	2708	2709	2710	2711	2712	2713	2714	2715	2716	2717	2718	2719
AA_	2720	2721	2722	2723	2724	2725	2726	2727	2728	2729	2730	2731	2732	2733	2734	2735
AB_	2736	2737	2738	2739	2740	2741	2742	2743	2744	2745	2746	2747	2748	2749	2750	2751
AC_	2752	2753	2754	2755	2756	2757	2758	2759	2760	2761	2762	2763	2764	2765	2766	2767
AD_	2768	2769	2770	2771	2772	2773	2774	2775	2776	2777	2778	2779	2780	2781	2782	2783
AE_	2784	2785	2786	2787	2788	2789	2790	2791	2792	2793	2794	2795	2796	2797	2798	2799
AF_	2800	2801	2802	2803	2804	2805	2806	2807	2808	2809	2810	2811	2812	2813	2814	2815
B0_	2816	2817	2818	2819	2820	2821	2822	2823	2824	2825	2826	2827	2828	2829	2830	2831
B1_	2832	2833	2834	2835	2836	2837	2838	2839	2840	2841	2842	2843	2844	2845	2846	2847
B2_	2848	2849	2850	2851	2852	2853	2854	2855	2856	2857	2858	2859	2860	2861	2862	2863
B3_	2864	2865	2866	2867	2868	2869	2870	2871	2872	2873	2874	2875	2876	2877	2878	2879
B4_	2880	2881	2882	2883	2884	2885	2886	2887	2888	2889	2890	2891	2892	2893	2894	2895
B5_	2896	2897	2898	2899	2900	2901	2902	2903	2904	2905	2906	2907	2908	2909	2910	2911
B6_	2912	2913	2914	2915	2916	2917	2918	2919	2920	2921	2922	2923	2924	2925	2926	2927
B7_	2928	2929	2930	2931	2932	2933	2934	2935	2936	2937	2938	2939	2940	2941	2942	2943
B8_	2944	2945	2946	2947	2948	2949	2950	2951	2952	2953	2954	2955	2956	2957	2958	2959
B9_	2960	2961	2962	2963	2964	2965	2966	2967	2968	2969	2970	2971	2972	2973	2974	2975
BA_	2976	2977	2978	2979	2980	2981	2982	2983	2984	2985	2986	2987	2988	2989	2990	2991
BB_	2992	2993	2994	2995	2996	2997	2998	2999	3000	3001	3002	3003	3004	3005	3006	3007
BC_	3008	3009	3010	3011	3012	3013	3014	3015	3016	3017	3018	3019	3020	3021	3022	3023
BD_	3024	3025	3026	3027	3028	3029	3030	3031	3032	3033	3034	3035	3036	3037	3038	3039
BE_	3040	3041	3042	3043	3044	3045	3046	3047	3048	3049	3050	3051	3052	3053	3054	3055
BF_	3056	3057	3058	3059	3060	3061	3062	3063	3064	3065	3066	3067	3068	3069	3070	3071

	0	1	2	3	4	5	6	7	8	9	A	B	C	D	E	F
C0_	3072	3073	3074	3075	3076	3077	3078	3079	3080	3081	3082	3083	3084	3085	3086	3087
C1_	3088	3089	3090	3091	3092	3093	3094	3095	3096	3097	3098	3099	3100	3101	3102	3103
C2_	3104	3105	3106	3107	3108	3109	3110	3111	3112	3113	3114	3115	3116	3117	3118	3119
C3_	3120	3121	3122	3123	3124	3125	3126	3127	3128	3129	3130	3131	3132	3133	3134	3135
C4_	3136	3137	3138	3139	3140	3141	3142	3143	3144	3145	3146	3147	3148	3149	3150	3151
C5_	3152	3153	3154	3155	3156	3157	3158	3159	3160	3161	3162	3163	3164	3165	3166	3167
C6_	3168	3169	3170	3171	3172	3173	3174	3175	3176	3177	3178	3179	3180	3181	3182	3183
C7_	3184	3185	3186	3187	3188	3189	3190	3191	3192	3193	3194	3195	3196	3197	3198	3199
C8_	3200	3201	3202	3203	3204	3205	3206	3207	3208	3209	3210	3211	3212	3213	3214	3215
C9_	3216	3217	3218	3219	3220	3221	3222	3223	3224	3225	3226	3227	3228	3229	3230	3231
CA_	3232	3233	3234	3235	3236	3237	3238	3239	3240	3241	3242	3243	3244	3245	3246	3247
CB_	3248	3249	3250	3251	3252	3253	3254	3255	3256	3257	3258	3259	3260	3261	3262	3263
CC_	3264	3265	3266	3267	3268	3269	3270	3271	3272	3273	3274	3275	3276	3277	3278	3279
CD_	3280	3281	3282	3283	3284	3285	3286	3287	3288	3289	3290	3291	3292	3293	3294	3295
CE_	3296	3297	3298	3299	3300	3301	3302	3303	3304	3305	3306	3307	3308	3309	3310	3311
CF_	3312	3313	3314	3315	3316	3317	3318	3319	3320	3321	3322	3323	3324	3325	3326	3327
D0_	3328	3329	3330	3331	3332	3333	3334	3335	3336	3337	3338	3339	3340	3341	3342	3343
D1_	3344	3345	3346	3347	3348	3349	3350	3351	3352	3353	3354	3355	3356	3357	3358	3359
D2_	3360	3361	3362	3363	3364	3365	3366	3367	3368	3369	3370	3371	3372	3373	3374	3375
D3_	3376	3377	3378	3379	3380	3381	3382	3383	3384	3385	3386	3387	3388	3389	3390	3391
D4_	3392	3393	3394	3395	3396	3397	3398	3399	3400	3401	3402	3403	3404	3405	3406	3407
D5_	3408	3409	3410	3411	3412	3413	3414	3415	3416	3417	3418	3419	3420	3421	3422	3423
D6_	3424	3425	3426	3427	3428	3429	3430	3431	3432	3433	3434	3435	3436	3437	3438	3439
D7_	3440	3441	3442	3443	3444	3445	3446	3447	3448	3449	3450	3451	3452	3453	3454	3455
D8_	3456	3457	3458	3459	3460	3461	3462	3463	3464	3465	3466	3467	3468	3469	3470	3471
D9_	3472	3473	3474	3475	3476	3477	3478	3479	3480	3481	3482	3483	3484	3485	3486	3487
DA_	3488	3489	3490	3491	3492	3493	3494	3495	3496	3497	3498	3499	3500	3501	3502	3503
DB_	3504	3505	3506	3507	3508	3509	3510	3511	3512	3513	3514	3515	3516	3517	3518	3519
DC_	3520	3521	3522	3523	3524	3525	3526	3527	3528	3529	3530	3531	3532	3533	3534	3535
DD_	3536	3537	3538	3539	3540	3541	3542	3543	3544	3545	3546	3547	3548	3549	3550	3551
DE_	3552	3553	3554	3555	3556	3557	3558	3559	3560	3561	3562	3563	3564	3565	3566	3567
DF_	3568	3569	3570	3571	3572	3573	3574	3575	3576	3577	3578	3579	3580	3581	3582	3583

	0	1	2	3	4	5	6	7	8	9	A	B	C	D	E	F
E0_	3584	3585	3586	3587	3588	3589	3590	3591	3592	3593	3594	3595	3596	3597	3598	3599
E1_	3600	3601	3602	3603	3604	3605	3606	3607	3608	3609	3610	3611	3612	3613	3614	3615
E2_	3616	3617	3618	3619	3620	3621	3622	3623	3624	3625	3626	3627	3628	3629	3630	3631
E3_	3632	3633	3634	3635	3636	3637	3638	3639	3640	3641	3642	3643	3644	3645	3646	3647
E4_	3648	3649	3650	3651	3652	3653	3654	3655	3656	3657	3658	3659	3660	3661	3662	3663
E5_	3664	3665	3666	3667	3668	3669	3670	3671	3672	3673	3674	3675	3676	3677	3678	3679
E6_	3680	3681	3682	3683	3684	3685	3686	3687	3688	3689	3690	3691	3692	3693	3694	3695
E7_	3696	3697	3698	3699	3700	3701	3702	3703	3704	3705	3706	3707	3708	3709	3710	3711
E8_	3712	3713	3714	3715	3716	3717	3718	3719	3720	3721	3722	3723	3724	3725	3726	3727
E9_	3728	3729	3730	3731	3732	3733	3734	3735	3736	3737	3738	3739	3740	3741	3742	3743
EA_	3744	3745	3746	3747	3748	3749	3750	3751	3752	3753	3754	3755	3756	3757	3758	3759
EB_	3760	3761	3762	3763	3764	3765	3766	3767	3768	3769	3770	3771	3772	3773	3774	3775
EC_	3776	3777	3778	3779	3780	3781	3782	3783	3784	3785	3786	3787	3788	3789	3790	3791
ED_	3792	3793	3794	3795	3796	3797	3798	3799	3800	3801	3802	3803	3804	3805	3806	3807
EE_	3808	3809	3810	3811	3812	3813	3814	3815	3816	3817	3818	3819	3820	3821	3822	3823
EF_	3824	3825	3826	3827	3828	3829	3830	3831	3832	3833	3834	3835	3836	3837	3838	3839
F0_	3840	3841	3842	3843	3844	3845	3846	3847	3848	3849	3850	3851	3852	3853	3854	3855
F1_	3856	3857	3858	3859	3860	3861	3862	3863	3864	3865	3866	3867	3868	3869	3870	3871
F2_	3872	3873	3874	3875	3876	3877	3878	3879	3880	3881	3882	3883	3884	3885	3886	3887
F3_	3888	3889	3890	3891	3892	3893	3894	3895	3896	3897	3898	3899	3900	3901	3902	3903
F4_	3904	3905	3906	3907	3908	3909	3910	3911	3912	3913	3914	3915	3916	3917	3918	3919
F5_	3920	3921	3922	3923	3924	3925	3926	3927	3928	3929	3930	3931	3932	3933	3934	3935
F6_	3936	3937	3938	3939	3940	3941	3942	3943	3944	3945	3946	3947	3948	3949	3950	3951
F7_	3952	3953	3954	3955	3956	3957	3958	3959	3960	3961	3962	3963	3964	3965	3966	3967
F8_	3968	3969	3970	3971	3972	3973	3974	3975	3976	3977	3978	3979	3980	3981	3982	3983
F9_	3984	3985	3986	3987	3988	3989	3990	3991	3992	3993	3994	3995	3996	3997	3998	3999
FA_	4000	4001	4002	4003	4004	4005	4006	4007	4008	4009	4010	4011	4012	4013	4014	4015
FB_	4016	4017	4018	4019	4020	4021	4022	4023	4024	4025	4026	4027	4028	4029	4030	4031
FC_	4032	4033	4034	4035	4036	4037	4038	4039	4040	4041	4042	4043	4044	4045	4046	4047
FD_	4048	4049	4050	4051	4052	4053	4054	4055	4056	4057	4058	4059	4060	4061	4062	4063
FE_	4064	4065	4066	4067	4068	4069	4070	4071	4072	4073	4074	4075	4076	4077	4078	4079
FF_	4080	4081	4082	4083	4084	4085	4086	4087	4088	4089	4090	4091	4092	4093	4094	4095

Hexadecimal and Decimal Integer Conversion Table

HALFWORD								HALFWORD							
BYTE				BYTE				BYTE				BYTE			
BITS: 0123		4567		0123		4567		0123		4567		0123		4567	
Hex	Decimal	Hex	Decimal	Hex	Decimal	Hex	Decimal	Hex	Decimal	Hex	Decimal	Hex	Decimal	Hex	Decimal
0	0	0	0	0	0	0	0	0	0	0	0	0	0	0	0
1	268,435,456	1	16,777,216	1	1,048,576	1	65,536	1	4,096	1	256	1	16	1	1
2	536,870,912	2	33,554,432	2	2,097,152	2	131,072	2	8,192	2	512	2	32	2	2
3	805,306,368	3	50,331,648	3	3,145,728	3	196,608	3	12,288	3	768	3	48	3	3
4	1,073,741,824	4	67,108,864	4	4,194,304	4	262,144	4	16,384	4	1,024	4	64	4	4
5	1,342,177,280	5	83,886,080	5	5,242,880	5	327,680	5	20,480	5	1,280	5	80	5	5
6	1,610,612,736	6	100,663,296	6	6,291,456	6	393,216	6	24,576	6	1,536	6	96	6	6
7	1,879,048,192	7	117,440,512	7	7,340,032	7	458,752	7	28,672	7	1,792	7	112	7	7
8	2,147,483,648	8	134,217,728	8	8,388,608	8	524,288	8	32,768	8	2,048	8	128	8	8
9	2,415,919,104	9	150,994,944	9	9,437,184	9	589,824	9	36,864	9	2,304	9	144	9	9
A	2,684,354,560	A	167,772,160	A	10,485,760	A	655,360	A	40,960	A	2,560	A	160	A	10
B	2,952,790,016	B	184,549,376	B	11,534,336	B	720,896	B	45,056	B	2,816	B	176	B	11
C	3,221,225,472	C	201,326,592	C	12,582,912	C	786,432	C	49,152	C	3,072	C	192	C	12
D	3,489,660,928	D	218,103,808	D	13,631,488	D	851,968	D	53,248	D	3,328	D	208	D	13
E	3,758,096,384	E	234,881,024	E	14,680,064	E	917,504	E	57,344	E	3,584	E	224	E	14
F	4,026,531,840	F	251,658,240	F	15,728,640	F	983,040	F	61,440	F	3,840	F	240	F	15
8		7		6		5		4		3		2		1	

TO CONVERT HEXADECIMAL TO DECIMAL

1. Locate the column of decimal numbers corresponding to the left-most digit or letter of the hexadecimal; select from this column and record the number that corresponds to the position of the hexadecimal digit or letter.
2. Repeat step 1 for the next (second from the left) position.
3. Repeat step 1 for the units (third from the left) position.
4. Add the numbers selected from the table to form the decimal number.

EXAMPLE	
Conversion of Hexadecimal Value	D34
1. D	3328
2. 3	48
3. 4	4
4. Decimal	3380

TO CONVERT DECIMAL TO HEXADECIMAL

1. (a) Select from the table the highest decimal number that is equal to or less than the number to be converted.
   (b) Record the hexadecimal of the column containing the selected number.
   (c) Subtract the selected decimal from the number to be converted.
2. Using the remainder from step 1(c) repeat all of step 1 to develop the second position of the hexadecimal (and a remainder).
3. Using the remainder from step 2 repeat all of step 1 to develop the units position of the hexadecimal.
4. Combine terms to form the hexadecimal number.

EXAMPLE	
Conversion of Decimal Value	3380
1. D	-3328
	52
2. 3	-48
	4
3. 4	-4
4. Hexadecimal	D34

To convert integer numbers greater than the capacity of table, use the techniques below:

HEXADECIMAL TO DECIMAL

Successive cumulative multiplication from left to right, adding units position.

Example: $D34_{16} = 3380_{10}$

```
D =   13
     x16
     208
3 =  + 3
     211
     x16
    3376
4 =   +4
    3380
```

DECIMAL TO HEXADECIMAL

Divide and collect the remainder in reverse order.

Example: $3380_{10} = X_{16}$

```
16 | 3380        remainder
16 | 211    ->  4
16 | 13     ->  3
            ->  D

3380₁₀ = D34₁₆
```

$3380_{10} = D34_{16}$

POWERS OF 16 TABLE

Example: $268,435,456_{10} = (2.68435456 \times 10^8)_{10} = 1000\ 0000_{16} = (10^7)_{16}$

16^n	n
1	0
16	1
256	2
4 096	3
65 536	4
1 048 576	5
16 777 216	6
268 435 456	7
4 294 967 296	8
68 719 476 736	9
1 099 511 627 776	10 = A
17 592 186 044 416	11 = B
281 474 976 710 656	12 = C
4 503 599 627 370 496	13 = D
72 057 594 037 927 936	14 = E
1 152 921 504 606 846 976	15 = F

Decimal Values

Hexadecimal and Decimal Fraction Conversion Table

HALFWORD													
BYTE					BYTE								
BITS 0123		4567			0123				4567				
Hex	Decimal	Hex	Decimal		Hex	Decimal			Hex	Decimal Equivalent			
.0	.0000	.00	.0000	0000	.000	.0000	0000	0000	.0000	.0000	0000	0000	0000
.1	.0625	.01	.0039	0625	.001	.0002	4414	0625	.0001	.0000	1525	8789	0625
.2	.1250	.02	.0078	1250	.002	.0004	8828	1250	.0002	.0000	3051	7578	1250
.3	.1875	.03	.0117	1875	.003	.0007	3242	1875	.0003	.0000	4577	6367	1875
.4	.2500	.04	.0156	2500	.004	.0009	7656	2500	.0004	.0000	6103	5156	2500
.5	.3125	.05	.0195	3125	.005	.0012	2070	3125	.0005	.0000	7629	3945	3125
.6	.3750	.06	.0234	3750	.006	.0014	6484	3750	.0006	.0000	9155	2734	3750
.7	.4375	.07	.0273	4375	.007	.0017	0898	4375	.0007	.0001	0681	1523	4375
.8	.5000	.08	.0312	5000	.008	.0019	5312	5000	.0008	.0001	2207	0312	5000
.9	.5625	.09	.0351	5625	.009	.0021	9726	5625	.0009	.0001	3732	9101	5625
.A	.6250	.0A	.0390	6250	.00A	.0024	4140	6250	.000A	.0001	5258	7890	6250
.B	.6875	.0B	.0429	6875	.00B	.0026	8554	6875	.000B	.0001	6784	6679	6875
.C	.7500	.0C	.0468	7500	.00C	.0029	2968	7500	.000C	.0001	8310	5468	7500
.D	.8125	.0D	.0507	8125	.00D	.0031	7382	8125	.000D	.0001	9836	4257	8125
.E	.8750	.0E	.0546	8750	.00E	.0034	1796	8750	.000E	.0002	1362	3046	8750
.F	.9375	.0F	.0585	9375	.00F	.0036	6210	9375	.000F	.0002	2888	1835	9375
1		2			3				4				

TO CONVERT .ABC HEXADECIMAL TO DECIMAL

Find .A	in position 1	.6250
Find .0B	in position 2	.0429 6875
Find .00C	in position 3	.0029 2968 7500
.ABC Hex is equal to		.6708 9843 7500

TO CONVERT .13 DECIMAL TO HEXADECIMAL

1. Find .1250 next lowest to subtract
   .1300
   -.1250 = .2 Hex
2. Find .0039 0625 next lowest to
   .0050 0000
   -.0039 0625 = .01
3. Find .0009 7656 2500
   .0010 9375 0000
   -.0009 7656 2500 = .004
4. Find .0001 0681 1523 4375
   .0001 1718 7500 0000
   -.0001 0681 1523 4375 = .0007
   .0000 1037 5976 5625 = .2147 Hex
5. .13 Decimal is approximately equal to ——→ .2147 Hex

To convert fractions beyond the capacity of table, use techniques below:

HEXADECIMAL FRACTION TO DECIMAL

Convert the hexadecimal fraction to its decimal equivalent using the same technique as for integer numbers. Divide the results by 16^n (n is the number of fraction positions).

Example: $.8A7 = .540771_{10}$

$8A7_{16} = 2215_{10}$

$16^3 = 4096$

$$\frac{2215.000000}{4096} = .540771$$

DECIMAL FRACTION TO HEXADECIMAL

Collect integer parts of product in the order of calculation.

Example: $.5408_{10} = .8A7_{16}$

```
        .5408
          x16
8  ←  [8].6528
          x16
A  ←  [10].4448
          x16
7  ←  [7].1168
```

Hexadecimal Addition and Subtraction Table

Example: 6 + 2 = 8, 8 − 2 = 6, and 8 − 6 = 2

	1	2	3	4	5	6	7	8	9	A	B	C	D	E	F
1	02	03	04	05	06	07	08	09	0A	0B	0C	0D	0E	0F	10
2	03	04	05	06	07	08	09	0A	0B	0C	0D	0E	0F	10	11
3	04	05	06	07	08	09	0A	0B	0C	0D	0E	0F	10	11	12
4	05	06	07	08	09	0A	0B	0C	0D	0E	0F	10	11	12	13
5	06	07	08	09	0A	0B	0C	0D	0E	0F	10	11	12	13	14
6	07	08	09	0A	0B	0C	0D	0E	0F	10	11	12	13	14	15
7	08	09	0A	0B	0C	0D	0E	0F	10	11	12	13	14	15	16
8	09	0A	0B	0C	0D	0E	0F	10	11	12	13	14	15	16	17
9	0A	0B	0C	0D	0E	0F	10	11	12	13	14	15	16	17	18
A	0B	0C	0D	0E	0F	10	11	12	13	14	15	16	17	18	19
B	0C	0D	0E	0F	10	11	12	13	14	15	16	17	18	19	1A
C	0D	0E	0F	10	11	12	13	14	15	16	17	18	19	1A	1B
D	0E	0F	10	11	12	13	14	15	16	17	18	19	1A	1B	1C
E	0F	10	11	12	13	14	15	16	17	18	19	1A	1B	1C	1D
F	10	11	12	13	14	15	16	17	18	19	1A	1B	1C	1D	1E

Hexadecimal Multiplication Table

Example: 2 x 4 = 08, F x 2 = 1E

	1	2	3	4	5	6	7	8	9	A	B	C	D	E	F
1	01	02	03	04	05	06	07	08	09	0A	0B	0C	0D	0E	0F
2	02	04	06	08	0A	0C	0E	10	12	14	16	18	1A	1C	1E
3	03	06	09	0C	0F	12	15	18	1B	1E	21	24	27	2A	2D
4	04	08	0C	10	14	18	1C	20	24	28	2C	30	34	38	3C
5	05	0A	0F	14	19	1E	23	28	2D	32	37	3C	41	46	4B
6	06	0C	12	18	1E	24	2A	30	36	3C	42	48	4E	54	5A
7	07	0E	15	1C	23	2A	31	38	3F	46	4D	54	5B	62	69
8	08	10	18	20	28	30	38	40	48	50	58	60	68	70	78
9	09	12	1B	24	2D	36	3F	48	51	5A	63	6C	75	7E	87
A	0A	14	1E	28	32	3C	46	50	5A	64	6E	78	82	8C	96
B	0B	16	21	2C	37	42	4D	58	63	6E	79	84	8F	9A	A5
C	0C	18	24	30	3C	48	54	60	6C	78	84	90	9C	A8	B4
D	0D	1A	27	34	41	4E	5B	68	75	82	8F	9C	A9	B6	C3
E	0E	1C	2A	38	46	54	62	70	7E	8C	9A	A8	B6	C4	D2
F	0F	1E	2D	3C	4B	5A	69	78	87	96	A5	B4	C3	D2	E1

appendix G
EBCDIC character codes

The following conversion table shows the 8-bit binary code with its corresponding punch combination, decimal value, hexadecimal value, and printed character (if any).

8-Bit BCD Code	Character Set Punch Combination	Decimal	Hexa-decimal	Printer Graphics
00000000	12,0,9,8,1	0	00	
00000001	12,9,1	1	01	
00000010	12,9,2	2	02	
00000011	12,9,3	3	03	
00000100	12,9,4	4	04	
00000101	12,9,5	5	05	
00000110	12,9,6	6	06	
00000111	12,9,7	7	07	
00001000	12,9,8	8	08	
00001001	12,9,8,1	9	09	
00001010	12,9,8,2	10	0A	
00001011	12,9,8,3	11	0B	
00001100	12,9,8,4	12	0C	
00001101	12,9,8,5	13	0D	
00001110	12,9,8,6	14	0E	
00001111	12,9,8,7	15	0F	
00010000	12,11,9,8,1	16	10	
00010001	11,9,1	17	11	
00010010	11,9,2	18	12	
00010011	11,9,3	19	13	
00010100	11,9,4	20	14	
00010101	11,9,5	21	15	
00010110	11,9,6	22	16	
00010111	11,9,7	23	17	
00011000	11,9,8	24	18	
00011001	11,9,8,1	25	19	
00011010	11,9,8,2	26	1A	
00011011	11,9,8,3	27	1B	
00011100	11,9,8,4	28	1C	
00011101	11,9,8,5	29	1D	
00011110	11,9,8,6	30	1E	
00011111	11,9,8,7	31	1F	
00100000	11,0,9,8,1	32	20	
00100001	0,9,1	33	21	
00100010	0,9,2	34	22	
00100011	0,9,3	35	23	
00100100	0,9,4	36	24	
00100101	0,9,5	37	25	
00100110	0,9,6	38	26	
00100111	0,9,7	39	27	
00101000	0,9,8	40	28	
00101001	0,9,8,1	41	29	
00101010	0,9,8,2	42	2A	
00101011	0,9,8,3	43	2B	
00101100	0,9,8,4	44	2C	
00101101	0,9,8,5	45	2D	
00101110	0,9,8,6	46	2E	
00101111	0,9,8,7	47	2F	
00110000	12,11,0,9,8,1	48	30	
00110001	9,1	49	31	
00110010	9,2	50	32	

8-Bit BCD Code	Character Set Punch Combination	Decimal	Hexa-decimal	Printer Graphics
00110011	9,3	51	33	
00110100	9,4	52	34	
00110101	9,5	53	35	
00110110	9,6	54	36	
00110111	9,7	55	37	
00111000	9,8	56	38	
00111001	9,8,1	57	39	
00111010	9,8,2	58	3A	
00111011	9,8,3	59	3B	
00111100	9,8,4	60	3C	
00111101	9,8,5	61	3D	
00111110	9,8,6	62	3E	
00111111	9,8,7	63	3F	
01000000		64	40	blank
01000001	12,0,9,1	65	41	
01000010	12,0,9,2	66	42	
01000011	12,0,9,3	67	43	
01000100	12,0,9,4	68	44	
01000101	12,0,9,5	69	45	
01000110	12,0,9,6	70	46	
01000111	12,0,9,7	71	47	
01001000	12,0,9,8	72	48	
01001001	12,8,1	73	49	
01001010	12,8,2	74	4A	
01001011	12,8,3	75	4B	. (period)
01001100	12,8,4	76	4C	<
01001101	12,8,5	77	4D	(
01001110	12,8,6	78	4E	+
01001111	12,8,7	79	4F	
01010000	12	80	50	&
01010001	12,11,9,1	81	51	
01010010	12,11,9,2	82	52	
01010011	12,11,9,3	83	53	
01010100	12,11,9,4	84	54	
01010101	12,11,9,5	85	55	
01010110	12,11,9,6	86	56	
01010111	12,11,9,7	87	57	
01011000	12,11,9,8	88	58	
01011001	11,8,1	89	59	
01011010	11,8,2	90	5A	
01011011	11,8,3	91	5B	$
01011100	11,8,4	92	5C	*
01011101	11,8,5	93	5D	)
01011110	11,8,6	94	5E	
01011111	11,8,7	95	5F	
01100000	11	96	60	—
01100001	0,1	97	61	/
01100010	11,0,9,2	98	62	
01100011	11,0,9,3	99	63	
01100100	11,0,9,4	100	64	
01100101	11,0,9,5	101	65	
01100110	11,0,9,6	102	66	
01100111	11,0,9,7	103	67	
01101000	11,0,9,8	104	68	
01101001	0,8,1	105	69	
01101010	12,11	106	6A	
01101011	0,8,3	107	6B	, (comma)

8-Bit BCD Code	Character Set Punch Combination	Decimal	Hexa-decimal	Printer Graphics
01101100	0,8,4	108	6C	%
01101101	0,8,5	109	6D	
01101110	0,8,6	110	6E	
01101111	0,8,7	111	6F	
01110000	12,11,0	112	70	
01110001	12,11,0,9,1	113	71	
01110010	12,11,0,9,2	114	72	
01110011	12,11,0,9,3	115	73	
01110100	12,11,0,9,4	116	74	
01110101	12,11,0,9,5	117	75	
01110110	12,11,0,9,6	118	76	
01110111	12,11,0,9,7	119	77	
01111000	12,11,0,9,8	120	78	
01111001	8,1	121	79	
01111010	8,2	122	7A	
01111011	8,3	123	7B	#
01111100	8,4	124	7C	@
01111101	8,5	125	7D	' (apostrophe)
01111110	8,6	126	7E	=
01111111	8,7	127	7F	
10000000	12,0,8,1	128	80	
10000001	12,0,1	129	81	a
10000010	12,0,2	130	82	b
10000011	12,0,3	131	83	c
10000100	12,0,4	132	84	d
10000101	12,0,5	133	85	e
10000110	12,0,6	134	86	f
10000111	12,0,7	135	87	g
10001000	12,0,8	136	88	h
10001001	12,0,9	137	89	i
10001010	12,0,8,2	138	8A	
10001011	12,0,8,3	139	8B	
10001100	12,0,8,4	140	8C	
10001101	12,0,8,5	141	8D	
10001110	12,0,8,6	142	8E	
10001111	12,0,8,7	143	8F	
10010000	12,11,8,1	144	90	
10010001	12,11,1	145	91	j
10010010	12,11,2	146	92	k
10010011	12,11,3	147	93	l
10010100	12,11,4	148	94	m
10010101	12,11,5	149	95	n
10010110	12,11,6	150	96	o
10010111	12,11,7	151	97	p
10011000	12,11,8	152	98	q
10011001	12,11,9	153	99	r
10011010	12,11,8,2	154	9A	
10011011	12,11,8,3	155	9B	
10011100	12,11,8,4	156	9C	
10011101	12,11,8,5	157	9D	
10011110	12,11,8,6	158	9E	
10011111	12,11,8,7	159	9F	
10100000	11,0,8,1	160	A0	
10100001	11,0,1	161	A1	
10100010	11,0,2	162	A2	s
10100011	11,0,3	163	A3	t
10100100	11,0,4	164	A4	u

8-Bit BCD Code	Character Set Punch Combination	Decimal	Hexa-decimal	Printer Graphics
10100101	11,0,5	165	A5	v
10100110	11,0,6	166	A6	w
10100111	11,0,7	167	A7	x
10101000	11,0,8	168	A8	y
10101001	11,0,9	169	A9	z
10101010	11,0,8,2	170	AA	
10101011	11,0,8,3	171	AB	
10101100	11,0,8,4	172	AC	
10101101	11,0,8,5	173	AD	
10101110	11,0,8,6	174	AE	
10101111	11,0,8,7	175	AF	
10110000	12,11,0,8,1	176	B0	
10110001	12,11,0,1	177	B1	
10110010	12,11,0,2	178	B2	
10110011	12,11,0,3	179	B3	
10110100	12,11,0,4	180	B4	
10110101	12,11,0,5	181	B5	
10110110	12,11,0,6	182	B6	
10110111	12,11,0,7	183	B7	
10111000	12,11,0,8	184	B8	
10111001	12,11,0,9	185	B9	
10111010	12,11,0,8,2	186	BA	
10111011	12,11,0,8,3	187	BB	
10111100	12,11,0,8,4	188	BC	
10111101	12,11,0,8,5	189	BD	
10111110	12,11,0,8,6	190	BE	
10111111	12,11,0,8,7	191	BF	
11000000	12,0	192	C0	
11000001	12,1	193	C1	A
11000010	12,2	194	C2	B
11000011	12,3	195	C3	C
11000100	12,4	196	C4	D
11000101	12,5	197	C5	E
11000110	12,6	198	C6	F
11000111	12,7	199	C7	G
11001000	12,8	200	C8	H
11001001	12,9	201	C9	I
11001010	12,0,9,8,2	202	CA	
11001011	12,0,9,8,3	203	CB	
11001100	12,0,9,8,4	204	CC	
11001101	12,0,9,8,5	205	CD	
11001110	12,0,9,8,6	206	CE	
11001111	12,0,9,8,7	207	CF	
11010000	11,0	208	D0	
11010001	11,1	209	D1	J
11010010	11,2	210	D2	K
11010011	11,3	211	D3	L
11010100	11,4	212	D4	M
11010101	11,5	213	D5	N
11010110	11,6	214	D6	O
11010111	11,7	215	D7	P
11011000	11,8	216	D8	Q
11011001	11,9	217	D9	R
11011010	12,11,9,8,2	218	DA	
11011011	12,11,9,8,3	219	DB	
11011100	12,11,9,8,4	220	DC	
11011101	12,11,9,8,5	221	DD	

8-Bit BCD Code	Character Set Punch Combination	Decimal	Hexa-decimal	Printer Graphics
11011110	12,11,9,8,6	222	DE	
11011111	12,11,9,8,7	223	DF	
11100000	0,8,2	224	E0	
11100001	11,0,9,1	225	E1	
11100010	0,2	226	E2	S
11100011	0,3	227	E3	T
11100100	0,4	228	E4	U
11100101	0,5	229	E5	V
11100110	0,6	230	E6	W
11100111	0,7	231	E7	X
11101000	0,8	232	E8	Y
11101001	0,9	233	E9	Z
11101010	11,0,9,8,2	234	EA	
11101011	11,0,9,8,3	235	EB	
11101100	11,0,9,8,4	236	EC	
11101101	11,0,9,8,5	237	ED	
11101110	11,0,9,8,6	238	EE	
11101111	11,0,9,8,7	239	EF	
11110000	0	240	F0	00
11110001	1	241	F1	1
11110010	2	242	F2	2
11110011	3	243	F3	3
11110100	4	244	F4	4
11110101	5	245	F5	5
11110110	6	246	F6	6
11110111	7	247	F7	7
11111000	8	248	F8	8
11111001	9	249	F9	9
11111010	12,11,0,9,8,2	250	FA	
11111011	12,11,0,9,8,3	251	FB	
11111100	12,11,0,9,8,4	252	FC	
11111101	12,11,0,9,8,5	253	FD	
11111110	12,11,0,9,8,6	254	FE	
11111111	12,11,0,9,8,7	255	FF	

Special Graphic Characters

¢	Cent Sign	*	Asterisk	>	Greater-than Sign
.	Period, Decimal Point	)	Right Parenthesis	?	Question Mark
<	Less-than Sign	;	Semicolon	:	Colon
(	Left Parenthesis	¬	Logical NOT	#	Numb Sign
+	Plus Sign	-	Minus Sign, Hyphen	@	At Sign
|	Vertical Bar, Logical OR	/	Slash	'	Prime, Apostrophe
&	Ampersand	,	Comma	=	Equal Sign
!	Exclamation Point	%	Percent	"	Quotation Mark
$	Dollar Sign	_	Underscore		

Examples	Type	Bit Pattern *Bit Positions* 01 23 4567	Hole Pattern	
			Zone Punches	*Digit Punches*
PF	Control Character	00 00 0100	12-9-4	
%	Special Graphic	01 10 1100	0-8-4	
R	Upper Case	11 01 1001	11-9	
a	Lower Case	10 00 0001	12-0-1	
	Control Character, function not yet assigned	00 11 0000	12-11-0-9-8-1	

appendix H

computer audit packages

Extraction

The extraction function should enable the user to select only those records that meet predetermined criteria. These criteria should be changeable by means of control card entries, which can be readily changed to fit shifting demands. These criteria should allow the selection of records on the basis of their data's inclusion or exclusion within a range of values or on a match with exact values. The possible combinations for extraction should be further expanded by AND/OR relationship tests for selection of records meeting required combinations of criteria. In addition, the ability to apply different sampling intervals to each type of extracted record is often most useful.

Mathematics

The mathematical function should allow the user to enter mathematical formulas of the user's own description for calculation. Possible applications are summation of payroll deductions, cross footing and balancing, checking extensions, to name only a few.

Surveying (Frequency Distribution)

The surveying function allows the auditor to take item and amount totals of all records meeting a certain criterion, without extracting the individual records. On this basis, file characteristics can be stratified without selecting the actual records for audit. For instance, in an accounts receivable application, the auditor may be interested in determining the number and dollar ranges $.01 to 50.00, and $50.01 to 500.00.

Totaling

The subtotaling function allows for printing subtotal amounts when there is a change in the given file sequence. As many levels of subtotals should be provided as the auditor deems necessary for the applications. Final trial totals should, of course, also be provided. A possible application should be the subtotaling of a payroll file, which is in order by branch, department, and section.

The aging function should make possible a comparison of the dates in the records to a given date, and the stratification of each record into selected categories, such as current, 31–60 days, 61–90 days, 91–120 days, and over 120 days.

Aging

The sampling functions can be used to select records based on a sequential interval or based on random numbers. Both are useful to the auditor and will be used in different types of audit situations.

Sampling

The comparison should allow the user to match two files on a given sequence and compare the data in one file to that of the other. In addition, in the case of information split between two files (one file of account numbers or transactions), and the other, a corresponding name file, both files can be used simultaneously to include more meaningful data on printed reports and other reports.

Comparison of Two Files

The package should provide multiple output types, such as report, file, and confirmations. All should be free format and under the auditor's control.

Printer-File and Confirmation Outputs

These provide the auditor with the ability to extend the capabilities of a system in new and unique areas of the user's own design.

User Exits

In order to test the content and format of the audit results prior to processing the entire file, the auditor may wish to run a test audit on a portion of the file.

Test Auditing

In order to prevent an audit from terminating because of invalid data (fields intended to be numeric and are not), the auditor should have the ability to bypass and print out invalid data.

Bypass Invalid Data

glossary

Abacus	The earliest known calculating device still used today by over half of the world's population, chiefly in the Far East.
ABEND (Abnormal End of Task)	Termination of a task prior to its completion because of an error condition that cannot be resolved by recovery facilities while the task is executing.
*Absolute Address	(1) (ISO) An *address* in a *computer language* that identifies a *storage location* or a device without the use of any intermediate reference. (2) An *address* that is permanently assigned by the machine designer to a *storage location.* (3) Synonymous with explicit address, machine address, specific address.
*Access Time	(1) (ISO) The time interval between the instant at which an *instruction control unit* initiates a call for *data* and the instant at which delivery of the data is completed. Access time equals *latency* plus *transfer time.* (2) The time interval between the instant at which *data* are requested to be *stored* and the instant at which *storage* is started. (3) (ISO) Deprecated term for *cycle time.*
*Accounting Machine	(1) A keyboard-actuated machine that prepares accounting *records.* (2) A machine that *reads data* from external *storage* media, such as cards or tapes, and automatically produces accounting records or tabulations, usually on continuous forms.
Acronym	A word formed from the first letter or letters of the words in a name or phrase; for example, COBOL from *CO*mmon *B*usiness *O*riented *L*anguage.
Activity	The percentage of records in a file that are processed in a run. *See also* Volatility.
Adder	Performs arithmetic functions to the extent that it accumulates the value of two data items and sends the results to an accumulator or register.

(ISO) Definitions bearing the source label (ISO) are based on material developed by the International Organization for Standardization.

(1) (ISO) A *character* or group of characters that identifies a *register*, a particular part of *storage*, or some other *data* source or destination. (2) (ISO) To refer to a device or an *item* of *data* by its *address*.	*Address
A *language* used to express *computer programs* by *algorithms*.	*ALGOL (*Algo*rithmic *L*anguage)
(ISO) A finite *set* of well-defined rules for the solution of a problem in a finite number of steps, e.g., a full statement of an arithmetic *procedure* for evaluating sin *x* to a stated *precision*.	*Algorithm
To grant a resource to, or reserve it for, a job or task.	Allocate
(ISO) A *character set* that contains *letters* and may contain *control characters, special characters,* and the *space character,* but not *digits*.	*Alphabetic Character Set
A code whose set consists only of letters and associated special characters.	Alphabetic Code
See Alphanumeric.	Alphameric
Pertaining to a character set that contains letters, digits, and usually other characters, such as punctuation marks. Synonymous with alphameric.	Alphanumeric
(ISO) A *character set* that contains both *letters* and *digits* and may contain *control characters, special characters,* and the *space character*.	*Alphanumeric Character Set
See Arithmetic Unit.	ALU (*A*rithmetic and *L*ogic *U*nit)
(1) (ISO) A *computer* in which *analog* representation of *data* is mainly used. (2) A *computer* that operates on *analog data* by performing physical processes on these data. (3) Contrast with *digital computer*.	*Analog Computer
The methodical investigation of a problem, and the separation of the problem into smaller related *units* for further detailed study.	*Analysis
(ISO) A person who defines problems and develops *algorithms* and *procedures* for their solution.	*Analyst
An added descriptive comment or explanatory note.	*Annotation
An organization sponsored by the *B*usiness *E*quipment *M*anufacturers (BEMA) for the purpose of establishing voluntary industry standards.	ANSI (*A*merican *N*ational *S*tandards *I*nstitute)
A problem-solving language designed for use at remote terminals. It offers special capabilities for handling arrays and for performing mathematical functions.	APL (*A* *P*rogramming *L*anguage)
Includes the activities relative to the selection and definition of data-processing applications which fulfill the objectives of an enterprise.	Application Selection
(1) (ISO) An independent *variable*. (2) (ISO) Any value of an independent *variable*.	*Argument

Arithmetic Operation	Any of the fundamental operations of arithmetic; for example, the binary operations of addition, subtraction, multiplication, and division and the monadic operations of negation and absolute value.
*Arithmetic Unit	(ISO) A part of a *computer* that performs *arithmetic operations* and related *operations.*
*Array	An arrangement of *elements* in one or more dimensions.
*Artificial Intelligence	The capability of a device to perform *functions* that are normally associated with human intelligence, such as reasoning, learning, and self-improvement.
*ASCII (*A*merican *N*ational *S*tandard *C*ode for *I*nformation *I*nterchange)	The standard code, using a *coded character set* consisting of 7-bit coded characters (8-bits including *parity check*), used for *information* interchange among *data processing systems, data communication systems,* and associated equipment. The ASCII set consists of *control characters* and *graphic characters.*
*Assembly Language	(1) (ISO) A *computer-oriented language* whose *instructions* are usually in one-to-one correspondence with *computer instructions* and that may provide facilities such as the use of *macroinstructions.* (2) A *computer programming language* whose *statements* may be *instructions* or *declarations.* The instructions usually have a one-to-one correspondence with machine instructions. Synonymous with computer-dependent language, computer-oriented language.
Attribute	A characteristic; for example, attributes of data include record length, record format, data set name, associated device type, and volume identification.
*Automatic	(ISO) Pertaining to a *process* or *device* that, under specified conditions, *functions* without intervention by a human operator.
*Automation	(1) (ISO) The implementation of *processes* by *automatic* means. (2) (ISO) The conversion of a *procedure,* a *process,* or equipment to *automatic* operation. (3) The theory, art, or technique of making a *process* more *automatic.* (4) The investigation, design, development, and application of methods of rendering processes *automatic,* self-moving, or self-controlling.
*Auxiliary Storage	(1) (ISO) A *storage device* that is not *main storage.* (2) *Storage* that supplements another storage. (3) Contrast with *main storage.*
Babbage	Invented large-scale calculating machines in the middle of the nineteenth century. His basic concepts of computing were used a hundred years later in the development of the computer.
*Background Processing	(1) The *execution* of lower priority *computer programs* when higher priority programs are not using the *system* resources. (2) Contrast with *foreground processing.*
*Base	(1) (ISO) In the *numeration system* commonly used in scientific papers, the *number* that is raised to the power denoted by the *exponent* and then multiplied by the *mantissa* to determine the *real number* represented, e.g., the number 6.25 in the expression $2.7 \times 6.25^{1.5} = 42.1875$. (2) A reference value. (3) A *number* that is multiplied by itself as many times as indicated by an *exponent.*

(1) (ISO) A *numeric* value that is used as a reference in the calculation of *addresses* in the *execution* of a *computer program*. (2) A given *address* from which an *absolute address* is derived by combination with a *relative address*.	*Base Address
A widely used programming language for conversational time sharing.	BASIC (*B*eginner's *A*ll-Purpose *S*ymbolic *I*nstruction *C*ode)
(1) The *processing* of *data* or the accomplishment of *jobs* accumulated in advance in such a manner that each accumulation thus formed is processed or accomplished in the same *run*. (2) The *processing* of *data* accumulated over a period of time. (3) Loosely, the *execution* of *computer programs serially*. (4) Pertaining to the technique of *executing a set* of *computer programs* such that each is completed before the next program of the set is started. (5) Pertaining to the *sequential input* of *computer programs* or *data*.	*Batch Processing
(1) A *unit* of *signalling* speed equal to the number of *discrete* conditions or signal events per second. For example, one baud equals one-half dot cycle per second in Morse code, one bit per second in a train of *binary* signals, and one 3-bit value per second in a train of signals each of which can assume one of eight different states. (2) In asynchronous *transmission*, the *unit* of modulation rate corresponding to one unit interval per second, i.e., if the duration of the unit interval is 20 milliseconds, the modulation rate is 50 baud.	*Baud
(1) A problem used to evaluate the performance of *hardware* or *software* or both. (2) A problem used to evaluate the performance of several *computers* relative to each other, or a single computer relative to *system* specifications.	*Benchmark Problem
(1) (ISO) Pertaining to a selection, choice, or condition that has two possible different values or states. (2) (ISO) Pertaining to a *fixed radix numeration system* having a *radix* of two.	*Binary
(ISO) A *binary-coded notation* in which each of the *decimal digits* is represented by a *binary numeral*, e.g., in binary-coded decimal notation that uses the *weights* 8–4–2–1, the number "twenty-three" is represented by 0010 0011 (compare its representation 10111 in the *pure binary numeration system*). Synonymous with binary-coded decimal code, binary-coded decimal representation, coded decimal notation.	**B*inary-*C*oded *D*ecimal Notation (BCD)
(ISO) (1) In *binary notation*, either of the *characters*, 0 or 1. (2) Synonym for *bit*.	*Binary Digit (Bit)
(1) (ISO) Any *notation* that uses two different *characters*, usually the *binary digits* 0 and 1, e.g., the *gray* code. The gray code is a binary notation but not a *pure binary numeration system*. (2) *Fixed-radix notation* where the *radix* is two. For example, in *binary notation* the *numeral* 110.01 represents the *number* 1 × 2 squared plus 1 × 2 to the first power plus 1 × 2 to the minus 2 power, that is, six and a quarter.	*Binary Notation
Conversion of a binary number to the equivalent decimal number; that is, a base two number to a base ten number.	Binary-to-Decimal-Conversion
The smallest unit of information in a binary system. A bit may be either of the characters 0 or 1.	BIT (*BI*nary digi*T*)

*Blank — A part of a *data medium* in which no *characters* are recorded.

*Block — (1) (ISO) A *string* of *records*, a string of *words*, or a *character string*, formed for technical or logic reasons to be treated as an entity. (2) A set of things, such as *words*, *characters*, or *digits*, handled as a *unit*. (3) A collection of contiguous *records* recorded as a unit. Blocks are separated by *interblock gaps* and each block may contain one or more records. (4) A group of *bits*, or *n-ary digits*, *transmitted* as a unit. An *enclosing procedure* is generally applied to the group of bits or n-ary digits for *error*-control purposes.

Block Diagram — A diagram of a system, instrument, or computer, in which the principal parts are represented by suitably associated geometrical figures to show both the basic functions and the functional relationships among the parts. Contrast with Flowchart.

Blocking — Combining two or more records into one block.

*Block Length — (1) (ISO) The number of *records*, *words*, or *characters* in a *block*. (2) A measure of the size of a *block*, usually specified in *units* such as *records*, *words*, *computer words*, or *characters*.

Boolean — (1) Pertaining to the processes used in the algebra formulated by George Boole. (2) Pertaining to the operations of formal logic.

*Bootstrap — (1) (ISO) An existing version, perhaps a primitive version, of a *computer program* that is used to establish another version of the program. (2) A technique or device designed to bring itself into a desired state by means of its own action, e.g., a machine *routine* whose first few *instructions* are sufficient to bring the rest of itself into the *computer* from an *input device*. (3) That part of a *computer program* used to establish another version of the computer program. (4) (ISO) To use a bootstrap.

Boundary Alignment — The positioning in main storage of a fixed-length field, such as a halfword or doubleword on an integral boundary for that unit of information.

BPS (*B*its *p*er *S*econd) — In serial transmission, the instantaneous bit speed with which a device or channel transmits a character.

*Branch — (1) A *set* of *instructions* that are executed between two successive *branch instructions*. (2) A direct path joining two nodes of a network or graph. (3) Loosely, a *conditional jump*. (4) (ISO) In the *execution* of a *computer program*, to select one from a number of alternative *sets* of *instructions*. (5) To select a branch as in (1).(6) (ISO) Deprecated term for *jump*.

Bubble Storage — Tiny magnetized areas that can be generated, moved, and detected in a specialized crystalline material. Bubbles offer moderately fast data retrieval, use less power, give off less radiant heat, and hold onto stored information in case of power failure.

*Buffer — (1) A *routine* or *storage* used to compensate for a difference in rate of flow of *data*, or time of occurrence of events, when *transferring* data from one device to another. (2) An isolating circuit used to prevent a driven circuit from influencing the driving circuit. (3) To allocate and schedule the use of *buffers*.

*Bug — A *mistake* or *malfunction*.

The necessary activities, such as payroll preparation, inventory control, sales analysis, and general accounting files, that are processed, and the required outputs of statements and reports that are prepared. Business data processing is characterized by the processing of many files, used repeatedly, requiring few calculations and many output reports.	Business Data Processing
(1) A sequence of adjacent binary digits operated upon as a unit and usually shorter than a computer word. (2) The representation of a character, usually the smallest addressable unit in the system.	Byte
(1) (ISO) A *data processor,* especially suitable for performing *arithmetical operations,* that requires frequent intervention by a human *operator.* (2) A device for carrying out logic and arithmetical *digital operations* of any kind.	*Calculator
(1) (ISO) The action of bringing a *computer program,* a *routine,* or a *sub*routine into effect, usually by specifying the *entry conditions* and *jumping* to an *entry point.* (2) In *data communication,* the action performed by the calling party, or the operations necessary in making a call, or the effective use made of a connection between two stations. (3) (ISO) In *computer programming,* to *execute* a *call.* (4) To transfer control to a specified *closed subroutine.*	*Call
The combinations of punched holes that represent characters in a punched card; for example, letters or digits.	Card Code
One of the vertical lines of punching positions on a punched card.	Card Column
One or more consecutive card columns assigned to data of a specific nature; for example, card columns 15–20 can be assigned for identification.	Card Field
(1) (ISO) The part of a card-*processing* device that holds the cards to be processed and makes them available to a *card feed* mechanism. (2) Contrast with *card stacker.*	*Card Hopper
(1) A device that *punches* holes in a card to represent *data.* (2) (ISO) Deprecated term for *keypunch.*	*Card Punch
(1) (ISO) A device that *reads* or senses the holes in a *punched card, transforming* the *data* from *hole patterns* to electrical *signals.* (2) An *input device* that senses *hole patterns* in a *punched card* and translates them into *machine language.* Synonymous with punched card reader.	*Card Reader
(1) (ISO) The part of a card-*processing* device that receives the cards after they have been *processed.* (2) Contrast with *card hopper.*	*Card Stacker
Pertains to equipment that transfers information directly from punched cards to punched or magnetic tape.	Card-to-Tape
(1) A tape that is used to control vertical tabulation of printing positions or *display* positions. (2) A tape that contains line feed control *data* for a printing device.	*Carriage Control Tape
(ISO) An *electrostatic storage* that uses a cathode ray beam for access to *data.*	*Cathode Ray Storage

***Cathode Ray Tube Display (CRT Display)** (1) A device that presents *data* in visual form by means of controlled electron beams. (2) The *data display* produced by the device as in (1).

Central Processing Unit A unit of a computer that includes the circuits controlling the interpretation and execution of instructions. Synonymous with Main Frame. Abbreviated CPU.

Centralized Data-Processing Unit The data-processing department is independent but at the same level with the departments it is servicing.

Chaining A system of storing records in which each record belongs to a list or group of records and has a linking field for tracing the chain.

***Chain Printer** (ISO) An *impact printer* in which the type slugs are carried by the links of a revolving chain.

***Channel** (1) A path along which *signals* can be sent, e.g., *data* channel, *output channel.* (2) The portion of a *storage medium* that is accessible to a given *reading* or *writing* station, e.g., *track, band.* (3) (ISO) In *information theory,* that part of a communication *system* that connects the *message source* with the *message sink*. Mathematically, this part can be characterized by the *set* of conditional probabilities of occurrence of all the possible *messages* received at the message sink when a given message emanates from the message source. (4) In *data communication,* a means of one-way transmission. Contrast with *circuit.*

***Character** (1) (ISO) A member of a *set* of *elements* upon which agreement has been reached and that is used for the organization, control, or representation of *data. Characters* may be *letters, digits,* punctuation marks, or other *symbols,* often represented in the form of a spatial arrangement of adjacent or connected strokes or in the form of other physical conditions in *data media.* (2) A *letter, digit,* or other *symbol* that is used as part of the organization, control, or representation of *data.* A character is often in the form of a spatial arrangement of adjacent or connected strokes.

***Character Printer** (1) (ISO) A device that prints a single *character* at a time, e.g., a typewriter. Synonymous with character-at-a-time printer. (2) Contrast with *line printer, page printer.*

Character Recognition The identification of graphic, phonic, or other characters by automatic means. *See* Magnetic-Ink Character Recognition and Optical Character Recognition.

***Character Set** (1) (ISO) A finite *set* of different *characters* upon which agreement has been reached and that is considered complete for some purpose, e.g., each of the character sets in ISO Recommendation R646 "6- and 7-bit coded character sets for information processing interchange." (2) An *ordered set* of unique representations called *characters,* e.g., the 26 *letters* of the English *alphabet, Boolean* 0 and 1, the set of symbols in the Morse code, and the 128 ASCII characters.

***Character String** (ISO) A *string* consisting solely of *characters.*

Charged Coupled-Storage Devices Store information as packets of charges within a semiconductor charge. These charge packets are manipulated by applying voltage to a routing pattern inscribed on the chip's surface.

***Check Bit** A *binary* check *digit,* e.g., a *parity bit.*

(ISO) A place in a *computer program* at which a *check* is made or at which a recording of *data* is made for *restart* purposes.	*Checkpoint
A point through which every document flows.	Checkpoint Controls
(1) A minute piece of semiconductive material used in the manufacture of electronic components. (2) An integrated circuit on a piece of semiconductive material. (3) In *micrographics*, a piece of *microfilm* smaller than a *microfiche* containing *microimages* and *coded* identification.	*Chip
(1) In *data communication*, a means of two-way communication between two *data terminal installations*. (2) Contrast with *channel*.	*Circuit
To arrange into classes of information according to a system or method.	Classify
(1) (ISO) To put one or more *storage locations* or *registers* into a prescribed state, usually that denoting *zero*. (2) (ISO) To cause one or more *storage locations* to be in a prescribed state, usually that corresponding to zero or that corresponding to the *space character*.	*Clear
Errors in a program that result from poor coding.	Clerical Errors
(1) (ISO) A device that generates periodic *signals* from which synchronism may be maintained. (2) A device that measures and indicates time. (3) A *register* whose content changes at regular intervals in such a way as to measure time. (4) (ISO) Deprecated term for *timer*.	*Clock
(ISO) A loop that has no *exit* and whose *execution* can be *interrupted* only by intervention from outside the *computer program* in which the loop is included.	*Closed Loop
(1) Pertaining to the *operation* of a *computer* facility in which most productive problem *programming* is performed by a group of programming specialists rather than the problem originators. The use of the computer itself may also be described as closed shop if full-time trained *operators*, rather than user/programmers, serve as the operators. (2) Contrast with *open shop*.	*Closed Shop
(1) (ISO) A *subroutine* of which one replica suffices for the subroutine to be *linked* by *calling sequences* for use at more than one place in a *computer program*. (2) Contrast with *open subroutine*.	*Closed Subroutine
A programming language designed for business data processing.	*COBOL (Common Business Oriented Language)
(1) (ISO) A *set* of unambiguous rules specifying the manner in which *data* may be represented in a *discrete* form. Synonymous with coding scheme. (2) A *set* of *items*, such as abbreviations, representing the members of another set. (3) (ISO) To represent *data* or a *computer program* in a symbolic form that can be accepted by a *data processor*. (4) To write a *routine*. (5) (ISO) Deprecated term for *coded representation*, *code set*. (6) (ISO) Synonym for *coded representation*. (7) Synonym for *coded character set*.	*Code

*Coder — A person who writes but does not usually design *computer programs.*

*Collate — (1) (ISO) To alter the arrangement of a *set* of *items* from two or more *ordered subsets* to one or more other subsets each containing a number of items, commonly one, from each of the original subsets in a specified order that is not necessarily the order of any of the original subsets. (2) *See also* Merge.

*Collator — A device that *collates, merges,* or *matches sets* of *punched cards* or other *documents.*

*Column — (1) A vertical arrangement of *characters* or other expressions. (2) Contrast with *row.*

*Command — (1) A control *signal.* (2) Loosely, an *instruction.* (3) Loosely, a mathematical or logic *operator.* (4) Deprecated term for *instruction.*

Communication Link — The physical means of connecting one location to another for the purpose of transmitting and receiving data.

Communications Network — The computers are usually long distances apart and are connected by common-carrier telephone lines.

*Compile — (1) (ISO) To *translate* a *computer program* expressed in a *problem-oriented language* into a *computer-oriented language.* (2) To prepare a *machine language* program from a *computer program* written in another *programming language* by making use of the overall logic structure of the program, or *generating* more than one *computer instruction* for each *symbolic statement,* or both, as well as performing the *function* of an *assembler.*

*Compiler — (ISO) A *computer program* used to *compile.* Synonymous with compiling program.

*Complement — (1) (ISO) In a *fixed-radix numeration system,* a *numeral* that can be derived from a given numeral by *operations* that include subtracting each *digit* of the *digital representation* of the given *number* from the corresponding digit of the digital representation of a specified number. (2) A *number* that can be derived from a specified number by subtracting it from a second specified number. For example, in *radix notation,* the second specified number may be a given power of the *radix* or one less than a given power of the radix. The negative of a number is often represented by its complement.

*Computer — (ISO) A *data processor* that can perform substantial computation, including numerous *arithmetic operations* or *logic operations,* without intervention by a human *operator* during a *run.*

Computer Abuse — Those incidents caused by intentional acts, negligent acts, or accidental occurrences in which a person realized a gain and/or a victim suffered or could have suffered a loss.

Computer-Assisted Instruction — A data-processing application in which a computing system is used to assist in the instruction of students. The application usually involves a dialog between the students and the computer program which informs them of their mistakes as they make them. Abbreviated CAI.

Computer Audit Packages — Generalized computer programs designed to satisfy the particular needs of the auditor.

A complex consisting of two or more interconnected *computers*.	*Computer Network
(1) (ISO) A *programming language* that reflects the structure of a given *computer* or that of a given class of computers. (2) A *programming language* whose *words* and *syntax* are designed for use on a specific class of *computers*. Synonymous with machine-oriented language.	*Computer-Oriented Language
The physical security of the computer or the data-processing installation and the security of vital data, files, records, and programs.	Computer Security
(1) (ISO) A *word stored* in one *computer location* and capable of being treated as a *unit*. Synonymous with fullword, machine word. (2) *See also* Halfword.	*Computer Word
(1) (ISO) Pertaining to the occurrence of two or more activities within a given interval of time. (2) Contrast with *simultaneous*.	*Concurrent
(ISO) A *jump* that takes place only when the *instruction* that specifies it is *executed* and specified conditions are satisfied.	*Conditional Jump
A *statement* used to express an assignment or *branch*, based in specified criteria, e.g., an IF-THEN statement.	*Conditional Statement
(ISO) A *flowchart symbol* that represents a break in a *flowline*, the same flowline being continued elsewhere.	*Connector
(1) (ISO) Pertaining to the occurrence of two *sequential* events without the intervention of any other such event. (2) Contrast with *sequential*.	*Consecutive
A part of a *computer* used for communication between the *operator* or *maintenance* engineer and the computer.	*Console
A fixed or invariable value or data item.	Constant
Provides the unbiased opinion and excellent cross-check on the existing procedures.	Consultant
A punched card containing input data or parameters for initializing or modifying a program.	Control Card
A *computer program* designed to schedule and supervise the *execution* of all the *programs, routines,* and *subroutines* of a computing *system*.	*Control Program
A sum resulting from the addition of a specified field from each record in a group of records, used for checking machine, program, and data reliability.	Control Total
A device that controls input/output operations at one or more devices.	Control Unit
Pertaining to a program or a system that carries on a dialog with a terminal user, alternately accepting input and then responding to the input quickly enough for the user to maintain a train of thought. *See also* Interactive.	Conversational
A mode of *operation* of a *data processing system* in which a *sequence* of alternating entries between a user and the system takes place in a manner similar to a conversation between two persons.	*Conversational Mode

Conversion	(1) The process of changing from one method of data processing to another or from one data-processing system to another. (2) The process of changing from one form of representation to another; for example, to change from decimal representation to binary representation. *See also* Translate.
Core Storage	A form of high-speed storage using magnetic cores. Tiny "donuts" of magnetized material that can store binary information.
*Counter	(ISO) A device whose state represents a number and that, on receipt of an appropriate *signal,* causes the *number* represented to be increased by a unit or by an arbitrary constant; the device is usually capable of bringing the number represented to a specified value, e.g., zero.
Cursor	A movable spot of light on the cathode-ray tube of a console or display unit that indicates where the next character will be entered.
*Cycle	(1) An interval of space or time in which one *set* of events or phenomena is completed. (2) Any set of *operations* that is repeated regularly in the same *sequence.* The operations may be subject to variations on each repetition.
Cylinder	The tracks of a disk storage device that can be accessed without repositioning the access mechanism.
*Data	(1) (ISO) A representation of facts, concepts, or *instructions* in a formalized manner suitable for communication, interpretation, or processing by humans or by *automatic* means. (2) Any representations such as *characters* or *analog* quantities to which meaning is or might be assigned.
*Data Bank	(1) (ISO) A *set* of *libraries* of *data.* (2) A comprehensive collection of *libraries* of *data.* For example, one line of an invoice may form an *item,* a complete invoice may form a *record,* a complete set of such records may form a *file,* the collection of inventory control files may form a *library,* and the libraries used by an organization are known as its data bank.
*Data Base	(1) (ISO) A *set* of *data,* part or the whole of another set of data, and consisting of at least one *file,* that is sufficient for a given purpose or for a given *data processing system.* (2) A collection of *data* fundamental to a *system.* (3) A collection of *data* fundamental to an enterprise.
Data Base Administrator	Manages all data for the production and control of business information. Abbreviated DBA.
Data Base Management System	A computerized system consisting of numerous components which have as their collective purposes, the implementation, management, and protection of large-scale data bases. Abbreviated DBMS.
Data Cell	A direct access storage volume containing strips of magnetic tape that store data.
Data Collection	A telecommunications application in which data from several locations is accumulated at one location before processing.
*Data Communication	(1) The *transmission* and reception of *data.* (2) The *transmission,* reception, and *validation* of *data.*

Data Control — The responsibility for seeing that data is prepared as the user submits it and accuracy of processing through the data center.

Data Dictionary — A well-organized, up-to-date notebook containing basic information about data elements. It becomes the central authority source for all information about the data itself.

Data Flow Controls — The recording of input/output through log sheets, registers, and documents.

***Data Management** — (1) The function of controlling the acquisition, *analysis, storage,* retrieval, and distribution of *data.* (2) In an *operating system,* the *computer programs* that provide access to *data,* perform or monitor *storage* of data, and control *input-output* devices.

Data Organization — The arrangement of information in a data set; for example, sequential, indexed sequential, and direct or partitioned organization.

***Data Processing** — (ISO) The *execution* of a systematic sequence of *operations* performed upon *data,* e.g., handling, *merging, sorting,* computing. Synonymous with information processing.

***Data Processing System** — (ISO) A collection of methods, *procedures,* or techniques united by regulated interaction to form an organized whole.

***Data Processor** — (ISO) A device capable of performing *data processing,* such as a desk *calculator,* a *punched* card machine, or a *computer.* Synonymous with processor.

Data Set — (1) The major unit of data storage and retrieval in the operating system, consisting of a collection of data in one of several prescribed arrangements and described by control information in which the system has access. (2) A device that performs the modulation/demodulation and control functions necessary to provide compatibility between business machines and communication facilities.

Data Transmission — The sending of data from one part of a system to another part. *See also* Data Communication.

***Debug** — (ISO) To detect, to trace, and to eliminate *mistakes* in *computer programs* or in other *software.* Synonymous with checkout.

Decentralized Data-Processing Unit — The data-processing department is within a larger unit, which is its major customer. This unit can be located at a variety of sites rather than a single one.

***Decimal** — (1) (ISO) Pertaining to a selection, choice, or condition that has ten possible different values or states. (2) (ISO) Pertaining to a *fixed-radix numeration system* having a *radix* of ten. Synonymous with denary. (3) *See* Binary-coded Decimal Notation.

***Decimal Digit** — (ISO) In *decimal notation,* or in the *decimal numeration system,* one of the *digits* 0 to 9.

Decision — A determination of future action.

***Decision Table** — (1) (ISO) A table of all contingencies that are to be considered in the description of a problem together with the actions to be taken. (2) A presentation in either matrix or tabular form of a *set* of conditions and their corresponding actions.

Default Value — The choice among exclusive alternatives made by the system when no explicit choice is specified by the user.

***Delimiter** — A *flag* that separates and organizes *items* of *data.* Synonymous with punctuation symbol, separator.

***Destructive Read** — (ISO) A *reading* that also *erases* the *data* in the source *location.*

***Diagnostic** — Pertaining to the detection and isolation of a *malfunction* or *mistake.*

***Digit** — (1) (ISO) A *graphic character* that represents an integer, e.g., one of the characters 0 to 9. (2) A *symbol* that represents one of the nonnegative *integers* smaller than the radix. For example, in *decimal notation,* a digit is one of the *characters* from 0 to 9. (3) (ISO) Synonymous with numeric character.

***Digital Computer** — (1) (ISO) A *computer* in which *discrete representations* of *data* are mainly used. (2) A *computer* that operates on *discrete data* by performing arithmetic and logic processes on these data. (3) Contrast with *analog computer.*

Diode — An electronic device used to permit current flow in one direction and to inhibit current flow in the other.

***Direct Access** — (1) (ISO) The facility to obtain *data* from *storage devices* or to enter data into a storage device in such a way that the *process* depends only on the location of that data and not on a reference to data previously accessed. (2) Contrast with *serial access.*

Direct Organization — A file organization in which, for purposes of storage and retrieval, there is a direct relationship between the contents of the records and their addresses on disk storage. *See also* Sequential, Indexed Sequential, and Partitioned Organizations.

***Disk** — (ISO) Synonym for *magnetic disk.*

Disk Operating System — A disk resident programming system that provides operating system capabilities for computers. Abbreviated DOS.

***Disk Pack** — (1) (ISO) A removable assembly of *magnetic disks.* (2) A portable *set* of flat, circular recording surfaces used in a *disk storage* device.

***Display** — (1) (ISO) A visual presentation of *data.* (2) (ISO) Loosely, a *display device.* (3) *See* Cathode Ray Tube Display.

Distributed Data Processing — The processing power of the computer is placed at points where the data is needed for supervision and management.

Distributed Processing Network — The total data-processing load is shared functionally among the computers in the network.

***Document** — (ISO) A *data medium* and the *data* recorded on it, that generally has permanence and that can be *read* by man or machine.

***Documentation** — (1) (ISO) The management of *documents* which may include the actions of identifying, acquiring, *processing, storing,* and disseminating them. (2) (ISO) A collection of *documents* on a given subject.

(*D*isk *O*perating *S*ystem)	DOS
(ISO) Pertaining to the use of two *computer words* to represent a *number* in accordance with the required *precision*.	*Double Precision
More than one numeric punch in any one column of a punched card.	Double Punch
A contiguous *sequence* of *bits* or *characters* which comprises two *computer words* and is capable of being *addressed* as a *unit*.	*Doubleword
The time during which a *functional unit* is inoperable due to a *fault*.	*Downtime
A direct access storage device that records data magnetically on a rotating cylinder. A type of addressable auxiliary storage associated with some computers.	Drum Storage
(1) (ISO) *Data* that have been dumped. (2) (ISO) To *write* the contents of a *storage*, or of part of a storage, usually from an *internal storage* to an external *medium*, for a specific purpose such as to allow other use of the storage, as a safeguard against *faults* or *errors*, or in connection with *debugging*.	*Dump
(ISO) To *copy* from a source to a destination that has the same physical form as the source, e.g., to *punch* new *punched cards* with the same pattern of holes as an original punched card. Synonymous with reproduce.	*Duplicate
(1) The change of a virtual storage address to a real storage address during the execution of an instruction. (2) A hardware feature that performs the translation. Abbreviated DAT.	Dynamic Address Translation
Pertaining to a data-processing equipment that is predominantly electromechanical, such as card punch, mechanical sorter, collator, and accounting machine.	EAM (*E*lectrical *A*ccounting *M*achine)
A *coded character set* consisting of 8-bit *coded characters*.	*EBCDIC (Extended Binary-Coded Decimal Interchange Code)
(ISO) To prepare *data* for a later *operation*. Editing may include the rearrangement or the addition of data, the deletion of unwanted data, *format* control, *code conversion*, and the application of standard *processes* such as *zero suppression*.	*Edit
Electronic data processing.	*EDP
One who evaluates controls to assure the accurate input and processing of financial data.	EDP Auditor
Pertaining to *data processing* equipment that is predominantly electromechanical such as keypunches, mechanical sorters, collators, and *tabulators*.	*Electrical Accounting Machine (EAM)
(ISO) *Data processing* largely performed by electronic devices.	*Electronic Data Processing (EDP)

Electronic Funds Transfer System	A system that is used to facilitate the exchange of monetary values by electronic means. Terminals are linked to bank computers for use by customers at remote locations. Abbreviated EFTS.
*Eleven-Punch	A *punch* in the second *row* from the top, on a *Hollerith card.* Synonymous with x-punch.
End-of-File Mark	A code that signals that the last record of a file has been read. Abbreviated EOF.
*End-of-Tape Marker (EOT)	A marker on a *magnetic tape* used to indicate the end of the permissible recording area, e.g., a photo reflective strip, a transparent section of tape, a particular *bit* pattern.
*ENIAC (*E*lectronic *N*umerical *I*ntegrator *a*nd *C*alculator)	The first electronic computer and the first to use stored programs (programs stored internally in the machine).
*Erase	(ISO) To remove all previous *data* from *magnetic storage* by changing it to a specified condition; that may be an unmagnetized state or a predetermined magnetized state.
*Error	(1) (ISO) A discrepancy between a computed, observed, or measured value or condition and the true, specified, or theoretically correct value or condition. (2) (ISO) Deprecated term for *mistake.* (3) Contrast with *failure, fault, malfunction, mistake.*
*Execute	(1) (ISO) In *programming,* to change the state of a *computer* in accordance with the rules of the *operations* it recognizes. (2) (ISO) To perform the execution of an *instruction* or of a *computer* program.
*Execution	(1) (ISO) In *programming,* the process by which a *computer program* or *subroutine* changes the state of a *computer* in accordance with the rules of the *operations* that a computer recognizes. (2) (ISO) The *process* of carrying out an *instruction* by a *computer.* (3) (ISO) The *process* of carrying out the *instructions* of a *computer program* by a *computer.*
Execution Cycle	The time during which an instruction is decoded and performed.
Extended Binary Coded Decimal Interchange Code	A set of 256 characters, each represented by eight bits. Abbreviated EBCDIC.
*External Storage	(ISO) In a hierarchy of *storage devices* of a *data processing system,* any storage device that is not *internal storage.* External storage and internal storage are terms which take on precise meanings only with reference to a particular configuration.
*Extract	(ISO) To select and remove from a *set* of *items* those items that meet some criteria, e.g., to obtain certain specified *digits* from a *computer word* as controlled by an *instruction* or a *mask.*
Feasibility Study	A study that provides management with enough information about the proposed system project so an objective decision can be made regarding its value.

***Field** — (1) (ISO) In a *record,* a specified area used for a particular category of *data,* e.g., a group of *card columns* in which a wage rate is *recorded.* (2) A group of adjacent *card columns* on a *punch card.*

***Figurative Constant** — (1) (ISO) A *data name* that is reserved for a specified *constant* in a specified *programming language.* (2) (ISO) Deprecated term for *literal.*

***File** — (ISO) A *set* of related *records* treated as a *unit,* e.g., in stock control, a file could consist of a set of invoices.

***File Maintenance** — (ISO) The activity of keeping a *file* up to date by adding, changing, or deleting *data.*

File Protection Ring — A plastic ring placed around the hub of a reel of magnetic tape that allows the tape to be written on. It prevents accidental erasure of data on the magnetic tape.

Filemaking — Involves the construction of records used for reference to obtain information or to accumulate data.

First-Generation Computer — A computer utilizing vacuum tube components.

Fixed-Length Record — A record having the same length as all other records with which it is logically or physically associated. Contrast with Variable-Length Record.

***Fixed-Point Representation System** — (ISO) A *radix numeration system* in which the *radix point* is implicitly fixed in the series of *digit places* by some convention upon which agreement has been reached.

Fixed-Word Length Computer — A computer in which data is treated in units of a fixed number of characters or bits.

***Flag** — (1) Any of various types of *indicators* used for identification, e.g., a *word mark.* (2) A *character* that signals the occurrence of some condition, such as the end of a *word.* (3) (ISO) Deprecated term for *mark.* (4) (ISO) Synonym for *switch indicator.* (5) Synonymous with sentinel.

***Flip-Flop** — A *circuit* or device containing active elements, capable of assuming either one of two stable states at a given time. Synonymous with bistable circuit, toggle.

***Floating-Point Representation** — (1) (ISO) A representation of a *real number* in a *floating-point representation system,* e.g., a floating-point representation of the number 0.0001234 is 0.1234–3, where 0.1234 is the *fixed-point part* and –3 is the *exponent.* The *numerals* are expressed in the *variable-point decimal numeration system.* (2) Contrast with *variable-point representation.*

Floppy Disk — A low-cost, compact, flexible storage device resembling a 45 RPM phonograph record used primarily for storage and retrieval of data in low-cost handling systems.

***Flowchart** — (ISO) A *graphical* representation of the definition, *analysis,* or method of solution of a problem, in which *symbols* are used to represent *operations, data,* flow, equipment. etc.

***Flowchart Symbol** — (ISO) A *symbol* used to represent *operations, data,* flow or equipment on a *flowchart.*

*Foreground Processing	(1) (ISO) The *execution* of a *computer program* that preempts the use of *computer* facilities. (2) Contrast with *background processing.*
*Format	(ISO) The arrangement or layout of *data* in or on a *data medium.*
*FORTRAN (FORmula TRANslation)	A *programming language* primarily used to express *computer programs* by arithmetic formulas.
*Function	(1) (ISO) A mathematical entity whose value, i.e., the value of the dependent *variable,* depends in a specified manner on the values of one or more independent variables, not more than one value of the dependent variable corresponding to each permissible combination of values from the respective *ranges* of the independent variables. (2) A specific purpose of an entity, or its characteristic action. (3) In *data communication,* a machine action such as *carriage return* or *line feed.* (4) In *computer programming,* synonym for *procedure.*
*Gang Punch	To *punch* identical *data* into a *card deck.*
*General Purpose Computer	(ISO) A *computer* that is designed to operate upon a wide variety of problems.
*Generator	A controlling *routine* that performs a *generating function,* e.g., report generator, I/O generator.
*Graphic	(ISO) A *symbol* produced by a *process* such as handwriting, drawing, or printing. Synonymous with graphic symbol.
Graphic Processing	The ability to produce a great variety of information in the form of graphics, charts, pictures, maps, etc.
Group Indicate	The printing of indicative information from only the first record of a group.
Half-Adjust	To round by one half of the maximum value of the number base of the counter.
Halfword	A contiguous sequence of bits or characters that comprises half of a computer word and is capable of being addressed as a unit.
Hard Copy	A printed copy of machine output in visually readable form; for example, printed reports, listings, documents, summaries, etc.
*Hardware	(1) (ISO) Physical equipment used in *data processing,* as opposed to *computer programs, procedures,* rules and associated documentation. (2) Contrast with *software.*
*Hash Total	The *result* obtained by applying an *algorithm* to a *set* of *data* for checking purposes, e.g., a summation obtained by treating *data items* as *numbers.*
*Header Card	A card that contains *information* related to the *data* in cards that follow.
Hexadecimal	Pertaining to a number system with a base of sixteen; valid digits range from 0 through F, where F represents the highest units position (15). Synonymous with sexadecimal.
Hierarchical Network	The interrelationship of computers of different capacities and levels of data-processing responsibility at successively higher levels in a business organization.

Hierarchy Plus Input-Process-Output — An approach to functional specification and documentation of a program. It is a method of graphically describing a program entity as an arrangement of functions to be performed. Abbreviated as HIPO.

***High-Level Language** — (ISO) A *programming language* that does not reflect the structure of any one given *computer* or that of any given class of computers.

***Hollerith** — Pertaining to a particular type of *code* or *punched card* utilizing 12 *rows* per *column* and usually 80 columns per card.

Host Computer — (1) The primary or controlling computer in a multiple computer operation. (2) A computer used to prepare programs for use on another computer or data-processing system; for example, a computer used to compile, link edit, or test programs to be used on another system.

***Housekeeping Operation** — (ISO) An *operation* that facilitates the *execution* of a *computer program* without making a direct contribution. For example, initialization of *storage* areas; the execution of a *calling sequence*. Synonymous with overhead operation.

***Identifier** — (ISO) A *character* or group of characters used to identify or name an *item* of *data* and possibly to indicate certain properties of that data.

Impact Printers — These printers perform printing operations by transferring ink to paper by striking the ribbon against the paper for each character.

***Index** — (1) (ISO) In *programming,* a *subscript,* of *integer* value, that identifies the *position* of an *item* of *data* with respect to some other item of data. (2) (ISO) A *list* of the contents of a *file* or of a *document,* together with *keys* or references for locating the contents. (3) A *symbol* or a *numeral* used to identify a particular quantity in an *array* of similar quantities. For example, the terms of an array represented by X1, X2, . . ., X100 have the indexes 1, 2, . . ., 100 respectively. (4) In *micrographics,* a guide for locating information on a roll of *microfilm* using targets, flash cards, lines, bars, or other optical *codes.* (5) To prepare a *list* as in (2). (6) To move a machine part to a predetermined position, or by a predetermined amount, on a *quantitized* scale.

Indexed Sequential Organization — A file organization in which records are arranged in logical sequence by key. Indexes to these keys permit direct access to individual records.

***Index Register** — (ISO) A *register* whose contents may be used to modify an *operand address* during the *execution* of *computer instructions,* so as to operate as a *clock* or *counter.* An index register may be used to control the execution of a *loop,* to control the use of an *array,* as a *switch,* for *table lookup,* as a pointer, etc. Synonymous with modifier register.

***Indicator** — (1) (ISO) A device that may be *set* into a prescribed state, usually according to the result of a previous *process* or on the occurrence of a specified condition in the equipment, and that usually gives a visual or other indication of the existence of the prescribed state, and that may in some cases be used to determine the selection among alternative next processes, e.g., an *overflow* indicator. (2) An *item* of *data* that may be interrogated to determine whether a particular condition has been satisfied in the *execution* of a *computer program,* e.g., a *switch indicator,* an *overflow* indicator.

*Information	(ISO) The meaning that a human assigns to *data* by means of the known conventions used in their representation.
*Information Processing	(ISO) Synonym for *data processing.*
*Information Retrieval	(1) (ISO) The action of recovering specific *information* from *stored data.* (2) (ISO) Methods and *procedures* for recovering specific *information* from *stored data.*
*Initialize	(1) To *set counters, switches, addresses,* or contents of *storage* to *zero* or other starting values at the beginning of, or at prescribed points in, the *operation* of a *computer routine.* (2) Contrast with *prestore.*
Inline Processing	The processing of data in random order, not subject to preliminary editing or sorting.
*Input	(1) One, or a *sequence* of, *input states.* (2) (ISO) Pertaining to a device, *process,* or *channel* involved in an *input process,* or to the *data* or states involved in an input process. In the English *language,* the adjective input may be used in place of input data, input signal, input terminal, etc., when such usage is clear in a given context. (3) (ISO) Synonym for *input data, input process.* (4) Synonym for *input channel.*
Input Area	An area of storage reserved for input.
Input Device	The device or collective set of devices used for conveying data into another device.
*Input/Output (I/O)	(1) (ISO) Pertaining to a device or to a *channel* that may be involved in an *input process* and, at a different time, in an *output process.* In the English *language,* input-output may be used in place of input-output *data,* input-output *signal,* input-output terminals, etc., when such usage is clear in a given context. (2) (ISO) Pertaining to a device whose parts can be performing an *input process* and an *output process* at the same time. (3) Pertaining to either *input* or *output,* or both.
Input/Output Control	The receiving, logging, controlling, and coordinating of documents and input/output devices.
Input/Output Control System	A group of routines provided by the computer manufacturer for handling transfer of data between main storage and auxiliary storage. Abbreviated IOCS.
Input/Output Device	A unit for putting or getting data out of a storage unit. Commonly called I/O.
Input Preparation	The translation of input data into codes and formats suitable for data processing.
*Input Process	(1) (ISO) The *process* that consists of the reception of *data* into a *data processing system,* into a subsystem, or into a device. Synonymous with input. (2) The *process* of *transmitting data* from *peripheral equipment,* or *external storage,* to *internal storage.* (3) The *process* of receiving *data* by a device.
Inquiry	A request for information from storage; for example, a request for the number of available airline seats or a machine statement to initiate a search of library documents.

The organization and scheduling of human resources and mechanical resources into an effective plan for establishing or changing a data-processing activity. **Installation Planning**

Time spent in installing and testing *hardware* or *software*. ***Installation Time**

(ISO) In a *programming language,* a meaningful *expression* that specifies one *operation* and identifies its *operands,* if any. ***Instruction**

The time during which an instruction is fetched from the main storage of computer into an instruction register. **Instruction Time**

A whole number, positive or negative, without a decimal point. **Integer**

(ISO) *Data processing* in which the coordination of *data* acquisition and other stages of data processing are combined in a coherent *data processing system.* ***Integrated Data Processing (IDP)**

The terminals possess program capability from the use of integrated processors or built-in microcomputers. The "intelligent" terminal can interface with communications networks employing such different protocols as storing, retrieving, and editing text locally without having to depend on the remote processor, process data locally beyond making simple edit checks, and define display formats locally. **Intelligent Terminals**

Pertaining to an application in which each entry elicits a response, as in an inquiry system or an airline reservation system. An interactive system may also be conversational, implying a continuous dialog between the user and the system. **Interactive**

A structured programming technique used for repeated execution of code while a condition is true (or false). **Interation Structure**

(1) (ISO) A space between *blocks* on *magnetic tape.* (2) An area on a *data medium* used to indicate the end of a *block* or *physical record.* (3) Synonymous with block gap. ***Interblock Gap**

A shared boundary. An interface might be a *hardware* component to link two devices or it might be a portion of *storage* or *registers* accessed by two or more *computer programs.* ***Interface**

(ISO) A *storage device* directly controlled by the *central processing unit* of a *digital computer.* ***Internal Storage**

(1) (ISO) A *computer program* used to *interpret.* Synonymous with interpretive program. (2) (ISO) In *punched card* operations, a device that prints on a punched card the characters equivalent to the *hole patterns* punched in the card. ***Interpreter**

(ISO) Deprecated term for *interblock gap.* ***Interrecord Gap**

To stop a *process* in such a way that it can be resumed. ***Interrupt**

(1) (ISO) One member of a group. A *file* may consist of a number of items such as *records* which in turn may consist of other items. (2) A collection of related *characters* treated as a *unit.* ***Item**

Jacquard Developed the punched-card principle used for weaving in the textile industry, which was later used by Babbage and Hollerith in calculating machines.

***Job** A set of *data* that completely defines a unit of work for a *computer.* A job usually includes all necessary *computer programs, linkages, files,* and *instructions* to the *operating system.*

***Job Control Language (JCL)** A *problem-oriented language* designed to express *statements* in a *job* that are used to identify the job or describe its requirements to an *operating system.*

***Job Control Statement** A *statement* in a job that is used for identifying the job or describing its requirements to the *operating system.*

Job Management A general term that collectively describes the functions of job scheduling and command processing. It provides the facilities to read, interpret, initiate, and terminate jobs submitted for processing.

Job Processing The reading of job control statements and data from an input stream, the initiating of job steps defined in the statements, and the writing of system output messages.

***Job Step** The *execution* of a *computer program* explicitly identified by a *job control statement.* A *job* may specify that several job steps be executed.

***Jump** (ISO) In the *execution* of a *computer program,* a departure from the implicit or declared *order* in which *instructions* are being executed.

***Justify** (1) (ISO) To control the printing *positions* of *characters* on a page so that both the left-hand and right-hand margins of the printing are regular. (2) (ISO) To *shift* the contents of a *register,* if necessary, so that the *character* at a specified end of the *data* that has been *read* or *loaded* into the register is at a specified *position* in the register. (3) To align *characters* horizontally or vertically to fit the *positioning* constraints of a required *format.*

K (Kilo) One thousand (1000) in decimal notation.

***Key** (ISO) One or more *characters,* within a set of *data,* that contains *information* about the set, including its identification.

***Keypunch** (ISO) A keyboard-actuated device that punches holes in a *punch card* or *punched card.* Synonymous with keyboard punch.

***Label** (1) (ISO) One or more *characters,* within or attached to a *set* of *data,* that contains *information* about the set, including its identification. (2) (ISO) In *computer programming,* an *identifier* of an *instruction.*

***Language** (ISO) A *set* of *characters,* conventions, and rules, that is used for conveying *information.* The three aspects of language are *pragmatics, semantics,* and *syntax.*

***Language Processor** (ISO) A *computer program* that performs such *functions* as *translating* and *interpreting* and other tasks required for *processing* a specified *programming language.*

Language Translator A general term for any assembler, compiler, or other routine that accepts statements in one language and produces equivalent statements in another language.

Learning Curves It takes the employees longer to do a new job than it took to do the old job.

***Library** (1) A collection of related *files.* For example, one line of an invoice may form an *item,* a complete invoice may form a file, the collection of inventory control files may form a library, and the libraries used by an organization are known as its *data bank.* (2) A repository for dismountable recorded media, such as *magnetic disk packs* and *magnetic tapes.*

***Library Routine** A proven *routine* that is maintained in a *program library.*

***Linear Programming (LP)** (ISO) In *operations research,* a procedure for locating the maximum or minimum of a linear *function* of *variables* that are subject to linear constraints. Synonymous with linear optimization.

***Line Printer** (1) (ISO) A device that prints a line of *characters* as a unit. Synonymous with line-at-a-time printer. (2) Contrast with *character printer, page printer.*

***Link** (1) (ISO) In *computer programming,* the part of a computer program, in some cases a single *instruction* or an *address,* that passes control and *parameters* between separate portions of the computer program. (2) (ISO) In *computer programming,* to provide a link. (3) (ISO) Synonymous with linkage.

***Linkage Editor** (1) A *utility routine* that creates a *loadable computer program* by combining independently *translated* computer program *modules* and by resolving cross references among the modules. (2) Contrast with *editor program.*

***List** (1) (ISO) An *ordered set* of *items* of *data.* (2) To print or otherwise *display items* of *data* that meet specified criteria. (3) (ISO) Deprecated term for *chained list.*

***Literal** (ISO) In a *source program,* an explicit representation of the value of an *item,* which value must be unaltered during any *translation* of the source program, e.g., the word FAIL in the *instruction:* "IF X = 0 PRINT FAIL."

***Load** (ISO) In *computer programming,* to enter *data* into *storage* or working *registers.*

***Loader** A *routine,* commonly a *computer program,* that *reads data* into *main storage.*

Load Module The output of the linkage editor; a program in a format suitable for loading into main storage for execution.

Lockword It permits access to a portion of file or to accept modification of that file.

Logical Errors Errors in a program that result from poor analysis.

***Logical Record** A *record* independent of its physical environment. Portions of the same logical record may be located in different physical records, or several logical records or parts of logical records may be located in one physical record.

***Loop** (ISO) A *set* of *instructions* that may be *executed* repeatedly while a certain condition prevails. In some implementations, no test is made to discover whether the condition prevails until the loop has been executed once.

***Machine Language** (1) A *language* that is used directly by a machine. (2) (ISO) Deprecated term for *computer instruction code.* (3) (ISO) Synonym for *computer language.*

*Machine-Oriented Language	Synonym for *computer-oriented language.*
*Macroinstruction	(ISO) An *instruction* in a *source language* that is to be replaced by a defined *sequence* of instructions in the same source language. The macroinstruction may also specify values for *parameters* in the instructions that are to replace it.
*Magnetic Card	A card with a magnetic surface on which *data* can be *stored* by *magnetic recording.*
*Magnetic Core	(1) (ISO) A piece of magnetic material, usually toroidal in shape, used for *storage.* (2) A configuration of magnetic material that is, or is intended to be, placed in a spatial relationship to current-carrying conductors and whose magnetic properties are essential to its use. It may be used to concentrate an induced magnetic field as in a transformer induction coil, or armature, to retain a magnetic polarization for the purpose of *storing data,* or for its nonlinear properties as in a *logic element.* It may be made of such material as iron, iron oxide, or ferrite and in such shapes as wires, tapes, toroids, rods, or thin film.
*Magnetic Core Storage	(ISO) A *magnetic storage* in which *data* are *stored* by the selective polarization of *magnetic cores.*
*Magnetic Disk	(ISO) A flat circular plate with a magnetic surface layer. Synonymous with disk.
*Magnetic Disk Storage	(ISO) A *magnetic storage* in which *data* are *stored* by the selective polarization of portions of magnetic material on the flat surface of one or more disks that rotate in use.
*Magnetic Drum	(ISO) A right circular cylinder with a magnetic surface layer.
*Magnetic Drum Storage	(ISO) A *magnetic storage* in which *data* are *stored* by the selective polarization of portions of magnetic material of the curved surface of a cylinder that rotates in use.
*Magnetic Ink Character Recognition (MICR)	(1) *Character recognition* of *characters* printed with ink that contains particles of a magnetic material. (2) Contrast with *optical character recognition.*
*Magnetic Storage	A *storage device* that utilizes the magnetic properties of certain materials.
*Magnetic Tape	(1) (ISO) A tape with a magnetic surface layer. (2) A tape of magnetic material used as the constituent in some forms of *magnetic cores.*
*Magnetic Tape Storage	A *magnetic storage* in which *data* are *stored* by the selective polarization of portions of magnetic material on the surface of a tape that moves longitudinally in use.
*Main Frame	Synonym for *central processing unit.*
*Main Storage	(ISO) A *storage device* whose *storage cells* can be *addressed* by a *computer program* and from which *instructions* and *data* can be *loaded* directly into *registers* from which the instructions can be *executed* or from which the data can be *operated* upon.
*Maintenance	(ISO) Any activity, such as tests, measurements, replacements, adjustments, and repairs, intended to eliminate *faults* or to keep a *functional unit* in a specified state.

Management by Exception — This technique is used by many companies to reduce the amount of detail that the decision maker is faced with. In this concept, only the exceptional facts are drawn to the attention of these executives.

***Management Information System (MIS)** — (1) (ISO) Management performed with the aid of *automatic data processing.* (2) An *information system* designed to aid in the performance of management *functions.*

Mandatory Reports — The necessary reports that are required by governmental agencies, stockholders, customers, etc. These reports must be prepared in a fixed format according to the needs of the user.

***Manual Input** — (1) The entry of *data* by hand into a device. (2) The *data* entered as in (1).

Mark 1 — The world's first automatic computer, in that it had an automatic sequence-controlled calculator operated entirely by mechanical switches.

***Mark Sensing** — (1) The electrical sensing of manually recorded conductive marks on a nonconductive surface. (2) The automatic sensing of manually recorded marks on a *data medium.*

***Mass Storage Device** — A device having a large *storage capacity,* e.g., *magnetic disk, magnetic drum.*

Mass Storage (Online) — The storage of a large amount of data which is also readily accessible to the central processing unit of a computer.

***Mathematical Model** — A mathematical representation of a *process,* device, or concept.

***Matrix** — (1) (ISO) A rectangular array of elements, arranged in rows and columns, that may be manipulated according to the rules of matrix algebra. (2) In *computers,* a logic network in the form of an array of *input* leads and *output* leads with *logic elements* connected at some of their intersections. (3) By extension, an array of any number of dimensions.

Medium — The material, or configuration thereof, on which data is recorded; for example, paper tape, cards, magnetic tape, etc. Synonymous with data medium.

Memory — Same as Storage.

***Merge** — (ISO) To combine the *items* of two or more *sets* that are each in the same given *order* into one set in that order.

MFT — Multiprogramming with a fixed number of tasks.

MICR — (*M*agnetic-*I*nk *C*haracter *R*ecognition)

Microcomputer — A computer that incorporates a microprocessor as its major component.

Microfiche — Data is maintained on a single sheet and new documents can be added to unused portions at any time and the film can be accessed randomly.

Microfilm — Data is maintained on a spool of film that can be recorded, updated, and retrieved sequentially, as on magnetic tape.

Microprocessor	The central processing unit of a microcomputer that is implemented in a single or very small number of integrated circuits that perform all data manipulation, programs, and decision-making logic and arithmetic logic functions.
*Microprogram	(ISO) A *sequence* of elementary *instructions* that correspond to a *computer operation,* that is maintained in special *storage*, and whose *execution* is initiated by the introduction of a *computer instruction* into an *instruction register* of a *computer.*
*Micro-programming	(ISO) The preparation or use of *microprograms.*
Microsecond	One millionth of a second.
Millisecond	One thousandth of a second.
Minicomputer	A stand-alone system, capable of operating independently, having a large number of peripheral devices and supported by a large number of software packages, competing with conventional computers.
Minor Total	The result when a summation is terminated by the least significant change of group.
*Mnemonic Symbol	(ISO) A *symbol* chosen to assist the human memory, e.g., an abbreviation such as "mpy" for "multiply."
Modem	(*Mo*dulator-*Dem*odulator) A device that modulates and demodulates signals transmitted over communication lines.
*Module	(1) A *program unit* that is discrete and identifiable with respect to *compiling,* combining with other units, and *loading,* e.g., the *input* to, or *output* from, an *assembler, compiler, linkage editor,* or *executive routine.* (2) A packaged functional *hardware unit* designed for use with other components.
*Monitor	(1) (ISO) A device that observes and verifies the operations of a *data processing system* and indicates any significant departure from the norm. (2) *Software* or *hardware* that observes, supervises, controls, or verifies the operations of a *system.*
*Monte Carlo Method	(ISO) A method of obtaining an approximate solution to a numerical problem by the use of *random numbers,* e.g., the *random walk* method, or a *procedure* using a *random number sequence* to calculate an integral.
*Multiple Punching	The *punching* of more than one hole in the same *card column* by means of more than one keystroke, usually in order to extend the *character set* of the punch.
*Multiplex	To *interleave* or simultaneously *transmit* two or more messages on a single *channel.*
*Multiprocessor	A *computer* employing two or more *central processing units* under integrated control.
*Multiprogramming	(1) A mode of *operation* that provides for the *interleaved* execution of two or more *computer programs* by a single *central processing unit.* (2) Pertaining to the *concurrent execution* of two or more *computer programs* by a *computer.*
Nanosecond	One billionth of a second.
Networks	Two or more processors linked together by communication lines used to distribute high-speed computing services to a large number of users.

Nonimpact Printers — These printers use special coated paper that responds to thermal or electrostatic stimuli to form an image.

***Number Representation** — (ISO) A representation of a *number* in a *numeration system*. Synonymous with numeration.

***Numeric** — (ISO) Pertaining to *data* or to physical quantities represented by *numerals*. Synonymous with numerical.

***Object Code** — *Output* from a *compiler* or *assembler* which is itself *executable machine code* or is suitable for *processing* to produce executable machine code.

Objectives — The basic goals of the organization.

***Object Module** — A *module* that is the *output* of an *assembler* or *compiler* and is *input* to a *linkage editor*.

***Object Program** — (1) (ISO) A fully *compiled* or *assembled program* that is ready to be *loaded* into the *computer*. (2) Synonym for *target program*. (3) Contrast with *source program*.

***OCR** — *Optical character recognition.*

***Octal** — (ISO) Pertaining to a *fixed-radix numeration system* having a *radix* of eight.

***Offline** — Pertaining to equipment or devices not under control of a *central processing unit*.

***Offline Storage** — *Storage* not under control of the *central processing unit*.

Offline System — In teleprocessing, that kind of a system in which human operations are required between the original recording functions and the ultimate data-processing function. This includes conversion operations as well as the necessary loading and unloading operations incident to the use of point-to-point or data-gathering systems. Contrast with Online System.

***Online** — (1) Pertaining to equipment or devices under the direct control of a *central processing unit*. (2) Pertaining to a user's ability to interact with a *computer*. (3) Pertaining to the user's access to a *computer* via a *terminal*.

***Online Storage** — *Storage* under control of the *central processing unit*.

Online System — (1) In teleprocessing, a system in which the input data enters the computer directly from the point of origin or in which output data is transmitted directly to where it is used. (2) In telegraph usage, a system of transmitting directly into the system. Contrast with Offline System.

***Open Shop** — (1) Pertaining to the *operation* of a *computer* facility in which most productive problem *programming* is performed by the problem originator rather than by a group of programming specialists. The use of the computer itself may also be described as open shop if the user/*programmer* also serves as the *operator*. (2) Contrast with *closed shop*.

***Open Subroutine** — (1) (ISO) A *subroutine* of which a replica must be inserted at each place in a *computer program* at which the subroutine is used. Synonymous with direct insert subroutine. (2) Contrast with *closed subroutine*.

***Operand** (1) (ISO) An entity to which an *operation* is applied. (2) That which is *operated* upon. An operand is usually identified by an *address part* of an *instruction.*

***Operating System** (ISO) *Software* that controls the *execution* of *computer programs* and that may provide scheduling, *debugging, input-output* control, accounting, *compilation, storage* assignment, *data* management, and related services.

***Operation** (1) (ISO) A well-defined action that, when applied to any permissible combination of known entities, produces a new entity. (2) A defined action, namely, the act of obtaining a *result* from one or more *operands* in accordance with a rule that completely specifies the result for any permissible combination of operands. (3) A *program* step undertaken or *executed* by a *computer*, e.g., addition, multiplication, *extraction, comparison, shift, transfer.* The *operation* is usually specified by the *operator* as part of an *instruction.* (4) The event or specific action performed by a *logic* element.

Operational Reports The reports that aid management in making the many necessary decisions in everyday business operations.

***Operation Code** (ISO) A *code* used to represent the *operations* of a *computer.*

***Operations Research (OR)** (ISO) The application of scientific methods to the solution of complex problems concerning the optimal allocation of available resources. Synonymous with operations analysis.

***Operator** (1) (ISO) A *symbol* that represents the action to be performed in a mathematical *operation.* (2) In the description of a *process*, that which indicates the action to be performed on *operands.* (3) A person who *operates* a machine.

***Optical Character Recognition (OCR)** (1) The machine identification of printed *characters* through use of light sensitive devices. (2) Contrast with *magnetic ink character recognition.*

***Optical Scanner** (1) (ISO) A *scanner* that uses light for examining patterns. (2) A device that scans optically and usually generates an *analog* or *digital signal.*

OS (Operating System)

***Output** (ISO) Pertaining to a device, process, or *channel* involved in an *output process,* or to the *data* or states involved in an output process.

Overflow That portion of the result of an operation that exceeds the capacity of the intended unit of storage.

Overlap To do something at the same time that something else is being done; for example, to perform input/output operations while instructions are being executed by the central processing unit.

***Overlay** (1) (ISO) In a *computer program,* a *segment* that is not permanently maintained in *internal storage.* (2) The technique of repeatedly using the same areas of *internal storage* during different stages of a *program.* (3) (ISO) In the *execution* of a *computer program,* to *load* a *segment* of the computer program in a *storage* area hitherto occupied by parts of the computer program that are not currently needed.

***Overpunch** (1) To add holes in a *card column* that already contains holes. Overpunches are often used to represent *special characters.* (2) To add holes to *perforated tape* to change a *character,* especially to produce a *delete character.* (3) Synonym for *zone punch.*

***Pack** (ISO) To *store data* in a compact form in a *storage medium* by taking advantage of known characteristics of the data and the storage medium, in such a way that the original form of the data can be recovered, e.g., to make use of *bit* or *byte locations* that would otherwise go unused.

***Page Printer** (1) A device that prints one page at a time, e.g., xerographic printer, cathode ray tube printer, film printer. Synonymous with page-at-a-time printer. (2) Contrast with *character printer, line printer.*

Paper Tape Reader A device that senses and translates the holes in perforated tape into electrical signals.

***Parallel** (1) Pertaining to the *concurrent operation* or *simultaneous operation* of two or more devices or to the concurrent performance of two or more activities in a single device. (2) Pertaining to the *concurrent* or *simultaneous* occurrence of two or more related activities in multiple devices or *channels.* (3) Pertaining to the *simultaneity* of two or more *processes.* (4) Pertaining to the *simultaneous processing* of the individual parts of a whole, such as the *bits* of a *character* and the characters of a *word,* using separate facilities for the various parts. (5) Contrast with *serial.*

***Parallel Processing** (1) The *concurrent* or *simultaneous execution* of two or more processes in a single *unit.* (2) Contrast with *serial processing.*

***Parameter** (ISO) A *variable* that is given a constant value for a specified application and that may denote the application.

***Parity Bit** A *check bit* appended to an *array* of *binary digits* to make the *sum* of all the binary digits, including the check bit, always odd or always even.

***Parity Check** A *check* that tests whether the number of ones (or *zeros*) in an *array* of *binary digits* is odd or even. Synonymous with odd-even check.

Partitioned Data Organization A data set in direct access storage that is divided into partitions, called members, each of which can be a program or part of a program. Each partitioned data set contains a directory (or index) that the control program can use to locate a program in the library. Abbreviated PDS. Synonymous with Program Library.

Password (1) A unique string of characters that a program or computer operator, or user, must supply to meet security requirements before gaining access to data. (2) In systems with time sharing, a one-to-eight character symbol that the user may be required to supply while logging on the system. The password is confidential, as opposed to the user identification.

***Patch** (1) A temporary electrical connection. (2) (ISO) To make an improvised modification. To modify a *routine* in a rough or expedient way.

***Pattern Recognition** (ISO) The identification of shapes, forms, or configurations by *automatic* means.

*Peripheral Equipment — (ISO) In a *data processing system,* any equipment, distinct from the *central processing unit,* that may provide the system with outside communication or additional facilities.

Personal Computers — Microcomputers that can be used in the home or business, that are programmable, that can be used for games, educational tools, small businesses, etc.

Physical IOCS — Supervisory routines that schedule and supervise the execution of channel programs. Physical IOCS controls the actual transfer of records between external storage and main storage and provides I/O device error recovery.

Physical Record — A record from the standpoint of the manner or form in which it is stored, retrieved, and moved; that is, one defined in terms of physical qualities. A physical record may contain all or part of one or more logical records.

Picosecond — One trillionth of a second.

PL/1 — A high-level programming language, designed for use in a wide range of commercial and scientific computer applications.

Plotter — Produces a recording of the pen movement on the surface of paper, three-dimensional drawings, color plotting, microfilm recording, etc.

*Plugboard — (ISO) A perforated board into which plugs or pins may be placed to control the *operation* of equipment. Synonymous with control panel, pinboard.

Point-of-Sale — The electronic control of credit and the electronic capture of merchandise information at the point of sale. This system has replaced the conventional cash register and provides control totals, operating statistics, data-processing flexibility, and an economical approach to retail data processing. Abbreviated POS.

Positional Notation — A number representation system in which a number is represented by means of an ordered set of digits, such that the value contributed by each digit depends on its position as well as upon its value. Synonymous with positional representation.

*Preventive Maintenance — (1) *Maintenance* specifically intended to prevent *faults* from occurring. Corrective maintenance and preventive maintenance are both performed during *maintenance time.* (2) Contrast with *corrective maintenance.*

Primary Storage — The main internal storage.

Printer — A device that writes output data from a system on paper or other media.

Privacy — The right of an individual to be free in private affairs from surveillance and intrusion; to be free to keep private affairs private, and to be free from compulsion in action, thought, and expression.

*Problem Description — (ISO) A statement of a problem, perhaps including a description of the method of solving it, the *procedures* and *algorithms,* etc.

Problem-Oriented Language — A programming language designed for the convenient expression of a given class of problems.

Any program that is executed when the central processing unit is in the problem state; that is, any program that does not contain privileged instructions. (A privileged instruction is an instruction that can be executed only when the processing unit is in the supervisor state.) — **Problem Program**

A programming language designed for the convenient expression of procedures used in the solution of a wide class of problems. — **Procedure-Oriented Language**

(1) A course of events occurring according to an intended purpose or effect. (2) A *systematic sequence* of *operations* to produce a specified *result*. (3) To perform operations on *data*. — ***Process**

(1) A general term for any program that is not a control program. (2) Any program capable of operating in the problem program state. — **Processing Program**

(1) In *hardware*, a *data processor*. (2) In *software*, a *computer program* that performs *functions* such as *compiling, assembling*, and *translating* for a specific *programming language*. — ***Processor**

(1) (ISO) A schedule or plan that specifies actions that may or may not be taken. (2) Loosely, a *routine*. (3) (ISO) To design, write, and test *computer programs*. (4) Loosely, to write a *routine*. — ***Program**

A graphic representation of the procedures, step-by-step, in sequence, by which data is to be processed. — **Program Flowchart**

(1) (ISO) An organized collection of *computer programs* that are sufficiently *documented* to allow them to be used by persons other than their authors. (2) A collection of available *computer programs* and *routines*. — ***Program Library**

Typically used to provide permanent instruction capability to the microprocessor in the functions it performs each time it is used. It does not lose the data and/or instructions it has stored when power is removed from the system. Unlike RAM memory, PROM memory can only be read and not used for any reading of the system. Abbreviated PROM. — **Programmable Read-Only Memory**

The making of relatively minor changes in operating programs to update them, solve program-operating problems, adapt to scheduling changes, and correct errors found in programs after they have gone into an operating state. — **Program Maintenance**

A person who designs, writes, and tests *computer programs*. — ***Programmer**

(ISO) The designing, writing, and testing of *programs*. — ***Programming**

(ISO) An *artificial language* established for expressing *computer programs*. — ***Programming Language**

(1) A device for making holes in a *data medium*. (2) A perforation, as in a *punched card* or paper tape. — ***Punch**

A card *punched* with *hole patterns*. — ***Punched Card**

The procedure of recording, manipulating, and reporting information through the use of holes punched in a card. — **Punched-Card Data Processing**

Punched Tape A tape on which a pattern of holes or cuts is used to represent data.

Queue (1) A waiting line or list formed by items in a system waiting for service; for example, tasks to be performed or messages to be transmitted in message switching system. (2) To arrange in or form a queue.

***Radix** (1) (ISO) Of a *digit* place in a *radix numeration system,* the positive *integer* by which the *weight* of the digit place is multiplied to obtain the weight of the digit place with the next higher weight, e.g., in the *decimal numeration system* the radix of each digit place is 10, in a biquinary code the radix of each fives position is 2. (2) (ISO) Deprecated term for *base.*

Random Access Same as Direct Access.

Random Access Memory The direct equivalent of core memory used in microcomputers. This type of memory is fast and economical and usually provides the bulk of the microcomputer's internal storage. Abbreviated RAM.

Random Access Units Devices that process data randomly; that is, records can be accessed without reading from the beginning of a file to find them.

Random Processing The processing of detail transactions against a master file, regardless of sequence of the input documents. It does not require all records to be examined, only those that need updating.

***Range** (1) (ISO) The *set* of values that a quantity or *function* may take. (2) The difference between the highest and lowest value that a quantity or *function* may assume. (3) (ISO) Deprecated term for *span.*

***Read** (ISO) To acquire or to interpret *data* from a *storage device,* from a *data medium,* or from another source.

Read-Only Memory A system on a chip for controlling the functions of the microcomputer. For example, by defining the instruction that will be executed, the characteristics of a machine can be appreciably altered by inserting a different ROM. Abbreviated as ROM.

***Real Time** (1) Pertaining to the actual time during which a physical *process* transpires. (2) Pertaining to the performance of a computation during the actual time that the related physical *process* transpires, in order that *results* of the computation can be used in guiding the physical process.

***Record** (ISO) A collection of related *data* or *words* treated as a *unit,* e.g., in stock control, each invoice could constitute one record.

***Record Gap** (ISO) Deprecated term for *interblock gap.*

***Record Layout** (ISO) The arrangement and structure of *data* or *words* in a *record* including the order and size of the components of the record.

***Record Length** (ISO) The number of *words* or *characters* forming a *record.*

***Register** (ISO) In a *computer,* a *storage device,* usually intended for some special purpose, capable of storing a specified amount of *data* such as a *bit* or a *word.*

Relational Operator — An operator that can be used in arithmetic or character relation to indicate the comparison to be performed between the terms in the relation. The relational operators are equal to, greater than or equal to, greater than, less than, less than or equal to, or not equal to.

Relocate — In computer programming, to move a routine from one portion of storage to another and to adjust the necessary address references so that the routine, in its new location, can be executed.

***Remote Access** — Pertaining to communication with a *data-processing* facility through a *data link*.

Remote Batch Terminals — These terminals transmit large amounts (batches) of data at a high speed to a central computer. They may include fast printers (that can use the entire range of business forms), card readers, and high-speed data-processing facilities, and can contain processors that enable them to do things that most small terminals can't do by themselves. They extend the processing capability of the larger control computer, via communication lines, to a distant site. They differ from other terminals in that they handle large amounts (batches) of important day-to-day operational data at a high speed with outputs comparable to those attainable at the computer site itself.

***Remote Job Entry (RJE)** — (ISO) Submission of *jobs* through an *input unit* that has access to a *computer* through a *data link*.

Report Generation — A technique for producing complete machine reports from information that describes the input file and the format and content of the output format.

Report Program Generator — A processing program that can be used to generate object programs that produce reports from existing sets of data. Abbreviated RPG.

Reproduce — To prepare a duplicate of stored information, especially for punched cards, punched paper tape, or magnetic tape.

Reproducer — A device that will duplicate, in one card, all or part of the information contained in another card.

***Rerun** — (1) (ISO) A repeat of a machine *run* from its beginning, usually made desirable or necessary by a false start, by an *interruption*, or by a change. (2) (ISO) To perform a rerun.

Resource-Sharing Network — A number of remote minicomputers with limited local capacity can draw the greater power of a larger minicomputer or large-scale host computer to handle the services available to a local user.

***ROM** — (ISO) *Read-only memory*.

***Round** — (1) (ISO) To delete or omit one or more of the least significant *digits* in a *positional representation* and to adjust the part retained in accordance with some specified rule. The purpose of rounding is usually to limit the *precision* of the *numeral* or to reduce the number of *characters* in the numeral, or to do both. The most common forms of rounding are *rounding down, rounding up,* and *rounding off*. (2) Contrast with *truncation*.

***Routine** — (ISO) An *ordered set* of *instructions* that may have some general or frequent use.

*Row	(1) A horizontal arrangement of *characters* or other expressions. (2) Contrast with *column.*
*RPG	Report program generator.
*Run	(1) (ISO) A single performance of one or more *jobs.* (2) A single, continuous performance of a *computer program* or *routine.*
Satellite Computer	(1) A computer that is under the control of another computer and performs subsidiary operations. (2) A computer that depends on a host computer for guidance in a distributed data-processing system.
Scientific Data Processing	The analysis of the data required and used for engineering and research purposes. It is mathematically oriented, nonrepetitive in nature, or file-oriented, requiring small amounts of input and output data with many calculations.
*Search	(1) (ISO) The examination of a *set* of *items* for one or more having a given property. (2) (ISO) To examine a *set* of *items* for one or more having a given property.
Secondary Storage	Same as Auxiliary Storage.
Second-Generation Computer	A computer utilizing solid-state components.
*Segment	(1) (ISO) A self-contained portion of a *computer program* that may be *executed* without the entire computer program necessarily being maintained in *internal storage* at any one time. (2) (ISO) To divide a *computer program* into segments.
Selection Structure	In structured programming, the choice is between two actions based on a condition encountered during the processing.
*Sequence	(1) (ISO) A series of *items* that have been sequenced. (2) An arrangement of *items* according to a specified set of rules, e.g., items arranged alphabetically, numerically, or chronologically. (3) (ISO) Deprecated term for *order.* (4) Synonym for *collating sequence.*
Sequence Structure	In structured programming, in the absence of instructions to the contrary, statements are executed in the order in which they are written.
Sequential Access Units	Process data sequentially; that is, each record must be read from the beginning of the file to find the desired record.
Sequential Organization	Records are organized solely on the basis of their successive physical locations in the file.
*Serial	(1) (ISO) Pertaining to the *sequential* performance of two or more activities in a single device. In English, the modifiers serial and parallel usually refer to devices, as opposed to sequential and consecutive, which refer to processes. (2) Pertaining to the *sequential* or *consecutive* occurrence of two or more related activities in a single device or *channel.* (3) Pertaining to the *sequential processing* of the individual parts of a whole, such as the *bits* of a character or the characters of a *word,* using the same facilities for successive parts. (4) Contrast with *parallel.*

***Serial Access** (1) (ISO) The facility to obtain *data* from a *storage device* or to enter data into a storage device in such a way that the process depends on the location of that data and on a reference to data previously accessed. (2) Pertaining to the *sequential* or *consecutive transmission* of *data* to or from *storage.* (3) Contrast with *direct access.*

Service Routine A routine in general support of the operation of a computer; for example, input/output, diagnostic, tracing, or monitoring routines. Synonymous with utility routine.

***Setup** (1) (ISO) In a *computer* which consists of an assembly of individual computing *units,* the arrangement of interconnections between the units, and the adjustments needed for the computer to *operate* upon a given problem. (2) An arrangement of *data* or devices to solve a particular problem.

Setup Time The time required by an operator to prepare a computing system to perform a job or job step.

Shared Processor Data Terminal System A number of data entry stations that share a minicomputer.

***Sight Check** A *check* performed by sighting through the holes of two or more aligned *punched cards* toward a source of light to verify the punching, e.g., to determine if a hole has been punched in a corresponding *punch position* on all cards in a card deck.

Significance In positional representation, the factor, dependent on the digit place, by which a digit is multiplied to obtain its additive contribution in the representation of a number.

***Sign Position** (ISO) A *position,* normally located at one end of a *numeral,* that contains an indicator denoting the algebraic sign of the *number* represented by the numeral.

***Simulation** (ISO) The representation of certain features of the behavior of a physical or abstract system by the behavior of another system, e.g., the representation of physical phenomena by means of *operations* performed by a *computer* or the representation of operations of a computer by those of another computer.

Small Business Computer A stand-alone data-processing system, built around a general-purpose computer, dedicated to the processing of standard business applications, that can handle inputs from mass storage devices costing less than \$100,000 complete, including all hardware and software.

***Software** (1) (ISO) *Computer programs, procedures,* rules, and possibly associated *documentation* concerned with the *operation* of a *data-processing system.* (2) Contrast with *hardware.*

***Solid State Component** A component whose *operation* depends on the control of electric or magnetic phenomena in solids, e.g., a transistor, crystal diode, *ferrite* core.

***Sort** (1) The *operation* of sorting. (2) (ISO) To segregate *items* into groups according to specified criteria. Sorting involves *ordering,* but need not involve *sequencing* for the groups may be arranged in an arbitrary order. (3) To arrange a *set* of *items* according to *keys* which are used as a basis for determining the *sequence* of the items, e.g., to arrange the records of a personnel *file* into alphabetical sequence by using the employee names as *sort keys.* (4) Synonym for order.

*Sorter — (1) (ISO) A device that deposits *punched cards* in *pockets* selected according to the *hole patterns* in the cards. (2) A person, device, or *computer routine* that *sorts*. (3) (ISO) Deprecated term for *sort program*.

*Source Language — (ISO) A *language* from which *statements* are *translated*.

Source Module — The source statements that constitute the input to a language translator for a particular translation.

*Source Program — (1) (ISO) A *computer program* expressed in a *source language*. (2) Contrast with *object program*.

*Special Purpose Computer — (ISO) A *computer* that is designed to *operate* upon a restricted class of problems.

*Spooling — (ISO) The *reading* of *output* from and the *writing* of input onto *auxiliary storage concurrently* with *job execution* in a form suitable for later processing or output operations.

*Statement — (1) (ISO) In a *programming language*, a meaningful *expression* that may describe or specify *operations* and is complete in the context of this programming language. (2) In *computer programming*, a *symbol string* or other arrangement of symbols. (3) (ISO) Deprecated term for *instruction*.

Static File — A file that has a low percentage of additions and deletions.

*Storage — (1) (ISO) The action of placing *data* into a *storage device* and retaining them for subsequent use. (2) The retention of *data* in a *storage device*. (3) A *storage device*.

*Stored Program Computer — (ISO) A *computer* controlled by *internally stored instructions*, that can synthesize and store instructions, and that can subsequently *execute* these instructions. Synonymous with programmed computer.

Structured Programming — A style of programming in which the structure of a program (that is, the interrelationship of its parts) is made as clear as possible by restricting control logic to just three structures.

*Subroutine — (1) (ISO) A *sequenced set* of *statements* that may be used in one or more *computer programs* and at one or more points in a computer program. (2) A *routine* that can be part of another routine.

Subsystem — A secondary or subordinate system, usually capable of operating independently of, or asynchronously with, a controlling system.

*Summary Punch — (ISO) A *card punch* that may be connected to another device, such as a tabulator, to enter *data* that was calculated or summarized by the other device.

Supervisor — The part of a control program that coordinates the use of resources and maintains the flow of CPU operations.

*Supervisory Program — (ISO) A *computer program*, usually part of an *operating system*, that controls the *execution* of other computer programs and regulates the flow of work in a *data processing system*. Synonymous with executive program supervisor.

A preliminary study undertaken by company personnel to determine whether or not a proposed computer system is feasible and whether or not it will give improved operation at a lower cost.	Survey
(1) (ISO) A conventional representation of a concept or a representation of a concept upon which agreement has been reached. (2) A representation of something by reason of relationship, association, or convention.	*Symbol
(ISO) An *address* expressed in a form convenient for *computer programming.*	*Symbolic Address
(1) (ISO) The relationship among *characters* or groups of characters, independent of their meanings or the manner of their interpretation and use. (2) The structure of *expressions* in a *language.* (3) The rules governing the structure of a *language.* (4) The relationships among *symbols.*	*Syntax
(ISO) In *data processing,* a collection of men, machines, and methods organized to accomplish a *set* of specific *functions.*	*System
A set of steps required to examine an existing system in order to identify the problems causing inefficiency or inaccuracy.	System Analysis
The analysis of the present methods, applications, objectives, and all pertinent data, followed by a design of improved systems using data-processing equipment and techniques.	System Analysis and Design
To determine the relationship between all parts of the system.	System Design
An overall visual of the system showing the flow of information from the input to output media without detailing the steps involved. It is a diagram that illustrates the flow of data into, through, and out of a system of programs.	System Flowchart
The responsibility for (1) generating and maintaining the operating system, (2) optimizing the performance of the computer through software and hardware monitoring, (3) identifying inefficient programs in terms of usage made of computer resources, and (4) creating operating standards for the allocation of files, the number of devices that can be used, and the operating practices.	Systems Programming
(1) (ISO) An *array* of *data* each *item* of which may be unambiguously identified by means of one or more *arguments.* (2) A collection of *data* in which each *item* is uniquely identified by a *label,* by its *position* relative to the other items, or by some other means. Synonymous with dictionary.	*Table
(ISO) A *procedure* for obtaining the value corresponding to an *argument* from a *table* of values.	*Table Lookup
(1) To format *data* into a *table.* (2) To print totals.	*Tabulate
(ISO) A device containing a *tape drive,* together with *read heads* and *write heads* and associated controls.	*Tape Unit
(1) The basic unit of work from the standpoint of a *control program.* (2) In a *multiprogramming* or *multiprocessing* environment, a *computer program,* or portion thereof, capable of being specified to the *control program* as a *unit* of work. Tasks compete for *system* resources.	*Task

Task Management	Those functions of the control program that regulate the use by tasks of the central processing unit and other resources, except for input/output devices.
*Tele-communication	(ISO) The *transmission* of *signals* over long distances, such as by telegraph, radio, or television.
*Terminal	A point in a *system* or communication network at which *data* can either enter or leave.
Third-Generation Computer	A computer utilizing solid logic technology components.
*Throughput	A measure of the amount of work performed by a *computing system* over a given period of time, e.g., *jobs* per day.
*Time Sharing	(1) (ISO) A mode of *operation* that provides for the *interleaving* of two or more independent *processes* on one *functional unit.* (2) Pertaining to the *interleaved* use of time on a *computing system* that enables two or more users to *execute computer programs concurrently.* (3) (ISO) Deprecated term for *conversational mode.*
*Track	The portion of a moving *data medium,* such as a drum, tape, or *disk*, that is accessible to a given *reading head position.*
*Transaction File	(ISO) A *file* containing relatively transient *data,* that, for a given application, is *processed* together with the appropriate *master file.* Synonymous with detail file.
*Transcribe	(ISO) To *transmit data* from one *data medium* to another, *converting* them as necessary for acceptance by the receiving medium.
Transistor	A small solid-state, semiconducting device, ordinarily using germanium, that performs nearly all the functions of an electronic tube, especially amplification.
*Translate	(ISO) To *transform data* from one *language* to another.
*Translator	(ISO) A *computer program* that translates from one *language* into another language and in particular from one *programming language* into another programming language. Synonymous with translating program.
Troubleshoot	Same as Debug.
*Truncate	To terminate a computational *process* in accordance with some rule, e.g., to end the evaluation of a power series at a specified term.
*Truncation	(1) (ISO) The deletion or omission of a leading or of a trailing portion of a *string* in accordance with specified criteria. (2) (ISO) The termination of a computation *process,* before its final conclusion or natural termination, if any, in accordance with specified rules. Contrast with *round.*
*Turnaround Time	(ISO) The elapsed time between submission of a *job* and the return of complete results.
Turnkey Black Box	A system whose input and output are specified in detail, but whose internal mechanism remains a mystery to the purchaser.
*Twelve-Punch	A *punch* in the top row of a *Hollerith card.* Synonymous with y-punch.
*Twos Complement	(ISO) The *radix complement* in the *pure binary numeration system.* Synonymous with complement-on-two.

A linear-type element containing printable symbols.	Typebar
The information concerning a single transaction is usually recorded in one punched card.	Unit Record Principle
The first commercial computer.	UNIVAC 1
A block of strange little lines and numbers on products which are passed over a scanner which tells the computer who made the product, describes the size, flavor, date of manufacture, price, etc., and at the same time, produces, for the customer, a printed tape which lists the name of the items as well as the price. Abbreviated UPC.	Universal Product Code
To modify a master file with current information according to a specified procedure.	Update
Same as ASCII.	USACII
Anyone who requires the services of a computing system.	User
A problem program designed to perform an everyday task, such as transcribing data from one storage device to another.	Utility Program
(1) (ISO) In *computer programming,* a *character* or group of characters that refers to a value and, in the *execution* of a *computer program,* corresponds to an *address.* (2) A quantity that can assume any of a given *set* of values.	*Variable
Pertaining to a *file* in which the *records* need not be uniform in length.	*Variable-Length Record
(ISO) A device that checks the correctness of transcribed *data,* usually by *comparing* with a second transcription of the same data or by comparing a retranscription with the original data.	*Verifier
(1) To determine whether a transcription of *data* or other *operation* has been accomplished accurately. (2) To *check* the *results* of *keypunching.*	*Verify
The notion of space on *storage devices* that may be regarded as *main storage* by the user of a computing system, in which *virtual addresses* are mapped into *real addresses.* The size of the virtual storage is limited only by the *addressing* scheme of the computing system and by the amount of *auxiliary storage* available, rather than by the actual number of main *storage locations.*	*Virtual Storage
The ability to speak directly into the computer. The systems use "discrete" or "isolated" word recognition systems. The speaker must pause briefly between words. The user must "train" the system to recognize his/her enunciation of the words in the vocabulary. This is done through repetitive utterances of these words to produce a reference pattern that can be stored in the main memory, or on a disk or cassette.	Voice Recognition Systems
The percentage of records on a file that are added or deleted in a run.	Volatility
(1) That portion of a single unit of storage which is accessible to a single read/write mechanism; for example, a drum, a disk pack, or part of a disk storage module. (2) A recording medium that is mounted and demounted as a unit; for example, a reel of magnetic tape, a disk pack, or a data cell.	Volume

*Word	(1) (ISO) A *character string* or a *binary element string* that is convenient for some purpose to consider as an entity. (2) A *character string* or a *bit string* considered as an entity.
*Word Length	(ISO) The number of characters or of *binary elements* in a *word.*
*Write	(ISO) To make a permanent or transient *recording* of *data* in a *storage device* or on a *data medium.*
*X-Punch	Synonym for *eleven-punch.*
*Y-Punch	Synonym for *twelve-punch.*
*Zero Suppression	(ISO) The elimination from a *numeral* of *zeros* that have no *significance* in the numeral. Zeros that have no significance include those to the left of the nonzero *digits* in the integral part of a numeral and those to the right of the nonzero digits in the fractional part.
*Zone Punch	(1) (ISO) A hole *punched* in one of the upper three *card rows* of a twelve-row *punch card.* Synonymous with overpunch. (2) A hole *punched* in one of the *punch rows* designated as twelve, eleven, or zero, and sometimes eight or nine. A *zero punch,* and sometimes a ninepunch, by itself, is considered a *numeric punch.* (3) A *zero punch* in combination with a *numeric punch.* (4) Contrast with *digit punch.*

index

Operation, 148, 272

Advance Praise for *Head First Physics*

"If you want to learn some physics, but you think it's too difficult, buy this book! It will probably help, and if it doesn't, you can always use it as a doorstop or hamster bedding or something. I wish I had a copy of this book when I was teaching physics."

— John Allister, physics teacher

"*Head First Physics* has achieved the impossible - a serious textbook that makes physics fun. Students all over will be thinking like a physicist!"

— Georgia Gale Grant, freelance science writer, communicator and broadcaster

"Great graphics, clear explanations and some crazy real world problems to solve! This text is full of strategies and tips to attack problems. It encourages a team approach that's so essential in today's work world."

— Diane Jaquith, high school physics, chemistry and physical science teacher

"This is an outstandingly good teacher masquerading as a physics book! You never feel phased if you don't quite understand something the first time because you know it will be explained again in a different way and then repeated and reinforced. "

— Marion Lang, teacher

"This book takes you by the hand and guides you through the world of physics."

— Catriona Lang, teacher

"*Head First Physics* really rocks - I never thought it was possible to enjoy learning physics so much! This book is about understanding and not about rote learning, so you can get to grips with the physics and remember it much better as a result."

— Alice Pitt-Pitts

Praise for other *Head First* academic titles

"Head First Statistics is by far the most entertaining, attention-catching study guide on the market. By presenting the material in an engaging manner, it provides students with a comfortable way to learn an otherwise cumbersome subject. The explanation of the topics is presented in a manner comprehensible to students of all levels."

— Ariana Anderson, Teaching Fellow/PhD candidate in Statistics, UCLA

"Head First is an intuitive way to understand statistics using simple, real-life examples that make learning fun and natural."

— Michael Prerau, computational neuroscientist and statistics instructor, Boston University

"Thought Head First was just for computer nerds? Try the brain-friendly way with statistics and you'll change your mind. It really works."

— Andy Parker

"This book is a great way for students to learn statistics—it is entertaining, comprehensive, and easy to understand. A perfect solution!"

— Danielle Levitt

"Down with dull statistics books! Even my cat liked this one."

— Cary Collett

Praise for the *Head First* Approach

"There are books you buy, books you keep, books you keep on your desk, and thanks to O'Reilly and the Head First crew, there is the ultimate category, Head First books. They're the ones that are dog-eared, mangled, and carried everywhere. Head First SQL is at the top of my stack. Heck, even the PDF I have for review is tattered and torn."

— Bill Sawyer, ATG Curriculum Manager, Oracle

"Elegant design is at the core of every chapter here, each concept conveyed with equal doses of pragmatism and wit."

— Ken Goldstein, Executive Vice President, Disney Online

"I feel like a thousand pounds of books have just been lifted off of my head."

—Ward Cunningham, inventor of the Wiki and founder of the Hillside Group

"This book's admirable clarity, humor and substantial doses of clever make it the sort of book that helps even non-programmers think well about problem-solving."

— Cory Doctorow, co-editor of Boing Boing
Author, *Down and Out in the Magic Kingdom*
and *Someone Comes to Town, Someone Leaves Town*

"It's fast, irreverent, fun, and engaging. Be careful—you might actually learn something!"

—Ken Arnold, former Senior Engineer at Sun Microsystems
Co-author (with James Gosling, creator of Java), *The Java Programming Language*

"I received the book yesterday and started to read it...and I couldn't stop. This is definitely très 'cool.' It is fun, but they cover a lot of ground and they are right to the point. I'm really impressed."

— Erich Gamma, IBM Distinguished Engineer, and co-author of *Design Patterns*

"One of the funniest and smartest books on software design I've ever read."

— Aaron LaBerge, VP Technology, ESPN.com

"I ♥ Head First HTML with CSS & XHTML—it teaches you everything you need to learn in a 'fun coated' format."

— Sally Applin, UI Designer and Artist

Author of Head First Physics

Heather Lang

Heather studied physics in Manchester, gaining a first class honours degree. She likes explaining how stuff works and persuading people to send her chocolate in the post. Her first foray into science communication was via the BaBar Particle Physics Teaching Package. She followed this up with a Ph.D. in the grey area between physics and biochemistry, but got fed up of sharing a fridge with petri dishes and moved on from the lab into education and Head First Physics.

When not explaining how stuff works, Heather likes to play extreme sports such as chess and cricket, play with sliders on a sound desk, or play the fool while running school chess clubs (in the name of teaching of course).

, Ph.D.

O'REILLY®

Köln • Sebastopol • Tokyo

Head First Physics

A learner's companion to mechanics and practical physics

Heather Lang

Beijing • Cambridg

Table of Contents (Summary)

Table of Contents (the real thing)

Intro

Your brain on Physics. Here *you* are trying to *learn* something, while here your *brain* is doing you a favor by making sure the learning doesn't *stick*. Your brain's thinking, "Better leave room for more important things, like which wild animals to avoid and whether naked snowboarding is a bad idea." So how *do* you trick your brain into thinking that your life depends on knowing physics?

1 think like a physicist

In the beginning ...

Physics is about the world around you and how everything in it works. As you go about your daily life, you're **doing** physics all the time! But the thought of actually **learning** physics may sometimes **feel** like falling into a bottomless pit with no escape! Don't worry... this chapter introduces how to **think like a physicist**. You'll learn to step into problems and to use your **intuition** to spot **patterns** and '**special points**' that make things much easier. By **being** part of the problem, you're one step closer to getting to the solution...

Go to the start of the problem then BE a part of it!

2 making it all MEAN something

Units and measurements

How long is a piece of string? Physics is based on making **measurements** that tell you about **size**. In this chapter, you'll learn how to use **units** and **rounding** to avoid making mistakes - and also why **errors** are OK. By the time you're through, you'll know when something is **significant** and have an opinion on whether size really **is** everything.

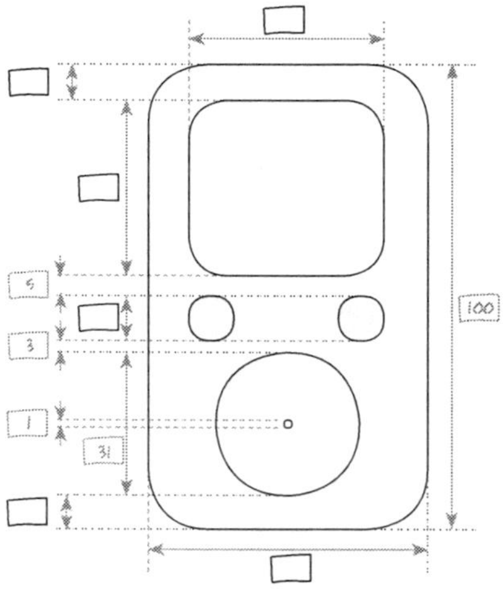

Length

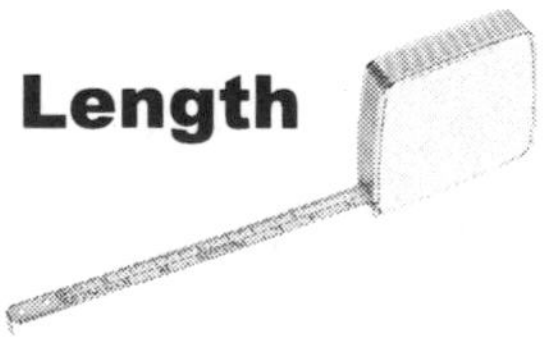

Time

Mass

3 scientific notation, area, and volume

All numbers great and small

In the real world, you have to deal with all kinds of numbers, not just the ones that are easier to work with. In this chapter, you'll be taking control of unwieldy numbers using scientific notation and discovering why rounding a large number doesn't mean having to write a zillion zeros at the end. You'll also use your new superpowers to deal with units of area and volume - which is where scientific notation will save you lots of grief (and time) in the future!

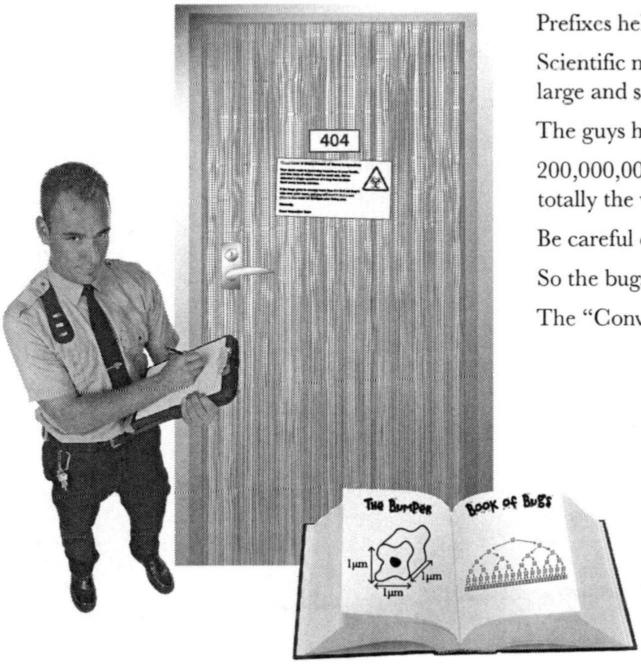

4

equations and graphs

Learning the lingo

Communication is vital. You're already off to a good start in your journey to truly think like a physicist, but now you need to **communicate your thoughts**. In this chapter, you're going to take your first steps in two universal languages - **graphs** and **equations** - pictures you can use to *speak a thousand words* about experiments you do and the physics concepts you're learning. *Seeing is believing.*

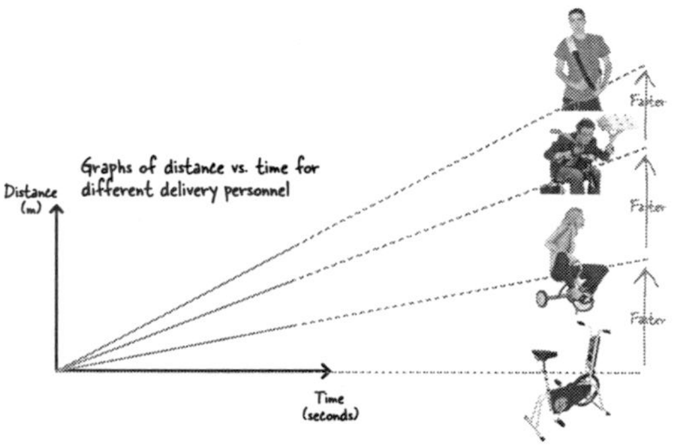

5 dealing with directions

Vectors

Time, speed, and distance are all well and good, but you really need DIRECTION too if you want to get on in life.

You now have multiple physics superpowers: You've mastered graphs and equations, and you can estimate how big your answer will be. But **size** isn't everything. In this chapter, you'll be learning about **vectors**, which give **direction** to your answers and help you to find **easier shortcuts** through complicated-looking problems.

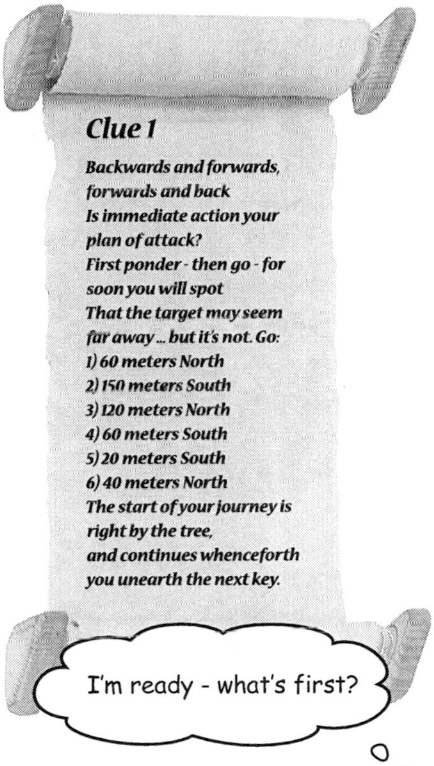

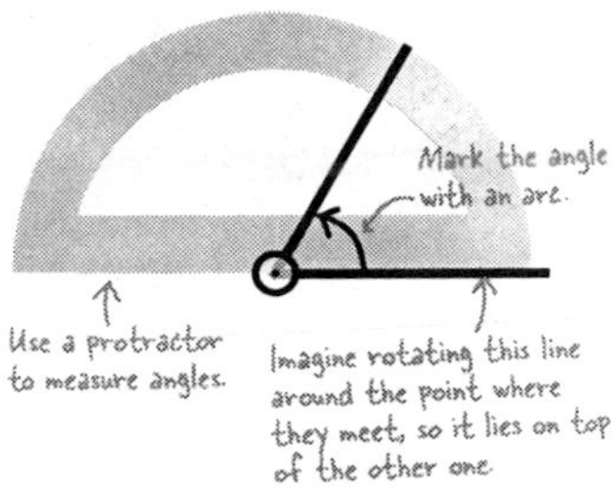

6 Displacement, Velocity, and Acceleration

What's going on?

It's hard to keep track of more than one thing at a time.

When something falls, its displacement, velocity, and acceleration are all important at the same time. So how can you pay attention to all three without missing anything? In this chapter, you'll increase your experiment, graph, and slope superpowers in preparation for bringing everything together with an equation or two.

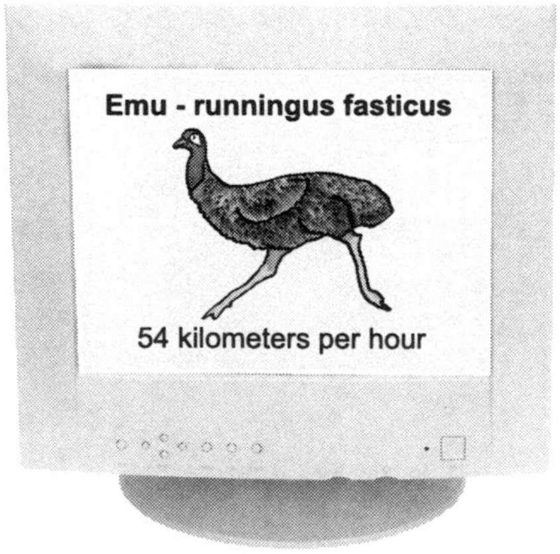

7 Equations of motion (part 1)

Playing With Equations

It's time to take things to another level.

So far, you've done experiments, drawn graphs of their results, and worked out equations from them. But there's only so far you can go since sometimes your graph isn't a straight line. In this chapter, you'll expand your math skills by making **substitutions** to work out a key **equation of motion** for a curved displacement-time graph of a falling object. And you'll also learn that **checking** your GUT reaction to an answer can be a good thing.

8 equations of motion (part 2)

Up, up, and... back down

You already know how to deal with things that are falling down, which is great. But what about the other half of the bargain - when something's launched up into the air? In this chapter, you'll add a third key equation of motion to your armory which will enable you to deal with (just about) anything! You'll also learn how looking for a little symmetry can

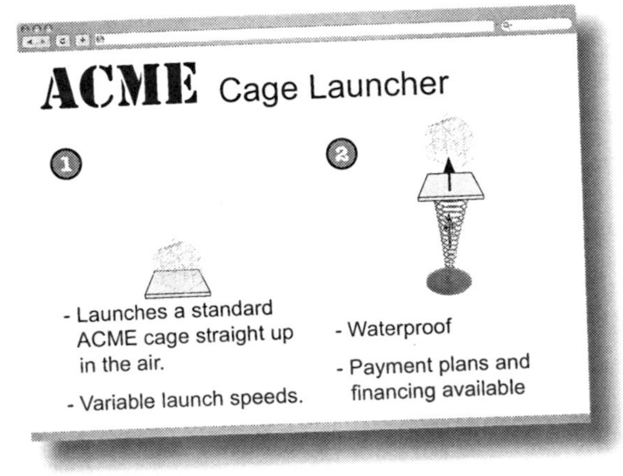

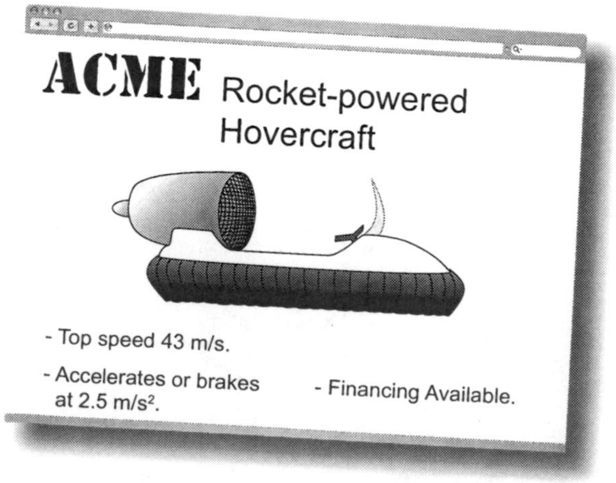

9 triangles, trig and trajectories

Going two-dimensional

So you can deal with one dimension. But what about real life?

Real things don't just go up or down - they go sideways too! But never fear - you're about to gain a whole new bunch of **trigonometry** superpowers that'll see you spotting **right-angled triangles** wherever you go and using them to **reduce complicated-looking problems into simpler ones that you can already do**.

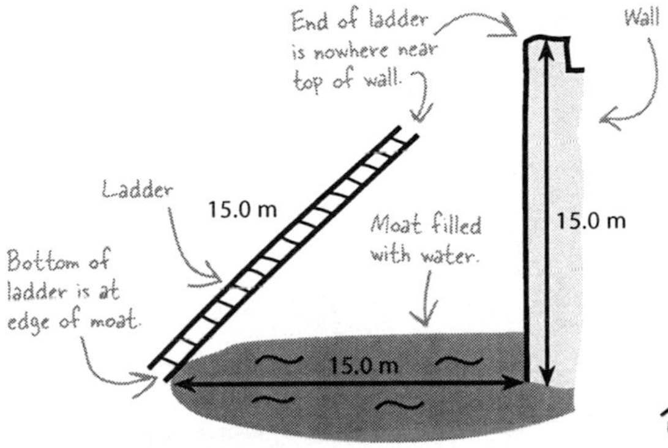

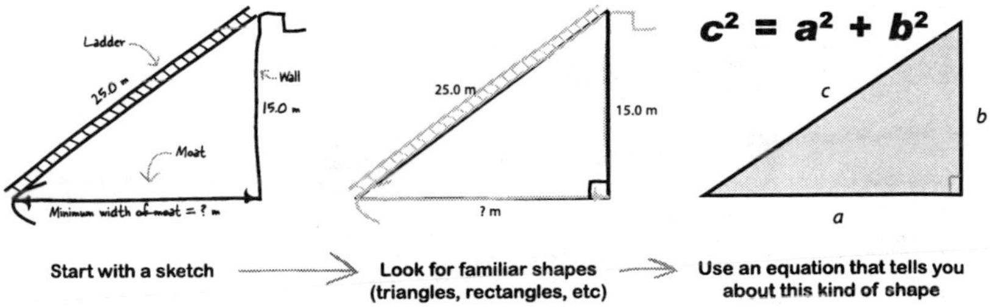

momentum conservation

10 What Newton Did

No one likes to be a pushover. So far, you've learned to deal with objects that are already moving. But what makes them go in the first place? You know that something will move if you push it - but *how* will it move? In this chapter, you'll overcome **inertia** as you get acquainted with some of **Newton's Laws**. You'll also learn about **momentum**, why it's **conserved**, and how you can use it to solve problems.

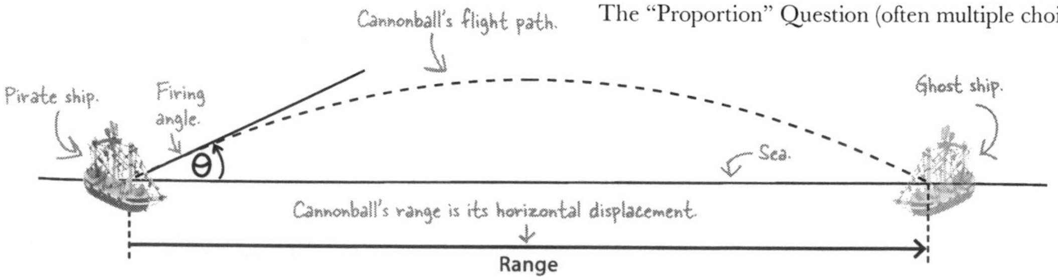

11 weight and the normal force

Forces for courses

Sometimes you have to make a statement forcefully.

In this chapter, you'll work out **Newton's 2nd Law** from what you already know about momentum conservation to wind up with the key equation, $\mathbf{F_{net}} = \boldsymbol{ma}$. Once you combine this with spotting **Newton's 3rd Law force pairs**, and drawing **free body diagrams**, you'll be able to deal with (just about) anything. You'll also learn about why mass and **weight** aren't the same thing, and get used to using the **normal force** to support your arguments.

12 using forces, momentum, friction and impulse
Getting on with it

You already know about equations of motion, component vectors, momentum conservation, free body diagrams and Newton's Laws. In this chapter, you'll learn how to fit all of these things together and apply them to solve a much wider range of physics problems. Often, you'll spot when a problem is like something you've seen before. You'll also

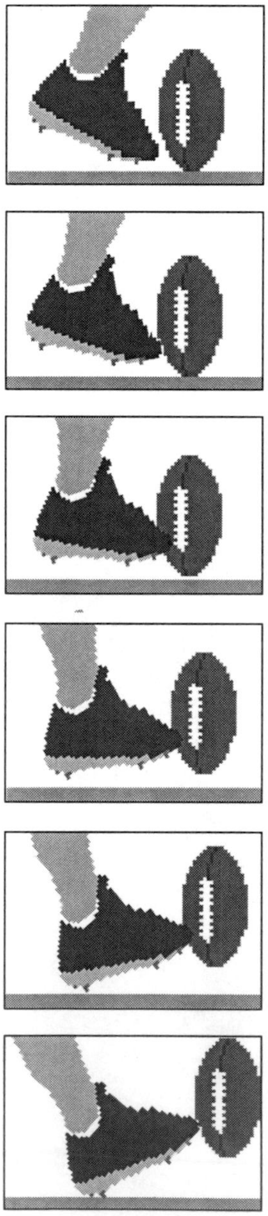

13 torque and work

Getting a lift

You can use your physics knowledge to do superhuman feats.

In this chapter, you'll learn how to harness torque to perform amazing displays of strength, by using a lever to exert a much larger force than you could on your own. However, you can't get something for nothing - **energy** is always **conserved** and the amount of **work** you do to give something **gravitational potential energy** by lifting it doesn't change.

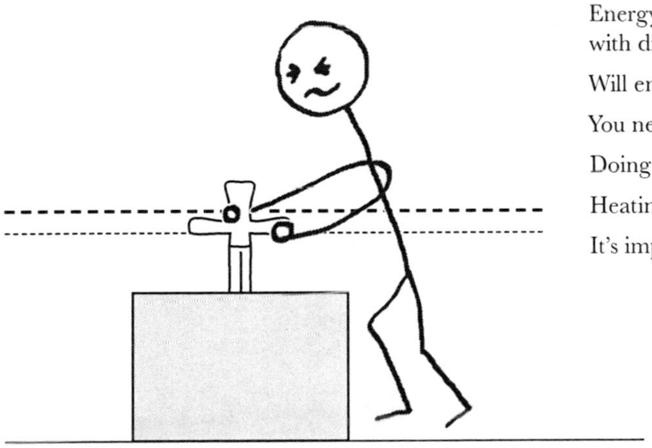

14 energy conservation

Making your life easier

Why do things the hard way when there's an easier way?

So far, you've been solving problems using equations of motion, forces and component vectors. And that's great - except that it sometimes takes a while to crunch through the math. In this chapter, you'll learn to spot where you can use **energy conservation** as a shortcut that lets you solve complicated-looking problems with relative ease.

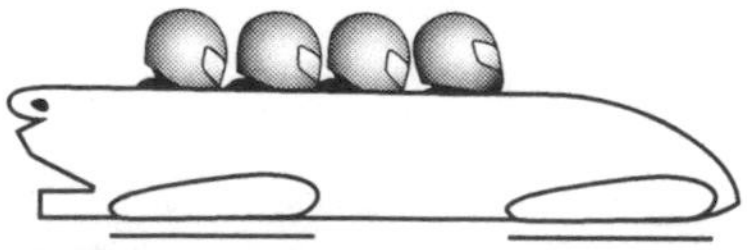

tension, pulleys and problem solving

15 Changing direction

So far, you've been using forces, free body diagrams and energy conservation to solve problems. In this chapter you'll take that further as you deal with ropes, pulleys, and yes, tension. Along the way, you'll also practise looking for familiar signposts to help navigate your way through

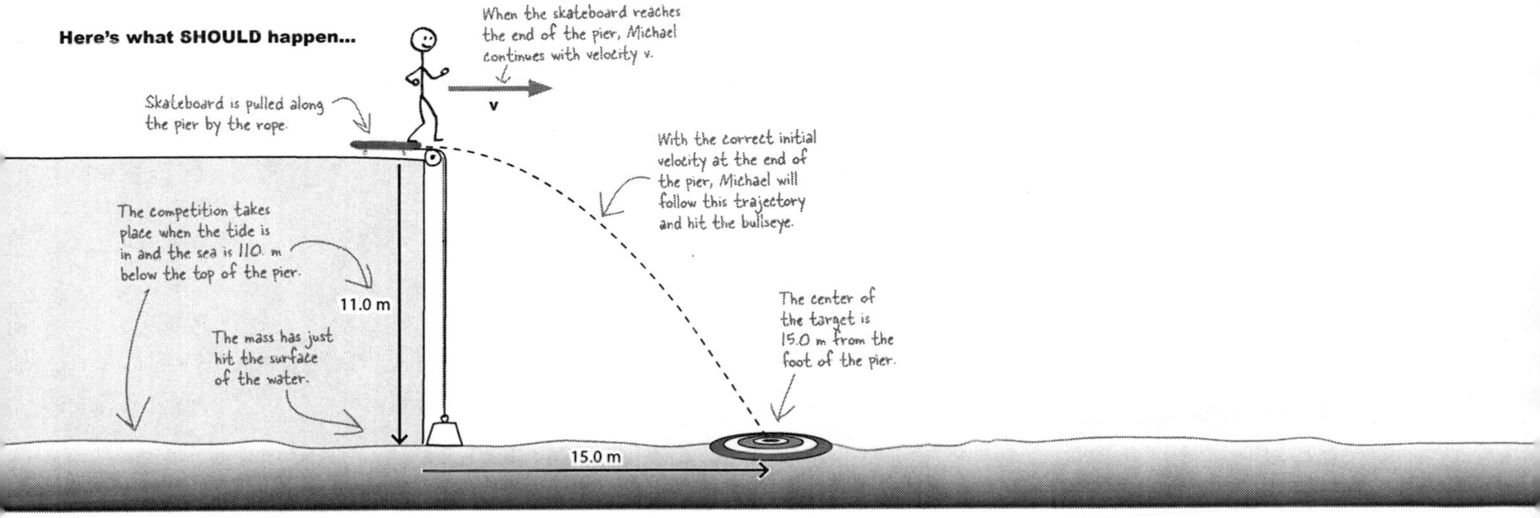

circular motion (part 1)

16 From α to ω

You say you want a revolution? In this chapter, you'll learn how to deal with **circular motion** with a crash course in **circle** anatomy, including what the **radius** and **circumference** have to do with pies (or should that be ϖs). After dealing with **frequency** and **period**, you'll need to switch from the **linear** to the **angular**. But once you've learned to use **radians** to measure angles, you'll know it's gonna be alright.

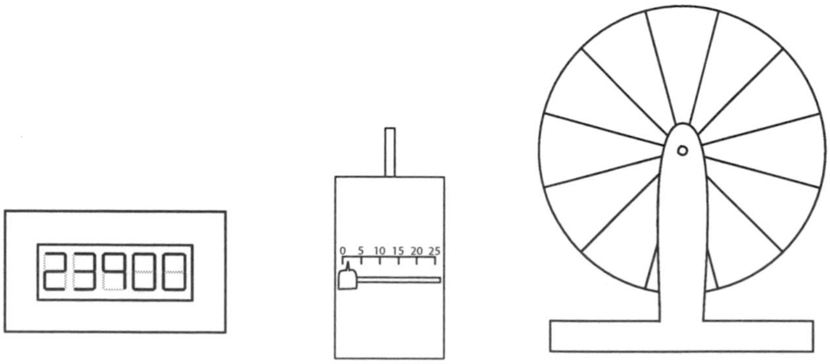

17 circular motion (part 2)

Staying on track

Ever feel like someone's gone off at a tangent? That's exactly what happens when you try to move an object along a **circular** path when there's not enough **centripetal force** to enable this to happen. In this chapter, you'll learn exactly what centripetal force is and how it can keep you on track. Along the way, you'll even solve some pretty serious problems with a certain Head First space station. So what are you waiting for? Turn the page, and let's get started.

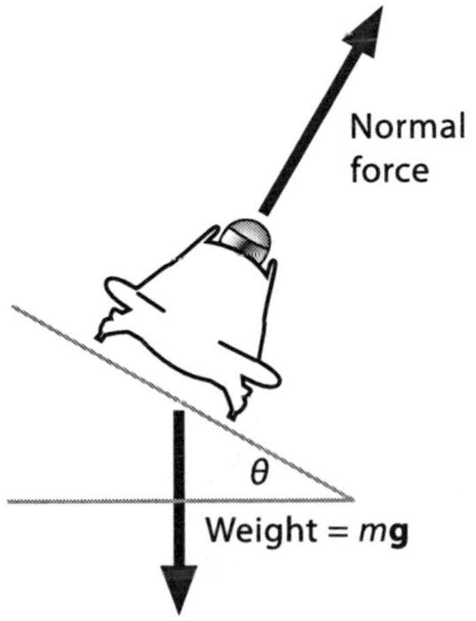

18 gravitation and orbits

Getting away from it all

- but what happens to the attraction as your feet leave the ground? In this chapter, you'll learn that gravitation is an inverse square law, and harness the power of gravitational potential to take a trip to infinity... and beyond. Closer to home, you'll learn how to deal with orbits - and learn how

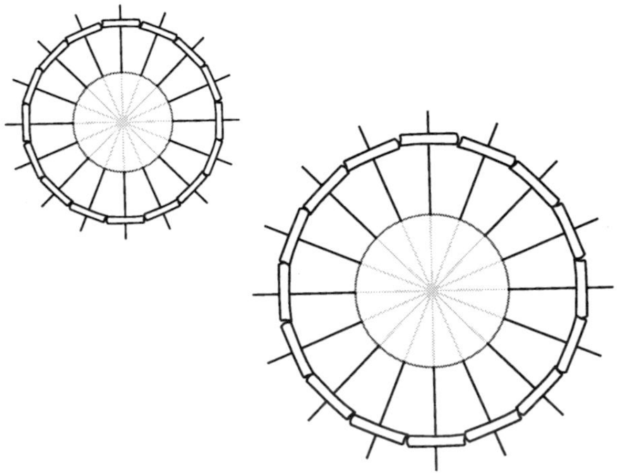

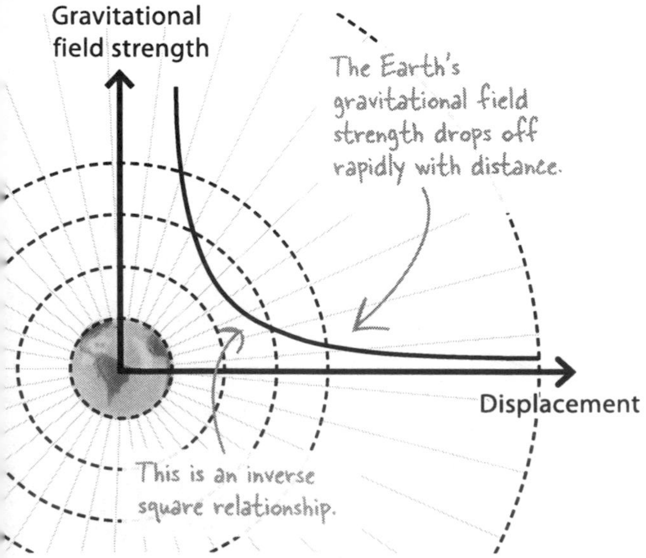

19 Oscillations (part 1)

Round and round

Things can look very different when you see them from another angle. So far you've been looking at circular motion from above - but what does it look like from the side? In this chapter, you'll tie together your **circular motion** and **trigonometry** superpowers as you learn extended definitions of **sine** and **cosine**. Once you're done, you'll be able to deal with anything that's moving around a circle - whichever way you look at it.

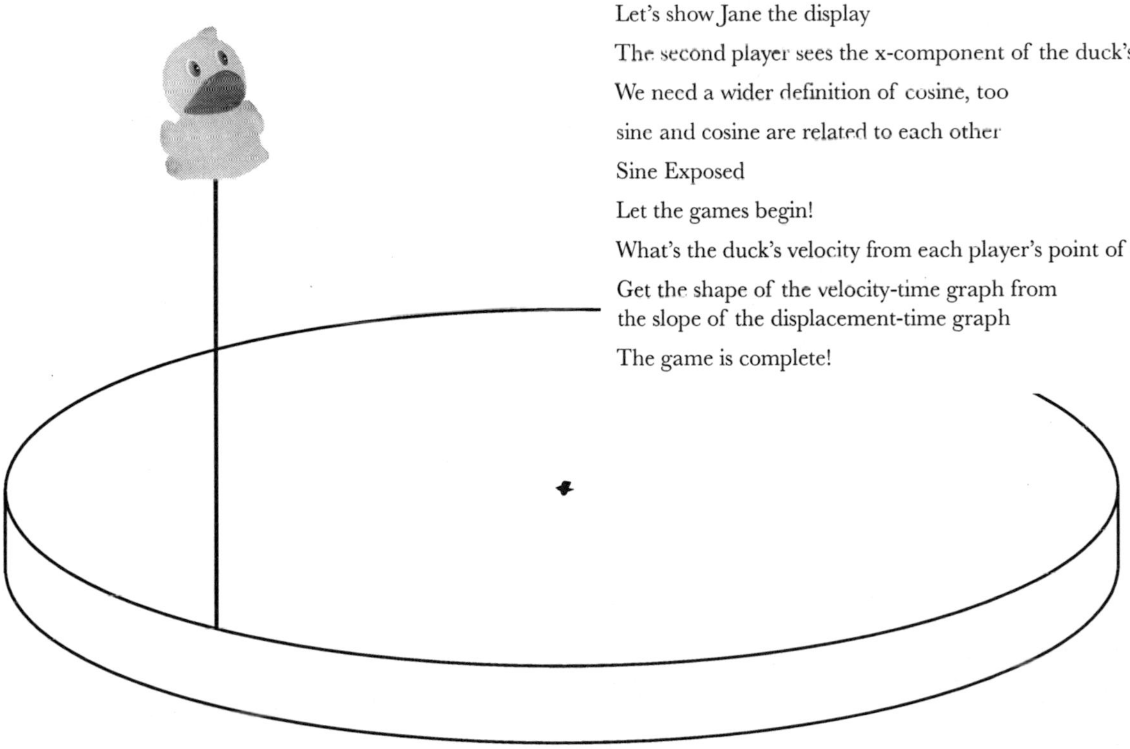

20 Oscillations (part 2)

Springs 'n' swings

This chapter is about dealing with oscillations, and helps you see the big picture. You'll put together what you know about graphs, equations, forces, energy conservation and periodic motion as you tackle springs and pendulums that move with simple harmonic motion to get the ultimate "I rule"

21 think like a physicist

It's the final chapter

It's time to hit the ground running. Throughout this book, you've been learning to **relate** physics to **everyday life** and have absorbed **problem solving** skills as you've gone along. In this final chapter, you'll use your new set of **physics tools** to dig into the problem we started off with - the bottomless pit through the center of the earth. The key is the question: "How can I use what I know to work out what I don't know (yet)?"

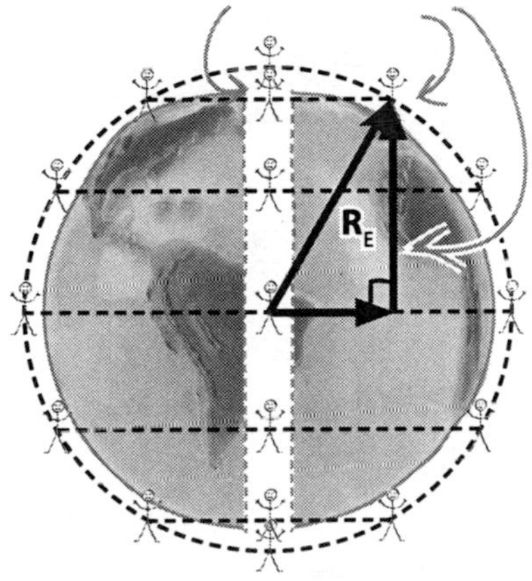

leftovers

The Top Six Things (we didn't cover)

No book can ever tell you everything about everything.

We've covered a lot of ground, and given you some great thinking skills and physics knowledge that will help you in the future, whether you're taking an exam or are just curious about how the world works. We had to make some really tough choices about what to include and what to leave out. Here are some topics that we didn't look at as we went along, but are still **important** and **useful**.

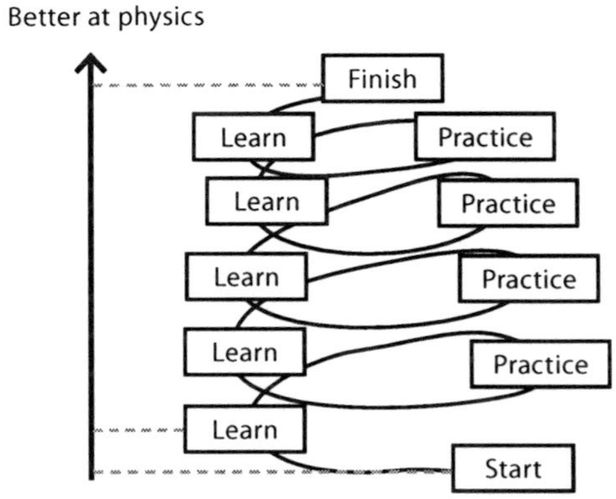

equation table

Point of Reference

It's difficult to remember something when you've only seen it once.

Equations are a major way of describing what's going on in physics. Every time you use equations to help **solve a problem**, you naturally start to become familiar with them without the need to spend time doing rote memorization. But before you get to that stage, it's good to have a place you can **look up** the equation you want to use. That's what this **equation table** appendix is for - it's a point of reference that you can turn to at any time.

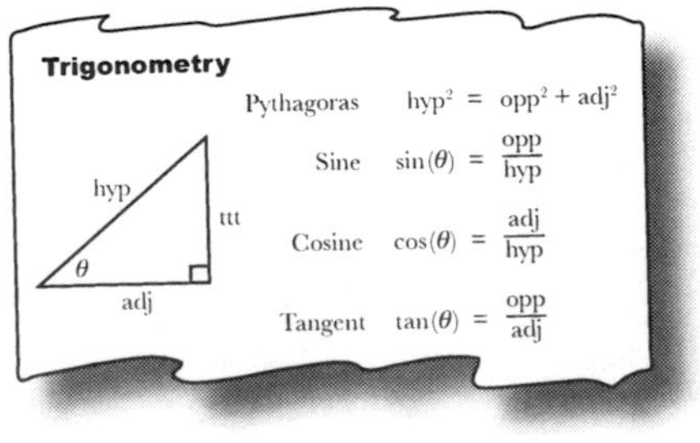

how to use this book

Intro

In this section we answer the burning question:
"So why DID they put that in a physics book?"

Who is this book for?

If you can answer "yes" to all of these:

1. Do you have access to a **pen** and a **scientific calculator**?

Don't worry if you're missing the calculator – they only cost a few dollars.

2. Do you want to **learn** and **understand physics** by **doing**, rather than by reading, whether you need to **pass an exam at the end** or not?

3. Do you prefer **chatting with friends about interesting things** to **dry**, **dull**, **academic lectures**?

this book is for you.

Who should probably back away from this book?

If you can answer "yes" to any of these:

1. **Are you someone who's never studied basic algebra?**

   (You don't need to be advanced, but you should be able to add, subtract, multiply and divide. We'll cover everything else you need to know about math and physics.)

2. Are you a physics ninja looking for a ***reference*** **book**?

3. Are you **afraid to try something different**? Would you rather have a root canal than mix stripes with plaid? Do you believe that a physics book can't be serious if it involves implementing a training schedule for thoroughbred hamster racing?

this book is not for you.

[Note from marketing: this book is for anyone with the cash to buy it.]

We know what you're thinking

"How can *this* be a serious physics book?"

"What's with all the graphics?"

"Can I actually *learn* it this way?"

We know what your *brain* is thinking

Your brain craves novelty. It's always searching, scanning, *waiting* for something unusual. It was built that way, and it helps you stay alive.

So what does your brain do with all the routine, ordinary, normal things you encounter? Everything it *can* to stop them from interfering with the brain's *real* job—recording things that *matter*. It doesn't bother saving the boring things; they never make it past the "this is obviously not important" filter.

How does your brain *know* what's important? Suppose you're out for a day hike and a tiger jumps in front of you, what happens inside your head and body?

Neurons fire. Emotions crank up. *Chemicals surge.*

And that's how your brain knows...

This must be important! Don't forget it!

But imagine you're at home, or in a library. It's a safe, warm, tiger-free zone. You're studying. Getting ready for an exam. Or trying to learn some tough technical topic your boss thinks will take a week, ten days at the most.

Just one problem. Your brain's trying to do you a big favor. It's trying to make sure that this *obviously* non-important content doesn't clutter up scarce resources. Resources that are better spent storing the really *big* things. Like tigers. Like the danger of fire. Like how you should never have posted those photos on your Facebook page.

And there's no simple way to tell your brain, "Hey brain, thank you very much, but no matter how dull this book is, and how little I'm registering on the emotional Richter scale right now, I really *do* want you to keep this stuff around."

We think of a "Head First" reader as a learner.

So what does it take to *learn* something? First, you have to *get* it, then make sure you don't *forget* it. It's not about pushing facts into your head. Based on the latest research in cognitive science, neurobiology, and educational psychology, *learning* takes a lot more than text on a page. We know what turns your brain on.

Some of the Head First learning principles:

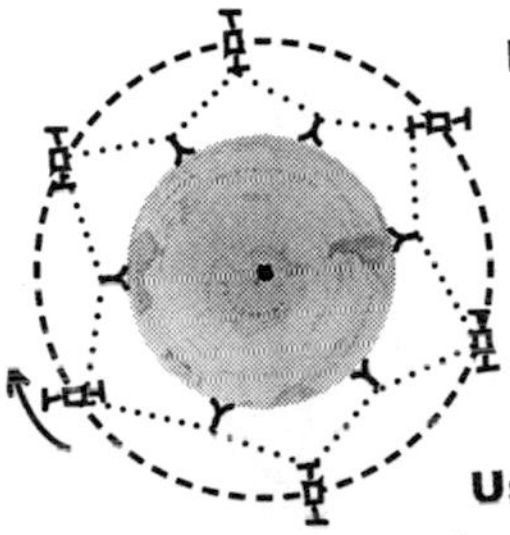

Make it visual. Images are far more memorable than words alone, and make learning much more effective (up to 89% improvement in recall and transfer studies). It also makes things more understandable. **Put the words within or near the graphics** they relate to, rather than on the bottom or on another page, and learners will be up to *twice* as likely to solve problems related to the content.

Use a conversational and personalized style. In recent studies, students performed up to 40% better on post-learning tests if the content spoke directly to the reader, using a first-person, conversational style rather than taking a formal tone. Tell stories instead of lecturing. Use casual language. Don't take yourself too seriously. Which would *you* pay more attention to: a stimulating dinner party companion, or a lecture?

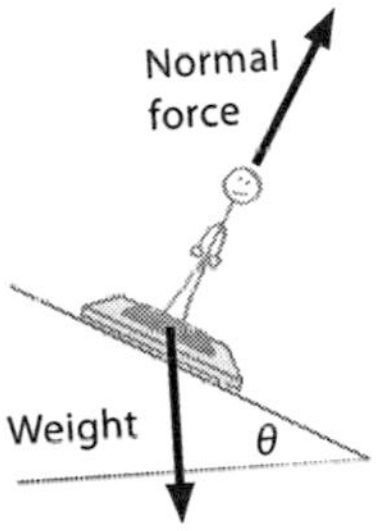

Get the learner to think more deeply. In other words, unless you actively flex your neurons, nothing much happens in your head. A reader has to be motivated, engaged, curious, and inspired to solve problems, draw conclusions, and generate new knowledge. And for that, you need challenges, exercises, and thought-provoking questions, and activities that involve both sides of the brain and multiple senses.

Get—and keep—the reader's attention. We've all had the "I really want to learn this but I can't stay awake past page one" experience. Your brain pays attention to things that are out of the ordinary, interesting, strange, eye-catching, unexpected. Learning a new, tough, technical topic doesn't have to be boring. Your brain will learn much more quickly if it's not.

Touch their emotions. We now know that your ability to remember something is largely dependent on its emotional content. You remember what you care about. You remember when you *feel* something. No, we're not talking heart-wrenching stories about a boy and his dog. We're talking emotions like surprise, curiosity, fun, "what the...?" , and the feeling of "I Rule!" that comes when you solve a puzzle, learn something everybody else thinks is hard, or realize you know something that "I'm more technical than thou" Bob from engineering *doesn't*.

Metacognition: thinking about thinking

If you really want to learn, and you want to learn more quickly and more deeply, pay attention to how you pay attention. Think about how you think. Learn how you learn.

Most of us did not take courses on metacognition or learning theory when we were growing up. We were *expected* to learn, but rarely *taught* to learn.

But we assume that if you're holding this book, you really want to learn how to do physics. And you probably don't want to spend a lot of time. If you want to use what you read in this book, you need to *remember* what you read. And for that, you've got to *understand* it. To get the most from this book, or *any* book or learning experience, take responsibility for your brain. Your brain on *this* content.

The trick is to get your brain to see the new material you're learning as Really Important. Crucial to your well-being. As important as a tiger. Otherwise, you're in for a constant battle, with your brain doing its best to keep the new content from sticking.

So just how *DO* you get your brain to treat physics like it was a hungry tiger?

There's the slow, tedious way, or the faster, more effective way. The slow way is about sheer repetition. You obviously know that you *are* able to learn and remember even the dullest of topics if you keep pounding the same thing into your brain. With enough repetition, your brain says, "This doesn't *feel* important to him, but he keeps looking at the same thing *over* and *over* and *over*, so I suppose it must be."

The faster way is to do ***anything that increases brain activity,*** especially different *types* of brain activity. The things on the previous page are a big part of the solution, and they're all things that have been proven to help your brain work in your favor. For example, studies show that putting words *within* the pictures they describe (as opposed to somewhere else in the page, like a caption or in the body text) causes your brain to try to makes sense of how the words and picture relate, and this causes more neurons to fire. More neurons firing = more chances for your brain to *get* that this is something worth paying attention to, and possibly recording.

A conversational style helps because people tend to pay more attention when they perceive that they're in a conversation, since they're expected to follow along and hold up their end. The amazing thing is, your brain doesn't necessarily *care* that the "conversation" is between you and a book! On the other hand, if the writing style is formal and dry, your brain perceives it the same way you experience being lectured to while sitting in a roomful of passive attendees. No need to stay awake.

But pictures and conversational style are just the beginning…

Here's what WE did:

We used ***pictures***, because your brain is tuned for visuals, not text. As far as your brain's concerned, a picture really *is* worth a thousand words. And when text and pictures work together, we embedded the text *in* the pictures because your brain works more effectively when the text is *within* the thing the text refers to, as opposed to in a caption or buried in the text somewhere.

We used ***redundancy***, saying the same thing in *different* ways and with different media types, and *multiple senses*, to increase the chance that the content gets coded into more than one area of your brain.

We used concepts and pictures in ***unexpected*** ways because your brain is tuned for novelty, and we used pictures and ideas with at least *some* ***emotional*** *content*, because your brain is tuned to pay attention to the biochemistry of emotions. That which causes you to *feel* something is more likely to be remembered, even if that feeling is nothing more than a little ***humor***, ***surprise***, or ***interest.***

We used a personalized, ***conversational style***, because your brain is tuned to pay more attention when it believes you're in a conversation than if it thinks you're passively listening to a presentation. Your brain does this even when you're *reading*.

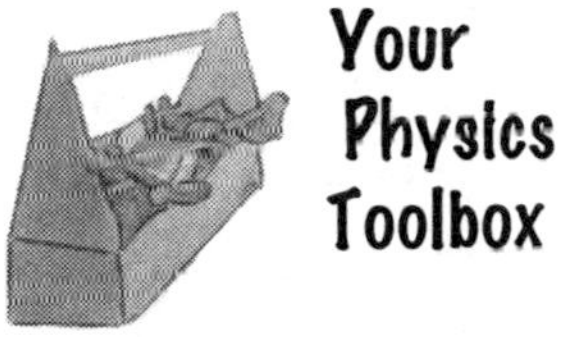

We included more than 80 ***activities***, because your brain is tuned to learn and remember more when you ***do*** things than when you *read* about things. And we made the exercises challenging-yet-do-able, because that's what most people prefer.

We used ***multiple learning styles***, because *you* might prefer step-by-step procedures, while someone else wants to understand the big picture first, and someone else just wants to see an example. But regardless of your own learning preference, *everyone* benefits from seeing the same content represented in multiple ways.

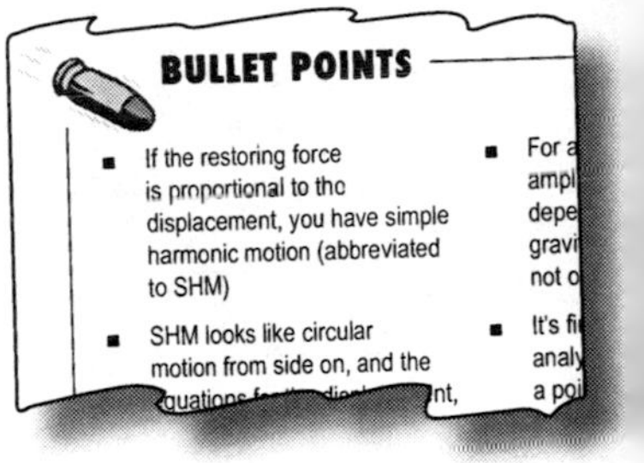

We include content for ***both sides of your brain***, because the more of your brain you engage, the more likely you are to learn and remember, and the longer you can stay focused. Since working one side of the brain often means giving the other side a chance to rest, you can be more productive at learning for a longer period of time.

And we included ***stories*** and exercises that present ***more than one point of view,*** because your brain is tuned to learn more deeply when it's forced to make evaluations and judgments.

We included ***challenges***, with exercises, and by asking ***questions*** that don't always have a straight answer, because your brain is tuned to learn and remember when it has to *work* at something. Think about it—you can't get your *body* in shape just by *watching* people at the gym. But we did our best to make sure that when you're working hard, it's on the *right* things. That ***you're not spending one extra dendrite*** processing a hard-to-understand example, or parsing difficult, jargon-laden, or overly terse text.

We used ***people***. In stories, examples, pictures, etc., because, well, because *you're* a person. And your brain pays more attention to *people* than it does to *things*.

Here's what YOU can do to bend your brain into submission

So, we did our part. The rest is up to you. These tips are a starting point; listen to your brain and figure out what works for you and what doesn't. Try new things.

Cut this out and stick it on your refrigerator.

1 Slow down. The more you understand, the less you have to memorize.

Don't just *read*. Stop and think. When the book asks you a question, don't just skip to the answer. Imagine that someone really *is* asking the question. The more deeply you force your brain to think, the better chance you have of learning and remembering.

Do the exercises. Write your own notes.

We put them in, but if we did them for you, that would be like having someone else do your workouts for you. And don't just *look* at the exercises. **Use a pencil.** There's plenty of evidence that physical activity *while* learning can increase the learning.

3 Read the "There are No Dumb Questions"

That means all of them. They're not optional sidebars—***they're part of the core content!*** Don't skip them.

4 Make this the last thing you read before bed. Or at least the last challenging thing.

Part of the learning (especially the transfer to long-term memory) happens *after* you put the book down. Your brain needs time on its own, to do more processing. If you put in something new during that processing time, some of what you just learned will be lost.

5 Drink water. Lots of it.

Your brain works best in a nice bath of fluid. Dehydration (which can happen before you ever feel thirsty) decreases cognitive function.

6 Talk about it. Out loud.

Speaking activates a different part of the brain. If you're trying to understand something, or increase your chance of remembering it later, say it out loud. Better still, try to explain it out loud to someone else. You'll learn more quickly, and you might uncover ideas you hadn't known were there when you were reading about it.

7 Listen to your brain.

Pay attention to whether your brain is getting overloaded. If you find yourself starting to skim the surface or forget what you just read, it's time for a break. Once you go past a certain point, you won't learn faster by trying to shove more in, and you might even hurt the process.

Feel something.

Your brain needs to know that this *matters*. Get involved with the stories. Make up your own captions for the photos. Groaning over a bad joke is *still* better than feeling nothing at all.

9 Do lots of physics!

The main way to learn how to do physics is by... doing physics. And that's what you're going to do throughout this book. We're going to give you a lot of practice: every chapter has exercises that pose problems for you to solve. Don't just skip over them—a lot of the learning happens when you solve the exercises. We included a solution to each exercise—don't be afraid to **peek at the solution** if you get stuck! Look at the first couple of lines, then turn back and take it from there yourself! But try to solve the problem before you look at the solution. And definitely make sure you understand the solution before you move on to the next part of the book.

Read Me

This is a learning experience, not a reference book. We deliberately stripped out everything that might get in the way of learning whatever it is we're working on at that point in the book. And the first time through, you need to begin at the beginning, because the book makes assumptions about what you've already seen and learned.

We begin with experiments, measurements, graphs and equations, then move on to forces and energy conservation, and then more advanced topics such as gravitation and simple harmonic motion.

It's important to start with a firm foundation. We start out with the building blocks and tools of physics – experiments, measurements, graphs, equations – and most importantly, how to approach problems by thinking like a physicist. But this is no dry, theoretical introduction. Right from the word go, you'll be picking up these important skills by *solving problems yourself.* As the book goes on, your brain is freed up to learn new concepts such as Newton's Laws and energy conservation because you've already absorbed and practiced the fundamentals. By the time you reach the end of the book, you'll even be sending people into space. We teach you what you need to know at the point where it becomes important, as that's when it has the most value. Yes - even the math!

We cover the same general set of topics that are in the mechanics sections of the AP Physics B and A Level curriculums

While we focus on the overall learning experience rather than exam preparation, we provide good coverage of the mechanics sections of the AP Physics B and A Level curriculums, as well as the practical side of experiments and data analysis in physics. This means that as you work your way through the topics, you gain a deeper understanding that will help you get a good grade in whatever exam you're taking. You'll also learn how to break down complicated problems into simpler ones that you already know how to do. This is a far more effective way of learning physics than rote memorization, as you'll feel confident about tackling *any* problem even when you haven't seen one exactly like it before.

We help you out with online resources.

Our readers tell us that sometimes you need a bit of extra help, so we provide online resources, right at your fingertips. We give you an online forum where you can go to seek help, and other resources too. The starting point is

http://www.headfirstlabs.com/books/hfphy/

The activities are NOT optional.

The exercises and activities are not add-ons; they're part of the core content of the book. Some of them are to help with memory, some are for understanding, and some will help you apply what you've learned. ***Don't skip the exercises.*** The crossword puzzles are the only thing you don't *have* to do, but they're good for giving your brain a chance to think about the words and terms you've been learning in a different context.

The redundancy is intentional and important.

One distinct difference in a Head First book is that we want you to *really* get it. And we want you to finish the book remembering what you've learned. Most reference books don't have retention and recall as a goal, but this book is about *learning*, so you'll see some of the same concepts come up more than once.

The Brain Power exercises don't have answers.

For some of them, there is no right answer, and for others, part of the learning experience of the Brain Power activities is for you to decide if and when your answers are right. In some of the Brain Power exercises, you will find hints to point you in the right direction.

The technical review team

John Allister

Scott Donaldson

Georgia Gale Grant

Diane Jaquith

Not pictured (but just as awesome):
Philip Kromer
Janet Painter
Don Wilke

Marion Lang

Catriona Lang

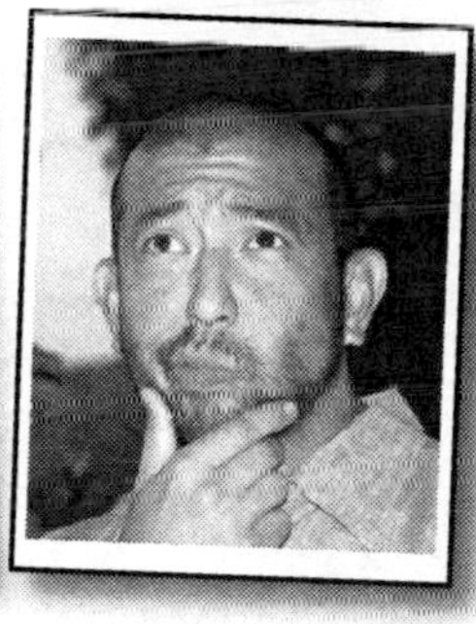
Michael Lew

Bill Mietelski

Alice Pitt-Pitts

Technical Reviewers:

John Allister has degrees from both Oxford and Cambridge universities, including a Master's in Experimental and Theoretical Physics. He taught physics for 5 years and is currently training for ordination in the Church of England.

Scott Donaldson is an editor, do-it-yourselfer, and all around lover of science and mathematics, with special focus on mechanics and biology.

Georgia Gale Grant is a freelance science writer, communicator and broadcaster. She read Chemistry at Oxford University before an MSc in Science Communication at Imperial College London.

Diane Jaquith earned her Master's degree in Physics at Wesleyan University. She taught physics, chemistry, and physical science at Durham High School, Durham, CT. She later taught chemistry at Notre Dame College and Pinkerton Academy in Derry, NH.

Catriona Lang studied singing at Birmingham Conservatoire. She currently earns her living as a singing teacher.

Marion Lang is a Classics graduate from St Andrews University who now works as a Nursery Teacher and also runs NYCoS Mini Music Makers classes. She is a member of Stirling Gaelic Choir.

Bill Mietelski is a Software Engineer and a huge Head First & Kathy Sierra fan. He plans on putting the things he learned in Head First Physics to good use while improving his golf game.

Michael Lew is an AP* Physics and Computer Science teacher at Loyola High School in Los Angeles, CA and has been teaching since 1991. In his spare time, he enjoys spending time with his wife, Britt, and his three children, Mike, Jade, and Dane.

Alice Pitt-Pitts enjoyed being a guinea pig reviewer for *Head First Physics*. She also likes reading, cycling and ice cream and now knows that all of these involve energy conservation!

*AP is a registered trademark of the College Board

Acknowledgments

Catherine Nolan

The editors:

Thanks go to **Catherine Nolan** and **Brett McLaughlin**, who were editors on this project at various points, and coped admirably with the US-UK time difference. Thanks also to **Mike Loukides** for starting the whole thing off as far as Head First Physics was concerned.

Brett McLaughlin

Lou Barr

The O'Reilly team:

Thanks go to **Lou Barr** for turning my "wouldn't it be dreamy if..." thoughts into reality with any artwork that's more complicated than a line drawing. And also to **Brittany Smith**, who pulled off the impossible in the final stages of production. Plus **Laurie Petrycki**, **Caitrin McCullough, Sanders Kleinfeld, Julie Hawks, Karen Shaner** and **Keith McNamara**.

The reviewers:

Thanks to everyone on the opposite page. In particular, I'd like to mention **Donald Wilke** for his extremely detailed physics-specific comments and **John Allister** for a physics educator point of view that spanned the whole book. A lot of improvements post tech review were down to the comments of physics guinea-pigs **Marion Lang**, **Catriona Lang** and **Alice Pitt-Pitts**, who did a sterling job of pointing out where things could be clearer.

Like distributed computing, but with a physics book.

The distributed.physics project:

As well as to say: "thanks," this is an experiment to test the theory that everyone mentioned in a book will buy a copy.

Between them, these heros and heroines got through a draft of the entire book in a single day...

Alice Pitt-Pitts, Andrew Lynn, Brian Widdas, Catriona Lang, Emma Simmons, Gareth Poulton, Graham Wood, Hazel Rostron-Wood, Jason Williams, John Vinall, Marion Lang, Peter Scandrett, Robin Lang, Roger Thetford, Stephen Swain, Tim Bannister, Tim Dickinson and **Will Burt**.

Safari® Books Online

When you see a Safari® icon on the cover of your favorite technology book that means the book is available online through the O'Reilly Network Safari Bookshelf.

Safari offers a solution that's better than e-books. It's a virtual library that lets you easily search thousands of top tech books, cut and paste code samples, download chapters, and find quick answers when you need the most accurate, current information. Try it for free at `http://safari.oreilly.com`.

1 think like a physicist

In the beginning ...

Physics is about the world around you and how everything in it works. As you go about your daily life, you're **doing** physics all the time! But the thought of actually **learning** physics may sometimes **feel** like falling into a bottomless pit with no escape! Don't worry... this chapter introduces how to **think like a physicist**. You'll learn to step into problems and to use your **intuition** to spot **patterns** and '**special points**' that make things much easier. By **being** part of the problem, you're one step closer to getting to the solution...

Physics is the world around you

Physics is about **the world around you** and how stuff in the world **actually works**. How do you aim a cannon with no direct line of sight? How can a satellite orbit the earth without falling back down? Will you win a prize shooting ducks at the fairground? Will the Dingo catch the Emu...

All of this **should** be really interesting... except that opening a normal physics textbook can make you feel rather like you've just fallen into a bottomless pit....

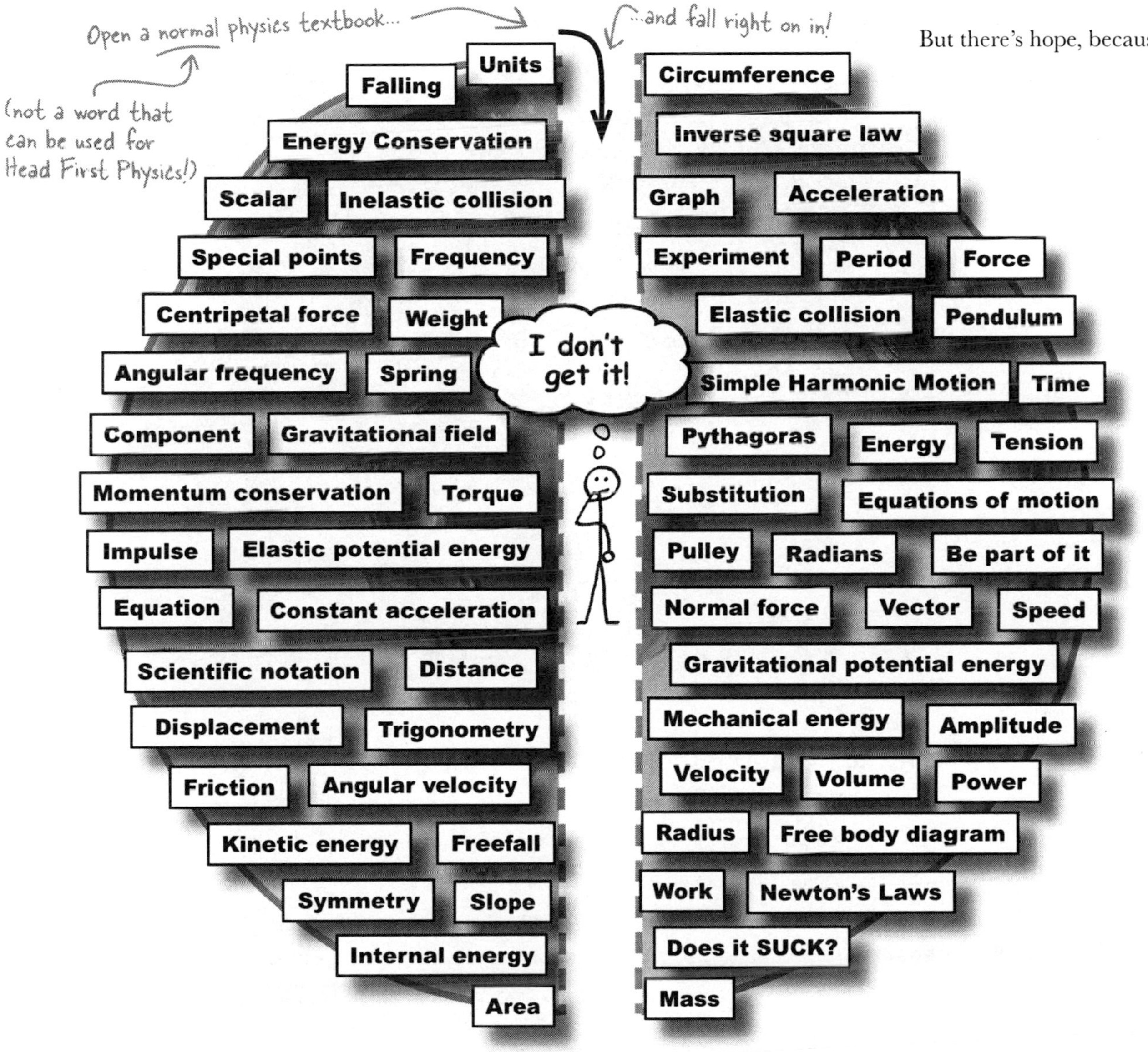

But there's hope, because...

You already know more than you think you do!

Honest!

Imagine you're part of a physics problem. What would you feel?

- [x] **You can get a feel for what's going on by being a part of it.**

Places where important or interesting things happen.

- [x] **You can use your intuition to spot special points.**

Where have you seen or experienced something like this before?

- [x] **You can use your life experience to spot what things are like.**

You don't pass physics by memorizing things. You pass physics by learning how to think about it.

This book is all about learning to think like a physicist.

You can get a feel for what's happening by being a part of it

The best way to get started with any kind of physics is to imagine that you're there, in the middle of it. Maybe you're a block, or a car, or a racing driver. Then ask yourself, "**What would I feel?**"

Which direction am I moving in?

Am I speeding up or slowing down?

Is there anything pushing or pulling me?

(and so on...)

Be a part of it!

Go to the start of the problem then BE a part of it!

So - could you ever escape from the bottomless pit?

Suppose you really **are** falling into a bottomless pit that runs from one side of the world to the other. What do you think would happen (assuming that the earth isn't hot and molten inside)?

Not sure where to start? That's okay ... break it down and go right back to the beginning. **Be a part of the problem!** Ask yourself, "What would I feel just after I step into the tunnel?"

BE part of it

Your job is to imagine you just stepped out over a bottomless pit. What would you feel if you were part of the scenario? Which direction are you moving in? Are you speeding up or slowing down?

WHY are you feeling that?

DIRECTION: ....

....

SPEED: ....

....

WHY: ....

....

Ask yourself, "What would I FEEL if I was part of the scenario?"

BE part of it - Solution

Your job is to imagine you just stepped out over a bottomless pit. What would you feel if you were part of the scenario? Which direction are you moving in? Are you speeding up or slowing down?

WHY are you feeling that?

DIRECTION: I fall down, into the tunnel.

SPEED: I get faster as I fall.

WHY: Gravity attracts me into the earth.

Normally the solutions aren't visible when you're working on the problem... but we're just getting started.

Relax

Don't worry if you wrote down something a bit different.

This is what we wrote. Your answers should be similar, but maybe not identical.

there are no Dumb Questions

Q: But all I've done is write down what I already knew and what was really obvious! I haven't worked out what happens inside the earth at all!

A: Physics is about being able to put yourself into a problem and asking "What would I feel?" When you're doing this, you need to start at the start - with what's initially going on.

Q: Why? It hasn't helped me get a final answer!

A: Starting off a question with 'obvious' things gives your brain time to calm down and settle. It's the first step towards solving a more complicated problem. Once you've made a start, you can build on it by using your intuition and experience to spot 'special points' (where important or interesting things happen) and similarities to problems you've seen before.

Q: What if I start out OK then get stuck or make a mistake? Surely I've completely failed if I don't get the right answer at the end?

A: Usually people grading exams are more interested in whether you **understand** the physics, even though the math part is important too. So, if you're able to start off in the right direction and show that you understand the important physics principles, you'll get credit for it even if you get stuck or make a mistake later on.

Q: But I still have no idea what happens next here!

A: You've already realized that **gravity** is important. And that you'll fall **faster** as you fall into the tunnel. That's a great start for you to build on.

Use your intuition to look for 'special points'

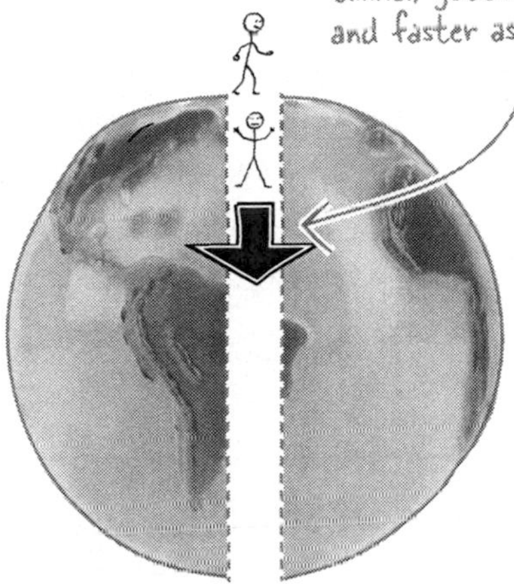

You've just started off the bottomless pit problem by **being a part of it**. You started at the start, imagined you'd just stepped over the edge, and asked yourself "What would I feel?" And you know that you'll fall into the tunnel, getting faster as you go.

But what happens next?

The key is to use your intuition to look for **'special points'** – places where important or interesting things happen.

For example, the **edge** of a cliff is a special point because that's where you change from being supported by the ground to being unsupported. And the **center** of a seesaw is a 'special point' because it's the only place on the seesaw that one person can stand without either side going up or down.

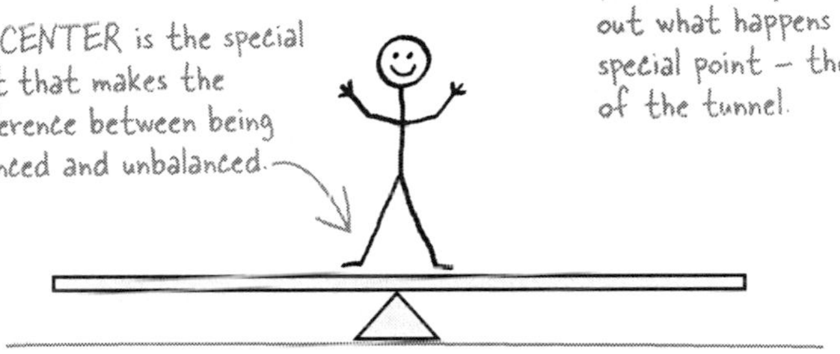

Spotting special points then asking "**What would I feel** if I was there?" helps you to understand what's going on.

You already did that for one special point - at the **edge** of the tunnel. Now it's time to look out for more special points in this problem, so you can think about what's going on there.

Once you know what's happening at each special point you can play connect the dots and work out what's happening in between too.

In physics, the 'special points' where things happen are usually at the <u>EDGES</u> and in the <u>CENTER</u>.

BRAIN POWER

The **edge** of the tunnel is a special point. Can you spot any other special points in this problem?

Jill: I have a hunch that the **center** of the earth must be important - it just looks like it must be!

Frank: Yeah. Even though we're assuming the center of the earth isn't hot (because we're dealing with an Earth which has lots of physics words written on it), the center still looks really important!

Jill: But what's gonna happen there?

Frank: I'm not sure. I guess that either you stop, or you keep on falling. But that's not narrowing it down all that much!

Jill: Maybe we can use **what we already figured out**? Didn't we say that when you're at the surface and step over the edge of the tunnel, you fall down into the tunnel because of **gravity**?

Frank: Yeah, that's right. I guess that the earth attracts you because it's so big. Gravity is the stuff the earth's made of and the stuff you're made of attracting each other, right?

Jill: And when you're at the surface - at the edge of the tunnel - the whole of the earth is under you. So gravity attracts you downwards.

Frank: Yeah, that makes sense. So what's going on in the center? The whole Earth isn't under you any more - it's kinda all around you. There's the same amount of Earth around you in all directions!

Jill: Then you must get pulled in all directions at once. Ouch! Sounds like you'd get torn apart or something!

Frank: Hmm. The Earth's gravity isn't strong enough to pull my atoms apart when I'm standing on the surface. I have a feeling it'll be more **like** standing in the exact center of a seesaw.

Jill: You mean, kinda like a **balance** point? I guess if you were at either **end** of the seesaw - or at either end of the tunnel - you'd move. But if you're in the center of the seesaw - or the center of the earth, you're balanced.

Frank: Yeah. With the seesaw, it's like you have one foot 'pulling' you an equal amount each way, so you stay balanced. And in the center of the earth, you have half the earth on one side and half the earth on the other side. That's balanced too.

Jill: So you must stop when you reach the center of the earth if you balance there. We solved the problem - you never get out!

Frank: Hmm... but didn't we say before that you're **already** moving **very fast** by the time you reach the center?

Once you've found a special point, ask yourself: "What would I FEEL there?" and "What is being there LIKE?"

What's it SIMILAR to?

The center of the earth is a special point

As Frank and Jill have worked out, the **center** of the earth is a special point where important or interesting things might happen. Maybe your eye was drawn to the center because of the **symmetry**, as there's the same amount of Earth around you in all directions.

So - be a part of it! Imagine yourself at the center of the earth. What would I feel there? What is being there **like**?

At the **first special point**—the **edge** of the tunnel—you're pulled downwards into the tunnel by gravity. This is because of the attraction between the "stuff" the earth's made of and the "stuff" you're made of.

(Stuff isn't a particularly technical term - we're basically using it to mean all of your atoms.)

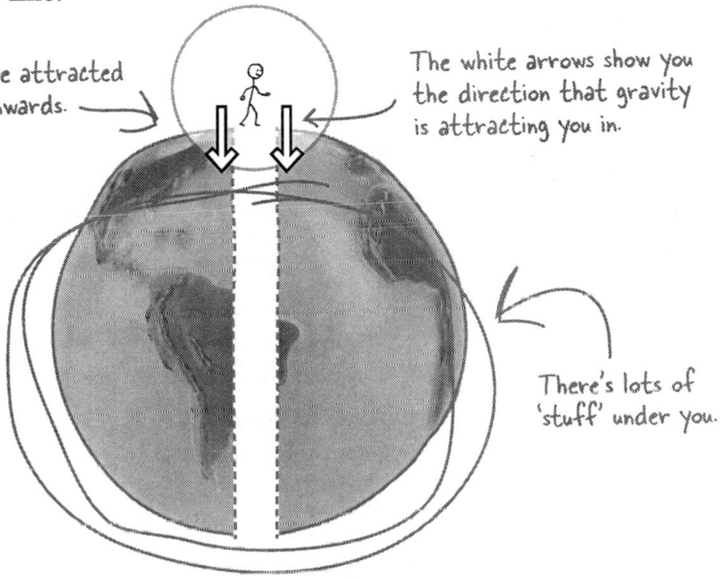

At the **second special point**, in the **center** of the earth, all of your atoms are pulled equally in all directions. You aren't attracted in any direction more strongly that you are in any other direction.

Being attracted in all directions at once may not sound like fun - but you're made of stronger stuff. The Earth's gravity isn't strong enough to pull your atoms apart. This means that all of the attractions **balance** each other out.

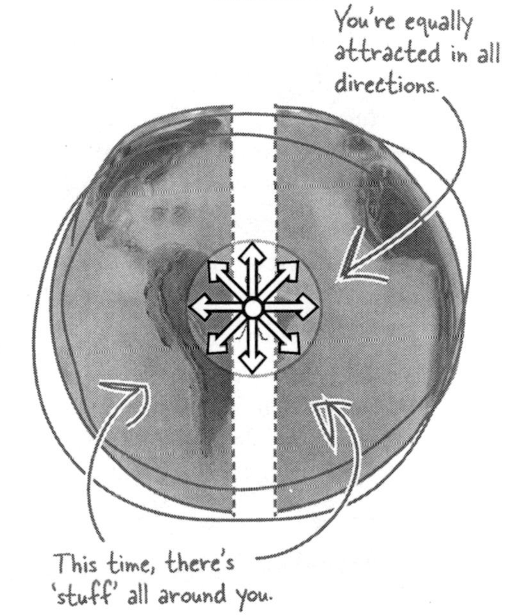

At the center, you're equally attracted in all directions - so all the gravitational attractions balance out.

Ask yourself "What am I ALREADY doing as I reach the special point?"

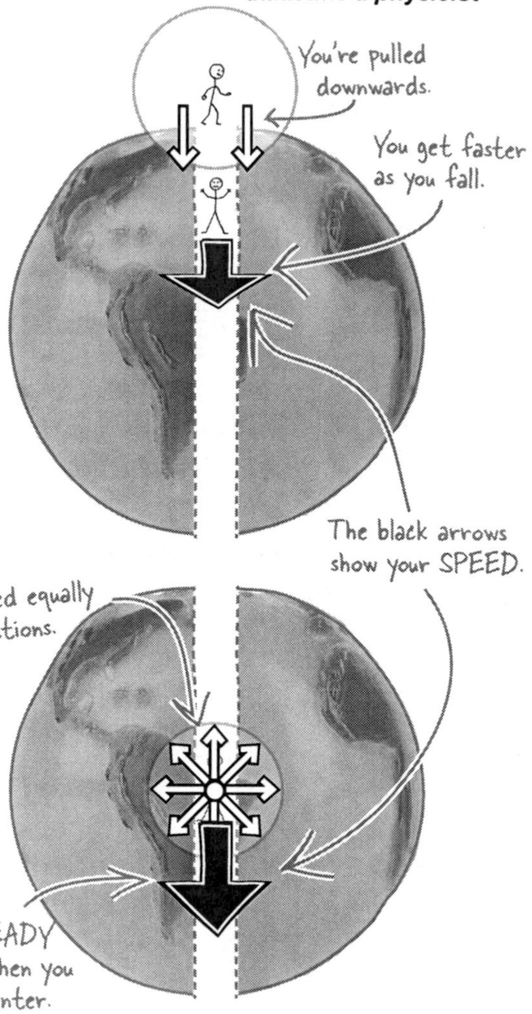

But Frank and Jill nearly made a big mistake when they were thinking about out what it would **feel like** in the center of the earth. At first, they thought that if all the gravitational attractions **balance** out, then you'll be stationary in the center of the earth, like you are when you balance yourself on the center of a seesaw.

But is that really true? You're **already** going very fast when you reach the center of the earth. You've fallen a very long way to get there, moving faster and faster all the time. **If all the attractions balance out, what is there to slow you down?**

What is it **like** to be already going fast when there's nothing pulling or pushing you?

When you put yourself in a problem, try to imagine what you're ALREADY doing when you reach the special point before going on to think about what happens next.

BE part of it

Your job is to imagine that you're going very fast. Maybe you're a car or a speed skater. What it is LIKE to be going very fast when nothing can pull or push you, and you can't pull or push on anything either? That means no brakes and no grabbing on to something to slow down. Does this give you any clues about what it will be LIKE at the center of the earth when all the attractions balance out?

....

....

....

....

....

....

....

BE part of it - Solution

Your job is to imagine that you're going very fast. Maybe you're a car or a speed skater. What it is LIKE to be going very fast when nothing can pull or push you, and you can't pull or push on anything either? That means no brakes and no grabbing on to something to slow down. Does this give you any clues about what it will be LIKE at the center of the earth when all the attractions balance out?

If I can't brake or grab onto anything, then I can't slow down. I'll just keep on going really fast.
I think the same thing will happen in the center of the earth. None of the directions of attraction will "win", and I'll just keep on going at the same speed.

You might have said that it was LIKE something else. That's OK. The main thing is that you keep on going at the SAME SPEED if there's nothing pushing or pulling on you.

Isn't this all a bit ridiculous? You wouldn't go at the same speed-you'd slow down from air resistance or bumping into the sides of the tunnel...or something like that... especially as the earth turns!

That's right - we've made some assumptions to turn the problem into a simpler version

We already made an **assumption** back on page 4 that (for this problem) the earth is solid and isn't hot in the middle, as getting fried isn't helpful.

And quite right - we're also assuming that air resistance doesn't slow you down and that the pit goes between the North and South poles, so you don't hit the sides as the earth turns.

In physics, the way of solving a complex problem is often to make approximations or assumptions to turn it into a simpler problem. That's OK, as you can ask yourself later on what the difference would be if you hadn't made the assumption. But only once you've got to come to grips with the simpler version.

Sometimes, including all the hard stuff right from the start makes the problem impossible to solve.

In physics, you sometimes make approximations or assumptions to turn a complex problem into a simpler version.

Understanding the simpler version helps you with the complex version.

Where you're at - and what happens next?

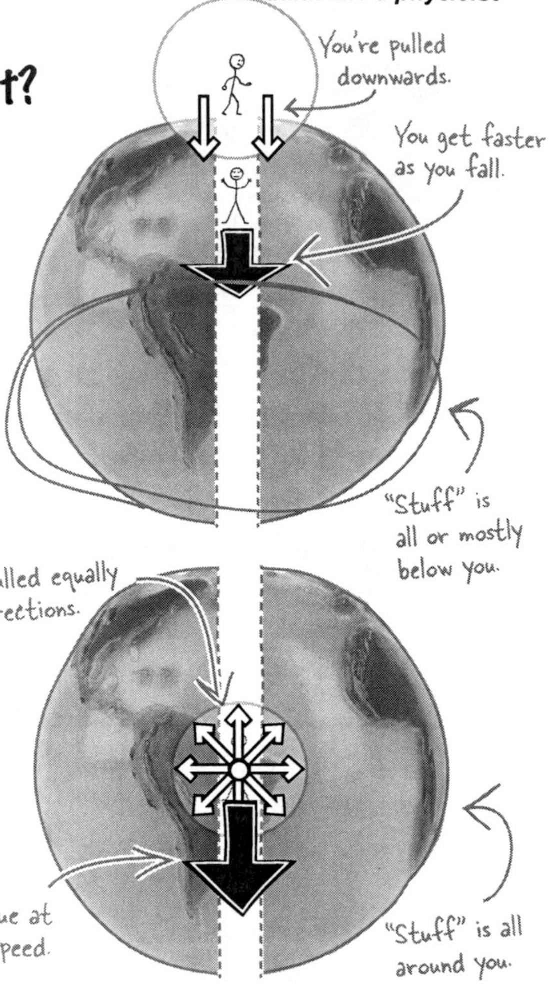

You've learned to step into the problem, so you can **be a part of it** and ask "**What would I feel**" and "**What's it like.**" This is a good way to start off and helps you see what the important things in the problem are. Here, you realized that **gravity** is important, and that you fall towards the center of the earth, getting faster and faster as you go.

You've also used your intuition to spot '**special points.**' You've spotted that the **center** of the earth is a place where the gravitational attraction between the stuff you're made of and the stuff the earth's made of is the same in all directions.

And you worked out that this means you just keep on going at the **same speed** you were already going at as you pass through the center because there's nothing to slow you down! So you're going quickly, but you aren't getting faster and faster anymore.

But now you're through the center, **what happens next**? What would you feel? What's it like? You already know that gravity is important and that its influence depends on where you and the earth are compared to each other. So - what happens next?

Sharpen your pencil

What do you think happens after you pass through the center of the earth? Do you continue at the same speed? Do you start falling faster? Do you slow down? How far do you think you keep falling? Or do you think something else happens?

Draw a picture then write down any ideas you have.

Write things on your sketch to help explain!

....

....

....

....

....

Hint: Think about where the majority of the earth's "stuff" is when you're at various points in the tunnel.

Sharpen your pencil Solution

What do you think happens after you pass through the center of the earth? Do you continue at the same speed? Do you start falling faster? Do you slow down? How far do you think you keep falling? Or do you think something else happens?

Draw a picture then write down any ideas you have.

I think that after passing through the center there starts to be more Earth above you than there is below you.
This acts a bit like brakes – you're moving away from the center but gravity's attracting you back in. The further from the center you are, the more Earth's above you, so the more you slow down.
I think you'll be moving slower and slower until you reach the other side of the tunnel.

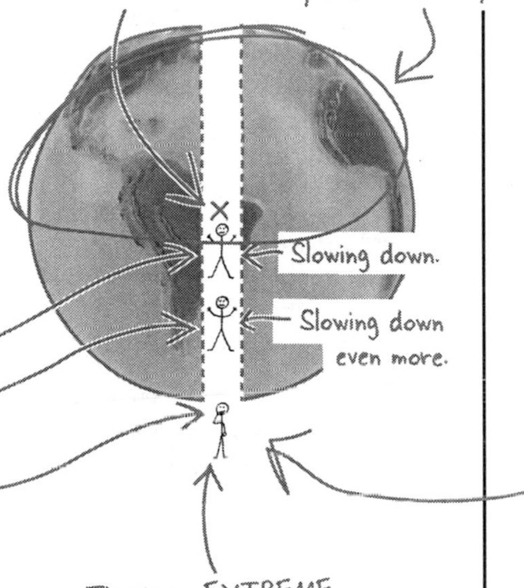

You should never be afraid to ask questions!

there are no Dumb Questions

Q: I thought that gravity always speeds you up when you fall. Now you're saying it can slow you down?

A: Things are always attracted towards each other by gravity. Whether you're already moving away from the earth or moving towards it, you'll always be attracted towards the center of the earth.

Q: But that doesn't say anything about speeding up or slowing down!

A: You need to think about the speed and direction you're already traveling in. If you throw a ball up, it's moving away from the center of the earth, and it gets slower. When it comes back down again, it's moving towards the center of the earth, and it gets faster.

It looks like you're **always** attracted towards the center, right?

You're always attracted towards the center unless you're already in the center.

Right. When you're on the surface at the start, there's a lot more Earth under you than there is on top of you, and you're attracted towards the center. This makes you speed up.

When you're in the center, the attractions all cancel each other out, and you keep going at the same speed.

As you move through the center towards the other side, there's more and more Earth above you than there is below you. So you start being attracted back towards the center, which slows you down.

Now put it all together

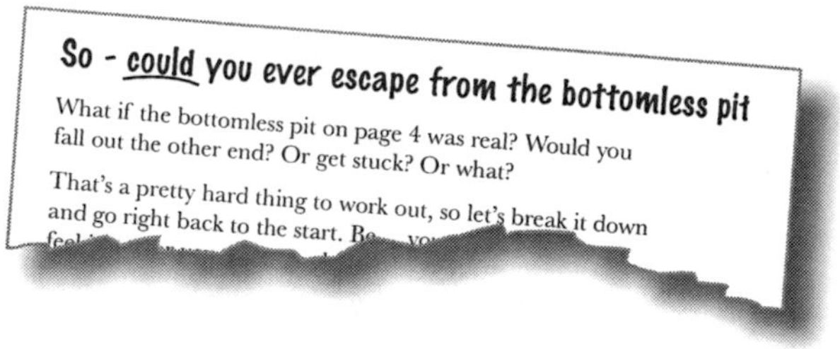
So - could you ever escape from the bottomless pit

What if the bottomless pit on page 4 was real? Would you fall out the other end? Or get stuck? Or what?

That's a pretty hard thing to work out, so let's break it down and go right back to the start.

Back on page 4, you wondered if you could ever escape from the bottomless pit. Being able to step out at the other side of the earth doesn't really count as escaping, as you'd be a very long way from where you started!

So - are you going to be able to get back home again, or are you doomed to hang out at the other end of the bottomless pit forever?

Sharpen your pencil

Could you ever get back home again - back to where you started before you fell in??

The pictures show what you've worked out for three special points so far. Use them to explain whether you think you'll ever be able to make it back home again.

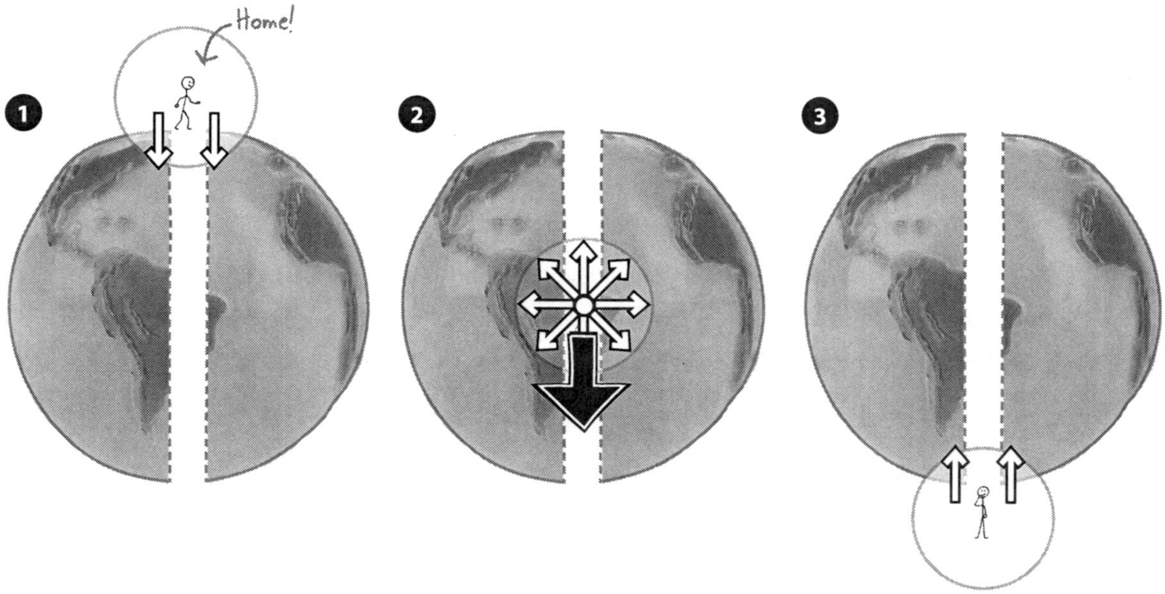

....

....

....

Hint: Turn the book upside-down. What's it LIKE?

Sharpen your pencil Solution

Could you ever get back home again - back to where you started before you fell in??

The pictures show what you've worked out for three special points so far. Use them to explain whether you think you'll ever be able to make it back home again.

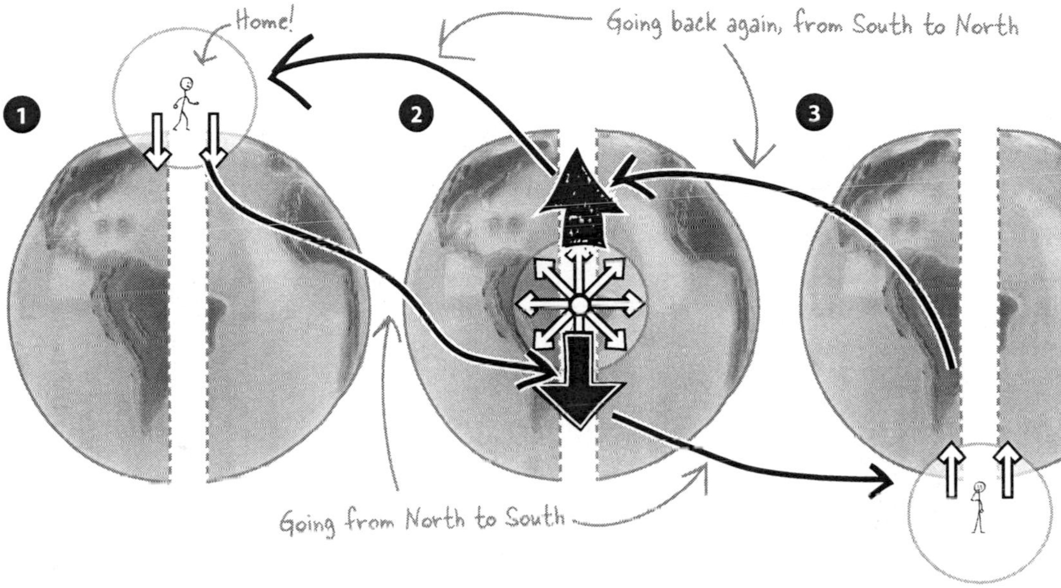

If you're at the other end of the tunnel, you can just step back in again and do the entire journey in the opposite direction! It's all exactly the same as your original trip through the earth – speed up, through center, slow down, emerge – except you're going back the way you came.

Though do be careful – if you forget to step off the Earth Express at the other end, you'll fall back into the tunnel again and keep on falling to and fro through it!

Not only can you escape, you end up on top of the world!

(As long as you remember to step off here!)

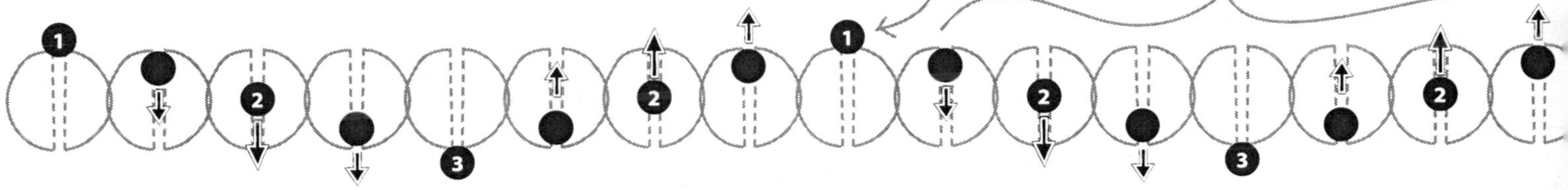

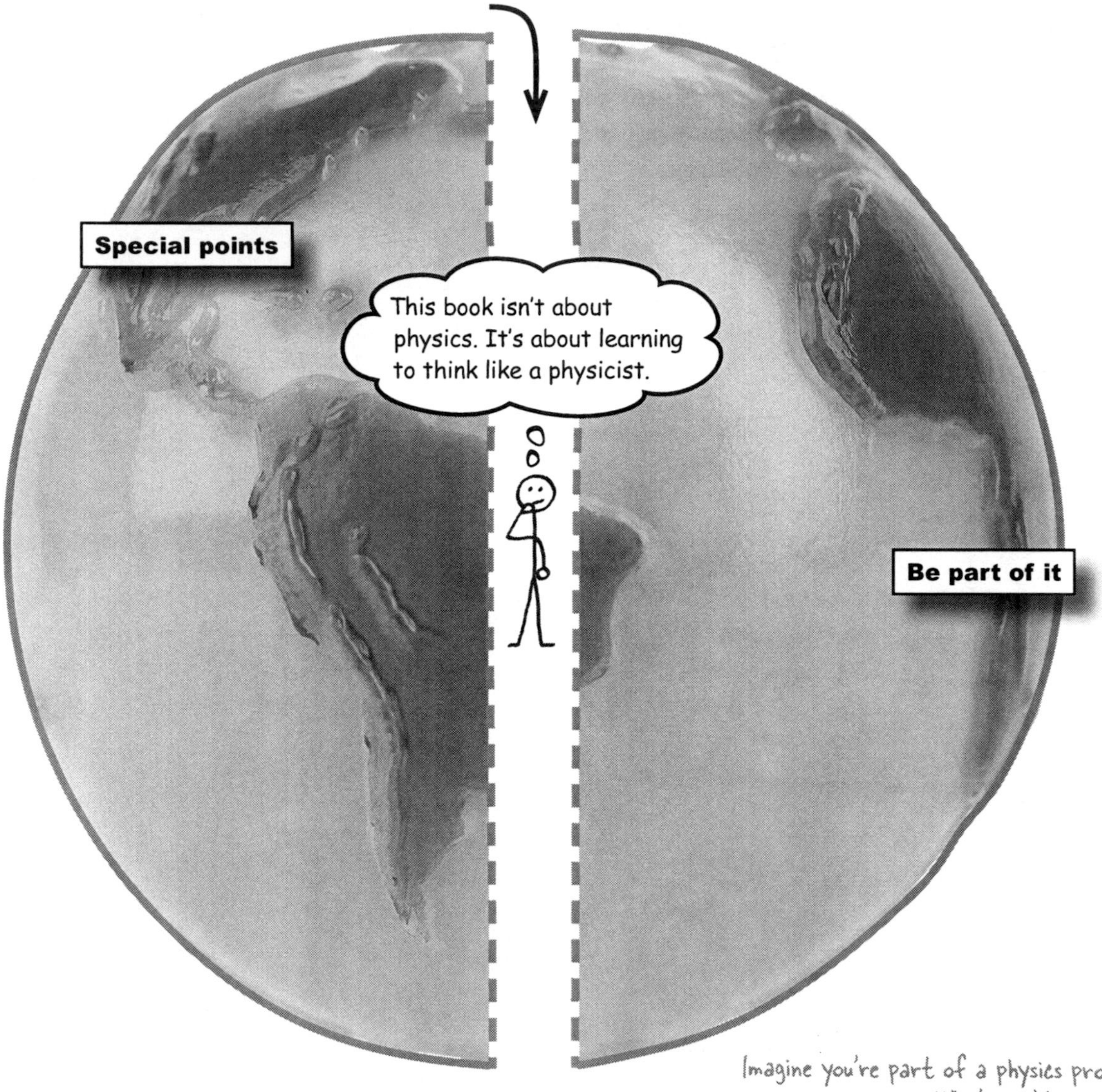

Imagine you're part of a physics problem. What would you feel?

- [x] **You can get a feel for what's going on by being a part of it.**

Places where important or interesting things happen.

- [x] **You can use your intuition to spot special points.**

Where have you seen or experienced something like this before?

- [x] **You can use your life experience to spot what things are like.**

Your Physics Toolbox

You've got Chapter 1 under your belt, and you've added some problem-solving concepts to your toolbox.

Be Part of It

Putting yourself in the heart of the problem often gives you clues about what might be happening.

You can draw on your experience because physics is all about how the world works, and you've got plenty of experience there. Imagine yourself in the scenario and ask "What would I feel?"

What's it LIKE?

You can get a long way with physics problems by asking yourself what the situation is LIKE.

It may look very different on the surface – but if you can spot an analogy or pattern and can connect the situation to something you already know how to deal with, you're sorted.

Special Points

Special points are extremes, places where important or interesting things happen.

If you work out what's going on at "special points," you can go on to "connect-the-dots" and work out what's going on in between as well.

Be visual!

Engage the whole of your brain by "thinking aloud" in pictures as well as in words. Drawing the scenario and then annotating it with what you know is one of the most powerful tools in your toolbox.

You already know more than you think you do

Above all else, don't panic or worry about physics. You already know more than you think you do from your real life experience. And by the end of this book you'll know – and understand – a whole lot more.

2 making it all MEAN something

Units and measurements

How long is a piece of string? Physics is based on making **measurements** that tell you about **size**. In this chapter, you'll learn how to use **units** and **rounding** to avoid making mistakes - and also why **errors** are OK. By the time you're through, you'll know when something is **significant** and have an opinion on whether size really **is** everything.

It's the best music player ever, and you're part of the team!

Introducing the myPod - a revolution in portable music players!

Your design team has just finished the final case prototype. Now you need to draw up the blueprints to be sent to the factory that's manufacturing the cases.

MEMO

From: myPod Case Design Team

We've just sent over the latest, and hopefully final, model myPod case design.

Could you draw up the plans and send them to factory where the cases are being manufactured? And send us back the myPod model when you're done.

You will, of course, receive one of the limited edition numbered myPods for your troubles if you manage to turn this around quickly!

So you get on with measuring the myPod case

The quicker the factory gets the plans, the better.

Sharpen your pencil

Here's the myPod case with various lengths marked out that you'll need to measure. Cut out the ruler (or just use your own that looks similar to ours) and write in the lengths. (The myPod design team already started writing them on for you.)

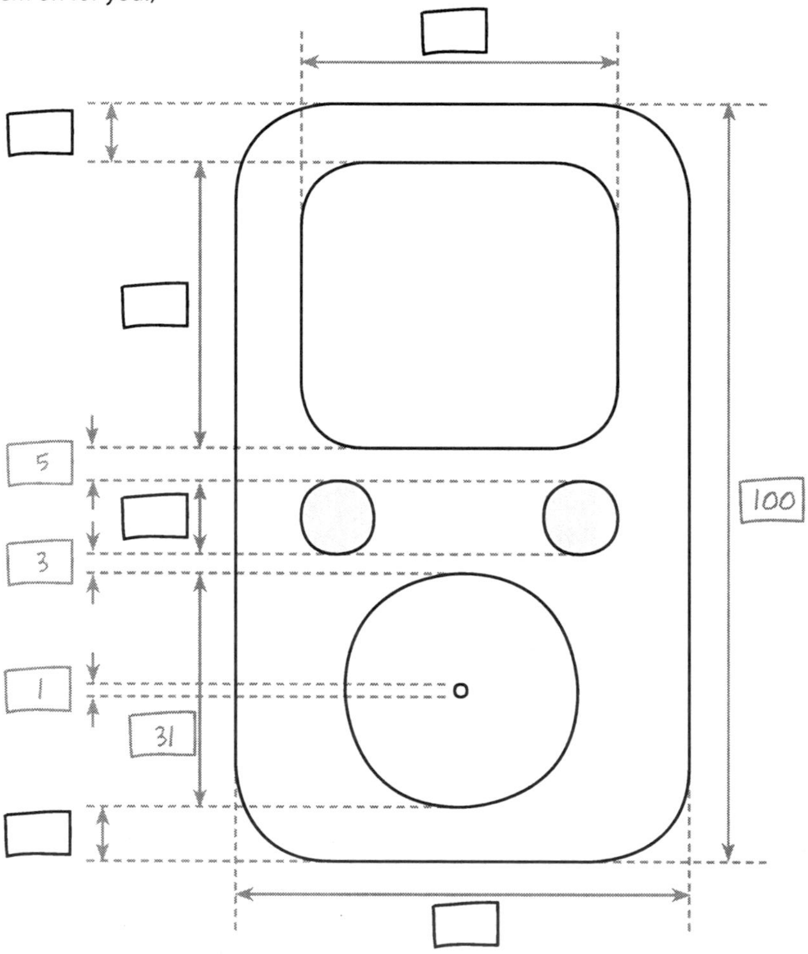

When the myPod case comes back from the factory...

After a lightning-quick turnaround, the myPod case comes back from the factory. But there's a problem.

Sharpen your pencil Solution

Here's the myPod case with various lengths marked out that you'll need to measure. Cut out the ruler (or just use your own that looks similar to ours) and write in the lengths. (The myPod design team already started writing them on for you.)

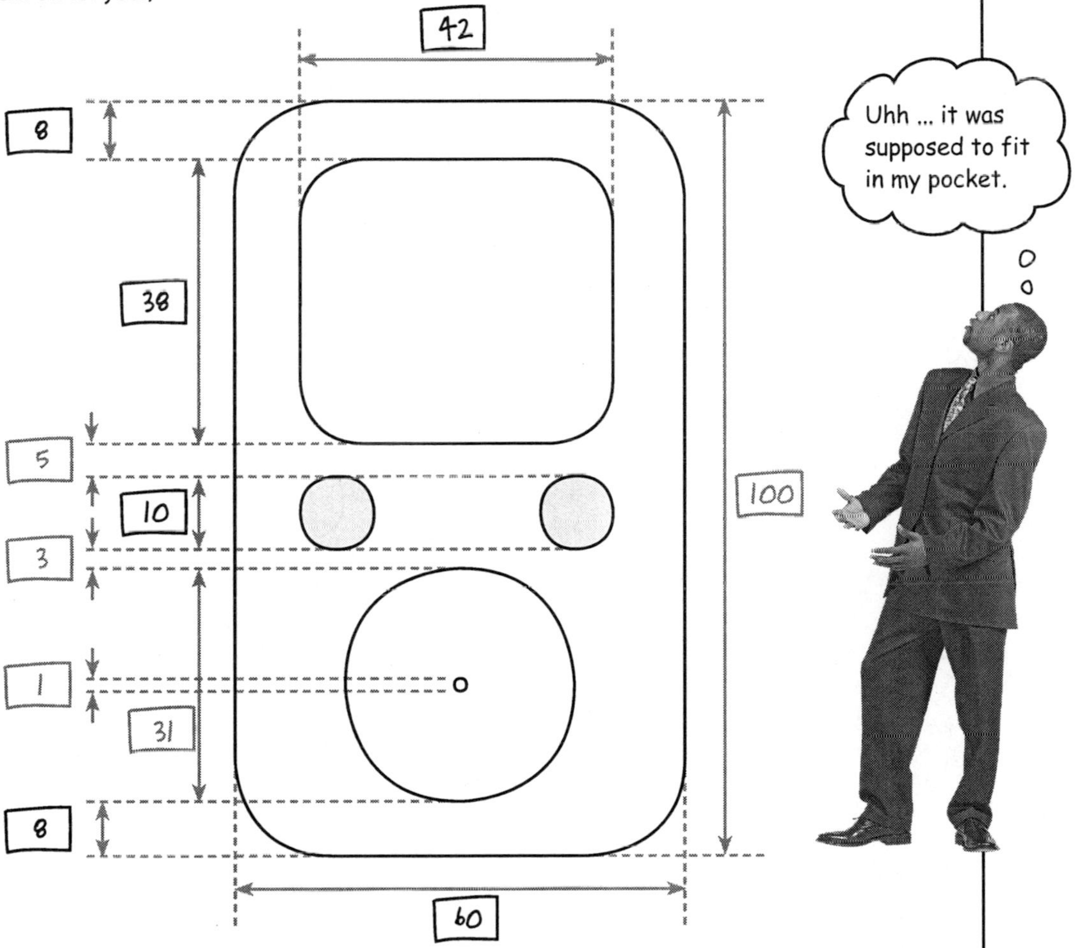

... it's waaay too big!

The myPod case is huge. Massive. Rocket-sized, not pocket-sized.

But when you give the factory a call, they say they followed your instructions exactly.

BRAIN POWER

Something's obviously gone very wrong. But what?!

Have another look at your blueprint, and see if it could be interpreted differently.

There aren't any UNITS on the blueprint

The ruler you used is marked off in millimeters (mm)- but there aren't any notes on the blueprint that say this. The factory is used to working in inches and assumed it was a giant promotional item. Inches are around 25 times bigger than millimeters, so the myPod has come back MUCH bigger than expected!

In physics, it's really important to say what the **units** are any time you write down a number. Units give numbers meaning, so you know whether the number represents millimeters or inches, or something else entirely.

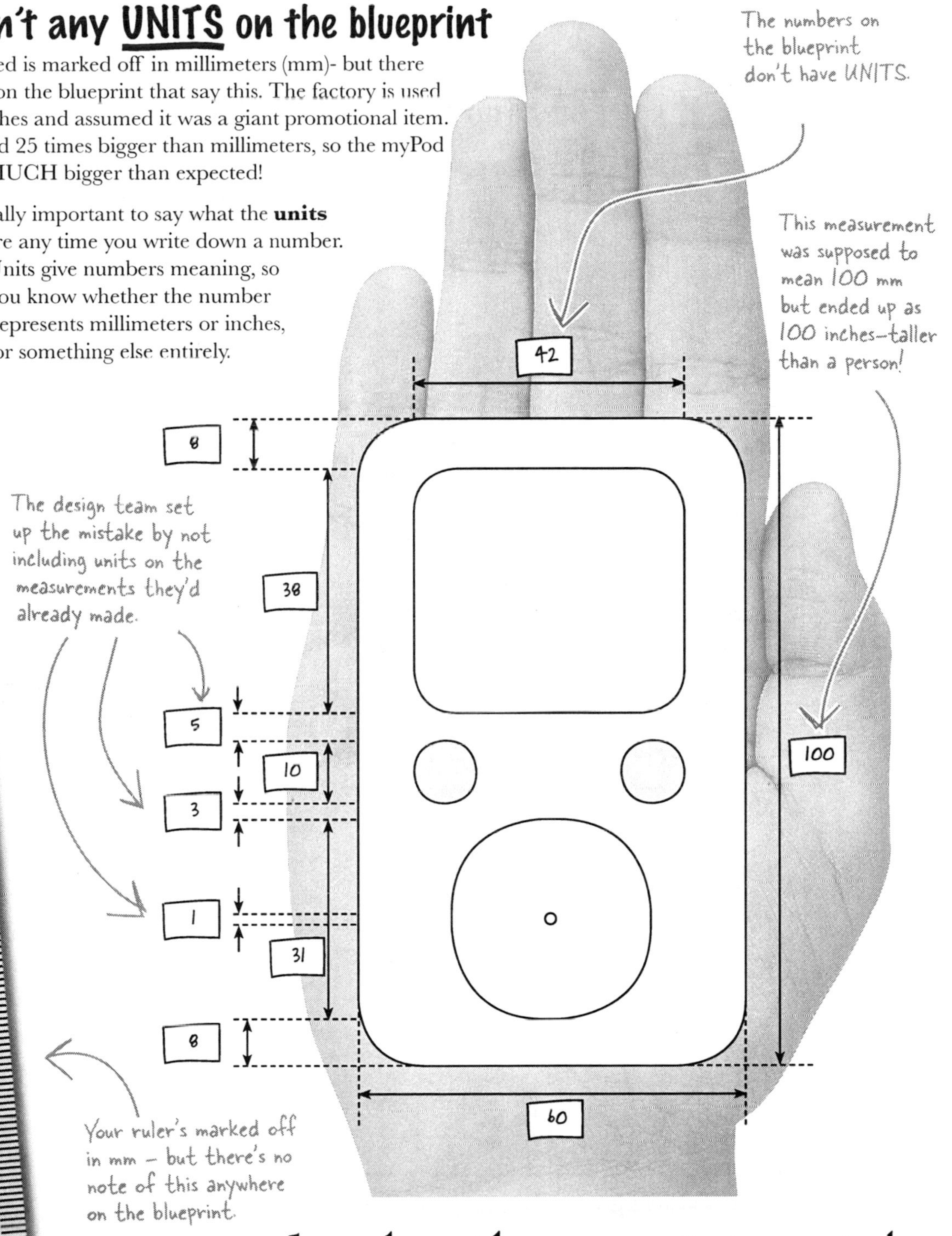

A number without any units is meaningless.

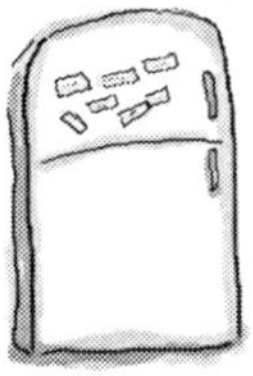

Units Magnets

Throughout the book, you'll be attaching lots of different units to numbers to give them meaning. Your job is to match the units with the kind of quantity they measure. You might not have heard of all of these, but give it a shot.

Length

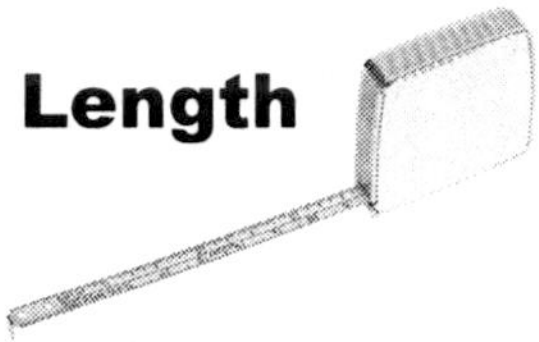

Time

Mass

Use these spaces to draw the magnets in the right columns.

inches

yards

milliseconds

milligrams

years

meters

feet

minutes

tonnes

millimeters

kilometers

hours

seconds

grams

kilograms

days

Units Magnets Solution

Check your work; were you able to match these up correctly?

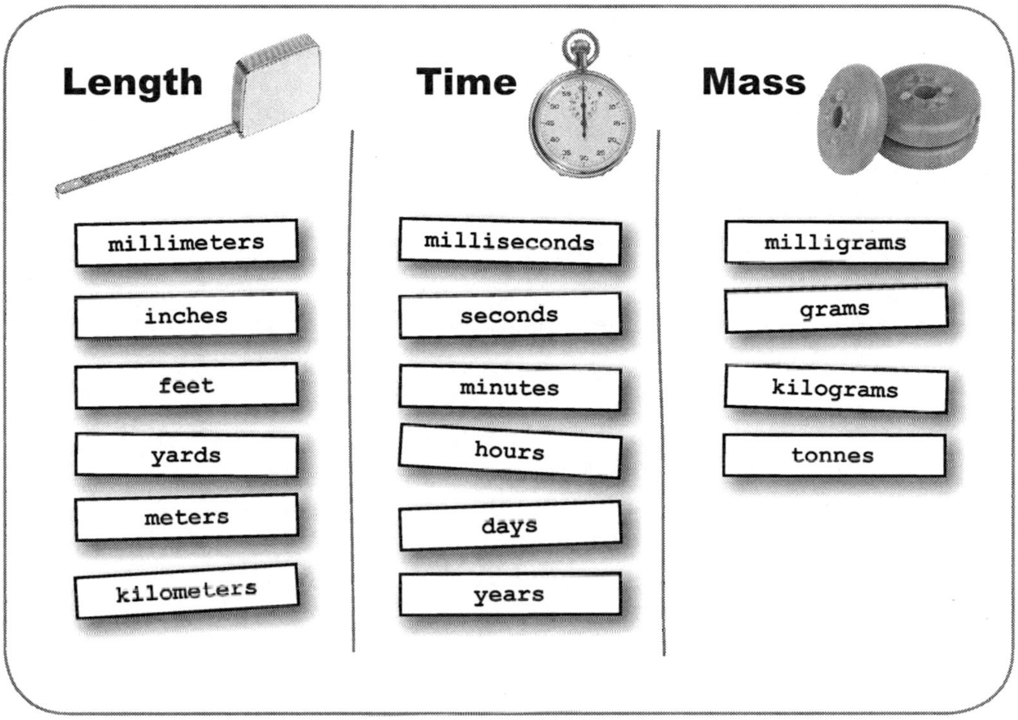

Relax

Don't worry if you're not familiar with all of these units just quite yet.

't have to work with all of these unfamiliar units ›ut the book! Instead, you'll be sticking with the system ...ldwide, which is what the next couple of pages are all about!

Plus you can always look up unfamiliar units.

You'll use SI units in this book (and in your class)

AP Physics B or UK A Level

The system of units used in physics worldwide is called SI (short for Système Internationale). They're much easier to use since they go up in multiples of 1000 for each 'step.'

If you're working with **lengths**, instead of having to do calculations using 12 inches in a foot, 3 feet in a yard, and 1760 yards in a mile, you have 1000 millimeters in a meter, 1000 meters in a kilometer, and so on and so forth.

Working with lengths is much easier in SI.

And with **masses**, instead of having to remember that there are 16 ounces in a pound and 2000 pounds in a ton, you have 1000 milligrams in a gram, 1000 grams in a kilogram (about the equivalent of three cans of soda), and so on. The only SI unit which doesn't follow this convention is **time**.

And working with masses is easier too.

But time is so widely agreed on; it'd be silly to reinvent it!

Multiplying and dividing by 1000 is more straightforward mental arithmetic, so calculations involving SI units are quicker and easier than calculations with other unit systems. If you're converting meters to kilometers, you divide by 1000 (easier), but going from yards to miles involves dividing by 1760 (not straightforward, and definitely not mental arithmetic!).

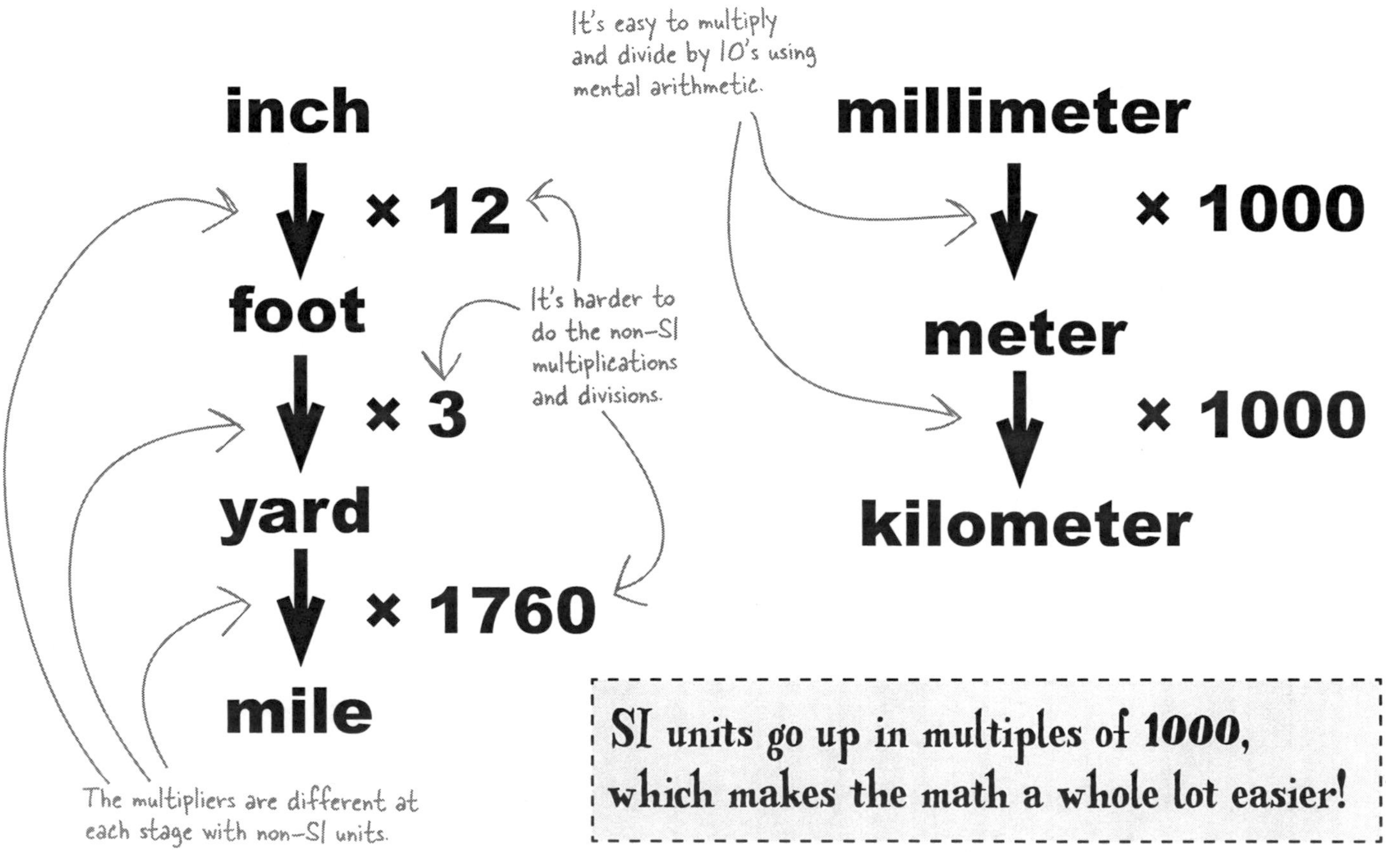

SI units go up in multiples of 1000, which makes the math a whole lot easier!

there are no Dumb Questions

Q: Run it past me again - why am I being forced to use SI units when I'm more used to yards and miles? I really have no idea how much a kilogram is!

A: SI units have been used throughout the world as the basic standard in physics since 1960. SI units are an agreed worldwide standard and make sure that everyone is using the same words and definitions when they make measurements.

Q: But I don't see why I can't just use the units I'm more familiar with. Surely I'm less likely to make mistakes in calculations if I use units I'm used to?

A: SI units actually make calculations easier. Instead of having to use all sorts of weird ratios to move between units (like inches, feet, yards, miles), you'll use tens. So even if they're less familiar at first, they'll be quicker and easier in the long run.

Q: But I'm not at all familiar with SI units at the moment. What kinds of units am I going to come across?

A: It's funny you should ask ...

Here are the SI units you'll use the most

Length

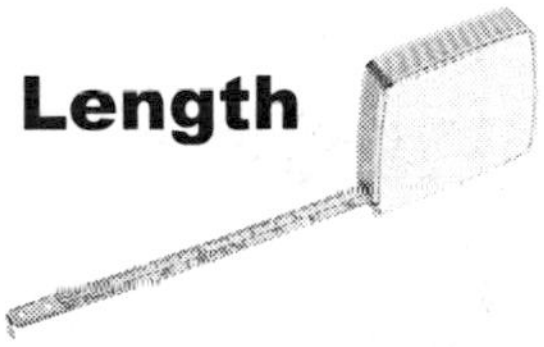

The SI unit of length is the **meter**.

Other related units are the **millimeter** (1000th of a meter), **centimeter** (100th of a meter), and **kilometer** (1000 meters).

Time

The SI unit of time is the **second**.

To work with time units, you'll just use common sense. There are 60 seconds in a **minute**, 60 minutes in an **hour**, 24 hours in a **day**, and 365 days in a **year**.

Mass

The SI unit of mass is the **kilogram**.

Other related units are the **gram** (1000th of a kilogram) and the **milligram** (1000th of a gram).

If you use SI units, people all over the world will understand your measurements.

there are no Dumb Questions

Q: It's a real pain to have to write out 'millimeters' or whatever every time. At least the units I'm used to have abbreviations - like lb for pounds.

A: SI units have abbreviations too! Generally, you just use the first letter of the unit - m for meters, s for seconds, and so on.

Q: OK, but what about things that start with the same letter - meters and minutes, for example?

A: The main SI unit takes precedence. The main unit for length is the meter, so it gets abbreviated to 'm'. The main SI unit for time is the second - the minute is defined as 60 seconds, so it isn't as important and usually gets abbreviated as 'min'.

Q: OK, so what about kilometers and kilograms. They start with the same FOUR letters!

A: The 'kilo' is a **prefix** that goes in front of the unit. A kilogram is 1000 times more than a gram; a kilometer is 1000 times further than a meter. The abbreviation includes the prefix as well, so kilograms are 'kg' and kilometers are 'km'.

It's easier when everyone uses SI units.

Q: So "kilo" means 1000, right? But what does 'milli' mean, then? It sure meant 1000 when the millennium came around, but a millimeter and kilometer are different things, right?!

A: Great observation! Kilo is Greek for 1000, and milli is Latin for 1000. In the SI system, 'kilo' in front of a unit means it's 1000 times as big - so a kilogram is 1000 grams. And 'milli' in front of a unit means it's 1000 times smaller - so a millimeter is 1/1000th of a meter.

Q: I was kind of wondering something. The meter is the main SI unit, and it doesn't have a prefix before the unit. So why is the kilogram the main SI unit and not the gram? That's plain weird!

A: Most everyday physics things like cars, people, and such have masses that are a nice manageable number of kilograms, but thousands, or even millions, of grams. It was a convention that everyone ended up using from 1960 onwards. It's easier when everyone does the same thing!

BRAIN POWER

How would you convert the measurements you've already made into inches **without remeasuring**?

Joe: Yeah. I guess we can remeasure the myPod using a ruler marked off in **inches** and make a new blueprint.

Frank: That sounds like an awful lot of work. It took ages to measure all the lengths in the first place, and I can't face having to do it all over again with inches instead of mm.

Joe: Do we definitely have to remeasure though? Can we do something with the measurements we already made instead?

Jim: It would be nice if they wanted the blueprint in centimeters instead. Then we'd just have to multiply each measurement by 0.1 to **convert** it from mm to cm.

Frank: How does that work?

Jim: We already know that there are 10 mm in 1 cm, which means that 1 mm = 0.1 cm. For every mm, you have 0.1 cm. So if you multiply the number of mm by 0.1, you get the number of cm.

Frank: You mean if the measurement is 23 mm, you multiply the number of mm in the measurement by the number of cm that's equivalent to 1 mm. So 23 × 0.1 = 2.3 cm. But what about the blueprint? That needs to be in **inches**, not cm, right?

Joe: What if we find out **how may inches 1 mm is**? Can't we do exactly the same thing we just did going from mm to cm?

Jim: Hmm ... Yes, I think we could.

Frank: So we'd multiply the length in mm by the number of inches that's equivalent to 1 mm. It's the same thing that we did to **convert** a measurement from mm to cm, but it's more useful, as it's what we're actually supposed to be doing!

Joe: So we can just use a calculator to do the new plans without remeasuring. That rocks!

Jim: Let's get to it!

If you know how many inches 1 mm is, you can CONVERT your measurements from mm to inches.

You use conversion factors to change units

At the moment you have a myPod blueprint measured in millimeters that you want to convert to inches. Although the **numbers** you've written down on the blueprint will change, converting the **units** of a measurement doesn't change its **size**. The myPod still fits comfortably in your pocket whether its size is described using millimeters or inches!

A meaningful measurement consists of both a number and its units. A **conversion factor** is the number you need to multiply your measurement by to convert it from one set of units to another. For example, if you want to convert measurements from mm to cm, you multiply by 0.1, as 1 mm = 0.1 cm.

Most physics books have a table you can use to look up less obvious conversion factors (for example, to convert non-SI units to SI units). Google Calculator can also do the same job. If you don't have access to a computer, we've also included some conversion factors in Appendix B.

"Just Google it"

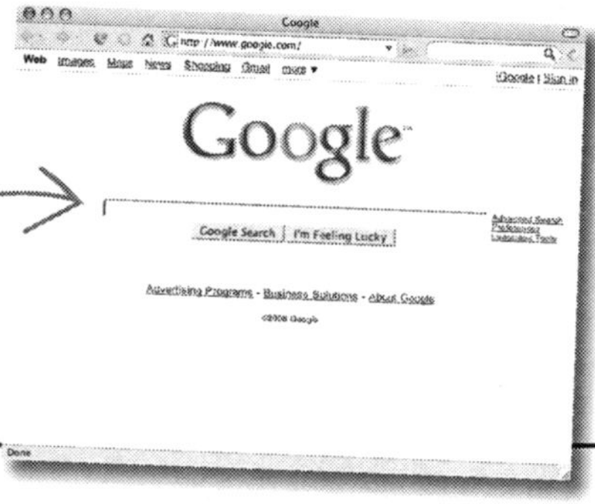

Type what you want to know into the search box on the Google homepage, www.google.com.

If you're at home or in class, the quickest way of looking up a conversion factor is to use Google! You can type things like 1 mm in inches or 1 kilogram in pounds into the search box, and it automatically runs Google Calculator for you and gives you an answer!

Sharpen your pencil

Time to work out a conversion factor to change the myPod blueprint from mm to inches!

Type 1 mm in inches into Google (or look it up in a book).

Write how many inches 1 mm is here:

....

Make sure you don't put "quotes" around this, or Google will look for web pages containing that phrase instead of looking up the conversion factor.

Remember to give your answer MEANING and CONTEXT by mentioning its UNITS.

Sharpen your pencil Solution

Time to work out a conversion factor to change the myPod blueprint from mm to inches!

Type 1 mm in inches into Google (or look it up in a book).

Write how many inches 1 mm is here:

1 millimeter is the same as 0.0393700787 inches.

This is how you should answer exam questions– give UNITS and a CONTEXT so that your answer has MEANING.

Never ever give just a number... or this happens!

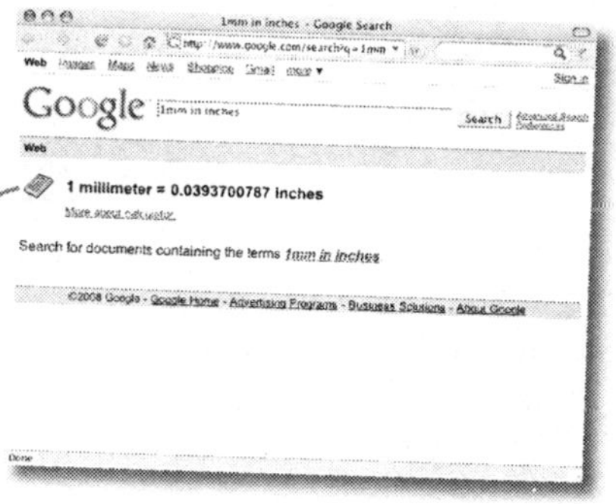

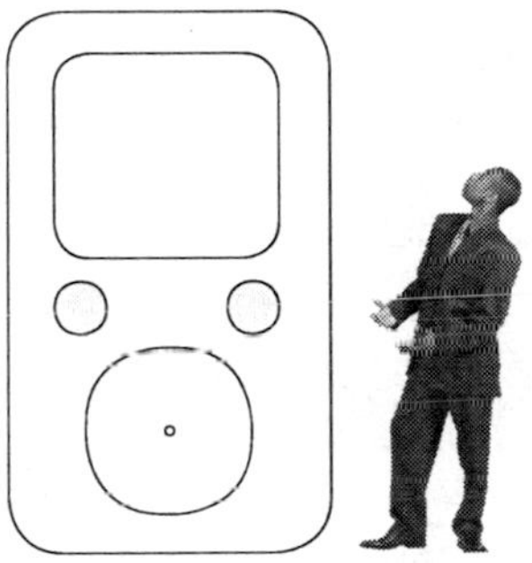

You can write a conversion factor as a fraction

Now that you know that 1 millimeter is the same as 0.0393700787 inches, you need to do some math to convert the other myPod measurements to inches.

The key is writing your conversion factor as a **fraction** so that the top and bottom of the fraction are both the same size:

$$\frac{0.0393700787 \text{ inches}}{1 \text{ millimeter}}$$

These two lengths are equivalent.

This fraction = 1, as the top and bottom are both the same size.

You can then multiply your measurement by the conversion factor fraction. Since the top and bottom of the fraction are the same size (or length), multiplying by the fraction is the same as multiplying by 1, and the **size** of your measurement doesn't change.

But multiplying by the conversion factor will change the **units** of your measurement, which is what you want to do!

If you multiply a measurement by a conversion factor, you don't change its size, but DO change its UNITS.

I guess the conversion factor fraction could be written either way- with the inches on the top or the millimeters on the top. So I need to think about which way to write it.

With fractions, you can divide out units like you'd divide out numbers.

You can write the conversion factor fraction either way up:

$$\frac{1 \text{ millimeter}}{0.0393700787 \text{ inches}} = \frac{0.0393700787 \text{ inches}}{1 \text{ millimeter}} = 1$$

The top and bottom are both the same size.

To work out the width of the player (60 mm) in inches, we want to end up with units in inches at the end, so use the conversion factor fraction that makes the millimeters divide out.

You have millimeters on the top and millimeters on the bottom, so they divide out.

$$60 \text{ millimeters in inches} = 60 \cancel{\text{millimeters}} \times \frac{0.0393700787 \text{ inches}}{1 \cancel{\text{millimeter}}}$$

$$= 2.362204722 \text{ inches}$$

The only units you're left with are inches - which is what you want.

Think about the SIZE of your answer. You're expecting a number less than 60, so this looks OK.

there are no Dumb Questions

Q: I don't get the "conversion factor is equal to 1" thing. How can that be when there are different numbers on the top and bottom?

A: There aren't just different **numbers** on the top and bottom of the fraction - there are also different **units**.

The top and bottom of the fraction are exactly the same **size**, so the fraction equals 1. The **numbers** are different because they're expressed in different **units**.

Q: And being able to write the fraction in two different ways isn't a problem because I can work out which one to use from the units?

A: Yes. You want the old units to divide out so that you're just left with the new units. Set up your fraction in a way that ensures this will happen.

Or you can think, "Do I expect the answer to be bigger or smaller than the number I started with?" That works too.

Q: So far, we've wanted to go from millimeters to inches. But if I wanted to go FROM inches TO millimeters, would I just turn the fraction the other way up?

A: Absolutely! Though always do an error-check just in case. Ask yourself if the units are going to divide out, and check that the answer's around the size you expected.

Units help you keep track of trickier problems.

Here you're only converting one set of units. But sooner than you think, you'll be asked to work out how many seconds are in a year, which will involve you converting to minutes, then hours, then days, and finally years - a calculation that uses five different units in total!

So it's best to practice simpler problems using the same techniques you'd have to use for more difficult problems. It's like practicing individual tennis shots over and over to perfect your technique. Then when you face a difficult opponent, the shot is totally second nature, and your brain is free to think about the match situation.

There's also the fact that **examiners will reward you for showing your work**, even if you get the final answer wrong! In your exam, you get rewarded for demonstrating that you **understand the physics** - and that means you must show the examiners how you worked out your answer.

Now you can use the conversion factor to update the blueprint

OK, so you used Google Calculator to find out that **1 mm = 0.0393700787 inches**. Now it's time to modify the blueprint so that it uses inches instead of millimeters, and the factory can cope with it.

Sharpen your pencil

Here's the blueprint with some of the millimeter lengths marked. **Convert** them to inches and earn that limited edition player! Remember to **show your work** (there's space down the right for that).

There's some space over here for your work.

Remember to write the UNITS on the blueprint!

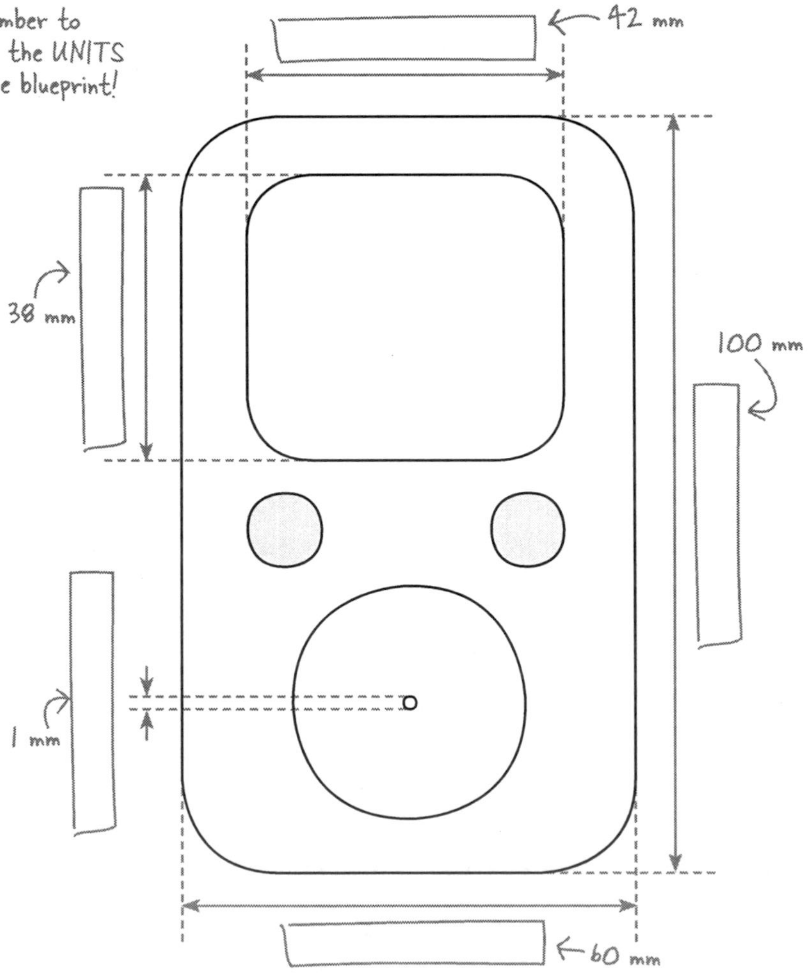

Sharpen your pencil Solution

Here's the blueprint with some of the millimeter lengths marked. **Convert** them to inches and earn that limited edition player! Remember to **show your work** (there's space down the right for that).

Make sure you lay out your work, so it's obvious which bit of the problem you're doing.

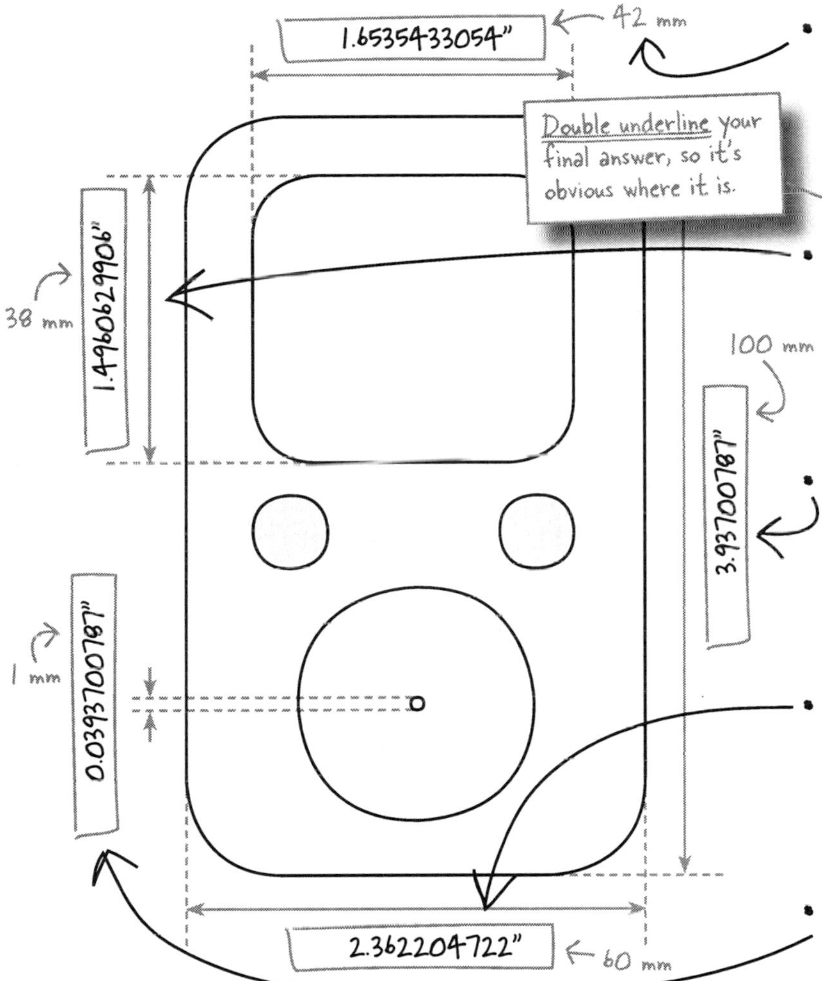

Double underline your final answer, so it's obvious where it is.

- 42 mm in inches

$= 42\ mm \times \frac{0.0393700787''}{1\ mm}$

$= 1.6535433054''$

- 38 mm in inches

$= 38\ mm \times \frac{0.0393700787''}{1\ mm}$

$= 1.4960629906''$

- 100 mm in inches

$= 100\ mm \times \frac{0.0393700787''}{1\ mm}$

$= 3.93700787''$

- 60 mm in inches

$= 60\ mm \times \frac{0.0393700787''}{1\ mm}$

$= 2.362204722''$

- 1 mm in inches – already know that 1 mm = 0.0393700787"

If you need to change units during a problem, look up a conversion factor to help, and show your work when you do it!

You just converted the units for the entire blueprint!

After **converting** all measurements from mm to inches and checking that the **units** are written at the end of **every** number, you send the blueprints off to the factory and dream of your limited edition myPod ...

It's important to make sure you include the units EVERY time you write down a number as a final answer.

What kind of ruler are you using anyway? There's no way we can measure a length like 2.362204722 inches!

But there's STILL a problem ...

A couple of hours after mailing the blueprints, you get a call from the factory. They're saying that they can't follow the instructions on the blueprint, as they're not capable of manufacturing the myPod case to the nearest 0.0000000001 inch!

BRAIN POWER

What could have caused this new problem?
And how can you fix it?

What to do with numbers that have waaaay too many digits to be usable

Right now your problem is that the numbers on the blueprint have **too many digits**. The blueprint says that the myPod is 2.362204722 inches wide, which implies that you measured it to the nearest 0.000000001 inch. But unless you have a ruler that can measure individual atoms, you didn't!

Don't worry if you've heard this called 'significant figures' in the past. Significant digits and significant figures are two different names for exactly the same thing.

You have to decide how many of the digits in your answers are **significant**. A number's most significant digit is the one that tells you the most about **how big the number is** - usually the **first non-zero digit**. The next-most significant digit is the next one along, and so on.

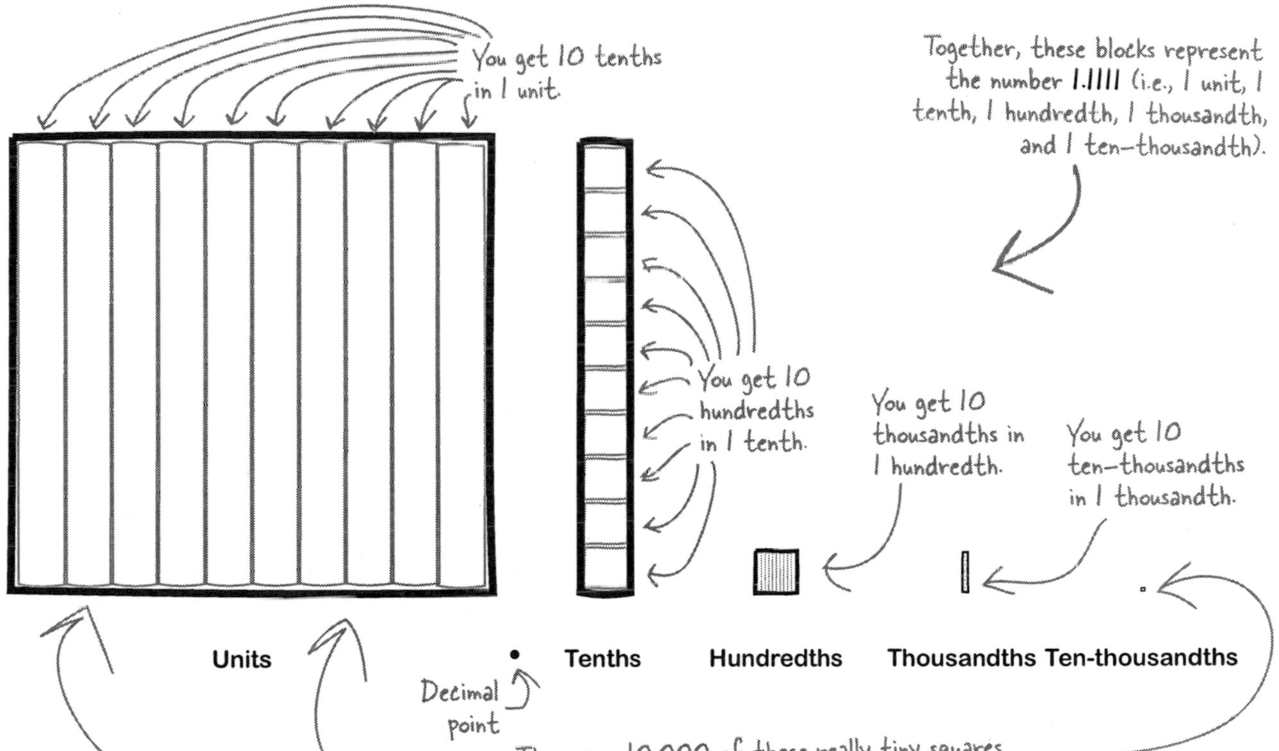

The most significant digit is the one that tells you the most about the SIZE of the number. The most significant digit in this number is the units digit.

If your number is 0.0022, then it's the thousandths digit that's the most significant.

The most significant digit is the one that tells you the most about the SIZE of the number.
So the first non-zero digit is the most significant.

How many digits of your measurements <u>look</u> significant?

Since the numbers on your blueprint have too many digits, it makes sense to **round** them to get rid of some of the less significant digits. For instance, if you round 2.362204722 inches to one significant digit, it's 2 inches (since it's closer to 2 than it is to 3); to two significant digits it would be 2.4 inches (since it's closer to 2.4 than it is to 2.3).

Don't worry too much about this – you'll be looking at rounding numbers on the next couple of pages.

But **how many significant digits** should you round your measurements to?

Sharpen your pencil

Use the grid to draw squares and columns that represent 2.362204722 inches (your measurement of the myPod's width) in the same way as on the opposite page. Beside it, write the digit that each group of squares or columns represents. (There may not be space to draw things for all of the digits in your number.)

How many digits of your measurement do you think **look significant,** or how many digits make an appreciable difference to the **size** of the number? Write your answer in the space below.

....

....

....

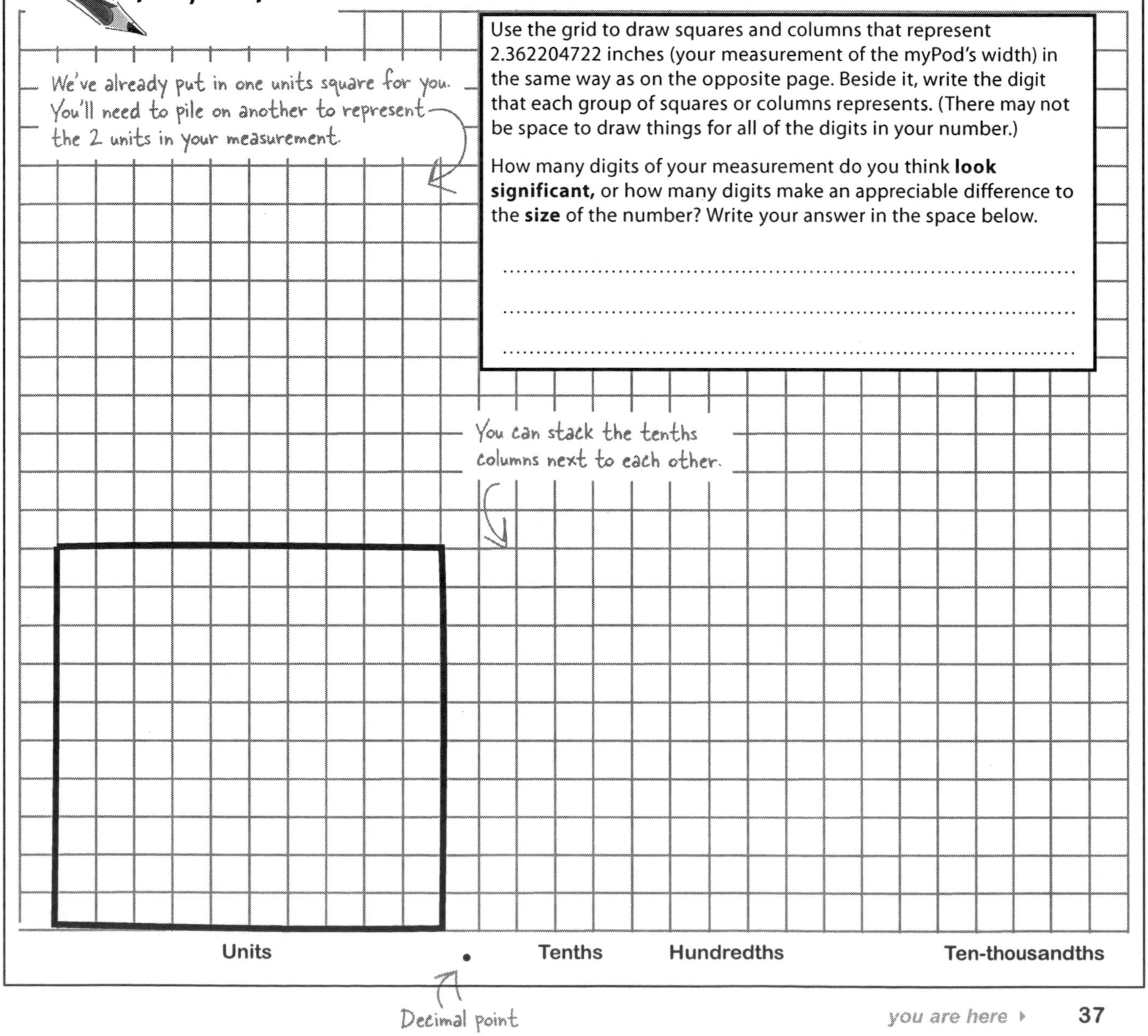

Sharpen your pencil Solution

Use the grid to draw squares and columns that represent 2.362204722 inches (your measurement of the myPod's width) in the same way as on the opposite page. Beside it, write the digit that each group of squares or columns represents. (There may not be space to draw things for all of the digits in your number.)

How many digits of your measurement do you think **look significant,** or how many digits make an appreciable difference to the **size** of the number? Write your answer in the space below.

Only the first three digits really contribute towards the size of the answer. The thousandths and ten-thousandths don't really. So I think I should round to 3 significant digits.

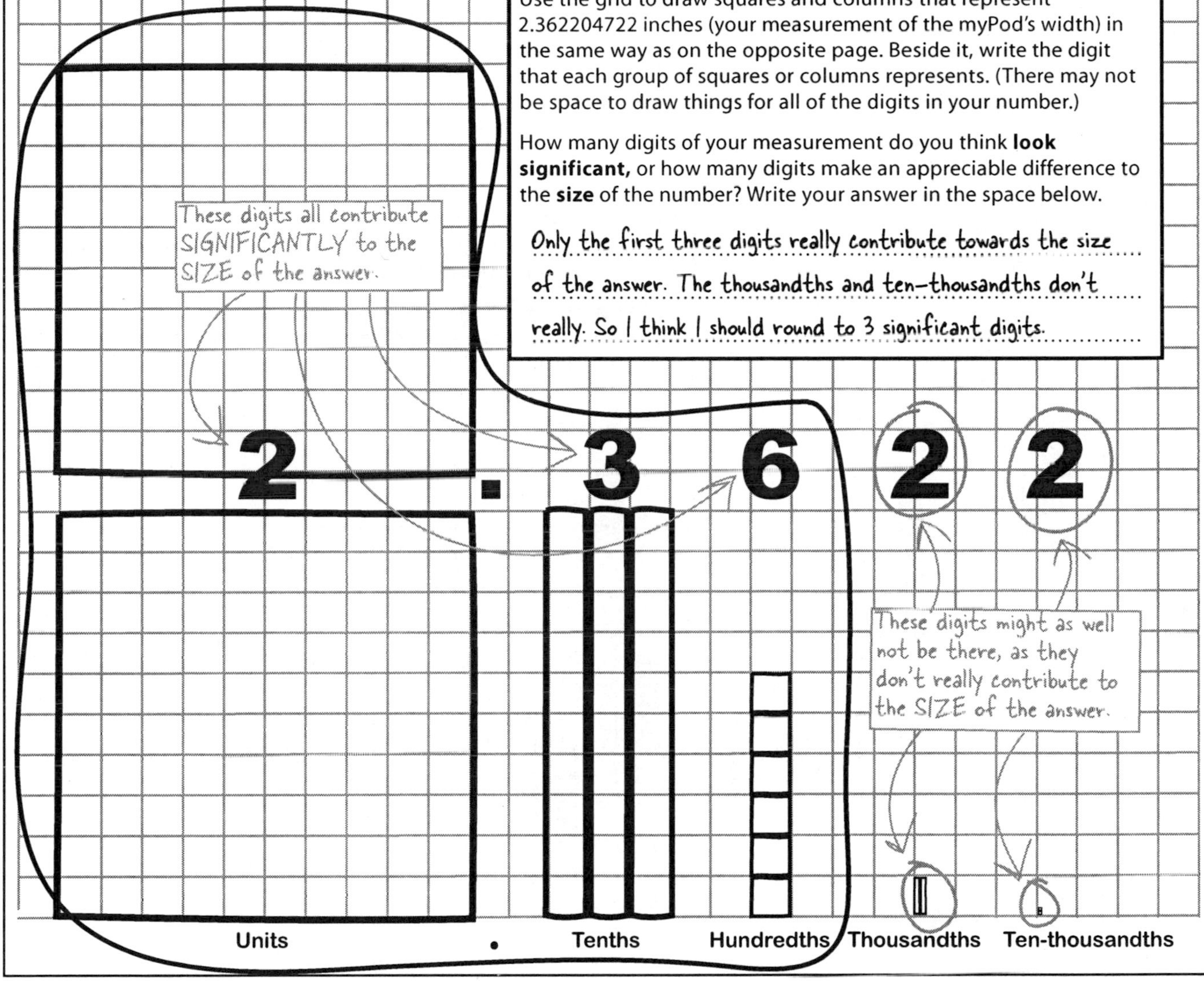

The first THREE digits of a number are the most significant. The other digits don't contribute much to the SIZE of the number.

Generally, you should round your answers to <u>three</u> significant digits

Unless you have extra information you can use to help, you should **round** your final answers for any calculation to **three significant digits**. The other digits in the number don't really contribute towards the size of the number.

You need to follow certain rules when you're rounding answers

When you're rounding a number, look at the digit to the **right** of the final significant digit that you want to round to. If this digit is 4 or less, then round down. If it's 6 or more, then round up.

So you would **round down** the width of the myPod, 2.3622... inches, to 2.36 inches, as it's closer to 2.36 than it is to 2.37. But you'd **round up** a measurement of 4.5874... inches to 4.59 inches, as it's closer to 4.59 than it is to 4.58.

If the digit to the right of your final significant digit is a 5, then look to see if there's another digit after the 5. If there is, round up. If there isn't, round upor down to the nearest even digit. So 2.365 would round down to 2.36, and 2.375 would round up to 2.38.

Once you've rounded your answer, always say how many significant digits you've rounded to, for example, by writing 2.36 (3 sd).

sd stands for "significant digits."

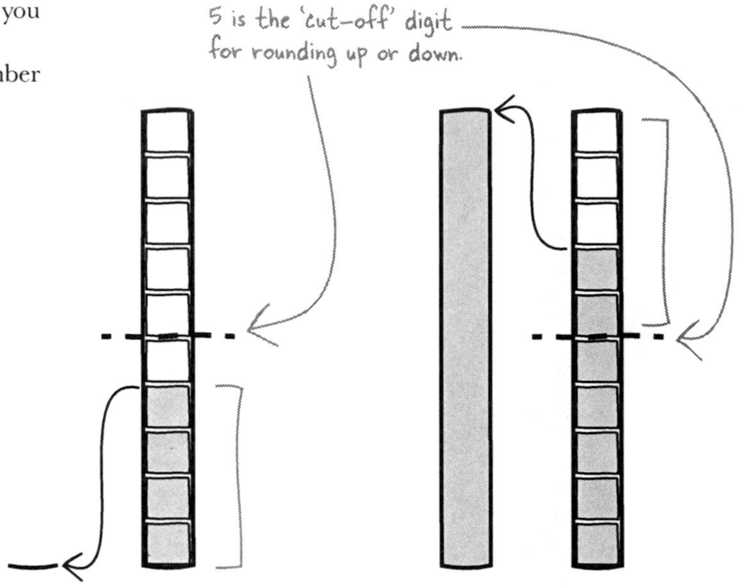

If the digit to the right of your last significant digit is 4 or less, round down.

If the digit to the right of your last significant digit is 6 or more, round up.

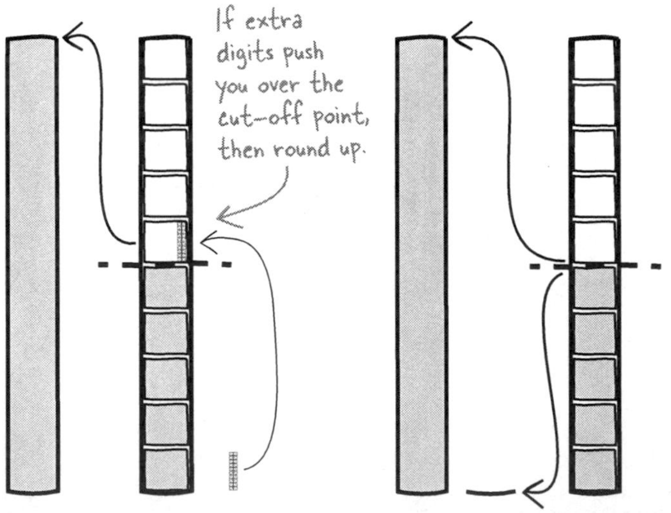

If the digit to the right of your last significant digit is a 5 and there are other digits after it, round up.

If the digit to the right of your last significant digit is 5 and there aren't any more digits, round up or down to the nearest even number.

When you're rounding a number, the digit to the <u>right</u> of your final significant digit tells you what to do.

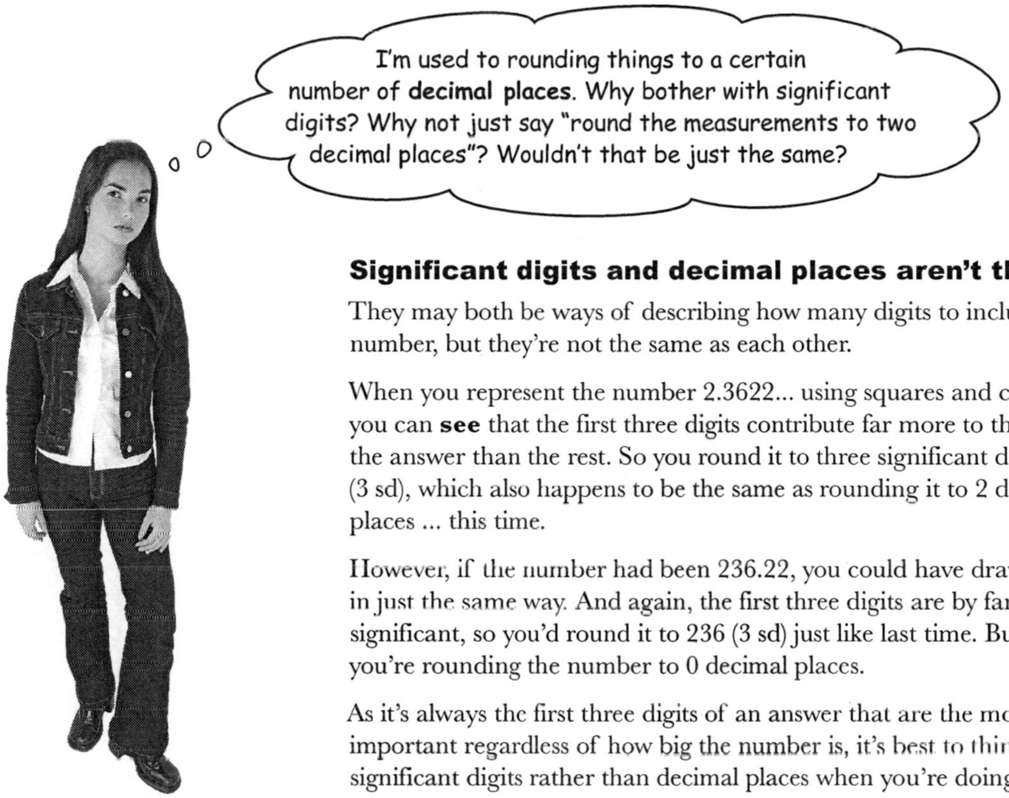

Significant digits and decimal places aren't the same

They may both be ways of describing how many digits to include in a number, but they're not the same as each other.

When you represent the number 2.3622... using squares and columns, you can **see** that the first three digits contribute far more to the size of the answer than the rest. So you round it to three significant digits, 2.36 (3 sd), which also happens to be the same as rounding it to 2 decimal places ... this time.

However, if the number had been 236.22, you could have drawn it out in just the same way. And again, the first three digits are by far the most significant, so you'd round it to 236 (3 sd) just like last time. But this time, you're rounding the number to 0 decimal places.

As it's always the first three digits of an answer that are the most important regardless of how big the number is, it's best to think about significant digits rather than decimal places when you're doing physics.

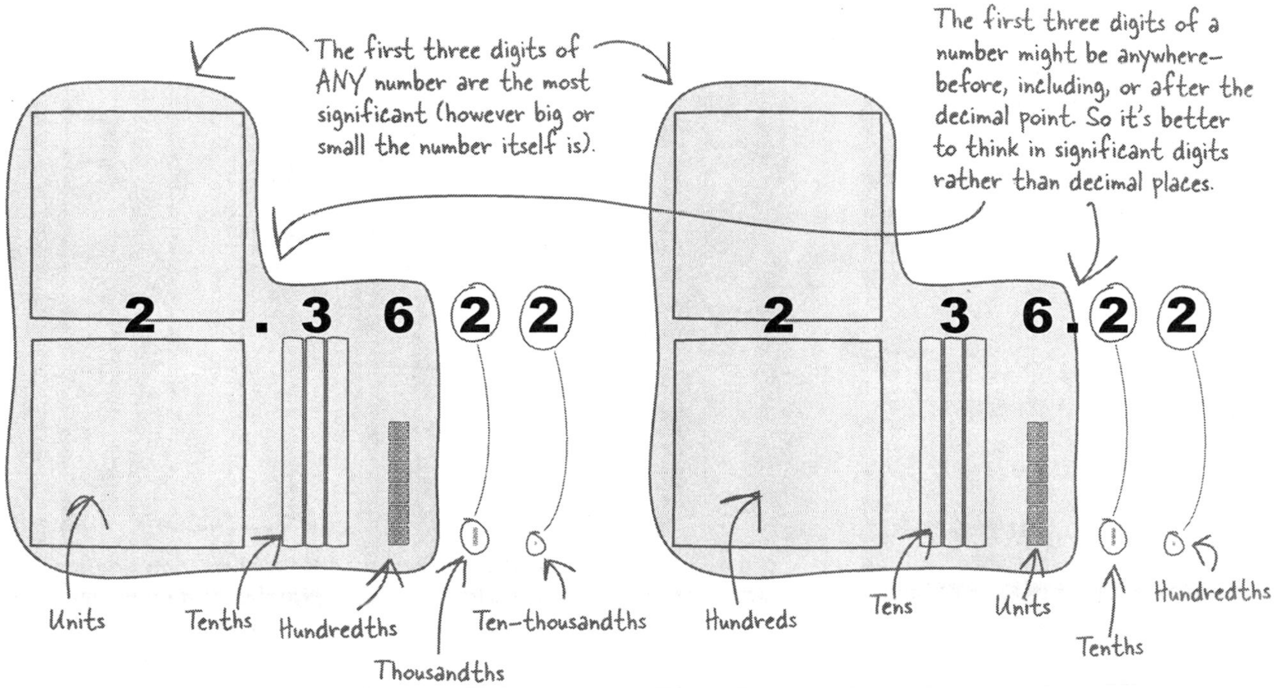

Is it OK to round the myPod blueprint to three significant digits?

You've already come a long way towards earning that free limited edition myPod! First, you measured the myPod case with your ruler and produced a blueprint so that the factory could produce the cases.

After a blip where the case came back 25 times too big (because there weren't any **units** on the blueprint, the factory assumed it was a giant promotional item), you came storming back and learned that with **conversion factors**, you can change the mm to inches without remeasuring the myPod.

Then, the factory pointed out that the converted measurements had **too many digits** in them - don't believe everything your calculator tells you! But you realized that some digits are more **significant** than others, as they tell you the most about the **size** of the number. And you learned that, in general, you should round calculations to **three significant digits**. So ... are you set to go?

I guess that rounding answers to three significant digits is the **general** rule in physics. But what if I **know more** about how a **specific** measurement was made. Does that affect what I should do?

Generally, you should round your answers to three significant digits

Unless you have extra information you can use to help, you should **round** your final answers for any calculation to **three significant digits**. The other digits in the number don't really contribute towards the size of the number.

BRAIN POWER

How might the way the original measurement was made affect the number of significant digits you round your converted answer to?

You ALREADY intuitively rounded your original myPod measurements!

When you were measuring the myPod to draw your original plan, you probably found that some of the dimensions weren't a whole number of millimeters long. The thing you were measuring didn't **exactly** line up with one of the scale divisions on your ruler.

When this happened, you may have intuitively rounded it to the nearest mm. If a measurement is between 6.5 and 7 mm, you'd round up to 7 mm. And if it's between 7 and 7.5 mm, you'd round down to 7 mm.

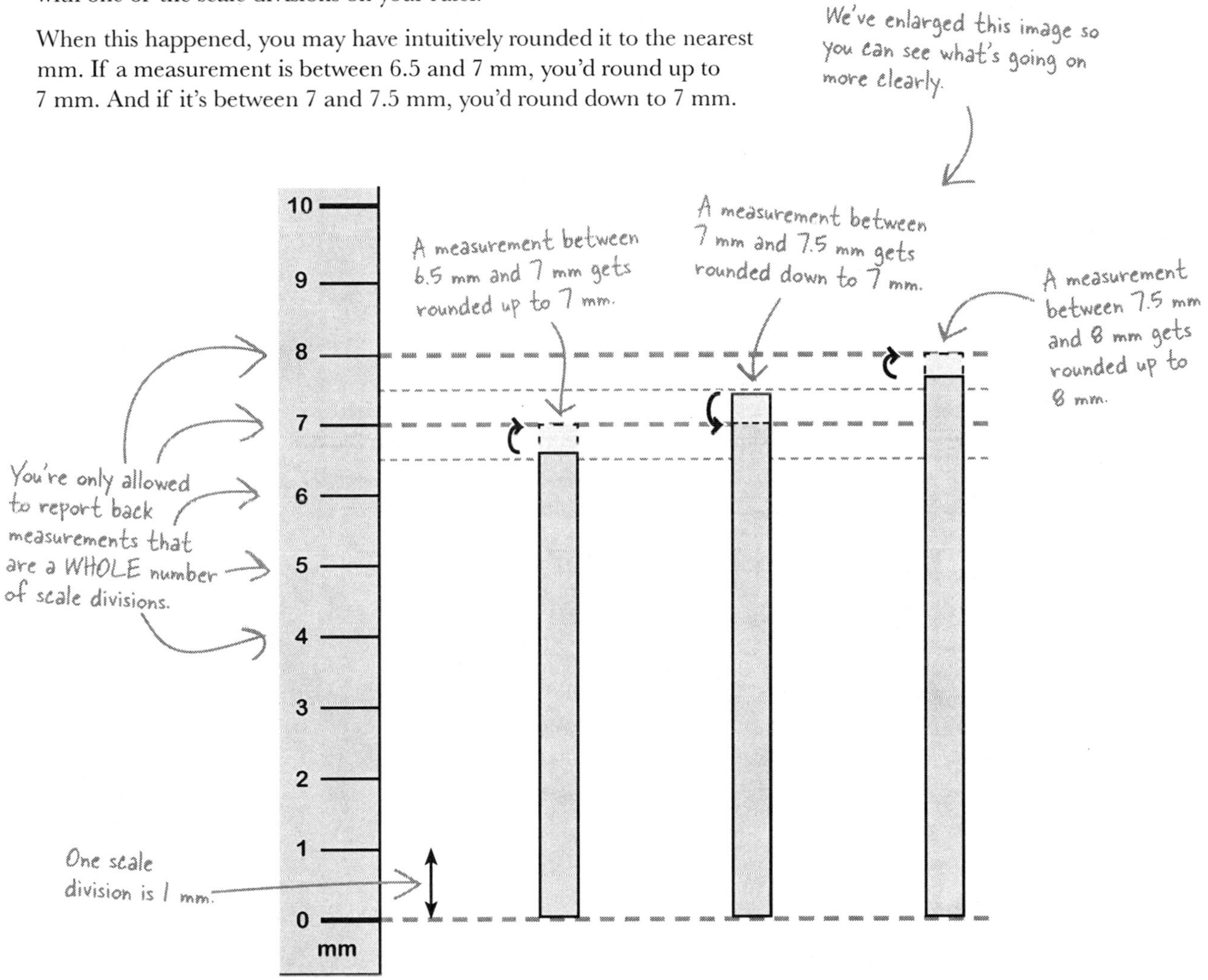

You should always round your measurement to the nearest scale division on your measuring apparatus.

Any measurement you make has an error (or uncertainty) associated with it

Any time you make a measurement, you intuitively **round** it to the nearest scale division on your measuring apparatus. But this means that a measurement you make with your ruler and write down as "7 mm" could actually **range** from just over 6.5 mm to just under 7.5 mm.

If you make a measurement, it's important that you (and any others using it) know how much **uncertainty** or **error** is associated with it. Was the 7 mm length measured using a ruler with a scale division of 1 mm, or with a micrometer with a scale division of 0.001 mm?

If you make a drawing of the thing you're measuring, you can show the range that the measurement may lie in using **error bars**, which mark the range's extremes.

If you write down your measurement, you can show the margin of error using numbers. The 7 mm measurement made using the ruler might be up to 0.5 mm larger (and rounded down to 7 mm) or 0.5 mm smaller (and rounded up to 7 mm). You write this as 7.0 mm ± 0.5 mm.

Because you round your measurements to the nearest scale division, the associated error is always **± half a scale division**.

You say this as "plus or minus."

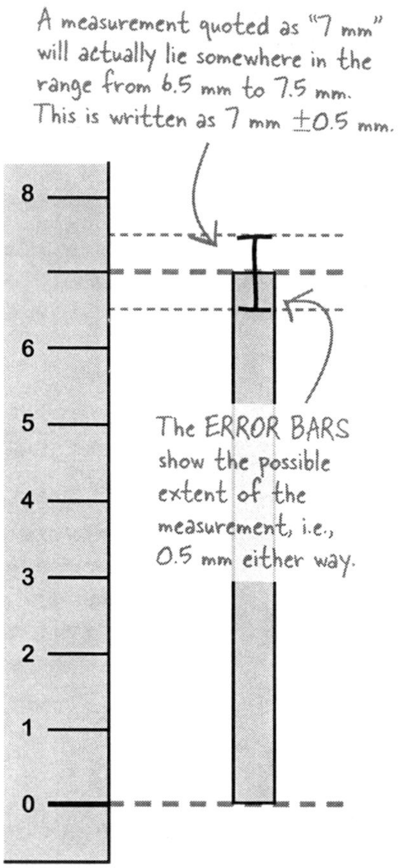

there are no Dumb Questions

Q: If my measurement has an error, does that mean I did something wrong?

A: No! In this context, "error" is another word for "uncertainty" - the range that your measurement might fall into.

Q: I can eliminate the error on a measurement completely if I have a good enough measuring device, right?

A: Not really. You can reduce it, like by using a micrometer where the error is ±0.0005 mm instead of a ruler where it's ±0.5 mm. But no surface is ever perfectly smooth at the atomic level, so you'd never be able to completely eliminate uncertainty.

Q: So is trying to reduce errors associated with measurements a good thing, or is that just being a perfectionist?

A: The smaller the error on your measurements, the more certain you can be of your results.

Q: OK. But a couple of pages ago, we decided we should round calculations to 3 significant digits. But now we're making measurements like 7.0 mm ± 0.5 mm. Neither the measurement nor the error have three significant digits!

A: That (general) rule was for **calculations**, not for raw measurements.

Q: But if we know how the measurements were originally made, surely that affects how I round the converted values on the blueprint?

A: Yes. Rounding to three significant digits is a **general** rule when you don't know how the measurements you used in your calculation were made. But when you have more information about the error, you can **propagate** that through the unit conversion.

Q: That kinda makes sense, but how do I actually DO it?

A: It's funny you should ask - that's what we're just getting on to now.

The error on your original measurements should propagate through to your converted blueprint

You already used your ruler to round the myPod measurements to the nearest mm. This gives you the **error** associated with each measurement.

To work out the equivalent to rounding like this using inches, you need to **convert your error** from mm to inches. Then you can write your final answers in inches, along with their errors in inches, so the factory knows how well they have to measure.

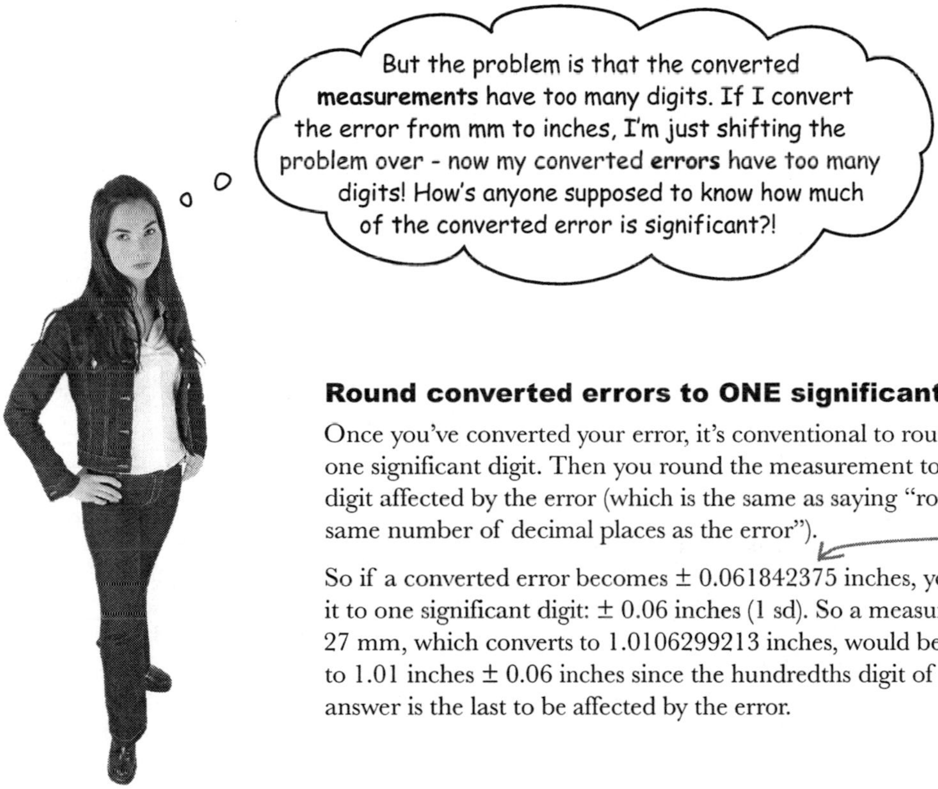

Round converted errors to ONE significant digit.

Once you've converted your error, it's conventional to round it to one significant digit. Then you round the measurement to the last digit affected by the error (which is the same as saying "round to the same number of decimal places as the error").

This is just an example - it's not what your myPod error converts to!

So if a converted error becomes $\pm$ 0.061842375 inches, you'd round it to one significant digit: $\pm$ 0.06 inches (1 sd). So a measurement of 27 mm, which converts to 1.0106299213 inches, would be rounded to 1.01 inches $\pm$ 0.06 inches since the hundredths digit of the answer is the last to be affected by the error.

It's conventional to round converted errors to ONE significant digit, then round converted measurements to the last digit affected by the error.

Right! Time to attack the blueprint again!

Now that you know how to convert measurements and how many significant digits to include, it's time to attack the blueprint again!

Sharpen your pencil

Use the page opposite to work out how many significant digits to quote the measurements to. Write your rounded answers in the boxes! Remember, you originally measured the myPod to the nearest mm, and Google Calculator told you that 1 mm = 0.0393700787 inches.

Remember to state the **error** on your measurements.

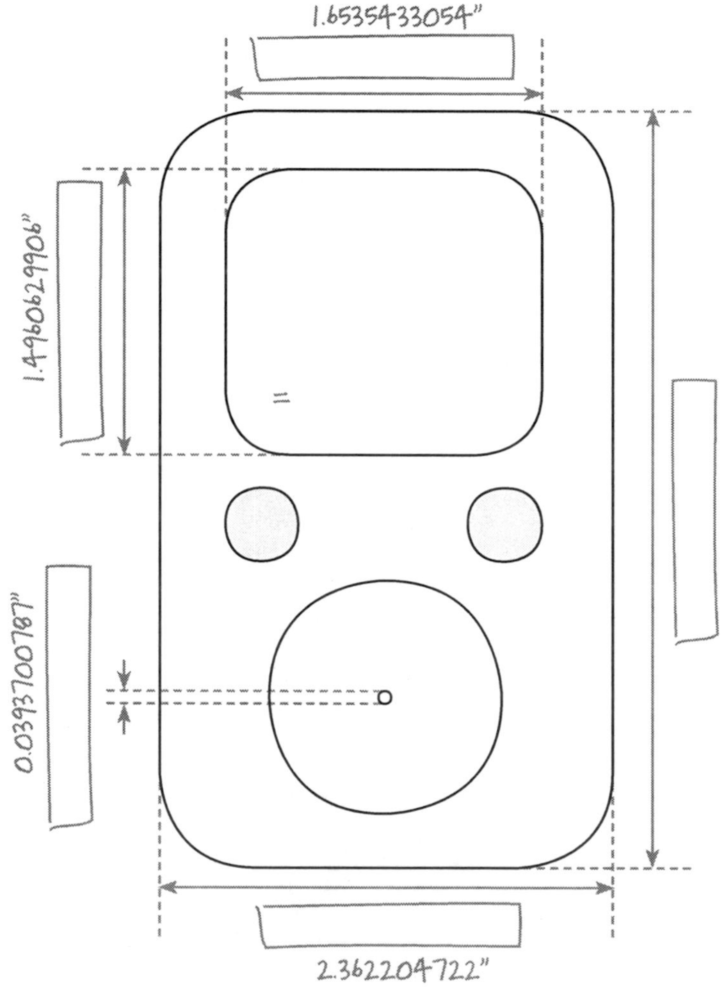

There's some space down here for you to work out the error on your measurements. Make sure you explain the stages you're going through.

Sharpen your pencil Solution

Use the page opposite to work out how many significant digits to quote the measurements to. Write your rounded answers in the boxes! Remember, you originally measured the myPod to the nearest mm, and Google Calculator told you that 1 mm = 0.0393700787 inches.

Remember to state the **error** on your measurements.

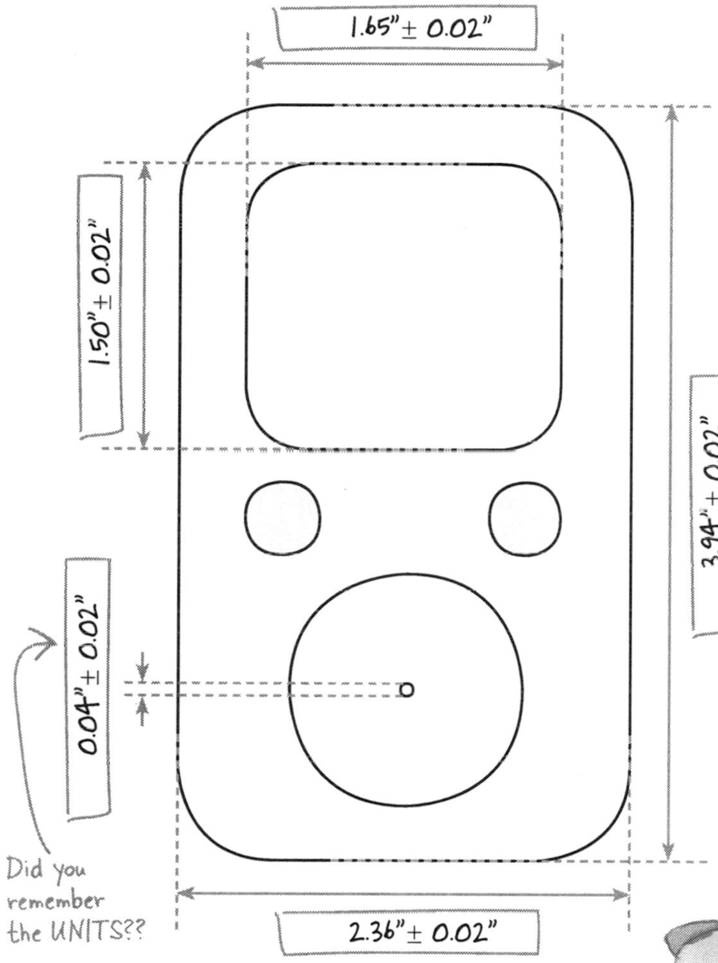

There's some space down here for you to work out the error on your measurements. Make sure you explain the stages you're going through.

Scale division on original ruler is 1 mm, so error on measurement is ± 0.5 mm.

Convert error: 0.5 mm in inches

$$= 0.5\ \text{mm} \times \frac{0.0393700787''}{1\ \text{mm}}$$

$$= 0.01968503935''$$

Round error to 1 sd:

Error = ± 0.02" (1 sd)

So quote myPod measurements to the same number of decimal places. (In this case, 2 decimal places.)

Hey ... are you ready to email those blueprints over yet? I'm kinda starting to worry that we might not fix this in time ...

STOP!! Before you hit send, do your answers SUCK?!

What's happened so far has probably convinced you that it's a good idea to **check over your answers** before you turn them in. So - **does your answer SUCK**?

S is for Size– How big/small are you expecting the answer to be?

U is for Units– Does the answer have units, and are they what was asked for?

C is for Calculations– Check them over and look out for silly mistakes!

K is for 'K'ontext– Go back to the big picture - what are you trying to do, and is it the same as what you actually did to get your answer?

Always check your answers before moving on.

Sharpen your pencil

Fill in the sections to see if your myPod blueprint **SUCK**s!

This is so you don't lose points in exams for doing 'silly things' that you could have avoided.

S

SIZE– Are the answers the size you're expecting?

....

....

U

UNITS– Do they have units, and are they what you were asked for?

....

....

C

CALCULATIONS– Did you do the math right?

....

....

K

"K'ONTEXT– What are you trying to do, and is it the same as what you actually did?

....

....

Sharpen your pencil Solution

Fill in the sections to see if your answer SUCKs.

This is an EXTREMELY useful way of checking if your answer is plausible.

S

SIZE– Are the answers the size you're expecting?

Well, inches are bigger than millimeters, so the inches measurements will be smaller numbers than the millimeter measurements. They seem about right for a music player.

U

UNITS– Do they have units, and are they what you were asked for?

The factory need inches, and I converted the lengths to inches. I also used the right number of significant digits.

C

CALCULATIONS– Did you do the math right?

I think so. The conversion factor is the right way up (so the units divide out) and the sizes already checked out OK.

K

"K'ONTEXT– What are you trying to do, and is it the same as what you actually did?

I want to convert measurements from mm to inches using the correct number of significant digits (based on the error associated with the original measurements).

ALWAYS ask yourself: "Does my answer SUCK?" before you move on to something else

You nailed it!

The blueprints are right at last, and the factory is happy! Before you know it, you're relaxing by the pool with your limited edition myPod.

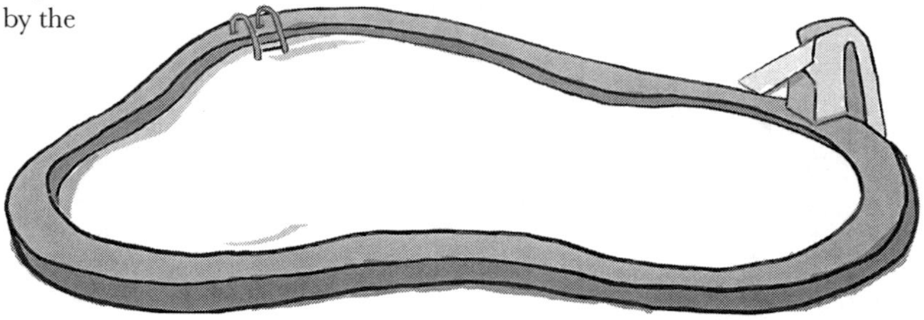

But what about the giant myPod case the mailman delivered? It was used for an even more limited edition supergiant version that sold for thousands of dollars in an online auction, with massive publicity.

Not so fast! I think I've spotted something. I put 1.5" for the height of the screen instead of 1.50". The 0 doesn't add any information to the measurement, and there's no point in wasting ink, right? So why's it in the blueprint?

The zero gives you extra information.

The number of significant digits you include in an answer implies the size of the error. The final digit you include is the one that is uncertain.

Here, your error is ± 0.02 inches - the length could be up to two hundredths of an inch either way. Writing down the measurement as 1.50 inches correctly implies that the hundredths digit is uncertain. But writing down 1.5 inches implies that the tenths digit is uncertain, as it's the last digit in the answer.

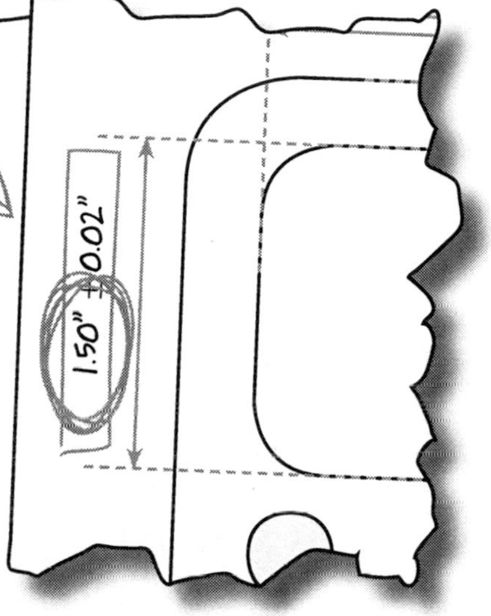

What do we do if we don't know anything about the errors of the measurement we are using in a calculation?

If you don't know what the errors are, use the same number of significant digits in the problem.

The first three digits of a number are the ones that are significant enough to be worth keeping when you round an answer. This means that most of the numbers you are given to work with are usually rounded to three significant digits.

So when you come up with an answer, you should also round it to three significant digits to preserve what was originally done to the number before you were given it.

Answers should have the same number of significant digits that you were provided with in the question.

When you write down a measurement, you need the right number of significant digits

If you write down a measurement of 1.5 inches, you're implying that it was measured to the nearest 0.1 inch (at best), i.e., the error is ± 0.05 inches.

If you write down a measurement of 1.50 inches, you're implying that it was measured to the nearest 0.01 inch (at best), i.e., the error is ± 0.005 inches.

So if you write down 1.5 inches when you should have written down 1.50 inches, you're implying that the measurement is **TEN times worse** than it actually is.

We've enlarged this image, so you can see what's going on more clearly.

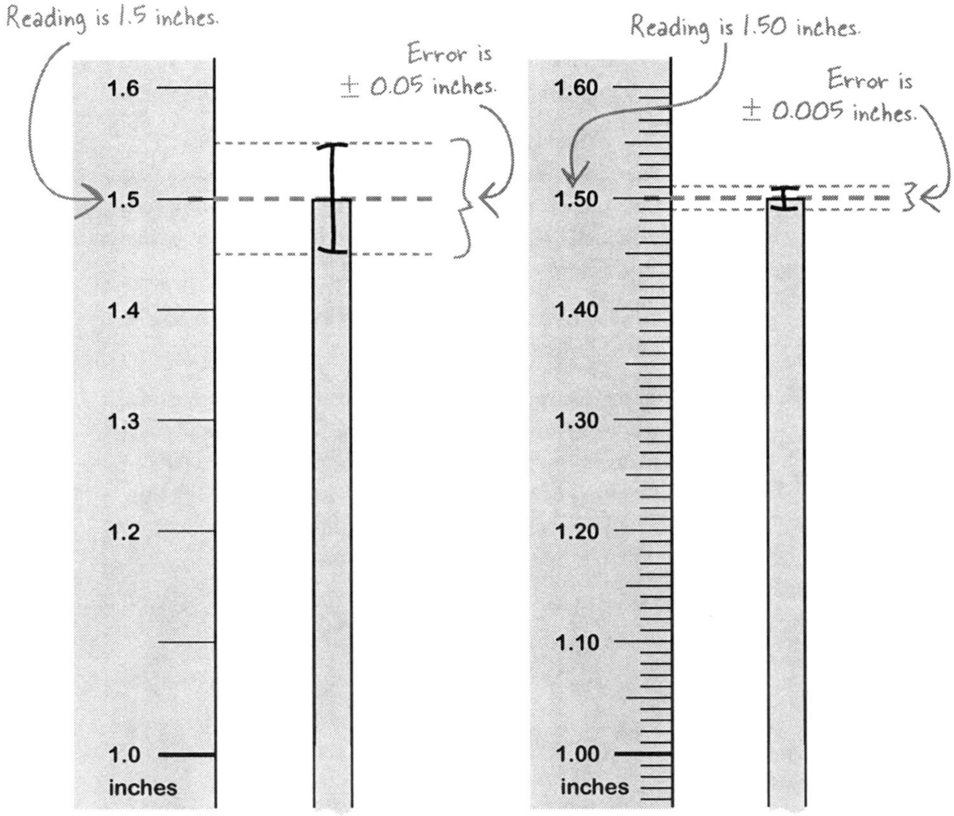

If you leave out a zero that would be affected by the error, you're implying that your measurement is TEN times worse than it actually is!

there are no Dumb Questions

Q: In some physics books, there are tables of constants with lots of significant digits, like the speed of light = 29979245.8 meters per second. That implies an error of ± 0.05 meters per second. Am I really supposed to write down NINE significant digits when the error propagates through to my answer?

A: When you're asked to work with numbers like that, don't round anything until you reach the end of your calculation. It's normal then to round your **final answer** to **three** significant digits.

Q: I'm a bit confused about zeros now. At first I thought they were just placeholders, but now you're saying they're sometimes significant. The zeros in the number 0.005 aren't significant, right? So how can I tell whether a zero is significant or not?

A: We're just going to interview a zero to get it all straightened out ...

Zeros Exposed

This week's interview: Hero or Zero?

Head First: Now, onto today's special guest - a very well known figure. As one of the papers asked recently - hero or a lot of fuss about nothing? So, Zero, what's your take on this debate about your importance?

Zero: Well, the short answer to your question is that my significance kinda depends on where I am in a situation.

Head First: How do you mean? Surely you'll be equally significant - or might that be insignificant - to anyone doing math all around the world? What's location gotta do with it?

Zero: I don't mean where in the world you find me. I mean **where in the number** you find me!

Head First: So, you reckon your significance depends on where in a number you are. But surely zero is zero, whether it's zero units, zero tenths, or so forth?

Zero: Well, yes, that's why I was originally invented - so you wouldn't lose your place in a number.

Head First: So you're just a placeholder, right?

Zero: Oh no, not at all! Sometimes I'm a placeholder, but sometimes I'm really significant!

Head First: You're gonna have to help me here ...

Zero: Well, I'm a placeholder if I'm at the left of a decimal point in a number that's less than 1. Like in 0.00123, the zeros at the start of the number are just padding so that the rest of the digits fall into the right place.

Head First: And when aren't you just padding?

Zero: If I'm not at the start of the number, then I'm significant. Especially if I'm part of a measurement.

Head First: Why are measurements special?

Zero: Measurements are quoted to the same number of significant digits as your measuring device. So if your ruler's in mm and you measure something 5 mm long, then you write 5 mm ...

Head First: ... but there's no zero there ...

Zero: ... and if your ruler was marked off in tenths of a mm, you'd write 5.0 mm.

Headfirst: But why write the extra zero at the end when it's just the same thing? It's still 5 mm long!

Zero: Because you've measured it to a tenth of a millimeter this time. So you need to have a figure in there to say how many tenths there are. The number of tenths is highly significant!

Head First: But there weren't any tenths! So 5 mm and 5.0 mm are just the same number, aren't they?

Zero: But they don't have the same meaning. **Measurements have meaning!** If it has a decimal point, then the last figure of the measurement tells you about the size of the error. So the last figure is always significant - even if it's a zero!

Head First: And if there's no decimal point, say in a number like 1000?!

Zero: Then it's ambiguous - you don't know exactly where it was rounded. Was the 1000 originally 501 rounded to the nearest thousand (1 sd), or 1000.1 rounded to the nearest unit (4 sd)? That's why you should always mention the number of sd when you make a measurement or give an answer.

Head First: Well, thank you, Zero, for coming in today and explaining what you do.

Measurements have MEANING! Zeros are significant when they show you the error on a measurement.

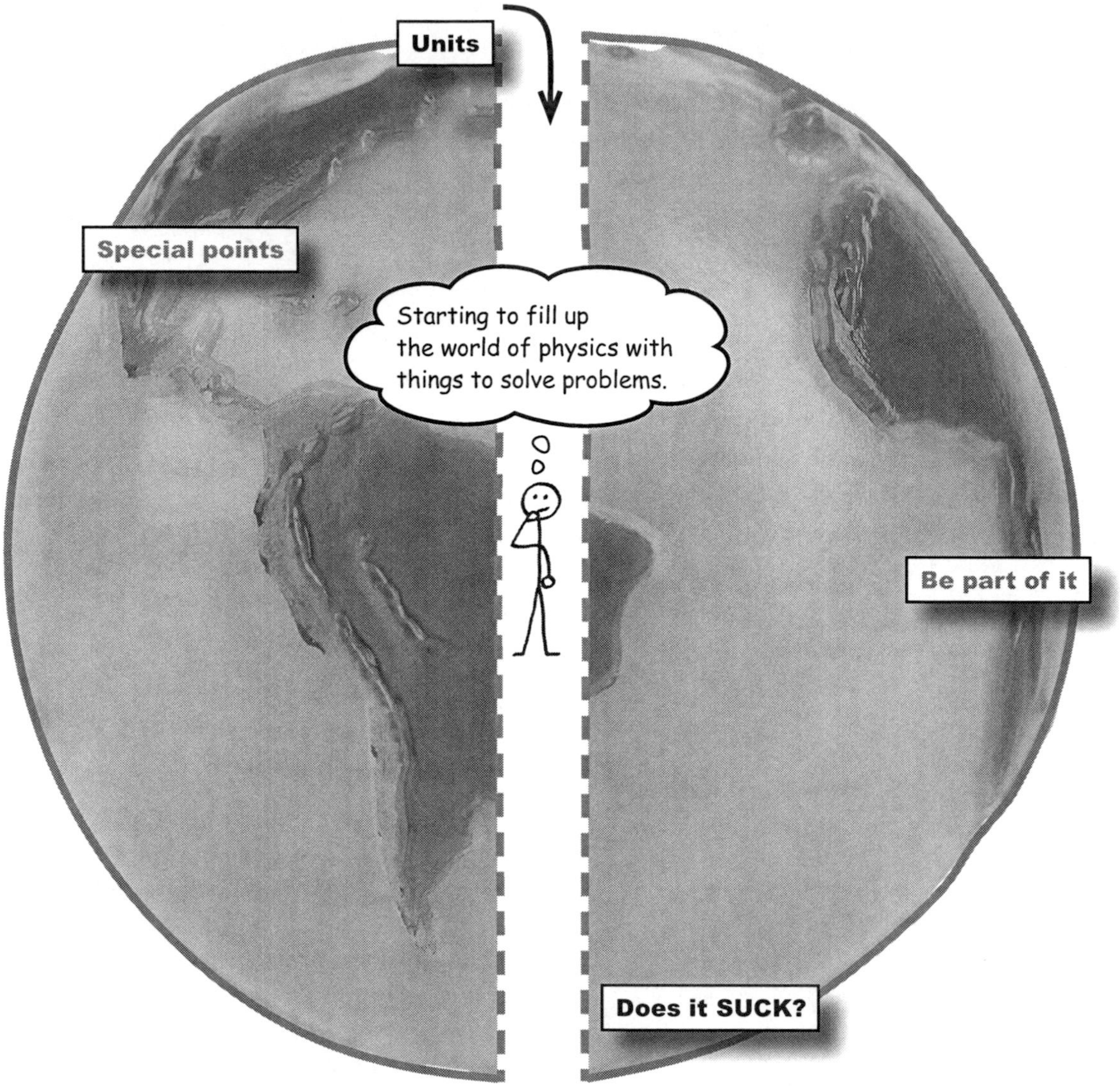

☑	**Units**	**Reference standards for measurements. For example, meters for distance and seconds for time.**
☑	**Does it SUCK?**	**Check the Size, Units, Calculations, and Kontext of your answers to see if they make sense.**

Your Physics Toolbox

You've got Chapter 2 under your belt, and you've added some terminology and answer-checking skills to your tool box.

Units

A number needs to have units for it to mean something.

You're only allowed to add things together if they have the same units.

Errors

Any measurement you make has an error associated with it that reflects the uncertainly in the measurement.

Don't worry – they're not called errors because you did something wrong!

Converting units

To convert an answer from one unit to another you need to multiply it by a conversion factor.

This is a fraction where the top and bottom are both equal sizes – but are expressed in different units.

Arrange things so that the units you don't want divide out when you multiply your answer by the conversion factor.

Also, think about whether you expect the number part of your converted answer to be bigger or smaller than what you currently have.

Significant digits

Any time your calculator gives you an answer, you'll need to round it.

Round your answer to the same number of significant digits as the least precise number you were given to work with.

(Usually this will be 3 significant digits.)

Does it SUCK?

Memory aid to see if your answer makes sense.

Size – How big did you expect your answer to be?

Units – Does your answer have the correct units?

Calculations – Did you do the math right?

'K'ontext – What are you trying to do – and is that what you actually did?

3 scientific notation, area, and volume

In the real world, you have to deal with all kinds of numbers, not just the ones that are easier to work with. In this chapter, you'll be taking control of unwieldy numbers using **scientific notation** and discovering why rounding a large number doesn't mean having to write a zillion zeros at the end. You'll also use your new superpowers to deal with units of **area** and **volume** - which is where scientific notation will save you lots of grief (and time) in the future!

A messy college dorm room

Well, actually a particularly filthy college dorm room Matt and Kyle probably wouldn't know one end of a vacuum cleaner from the other, and the idea of cleaning has never entered their heads.

But the Dorm Inspector has had enough...

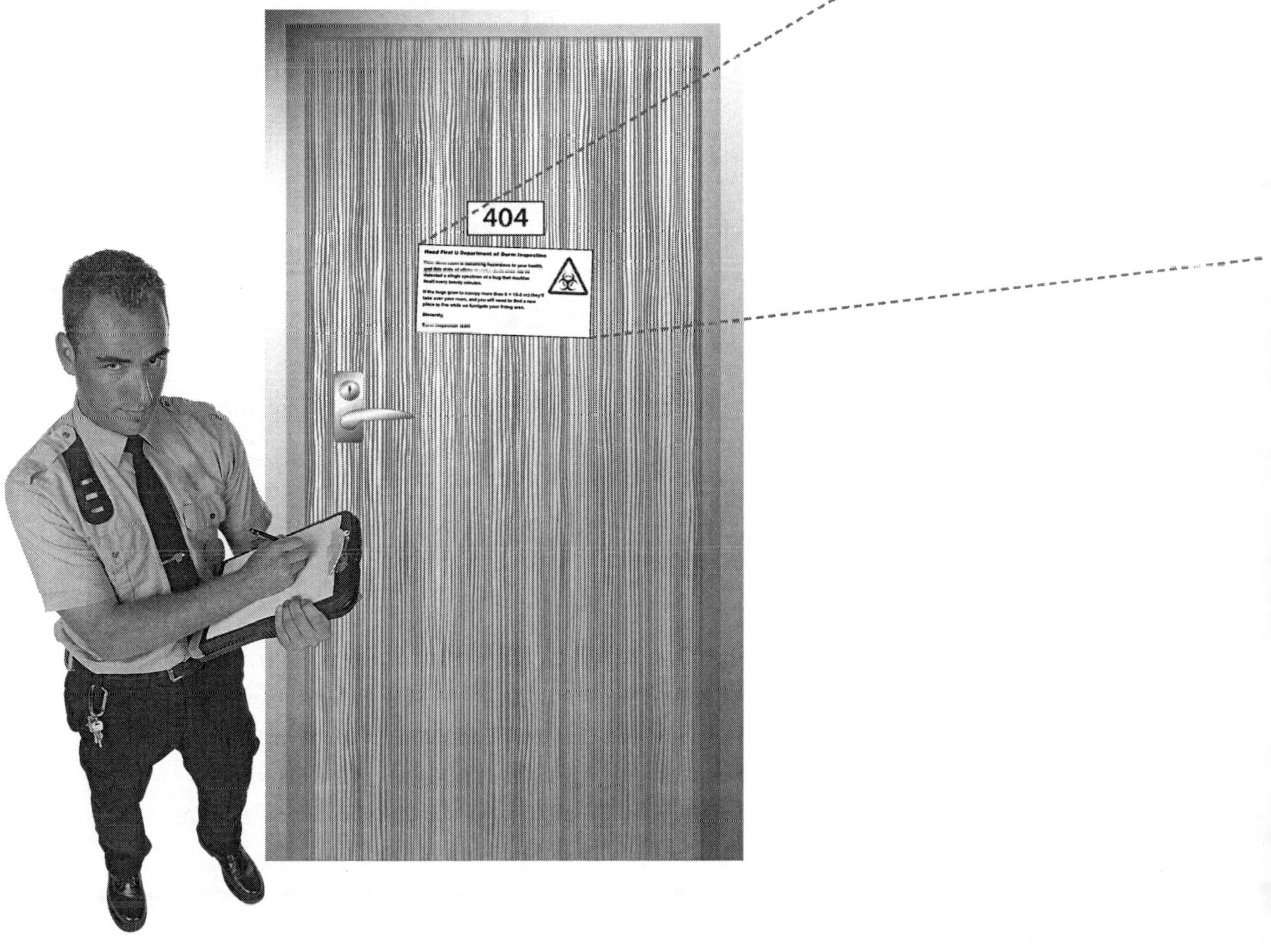

Your dorm room is becoming hazardous to your health, and this state of affairs must be dealt with. We've detected a single specimen of a bug that doubles in number every twenty minutes.

If the bugs grow to occupy more than 6×10^{-5} m^3, they'll take over your room, and you will need to find a new place to live while we fumigate your living area.

Sincerely,

Dorm Inspection Team

So how long before things go really bad?

BRAIN POWER

Every 20 minutes, the bugs will divide in two. So the total number of bugs will double every 20 minutes.

How many do you think there will be by tomorrow (12 hours later) - and how might you work that out?

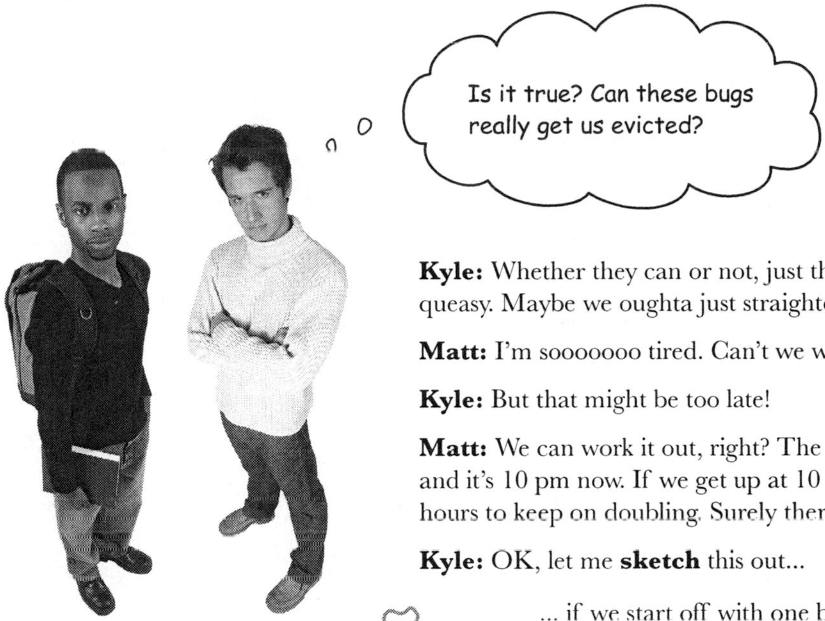

Kyle: Whether they can or not, just the thought of it makes me queasy. Maybe we oughta just straighten this place up now.

Matt: I'm sooooooo tired. Can't we wait until tomorrow?

Kyle: But that might be too late!

Matt: We can work it out, right? The bug doubles every 20 minutes, and it's 10 pm now. If we get up at 10 am, we've given the bug 12 hours to keep on doubling. Surely there can't be that many by then?

Kyle: OK, let me **sketch** this out...

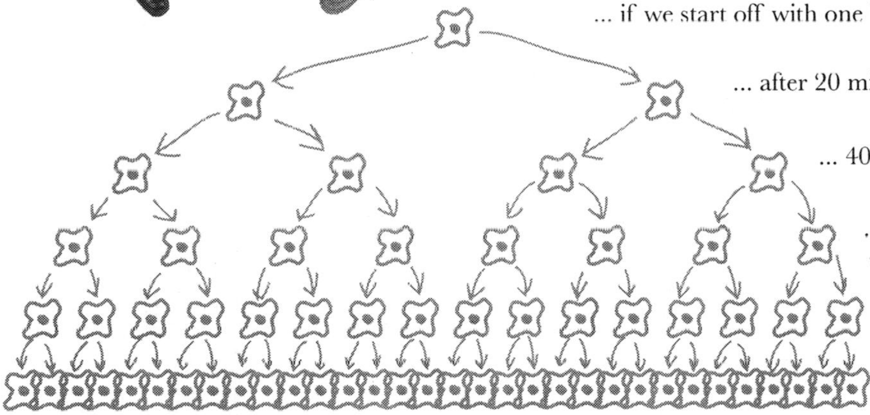

... if we start off with one bug ...

... after 20 minutes, there'll be two of them ...

... 40 minutes = 4 bugs ...

... 1 hour = 8 bugs - not that many and we only need to give it 12 hours ...

... 1 hour 20 minutes = 16 bugs ...

... 1 hour 40 minutes = ...

Kyle: ... hmmm, I'm not sure - my drawing's getting messy!

Matt: Yeah, the drawing will take forever. There's gotta be a **math** way to figure out how many bugs there'll be after 12 hours.

Kyle: Yeah, OK.

Matt: Hmmm. I can't think of an equation for "the bugs double every 20 minutes," but we could just make a table to keep track of things and keep on doubling until 12 hours are up. Then we'll know how many bugs there'll be by the morning.

Kyle: I think that'll work, but there's still that funny phrase in the note, "If the bugs grow to occupy more than 6×10^{-5} m^3." I don't know what that is, but it sure ain't a number of bugs.

Matt: Why don't we worry about that later, once we know **how many** bugs there'll be...

Sharpen your pencil

Matt and Kyle have drawn up the table below and started doubling the bugs. Your job is to finish off the table to see how many bugs there'll be after 12 hours.

You start off with 1 bug. After 20 minutes, it's doubled once, and there are 2 bugs.

This is as far as they got with their sketch.

Number of doublings	Elapsed time	Number of bugs
1	20 min	2
2	40 min	4
3	1 h	8
4	1 h 20 min	16
5	1 h 40 min	

Number of doublings	Elapsed time	Number of bugs

There are a lot of doublings in 12 hours, so we've given you space to continue the table.

Sharpen your pencil Solution

Matt and Kyle have drawn up the table below and started doubling the bugs. Your job is to finish off the table, to see how many bugs there'll be after 12 hours.

You start off with 1 bug. After 20 minutes, it's doubled once, and there are 2 bugs.

This is as far as they got with their sketch.

Number of doublings	Elapsed time	Number of bugs
1	20 min	2
2	40 min	4
3	1 h	8
4	1 h 20 min	16
5	1 h 40 min	32
6	2 h	64
7	2 h 20 min	128
8	2 h 40 min	256
9	3 h	512
10	3 h 20 min	1024
11	3 h 40 min	2048
12	4 h	4096
13	4 h 20 min	8192
14	4 h 40 min	16384
15	5 h	32768
16	5 h 20 min	65536
17	5 h 40 min	131072
18	6 h	262144

Number of doublings	Elapsed time	Number of bugs
19	6 h 20 min	524288
20	6 h 40 min	1048576
21	7 h	2097152
22	7 h 20 min	4194304
23	[illegible]	[illegible]
24	[illegible]	[illegible]
25	[illegible]	[illegible]
26	8 h 40 min	67108864
27	9 h	[illegible]
28	9 h 20 min	[illegible]
29	9 h 40 min	[illegible]
30	10 h	[illegible]
31	10 h 20 min	[illegible]
32	10 h 40 min	[illegible]
33	11 h	[illegible]
34	11 h 20 min	[illegible]
35	11 h 40 min	[illegible]
36	12 h	[illegible]

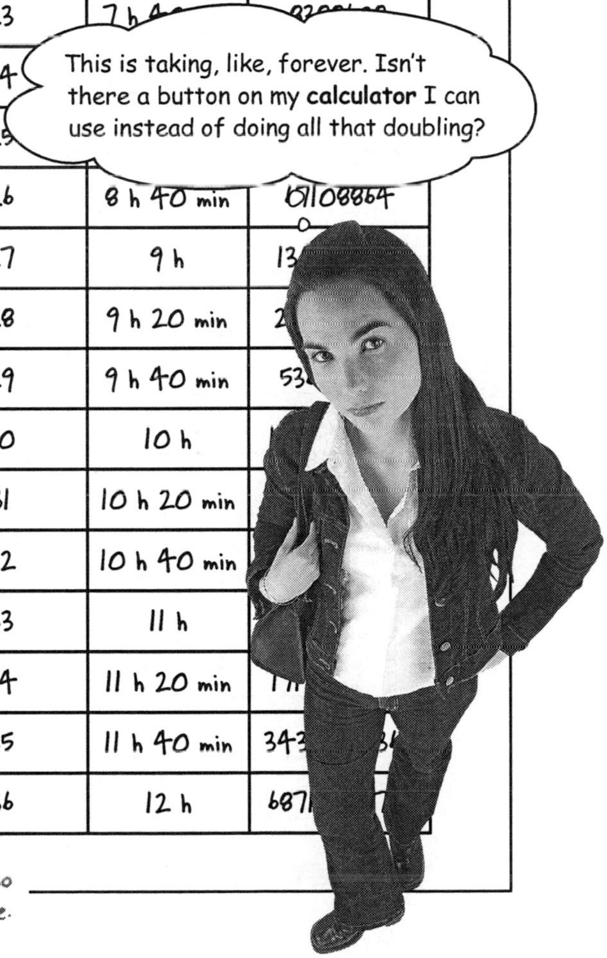

There are a lot of doublings in 12 hours, so we've given you space to continue the table.

Power notation helps you multiply by the same number over and over

If you want to multiply by the same number several times over, you can write it down using **power notation**. This means that $2 \times 2 \times 2 \times 2 \times 2$ becomes 2^5, as there are five instances of 2. When you say 2^5 out loud, you say "two to the power of five" or sometimes just "two to the five." The five part is called the **index**.

$$2^5$$

This whole term is the same as $2 \times 2 \times 2 \times 2 \times 2$

Number that you're multiplying by lots of times.

How many times you're multiplying by it. This is called the INDEX.

Your calculator's power button gives you superpowers

You can use the **power button** on your calculator to multiply by the same number lots of times without having to type it all out. Usually, you type in the number you want to multiply by, then press the power button, then type the number of times you want to multiply by it.

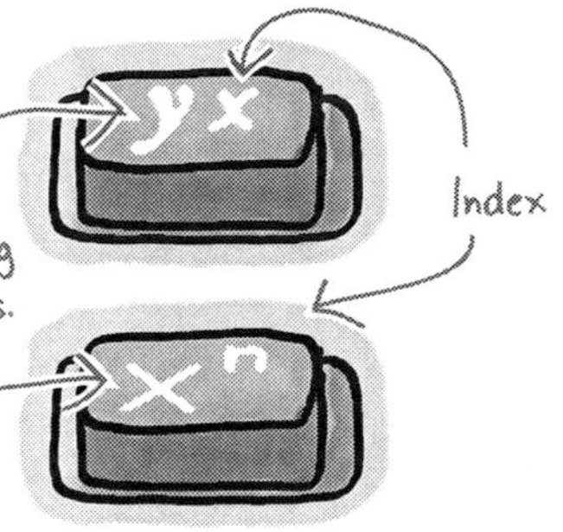

Watch out though - different calculators have different things written on the power button! Make sure you know what yours looks like and how it works before you try to use it!

If your calculator doesn't have a power button, then you'll need to get a scientific calculator. It'll help you out in the long run as you move onto solving more sophisticated and complicated physics problems.

Sharpen your pencil

There's space here to explain what you're doing.

(a) The number of bugs doubles every 20 minutes. How many times do you need to multiply by 2 to get the total number of bugs after 12 hours?

(b) How many bugs will there be after 12 hours?

Power notation makes multiplying by the same number over and over less prone to mistakes.

Sharpen your pencil Solution

Take time to jot down what you're doing and why. It helps you to stay on track..

(a) The number of bugs doubles every 20 minutes. How many times do you need to multiply by 2 to get the total number of bugs after 12 hours?

(b) How many bugs will there be after 12 hours?

(a) There are 3 lots of 20 minutes in an hour. In 12 hours there are 3 × 12 = 36 periods of 20 minutes, so they double 36 times.

(b) Number of bugs after 12 h = number at the start × 36 groups of 2.

Number $= 1 \times 2^{36} =$ ______

Write what YOUR calculator said in here.

Don't just copy answers down and move on.

It's important to understand the answers your calculator gives you.

Your calculator displays big numbers using scientific notation

Sometimes, an answer has too many digits to fit on your calculator's screen. When that happens, your calculator displays it using **scientific notation**. Scientific notation is an efficient and shorter way of writing very long numbers.

In math, scientific notation is often called standard form. Don't worry, they're the same thing.

The value of 2^{36} has 11 digits in it, but a calculator doesn't have enough space to display all of the digits. So instead, they've **rounded** the answer to the number of **significant digits** that they can fit on the screen.

Answers written in scientific notation have two parts.

The **first** part of the number on the screen is for the part that starts 6.87...

But there were already 8 bugs after an hour. 8 is more than 6.87, so how can the answer to 2^{36} possibly be that small?!

The second part of the number tells you the size of the first part.

Numbers written in scientific notation have two parts.

The **first** part is a number with **one significant digit before the decimal point** and the rest of the number after the decimal point.

The **second** part tells you the **number of 10's you have to multiply the first part by** to make your answer the correct **size**.

This part tells you how many 10's to multiply the first part by.

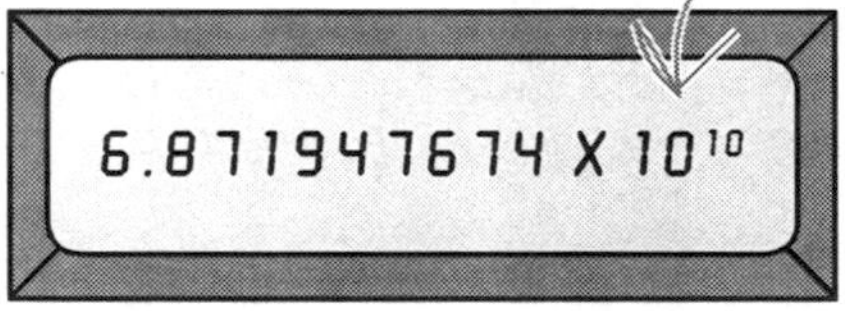

The first calculator's given an answer of $6.871947674 \times 10^{10}$. It's given you 10 significant digits, and the number is the same as writing $6.871947674 \times 10 \times 10 \times 10 \times 10 \times 10 \times 10 \times 10 \times 10 \times 10 \times 10$, which is 68719476740.

The second calculator has displayed 6.871947E10, which is 68719470000- it's rounded the answer to seven significant digit and used an E to indicate the second part of the number because of the limits of its display.

Scientific notation uses powers of 10 to write down long numbers

So you don't have to write them out the long way if they have 28 digits or something!

You calculator's given you the answer $2^{36} = 6.871947674 \times 10^{10}$. You know that to get this into the form you're used to, you need to multiply the first part of the number by ten groups of 10.

Each time you multiply by 10, the number's digits **shift along one place to the left** so that each digit is worth 10 times more than it was before.

But it's quite hard for you to draw that, so practically speaking, you can get to the same place by **hopping the decimal point** the correct number of times to the right. Then the number becomes 68719476740.

You can work out where the number's digits should lie by 'hopping' the decimal point.

Each time you multiply by 10, the decimal point hops along one place to make the number bigger.

1 2 3 4 5 6 7 8 9 10

This bit tells you how many 10's to hop along by.

$$6.871947674 \times 10^{10}$$

Decimal point is now here.

$$68719476740.$$

You need to put a placeholding zero in here for this hop.

You should round your answers to **three significant digits**, like you did in Chapter 2.

But numbers like that are really annoying to round. There are **so many zeros** to write in at the end; I always lose count. Does it work out as 6870000000 or 68700000000?!

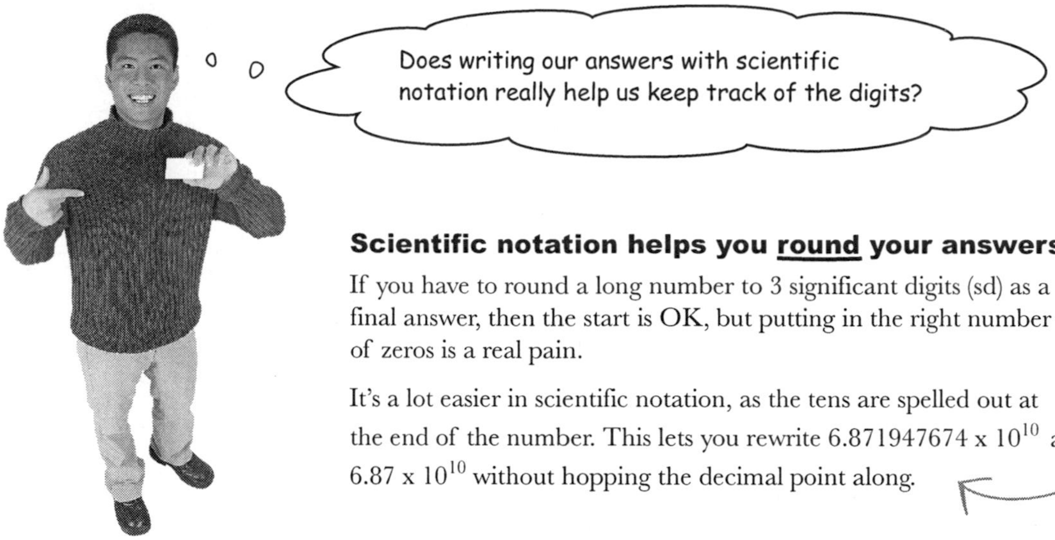

Scientific notation helps you round your answers.

If you have to round a long number to 3 significant digits (sd) as a final answer, then the start is OK, but putting in the right number of zeros is a real pain.

It's a lot easier in scientific notation, as the tens are spelled out at the end of the number. This lets you rewrite $6.871947674 \times 10^{10}$ as 6.87×10^{10} without hopping the decimal point along.

Strictly speaking, it's the digits that move, not the decimal point, but that's much harder for you to draw!

To convert a normally-written number into scientific notation, count how many hops until only one digit is left in front of the decimal point, and multiply the number by that many 10's.

You can just start here, as this is the answer your calculator gave you.

$$6.871947674 \times 10^{10}$$

3 significant digits

The less significant digits – round to get rid of them.

$$6.87 \times 10^{10} \text{ (3 sd)}$$

You don't need placeholding zeros after a decimal point.

Scientific notation helps you to round your answers to 3 significant digits without making mistakes.

Or however many sd is appropriate for your answer.

there are no Dumb Questions

Q: I thought what you're calling 'scientific notation' is actually called 'standard form.' What gives?

A: They're both the same thing. Scientists use the term 'scientific notation' and mathematicians 'standard form.'

Q: Why should I bother with scientific notation when I'm really careful about how I type numbers into my calculator?

A: Your calculator screen might not be big enough to display an answer that's either really big or really small. So you need to understand scientific notation, or it won't make sense.

Q: But I have a super duper flashy calculator that'll display lots and lots of digits on its humongous screen. So if I'm careful, why would I ever need scientific notation?

A: You could be given a number in scientific notation to work with - in an exam question or when you look something up to find out how big it is.

Q: How big are we talking about?

A: Well, the earth's mass is 5.97×10^{24} kilograms. That's a very big number with a lot of zeros at the end if you write it out longhand.

Q: OK, I can see why I might not be happy handling over 20 zeros at the end. But why would I ever want to write an answer I've worked out myself in scientific notation?

A: If you're rounding your answer to 3 significant digits (like you'll do in your exam), then it's much easier to use scientific notation than it is to scrawl a whole lot of zeros across your page.

You can just take the number your calculator gives you, for example, $6.871947674 \times 10^{10}$, and write 6.87 × 1010 without having to do anything else to it?

Q: So are you saying that scientific notation isn't just there because my calculator's screen isn't big enough - it helps me as well?

A: Yep, scientific notation helps you to write and round very long numbers in a much shorter form. So it's not just about calculators - it's about making your life easier.

Q: So which came first - small calculator screens or scientific notation.

A: Scientific notation came first by several hundred years!

Q: I have one more question. Are numbers in scientific notation always written with one digit in front of the decimal point? Couldn't you equally write 6.87×10^{10} as 687×10^{8}?

A: Conventionally, they're written with one digit in front of the decimal point. Your brain will soon get used to estimating the size of the number from the tens part, so sticking to the convention is best.

Scientific notation helps you to handle very long numbers that would otherwise have many digits, even when you've round them.

So the weird number in the eviction notice is in scientific notation. But it's 6 x 10⁻⁵. How do you multiply by a **negative** number of tens???
Head First U Department
Inspection
Your dorm room is becc
ealth,
and this state of affair
detected a single sp
itself every twenty
If the bugs grow to
take over your roon
place to live while w
han 6 × 10-5
need to fin
Sincerely,
Dorm
Team
This sure looks like scientific notation, but what does it mean?

Scientific notation helps you with small numbers as well

The number in the Dorm Inspection note is 6×10^{-5}. It's scientific notation alright - but there's a **negative** power of 10. This is the conventional way of showing you that you should **divide** by the 10's instead of multiplying.

Every time you divide by 10, the number's digits shift along one place to the right, so each digit is worth 10 times less than it was before.

It's difficult for you to draw that, but practically speaking, you can get to the same place if you hop the decimal point the correct number of times to the left. So 6×10^{-5} works out as 0.00006.

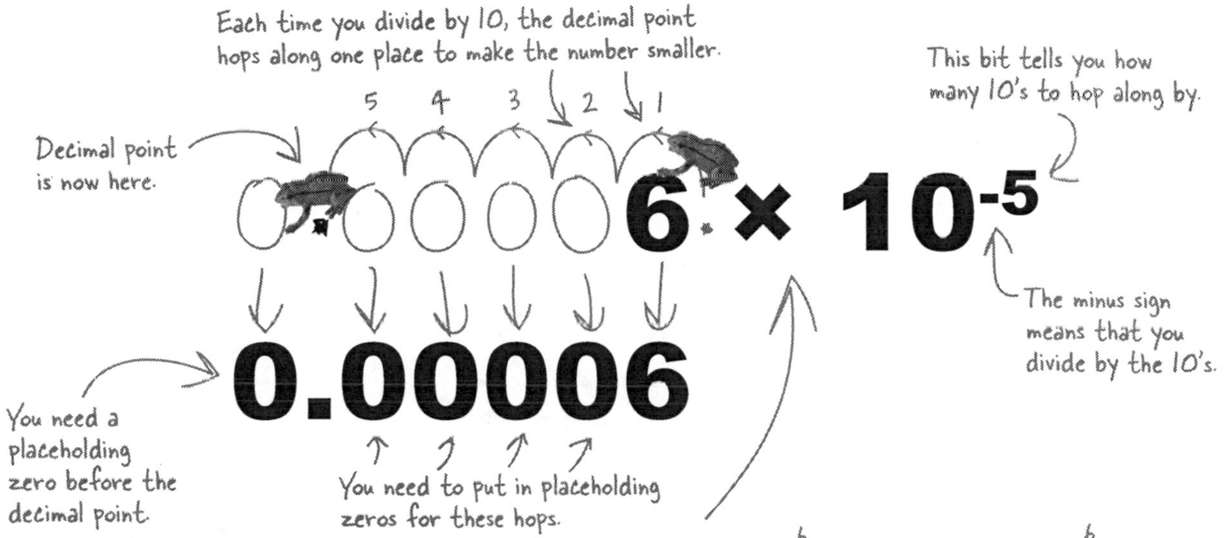

6×10^{-5} and $\frac{6}{10^5}$ both mean: $\frac{6}{10 \times 10 \times 10 \times 10 \times 10}$ ← You're dividing by 10 five times.

Another way of showing this is as a **fraction**, by writing $\frac{6}{10^5}$.

This makes it more obvious that you're dividing by all the 10's, as they appear on the bottom of a fraction.

$$\frac{6}{10^5}$$

If the 10's are on the bottom of the fraction, you're obviously dividing by them, so you don't need to put in the minus sign.

The key thing with scientific notation is to rewrite the number with ONE digit before the decimal point, then multiply or divide by the correct number of 10's.

The minus sign is part of a pattern

The convention of using a minus (or negative) sign in the index to say you're dividing by that number of 10's comes from a pattern that you're about to discover for yourself...

In this exercise, spot the pattern behind the convention of using a negative index (6×10^{-5}) to represent dividing by a series of 10's.

Original number	In scientific notation	Number of 10's you're multiplying or dividing by.
10000	10^4	4 (multiplying)
1000		
100		
10		
1		
0.1		
0.01	10^{-2}	2 (dividing)
0.001		
0.0001		

(Beside each step down the table: Divide by 10.)

This is a negative index, like in the Dorm Inspector's note.

Write down any patterns you spot.

....

....

Is there anything in your table that looks a bit unusual?

....

....

Exercise Solution

In this exercise, you're going to spot patterns that'll help you write very small numbers in scientific notation even more efficiently than we've done over there.

Original number	In scientific notation	Number of 10's you're multiplying or dividing by.
10000	10^4	4 (multiplying)
1000	10^3	3 (multiplying)
100	10^2	2 (multiplying)
10	10^1	1 (multiplying)
1	10^0	0
0.1	10^{-1}	1 (dividing)
0.01	10^{-2}	2 (dividing)
0.001	10^{-3}	3 (dividing)
0.0001	10^{-4}	4 (dividing)

Divide by 10. (between each row)

UNUSUAL: Any number to the power of 0 is 1. This is a math convention, but the table should help you see why it's sensible.

The PATTERN is that every time you divide by 10 to make the number smaller, the index of the scientific notation version decreases by 1.

Right. And it helps you estimate the size of the number too.

If the number in scientific notation is **greater** than 1, then it'll be **multiplied** by 10's, and if it's **less** than 1, it'll be **divided** by 10's.

So you can instantly see whether a number is larger or smaller than 1 by looking at the **sign** of the index. And you can see how large or small it is by looking at the **size** of the index, that is, the number of 10's that are doing the multiplying or dividing.

You can estimate the size of a number written in scientific notation by looking at the sign and size of the index.

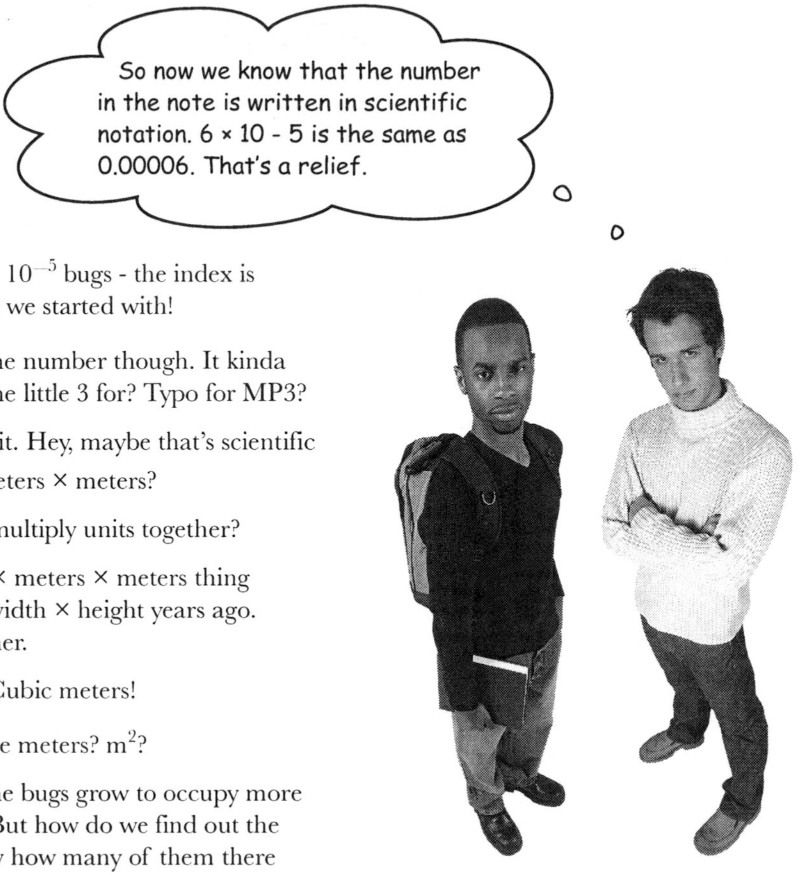

Kyle: But 6×10^{-5} what?? It can't be 6×10^{-5} bugs - the index is negative so that's much less than the 1 bug we started with!

Matt: There's that funny m^3 thing after the number though. It kinda looks like it might be meters - but what's the little 3 for? Typo for MP3?

Kyle: I don't see where music comes into it. Hey, maybe that's scientific notation as well. Could m^3 be meters × meters × meters?

Matt: But when would you ever want to multiply units together?

Kyle: Hmm, good point. But the meters × meters × meters thing reminds me of doing stuff with length × width × height years ago. That's three lengths multiplied by each other.

Matt: And that would make a **volume**! Cubic meters!

Kyle: Like how **area**'s measured in square meters? m^2?

Matt: Yeah. So the note's saying that if the bugs grow to occupy more than that volume, we wind up in trouble. But how do we find out the volume that all the bugs take up? We know how many of them there are after 12 hours, but that doesn't say how big they are all together.

Kyle: I wonder if there's anywhere we can **look up** the volume of one bug? Then we can multiply that by the number of bugs to get the total volume.

Matt: Sweet!

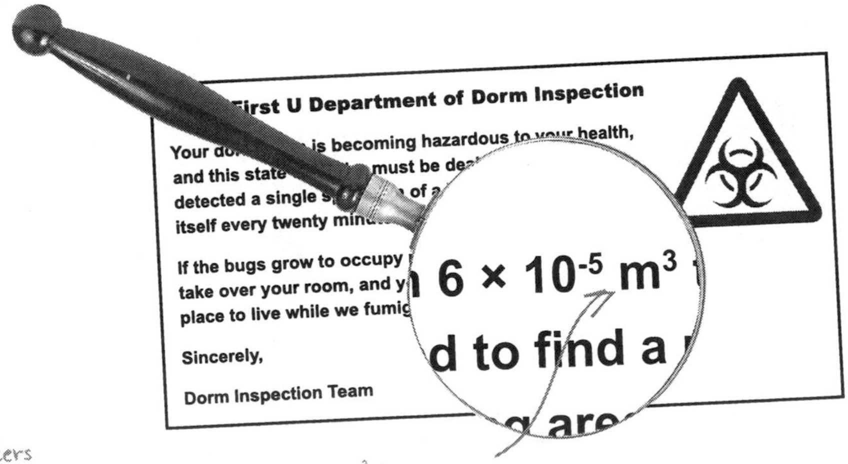

m^3 is m × m × m
i.e., length × width × height, so represents a VOLUME.

You can write units in scientific notation, e.g. area (m^2) or volume (m^3).

Square meters

Cubic meters

You'll often need to work with area or volume

The guys have decided that if they can find out the **volume** of one bug, they can multiply that by the total number of bugs to get the total volume.

Area is the amount of space something occupies in **two dimensions**. In SI units, it's measured in m^2 (if you say it out loud, this is "meters squared" or "square meters").

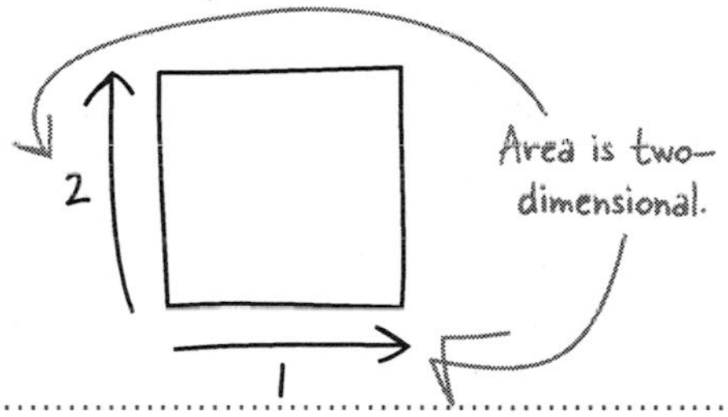

Volume is the amount of space something occupies in **three dimensions**. In SI units, it's measured in m^3 (if you say it out loud, this is "meters cubed" or "cubic meters").

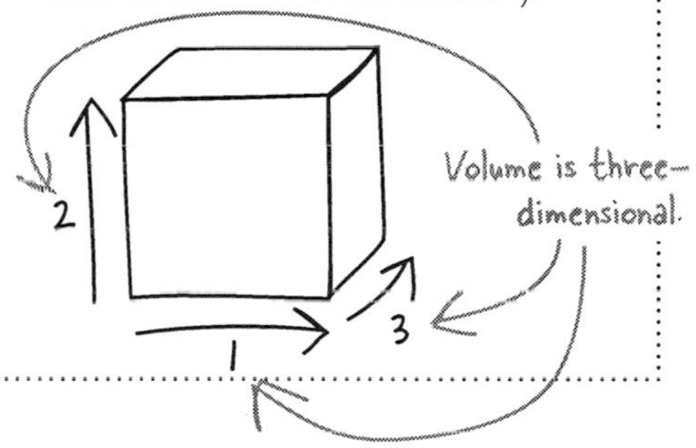

Area and volume units based on length help you visualize how big things are.

There are lots of other units that people can use for areas and volumes. But in your physics course, it makes the most sense to use units based on **length**.

For a start, this makes it easier to **visualize** how big an area or volume is. If you can imagine a meter, then you can also imagine a square meter or cubic meter. And if you know a football field is approximately 90 m long and 50 m wide, then you have a good idea of what $90 \times 50 = 4500\ m^2$ looks like!

Also, in physics you'll sometimes need to work out the area or volume of something when you know how long it is in different directions. It's far easier to use volume units based on the lengths you already know than it is to introduce even more conversion factors.

Look up facts in a book (or table of information)

You'll have a table of information in your exam. There's one a bit like it in Appendix B, but it's best for you to go to the AP Central website to download and practice with the one you'll actually have, so it's familiar.

If you're taking a test, you're not completely on your own. In both the multiple choice and the free response sections of the AP Physics B exam, you'll get a **table of information**.

The stuff in the table is there to prevent you from having to **memorize** lots of values (like the mass of an electron) that are vital for certain parts of a question, but don't help you **understand** the physics.

The table of information doesn't have anything in it about bugs, but Matt and Kyle find something that does. The Big Book of Bugs says that the particular strain of bug the Inspector found in their room is about 1 μm long by 1 μm wide by 1 μm high.

The only problem is, what on earth is a μm?

Tables of information and references leave your brain free to understand physics instead of memorizing lots of values that you can easily look up.

Prefixes help with numbers outside your comfort zone

Back in Chapter 2, you learned that you can put **prefixes** in front of units to show how big or small the units are. A kilometer is 1000 meters (10^3 meters), a millimeter is 0.001 of a meter (10^{-3} meters), and so forth.

There are several other SI unit prefixes. The μ prefix in the bug book is the Greek letter 'mu,' and is short for 'micro.' One μm is one millionth of a meter (10^{-6} meters).

That's not exactly the size of number you're used to working with from day to day! Your brain is happier with numbers closer to 1, so it feels better to say that the bug is 1 μm long instead of 0.000001 m long (or 10^{-6} m long).

You usually get a new prefix when something becomes 1000 times bigger, at 10^3, 10^6, 10^9, etc. The exception is 'centi,' which means 10^{-2} and is commonly used in the context of centimeters.

These are the SI prefixes you'll come across most often. (There are more of them, but there's no point in knowing what they all are if you'll never use them).

Power of 10	SI Prefix	Symbol
10^{12}	tera	T
10^{9}	giga	G
10^{6}	mega	M
10^{3}	kilo	k
10^{-2}	centi	c
10^{-3}	milli	m
10^{-6}	micro	μ
10^{-9}	nano	n
10^{-12}	pico	p

The little tail is very important, as this is μ, not u.

You usually get a new prefix every 10^3.

there are no Dumb Questions

Q: So why bother with scientific notation at all when you can just incorporate all the 10's into the prefix, and say μm instead of 1×10^{-6} m?

A: There are equations you'll come across later on that only work when you're measuring distance in meters, mass in kilograms, and so on. So you end up converting everything into meters (usually using scientific notation) anyway.

Scientific notation also makes calculations easier - as you'll see in a moment ...

Q: So why bother with μm and all those prefixes then?

A: Mainly ease of use. In everyday life, it's far easier to talk about "1 millimeter" or "10 kilometers" than it is to talk about "1×10^{-3} meters" or "1×10^4 meters."

Q: But why is that easier?

A: People usually have a better feel for numbers that are similar to the numbers of objects they can count.

Q: So that's why you get things like 'nanotechnology' - it's easier to talk about numbers that are close to everyday counting numbers than it is to say 'thousand-millionth technology'!

A: Yes. When speaking out loud, a physicist will prefer to say that something is 100 nm long rather than 0.0000001 m or 1×10^{-7} m. Once you get used to how big a nanometer is, your brain is happy to use it as a starting point.

Kyle: Yeah, a millionth of a meter. That sure is tiny - I can't even picture it in my head!

Matt: So if one bug is so small, maybe we can get away with cleaning even later! There's a game on tomorrow - If we figure out how many bugs there will be after 16 hours, we could maybe catch that before cleaning.

Kyle: 16 hours is $16 \times 3 = 48$ groups of 20 minutes, so they double in number 48 times. My calculator says that $2^{48} = 2.81 \times 10^{14}$ (to 3 significant digits). So there'd be 2.81×10^{14} bugs.

Matt: And after 12 hours, there were 6.87×10^{10} bugs. So what we really want to do is work out what **volume** these bugs take up and compare it with the volume in the Dorm Inspector's note.

Kyle: That's pretty simple. One bug = 1 μm^3, right? So 6.87×10^{10} bugs is $6.87 \times 10^{10}\ \mu m^3$, and 2.81×10^{14} bugs is $2.81 \times 10^{14}\ \mu m^3$.

Matt: Uhhh, not so fast. The volume in the note is measured in m^3, not μm^3. So we have to convert the **units** of our answers to m^3 to be able to compare them.

Kyle: Ah, good point. It looks like we're gonna have to do some **calculations** using numbers in scientific notation, keeping in mind that 1 m is the same as 1×10^6 μm. I've no idea how to do that.

Matt: Me neither.

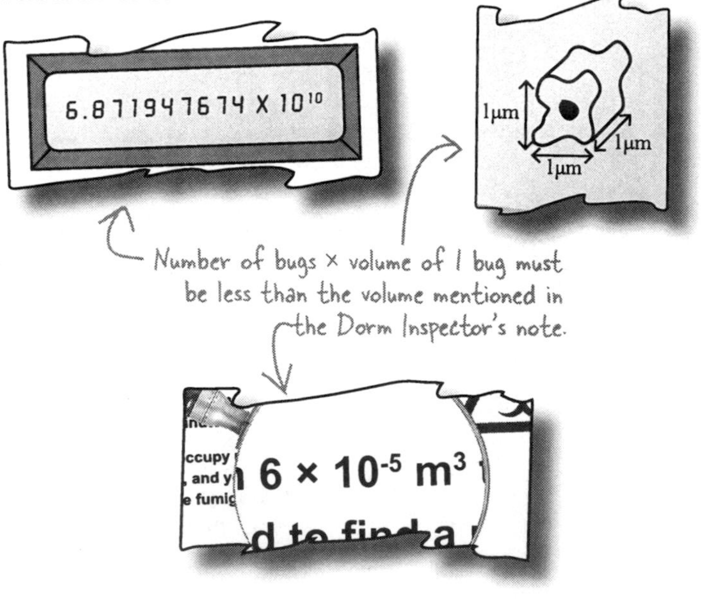

BRAIN POWER

How might scientific notation help you to multiply a very large number and a very small number together?

Scientific notation helps you to do calculations with large and small numbers

There are 6×10^{22} helium atoms in the balloon.

One helium atom has a mass of 6.65×10^{-27} kg.

Writing down numbers in scientific notation really helps you do calculations that involve big numbers, small numbers, or both.

Suppose someone asks you to work out the mass of all the atoms in a balloon. They tell you that there are 6×10^{22} atoms in the balloon, and each atom has a mass of 6.65×10^{-27} kg.

If you don't use scientific notation, you end up with a horrendous bout of calculator-bashing:

The mass of all the atoms is the number of atoms times the mass of one atom :

Mass of all atoms = 60000000000000000000000 × 0.00000000000000000000000000665 kg

This is a horrible-looking calculation!

I guess we should keep the numbers in scientific notation to make the calculation easier - right?

Powers of 10 make calculations easier.

If you're multiplying together two numbers written in power notation, you can **add the indices**.

Add the indices: $5 + 3 = 8$

$$10^5 \times 10^3 = 10^8$$

Here you're multiplying by five lots of 10, and then multiplying by another three lots of 10. So you're multiplying by eight lots of 10 in total, or 10^8.

$\frac{1}{10^{-3}}$ is the same as 10^3

$$\frac{10^5}{10^{-3}} = 10^8$$

If there's a division sign in your calculation, it's easiest to rewrite it as a multiplication. You can rewrite this as $10^5 \times 10^3 = 10^8$.

Add the indices: $5 + (-3) = 2$

$$10^5 \times 10^{-3} = 10^2$$

$5 + (-3)$ is the same as $5 - 3$.

Here you're multiplying by five lots of 10, and dividing by three lots of 10. This is the same as multiplying by two lots of 10 in total, or 10^2.

$\frac{1}{10^3}$ is the same as 10^{-3}.

$$\frac{10^5}{10^3} = 10^2$$

You can rewrite this as $10^5 \times 10^{-3} = 10^2$.

Pool Puzzle - Powers of 10

Here's the chance to practice working with powers of 10 with some calculations. Your **job** is to take numbers from the pool and place them into the boxes in these statements. You may **not** use the same number more than once, and you won't need to use all the numbers.

$\frac{1}{10^{-24}}$ is the same as 10^{24}.

$\frac{10^{-12}}{10^{-24}} = \square$

Rewrite this as a multiplication (rather than a division) before you work out the answer.

$10^4 \times 10^{-16} = \square$

The vast majority of people have $\square$ nose.

One divided by a million = $\square$

$\frac{10^{-12}}{10^{24}} = \square$

$\frac{1}{10^{24}}$ is the same as 10^{-24}.

$10^5 \times 10^{-13} \times 10^4 = \square$

The two biggest numbers in the pool are $\square$ and $\square$.

10000 is the same as $\square$.

A millionaire is likely to have at least \$ $\square$ dollars in the bank.

There are $\square$ meters in a kilometer.

$\frac{10^{14}}{10^{-3}} \times 10^{-6} \times 10^7 = \square$

0.000001 is the same as $\square$.

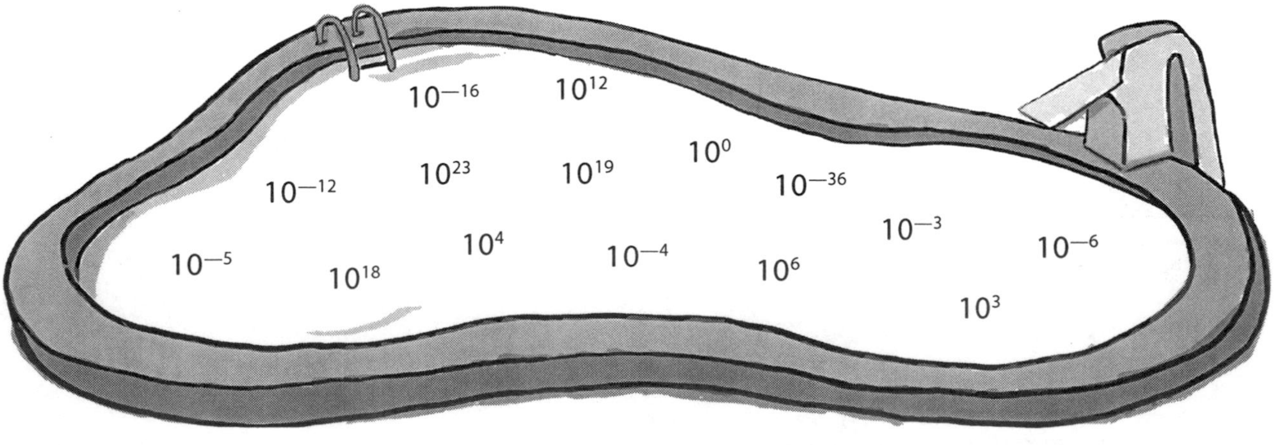

Pool Puzzle - Powers of 10 - SOLUTION

Here's the chance to practice working with powers of 10 with some calculations. Your **job** is to take numbers from the pool and place them into the boxes in these statements. You may **not** use the same number more than once, and you won't need to use all the numbers.

$\frac{1}{10^{-24}}$ is the same as 10^{24}.

$\frac{10^{-12}}{10^{-24}} = 10^{12}$

This is the same as $10^{-12} \times 10^{24}$.

$10^4 \times 10^{-16} = 10^{-12}$

The vast majority of people have 10^0 nose.

One divided by a million = 10^{-6}

$\frac{10^{-12}}{10^{24}} = 10^{-36}$

This is the same as $10^{-12} \times 10^{-24}$.

$10^5 \times 10^{-13} \times 10^4 = 10^{-4}$

The two biggest numbers in the pool are 10^{23} and 10^{19}.

10000 is the same as 10^4.

A millionaire is likely to have at least \$ 10^6 dollars in the bank.

There are 10^3 meters in a kilometer.

This is the same as $10^{14} \times 10^3 \times 10^{-6} \times 10^7$.

$\frac{10^{14}}{10^{-3}} \times 10^{-6} \times 10^7 = 10^{18}$

0.00001 is the same as 10^{-5}

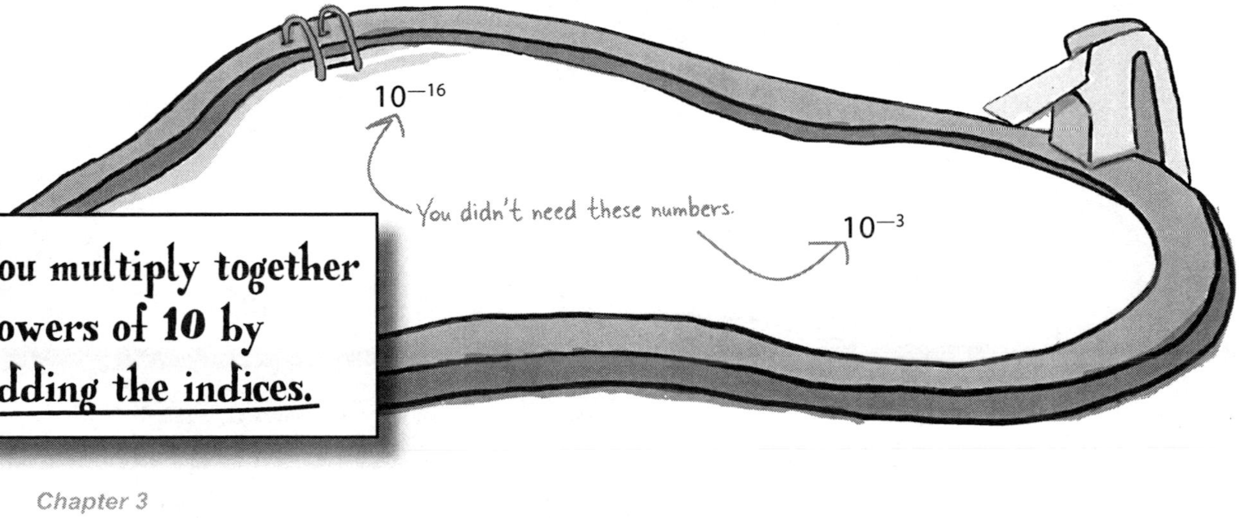

You multiply together powers of 10 by adding the indices.

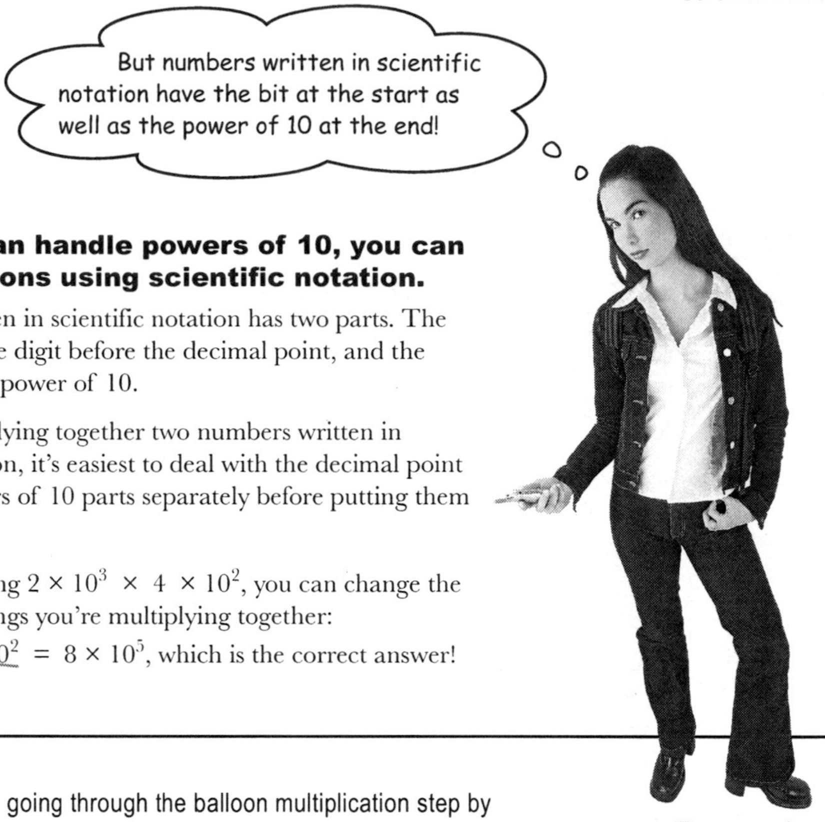

Once you can handle powers of 10, you can do calculations using scientific notation.

A number written in scientific notation has two parts. The first part has one digit before the decimal point, and the second part is a power of 10.

If you're multiplying together two numbers written in scientific notation, it's easiest to deal with the decimal point parts and powers of 10 parts separately before putting them back together.

So if you're doing $2 \times 10^3 \times 4 \times 10^2$, you can change the order of the things you're multiplying together:

$2 \times 4 \times \underline{10^3 \times 10^2} = 8 \times 10^5$, which is the correct answer!

Rewrite the order of the parts in the multiplication so that the powers of 10 are all together.

Exercise

Spend some time going through the balloon multiplication step by step before going back to the bug problem.

a. There are 6×10^{22} helium atoms in the balloon. 1 helium atom has a mass of 6.65×10^{-27} kg. Write down the multiplication you'd do to find the mass of all the atoms in the balloon.

b. You are allowed to multiply numbers together in any order. Change the order of the things you're multiplying together so that the powers of 10 are next to each other.

c. Multiply together the two 'decimal point' parts. Then multiply together the two 'powers of 10' parts. This should give you an answer with one decimal point part and one power of 10 part.

d. Rewrite your answer from part c. so that the decimal point part has one digit in front of the decimal point. (You'll need to adjust the power of 10 part.)

Spend some time going through the balloon multiplication step by step before going back to the bug problem.

a. There are 6×10^{22} helium atoms in the balloon. 1 helium atom has a mass of 6.65×10^{-27} kg. Write down the multiplication you'd do to find the mass of all the atoms in the balloon.

Mass of all atoms $= 6 \times 10^{22} \times 6.65 \times 10^{-27}$ kg

b. You are allowed to multiply numbers together in any order. Change the order of the things you're multiplying together so that the powers of 10 are next to each other.

Mass of all atoms $= 6 \times 6.65 \times 10^{22} \times 10^{-27}$ kg

c. Multiply together the two 'decimal point' parts. Then multiply together the two 'powers of 10' parts. This should give you an answer with one decimal point part and one power of 10 part.

Mass of all atoms $= 39.9 \times 10^{-5}$ kg

d. Rewrite your answer from part c. so that the decimal point part has one digit in front of the decimal point. (You'll need to adjust the power of 10 part.)

Mass of all atoms $= 3.99 \times 10^{-4}$ kg

Your answer needs to stay the same size.

If you wind up with the answer 39.9×10^{-5}, you need to rewrite it in scientific notation as a number that has a part with **one digit in front of the decimal point** and a power of 10 part.

You need to divide the 39.9 part of the number by 10 to get 3.99. But the number must remain the same size- so you need to multiply the second part by 10.

$$39.9 \times 10^{-1} \times 10^{-5} \times 10^{1} = 3.99 \times 10^{-4}$$

You need to divide the first part by 10 (same as multiplying by 10^{-1}) to get one digit in front of the decimal point.

So you need to multiply the second part by 10 to keep your answer the same size.

The guys have it all worked out

Well, they hope they do...

Matt and Kyle have had a go at working out the volume of the bugs using scientific notation. But have they done it correctly?

Sharpen your pencil

Matt and Kyle have had a go at working out the volume of bugs in m^3 that there'll be after 12 and 16 hours. Your job is to see if you agree with their calculations, and decide whether their final answer SUCKs (Size, Units, Calculations, 'K'ontext).

Look at the **Size** of their answer - if it feels wrong, then look to see if there's a mistake with the **Units** or **Calculations**.

There are 10^6 μm in 1 m.

We'll use this as the conversion factor for the volume.

After 12 hours:

$$\text{Volume of bugs} = 6.87 \times 10^{10}\ \mu m^3$$

$$= 6.87 \times 10^{10}\ \cancel{\mu m^3} \times \frac{1\ m^3}{10^6\ \cancel{\mu m^3}}$$

$$= 6.87 \times 10^{10} \times 10^{-6}\ m^3$$

$$= \underline{\underline{6.87 \times 10^4\ m^3}}$$

After 16 hours:

$$\text{Volume of bugs} = 2.81 \times 10^{14}\ \mu m^3$$

$$= 2.81 \times 10^{14}\ \cancel{\mu m^3} \times \frac{1\ m^3}{10^6\ \cancel{\mu m^3}}$$

$$= 2.81 \times 10^{14} \times 10^{-6}\ m^3$$

$$= \underline{\underline{2.81 \times 10^8\ m^3}}$$

there are no Dumb Questions

Q: My calculator has a button that lets me input numbers in scientific notation. Why can't I just use that?

A: Sometimes you don't get to use a calculator, like in the multiple choice part of the AP exam!

Plus doing the calculation like this helps you to see the **size** of answer you're expecting, and you're more likely to spot silly mistakes when you ask yourself if your answer SUCKs.

Q: But when will I ever see numbers like this in my exam?

A: There are lots of very big or very small numbers in physics - the size of an electron, the mass of the earth, etc.

If you're doing a calculation with numbers written in scientific notation, you should separate out the powers of 10 to add the indices before recombining them with the rest of the numbers.

Sharpen your pencil Solution

Matt and Kyle have had a go at working out the volume of bugs in m^3 that there'll be after 12 and 16 hours. Your job is to see if you agree with their calculations, and decide whether their final answer SUCKs (Size, Units, Calculations, 'K'ontext).

Look at the **Size** of their answer - if it feels wrong, then look to see if there's a mistake with the **Units** or **Calculations**.

There are 10^6 μm in 1 m.

We'll use this as the conversion factor for the volume.

This is the problem! There are 10^6 μm in 1 m, but that's LENGTH, not VOLUME. You can't use it as a conversion factor for volume.

Volume is length × length × length and has units of m^3, not m. Converting between μm^3 and m^3 is different from converting between μm and m.

After 12 hours:

Volume of bugs = $6.87 \times 10^{10}\ \mu m^3$

$= 6.87 \times 10^{10}\ \mu m^3 \times \frac{1\ m^3}{10^6\ \mu m^3}$

$= 6.87 \times 10^{10} \times 10^{-6}\ m^3$

$= 6.87 \times 10^4\ m^3$

These answers are totally the wrong SIZE!

$2.81 \times 10^8\ m^3$ is the same volume as 2000 giant football stadiums!

After 16 hours:

Volume of bugs = $2.81 \times 10^{14}\ \mu m^3$

$= 2.81 \times 10^{14}\ \mu m^3 \times \frac{1\ m^3}{10^6\ \mu m^3}$

$= 2.81 \times 10^{14} \times 10^{-6}\ m^3$

$= 2.81 \times 10^8\ m^3$

200,000,000 meters cubed bugs after only 16 hours is totally the wrong size of answer!

The **size** of Matt and Kyle's answer is waaay off - if you spotted that, well done! It just doesn't make sense to say that the bugs will occupy a volume of two hundred million cubic meters after only 16 hours - **especially if you can visualize the size of just one cubic meter**!

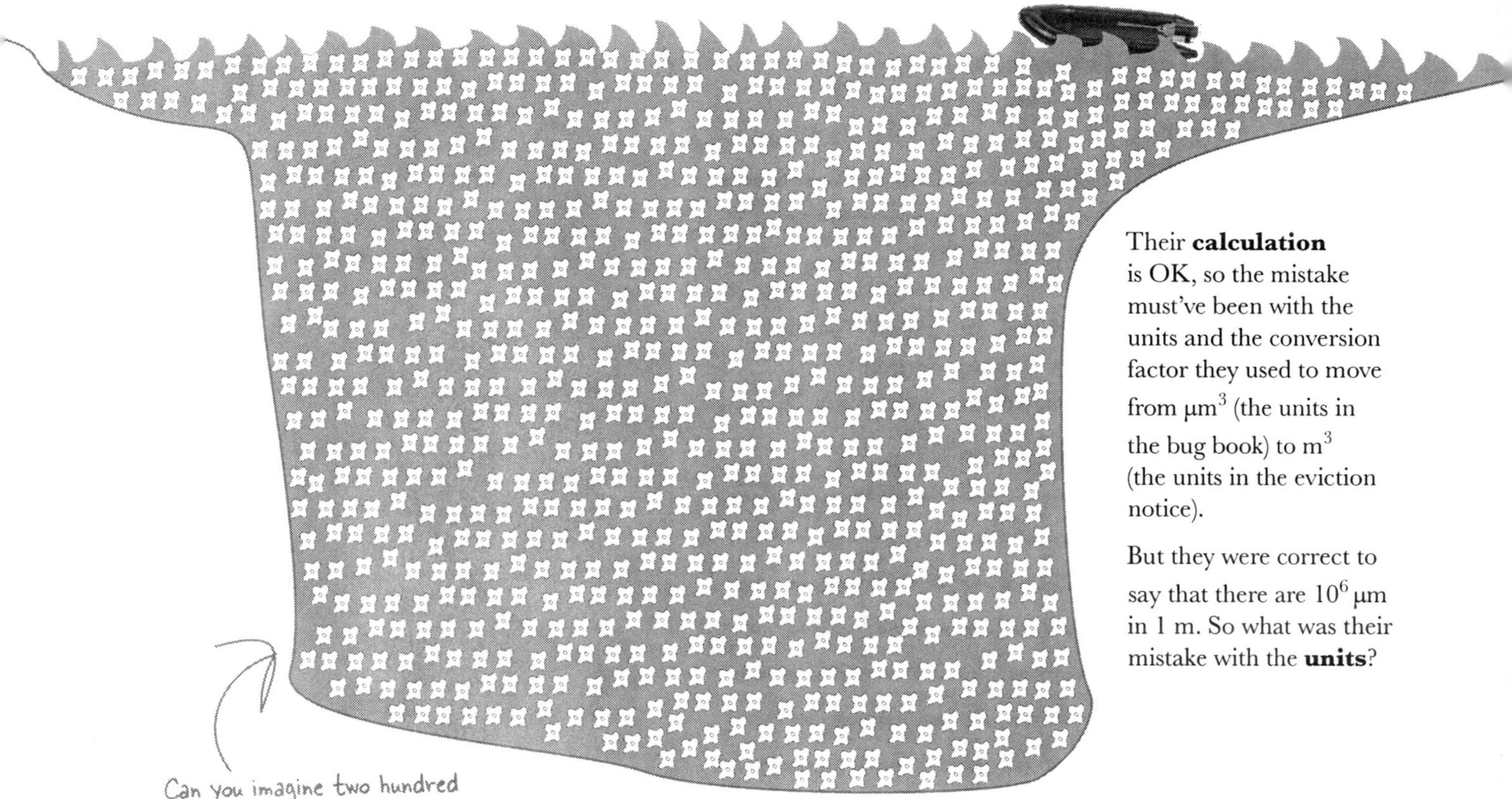

Their **calculation** is OK, so the mistake must've been with the units and the conversion factor they used to move from μm^3 (the units in the bug book) to m^3 (the units in the eviction notice).

But they were correct to say that there are 10^6 µm in 1 m. So what was their mistake with the **units**?

Can you imagine two hundred million cubic meters of bugs? Think of an enormous sea of bugs....eww.

BRAIN POWER

There **are** 10^6 µm in a m - that part is correct.

So why has there been such a problem converting the units from μm^3 to m^3?

Be careful converting units of area or volume

Although there are 1×10^6 μm in a m, there aren't 1×10^6 μm^3 in a m^3. This is difficult to see because the numbers are so big - and it's what the guys missed. They've ended up saying that the bugs will occupy a volume of two hundred million cubic meters after only 16 hours, which must be nonsense!

A μm is so small; it's easier to visualize how this happened using mm and cm to measure area and volume.

Length is **one-dimensional**.
There are 10 mm in 1 cm.

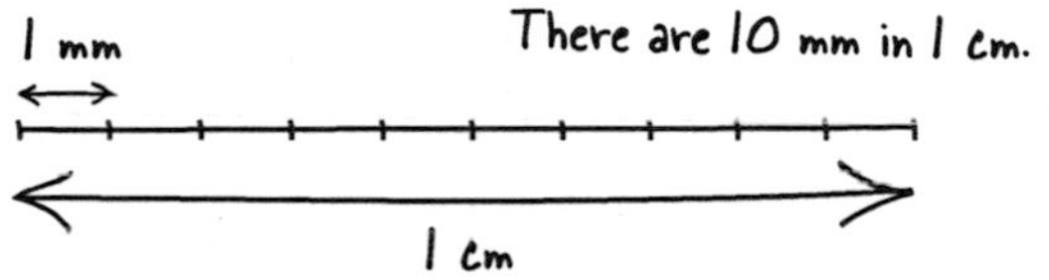

All these pictures are magnified from actual size!

Area is **two-dimensional**, i.e., length × width.
So there are $10 \times 10 = 100$ mm^2 in 1 cm^2.
Or in scientific notation: $10^1 \times 10^1 = 10^2$ mm^2 in 1 cm^2.

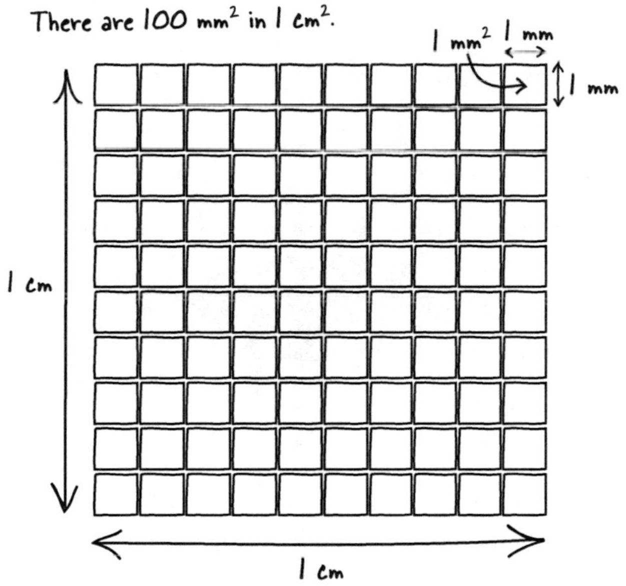

Area and volume are NOT the same as length.

Volume is **three-dimensional**, i.e., length × width × height.
So there are $10 \times 10 \times 10 = 1000$ mm^3 in 1 cm^3.
Or in scientific notation: $10^1 \times 10^1 \times 10^1 = 10^3$ mm^3 in 1 cm^3.

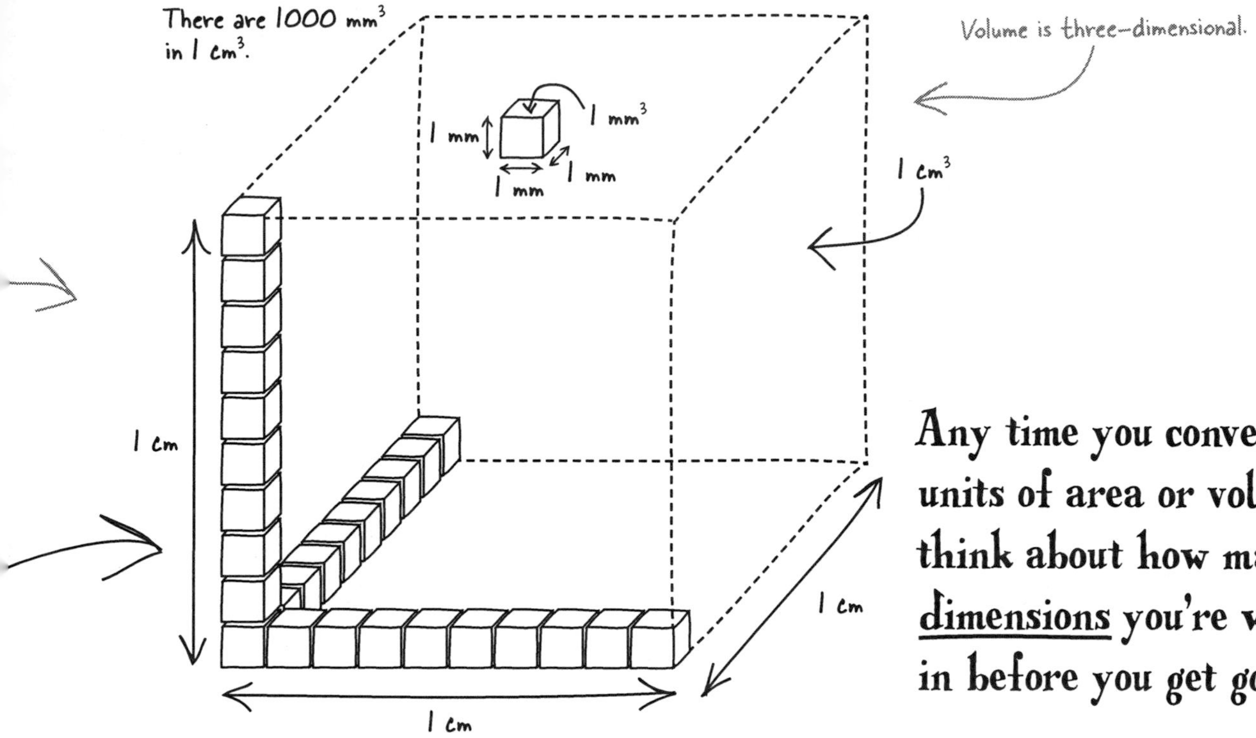

Any time you convert units of area or volume, think about how many dimensions you're working in before you get going!

Sharpen your pencil

The bugs occupy 6.87×10^{10} μm³ after 12 h and 2.81×10^{14} μm³ after 16 h. How many m³ is that, and how does this compare with the 6×10^{-5} m³ mentioned in the note? (There are 10^6 μm in 1 m.)

Sharpen your pencil Solution

The bugs occupy $6.87 \times 10^{10}\ \mu m^3$ after 12 h and $2.81 \times 10^{14}\ \mu m^3$ after 16 h. How many m^3 is that, and how does this compare with the $6 \times 10^{-5}\ m^3$ mentioned in the note? (There are $10^6\ \mu m$ in 1 m.)

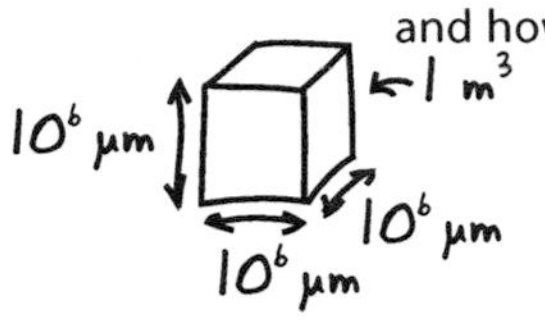

There are $10^6\ \mu m$ in 1 m. Volume is three-dimensional.

So there are $10^6 \times 10^6 \times 10^6 = 10^{18}\ \mu m^3$ in $1\ m^3$.

After 12 hours:

$$\text{Volume of bugs} = 6.87 \times 10^{10}\ \mu m^3 = 6.87 \times 10^{10}\ \cancel{\mu m^3} \times \frac{1\ m^3}{10^{18}\ \cancel{\mu m^3}} = 6.87 \times 10^{10} \times 10^{-18}\ m^3 = \underline{\underline{6.87 \times 10^{-8}\ m^3}}$$

This is less than $6 \times 10^{-5}\ m^3$.

After 16 hours:

$$\text{Volume of bugs} = 2.81 \times 10^{14}\ \mu m^3 = 2.81 \times 10^{14}\ \cancel{\mu m^3} \times \frac{1\ m^3}{10^{18}\ \cancel{\mu m^3}} = 2.81 \times 10^{14} \times 10^{-18}\ m^3 = \underline{\underline{2.81 \times 10^{-4}\ m^3}}$$

This is more than $6 \times 10^{-5}\ m^3$.

So the bugs won't take over ... unless the guys sleep in!

You just worked out that if the guys remember to set their alarms for 12 hours from now, the bugs won't reach the tipping point and get the guys evicted.

But if the guys try waiting 16 hours to catch the football game, the Dorm Inspector will turf them out. Unfortunately...

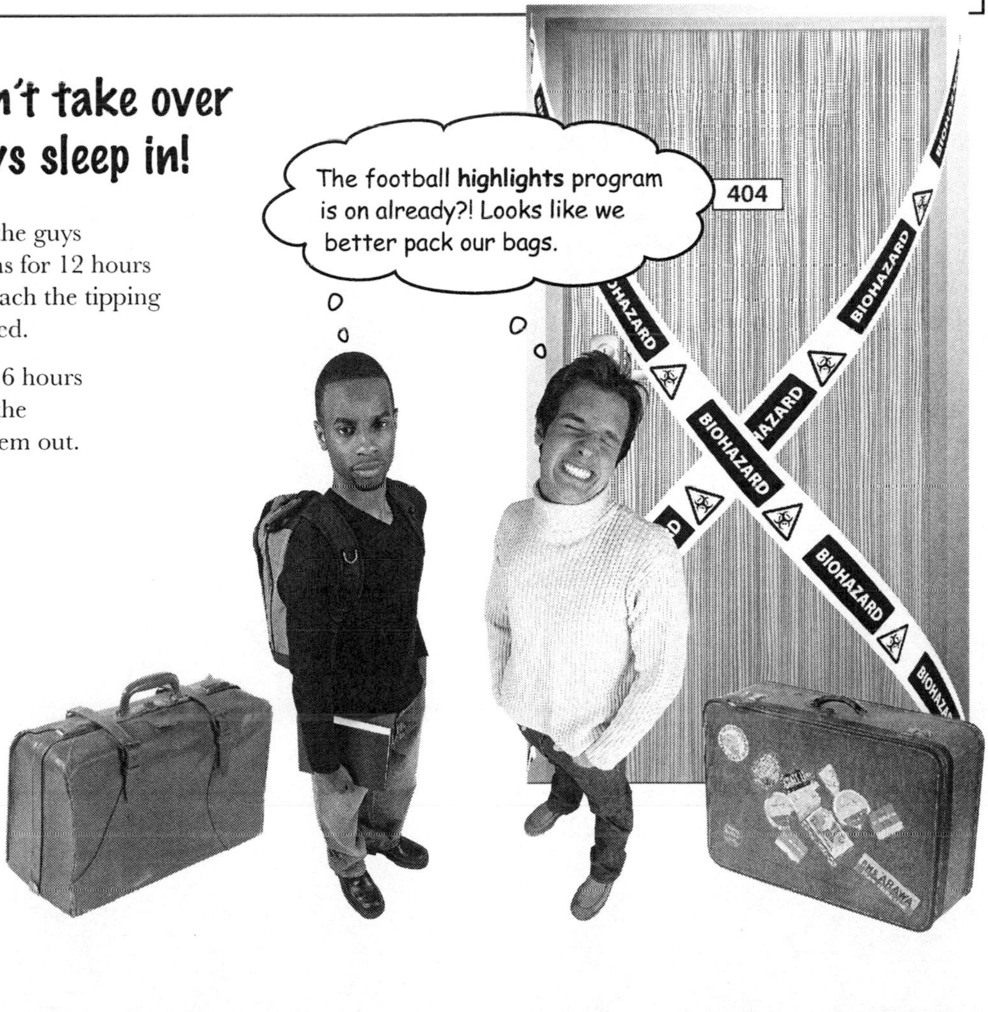

Question Clinic: The "Converting units of area or volume" Question

In the course of doing another question, you'll often find yourself having to **convert units of area or volume**. As soon as you see areas or volumes mentioned, think of the bugs occupying 2000 football stadiums - you don't want to majorly mess up like that! Keep your cool, and think about what area and volume actually **are** to convert the units.

These are all LENGTHS, and they're all in mm.

But you're asked for a VOLUME in m^3, not mm^3.

4. A treasure chest is 800 mm long, 400 mm wide, and 500 mm high.

a. What is its volume in m^3?

b. How many gold blocks measuring 20 cm by 10 cm by 5 cm could fit in the chest? (Assume that you're allowed to melt down the gold so that it will fit exactly.)

It's probably best to work through the whole question in m^3, as this is the unit you're asked to give your answers in.

Here's yet another way of measuring length (cm) that needs to be converted into a volume.

With volume questions, you sometimes have to think of how many blocks you could stack in each direction before you reach the side of the container. This bit lets you know that you don't need to allow for that.

It's often easiest to convert the lengths to m first and work out the volume in m^3. (Though you could also work out the area in cm^3 and convert that to m^3 at the end.)

When you have to convert units of area or volume, draw a little **sketch** to make sure the powers of 10 work out OK in your conversion factor.

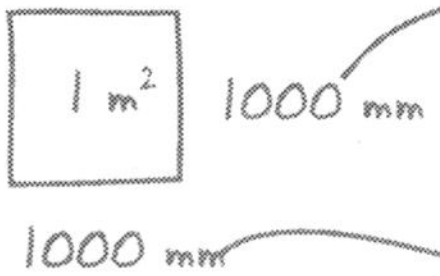

$$1\ m^2 = 1000\ mm \times 1000\ mm = 10^3\ mm \times 10^3\ mm = 10^6\ mm^2$$

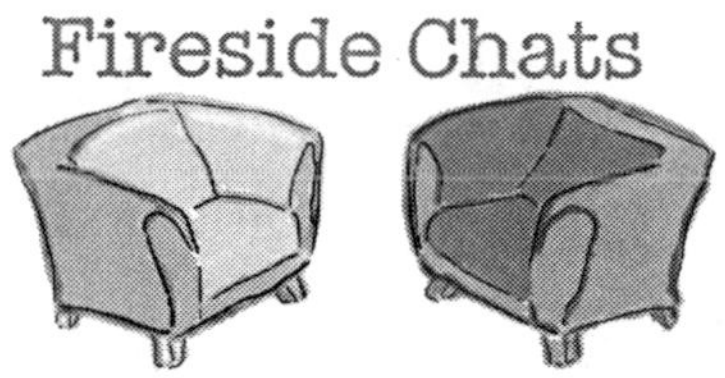

Tonight's talk: **A normal number and one written in scientific notation go head-to-head. Who will be the last one standing when the revolution comes.**

Normal number:	**Scientific notation number:**
Well, well, Mr. Obscurity. Lovely to meet you at last!	
	Less of that! I know most people go 16+ years before they meet me, but I'm well worth the wait!
You hide for decades while I do all the counting, shopping, algebra, and so on. Then, suddenly you show up and expect to take center stage. It's just plain rude!	
	You can still do all the stuff you've always done – I'm not trying to steal your thunder. But the fact is that I am naturally better at some things.
Yeah? Show me one thing you can do that I can't!	
	OK, what about writing out Bill Gates' fortune nicely? 5×10^{10} dollars.
No way! "50 billion dollars" gives you a much better idea of size than these silly little numbers by the ten.	
	Well, my way is really obviously "5" with ten zeros after it – what's so difficult about that?
It's not what people are used to! They've been doing it my way all their lives, and you've totally failed to show that your way is better.	
	Well then, Mister "They're used to me," how would you talk about the mass of a proton?
Um, let me look up my table of information. That'd be 0.00000000000000000000000000167 kilograms.	
	When have people ever seen silly numbers like that? They're not used to them at all! They're better off writing it my way – 1.67×10^{-27} kilograms.
But they can still count up my zeros to get the size.	
	Well, yeah, but who's going to bother with that?
Um, OK. I guess you are the master of showing big or small numbers. So ... do you plan to take over completely?	

Normal number

Scientific notation number:

Not completely. People still prefer doing things your way if they can! They've even invented a whole load of units so they don't have to go around saying "blah times ten to the power of whatever" all the time. Like nanometers, kilograms, and such.

I told you they like me more!

Actually, all I've said is that people like numbers they feel comfortable with. But when it comes to doing **calculations** with the numbers, that's when I shine.

Yeah, right. Every calculator manufacturer has a different way to input you, especially your 10 to the power of negative thingamajiggers.

Ah, but the humans don't have to do that if they're multiplying or dividing numbers like me. They only type the first bit into their calculators, the 1.67 or whatever. Then they do the tens part separately, on paper (which is just simple adding).

Sorry? You can multiply by adding? Sounds a bit suspicious to a purist like me.

Yes, if you're multiplying lots of tens parts together, all you need to do is add the indices. $10^2 \times 10^3 = 10^5$ can be broken down into "$10^2 = 10 \times 10$" and "$10^3 = 10 \times 10 \times 10$." Together, they make "$10 \times 10 \times 10 \times 10 \times 10$." Five lots of 10 is 10^5.

So you're saying that the first bit of you is easy to deal with (but only because people have practiced with me), and the second bit is easy because they're used to adding sums (again, because of me)?

I suppose you could put it like that. Maybe we need each other more than we realized in the beginning.

The giant who came for breakfast

Once upon a time, long long ago, a refugee from the land of the giants came to the king's palace. He was hungry. Now, when I say hungry, I don't just mean the kind of hunger you feel in between meals. The giant was twice as tall as a normal person...and starving.

The king sighed with relief when he realized that the giant wasn't about to gobble him up, but instead was far more interested in a hearty meal of sausage, bacon, and eggs.

"But if it's paltry food you bring, I'll eat the servants, then the king!" he concluded.

The smile froze on the king's lips, becoming the kind of grimace you might muster when face-to-face with a hungry giant who'd just threatened to turn you into a tasty snack.

The king gathered his advisers around him to ask them for advice (which advisers generally provide).

"Your highness," they began. "Since the giant is twice a tall as a normal person and perfectly in proportion, we should serve him twice as much breakfast...maybe with a couple of extra pieces of toast just in case."

Should the king listen, and agree to feed the giant twice as much as a normal person because he's twice as tall?

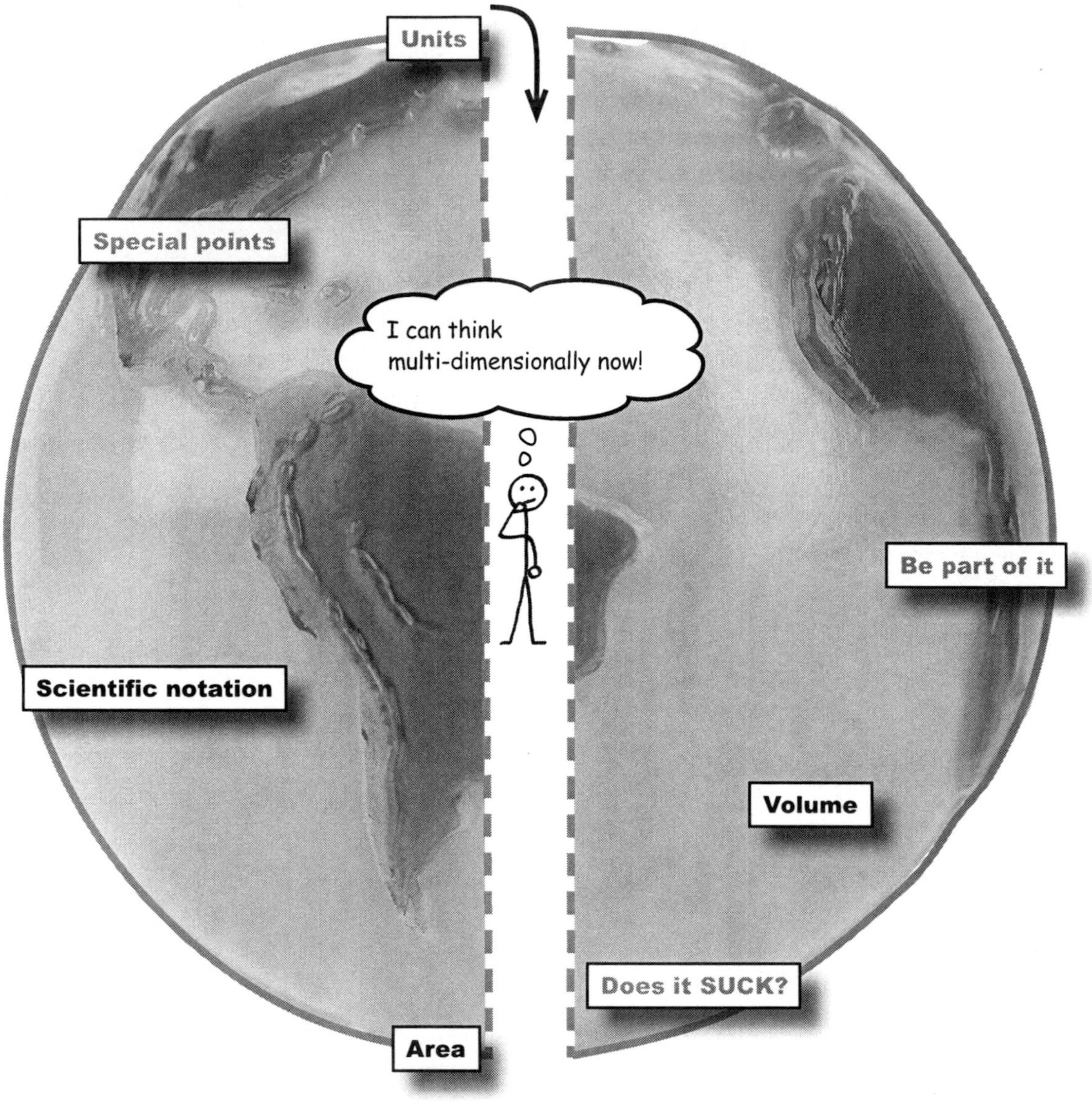

- [x] **Scientific notation** — **A method of representing long numbers using powers of 10.**
- [x] **Area** — **Two-dimensional space.**
- [x] **Volume** — **Three-dimensional space.**

CHAPTER 3

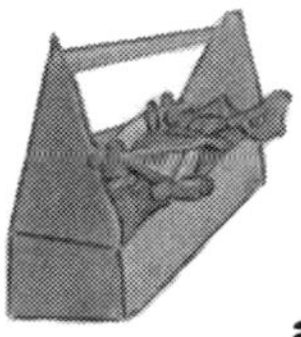

Your Physics Toolbox

You've got Chapter 3 under your belt, and you've added some terminology and answer-checking skills to your toolbox.

Power notation

Power notation is a way of showing that you're multiplying or dividing by the same number over and over again.

For example, if you have 10^6, it means you're multiplying by 10 six times over.

And if you're dividing by the same number several times, you can show this using a negative index, e.g., 10^{-7}.

Multiplying powers of 10 by each other

Multiply together different powers of 10 by adding the indices.

For example, $10^5 \times 10^{-2} = 10^3$ because $5 + (-2) = 3$

Dividing powers of 10 by each other

If you're dividing by a power of 10, it's easiest to rewrite this as a power of 10 you're multiplying by, then add the indices as before.

For example:

$$\frac{10^5}{10^2} = 10^5 \times 10^{-2} = 10^3$$

Scientific notation

Scientific notation is a way of writing really long numbers using two parts multiplied together.

The first part is written as a number with one digit in front of the decimal point.

The second part is a power of 10.

For example, $5 \times 10^3 = 5000$

Calculations using scientific notation

If you have to multiply together several numbers written in scientific notation, it's easiest to treat the powers of 10 separately before putting the number back together.

Converting units of area and volume

Areas are based on lengths – you can imagine what a m^2 or a m^3 looks like and see if your answer makes sense.

Start any units conversion of area or volume with a sketch to make sure you use the correct conversion factor.

This will often involve multiplying or dividing powers of 10 by each other.

The giant who came for breakfast

Should the king listen, and feed the giant twice as much because he's twice as tall as a normal person?

The king needs to make sure that the giant's stomach ends up full of food, so there's no room left in there for him or his advisors!

If the giant's twice as tall as a normal man and in proportion, then he's also twice as wide from side to side, and twice as deep from front to back.

So the giant's stomach is twice as high, twice as wide and twice as deep as a normal man's and is $2 \times 2 \times 2 = 8$ times larger -so the king should order **eight** breakfasts for the giant to be on the safe side.

4 equations and graphs

Learning the lingo

Communication is vital. You're already off to a good start in your journey to truly think like a physicist, but now you need to **communicate your thoughts**. In this chapter, you're going to take your first steps in two universal languages - **graphs** and **equations** - pictures you can use to *speak a thousand words* about experiments you do and the physics concepts you're learning. *Seeing is believing.*

The new version of the Break Neck Pizza website is nearly ready to go live ...

Break Neck Pizza already revolutionized pizza delivery through its patented "just in time" cooking process and its large fleet of delivery bicycles.

But now it's even better! The award-winning Break Neck website has just been upgraded to give each customer a **delivery time** for their order.

... but you need to work out how to give the customer their delivery time

You've been called in to figure out what time the website should quote each customer. The web programmers are happy to implement your solution, and you also have Alex, the top Break Neck delivery guy, on hand to help. He knows how long it takes him to get to some houses, but you'll need another way to work out the delivery time to new, unknown neighborhoods.

Sharpen your pencil

Write down everything you can think of that might affect the delivery time the website should give to a customer.

How fast Alex can cycle ....

....

....

....

....

....

....

Sharpen your pencil Solution

Write down everything you can think of that might affect the delivery time the website should give to a customer.

- Alex's cycling speed
- Distance from Break Neck to the customer
- Can all the pizzas be cooked at once?
- Deep pan or Italian base?
- How long it takes the website to process the order
- Whether the customer enters their address correctly

These both have to do with the time it takes Alex to reach the house.

Both of these affect the time it takes for the pizza to cook.

It's fine if you had some other answers – like the amount or type of topping – that we haven't jotted down here.

It's OK to assume that the web guys have already dealt with these. You only need to think about the physics!

If you write the delivery time as an equation, you can see what's going on

The total delivery time is the time Alex spends cycling to the customer's house plus the cooking time for the pizza.

It takes a lot of words to describe this, and it's difficult to tell what's going on without reading the whole thing. This is why in physics, people use **equations** to describe how the world works.

You can use **letters** with subscripts as symbols to represent each of the times:

t_{total} for the total delivery time.

t_{cyc} for Alex's cycling time.

t_{cook} for the cooking time.

Use 't' to show that a symbol represents a time, and use subscripts to indicate which time, e.g., t_{cook}

Then you can write down the equation $t_{total} = t_{cyc} + t_{cook}$. This says exactly the same thing as "The total delivery time is equal to the time Alex spends cycling to the customer's house plus the cooking time for the pizza." Except the equation lets you see that at a glance.

We're using italics here to represent variables. You don't have to do this when you're writing them down!

Equations let you represent the real world symbolically.

Use variables to keep your equation general

So you can reuse it for ANY customer who orders pizza.

An equation like $t_{total} = t_{cyc} + t_{cook}$ is **general** because it isn't tied to any particular values for the cycling or cooking times. This means you can use the same equation for any order. Any quantity represented by a letter rather than a number is called a **variable**. Here it's good for t_{total}, t_{cyc}, and t_{cook} to be variables because their values will vary for each customer.

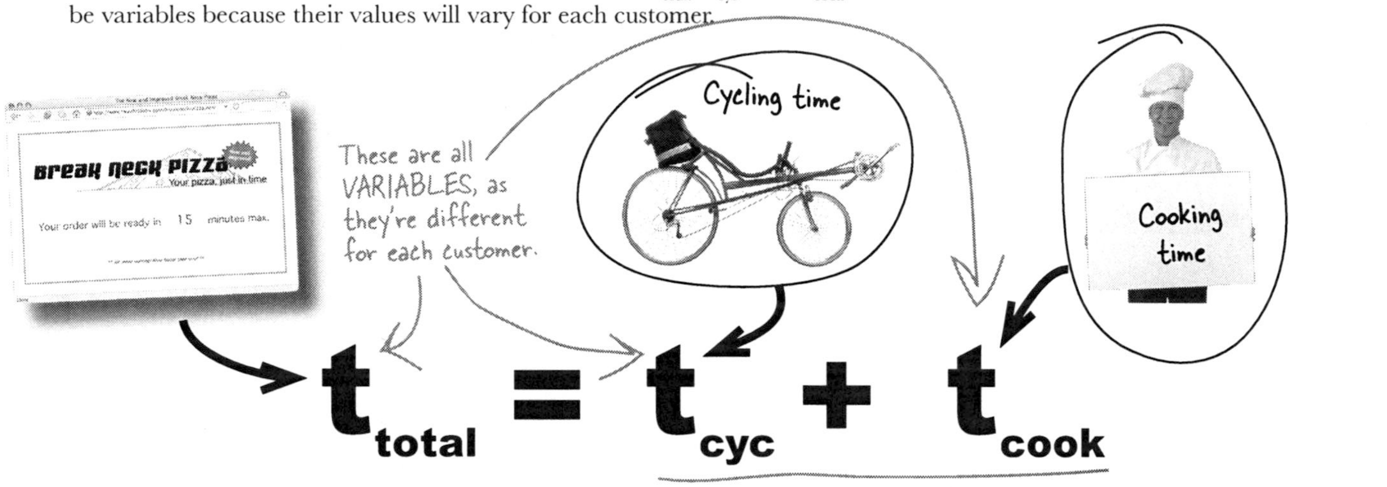

The order you add in doesn't matter. You could also write $t_{total} = t_{cook} + t_{cyc}$.

there are no Dumb Questions

Q: Why bother with an equation when a description will do just as well?

A: Descriptions are good because if you can explain something in words, you know you've got it. But equations are also good because they let you be short and sweet when you're explaining things.

Q: But the equations use letters in them. Surely that makes things harder because you have to explain what each of the letters means before anyone else can understand what the equation says.

A: That's true - but once you know what the letters represent, they're much quicker to write down and take in than a load of words.

Q: But why use letters in the equation at all? Surely it would be easier to get the delivery time if we write numbers in there from the start?

A: You're right, that would work - but only for one particular house! You'd need to start over again for each new delivery.

Q: Can't I use different letters to represent each thing instead of using *t* all the time?

A: Each of the variables in your equation is a time. It's conventional to use the letter *t* to represent a time, and use subscripts to indicate which time that variable represents.

Q: But why use subscripts rather than using two letters next to each other? Surely using initials like 'dt' for delivery time would be clearer?

A: One reason is that in physics and math, you indicate that you're multiplying two variables together by writing them next to each other. So you write $a \times b$ as ab. The second is that '*dt*' is already reserved for something else (which you'll come across later on in the book).

Q: Oh yeah, I kinda remember that from math. Why is it useful?!

A: It helps you to see the building blocks of your equation more easily. We're just getting to that ...

Equations Up Close

An equation uses symbols to show you that two things are **equal** to each other.

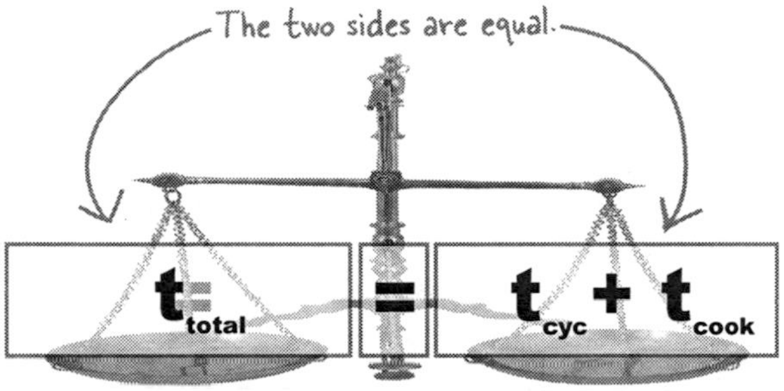

An equation must have an equal sign!

If it doesn't, it's not an EQUAtion!

In an equation, each of the blocks you add together or subtract from each other is called a **term**. A term can be a number, a single variable, or several numbers and variables multiplied or divided by each other.

$$t_{total} = t_{cyc} + t_{cook}$$

These are terms.

A TERM is one of the building blocks that you add or subtract.

You can break down equations by thinking about them **one term at a time**. If a term is more complicated than a single variable, you need to do all the calculations (multiplying, dividing, and so forth) within a term before you add it to or subtract it from other terms. So that you can spot terms easily, it's usual to use a shorthand for multiplication, like *bz* instead of *b* × *z* since this groups together all the variables in each term.

$$x = y + bz$$

This term is two variables multiplied together. If you're putting numbers into your equation, you need to work out bz before you add the term to the others.

Think about equations one term at a time

You need to work out Alex's cycling time

Your equation for the delivery time is $t_{total} = t_{cyc} + t_{cook}$. There are two terms on the right hand side: t_{cyc} for the cycling time, and t_{cook} for the cooking time. You can make the job of working out the total time, t_{total}, easier for yourself by thinking about t_{cyc} and t_{cook} one at a time.

You already made great progress with t_{cyc} (Alex's cycling **time**) when you intuitively realized that t_{cyc} must depend on the **speed** at which Alex cycles and the **distance** the customer's house is from Break Neck. But **how** do the speed and distance affect the cycling time?

What do you expect to happen for **extremes**, like a short distance or a high speed?

Sharpen your pencil Solution

Write down everything you can think of that migl time the website should give to a customer.

How fast Alex can cycle

Distance from Break Neck to the customer

Part of your Sharpen answer from page 98.

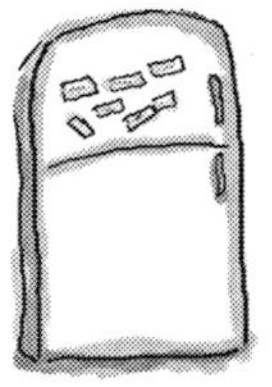

Pizza Delivery Magnets

Your job is to use the magnets to explain **how** the **distance** to the house and the **speed** at which Alex cycles affect the **time** it takes him to get there. There are only two words on the magnets, but they all have a place on the pictures.

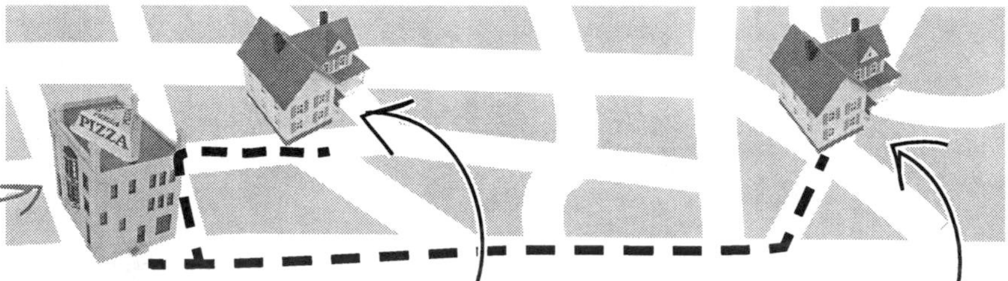

Break Neck Pizza HQ

Remember – t_{cyc} is the time it takes Alex to cycle there.

If the distance is .... then t_{cyc} is ....

If the distance is .... then t_{cyc} is ....

If the speed is .... then t_{cyc} is ....

If the speed is .... then t_{cyc} is ....

higher | higher | lower | higher | lower | lower | higher | lower

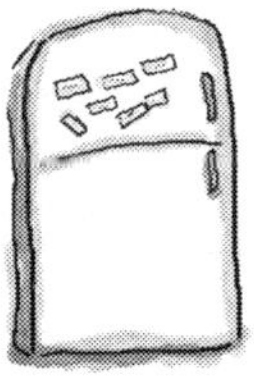

Pizza Delivery Magnets Solution

Your job is to use the magnets to explain how the **distance** to the house and the **speed** at which Alex cycles affect the **time** it takes him to get there. There are only two words on the magnets, but they all have a place on the pictures.

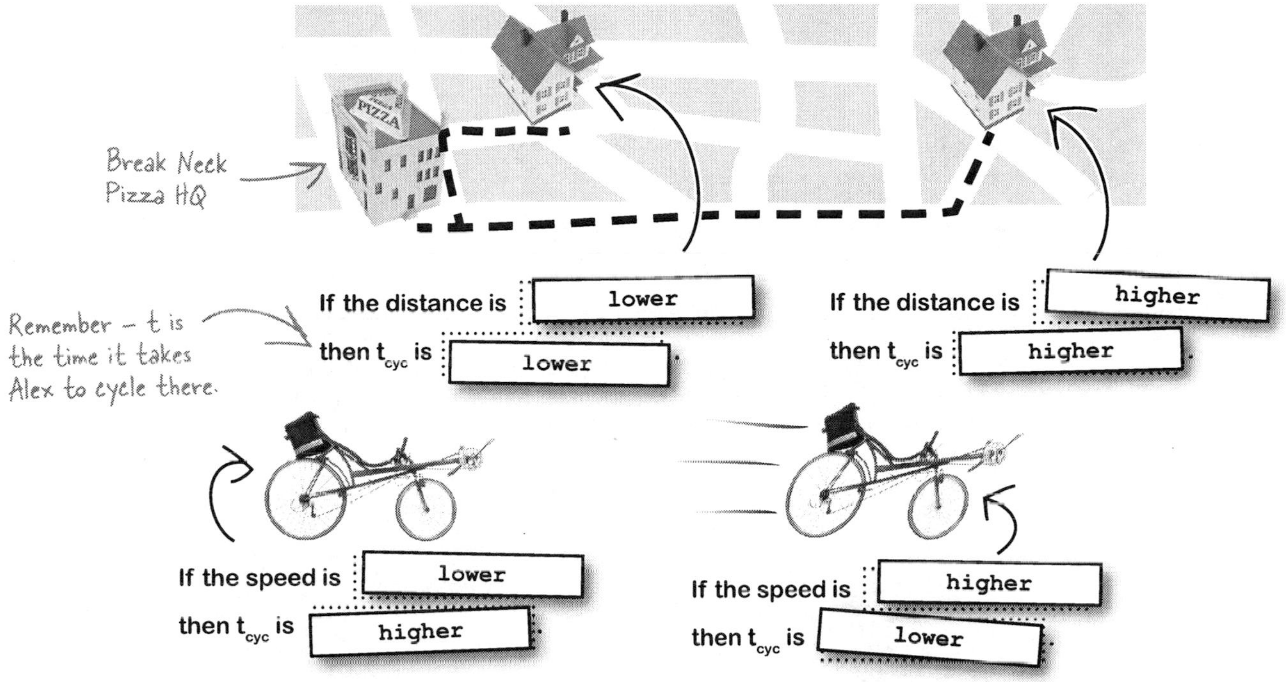

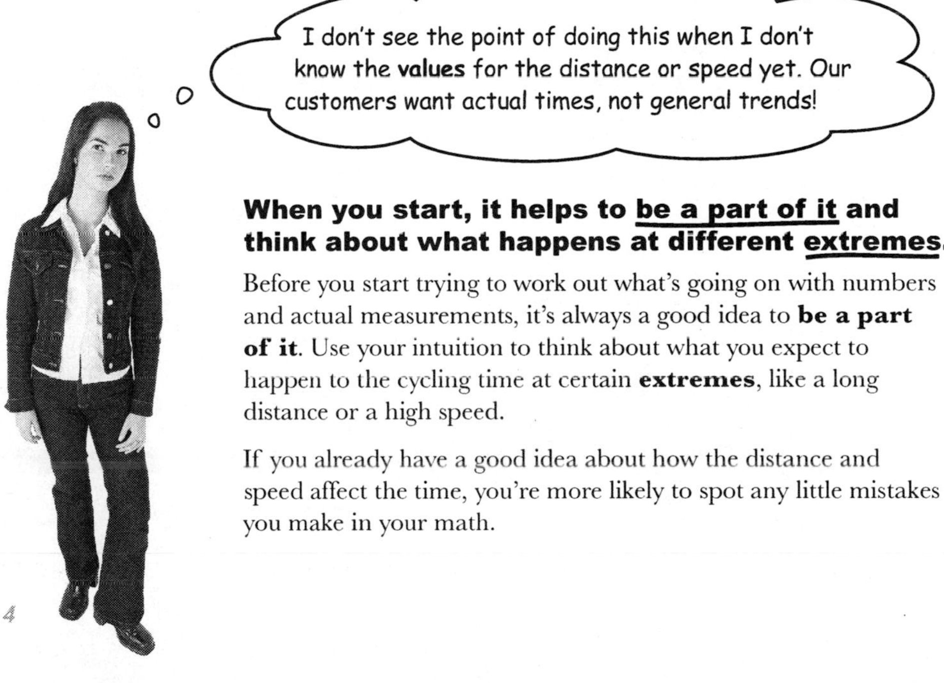

When you start, it helps to <u>be a part of it</u> and think about what happens at different <u>extremes</u>.

Before you start trying to work out what's going on with numbers and actual measurements, it's always a good idea to **be a part of it**. Use your intuition to think about what you expect to happen to the cycling time at certain **extremes**, like a long distance or a high speed.

If you already have a good idea about how the distance and speed affect the time, you're more likely to spot any little mistakes you make in your math.

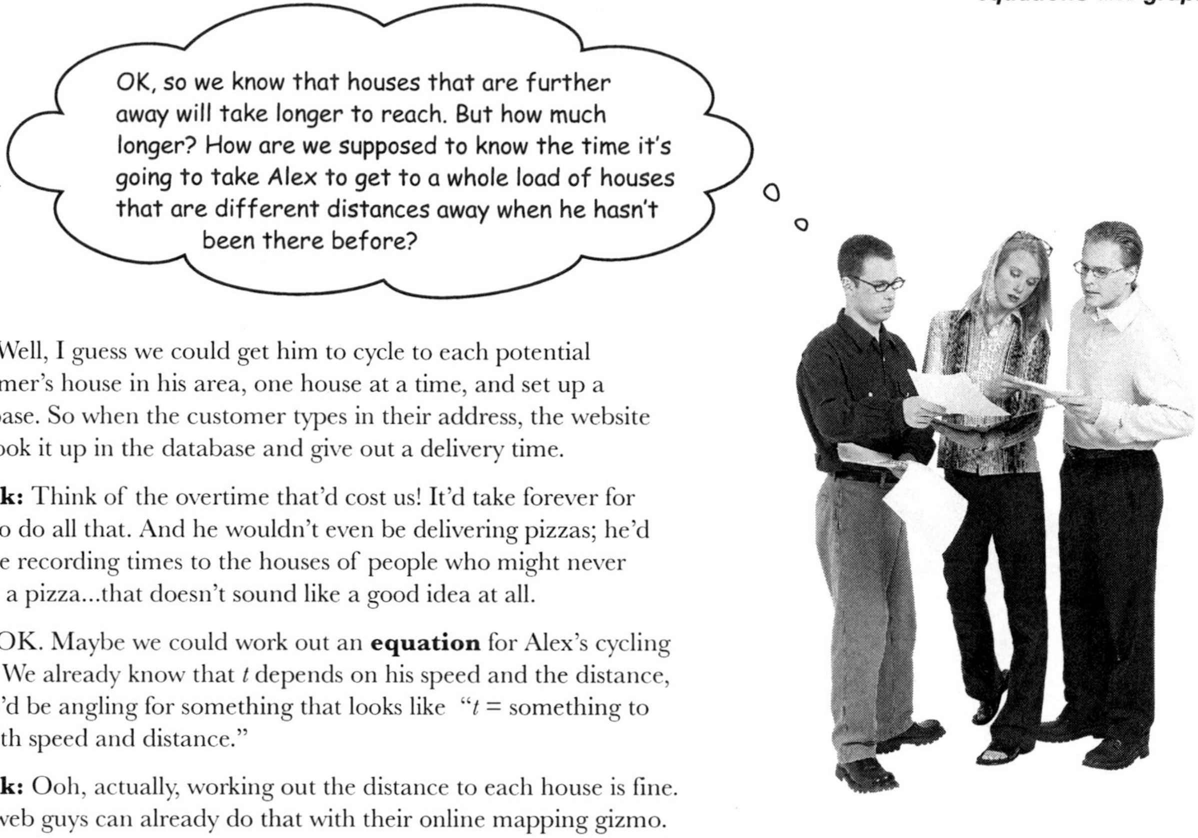

Joe: Well, I guess we could get him to cycle to each potential customer's house in his area, one house at a time, and set up a database. So when the customer types in their address, the website can look it up in the database and give out a delivery time.

Frank: Think of the overtime that'd cost us! It'd take forever for him to do all that. And he wouldn't even be delivering pizzas; he'd just be recording times to the houses of people who might never order a pizza...that doesn't sound like a good idea at all.

Joe: OK. Maybe we could work out an **equation** for Alex's cycling time. We already know that t depends on his speed and the distance, so we'd be angling for something that looks like "t = something to do with speed and distance."

Frank: Ooh, actually, working out the distance to each house is fine. The web guys can already do that with their online mapping gizmo.

Joe: We now need to work out Alex's speed, so we can try to use it in an equation. I know this sounds weird ... but we might try **being** Alex. Putting yourself in someone else's shoes is supposed to help you solve problems.

Frank: Like "Alex pushes the pedals, and the bike goes forward"? OK, let's brainstorm. So say I'm Alex, out delivering pizzas all evening. I don't want to ride too fast, or I'll get tired.

Joe: But I also don't want to ride too slow, or I won't deliver that many pizzas and won't get as many tips.

Frank: But I'm the top delivery guy, so I have the experience to start off riding at the best speed and to keep up that speed for the whole evening.

Jill: So Alex always rides at the **same speed**. Hmm, if we can work out his speed, could we use that and the **distances** from the mapping gizmo to work out the **time** it takes him reach a house?

Frank: I think you might be right. But how on earth are we supposed to work out what speed Alex rides at? And how do we use that to get a delivery time?

It usually helps to BE someone (or something), so you see what the physics looks like from inside the problem.

BRAIN POWER

How might it be possible to **measure** Alex's speed, so you can use it to work out cycling times for deliveries?

Joe: Well, if Alex always rides at the **same speed**, he should always cover the **same distance** in the **same amount of time**.

Frank: Ah ... I think I see what you mean. If Alex always goes at the same speed, and we **measure** his time for 1 km, it'll always take him that amount of time to cycle 1 km. But wouldn't we still need to time him over all possible distances to keep our bases covered?

Joe: I don't think we need to time Alex over lots of distances. If we time how long it takes him to cycle 1 km, we know, without having to time him again, that it'll take him twice as long to go 2 km.

Frank: Then, we can take his time for 1 km and say it'll take him half as long to go 0.5 km, and three times as long to go 3 km. I get it! So we only need to time him once to get his time for **any** distance.

Jill: I'm not so sure about only timing him once. A lot hangs on this- if we get the delivery times wrong, the customers get free pizza, and that's very expensive. Why don't we time him more than once over 1 km and take an **average** of all his times in case there's a bit of fluctuation between one run and the next?

Joe: A bit of **uncertainty**, you mean? That makes sense. And why don't we cover our bases by timing Alex over a variety of distances to make sure he does always ride at the same speed?

Jill: Sounds good to me.

Frank: Aren't we giving ourselves a harder calculation to do at the end though? If we just time Alex once over 1 km, it's easy to scale the time for a different distance - 2 km takes twice as long, 0.5 km takes half as long, and so forth. If we time him more than once over a variety of distances, how can we work them out?

Jill: If we work out Alex's speed in meters per second, we can use that to work out the time. So suppose he goes at 10 m/s; he'd cover 100 m in 10 s, 1 km in 100 s, and so on. We can estimate his time for any distance if it follows the same pattern.

Frank: OK, I think you've managed to convince me - especially since the town is relatively flat, so there aren't any hills to mess things up. Let's go **design** an experiment!

When you do an experiment, you should make multiple measurements so you get the best average possible.

I'm still not convinced about needing to make more than one measurement. Why would taking an average help me?

Making multiple measurements gives you an idea of how widely your results are spread out.

At the moment, you're assuming that Alex always rides at the same speed. But what if he doesn't, or if his speed varies between trips or at different distances?

If you only time Alex once, you have no idea how consistent his speed is. If you time him more than once, and his results have a wide **spread**, then you'll probably need to think again. But if his times are all similar to each other and close to the margin of **error** of your stopwatch, then you're good to go with their **average**.

The margin of error for a measuring device is ± half a scale division.

When you design an experiment, think about what might go wrong!

Making more than one measurement is just one way of **improving** your experiment. Everything in your experiment - Alex, the road, your tape measure, and your stopwatch - could cause you problems! If you don't think about the worst that could happen before you start, you could end up with useless results and no chance to repeat the experiment.

Would you really ask Alex to do it all again?

Sharpen your pencil

Think about what might go wrong with all the things in your experiment - and how you would make sure the worst didn't happen.

Item involved in experiment	Potential source(s) of error	How to deal with this
Alex and his bike	Alex's speed is inconsistent.	Time him more than once over a distance, and take an average.
The road		
Tape measure		
Stopwatch	The watch doesn't start at the right time.	

There might be more than one thing that could go wrong with each item.

Design experiment

Sharpen your pencil Solution

Think about what might go wrong with all the things in your experiment - and how you would make sure the worst didn't happen.

Item involved in experiment	Potential source(s) of error	How to deal with this
Alex and his bike	Alex's speed is inconsistent. Alex gets tired as he cycles longer.	Time him more than once over a distance and take an average. Time him over both long and short distances.
The road	The road might not be flat. Alex would be slower uphill and faster downhill.	Make sure you do the experiment on a flat piece of road.
Tape measure	The tape measure might have stretched with use and not be accurate.	Test it against something you know is OK before you use it.
Stopwatch	The watch doesn't start at the right time. The watch doesn't stop at the right time.	Make sure you and Alex agree on a timing protocol before you start.

Don't worry if you said some other things, or if you didn't come up with every single one of these possibilities.

Most of the sources of error in the table would **bias** the results in one particular direction. I'm not sure I can sort that out by making lots of measurements and taking averages.

There are two different types of errors- random and systematic.

You already realized that if Alex's speed isn't 100% consistent, his times will be **spread** around. This is similar to the range that a measurement may fall into due to your measuring device having scale divisions (like your myPod measurements). If Alex's times aren't too different for each ride, you can reduce the **random error** by making **several measurements** and taking an **average**.

Some sources of error are built into the system. If you time Alex going downhill, he will be faster than he would around the town, which is mostly flat. If the tape measure has stretched, the actual distance will be shorter than you think it is. Errors like these are called **systematic errors,** and they **bias** the results in one particular direction. Taking averages doesn't help reduce bias, as all the results will be higher (or lower) in the direction of the bias. You need to spot them in advance and **plan ahead** to minimize them.

Random errors involve SPREAD. Minimize them by AVERAGING.

Systematic errors involve BIAS. Minimize them by PLANNING ahead.

OK - time to recap where you're at...

Exercise

You're designing an experiment to help Break Neck Pizza with their website, on a spare napkin (as all good physicists do), but unfortunately, some of the words have succumbed to pizza grease.

Fill in the blanks using the words at the bottom of the box.

You might not use all of the words, and you may use some more than once!

Experiment to help Break Neck Pizza find out the ____ it takes Alex to cycle any ____

Although I really want a delivery ____ I think the best way to do this is to work out Alex's ____ - he says he cycles at a constant ____ all evening.

I'm going to measure out several ____ with a tape measure, making sure the ground is ____ and that the tape measure isn't warped to reduce ____ errors.

I'm going to ____ each measurement ____ and take an ____ to try to cut down on ____ errors.

Then I can ____ from the ____ and ____ I measured to work out a delivery ____ for any house, any ____ away.

This means use the results you already have for some values to work out what the result would be for any value.

Missing words: **speed, three times, extrapolate, direction, systematic, distance, once, repeat, average, time, distances, random, flat, times**

Conduct an experiment to find out Alex's speed

You need to give Break Neck Pizza's customers a delivery **time**. It's important not to get this wrong since you'll have to give out free pizza if you do!

You've decided to do an **experiment** to find out Alex's speed when he's out delivering pizzas. Then you can use that to work out the **time** it takes him to cover any **distance**.

You're timing Alex over three different distances, three times for each distance. That way you'll be able to spot how consistent Alex's speed is and smooth over **random errors**. These crop up because you can't recreate exactly the same conditions each time, and because your measuring devices can't possibly be accurate to the nearest fraction of an atom! You've also thought of possible sources of **systematic** error and made sure your equipment is up to scratch.

Experiment to help Break Neck Pizza find out the time it takes Alex to cycle any distance.

Although I really want a delivery time, I think the best way to do this is to work out Alex's speed – he says he cycles at a constant speed all evening.

I'm going to measure out several distances with a tape measure, making sure the ground is flat and that the tape measure isn't warped to reduce systematic errors.

I'm going to repeat each measurement three times and take an average to try to cut down on random errors.

Then I can extrapolate from the times and distances I measured to work out a delivery time for any house, any distance away.

Exercise Solution

Here's what happens:

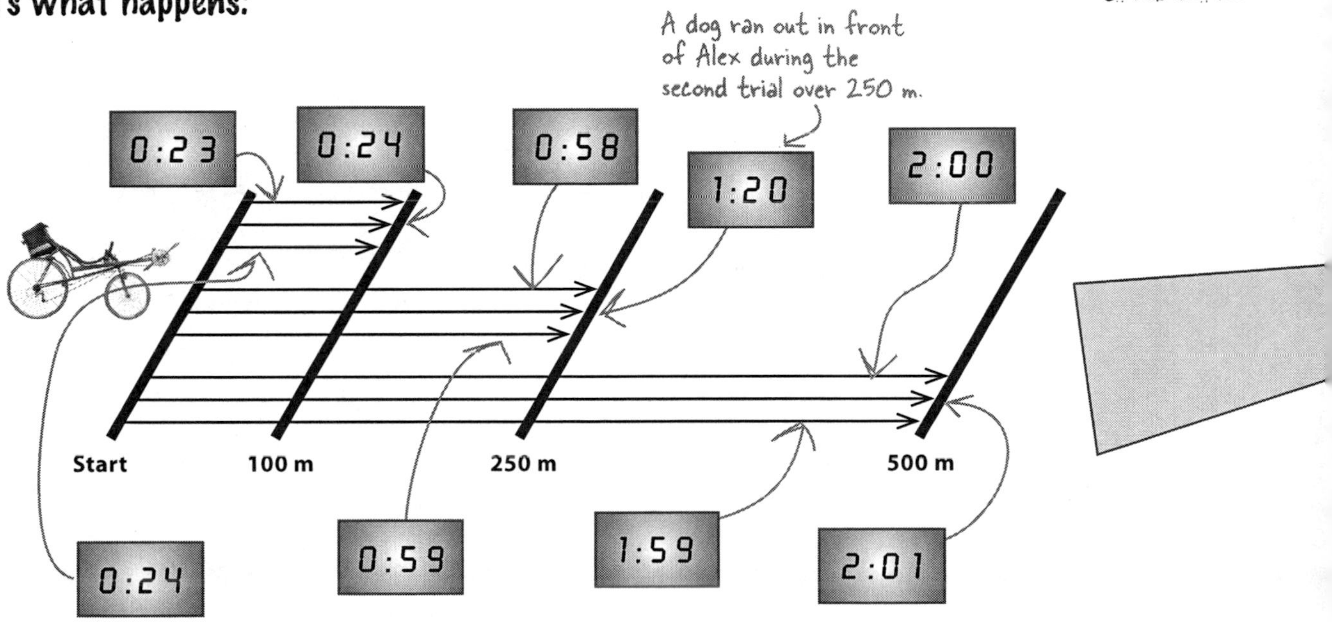

Write down your results... in a table

As you're doing your experiment, write your results down in a **table.** This keeps all your related pieces of information next to each other, in rows or columns. You're less likely to make a mistake writing down a measurement if you use a table. It's also much easier to see what's going on and **spot patterns** in your experiment

The **headings** for your table should go in the top row, with the thing you're changing on the left, and the thing(s) you're measuring to the right. You should put the **units** of each column in the headings.

As you make measurements for your experiment, write them down in a TABLE.

Sharpen your pencil

Put units in the headings so that the table just has numbers in it.

Fill in the table using the results shown on the opposite page.
You'll need to add some extra information to the table headers as well.

Put your headings in the top row.

Your values go in these rows.

Distance Alex cycles ( )	Time 1 (s)	Time 2 ( )	Time 3 ( )	Average time ( )
500	120			

Put the thing you're varying in the left hand column, in order of size.

Anything you're measuring should go in columns to the right.

If you're averaging your measurements, this should be to the right of the measurements themselves.

Transfer your experimental results into the table.

Tables help you keep your results ordered and make it easier for you to spot patterns.

Design experiment | Carry out experiment | **Look at results**

Sharpen your pencil Solution

Is it fair to include the 80 seconds in this average, considering a dog got in his way and slowed him down?

Fill in the table using the results shown on the opposite page.
You'll need to add some extra information to the table headers as well.

Distance Alex cycles (m)	Time 1 (s)	Time 2 (s)	Time 3 (s)	Average time (s)
100	23	24	24	23.7 (3 sd)
250	58	80	59	~~65.7~~ (3 sd) 58.5
500	120	121	119	120 (3 sd)

Remember to say what UNITS you're using.

You'll usually lose points every time you don't mention units. That adds up pretty quickly!

If you don't include the off measurement, then the average time for 250 m becomes 58.5 s.

Look out for measurements that don't fit.

One of the reasons for timing Alex more then once over each distance was to assess the **spread** (or **scatter**) of his results. If he can't ride at a consistent speed, you'll have to think again about your whole approach.

In this experiment, all of the times for each distance are close together, with a spread similar to your stopwatch's margin of error. However, there's one time that's way off. The 80 s measurement for Alex going 250 m sticks out, and you need to think about why. Is it because Alex isn't very consistent - or did something go wrong just that one time?

If the measurements are spread out because Alex is **inconsistent**, you should probably make more and more measurements at each distance, so you can get a better idea of the spread and take a better **average**.

If there's a good **reason** for the outlying data (which there is here because a dog ran out in front of him), then it's OK to **discard** the measurement since it's not representative.

But if you don't have a good reason to discard it, then it's gotta stay in there!

Thinking about where your outliers may have come from will help you to improve your experimental setup and reduce errors.

If a measurement doesn't fit, think about WHY it doesn't before deciding what to do with it.

Use the table of distances and times to work out Alex's speed

Now that you have a table of distances and times, you can work out Alex's speed. Speed is measured in miles per hour, kilometers per hour, or meters per second. "Per" means "divided by," so whatever the **units**, the **dimensions** of speed are **distance divided by time**. And the speed itself is the change in the distance Alex has gone since he started divided by the change in the time that's gone by since he started.

Don't worry too much about the 'change in' bit for now. You'll see why it's really important later on in the chapter.

$$\text{speed} = \frac{\text{(change in) distance}}{\text{(change in) time}}$$

kilometers per hour

You already knew this equation because you already knew the units!

Once you've worked out Alex's speed, you can give the customer a delivery time for any distance.

Sharpen your pencil

Using the equation above, work out Alex's speed for each of the distances in the table.

Distance Alex cycles (m)	Average time (s)	Average speed (meters per second)
100	23.7	
250	58.5	
500	120.0	

There's space down here for your WORK (doing the speed calculations and converting the units).

You can work out the equation for speed using its UNITS - "miles per hour," "kilometers per hour," and so on. Speed is distance divided by time.

Strictly speaking, this reasoning only works for simple equations. But here you intuitively know it's right.

Sharpen your pencil Solution

Using the equation, work out Alex's speed for each of the distances in the table:

$$\text{speed} = \frac{\text{(change in) distance}}{\text{(change in) time}}$$

Distance Alex cycles (m)	Average time (s)	Average speed (meters per second)
100	23.7	4.22 (3 sd)
250	58.5	4.27 (3 sd)
500	120.0	4.17 (3 sd)

3 sd means "3 significant digits."

Remember to EXPLAIN what you're doing.

For the 100 m distance:

$$\text{speed} = \frac{\text{distance}}{\text{time}} = \frac{100 \text{ m}}{23.7 \text{ s}} = 4.22 \text{ meters per second}$$

For the 250 m distance:

$$\text{speed} = \frac{\text{distance}}{\text{time}} = \frac{250 \text{ m}}{58.5 \text{ s}} = 4.27 \text{ meters per second}$$

For the 500 m distance:

$$\text{speed} = \frac{\text{distance}}{\text{time}} = \frac{500 \text{ m}}{120.0 \text{ s}} = 4.17 \text{ meters per second}$$

How can there be a different answer every time for the average speed? There must have been something **wrong** with the experiment!

It's OK - there will be some spread in your experimental results due to random errors.

For a start, the error on each of your measurements is ± half a scale division. Then there are random fluctuations in things you don't have control over - tiny changes in wind speed, the exact state of Alex's tires, tiny changes in the surface of the road, and so on.

When you measure the same thing more than once, you shouldn't expect exactly the same answer each time.

Random errors mean that results will be spread out

Random errors mean that your experimental results will be **spread** around an **average**. If they're not spread out very much, your results are said to be **precise**.

However, if you have an underlying **systematic** error that's biasing your results in one particular direction (like if the stopwatch is consistently started at the wrong time), then you won't be able to work out an **accurate** value by taking an **average**.

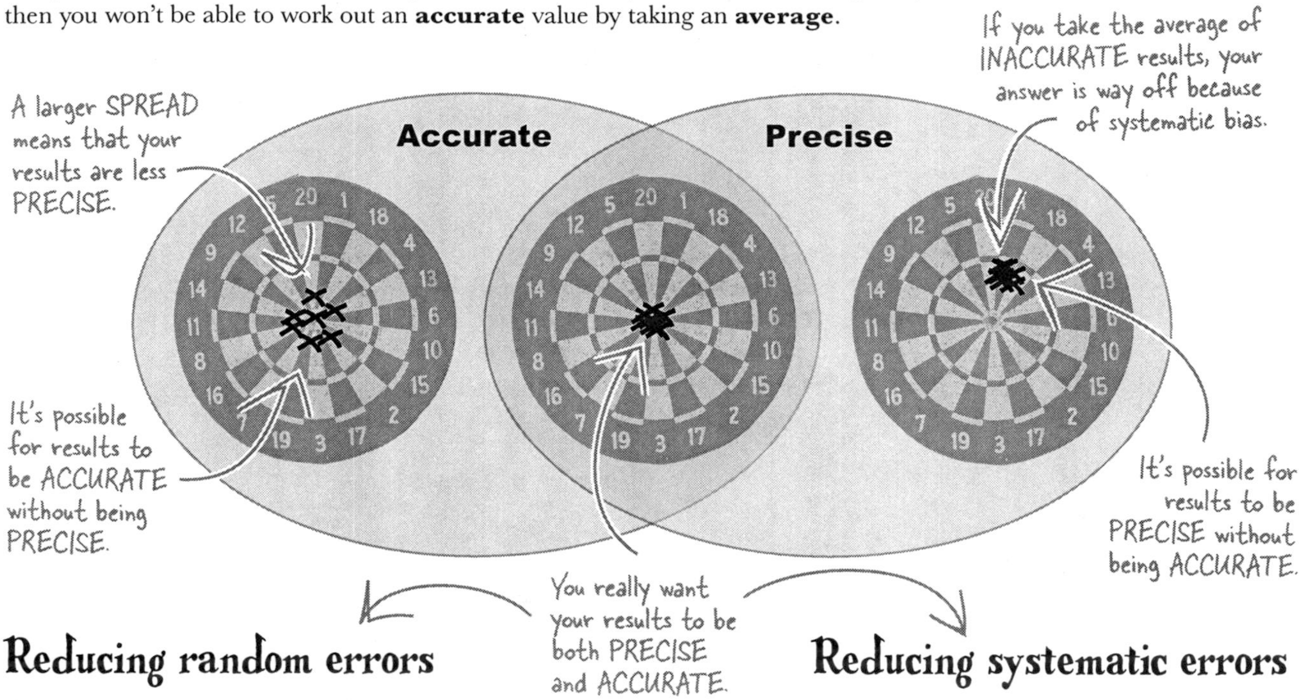

Reducing random errors improves your precision.

Reducing systematic errors improves your accuracy.

there are no Dumb Questions

Q: So I can reduce random errors by choosing a more accurate measuring device?

A: You mean a more precise measuring device. Smaller scale divisions mean a smaller spread and lead to greater precision. A more accurate device would be one that reads true values.

Q: So could I get perfect precision as long as I use a fine enough scale division?

A: Not quite. At very small scale divisions, you get **random** fluctuations (errors), e.g., the distance read by a micrometer is affected by surface imperfections, and the reading on a balance by tiny air currents.

Q: OK, but the spread in Alex's speeds isn't because of things like that, is it?

A: It's impossible to set up your experiment with exactly the same initial conditions, right down to the position of every atom, each time. Your results will always have some kind of spread whatever you do.

Q: That's annoying. I worked out an average speed over three distances, and it came out different each time. How do I decide what the best average is?

A: You really need **a better way of taking averages**. We're just getting on to that now ...

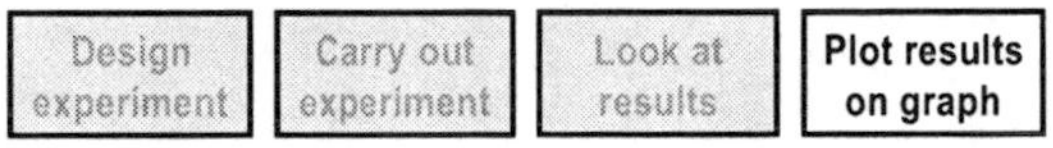

A graph is the best way of taking an average of ALL your results

So far you've been taking the average of one set of results at a time - but the average times (and, therefore, average speeds) for each distance are slightly different. You can kind of think of this as a 'one-dimensional' average.

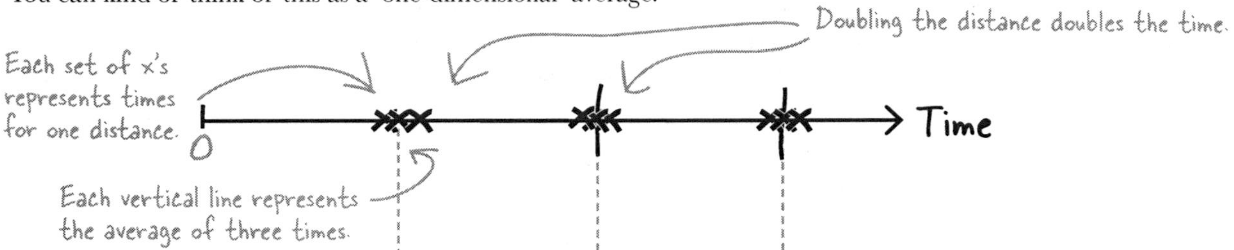

The best way to work out the average speed across **all** of your results is to draw a **graph**. Since you're expecting the time to double every time you double the distance, triple every time you triple the distance, and so on, your measurements will lie along a **straight line**. You can kind of think of this as taking a 'two-dimensional' average, as you're using two axes for your plot and are able to include measurements made for different distances on the same graph.

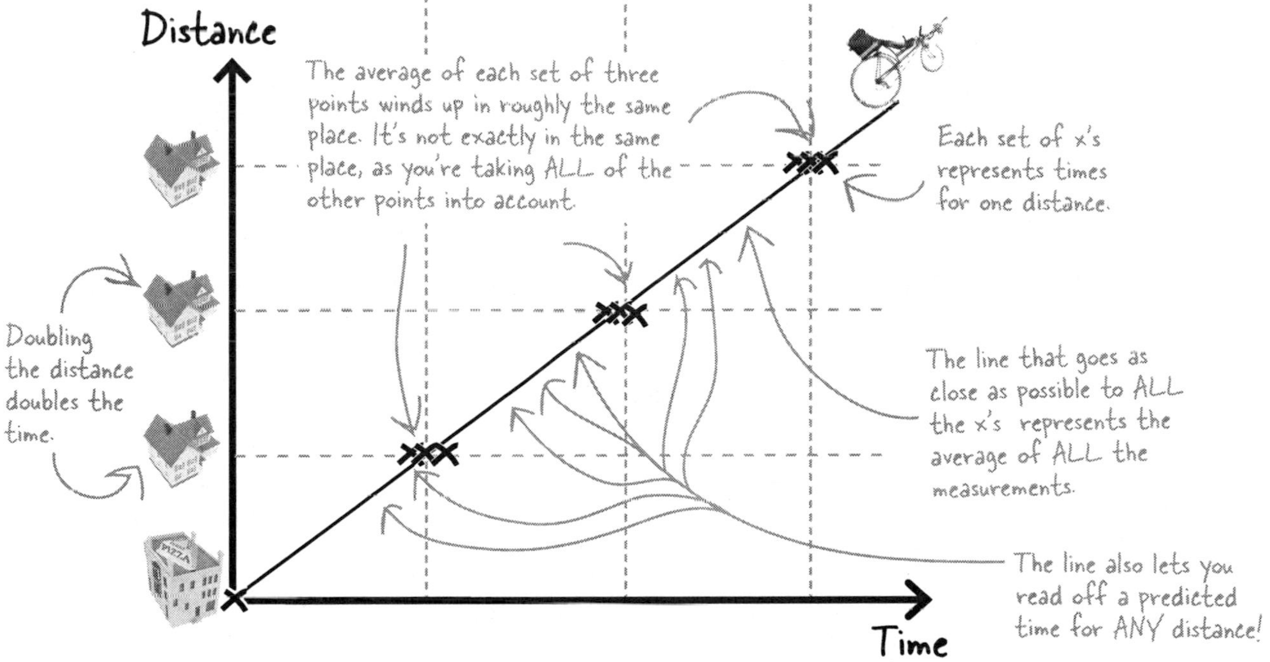

This also has the advantage of giving you a way of reading off the time it should take to cover any distance.

As is often the case in physics, a picture speaks a thousand words!

A Graph Up Close

You've probably drawn graphs before, so here's a quick refresher.

The most important thing is to make it clear **what** your graph is representing! That means you need a **title**, **labels** for each of your axes, and **units** along each axis.

Plot your points by putting the center of an '**x**' exactly where your measurement is.

If you're expecting each thing you've plotted to double when you double the other thing, draw the best **straight line** you can through **all the points** on your graph. This takes the best **average** possible of all your data and allows you to read off extra values by **interpolating** (for values that lie between your measurements) or **extrapolating** (for points that lie beyond the range of your measurements).

This graph isn't of the experiment you did with Alex - that's your job on the next page! It's another graph where the doubling thing happens - the cost vs. volume of pizza sauce!

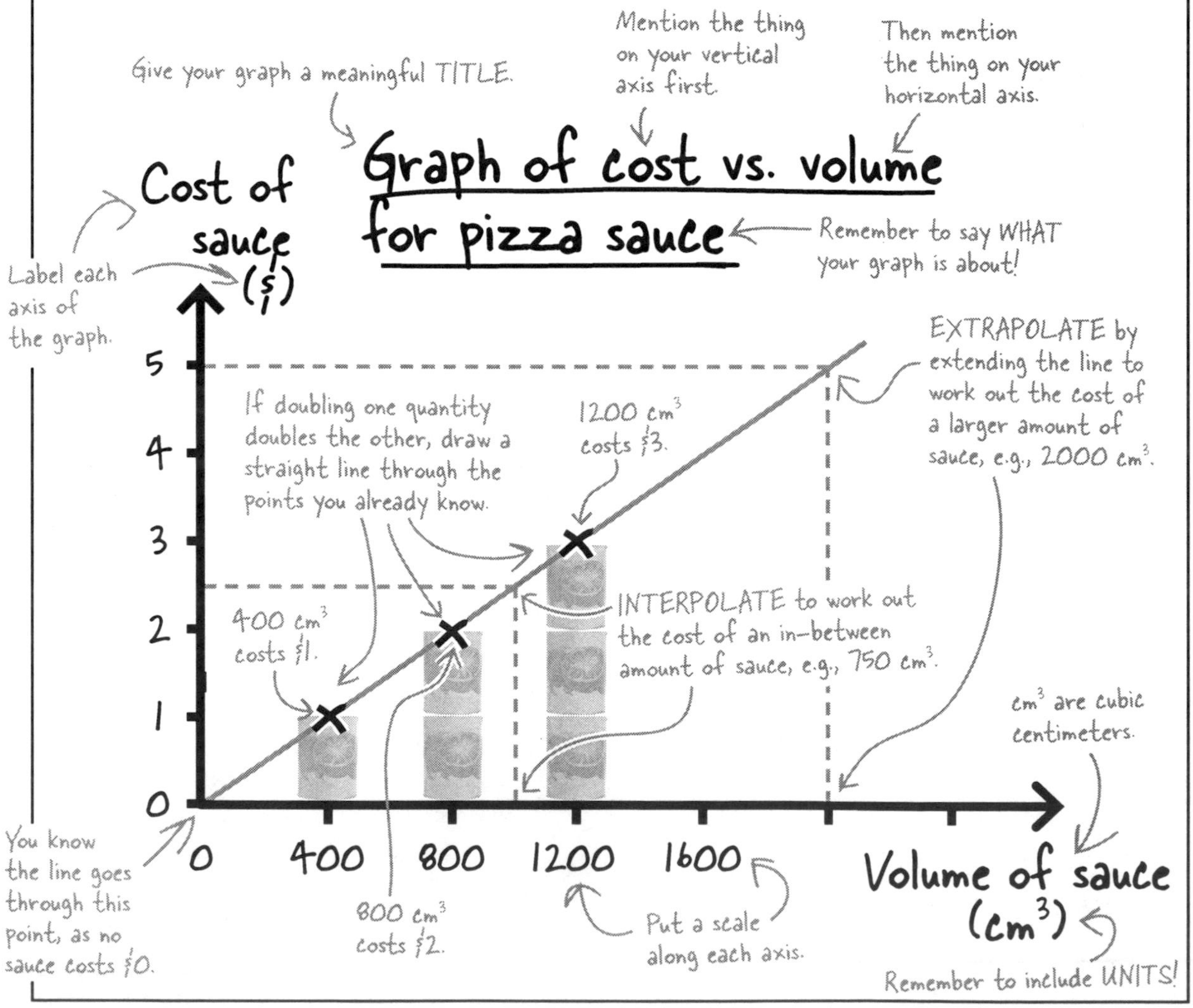

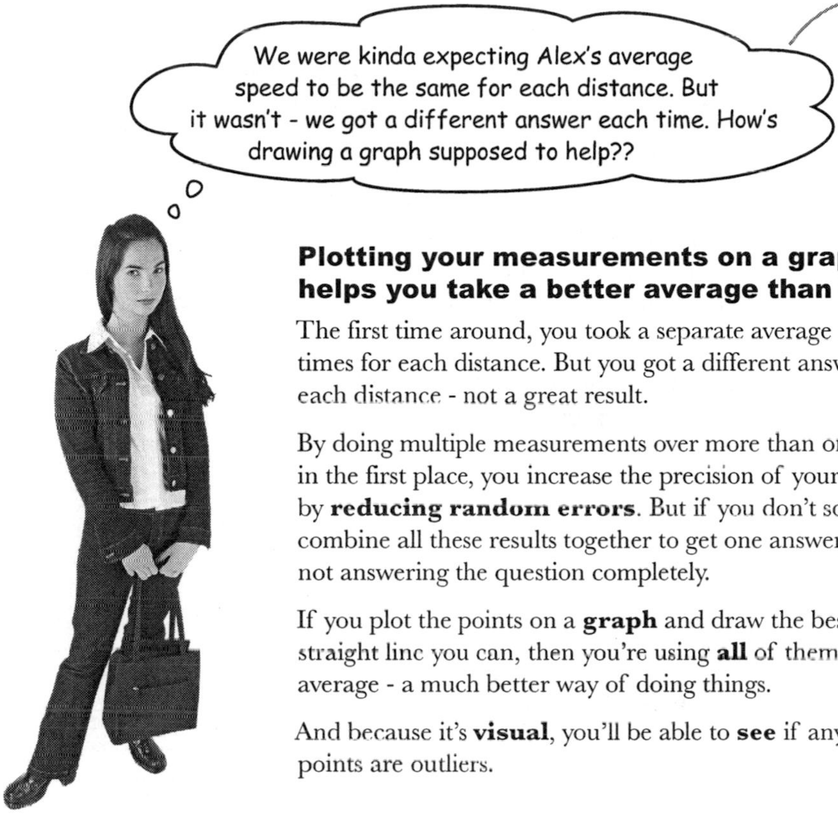

(s)	Average speed (meters per second)
	4.22 (3 sd)
	4.27 (3 sd)
	4.17 (3 sd)

Plotting your measurements on a graph helps you take a better average than before.

The first time around, you took a separate average of Alex's times for each distance. But you got a different answer for each distance - not a great result.

By doing multiple measurements over more than one distance in the first place, you increase the precision of your result by **reducing random errors**. But if you don't somehow combine all these results together to get one answer, you're not answering the question completely.

If you plot the points on a **graph** and draw the best-fitting straight line you can, then you're using **all** of them to take an average - a much better way of doing things.

And because it's **visual**, you'll be able to **see** if any of your points are outliers.

Fitting a line to a graph is like taking an 'informed average.'

Graph-drawing Tips

- If you're plotting how something changes with time, then **time always goes along the horizontal axis**.
- Look at the **extremes** of your data - the largest and smallest numbers. Choose a scale that allows you to use most of the paper.
- Remember to mention your **units** on the axes!
- Plot points using a small **x** (not a dot), so you can still see the points after you have joined them up.
- Join the points freehand with a **smooth line** unless you know that a straight line is more appropriate (e.g., if someone went at a steady speed).
- Drawing a straight line through your points is like taking an **average**, except in a better, more visual way than you did before in your table.
- Give your graph a meaningful **title** that makes its **context** clear.

Use these tips to help you with this exercise.

Use a graph to show Alex's time for ANY distance

Alex is good at sticking to the same speed. This means that if you double the distance, then the time he takes to cover the new distance will double accordingly.

In other words, the distance and time points should lie along a **straight line** when you plot them on a graph (give or take experimental error). And once you've plotted a graph, you can read off Alex's time for **any** distance.

Just like the cost and amount of sauce did

Sharpen your pencil

Distance Alex cycles (m)	Time 1 (s)	Time 2 (s)	Time 3 (s)
100	23	24	24
250	58	80	59
500	120	121	119

a) Plot the measurements from the table as points on the graph (you can skip the outliers).

b) Then draw a **best fit straight line** through the points so that you can read off the time it'll take Alex to travel **any** distance.

c) How long do you think it'll take Alex to travel 400 m?

....

d) And how would you work out his time for a house 1040 m away?

....

....

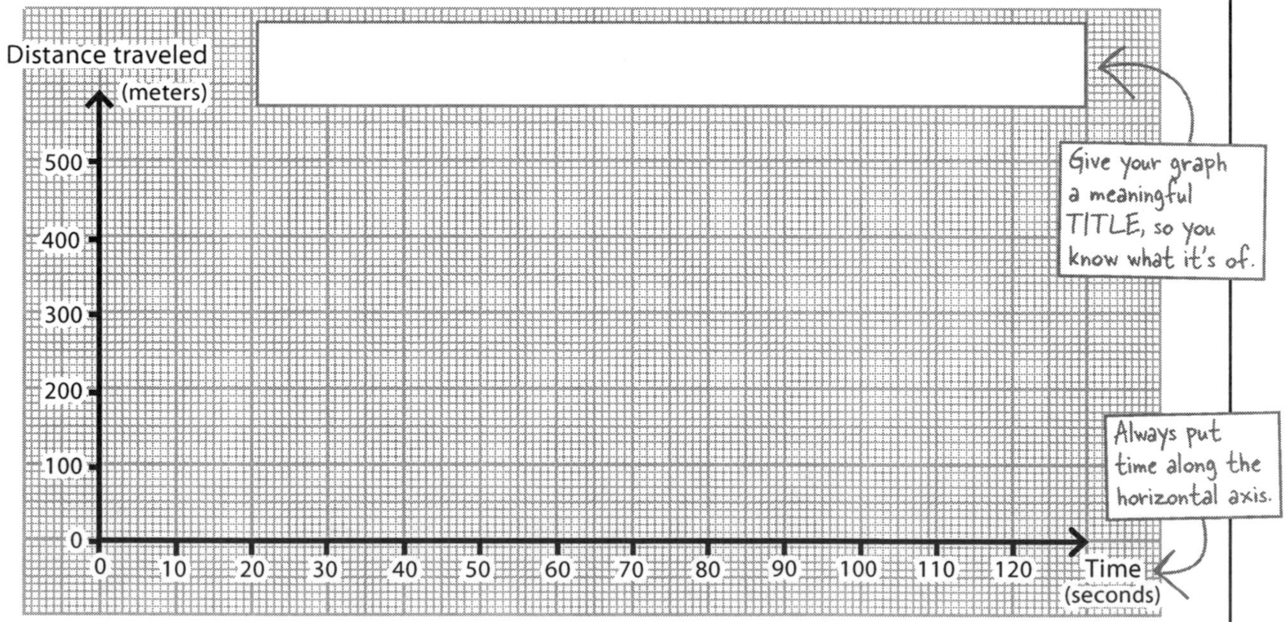

The line on the graph is your best estimate for how long Alex takes to cycle ANY distance

Now that you've drawn a graph, you can use it to read off ANY distance Alex may have to travel by extending the straight line you drew, and estimating the pattern or **extrapolating** from that.

So for example, if a house is 1040 m away (much further than any of the distances we got Alex to bike in the experiment), you can extend the graph and straight line to find out that it would take him 250 seconds to get there. The graph works!

There's only one problem - how to get the graph "into" the Break Neck website, so it can give the time to the customer.

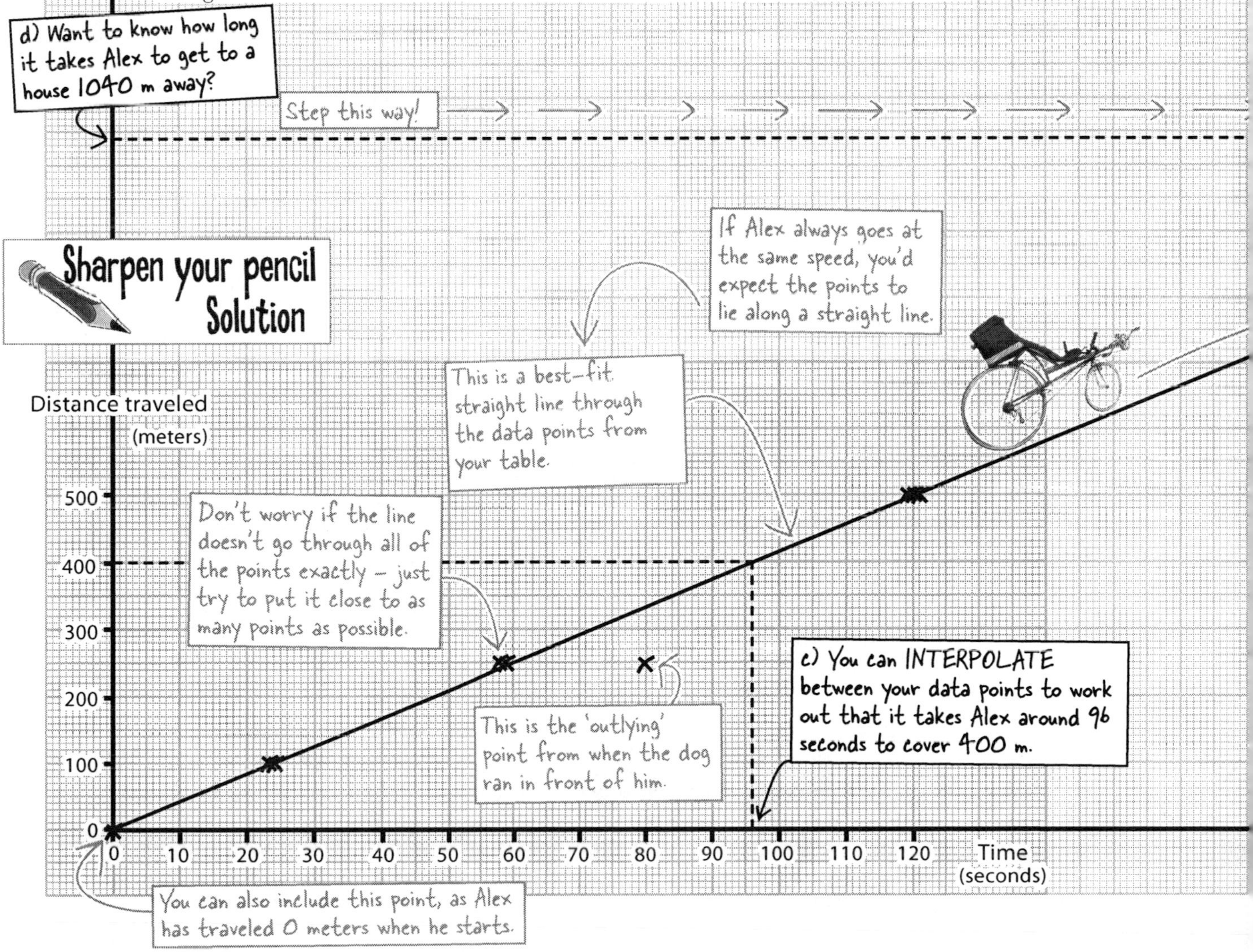

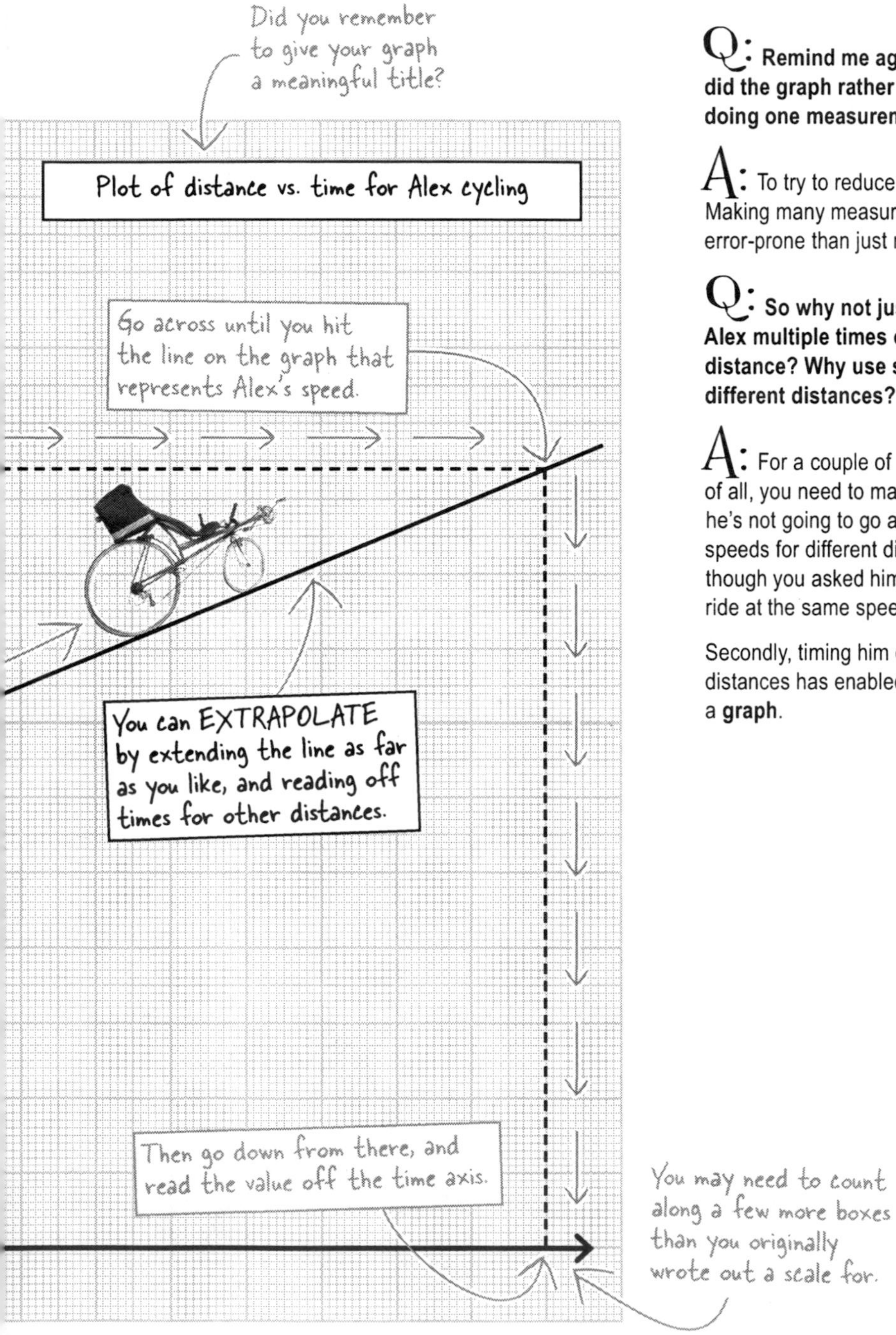

there are no Dumb Questions

Q: Remind me again why we did the graph rather than just doing one measurement?

A: To try to reduce the errors. Making many measurements is less error-prone than just making one.

Q: So why not just measure Alex multiple times over one distance? Why use several different distances?

A: For a couple of reasons. First of all, you need to make sure that he's not going to go at different speeds for different distances (even though you asked him to try and ride at the same speed each time).

Secondly, timing him over several distances has enabled you to draw a **graph**.

Q: So why not be like a spreadsheet program and join the points properly? Why draw a line that doesn't even go through some of the points?

A: Doing a best-fit straight line effectively takes an **average** of your measurements. If Alex goes at the same speed the whole way, you'd expect the points to all lie along a straight line. Errors mean that they don't. You're trying to 'find' the line that the errors have obscured. A graph allows you to see where **outlying** points are. You can then make them count less by not going so near them with your line.

You can see Alex's speed from the steepness of the distance-time graph

If you SEE it, you get it!

The distance-time graph not only lets you read off values, but it also lets you **see** how fast something's going at a glance.

The faster someone is, the greater the distance they go in a set time. When you plot their distance-time graph, you'll see its **slope** (or **gradient**) is steeper compared to someone who's slower. The **higher** the speed, the **steeper** the slope of the distance-time graph.

So if Alex raced against the delivery personnel from some of Break Neck's rivals (all going at their steady delivery speed), you'd be able to pick the winner in advance from the slope of their distance-time graphs.

In physics, the steepness of a graph is called its SLOPE.

The slope can also be called the gradient – they're the same thing.

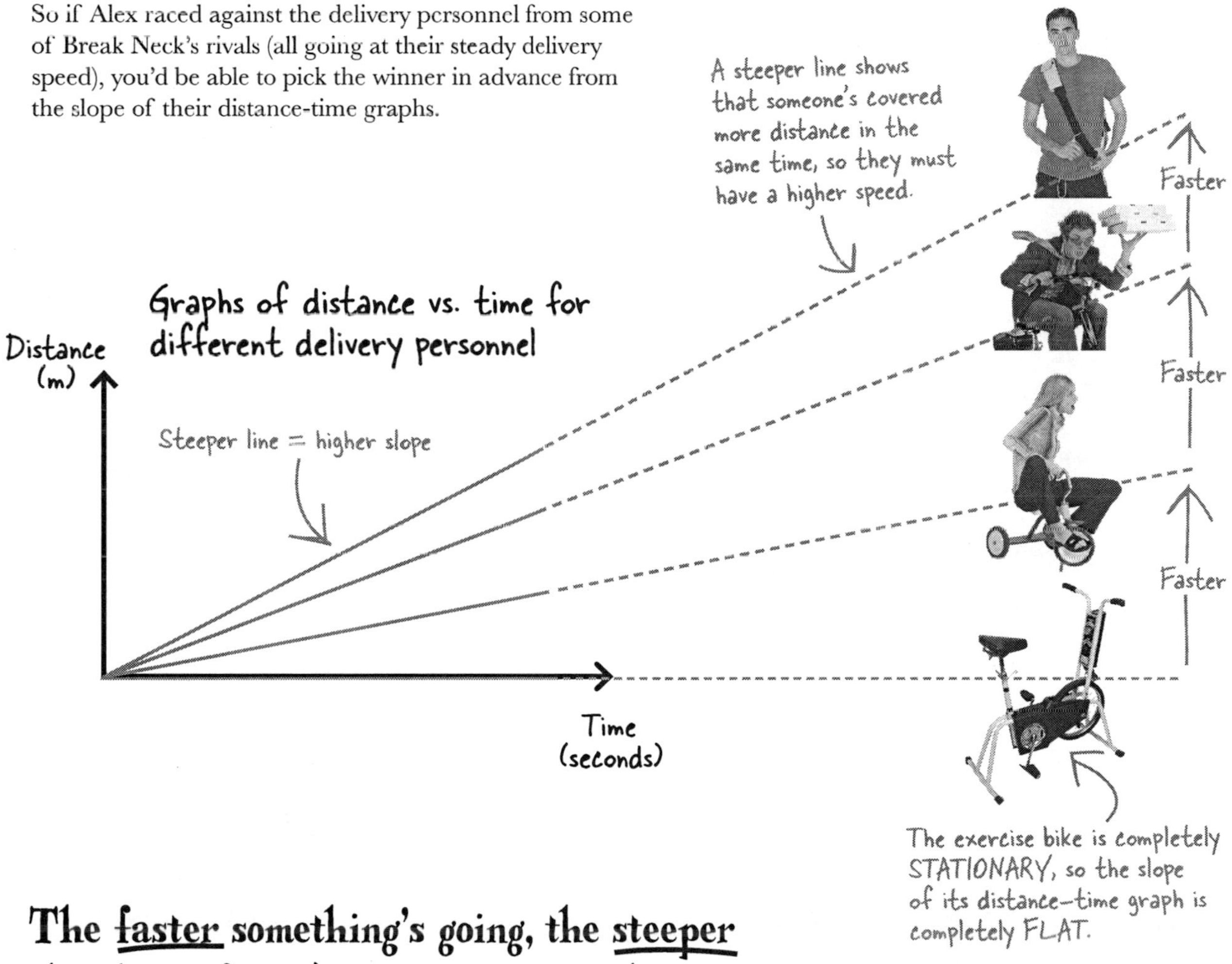

The faster something's going, the steeper the slope of its distance-time graph.

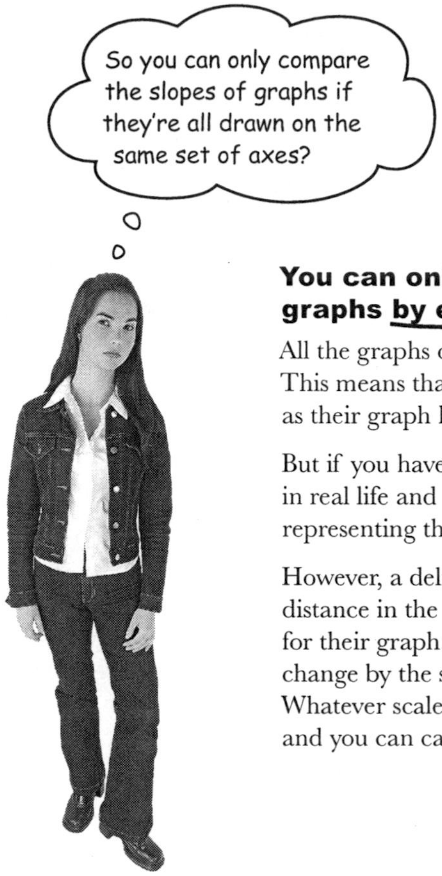

You can only compare the slopes of graphs by eye if they have the same scale.

All the graphs on the opposite page have the same **scale**. This means that you can just **see** who's going the fastest, as their graph has the steepest slope.

This is being qualitative, like saying "this one's faster" or "this one's slower" but without mentioning any numbers.

But if you have one graph where 1 cm on paper = 200 m in real life and another where 1 cm = 10 m, then a line representing the same thing will look very different.

Which means to do things with numbers so that the website can give the customer a delivery time

However, a delivery person will still cover the same distance in the same time no matter which scale you use for their graph. So the distance on their graph will still change by the same number of meters in the same time. Whatever scale it's drawn at, the numbers don't change, and you can calculate a value for the slope.

This means doing things with numbers (so that the website can give the customer a delivery time).

To be quantitative, you have to calculate the slope of your graph using numbers.

If you calculate the slope of your distance-time graph, it'll give you an **equation** which will show you how the distance and time relate to each other. And as Alex's **speed** is (change in) distance divided by (change in) time, you'll be able to work that out. This is what you really want for the Break Neck Pizza website!

When you calculate the slope of a graph, you get an equation which shows you how the two things you plotted on the graph relate to each other.

Alex's speed is the slope of the distance-time graph

To calculate the slope of a straight line graph, pick two points on it, and work out the **change in the vertical direction** divided by the **change in the horizontal direction**. The steeper the graph, the larger the slope.

On your graph, the vertical axis is distance, and the horizontal axis is time. So the slope of your graph is **change in distance** divided by **change in time** - exactly the same as your equation for Alex's **speed**.

To save time, you can use shorthand 'Δ' which means "change in." So "change in distance" is Δ distance.

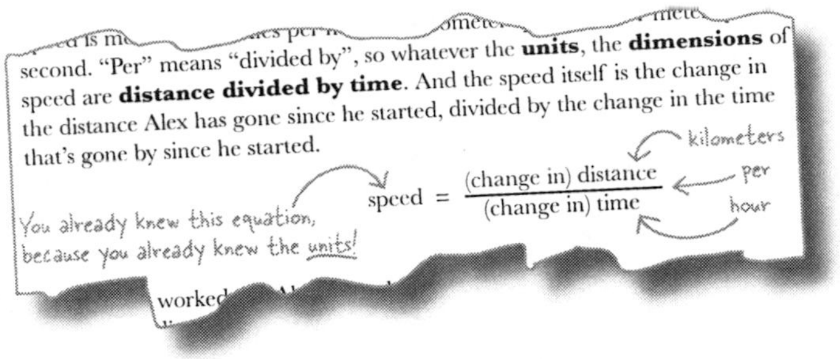

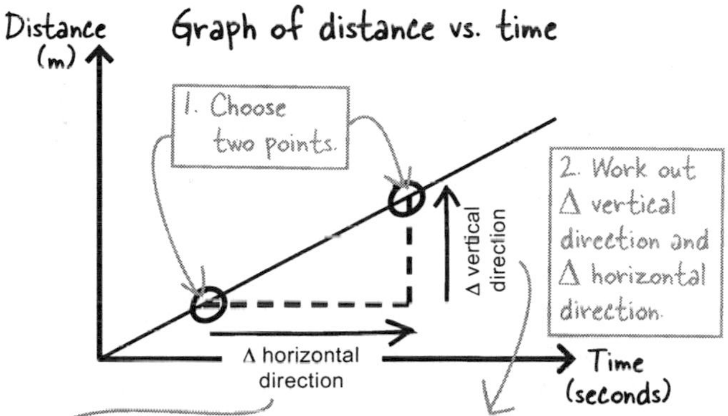

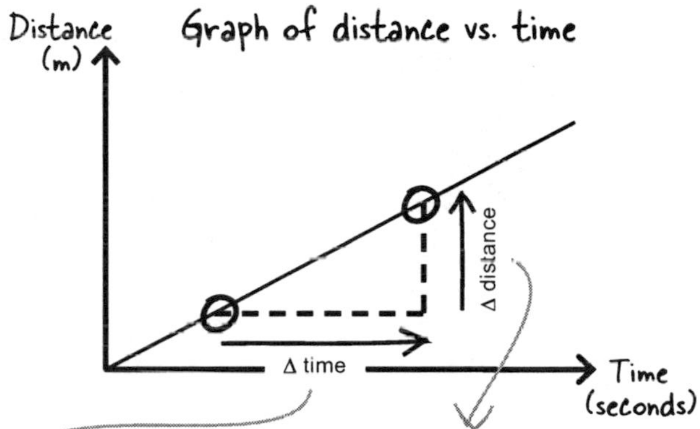

$$\text{Slope} = \frac{\Delta \text{ vertical direction}}{\Delta \text{ horizontal direction}}$$

$$\text{Speed} = \frac{\Delta \text{ distance}}{\Delta \text{ time}}$$

Slope-calculating tips

- You need to choose **two** points **on your line** to calculate its slope.
- Try to find points where your line crosses the gridlines on the graph paper so that the numbers you use are whole numbers of gridline divisions.
- Choose two points that are far apart from each other - this makes your calculation more accurate.
- The slope is the change in the vertical direction (between your two points) divided by the change in the horizontal direction (between your two points).
- Remember to write down the equation for the slope before putting the numbers in.
- Always subtract the coordinates of the left-most point from the coordinates of the right-most point.
- When you've calculated the slope, look back at the graph to see if your answer SUCKs. A slope of 2 would mean that the graph goes up 2 for every 1 you go across. Does your graph look the same as your numerical answer?
- Remember to include units in your answer.

Use these tips to help you work out the slope of Alex's distance-time graph.

Now work out Alex's average speed from your graph

Sharpen your pencil

a. Choose two points on the line, and calculate the **slope** of the distance-time graph. Use the tips on the opposite page to help you.

b. What do you notice about the **units** of your answer?

This may just have something to do with Alex's speed ...

Design experiment | Carry out experiment | Look at results | Plot results on graph | **Calculate slope**

Sharpen your pencil Solution

a. Choose two points on the line, and calculate the **slope** of the distance-time graph.

b. What do you notice about the **units** of your answer?

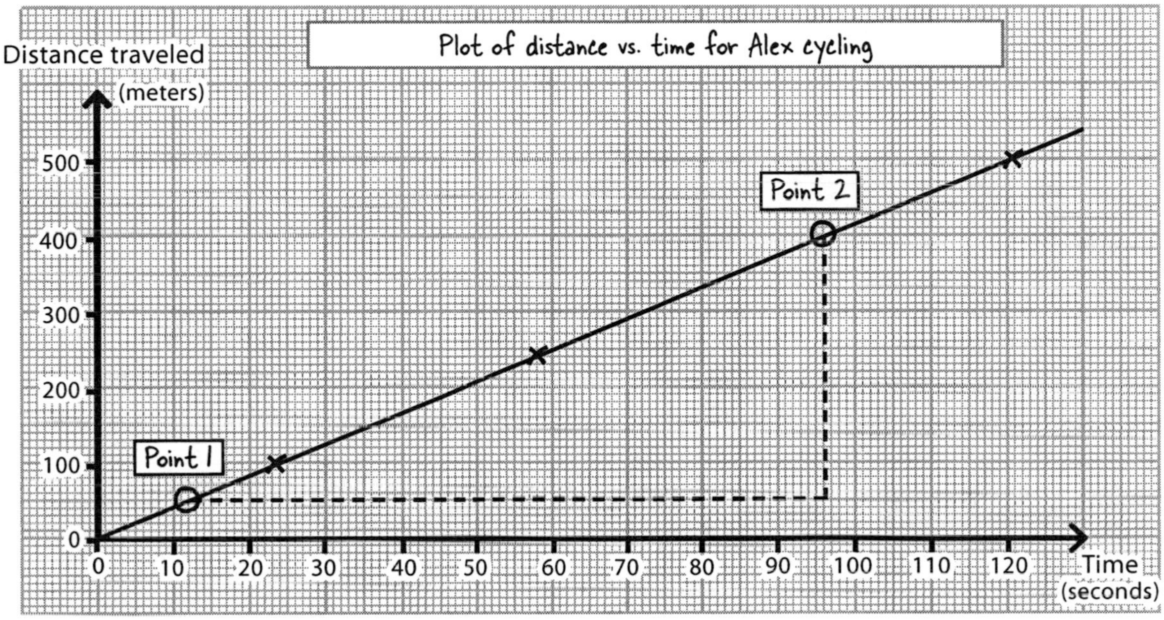

a. Point 1 is (12 s , 50 m), Point 2 is (96 s , 400 m)

Slope is $\frac{\Delta \text{ vertical}}{\Delta \text{ horizontal}} = \frac{\Delta \text{ distance}}{\Delta \text{ time}}$

This is the same as your equation for speed!

(Putting numbers in) $= \frac{400 \text{ m} - 50 \text{ m}}{96 \text{ s} - 12 \text{ s}} = \frac{350 \text{ m}}{84 \text{ s}} =$ 4.17 meters per second (3 sd)

Don't worry if you picked different points or got a slightly different answer.

b. The units of the slope (meters per second) are the same as the units for speed – distance divided by time.

This makes sense, as the equation for slope of the graph is the same as working out the distance covered per amount of time. The slope of the distance-time graph is the speed!

The slope of the distance-time graph is the speed.

there are no Dumb Questions

Q: Way back on page 112, I worked out Alex's speed for each of the measurements we made, and it always worked out somewhere close to 4.17 meters per second (the answer I just got from the graph). So what's the point of doing a graph when it just gives me close to the same answer again?

A: The main reason is that by plotting the points and drawing a best-fit straight line, you take a better and more informed **average** of your experimental results than you'd be able to otherwise. The speed you got from doing the graph is more **accurate** than what you'd get from a single measurement.

A graph helps you **see** what's going on. If you see it, you get it.

Q: I got a slightly different answer from you. Is that OK?

A: You probably drew a slightly different 'best-fit' line through your points. That's fine.

Q: But there must be an actual best-fit line?

A: Yes, if you use special statistical software to draw the line, you always get the same answer. But you don't have that on hand during an exam!

Q: OK. But what about Alex's speed and the slope of the graph? How can you say they're the same thing?

A: Alex's average speed is Δ distance divided by Δ time - e.g., meters per second. The slope of any graph is Δ vertical direction divided by Δ horizontal direction.

So if you draw a graph of Alex's distances and times with distance on the vertical axis and time on the horizontal axis, then its slope is the same as Alex's average speed.

You need an equation for Alex's time to give to the web guys

You've used the results of your experiment to draw a distance-time graph and calculate its slope, which is the same as Alex's speed. That's fantastic!

But the web guys need to be able to use Alex's speed and the distance to a house to work out the **time** it takes Alex to get there. And they're asking you for an **equation** that they can plug the distance and speed into to get the time.

You already have an equation that involves speed, distance, and time, which you worked out from the units of speed:

$$\text{speed} = \frac{\Delta\ \text{distance}}{\Delta\ \text{time}}$$

meters
per
second

This gives you the average speed at which something travels between two points. But the equation says "speed = " on the left hand side, allowing you to work out a speed if you know a distance and a time. What the web guys want is an equation that says "**Δ time =** " on the left hand side, so they can work out a time from the map distance and Alex's speed.

How are you going to get an equation that the web guys can use?

Rearrange the equation to say "Δtime = something"

If you have an equation where the thing you want isn't on the left hand side all by itself, you'll have to **rearrange** the equation so that it is.

The top thing to remember when rearranging equations is that you must do the same thing to each term on both sides of the equation or else the two sides won't be equal (or balance) anymore. The huge advantage of this is that you don't have to remember lots and lots of equations, as you can rearrange the ones you know to figure out what you need.

For time, speed, and distance, you only need ONE equation, which you ALREADY know (from the units of speed).

You can rearrange your equation to say "**Δ** time = something" like this:

1

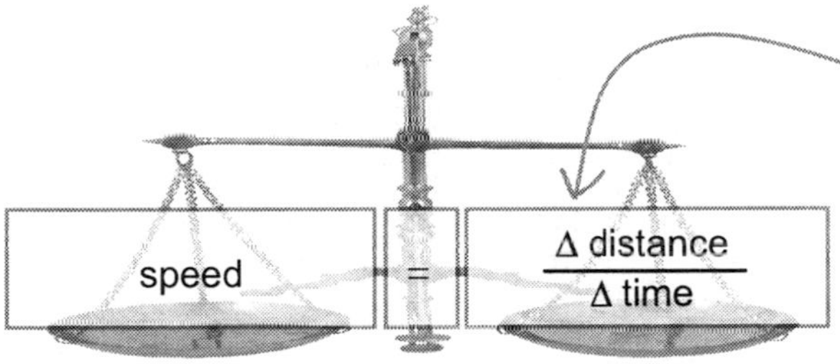

Δ is short for 'change in.' It's a Greek letter called 'delta'.

At the moment you're dividing by **Δ** time. You want an equation that says "**Δ** time = something." So multiply both sides by **Δ** time to get it off the bottom.

2

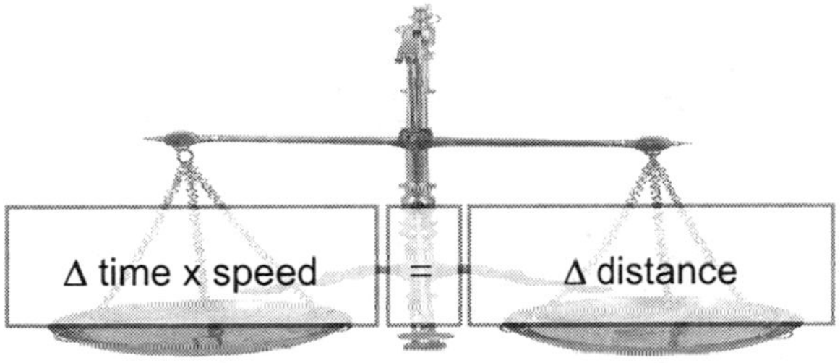

If you're adding or subtracting, that's a whole new term that you need to add/subtract from each side.

If you're multiplying or dividing, you need to do the same thing to each TERM on both sides.

You now have **Δ** time where you want it, but at the moment it's being multiplied by speed. So divide both sides by speed to sort that out.

When you rearrange an equation, always make sure you do the <u>same thing</u> to each side so that the equation remains BALANCED

3

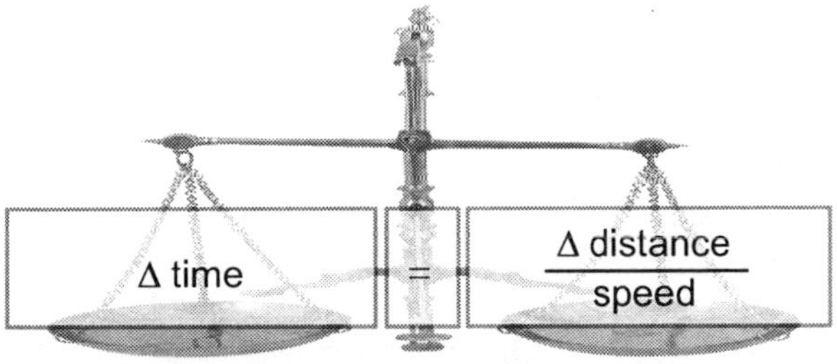

An equation that says "**Δ time = something**" that you can use for the Break Neck website. Sorted!

1

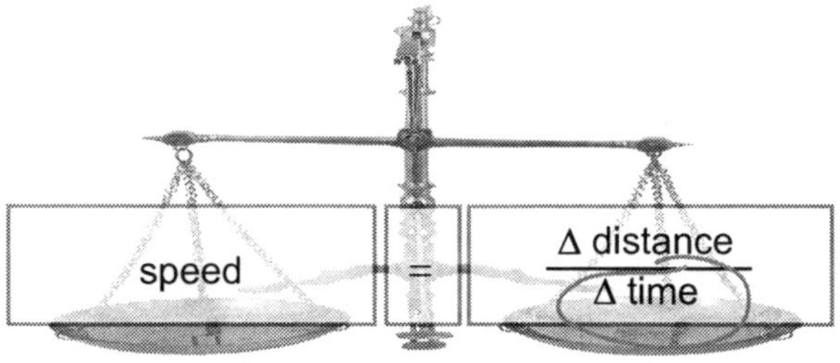

At the moment you're dividing by Δ time. You want an equation that says "Δ time = something." So multiply both sides by Δ time to get it off the bottom.

Multiply both sides by Δ time.

$$\Delta\text{ time} \times \text{speed} = \frac{\Delta\text{ distance} \times \Delta\text{ time}}{\Delta\text{ time}}$$

$$\Delta\text{ time} \times \text{speed} = \frac{\Delta\text{ distance} \times \cancel{\Delta\text{ time}}}{\cancel{\Delta\text{ time}}}$$

These Δ times divide out.

2

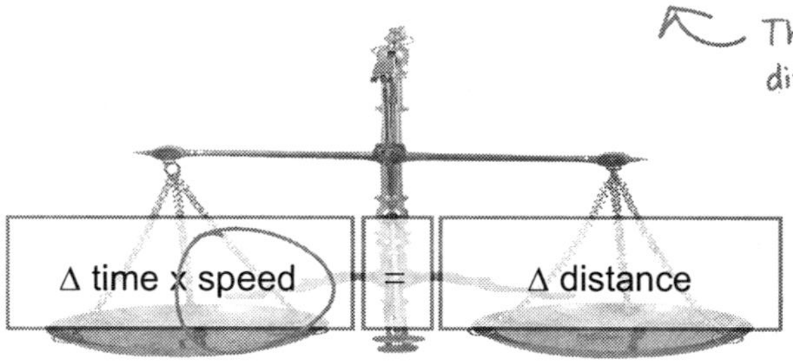

You now have Δ time where you want it, but at the moment it's being multiplied by speed. So divide both sides by speed to sort that out.

$$\frac{\Delta\text{ time x speed}}{\text{speed}} = \frac{\Delta\text{ distance}}{\text{speed}}$$

Divide both sides by speed.

$$\frac{\Delta\text{ time x } \cancel{\text{speed}}}{\cancel{\text{speed}}} = \frac{\Delta\text{ distance}}{\text{speed}}$$

These speeds divide out.

3

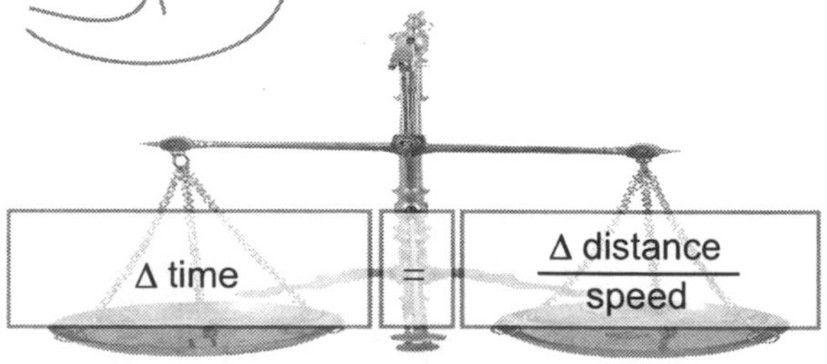

An equation that says "Δ time = something" that you can use for the Break Neck website.

When you rearrange an equation, show your work ...

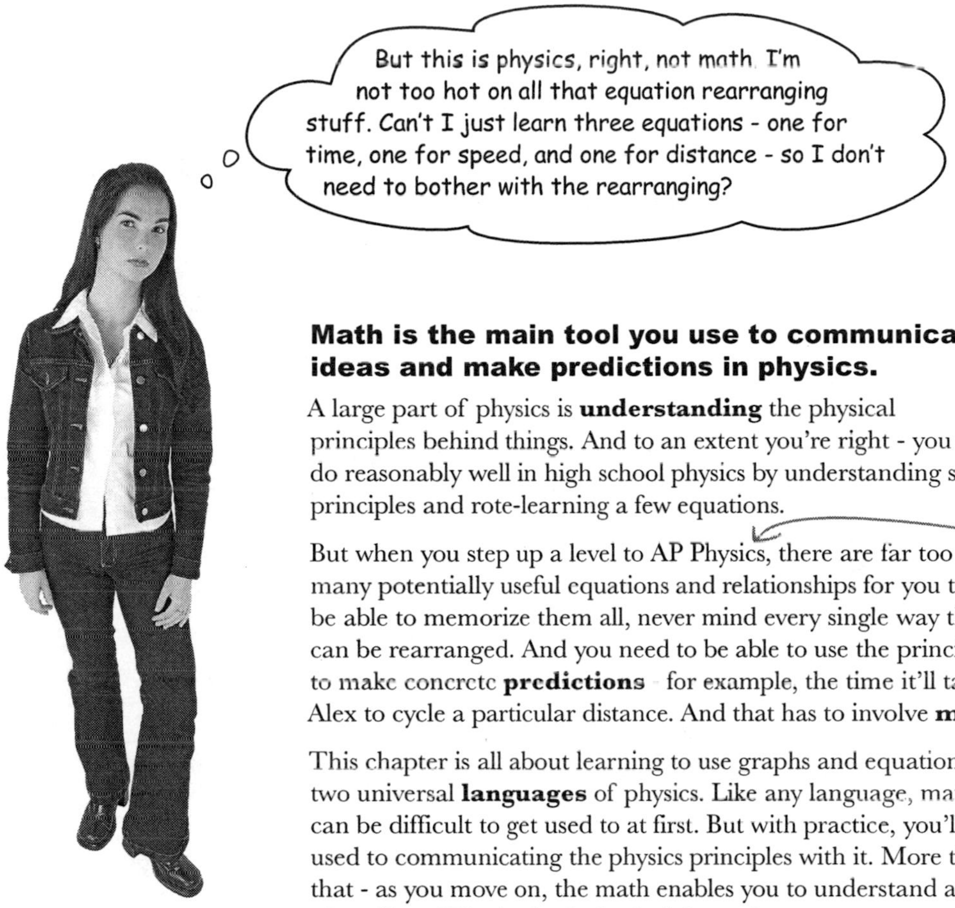

Math is the main tool you use to communicate ideas and make predictions in physics.

A large part of physics is **understanding** the physical principles behind things. And to an extent you're right - you can do reasonably well in high school physics by understanding some principles and rote-learning a few equations.

But when you step up a level to AP Physics, there are far too many potentially useful equations and relationships for you to be able to memorize them all, never mind every single way they can be rearranged. And you need to be able to use the principles to make concrete **predictions** - for example, the time it'll take Alex to cycle a particular distance. And that has to involve **math**.

Or the UK equivalent - A level

This chapter is all about learning to use graphs and equations, two universal **languages** of physics. Like any language, math can be difficult to get used to at first. But with practice, you'll get used to communicating the physics principles with it. More than that - as you move on, the math enables you to understand and **visualize** difficult physical principles and concepts.

At AP level, being able to rearrange equations yourself is a must, so stick at it. The **rewards** are massive, as you'll only need to learn relatively few fundamental equations, which you can then rearrange to get any other equation you might need. Thinking like a physicist isn't about rote memorization. So hang in there - it will get easier!

That's a promise!

In physics, math is a vital tool for making predictions and communicating principles.

Use your equation to work out the time it takes Alex to reach each house

You now have an **equation** that lets you **predict** how long it takes Alex to get to each of Break Neck's potential customers!

First, you designed and carried out an **experiment**. After looking at the results to see how spread out they were, you plotted the results on a **graph**, drew a best-fit straight line, and calculated the **slope** of the line to find Alex's **speed** in terms of the change in distance and change in time. Phew!

And you've just **rearranged** the speed equation so that you can put in a speed and distance to calculate the time it takes Alex to travel that distance at that speed:

$$\Delta \text{ time} = \frac{\Delta \text{ distance}}{\text{speed}}$$

So now you can do a **test run** with some random addresses to catch any potential problems before the site goes live.

This involves putting in some numbers to see if what comes out is sensible.

A 'test run' is an important part of seeing if your answer's correct.

Sharpen your pencil

Use Alex's speed (4.17 meters per second) and the equation you worked out to give these Break Neck customers a delivery time.

Customer's address	Distance (m)	Calculation	Time (s)
57 Mt. Pleasant Street	1000		
710 Ashbury	3500		
29 Acacia Road	5100		

Sharpen your pencil Solution

Use Alex's speed (4.17 meters per second) and the equation you worked out to give these Break Neck customers a delivery time.

Customer's address	Distance (m)	Calculation	Time (s)
57 Mt. Pleasant Street	1000	$\Delta \text{time} = \frac{\Delta \text{distance}}{\text{speed}} = \frac{1000}{4.17}$	240 (3 sd)
710 Ashbury	3500	$\Delta \text{time} = \frac{\Delta \text{distance}}{\text{speed}} = \frac{3500}{4.17}$	840 (3 sd)
29 Acacia Road	5100	$\Delta \text{time} = \frac{\Delta \text{distance}}{\text{speed}} = \frac{5100}{4.17}$	1220 (3 sd)

So you do a test run with the website ...

... but there's a problem. The programmers set the website up to display delivery times in units of **minutes**. Your calculation used **seconds**, but the units weren't **converted** before being displayed.

Doing the question right, but giving the wrong UNITS in your answer is a common, but avoidable, error.

Design experiment | Carry out experiment | Look at results | Plot results on graph | Calculate slope | Rearrange equation | ~~Use equation~~ | **CHECK EQUATION!**

So just convert the units, and you're all set...right?

Not so fast! Any time you think you're ready to roll with an important website (or even an answer on your exam), take a look from 20,000 feet away and ask yourself: Does this **SUCK**?

You're never finished until you've asked: "Does it SUCK?"

Sharpen your pencil

Change the units for this customer's delivery time to minutes, then step back to see if it SUCKs.

Customer's address	Time (s)	Calculation	Time (minutes)
57 Mt. Pleasant Street	240		

S

SIZE - Are the answers the size you're expecting?

....

....

U

UNITS - Do they have units, and are they what you were asked for?

....

....

C

CALCULATIONS - Did you do the math right?

....

....

K

"K'ONTEXT - What are you trying to do, and is it the same as what you actually did?

....

....

Design experiment	Carry out experiment	Look at results	Plot results on graph	Calculate slope	Rearrange equation	~~Use equation~~	CHECK EQUATION!

Sharpen your pencil Solution

Change the units for this customer's delivery time to minutes, then step back to see if it SUCKs.

Customer's address	Time (s)	Calculation	Time (minutes)
57 Mt. Pleasant Street	240	$240\ s = 240\ s \times \frac{1\ min}{60\ s}$ ← conversion factor	4

S

SIZE - Are the answers the size you're expecting?

Well, 4 minutes is plausible for pizza delivery in a way that 240 minutes isn't!

U

UNITS - Do they have units, and are they what you were asked for?

They asked for minutes, and they've got minutes. (Well, they do now!)

C

CALCULATIONS - Did you do the math right?

The first equation I wrote down was $t_{tot} = t_{cyc} + t_{cook}$, where t_{cyc} was the cycling time, and t_{cook} the cooking time. OH NO, I FORGOT ABOUT THE COOKING TIME!!

K

"K'ONTEXT - What are you trying to do, and is it the same as what you actually did?

Apart from using the wrong units originally, and forgetting the cooking time, I think the rest is OK.

Doing part of the problem right, then writing the 'interim' answer to that part as your final answer by mistake is another common (and very avoidable) error!

Design experiment | Carry out experiment | Look at results | Plot results on graph | Calculate slope | Rearrange equation | ~~Guess equation~~ | CHECK EQUATION! | **Use equation**

Include the cooking time in your equation

The original equation included both a delivery time **and** a cooking time. You did a fantastic job of working out the hard part - the delivery time - but forgot to add on the cooking time at the end.

An Italian pizza takes 10 minutes to cook, and a deep pan pizza takes 13 minutes. I can cook them all at the same time.

Total delivery time — Cycling time — Cooking time

$$t_{total} = t_{cyc} + t_{cook}$$

This is the total delivery time the website should give the customer.

$$\Delta \text{time} = \frac{\Delta \text{distance}}{\text{speed}}$$

From the online maps

4.17 meters per second

Sharpen your pencil

Work out the cooking time and total delivery time for each of the orders.

Work out the cooking time from what the chef tells you.

Customer's address	Distance (m)	Order	Road time (s)	Road time (min)	Cooking time (min)	Delivery time (min)
57 Mt. Pleasant Street	1000	1 Italian	240	4		
710 Ashbury	3503	2 deep pan	840			
29 Acacia Road	5100	1 Italian 1 deep pan	1220			

Design experiment | Carry out experiment | Look at results | Plot results on graph | Calculate slope | Rearrange equation | ~~Use equation~~ | CHECK EQUATION! | **Use equation**

Sharpen your pencil Solution

Work out the cooking time and total delivery time for each of the orders.

Customer's address	Distance (m)	Order	Road time (s)	Road time (min)	Cooking time (min)	Delivery time (min)
57 Mt. Pleasant St.	1000	1 Italian	240	4	10	14
710 Ashbury	3500	2 deep pan	840	14	13	27
29 Acacia Road	5100	1 Italian 1 deep pan	1220	20 m 20 s	13	33 m 20 s

This answer works out at 20.3333333... minutes. The fraction at the end is a third of a minute, which is 20 seconds (not 33 seconds) Don't forget that there are 60 seconds in a minute (and not 100), so you need to convert the fraction of a minute into seconds at the end.

The Break Neck website goes live, and the customers love it!

You've done it! Break Neck have a shiny new website thanks to your experiment, graph, equation, and units conversion. Every time a customer makes an order, they're given a delivery time that they can plan their evening around.

The customers are delighted, and word's starting to get around. Alex is pleased too. He's getting more tips and has nearly saved up enough for the new myPod he has his eye on.

A few weeks later, you hear from Break Neck again

Most of the pizzas are still arriving on time ... but some of the pizzas are **late,** and the customers are starting to get impatient with Break Neck. The worst thing that could happen would be customers switching to one of Break Neck's competitors because of a bug in the website.

So Break Neck has asked you to come back on a new contract to see if you can work out what the problem is.

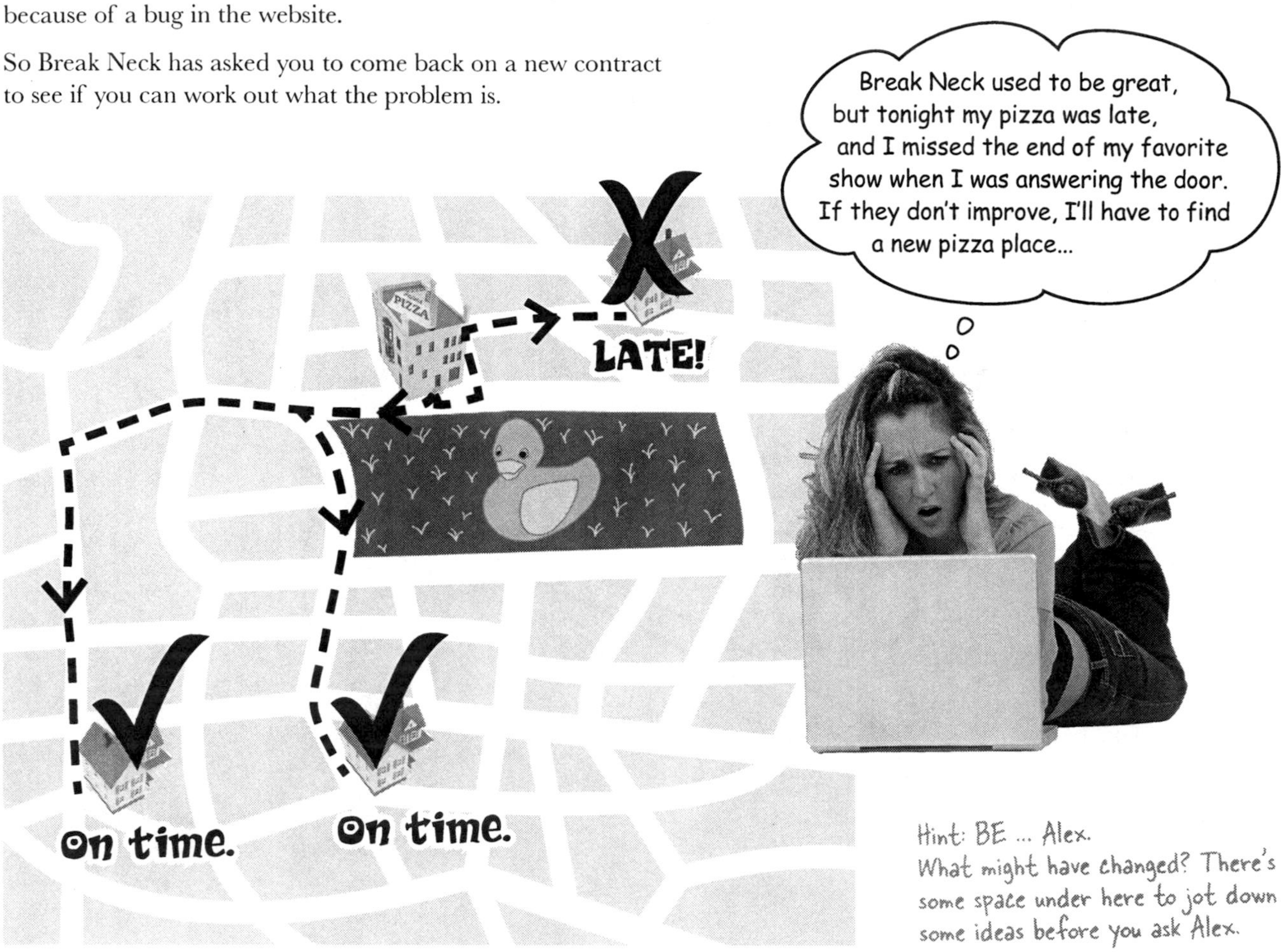

Hint: BE ... Alex.
What might have changed? There's some space under here to jot down some ideas before you ask Alex.

BRAIN POWER

But why are only **some** pizzas now arriving late when the rest are still arriving on time?

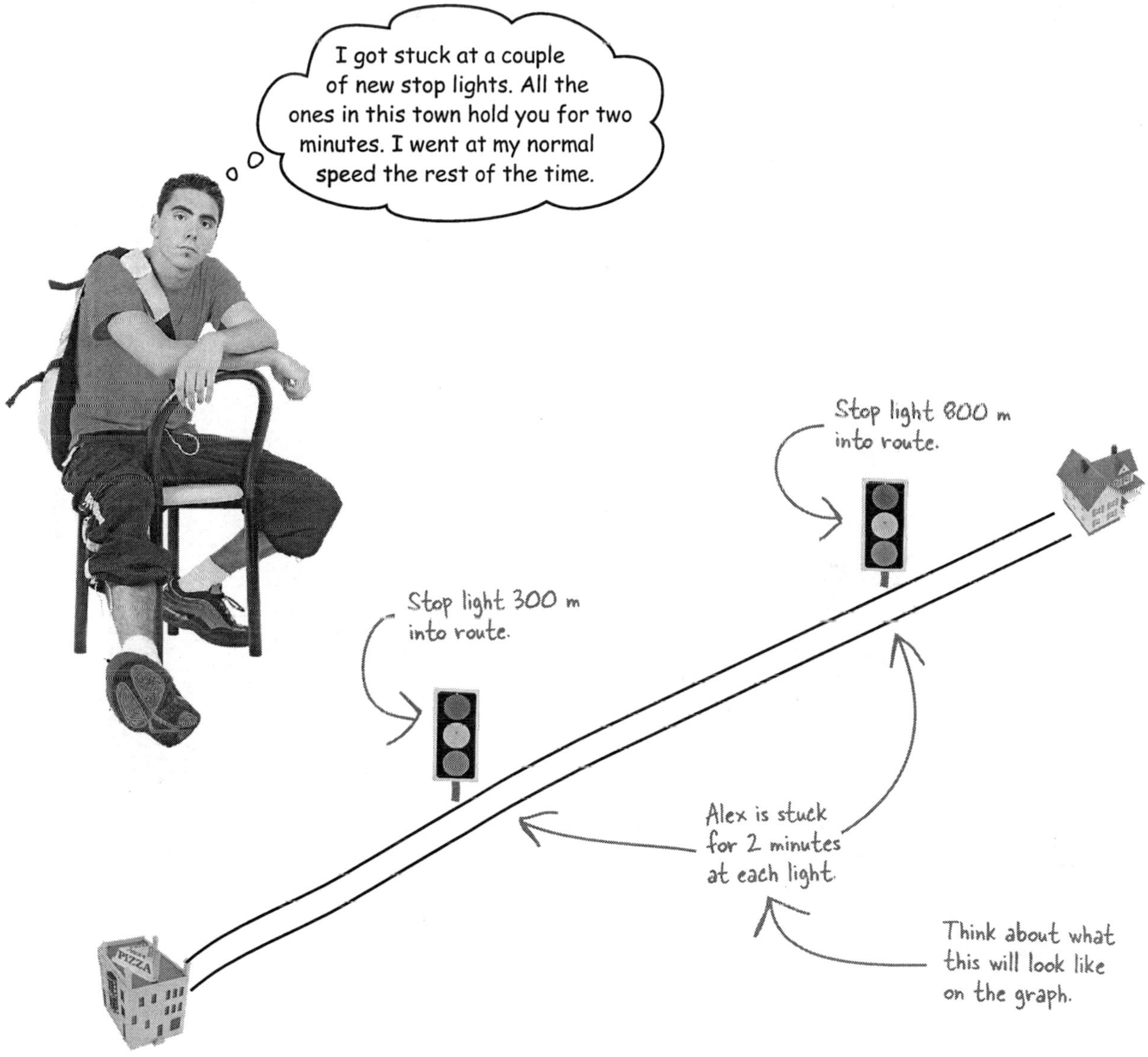
I got stuck at a couple of new stop lights. All the ones in this town hold you for two minutes. I went at my normal speed the rest of the time.
Stop light 800 m into route.
Stop light 300 m into route.
Alex is stuck for 2 minutes at each light.
Think about what this will look like on the graph.

A graph lets you see the difference the stop lights made

If you can **see the difference** the stop lights made to Alex's journey, you're more likely to be able to work out what to do about it.

Sharpen your pencil

The line already on the graph represents what we expected Alex to do - travel at a constant speed without stopping, so he reaches the house in four minutes.

Draw Alex's actual journey (which he describes over there on page 136) on the graph to **show** and compare the difference that the stop lights made.

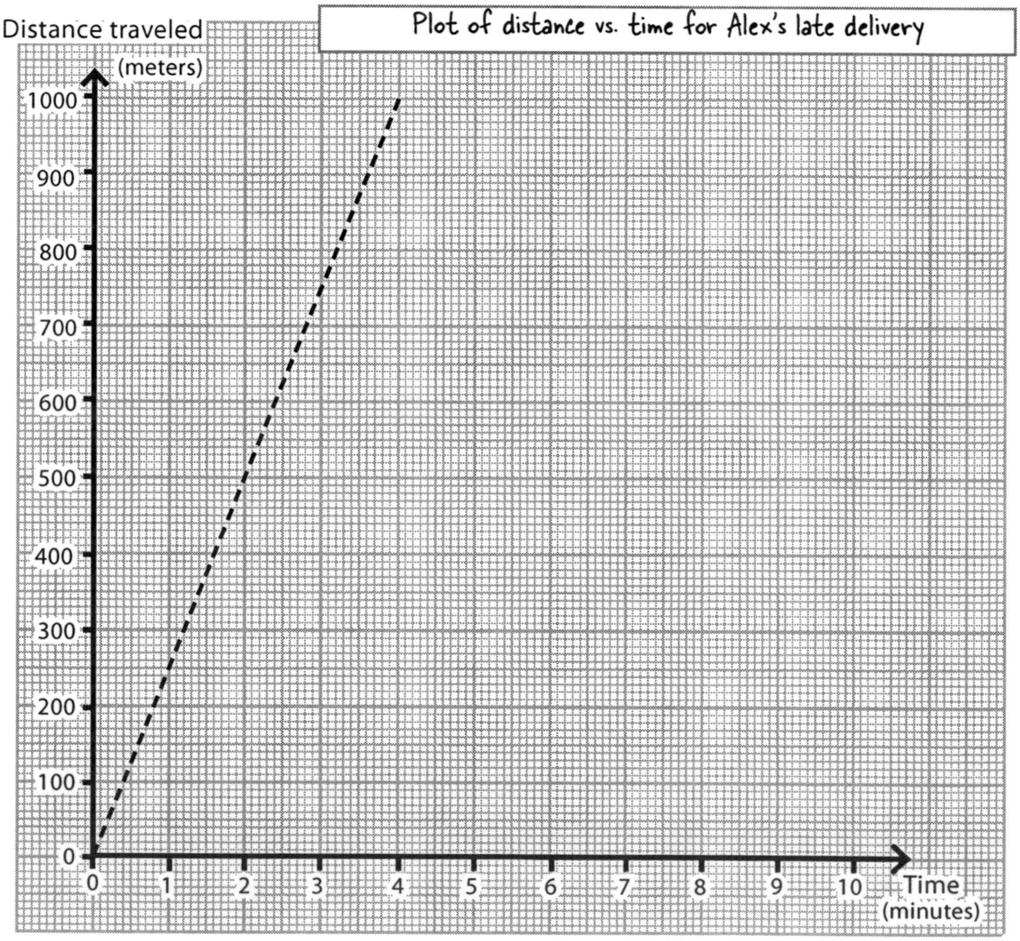

Sharpen your pencil Solution

The line already on the graph represents what we expected Alex to do - travel at a constant speed without stopping, so he reaches the house in four minutes.

Draw Alex's actual journey (which he describes over there on page 136) on the graph to **show** and compare the difference that the stop lights made.

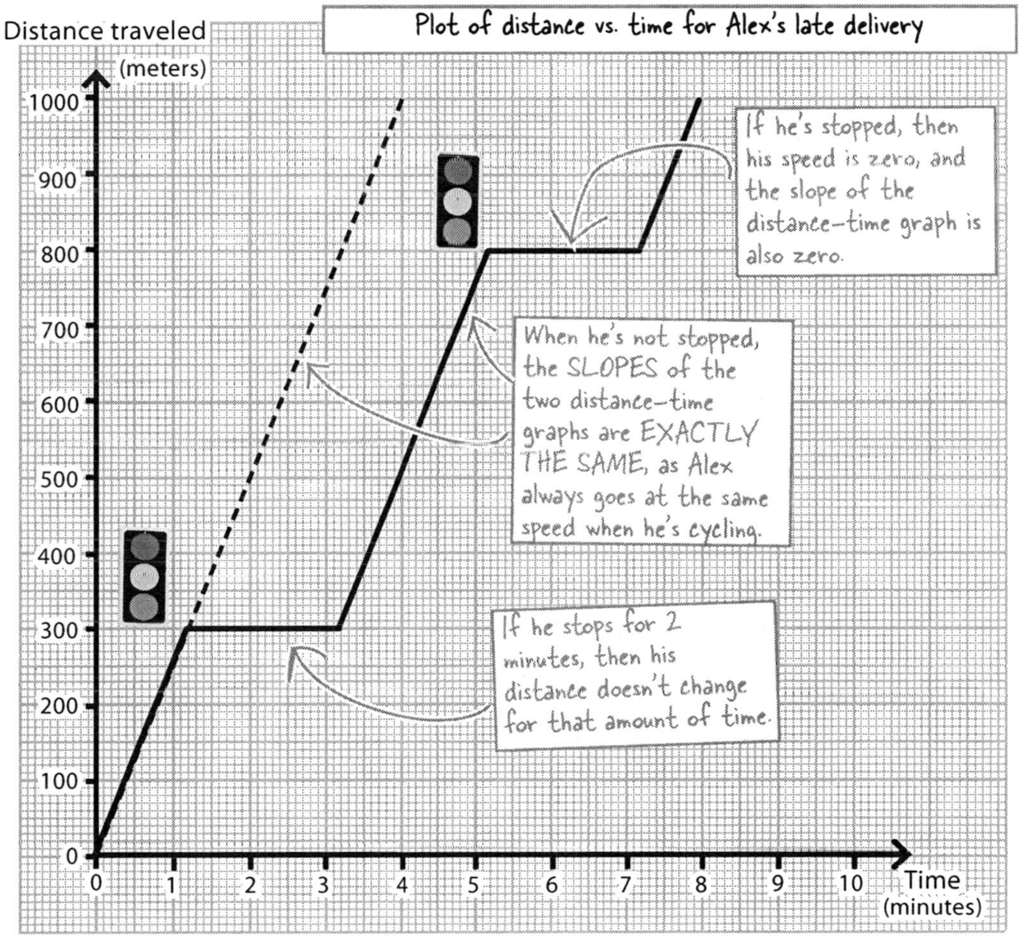

It's easy to tell when something's sitting still, as the slope of its distance-time graph is zero (or a flat line).

The stop lights change Alex's average speed

The **average** speed for a trip is the constant speed at which you could have traveled to cover the same **total** distance in the same total time. So Alex's average speed is the **slope** of a line between his start and end points on his distance-time graph since the slope of a distance-time graph is the speed.

Sharpen your pencil

a. Draw a line on the graph to represent Alex's average speed.

b. Calculate Alex's **average** speed for the delivery in meters per second (show your work down the side).

c. Does Alex ever actually travel at his average speed?

Plot of distance vs. time for Alex's late delivery

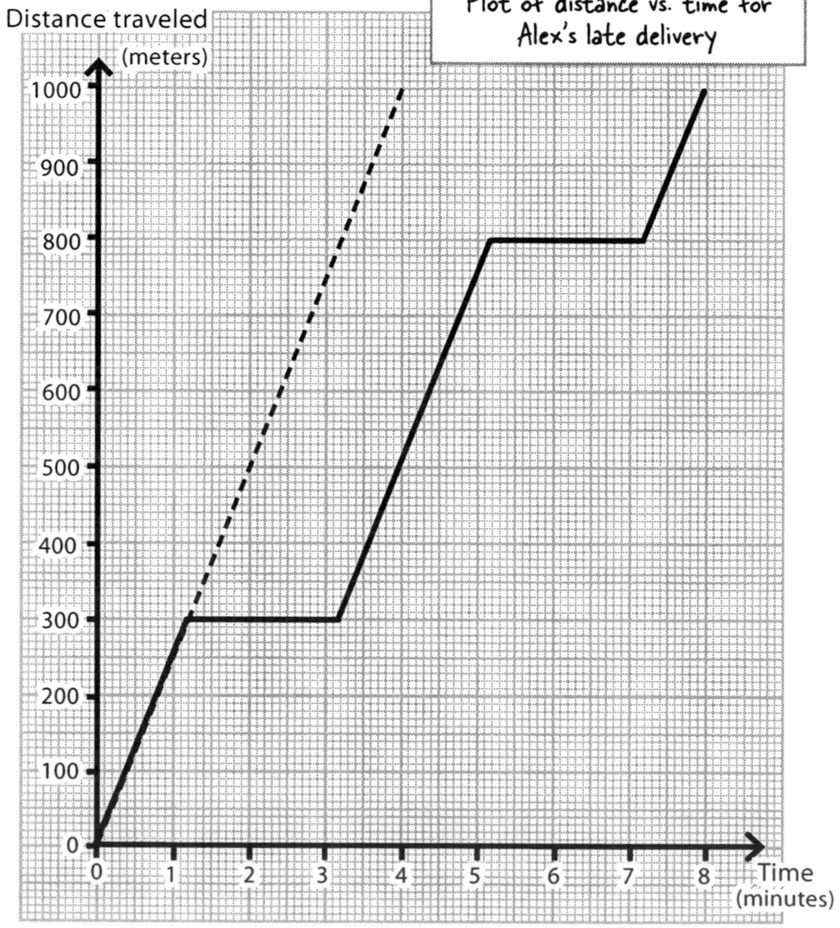

Space for part b work.

Space for part c answer.

Sharpen your pencil Solution

a. Draw a line on the graph to represent Alex's average speed.

b. Calculate Alex's **average** speed for the delivery in meters per second (show your work down the side).

c. Does Alex ever actually travel at his average speed?

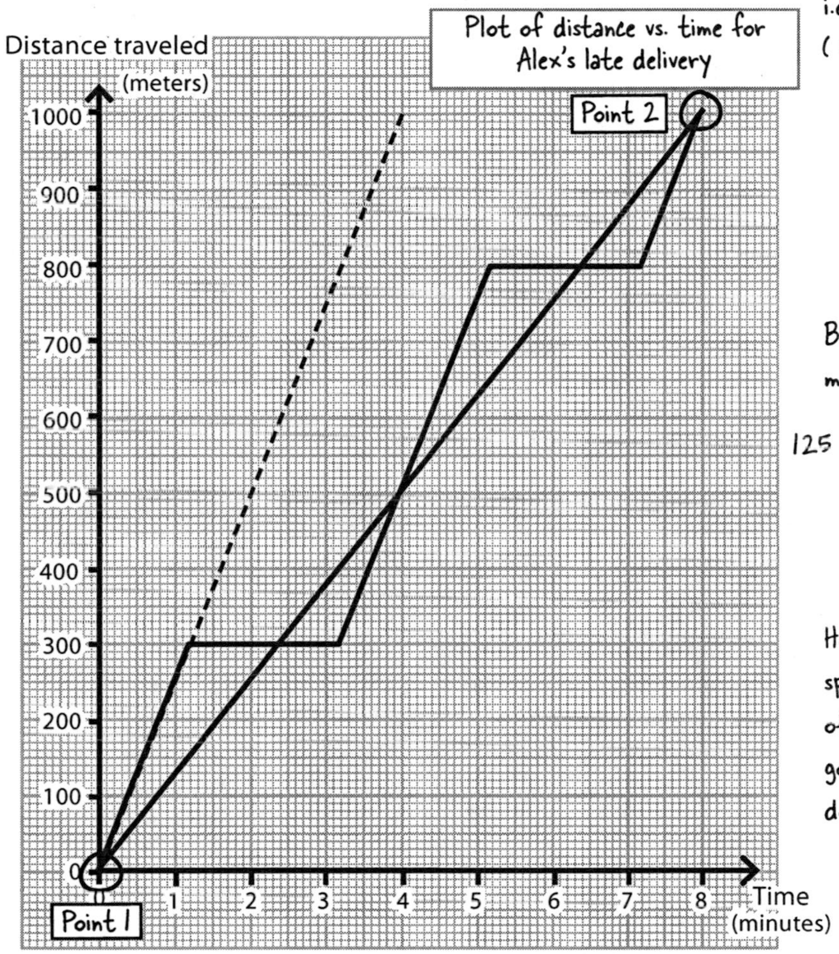

Space for part b work.

Choose point 1 to be the start of the run, and point 2 the end.

i.e., (0 min , 0 m)

(8 min , 1000 m)

$$\text{speed} = \frac{\Delta \text{ distance}}{\Delta \text{ time}} = \frac{1000 \text{ m}}{8 \text{ min}} = 125 \text{ meters per min}$$

But was asked for speed in meters per second:

$$125 \frac{\text{meters}}{\text{min}} = 125 \frac{\text{meters}}{\cancel{\text{min}}} \times \frac{1 \cancel{\text{min}}}{60 \text{ s}} = 2.08 \text{ meters per second (3 sd)}$$

Space for part c answer.

He never travels at the average speed for any significant length of time (though he must briefly go at it as he speeds up/slows down for each light).

With an AVERAGE speed, it's the changes in total distance and total time that are important.

Add on two minutes per stop light to give the customer a maximum delivery time ...

Trying to do something with the average speed will be too difficult at this stage; this is simpler.

In physics, simpler is usually clearer – and, therefore, better!

So you - and Alex - have reached the end of the road. You realized that the stop lights slow him down. But you were able to get the online map to consider the number of stop lights on his route when giving the customer a maximum delivery time.

If the lights are red, that's OK because you planned for that to happen. If the lights are green, and Alex isn't slowed down, then the pizza arrives early, and the customer is still happy.

... the customers are extremely happy ...

The 14 minutes you calculated before plus up to 2 minutes for each of the 2 stop lights.

... and you're invited to the Pizza Party

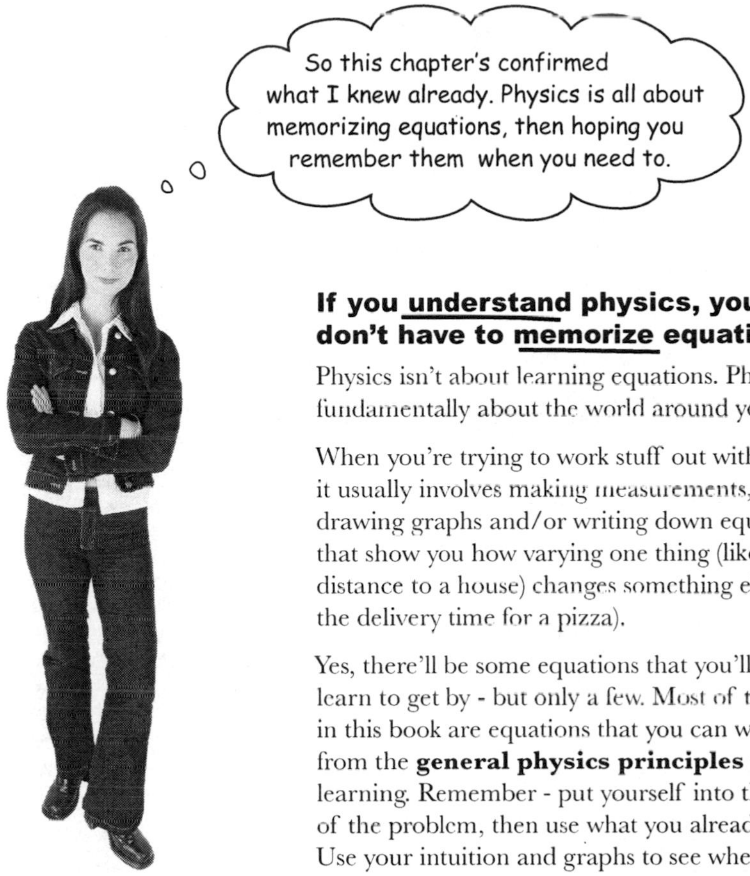

If you understand physics, you don't have to memorize equations!

Think like a physicist!

Physics isn't about learning equations. Physics is fundamentally about the world around you.

When you're trying to work stuff out with physics, it usually involves making measurements, then drawing graphs and/or writing down equations that show you how varying one thing (like the distance to a house) changes something else (like the delivery time for a pizza).

Yes, there'll be some equations that you'll have to learn to get by - but only a few. Most of the ones in this book are equations that you can work out from the **general physics principles** you're learning. Remember - put yourself into the heart of the problem, then use what you already know! Use your intuition and graphs to see whether you expect something to get bigger or smaller when you change another thing.

In physics, memorizing is the opposite of understanding!

If you see it, you get it!

I guess there are a few equations that are kind of common sense, so you don't need to memorize them if you just think about **where** they come from?

You <u>already</u> knew the two equations you've used in this chapter!

The first equation you used was:

$$\text{speed} = \frac{\Delta \text{ distance}}{\Delta \text{ time}}$$

meters per second

But that was **something you already knew**! Every time you say something has a speed of "70 miles per hour," you're quoting **units** that you can use to write down that equation straight out of your head!

Then you can rearrange it to get what you want.

The second equation you used was:

$$\text{slope} = \frac{\Delta \text{ vertical direction}}{\Delta \text{ horizontal direction}}$$

But you already knew that one too! **Steep hills have big slopes**. So you can use your intuition to work out that Δ vertical must be on the top of the fraction so that you get a big value for a big slope.

A steep hill has a big slope.

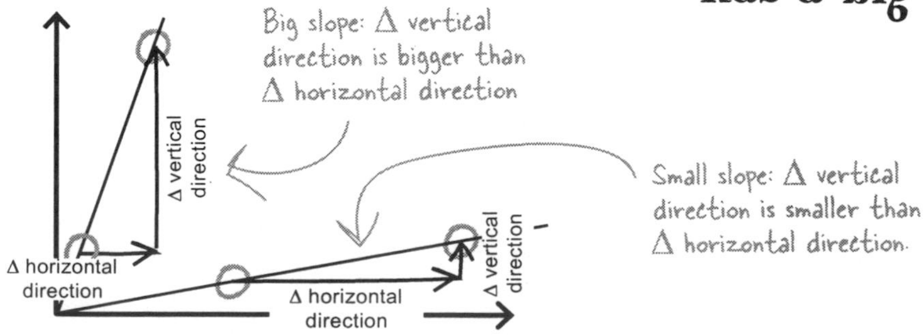

Fireside Chats

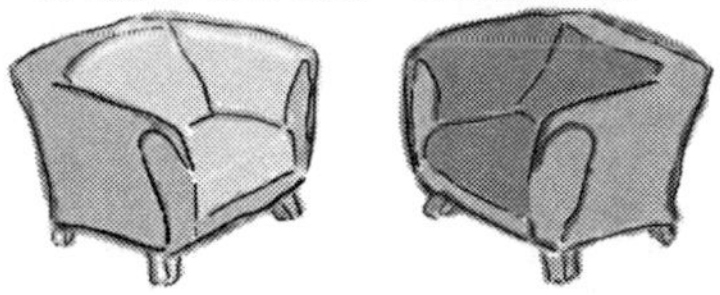

Tonight's talk: **Graph and Equation debate who's best at getting the point across.**

Graph

You've heard it said - "A picture speaks 1000 words," and "If you see it, you get it." Which kinda makes me wonder - what on earth are you doing here in my chapter, Equation?

Equation

Well, that's a nice way to draw me into the conversation considering the chapter title actually names me first - "equations and graphs," it says there.

Graph

Obviously one that got past the editor! I mean, in a chapter that's mostly about visualizing things, what role do you have to play?

Equation

I'm just a different way of visualizing things. With me, it's easy to see, at a glance, when two things are equal to each other - you can't do that.

Graph

But with me, you can see how two things relate to each other-how one thing responds when the other thing changes.

Equation

But I can do that too. All you need to do is think what'll happen to the stuff on the other side of the equation when you change the value of one of the variables.

Graph

Huh? Variables, which you have to look up before you make any sense whatsoever! All those symbols and letters, whereas I'm easily accessible from the start!

Equation

I disagree- you only make sense once someone's gotten used to working with graphs! Anything strange can become familiar if you use it a lot. Once you're used to my kind of shorthand, you'll be able to use it to convey a lot of information in a very small space and short amount of time.

Graph	Equation
And random letters are easy to get used to, are they?	
	They're not random, actually. Physicists always choose the same letter to mean the same one thing in equations. So once you've learned the lingo, it's not as hard as you make it out to be.
But can you do slopes?! Can you display experimental results? Do people plant little kisses on you, like this ✕ ? In short, are you loved?	
	Has it ever occurred to you that a graph and an equation are just different ways of saying these same things?
Uhhhhh - how do you mean?	
	Take that distance-time graph from earlier on in the chapter. It's the same as the equation Δdistance = speed $\times$ Δtime except drawn out. (But it's not as long-winded!)
I think not! I have a slope, and you have ... well, you have nothing of great interest.	
	Oh, but this equation tells you all about the slope of the graph. You have to work out your slope using an equation in the first place, don't you? And if you've plotted a distance-time graph, then it's the same equation as I already said.
No, it's not! The slope is Δ vertical direction divided by Δ horizontal direction, and there's no division sign in your equation!	
	Ah, but equations can be rearranged to give you anything you want (as long as it was in or related to the equation in the first place).
Well, I guess you might just be a teeny bit more versatile. But I'm still the best for visualizing things!	
	I'm not denying that - just pointing out that I'm not entirely useless, you know!

Question Clinic: The "Did you do what they asked you" Question

Some questions will give you one **unit** (like minutes) - but ask for your answer in another unit (like seconds). And some questions have some harder intermediate steps before a more simple step to give the **final** answer. Always check that you've done what they asked you! Otherwise you'll lose credit for 'little' mistakes on questions that you mostly did right!

This question contains two different units of distance.

It also contains two different units of time.

2. A runner jogs one kilometer to a 400 m track, where he starts doing laps. For the first half hour, he passes the finish line every 90 seconds. After this, he does four more laps in 75 seconds each.

a. How far does he run in the first 30 minutes of his training session?

b. If he started his training session at 1:00 pm, what time does he finish at?

c. If he takes the bus home, how far has he run in total that day?

This distance is written in words rather than figures, which makes it more difficult to spot!

And here's yet another unit of time!

And another way of writing down a time!

One more unit of time to finish off with!

By the time you've done the whole question, have you forgotten about the 1 km he jogged to get to the track in the first place?

The first type of "Did you do what they asked you?" question is there to make sure you **think about the physics** (and **units**) involved rather than just plugging numbers into a formula. The other type makes sure you **read the whole question** and can follow things through to the very end.

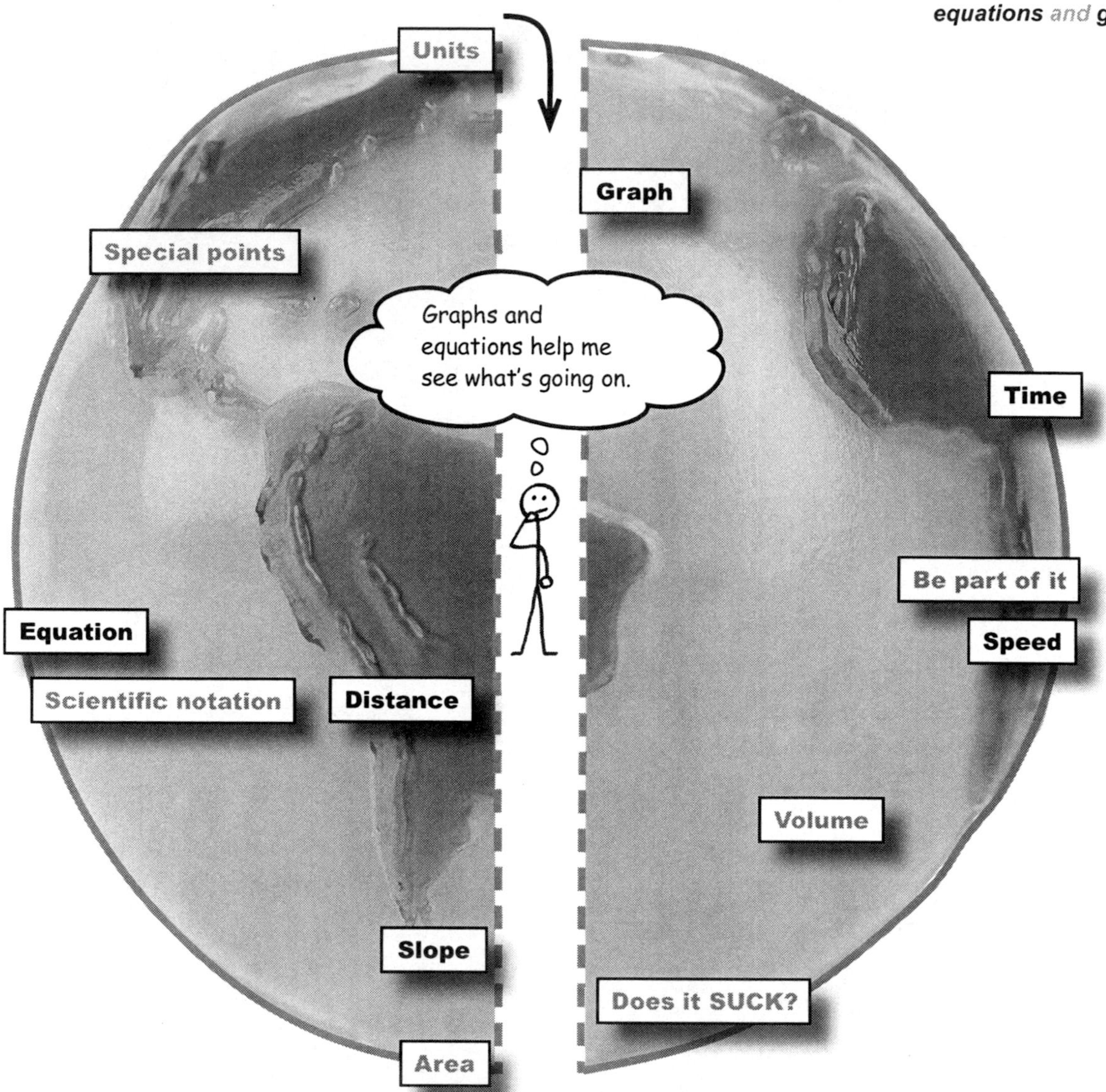

☑	**Distance**	**A length; the number of meters (or miles, or so forth) you cover when you take a particular route between two points.**
☑	**Time**	**How long something takes; how many seconds (or minutes, and so on) that elapse between two moments you're interested in.**
☑	**Speed**	**How fast something's going - the rate of change of distance with time.**
☑	**Graph**	**A visual representation of how two variables depend on each other.**
☑	**Equation**	**A mathematical representation of how variables depend on each other.**
☑	**Slope**	**The steepness of a graph; the change in the vertical direction divided by the change in the horizontal direction.**

Your Physics Toolbox

You've got Chapter 4 under your belt, and you've added some terminology and answer-checking skills to your toolbox.

Do an experiment

An experiment enables you to find out how two variables depend on each other – like distance and time in this chapter.

Think about errors

Think about sources of experimental error at the design stage.

Reduce systematic errors by planning ahead.

Reduce random errors by making multiple measurements and averaging (either mathematically or by drawing a graph).

Draw a graph

A graph visually shows you how two variables relate to each other.

You'll usually want to know how something varies as time goes on.

ALWAYS put time on the horizontal axis of your graph.

The slope of a graph

You can use the equation

$$\text{slope} = \frac{\Delta \text{ vertical direction}}{\Delta \text{ horizontal direction}}$$

to compare the two variables you've plotted on your graph to each other.

Work out an equation

An equation shows you how variables relate to each other mathematically.

Use the same letter for the same 'type' of thing, e.g., 't' for a time.

Use subscripts to represent different things of the same 'type', like you did with t_{cook}, t_{total}, and t_{cyc}.

Rates and slopes

When you've plotted time along the horizontal axis, the slope of the graph gives you the rate at which the variable on the vertical axis changes with time.

So the slope of a distance – time graph gives you the speed, as speed is rate of change of distance with time.

Rearrange your equation

If the equation you come up with doesn't have the variable you want to work out on its own on the left hand side, you have to rearrange your equation.

Make sure you always do the same thing to both sides at each stage so that your equation stays balanced.

It's safer to show more work than it is to show no work at all.

5 dealing with directions

Vectors

Time, speed, and distance are all well and good, but you really need DIRECTION too if you want to get on in life.

You now have multiple physics superpowers: You've mastered graphs and equations, and you can estimate how big your answer will be. But **size** isn't everything. In this chapter, you'll be learning about **vectors**, which give **direction** to your answers and help you to find **easier shortcuts** through complicated-looking problems.

The treasure hunt

It's treasure time. You and your teammate, Annie, are part of a scavenger hunt. To be the first team to reach the prize at the end of the game, you have to follow four clues.

Here's the first clue ...

Clue 1

Backwards and forwards,
forwards and back
Is immediate action your
plan of attack?
First ponder - then go - for
soon you will spot
That the target may seem
far away ... but it's not. Go:
1) 60 meters North
2) 150 meters South
3) 120 meters North
4) 60 meters South
5) 20 meters South
6) 40 meters North
The start of your journey is
right by the tree,
and continues whenceforth
you unearth the next key.

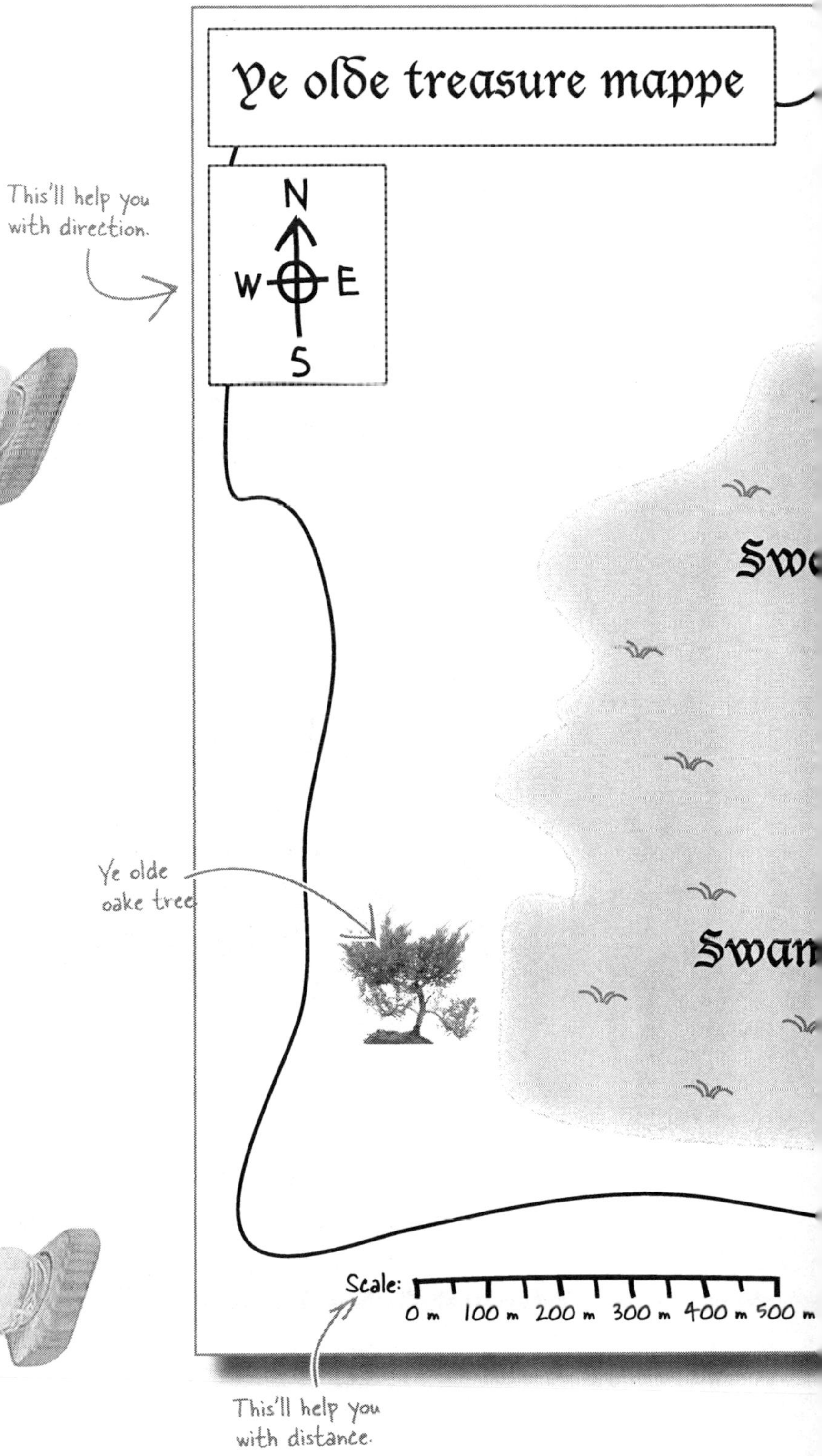

BRAIN POWER

What do you think is the best way to guide Annie to the next clue **as quickly as possible**?

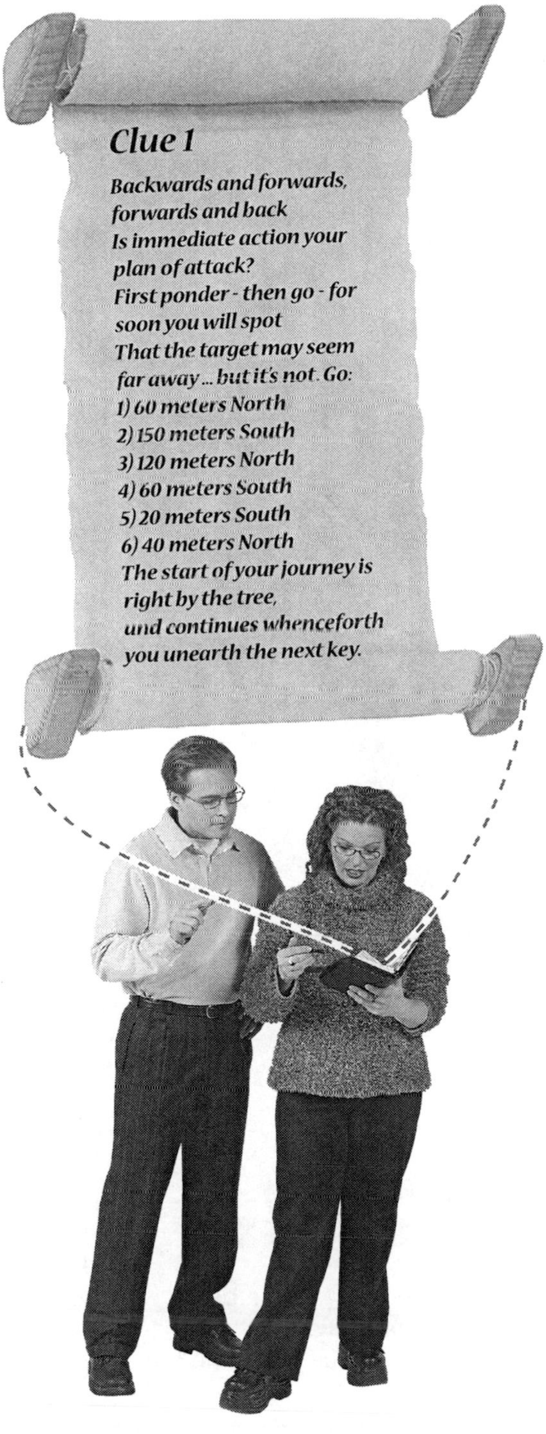

Joe: I say we just tell Annie to get going and follow the directions as quickly as possible!

Mary: Hang on, the clue says to "first ponder - then go."

Joe: Hmmm?

Mary: I mean, we should think first rather than rushing into it. The directions do seem to be a bit...uh... repetitive. It's silly to do the same thing over and over again if we don't have to.

Joe: Oh yeah, I see what you mean. The first instruction sends us off to the North - and then the next one makes us retrace our steps back to the South again!

Mary: All of the directions in the clue are either North or South. So we're just running up and down the same line until we get to the end of the directions.

Joe: So following the instructions exactly isn't the quickest way after all.

Mary: What if we try to imagine the directions first - that'll be quicker than doing all that running backwards and forwards. So that's 60 m North, then 150 m South, then ...

Joe: Isn't it better to sketch them out? It'll be much easier to see what's going on than trying to hold onto all these directions in our heads.

Mary: I guess so - let's get to work!

ALWAYS start with a sketch!

Sketching things out on paper leaves room in your brain to think about physics.

Sharpen your pencil

Your team already started a sketch of the instructions in clue 1, but they haven't managed to finish it off yet.

That's your job.

They've decided to represent each leg of the instructions using an arrow so that 1 cm represents 20 m. They've also decided to spread the arrows out a bit, so they aren't all drawn on top of each other.

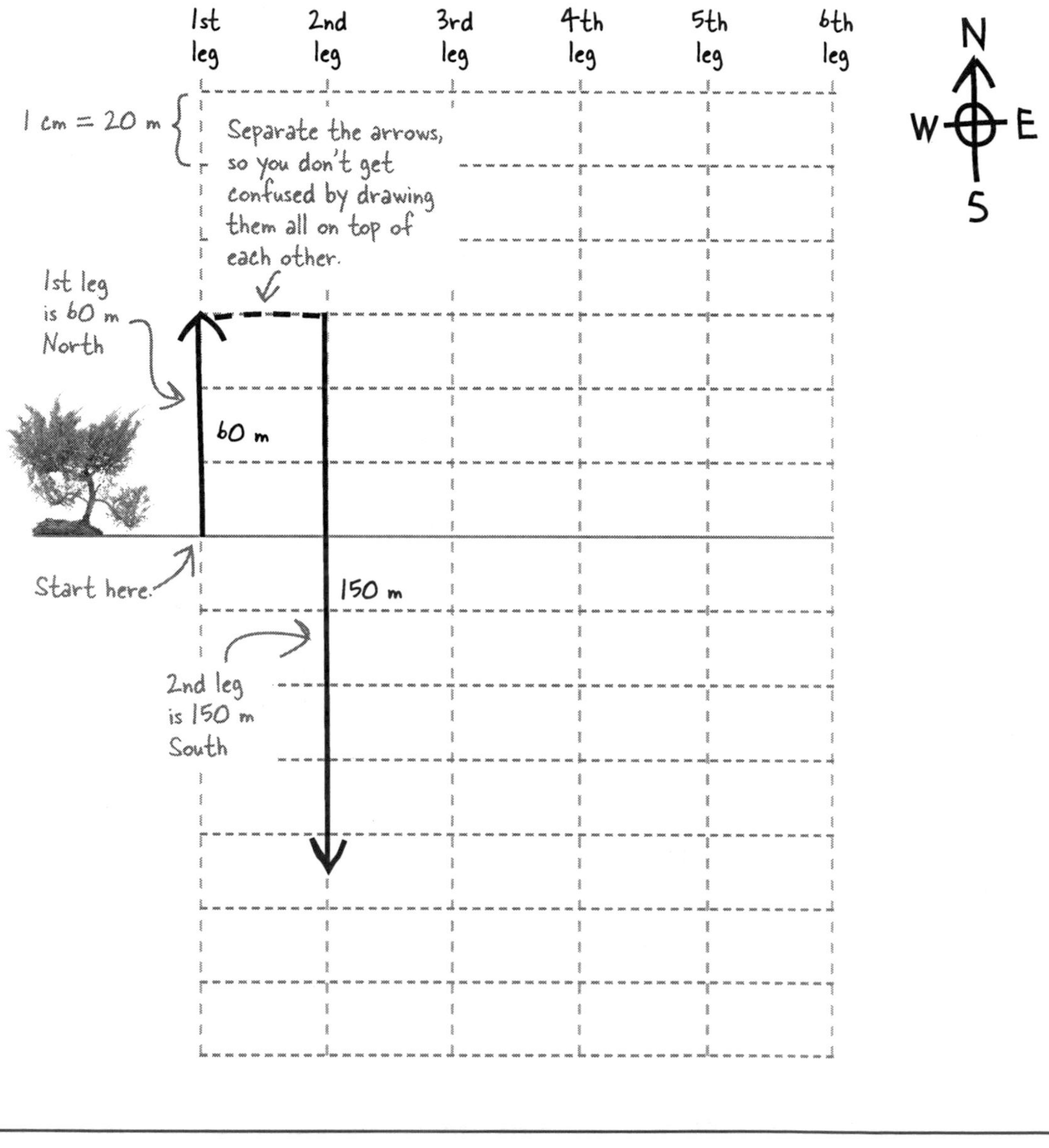

Sharpen your pencil Solution

Your team already started a sketch of the instructions in clue 1, but they haven't managed to finish it off yet.

That's your job.

They've decided to represent each leg of the instructions using an arrow so that 1 cm represents 20 m. They've also decided to spread the arrows out a bit, so they aren't all drawn on top of each other.

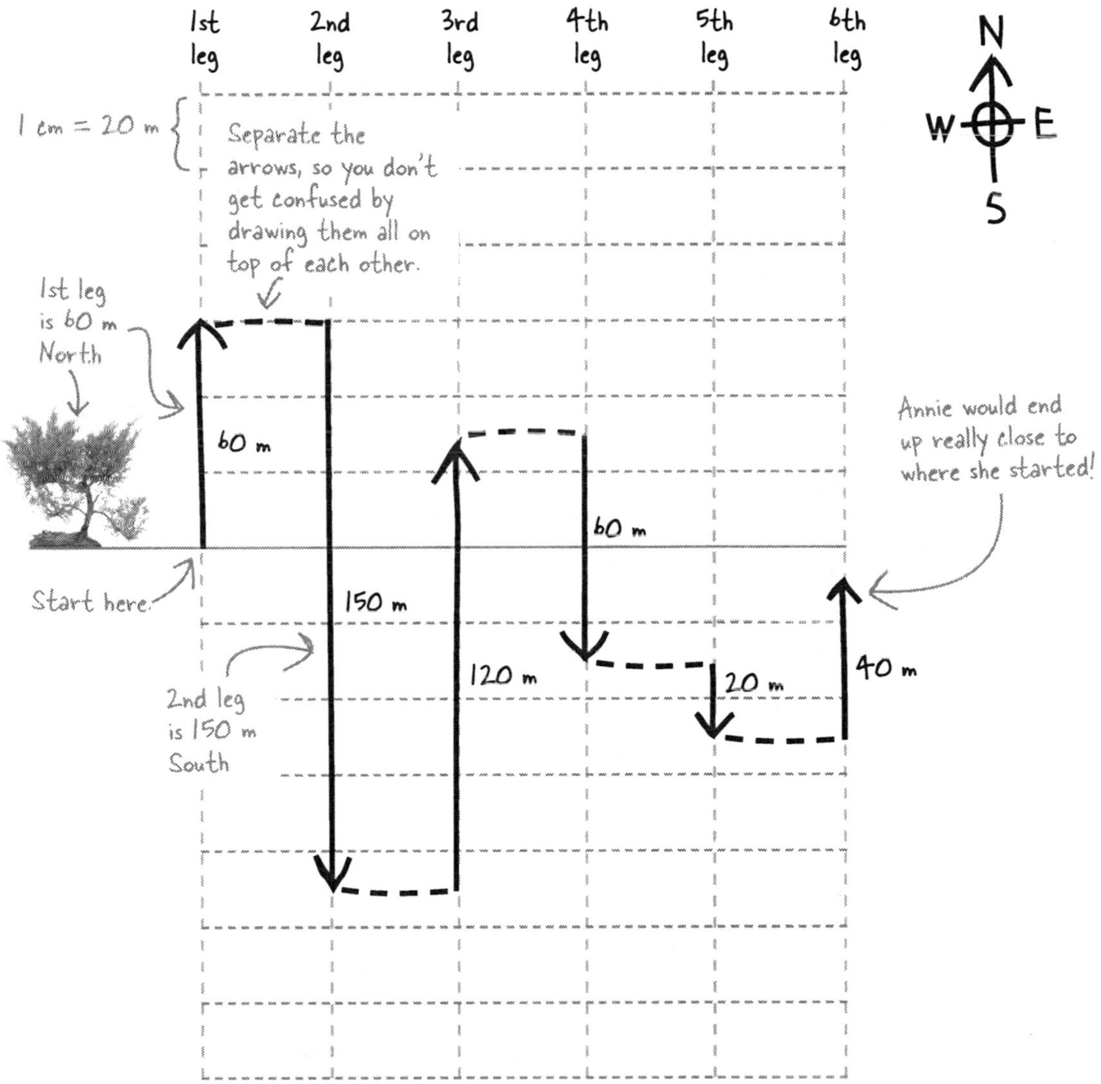

Displacement is different from distance

You've just worked out that Annie will end up very close to the tree if she follows the directions in the clue line by line. This illustrates the **difference between distance and displacement.**

Distance is the actual total distance traveled. If you walk 70 m North, then 30 m South, you travel a **total distance** of 100 m.

This is just a number with units - a size with no indication of direction.

But **displacement** is the change in **position** between two points regardless of the route you take to get there. If you walk 70 m North, then 30 m South, you wind up 40 m North of where you started. So your displacement is 40 m North.

This has both a size and a direction.

Sharpen your pencil

a. Work out the **distance** Annie would travel if she followed the instructions in the clue exactly.

b. Work out Annie's **displacement** - the size and direction of the change in position between her start and finish points.

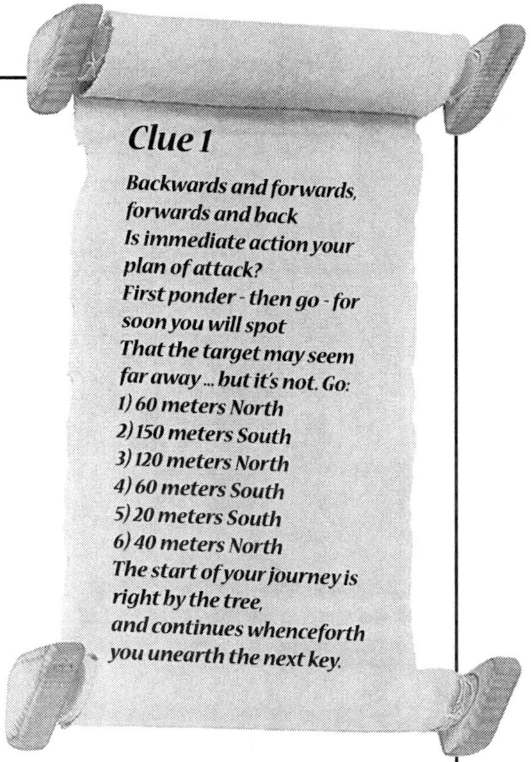

Sharpen your pencil Solution

a. Work out the **distance** Annie would travel if she followed the instructions in the clue exactly.

Distance = 60 + 150 + 120 + 60 + 20 + 40

= 450 m

She'd travel 450 m if she followed the instructions in the clue exactly.

b. Work out Annie's **displacement** - the size and direction of the change in position between her start and finish points.

The picture with the arrows on it shows that she ends up 10 m South of where she started.

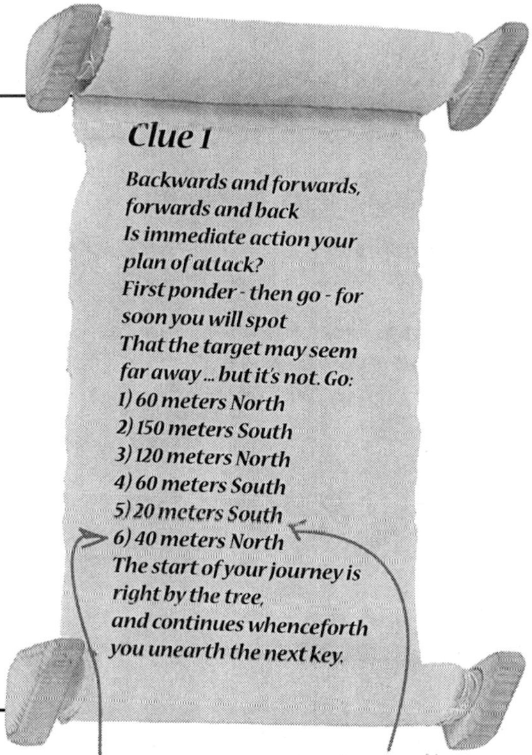

Each of the instructions in the clue is a displacement – with a SIZE and a DIRECTION.

there are no Dumb Questions

Q: So Annie ends up 10 m South of where she started! Isn't the clue a lot of fuss about nothing?!

A: The point of the clue is thinking before you act. If you set out instantly to try and save time, you actually end up running much further.

Q: We've done a lot with units in the past. Are the units of distance and displacement the same?

A: Distance and displacement are both measured in meters (or other units of length).

Q: How can distance and displacement be different things when they both have the same units?

A: Displacement has a direction attached to it - distance doesn't.

Q: Doesn't a direction have units too?

A: No. North, South, left, right, horizontal, vertical ... etc. None of them have units.

Q: OK, I think I'm getting it now. Distance and displacement are different because distance is just a size - but with displacement there's also a direction.

A: That's right ... and we're just getting to that now.

Distance has a size.

Displacement has a size and a direction.

Distance is a scalar; displacement is a vector

Distance is an example of a **scalar** quantity in physics. Scalars only have a **size**, like 10 meters.

Displacement is an example of a **vector** quantity in physics.

Vectors have a **size** and a **direction**, for instance 10 meters South.

The instructions in the clue are all vectors, as they have a size and a direction. The route you take to get to the next clue isn't important - all you're really interested in is the change in position between the start and end points.

Scalars only have a SIZE.

Vectors have a SIZE and a DIRECTION.

You can represent vectors using arrows

You can represent a vector quantity using an **arrow**, where the length of the arrow is proportional to the vector's size, and the arrow points in the vector's direction. You already did this when you were solving the clue.

You also intuitively added the vectors correctly, lining them up "**nose-to-tail**" by putting the tail of the next vector by the nose of the previous one.

If the vectors all lie along a straight line (like the ones here) it can be confusing just to draw them all on top of each other. It's easy to lose track of where you are. So sometimes it's appropriate to line them up next to each other (like you already did) with the understanding that they're actually all on top of each other.

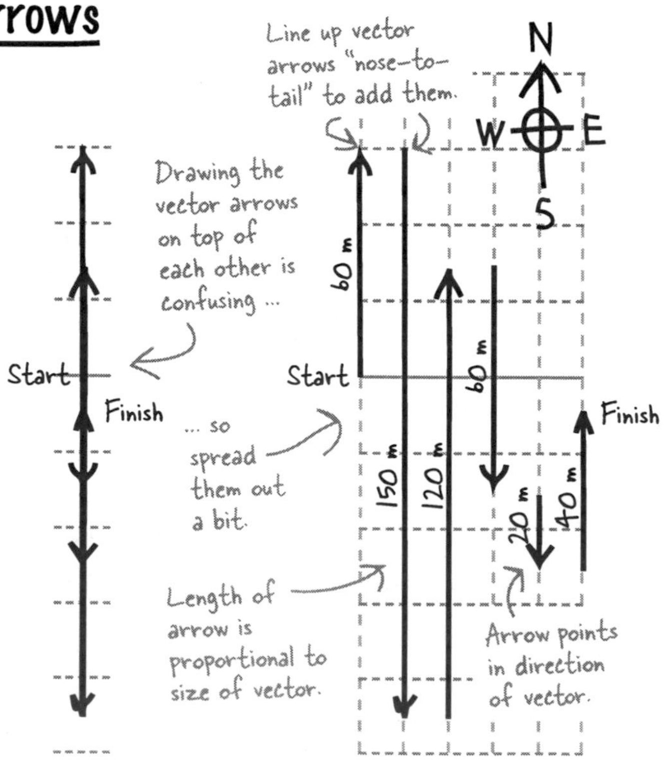

You can add vector arrows by lining them up "nose-to-tail."

Nope. The only thing that matters is adding vectors "nose-to-tail."

When you're adding vectors together, you should always line them up "nose to tail." This is what's important - it doesn't matter which **order** you add the vectors in.

Practically speaking, it might be easier to add together all the Norths first, then all the Souths, since the overall displacement is still the same.

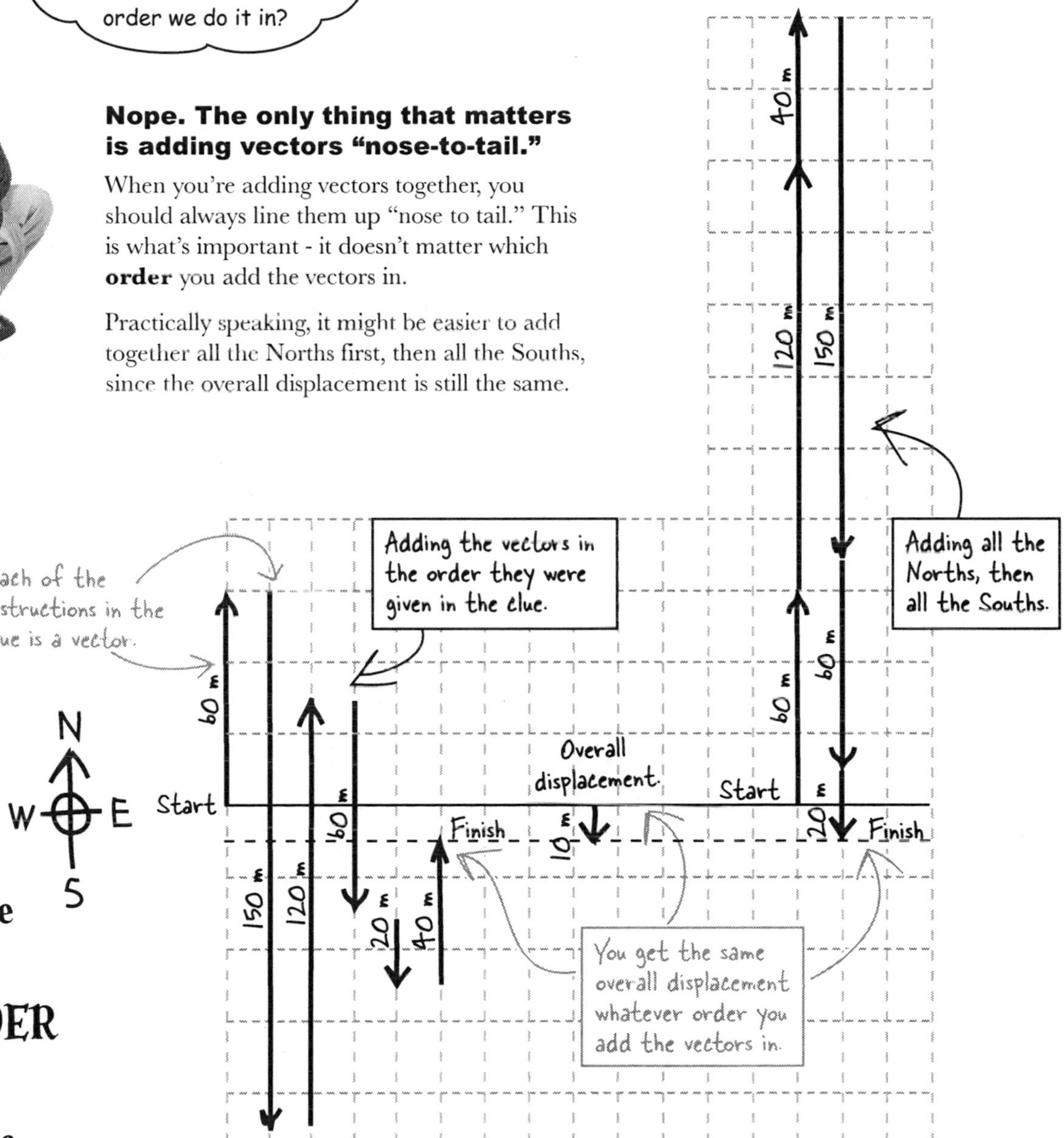

Adding the vectors in ANY ORDER will result in the same overall displacement.

Why take all that time to draw the vector arrows? If I'm **adding** them, can't I do it faster using math?!

You can add vectors quickly using math.

If you go 60 m North, and then 60 m South, your displacement is zero since you're back where you started.

North and South are **opposite directions** - so you can use **opposite signs** to represent them mathematically. Suppose you decide that traveling North is positive, and traveling South is negative. So 60 m North, then 60 m South is a displacement of 60 - 60 = 0 m (or 60 + -60 = 0).

When you were working out the displacement, you might already have intuitively done something like this (by making North the positive direction), like 60 - 150 + 120 - 60 - 20 + 40 = -10 m, which is the same as 10 m South of where you started. Or you may have added together all the Norths, then all the Souths, like the vector diagram on the other page.

You can use opposite <u>signs</u> to mean opposite <u>directions</u>.

This ONLY works if you have two opposite directions, like North-South, up-down, left-right, and so forth.

there are no Dumb Questions

Q: If vectors add "nose-to-tail," then how do scalars add?

A: The same way they always have - you just add the numbers together.

Q: Are there any other vector quantities apart from displacement?

A: Yes - we'll meet some others soon ...

Q: Don't you need to define a starting point before you add your vectors?

A: Yes, that's right. Sometimes there'll be an obvious starting point - like a tree! Sometimes you'll need to define one. For example, if you're describing heights, it's conventional to make 0 m equal to sea level and measure everything else in reference to that.

Q: How do you decide which way is positive and which way is negative?

A: It's up to you - as long as you choose a direction and stick with it, the math will work out the same. If you make North positive and your answer is -10 m, it means 10 m South. And if you make South positive and get the answer 10 m, that means 10 m South as well. You just need to remember how to **interpret the sign** of your answer at the end.

You found the next clue...

But there's a problem ...

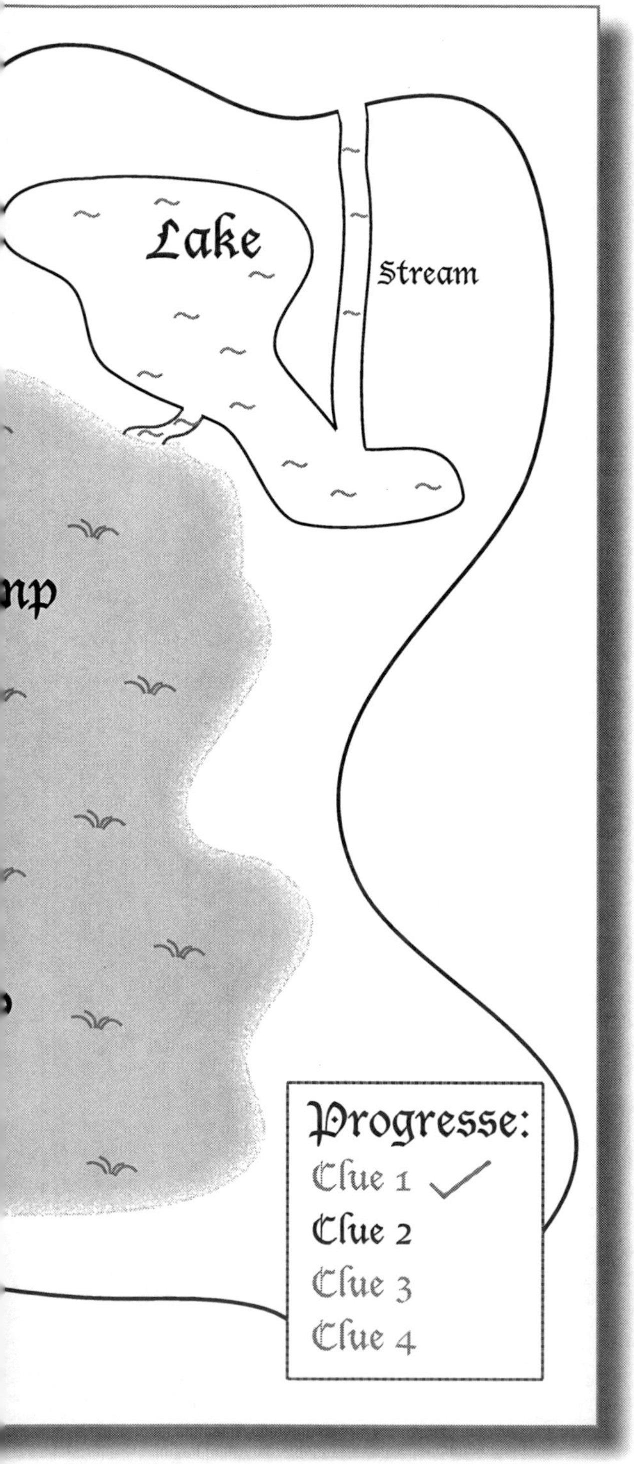

Sharpen your pencil

a. Draw the instructions from the clue on the map using vector arrows.

b. "Do not be swamped" is an important part of the clue. Write down your ideas about how you might achieve this.

....

....

....

....

....

Sharpen your pencil Solution

a. Draw the instructions from the clue on the map using vector arrows.

b. "Do not be swamped" is an important part of the clue. Write down your ideas about how you might achieve this.

Going East then North is impossible because of the swamp. But you can get to exactly the same place by going 1100 m North, then 700 m East. – you can follow the instructions either way around.

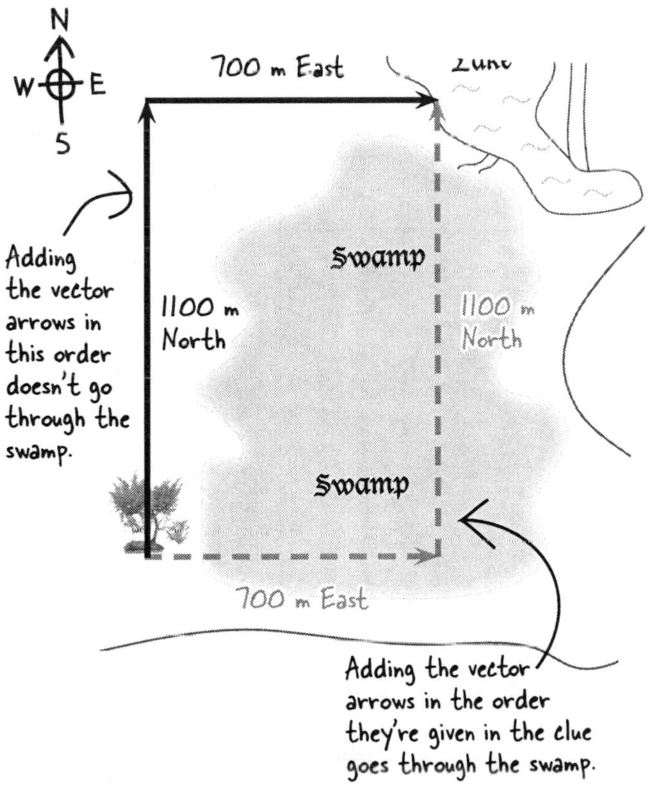

You can add vectors in any order

Even when vectors aren't pointing along the same line, you can still add them together by lining them up "nose-to-tail."

Whichever order you add them in, you always end up with the same difference in position between the start and finish points.

So you can send Annie 1100 m North first, then 700 m East. This way, she'll find the next clue without getting swamped.

there are no Dumb Questions

Q: So you're saying that even if I have hundreds of vectors, it doesn't matter what order I add them in?

A: Exactly! As long as you line the vectors up "nose-to-tail," you'll always end up with the same resultant vector at the end.

Q: Wait, what's a resultant vector?!

A: It's just another way of saying "answer vector." A resultant vector is what you get when you add together other vectors.

Q: So if I add together vectors, do I always get a resultant vector as my answer?

A: Yes. If you're adding vectors, your answer must also be a vector.

Q: Can a vector equal zero? Is that still a vector?

A: Yep, in the context of vector addition, you get a special vector called the "zero vector."

Q: It's OK to use a different sign for two directions when they're total opposites, like North and South, isn't it? But what about when they're not opposites - like North and East in this clue. How do I add the vectors using math then?

A: Great question - and something you'll learn all about in chapter 9.

When you add vectors together, your answer can be called the resultant vector.

BULLET POINTS

- Scalars have size. Distance is an example of a scalar.
- Vectors have both size and direction. Displacement is an example of a vector.
- You can represent vectors using arrows.
- The length of a vector arrow is equal to the size of the distance.
- The direction of a vector arrow is equal to direction of movement.
- You add vectors by lining them up "nose-to-tail" and following the arrows from start to finish.
- If your vectors all lie along a straight line, you can add them quickly using math by defining one direction as positive and the other direction as negative.
- If your vectors point in different directions, you can still add them by lining them up nose-to-tail, and following the arrows.
- You can add vectors in any order regardless of which direction they point in.

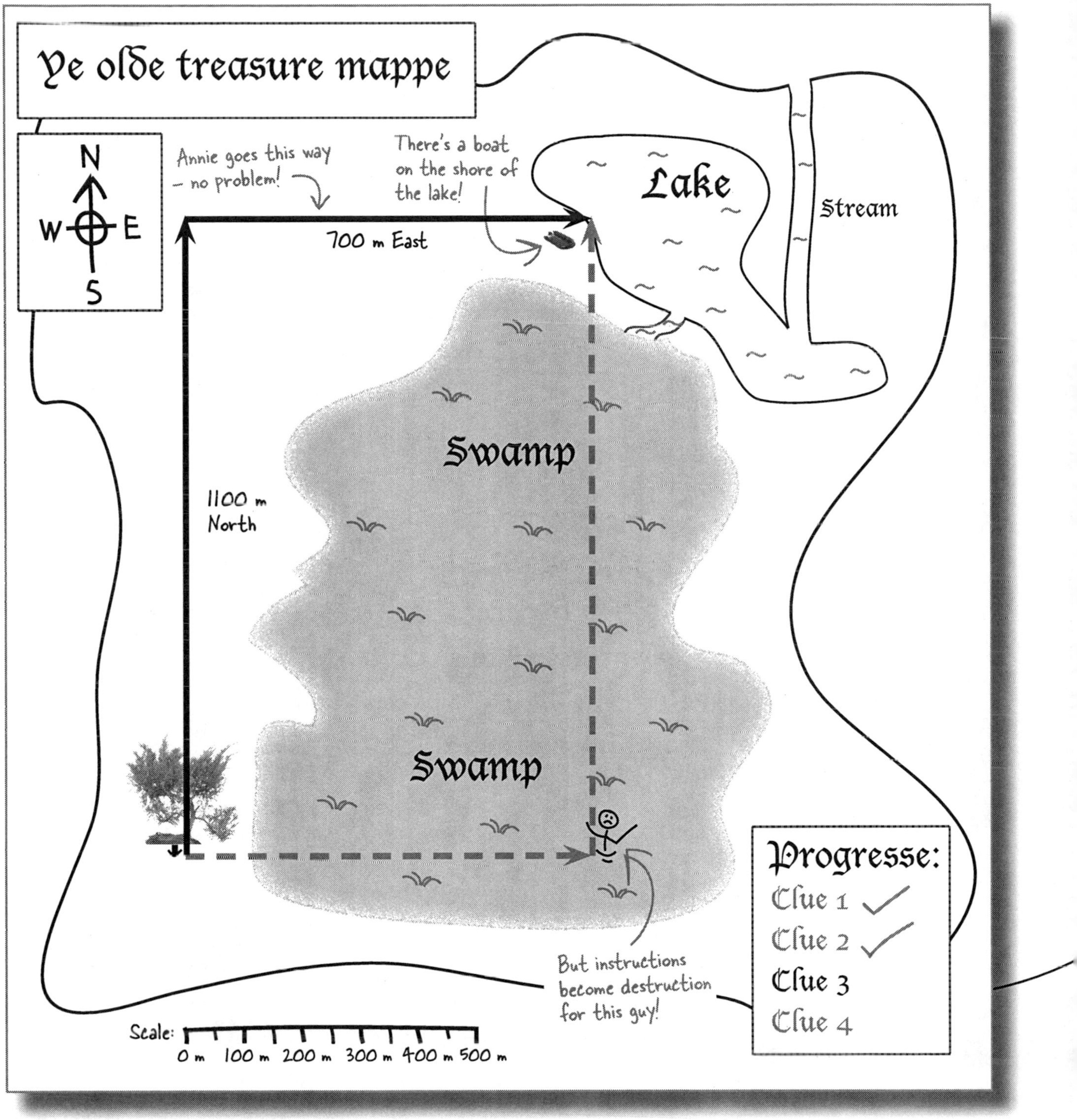

Ye olde treasure mappe
N
W
E
S
Annie goes this way – no problem!
There's a boat on the shore of the lake!
Lake
Stream
700 m East
1100 m North
Swamp
Swamp
Progresse:
Clue 1
Clue 2
Clue 3
Clue 4
But instructions become destruction for this guy!
Scale:
0 m 100 m 200 m 300 m 400 m 500 m

Well done - you've found the third clue!

And along with the third clue at the shore of the lake is a motor boat. There's a problem though - the clue has a lot of numbers and technical jargon in it.

To pick your way through it, first, work out **what** you're supposed to do. Once that's clear, think about **how** you might do it.

First what, then how.

Sharpen your pencil

Think - first **what**, then **how**.

Underline the parts of the clue that give you the "what," then use your own words to write down what you're supposed to do - and also how you might do it.

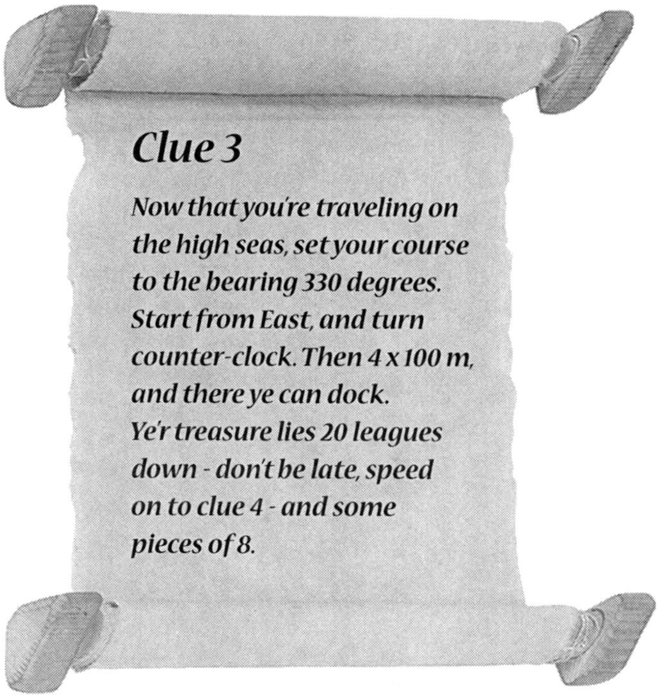

Question Clinic: The "Wheat from the chaff" Question

Sometimes a question will have a lot of unfamiliar words or jargon in it. Don't panic! Often a complicated-looking build-up leads into a straightforward question to test your ability to sort out the stuff that actually matters. The question may give you more information than you need to actually solve the problem, so don't worry if you don't use everything you're given.

Parts of the question contain irrelevant information and unfamiliar words. Don't let that stress you out or make you think you can't do it.

Here's some relevant information!

Clue 3

Now that you're traveling on the high seas. Set your course to the bearing 330 degrees. Start from East, and turn counter-clock. Then 4 x 100 m, and there ye can dock. Ye'r treasure lies 20 leagues down - don't be late, Speed on to clue 4 - and some pieces of 8.

Sometimes there'll be a line break in the middle of something relevant. Don't let that put you off!

As long as you can sort out the wheat from the chaff – or the important information from the irrelevant padding – you'll be fine.

Here are some numbers that you don't actually need to use to get your answer.

Look out for direction as well as size.

First what - then how! Start off by looking at the end of the question to see what you're actually being asked. Sometimes extra numbers or information are included in a simple factual question to test your understanding of the physics.

Sharpen your pencil Solution

Think - first **what**, then **how**.

Underline the parts of the clue that give you the "what," then use your own words to write down what you're supposed to do - and also how you might do it.

Clue 3

Now that you're traveling on the high seas, set your course to the bearing <u>330 degrees</u>. <u>Start from East</u>, and <u>turn counter-clock</u>. Then <u>4 x 100 m</u>, and there ye can dock. Ye'r treasure lies 20 leagues down - don't be late, speed on to clue 4 - and some pieces of 8.

WHAT – 4 x 100 m is 400 m

A bearing of 330 degrees sounds like an angle.

Measure it counter-clockwise from the East.

HOW – Protractor measures 330° counter-clockwise from the East, and a ruler plus the scale on the map measures the 400 m.

Don't worry if you've forgotten a lot about angles. We'll spend a while going over them on the next few pages.

Look out for questions on 'hard topics' (like particle physics) that you don't think you know much about. Often they're just questions about simpler stuff disguised to make them look 'difficult.' You may already know how to do them, so don't get psyched out at the start.

First WHAT - then HOW!

Angles measure rotations

Angles measure rotations, how far you have to rotate a line so that it lies on top of another line.

You've probably already come across a common way of measuring angles - in **degrees** (symbol: °).

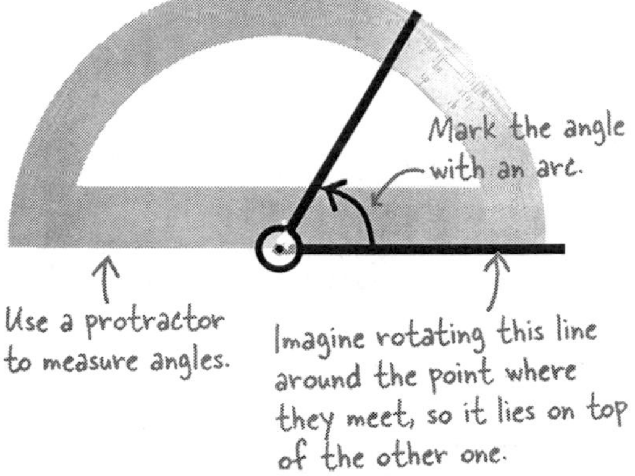

You measure angles with a **protractor**. It's marked off in degrees, so you can line it up and read off the size of the angle just like you would with a ruler.

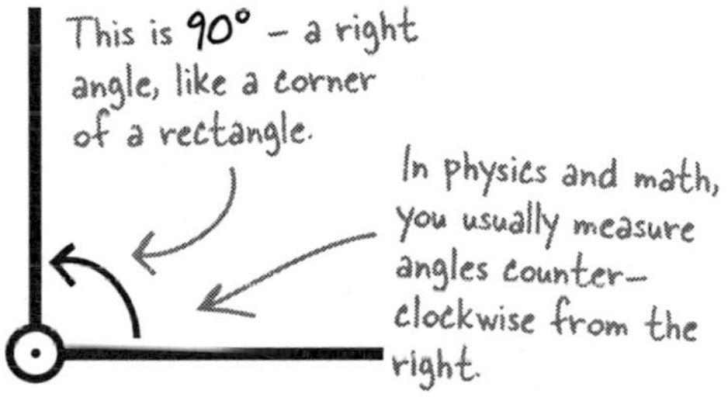

An angle that comes up a lot in physics is the **right-angle**, which is **90°**. It's a quarter of a revolution, and it's the angle you find in the corners of a rectangle. So you see right-angles everywhere you go - between the ground and anything standing on it (chair, table, building, and so forth).

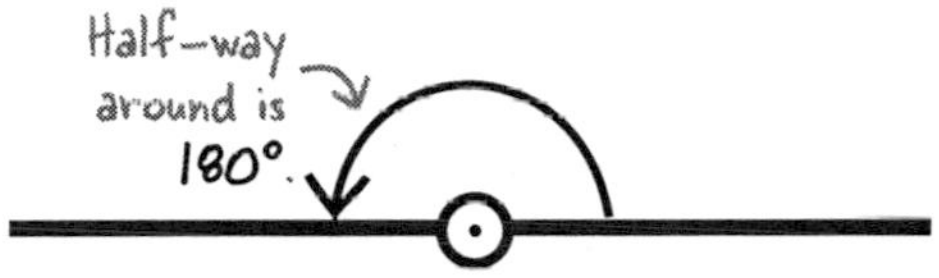

Half a revolution is **180°**, and it's called a straight angle. So anything that does a U-turn to go in the opposite direction has rotated 180°. It looks like a straight line.

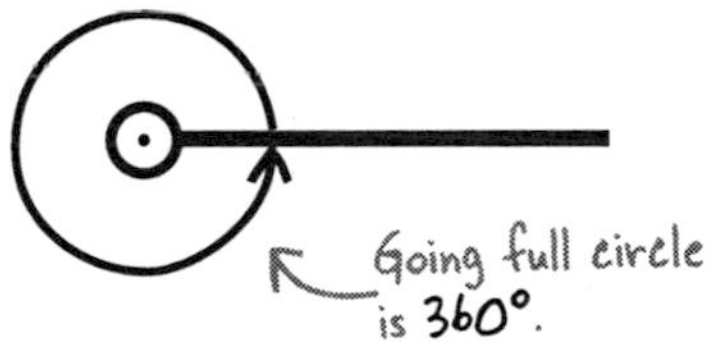

There are 360° in a complete revolution - if you go all the way around, so the line ends up back on top of itself, that's an angle of 360°.

90° = a right angle
180° = halfway around
360° = a full revolution

there are no Dumb Questions

Q: Why 360° in a full rotation? That seems a bit random. I mean - why not a nicer number like 100° or 1000°? Doesn't that fit in better with SI units?

A: The rotation originated from ancient civilizations thousands of years ago. But the most practical reason is that 360 divides exactly by a lot of useful numbers.

Q: But that works just as well if there are 100 degrees in a circle. Half a rotation would be 50, and a quarter would be 25 ...

A: Yes, we were just getting to that. With 360° in a rotation, a third of a rotation is 120°, and a sixth is 60°. Now, try doing that with 100 degrees in a circle- 33.33333333... degrees in a third of a rotation, anyone?

Q: Can you get angles bigger than 360° if something keeps on going round and round? Or does the angle 'reset' itself to 0° when you get back to where you started?

A: It depends on what you're trying to do - sometimes talking about the total rotation is useful; other times 'resetting' the angle when you get back to the start is useful.

Q: Is an angle a scalar or a vector?

A: Good question! It can be either, depending on whether you're talking about the total rotation (scalar) or the rotation distance between the start and finish points.

Q: Vectors are represented by straight arrows, where the length is proportional to the size. But how do you use a straight vector arrow to give the direction of an angle that's kinda curved?!

A: Yes - you can't directly represent an angle using a vector arrow. It's a valid question, but you don't have to worry about it for the moment, as we'll get on to representing angular quantities with vector arrows in chapter 12.

Now you can get on with clue 3!

You've worked out that you need to start off facing East, and rotate counter-clockwise through an angle of 330°. Once you've done that, you'll travel 400 m in the direction you're now facing to reach clue 4.

400 m on a bearing of 330 counter-clockwise from East is a displacement, not a distance, as it has both a size (400 m) and a direction (330° counter-clockwise from the East).

You can use an angle to indicate direction.

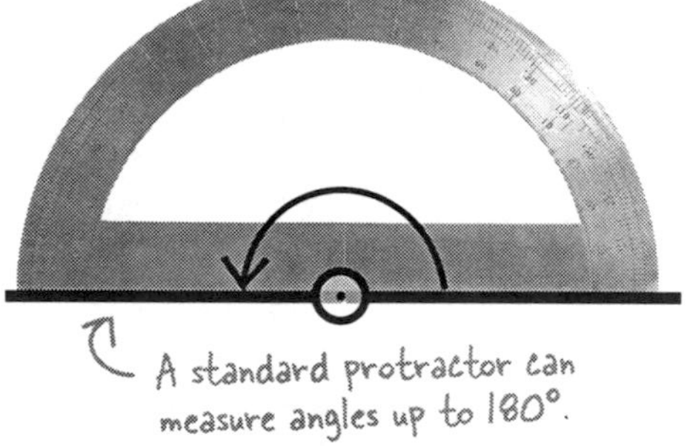

BRAIN POWER

How can **you** measure an angle of 330° when your protractor only goes up to 180°?

If you can't deal with something big, break it down into smaller parts

If you're measuring something with your ruler, and it's too long, you can start off by measuring along as far as you can. Then, you can make a mark, move the ruler along, and measure the next part. And so on.

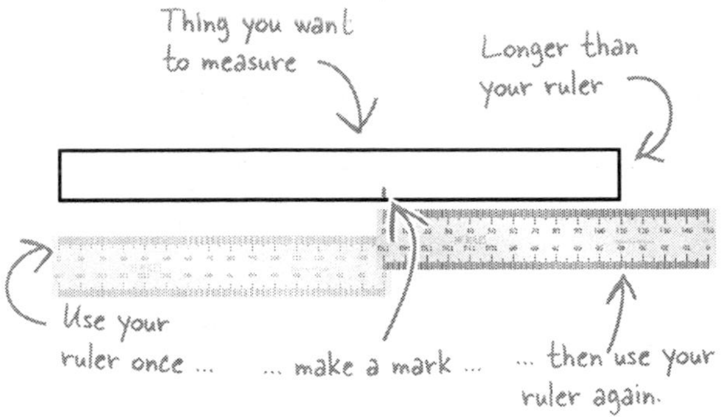

The underlying principle is one that's essential for physics - especially when it gets more complicated! If something's too big for you to deal with it all at once, **break it down into smaller parts** that you can deal with.

There are two ways you can do this with a standard 180° protractor - do whatever you're most comfortable with:

You can use your protractor twice to break down the angle

You can do exactly the same as you would with a ruler, and use your protractor twice. It goes up to 180°, so measure that far first.

To work out how much further to go, you can say 330° - 180° = 150°, then measure around another 150° from where you stopped.

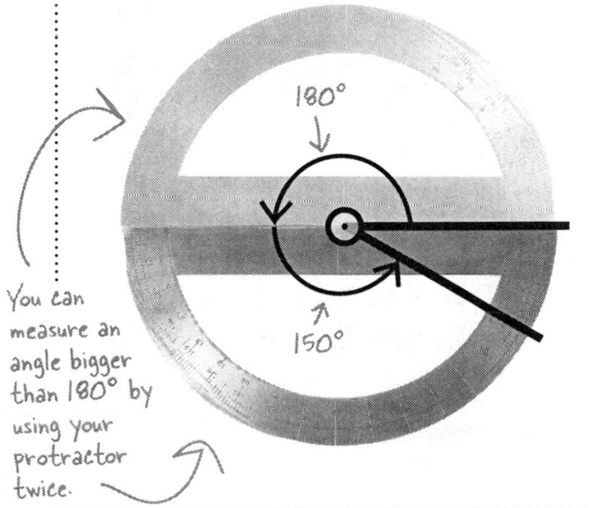

You can measure your angle the other way around

You can also say, "330° is only 30° short of being a full 360° circle." So turning 330° counterclockwise is the same as turning 30° clockwise.

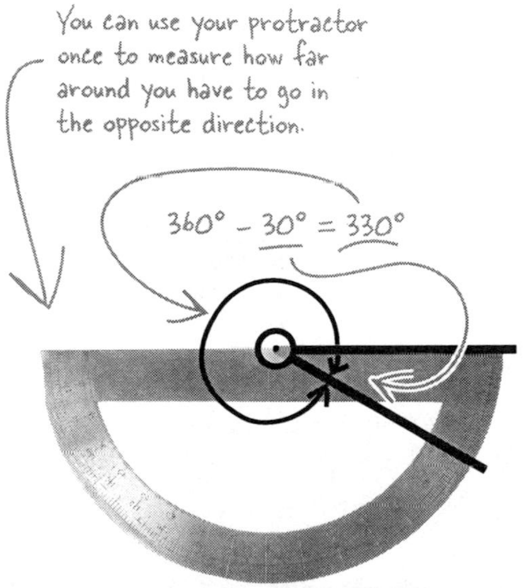

Sharpen your ~~pencil~~ protractor

Sharpen your protractor, follow the instructions in the clue, and draw Annie's route on the lake.

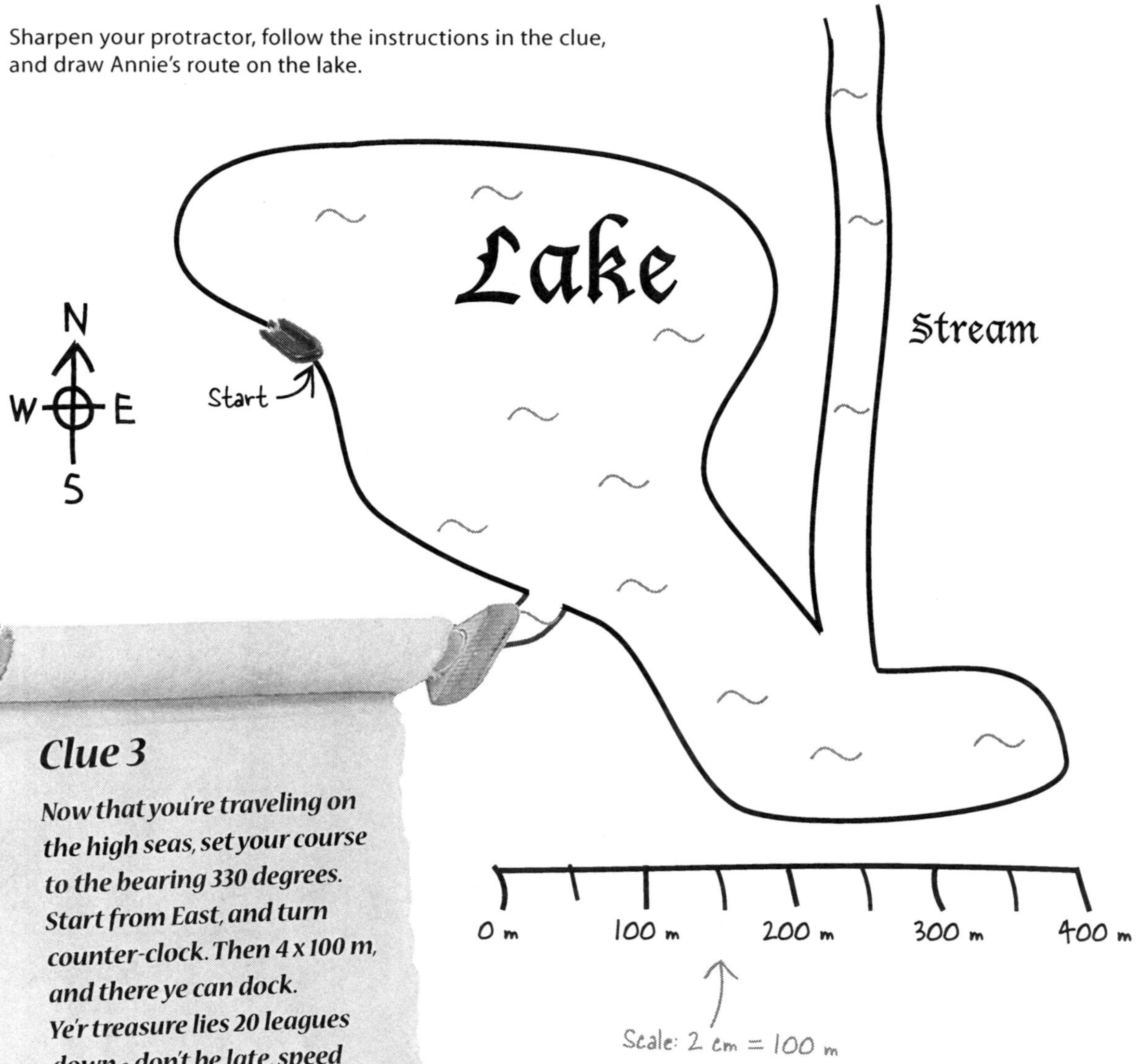

Clue 3

Now that you're traveling on the high seas, set your course to the bearing 330 degrees. Start from East, and turn counter-clock. Then 4 x 100 m, and there ye can dock. Ye'r treasure lies 20 leagues down - don't be late, speed on to clue 4 - and some pieces of 8.

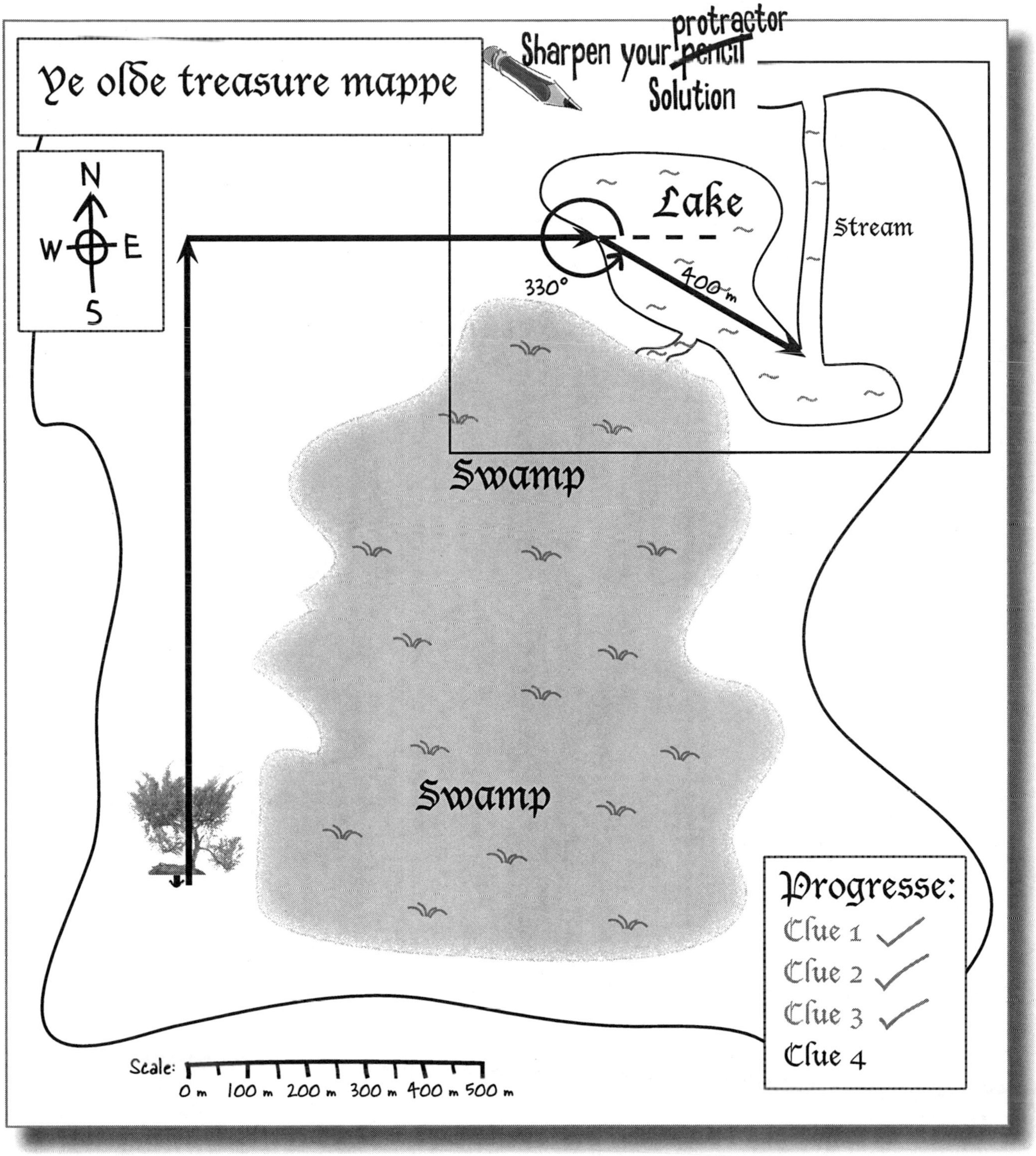
Ye olde treasure mappe
Sharpen your ~~pencil~~ protractor
Solution
N
W
E
S
Lake
Stream
330°
400 m
Swamp
Swamp
Progresse:
Clue 1
Clue 2
Clue 3
Clue 4
Scale:
0 m 100 m 200 m 300 m 400 m 500 m

You move onto the fourth clue...

You got the angle right because Annie's found a sign sticking out of the water with the fourth clue on it!

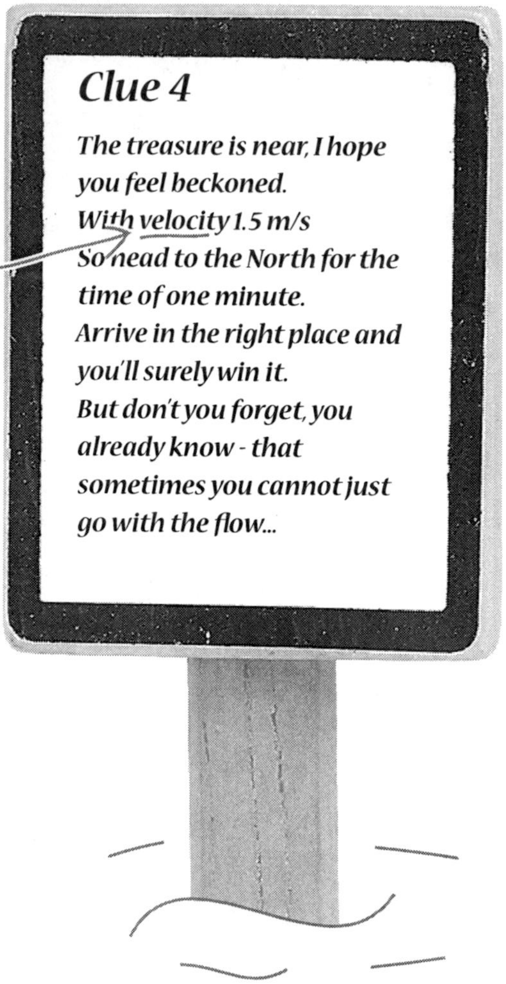

A word you've not seen yet in this book

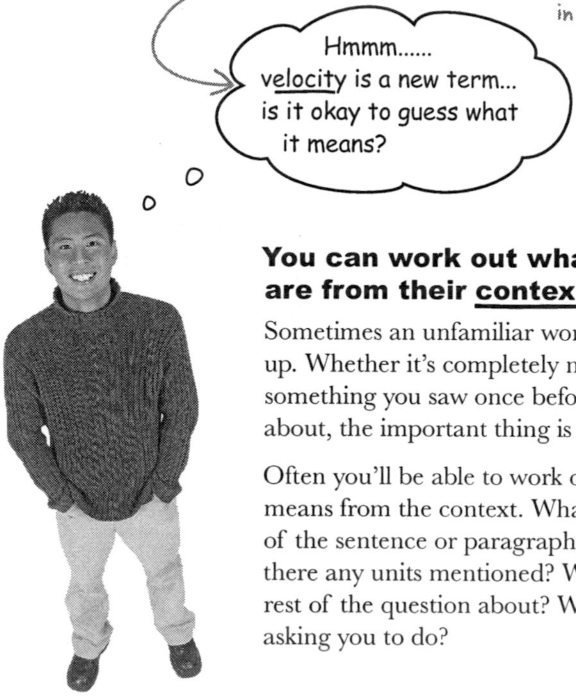

You can work out what things are from their context.

Sometimes an unfamiliar word comes up. Whether it's completely new to you or something you saw once before then forgot about, the important thing is **not to panic.**

Often you'll be able to work out what it means from the context. What is the rest of the sentence or paragraph about? Are there any units mentioned? What is the rest of the question about? What are they asking you to do?

Sharpen your pencil

See if you can work out what a velocity might be from the context.

If you already know what a velocity is, then write down how someone who doesn't could work it out from the context.

....

....

....

....

Sharpen your pencil Solution

See if you can work out what a velocity might be from the context.

If you already know what a velocity is, then write down how someone who doesn't could work it out from the context!

Velocity has UNITS of m/s, which looks like meters divided by seconds.

That's the same units as speed.

There's also a DIRECTION mentioned–North.

I think that velocity might be a vector version of speed, with both a size and a direction.

Just like displacement is the vector version of distance.

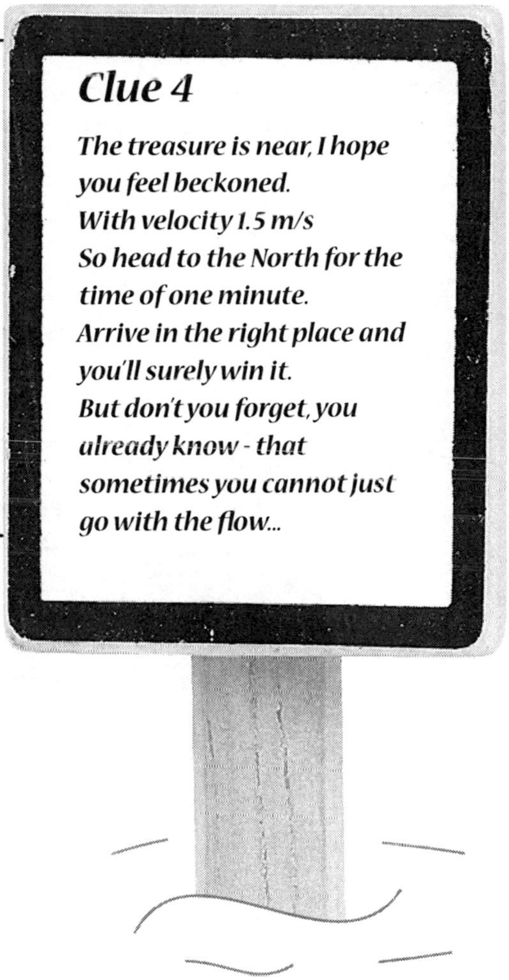

Velocity is the 'vector version' of speed

Velocity is measured in meters per second - which is exactly the same units as speed. Velocity is the 'vector version' of speed - it has a **direction** as well as a **size**.

Speed is a scalar - "I'm traveling at 1.5 m/s."

Velocity is a vector - "I'm traveling North at 1.5 m/s."

Same units

Direction

Size

So the clue is asking you to go North at 1.5 m/s for a minute.

Scalar → **Speed is rate of change of distance.** ← Scalar

Vector → **Velocity is rate of change of displacement.** ← Vector

Write units using shorthand

You've spotted that the units of velocity are written as m/s in the clue. This is a more concise way of writing meters per second. The '/' means 'per' or 'divided by.'

Meters per second is the same as meters divided by seconds. So when you use the standard letters to abbreviate the units, you get m/s.

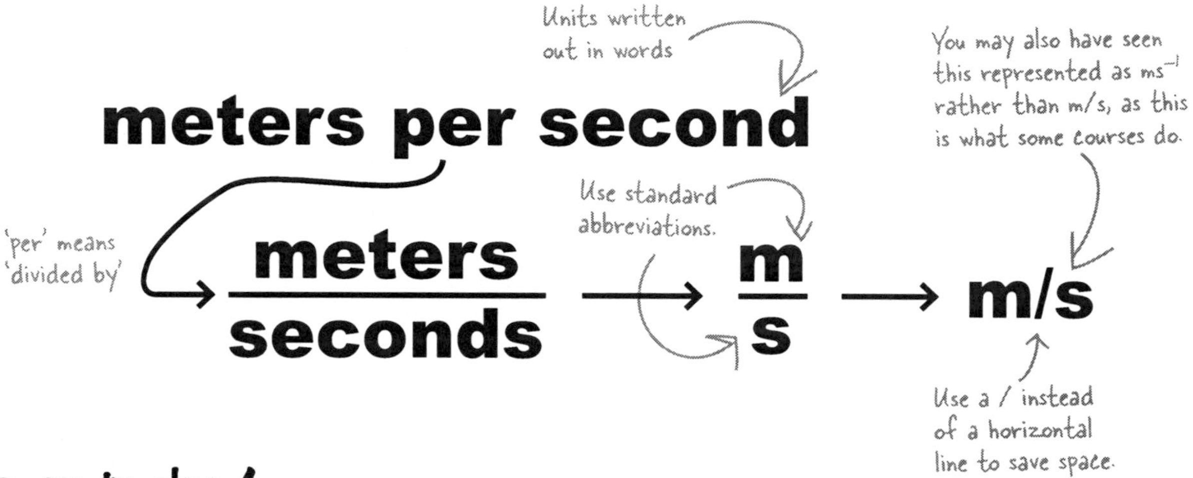

So, on to clue 4 ...

Now that you know that velocity is the vector version of speed, you tell Annie to point the boat North, set the controls to 1.5 m/s, and travel for a minute before dropping the anchor.

But when she arrives, there's no treasure.

BRAIN POWER

What do you think's gone wrong?

You need to allow for the stream's velocity too!

Clue 3 took place entirely on a still lake. So when the boat was set to go at a certain velocity relative to the water, that was the velocity it went at.

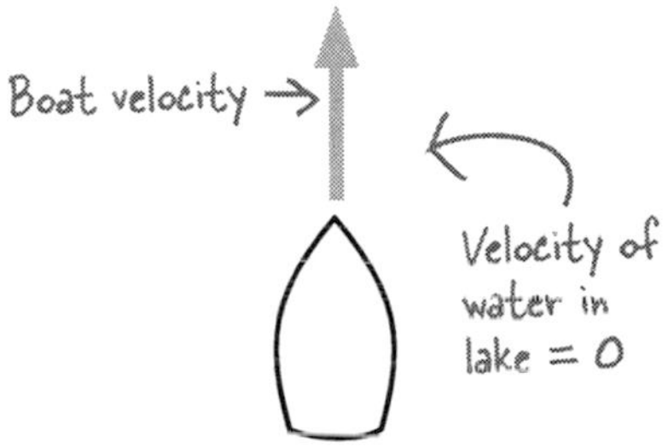

Going North from the Clue 4 sign involves going downstream, towards the sea. If Annie didn't start the motor, the boat would move North with the same velocity as the stream.

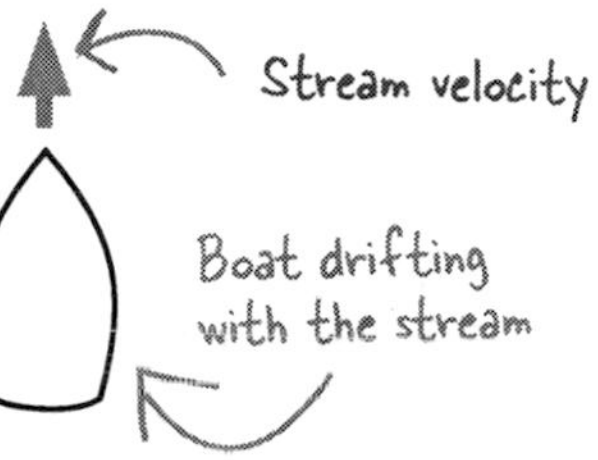

But Annie did start the motor - and the boat moved North with a reading of 1.5 m/s on its speedometer. But the speedometer tells you how fast the boat's going **relative** to the water. This means that Annie went faster than the clue said she should, at 1.5 m/s plus the velocity of the stream.

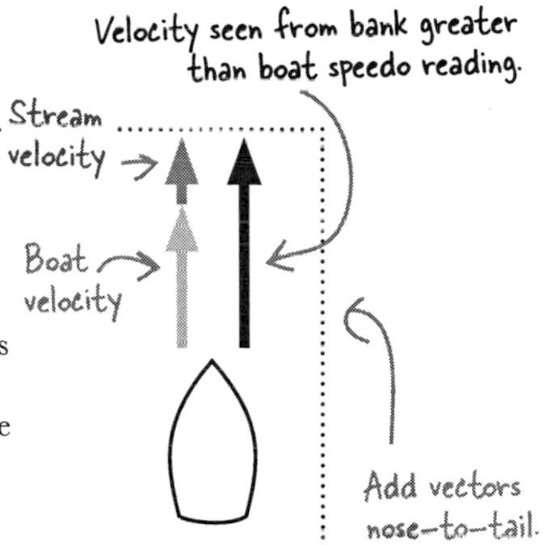

If the upstream current was really, really fast, the boat would go backwards even if the reading on its speedometer said it was going forwards!

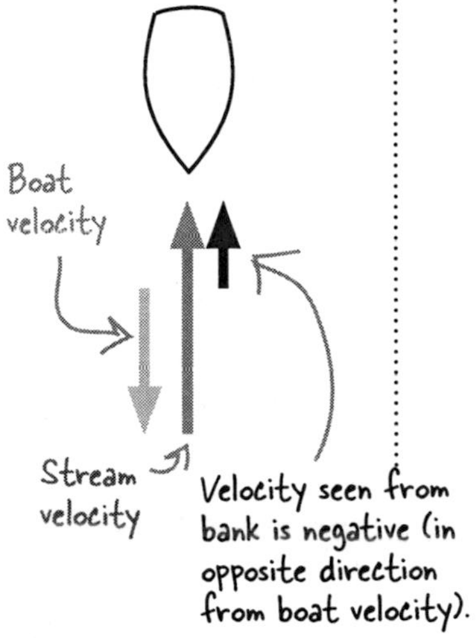

If Annie had been going South, upstream, the boat and stream velocity vectors would point in different directions. So the overall velocity of the boat as seen from the bank would be less than the reading on its speedometer.

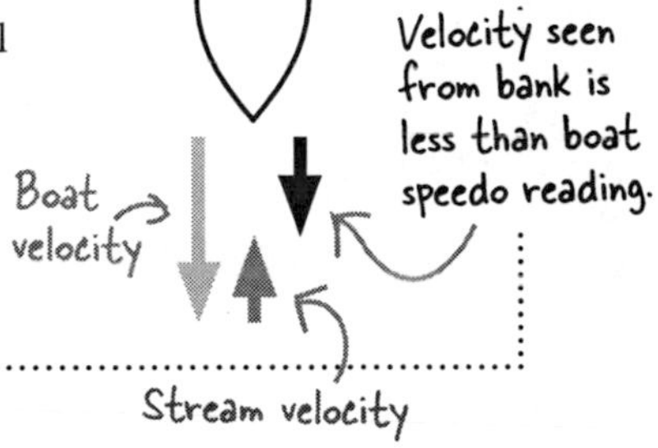

If you can find the stream's velocity, you can figure out the velocity for the boat

It's possible to add velocity vectors by lining them up nose-to-tail in the same way you added up the displacement vectors earlier on.

You know that the overall velocity of the boat needs to be 1.5 m/s to the North. And Annie works out a way of measuring the velocity of the stream by dropping leaves in it.

Now, you only need to do the calculation, send Annie on her way, and the treasure is yours ...

Sharpen your pencil

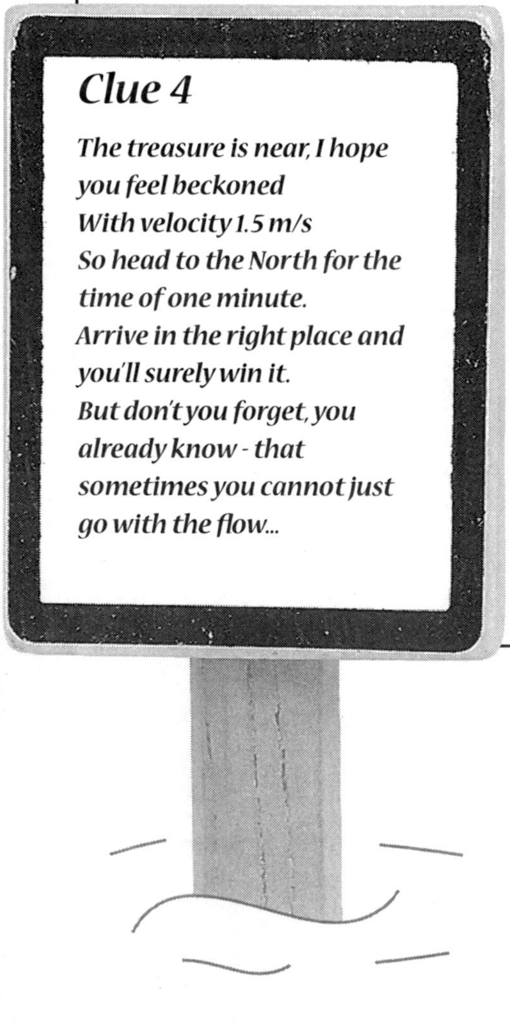

The boat needs to go North with an overall velocity of 1.5 m/s for a minute.

a. If the leaves Annie throws into the stream travel 10 m North in 20 s, what's the velocity of the stream?

b. What speed should Annie set on the boat's speedometer to solve the clue and find the treasure? (You may find it helpful to use vector arrows to visualize this.)

Sharpen your pencil Solution

The boat needs to go North with an overall velocity of 1.5 m/s for a minute.

a. If the leaves Annie throws into the stream travel 10 m North in 20 s, what's the velocity of the stream?

b. What speed should Annie set on the boat's speedometer to solve the clue and find the treasure? (You may find it helpful to use vector arrows to visualize this.)

a. Leaves travel 10 m North in 20 s.

$$\text{Velocity} = \frac{\text{Change in displacement}}{\text{Change in time}} = \frac{10\text{ m}}{20\text{ s}} = \underline{\underline{0.5\text{ m/s North}}}$$

b. Annie wants to go North at 1.5 m/s.

Stream will 'provide' 0.5 m/s of this velocity.

So the boat should go North at 1.0 = m/s (relative to the stream).

If you're asked for a vector quantity, remember to give a DIRECTION as well as a size.

A sketch makes everything clearer!

there are no Dumb Questions

Q: So basically a vector is something I can draw as an arrow, right?

A: Yes - the length of the arrow represents the size, and the direction of the arrow represents the direction.

Q: I was fine with displacement, where the length of the arrow represents an ACTUAL length. But I'm kinda finding it hard to visualize a velocity.

A: Something's overall velocity vector points in the direction that it's currently moving in. If it's going fast, you draw a long arrow, and if it's going slow, a shorter arrow.

Q: Right - so something going fast to the North would have a long arrow pointing North, and something moving slowly to the East would have a short arrow pointing East.

A: Exactly.

The overall velocity vector points in the direction the thing's currently moving in.

A speedometer gives the velocity RELATIVE to the water. But you're interested in the velocity RELATIVE to the bank

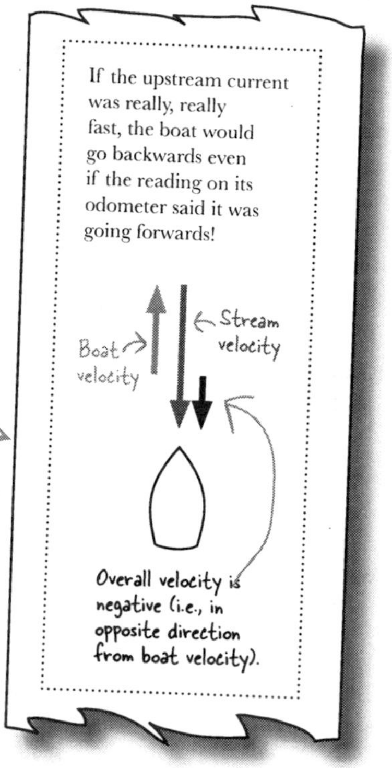

Q: How do you mean? Surely the boat can only have one velocity?

A: The boat's speedometer tells you how fast it's going relative to the water. But if the water is also moving, then the boat's velocity vector, as seen from the bank of the stream, will be different. It points in the direction that the boat is currently moving in. The velocity of the boat as seen from the bank is equal to the boat's velocity relative to the water plus the water's velocity.

Q: But that doesn't make sense.

A: You know the moving walkway at the airport that helps you travel long distances more quickly? What happens if you turn around and start walking in the opposite direction of the walkway's motion? You start moving backwards relative to the rest of the building, but you're actually moving forwards relative to the walkway. The walkway moves you backwards more quickly than you're walking forwards.

It's the same with the boat and the stream.

So Annie goes North at 1.0 m/s for 1 minute ...

... but doesn't find any treasure this time either.

BRAIN POWER

Annie did exactly what you asked her to, but it hasn't worked out again. Any ideas why?

It takes the boat time to accelerate from a standing start

Although Annie pointed the boat North and set the controls for 1.5 m/s, the boat takes time to get up to that speed from standing still. It takes time to **accelerate** from 0 m/s to 1.5 m/s.

Annie started timing the boat before it had accelerated up to 1.5 m/s. So it didn't go at 1.5 m/s for the whole minute - and didn't go as far as it should have.

It's OK if you didn't think of the boat accelerating – this one was pretty tricky!

The boat spent part of the minute accelerating from 0 m/s to 1.5 m/s ...

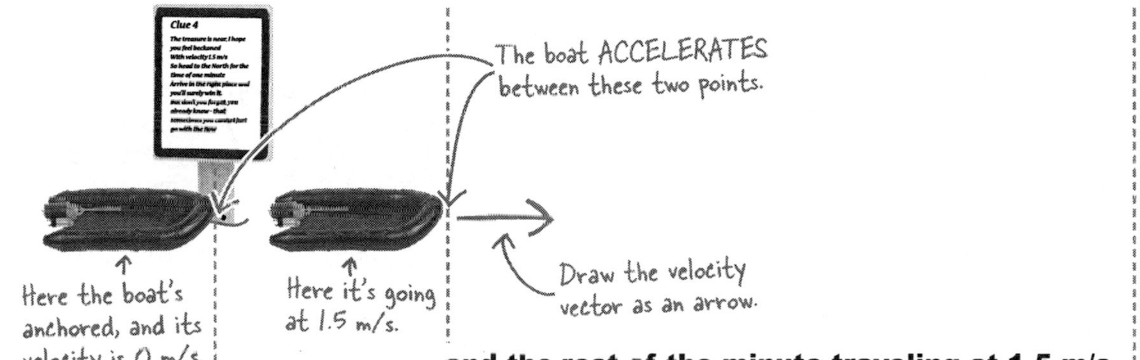

... and the rest of the minute traveling at 1.5 m/s.

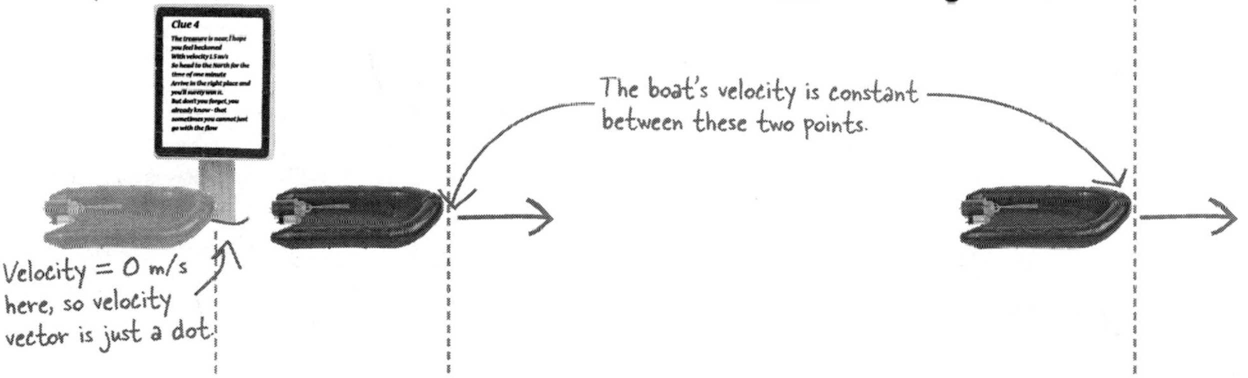

If it had spent the WHOLE MINUTE traveling at 1.5 m/s, it would've gone even further.

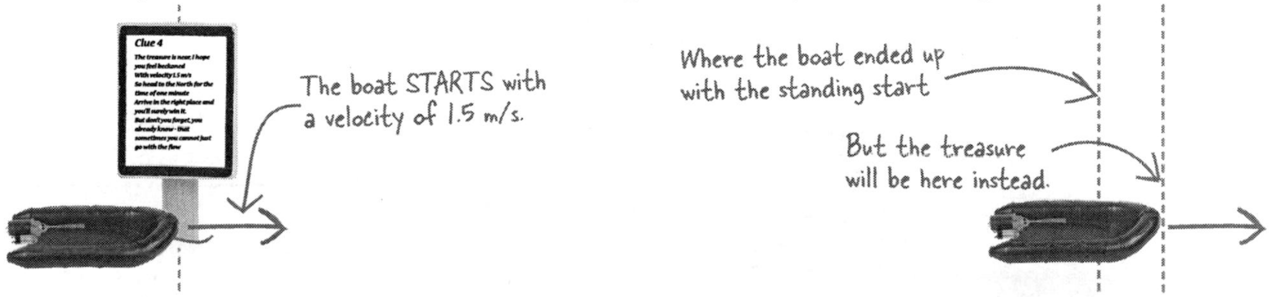

How do you deal with acceleration?

Acceleration is the rate of change of velocity - if something is accelerating, it means that its velocity is changing. Acceleration is a vector with a size and a direction.

If the boat is going forwards, and you open up the throttle, it accelerates in the same direction you're already going in. Its acceleration vector points forwards.

If a boat's going forwards, and you drop the anchor, it decelerates. You can think of this as acceleration in the opposite direction from the one it's already traveling in, so its acceleration vector points backwards.

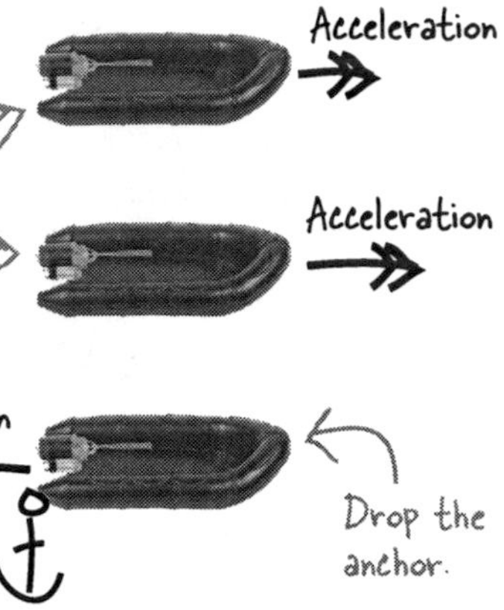

Acceleration is the rate of change of velocity.

Exercise

Draw the directions of the velocity vector and acceleration vector for each of these things, showing what they'll look like at the very moment when the acceleration that's described starts to happen.

We gave the acceleration vector a second arrowhead, so you can tell the difference between it and velocity or displacement vectors.

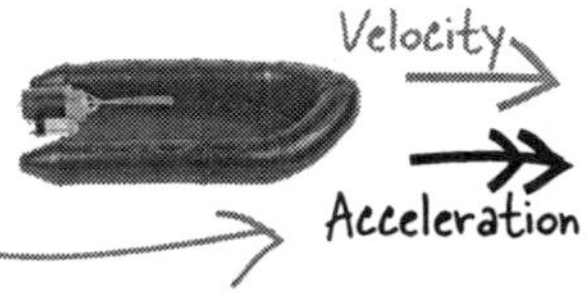

The boat is traveling forwards, and you open up the throttle.

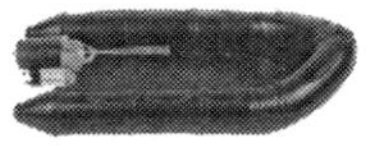

The boat is drifting backwards, and you open up the throttle.

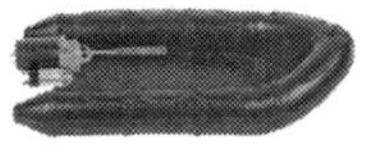

The boat is going forwards, and you drop the anchor.

The boat is going backwards, and you drop the anchor.

The duck is going from right to left, and it just hit the edge.

The duck is going forwards and is pushed by a current coming from the right.

Your right, as you look straight at the duck, that is.

Sharpen your pencil Solution

Velocity vector is gray.

Acceleration vector is black with two arrowheads.

Draw the directions of the velocity vector and acceleration vector for each of these things, showing what they'll look like at the very moment when the acceleration that's described starts to happen.

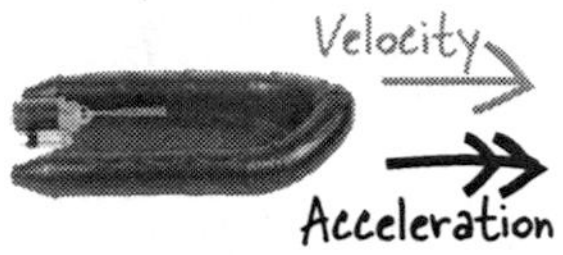

The boat it traveling forwards, and you open up the throttle.

The boat is drifting backwards, and you open up the throttle.

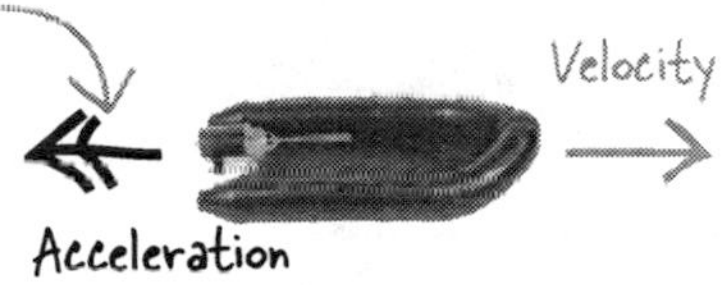

The boat is going forwards, and you drop the anchor.

The boat is going backwards, and you drop the anchor.

The duck is going from right to left, and it has just hit the edge.

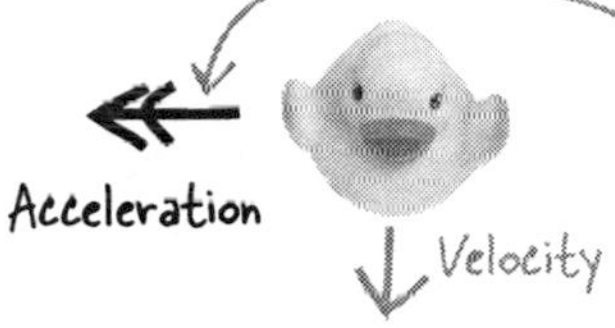

The duck is going forwards and is pushed by a current coming from the right.

there are no Dumb Questions

Q: Isn't it confusing to represent the displacement, velocity, and acceleration all with arrows?

A: It's only confusing if you don't label your sketches with what's going on.

Q: How can the anchor make the boat accelerate when it slows it down?

A: The anchor changes the velocity of the boat. Acceleration is rate of change of velocity. So even slowing down is still an acceleration.

Q: But wouldn't that be a DEceleration then?!

A: The 'de' means the acceleration and velocity are in **opposite directions**. So when you do math, the acceleration and velocity vectors will have **opposite signs**.

Q: Ah math, lovely. Shouldn't I know the units of acceleration to do that?

A: Acceleration is the rate of change of velocity. You'll work out the units in chapter 6; right now, we're just dealing with the concept.

So it's back to the boat ...

You told Annie to start at the Clue 4 sign, set the controls for 1.0 m/s, and go North for a minute. But because the boat took time to accelerate from a standing start, it didn't go the whole way at 1.0 m/s, and Annie ended up in the wrong place.

Now that you know that the boat's acceleration could be a problem, how are you going to guide Annie to the treasure?

Sharpen your pencil

Can you think of how to make sure Annie ends up where the treasure is?

Draw / write / explain / calculate in the space below.

We're not telling you which of these you'll have to do – that's up to you! The main thing is to explain your idea as clearly as possible.

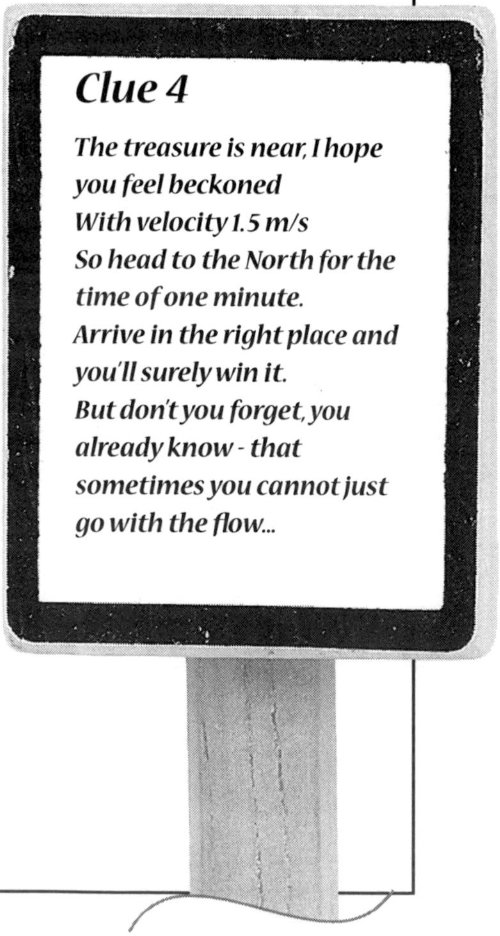

Sharpen your pencil Solution

Can you think of how to make sure Annie ends up where the treasure is?

Draw / write / explain / calculate in the space below.

We're not telling you which of these you'll have to do – that's up to you! The main thing is to explain your idea as clearly as possible.

There are TWO ways you could have done this problem.

<u>You can do this by working out the DISPLACEMENT.</u>

The boat needs to travel at 1.5 m/s for 60 s to reach the treasure.

In 1 s, the boat travels 1.5 m.

So in 60 s, the boat travels 1.5 × 60 = 90 m

So tell Annie to go <u>90 m North</u> of the clue 4 sign.

The principle for velocity and displacement is exactly the same as for speed and distance.

If you forget a formula, you'll often be able to work it out using common sense, like this. So don't panic!

<u>You can also do this with a 'rolling start.'</u>

If the boat's ALREADY going at the correct velocity when it passes the clue 4 sign, then going for a minute, as per the clue, will work out fine.

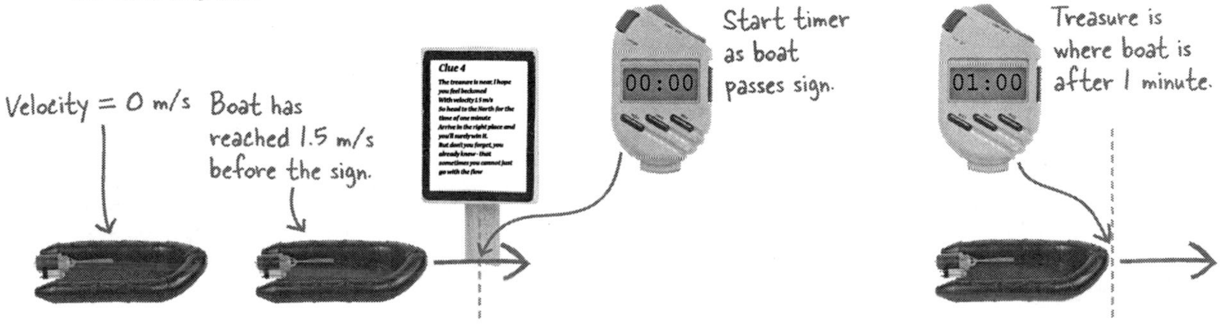

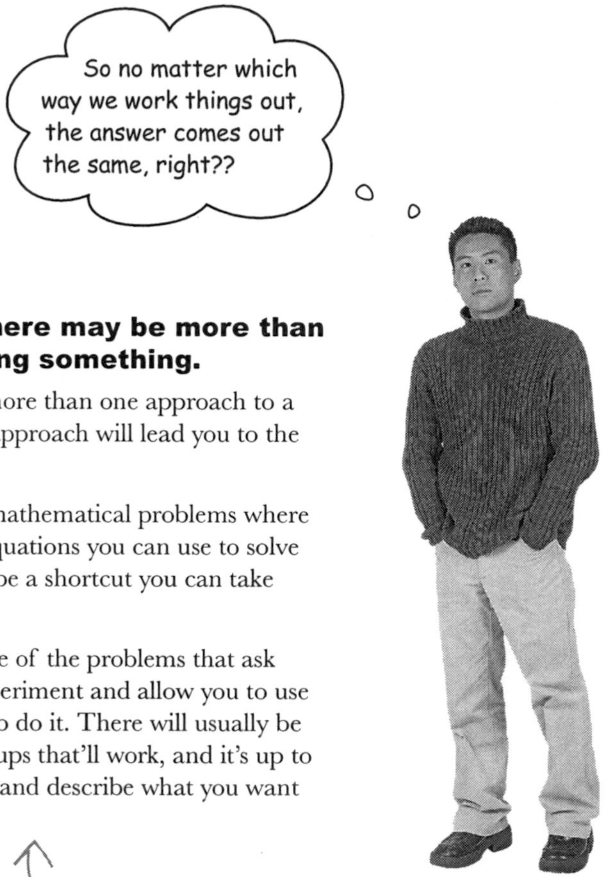

That's right - there may be more than one way of doing something.

Sometimes there's more than one approach to a problem, and each approach will lead you to the same answer.

This is the case for mathematical problems where there are multiple equations you can use to solve them, or there may be a shortcut you can take that'll save you time.

This is especially true of the problems that ask you to design an experiment and allow you to use a lot of equipment to do it. There will usually be several different set-ups that'll work, and it's up to you to design, draw, and describe what you want to do.

Like you just did here!

Problem Solving 101: Understand WHAT's going on, then work out HOW to do it.

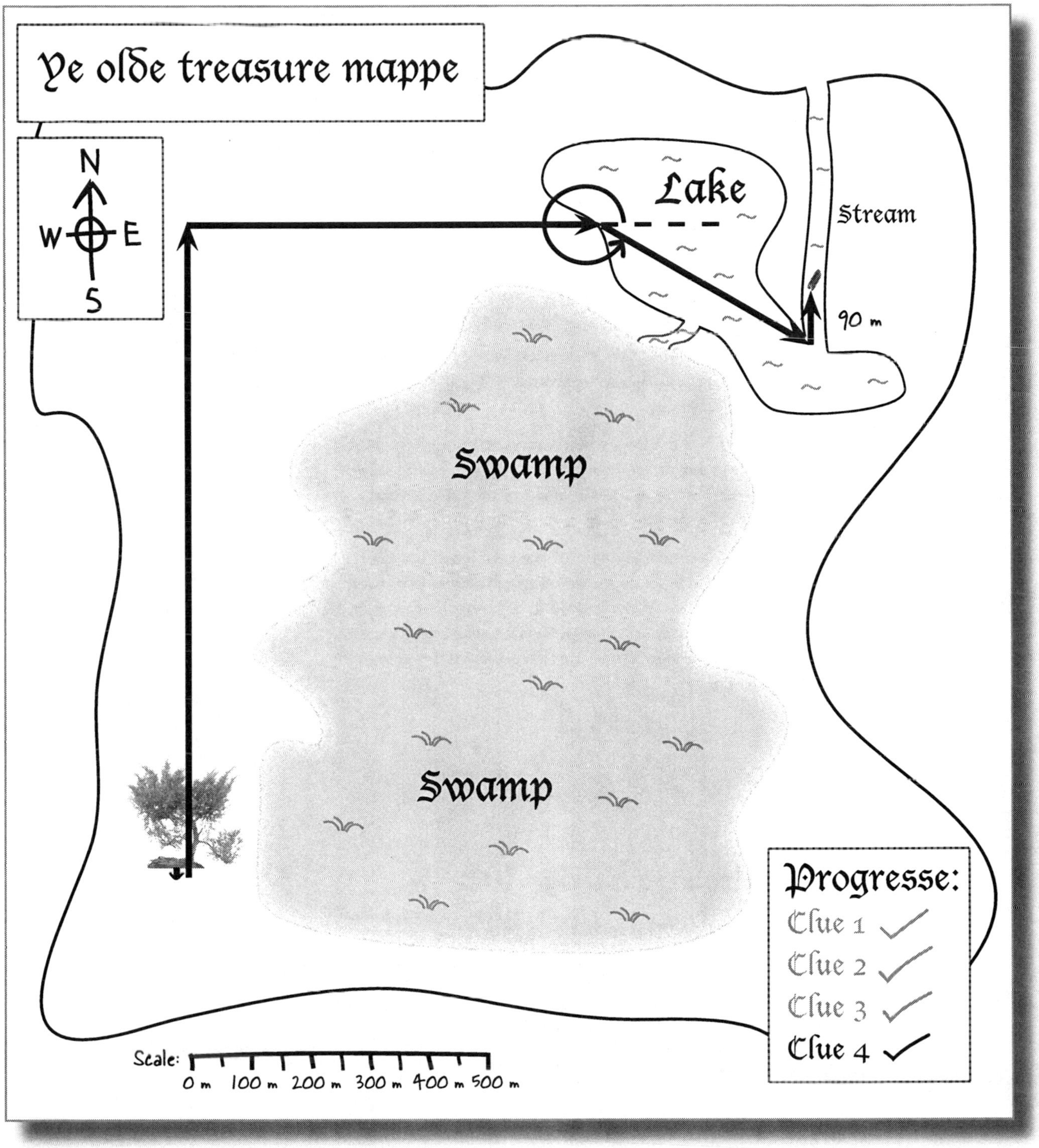
Ye olde treasure mappe
N
W
E
S
Lake
Stream
90 m
Swamp
Swamp
Progresse:
Clue 1
Clue 2
Clue 3
Clue 4
Scale:
0 m 100 m 200 m 300 m 400 m 500 m

Vector, Angle, Velocity, Acceleration = WINNER!!!

Clue 1

Direction is important.

Displacement is the 'vector version' of distance. It has both a size and a direction.

You can represent opposite directions using vector arrows or math signs.

Clue 2

You can add vectors that don't lie along a straight line by drawing them out and adding 'nose-to-tail.'

It doesn't matter which order you add vectors in as long as you line them up 'nose-to-tail.'

Clue 3

In physics, you measure angles counter-clockwise from the horizontal.

Clue 4

Velocity is the 'vector version' of speed. It has both a size and a direction.

You can add velocity vectors by lining them up 'nose-to-tail.'

Be careful about what a velocity is relative to; for example, a boat's velocity could be relative to the stream or the bank.

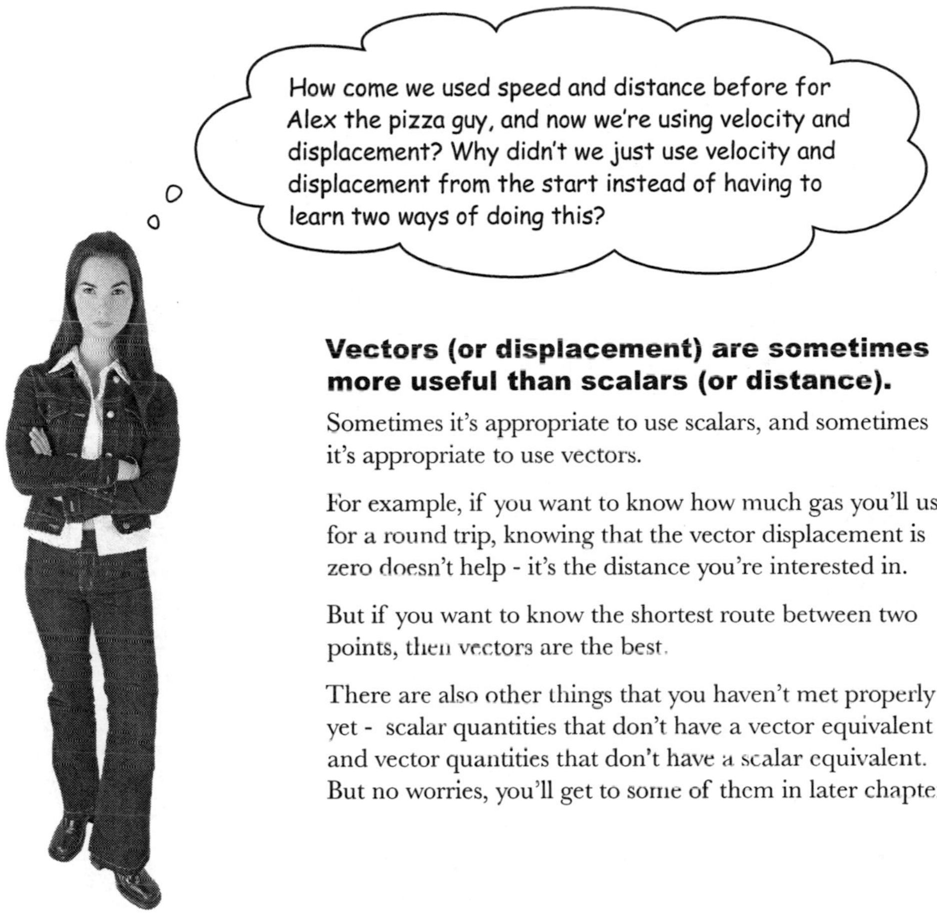

Vectors (or displacement) are sometimes more useful than scalars (or distance).

Sometimes it's appropriate to use scalars, and sometimes it's appropriate to use vectors.

For example, if you want to know how much gas you'll use for a round trip, knowing that the vector displacement is zero doesn't help - it's the distance you're interested in.

But if you want to know the shortest route between two points, then vectors are the best.

There are also other things that you haven't met properly yet - scalar quantities that don't have a vector equivalent and vector quantities that don't have a scalar equivalent. But no worries, you'll get to some of them in later chapters.

It's up to you to decide which is best for any situation.

Sometimes it's appropriate to use vectors.
Sometimes it's appropriate to use scalars.

Sharpen your pencil

Here's a map of one of Alex's pizza deliveries from the pizza shop to a customer's house.

a. Draw his route to show his overall distance, and draw a vector arrow to show his overall displacement.

b. Draw vector arrows to represent his velocity at each of the X's on the road.

c. Explain why it was more appropriate to use distance and speed to deal with Alex rather than displacement and velocity.

....

....

....

....

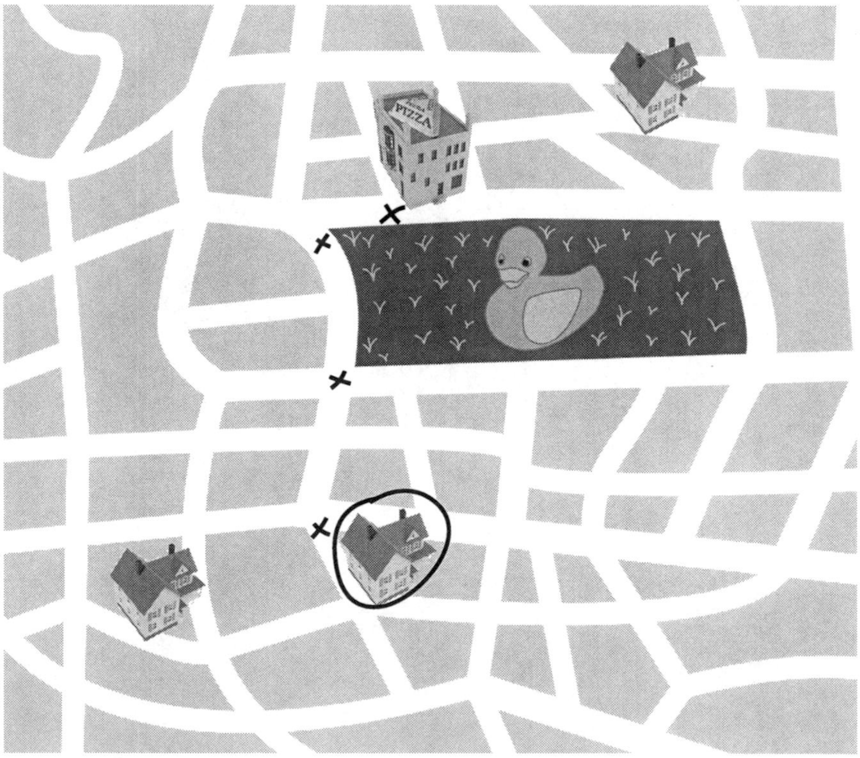

Sharpen your pencil Solution

Here's a map of one of Alex's pizza deliveries from chapter 3.

a. Draw his route to show his overall distance, and draw a vector arrow to show his overall displacement.

b. Draw vector arrows to represent his velocity at each of the X's on the road.

c. Explain why it was more appropriate to use distance and speed to deal with Alex rather than displacement and velocity.

Alex can't go directly through buildings or duckponds works – but the displacement vector does. So it would be silly to talk about displacement instead of distance. And he always covers the distance at the same speed even though the direction of his velocity changes. So there's no point in talking about velocity either.

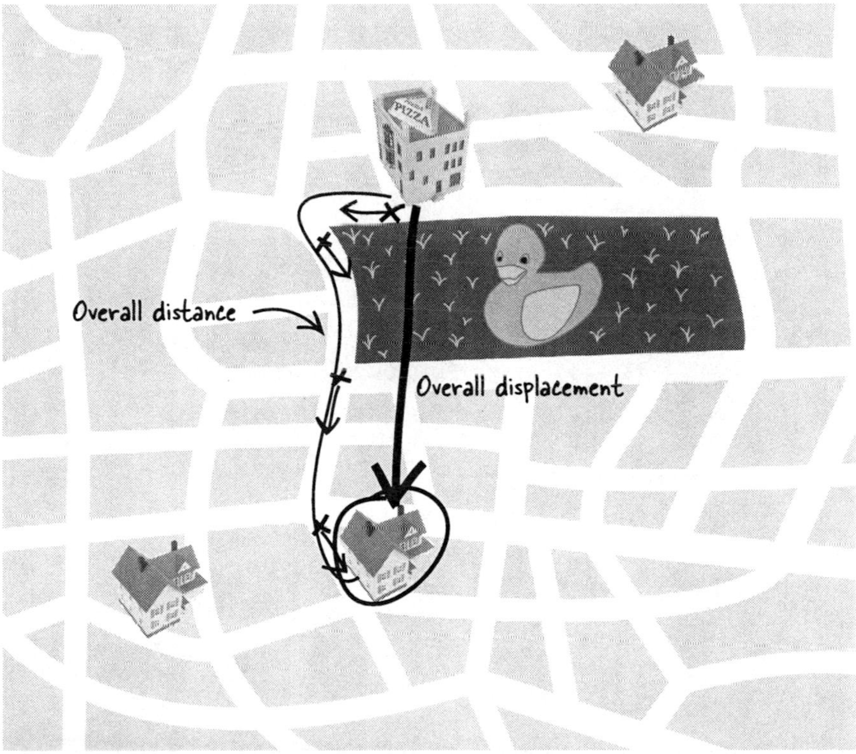

You only use distance and speed if direction isn't important.

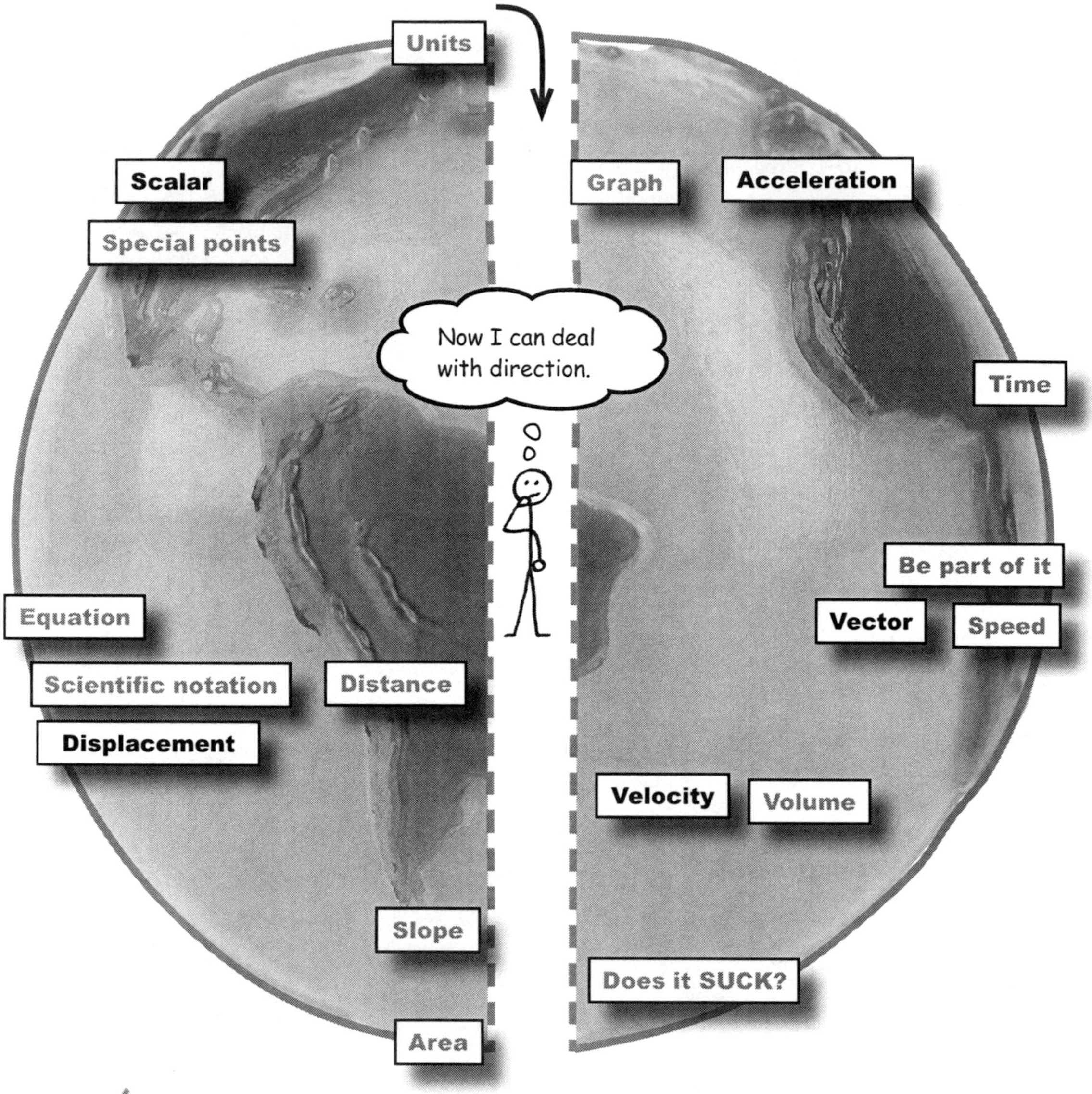

☑	**Scalar**	**A quantity that just has a size.**
☑	**Vector**	**A quantity with both a size and a direction.**
☑	**Displacement**	**The "vector version" of distance. The change in position between two points.**
☑	**Velocity**	**The "vector version" of speed. The rate of change of displacement.**
☑	**Acceleration**	**The rate of change of velocity.**

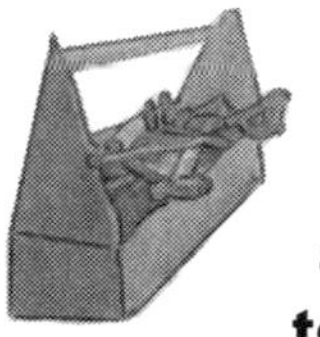

Your Physics Toolbox

You've got Chapter 5 under your belt and added some terminology and math skills to your toolbox.

Start with a sketch

Start every physics problem with a sketch. No, really – start every physics problem with a sketch!

A sketch gathers everything you know into one place in a visual way, so your brain is free to think about physics.

Is direction important?

Ask yourself, "Is direction important?"

Then you'll know whether to use scalars (like distance and speed) or vectors (like displacement and velocity).

Measuring angles

In physics, you measure angles counter-clockwise from the horizontal.

You can measure angles greater than 180° with your protractor either by thinking of how much greater than 180° the angle is, or how much less than 360° it is.

First what, then how

Before you start to work on a problem, work out what it is you're supposed to be doing.

Go through the question and underline the important parts.

Only think about how you'll do the problem once you've worked out what they're looking for.

Math with vectors

Add vector arrows by lining them up "nose-to-tail."

OR

If your vectors all lie along the same line, define one direction as positive and the other as negative.

Add the sizes of the vectors, making sure you get the signs correct.

Direction of velocity and acceleration vectors

An object's velocity vector points in the direction it's currently moving in.

An object's acceleration vector points in the direction the velocity is currently changing in. If the velocity is being changed by a push, the acceleration vector points in the direction of the push.

You're right. Experiments are valuable tools for observation.

The next few pages will show you an experimental design set-up…but put yourself in the problem, and try it on your own first. Don't worry, you already know more than you think you do.

Try it

An electromagnet is a magnet that can be switched on and off using electricity.

You have a steel ball-bearing, a tape measure, a timer, and an electromagnet that you can rig to switch off when the timer starts. Your challenge is to design an experiment which will enable you to draw a graph of displacement vs. time for a falling object.

a. List any additional equipment you would like to use.

Don't be afraid to try this! The next few pages will take you through it ... but you already know more than you think you do!

b. Draw and label a diagram of your experimental design.

c. Briefly describe how you would carry out your experiment. You should mention what measurements you will make, and how you will use them to draw graphs that will show you a value for the displacement at any time.

Question Clinic: The "Design an experiment" Question

Physics is based on experimental results, so it's important to be able to design an experiment yourself. There are often several good ways to do this. Some problems will give you a list of equipment, but you may not need to use it all, depending on what you decide to do.

The AP Physics B free response paper ALWAYS includes at least one question that asks you to design or analyze an experiment.

These types of questions always give you a list of available equipment, and may say that additional items are available if you can think of any you'd like to use.

6. You have a steel ball-bearing, a tape measure, a timer and an electromagnet that you can rig to switch off when the timer starts. Your challenge is to design an experiment which will enable you to draw a graph of displacement vs. time for a falling object.

a. List any additional equipment you would like to use.

b. Draw and label a diagram of your experimental design.

c. Briefly describe how you would carry out your experiment. You should mention what measurements you will make, and how you will use them to draw a graph that shows you a value for the displacement at any time.

If you're plotting any graph involving time, then time should be on the horizontal axis.

These types of questions also contain buzzwords that tell you exactly what you're supposed to do. So be careful – if it says 'draw' and you don't, you'll automatically lose points!

When you see a **"design an experiment" question,** make sure you **underline everything you're supposed to do** to separate out the wheat from the chaff and clarify the task in hand.

WHO DOES WHAT?

Match each **term** to its description, which says what you **have to do** when you answer the question.

Term	Description that says what you have to do
design	A number with units. The reason you're doing your experiment - you can work it out from your results.
describe how you would carry out ...	Words that say how you set up your experiment.
	Annotation with arrow describing part of a drawing.
draw a graph	
label	Make a picture of how the equipment you're using works together.
measurement	Make a plot of one set of measurements against another set of measurements.
a value for ...	Words that say what you do with the equipment you've set up.
draw a diagram	
	A number, with units, that you read from a scale or a meter in the course of your experiment.

WHO DOES WHAT?

Match each **term** with its description, which says what you **have to do** when you answer the question.

Buzzword	Description that says what you have to do
design	A number, with units. The reason you're doing your experiment - you can work it out from your results.
describe how you would carry out ...	Words that say how you set up your experiment.
draw a graph	Annotation with arrow describing part of a drawing.
label	Make a picture of how the equipment you're using works together.
measurement	Make a plot of one set of measurements against another set of measurements.
a value for ...	Words that say what you do with the equipment you've set up.
draw a diagram	A number, with units, that you read from a scale or a meter in the course of your experiment.

6. You have a steel ball-bearing, a tape measure, a timer, and an electromagnet that you can rig to switch off when the timer starts. Your challenge is to design an experiment which will enable you to draw a graph of displacement vs. time for a falling object.

Sharpen your pencil

Here are all the pieces of equipment mentioned in the question. Your job is to write down what quantity you can **measure** with it, and what you can **do** with it in the experimental setup.

You should also write down what it is you're being asked to find by doing your experiment, plus any relationships between the **units** of what you can measure and what you're being asked to work out.

Piece of equipment	What can you measure / do with it?
Steel ball-bearing	
Tape measure	
Timer	
Electromagnet	

What I'm supposed to do:

Relationships between what the items in the table can measure and what I'm being asked to work out:

Any other equipment you'll need to be able to do the experiment:

If you have a list of equipment, ask yourself: "What can I DO with this stuff?" and "How can these items work together?"

Sharpen your pencil Solution

You wouldn't draw out a table like this in an exam – just annotate the equipment list you're given!

Here are all the pieces of equipment mentioned in the question. Your job is to write down what quantity you can **measure** with it, and what you can **do** with it in the experimental setup.

You should also write down what it is you're being asked to find by doing your experiment, plus any relationships between the **units** of what you can measure and what you're being asked to work out.

Piece of equipment	What can you measure / do with it?
Steel ball-bearing	I can drop it so that it falls downwards.
Tape measure	I can measure the height that the ball-bearing falls from.
Timer	I can time how long the ball-bearing takes to fall.
Electromagnet	It can hold the ball-bearing then drop it when it switches off. The timer starts when the magnet switches off.

What I'm supposed to do	Draw a graph of displacement vs. time.
Relationships between what the items in the table can measure and what I'm being asked to work out:	I can measure displacement (m) with the tape measure and time (s) with the timer.
Any other equipment you'll need to be able to do the experiment:	Something to hold the electromagnet. And a way to stop the timer when the ball lands.

Look at the UNITS of what you can measure and what you're being asked to work out. How do they relate to each other?

This particular question asks if you'd like to use any other equipment. So do the 'ideal world' test - in an ideal world, what would you need to measure the values as accurately as possible? Then, you actually need to design the experiment in your head before you can describe, draw, or label it!

You need extra equipment to stop the timer and to hold the electromagnet

You can measure displacement and time using the tape measure and timer. And the question says that the electromagnet can be rigged up to release the ball-bearing when the timer starts.

All you need then is to stop the timer when the ball lands - which will need an extra piece of equipment, for instance a switch plate rigged up to stop the timer when the ball lands on it.

Sharpen your pencil

Is the experimental setup you now have in mind similar to what you drew at the start, or is it different?

If it's different, draw and label a diagram of your new experimental setup, and explain how you'll use it to make measurements and draw a graph that shows you a value for the displacement at any time.

You might not have any changes, and if you don't...that's okay too...

Try it

You have a steel ball-bearing, a tape measure, a timer, and an electromagnet that you can rig to switch off when the timer starts. Your challenge is to design an experiment which will enable you to draw a graph of displacement vs. time for a falling object.

a. List any additional equipment you would like to use.

b. Draw and label a diagram of your experimental design.

c. Briefly describe how you would carry out your experiment. You should mention what measurements you will make, and how you will use them to draw graphs that will show you a value for the displacement at any time.

Sharpen your pencil Solution

Is the experimental setup you now have in mind similar to what you drew at the start, or is it different?

If it's different, draw and label a diagram of your new experimental setup, and explain how you'll use it to make measurements and draw a graph that shows you a value for the displacement at any time.

You might not have any changes, and if you don't...that's okay too...

Make sure you include labels so it's clear what everything is.

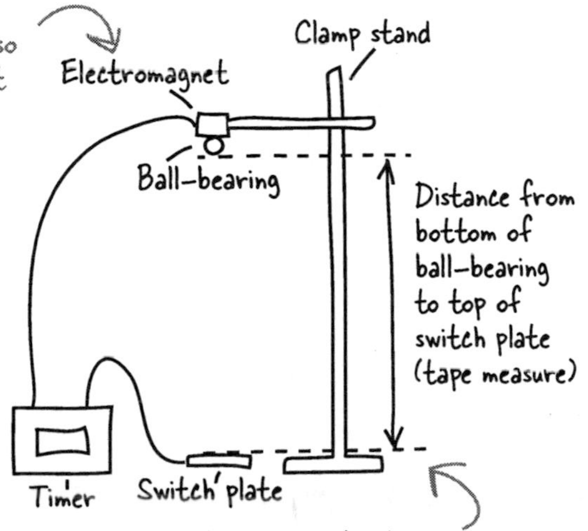

Don't spend too much time making your diagram look pretty.

Use the clamp stand and the tape measure to set the height of the ball-bearing. Time how long it takes to fall from that height using the timer, electromagnet and switch plate. Use a range of heights, from the smallest the timer can measure to the height of the ceiling, and several heights in between as well. And time each height two or three times to reduce random errors.

Then, plot a graph with the time along the horizontal axis and the distance up the vertical axis. Draw a smooth line through the data points. The graph lets you read off the time it'll take for the ball-bearing to fall any distance.

On your graphs, time should always be along the horizontal axis.

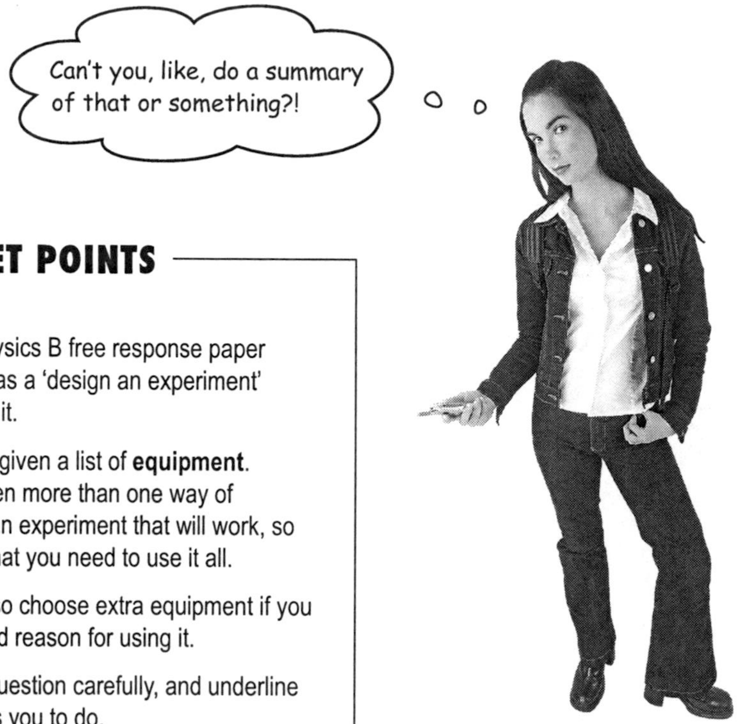

BULLET POINTS

- The AP Physics B free response paper ALWAYS has a 'design an experiment' question in it.
- You will be given a list of **equipment**. There's often more than one way of designing an experiment that will work, so don't feel that you need to use it all.
- You can also choose extra equipment if you have a good reason for using it.
- **Read** the question carefully, and underline what it asks you to do.
- If the question asks you to **design**, **describe**, **draw**, **label** or **explain**, that's what you get points for!
- You may find it useful to jot down what you can **measure** or **do** with each piece of equipment to get your creative juices flowing.
- Remember to explain clearly **what** you'll do in your experiment - **how** you'll use your equipment, and what you'll plot on a graph.
- If you're plotting a graph, **time** always goes along the **horizontal axis**.

Remember to explain clearly what you'll do in your experiment!

6 Displacement, Velocity, and Acceleration

What's going on?

It's hard to keep track of more than one thing at a time.

When something **falls**, its **displacement**, **velocity,** and **acceleration** are all important at the same **time**. So how can you pay attention to all three without missing anything? In this chapter, you'll increase your **experiment**, **graph,** and **slope** superpowers in preparation for bringing everything together with an **equation** or two.

Just another day in the desert ...

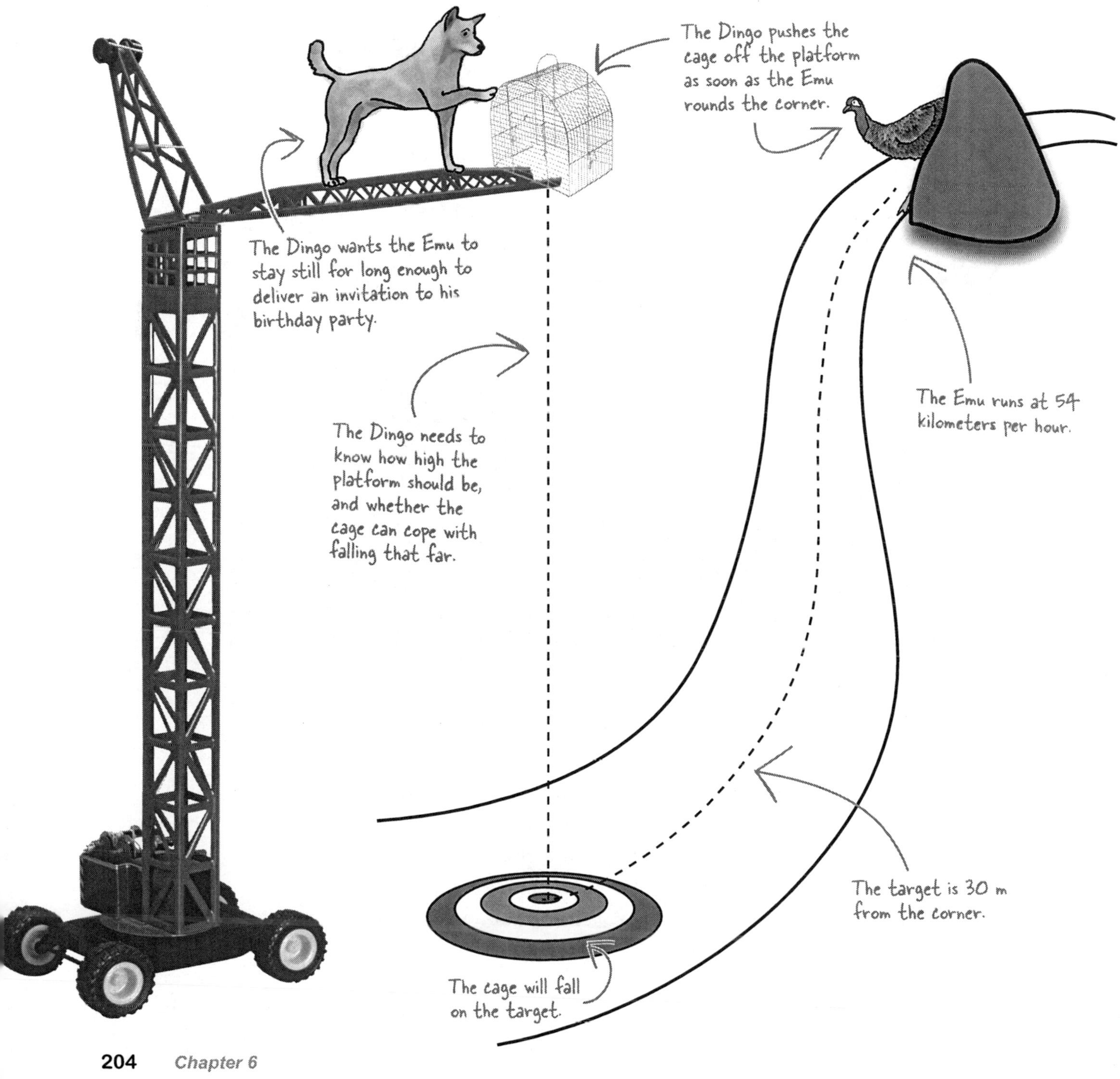

... and another Dingo-Emu moment!

Every year it's the same. The Dingo wants to invite the Emu to his birthday party - but the daft bird won't stop running for long enough for him to deliver the invitation. So this year, the Dingo's decided that extending a paw of friendship needs drastic measures. He's hired a crane, and wants to push a cage off the platform the moment the Emu rounds the bend. But is this practical? **What height does the platform need to be, and will the cage be able to handle hitting the ground at a high speed?**

So the Dingo calls the crane company's customer service department to ask some questions ...

Crane Company Magnets

The crane company gets to work on the problem. But we accidentally dropped their memo and some of the words fell off. Your job is to put them back in the right places. You might use some magnets more than once, and some not at all.

Also, **underline the most important parts** in the memo to separate the important stuff from the fluff - the wheat from the chaff.

To: Dingo Re: Cage

Hmmm, falling cage landing exactly on running ______ , tricky! The Emu's ______ is on the computer up there - ______ - and we set up the crane and target ______ past the corner. The ______ falls at the same time as the ______ rounds the corner. If we work out the ______ the cage falls in the ______ it takes the Emu to run ______ ,we can set the crane to that ______ and take home a fat ______ . Be careful - the ______ is only guaranteed if it hits the ground at less than 25 m/s.

30 m | 54 m/s | time | height | commission | cage | velocity | Emu | 54 km/h | speed | distance | 30 km

Crane Company Magnets - Solution

The crane company gets to work on the problem. But we accidentally dropped their memo and some of the words fell off. Your job is to put them back in the right places. You might use some magnets more than once, and some not at all.

Also, **underline the most important parts** in the memo to separate the important stuff from the fluff - the wheat from the chaff.

To: Dingo Re: Cage

Hmmm, falling cage landing exactly on running [Emu], tricky! The Emu's [speed] is on the computer up there - [54 km/h] - and we set up the crane and target [30 m] past the corner. The [cage] falls at the same time as the [Emu] rounds the corner. If we work out the [distance] the cage falls in the [time] it takes the Emu to run [30 m], we can set the crane to that [height] and take home a fat [commission]. Be careful - the [cage] is only guaranteed if it hits the ground at less than 25 m/s.

[30 km]

[54 m/s]

These didn't get used because the units are wrong.

[velocity]

The Emu's speed, rather than his velocity, is important, as the road is curved.

NOTES

- What time does the cage fall for?
- What height should the crane be?
- Will the cage be going faster than 25 m/s when it hits the ground?

BRAIN POWER

Which of these would you try to work out first?

How can you use what you know?

The Dingo drops the cage as soon as the Emu rounds the corner. Then, the cage falling and the Emu running both take the same **time** to reach the target.

The **time** that the Emu takes to arrive depends on the **speed** he runs at and the **distance** he covers from the corner to the target. As the Emu always runs with a **constant speed**, you already know an **equation** you can use to do this.

Once you know the time it takes the Emu to arrive, you'll have to figure out how far the cage **falls** during that time. This will give the Dingo the height that he needs to set the platform at.

However, if the cage travels faster than 25 m/s in the time it takes for the Emu to reach the target, this plan won't work because the cage will hit the ground and be destroyed upon impact.

You haven't dealt with falling things yet – but don't worry, that's what this chapter's about!

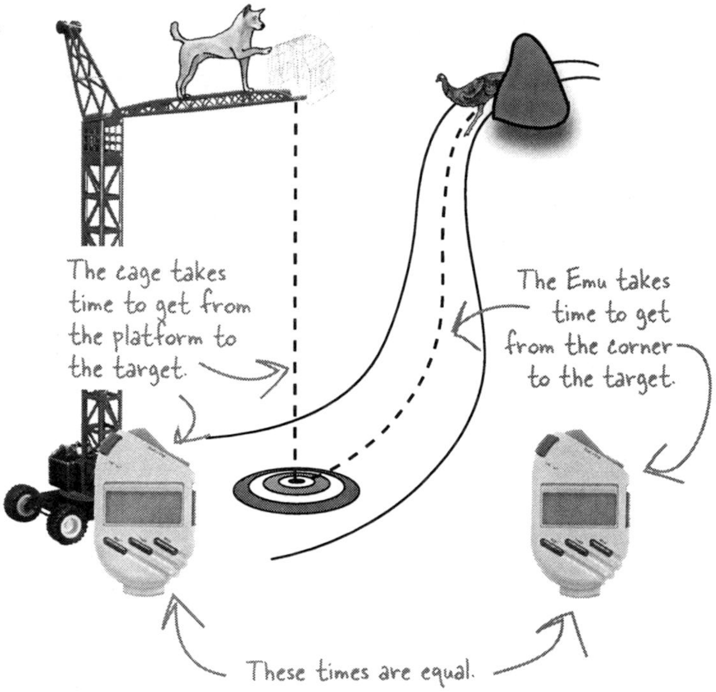

Sharpen your pencil

First things first. Work out the time it takes the Emu to cover 30 m from the corner to the target at a speed of 54 km/h.

Hint: You'll need to convert units.

Sharpen your pencil Solution

Work out the time it takes the Emu to cover 30 m from the corner to the target at a speed of 54 km/h.

Convert units: km/h to m/s

$$54 \text{ km/h in m/s} = 54\,\frac{\text{km}}{\text{hours}} \times \frac{1000\text{ m}}{1\text{ km}} \times \frac{1\text{ hour}}{60\text{ mins}} \times \frac{1\text{ min}}{60\text{ s}}$$

$$= 15 \text{ m/s}$$

After stringing together conversion factors, you're left with meters on the top and seconds on the bottom – m/s.

If you don't feel so confident about stringing them together, you can do the units conversion one step at a time. That's fine too.

This symbol means 'implies that'. You can use it going from one line to the next as you rearrange an equation.

Work out the time it takes:

$$\text{speed} = \frac{\Delta\text{ distance}}{\Delta\text{ time}}$$

Equation comes from the units of speed. Meters per second is a distance divided by a time.

$$\Rightarrow \text{speed}\ \Delta\text{ time} = \Delta\text{ distance}$$

$$\Rightarrow \Delta\text{ time} = \frac{\Delta\text{ distance}}{\text{speed}} = \frac{30\text{ m}}{15\text{ m/s}} = \underline{\underline{2.0\text{ seconds}}}\ (2\text{ sd})$$

Rearrange equation to get Δ time = ...

The problem gave numbers with 2 significant digits to work with, so your answer should have 2 sd.

The Emu takes 2.0 seconds to reach the target - so the cage needs to take 2.0 seconds to reach the target as well.

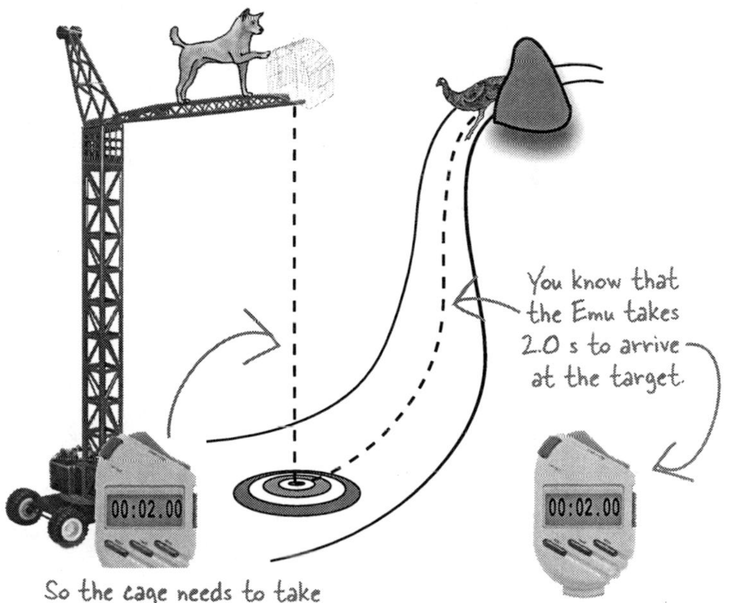

NOTES

1. ✓ What time does the cage fall for?
   The cage falls for 2.0 s.
- What height should the crane be?
- Will the cage be going faster than 25 m/s when it hits the ground?

2

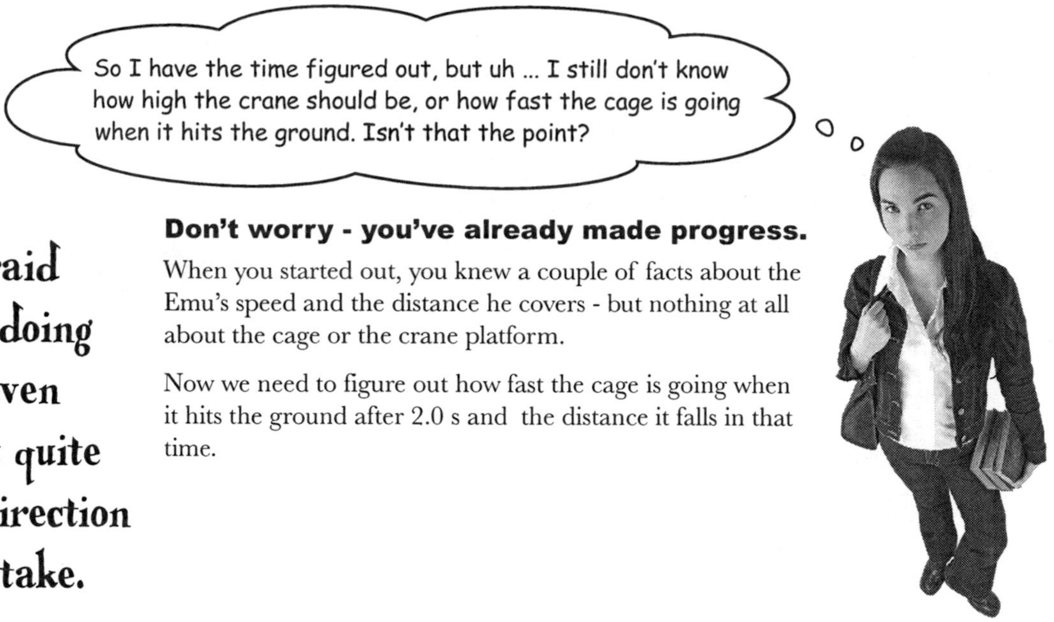

Don't be afraid to start out doing a question, even if you're not quite sure what direction it's going to take.

Don't worry - you've already made progress.

When you started out, you knew a couple of facts about the Emu's speed and the distance he covers - but nothing at all about the cage or the crane platform.

Now we need to figure out how fast the cage is going when it hits the ground after 2.0 s and the distance it falls in that time.

BE the cage

Your job is to imagine that you're the cage. What do you feel at each of the points in the picture? Which direction are you moving in? Are you speeding up or slowing down? Why are you moving like this?

At Point 1: ....

....

At Point 2: ....

....

At Point 3: ....

....

At Point 4: ....

....

Why: ....

....

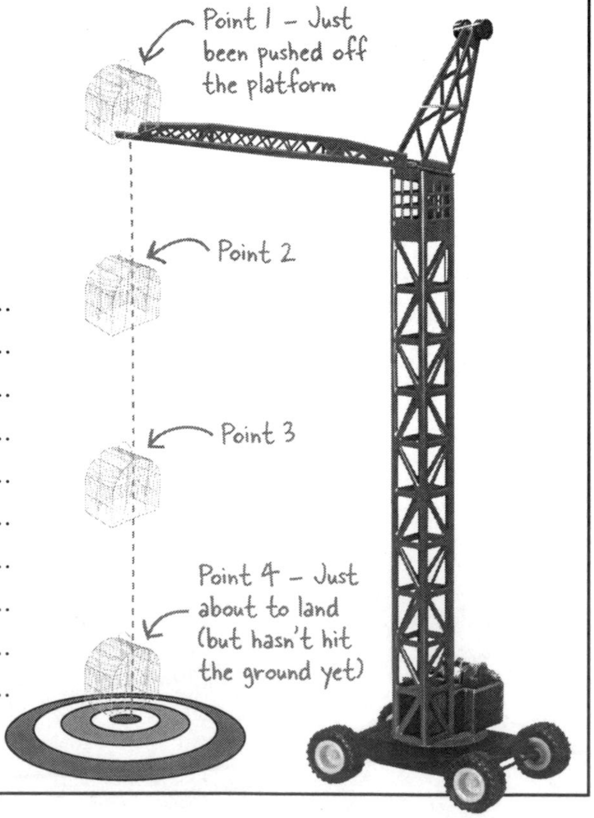

BE the cage - SOLUTION

Your job is to imagine that you're the cage. What do you feel at each of the points in the picture? Which direction are you moving in? Are you speeding up or slowing down? Why are you moving like this??

At Point 1: A 'special point', as I'm suddenly going from standing still to starting to move downwards.

At Point 2: Falling down faster than I was at point 1.

At Point 3: Falling down even faster than I was at point 2.

At Point 4: This is the fastest I'll be going before I hit the ground (I'll be here after 2.0 seconds if the height is right).

Why: Gravity's accelerating me downwards.

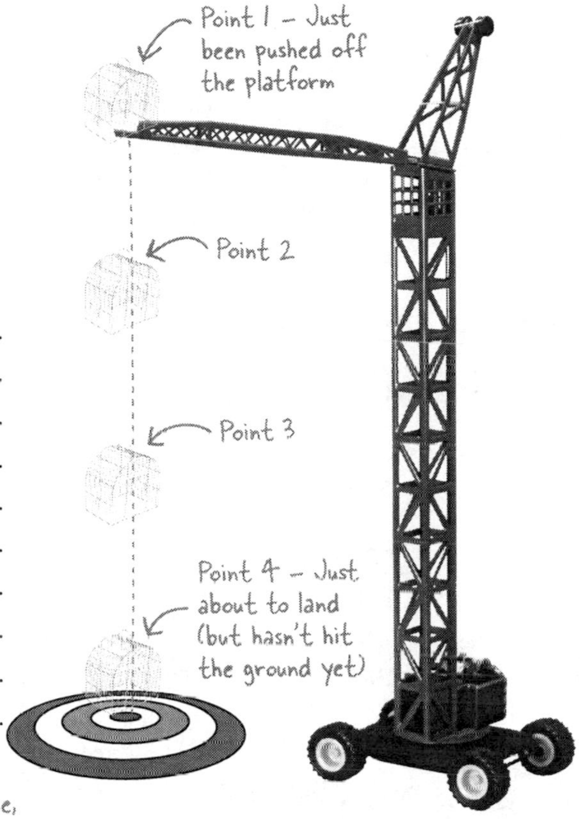

In this problem, we gave you headings to use, but it's always a good idea to make it clear which part of the problem you're answering at each stage!

The cage accelerates as it falls

You've spotted that the cage **accelerates** as it falls. Acceleration is the **rate of change of velocity**. You can tell that the cage is accelerating because its velocity is continually changing. It starts off with zero velocity, then gets faster and faster until it hits the ground.

With that in mind, it's on to working out the cage's **velocity** after 2.0 seconds and its **displacement** in that time so that the Dingo knows whether the idea's a starter - and if so, how high to make the platform.

We're going to talk about the cage's displacement and velocity, as the DIRECTION is starting to become important - the cage isn't being launched up into the air, just dropped!

You know that something is accelerating if its velocity is changing.

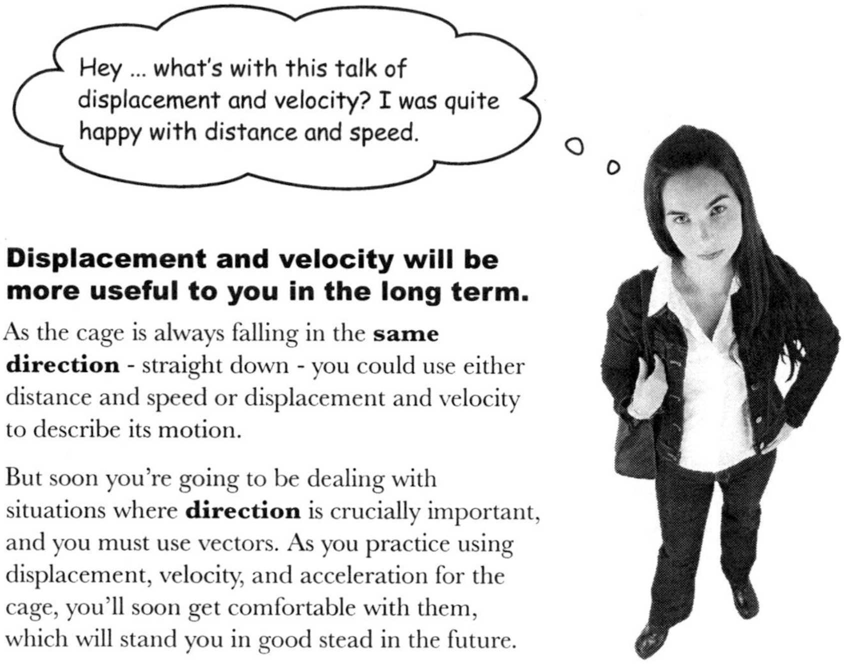

Displacement and velocity will be more useful to you in the long term.

As the cage is always falling in the **same direction** - straight down - you could use either distance and speed or displacement and velocity to describe its motion.

But soon you're going to be dealing with situations where **direction** is crucially important, and you must use vectors. As you practice using displacement, velocity, and acceleration for the cage, you'll soon get comfortable with them, which will stand you in good stead in the future.

–Displacement, Velocity, and Acceleration Up Close

Displacement is the 'vector version' of distance and is represented by the letter **x** in equations (or the letter **s** in some courses).

Velocity is rate of change of displacement - the 'vector version' of speed. It is represented by the letter **v** in equations.

Acceleration is rate of change of velocity, represented by **a**, and doesn't have a scalar equivalent. If an object's velocity is changing, you need to know which **direction** the velocity is changing in for the statement to have meaning. Otherwise, you don't know if the object's speeding up, slowing down, or changing direction - which are all ways that an object's velocity can change.

'Vectorize' your equation

You've already used the equation

$$\text{speed} = \frac{\Delta\ \text{distance}}{\Delta\ \text{time}}$$

to work out that it takes the Emu 2.0 seconds to reach the target.

Δ means 'change in'

The 'vector version' of this equation is

$$\text{velocity} = \frac{\Delta \text{displacement}}{\Delta\ \text{time}}, \text{ or } \mathbf{v} = \frac{\Delta \mathbf{x}}{\Delta t}.$$

It's fundamentally the same, except that it involves velocity and displacement instead of speed and distance.

$$\mathbf{v} = \frac{\Delta \mathbf{x}}{\Delta t}$$

velocity

change in displacement

change in time

We're using bold letters, like **x** and **v**, to represent vectors and italic letters, like *t*, to represent scalars.

So we need to work out the **displacement** of the cage after 2.0 seconds. That doesn't sound too bad.

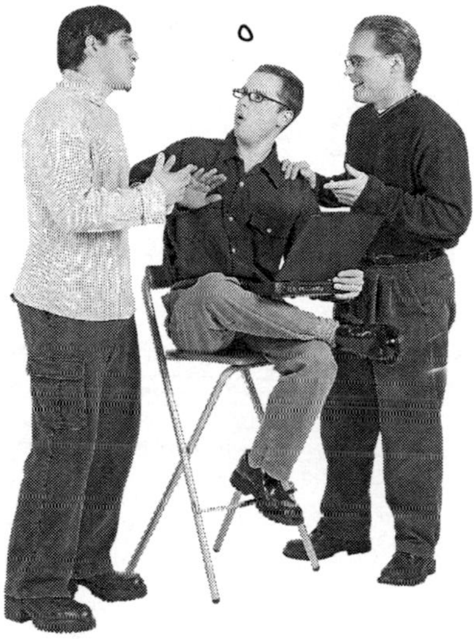

Jim: We also need to work out what its **velocity** will be when it hits the ground. If that's more than 25 m/s, then the cage will shatter.

Joe: Why don't we work out the velocity first? That way, if it turns out that the cage is going too fast after it's been falling for 2.0 seconds, we won't have to bother working out the displacement as well.

Frank: Sounds good. I'm all for spotting shortcuts!

Jim: Well, we've done something similar before with that cyclist who rode everywhere at the same speed. Can't we use the **equation** $\mathbf{v} = \frac{\Delta \mathbf{x}}{\Delta t}$ to work out the cage's velocity

Frank: Yeah, let's just use that equation! We want to know the velocity, and that equation says "**v** =" on the left hand side. **v** for velocity. It's perfect!

Joe: Um, I'm not so sure. The cage doesn't have the same velocity all the time - it accelerates as it falls.

Jim: But we can still use that equation, right? If we work out the displacement, we can divide it by the time to get the velocity.

Joe: I don't think so. If the cage always had the same velocity, then, fair enough, that would work. But the cage's velocity is always changing because it's **accelerating** - it isn't **constant**. We want to know what its velocity is at the very end, as it hits the ground.

Frank: Oh ... and when it hits the ground, it's only been traveling at that velocity for a split second.

Jim: Yeah, as it gets closer to the ground its velocity increases, so it covers more and more meters per second. If we divided the total displacement by the total time, we'd get the cage's **average** velocity.

Joe: But we need to know what the velocity is the **instant** it hits the ground. An average velocity's no good to us.

Frank: I guess we need to do something different ...

NEVER blindly stick numbers into an equation. Always ask yourself "What does this equation MEAN?"

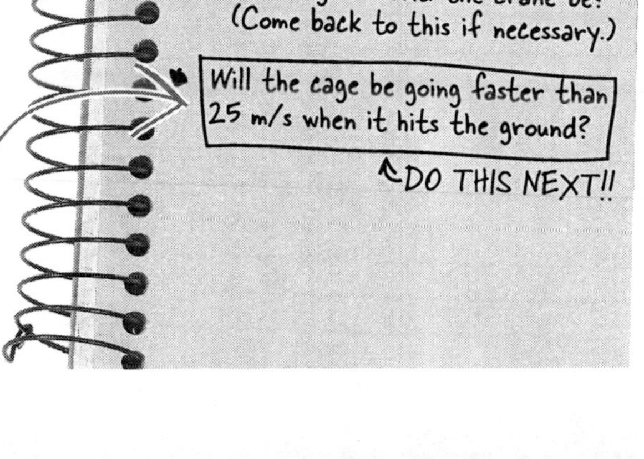

If you calculate the cage's velocity first, you won't have to bother calculating its displacement if it turns out that the cage will break.

You want an instantaneous velocity, not an average velocity

The equation $\mathbf{v} = \frac{\Delta \mathbf{x}}{\Delta t}$ works fine if you have something traveling at a constant velocity. But the cage gets faster and faster as it falls - and you want to know what its velocity is the **instant** it hits the ground.

The best you can do with the equation is to work out the cage's **average** velocity, which is the **constant** velocity it would need to travel with to cover that displacement in that time. But since the cage isn't traveling with a constant velocity, this value won't help you out.

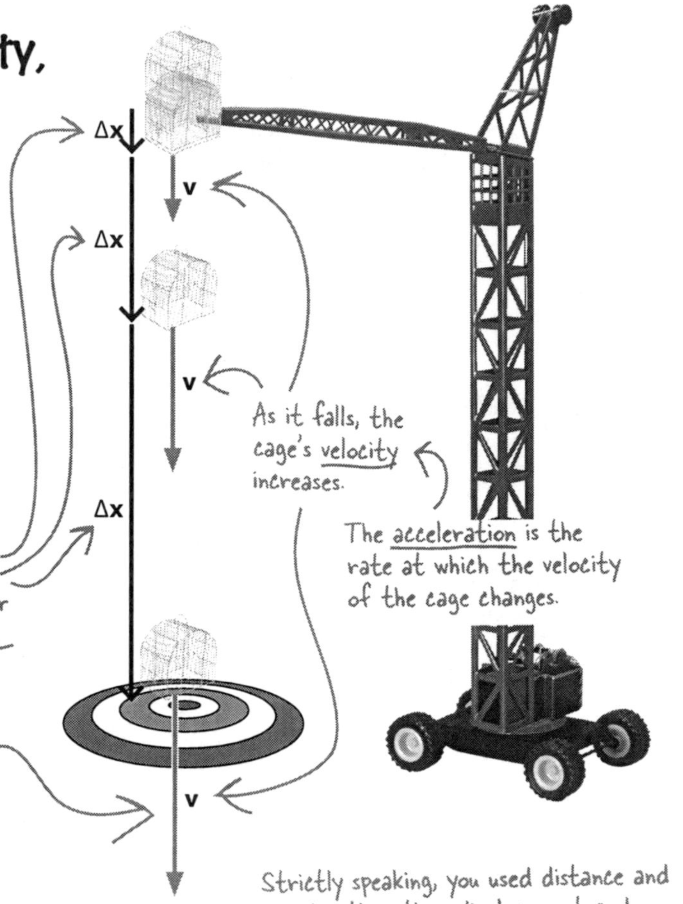

This is the graph for the cyclist in chapter 4.

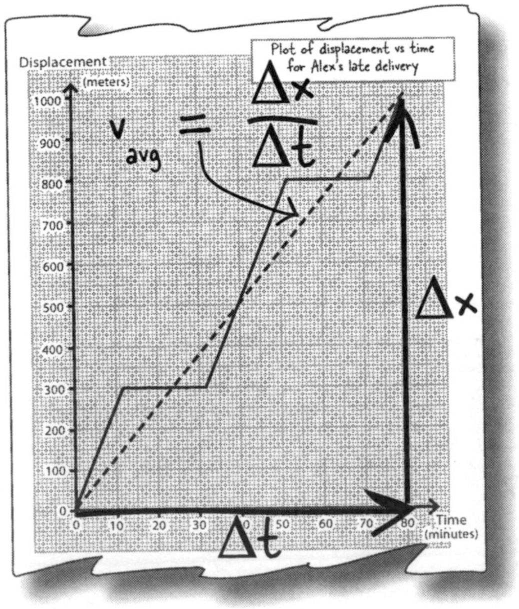

Strictly speaking, you used distance and speed rather than displacement and velocity, but the principle is the same.

You've previously used the equation $\mathbf{v} = \frac{\Delta \mathbf{x}}{\Delta t}$ to work out the **average** velocity of a cyclist who was slowed down by stop lights, and it gave you the slope of a straight line between the start and end points of his displacement-time graph. Using the **slope** of his displacement-time graph at that point, you were also able to work out his **instantaneous** velocity at any point.

BRAIN POWER

How might you try to work out a value for the **instantaneous** velocity of the cage just before it hits the ground.

You may be able to use the same <u>method</u> even if you can't use the same equation.

As the cage doesn't fall with a constant velocity, the best you can do with the equation $\mathbf{v} = \frac{\Delta \mathbf{x}}{\Delta t}$ is work out its **average** velocity - which isn't what you want. You can't reuse this equation to work out the cage's **instantaneous** velocity because the **context** is different.

But you can use the same **method** even if you can't directly reuse the same equation. If you draw a displacement-time graph for a falling thing and are able to calculate its slope at t = 2.0 s, this will give you the instantaneous velocity of the cage. As long as you understand the physics, you can work out how to do a problem even if you can't directly use an equation you already know.

Though you still need to design the experiment...

Understanding the physics helps you to work out how to solve a problem even if you can't directly use an equation you already know.

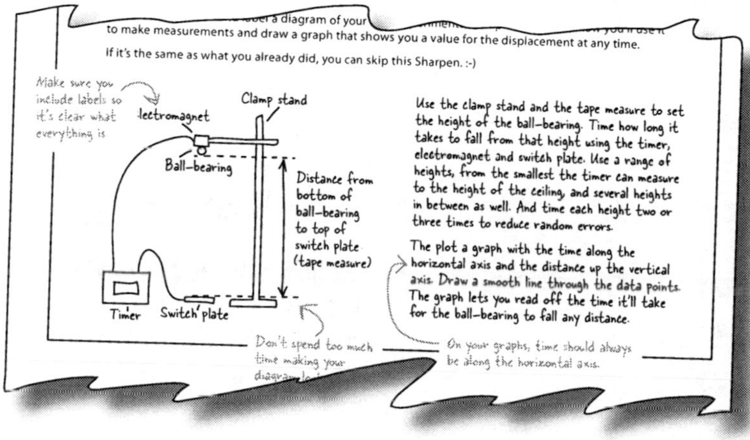

Sharpen your pencil

When you carry out the experiment with the falling ball-bearing, electromagnet, and timer that you designed earlier, you get the results shown in the table.

Use these measurements to draw a displacement-time graph for the falling ball-bearing.

(Don't worry about calculating the slope of your graph for now - you'll do that next.)

Displacement of ball (m)	Time 1 (s)	Time 2 (s)
0.10	0.142	0.150
0.25	0.228	0.224
0.50	0.316	0.319
0.75	0.387	0.390
1.00	0.456	0.451
1.50	0.552	0.556
2.00	0.639	0.637
2.50	0.712	0.712
3.00	0.779	0.782

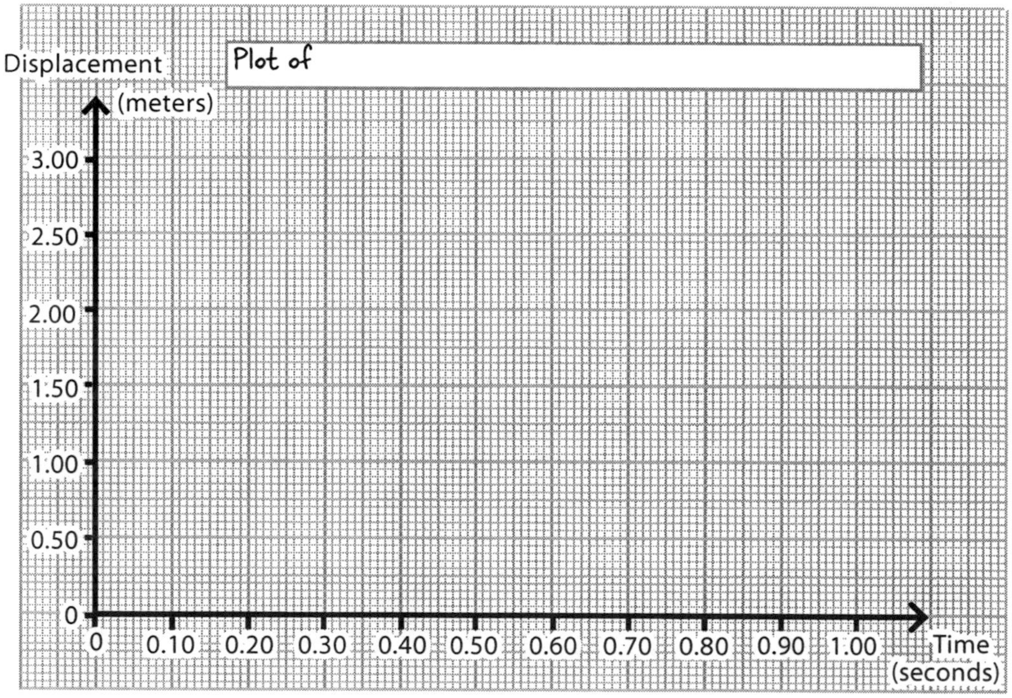

Sharpen your pencil Solution

When you carry out the experiment with the falling ball-bearing, electromagnet, and timer that you designed earlier, you get the results shown in the table.

Use these measurements to draw a displacement-time graph for the falling ball-bearing.

(Don't worry about calculating the slope of your graph for now - you'll do that next.)

Displacement of ball (m)	Time 1 (s)	Time 2 (s)
0.10	0.142	0.150
0.25	0.228	0.224
0.50	0.316	0.319
0.75	0.387	0.390
1.00	0.456	0.451
1.50	0.552	0.556
2.00	0.639	0.637
2.50	0.712	0.712
3.00	0.779	0.782

It's important to mention that this object is falling.

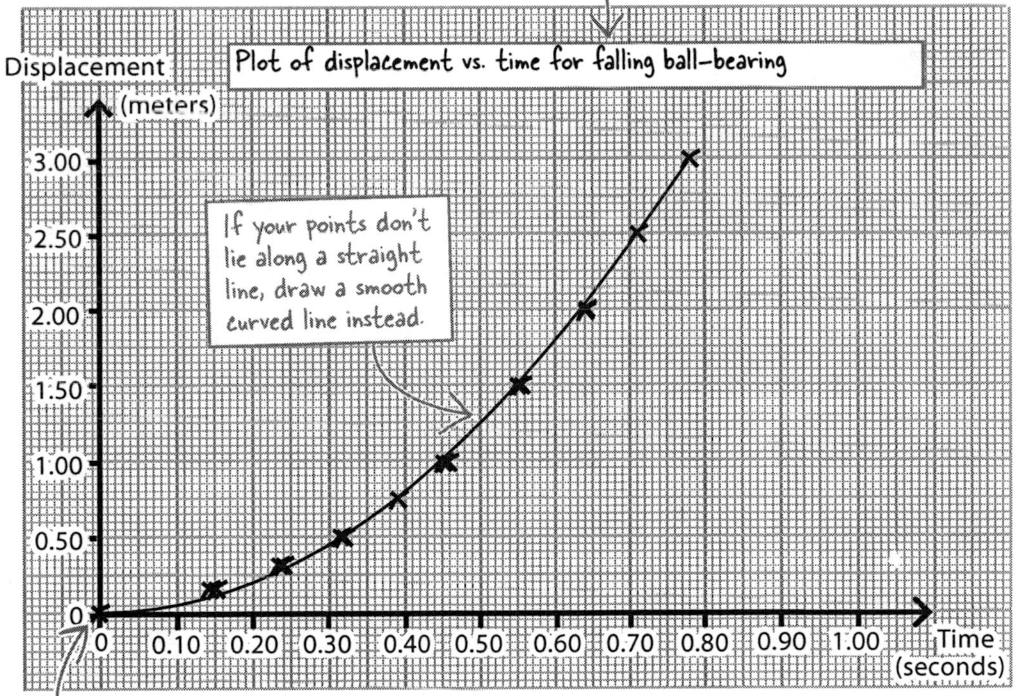

Remember to include the point (0, 0) – the ball-bearing has zero displacement at $t = 0$.

Never play 'connect the dots' with your points. Always use a smooth line (whether it's straight or curved).

Look at where the points are to work out what type of line to draw

If your points look like they ought to lie along a straight line, then draw a straight line that passes as close to as many points as possible.

If your points look like they ought to lie along a curve, then draw a smooth curve that passes as close to as many points as possible.

But never play 'connect the dots'!

there are no Dumb Questions

Q: So ... why am I drawing a displacement-time graph when I want to know the cage's velocity after 2.0 s?

A: You can use the displacement-time graph to get the cage's velocity after 2.0 s.

Q: But what does velocity have to do with displacement?

A: Velocity is rate of change of displacement. That means that the slope at a point on a displacement-time graph is the same as the velocity at that point.

Q: Velocity and displacement are vectors, right? Do I have to write them in bold letters like in the book?

A: Not if you're just handwriting them. We've made the vectors bold so you get used to thinking of them the right way, but you don't have to do that in your solutions.

Q: Why does the slope of a graph matter? How does it help me?

A: The slope of a graph is the change in the vertical direction divided by the change in the horizontal direction. On a displacement-time graph, displacement is on the vertical axis, and time is on the horizontal axis.

So the equation for the slope gives you change in displacement divided by change in time - which is the same as the equation for velocity.

Q: OK, so I see why the displacement-time graph is important. But why haven't I drawn a straight line on it this time?

A: Last time, the points on your graph lay along a straight line. But this time it's obvious that they don't.

Q: So should I mimic a spreadsheet program, using my ruler to draw straight lines from point to point?

A: No, not in physics. The cage doesn't move jerkily from point to point - it moves smoothly. So you should draw a **smooth** line that goes as close to as many of the points as possible.

Q: OK, so the displacement-time graph is curved. I can work out the slope of a straight line graph, it's $\frac{\Delta x}{\Delta t}$.

But how can I work out the slope of the curved graph when it won't "sit still" for long enough for me to work out $\frac{\Delta x}{\Delta t}$ for a straight portion?

A: Funny you should ask ...

You already know how to calculate the slope of a straight line...

In Chapter 4, you calculated the slope of a straight line graph by picking two points on it, and calculating $\frac{\Delta \text{ vertical direction}}{\Delta \text{ horizontal direction}}$.

If the graph is plotted with displacement, **x**, on the vertical axis and time, t, on the horizontal axis, this expression for the slope becomes $\frac{\Delta \mathbf{x}}{\Delta t}$, which is the velocity.

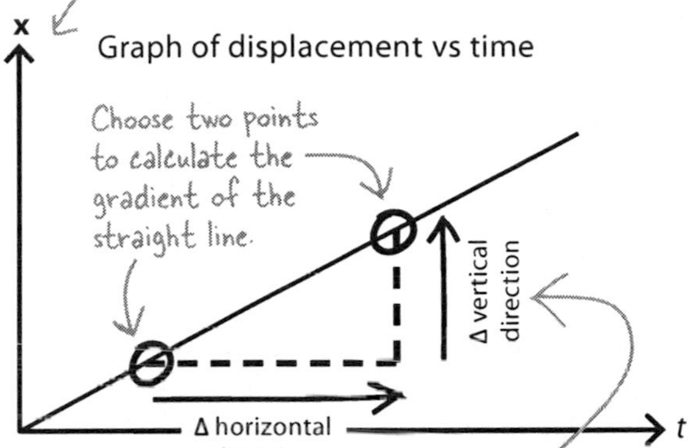

$$\text{Slope} = \frac{\Delta \text{ vertical direction}}{\Delta \text{ horizontal direction}}$$

$$\text{Slope} = \frac{\Delta x}{\Delta t}$$

$$\text{Slope} = \text{Velocity}$$

Velocity is rate of change of displacement with time.

Work out the slope of the tangent the same way you worked out the slope of a straight line graph.

A point on a curved line has the same slope as its tangent

You can calculate the slope at a point on a curved graph by drawing a **tangent**. This is a straight line that touches a curve at only that point without crossing the curve.

This means that the tangent has the same slope as the curve at that point - so calculating the slope of the tangent tells you the slope of the curve at that point.

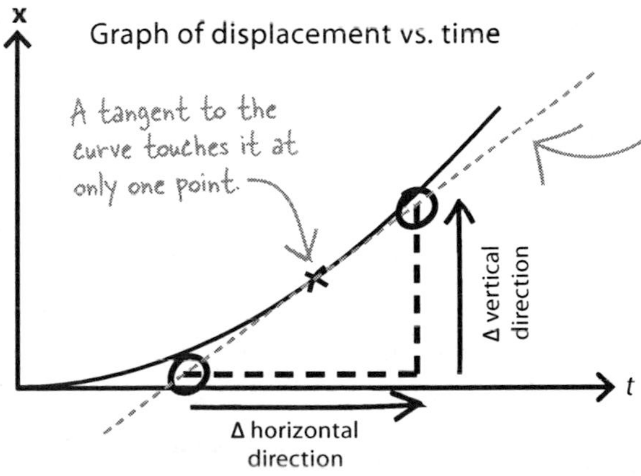

A tangent is a line that touches a curve at one point without crossing it.

there are no Dumb Questions

Q: Isn't a tangent something to do with circles?

A: In this context, a tangent is a straight line that touches a curve at one point but doesn't intersect it. The tangent has the same slope as the curve at that point. You can also talk about a tangent to a circle - a straight line that touches it at one point.

Q: Aren't there tangents in trigonometry as well?

A: 'Tangent' means something different in the context of trigonometry. The definition there is related to this one. You'll learn more about the other meaning in chapter 9.

Q: So here, I can draw a tangent that touches my curve at a point and use it to work out the velocity at that point?

A: Yes - the slope of a displacement-time graph gives you the rate of change of distance with time, which is the same as the velocity.

Q: But the graph I've drawn only goes up to 0.78 s, and I want to know the velocity after 2.0 s. Do I have to extrapolate my graph out to 2.0 s or something?

A: Let's try it ...

Sharpen your pencil

When you drew the displacement-time graph for the cyclist, you were able to **extrapolate** it further than the measurements you'd originally made.

Now you can extrapolate your graph for the ball bearing experiment. Your set of measurements goes up to 0.78 s, but you're interested in what's going on after it's been falling for 2.0 s. We've redrawn it to give you more space.

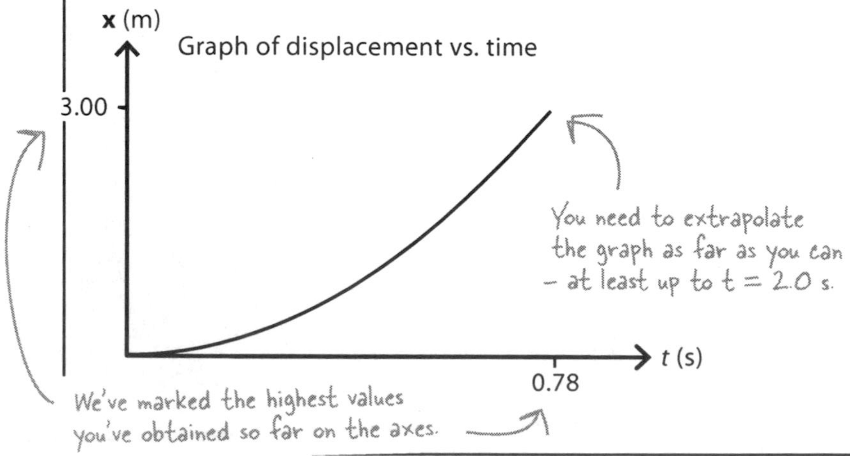

Sharpen your pencil Solution

When you drew the displacement-time graph for the cyclist, you were able to **extrapolate** it further than the measurements you'd originally made.

Now you can extrapolate your graph for the ball bearing experiment. Your current set of measurements goes up to 0.78 s but you're interested in what's going on after it's been falling for 2.0 s. We've redrawn it to give you more space.

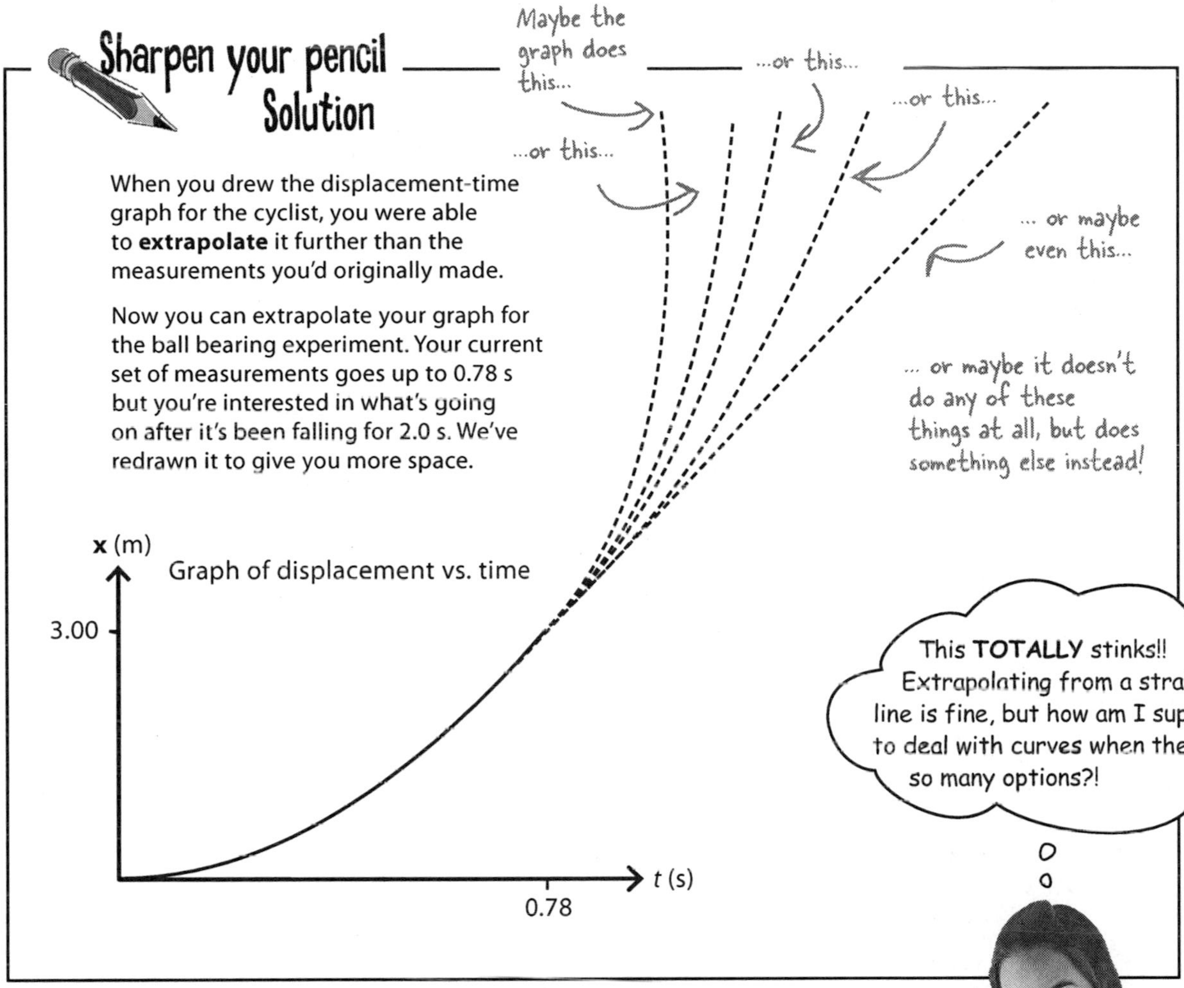

It's only meaningful to extrapolate a graph if its points lie along a straight line.

It's nearly impossible to extrapolate a curve accurately.

It turns out that this method isn't so hot after all. Drawing the displacement-time graph was fine, but this time, instead of being a straight line, it's a curve.

With a straight line displacement-time graph, its easy to use a ruler to continue the straight line as far as you need to.

But you can't extrapolate from a curved graph in the same way, as it's almost impossible to tell exactly how the curve will continue.

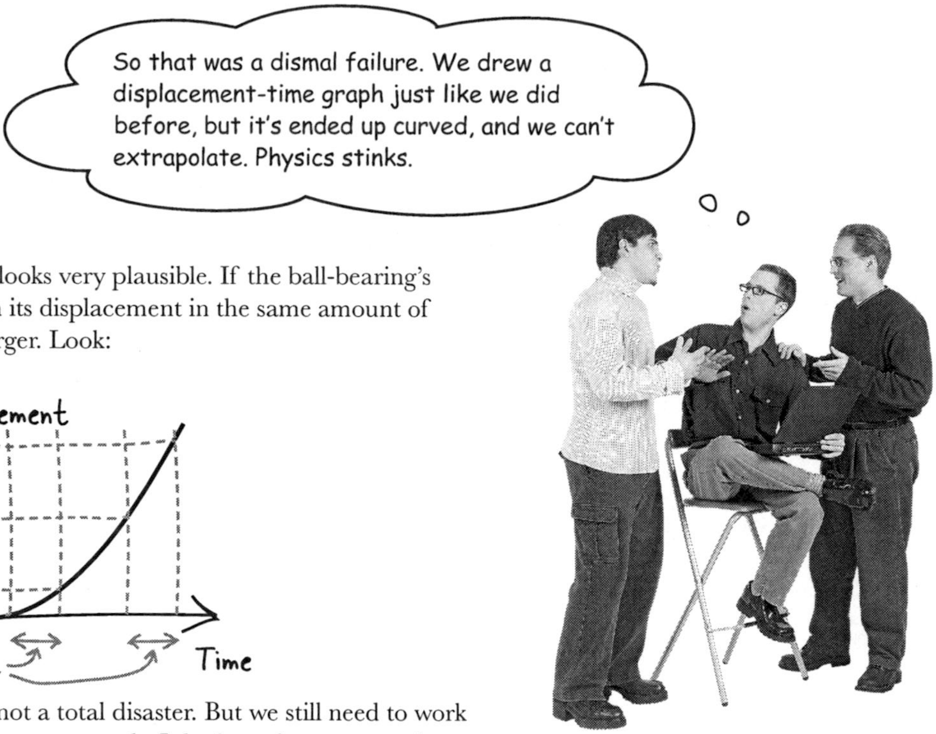

Joe: But our curved graph looks very plausible. If the ball-bearing's getting faster as it falls, then its displacement in the same amount of time will keep on getting larger. Look:

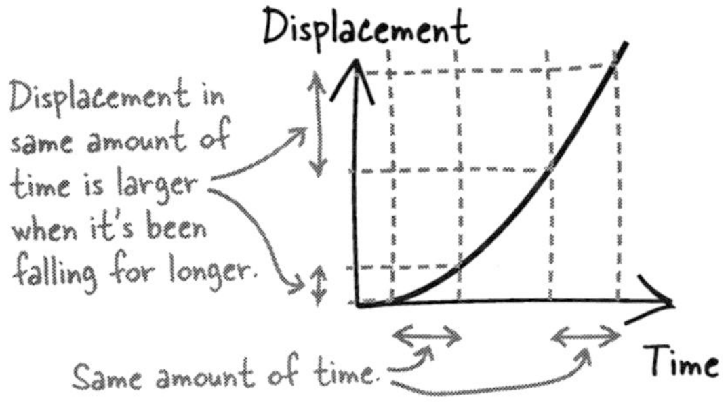

Frank: OK, so maybe it's not a total disaster. But we still need to work out the cage's **velocity** after two seconds. I don't see how we can do that - without dropping the actual cage from a distance high enough to make it fall for 2.0 s. That sounds tough. Even in a room with a 3 meter ceiling, we didn't get the ball-bearing to fall for more than 0.78 seconds.

Joe: We can't keep on dropping the cage - we might break it, which is what we're trying to avoid! Plus there'd be the repair bill for the road.

Jim: Hmmm. When we were drawing a displacement-time graph for a cyclist, we didn't ever need him to ride long distances, just short ones.

Frank: That's because we were able to **extrapolate** his displacement-time graph. But we already said we can't do that here!

Jim: The last time we drew a displacement versus time graph, we calculated its **slope** to work out the pizza guy's **velocity**. And then we used that in an **equation** to work out his time for any distance.

Frank: But here the velocity's changing - it doesn't have one single value. We already said we can't use the equation we worked out then.

Joe: But what if we use the slope of our displacement-time graph at various points to plot a **velocity-time graph**? If it's a nice shape, we might be able to extrapolate it and use it to get the velocity after 2.0 s

Jim: Yeah, if we draw some **tangents** on our displacement - time graph, we could do that. It might just work ...

Usually when you do an experiment, you'll use the results to draw a graph - then use the graph to work out an EQUATION.

Sharpen your pencil

You want to plot the velocity-time graph for the ball-bearing. You can get values for its velocity at various points in time from the **slope** of your displacement-time graph at each point in time. As this is a curved graph, we've already selected some regularly-spaced points on it and sketched in their **tangents** for you.

a. Fill in the table by choosing two points on each tangent and working out its slope - and, therefore, the velocity of the ball-bearing at each point.

b. Use the velocities you've calculated to plot the velocity-time graph for the ball-bearing. You'll need to write in all the labels yourself and choose your own scale for the vertical axis.

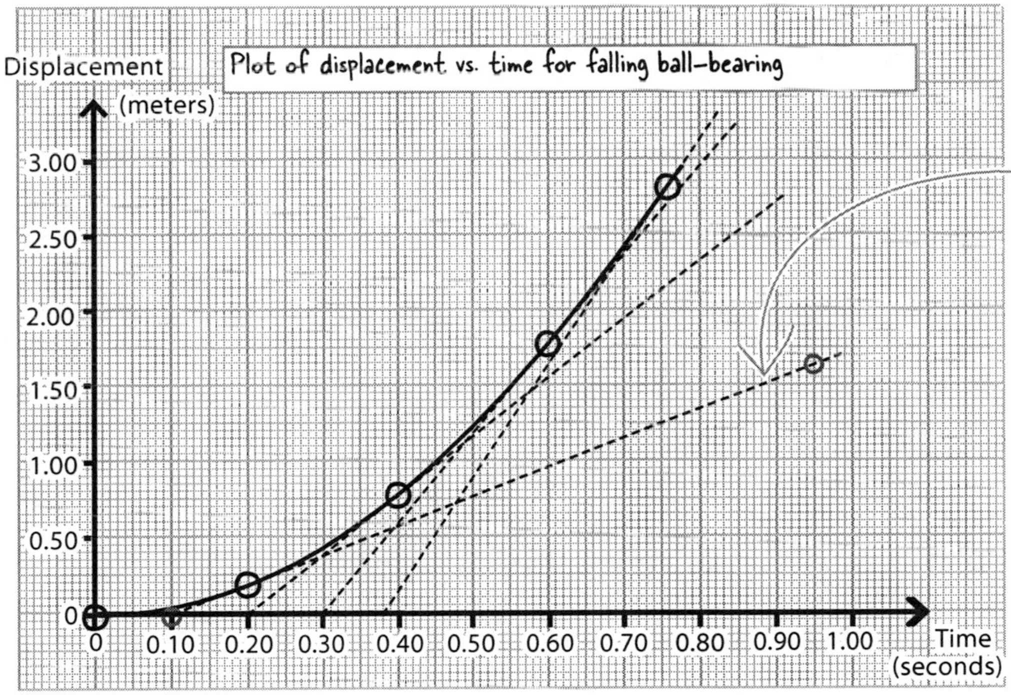

We already selected two points on this tangent and calculated the slope at $t = 0.20$ s.

You might like to go over the tangents with your ruler and different-colored pens so you can tell them apart!

You can work out something's velocity at any point in time from the slope of its displacement-time graph.

This is Δx between two points you pick on the tangent.

This is Δt between two points you pick on the tangent.

a.

Time at point (s)	Δx (m)	Δt (s)	Velocity = $\frac{\Delta x}{\Delta t}$ (m/s)
0.00			
0.20	1.65 - 0.00 = 1.65	0.95 - 0.10 = 0.85	$\frac{1.65}{0.85}$ = 1.94 (3 sd)
0.40			
0.60			
0.76			

b.

Plot of

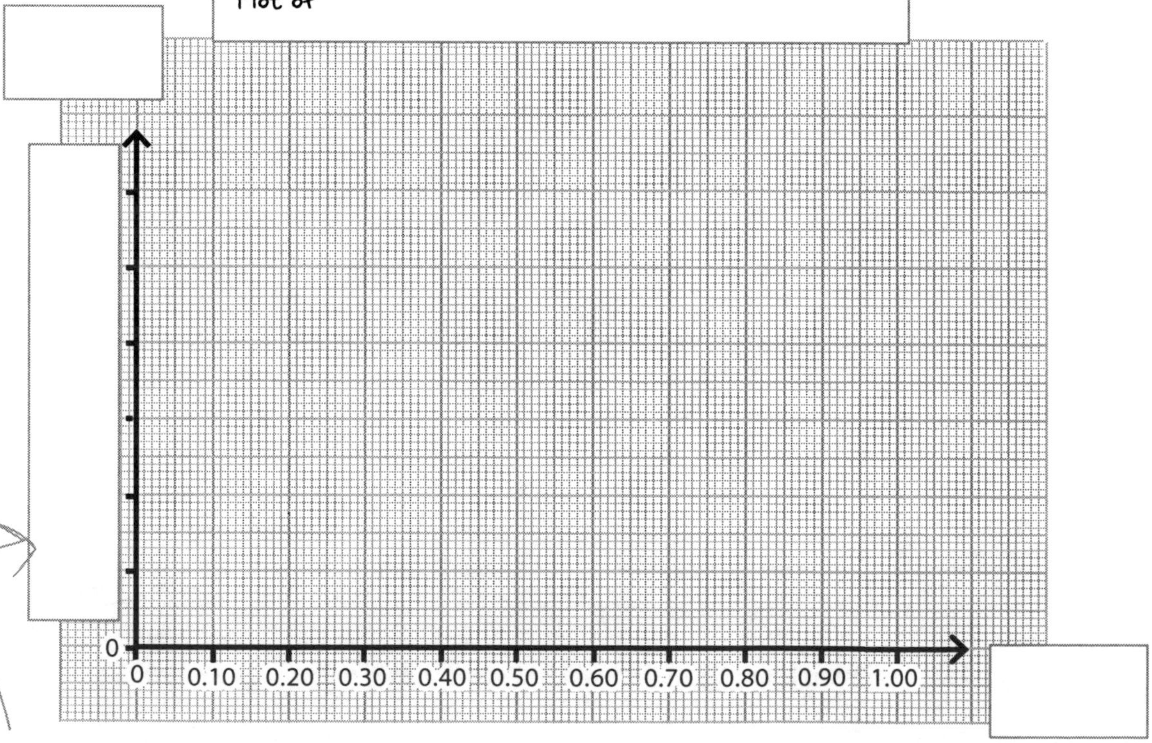

You'll need to pick a suitable scale for your vertical axis.

Sharpen your pencil Solution

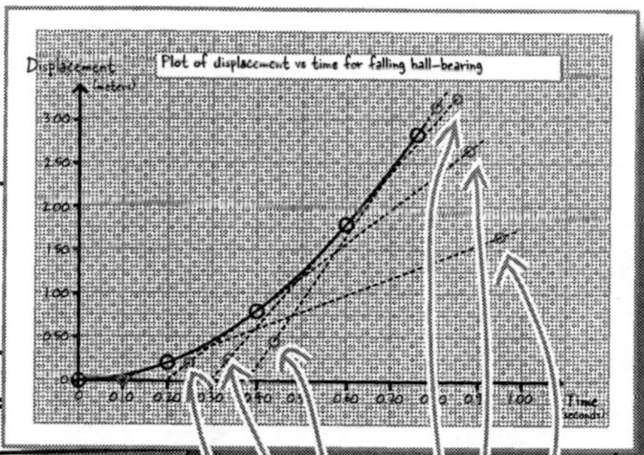

These are the points we chose to use. If you chose slightly different points or got slightly different values for the velocities, then don't worry as long as you were close!

a.

Time at point (s)	Δx (m)	Δt (s)	Velocity =
0.00	0	1	$\frac{0}{1} = 0$
0.20	1.65 - 0.00 = 1.65	0.95 - 0.10 = 0.85	$\frac{1.65}{0.85} = 1.94$ (3 sd)
0.40	2.65 – 0.20 = 2.45	0.88 – 0.25 = 0.63	$\frac{2.45}{0.63} = 3.89$ (3 sd)
0.60	3.25 – 0.25 = 3.00	0.85 – 0.34 = 0.51	$\frac{3.00}{0.51} = 5.88$ (3 sd)
0.76	3.15 – 0.45 = 2.70	0.80 – 0.44 = 0.36	$\frac{2.70}{0.36} = 7.50$ (3 sd)

b.

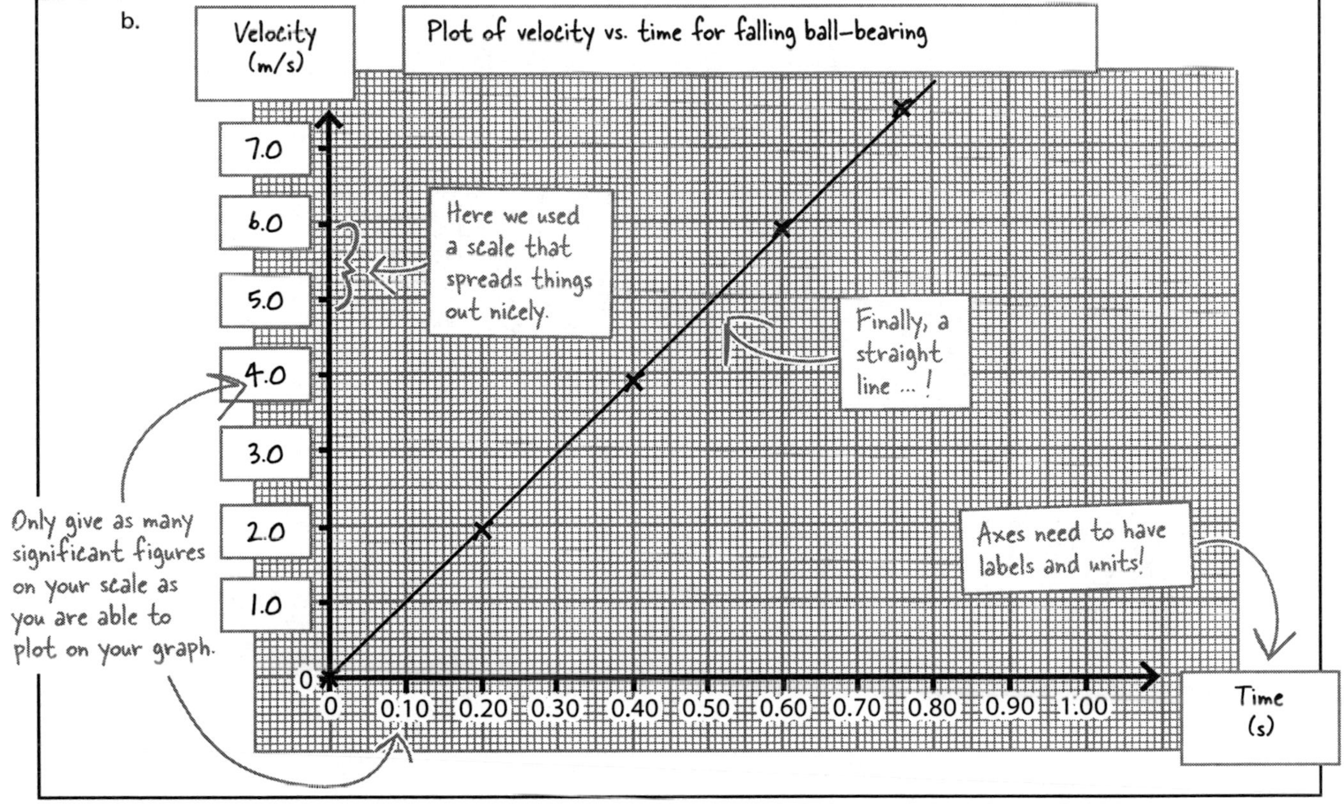

Jim: That looks, hmmm, nice. I'm starting to find straight lines strangely comforting, like they're somehow meant to be.

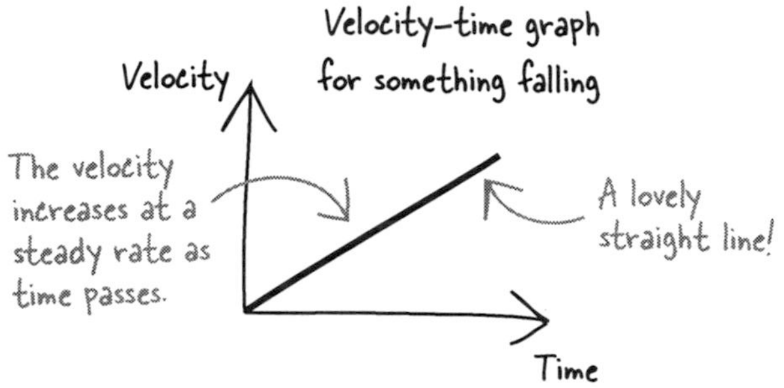

Frank: But what now? We still need to work out what the velocity will be after 2.0 s. Our graph only goes up to 0.78 s.

Jim: We can always **extrapolate** the graph out to 2.0 s and read off the velocity. It's OK to extrapolate straight line graphs!

Joe: Yeah ... but it would be kinda nice to come up with an **equation** if we can, so we can quickly work out the velocity at any time. Like, what if the Dingo wants to put the crane somewhere else?

Frank: With the cyclist, we used the slope of his displacement-time graph to work out the equation $\mathbf{v} = \frac{\Delta \mathbf{x}}{\Delta t}$.

Jim: The cyclist's displacement-time graph was a lovely straight line, like this one. Except this is a velocity-time graph. I wonder if we can use it to work out an equation in a similar way.

Joe: Well, the slope of the velocity-time graph will be $\frac{\Delta \mathbf{v}}{\Delta t}$ because velocity is on the vertical axis this time. So the slope would be the rate of change of velocity ...

Frank: Hey! Didn't we say before that the acceleration is the rate of change of velocity? So we can use the slope to get the equation $\mathbf{a} = \frac{\Delta \mathbf{v}}{\Delta t}$.

Jim: Ooh - because it's a lovely straight line graph, the slope is constant. So the acceleration must be constant. Which means we can use the graph to calculate the acceleration - then use the acceleration to work out the velocity after any time!

The slope of a 'something'-time graph tells you the rate at which the 'something' changes with time.

Velocity is rate of change of displacement.

$$\mathbf{v} = \frac{\Delta \mathbf{x}}{\Delta t}$$

Acceleration is rate of change of velocity.

$$\mathbf{a} = \frac{\Delta \mathbf{v}}{\Delta t}$$

The slope of something's velocity-time graph lets you work out its acceleration

Acceleration is rate of change of velocity with time. So the slope of a velocity-time graph is the acceleration.

The pizza guy goes at a **constant velocity**, so his displacement-time graph has a **constant slope**. His velocity-time graph is a flat line, as his velocity is constant at all times. The slope of his velocity-time graph is zero, so his acceleration is zero.

The falling thing's velocity-time graph is a straight line with a **constant slope**. As acceleration is rate of change of velocity, this means that it has a **constant acceleration**, equal to the slope of the velocity-time graph $\mathbf{a} = \frac{\Delta \mathbf{v}}{\Delta t}$.

The slope of a velocity-time graph is the acceleration.

$$\mathbf{a} = \frac{\Delta \mathbf{v}}{\Delta t}$$

Acceleration

Slope of velocity-time graph

Graphs for Alex the cyclist (constant velocity)

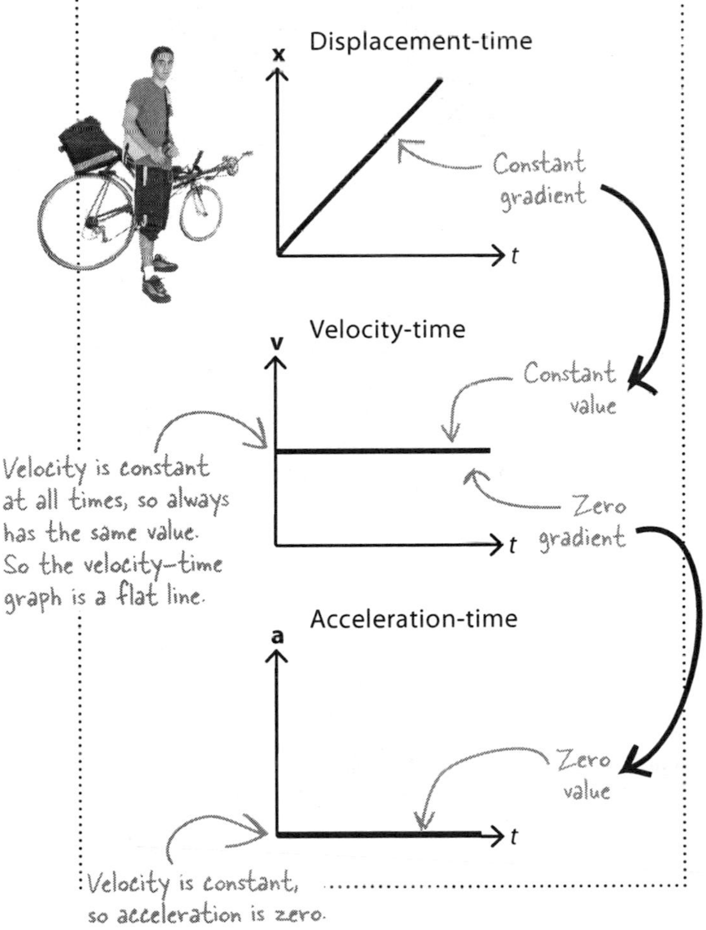

Graphs for a falling object (constant acceleration)

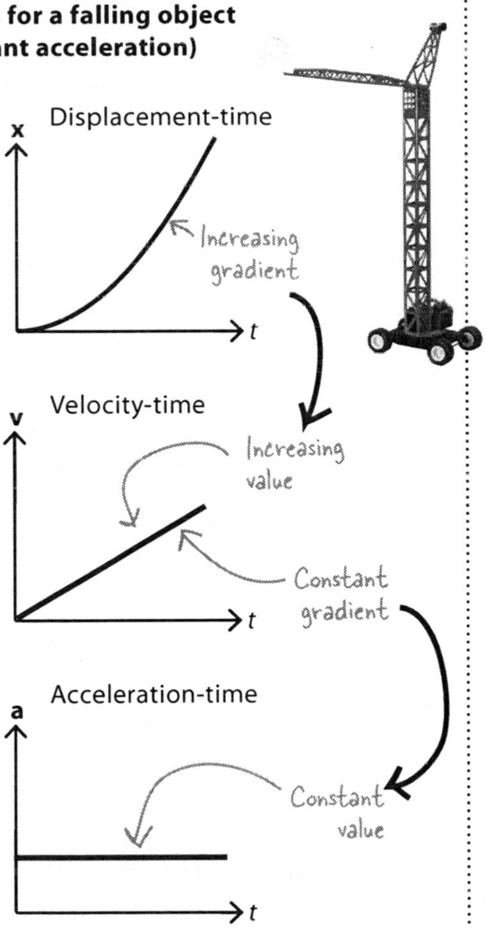

there are no Dumb Questions

Q: Why do the graphs over there on the opposite page not have any numbers or units on them?

A: Because these are 'sketch graphs' where the **shape** is the most important thing. The **x**-*t*, **v**-*t* and **a**-*t* graphs for something with a constant velocity will always have the same shape, no matter what that constant velocity is. Same goes for anything with constant acceleration.

You'll sometimes see graphs like this on an exam - these allow you to show that you understand physics principles by choosing, drawing, or explaining the shape of a graph.

Q: I don't get why Alex's acceleration-time graph is a flat line.

A: Alex cycles with a constant velocity. So at each point in time, his velocity is always the same. So the graph doesn't go up or down - the value stays the same.

Q: And how do you get from that to 'zero value' for the acceleration?

A: Acceleration is rate of change of velocity. The velocity-time graph shows that his velocity isn't changing. So his acceleration must be zero.

Q: OK, I think I get Alex's graphs now. But I'm still puzzled about how the falling thing's displacement-time graph turned into a straight line velocity-time graph.

A: Velocity is the rate of change of displacement. As the curve gets steeper, its slope gets larger. So you know that the velocity increases as time goes on, and the velocity-time graph you just drew showed that the increases form a straight line.

Q: So, what are the units of acceleration, anyway? Surely I need to know that to be able to do calculations?

A: Funny you should ask ...

Work out the units of acceleration

Velocity is rate of change of displacement, in other words how something's displacement varies with time. You already worked out that its units are meters per second (m/s).

Acceleration is rate of change of velocity, or how something's velocity varies with time. Although you've met acceleration as a concept before, you now need to deal with acceleration in calculations. Which means that you need to know about its **units**.

Sharpen your pencil

Hint: It's easiest to write the units as fractions to work them out before changing them to the 'inline' style of m/s at the very end.

Fill in the blanks in the table to work out the units of acceleration.

Quantity	is rate of change of	Units of the changing thing	Units of time	Units of quantity
Velocity	Displacement	m	s	$\frac{m}{s}$ = m/s
Acceleration				

Sharpen your pencil Solution

Fill in the blanks in the table to work out the units of acceleration.

Quantity	is rate of change of	Units of the changing thing	Units of time	Units of quantity
Velocity	Displacement	m	s	$\frac{m}{s}$ = m/s
Acceleration	Velocity	m/s	s	$\frac{\frac{m}{s}}{s} = \frac{m}{s^2} = m/s^2$

You're dividing by seconds twice, so it works out as m/s^2.

s^2 is a weird unit. I guess I should think of them as something other than 'square seconds,' right?

Think of m/s^2 as (meters per second) per second

Velocity is the rate of change of displacement, so its units are meters per second, or m/s.

Acceleration is the rate of change of velocity, so its units are [velocity] per second, or meters per second per second, or m/s^2.

This might seem weird at first, as m^2 is a visible area in 'square meters,' but there's no such thing as a 'square second'! But if you instead think of the units as (meters per second) per second, it makes a lot more sense.

Square brackets around something is shorthand for 'units of'. So [velocity] means 'units of velocity'.

The units of acceleration are m/s^2, or (meters per second) per second.

'per' means 'divided by'

Sharpen your pencil

a. Use your velocity-time graph to get a value for the acceleration of a falling object.

b. Use that to work out the cage's velocity when it's been falling for 2.0 s. Is this less than 25 m/s?

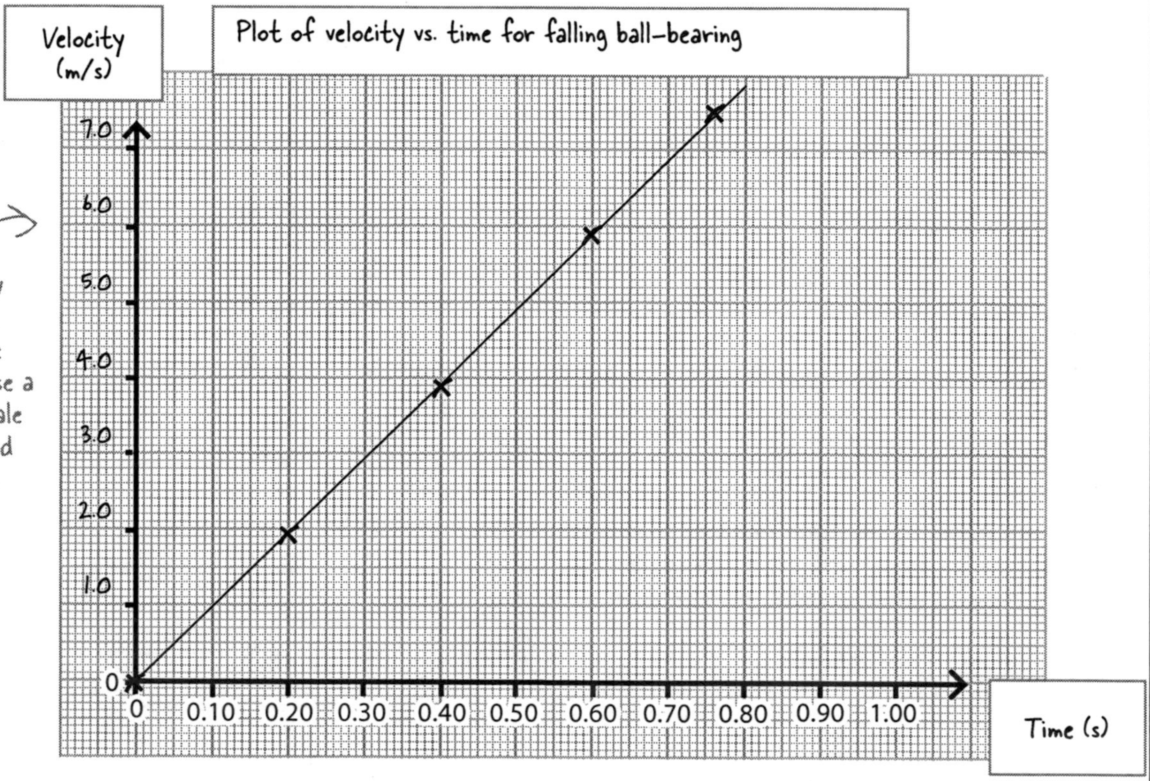

You already titled and labeled the graph, chose a vertical scale and plotted the points.

There's space down here for you to show your work.

Sharpen your pencil Solution

a. Use your velocity-time graph to get a value for the acceleration of a falling object.

b. Use that to work out the cage's velocity when it's been falling for 2.0 s. Is this less than 25 m/s?

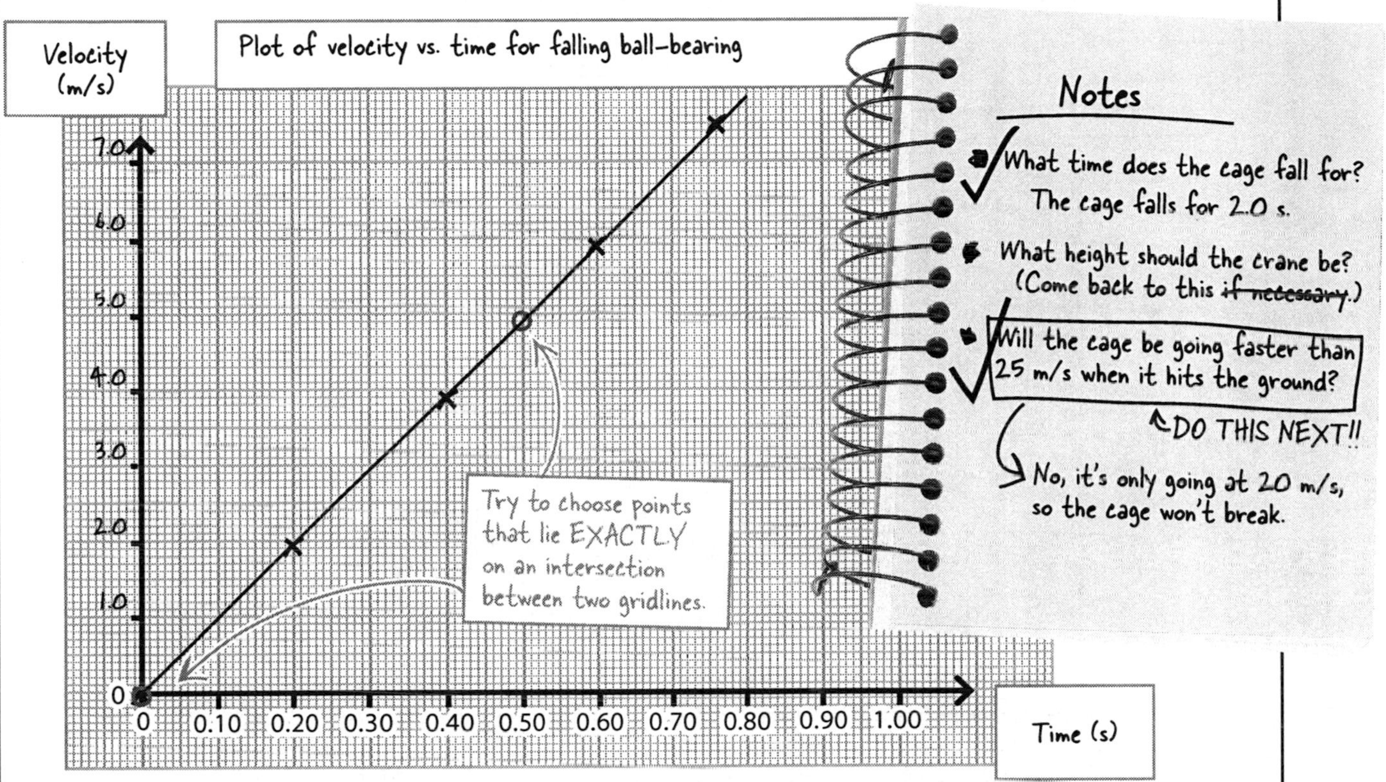

a. Acceleration = Rate of change of velocity

$$a = \frac{\Delta v}{\Delta t}$$

$$a = \frac{4.9 - 0.0}{0.50 - 0.00}$$

$$a = 9.8\ m/s^2\ (2\ sd)$$

Remember to write down what it is you're actually doing!

These were the points we chose – if you chose slightly different points and got a slightly different answer, that's OK.

You can only quote the answer to 2 sd as the velocities are only plotted on the graph to 2 sd.

b. Velocity after 2.0 s:

$$a = \frac{\Delta v}{\Delta t}$$

$$\Rightarrow \Delta v = a\Delta t = 9.8 \times 2.0 = 19.6 = 20\ m/s\ (2\ sd)$$

The cage starts off with zero velocity. So a 20 m/s change in velocity means it ends up going at 20 m/s.

Your final answer should have 2 sd, as the numbers you were working with only have 2 sd.

This is less than 25 m/s, so the cage won't break, and the plan is a go.

Success! You worked out the velocity after 2.0 s - and the cage won't break!

You've just worked out that the cage will be going at 20 m/s after 2.0 s, so the cage won't break. - and the Dingo will be able to stop the Emu for long enough to deliver his party invitation! You got here by designing an **experiment,** which let you draw the **displacement-time graph** for a falling object.

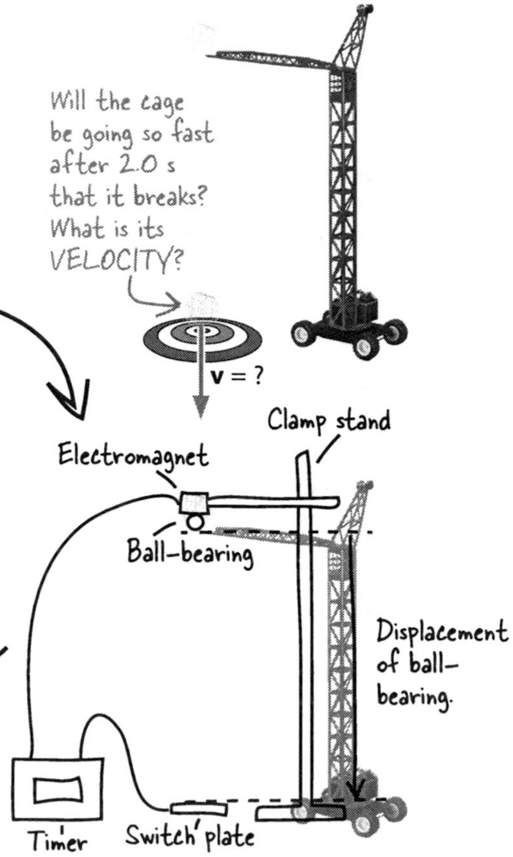

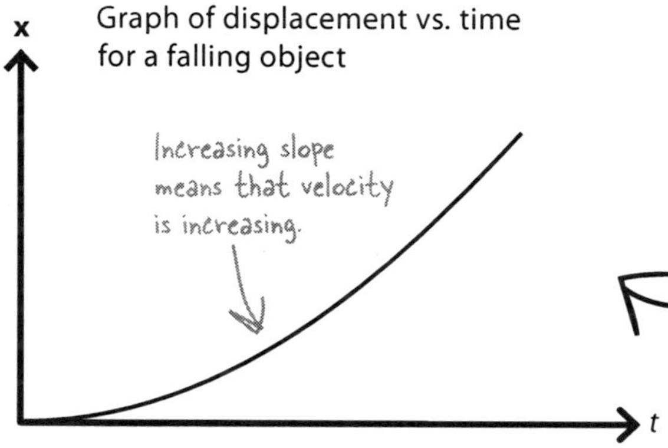

Then, you used the **slope** at various points of the displacement-time graph to draw a **velocity-time graph**.

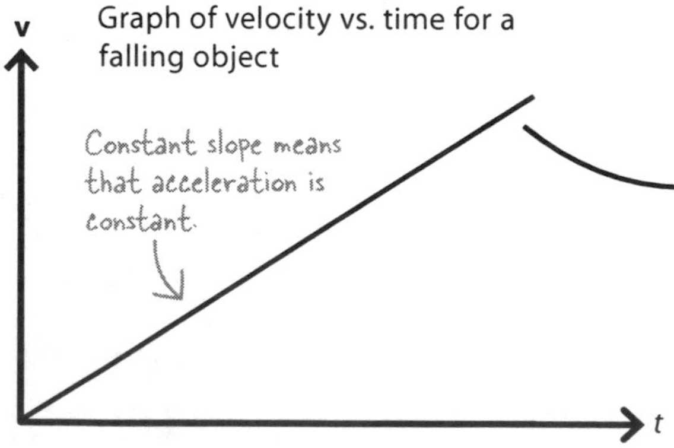

Then, you used the slope of the velocity-time graph to calculate a value for the **acceleration due to gravity, 9.8 m/s^2**.

Finally you used that value in the **equation** $\mathbf{a} = \frac{\Delta \mathbf{v}}{\Delta t}$, which you rearranged to calculate the cage's velocity.

The velocity is less than 25 m/s, so the cage won't break.

The Earth's gravity accelerates falling objects at a constant rate of 9.8 m/s^2.

there are no Dumb Questions

Q: I've seen values of 10 m/s^2 or 9.81 m/s^2 for acceleration due to gravity used in other books. These values are both close to 9.8 m/s^2 but...

A: The AP Physics B table of information gives the value of acceleration due to gravity as 9.8 m/s^2. That's what we're going to use in this book.

Q: But surely I should practice with the value I'll use in my exam?

A: Yes, that'll be fine. Your answers won't work out too different from ours, and the exact value you're supposed to use will become second nature to you.

Q: I'm worried about the AP B multiple choice exam though. Doing calculations involving 9.8 without a calculator is a bit time-consuming, to say the least!

A: That's right - in the AP B multiple choice exam, you need to do mental arithmetic because you're not allowed to use a calculator. But at the start of the multiple choice exam, it says 'Note: To simplify calculations, you may use **g** = 10 m/s^2 in all problems.'

Multiplying and dividing by 10 is much, much easier than dealing with 9.8 s, so there's no need to worry about that.

Q: Hmmm. Why do you use '$/s^2$' to indicate dividing by s^2 with units, but use 10^{-2} to indicate dividing by 10^2 in scientific notation?

A: These are the conventions that the AP physics course, table of information, and exam all use. It's also possible to write m/s^2 as ms^{-2} - using the same convention as you do for scientific notation. If this is what you're more used to, then do feel free to write your units like this instead.

Q: OK, so I got the value for the cage's acceleration - but what about its displacement after 2.0 seconds?!

A: You'll work that out in chapter 7 ...

Gravity accelerates everything at the same rate (if air resistance is minimal)

Although everyday experience might lead you to think otherwise, the earth's gravity accelerates everything at the same rate of 9.8 m/s^2 if you ignore the effect of air resistance.

The reason 'light' things like feathers fall more slowly than 'heavy' things like ball-bearings or cages is because they're falling through the air. The feather has a large surface area compared to its weight, so it's held up more by the air. If the air wasn't there, the feather and ball-bearing would land at the same time.

Most of the time in physics, you'll be dealing with things like cages and ball-bearings, which have small surface areas compared to their weight. Unless a question states otherwise, you can safely ignore air resistance.

Sometimes it's useful to make an assumption that simplifies a problem so you can solve the easier version.

While we're here, I've been wondering how it's possible to calculate an 'instantaneous' velocity at a single point on a displacement-time graph. Surely you need to use **two** points, so you can work out the change that happens **between** them?!

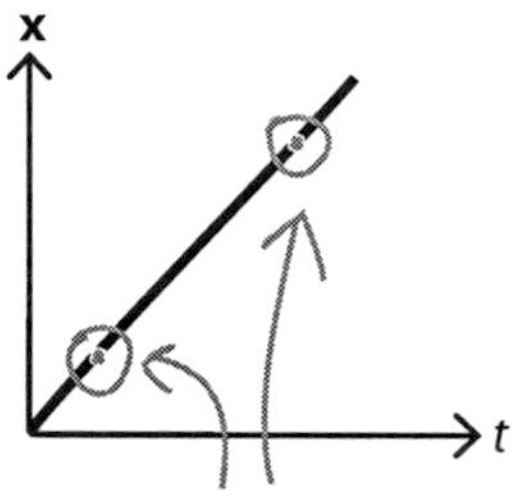

You do need two points - but they can be really really close together

The first time you calculated a velocity from a displacement-time graph, it was for a cyclist who traveled with a constant velocity. So the graph had a constant slope, and it didn't matter which two points you chose to use to calculate $\Delta \mathbf{x}$ and Δt since the value of the slope (and, therefore, the velocity) was always the same.

Now, you've had to deal with a falling thing for which the velocity is continually increasing. This produced a curved displacement-time graph where the slope was never the same from one moment to the next.

You can think of calculating the slope at a single **point** on this graph as calculating $\Delta \mathbf{x}$ and Δt over a very, very small interval, using two points infinitesimally close to the point you're interested in.

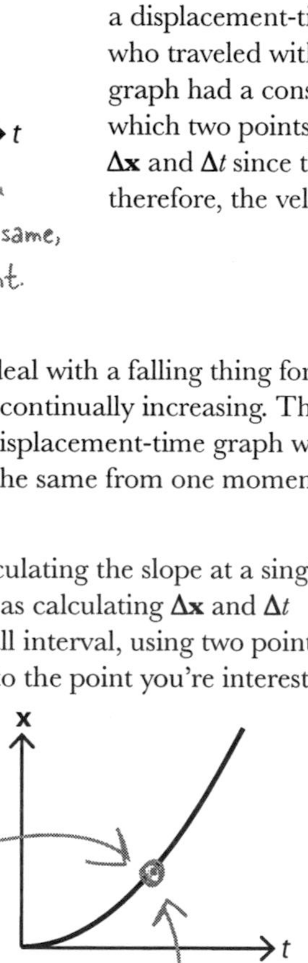

A capital Δ implies that you mean a reasonable-sized change in a quantity.

This means "smaller than any possible measure".

If you're talking about an **instantaneous** velocity at a single point like this, a more 'correct' way of writing your equation is to use a small letter 'd' to mean 'change in' instead of a capital 'Δ'. This means that the change is infinitesimally small.

So you'd write the equation for instantaneous velocity as $\mathbf{v} = \frac{d\mathbf{x}}{dt}$ to make it clear that you mean an instantaneous velocity measured over a tiny, tiny change in **x** and t rather than the larger change that using $\Delta \mathbf{x}$ and Δt would imply.

Practically speaking, there are two ways of calculating $\frac{d\mathbf{x}}{dt}$: drawing a tangent (as you've already done) and using calculus (which isn't part of this book).

Now onto solve for the displacement!

You know that the cage **won't** be going fast enough to break when it hits the ground 2.0 s after being dropped, so it's OK to go ahead with the plan. The notebook summarizes everything you've learned in this chapter about falling objects.

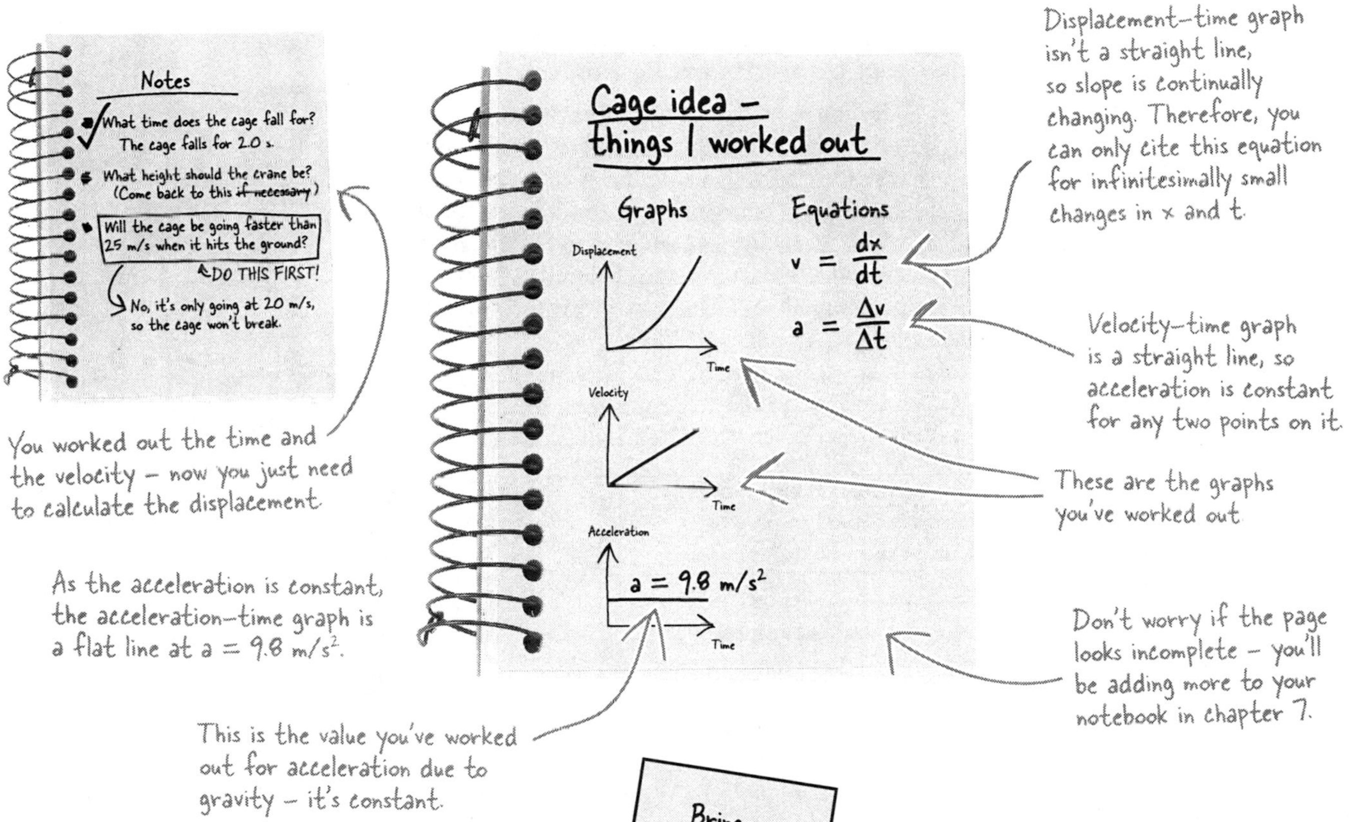

The Dingo's plan to stop the Emu and invite him to the birthday party is taking shape!

So it's on to chapter 7 - where you'll calculate the cage's **displacement** after 2.0 s. so that the Dingo knows how high to set the crane platform ...

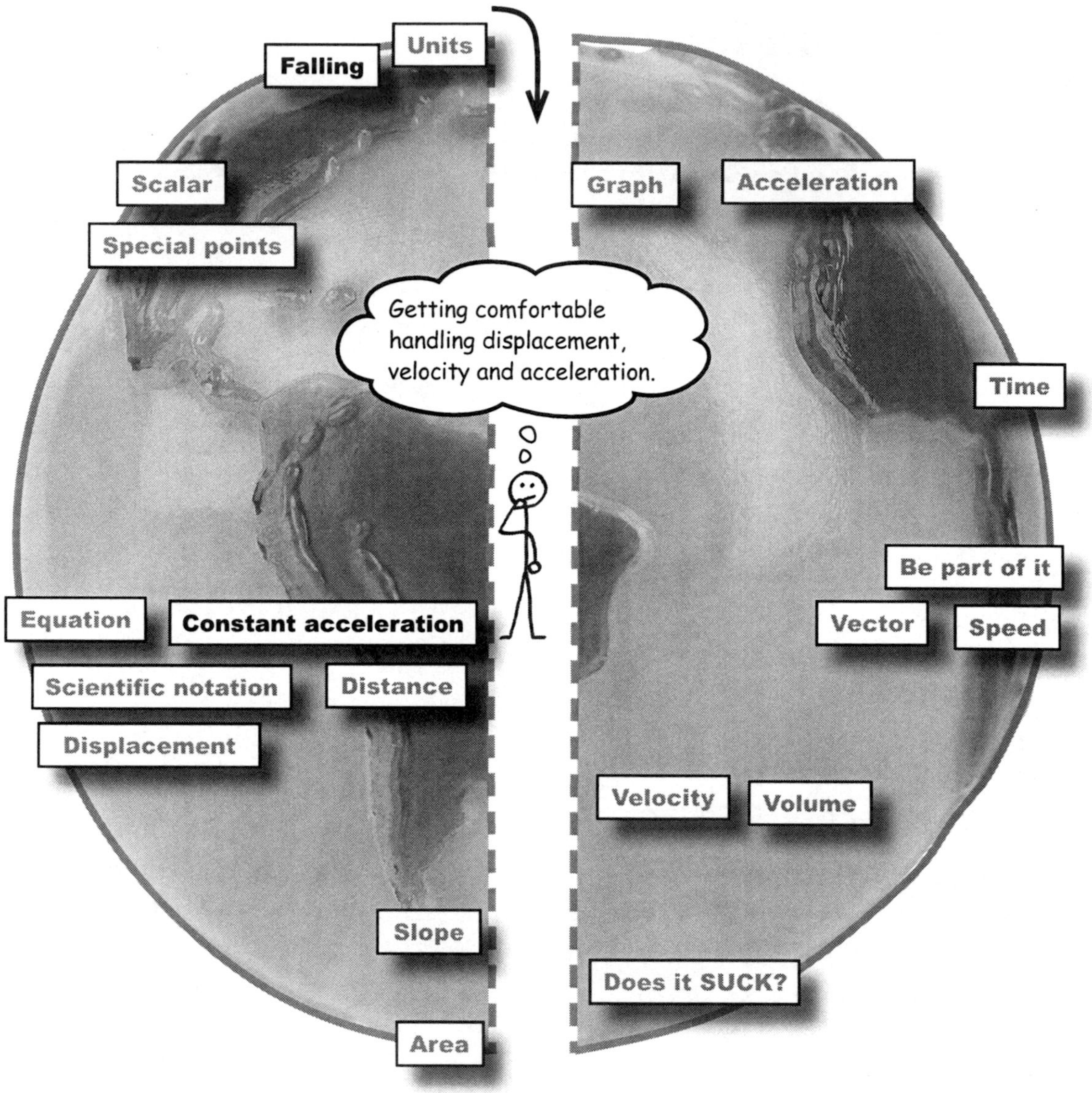

☑	**Constant acceleration**	**Something with constant acceleration has a straight line velocity-time graph described by the equation $a = \frac{\Delta v}{\Delta t}$**
☑	**Falling**	**Something falling close to the Earth is accelerated by gravity at a constant rate of 9.8 m/s^2.**

Your Physics Toolbox

You've got Chapter 6 under your belt, and you've added some terminology and problem-solving skills to your toolbox.

Experiment -> graph -> equation

When you do an experiment, you'll usually use the results to draw a graph, then use the slope of the graph to work out an equation.

Slope of a graph

The slope of a displacement-time graph is equal to the velocity.

The slope of a velocity-time graph is equal to the acceleration.

Constant velocity

If something has constant velocity, its displacement increases at a steady rate.

This means that its displacement-time graph has a constant slope equal to its velocity.

Something with a constant velocity has an acceleration of zero, as its velocity isn't changing.

Constant acceleration

If something has constant velocity, its displacement increases more and more each second as time goes on.

Its velocity-time graph has a constant slope equal to its acceleration.

Falling object

A falling object is accelerated by gravity – so has a constant acceleration of 9.8 m/s^2 downwards close to the the Earth's surface..

Acceleration due to gravity

Acceleration due to gravity has a value of 9.8 m/s^2 downwards when you're close to the Earth's surface.

7 Equations of motion (part 1)

Playing With Equations

It's time to take things to another level.

So far, you've done experiments, drawn graphs of their results and worked out equations from them. But there's only so far you can go, since sometimes your graph isn't a straight line. In this chapter, you'll expand your math skills by making **substitutions** to work out a key **equation of motion** for a curved displacement - time graph of a falling object. And you'll also learn that **checking** your GUT reaction to an answer can be a good thing.

How high should the crane be?

The Dingo wants to invite the Emu to his birthday party - but the only way he'll get him to stay still for long enough is by catching him in a cage!

In chapter 6, you figured out that it takes the Emu 2.0 s to get from the corner to the target on the road while running at his constant speed.

You also figured out that the cage's **velocity** after 2.0 s won't lead to it shattering on impact, by drawing its **velocity - time graph** and working out the **equation** $\mathbf{a} = \frac{\Delta \mathbf{v}}{\Delta t}$.

But the Dingo wants to know how high to set the crane. Which means that you now need to work out the cage's **displacement** after it's been falling for 2.0 s.

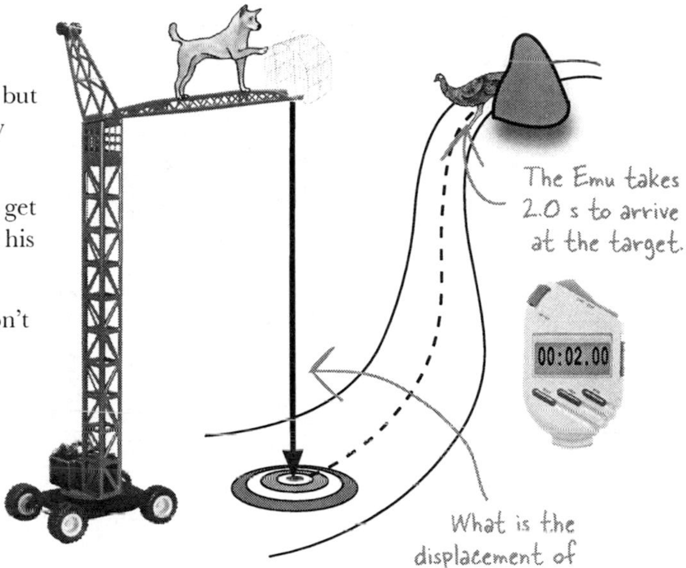

The falling cage's displacement - time graph is curved, so you can't extrapolate

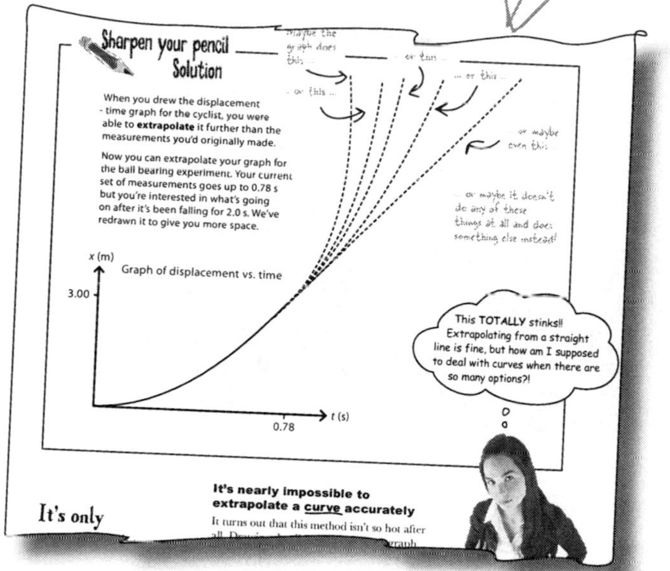

You already drew a **displacement - time graph** for a falling object, but you can't **extrapolate** it to read off the displacement after 2.0 s because the graph is curved.

BRAIN POWER

If you can't read the value for the displacement after 2.0 s off your graph, what can you do?

OK, so we have to figure out the cage's displacement after it's been falling for 2.0 s. Are we absolutely sure we can't just extrapolate the displacement-time graph we drew before?

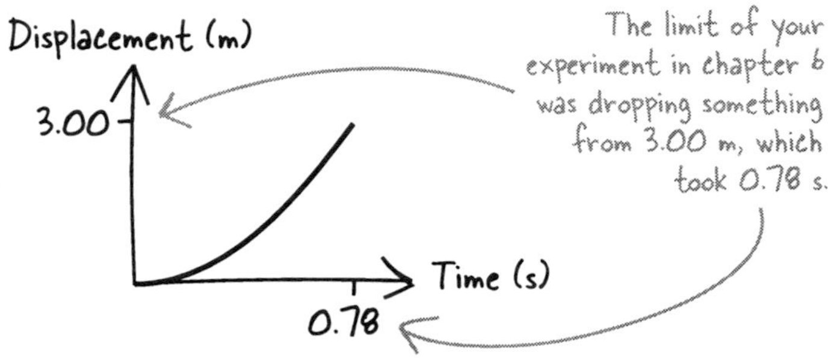

Jim: It's a **curve**, so we don't really know what it's going to do next. If the last point we'd plotted was close to 2.0 s we could probably make an educated guess, but not when we're so far away.

Frank: But 0.78 s is only a little bit less than 2.0 s. We'd only need to continue the graph for another 1.22 s - that's hardly any time at all!

Jim: It's a lot of time compared to what we already have. We've plotted less than half the graph between $t = 0.0$ s and $t = 2.0$ s.

Joe: Maybe we could try working out an **equation**, like we did before to get a value of the cage's velocity from its velocity - time graph?

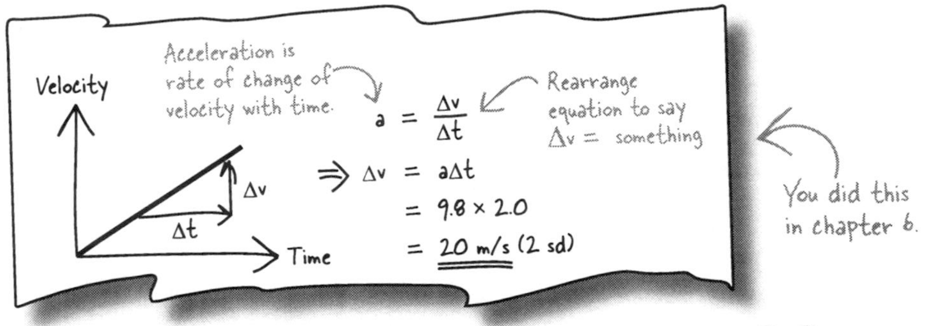

Graphs and equations are both ways of representing reality.

Frank: But the velocity - time graph is a **straight** line. Our displacement - time graph is a **curved** line!

Jim: Yeah, I dunno if it's possible for a curved graph to be represented by an equation.

Joe:: I'm sure it must be possible, if graphs and equations are both ways of representing reality ...

BRAIN POWER

Do you think it's possible for a curved graph to be represented by an equation?

Graphs and equations both represent the real world

Graphs are a way of representing the real world visually. **Equations** are a way of representing the real world symbolically. They both allow you to **predict** what will happen to a quantity when other things that affect it change as well.

For example, $\mathbf{a} = \frac{\Delta \mathbf{v}}{\Delta t}$ is the equation for the cage's velocity-time graph. The equation and the graph both represent the same physical reality. The equation shows you symbolically how the velocity, acceleration and time interrelate when the acceleration is constant. If you know values for two of the quantities in the equation, you can use the equation to calculate the third by **rearranging** the equation.

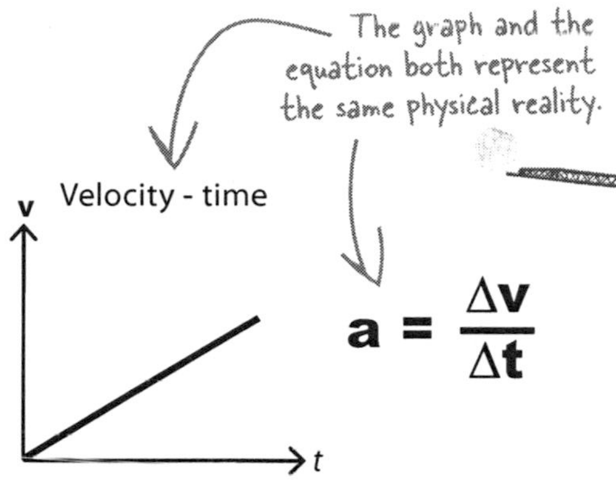

$$\mathbf{a} = \frac{\Delta \mathbf{v}}{\Delta \mathbf{t}}$$

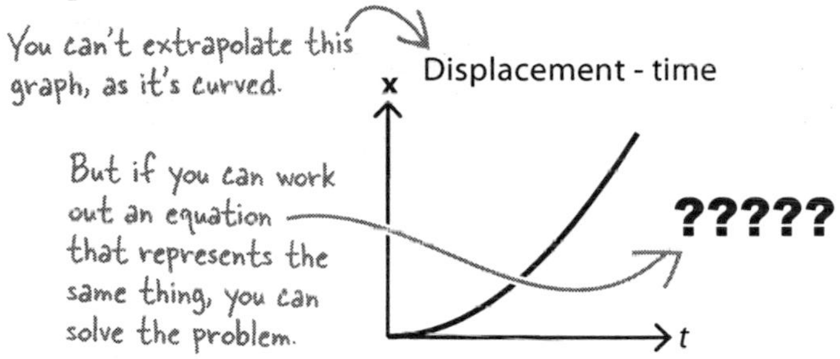

So, if you can work out the **equation that represents your displacement - time graph**, you'll be able to use it to solve the problem of how high the cage needs to be.

That's right - we're not going to use Δx and Δt this time.

Originally, **Δx** and Δ*t* helped with the concept of finding the **slope** of a graph using the change in **x** and *t* between two points. But as the slope of this graph is continually changing, you'd have to put the two points so close together it'd be impossible to measure the changes!

Instead, you'll use a different **variable** to represent the displacement and time at **each point** you're interested in.

Use a different variable to represent each of the values at the points you're interested in.

You're interested in the start and end points

We're only really interested in two points in the cage's motion - the **start** (when it's on the platform) and the **end** (when it hits the ground) - as we want to calculate the cage's displacement between these points.

In the equation you work out for your curved displacement - time graph we're going to use variables to represent every value we might be interested in at these start and end points:

$\mathbf{x}_0$ is the displacement at the start (when $t = 0$).
$\mathbf{v}_0$ is the velocity at the start (when $t = 0$).
x is the displacement at the end.
v is the velocity at the end.
a is the acceleration (which you already know is constant).

You call this "v nought" if you're speaking out loud.

You can tell that v and v_0 are both displacements because they use the letter v. But that they're different quantities because they have different subscripts.

The little '0' is part of the variable name, and is called a subscript.

There's no point in having a_0 and a, as the value for the acceleration is always the same.

Use the same letter to represent the same type of thing, and subscripts to say which is which.

Sharpen your pencil

We've drawn in the interesting start and end points on your velocity - time graph.

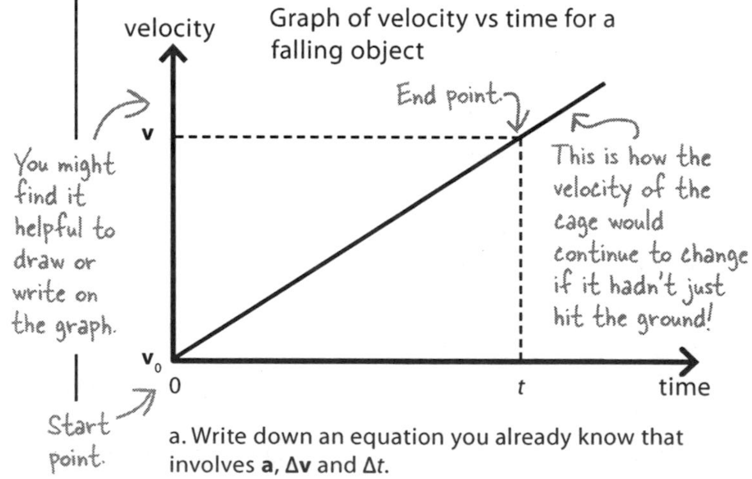

a. Write down an equation you already know that involves **a**, **Δv** and Δ*t*.

b. Use the values on the graph to rewrite this equation as an equation involving **a**, $\mathbf{v}_0$, **v** and *t*.

c. Rearrange your equation so that it says "**v** = something".

Sharpen your pencil Solution

We've drawn in the start and end points we're interested in on your velocity - time graph.

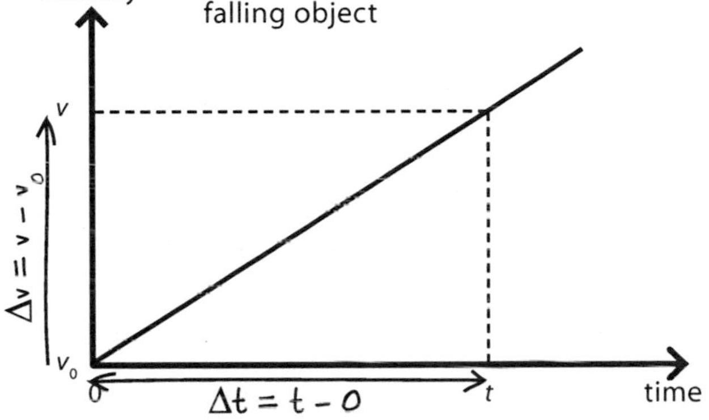

a. Write down an equation you already know that involves **a**, **Δv** and Δ*t*.

Acceleration = Rate of change of velocity

$$a = \frac{\Delta v}{\Delta t}$$

b. Use the values on the graph to rewrite this as an equation involving **a**, $\mathbf{v_0}$, **v** and *t*.

$$a = \frac{\Delta v}{\Delta t} = \frac{v - v_0}{t - 0}$$

$$a = \frac{v - v_0}{t}$$

c. Rearrange your equation so that it says "**v** = something".

$$a = \frac{v - v_0}{t}$$

Multiply both sides by t.

$$at = \frac{v - v_0}{t} \times t$$

Add v_0 to both sides.

$$v_0 + at = v - v_0 + v_0$$

Swap the sides over.

$$v = v_0 + at$$

Now you have v on its own.

You want your equation to be as general as possible so you can use it elsewhere.

At the moment, you're dealing with a falling cage. You could stick in the numbers you already know (t = 2.0 s, **a** = 9.8 m/s^2) but then you'd end up with an equation that you can only use once.

If you leave everything as letters for now and only put the numbers in at the end, you'll end up with a **general** equation you can use to deal with falling things, jet skis, racing cars ... anything that has a period of **constant acceleration**.

If your equation is general, you can reuse it in other problems.

there are no Dumb Questions

Q: Why did you choose particular variable names, like v (with no subscripts) for the final velocity and v_0 for the initial velocity?

A: It's a common convention to use $\mathbf{x}_0$ and $\mathbf{v}_0$ for the initial values of displacement and velocity and **x** and **v** for the final values. It's what's used in lots of textbooks, as well as the AP Physics B exam.

Q: But the convention isn't consistent! The initial velocity is called v_0, but the initial time doesn't even have a symbol - we just put in its value of 0.

A: The convention assumes that everything you're interested in starts at t=0. The '0' subscript in $\mathbf{v}_0$ stands for 'at t=0'', so you can read $\mathbf{v}_0$ as "the velocity at t=0". Similarly, t_0 would stand for "the time at t=0". So there's no need to bother with a t_0 symbol, as you already know that t=0 when t=0!

Q: Do I have to use these letters? Before, I've used s instead of x for displacement, and u instead of v_0 for initial velocity. I'm finding this confusing!

A: The main thing is that you understand the **physics concepts** that lie behind the equations. It doesn't matter which set of letters you use for that. It's fine to show your work using the letters you're more familiar with that already make sense for you!

Q: So what physics concepts are the most important here?

A: A graph and an equation can represent the same thing in real life. In this problem, they both describe what happens to the velocity of the falling cage as time passes.

Q: OK. But why have I used letters in the equation when I already worked out all the values of the things in the equation?! I know what v, v_0, a and t are for the falling cage!

A: One reason is that you can reuse a general equation again and again. If the crane is a different distance away from the corner, the cage would fall for a different time. Your general equation, $\mathbf{v} = \mathbf{v}_0 + \mathbf{a}t$, will give you the value of **v** for any time. All you need to do is put in the new numbers.

Q: And the other reason for not putting in the values yet?

A: If you keep the equation **general**, you'll be able to use it for anything with constant acceleration, even if it isn't 9.8 m/s^2. All you need to do is to put in the new numbers for your new problem.

The equation shows how different variables depend on one another. You can use it as a stepping stone to get what you really want.

Your equation $\mathbf{v} = \mathbf{v}_0 + \mathbf{a}t$ shows you how the variables $\mathbf{v}$, $\mathbf{v}_0$, **a** and t depend on each other. But it doesn't have an **x** in it, so you can't use it to directly calculate a value for the displacement,

However, as displacement is rate of change of velocity, the displacement and the velocity must depend on each other. So although you can't use this equation directly, you'll be able to use it as a stepping stone towards calculating the displacement of the cage after 2.0 s.

You have an equation for the velocity - but what about the displacement?

You've worked out the equation $\mathbf{v} = \mathbf{v}_0 + \mathbf{a}t$, which comes from the slope of your velocity - time graph. It gives you an object's **velocity**, **v**, after a certain amount of time (if you know its initial velocity, $\mathbf{v}_0$, and its acceleration, **a**).

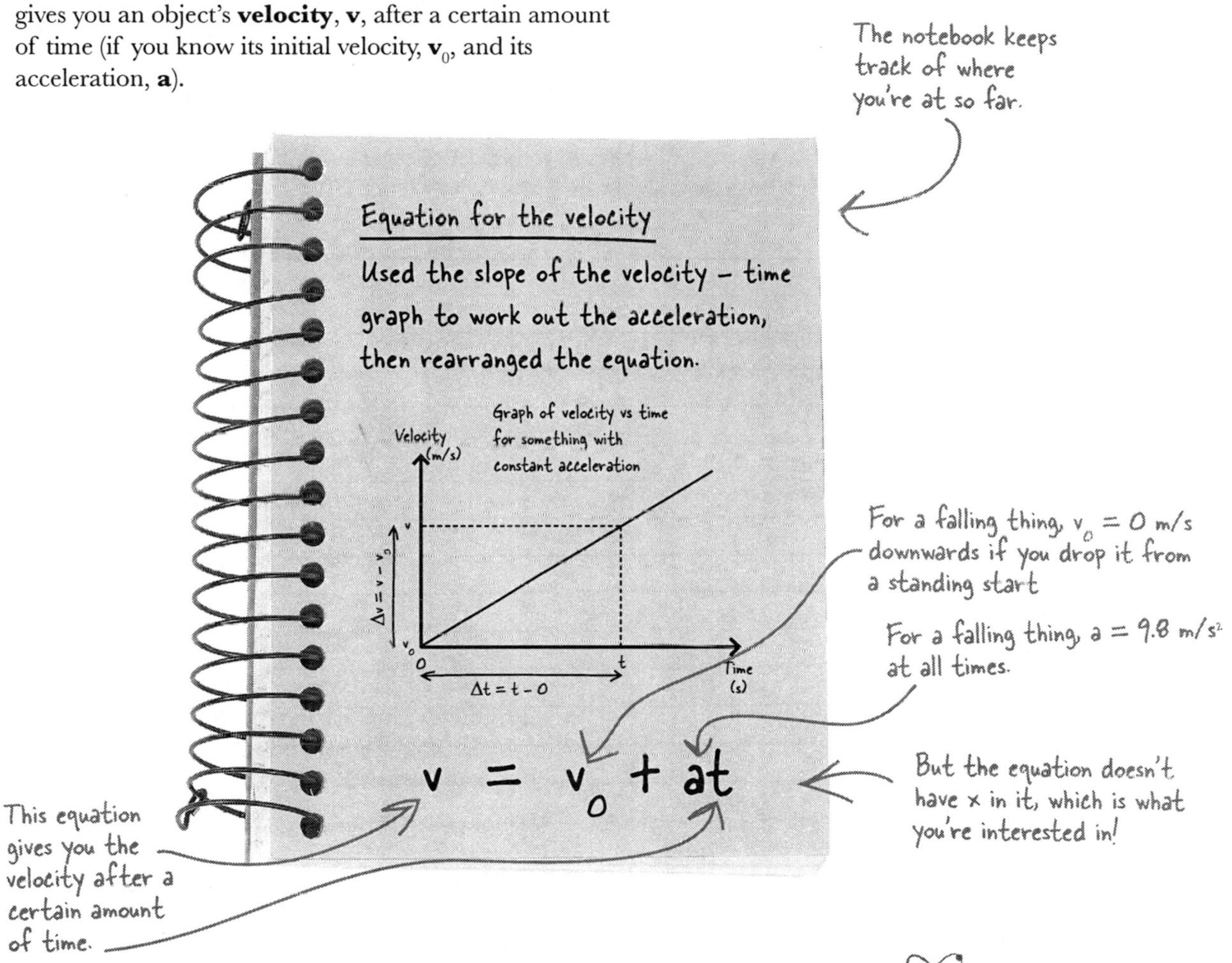

But what we're really interested in is the **displacement**, **x**, after a certain amount of time. If you have an equation for that, you can say how far the cage will fall in 2.0 s.

The velocity equation might be useful later on, as velocity and displacement must be related somehow. But right now, you really need an equation with an **x** in it to move forward ...

BRAIN POWER

How might you get an equation that involves the displacement?

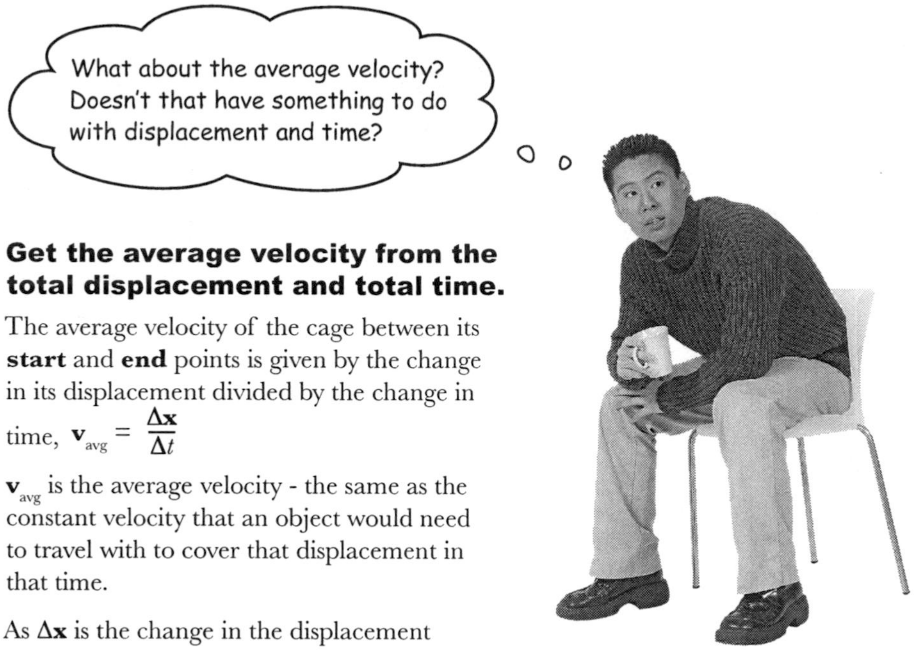

The average velocity is the same as the constant velocity you could have gone at to cover the displacement between your start and end points in the same time

Get the average velocity from the total displacement and total time.

The average velocity of the cage between its **start** and **end** points is given by the change in its displacement divided by the change in time, $\mathbf{v}_{avg} = \frac{\Delta \mathbf{x}}{\Delta t}$

$\mathbf{v}_{avg}$ is the average velocity - the same as the constant velocity that an object would need to travel with to cover that displacement in that time.

As $\Delta\mathbf{x}$ is the change in the displacement between the start and end points, the equation for the average velocity will have an **x** in it - which is what you want to calculate!

x is the displacement at the end point.

Sharpen your pencil

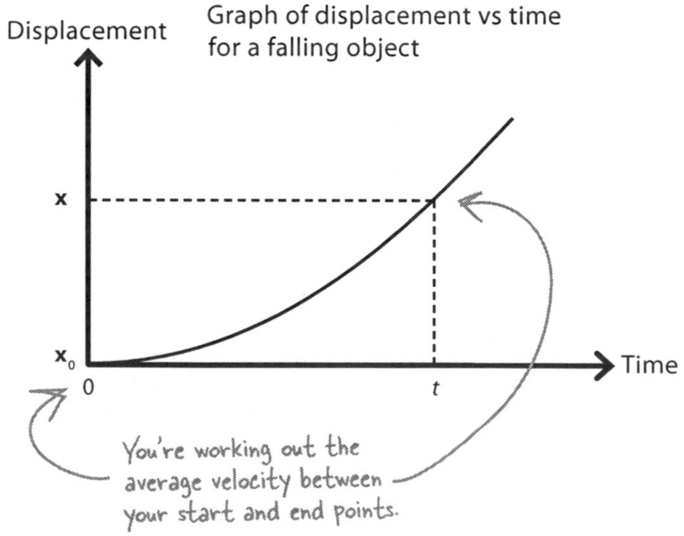

a. Draw a line on your displacement - time graph to represent the cage's average velocity between times 0 and *t*.

b. Use the graph to come up with an equation for the average velocity, $\mathbf{v}_{avg}$, in terms of $\mathbf{x}_0$, **x** and *t*.

Sharpen your pencil Solution

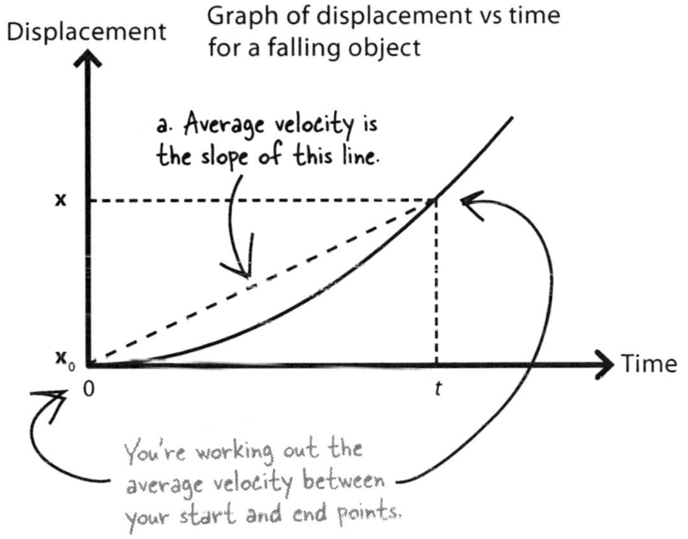

a. Draw a line on your displacement - time graph to represent the cage's average velocity between times 0 and *t*.

b. Use the graph to come up with an equation for the average velocity, $\mathbf{v}_{avg}$, in terms of $\mathbf{x}_0$, $\mathbf{x}$ and *t*.

$$\text{Average velocity} = \frac{\text{Total displacement}}{\text{Total time}}$$

$$v_{avg} = \frac{\Delta x}{\Delta t} = \frac{x - x_0}{t - 0}$$

$$v_{avg} = \frac{x - x_0}{t}$$

Equation for the velocity

Used the slope of the velocity - time graph to work out the acceleration, then rearranged the equation.

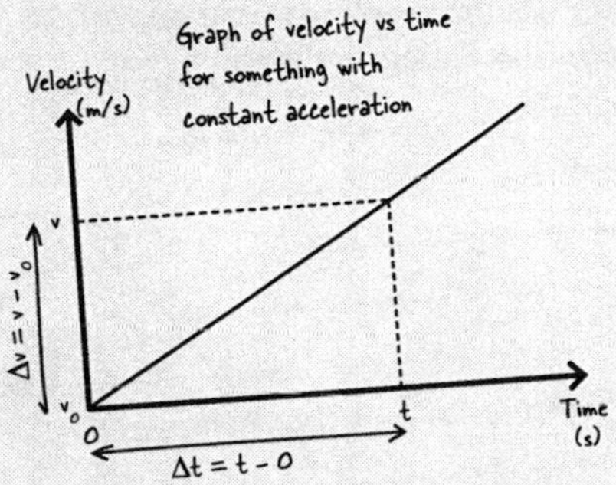

$$v = v_0 + at$$

Equation for the average velocity

Used the displacement - time graph to work out the average velocity.

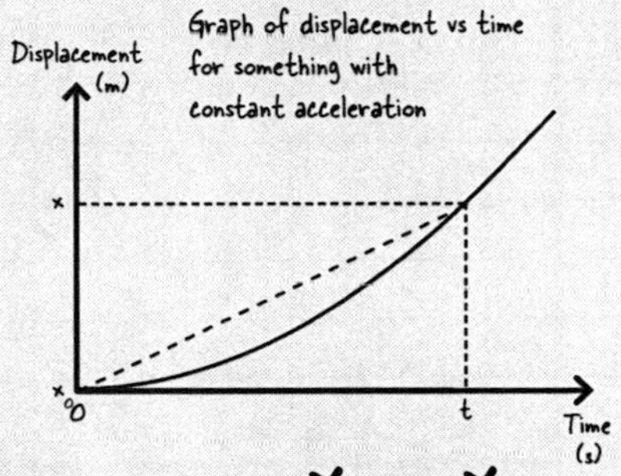

$$v_{avg} = \frac{x - x_0}{t}$$

An equation with x in it, which is what I want!

This stinks! Now we've got an equation with an x in it, but it's got the cage's average velocity in it as well - and we don't know what that is!! So we can't work out the value of the displacement. How's that supposed to help?!

That's right - we don't know the value of the average velocity.

You've come a long way, and have two equations from the graphs you drew:

$\mathbf{v} = \mathbf{v}_0 + \mathbf{a}t$ and $\mathbf{v}_{avg} = \frac{\mathbf{x} - \mathbf{x}_0}{t}$.

The second of these equations has an **x** in it, which is what you want - but it also has $\mathbf{v}_{avg}$, the average velocity, in it.

Since you don't know what the average velocity is, you can't use this equation to calculate **x** and tell the Dingo how high to put the crane platform right now. But **you're definitely making progress** ...

Wouldn't it be dreamy if we could calculate the value of the average velocity a different way. But I know it's just a fantasy ...

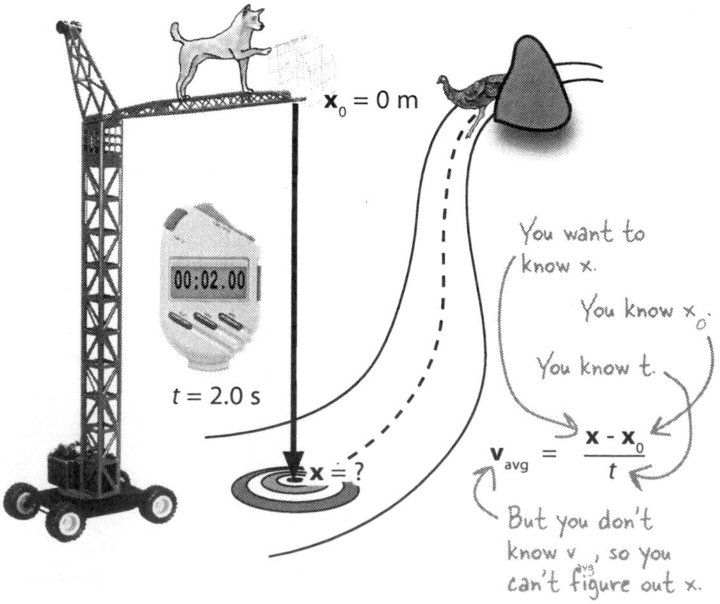

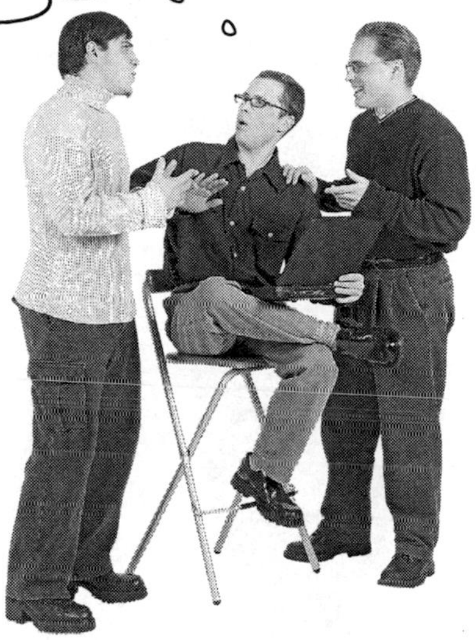

$$v = v_0 + at \qquad v_{avg} = \frac{x - x_0}{t}$$

Jim: Let's just see how they help us. I'm gonna put a question mark by the x, because we want to work that out. Then I'll tick what we already know values for, and cross the variables we don't know ...

$$v = v_0 + at \qquad v_{avg} = \frac{?x - x_0}{t}$$

Jim: ... hmmm, neither equation helps us. The one on the left is for the velocity, **v**, which we're not interested in. The one on the right has the displacement, **x**, in it, which is what we want to work out ... but it also has the average velocity, $\mathbf{v}_{avg}$, in it. And we don't know what $\mathbf{v}_{avg}$ is.

Joe: Is there another equation we can use?

Frank: What do you mean?

Joe: Our problem is $\mathbf{v}_{avg}$, right? We can't just rearrange the equation to say "**x** = something" and put in the values for the other variables because we don't have a value for $\mathbf{v}_{avg}$. But what if there was another equation we could use to calculate the value of $\mathbf{v}_{avg}$?

Frank: I like your thinking. But we already worked out $\mathbf{v}_{avg}$ the only way we know how - from the slope of our **displacement - time graph**.

Jim: Hang on! What about our **velocity - time graph**? Maybe if we look at that, we can eyeball a second equation for $\mathbf{v}_{avg}$.

Joe: You might be on to something there ... let's try it!

If you don't know the value for a variable in your equation, try to find another equation which includes that variable.

See the average velocity on your velocity-time graph

You've already worked out one equation for the falling cage's average velocity, $\mathbf{v}_{avg}$, from its **displacement - time graph**.

Now you can use your **intuition** to spot $\mathbf{v}_{avg}$ on the cage's **velocity - time graph** , which will lead you to a second equation for the cage's average velocity.

(And once you know the cage's average velocity, you can use that to get its displacement, which is what you really want to know!)

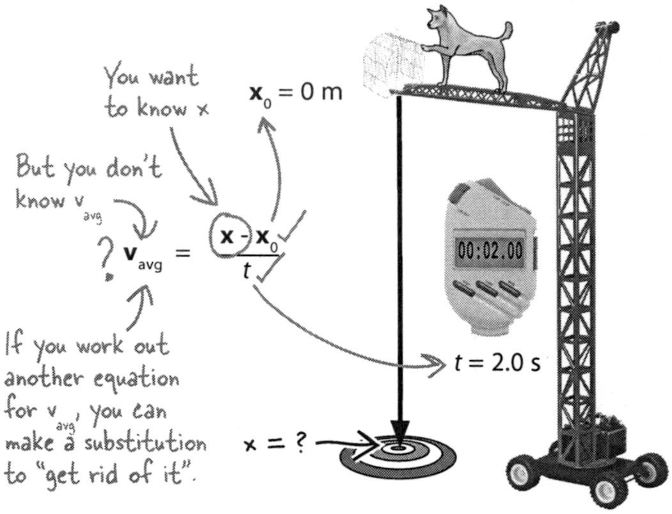

Sharpen your pencil

It'll be somewhere between v_0 and v.

a. On your graph, draw in where you think the cage's average velocity is between times 0 and *t*.

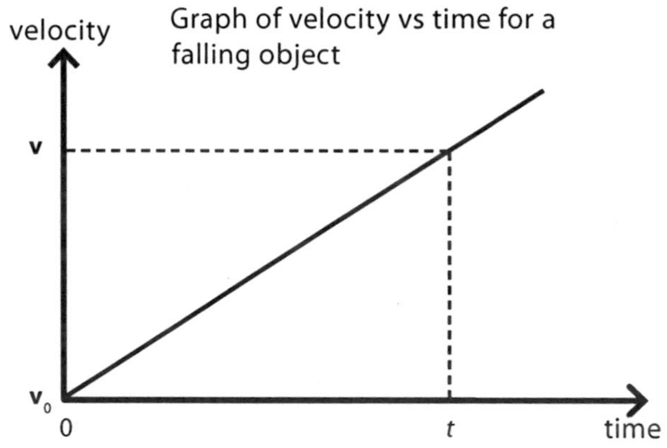

b. Explain how you worked that out visually.

c. Circle the equation from the choices on the right that matches most closely with your ideas.

$$v_{avg} = \frac{v - v_0}{2}$$

$$v_{avg} = \frac{v + v_0}{t}$$

$$v_{avg} = \frac{v - v_0}{t}$$

$$v_{avg} = \frac{v + v_0}{2}$$

Sharpen your pencil Solution

It'll be somewhere between v_0 and v.

a. On your graph, draw in where you think the cage's average velocity is between times 0 and *t*.

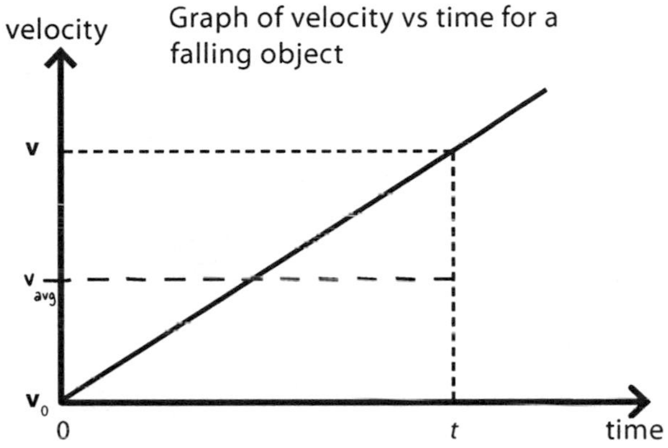

b. Explain how you worked that out visually.

I think that v_{avg} will be halfway between v_0 and v.

In fact it'll be the average of v_0 and v!

The equation I've picked adds together v_0 and v then divides by 2, which is how you take an average of 2 numbers.

c. Circle the equation from the choices on the right that matches most closely with your idea.

$$v_{avg} = \frac{v - v_0}{2}$$

$$v_{avg} = \frac{v + v_0}{t}$$

$$v_{avg} = \frac{v - v_0}{t}$$

$$v_{avg} = \frac{v + v_0}{2}$$

The right equation will work for ALL values of v_0 and t.

If you tried putting in the Dingo's values for $\mathbf{v}_0$ and *t* into the equations, then **well done**. You're definitely thinking along the right lines.

If you're still not sure which equation is correct, the next thing to do is to try some different numbers for $\mathbf{v}_0$ and *t* and see what happens.

Even if you think you already know which equation is right, it's always a good idea to double-check it with some numbers.

Test your equations by imagining them with different numbers

If you're not sure whether an equation's right and want to test it, you can **try some numbers in it** to see if the answers you get are plausible.

You have four different equations for $\mathbf{v}_{avg}$ to choose from. They can't all be right! So it's time to try some different values for $\mathbf{v}$, $\mathbf{v}_0$ and t in each equation to see which gives you consistently sensible answers that are the right **size**.

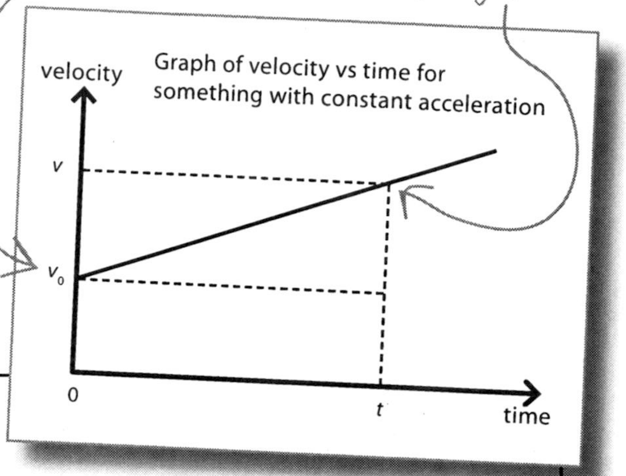

v_0 may not be 0 m/s. if the thing is already falling when you start the timer.

t could be anything at all, not just 2.0 s.

Sharpen your pencil

Fill in the table to show the value for $\mathbf{v}_{avg}$ given by each of these equations for various values of $\mathbf{v}_0$, $\mathbf{v}$ and t.

Is the average velocity the size you'd expect it to be?

Does the equation have the right units?

Possible equation for v_{avg}	v_0 = 0 m/s v = 10 m/s t = 5 s	v_0 = 0 m/s v = 10 m/s t = 100 s	v_0 = 9 m/s v = 10 m/s t = 5 s	Does this equation SUCK?
$\frac{v - v_0}{2}$	$\frac{10 - 0 \text{ m/s}}{2} = 5 \text{ m/s}$			
$\frac{v + v_0}{t}$				
$\frac{v - v_0}{t}$				
$\frac{v + v_0}{2}$				

Sharpen your pencil Solution

Fill in the table to show the value for v_{avg} given by each equation for various values of v_0, v and t.

Possible equation for v_{avg}	$v_0 = 0$ m/s, $v = 10$ m/s, $t = 5$ s	$v_0 = 0$ m/s, $v = 10$ m/s, $t = 100$ s	$v_0 = 9$ m/s, $v = 10$ m/s, $t = 5$ s	Is this equation plausible?
$\frac{v - v_0}{2}$	$\frac{10 - 0 \text{ m/s}}{2} = 5$ m/s	$\frac{10 + 0 \text{ m/s}}{2} = 5$ m/s	$\frac{10 - 9 \text{ m/s}}{2} = 0.5$ m/s	No. In the 3rd answer the average must be between 9 and 10. It isn't!
$\frac{v + v_0}{t}$	$\frac{10 + 0 \text{ m/s}}{5 \text{ s}} = 2$ m/s^2	$\frac{10 + 0 \text{ m/s}}{100 \text{ s}} = 0.1$ m/s^2	$\frac{10 + 9 \text{ m/s}}{5 \text{ s}} = 3.8$ m/s^2	No. The units are wrong and the 2nd and 3rd answers are way too low.
$\frac{v - v_0}{t}$	$\frac{10 - 0 \text{ m/s}}{5 \text{ s}} = 2$ m/s^2	$\frac{10 - 0 \text{ m/s}}{100 \text{ s}} = 0.1$ m/s^2	$\frac{10 - 9 \text{ m/s}}{5 \text{ s}} = 3.8$ m/s^2	No. The units are wrong and the 2nd and 3rd answers are way too low.
$\frac{v + v_0}{2}$	$\frac{10 + 0 \text{ m/s}}{2} = 5$ m/s	$\frac{10 + 0 \text{ m/s}}{2} = 5$ m/s	$\frac{10 + 9 \text{ m/s}}{2} = 9.5$ m/s	Yes. All of the answers for v_{avg} are between v_0 and v, which is sensible.

The right equation for v_{avg}

The equation only works when the acceleration's constant, right?

That's right - the average velocity will be different if the acceleration isn't constant.

This equation only works because your velocity - time graph is a straight line (your object, the cage, has constant acceleration).

If you didn't know what happened in between the initial and final velocities $\mathbf{v}_0$ and v, you couldn't work out the average velocity. If someone goes at 1 m/s for most of the time then at 5 m/s right at the end, they won't have an average velocity of 3 m/s as they spent most of their time travelling slowly.

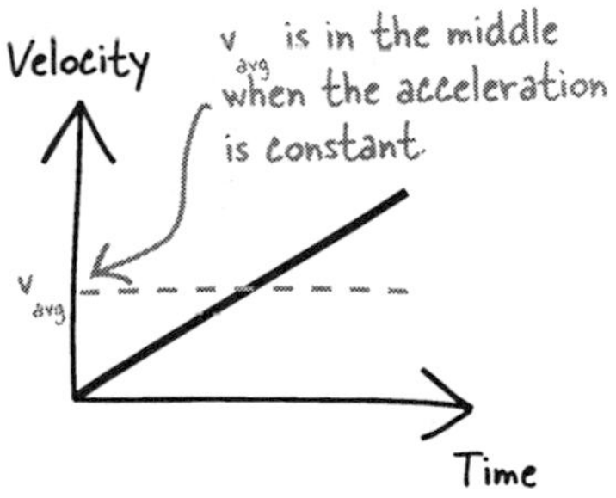

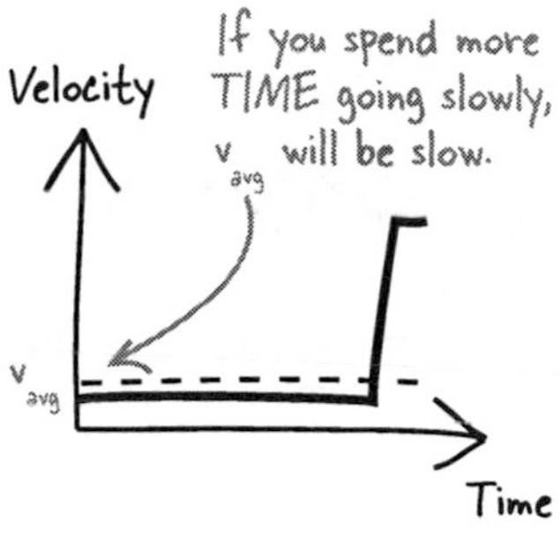

Calculate the cage's displacement!

You've used your displacement - time and velocity - time graphs to work out some equations that describe what the cage is doing as it falls towards the ground.

Now, you can use them to calculate a value for the cage's displacement after 2.0 s!

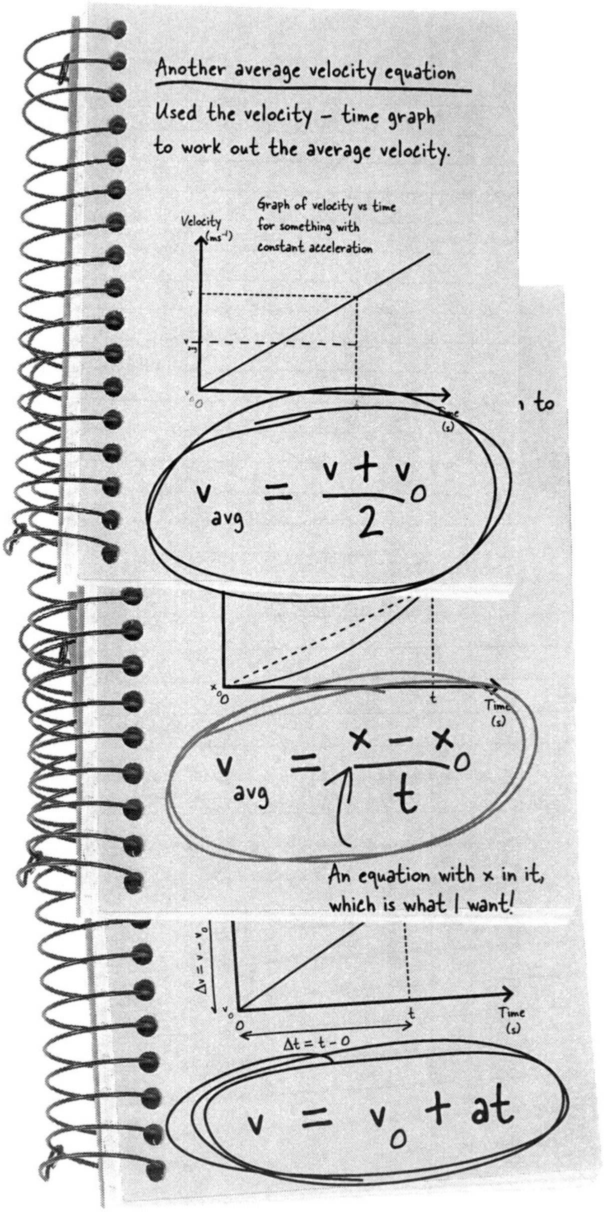

Sharpen your pencil

a. Draw a sketch of the cage and platform, with values and/or vector arrows representing what you already know about **x**, $\mathbf{x}_0$, $\mathbf{v}_0$, **v**, **a** and *t*.

This collates together all the information you already know in a visual format.

The cage has to fall for 2.0 seconds, and acceleration due to gravity is 9.8 m/s².

b. Use what you already know to calculate **v**.

c. Use your answer from part b. to calculate $\mathbf{v}_{avg}$.

d. Use your answer from part c. to calculate **x**.

Sharpen your pencil

The cage has to fall for 2.0 seconds, and acceleration due to gravity is 9.8 m/s².

a. Draw a sketch of the cage and platform, with values and/or vector arrows representing what you already know about **x**, $\mathbf{x_0}$, $\mathbf{v_0}$, **v**, **a** and *t*.

This collates together all the information you already know in a visual format.

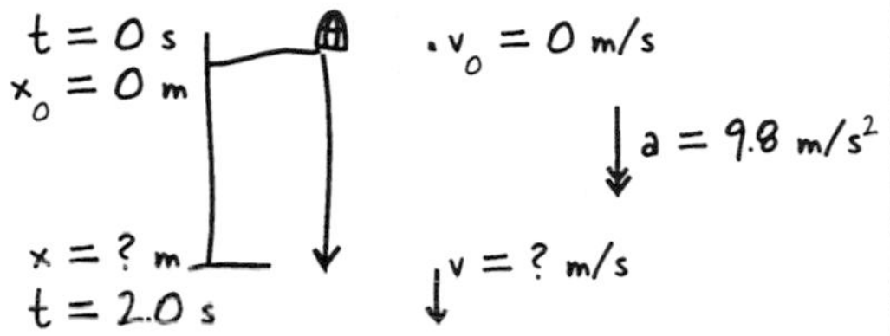

b. Use what you already know to calculate **v**.

$$v = v_0 + at$$
$$v = 0 + 9.8 \times 2.0$$
$$v = 19.6 \text{ m/s} = \underline{\underline{20 \text{ m/s}}} \text{ (2 sd)}$$

It's also OK to write in the value you calculated in chapter 6.

c. Use your answer from part b. to calculate $\mathbf{v}_{avg}$.

$$v_{avg} = \frac{v + v_0}{2} = \frac{20 + 0}{2}$$
$$v_{avg} = \underline{\underline{10 \text{ m/s}}} \text{ (2 sd)}$$

d. Use your answer from part c. to calculate **x**.

$$v_{avg} = \frac{x - x_0}{t}$$
$$x - x_0 = v_{avg} t$$
$$x = v_{avg} t + x_0$$
$$x = 10 \times 2.0 + 0$$
$$x = \underline{\underline{20 \text{ m}}} \text{ (2 sd)}$$

Each part of this problem involves using a different equation that you originally worked out from your graphs.

You know how high the crane should be!

You've calculated the cage's displacement after 2.0 s, so you know how high the crane should be - an awesome result!

At last, the Dingo will be able to make the Emu pause for long enough to invite him to his birthday party ...

Start every problem with a sketch to bring together everything you know in a visual way.

Then use what you already know to work out what you don't know.

But now the Dingo needs something more general

But the Dingo's soon back, with the sad news that his crane won't go high enough! What's more, he's not sure where he's going to find another spot for the crane, so has to stay flexible.

The Dingo really needs to be able to work out the cage's displacement for **any** time that the Emu might take to get to the target.

You don't want to do all of that every time when you just want the displacement!

You're right - you can do this by calculating intermediate values for **v** and $\mathbf{v}_{avg}$ every time you want to know a new value for **x**. But to go through all of that every time you want to calculate a displacement isn't very efficient, and will take a long time.

This is exactly what you did on the opposite page.

What you really want is an equation that says "**x** = something" where the right hand side only contains variables that you already know values for ($\mathbf{x}_0$, **a** and *t*). Somehow, we need to "get rid" of the intermediate variables **v** and $\mathbf{v}_{avg}$ from your equations to come up with a general equation for the displacement that you'll be able to use again and again.

The time you spend getting your equations into this form will be made up by the time you save by using the new equation!

BRAIN POWER

Can you think of any way of using the equations you already have to "get rid of" **v** and $\mathbf{v}_{avg}$, the variables you don't know - and don't want?

A substitution will help

Suppose you have two equations, that say "$e = 2b$" and "$e = c + d$" respectively. By definition, the two sides of an equation are equal.

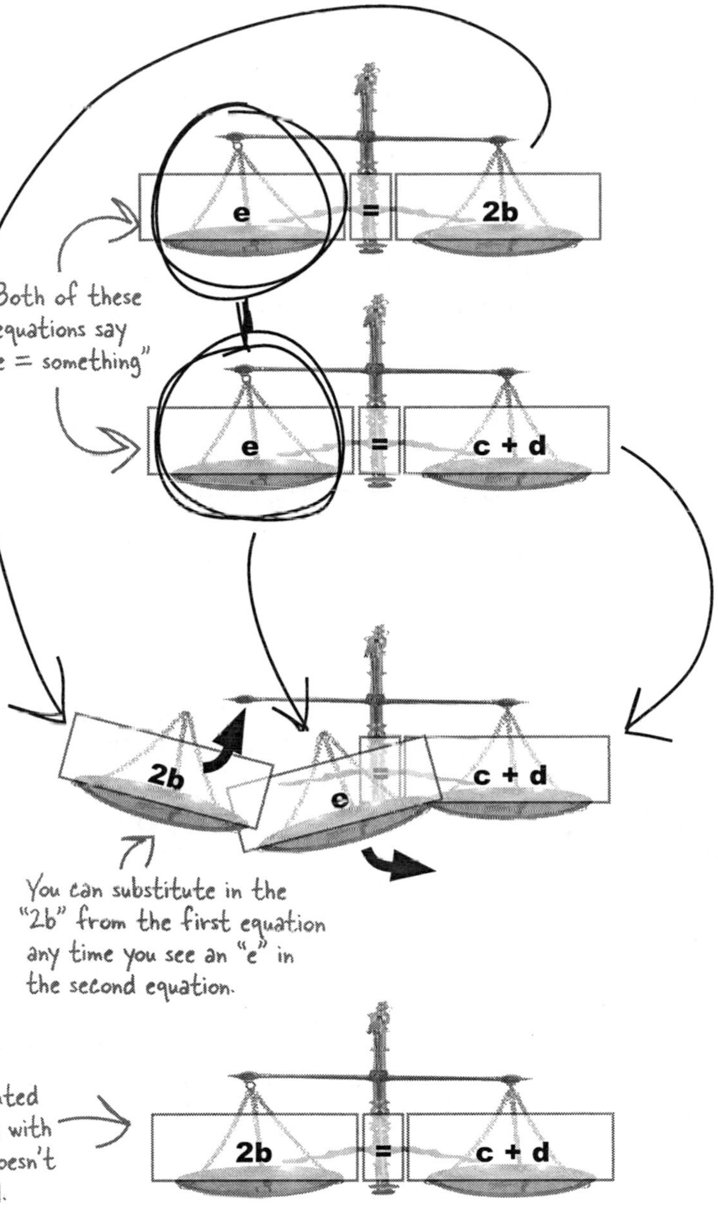

Both equations say "$e =$" on one side. So $2b$ is equal to e and $c + d$ is also equal to e.

Therefore, we can write down the new equation: $2b = c + d$. This works because if $2b$ **and** $c + d$ are both equal to e, they must also be equal to each other.

This is called making a **substitution** because the equation you're left with doesn't have any mention of e in it. It's like the e has been substituted and gone off the playing field, like substitutes do in sports.

You can get rid of a variable that isn't helpful to you by making a substitution.

Substitution can be useful if e is a quantity that's difficult to measure, but you're interested in the other variables in the equations. Instead of having two equations which both have an e in them, you can combine them to completely get rid of the e by doing a substitution.

Don't worry if you're not sure how a substitution will help you with the crane problem yet. We're almost there...

there are no Dumb Questions

Q: Can I do substitutions with any equations I like?

A: Only with equations where there's some form of overlap between the variables. In the same way that some dominos don't match, some equations don't have any variables in common.

So if your equations are $a = b$ and $c = d$, you can't make any substitutions because there's no common ground.

Q: What if I have two equations, but the letters mean different things. Like in one equation "*a*" means acceleration but in another "*a*" means altitude?

A: Then you can't make a substitution. The letters need to represent the same thing each time for it to be **meaningful**.

Q: If I'm given some equations to use in a test, how am I supposed to know what the letters in them represent?

A: Many exam boards provide an equation sheet. For example, the AP Equation Table gives you a list of what the letters stand for in the equations for each section of the syllabus. You're doing Newtonian Mechanics at the moment, so should look in that section to find out what the symbols mean.

Q: But I don't really want to look backwards and forwards to an equation table all the time to look up what the letters mean.

A: That's why we've mentioned what each symbol means as we've introduced it, and keep on slipping in hand-written reminders when they come up again. You'll pick a lot up as you go along, which is great if you're doing the AP course as you don't get an equation table at all in the multiple choice part!

Q: So if I get used to the equations by USING them, I won't really need the table at all and can go a lot faster?

A: You got it! It can be nice to have the equation table to double-check what you think you can remember, to check units or simply for inspiration if you're not sure where to go with a problem.

But learning the equations through **understanding** and **using** them is the most successful route.

Q: But the equations on the scales over there aren't physics equations!

A: OK, so it's time to get back to the Dingo's crane where your substitution skills are about to come in handy ...

You can only substitute one equation into another if they have at least one variable in common between them.

If you're working with more than one equation, make sure that the same letter represents the same thing in all of them!

But what if I want to get rid of a variable that isn't sitting on its own on one side of an equation. How do I do a substitution then?

You can rearrange one equation so the thing you want to get rid of is on its own

If the equations you're dealing with don't have $\mathbf{v}_{avg}$ on its own, you'll have to **rearrange** at least one of them before you can make a substitution.

But once you've rearranged one of your equations to say "$\mathbf{v}_{avg}$ = something", you can insert the "something" into your second equation every time you see $\mathbf{v}_{avg}$ mentioned.

You can make substitutions using any equation as long as you're able to rearrange it.

there are no Dumb Questions

Q: Why is it useful for me to make a substitution?

A: Sometimes the equation you want to use has a variable in it that you don't have a value for. If you do a substitution to get rid of that variable, you'll be able to use the new equation to get what you want.

Q: How do I get rid of a variable by making a substitution?

A: You also need a second equation that contains that variable. If you rearrange that equation so that the variable you want to get rid of is on its own on the left, you can then substitute in everything on the right hand side every time you see that variable in your original equation.

Q: What's wrong with just calculating a value for the variable and putting that in the original equation instead?

A: There's nothing inherently wrong with that - but it's a process you'll have to repeat again and again in the future if you want to do the same calculation using different numbers. You also might run into problems with rounding your intermediate values, or making a calculator typing mistake.

Q: So is making a substitution kind-of the same as calculating an intermediate value, except with letters not numbers?

A: Great spot! Instead of substituting in a value for the variable, you'll be substituting in some other variables that it's equal to.

Making a substitution instead of calculating intermediate values saves you time in the long run.

Get rid of the variables you don't want by making substitutions

You've managed to work out three different equations from your graphs.

But there are a couple of variables, **v** and $\mathbf{v}_{avg}$, which you didn't know at the start, and it would be good to get rid of them by making substitutions so that you don't have to spend time calculating them.

If you can do that, you'll be left with a **general equation** that gives you the displacement after any time, but doesn't include $\mathbf{v}_{avg}$ or **v**. You'll be able to use this equation to work out how far the cage falls in any time - and also for any problem where an object has constant acceleration.

So, it's time to get on with making some substitutions to get rid of the variables you don't want, **v** and $\mathbf{v}_{avg}$.

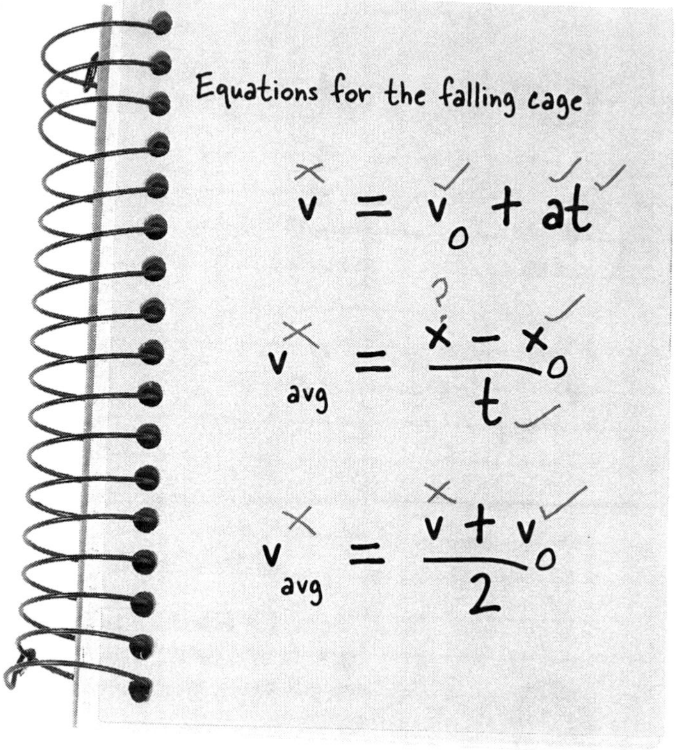

Sharpen your pencil

The equations you've worked out so far (with the variables you knew values for at the start checked off) are in the notebook above.

Decide which of $\mathbf{v}_{avg}$ and **v** is the easiest to get rid of first by making a substitution. Then go ahead and do the substitution!

Sharpen your pencil Solution

$$v = v_0 + at$$

$$v_{avg} = \frac{x - x_0}{t}$$

$$v_{avg} = \frac{v + v_0}{2}$$

The equations you've worked out so far (with the variables you knew values for at the start checked off) are in the notebook above.

Decide which of $\mathbf{v}_{avg}$ and $\mathbf{v}$ is the easiest to get rid of first by making a substitution. Then go ahead and do the substitution!

I already have two equations that say "v_{avg} = something", so make the substitution to get rid of v_{avg} first.

$$v_{avg} = \frac{v + v_0}{2} \quad \text{and also} \quad v_{avg} = \frac{x - x_0}{t}$$

$$\Rightarrow \frac{v + v_0}{2} = \frac{x - x_0}{t}$$

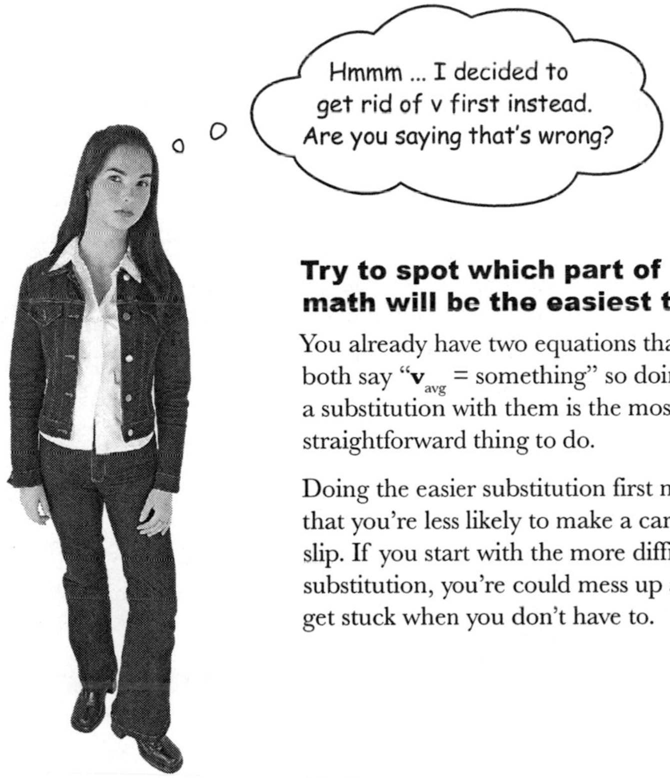

Try to spot which part of the math will be the easiest to do.

You already have two equations that both say "$\mathbf{v}_{avg}$ = something" so doing a substitution with them is the most straightforward thing to do.

Doing the easier substitution first means that you're less likely to make a careless slip. If you start with the more difficult substitution, you're could mess up and get stuck when you don't have to.

If you can choose which order to do the math in, always try to spot the easier part and do it first.

Continue making substitutions ...

Now that you've made one substitution, your equation with **x** and *t* in it doesn't have $\mathbf{v}_{avg}$ in it anymore But in addition to $\mathbf{v}_0$ and *t* (which you've known values for from the start) the equation contains the variable **v**.

Since we're deriving a general equation for **x** that doesn't require you to know a value for **v**, you can use the other equation to make a substitution that 'gets rid' of the **v** as well.

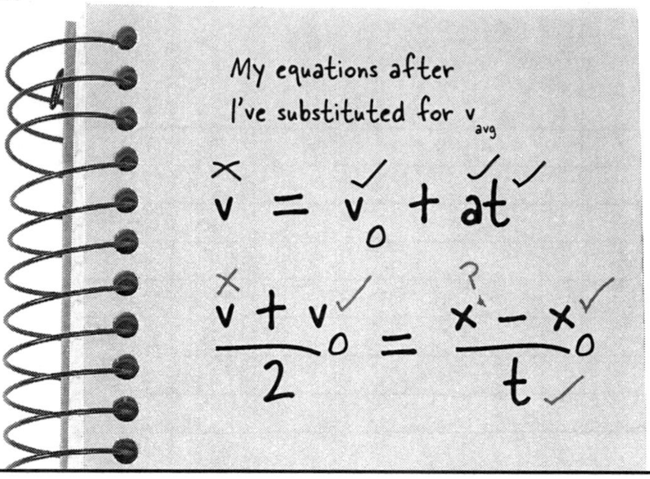

Sharpen your pencil

a. Using your two equations, make a substitution to 'get rid' of the variable **v**.

b. Then rearrange your new equation into the form "**x** = something".

Sharpen your pencil Solution

a. Using your two equations, make a substitution to 'get rid' of the variable **v**.

$$v = v_0 + at \quad (1)$$

$$\frac{v + v_0}{2} = \frac{x - x_0}{t} \quad (2)$$

It's a good idea to number your equations (1) and (2) so you can refer to them later on.

Equation (1) already says "v = something".

$$v = v_0 + at$$

Remember to explain what you're doing and why.

Rearrange equation (2) to say "v = something".

$$\frac{v + v_0}{2} = \frac{x - x_0}{t}$$

Multiply both sides by 2.

$$= \quad v + v_0 = \frac{2(x - x_0)}{t}$$

Subtract v_0 from both sides.

$$\Rightarrow \quad v = \frac{2(x - x_0)}{t} - v_0$$

Make a substitution:

$$\frac{2(x - x_0)}{t} - v_0 = v_0 + at$$

If the x starts off on the left, it's easier to rearrange the equation to say "x = something".

b. Then rearrange your new equation into the form "**x** = something".

$$\frac{2(x - x_0)}{t} - v_0 = v_0 + at$$

Add v_0 to both sides so that there's only the term that contains x on the left hand side.

$$\frac{2(x - x_0)}{t} = 2v_0 + at$$

Multiply both sides by t so that the $x - x_0$ bit isn't divided by anything.

$$2(x - x_0) = 2v_0t + at^2$$

Divide both sides by 2 so that the $x - x_0$ is left on its own.

$$x - x_0 = v_0t + \tfrac{1}{2}at^2$$

Add x_0 to both sides so that you have x on its own.

$$x = x_0 + v_0t + \tfrac{1}{2}at^2$$

Your final answer should be in the simplest form possible.

Can we save time by making substitutions without rearranging **both** equations to say "v = something"?

It's OK to do substitution in a different way as long as you understand what's going on.

If you want to rearrange just one of your equations to say "**v** = something" then substitute the "something" in every time you see **v** in your other equation, then that's fine.

Doing it this way would look like this:

$$v = v_0 + at \qquad (1)$$

Substitute $v_0 + at$ for v in equation (2):

$$\frac{v + v_0}{2} = \frac{x - x_0}{t} \qquad (2)$$

$$\frac{(v_0 + at) + v_0}{2} = \frac{x - x_0}{t}$$

Then you'd go on to rearrange the equation to say $\mathbf{x} = \mathbf{x}_0 + \mathbf{v}_0 t + \frac{1}{2}\mathbf{a}t^2$ as you did before.

Doing the math this way is fine. The main thing is that you always **understand** what you're doing and why.

Sharpen your pencil

This is the equation you've worked out. But is it right?

$$x = x_0 + v_0 t + \frac{1}{2}at^2$$

You've made a lot of substitutions, and come up with a nice-looking equation for x that only involves variables you already knew the values for at the start.

But does your equation SUCK?

Use the space on the right to jot down as many different ways you can think of to **check over** your equation, which is supposed to work OK for any values of the variables in it.

Don't worry if you're not sure how to do a particular check yet. Just say what you'd like to do if possible.

Sharpen your pencil Solution

This is the equation you've worked out. But is it right?

$$x = x_0 + v_0 t + \frac{1}{2}at^2$$

You've made a lot of substitutions, and come up with a nice-looking equation for x that only involves variables you already knew the values for at the start.

But does your equation SUCK?

Use the space on the right to jot down as many different ways you can think of to check over your equation, which is supposed to work OK for any values of the variables in it.

S – Size. I guess I could try the value $t = 2.0$ s in the equation to see if it gives the same answer as it did before. And maybe try some other values as well.

U – Units. I'd like to check the units, but I'm not sure how to do that.

C – Calculations. I think I did the substitutions OK.

K – 'K'ontext. The equation says that x depends on v_0, a and t, which it probably should!

You did it - you derived a useful equation for the cage's displacement!

The equation you've worked out for the displacement after a certain amount of time is $\mathbf{x} = \mathbf{x}_0 + \mathbf{v}_0 t + ½\mathbf{a}t^2$. With not a **v** or $\mathbf{v}_{avg}$ to be seen anywhere!

But **is your equation correct**? You don't want the Dingo's birthday plans to go wrong because of a calculation error.

When you work out an equation, you should check it over before you use it.

When you're checking over a numerical answer, asking yourself if it SUCKs is a good tool. But not all of the parts of SUCK are applicable to an equation.

So instead, we're going to think GUT.

G - Graph. Does your equation describe the graph?

U - Units. Does each term have the same units?

T - Try out extreme values (or values you already know the answer for) in your equation.

We're going to do the units part first, as it's the quickest check you can do once you've got used to how it works.

Check your equation using Units

A quick way of checking your equation is to think about the **units** of each of its **terms** (a term is one of the chunks in your equation that you **add** or **subtract**).

You're only allowed to add or subtract things that have the same units, as something like "2 seconds + 3 meters" is meaningless. So **every term in your equation must have the same units**.

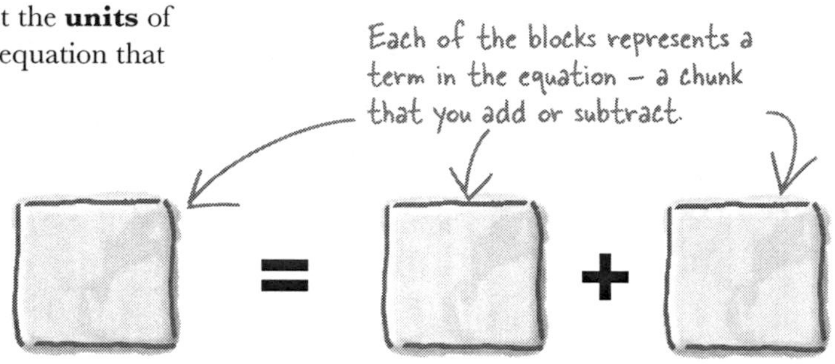

Every term in your equation must have the same units, so you can add or subtract them.

A term can be anything from a single variable to a group of variables and numbers multiplied together. You need to keep track of the units of each variable to make sure that each term has the same units.

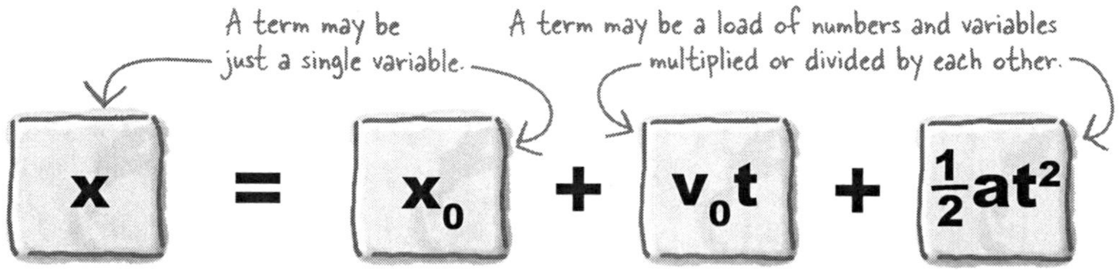

A term can be anything from a single variable to a group of variables and numbers multiplied together.

Sharpen your pencil

Does your equation make sense - do all of its terms have the same units? Fill in the table to find out.

Some answers are already filled in for you.

Square brackets means 'units of'. So [x] = meters.

As these variables are multiplied together, you can work out the units of the term by multiplying the units of each variable together.

Term	x	x_0	v_0t		$\frac{1}{2}at^2$		
Units of variable	[x]	$[x_0]$	$[v_0]$	[t]	[½]	[a]	[t]
			m/s	s			
Units of term	[x]	$[x_0]$	$[v_0t]$ = m/s × s		$[\frac{1}{2}at^2]$ = ...		
			$\frac{m}{\not s} \times \not s = m$				

Sharpen your pencil Solution

Does your equation make sense - do all of its terms have the same units? Fill in the table to find out.

Term	x	x_0	v_0t		½at^2		
Units of variable	[x]	[x_0]	[v_0]	[t]	[½]	[a]	[t]
	m	m	m/s	s	No units.	m/s^2	s^2
Units of term	[x]	[x_0]	[v_0t] = m/s × s		[½at^2] = $m/s^2 \times s^2$		
	m	m	$\frac{m}{s} \times s$		$\frac{m}{s^2} \times s^2 = m$		

Square brackets means 'units of'. So [x] = meters.

Numbers are dimensionless and don't have units.

All of the terms have units of m, so the equation's units check out OK.

All of the terms in your equation have the same units (meters) so your equation makes sense.

All of the terms in your equation have the same units.

$$x = x_0 + v_0t + \frac{1}{2}at^2$$

If a term in your equation has different units, then you know there MUST be something weird going on, as the equation doesn't make sense.

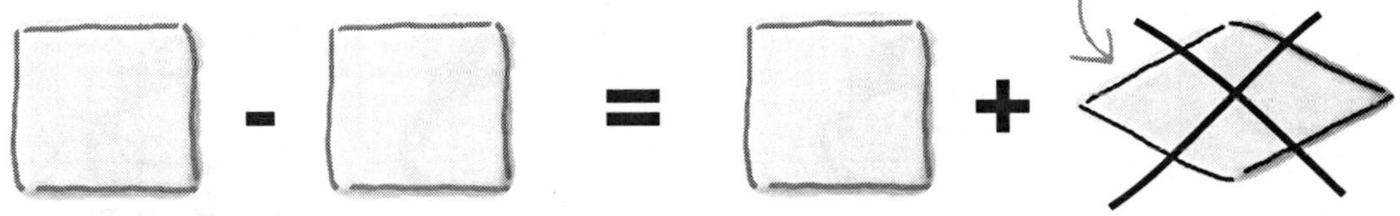

Anything you add or subtract must have the same UNITS.

Each TERM in the equation

there are no Dumb Questions

Q: Why is it important for all the terms in an equation to have the same units?

A: You can't add things together which have different units. The question "What is 2.0 seconds + 3 meters?" is meaningless, because you can't add meters to seconds.

Q: But you can multiply and divide things that have different units, right?

A: Yes - for example, when you divide a displacement by a time to work out something's velocity in meters per second.

Q: What would I do if it turned out that one of the terms in my equation had different units from the rest?

A: If one of the terms has different units from the others, you probably made a little slip with the math when you were rearranging an equation.

Q: What kinds of mathematical slips should I be on the lookout for?

A: If one of the terms sticks out when you compare the units, look back and see if you made a slip with that term when you were rearranging your equation.

For example, maybe you meant to multiply everything by t when you were rearranging your equation, but missed doing that to one of the terms.

Q: Does checking the units like this guarantee 100% that my equation's right?

A: No, not totally. Thinking about the units of each term of your equation will help to catch any mistakes that altered the units.

Q: What kinds of mistakes don't alter the units?

A: Perhaps you meant to multiply everything by 2 when you were rearranging your equation. Since 2 is just a number, it doesn't have any units, so this method wouldn't pick up on that.

The other thing that sometimes happens is missing off a subscript, like writing x instead of x_0. As x and x_0 both have the same units, this wouldn't get picked up.

Q: How would I find a mistake if it doesn't involve units?

A: You can compare your equation with your graph and try out some extreme values in it to see if it really does describe reality ...

If all of the terms in your equation that need to be added to or subtracted from each other have the same units, you're doing great!

Check your equation by trying out some extreme values

You've worked out an equation that describes the displacement - time graph for a falling object: $\mathbf{x} = \mathbf{x}_0 + \mathbf{v}_0 t + \frac{1}{2}\mathbf{a}t^2$. And you've just confirmed that each term in the equation has the same **units**.

But that doesn't totally guarantee that the equation is right.

It's also a good idea to check your equation by trying out some **extreme numbers** in it, and comparing what your equation says to what would happen in real life. So ask yourself things like "what would happen if the time was **zero**?" or "what would happen if the initial velocity was **very large**?"

In real life, if the time was zero, then you wouldn't have time to go anywhere. Your displacement would be the same as $\mathbf{x}_0$, your initial displacement.

Your equation says $\mathbf{x} = \mathbf{x}_0 + \mathbf{v}_0 t + \frac{1}{2}\mathbf{a}t^2$. But if t = 0, then the term $\mathbf{v}_0 t$ is 0 because anything multiplied by zero is zero. Similarly, the term $\frac{1}{2}\mathbf{a}t^2$ is zero. So your equation becomes $\mathbf{x} = \mathbf{x}_0 + 0 + 0$, or just $\mathbf{x} = \mathbf{x}_0$. Which is what you already worked out would happen in real life!

If a variable is zero, then any term where it's multiplying must also be zero.

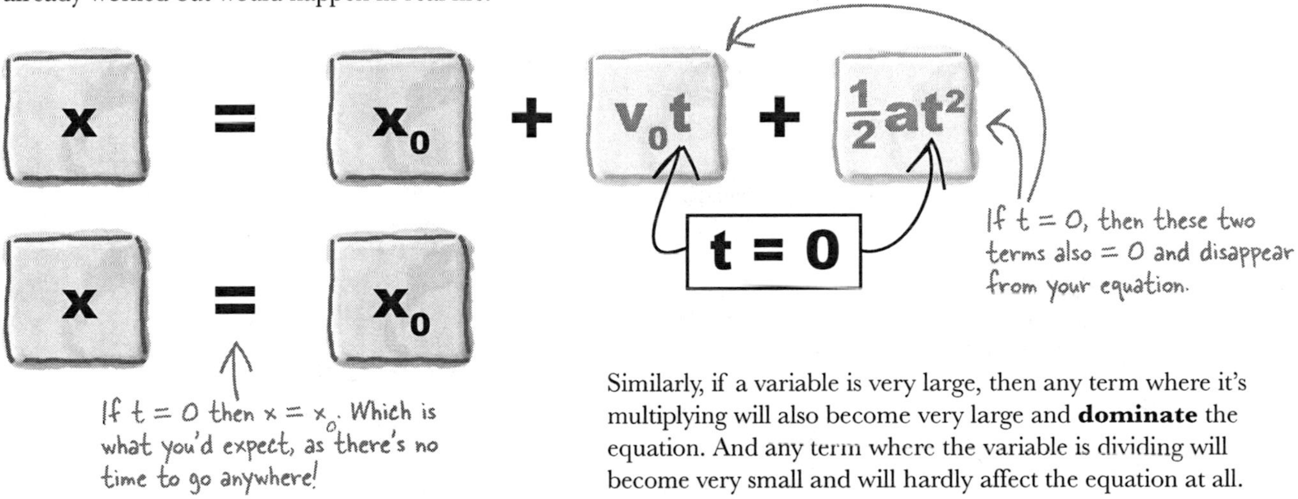

If a variable is very large, then any term where it's multiplying must also be very large. And any term where it's dividing must be very small.

Similarly, if a variable is very large, then any term where it's multiplying will also become very large and **dominate** the equation. And any term where the variable is dividing will become very small and will hardly affect the equation at all. This is because dividing by a very large number gives you a very small answer.

In real life, if the initial velocity was very large, you'd expect the displacement to be very large as well.

Your equation says $\mathbf{x} = \mathbf{x}_0 + \mathbf{v}_0 t + \frac{1}{2}\mathbf{a}t^2$. If $\mathbf{v}_0$ is very large, then the $\mathbf{v}_0 t$ term will also be very large and will dominate the equation. So your equation would become "$\mathbf{x}$ = something very large", which is what you know will happen in real life.

BE the equation

Your job is to imagine you're the equation. What's going to happen to you at various EXTREMES? When the acceleration is zero? When the acceleration is very large? When the time is zero? When the time is very large? How does v_0 affect you? And most importantly - do you describe reality?!

$$x = x_0 + v_0 t + \frac{1}{2}at^2$$

Extreme	What happens in real life?	What happens to your equation?	Does your equation describe what happens in real life?
$t = 0$	You've had no time to move, so you won't have gone anywhere.		
t is large		x is large because the v_0t and the $\frac{1}{2}at^2$ terms dominate.	
$a = 0$			
a is large			
v_0 is zero		The equation becomes $x = x_0 + \frac{1}{2}at^2$	
v_0 is large	Your displacement is large, as you're going really fast right from the start.		

BE the equation - SOLUTION

Your job is to imagine you're the equation. What's going to happen to you at various EXTREMES? When the acceleration is zero? When the acceleration is very large? When the time is zero? When the time is very large? How does v_0 affect you? And most importantly - do you describe reality?!

$$x = x_0 + v_0 t + \frac{1}{2}at^2$$

Extreme	What happens in real life?	What happens to your equation?	Does your equation describe what happens in real life?
$t = 0$	You've had no time to move, so you won't have gone anywhere.	$x = x_0$	Yes – it says that you stay where you started and don't go anywhere.
t is large	Your displacement is large because you travel for a long time.	x is large because the v_0t and the $\frac{1}{2}at^2$ terms dominate.	Yes – it predicts that your displacement is large.
$a = 0$	The velocity is constant.	The equation becomes $x = x_0 + v_0t$	Yes. This is similar to the equation distance = speed × time except with vectors and the initial displacement, x_0, in there.
a is large	The velocity will get faster and faster more quickly.	The $\frac{1}{2}at^2$ term dominates more and more as t^2 increases.	Yes – it says that you get faster more quickly.
v_0 is zero	x will depend only on the acceleration and x_0 as you have no velocity at the start.	The equation becomes $x = x_0 + \frac{1}{2}at^2$	Yes – displacement only depends on acceleration and x_0, and not on v_0.
v_0 is large	Your displacement is large, as you're going really fast right from the start.	x is large because the v_0t term dominates.	Yes – it predicts that you go a long way.

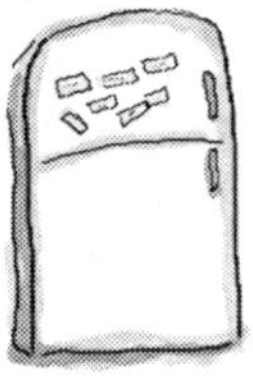

Graph and equation story magnets

As graphs and equations both represent reality, a third (and final) way you can check your equation is to see if it **tells the same story as your graph**.

Your job is to match up each graph and an equation with a story. Each magnet will be used exactly once.

All of the equations are based on the equation you worked out, $x = x_0 + v_0t + \frac{1}{2}at^2$ but with some of the variable equal to zero (like you've just been thinking about) which leads to some of the terms being missing.

A couple of the story magnets have been left blank so that you can make up your own stories to describe the graphs! Think about using phrases like "constant velocity", "zero velocity", "constant acceleration" or "zero acceleration" in your stories.

Write your own stories on the blank magnets.

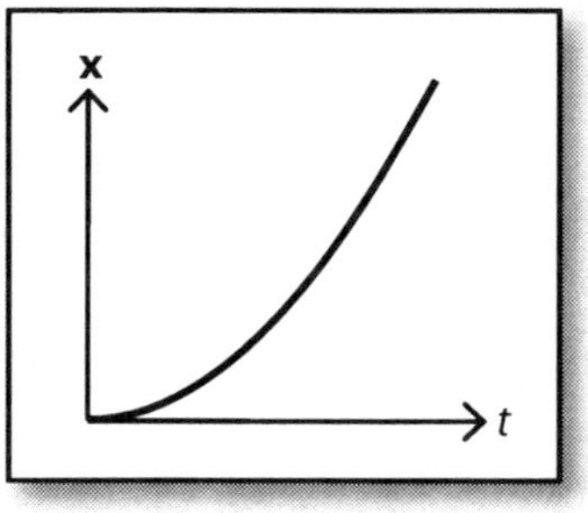

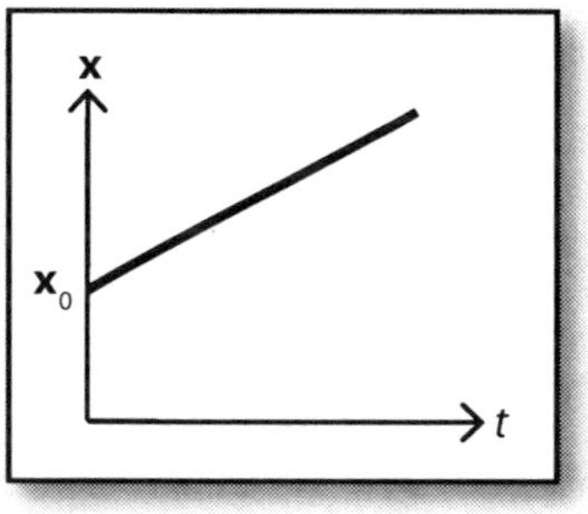

A car sitting at traffic lights at displacement x_0 from home pulls away with constant acceleration.

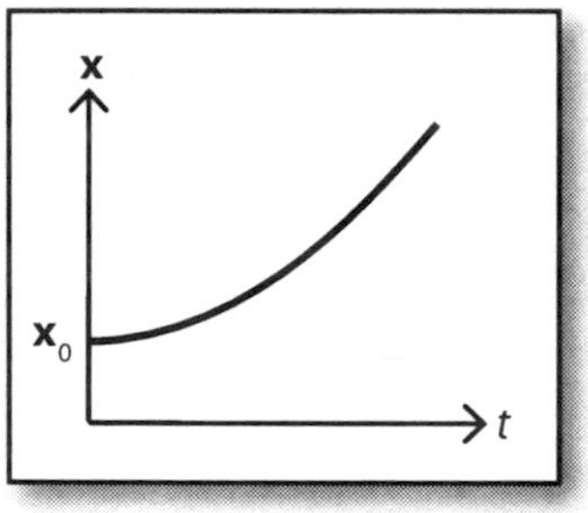

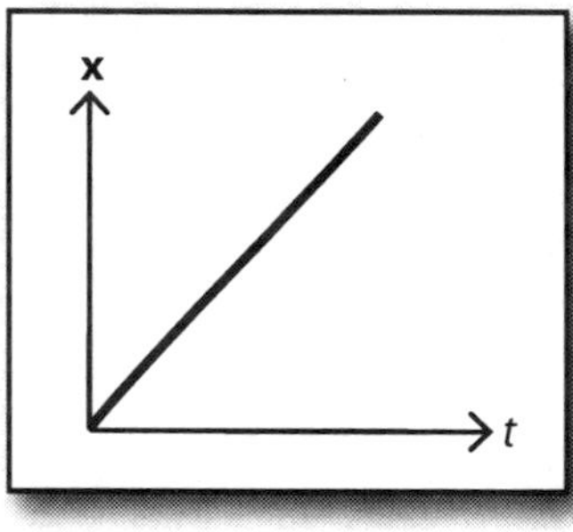

A person in an office sits in the same position for a long time.

A cage is dropped from a crane from initial displacement $x_0 = 0$.

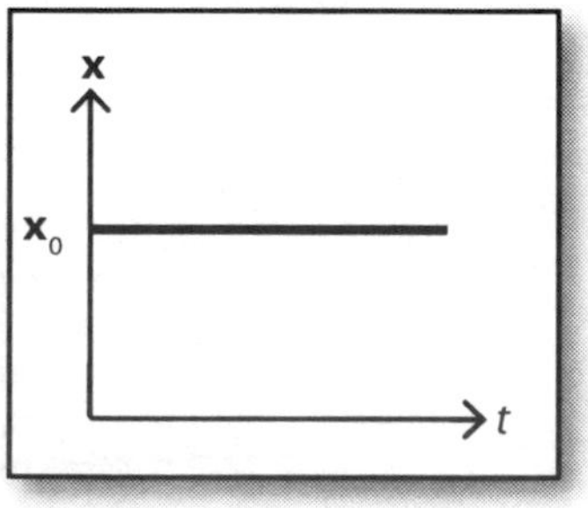

$x = x_0$

$x = x_0 + v_0t$

$x = v_0t$

$x = \frac{1}{2}at^2$

$x = x_0 + \frac{1}{2}at^2$

Graph and equation story magnets - SOLUTION

As graphs and equations both represent reality, a third (and final) way you can check your equation is to see if it **tells the same story as your graph.**

Your job is to match up each graph and an equation with a story. Each magnet will be used exactly once.

All of the equations are based on the equation you worked out, $x = x_0 + v_0t + ½at^2$ but with some of the variable equal to zero (like you've just been thinking about) which leads to some of the terms being missing.

A couple of the story magnets have been left blank so that you can make up your own stories to describe the graphs! Think about using phrases like "constant velocity", "zero velocity", "constant acceleration" or "zero acceleration" in your stories.

$x = x_0$

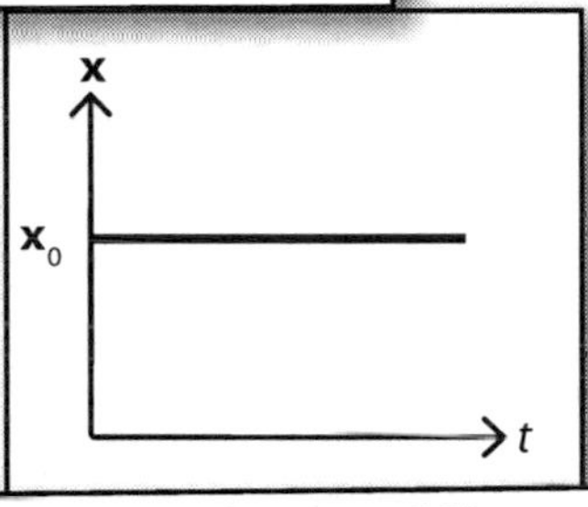

A person in an office sits in the same position for a long time.

The equation doesn't have the variable t in it. If x doesn't depend on t, then x must be constant.

$x = v_0t$

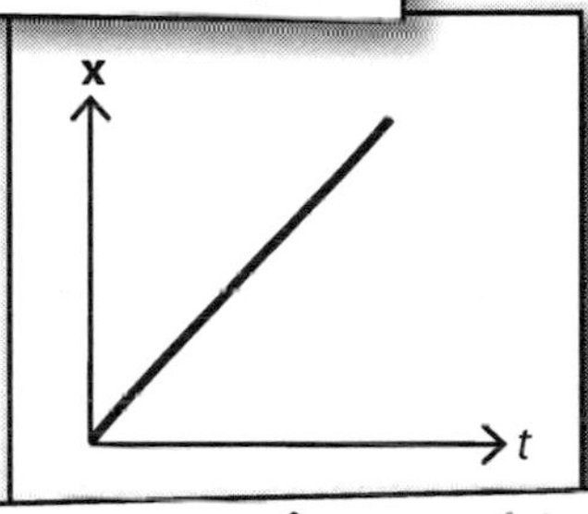

A person walks from home (where x = 0) to work at a constant velocity (with zero acceleration).

$x = x_0 + v_0t$

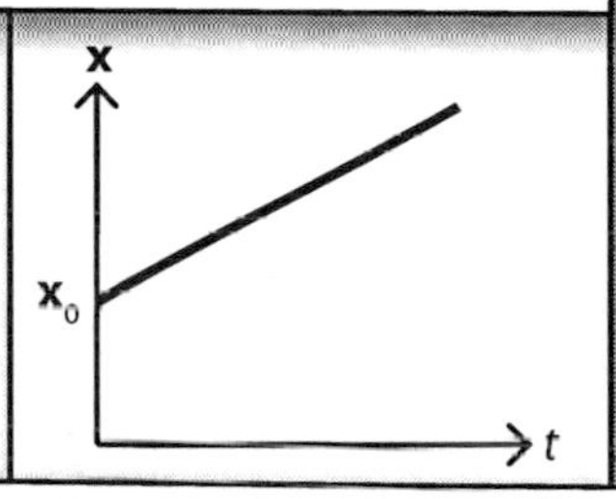

A car joins a long straight freeway at position $x = x_0$, and hits cruise control to travel at a constant velocity (zero acceleration)..

It doesn't matter what story you made up, as long as you realized that a constant slope on the x–t graph means a constant velocity.

Think of graphs and equations "telling stories" about what happens.

$x = ½at^2$

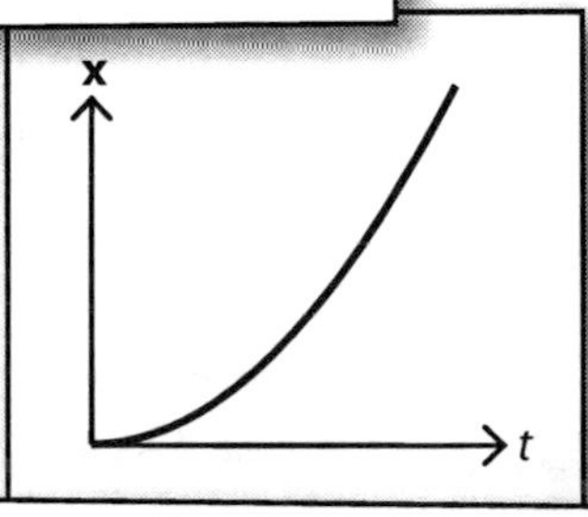

A cage is dropped from a crane from initial displacement $x_0 = 0$.

These graphs are curved because of the t^2 part of the equation. $1^2 = 1$, $2^2 = 4$, $3^2 = 9$, and so on. As t increases, the t^2 term dominates and makes the graph get steeper and steeper.

$x = x_0 + ½at^2$

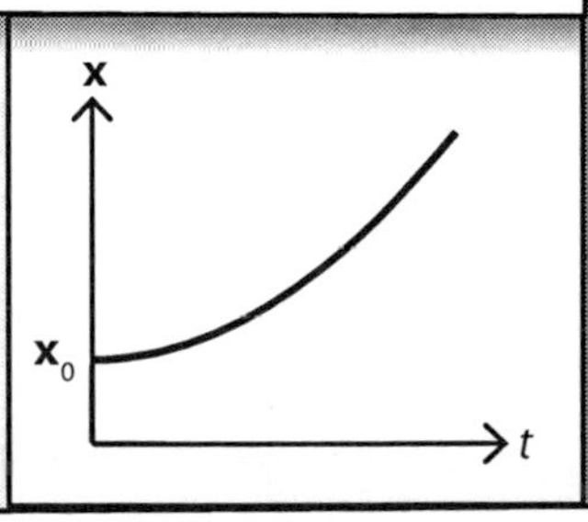

A car sitting at traffic lights at displacement x_0 from home pulls away with constant acceleration.

Your equation checks out!

Your equation $\mathbf{x} = \mathbf{x}_0 + \mathbf{v}_0 t + \frac{1}{2}\mathbf{a}t^2$ passes all of the tests you've done on it.

To check your equation over, check your GUT.

G The **graph** and the equation both tell the same story.

The t^2 part means that the x–t graph is curved.

$$x = x_0 + v_0 t \ \tfrac{1}{2}at^2$$

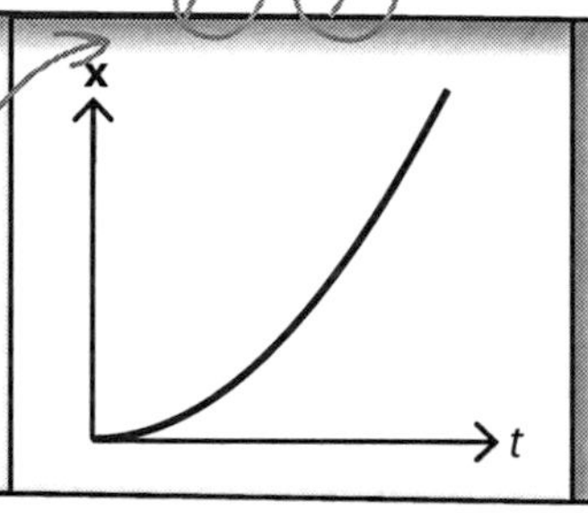

A cage is dropped from a crane from initial displacement $x_0 = 0$.

On this occasion, $x_0 = 0$ (so the graph starts at $x = 0$) and $v_0 = 0$ (as you're dropping it from a standing start).

U All of the terms in the equation have the same **units** (meters).

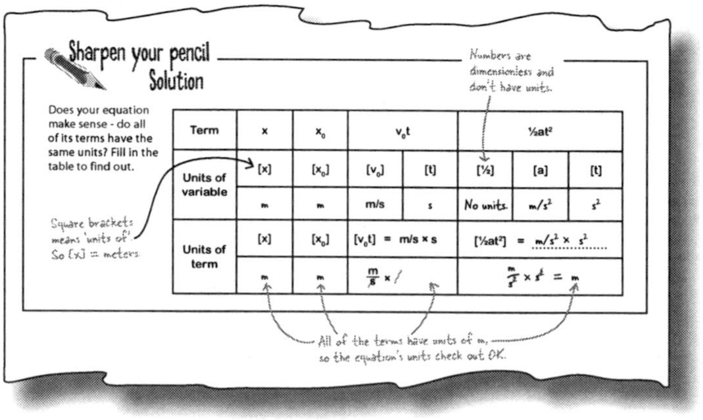

Sharpen your pencil Solution

Does your equation make sense - do all of its terms have the same units? Fill in the table to find out.

Term	x	x_0	v_0t		$\frac{1}{2}at^2$		
Units of variable	[x]	[x_0]	[v_0]	[t]	[½]	[a]	[t]
	m	m	m/s	s	No units	m/s^2	s^2
Units of term	[x]	[x_0]	[v_0t] = m/s × s		[½at^2] = m/s^2 × s^2		
	m	m	$\frac{m}{s}$ × s		$\frac{m}{s^2}$ × s^2 = m		

Numbers are dimensionless and don't have units.

Square brackets means 'units of'. So [x] = meters.

All of the terms have units of m, so the equation's units check out OK.

T When you **try** out extreme values, the equation corresponds to reality.

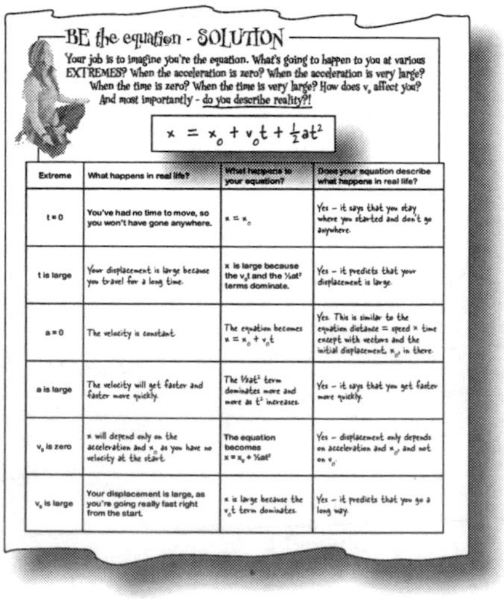

BE the equation - SOLUTION

Your job is to imagine you're the equation. What's going to happen to you at various EXTREMES? When the acceleration is zero? When the acceleration is very large? When the time is zero? When the time is very large? How does v_0 affect you? And most importantly - do you describe reality?!

$$x = x_0 + v_0t + \tfrac{1}{2}at^2$$

Extreme	What happens in real life?	What happens to your equation?	Does your equation describe what happens in real life?
t = 0	You've had no time to move, so you won't have gone anywhere.	$x = x_0$	Yes – it says that you stay where you started and don't go anywhere.
t is large	Your displacement is large because you travel for a long time.	x is large because the v_0t and the ½at^2 terms dominate.	Yes – it predicts that your displacement is large.
a = 0	The velocity is constant.	The equation becomes $x = x_0 + v_0t$	Yes. This is similar to the equation distance = speed × time except with vectors and the initial displacement, x_0, in there.
a is large	The velocity will get faster and faster more quickly.	The ½at^2 term dominates more and more as t^2 increases.	Yes – it says that you get faster more quickly.
v_0 is zero	x will depend only on the acceleration and x_0, as you have no velocity at the start.	The equation becomes $x = x_0 + \frac{1}{2}at^2$	Yes – displacement only depends on acceleration and x_0, and not on v_0.
v_0 is large	Your displacement is large, as you're going really fast right from the start.	x is large because the v_0t term dominates.	Yes – it predicts that you go a long way.

Sharpen your pencil

The Dingo now wants the cage to fall for 1.5 s. How high should he set the platform of the crane?

Sharpen your pencil Solution

The Dingo now wants the cage to fall for 1.50 s.
How high should he set the platform of the crane?

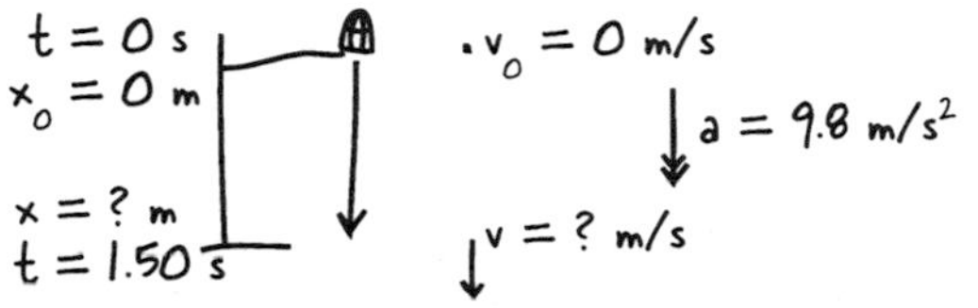

$$x = x_0 + v_0 t + \frac{1}{2}at^2$$

$$x = 0 + 0 + 0.5 \times 9.8 \times 1.50^2$$

$$x = \underline{\underline{11.0\ m}}\ (3\ sd)$$

So the Dingo drops the cage ...

... but as the dust clears ...

To be continued ...

Question Clinic: The "Substitution" Question

A question that asks you to find an "equation", "expression" or "formula" for something often involves manipulating equations you already know or are given in the question. The main thing is not to panic, especially if you're given equations you've not seen before, and to identify the variables that need to be eliminated from the final equation.

This indicates that you probably don't have to work out any extra equations apart from the ones they give you.

If you're aware of the units of your variables, you can test your final answer by making sure each term in your equation has the same units (see page 266).

7. Given the equations:

$$v = v_0 + at \qquad v_{avg} = \frac{x - x_0}{t} \qquad v_{avg} = \frac{v + v_0}{2}$$

a. Write down what each of these symbols conventionally means / represents in physics, and give their units.

b. Find an expression for **x** in terms of x_0, v_0, **a** and *t*.

Always remember that physics equations MEAN something and aren't just meaningless letters to do algebra with.

This means that they want an equation that says "x = something", i.e. the x is on its own on the left hand side.

This means that they want the right-hand side to only have x_0, v_0, a and t in it, and NO other variables.

Watch for the variables that you DON'T want in the final equation, and try to work out how to make substitutions that get rid of them.

These questions are mostly algebra and involve substitution to get rid of the variables you don't want in the final equation. Don't forget to check your equation, using GUT - Graphs, Units and Trying some extreme numbers - to make sure your equation represents reality!

Try to get a FEEL for what your equation is saying at the extremes of variables. Does it represent reality?

Question Clinic: The "Units" or "Dimensional analysis" Question

Sometimes you'll be asked to show that an equation makes sense by using "dimensional analysis" or by "considering the units". You do this by figuring out the units of each term in the equation. All terms must have the same units, as you're not allowed to add or subtract terms that have different units. The main thing you need to be able to do is to handle units written in scientific notation. This is basically the same as being able to handle numbers written in scientific notation - go back to Chapter 3 if you feel you need a review.

Each TERM in the equation must have the same units.

You're only given the units of t and x, not v_0 or x_0 or a. But you only need the units of one of the terms, and as x is a term you're fine.

8. In the equation $x = x_0 + v_0t + \frac{1}{2}at^2$, the units of t are seconds and the units of x are meters. What are the units of a?

9. In the equation $x = x_0 + v_0t + \frac{1}{2}at^2$, t has dimensions of time and x has dimensions of length. What are the dimensions of a?

Look carefully to see whether the question asks you to give your answer in terms of UNITS or DIMENSIONS.

A question that asks you about dimensions is exactly the same as one that asks you about units, except that you need to give a final answer of "length" instead of "meters", or "time" instead of "seconds" etc.

Some questions may ask you about DIMENSIONS (length, time) instead of units (meters, seconds). The easiest thing to do is to do all your work with units (which you've practiced with more), then give your final answer in dimensions, for example if your answer has units of m/s^2, its dimensions are length/time^2.

Honest Harry has a problem

At Honest Harry's Autos, they're always thinking of new ways to make their second-hand cars stand out from the competition. Detailed specs on their website, a one year guarantee, and fluffy dice all help them to stay ahead of the rest.

But Harry's latest idea has got him into trouble.

Five Minute Mystery

"Most dealers have the car's acceleration from 0-60 miles per hour in their specs," he explains. "But you can go at 80 mph on the freeway. So I decided to come up with specs for acceleration between 60-80 mph myself. No one else has that!"

But his figures got Harry into hot water when scores of angry motorists returned their cars threatening to sue him for misinformation, as the car's performance from 60-80 mph was far poorer than he'd claimed.

"I dunno what went wrong," Harry says mournfully. "I set things up to plot the speedometer reading on a graph as I accelerated from 60 to 80 mph. Then I drew a best fit straight line through my data points, making sure it went through the origin, and used the slope of that to work out the acceleration that went on the spec sheet."

Why did Harry calculate the wrong acceleration?

The origin of Harry's problem ... is the origin!

Why did Harry calculate the wrong acceleration?

Harry drew his straight line through the origin of his graph (where the velocity is 0 mph and the time is 0 s). But the car's speed at t = 0 was actually 60 mph, so the line he drew should have crossed the vertical axis at 60 mph, not at the origin.

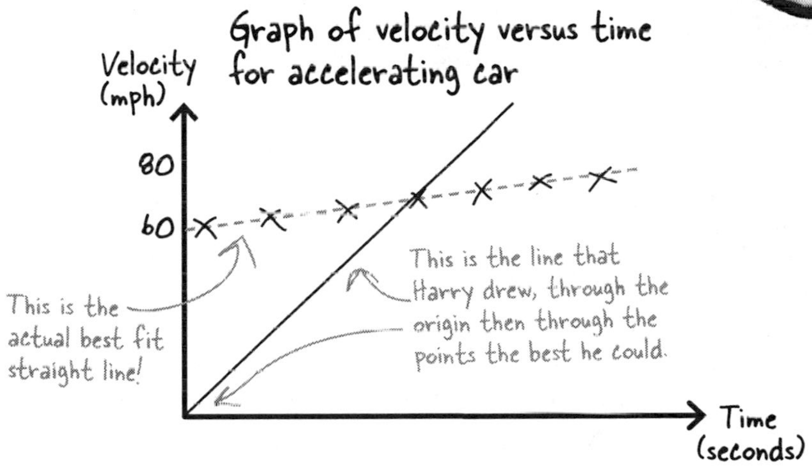

This meant that the slope of his line was much steeper than it should have been - so his values for the acceleration of each car were far too high. No wonder Harry's customers came back to complain!

The equation for the graph is $v = v_0 + at$. where v_0 is the velocity at $t = 0$. Harry's right that he can work out the car's acceleration from the slope of a best fit straight line - but only if the line he draws passes through v_0!

A best fit straight line doesn't need to go through the origin.

Do I really need to **memorize** all of this chapter for my exam? Dude, that was tough!

You only need to memorize a couple of this chapter's equations for your exam

The two important equations from this chapter are $\mathbf{v} = \mathbf{v}_0 + \mathbf{a}t$ and $\mathbf{x} = \mathbf{x}_0 + \mathbf{v}_0 t + \frac{1}{2}\mathbf{a}t^2$. These are the two things you need to memorize for your exam - so that **you can solve all kinds of problems similar to this one**!

And don't worry - you'll pick the equations up soon enough by **using** them to do problems. As long as you practice, there'll be no need for you to do any rote memorization.

Think like a physicist!

If you practice your tennis forehand, you can guarantee that your tennis results will improve even though you'll never play two identical forehands because each game situation is unique.

In a similar way to your forehand. you can also develop your equation-handling skills to enable you to solve all kinds of problems that are **like** this one, even if they're not exactly the same.

Grooving your physics skills means that you can solve all kinds of problems, not just ones you've memorized.

Throughout your physics career (and definitely in your exam) you'll be interpreting graphs and working out equations from them. If you want to understand what's going on and do well in physics, you need to be able to **rearrange equations**, make **substitutions** and **check your answers**. Which is what you've been practicing in this chapter.

Now you can solve all kinds of problems that are <u>like</u> this one.

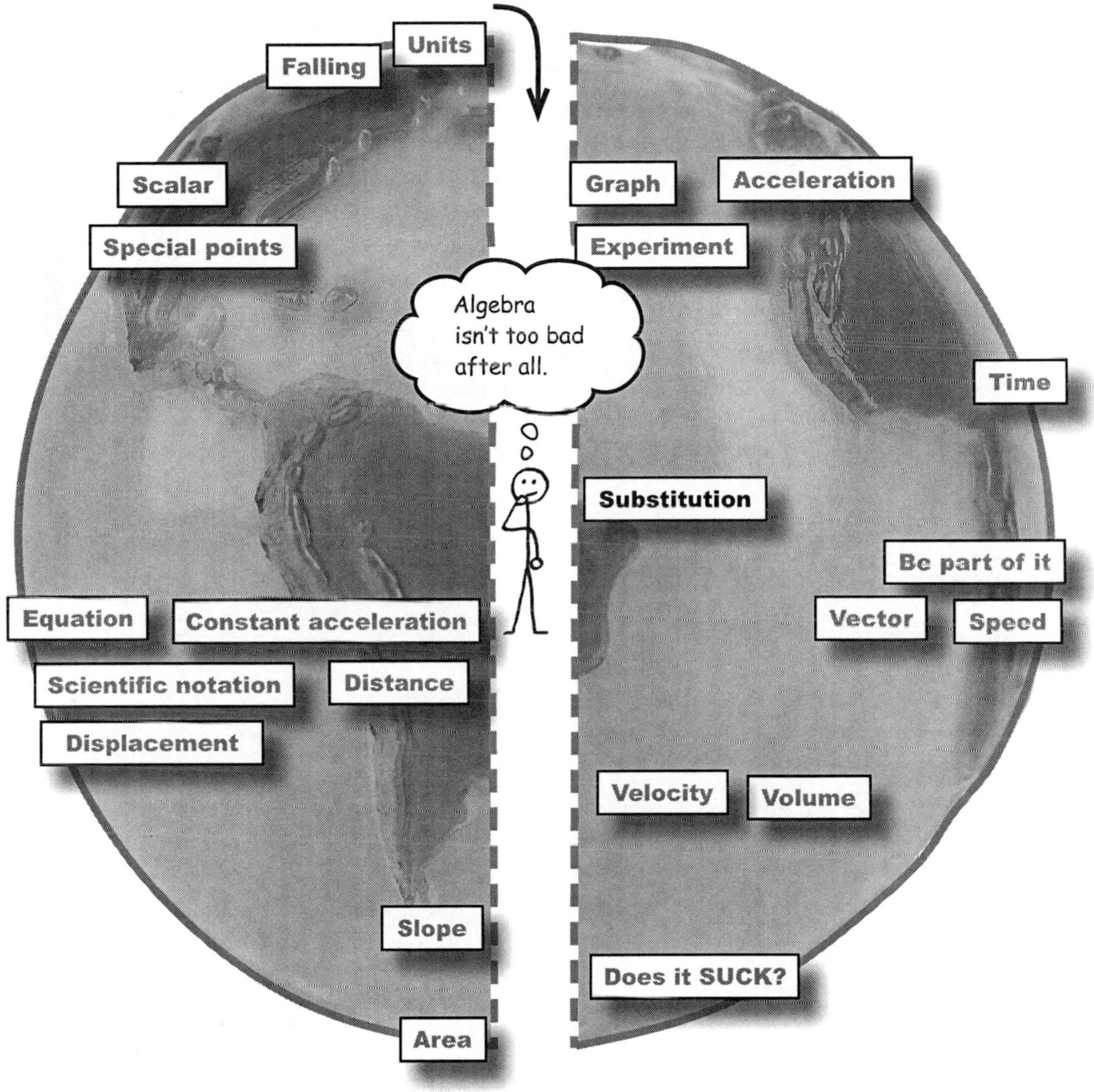

Substitution **Making a substitution is 'getting rid' of a variable from an equation by replacing it with an expression it's equal to (usually from a second equation).**

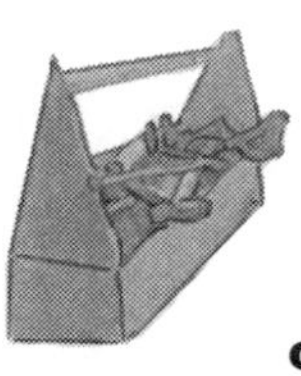

Your Physics Toolbox

You've got Chapter 7 under your belt and added some problem-solving and answer-checking skills to your toolbox.

Equation of a graph

The equation of a graph has the form:

vertical = something to do with horizontal

A fundamental equation of motion

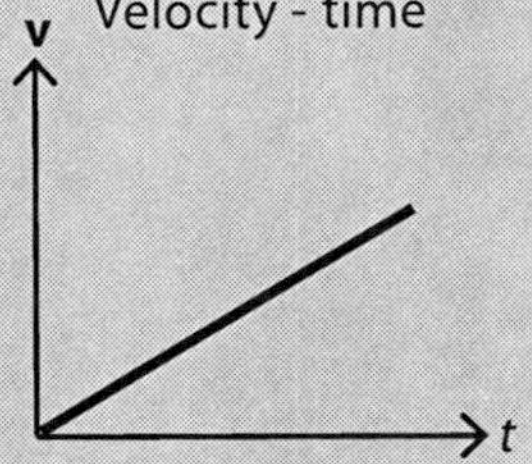

$$v = v_0 + at$$

Another fundamental equation of motion

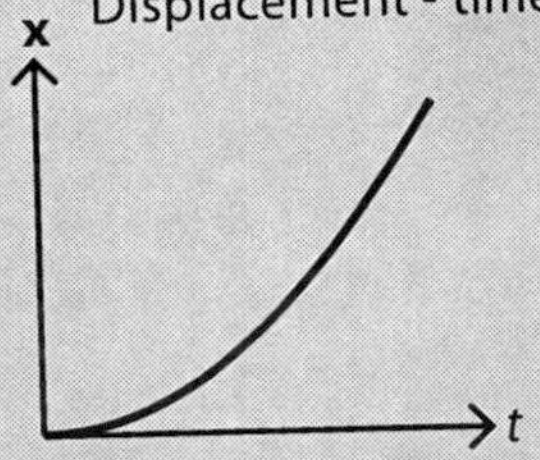

$$x = x_0 + v_0 t + \frac{1}{2}at^2$$

GUT check

Graph – Do your equation and graph tell the same story?

Units – Do all the terms in your equation have the same units?

Try extreme values – Does your equation mirror reality when you make the variables zero or very large one at a time?

Substitution

Making a substitution is replacing a variable in an equation with an expression that's equal to it.

This can be useful if you have a variable in your equation that you don't know a value for.

8 equations of motion (part 2)

Up, up, and... back down

What goes up must come down. You already know how to deal with things that are falling **down**, which is great. But what about the other half of the bargain - when something's launched **up** into the air? In this chapter, you'll add a third key **equation of motion** to your armory which will enable you to **deal with** (just about) **anything**! You'll also learn how looking for a little **symmetry** can turn impossible tasks into manageable ones.

Previously ...

Now ACME has an amazing new cage launcher

But you can't keep the Dingo down for long - especially when ACME has an amazing new cage launcher! Once installed, it'll propel a standard ACME cage straight up in the air at a speed of your choice.

It's ideal for a more subtle approach - you can launch the cage from ground level, instead of having a big crane that the Emu will spot.

You just need to work out what velocity to launch it at so that it lands back on the target when the Emu arrives, exactly 2.0 s after you launched it.

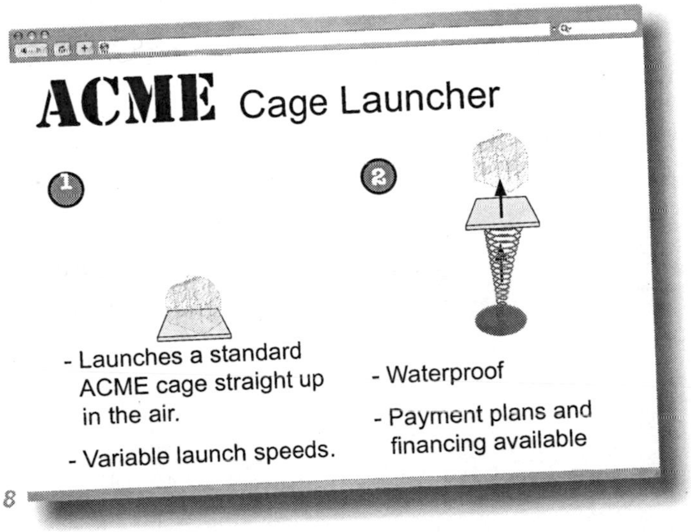

So we have to launch the cage up in the air so that it lands 2.0 s later. That sounds a lot harder than just dropping it.

Joe: Hmm, could we try using the equation we worked out in chapter 7? Y'know, $\mathbf{x} = \mathbf{x}_0 + \mathbf{v}_0 t + \frac{1}{2}\mathbf{a}t^2$.

Frank: But that was for a **falling** thing. This time, the cage is **going up**. It's not the same thing.

Joe: But once the cage gets to its maximum height, it falls back down again. So it's kinda the same. Or, well, at least the falling down part of it is!

Frank: But what about the first half, when the cage is going up?

Jim: Actually, the equation might work OK then too. It's supposed to work in any situation where the acceleration's constant, right? And I think that the acceleration due to gravity is constant, whatever direction you're moving in.

Frank: But how can the cage be accelerating downwards, when it's moving upwards?

Joe: Acceleration is rate of change of velocity, right? And the cage gets **slower** as it goes up. So the acceleration vector must be pointing downwards, or else it wouldn't get slower.

Frank: I think I'd find it easier to visualize with a sketch ...

Always start with a sketch!

Sharpen your pencil

Draw a sketch of the cage just after it's been launched straight up in the air. Mark on the initial velocity vector $\mathbf{v}_0$, the acceleration vector $\mathbf{a}$, and any other information you know about the problem.

Do you think it's going to be OK to reuse the equation $\mathbf{x} = \mathbf{x}_0 + \mathbf{v}_0 t + \frac{1}{2}\mathbf{a}t^2$ in this new scenario? Why / why not?

Sharpen your pencil Solution

Draw a sketch of the cage just after it's been launched straight up in the air. Mark on the initial velocity vector $\mathbf{v}_0$, the acceleration vector **a**, and any other information you know about the problem.

Cage takes t = 2.0 s to go up then down.

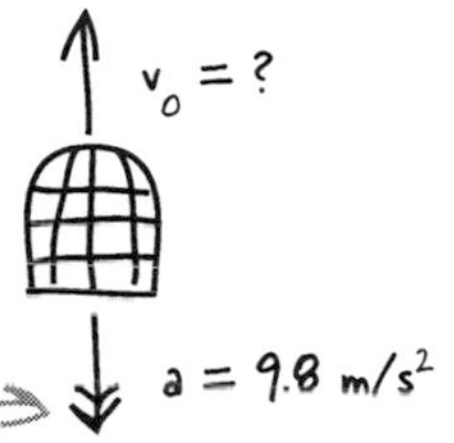

Do you think it's going to be OK to reuse the equation $\mathbf{x} = \mathbf{x}_0 + \mathbf{v}_0 t + \frac{1}{2}\mathbf{a}t^2$ in this new scenario? Why / why not?

The acceleration vector points down regardless of the direction of the cage's velocity.

The acceleration will be constant at 9.8 m/s² downwards. The equation's supposed to be used for constant acceleration, so it'll probably work.

The acceleration due to gravity is constant

The **equation of motion** you worked out last time, $\mathbf{x} = \mathbf{x}_0 + \mathbf{v}_0 t + \frac{1}{2}\mathbf{a}t^2$, is supposed to be OK in any situation where the **acceleration is constant**.

If you can reuse this equation, it'll be much much faster than going through the rigmarole of trying to design and carry out an experiment where you shoot things straight up into the air.

If an object is acted on ONLY BY GRAVITY, it has an acceleration of 9.8 m/s² downwards, whatever its velocity is.

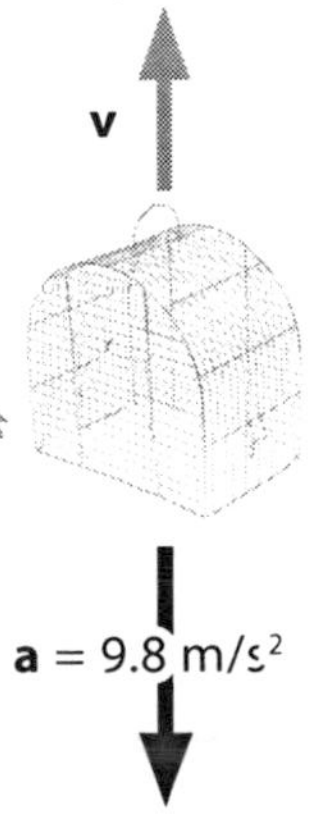

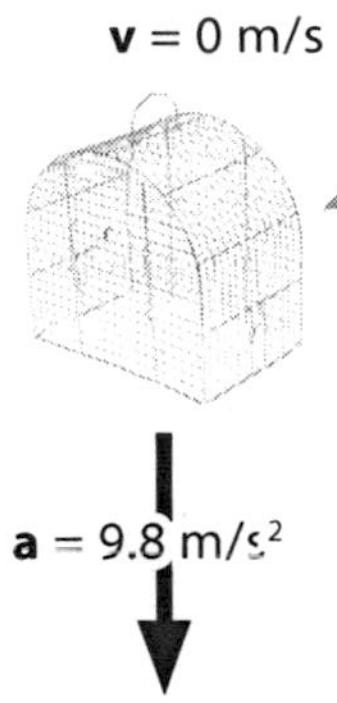

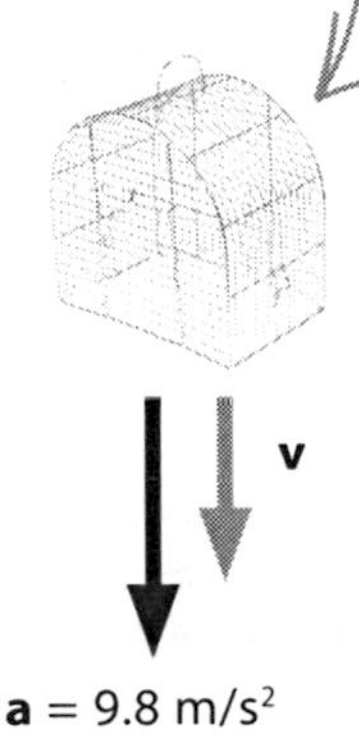

Although you originally worked out this equation from a graph you plotted by dropping things down from a height, any object that's accelerated only by gravity has a **constant acceleration of 9.8 m/s² downwards.** It doesn't matter whether its velocity vector points up, down, sideways, or at an angle.

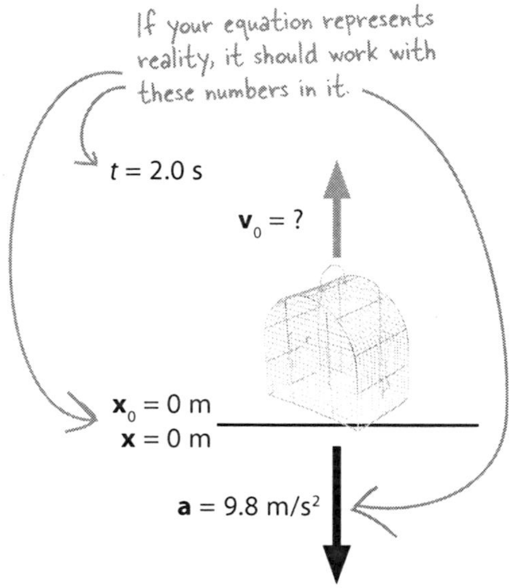

Good thinking - try to imagine your equation with some numbers in it.

The cage starts and finishes at ground level. This means that both $\mathbf{x}$ and $\mathbf{x}_0$ are zero, and your equation becomes $0 = 0 + \mathbf{v}_0 t + \frac{1}{2}\mathbf{a}t^2$ when you put these values in.

So for the equation to be true, the two terms on the right hand side, $\mathbf{v}_0 t$ and $\frac{1}{2}\mathbf{a}t^2$, must add up to zero. But how can two terms added together be zero? It's time to ...

BE the equation

Your job is to imagine you're the equation. Here, both x and x_0 are 0 because the cage starts and finishes in the same place. This means that the left hand side of the equation = 0, and on the right hand side, there are two non-zero terms ADDED together. Is there any way this is possible, or will we need to work out a different equation for the cage?

$$x = x_0 + v_0 t + \frac{1}{2}at^2$$

BE the equation - SOLUTION

Your job is to imagine you're the equation. Here, both x and x_0 are 0 because the cage starts and finishes in the same place. This means that the left hand side of the equation = 0, and on the right hand side, there are two non-zero terms ADDED together? Is there any way this is possible, or will we need to work out a different equation for the cage?

$$x = x_0 + v_0 t + \frac{1}{2}at^2$$

Velocity and acceleration are vectors.

v_0 is upwards, and a is downwards – as they point in opposite directions, they'll have opposite signs.

It IS possible for a positive number and a negative number to equal zero when you add them together. So the equation could be OK.

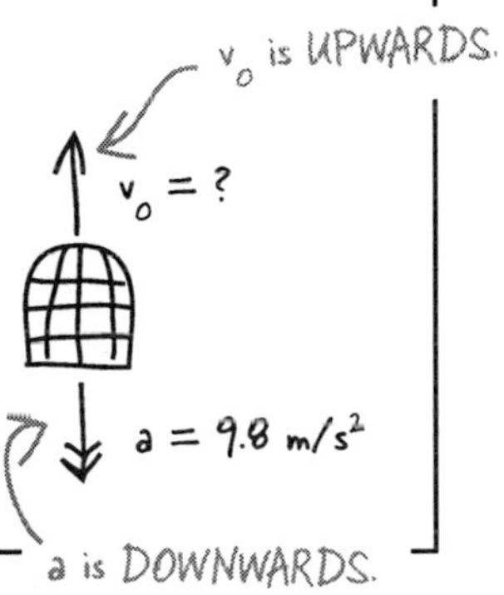

Velocity and acceleration are in opposite directions, so they have opposite signs

When **x** and $\mathbf{x}_0$ are both zero, your equation becomes $0 = 0 + \mathbf{v}_0 t + \frac{1}{2}\mathbf{a}t^2$. So the terms on the right hand side of your equation, $\mathbf{v}_0 t$ and $\frac{1}{2}\mathbf{a}t^2$, must add up to zero. You're interested in what's happening at $t = 2.0$ s, so both t and t^2 are positive. Therefore, the signs of the terms $\mathbf{v}_0 t$ and $\frac{1}{2}\mathbf{a}t^2$ are determined by the signs of $\mathbf{v}_0$ and **a**.

You're working with **vectors**! So as well as having a **size**, $\mathbf{v}_0$ and **a** have a **direction**. The acceleration due to gravity, **a**, always acts **downwards**. But the initial velocity, $\mathbf{v}_0$, is **upwards**. So $\mathbf{v}_0$ and **a** have opposite **signs**. One is positive and the other is negative.

As $\mathbf{v}_0$ and **a** have opposite signs, it's perfectly reasonable to say that there's a certain value for $\mathbf{v}_0$ where $\mathbf{v}_0 t + \frac{1}{2}\mathbf{a}t^2 = 0$. And that's the value you want to work out, as it's the launch velocity for the cage!

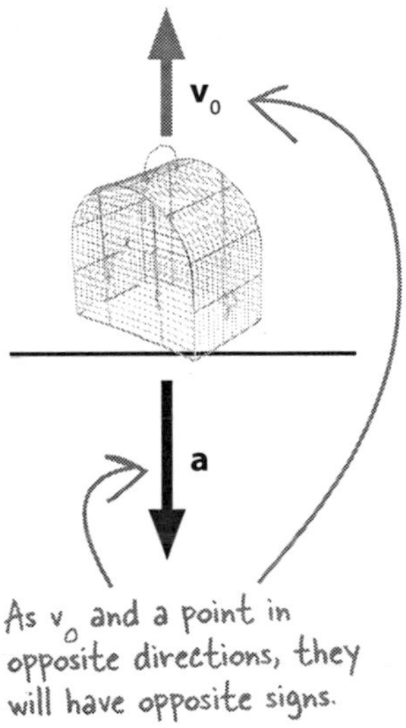

Vectors have DIRECTION!

You use positive and negative signs to show the direction.

Do we get to decide which **direction** is positive and which is negative? So this is just another way to use vectors?

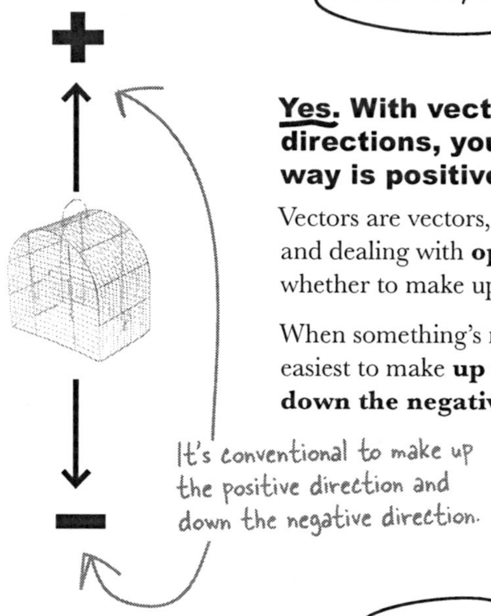

Yes. With vectors that point in opposite directions, you get to decide which way is positive and which is negative.

Vectors are vectors, so as long as you are consistent and dealing with **opposites**, you get to choose whether to make up or down the positive direction.

When something's moving through the air, it's usually easiest to make **up the positive direction** and **down the negative direction**.

But when we were **dropping** the cage, we said that down was positive. Why suddenly change now to make up positive - it's confusing!

Choose the direction that makes the math easier.

It's easy to 'lose' or forget about **minus signs** when you're doing calculations and end up with the wrong answer. When you dropped the cage, its displacement, velocity and acceleration all pointed in the **same direction** - downwards. So by making down the positive direction, you didn't have to deal with minus signs.

But now that the cage is going up then down, with $\mathbf{v}_0$ and **a** pointing in **opposite directions**, you've nothing to gain by making down positive. You're better off sticking with the convention of making up positive so that when you draw a displacement-time graph, up on the graph is the same direction as up in the real world.

You're less prone to making mistakes when doing math with only positive numbers than you are when there are negative numbers around.

there are no Dumb Questions

Q: I still don't get how you can add two numbers together and get zero as your answer.

A: Numbers can be negative as well as positive. If one of the numbers is negative, it can work out like that. For example, if $\mathbf{v}_0 t = -2$ and $\frac{1}{2}\mathbf{a}t^2 = 2$, then you have $-2 + 2 = 0$.

Q: Sorry ... I still don't quite see how two numbers added together can be zero?

A: Suppose you spend \$10 entering a competition, then win a \$10 prize in it. You've earned (-10) + 10 = 0 dollars. The sum of the (negative) entry fee and the (positive) prize win comes out to a zero balance.

Q: Why would I want to add a negative number to a positive number when I can just do a subtraction?

A: Because when you have an equation like $\mathbf{x} = \mathbf{x}_0 + \mathbf{v}_0 t + \frac{1}{2}\mathbf{a}t^2$, you don't know in advance which variables are positive and which are negative. But when you put the numbers in, it'll work out as long as you get the minus signs right.

Q: So the variables x_0, x, v_0, v and a could all be negative because they're vectors?

A: Yes, vectors have both a size and a direction. When all of your vectors lie along one line (like in this case, they're either pointing up or down) then you can choose to make one direction positive and the other direction negative.

Q: And I get to choose whatever direction I want to be positive? Either up or down?

A: Yes, as long as you're **consistent** throughout. But it's usual to make up the positive direction so that when you plot a graph, up on the graph corresponds to up in real life.

Q: What would happen if I made down the positive direction instead?

A: The math would all still work out, as long as you make sure you're consistent. You just have to be careful to do the right thing when you're adding or subtracting a negative number.

Q: How would I figure out if I'd made a mistake with the minus signs?

A: You can see if your answer SUCKs. If a minus sign has gone astray, then the answer may end up a very different size from what you'd expect. So make sure you have a rough idea of what size your answer's going to be at the back of your mind, then compare it with the result of your calculation.

Q: OK, so I think I have the negative numbers, vectors and directions all figured out. Is there anything else I should do?

A: As you've never used this equation before to deal with something going up then down, it wouldn't hurt to sketch some graphs to confirm that it's going to be OK ...

Vectors in opposite directions have opposite signs.

Frank: I guess we need to do some graphs that **show** it's OK to use the equation to deal with the cage going straight up in the air and back down again.

Jim: But that's gonna be difficult. We usually draw graphs of **experimental** results, but I don't think we can do that this time. We only get one shot at launching the cage, and if we miniaturize the experiment, we can't really measure the launch speed.

Joe: Hmmm. Maybe we could **sketch graphs** of what we know happens to something that goes up and down. Then put some numbers into the equation and plot it to see if it comes out the same **shape** - like doing that GUT check thing - comparing the equation with the **g**raph by **t**rying out some values.

Frank: But how do we sketch a displacement-time graph for something that goes up then down? Is it curved? Is it straight? Does the shape depend on whether it's going up or down? I don't think we can do that straight off.

Joe: We could start off with the **acceleration-time graph**. We know that has a constant value of 9.8 m/s^2.

Jim: You mean **-**9.8 m/s^2 ... up is positive, so down is negative!

Joe: Yeah, well, acceleration is rate of change of velocity. So the value of the acceleration is the slope of the velocity-time graph. The value of the acceleration is constant: -9.8 m/s^2, so the **slope** of the **velocity-time graph** must also be constant at -9.8 m/s^2.

Frank: Err, a **negative slope**?! What would that look like?!

Jim: I guess it would go the other way, down from left to right instead of up?! Like going downhill instead of uphill?

Joe: That sounds about right. Then when we have the velocity-time graph, we can use the fact that velocity is rate of change of displacement. So the value of the velocity is the slope of the **displacement-time** graph.

Frank: Which lets us draw a displacement-time graph as well.

Jim: Great!

Equations represent reality. If you sketch a graph of what happens in real life, it should be the same shape as the graph for your equation.

BRAIN POWER

What might the velocity-time and displacement-time graphs look like?

Don't worry about numbers here – the important thing is the SHAPES of the graphs.

Slope Up Close

The same principle applies to the slope of a displacement-time graph and the value of the velocity.

Since velocity is a **vector**, it can be either positive or negative. The **slope** of a velocity-time graph shows you the **value** of the acceleration.

If the change in velocity is positive, then the graph slopes **up,** and the acceleration is **positive**. If the change in velocity is **negative**, then the graph slopes down, and the acceleration is **negative**.

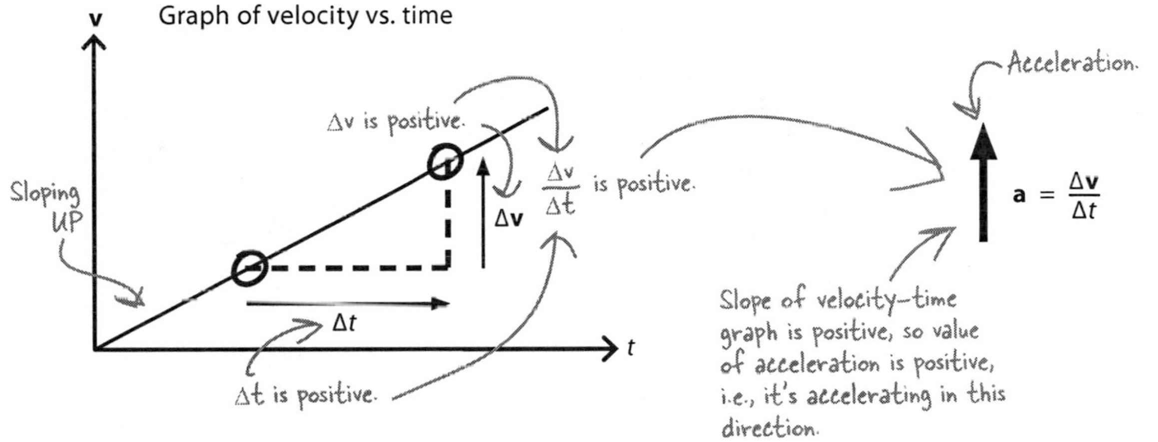

If a graph goes up, its slope is positive.

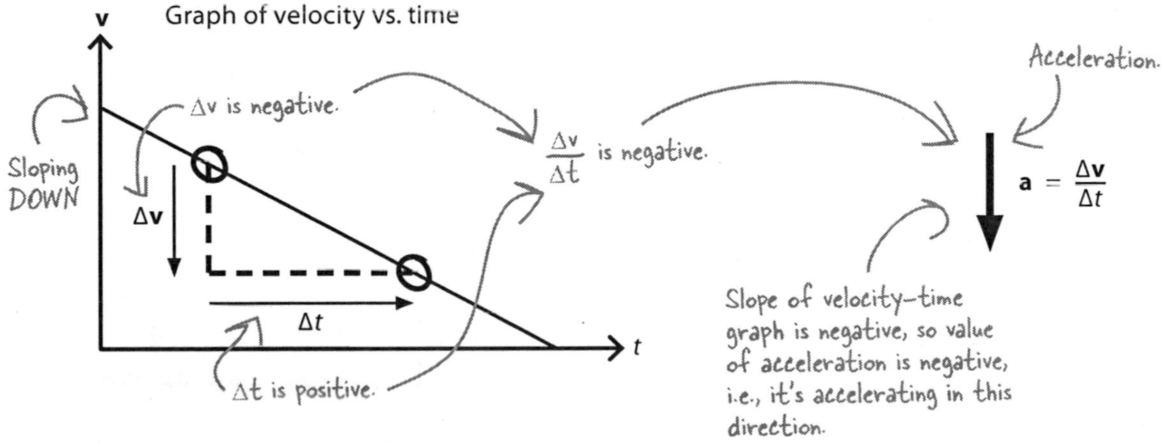

If a graph goes down, its slope is negative.

You already sketched graphs by thinking about values and slopes. What you're doing here isn't too different.

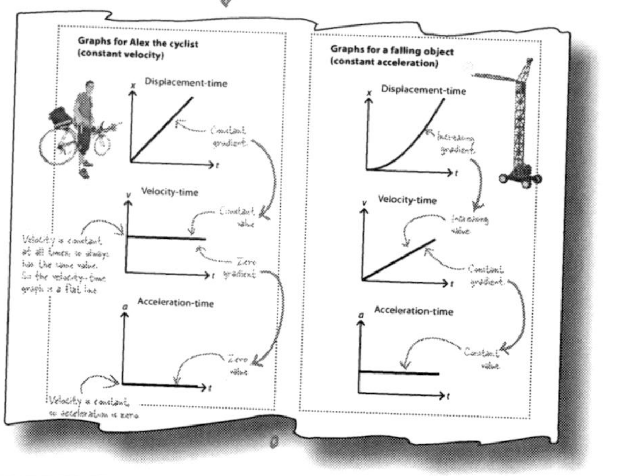

You can use one graph to work out the shapes of the others

Acceleration, velocity, and displacement are all related to each other. If you have the graph of one of them and some initial values for the others, you can use these to sketch the shapes of the other graphs.

You know that the launched cage has a constant acceleration of -9.8 m/s^2. Since the **value** of the acceleration is constant and negative, the **slope** of the velocity-time graph must be constant and negative too.

Sharpen your pencil

Use the value of your acceleration-time graph to sketch the shape of the velocity-time graph. Try to imagine the velocity of the cage as it goes up then back down again. The first dotted line is the top of its flight, and the second one is when it lands again.

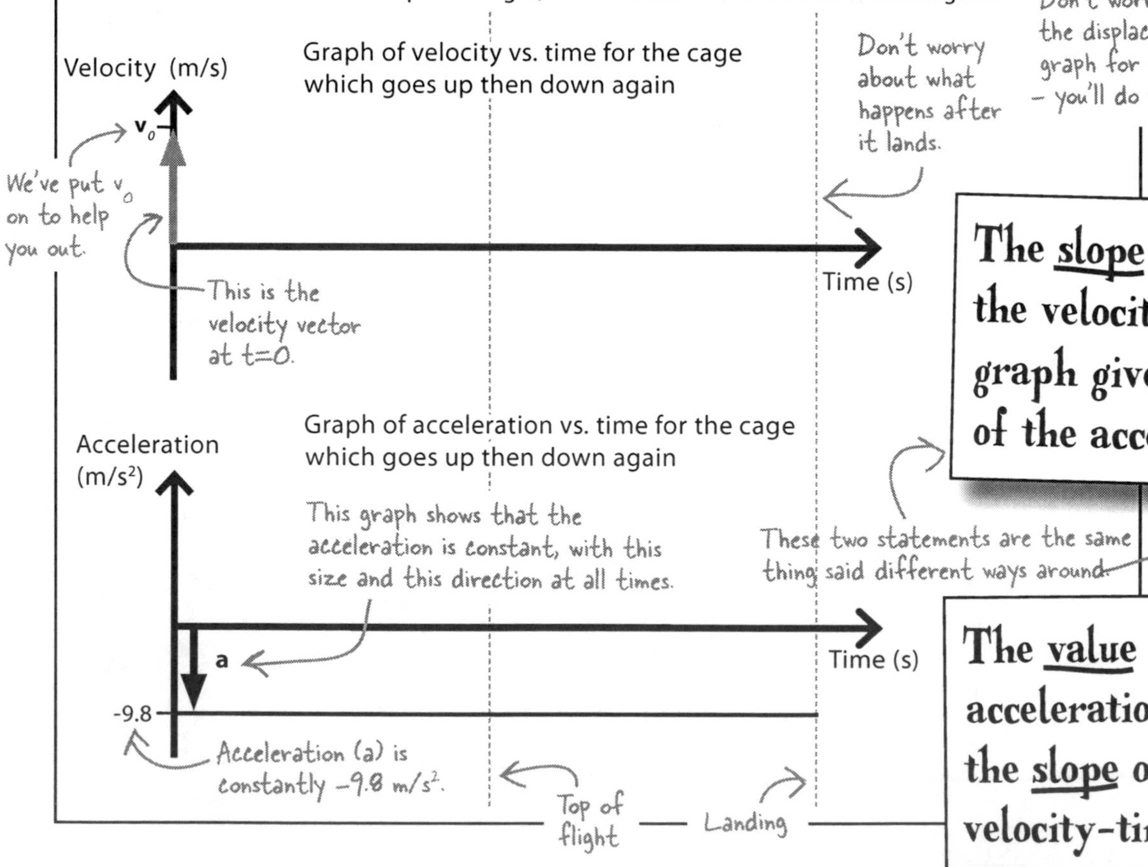

The slope of the velocity-time graph gives the value of the acceleration.

The value of the acceleration gives the slope of the velocity-time graph.

Sharpen your pencil Solution

Use the value of your acceleration-time graph to sketch the shape of the velocity-time graph. Try to imagine the velocity of the cage as it goes up then back down again. The first dotted line is the top of its flight, and the second one is when it lands again.

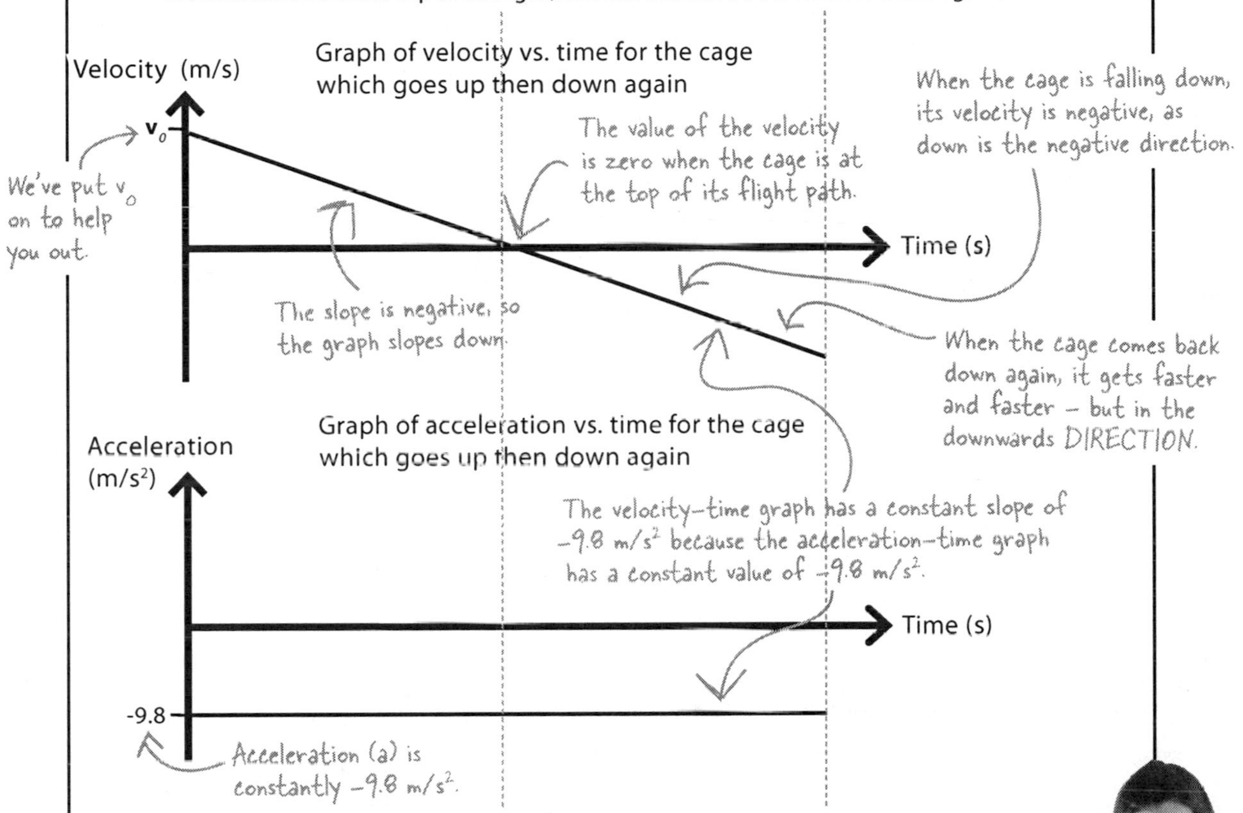

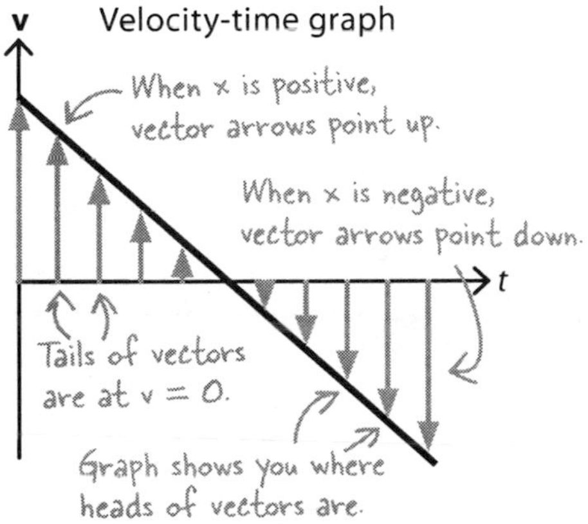

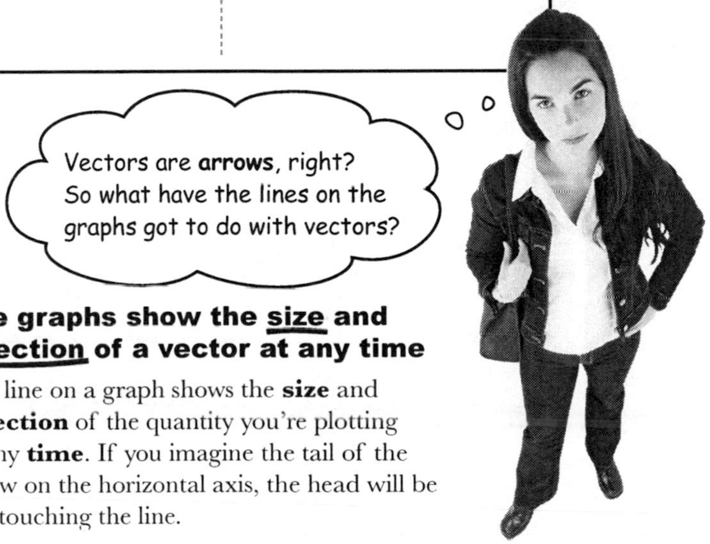

The graphs show the size and direction of a vector at any time

The line on a graph shows the **size** and **direction** of the quantity you're plotting at any **time**. If you imagine the tail of the arrow on the horizontal axis, the head will be just touching the line.

Sharpen your pencil

Now it's time for you to sketch the displacement-time graph for the cage, then annotate it to explain what you've done. The first dotted line is the top of its flight, and the second one is when it lands again.

Another way to do this (or to check over your answer) is to "be the cage" and think about what's going on as you go up then down again.

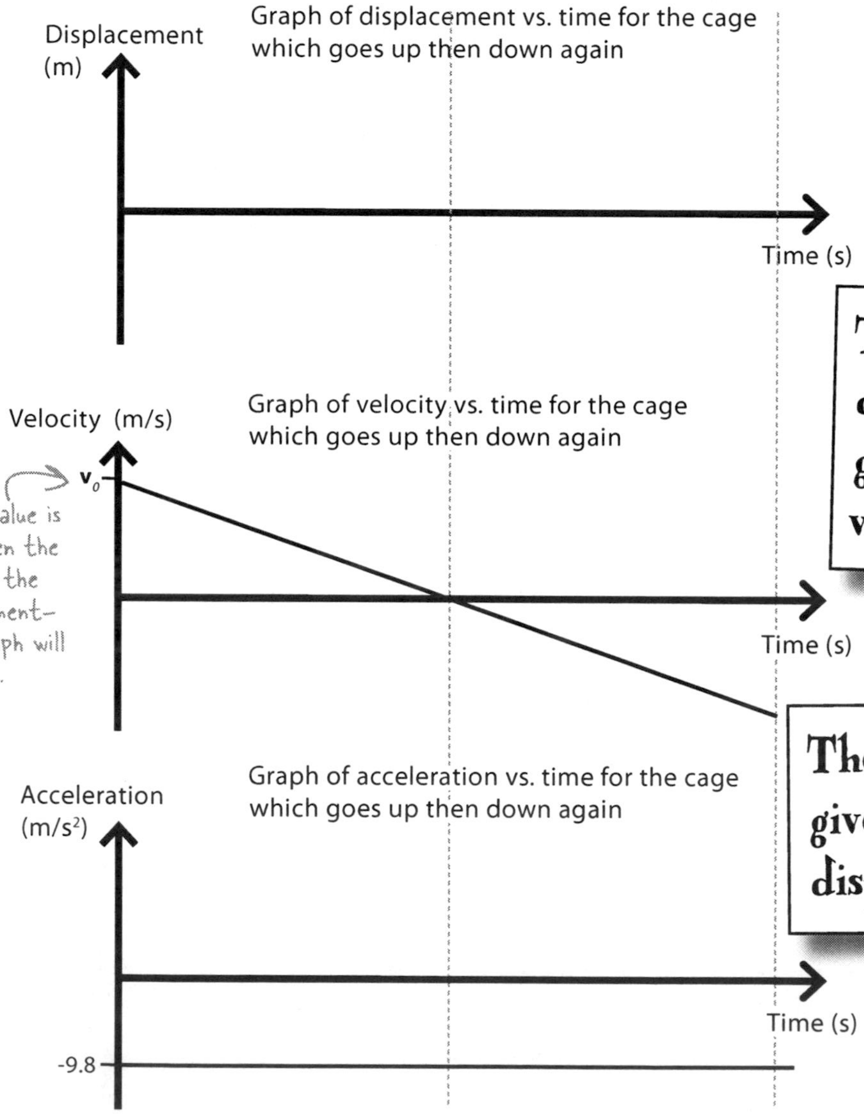

If this value is high, then the slope of the displacement-time graph will be steep.

The slope of the displacement-time graph gives the value of the velocity.

These two statements are the same thing, said different ways around.

The value of the velocity gives the slope of the displacement-time graph.

Sharpen your pencil Solution

Now it's time for you to sketch the displacement-time graph for the cage, then annotate it to explain what you've done. The first dotted line is the top of its flight, and the second one is when it lands again.

You might be used to using the word 'gradient' to indicate the steepness of a graph. In this book, we're using the word 'slope' to indicate the steepness of a graph.

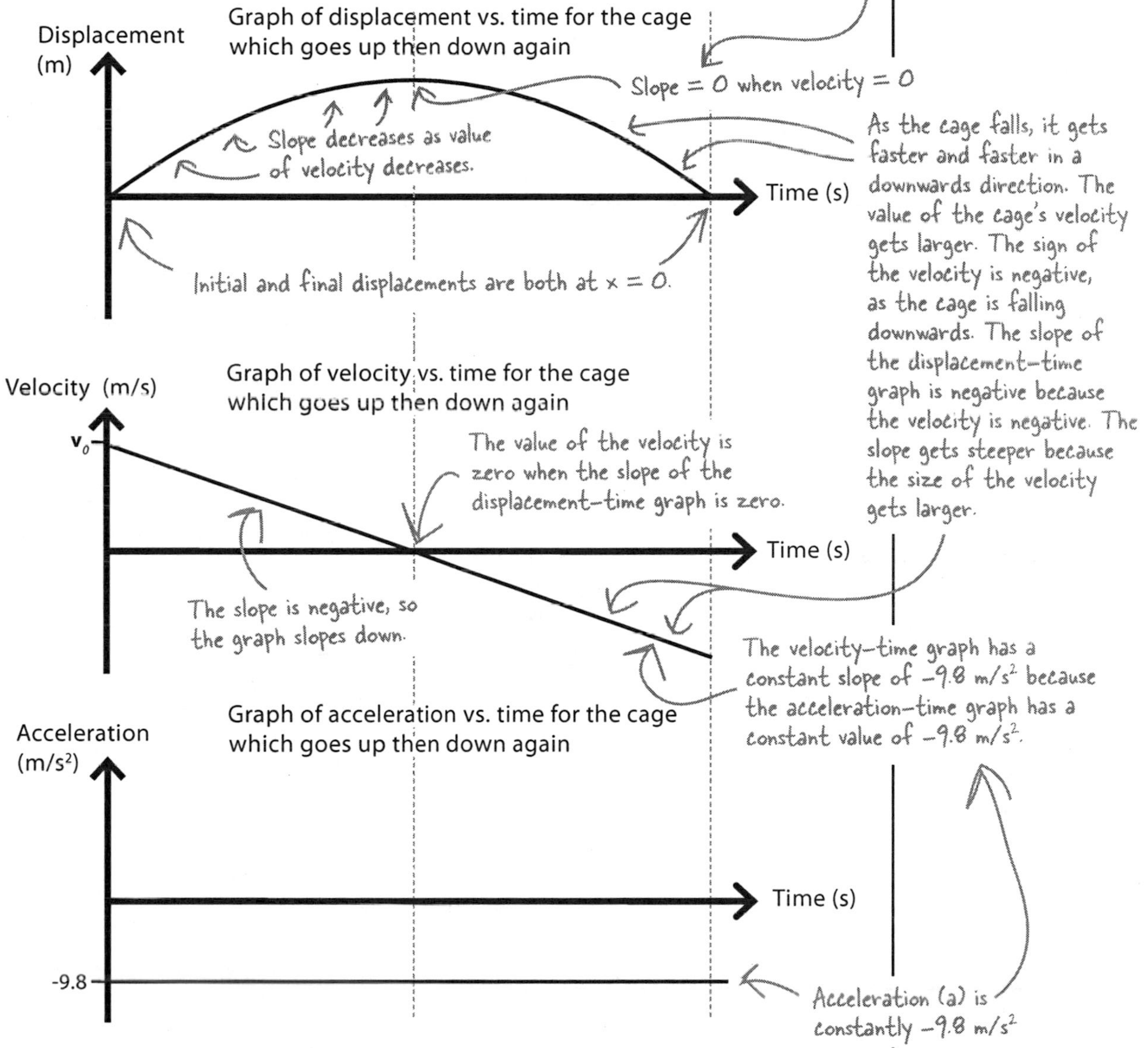

If you launch an object straight up, the object's velocity = 0 at the top of its flight.

Yes. The second half is like dropping something from a stationary start.

What goes up must come down! At its highest point, the cage isn't going up any more and hasn't quite started coming down yet. The top of its flight is a 'special point' where its velocity is zero.

So for the second part of its motion, when it's coming back down, the cage behaves exactly as if it's been dropped from its maximum height.

The graph is the same shape as last time, though it's the other way up because this time up is positive.

there are no Dumb Questions

Q: I can't quite believe that the velocity-time graph is just a diagonal line like that. It seems too perfect.

A: The acceleration is constant and negative. So the slope of the velocity-time graph also has to be constant and negative. This is another way of saying that the velocity-time graph is a straight line graph that slopes downwards.

Q: How do you know where to start drawing the diagonal line? You could put it anywhere on the velocity-time graph!

A: Good point! If you didn't know that the initial velocity was $\mathbf{v_0}$, then you wouldn't know where to start drawing the graph.

Q: How do you know what angle to slope the velocity-time graph at?

A: This is just a sketch graph, with no scales on the axes, so the angle doesn't matter much here. Just make sure the line goes through **v**= 0 when the object is at the top of its flight.

If you were plotting a velocity-time graph with values on your axes, then you'd make its slope the same as the value of the acceleration-time graph.

Q: You said that the line should go through v = 0 when the object is at the top of its flight. How can something's velocity be zero when it's up in the air?

A: There's a split second when the object reaches its maximum height. There, the object's just stopped going up and is just about to come down. At that point, the velocity is zero.

Q: So when the velocity of a launched object is zero, does that mean the displacement's zero as well?

A: No ... it means that the **slope** of the displacement-time graph is zero.

Q: So you're saying that we can work backwards from the acceleration-time graph to draw the other graphs?

A: Close but not quite - the cage started with velocity $\mathbf{v_0}$ and at $\mathbf{x_0}$ = 0. If you hadn't known these initial values, you wouldn't have known where to start sketching the graphs.

Q: But I knew some start values, so the sketches are OK. Can I get on with plotting the equation $x = x_0 + v_0t + \frac{1}{2}at^2$ to see if it's the same shape as the sketch?

A: Well, alright then ...

Is a graph of your equation the same shape as the graph you sketched?

You can work out whether it's OK to use the equation $\mathbf{x} = \mathbf{x}_0 + \mathbf{v}_0 t + \frac{1}{2}\mathbf{a}t^2$ by **plotting** it on a graph. If the **shape** is the same as the shape of the graph you already sketched, then you're good to go!

You're already reasonably sure that it's OK to use the equation, as it's supposed to work when the acceleration is constant. But you want to make ABSOLUTELY sure!

As you're just doing a GUT check by drawing a **g**raph and **t**rying some values to see the shape of the graph, it's OK to just choose a value for $\mathbf{v}_0$. After all, you're expecting the cage to go up and eventually come back down again whatever $\mathbf{v}_0$ is (as long as it's positive!), so if the equation gives you that shape, it'll be fine to use it to give the Dingo an answer.

Back in chapter 7, we tried out extreme values for the 'T' of GUT to make sure that the equation we worked out there wasn't completely ridiculous. Here, we're trying some reasonable values to draw a graph. The principle is the same.

Sharpen your pencil

You want to plot a graph of your equation $\mathbf{x} = \mathbf{x}_0 + \mathbf{v}_0 t + \frac{1}{2}\mathbf{a}t^2$ to see if it's the same shape as the displacement an object has when it goes up then down in real life.

If the equation is correct, then it should produce the same **shape** of graph whatever value of $\mathbf{v}_0$ you choose. We're going to get you to plot the graph of the equation using $\mathbf{v}_0$ **= 15 m/s.**

a. Fill in the table of values.

b. Plot the graph. Is it the same shape as your sketch graph?

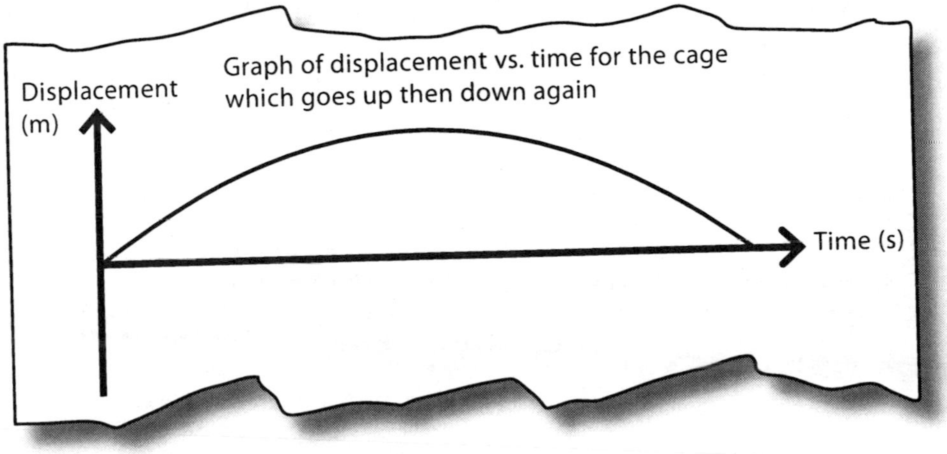

This is the sketch graph you already did a couple of pages ago.

Horizontal axis

We're trying $v_0 = 15$ m/s

Remember $a = -9.8$ m/s²

Vertical axis

time (s)	v_0t	$\frac{1}{2}at^2$	$x = x_0 + v_0t + \frac{1}{2}at^2$
0.0	15 × 0 = 0	0.5 × (-9.8) × 0² = 0	0 + 0 = 0
0.5			
1.0			
1.5			
2.0			
2.5			
3.0			

Plot of

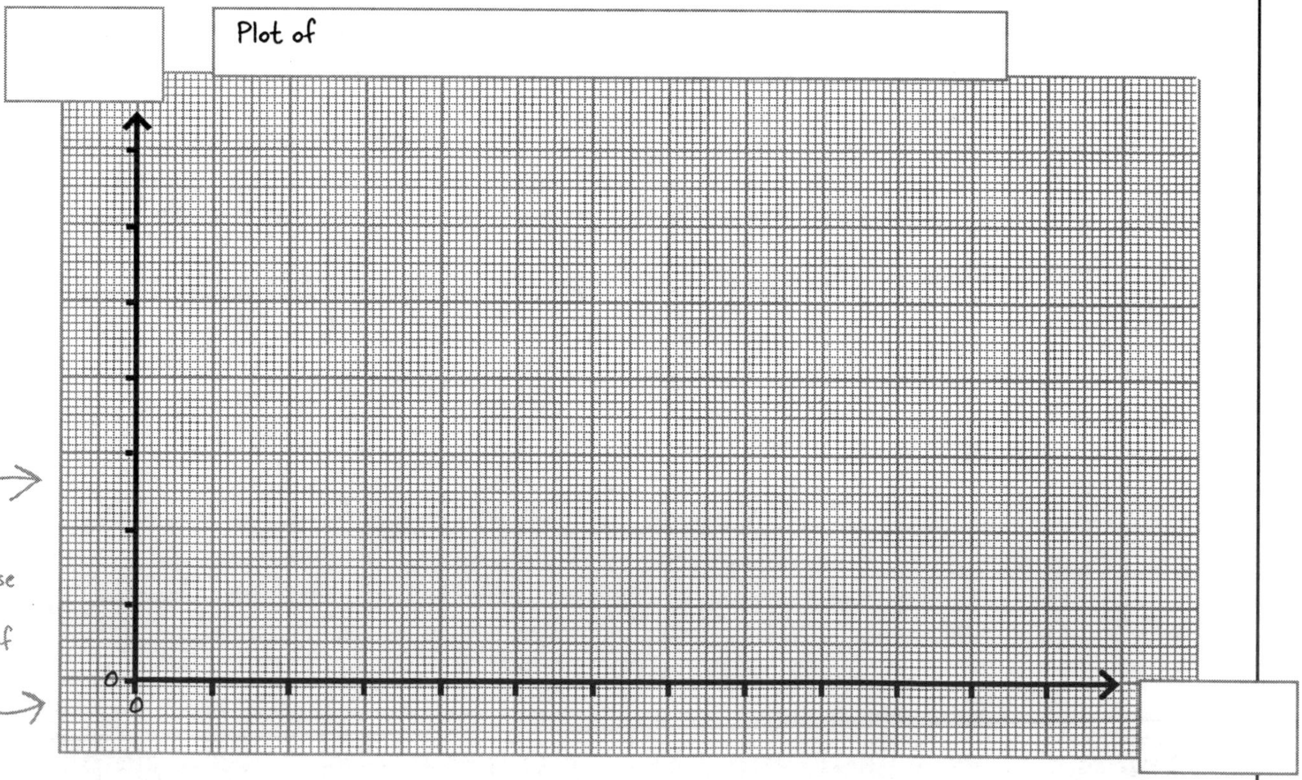

It's up to you to choose a scale for both axes of your graph.

Sharpen your pencil Solution

If you're adding or subtracting, quote your answers to the same number of decimal places as the least precise number.

You want to plot a graph of your equation $\mathbf{x} = \mathbf{x}_0 + \mathbf{v}_0 t + \frac{1}{2}\mathbf{a}t^2$ to see if it's the same shape as the displacement an object has when it goes up then down in real life.

If the equation is correct, then it should produce the same **shape** of graph whatever value of $\mathbf{v}_0$ you choose. We're going to get you to plot the graph of the equation using $\mathbf{v}_0 = \mathbf{15\ m/s}$.

a. Fill in the table of values.

b. Plot the graph. Is it the same shape as your sketch graph?

It's the same shape as the sketch graph, so it's OK to use the equation!

time (s)	v_0t	$\frac{1}{2}at^2$	$x = x_0 + v_0t + \frac{1}{2}at^2$
0.0	15 × 0 = 0	0.5 × (-9.8) × 0² = 0	0 + 0 = 0
0.5	15 × 0.5 = 7.5	0.5 × (–9.8) × 0.5² = –1.23	7.5 + (–1.23) = 6.3 (1 dp)
1.0	15 × 1.0 = 15.0	0.5 × (–9.8) × 1.0² = –4.90	15.0 + (–4.90) = 10.1 (1 dp)
1.5	15 × 1.5 = 22.5	0.5 × (–9.8) × 1.5² = –11.0	22.5 + (–11.0) = 11.5 (1 dp)
2.0	15 × 2.0 = 30.0	0.5 × (–9.8) × 2.0² = –19.6	30.0 + (–19.6) = 10.4 (1 dp)
2.5	15 × 2.5 = 37.5	0.5 × (–9.8) × 2.5² = –30.6	37.5 + (–30.6) = 6.9 (1 dp)
3.0	15 × 3.0 = 45.0	0.5 × (–9.8) × 3.0² = –44.1	45.0 + (–44.1) = 0.9 (1 dp)

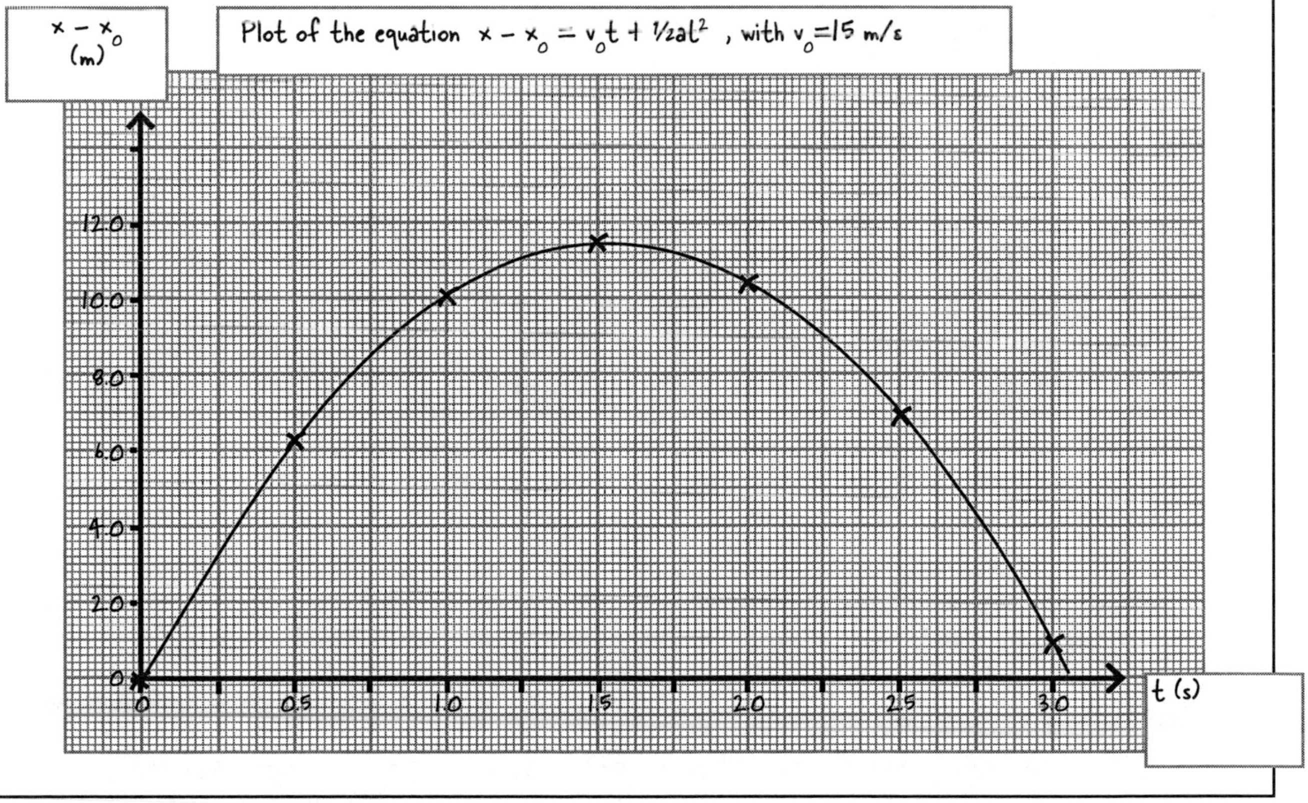

You can check equations by picking values and plotting a graph.

Ready to launch the cage!

The cage is ready for lift-off! You've sketched graphs and tried numbers to confirm that the equation of motion $\mathbf{x} = \mathbf{x}_0 + \mathbf{v}_0 t + \frac{1}{2}\mathbf{a}t^2$ works in any situation where the acceleration is constant - whether the cage starts off falling or going up.

So you're ready to rock and roll and work out a launch velocity for the Dingo!

Once the launch velocity's input, all he needs to do is sit and wait for the Emu ...

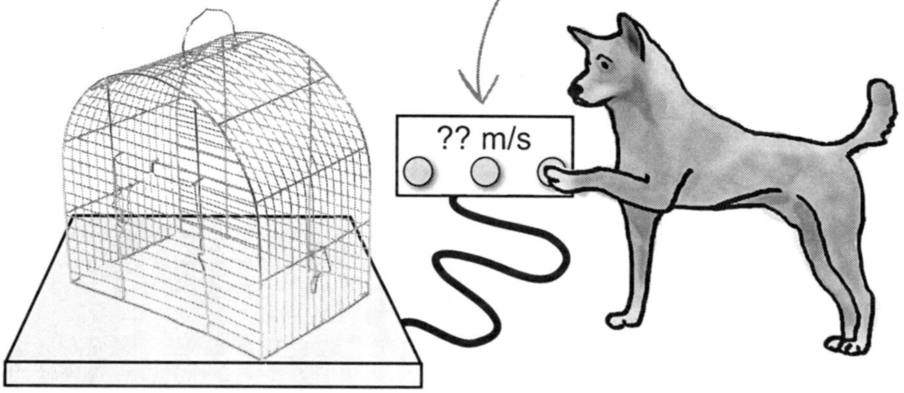

Sharpen your pencil

The Dingo wants to catch the Emu by launching a cage straight up in the air as the Emu rounds a bend. The cage needs to land 2.0 s later, when the Emu reaches the launch site.

What should the initial launch velocity be?

$t = 0$ s at start and
$t = 2.0$ s at end.

Up is positive direction.

This is a typical question. We've included the sketch you drew before so that you don't have to do that again.

Sharpen your pencil Solution

The Dingo wants to catch the Emu by launching a cage straight up in the air as the Emu rounds a bend. The cage needs to land 2.0 s later, when the Emu reaches the launch site.

What should the initial launch velocity be?

$t = 0$ s at start and
$t = 2.0$ s at end.

Up is positive direction.

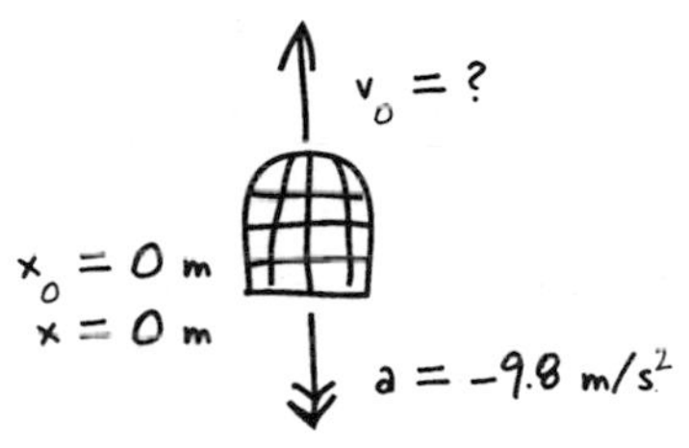

Need to know what v_0 is for x to be 0 after 2.0 seconds.

$$x = x_0 + v_0 t + \frac{1}{2}at^2$$

Rearrange equation to say "v_0 = something."

$$v_0 t = x - x_0 - \frac{1}{2}at^2$$

$$v_0 = \frac{x - x_0 - \frac{1}{2}at^2}{t}$$

Put in numbers.

$$v_0 = \frac{0 - 0 - 0.5 \times (-9.8) \times 2^2}{2}$$

Two negative numbers multiplied together is a positive number.

$$v_0 = 9.8 \text{ m/s (2 sd)}$$

The initial launch velocity should be 9.8 m/s (2 sd).

BULLET POINTS

- **Always start with a sketch**. Draw in all the **sizes** and **directions** of the things you already know plus the ones you want to find out.
- If your equations involve **vectors**, make sure you decide **which direction is positive** and stick to it!
- Be very careful when you're dealing with **negative numbers**!!
- If you already have any one of the displacement-time, velocity-time or acceleration-time **graphs**, you can work out the other two (though sometimes you may need initial values to know where to start drawing the other graphs).
- Before you 'reuse' an equation, think about the **context** you're trying to reuse it in. For instance, does it only work when the velocity is constant, and is the velocity constant in your situation?
- You can use your key **equations** $v = v_0 + at$ and $x = x_0 + v_0 t + \frac{1}{2}at^2$ in any situation where there's **constant acceleration**.

there are no Dumb Questions

Q: I did exactly the same as you did when I rearranged the equation to say "v_0 = something" but got a different answer when I put the numbers in. Why was that?

A: You might need to spend a bit more time practicing with your calculator.

Q: It doesn't seem fair that I do all that work then get marked wrong because I typed something in wrong.

A: Understanding the physics is the most important thing - you won't get marked wrong for the whole problem. In many mark schemes, including AP Physics B, you get most of your points for setting up the answer using the fact that you understand the physics.

Q: Is that why everyone's always going on about how I should show my work and not just write down an equation or an answer?

A: Partly. If you show your work, it's easier for you to spot any little slip you might have made on the way through that caused your answer to turn out wrong.

Q: But people who are good at doing physics and math don't make little slips like losing minus signs or typing in the numbers wrong ... do they?

A: You'd be surprised! That's why we've been practising checking over your answers a lot, using things like SUCK and GUT. If you get into thinking in this way, it's like having a second line of defense against little mathematical slips.

Q: So you're saying that people who've more experience of physics than me make this kind of mistake as well? That's a relief!

A: Oh yes!

Q: So the main thing is that if I show my work, then I can go back and try to fix it if I spot something's not quite right with my final answer?

A: Exactly! It might be something as simple as inserting a minus sign and retyping the numbers into your calculator.

Q: Can we go see how the Dingo's getting on with the launcher?

A: Oh yes ...

If you show your work, it's easier to spot - and fix - little mathematical slips.

Your launch velocity of 5.0 m/s is definitely right!

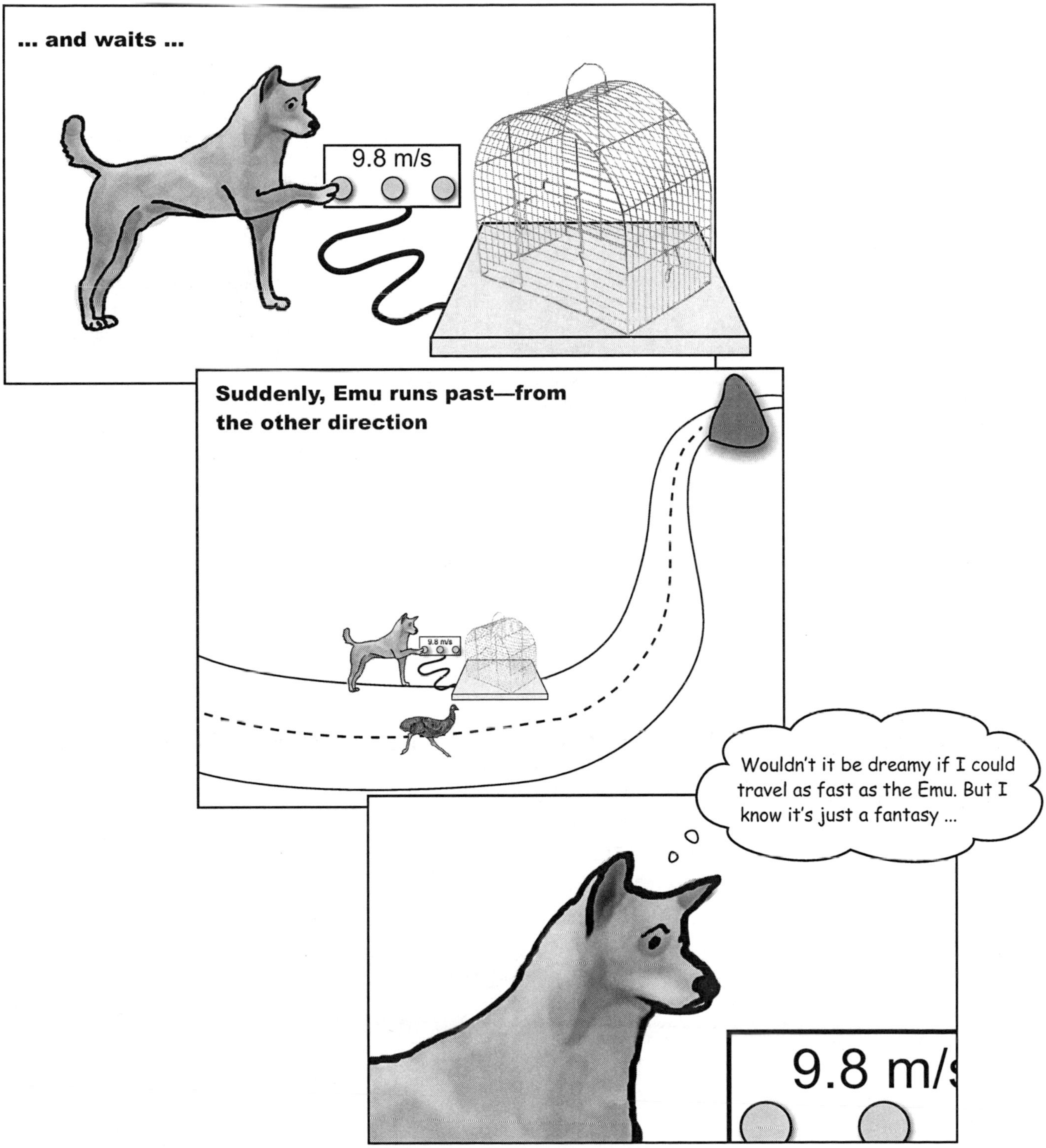
... and waits ...
9.8 m/s
Suddenly, Emu runs past—from the other direction
9.8 m/s
Wouldn't it be dreamy if I could travel as fast as the Emu. But I know it's just a fantasy ...
9.8 m/

Fortunately, ACME has a rocket-powered hovercraft!

The Dingo goes back to ACME and discovers a rocket-powered hovercraft, which is tailor-made for his needs! Usually, he can't run as fast as the Emu can, but now he can set the hovercraft to any **speed** he likes and use it to catch up with the Emu. More importantly, he can exactly match his speed with the Emu by setting the controls to 15 m/s. Perfect for passing on a party invitation!.

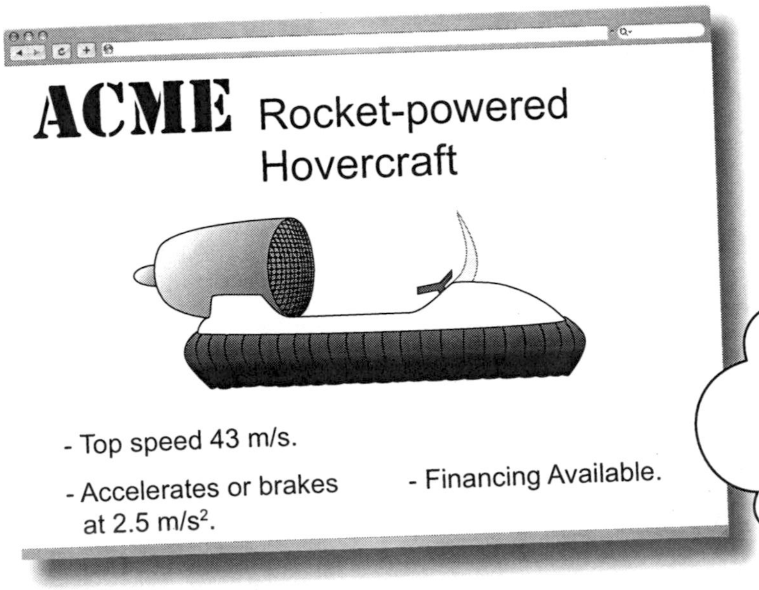

However, the Dingo's a bit nervous, as he's tried this kind of thing before and it didn't go well. Before he goes anywhere near the hovercraft, he wants to know its **stopping distance** (the distance that it travels between applying the brake and the hovercraft actually stopping).

Sharpen your pencil

You need to figure out the stopping distance of the hovercraft. So start off by drawing a **sketch** of the hovercraft. Do one sketch showing the moment that it puts on the brakes while traveling at 15 m/s. Do another sketch showing the moment that the hovercraft comes to a halt (before you release the brakes). Put on all the values you already know, plus the ones you want to find out.

You're only going to do the sketch now. You'll do the calculation later.

There are various values on the website above.

Hint: Draw two separate hovercraft drawings – one with all the values at the start next to it and the other with all the values at the end next to it.

Sharpen your pencil Solution

You didn't use all of the values on the hovercraft website – for example, the hovercraft's top speed That's OK – sometimes you won't need to use all the values you're given.

You need to figure out the stopping distance of the hovercraft. So start off by drawing a **sketch** of the hovercraft. Do one sketch showing the moment that it puts on the brakes while traveling at 15 m/s. Do another sketch showing the moment that the hovercraft comes to a halt (before you release the brakes). Put on all the values you already know, plus the ones you want to find out.

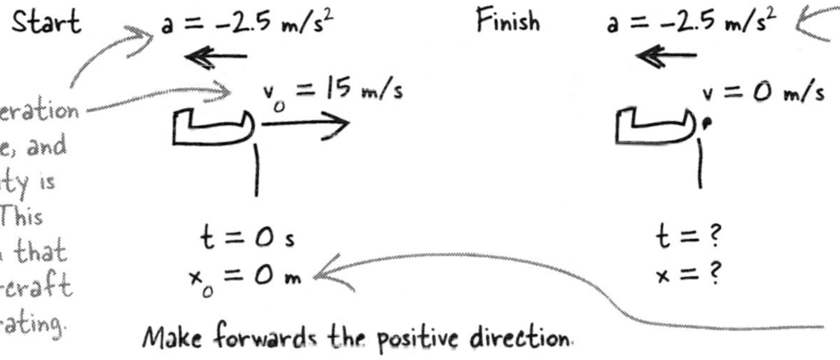

The acceleration is negative, and the velocity is positive. This shows you that the hovercraft is decelerating.

The acceleration is backwards because putting on the brakes makes the hovercraft's velocity change in the opposite direction from the direction the hovercraft is currently traveling in.

It's nearly always best to define $x_0 = 0$ as your starting point.

You don't know the time it takes to stop!

The equation you used before, $\mathbf{x} = \mathbf{x}_0 + \mathbf{v}_0 t + \frac{1}{2}\mathbf{a}t^2$, has several variables in it: $\mathbf{x}$, $\mathbf{x}_0$, $\mathbf{v}_0$, t, and $\mathbf{a}$. You're trying to work out the stopping distance, $\mathbf{x}$, and you already know $\mathbf{v}_0$ and $\mathbf{a}$. So far, so good.

But you don't know t! If you have **one equation** with **two unknowns**, you can't use it (on its own) to work out either of the things you don't know.

Before you try to use an equation, make sure that the value you want to find out is the ONLY variable you don't already know.

Jim: The equation we used last time is $\mathbf{x} = \mathbf{x}_0 + \mathbf{v}_0 t + \frac{1}{2}\mathbf{a}t^2$, but we can't use that equation here because we don't know what t is.

Frank: Yeah, if there are **two** values you don't know and only **one** equation, then you can't work out what either value is.

Joe: The hovercraft's acceleration's **constant** at 2.5 m/s^2, isn't it?

Jim: MINUS 2.5 m/s^2 ! We made forwards the **positive direction**.

Joe: OK, the acceleration's -2.5 m/s^2 then, but it's still constant, right? So there's a second key **equation of motion** we can use, $\mathbf{v} = \mathbf{v}_0 + \mathbf{a}t$

Frank: I don't see how it helps - that equation doesn't have an x in it, which is what we want to work out!

Joe: But it does have t in it. We know $\mathbf{v}_0$, we know $\mathbf{v}$, and we know $\mathbf{a}$ - the only other variables in the equation. So we could use this equation to work out a value for t to use in the other equation.

Jim: That sounds good, but I don't want to have to work out an **intermediate value** for t every time I want to do something like this. Is there any way we could make a **substitution** to get a more **general equation** that we could use to work out something's displacement when we don't know the time interval? That would be really useful!

Joe: OK, I think you're right about trying to be general. It's more efficient, and we can use our new equation again and again to solve **similar problems**. But how are we going to wind up with an equation for **x** that doesn't involve t ?

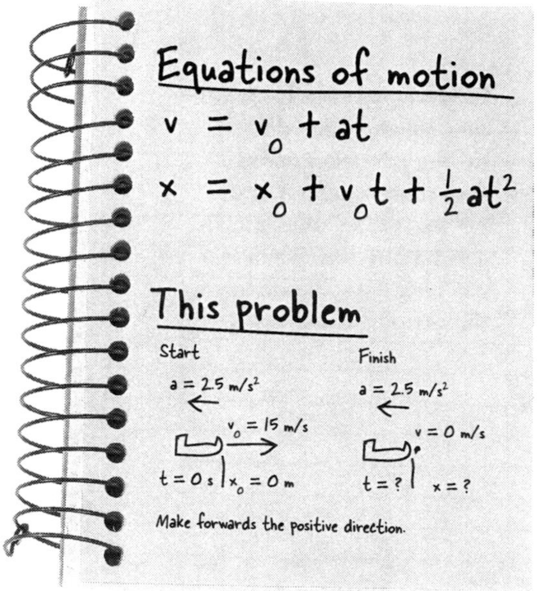

BRAIN POWER

How might you use your two equations, $\mathbf{v} = \mathbf{v}_0 + \mathbf{a}t$ and $\mathbf{x} = \mathbf{x}_0 + \mathbf{v}_0 t + \frac{1}{2}\mathbf{a}t^2$, to come up with a general equation that lets you work out **x** when you don't know what t, the time interval is?

Working out a general equation is better than scribbling down a whole lot of intermediate values.

You can work out a new equation by making a substitution for t

So far, you know two key equations of motion:

$\mathbf{v} = \mathbf{v}_0 + \mathbf{a}t$ and $\mathbf{x} = \mathbf{x}_0 + \mathbf{v}_0 t + \frac{1}{2}\mathbf{a}t^2$

You want to work out x, the stopping distance for the Dingo's hovercraft. The hovercraft is traveling with a particular **velocity** and braking with a particular **acceleration**. However, you don't know the **time** the hovercraft takes to stop, so you can't use $\mathbf{x} = \mathbf{x}_0 + \mathbf{v}_0 t + \frac{1}{2}\mathbf{a}t^2$ directly.

However, you can form a new equation that doesn't involve t by **rearranging** your other equation to say "t = something" then making a **substitution**. Then you can plug the values in to get the stopping distance.

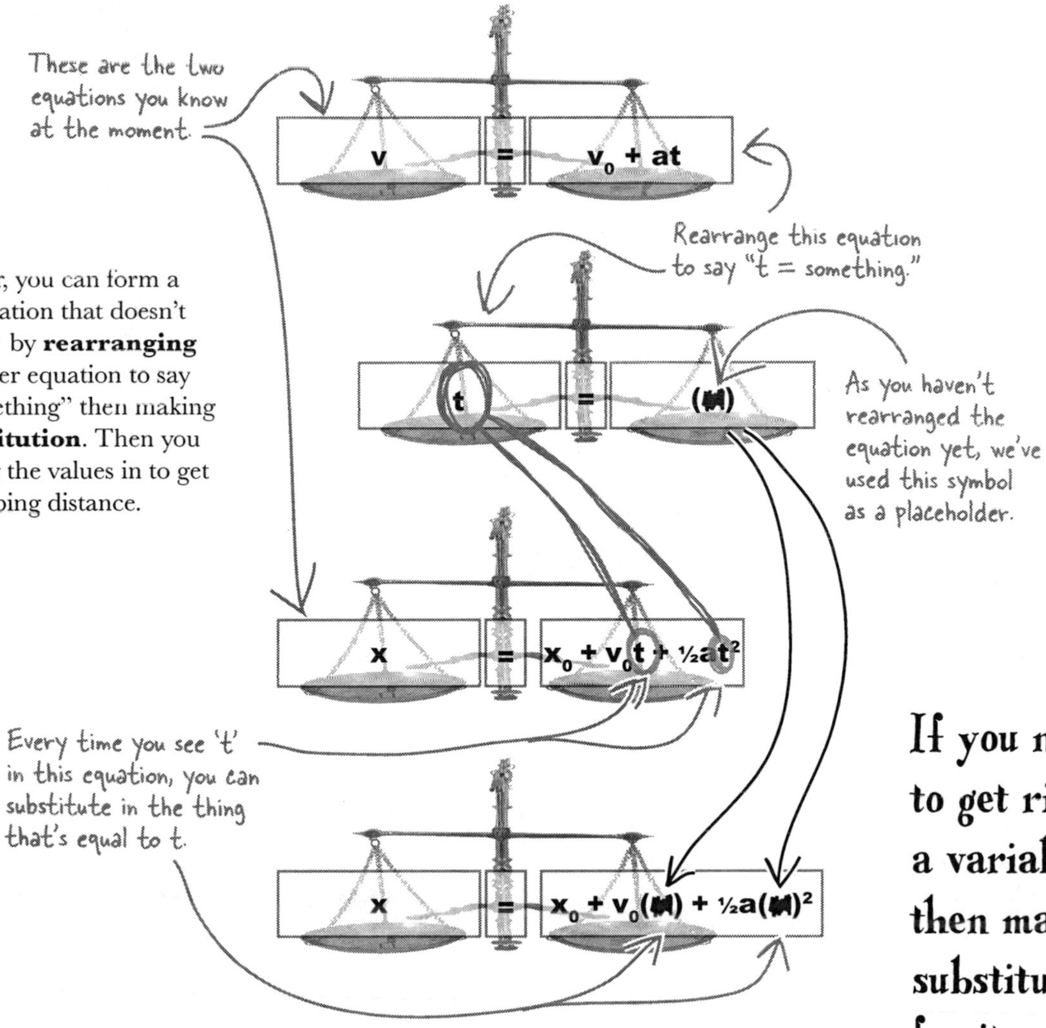

If you need to get rid of a variable, then make a substitution for it.

Sharpen your pencil

Rearrange the equation $\mathbf{v} = \mathbf{v}_0 + \mathbf{a}t$ so that you can substitute for t in the equation $\mathbf{x} = \mathbf{x}_0 + \mathbf{v}_0 t + \frac{1}{2}\mathbf{a}t^2$ and end up with an equation for $\mathbf{x}$ in terms of $\mathbf{v}_0$, $\mathbf{v}$, and $\mathbf{a}$.

You may find it helpful if you use **parentheses** (also called brackets) when you make the substitution, to keep everything that's equal to t together.

We're only asking you to make the substitution at the moment. You don't need to simplify the equation once you've substituted for t – we'll do that next.

Sharpen your pencil Solution

Rearrange the equation $v = v_0 + at$ so that you can substitute for t in the equation $x = x_0 + v_0t + \frac{1}{2}at^2$ and end up with an equation for x in terms of v_0, v, and a.

You may find it helpful if you use **parentheses** (also called brackets) when you make the substitution, to keep everything that's equal to t together.

I have two equations to rearrange, then substitute to get rid of t:

Remember to EXPLAIN what you're doing at each stage.

$$x = x_0 + v_0t + \frac{1}{2}at^2 \quad (1)$$

$$v = v_0 + at \quad (2)$$

If you number your equations, it makes it easier for you to refer to them in your explanations.

Rearrange (2) to say "t = something" then substitute it into (1).

$$at = v - v_0$$

$$t = \frac{v - v_0}{a} \quad (2')$$

Number this equation 2' to show it's a rearranged version of 2, not an entirely new equation.

Substitute (2') into (1).

$$x = x_0 + v_0\left(\frac{v - v_0}{a}\right) + \frac{1}{2}a\left(\frac{v - v_0}{a}\right)^2$$

Put this in parentheses to make it clear that EVERYTHING in the parentheses is to be multiplied by the other part of the term.

Remember to include the ^{2} part, as the t you replaced was squared.

That's a very complicated-looking equation. Can we try to **simplify** it a bit by **multiplying out the parentheses**?

If you're asked to work out an equation, always give it in its most simple form.

Often when you do a substitution, you're left with a complicated-looking equation with some **parentheses** in it. You can make life a lot easier for yourself by multiplying out the parentheses and seeing if some of the terms in the equation **cancel** by dividing out or adding to zero.

You're going to spend the next few pages making this ugly equation more clear and simple so that you're less likely to make mistakes when you use it in the future.

Clear, simple equations are nicer to work with than ugly, complicated equations.

Multiply out the parentheses in your equation

You need to know how to deal with an equation where you have stuff inside parentheses that you need to multiply by something that's outside the parentheses.

For example, $a(b + c) = ab + ac$

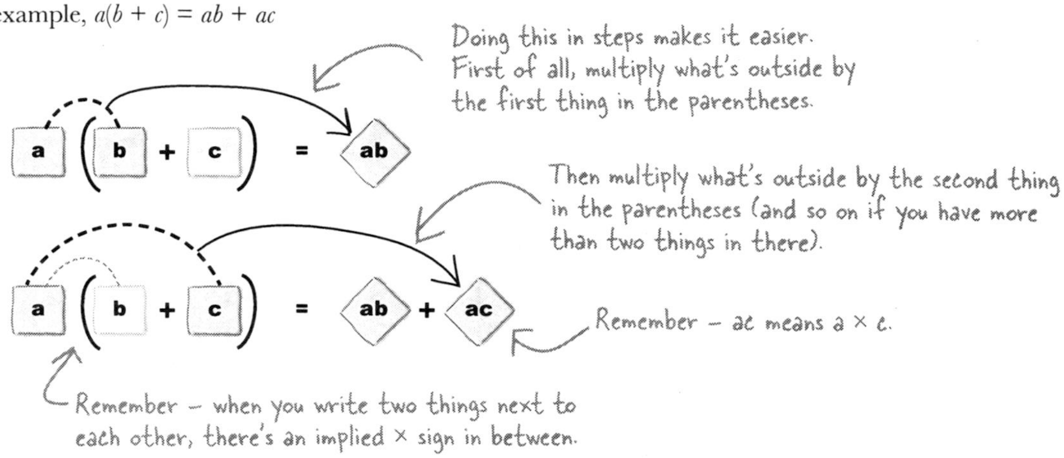

You can sort out one of the terms on the right hand side like this

The first term on the right hand side of your equation is:

$$\mathbf{v}_0\left(\frac{\mathbf{v} - \mathbf{v}_0}{\mathbf{a}}\right)$$

When you write two things next to each other like this, there's an implied × sign in between.

Everything **inside** the parentheses needs to be multiplied by $\mathbf{v}_0$, which is **outside** the parentheses.

Sharpen your pencil

Multiply out the parentheses for this term on the right hand side of your equation.

$$x = x_0 + v_0\left(\frac{v - v_0}{a}\right) + \tfrac{1}{2}a\left(\frac{v - v_0}{a}\right)^2$$

You can leave the terms we've greyed out as they are for the moment.

Sharpen your pencil Solution

Multiply out the parentheses for the first term on the right hand side of your equation.

$$x = x_0 + v_0\left(\frac{v - v_0}{a}\right) + \frac{1}{2}a\left(\frac{v - v_0}{a}\right)^2 \Rightarrow x = x_0 + \frac{v_0 v - v_0^2}{a} + \frac{1}{2}a\left(\frac{v - v_0}{a}\right)^2$$

When you multiply a fraction by a number that's not a fraction, you only multiply the bit on the top of the fraction. So the bit on the bottom stays as 'a,' and doesn't become '$v_0 a$.'

You have two sets of parentheses multiplied together

The other nasty-looking term on the right hand side of your equation involves something inside parentheses squared. If you square something, it means you multiply it by itself.

For example, if you have $(a + b)^2$, it's the same as $(a + b)(a + b)$. You need to multiply everything in the first set of parentheses by everything in the second set of parentheses. This gives you $a^2 + ab + ab + b^2$, which simplifies to $a^2 + 2ab + b^2$ when you add the two lots of ab together.

$$(a + b)(a + b) = a^2$$

Doing this in steps makes it easier. First of all, multiply the first thing in the first bracket by the first thing in the second bracket.

$$(a + b)(a + b) = a^2 + ab$$

Then multiply the first thing in the first bracket by the second thing in the second bracket

$$(a + b)(a + b) = a^2 + ab + ab$$

Then do the same with the second thing in the first bracket.

$$(a + b)(a + b) = a^2 + ab + ab + b^2$$

$$(a + b)(a + b) = a^2 + 2ab + b^2$$

You can simplify your answer a bit by adding the two lots of ab together.

Multiply every term in the second set of parentheses by every term in the first set of parentheses, one term at a time.

Then you can figure out your second term on the right hand side

The second term on the right hand side of your equation is:

$$\tfrac{1}{2}\mathbf{a}\left(\frac{\mathbf{v} - \mathbf{v}_0}{\mathbf{a}}\right)^2$$

Because the stuff in the parentheses is squared, this is the same as writing

$$\tfrac{1}{2}\mathbf{a}\left(\frac{\mathbf{v} - \mathbf{v}_0}{\mathbf{a}}\right)\left(\frac{\mathbf{v} - \mathbf{v}_0}{\mathbf{a}}\right)$$

Everything in the second set of parentheses needs to be multiplied by **everything in the first set of parentheses**, like in the example on the opposite page.

Do the top of the fractions first. Multiply everything on the top by everything on the top. Then do the bottom of the fractions. Multiply everything on the bottom by everything on the bottom.

Sharpen your pencil

Multiply out the parentheses for the second term on the right hand side of your equation.

It's probably easiest to do the squared part inside the parentheses first (similar to the example on the opposite page), then multiply everything through by ½**a**, which is outside the parentheses.

$$x = x_0 + \frac{v_0 v - v_0^2}{a} + \tfrac{1}{2}a\left(\frac{v - v_0}{a}\right)^2$$

It's easiest to write out the thing in the parentheses × itself first, so you can multiply out the parentheses more easily.

You can leave the terms we've greyed out as they are for the moment.

Sharpen your pencil Solution

Multiply out the parentheses for the second term on the right hand side of your equation.

It's probably easiest to do the squared part inside the parentheses first (similar to the example on the opposite page), then multiply everything through by ½*a*, which is outside the parentheses.

$$x = x_0 + \frac{v_0 v - v_0^2}{a} + \tfrac{1}{2}a\left(\frac{v - v_0}{a}\right)^2$$

It's easiest to write out the thing in the parentheses × itself like this, so you can multiply out the parentheses more easily.

$$x = x_0 + \frac{v_0 v - v_0^2}{a} + \tfrac{1}{2}a\left(\frac{v - v_0}{a}\right)\left(\frac{v - v_0}{a}\right)$$

negative × negative = positive

so $(-v_0) \times (-v_0) = v_0^2$

$$x = x_0 + \frac{v_0 v - v_0^2}{a} + \tfrac{1}{2}a\left(\frac{v^2 - 2vv_0 + v_0^2}{a^2}\right)$$

On the bottom of the fraction, $a \times a = a^2$

Now you have to multiply everything inside the brackets by ½a ...

$$x = x_0 + \frac{v_0 v - v_0^2}{a} + \frac{\tfrac{1}{2}v^2 - vv_0 + \tfrac{1}{2}v_0^2}{a}$$

... but the a on the top and the a^2 on the bottom cancel to leave everything divided by a.

You can still pass physics, but algebra is important too.

In your exam you get points for **understanding physics concepts** - but you also get points for being able to **explain** physics using **graphs** and **equations**.

For much of your course, you won't need to do that much algebra. But if you need to **rearrange** equations and make **substitutions** to get a solution, you won't get full credit if your algebra is a bit hazy - though you can probably score enough points to pass if you can explain **how** you would do the question.

Your priority is definitely understanding the physics. There aren't that many patches of nasty algebra in the rest of this book, so hang in there!

Where you're at with your new equation

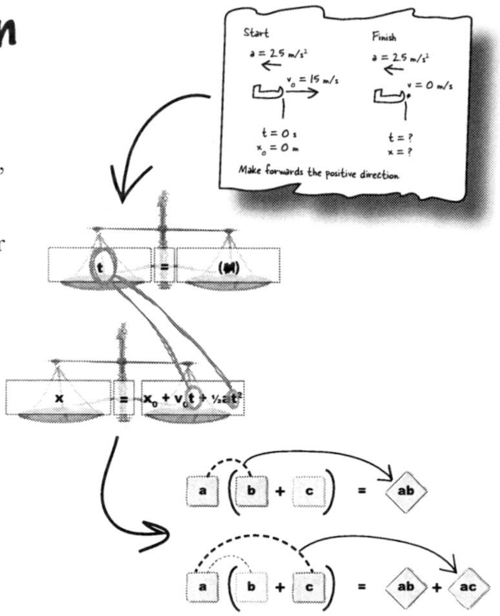

You're working out an **equation** that'll give you the stopping distance for the Dingo's new rocket-powered sled given $\mathbf{v}_0$, its initial velocity. However, the only equation you had for **x**, the displacement, included *t*, the time it would take to stop. But you don't know what *t* is.

You're already most of the way through working out a new equation for **x** that doesn't involve *t* by **rearranging** some equations you already knew and **substituting** in for the variable *t* to get rid of it.

You want the equation to be as clear and simple as possible so that you're less likely to make mistakes when you use it. You just multiplied out the parentheses to try to simplify the equation. But it doesn't look particularly simple at the moment!

You need to simplify your equation by grouping the terms

Now that you've multiplied out the parentheses, your equation has a lot of terms in it! If you **group** together all the terms that are the same letter (or letters multiplied together), you'll be able to **simplify** your equation.

For example, if you have the equation $a = b + c - b - 2c$, you have b and $-b$ on the right hand side. When you group them together, they become $b - b = 0$. You also have c and $-2c$. When you group them together, they become $c - 2c = -c$

Written out, the work looks like:

$$a = b + c - b - 2c$$

$$a = b - b + c - 2c$$

$$a = -c$$

If you do something similar with the equation for the hovercraft's stopping distance, it'll be a lot clearer to work with and less prone to error. We don't want the Dingo to get hurt when he only wants to invite the Emu to his birthday party.

Sharpen your pencil

Group together the similar terms on the right hand side of your equation, and simplify it down.

(We've already started by joining together the terms that were all being divided by a).

$$x = x_0 + \frac{v_0v - v_0^2 + ½v^2 - vv_0 + ½v_0^2}{a}$$

Sharpen your pencil Solution

Group together the similar terms on the right hand side of your equation, and simplify it down.

(We've already started by joining together the terms that were all being divided by a).

$$x = x_0 + \frac{v_0 v - v_0^2 + 1/2v^2 - vv_0 + 1/2v_0^2}{a}$$

$$x = x_0 + \frac{v_0 v - vv_0 + 1/2v^2 - v_0^2 + 1/2v_0^2}{a}$$

$$x = x_0 + \frac{1/2v^2 - 1/2v_0^2}{a}$$

$$x = x_0 + \frac{v^2 - v_0^2}{2a}$$

We've spaced the lines of the answer out so that the annotations can fit!

Did you spot that vv_0 and $v_0 v$ are just the same thing written in a different order?

On this line, the similar terms are grouped together.

These two terms add up to zero and cancel each other out.

This is what happens when you group together the v_0^2 terms.

It's nicer to write $1/2v^2 - 1/2v_0^2$ than it is to write $-1/2v_0^2 + 1/2v^2$.

This is just a neater way of writing the same thing that you have in the line above.

This equation is usually rearranged on equation tables to say:

$v^2 = v_0^2 + 2a(x - x_0)$

Relax

You won't need to do all that again!

We've been working out this key equation as an opportunity to practice the **kind of math** you'll come across while you're doing some parts of physics. Now that you know the equation, you can use it time and time again - either from memory (in your multiple choice paper) or by looking it up on your equation table (in the free response section).

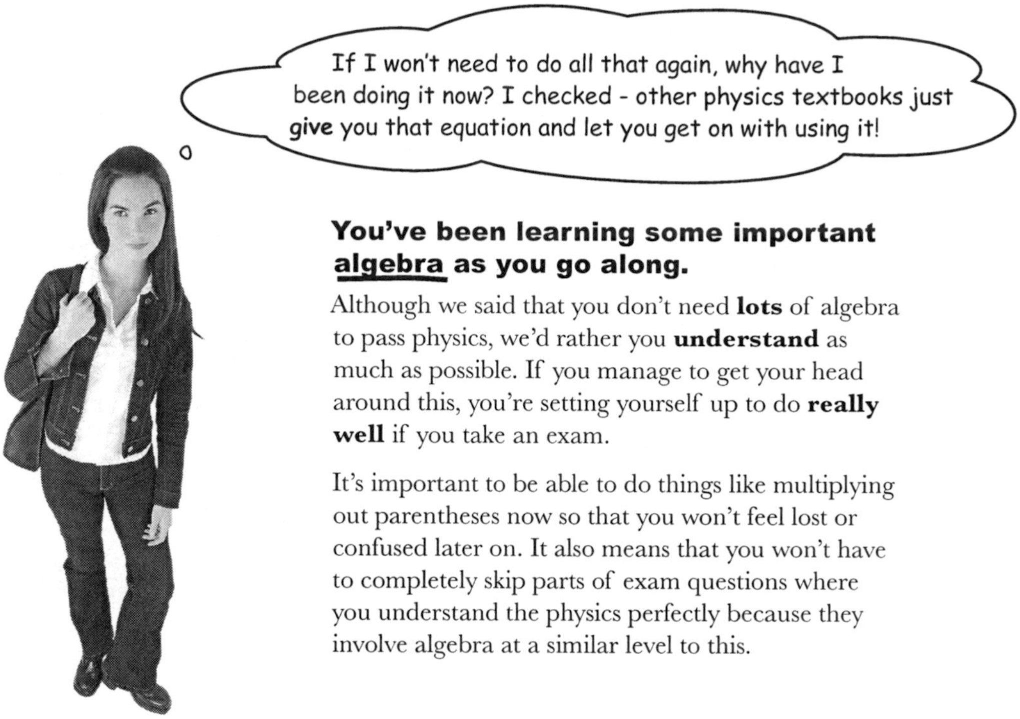

You've been learning some important algebra as you go along.

Although we said that you don't need **lots** of algebra to pass physics, we'd rather you **understand** as much as possible. If you manage to get your head around this, you're setting yourself up to do **really well** if you take an exam.

It's important to be able to do things like multiplying out parentheses now so that you won't feel lost or confused later on. It also means that you won't have to completely skip parts of exam questions where you understand the physics perfectly because they involve algebra at a similar level to this.

You can use your new equation to work out the stopping distance

You've worked out an equation you can use to calculate the stopping distance of the hovercraft for the Dingo.

$$x = x_0 + \frac{v^2 - v_0^2}{2a}$$

This is the sketch of the problem that you drew before.

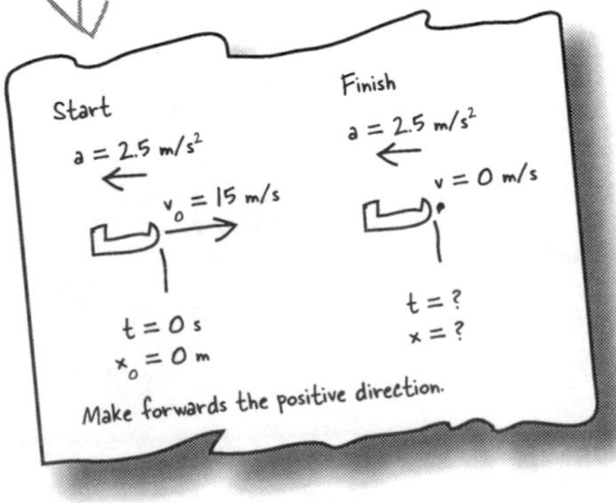

Sharpen your pencil

A rocket-powered hovercraft is traveling at 15 m/s. When the brakes are applied, it decelerates at a rate of 2.5 m/s^2. What is its stopping distance?

Sharpen your pencil Solution

A rocket-powered hovercraft is traveling at 15 m/s. When the brakes are applied, it decelerates at a rate of 2.5 m/s². What is its stopping distance?

$$x = x_0 + \frac{v^2 - v_0^2}{2a} \Rightarrow x = 0 + \frac{0^2 - 15^2}{2 \times (-2.5)}$$

$$x = 45 \text{ m (2 sd)}$$

The stopping distance is 45 meters (2 sd).

$$x = x_0 + \frac{v^2 - v_0^2}{2a}$$

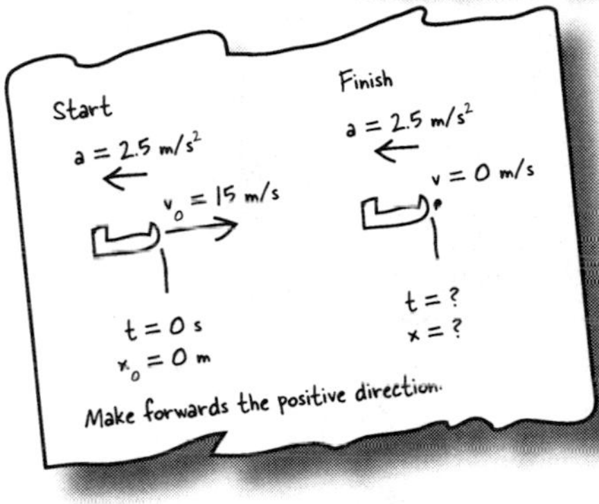

There are THREE key equations you can use when there's constant acceleration

As well as a stopping distance to pass onto the Dingo, you now know the **three key equations** that will enable you to deal with **any** problem where the acceleration is constant.

Falling things, launched things, rocket hovercrafts, cars, boats - you name it.

Now **that's a real superpower!**

$$x = x_0 + \frac{v^2 - v_0^2}{2a}$$

This is the equation you just worked out. it's sometimes called the "no time" equation because the variable 't' doesn't appear in the equation.

This is exactly the same equation, but rearranged so that there are no fractions in it. We've mentioned it here because it's the version of the equation you'll find on equation sheets.

Equations of motion

The three key equations for something with constant acceleration.

$$v = v_0 + at$$

$$x = x_0 + v_0 t + \frac{1}{2}at^2$$

$$v^2 = v_0^2 + 2a(x - x_0)$$

So the bottom line with the math stuff is that if I can **use** these equations, I'll do **OK**. But if I can rearrange, substitute, multiply out parentheses, and simplify equations, I can do even better?

That's right - math is just another tool to help you get better at physics.

Most physics books assume you can already do algebra to use the equations they give to you ready-baked. This book is different. You've gradually been introduced to a lot of algebra **in the context of physics** so that you can use it as a tool to help you **understand** physics the best you can.

If you're not so sure of some of the math, you can still do OK, but it's up to you to **practice** anything you initially find difficult until you get better at it.

there are no Dumb Questions

Q: So am I supposed to memorize all of these equations? That's an awful lot! I thought this was supposed to be about understanding, not memorization!

A: The first equation, $\mathbf{v} = \mathbf{v}_0 + \mathbf{a}t$, says that your new velocity is the same as your old velocity, plus the effect of your acceleration. You don't care about $\mathbf{x}_0$ or $\mathbf{x}$.

The second equation, $\mathbf{x} = \mathbf{x}_0 + \mathbf{v}_0 t + \frac{1}{2}\mathbf{a}t^2$, says that your new displacement depends on your old displacement, your initial velocity and your acceleration, as well as the length of time you've been going for. You don't care about **v**.

The third equation, $\mathbf{v}^2 = \mathbf{v}_0^2 + 2\mathbf{a}(\mathbf{x}-\mathbf{x}_0)$, is the one you just worked out. It gives you your final velocity when you don't know *t*, the time you're traveling for.

Or don't care about t!

Q: So if the best way to learn equations is to do lots and lots of problems, how come Head First Physics doesn't have hundreds of examples at the end of each chapter, like most other physics books do?

A: One reason is that you're learning and doing problems throughout each chapter.

This book is about trying things out while you're learning. You use the concepts as you go along so that you really understand the physics, rather than the 'read along and nod' method that most textbooks use. There are plenty of resources with practice questions out there - do spend time working through lots of problems to reinforce what you're learning here.

Q: So if I keep a lookout on the Head First website, will there be something up there to help me practice?

A: Yes, we'll be producing some online resources to go with the book.

OK, here we go ...

The rocket-powered hovercraft is a great success...
Stopping distances aren't much good if you don't look where you're going.
Splat!
Cage
Dingo
Top of cliff 7 m

You need to work out the launch velocity that gets the Dingo out of the Grand Canyon!

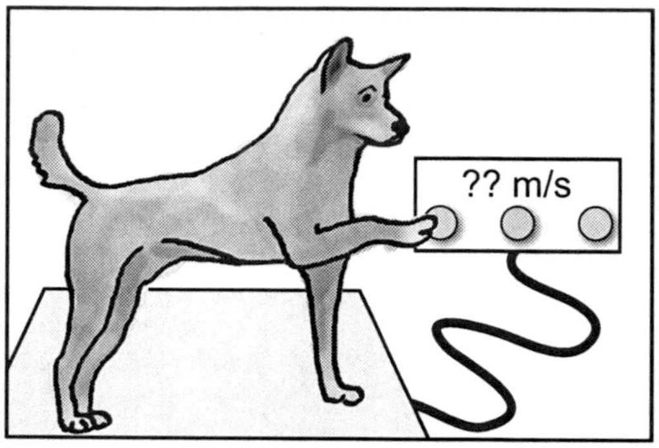

The Dingo's fallen over a cliff, but he had a soft splash landing. Fortunately, he still has his ACME launcher. And a new idea! If he launches himself into the air so that the top of his flight is exactly level with the top of the cliff, he should be able to pass the Emu the party invitation - but in a situation where the Emu doesn't feel scared.

The thing is that the Dingo doesn't know what what his launch **velocity** should be. If he sets the launch velocity too low, he won't make it up to the edge. If he sets the launch velocity too high, he'll still be going up when he reaches the edge and might not have time to pass on the invitation.

What should the Dingo set as the launch velocity this time?

Sharpen your pencil

Do as much of this as you can from memory, then turn back to page 314 to copy them down.

The Dingo is stuck at the bottom of the cliff with a launcher. If the cliff is 7.00 m high at this point, what launch speed will mean that the top of his flight is at the top of the cliff?

a. Start with a sketch! Draw everything you already know about.

b. Write down your three key equations for doing these kinds of problems. Next to each variable in each equation, put a ? if you want to find it out, a tick if you know it, and a cross if you don't know it.

This is an important problem-solving skill.

c. Do you think you can do this problem straight off, or do you need some extra information?

Sharpen your pencil Solution

Do as much of this as you can from memory, then turn back to page 314 to copy them down.

The Dingo is stuck at the bottom of the cliff with a launcher. If the cliff is 7.00 m high at this point, what launch speed will mean that the top of his flight is at the top of the cliff?

a. Start with a sketch! Draw everything you already know about.

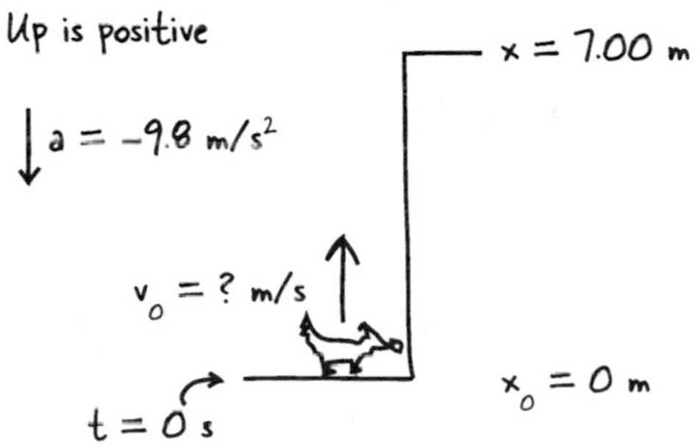

b. Write down your three key equations for doing these kinds of problems. Next to each variable in each equation, put a ? if you want to find it out, a tick if you know it, and a cross if you don't know it.

This is an important problem-solving skill.

$$x = x_0 + v_0 t + \tfrac{1}{2}at^2$$
(x ✓, x_0 ✓, v_0 ?, t ✗, a ✓, t^2 ✗)

$$v = v_0 + at$$
(v ✗, v_0 ?, a ✓, t ✗)

$$v^2 = v_0^2 + 2a(x - x_0)$$
(v ✗, v_0 ?, a ✓, $(x - x_0)$ ✓)

If you don't know which equation to use, you should always have a go at doing this.

c. Do you think you can do this problem straight off, or do you need some extra information?

All of the equations have something else in them that I don't know (either v or t, or both!), as well as v_0 (which is what I want to find out). So I need some extra information to do the problem.

Wouldn't it be dreamy if I could work out v or t somehow, so I could use the equations to get v_0. But I know it's just a fantasy ...

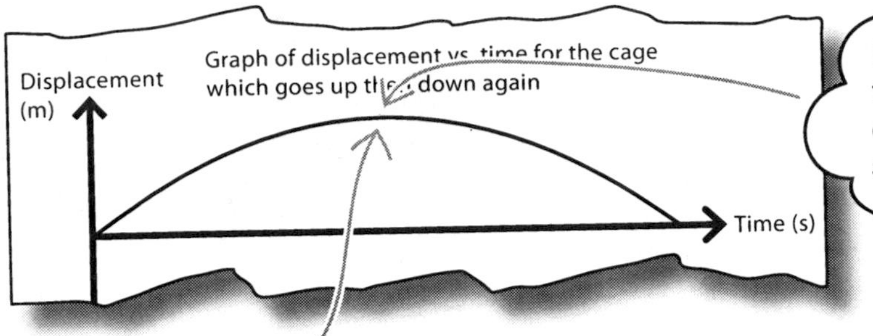

Slope of displacement-time graph is zero, so velocity MUST be zero.

Sometimes you'll need to spot a 'special point.'

Don't settle just for the information you're given in a problem. Start with a sketch. Be the Dingo. **Spot the 'special point'**!

You've just realized that the top of something's flight is a special point where it's stopped going up but hasn't quite started going down again. So the velocity is zero there.

This is a value you can use in your equations to help you work out other things.

Sharpen your pencil

Now that you've spotted the special point, use your extra information that **v** = 0 at the top of the Dingo's flight together with what you did on the opposite page to calculate what his launch velocity should be.

You should add v = 0 to your sketch, and tick 'v' every time you see it in an equation.

Sharpen your pencil Solution

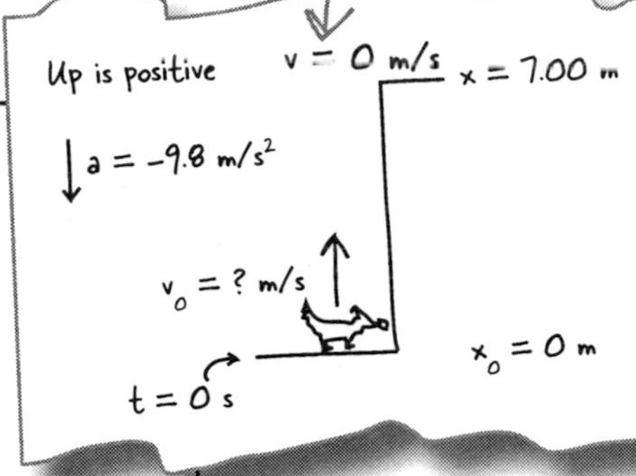

Now that you've spotted the special point, use your extra information that v = 0 at the top of the Dingo's flight together with what you did on the opposite page to launch him out of the Grand Canyon.

$$v^2 = v_0^2 + 2a(x - x_0)$$

v_0 is now the only unknown in this equation.

Extra information: v = 0 m/s at the top.

Rearrange to say "v_0 = something"

$$v_0^2 = v^2 - 2a(x - x_0)$$

This works out as negative × negative × positive = positive

$$v_0 = \sqrt{v^2 - 2a(x - x_0)} = \sqrt{0^2 - 2 \times (-9.8) \times (7.00 - 0)} = \sqrt{137.2}$$

$$v_0 = 11.7 \text{ m/s (3 sd)}$$

The Dingo needs to be launched at 11.7 m/s (3 sd).

Extra information: you know what v is.

$$x = x_0 + v_0 t + \tfrac{1}{2}at^2$$

$$v = v_0 + at$$

$$v^2 = v_0^2 + 2a(x - x_0)$$

The launch velocity's right!

You just used the fact that **v** = 0 m/s at the top of the cliff to work out that the Dingo's launch velocity should be 11.7 m/s.

I wanna know the time it takes for me to go up then back down to the bottom of the cliff. Is it long enough for my safety thingy to inflate?

While he's in the air, a safe landing area inflates.

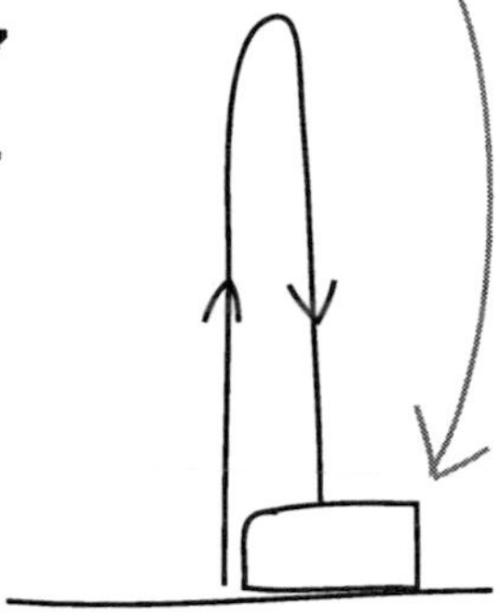

But the Dingo doesn't like getting wet, and wants a better plan for landing than splashing into the river again. He has an ACME inflatable landing area and wants to press its inflate button at the same time as launching himself up in the air.

The landing area takes 1.00 s to inflate. How long will the Dingo be in the air for? Will the landing area have enough **time** to inflate before he comes back down?

So we need to work out the **time** the Dingo will be in the air for. That shouldn't be too bad.

Jim: Yeah, we already know a lot of values! $\mathbf{x}_0$ and $\mathbf{x}$ will both be zero (as he's starting and finishing at the bottom of the canyon). And $\mathbf{v}_0 = 11.7$ m/s.

Joe: Not forgetting $\mathbf{a} = -9.8$ m/s^2. I think we know more values right now than we've done for any other problem!

Frank: So which equation can we use? We don't know what v is, so we can't use either of the equations with v in them.

Jim: Well, that leaves $\mathbf{x} = \mathbf{x}_0 + \mathbf{v}_0 t + \frac{1}{2}\mathbf{a}t^2$, which should be cool. We know $\mathbf{x}$, $\mathbf{x}_0$, $\mathbf{v}_0$, and $\mathbf{a}$ ... that leaves only t, which is what we want to calculate!

Joe: One equation, one unknown - sounds ideal!

Frank: So I guess we rearrange the equation so that it says "t = something."

Jim: Yeah, let's get on with it!

Important problem-solving skill!

Write down your equations, and tick or cross the variables you know or don't know.

Sharpen your pencil

a. Try rearranging the equation $\mathbf{x} = \mathbf{x}_0 + \mathbf{v}_0 t + \frac{1}{2}\mathbf{a}t^2$ to say "t = something," so you can use it to work out the time it takes the Dingo to go up and back down again.

b. Write down your thoughts about whether this idea will work or not.

Sharpen your pencil Solution

a. Try rearranging the equation $\mathbf{x} = \mathbf{x}_0 + \mathbf{v}_0 t + \frac{1}{2}\mathbf{a}t^2$ to say "t = something," so you can use it to work out the time it takes the Dingo to go up and back down again.

$$x = x_0 + v_0 t + \tfrac{1}{2}at^2$$

Try to get this t on its own to say "t = something"

$$v_0 t = x - x_0 - \tfrac{1}{2}at^2$$

$$t = \frac{x - x_0 - \tfrac{1}{2}at^2}{v_0}$$

But now there's a t^2 over here, so that doesn't work.

b. Write down your thoughts about whether this is a good idea or not.

This isn't going to work. If you try to rearrange to say "t = something," there's a t^2 on the other side. And if you get the t^2 on its own to take a square root, there'll still be the t on the other side. You can't simplify the equation enough to say "t = something."

Strictly speaking, this is possible if you use something called the quadratic formula. If you already know how to do this, then feel free to use this method. But if you've never heard of the quadratic formula before, don't worry. You're about to learn a much less complicated way ...

You need to find another way of doing this problem

Your equation $\mathbf{x} = \mathbf{x}_0 + \mathbf{v}_0 t + \frac{1}{2}\mathbf{a}t^2$ contains **two terms with *t* in them**, $\mathbf{v}_0 t$ and $\frac{1}{2}\mathbf{a}t^2$. Because one of the terms has t in it, and the other has t^2 in it, there's no easy way to rearrange your equation to say "t = something" because the t and t^2 won't cancel by adding to zero.

However, if either $\mathbf{v}_0 = 0$ or $\mathbf{a} = 0$, then one of these terms would **disappear**. This means you'd be able to rearrange the equation to say "t = something" and use it to calculate the value of t.

If any variable that's multiplying a term is zero, then the whole term is zero and disappears.

$$x = x_0 + v_0 t + \tfrac{1}{2}at^2$$

If $v_0 = 0$, the equation becomes $x = x_0 + \frac{1}{2}at^2$

If $a = 0$, the equation becomes $x = x_0 + v_0 t$

What would happen to your equation if different variables were zero? Would this make the equation easier to solve?

If $\mathbf{a} = 0$, then the equation becomes $\mathbf{x} = \mathbf{x}_0 + \mathbf{v}_0 t$, which is the equation you worked out before for something that moves with a constant velocity without accelerating. But the acceleration isn't zero in this scenario.

But if $\mathbf{v_0} = \mathbf{0}$, then the equation would simplify to $\mathbf{x} = \mathbf{x}_0 + \frac{1}{2}\mathbf{a}t^2$, which you can rearrange to say "t = something." That's incredibly useful!

If only there was a way of reframing the problem so that $\mathbf{v}_0 = 0$, then all of this would be possible ...

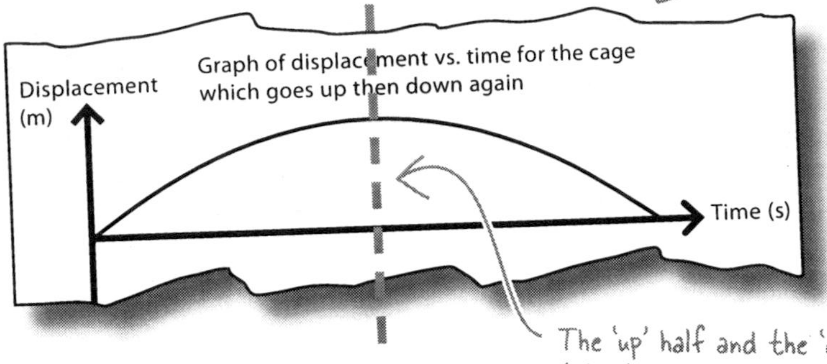

The 'up' half and the 'down' half take the same amount of time

Sharpen your pencil

A dingo is launched with an initial velocity of 11.7 m/s upwards. The top of his flight path is 7.00 m from the level he started at.

a. Use **symmetry** to make a new problem where $\mathbf{v}_0 = 0$. This will enable you to rearrange the equation $\mathbf{x} = \mathbf{x}_0 + \mathbf{v}_0 t + \frac{1}{2}\mathbf{a}t^2$ to say "t = something." Use this equation to calculate the time it takes for the Dingo to return to the bottom of the cliff.

You're creating a new problem, so start with a new sketch.

b. The Dingo's safety device takes 1.00 s to inflate. Will the safety device have inflated before the Dingo lands?

Look out for <u>symmetry</u> that might make a hard problem easier ...

Sharpen your pencil Solution

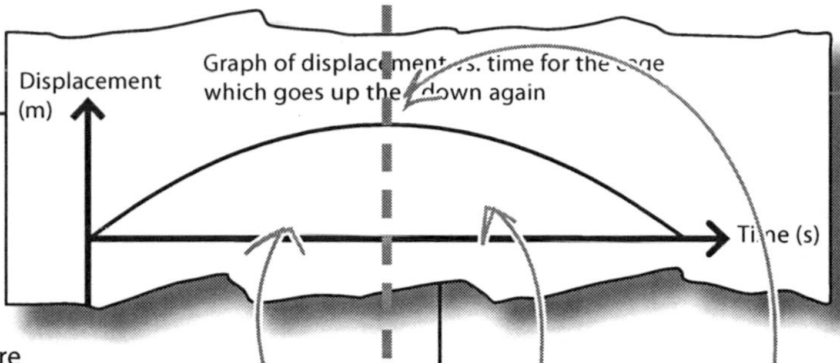

A dingo is launched with an initial velocity of 11.7 m/s upwards. The top of his flight path is 7.00 m from the level he started at.

a. Use **symmetry** to make a new problem where $\mathbf{v}_0 = 0$. This will enable you to rearrange the equation $\mathbf{x} = \mathbf{x}_0 + \mathbf{v}_0 t + \frac{1}{2}\mathbf{a}t^2$ to say "t = something." Use this equation to calculate the time it takes for the Dingo to return to the bottom of the cliff.

Work out the time it takes him to fall 7.00 m, then double it to get the time it takes him to go up then down.

Down is positive $v_0 = 0$ m/s

$x_0 = 0$ m, $t = 0$ s

$\downarrow a = 9.8$ m/s²

Now that you're ONLY dealing with vectors pointing downwards, you can make down the positive direction so that the math is easier.

$t = ?$ s, $x = 7.00$ m

$$x = x_0 + v_0 t + \frac{1}{2}at^2$$ Rearrange this to say "t = something"

$v_0 = 0$ so this term is zero.

$$\frac{1}{2}at^2 = x - x_0$$

$$at^2 = 2(x - x_0)$$

Now there's only t^2 and no t, so this is an equation you can solve.

$$t = \sqrt{\frac{2(x - x_0)}{a}} = \sqrt{\frac{2(7.00 - 0)}{9.8}} = 1.20 \text{ s (3 sd)}$$

You get the same answer if you make "up" the positive direction, but there's more risk of making a mistake with minus signs.

b. The Dingo's safety device takes 1.00 s to inflate. Will the safety device have inflated before the Dingo lands?

Yes, the safety device inflates before the Dingo lands. Result!

The top of the flight path is exactly HALFWAY through the flight.

The time it takes to go up and down is DOUBLE the time it takes to fall from the top of the flight path.

If it's **symmetrical**, does that mean that you have the **same speed** when you hit the bottom as you did when you were launched, but in the opposite **direction**?

At a single height, a launched object has the same speed whether it's going up or down.

The Dingo left the ground with a speed of 11.7 m/s and a velocity of 11.7 m/s upwards. Since going up then down again is symmetrical, his speed at the bottom will also be 11.7 m/s, and his velocity will be 11.7 m/s downwards.

Also, at any displacement in his flight, his speed will be the same whether he's going up or down. This is another special **symmetry** thing that you can sometimes use to solve problems. If you start and end at the same height, then $\mathbf{v} = -\mathbf{v}_0$.

there are no Dumb Questions

Q: So why was I trying to find a special point where $v_0 = 0$? I wasn't quite sure about that bit.

A: You want to use the equation $\mathbf{x} = \mathbf{x}_0 + \mathbf{v}_0 t + \frac{1}{2}\mathbf{a}t^2$ to calculate t. But because it has both t and t^2 in it, you can't easily rearrange it to say "t = something."

But the term with the t in it is actually $\mathbf{v}_0 t$. So if you can reframe the problem into one where $\mathbf{v}_0$ is zero, you lose that term entirely and can solve the equation to find t.

Q: But couldn't I just use the quadratic formula to solve for t without having to do all of that symmetry stuff?

Don't worry about what this is if you don't already know. You won't need to use it if you can spot symmetry in problems!

A: If you already know how to solve quadratic equations like this one, that's fine. Feel free to use any method you understand.

But spotting the symmetry and working out how long it takes to fall, then doubling it is actually easier mathematically and a very useful shortcut to know about. Symmetry makes hard problems easier.

Q: But what if I'm in a situation where I can't make $v_0 = 0$? How do I solve that kind of equation then?

A: In that case, it's usually most straightforward to work out a value for **v**, so you can use the simpler equation $\mathbf{v} = \mathbf{v}_0 + \mathbf{a}t$. You'd do this using the other one of the three key equations, $\mathbf{v}^2 = \mathbf{v}_0^2 + 2\mathbf{a}(\mathbf{x} - \mathbf{x}_0)$.

Q: Ack. I have trouble remembering these equations.

A: Don't worry - it's on your equation table. And you'll naturally memorize it as you practice using it.

You'll also learn another approach to doing a problem like this in chapter 14, which you can use instead if you want to.

Symmetry makes hard problems easier.

The start of a beautiful friendship

Thanks to you, the Dingo has managed to deliver his party invitation. And the party marks the start of a beautiful friendship.

Question Clinic: The "Sketch a graph" or "Match a graph" Question

Sometimes you'll be asked to sketch a graph or match a sketched graph with an equation or story. The point is to show that you understand what's going on. Sketching a graph will usually be part of a free response question, and choosing graphs that match stories or scenarios is a standard style of multiple choice question.

ALWAYS START WITH A SKETCH!! Even if you're asked for a graph, sketch the situation to get your whole brain zoned in on the job.

Make a note of initial DIRECTIONS, and decide which direction to make positive.

2. A cage is propelled straight up from ground level by a launcher with initial velocity v_0. Sketch graphs of:

a. The displacement

b. The velocity

c. The acceleration

of the cage with respect to time, from the moment it's launched until it hits the ground again. State any assumptions you make.

Make a note of any initial VALUES, as you should include them on your graph.

You don't have to actually draw the graphs in this order. The easiest one is the acceleration, as it's a constant $-9.8\ m/s^2$. So start with that and work backwards.

This tells you where your sketch should end.

This tells you what to put on the horizontal axis.

This means get the SHAPE right. Don't plot only put on values you know/have been given.

Don't forget to do this bit, or you'll lose points!

If you're asked to sketch more than one graph (like displacement, velocity, and acceleration), it's usually best to work out which graph is easiest to draw, and start with that one. You can then work out what the others look like by thinking about values and slopes.

Question Clinic: The "Symmetry" and "Special points" Questions

Some of the questions you'll be asked about moving things will have one simple step. But in many, you'll have to spot symmetry to take a shortcut - or to make the problem solvable at all. You may also need to spot 'special points' that give you extra information because of symmetry - like **v** = 0 at the top of something's flight, or the fact that something's speed will be identical at the same height whether it's going up or coming down (though the direction of the velocity is different).

ALWAYS START WITH A SKETCH!!

It starts and finishes at the same HEIGHT, so it will have the same SPEED both times, just in opposite directions.

3. A cage is propelled straight up from ground level by a launcher with initial velocity v_0 = 10 m/s. If it goes up then comes back down again to ground level,

a. What is the value of its velocity just before it hits the ground

b. How long does it remain in the air for?

c. What is the maximum height it reaches?

This is asking for a time. If you already know the height, you could work out how long it takes to fall that far and double it.

But here you know v and v_0 already (as $v_0 = -v$), so you can use $v = v_0 + at$.

You know that the maximum height is a 'special point' where the velocity is zero and that it gets there in half the time it takes to go up and down..

DO ANOTHER SKETCH!! As this part of the problem has a DIFFERENT END POINT (the top of the flight path instead of ground level), some of your variables will have different values.

The secret is to keep calm and **start with a sketch**. Write down the three key equations, add in 'special points' to your sketch, then play with the terms and the variables in your equations until you know which of them to use to get the answer you want.

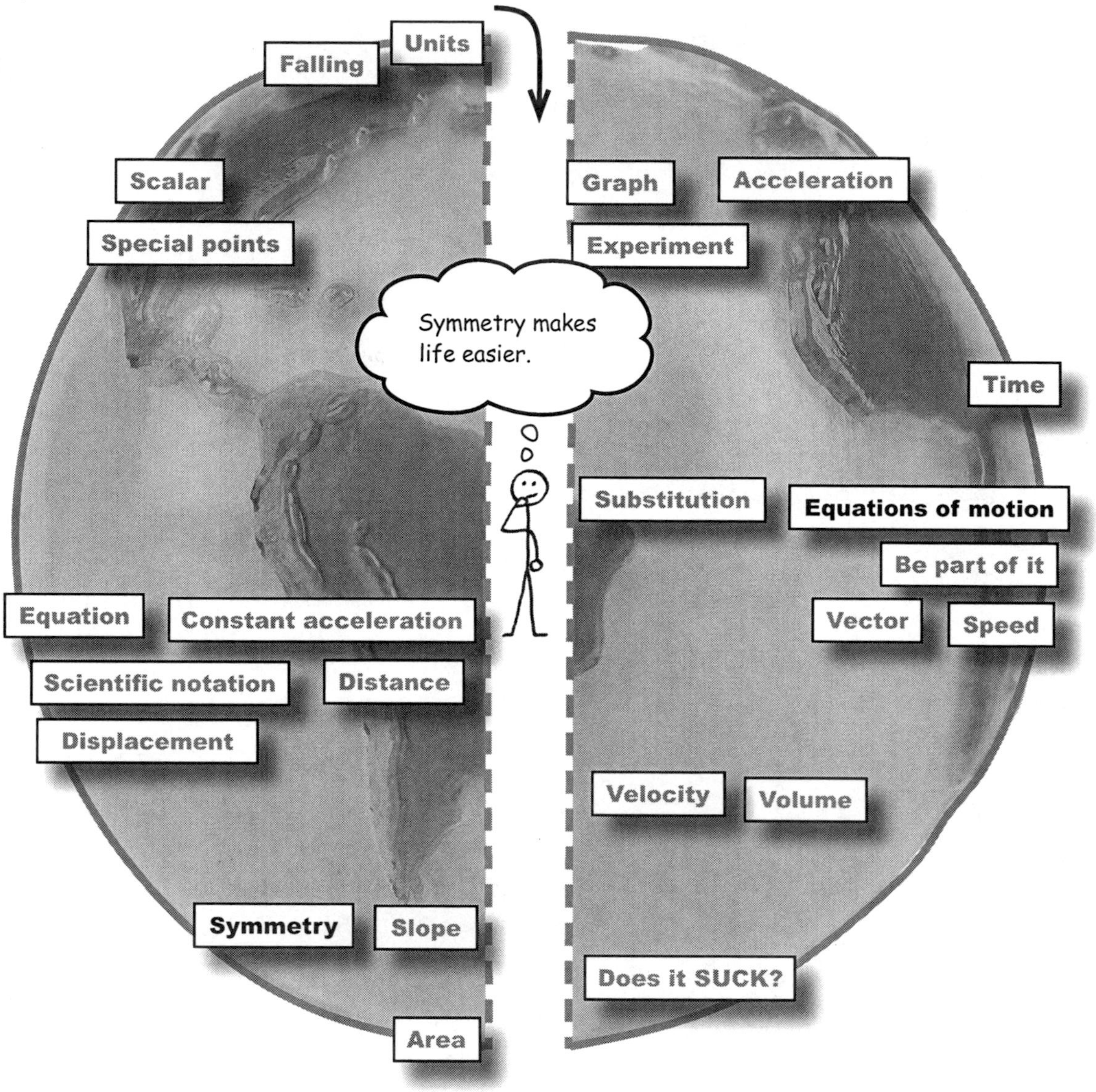

✓	**Equations of motion**	**Three equations that you can use to calculate the motion of an object that is moving with constant acceleration.**
✓	**Symmetry**	**In physics, the second half of something's motion sometimes mirrors the first. For example, going up into the air then back down again is symmetrical.**

Your Physics Toolbox

You've got Chapter 8 under your belt and added some equations, math techniques and problem-solving skills to your tool box.

Vectors: positive direction

When you're dealing with vectors that all lie along one line, you have to decide which direction is positive.

Usually, you'd make up positive so that your graphs come out the same way round as real life.

If all your vectors point down (e.g., if an object is falling), then making down positive helps to reduce errors with minus signs.

Equations of motion

The three key equations for something with constant acceleration.

$$v = v_0 + at$$

$$x = x_0 + v_0 t + \frac{1}{2}at^2$$

$$v^2 = v_0^2 + 2a(x - x_0)$$

Parentheses

When you're multiplying out parentheses, you multiply every term inside by every term outside:

$$a(b + c) = ab + ac$$

$$(a + b)(a + b) = a^2 + 2ab + b^2$$

Which equation of motion should I use?

If you don't know which equation of motion to use, write down all three of them. Tick the variable you know values for, cross the variables you don't know, and put a ? by the variable you want to find out. For example:

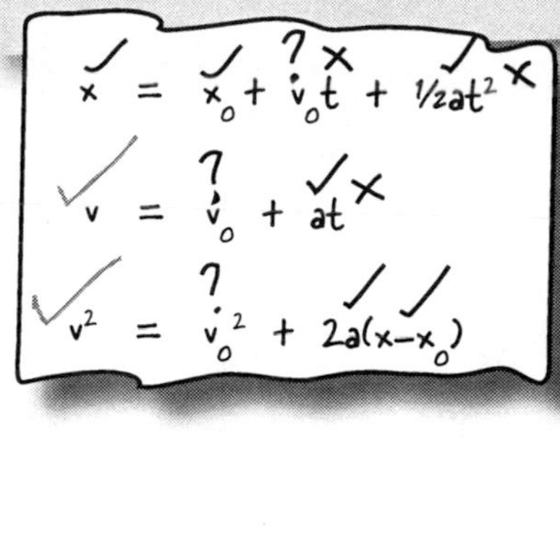

Special points

Special points help you to simplify and solve problems.

Vertical velocity = 0 at the top of an object's flight.

The object may also be moving horizontally. We'll talk about this in chapter 9 ...

Symmetry

When an object goes up then down, the up part and the down part of its motion both take the same TIME.

When something goes up then down, its VELOCITY has the same size at any one height regardless of whether the direction of the velocity is up or down.

9 triangles, trig and trajectories

Going two-dimensional

So you can deal with one dimension. But what about real life?

Real things don't just go up or down - they go sideways too! But never fear - you're about to gain a whole new bunch of **trigonometry** superpowers that'll see you spotting **right-angled triangles** wherever you go and using them to **reduce complicated-looking problems into simpler ones that you can already do**.

Camelot - we have a problem!

The Head First castle is in imminent danger! Back when it was built, the longest ladder available from Sieges-R-Us was 15.0 m long. So the castle was designed with a moat 15.0 m wide and a wall 15.0 m high, making it impossible for anyone to put a ladder from the edge of the moat to the top of the wall.

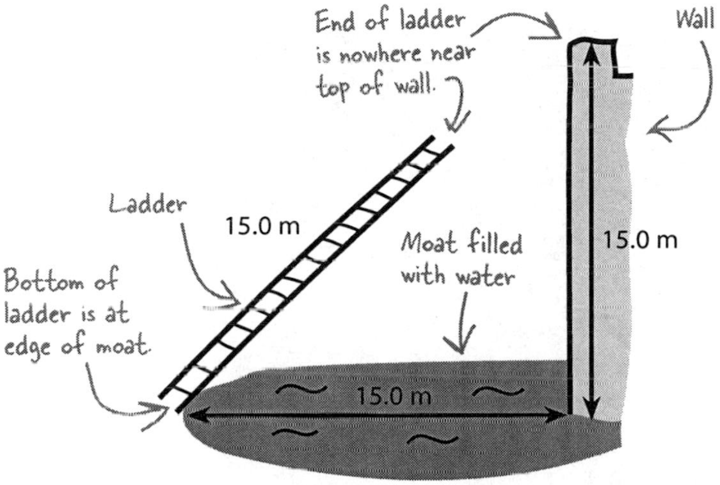

But the Sieges-R-Us website has just been updated with a new top of the range 25.0 m ladder. It's only a matter of time before someone comes to attack your castle armed with the new ladder, and your current defense system just isn't big enough...

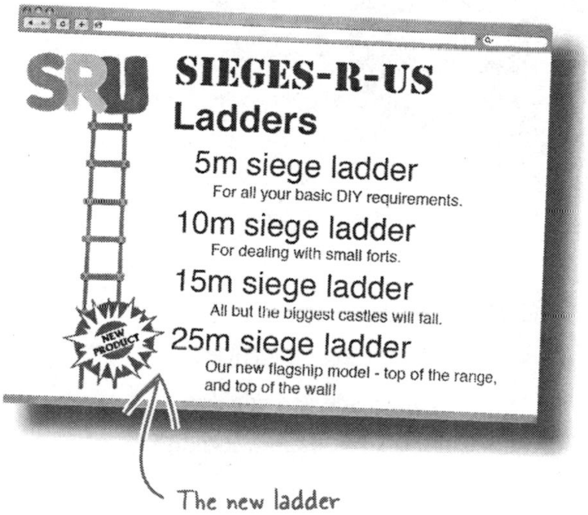

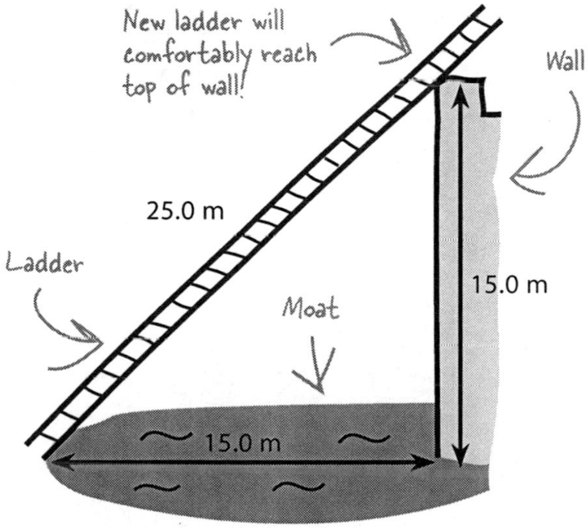

If you don't act quickly, someone will turn up with the new ladder, and you'll be toast. It's time to **design a new castle defense system**!

Sharpen your pencil

Check the box next to the idea you think is best.

Here are some ideas for a new castle defense system. Unfortunately, you don't have many spare stones lying around, only some shovels and food.

Write down at least one advantage and disadvantage of each idea, and check the box next to the idea you think is the best.

☐ **Coat the top of the wall with something slippery.**

Advantage(s)	Disadvantage(s)
....	....
....	....

☐ **Make the moat wider.**

Advantage(s)	Disadvantage(s)
....	....
....	....

☐ **Run away! Run away!**

Advantage(s)	Disadvantage(s)
....	....
....	....

☐ **Make the wall higher.**

Advantage(s)	Disadvantage(s)
....	....
....	....

☐ **Put a health and safety rep on the top of the wall to recite the working height directive repeatedly to anyone who gets higher than 2 m. Also to ask when their ladders were last inspected and if they have been trained in the proper use of ladders. And insist that they all wear safety harnesses, hard hats, ear defenders, goggles, gloves and toe protectors.**

Advantage(s)	Disadvantage(s)
....	....
....	....
....	....

Sharpen your pencil Solution

Here are some ideas for a new castle defense system. Unfortunately, you don't have many spare stones lying around, only shovels and food.

Write down at least one advantage and disadvantage of each idea, and check the box next to the idea you think is the best.

☐ **Coat the top of the wall with something slippery.**

Advantage(s)	Disadvantage(s)
Ladders will slip, it might delay them a bit.	Washes off in the rain, attracts cats, not a long-term solution.

☑ **Make the moat wider.**

Advantage(s)	Disadvantage(s)
I have a shovel to dig a wider moat.	I'm not sure how wide to make the moat.

It's a lot easier to dig a wider moat than it is to build a higher wall.

☐ **Run away! Run away!**

Advantage(s)	Disadvantage(s)
I won't be there when they get into the castle.	They'll get into the castle.

☐ **Make the wall higher.**

Advantage(s)	Disadvantage(s)
This would definitely keep them out of the castle ...	... but there's no stone available to build a higher wall.

☐ **Put a health and safety rep on the top of the wall to recite the working height directive repeatedly to anyone who gets higher than 2 m. Also to ask when their ladders were last inspected and if they have been trained in the proper use of ladders. And to Insist that they all wear safety harnesses, hard hats, ear defenders, goggles, gloves and toe protectors.**

Advantage(s)	Disadvantage(s)
The attackers might get bored and attack a different castle.	By wearing ear defenders, they can ignore him and continue attacking the castle anyway.

How wide should you make the moat?

The best way of defending the castle against the 25.0 m ladder is to make the moat wider. The moat is already 15.0 m wide—so how much wider do you need to make it?

You could try making the moat the same size as the ladder —25.0 m— so that the distance from the edge of the moat to the bottom of the wall is the same length as the ladder. That would make sure that attackers couldn't simultaneously put one end of the ladder at the edge of the moat and the other end on the top of the wall.

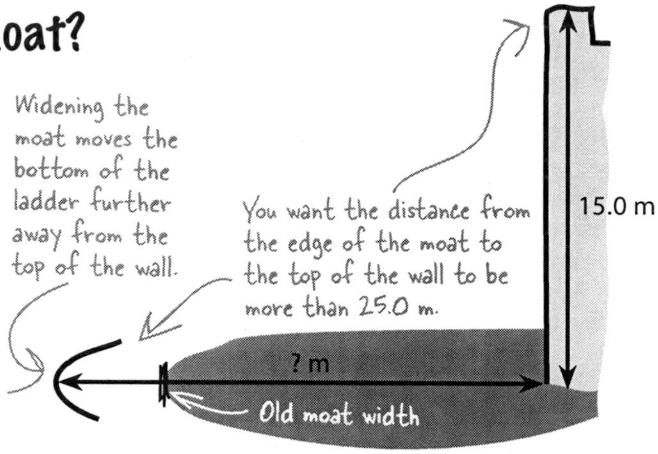

But time is of the essence, and you don't want to start out digging a 25.0 m moat if a narrower moat will do the same job. The important thing is the **distance from the edge of the moat to the top of the wall.** If that's more than 25.0 m, there won't be anything to lean the ladder on. And you might be able to achieve that with a narrower moat... a **sketch** should help.

Sharpen your pencil

a. Draw a sketch of the 15.0 m castle wall, 25.0 m ladder, and extended moat, where the ladder is only just too short to reach the top of the wall from the side of the moat.

(This sketch is just a quick drawing to get the visual parts of your brain working—the lengths on it don't have to be accurate as long as everything's labelled correctly.)

b. What shape does your sketch resemble?

....

Sharpen your pencil Solution

a. Draw a sketch of the 15.0 m castle wall, 25.0 m ladder, and extended moat, where the ladder is only just too short to reach the top of the wall from the side of the moat.

(This sketch is just a quick drawing to get the visual parts of your brain working—the lengths on it don't have to be accurate as long as everything's labelled correctly.)

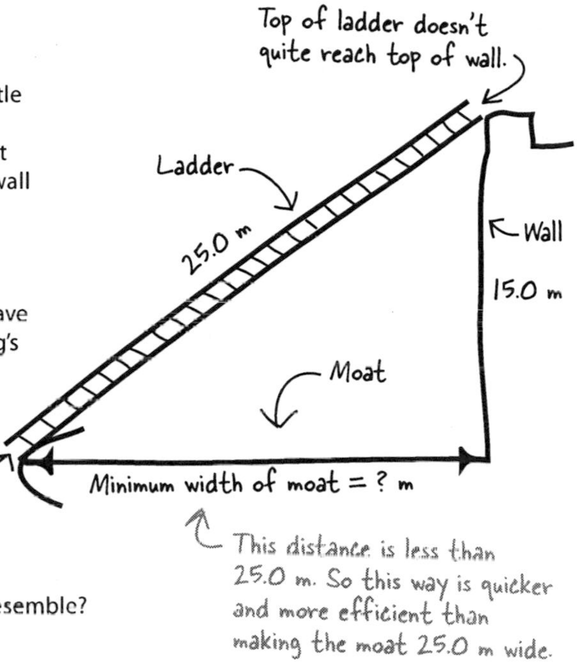

b. What shape does your sketch resemble?

It looks like a triangle.

Looks like a triangle, yeah?

You can turn your complicated-looking castle, ladder, and moat sketch into a more simple picture of a **right-angled triangle**, with a 90° angle (a right angle) between the wall and the moat. You already know the lengths of two of the triangle's sides and want to find out how long the third side is.

You could figure this out by ordering a 25.0 m ladder, putting one end at the top of the wall, and seeing where the ladder touches the ground. But the attackers might arrive with their new ladder first!

If you don't want to wait, you can measure 25.0 m of rope, tie one end to the top of the wall, and see where it touches the ground when you pull it tight.

But that still involves a lot of steps and equipment.

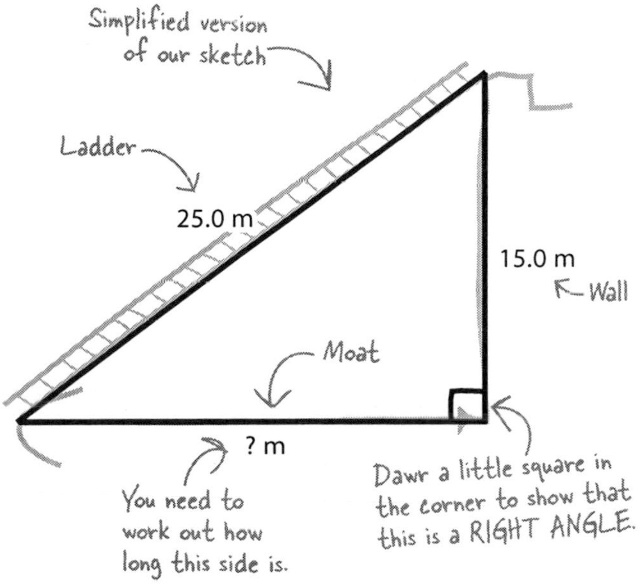

Wouldn't it be dreamy if you could just work out the smallest moat width from the triangle drawing, without having to climb the wall and make a lot of measurements? But I know it's just a fantasy...

A scale drawing can solve problems

This is one way of getting the best moat width from a triangle drawing. But it's not the best way.

At the moment, your drawing is only a **sketch**—the triangle's side lengths aren't to **scale** (though the lengths you've written beside them are correct).

A **scale drawing** is one where you say something like "1 cm on the drawing = 1 m in real life." You can then do the same as you would with the 15.0 m castle wall and 25.0 m ladder, except with 15 cm and 25 cm!

Start off by making a right-angle to represent where the wall meets the moat. Then measure up 15 cm to represent the wall.

Now, you want to swing the ladder down and see where it hits the ground. So set a pair of compasses to 25 cm...

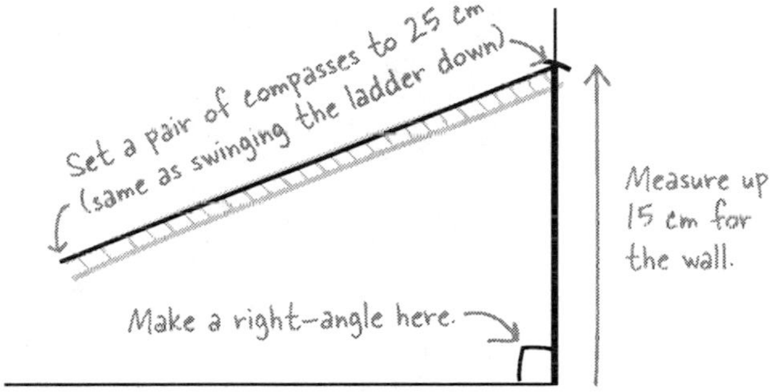

... and swing down from the top of the wall to meet the ground line. Now you can measure the most economical moat width.

That's a lot of effort just to work out a simple length though ...

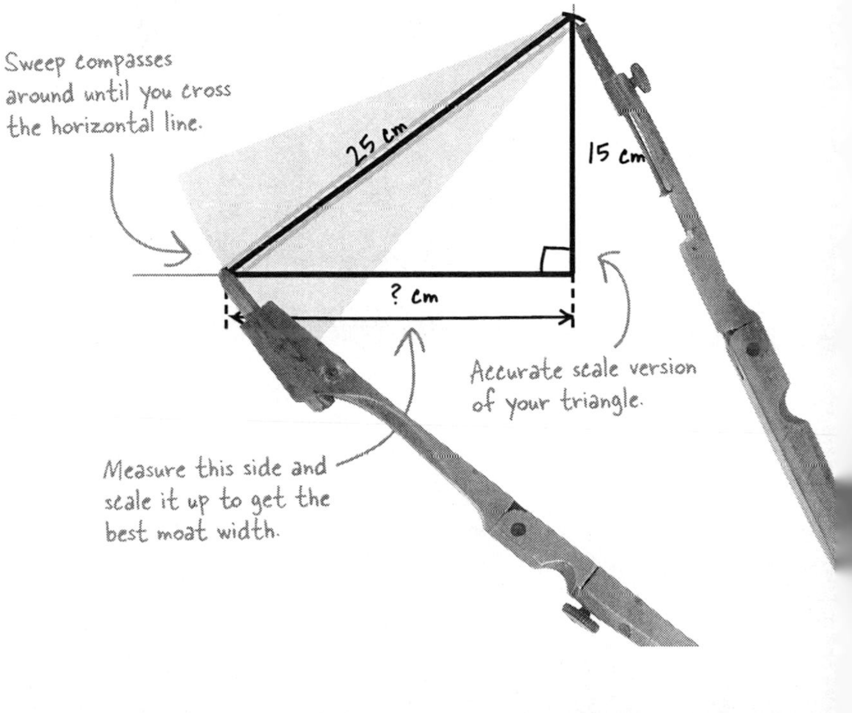

You can solve some problems with scale drawings, but it takes time and effort.

Pythagoras' Theorem lets you figure out the sides quickly

Pythagoras' theorem is an **equation** for solving this kind of problem without waving ladders around or making a super-accurate drawing. You only need to know the lengths of two sides, and the equation will tell you the third.

The longest side of the triangle is opposite the biggest angle (the right angle). This side has a special name and gets called the **hypotenuse**.

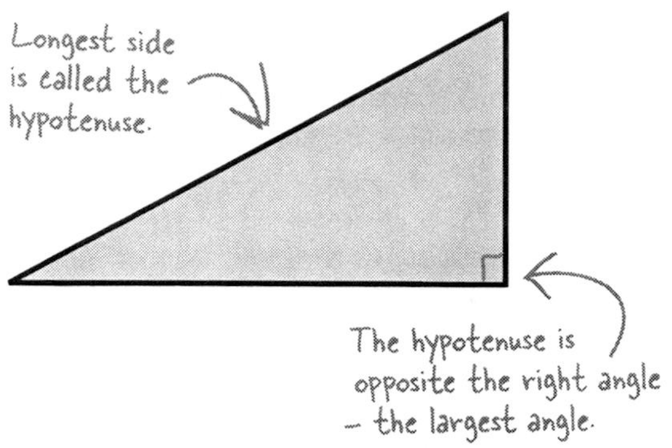

If you square the length of the hypotenuse, the answer is equal to the answer you get if you square the length of the other two sides individually, then add the squares together.

That's very wordy. So here's the equation - if you label the sides of your triangle a, b and c (where c is the hypotenuse) then Pythagoras' Theorem says:

$$c^2 = a^2 + b^2$$

It doesn't really matter which letters you use for the sides. We've chosen the same letters as the AP physics equation table.

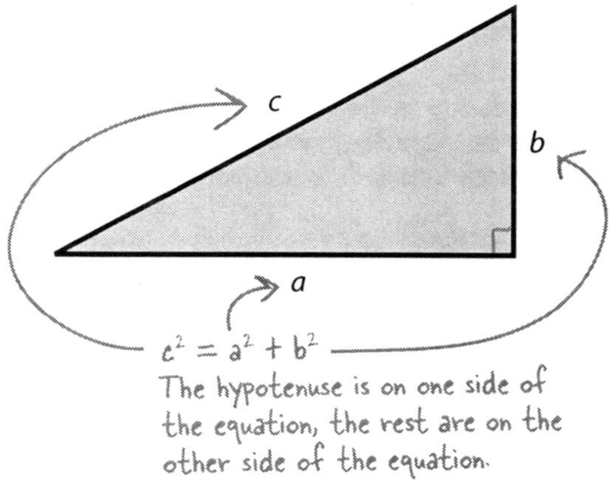

Pythagoras' Theorem **only works for right-angled triangles**. You can't use it if your triangle doesn't have a right angle.

Pythagoras only works for right-angled triangles.

If you already know two sides of the right-angled triangle, Pythagoras gets you the third.

If the triangle is right-angled:

The square of the hypotenuse is equal to the sum of the other two sides squared:

$$c^2 = a^2 + b^2$$

there are no Dumb Questions

Q: You've called Pythagoras a theorem and an equation so far. And I've seen things like that called a formula too. So which is it?

A: Equation, formula, and theorem mean the same thing really. They all describe relationships where you write down "something = another thing."

Q: How do I try to remember Pythagoras? I mean, how do I remember which sides are *a*, *b* and *c*, then what order to put them in the equation?

A: If you can remember the form of the equation, you don't need to remember the letters. The hypotenuse is the longest side, whatever letter you use to name it. So hypotenuse goes on the left of the equation.

And on the right of the equation, you square each of the other sides, then add them together. You can think about the S in SUCK - size matters. So it's the square of the longest side that goes on its own.

Q: What if I know the hypotenuse and want to calculate the length of one of the other sides?

A: You can rearrange the equation so that the side you don't know is on its own on the left.

Q: So where does Pythagoras' Theorem come from? Aren't we going to go through proving it?

A: It's only really worth going into understanding where an equation comes from if the understanding you gain helps you see how the world works, so you can solve physics problems (and other problems) better.

Being able to prove Pythagoras' Theorem doesn't help with this, so we've not gone into that here.

You'll spot many right angles between the horizontal and vertical

Right-angled triangles are going to be one of your most important physics tools. There are lots of right angles in physics, often between the horizontal ground and vertical walls or vertical acceleration vectors that exist as a result of gravity.

Keep your eyes open for them as this chapter progresses ...

Sketch + shape + equation = Problem solved!

Back to the castle and the new Sieges-R-Us ladder!

You started with a **sketch** and spotted a right-angled triangle **shape** in it. After toying with the idea of a scale drawing, Pythagoras popped up with an **equation**!

So now you can work out the best moat width—and save the castle!

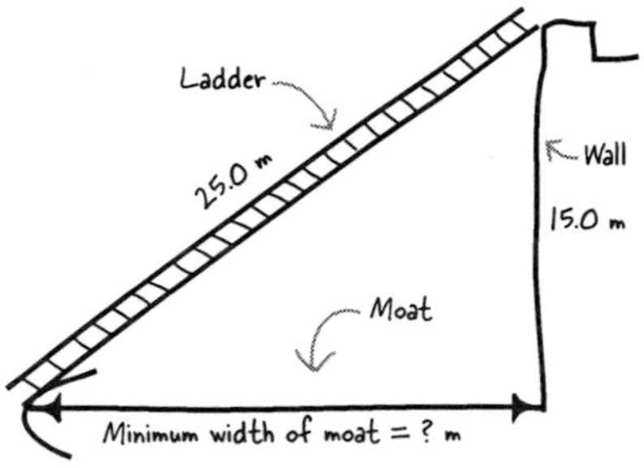

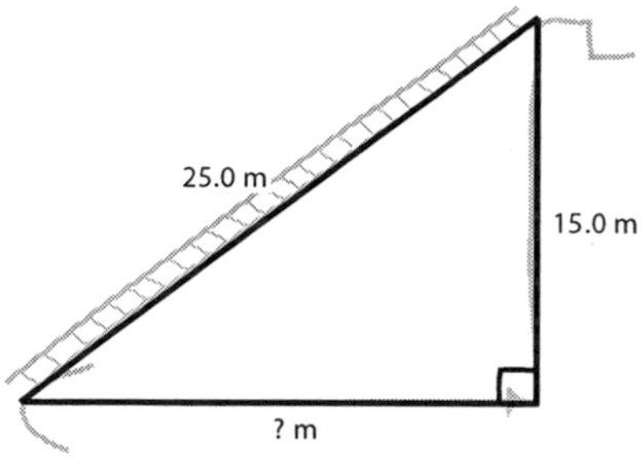

$$c^2 = a^2 + b^2$$

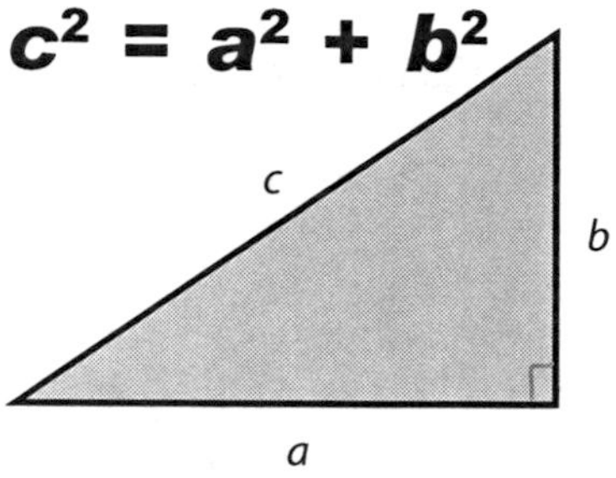

Start with a sketch → **Look for familiar shapes (triangles, rectangles, etc)** → **Use an equation that tells you about this kind of shape**

Sharpen your pencil

Solve your problem!

A castle is built on flat ground with 15.00 m walls. How wide must the moat be to ensure that a 25.00 m ladder only just touches the top of the wall? Assume that the base of the ladder is placed at the edge of the moat.

Sharpen your pencil Solution

A castle is built on flat ground with 15.00 m walls. How wide must the moat be to ensure that a 25.00 m ladder only just touches the top of the wall? Assume that the base of the ladder is placed at the edge of the moat.

Start with a sketch:

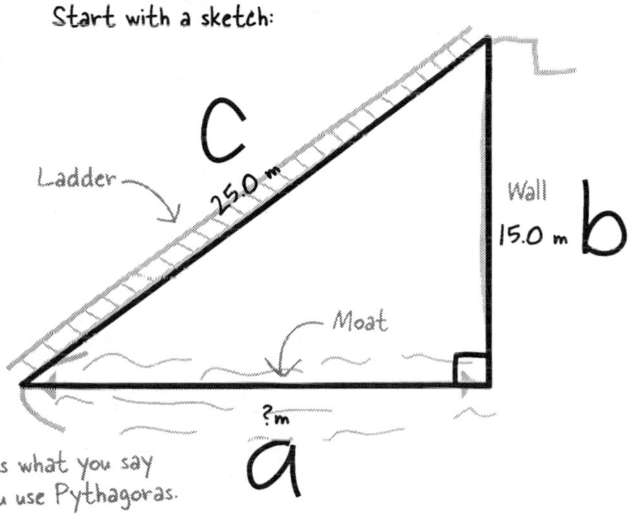

This is what you say if you use Pythagoras.

Want to know a, the width of the moat.

By Pythagoras, $c^2 = a^2 + b^2$

Rearrange equation for the side you want. $a^2 = c^2 - b^2$

$a^2 = 25^2 - 15^2$

$a^2 = 400$

$a = \sqrt{400} = 20.0$ m

So the best moat width is 20.0 m (3 sd).

Values in your question were given to 3 sd, so your answer should have 3 sd too.

there are no Dumb Questions

Q: There were square roots in that solution, but it's been a while since I used these, and they're a bit hazy. Remind me how they work again?

A: As we saw in chapter 3, the square of a number is the number times itself.

or $3^2 = 3 \times 3 = 9$.

If you take the square root (√) of a number, the answer you get is the number you'd have to square to get the one you started off with. For example, $\sqrt{9} = 3$ because $3^2 = 9$.

Q: I noticed that I got nice round numbers – 15.0, 20.0 and 25.0 – for the side lengths. Does that always happen with right-angled triangles?

A: Here, the wall, ladder and moat formed a right-angled triangle which has nice side lengths in a 3:4:5 ratio. $3^2 + 4^2 = 5^2$, and a 15:20:25 ratio is just a 3:4:5 ratio multiplied by 5.

But usually that doesn't happen - your calculator will give you answers that you'll have to round to the same number of significant digits as the values you were initially given to work with.

You kept them out!

Under your instructions, the castle workmen start digging your 20.0 m wide moat immediately.

A couple of hours after they've finished, some attackers come along with the new 25.0 m ladder ... and have an unexpected bath!

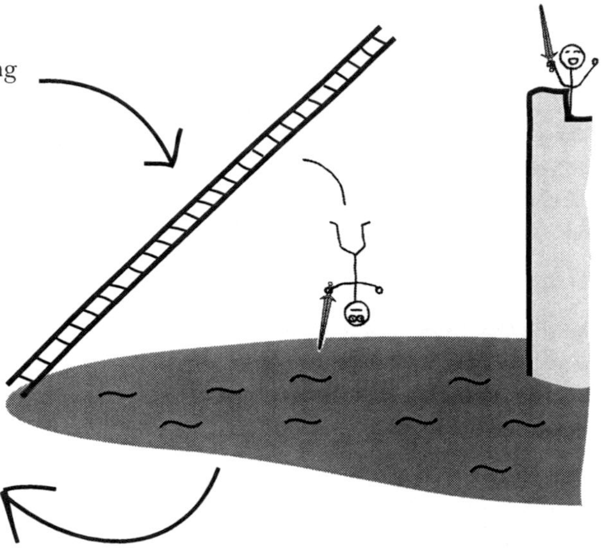

But the attackers get smarter!

BRAIN POWER

Phoning for a pizza just isn't an option. How could you try to scare them away so you can get more supplies in?

BULLET POINTS

- The routine
  SKETCH
  SHAPE
  EQUATION
  is an excellent one!
- You'll often see **right-angled triangles**, as the ground is **horizontal** and walls, gravity and such operate **vertically**.
- The **hypotenuse** is the side opposite the right angle.
- Pythagoras' Theorem is an **equation** you can use to get the third side of a right-angled triangle if you already know the other two.
- Pythagoras' Theorem **only** works on right-angled triangles!
- If you spot a triangle with side lengths in a 3:4:5 ratio, then you know it must be right-angled (because Pythagoras' Theorem only works on right-angled triangles).
- If you forget which way around Pythagoras is, then think about the lengths of the sides and what makes sense. Or sketch out a 3:4:5 triangle and work out what Pythagoras must be from that.

Camelot ... we have ANOTHER problem!

You dealt with the new ladders—and gave the attackers an early bath by widening the moat.

But now they're camped at the edge of the moat, waiting for you to run out of food and surrender. It would be someone else's problem ... if you weren't stuck in the castle too!

On the bright side—you have a cannon!

On the not-so-bright side, you need to aim before you fire. And you can't look over the top of the wall to aim the cannon, as they'll probably shoot at you before you can aim at them...

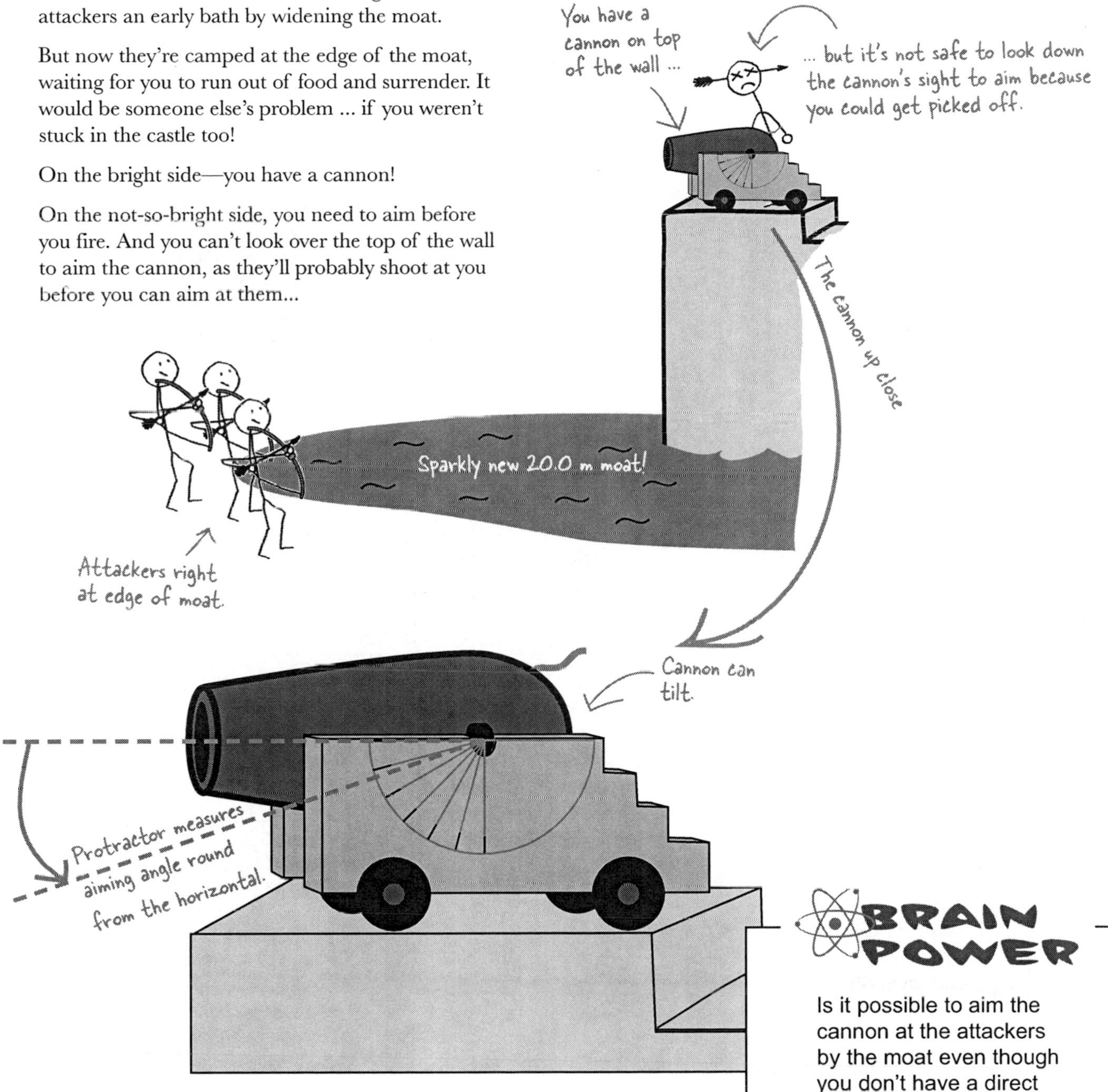

BRAIN POWER

Is it possible to aim the cannon at the attackers by the moat even though you don't have a direct line of sight?

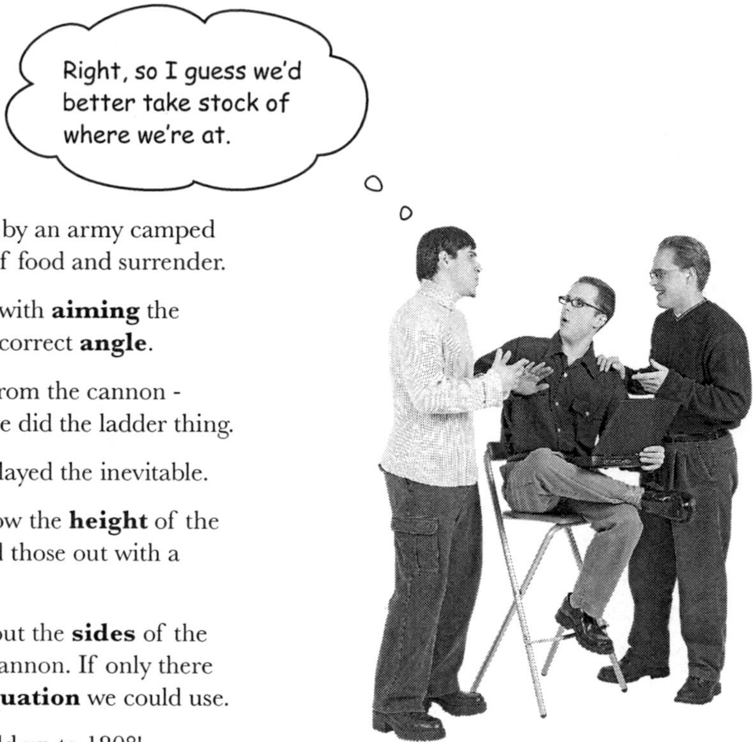

Frank: That's easy! In a castle, surrounded by an army camped at the edge of our moat... until we run out of food and surrender.

Jim: Uhhhh. I kinda meant where we're at with **aiming** the cannon, when we can't see to point it at the correct **angle**.

Joe: Well, we know the **distance** they are from the cannon - 25.0 m! We already worked that out when we did the ladder thing.

Frank: Oh yeah ... well looks like it only delayed the inevitable.

Joe: Think positive - we can do this! We know the **height** of the wall and the **width** of the moat. We worked those out with a sketch and Pythagoras' Theorem.

Jim: Yeah, we know all there is to know about the **sides** of the triangle. But we need an **angle** to aim the cannon. If only there was some kind of 'Pythagoras for angles' **equation** we could use.

Joe: But there is! The angles in a triangle add up to 180°!

Jim: And we already know that the right angle is 90°, so the other two angles must add up to 180° - 90° = 90°. That's progress!

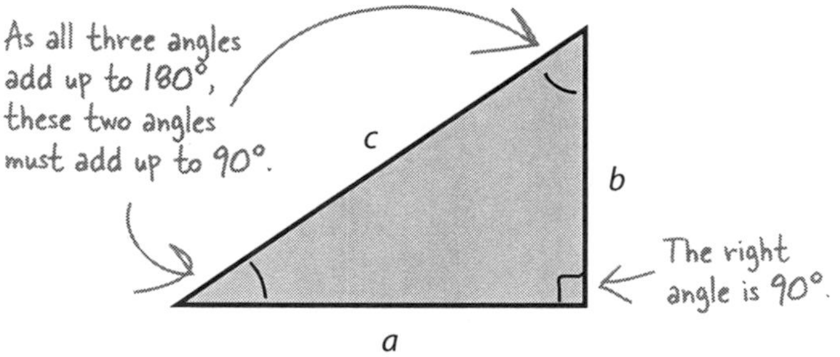

The three angles in a triangle add up to 180°.

Frank: Not a lot of progress though. The other two angles could be 1° and 89°, or 45° and 45°, or 18.2° and 71.8°.

Jim: Oh yeah. You can't find out **two** things you don't know if you only have **one** equation to work with.

Joe: Well, since we only have one equation at the moment, maybe we can do an **experiment** with some different right-angled triangles and see if we can figure something out?

Frank: OK, that kinda thing's worked for us before ...

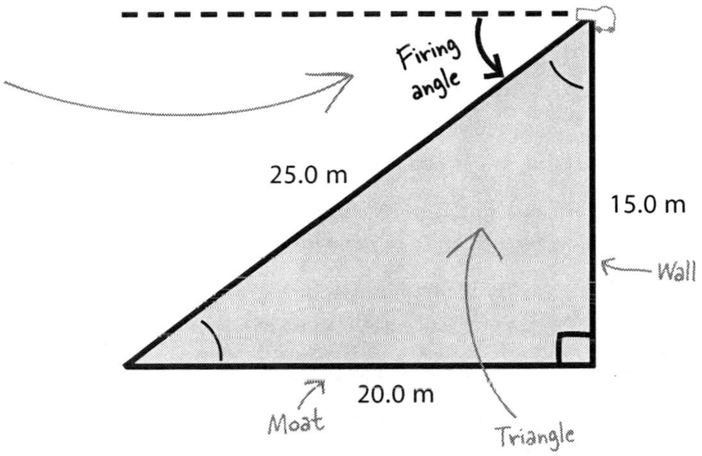

The angle you want might be the SAME SIZE as one of the angles in your triangle.

When there are right-angled triangles around, you'll often find **complementary** and/or **supplementary** angles.

You don't need to remember which is which to be able to actually USE them!

Complementary angles add up to 90°, and supplementary angles add up to 180°. They're useful because they help you work out the sizes of angles that aren't in your triangle.

Try to spot angles that add up to 90° or 180° in and around your right-angled triangles.

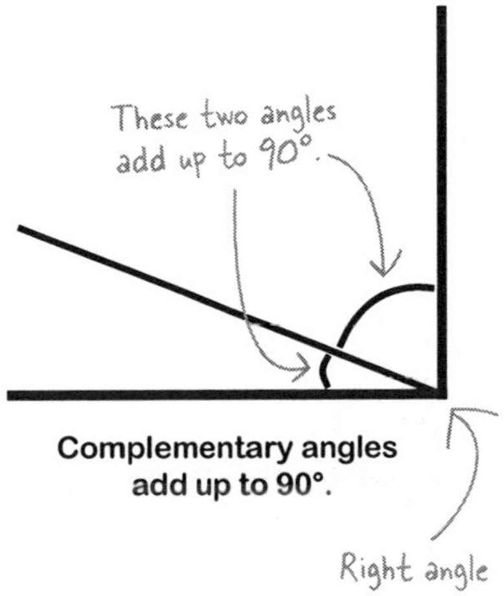

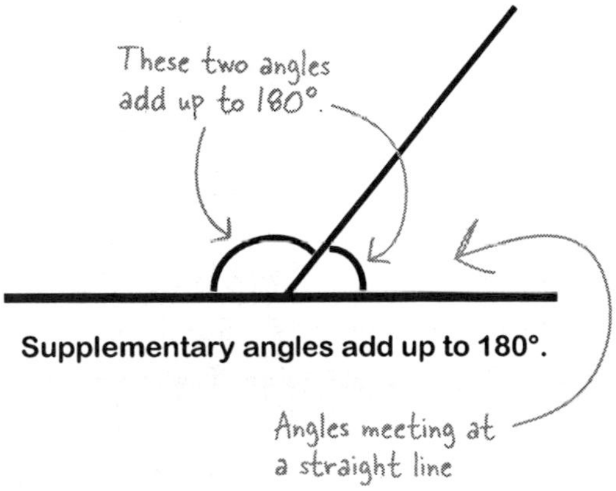

Relate your angle to an angle inside the triangle

We're going to give the firing angle the symbol θ. This is the Greek letter theta and is often used in physics to represent an angle that you're interested in.

You want to calculate the firing angle - but it isn't part of your triangle. However, when there are right-angled triangles around, there are often angles that add up to 90° or 180° that you can use to work out the angle you're interested in. Here, the firing angle and the angle at the top of your triangle add up to 90°.

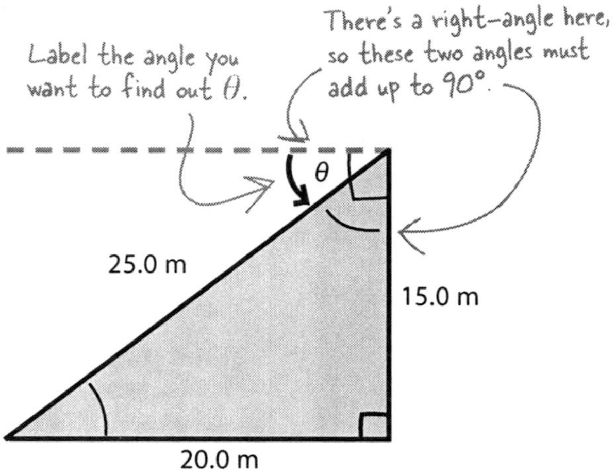

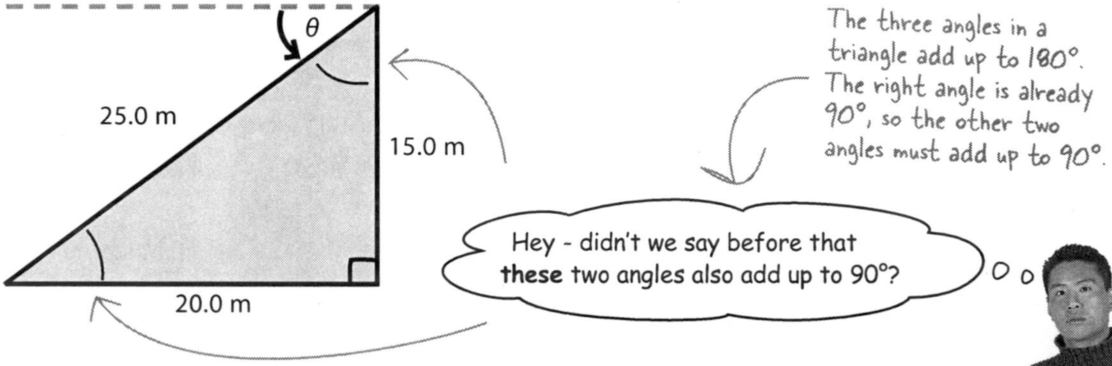

The firing angle is the same size as an angle in your triangle.

Now you have two sets of angles that add up to 90°. The first set is the firing angle, θ, and the angle at the top of the triangle. The second set is the angles at the bottom and top of the triangle.

This means that θ and the angle at the bottom of the triangle must both be the same size. So you can label the angle at the bottom of the triangle θ as well, and get on with trying to work out what size it should be to fire the cannonball ...

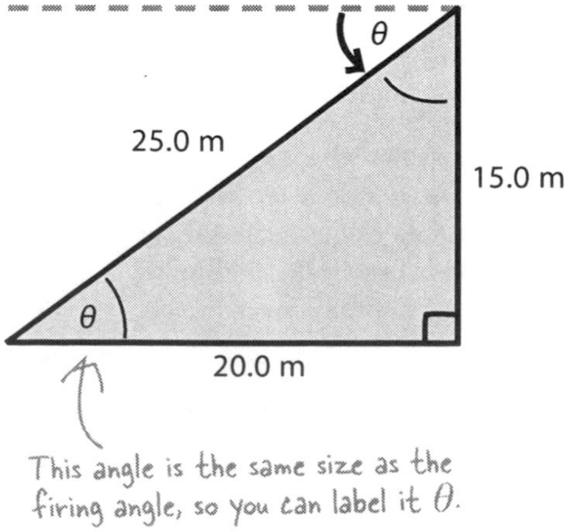

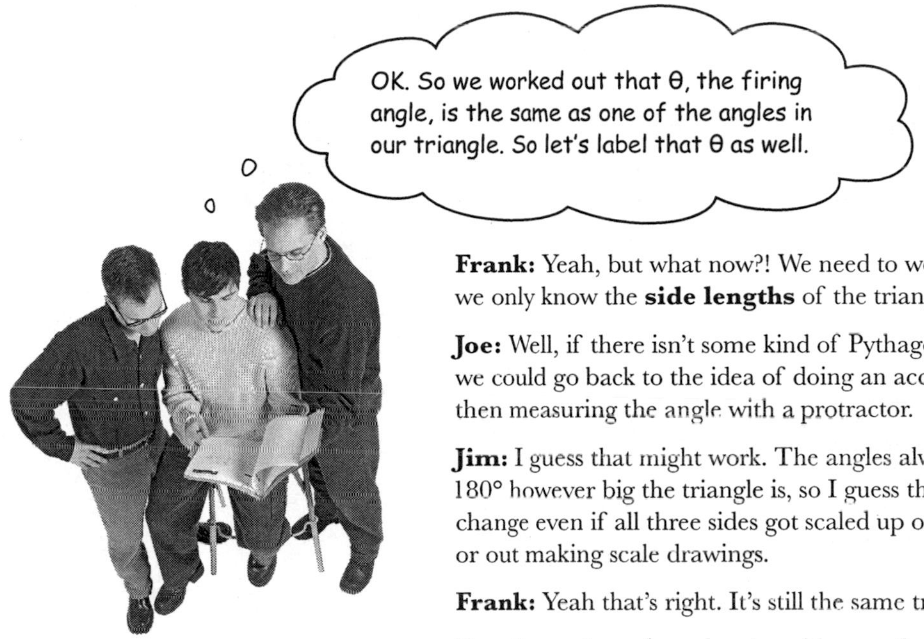

Frank: Yeah, but what now?! We need to work out an **angle** - but we only know the **side lengths** of the triangle.

Joe: Well, if there isn't some kind of Pythagoras for angles, maybe we could go back to the idea of doing an accurate scale drawing, then measuring the angle with a protractor.

Jim: I guess that might work. The angles always have to add up to 180° however big the triangle is, so I guess that the angles wouldn't change even if all three sides got scaled up or down as we zoom in or out making scale drawings.

Frank: Yeah that's right. It's still the same triangle!

Jim: It says here that triangles with **equal angles** (but different side lengths) are called **similar triangles**.

Joe: So the scale drawing would be of a similar triangle. And the angles would be the same as the original, big triangle. Cool!

Frank: But what if the attackers move? We'd have to do another scale drawing, and that's gonna take time.

Jim: We can do that in advance. We can draw all the right-angled triangles that you could ever get and measure their angles.

Joe: Yeah, we can make the information into a **table** so that you can look up the angles of any right-angled triangle without having to measure them. And we could get a computer or a calculator to **look up** the angles when we tell it the sides—that bit would be really quick.

Frank: But if we were drawing all possible right-angled triangles, some of them would be really huge, like, miles long!

Jim: Not necessarily. We just worked out that **the angles of similar triangles are always the same**. So if we have a triangle in the table with side lengths 3 cm, 4 cm, and 5 cm, we don't also need one with 3 miles, 4 miles, 5 miles or 1500 miles, 2000 miles, 2500 miles, etc, as they're all just the same triangle, except zoomed in or out a bit.

Joe: Cool! Let's get cracking!

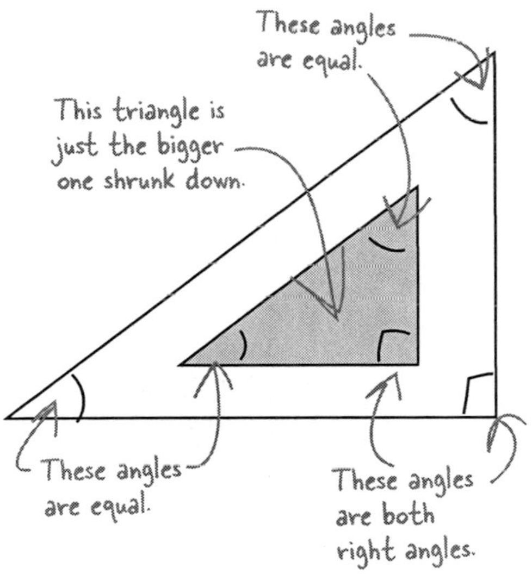

Triangles with equal angles are called similar triangles.

You can classify triangles by their shape - but need a way of looking them up later on.

Using **similar triangles** in your table is the best bet, so each type of triangle only needs to appear in the table once. For example, instead of the table including lots of different triangles with side lengths in a ratio of 3:4:5, it only needs to include one.

But the problem now is how to arrange or **index** the table. How are you actually going to **find** the triangle when you go to look it up?

The problem is that the triangle someone wants to look up could be any SIZE or zoomed in or out from the SHAPE of its entry in the table. So how on earth can you ever find the row with the right SHAPE in it?

Triangle shape	Angle θ (°)	Other angle (°)
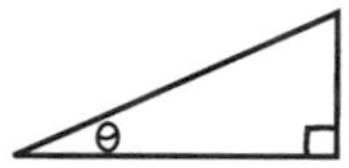	24.6	65.4
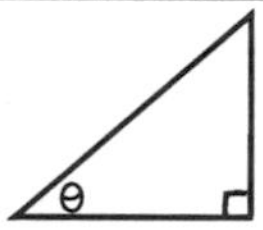	40.6	49.4
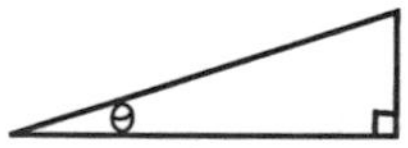	18.5	71.5

If you look up the shape of your triangle, the table will give you its angles.

The angles in this table have 3 significant digits because that's easier to write - but the angles in the completed table could have more significant digits.

You need some way to classify the SHAPE of a triangle that doesn't involve its angles (which are what you want to look up).

BRAIN POWER

How might you classify the **shapes** of the triangles in your table?

Classify similar triangles by the ratios of their side lengths

If you take a triangle and magnify or reduce it (zoom in or out), you make a **similar triangle** which has the same angles as the triangle you started off with. For example, a scale drawing of a bigger triangle is a similar triangle.

Similar triangles don't have the same side lengths, but they do have the same **ratios** of side lengths. To work those out, you have to decide on a way of naming the sides so that everyone knows what you're talking about:

The hypotenuse it labelled '**hypotenuse.**'
The side opposite 'your' angle is labelled '**opposite.**'
And you label the third side '**adjacent.**'

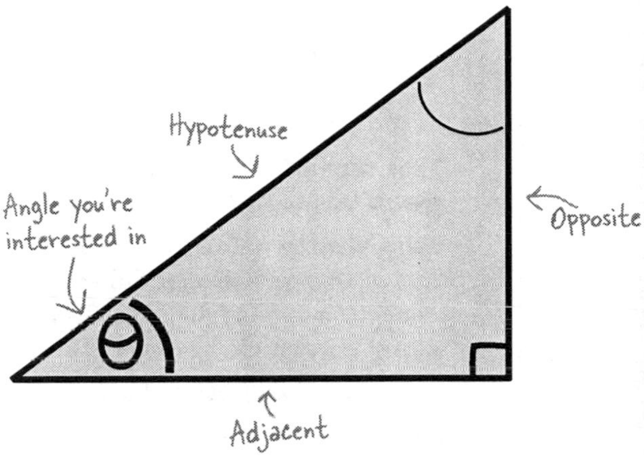

Label the sides the same way every time.

The **ratio** of two side lengths is simply **one side length divided by the other side length**. There are three sides and three ratios, which all have names:

Sine (pronounced "sign")

Cosine (pronounced co-sign)

Tangent

When you're writing these as part of an equation, sine is abbreviated to sin, cosine becomes cos and tangent becomes tan.

If you were saying this out loud, it would be "sine theta."

$$\sin(\theta) = \frac{\textbf{opposite}}{\textbf{hypotenuse}}$$

The RATIO of two side lengths is one side length divided by another side length.

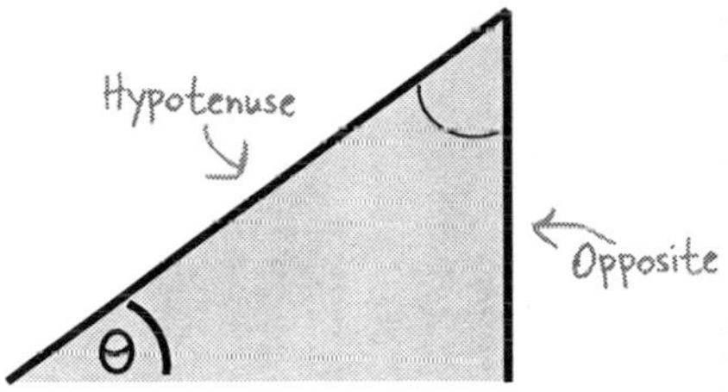

$$\cos(\theta) = \frac{\textbf{adjacent}}{\textbf{hypotenuse}}$$

Don't worry about remembering which name is which ratio at the moment.

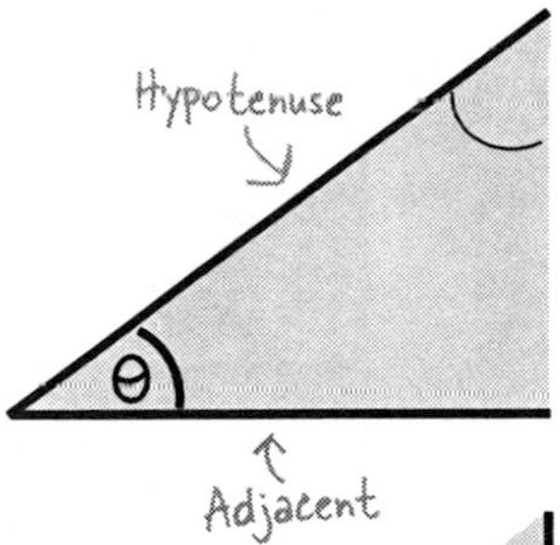

$$\tan(\theta) = \frac{\textbf{opposite}}{\textbf{adjacent}}$$

The angle you are interested in goes in brackets after the name of the ratio.

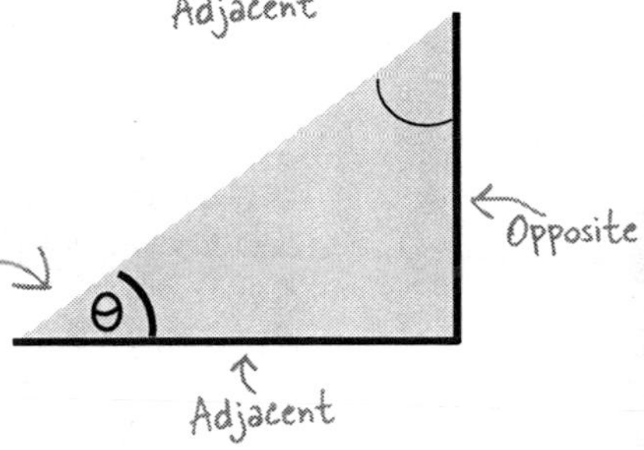

Similar triangles have the same RATIOS of side lengths. Sine, cosine, and tangent are RATIOS.

Tangent has the same name as the tangent to a curve – which can be confusing at first. But it's always abbreviated to 'tan' in equations.

Sine, cosine and tangent connect the sides and angles of a right-angled triangle

The ratios sine, cosine and tangent are a way of classifying the similar triangles in your table. Suppose you have two **similar triangles**, one with side lengths 3 cm, 4 cm and 5 cm, and the other with side lengths 15.0 m, 20.0 m and 25.0 m. As they're similar triangles, you know that their **angles** must be equal.

And although their sides aren't equal, the **ratios** of their sides are. In the first triangle, the ratio of the two shortest sides is $\tan(\theta) = \frac{3}{4} = 0.75$; in the second triangle, $\tan(\theta) = \frac{15}{20} = 0.75$.

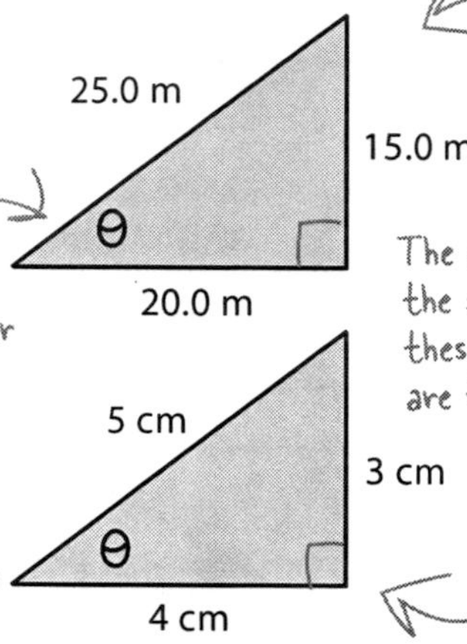

These are similar triangles with the same sizes of angles.

The ratios of the sides of these triangles are the same.

Exercise

Label the sides of these right-angled triangles with '**h**' (hypotenuse), '**o**' (opposite), and '**a**' (adjacent), then fill the blanks in the table below. If a side length is missing, then use Pythagoras to work it out in the space under the table. The angle θ is the one you're interested in.

	Triangle	sin(θ)	cos(θ)	tan(θ)
a	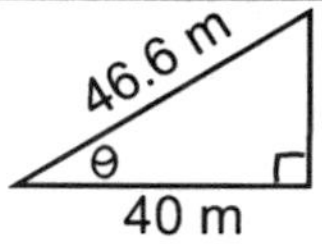	$\frac{o}{h} = \frac{24}{46.6} = 0.515$		
b	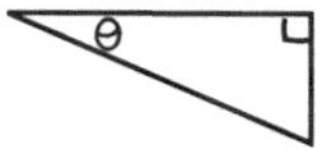			
c	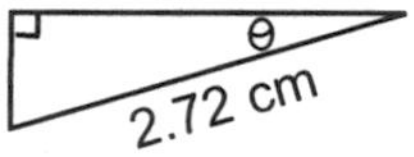			
d	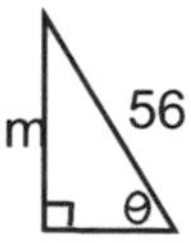			

Use the definitions of sine, cosine and tangent on the opposite page to fill in these boxes.

Space for working out the missing side lengths using Pythagoras.

At the moment, this table just has ratios in it. The final table will have the angle that each ratio corresponds to, so you can look up an ANGLE if you have a RATIO, and vice versa.

Exercise Solution

Label the sides of these right-angled triangles with 'h' (hypotenuse), 'o' (opposite), and 'a' (adjacent), then fill the blanks in the table below. If a side length is missing, then use Pythagoras to work it out in the space under the table. The angle θ is the one you're interested in.

	Triangle	sin(θ)	cos(θ)	tan(θ)
a	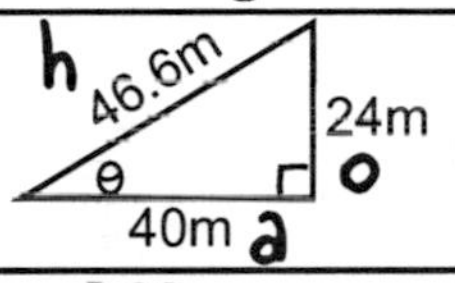	$\frac{o}{h} = \frac{24}{46.6} = 0.515$	$\frac{a}{h} = \frac{40}{46.6} = 0.858$	$\frac{o}{a} = \frac{24}{40} = 0.600$
b	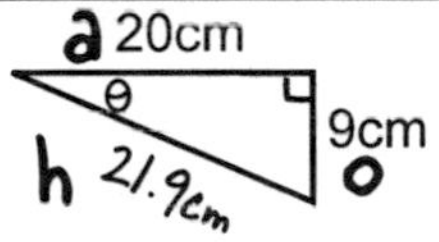	$\frac{o}{h} = \frac{9}{21.9} = 0.411$	$\frac{a}{h} = \frac{20}{21.9} = 0.913$	$\frac{o}{a} = \frac{9}{20} = 0.45$
c	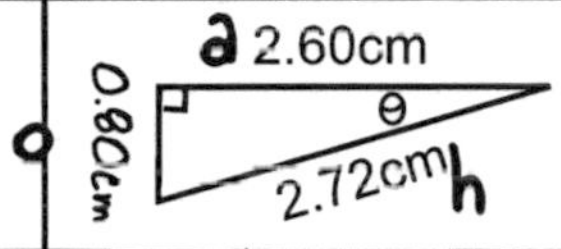	$\frac{o}{h} = \frac{0.80}{2.72} = 0.294$	$\frac{a}{h} = \frac{2.60}{2.72} = 0.956$	$\frac{o}{a} = \frac{0.80}{2.60} = 0.308$
d	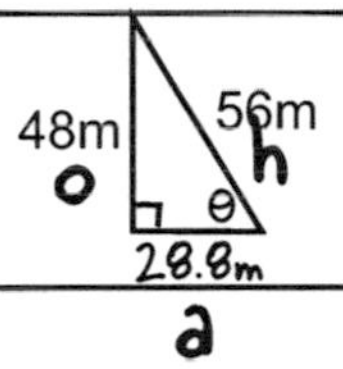	$\frac{o}{h} = \frac{48}{56} = 0.857$	$\frac{a}{h} = \frac{28.8}{56} = 0.514$	$\frac{o}{a} = \frac{48}{28.8} = 1.67$

The ratios don't have units, as $\frac{\text{length}}{\text{length}}$ is dimensionless.

By Pythagoras, $h^2 = o^2 + a^2$

Triangle b:

$h^2 = 20^2 + 9^2$

$\Rightarrow h = \sqrt{481} = 21.9 \text{ cm (3 sd)}$

Triangle c:

$o^2 = h^2 - a^2$

$o^2 = 2.72^2 - 2.60^2$

$\Rightarrow o = \sqrt{0.6384} = 0.80 \text{ cm (3 sd)}$

Triangle d:

$a^2 = h^2 - o^2$

$a^2 = 56^2 - 48^2$

$\Rightarrow a = \sqrt{832} = 28.8 \text{ m (3 sd)}$

The units are important, as some triangles are in m and some are in cm.

When you've labelled your triangle 'h', 'o' and 'a' (hypotenuse, opposite and adjacent) it's fine to use these letters instead of a, b and c in Pythagoras' Theorem.

The side length ratios - sine, cosine and tangent - are always the same for similar triangles.

How to remember which ratio is which??

The mnemonic 'SOH CAH TOA' helps you to remember which ratio involves which sides.

SOH - **S**ine is **O**pposite divided by **H**ypotenuse.

CAH - **C**osine is **A**djacent divided by **H**ypotenuse.

TOA - **T**angent is **O**pposite divided by **A**djacent.

SOH

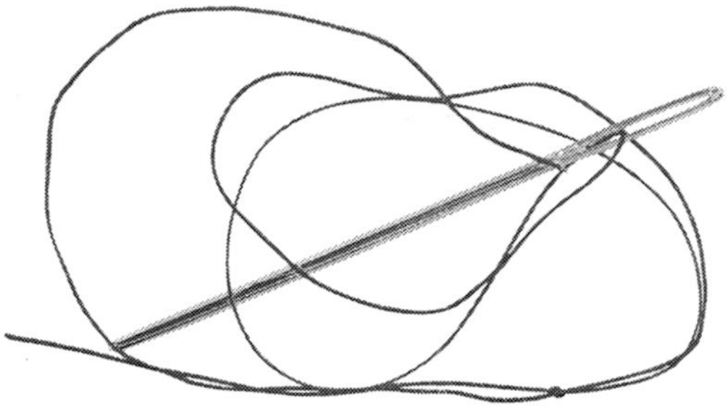

$$\sin(\theta) = \frac{\text{opposite}}{\text{hypotenuse}}$$

CAH

Like they say it in Boston.

$$\cos(\theta) = \frac{\text{adjacent}}{\text{hypotenuse}}$$

TOA

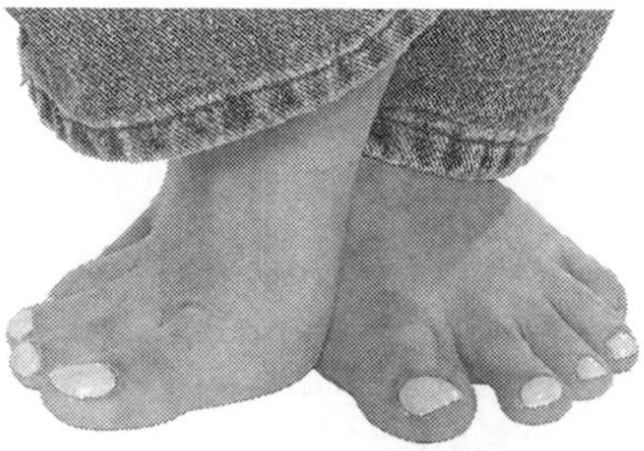

$$\tan(\theta) = \frac{\text{opposite}}{\text{adjacent}}$$

Say it a few times before you turn the page to help you remember.

"SOH CAH TOA"
"SOH CAH TOA"
"SOH CAH TOA"
"SOH CAH TOA"
"SOH CAH TOA"

If you forget which sides go with which ratio, write down this mnemonic, and go on from there.

Sine Exposed

This week's interview:
sine is mighty fine!

Interviewer: So, sine, would you say that your bad reputation is justified?

sine: Sigh. The problem is that I'm sometimes get called 'sin.' But I'm still pronounced sin**e** - with an 'e' - like 'pine.' I'm not bad—I'm a **trigonometric function**!

Interviewer: Err ... a trigono-what-now?!

sine: Trigonometric - that means I help you with triangles. And I'm a function, so you give me a number, and I give you a different number back.

Interviewer: Hmmm. No, sorry, you've lost me. Why would I ever want to swap numbers with you?

sine: Well, the number you give me is an **angle**, from a right-angled triangle. I give you back the **ratio** of the side opposite the angle divided by the hypotenuse.

Interviewer: Riiiiight. I'm not sure why I'd ever care about that, but there you go.

sine: I'm the missing link! I'm what connects what you can know about the **lengths of a triangle's sides** to what you can know about the sizes of its **angles**.

Interviewer: Hmm. So what?

sine: Right angled triangles and angles are very important in physics. In fact, I'm one of the most important things in your entire physics toolbox!

Interviewer: So, without you, people wouldn't be able to do most of the stuff in the rest of this book.

sine: Exactly!

Interviewer: You sound extremely important then. Can you just run past us again how you work?

sine: You give me an angle–probably one you found in a right-angled triangle. And I give you a number back, which is the ratio of the side opposite the angle divided by the hypotenuse. Like this:

$$\sin(\theta) = \frac{\textbf{opposite}}{\textbf{hypotenuse}}$$

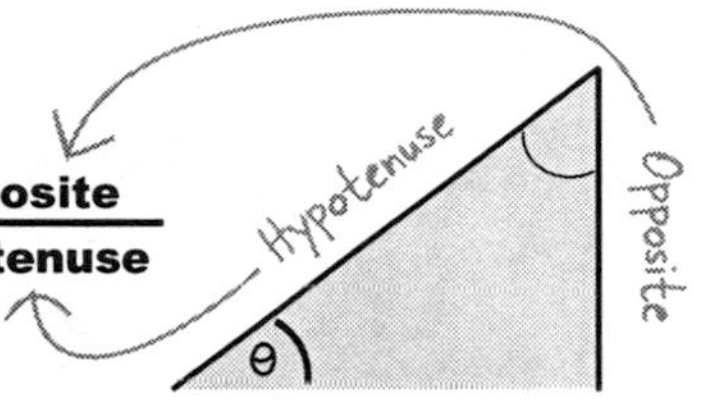

Interviewer: But I don't really see how that helps.

sine: Well, if you already know the angle and the side opposite it, you can rearrange that equation to get the hypotenuse. And if you already know the angle and the hypotenuse, you can get the opposite side.

Interviewer: But what if I know the length of the adjacent side, plus one other side? Should I get Pythagoras to work out the missing side before calling on you to help?

sine: Not necessarily—you could call on my close relatives cosine or tangent.

Interviewer: And what do they do?

sine: Well, cosine is the ratio of the side adjacent to the angle divided by the hypotenuse. And tangent is the opposite divided by the adjacent.

Interviewer: Oh, so you guys cover all possible combinations of two sides of the triangle between you. So if I already know an angle and a side, I can get the length of any other side in one step. Cool. But what if I don't know any angles at all? Can I use you to work out the **angles** in a triangle too?

sine: Going the other way - from side lengths to angles?

Interviewer: That's right - some guys in a castle were trying to do that just before we went on air.

sine: You'll want my **inverse** to go the other way. He looks up the table of angles and ratios in the opposite direction. So you give my inverse a ratio, and he gives you the angle that the ratio corresponds to.

Interviewer: That sure sounds useful. Thank you, sine, you've been just swell.

there are no Dumb Questions

Q: Why choose to have three different ratios? Why not one, or two ... or five or six?

A: Suppose you only know two sides of your right-angled triangle, and want to find out one of the angles. If there were only one or two ratios in your calculator's table, you'd often have to work out the third side using Pythagoras before you could work out a ratio to get the angle. Having three ratios in the table covers all the different combinations of two sides.

Q: And why not five or six? You could have hypotenuse divided by adjacent, for example.

A: There are special names for these other ratios, but they're not important right now. You'll never need to use them on your physics course.

Q: OK. Now, I was wondering something else about 'tan' - or tangent, to give it its full name. I did tangents before, right? But that was something to do with working out the gradient of a curve, wasn't it?

A: Good point. **Very** good point! A tangent is a straight line that only touches a curve at one point - and you did use one to work out the slope of a line in chapter 7:

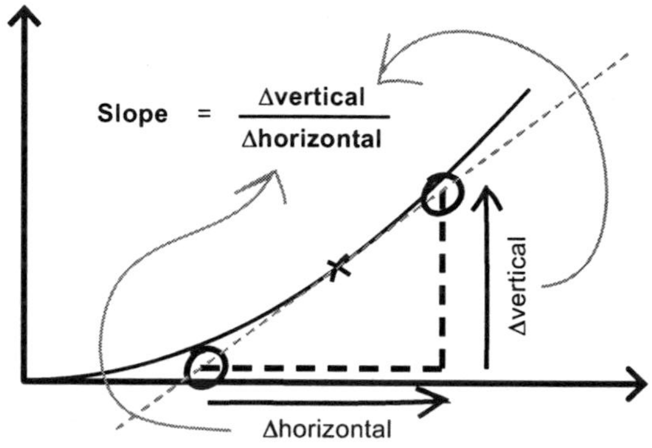

Your formula for tan(θ) is basically a rewrite of the "slope of a line" equation, which is where the name 'tangent' comes from.

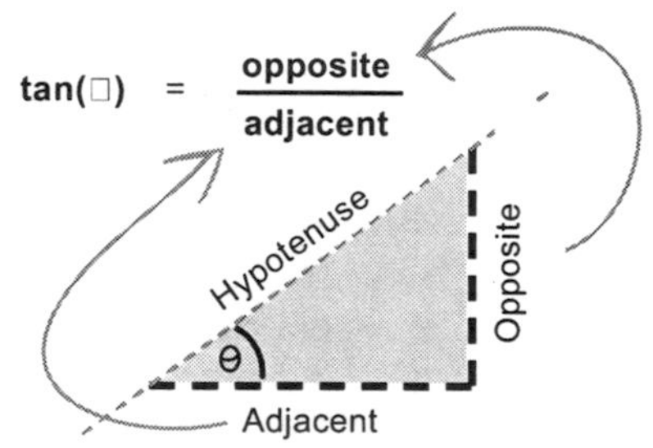

The trigonometric functions sine, cosine and tangent connect what you know about the <u>sides</u> of a right-angled triangle to what you know about its <u>angles</u>.

If you put a value into a function, then it gives you a different value back. For example, if you give an angle to the sine function, it gives you back the ratio of the opposite and hypotenuse.

Q: Suppose I work out a ratio (sine, cosine or tangent) from two of the sides of my triangle. How do I use that to get an angle?

A: You need to calculate the firing angle for the cannon using the ratio of two sides of the moat-wall triangle. We're just getting on to that ...

Calculators have sin(Θ), cos(Θ) and tan(Θ) tables built in

Your calculator already contains a table a bit like the one you've been filling in, where the angles of similar triangles are indexed using the ratios sine, cosine and tangent.

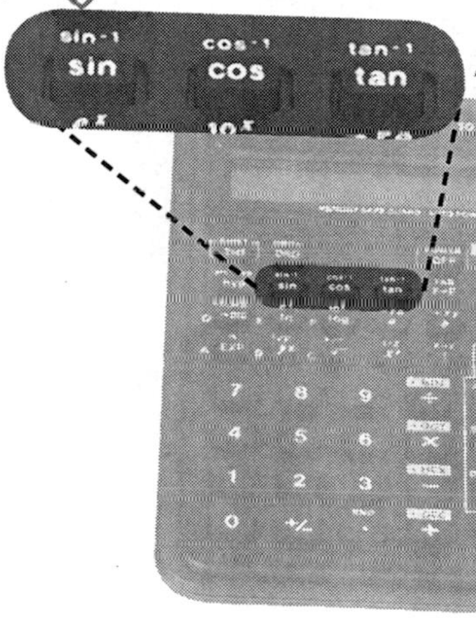

To get a ratio when you have an angle, use the sin(θ), cos (θ) and tan (θ) functions. They're usually printed on a calculator button.

To get an angle when you have a ratio, you need to use the **inverse** sine, cosine and tangent functions. They're usually written above the 'sin' 'cos' and 'tan' buttons. You use the inverse functions by pressing the 'shift' or '2nd fn' button first.

The inverse functions are usually called $\sin^{-1}$, $\cos^{-1}$ and $\tan^{-1}$. This is weird, as at first glance the '$^{-1}$' bit looks like scientific notation. But it's not - it's just a convention for indicating an inverse function that you'll unfortunately need to get used to.

Sometimes the inverse functions are called arcsine, arccosine and arctangent. These are abbreviated to asin, acos and atan on calculators. Make sure you know what they're called on your calculator!

Make sure your calculator's set to degrees!

If you and your calculator are speaking different languages, there's no way you're going to get the right answer. There's more than one way of measuring angles. Right now, make sure your calculator's set to work in degrees.

Usually, there'll be a switch or a button with a 'deg' or ° sign on it that you can use to sort this out.

It's also good to spend time playing with your calculator to see which **order** you need to press the buttons in. On some calculators, you type the number in, then press the button for the function you want. Other, more expensive, calculators let you type things in the same order you'd write them.

Play with your calculator, and make sure you know how it works before you go on to find the firing angle.

Know how your calculator works and inwhich order you should press the buttons!

Then the calculator will do what you want it to.

Exercise

Here's the table you already started filling in on pages 351-352. It's similar to the kind of table in your calculator, and it's time to practice moving smoothly between sides and angles before you do the critical mission of calculating the angle back at the castle.

The side lengths you were originally given are written in type. Your job is to skip the Pythagoras step and use the appropriate **ratio** — sin(θ), cos (θ) or tan (θ) — to get from the two given sides to find the angle θ. Show which ratio you'd use by circling it.

Once you've worked out θ, try to spot a quick way of calculating β for each triangle as well.

We've used another Greek letter, β (beta), to represent the other angle.

	Triangle	sin(□)	cos(□)	tan(□)	Angle □ (°)	Angle □ (°)
a	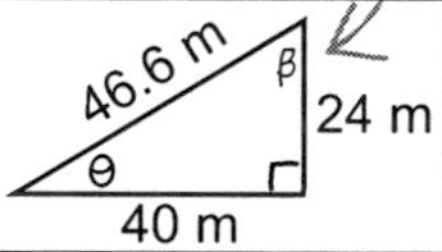	0.515	0.858	0.6	31.0	
b	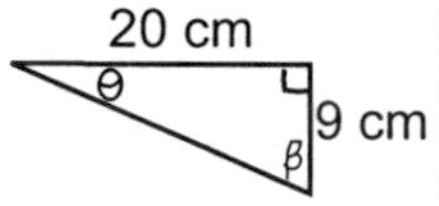	0.411	0.913	0.45		
c	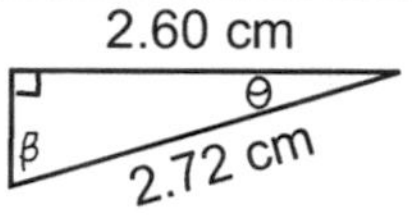	0.294	0.956	0.308		
d	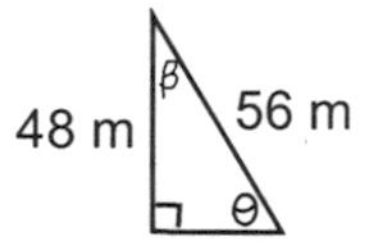	0.857	0.514	1.67		

Triangle a – could use any two of three given sides.
Use tangent with opp and adj.

$$\theta = \tan^{-1}(0.6) = 31.0° \text{ (3 sd)}$$

If you're not sure what to do with your calculator, play with the one we've already done, and see which buttons you need to press to get the same answer.

Exercise Solution

Here's the table you already started filling in on pages 351-352.

The side lengths you were originally given are written in type. Your job is to skip the Pythagoras step and use the **ratio** (sin, cos or tan) you can get from the two given sides to find the angle α. Show which ratio you'd use by circling it.

Once you've worked out θ,try to spot a quick way of getting β for each triangle as well.

	Triangle	sin(□)	cos(□)	tan(□)	Angle □ (°)	Angle □ (°)
a	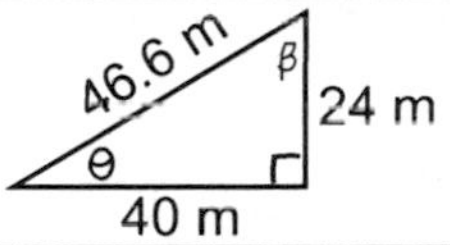	(0.515)	(0.858)	(0.6)	31.0	59.0
b	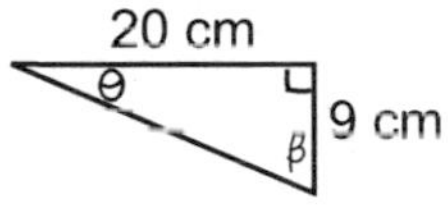	0.411	0.913	(0.45)	24.2	65.8
c	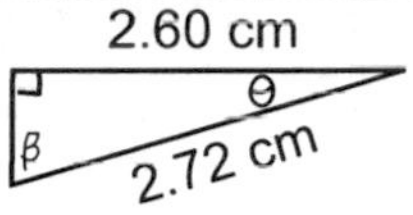	0.294	(0.956)	0.308	17.1	72.9
d	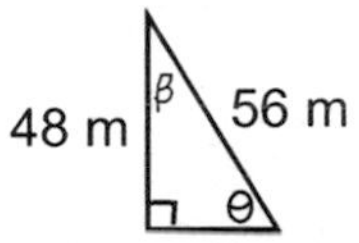	(0.857)	0.514	1.67	59.0	31.0

Triangle a: could use any two of three given sides.
Use tangent with opp and adj.

$\theta = \tan^{-1}(0.6) = 31.0°$ (3 sd)

Triangle b: $\theta = \tan^{-1}(0.45) = 65.8°$ (3 sd)

Triangle c: $\theta = \cos^{-1}(0.956) = 17.1°$ (3 sd)

Triangle d: $\theta = \sin^{-1}(0.857) = 59.0°$ (3 sd)

Slow way of getting β: find sine, cosine or tangent of β.

Quick way of getting β: $\theta + \beta = 90°$

there are no Dumb Questions

Q: I was playing with my calculator and typed in sin⁻¹ (random number), and it gave me an error instead of an angle. Why was that?

A: It's great that you took the time to play with your calculator. Since the hypotenuse is the longest side, the length of any other side divided by the length of the hypotenuse must always be less than 1. So if you type in $\sin^{-1}$ of a random number bigger than 1, it's not in the table, and the calculator gives you an error.

Back at the castle, everyone's depending on you!

Back at the castle, things are starting to get slightly desperate. The supply of food has just run out, and morale is low.

We're running out of time, and we'll need to work out how to aim the cannon and make the attackers retreat.

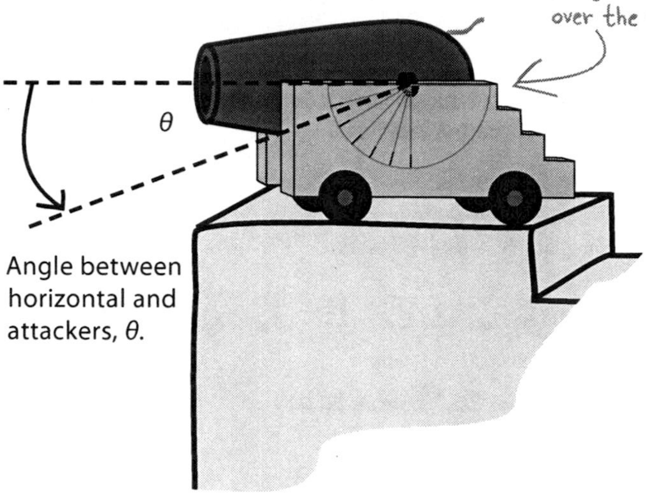

The trigonometric functions sine, cosine and tangent let you work out angles from side lengths, and vice-versa.

Sharpen your pencil

This is how it might be worded in a physics exam.

A cannon sits on top of a 15.0 m castle wall. Outside the castle, at the edge of its 20.0 m moat, are some attackers. What angle should the cannon make with the horizontal if it is to be pointed directly at the attackers?

Sharpen your pencil Solution

A cannon sits on top of a 15.0 m castle wall. Outside the castle, at the edge of its 20.0 m moat, are some attackers. What angle should the cannon make with the horizontal if it is to be pointed directly at the attackers?

The firing angle is the same as the angle θ in the triangle.

$$\tan(\theta) = \frac{o}{a} = \frac{15.0}{20.0} = 0.75$$

Then use $\tan^{-1}$ button to look up table in calculator:

$$\theta = \tan^{-1}(0.75) = 36.9° \text{ (3 sd)}$$

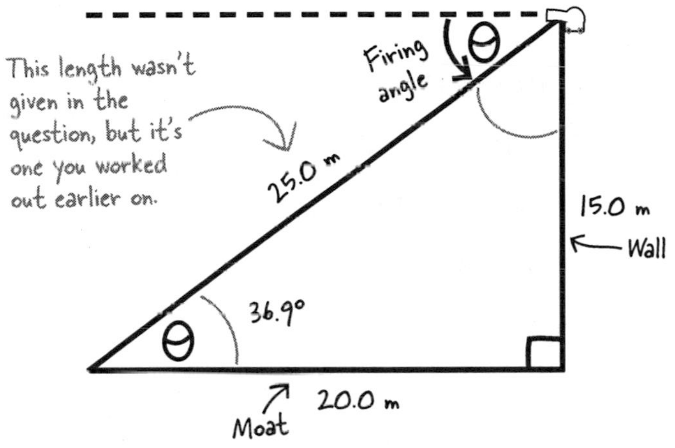

The cannon points at the attackers if it's aimed at 36.9° below horizontal.

Remember to give some MEANING to your answer – it's more than a number.

You can know everything! *

When you have a **right-angled triangle** and know the length of one **side**, plus **one other fact** (either another side length or an angle), you now have superpowers that enable you to work out **all** the other sides and angles.

You're going to see a lot of right-angled triangles through the rest of the book since the ground is horizontal and gravity accelerates things vertically at right-angles to the ground.

If you know ONE SIDE, plus ONE OTHER FACT (a side or an angle), you can work out EVERYTHING about a right-angled triangle using sine, cosine, tangent and Pythagoras.

*** Well, everything about a right-angled triangle at least!**

Does your answer SUCK?

Remember to check your answer once you've got it! Does the angle feel like it's the right kind of **size**? Did you remember the **units**? How about the **calculations**? And what about the '**kontext**' - stepping back and thinking about the big picture before moving on.

Well done if you already did this automatically when you worked it out!

Sharpen your pencil

Fill in the sections to see if your answer to the cannon question SUCKs. Remember to think about the 'k'ontext of what you're actually being asked to do!

S

SIZE ....

....

....

U

UNITS ....

....

....

C

CALCULATIONS ....

....

....

K

"K'ONTEXT ....

....

....

Sharpen your pencil Solution

This is an EXTREMELY useful way of checking if your angle is plausible.

Fill in the sections to see if your answer to the cannon question SUCKs. Remember to think about the 'k'ontext of what you're actually being asked to do!

S

SIZE I'm expecting an angle less than 45°, as it's opposite the smallest side of the triangle. So 36.9° is very plausible, as the smallest side isn't that much smaller than the other two, and my angle isn't that much less than 45°.

U

UNITS I've put them in – it's an angle, measured in degrees.

C

CALCULATIONS Well, they look OK. I rearranged the equation and used the inverse sine button OK (I didn't press the normal sine one by mistake).

K

"K'ONTEXT It's a cannon firing a cannonball from the top of a wall, so it goes along a straight line that's the hypotenuse of a right-angled tri ... hang on.
OH NO – WE FORGOT ABOUT GRAVITY!!

Before you launch in, think:
"Am I actually answering the question I was asked?"

It saves time to do this BEFORE starting on the math rather than afterwards.

Uh oh. Gravity...

Everyone forgot about **gravity**! The calculations assumed that the cannonball's going to follow the same **straight** path as the ladder. So although you got an answer which was the correct size with correct units and flawless calculations, it wasn't the answer to the problem we have to solve!

Gravity makes objects like baseballs and footballs travel along **curves** as they fly through the air. So the cannonball's going to curve too because gravity will **accelerate it downwards**.

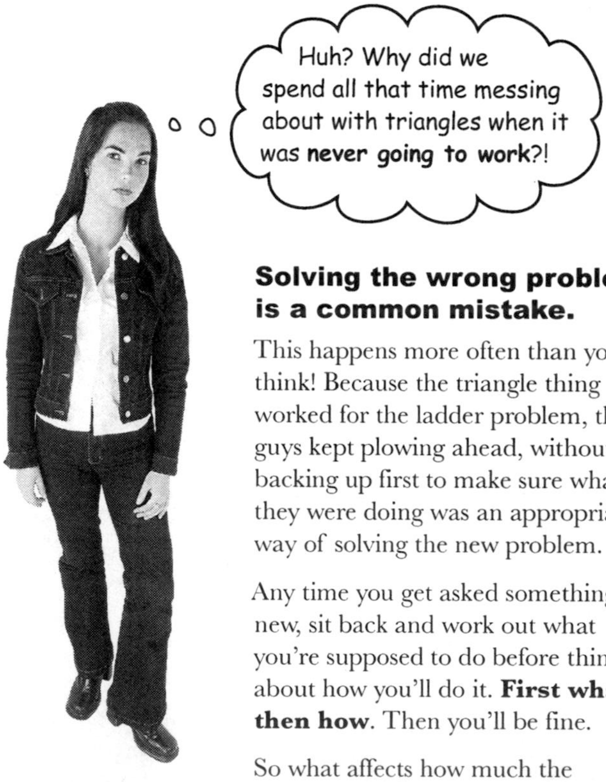

Solving the wrong problem is a common mistake.

This happens more often than you'd think! Because the triangle thing worked for the ladder problem, the guys kept plowing ahead, without backing up first to make sure what they were doing was an appropriate way of solving the new problem.

Any time you get asked something new, sit back and work out what you're supposed to do before thinking about how you'll do it. **First what, then how**. Then you'll be fine.

So what affects how much the cannonball curves? A baseball and a bullet appear to curve by different amounts. So maybe the firing angle will be OK after all if the cannonball doesn't deviate from its part all that much. To work out if the angle's OK, it's time to **be** the cannonball!

BE the cannonball

Your job is to imagine you're the cannonball. What makes you change direction as you go through the air.? And what affects how much you deviate from a straight line?

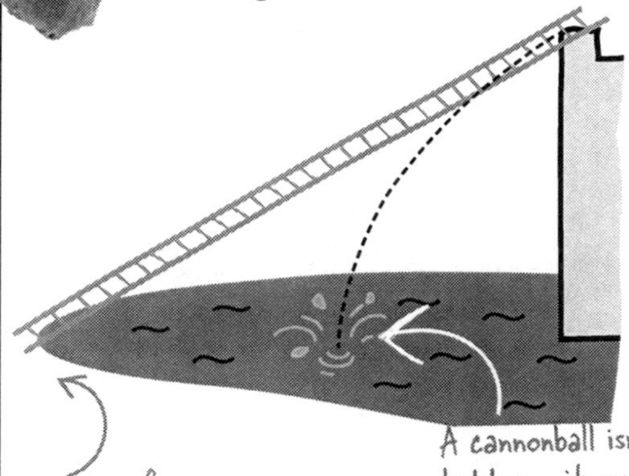

BE the cannonball - SOLUTION

Your job is to imagine you're the cannonball. What makes you change direction as you go through the air? And what affects how much you deviate from a straight line?

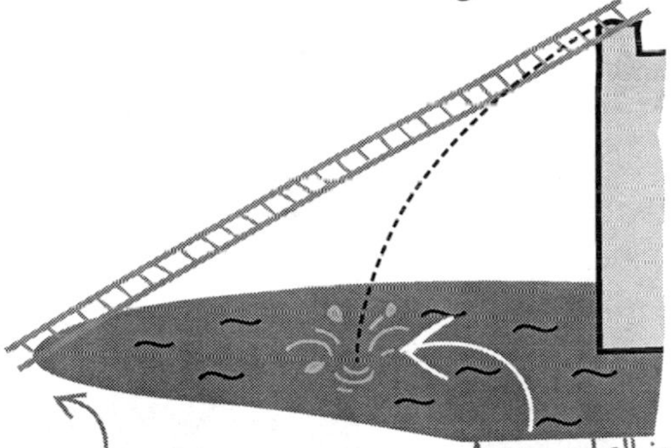

I'm being accelerated downwards by gravity.

If I was going slowly, I'd land very close to the wall.

If I was going quickly, I'd land further out.

If I was going really quickly, I'd almost go along a straight line.

My velocity affects how much I deviate from a straight line.

Jim: We might still be OK though. I just looked up the cannon on the Sieges-R-Us website, and its muzzle **velocity** is 90 m/s! That's high compared with the distance it's traveling, so maybe there won't be time for it to deviate from its original path too much.

Joe: We could use our **equations of motion**... except that we don't know the cannonball's total **displacement**! We know that the straight line distance from the cannon to the enemy is 25.0 m. But how do we get the length of its curved path?

Jim: Maybe that doesn't matter though. Back in the desert, we didn't need to know everything about the cage to be able to use equations of motion to work things out.

Joe: So ... what do we know? The cannonball's initial velocity ($\boldsymbol{v}_0$), its initial displacement ($\boldsymbol{x}_0$) and the acceleration due to gravity ($\boldsymbol{a}$).

Frank: Except - how are we going to put the numbers into the equations? Before, the acceleration and velocity vectors were always along the same straight line, either in the same direction or in opposite directions. So we defined one direction as positive and the other as negative. But with the cannon, the acceleration vector points down, and the velocity vector points at an angle. They're not opposites! How do we deal with that?

Joe: Ah ... I see what you mean. And it's even worse - the direction the cannonball's going in keeps changing. So both the size and the direction of the velocity vector are changing all the time!

Jim: Mm-hm. How on earth are we gonna deal with that?

Joe: We could always go back to the experiment idea since we're doing something totally new now ...

The cannonball's velocity and acceleration vectors point in different directions

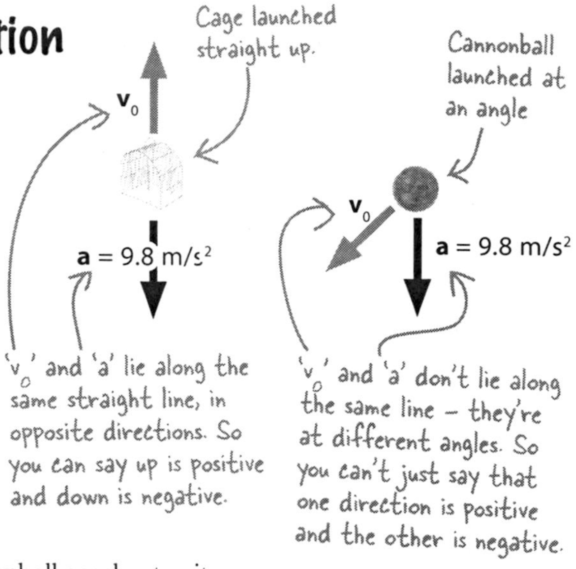

There's a big difference between the cannonball and an object launched vertically. The cannonball's velocity and acceleration vectors point in **different directions**. Not opposite directions - they're at completely different **angles**.

This creates a problem with the math. Before, we defined 'up' as the positive direction, and 'down' as the negative direction. This was because a launched object's velocity vector points up, and its acceleration vector points down. But the cannonball's velocity doesn't point up or down—it's at an angle—so you can't do that.

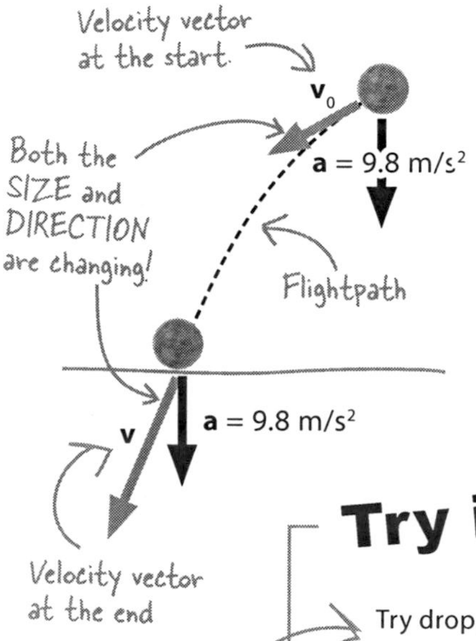

And even worse - as the cannonball accelerates, it **changes direction** and curves towards the ground. As time goes on, the direction of the velocity vector changes to point more and more towards the ground. That sounds difficult to deal with.

What IS possible is to **try** things out. You can see if there's any difference between how gravity acts on an object that is dropped versus an object that is already moving horizontally (like the cannonball is) before it falls.

Try it!

Try dropping two balls off the edge of a table at the same time, one with a little push and one with a big push. Keep the pushes horizontal for now so you're not 'helping' either of them downwards by pushing them towards the ground.

Look out for where they land - and when they land - and write down anything you notice.

Or you could use two pens instead - the type of object doesn't matter.

....

....

....

....

Gravity accelerates everything downwards at 9.8 m/s^2

Back when you were thinking about the Dingo dropping/launching his cage, you worked out that **gravity** always **accelerated** the cage **vertically** at 9.8 m/s^2, whether the cage was going up or coming back down again.

This is also the case if an object's velocity has a **horizontal** part (or component). Gravity accelerates **everything** downwards at the same rate of 9.8 m/s^2.

Tried it!

You've just been pushing two things off a table at the same time, but with different horizontal velocities, and seeing which hit the ground first.

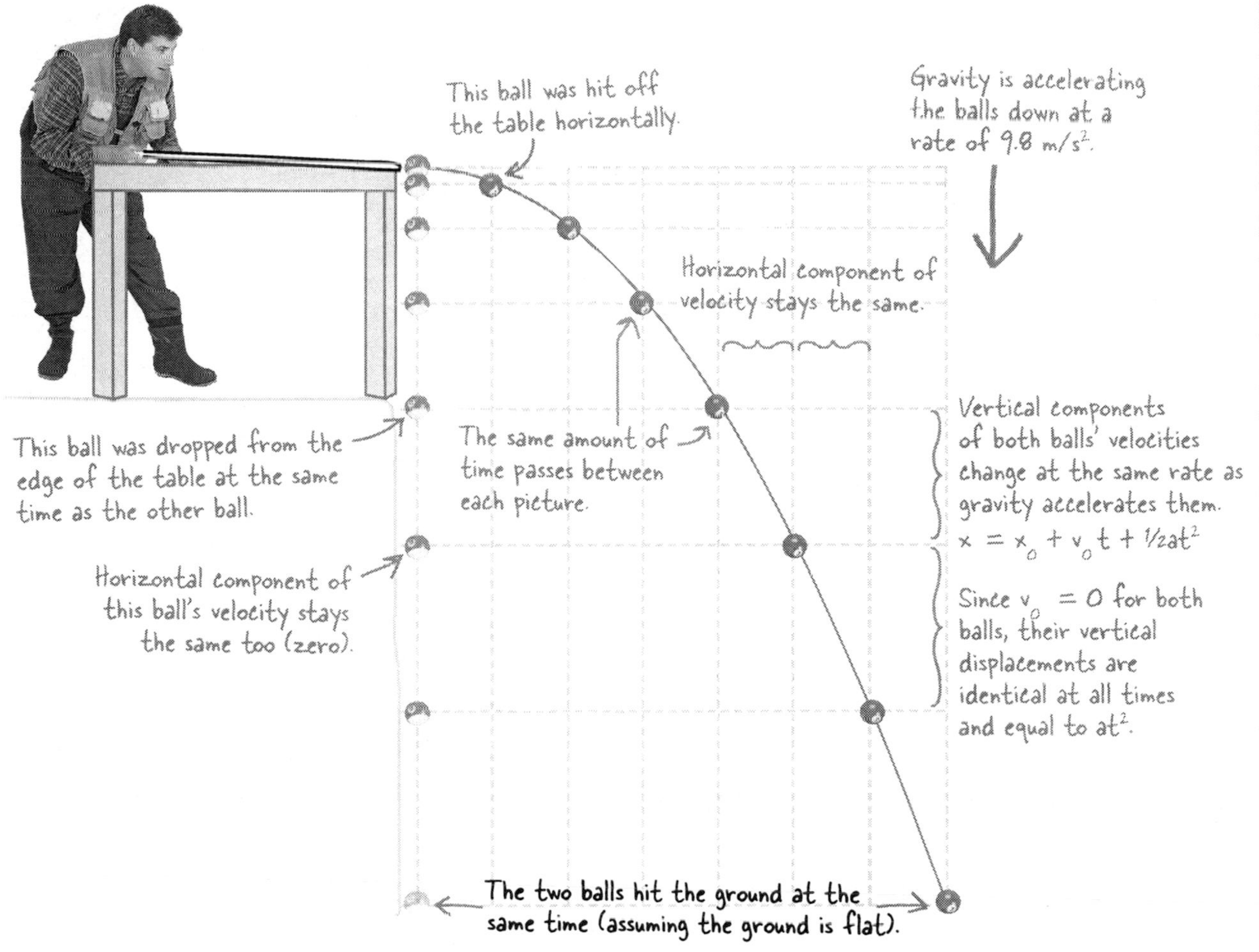

The horizontal component of the velocity can't change once you've let go

Gravity accelerates things downwards at a rate of 9.8 m/s^2. When something moves through the air, gravity is the only thing affecting it (assuming that it doesn't have an engine like an airplane). The cannonball doesn't have an engine, so gravity changes the **vertical component** of its velocity at a rate of 9.8 m/s^2.

The technical term for 'something moving through the air' is a PROJECTILE.

Once you've launched the cannonball, nothing affects the **horizontal component** of its velocity. It will keep on doing exactly what it was doing.

Strictly speaking, there'll be air resistance, but for a cannonball, this will be tiny, and you can ignore it for now.

That's why the two objects you knocked off the table hit the ground at the same time, even though you gave one object a big horizontal push and let the other object drop straight down vertically.

The **vertical components** of both objects' velocities were zero at the start - they weren't falling before they left the table. Gravity accelerated both objects downwards at the same rate of 9.8 m/s^2, changing the horizontal components of each object's velocity by the same amount.

The **horizontal component** of both objects' velocities were unaffected by gravity. The dropped object landed directly under where it started, but the pushed object landed further away.

But the cannonball is launched at an **angle** - so its velocity initially has both horizontal and vertical components. What happens to something like that? Time to try it ...

Try it!

Get a ball, and throw it straight up in the air while standing still.

Now start to walk along a straight line, still throwing the ball in the same way you were before. Walking forwards gives the ball a **horizontal velocity component** which is the same as your walking velocity. Throwing the ball upwards gives it a **vertical velocity component**.

Write and sketch anything you notice.

Gravity only affects the vertical component of the velocity.

The horizontal component of a projectile's velocity is constant

A ball you throw straight up comes straight back down into your hand for you to catch.

A ball you throw straight up while moving forwards also comes back down into your hand. Even though your hand stays the same distance away from your body as you throw the ball (so you throw it straight up), the ball's velocity also has a **horizontal component** . This is because you're moving forwards at the time that you throw the ball.

A "horizontal component" is sometimes called a "horizontal component vector."

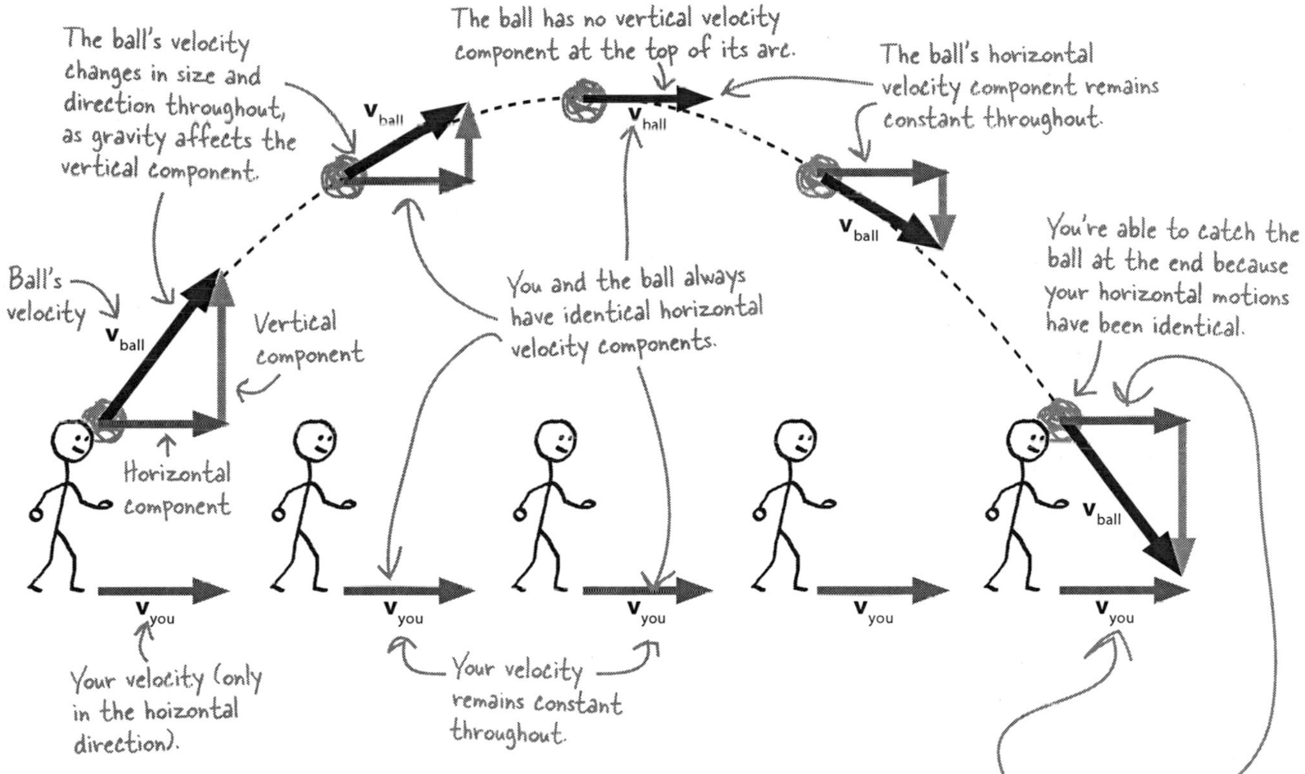

Throughout the ball's flight, the **horizontal component** of your velocity and the horizontal component of the ball's velocity are exactly the same. The horizontal component of the ball's velocity doesn't change even though the ball's going up and down.

Would you, could you, on a plane?

OK, so imagine yourself on an airplane, traveling horizontally through the sky. If you throw a ball straight up in the air, it comes straight back down again.

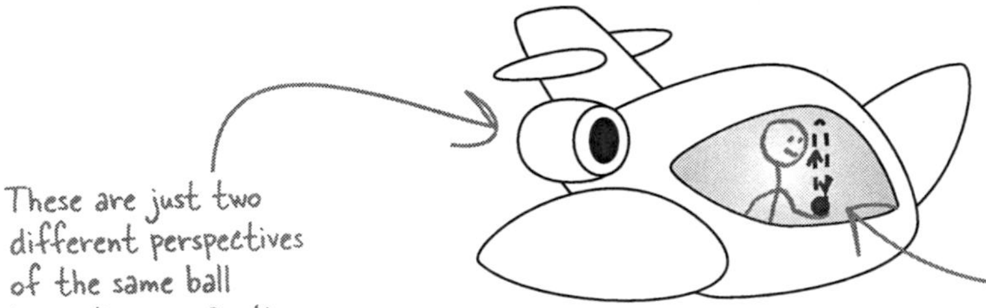

Now, imagine that you're looking at the airplane from outside. You see the ball following a **curved** path. Relative to the inside of the plane, the ball goes straight up and down. But **relative** to a person outside, the ball moves horizontally with the same velocity as the plane.

The **horizontal component** of the ball's velocity is **constant** throughout the balls' motion.

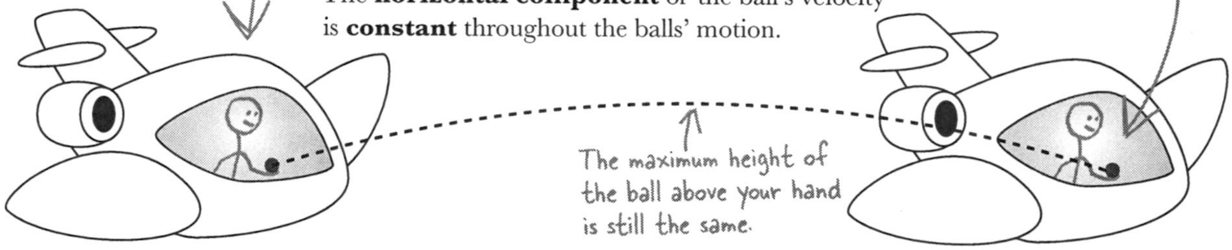

The horizontal component of a projectile's velocity isn't affected by gravity, so is CONSTANT throughout the projectile's flight.

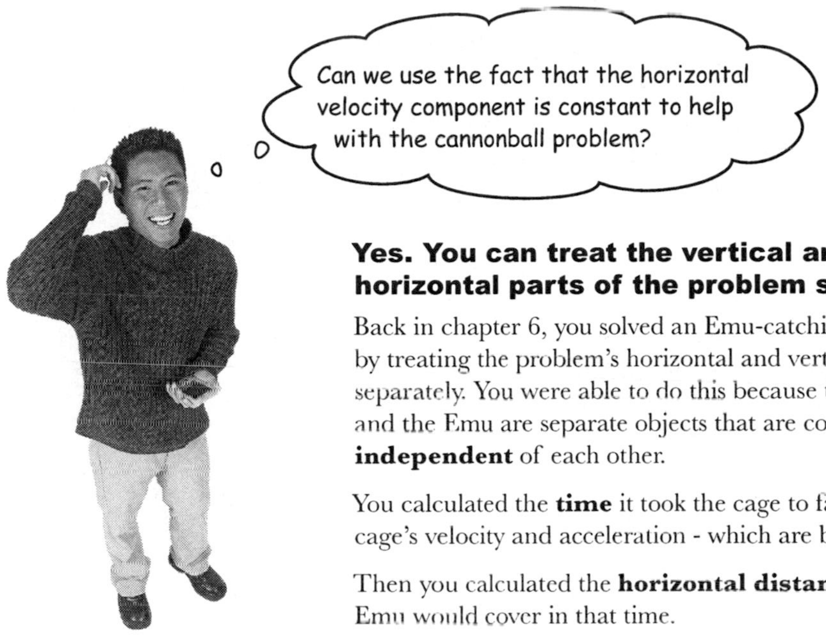

Yes. You can treat the vertical and horizontal parts of the problem separately.

Back in chapter 6, you solved an Emu-catching problem by treating the problem's horizontal and vertical parts separately. You were able to do this because the cage and the Emu are separate objects that are completely **independent** of each other.

You calculated the **time** it took the cage to fall using the cage's velocity and acceleration - which are both **vertical**.

Then you calculated the **horizontal distance** that the Emu would cover in that time.

As the horizontal and vertical components of the cannonball's velocity are completely **independent**, you can do the cannonball problem the same way you did the Emu problem.

You can calculate the time it **takes** for the cannonball to land by thinking about the **vertical component** of the cannonball's velocity and the cannonball's acceleration, which is also vertical.

Then you can calculate the **horizontal displacement** that the cannonball has in that time using the horizontal component of the cannonballs' velocity.

The vertical component of a projectile's velocity behaves like an object launched straight up or down at that velocity.

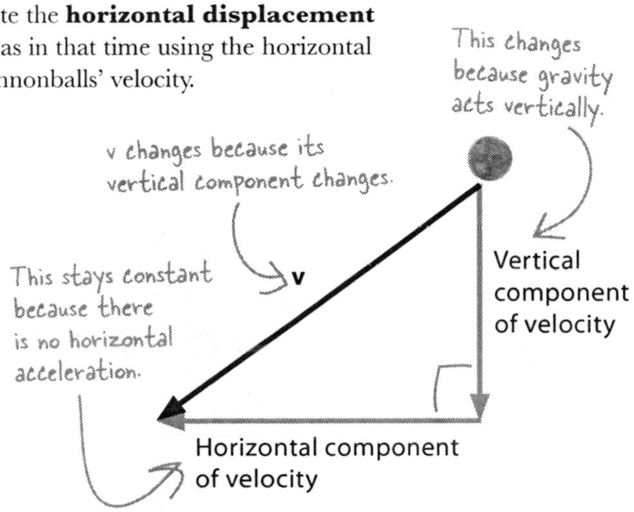

The same method solves both problems

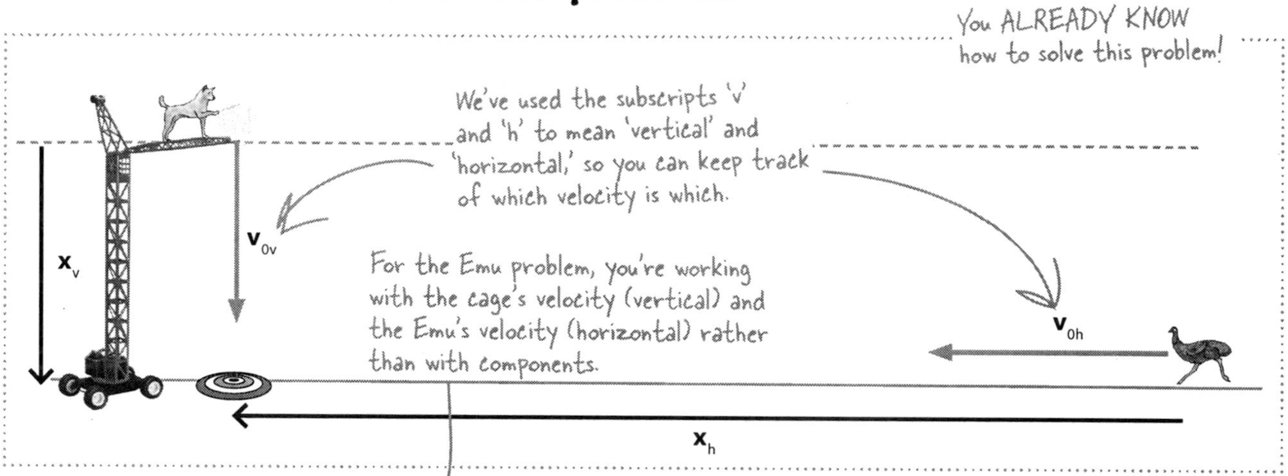

Step 1: Work out the vertical and horizontal **components** of the initial velocity, $\mathbf{v}_{0v}$ and $\mathbf{v}_{0h}$.

Step 2: Use the **vertical velocity component** and **vertical displacement** to work out the **time** the object is in the air for.

Step 3: Use the **horizontal velocity component** and the **time** to work out the object's horizontal displacement.

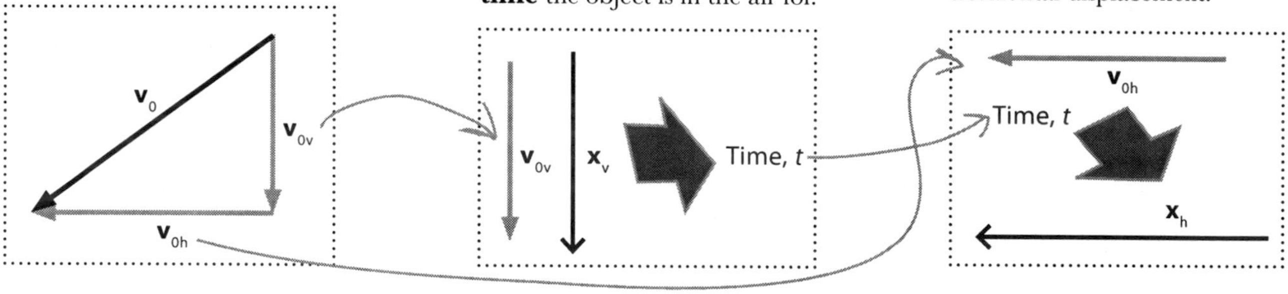

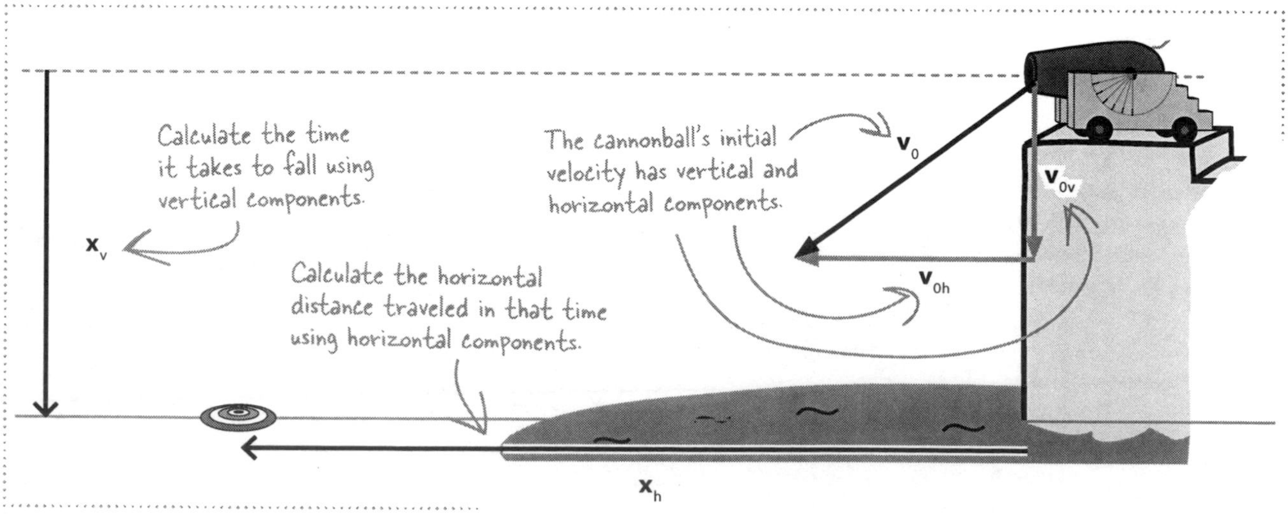

Question Clinic: The "Projectile" Question

Any question that involves an object projected through the air usually means you have to turn its velocity into horizontal and vertical components. Then you can use your right-angled triangle superpowers together with your equations of motion (from chapters 6, 7, and 8) to get your answers. The question presented here is a typical question.

This is just our problem worded differently.

Remember to start with a sketch, and to add information to the sketch as you work things out, so you have it all in one place.

You need to work out the vertical and horizontal velocity components first, before you do parts b and c.

5. You are in a castle where the wall is 15.0 m high. A cannon at the top of the wall is aimed directly at an enemy 20.0 m from the base of the castle wall. The cannon's muzzle velocity is 90.0 m/s.

a. What angle does the cannon make with the ground?

b. How long does it take for the cannonball to reach the ground?

c. How far from the attackers does the cannonball land?

You've already done part a of the question with the displacement vector triangle.

When you see the word 'angle,' start trying to spot right-angled triangles, and thinking about "sin, cos, tan & Pythagoras." Use the displacement triangle to calculate the angle.

This involves using the VERTICAL component of the cannonball's velocity to see how long it takes to fall vertically.

This involves using the HORIZONTAL component of the cannonball's velocity to see how far it travels horizontally in that time.

The word 'angle' also gives you the hint that component vectors might be important.

The projectile question almost always requires you to work out the **time** it takes for an object to fall (using the **vertical** velocity component), and then the **distance** it travels horizontally in that time (using the horizontal velocity component).

Step 1: Work out the vertical and horizontal **components** of the initial velocity, $\mathbf{v}_{0v}$ and $\mathbf{v}_{0h}$.

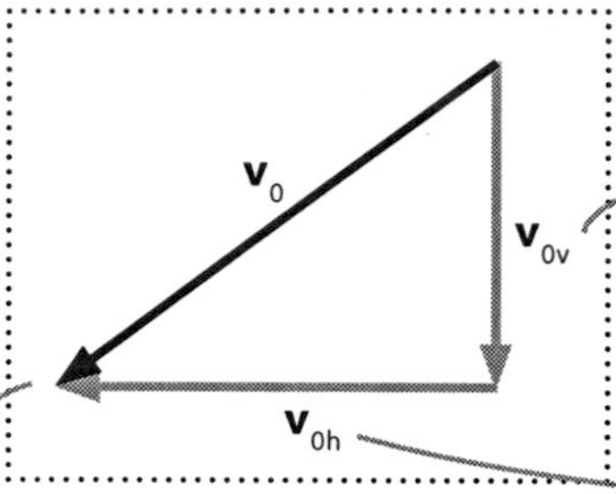

Step 2: Use the **vertical velocity component** and **vertical displacement** to work out the **time** the object is in the air for.

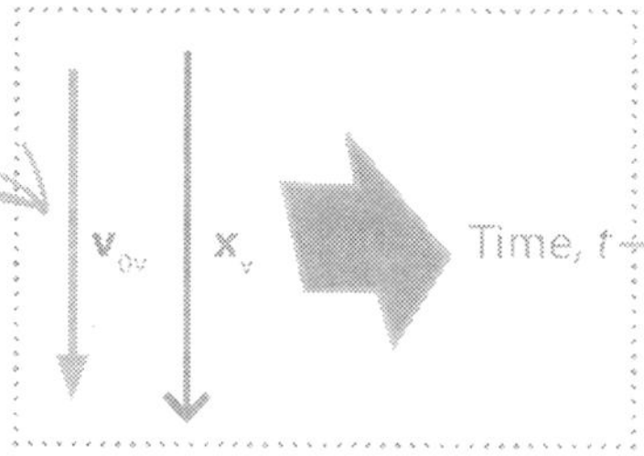

Step 3: Use the **horizontal velocity component** and the **time** to work out the object's horizontal displacement.

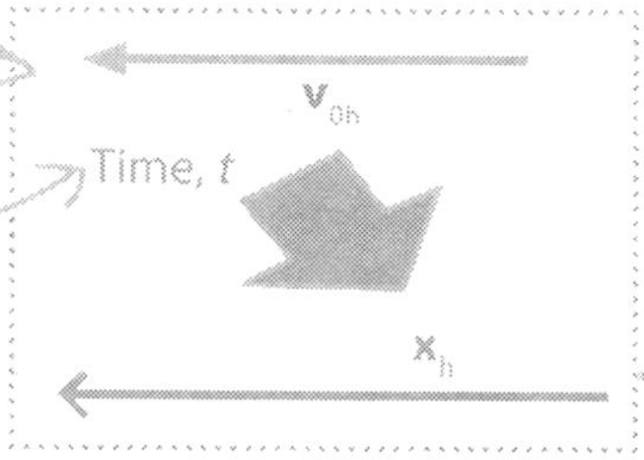

Sharpen your pencil

You are in a castle where the wall is 15.0 m high. A cannon at the top of the wall is aimed directly at an enemy 20.0 m from the base of the castle wall. The cannon's muzzle velocity is 90.0 m/s.

You've already worked out that the cannon makes an angle of 36.9° with the horizontal.

Now it's time to work out the **vertical and horizontal components of the cannonball's velocity.** Use subscripts in your symbols, $\mathbf{v}_v$ for the vertical component and $\mathbf{v}_h$ for the horizontal component.

This is a displacement vector triangle. You need to draw a velocity vector triangle and work out the lengths of its sides.

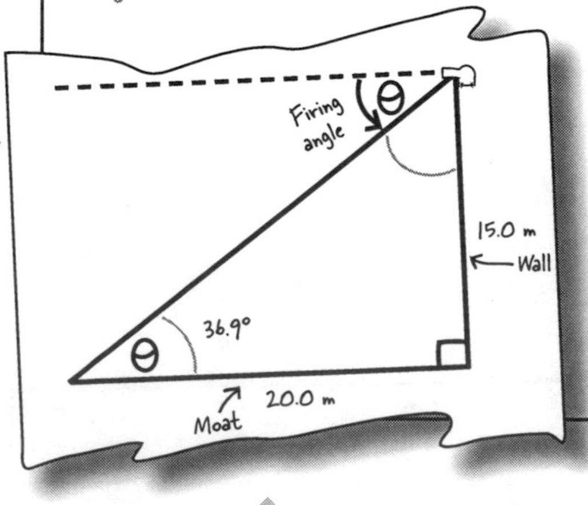

Sharpen your pencil Solution

You are in a castle where the wall is 15.0 m high. A cannon at the top of the wall is aimed directly at an enemy 20.0 m from the base of the castle wall. The cannon's muzzle velocity is 90.0 m/s.

You've already worked out that the cannon makes an angle of 36.9° with the horizontal.

Now it's time to work out the **vertical and horizontal components of the cannonball's velocity.** Use subscripts in your symbols, $\mathbf{v}_v$ for the vertical component and $\mathbf{v}_h$ for the horizontal component.

There are TWO different ways of doing this question!

It doesn't matter which one you used – they both work!

Doing it using sine, cosine and tangent.

This way would be the quickest if you hadn't already been playing with the displacement triangle earlier on.

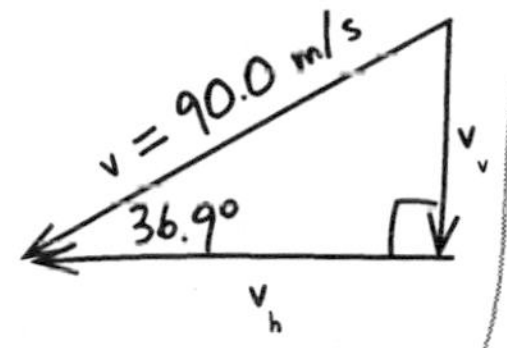

Start by writing out the equation.

Vertical component

$$\sin(36.9°) = \frac{opp}{hyp} = \frac{v_v}{90}$$

Then put the numbers in/rearrange it.

$$\Rightarrow v_v = 90\sin(36.9°) = 54.0 \text{ m/s (3 sd)}$$

Make sure you use headings, so you and others know what you're trying to do.

Horizontal component

$$\cos(36.9°) = \frac{adj}{hyp} = \frac{v_h}{90}$$

$$\Rightarrow v_h = 90\cos(36.9°) = 72.0 \text{ m/s (3 sd)}$$

Doing it using similar triangles

The position and velocity triangles are SIMILAR TRIANGLES.

Their angles are the same, as they both have a 90° angle and a 36.9° angle.

Velocity

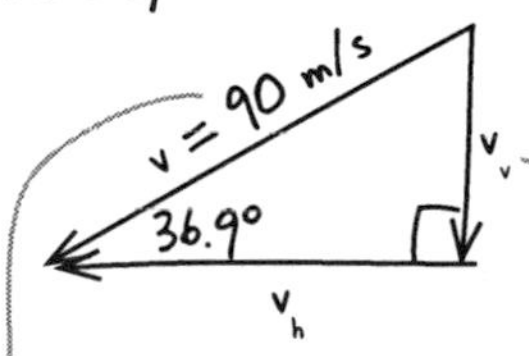

Displacement

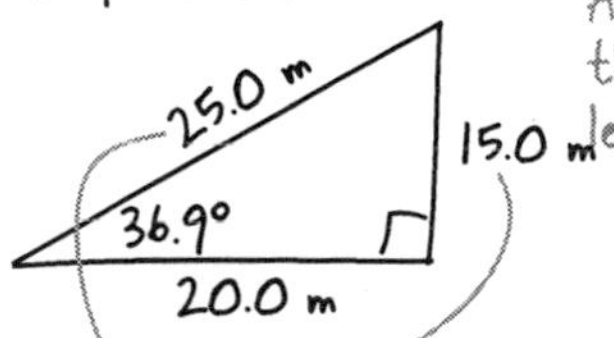

As they're similar triangles, the ratios of their side lengths are identical.

Vertical component: $\frac{v_v}{90} = \frac{15}{25} \Rightarrow v_v = \frac{15 \times 90}{25} = 54 \text{ m/s}$

Horizontal component: $\frac{v_h}{90} = \frac{20}{25} \Rightarrow v_v = \frac{20 \times 90}{25} = 72 \text{ m/s}$

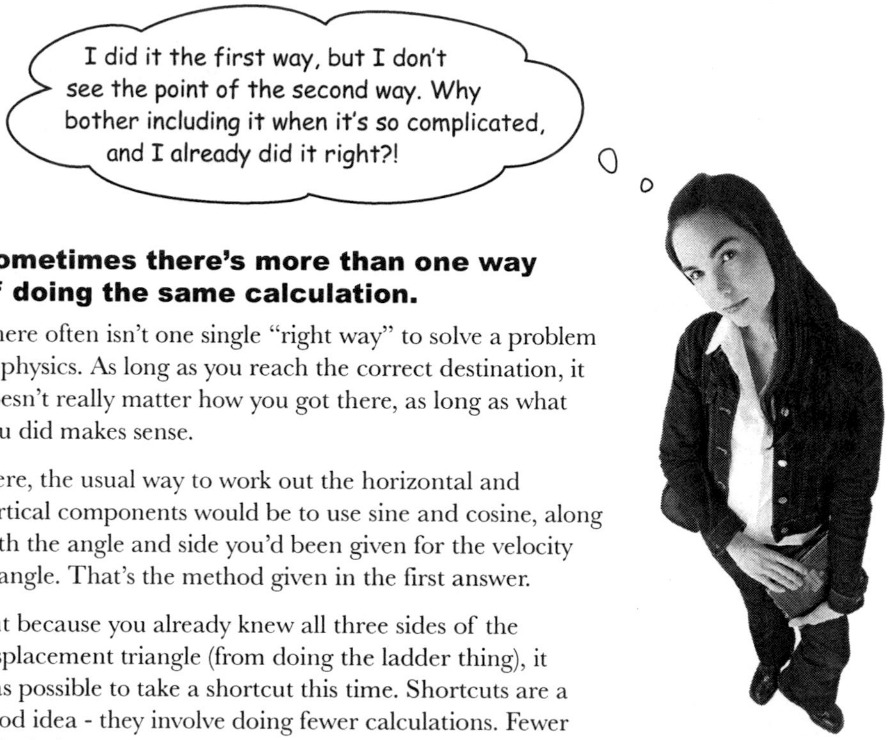

Sometimes there's more than one way of doing the same calculation.

There often isn't one single "right way" to solve a problem in physics. As long as you reach the correct destination, it doesn't really matter how you got there, as long as what you did makes sense.

Here, the usual way to work out the horizontal and vertical components would be to use sine and cosine, along with the angle and side you'd been given for the velocity triangle. That's the method given in the first answer.

But because you already knew all three sides of the displacement triangle (from doing the ladder thing), it was possible to take a shortcut this time. Shortcuts are a good idea - they involve doing fewer calculations. Fewer calculations mean you type less into your calculator - and there's a smaller chance that you'll mess up by accidentally typing the wrong thing.

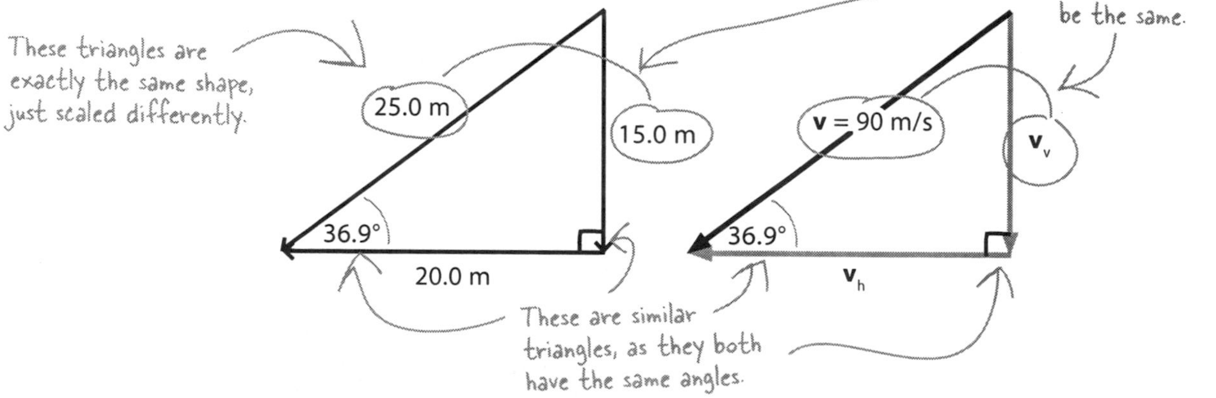

This particular shortcut works because the displacement and velocity triangles are similar triangles. You already know that the ratios of their side lengths will be the same. $\frac{15}{25}$ in the first triangle $= \frac{\mathbf{v}_v}{90}$ in the second triangle. You don't need to use the angle and sine, cosine or tangent to calculate the ratios of the side lengths.

5. You are in a castle where the wall is 15.0 m high. A cannon at the top of the wall is aimed directly at an enemy 20.0 m from the base of the castle wall. The cannon's muzzle velocity is 90 m/s.

a. What angle does the cannon make with the ground?

b. How long does it take for the cannonball to reach the ground?

c. How far from the attackers does the cannonball land?

Now it's time to get on with part b of the original problem!

Calculating the horizontal and vertical components of the cannonball's velocity wasn't part of the original question. Is there a way of spotting that we need to do that?

Sometimes you have to work out the intermediate steps yourself.

Many processes in life involve a series of **intermediate steps** to get from where you are to where you want to be. To get into your house, first of all you need to find your keys! Physics problems can be like this too.

In order to calculate the time it takes for the cannonball to fall, you need the vertical component of the cannonball's velocity. And to calculate the horizontal displacement, you need the horizontal component of the cannonball's velocity.

Spotting these intermediate steps comes with experience and practice with a variety of physics problems. You've been building up the ability to spot what you need to do to solve a problem as you've been learning to think like a physicist. But using what you've learned in this book to do practice problems and exam questions from elsewhere is important too.

In the Question Clinics throughout the book, we've taken several typical exam-style questions and broken them down to tell you what kinds of clues to look out for.

Step 1: Work out the vertical and horizontal **components** of the initial velocity, $\mathbf{v}_{0v}$ and $\mathbf{v}_{0h}$.

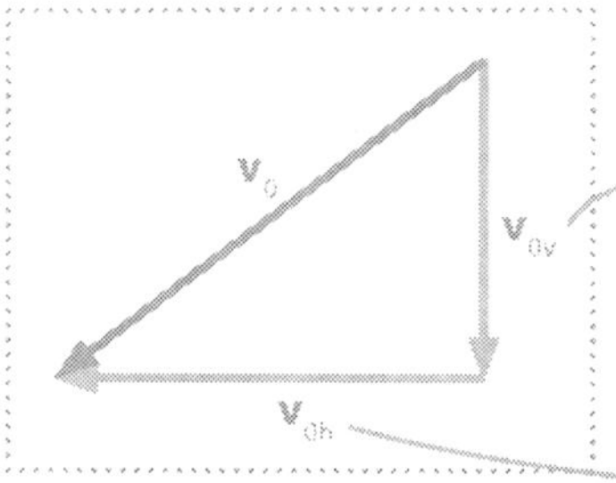

Step 2: Use the **vertical velocity component** and **vertical displacement** to work out the **time** the object is in the air for.

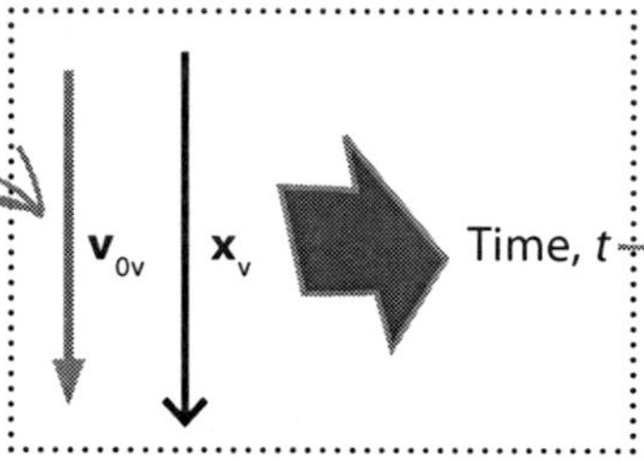

Step 3: Use the **horizontal velocity component** and the **time** to work out the object's horizontal displacement.

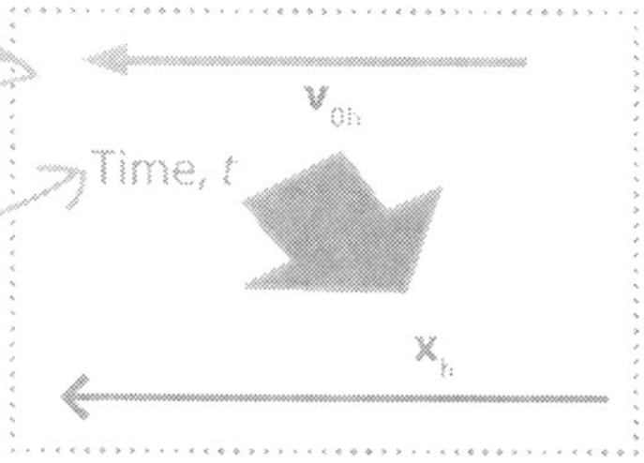

Sharpen your pencil

b. How long does it take for the cannonball to reach the ground?

Hint: Treat the cannonball like something launched directly downwards with the vertical component of the cannonball's velocity. Do a sketch that only deals with the VERTICAL direction and go on from there.

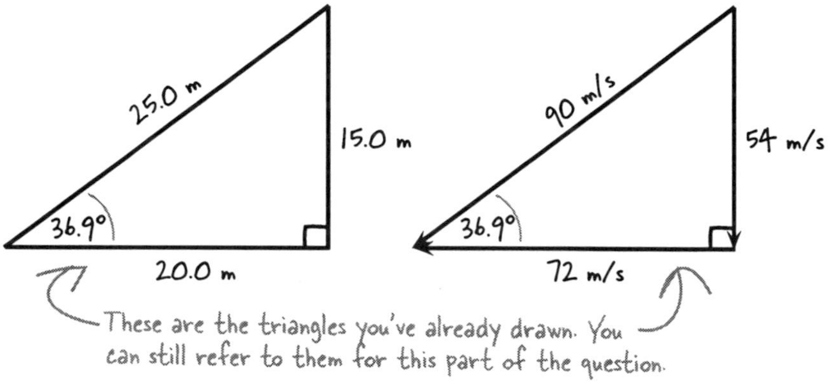

Hint: You may need to use more than one equation of motion to solve this problem.

Sharpen your pencil Solution

b. How long does it take for the cannonball to reach the ground?

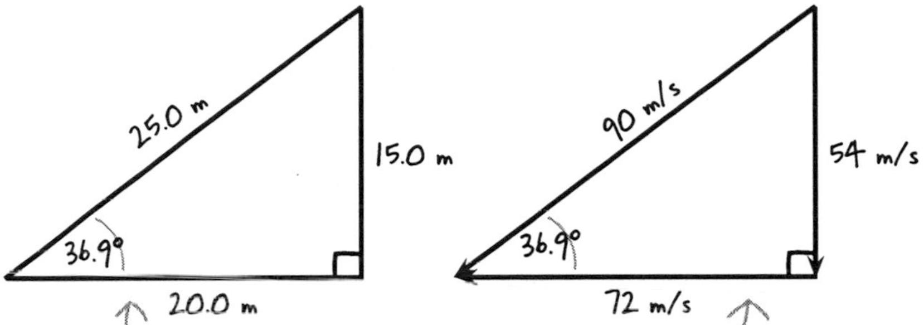

These are the triangles you'd already have drawn on your page during earlier parts of the question.

This is a sketch that only deals with the vertical direction. It's much clearer to do this than it is to try to work with parts of triangles.

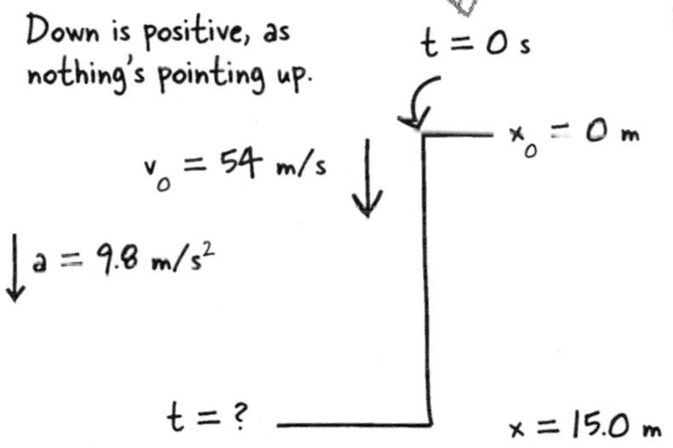

$$x - x_0 = v_0 t + \frac{1}{2}at^2$$

$$v = v_0 + at$$

$$v^2 = v_0^2 + 2a(x - x_0)$$

Write down your three key equations, and make a note of what you do and don't know.

In the first equation, the only thing I don't know is t. But there's both t and t^2 in the equation, and I can't rearrange it to say "t = something."

So use third equation to work out v, then use that value in $v = v_0 + at$ to work out t.

$$v^2 = v_0^2 + 2a(x - x_0)$$

$$v = \sqrt{54^2 + (2 \times 9.8 \times 15)} = 56.7 \text{ m/s (3 sd)}$$

If you're only dealing with one component (in this case the vertical component) of the displacement, velocity and acceleration, you can omit the 'horizontal' and 'vertical' subscripts from your variables to reduce the clutter in your work.

Use this value in $v = v_0 + at$ to work out t.

$$v = v_0 + at$$

$$at = v - v_0$$

$$t = \frac{v - v_0}{a} = \frac{56.7 - 54}{9.8} = 0.276 \text{ s (3 sd)}$$

It takes 0.276 s (3 sd) for the cannonball to reach the ground.

Step 1: Work out the vertical and horizontal **components** of the initial velocity, $\mathbf{v}_{0h}$ and $\mathbf{v}_{0v}$.

Step 2: Use the **vertical velocity component** and **vertical displacement** to work out the **time** the object is in the air for.

Step 3: Use the **horizontal velocity component** and the **time** to work out the object's horizontal displacement.

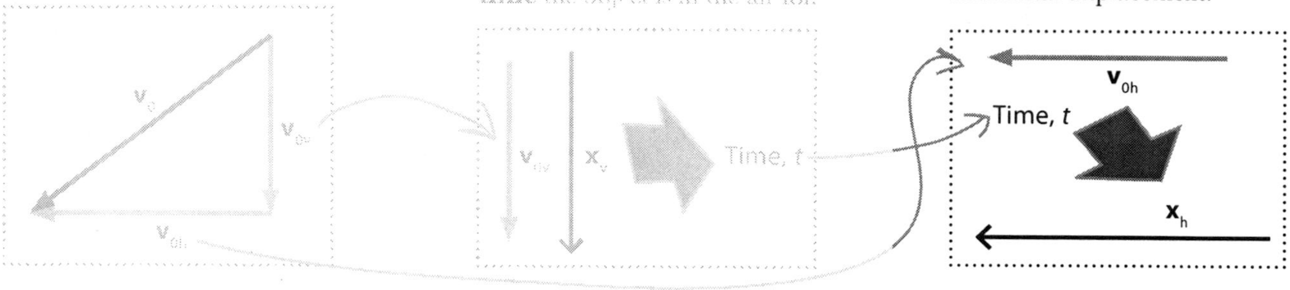

Sharpen your pencil

Now for part c (or step 3 in the illustration above). Hang in there; you're nearly done!

c. How far from the attackers does the cannonball land? (The attackers are at the edge of the moat, 20.0 m from the base of the wall.)

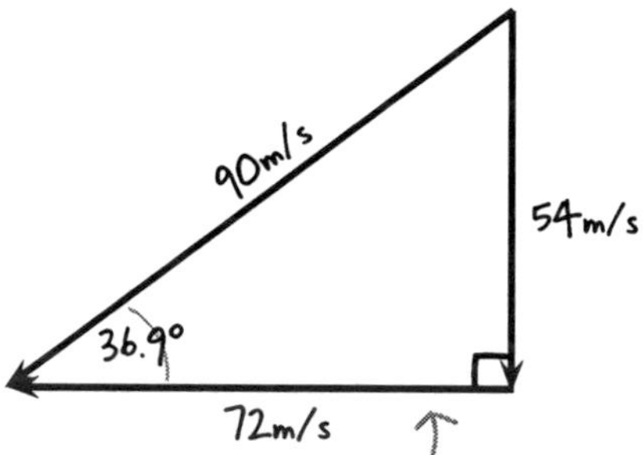

Hint: Treat the cannonball like something launched horizontally with the horizontal component of the cannonball's velocity. Do a sketch that only deals with the HORIZONTAL direction and go on from there.

You'll need to use the velocity triangle you already worked out and the time from part b (it takes 0.276 s for the cannonball to reach the ground).

Sharpen your pencil Solution

c. How far from the attackers does the cannonball land?
(The attackers are at the edge of the moat, 20.0 m from the base of the wall.)

$t = 0.276$ s

$v = 72$ m/s ← This is the horizontal component of the cannonball's velocity.

Distance = ?

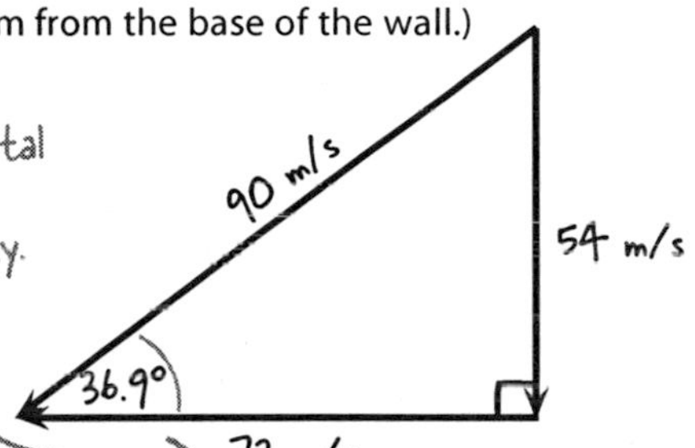

You worked this out in part b.

Cannonball takes 0.276 s to reach the ground.

Horizontal component of velocity = 72 m/s. ← You worked this out in the 'missing step' between parts a and b.

Horizontal distance traveled in this time = speed × time ← This is the right method – once you know how long it takes to reach the ground VERTICALLY, work out how far the cannonball travels HORIZONTALLY in this time.

= 72 × 0.276

= 19.9 m (3 sd)

Attackers are 20.0 m away from the foot of the castle wall. This is another way of saying that they are 20.0 m horizontally from the cannon.

So the cannonball lands 20.0 – 19.9 = 0.1 m short of the attackers, but probably gets them running scared ...

Did you answer the question you were ACTUALLY ASKED (distance from the attackers) or did you leave it as 19.9 m (distance from the wall)?

Check: "Have I actually answered the question I was asked?"

Make sure you don't forget to do something simple at the end, like convert units or subtract one length from another.

And so they ran away ...

The cannonball lands only 10 cm away from the attackers and soaks them! They didn't know you had a cannon up your sleeve (as well as your shovels). And and they're not waiting around to see what you do next - so make a very hasty retreat!

BULLET POINTS

- With a right-angled triangle where you know the length of **one side plus one other fact** (a side length or an angle), you can work out all the other sides and angles using sine, cosine, tangent and Pythagoras.
- Similar triangles have the same sizes of angles.
- Similar triangles are useful because the **ratios** of the similar sides are the same. This means you can often find side lengths without having to work out an angle.
- If something's velocity is in a different direction from its acceleration, try breaking the velocity down into vector **components** parallel to and perpendicular to the acceleration.
- Vectors should always be added **nose to tail**.
- Once your displacement/velocity/acceleration vectors are broken down into components at 90° to each other, you can treat the two directions **independently**.
- You might want to work out the **time** it takes something to happen from one component, then use that in an equation involving the other component.
- Add together the component vectors at the end to find out what's happened to the original vector.

If you're doing the AP Physics exam, you're not allowed a calculator in the multiple choice section. So they give you a table – like the one you worked out earlier – of values for sine, cosine and tangent for certain 'common angles.'

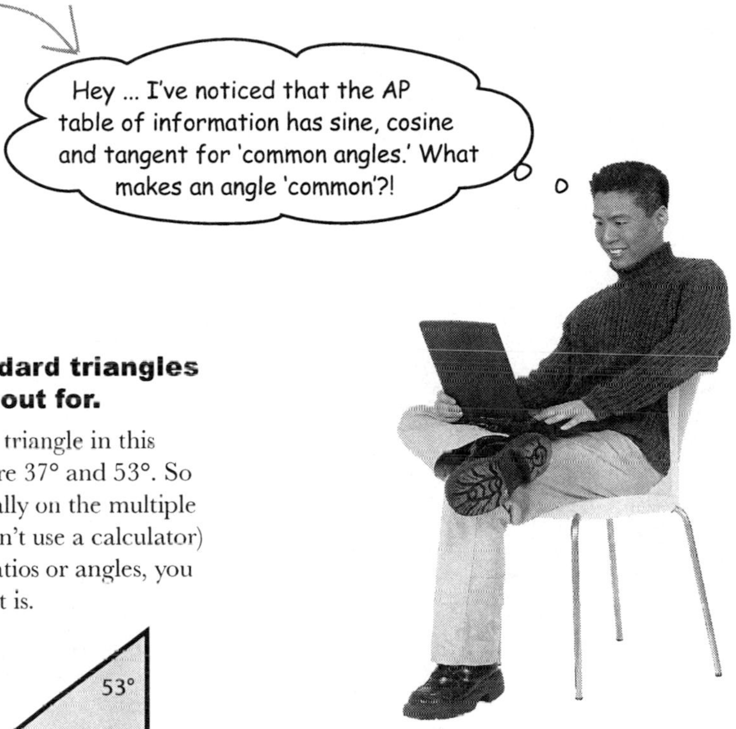

There are some standard triangles that you should look out for.

You've already met the 3:4:5 triangle in this chapter. Its angles (to 2 sd) are 37° and 53°. So if you see a question, especially on the multiple choice section (where you can't use a calculator) involving these side length ratios or angles, you know what kind of triangle it is.

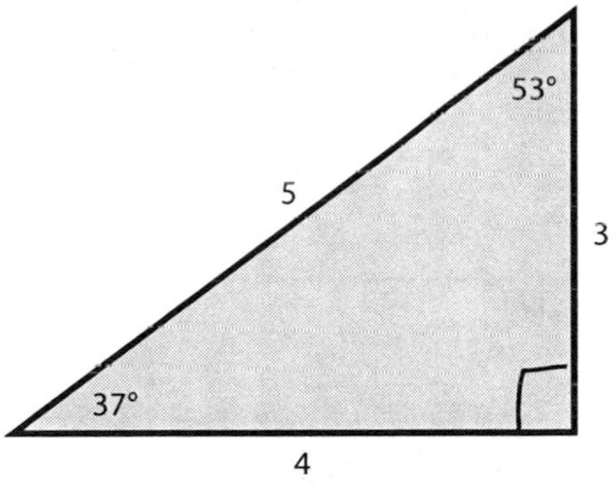

Note that the smallest side is always opposite the smallest angle, and the largest side is opposite the largest angle.

Another standard triangle is the 1:1:√2 triangle.. It has two sides that are the same length, so the two angles opposite them are the same size - 45°.

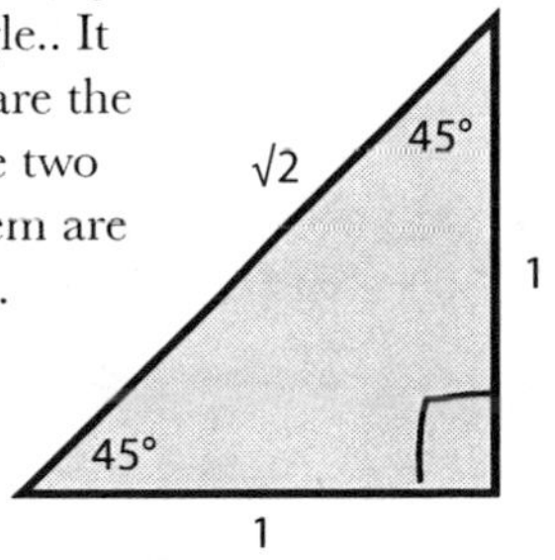

The third standard triangle in the table is the 1:2:√3 triangle. Its angles are 30° and 60°.

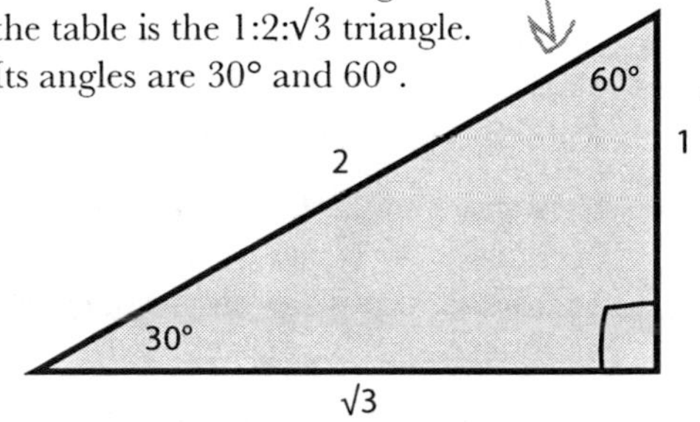

Question Clinic: The "Missing steps" Question

Often, you'll get a multi-part question, which doesn't directly ask you to carry out some of the steps you need to get from one bit of the question to the next. So there are **missing steps** that you need to figure out yourself. If you're familiar with the methods that are used in certain **types** of questions, you'll be fine with this.

The way the question is set up at the start, it could be a 'wheat from the chaff' one where these details are irrelevant and just in there to distract you.

So you start with a sketch and do the first bit with trigonometry (sine, cosine and tangent) which may make you think Pythagoras will be next.

5. You are in a castle where the wall is 15.0 m high. A cannon at the top of the wall is aimed directly at an enemy 20.0 m from the base of the castle wall. The cannon's muzzle velocity is 90 m/s.

a. What angle does the cannon make with the ground?

Work out the horizontal and vertical components of the cannonball's velocity.

b. How long does it take for the cannonball to reach the ground?

c. How far from the attackers does the cannonball land?

This is the missing step and the KEY to being able to do the question.

If you don't realize that this is REALLY important, you might wrongly try to do the question using Pythagoras and a straight flight path along the hypotenuse of a right-angled triangle, like we did earlier.

Parts b and c need you to use equations of motion – and you MUST carry out the missing step to be able to do them correctly.

This shows you how important it is to practice thinking about and doing certain **types** of questions, so that the in-between steps become something you'd do naturally, and you don't get stuck or waste time going down the wrong path.

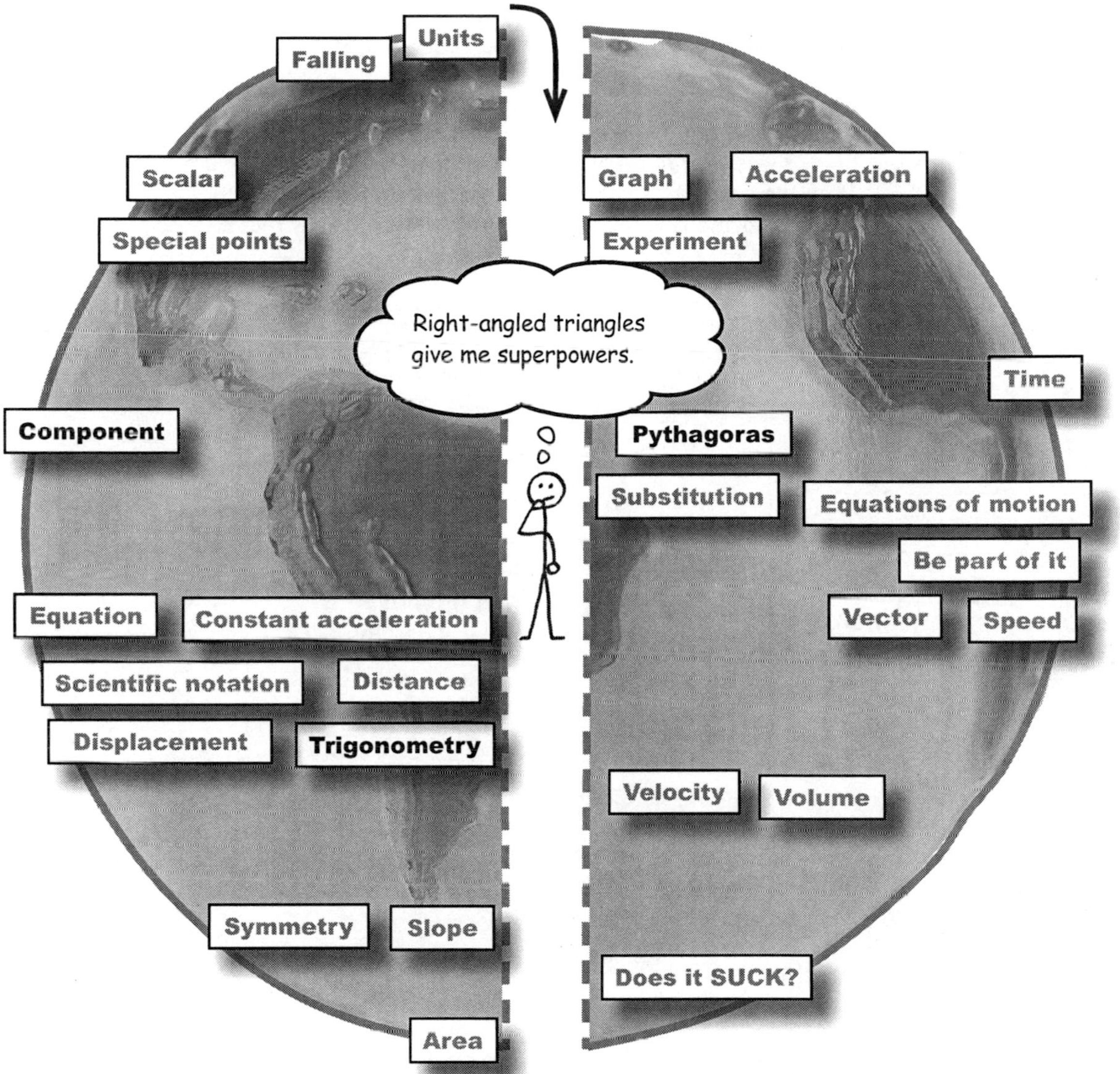

☑	**Pythagoras**	**An equation that you can use to find the third side of a right-angled triangle when you already know two sides.**
☑	**Trigonometry**	**Using the ratios sine, cosine and tangent to relate ratios of side lengths to angles.**
☑	**Component**	**'Part' of a vector. For example, you can turn a vector that's at an angle into horizontal and vertical conponent vectors.**

Your Physics Toolbox

You've got Chapter 9 under your belt and added some terminology and answer-checking skills to your tool box.

Spot the triangle

Anytime you do a sketch that involves two dimensions, look out for triangles.

Keep a special look out for right-angled triangles formed when there are things going on both horizontally and vertically.

Pythagoras' Theorem

If you know the lengths of two sides of your right-angled triangle, you can calculate the length of the third side.

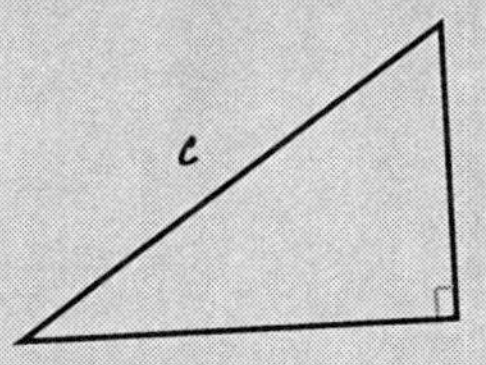

$$c^2 = b^2 + a^2$$

sine, cosine and tangent

sine, cosine and tangent are ratios of the sides of a right-angled triangle.

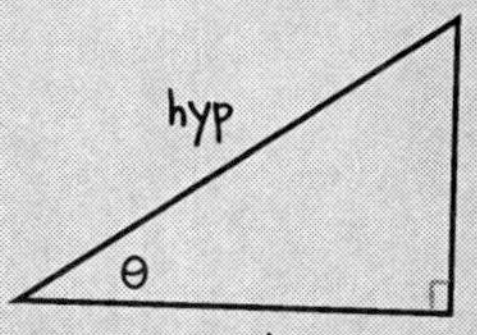

$$\sin(\theta) = \frac{opp}{hyp}$$

$$\cos(\theta) = \frac{adj}{hyp}$$

$$\tan(\theta) = \frac{opp}{ajd}$$

Right-angled triangle facts

If you know one side and one other fact (either a side or an angle), then you can work out EVERYTHING there is to know about a right-angled triangle using Pythagoras and sine, cosine and tangent.

Component vectors

If an object is moving at an angle, it can be useful to break down its velocity vector into horizontal and vertical component vectors.

The horizontal component remains constant.

The vertical component is affected by gravity.

This lets you break down a complicated problem into two simpler problems that you already know how to do.

TOP TIP – Make sure you know how your calculator works! Do you have to press the 'sin,' 'cos' or 'tan' button before or after entering the angle? Is your calculator definitely in the degree mode of measuring angles? It's annoying to understand the physics only to get the problem wrong by making silly mistakes!

CHAPTER 9

10 momentum conservation

What Newton Did

No one likes to be a pushover. So far, you've learned to deal with objects that are already moving. But what makes them go in the first place? You know that something will move if you push it - but *how* will it move? In this chapter, you'll overcome **inertia** as you get acquainted with some of **Newton's Laws**. You'll also learn about **momentum**, why it's **conserved**, and how you can use it to solve problems.

The pirates be havin' a spot o' bother with a ghost ship ...

The pirate captain is being chased across the seas by a ghost ship and needs to make sure it keeps its distance.

His ship's fitted with some Sieges-R-Us battle cannons. The captain wants to know the maximum **range** of his cannons - the maximum horizontal distance he can fire a cannonball, and you've been called in as the expert.

But the supply of cannonballs is limited at sea - so he won't actually be able to fire a cannon until you've got it all worked out.

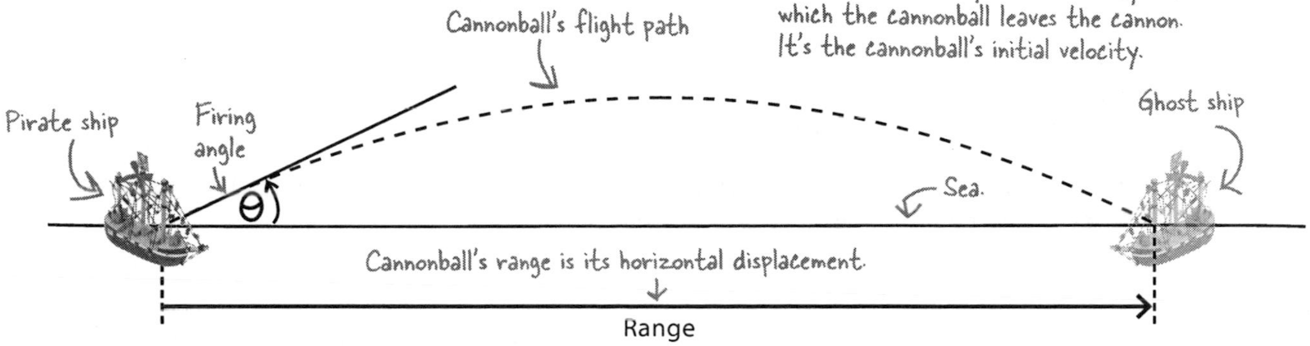

Whiteboard Wipeout - Cannonball

Time to get the hang of what the cannonball's doing. Your job is to sketch graphs that show how the horizontal and vertical components of the displacement, velocity and acceleration change with time. Think about it one component at a time, and do the easier graphs first!

Hint: Start off by thinking about what the cannonball's horizontal acceleration and vertical acceleration are first.

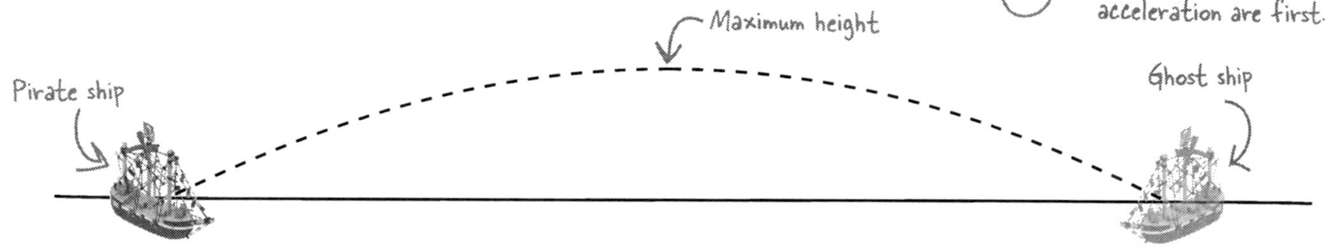

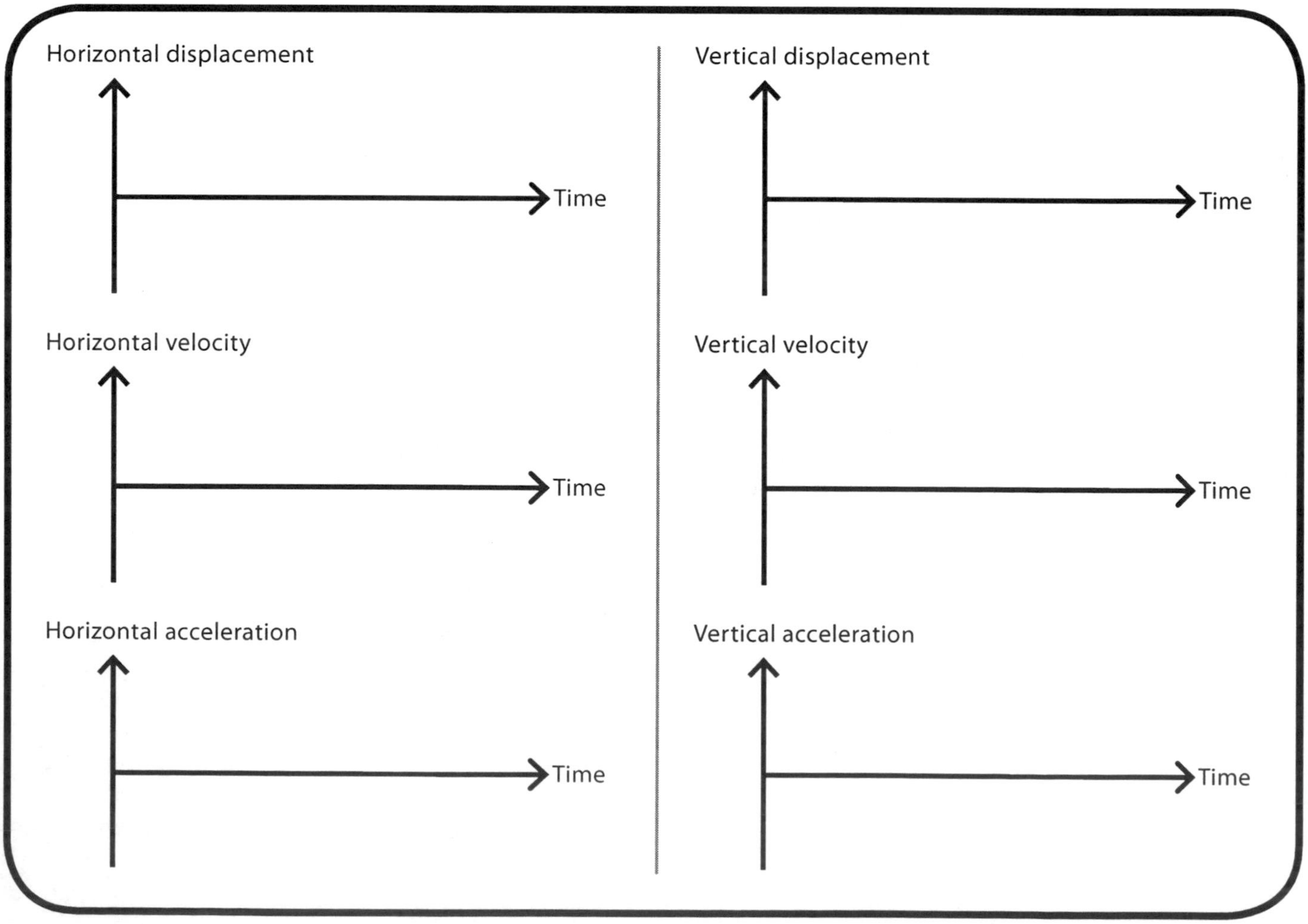

Whiteboard Wipeout - Cannonball SOLUTION

Time to get the hang of what the cannonball's doing. Your job is to sketch graphs that show how the horizontal and vertical components of the displacement, velocity and acceleration change with time. Think about it one component at a time, and do the easier graphs first!

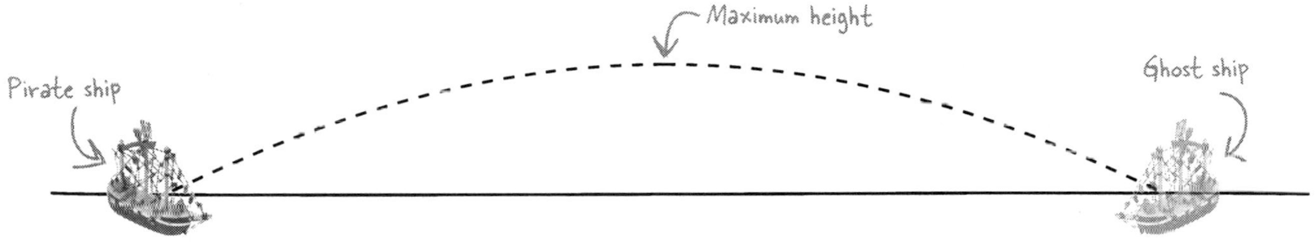

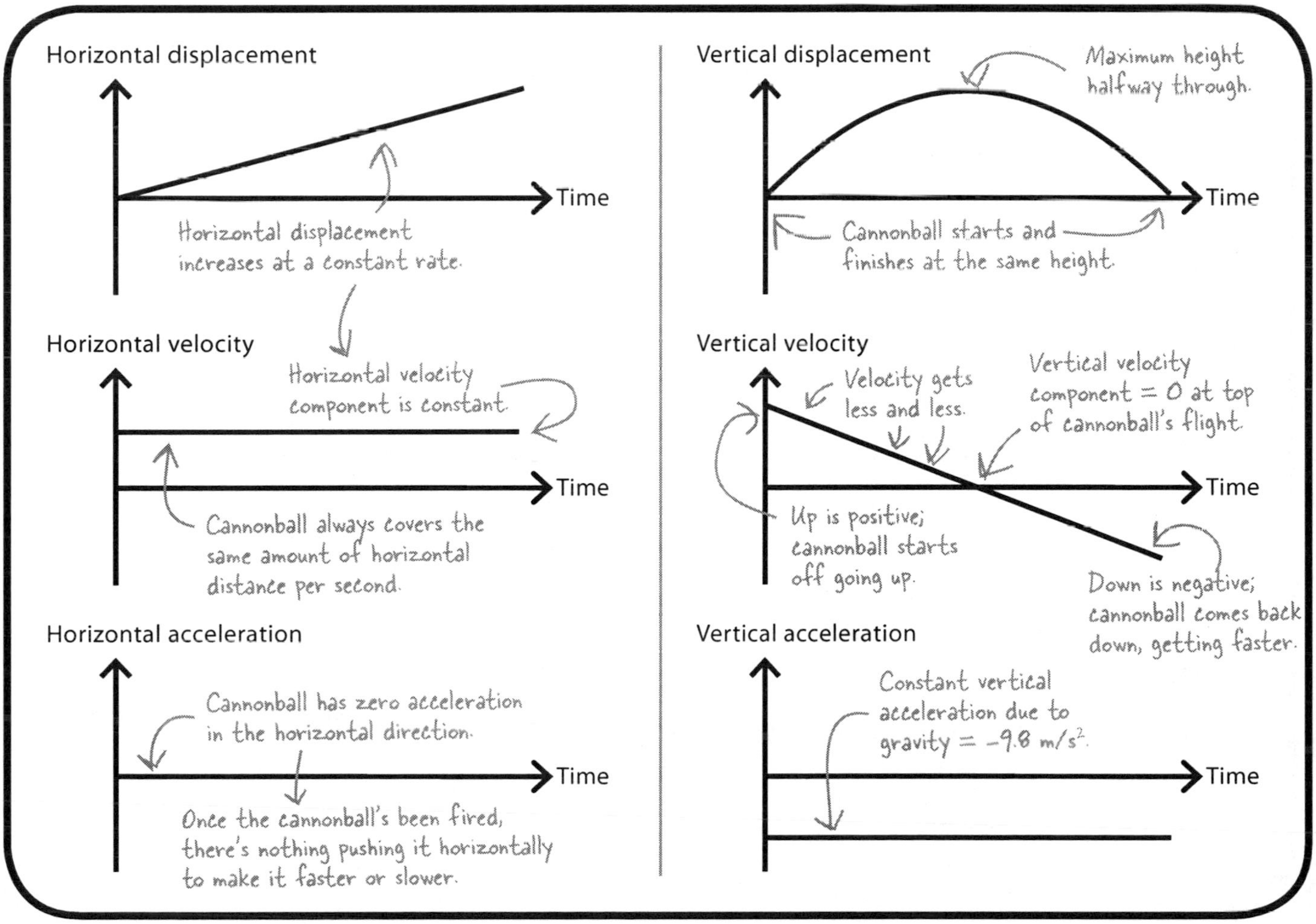

What does the maximum range depend on?

Now that you've sketched the graphs of its component vectors, you can think which **variables** may affect the maximum range of the cannonball.

For example, you already know from the last chapter that the firing **angle** will make a difference to the range. But what angle will be the best? Can you figure it out by thinking about what will happen at the **extremes** of the range of angles you could fire the cannonball at? And is there anything else you might need to take into account?

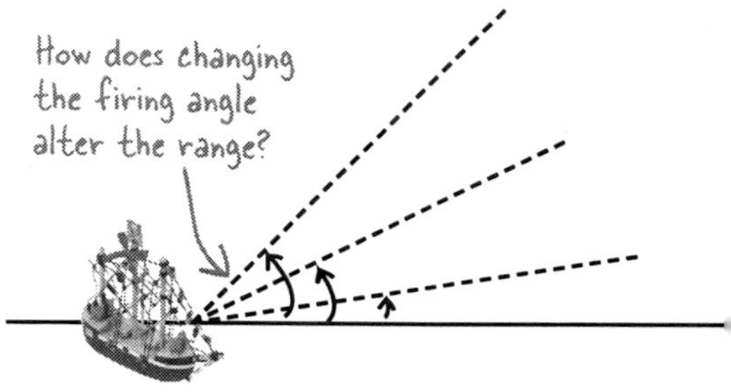

Sharpen your pencil

a. Write down all the things that could possibly affect the range of the cannonball.

Now think about some **extreme** angles to help you work out what's important.

b. Imagine - and draw - what will happen for **small firing angles** (close to 0° or horizontal) and describe this in terms of horizontal and vertical velocity components.

Space to draw.

c. Imagine - and draw - what will happen for **large firing angles** (close to 90° or vertical) and describe this in terms of horizontal and vertical velocity components.

Space to write in.

d. What do you think the **optimal firing angle** will be to give the **maximum range**? (You don't have to be right - just guess and trust your instincts).

Sharpen your pencil Solution

a. Write down all the things that could possibly affect the range of the cannonball.

Firing angle

Velocity of ship

Velocity of cannonball

A big wave could change the angle / velocity

Wind speed and direction

Now think about some **extreme** angles to help you work out what's important.

b. Imagine - and draw - what will happen for **small firing angles** (close to 0° or horizontal) and describe this in terms of horizontal and vertical velocity components.

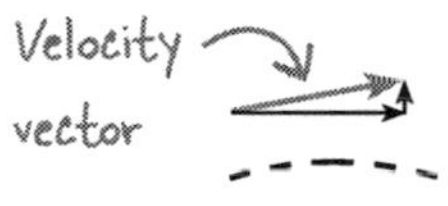

If the firing angle is small, then the horizontal component is large, and the vertical component is small. Although it's going fast horizontally, it isn't spending much time in the air because the vertical component is so low.

c. Imagine - and draw - what will happen for **large firing angles** (close to 90° or vertical) and describe this in terms of horizontal and vertical velocity components.

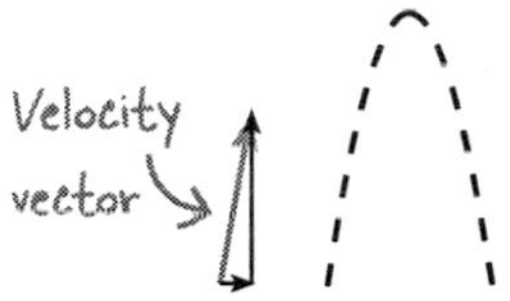

If the firing angle is large, then the vertical component is large, and the horizontal component is small. So the cannonball spends a long time off the ground – but doesn't travel very far horizontally in that time.

d. What do you think the **optimal firing angle** will be to give the **maximum range**? (You don't have to be right - just guess and trust your instincts.

The optimal firing angle will be between these two extremes – probably at around 45°.

Firing at 45° maximizes your range

An **angle of 45°** gives you the best balance between **time** in the air (vertical component of velocity) and **distance** covered horizontally in that time (horizontal component of velocity).

So you end up with the maximum range possible for that velocity.

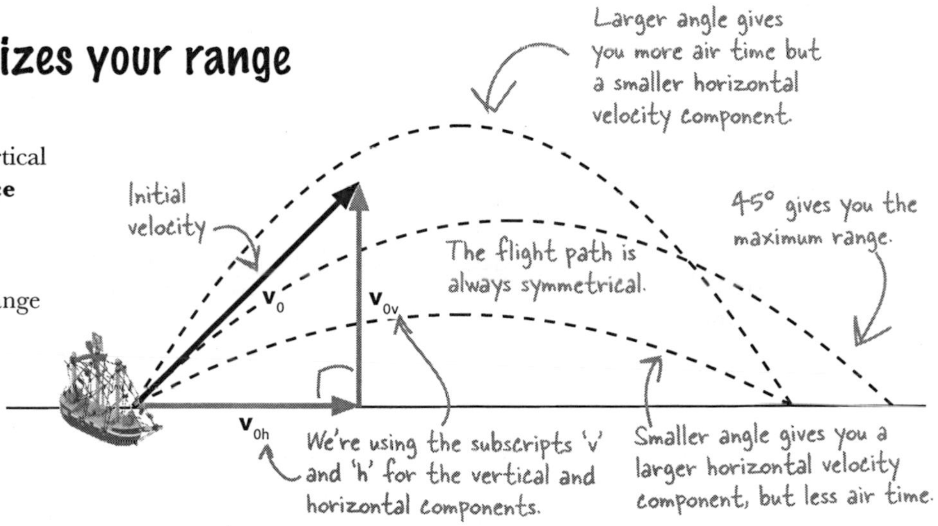

You can't do everything that's theoretically possible - you need to be practical too

The pirate captain is delighted at your suggestion of achieving a maximum range using a 45° firing angle. Unfortunately, the pirates aren't able to aim properly for angles greater than 10°, so a 45° firing angle isn't **practical**. Sometimes what would be **theoretically** possible is restricted by what's physically possible.

But on the bright side, you know that if the pirates fire their cannon at 10°, the cannonball will go further than it would for any other possible angle, as 10° is the closest to 45° you can practically get. So you can **calculate the range** ...

Sharpen your pencil

Work out the maximum range of the cannon when it's fired at an angle of 10° with an initial velocity of 90.0 m/s. (Assume that the cannonball is fired from sea level to sea level.)

Remember to start with a sketch, and say which direction is positive. You might want to use subscripts to represent the vertical and horizontal components, like v_h and v_v.

Page 328 in chapter 8 and page 375 in chapter 9 should help you if you're not sure how to break this problem down into smaller parts.

Sharpen your pencil Solution

Work out the maximum range of the cannon when it's fired at an angle of 10° with an initial velocity of 90.0 m/s. (Assume that the cannonball is fired from sea level to sea level.)

Start off by working out horizontal and vertical velocity components.

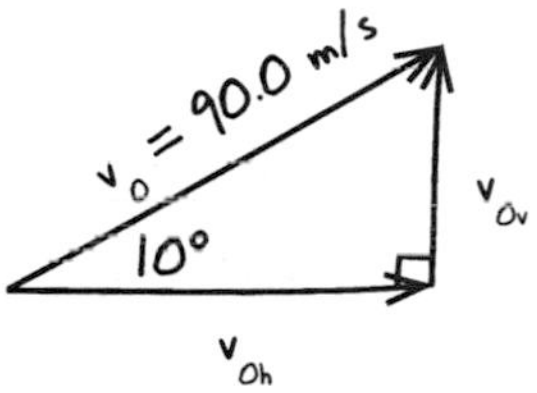

$$\sin(10°) = \frac{opp}{hyp} = \frac{v_{0v}}{v_0} \quad \Rightarrow v_{0v} = v_0 \sin(10°) = 15.6 \text{ m/s (3 sd)}$$

$$\cos(10°) = \frac{adj}{hyp} = \frac{v_{0h}}{v_0} \quad \Rightarrow v_{0h} = v_0 \cos(10°) = 88.6 \text{ m/s (3 sd)}$$

Either use subscripts like this, or be very very careful when you treat the vertical and horizontal components separately!

Get time from vertical velocity component (working ONLY with vertical components):

$a_v = -9.8 \text{ m/s}^2$ Up is positive

$x_v - x_{0v} = 0$ m

$v_{0v} = 15.6$ m/s ↑

$t = ?$

↓ $v_v = -15.6$ m/s

$$v_v = v_{0v} + at \quad (✓ \; ✓ \; ✓?)$$

$$\Rightarrow at = v_v - v_{0v}$$

$$\Rightarrow t = \frac{v_v - v_{0v}}{a_v} = \frac{(-15.6) - (15.6)}{-9.8} = 3.18 \text{ s (3 sd)}$$

Work out horizontal change in position during that time using horizontal velocity component

$v_h = 88.6$ m/s

O ⟶

No acceleration in horizontal direction.

$t = 3.18$ s

$x_{0h} = 0$ m

$x_h = ?$

$$v_h = \frac{\Delta x_h}{\Delta t} = \frac{x_h - x_{0h}}{t - 0} = \frac{x_h}{t}$$

$$\Rightarrow x_h = v_h t = 88.6 \times 3.18 = 282 \text{ m (3 sd)}$$

The range of the cannonball fired at 10° is 282 m (3 sd)

Spotting that the initial and final vertical velocity components are the same **size** (although in **opposite directions**) is pretty useful, right?

Look out for shortcuts involving symmetry.

Symmetry is often a useful shortcut - especially if the overall vertical displacement is zero.

Sometimes you can use the fact that a projectile takes **equal times to go up and down** as a shortcut.

And sometimes you can use the fact that the **vertical components of v_0 and v have the same size** (but opposite directions) at the same height.

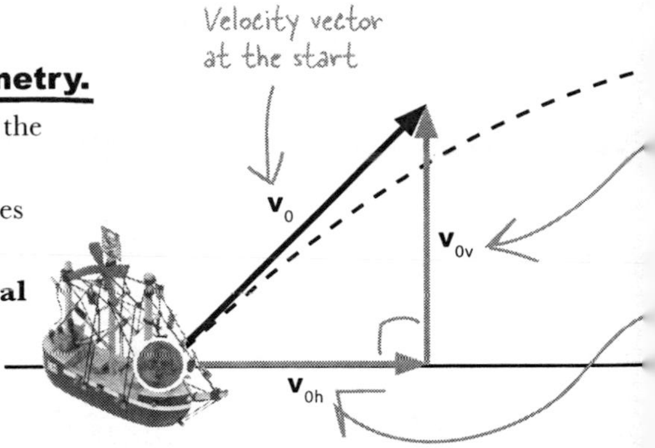

there are no Dumb Questions

Q: Is it OK if I didn't spot the symmetry but still got most of the way through the problem?

A: Yes, it's absolutely fine. But it's always a good idea to keep on the lookout for symmetry, because it sometimes lets you solve problems more quickly.

Q: Can you still get the right answer to a problem like this even if you don't spot the symmetry?

A: Yes - you can use the equation $v^2 = v_0^2 + 2(x - x_0)$. Here, $x - x_0 = 0$ because the cannonball starts and finishes at the same height. So the equation simplifies to $v^2 = v_0^2$.

Q: If I have the equation $v^2 = v_0^2$, doesn't that mean that $v = v_0$?

A: Not necessarily. If you multiply two negative numbers together, then you get a positive number. So the solution to the equation $v^2 = v_0^2$ could either be $v = v_0$ or $v = -v_0$.

Q: If I have an equation with two possible solutions, how do I work out which solution is correct?

A: Look at the context (or 'k'ontext). Here, the vertical component of the cannonballs' velocity points up at the start and down at the end. So they're in opposite directions. Therefore, the solution must be the one where the vertical velocity components point in opposite directions: $v = -v_0$.

Q: I noticed that there were some subscripts used in the sharpen answer. Should I use subscripts too?

A: Subscripts sometimes help you keep track of things - and sometimes make things look messy! As long as you stay organized and write out what you're doing, you'll be OK.

Q: What if the ghost ship's more than 282 m away? I guess the pirates can't just get new cannons that have a higher muzzle velocity?

A: The pirates have to stick with the same cannons. But the website does say that the muzzle velocity is for a **standard** iron cannonball ...

If a projectile starts and finishes at the same height, the vertical component of its velocity has the same size, but the opposite direction, at the start and finish.

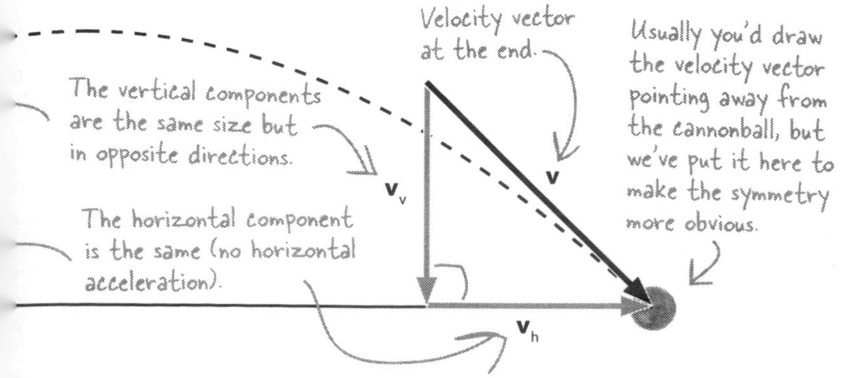

Sieges-R-Us has a new stone cannonball, which they claim will increase the range!

The Sieges-R-Us website has just been updated! As well as the standard iron cannonball, they now have a stone cannonball. Although both cannonballs are the same size, the stone cannonball is only a third of the **mass** of the iron cannonball because they're made from different materials.

An object's **mass** is a measure of the amount of stuff it's made from. Both cannonballs are the same size and have the same volume (so fit in the same cannon), but the iron one has more material in it.

The website claims that the stone cannonball has a longer range than the iron one if you fire it out of the same cannon. But the stone cannonball is so new that there are no tech specs - like the muzzle velocity.

So... **does the stone cannonball actually go further**, or is it all hype?

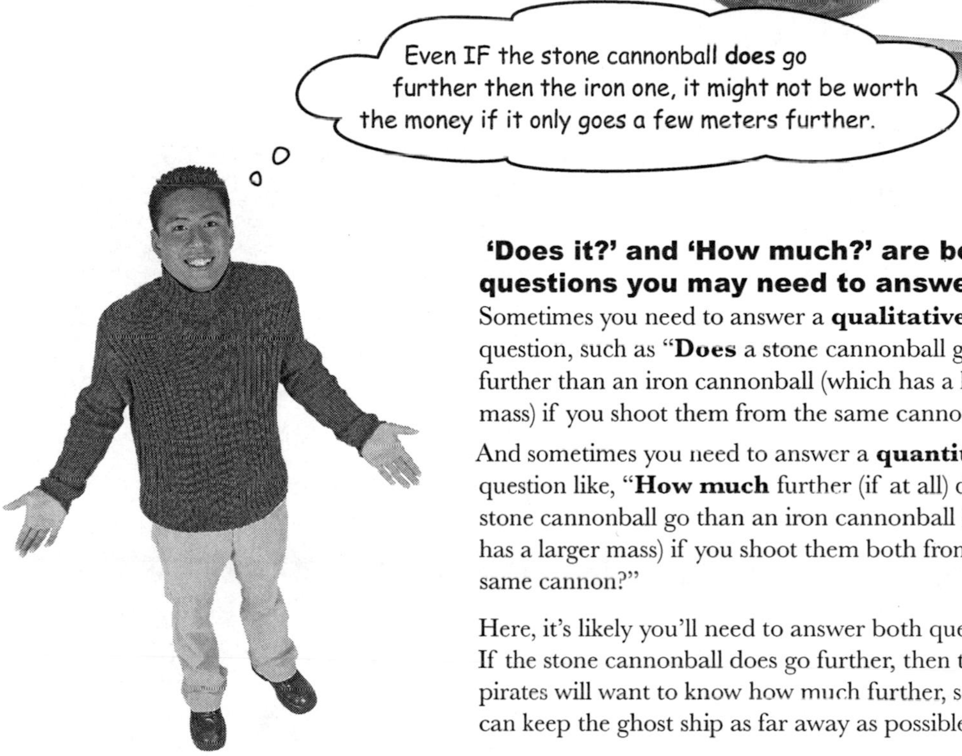

'Does it?' and 'How much?' are both questions you may need to answer.

Sometimes you need to answer a **qualitative** question, such as "**Does** a stone cannonball go further than an iron cannonball (which has a larger mass) if you shoot them from the same cannon?"

And sometimes you need to answer a **quantitative** question like, "**How much** further (if at all) does a stone cannonball go than an iron cannonball (which has a larger mass) if you shoot them both from the same cannon?"

Here, it's likely you'll need to answer both questions. If the stone cannonball does go further, then the pirates will want to know how much further, so they can keep the ghost ship as far away as possible.

Jim: Yeah, they don't even have any tech specs on there about the **velocity** the stone cannonball will travel at - only the fact that it's a third of the **mass** of the iron cannonball.

Frank: But the two cannonballs must have the same **size** if they both fit in the same cannon - so how can they have different masses?

Joe: 1 cm^3 of iron has a larger mass than 1 cm^3 of stone, doesn't it? If you have the same **volumes** of iron and stone, it takes more effort to lift the iron. So if the two cannonballs are the same size, then the iron cannonball must have a larger mass. The website's right about that!

Jim: But didn't we say before that all falling objects accelerate at the same rate no matter what their masses are? So there wouldn't be any difference for the stone and iron cannonballs.

Joe: Hmmm. But the cannonballs are coming out of the cannon before gravity takes over, aren't they? There'd be the same explosion to **push** them out of the cannon each time.

Frank: And I guess that's different from gravity - the explosion pushes the cannonball, but gravity doesn't have to make **contact** with the cannonball to accelerate it.

Jim: Maybe we could **be** the cannon. We could imagine pushing the stone and iron cannonballs to see what we think would happen.

Joe: But to us, both cannonballs are difficult to push. Maybe this is a good place to think in **extremes** - like pushing a large mass versus pushing a small mass ... pushing an elephant versus pushing a mouse ...

The cannon is different from gravity because it pushes the cannonball by making contact with it.

BE ... someone pushing something

Your job is to imagine pushing an elephant, then pushing a mouse with the same strength of push. You might want to think about each animal being on a skateboard so that you can actually see the effect of pushing them. How do their velocities vary?

BE ... someone pushing something - SOLUTION

Your job is to imagine pushing an elephant, then pushing a mouse with the same strength of push. You might want to think about each animal being on a skateboard so that you can actually see the effect of pushing them. How do their velocities vary?

If I push the mouse hard, it'll go really fast.

It's harder to get the elephant going because it has a larger mass. If I give it the same push I give the mouse, it'll hardly move at all.

The object with a lower mass has a higher velocity for the same push.

Massive things are more difficult to start off

If you stand an elephant and a mouse on a skateboard and give each the same size of push to make them move, then the mouse ends up traveling at a higher velocity than the elephant. Because the elephant has a larger mass, it's more difficult to change its velocity.

The elephant and the mouse both start with zero velocity.

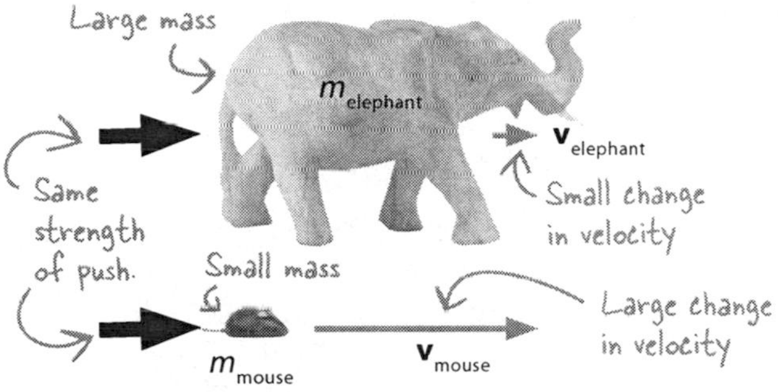

The larger an object's mass, the more difficult it is to change its velocity.

This is true if the object's initial velocity is zero. It's also true if the object is moving.

Massive things are more difficult to stop

If the elephant and the mouse are already traveling with the same velocity, the elephant is more difficult to stop. This is because its greater **mass** means it has a greater tendency to continue at its current velocity when you give it the same strength of push.

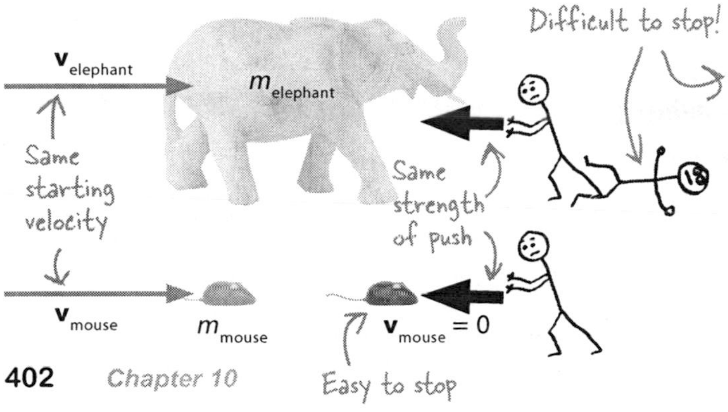

This is true if the object's current velocity is zero. It's also true if the object is moving.

Objects enjoy continuing at their current velocity.

Newton's First Law

You might have heard the saying "An object at rest tends to stay at rest; an object in motion tends to stay in motion." Newton's 1st Law takes this further.

Objects have **inertia**, which means that they will keep on moving with their **current velocity** unless you act on them with a **force** (for example, by giving them a push). A stationary object remains stationary unless something happens to make it move. And a moving object continues to move with its current velocity unless something happens to speed it up, slow it down, or change its direction of movement.

Another way of putting this is **Newton's First Law**, which says that an object will continue on with a **constant velocity** unless there's a **net force** acting on it.

'Net force' means total overall force.

Newton's First Law says that an object will carry on with the same velocity unless there's a net force acting on it.

The same SPEED in the same DIRECTION

We'll talk about this more later on.

there are no Dumb Questions

Q: If this is Newton's FIRST Law, does that mean there are others? How many are there?

A: You'll meet Newton's three Laws of Motion in this chapter and the next.

Q: I've heard something about Galileo's Law of Inertia, which sounds very similar to Newton's First Law. Do I need to know about that as well?

A: Galileo's Law of Inertia and Newton's First Law both say the same thing, there's no need to worry.

Q: OK, so does it matter what I call these laws? Do I have to learn their names or is it enough to understand the physics concepts?

A: Understanding the concepts is the most important thing, but in an exam, you may be asked to explain what's happening in terms of Newton's three laws. Then you'd have to remember which is which.

Q: If an object continues on with "constant velocity," it could either already be moving, or it could be completely still and have a velocity of zero, right?

A: Yes, that's correct. Whether something's stationary or moving, you need a net force to change its velocity.

Q: If its velocity changes, that means it speeds up or slows down, right?

A: Velocity is a vector, so as well as speeding up or slowing down, a change in velocity could be a change in direction without a change in speed.

Q: What does 'net' force mean?

A: There might be more than one force acting on an object at the same time. The 'net' force is what you get when you add all the forces acting on an object together. Just like a company's net profit (or net loss) is when you add together all its incomings and (negative) outgoings.

Friction is a force.

Friction is a force that you get when things are in contact with one another. Newton's First Law says that an object will move at a constant velocity unless acted on by a net force.

As friction is a force, it is able to change the object's velocity, for example by slowing it down, which is why moving objects often appear to slow down naturally when you don't interfere with them.

You'll learn more about friction in chapter 12.

Mass matters

If you push an elephant and a mouse with the same **force** each time, the mouse ends up with a larger **velocity** than the elephant because it has a smaller **mass**. And if you try to stop an elephant and a mouse that are already traveling with the same velocity, you'll get flattened by the elephant if you push it with the same force that you need to stop the mouse.

The more massive something is, the greater its **inertia**, or tendency to continue with its current velocity, and the larger the force you have to push it with to produce the same change in velocity.

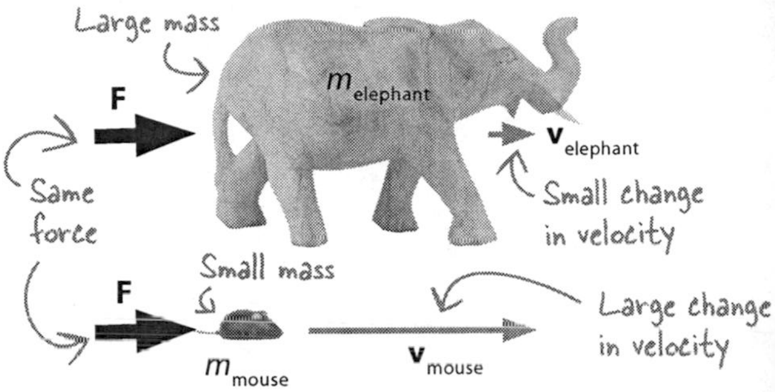

there are no Dumb Questions

Q: Does this mean I have to do math with forces? How do I do that?

A: That's something for later on. Right now, you're not doing calculations with forces, just working out some general physics principles involving them.

Q: I've heard the word 'inertia' used to mean reluctance. Like, "I had to overcome a lot of inertia to get out of bed on a cold morning." Is this another meaning for the same word?

A: It's kind of similar actually. An object's inertia is its tendency to continue at its current velocity. In the example you mention, your inertia is your tendency to continue in your current sleeping place. So the usage is kind-of similar!

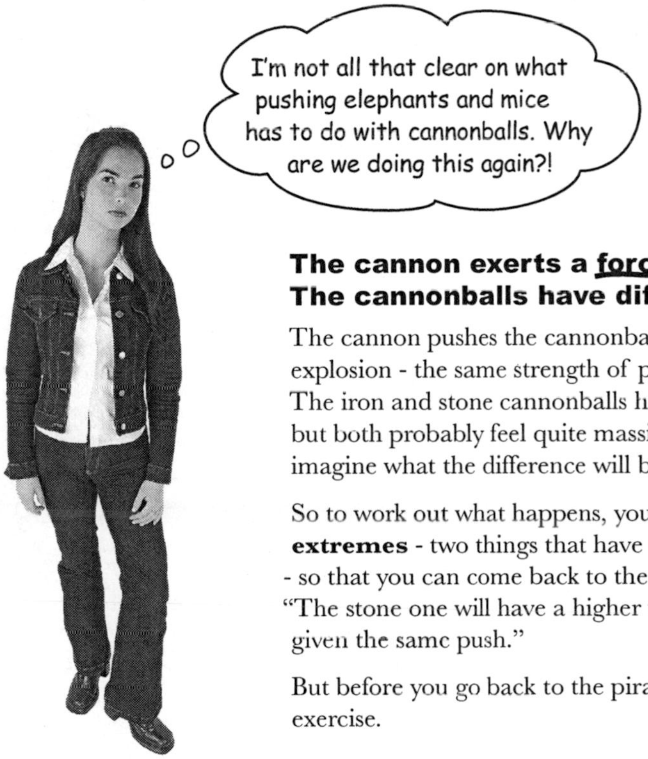

The cannon exerts a force.
The cannonballs have different masses.

The cannon pushes the cannonballs with the same explosion - the same strength of push, the same **force**. The iron and stone cannonballs have different masses, but both probably feel quite massive to you. It's hard to imagine what the difference will be.

So to work out what happens, you've been thinking about **extremes** - two things that have **very** different masses - so that you can come back to the cannonballs and say, "The stone one will have a higher velocity if they're both given the same push."

But before you go back to the pirate ship, here's a quick exercise.

Get used to thinking in extremes to work out what will happen in your situation.

Exercise

In this exercise, you have three coffee machine cups. One has an iron cannonball balanced on top, the next has a less massive stone cannonball on top, and the third has an even less massive wood ball balanced on top.

The same brick is dropped directly onto each ball from the same height each time.

Which cup is damaged the least, and why?

Relax – we're looking for a prediction, so don't worry if you're not sure what will happen.

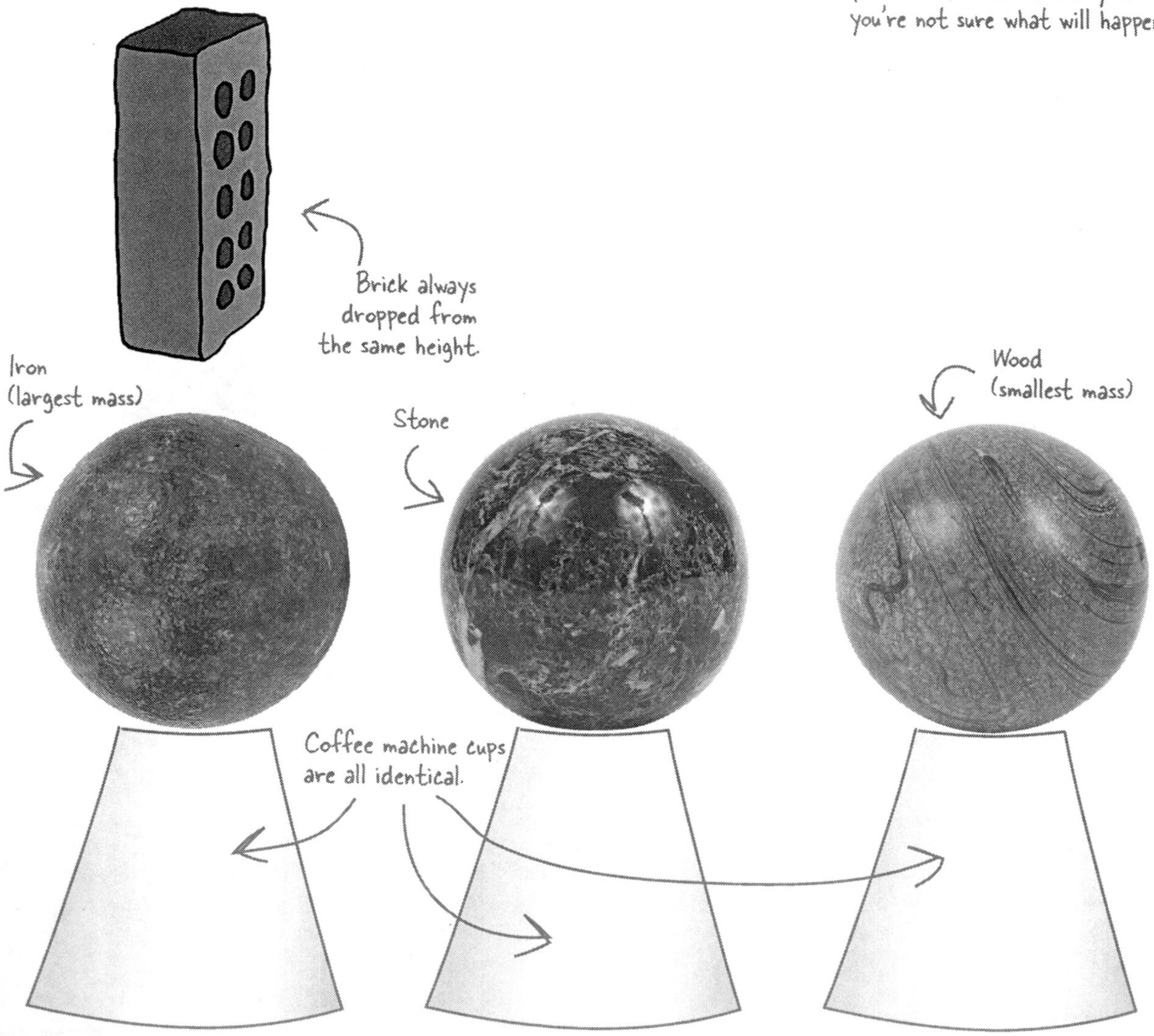

In this exercise, you have three coffee machine cups. One has an iron cannonball balanced on top, the next has a less massive stone cannonball on top, and the third has an even less massive wood ball balanced on top.

The same brick is dropped directly onto each ball from the same height each time.

Which cup is damaged the least, and why?

Newton's first law says that objects continue at the velocity they already have unless acted on by a net force. All of the balls have zero velocity. The more massive something is, the more force you need to change its velocity. So it's most difficult to get the iron cannonball moving when you drop the brick on it, as it has the most mass. By being difficult to shift, it kind of protects the cup.
Therefore, the cup under the iron ball is damaged the least.

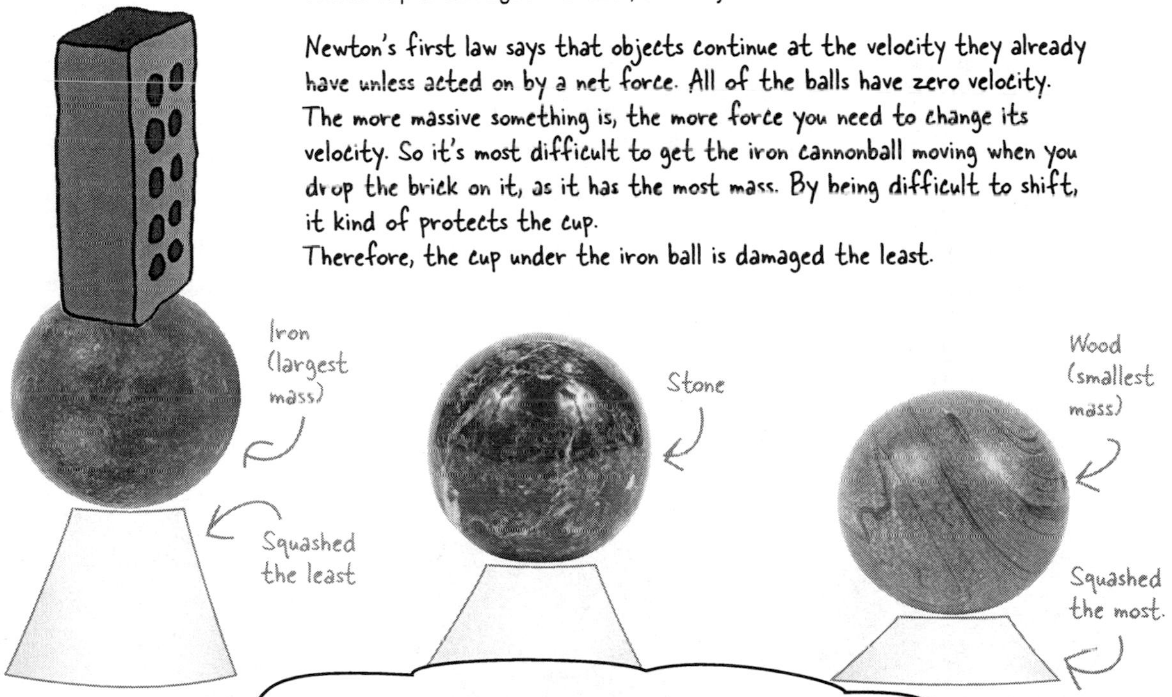

The larger an object's mass, the more difficult it is to change the object's velocity.

Massive things are more difficult to shift.

If an elephant was sliding towards you, which would you rather it hit first - a solid wall or a sheet of paper? With this setup, the balls are actually **protecting** the cups from the impact of the brick like a wall would protect you from an elephant. The cup under the iron ball suffers the least damage because the iron ball has the largest **mass**.

If we dropped the balls themselves directly onto the cups, the iron ball would do the most damage since it takes more force to bring it to a standstill (the cup can't exert enough force to stop the ball ... but the ground can).

A stone cannonball has a smaller mass - so it has a larger velocity. But how much larger?

As the stone cannonball has a smaller **mass** than the iron one, it will come out of the cannon with a greater **velocity**.

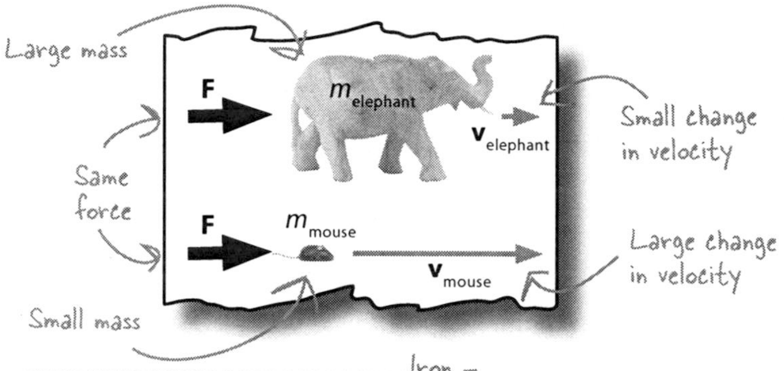

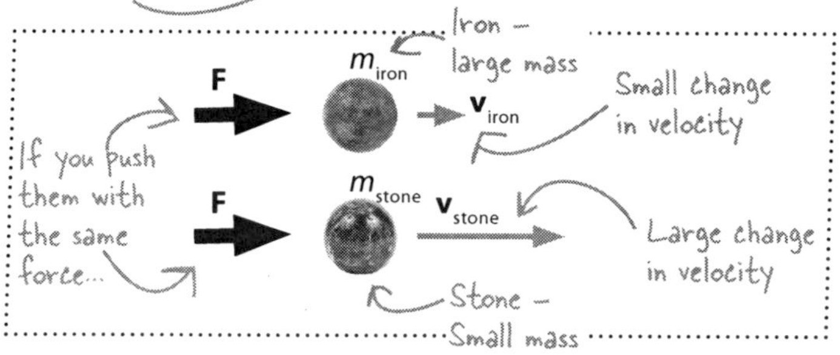

However, the only thing you know about a stone cannonball is that it's a quarter of the **mass** of an iron cannonball. The pirate captain wants to know the range of a stone cannonball fired at 10°, but will only let you fire a stone cannonball horizontally.

Firing horizontally doesn't sound like it'll help, as you can't measure the **distance** the cannonball goes out to sea, and the cannonball's **velocity** will be far too high to measure directly.

You can't measure the distance when you're at sea!

If you know the velocity, you can calculate the range.

BRAIN POWER

Is there any way of working out the **range** or **velocity** for a stone cannonballs fired at 10° when you can only measure things that are actually on the ship?

So the stone cannonball will go further. Since the stone cannonball has less **mass** than the iron cannonball, the stone cannonball will come out of the cannon with a higher **velocity**.

Jim: Yeah, if the stone cannonball has a higher velocity, the vertical velocity **component** will be larger, so the cannonball will stay off the ground for longer. And the horizontal velocity component will also be larger, so the cannonball will go even further in that **time**.

Joe: So we've answered the "**Does it?**" question - it does go further. But now we need to answer the "**How much?**" question - how much further than the iron cannonball will the stone cannonball go?

Frank: But the stupid Sieges-R-Us website still hasn't been updated with proper tech specs. If we knew the muzzle **velocity** for the stone cannonball, it'd be easy. We might be able to do something if we knew the actual **masses** of the cannonballs. But all the website says is that the stone one is four times lighter than the iron one.

Joe: Maybe we could do some kind of **experiment**?

Frank: But the pirates won't let us fire their cannons at the ghost ship - they want the element of surprise...

Joe: I mean, maybe we could miniaturize things to do a small experiment then scale it up, like we've done before.

Jim: With a toy cannon, perhaps. We could make it fire two different objects, one four times the mass of the other.

Frank: I'm not sure how practical it is to calibrate a toy cannon. How about we use a **spring** to push an object horizontally? Then we're only thinking about one **dimension** - we can always extrapolate to two dimensions later on by using component vectors.

Joe: But if we push an object horizontally, they'll soon grind to a halt because of the **friction** between them and the table. There's relatively little friction when a cannonball goes through the air. It wouldn't be the same.

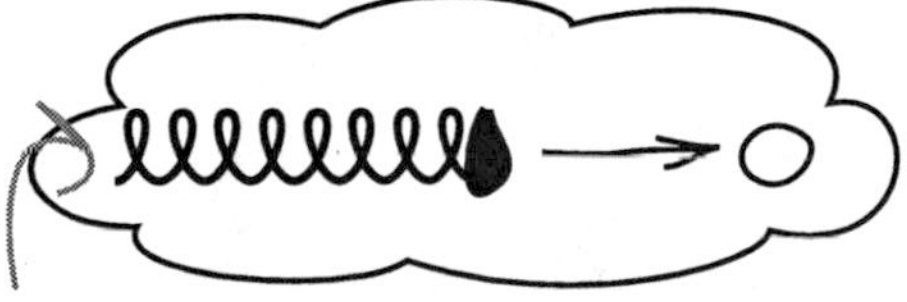

Jim: Hmm, air. Can we make some kind of hovercraft thingy to push with the spring? That floats on a cushion of air.

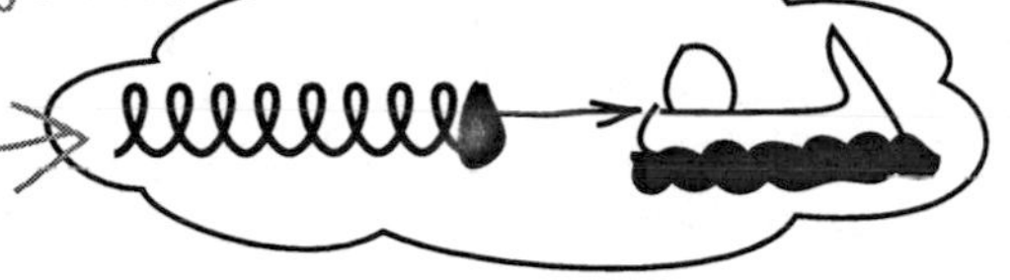

Frank: Or, no ... even better - can we use an air hockey table to reduce friction? We can push an object horizontally across an air hockey table, using a spring to make sure we use the same force each time.

Joe: I just thought of something else. Cannons **recoil**, right?

Jim: What do you mean?!

Joe: When you fire a cannon or a gun, the force of the explosion makes it kick back. That's why the pirates' cannon has wheels.

Frank: So how about putting the spring between **two** objects on the air hockey table. One has a large mass, like the cannon. The other has a smaller mass, like the cannonball. Then we get a **recoil** when we let the spring do its thing?

Joe: That sounds good, but I've also been thinking - how do we **measure velocity**? That's what we actually want to find out for the things with different masses - so we can scale it up for the two cannonballs and work out the range of the stone cannonball.

Jim: I guess we could mark out a **distance** we know, and **time** how long it takes for the thing we're pushing to cover it. We can work out a **velocity** from that.

Joe: But it's going to be difficult to do that **precisely**. It's not like we can use a regular stopwatch because the times here are going to be very short, maybe less than half a second and difficult to do by hand.

Frank: I've seen this thing in a physics lab before. It's a beam of light, and when something goes through and breaks the beam, a timer starts. Then when the beam's restored, the timer stops.

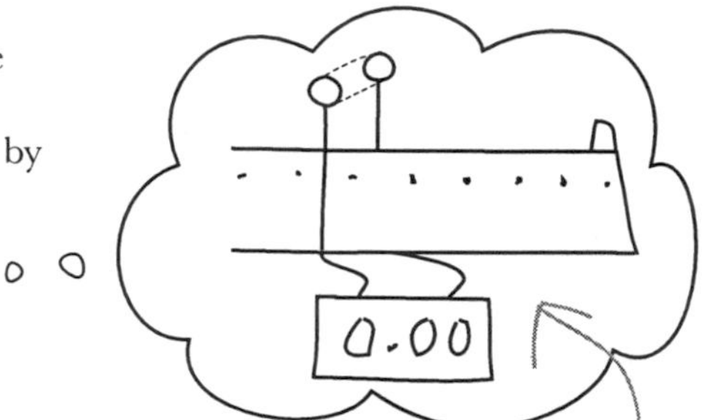

Jim: But there's only one beam, right? So how can we **time** something over a certain distance when the beam's always in the same place?

Frank: If we know the **length** of the object going through the beam, then we know that it's gone exactly that **distance** while breaking the beam. So we can work out the velocity.

Joe: And we could do that for both the small object (cannonball) and large object (cannon) so we get the **recoil velocity** as well.

Jim: Let's go see what equipment we've got in the lab ...

When you design an experiment, try to make it LIKE the situation you're modelling.

Here's your lab equipment

Here are the things you need for this experiment:

You need **a way of reducing friction**. You have an air track, which is like an air hockey table because it has small holes in it all the way along its length to create a 'cushion' of air and reduce friction as much as possible.

You need **objects to represent the cannon and cannonball**. The air track has specially-designed vehicles that sit on it.

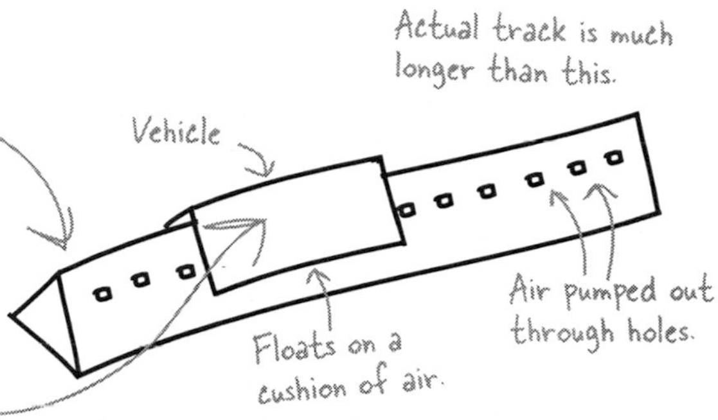

An air track reduces friction, and the vehicles represent the cannon and cannonball.

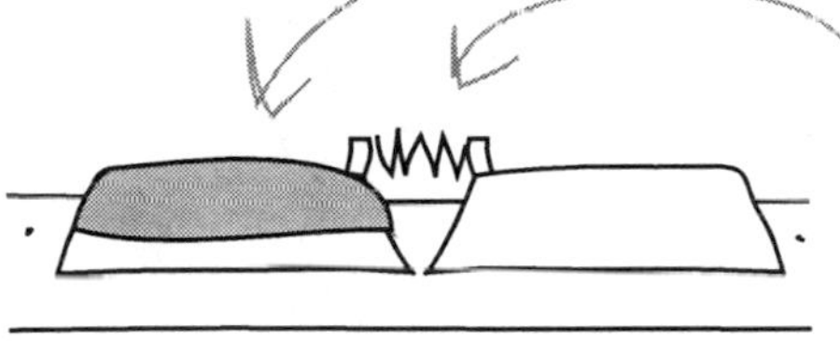

You can add masses to the vehicles and push them apart with a spring

You need a way of **changing and measuring the vehicles masses**. The air track vehicles come with a set of masses that you can stack on top of them - both these and the vehicle are marked with their masses. So one vehicle can represent the cannonball and the other one the cannon.

You need something to **push the vehicles apart with the same force each time**. You can use a spring, which you push in to the same place every time. Then when you let go of the spring, it pushes the vehicles apart.

You need a way of **measuring velocity**. You can measure pieces of card and attach them along the length of each vehicle.

Then set up a light gate (sometimes called a photogate) for each vehicle to pass through. When the card breaks the beam, it starts a timer, and when the card has passed all the way through, the beam is restored and the timer stops. This gives you the **time** it took for the vehicle to go the same **distance** as the length of the card, which you can use to calculate the **velocity**.

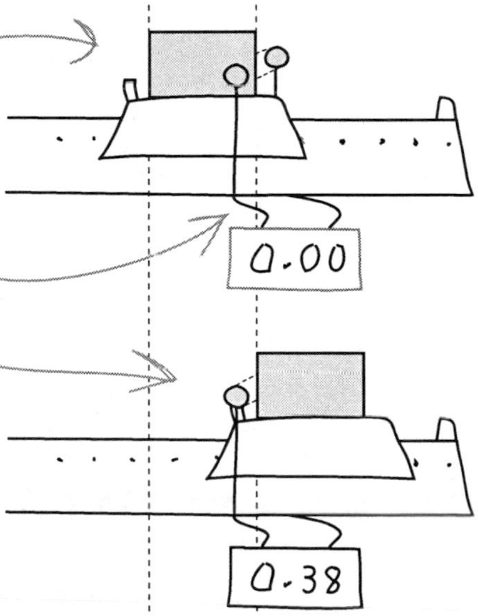

You can add a piece of card to a vehicle and time it with a light gate to work out its velocity.

Think about what you NEED to do. Then about what equipment you HAVE available to do it.

How are force, mass and velocity related?

You now **have** all the equipment you **need** to **design** an experiment that will let you work out the effect that a cannonball's mass has on its muzzle velocity. But you need to put the equipment together in an **experimental setup**.

The other important thing at this stage is to work out what **variables** you can change during the course of your experiment. These are all the different things that might affect what you are measuring (in this case, the velocities of the vehicles).

Any time you design an experiment, think about what your VARIABLES are.

Sharpen your pencil

a. Design and draw an experimental setup with the equipment on the opposite page (plus anything else you'd like to use) to replicate a scenario where a force pushes apart a cannon and a cannonball, so that they both experience a change in velocity. Your aim is to see how the velocity of the cannonball varies with its mass (and whether this also affects the recoil velocity of the cannon).

b. Identify the things in your experimental setup that you can **vary** in order to produce a set of results. (At this stage you're not being asked how you would vary them.)

c. Explain what **measurements** you would make for one trial of your experiment, and how you would use them to fill in a table of masses and velocities.

Sharpen your pencil Solution

a. Design and draw an experimental setup with the equipment on the opposite page (plus anything else you'd like to use) to replicate a scenario where a force pushes apart a cannon and a cannonball, so that they both experience a change in velocity. Your aim is to see how the velocity of the cannonball varies with its mass (and whether this also affects the recoil velocity of the cannon).

b. Identify the things in your experimental setup that you can **vary** in order to produce a set of results. (At this stage you're not being asked how you would vary them.)

c. Explain what measurements you would make for one trial of your experiment, and how you would use them to fill in a table of masses and velocities.

a.

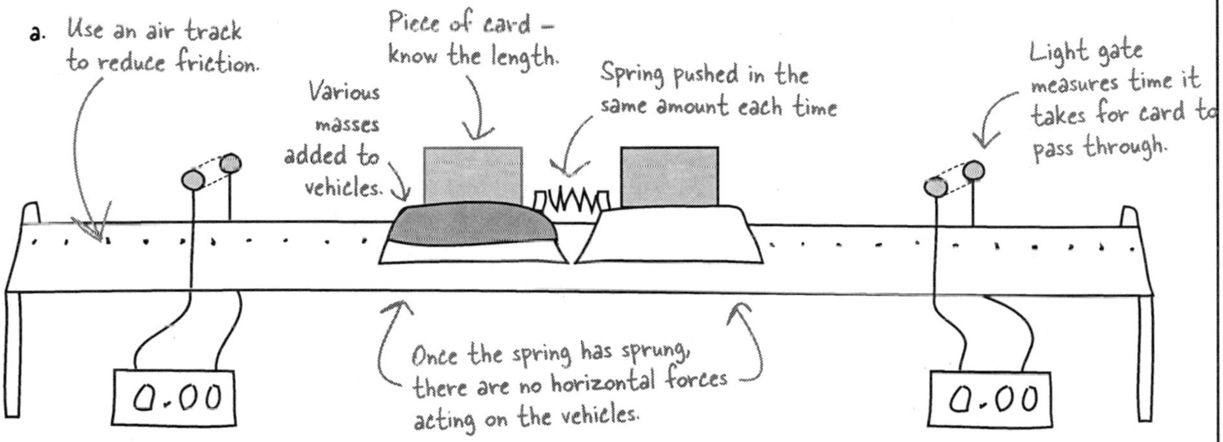

b. I can vary the mass of each vehicle, and the strength of the spring.

c. For one trial, I would put masses on each vehicle. Then I'd use scales to find the mass of the vehicle plus the masses. I would use the light gates to measure the time it takes for each vehicle to pass through. Then I would use the length of the card and the time to work out each vehicle's velocity

there are no Dumb Questions

Q: Why am I using two vehicles again?

A: Cannons recoil. As well as the cannonball going forwards, the cannon goes backwards. So you're replicating that.

Q: Why am I measuring the 'cannon' vehicle's velocity when I'm only interested in the cannonball's velocity?

A: You never know what might be useful...

Q: But that's just extra work!

A: The spring pushes **both** vehicles, so knowing both velocities might help you come to a better conclusion than only knowing one.

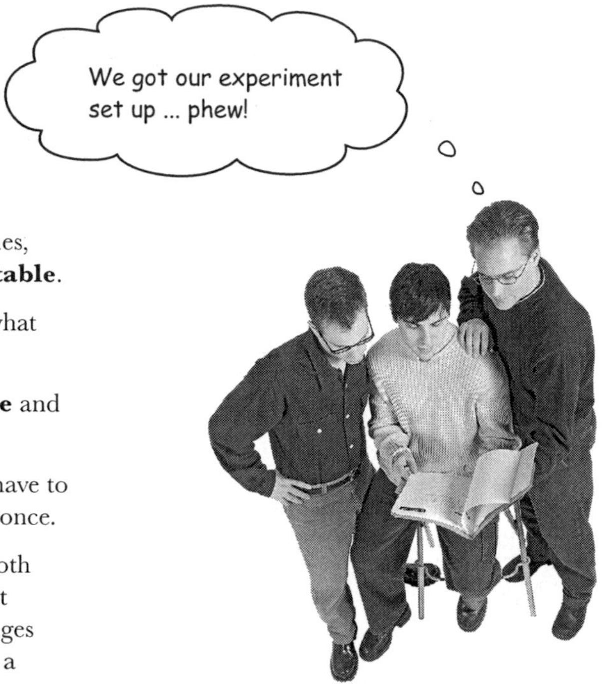

Frank: Yeah, but what do we do now?

Jim: I guess we push the vehicles apart, measure some times, use them to work out velocities and write them down in a **table**.

Frank: But we gotta be more organized than that. Like, what will we **change** in between one trial and the next?

Joe: We can change the **mass of the "cannon" vehicle** and the **mass of the "cannonball" vehicle**.

Jim: So we just change both masses each time. We won't have to do so many trials that way, as we can change two things at once.

Joe: I'm not sure that's a good idea. Suppose we change both masses and get a different result for the velocities. We won't know why we got a different result. Which of the two changes was responsible for the difference - or did it come about as a result of both changes working together somehow?

Frank: Yeah, that's a good point. In real life, the cannon's mass doesn't change. I think we should give one of the vehicles a really large mass - like the cannon has compared to the cannonball - then vary the mass of the other vehicle each time. we do a trial.

Jim: But what if we just happen to choose a mass for our 'cannon' vehicle that produces a special result. I think we need to change that mass as well, to make sure anything we work out isn't a special case.

Joe: So why don't we do one set of trials with a fixed 'cannon' mass and change the 'cannonball mass' each time, then do another set with a different fixed 'cannon' mass to see if that makes a difference?

Frank: And then do another lot with a different spring, to make sure that's not a special case too.

Jim: OK, I see what you mean. **Changing only one thing at a time** must be the best way of doing it. If something different happens, you know for sure that the thing you changed is what caused the difference.

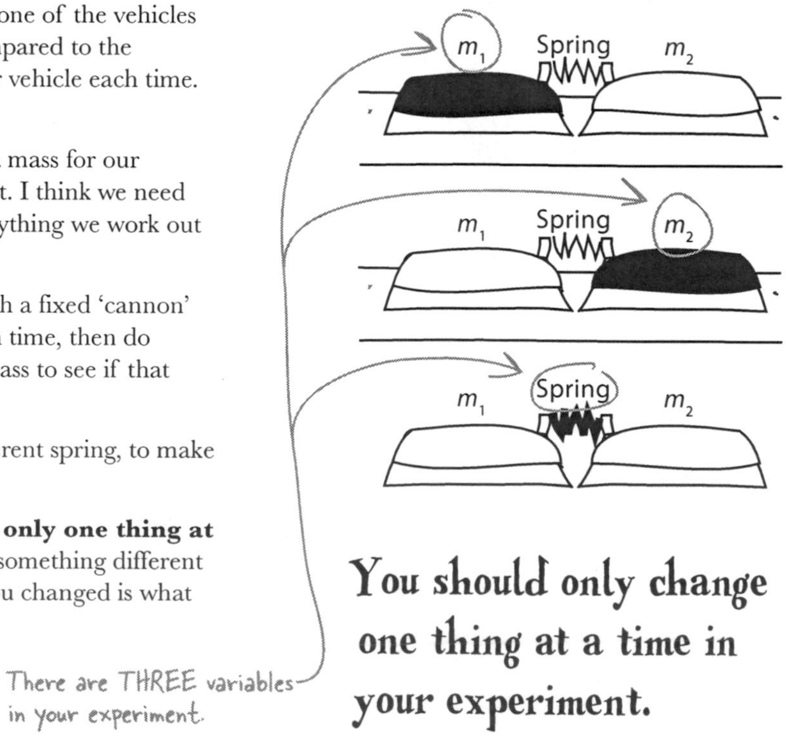

You should only change one thing at a time in your experiment.

Vary only one thing at a time in your experiment

The point of doing an experiment is to find out what happens to one quantity if you **vary** another quantity. In this experiment, we want to find out what happens to the **velocities** of two objects that are pushed apart by a **force** when you vary the objects' **masses**. Then you can **extrapolate** your results to predict what will happen to the velocities of a cannon and cannonball when they're forced apart by an explosion.

If you vary both masses for each trial of your experiment, it'll be difficult to spot patterns in your results. You won't know which change had the most effect on your results - or if the changes somehow canceled each other out.

So by varying only **one** mass at a time then changing the other mass and doing it again will make sure that it'll be OK to extrapolate your findings to **any** two masses.

An experiment shows you what happens to one quantity when you vary another quantity.

Sharpen your pencil

Here are the results of your experiment. We've annotated the diagram with all of the relevant details like labelling which light gate is which, and the length of the pieces of card (10 cm). Be careful with the direction that each velocity is in!

Fill in the missing boxes in the table, and **use the space below to write down any patterns you see.**

....

....

....

....

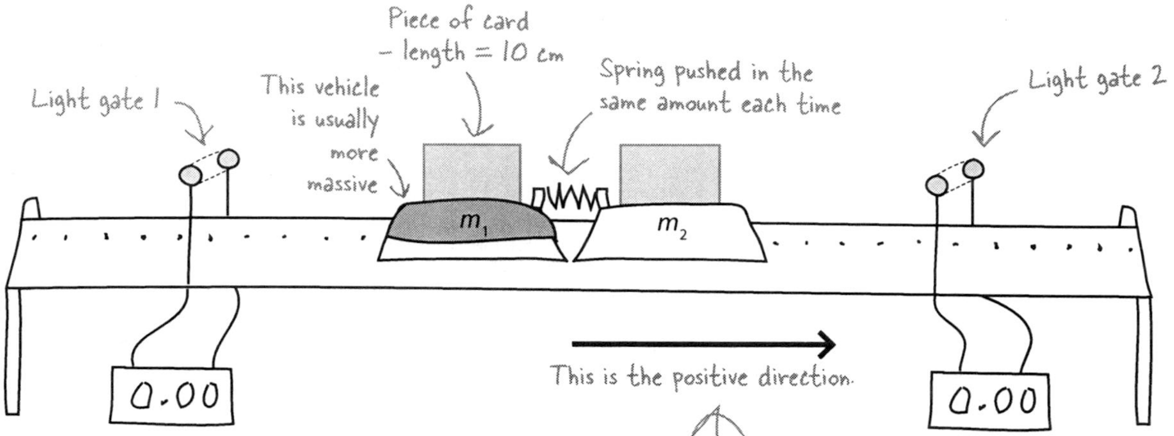

Be careful with the minus signs that show the direction of each vehicle's displacement and velocity vectors.

Times measured to 2 sd so you should only quote your velocities to 2 sd.

Mass 1 (kg)	Mass 2 (kg)	LG 1 time (s)	LG 2 time (s)	Velocity 1 = $\frac{\Delta x}{\Delta t}$ (m/s)	Velocity 2 = $\frac{\Delta x}{\Delta t}$ (m/s)
0.150	0.150	0.19	0.20	$\frac{-0.10}{0.19}$ = -0.53 (2 sd)	$\frac{0.10}{0.20}$ = 0.50 (2 sd)
0.150	0.300	0.17	0.35		
0.150	0.450	0.16	0.48		
0.300	0.150	0.34	0.17		
0.300	0.300	0.27	0.26		
0.300	0.450	0.25	0.38		
0.450	0.150	0.47	0.16		
0.450	0.300	0.37	0.25		
0.450	0.450	0.34	0.33		

Repeat experiment with masses the other way round in case of systematic error/BIAS, e.g. the air track being on a slight slope.

Sharpen your pencil Solution

Here are the results of your experiment. We've annotated the diagram with all of the relevant details like labelling which light gate is which. Note: The pieces of card on the vehicles are 10 cm long.

Fill in the missing boxes in the table, and use the space below to write down any patterns you see.

Mass 1 (kg)	Mass 2 (kg)	LG 1 time (s)	LG 2 time (s)	Velocity 1 = $\frac{\Delta x}{\Delta t}$ (m/s)	Velocity 2 = $\frac{\Delta x}{\Delta t}$ (m/s)
0.150	0.150	0.19	0.20	$\frac{-0.10}{0.19}$ = -0.53 (2 sd)	$\frac{0.10}{0.20}$ = 0.50 (2 sd)
0.150	0.300	0.17	0.35	$\frac{-0.10}{0.17}$ = -0.59 (2 sd)	$\frac{0.10}{0.35}$ = 0.29 (2 sd)
0.150	0.450	0.16	0.48	$\frac{-0.10}{0.16}$ = -0.63 (2 sd)	$\frac{0.10}{0.48}$ = 0.21 (2 sd)
0.300	0.150	0.34	0.17	$\frac{-0.10}{0.34}$ = -0.29 (2 sd)	$\frac{0.10}{0.17}$ = 0.59 (2 sd)
0.300	0.300	0.27	0.26	$\frac{-0.10}{0.27}$ = -0.37 (2 sd)	$\frac{0.10}{0.26}$ = 0.38 (2 sd)
0.300	0.450	0.25	0.38	$\frac{-0.10}{0.25}$ = -0.40 (2 sd)	$\frac{0.10}{0.38}$ = 0.26 (2 sd)
0.450	0.150	0.47	0.16	$\frac{-0.10}{0.47}$ = -0.21 (2 sd)	$\frac{0.10}{0.16}$ = 0.63 (2 sd)
0.450	0.300	0.37	0.25	$\frac{-0.10}{0.37}$ = -0.27 (2 sd)	$\frac{0.10}{0.25}$ = 0.40 (2 sd)
0.450	0.450	0.34	0.33	$\frac{-0.10}{0.34}$ = -0.29 (2 sd)	$\frac{0.10}{0.33}$ = 0.30 (2 sd)

When the masses are the same, the velocities are roughly the same magnitude. i.e. the same size – magnitude is another word for size.

When the masses are the same but both heavier than another trial, their velocities are smaller.

When the masses are different, the smaller one always has a higher magnitude of velocity.

The size of mass × velocity is the same for both vehicles, whether the masses are the same or not.

mass x velocity is always the same size for both vehicles in any one trial.

Don't worry if you didn't spot this last pattern. It's more difficult to see than the others.

there are no Dumb Questions

Q: I looked really hard for the pattern but didn't spot it. Is that OK?

A: If you spotted that when the mass of the vehicle is smaller its velocity is larger (as long as the other vehicle still has the same mass) then that's the main thing. Spotting that mass × velocity always has the same value was the bonus.

Q: So if I hadn't kept one vehicle's mass constant, I might not have spotted the pattern for the other vehicle so clearly?

A: That's right. Before you started actually doing your experiment, you worked out what things you are able to **vary**. Then you made sure that you varied only one thing at a time.

Keeping the mass of one of the vehicles constant enabled you to see the effect that varying the other vehicle's mass had. You were able to spot the pattern because you only changed one variable at a time.

Q: So I should turn all but one of the variables into constants for each trial - each set of measurements - that I make?

A: Precisely - just like you did in this experiment. Your first set of trials were for one mass of 'cannon' vehicle and your second set of trials for another.

Change only one variable at a time and keep the others constant when you do an experiment. This helps you reach better conclusions.

Q: And that was so I didn't inadvertently draw conclusions from just one set of trials, when the results might have looked different for a different 'cannon' vehicle mass?

A: You got it!

Q: Why are we using a 'cannon' vehicle and measuring its velocity in the first place? Why not just push the 'cannonball' vehicle off of a solid wall or something?

A: Because of the observation that cannons **recoil**. When the cannonball goes forward, the cannon rolls backwards - that's why they have wheels!

Q: So we're trying to replicate the 'big' scenario the best we can with our experiment?

A: Yeah, that's the idea.

Q: And now I get to use the results to come up with an equation that helps to work out the difference between firing the iron and stone cannonballs?

A: You got it!

Mass × velocity is the same **size** for both of the vehicles, but the two velocity vectors point in opposite **directions**. So we should be careful with negative signs, right?

Any time you're dealing with vectors, think about signs!

When you filled in your table of experimental results, you were talking about velocity, not speed. So each velocity should have a **sign** corresponding to the **direction** the vehicle is going in.

So far we've been saying that both vehicles have the same **size** of mass × velocity. But you're right, the **direction** of the vectors is about to become really important ...

Mass x velocity - momentum - is conserved

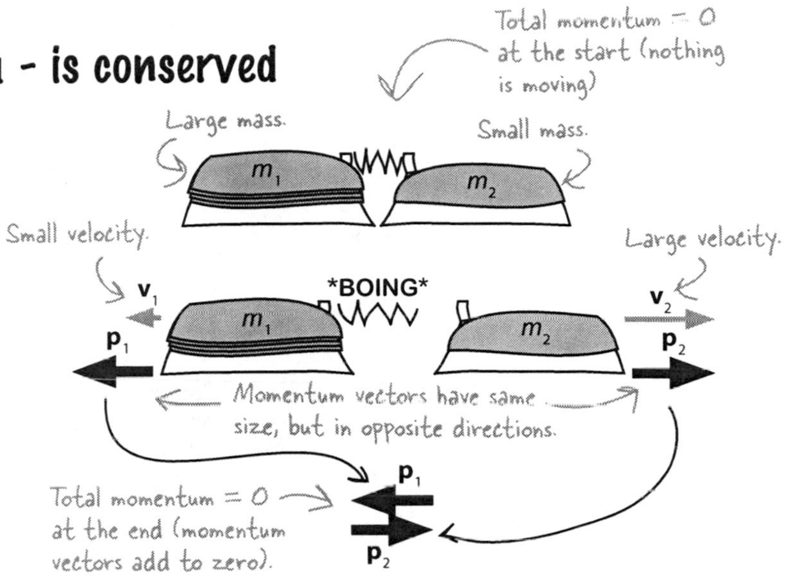

From your experiment, you've worked out that when you push two objects apart, they end up with the same size of mass × velocity. The name given to mass × velocity is **momentum**. Momentum is given the symbol **p**.

An object's momentum is a **vector** that points in the same direction as its velocity vector. Your experiment has told you that **momentum is conserved** in this interaction when two things are pushed apart, as the total momentum is the same both before and after.

Mass is measured in kg and velocity in m/s. This means that momentum has units of kg·m/s The · between 'kg' and 'm' means 'multiplied by' The · helps to reduce confusion by keeping the 'kg' and the 'm' distinct

The total momentum is conserved in any interaction between different objects.

At the **start** of your experiment, the total momentum of the system is **zero**, as nothing's moving at all. Once the vehicles have been pushed apart, the total momentum of the system is still zero, as the two equally-sized momentum vectors point in **opposite directions** and cancel when you add them 'nose to tail'.

Momentum is always conserved in **any** interaction between two (or more) objects.

there are no Dumb Questions

Q: How can you say momentum is conserved? At the start, the vehicles don't have any momentum - they're sitting still. After they're pushed apart, they're moving, so they both have momentum.

A: If you just think about each vehicle individually, then you're right - at the start they have no momentum and at the end they do.

But when you add up the **total** momentum of all the individual objects involved in the experiment, then it's the same both before and after the interaction

Q: But I thought we said before that mass × velocity is the same for both vehicles once they're pushed apart. How can two things that are the same be zero when they're added together?

A: We said that the **size** of mass × velocity is the same for both vehicles. But as they're traveling away from each other in opposite **directions**, their velocity vectors - and momentum vectors - point in opposite directions.

Momentum is a vector!

Q: So when I add together two vectors that are the same size but point in opposite directions, the answer is zero?

A: Yes, that's right. Vectors add 'nose-to tail'. When you line up two vectors that are the same size and point in opposite directions, you end up where you started so the answer is zero.

Q: So now I've got my head around momentum conservation, do I get to play with equations to try and solve the stone cannonball problem?

A: Absolutely!

Good point - you need to work out what happens when the force is different

When you were designing the experiment, you realized that there are three things you can vary - the mass of vehicle 1, the mass of vehicle 2 and the strength of the spring that pushes them apart.

To make your experiment complete, you'd usually have to repeat it with a couple of different springs. But this time around, you're going to use your physics **intuition** to predict what would happen if you used a stronger spring ...

BE the experiment

Your job is to be the experiment you've just been doing, and imagine what will happen if you use an even stronger spring to push the two vehicles apart. How will the increased strength of spring affect mass x velocity for the vehicles?

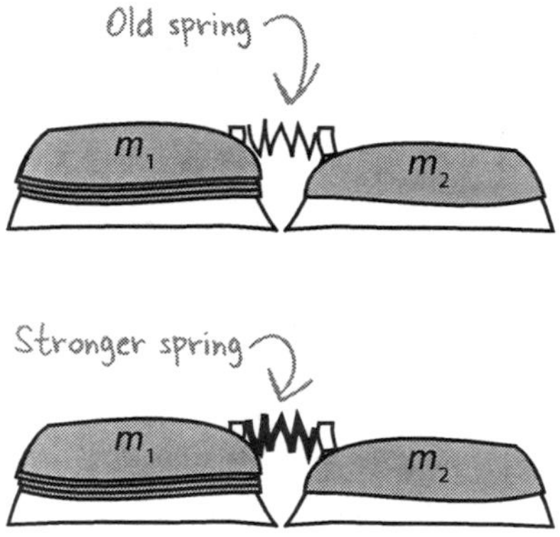

....

....

....

....

....

....

....

BE the experiment - SOLUTION

Your job is to be the experiment you've just been doing, and imagine what will happen if you use an even stronger spring to push the two vehicles apart. How will the increased strength of spring affect mass x velocity for the vehicles?

A stronger spring will push the two vehicles apart with a bigger force. So it'll have a bigger effect on the velocity of each vehicle. I think that momentum will still be conserved but the mass x velocity for each vehicle will be bigger, as they were pushed with a bigger force.

Pushing with a greater force for the same amount of time, leads to a greater change in momentum.

A greater force acting over the same amount of time gives a greater change in momentum

If you use a stronger spring, you increase the **force** that pushes the two vehicles apart. If you apply this larger force for the same time that you were applying the smaller force, it leads to a greater **change of momentum** for each vehicle. If both vehicles are still the same mass, their velocities will both be larger than before.

Small force, smaller change in momentum (when force is applied for the same time).

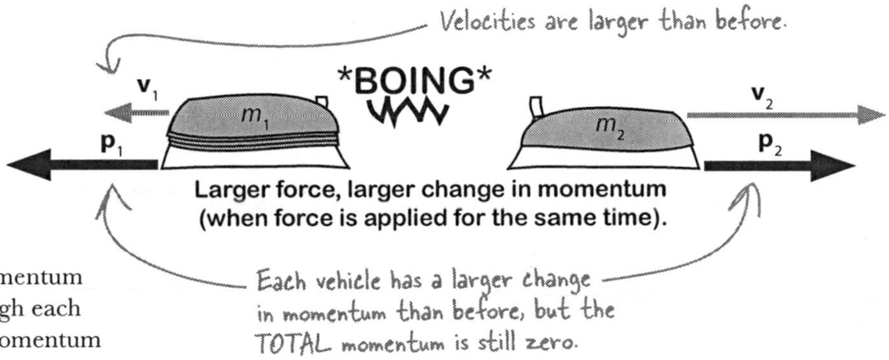

Larger force, larger change in momentum (when force is applied for the same time).

But because of **momentum conservation**, the **total** momentum is still equal to zero, even though each individual vehicle has more momentum than it did previously.

Write momentum conservation as an equation

The symbol for momentum is **p**, so you can write the equation $\mathbf{p} = m\mathbf{v}$ (momentum = mass × velocity).

When you're dealing with more than one object, you'll typically see **subscripts** to make it clear which object you're talking about. So vehicle 1 has mass m_1, velocity $\mathbf{v}_1$, and momentum $\mathbf{p}_1$. Vehicle 2 has mass m_2, velocity $\mathbf{v}_2$, and momentum $\mathbf{p}_2$.

We've not drawn in the spring this time, to make what's going on with the vehicles a bit clearer.

The total momentum is always $\mathbf{p}_{total} = \mathbf{p}_1 + \mathbf{p}_2$ - this is what's **conserved**.

At the start

$\mathbf{p}_{total} = \mathbf{p}_1 + \mathbf{p}_2$

$\mathbf{p}_{total} = 0$

At the start of your experiment, $\mathbf{v}_1$ and $\mathbf{v}_2$ are both 0, therefore $\mathbf{p}_1$ and $\mathbf{p}_2$ are both zero so $\mathbf{p}_{total} = 0$.

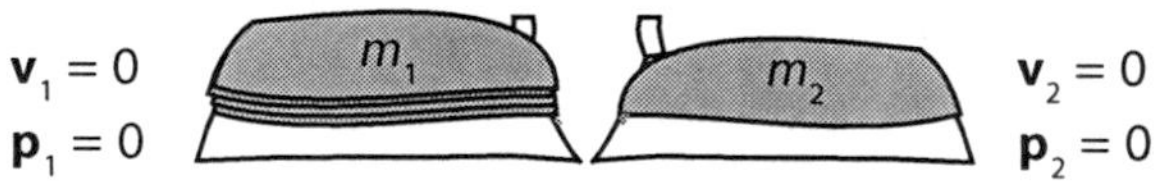

At the end

$\mathbf{p}_{total} = \mathbf{p}_1 + \mathbf{p}_2$

$\mathbf{p}_{total} = 0$

At the end of your experiment, the massive vehicle is moving slowly to the left, and the less massive vehicle is moving more quickly to the right. $\mathbf{p}_{total}$ is still 0, as momentum is conserved.

The symbol for momentum is p.

So you can write down the equation:

$$\mathbf{p}_{total} = \mathbf{p}_1 + \mathbf{p}_2 = 0$$

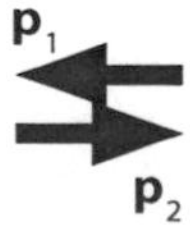

$p_{total} = 0$, as the momentum vectors add to zero when you line them up nose to tail.

The total momentum is the same before and after.

You can also write the equation this way, which will be very useful for working with **masses** and **velocities**:

$$\mathbf{p}_{total} = m_1\mathbf{v}_1 + m_2\mathbf{v}_2 = 0$$

$p_1 = m_1v_1$ $p_2 = m_2v_2$

This is zero because the total momentum was zero at the start. If the total momentum had a different value at the start, that value would be here instead.

There is a second law too – you'll meet that later.

Momentum conservation and Newton's Third Law are equivalent

Newton's Third Law says that if you push something, it pushes back at you with an equal size of force in the opposite direction.

Imagine that instead of being separate, the spring is attached to the left hand vehicle, so the left hand vehicle 'pushes' the right hand vehicle. Then imagine that the spring is attached to the right hand vehicle, so that it 'pushes' the left-hand vehicle.

It actually doesn't make any difference which vehicle is "doing the pushing" - they still move apart in the same way. The size of each vehicle's **change in momentum** is the same, though their momentum vectors point in opposite directions. So both vehicles must have experienced the same size of **force** for the same amount of time, though in **opposite directions**. This is the case whichever vehicle you think of as "doing the pushing". Both vehicles experience the same size of force, but in opposite directions, as a result of their interaction.

In any interaction between two objects, they both experience the same <u>size</u> of force, but in opposite <u>directions.</u>

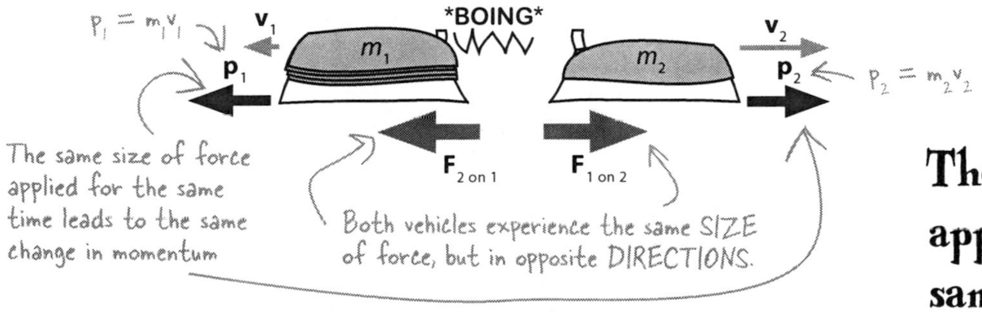

Newton's third law and momentum conservation mean that the cannon and cannonball exert the same **force** on each other when the cannon is fired. So the change in the cannonball's momentum is the **same size** as the change in the cannon's momentum. These changes in momentum happen in **opposite directions**, as the force that the cannon exerts on the cannonball is in the opposite direction from the force that the cannonball exerts on the cannon.

The same force applied for the same amount of time always produces the same change in momentum.

If the cannon's attached to the ground, you make the EARTH move backwards!

Momentum is **always** conserved in interactions between two or more objects. If the cannon exerts a force on the cannonball, then the cannonball exerts an equal-sized force on the cannon in the opposite direction.

This is Newton's Third Law.

If the cannon is on wheels, this force makes it recoil and roll backwards. But if the cannon is attached to the earth, then the whole earth experiences the force from the cannonball! Since momentum is conserved, the earth must recoil backwards - but because the earth is so massive, its recoil velocity is incredibly small. You can work out how small it is ...

Sharpen your pencil

The Sieges-R-Us website doesn't give its mass, but it feels like it's around 1 kg.

Use momentum conservation to work out the approximate velocity that the earth would 'recoil' with if the cannon is firmly attached to it when it is fired.

The cannonball has a velocity of 90.0 m/s and a mass of around 1 kg.

The earth's mass is 5.97×10^{24} kg.

If you need a refresher in scientific notation, turn to chapter 3.

Why don't you notice the earth recoiling like this?

Remember to start with a labelled sketch!

Sharpen your pencil Solution

Use momentum conservation to work out the approximate velocity that the earth would 'recoil' with if the cannon is firmly attached to it when it is fired.

The cannonball has a velocity of 90.0 m/s and a mass of around 1 kg.

The earth's mass is 5.97×10^{24} kg.

Why don't you usually notice the earth recoiling like this?

Total momentum of earth and cannonball at start = 0

Total momentum of earth and cannonball after firing = 0 (momentum conservation)

$$p = m_1 v_1 + m_2 v_2 = 0$$

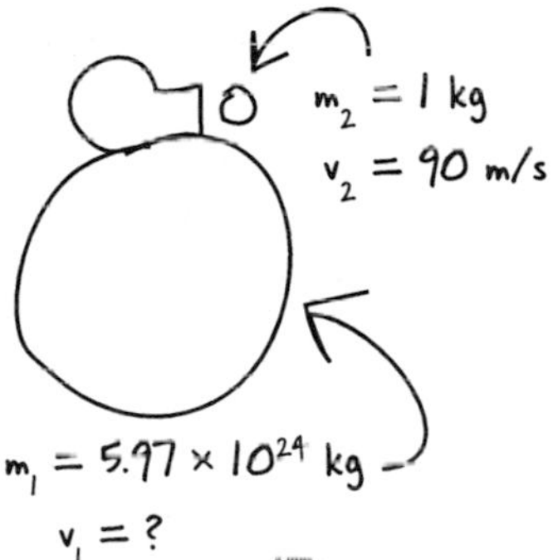

Want to know v_1, so rearrange equation.

$$m_1 v_1 = -m_2 v_2$$

$$v_1 = \frac{-m_2 v_2}{m_1} = \frac{-(1 \times 90)}{5.97 \times 10^{24}}$$

$$v_1 = -1 \times 10^{-23} \text{ m/s (1 sd)}$$

The Earth's velocity is negative, as it moves in the opposite direction to the cannonball.

Remember to draw a labelled sketch, so that it's easy for you (and your examiner) to work out what m_1, v_2 etc are.

The earth's recoil velocity is around 1×10^{-23} m/s in the opposite direction to the cannonball's velocity.

You don't notice this because it would take an incredibly long time to travel any noticeable distance at this velocity!

This answer should only be quoted to 1 sd as the cannonball's mass is listed as 'around 1 kg,' so has 1 sd.

there are no Dumb Questions

Q: Momentum is always conserved, even when it doesn't look like it is?

A: That's right - it's easy to see a cannon recoil. But impossible to see the earth recoil!

Q: When am I allowed to use momentum conservation?

A: Any time two (or more) objects interact, momentum is conserved, so you can say $p_{before} = p_{after}$. As long as you keep track of which mass and velocity is which, you're fine.

Q: So I guess I can use the same type of calculation to work out what happens with the stone cannonball?

A: Yes - momentum conservation is the vital key to working out what happens there. Speaking of which ...

Sometimes you can do this using an experiment (like here). Sometimes you'll need to think through assumptions using words, graphs or equations.

Test out any assumptions you have

If the cannon exerts the same force for the same amount of time on the stone cannonball as it does on the iron cannonball, the change in momentum would be the same for both cannonballs.

But right now this is an **assumption**, as the cannon may not always exert the same force for the same amount of time.

To investigate this further, you can revisit the experiment you did earlier...

Sharpen your pencil

The same size of **force** applied for the same amount of **time** always leads to the same **change in momentum**.

Therefore, if a spring pushing two vehicles apart always exerts the same force on both vehicles for the same amount of time, then each individual vehicle will experience the same change in momentum every time you do the experiment.

a. The table below is taken from your experiment a few pages ago, where you pushed two vehicles of varying masses apart with the same spring. Complete the table to show the change in momentum for each vehicle.

Mass 1 (kg)	Mass 2 (kg)	Velocity 1 (m/s)	Velocity 2 (m/s)	Change in momentum 1 $p_1 = m_1v_1$ (kg.m/s)	Change in momentum 2 $p_1 = m_1v_1$ (kg.m/s)
0.450	0.150	-0.21	0.63	0.450 × -0.21 = 0.094 (2 sd)	
0.450	0.300	-0.27	0.40		
0.450	0.450	-0.29	0.30		

b. Is the change in momentum of a single vehicle always the same in each trial of the experiment?

c. Try to think of reasons to explain the result you described in part b. Does this have implications for the iron and stone cannonballs, which are fired separately and have different masses?

Sharpen your pencil Solution

The same size of **force** applied for the same amount of **time** always leads to the same **change in momentum**.

Therefore, if a spring pushing two vehicles apart always exerts the same force on both vehicles for the same amount of time, then each individual vehicle will experience the same change in momentum every time you do the experiment.

a. The table below is taken from your experiment a few pages ago, where you pushed two vehicles of varying masses apart with the same spring. Complete the table to show the change in momentum for each vehicle.

Mass 1 (kg)	Mass 2 (kg)	Velocity 1 (m/s)	Velocity 2 (m/s)	Change in momentum 1 $p_1 = m_1v_1$ (kg.m/s)	Change in momentum 2 $p_1 = m_1v_1$ (kg.m/s)
0.450	0.150	-0.21	0.63	0.450 × -0.21 = 0.094 (2 sd)	0.150 × 0.63 = 0.094 (2 sd)
0.450	0.300	-0.27	0.40	0.450 × -0.27 = 0.12 (2 sd)	0.300 × 0.40 = 0.12 (2 sd)
0.450	0.450	-0.29	0.30	0.450 × -0.29 = 0.13 (2 sd)	0.450 × 0.30 = 0.14 (2 sd)

b. Is the change in momentum of a single vehicle always the same in each trial of the experiment?

No, the change in momentum isn't the same. It seems to get larger as the masses of the vehicles get larger.

c. Try to think of reasons to explain the result you described in part b. Does this have implications for the iron and stone cannonballs, which are fired separately and have different masses?

The change in momentum is only the same on different occasions if the same force is applied for the same time.

As the masses of the vehicles get larger, the change in momentum increases. The larger a vehicle's mass, the more difficult it is to get the vehicle going. So maybe the vehicles with larger masses spend more time in contact with the spring, so the force isn't applied over the same time.

The iron cannonball has a larger mass than the stone cannonball. This means that it's more difficult to get it going. So it may spend a longer time inside the cannon, and end up with a larger momentum.

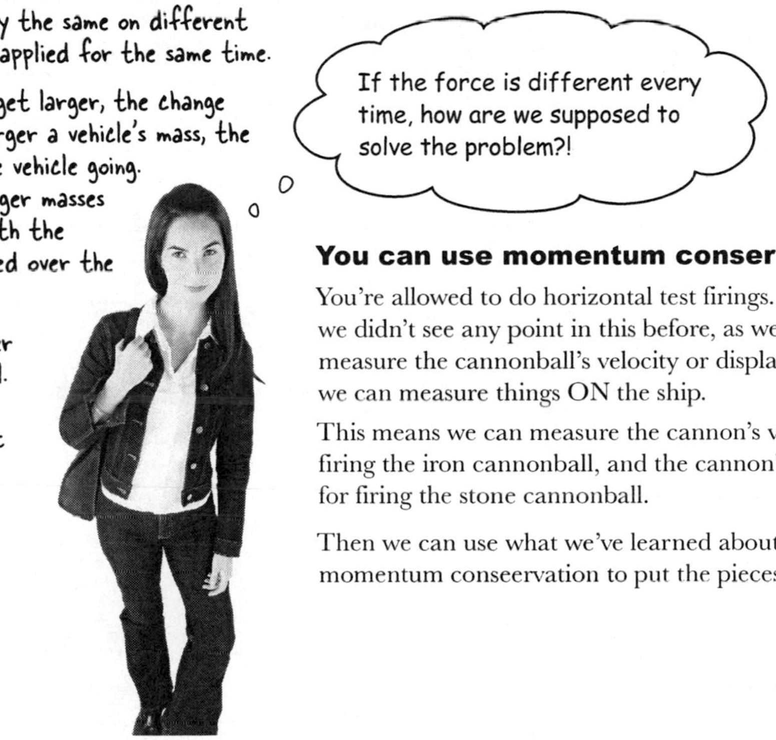

You can use momentum conservation

You're allowed to do horizontal test firings. Although we didn't see any point in this before, as we can't measure the cannonball's velocity or displacement, we can measure things ON the ship.

This means we can measure the cannon's velocity for firing the iron cannonball, and the cannon's velocity for firing the stone cannonball.

Then we can use what we've learned about momentum conseervation to put the pieces together ...

Yaar, we can test-fire the cannon - as long as we aim it horizontally and away from the ghost ship!

Sharpen your pencil

This is the value given for this particular cannon and cannonball on the website.

Here are the results of two horizontal test firings, where the cannon's recoil velocity was measured.

Iron cannonball: Cannon velocity = 0.126 m/s, Cannonball velocity = 90.0 m/s

Stone cannonball: Cannon velocity = 0.063 m/s

The only other fact you know is that the mass of the iron cannonball is four times the mass of the stone cannonball. If you knew the mass of the cannon you'd be fine, but it's far too heavy to measure using scales. But there's another way to measure the mass of the cannon...

a. Use momentum conservation to calculate m_c the mass of the cannon, in terms of m_i the mass of the iron cannonball.

You won't be able to give your answer as just a number. Your answer will look something like $m_c = 400m_i$ which would tell you that the cannon has 400 times the mass of the iron cannonball.

By the way, this isn't the correct answer, it's just an example of what an answer would look like!

b. Use momentum conservation and your answer from part a. to calculate the velocity of the stone cannonball. The stone cannonball's mass is a quarter of the mass of the iron cannonball.

Don't worry about calculating the range yet - you'll do that next.

Sharpen your pencil Solution

Iron cannonball: Cannon velocity = 0.126 m/s, Cannonball velocity = 90.0 m/s
Stone cannonball: Cannon velocity = 0.063 m/s.

a. Use momentum conservation to calculate m_c the mass of the cannon, in terms of m_i the mass of the iron cannonball.

b. Use momentum conservation and your answer from part a. to calculate the velocity of the stone cannonball. The stone cannonball's mass is a quarter of the mass of the iron cannonball.

Iron cannonball

$m_c = ?$, $v_c = -0.126$ m/s; $m_i = ?$, $v_i = 90.0$ m/s

$$p = m_c v_c + m_i v_i = 0$$

$$m_c v_c = -m_i v_i$$

$$m_c = \frac{-m_i v_i}{v_c}$$

$$m_c = \frac{-m_i \times 90v_i}{-0.126}$$

$$m_c = 714 m_i \text{ (3 sd)}$$

Sometimes you'll be asked to do a problem where your final answer isn't a number. That's OK.

Don't put units on an answer like this. The units of m_c will depend on the units that m_i is measured in.

Stone cannonball

$m_c = 714 m_i$, $v_c = -0.063$ m/s; $m_s = \frac{m_i}{4} = 0.25 m_i$, $v_s = ?$ m/s

$$p = m_c v_c + m_s v_s = 0$$

You don't know actual values for any of the masses – but the terms in the momentum conservation equation all mention masses.

$$m_s v_s = -m_c v_c$$

$$v_s = \frac{-m_c v_c}{m_s}$$

If you know what all the masses are relative to each other, for example in terms of m_i, all mention of mass in your equation will divide out and cancel.

Make substitutions for m_c and m_s in terms of m_i.

$$v_s = \frac{-714 m_i v_c}{0.25 m_i}$$

$$v_s = \frac{-714 \times (-0.063)}{0.25}$$

$$v_s = 180 \text{ m/s (2 sd)}$$

Even though we **didn't know** the masses of the cannonballs, we could still do the question because the masses we didn't know divided out and cancelled.

Try the variables from your sketch in equations to see what happens

Often, you won't know how a problem's going to work out until you start writing down equations and playing with them.

So don't get stressed if you don't know many values at the start. Do your sketch, write down everything you know, and jot down **how** you'd do the problem and which equation(s) you'd use.

Then play with the equations! You'll often find that variables cancel and the equation simplifies down to a calculation you're able to do.

If you don't know values for the variables you're working with, play with the equations. Some of the variables may divide out and cancel.

You've calculated the stone cannonball's velocity...

Although the cannon doesn't always exert the same force on a cannonball, **momentum** is always conserved on every occasion that the cannon is fired.

You've just used **momentum conservation** twice. The first time was for firing the iron cannonball, which allowed you to calculate the **mass** of the cannon. The second time was for the stone cannonball, which allowed you to calculate the **velocity** of the stone cannonball: 180 m/s.

Momentum conservation allows you to calculate masses or velocities that you don't already know.

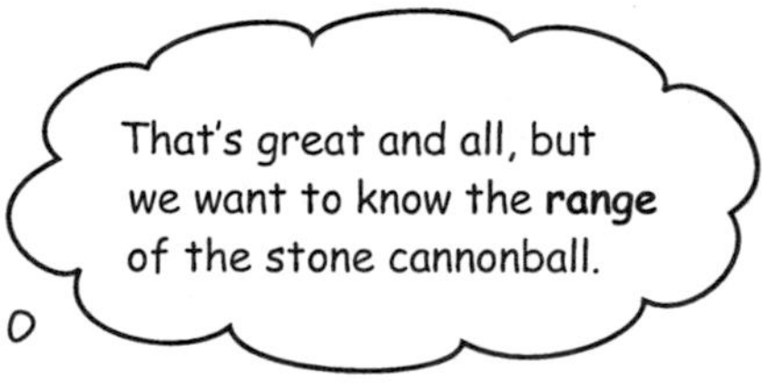

... but you want the new range!

You already know that you can work out the cannonballs' **range** if you know its **velocity** - you already did that for the iron cannonball.

But that was a long, involved calculation which took you quite a while.

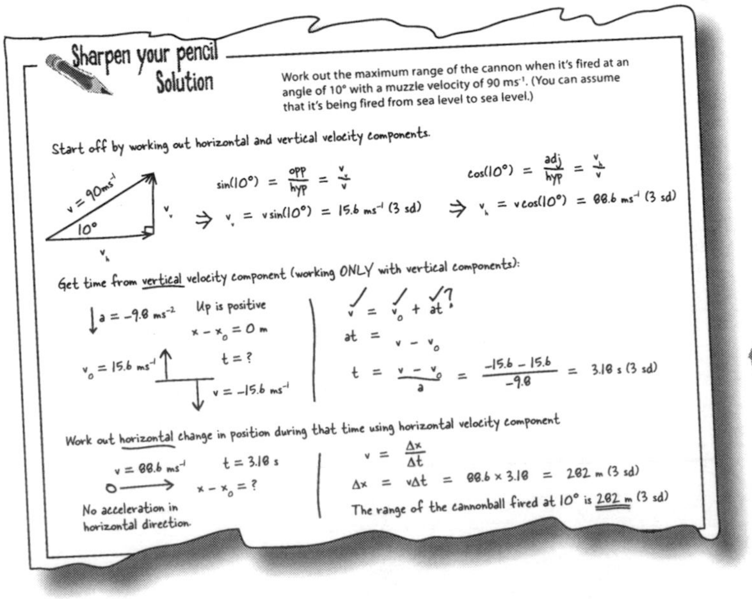

This is what you did to work out the iron cannonball's range.

Wouldn't it be dreamy if you could work out the new range without having to redo the whole calculation all over again with different numbers. But I know it's just a fantasy...

You used subscripts to keep track of which component is which.

Use proportion to work out the new range

Your earlier calculation to work out the range of the iron cannonball had three parts:

Part a: Work out the vertical and horizontal **components** of the initial velocity, $\mathbf{v}_{0v}$ and $\mathbf{v}_{0h}$.

Part b: Use the **vertical component** and the equation $\mathbf{v}_v = \mathbf{v}_{0v} + \mathbf{a}_v t$ to work out the **time** the cannonball is in the air for.

Part c: Use the **horizontal component** and the equation $\Delta\mathbf{x}_h = \mathbf{v}_{0h}\Delta t$ to work out the cannonball's horizontal displacement in that time.

You've calculated that the stone cannonball's initial velocity $\mathbf{v}_0$ is two times greater than the iron cannonballs' velocity.

So rather than doing the entire calculation again with a different value for $\mathbf{v}_0$, you can use **proportion** to work out the new range ...

Sharpen your pencil

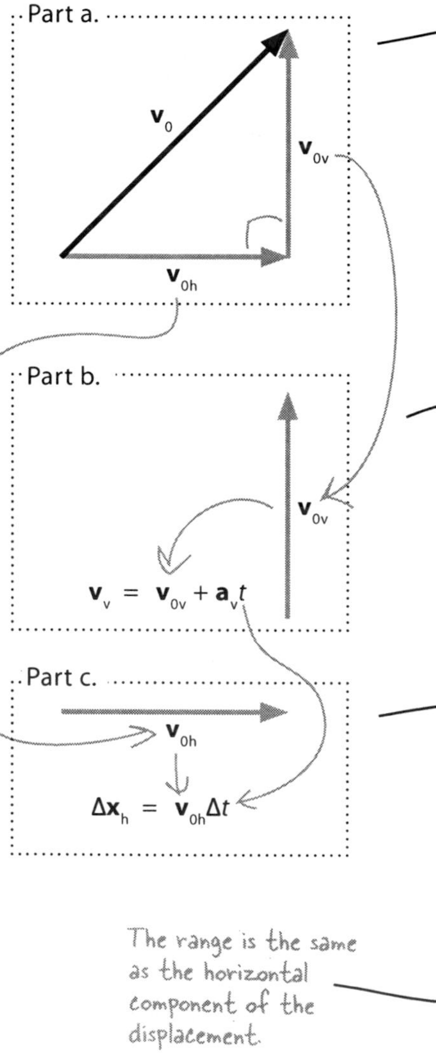

a. If the initial velocity is 2 times greater than before, how many times greater are its horizontal and vertical components?

b. The vertical component of the velocity is used in the equation $\mathbf{v} = \mathbf{v}_0 + \mathbf{a}t$ to work out the time in the air. How many times greater is the time in the air with the new cannonball?

c. The horizontal component of the velocity and the time in the air are used in the equation $\Delta \mathbf{x}_h = \mathbf{v}_h \Delta t$ to work out the range. How many times greater is the range with the new cannonball?

d. The range of the iron cannonball fired at 10° is 282 m. What is the range of the stone cannonball when it's fired at 10°?

Sharpen your pencil Solution

a. If the initial velocity is 2 times greater than before, how many times greater are its horizontal and vertical components?

The angle is still the same, so they're similar triangles. If one side is two times longer, the other sides are too.

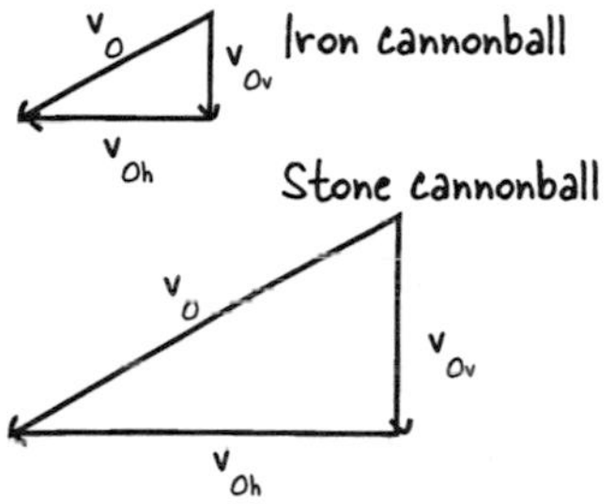

Both components are 2 times greater than before.

b. The vertical component of the velocity is used in the equation $\mathbf{v}_v = \mathbf{v}_{0v} + \mathbf{a}_v t$ to work out the time in the air. How many times greater is the time in the air with the new cannonball?

Both v_v and v_{0v} are 2 times larger. When you rearrange the equation to say "t = something" it becomes $t = \frac{v_v - v_{0v}}{a_v}$

When you're adding or subtracting (which you are before you divide by a_v) and the numbers you're dealing with become two times larger, your answer also becomes two times larger.

c. The horizontal component of the velocity and the time in the air are used in the equation $\Delta \mathbf{x}_h = \mathbf{v}_h \Delta t$ to work out the range. How many times greater is the range with the new cannonball?

Both v_h and t are 2 times greater then before.

As they're multiplied together to give Δx_h, this means that Δx_h is 4 times greater than before, as $2 \times 2 = 4$.

d. The range of the iron cannonball fired at 10° is 282 m. What is the range of the stone cannonball when it's fired at 10°?

New range is 4 times greater than old range.

New range $= 4 \times 282 =$ 1130 m (3 sd)

there are no Dumb Questions

Q: What's the 'similar triangles' thing again? It rings a bell ...

A: If two triangles have identical angles, then the ratios of their sides are equal. You used that before to work out sin, cos, and tan.

Here, if you make the velocity two times larger, then the whole triangle also becomes two times larger - as do the components.

Q: Oh yeah. But what's this bit about adding rather than multiplying v_v and v_{0v}?

A: The rearranged equation is $t = \frac{\mathbf{v}_v - \mathbf{v}_{0v}}{\mathbf{a}_v}$

Since $\mathbf{v}_{0v} = -\mathbf{v}_v$ (they have the same size but are in opposite directions), the bit on top of the fraction is 2 times greater than it was before. And since **a** is constant, *t* is also 2 times greater than before.

Q: What about part c?

A: That equation is $\Delta \mathbf{x}_h = \mathbf{v}_h \Delta t$. You're now dealing with the horizontal component of the velocity, $\mathbf{v}_h$, which is two times greater than before. And the time, *t*, is also two times greater than before. So the term **v**Δ*t* is **four** times greater, as 2×2 = 4.

Using proportion to work out the answer to a question that's similar to one you already did can be a good shortcut.

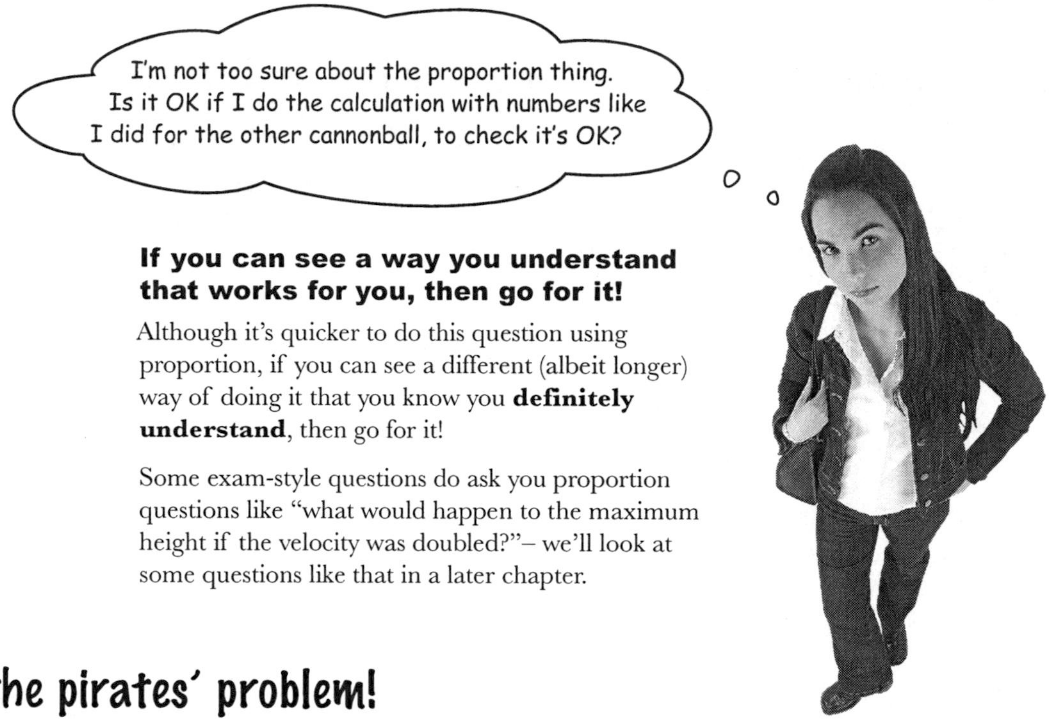

If you can see a way you understand that works for you, then go for it!

Although it's quicker to do this question using proportion, if you can see a different (albeit longer) way of doing it that you know you **definitely understand**, then go for it!

Some exam-style questions do ask you proportion questions like "what would happen to the maximum height if the velocity was doubled?"– we'll look at some questions like that in a later chapter.

You solved the pirates' problem!

The Sieges-R-Us hype is justified! The **vertical component** of the stone cannonball's velocity is **two** times greater than for the iron cannonball, so the **time** in the air is **two** times greater as well. If the horizontal component of the velocity was the same for both cannonballs, then the stone cannonball would go two times as far (as it's in the air for two times as long).

But the **horizontal component** of the stone cannonball's velocity is also **two** times greater than the horizontal component of the iron cannonballs' velocity. So the stone cannonball's **range** is a massive **four** times further than the iron cannonball's!

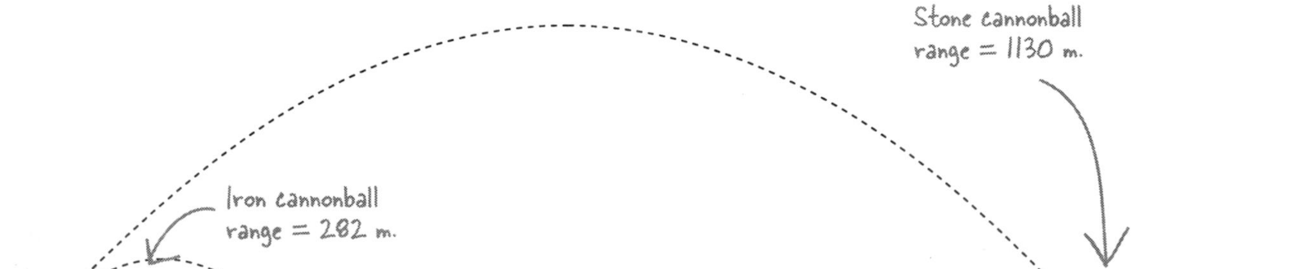

So the ghost ship has to stay 4 × 282 m = 1130 m away - where it doesn't cause problems any more. **Another job well done!**

Question Clinic: The "Proportion" Question (often multiple choice)

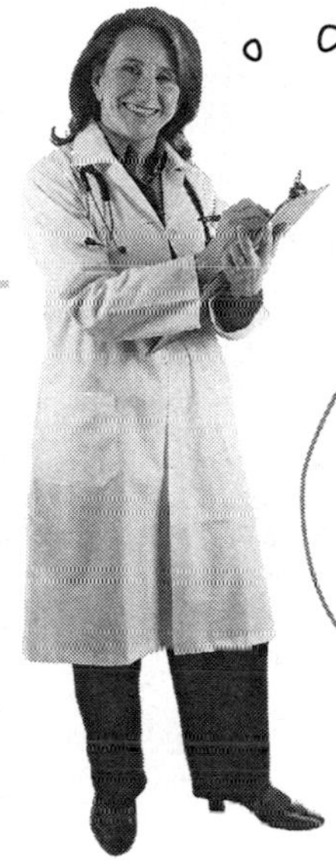

You will sometimes come across questions, especially in a multiple choice exam, which don't give you numerical values. Instead they may say that something is 'three times the mass' or has 'double the momentum' of something else. These are designed to test your understanding of the physics, rather than your ability to press buttons on a calculator.

Start with a sketch! Then you'll spot that this question is about momentum conservation.

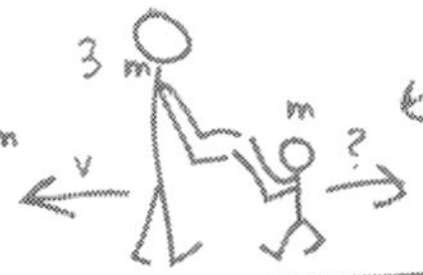

Write what you know on your sketch.

This tells you that you can ignore the effect of friction.

2. An adult and a child are on an ice rink. The child has mass m and the adult has mass 3 m. The child pushes the adult, and as a result the adult slides backwards with velocity v. What is the size of the child's velocity?

a. v

b. $\frac{v}{3}$

c. $3v$

d. $\frac{v}{2}$

e. $9v$

This tells you that it's a proportion question, so don't worry about not knowing any values.

The child has a lower mass, so it will go faster than the adult when they push with the same force. So you can already eliminate any answer where the child is going slower than the adult, or at the same speed.

Velocity is a vector, but this question only wants the size, not the direction.

The adult and child experience the same force for the same amount of time (Newton's 3rd Law). So mass × velocity should have the same size for the adult and the child. As the child is a third of the mass of the adult, the child's velocity needs to be three times greater than the adult's velocity.

The 'proportion' question may look like it's from a 'weird' part of physics - for instance a question about an atomic nucleus that splits into two parts. The key is to see past the story - **start with a sketch** - what is it **like**? When you do this, you'll realize that it's the same as two things being pushed apart and you can use momentum conservation to solve the problem.

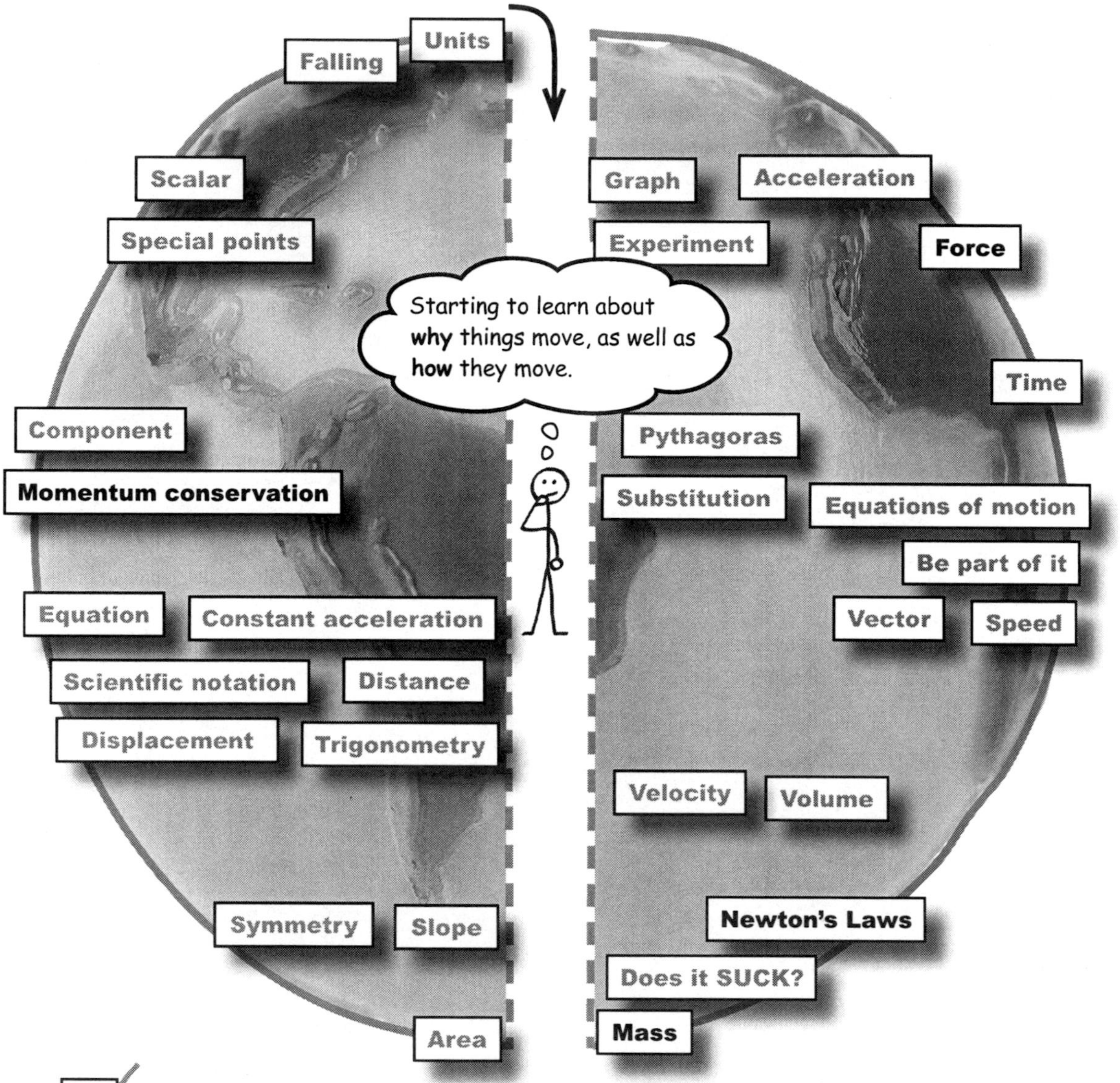

☑	**Mass**	**The amount of 'stuff' that something is made from.**
☑	**Momentum conservation**	**Momentum is mass × velocity. When two (or more) objects interact, the total momentum is the same both before and after.**
☑	**Force**	**Something that causes a change in an object's momentum, for example a push or a pull (though there are also other types of forces).**
☑	**Newton's Laws**	**Three laws that tell you how objects move in the presence (or absence) of forces.**

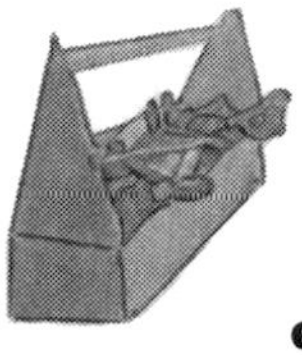

Your Physics Toolbox

You've got Chapter 10 under your belt and added some problem-solving skills to your ever-expanding toolbox.

Vary one thing at a time

If you're doing an experiment, you should only vary one thing at a time.

This means that you can know for certain what has caused any change to your results that you observe.

Newton's 1st law

An object continues with its current velocity unless it's acted on by a force.

In everyday life, things appear to slow down as time passes, but that's because of the force of friction.

Proportion

If you have an equation, you can work out what happens to the answer you get if you change one of the variables by a certain amount (e.g., doubling, tripling or halving it).

If you've already used the equation, this can be faster than redoing the same calculation with different values.

Momentum conservation

Momentum is mass × velocity, $p = mv$

Momentum is a vector that has the same direction as an object's velocity vector.

The same force always causes the same change in momentum

If two (or more) objects interact, their total momentum is the same both before and after the interaction. You can work out the total momentum by adding the momentum vectors 'nose-to-tail.'

Newton's 3rd law

When two objects interact, each experiences an equal force, but in opposite directions.

This is a direct consequence of momentum conservation. As the same force always causes the same change in momentum, and momentum is conserved, then the two objects must experience equal (but opposite) forces so that the total momentum is the same before and after.

Newton's 2nd law is in chapter 11!

11 weight and the normal force

Forces for courses

Sometimes you have to make a statement forcefully.

In this chapter, you'll work out **Newton's 2nd Law** from what you already know about momentum conservation to wind up with the key equation, $\mathbf{F}_{net} = m\mathbf{a}$. Once you combine this with spotting **Newton's 3rd Law force pairs**, and drawing **free body diagrams**, you'll be able to deal with (just about) anything. You'll also learn about why mass and **weight** aren't the same thing, and get used to using the **normal force** to support your arguments.

WeightBotchers are at it again!

WeightBotchers claim that their new product guarantees instant weight loss. It's been difficult to miss their brash advertisements since the campaign launched last week.

But the TV show FakeBusters doesn't buy those claims, and want you to investigate the details. If you can prove that the WeightBotchers machine is a hoax, your work will be featured in a special episode in their next series.

Memo

From: FakeBusters

Re: WeightBotchers

We're planning to include a 10 minute slot in our next series looking into the claims made by WeightBotchers about their latest product.

If you can bust the fake with physics, we'd love to have you on our show.

Is it really possible to lose weight instantly?!

Here's the deal. The machine has a platform at the top with some scales on it. When you stand on the scales, they read the same number of kilograms as they usually would in your bathroom. No surprises there.

But then the platform you're standing on suddenly moves downwards - and the reading on the scales becomes lower. Numbers don't lie - so if the reading's gone down then you must have lost weight. Right?

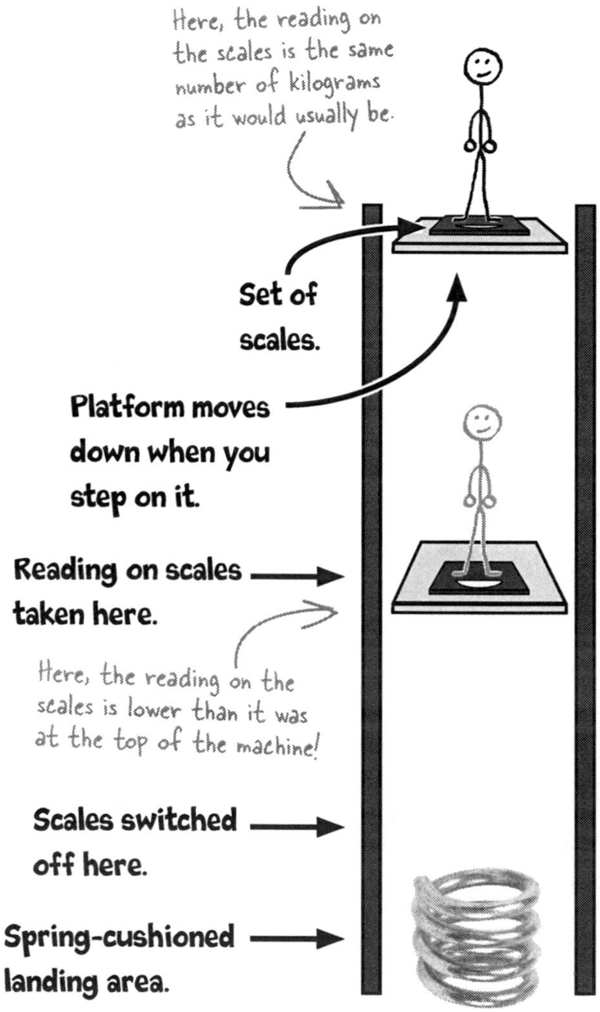

Just before you reach the bottom of the machine, the scales are switched off to protect them from the impact with the cushioned landing area.

There must be a trick involved somewhere... but what is it? The scales don't look fake and read the same number of kilograms as usual when they're not on the machine.

So maybe it's something to do with what the machine does and **how the scales produce a measurement.**

BRAIN POWER

How do you think the machine works?

(How do scales actually produce a **measurement**?)

Scales work by compressing or stretching a spring

Some scales work by **compressing** a spring. If you put pieces of fruit on top that are all more or less the same size, the spring will compress by the same amount each time you add another piece. The **change in length** of the spring is **converted** into a reading in **kilograms**.

Another type of scales works by **stretching** a spring. This is exactly the same principle as compressing a spring, except that you hang an object from the spring rather than putting it on top. Again, a change in length is converted into a reading in kilograms.

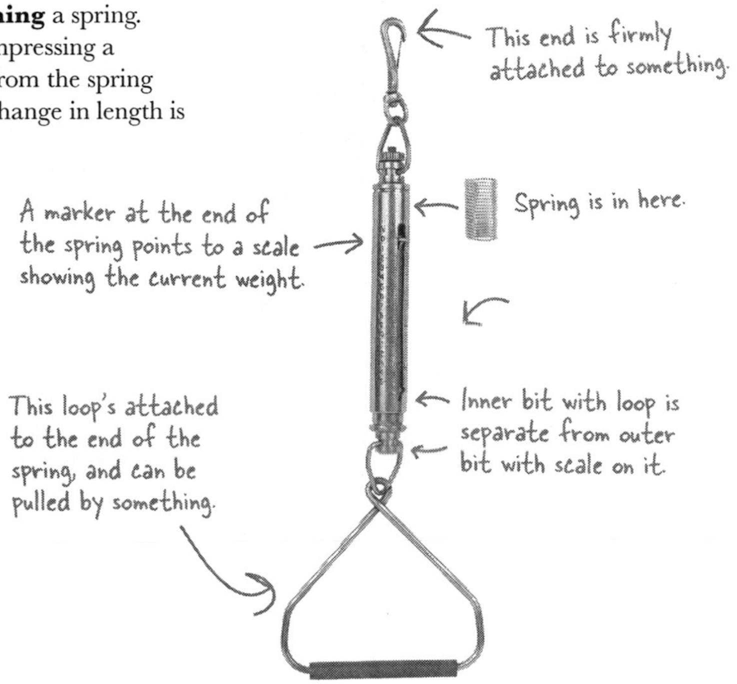

A spring will always compress/ stretch by the same amount for the same load, to give a consistent reading.

Jim: Yeah, I'm struggling as well. I don't see how the person's lost weight. It's not like they were wearing a rucksack full of boulders that they suddenly took off, or anything.

Joe: Maybe it's something to do with how the scales make their **measurements**. Scales don't measure the number of kilograms directly - scales measure the **change in length** of a spring.

Frank: Hmmm. You mean if I put the scales against the wall and **pushed** them with my hand, they'd register a number of kilograms. Yeah, I can see that.

If you know HOW your measuring devices work, you can trouble-shoot your experiments when unexpected things happen.

Jim: That's weird. **Kilograms** are units of **mass**, right? Mass is the amount of 'stuff' something's made from. But if you push the scales sideways like that, the reading depends on the **force** that you push with, not on the amount of stuff your hand's made from.

Joe: I guess that's because the scales don't really measure kilograms directly - they measure the **change in the length** of the spring. And that must depend on the **force** that the spring's pushed with.

Frank: If I'm standing on the scales, I'm kinda pushing down on the spring inside them because of gravity. I guess that because of gravity, a certain number of kilograms must produce a certain force - and a certain change in length of the spring. So the scales always assume that you're standing on them when making a measurement.

Joe: So if you use the scales differently from how the manufacturer intended - by pushing them against the wall, or perhaps by making them move down like the WeightBotchers machine does - then you get a flakey reading.

Frank: That sounds plausible - but personally I'd like to get my head around how force (which seems to do with pushing) and mass (which is to do with the 'stuff' you're made of) are connected ...

Mass is a measurement of "stuff"

Mass is an indication of how much 'stuff' something is made from, and is measured in **kilograms**. Mass is a **scalar**, as 'stuff' can't have a direction - it's just what's there.

Even though the scales indicate otherwise, the person on the WeightBotchers machine always has the same mass - it's not like they took off a rucksack or had a haircut halfway down and lost a whole lot of matter.

MASS is how much "stuff" something's made of. It's a scalar, because 'stuff' doesn't have a direction.

Weight is a force

If you put the scales against the wall, you can exert a horizontal **force** on them by pushing them with your hand and compressing the spring.

Force is a **vector** because it has direction - the direction that you're pushing the spring in.

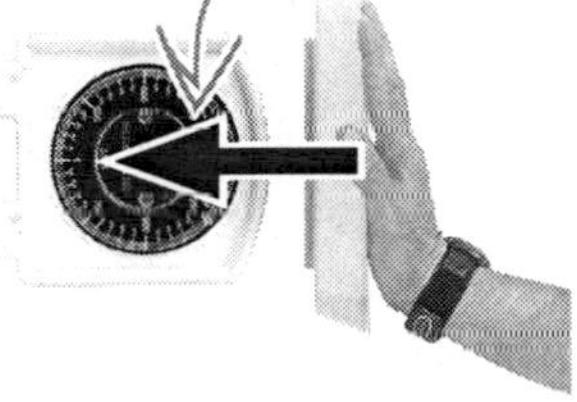

Applying a force in this direction compresses the spring and makes the dial go round.

The force vector of the fruit's weight points in this direction.

Although the scales give a reading in kilograms, they actually make measurements based on the **change in length** of the spring. So if you put fruit on the scales and the spring's length changes, there must be a force involved.

The change in length comes about because the spring has to counteract the fruit's **weight**, which is there because the fruit is in the earth's gravitational field. The fruit's weight is the **force** exerted on it by the earth's gravitational pull. You can draw the fruit's weight as a force vector arrow pointing down, towards the center of the earth.

WEIGHT is the FORCE you experience as a result of being in a gravitational field.

As weight is a force, this is a force vector.

On Earth, your weight vector points down, towards the center of the earth.

But people say things like "I weigh 60 kilograms" all the time. How can you say that mass and weight are different?

Mass and weight are different!

In everyday speech, people use the words "mass" and "weight" like they're the same thing. But in physics we need use these words more carefully.

Mass. Stuff. Scalar.

If you go to the moon, your **mass** is the same number of kilograms as it is on earth, as you're still made from the same amount of 'stuff'.

Weight. Force. Vector.

But **weight** is the force you experience as a result of being in a **gravitational field**. And as the moon's gravitational field is smaller than the earth's, your weight is less on the moon than it is on Earth even though your mass is still the same.

So the scales measure the force it takes to compress a spring, then **convert** the force that causes a certain change in spring length into kilograms? It sounds like the **relationship** between mass and weight is really important here.

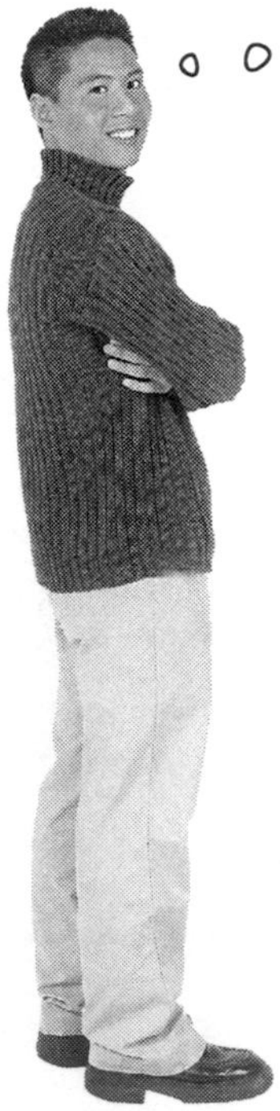

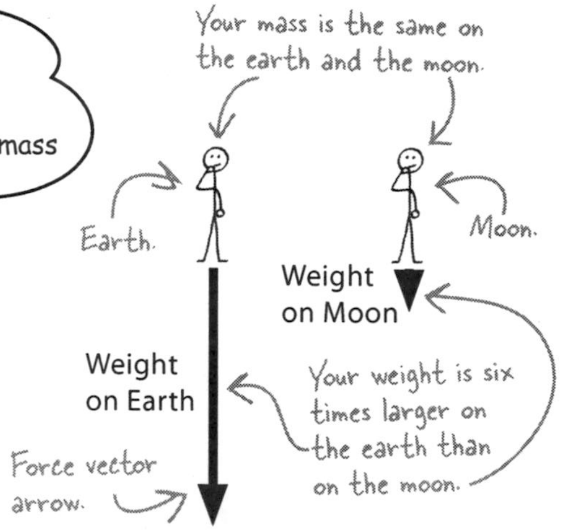

The way that the scales convert a force into a reading in kg is crucial.

If you stand on the scales on the moon, the scales will read the wrong number of kilograms - even though your mass hasn't changed. This is because the scales assume you're on earth when they **convert** the change in length (as a result of an applied force) into a reading in kilograms.

If you can work out the **relationship between force and mass** that the scales use to do this conversion, you'll be able to debunk the WeightBotchers machine.

BRAIN POWER

Have you seen an equation that involves both **force** and **mass** somewhere before?

The relationship between force and mass involves momentum

In chapter 10, you figured out that when you apply the same **force** for the same amount of **time** to any object, you always give it the same **change in momentum**. As long as there are no other forces acting on the object, you can write this as an equation:

$$\mathbf{F}\Delta t = \Delta\mathbf{p}$$

Force applied ... for a period of time ... gives a change in momentum.

But momentum is mass × velocity. So you can substitute in $m\mathbf{v}$ every time you see a $\mathbf{p}$ and rewrite this equation as:

$$\mathbf{F}\Delta t = \Delta(m\mathbf{v})$$

Momentum, p = mv

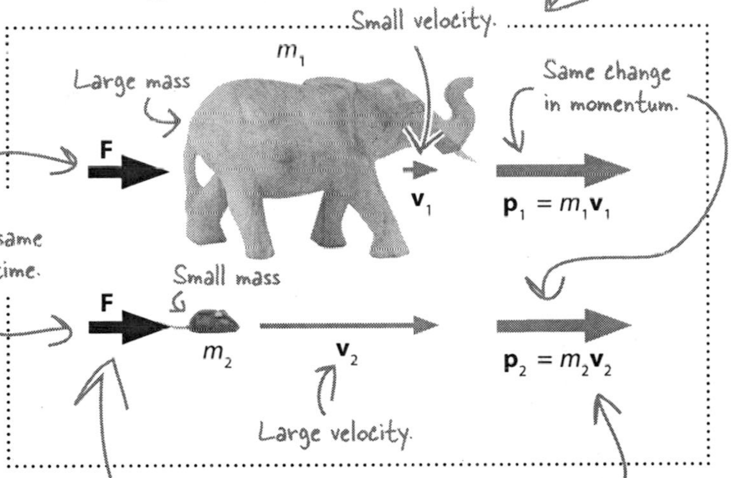

Same force applied for same amount of time.

Here, we've called the elephant object 1, so it has mass m_1 and velocity v_1. Using numbers in subscripts is a common way of distinguishing between objects in physics.

Using numbers in subscripts makes equations more general. We could still write down the same equation, $p_1 = m_1v_1$ if we swapped the elephant for a duck, whereas $p_e = m_ev_e$ would be confusing.

$$\mathbf{F\Delta t = \Delta(mv)}$$

This equation works if F is the only force acting on the object.

Momentum, p = mv

This equation works for ANY object. We don't have a specific object in mind here, so there are no subscripts on the 'm' or 'v'.

This is **Newton's Second Law**. It shows that objects with more mass have more **inertia**, or more resistance to changing how they're currently moving. If you apply the same force for the same time to push two different objects, the object with the larger mass is more 'resistant to change' and has a smaller change in velocity at the end.

The equation $\mathbf{F}\Delta t = \Delta(m\mathbf{v})$ gives you a **relationship between force and mass** that you can use to work out what's going on with the WeightBotchers machine.

Newton's Second Law:

If you apply a NET force to any object for a period of time, the change in the object's momentum always has the same value.

$$F_{net}\Delta t = \Delta(mv)$$

This equation works for any number of forces acting on the object added together to make the net force, F_{net}.

It's the net force that matters.

Two people pushing the mouse with equal forces in opposite directions looks like this:

When you add together these force vectors by lining them up 'nose to tail', the overall, or **net** force you end up with is zero. And the mouse doesn't go anywhere, so its momentum doesn't change.

But if the left-to-right force became larger, it would start to 'overpower' the right-to-left force, and there'd be a net force to the right. So the mouse would start moving to the right - its momentum would change in the direction of the net force.

Sharpen your pencil

a. After introducing a subscript to make it clear that it is the **net force** that causes the change in momentum, the equation on the opposite page, $\mathbf{F}_{net}\Delta t = \Delta(m\mathbf{v})$ can be rearranged to say $\mathbf{F}_{net} = \frac{\Delta(m\mathbf{v})}{\Delta t}$ Use this equation to work out the units of force.

b. Your equation contains the term $\frac{\Delta(m\mathbf{v})}{\Delta t}$. Do both m and $\mathbf{v}$ change with time while a force is applied? (Assume that the situation is one where an elephant or mouse has been pushed with a net force.)

c. Does your answer to part b give you any ideas about how you might simplify your equation $\mathbf{F}_{net} = \frac{\Delta(m\mathbf{v})}{\Delta t}$

Hint: What other equations do you know where a variable changes with time?

Sharpen your pencil Solution

a. After introducing a subscript to make it clear that it is the **net force** that causes the change in momentum, the equation on the opposite page, $\mathbf{F}_{net}\Delta t = \Delta(m\mathbf{v})$ can be rearranged to say $\mathbf{F}_{net} = \frac{\Delta(m\mathbf{v})}{\Delta t}$
Use this equation to work out the units of force.

$[m] = kg \quad [t] = s \quad [F] = \frac{kg.m/s}{s} = kg.m/s^2$ ← If you say this out loud, it's: "kilogram-meters per second squared"

$[v] = m/s$

b. Your equation contains the term $\frac{\Delta(m\mathbf{v})}{\Delta t}$. Do both m and $\mathbf{v}$ change with time while a force is applied?
(Assume that the situation is one where an elephant or mouse has been pushed with a net force.)

The velocity changes but the mass doesn't change.

c. Does your answer to part b. give you any ideas about how you might simplify your equation $\mathbf{F}_{net} = \frac{\Delta(m\mathbf{v})}{\Delta t}$

You could turn it into $F = m\frac{\Delta v}{\Delta t}$ as the mass is constant.

And $\frac{\Delta v}{\Delta t}$ is the acceleration. So it could become $F = ma$. ← Don't worry if you didn't spot this.

If the object's mass is constant, $F_{net} = ma$

Newton's Second Law says that if you apply a net force to an object for a period of time, then its momentum changes. So **force is the rate of change of the momentum** of an object:

$$\mathbf{F}_{net} = \frac{\Delta(m\mathbf{v})}{\Delta t}$$ ← Rate of change of momentum

Typically, the **mass** of an object doesn't change during the time that the force is applied. This means that m is constant and only $\mathbf{v}$ changes with time. And you already know that $\frac{\Delta \mathbf{v}}{\Delta t}$ is the rate of change of velocity - in other words, the **acceleration**.

So you can rewrite Newton's Second Law as:

$$\mathbf{F}_{net} = m\mathbf{a}$$

This shows you that the units of force are $kg.m/s^2$. However, as this is a rather unwieldy unit to write out, physicists have come up with a new unit, the **Newton** (N) where $1\ N = 1\ kg{\cdot}m/s^2$.

So if you do a calculation to work out a force where the mass is in kg and the acceleration is in m/s^2, you'd write your answer as 10 N instead of $10\ kg.m/s^2$.

The form of Newton's Second Law that you'll use the most is:

$$\mathbf{F}_{net} = \mathbf{ma}$$

Net force → F_{net}; Mass → m; Acceleration → a

there are no Dumb Questions

Q: So why not just say "$F_{net} = ma$" from the start? Why all this stuff about momentum first?

A: This book is about **understanding** physics. Rather than nodding and accepting "$F_{net} = ma$" with no reason for it, we went back to what you discovered about momentum in chapter 10, when you used a force to change the momentum of various objects. You've just used what you already knew about momentum to work out this form of Newton's Second Law for yourself.

Q: Won't the mass of an object always be constant? So you can always use $F_{net} = ma$?

A: Sometimes, both the mass and velocity of an object can change. For example, a rocket going into space carries a large mass of fuel, which it continually burns. As time goes on, its velocity gets larger, but its mass gets smaller as the fuel gets used up. So both the mass and velocity change with time, which means that you'd need to treat the $\Delta(mv)$ part of the equation $F_{net}\Delta t = \Delta(mv)$ differently.

But you don't need to worry about this too much, since it's not the part of the physics that we'll cover in this book.

Q: If an object's mass stays the same, you can say $F_{net} = ma$. But if its mass changes, you have to say $F_{net}\Delta t = \Delta(mv)$?

A: Yes. The equation $F_{net}\Delta t = \Delta(mv)$ works for **any** object, whether its mass is constant or not.

The equation $F_{net} = ma$ only works for an object whose mass is constant.

Q: But how do I know which equation to use?

A: If you're interested in the object's **velocity** or **momentum** rather than its acceleration, $F_{net}\Delta t = \Delta(mv)$ is the most useful form of Newton's Second Law.

If you're interested in the object's **acceleration**, then $F_{net} = ma$ its the most useful form of Newton's Second Law (as long as the mass of the object is constant).

But we're interested in **weight**! When I put an apple on scales, its velocity doesn't change and it doesn't accelerate, but it still has a weight!

g is the gravitational field strength.

On earth, $g = 9.8\ m/s^2$

Different physics courses use slightly different values for g. AP Physics uses $9.8\ m/s^2$

Weight = mg

Weight is the force that causes an object to accelerate when it falls.

If you drop an apple, it **accelerates** at a rate of $9.8\ m/s^2$. This is because the earth's gravitational field strength is $9.8\ m/s^2$. You now know that for something to accelerate, a **net force** must act on it.

The only force acting on the falling apple is its **weight**. You can think of this as a **gravitational force** which results from the stuff that the earth's made of and the stuff that the apple's made of attracting each other.

Even when the apple isn't falling, it's still subject to the same gravitational force, so it still has the same weight - its mass × the gravitational field strength, or $m\mathbf{g}$ (we use the letter **g** to represent the gravitational field strength).

So where have we got to now? Weight is a force, right?

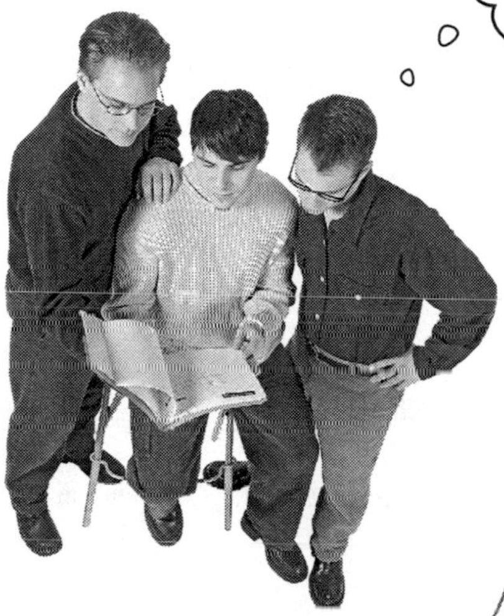

Jim: Right - and my **weight** is due to the "stuff" I'm made of and the "stuff" the earth's made of attracting each other. So we can think of weight as being a **gravitational force**.

Joe: Yeah, your weight is the reason you **accelerate** towards the ground at 9.8 m/s^2 when there's nothing to support you. And $\mathbf{F}_{net} = m\mathbf{a}$, so if I have a mass of 80.0 kg, my weight must be $80 \times 9.8 = 784$ N as that's the gravitational force on me.

Frank: Yeah, and if you're not accelerating, that force of your weight's still there, and is still 784 N, as **weight** = $m\mathbf{g}$. I guess that means that if my mass is constant, then the force of my weight is constant whatever's going on - my weight is still $m\mathbf{g}$.

Jim: But the force that the WeightBotchers machine measures goes down when the scales move downwards!

Jim: Yeah, that's a puzzle. The scales can't be measuring weight directly, or else they would always have the same reading. So if the scales don't measure weight, what force do the scales measure?!

Joe: I think the key thing might be that the scales on the WeightBotchers machine are accelerating towards the ground when the reading changes.

Frank: But why would that change the reading?

Joe: I guess that the scales aren't **supporting** you as much as they were before they started to move.

Jim: Yeah ... when you stand on the scales, the spring inside the scales compresses until it provides enough force to support you - to stop you moving down any further. And it's the compression of the spring that the scales measure.

Joe: Yeah, the scales measure the support force!

Frank: So if the scales aren't totally supporting your weight, the reading would be less?

Joe: I think that's probably right.

Practical point: Different physics courses use slightly different values for g. AP Physics uses 9.8 m/s^2 - but generally expects you to quote answers to 3 significant digits even though this value for g given in the AP table of information only has 2 significant digits.

If the scales (or the earth) didn't provide a support force, you'd just keep on falling!

The scales measure the support force

Your weight is always $m\mathbf{g}$. If you're falling, then the force of your weight causes you to accelerate. But if you're stationary, the thing you're standing on must be exerting a **support force** on you in the opposite direction from your weight - otherwise you'd be falling!

When you stand on scales that are sitting on the ground, you compress the spring and continue to move down slightly until the spring is compressed enough to exert a support force on you that's equal to your weight. Then the net force on you is zero.

If you are stationary, the net force acting on you must be zero.

Sharpen your pencil

a. What is the weight of an 80 kg person?

b. An 80 kg person stands stationary on some scales that are sitting on the ground. What support force do the scales need to exert on the person to prevent them from breaking or falling through the scales?

c. What is the net force on the person?

d. Draw a sketch of the person showing all of the forces acting on them. Use labeled vector arrows pointing away from the person to represent the forces.

ONLY draw the person - don't draw the scales or the earth or anything else.

e. Now, imagine that the person on the scales grabs onto a couple of rings hanging from the ceiling, and pulls down on them with a force of 200 N. Draw a sketch showing all the forces acting on the person, including both the support force provided by the rings, and the support force provided by the scales.

f. What reading (in kg) do the scales show when the person is partially supported by the rings, as described in part e?

Sharpen your pencil Solution

a. What is the weight of an 80 kg person?

weight = mass × gravitational field strength

= 80.0 × 9.8

weight = 784 N

b. An 80 kg person stands stationary on some scales that are sitting on the ground. What support force do the scales need to exert on the person to prevent them from breaking or falling through the scales?

The person's weight is 784 N. So to stop them breaking the scales, the support force needs to be 784 N.

c. What is the net force on the person?

The net force is 0 N, as the weight acts downwards, the support force acts upwards, and the weight and support force are equal sizes.

d. Draw a sketch of the person showing all of the forces acting on them. Use labeled vector arrows pointing away from the person to represent the forces.

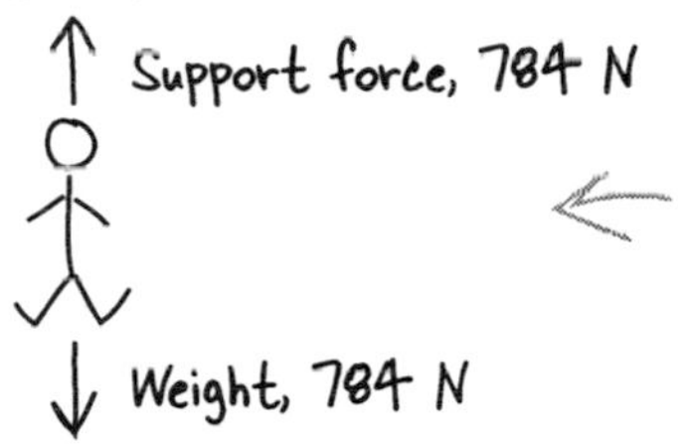

ONLY draw the person – don't draw the scales or the earth or anything else.

e. Now, imagine that the person on the scales grabs onto a couple of rings hanging from the ceiling, and pulls down on them with a force of 200 N. Draw a sketch showing all the forces acting on the person, including both the support force provided by the rings, and the support force provided by the scales.

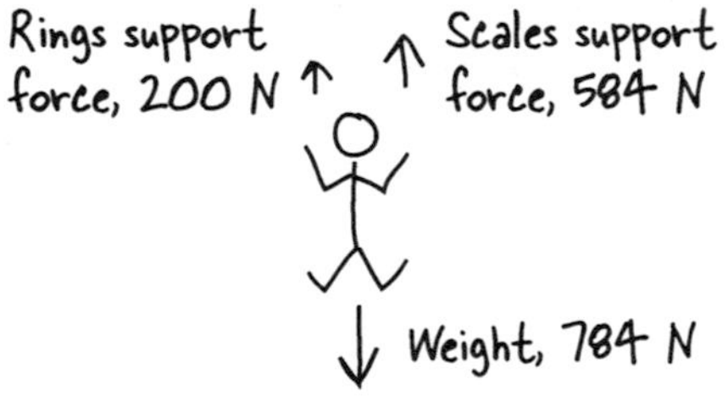

f. What reading (in kg) do the scales show when the person is partially supported by the rings, as described in part e?

Scales provide a support force of 584 N and assume that $F = mg$

$$\Rightarrow m = \frac{F}{g} = \frac{584}{9.8}$$

$$m = 59.6 \text{ kg (3 sd)}$$

Scales measure the **support force** provided by the spring, then convert this into kilograms using $\mathbf{F} = m\mathbf{g}$ to tell you what your mass is.

If, for some reason, the support force isn't equal to your weight, then the scales will still convert the support force into kilograms. However, this reading in kilograms will not be equal to your mass, as the support force wasn't the same size as your weight.

Scales measure the support force.

Now you can debunk the machine!

You've worked out that the scales measure the support force - and that if the support force is less than your weight, the reading on the scales will be less than your mass.

One of the tools you've used to do this is a **free body diagram**. This is just another name for a sketch of an object showing all of the forces acting on it, and it's a very useful way of analyzing forces.

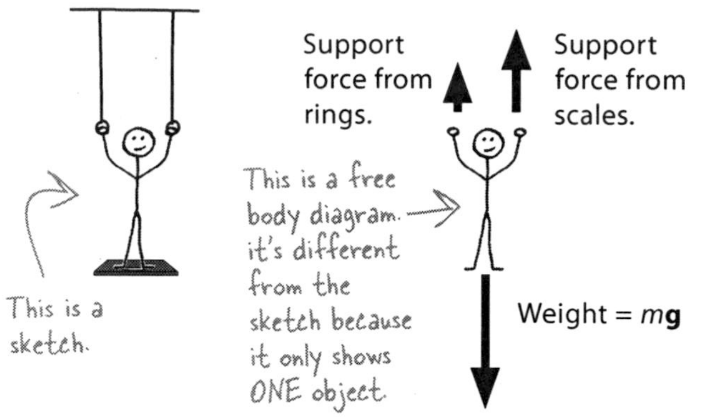

A free body diagram shows an object plus all of the forces acting on it, and nothing else.

Speaking of analysis, the FakeBusters team think they've made a breakthrough! They've looked at the advertisement and worked out that the machine is accelerating downwards at a rate of 2.0 m/s^2 while the low reading is being taken.

You can use this fact to demonstrate why the WeightBotchers machine gives false readings.

A free body diagram only shows one object. So only draw the person – not the scales or the machine.

Sharpen your pencil

a. Draw a free body diagram for the person, mass m, on the WeightBotchers machine, inside the box to the right.

(There's no need to include the values of forces you've not calculated yet, just words to describe what they are.)

b. Newton's Second Law, $\mathbf{F}_{net} = m\mathbf{a}$, says that an object accelerates if all of the forces acting on it **add up** to a non-zero net force. The person on the machine accelerates downwards at a rate of 2.0 m/s^2. Use these facts to derive an equation for the support force from the scales.

Hint: The scales assume that they are measuring the force mg and convert that to kilograms.

c. The scales will give a reading in kg. What will this reading be?

Your answer won't be a pure number. It will still have m, the mass of the person, in it. For example 0.5 m kg means that the scales will give a reading that's half the person's mass.

d. Explain why the reading on the scales is lower than it would be if the scales were stationary.

Be careful not to get the variable used to represent mass and the unit of meters mixed up. They are both represented by the letter 'm' (but in different contexts).

Sharpen your pencil Solution

a. Draw a free body diagram for the person, mass m, on the WeightBotchers machine, inside the box to the right.

(There's no need to include the values of forces you've not calculated yet, just words to describe what they are.)

b. Newton's Second Law, $\mathbf{F}_{net} = m\mathbf{a}$, says that an object accelerates if all of the forces acting on it **add up** to a non-zero net force. The person on the machine accelerates downwards at a rate of 2.0 m/s². Use these facts to derive an equation for the support force from the scales.

Make down the positive direction. ← Force is a vector, so you need to get the signs right.

The net force is the weight and the support force added together.

$$F_{net} = ma$$

$$\Rightarrow mg - F_s = 2.0\,m$$

$$F_s = mg - 2.0\,m$$

Start with Newton's 2nd Law, then substitute in.

We chose this symbol for support force.

c. The scales will give a reading in kg. What will this reading be?

Scales assume that measured F = mg, so divide support force by g to get mass in kg.

$$\text{Reading} = \frac{mg - 2.0\,m}{g}$$

$$\text{Reading} = m - \frac{2.0\,m}{g}$$

$$\text{Reading} = m - \frac{2.0\,m}{9.8} = m - 0.204\,m$$

This is like $(1 - 0.204)\,m$

$$\text{Reading} = 0.80\,m \text{ kg} \quad (2 \text{ sd})$$

d. Explain why the reading on the scales is lower than it would be if the scales were stationary.

As the person is accelerating downwards, there must be a net downwards force. This means that the support force (what the scales measure) is less than the person's weight.

The scales are only partially supporting the person.

The machine reduces the support force

The WeightBotchers machine 'works' because scales measure the support force that the scales exert on the person that stands on them. If the support force is less than your weight, then the reading on the scales is also less then your weight.

The machine **accelerates** you downwards. This means that there must be a **net force** acting on you to produce the acceleration, as $\mathbf{F}_{net} = m\mathbf{a}$. The only force acting downwards on you is your weight, and the only force acting upwards is the support force.

So if you're accelerating downwards, the support force must be less than your weight and the scales will in turn have a lower reading - that's how WeightBotchers are doing it.

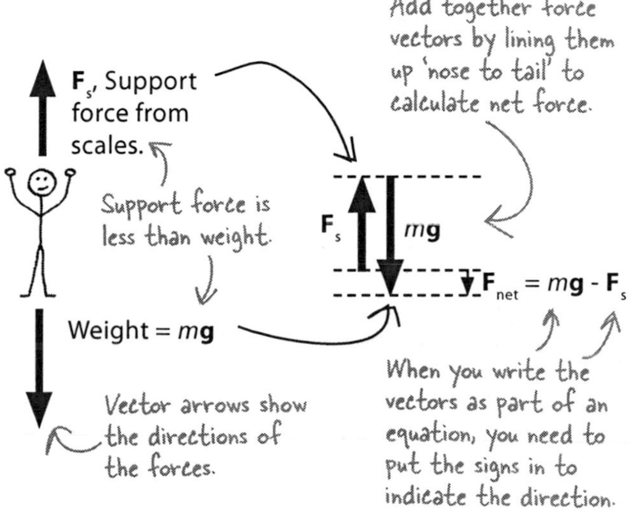

there are no Dumb Questions

Q: So the scales don't measure my mass ... and they don't even measure my weight?!

A: The scales measure the force that the spring is exerting on you, which we've called the support force here. They calculate the support force from the change in the length of the spring.

Q: So how is it possible for the scales to measure a support force that's less than my weight?

A: If the scales are only partially supporting you (for example, if you're partially pulling yourself up using rings, or you have one foot on the scales and one foot on the floor) then they will provide only part of the supporting force.

Q: So if I'm being supported by more than one thing, all of the supporting forces will add up to my weight?

A: If you're not being **accelerated** then yes, the supporting forces will add up to your weight because the net force on you is zero.

Q: Why does being accelerated change the supporting force?

A: Good question! But don't think of an acceleration 'causing' or 'changing' a force. It's the other way around - a non-zero net force causes an acceleration.

If you're accelerating, there must be a non-zero net force on you, because $\mathbf{F}_{net} = m\mathbf{a}$. If you're accelerating downwards, your weight (which points down) must be greater than the supporting force (which points up) to have a net downwards force that causes your acceleration.

Q: What would happen if the upwards force was larger than my weight? Like if I sat on a rocket or something?

A: Then there'd be a net force upwards, so you would accelerate upwards.

Q: I've a question about free body diagrams. Why do the force vector arrows always point away from the object, even when some of them act from underneath (like the support force from scales does)?

A: If you're drawing a free body diagram with several different forces on it, this convention helps you to see at a glance which directions forces are operating in. An arrow above the object must be a force acting upwards, and so on.

Q: Now I've debunked the WeightBotchers machine, do I get to go on television?

A: Well ...

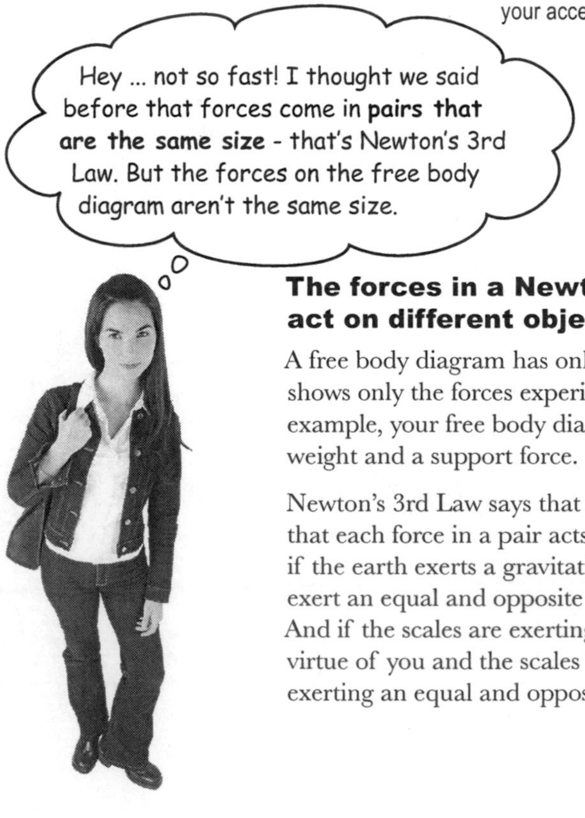

The forces in a Newton's 3rd Law pair act on different objects.

A free body diagram has only **one** object in it, and shows only the forces experienced by that object. For example, your free body diagram might show your weight and a support force.

Newton's 3rd Law says that forces come in **pairs** - and that each force in a pair acts on **different** objects. So if the earth exerts a gravitational force on you, you exert an equal and opposite gravitational force on it. And if the scales are exerting a support force on you (by virtue of you and the scales being in contact), you're exerting an equal and opposite **contact force** on them.

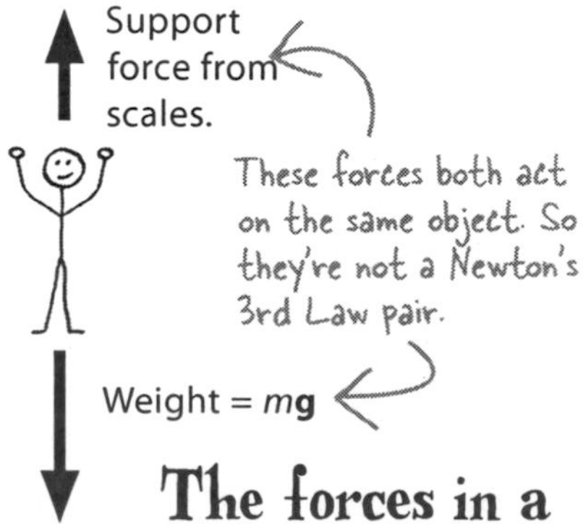

The forces in a Newton's 3rd Law pair act on different objects.

Force pairs help you check your work

You need to make sure you worked out the forces involved in the WeightBotchers machine correctly before you present your findings to FakeBusters. And the best way to do that is to make sure that each force you've drawn on your free body diagram is part of a **Newton's 3rd Law pair of forces.**

You originally met Newton's 3rd Law back in chapter 10 when you were dealing with pushing two objects apart. In order for momentum to be conserved (an experimental result that you worked out), each object must experience the **same size of force** but in **opposite directions** when they interact.

If the objects are "1" and "2" the pair of forces is:

The force that object 1 exerts on object 2.
The force that object 2 exerts on object 1.

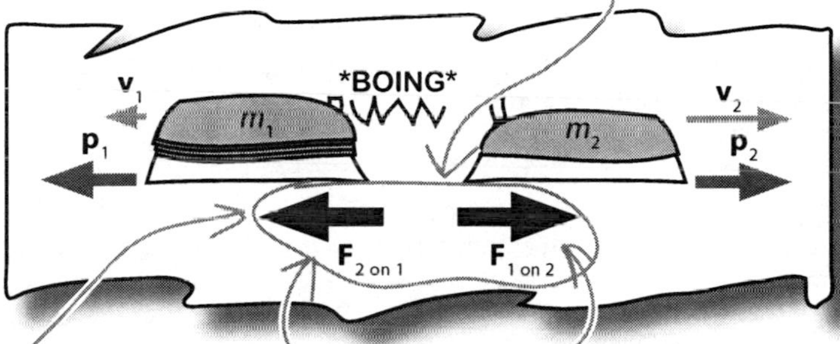

If you draw a **free body diagram** of a person standing on scales, there are two forces acting on the person - their weight and the support force.

Although these forces are equal in size and in opposite directions, they are not a Newton's 3rd Law pair of forces, as both forces act on the same object.

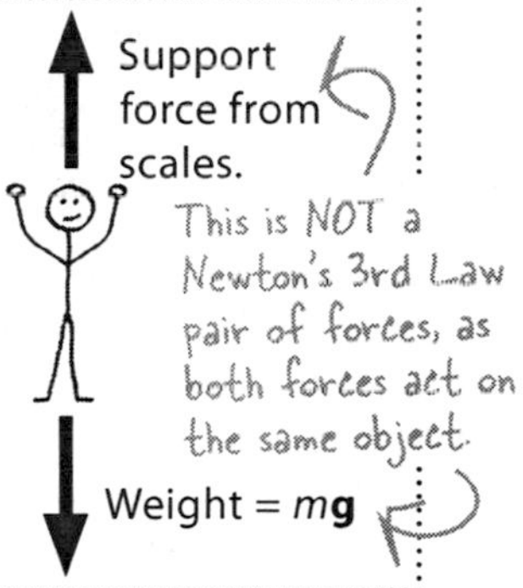

You can check your work by seeing if each of the forces you've drawn on the free body diagram is part of a Newton's 3rd Law pair.

To do this, you need to work out what the other object in each pair would be:

The force that pairs with your weight is the gravitational force that you exert on the earth - as the stuff you're made from and the stuff that the earth's made from mutually attract each other.

This pair of forces will also exist at a distance, even if you're not in contact with the earth.

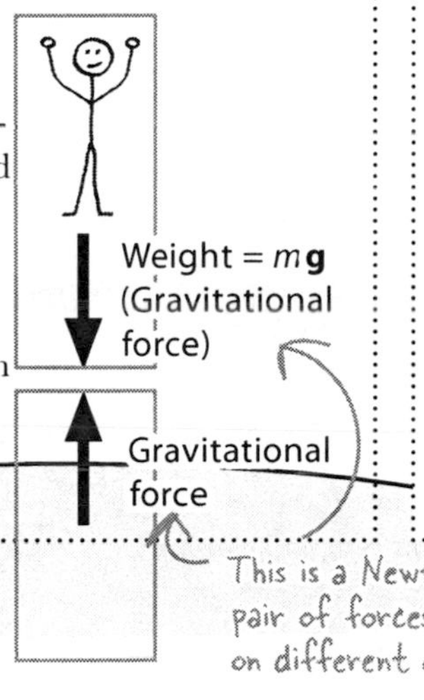

The force that pairs with the support force from the scales is the **contact force** that you exert on the scales.

Neither the support force that the scales exert on you nor the contact force that you exert on the scales would exist if there was no contact.

It's only meaningful to add together forces that act on the same object.

Your weight is a force that acts on you.

Your weight is a force that acts on you. It must act on you or else you wouldn't fall through the air as a result of it. It points downwards. If it helps, think of it as "gravitational attraction."

The contact force between you and the scales acts on the scales. It also points downwards - but it acts on the scales, not on you.

You can only add together forces if they act on the same object. As these two downwards forces act on different objects, you can't add them together.

There's a distinction between contact forces and non-contact forces

Gravitational forces are **non-contact** forces, which can act at a distance. The earth exerts a gravitational force on you whether you're in contact with it or not.

Contact forces only exist if there is contact between two objects. If you stand on the ground you're not accelerating. The net force on you is zero, so your weight and the support force that the ground exerts on you must add to zero.

Newton's 3rd Law says that if the ground is exerting a contact force to support you, then you must be exerting a contact force on it. This makes sense - you can only squash a bug by stepping on it, which involves contact. This can't be done by the force of your weight - as this is a force that acts on you, not on the bug. But it can be done by the contact force that pairs with the support force that the ground exerts on you.

The forces in a Newton's 3rd Law pair must both be of the same type (for example, both contact or both non-contact).

there are no Dumb Questions

Q: Why is it useful to think about Newton's 3rd Law pairs of forces?

A: When you draw a free body diagram, you're drawing only the forces that act on a single object. Each of these forces must be one of a pair - as when two objects interact, each of them experiences an equal-sized force in opposite directions.

Q: So when I draw a free body diagram, I should think about what the other force in the pair is?

A: That's right - and you should also think about which two objects are involved in the interaction. This prevents you from accidentally drawing two forces on your free body diagram that act on different objects.

Q: Where does this idea of a 'contact force' with the ground come from? I thought that the Newton's 3rd Law force pair was my weight and the support force.

A: Both your weight and the support force that the scales exert are forces that act on you. They can't be a Newton's 3rd Law force pair, as they don't act on different objects.

Q: Is there any other way for me to work out what forces might be in a pair?

A: The forces in a Newton's 3rd Law force pair must be of the same type. So either they both have to be contact forces, or they both have to be non-contact forces.

Q: Why doesn't the contact force I exert on the earth (via the scales, which are attached to the earth) lead to the earth accelerating? Don't I exert a net force on the earth?

A: As well as the contact force you exert on the earth, you also exert an attractive gravitational force on it, in the opposite direction. So the net force on the earth as a result of you being there is zero, and the earth doesn't accelerate.

Q: What if I wasn't standing on the earth? Then the gravitational force that the earth experiences as a result of me being there must accelerate the earth towards me, right?

A: That's completely spot on, and a great observation. When you're not standing on the earth, there's a gravitational force pair. The gravitational force on you (your weight) accelerates you towards the earth. And the gravitational force on the earth accelerates it towards you.

Q: So why don't I notice the earth accelerating towards me?

A: Newton's 2nd Law says that $\mathbf{F} = m\mathbf{a}$. Therefore, $\mathbf{a} = \frac{\mathbf{F}}{m}$. As the earth has a much much larger mass than you, its acceleration is very small compared to yours. So it's not something you'd notice.

Thinking about Newton's 3rd Law pairs of forces helps you make sure your free body diagram is correct.

You debunked WeightBotchers!

Your free body diagram of the person on the scales is correct. The support force exerted by the scales on the person is less than the person's weight.

This means that the net force on the person is not zero. A non-zero net force produces an acceleration: $\mathbf{F}_{net} = m\mathbf{a}$. The net force leads to the person accelerating downwards, as observed on the advert.

The scales measure the support force, and convert it to a mass by assuming that $\mathbf{F} = \mathbf{weight} = m\mathbf{g}$. If the support force is less than the person's weight, then the scales read a smaller number of kilograms than they would if there was no acceleration.

FakeBusters are soon back in touch to congratulate you, and arrange for your segment of the show to be filmed.

But WeightBotchers are back!

We spoke too soon. WeightBotchers are back with a new machine - though only the magazine ads for it have appeared so far.

This time, the person on the scales is sliding down a hill. And miraculously (or so it seems), the scales read lower than they did when the person was standing on flat ground.

FakeBusters wants your help busting the new scam with science once again.

Memo

From: FakeBusters

Re: WeightBotchers

Great work busting WeightBotchers... but they're back.

Could you investigate WeightBotchers' latest machine, and work out how it produces the results it does? We've enclosed a copy of their ad. If you can bust the fake we'd love to have you back on the show.

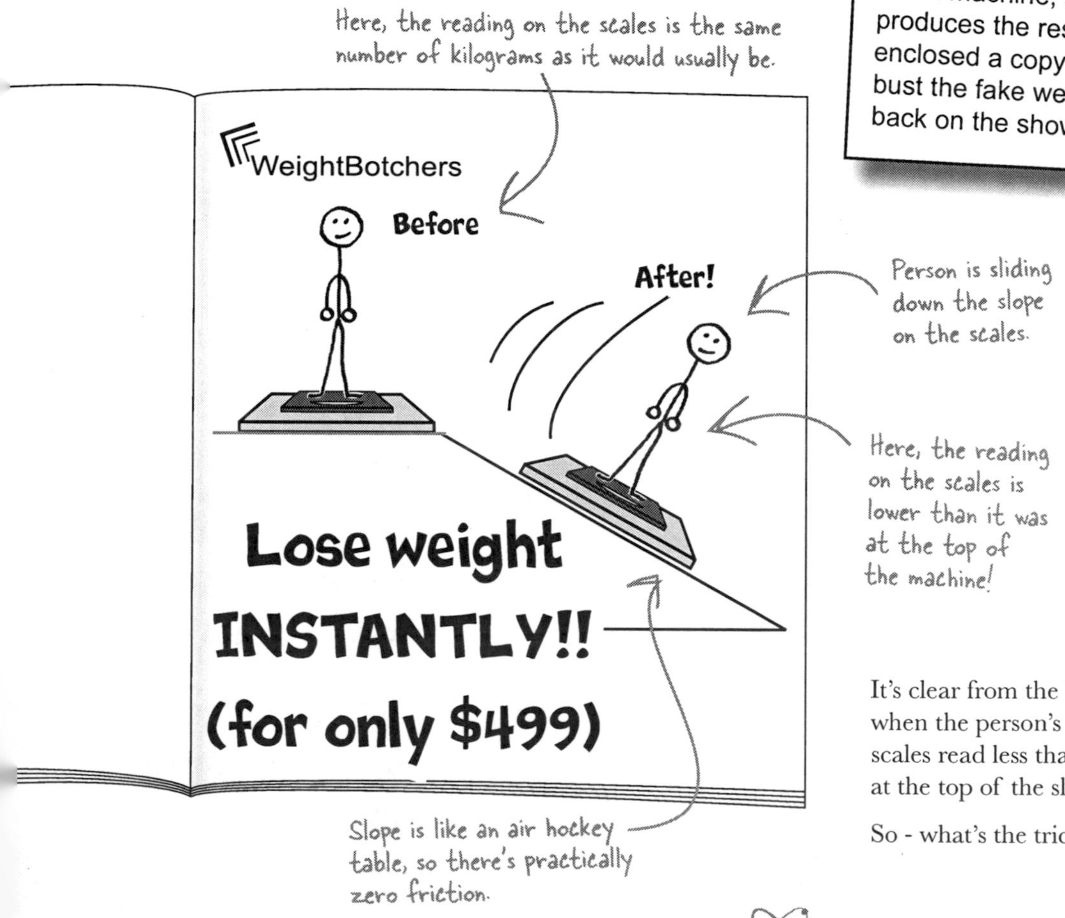

It's clear from the WeightBotchers ad that when the person's going down the slope, the scales read less than they did on the flat ground at the top of the slope.

So - what's the trick this time?!

BRAIN POWER

How do you think the new machine works?

A surface can only exert a force perpendicular (or normal) to it

If you're standing on a **horizontal** surface, you don't accelerate. This is because the surface exerts a vertical **contact force** on you, **perpendicular** to the surface.

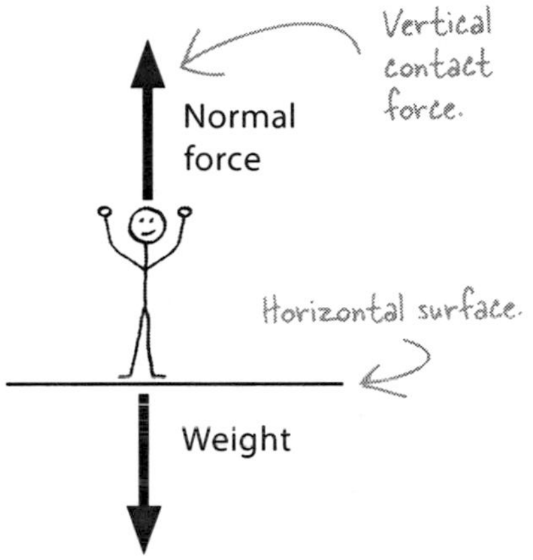

Up until now, we've been calling a perpendicular contact force exerted by a surface a "support force". But a more accurate name for the perpendicular contact force exerted by a surface is the **normal force**.

This is because whatever angle a surface is at, the surface can only exert a contact force perpendicular, or **normal**, to itself. Depending on the situation, the normal force may not be supporting an object's weight.

If you try to "stand" on a **vertical** surface (like a wall), you just fall straight down, as the vertical surface can only produce a horizontal normal force. The vertical surface is unable to provide any support for your weight.

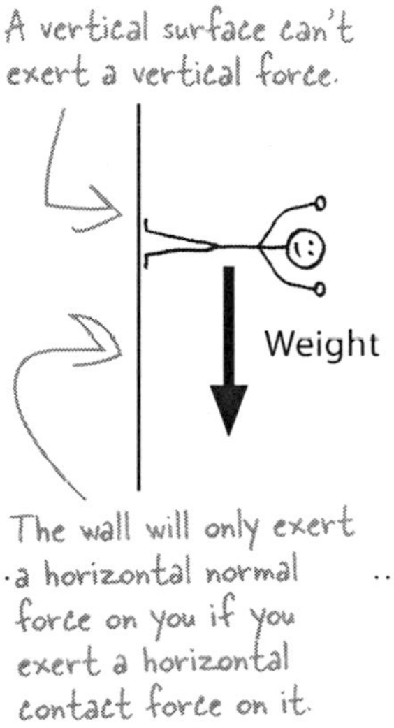

If you throw a ball horizontally at a vertical wall, it experiences a horizontal **normal force** from the wall that makes it bounce.

The ball also experiences the force of its weight, but as the ball's weight is parallel to the wall, it doesn't affect the size of the normal force.

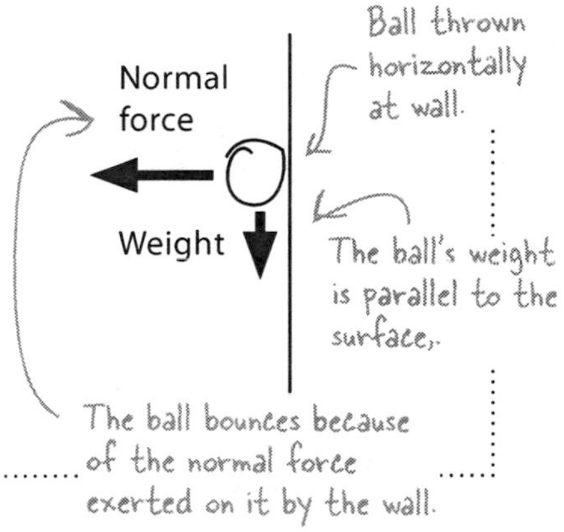

The normal force that a surface exerts on you is the same size as the <u>perpendicular</u> force that you exert on the surface, but in the opposite direction.

The normal force that a surface exerts on you is the same size as the **perpendicular** force you are exert on it, but in the opposite direction. If you are stationary on a horizontal surface, the normal force is equal to your weight. If you push a wall horizontally with a force of 50 N, the normal force is 50 N.

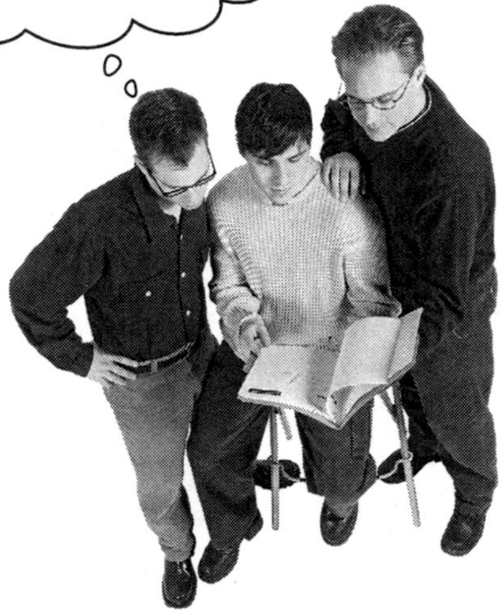

Jim: Yeah, the spring in the scales that makes the measurement can only be compressed perpendicular - or normal - to the slope.

Joe: But how do we calculate the **normal force** this time? Last time we got data from the TV ad, but there's only a magazine ad this time. We need to do this before the deadline for FakeBusters.

Frank: I guess we can measure the **angle** of the slope...

Jim: How does the angle help us to calculate the normal force?

Joe: It says here: "the normal force that a surface exerts on you is the same size as the perpendicular force that you exert on the surface, but in the opposite direction."

Frank: I think that means we need to think in terms of **forces** that are **parallel** and **perpendicular** to the slope.

Jim: Yeah, I'm sure the **net force** and the equation $\mathbf{F}_{net} = m\mathbf{a}$ will come in to it somewhere. Though I'm not really sure where yet...

Sharpen your pencil

Hint: An object's acceleration must be in the same direction as the net force acting on the object, since $F_{net} = ma$ is a vector equation.

a. If a car accelerates horizontally, parallel to the ground, does its acceleration have a component perpendicular to the surface?

b. If a person on a sloped surface accelerates down the slope, parallel to it, does their acceleration have a component perpendicular to the surface?

c. If an object has zero acceleration, what can you say about the net force acting on it?

d. If one component of an object's acceleration is zero, what can you say about the net force acting in the direction of that component?

e. Do your answers to parts a-d give you any ideas about how to deal with the person on the WeightBotchers machine accelerating down the slope?

Sharpen your pencil Solution

Hint: An object's acceleration must be in the same direction as the net force acting on the object, since $F_{net} = ma$ is a vector equation.

a. If a car accelerates horizontally, parallel to the ground, does its acceleration have a perpendicular component?

No, it only has a parallel (horizontal) component as it is accelerating parallel to the surface.

b. If a person on a sloped surface accelerates down the slope, parallel to it, does their acceleration have a component perpendicular to the surface?

No, they only have a parallel component, as they are accelerating parallel to the surface.

c. If an object has zero acceleration, what can you say about the net force acting on it?

$F = ma$ so if the acceleration is zero then the net force is zero (even though there may be several forces acting on the object).

d. If one component of an object's acceleration is zero, what can you say about the net force acting in the direction of that component?

If the component of the acceleration in that direction is zero, then the net force in that direction must be zero.

e. Do your answers to parts a-d give you any ideas about how to deal with the person on the WeightBotchers machine accelerating down the slope?

The person is accelerating parallel to the slope but not perpendicular to the slope. If we think about acceleration and force components parallel and perpendicular to the slope, it might work out well, because the perpendicular components will all be zero.

there are no Dumb Questions

Q: I just want to get some terminology straight. Are the normal force and a support force the same thing or not?

A: The normal force is the contact force that a surface exerts on you. The normal force always acts perpendicular to the surface, and depends on the force you are exerting perpendicular to the surface

What we were calling the support force earlier on was a specific example of a normal force. We called it a "support force" because it was supporting your weight, which acts perpendicular to a horizontal surface. "Support force" was a good mental image to have when you were getting to grips with how scales work.

Q: Why are we now using the term 'normal force' instead of 'support force'?

A: Now, the surface isn't horizontal any more - it's at an angle. The normal force always acts perpendicular to the surface. So the normal force doesn't point in the opposite direction from your weight any more - it's at an angle because the surface is at an angle.

You can't think of the normal force as "supporting" your weight in quite the same way, as the weight vector and normal force vector are not parallel to each other. So it's best to use the term "normal force" rather than "support force" to avoid getting confused.

Q: We've always talked about horizontal and vertical vector components in earlier chapters. Why are we talking about parallel and perpendicular vector components now?

A: When you're dealing with projectiles, the net force that causes the projectile to accelerate at 9.8 m/s^2 is the gravitational force. The net force acts vertically, so the projectile accelerates vertically. There's zero net force in the horizontal direction.

When you're dealing with an object accelerating down a slope, the net force acts down the slope, so the object accelerates down the slope. The net force acts parallel to the slope. There's zero net force in the perpendicular direction.

When you slide downhill, there's zero perpendicular acceleration

The person on the slope has two forces acting on them: their **weight** and the **normal force** from the slope.

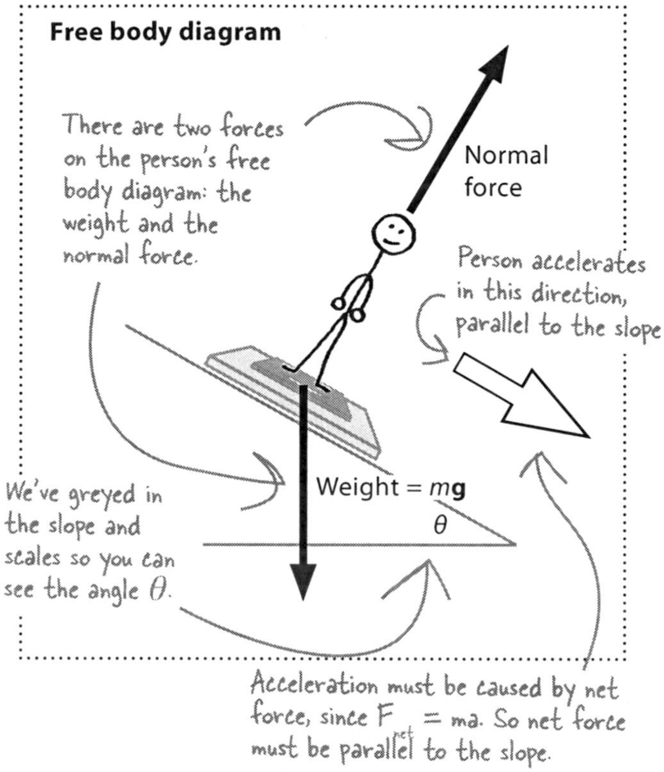

The person slides down the slope, accelerating parallel to the slope. This means that the net force must act parallel to the slope, because Fnet = ma.

This means that the components of the forces perpendicular to the slope must add up to zero.

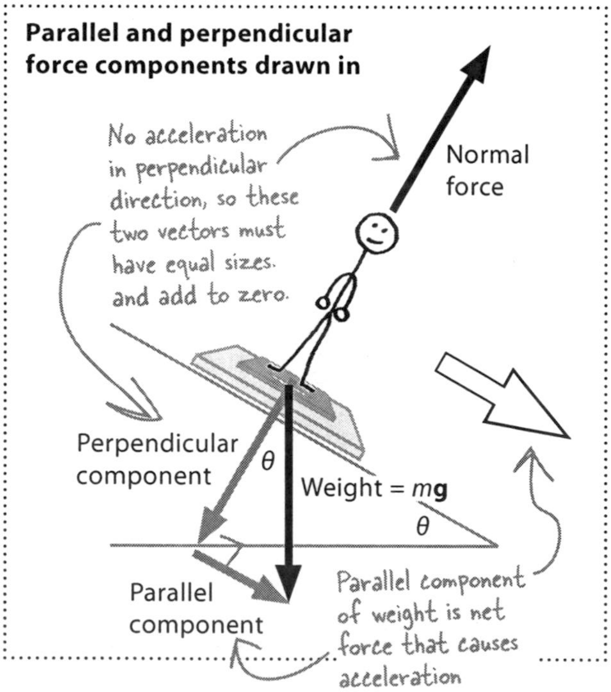

The NORMAL force, F_N, is always perpendicular to a surface.

The NET force, F_{net}, always points in the same direction as the acceleration it causes.

The only two forces with components perpendicular to the slope are the **weight** and the **normal force**. Therefore, the perpendicular component of the weight and the normal force must add up to zero, so that **the net force is parallel** to the slope.

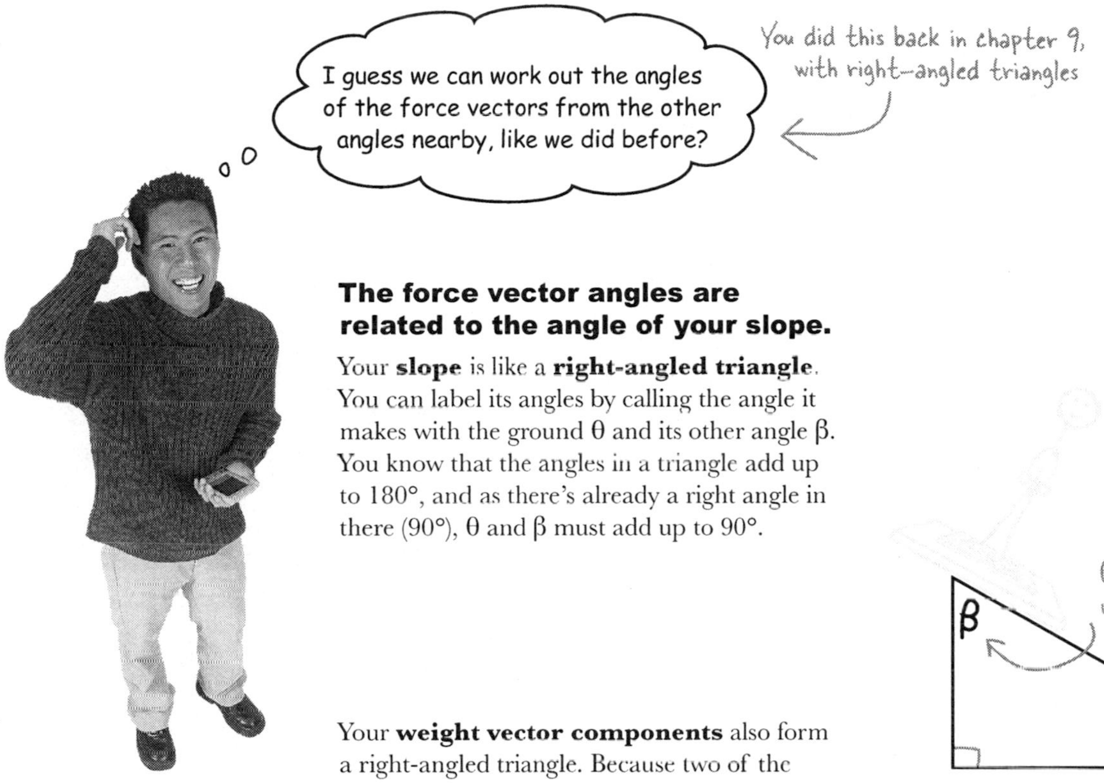

The force vector angles are related to the angle of your slope.

Your **slope** is like a **right-angled triangle**. You can label its angles by calling the angle it makes with the ground θ and its other angle β. You know that the angles in a triangle add up to 180°, and as there's already a right angle in there (90°), θ and β must add up to 90°.

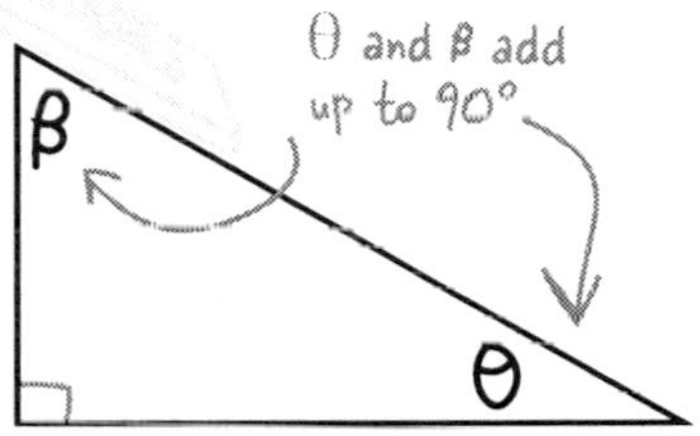

Your **weight vector components** also form a right-angled triangle. Because two of the sides of the weight vector triangle are parallel and perpendicular to the slope, the slope triangle and weight vector triangle are **similar triangles**. So the angle *θ* from your slope will also appear in your weight vector component triangle.

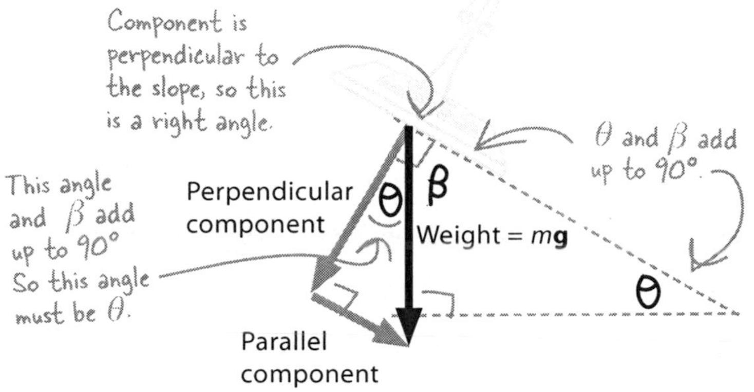

If a problem involves parallel components, perpendicular components and angles, look for similar triangles.

Use parallel and perpendicular force components to deal with a slope

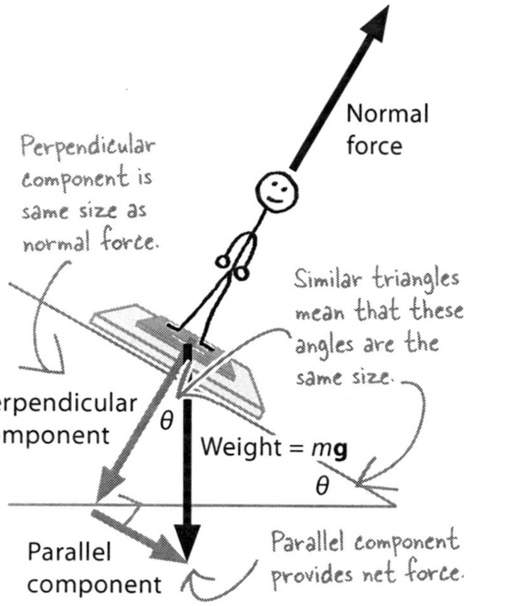

The reading on the scales is the **normal force**, which is the same size as the **perpendicular componen**t of your weight. This is because the normal force always acts perpendicular to a surface, and always exerts the same size of force on you as you exert on the surface.

The **parallel component** of your weight is is the **net force** that leads to you accelerating down the slope.

Time to get on TV ...

Sharpen your pencil

The WeightBotchers ad shows an "instant 5% reduction" when the person goes down the slope. You're going to calculate the angle the slope would need to be to produce this reduction. Then the Fakebusters team will compare your theoretical calculation with the angle of the slope in the ad.

a. Draw a big vector triangle showing the weight and its components of the weight parallel and perpendicular to the slope, so you can write things on it.

b. If the WeightBotchers scales show a 5% reduction in someone's mass, what's the angle of the slope? (Assume that the person has mass *m*, and that the gravitational field strength is **g**.)

Hint: a 5% reduction means that the normal force is 95% of the person's actual weight.

c. What is the person's acceleration down the slope?

Hint: Calculate the net force down the slope, and use $F_{net} = ma$

Sharpen your pencil

The WeightBotchers ad shows an "instant 5% reduction" when the person goes down the slope. You're going to calculate the angle the slope would need to be to produce this reduction. Then the Fakebusters team will compare your theoretical calculation with the angle of the slope in the ad.

a. Draw a big vector triangle showing the weight and its components of the weight parallel and perpendicular to the slope, so you can write things on it.

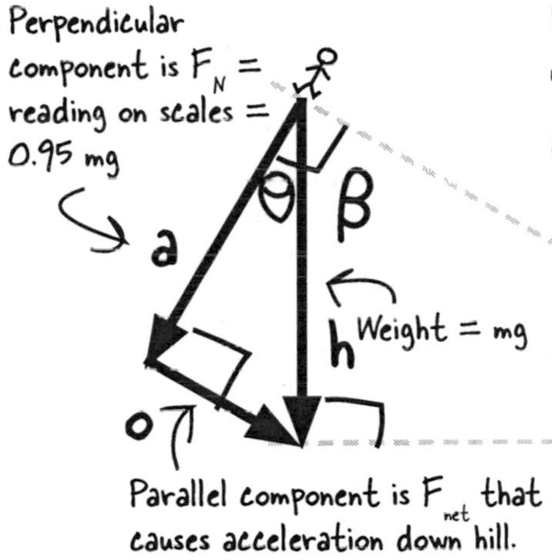

b. If the WeightBotchers scales show a 5% reduction in someone's mass, what's the angle of the slope? (Assume that the person has mass *m*, and that the gravitational field strength is **g**.)

Hint: a 5% reduction means that the normal force is 95% of the person's actual weight.

Weight = mg.

5% reduction means that normal force = 0.95 mg

Using triangle:

$$\cos(\theta) = \frac{a}{h} = \frac{0.95\,mg}{mg} = 0.95$$

$$\theta = \cos^{-1}(0.95) = 18.2° \text{ (3 sd)}$$

'mg' is on the top and bottom of the fraction so it divides out and cancels.

The angle doesn't depend on the person's mass.

c. What is the person's acceleration down the slope?

Calculate net force then use $F_{net} = ma$ to get acceleration

Using triangle to work out net force (which is opp side)

$$\sin(\theta) = \frac{o}{h} = \frac{F_{net}}{mg}$$

$$F_{net} = mg\sin(18.2)$$

$$F_{net} = 0.312\,mg$$

$$ma = 0.312\,mg$$

'm' is multiplying both sides of the equation, so it divides out and cancels.

$$a = 0.312 \times 9.8 = 3.06\ m/s^2 \text{ (3 sd)}$$

The acceleration doesn't depend on the person's mass.

Another fake busted!

There are two forces acting on you when you stand on the second WeightBotchers machine - your **weight** and the **normal force** from the surface.

Your weight vector points straight down, but the normal force points **perpendicular** to the surface.

You accelerate down the slope, parallel to the surface. This means that the **net force** acting on you must be **parallel** to the surface, because $\mathbf{F}_{net} = m\mathbf{a}$. And the **perpendicular** components of the forces must add to zero.

When you draw in the parallel and perpendicular components of your weight vector, you see that the parallel component of your weight provides the parallel net force.

The net perpendicular force on you is zero. Therefore, the normal force and the perpendicular component of your weight must add to zero. As the scales measure the normal force, and the normal force is only a component of your weight, the scales don't register your full weight. The reading on the scales is lower than it would be on a horizontal surface.

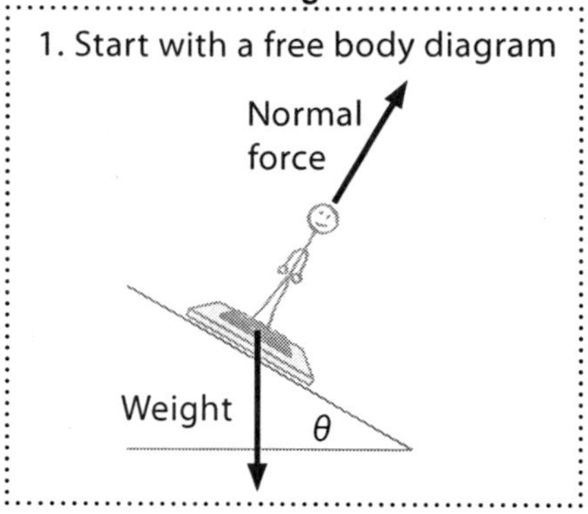

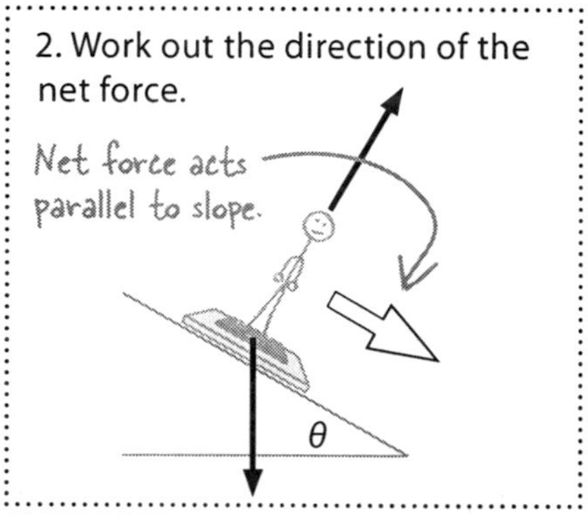

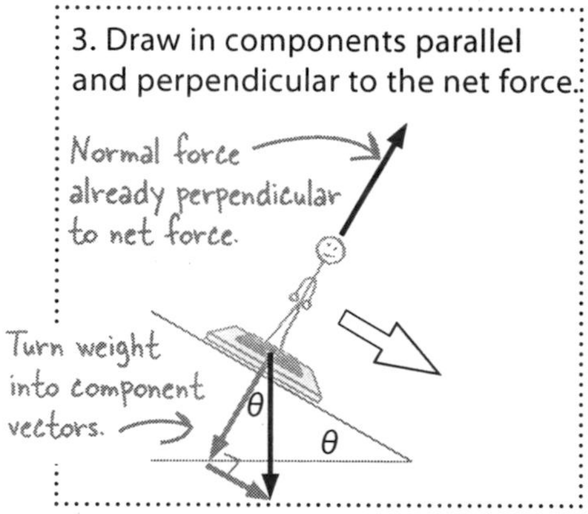

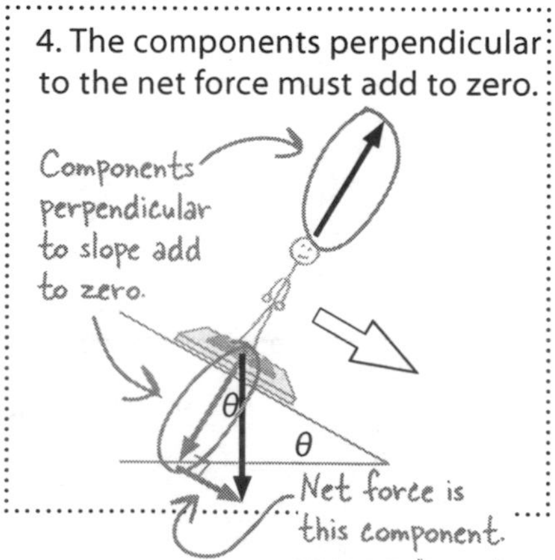

Question Clinic: The "Free body diagram" Question

Any time you have a problem that involves forces, always, always, ALWAYS start with a free body diagram! To do this, think of all the Newton's 3rd Law pairs of forces that the object is involved in. Then draw in all the forces from the pairs that act ON the object (but not the forces that the object exerts on other things).

If you know the mass, you might be able to use it to work out the net force ($F = ma$) or the momentum ($p = mv$) later on.

This should immediately get you thinking about horizontal and vertical components.

5. A hot air balloon, mass 3500 kg, travels horizontally at a constant speed of 2.0 m/s.

a. Draw a free body diagram for the balloon, clearly labelling all the forces acting on it.

b. If sandbags with a mass of 200 kg are dropped from the basket, draw the new free body diagram for the balloon.

c. What is the acceleration of the balloon after the sandbags are removed?

This means that you should write down what your force vector arrows represent next to them.

This means that there is no net force acting on the balloon, causing it to accelerate.

This changes the weight of the balloon.

If there's no net force, then the weight and the buoyant force must be equal.

There's now a net force, as the buoyant force that holds up the balloon is greater than the new weight. So you can use $F_{net} = ma$ to work out the acceleration.

Remember to use the new mass without the ballast!

This will be the same as your old one, but with the new weight.

Remember - if the object is stationary or moving with a constant velocity, there's no net force acting on it - it's not accelerating. So all the forces you draw must add to zero when you line them up 'nose-to-tail'. This will help you not to forget forces that you should include on your free body diagram.

Question Clinic: The "Thing on a slope" Question

Sometimes, you'll be asked a question about an object on a slope. You should always **start with a sketch** - draw the slope, and write on all the information you know. If the question is about **forces** and **acceleration**, then make sure you draw a **free body diagram** as well. Look carefully to see if the wording of the question implies that there's a net force

These are the values you know at the start of the problem.

This means that there is a net force acting on the person.

This gives you the direction of the net force – parallel to the slope.

5. A person, mass m, stands on scales that accelerate down a slope. The slope makes an angle θ with the ground.

a. Draw a free body diagram for the person, clearly labelling all the forces acting on them.

b. Calculate the normal force in terms of m, θ and **g**, the gravitational field strength.

c. What mass do the scales say the person is?

d. If the person accelerates down the slope at 3 m/s², what is θ?

e. If there was no slope and the person was just falling, what would the reading on the scales be?

A simple free body diagram shouldn't contain components – just the actual forces.

Work with components perpendicular to the slope.

This means that you're using the variables m, θ and g rather than numerical values, which tests your understanding of the physics more.

Note when you're asked for a mass rather than a weight.

Draw a new free body diagram. There's no normal force, so the scales will read zero.

Use $F = ma$ and components.

It's very important to resolve your force vectors into **components** parallel and perpendicular to the slope - especially the object's **weight** vector. This is because an object moving down a slope experiences no net force perpendicular to the slope. So drawing in the components of your forces helps you calculate the correct value for the normal force, and provides a way of working out the net force as well.

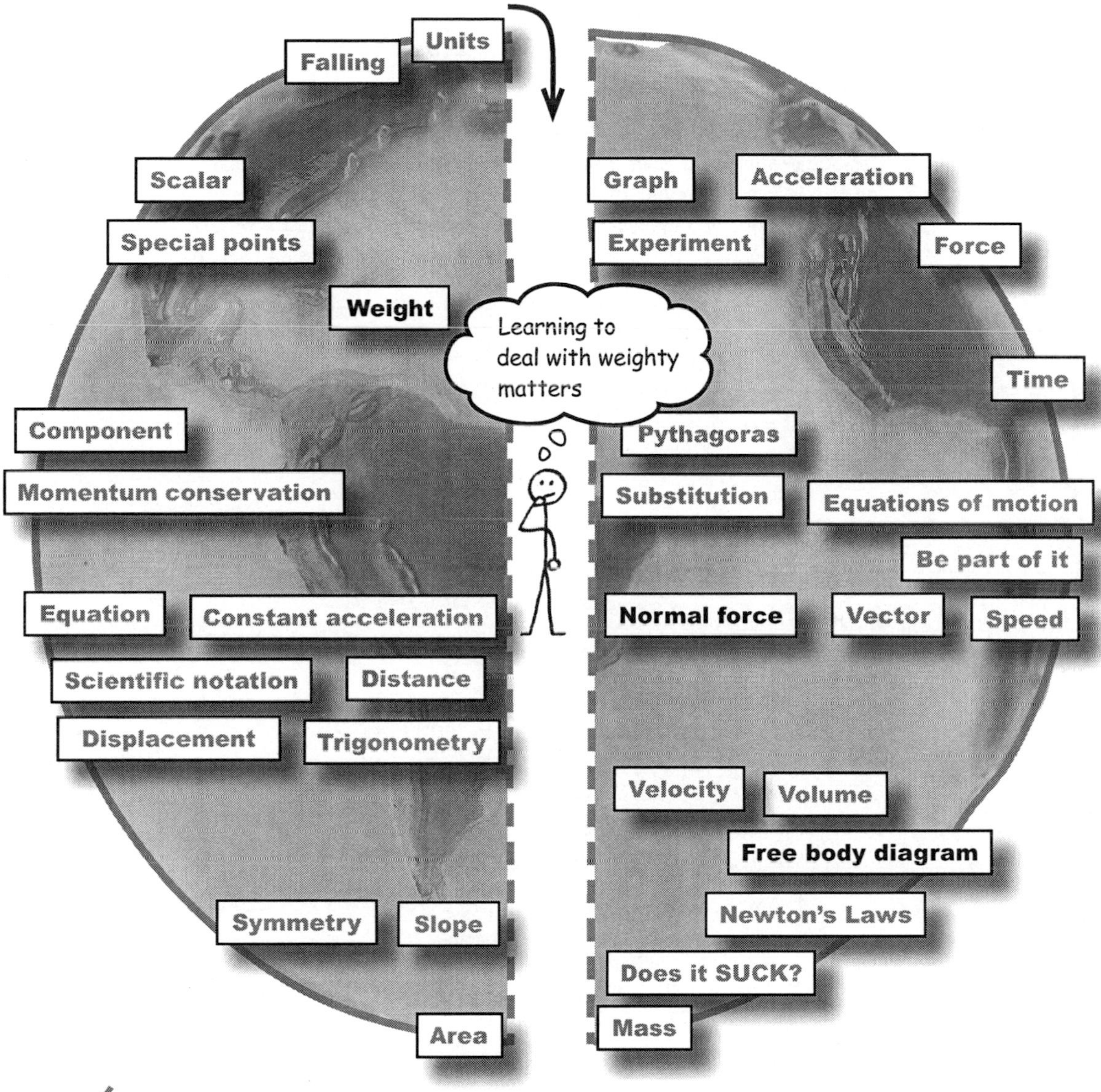

☑	**Weight**	**The gravitational force exerted on an object by a much larger object, such as the earth. Weight = mg, where m is the mass and g is the gravitational field strength.**
☑	**Free body diagram**	**A diagram showing only one object, and all of the forces acting on it.**
☑	**Normal force**	**The contact force exerted by a surface on an object. This force is always perpendicular (or normal) to the surface**

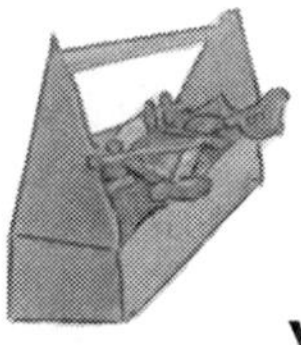

Your Physics Toolbox

You've got Chapter 11 under your belt and added some problem-solving concepts to your toolbox.

CHAPTER 11

Free body diagram

For any problem that involves forces, you should always draw a free body diagram, giving the size and direction of every force acting on a single body.

Draw your force vector arrows pointing away from the object.

Net force

You can work out the net force on an object by adding together all the force vectors from its free body diagram by lining them up "nose to tail."

If the net force is zero, the object isn't accelerating.

If there is a non-zero net force, the object accelerates in the direction of the net force.

Newton's 2nd law

A net force applied for a time always leads to the same change in momentum:

$$F_{net}\Delta t = \Delta(mv)$$

If the mass of an object is constant, this can simplify to:

$$F_{net} = ma$$

Newton's 3rd Law pairs of forces

Newton's 3rd Law pairs of forces exist where two objects interact.

Both forces in the pair must be of the same type (contact or non-contact).

Each force in the pair must act on a different object.

Each force in the pair will have the same size, but the forces will be in opposite directions.

Object on a slope

If you have an object on a slope, the normal force and the perpendicular component of the weight are equal sizes.

The net force and the parallel component of the weight are equal sizes.

Choosing component directions

If you have a problem where the net force is zero in one particular direction (e.g. perpendicular to a slope) then choose component vectors parallel and perpendicular to this direction to make your calculations easier.

12 using forces, momentum, friction and impulse

Getting on with it

It's no good memorizing lots of theory if you can't apply it.

You already know about equations of motion, component vectors, momentum conservation, free body diagrams and Newton's Laws. In this chapter, you'll learn how to fit all of these things together and apply them to solve a much **wider range** of physics problems. Often, you'll spot when a problem is **like** something you've seen before. You'll also add more realism by learning to deal with **friction** - and will see why it's sometimes appropriate to act on **impulse**.

It's ... SimFootball!

You've been contacted by the SimFootball team, who need your help with some of the physics in their video game. If you can help them figure out why the characters in the game aren't behaving like they would in real life - you'll get an all expenses paid trip to the X-Force Games.!

Memo

From: SimFootball

Re: Physics in our new game

We saw you on FakeBusters the other night, and thought you might like to be a consultant on our latest game.

We already have the graphics in place, but need advice on the **physics** engine for many of the components of the game - passing, tackling, tire drag (in training mode) and kicking. You will work closely with one of our programming team.

If you can help us get this all together in time, we'll send you to the X-Force Games...all expenses paid.

Sharpen your pencil

The SimFootball programming team have come up with a list of things they need physics advice on for their game. Your first job is to outline the physics you think you'll need to use.

So **start with a sketch** of each item to reduce it to its 'bare bones' and see if it's **like** something you already know how to do. Label things like velocity, acceleration, force etc where appropriate. And give a brief **outline** of the kind of physics you might use to solve each problem.

a. **Passing** - Working out the path of a ball that has been thrown through the air at a known angle with a known initial velocity.

b. **Tackling** - Players with known masses each running with a certain velocity collide with each other and grab on.

c. **Tire drag** - In training mode, a player with a rope around his waist runs, dragging a tire along the ground.

d. **Kicking** - Moving foot kicks stationary ball with a force, and is in contact for a known period of time.

Relax

Don't worry if you don't know much about football.

Each of the game elements are explained in the 'Sharpen your pencil'. You're only going to be working with the physics, so it doesn't matter if you don't know much about the rules.

This is American football, not soccer. But whatever you call it, don't worry!

Sharpen your pencil Solution

The SimFootball programming team have come up with a list of things they need physics advice on for their game. Your first job is to outline the physics you think you'll need to use.

So **start with a sketch** of each item to reduce it to its 'bare bones' and see if it's **like** something you already know how to do. Label things like velocity, acceleration, force etc where appropriate. And give a brief **outline** of the kind of physics you might use to solve each problem.

a. **Passing** - Working out the path of a ball that has been thrown through the air at a known angle with a known initial velocity.

This looks like a projectile fired through the air at an angle. Use equations of motion and treat horizontal and vertical components separately.

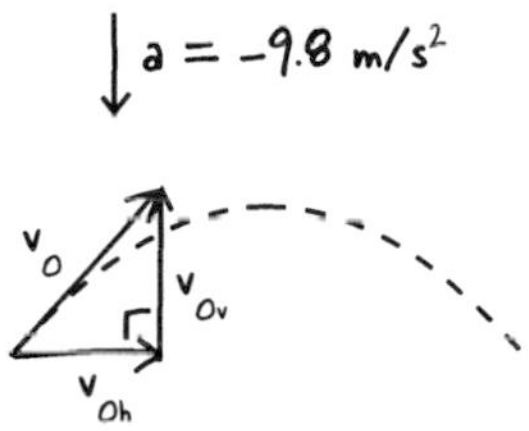

b. **Tackling** - Players with known masses each running with a certain velocity collide with each other and grab on.

Players both have mass and velocity, so both have momentum before collision.

Momentum is conserved so it must be the same before and after.

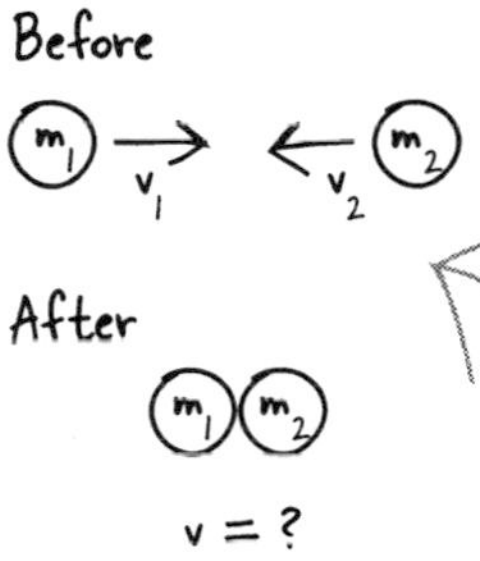

c. **Tire drag** - In training mode, a player with a rope around his waist runs, dragging a tire along the ground with a constant velocity.

The tire is being pulled at an angle, so you can maybe make a right-angled triangle and use component vectors of forces to work this out.

d. **Kicking** - Moving foot kicks stationary ball with a force, and is in contact for a known period of time.

Foot and ball both have a mass and a velocity, and again momentum must be conserved.

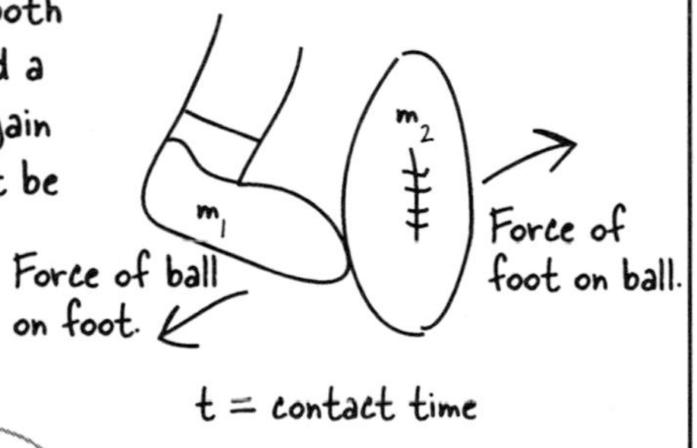

You don't know exactly how to do some of these problems yet, but don't worry – you've already got off to a great start!

If two objects interact, look out for being able to use momentum conservation or a form of Newton's 2nd Law (either $F = ma$ or $F\Delta t = \Delta p$) as both objects experience the same size of force.

If you're given a story, start with a sketch to work out what physics the story involves. What's it LIKE?

Jim: Yeah, but what about tackling? The players usually hit head on and grab on to each other. In the game we know their **masses** and **velocities** before the tackle. Ow!!! What are you doing?!

Joe: Just being a part of it! Looks like if I'm running faster when I tackle you, we move faster afterwards than when I run slowly.

Frank: And if your mass was larger, Jim would have gone flying!

Joe: The total **momentum**, mass × velocity, will be the same before and after - right?

Jim: I'm glad we're back to math now! Yeah, the game would need to move the players with the correct **velocity** after the tackle. We know the **mass** and velocity of each player before the tackle, so using **momentum conservation** sounds about right.

Sharpen your pencil

Two football players hit each other head on. One has a mass of 95.0 kg and is running from left to right at 8.50 m/s. The other has a mass of 120.0 kg and is running from right to left at 3.80 m/s

If the players lock together in the tackle, what velocity do they move with in the split second after the tackle?

Hint: If the players lock together, they move as one mass after the tackle

Sharpen your pencil Solution

Two football players hit each other head on. One has a mass of 95.0 kg and is running from left to right at 8.50 m/s. The other has a mass of 120.0 kg and is running from right to left at 3.80 m/s

If the players lock together in the tackle, what velocity do they move with in the split second after the tackle?

Before: $m_1 = 95.0$ kg $m_2 = 120.0$ kg

$v_1 = 8.5$ m/s $v_2 = -3.8$ m/s

After: $m_3 = 95.0 + 120.0 = 215.0$ kg

$v_3 = ?$

Left to right is positive.

Momentum is a VECTOR so you need to choose which DIRECTION to define as positive.

Use momentum conservation to work out v_3:

total momentum before = total momentum after.

$$m_1v_1 + m_2v_2 = m_3v_3$$

$$v_3 = \frac{m_1v_1 + m_2v_2}{m_3}$$

It's safest to rearrange your equation before you put the values in.

$$v_3 = \frac{95.0 \times 8.50 - 120.0 \times 3.80}{215.0}$$

$$v_3 = 1.63 \text{ m/s (3 sd)}$$

They go from left to right at 1.63 m/s (3 sd).

Momentum is conserved in a collision

Momentum is always conserved in an interaction between two or more objects. So when the two players **collide** in the tackle, the total momentum must be the same afterwards as it was before the collision.

This happens because each player experiences the same size of **force** when they collide, but in opposite directions - a **Newton's Third Law pair of forces**. The same size of force always causes the same change in momentum.

So the first object has its momentum changed in the direction of the force acting on it - and the second object has its momentum changed in the direction of the force acting on it.

But the forces are equal sizes and in opposite directions. So the changes in momentum are equal sizes and in opposite directions. This means that the total momentum is the same both before and after the collision. The changes in momentum make no difference to the total when you add them together.

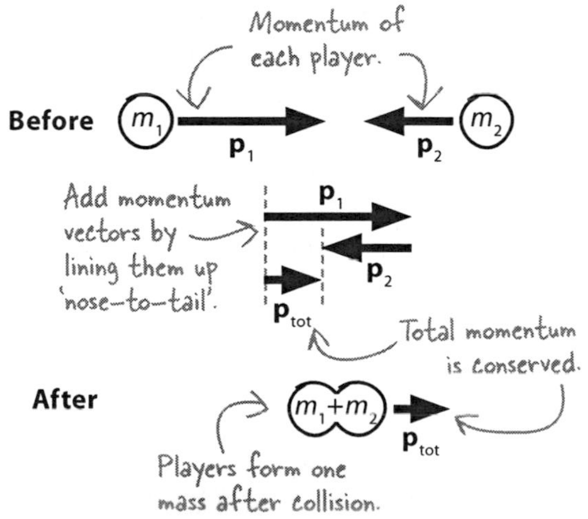

When two objects collide, think about what happens. Do they become one object?

there are no Dumb Questions

Q: How do you know that the two masses that exist before the collision have turned into one mass afterwards?

A: You'll often do problems where two masses stick together after colliding. This means that they no longer move as two separate masses, but as one mass with a single velocity. Read the question carefully!

Q: Are there any buzzwords that indicate that the objects stick together?

A: Sometimes the term "inelastic" is used to indicate a situation where two objects collide without bouncing (in an "elastic" way).

Q: Is momentum always conserved? Or does that only happen when the objects stick together?

A: Momentum is always conserved in any interaction between two objects, whether they stick together or bounce off of each other. This happens because each object experiences an equal-sized forces in opposite directions as a result of the collision. The same size of force always leads to the same change in momentum.

So if one object's momentum changes by +10 kg.m/s and the other object's by -10 kg.m/s, the total momentum is still the same. The +10 and -10 add to zero when you add the "after" momentums together.

Q: So that happens because of a Newton's Third Law pair of forces?

A: Spot on! Newton's 3rd Law and momentum conservation are two sides of the same coin.

Q: What if the football player had a collision with an advertising billboard that stopped him completely? Where's the momentum conservation there?

A: The advertising billboard is attached to the Earth, which has a huge mass compared to the player. As momentum is mass × velocity, the Earth's huge mass means that the change in its velocity is far too small for you to notice.

But the collision might be at an angle

The SimFootball team are really happy with what you told them about tackling, and write it into the game!

But they soon realize that the problem's more involved than they first thought. The players don't always collide head on - sometimes they hit each other at an **angle**. And they don't know how to deal with that.

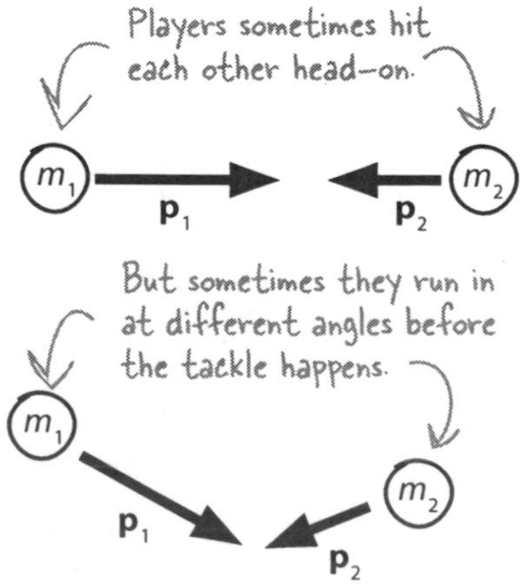

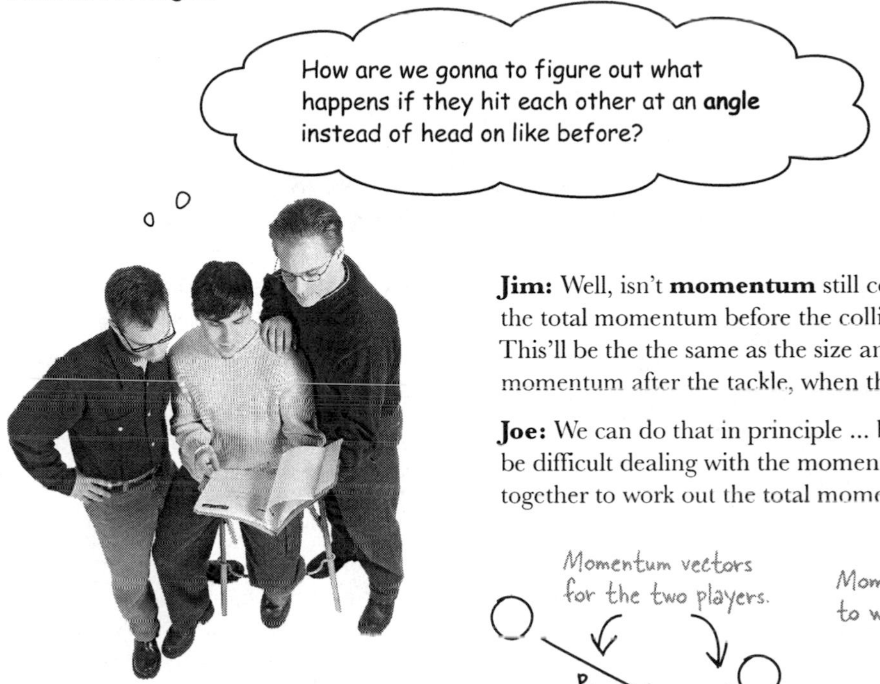

Jim: Well, isn't **momentum** still conserved? We can figure out the total momentum before the collision just like we did before. This'll be the the same as the size and direction of the players' total momentum after the tackle, when they stick together.

Joe: We can do that in principle ... but in practice it's going to be difficult dealing with the momentum vectors if we add them together to work out the total momentum at the start. Look:

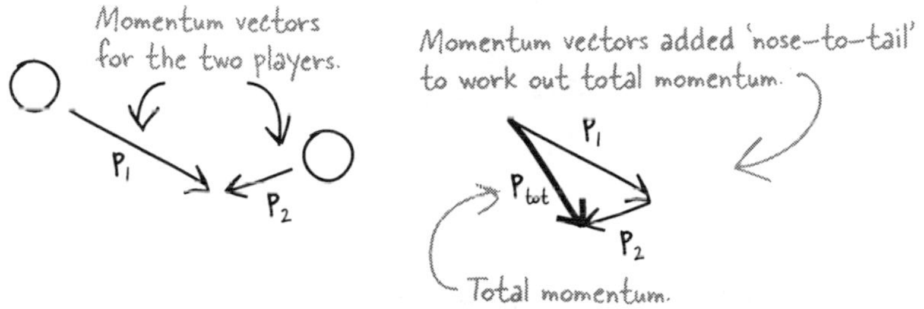

When you draw a sketch, make sure you think about angles.

You can't use what you know of Pythagoras, sine, cosine or tangent unless your triangle is right-angled.

Frank: But what's the big deal? The vectors make a **triangle** - and we can deal with triangles!

Jim: Correction ... we can deal with **right-angled triangles**. But that triangle sure ain't right-angled.

Frank: Oh yeah. When the players hit head on, we didn't need to think about angles, because all the action was taking place along a straight line that ran from left to right.

Jim: But can't we just use Pythagoras etc?

Joe: Pythagoras only works for right-angled triangles. And what we know about sine, cosine and tangent only works for right-angled triangles. I guess we could try to work out something that works for other triangles, but that sounds waaay hard.

Frank: Hmmm, a triangle with no right-angles like the one we're stuck with sure is awkward.

Jim: I wonder if we could somehow flip things around so that there are some right-angled triangles ..

A triangle with no right angles is awkward

The main problem with this collision is that the players are running in at different **angles**. You can add together the players' **momentum** vectors to get the total momentum before the collision by lining them up nose-to-tail, like we've done here.

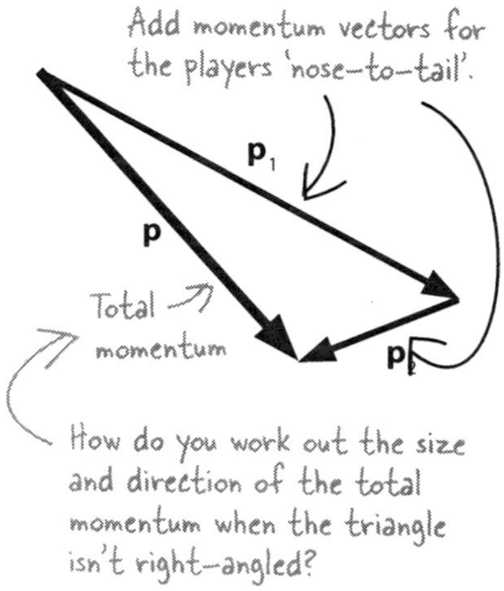

But the triangle formed by the players' momentum vectors isn't right-angled. This makes it difficult for you to calculate the total momentum. Pythagoras, sine, cosine and tangent only work with a right-angled triangle. A triangle with no right angles is awkward!

Use component vectors to create some right-angled triangles

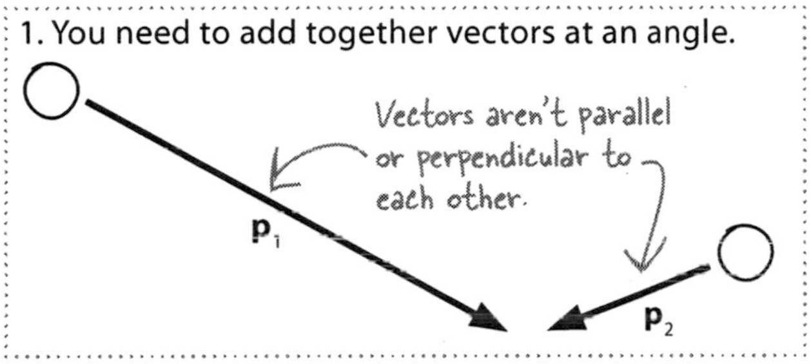

If your problem has two dimensions, think component vectors.

You can redraw any vector as two **component vectors** at **right-angles** to each other. This is especially useful if you have to **add two vectors together** that aren't parallel or perpendicular to each other.

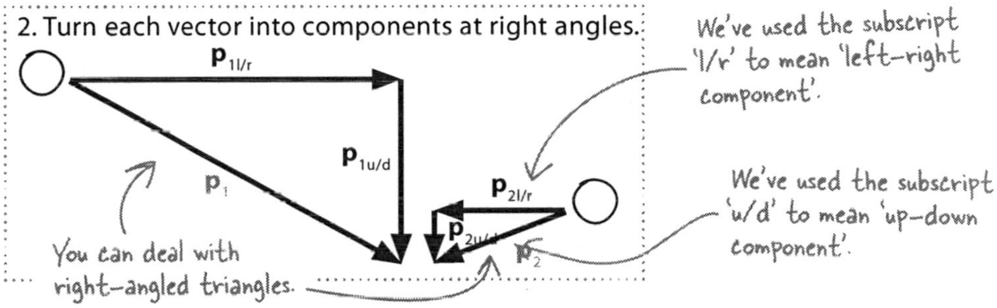

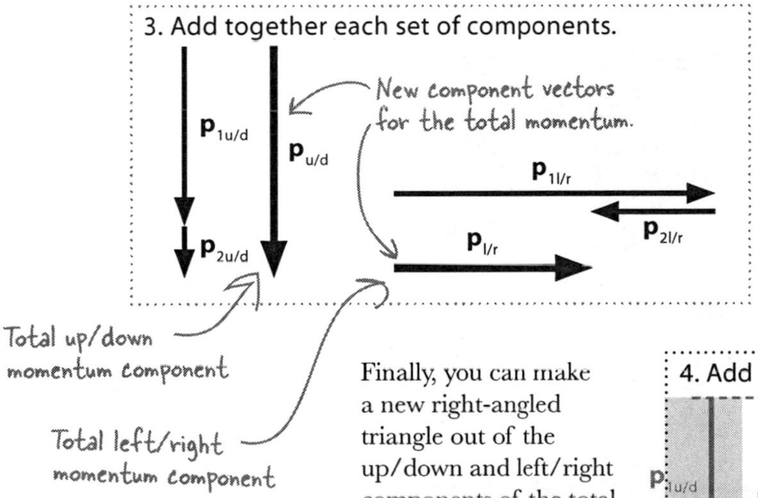

Now work with the components! Use right-angled triangles to add together the up/down and left/right components of each momentum vector separately.

This gives you the up/down and left/right components of the total momentum vector.

Finally, you can make a new right-angled triangle out of the up/down and left/right components of the total momentum, and use it to calculate the **total momentum** (which will be the same before and after the collision)

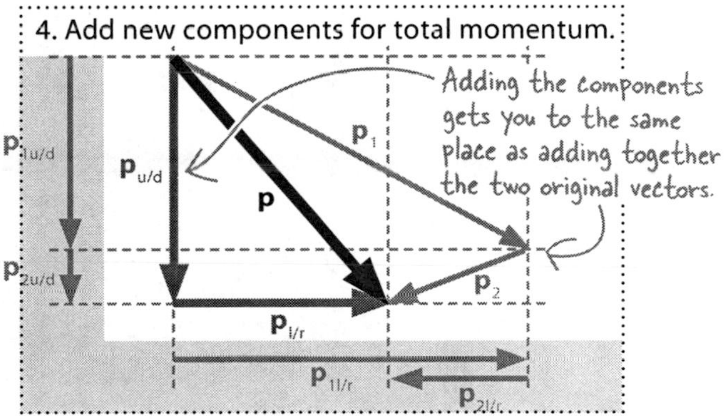

Sharpen your pencil

Two players in the "SimFootball" game collide in a tackle and grab on to each other. Their masses and velocity vectors are shown here:

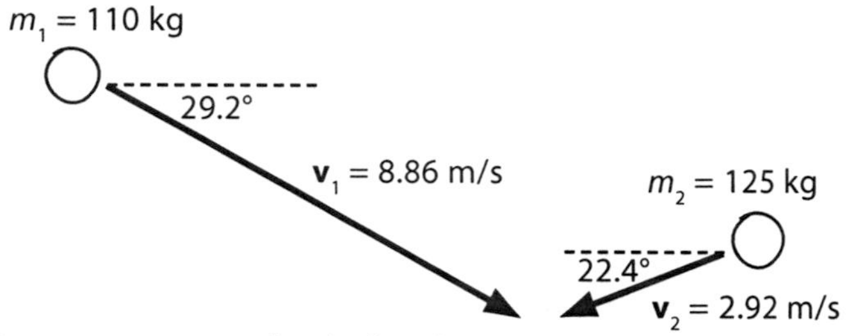

a. Calculate the size of the momentum vector for each player.

b. Draw a sketch to show the left/right and up/down components of each player's momentum, and calculate the sizes of these components.

c. Calculate the size and direction of the total momentum vector using your results from part b.

d. What velocity do the players move with after the tackle?

Sharpen your pencil Solution

Two players in the "SimFootball" game collide in a tackle and grab on to each other. Their masses and velocity vectors are shown here:

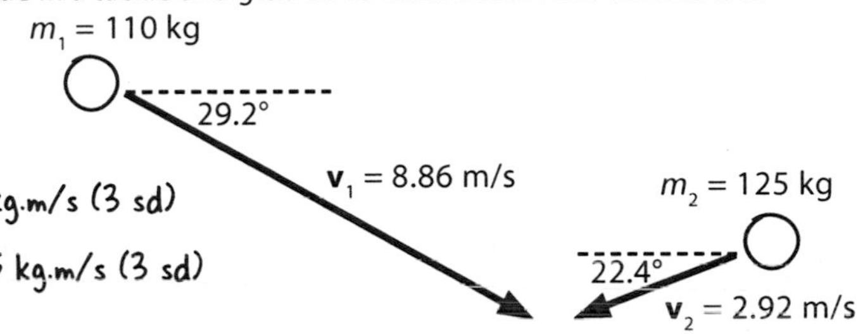

a. Calculate the size of the momentum vector for each player.

$p_1 = m_1 v_1 = 110 \times 8.86 = 975$ kg.m/s (3 sd)

$p_2 = m_2 v_2 = 125 \times 2.92 = 365$ kg.m/s (3 sd)

b. Draw a sketch to show the left/right and up/down components of each player's momentum, and calculate the sizes of these components.

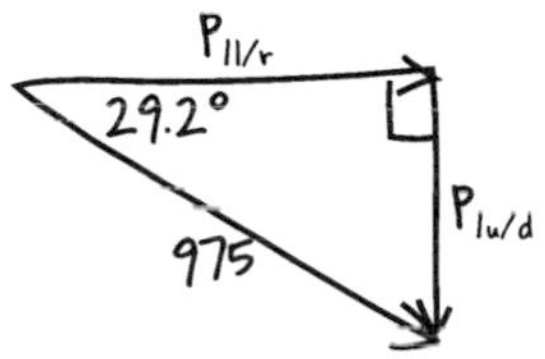

$\cos(29.2) = \frac{a}{h} = \frac{p_{1l/r}}{975}$

$p_{1l/r} = 975\cos(29.2)$

$p_{1l/r} = 851$ kg.m/s (3 sd) right

$\sin(29.2) = \frac{o}{h} = \frac{p_{1u/d}}{975}$

$p_{1u/d} = 975\sin(29.2)$

$p_{1u/d} = 476$ kg.m/s (3 sd) down

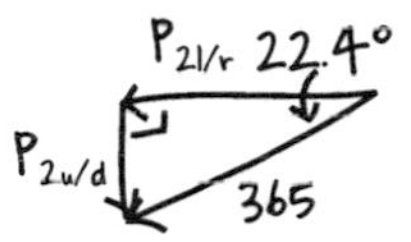

$\cos(22.4) = \frac{a}{h} = \frac{p_{2u/d}}{365}$

$p_{2l/r} = 365\cos(22.4)$

$p_{2l/r} = 337$ kg.m/s (3 sd) left

$\sin(22.4) = \frac{o}{h} = \frac{p_{2u/d}}{365}$

$p_{2u/d} = 365\sin(22.4)$

$p_{2u/d} = 139$ kg.m/s (3 sd) down

c. Calculate the size and direction of the total momentum vector using your results from part b.

Left/ right components: $851 - 337 = 514$ kg.m/s right

Up / down components: $476 + 139 = 615$ kg.m/s down

Size: By Pythagoras, $p^2 = p_{l/r}^2 + p_{u/d}^2 = 514^2 + 615^2$

$p = \sqrt{514^2 + 615^2} = 802$ kg.m/s (3 sd)

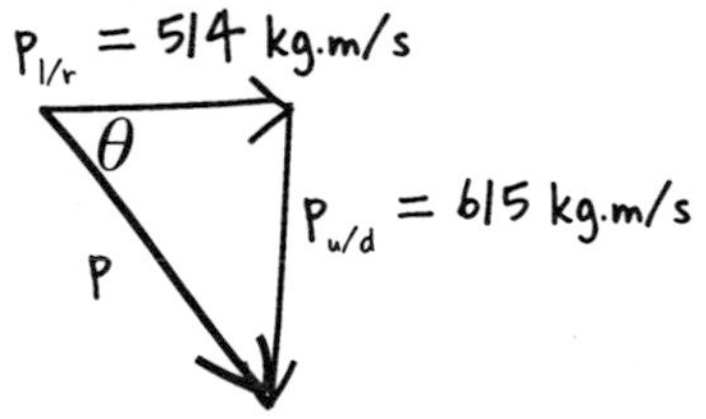

Direction: Given angles all measured from the horizontal, so do this too.

$\tan(\theta) = \frac{o}{a} \Rightarrow \theta = \tan^{-1}\left(\frac{615}{514}\right) = 50.1°$ (3 sd) from the horizontal, left to right.

d. What velocity do the players move with after the tackle?

m = total mass $= 110 + 125 = 235$ kg

$p = mv \Rightarrow v = \frac{p}{m} = \frac{802}{235} = 3.41$ m/s (3 sd) at 50.1° (3 sd) from the horizontal, left to right.

there are no Dumb Questions

Q: That was a lot of math to go through with all the component vectors!!

A: It wasn't any more difficult than what you've done previously. It's just that you had to calculate a number of sides and angles! But as long as you manage to organize your work so that you don't get mixed up, you're fine. Now you can handle component vectors and right-angled triangles, you have superpowers that let you deal with two-dimensional situations.

Q: How often will I need to do a problem involving momentum conservation like this one?

A: You may not come across many problems exactly like this. But the **general skill** of being able to turn vectors at awkward angles into component vectors so you can add them together is one you can use again and again with any vectors.

Q: I was just thinking ... what happens if the players bounce off each other after the tackle? Then I'd have two momentum vectors to deal with after the collision!

A: Great spot! You're right - this would be a more difficult problem, and you'll need to learn about energy before you can solve it. You'll come back to a similar scenario in a later chapter, so don't worry about it for now.

To add together two vectors at different angles, resolve the vectors into components at right-angles, then add together the components.

The programmer includes 2D momentum conservation ...

The SimFootball programmer gets to work, and quickly codes up what you've learned about 2D collisions using momentum conservation. Now the players move realistically for the split second after the tackle ...

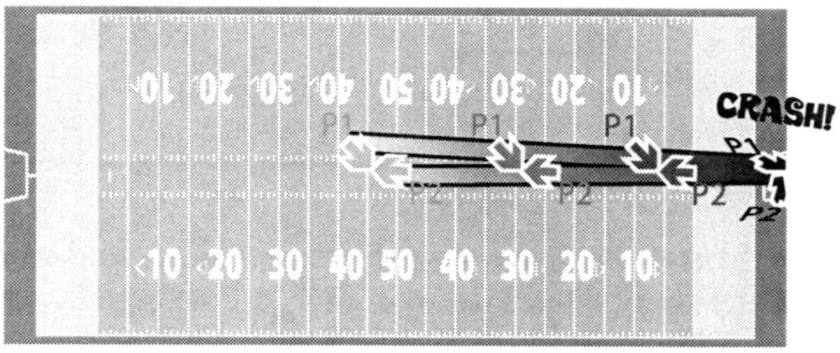

... but the players keep on sliding for ever!

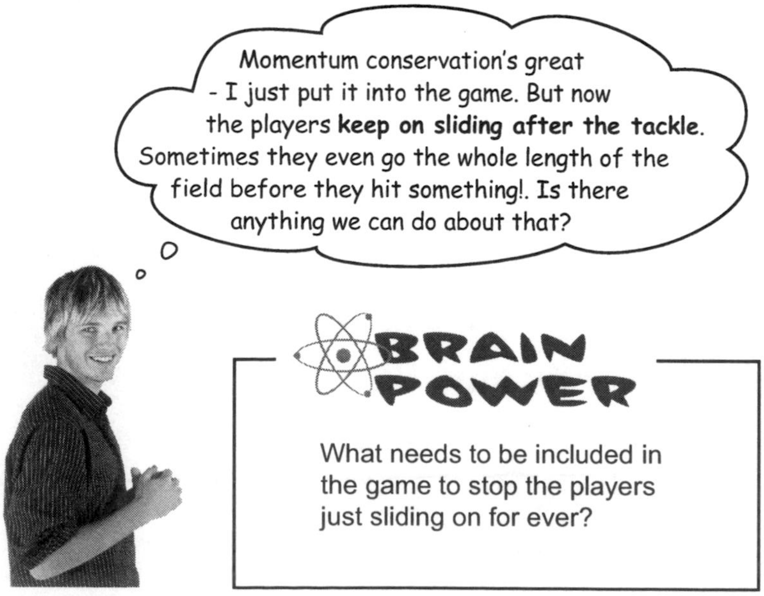

BRAIN POWER

What needs to be included in the game to stop the players just sliding on for ever?

In real life, the force of friction is present

Newton's First Law says that an object will continue on at the same velocity unless acted on by a net force. At the moment, the SimFootball game isn't finished, and the only way sliding players can be stopped is if they crash into the advertising billboards or a goalpost.

So at the moment, the players just continue along at the same velocity after the tackle until they hit something.

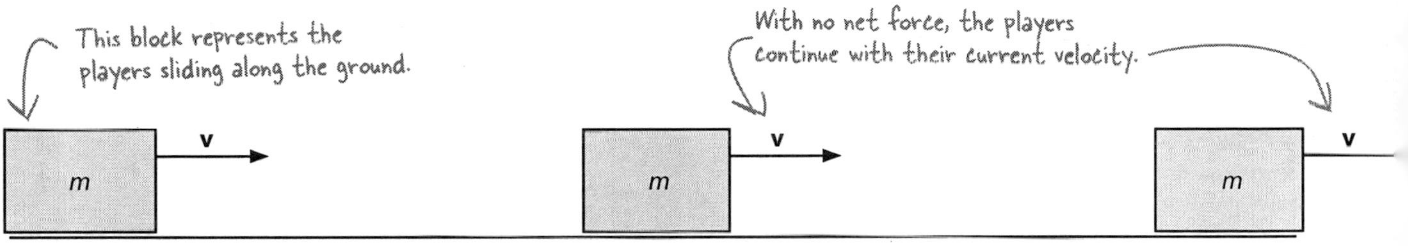

In the real world, **moving** objects slow down and eventually stop because of the force of **friction** (symbol $\mathbf{F}_{fric}$). Friction only comes about when two surfaces are in **contact** with each other, and the frictional force always acts to **oppose motion**. If an object is sliding along a surface, the frictional force always acts **parallel** to the surface.

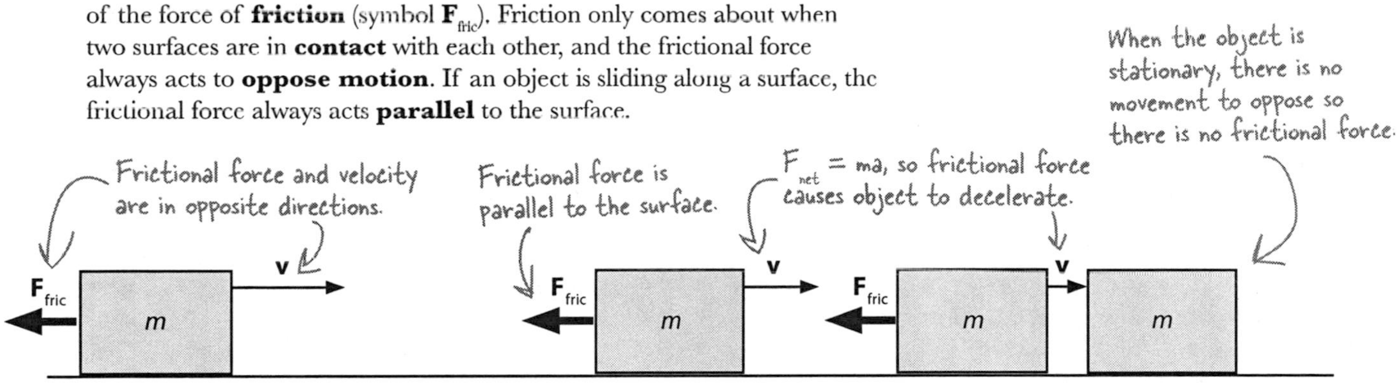

Friction always acts to OPPOSE motion. If an object is sliding along a surface, the frictional force on it acts PARALLEL to the surface.

If the object is **stationary**, its velocity is constant (zero) therefore there is no net horizontal force. If no other horizontal forces are present, and therefore no friction if there are no other horizontal forces.

If you start to gently push a stationary object, it won't move, as friction always opposes motion. But if you keep on pushing harder, you'll eventually manage to exert a larger force than the frictional force, and the object will move.

No-one knows for sure exactly how friction works. It's definitely a contact-dependent force, which you see when you try to slide one surface over another. Interactions between the surfaces act to oppose the motion until, eventually, the two surfaces end up at rest. But the exact nature of these interactions hasn't yet been pinned down.

Jim: How are we gonna calculate that?! I don't know where to start.

Joe: How about we think of all the things that might affect the size of the frictional force. We can be **qualitative** even if we don't know how to be **quantitative** yet.

Frank: Well, there's the **roughness** of the surface for a start. I think grass and astroturf will produce different results.

Jim: How about the **mass** of the players.

Joe: Yeah, and the **velocity** they're going at when they start to slide. Plus some football fields **slope** a little - that might make a difference.

Frank: I guess we'd better have a go at **being** a sliding object, to see how each of these variables might affect the frictional force.

BE the sliding object

Your job is to be a sliding object. We've drawn an experiment here that you can do yourself - or you can put yourself in the place of the sliding object / player. Write down the effect you think each factor will have on the size of the frictional force and give reasons for your answers.

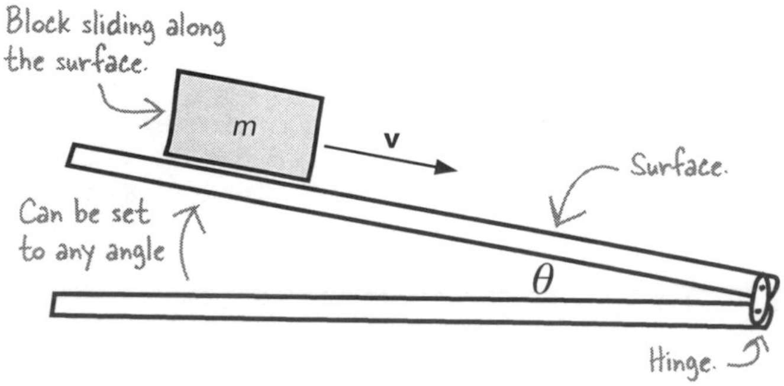

a. Materials block and surface are made from.

....

....

....

b. Mass / weight of block.

....

....

....

c. Angle / slope of surface.

....

....

....

d. Velocity of block.

....

....

....

BE the sliding object - SOLUTION

Your job is to be a sliding object. We've drawn an experiment here that you can do yourself - or you can put yourself in the place of the sliding object / player. Write down the effect you think each factor will have on the size of the frictional force and give reasons for your answers.

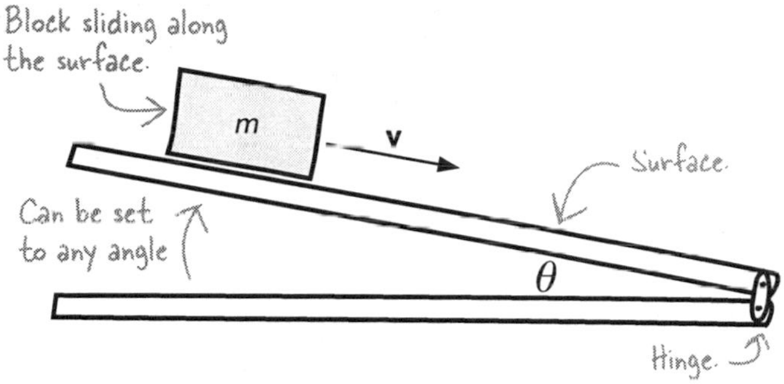

a. Materials block and surface are made from.

Some surfaces will have more friction than others. Players slide further on grass than on astroturf so frictional force is smaller.

b. Mass / weight of block.

The heavier something is, the harder it is to slide, as it's "pushed into" the surface. So a larger mass leads to a larger frictional force.

c. Angle / slope of surface.

The larger the angle, the smaller the frictional force, because the block isn't "pushed into" the surface so much.

d. Velocity of block.

It's difficult to tell what effect the velocity has on the friction without making more accurate measurements.

there are no Dumb Questions

Q: So the amount of friction depends on how rough the surfaces are, right? Like, sandpaper on sandpaper creates a lot of friction, but there's less friction with smooth surfaces?

A: Not quite. As anyone who's ever worn through their bicycle brakes may have spotted, there's actually more friction with two perfectly smooth surfaces (steel on steel) than with sandpaper, or rubber brake blocks on steel! Friction depends on the type of surface, but not necessarily on roughness.

Q: But everyone knows that when you oil something (i.e. make its surface more smooth) then there's less friction.

A: Friction occurs when two surfaces are in **contact** with each other. Oiling introduces a **layer** in between the two surfaces, which increases the **distance** between them. Oiling doesn't change the smoothness of the surfaces themselves.

Friction is a contact-dependent force.

Q: What about something moving through the air? It's not close to any surfaces, but it still slows down.

A: That's mainly air resistance, which isn't quite the same as friction. The force of friction experienced by an object sliding across a surface actually doesn't depend on its velocity. But the resistive force that something moving through the air experiences increases when its velocity increases, as the faster it goes, the more air molecules it has to 'push aside' every second to make progress.

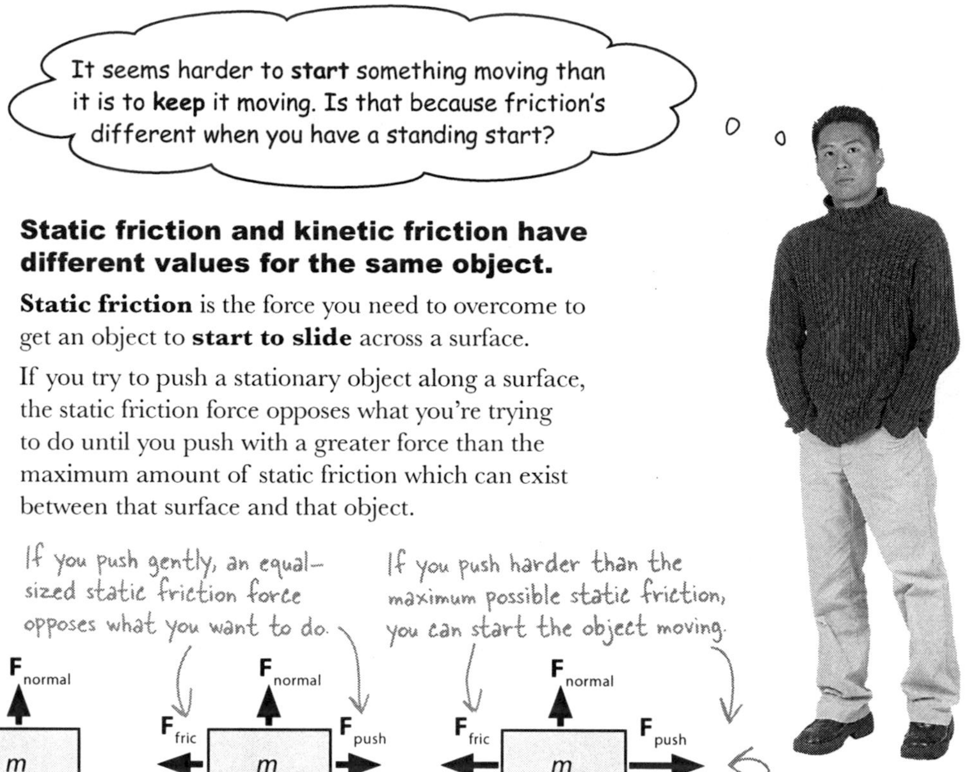

Static friction and kinetic friction have different values for the same object.

Static friction is the force you need to overcome to get an object to **start to slide** across a surface.

If you try to push a stationary object along a surface, the static friction force opposes what you're trying to do until you push with a greater force than the maximum amount of static friction which can exist between that surface and that object.

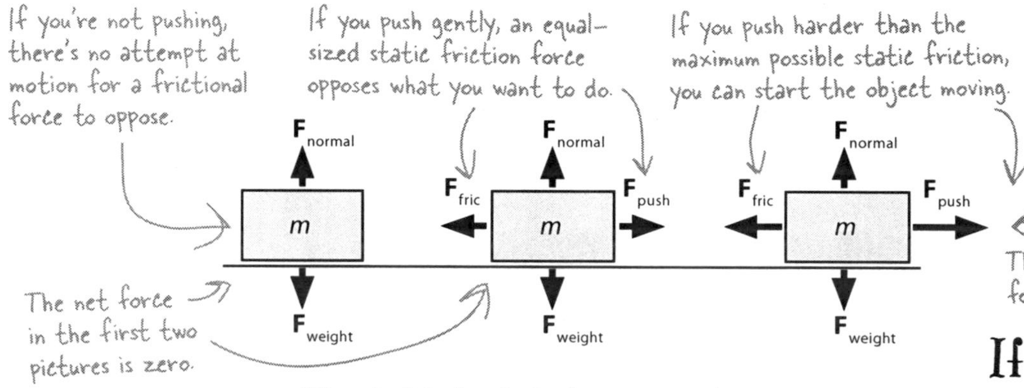

Kinetic friction is the force you need to overcome to keep an object moving. If an object is already moving and you push with a force equal to the kinetic friction, the object will move with a constant velocity, since there is no net force. The amount of friction doesn't depend on the object's velocity.

Newton's 1st Law says that an object will move with a constant velocity unless there is a net force acting on it.

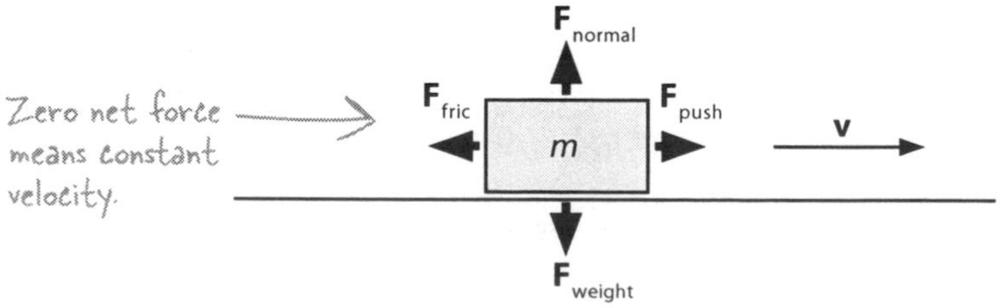

Static friction is greater than kinetic friction between the same two surfaces. So you need a larger force to start something moving than you need to keep it moving.

If the parallel component of the pushing force and the kinetic friction are equal in size, your object will move with a constant velocity, since there is no net force.

So there are grass and astro fields in SimFootball. We need to be able to **calculate** the friction for each so that the game knows how the players should move.

Friction depends on the types of surfaces that are interacting

The frictional force that a moving object (such as two football players sliding after a tackle) experiences depends on the nature of the two surfaces that are interacting. In physics, this is expressed by the **coefficient of friction**, μ. The greater the value of μ, the greater the amount of friction. Values of μ can range from around 0.05 for two teflon surfaces to around 1.7 for a rubber tire on a road.

For the football pitch surfaces, $\mu = 0.8$ for astro and $\mu = 0.5$ for grass. So you can see that the frictional force as the players slide along astroturf will be higher than the frictional force from grass.

μ is the Greek letter 'mu' and is pronounced 'mew'.

The larger the coefficient of friction, μ, the larger the frictional force.

Friction depends on the normal force

The frictional force that a moving object experiences depends on how much the object is "pushed into" the surface. This is another way of saying that friction depends on the **normal force** that a surface exerts on the object. **The greater the normal force, the greater the amount of friction.**

The **equation** for the size of the frictional force experienced by an object is:

$$F_{fric} = \mu F_N$$

Frictional force → F_{fric}; Coefficient of friction → μ; Normal force → F_N

This is just an equation for the **size** of the frictional force. $\mathbf{F}_{fric}$ will always oppose the direction of motion (or attempted motion) parallel to the surface. So to get the **direction** of $\mathbf{F}_{fric}$, you need to look at the velocity of the object (for kinetic friction) or the parallel component of a pushing force (for static friction).

When you know the direction of $\mathbf{F}_{fric}$, you can use $\mathbf{F}_{net} = m\mathbf{a}$ to calculate the players' **acceleration**. You can then use the acceleration in equations of motion to see how the players move.

The larger the normal force, the larger the frictional force.

This applies to size. The normal force is perpendicular and the frictional force is parallel.

Be careful when you calculate the normal force

The normal force is always **perpendicular** to a surface. It should be the last force you add to a free body diagram, as it is the force exerted by the surface on an object so as to make the **net perpendicular force equal to zero**.

If the net perpendicular force wasn't zero, the object would either crash through the surface, burrow into the surface or bounce off the surface.

If surface is horizontal and there are no other forces acting on the object then the normal force is exactly the same as the object's weight.

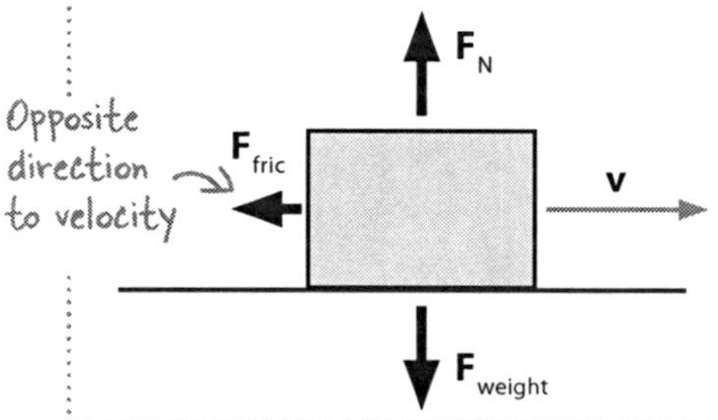

If the surface is at an angle, the normal force is also at an angle, as it is always perpendicular.

If there are other forces acting on the object (for example, a player may be pushed into the ground by another player), then you need to ensure that you draw on the normal force so as to make the net perpendicular force equal to zero.

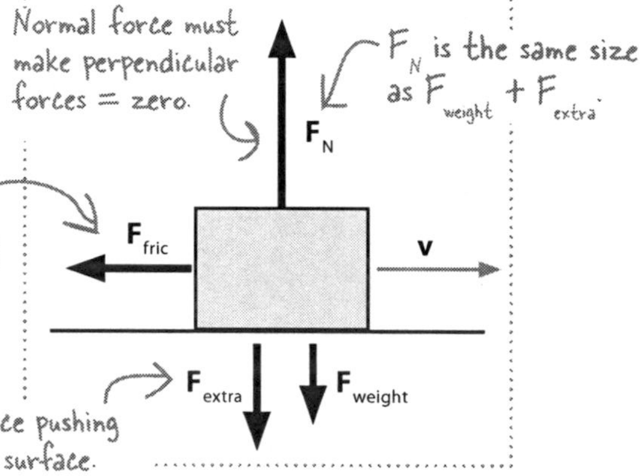

The normal force ensures that the net force perpendicular to the surface is zero.

If the object is on a **slope** then you'll have to work out the **perpendicular components** of all the forces acting on the object. Usually, this will just involve the object's weight, but it can sometimes involve extra forces if something else is pushing or pulling the object.

If there are other forces with perpendicular components in addition to the weight, you'll need to calculate the size of the normal force that makes the net perpendicular force equal to zero.

You already know how to calculate the normal force when an object is on a slope.

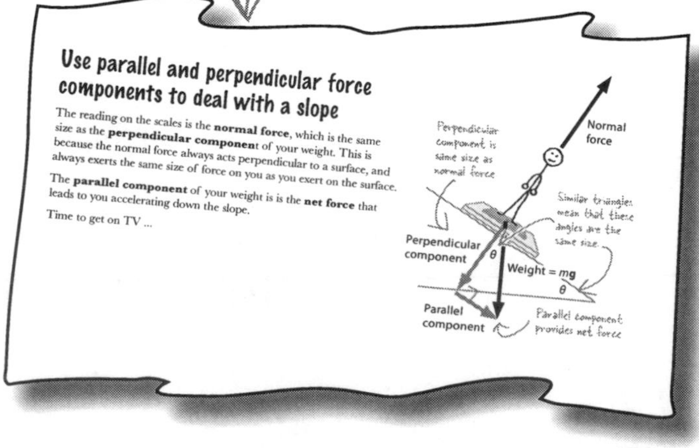

Use parallel and perpendicular force components to deal with a slope

The reading on the scales is the **normal force**, which is the same size as the **perpendicular component** of your weight. This is because the normal force always acts perpendicular to a surface, and always exerts the same size of force on you as you exert on the surface.

The **parallel component** of your weight is the **net force** that leads to you accelerating down the slope.

Time to get on TV ...

Frictional force doesn't depend on surface area!

Since friction is a force that depends on **contact** between two surfaces, it seems logical to assume that you will have a greater value of friction when the surface area is greater.

But think of it this way instead. If you have a flat-sided brick, there are three different ways you can put it on a flat surface. The normal force is always the same each time, since the weight of the brick doesn't change. So if you maximize the contact surface area, you might think that the quantity of friction will increase.

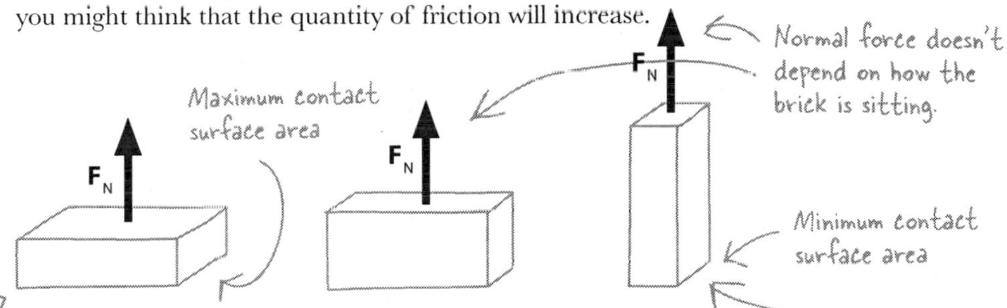

However, if you increase the surface area, you also reduce the **pressure** (force per bit of area) that the brick exerts on the surface. So the brick with a large contact surface area won't 'dig in' to the surface as much as one on its end - in the same way as flat-soled shoes don't 'dig in' to a surface as much as high heels do.

It turns out that these two effects - increasing the surface area and reducing the pressure - exactly cancel each other out when it comes to their effect on the frictional force experienced by the brick. The frictional force depends **only** on the coefficient of friction and the normal force, i.e. $\mathbf{F}_{fric} = \mu \mathbf{F}_N$

The frictional force ONLY depends on the coefficient of friction and the normal force.

You're ready to use friction in the game!

You should start any problem that involves forces with a **free body diagram**. This is even more important if **friction** is involved. Remember that friction always acts to oppose motion, so you need to think about the object's **velocity** to get the direction of the frictional force.

Think about which direction the object is **accelerating** in (if any). If it isn't accelerating perpendicular to the surface, then all of the perpendicular force **components** will cancel each other out so that there is no net force in that direction. The value of the normal force will be whatever makes the net perpendicular force equal to zero.

Look at the pictures on page 489 if this sounds mind-boggling.

If a problem involves forces, start by drawing a free body diagram.

Sharpen your pencil

After a tackle, two players with a combined mass of 215 kg slide horizontally along the ground with an initial velocity of 3.70 m/s.

How long does it take for them to come to a complete stop on a. Astroturf ($\mu = 0.80$) and b. grass ($\mu = 0.50$)?

Hint: Use the normal force to calculate the frictional force. Work out the acceleration that the frictional force produces using $F_{net} = ma$. Then use the acceleration and equations of motion to calculate the stopping time.

Hint: Draw a free body diagram to get the forces right. Draw a separate sketch to use with equations of motion.

Sharpen your pencil Solution

After a tackle, two players with a combined mass of 215 kg slide horizontally along the ground with an initial velocity of 3.70 m/s.

How long does it take for them to come to a complete stop on a. Astroturf ($\mu = 0.80$) and b. grass ($\mu = 0.50$)?

Free body diagram

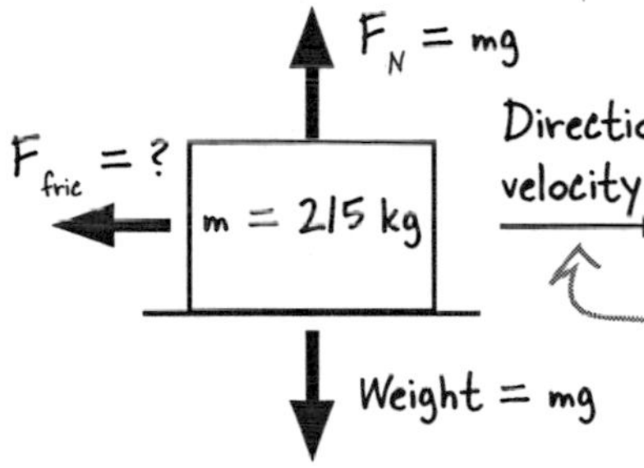

Want to work out time. Use $F_{net} = ma$ to work out acceleration then equations of motion to get t.

$$F_{net} = ma$$

$$F_{net} = F_{fric} = \mu F_N$$

The net force is the frictional force.

$$\mu F_N = ma$$

$$a = \frac{F_{net}}{m} = \frac{\mu F_N}{m} = \frac{\mu \cancel{m} g}{\cancel{m}} = \mu g$$

Equations of motion sketch

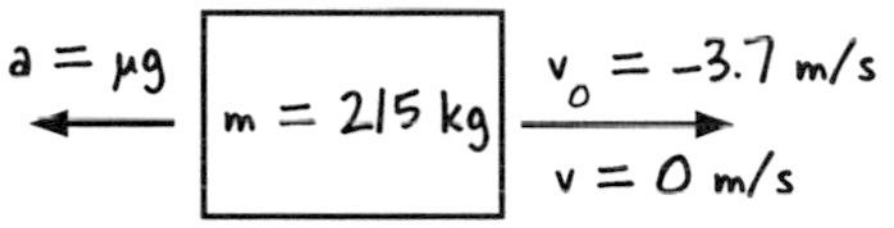

Right to left is positive.

Choose a positive direction and stick with it.

$$v = v_0 + at \Rightarrow t = \frac{v - v_0}{a} = \frac{v - v_0}{\mu g}$$

a. For astro: $t = \frac{v - v_0}{\mu g} = \frac{0 - (-3.70)}{0.80 \times 9.8} = \underline{\underline{0.47\text{ s}}}$ (2 sd)

b. For grass: $t = \frac{v - v_0}{\mu g} = \frac{0 - (-3.70)}{0.50 \times 9.8} = \underline{\underline{0.76\text{ s}}}$ (2 sd)

Including friction stops the players from sliding forever!

You explain to the programmer that the players sliding along a surface will experience a frictional force that opposes their current velocity, with size $\mathbf{F}_{fric} = \mu\mathbf{F}_N$.

When he includes this in the game, the players stop sliding endlessly, and come to a stop like you'd expect them to in real life. Which is great!

The sliding players are fine - but the tire drag is causing problems

Soon, the SimFootball team have another problem that involves **friction**. In training mode, the players can run dragging a tire behind them.

The programmer's tried working out the weight of the tire and making the normal force the same size as the tire's weight to calculate the friction. But the computer-generated players aren't behaving the way the programmer expects them to.

The frictional force that the game calculates appears to be larger than the frictional force actually is is in real life.

BRAIN POWER

What could be behind the game calculating too high a value for the friction?

So the frictional force doesn't come out right when you say that the **normal force** is equal to the weight of the tire then use that to calculate the size of the **friction** with $\mathbf{F}_{fric} = \mu\mathbf{F}_N$. Hmmm.

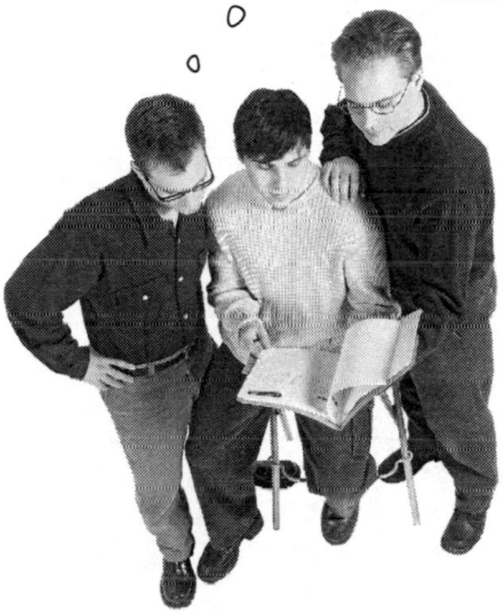

Jim: Do we have the right value for μ, the coefficient of friction? And is the field totally flat?

Joe: Yeah the game's using flat astroturf, and the experiment involving the real player was done on astroturf too, with no slope.

Frank: I guess we'd better do a **sketch** - we might have some more ideas about what's going on if we can actually see this.

Jim: Ooh, the rope's tied to the player's waist, isn't it?

Joe: Yeah, the force that the player exerts on the tire via the rope acts at an **angle**.

Frank: Will that make the normal force different somehow?

Jim: I think so - the player's kind-of pulling the tire up as well as along. Look at the **components** of the pulling force:

If forces act at angles, think about resolving them into components that are parallel and perpendicular to a surface.

Joe: The rope's **supporting** the tire vertically as well as pulling it horizontally. The normal force will be smaller than the tire's weight.

Frank: So how do we work with that?

Jim: Well, the tire's weight vector points downwards. The vertical component of the force from the rope points upwards. And the normal force points upwards. The tire isn't rising or burrowing down - there's no net perpendicular force. So the tire's weight, the vertical force from the rope and the normal force must add to zero.

Joe: And the tire's moving horizontally with a **constant velocity,** so the frictional force and the horizontal component of the force from the rope must add to zero, so that there's **zero net horizontal force**. Or else the tire would accelerate.

Sharpen your pencil

A football player has one end of a rope tied around his waist; the other end is attached to a tire. The programmer has done a brief experiment involving a real player and tire, and wants to calculate the force that the player exerts on the tire via the rope so he can use it in the game.

a. Draw a free body diagram of the tire when it is dragged along the ground with a constant velocity. Use $\mathbf{F}_r$ to represent the force that the player exerts on the tire via the rope.

Don't put on any values yet, just draw the force vector arrows and say what they represent.

b. Draw a new sketch showing the horizontal and vertical components of all the forces acting on the tire.

c. Use the vertical components to work out an equation for the normal force, $\mathbf{F}_N$.

d. Use the fact that the frictional force, $\mathbf{F}_{fric} = \mu\mathbf{F}_N$ to arrive at an equation that only involves the components of $\mathbf{F}_{fric}$, the mass of the tire, the coefficient of friction and **g**, the gravitational field strength.

e. The tire has a mass of 10.0 kg, the rope is 2.00 m long and the player's belt is 120 cm above the ground, which is astro with $\mu = 0.80$. Use your equation from part d to work out $\mathbf{F}_r$, the force that the player exerts on the tire via the rope.

Sharpen your pencil Solution

A football player has one end of a rope tied around his waist; the other end is attached to a tire. the programmer has done a brief experiment involving a real player and tire, and wants to calculate the force that the player exerts on the tire via the rope so he can use it in the game.

a. Draw a free body diagram of the tire when it is dragged along the ground with a constant velocity. Use $\mathbf{F}_r$ to represent the force that the player exerts on the tire via the rope.

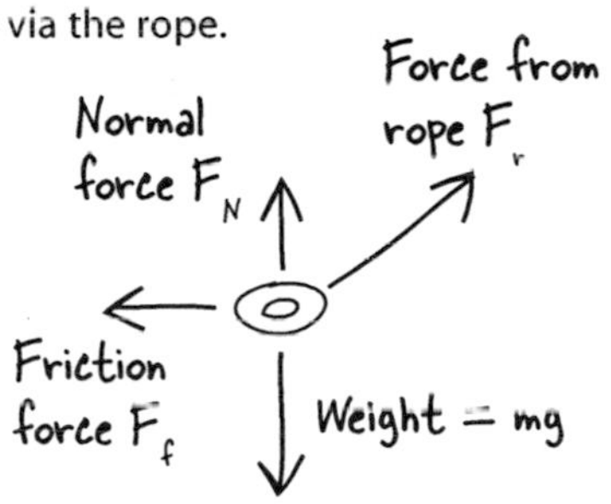

b. Draw a new sketch showing the horizontal and vertical components of all the forces acting on the tire.

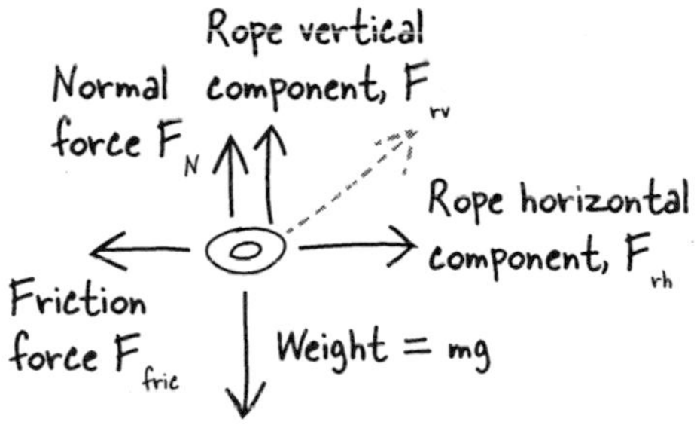

c. Use the vertical components to work out an equation for the normal force, $\mathbf{F}_N$.

Up is the positive direction.

No net force so $F_N + F_{rv} - mg = 0$

$$F_N = mg - F_{rv}$$

d. Use the fact that the frictional force, $\mathbf{F}_{fric} = \mu\mathbf{F}_N$ to arrive at an equation that only involves the components of $\mathbf{F}_{fric}$, the mass of the tire, the coefficient of friction and **g**, the gravitational field strength.

Right is the positive direction.

Constant velocity so $F_{rh} + (-F_{fric}) = 0$ (There's zero net horizontal force.)

$$F_{fric} = F_{rh}$$

But also $F_{fric} = \mu F_N = \mu(mg - F_{rv})$

$$\Rightarrow \mu(mg - F_{rv}) = F_{rh}$$

e. The tire has a mass of 10.0 kg, the rope is 2.0 m long and the player's belt is 120 cm above the ground, which is astro with $\mu = 0.80$. Use your equation from part d to work out $\mathbf{F}_r$, the force that the player exerts on the tire via the rope.

Rope distance triangle and force triangle are similar triangles.

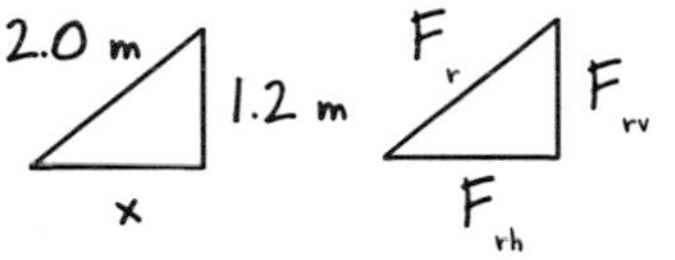

By Pythagoras, $x^2 + 1.2^2 = 2.0^2 \Rightarrow x = 1.6$ m

Similar triangles: $\frac{F_{rv}}{F_r} = \frac{1.2}{2.0} \Rightarrow F_{rv} = 0.60F_r$

$\frac{F_{rh}}{F_r} = \frac{1.6}{2.0} \Rightarrow F_{rh} = 0.80F_r$

Equation: $\mu(mg - F_{rv}) = F_{rh}$

$\Rightarrow \mu(mg - 0.60F_r) = 0.80F_r$

$\Rightarrow \mu mg - 0.60\mu F_r = 0.80F_r$

$\Rightarrow \mu mg = F_r(0.60\mu + 0.80)$

$\Rightarrow F_r = \frac{\mu mg}{0.60\mu + 0.80} = \frac{0.80 \times 10 \times 9.8}{(0.60 \times 0.80) + 0.80}$

$F_r = 61$ N (2 sd)

Using components for the tire drag works!

Now that the programmer knows how to calculate the normal force, there's no stopping him, and the parts of the game that are affected by friction are soon in place.

And as well as sliding players and dragging tires, the game can even deal with dragging tackles!

there are no Dumb Questions

Q: What do I need to know in order to calculate the force of friction?

A: The equation for the size of the frictional force is $F_{fric} = \mu F_N$. So you need to know the coefficient of friction for the surfaces you have, and the normal force.

Q: How do I find out what the coefficient of friction is?

A: You can look it up in a book or on the web. And if you're taking a test, μ will either be something you're given or something you're asked to work out from the values of various forces.

Q: How do you get the normal force?

A: The object isn't accelerating into the surface, so the perpendicular components of the forces acting on it must add to zero. The normal force will have the value that makes this possible

Q: I've noticed that an object travelling at a constant velocity has come up more than once. Is there a reason for that, and what's the best way of dealing with it?

A: There are many situations where you'd want something to travel with a constant velocity. A constant velocity means that there's no net force on an object (Newton's 1st Law) - you'll be fine if you remember this.

Q: What if there is a frictional force acting on an object? How do you get a situation where there is no net force?

A: Either by pushing or pulling the object with a force equal to the frictional force, or by tipping the surface to a greater angle, so that the normal force (and therefore the frictional force) is smaller, and the component of the object's weight accelerating it down the slope is greater.

Q: Does the tire experience the same frictional force when it rolls?

A: No. It experiences a relatively small amount of rolling friction, due to the part of the tire in contact with the surface deforming.

Friction Exposed

This week's interview:
Getting to grips with friction.

HeadFirst: So, friction, you're a bit of an enigma, aren't you? Like, no-one really knows where you come from. What's your take on that?

Friction: Yeah, it's true that people don't really know why I'm around. But the important thing is that I'm here!

HeadFirst: But you're a bit of a stick-in-the-mud, aren't you? You always oppose everything!

Friction: It's true that I always **oppose motion**, but it's not something you should take personally.

HeadFirst: And you're a little without direction, aren't you? I mean, you always depend on what everyone else is doing!

Friction: OK, well I guess that's true. Because I'm a force that always opposes motion, I don't actually appear until something actually moves, or tries to move. But as long as you're watching closely, that shouldn't be a problem.

HeadFirst: So are you in surfaces all the time, just hiding and waiting to come out?

Friction: Not at all. I'm just not there unless something's moving or trying to move.

HeadFirst: You've used that phrase "moving or trying to move" a couple of times now. What do you mean by it?

Friction: Well, I come in a couple of different varieties. If you're already moving, the force that opposes this motion is called **kinetic friction**.

HeadFirst: Why is it called that?

Friction: Kinetic means "moving"!

HeadFirst: And what if an object's stationary then someone comes along and tries to move it?

Friction: Then there's **static friction**. I guess the two surfaces have longer to interact with each other because they're stationary, and so the frictional force you have to overcome is greater.

HeadFirst: But kinetic friction doesn't depend on velocity, right?

Friction: Right. That's why having a mental picture of "bonds forming and breaking" or something like that can be misleading

HeadFirst: So what's this about you and the normal force?

Friction: I was wondering when that would come up! I can only oppose motion if two surfaces are actually touching. And the more they're "pushed together" the larger the frictional force between them. The **normal force** is a measure of how hard the two surfaces are being "pushed together."

HeadFirst: And how might the normal force vary?

Friction: If the surface is at an **angle**, and there are no other forces present, then the normal force will be less than the weight of the object.

HeadFirst: Is it only the angle of the surface that affects the normal force?

Friction: No - if there are extra forces acting on the object as well as its weight and the normal force, then the perpendicular components all have to add to zero.

HeadFirst: Why is that?

Friction: If the object isn't burrowing into or bouncing off the surface, there's no net perpendicular force. So the perpendicular components of the forces acting on the object have to add to zero. The normal force is whatever it needs to be for that to be true.

Question Clinic: The "Friction" Question

Sometimes, you will be presented with a problem where friction plays a vital role. The main thing in this type of problem is to work out the normal force (which you can then multiply by μ to get the frictional force) - so always start with a free body diagram. NB: This example question has these 'intermediate steps' filled in for you; in other questions you may need to carry them out unprompted as you home in on your final answer.

If the overall velocity is constant (or zero), this means that there is no net force acting on the object.

Friction always opposes motion, so the frictional force will be in the opposite direction from the velocity.

2. A tire attached to a rope is dragged along the ground by a player. with a constant velocity. The tire has a mass of 10 kg, the rope is 2.0 m long and the player's belt is 120 cm above the ground, which is Astroturf with μ = 0.8

a. Draw a free body diagram for the tire.

b. Draw in the components parallel and perpendicular to the ground for any forces that aren't entirely parallel or perpendicular.

c. Use the perpendicular components to work out the normal force and hence the frictional force in terms of F, the force the player exerts on the tire via the rope.

d. Use the parallel components to work out a value for F.

The normal force acts perpendicular to the surface – so you'll need to turn any vector that's not already perpendicular or parallel to the surface into components.

As the normal force depends on all of the other force components perpendicular to the surface (as it needs to balance them all so that the net force in the direction is zero), it should be the last thing you calculate.

If the velocity in a particular direction is constant (or zero) then there is no net force in that direction, i.e. all the components must add up to zero.

An important thing to remember when doing problems that involve forces is that 'constant velocity' is shorthand for 'no net force'. Usually, this means that the frictional force will have the same size as the component of the force that's causing the object to move.

How does kicking a football work?

So the game's nearly complete ... but the SimFootball team want to make kicking the football as realistic as possible. They've got their hands on some freeze frame footage - and have worked out the ball's **velocity** as it heads for goal. But they need you to work out the **average force** of the kick so they can program it in

But how are you going to do that when you don't know the ball's **acceleration**, can't use $\mathbf{F}_{net} = m\mathbf{a}$?

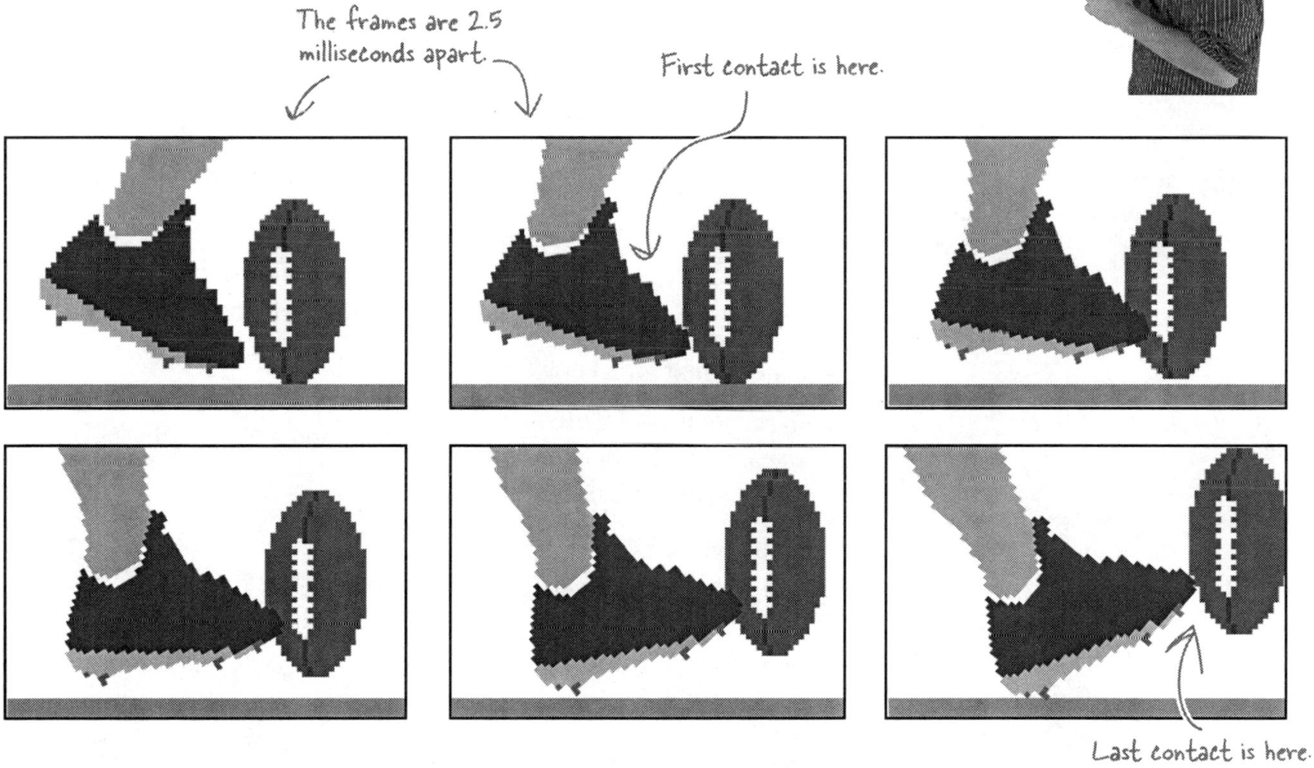

BRAIN POWER

What might you be able to do with the images to work out the average force that the ball experiences when the player kicks it?

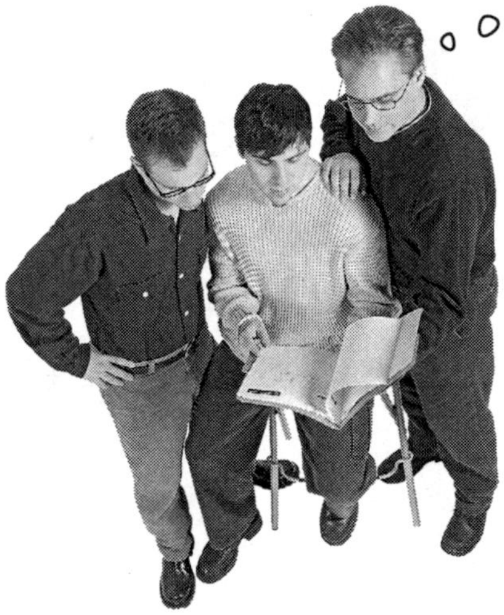

Jim: But we don't know the football's **acceleration** - we only know the **velocity** that it takes off with.

Frank: Hmm, good point.

Jim: Can we somehow use the freeze frame footage to work out the acceleration?

Joe: I think that's gonna be difficult. The ball deforms when it's kicked, then expands to its normal shape again. Which part of the ball would we use to work out the acceleration, when different parts are moving in different ways?!

Frank: But we **can** use the freeze frames to work out the **time** that the foot's in contact with the ball for. It looks like it's around 10 milliseconds... if we can use the time, it might help us somehow.

Joe: Oh ... hang on! Newton's second Law isn't actually $\mathbf{F}_{net} = m\mathbf{a}$, is it? In its purest form, it actually says that when you apply a force for a period of time, then it causes a **change in momentum**.

Jim: So you're saying that we can use $\mathbf{F}_{net}\Delta t = \Delta\mathbf{p}$ (where $\mathbf{p} = m\mathbf{v}$)? That's cool: momentum is mass × velocity, and we know what both of these are for the football!.

Frank: And we can get the time of contact from the freeze frame! That's the time that the force acts for, isn't it? 10 milliseconds?

Jim: Yeah, that sounds good. Though the force doesn't look like it'll be the same all the time. I'm sure the middle of the kick exerts more force than the start or end of it ...

Joe: But we've been asked to find the **average force**. When we were finding average speeds it was only the overall change in position that counted. So with the football, we can use the overall change in momentum to work out the average force.

Frank: So we are using Newton's Second Law like I suggested all along - but just a **different form** of it.

Jim: Yeah. Come on - let's do it!

Earlier on, you rewrote Newton's Second Law, having originally worked it out from momentum conservation.

You can rewrite Newton's Second Law as F

Newton's Second Law says that if you apply a net force to an object for a period of time, then its momentum changes. So force is rate of change of momentum:

$$F = \frac{\Delta(mv)}{\Delta t}$$ ← Rate of change of momentum

Usually the mass of an object doesn't change during the time that the force is applied. This means that m is constant, so you can rewrite the equation as:

$$F = m\frac{\Delta v}{\Delta t}$$ (m is constant; v changes with time)

But you already know that $\frac{\Delta v}{\Delta t}$ is the rate of change of velocity - i.e. acceleration.

So you can rewrite your equation as:

F = ma

This is the form of Newton's Second Law you'll use on your course.

Newton's Second Law in its purest form is:

$$F_{net} = \frac{\Delta p}{\Delta t}$$

$F\Delta t$ is called impulse

You can work out the force of the kick using a slightly different form of Newton's Second Law, $\mathbf{F}\Delta t = \Delta\mathbf{p}$. The quantity $\mathbf{F}\Delta t$ is also called **impulse**, and the equation says that impulse is equal to the change in something's **momentum**.

If you have a problem where your first instinct is to use $\mathbf{F}_{net} = m\mathbf{a}$ but you don't know the acceleration, look to see if you know the **mass** and **velocity** at the start and at the end.

If you do, you can work out the change in momentum, which is equal to the impulse, and then get the force from that.

Foot is in contact with ball for time Δt during which it exerts force F on it.

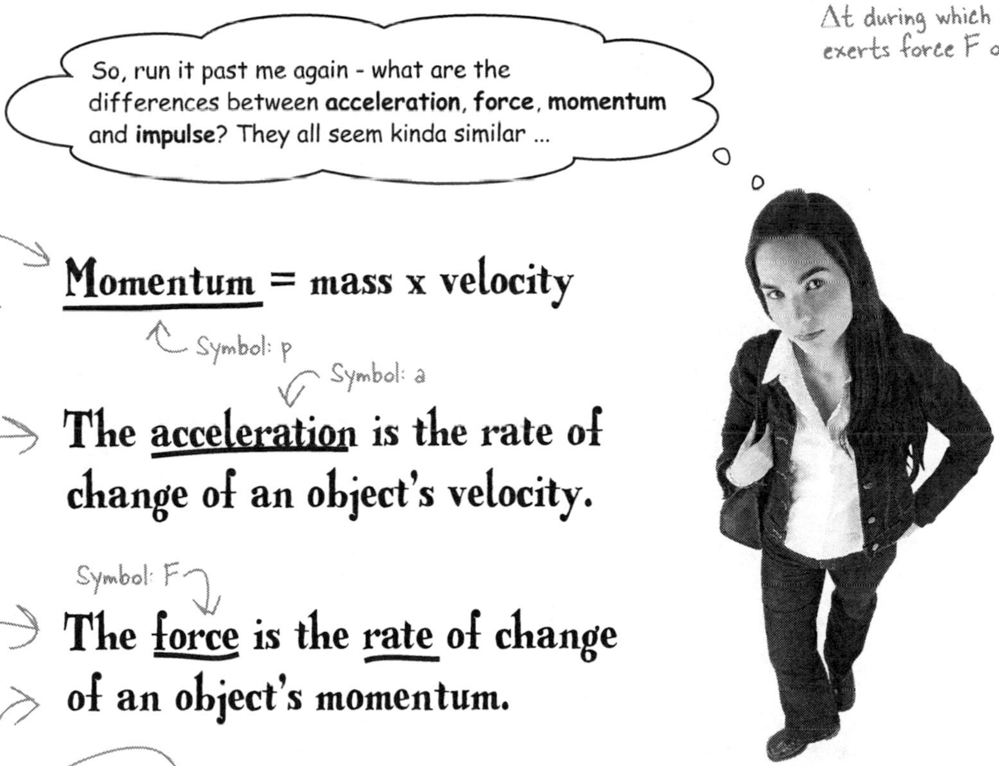

The total momentum of everything taking part in an interaction is conserved.

Momentum = mass x velocity

Symbol: p

Symbol: a

The acceleration is the rate of change of an object's velocity.

These are related by the equation $F_{net} = ma$

Symbol: F

The force is the rate of change of an object's momentum.

If you apply a force for a short time, you get a smaller change in momentum than if you apply it for a long time.

The impulse is the actual change in an object's momentum.

Δp also happens to be called impulse. And you can write down the equation $F\Delta t = \Delta p$

Some people give impulse the symbol J, many others don't bother with a symbol.

Sharpen your pencil

a. The programmer wants to know the average force of the kick. The football has a mass of 400 grams and from the freeze frames, you can tell that the foot and ball are in contact for 10 ms (milliseconds). If the ball leaves the boot at an angle of 45° and travels 60 m, work out the force of the kick.

Hint: 45° is when the horizontal and vertical components of the ball's velocity are equal.

Hint: Use equations of motion to calculate the initial velocity. Look back at pages $$-$$ of chapter 10 if you get stuck, as the problem there is very similar.

Hint: Once you know the initial velocity, you can use $\mathbf{F}\Delta t = \Delta\mathbf{p}$. (Remember that $\mathbf{p} = mv$)

b. Experiencing a large net contact force hurts! Explain, using impulse, why football players wear padding.

Sharpen your pencil Solution

a. The programmer wants to know the average force of the kick. The football has a mass of 400 grams and from the freeze frames, you can tell that the foot and ball are in contact for 10 ms (milliseconds). If the ball leaves the boot at an angle of 45° and travels 60 m, work out the force of the kick.

Hint: 45° is when the horizontal and vertical components of the ball's velocity are equal.

Hint: Use equations of motion to calculate the initial velocity. Look back at pages $$-$$ of chapter 10 if you get stuck, as the problem there is very similar.

Hint: Once you know the initial velocity, you can use $\mathbf{F}\Delta t = \Delta \mathbf{p}$. (Remember that $\mathbf{p} = mv$)

Use $F\Delta t = \Delta mv$ to work out the force. So work out the initial velocity, v_0, from 60 m range.

45° angle, so $v_{0h} = v_{0v}$ Pythagoras: $v_0^2 = v_{0h}^2 + v_{0v}^2$

$\Rightarrow v_0^2 = 2v_{0v}^2$

$v_0 = \sqrt{2}\, v_{0v}$

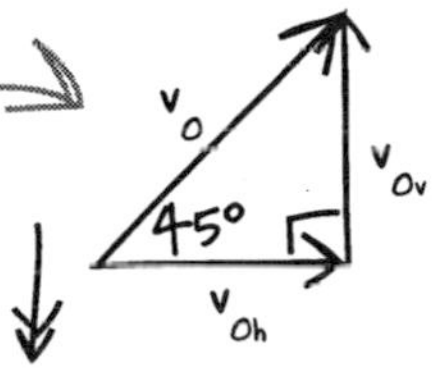

Symmetry: Replace v_v with $-v_{0v}$ in every equation you use

$a = -9.81\ m/s^2$

$x_0 = 0\ m$

$x = 60\ m$

UP is positive

RIGHT is positive

Get time from vertical component, then distance in that time from horizontal.

Vertically: $v_v = -v_{0v}$ because of symmetry. Use this in equation of motion:

$v_v = v_{0v} + at$

$t = \dfrac{-v_{0v} - v_{0v}}{a} = \dfrac{-2v_{0v}}{-9.8} = 0.204v_{0v}$

Negative divided by negative is positive.

Use this value for t with horizontal component of velocity.

Horizontally: $v_{0h} = v_{0v} = \dfrac{x - x_0}{t}$

v_{0h} and v_{0v} are the same size. A right-angled triangle with two equal 45° angles has two equal sides.

$v_{0v} = \dfrac{60 - 0}{0.204v_{0v}}$

There's a v_{0v} on both sides, so you can solve for v_{0v}, and then for v.

Multiply both sides by v_{0v} → $v_{0v}^2 = 294 \Rightarrow v_{0v} = 17.1\ m/s$ (3 sd)

From 45° triangle, $v_0 = \sqrt{2}\, v_{0v} \Rightarrow v_0 = \sqrt{2} \times 17.1 = 24.2\ m/s$ (3 sd)

This is contact time for foot and ball, not flight time!

Rearrange $F\Delta t = \Delta mv$ to get F: $F = \dfrac{\Delta mv}{\Delta t} = \dfrac{0.4 \times 24.2}{10 \times 10^{-3}} = 968\ N$

Force is measured in Newtons.

The average force of the kick is 970 N (2 sd).

b. Experiencing a large net contact force hurts! Explain, using impulse, why football players wear padding.

If you have velocity v and are tackled so that your final velocity = 0, your momentum has changed from mv to 0. And Newton's Second Law / impulse says that $F\Delta t = mv$

If you're not wearing padding, then this happens over a short time. So F is high and it hurts.

If you're wearing padding, then this happens over a longer period of time, as the padding deforms. So F is lower than if you weren't wearing any padding at all and it hurts less.

If a collision takes more time, the average force is lower - and it hurts less!

there are no Dumb Questions

Q: So why does this thing have the special name "impulse"? Why can't I just call it "change in momentum" like we've been doing all along?

A: Because "impulse" is what it's called! If you understand how it works that's great - but you need to be able to communicate with other people who call it impulse.

Q: But if I explain what I mean, won't they get it?

A: If your exam question asks you to explain something using impulse (like the question about padding did) then you need to know what impulse is.

Q: Yeah, the question about padding. Surely padding works because it absorbs some of the hit so you don't feel it as much by the time it gets to you? What does that have to do with impulse?

A: You just said "the time it gets to you". If the interaction takes place over a longer time, the average force is lower.

Q: What does that have to do with it?

A: Big forces hurt! If you were wearing a suit of armor instead of padding, it wouldn't deform. The collision would take the same time as it did before, and it would hurt just as much.

The game's great - but there's just been a spec change!

You and the SimFootball team have come up with a realistic game that's also fun to play! Big win! But before you all collect your VIP passes, the CEO takes a look at the game - and decides he wants to have a mode where you can play football on the moon!

The strength of the moon's gravitational field is lower then the Earth's

The moon is smaller and less massive than the Earth, so the gravitational force it exerts on objects is less, which means its gravitational field strength is less. You need to work out how this will affect the physics of the game

The players will be in a pressurized dome where there's plenty of air, so you don't need to worry about anything medical!

BRAIN POWER

How is being on the moon going to affect the game (if at all)?

Sharpen your pencil

Which aspects of the game will change as a result of being on the moon and which will stay the same? The SimFootball programming team have already had a go at guessing what will happen - and you need to decide whether each of these statements is correct or not.

If you think a statement and the reasoning is correct, please explain why, using physics.

If a statement is incorrect, or an incorrect reason is given for a correct statement, then please explain why using physics - to debunk the myth! Use relevant equations wherever you can.

a. The ball will go further when passed horizontally because it weighs less so is easier to throw.

b. The ball will go further when passed horizontally because it weighs less so spends longer in the air.

c. The ball will go further when passed horizontally because the gravitational field strength is less.

d. There will be less friction in the game so the players will slide further.

e. Tackles will involve less force because the players weight less.

f. The optimal angle where punts go furthest won't be 45° any more because the ball weighs less.

g. The ball will have a higher velocity when it leaves a player's boot because it weighs less.

h. If a player runs into and collides with a goalpost, it will hurt less because they weigh less.

Sharpen your pencil Solution

Which aspects of the game will change as a result of being on the moon and which will stay the same? The SimFootball programming team have already had a go at guessing what will happen - and you need to decide whether each of these statements is correct or not.

If you think a statement and the reasoning is correct, please explain why, using physics.

If a statement is incorrect, or an incorrect reason is given for a correct statement, then please explain why using physics - to debunk the myth! Use relevant equations wherever you can.

a. The ball will go further when passed horizontally because it weighs less so is easier to throw.

No – wrong reason! The ball still has the same mass. Throwing force $F_{net} = ma$ so the acceleration (and velocity) depend on the ball's mass, not its weight, if it's thrown horizontally.

b. The ball will go further when passed horizontally because it weighs less so spends longer in the air.

Yes. The ball accelerates vertically because of its weight. On the moon, the ball weighs less. Therefore it will go further, as it'll have a longer time to travel horizontally.

c. The ball will go further when passed horizontally because the gravitational field strength is less.

Yes. This is just another way of wording the statement in b.

d. There will be less friction in the game so the players will slide further.

Yes. If the gravitational field strength is less, the players weigh less, and the normal force is less. Therefore, there will be less friction in the game and the players will slide further.

e. Tackles will involve less force because the players weight less.

No. Newton's 2nd Law is $F_{net} = ma$. Tackling is horizontal. So their weights have nothing to do with it (weight would only have an effect if they were tackling vertically!).

f. The optimal angle where punts go furthest won't be 45° any more because the ball weighs less.

No. The optimal angle is always 45° whatever planet you're on!

g. The ball will have a higher velocity when it leaves a player's boot because it weighs less.

No. $F\Delta t = \Delta(mv)$. Force, time and mass are still the same, so the velocity is still the same.

h. If a player runs into and collides with a goalpost, it will hurt less because they weigh less.

No. Same reason as a, e and g. Any time the change is in the horizontal direction but not the vertical direction, the important thing is the mass, not the weight.

For added realism, sometimes the players should slip

After successfully adding the 'moon mode', the SimFootball team have decided that the game needs one more element. At the moment, the players are able to make impossibly tight turns and **change direction** more or less instantly. But if they tried that in real life, they would **slip**.

But what makes someone slip? Or rather - what makes someone able to change direction in the first place? A change of direction means a change in velocity. Newton's First Law says that for a velocity to change, there must be a net force. But where does the force that enables a player to change direction come from?

Sharpen your pencil

a. If a player changes direction, they change velocity, so there must be a net force acting on them in the same direction as the change in velocity.

Explain where this force comes from, and why a player might slip in real life.

b. Describe in words how you'd go about working out whether a player will slip when they change direction.

Sharpen your pencil Solution

a. If a player changes direction, they change velocity, so there must be a net force acting on them in the same direction as the change in velocity.

Explain where this force comes from, and why a player might slip in real life.

The player can change direction because of friction between their foot and the ground.

If the player exerts a force on the ground with their foot, the ground exerts an equally-sized force on the player in the opposite direction – a Newton's Third Law pair of forces.

If the force required for the change in direction is smaller than the force that can be provided by friction, then the player will slip.

b. Describe in words how you'd go about working out whether a player will slip when they change direction.

Work out what the player's change in momentum is when they change direction.

Work out what the maximum friction force is given the player's weight, the normal force and the surface he's playing on.

$F\Delta t = \Delta p$ Use what you worked out for F and Δp to work out how long the player's foot needs to be in contact with the ground to provide this change in momentum.

Estimate whether this is reasonable or not.

You can change only direction horizontally on a flat surface because of friction

If you're trying to change direction horizontally on a flat surface, friction is the only thing that can provide the force you require to change your momentum. Otherwise, you would slip (unless there's a convenient wall or curb you can push against instead).

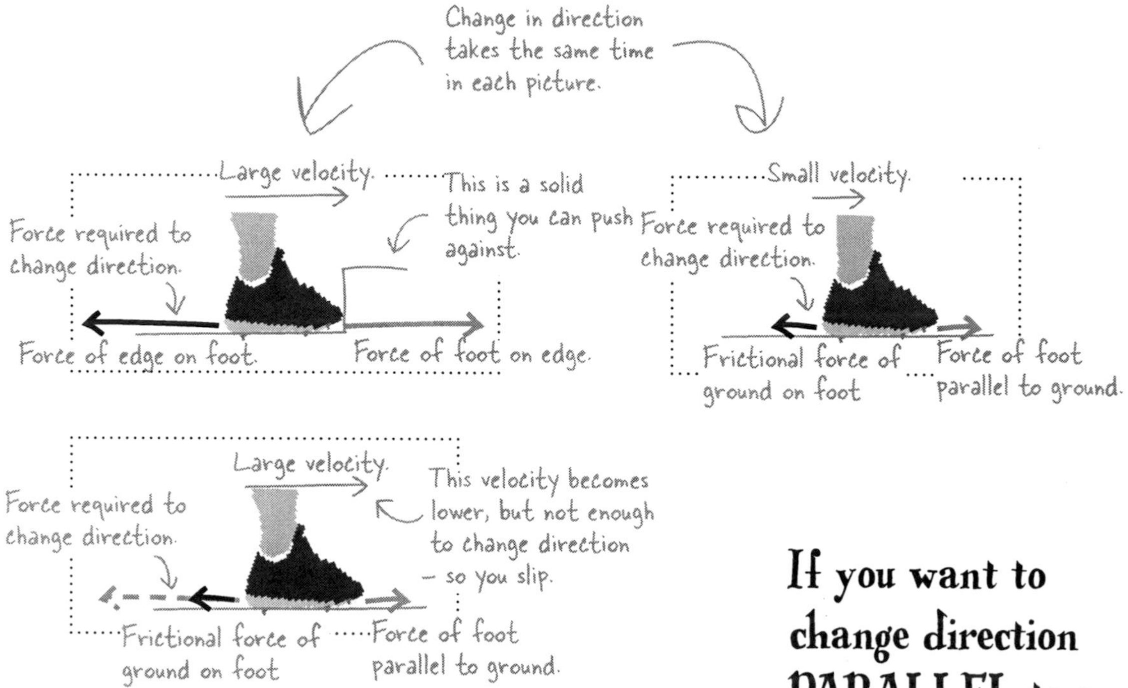

If you want to change direction PARALLEL to a surface, friction is the only thing that can provide the force you require.

The game is brilliant, and going to X-Force rocks!

SimFootball is a success! Using physics, you were able to turn the real game into a computer game. Everything acts just like it should - on Earth and on the moon!

Newton's Laws give you awesome powers

You can use momentum conservation, Newton's Laws and free body diagrams to work out problems that involve forces.

The fundamental thing you can work out from experiments.

Total momentum is conserved.

Constant velocity (or zero velocity) means no net force.

Newton One: Things carry on.

This comes from momentum conservation

Newton Two: $F_{net} = ma$

Draw a FREE BODY DIAGRAM to work out the net force.

This comes from momentum conservation.

Newton Three: Push you, push me.

Forces come in pairs that are the same size in opposite directions and act on different objects.

BULLET POINTS

- Always start with a free body diagram of all the forces acting on an object.
- Mark on all the forces.
- Is there a net force?
- Work out forces you don't know.
- Use $\mathbf{F}_{net} = ma$ to determine how the object moves.
- Remember the impulse form of Newton's Second Law: $\mathbf{F}_{net}\Delta t = \Delta \mathbf{p}$
- Total momentum is conserved!

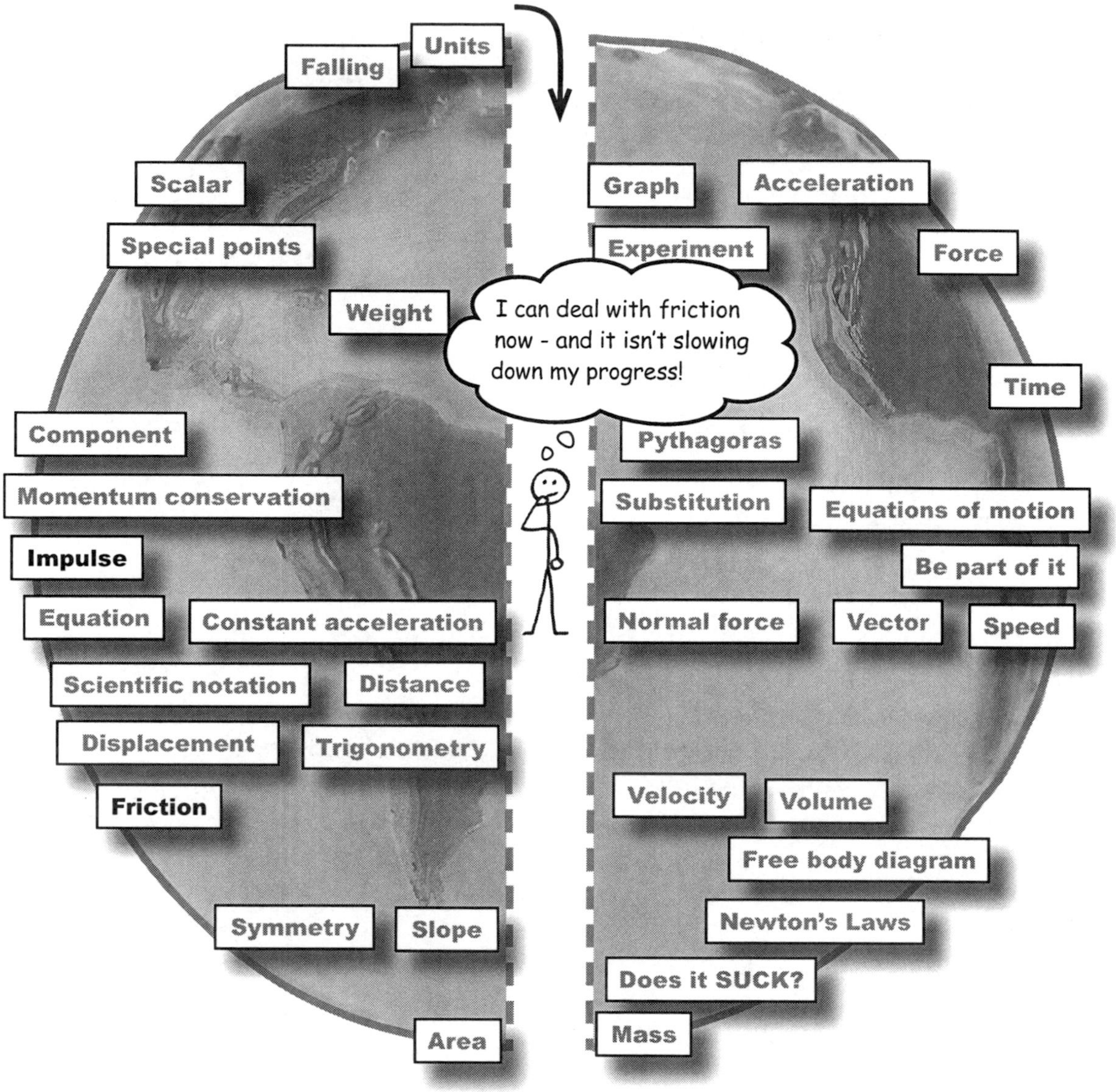

☑ **Friction** — **A contact-dependent force that opposes motion.**

☑ **Impulse** — **Impulse is equal to the change in momentum, $F_{net}\Delta t$. Impulse is sometimes given the symbol J.**

CHAPTER 12

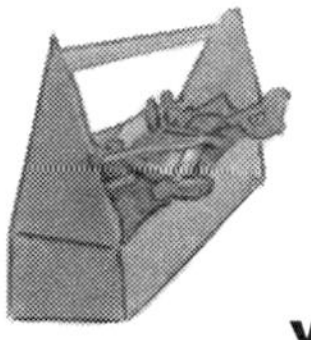

Your Physics Toolbox

You've got Chapter 12 under your belt and added some problem-solving concepts to your toolbox.

How many objects?

Before you start a problem, think about how many objects there are interacting in it.

If there is only one object, you can probably use equations of motion to work out what happens

But if there are two or more objects, or if there are forces involved, then look to use Newton's Laws, momentum conservation or impulse (or a combination of these).

Working with forces and equations of motion

A common way of making progress on a problem is to use Newton's 2nd Law (usually in the form $F_{net} = ma$, though occasionally in the form $F_{net}\Delta t = \Delta p$) to calculate the acceleration (or velocity) an object experiences.

Then you can use this value in your equations of motion to find out how the object moves as a result of the force.

Calculating friction

The friction experienced by an object on a surface depends on the normal force and the coefficient of friction, μ, for that object and that surface.

$$F_{fric} = \mu F_N$$

The normal force

Be careful when calculating the normal force as part of a friction problem (or indeed any problem).

The normal force is perpendicular to a surface. As long as the object in contact with the surface isn't accelerating in the perpendicular direction, the normal force has the right size to make the net perpendicular force equal to zero.

"Constant velocity"

If an object moves with "constant velocity", it means that there is no net force on an object

To solve a problem where an object moves with constant velocity, you should draw a free body diagram and start equating forces and/or components of forces.

13 torque and work

Getting a lift

You can use your physics knowledge to do superhuman feats.

In this chapter, you'll learn how to harness torque to perform amazing displays of strength, by using a lever to exert a much larger force than you could on your own. However, you can't get something for nothing - **energy** is always **conserved** and the amount of **work** you do to give something **gravitational potential energy** by lifting it doesn't change.

Half the kingdom to anyone who can lift the sword in the stone ...

The sword in the stone has acquired near-legendary status. But now, in a shock move, anyone can attempt to lift it.

There are rules of course - but the promise of half the kingdom for anyone who succeeds is completely genuine.

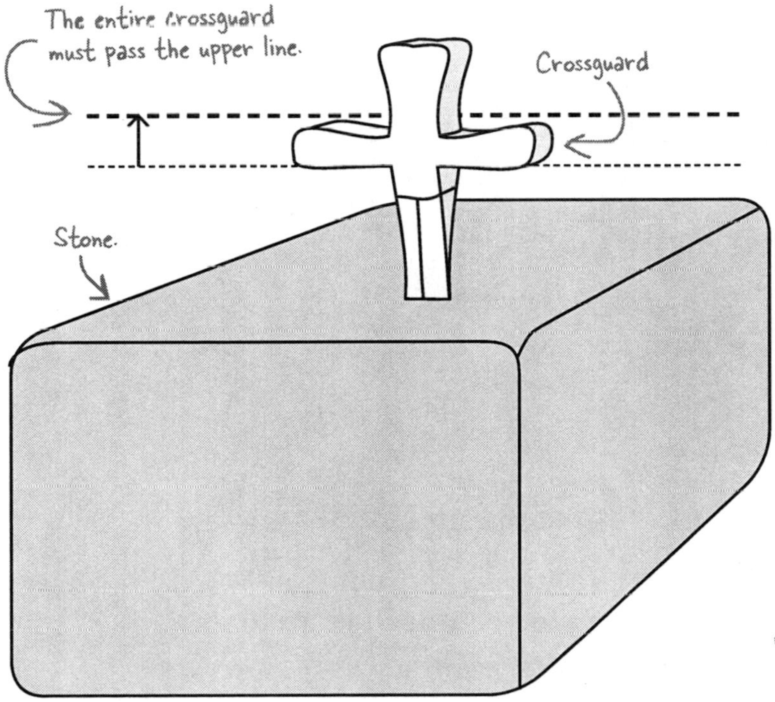

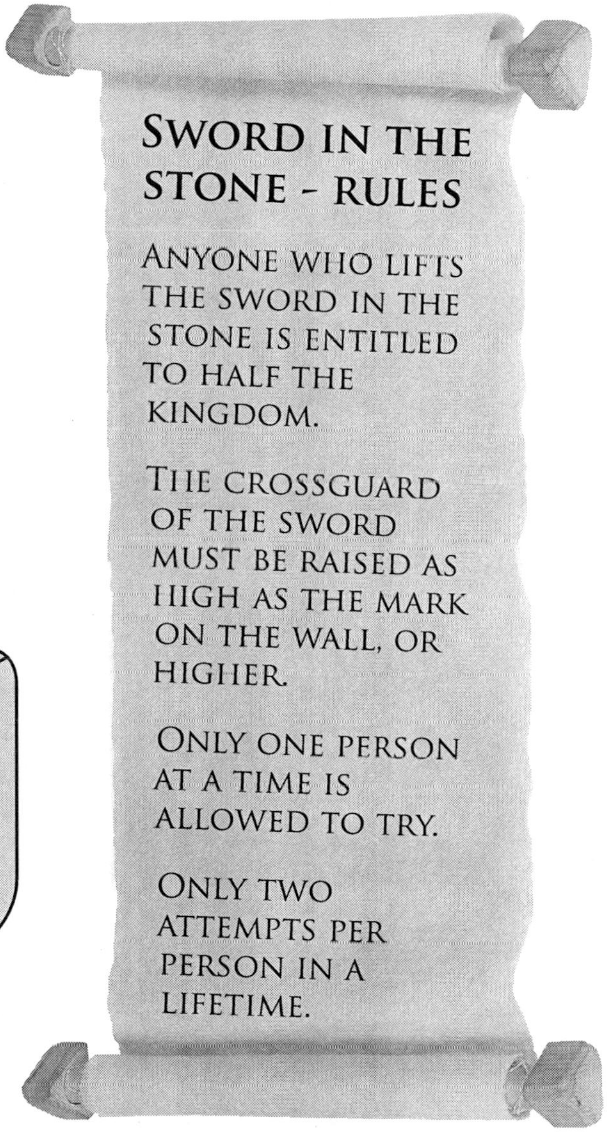

Can physics help you to lift a heavy object?

The rules say that the crossguard of the sword must go up by at least 10.0 cm to reach the line. But they don't say anything about whether the sword needs to be detached from the stone at the time!

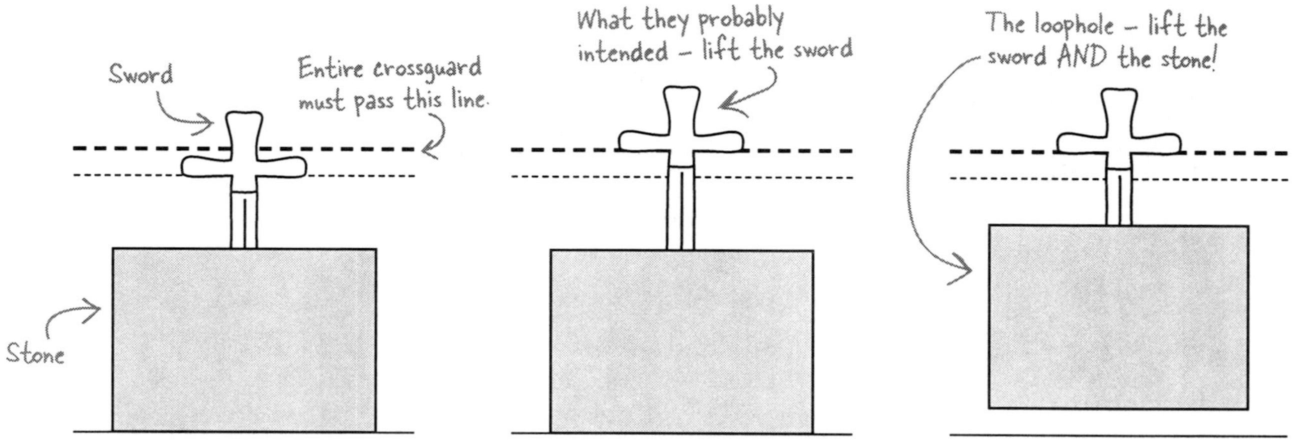

If you can use **physics** to lift both the sword **and** the stone 10.0 cm off the ground, you'll win. The only thing is the stone is far too **heavy** for one person to lift on their own, and it's not like you can take it to the moon to reduce its weight or use something like a crane that hasn't been invented yet...

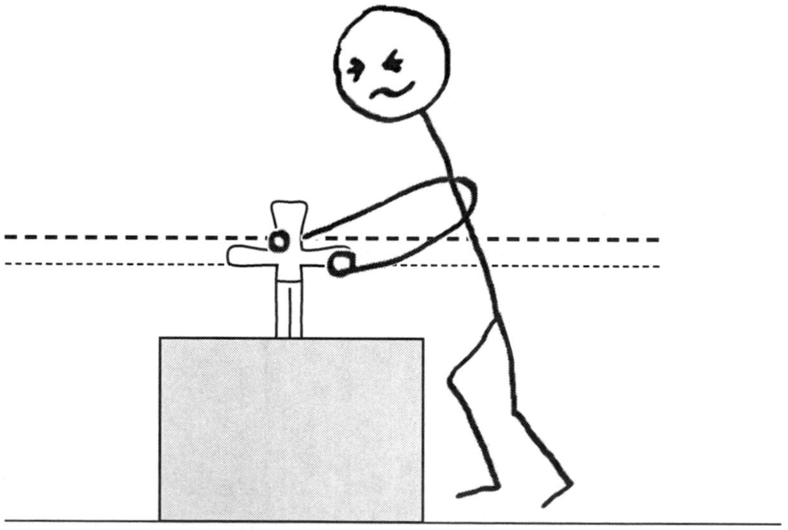

BRAIN POWER

Think about the physics you've learned so far. How might you be able to lift the sword and the stone?

Jim: So how are we gonna do it? How do people use physics to lift heavy objects. **What's it like** ... ?

Joe: Maybe "how do people lift heavy objects" is the wrong question. Lifting involves applying an upwards **force** at least equal to the **weight** of the thing you're trying to lift. So maybe we should be thinking about how people apply large forces to objects.

Frank: That's a really good point.

Jim: Um ... how can we say that an **equal** force will lift it? Wouldn't we need to apply a force **greater** than the sword and stone's weight to get it to move upwards?

Joe: Once you've got the sword and stone going (with a force slightly larger than its weight) the most efficient way to lift it is to use a force equal to its weight. If there's no net force, it'll go up with a constant velocity.

Jim: Ah - I forgot about that Newton stuff. So if we can somehow apply a force equal to the sword and stone's weight, we'll be OK.

Frank: So how do people apply large forces? What circumstances might I want to use a large force in? **What's it like?**

Frank: Well, I guess that if you want to get through a locked door without a key, you could pry it open. You'd use a **crowbar** for that - to apply a large enough force to break either the door or the lock.

Joe: So how does that work?! I guess it has a long handle and a short claw ... you use it like a **lever**. You push down on the long end, and the short end does a lot of damage!

Jim: Yeah - far more damage than your pushing force would do if you just pushed on the door directly. Somehow, the force that the lever exerts on the door is greater than the force you exert on it.

Frank: So maybe we can rig up a lever with a long end and a short end to exert a larger force on the sword and stone than we can manage directly. I think we're on to something here ...

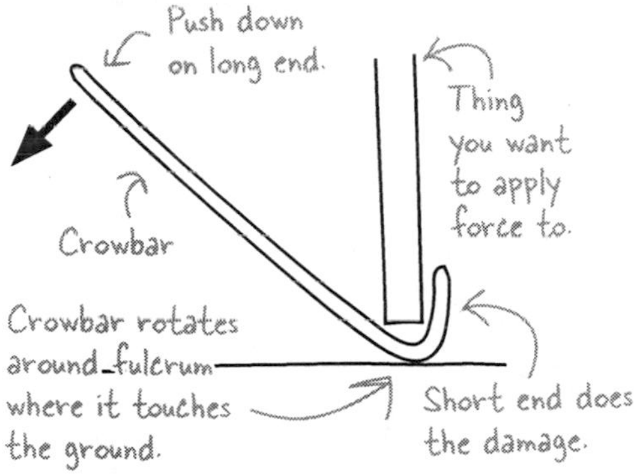

If you're asking "what's it like?" try to <u>generalize</u>. Ask "How can I apply a large force?" instead of "How can I lift a heavy thing?"

Use a lever to turn a small force into a larger force

It's just not possible for one person to generate enough force on their own to lift the sword and the stone - it weighs too much.

But by using a **lever**, you can exert a greater force on the sword and stone than you can manage by grabbing and pulling. You can use physics to **increase the force** you can generate.

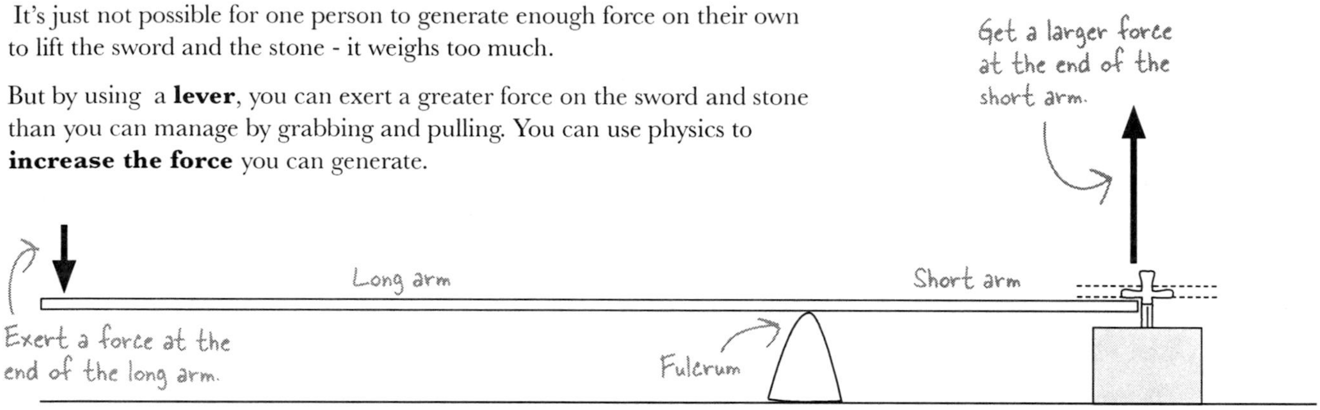

A lever is a bit like a seesaw - a rigid bar that can **rotate** about a **fulcrum** (or pivot point). If you push down on one end, the other end goes up.

In physics, the two sides of the lever are called the **arms**. If the lever arms are different **lengths**, you can use the lever to exert a large force at the end of the short arm by pushing down on the long arm.

But what size of force do you need to generate to lift the sword and stone?

Use a lever to exert a larger force than you could on your own.

A lever's arms aren't like your arms – they always move together and can't move independently.

Sharpen your pencil

The stone is granite. We looked it up, and 1.00 cm^3 of this granite has a mass of 2.680 grams.

a. The stone is 1.0000 m by 0.8100 m by 0.6900 m. What is the mass of the stone?

Hint: Be careful with the units!

b. The sword's mass is 2.2 kg. What is the minimum force required to lift the sword and stone?

Sharpen your pencil Solution

The stone is granite. We looked it up, and 1.00 cm^3 of this granite has a mass of 2.680 grams.

a. The stone is 1.0000 m by 0.8100 m by 0.6900 m. What is the mass of the stone?

Work out volume of block in cm^3 then multiply that by 2.680 grams to get mass.

$$\text{Volume} = 100.0 \times 81.0 \times 69.0 = 558900 \text{ cm}^3$$

$$\text{Mass} = 560000 \times 2.68 = 1500000 \text{ g} = \underline{\underline{1498 \text{ kg}}} \text{ (4 sd)}$$

It's generally best to give your answers in SI units - in this case, kg rather than grams.

b. The sword's mass is 2.2 kg. What is the minimum force required to lift the sword and stone?

$$\text{Total mass} = 1498 + 2.2 = 1500 \text{ kg (4 sd)}$$

Minimum force will be the same size as the sword and stone's weight.

$$\text{Weight} = mg = 1500 \times 9.8 = \underline{\underline{14700 \text{ N}}} \text{ (3 sd)}$$

Zero net force (weight + lifting force) means that you can lift the sword and stone with a constant velocity - Newton's 1st Law.

Be careful not to get 'g' (grams) and 'g' (gravitational field strength) mixed up!

there are no Dumb Questions

Q: We've assumed that the minimum force required to lift an object is equal to its weight. But surely you need to use a larger force?

A: Newton's 1st Law says that if the net force is zero, an object will move at a constant velocity. So the most efficient way to lift something is to exert a force on it that's a tiny bit larger than its weight for a short time. This gives it a small upwards velocity. Then you can continue with a force **equal** to its weight, so the object continues to move upwards with this velocity.

Q: So you DO need a force larger than the object's weight!

A: Yes, but only slightly larger and for a very short period of time to get it started. You can approximate this to a force equal to the object's weight (with an extra initial 'nudge').

Q: We've called the two ends of the lever "arms". But doesn't that imply that they can move independently (like my own two arms)?

A: Talking about the "arms" of a lever is physics terminology. Each side of the lever is an arm - but they're connected together and can't move independently.

Q: The whole setup looks like a seesaw, with two arms and a fulcrum. But how can you increase the force at the other end? Everyone knows that to balance a seesaw, you need the same weight - the same force - at each end.

A: If you have an adult and a child on a seesaw, you can balance them by moving the adult closer to the center. The force of the child's weight is smaller than the force of the adult's weight, but they can still balance.

Q: OK, but the two sides of the seesaw are still the same length, right?

A: Yes, but the distance between the adult and the fulcrum has changed. So the child's small weight is able to provide enough force to lift the adult's larger weight (by balancing then doing a small initial 'nudge' to get going) - just like you'd like to do with the sword and stone.

Q: So you mean that if you get the adult and child to balance, then saw off the 'extra' bit of seesaw behind the adult, I get a lever where the two arms are different lengths, like we were already talking about?

A: You got it! Though you may have to reposition the adult slightly, to compensate for the missing bit of seesaw.

Do an experiment to determine where to position the fulcrum

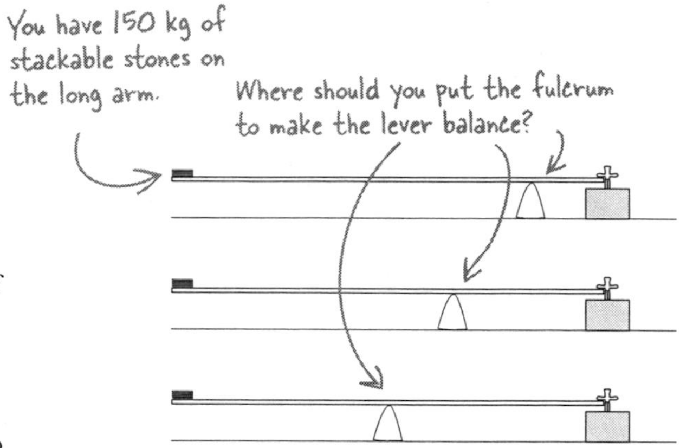

If we use a **lever** to lift the sword and stone, a small force applied to the long arm will be able to exert a large force at the short arm. A quick look on the Sieges-R-Us website reveals that they have ten 15 kg stackable stones in stock - giving us a total of $10 \times 15 = 150$ kg we can place on the long arm.

But where should we put the fulcrum? The rules say only one attempt per lifetime! We need to make sure we have the fulcrum in the right spot before actually trying to use the lever to lift the sword and stone.

Time to design an experiment!

A small force on the long arm can balance out a large force on the short arm.

Sharpen your pencil

Don't worry if you're not sure what some of these items are. Just do your best!

Design an experiment that will allow you to determine the relationship between the two forces required to balance a lever and the distance from the fulcrum to the point each force is applied at.

a. Underline the items of equipment you will use to obtain the data: Stopwatch, Metal ruler, Scales, Protractor, Double-sided tape, Pipette, Triangular prism, Air track, Set of identical masses

b. On the tabletop below, sketch the setup you will use to obtain the data, labelling the fulcrum and any relevant forces and distances.

Table top.

c. Explain how you will carry out the experiment.

Sharpen your pencil Solution

Design an experiment that will allow you to determine the relationship between the two forces required to balance a lever and the distance from the fulcrum to the point each force is applied at.

a. Underline the items of equipment you will use to obtain the data: Stopwatch, Metal ruler, Scales, Protractor, Double-sided tape, Pipette, Triangular prism, Air track, Set of identical masses

b. On the tabletop below, sketch the setup you will use to obtain the data, labelling the fulcrum and any relevant forces and distances.

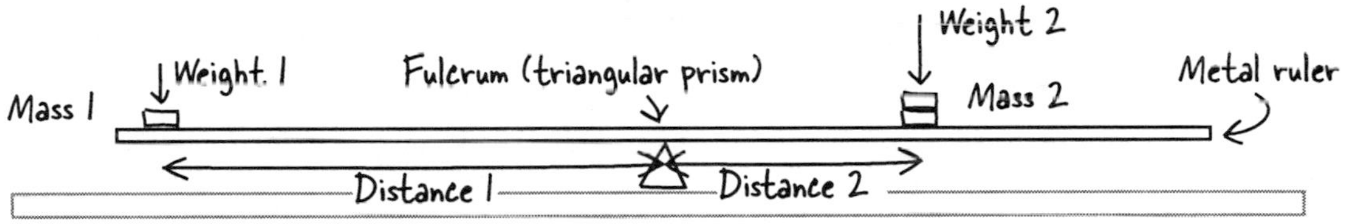

c. Explain how you will carry out the experiment.

Use the prism as the fulcrum and the ruler as the lever. Have the fulcrum in the middle of the ruler (so that the two halves of ruler balance), and put the masses at different distances from the fulcrum. Pile the masses on top of each other so that they press down on the same point, and use small amounts of blutac to avoid them slipping.

Start with one mass at the far end, and make sure one mass an equal distance away balances it. Then try moving two masses up and down to find the balance point. Repeat with three and so on.

Draw a table of results (mass 1, distance 1, mass 2, distance 2) and look for a pattern.

You get credit for any experimental setup that works.

Many 'design an experiment'-style questions are open-ended. You will be provided with a range of equipment, and there may be more than one way of investigating what you've been asked about.

As long as you **describe** what you want to do and **draw** a clearly labelled diagram, you'll get the points if your experiment would work.

When designing an experiment, think about what you can DO with each piece of equipment.

Try it!

We've put the larger mass on the right in the experiment, because the larger mass (sword and stone) is on the right in the other picture.

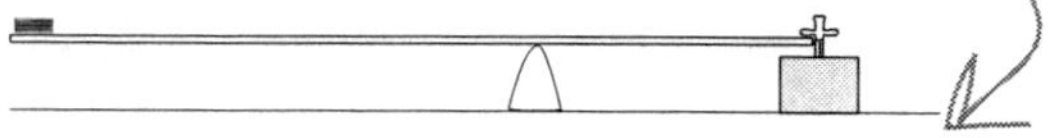

Now you can get on with doing this experiment! Your job is to find the balance point of the ruler when different weights are applied to each arm.

Find five large coins that all have the same value - you'll use these as your weights. You don't need to know the force exerted by a single coin in SI units, as you can use your own unit, the "coin-weight"!

Stick a round pen to a tabletop to use as your fulcrum. Keep it in the center of the ruler, and the smaller weight at one end, then slide the larger pile of coins up and down until the two sides balance. Use the measurements on the ruler to read off the distances between the center of each stack of coins and the fulcrum, and fill in the table below.

Keep this at the end of the ruler

Slide this mass to and fro until the lever balances.

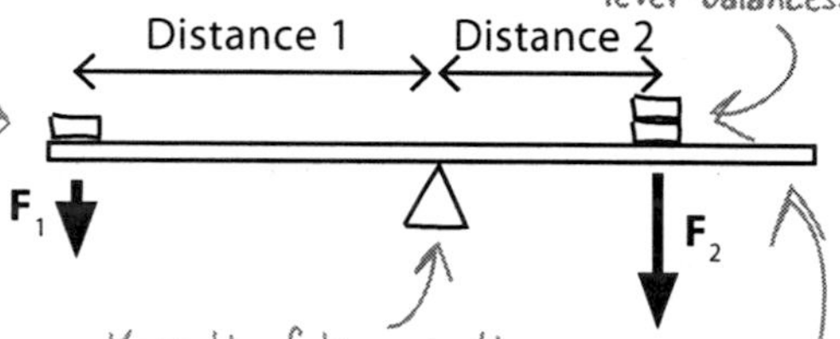

Keep the fulcrum in the center of the ruler

Use a 30 cm (or longer) ruler as your lever.

You can use "coin-weights" as a unit because all of the coins have the same weight.

Force 1 (coin-weights)	Force 2 (coin-weights)	Distance 1 (cm)	Distance 2 (cm)
1	1	15	
1	2	15	
1	3	15	
1	4	15	

We chose 15 cm for Distance 1 because it's halfway along a 30 cm ruler. If your ruler is a different length, then change the value in this column to halfway along your ruler.

Do you see a pattern? Write down anything you notice about the forces and their distances from the fulcrum if the ruler is to balance.

Tried it!

Now you can get on with doing this experiment! Your job is to find the balance point of the ruler when different weights are applied to each arm.

Find five large coins that all have the same value - you'll use these as your weights. You don't need to know the force exerted by a single coin in SI units, as you can use your own unit, the "coin-weight"!

Stick a round pen to a tabletop to use as your fulcrum. Keep it in the center of the ruler, and the smaller weight at one end, then slide the larger pile of coins up and down until the two sides balance. Use the measurements on the ruler to read off the distances between the center of each stack of coins and the fulcrum, and fill in the table below.

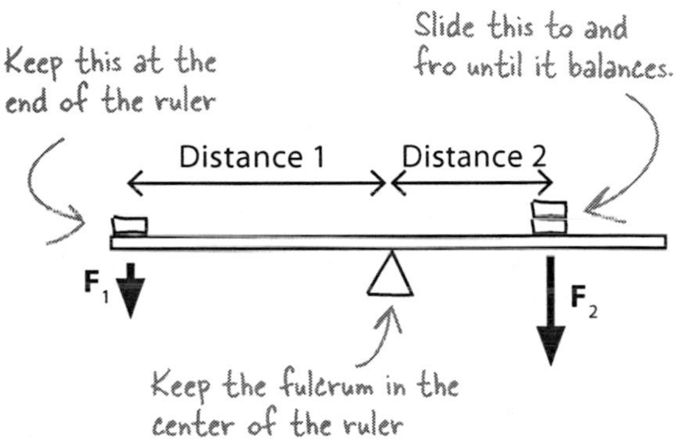

Force 1 (coin-weights)	Force 2 (coin-weights)	Distance 1 (cm)	Distance 2 (cm)
1	1	15	15
1	2	15	7.5
1	3	15	5.0
1	4	15	3.8

These are our results – it's OK if yours are slightly different.

Do you see a pattern? Write down anything you notice about the forces and their distances from the fulcrum if the ruler is to balance.

If I double the force (e.g. by using two coins instead of one) then I need to half the distance between it and the fulcrum to keep the ruler balanced.

I also noticed that number of coins × distance from fulcrum is the same for both sides when the ruler is balanced.

Zero net torque causes the lever to balance

A **torque** is like a 'turning force.' The greater the torque, the greater the effect it has on the **rotational** motion of the object that the torque is applied to. (A torque can also be referred to as a turning moment.)

You might not have thought of the lever rotating - but that's exactly what it would do if the ground wasn't there, but the lever was still supported by its fulcrum.

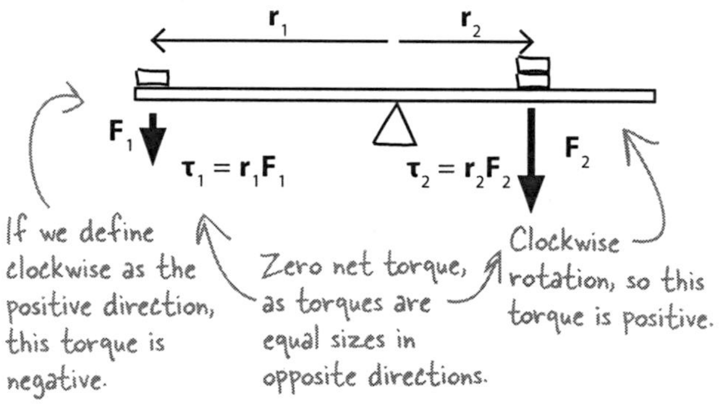

Torque is a **vector** - you define clockwise as positive and counter-clockwise as negative. The direction of rotation depends on the direction of the force and the direction of the displacement. If two torques are the same size but would cause rotation in opposite **directions**, there's zero net torque on the lever, and the lever balances.

The experiment you just did shows that the **size of a torque** is proportional to both the **size of the force** and the **distance from the fulcrum**. So if you double the force, the torque doubles. Or if you double the distance from the fulcrum, the torque doubles.

In physics, the Greek letter **τ** (pronounced 'tau') is used to represent a torque. When you have a fulcrum, torque is defined as the **displacement** from the fulcrum a force is applied at × the component of the **force** perpendicular to the lever. You can write this as an equation: $\boldsymbol{\tau} = \mathbf{r}\mathbf{F}_\perp$

$$\tau = rF_\perp$$

Torque → τ

Displacement from fulcrum to point where force is applied → r

Force perpendicular to lever → $F_\perp$

This symbol means perpendicular. → ⊥

Use **torque** to explain:

a. Why you can lift the sword and stone using a force smaller than their weight.

....

....

....

....

b. Why door handles are positioned far away from the hinges.

....

....

....

....

c. Why a wrench (used to undo nuts and bolts) has a long handle.

....

....

....

....

Exercise Solution

Use **torque** to explain:

a. Why you can lift the sword and stone using a force smaller than their weight.

If you use a lever whose arms are different lengths, a small force acting on the long end can produce the same torque as a large force acting on the short end, as torque = distance from fulcrum × force. So you can use a small force to lift a large weight.

b. Why door handles are positioned far away from the hinges.

To open a door, you need to produce a torque, so that the door rotates round its hinges (fulcrum). If the door handle is far away from the hinges, you need a smaller force to produce the same torque, as the same force applied a greater distance from the fulcrum produces a greater torque.

c. Why a wrench (used to undo nuts and bolts) has a long handle.

You use the handle of the wrench to apply a torque to a nut (the fulcrum is the center of the nut). The longer the handle, the smaller the force you need to apply to produce the same torque.

there are no Dumb Questions

Q: Why are we calling a torque a "turning force" when the seesaw isn't turning - it's just swinging up and down?

A: Swinging is just turning, but not full circle! A seesaw swings around a fulcrum, and if the ground wasn't there it would be able to rotate all the way round.

Q: What's the difference between a force and a torque?

A: To exert a torque on an object, there needs to be a fulcrum that it can rotate about. A torque is a force applied to the object at a distance from the fulcrum, with a component that's perpendicular to the axis of the lever.

There's a picture of this on the opposite page.

Q: In the equation $\tau = rF_{\perp}$, why is the letter r used to represent a displacement instead of x, the letter we usually use?

A: A torque produces a rotation. If you imagine the seesaw rotating all the way around, it would trace out a circle with the fulcrum at the center. The '**r**' stands for 'radius', as the radius of a circle is the distance from its centre to its edge.

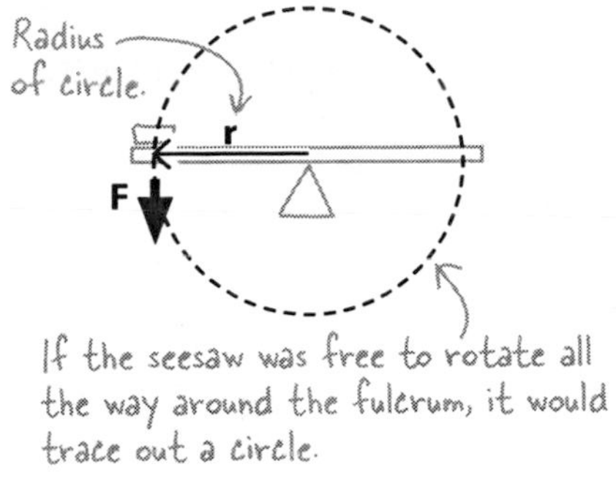

Q: It's confusing to use different letters to represent displacements. Why are we doing that?

A: Using '**r**' in this equation is a physics convention that's followed any time circular motion is involved. It makes you think about the fact that the displacement is a radius, and that rotation is involved.

A torque causes an object to rotate about a fulcrum.

It's the perpendicular component of a force that produces a torque.

Only the force component perpendicular to the lever produces a torque.

In your experiment, the vertical forces you applied always acted perpendicular to the horizontal lever. But sometimes a force will be applied to a lever at an **angle**.

If a force is applied **parallel** to the lever, it won't rotate at all, and the torque will be zero.

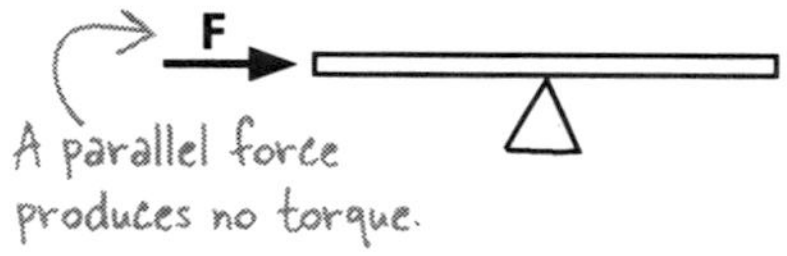

If a force, **F**, is applied at an angle, θ, to the lever, only the **perpendicular component** of **F** will produce a torque.

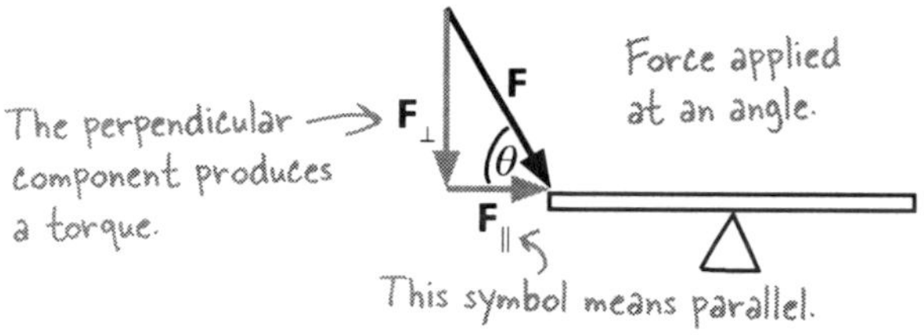

Sharpen your pencil

A force, **F**, is applied to a horizontal lever at a point displacement **r** from the fulcrum. The force is applied in such a way as to make the angle θ with the horizontal.

a. Draw a large sketch showing the lever and the relevant components of **F**.

The sketch will be a large version of this one.

b. Use your sketch to derive an equation for the torque, $\tau = rF_\perp$, in terms of **r**, **F** and θ.

Sharpen your pencil Solution

A force, **F**, is applied to a horizontal lever at a point displacement **r** from the fulcrum. The force is applied in such a way as to make the angle θ with the horizontal.

a. Draw a large sketch showing the lever and the relevant components of **F**.

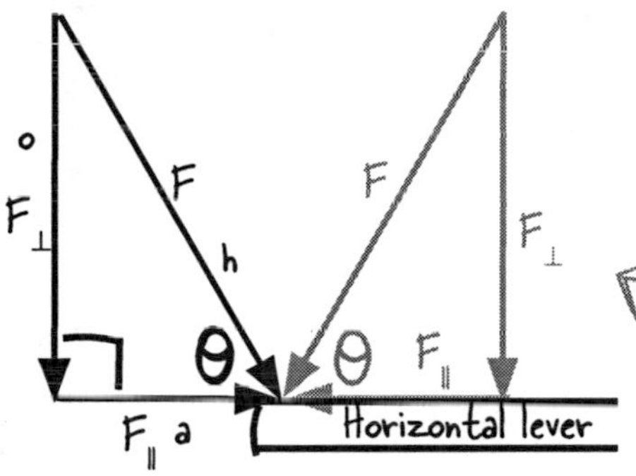

It doesn't matter if the force is pointing "outwards" or "inwards" – the perpendicular component still has the same size and direction.

b. Use your sketch to derive an equation for the torque, $\tau = rF_{\perp}$, in terms of **r**, **F** and θ.

Force is applied at angle θ.

Perpendicular component is opposite side.

$$\sin(\theta) = \frac{o}{h} = \frac{F_{\perp}}{F}$$

$$\Rightarrow \quad F_{\perp} = F\sin(\theta)$$

$$\tau = rF_{\perp}$$

$$\Rightarrow \quad \tau = rF\sin(\theta)$$

This is the equation for torque given on many equation sheets. However, we'd recommend working it out for yourself with triangles, as the equation doesn't make it crystal clear how the angle θ is measured.

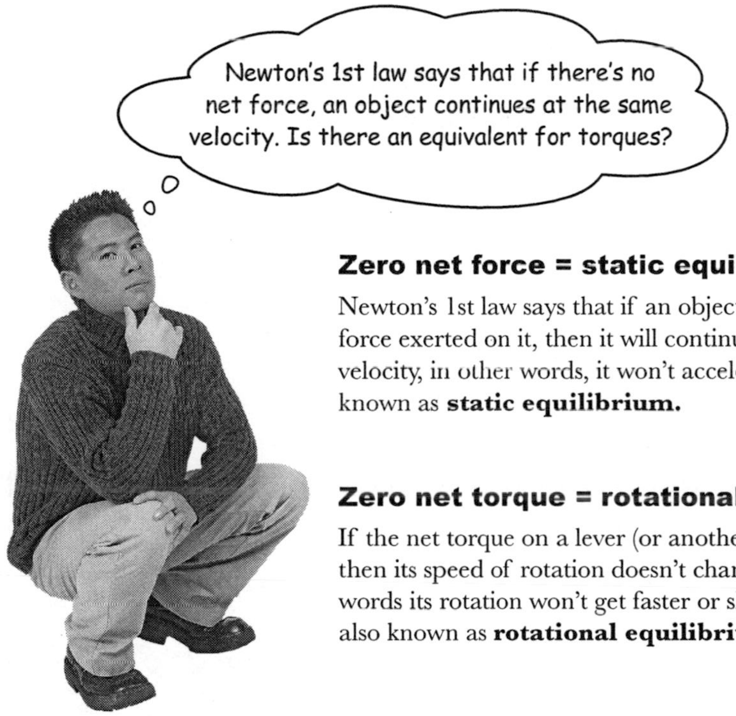

Zero net force = static equilibrium

Newton's 1st law says that if an object has zero net force exerted on it, then it will continue at its current velocity, in other words, it won't accelerate. This is also known as **static equilibrium.**

Zero net torque = rotational equilibrium

If the net torque on a lever (or another object) is zero, then its speed of rotation doesn't change, in other words its rotation won't get faster or slower. This is also known as **rotational equilibrium**.

If a lever isn't rotating (or is spinning at a constant rate) the net torque must be zero.

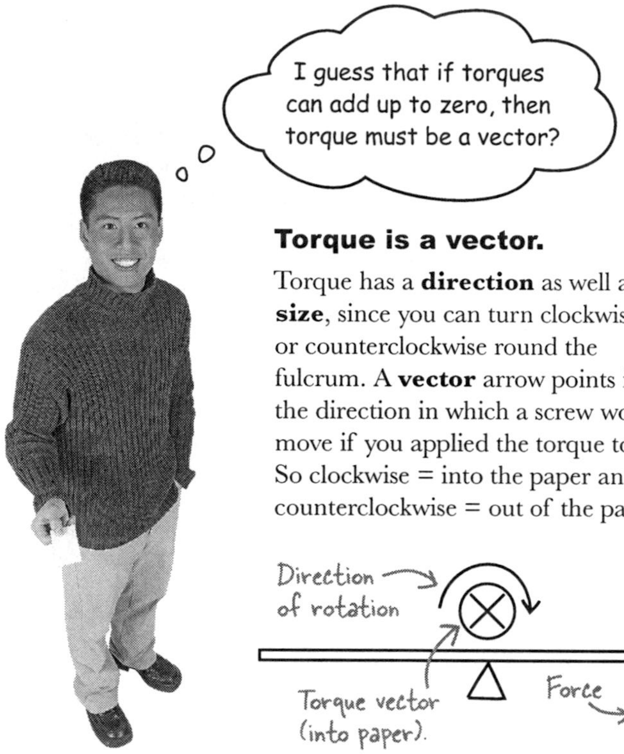

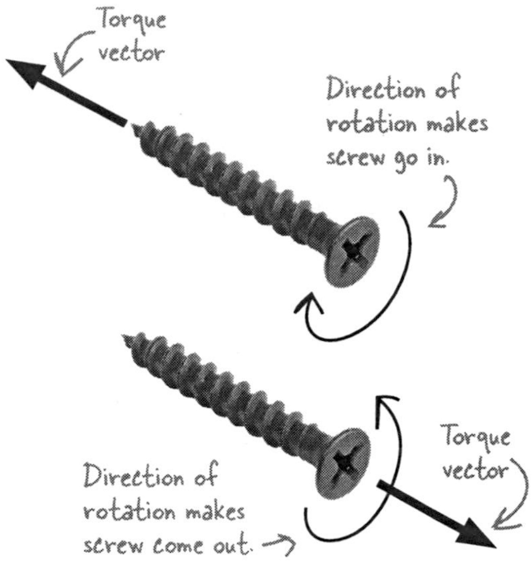

Torque is a vector.

Torque has a **direction** as well as a **size**, since you can turn clockwise or counterclockwise round the fulcrum. A **vector** arrow points in the direction in which a screw would move if you applied the torque to it. So clockwise = into the paper and counterclockwise = out of the paper.

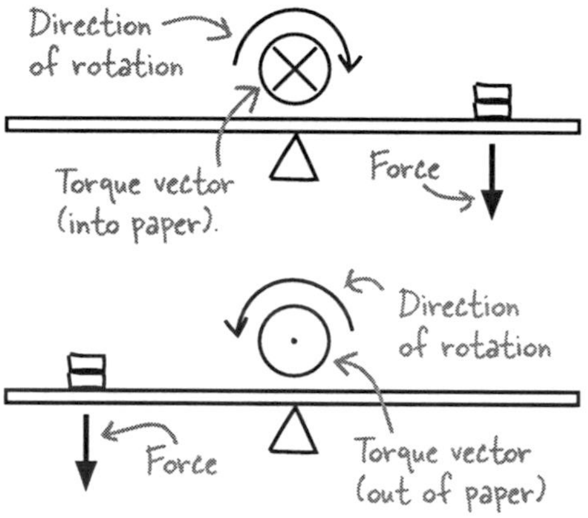

This sounds difficult to draw in only two dimensions, but there's a standard convention that helps.

The symbol for a vector going into the paper is ⊗ (like the head-on view of a screw) and for one coming out of the paper is ⊙, (like the view of the screwpoint).

If you can't imagine which way a screw would move if a torque was applied, then do a 'thumbs up' with your **right hand.** If you curl your fingers in the direction that the object's turning in, then your thumb points in the direction of the torque vector.

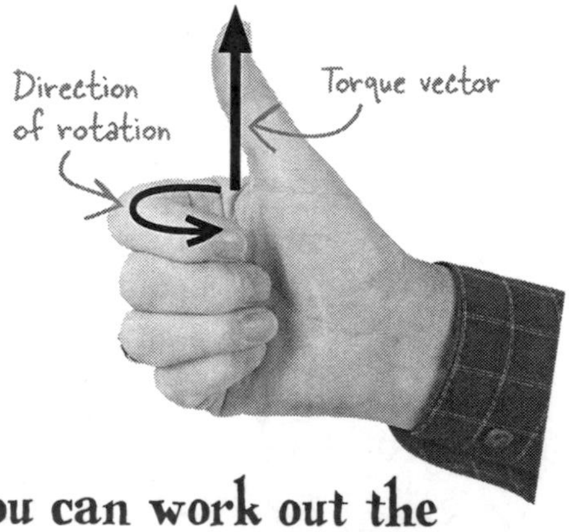

You can work out the direction of the torque vector by doing a 'thumbs up' with your right hand.

there are no Dumb Questions

Q: Can I just memorise the equation $\tau = rF\sin(\theta)$ or look it up on my equation sheet rather than working it out with triangles each time?

A: You can if you like ... but what if you come across a problem where you're given the angle that the force makes with the vertical, rather than the angle it makes with a horizontal lever. If you're used to starting with triangles you can work that out, but if you just assume the equation will be the same, you'll come undone.

Q: What is equilibrium?

A: Equilibrium is another word for balance. Static equilibrium is when forces are balanced - in other words, when the net force is zero. Rotational equilibrium is when the torques are balanced - in other words the net torque is zero.

Equilibrium is another word for balance.

Q: Why is there a distinction between static and rotational equilibrium? Equilibrium's just equilibrium, right?!

A: A rocket firework that's just been started off is in rotational equilibrium, as there's no torque on it. But it isn't in static equilibrium as it's accelerating.

A Catherine-wheel firework that's just been started off isn't in rotational equilibrium, as it's spinning faster and faster due to a non-zero net torque. But it is in static equilibrium - as it isn't going anywhere, the net force on the firework must be zero.

Use torque to lift the sword and the stone!

The force you need to lift the sword and the stone is equal to its weight, which is very, very large! But you can use physics to make it easier by designing a **lever**.

A lever consists of two arms of different lengths which can rotate around a **fulcrum**. Applying a force produces a **torque**, which can cause the lever to rotate around the fulcrum.

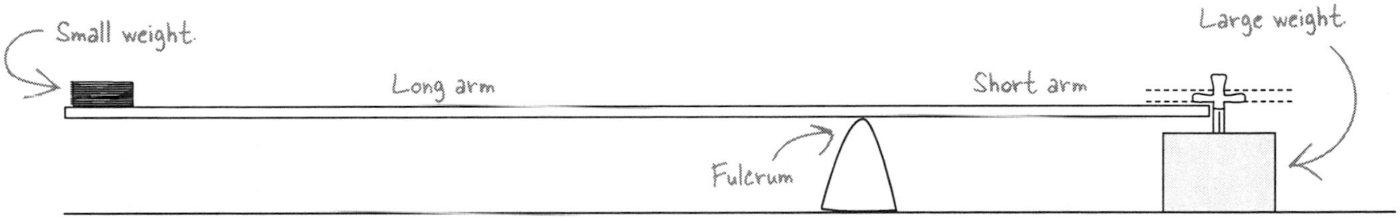

If an object will rotate around a fixed point, see if you can use torque to solve problems.

The equation for torque is $\boldsymbol{\tau} = \mathbf{rF}_{\perp}$.

So if you make a lever and put the sword and stone (which exerts a large force due to its weight) at the end of a short arm then apply an equal torque on a long arm using stackable stones, you'll be able to arrange a setup where there is **zero net torque** on the lever, which is therefore in **rotational equilibrium**. From there, a tiny nudge will be enough to lift the sword and stone. Fame and fortune beckon ... you just need to work out where to put the fulcrum.

Sharpen your pencil

A lever, length L, has two masses on it. At one end is a sword and stone, mass m_1 and displacement $\mathbf{r}_1$ from the fulcrum. At the other end of the lever is a stack of stones, mass m_2 and displacement $\mathbf{r}_2$ from the fulcrum.

a. Write down an equation for **L**, the total length of the lever, in terms of $\mathbf{r}_1$ and $\mathbf{r}_2$. (Make left-to-right the positive direction, and make **L** a positive vector. $\mathbf{r}_1$ and $\mathbf{r}_2$ are also vectors - do a sketch and be VERY careful with signs!)

b. Write down the condition for the rotational equilibrium of the lever (from where a small nudge will allow you to lift the sword and stone).

c. Use these two equations to work out an equation for $\mathbf{r}_1$ in terms of m_1, m_2 and **L**.

d. If the lever is 10.00 m long, the sword and stone have a mass of 1500 kg and the stackable stones a mass of 150 kg, how far from the sword and stone end should the fulcrum be placed?

Sharpen your pencil Solution

A lever has two masses on it. At one end is a sword and stone, mass m_1 and displacement $\mathbf{r}_1$ from the fulcrum. At the other end of the lever is a stack of stones, mass m_2 and displacement $\mathbf{r}_2$ from the fulcrum.

a. Write down an equation for **L**, the total length of the lever, in terms of $\mathbf{r}_1$ and $\mathbf{r}_2$. (Make left-to-right the positive direction, and make **L** a positive vector. $\mathbf{r}_1$ and $\mathbf{r}_2$ are also vectors - do a sketch and be VERY careful with signs!)

Make left to right the positive direction, and make L a vector going from left to right.

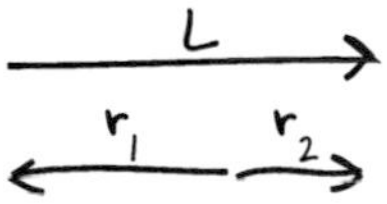

$$L = r_2 - r_1$$

If you chose a different way of defining the positive direction, your answer will work out the same in the end, but some of the minus signs in the algebra may be different.

b. Write down the condition for the rotational equilibrium of the lever (from where a small nudge will allow you to lift the sword and stone).

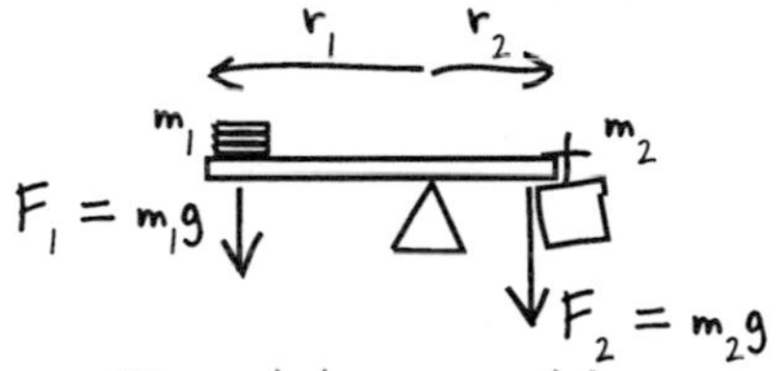

The net torque must be zero.

$$r_1F_1 + r_2F_2 = 0$$

$$\Rightarrow r_1m_1g + r_2m_2g = 0$$

$$\Rightarrow r_1m_1 + r_2m_2 = 0$$

Both terms are multiplied by g, so g divides out and cancels.

c. Use these two equations to work out an equation for $\mathbf{r}_1$ in terms of m_1, m_2 and **L**.

Need to make a substitution to get rid of r_2.
Rearrange equation from part a:

$$r_2 = L + r_1$$

Substitute this into equation from part b:

$$r_1m_1 + (L + r_1)m_2 = 0$$

$$r_1m_1 + Lm_2 + r_1m_2 = 0$$

$$r_1m_1 + r_1m_2 = -Lm_2$$

$$r_1(m_1 + m_2) = -Lm_2$$

$$r_1 = \frac{-Lm_2}{(m_1 + m_2)}$$

Put brackets in, so there's only one occurrence of r_1 on the left hand side.

d. If the lever is 10.00 m long, the sword and stone have a mass of 1500 kg and the stackable stones a mass of 150 kg, how far from the sword and stone end should the fulcrum be placed?

Use equation from part c. with values (m_1 is stackable stones and m_2 is sword and stone)

$$r_1 = \frac{-Lm_2}{(m_1 + m_2)}$$

$$r_1 = \frac{-10 \times 1500}{(150 + 1500)} = -9.09 \text{ m (3 sd)}$$

This is negative as we made left to right the positive direction.

r_1 is the displacement from the stackable stones end – need to work out r_2.

Displacement from sword and stone end will be:

$$r_2 = L + r_1$$

$$r_2 = 10 - 9.09 = 0.91 \text{ m (3 sd)}$$

The question asks for the displacement of the sword and stone from the fulcrum.

Question Clinic: The "Two equations, two unknowns" Question

If you have one equation, you can use it to work out the value of one unknown variable as long as you know values for the others. If you have two equations, you can use them to work out two unknowns (as long as it's the same two unknowns in both equations!)

Always, always, always start with a sketch!

The buzzwords 'lever' and 'fulcrum' tell you that torque is involved.

2. A lever has two masses on it. At one end is a sword and stone, mass m_1 and displacement r_1 from the fulcrum. At the other end of the lever is a stack of stones, mass m_2 and displacement r_2 from the fulcrum.

a. Write down an equation for **L** in terms of $\mathbf{r}_1$ and $\mathbf{r}_2$.

b. Write down the condition for the rotational equilibrium of the lever.

c. Use these two equations to work out an equation for $\mathbf{r}_1$ in terms of m_1, m_2 and **L**.

If the question gives you variable names, make sure you use the same ones in your answer.

You may be expected to spot this is useful from your sketch, rather than being asked explicitly to do it.

'Condition' probably means equation in this context, though you should write it in words as well as you get points for it!

Work out what variable(s) you need to get rid of, and make sure you do what they ask you to!

In this book we've concentrated on making substitutions, but if there's another way that makes sense for you, then go for it!

You can solve for two unknowns either by using a **substitution** or by setting up **simultaneous equations**. These methods are effectively the same, and it's up to you which to choose. If one of your unknowns is 'buried' deep inside a term, it's probably easiest to do a substitution. If both unknowns are terms in their own right (or are multiplied by just a number) then simultaneous equations will be quicker - but a substitution will still work.

BULLET POINTS

- The **size** of a **torque** is equal to the component of the force perpendicular to the lever × the displacement from the fulcrum.
- You can work out the perpendicular force component using trigonometry.
- If a problem involves something turning, you need to work out where the fulcrum is.
- Torque is a vector - the **direction** you're turning in matters.
- If you curl the fingers of your right hand in the direction you're turning in, your thumb points in the direction of the torque vector.
- If an object is in rotational equilibrium, it means that vector sum of all the torques on the object is zero.

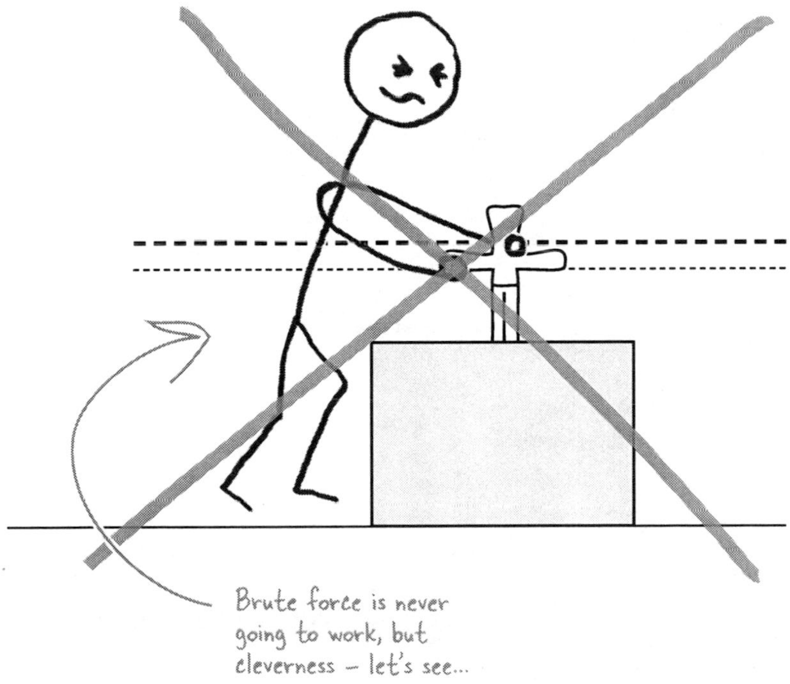

Time to try using a lever to lift the sword and stone. Hopefully, by using physics, you'll be more successful than than the person who tried before you ...

So you lift the sword and stone with the lever ...

You've used what you know about **torque** to predict that you can lift a 1500 kg sword and stone by using only 150 kg of stackable stones to generate a force much larger than their weight with a lever.

So you set everything up, and as you lift the final stone into place, the sword and stone begin to move...

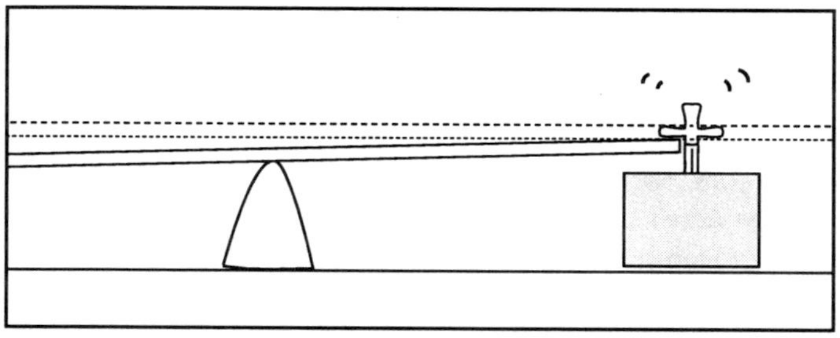

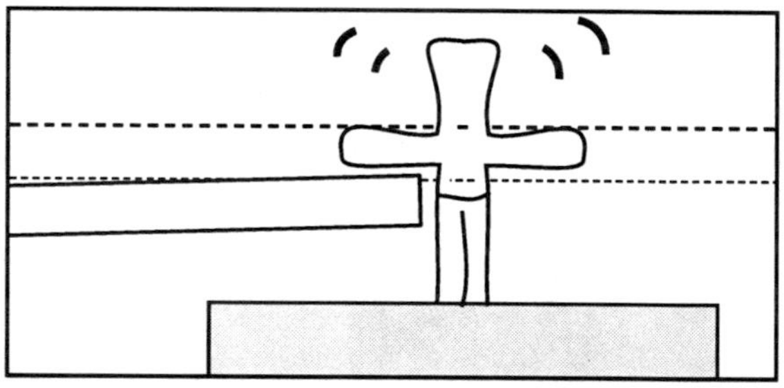

... but they don't go high enough!

Although the sword and the stone get off ground, they don't go high enough. The crossguard of the sword needs to be raised by 10 cm for the lift to count, but it only went up by around 1 cm.

The stackable stones have definitely gone down by 10 cm at the other end of the lever - but the sword and stone haven't gone up by the same amount. What's going on?!

BRAIN POWER

The stackable stones have gone down by 10 cm. So why haven't the sword and the stone gone up by 10 cm?

Jim: But it didn't reach the line!. The stone end went down by 10 cm - why didn't the sword and stone end go up by 10 cm?

Joe: Hang on while I do a quick sketch ...

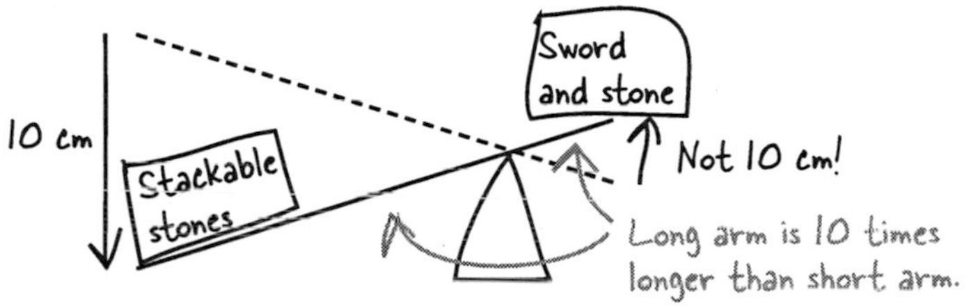

Frank: Ooh, triangles!

Joe: Yeah, **similar triangles**! Look - the stackable stones lever arm is ten times longer than the sword and stone lever arm. So if the stackable stones side goes down 10 cm, the sword and stone end only goes up a tenth of that distance - 1 cm.

Jim: If the stackable stones going down by 10 cm causes the sword and stone to rise by 1 cm, then I guess the stackable stones need to go down by 100 cm to make the sword and stone rise by 10 cm.

Frank: That sounds like an awful lot of **work** to lift the stackable stones that high in the first place! Maybe it's easier to make the two arms of the lever equal lengths. Then we only need to lift the stackable stones 10 cm - a much smaller **distance**.

Joe: But we'd need 1500 kg of stackable stones to lift the sword and stone, instead of 150 kg. That's ten times as many stackable stones! Even though you only have to lift them a tenth of the **distance**, you're lifting ten times more **weight** than you were before.

Jim: I'm kinda starting to think that you can't get something for nothing. We either lift a tenth of the weight ten times the distance, or the same weight the same distance.

Joe: Yeah, it's hard work either way around!

Always look out for triangles - and especially similar triangles!

Similar triangles don't have to be right-angled. They just need to have the same angles as each other.

BRAIN POWER

Which do you think involves more work - lifting 10 stackable stones 1 m each, or 100 of them 10 cm each?

You can't get something for nothing

You can't get something for nothing. If you use 150 kg of stackable stones to lift a 1500 kg sword and stone, the long lever arm needs to be 10 times the length of the short one. But that means the sword and stone only get lifted a tenth of the distance that the stackable stones move through.

So to lift the 1500 kg sword and stone 0.10 m (10 cm) off the ground, you need to lift the 150 kg of stackable stones 1.00 m off the ground to start off with - 10 times as high. That's a lot of work for you!

We've now redesigned the lever as a pan balance. This is so that you only have to lift the stackable stones the minimum height necessary (onto the pan) and not all the way up to the top of the lever.

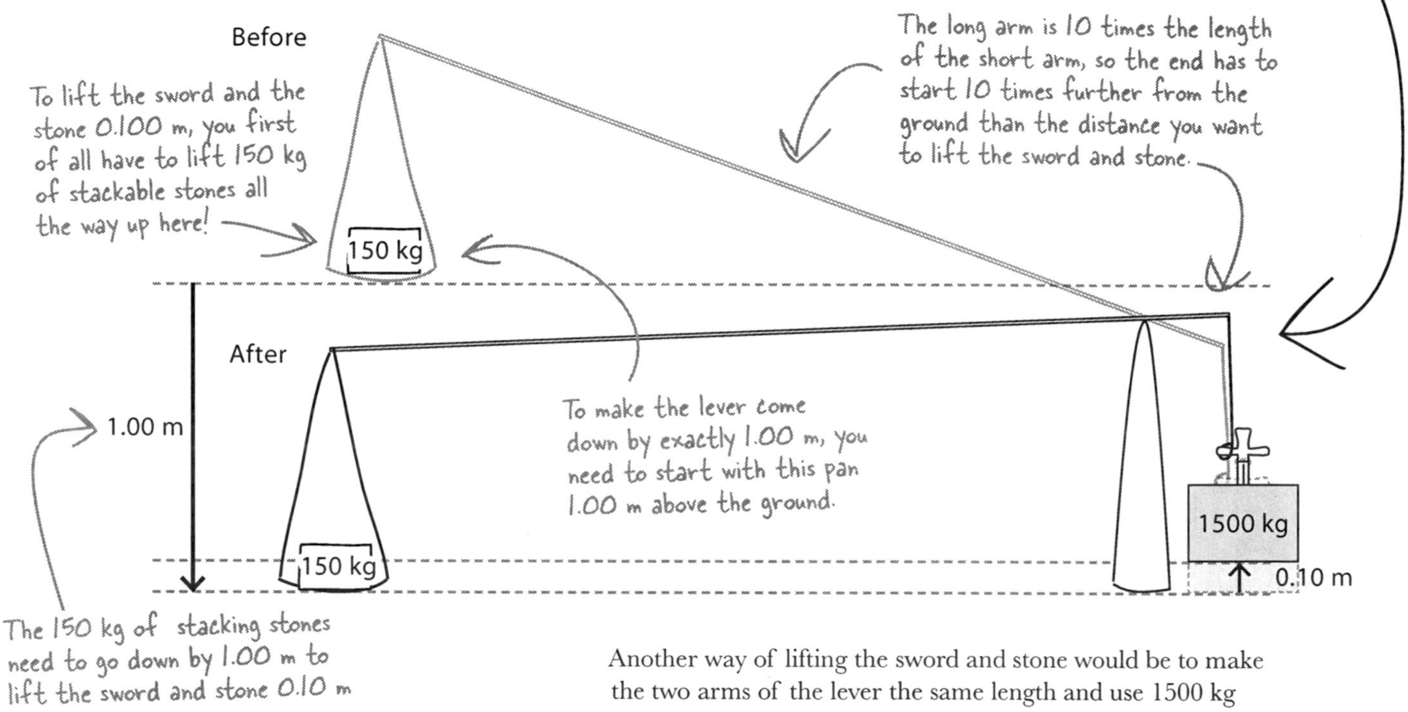

Another way of lifting the sword and stone would be to make the two arms of the lever the same length and use 1500 kg of stackable stones. You only have to lift the stacking stones 0.100 m instead of 1.00 m - but you have to lift 10 times as much weight to take advantage of the smaller displacement!

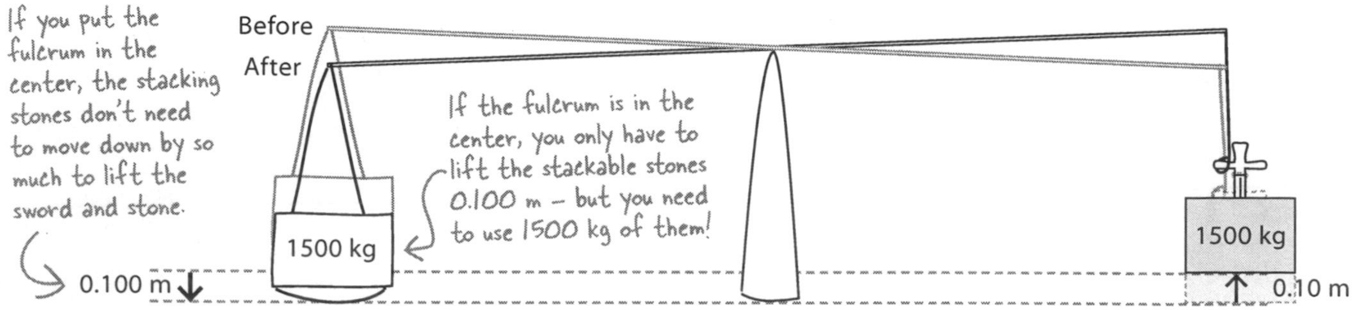

When you move an object against a force, you're doing work

You have a job to do - lift the 1500 kg sword and stone 0.100 m in the air by overcoming the gravitational force on it. In physics, if you **displace** an object in the **opposite** direction from a **force** that's acting on the object, you're said to be **doing work** on the object against the opposing force.

So when you lift a stackable stone, you **do work on** it against the force of gravity. And if a pile of stackable stones lifts the sword and stone (using a lever) then the stackable stones **do work on** the sword and stone against the force of gravity.

To do WORK on an object, you need to use a FORCE to DISPLACE the object in the opposite direction from another force that's acting on the object.

The work you need to do a job = force x displacement

In physics, the word **work** has a very specific meaning. When you do work on something against a force (e.g. by lifting it against the force of gravity), the amount of work you do depends on two things:

The component of the **force** you exert on the object that's **parallel** to other force you're working against. When you're lifting something against the force of gravity, this is the vertical component of the lifting force.

The **displacement** of the object in the same direction. When you're lifting something against the force of gravity, this is the vertical component of the displacement.

Work done on object

Component of the force you exert on it that's parallel to the force opposing it.

$$W = F_{||}\Delta x$$

Be careful – work begins with the same letter as weight!

This symbol means 'parallel'.

Displacement in same direction as $F_{||}$

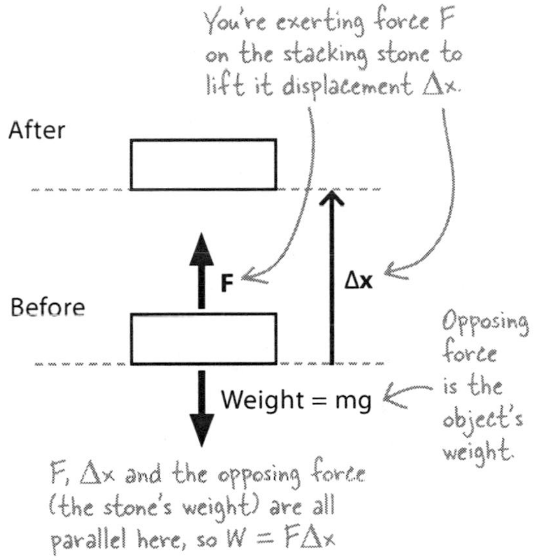

The **work** you do on the object is defined as the he parallel component of the **force** you use to move the object × its **displacement**. This can be written as:

$$W = \mathbf{F}_{||}\mathbf{\Delta x}$$

where W is the work, $\mathbf{\Delta x}$ is the displacement and $\mathbf{F}_{||}$ is the component of the force you're exerting on the object parallel to the object's displacement.

Which method involves the least amount of work?

You've come up with two different ways of lifting the sword and stone using a lever and some stackable stones. You can either lift 150 kg of stones 1.00 m, or 1500 kg of stones 0.100 m (depending on where you put the fulcrum) to enable the stacking stones to lift the sword and stone.

When you lift an object, you do work on it by displacing it upwards with an upwards force that counters the downwards gravitational force.

150 kg of stackable stones lifted 1.00 m.

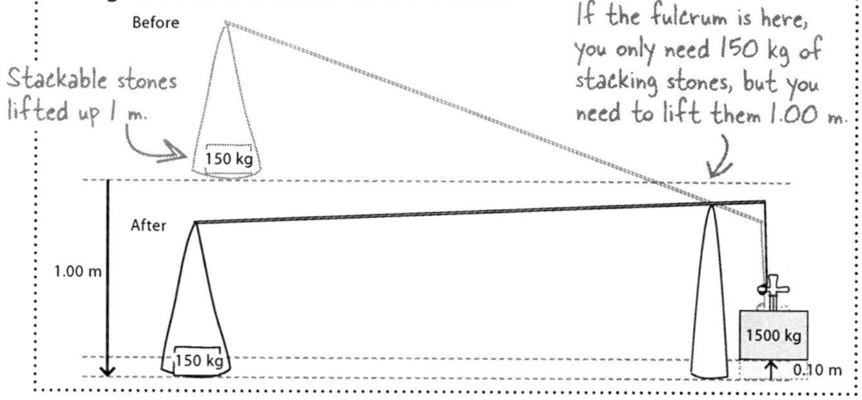

1500 kg of stackable stones lifted 0.100 m.

It would make sense to choose the easier method - the one that involves you having to do less work on the stackable stones in order to get them from the ground into a position where they can lift the sword and stone.

Sharpen your pencil

You need to do work on the stackable stones before they can do work on the sword and stone. But which method involves doing more work? Calculate the amount of work you need to do to:

a. Lift 150 kg of stackable stones 1.00 m.

b. Lift 1500 kg of stackable stones 0.100 m.

c. Comment on the sizes and the units of your answers.

Hint: Get the units of work from the units of the variable on the right hand side of the equation you use to calculate the work.

Sharpen your pencil

You need to do work on the stackable stones before they can do work on the sword and stone. But which method involves doing more work? Calculate the amount of work you need to do to:

a. Lift 150 kg of stackable stones 1.00 m.

Lifting force same size as weight, so $F = mg$

$W = F\Delta x = 150 \times 9.8 \times 1.00$

$W = 1470$ Nm (3 sd)

b. Lift 1500 kg of stackable stones 0.100 m.

Lifting force same size as weight, so $F = mg$

$W = F\Delta x = 1500 \times 9.8 \times 0.100$

$W = 1470$ Nm (3 sd)

c. Comment on the sizes and the units of your answers.

Both ideas involve doing the same amount of work on the stackable stones. The units of work are force × displacement. Force is measured in Newtons and displacement in meters, so the units of work are Nm.

You say "Newton meters" if you're saying this unit out loud.

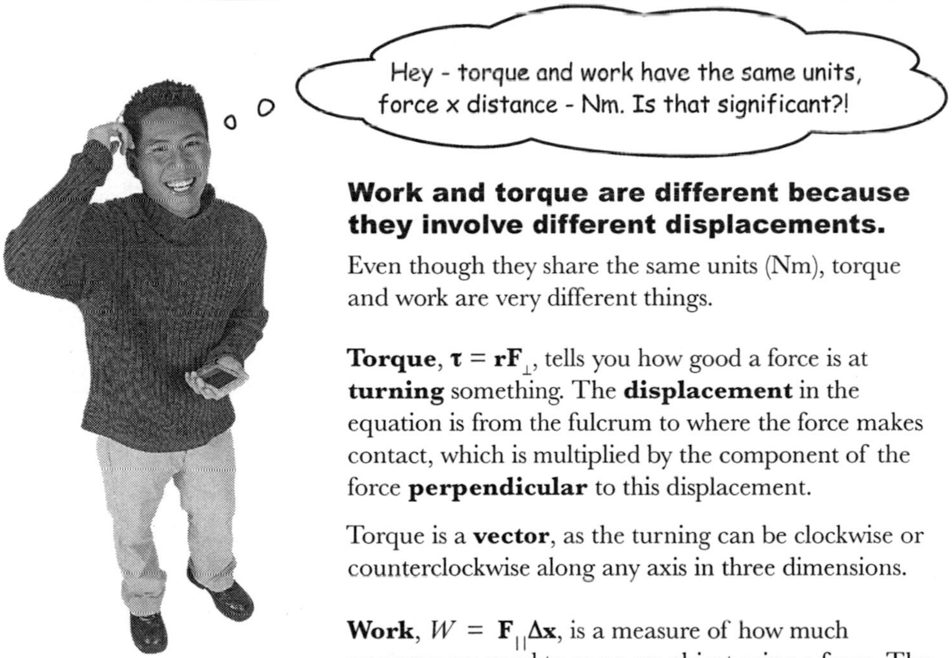

Work and torque are different because they involve different displacements.

Even though they share the same units (Nm), torque and work are very different things.

Torque, $\tau = rF_{\perp}$, tells you how good a force is at **turning** something. The **displacement** in the equation is from the fulcrum to where the force makes contact, which is multiplied by the component of the force **perpendicular** to this displacement.

Torque is a **vector**, as the turning can be clockwise or counterclockwise along any axis in three dimensions.

Work, $W = F_{||}\Delta x$, is a measure of how much **energy** you need to move an object using a force. The **displacement** in the equation is the displacement of the moved object, which is multiplied by the component of the force **parallel** to this displacement.

Work is also a **scalar**, as the same amount of work will be done by the same size of force moving something the same distance, regardless of direction.

Torque is a vector, work is a scalar.

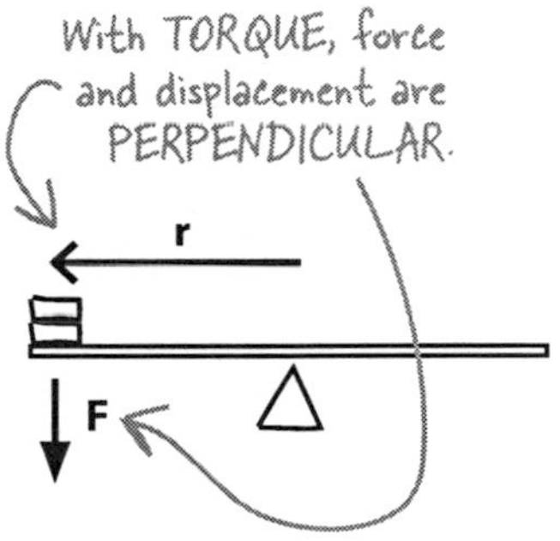

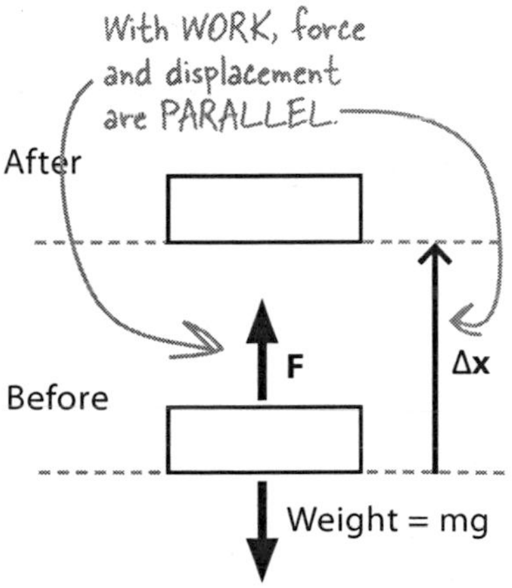

Work has units of Joules

To avoid getting confused because torque and work have the same units, scientists measure work in something called **Joules** (J) where 1 J = 1 Nm. If you're answering a question about work, you should always give your answer in Joules.

Work is measured in Joules.

Power is the rate at which you do work.

Power's measured in Joules per second, J/s

If you lift something in a shorter time, your power output is higher.

Work is measured in Joules. You do the same amount of work to lift the stone the same distance each time, regardless of the time it takes.

The difference is your **power** output. Power is the **rate** at which you do work and is measured in Joules per second (J/s).

Because of how your body functions, you get more tired if you do the same work in a shorter time with a higher power output. So how **tired** you feel won't always correlate with the amount of work you've done.

there are no Dumb Questions

Q: I don't like how physics steals words like 'work' and 'power' and makes them mean different things from usual.

A: Many words can be used in a variety of ways in everyday speech. You're right that in physics, words like work, power, and force have very **specific** meanings, but they have to so that people know exactly what you're talking about.

Q: I can make myself tired without doing any work at all if I hold my arm out at shoulder height with an object in my hand. The weight's not moving, so I'm not doing work on it. What's that all about?!

A: The fibers in your muscles are continually expanding and contracting (moving as a result of a force) to enable you to do that. You **are** doing work, but on your muscle fibers, not the object! A table can support the object quite happily without doing any work on it!

Q: You said over there that "work is a measure of how much energy you need to move something with a force." Is 'energy' another of these physics words with a very specific meaning?

A: It sure is - and you're going to be doing a lot with energy in the next few chapters, starting now...

Energy is the capacity that something has to do work

If something has the **capacity** to do work, it means that it is able to exert a force to displace an object. But how much work might it be able to do?

Energy is the capacity that something has to do work. By lifting 150 kg of stackable stones 1.00 m, you are giving them the capacity to do $\mathbf{F}_{||}\mathbf{\Delta x} = 150 \times 9.8 \times 1.00 = 1470\,\text{J}$ of work.

Another way of putting this is that you have given the stackable stones 1470 J of **gravitational potential energy**.

Energy is conserved

The total energy of everything in the entire universe is always constant. Closer to home, the total energy of an isolated system (for instance you, stackable stones, lever, sword and stone, plus surroundings) is always the same, or in other words energy is **conserved**.

Energy is conserved.

Lifting stones is like transferring energy from one store to another

The gravitational potential energy that the stackable stones gain when you lift them doesn't just 'appear' from nowhere. You can think of the food you eat as a store of **chemical potential energy**, which your body can tap into to do work.

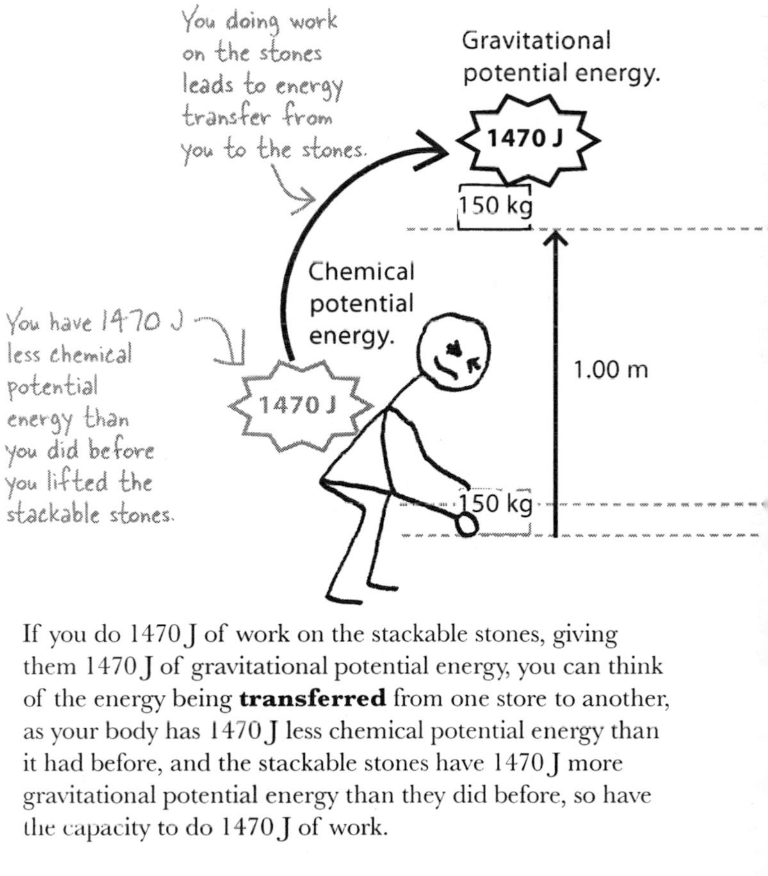

If you do 1470 J of work on the stackable stones, giving them 1470 J of gravitational potential energy, you can think of the energy being **transferred** from one store to another, as your body has 1470 J less chemical potential energy than it had before, and the stackable stones have 1470 J more gravitational potential energy than they did before, so have the capacity to do 1470 J of work.

Doing work is a way of transferring energy.

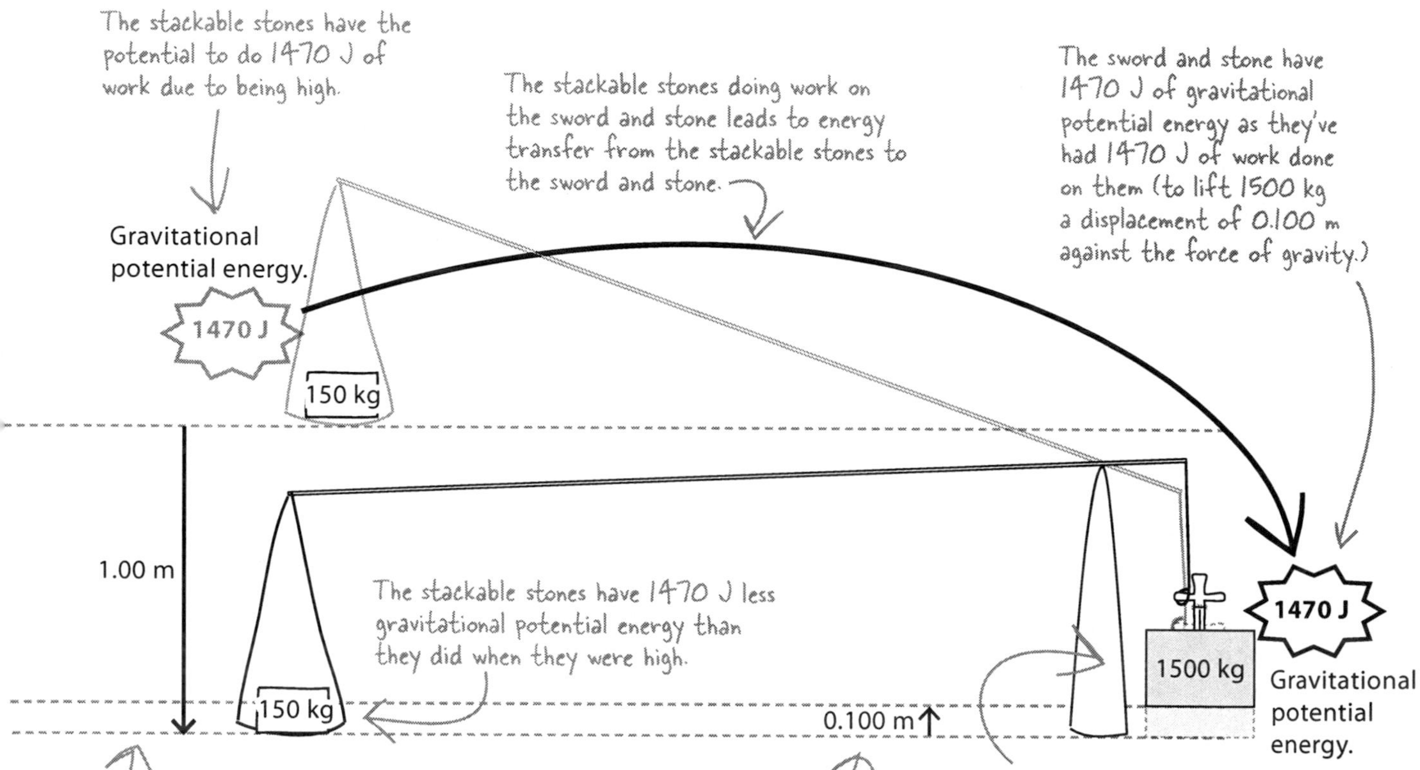

If the stackable stones then do 1470 J of work on the sword and stone (via the lever), you can also think of that as 1470 J of energy being **transferred** from one store to another.

The 1470 J that started out as chemical potential energy in your body has ended up being transferred to gravitational potential energy in the sword and stone (via the stackable stones).

You can think about any physical process that involves change in terms of energy transfer.

Energy conservation allows you to solve tough-looking problems quickly.

Back on page 528, you used forces, torques, similar triangles, substitution, etc to calculate the best way to lift a 1500 kg sword and stone using 150 kg of stackable stones and a lever.

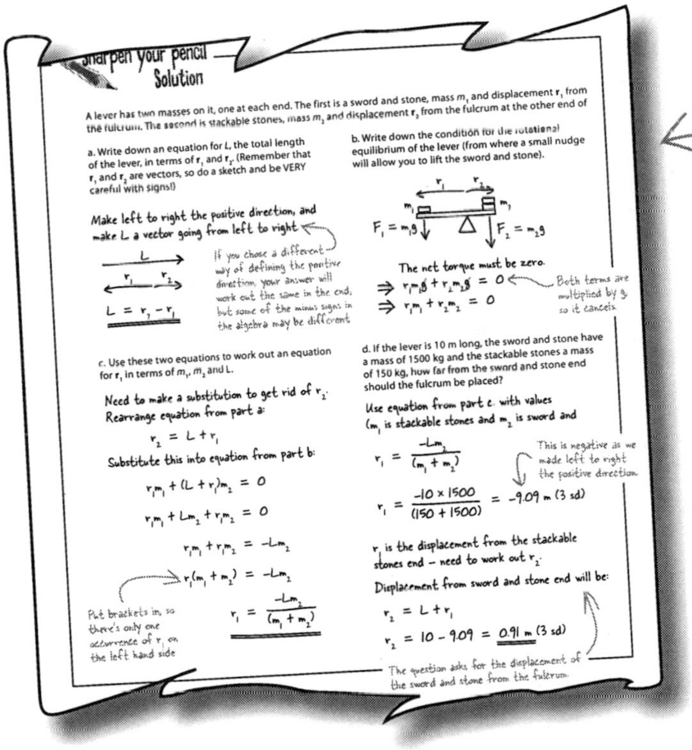

Sharpen your pencil Solution

A lever has two masses on it, one at each end. The first is a sword and stone, mass m_1 and displacement $\mathbf{r}_1$ from the fulcrum. The second is stackable stones, mass m_2 and displacement $\mathbf{r}_2$ from the fulcrum at the other end of the lever.

a. Write down an equation for L, the total length of the lever, in terms of $\mathbf{r}_1$ and $\mathbf{r}_2$. (Remember that $\mathbf{r}_1$ and $\mathbf{r}_2$ are vectors, so do a sketch and be VERY careful with signs!)

Make left to right the positive direction, and make L a vector going from left to right

If you chose a different way of defining the positive direction, your answer will work out the same in the end, but some of the minus signs in the algebra may be different

$L = r_2 - r_1$

b. Write down the condition for the rotational equilibrium of the lever (from where a small nudge will allow you to lift the sword and stone).

$F_1 = m_1 g$, $F_2 = m_2 g$

The net torque must be zero.

$\Rightarrow r_1 m_1 g + r_2 m_2 g = 0$ — Both terms are multiplied by g, so it cancels.

$\Rightarrow r_1 m_1 + r_2 m_2 = 0$

c. Use these two equations to work out an equation for $\mathbf{r}_1$ in terms of m_1, m_2 and L.

Need to make a substitution to get rid of r_2. Rearrange equation from part a:

$r_2 = L + r_1$

Substitute this into equation from part b:

$r_1 m_1 + (L + r_1) m_2 = 0$

$r_1 m_1 + L m_2 + r_1 m_2 = 0$

$r_1 m_1 + r_1 m_2 = -L m_2$

$r_1(m_1 + m_2) = -L m_2$

Put brackets in, so there's only one occurrence of r_1 on the left hand side

$r_1 = \frac{-L m_2}{(m_1 + m_2)}$

d. If the lever is 10 m long, the sword and stone have a mass of 1500 kg and the stackable stones a mass of 150 kg, how far from the sword and stone end should the fulcrum be placed?

Use equation from part c with values (m_1 is stackable stones and m_2 is sword and stone)

$r_1 = \frac{-L m_2}{(m_1 + m_2)}$

This is negative as we made left to right the positive direction.

$r_1 = \frac{-10 \times 1500}{(150 + 1500)} = -9.09 \text{ m (3 sd)}$

r_1 is the displacement from the stackable stones end – need to work out r_2.

Displacement from sword and stone end will be:

$r_2 = L + r_1$

$r_2 = 10 - 9.09 = 0.91 \text{ m (3 sd)}$

The question asks for the displacement of the sword and stone from the fulcrum.

You don't want to have to go through all of this (and still not quite get the correct answer) when there's an easier way ...

But that was a complicated calculation where you had to be very careful with minus signs! And what's more - it wasn't obvious what height the stackable stones should start off at to lift the sword and stone the correct height (0.100 m off the ground) even when you'd worked out where to put the fulcrum.

Energy conservation helps you to solve problems with differences in height

The stackable stones are able to lift the sword and stone because of the **difference in height** between them.

With the lever in place, this difference in height causes a **change in height** for both the stackable stones and the sword and stone. This process involves **energy transfer**, from the stackable stones to the sword and stone.

You give an object gravitational potential energy by doing work on it, $W = \mathbf{F}_{||}\mathbf{\Delta x}$. As the force you're working against is the object's weight, $m\mathbf{g}$, and you're lifting it to a height, **h**, the gravitational potential energy you give the object is $U_g = m\mathbf{gh}$.

Differences drive changes that lead to energy transfer.

Potential energy has the symbol *U*.

mg is the object's weight – the force you're doing work against.

$$U_g = mgh$$

The 'g' subscript shows you it's gravitational potential energy.

Here, the displacement is a height, so gets symbol 'h' to remind you of this.

One of our stackable stones is missing ...

Unfortunately, in between your first attempt at lifting the sword and stone (where it lifted but didn't go high enough) and this one, a stackable stone has gone missing. Now you only have 9 stones each with a mass of 15 kg instead of 10 ...

Sharpen your pencil

You are using a lever to lift the sword and stone (mass 1500 kg) a height of 0.100 m off the ground.

a. How much gravitational potential energy are you giving the sword and stone?

b. You have 9 stackable stones available to put on the other end of the lever, each with a mass of 15.0 kg. How much gravitational potential energy do you need to give the stackable stones in order for them to be able to lift the sword and stone to the required height?

c. What height do you need to lift the stackable stones to?

Sharpen your pencil Solution

You are using a lever to lift the sword and stone (mass 1500 kg) a height of 0.10 m off the ground.

a. How much gravitational potential energy are you giving the sword and stone?

$$U_g = mgh$$
$$U_g = 1500 \times 9.8 \times 0.10$$
$$U_g = 1470 \text{ J (3 sd)}$$

You need to give the sword and stone 1470 J of gravitational potential energy.

b. On the other side of the lever, you have 9 stackable stones, each with a mass of 15 kg. How much gravitational potential energy do you need to give them in order for them to be able to lift the sword and stone the required distance?

The stackable stones need to be able to do 1470 J of work on the sword and stone. Therefore you need to give them 1470 J of gravitational potential energy.

c. What height do you need to lift the stackable stones to?

Mass of stacking stones $= 9 \times 15 = 135$ kg.

$$U_g = mgh$$
$$\Rightarrow h = \frac{U_g}{mg} = \frac{1470}{135 \times 9.8} = 1.11 \text{ m (3 sd)}$$

This makes sense, as it's more than 1.00 m (the height you'd have needed to lift 10 stones).

there are no Dumb Questions

Q: Why are energy and work useful?

A: Using energy conservation and work to do problems is often more straightforward than using forces.

Q: Can you give an example of where using energy conservation to do a problem is easier than using forces?

A: If the problem involves **differences** in heights, for example if you need to lift an object, then using energy conservation is faster than using forces.

Any time there are differences that drive change, think about using energy conservation to solve problems.

Q: So what IS energy? It has the same units as work - does that mean they're both the same thing?

A: Not quite. Energy is the **capacity** that something has to do work.

Q: But I thought that energy was something to do with electricity? Like when you use a food mixer or boil a kettle, you're using energy, aren't you?!

A: Energy can be stored in a number of different ways - we've already mentioned gravitational potential and chemical potential energy. Electrical potential energy is another way - but we won't be dealing with that in this chapter.

Think - what was the difference at the start, what change did it cause, and where has energy transfer taken place?

Will energy conservation save the day?

You've just calculated that lifting 135 kg of stackable stones 1.11 m gives them 1470 J of gravitational potential energy. This allows the stackable stones to do the 1470 J of work required to lift 1500 kg of sword and stone 0.100 m.

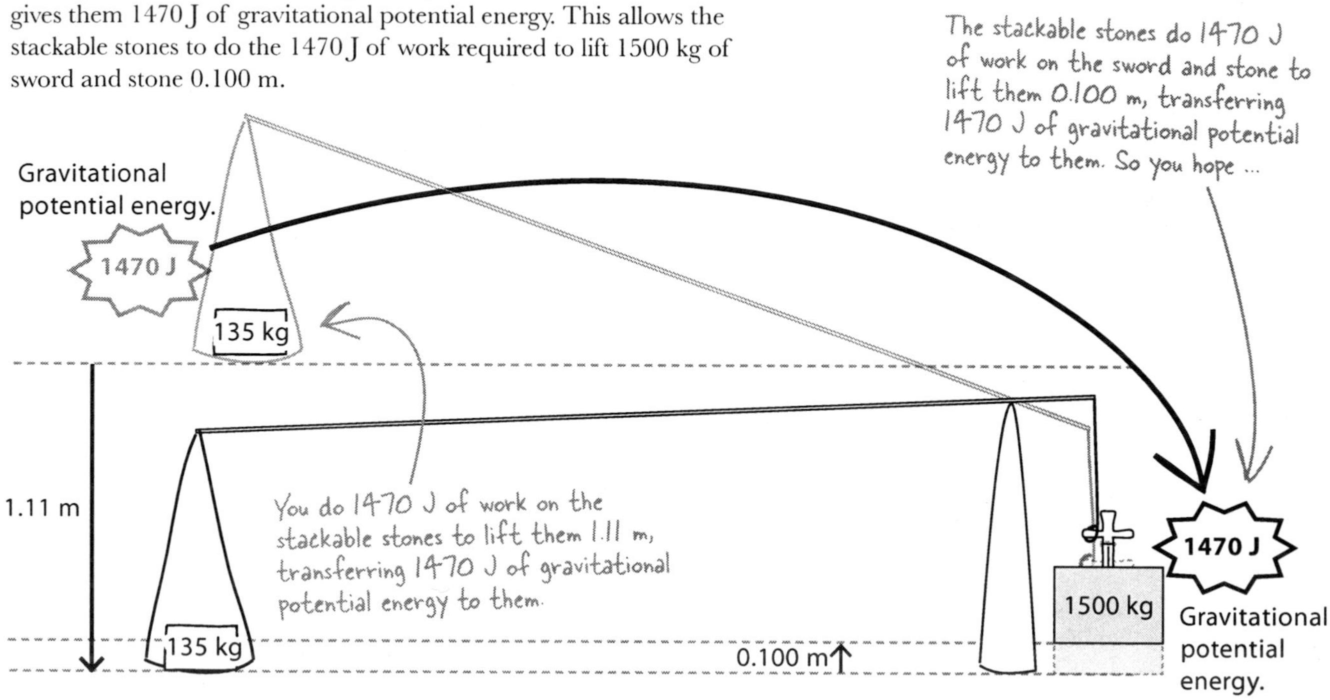

The rules say that you're allowed to have two attempts per lifetime, and this is your second attempt. Here goes ...

Oh. The sword and stone wobble a little, but **don't go up in the air**. They're very close to leaving the ground, but haven't quite made it.

If you can think quickly and work out what's gone wrong and how much extra you need to add to the stone side of the lever, there's still time to rescue the situation and claim your half of the kingdom!

BRAIN POWER

You've done the same amount of work on the stackable stones as you want them to do on the sword and stone. So why haven't you managed to lift the sword and stone?

Jim: Might it be a **rounding** thing - like, we calculated the amount of work we'd need to do on the sword and stone then rounded down to 3 significant digits, so didn't do quite enough work on the stackable stones?

Joe: I don't think it's that. We did calculate the energy at one point, but we didn't use the rounded value to work out the height. We just used proportion - a tenth of the weight meant ten times the height.

Frank: Hang on ... you said '**weight**' didn't you?! Look! Now that the lever's at a much bigger angle, the force of the stackable stones' weight isn't perpendicular to the lever any more - look! So we're using less **torque** than we thought.

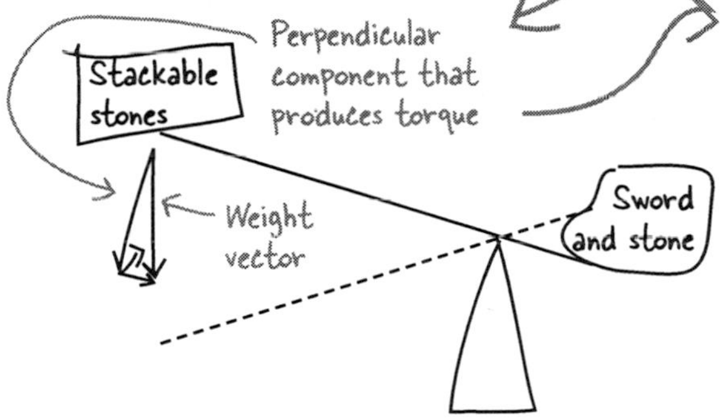

Jim: But the weight vector of the sword and stone isn't perpendicular to the lever either. So its torque is less too. And as both force vectors make the **same angle** with the lever, the torques they produce will still be the same whatever angle the lever's at.

Frank: Hmmm. I think you're right. There must be another reason that we've not managed to do enough work on the sword and stone to lift it properly.

Joe: Wait...this isn't an ideal situation...what about friction?

Frank: How do you mean?

Joe: Well, if there's some **friction** in the fulcrum, we'd need to use more **force** to overcome it than if it's perfectly frictionless.

Frank: Ahh ... we'd be doing **work** against the force of friction as well as doing work against the force of gravity!

Jim: But how can you tell? It's not like the fulcrum gets lifted up.

Joe: Right...but before, we were expecting to use 100% of the stackable stones' gravitational potential energy to do work against gravity to lift the sword and stone. But we also need to do work against friction in the fulcrum. So not all of the stackable stones' energy is available to lift the sword and stone. Quick - find something else we can put on the lever ...

You need to do work against friction as well as against gravity

The sword and stone are teetering on the brink because it's impossible to be 100% **efficient**.

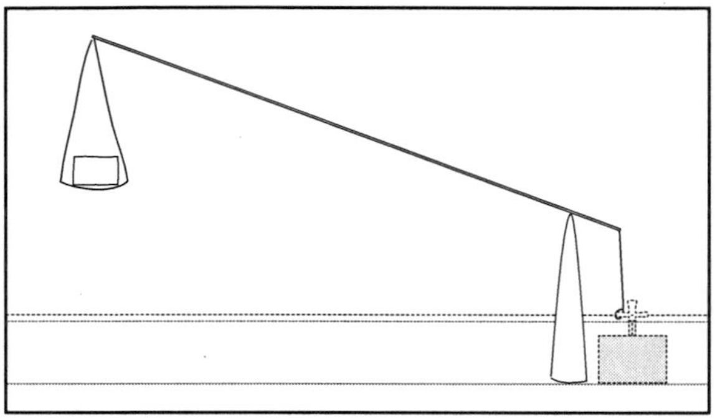

Your calculation assumed that all of the gravitational potential energy in the stackable stones would be available to do **work** on the sword and stone, so that all the stored energy you started with would be **transferred** in this way.

But there will be **friction** in the fulcrum of the lever, and some of the stackable stones' gravitational potential **energy** will go towards increasing the fulcrum's **internal energy** as you do work against the force of friction.

But as long as there isn't too much friction, it shouldn't be too difficult to tip the balance ...

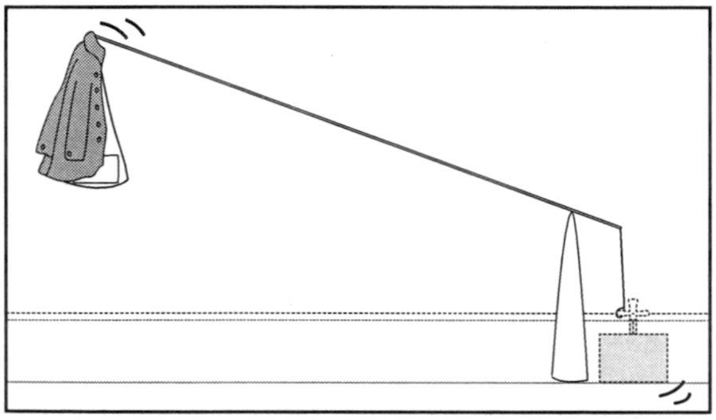

Fortunately, the fulcrum's well-oiled, and the simple act of hanging your coat on the stackable stones is enough to tip the lever, lift the sword and stone, and gain you half the kingdom!

Result!

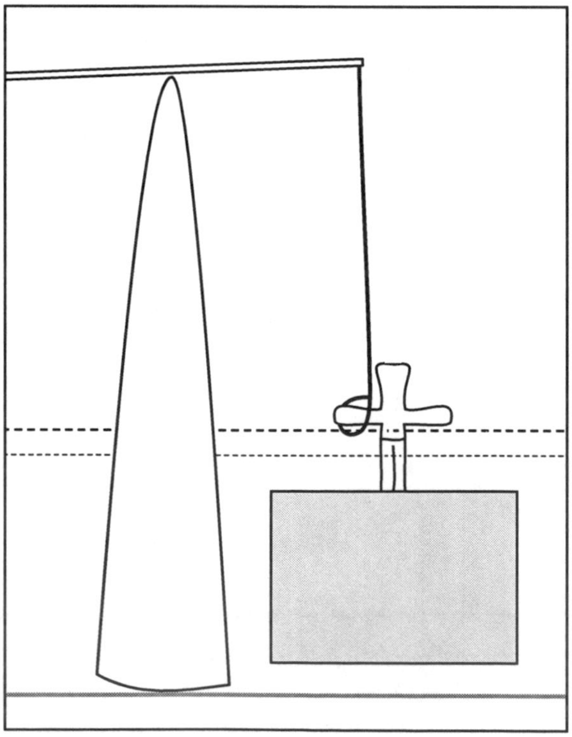

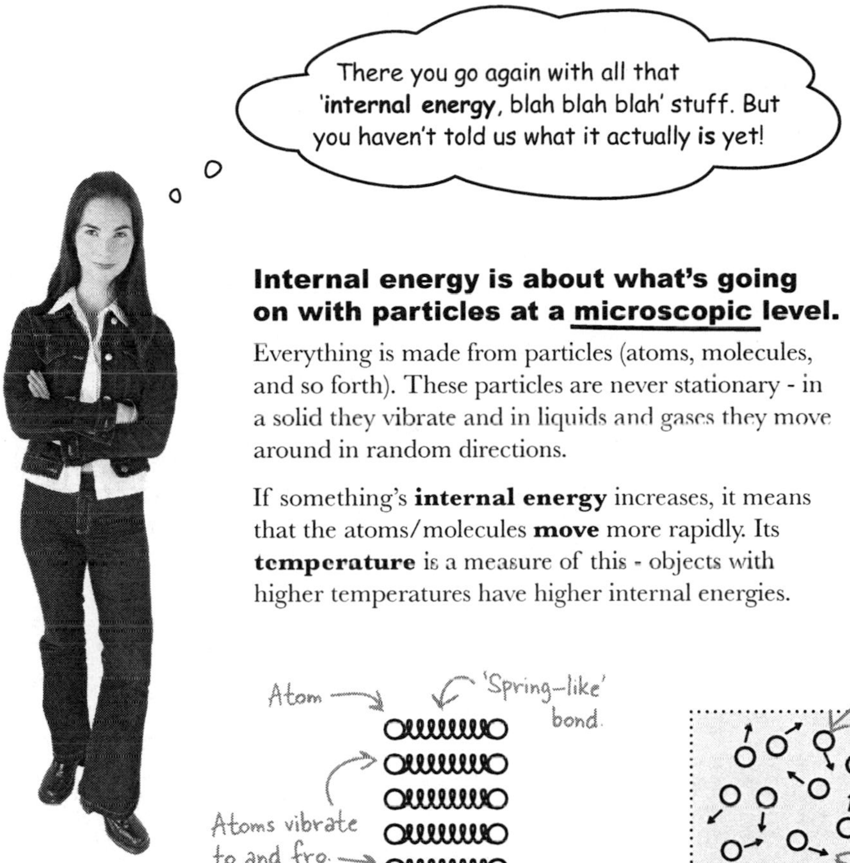

Internal energy is about what's going on with particles at a microscopic level.

Everything is made from particles (atoms, molecules, and so forth). These particles are never stationary - in a solid they vibrate and in liquids and gases they move around in random directions.

If something's **internal energy** increases, it means that the atoms/molecules **move** more rapidly. Its **temperature** is a measure of this - objects with higher temperatures have higher internal energies.

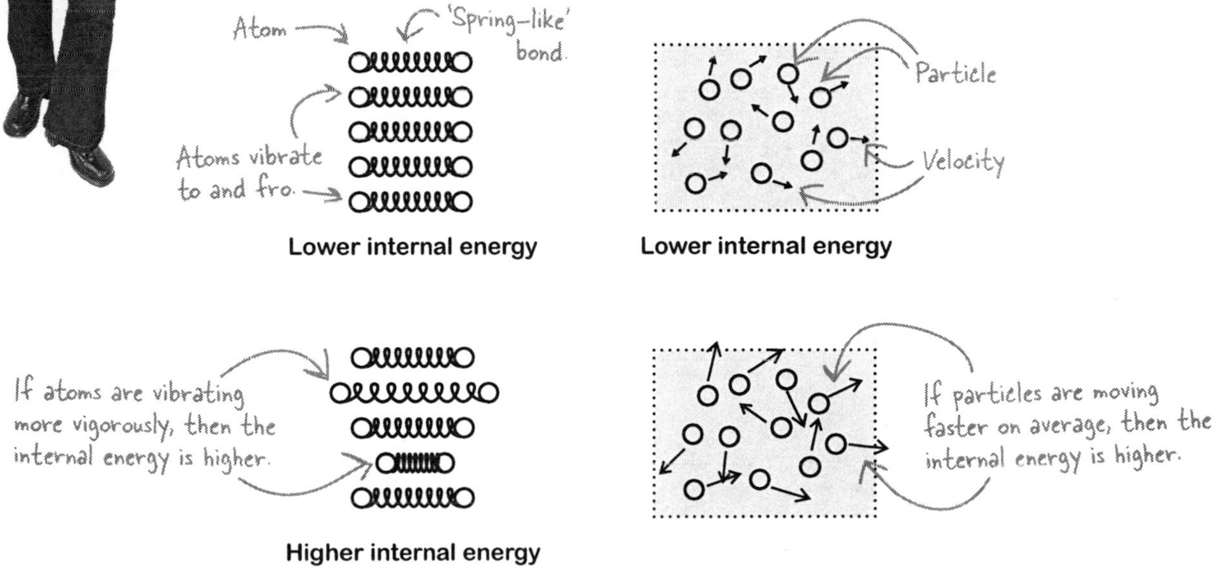

The higher something's temperature, the higher its internal energy.

Temperature is a measure of internal energy.

Doing work against friction increases internal energy

It's possible to increase something's internal energy by doing **work** on it against the force of **friction**. The most obvious way of seeing this is by pushing something along the ground. If you push it long enough, its temperature will increase (and so will the temperature of the ground).

If you think about the particles as marbles, the two surfaces moving over each other is a bit like like jiggling and jostling a tray of marbles around so that the marbles end up with a greater average speed, and therefore a greater **internal energy**.

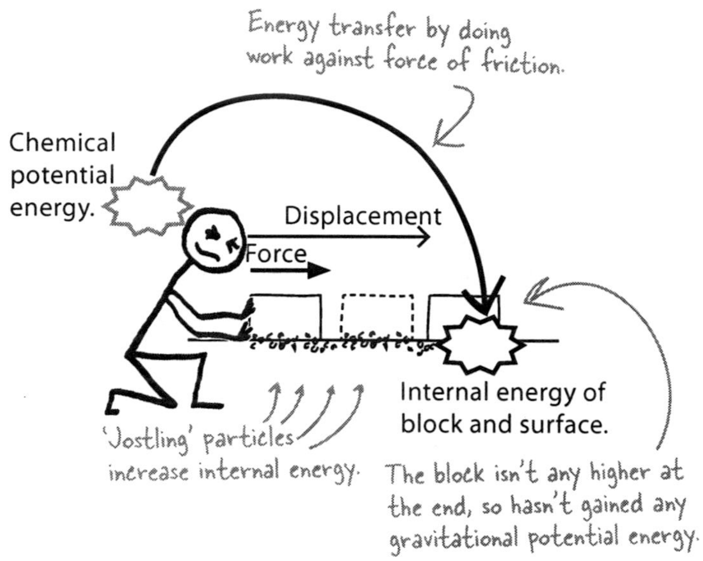

Something similar happens in the fulcrum of the lever, where the moving parts rub together. This time, most of the gravitational potential energy in the stackable stones does work against gravity and is transferred to gravitational potential energy in the sword and stone.

But work is also done against the **friction** that comes from the moving parts of the fulcrum rubbing together. This leads to some of the stackable stones' gravitational potential energy being transferred to the **internal energy** of the fulcrum.

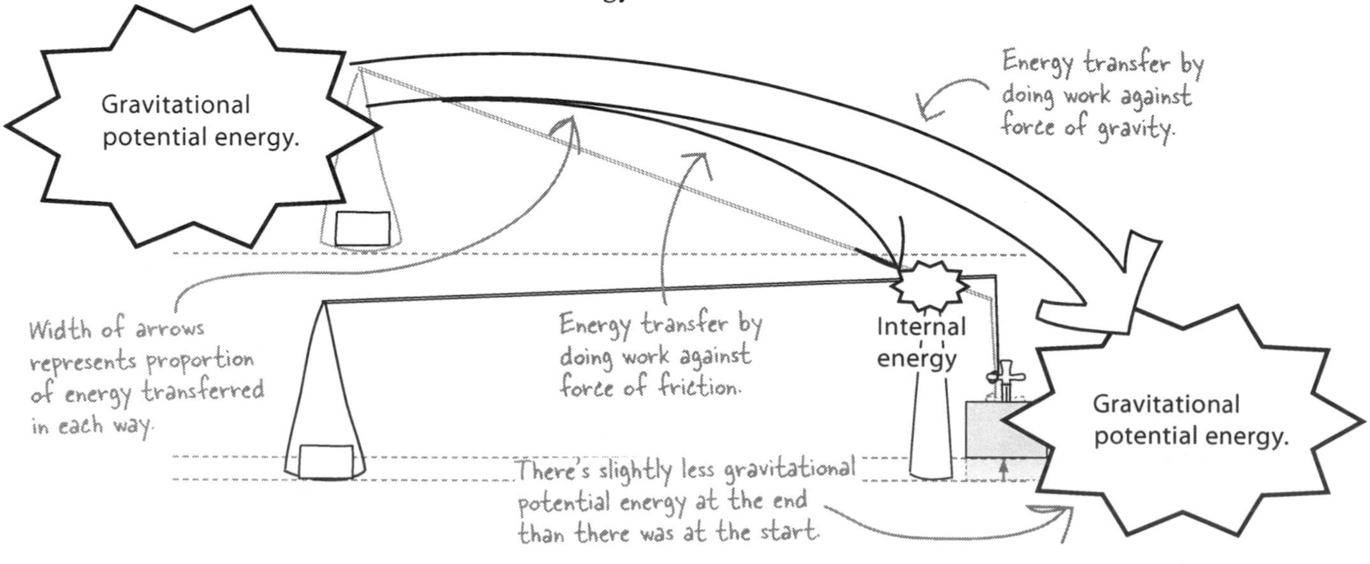

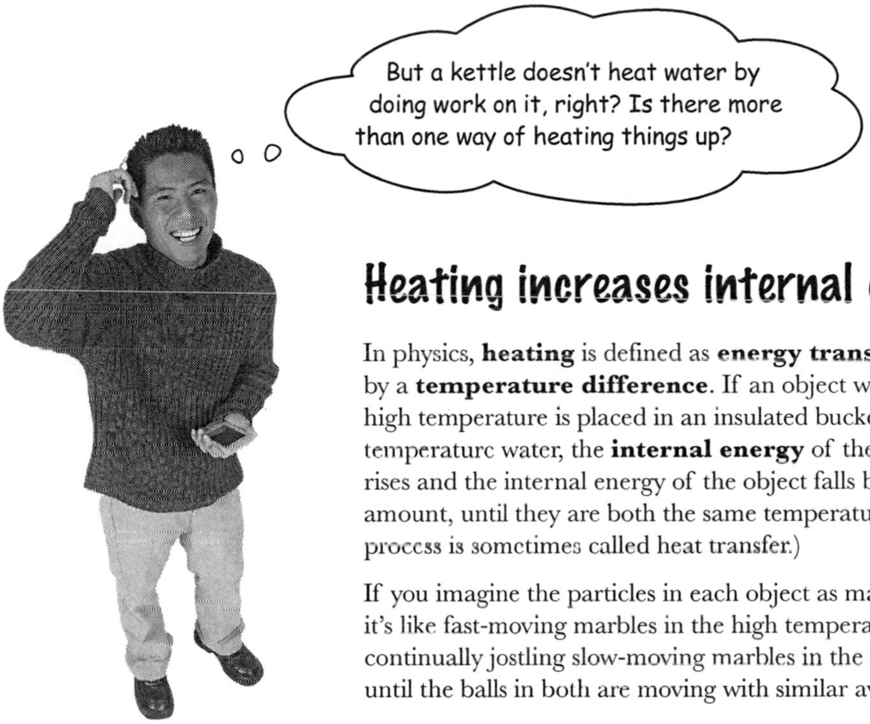

Heating increases internal energy

In physics, **heating** is defined as **energy transfer** caused by a **temperature difference**. If an object with a high temperature is placed in an insulated bucket of low temperature water, the **internal energy** of the water rises and the internal energy of the object falls by the same amount, until they are both the same temperature. (This process is sometimes called heat transfer.)

If you imagine the particles in each object as marbles, then it's like fast-moving marbles in the high temperature object continually jostling slow-moving marbles in the cold water, until the balls in both are moving with similar average speeds.

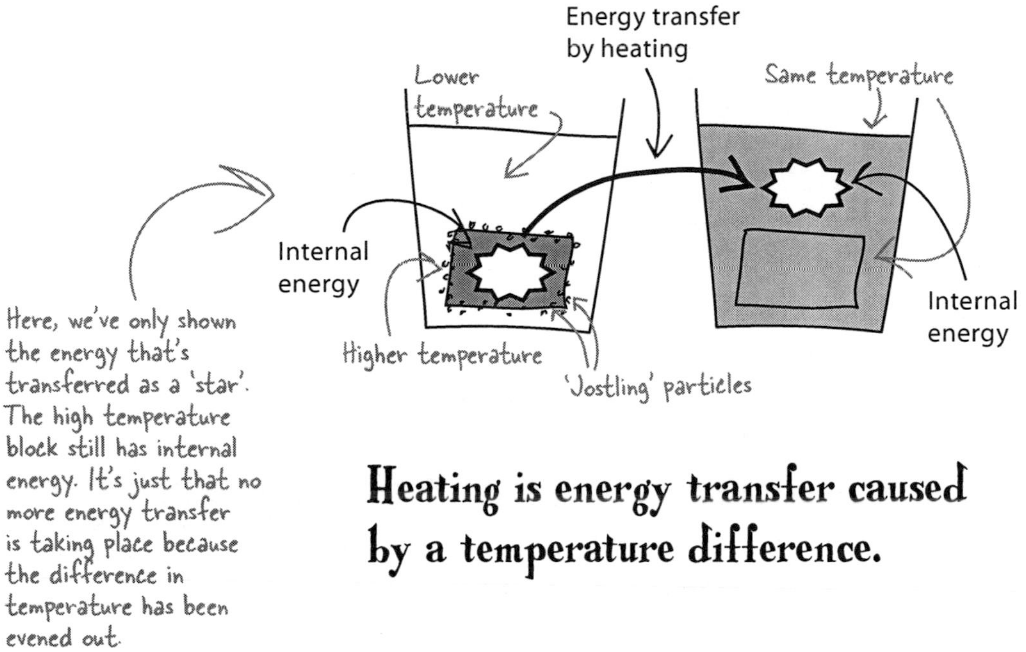

Heating is energy transfer caused by a temperature difference.

It's impossible to be 100% efficient

Back with the sword and stone, you've realized that not all of the gravitational potential energy in the stackable stones will be available to do work against the force of gravity by lifting the sword and stone. You also need to do work against the force of friction in the fulcrum - which you've successfully done by hanging your coat on the stackable stones!

The **efficiency** of your lever is the **fraction** of energy that it can **usefully** transfer to the sword and stone. Increasing the internal energy of the fulcrum isn't useful to you! The total energy is always conserved - some is transferred to the sword and stone and some to the fulcrum.

It's like having a banking system where you're not able to transfer dollar bills from one place to another without some of them going through a shredder! You could try not transferring any of your money - but then you'll never be able to do anything **useful** with it!

Efficiency is the fraction of energy you can usefully transfer.

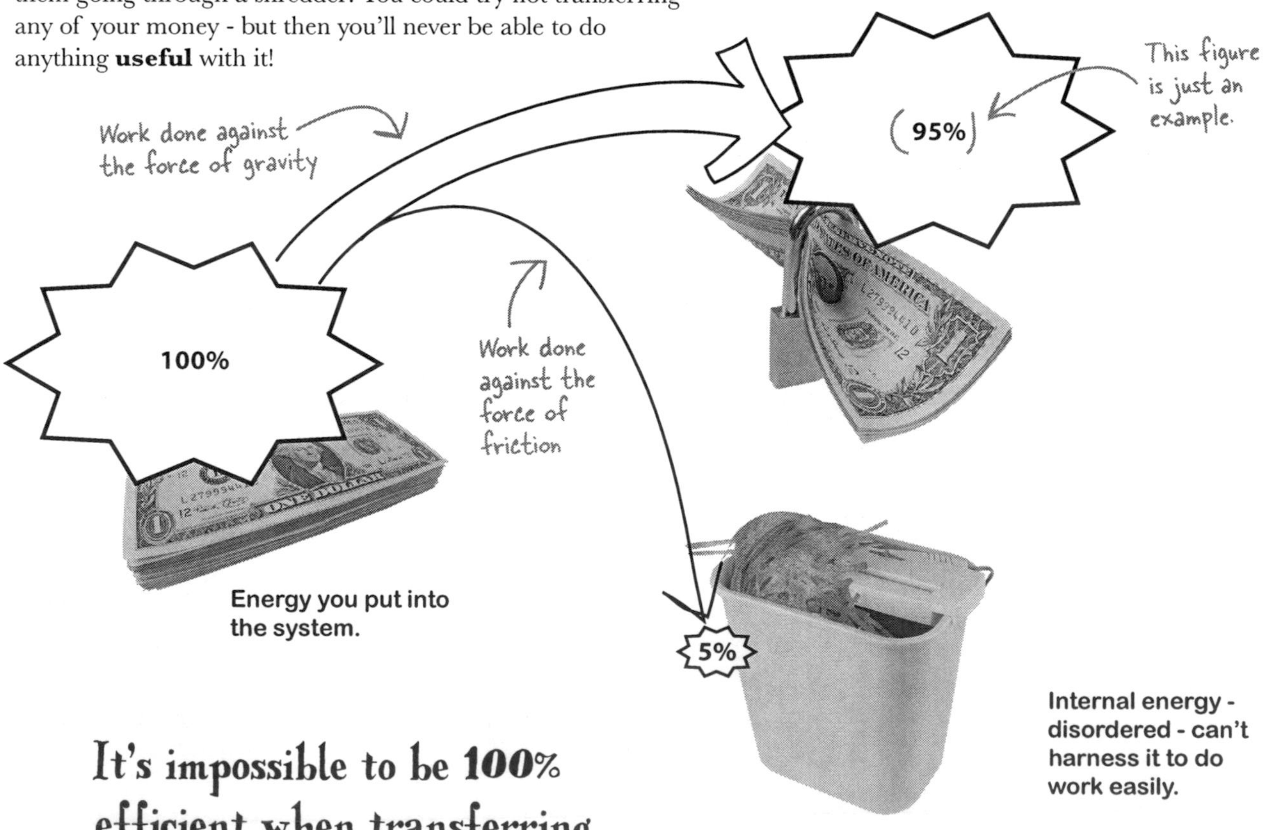

It's impossible to be 100% efficient when transferring energy from one store to another.

Fireside Chats

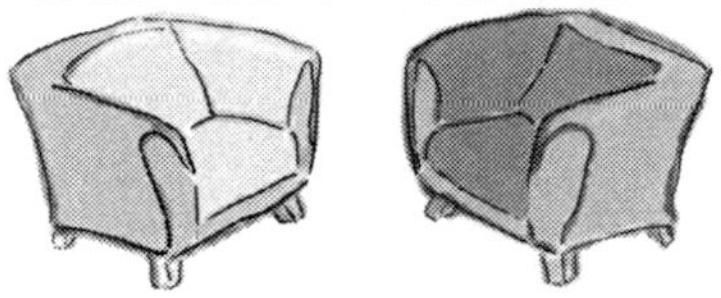

Tonight's talk: **Energy and Work go head to head.**

Energy: Oh hi work, what are you up to today?

Work: Whatever it is ... it'll be more useful than what you're up to, I'm sure!

Energy: Hey - there's no need to get so hot under the collar! What's up?

Work: Well, to tell you the truth, I'm feeling a little left out. It was great back at the start of the chapter when I was the star of the show. I loved the attention. But now you've come along, people are thinking almost exclusively about you instead.

Energy: Oh yes, I have rather hogged the limelight recently!

Work: Yeah, and it's me who's the useful one! If you want to get something moved by applying a force, I'm right in there!

Energy: Well, to be fair ... I'm in there too!

Work: But only as a noun - not a verb. If work is done on something, the energy is transferred. See?

Energy: But if it wasn't for me, you wouldn't be able to happen at all!

Work: Err ... I don't think so. How can you say that I depend on you?

Energy: Well, energy is the capacity that something has to do work. If something doesn't have a capacity to do work, then it can't do work. No me - no you!

Work: There you go - playing with words as usual and not letting yourself be pinned down. At least I know what I am - a displacement × the component of a force in the same direction. But what are you?

Energy: I'm the capacity that something has to do work!

Work: That's not what you are though - that's just words!

Energy: OK then - I'm always conserved, and I can't be created or destroyed. How about that then?!

Work: Well, it sounds a bit metaphysical - but is it physics?! And it still doesn't tell me what you actually are!

Energy: I guess that's because you can't pin me down really. You can't measure me directly. You can only measure changes as I'm transferred from one thing to another.

Work: Ha! Now there's where you can't get on with your life without me!! You need me!

Energy: Meaning ...

Work: Well, when work is done, energy is transferred. If it wasn't for me, you'd be totally stuck in one place all the time. No holidays, no day trips - just stuck.

Energy: That's not entirely true. Yes, doing work is one way of transferring energy, but I can also be transferred through heating, if there's a temperature difference between two things. The hot one gets cooler (so its internal energy gets lower) and the cool thing gets hotter (so its internal energy gets higher, until they both have the same temperature

Work: But that's all the same, isn't it? Where's the excitement?! At least when I act on something, you usually get transferred in a different way - like into something's potential energy. I give your life variety!

Energy: Yeah, but sometimes you do transfer me to raise something's internal energy as well - when there's friction involved.

Work: Ah yes, friction. I hate him. Y'know, the reason I didn't get a bonus this year was because I wasn't efficient enough. And guess whose fault that was!

Energy: Yeah ... I guess that's something we agree on. I don't get to go to such interesting places if there's too much friction.

Work: But I'm still more useful than you!

Energy: And you still couldn't do anything without me - so there!

Work: Whaaatever.

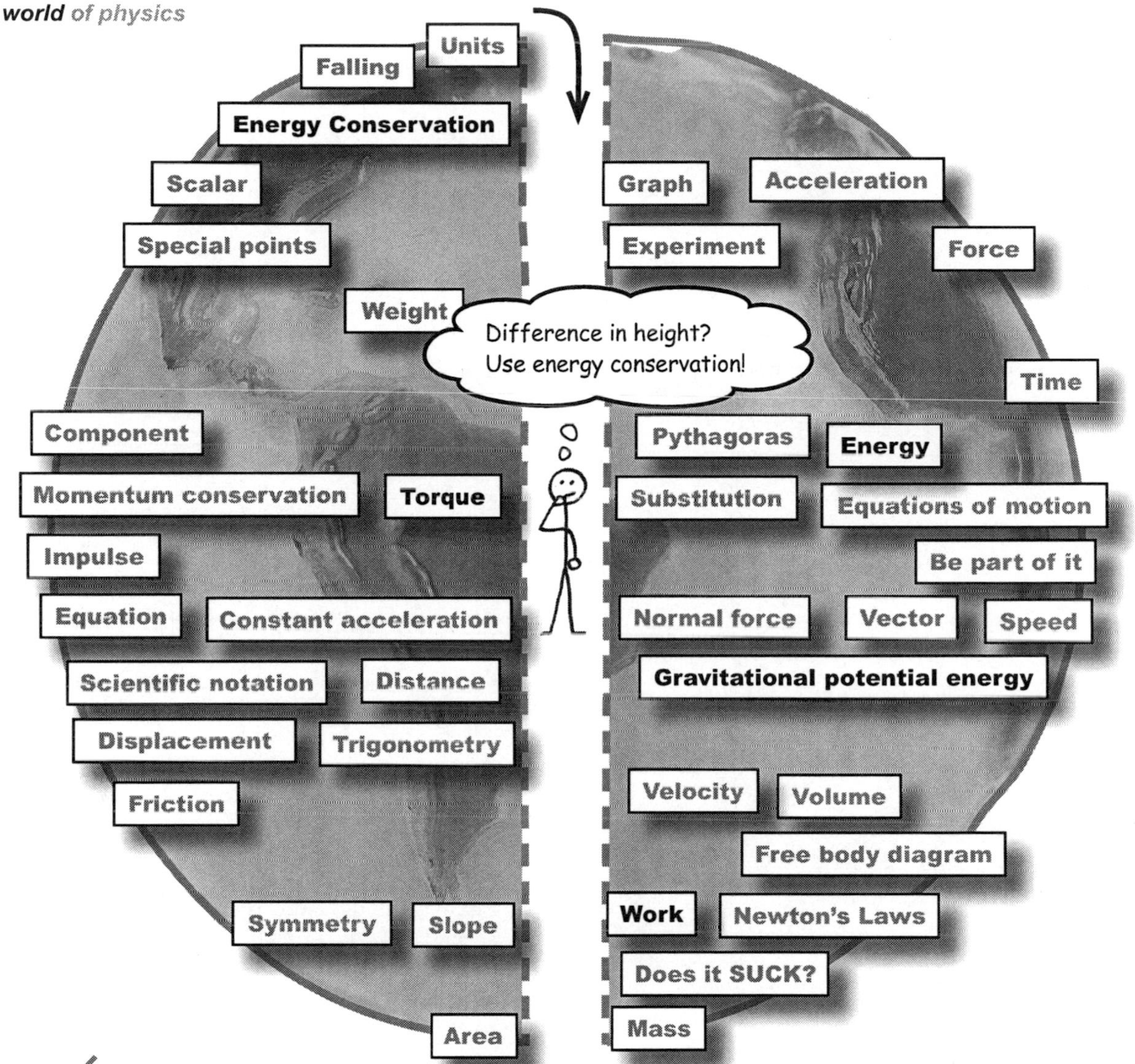

☑	**Torque**	**A "turning force" equal to component of force perpendicular to arm × distance from the fulcrum**
☑	**Work**	**When moving an object in the opposite direction from a force, work done = force × displacement parallel to force**
☑	**Energy**	**The capacity that something has to do work.**
☑	**Potential energy**	**The capacity something has to do work due to its increased height.**
☑	**Energy conservation**	**The total energy of a system must be the same before and after a change to the system, as energy is conserved.**

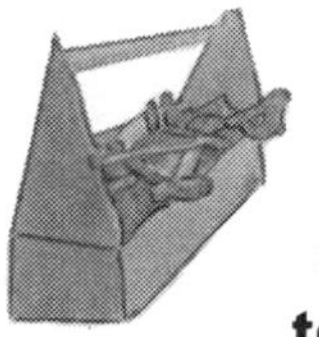

Your Physics Toolbox

You've got Chapter 13 under your belt and added some problem-solving tools to your toolbox.

CHAPTER 13

Lifting an object

If you have to lift an object in a physics problem, you should assume that the minimum force you require is equal to the object's weight (unless there is friction involved).

This is because Newton's 1st Law says that with zero net force, an object continues with a constant velocity. So once you've got it going upwards with an extra little 'nudge', you only need to exert a force equal to its weight to maintain its velocity.

"Zero net torque"

If you have a problem where something could potentially rotate and you have to work out the force you need to apply to make sure it doesn't, then you are being asked what force is required for there to be zero net torque.

When you're working with torques, take care to make one direction of rotation positive and stick with it.

Doing work

Doing work is a way of transferring energy from one store to another.

If you do work against a gravitational force by lifting an object, you increase its gravitational potential energy.

If you do work against a frictional force by pushing an object, you increase the internal energy of the object and of the surface it's in contact with.

"Spot the difference"

Differences drive changes that lead to energy transfer.

If there's a difference in the height of an object between the start and finish of a problem, look and see if you can use energy conservation instead of forces to solve it.

14 energy conservation

Making your life easier

Why do things the hard way when there's an easier way?

So far, you've been solving problems using equations of motion, forces and component vectors. And that's great—except that it sometimes takes a while to crunch through the math. In this chapter, you'll learn to spot where you can use **energy conservation** as a shortcut that lets you solve complicated-looking problems with relative ease.

The ultimate bobsled experience

The fairground has designed a unique new state-of-the-art bobsled track that's due to open soon. But before anyone can use it, it has to be designated as safe to ride. That's your job. Even though you're not a bobsledder, you can still use physics to figure out whether or not any adjustments have to be made.

From the start to checkpoint 1, the track has a **uniform slope**. Between checkpoints 1 and 2, the track **drops 30.0 m**, but the track **undulates**—the bobsled's even going uphill for a bit! Then the third part of the track is totally flat—where the bobsled is **stopped** by applying its brake to the ice.

Your job is to work out what the bobsled's **speed** will be at each checkpoint, and how hard you need to brake at the end.

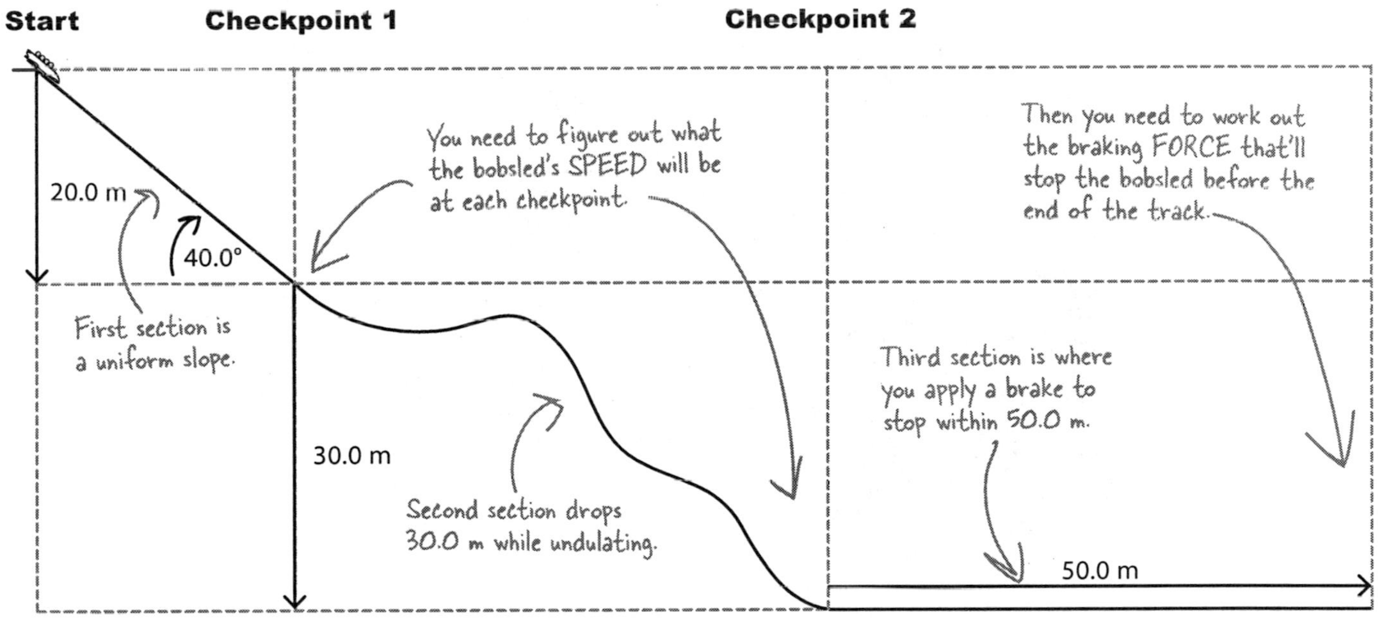

Start any problem with a sketch and by asking yourself "What's it LIKE?".

BRAIN POWER

Can you see any parts of the bobsled track that you **already know** how to deal with?

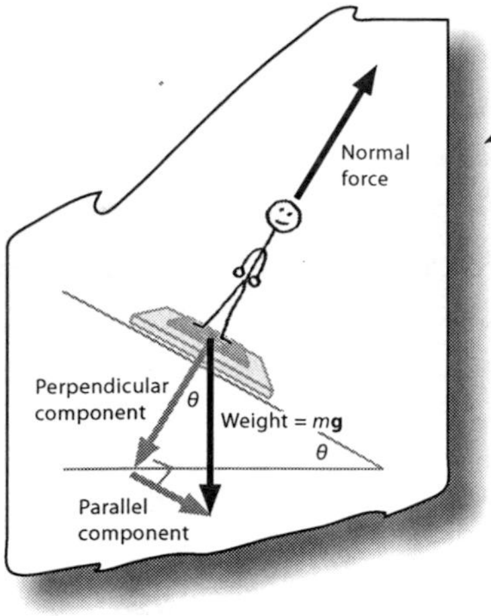

Hey... haven't we seem something going down a uniform slope before?!

You are here.

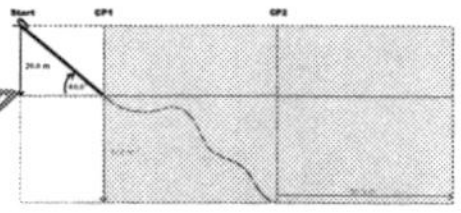

You already know how to do this!

The **first** section of track looks like the WeightBotchers machine from chapter 11 where the person on a set of scales slides down a slope.

Even if the later parts of the track look tough, you can still start with what you can **already** do!

Sharpen your pencil

You can already handle the first part of the track.

A bobsled, mass m, travels down a uniform slope that makes an angle of 40.0° with the horizontal and drops 20.0 m in height between the start and the first checkpoint.

a. What distance does the bobsled travel between the start and the first checkpoint?

b. What is the component of the bobsled's weight parallel to the slope?

Hint: You don't know a value for the bobsled's mass, so this answer won't be purely numerical and will have 'm' in it

c. What is the bobsled's speed at the first checkpoint?

Hint: Use Newton's 2nd Law to move from net force to acceleration, then use equations of motion to calculate the speed.

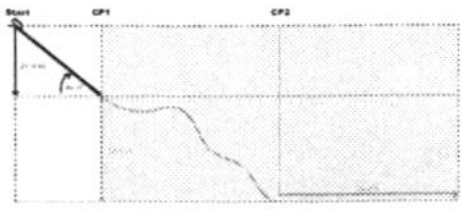

Sharpen your pencil Solution

A bobsled, mass *m*, travels down a uniform slope that makes an angle of 40.0° with the horizontal and drops 20.0 m in height between the start and the first checkpoint.

a. What distance does the bobsled travel between the start and the first checkpoint?

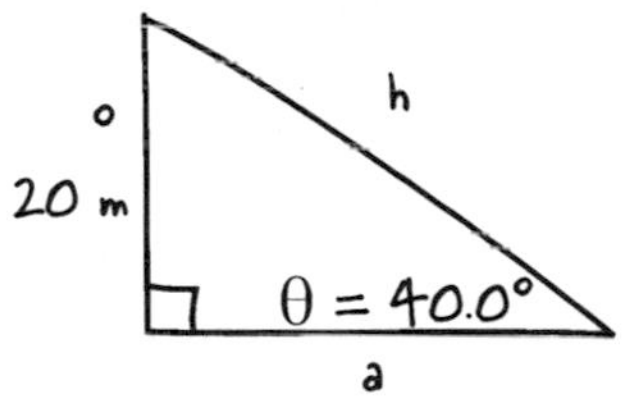

$$\sin(\theta) = \frac{o}{h}$$

$$h = \frac{20.0}{\sin(40.0)}$$

$$h = \underline{31.1\text{ m}}\ (3\text{ sd})$$

b. What is the component of the bobsled's weight parallel to the slope?

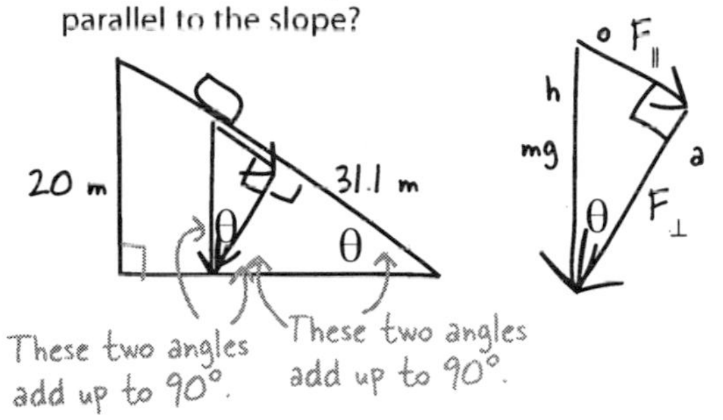

Bobsled's weight = mg

$F_{\parallel}$ component down the slope is the side opposite θ.

Use similar triangles to calculate side:

$$\frac{F_{\parallel}}{mg} = \frac{20.0}{31.1}$$

$$F_{\parallel} = \underline{0.643\ mg}\ (3\text{ sd})$$

If your answer contains variables, such as 'm' and 'g', you don't need to put in units at the end, as the variables already have units. But you still need units for a purely numerical answer.

c. What is the bobsled's speed at the first checkpoint?

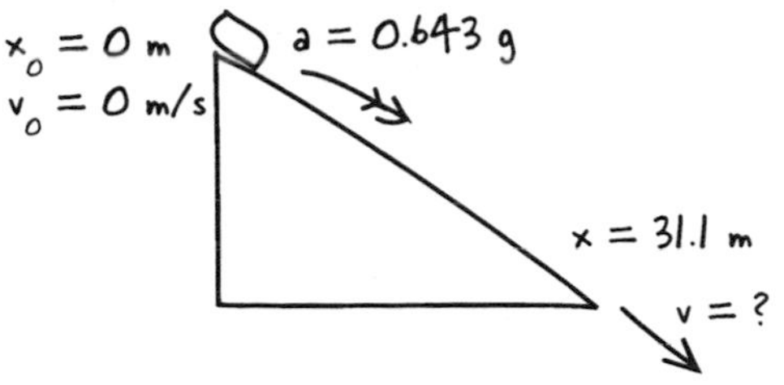

$$F_{net} = ma$$

$$0.643\ mg = ma$$

$$a = 0.643\ g$$

The acceleration is 0.643 g, so remember to put in the 9.8.

$$v^2 = v_0^2 + 2a(x - x_0)$$

$$v = \sqrt{0 + 2 \times 0.643 \times 9.8 \times 31.1} = \underline{19.8\text{ m/s}}\ (3\text{ sd})$$

Triangle Tip: sketch extreme angles

If you're not sure which angle in your force vector triangle corresponds to the angle of your slope, sketch a slope with a **small angle**, □.

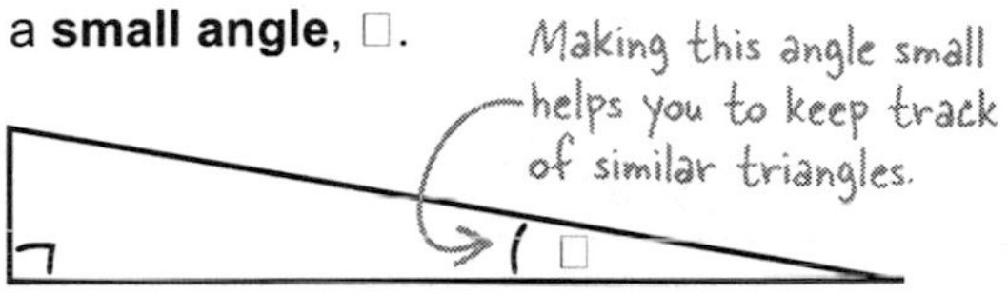

Now draw the force triangle. Draw on the weight pointing straight down. Then draw in the parallel and perpendicular components. It doesn't matter which way around you draw the components, as the triangle's sides will still be the same length.

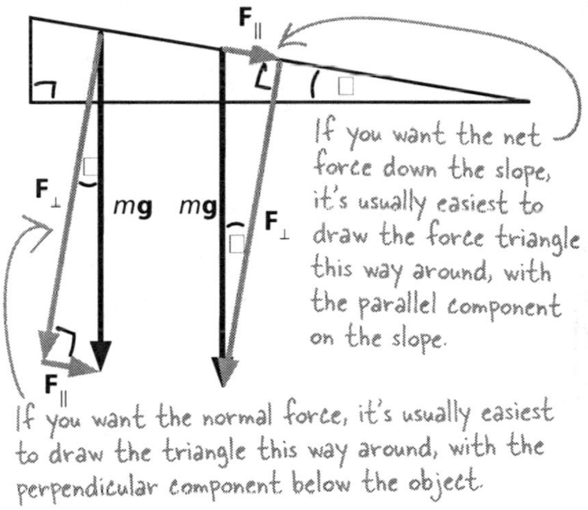

□ is the small angle in the slope triangle - so □ will also be the small angle in the force triangle.

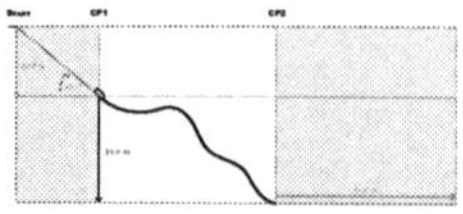

Forces and component vectors solve the first part...

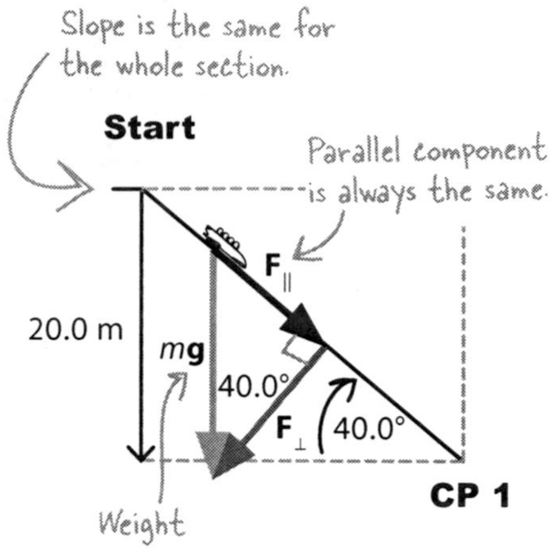

The first part of the track has a **uniform slope** that always makes the same angle with the horizontal. This means that the bobsled always experiences the same **net force** down the slope, as the component of the bobsled's weight **parallel** to the slope is constant.

And you've just worked out that the bobsled will have reached a speed of 19.8 m/s when it reaches the first checkpoint. So far, so good...

You want to know the bobsled's speed at each checkpoint.

...but the second part doesn't have a uniform slope

However, the second part of the bobsled run isn't quite as straightforward. Although the track drops 30.0 meters further, the slope definitely isn't uniform—it has peaks and dips along the way. Sometimes bobsleds even going uphill!

Any time the **angle** of the slope changes, the component of its weight parallel to the slope also changes. This means that the net force on the bobsled changes, so the size and direction of its **acceleration changes**.

This is a problem because the equations of motion only work when an object's acceleration is constant. So you can't use the same method as you did for the uniform slope.

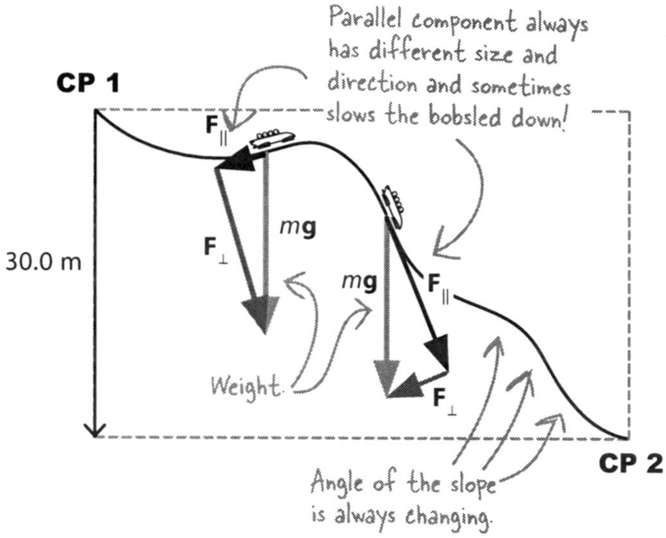

An object moving down a slope is accelerated by the component of its weight parallel to the slope.

> **BRAIN POWER**
>
> How can you deal with an **undulating** slope when all you know is that the bobsled drops 30.0 meters between the the first and second checkpoints?

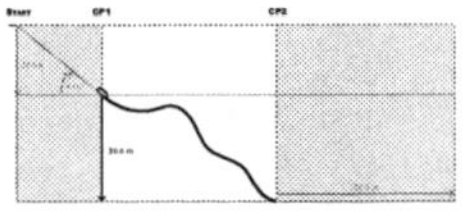

Joe: But the next section's more difficult—the slope changes all the time! The bobsled's acceleration won't be constant.

Jim: Maybe we can split the section up into lots of tiny sections? If the slope is uniform for a couple of meters, we could do a calculation for that, and then for the next bit, and then for the next bit, and so on. Then add together all the changes in speed to get our final answer.

Joe: That'll take forever! I don't think you could do it by hand.

Frank: You could probably program a computer to do that kinda job... but I've no idea how to do that.

Jim: Maybe we're going about this the wrong way. We've been thinking in terms of **forces** so far, but what about **energy**?

Joe: Hmmm. The bobsled loses 30.0 m of height. So the bobsled has more **gravitational potential energy** at the start of the section than it does at the end because of the **difference in height**.

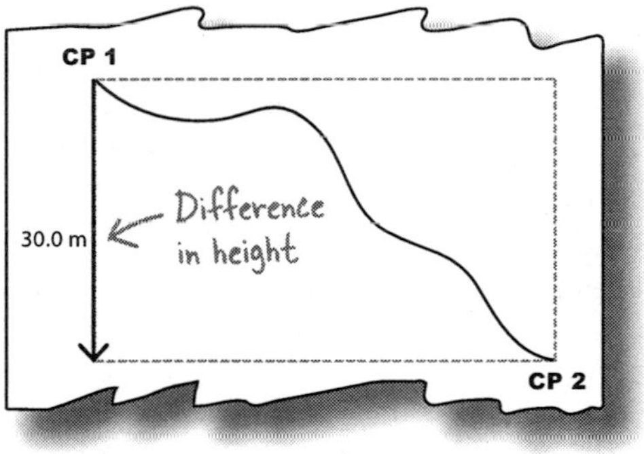

Any time you see a change in height, think about using energy conservation.

Frank: But how do we do a calculation with that? I'm not sure where that energy's been transferred to!

Jim: Yea, but **energy's conserved**, right?! So the energy must be transferred in some way when the bobsled goes down the slope!

Jim: I wonder if we can say that the bobsled has energy because it's **moving**?! Energy's the capacity something has to do work, right?

Frank: Yeah... if a moving object hits another object, the first object will exert a **force** that **displaces** the second object. So work gets done. A hammer! A moving hammer exerts a force to displace a nail into wood. That's doing work, isn't it?

Joe: I think we'd better take this further!

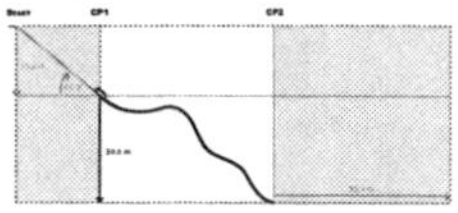

A moving object has kinetic energy

At the top of the slope, the bobsled has more **gravitational potential energy** than it does part-way down or at the bottom because of the difference in **height**.

Moving objects are said to have **kinetic energy**. They're able to do work by exerting a force that displaces something—that's how hammering in a nail works. If the hammer was stationary and didn't have a **velocity**, you couldn't use it to do work on the nail!!

Differences drive changes that involve energy transfer. The difference in **height** leads to a change in the **velocity** of the bobsled. This means that the bobsled gains kinetic energy as it loses potential energy. If the bobsled's potential energy goes down by 1000 J due to the difference in height, its kinetic energy increases by 1000 J.

If you can work out an **equation** for the kinetic energy, you'll be able to use **energy conservation** to calculate the bobsled's velocity at checkpoint 2 due to its change in height.

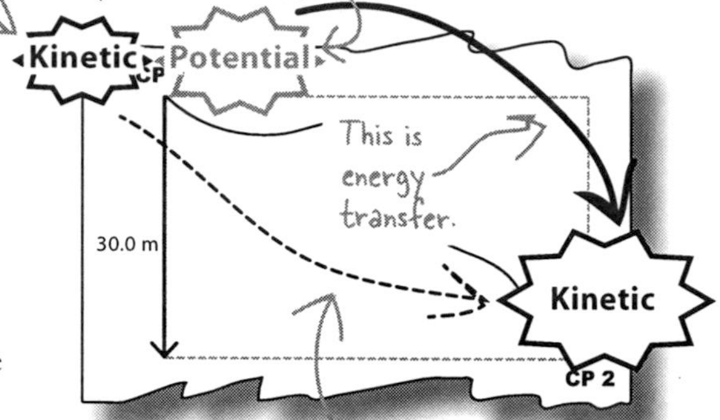

The change in potential energy is the same size as the change in kinetic energy because energy is conserved.

This is assuming there's no friction - and there won't be that much on ice.

Sharpen your pencil

This is doing work: Work = $F\Delta x$

a. Imagine a **moving** hammer doing work on a nail by exerting a force on it to move it a displacement into a piece of wood. The more **kinetic energy** the hammer has, the more work it can do. With this in mind, what variables do you think the hammer's kinetic energy might depend on, and why?

Now you can collect useful equations that will help you work out an equation for kinetic energy. In this "Sharpen your pencil," you're only writing the equations down—you'll do the rearranging and substituting on the next page. If you can't remember the equations, it's OK to look them up in appendix ii.

b. Write down an equation for the gravitational potential energy of the bobsled, mass *m*, at its highest point, height **h**.

c. Write down an equation of motion for a falling object that involves **x**, $\mathbf{x_0}$, $\mathbf{v_0}$, **v** and **a**.

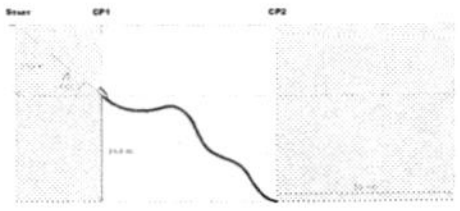

Sharpen your pencil Solution

a. Imagine a **moving** hammer doing work on a nail by exerting a force on it to move it a displacement into a piece of wood. The more **kinetic energy** the hammer has, the more work it can do. With this in mind, what variables do you think the hammer's kinetic energy might depend on, and why?

The hammer will do more work if it has a high speed.

The hammer will do more work if it has a large mass.

So kinetic energy must depend on both mass and velocity.

The more work the hammer does with each hit, the larger the displacement of the nail with each hit.

Now you can collect useful equations that will help you work out an equation for kinetic energy. In this "Sharpen your pencil," you're only writing the equations down—you'll do the rearranging and substituting on the next page. If you can't remember the equations, it's OK to look them up in appendix ii.

b. Write down an equation for the gravitational potential energy of the bobsled, mass *m*, at its highest point, height **h**.

$$U_g = F\Delta x = mgh$$

This gives you an expression for the potential energy that will be transferred to kinetic energy.

c. Write down an equation of motion for a falling object that involves **x**, $\mathbf{x_0}$, $\mathbf{v_0}$, **v** and **a**.

$$v^2 = v_0^2 + 2a(x - x_0)$$

This will help you to connect the difference in height with the speed.

there are no Dumb Questions

Q: If I know the difference in height between the start and end of a uniform slope, I can work out an object's velocity at the end, right?

A: Yes. If a slope is uniform and always at the same angle (like the first part of the track was), you can use forces and component vectors to calculate the net force on an object and, therefore, its acceleration and final velocity.

Q: What about an undulating slope? Can I do the same to solve that problem?

A: You could in theory... though not easily. You'd need to work out the net force on the object for every tiny part of the slope. This is practically impossible unless you program a computer do to it for you.

Q: Does a problem with an undulating slope always need a computer to solve it?

A: No. You can use energy conservation. The **potential** energy that the object has at the top of the slope must be transferred to **kinetic** energy as the object goes down the slope.

Q: What's kinetic energy?

A: The capacity that something has to do work due to its velocity. Moving things have kinetic energy.

Q: I know that the potential energy is mgh, but what's the equation for kinetic energy?

A: That's what you're in the process of working out. So far, you've realized that an object's kinetic energy must depend on its mass and velocity. And you're about to do some substitutions to see exactly how...

The kinetic energy is related to the velocity

Moving objects have **kinetic energy**.

As the bobsled gets lower down the track, some of the **potential energy** it had at the start will be **transferred** to kinetic energy. The kinetic energy the bobsled gains must be **equal** to the potential energy that it loses.

The kinetic energy must depend somehow on the **mass** and **velocity** of the bobsled. If you can work out an equation for the change in kinetic energy, you can use it to calculate the bobsled's change in velocity between the first and second checkpoints—and, therefore, its velocity at the second checkpoint.

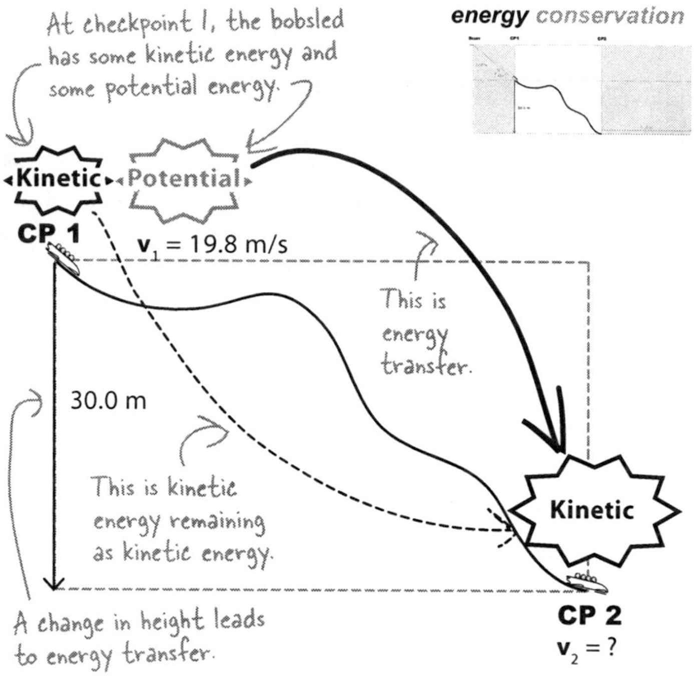

Sharpen your pencil

a. The two equations you wrote down on the previous page, $U_g = mgh$ and $\mathbf{v}^2 = \mathbf{v}_0^2 + 2\mathbf{a}(\mathbf{x} - \mathbf{x}_0)$, are both written down in the form that you'll find them on equation sheets - but they use different letters to represent the same quantities. If you're dealing with an object dropped straight down and accelerated by gravity, which variables in the equations are equivalent to each other?

b. By making a substitution for the change in height, show that the kinetic energy (K) of an object dropped straight down from a stationary start at height **h** which started with potential energy $U_g = m\mathbf{g}\mathbf{h}$ is $K = ½m\mathbf{v}^2$.

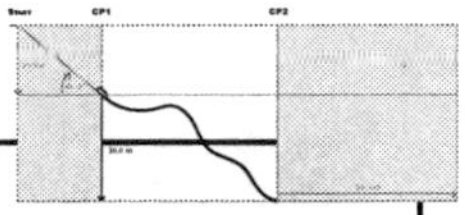

Sharpen your pencil Solution

a. The two equations you wrote down on the previous page, $U_g = m\mathbf{gh}$ and $\mathbf{v}^2 = \mathbf{v}_0^2 + 2\mathbf{a}(\mathbf{x} - \mathbf{x}_0)$, are both written down in the form that you'll find them on equation sheets - but they use different letters to represent the same quantities. If you're dealing with an object dropped straight down and accelerated by gravity, which variables in the equations are equivalent to each other?

$U = mgh \qquad v^2 = v_0^2 + 2a(x - x_0)$

In the first equation, the displacement is h; in the second it's $x - x_0$.

In the first equation, the acceleration is g; in the second it's a.

b. By making a substitution for the change in height, show that the kinetic energy (K) of an object dropped straight down from a stationary start at height **h** which started with potential energy $U_g = m\mathbf{gh}$ is $K = ½m\mathbf{v}^2$.

Stationary start, so $v_0 = 0$

Energy is conserved, so $U_{start} = K_{end}$

The change in height, h, is $x - x_0$ so rearrange and substitute.

Substitute 'g' for 'a'. → $v^2 = 2g(x - x_0)$

$(x - x_0) = \frac{v^2}{2g}$

Substitute 'h' for 'x − x_0' → $h = \frac{v^2}{2g}$ ← Substitute for 'h'

$K_{end} = U_{start} = mgh = mg\frac{v^2}{2g}$

$K_{end} = ½mv^2$

It's sometimes a good idea to drop the 'g' subscript from U_g, the gravitational potential energy.

This is because the subscript is only to distinguish gravitational potential energy from U_s, the elastic potential energy of a spring.

In a situation where there are no springs and there could be confusion with 'g', the gravitational field strength, it's best just to use the symbol 'U' with no subscript for gravitational potential energy. This also allows you to write U_{start} and U_{end} more easily.

But that equation's for something that falls straight down, right? The bobsled doesn't do that!

The same change in height always leads to the same change in potential energy, regardless of path.

The amount of energy transferred only depends on the change in height.

The bobsled has a certain store of **potential energy** as a result of being at a certain height. Its potential energy store doesn't depend on what path it took to get up there in the first place.

The same change in height always leads to the same change in potential energy when the bobsled's going down as well as when it's going up. So that change in potential energy must be transferred to **kinetic energy**, whatever path the bobsled takes (assuming there's no friction). The bobsled will always have the same change in kinetic energy for the same change in height.

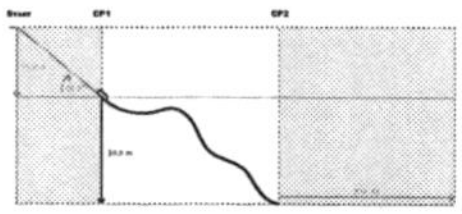

Calculate the velocity using energy conservation and the change in height

The kinetic energy of a moving object is given by the equation

$$K = \frac{1}{2}m\mathbf{v}^2$$

This means that if you know the bobsled's **mass** and **kinetic energy**, you can use them to calculate the bobsled's **velocity**.

Kinetic energy → $$K = \frac{1}{2}mv^2$$ ← Mass, Velocity

You can calculate the bobsled's kinetic energy using energy conservation. The difference in its speed between checkpoint 1 and checkpoint 2 is because of the difference in height between the two checkpoints. So the change in **potential** energy and the change in **kinetic** energy must be the same size.

Sharpen your pencil

A bobsled travelling down a track has just reached its first checkpoint (CP1). The second checkpoint (CP2) is at the bottom of the slope, 30.0 m lower than the first.

If the bobsled has a speed of 19.8 m/s at CP1, what is its speed at CP2? (The bobsled's potential + kinetic energy at the start will be equal to its kinetic energy at the end.)

Hint: It's a good idea to use subscripts to represent energy at each checkpoint, for example K_1, U_1, K_2, U_2, etc.

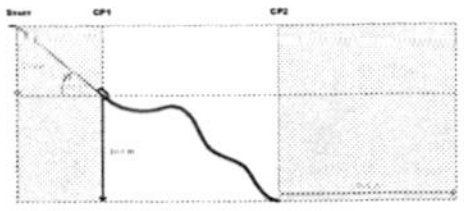

Sharpen your pencil Solution

A bobsled travelling down a track has just reached its first checkpoint (CP1). The second checkpoint (CP2) is at the bottom of the slope, 30.0 m lower than the first.

If the bobsled has a speed of 19.8 m/s at CP1, what is its speed at CP2? (The bobsled's potential + kinetic energy at the start will be equal to its kinetic energy at the end.)

$$CP1:\ K_1 + U_1 = mgh + \tfrac{1}{2}mv_1^2$$

$$CP2:\ K_2 = \tfrac{1}{2}mv_2^2$$

$$\tfrac{1}{2}mv_2^2 = mgh + \tfrac{1}{2}mv_1^2$$

$$v_2^2 = 2gh + v_1^2$$

$$v_2 = \sqrt{2gh + v_1^2}$$

$$v_2 = \sqrt{(2 \times 9.8 \times 30) + 19.8^2}$$

$$v_2 = 31.3\ \text{m/s (3 sd)}$$

$v_1 = 19.8$ m/s

$h = 30$ m

$v_2 = ?$

Each term is multiplied by 'm'. So 'm' divides out and cancels.

If you can use energy conservation to do a problem, it's less complicated than using forces.

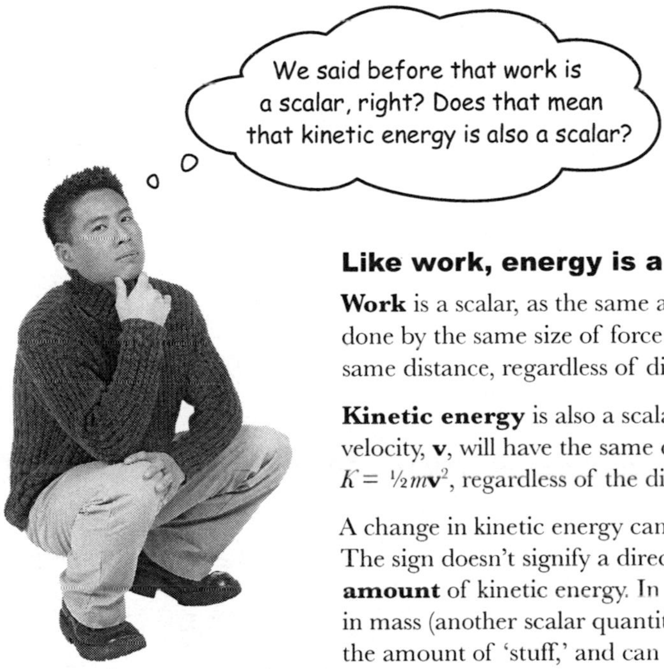

Like work, energy is a scalar quantity.

Work is a scalar, as the same amount of work will be done by the same size of force moving an object the same distance, regardless of direction.

Kinetic energy is also a scalar, as an object with velocity, **v**, will have the same quantity of kinetic energy, $K = \tfrac{1}{2}m\mathbf{v}^2$, regardless of the direction of its velocity.

A change in kinetic energy can be positive or negative. The sign doesn't signify a direction, just a change in the **amount** of kinetic energy. In the same way, a change in mass (another scalar quantity) signifies the change in the amount of 'stuff,' and can be positive or negative.

When you have a vector, its direction is shown by its sign. But when you square a number, the result is always positive. Therefore, v^2 is a scalar because the information about the direction of v (its sign) has been lost. This means that kinetic energy must also be a scalar, as $K = \tfrac{1}{2}mv^2$.

Same velocity means same kinetic energy, regardless of direction.

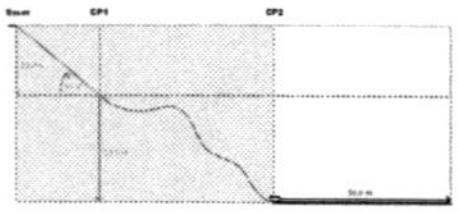

You've used energy conservation to solve the second part

You've used energy conservation to work out that the bobsled has a speed of 31.3 m/s when it hits the second checkpoint, 30.0 m below the first.

The same **change in height** will always leads to the same **change in potential energy**—and to the same **change in kinetic energy** if there's no friction.

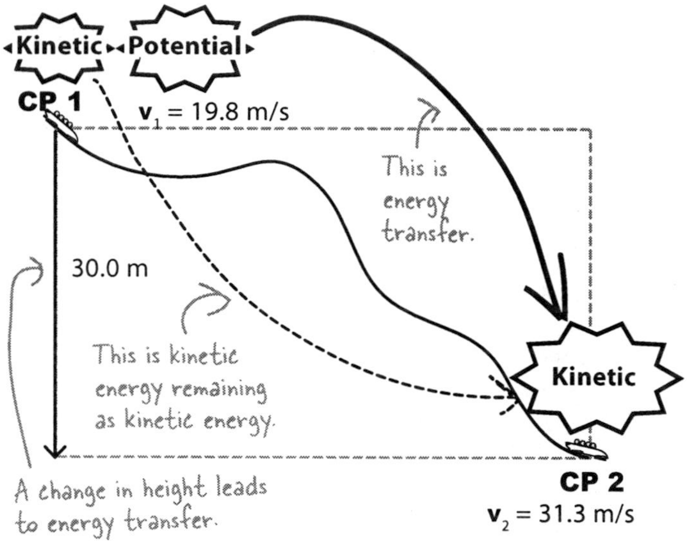

In the third part, you have to apply a force to stop a moving object

The third part of the track is flat and is the stretch where the bobsled must be brought to a halt by applying a brake to the ice. The track design states that the 630 kg bobsled must be stationary by the time it's covered 50.0 m.

630 kg is the maximum mass the bobsled is allowed to have when there are people in it.

How should you go about calculating the **force** you need to apply with the brake?

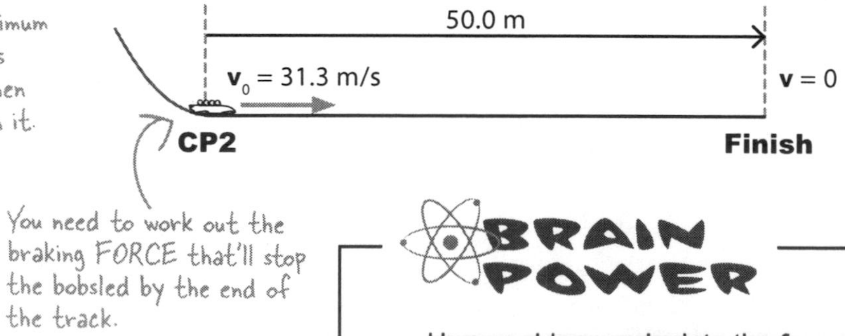

BRAIN POWER

How could you calculate the **force** you need to apply with the brake to stop the bobsled?

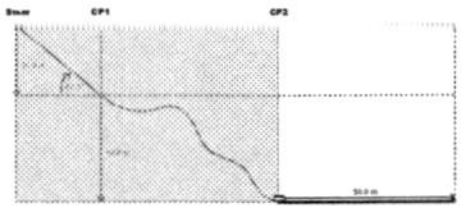

Jim: Well, there's no change in height, so we can't do anything with energy. I guess we can use **equations of motion** to work out the **acceleration**, and then Newton's Second Law, $\mathbf{F}_{net} = m\mathbf{a}$, to calculate the **force**. That would work!

Joe: But it would be a lot of calculations. Are you **sure** we can't do something with **energy conservation**? That was easier than using equations of motion for the previous part of the track.

Jim: Well, fairly sure. There's no change in height, so there's no change in potential energy. So how would we use energy conservation?

Joe: I was thinking, we need to stop the bobsled within a certain **distance** by applying a **force**. That sounds like doing **work** to me!

Frank: Yeah, you do work on something by applying a force. But I thought you actually had to displace something with the force—not just shove a brake down as you slide along some ice!

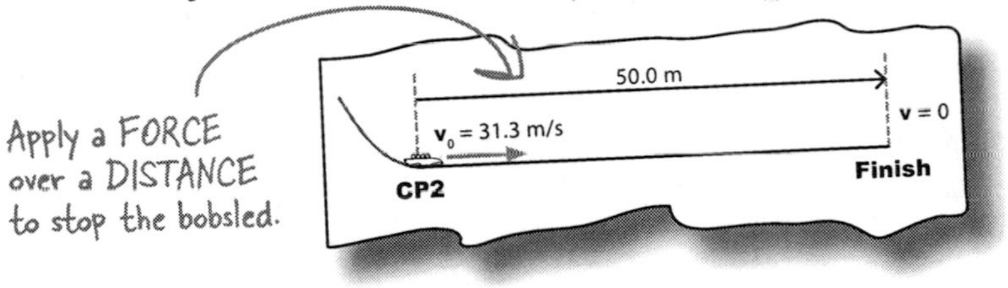

Any time you apply a <u>force</u> over a <u>distance</u>, think <u>work and energy</u>!

Jim: Wait, he might be right. When you catch a baseball, you exert a force on it with your hand. And your hand moves backwards as you catch it, so you apply the force over a distance. And that changes the kinetic energy of the ball.

Joe: So can we use the same kind of principle with calculating the force we need to stop the bobsled? We know its mass and velocity, so we can calculate its **kinetic energy**. AND we also know the distance that we need to apply the force over—50.0 m.

Frank: But where does the kinetic energy of the bobsled—or the baseball for that matter—go when you stop it?! It's not like it gets transferred to potential energy, is it?

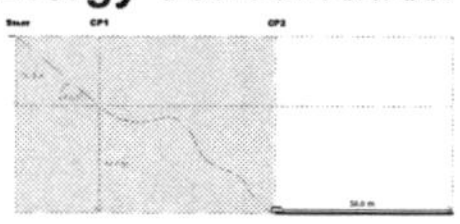

Putting on the brake does work on the track

You need to stop the bobsled by applying the brake before it reaches the end of the course. You have 50.0 m to stop it, but you need to know what **force** to apply with the brake.

One way of doing this problem would be to calculate the acceleration that the bobsled experiences as is slows down, then use $\mathbf{F}_{net} = m\mathbf{a}$ to calculate the force required. This method is fine and will give you the correct answer.

Do problems using energy conservation if possible.

However, for the earlier parts of this problem, you've discovered that using **energy conservation** to do a calculation can be a lot quicker and easier than using forces. Work = $\mathbf{F}\Delta\mathbf{x}$, so applying a force with the brake over the 50.0 m distance will do work.

But how is **energy transferred** from the moment the brake is applied to the moment the bobsled stops moving?

BE the brake

Your job is to imagine that you're the brake. What happens in terms of energy transfer from the moment that the brake is applied to the track to the moment that the bobsled comes to a complete stop? Write notes on the picture and give a written explanation below.

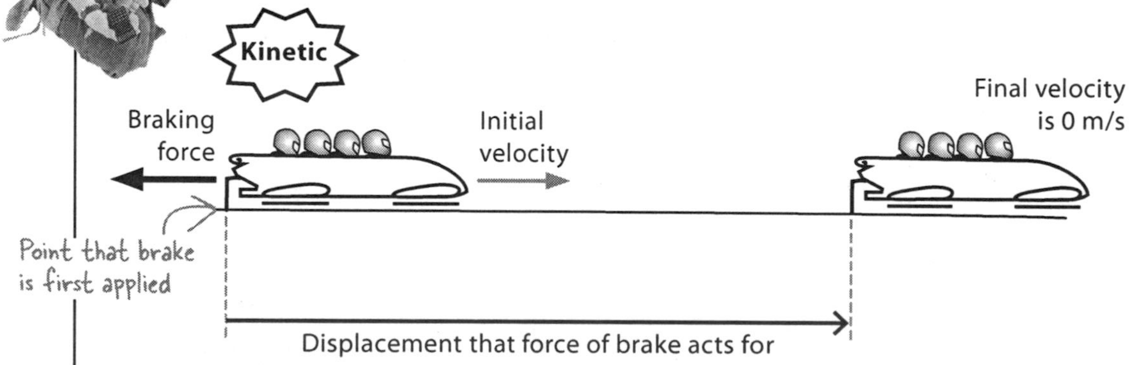

....

....

....

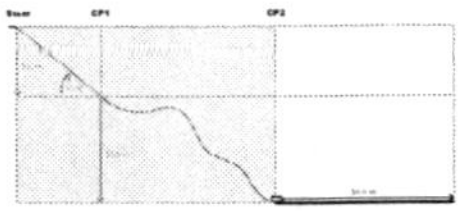

BE the brake - SOLUTION

Your job is to imagine that you're the brake. What happens in terms of energy transfer from the moment that the brake is applied to the track to the moment that the bobsled comes to a complete stop? Write notes on the picture and give a written explanation below.

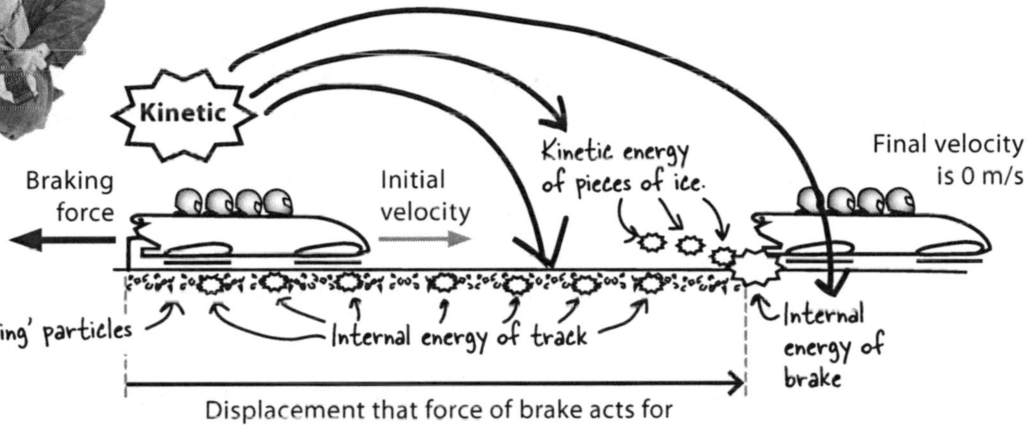

At the start the bobsled has kinetic energy; at the end its kinetic energy is zero.
The kinetic energy is transferred to the internal energy of the brake and the track, as the brake does work against friction. The movement of the brake over the track kind of 'jostles' the particles and makes them move around more vigorously inside the brake and the track.

Doing work against friction increases the internal energy

When you put on the brake, you **transfer** some of the bobsled's **kinetic** energy to the **internal** energy of the brake and the track by doing work against friction. This reduces the kinetic energy of the bobsled and also its speed, as $K = \frac{1}{2}mv^2$.

Energy transfer also happens when small pieces of ice spray up from the track. Each individual piece of ice has a small amount of **kinetic** energy. It's not much compared with the bobsled's kinetic energy, this will have an effect over a distance of 50.0 m.

When you do work against friction, you increase the INTERNAL ENERGY of the surfaces that are moving over each other.

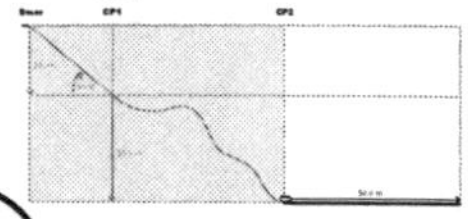

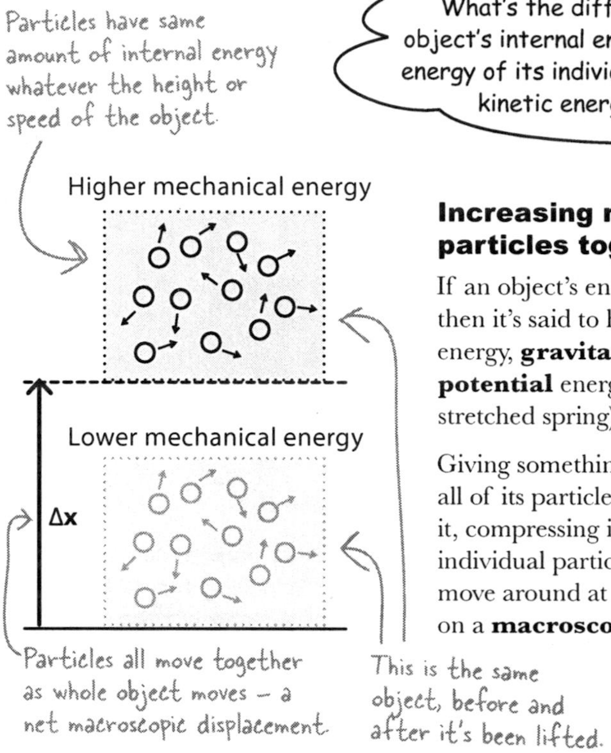

Increasing mechanical energy moves particles together in an ordered way.

If an object's energy store can easily be used to do work, then it's said to have **mechanical energy**. **Kinetic** energy, **gravitational potential** energy, and **elastic potential** energy (which is like a compressed or stretched spring) are all examples of mechanical energy.

Giving something mechanical energy involves moving all of its particles **together**, for example, by lifting it, compressing it, or giving it a velocity. Although the individual particles inside the object will continue to move around at random, there's a **net displacement** on a **macroscopic scale** (large scale).

With potential or kinetic energy, the whole object moves in an ordered way.

Increasing internal energy makes particles move more vigorously in a disordered way.

If you increase something's internal energy, you make the **random** motion of its particles more pronounced.

If it's a liquid or a gas, you can think of this as increasing the kinetic energy of each individual particle as they move around.

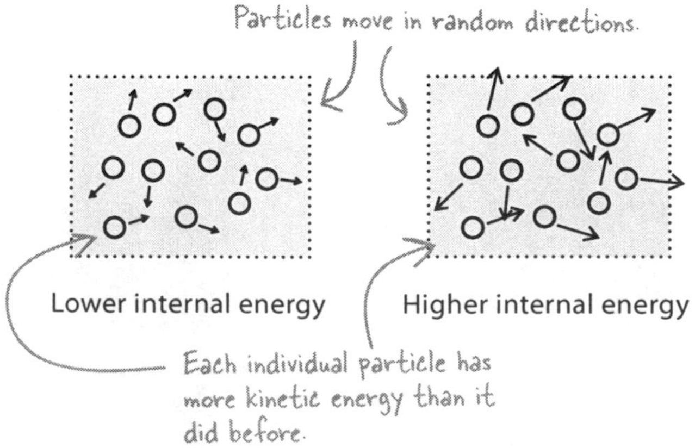

If it's a solid, you can think of this as increasing the intensity with which atoms vibrate. This is like giving the atoms kinetic energy and their bonds potential energy (like springs).

Increasing internal energy involves many tiny increases of kinetic or potential energy on a **microscopic scale**. But as these changes occur in **random directions**, they don't lead to a change in mechanical energy on a macroscopic scale because there's **no overall net displacement**.

there are no Dumb Questions

Q: So what's the difference between mechanical energy and kinetic energy? The names sound kinda similar.

A: Mechanical energy is a catch-all term for kinetic energy and potential energy—the kinds of energy stores that can be easily harnessed to do work.

Q: How do I calculate the mechanical energy of a system?

A: The mechanical energy is the total potential energy plus the total kinetic energy.

Q: Why is mechanical energy useful?

A: If there's no friction, the total mechanical energy is conserved. For example, you can work out the speed of an object that's at a lower height than it started off at by working out the change in its potential energy. This must be the same size as its change in kinetic energy, which you can use to calculate its speed.

Q: What is internal energy?

A: Every object or substance has internal energy due to the movement of the particles it's made from. Particles in a solid vibrate; particles in a liquid or gas move around.

Q: Why is internal energy different from mechanical energy?

A: An object's mechanical energy changes when all of its particles experience the same movement on a macroscopic (large) scale.

For example, if an object is lifted to a new height, its particles all move together in an ordered way and its potential energy increases. And if an object gets faster, its particles all move together in an ordered way and its kinetic energy increases.

Q: But internal energy also involves the movement of particles, which have individual stores of kinetic or potential energy themselves. Why is it different from the movement of particles in mechanical energy?

A: The particles move or vibrate in a random, disordered way. When you increase the internal energy of an object, its particles don't suddenly relocate all together. They do move with greater individual energies on a microscopic scale. But on a macroscopic scale, the object as a whole stays where it is!

Mechanical energy is about changes on a <u>macroscopic</u> scale.

Internal energy is about changes on a <u>microscopic</u> scale.

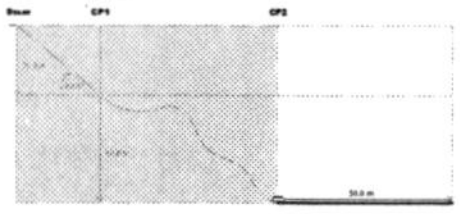

Sharpen your pencil

A 630 kg bobsled going at 31.3 m/s is to be brought to a halt by a brake applied to the ice track.

a. Describe this process in terms of energy transfer.

b. If the bobsled is to be stopped in 50.0 m, what force needs to be used?

c. Another way of helping to stop the bobsled is for the final part of the track to be slightly uphill. If the track goes up by 10.0 m during the final 50.0 m, what force would be required from the brake then?

d. If the bobsled is to be returned to the top of the track (50.0 m above the bottom), what is the minimum time it would take a 10.0 kW engine to lift it the requisite height (assuming 90% efficiency)?

Watts (W) are a measure of power. 1 Watt = 1 Joule per second.

This means that only 90% of the engine's energy is used 'usefully.' The rest goes towards increasing the internal energy of various moving parts.

Hint: Assume that there's no friction, so the engine only has to do work against gravity.

Hint: Calculate the total energy required, then see how many seconds it takes the engine to produce that amount of energy.

Sharpen your pencil Solution

A 630 kg bobsled going at 31.3 m/s is to be brought to a halt by a brake applied to the ice track.

a. Describe this process in terms of energy transfer.

The moving bobsled has kinetic energy. As it slows down, energy is transferred and the internal energy of the brake and the track increase. When the bobsled is stationary, the brake and the track will be hotter than they were before due to their increase in internal energy.

b. If the bobsled is to be stopped in 50.0 m, what force needs to be used?

$$\text{Work done} = F\Delta x \qquad K = \tfrac{1}{2}mv^2$$

Need to 'get rid of' all the bobsled's kinetic energy by doing work against friction.

$$F\Delta x = \tfrac{1}{2}mv^2$$

$$F = \frac{\tfrac{1}{2}mv^2}{\Delta x} = \frac{0.5 \times 630 \times 31.3^2}{50.0} = \underline{\underline{6170\text{ N}}} \text{ (3 sd)}$$

c. Another way of helping to stop the bobsled is for the final part of the track to be slightly uphill. If the track goes up by 10.0 m during the final 50.0 m, what force would be required from the brake then?

Some kinetic energy transferred to potential energy. Transfer the rest by doing work against friction.

$$F\Delta x + mgh = \tfrac{1}{2}mv^2$$

$$F = \frac{\tfrac{1}{2}mv^2 - mgh}{\Delta x} = \frac{(0.5 \times 630 \times 31.3^2) - (630 \times 9.8 \times 10.0)}{50.0}$$

$$F = \underline{\underline{4940\text{ N}}} \text{ (3 sd)}$$

d. If the bobsled is to be returned to the top of the track (50.0 m above the bottom), what is the minimum time it would take a 10.0 kW engine to lift it the requisite height (assuming 90% efficiency)?

$$\text{Work required to lift bobsled} = mgh = 630 \times 9.8 \times 50.0 = 309000\text{ J (3 sd)}$$

Engine produces 10000 Joules per second; 9000 Joules per second are useful.

$$\text{Time taken} = \frac{309000}{9000} = 34.3\text{ s (3 sd)}$$

It doesn't matter how far the bobsled travels horizontally. As long as it ends 50.0 m higher than it starts, this is the energy required to get it up there.

there are no Dumb Questions

Q: If energy conservation lets me do complicated questions this easily, what's the point of equations of motion and force?

A: To understand energy conservation, you needed to build on top of a base of the other things you mention. And you can't solve every problem using energy conservation! It's another tool in your toolkit, but not one you'll be able to use exclusively.

Q: But I will be using it a lot, right?

A: Yes ... but when it's appropriate! A lot of scenarios will involve collisions where mechanical energy isn't conserved, and you can't directly calculate the change in internal energy. You'll have to use other tools as well as energy for dealing with problems like that.

Energy conservation helps you to do complicated problems in a simpler way

You've just used energy conservation to solve complicated and even impossible-looking problems in a simpler way.

If you have something moving down or up a slope, then you can work out the change in its **potential energy**—and hence the change in its **kinetic energy** and speed—from the change in its **height**, no matter what path it takes.

And if there's friction involved, you can think of it in terms of **energy transfer** rather than forces if you're interested in displacement. This gives you the braking force of 6170 N that you need.

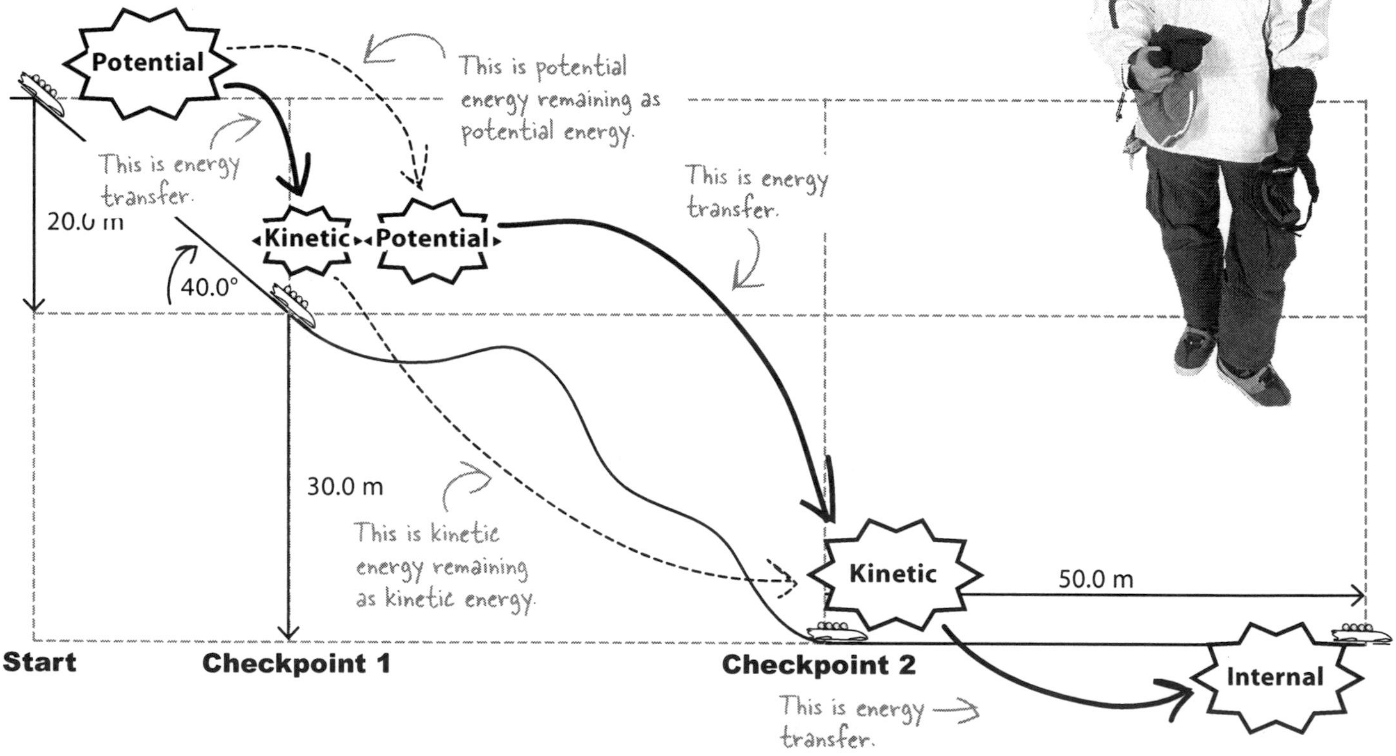

Look out for <u>differences</u> in height, velocity, etc. between the start and end of your problem that may allow you to use <u>energy conservation</u>.

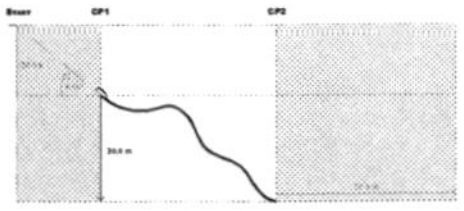

I'm not clear on the **difference** between momentum (mv) and kinetic energy ($\frac{1}{2}mv^2$). A moving object has both. Their equations look similar and they're both conserved. So aren't they just different ways of saying the same thing?!

Not quite. Momentum and kinetic energy are different.

If something is stationary, you can get it going by giving it a push, i.e., applying a force.

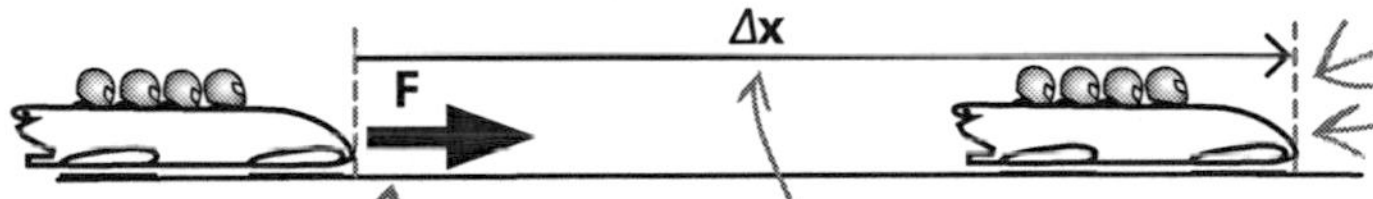

The **momentum-impulse** equation says that if you apply a net **force** for a period of **time**, it causes a change in momentum, $\mathbf{F}\Delta t = \Delta\mathbf{p} = \Delta(m\mathbf{v})$.

$$\mathbf{F}\Delta t = \Delta\mathbf{p}$$

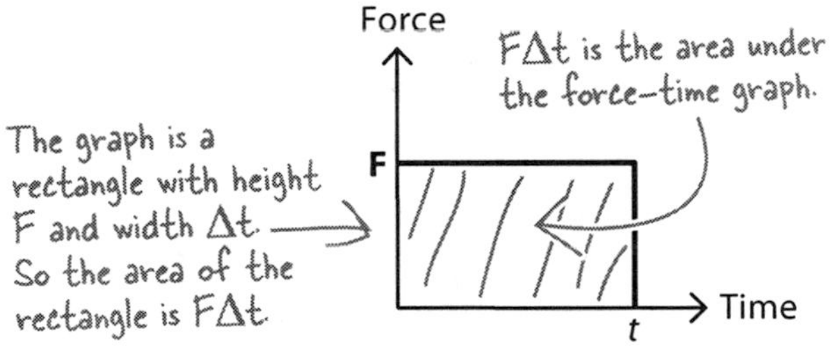

You get something's <u>momentum</u> from the <u>time</u> a force is applied for.

The **kinetic energy** equation says that if you do work on an object by applying a **force** for a certain **displacement**, it gains kinetic energy, $\mathbf{F}\Delta\mathbf{x} = \Delta K = \frac{1}{2}m\mathbf{v}^2$.

$$\mathbf{F}\Delta\mathbf{x} = \Delta K$$

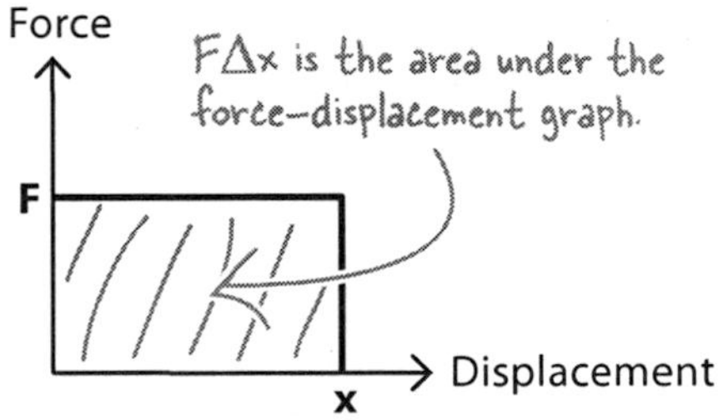

You get something's <u>kinetic energy</u> from the <u>displacement</u> a force is applied for.

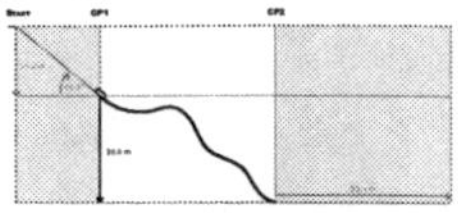

There's a practical difference between momentum and kinetic energy

To think about **pushing** an object to start it off is a bit abstract. A more practical way of seeing the difference between momentum and kinetic energy is to think about **stopping** a moving object.

Imagine catching a ball thrown to you. The ball has a mass and a velocity, and you need to apply a **force** with your hand to stop it. The amount of **time** you need to apply the force for depends on the ball's **momentum**. The **displacement** you need to apply the force over depends on the ball's **kinetic energy**. In stopping the ball, it does work on you to deform the glove and stretch your arm, which reduces the ball's kinetic energy to zero.

The exercise is about the **practical** difference between the **time** and the **displacement** it takes to stop an object, which illustrates the difference between its momentum and its kinetic energy.

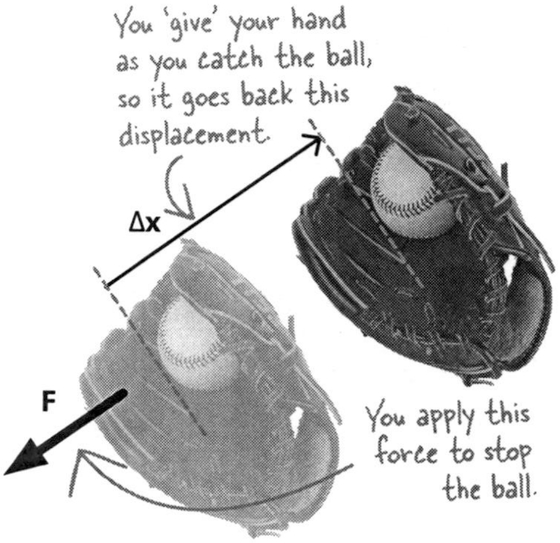

Exercise

a. A baseball with a mass of 145 g is pitched at 35.8 m/s. Calculate (i) its momentum and (ii) its kinetic energy.

b. A bullet with a mass of 3.45 g is fired at 1500 m/s. Calculate (i) its momentum and (ii) its kinetic energy

c. You can catch the baseball by exerting a force on it with your hand. Use physics to explain why you couldn't practically stop the bullet by exerting the same force. (Assume that by using 'soft hands' as you catch the ball, you apply the force and bring the ball to a stop over a displacement of 30 cm.)

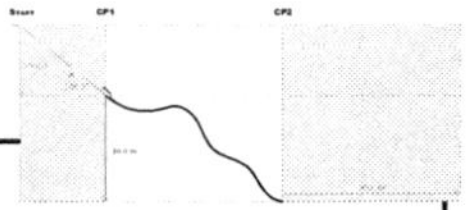

Exercise Solution

a. A baseball with a mass of 145 g is pitched at 35.8 m/s. Calculate (i) its momentum and (ii) its kinetic energy.

(i) $p = mv = 0.145 \times 35.8$

$p = \underline{5.19 \text{ kg.m/s}}$ (3 sd)

(ii) $K = \frac{1}{2}mv^2 = 0.5 \times 0.145 \times 38.5^2$

$K = \underline{107 \text{ J}}$ (3 sd)

b. A bullet with a mass of 3.45 g is fired at 1500 m/s. Calculate (i) its momentum and (ii) its kinetic energy

(i) $p = mv = 0.00345 \times 1500$

$p = \underline{5.18 \text{ kg.m/s}}$ (3 sd)

(ii) $K = \frac{1}{2}mv^2 = 0.5 \times 0.00345 \times 1500^2$

$K = \underline{3880 \text{ J}}$ (3 sd)

c. You can catch the baseball by exerting a force on it with your hand. Use physics to explain why you couldn't practically stop the bullet by exerting the same force. (Assume that by using 'soft hands' as you catch the ball, you apply the force and bring the ball to a stop over a displacement of 30 cm.)

The bullet has around 35 times more kinetic energy than the ball. To stop a moving object, you need to do the same amount of work on it as its current kinetic energy.

So you need to do 35 times more work on the bullet than on the ball.

Work $= F\Delta x$. If you exert the same size of force on the bullet, you need to apply it over a displacement of 30×30 cm $= 900$ cm $= 9$ meters for the bullet. You can't physically do that, so the bullet goes through your glove (and worse). Not recommended.

there are no Dumb Questions

The distance required to stop an object depends on its kinetic energy.

Q: So even though the equations for momentum and kinetic energy look similar, they're different?

A: Yes. They're different quantities with different units.

Q: But momentum and kinetic energy are both conserved?

A: Momentum is always conserved. Total energy is also always conserved, but may be transferred between potential, kinetic and internal energy—it won't always be kinetic.

Q: If a baseball and a bullet both have the same momentum, how come a bullet does more damage?

A: Momentum depends on **v**, but kinetic energy depends on $\mathbf{v}^2$. If an object has a high velocity, then $\mathbf{v}^2$ really dominates. If the object is going three times faster, it'll have nine times as much kinetic energy! So the same force requires nine times as much displacement to stop it. That's part of the reason that a bullet will embed itself a large distance into a piece of wood, but a baseball with the same momentum will only make a small dent.

I've kinda been wondering ... I've been using energy for a couple of chapters now, but I still don't really know what it actually **is**.

Energy is the capacity something has to do work. Total energy is conserved.

The definition of energy is the capacity something has to do work—if all of the energy could be harnessed and used in this way.

You can measure changes in energy as it is transferred and use energy to do calculations.

So should I think about **changes** in energy rather than about the "total" energy something possesses?

Energy conservation is a law.

Energy conservation is a law of nature. A law isn't an object—you can't pick it up and put it in your pocket and say "this is energy conservation." But you can observe how things behave as a result of a law.

You can observe **changes** in kinetic energy, potential energy, internal energy, etc. When you look at all the changes in energy, you find that they add up to zero and the total energy is conserved. For example, a positive change in kinetic energy may be offset by a negative change in potential energy.

Even though you can't "see energy" directly, you can express the law using words or math and use energy conservation to work things out.

You deal with <u>changes</u> in potential, kinetic, internal, etc energy - not absolute values.

Question Clinic: The "Show that" Question

The "Show that" question is unusual in that it gives you the answer and asks you to show how you can get there from a given starting point. The key is to realize that it's OK to **work backwards** as well as forwards! Look at the equation you're supposed to end up with and figure out which variables you'll need to make substitutions for. Also look back at earlier parts of the question, since you have probably already been asked to do something with the equations you'll need to manipulate for the "Show that" question.

Be aware that the equations on your equation sheet may use different letters to represent the same thing.

a and g both represent acceleration.

h and $(x - x_0)$ both represent a change in displacement/position.

This is a buzzword which means "mechanical energy conservation."

2. A bobsled moves down a non-uniform, frictionless slope.

a. Using the equations $U = mgh$, and $v^2 = v_0^2 + 2a(x-x_0)$ and the fact that the potential energy, U, at the top is equal to the kinetic energy, K, at the bottom, show that $K = \frac{1}{2}mv^2$

b. The second checkpoint is 30.0 m lower than the first. If the bobsled has a speed of 19.8 m/s at the first checkpoint, what is its speed at the second?

This means that the question is about algebra – and you need to manipulate the equations you already have to get this one.

Part b. of a question doesn't exist on its own – it's usually related to part a. in some way. Here, you need to realize that part b. is about using the energy conservation equation you worked out in part a with some numbers included.

Even if you didn't manage the 'show that' part of the question, you're still allowed to USE the equation that you were supposed to derive in the second part.

If you spot a "Show that" question, look carefully at the parts of the question that came before to see what it would like you to use. If you get stuck and there's another part of the question that asks you to use the equation in the "show that" part, it's OK to use the equation to do a calculation even if you got stuck deriving the equation.

Question Clinic: The "Energy transfer" Question

Any time you see forces and displacements mentioned, you should immediately think about whether you can use energy as a way of solving the problem. Look out for differences in height - these should immediately scream "gravitational potential energy" at you! And look out for a net force being applied for a certain distance. This may lead to an object gaining kinetic energy or to work being done against friction, or both, depending on the circumstances.

The buzzword 'brake' means that kinetic energy will be transferred to internal energy when work is done against friction.

You need to explain that energy is conserved and where it is transferred from and to.

3. A 630 kg bobsled going at 31.3 m/s is to be brought to a halt by a brake applied to the track.

a. Describe this process in terms of energy transfer.

b. If the bobsled is to be stopped in 50.0 m, what force needs to be used?

c. Another way of helping to stop the bobsled is for the final part of the track to be slightly uphill. If the track goes up by 10.0 m during the final 50.0 m, what force would be required from the brake then?

Any time you see a force and a displacement, think about whether work is being done.

This means you're to use words to put across the physics concepts behind what happens.

When you see a change in height, think about gravitational potential energy.

The force will be different, as some of the kinetic energy is transferred to gravitational potential energy because of the change in height.

Always remember that it's the **total** energy that's conserved. if the question gives you reason to believe there's **no friction** , then this means the **mechanical** energy (i.e., kinetic + potential) is conserved . If there is friction, then energy may be transferred in more than one way at once, e.g., kinetic to both potential and internal.

After the roaring success of SimFootball, it's time for SimPool

A few weeks after your key role as physics consultant on the multi-million seller SimFootball game, the programmer is back in touch. They're working on a SimPool game but have run into a problem.

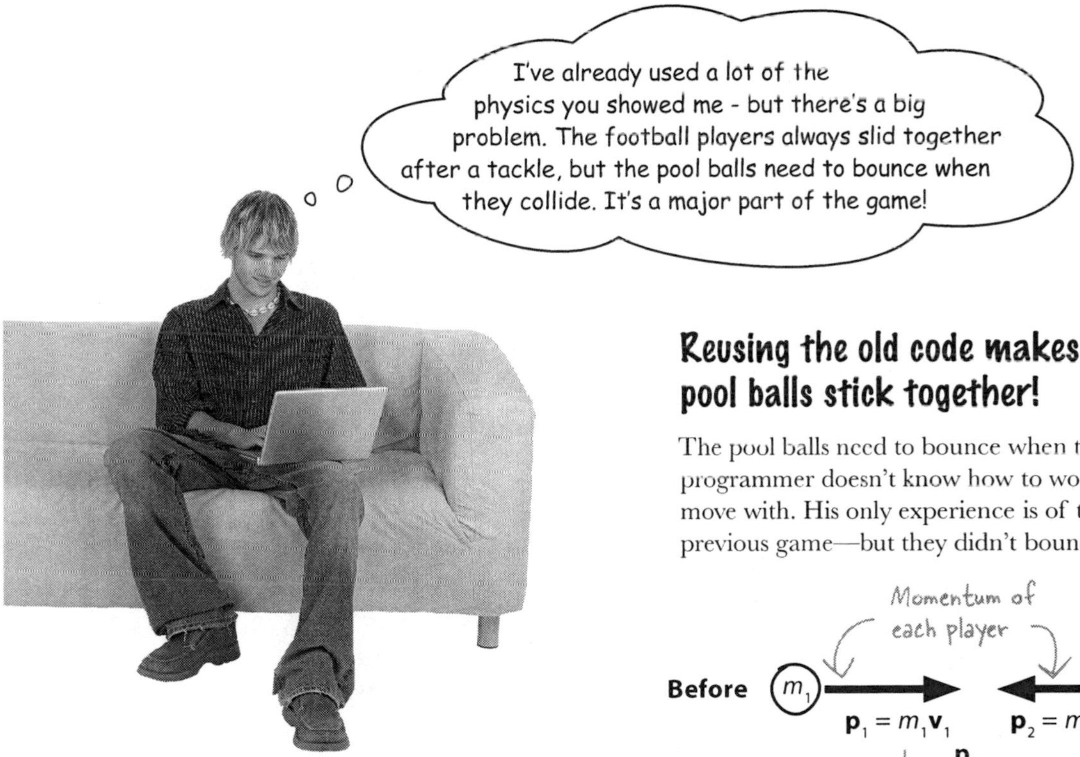

Reusing the old code makes the pool balls stick together!

The pool balls need to bounce when they collide, but the programmer doesn't know how to work out the velocity they move with. His only experience is of the football players in the previous game—but they didn't bounce when they collided.

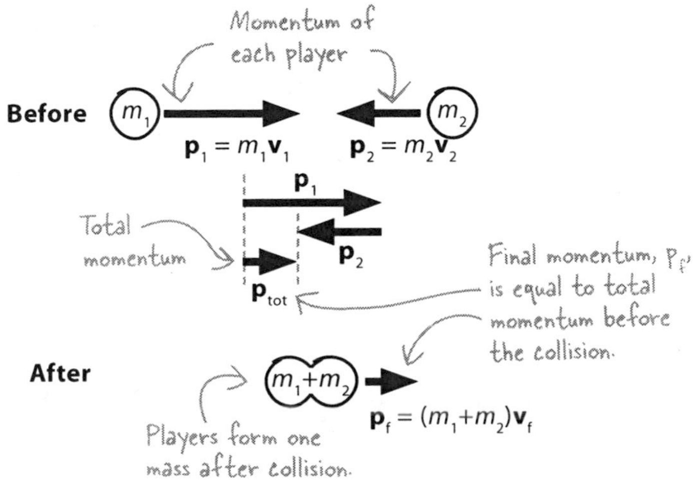

Reusing the football code in the pool game makes the pool balls stick together when they collide—which definitely isn't right!

Momentum conservation will solve an inelastic collision problem

The collision in the football game is called an **inelastic collision** because the players don't bounce off of each other in an elastic way.

Momentum is always conserved in a collision. Since you know the **mass** and **velocity** of each player before the collision, you have **one unknown** (the velocity of the stuck together players after the collision) which you can work out using **one equation** (the momentum conservation equation).

The football players become one mass with one velocity after the collision.

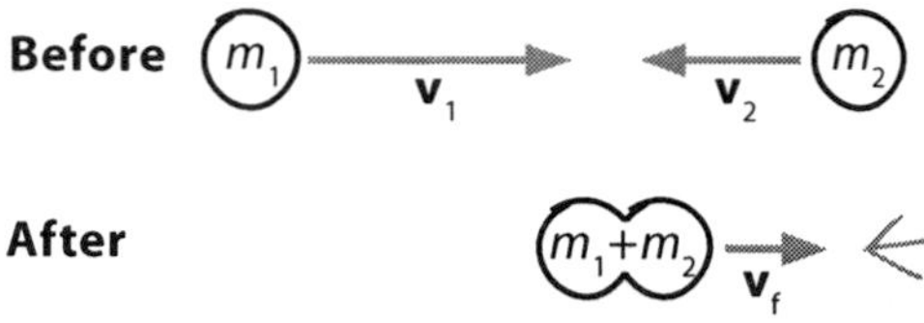

Momentum conservation:

$$m_1\mathbf{v}_1 + m_2\mathbf{v}_2 = (m_1+m_2)\mathbf{v}_f$$

v_f is the only unknown, so you can use this one equation to calculate it.

You need a second equation for an elastic collision

The collision in the pool game is called an **elastic collision** because the pool balls bounce off of each other in an elastic way.

With the completely inelastic collision, you had a single mass moving with a single velocity after the collision. But with this elastic collision, you have two masses, each with their own velocity. You don't know either of the velocities, so this time there are two unknowns that you need to calculate.

Momentum is always conserved in a collision, but with two unknowns, a single momentum conservation equation is not enough. We'll need to come up with a second equation to fix the pool game. If you have two equations, you can work out two unknowns.

v_{10} means 'initial velocity of object 1.' v_{1f} means 'final velocity of object 1.' The subscripts help you to keep track of which object is which.

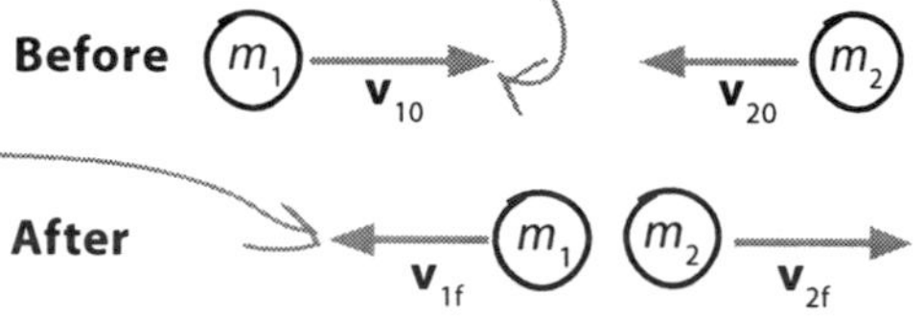

Momentum conservation:

$$m_1\mathbf{v}_{10} + m_2\mathbf{v}_{20} = m_1\mathbf{v}_{1f} + m_2\mathbf{v}_{2f}$$

You don't know v_{1f} or v_{2f}. As there are two things you don't know, you can't work either of them out when you just have one equation.

To solve for <u>two unknowns</u>, you need <u>two equations</u>.

BRAIN POWER

Where might you get a second equation from so you can solve for the two unknown velocities?

We soooo need to fix that pool game. The pool balls definitely shouldn't stick together—it's an **elastic** collision!

Jim: Yeah, but that gives us a problem that we didn't have with the **inelastic collision**. We wind up with two **velocities** after the collision instead of only one.

Joe: We can't use **momentum conservation** on its own to solve the problem this time. You can't get the values of two unknowns from one equation.

Frank: Yeah, but momentum is still conserved in an elastic collision, right? So we need to think of a second equation we can use alongside momentum conservation to solve the problem.

Jim: What about **energy conservation**? That's been useful to us before.

Joe: I'm not sure about that. It's not like the pool ball's height changes. We can't do anything with potential energy.

Frank: But the pool balls are moving, right? What about their **kinetic energy**?

Jim: Yeah, the pool balls are moving before and after the collision, so they must have kinetic energy before and after.

Joe: How do we know for sure that some of the kinetic energy isn't transferred to internal energy when the pool balls collide?

Frank: Well, it's not like the pool balls get really hot, like a brake would when you apply it to slow down.

Jim: And it's not like the pool balls deform and the arrangement of the particles inside them gets messed up.

Joe: Yeah, I think you might be right. The collision's elastic, right? And energy must be conserved. There's kinetic engergy before and after. If the change in internal energy is minimal, we can say that there's the same amount of kinetic energy before and after the collision.

Frank: So, momentum is conserved—that's one equation.

Jim: And the kinetic energy's the same before and after because the collision is elastic—that's a second equation!

Joe: And both of the equations have the pool balls' velocities in them, so we can use the two equations to solve the problem!

Momentum is conserved in an inelastic collision.

Momentum and kinetic energy are conserved in an elastic collision.

Energy conservation gives you the second equation that you need!

The pool balls hit each other in an **elastic collision**. This means that their internal energies don't increase significantly as a result of the collision, because they don't deform in any way (unlike the football players, whose padding deforms and doesn't bounce back when they collide).

Since the internal energy doesn't change, the **total kinetic energy** of the two pool balls is the same before and after the collision. This gives you a second equation you can use.

If you have **two equations** (momentum conservation and kinetic energy before and after the collision), you can work out **two unknowns**—the final velocities of the two pool balls.

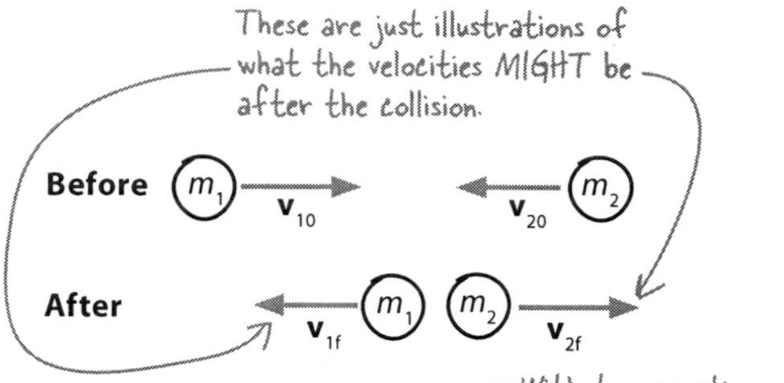

Momentum conservation:

With two equations, you can solve for two unknowns.

$$m_1\mathbf{v}_1 + m_2\mathbf{v}_2 = m_1\mathbf{v}_{1f} + m_2\mathbf{v}_{2f}$$

✓✓ ✓✓ ✓? ✓?

Energy conservation:

$$\tfrac{1}{2}m_1\mathbf{v}_1^2 + \tfrac{1}{2}m_2\mathbf{v}_2^2 = \tfrac{1}{2}m_1\mathbf{v}_{1f}^2 + \tfrac{1}{2}m_2\mathbf{v}_{2f}^2$$

✓✓ ✓✓ ✓? ✓?

Sharpen your pencil

This means that $m_1 = m_2 = m$

This means that $v_{20} = 0$, which should simplify the problem a bit.

Two pool balls both have the same mass, *m*. A moving ball with velocity $\mathbf{v}_{10}$ hits a second, **stationary,** ball head on. After the collision, the first ball has velocity $\mathbf{v}_{1f}$ and the second $\mathbf{v}_{2f}$.

a. Write down an equation showing that momentum is conserved.

b. Write down an equation showing that kinetic energy is conserved.

c. Eliminate the variable $\mathbf{v}_{2f}$ by rearranging your equation from part a and substituting it into your equation from part b so that you only have one unknown, $\mathbf{v}_{1f}$.

d. Multiply out the parentheses and simplify your new equation as much as you can. (Don't worry if you can't find a way to make it say "$\mathbf{v}_{1f}$ = something" yet—we'll do that on the next page.)

Sharpen your pencil Solution

This means that $m_1 = m_2 = m$

This means that $v_{20} = 0$, which should simplify the problem a bit.

Two pool balls both have the same mass, *m*. A moving ball with velocity $\mathbf{v}_{10}$ hits a second, **stationary**, ball head on. After the collision, the first ball has velocity $\mathbf{v}_{1f}$ and the second $\mathbf{v}_{2f}$.

a. Write down an equation showing that momentum is conserved.

$$mv_{10} + 0 = mv_{1f} + mv_{2f}$$

b. Write down an equation showing that kinetic energy is conserved.

$$\tfrac{1}{2}mv_{10}^2 + 0 = \tfrac{1}{2}mv_{1f}^2 + \tfrac{1}{2}mv_{2f}^2$$

$v_{20} = 0$, so it doesn't appear in either equation.

c. Eliminate the variable $\mathbf{v}_{2f}$ by rearranging your equation from part a and substituting it into your equation from part b so that you only have one unknown, $\mathbf{v}_{1f}$.

$$mv_{10} = mv_{1f} + mv_{2f} \quad \text{(a)}$$

All terms are multiplied by m, so you can divide it out and cancel it.

$$v_{10} = v_{1f} + v_{2f}$$

$$v_{2f} = v_{10} - v_{1f}$$

$$\tfrac{1}{2}mv_{10}^2 = \tfrac{1}{2}mv_{1f}^2 + \tfrac{1}{2}mv_{2f}^2 \quad \text{(b)}$$

All terms are multiplied by ½m, so you can divide it out and cancel it.

$$v_{10}^2 = v_{1f}^2 + v_{2f}^2$$

Substitute this into (b).

$$v_{10}^2 = v_{1f}^2 + (v_{10} - v_{1f})^2$$

The only unknown in this equation is v_{1f}.

d. Multiply out the parentheses and simplify your new equation as much as you can. (Don't worry if you can't find a way to make it say "$\mathbf{v}_{1f}$ = something" yet—we'll do that on the next page.)

$$v_{10}^2 = v_{1f}^2 + (v_{10} - v_{1f})^2$$

$$v_{10}^2 = v_{1f}^2 + v_{10}^2 - 2v_{10}v_{1f} + v_{1f}^2$$

There's a v_{10}^2 on each side, so it can be subtracted from both sides and canceled.

$$0 = 2v_{1f}^2 - 2v_{10}v_{1f}$$

You can divide every term in the equation by 2.

$$v_{1f}^2 - v_{10}v_{1f} = 0$$

This is the equation where all the terms with v_{1f} in them are on the left hand side.

So I end up with this thing $v_{1f}^2 - v_{10}v_{1f} = 0$ that I'm supposed to rearrange to say "v_{1f} = something." But how am I gonna do that?!

Factoring can also be called factorising.

Factoring your equation will help.

If rearranging your equation to say "$\mathbf{v}_{1f}$ = something" is difficult, then **factoring** it is another way of trying to solve it. Factoring involves spotting where you can put in some parentheses. It's basically the reverse of multiplying out parentheses.

If two things multiplied together equal zero, then at least one of the things must be zero. For example, if you have $xy = 0$, then either x or y (or perhaps both) must be 0. You have a zero on the righthand side of your equation, $\mathbf{v}_{1f}^2 - \mathbf{v}_{10}\mathbf{v}_{1f} = 0$.

So if you can factor the lefthand side of your equation so that it consists of two things multiplied together, you can say for sure that one of them **must be zero**. You can work out from the **context** which of them actually is zero.

If xy = 0, then either x or y (or maybe both) MUST be 0.

Factoring involves putting in parentheses

The terms ab and ac both have an 'a' in them that everything else in the term is multiplied by. The 'a' is called a **common factor** because it is common to both terms.

You can factor your terms by moving the common factor outside a set of parentheses. So $ab + ac$ becomes $a(b + c)$.

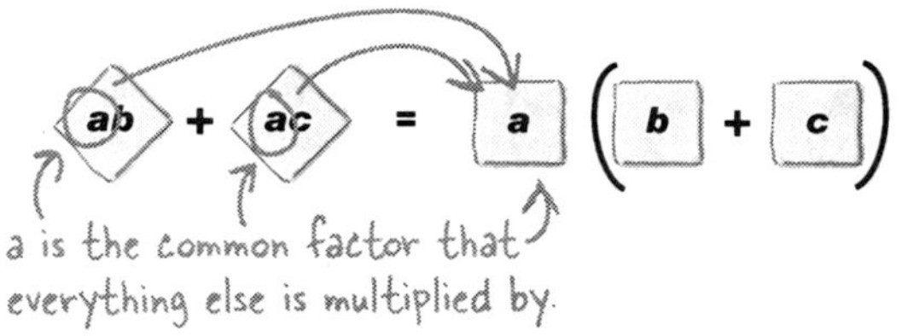

If you have the equation $a(b+c) = 0$, then either $a = 0$ or $(b+c) = 0$. This is because, if two things multiplied together = 0, then one (or both) of the things must be zero.

If more than one term has the same variable multiplying everything else in the term, you can factor your equation.

Sharpen your pencil

a. In your equation $\mathbf{v}_{1f}^2 - \mathbf{v}_{10}\mathbf{v}_{1f} = 0$, which variable appears in both terms so that everything else in the term is multiplied by it?

b. If you have parentheses, you can multiply them out, e.g., $a(b + c) = ab + ac$. The terms ab and ac both have the common factor 'a' in them which everything else in the term is multiplied by.

Use this information to write your equation $\mathbf{v}_{1f}^2 - \mathbf{v}_{10}\mathbf{v}_{1f} = 0$ in a form where the left hand side is a single term that involves parentheses.

c. If two things multiplied together equal 0, then one or both of the things must be zero. Use this fact to calculate two values that $\mathbf{v}_{1f}$ may have, then use the context to explain which value you think is correct.

Sharpen your pencil Solution

a. In your equation $\mathbf{v}_{1f}^2 - \mathbf{v}_{10}\mathbf{v}_{1f} = 0$, which variable appears in both terms so that everything else in the term is multiplied by it?

The variable v_{1f} appears in both terms.

b. If you have parentheses, you can multiply them out, e.g., $a(b + c) = ab + ac$. The terms ab and ac both have the common factor '*a*' in them which everything else in the term is multiplied by.

Use this information to write your equation $\mathbf{v}_{1f}^2 - \mathbf{v}_{10}\mathbf{v}_{1f} = 0$ in a form where the left hand side is a single term that involves parentheses.

$$v_{1f}^2 - v_{10}v_{1f} = 0$$

$$v_{1f}(v_{1f} - v_{10}) = 0$$

c. If two things multiplied together equal 0, then one or both of the things must be zero. Use this fact to calculate two values that $\mathbf{v}_{1f}$ may have, then use the context to explain which value you think is correct.

Either $v_{1f} = 0$ or $(v_{1f} - v_{10}) = 0$

If $(v_{1f} - v_{10}) = 0$, this means that $v_{1f} = v_{10}$. In other words, the first pool ball has continued at its original velocity as if it hadn't hit the other one. This is impossible.

The other possible solution is $V_{1f} = 0$. This looks right, as when you hit a pool ball straight at another, the first ball often stops.

You can deal with elastic collisions now

Momentum is conserved in all collisions, whether inelastic or elastic. **Energy** is always conserved as well, but if the collision is inelastic, some is transferred as internal energy. If the collision is elastic, then the total kinetic energy is conserved.

A rule of thumb is that any collision that involves an object being deformed in some way is inelastic, as the molecules in the object have been rearranged, which increases the internal energy of the object.

For any collision, use momentum conservation first. If the collision is elastic and you have two unknowns, use kinetic energy as well.

If you have a problem involving an **elastic** collision, you should always use **momentum conservation**. If you only have one unknown, then you're done.

If you have two unknowns, you can use **energy conservation** to give you a second equation that helps you to work out both unknowns.

In an elastic collision, the relative velocity reverses

You've worked out that when one pool ball hits a stationary pool ball head-on, the first pool ball stops and the second pool ball continues with the velocity that the first ball had.

Imagine sitting on top of the second pool ball. You see the first pool ball coming towards you with velocity $\mathbf{v}_{10}$. After the collision, it appears to you that the first pool ball is moving away from you with velocity $-\mathbf{v}_{10}$ (though it's actually the second ball that is moving).

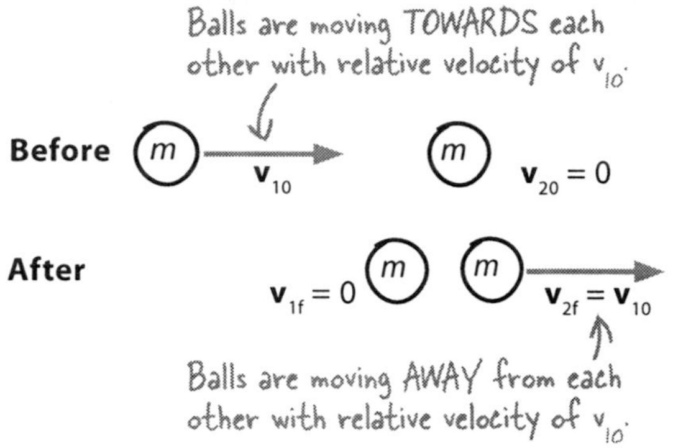

This also works in the opposite direction. If the relative velocity of the objects is reversed after the collision, then the collision must have been elastic.

This is a special case of a general rule for elastic collisions: the **relative velocity** of the two objects is **reversed** after the collision. This is also true if both objects were originally moving.

there are no Dumb Questions

Q: If a collision is elastic, do I always have to use momentum conservation AND energy conservation?

A: Not always. Sometimes you'll only start off with one unknown. Then you'd only need to use one equation.

Q: If I only have one unknown velocity, which equation is it better for me to use, momentum conservation or energy conservation?

A: It's better to use momentum conservation because direction is important. And the momentum conservation equation tells you the direction of the velocity as well as its size, as momentum is a vector.

Q: Does the kinetic energy equation tell me the direction of the velocity too?

A: No. Because kinetic energy is a scalar, an object of a certain mass will always have the same kinetic energy.

Q: Can't I get the velocity's direction from the kinetic energy equation?

A: Kinetic energy is $K = \frac{1}{2}mv^2$. The velocity is **squared**. If you multiply two positive numbers together, you get a positive number. And if you multiply two negative numbers together, you also get a positive number.

So whether **v** is positive or negative (an indication of direction), $\mathbf{v}^2$ will always be positive. This means that you can't work out the direction of the velocity (a vector) from the kinetic energy (a scalar). You can work out its size, though.

Q: In the problem I just did over there, there were two possible answers at the end. How do I pick between them?

A: There were two possible answers because the kinetic energy conservation equation involves $\mathbf{v}^2$. You then have to pick between them by thinking about the 'k'ontext of the problem. Choose the answer that makes the most physical sense.

Q: What if the collision happens at an angle instead of along a straight line?

A: The rule of thumb is always to use momentum conservation first. Break down the velocities you're given into components, then apply momentum conservation for each component (like you did in chapter 12).

Q: Does the relative velocity always reverse in an elastic collision even if the objects have different masses?

A: Yes. For example, a rubber ball hitting a wall with velocity **v** will rebound with velocity **-v** (assuming that the collision is completely elastic). And any two objects with less extreme masses will also have their relative velocity reversed after a collision.

The pool ball collisions work!

The programmer writes the elastic pool ball collisions into the game—exactly like you describe—and they work!

But a few days before the game is due to be released,

There's a gravity-defying trick shot to sort out ...

The game also has a trick shot mode, which uses some odd items you wouldn't usually see on a pool table. The programmer's stuck on one particular trick shot where the cue ball is hit into a padded 'bucket,' which then swings up and releases the cue ball—as long as it reaches exactly the right height at the top of its swing

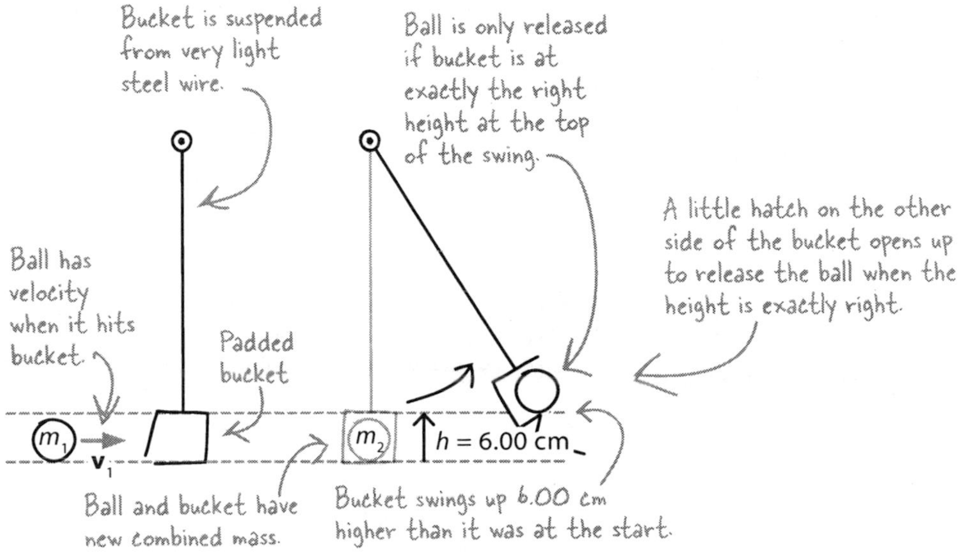

Where is the problem with the programmer's reasoning?

The programmer's been using what you taught him about **energy conservation** to work out the speed the player should hit the ball with.

He's assumed that the initial **kinetic energy** of the ball is being transferred to the final **potential energy** of the ball and bucket, which wind up 6.00 cm higher than they started (a problem that would be very, very difficult to do using forces and equations of motion!)

However, the velocity he's calculated is lower than a 'play tester' pool player has to hit the ball with to do the trick in real life. The real pool player needs to hit the ball with a higher velocity, and the programmer doesn't know why.

Sharpen your pencil

Your job is to work out what's going wrong. The programmer's math is to the right, and there's space for you to write down what might be going wrong.

The ball has a mass of 165 g and the bucket is 95 g.

(1) (2)

$m_1 = 0.165$ kg
$v_1 = ?$

$m_2 = 0.260$ kg
$v_2 = 0$ m/s
Height = 0.060 m

K of ball at (1) = U of ball and bucket at (2)

Use energy conservation

$$K = \tfrac{1}{2}m_1v_1^2 = m_2gh$$

$$v_1^2 = \frac{2m_2gh}{m_1}$$

$$v_1 = \sqrt{\frac{2m_2gh}{m_1}} = \sqrt{\frac{2 \times 0.260 \times 9.8 \times 0.060}{0.165}}$$

$$v_1 = 1.36 \text{ m/s (3 sd)}$$

But the real pool player doing the trick shot in real life has to hit the ball with a higher velocity than this – and I don't know why! Argh!

Sharpen your pencil Solution

Your job is to work out what's going wrong. The programmer's math is to the right, and there's space for you to write down what might be going wrong.

The ball has a mass of 165 g and the bucket is 95 g.

The programmer has assumed that all of the pool ball's kinetic energy is transferred to potential energy.

However, the bucket is padded. This means that the pool ball is colliding with it is an inelastic collision, so mechanical energy isn't conserved.

When the pool ball hits the bucket, the padding in the bucket deforms and its internal energy increases. So not all of the ball's kinetic energy is transferred to potential energy.

This is consistent with the real pool player having to hit the ball faster.

$m_1 = 0.165$ kg
$v_1 = ?$

$m_2 = 0.260$ kg
$v_2 = 0$ m/s
Height = 0.060 m

K of ball at (1) = U of ball and bucket at (2)

Use energy conservation

$$K = \frac{1}{2}m_1 v_1^2 = m_2 gh$$

$$v_1^2 = \frac{2m_2 gh}{m_1}$$

$$v_1 = \sqrt{\frac{2m_2 gh}{m_1}} = \sqrt{\frac{2 \times 0.260 \times 9.8 \times 0.060}{0.165}}$$

$$v_1 = 1.36 \text{ m/s (3 sd)}$$

But the real pool player doing the trick shot in real life has to hit the ball with a higher velocity than this - and I don't know why! Argh!

The initial collision is inelastic - so mechanical energy isn't conserved

When the ball hits the **padded** bucket, some of its kinetic energy is transferred to the bucket as **internal energy**. The collision is **inelastic**. The bucket is padded, so the mechanical energy of the system is reduced as the internal energy of the bucket increases due to the padding deforming.

Therefore, the programmer's assumption that the ball's initial kinetic energy will all be transferred to gravitational potential energy is incorrect.

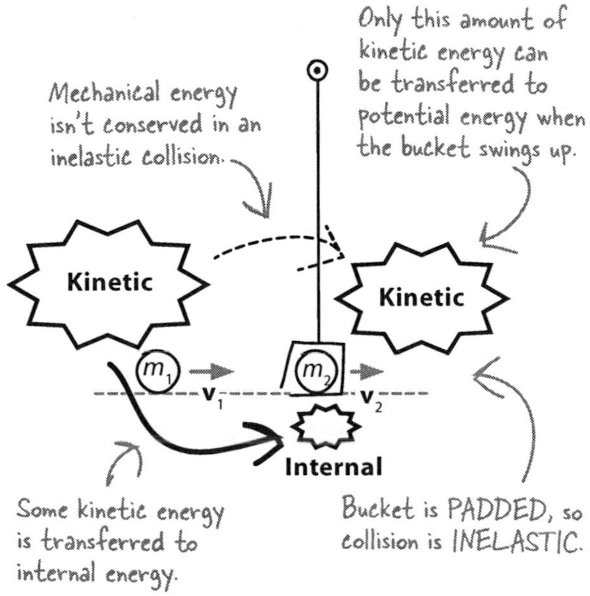

Before you do any math, think: "Is this collision elastic or inelastic?"

Use momentum conservation for the inelastic part

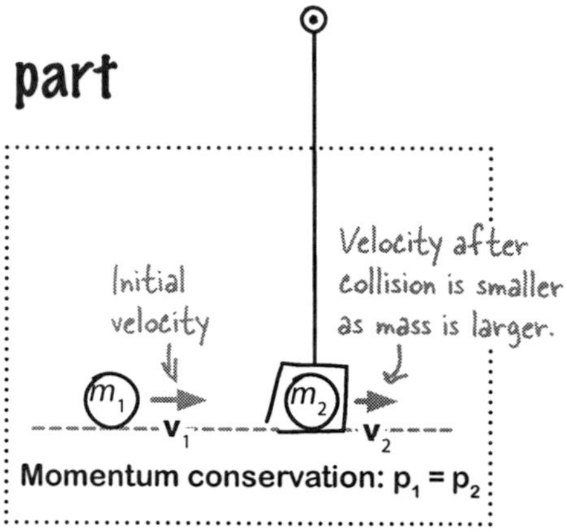

The trick with this trick shot is thinking about it in two stages.

The **first stage** is when the cue ball collides with the padded bucket. This is an **inelastic** collision, so momentum is conserved but mechanical energy isn't. As you know the masses of the ball and bucket, you can use momentum conservation to calculate their new velocity (and, hence, their kinetic energy) in terms of the cue ball's initial velocity.

The **second stage** is when the bucket containing the ball swings up. This involves the **kinetic energy** of the ball and bucket being transferred to **potential energy**. If you know the **height** that the bucket swings, you can work out its potential energy, the kinetic energy and velocity of the ball and bucket, and the initial velocity of the cue ball.

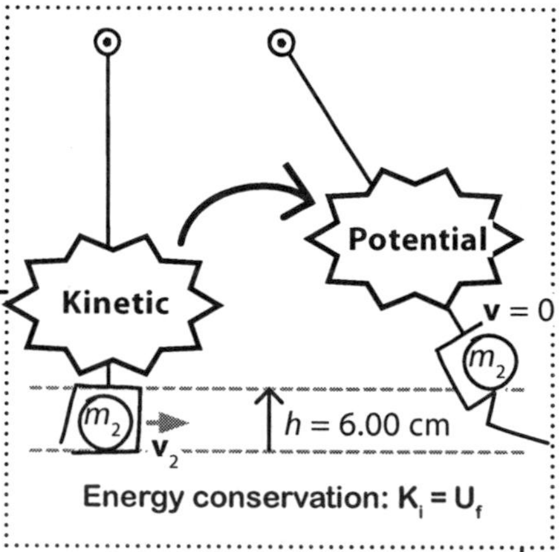

Now it's your turn!

Sharpen your pencil

A pool ball, mass 165 g, is played into a padded bucket, which is arranged so it can swing upwards on the end of some light steel wires. For the shot to work, the ball must be struck so that the top of the bucket's swing is 6.00 cm higher than it started.

Find the velocity that the ball must be struck with if the bucket has a mass of 95 g.

Hint: The quickest way of doing this is to calculate the velocity that the ball and bucket must have after the collision, then work backwards.

Sharpen your pencil Solution

A pool ball, mass 165 g, is played into a padded bucket, which is arranged so it can swing upwards on the end of some light steel wires. For the shot to work, the ball must be struck so that the top of the bucket's swing is 6 cm higher than it started.

Find the velocity that the ball must be struck with if the bucket has a mass of 95g.

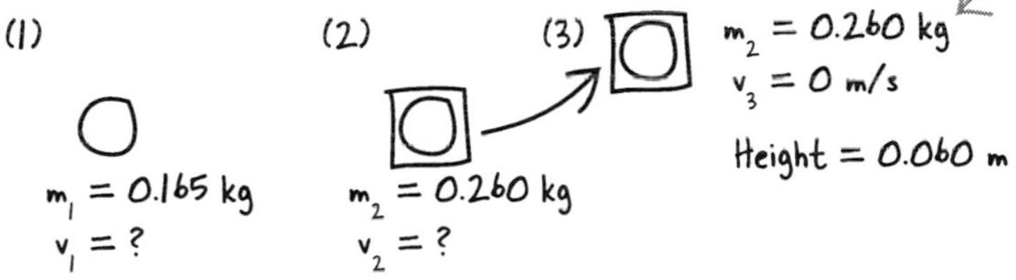

To get a velocity in m/s, make sure you work in kg and m, not g and cm.

K of ball and bucket at (2) = U of ball and bucket at (3)

Use energy conservation to get v_2.

$$K = \tfrac{1}{2} m_2 v_2^2 = m_2 g h$$

$$v_2 = \sqrt{2gh} = \sqrt{2 \times 9.8 \times 0.060} = 1.08 \text{ m/s (3 sd)}$$

This is different from the programmer's math, as the ball is already in the bucket before you do the energy conservation part.

Use momentum conservation to get v_1.

$$m_1 v_1 = m_2 v_2$$

$$v_1 = \frac{m_2 v_2}{m_1} = \frac{0.260 \times 1.08}{0.165} = \underline{\underline{1.70 \text{ m/s}}} \text{ (3 sd)}$$

there are no Dumb Questions

Q: So sometimes I can't just use energy conservation to do a problem?

A: That's right. If the internal energy increases in a way that's very difficult to measure (like when padding is deformed), then you know that energy is conserved but aren't able to do calculations with it!

Q: Does that mean there's a way that the internal energy can change that is easy to quantify?! Surely you can't see what's going on inside an object!

A: If the internal energy increases as a result of work being done entirely against friction, then the change in internal energy is equal to **FΔx**, the total quantity of energy transferred as a result of doing work against friction.

Q: What do I do if I can't calculate the increase in internal energy?

A: You need to use momentum conservation to deal with inelastic collisions. This will give you the velocity after the collision (after the inelastic deformation has taken place). It's this velocity that you should use to calculate the kinetic energy that remains in the system.

Question Clinic: The "Ballistic pendulum" Question

The pool ball trick shot is an example of the "ballistic pendulum" question. The name is taken from a technique used to find the velocity of a bullet by firing it into a wooden block suspended from wires, then measuring how high the block swings. The most important thing to remember is that if part of the process is inelastic, mechanical energy (i.e., kinetic + potential) won't be conserved as the internal energies of the block and bullet must increase as the bullet does work by tunnelling into the block.

This is a buzzword that may mean 'elastic collision' depending on what it collides with!

This is a buzzword that means 'inelastic collision'.

You can't use mechanical energy conservation for an inelastic collision, so you need to use momentum conservation for this part

3. A pool ball, mass 165 g, is played into a padded bucket, which is arranged so it can swing upwards on the end of some light steel wires. For the shot to work, the ball must be struck so that the top of the bucket's swing is 6.00 cm higher than it started.

Find the velocity that the ball must be struck with if the bucket has a mass of 95 g.

Some of the ball's initial kinetic energy will be transferred to internal energy.

This means that you don't have to take the mass of the wires into account in your calculation.

A difference in height should get you thinking about energy conservation.

Find the kinetic energy of the ball and bucket after the collision, since that is what is transferred to potential energy. And to do this, you must first use momentum conservation to work out the initial velocity of the ball.

The secret of doing this type of question is to ask yourself if an inelastic collision is involved before you go rushing into the math. Momentum is conserved in an inelastic collision, but the kinetic energy isn't the same before and after an inelastic collision. First you need to use momentum conservation to calculate the velocity and, therefore, kinetic energy of the new mass (block + bullet). Then you can use mechanical energy conservation to work out the height.

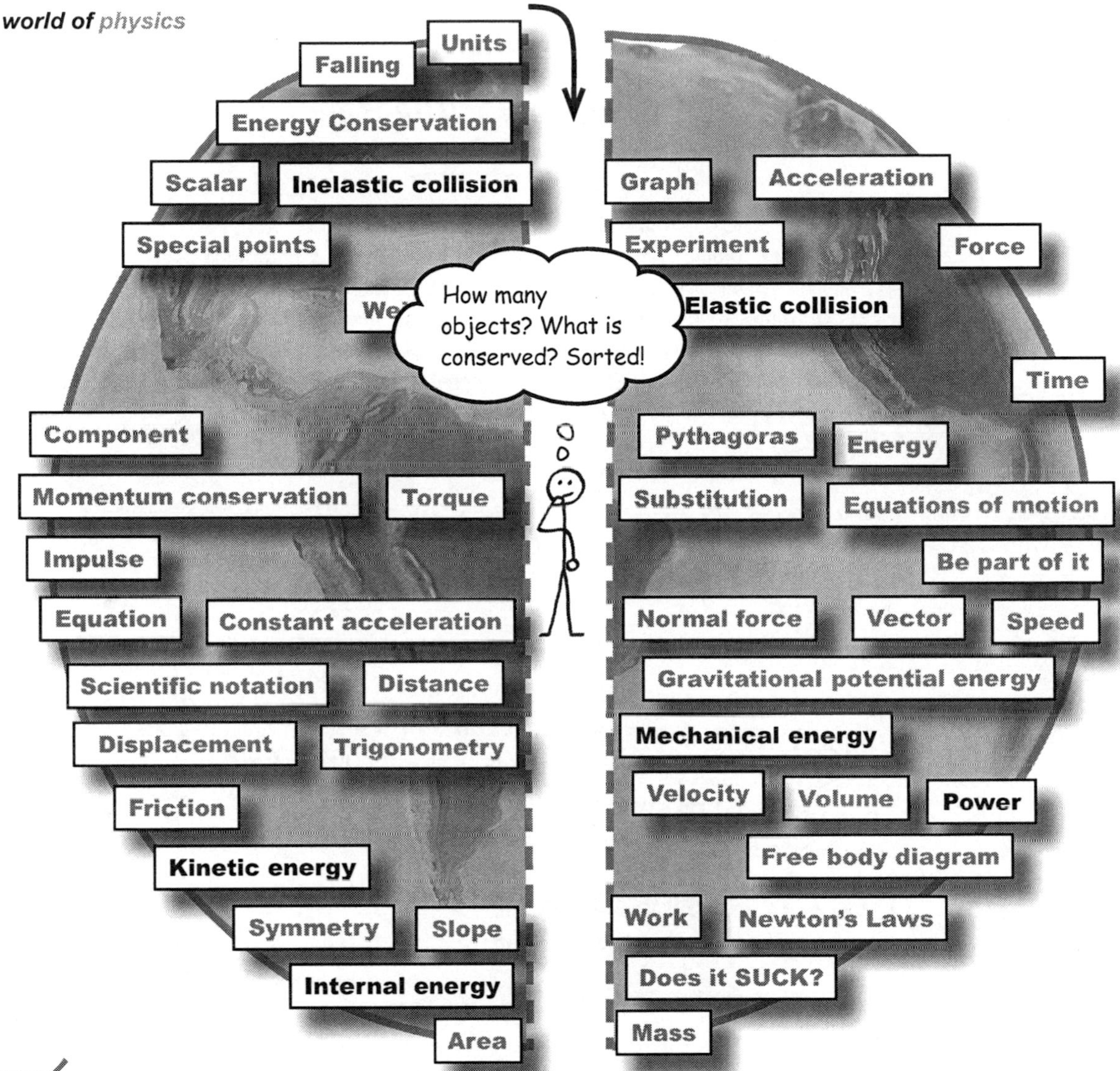

☑	**Kinetic energy**	**The capacity something has to do work due to its speed.**
☑	**Internal energy**	**The total kinetic and potential energy due to the random motion or vibration of particles on a microscopic scale**
☑	**Mechanical energy**	**The total kinetic + potential energy of a system on a macroscopic scale.**
☑	**Power**	**The rate at which energy is transferred or work is done. Measured in Watts (1 W = 1 Joule per second).**
☑	**Inelastic collision**	**A collision where momentum is conserved but kinetic energy is not conserved.**
☑	**Elastic collision**	**A collision where both momentum and energy are conserved**

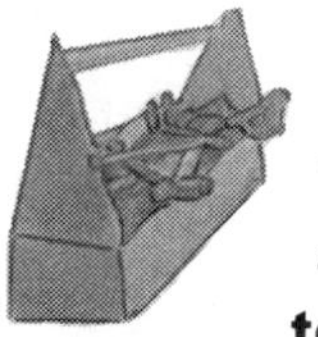

Your Physics Toolbox

You've got Chapter 14 under your belt and added some problem solving skills to your toolbox.

Momentum vs kinetic energy

You calculate the change in momentum by thinking about a force applied for a period of time.

You calculate the change in kinetic energy by thinking about a force applied for a displacement.

Inelastic collision

A collision is inelastic if one or both of the objects involved deform in some way, or if the objects stick together.

Momentum is conserved, but kinetic energy isn't conserved because the deformation of the object increases its internal energy.

Elastic collision

A collision is elastic if neither object is deformed and the objects bounce off of each other.

Mathematically, elastic collisions can be harder to deal with than inelastic collisions, as you still have two separate objects at the end.

However, both momentum and kinetic energy are conserved, which gives you two equations you can use to find two unknowns.

Difference in height

Any time a problem involves a difference in height, it's almost always easier to deal with it using energy conservation than with equations of motion.

The total energy is the same at the start and the end, so any change in potential energy will be accompanied by an equal change in kinetic energy.

Stopping an object

A quick way to determine the force required to stop an object at a certain displacement is to calculate its kinetic energy.

This is equal to the work you need to do against friction to stop it. As work = $F\Delta x$, this allows you to find the force quickly.

15 tension, pulleys and problem solving

Changing direction

Sometimes you need to deal with the tension in a situation

So far, you've been using forces, free body diagrams and energy conservation to solve problems. In this chapter, you'll take that further as you deal with ropes, **pulleys**, and, yes, **tension**. Along the way, you'll also practice looking for familiar signposts to help navigate your way through complicated situations.

It's a bird... it's plane... ...no, it's... a guy on a skateboard?!

A new high-risk sporting event has come to town. The challenge? Jump off an 11.0 m pier and hit a target floating in the sea 15.0 m from the foot of the pier. Michael, a daredevil and skateboarding fiend, plans to take home the first place prize.

Michael wants to give himself a predictable launch **velocity** so he can be sure of hitting the target in the water. He's attached a skateboard to one end of a rope, put a large stack of **masses** at the other end, and placed a **pulley** in between.

The problem is, Michael's not so great at physics. And that's where you come in... can you help Michael out?

Here's what SHOULD happen...

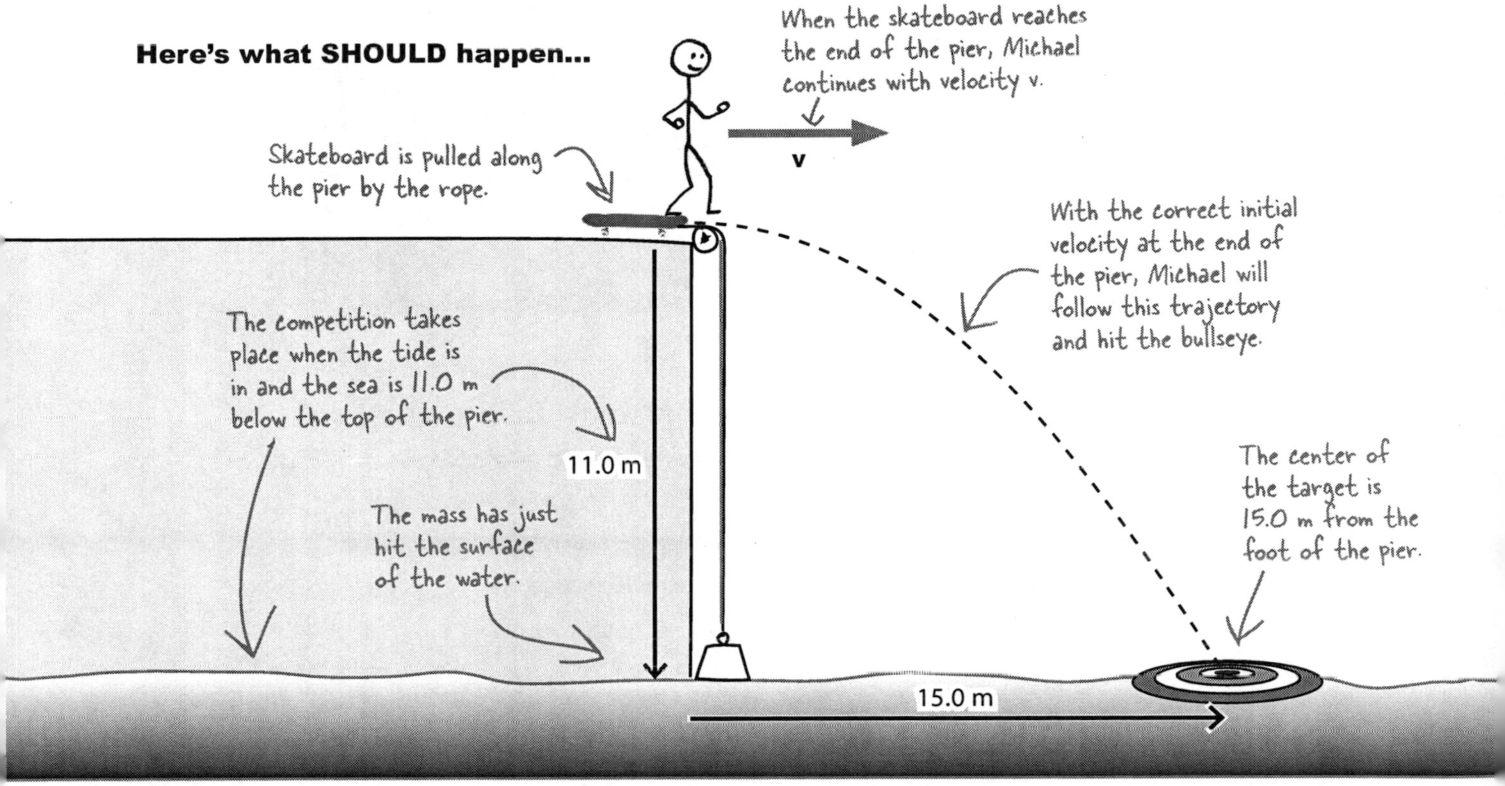

Always look for something familiar

This problem involves a skateboard, a person, a stack of masses, a rope, a pulley, gravity, the height of the pier, and the distance to the target. Plus it takes place in two dimensions. It's a complicated problem!

But you don't have to start the problem in the same place as Michael, with the rope, pulley and stack of masses. The best place for **you** to start tackling a problem is from a point where it looks **like** something you've seen before....

You can start at the point where Michael flies through the air with velocity **v**. That looks kinda familiar...

Break down a complicated problem into smaller parts, then look for something that's LIKE what you've seen before.

Sharpen your pencil

Suppose Michael is launched horizontally from the end of a pier. What velocity does he need to possess in order to hit a target in the water 15.0 m from the foot of the pier, which is 11.0 m high?

Always start with a sketch to help you figure a problem out.

Sharpen your pencil Solution

This part of the problem uses equations of motion. The key to solving it is to realize that you can do it separately from the rest of the problem, before you know anything about the stack of masses or the pulley.

Suppose Michael is launched horizontally from the end of a pier. What velocity does he need to possess in order to hit a target in the water 15.0 m from the foot of the pier, which is 11.0 m high?

Down is positive direction.

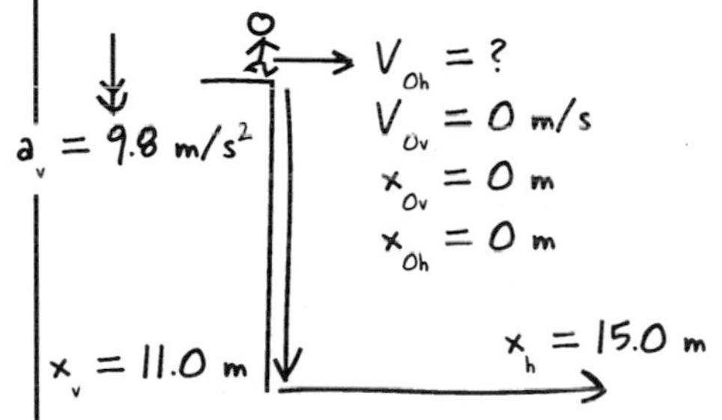

Get time from vertical components:

$$x_v = x_{0v} + v_{0v}t + \frac{1}{2}a_v t^2$$

These terms are both zero.

$$\Rightarrow \frac{1}{2}at^2 = x_v$$

$$\Rightarrow t = \sqrt{\frac{2x_v}{a_v}} = \sqrt{\frac{2 \times 11.0}{9.8}} = 1.50 \text{ s (3 sd)}$$

Get horizontal velocity from horizontal components:

$$v_{0h} = \frac{x_h}{t} = \frac{15}{1.50} = \underline{10.0 \text{ m/s (3 sd) left to right.}}$$

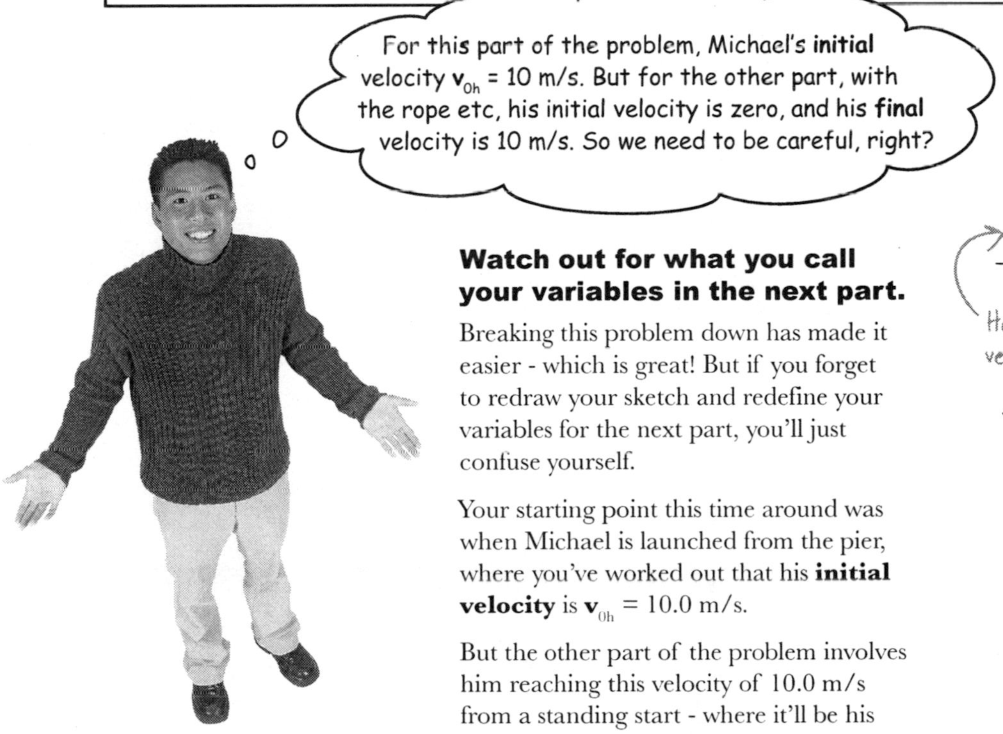

Watch out for what you call your variables in the next part.

Breaking this problem down has made it easier - which is great! But if you forget to redraw your sketch and redefine your variables for the next part, you'll just confuse yourself.

Your starting point this time around was when Michael is launched from the pier, where you've worked out that his **initial velocity** is $\mathbf{v}_{0h}$ = 10.0 m/s.

But the other part of the problem involves him reaching this velocity of 10.0 m/s from a standing start - where it'll be his **final velocity**. So be careful!

When you break up a problem, you might need to redefine variables as you move from part to part.

Jim: Yeah, and we've got that stack of weights on the other end of the rope to **accelerate** him with.

Frank: Yeah, the stack is falling, so it will accelerate at 9.8 m/s^2 and drag Michael along behind it. So Michael accelerates at 9.8 m/s^2, just like the stack. This is gonna be a piece of cake!

Joe: Um, I'm not so sure about that. The stack has to pull Michael along, so I don't think the stack will fall as fast as it would if it wasn't attached to the skateboard. I don't think it would accelerate at 9.8 m/s^2.

Frank: But if something's falling, its acceleration doesn't depend on its mass. Everything falls at the same rate, no matter what its mass is (as long as air resistance isn't a big factor).

Joe: But Michael isn't falling - he's travelling horizontally.

Jim: Oh yeah ... I guess if there was an elephant on the skateboard instead, the board would hardly accelerate at all.

Frank: Yeah, the **force** is due to the weight of the falling stack - but not Michael's weight, as he isn't falling.

Joe: This isn't so straightforward after all.

BE the skater

Your job is to imagine you're Michael on the skateboard. What happens to you as the mass at the other end of the rope falls? How will making the mass larger or smaller affect what happens to you?

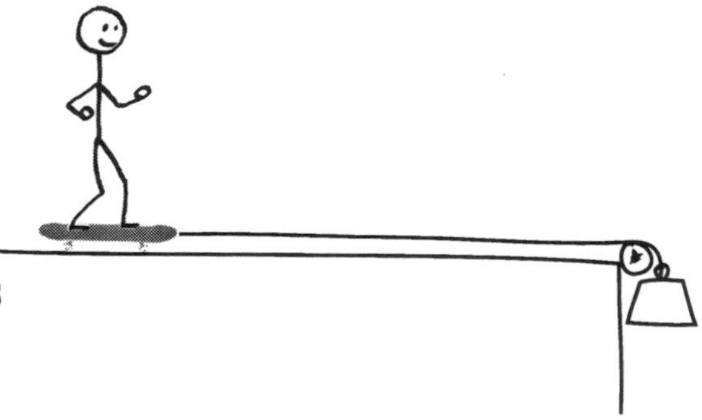

....

....

....

....

BE the skater - SOLUTION

Your job is to imagine you're Michael on the skateboard. What happens to you as the mass at the other end of the rope falls? How will making the mass larger or smaller affect what happens to you?

As the mass falls vertically, I accelerate horizontally because it pulls the skateboard.

If the mass is larger, I accelerate more quickly.

If the mass is smaller, I accelerate more slowly, and if the mass is a really small I might not accelerate at all.

Michael and the stack accelerate at the same rate

Michael and the stack are joined together by the rope, so they both **accelerate** at the same rate. This is because of the **tension** in the rope - the rope is pulled tight. If the rope wasn't there or wasn't pulled tight, there would be no tension and Michael wouldn't accelerate as the stack falls.

A stack with a larger mass on it will accelerate Michael more rapidly, and a smaller mass will accelerate him more slowly. This is something you can analyze by thinking about the tension in the rope.

A rope pulled tight can mediate a TENSION force.

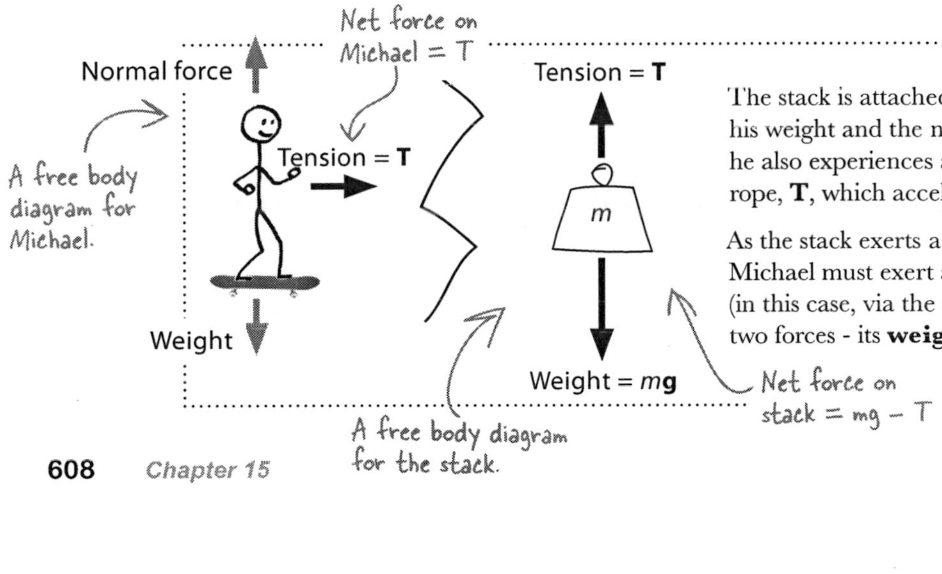

The stack is attached to Michael by a rope. As well as his weight and the normal force (which add to zero), he also experiences a net **tension** force from the rope, **T**, which accelerates him to the right.

As the stack exerts a force on Michael (via the rope) Michael must exert an equal-sized force on the stack (in this case, via the rope) . So the stack experiences two forces - its **weight** and the **tension**.

How can the tension act **horizontally** on one thing and **vertically** on the other? Doesn't Newton's 3rd Law say that pairs of forces need to act in **opposite** directions?

The pulley changes the direction that the tension force acts in.

If a rope experiences a pulling force at both ends that makes it tight (like the rope we have here) it's said to be in **tension**.

But a **pulley** changes the **direction** that the tension force acts in. The pulley is able to do this because it's firmly attached to the pier, which is able to provide a support force. Otherwise, the rope would just get pulled straight.

If you just draw the free body diagrams for Michael and the stack, it looks like you have a Newton's 3rd Law force pair that isn't acting in opposite directions. But when you include the free body diagram of the pulley, you can see that there are horizontal and vertical pairs of tension force pairs.

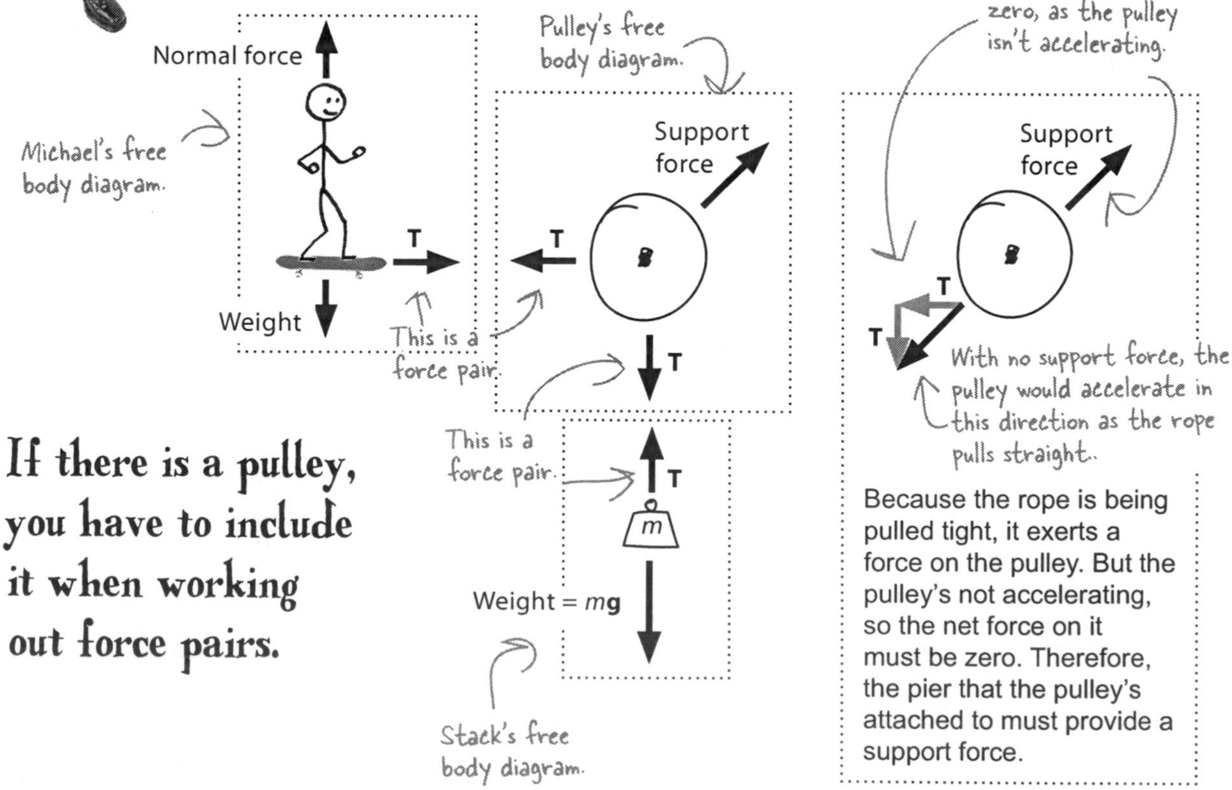

If there is a pulley, you have to include it when working out force pairs.

there are no Dumb Questions

Q: Why doesn't the stack just accelerate at 9.8 m/s^2, like it usually would if you dropped it?

A: It's attached to Michael (and his skateboard) by a rope. So the force of the stack's weight has to accelerate Michael's mass as well as the stack's own mass.

Q: But don't all falling objects accelerate at the same rate, whatever their mass?

A: Not if they're tied on to something else that isn't falling!

Q: So where does tension come in?

A: Tension is the name given to the force exerted at each end of a rope. For example, if the stack was hanging from a rope attached to the ceiling, the tension would be the same size as the stack's weight.

Q: Is the tension in a rope always the same size as the weight of the object it's supporting?

A: If an object is hanging straight down from a rope, then its acceleration is zero and the net force must be zero. So the tension in the rope must be the same size as the object's weight (in the opposite direction).

But if the object is accelerating downwards, (like the stack is here), the object's weight must be greater than the tension in the rope to produce a net downwards force.

Q: Is it OK to think of a tension force a bit like the normal force in other problems - as it's a support force?

A: As long as you remember that the tension always acts in the direction of the rope, that should be OK conceptually.

Q: Do I have to take into account the mass of the rope as well?

A: Great question! In real life you would, but in practice the mass of the rope has very little effect if it's much smaller than the masses it's attached to. So we're making the approximation that the rope is massless.

Q: How do you know that the two objects attached to the rope both accelerate at the same rate?

A: If the two objects are at either end of a rope which is pulled tight, they must always move with the same speed in order for the rope to remain tight. Therefore, they must also both accelerate at the same rate (though they may accelerate in different directions depending on how the rope is positioned).

When two objects are joined together and move together, they both accelerate at the SAME rate.

Use tension to tackle the problem

Because the stack and Michael are joined together by a rope under tension, they both accelerate at the same rate .You need to work out what **mass** the stack should have in order for both it and Michael to be going at 10.0 m/s after the stack has fallen 11.0 m from the top to the bottom of the pier.

If you draw separate free body diagrams for the stack and for Michael, showing all the **forces** acting on them, you can use these to work out the mass of the stack.

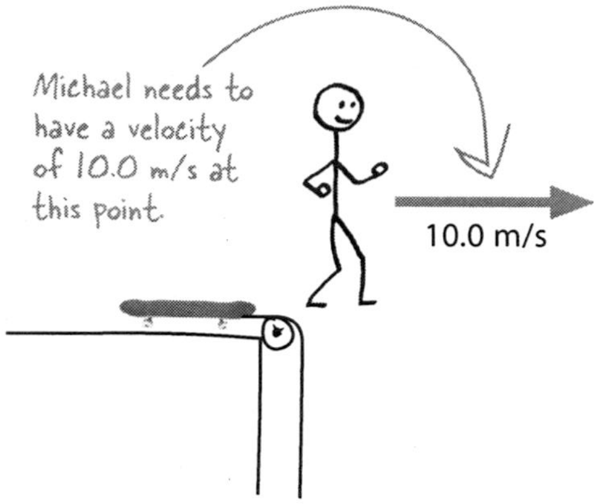

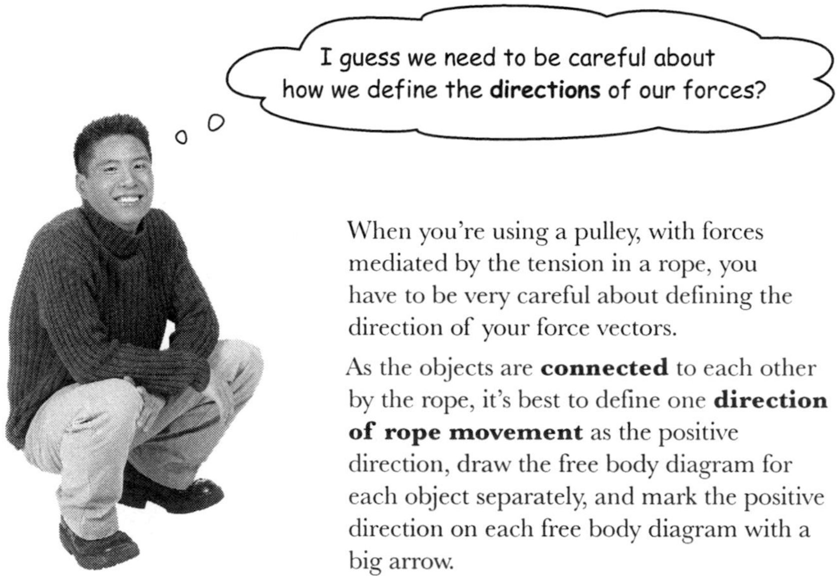

When you're using a pulley, with forces mediated by the tension in a rope, you have to be very careful about defining the direction of your force vectors.

As the objects are **connected** to each other by the rope, it's best to define one **direction of rope movement** as the positive direction, draw the free body diagram for each object separately, and mark the positive direction on each free body diagram with a big arrow.

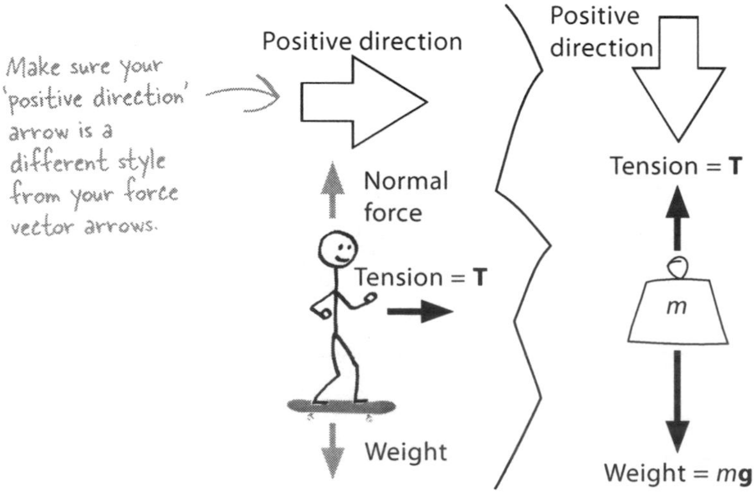

Define one direction of rope movement as positive and mark it on your free body diagrams.

Sharpen your pencil

Michael on a skateboard, mass M, is attached via a rope and a pulley to a stack of masses, mass m, as shown in the picture. When the stack is allowed to accelerate downwards in a gravitational field, strength **g**, the rope has tension, **T** and Michael also accelerates.

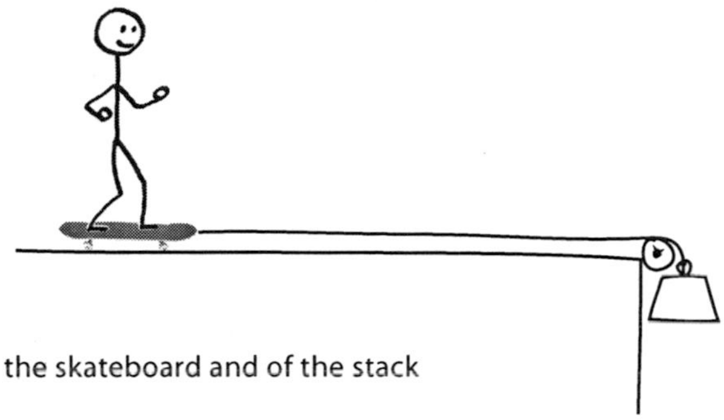

a. Draw separate free body diagrams of Michael on the skateboard and of the stack

b. Write down the size of the net force on Michael.

c. Write down the size of the net force on the stack.

d. Michael and the stack both accelerate with acceleration, **a**. Use Newton's 2nd Law to write down a separate expression for each of them that relates their mass, their acceleration and the net force on them.

e. The size of the tension in the rope is the same for both Michael and the stack. Make a substitution using your equations from part d. and rearrange your answer so that you have an equation for m, the mass of the stack, in terms of *M*, **g** and **a**.

Sharpen your pencil Solution

Michael on a skateboard, mass M, is attached via a rope and a pulley to a stack of masses, mass m, as shown in the picture. When the stack is allowed to accelerate downwards in a gravitational field, strength **g**, the rope has tension, **T** and the man also accelerates.

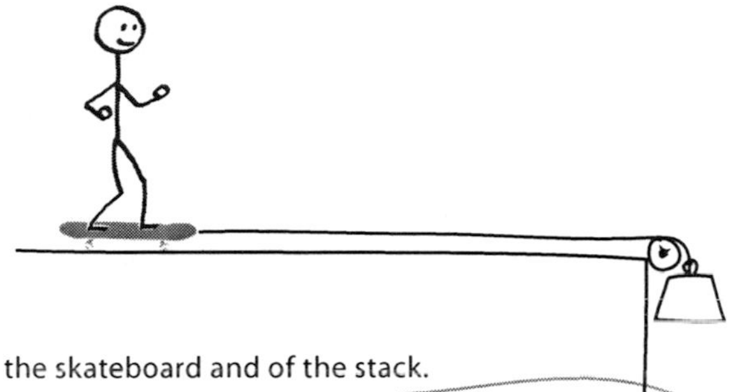

a. Draw separate free body diagrams of Michael on the skateboard and of the stack.

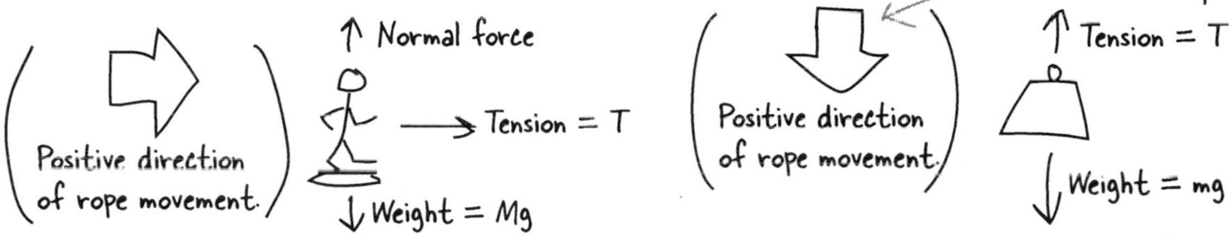

b. Write down the size of the net force on Michael.

Normal force and weight add to zero.

$F_{net} = T$

c. Write down the size of the net force on the stack.

$F_{net} = mg - T$

Drawing on the big arrow helps you get the signs correct in these equations

d. Michael and the stack both accelerate with acceleration, **a**. Use Newton's 2nd Law to write down a separate expression for each of them that relates their mass, their acceleration and the net force on them.

Man has mass M.

$F_{net} = ma$ becomes $T = Ma$

Stack has mass m.

$F_{net} = ma$ becomes $mg - T = ma$

Make substitutions.

e. The size of the tension in the rope is the same for both Michael and the stack. Make a substitution using your equations from part d. and rearrange your answer so that you have an equation for m, the mass of the stack, in terms of M, **g** and **a**.

$T = Ma$ (1)

$mg - T = ma$ (2)

Substitute the expression for T in (1) into (2)

$mg - Ma = ma$

Rearrange equation to say "m = ... "

$mg - Ma = ma$

$mg - ma = Ma$

$m(g - a) = Ma$

$m = \frac{Ma}{g - a}$

Then you can divide both sides by $(g - a)$ to get "m = ..."

Both the g and the a are multiplied by the m.

So you can introduce some parentheses so that there's only one instance of m on the left hand side.

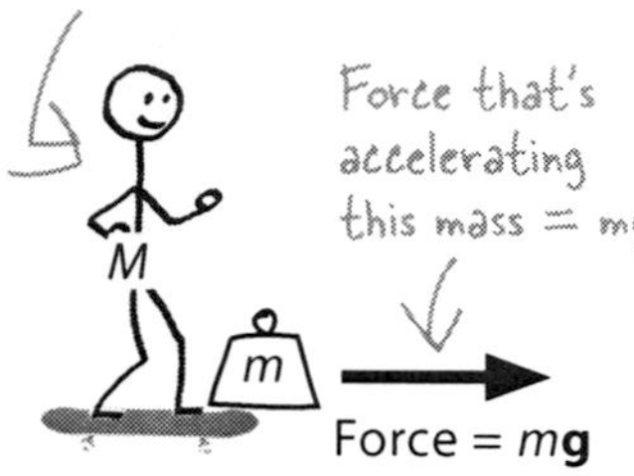

Could we also have treated the stack and Michael as one 'thing' with mass (M + m)? Would that have worked too?

Treating both objects as one single mass works here (but NOT always).

On this occasion, you can also treat Michael and the stack as one object with mass $(M + m)$ that's accelerated by the force $m\mathbf{g}$ (the weight of the stack). You'd write down:

$$\text{Force} = \text{mass} \times \text{acceleration}$$

$$m\mathbf{g} = (M + m)\mathbf{a}$$

When you rearrange this, you get the same equation as over there: $m = \dfrac{M\mathbf{a}}{\mathbf{g} - \mathbf{a}}$

This is NOT a shortcut that will always work. This problem is a special case.

So why bother with the tension at all, if we can do it that way instead?

If you're able to draw free body diagrams for problems that involve ropes and tension, you'll be able to solve **any** problem, not just this one.

For example, if Michael was being pulled up a ramp by the stack instead of being pulled horizontally, you'd have to think about Michael's weight vector as well. The only way of using forces and Newton's 2nd Law to deal with that is to draw a free body diagram for each object attached to the rope - which is fine if you understand the physics.

If you're analyzing a problem with ropes and pulleys using forces, ALWAYS start with individual free body diagrams, have a go at BEING each object, and go on from there.

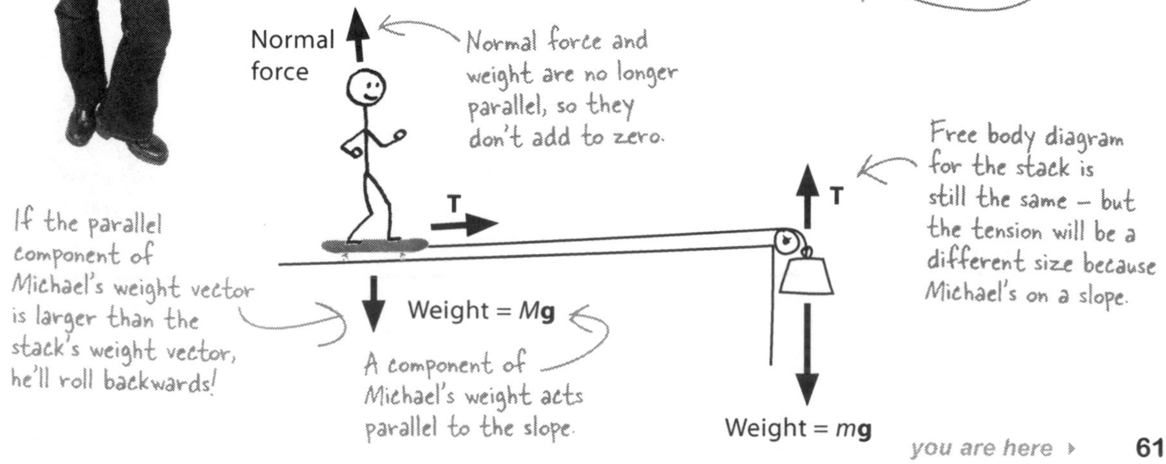

Frank: Right. All we need to do it to put the numbers into it:

$$m = \frac{M\mathbf{a}}{\mathbf{g} - \mathbf{a}}$$

Mass of stack. (m) — Mass of Michael and skateboard. (M)

Jim: Yeah, I just asked Michael, and he says that him plus the skateboard come to 80.0 kg, so we can put that in instead of M. And we already know that $\mathbf{g} = 9.8\ \text{m/s}^2$.

Joe: But what about **a**, the **acceleration**. We don't know that.

Frank: Can't we just put in $\mathbf{a} = 9.8\ \text{m/s}^2$ like we usually do?

Joe: Not this time! The **force** of the stack's weight has to accelerate both the stack's mass and Michael's mass. So the stack won't accelerate as quickly as it would if it was just falling on its own.

Jim: So we gotta work out a value for the acceleration first, before we can get a value for the mass. How are we gonna do that?

Joe: Well, there is the **sketch** we did earlier ...

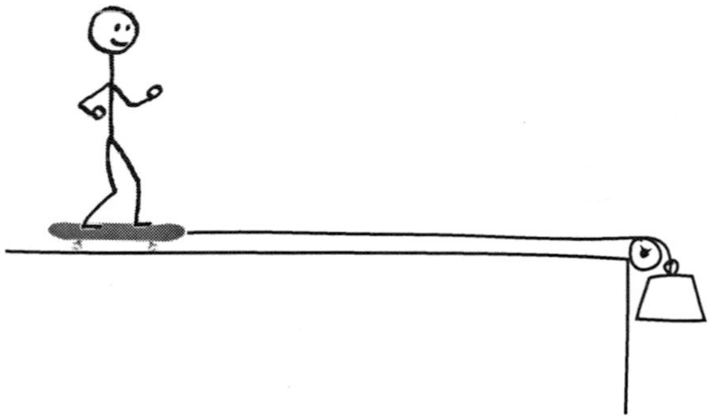

If you start with a sketch, you can always look back at it for inspiration if you're not sure what to do next.

The sketch acts as an anchor that reminds you of what you're working on - and also of ways you might solve your problem.

Jim: Can we just write things like $\mathbf{v}_0$, $\mathbf{v}$ and $\mathbf{x}$ on it, and use **equations of motion** to calculate **a**?

Frank: Oh yeah! I've been getting so wrapped up into working with masses and forces that I forgot we could just look at Michael's velocity, displacement and acceleration, without going into all the reasons behind them.

Joe: Cool, let's do it!

Look at the big picture as well as the parts

Right at the start, you broke down this complicated problem into two parts:

1. Work out the **velocity** Michael needs at the end of the pier to hit the target. You did this first because it involved **equations of motion**, and a scenario similar to others you'd **seen before**.

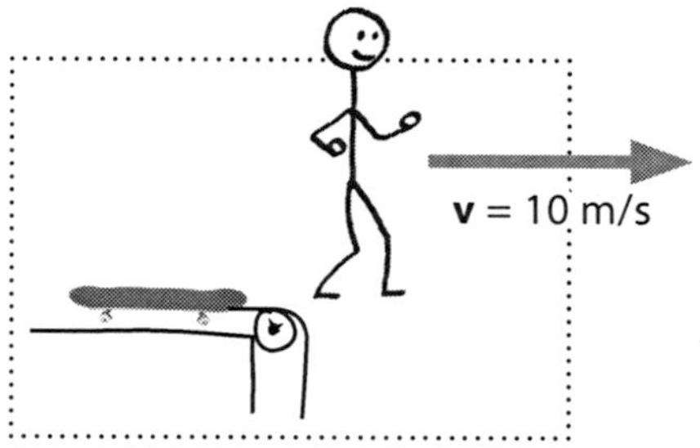

2. Work out what **mass** the stack needs to be for him to reach this velocity at the end of the pier. You've just used free body diagrams and Newton's 2nd Law to come up with an equation for the mass of the stack, $m = \frac{M\mathbf{a}}{\mathbf{g} - \mathbf{a}}$

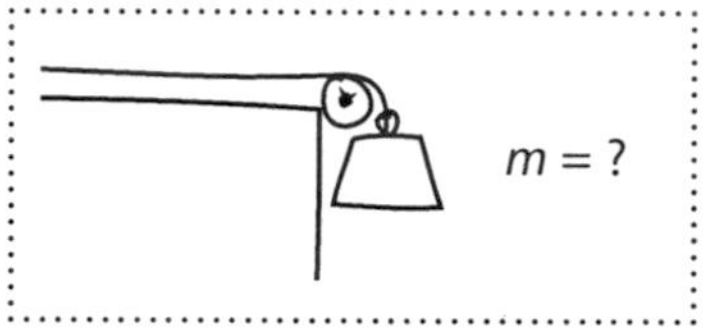

But now you've discovered that there's **another part** to this problem! You need to work out a value for the acceleration of Michael and the stack. The important thing is not to panic, and to step back and look at the **big picture**.

Then you'll see that you can use your **equations of motion** to calculate the acceleration. Once you have a value, you can calculate the mass of the stack, which is what you really want to know.

Though do be careful with how you define the variables you use.

Sharpen your pencil

Michael is to be launched horizontally from the end of a 11.0 m high pier with a velocity of 10.0 m/s. He stands on a skateboard, which is attached via a rope and pulley to a stack of masses that falls vertically downwards. Michael and the skateboard have a combined mass of 80.0 kg.

a. If Michael reaches the edge of the pier at the same time as the stack hits the water, what is his displacement?

b. Calculate Michael's acceleration.

c. Use the equation $m = \frac{M\mathbf{a}}{\mathbf{g} - \mathbf{a}}$ that you worked out before to calculate the mass that the stack needs to be in order to produce this acceleration. (The stack has mass *m*, Michael and his skateboard have mass *M*).

Sharpen your pencil Solution

Michael is to be launched horizontally from the end of a 11.0 m high pier with a velocity of 10.0 m/s. He stands on a skateboard, which is attached via a rope and pulley to a stack of masses that falls vertically downwards. Michael and the skateboard have a combined mass of 80.0 kg.

a. If Michael reaches the edge of the pier at the same time as the stack hits the water, what is his displacement?

The stack has fallen 11.0 m vertically.

So Michael has travelled 11.0 m horizontally, towards the edge of the pier.

b. Calculate Michael's acceleration.

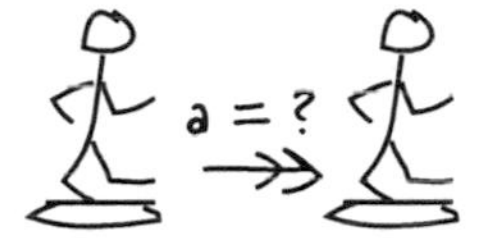

$x_0 = 0$ m $\quad x = 11.0$ m

$v_0 = 0$ m/s $\quad v = 10.0$ m/s

$$v^2 = v_0^2 + 2a(x - x_0)$$

But $v_0 = 0$ and $x_0 = 0$.

$$\Rightarrow v^2 = 2ax$$

$$\Rightarrow a = \frac{v^2}{2x} = \frac{10.0^2}{2 \times 11.0}$$

$$a = 4.54 \text{ m/s (3}$$

c. Use the equation $m = \frac{Ma}{g - a}$ that you worked out before to calculate the mass that the stack needs to be in order to produce this acceleration. (The stack has mass *m*, Michael and his skateboard have mass *M*).

$$m = \frac{Ma}{g - a}$$

$$m = \frac{80.0 \times 4.54}{9.8 - 4.54} = 69.0 \text{ kg (3 sd)}$$

So we should tell Michael to use a 69.0 kg stack – and let him know we want some of the credit when he wins first prize!

But the day before the competition ...

Michael's just been down to the venue to check it out - and he's discovered that the pier slopes up towards the sea at a slight **angle**. The angle is only 5.0° ... but that might be enough to throw out your careful calculations. On the bright side, it levels out just at the end, so at least he's still taking off horizontally, and the end of the pier is still 11.0 m above the water.

On top of that, Michael's checked the skateboard website and found out that its wheels have a coefficient of **friction**, $\mu = 0.0500$.

Your complicated problem just got a LOT more complicated ...

Sharpen your pencil

Michael on his skateboard, with a total mass M, is attached to a stack of masses, total mass m, via a rope and pulley, as shown in the picture. The wheels of the skateboard have coefficient of friction, μ, and the pier slopes up towards the sea at angle θ from the horizontal.

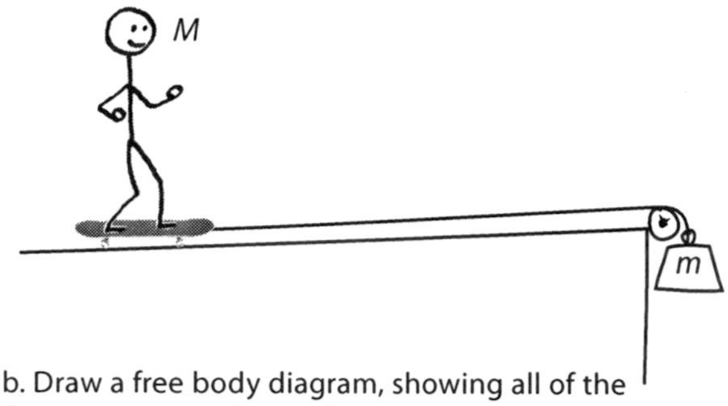

a. Draw a free body diagram, showing all of the forces acting on Michael.

b. Draw a free body diagram, showing all of the forces acting on the stack.

c. Outline what you would do to approach this problem. You don't need to do any math - just explain the process you'd go through.

Sharpen your pencil Solution

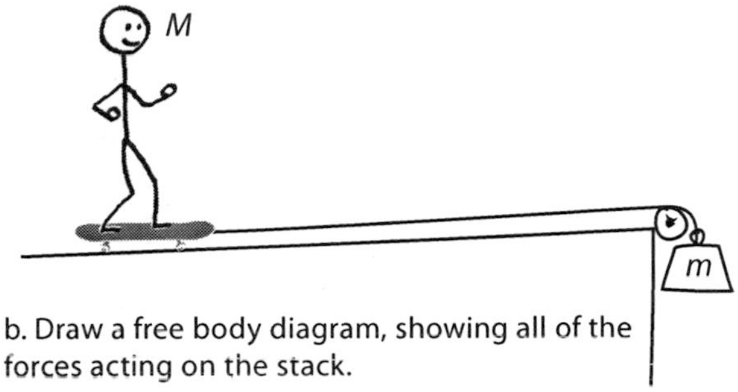

Michael on his skateboard, with a total mass M, is attached to a stack of masses, total mass m, via a rope and pulley, as shown in the picture. The wheels of the skateboard have coefficient of friction, μ, and the pier slopes up towards the sea at angle θ from the horizontal.

a. Draw a free body diagram, showing all of the forces acting on Michael.

b. Draw a free body diagram, showing all of the forces acting on the stack.

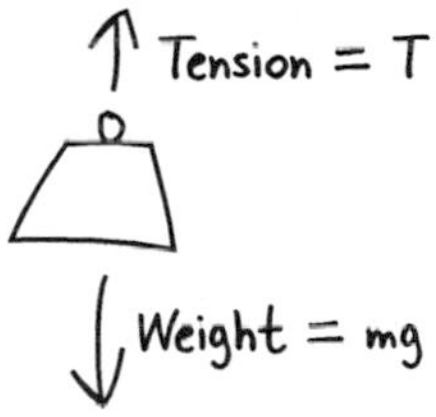

c. Outline what you would do to approach this problem. You don't need to do any math - just explain the process you'd go through.

Use triangles to calculate the parallel component of Michael's weight, $F_{\parallel}$. Also calculate the normal force (equal to the perpendicular component of Michael's weight) and use it to calculate the friction force, as $F_{fric} = \mu F_{normal}$. The net force on Michael is parallel to the pier, $F_{net} = T - F_{\parallel} + F_{fric}$. Then do $F_{net} = ma$ for both Michael and the stack. They both have the same acceleration so go on from there by substituting in for the tension, etc, similar to before.

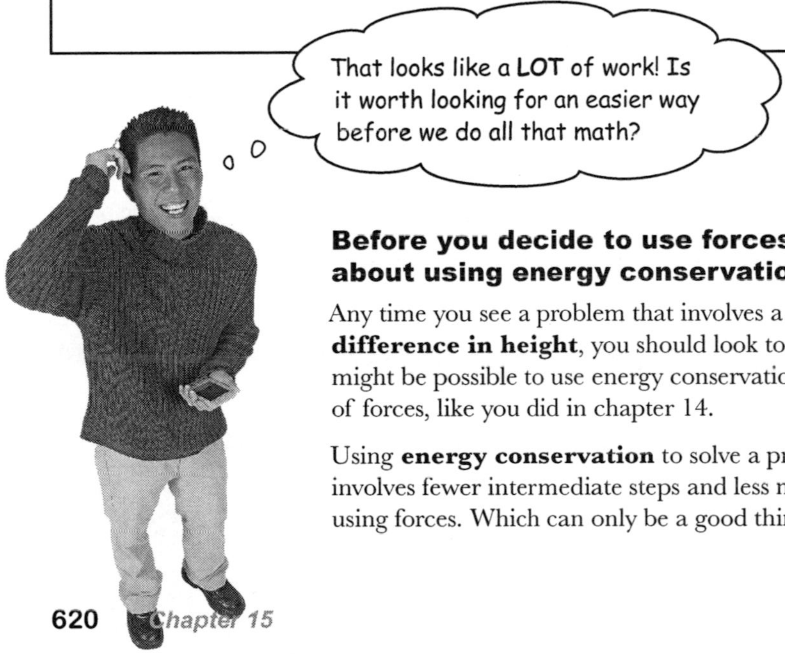

Before you decide to use forces, think about using energy conservation.

Any time you see a problem that involves a **difference in height**, you should look to see if it might be possible to use energy conservation instead of forces, like you did in chapter 14.

Using **energy conservation** to solve a problem involves fewer intermediate steps and less math than using forces. Which can only be a good thing!

If your problem involves a difference in height, look to see if you can use ENERGY CONSERVATION.

Using energy conservation is simpler than using forces

This is the kind of problem that lends itself to using **energy conservation** instead of forces, because it involves masses whose heights and velocities change, and work being done against friction.

The total energy of the system is always constant, and differences drive changes that lead to energy transfer. So if you **spot the differences** between the start (when you've just dropped the stack) and the end (when Michael has just launched horizontally from the skateboard) you'll know what to include in the energy conservation equation.

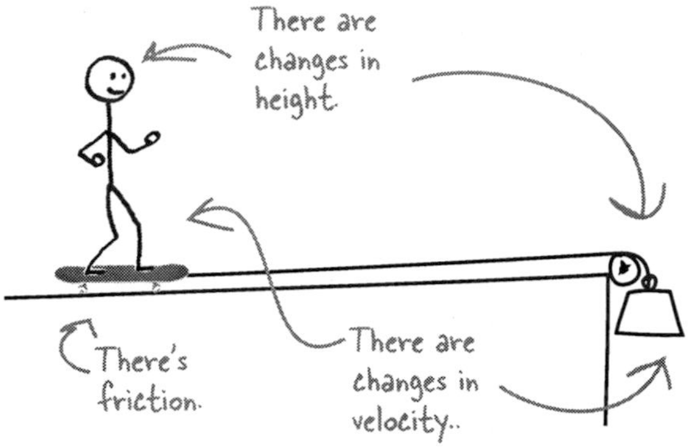

Spot the difference

a. Play "spot the difference" between the start and the end. Circle all the differences between the two pictures and write down what they are.

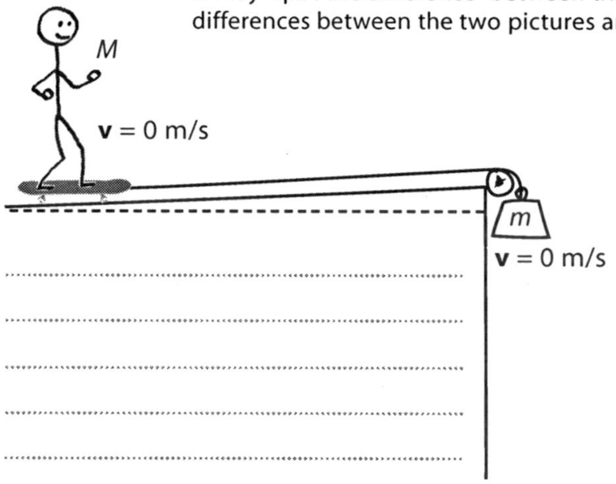

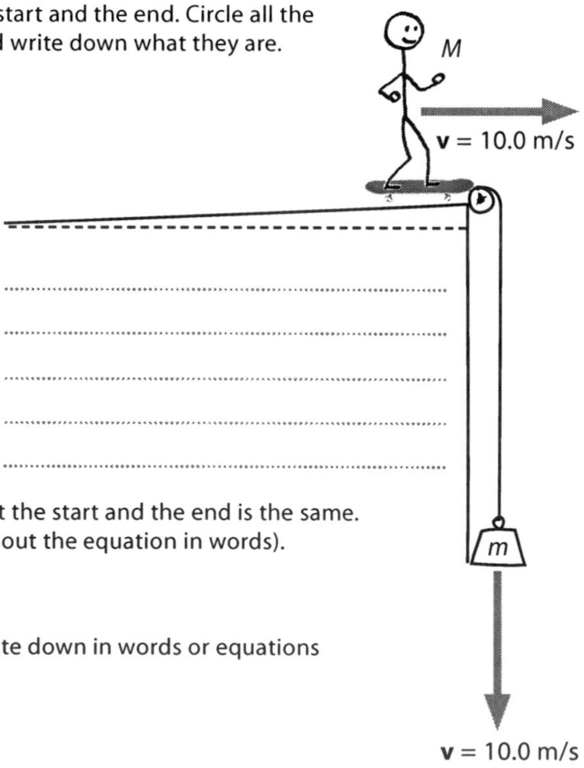

b. Write down an equation to show that the total energy at the start and the end is the same. (You can use any symbols and subscripts you like, or write out the equation in words).

c. For each term in your energy conservation equation, write down in words or equations how you would go about calculating it.

Spot the difference - SOLUTION

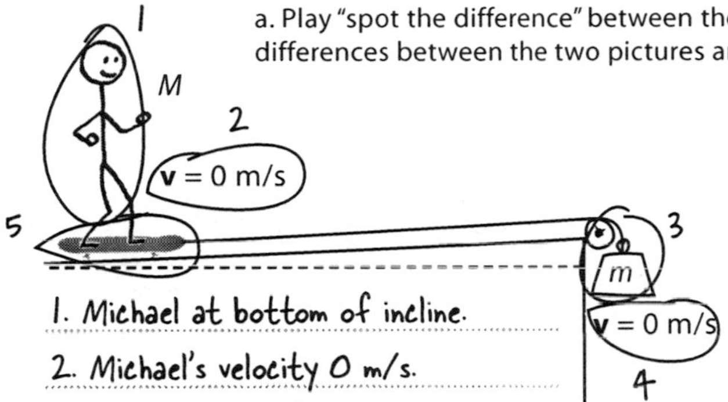

a. Play "spot the difference" between the start and the end. Circle all the differences between the two pictures and write down what they are.

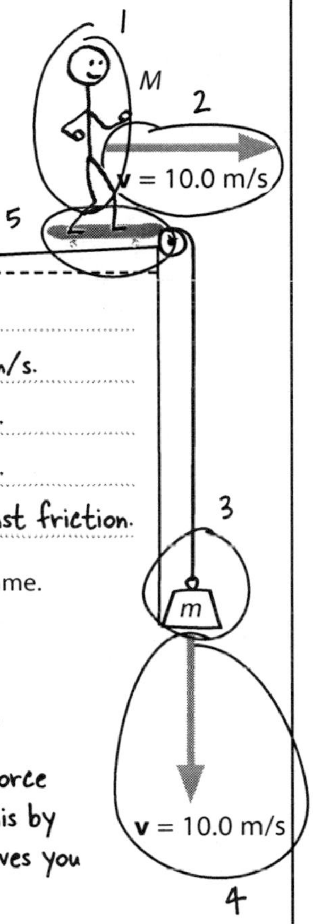

1. Michael at bottom of incline.
2. Michael's velocity 0 m/s.
3. Stack at top of pier.
4. Stack velocity 0 m/s.
5. No work done against friction.

1. Michael at top of incline
2. Michael's velocity 10.0 m/s.
3. Stack at bottom of pier.
4. Stack velocity 10.0 m/s.
5. Work has been done against friction.

b. Write down an equation to show that the total energy at the start and the end is the same. (You can use any symbols and subscripts you like, or write out the equation in words).

Energy at start = energy at end $\Rightarrow U_{stack} = U_{man} + K_{man} + K_{stack} + W_{friction}$

c. For each term in your energy conservation equation, write down in words or equations how you would go about calculating it.

$U = \text{mass} \times g \times h$
$K = \frac{1}{2} \times \text{mass} \times v^2$
} Same method for Michael and stack.

To calculate $W_{friction}$, calculate normal force using angle and weight and multiply this by μ, the coefficient of friction. This gives you the frictional force, $F_{friction}$.

Then $W_{friction} = F_{friction} \times$ displacement

By playing Spot the difference, we know that the **potential** energy that the stack has as a result of being 11.0 m higher at the start than it is at the end is transferred to:

- The **potential** energy Michael gains by going up the incline.
- The **kinetic** energy of Michael and the skateboard.
- The **kinetic** energy of the stack.
- The **work** done against the **friction** of the skateboard wheels.

It's time to put that all together ...

The easiest way to do energy conservation is to play "spot the difference."

Sharpen your pencil

Michael on his skateboard, with a total mass of 80.0 kg, is attached to a stack of masses, total mass m, via a rope and pulley. The wheels of the skateboard have coefficient of friction, $\mu = 0.0500$, and the board travels 11.0 m along a pier which slopes up towards the sea at angle $\theta = 5.0°$ from the horizontal as the stack goes 11.0 m straight down.

a. Calculate the difference in the height of Michael on the skateboard at the beginning and end of the pier.

b. Calculate the normal force exerted by the pier on Michael, and hence the work done against friction.

Remember that $F_{fric} = \mu F_N$

c. Michael needs to have a speed of 10.0 m/s at the end of the pier. Use energy conservation to work out the mass that the stack needs to have in order to achieve this.

Sharpen your pencil Solution

Michael on his skateboard, with a total mass of 80.0 kg, is attached to a stack of masses, total mass *m*, via a rope and pulley. The wheels of the skateboard have coefficient of friction, $\mu = 0.0500$, and the board travels 11.0 m along a pier which slopes up towards the sea at angle $\theta = 5.0°$ from the horizontal as the stack goes 11.0 m straight down.

a. Calculate the difference in the height of Michael on the skateboard at the beginning and end of the pier.

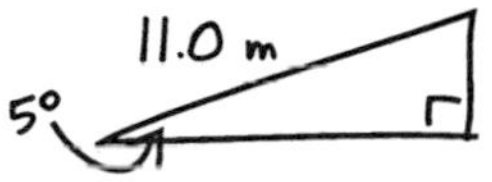

$$\sin(5.0°) = \frac{h_M}{11.0} \Rightarrow h_M = 11.0\sin(5.0°)$$

$$h_M = 0.959 \text{ m (3 sd)}$$

We're using a subscript here so that we don't get mixed up with the height of the pier. h_M is Michael's change in height.

b. Calculate the normal force exerted by the pier on Michael, and hence the work done against friction.

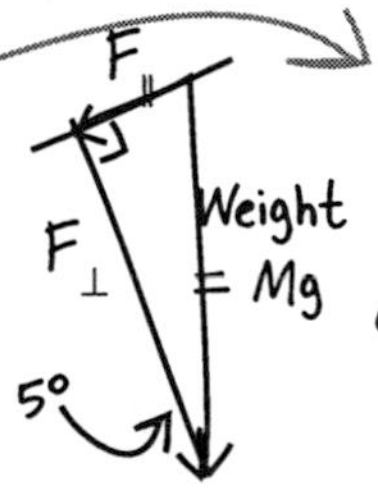

Normal force is same size as perpendicular component of weight.

$$\cos(5°) = \frac{F_\perp}{Mg}$$

Use these tips to get your triangles right.

$$\Rightarrow F_\perp = mg\cos(5.0°)$$

$$F_\perp = 80 \times 9.8 \times \cos(5.0°) = 781 \text{ N}$$

$$F_N = 781 \text{ N}$$

$$W_{friction} = \mu F_N \Delta x = 0.0500 \times 781 \times 11.0$$

$$W_{friction} = 430 \text{ J (3 sd)}$$

Michael doesn't float in the air or disappear through the ground. So the perpendicular components of the forces acting on him must add to zero.

Triangle Tip: sketch extreme angles

If you're not sure which angle in your force vector triangle corresponds to the angle of your slope, sketch a slope with a **small angle**, □.

Making this angle small helps you to keep track of similar triangles.

Now draw the force triangle. Draw on the weight pointing straight down. Then draw in the parallel and perpendicular components. It doesn't matter which way round you draw the components, as the triangle's sides will still be the same length.

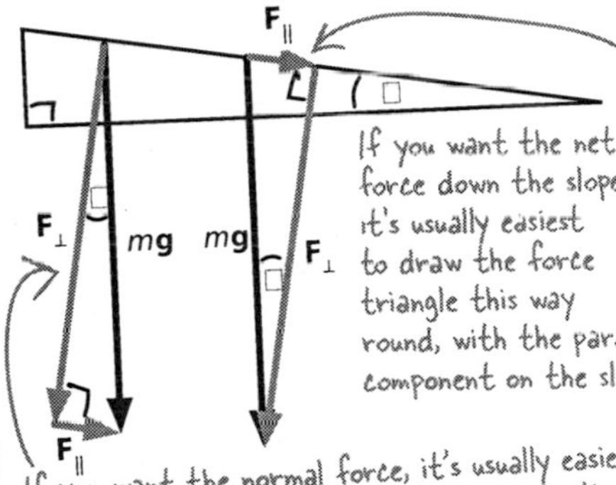

If you want the net force down the slope, it's usually easiest to draw the force triangle this way round, with the parallel component on the slope.

If you want the normal force, it's usually easiest to draw the triangle this way round, with the perpendicular component below the object.

□ is the small angle in the slope triangle - so □ will also be the small angle in the force triangle.

These also appeared in ch. 13.

c. Michael needs to have a speed of 10.0 m/s at the end of the pier. Use energy conservation to work out the mass that the stack needs to have in order to achieve this.

Energy at start = energy at end

$$U_{stack} = U_{man} + K_{man} + K_{stack} + W_{friction}$$

$$mgh = Mgh_M + \frac{1}{2}Mv^2 + \frac{1}{2}mv^2 + W_{friction}$$

$$mgh - \frac{1}{2}mv^2 = Mgh_M + \frac{1}{2}Mv^2 + W_{friction}$$

Introduce parentheses to leave one instance of m on the left hand side.

$$m(gh - \frac{1}{2}v^2) = Mgh_M + \frac{1}{2}Mv^2 + W_{friction}$$

$$m = \frac{Mgh_M + \frac{1}{2}Mv^2 + W_{friction}}{(gh - \frac{1}{2}v^2)}$$

$$m = \frac{(80 \times 9.8 \times 0.959) + (0.5 \times 80 \times 10^2) + 430}{(9.8 \times 11) - (0.5 \times 10^2)}$$

$$m = 89.7 \text{ kg (3 sd)}$$

This is larger then the mass you calculated last time, when there was no incline and no friction, which makes sense.

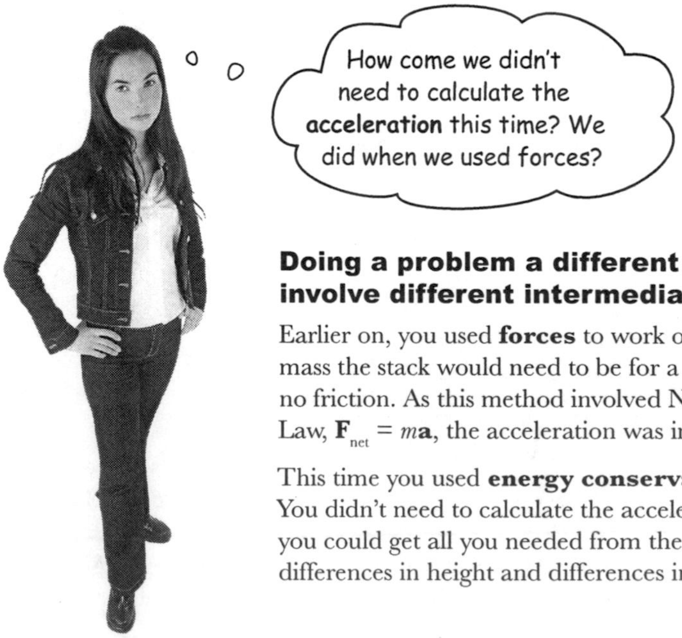

Doing a problem a different way may involve different intermediate steps.

Earlier on, you used **forces** to work out what mass the stack would need to be for a flat pier with no friction. As this method involved Newton's 2nd Law, $\mathbf{F}_{net} = m\mathbf{a}$, the acceleration was important.

This time you used **energy conservation**. You didn't need to calculate the acceleration, as you could get all you needed from the masses, differences in height and differences in velocity.

There goes that skateboard...

Michael's taken your advice, and he's off...
let's see how he does:

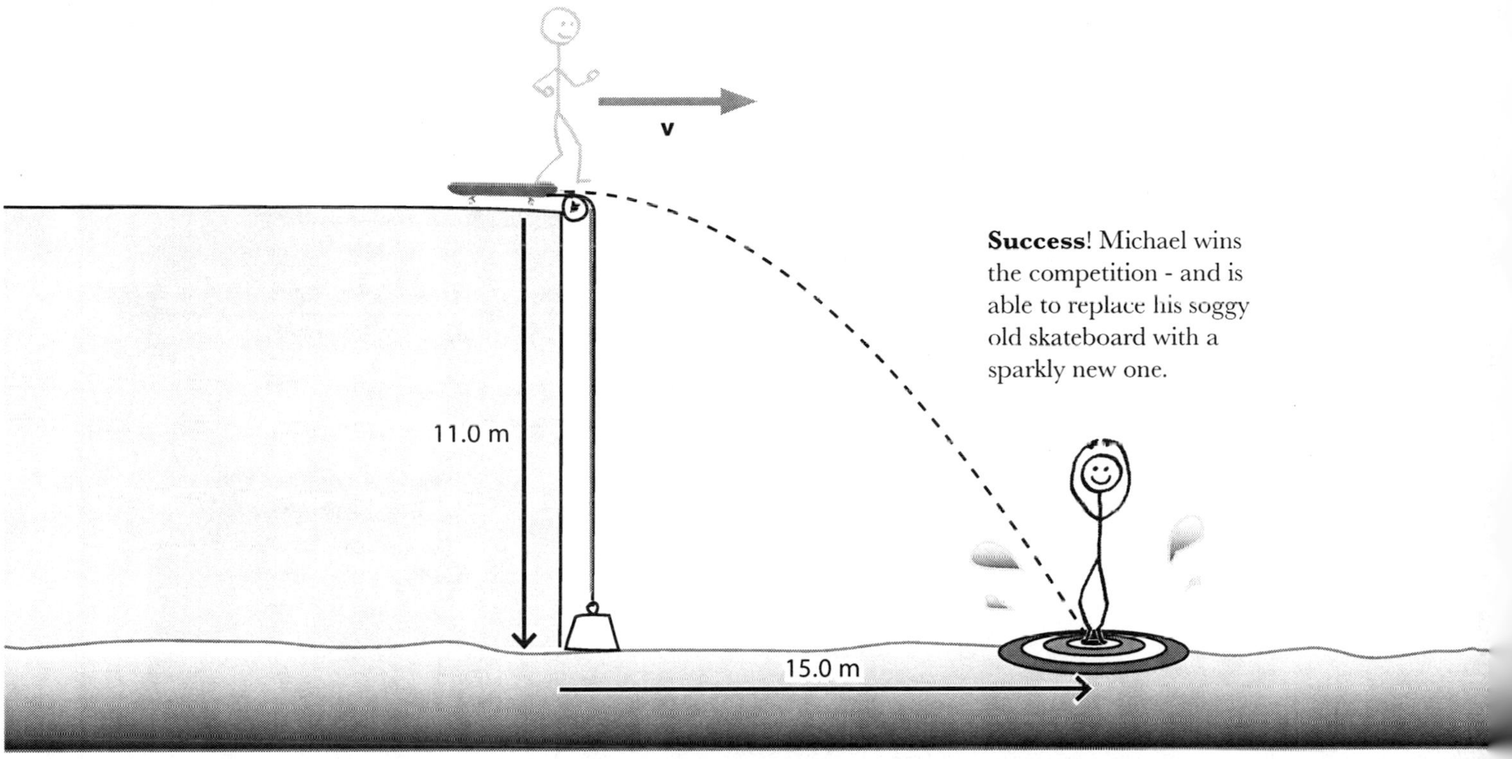

Success! Michael wins the competition - and is able to replace his soggy old skateboard with a sparkly new one.

BULLET POINTS

- When two objects are joined together by a rope that's pulled tight, they both accelerate at the same rate in the same direction that the rope moves in.
- The **tension** in a rope is the same at both ends.
- A mass won't accelerate at $9.8\ m/s^2$ when it falls if it is attached to another mass that isn't also falling with it.
- If you have more than one mass, draw a **free body diagram** for each ...
- ... but do also check to see if you can use **energy conservation** instead!
- Play "spot the difference" to make sure you spot all the **differences** that involve energy transfer before you write down any equations.

Five Minute Mystery

Problems with a punchbag

Geoff's Gym was becoming more and more popular - so much so that his customers were having to queue for each piece of apparatus. But being that popular also has its disadvantages - and many of Geoff's customers were talking of going somewhere more quiet once their current memberships had expired.

So Geoff brought in lots of new equipment - bikes, rowing machines, weights machines - some seriously complicated and expensive pieces of kit. But the item Geoff had the most problems with was the humble punchbag.

"I just don't know what went wrong," he explains. "The punchbag's 20 kg. So its weight is 196 N - call it 200 N to be on the safe side. I wasn't able to hang it straight down like I usually would because the girders in the roof are in the wrong place. So I decided to use two ropes to hang it from a couple of girders.

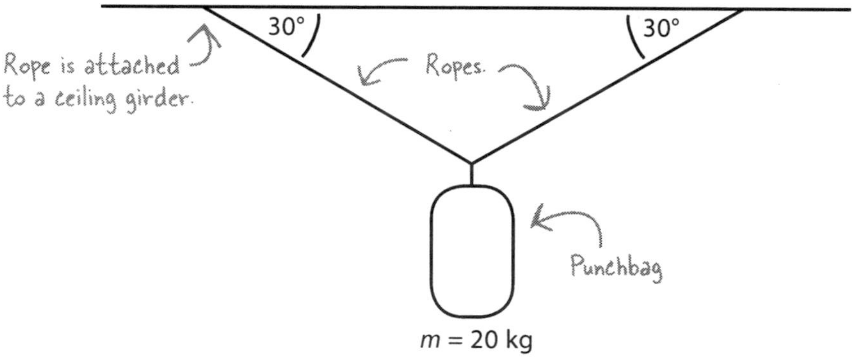

I thought that each rope will be supporting half of the weight. That must be 100 N per rope, as both ropes are at the same angle. The ropes I used to hang the punchbag were guaranteed to cope with a tension of up to 180 N ... or so the manufacturers claimed.

So I put the punchbag on top of a stepladder to set it at the right height, then went up and attached the ropes. But as soon as I took away the stepladder, one of the ropes broke! I couldn't believe it! And then of course the punchbag swung sideways and the other rope broke.

Why did the first rope break?

Problems with a punchbag

Why did the first rope break?

Geoff assumed that each rope would only have to provide enough tension force to prevent the punchbag from **falling**. But the tension force also needs to prevent the punchbag from **swinging**. which is what would happen if the other rope wasn't present.

Each rope exerts a tension force on the punchbag in the direction of the rope:

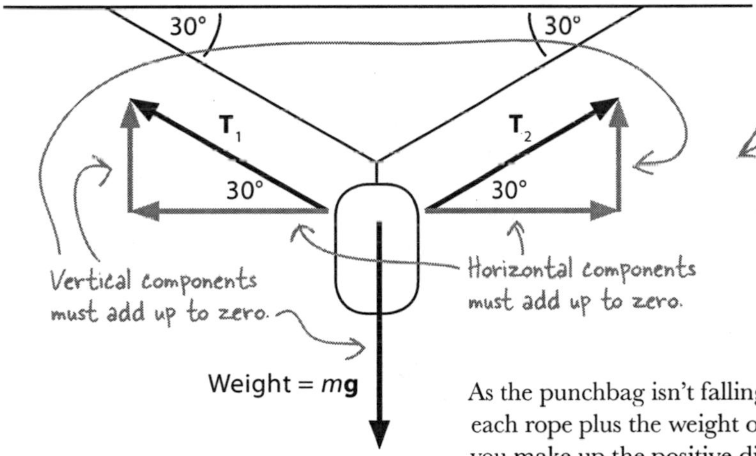

As the punchbag isn't falling, the vertical components of the tension in each rope plus the weight of the punchbag need to add up to zero. If you make up the positive direction:

$$\mathbf{T}_1\sin(30°) + \mathbf{T}_2\sin(30°) - 196\text{N} = 0$$

But for the punchbag to be stationary and not to swing, the horizontal components of the tension in each rope must also add up to zero. If you make left the positive direction:

$$\mathbf{T}_1\cos(30°) - \mathbf{T}_2\cos(30°) = 0$$

This gives you two equations to work out two unknowns, $\mathbf{T}_1$ and $\mathbf{T}_2$. When you solve them, the tension in each rope is an enormous 196 N - the same as the tension you'd need to hold up the punchbag using a single vertical rope. As each rope can only cope with a tension of 180N, one of them broke just before the other one would have.

Have a go at solving them yourself!

The high tension is because of the relatively small angle the ropes make with the horizontal - a lot of extra tension is needed to prevent the bag from swinging.

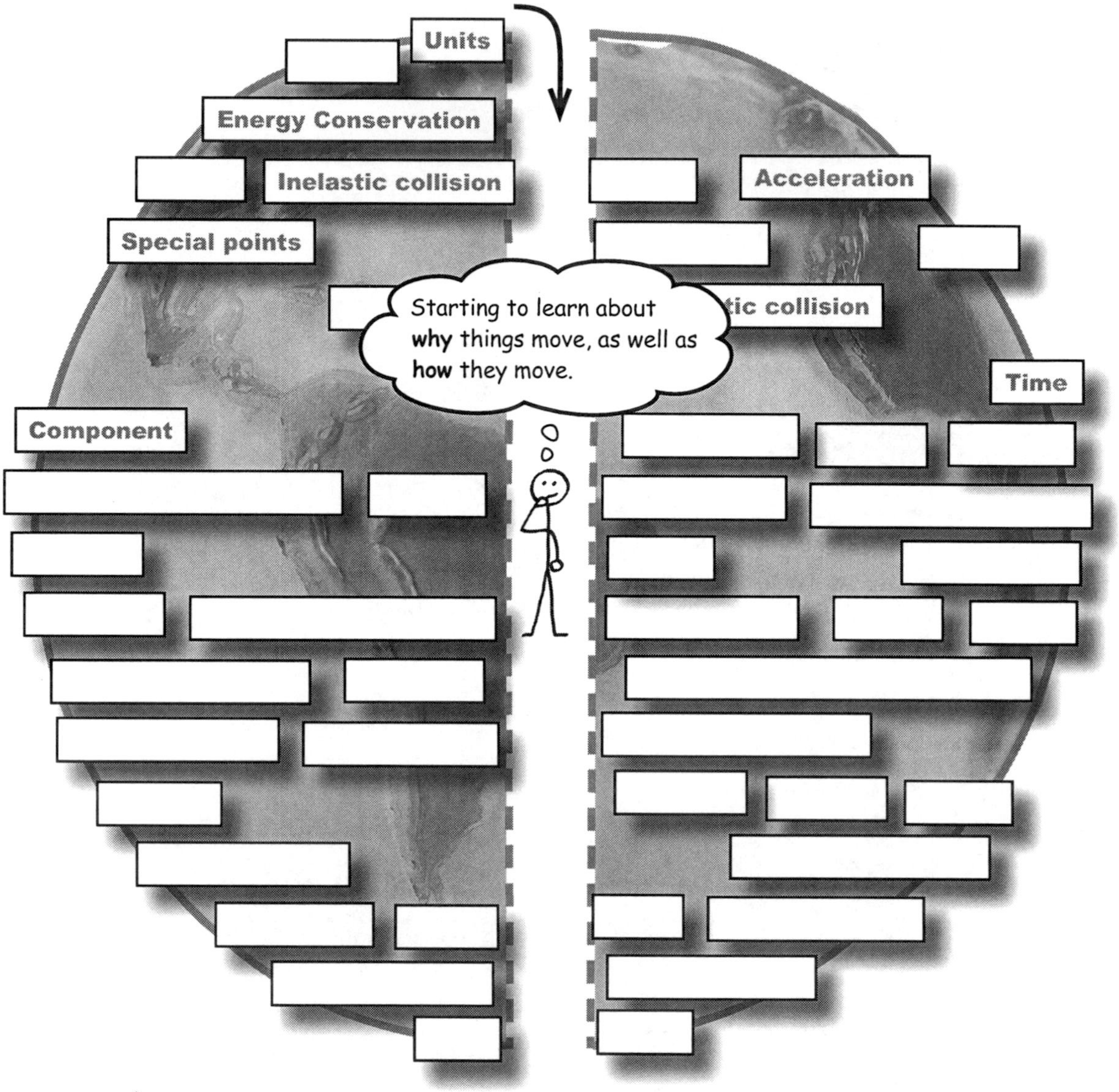

Tension — **Tension is the force that a rope can mediate when it's pulled tight. The tension force is the same at each end of the rope.**

Pulley — **A pulley allows you to "change" the direction of a force by providing a wheel that a rope can run around and providing a support force to prevent the rope from straightening.**

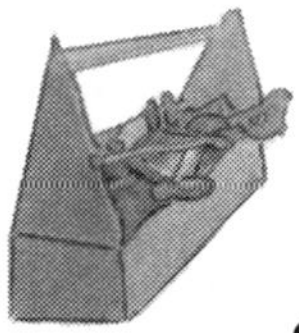

Your Physics Toolbox

You've got Chapter 15 under your belt and added some problem-solving skills to your ever-expanding toolbox.

Rope and pulley

If a problem involves a rope and a pulley, look to see if you're asked about forces. If so, you should draw a separate free body diagram for each object attached to the rope.

The size of the tension is the same at each end of the rope.

Both objects must have the same size of acceleration, as they are attached together.

Break down the problem into parts

When you have a complicated problem, try to break it down into parts.

Then start with the part that looks the easiest for you to solve!

Spot the difference

As well as differences in height, look out for differences in speed and work done against friction.

Play "spot the difference" like this before you write down an energy conservation equation to make sure you don't miss anything out.

Can you use energy conservation?

If you see a difference in height, you should immediately think about using energy conservation – especially if you're not asked about forces?

This involves less math than using forces – so takes you less time with less chance of slipping up.

16 circular motion (part 1)

From a to ω

You say you want a revolution? In this chapter, you'll learn how to deal with **circular motion** with a crash course in **circle** anatomy, including what the **radius** and **circumference** have to do with pies (or should that be ϖs). After dealing with **frequency** and **period**, you'll need to switch from the **linear** to the **angular**. But once you've learned to use **radians** to measure angles, you'll know it's gonna be alright.

Limber up for the Kentucky Hamster Derby

Universally acclaimed as the most exciting two minutes in a wheel, the Kentucky Hamster Derby is big business! You've been called upon by one of the biggest owners in the business to implement an exacting training programme that's been tailored for the big race.

At the moment, the hamsters aren't following their schedule. Some are slacking off, and others are over-working. It's up to you to make sure that the hamsters train exactly as they should.

Hamsters like to run all night in their wheels. The training schedule is a way of honing the kinds of distances and speeds they typically run at into training for a race.

Distance (km)	Speed (km/h)	Total number of revolutions	Motor setting ( )
15.00	3.00		
10.00	4.00		
2.00	5.50		

The hamsters are to do three different types of run, depending on which day of their schedule they're on. The hamster owner knows the **distances** he'd like the hamsters to cover and the **speeds** he'd like them to run at.

But he's not great at physics - which is where you come in!

You can revolutionize the hamsters' training

It's time to design the ultimate hamster training tool.
The equipment you have to achieve this is:

A standard hamster racing wheel with a **radius** of 10.0 cm. This means that it is 10 cm from the center of the wheel to the edge, where the hamster runs.

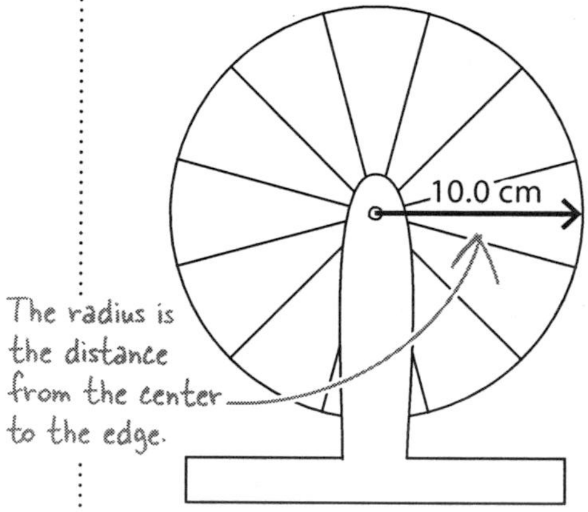

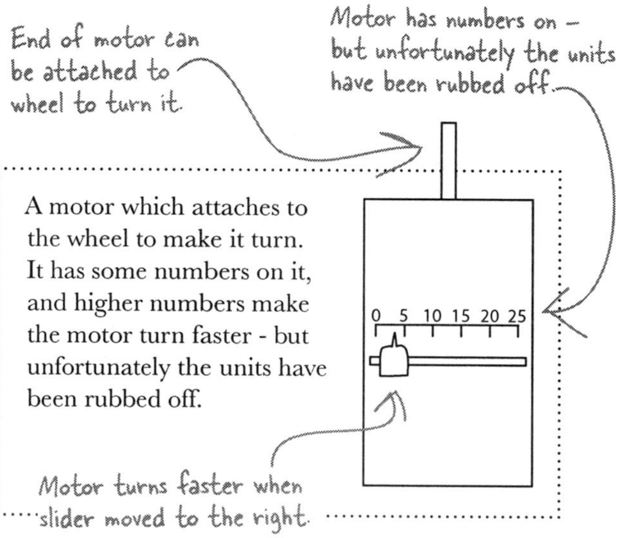

A motor which attaches to the wheel to make it turn. It has some numbers on it, and higher numbers make the motor turn faster - but unfortunately the units have been rubbed off.

A counter that counts wheel revolutions. You can use this to start the motor, then stop it after a certain number of wheel revolutions.

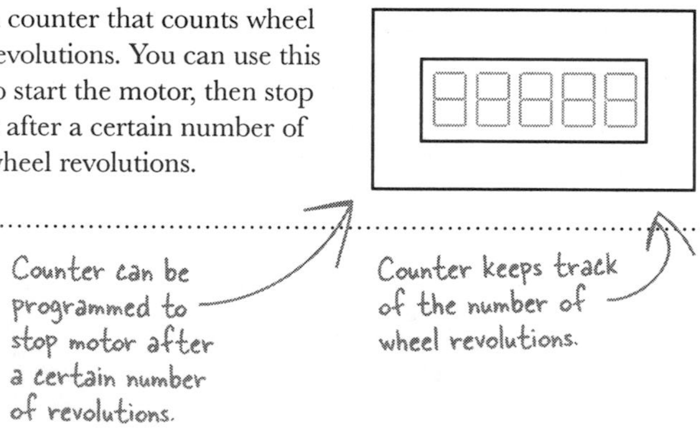

The schedule involves **linear** distances and speeds, which you'd usually measure along a straight line or by using component vectors.

But the hamster wheel is **circular**, and the counter keeps track of the number of **revolutions**. How are we going to go from the linear schedule to the circular equipment?

Circular motion is different from linear motion.

BRAIN POWER

The schedule is linear, but the equipment is **circular**. What are you going to do next?

Joe: Yeah - it's really important to get this training schedule automated and set up!

Jim: So I guess we use the motor to make the wheel turn at a certain **speed**, and have the timer switch it off when it's covered the right **distance**? That sounds pretty straightforward.

Frank: We already know the wheel's 10.0 cm all the way round ...

Jim: No - the **radius** of the wheel is 10.0 cm, but that's the distance from its center to its edge. We need to know the **distance** the outside of the wheel travels in one **revolution**.

Frank: Yeah, OK, so we need to figure out the distance a hamster runs for each revolution of the wheel. The counter counts the **number** of revolutions the wheel's made. So we work out the number of revolutions required to cover each distance, and we're fine.

Joe: But if we don't know the **circumference** of the wheel, we can't do anything with that.

Frank: What's a circumference?

Joe: The circumference is the special name for the **perimeter** of a circle - the distance all the way round the outside.

Jim: OK, so we need some way of working out the circumference. If we know what distance the hamster covers when the wheel goes round once, we can use that to work out how many **revolutions** the wheel needs to do to cover each distance.

Jim: And if we know that, then we can set the counter to turn the motor off once the wheel's done the correct number of revolutions.

Frank: I guess we need to work out what those numbers on the motor mean as well, so we can get the **speed** right. It's a shame the **units** got rubbed off.

Joe: Yeah, that's a good point.

Jim: Well, speed is distance divided by time, isn't it? So if we get the distance sorted out first, we can think about setting the right speed later.

Frank: Cool, let's go for it!

Circumference is a word that means the 'perimeter' of a circle.

The circumference of a circle is the DISTANCE something at the edge travels in one REVOLUTION.

You can also think of the circumference as the distance around the edge of a stationary circle, but in physics it's more useful to think about it in terms of a rotating circle.

Thinking through different approaches helps

You need to work out the hamster wheel's **circumference** (the distance all the way round the edge) so that you know how many **revolutions** are equal to each **distance** in the training schedule.

But all you know at the moment is that the wheel is a circle with a 10.0 cm **radius** (the distance from its center to its edge). How are you going to work out its circumference so that you can implement the training schedule?

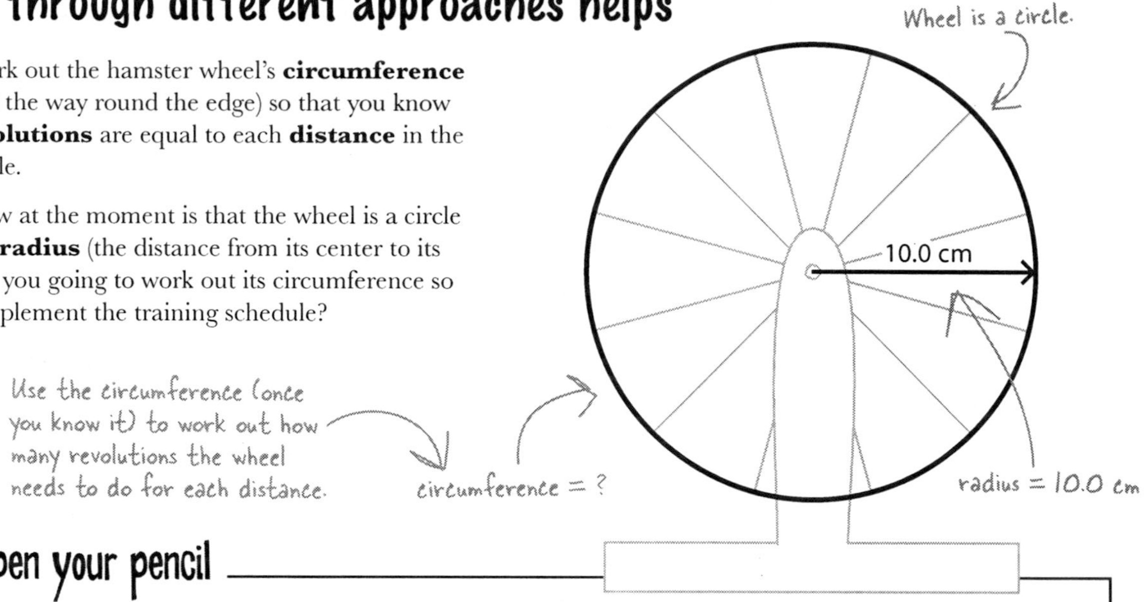

Sharpen your pencil

You have a hamster wheel and want to know the distance that the hamster will cover when the wheel goes round once - i.e., the circumference of the wheel (which has a 10.0 cm radius).

Write down as many methods as you can think of to work this out.

You're **describing** practical methods, not giving a numerical answer.

Sharpen your pencil Solution

You have a hamster wheel and want to know the distance that the hamster will cover when the wheel goes round once - i.e., the circumference of the wheel.

Write down as many methods as you can think of to work this out.

You're **describing** practical methods, not giving a numerical answer.

Get a piece of string, wrap it once round the wheel.

Mark where it comes to, then take the string off the wheel and measure it with a ruler.

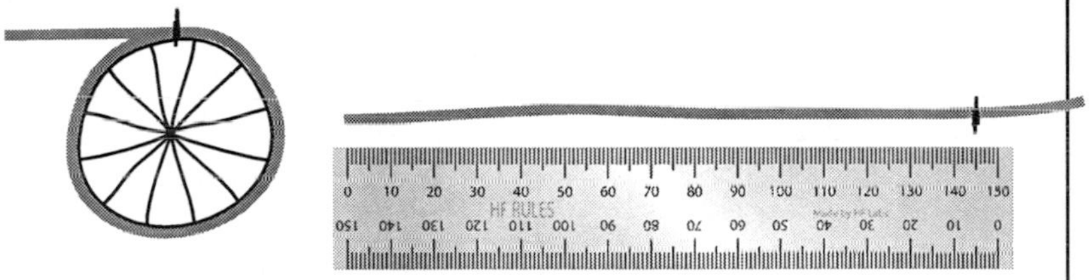

Remove the wheel from the stand and make a mark on it. Line up this mark with a mark on the ground.

Then roll the wheel along until the mark is touching the ground again.

Measure the distance between the first mark on the ground and the second mark on the ground.

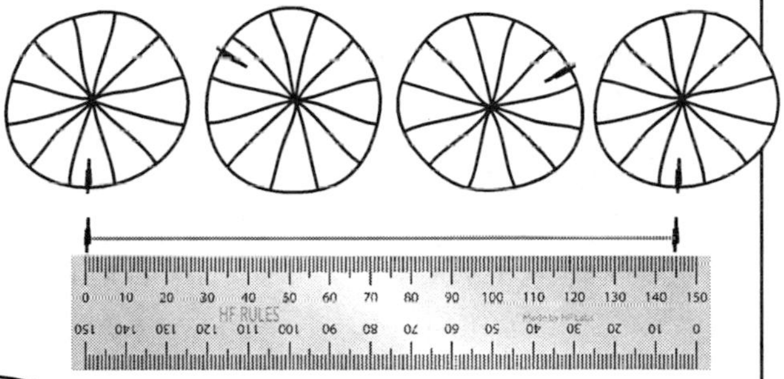

Equations save you time.

You can work out the distance around the hamster wheel by wrapping string around it or rolling it. But what if you need to deal with other circles in the future?

It's definitely easier to use a ruler to measure a **linear** distance (like the radius) than it is to measure a curved distance (like the circumference), so an equation linking the radius and circumference would be useful!

If you have to do a task more than once, try to work out an equation that'll save you time.

A circle's radius and circumference are linked by ϖ

All circles are similar. They're exactly the same shape zoomed in or out. Although they don't have 'sides', you can be sure that **the ratio of a circle's circumference to its radius** will always be the same. (Just like the sides of similar triangles always have the same ratios.)

This is another way of saying that whatever size the circle is, its radius will always fit around its circumference the same number of times.

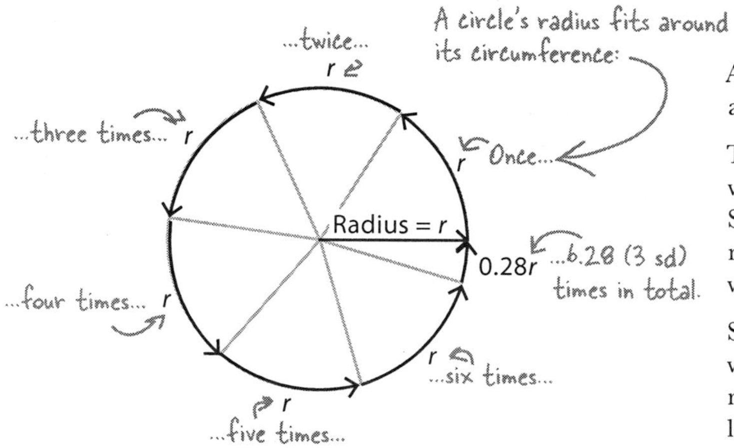

A circle's radius fits around its circumference approximately 6.28 times (3 sd).

The actual ratio of the lengths is a number with an infinite number of significant digits! So rather than writing "6.28 (3 sd)" as the ratio, there's a special abbreviation for it - 2ϖ, where $\varpi = 3.14$ (3 sd).

So you can write down the equation $C = 2\varpi r$, where C is the circumference and r is the radius. In other words, if a circle's radius is 1.00 m, its circumference is 6.28 m, and so on.

$$C = 2\varpi r$$

Circumference (C), *Radius* (r), $\pi = 3.14$ (3 sd)

> But that's just dumb! Why not make π twice as big, i.e. $\pi = 6.28...$, so that the ratio is π instead of 2π? If I get to make up a new number, surely it's easier not to have that 2 in there!

π was invented when the diameter was more interesting than the radius.

Mathematicians originally defined ϖ as the ratio between a circle's diameter (the distance across the circle) and its circumference. The diameter is twice the length of the radius, so $\varpi = 3.14$ (3 sd) as the diameter fits round the circumference 3.14 (3 sd) times. Once ϖ has been defined, you can't really go changing its value.

In physics, you're often a lot more interested in the radius of a circle than you are in its diameter (for example, torque = radius × force), so the value 2ϖ will often turn up in your equations.

$$\varpi = 3.14 \text{ (3 sd)}$$

In physics, the RADIUS is more interesting than the diameter.

For example, torque = radius x force

there are no Dumb Questions

Q: What are the units of π ?

A: π is a ratio of two lengths, the circumference and the diameter. It tells you the NUMBER of times the diameter fits into the circumference - 3.14 (3 sd) times. Length divided by length is dimensionless, so π is a NUMBER and doesn't have any units.

Q: Do I need to remember the value of π for my exam?

A: Knowing that π = 3.14 (3 sd) is useful. If you're doing AP Physics, you won't have a calculator in the multiple choice section, so the approximation π = 3 (1 sd) will help you to choose the option that's in the right ballpark.

Q: Can I use the [π] button on my calculator in the section where I'm allowed a calculator?

A: Yes, that's be fine - though you need to round your answer to an appropriate number of significant digits at the end.

Q: But why is π 3.14 (etc) in the first place, when that makes the ratio of a circle's radius to its circumference 2π?

A: π was originally coined to describe the ratio between a circle's circumference and its **diameter**: $C = \pi d$. Nowadays, the ratio of a circle's circumference to its **radius** is more often used in physics - but the value of π had already been decided.

The ratio of a circle's circumference to its diameter is π. As the radius is half the length of the diameter, the ratio of the circumference to the radius is 2π. So $C = 2\pi r$

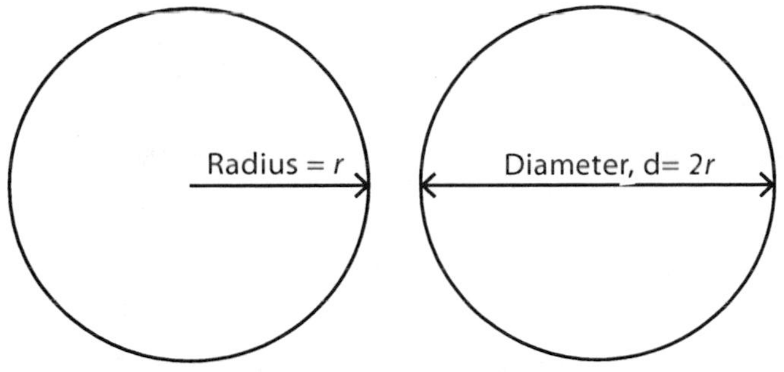

C = 2ϖr　　**C = ϖd**

Q: You said that π has an infinite number of digits? Surely it must end somewhere!

A: Nope! π is an irrational number, which means you can't write it down exactly.

Q: Is that why there's a symbol for it then? To avoid having to write more of it out than you really need to?

A: That's right. You can write the equation: circumference = $2\pi r$ and the '=' sign is true because when you use the symbol π it implies the full irrational number!

Otherwise you'd have to write circumference = $6.28r$ (3 sd) as you'd never be able to write down the exact value of the circumference as an equation.

Q: That all sounds a bit philosophical to me. I guess that in practice, I can write down circumference = $2\pi r$ when I'm showing my work, then at the very end I can use the value 3.14 (3 sd) for π when I'm actually putting the numbers In to work out an answer?

A: That's a very good way of thinking about it.

Q: So do I get to use π to design the hamster trainer now?

A: On you go then ...

π is the <u>ratio</u> of two lengths - it tells you the NUMBER of times the diameter fits into the circumference. Because π is a NUMBER, it has no units.

Convert from linear distance to revolutions

The hamster training schedule contains distances in km. Your job is to implement the schedule using the wheel and a counter that keeps track of the number of **revolutions**. So you need to work out how many circumferences - and therefore how many revolutions - each distance is equivalent to.

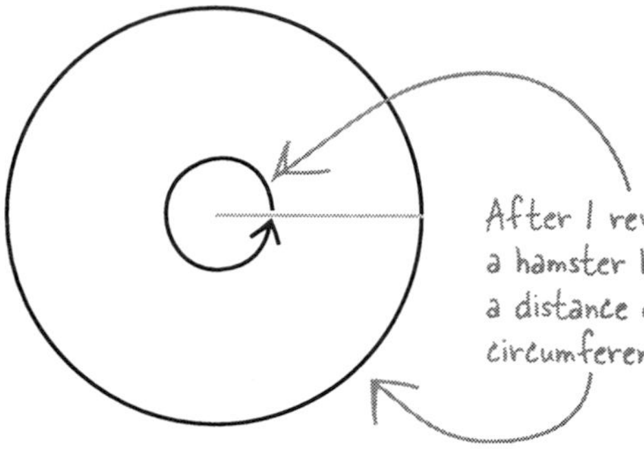

Sharpen your pencil

a. Assume you have a hamster wheel, radius r. Write down an equation in terms of r that gives you the distance that something on the edge of the circle will cover if the circle rotates once.

b. You would like the hamster to cover distance x. Write down an equation that gives you x in terms of r. and the total number of revolutions, N.

c. Your hamster wheel has a radius of 10.0 cm. Fill in the 'total number of revolutions' column for the distances shown in the hamster training schedule. There's space under the table for you to show your work.

Don't worry about this column yet, you'll fill it in later.

Distance (km)	Speed (km/h)	Total number of revolutions	Motor setting ( )
15.00	3.00		
10.00	4.00		
2.00	5.50		

Sharpen your pencil Solution

Don't worry about this column yet, you'll fill it in later.

a. Assume you have a hamster wheel, radius **r**. Write down an equation in terms of **r** that gives you the distance that something on the edge of the circle will cover if the circle rotates once.

Circumference $C = 2\pi r$

b. You would like the hamster to cover distance *x*. Write down an equation that gives you *x* in terms of *r*. and the total number of revolutions, *N*.

Number of revolutions is the same as the number of circumferences in distance x:

$N = \frac{x}{C}$ and $C = 2\pi r$

$\Rightarrow N = \frac{x}{2\pi r}$

$\Rightarrow \underline{x = 2\pi r N}$

c. Your hamster wheel has a radius of 10.0 cm. Fill in the 'total number of revolutions' column for the distances shown in the hamster training schedule. There's space under the table for you to show your work.

Distance (km)	Speed (km/h)	Total number of revolutions	Motor setting ( )
15.00	3.00	23900 (3 sd)	
10.00	4.00	15900 (3 sd)	
2.00	5.50	3180 (2 sd)	

$x = 2\pi r N \Rightarrow N = \frac{x}{2\pi r}$

If you have a mixture of distance units, it's usually safest to convert everything to meters.

15.00 km: $N = \frac{15.00 \times 10^3}{2 \times \pi \times 0.100}$

$\underline{N = 23900 \text{ revolutions}}$ (3 sd)

10.00 km: $N = \frac{10.00 \times 10^3}{2 \times \pi \times 0.100}$

$\underline{N = 15900 \text{ revolutions}}$ (3 sd)

2.00 km: $N = \frac{2.00 \times 10^3}{2 \times \pi \times 0.100}$

$\underline{N = 3180 \text{ revolutions}}$ (3 sd)

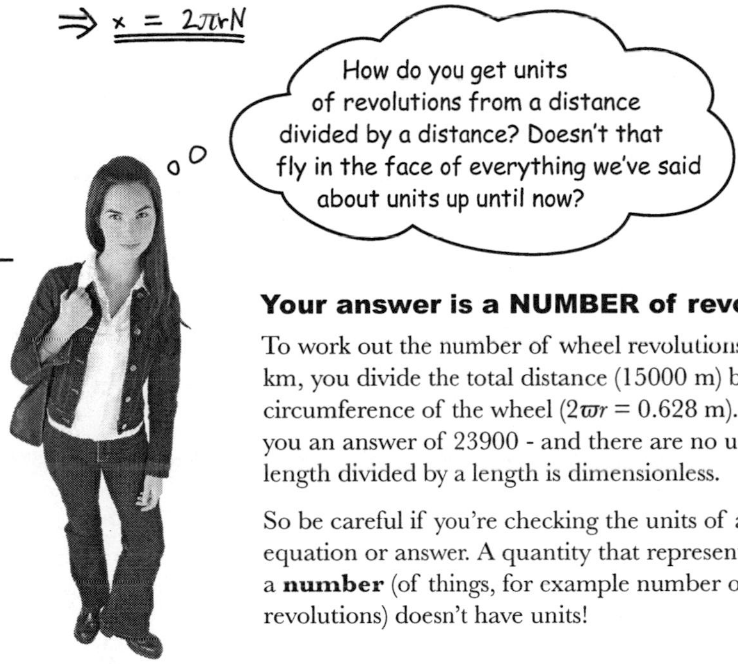

Your answer is a NUMBER of revolutions.

To work out the number of wheel revolutions in 15 km, you divide the total distance (15000 m) by the circumference of the wheel ($2\varpi r = 0.628$ m). This gives you an answer of 23900 - and there are no units, as a length divided by a length is dimensionless.

So be careful if you're checking the units of an equation or answer. A quantity that represents a **number** (of things, for example number of revolutions) doesn't have units!

The units divide out and cancel.

$\frac{15000 \text{ m}}{0.628 \text{ m}} = 23900$ (3 sd)

The final answer is a NUMBER with no units.

Convert the linear speeds into Hertz

The distances slot into the training schedule brilliantly - but the **speed** the hamsters train at for each session is also vital. You have a motor you can use to turn the wheel ... but the units have been rubbed off. However, the hamster owner thinks that the motor might be marked in **Hertz**.

Hertz is always capitalized, and can be abbreviated to Hz

Hertz is a unit of **frequency** that describes the number of times **per second** something regular happens. In physics, this is often referred to as the number of cycles per second.

So if the wheel goes round 5 times per second, you can say that it has a frequency, f, of 5 Hz.

The **period** of the wheel is the **time** the wheel takes to do one rotation, and is given the symbol T.

You can calculate the period from the frequency. If something happens 5 times per second (so has a frequency of 5 Hz), then it happens 5 times in 1 second. So its period must be $T = \frac{1}{5} = 0.2$ s.

$$f = \frac{1}{T} \qquad T = \frac{1}{f}$$

Frequency (f), Period (T)

Sharpen your pencil

Distance (km)	Speed (km/h)	Total number of revolutions	Motor frequency (Hz)
15.00	3.00	23900 (3 sd)	
10.00	4.00	15900 (3 sd)	
2.00	5.50	3180 (3 sd)	

a. What time, in seconds, does it take the hamsters to cover 15.00 km at 3.00 km/h?

b. You already worked out that this training plan involves the wheel doing a total number of 23900 revolutions. Calculate the period, T, and hence the frequency, f, of the wheel, and fill in the table.

c. Do similar calculations to fill in the rest of the table.

The period, T, is the time for one rotation of the wheel.

Sharpen your pencil Solution

Distance (km)	Speed (km/h)	Total number of revolutions	Motor frequency (Hz)
15.00	3.00	23900 (3 sd)	1.33 (3 sd)
10.00	4.00	15900 (3 sd)	1.77 (3 sd)
2.00	5.50	3180 (3 sd)	2.43 (3 sd)

a. What time, in seconds, does it take the hamsters to cover 15.00 km at 3.00 km/h?

$$\text{speed} = \frac{\text{distance}}{\text{time}} \Rightarrow \text{time} = \frac{\text{distance}}{\text{speed}}$$

$$\text{time} = \frac{15.00\ \text{km}}{3.00\ \text{km/hr}} = 5\ \text{hr}$$

$$5\ \text{hr} = 5\ \text{hr} \times \frac{60\ \text{min}}{1\ \text{hr}} \times \frac{60\ \text{s}}{1\ \text{min}} = 18000\ \text{s (3 sd)}$$

b. You already worked out that this training plan involves the wheel doing a total number of 23900 revolutions. Calculate the period, *T*, and hence the frequency, *f*, of the wheel, and fill in the table.

Period is time for 1 revolution.

23900 revolutions take 18000 s.

$$\Rightarrow T = \frac{18000}{23900} = 0.753\ \text{s (3 sd)}$$

$$f = \frac{1}{T} = \frac{1}{0.753} = 1.33\ \text{Hz (3 sd)}$$

c. Do similar calculations to fill in the rest of the table.

10.00 km at 4.00 km/h takes $\frac{10.00}{4.00} \times 60 \times 60 = 9000$ s.

$$T = \frac{9000}{15900} \qquad f = \frac{1}{T} = \frac{15900}{9000} = 1.77\ \text{Hz (3 sd)}$$

2.00 km at 5.50 km/h takes $\frac{2.00}{5.50} \times 60 \times 60 = 1310$ s.

$$T = \frac{1310}{3180} \qquad f = \frac{1}{T} = \frac{3180}{1310} = 2.43\ \text{Hz (3 sd)}$$

This is a shortcut that stops you having to calculate a value for T before you calculate a value for f.

there are no Dumb Questions

Q: What's the difference between the frequency and the period?

A: The frequency is the number of cycles per second - the number of times a regular thing happens per second.

The period is the number of seconds per cycle - the number of seconds that it takes for a regular thing to happen once.

Q: Why is frequency measured in Hz instead of however you'd write "per second" as a unit?

A: "Hz" is easier to write than "1/s" (which is the correct format) and less open to being misinterpreted.

Q: I've seen frequency written in units of s^{-1} in other books. Is that OK?

A: Yes, that's fine, and is another way of representing units using scientific notation. For example, other books may say ms^{-2} instead of m/s^2. As long as you use what you're comfortable with, you'll be fine.

Q: Why aren't the units of frequency written as cycles/s? Why just "1/s"?

A: Good question. The thing to remember is that frequency is the **number** (of things) per second. It could be the number of revolutions, or the number of waves that break on the beach or the number of times a dog barks. A number is dimensionless so has no units.

Q: What if the regular thing happens less than once per second?

A: Then the frequency would be smaller than 1. For example, something that happens every 5 s has a frequency of 0.2 Hz.

Q: Why does $f = \frac{1}{T}$ and $T = \frac{1}{f}$?

A: Frequency is cycles per second; period is seconds per cycle. "Per" means "divided by", so frequency and period are the "opposite way up" from each other.

For example, if something happens 5 times per second, it has a frequency of 5 Hz. Another way of putting it is that the thing happens every 0.2 s because $T = \frac{1}{f} = 0.2$ s.

So you set up the machine ...

You've used the fact that the **circumference** of a circle $C = 2\varpi r$ to convert the units in the training schedule (km and km/h) to units that are much easier for you to work with - **number of revolutions** and **Hertz**.

The motor has numbers on its dial, but the units have rubbed off. The hamster trainer is sure they must be Hertz, so you set up the machine to test the first training session on the schedule, using the data from your table ...

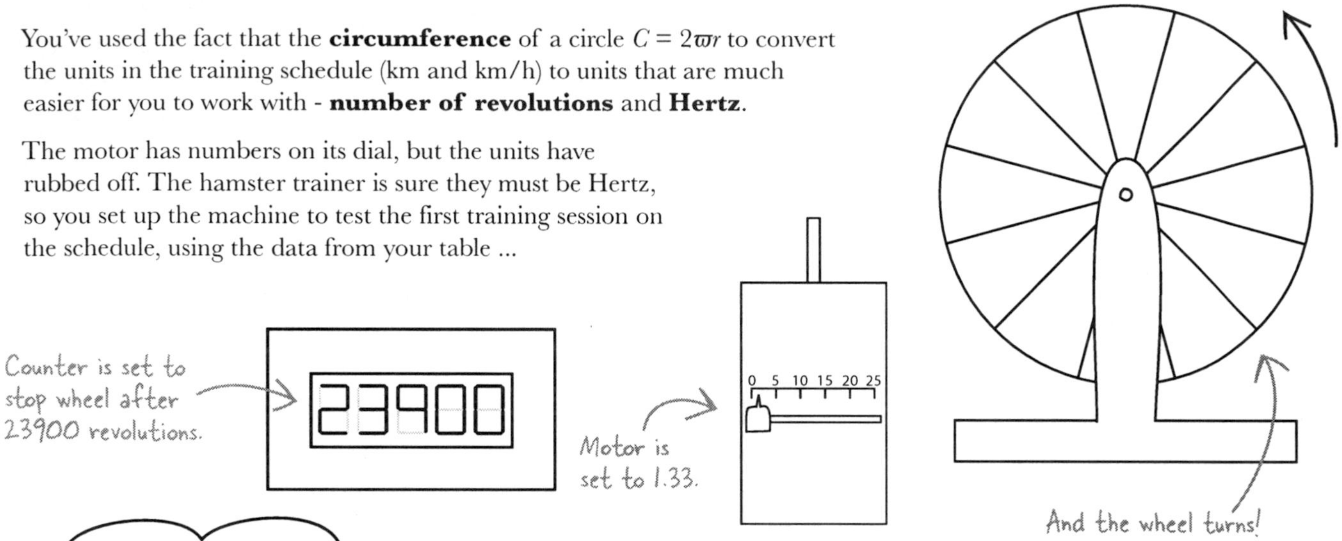

... but the wheel turns too slowly!

When the billionaire hamster owner comes to inspect your work, there's a problem. He says that the wheel's turning far **too slowly** - something's gone wrong and you need to fix it quickly if you're going to stand any chance in the race!

Sharpen your pencil

a. What do you think might have gone wrong?

b. How would you go about investigating and fixing it?

Sharpen your pencil Solution

a. What do you think might have gone wrong?

Maybe the owner got the units of the motor wrong, and they're something else instead of Hz

b. How would you go about investigating and fixing it?

Do some tests or experiments with the motor to count the number of revolutions it does in a certain time when set to a certain number, to try to work out what its units are and how to convert them to what we already know about.

Always make sure you know the UNITS of everything you're dealing with!

So it's running too slowly. Maybe we made a mistake with the math?

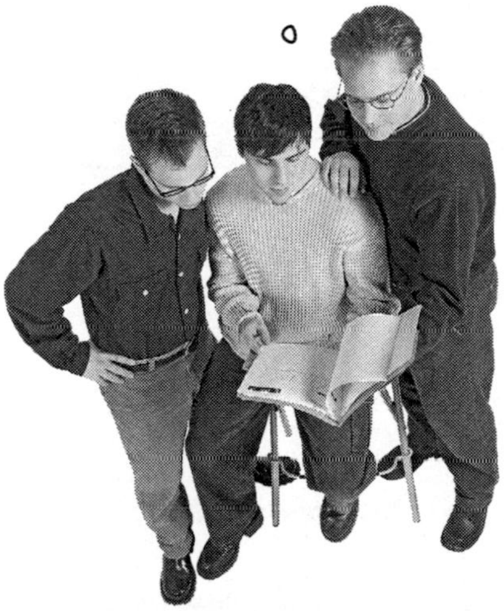

Jim: I already double-checked the math - and it's fine.

Joe: Hmm. Maybe we made a mistake with some **units**.

Jim: I already checked the units - they all work out.

Joe: No, I mean we assumed that the numbers written on the motor are in Hertz when the units had rubbed off. But what if the hamster owner's wrong about that?

Frank: So how are we going to work out what the numbers on the motor mean? I guess we could count how many times it actually goes round per second when it's set to 1.33 like it is now?

Jim: Why use a clumsy number like 1.33? Why don't we set it to '1.00' and see how long it takes to do 1 revolution like that. Then we'll be able to convert the frequency in Hertz we worked out to whatever units the numbers are in.

Joe: Yeah, '1' is an easier number to work with. I guess we could also move the slider to try and make the wheel go round exactly once per second. Then we have two values to work with.

Try some numbers to work out how things relate to each other

We originally assumed that the numbers on the motor represent revolutions per second (i.e. Hz) - but the wheel's going too slowly for that. What you need to do is try some 'nice' values on the control, and count how many revolutions per second they correspond to.

If you want to try things out, choose 'nice' numbers, like 1 or 10, to play with.

What if you set the motor to '1.0'?

When you set the control on the motor to 1.0, the wheel takes around 6.3 seconds to complete exactly 1 revolution.

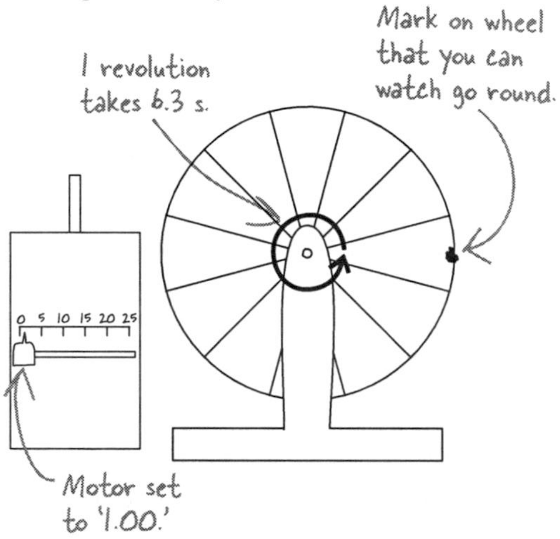

What if the wheel goes at 1.0 Hz?

Then you try to find the value on the motor where the wheel actually goes around once per second, i.e., with a frequency of 1.0 Hz. After playing a bit, you find that a setting of around 6.3 does the job.

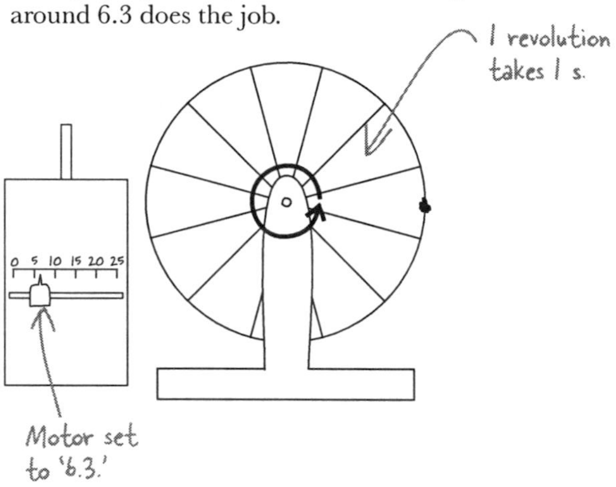

Sharpen your pencil

With the motor set at 1.0, 1.0 revolution takes 6.3 s. And with the motor set at around 6.3, 1.0 revolution takes 1.0 s.

Have you seen a number close to 6.3 somewhere else recently? Look back through this chapter if you can't remember.

What do you think the numbers on the motor might represent?

Sharpen your pencil Solution

With the motor set at 1.0, 1.0 revolution takes 6.3 s. And with the motor set at around 6.3, 1.0 revolution takes 1.0 s.

Have you seen a number close to 6.3 somewhere else recently? Look back through this chapter if you can't remember.

What do you think the numbers on the motor might represent?

The circumference of a circle is 2π – or 6.28 – times larger than the radius. So 1 revolution is around 6.3 radii. If you set the motor to 1, it takes about 6.3 seconds to do one revolution (i.e. 6.3 radii) And if you set the motor to 6.3, it does 1 revolution (i.e. 6.3 radii) in a second.

So maybe the units on the motor tell you how many radii per second the outside of the wheel does?

The units on the motor are radians per second

You've spotted that there are around 6.3 (2 sd) 'radii' in a circumference. When the motor is set to 6.3, the wheel goes at 1 revolution per second (i.e. 6.3 'radii' per second).

The numbers on the motor should have units of **radians**. A radian is a unit used to measure **angles**. If you rotate the wheel through an angle of 1 radian, the outside of the wheel travels a distance equal to the radius of the wheel.

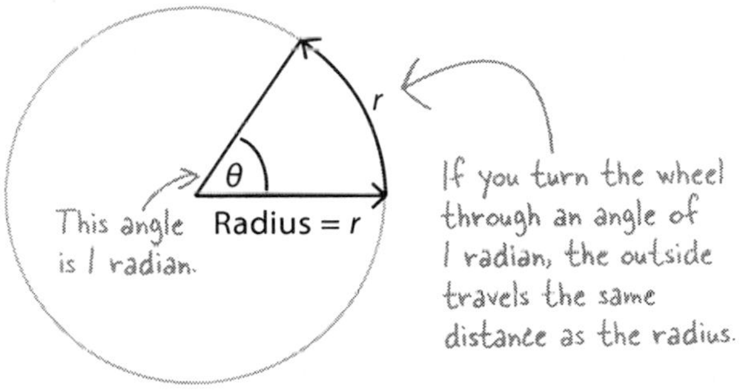

Radians are a way of measuring angles.

There are 2π radians in one complete revolution.

Radians are very helpful if you're trying to connect the **angle** a wheel's turned through and the **distance** the edge of the wheel has covered.

The edge of a wheel that's turned through an angle of 1 radian has covered a distance the length of the wheel's radius, r. If you turn the wheel an angle of 2 radians, the edge covers a distance of $2r$. If you turn the wheel by 2.4 radians, the edge covers a distance of $2.4r$. You **multiply the angle by the radius to get the distance**.

If you rotate the wheel through an angle of 2ϖ radians, the outside of the wheel travels a distance of $2\varpi r$, as the circumference of the circle $= 2\varpi r$. Therefore, there are 2ϖ radians in one revolution.

This fits with what you learned by experimenting with the motor. When the motor is set to 6.3 (2ϖ) radians per second, the wheel goes round at a rate of 1 revolution per second.

Radians are particularly useful when you're dealing with circles.

Degrees are only 'familiar' because you're already used to dealing with them. As you practice with radians, they'll become a whole lot more familiar.

Although you'll still use degrees when working with triangles, radians are particularly useful when you're dealing with circles, as you can move between angles and distances more quickly using the equation $x = r\theta$, where x is the distance covered round the edge of the circle as you rotate through angle θ.

$$x = r\theta$$

Linear distance. → x; Radius → r; Angle in radians → θ

This is a scalar equation

Exercise

When you're working with circles, radians help you to move between angles and distances quickly. Here's your chance to practice working with radians and compare it with working with degrees before you go on to do the 'mission-critical' bit with the hamster wheel.

Working with degrees

A hamster wheel with a radius of 0.100 m turns through an angle of 60°. What distance does the outside of the wheel cover?

Hint: What proportion of the circle's circumference is swept out by an angle of 60°?

Working with radians

A hamster wheel with a radius of 0.100 m turns through an angle of $\frac{\pi}{3}$ radians. What distance does the outside of the wheel cover?

Hint: Use the equation $x = r\theta$ where x is the distance covered for the angle θ.

Compare the math you've had to do to calculate a distance from an angle using degrees and using radians.

Exercise Solution

When you're working with circles, radians help you to move between angles and distances quickly. Here's your chance to practice working with radians and compare it with working with degrees before you go on to do the 'mission-critical' bit with the hamster wheel.

Working with degrees

A hamster wheel with a radius of 0.100 m turns through an angle of 60°. What distance does the outside of the wheel cover?

Angle of 60° is $\frac{60}{360}$ or $\frac{1}{6}$ of the circle.

Total circumference $= 2\pi r$

$\Rightarrow$ Distance covered $= \frac{1}{6} \times 2\pi r$

$= \frac{1}{6} \times 2 \times \pi \times 0.100$

Distance covered $= \underline{\underline{0.105\text{ m}}}$ (3 sd)

Working with radians

A hamster wheel with a radius of 0.100 m turns through an angle of $\frac{\pi}{3}$ radians. What distance does the outside of the wheel cover?

$x = r\theta$

$x = 0.100 \times \frac{\pi}{3}$

$x = \underline{\underline{0.105\text{ m}}}$ (3 sd)

Compare the math you've had to do to calculate a distance from an angle using degrees and using radians.

The final step of the math is more or less the same both times. But it takes much longer to get there from an angle in degrees than it does from an angle in radians.

there are no Dumb Questions

Q: Why would I want to use radians to measure angles?

A: If you're working with circles, radians simplify calculations greatly. In degrees, you first of all have to work out what fraction of the circle the angle is (for example, 60° is a sixth of a full circle), then multiply that by $2\pi r$ to get the distance. But in radians, this has already been done, and you only have to multiply the angle by the radius to get the distance.

Q: Will I be using radians for the rest of this book then?

A: For anything involving circles and regular motion, you'll be using radians. But you'll still be using degrees for triangles.

Q: How can I get used to using radians when they look so weird!

A: The big thing to remember is that there are 2π radians in one complete rotation. So there are π radians in half a rotation, $\frac{\pi}{2}$ radians in quarter of a rotation, $\frac{\pi}{3}$ radians in a sixth of a rotation, etc.

Q: Aren't fractions of π very awkward to work with, as π is an irrational number?

A: As long as you keep using fractions, like $\frac{\pi}{3}$ and $\frac{\pi}{2}$, then only put in the value of π at the end of a calculation, the fractions aren't difficult to work with.

Think of angles in radians in terms of fractions of π.

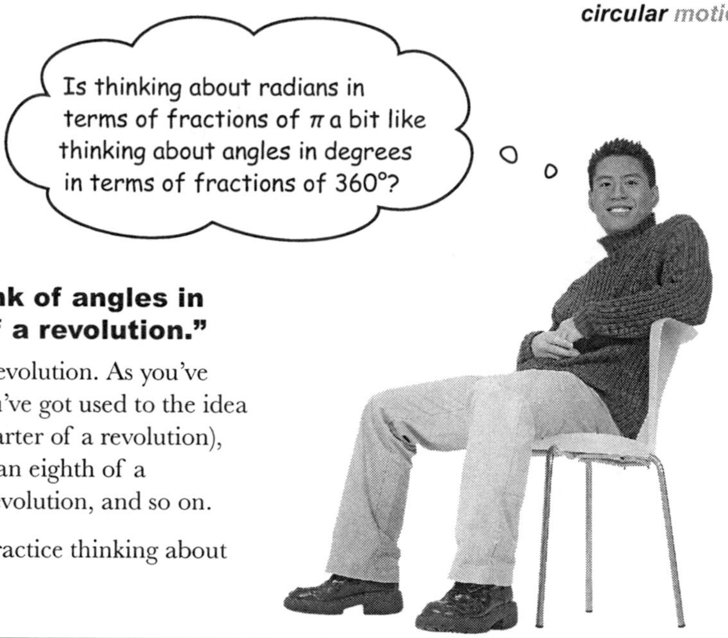

Yes - it's good to think of angles in terms of "fraction of a revolution."

There are 360° in one full revolution. As you've practiced using degrees, you've got used to the idea that 90° is a right angle (quarter of a revolution), 45° is half of a right angle (an eighth of a revolution), 180° is half a revolution, and so on.

Here's the opportunity to practice thinking about radians in a similar way:

Pool Puzzle - Radians

Your **job** is to take the angles measured in radians from the pool and place them into the boxes around the circle to indicate the size of each angle. You may **not** use the same angle more than once, and you won't need to use all the angles. Your **goal** is to become more familiar with using radians to measure angles.

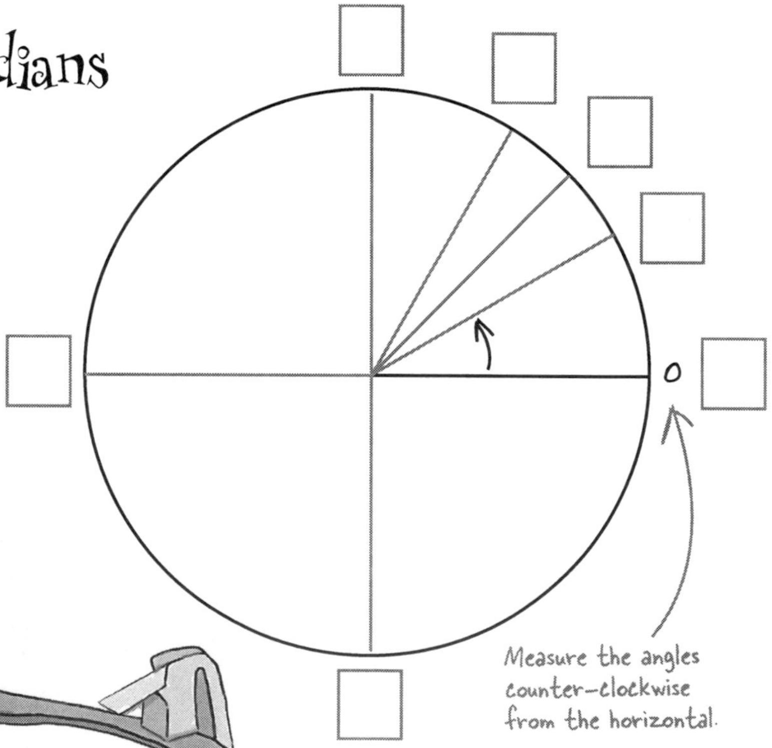

Note: each angle from the pool can only be used once!

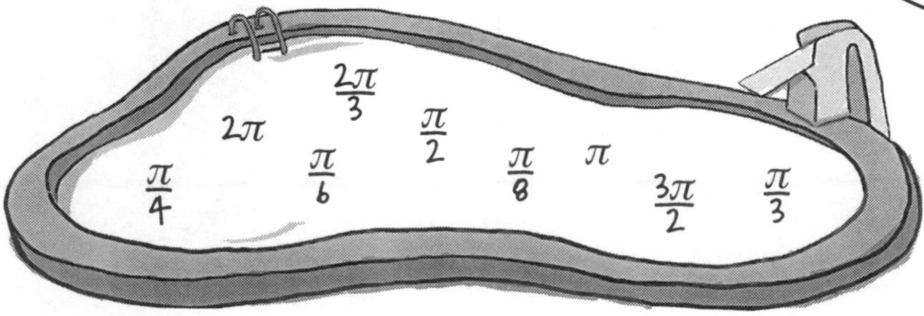

Pool Puzzle - Radians - SOLUTION

Your **job** is to take the angles measured in radians from the pool and place them into the boxes around the circle to indicate the size of each angle. You may **not** use the same angle more than once, and you won't need to use all the angles. Your **goal** is to become more familiar with using radians to measure angles.

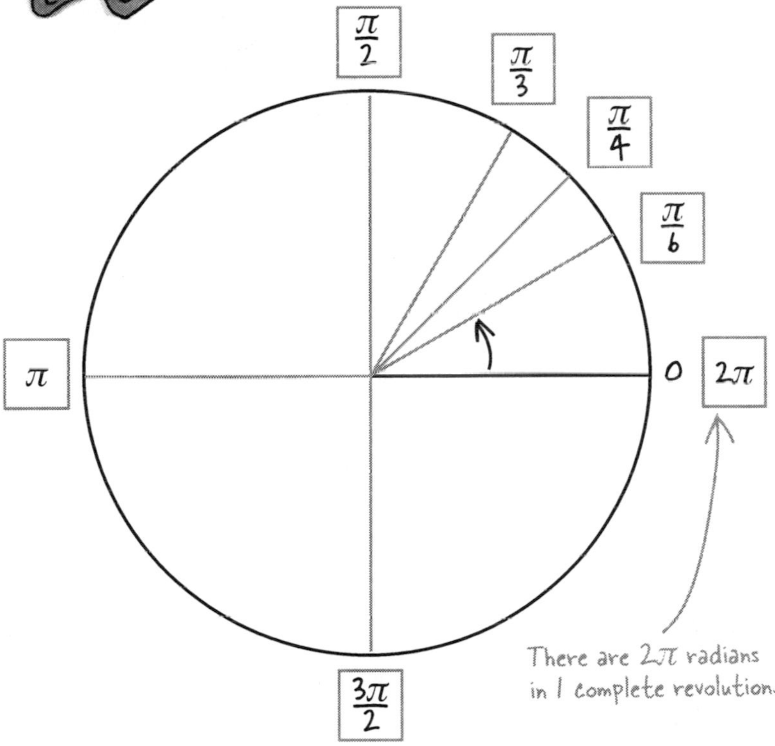

Note: each angle from the pool can only be used once!

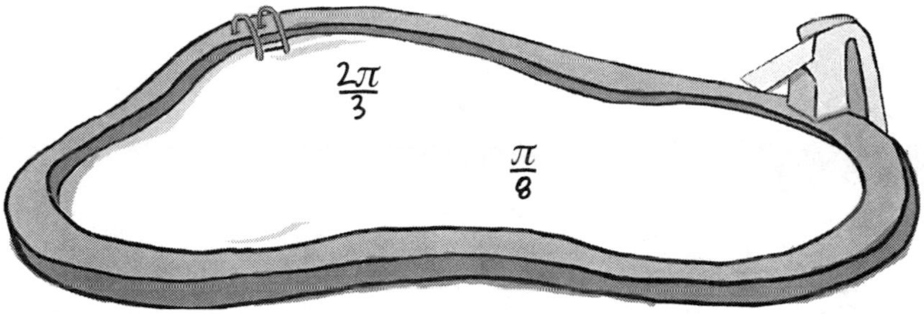

Convert frequency to angular frequency

You've worked out that the units on the motor are radians per second. This is known as the **angular frequency**, and is given the symbol ω (pronounced "omega"). So if you set the motor to 1.0, it will turn at a rate of 1.0 radian per second.

There are 2ϖ radians in one complete revolution. You already know the frequency, f, that the wheel needs to be set at for each run - this is the number of revolutions per second that the wheel does.

Angular frequency

$$\omega = 2\varpi f$$

Frequency

The angular frequency is the number of radians per second.

As there are 2ϖ radians in 1 complete revolution, you can use the equation $\omega = 2\varpi f$ to calculate the angular frequency that the motor needs to turn at for each of the hamsters' training sessions.

Sharpen your pencil

Complete the table by calculating the angular frequency that the wheel needs to turn at for each training session. There's space for your work under the table.

Distance (km)	Speed (km/h)	Total number of revolutions	Frequency (Hz)	Angular frequency (rad/s)
15.00	3.00	23900 (3 sd)	1.33 (3 sd)	
10.00	4.00	15900 (3 sd)	1.77 (3 sd)	
2.00	5.50	3180 (3 sd)	2.43 (3 sd)	

Sharpen your pencil Solution

Complete the table by calculating the angular frequency that the wheel needs to turn at for each training session. There's space for your work under the table.

Distance (km)	Speed (km/h)	Total number of revolutions	Frequency (Hz)	Angular frequency (rad/s)
15.00	3.00	23900 (3 sd)	1.33 (3 sd)	8.35 (3 sd)
10.00	4.00	15900 (3 sd)	1.77 (3 sd)	11.3 (3 sd)
2.00	5.50	3180 (3 sd)	2.43 (3 sd)	15.3 (3 sd)

$f = 1.33$ Hz: $\omega = 2\pi f = 2 \times \pi \times 1.33 = \underline{\underline{8.35 \text{ rad/s}}}$ (3 sd)

$f = 1.77$ Hz: $\omega = 2\pi f = 2 \times \pi \times 1.77 = \underline{\underline{11.1 \text{ rad/s}}}$ (3 sd)

$f = 2.43$ Hz: $\omega = 2\pi f = 2 \times \pi \times 2.43 = \underline{\underline{15.3 \text{ rad/s}}}$ (3 sd)

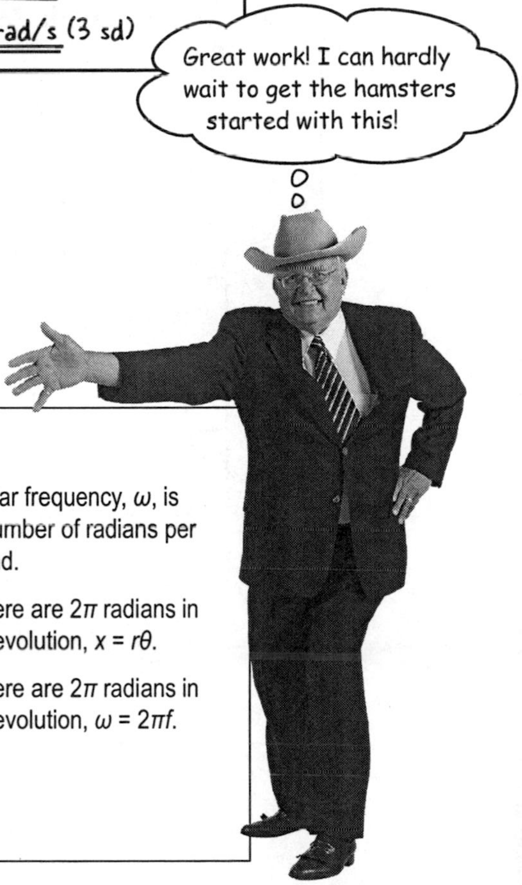

The hamster trainer is complete!

When you put the finishing touches to your hamster trainer by calculating the angular frequency, it's brilliant! After some hearty congratulations from the owner, you find yourself with a 20% stake in the thoroughbred hamster that's favorite to win next month's Kentucky Hamster Derby!

BULLET POINTS

- A circle's circumference is 2π times the size of its radius, $C = 2\pi r$.
- Frequency, f, is measured in cycles per second, or Hertz (Hz).
- Period, T, is the time it takes for one regular thing to happen. Think of it as "seconds per cycle."
- Radians are a way of measuring angles that are especially useful for doing calculations with circles. There are 2π radians in one revolution.
- It can sometimes be helpful to think about radians in terms of fractions of π.
- Angular frequency, ω, is the number of radians per second.
- As there are 2π radians in one revolution, $x = r\theta$.
- As there are 2π radians in one revolution, $\omega = 2\pi f$.

Fireside Chats

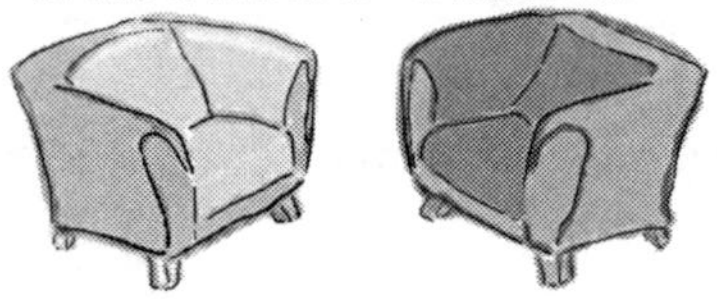

Tonight's talk: **Degree and Radian have a barney about who is better at measuring angles.**

Degree:

Well, hello radian. You're pretty late to the party, aren't you?!

Radian:

I wouldn't quite say that. Sure, you've been around for a bit longer than I have. But that doesn't mean you're inherently better - just over the hill!

Degree:

But I'm so easy to understand! None of those messy pies (or should I say ϖs) - just 360 degrees of goodness in every complete revolution. How much more straightforward can you get?

Radian:

OK, so I admit that the ϖs might take a little bit of getting used to. But once you've got your head around them, you have to admit that I have far greater superpowers than you do!

Degree:

Oh yeah?! Such as ... ?

Radian:

Well, it's really easy to calculate **distances** from **angles** when something's going round in a circle using me. Suppose a wheel goes round an angle of θ radians, and they want to know the distance the has wheel gone? No problem! Just multiply the angle by the distance you are from the center of the circle (the radius, r) to get the distance, $r\theta$.

Degree:

They can do that with me as well though! Suppose a wheel goes round 180°. They can work out that this is half the circle, as 180/360 = 0.5. And they know what the circumference of the circle is - $2\varpi r$. So they just multiply those together - $0.5 \times 2\varpi r$ to get ϖr which is the distance the wheel's gone. Sorted!

Radian:

Um ... you mean that if you go round ϖ radians (i.e. half a circle) you've travelled a distance of $r\theta = \varpi r$ I'm sorry, but my way is just a lot lot quicker!

Degree:

But your way is sooo anti-intuitive!

Radian:

I think you really mean that my way is much better once you've got used to it!

Degree:

Whaaaaatever!

A couple of weeks later ...

The hamsters are ready to move into the sprint training phase of their program. The owner explains that he wants the hamsters to be able to run at 3.00 m/s - and that he also wants an easy way to convert from speeds in m/s to "the numbers on that motor".

This means that you need to come up with a way of converting between meters per second (**linear speed**) to radians per second (**angular frequency**).

When you did this before, it involved several steps. First of all, you worked out the total number of revolutions for a training run, and the total time the run took. From these figures, you were able to calculate the frequency (revolutions per second) and from there the angular frequency (radians per second).

Sharpen your pencil Solution

Complete the table by calculating the angular frequency that the wheel needs to turn at for each training session. There's space for your work under the table.

Distance (km)	Speed (km/h)	Total number of revolutions	Frequency (Hz)	Angular frequency (rad/s)
15.00	3.00	23900 (3 sd)	1.33 (3 sd)	8.35 (3 sd)
10.00	4.00	15900 (3 sd)	1.77 (3 sd)	11.1 (3 sd)
2.00	5.50	3180 (3 sd)	2.43 (3 sd)	15.3 (3 sd)

That's a lot of steps!

But back then, you didn't know that the numbers on the motor were radians per second - you didn't know that's what you were aiming at. Now you know that you're aiming at radians per second ...

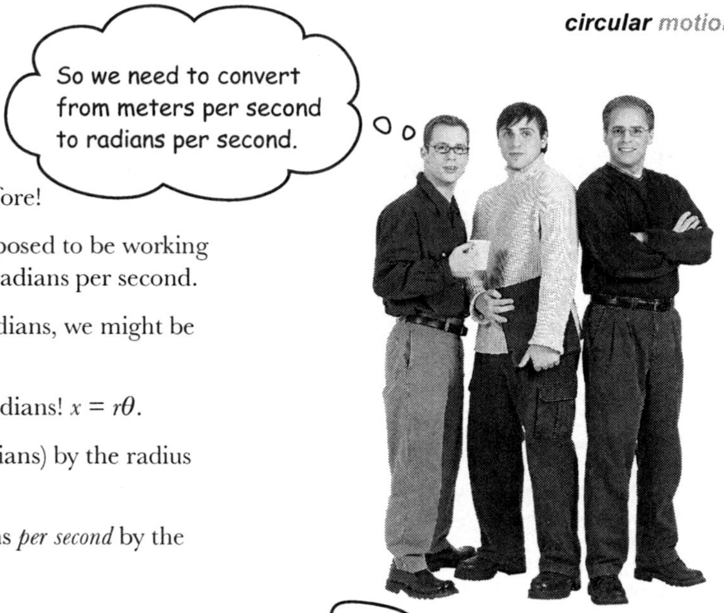

Jim: Yeah - but that took us a loooong time before!

Joe: I've noticed that both the things we're supposed to be working with are "per second". Meters per second and radians per second.

Frank: So if we can convert from meters to radians, we might be able to do it more quickly than we did before.

Jim: We can already go between meters and radians! $x = r\theta$.

Frank: Hmm. So multiplying the angle (in radians) by the radius gives you the distance in meters. $x = r\theta$.

Jim: I wonder if that means multiplying radians *per second* by the radius will give us meters *per second*.

Joe: Yeah ... maybe we can say that $v = r\omega$?

Jim: How do the units check out? If you multiply radians by the radius, you get meters. So if you multiply radians per second by the radius then you get distance per second.

Frank: And "distance per second" is just another way of saying velocity. Brilliant!

- Angular frequency, ω, is the number of radians per second.
- As there are 2π radians in one revolution, $x = r\theta$.

These are some of the things from earlier in the chapter that the guys are talking about.

Sharpen your pencil

a. Your hamster wheel has a radius of 10.0 cm. Use the equation $v = r\omega$ to calculate the angular frequency it would need to turn with to enable the hamster to run with a speed of 3.00 m/s.

b. Your motor can spin at any angular frequency up to 25.0 rad/s. How might you build a speed trainer capable of making a hamster run at 3.00 m/s if you don't have a faster motor available?

Sharpen your pencil Solution

a. Your hamster wheel has a radius of 10.0 cm. Use the equation $v = r\omega$ to calculate the angular frequency it would need to turn with to enable the hamster to run with a speed of 3.00 m/s.

$$v = r\omega$$

$$\Rightarrow \omega = \frac{v}{r} = \frac{3.00}{0.100}$$

$$\omega = \underline{\underline{30.0 \text{ rad/s}}} \text{ (3 sd)}$$

b. Your motor can spin at any angular frequency up to 25.0 rad/s. How might you build a speed trainer capable of making a hamster run at 3.00 m/s if you don't have a faster motor available?

$v = r\omega$. The speed depends on both the radius and the angular frequency.

If it's not possible to increase the angular frequency high enough, another way to get a higher speed is to increase the radius. So you could use a larger wheel with the same motor.

there are no Dumb Questions

Q: So radians help you to go straight from distance to angle, or from speed to angular frequency?

A: Yes - you can use the equations $x = r\theta$ and $v = r\omega$ to move quickly between linear and angular quantities.

Q: What if I want to know the speed of a point that's on the wheel, but not at the edge?

A: When the wheel spins, that point will 'sketch out' a circle with a radius the same as the distance that the point is from the center.

Q: Is it OK to use that value for the radius, even if it's not the radius of the wheel?

A: Yes - in this context, the radius is the distance from the center of the wheel to the point you're interested in.

Q: Will $x = r\theta$ and $v = r\omega$ only work if θ and ω are in terms of radians not degrees?

A: Correct. If θ is in degrees, then you need to work out what proportion of the circle's circumference is included by dividing the angle by 360°, then multiplying by 2π to get the distance the point's travelled. With radians, that's already been done for you.

You can increase the (linear) speed by increasing the wheel's radius

If you have a wheel turning at angular frequency ω, the whole wheel turns through the same **angle** in the same time. But parts of the wheel that are a greater **radius** from the center travel a greater **distance** in the same time, so have a greater **speed**, v.

This means that you can increase the maximum speed that your hamster trainer can cope with by increasing the radius of your wheel - without needing to change the angular frequency that it turns with.

Here, we're written v as a scalar to indicate that it's the size of the object's velocity. The direction of the velocity changes all the time as the wheel rotates.

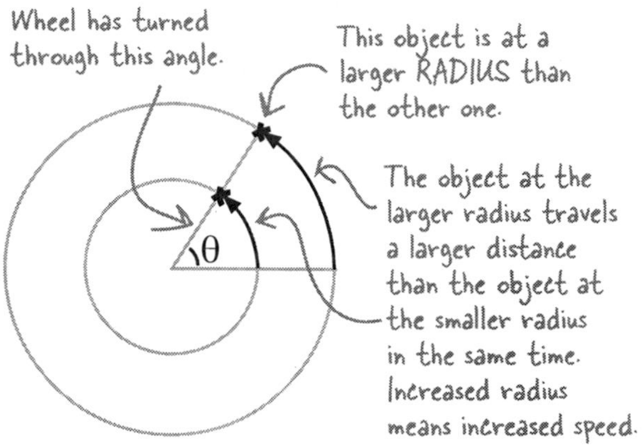

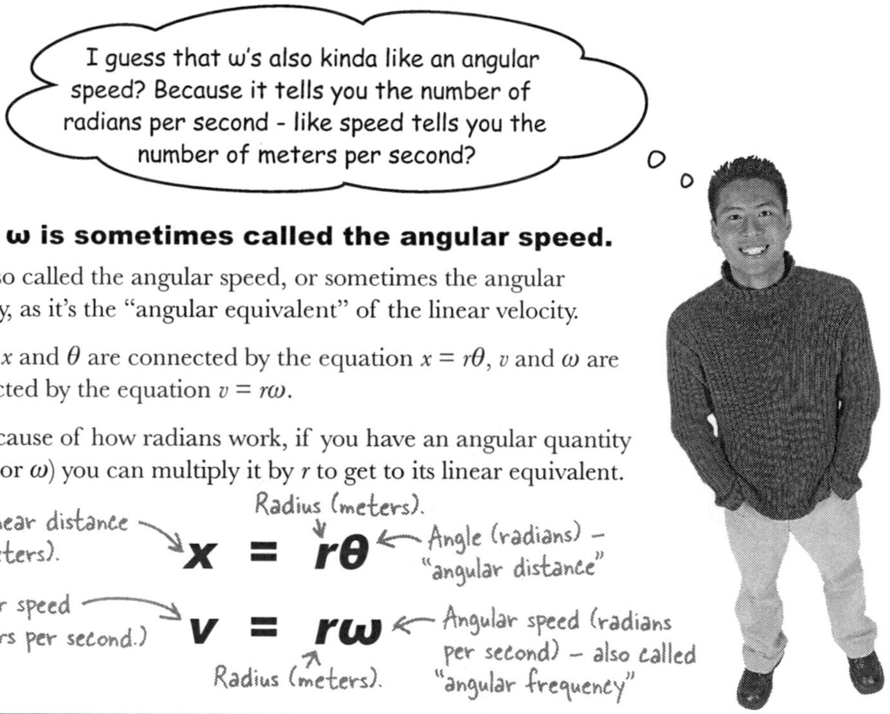

Multiply the linear quantity by the radius to get the equivalent angular quantity.

Yes - ω is sometimes called the angular speed.

ω is also called the angular speed, or sometimes the angular velocity, as it's the "angular equivalent" of the linear velocity.

Just as x and θ are connected by the equation $x = r\theta$, v and ω are connected by the equation $v = r\omega$.

So, because of how radians work, if you have an angular quantity (like θ or ω) you can multiply it by r to get to its linear equivalent.

$$x = r\theta$$

Linear distance (meters). Radius (meters). Angle (radians) – "angular distance"

$$v = r\omega$$

Linear speed (meters per second.) Radius (meters). Angular speed (radians per second) – also called "angular frequency"

Sharpen your pencil

You have a motor capable of turning at 25.0 rad/s, and wish to train a hamster that runs at 3.00 m/s.

What radius of wheel do you need to use?

Sharpen your pencil Solution

You have a motor capable of turning at 25.0 rad/s, and wish to train a hamster that runs at 3.00 m/s.

What radius of wheel do you need to use?

$v = r\omega$

$\Rightarrow r = \frac{v}{\omega} = \frac{3.00}{25.0}$

$r = \underline{\underline{0.120}}$ m (3 sd)

$\mathbf{x = r\theta}$

$\mathbf{v = r\omega}$

Linear quantity. Radius. Angular quantity.

Multiply the angular quantity by the radius to get the linear quantity.

With sprint training in a larger wheel added to their schedule, the hamsters are unbeatable, and win all of their races - including the Kentucky Hamster Derby!

BULLET POINTS

- You can go from an angle, θ, to the distance something r from the center of the circle has travelled by multiplying by the radius: $x = r\theta$.
- You can go from the angular frequency to the speed that something r from the center of the circle is moving at by multiplying by the radius, $v = r\omega$.
- The equation $v = r\omega$ only gives you the size of the velocity vector, not its direction. That's why v is written as a scalar.
- ω is also called the angular speed. This is the same thing as the angular frequency - radians per second.

OK, so in the equation x = rθ, x and r are both distances, right? But that implies that θ doesn't have any units - even though I know that θ is measured in radians! What gives?!

Think of radians as a clarification of scale rather than as a unit.

2ϖ is the ratio of a circle's radius to its circumference. This **ratio** is a length divided by a length. 2ϖ is the answer to the question "how many times does the radius fit into the circumference?" The answer is a **number** of times. 2ϖ is a number - it doesn't have units.

It so happens that this ratio, 2ϖ, is very useful as a measure of how far something has **rotated**. To make it clear that you're using 2ϖ to represent turning, rather than a number (of elephants, monkeys etc), you can append the word 'radians' to it. So turning 2ϖ radians is the same as turning a complete circle. The same applies to any other angle measured in radians.

This means that when you're thinking about the units of terms in an equation (doing dimensional analysis or units analysis), you should treat radians like a number without any units.

When you're thinking about the units of the terms in an equation, radians are dimensionless so don't have units.

Question Clinic: The "Angular quantities" Question

Any time something's going in a circle, you're almost certain to have to deal with quantities such as angular displacement θ, and angular speed, ω. The main things to remember is that there are 2π radians in one complete revolution and that the circumference of the circle = $2\pi r$. This means you can work out that you get the linear quantity by multiplying the angular quantity (e.g. $\theta = 2\pi$) by the radius, even if you forget the formulae $x = r\theta$ and $v = r\omega$.

'Wheel' is a buzzword that should get you thinking about rotational motion.

This question gives you the diameter. Be careful – all of your equations involve the RADIUS, so you'll need to use a value of 10.0 cm not 20.0 cm.

This is a LINEAR speed.

2. You need to arrange for a hamster wheel (diameter 20.0 cm) to turn so that the outside of the wheel goes at a speed of 3.00 km/h.

a. What angular frequency (in radians per second) does the wheel need to turn with to achieve this?

b. How many revolutions per second is this equivalent to?

c. If the motor driving the wheel is only capable of rotating it at 25 rad/s, what diameter would the wheel need to have in order to achieve a speed of 3 km/h?

Angular frequency and angular speed are both to do with how fast something is rotating in radians per second.

Remember that there are 2π radians in exactly 1 revolution. Ask yourself which number you're expecting to be bigger when you do the conversion.

The question asks you for a diameter when you've been working with a radius throughout. Make sure you give them what they asked for!

One thing to bear in mind with this kind of question is whether it talks about the frequency - number of revolutions per second - or the angular frequency, aka angular speed which is the number of radians per second. As there are 2π radians in one revolution you can convert from one to the other easily enough - as long as you pay attention to which units are involved in the first place!

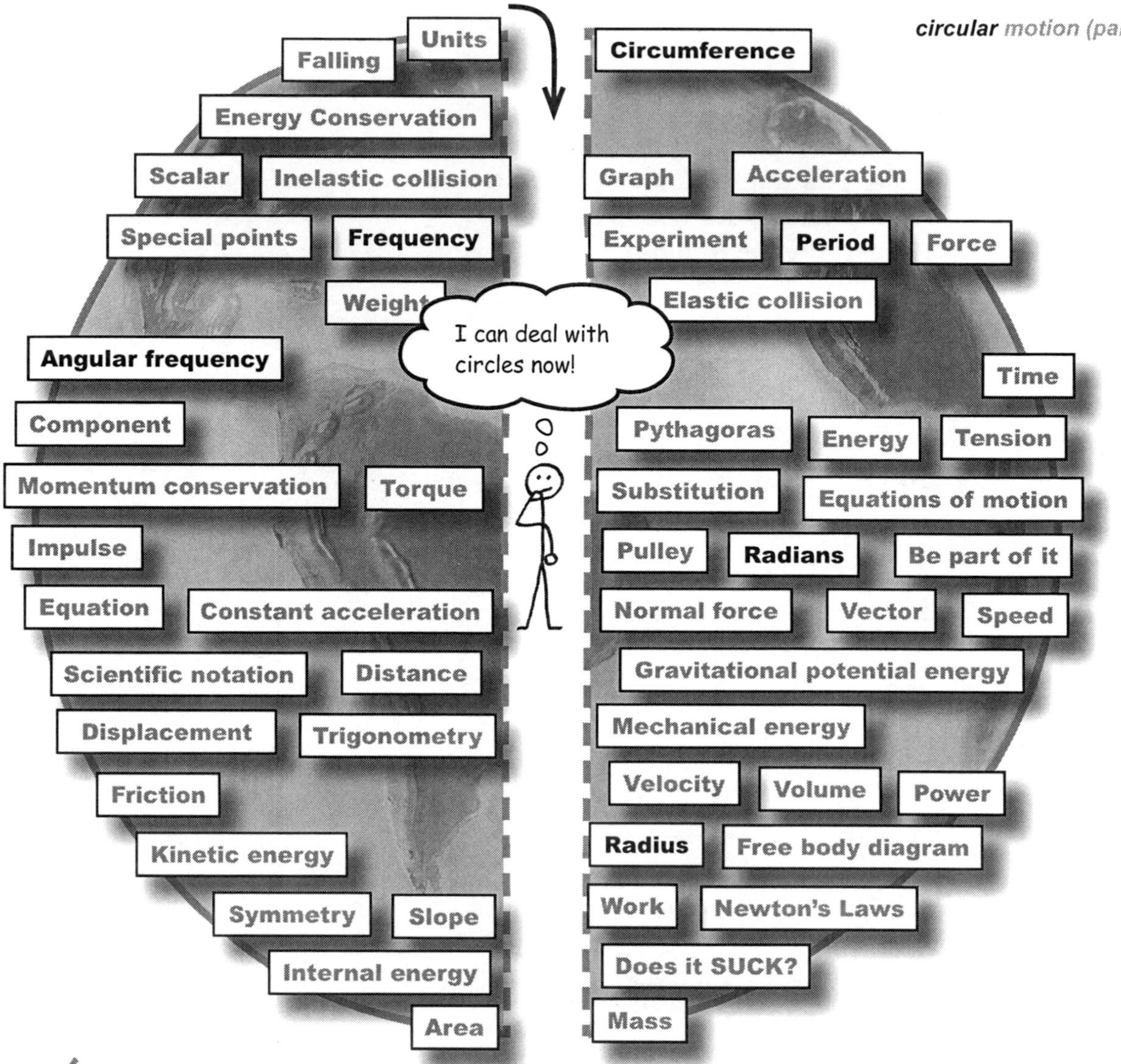

☑	**Radius**	**The distance from the center to the edge of a circle.**
☑	**Circumference**	**The distance round the outside of a circle.** $C = 2\pi r$
☑	**Frequency**	**The number of times something regular happens per second.**
☑	**Period**	**The number of seconds it takes for something regular to happen once.**
☑	**Radians**	**An alternative way of measuring angles. There are** 2π **radians is one complete revolution.**
☑	**Angular frequency**	**The number of radians per second. Also known as angular speed.**

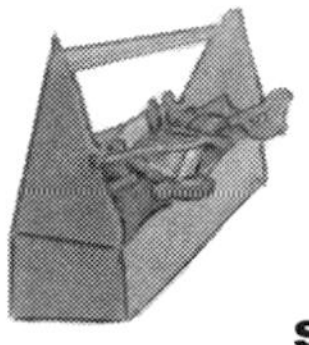

Your Physics Toolbox

You've got Chapter 16 under your belt and added some terminology and problem-solving skills to your tool box.

Radians

Radians are a way of measuring angles. They are especially useful for working with circles. There are 2π radians in 1 revolution. Think of other angles in terms of 'fractions of '2π.

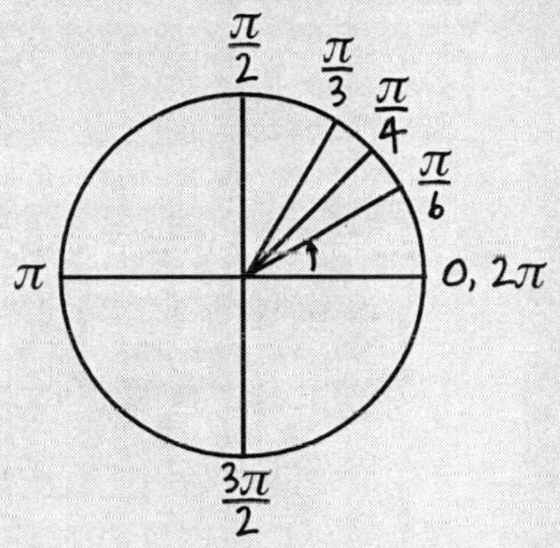

Frequency and period

Frequency, f, is cycles per second.

Period, T, is seconds per cycle.

$$T = \frac{1}{f} \qquad f = \frac{1}{T}$$

Angular frequency and angular speed

Angular frequency and angular speed both have the same size and both have units of radians per second. They're exactly the same thing,

You can get from the frequency, f, to the angular frequency, ω, with the equation:

$$\omega = 2\pi f$$

Linear and angular

You can get from the angle, θ, to the linear distance, x, with the equation:

$$x = r\theta$$

You can get from the angular speed, ω, to the linear speed, v, with the equation:

$$v = r\omega$$

17 circular motion (part 2)

Staying on track

Ever feel like someone's gone off at a tangent? That's exactly what happens when you try to move an object along a **circular** path when there's not enough **centripetal force** to enable this to happen. In this chapter, you'll learn exactly what centripetal force is and how it can keep you on track. Along the way, you'll even solve some pretty serious problems with a certain Head First space station. So what are you waiting for? Turn the page, and let's get started.

Houston ... we have a problem

Astronauts at the Head First space station are threatening to go on strike. They're fed up with floating around all the time. The astronauts want to be able to walk around the station just like they can on Earth.

You've been called in to create artificial gravity for an add-on to the station... and keep those astronauts happy.

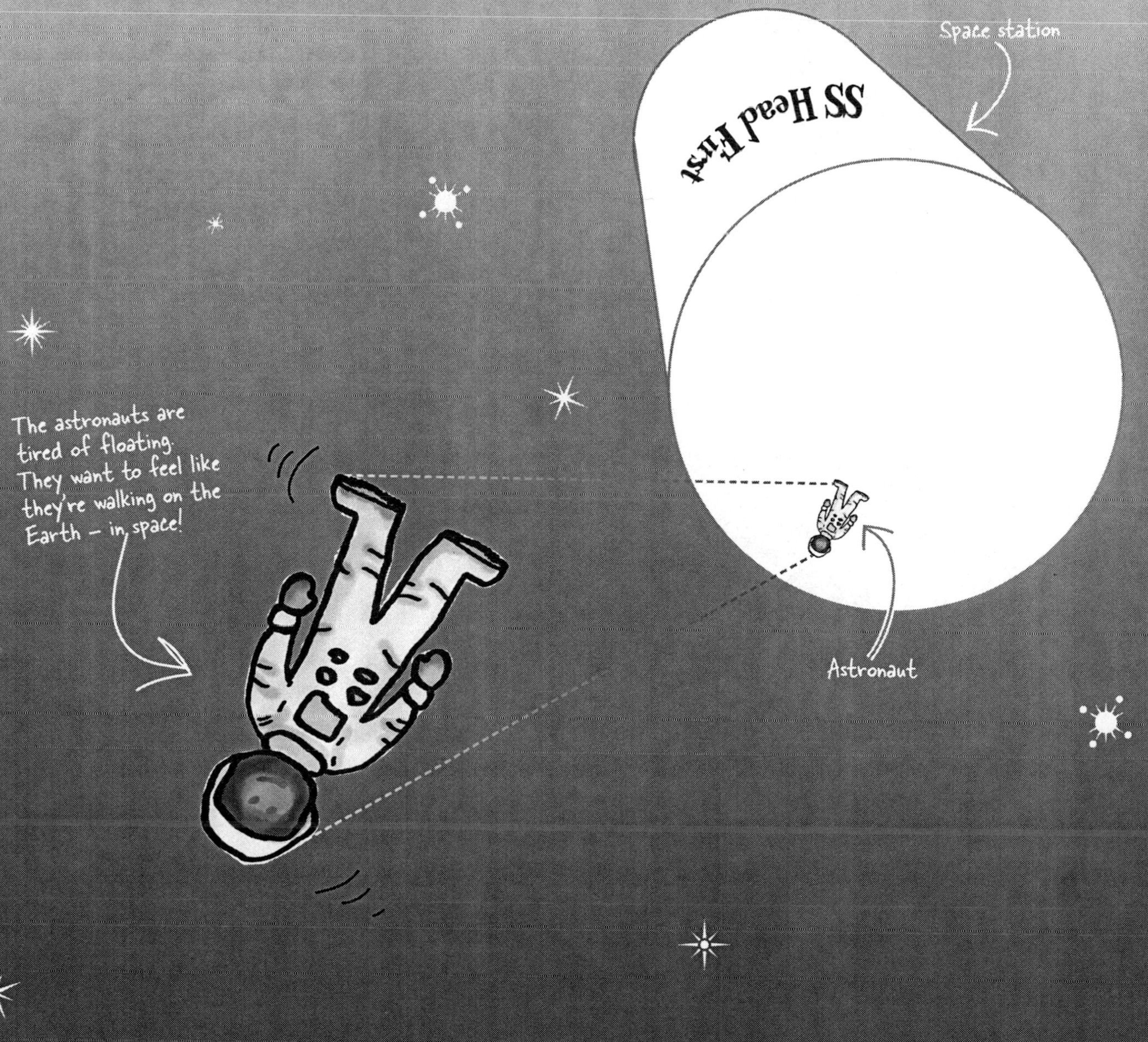

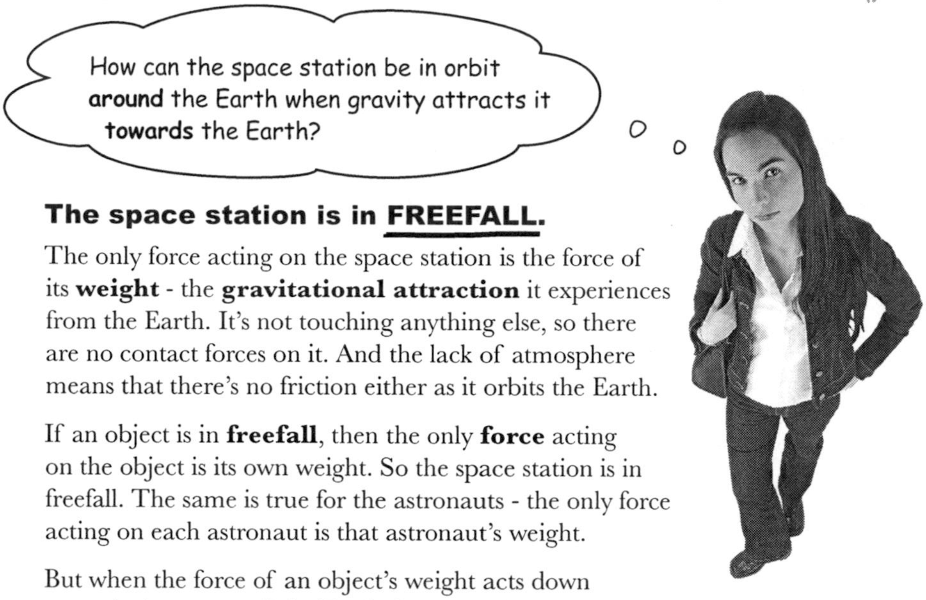

The space station is in FREEFALL.

The only force acting on the space station is the force of its **weight** - the **gravitational attraction** it experiences from the Earth. It's not touching anything else, so there are no contact forces on it. And the lack of atmosphere means that there's no friction either as it orbits the Earth.

If an object is in **freefall**, then the only **force** acting on the object is its own weight. So the space station is in freefall. The same is true for the astronauts - the only force acting on each astronaut is that astronaut's weight.

But when the force of an object's weight acts down towards the center of the Earth, how can the object possibly **orbit** the Earth by going around the Earth?!

If an object is in freefall, the only force acting on the object is its own weight.

1 Suppose you fire a cannon. The cannonball is in freefall, because the only force acting on the cannonball is its own weight. So the cannonball follows a **curved** path as it falls and hits the Earth.

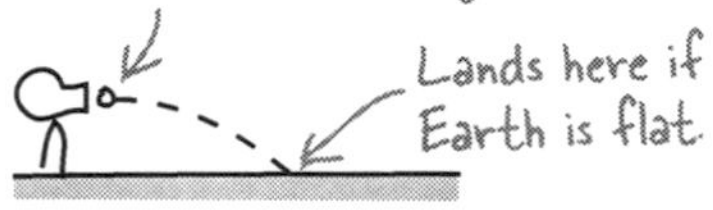

2 Locally, the Earth appears flat, but it's really round. If the cannonball is very fast or starts off very high, it goes further before it lands because the surface of the Earth curves away from the cannonball as it falls.

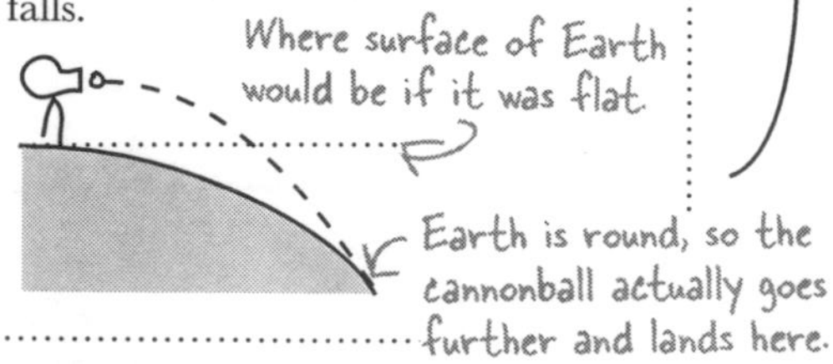

3 If the cannon is high enough and the cannonball is fast enough, the surface of the Earth keeps on curving away as the cannonball's flightpath curves down. The cannonball keeps on freefalling round the Earth - in **orbit** - just like the space station and astronauts.

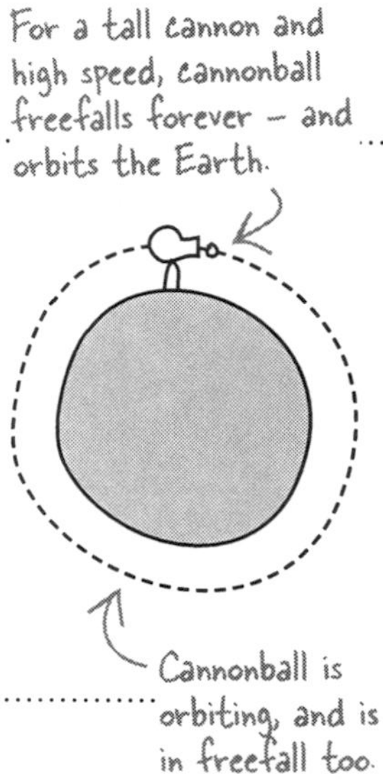

BRAIN POWER

The astronaut is in freefall - the only force acting on him is his weight. So why does he feel weightless in the space station?

When you're in freefall, objects appear to float beside you

Suppose you're midway through a parachute jump, but you haven't opened your chute yet. If you let go of an apple as you fall, the apple will **fall with the same velocity as you**. It looks like the apple's just floating there.

Of course, if you're doing a parachute jump, there are some clues that indicate that you and the apple are both falling. The Earth gradually looks bigger, and you can feel the wind rushing past you!

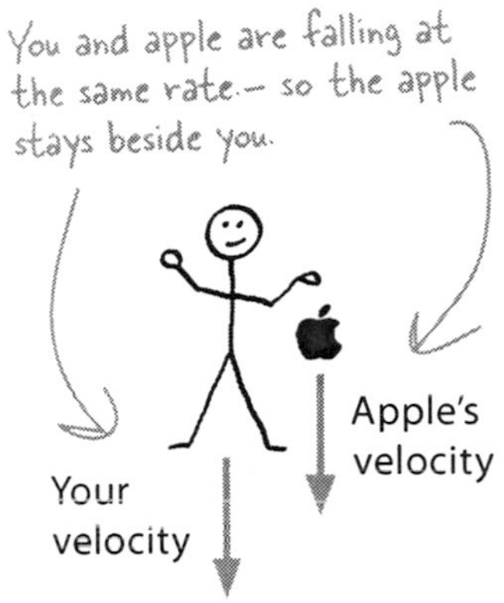

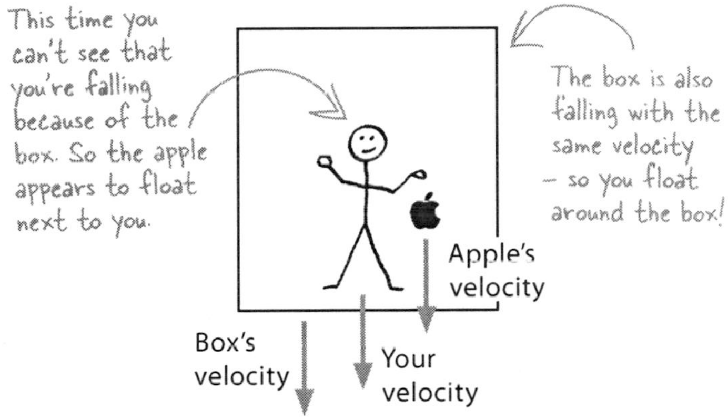

But if you and the apple were in a soundproof windowless box, you wouldn't have any visual or audible clues that you're falling. The apple would appear to float next to you! And as the box is also falling at the same rate as you, you would appear to float around inside the box. If you pushed yourself up off the floor, you wouldn't fall back down again like you would on Earth.

It's the same for an astronaut in the space station. He's continually falling around the Earth. So if he lets go of an apple, it floats around the space station rather than falling towards the ground.

This makes it look as though the apple is weightless - and as though the astronaut is weightless. The astronaut is used to the force of his weight attracting him towards the ground. But here, the "ground" (the wall of the spacestation) is falling at the same rate as the astronaut

This means that the astronaut can't walk around the space station like he can on Earth.

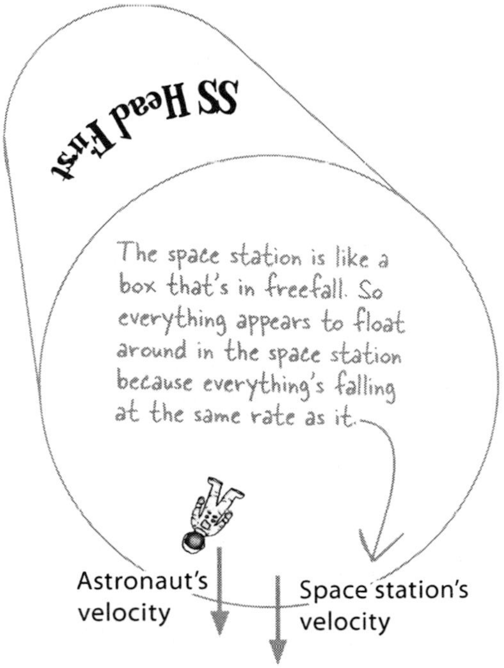

What's the astronaut missing, compared to when he's on Earth?

If an astronaut is in freefall, then he and the objects in the space station will appear to float around because everything's falling at the same rate.

But why does a dropped apple in an orbiting space station appear to act so differently from a dropped apple on Earth - when they're both falling because of the force of their weight, as usual? And why isn't it possible to walk around normally in the space station like you can on Earth?

When you're dealing with forces, always start with a free body diagram...

For problems involving forces, always start with a free body diagram.

Sharpen your pencil

a. Draw a free body diagram of all the forces the astronaut would experience while standing on Earth.

b. Draw a free body diagram of all the forces an astronaut would experience while in freefall.

c. When you compare the free body diagrams in parts a and b, which force is missing?

d. How does a person on Earth experience their weight differently from a person in freefall?

e. How might you introduce a new force to compensate for the missing one you spotted in parts c and d, so the astronaut can walk around as he would on Earth?

Sharpen your pencil Solution

a. Draw a free body diagram of all the forces the astronaut would experience while standing on Earth.

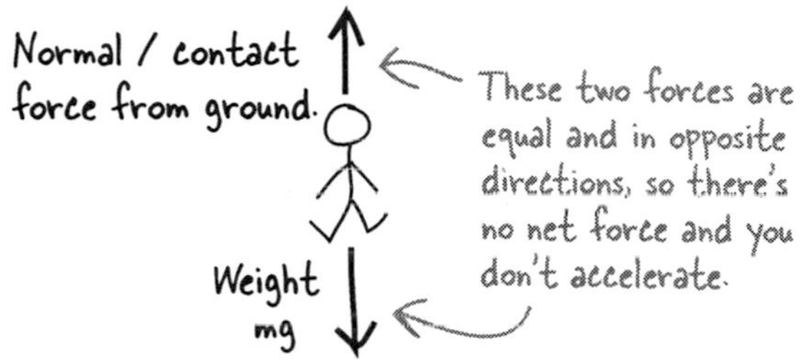

b. Draw a free body diagram of all the forces an astronaut would experience while in freefall.

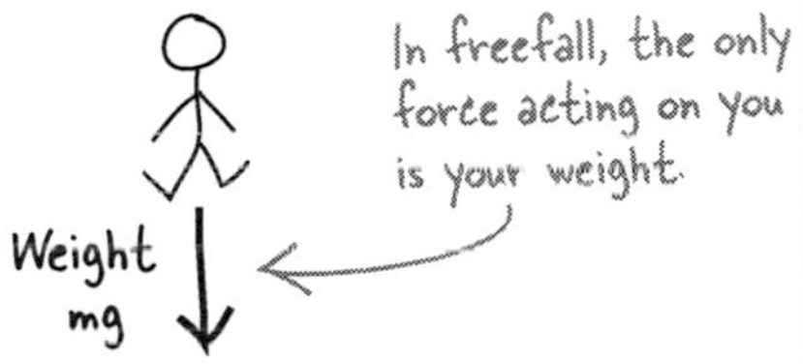

c. When you compare the free body diagrams in parts a and b, which force is missing?

The astronaut in the space station doesn't experience a contact force from the ground.

d. How does a person on Earth experience their weight differently from a person in freefall?

They don't feel a contact force from the ground – they're in freefall, and the only force they experience is their weight. This means that they can't walk around like they can on Earth, as you need a normal force to have enough friction to walk like they usually do.

e. How might you introduce a new force to compensate for the missing one you spotted in parts c and d, so the astronaut can walk around as he would on Earth?

Newton's 2nd law is $F = ma$. You could make the astronaut experience a force by accelerating the space station.

there are no Dumb Questions

Q: So why do we need artificial gravity when the space station still feels the effect of the Earth's gravity?

A: If you're in freefall, you feel weightless because you - and other objects - appear to float around, as they're not going anywhere with respect to each other.

Q: But you still have a weight, right?

A: Yes - just like someone doing a parachute jump still has a weight. It's the force of their weight that makes them fall!

Q: So why is someone in freefall called "weightless" when they have a weight? Isn't that confusing?

A: Yes, it is confusing! "Weightless" is an everyday way of saying that they aren't experiencing any kind of **contact force** from a surface as a result of their weight. If the person had scales under their feet, the scales would read zero.

Go back and look at the first WeightBotchers machine in chapter 11 if you're not sure why this is.

Can you mimic the contact force you feel on Earth?

The difference between standing on the ground and freefalling is the **contact force** that the ground exerts on you. This is the force that the astronauts want to experience.

If you can make each astronaut experience a contact force equal to the size of his **weight**, as he does on Earth, he should be able to walk around the space station just like he can on Earth.

But how can you make someone experience a contact force like this?

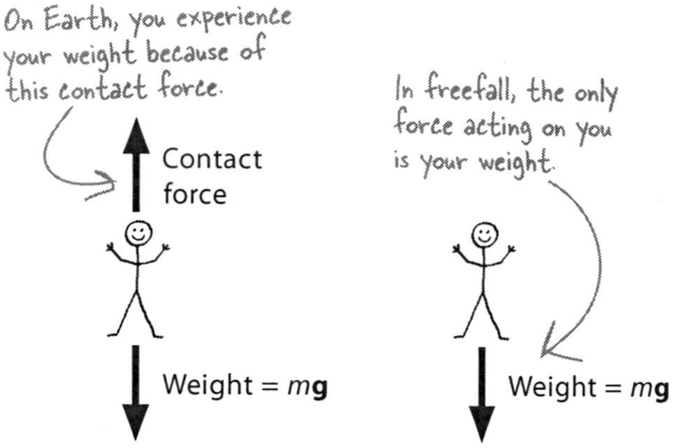

On Earth, you experience your weight because of a contact force from the ground.

Sharpen your pencil

The key thing is to close your eyes and ask "WHAT DO I FEEL PUSHING ON ME?"

Imagine yourself in these scenarios. Draw the contact force you experience in each situation as a result of the acceleration, and write down what you FEEL. For instance, "Something's pushing me in the back."

Train is sitting still, then accelerates to the right as it pulls out of a station.

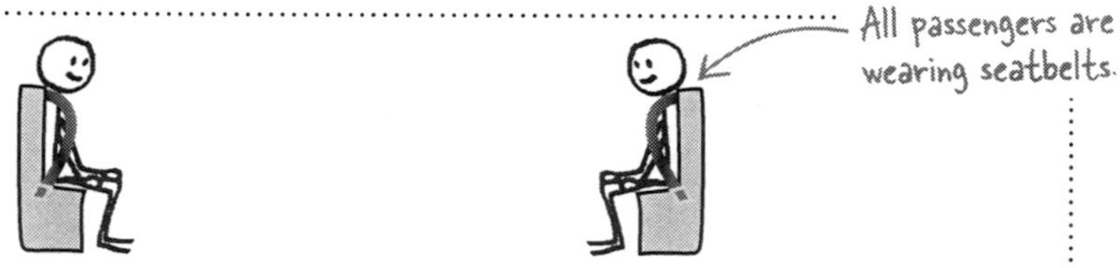

Train is moving to the right, then decelerates to a stop as it pulls into a station.

Does this give you an idea about how you might make the astronaut experience a contact force from the inside wall of the space station that would feel similar to the one he experiences on Earth?

Sharpen your pencil Solution

Imagine yourself in these scenarios. Draw the contact force you experience in each situation as a result of the acceleration, and write down what you FEEL. For instance, "Something's pushing me in the back."

All passengers are wearing seatbelts.

Train is sitting still, then accelerates to the right as it pulls out of a station.

The back of the seat is pushing on me.

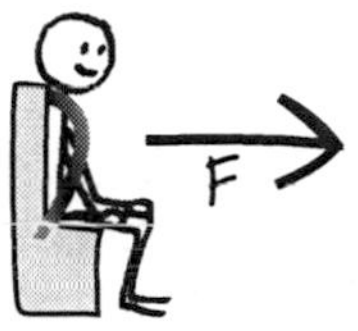

The seatbelt is digging into me.

Train is moving to the right, then decelerates to a stop as it pulls into a station.

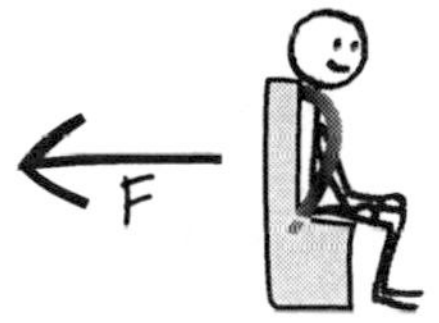

The seatbelt is digging into me.

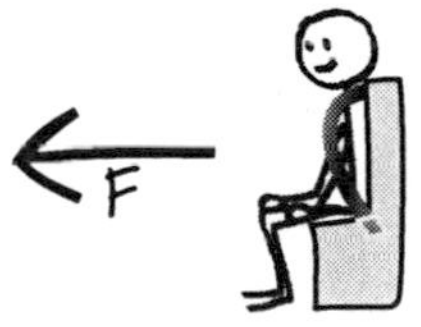

The back of the seat is pushing on me.

Does this give you an idea about how you might make the astronaut experience a contact force from the inside wall of the space station that would feel similar to the one he experiences on Earth?

You could accelerate the space station. That would make the astronaut experience a contact force – like I do when a train accelerates.

If you accelerate it at 9.8 m/s², then this contact force will be exactly the same size as the one he experiences on Earth.

there are no Dumb Questions

Q: I can imagine the seat pushing into my back when a train accelerates. But why does that happen?

A: Newton's 1st law says that an object will continue to move at a constant velocity unless it's acted on by a net force. If you were sitting on the platform, the fact that the train is accelerating wouldn't affect you, as there's no contact between you and it.

But because you're sitting on the train, the back of your seat is able to mediate a net contact force that causes you to accelerate. You feel the seat pushing into you.

In the context of forces, 'mediate' means 'transmit'.

Q: How large is the contact force?

A: Newton's 2nd Law says that **F** = *m***a**. You can work out the size of the contact force from your mass and your acceleration.

Q: How can I make the astronaut feel a contact force?

A: If you accelerate the space station upward, the astronaut will experience a contact force from its wall because he is inside it - just like you do when you're on the train.

Q: Why will accelerating the space station mean that a dropped apple will fall like it does on Earth?

A: The apple will continue at the velocity it already had (Newton's 1st Law), as there is no contact force on it while it is falling.

Meanwhile, the space station will accelerate up to meet it at a rate of 9.8 m/s². So if you're in the space station, it feels like you're on Earth (because of the contact force you experience), and it looks like you're on Earth because objects accelerate towards the ground at the same rate.

Accelerating the space station allows you to experience a contact force

If you lie on the ground with your eyes shut, you can feel a **contact force** from the ground pushing into your back.

If the train pulls away from the station with an acceleration of exactly **9.8 m/s²**, then you would feel exactly the **same size** of contact force as you do when you lie on the ground.

So if you accelerate the space station at a rate of 9.8 m/s², the astronauts will experience the same size of contact force as they usually experience when they're standing on Earth. This creates the artificial gravity that the astronauts want!

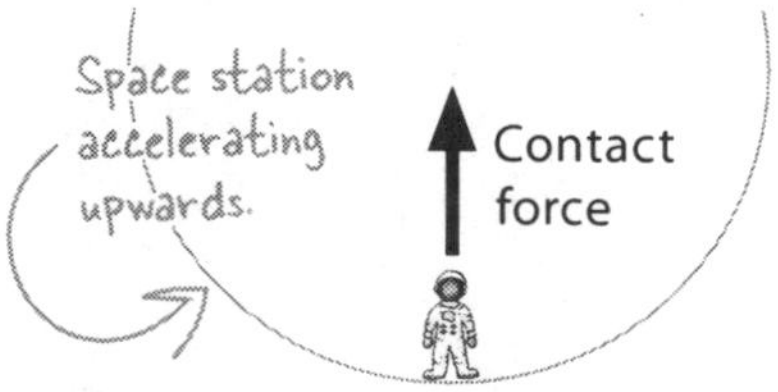

But how **practical** is this?

Sharpen your pencil

Don't be intimidated by the first four words of this problem!

a. Einstein's Theory of Relativity says that nothing can move faster than the speed of light, 3.0×10^8 m/s. If you accelerate a space station from rest at a rate of 9.8 m/s², what time would it take it to reach a speed of 3.0×10^8 m/s (assume for a moment that this is possible and there are no relativistic effects)?

b. What distance would the space station cover in that time?

c. The distance from the Earth to the Moon is 4×10^8 m (1 sd), and the distance to the edge of the Solar System is 5.7×10^{12} m. How does the distance you worked out in part b compare?

d. How practical do you think this idea is for creating artificial gravity in a space station?

Sharpen your pencil Solution

a. Einstein's Theory of Relativity says that nothing can move faster than the speed of light, 3.0×10^8 m/s. If you accelerate a space station from rest at a rate of 9.8 m/s², what time would it take it to reach a speed of 3.0×10^8 m/s (assume for a moment that this is possible and there are no relativistic effects)?

Work out t: $v = v_0 + at$

$v_0 = 0$ m/s

$v = 3.0 \times 10^8$ m/s

$a = 9.8$ m/s²

$t = ?$ $x - x_0 = ?$

But $v_0 = 0$

$$t = \frac{v}{a} = \frac{3.0 \times 10^8}{9.8}$$

$t = 3.1 \times 10^7$ s (2 sd)

b. What distance would the space station cover in that time?

Work out x:

$$x = x_0 + v_0 t + \tfrac{1}{2}at^2$$

$$x = 0 + 0 + 0.5 \times 9.8 \times (3.1 \times 10^7)^2$$

$$x = 4.7 \times 10^{15} \text{ m (2 sd)}$$

c. The distance from the Earth to the Moon is 4×10^8 m (1 sd), and the distance to the edge of the Solar System is 5.7×10^{12} m. How does the distance you worked out in part b compare?

This distance is around 10 million times greater than the Earth–Moon distance and a thousand times greater than the edge of the Solar System.

d. How practical do you think this idea is for creating artificial gravity in a space station?

It's not practical because it's not possible to sustain it for a good length of time, and you end up very far away from the Earth. It must take a lot of fuel too.

It's (theoretically) possible to make the astronaut experience a contact force similar to the one he experiences on Earth by accelerating the space station along a straight line at 9.8 m/s².

But it's not **practical**. It's impossible to do this indefinitely, since the space station can't go faster than the speed of light, you'd run out of fuel, and you'd wind up a ridiculously long way away from the Earth.

Linear means "along a straight line."

So if **linear acceleration** isn't practical, what might another option be?

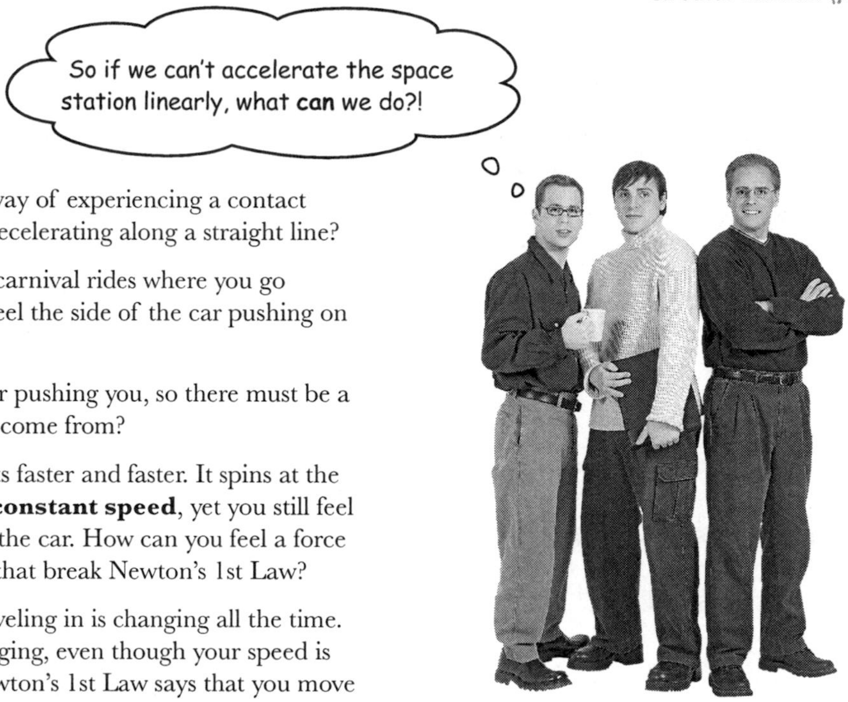

Jim: I wonder if there's another way of experiencing a contact force, apart from accelerating or decelerating along a straight line?

Joe: Hmmm ... what about those carnival rides where you go **around in a circle**? You kinda feel the side of the car pushing on you when they spin really fast ...

Frank: You feel the side of the car pushing you, so there must be a **contact force**. But where does it come from?

Jim: Yeah, it's not like the ride gets faster and faster. It spins at the same rate, so you keep going at a **constant speed**, yet you still feel this contact force from the side of the car. How can you feel a force if your speed is constant - doesn't that break Newton's 1st Law?

Joe: But the **direction** you're traveling in is changing all the time. That means your **velocity** is changing, even though your speed is constant. Velocity is a **vector**. Newton's 1st Law says that you move with a constant velocity unless there's a force acting on you.

Frank: So I guess the contact force **changes your direction** of travel - which changes your velocity - so causes you to **accelerate**.

Jim: But where does the force come from?! It's not like there's a train engine sitting behind you making you accelerate!

Frank: Well, you're thrown to the outside of the ride, aren't you? So there must be some kind of mysterious force pushing you outwards that's only there when you're spinning.

Frank: Hang on! When you're thinking about contact forces, you're meant to shut your eyes and ask, "What do I feel pushing on me?" And when I do that, I feel the side of the car pushing me **inwards**, not a 'ghost force' pushing me outwards.

Jim: But you slide kinda outwards across your seat before you make contact with the side of the car. If there isn't a force pushing you outwards, then why does that happen?!

Joe: If the side of the car wasn't there, you'd go straight on and fly out of the car. You only go in a circle because of the contact force from the side of the car pushing you inwards.

Frank: Ah ... you mean that sliding outwards feeling is just you continuing on at your current velocity (Newton's 1st Law) before you make contact with the side of the car - which exerts a force on you that lets you move in a circle?

If a contact force is acting on you, you can feel the direction it's pushing you in.

BRAIN POWER

Can you imagine yourself in the spinning carnival ride and the contact force acting on you?

You can only go in a circle because of a centripetal force

Newton's 1st Law says that you continue with a **constant velocity** unless there's a **net force** acting on you. In other words, you keep on going at the **same speed** in the **same direction.**

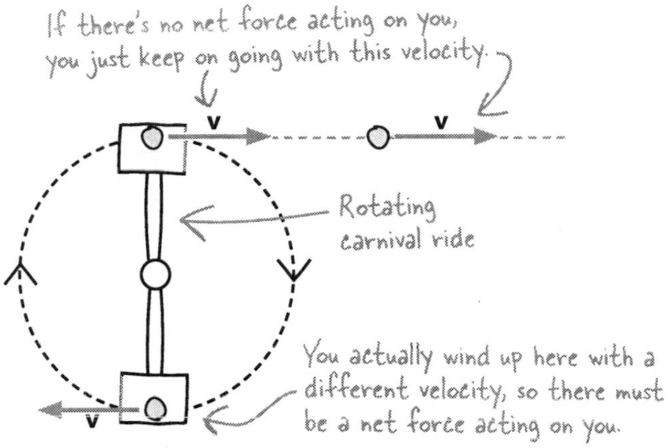

If you're going around in a circle, your speed may stay the same, but the direction of your velocity vector changes.

If you're going around in a circle, your speed may be constant, but the **direction** of your velocity is certainly changing! This means that a **force** must be acting on you in order to make you go around in a circle - and stop you from going off along a straight line with the velocity you already have.

A force that allows you to go in a circle like this is called a **centripetal force**.

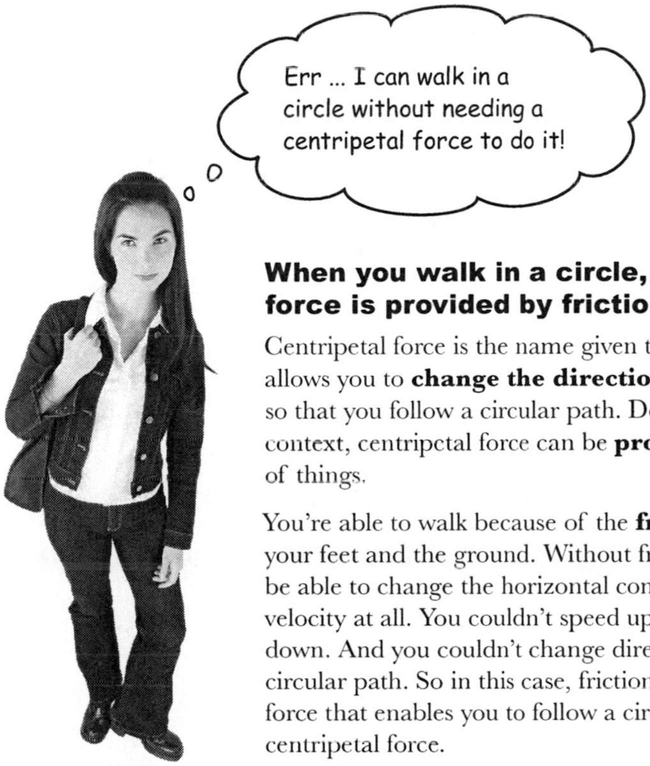

When you walk in a circle, the centripetal force is provided by friction.

Centripetal force is the name given to a **net force** that allows you to **change the direction of your velocity** so that you follow a circular path. Depending on the context, centripetal force can be **provided** by a number of things.

You're able to walk because of the **friction** between your feet and the ground. Without friction, you wouldn't be able to change the horizontal component of your velocity at all. You couldn't speed up. You couldn't slow down. And you couldn't change direction to follow a circular path. So in this case, friction provides the net force that enables you to follow a circular path - the centripetal force.

If the net force acting on you changes the direction of your velocity so that you travel in a circle, it's called a centripetal force.

there are no Dumb Questions

Q: Is centripetal force another category of force to add to a contact forces and gravitational forces?

A: No, not at all! Centripetal force is the name given to the net force when it enables you to follow a circular path instead of continuing along a straight line.

Q: So if a force is able to change my direction, it might be able to provide a centripetal force?

A: Yes, that's a good way to think about it.

Q: Where does a centripetal force come from?

A: The centripetal force required for you to follow a circular path may come from any source at all. It might be a contact force. It might be a frictional force. It might be a gravitational force.

Q: So it's not a "ghost force" that magically appears from nowhere?

A: That's right. If you draw a free body diagram of an object moving around in a circle, then the net force will be the centripetal force that causes the circular motion.

Q: Which direction does the centripetal force act in?

A: You're about to figure that out ...

Sharpen your pencil

Tip: Draw in the radius of the circle, from the center of each point. The velocity vector will be at 90° to the radius.

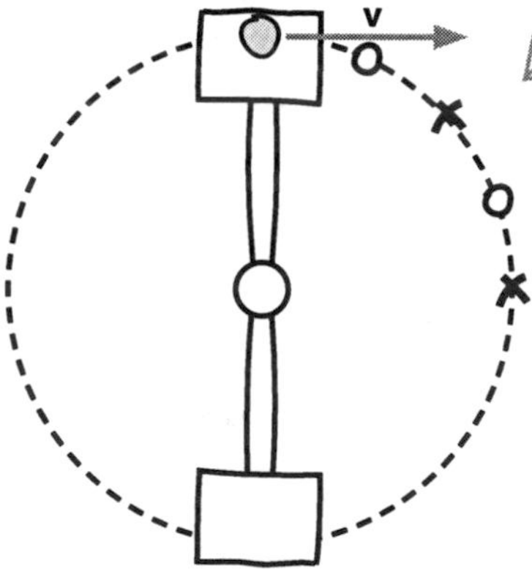

a. Draw the velocity vector at each of the points marked with an 'x' on the ride. Assume that the ride is rotating with a constant angular frequency.

b. In a different color, draw in the left-right and up-down components of the velocity vectors you drew in part a.

c. Describe how the velocity components have changed from one 'x' to the next. At each of the points marked 'o', draw in a vector representing a force that may have caused these changes.

Hint: the direction of the force may be changing as the ride rotates.

d. Which direction do you think the force vector will point in for other positions on the ride?

e. What is the source of this centripetal force that enables you to move in a circle?

Sharpen your pencil Solution

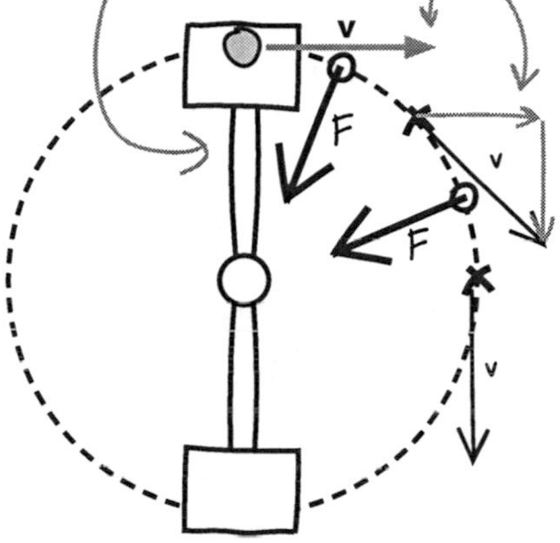

The force needs to have a large down component and a small left component to have made this change.

a. Draw the velocity vector at each of the points marked with an 'x' on the ride. Assume that the ride is rotating with a constant angular frequency.

b. In a different color, draw in the left-right and up-down components of the velocity vectors you drew in part a.

c. Describe how the components have changed from one snapshot to the next, and draw in a vector representing a force that may have caused these changes.

Between the 1st and 2nd snapshots, the down component got much larger and the right component a bit smaller. So the force must be acting down and left (with more down)

Between the 2nd and 3rd snapshots, the right component has disappeared and the down component has got a bit larger. So the force must be acting down and left (with more left).

Centripetal force acts towards the center of the circle.

d. Which direction do you think the force vector will point in for other positions on the ride?

I think the force vector will always point towards the center of the circle.

e. What is the source of this centripetal force that enables you to move in a circle?

The contact force of the outside wall of the car pushing in on me.

It's OK if you said "the arm that goes between the car and the center", as that exerts the centripetal force that stops the car from flying off along a straight line.

Always think "what contact force do I feel pushing me?"

The reason you slide towards the outside is that you want to keep on going in the direction you're already going in. That's Newton's 1st Law.

But the side of the car stops you from going any further and pushes you towards the center. This is where the **centripetal force** that makes you go round in a circle comes from.

Being thrown to the outside is an illusion. There's no force moving you in that direction - just your own momentum.

Centripetal force acts towards the center of the circle

If you're sitting in a rotating carnival ride, you experience a centripetal force, $\mathbf{F}_c$, towards the center of the ride. This is the force that enables you to continue traveling in a **circle**, instead of continuing at a constant speed in the same direction as you would if there was no force (Newton's 1st Law).

In the carnival ride, the centripetal force is **provided** by a **contact force** from the side of the car - you feel the side of the car pushing you towards the center of the circle as you go around..

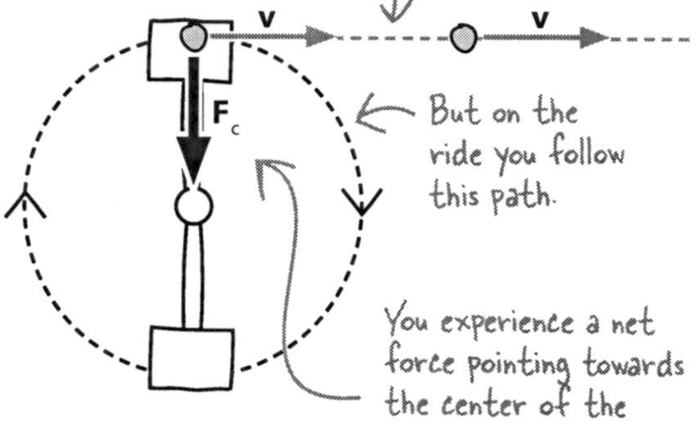

Centripetal force is always provided by the net force on your free body diagram. Otherwise you'd just go along a straight line.

"Centrifugal force" isn't a force.

"Centrifugal force" is the name commonly given to the sensation of being thrown to the outside when you're in something that's rotating (e.g., a centrifuge).

But as you've just learned, what is often referred to as centrifugal force isn't a force! It's just you **continuing at your current velocity** in the absence of a net force.

And once you're in CONTACT with the side of the centrifuge, the contact force can provide a centripetal force that makes you follow a circular path.

Never EVER talk about "centrifugal force."

BRAIN POWER

How can you use what you've figured out about centripetal force to help the astronauts?

The astronaut experiences a contact force when you rotate the space station

You can **rotate** the space station just like you rotate the carnival ride. Each astronaut will experience a **centripetal force** acting towards the center of the space station. This will be mediated by the **contact force** between his feet and the side of the space station. This will feel similar to the contact force he experiences on Earth.

As there's now a **contact force**, the astronauts will be able to walk around like they can on Earth - and won't go on strike!

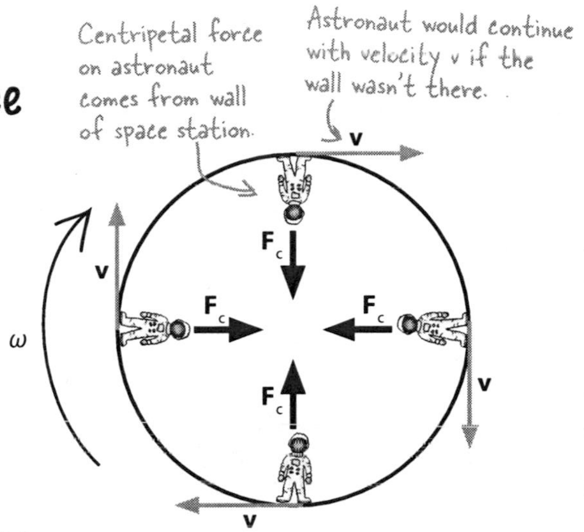

there are no Dumb Questions

Q: So anything that's rotating is subject to a centripetal force?

A: That's right. If the centripetal force wasn't there, the thing wouldn't rotate - it would travel along a straight line at its current speed.

Q: So why didn't the hamster running in the wheel in chapter 16 experience a centripetal force? Or did it?

A: Was the hamster rotating?

Q: No ... the hamster stayed in the same place, and the wheel rotated as its feet pushed it along. I guess the hamster didn't experience a centripetal force.

A: Yeah, that's right.

Q: But the wheel's rotating, so the wheel must experience a centripetal force - yes? But how? The outside of the wheel isn't in contact with anything!

A: Centripetal force doesn't always have to be provided by a contact force from the outside. All you need is a force that points towards the **center** of the circle.

Q: So I guess the struts in the hamster wheel are mediating the centripetal force?

A: Absolutely! If one of the struts broke, and part of the outside of the wheel flew off, then it wouldn't be moving in a circle anymore. The broken part would fly off along a straight line at a tangent to the circle with whatever velocity it had when it became detached.

Q: That's Newton's 1st Law, right?

A: Yep. It's also how hammer throwing works at the Olympics. The athlete spins round and round with the heavy ball on the end of a chain, then lets go. Without the centripetal force provided by the athlete pulling on the chain, the hammer flies off in a straight line.

If the centripetal force 'disappears', you'll go off at a <u>tangent</u> to the circle.

Q: Yeah, I've seen that before. So are you saying it's the same in the space station? If you rotate the space station, you're giving the astronaut the potential to go flying off into space if a door suddenly opens or something?

A: That's right. If the astronaut didn't experience the centripetal contact force from the side of the space station acting towards its center, he would go along a straight line.

Q: Hmmm. I guess there must be a centripetal force acting on the space station for it to have a circular orbit around the Earth in the first place?

A: Great spot! You'll be learning all about that in chapter 16.

Q: So I guess I need to work out how fast I need to rotate the space station to produce a centripetal force of mg, like an astronaut would feel on Earth?

A: Let's look at that now...

What affects the size of centripetal force?

Newton's 2nd Law tells you that the **centripetal force** the astronaut experiences will be equal to his mass × acceleration:

$$\mathbf{F}_c = m\mathbf{a}_c$$

The centripetal force depends on the centripetal acceleration.

You can write this because the centripetal force is the net force that causes the centripetal acceleration.

The acceleration that the centripetal force causes is called **centripetal acceleration**. Acceleration is the rate of change of velocity and points in the direction of that change:

$$\mathbf{a}_c = \frac{\Delta \mathbf{v}}{\Delta t}$$

The centripetal acceleration depends on the rate of change of velocity.

You want the centripetal acceleration that the astronauts experience to be equal to 9.8 m/s². This makes the contact force each astronaut experiences in the space station the same size as the contact force he experiences on Earth.

But what affects the **size** of the centripetal acceleration? If you can work that out, you can get an **equation** for the centripetal acceleration and stop the astronauts going on strike!

Sharpen your pencil

The equation from chapter 16 shows you what happens to v when you vary r and ω.

The sketch here could either be of a carnival ride or a space station - imagine it in the way that seems most natural to you. There are two 'pods' attached to the circle, one twice as far from the center as the other.

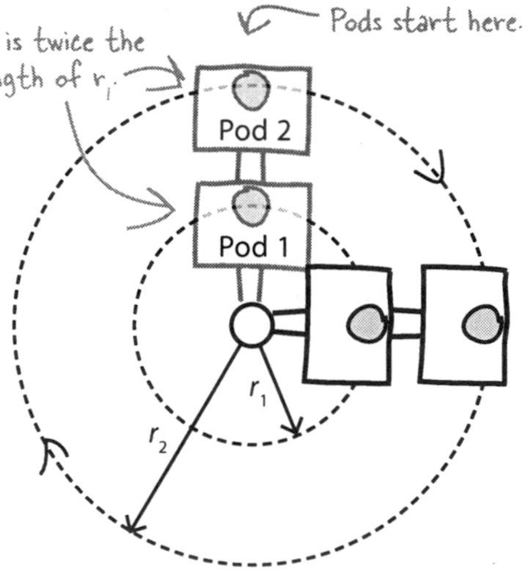

a. Bearing in mind that $v = r\omega$, draw in velocity vectors for the two pods at each position shown.

b. Which pod experiences the larger change in its velocity between the two positions?

c. Which pod experiences the greater centripetal acceleration between the two positions?

d. Can you think of another way of increasing the centripetal acceleration that the pods experience (assuming each pod's radius is fixed)?

Sharpen your pencil Solution

The sketch here could either be of a carnival ride or a space station - imagine it in the way that seems most natural to you. There are two 'pods' attached to the circle, one twice as far from the center as the other.

Twice the radius means double the velocity ($v = r\omega$)

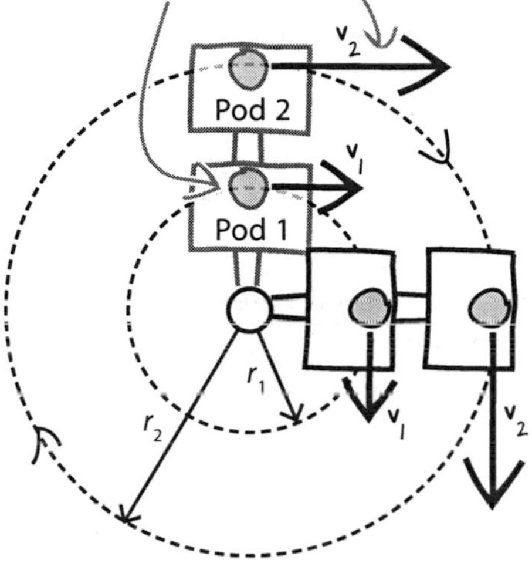

a. Bearing in mind that $v = r\omega$, draw in velocity vectors for the two pods at each position shown.

b. Which pod experiences the larger change in its velocity between the two positions?

Pod 2 (on the outside) has the bigger change in velocity because its velocity vectors are larger, but the change in direction is the same.

c. Which pod experiences the greater centripetal acceleration between the two positions?

Acceleration is rate of change of velocity. So pod 2 has the greatest centripetal acceleration since it has the greatest change in velocity.

d. Can you think of another way of increasing the centripetal acceleration that the pods experience (assuming each pod's radius is fixed)?

Spin the space station with a faster ω to increase all the velocities (as $v = r\omega$).

We're not looking for an equation for the centripetal acceleration yet - just working out which variables it must depend on.

ω is the number of radians per second. ω can be called the **angular frequency**, or the **angular speed**. It is also sometimes referred to as the **angular velocity**, with the understanding that when the variable is written as a scalar, ω, it only refers to the **size** of the angular velocity, and not its direction. As we will often be moving between v, the size of the linear velocity and ω, we will often refer to ω as the angular velocity to make the connection clearer.

Centripetal acceleration depends on both the radius and the angular velocity, as both of these affect the rate of change of velocity.

For the same angular velocity, a larger RADIUS means a larger centripetal acceleration.

For the same radius, a larger ANGULAR VELOCITY means a larger centripetal acceleration.

Spot the equation for the centripetal acceleration

A larger **centripetal acceleration** is required to move something in a circle when the **radius** is large, and when the **angular velocity** is large, because the rate of change of velocity is larger in both cases.

Deriving the equation for the centripetal acceleration from scratch is tricky and doesn't really help your understanding of the physics. So instead, **spot** the correct equation by **trying out extreme values** and looking at its **units**.

Check an equation by thinking about EXTREMES and working out its UNITS.

You've done this kind of thing before, don't worry!

Equation ID Parade

Here are six equations that all claim to be a formula that gives you the size of the centripetal acceleration of something rotating with angular velocity ω at radius r.

Annotate the equations to explain what will happen if r gets much bigger, or if ω gets much bigger. Use this information to cross out any equations that don't behave as you would expect them to.

For your remaining equations, check that the units on both sides are the same. This should leave you with just one equation. (Remember that radians are dimensionless.)

$$a_c = \frac{r}{\omega} \qquad a_c = \frac{\omega}{r} \qquad a_c = r^2\omega$$

$$a_c = r\omega^2 \qquad a_c = \frac{\omega^2}{r} \qquad a_c = \frac{r^2}{\omega}$$

These are all scalar equations as we're only talking about the SIZE of the centripetal acceleration.

Equation ID Parade SOLUTION

Here are six equations that all claim to be a formula that gives you the size of the centripetal acceleration of something rotating with angular velocity ω at radius r.

Annotate the equations to explain what will happen if r gets much bigger, or if ω gets much bigger. Use this information to cross out any equations that don't behave as you would expect them to.

For your remaining equations, check that the units on both sides are the same. This should leave you with just one equation. (Remember that radians are dimensionless.)

~~$a_c = \frac{r}{\ }$~~

a_c gets smaller as ω gets larger. So this is wrong.

~~$a_c = \frac{\omega}{r}$~~

a_c gets smaller as r gets larger. So this is wrong.

~~$a_c = r^2\omega$~~

a_c gets larger as ω and r get larger. So check units.

RHS: Units $= m^2 \times 1/s$
$= m^2/s$
Not units of acceleration.

Radians are dimensionless, the units of ω are $1/s$.

$a_c = r\omega^2$

a_c gets larger as ω and r get larger. So check units.

RHS: Units $= m \times /s^2$
$= m/s^2$
Units of acceleration! ✓

~~$a_c = \frac{\omega^2}{r}$~~

a_c gets smaller as r gets larger. So this is wrong.

~~$a_c = \frac{r^2}{\omega}$~~

a_c gets smaller as ω gets larger. So this is wrong.

there are no Dumb Questions

Q: I got the equation '$a_c = r\omega^2$' from the parade. Why doesn't the equation for 'a_c' have 'v' in it, when acceleration is rate of change of velocity?

A: Remember that $v = r\omega$. So you can make a substitution for the 'ω' in '$a_c = r\omega^2$' to express it as an equation that involves v.

ω is the rate of change of the angle θ.

Q: OK ... so I make that substitution and get the equation $a_c = \frac{v^2}{r}$. But that can't be right! a_c should get larger as r gets larger. But you're dividing by r, so a_c would get smaller as r gets larger.

A: But when r gets larger, v gets larger as well, because $v = r\omega$. And because the velocity is squared, the v^2 on the top of the fraction gets larger more rapidly than the r on the bottom of the fraction. So overall, a_c still gets larger as r gets larger.

Q: But what if $r = 0$ in $a_c = \frac{v^2}{r}$? I'm not sure I know how to divide by 0!

A: It's easier to look at the other form of the equation, $a_c = r\omega^2$. If $r = 0$ then $a_c = 0$.

Q: Isn' t acceleration is usually a vector? Why is $a_c = r\omega^2$ a scalar equation gives the size but not the direction?

A: The centripetal acceleration vector always points towards the center of the circle, so its direction is always changing. To avoid getting muddled up with direction, we're just dealing with scalar equations for the size of the acceleration.

Give the astronauts a centripetal force

The equation for the size of the centripetal acceleration is $a_c = r\omega^2$. The vectors $\mathbf{a}_c$ and $\mathbf{r}$ are always in opposite directions, but because the space station is spinning, we're using a scalar equation.

$$a_c = r\omega^2$$

Size of centripetal acceleration → a_c; Radius → r; Angular velocity → ω

Newton's 2nd Law is $\mathbf{F}_{net} = m\mathbf{a}$. The centripetal force is the net force that must be present for an object to follow a circular path. A substitution gives you the size of the centripetal force:

$$F_c = mr\omega^2$$

Size of centripetal force → F_c; Mass → m; $F_c = ma_c$

It's good to appreciate the directions of the vectors even though the equation only deals with the sizes.

Even though F_c and r are in opposite directions, their directions are always changing because the space station is spinning.

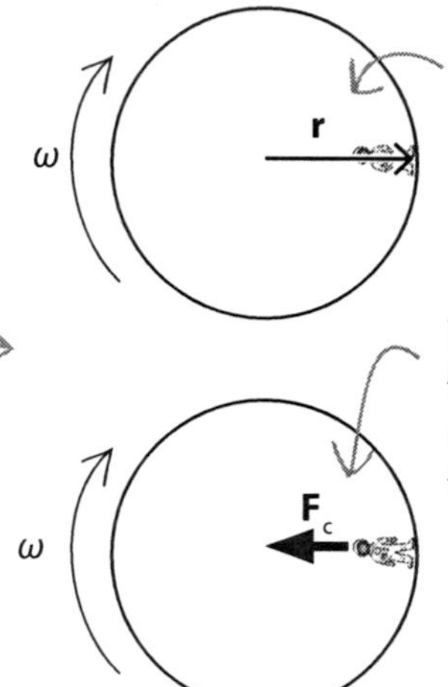

Sharpen your pencil

We're designing a spinning module for the existing space station, so that the astronauts can walk around. Two design candidates are cylinders with the same volume, but radii of 10.0 m and 100 m respectively.

a. Calculate the angular velocity required to produce a centripetal acceleration of 9.8 m/s² for (i) the 10.0 m radius module and (ii) the 100 m radius module.

ω can be called angular frequency, angular speed or angular velocity! It's always radians per second.

b. If a door in the space station opened, and the astronaut went through, what velocity (size and direction) would he travel AT if he'd been in (i) 10.0 m radius module and (ii) the 100 m radius modules?

Sharpen your pencil Solution

We're designing a spinning module for the existing space station, so that the astronauts can walk around. Two design candidates are cylinders with the same volume, but radii of 10.0 m and 100 m respectively.

a. Calculate the angular velocity required to produce a centripetal acceleration of 9.8 m/s² for (i) the 10.0 m radius module and (ii) the 100 m radius module.

Centripetal force: $F_c = mr\omega^2$

Centripetal acceleration: $F_c = ma_c$

$\Rightarrow a_c = r\omega^2$

$\Rightarrow \omega = \sqrt{\frac{a_c}{r}}$

(i) For 10.0 m radius:

$\omega = \sqrt{\frac{9.8}{10.0}}$

$\omega = 0.990$ rad/s (3 sd)

(ii) For 100 m radius:

$\omega = \sqrt{\frac{9.8}{100}}$

$\omega = 0.313$ rad/s (3 sd)

b. If a door in the space station opened, and the astronaut went through, what velocity (size and direction) would he travel AT if he'd been in (i) 10.0 m radius module and (ii) the 100 m radius modules?

(i) For 10.0 m radius:

$v = r\omega = 10.0 \times 0.990$

$v = 9.90$ m/s (3 sd)

(ii) For 100 m radius:

$v = r\omega = 100 \times 0.313$

$v = 31.3$ m/s (3 sd)

He'll keep on going with the same velocity he already had, at a tangent to the place he came out of the space station.

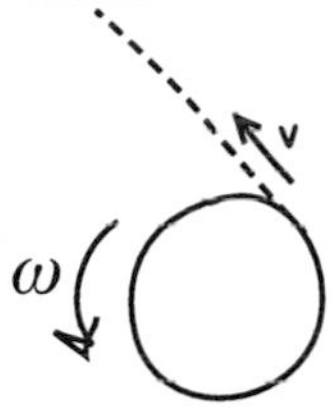

The velocity vector is always at a tangent to the circle.

The astronauts want as much floor space as possible

The two space station module designs have the same **volume** (90000 m³) and need to be spun at similar angular velocities to produce the same centripetal acceleration. The 10.0 m radius space station needs to be spun at a rate of 0.990 rad/s and the 100 m radius station would be spun at a rate of 0.313 rad/s.

How are you going to choose between the two competing designs? The astronauts can help. They want as much floor **area** to walk around on as possible. They really feel the need to stretch their legs and get some exercise when they've been in the space station for a while!

BRAIN POWER

Which space station do you think will have the most floor space?

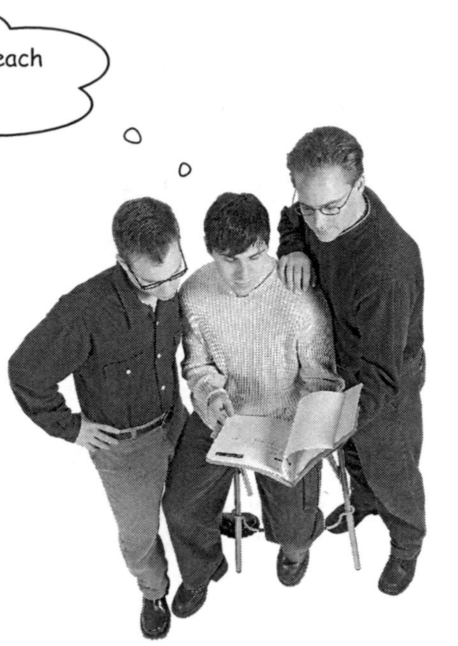

Frank: Well, duh, the 100 m radius space station must have a bigger floor area than the 10.0 m radius one, as it's a bigger circle!

Jim: I'm not so sure. The floor is actually the **side** of the cylinder, not the circular part at the ends.

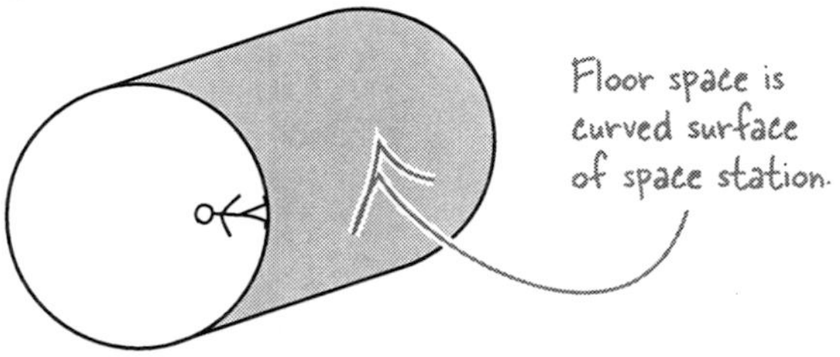

Frank: Ohhh ... good point. So how are we gonna do that? I don't think I know how to find the **area** of a curved surface!

Joe: Well, let's think this out. If we unroll the cylinder into simpler shapes what would they be?

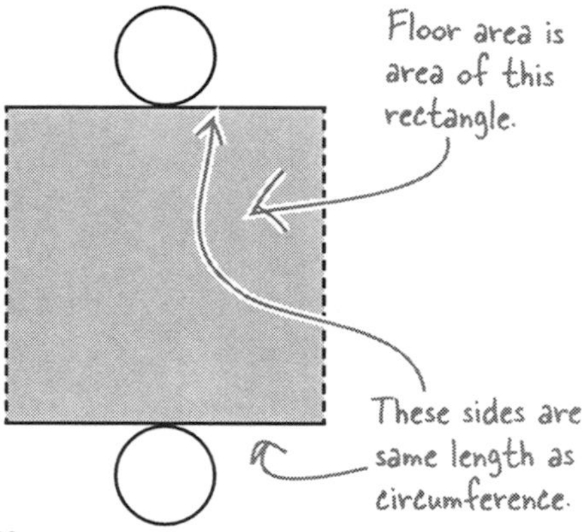

Jim: OK, the cylinder's basically a **circle** at each end and a **rectangle** rolled around them. And we know how to find the area of a rectangle - job done!

Frank: Hold up ... how do we figure out the **lengths** of the rectangle's sides? We need those to calculate its area.

Jim: Well, one of the sides is easy - it's the same length as the circumference. But there's no mention of how long the other side is for either of the space stations. Houston, we have a problem!

Joe: We DO know that each space station has the same **volume** - 90000 m^3. When something has straight sides and identical ends (like a cylinder), its volume is area of base × height. So we can use that to work out the height?

Jim: That seems right... but the base is a circle. Which means we need to calculate the **area of a circle**. That's gotta be tricky ...

If you're calculating the surface area of a 3D shape, imagine "unrolling" the shape so that the surfaces are flat.

Here, the floor space is the area of a cylinder's curved surface

The astronauts want the design with the larger floor space - which means that you need to calculate the **area** of the curved surface of each cylindrical space station.

If you're calculating a surface area, it's best to 'unroll' the shape so that the surfaces are flat. When you do this, the curved surface becomes a rectangle. That's great, because you already know how to work out the surface area of a rectangle: width × height.

One side of the rectangle is the same length as the circumference, and the other side is the height of the cylinder - so far, so good. But you don't know the cylinder's height, only its volume.

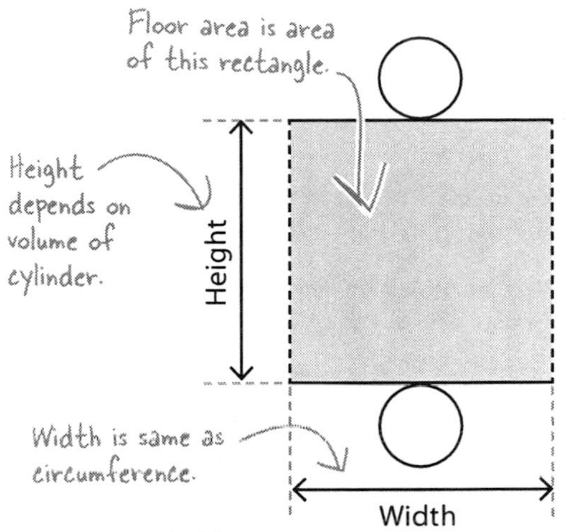

The area of a rectangle is width x height

Note the similarities between these two equations.

If you work out the volume, you can calculate the astronauts' floor space

If you have a 3D shape - like a cube or a cylinder - where the base and the top are the same shape with straight sides in between, its volume is **(area of base) × height**.

You already know that both space stations are cylinders with volumes of 90000 m^3. Which means that if you can work out the area of the base (i.e., the area of the circle), you can use the equation to determine the height of the cylinder. Which is great, as that's exactly what you need to calculate the astronauts' floor space.

If a 3D shape has two ends that are the same and straight sides between them, its volume is (area of base) x height

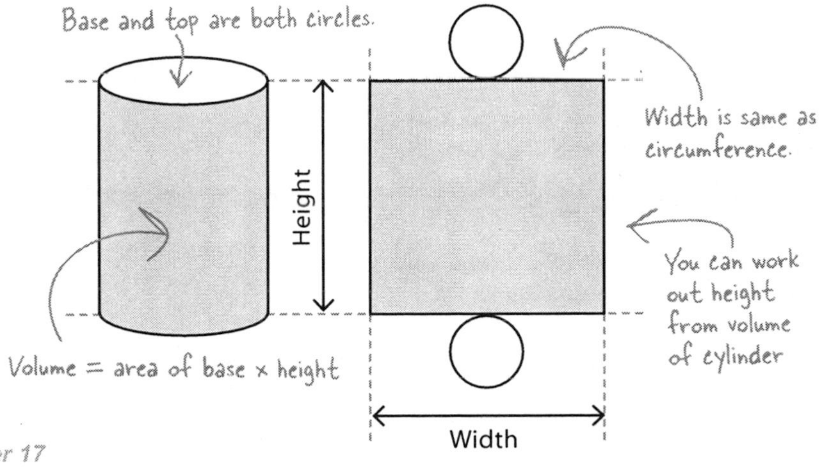

Sharpen your pencil

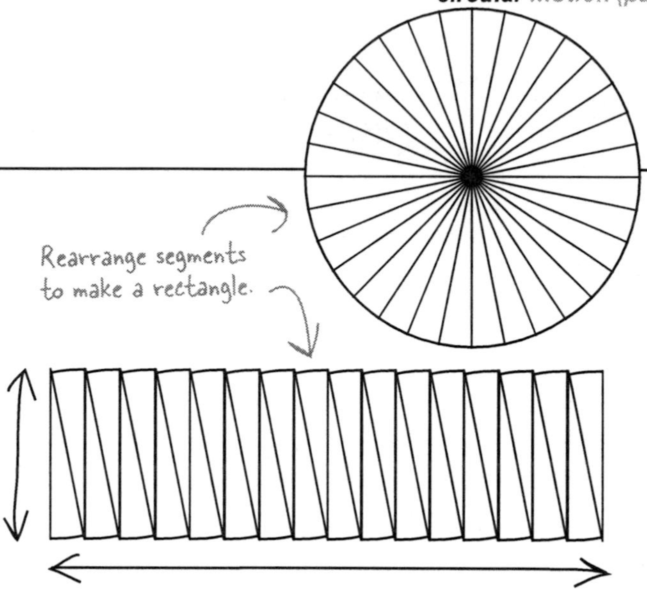

1. To find a circle's area, you can chop it up into tiny segments and reassemble it into a rectangle. In terms of the circle's radius:

In terms of *r:*

a. What is the height of the rectangle?

b. What is the width of the rectangle?

c. What is the area of the rectangle (and therefore the area of the circle)?

Remember to start with a sketch!

2. Two cylinders each have a volume of 90000 m^3.

a. The first cylinder has a radius of 10.0 m. What is the area of its circular base? What is its height?

b. The second cylinder has a radius of 100 m. What is the area of its circular base? What is its height?

c. What is the area of the curved surface of each cylinder... and which space station has a bigger floor area?

Sharpen your pencil Solution

1. To find a circle's area, you can chop it up into tiny segments and reassemble it into a rectangle. In terms of the circle's radius:

In terms of r:

a. What is the height of the rectangle?

b. What is the width of the rectangle?

c. What is the area of the rectangle (and therefore the area of the circle)?

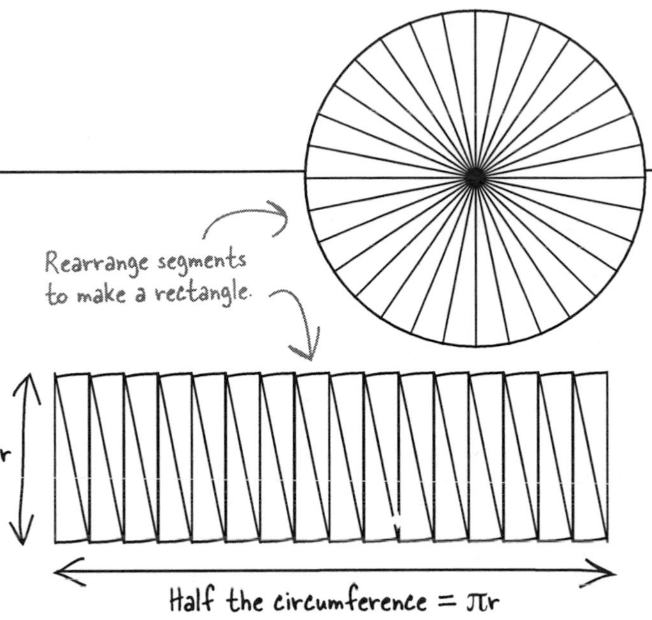

a. The height is the radius $= \underline{\underline{r}}$

b. The width is half the circumference $= \frac{1}{2} \times 2\pi r = \underline{\underline{\pi r}}$

c. The area is height × width $= r \times \pi r = \underline{\underline{\pi r^2}}$

Remember to start with a sketch!

2. Two cylinders each have a volume of 90000 m^3.

a. The first cylinder has a radius of 10.0 m. What is the area of its circular base? What is its height?

b. The second cylinder has a radius of 100 m. What is the area of its circular base? What is its height?

c. What is the area of the curved surface of each cylinder ... and which space station has a bigger 'floor' area?

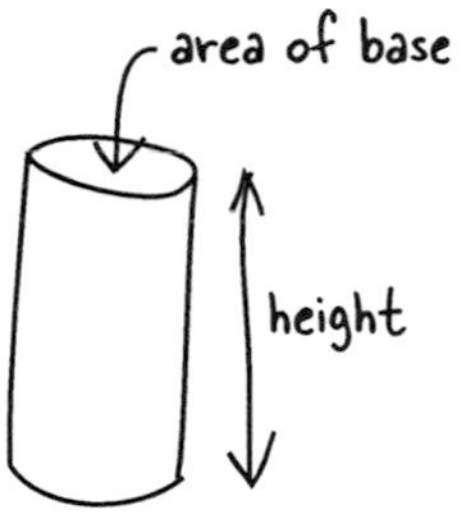

a. Area of base $= \pi r^2 = 3.14 \times 10.0^2 = 314\ m^2$ (3 sd)

Get height of cylinder from volume: volume = area of base × height

$$\Rightarrow \text{height} = \frac{\text{volume}}{\text{area of base}} = \frac{90000}{314} = \underline{\underline{287\ m}} \text{ (3 sd)}$$

b. Area of base $= \pi r^2 = 3.14 \times 100^2 = 31400\ m^2$ (3 sd)

$$\text{height} = \frac{\text{volume}}{\text{area of base}} = \frac{90000}{31400} = \underline{\underline{2.87\ m}} \text{ (3 sd)}$$

c. Curved surface is a rectangle: width = circumference $= 2\pi r$ height = height of cylinder

For 10 m radius design: Floor area $= 2 \times 3.14 \times 10.0 \times 287 = \underline{\underline{18000\ m^2}}$ (3 sd)

For 100 m radius design: Floor area $= 2 \times 3.14 \times 100 \times 2.87 = \underline{\underline{1800\ m^2}}$ (3 sd)

The 10 m radius design has 10 times the floor space of the 100 m radius one.

The area of a circle = πr^2

Let's test the space station...

As the tall narrow space station module (the one with the 10.0 m radius that needs to rotate at around 1 rad/s) has the larger floor area, you go ahead and build a test rig for the astronaut to try out.

But weird things are happening! When the astronaut drops an apple, it doesn't fall as you'd expect. And the astronaut's not feeling well either.

What's going on?!

Sharpen your pencil

Jot down some ideas that might help to explain why weird things are going on.

Would using the 100 m radius space station design instead of the 10.0 m space station design help to lessen the weird effects?

Don't worry if you're not sure why these things are happening – just throw some ideas around.

Don't worry if you didn't come up with all of these ideas!

Sharpen your pencil Solution

Jot down some ideas that might help to explain why weird things are going on.

- Maybe his balance or stomach can't cope with high angular velocity.

- His head and feet are at different distances from the center. So they must experience different centripetal accelerations.

- When he drops the apple, the space station keeps rotating, but the apple doesn't. So it looks like it follows a curved path.

Can't cope with rotation

Your sense of balance isn't designed to work well when you're rotated. Although people can adapt to being spun at low angular velocities, close to 1 rad/s is too fast and will produce nasty symptoms.

Apple falls straight while space station rotates

Someone looking at the space station from outside will see the apple moving along a straight line. But to the astronaut in his rotating frame of reference, it looks like the apple follows a curved path. Which looks very weird!

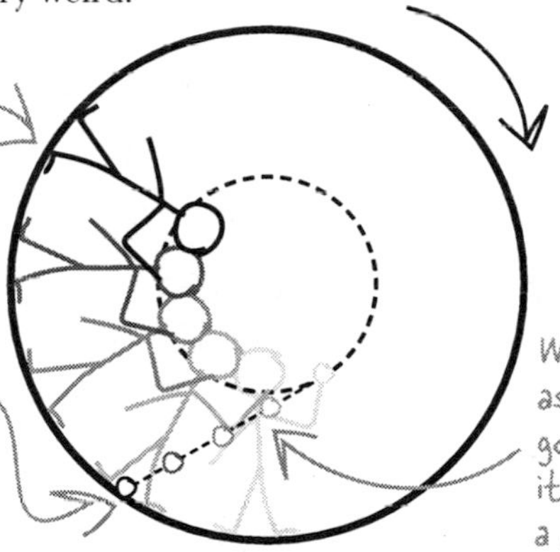

Head and feet at different radii

The centripetal force depends on the radius and is larger the further away something is from the center. So the astronaut will experience a smaller force at his head than he does at his feet. Which will feel a bit weird!

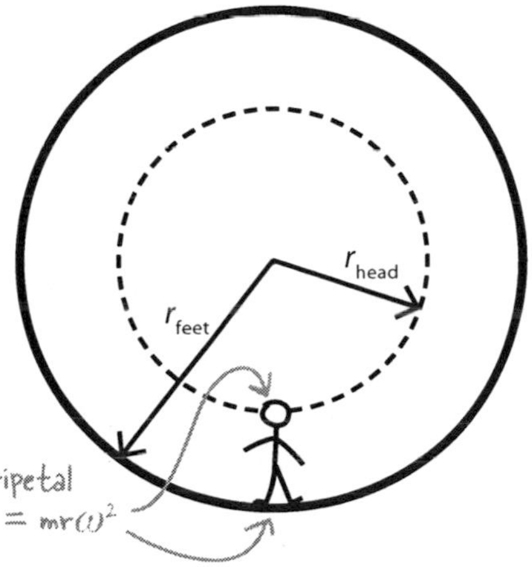

Fewer uncomfortable things happen with the 100 m radius space station

The space station module with the 100 m radius only needs to **rotate** at 0.313 rad/s, compared to the 0.990 rad/s of the module with the 10.0 m radius. This means that the astronaut has a much better chance of getting used to the rotation and feeling fewer ill effects.

The astronaut's head and feet are still **different radii** from the center of the space station, but compared to the radius of the wider space station, this difference is much less.

And when you drop an apple, the 100 m radius space station won't rotate through as great an **angle** as the 10.0 m radius space station, as the angular velocity is lower. Although the apple still won't fall exactly like it would on Earth, the curve in its path will be much less than it was.

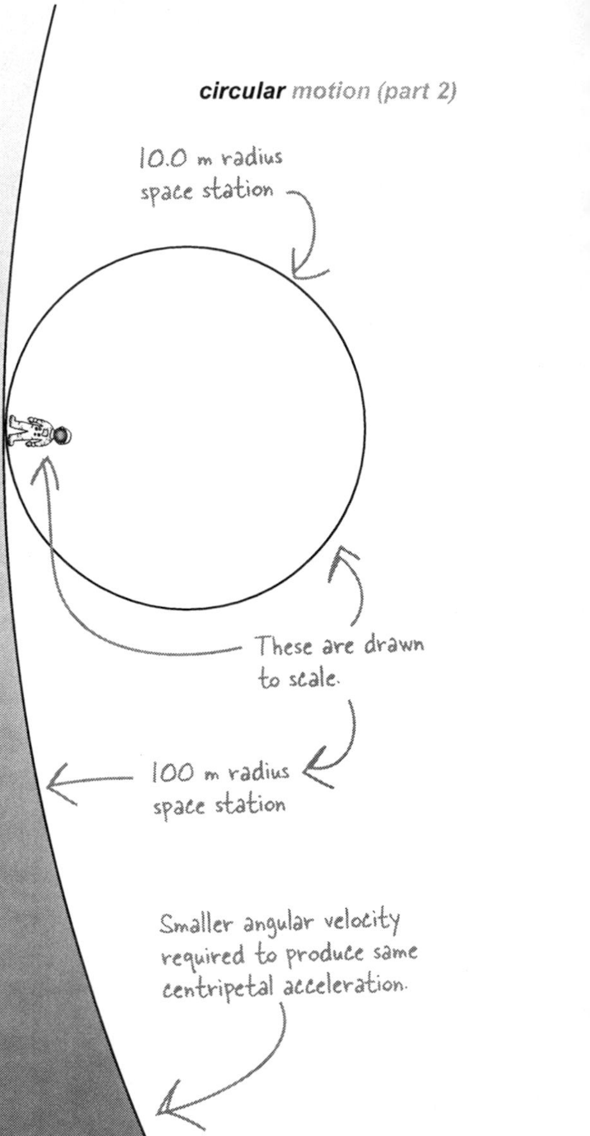

You've sorted out the space station design!

Success! When you spin the 100 m radius test rig, the astronauts are able to walk around on the curved surface without too many ill effects!

Not only have you worked out how to provide 'aritficial gravity' in space, you've also managed to understand enough of the physics to choose between two competing space station designs.

Result!

That's it from Head First in Space for now ... though the astronauts are starting to mutter something about going to infinity and beyond?!

Sound exciting? Stay tuned!

Question Clinic: The "Centripetal force" Question

Any time an object follows a curved path, ask yourself whether you may need to think about centripetal force. This is the force required for the object to move in this way: $F_c = mr\omega^2$. You can move between the velocity (v) and the angular velocity (ω) using the equation $v = r\omega$. The larger the radius and the larger the angular velocity, the greater the force required.

This should immediately get you thinking about centripetal force.

Be careful about whether you are being given the RADIUS or the DIAMETER of the circle. Make sure you use the correct value for the radius later on!

2. A carnival ride rotates in a horizontal circle with diameter 20.0 m. People sit in cars on the outside of the circle.

a. Draw a free body diagram for someone sitting on the ride while it isn't moving.

b. Draw a free body diagram for someone sitting on the ride while it is moving. Clearly mark the center of the ride on your diagram.

c. How many revolutions per minute must the ride spin with for the person in the car to experience a horizontal contact force equal to their weight?

Draw all the forces acting ON the person.

Make sure you follow the instructions exactly!

The net force is towards the center of the circle.

Draw all the forces acting ON the person. You know there will be a net centripetal force, but don't label the net force like that. Use a label like "contact force from side of car."

Be careful with units. ω is measured in radians per second.

Don't worry if you don't know the mass. When you say $mr\omega^2 = mg$, the m will divide out.

If you're asked to draw a free body diagram, never EVER label an arrow "centripetal force." The centripetal force is a net force toward the center of the circle that's provided by the forces already on your free body diagram. Oh, and some questions may ask about centripetal acceleration rather than centripetal force. You can just use Newton's 2nd Law, $F_c = ma_c$, to move between F_c and a_c.

there are no Dumb Questions

Q: How should I include the centripetal force when I'm drawing a free body diagram?

A: A free body diagram shows all of the forces acting on a single object. So far, you know about gravitational force (a non-contact force) plus a variety of contact forces - normal force, frictional force, and tension force (exerted by a rope).

Q: None of these forces are the centripetal force though. How do I include the centripetal force on my free body diagram?

A: If you have an object that's moving in a circle, you should include all the forces acting on the object in your free body diagram. When you add these forces together by lining them up nose to tail, there will be a net force on your object that makes it follow a circular path. This centripetal force (the force required to make the object follow a circular path) may be provided by a gravitational force, or a normal force, or a support force, or a tension force.

Q: Are you saying that I shouldn't draw an arrow on my free body diagram and label it centripetal force?

A: Spot on! Your free body diagram should indicate the **origin** of each force vector arrow - gravitational force, normal force, frictional force, tension force, etc.

Centripetal force is the name given to the net force on an object when the net force is making the object follow a circular path. It's not a "ghost force" that appears from nowhere on your free body diagram. So you're right - you shouldn't ever label an arrow on your free body diagram "centripetal force," as this tells you nothing about the origin of the force.

Q: What if the net force doesn't cause the object to follow a circular path?

A: Then it doesn't get called "centripetal force," as this its the term reserved for when the net force does make an object follow a circular path.

Hey ... I was just wondering if you could come and help us out back at the bobsled track?

Your free body diagram should indicate the ORIGIN of each of the force vector arrows - gravitational force, normal force, frictional force, tension force, etc.

The net force will provide the centripetal force. There shouldn't be any arrows on a free body diagram labelled 'centripetal force'.

Back to the track!

When you last checked in as the track's safety consultant, you were working out the speed the bobsled would have as it passed through various checkpoints.

But they just got a whole lot more ambitious ...

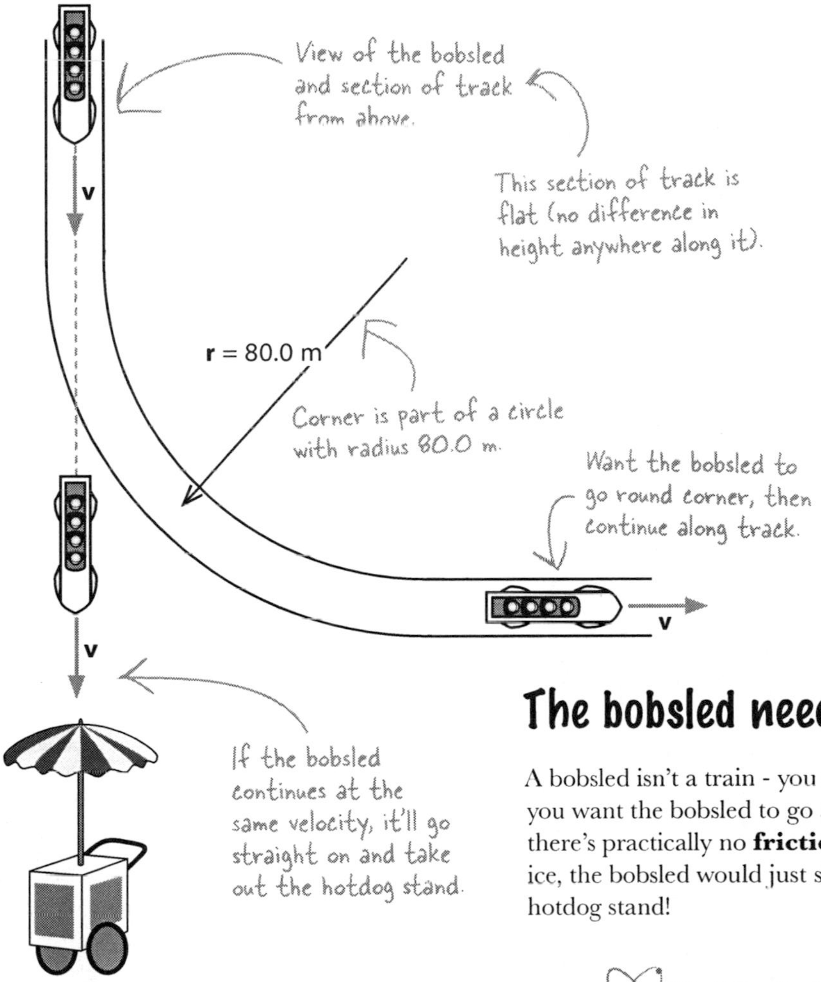

The bobsled needs to turn a corner

A bobsled isn't a train - you can't just point the track where you want the bobsled to go and expect it to follow! Since there's practically no **friction** between the bobsled and the ice, the bobsled would just slide straight on and demolish the hotdog stand!

BRAIN POWER

How might you persuade the bobsled to take the corner instead of going straight on?

Sharpen your pencil

a. The 630 kg bobsled has dropped 50.0 m from a standing start between the beginning of the track and the corner. What is its current speed?

b. The radius of the corner is 80.0 m. What size of centripetal force is required for the bobsled to be able to make it round the corner?

Hint: Think about the shape of a cycling velodrome or Indy car oval.

c. In what direction does there need to be a centripetal force to make the bobsled turn the corner?

d. How might the track be modified to provide the force the bobsled needs to make the turn? Draw force vector components to illustrate where the required force could come from if the track was modified.

Sharpen your pencil Solution

a. The 630 kg bobsled has dropped 50.0 m from a standing start between the beginning of the track and the corner. What is its current speed?

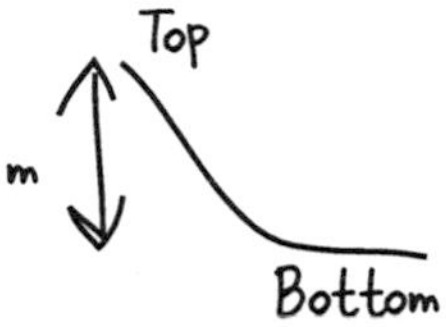

Use energy conservation

$U_{top} = K_{bottom}$

$\Rightarrow \cancel{m}gh = \frac{1}{2}\cancel{m}v^2$

$\Rightarrow v = \sqrt{2gh} = \sqrt{2 \times 9.8 \times 50.0}$

$v = 31.3$ m/s (3 sd)

No need to worry about direction as you're aked about SIZE of force.

b. The radius of the corner is 80.0 m. What size of centripetal force is required for the bobsled to be able to make it round the corner?

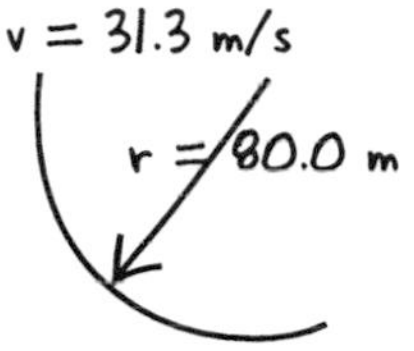

Calculate centripetal force, F_c

$F_c = mr\omega^2$

Use $v = r\omega$ to work out ω

$\Rightarrow \omega = \frac{v}{r} = \frac{31.3}{80.0} = 0.391$ rad/s

$F_c = mr\omega^2 = 630 \times 80.0 \times 0.391^2$

$F_c = 7710$ N (3 sd)

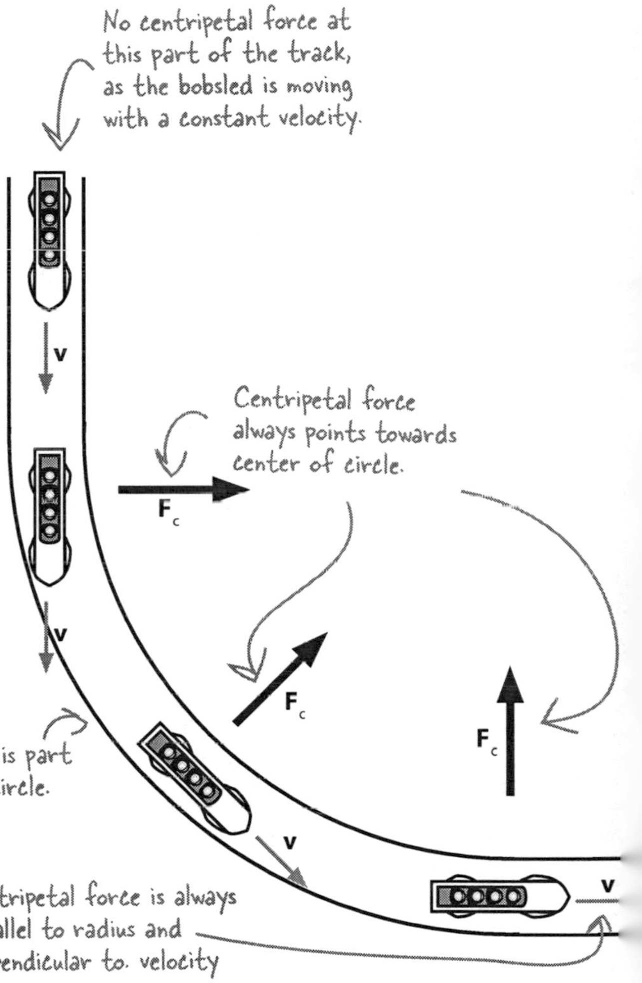

c. In what direction does there need to be a centripetal force to make the bobsled turn the corner?

There needs to be a centripetal force towards the center of the corner.

d. How might the track be modified to provide the force the bobsled needs to make the turn? Draw force vector components to illustrate where the required force could come from if the track was modified.

Banking the track towards the center of the corner to redirect the normal force might work, as there would be a component pointing towards the center of the corner.

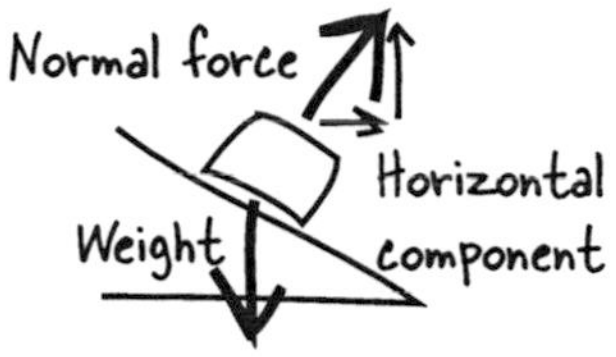

For the bobsled to go around a corner, you need a net force pointing towards the CENTER of the circle to provide a centripetal force.

Angling the track gives the normal force a horizontal component

There are two forces acting on the bobsled - its **weight** and the **normal force**. To make the bobsled turn the corner, you need to have a **net force** pointing **horizontally** towards the center of the circle, exerting a **centripetal force** on the bobsled that makes it turn.

The bobsled's weight points vertically downwards, so there's no way that any component of the weight can point horizontally. And if the track is horizontal, the normal force points verticallty upwards, with no horizontal component.

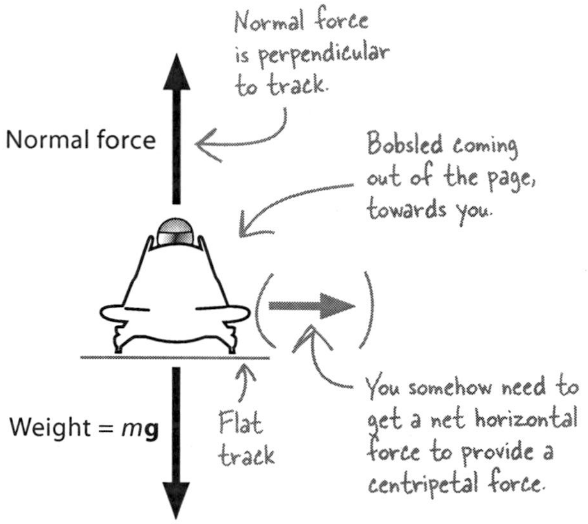

The normal force always acts **perpendicular** to the surface of the track. If the track is banked at an **angle**, towards the center of the circle, the normal force also points at an angle.

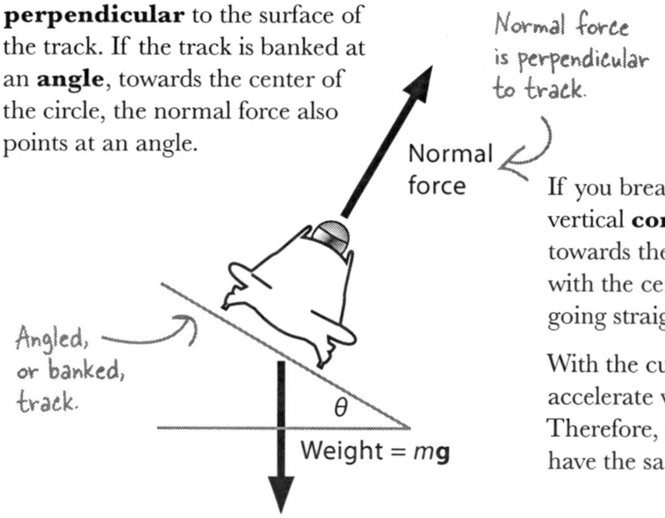

If you break the **normal force** down into horizontal and vertical **components**, the horizontal component points towards the **center** of the curve. This can provide the bobsled with the centripetal force it needs to take the corner instead of going straight on.

With the curve banked at the correct angle, the bobsled won't accelerate vertically and the net vertical force must be zero. Therefore, the vertical component of the normal force must have the same size as the bobsled's weight.

The normal force always acts PERPENDICULAR to a surface.

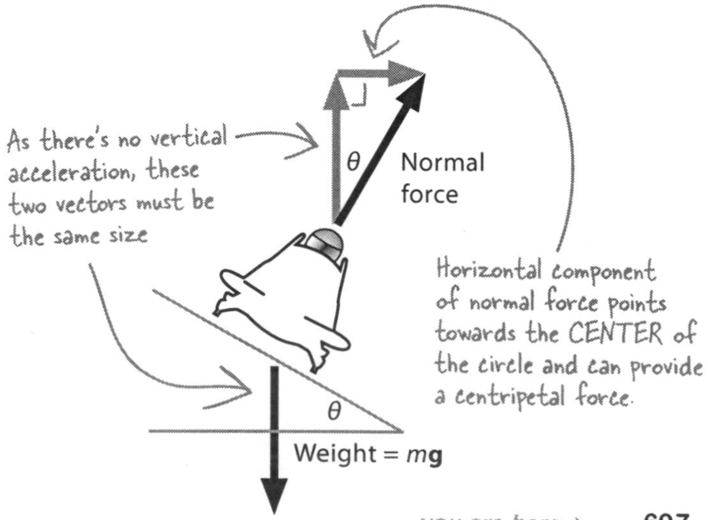

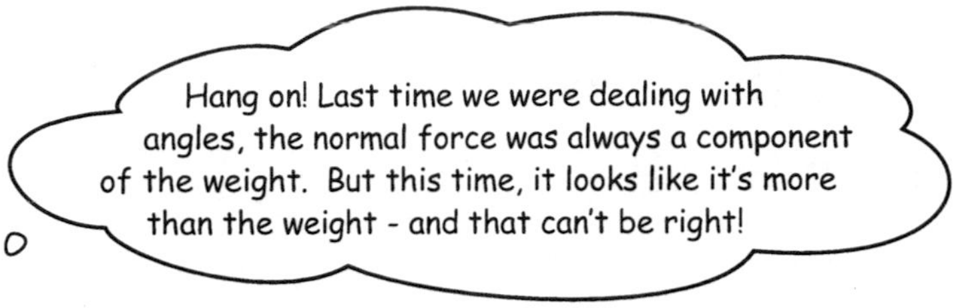

When you slide downhill, there's no perpendicular acceleration

The NET FORCE acts PARALLEL to the slope.

When an object slides down a slope, it accelerates parallel to the slope, **but doesn't accelerate perpendicular to the slope**. This means that the components of the forces perpendicular to the slope must add up to zero.

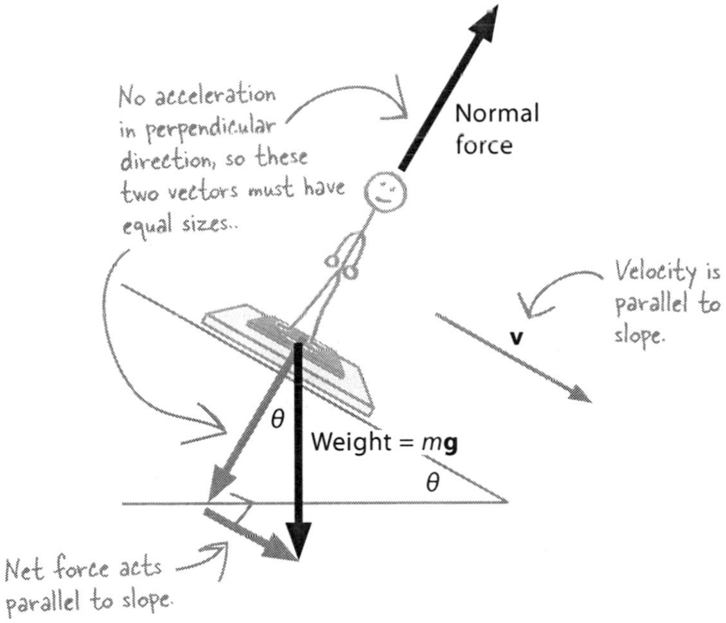

The only two forces with components perpendicular to the slope are the **weight** and the **normal force**. Therefore, the components of the weight and normal force, which are perpendicular to the slope, must add up to zero so that **the net force is parallel** to the slope.

When you turn a corner, there's no vertical acceleration

The NET FORCE acts HORIZONTALLY.

For the bobsled to go round the corner, there must be a net horizontal force acting on it to provide the centripetal force it requires.

This means that the bobsled **doesn't accelerate vertically**, only horizontally. So the vertical components of the forces acting on the bobsled must add up to zero.

The bobsled doesn't float in the air, or go down into the ground. We don't want it to slide UP or DOWN the banking either.

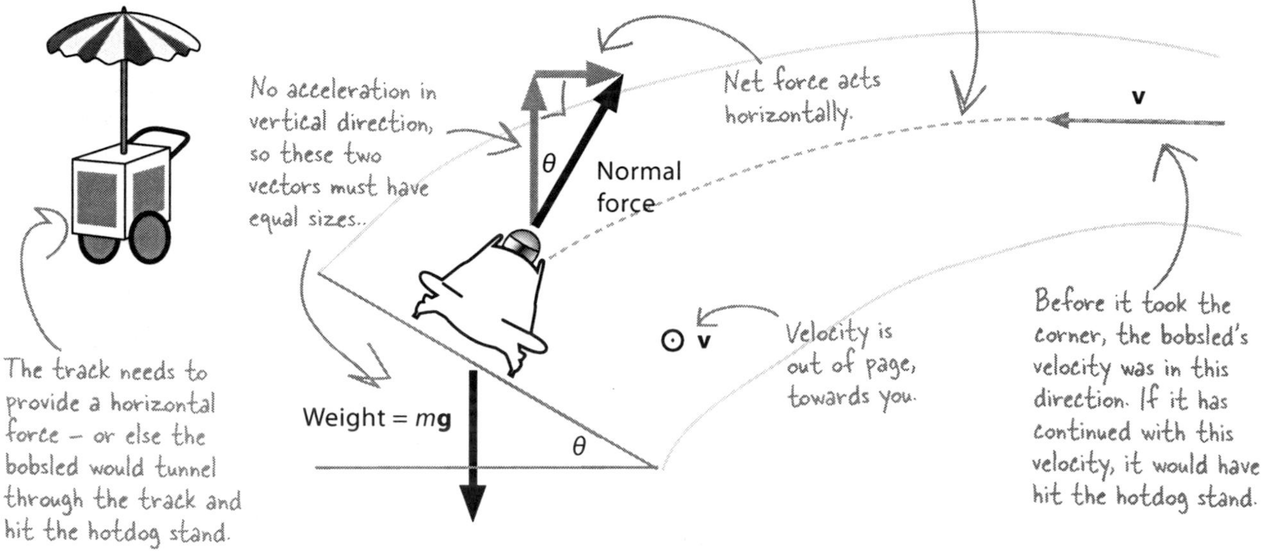

There's no acceleration in the direction 90° to the net force. So the forces in that direction must add to zero.

The only two forces with vertical components are the bobsled's **weight** and the **normal force**. Therefore, the vertical component of the normal force and the weight must add to zero so that **the net force is the horizontal centripetal force** the bobsled requires to take the corner.

Not only does the track have to support the bobsled's weight, it also has to prevent the bobsled from tunneling horizontally through the track, and into the hotdog stand. This is why the normal force has a horizontal component. The horizontal centripetal force is provided by the horizontal component of the normal force.

Because the normal force is doing these two jobs (supporting the bobsled's weight and preventing it from tunneling through the track), the size of the normal force must be larger than the size of the bobsled's weight.

How to deal with an object on a slope

1. Start with a free body diagram

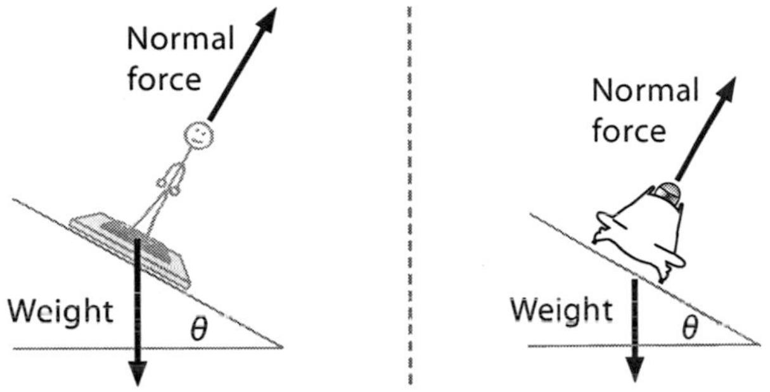

2. Work out the direction of the net force.

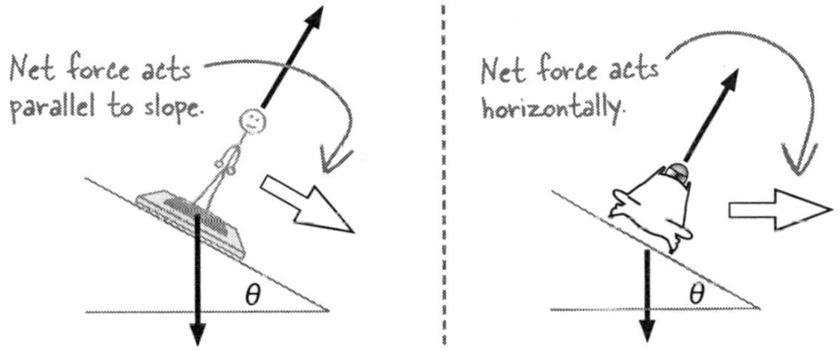

3. Draw in components parallel and perpendicular to the net force.

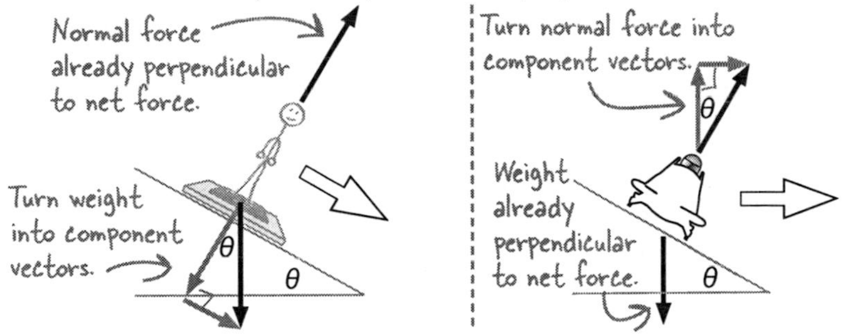

4. The components perpendicular to the net force must add to zero.

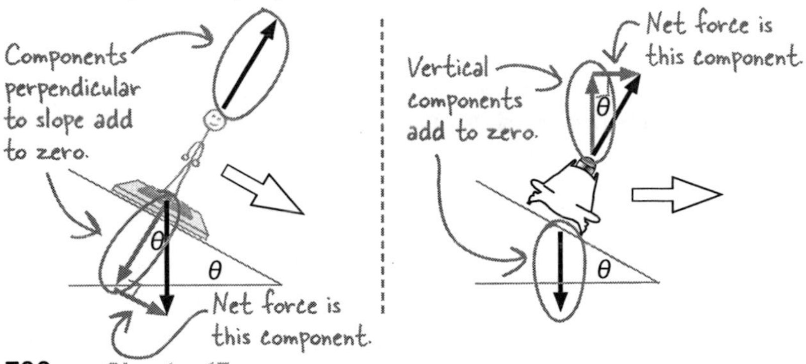

there are no Dumb Questions

Q: How can I work out which force components add to zero when an object is on a slope?

A: First of all, work out the direction of the net force. This is the direction that the object accelerates in. Then draw in components of forces parallel and perpendicular to the net force. The components perpendicular to the net force must add to zero.

Q: How can the normal force from a track be larger than an object's weight?

A: This can happen if the track is banked so that the object can take a corner. As well as providing a vertical force to support the object's weight, the track also needs to provide a horizontal force to stop the object from tunneling straight on through the track. So the total normal force - the normal force that the track exerts on the object - will have a vertical 'weight support' component and a horizontal 'anti-tunneling' component.

Q: How do you know the net force is horizontal for an object taking a corner?

A: The net horizontal force provides the centripetal acceleration **required** for the object to take the corner.

Start off with a free body diagram and work out which components ADD TO ZERO before you draw in the components.

Sharpen your pencil

You already worked this out earlier on.

A 630 kg bobsled traveling at 31.3 m/s requires a horizontal centripetal force of 7710 N to make it go around a corner with a radius of 80.0 m at a constant speed. You can provide the centripetal force by banking the track.

a. Draw a free body diagram of the bobsled taking the corner on an angled track, showing all the forces acting on it.

b. What is the weight of the bobsled?

c. What do the horizontal and vertical components of the normal force need to be for the bobsled to go around the corner without sliding up or down the banking?

d. What angle should the track make with the horizontal to achieve this?

Sharpen your pencil Solution

A 630 kg bobsled traveling at 31.3 m/s requires a horizontal centripetal force of 7710 N to make it go around a corner with a radius of 80.0 m at a constant speed. You can provide the centripetal force by banking the track.

a. Draw a free body diagram of the bobsled taking the corner on an angled track, showing all the forces acting on it.

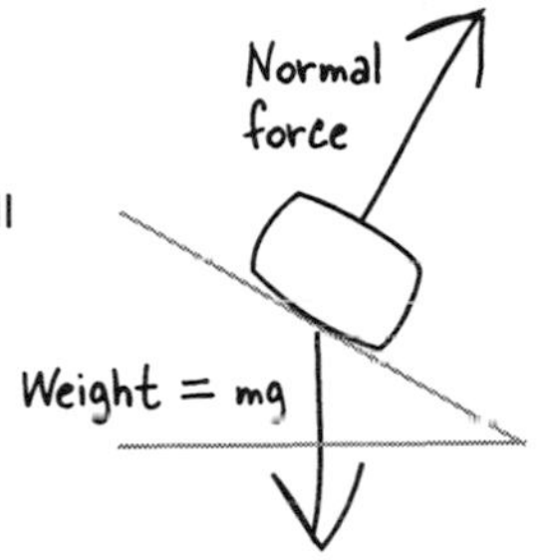

b. What is the weight of the bobsled?

Weight = mg

Weight = 630 × 9.8

Weight = 6180 N (3 sd)

c. What do the horizontal and vertical components of the normal force need to be for the bobsled to go around the corner without sliding up or down the banking?

Horizontal component = 7710 N (provides centripetal force)

Vertical component = 6180 N (must be same size as weight – no acceleration in vertical direction)

d. What angle should the track make with the horizontal to achieve this?

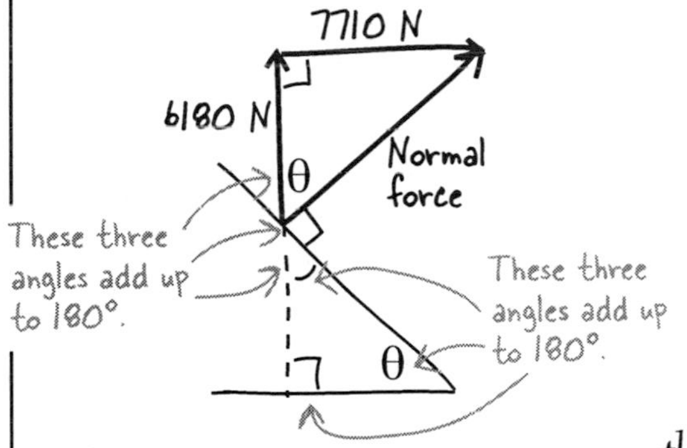

Banking angle of track:

$$\tan\theta = \frac{o}{a} = \frac{7710}{6180} = 1.25 \text{ (3 sd)}$$

$$\Rightarrow \theta = \tan^{-1}(1.25) = 51.3° \text{ (3 sd)}$$

See page 562 of chapter 14 for help with setting up triangles like this.

there are no Dumb Questions

Q: So - what if the bobsled was going faster or slower? Would the banking angle need to be different?

A: You originally worked out the **required** centripetal force using the bobsled's velocity and the radius of the curve. If the bobsled was going faster or slower, it would require more or less centripetal force.

Q: If the bobsled has a lower mass, will it require a smaller centripetal force?

A: Yes, that's right. But as the bobsled's weight is less, the normal force will also be less, and the banking angle will work out the same. The banking angle doesn't depend on the bobsled's mass - only on the bobsled's speed and the radius of the corner.

Q: So could the bobsled just go round and round forever if I closed off the curve to make a circle?

A: If there was no friction, then it could, but there's always some friction somewhere to transfer kinetic energy to internal energy. So it couldn't keep on going forever.

Banking the track works ...

Banking the track at 51.3° like you calculated does the trick! The hotdog stand is saved, and everyone at the bobsled track is happy. Though they've just come up with something even more ambitious ...

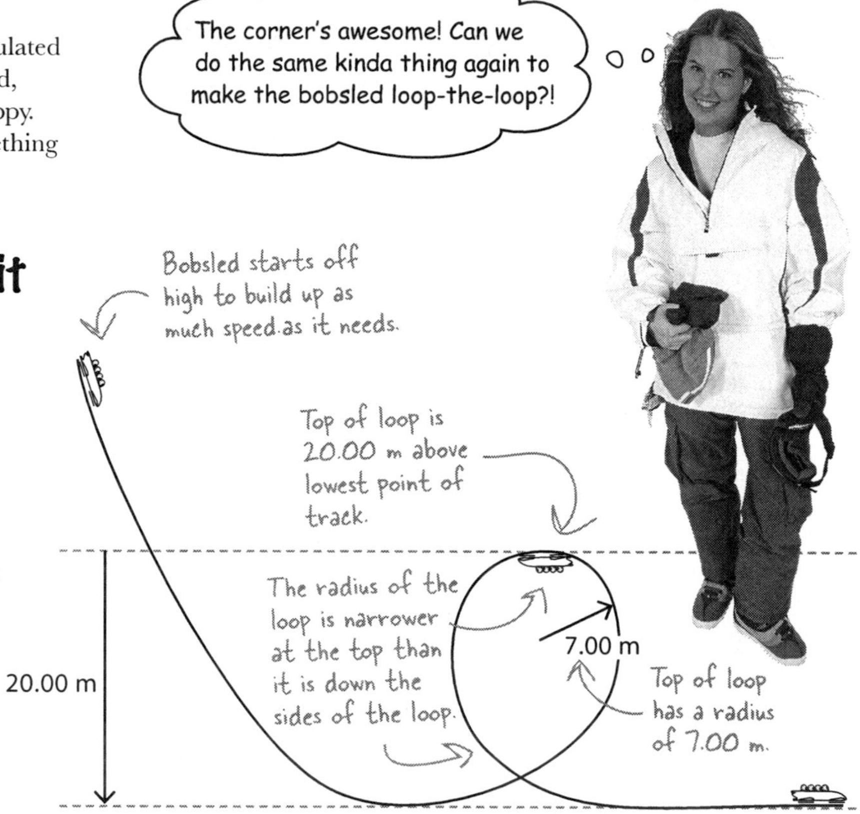

... but now they want it to loop-the-loop!

Inspired by the success of your corner, you've just been asked if you can make the bobsled loop-the-loop at the end of the track!

As the bobsled is traveling in a circle (just like it was for the corner), the track designers are confident that you can make it work ...

Try it!

Are horizontal and vertical circles the same? Try it! Tie an object to the end of a piece of string, and swing it **as slowly as possible** in horizontal and vertical circles. Feel what happens to the **tension** in the string as the tension provides a centripetal force.

How does the tension in the string vary at different points as you swing the object in horizontal and vertical circles? Do you need to pull harder or more gently when the object's at the top or bottom of the circle?

The "support force" (normal force or tension force) required for a vertical circle varies

For an object moving in a **horizontal circle**, the tension in the string provides the centripetal acceleration to keep the object moving. If the object moves at a constant speed, the **tension remains constant.**

This is the same as for the horizontal corner. The banking angle was the same all the way round, providing the same horizontal component of the normal force all the way round.

For a **vertical circle**, the tension in the string is less at the top of the circle than it is at the bottom - as long as the speed of the object remains the same throughout.

At the **top of the circle**, the force of the object's weight points towards the center of the circle, and can provide much of the centripetal force that the object needs to move in a circle (as long as the object's going at an appropriate speed). If the object's going faster than the minimum speed, the centripetal force will be provided by weight + tension in the string.

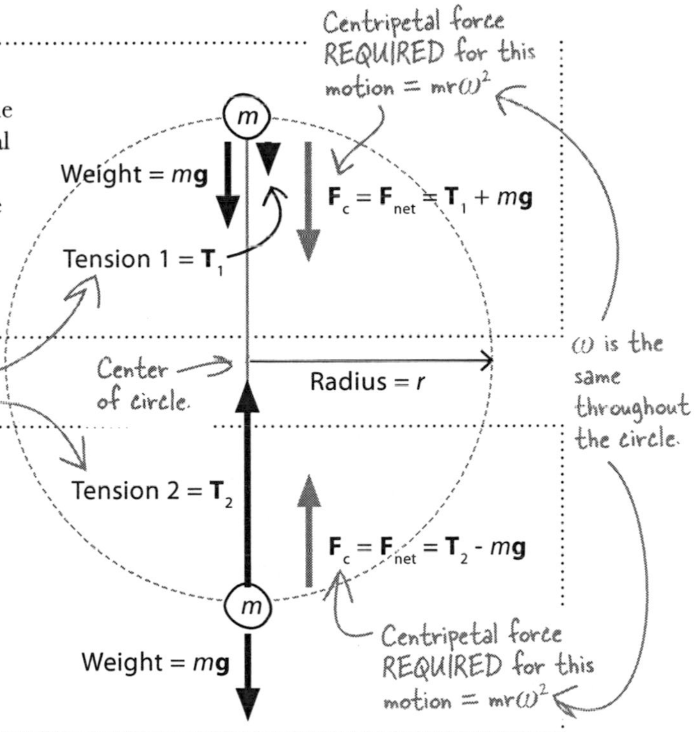

At the **bottom of the circle**, the object's weight points directly away from the center of the circle, so the centripetal force must all be provided by the tension in the string.

As the object's weight is pointing away from the center of the circle, the tension in the string must be equal to the weight + the required centripetal force.

You might have observed the object on the string kind-of "falling over the top" as you swung it slowly.

You might have noticed the object on the string "pulling against you" when it swung round the bottom of the circle.

At the top of the circle, the object's WEIGHT is able to provide some of the centripetal force, as the weight vector points towards the CENTER of the circle.

I don't agree. Surely there's more force at the top - because gravity's adding to the centripetal force from the string?

Centripetal force is required for circular motion and provided by existing forces

At the top of the circle, the object has a horizontal velocity. Without the string, the object would follow a curved path anyway (just not a circular one).

You mustn't think of centripetal force as a 'ghost force' that appears from nowhere when an object moves in a circle. Circular motion is only possible if a force capable of providing the centripetal force is **already present**.

At the top of the circle, the centripetal force can actually be entirely provided by the gravitational force, as it points towards the center of the circle. At the minimum speed for circular motion, the gravitational force, $m\mathbf{g}$, will **provide** all of the **required** centripetal force, so will be **equal** in size to $mr\omega^2$.

This exercise lets you get the hang of dealing with vertical circles before you tackle the bobsled track.

Exercise

You want to swing a bucket of water, mass *m*, in a vertical circle at a constant speed, *v*.

a. Write down an equation that relates the mass of the bucket, the length of your arm and the size of the required centripetal force.

b. If your arm has length *r*, what's the minimum speed, *v*, you need to swing it at so that you don't get wet when the bucket passes over your head?

At the minimum speed, the centripetal force is provided entirely by the gravitational force.

c. In terms of *m* and **g**, what force does the base of the bucket exert on the water at the top of the circle?

d. In terms of *m* and **g**, what force does the base of the bucket exert on the water at the bottom of the circle if you swing it at the same velocity round the whole circle?

Your arm exerts a force on the bucket – and the base of the bucket transmits that force to the water.

Draw a free body diagram to work each of these out! Look at the ones on the opposite page to help you.

You want to swing a bucket of water, mass *m*, in a vertical circle at a constant speed, *v*.

a. Write down an equation that relates the mass of the bucket, the length of your arm and the size of the required centripetal force.

$$F_c = mr\omega^2$$

m is mass of bucket.
r is length of arm.
ω is angular velocity.

b. If your arm has length r, what's the minimum speed, *v*, you need to swing it at so that you don't get wet when the bucket passes over your head?

$$F_c = mr\omega^2$$

$$v = r\omega \Rightarrow \omega = \frac{v}{r}$$

$$F_c = \frac{mv^2}{r}$$

Minimum force = $mg = F_c$

$$\Rightarrow mg = \frac{mv^2}{r}$$

$$v^2 = gr$$

$$v = \sqrt{gr}$$

c. In terms of *m* and **g**, what force does the base of the bucket exert on the water at the top of the circle?

Tension of force of string on bucket transmitted to water by base of bucket.

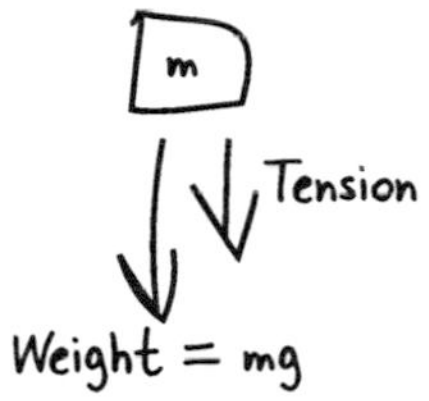

But net force is $F_c = mg$.
So tension = 0.

Force exerted by base of bucket on water = 0

d. In terms of *m* and **g**, what force does the base of the bucket exert on the water at the bottom of the circle if you swing it at the same velocity round the whole circle?

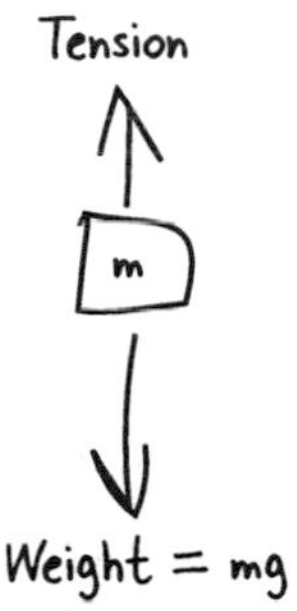

Continues at same speed, so $F_c = mg$ as centripetal force same for same speed.

F_c is net force, so Tension + Weight must be equal to F_c

Up positive direction: $T - mg = F_c$

But $F_c = mg \Rightarrow T - mg = mg$
make substitution

$$T = 2\,mg$$

Your free body diagram is key

When you draw a free body diagram, take special note of the forces pointing towards the **center** of the circle. These have the potential to contribute towards a net centripetal force that makes an object follow a circular path.

For the bobsled, the normal force from the track will point towards the center of the circle.

Any force that acts towards the center of the circle can provide a centripetal force

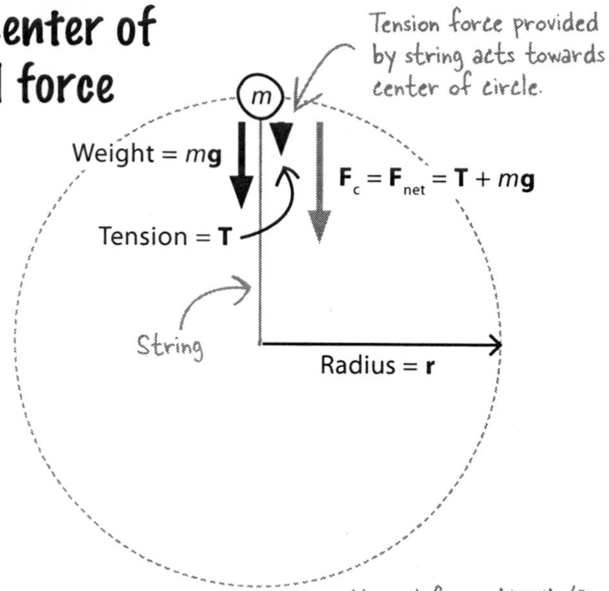

For an object on a string at the top of a circle, there are two forces that can point towards the center of the circle and, therefore, contribute towards a net centripetal force in that direction. One is the **tension** force from the string, and the other is the **gravitational** force - the object's **weight**.

The tension force + the component of the gravitational force that points towards the center of the circle will always add up the centripetal force required to move the object at that speed around a circle with that radius.

The components of all the forces that point towards the center of the circle must add up to the centripetal force.

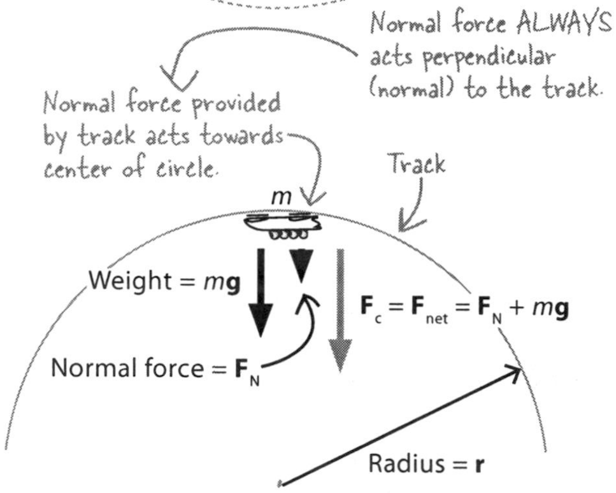

Think of the normal force provided by the track as an "anti-tunneling" force that stops the bobsled from tunneling through the track.

The bobsled's free body diagram is nearly identical to the object on the string, except that it's the **normal force** from the (circular) track that points towards the center of the circle instead of a tension force.

You can think of the normal force as an "anti tunneling" force. If the bobsled is going upwards with a high speed and the track is soft and can't provide enough normal force, the bobsled will tunnel into - and probably through - the track. The normal force provided by a solid track prevents the bobsled from tunneling, and provides some of the centripetal force that the bobsled requires to follow a circular path.

there are no Dumb Questions

Q: So how can the gravitational force provide a centripetal force?! Surely if that was happening, the bobsled would just fall straight down, off the track.

A: To make it around the loop, the bobsled must already be traveling very fast horizontally when it gets to the top of the circle. So it couldn't possibly fall straight down - even if the track wasn't there, it would move through the air like a projectile.

Q: But what if the bobsled wasn't going fast enough at the top of the loop?

A: Then there wouldn't be enough centripetal force to keep the bobsled on the track - it would curve down towards the ground faster than the curve of the track, and fall off the track.

Q: How do I know if the bobsled's going fast enough or not?

A: The size of the centripetal force is given by the equation $F_c = mr\omega^2$, which can also be written $F_c = \frac{mv^2}{r}$ by making a substitution using the equation $v = r\omega$.

The faster the bobsled's going, the larger the centripetal force required to make it travel in a circle with radius *t*.

Q: Doesn't that equation give you the value of the centripetal force?

A: Not quite. The equation gives you the value of the centripetal force that is **required** for the bobsled to move in that way. If the net force on the free body diagram isn't large enough, then the bobsled won't get round the loop safely.

Q: What else might the centripetal force be provided by, apart from gravity?

A: The normal force from the track always points perpendicular to the track. So when the bobsled is upside-down, the normal force points down.

Think of the normal force as an "anti-burrowing" force that prevents the bobsled from burrowing through the track if it's going really fast.

Q: How can I work out whether the track is safe or not?

A: Your job is to calculate the minimum speed that the bobsled needs to be going at to get around the loop safely. Which we're just getting on to now ...

The required centripetal force depends on the radius and speed.

How fast does the bobsled need to go?

Your job is to calculate the minimum speed that the bobsled needs to be going at to make it around the 7.00 m radius loop.

At the top of the circle, the bobsled's **weight** points towards the center and can provide all the centripetal force the bobsled needs to go in a circle - as long as it's going at just the right speed.

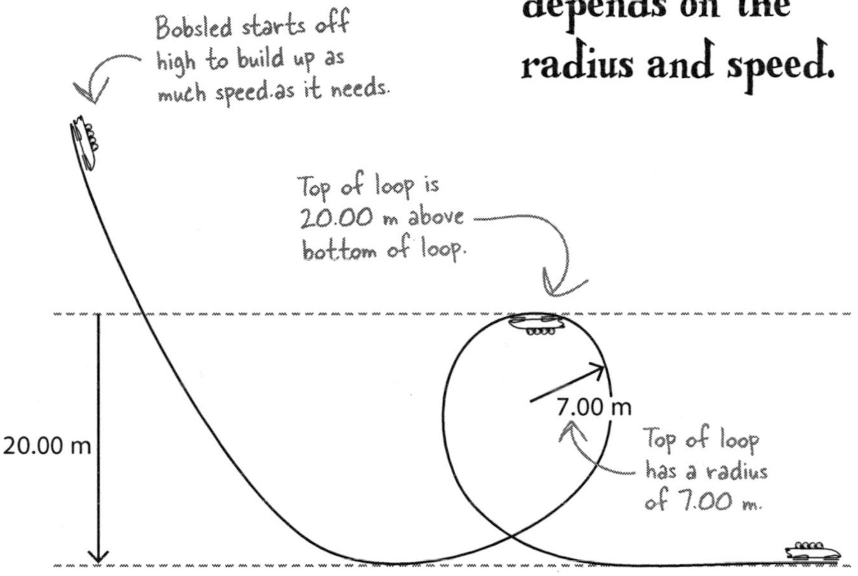

Sharpen your pencil

Hint: You have various differences in height here...

A 630 kg bobsled is to do a loop-the-loop. The loop has a 7.00 m radius at its top, which is 20.00 m higher than the bottom of the loop. The bobsled can start as high as you want it to above the bottom of the loop.

a. What is the minimum speed the bobsled needs to have at the top of the loop in order to make it around the loop successfully?

b. What speed does the bobsled need to have when it enters bottom of the loop in order to achieve this?

c. What is the minimum height the bobsled needs to start at to achieve these speeds?

d. Now assume that the bobsled is traveling at 10.0 m/s at the top of the loop (instead of the speed you calculated in part a). How large is the normal force that the track exerts on it?

The normal force is like an "anti-tunneling" force that provides a centripetal force and makes the bobsled follow the track instead of tunneling straight through the track.

Sharpen your pencil Solution

A 630 kg bobsled is to do a loop-the-loop. The loop has a 7.00 m radius at its top, which is 20.00 m higher than the bottom of the loop. The bobsled can start as high as you want it to above the bottom of the loop.

a. What is the minimum speed the bobsled needs to have at the top of the loop in order to make it around the loop successfully?

At minimum speed, all of F_c provided by weight.

$$F_c = mr\omega^2$$

$$v = r\omega \Rightarrow \omega = \frac{v}{r}$$

$$F_c = \frac{mv^2}{r}$$

$$F_c = \frac{mv^2}{r}$$

$$\Rightarrow \cancel{m}g = \frac{\cancel{m}v^2}{r}$$

$$v^2 = gr$$

$$v = \sqrt{gr} = \sqrt{9.8 \times 7.00} = \underline{\underline{8.28\ \text{m/s}}}\ (3\ \text{sd})$$

b. What speed does the bobsled need to have when it enters bottom of the loop in order to achieve this?

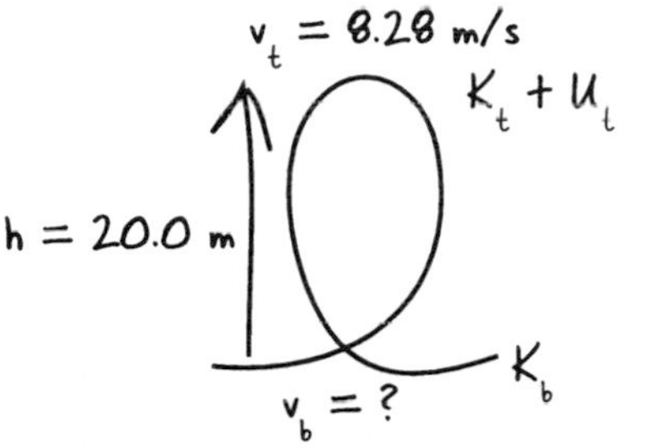

Energy conservation:

$$K_b = K_t + U_t$$

$$\tfrac{1}{2}\cancel{m}v_b^2 = \tfrac{1}{2}\cancel{m}v_t^2 + \cancel{m}gh$$

$$v_b^2 = v_t^2 + 2gh$$

$$v_b = \sqrt{v_t^2 + 2gh} = \sqrt{8.28^2 + 2 \times 9.8 \times 20.00} = \underline{\underline{21.5\ \text{m/s}}}\ (3\ \text{sd})$$

We've used the subscripts 't' and 'b' to mean 'top' and 'bottom' of the loop.

c. What is the minimum height the bobsled needs to start at to achieve these speeds?

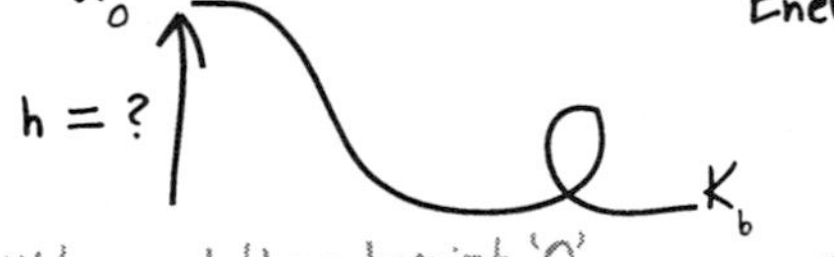

We've used the subscript 'O' to mean the initial conditions atthe start of the track.

Energy conservation:

$$U_0 = K_b$$

$$\cancel{m}gh = \tfrac{1}{2}\cancel{m}v_b^2$$

$$h = \frac{\tfrac{1}{2}v_b^2}{g} = \frac{0.5 \times 21.5^2}{9.8} = \underline{\underline{23.6\ \text{m}}}\ (3\ \text{sd})$$

d. Now assume that the bobsled is traveling at 10.0 m/s at the top of the loop (instead of the speed you calculated in part a). How large is the normal force that the track exerts on it?

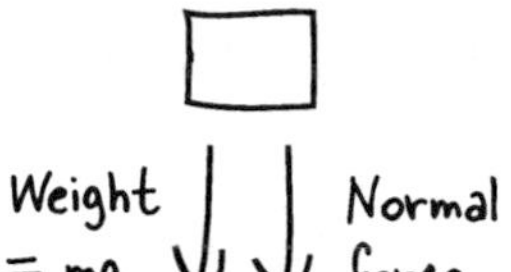

$$F_c = \frac{mv^2}{r} = \frac{630 \times 10^2}{7.00} = 9000\ \text{N}\ (3\ \text{sd})$$

$$F_c = \text{weight} + \text{normal force} = mg + F_N$$

$$F_N = F_c - mg = 9000 - 630 \times 9.8 = \underline{\underline{2830\ \text{N}}}\ (3\ \text{sd})$$

Normal force stops bobsled burrowing on upwards.

Question Clinic: The "Banked curve" Question

The banked curve question tests your understanding of forces, free body diagrams, components, Newton's laws, circles, and trigonometry - all in all, a good and varied workout! Usually, you'll need to calculate the centripetal force required in order for the object to make it around the curve, then make this equal to the net force that points towards the center of the circle, which comes from the horizontal component of the normal force.

Keep the mass as 'm' for the moment, to avoid numerical errors. It'll divide out later on, when you equate the centripetal force to the horizontal component of the normal force.

These figures give you the information you need to calculate the centripetal force, $F_c = mr\omega^2$

3. A 630 kg bobsled traveling at 31.3 m/s needs to go around a corner with a radius of 80.0 m at a constant speed.

a. What size and direction of centripetal force is required for the bobsled to be able to make it round the corner?

b. You can provide the required centripetal force by banking the track. Explain, using a diagram, why this is the case.

c. What angle should the track make with the horizontal to provide the centripetal force that is required?

Don't forget to say that the direction is horizontal, towards the center of the circle that the bend forms part of.

This means draw a free body diagram and show that the vertical components of the forces add to zero, leaving a net horizontal force that can provide the centripetal force.

Some questions may be about centripetal acceleration instead of centripetal force. Use Newton's 2nd Law, $F = ma$ to move between these two things.

Make sure you calculate the correct angle! Spot similar triangles then think to see if your answer SUCKs.

Any time you're dealing with a slope, start with a free body diagram and work out which direction there's no acceleration in. Then resolve your force vectors into components parallel and perpendicular to this direction. In the banked curve question, there's no acceleration in the vertical direction - which helps you to see that it's the horizontal component that you need to make equal to the centripetal force.

Question Clinic: The "Vertical circle" Question

The vertical circle question can lead to a lot of confusion about what forces are in play and the direction that they point in. The **normal force** is always **perpendicular** to the surface - even if something's upside-down! And the force of something's weight always points downwards. The vertical circle also involves a change in **height** - so be on the lookout for places you can use **energy conservation.**

The mass will divide out when you make the centripetal force equal the net force on your free body diagram.

Difference in height – think potential energy!

This is the value of radius you'll need to use for calculating the required centripetal force.

2. A 630 kg bobsled is to do a loop-the-loop. The loop has a 7.00 m radius at its top, which is 20.00 m higher than the bottom of the loop.

a. What is the minimum speed the bobsled needs to have at the top in order to make it around the loop successfully?

b. How fast does the bobsled need to be going when it enters the bottom of the loop in order to achieve this?

c. What is the minimum height the bobsled needs to start at to achieve these speeds?

d. Now assume that the bobsled is traveling at 10.0 m/s at the top of the loop (instead of the speed you calculated in part a). How large is the normal force that the track exerts on it?

This is when all the centripetal force is provided by the bobsled's weight.

This involves energy conservation.

You need to redo everything as the required centripetal acceleration for this speed will be greater. Part will come from its weight, and part from a normal force exerted by the track.

Always, always, always start with a **free body diagram**! Mark on the real **forces**, and work out which of them contribute towards the **centripetal** force. The **minimum speed** for a successful loop-the-loop is shorthand for saying that the object's **weight** provides all the centripetal force when the thing is upside-down. If it's going faster than that, then some of the centripetal force will be provided by the **normal force** from the track.

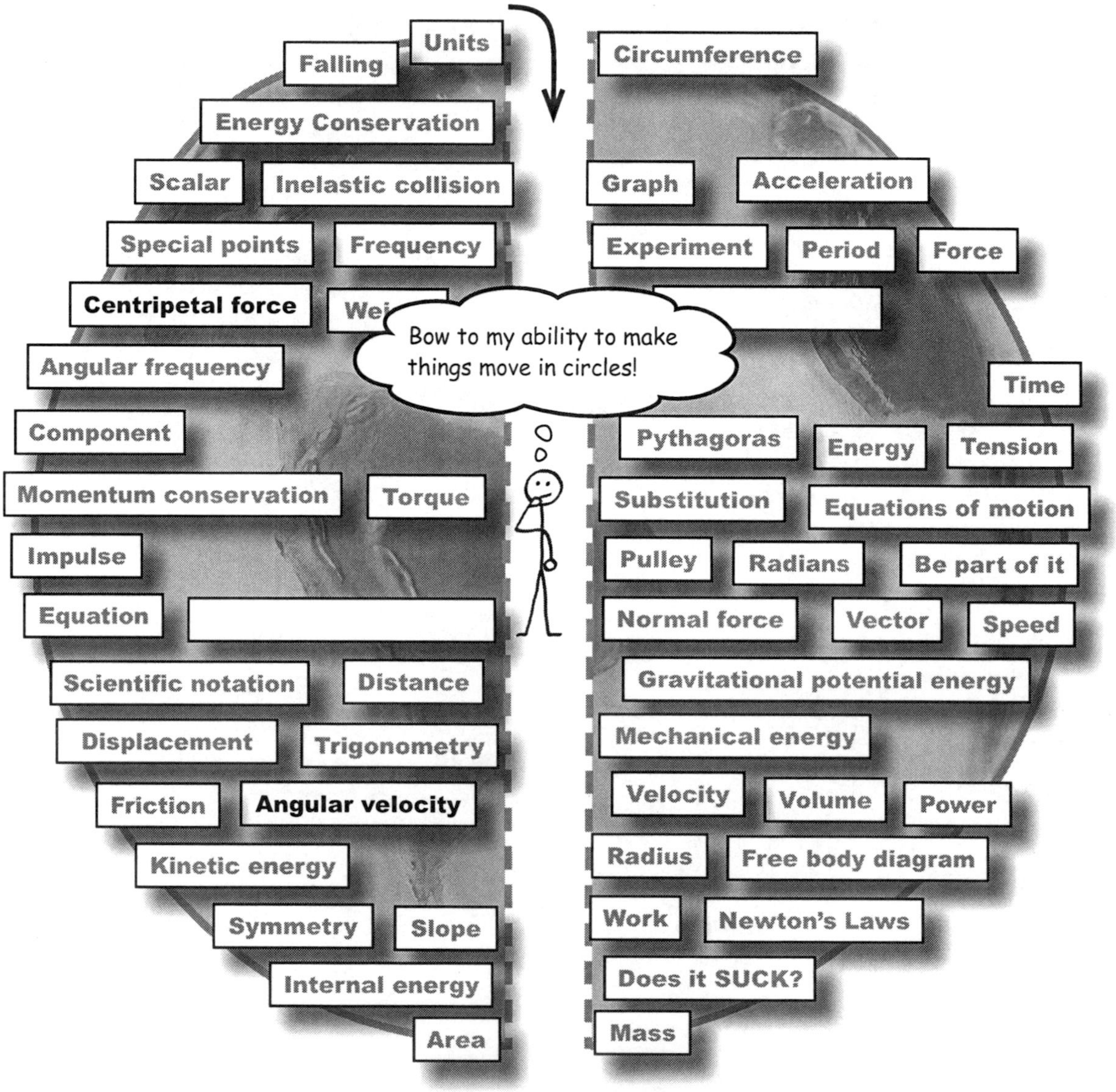

☑	**Centripetal force**	**The net force required to make an object travel along a circular path. Always points towards the center of the circle. Size given by $F_c = mr\omega^2$**
☑	**Angular velocity**	**The size of the angular velocity is exactly the same as the angular frequency or angular speed.**

Your Physics Toolbox

You've got Chapter 17 under your belt and added some terminology and problem-solving skills to your tool box.

Freefall

Something is said to be in freefall when the only force acting on it is its weight.

Examples of objects in freefall are a parachute jumper (if there's no air resistance) and an object orbiting the Earth.

"What's pushing me?"

This is the question you need to ask yourself in order to spot the contact forces that are present.

Shut your eyes and think "What's pushing me?"

You can't experience a non-contact force (such as your weight) in this way.

Volumes and areas

If you have a 3D shape, try to unfold it into 2D shapes you know how to deal with.

Area of circle = πr^2

For a 3D volume with straight sides and the same shape of flat base and top:

Volume = area of base × height

~~Centrifugal force~~

Don't talk about this. Naughty!!

Centripetal force

The force required to move an object round a curved path.

A greater centripetal force is required for a higher speed or a larger radius.

Equation: $F_c = mr\omega^2$

with $v = r\omega$.

Solving problems that involve a slope

Start with a free body diagram

Work out the direction of the net force (the direction that the object accelerates in).

Draw on components parallel and perpendicular to the net force.

The components perpendicular to the net force must add up to zero.

Solving centripetal force problems

Start with a free body diagram

The centripetal force doesn't appear from nowhere – it's the NET FORCE on your free body diagram and it acts towards the CENTER of the circle.

18 gravitation and orbits

Getting away from it all

So far, you've been up close and personal with gravity - but what happens to the attraction as your feet leave the ground? In this chapter, you'll learn that gravitation is an **inverse square law**, and harness the power of **gravitational potential** to take a trip to **infinity**... and beyond. Closer to home, you'll learn how to deal with **orbits** - and learn how they can revolutionize your communication skills.

Party planners, a big event, and lots of cheese

The local party planner is in need of your help. They're catering a big event, and the centerpiece is a huge, innovative globe of cheese.

But there's more... the planner has sent over instructions.

The notes include a cross-section of the cheese globe.

Once-in-a-lifetime cheese globe

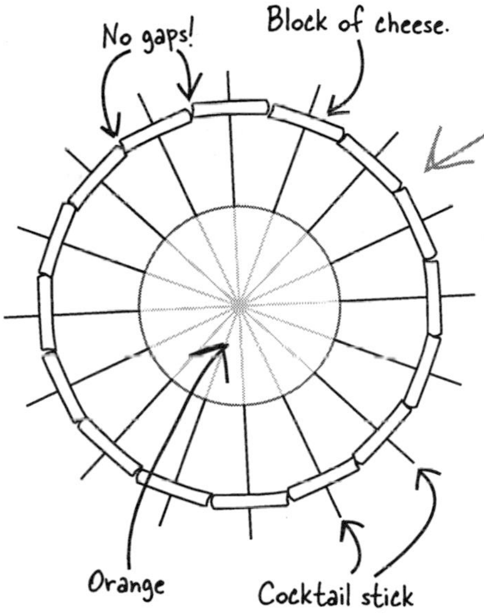

The center of the cheese globe is an orange.

Cocktail sticks are inserted into the center of the orange, and radiate outwards. At the outer ends of the sticks are blocks of cheese, all around the outside of the globe. The cheese forms a "shell" around the orange.

Cheese blocks must be 2.0 cm by 2.0 cm x 0.50 cm, with the square face outwards. Each cheese globe should have 500 blocks.

Each stick should protrude by 2.0 cm from the end of the cheese block, so party-goers can easily remove a block from the cheese globe.

THERE MUST BE NO GAPS VISIBLE BETWEEN THE BLOCKS OF CHEESE. THIS IS CRUCIAL!

Assume you've got a machine that can put the sticks in the orange at regular intervals.

Assume you've got a machine to insert sticks into cheese blocks easily.

The party planner already has a machine that will put cheese blocks onto cocktail sticks with 2.0 cm sticking out at the end. The machine is also able to put all 500 cocktail sticks into the center of the orange so that they're evenly spaced. You don't need to worry about how to do any of that.

What length should the cocktail sticks be?

Your job is to calculate the **length** that the cocktail sticks should be.

If the sticks are **too short**, there won't be space for you to fit on all 500 pieces of cheese, as the sticks won't spread out enough for the pieces of cheese to fit on next to each other.

But if the sticks are **too long**, they'll spread out too much and there'll be gaps in between the pieces of cheese.

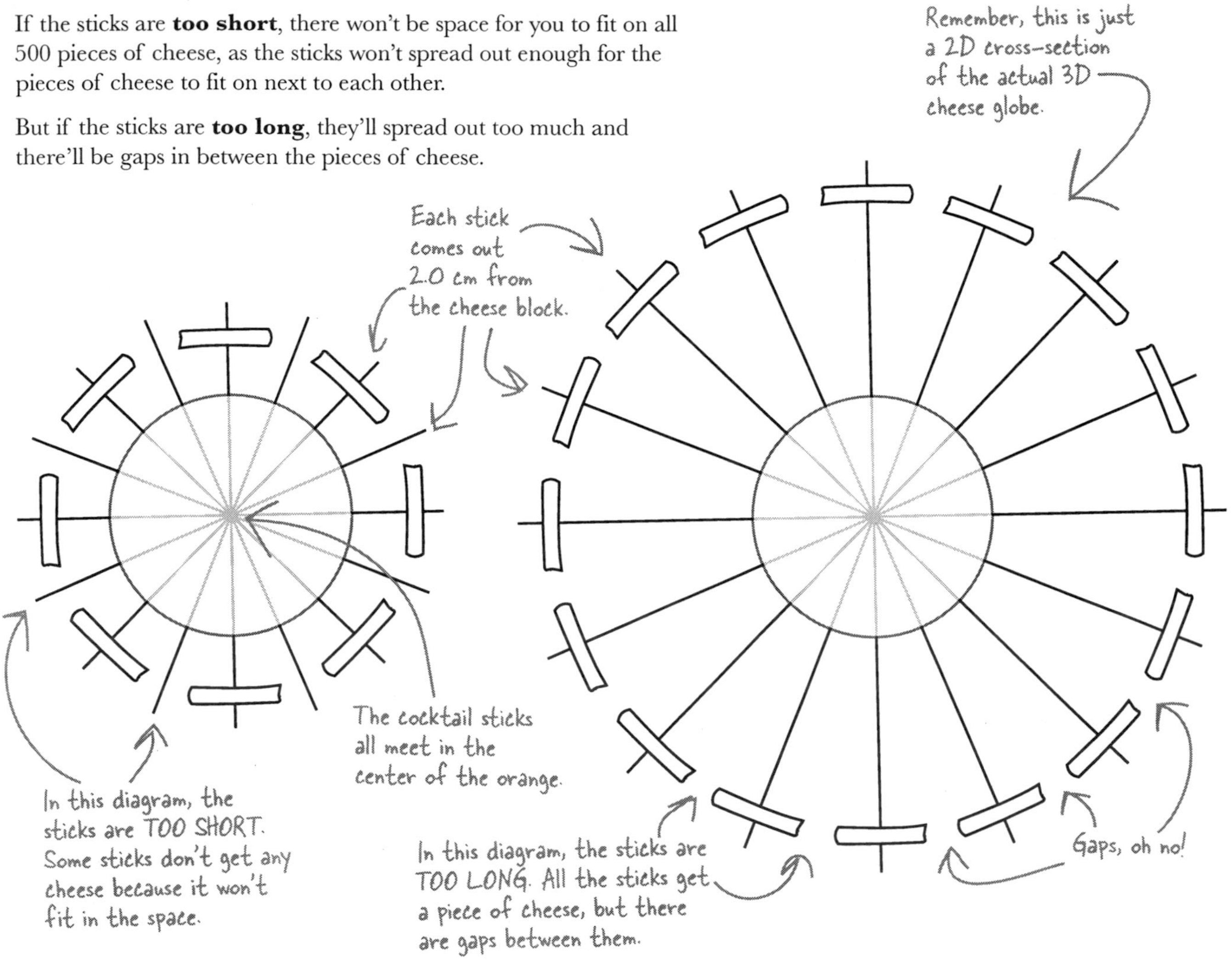

BRAIN POWER

What properties of the cheese blocks might be important when it comes to working out the length that the cocktail sticks should be?

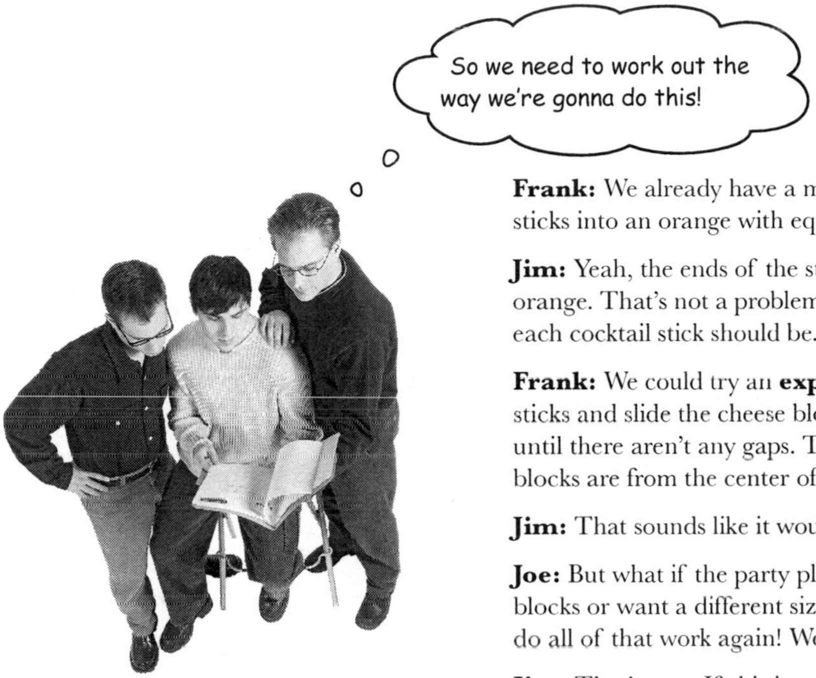

Frank: We already have a machine that can slam 500 cocktail sticks into an orange with equal spacing? Cool or what!

Jim: Yeah, the ends of the sticks all meet in the **center** of the orange. That's not a problem. But we don't know the **length** that each cocktail stick should be.

Frank: We could try an **experiment** - y'know, use really long sticks and slide the cheese blocks up and down the sticks by hand until there aren't any gaps. Then we could measure how far the blocks are from the center of the orange.

Jim: That sounds like it would work, sure.

Joe: But what if the party planners change the number of cheese blocks or want a different size of block in the future? We'd have to do all of that work again! We need to future-proof our solution.

Jim: That's true. If this is a success, the planners will want to milk this cheese globe for all it's worth. There must be a butter way.

Joe: Can we come up with an **equation** that tells us what length of cocktail stick to use?

Frank: OK, let's think about that. What's the cheese globe **like**?

Jim: Well, the finished cheese globe kinda looks like the cheese has coated a soccer ball with a bunch of little spikes s

Start solving a new problem by asking yourself, "What is this problem LIKE?"

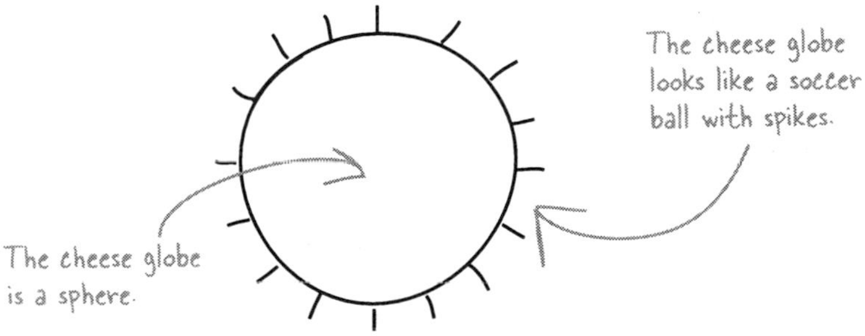

Joe: Right, the cheese globe's basically a **sphere**.

Jim: So maybe the **volume** that each cheese block takes up is important ...

Joe: ... or maybe the **surface area** of the cheese blocks is important ...

The cheese globe is a sphere

Because you start with a spherical orange and put all the cocktail sticks in the same distance, the cheese also makes a **sphere** shape. The larger the **radius** of the sphere, the larger the surface area, and the larger the volume.

But is it the **surface area** of the sphere that's important, or the **volume** ... or both? How are you going to figure that out?

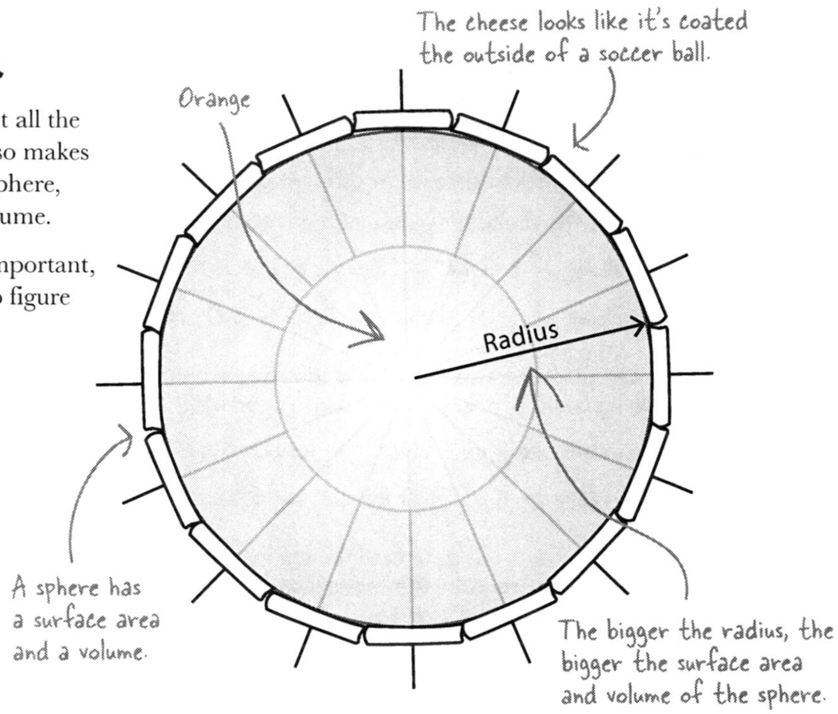

If a sphere has a big radius, then it also has a big surface area and a big volume.

Sharpen your pencil

A single block of cheese has dimensions of 2.0 cm by 2.0 cm by 0.50 cm. You have 500 of them.

a. Calculate the total volume of the cheese blocks in cm^3.

b. Calculate the area in cm^2 that the cheese blocks occupy when you arrange them on a flat surface with the square side of each block facing upwards.

c. Do you think the volume of the cheese blocks or their surface area - or both - is important for working out how long to make the cocktail sticks? Give a reason for your answer.

d. What other information might you need to be able to solve this problem?

Sharpen your pencil Solution

A single block of cheese has dimensions of 2.0 cm by 2.0 cm by 0.5 cm. You have 500 of them.

a. Calculate the total volume of the cheese blocks in cm^3.

Volume of 1 block = length × width × height = 2.0 × 2.0 × 0.50 = 2.0 cm^3 (2 sd)

Volume of 500 blocks = 500 × 2.0 = 1000 cm^3 (2 sd)

b. Calculate the area in cm^2 that the cheese blocks occupy when you arrange them on a flat surface with the square side of each block facing upwards.

Surface area of 1 block = length × width = 2.0 × 2.0 = 4.0 cm^2 (2 sd)

Surface area of 500 blocks = 500 × 4.0 = 2000 cm^2 (2 sd)

c. Do you think the volume of the cheese blocks or their surface area - or both - is important for working out how long to make the cocktail sticks? Give a reason for your answer.

I think the surface area is important, because the blocks have to cover a surface without any gaps in between them, not fill up a volume. The volume isn't important.

d. What other information might you need to be able to solve this problem?

An equation for the surface area of a sphere would be useful.

The surface area of the sphere is the same as the surface area of the cheese

If you were making a solid sphere of cheese, then the volume of the cheese and sphere would need to be equal.

But the cheese makes a spherical 'shell' - not a filled-in sphere. Therefore, the surface area of the cheese will be the same as the **surface area** of the sphere that it's coating.

Your table of information gives you an equation for the surface area of a sphere: $S = 4\pi r^2$.

Ready Bake Equation

Surface area of a sphere

$$S = 4\pi r^2$$

Surface area (S) — Radius (r)

Sharpen your pencil

You have 500 cheese blocks, measuring 2.0 cm by 2.0 cm by 0.50 cm, and are required to make a cheese sphere. You have 500 cocktail sticks, which start in the center of an orange and are equally spread across the orange. 2.0 cm of each stick should be visible on the outside of the sphere.

a. What length should the cocktail sticks be if the 500 pieces of cheese are to be arranged so as to leave no gaps in the surface of the cheese sphere?

b. Now, suppose you have 2000 pieces of cheese the same as before - 4 times as many. Without redoing the calculations you did above, use the equation for the surface area of a sphere to explain what radius of cheese globe you'd be able to make while leaving no gaps.

Sharpen your pencil Solution

You have 500 cheese blocks, measuring 2.0 cm by 2.0 cm by 0.50 cm, and are required to make a cheese sphere. You have 500 cocktail sticks, which start in the center of an orange and are equally spread across the orange. 2.0 cm of each stick should be visible on the outside of the sphere.

a. What length should the cocktail sticks be if the 500 pieces of cheese are to be arranged so as to leave no gaps in the surface of the cheese sphere?

Inside surface of cheese coats a sphere.

surface area of sphere = surface area of cheese

$\Rightarrow 4\pi r^2 = 2.0 \times 2.0 \times 500$

$r = \sqrt{\dfrac{2000}{4\pi}} = 12.6$ cm (3 sd)

You need to remember the thickness of the cheese as well as the bit at the end!

Length of cocktail stick:
Need to include 2.0 cm at end, and thickness of cheese.

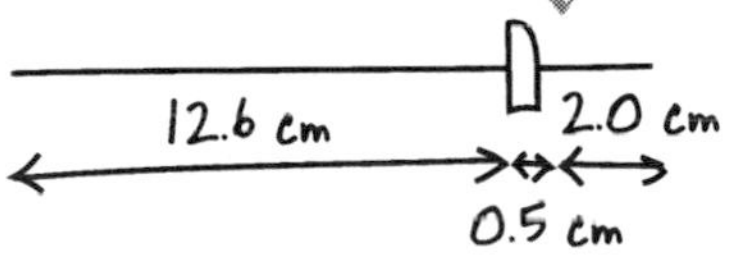

Length = 12.6 + 0.5 + 2.0 = 15.1 cm (3 sd)

Surface area of sphere.

$S = 4\pi r^2$

Radius of sphere.

Doubling the radius of a sphere QUADRUPLES the surface area of the sphere.

b. Now, suppose you have 2000 pieces of cheese the same as before - 4 times as many. Without redoing the calculations you did above, use the equation for the surface area of a sphere to explain what radius of cheese globe you'd be able to make while leaving no gaps.

The surface area is proportional to r^2, as $S = 4\pi r^2$. If S is 4 times larger, then $4\pi r^2$ will be four times larger. But 4 and π are constants. Therefore r^2 must be 4 times larger, so r must be 2 times larger

Inner radius = 12.6 × 2 = 25.2 cm.

there are no Dumb Questions

Q: How can I tell whether it's the volume or surface area that's important?

A: Ask yourself - "What's it **like**?" Here, arranging the cheese is like coating the surface of a soccer ball. This means that the surface area of the cheese is important.

If you were melting the cheese and filling the volume of a soccer ball, then the volume of the cheese would be the important thing.

Q: I thought that 3D objects have volumes, not surface areas?

A: Anything you can paint has a surface area - or else there'd be nowhere for the paint to go! A sphere has a surface area. It's a curved surface - and one you can't flatten out properly - but it's a surface nonetheless.

Q: How do you know what happens to the area when you change the radius?

A: In the equation $S = 4\pi r^2$, the area is **proportional** to r^2. If you double the radius, you quadruple the surface area, as $2^2 = 4$ Think about it like this: if the old radius is y and you double it, the new radius is $2y$.

Old: $S = 4\pi y^2$ ← Old surface area.

New: $S = 4\pi(2y)^2 = 4\pi 4y^2 = 4 \times 4\pi y^2$

So when you double the radius, the new surface area is four times the old surface area.

Let there be cheese...

Give your solutions to the party planners, and let's see what they come up with.

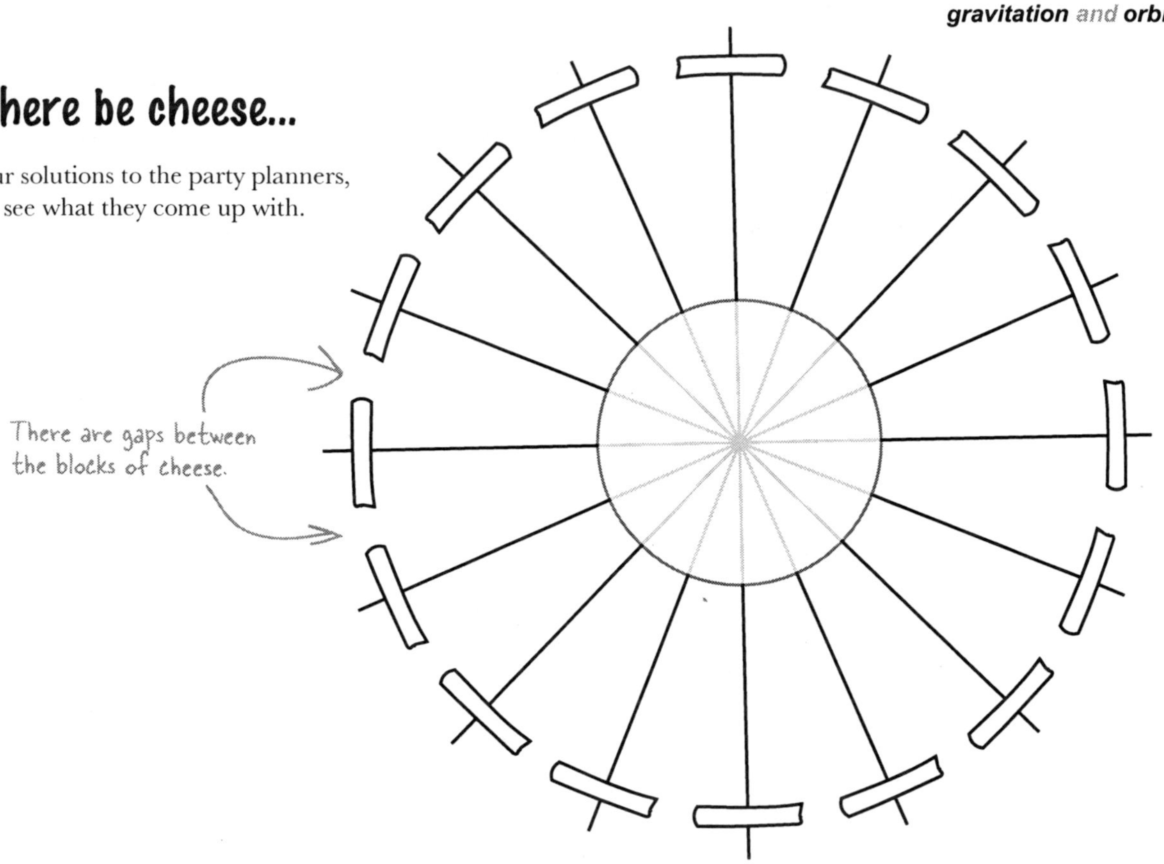

...but there are gaps in the globe!

Sharpen your pencil

Your solution on the opposite page is correct, but the party planners have gone wrong somewhere.

Circle the mistake in the notes that the machine programmer made and explain what went wrong.

Cheese globe notes

Set machine to put 500 sticks into orange, evenly-spaced with ends of sticks in center.

Machine puts 2.0 cm by 2.0 cm by 0.5 cm blocks on sticks, square side up, with 2.0 cm of stick protruding.

Set stick length so that 15.1 cm of stick is visible outside orange.

Press go.

Sharpen your pencil Solution

Your solution on the opposite page is correct, but the party planners have gone wrong somewhere.

Circle the mistake in the notes that the machine programmer made and explain what went wrong.

Cheese globe notes

Set machine to put 500 sticks into orange, evenly-spaced with ends of sticks in center.

Machine puts 2.0 cm by 2.0 cm by 0.5 cm blocks on sticks, square side up, with 2.0 cm of stick protruding.

~~Set stick length so that~~ 15.1 cm of stick is visible outside orange.

Press go.

I worked out the the sticks need to have a TOTAL length of 15.1 cm.

But the party planner has made 15.1 cm of stick visible on the outside of the orange.

This means that the sticks will be too long, as they will have alength of 15.1 cm + radius of orange.

If the sticks are too long, there will be gaps between the blocks of cheese.

This is the dstance you calculated to be 15.1 cm – the length of the entire cocktail stick – the RADIUS of the sphere. to the tips of the sticks.

This is the distance that the party planners accidentally programmed their machine with – the distance from the surface of the orange.

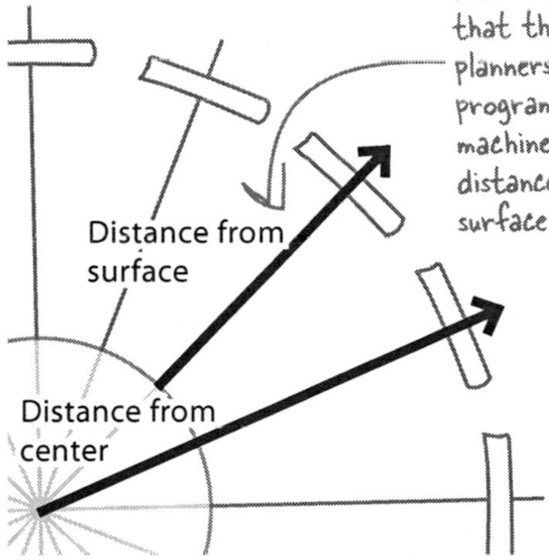

Accidentally working with the distance from the surface instead of the radius - or vice-versa - is a common mistake.

The party planners had programmed their machine incorrectly, using the **distance from the surface** of the orange.

They should have used the **radius** - the **distance from the center**.

Fortunately, it was only a prototype, and you soon have them back on track ...

The party's on!

The party planners are thrilled. In fact, they've already had more orders for different size cheese globes

With an ability to churn out different sizes thanks to your flexible equation for working out cocktail stick sizes, you're ready to turn these unique (and spiky) cheese globes into big business.

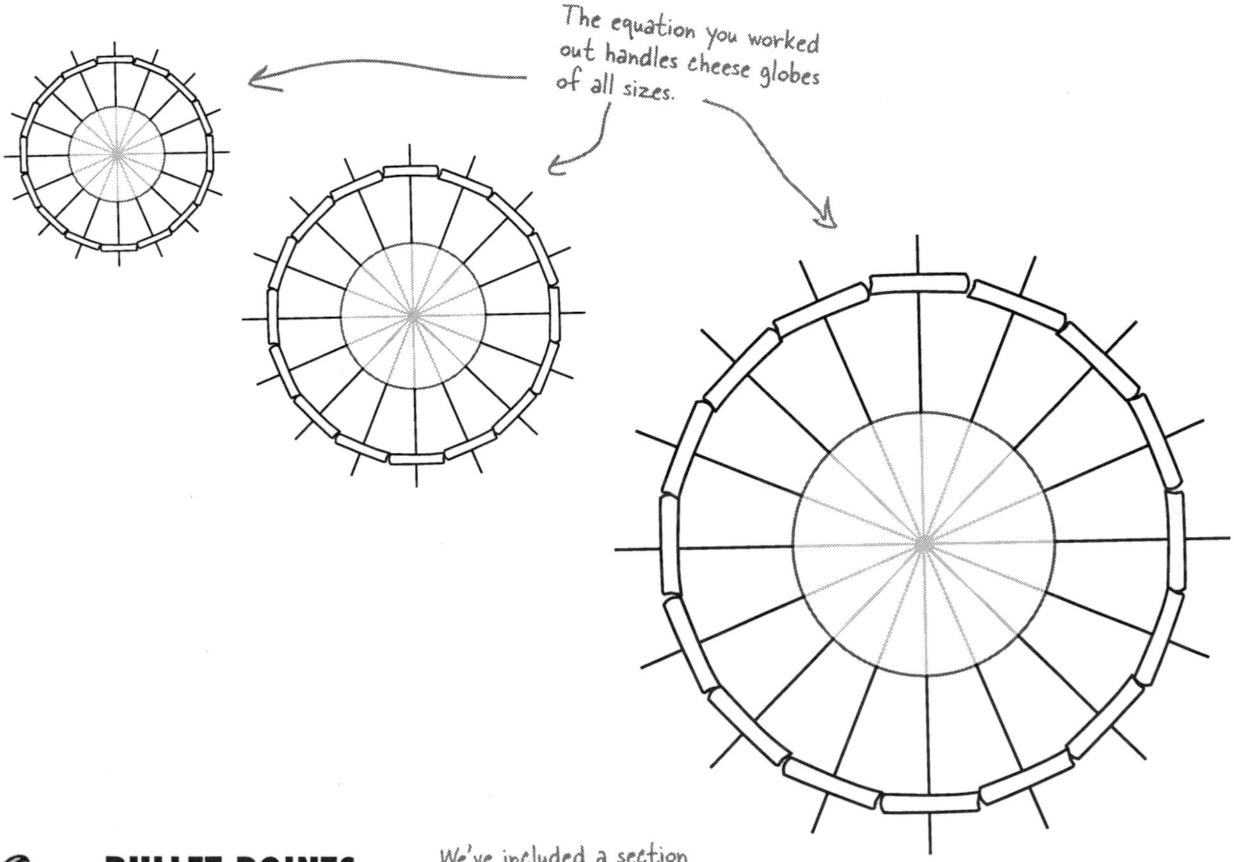

BULLET POINTS

We've included a section like this in appendix ii.

- If you're working with a 3D shape, think about whether it's surface area or volume that's important.
- If the shape will 'unroll' flat, you can work out its surface area by turning it into 2D shapes. *You did this in chapter 17.*
- If the shape won't 'unroll' flat, see if you can look it up in a book or table of information.
- On the AP course, the 'geometry and trigonometry' section of the table of information is the place to look.
- The surface area of a sphere is **proportional** to r^2.

To infinity - and beyond!

The lead astronaut on the Head First space station has been chosen to boldly go where no man has gone before - to the edge of the solar system! Your job is to work out how to get him there.

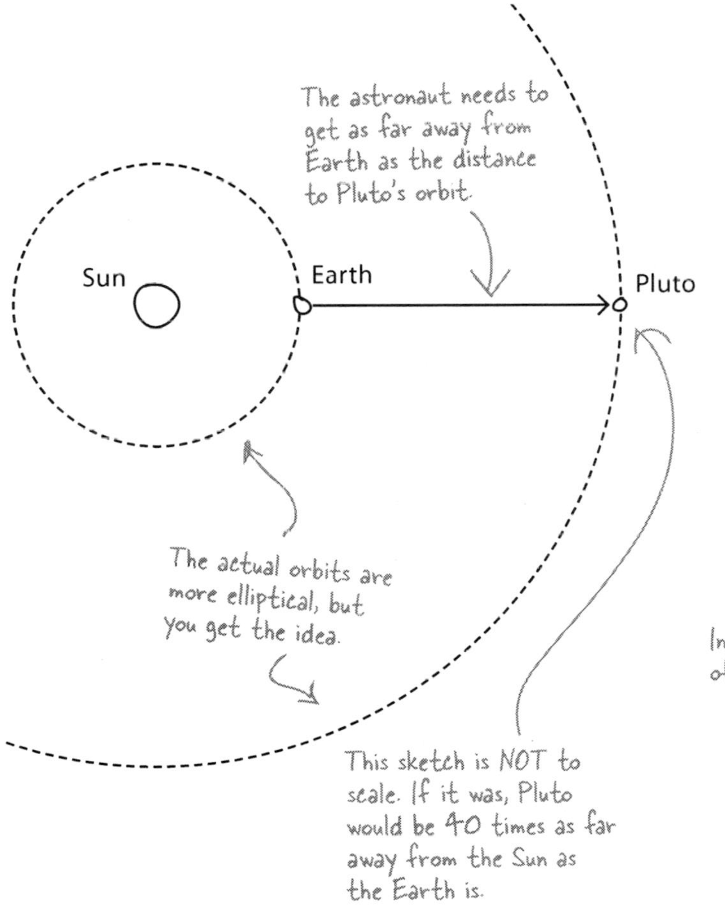

When you launch an object directly upwards, sooner or later it comes back down. If the astronaut is to make it to the edge of the solar system, he needs to be able to keep on going and going - without being brought back down to Earth!

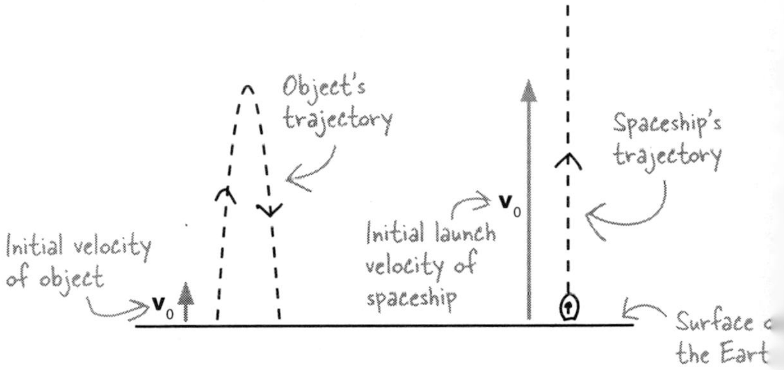

Since you're able to use a spaceship, this sounds easy at first - but you can't accelerate forever, as you'd run out of fuel! Your best strategy is to blast off to achieve as high a **velocity** as possible - after all, the greater the upwards velocity, the greater the time an object will spend away from the Earth.

The spaceship's acceleration due to gravity doesn't depend on its mass. So you don't need to worry about the mass of the spaceship changing as it burns fuel.

You need to calculate the **escape velocity** for the Earth - the velocity that the astronaut needs to reach at the start when he's close to Earth so as to not fall back down again. (You may need to work out other things for later on in the mission, but the escape velocity for the earth is enough to be getting on with for now!)

Jim: Yeah, we just need to run the spaceship's engine as hard as possible for as long as possible. That gives the astronaut the largest possible **velocity** at the start - and the best chance of making it.

Joe: But how do we guarantee that's going to be good enough? What if the astronaut falls back down to Earth again, like a football does when you throw it up in the air?

Frank: Well, let's work it out. I looked up the distance to Pluto's orbit, and it's around 6×10^{12} m...

Jim: ...and **acceleration** due to the Earth's gravity is 9.8 m/s^2...

Frank: Wait ... you mean **negative** 9.8 m/s^2, right? The acceleration needs to be negative if we're calling "away from the Earth" the positive direction.

Joe: OK, so we know the **displacement** and the **acceleration**, and let's say that he needs to have a **velocity** of 0 m/s when he reaches Pluto's orbit. That's the smallest velocity he could have by that point and still make it.

Jim: Let's get on with the calculation!

This distance is a million times grater than the radius of the Earth, and only has one significant digit. So it doesn't really matter if this distance is measured from the center or the surface of the Earth.

Sharpen your pencil

a. Pluto's orbit is 6×10^{12} m (1 sd) from Earth. If the acceleration due to the Earth's gravity is constant throughout the journey, work out the velocity that a spaceship needs to have at the start in order to escape from Earth.

b. How practical does your answer feel to you?

Sharpen your pencil Solution

a. Pluto's orbit is 6×10^{12} m (1 sd) from Earth. If the acceleration due to the Earth's gravity is constant throughout the journey, work out the velocity that a spaceship needs to have at the start in order to escape from Earth.

Suppose spaceship has velocity of 0 m/s by the time it reaches Pluto's orbit:

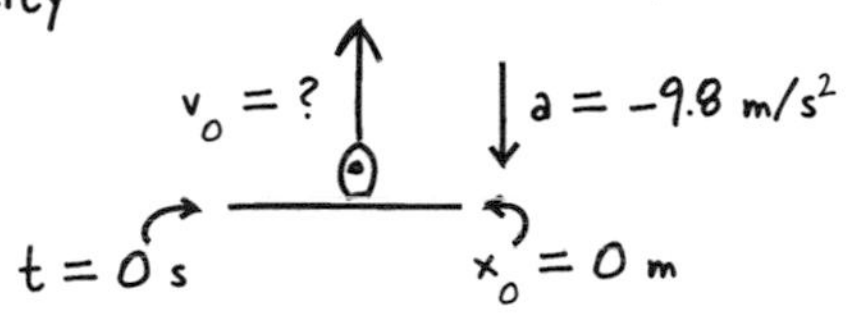

$$v^2 = v_0^2 + 2a(x - x_0)$$

$$v_0^2 = v^2 - 2a(x - x_0)$$

$$\Rightarrow v_0^2 = 0 - 2 \times (-9.8) \times (6 \times 10^{12} - 0)$$

$$v_0 = \underline{3 \times 10^{13} \text{ m/s (1 sd)}}$$

The speed of light is 3×10^8 m/s

b. How practical does your answer feel to you?

This is very, very, very fast. It's 100000 times faster than the speed of light (the largest speed a material body can have) so is just totally impossible!

Looks like the velocity's the wrong **size** - it's way too high!

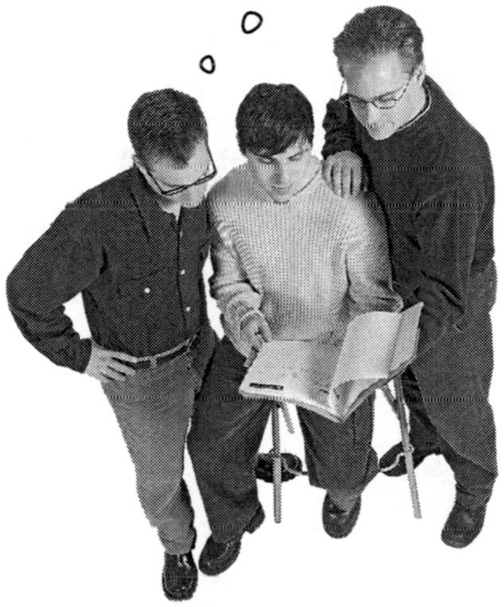

Jim: Yeah, you can't get a spaceship - or anything else to go faster than the speed of light!

Frank: But real space probes have gone past Pluto and even left the solar system before. So it must be possible ...

Joe: What if the **effect of the Earth's gravity gets less** as you go **further away**?

Frank: How do you mean?

Joe: Well, sounds are quieter if you're further away from their source. And lights are less bright. Maybe it's the same with gravity.

Jim: You mean your **acceleration due to gravity** might get smaller as you move further away?

Frank: Oh yeah ... the equations of motion we used assumed that the acceleration due to gravity was constant for the whole journey

Jim: Good point. If the acceleration changes as you get further away, we can't use those equations of motion - they only work for a situation with constant acceleration.

Joe: Let's try to work out **how** the acceleration changes as you get further away from the Earth ...

Your equations of motion only work if the acceleration is constant.

Earth's gravitational force on you becomes weaker as you go further away

When you're near the Earth, you experience a **gravitational force** because the stuff you're made of and the stuff the Earth's made of attract each other. But as the **distance** between you and the Earth **increases**, the **gravitational force gets weaker**. In the same way, sounds get quieter and lights get less bright as you increase the distance between yourself and the source of the sound or light.

As the gravitational force on you gets smaller, your **acceleration due to gravity** also decreases (as $\mathbf{F}_{net} = m\mathbf{a}$). So your acceleration isn't constant. That means you can't use your equations of motion here, as they only work when the acceleration is constant.

But **how** does the gravitational force change as you get further away?

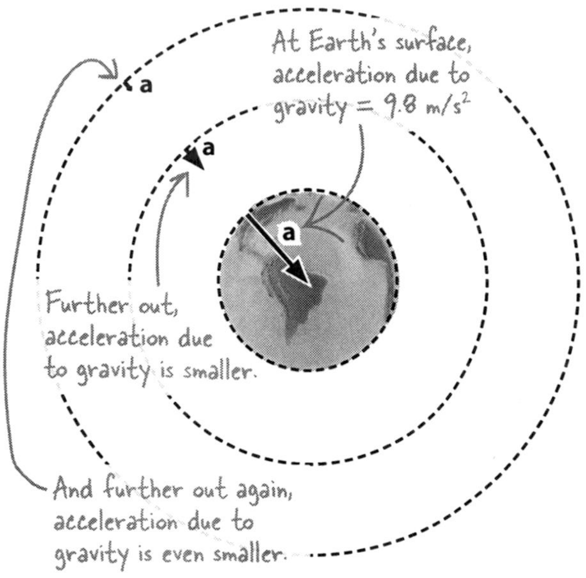

Sharpen your pencil

The brightness of a light becomes less as you get further away. In this picture, you have a spherical light that emits light equally in all directions, and you look at it with your eye from two different distances. Assume that the pupil of your eye (the bit that lets the light in) has the same area at both distances.

Explain why the light appears dimmer when you are further away.

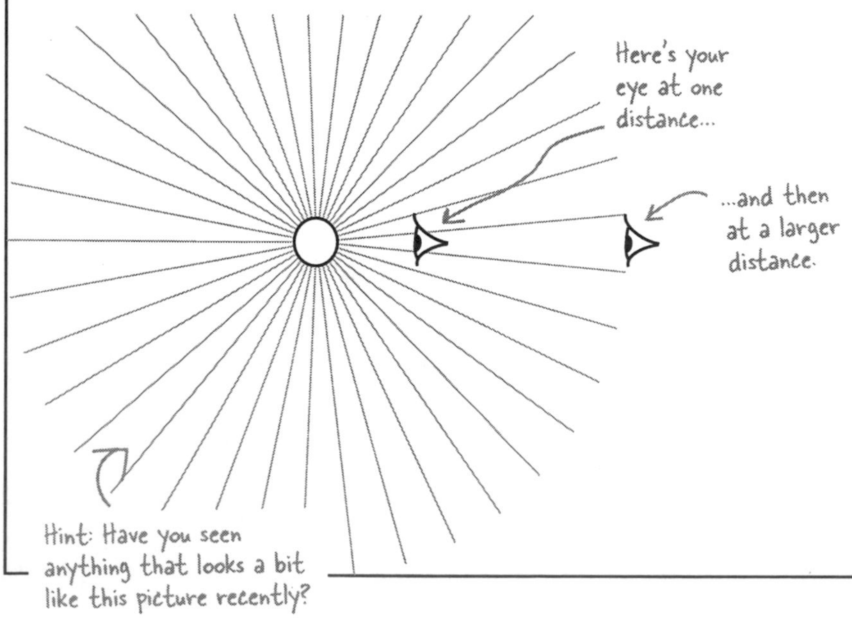

Sharpen your pencil Solution

The brightness of a light is something that becomes weaker as you get further away. In this picture, you have a spherical light that emits light equally in all directions, and you look at it with your eye from two different distances. Assume that the pupil of your eye (the bit that lets the light in) has the same area at both distances.

Explain why the light appears dimmer when you are further away.

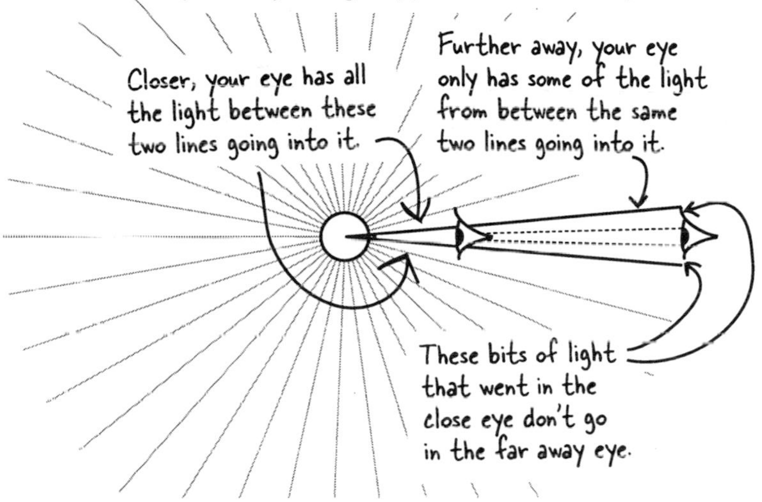

As the light goes away from the bulb, it spreads out more.

The close eye has all the light within the two heavy lines going into it.

The far away eye only has a part of this light going into it – so the bulb looks dimmer from further away.

At distance r_1, all of the light coming from the bulb is spread out over the area $4\varpi r_1^2$.

At distance r_2, the light is spread out over the area $4\varpi r_2^2$.

The same amount of light it spread out over each surface. However, at a greater distance there's less light available per square meter, as there are more square meters of surface for the light to spread out over.

So the light looks less bright from further away.

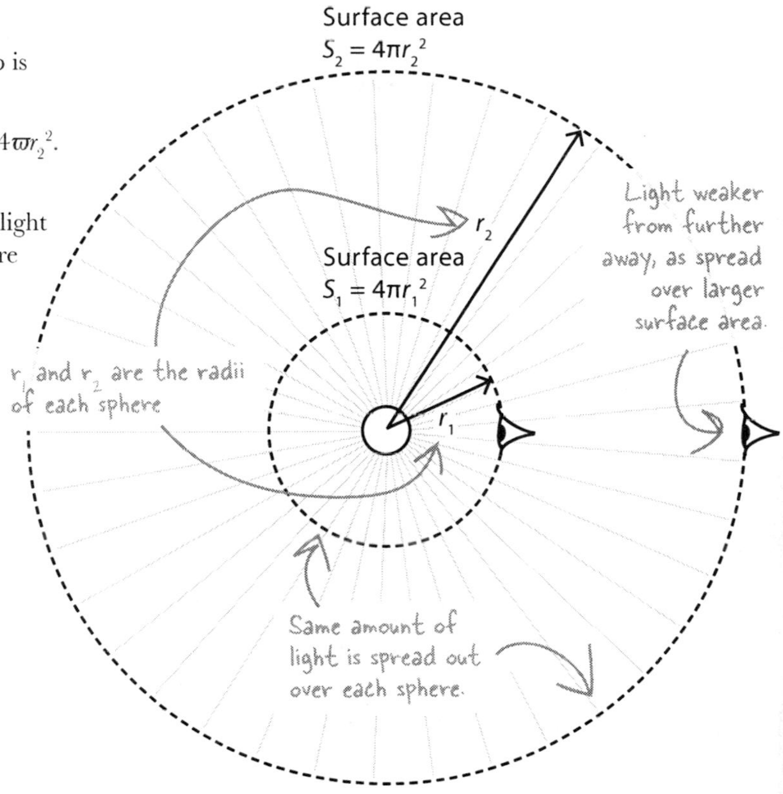

The further you are from a light, the greater the SURFACE AREA it's spread over.

Err ... what does light spreading out have to do with getting an astronaut to the edge of the solar system?

Light intensity and gravitational field strength both depend on the <u>surface area</u> of spheres.

You have been representing light using **rays** that start in the center and spread out. The rays show you the **direction** that the light is traveling in.

As light rays spread out, the **surface area** that the light's spread over increases. So the intensity of the light decreases.

You can represent the Earth's gravitational field in a similar way by using **gravitational field lines**. The lines show you the direction an object will accelerate in if the gravitational force is the only force acting on it. The object will accelerate along a line, moving closer to the Earth.

As the gravitational field lines spread out, the surface area of a sphere at that radius increases. So the **gravitational field strength** decreases.

The gravitational field strength is another name for the acceleration due to gravity.

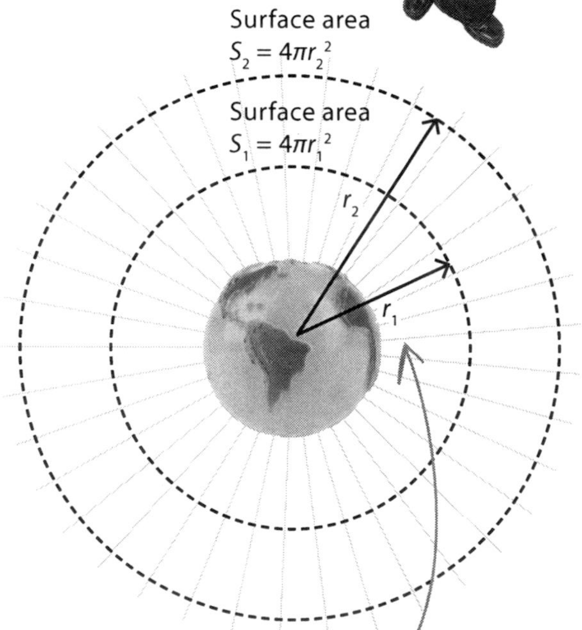

r_1 and r_2 are radius vectors pointing away from the center of the sphere. Most of the time we are interested in the distance, buit sometimes we will be interested in the direction, as r is in the opposite direction from the acceleration caused by the gravitational field.

Gravitational field lines show you the DIRECTION that an object will accelerate in.

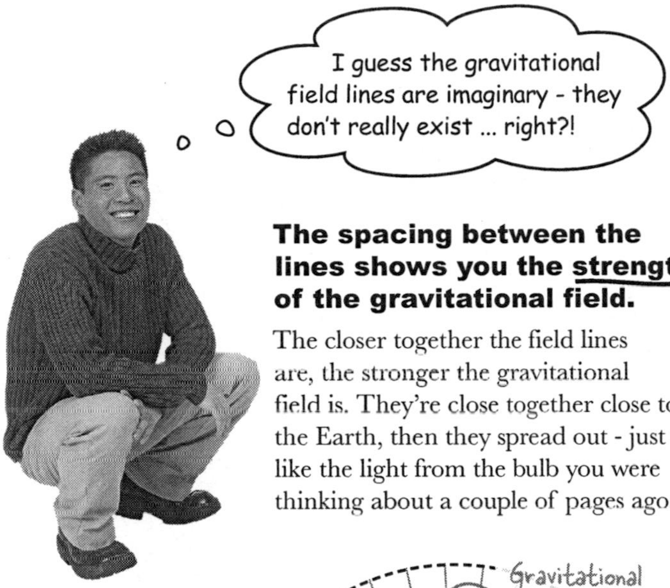

The spacing between the lines shows you the strength of the gravitational field.

The closer together the field lines are, the stronger the gravitational field is. They're close together close to the Earth, then they spread out - just like the light from the bulb you were thinking about a couple of pages ago.

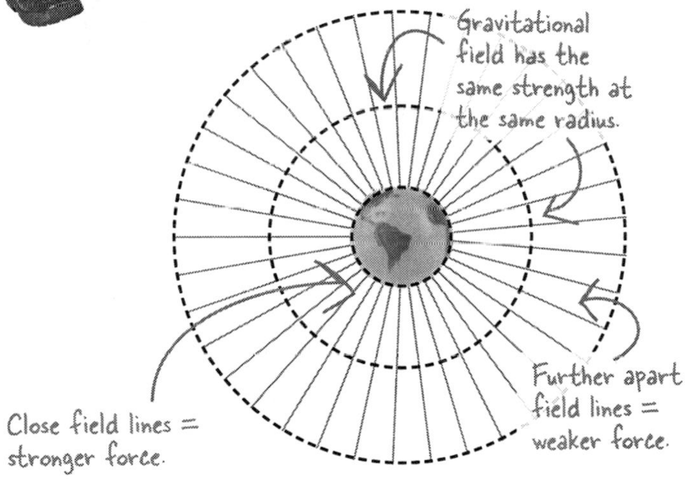

The field lines themselves don't physically exist. The field lines are a tool you can use to help you **visualize** what happens to the gravitational field.

The closer together the field lines, the stronger the field (so the greater the acceleration due to gravity).

there are no Dumb Questions

Q: Why is this called a gravitational field? Surely gravitational acceleration or gravitational force is a better?

A: The 'field' is a way of visualizing what's going on with the strength of the acceleration due to gravity. Gravitational field strength has units m/s^2, the same as acceleration. Close to the Earth, the gravitational field strength is $9.8\ m/s^2$, but further away it's lower.

Q: If I'm drawing gravitational field lines on a picture, is there a standard number of lines that I should draw? Should I always draw 32 lines, like in these pictures?

A: There's no strict rule - you should draw as many field lines as help you visualize what's happening. Probably at least eight is a good rule of thumb.

Q: So what's the connection between gravitational field and gravitational force?

A: The gravitational field represents the acceleration due to gravity that an object would experience if it was placed at that point. You can get from there to the gravitational force using $\mathbf{F}_{net} = m\mathbf{a}$

Q: And the gravitational force is just the same as an object's weight, right?

A: Absolutely! Though you now know that the force - and therefore the weight - will vary depending on the distance from Earth.

Q: So - what's the equation for that?

A: Funny you should ask ...

Sharpen your pencil

You want to work out an equation for the gravitational force that a spaceship experiences at any distance from the Earth

a. What happens to the surface area of a sphere if you double its radius?

b. The gravitational force depends on the distance something is from the Earth. If you're further away, will the gravitational force be larger or smaller?

c. The gravitational field gets 'spread out' over the surface area of a sphere as you get further away, in the same way as light does. What do you think will happen to the gravitational field strength if you double the distance between you and the Earth (i.e. double the radius)?

d. What do you think would happen to the gravitational force if you double your mass?

Hint: F=ma.

e. What do you think would happen to the gravitational force if you doubled the mass of the Earth?

f. Here are four equations. In each equation, *G* is a constant (and a conversion factor) that will make the numbers and units work out later on. For each equation, write down whether what happens to the size of the gravitational force, F_G, when you change *r* (the distance of the object from the Earth), m_1 (the mass of the Earth) or m_2 (the mass of the object) is what you'd expect in real life. Circle the equation you think is correct.

F_G points towards the Earth and r points away. In gravitation, it's conventional to include a minus sign to show the directions of F_G and r are opposite even though this is a scalar equation for the size of F_G.

In each equation, G is a constant that makes the units work out. So don't worry about units right now.

$$F_G = -Gm_1m_2r^2$$

$$F_G = -\frac{Gm_1r}{m_2}$$

$$F_G = -\frac{Gm_1m_2}{r}$$

$$F_G = -\frac{Gm_1m_2}{r^2}$$

Sharpen your pencil Solution

You want to work out an equation for the gravitational force that a spaceship experiences at any distance from the Earth

a. What happens to the surface area of a sphere if you double its radius?

If you double the radius, you quadruple the surface area, as $S = 4\pi r^2$ and $2^2 = 4$.

Look back at the No Dumb Questions on page 718 for an explanation.

b. The gravitational force depends on the distance something is from the Earth. If you're further away, will the gravitational force be larger or smaller?

If you're further away, the gravitational force will be smaller.

c. The gravitational field gets 'spread out' over the surface area of a sphere as you get further away, in the same way as light does. What do you think will happen to the gravitational field strength if you double the distance between you and the Earth (i.e. double the radius)?

If you double the radius, you quadruple the surface area that the field will be spread out over. So I think that the field strength would decrease by a factor of four.

d. What do you think would happen to the gravitational force if you double your mass?

If you double your mass, you double the force, as $F = ma$

Hint: $F=ma$.

e. What do you think would happen to the gravitational force if you doubled the mass of the Earth?

If you double the mass of the Earth, you double its gravitational attraction to you ($F = ma$). As gravitational forces exist in Newton's 3rd Law pairs, the force that the Earth exerts on you must also double.

f. Here are four equations. In each equation, G is a constant (and a conversion factor) that will make the numbers and units work out later on. For each equation, write down whether what happens to the size of the gravitational force, F_G, when you change r (the distance of the object from the Earth), m_1 (the mass of the Earth) or m_2 (the mass of the object) is what you'd expect in real life. Circle the equation you think is correct.

$$F_G = -Gm_1m_2r^2$$

Wrong – if you increase r, then size of F_G gets larger.

$$F_G = \frac{Gm_1r}{m_2}$$

Wrong – if you increase m_2, then size of F_G gets smaller.

$$F_G = \frac{Gm_1m_2}{r}$$

Wrong – if you double r, then the size of F_G only halves.

$$F_G = \frac{Gm_1m_2}{r^2}$$

Right – Doubling m_1 or m_2 doubles size of F_G. Doubling r quarters F_G.

Gravitation is an inverse square law

The gravitational force between two objects depends on $\frac{1}{r^2}$. If you double the distance, you decrease the force by a factor of 4. Something that behaves like this is said to follow an **inverse square law**.

This is because an inverse is 1 divided by something - in this case $\frac{1}{r^2}$ - and the square part comes from the fact that the thing doing the dividing is squared.

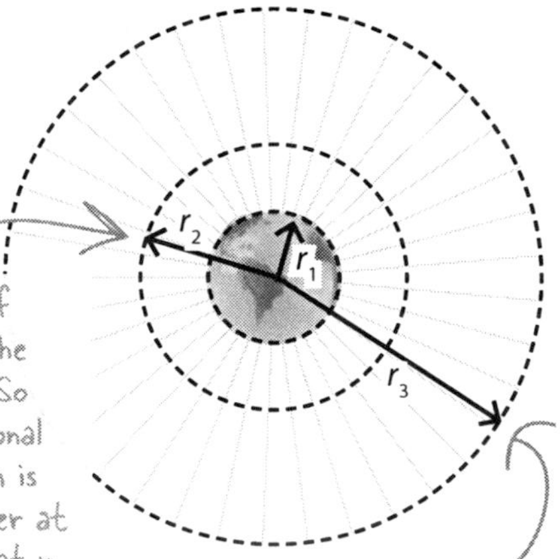

Thje length of r_2 is double the length of r_1. So the gravitational field strength is 4 times smaller at r_2 than it is at r_1.

The length of r_3 is four times the length of r_1. So the gravitational field strength is 16 times smaller at r_2 than it is at r_1, because $4^2 = 16$

there are no Dumb Questions

Q: But the surface of the Earth is the zero point for distance, right? Doesn't that equation go all weird with a zero on the bottom when you're at the surface?

A: *r* is the **distance from the CENTER of the Earth**, not the distance from the surface of the Earth. When you're at the surface of the Earth, *r* is just the radius of the Earth. And when you're further away, *r* is your distance from the center.

Q: Doesn't the force depend on $\frac{1}{4\pi r^2}$ rather than $\frac{1}{r^2}$, as the surface area is $4\pi r^2$?

A: The 4π is a **constant**. Whatever you do to *r* (double it, half it, etc), the 4π doesn't change. So it's not right to say that the gravitational force 'depends' on the 4π.

Q: What are the units of *G*?

A: You can work that out ...

Sharpen your pencil

You've realized that equation below does all the right things when you change the masses and the radius.

Work out what SI units *G* must have to make **both sides** of the equation have the **same units**.

$$F_G = -\frac{Gm_1m_2}{r^2}$$

Hint: Don't use Newtons for force. Work out more fundamental units for force (based on kg, m and s) using F = ma

Be very careful with m for mass and m for meters!

Sharpen your pencil Solution

You've realized that equation below does all the right things when you change the masses and the radius.

Work out what SI units *G* must have to make **both sides** of the equation have the **same units**.

$$F_G = -\frac{Gm_1m_2}{r^2}$$

Work out the units of each side individually first.

Write the units out using fractions rather than in "m/s" form, as it makes the algebra easier.

Units of left hand side:

$F = ma$

$[F] = [m][a] = \frac{kg.m}{s^2}$

Units of right hand side:

Equation is $\frac{Gm_1m_2}{r^2}$

Units are $\frac{[G][m_1][m_2]}{[r^2]} = \frac{[G].kg^2}{m^2}$

Units are same on both sides, so rearrange to solve for [G]:

$$\frac{kg.m}{s^2} = \frac{[G].kg^2}{m^2} \Rightarrow [G] = \frac{kg.m.m^2}{s^2.kg^2} = \frac{m^3}{kg.s^2} = m^3/kg.s^2$$

[G] means 'units of G'

When you're working with units, it's safest to put dots between them, as you may treat 'kg' like k × g, as if the k and the g are different variables.

You can rearrange units equations just like you can rearrange other equations.

G is like a conversion factor which makes the units and numbers correct.

If you're working in SI units, F_G will be in Newtons, m_1 and m_2 in kg and r in meters. The first job G does is to give both sides of the equation the same **units** - as you've just worked out.

The second job that G does is to make the **numbers** correct. If you just multiply m_1 and m_2 together then divide by r^2, the numerical answer you get won't be equal to the force in Newtons.

G is kinda like a conversion factor - a **constant** that makes the numbers correct as well. For this reason, G is called the **gravitational constant**.

G is the gravitational constant. It makes both the units and the numbers work out.

So we can calculate the force for any combination of masses and distances. That rocks!

Jim: Um, not quite. We don't know what G is in the equation. Well I mean, we know its **units**, but we don't know its **size**. If only we had a way of working that out.

Joe: Well, we've got one equation, and G is an unknown. As long as G is the only unknown, we can use the equation to calculate the value of G.

Frank: I guess we already know that **acceleration due to gravity at the Earth's surface** is 9.8 m/s^2. That's gotta give us a few things we can use in that equation.

Joe: And I just found the **radius** and **mass** of the Earth in a textbook. So we know those two things as well. I think that should be enough to work out the value of G...

Sharpen your pencil

a. By considering the acceleration due to gravity at the Earth's surface, use the equation and the ready-bake facts to work out the value of G, the gravitational constant.

Ready Bake Facts

Mass of the Earth:

5.97×10^{24} kg

Radius of the Earth:

6.38×10^{6} m

Gravitational force between two masses:

$$F_G = -\frac{Gm_1m_2}{r^2}$$

The minus sign is just a convention to show that F_G and r are in opposite directions. If you're working with the SIZE of F_G, you can leave the minus sign out of your calculations.

b. Use the value for G you worked out in part a to calculate the acceleration due to the Earth's gravity that a spaceship experiences at Pluto's orbit, which is 6×10^{12} m (1 sd) from Earth.

Sharpen your pencil Solution

a. By considering the acceleration due to gravity at the Earth's surface, use the equation and the ready-bake facts to work out the value of G, the gravitational constant.

Make m_1 the mass of an object and m_2 the mass of the Earth. $a = 9.8\ m/s^2$ at Earth's surface.

$$F = \cancel{m_1}a = \frac{G\cancel{m_1}m_2}{r^2}$$

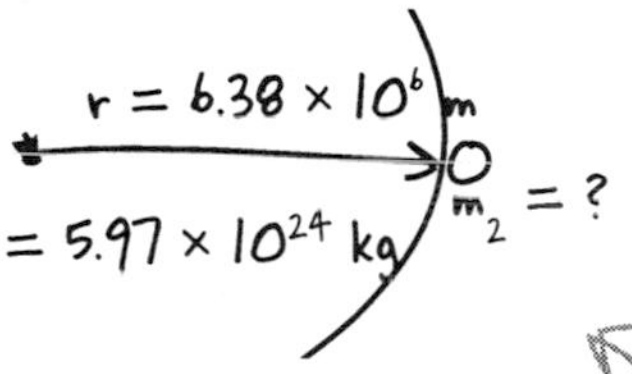

$$a = \frac{Gm_2}{r^2}$$

$$\Rightarrow G = \frac{ar^2}{m_2}$$

$$G = \frac{9.8 \times (6.38 \times 10^6)^2}{5.97 \times 10^{24}} = 6.68 \times 10^{-11}\ m^3/kg.s^2$$

b. Use the value for G you worked out in part a to calculate the acceleration due to the Earth's gravity that a spaceship experiences at Pluto's orbit, which is 6×10^{12} m (1 sd) from Earth.

$$F = \cancel{m_1}a = \frac{G\cancel{m_1}m_2}{r^2} \Rightarrow a = \frac{Gm_2}{r^2} = \frac{6.68 \times 10^{-11} \times 5.97 \times 10^{24}}{(6 \times 10^{12})^2} = 1 \times 10^{-11}\ m/s^2\ (1\ sd)$$

Ready Bake Facts

Mass of the Earth:

5.97×10^{24} kg

Radius of the Earth:

6.38×10^6 m

Gravitational force between two masses:

$$F_G = -\frac{Gm_1m_2}{r^2}$$

The minus sign shows that F_G and r are in opposite directions. Here, we've used the equation without the minus sign to calculate the SIZE of F_G

G is a constant that you can look up when you need it.

G is a fundamental **physical constant.** It's not a number you have to remember or calculate every time, and we've included its value in the appendix, so you can look it up if you need it.

If you're taking an exam, the value of *G* will be given in your table of information - so you can just look it up there and use the value in your equation.

there are no Dumb Questions

Q: How did people work out the mass of the Earth in the first place?

A: Historically, the mass of the Earth was worked out from *G*. *G* was originally worked out from experiments that measured the gravitational attraction between large masses, like cannonballs.

Q: You mean that it's not just the Earth that attracts things gravitationally?

A: Precisely! Everything that's made of stuff attracts everything else gravitationally. It's just that the effect isn't very large unless one of the objects you're dealing with has a very large mass (like the Earth), so you don't usually notice.

Sharpen your pencil

The minus sign shows that F_G and r are in opposite directions. Here, we've used the equation without the minus sign to calculate the SIZE of F_G, and therefore the size of a.

$F = m_1 a = \frac{G m_1 m_E}{r^2}$

Gravitation is an **inverse square law.** This means that if you double the distance that an object is from the Earth, it will only experience a quarter of the gravitational force that it did in its previous position.

But what does an inverse square law look like? A **graph** will help you visualize it.

a. Fill in the values of the gravitational field strength at a variety of distances from Earth. *G*, the gravitational constant, is 6.67×10^{-11} $m^3/kg.s^2$. m_E, the mass of the Earth, is 5.97×10^{24} kg. The radius of the Earth is 6.4×10^6 m (rounded to 2 sd) to make the figures easier.

Hint: look at how the values in the table increase...

Distance from Earth (m)	$a = \frac{Gm_E}{r^2}$ (m_E is the mass of the Earth.)
6.4×10^6	
1.28×10^7	
1.92×10^7	
2.56×10^7	
5.12×10^7	

b. Draw a graph with the distance from the Earth on the horizontal axis and the gravitational force on the vertical axis.

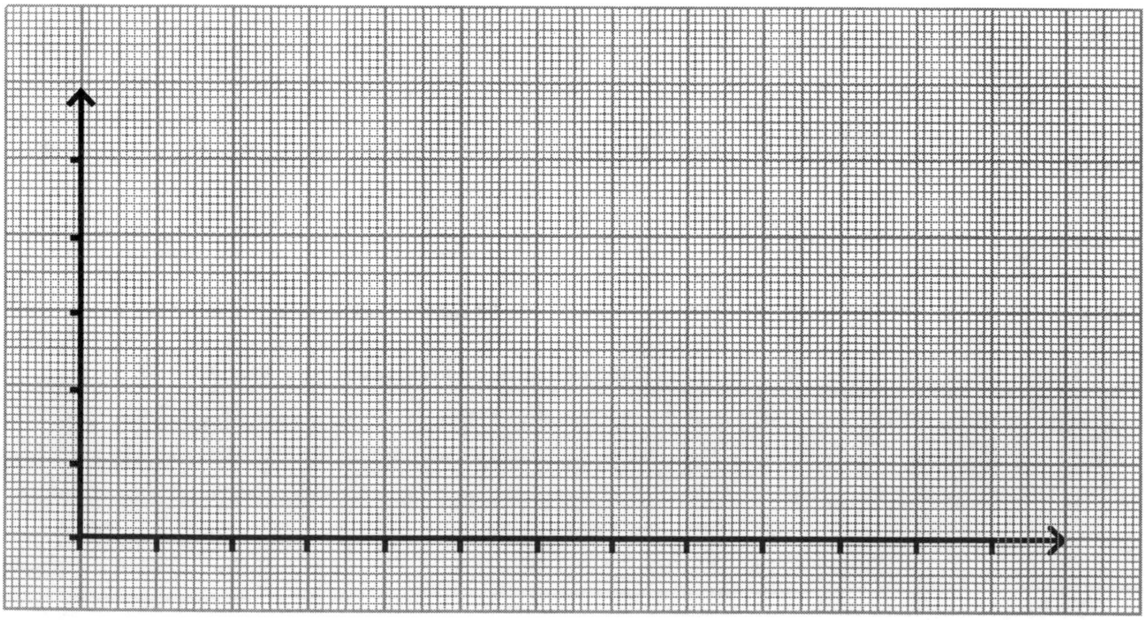

Sharpen your pencil Solution

You need to remember to square r.

You can either calculate each of these values individually, or use the inverse square relationship (double the distance, quarter the force) once you've calculated the first value.

Gravitation is an **inverse square law.** This means that if you double the distance that an object is from the Earth, it will only experience a quarter of the gravitational force that it did in its previous position.

But what does an inverse square law look like? A **graph** will help you visualize it.

a. Fill in the values of the gravitational field strength at a variety of distances from Earth. *G*, the gravitational constant, is 6.67×10^{-11} $m^3/kg.s^2$. m_E, the mass of the Earth, is 5.97×10^{24} kg. The radius of the Earth is 6.4×10^6 m (rounded to 2 sd) to make the figures easier.

Hint: look at how the values in the table increase...

Distance from Earth (m)	$a = \frac{Gm_E}{r^2}$ ← m_E is the mass of the Earth.
6.40×10^6	9.72 m/s^2 (3 sd)
1.28×10^7	2.43 m/s^2 (3 sd)
1.92×10^7	1.08 m/s^2 (3 sd)
2.56×10^7	0.608 m/s^2 (3 sd)
5.12×10^7	0.152 m/s^2 (3 sd)

b. Draw a graph with the distance from the Earth on the horizontal axis and the gravitational force on the vertical axis.

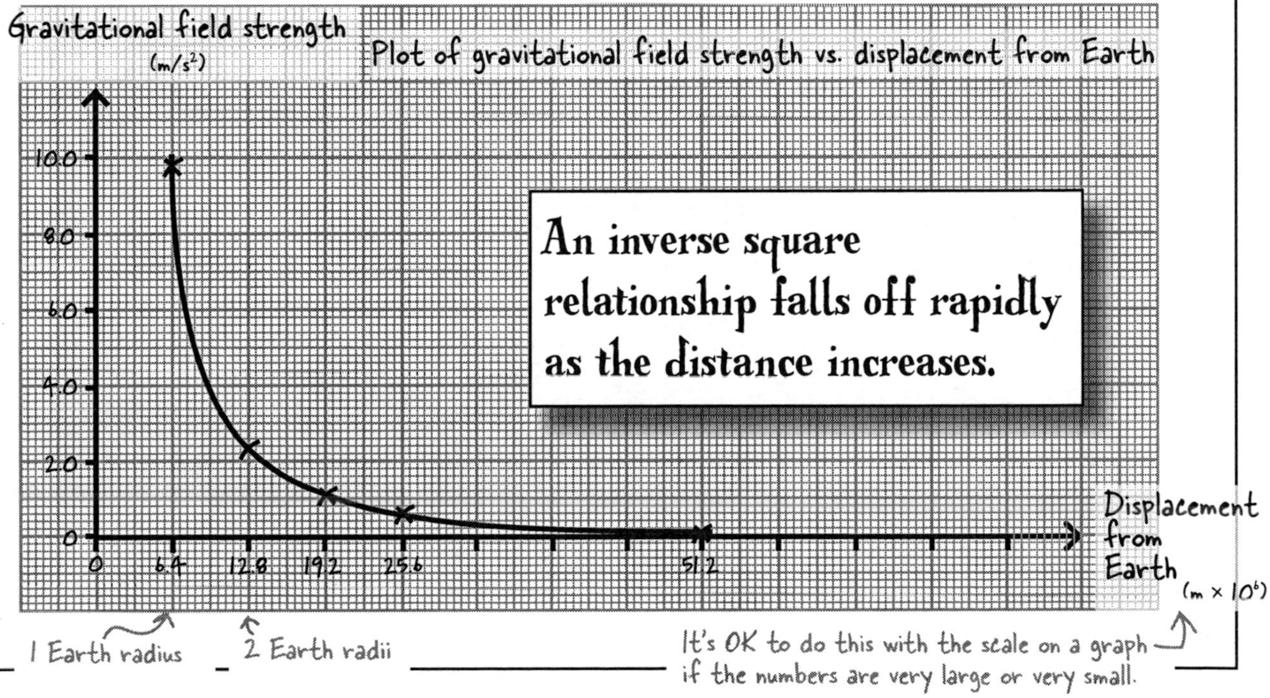

Now you can calculate the force on the spaceship at any distance from the Earth

An astronaut is going from the Earth to the outer reaches of the solar system. We're trying to calculate his **escape velocity** - the speed he needs to be going at so as to not fall back down to Earth again.

You've realized that the Earth's gravitational field must get smaller as you move further away from the Earth. This means that the **acceleration** of an astronaut's spaceship due to the gravitational field isn't constant - and, therefore, the **force** that the spaceship experiences isn't constant either.

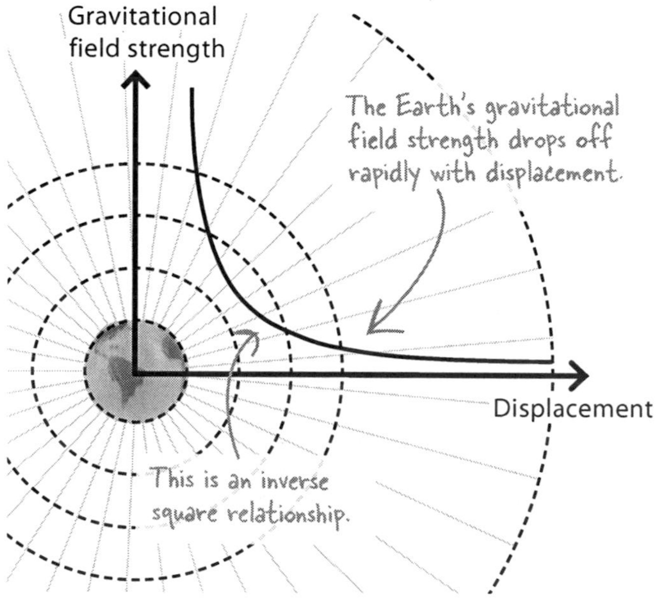

You've worked out that the gravitational field strength follows an **inverse square** relationship. If you double the displacement, you quarter the strength of the gravitational field - and also quarter the gravitational force that the spaceship experiences.

As the force (and acceleration) aren't constant, you can't use equations of motion to calculate the escape velocity.

You can only use equations of motion when the acceleration is constant.

BRAIN POWER

You have a problem where the **force** acting on the spaceship isn't constant - so its **acceleration** isn't constant and you can't use equations of motion.

Can you think of a different method you can use to calculate the escape velocity?

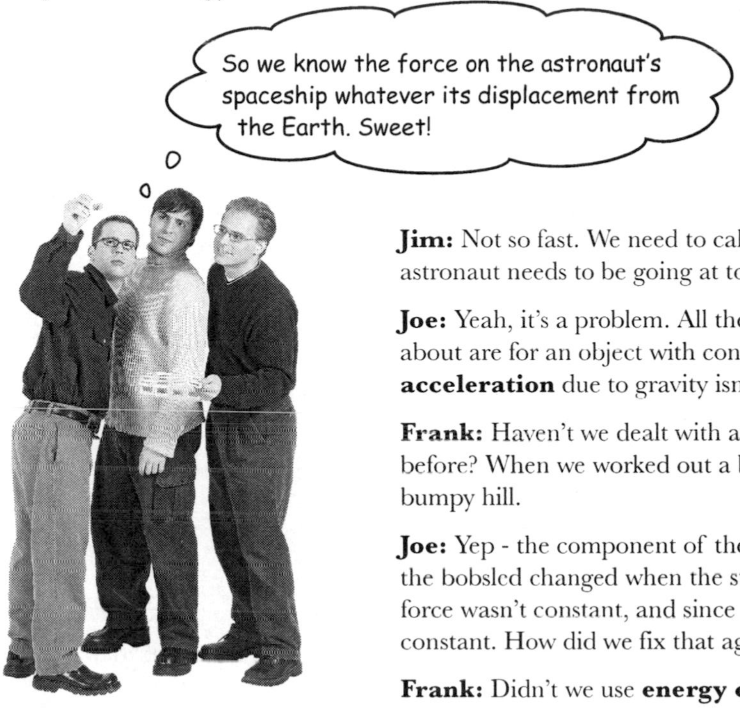

Jim: Not so fast. We need to calculate the **velocity** that the astronaut needs to be going at to escape from the Earth.

Joe: Yeah, it's a problem. All the equations of motion we know about are for an object with constant acceleration. But the **acceleration** due to gravity isn't constant

Frank: Haven't we dealt with a **non-constant acceleration** before? When we worked out a bobsled's velocity at the bottom of a bumpy hill.

Joe: Yep - the component of the gravitational **force** accelerating the bobsled changed when the steepness of the hill changed. So the force wasn't constant, and since $\mathbf{F}_{net} = m\mathbf{a}$, the acceleration wasn't constant. How did we fix that again?

Frank: Didn't we use **energy conservation**?

Joe: Yeah, we said that the bobsled's **potential energy** at the top of the slope was transferred to **kinetic energy** at the bottom of the slope - whatever the shape of the slope in between.

Frank: It was just the **difference in height** that was important.

Jim: Can we do the same for the spaceship? Can we pretend that it starts out very far away with lots of potential energy, then "falls" back down to Earth? It'd be **symmetrical**, right? **The velocity you need to escape from the Earth would be the same as the velocity you end up with when you fall to Earth.**

Joe: The change in potential energy is the same size as the change in kinetic energy, so we can use $K = \frac{1}{2}m\mathbf{v}^2$ to calculate the velocity!

Frank: Cool. So we just say $U_g = m\mathbf{gh}$ to calculate the change in potential energy, and we're nearly done!

Jim: Um ... I'm not so sure. The '**g**' in that equation is the acceleration due to gravity, isn't it? But that isn't constant here!

Joe: Hmm. The equation $U_g = m\mathbf{gh}$ originally comes from work = force × displacement, doesn't it. And it works over displacements on a scale of a few hundred meters. So can we break down the force-displacement graph into little portions of a few hundred meters each, calculate the work done for each portion, then add them together to get the total work done?

Frank: Or can we try to look up a book to get an equation for the gravitational potential energy when you're far away?

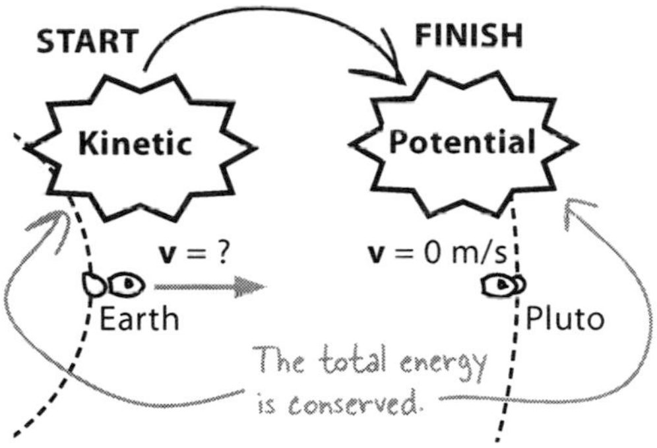

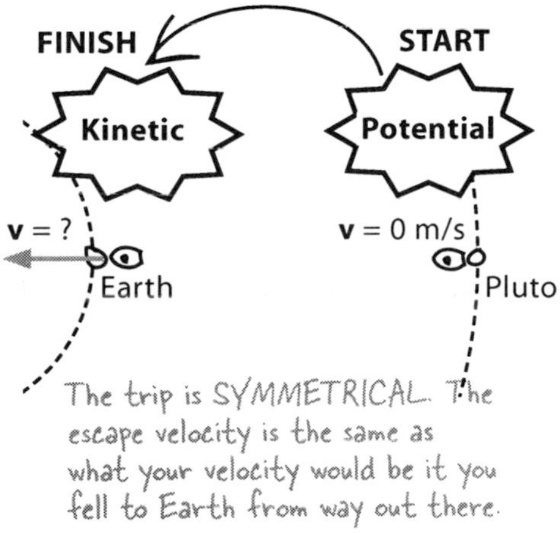

The potential energy is the area under the force-displacement graph

You give an object potential energy, U, by doing work on the object against the force of gravity. As Work = $\mathbf{F\Delta x}$, close to the Earth you can say $U = m\mathbf{gh}$, where $m\mathbf{g}$ is the gravitational force and **h** is the object's change in height.

A visual way of showing this is to say that the potential energy is equal to the **area under the force-displacement graph**.

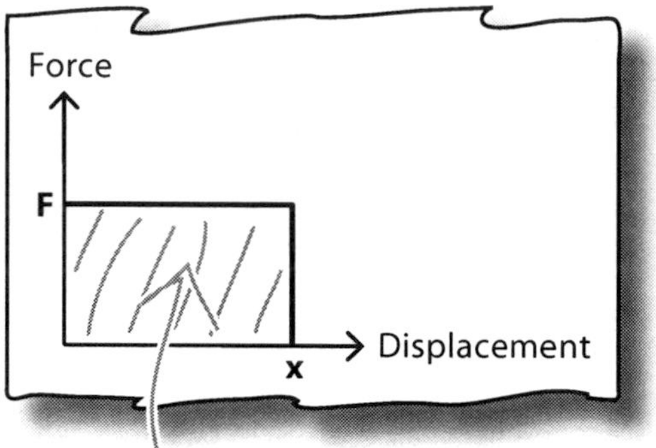

But if you're going a long way from the Earth, the force changes as the displacement changes. This means that it's not so easy to calculate the area under the force-displacement graph - and, therefore, not so easy to calculate the change in potential energy.

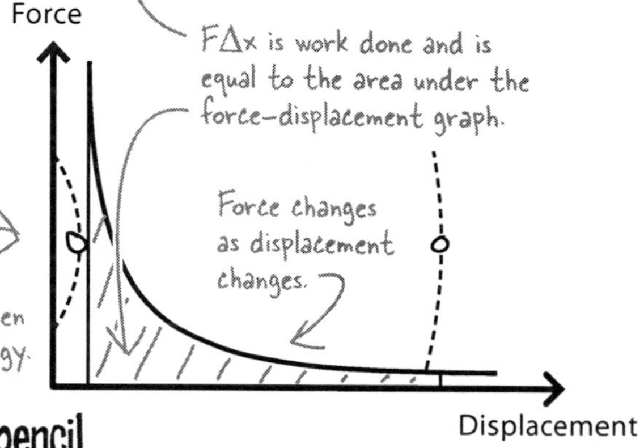

To save you having to calculate the area under the curved graph (difficult!) we've provided a ready-bake **equation** for the gravitational potential energy.

Ready Bake Equation

$$U_G = -\frac{Gm_1m_2}{r}$$

If you're taking an exam, you'll see this on your equation sheet.

Sharpen your pencil

a. According to the ready bake equation, what is the value of U when r is very, very large (i.e., infinite)?

b. According to the ready bake equation, what is the value of U at the Earth's surface for a 10.0 kg mass? (The radius of the Earth is 6.38×10^6 m and its mass is 5.97×10^{24} kg. G is 6.67×10^{-11} $m^3/kg.s^2$)

c. Comment on your answers.

Sharpen your pencil Solution

Ready Bake Equation

$$U_G = -\frac{Gm_1m_2}{r}$$

a. According to the ready bake equation, what is the value of U when r is very, very large (i.e., infinite)?

When r is very very large, $U = 0$ J, as you are dividing by a very very large number and r dominates.

b. According to the ready bake equation, what is the value of U at the Earth's surface for a 10.0 kg mass? (The radius of the Earth is 6.38×10^6 m and its mass is 5.97×10^{24} kg. G is 6.67×10^{-11} m^3/kg.s^2)

At Earth's surface, r is radius of Earth:

$$U = -\frac{Gm_1m_2}{r} = -\frac{6.67 \times 10^{-11} \times 10.0 \times 5.97 \times 10^{24}}{6.38 \times 10^6}$$

$$U = -6.24 \times 10^8 \text{ J (3 sd)}$$

c. Comment on your answers.

Weird! Last time, $U = 0$ at the surface, not at infinity. And what's with the negative number at the Earth's surface?!

It's the CHANGE in gravitational potential energy that allows you to do calculations, not the absolute values.

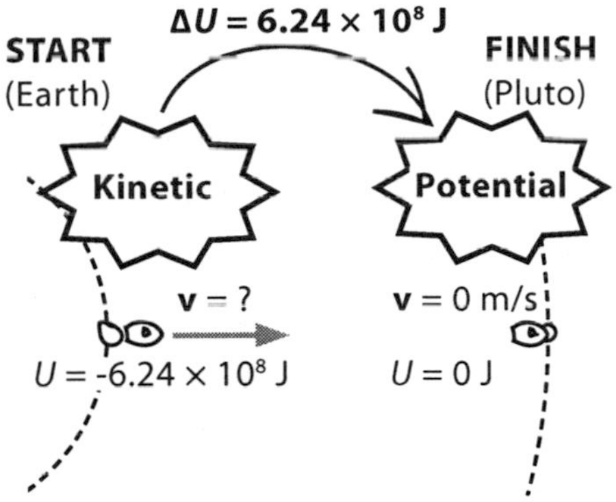

Didn't we say before that U = 0 at the Earth's surface - and what's with the negative numbers? The equation must be wrong!

You can only measure changes in energy.

If you know the **change in potential energy** between the surface of the Earth and the edge of the solar system, you can say that an identical amount of **kinetic energy** must be transferred to get there - then use this to work out the escape velocity, as $K = \frac{1}{2}m\mathbf{v}^2$.

As it's the **change** in potential energy that's important, it doesn't matter what the absolute values you calculate are - as long as the change is the same.

It's like putting an object part-way along a ruler. If one end of the object is at the mark that says 2.0 cm and the other end is at the 4.0 cm mark, you can see that the object is 2.0 cm long. Same goes if your object is between the 28.0 cm and 30.0 cm marks. The object is still 2.0 cm, long, and where you choose to count from on your **scale** doesn't affect this.

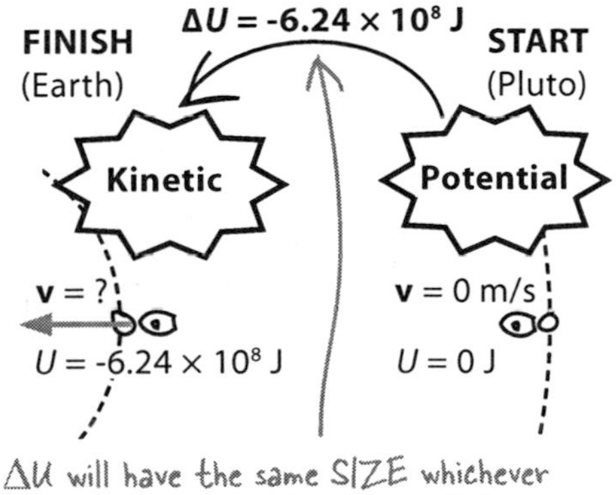

ΔU will have the same SIZE whichever direction you make the trip in, but in one direction the change will be positive (as you lose kinetic energy) and in the other direction the change will be negative (as you gain kinetic energy).

If $U = 0$ at infinity, the equation works for any star or planet

Saying that $U = 0$ at the Earth's surface is great if you're close to the Earth's surface, when you can take **g** = 9.8 m/s^2 to be a constant. In that context, you'd almost always define zero potential energy to be at ground level, as this is a common reference point for everything.

But if you're moving away from the Sun or another planet, the Earth's surface isn't a good reference point!

It's a bit like temperature. On Earth, it's convenient to have a scale defined by the freezing and boiling points of water on Earth, 0°C and 100°C. But that's not a very universal scale, as the reference point depends on you being on Earth.

Your have your maximum possible potential energy when you're at infinity.

For temperature, scientists use the Kelvin scale, where "absolute zero" is defined as the lowest temperature theoretically possible. No one has ever reached absolute zero – just like no one has ever reached infinity – but defining an unchanging common reference point like this gives you a benchmark you can measure everything else against.

So rather than having a different reference point for every one of the (estimated) 10^{22} stars and planets in the universe, it's better to use a **common reference point** that is the same for any star or planet, regardless of its mass and the distance an object is from it.

That common reference point is the place where you have **maximum gravitational potential energy**. This has to be when you have the **maximum possible displacement** from the Earth - and the Sun - and all the other stars. We call this reference point "being at **infinity**".

So ... you have your maximum potential energy when r is very large. And the equation tells us that U = 0 when r is very large. So your **maximum** potential energy is zero?! Doesn't that mean your potential energy will be **negative** if you're not at infinity?

$U = 0$ at infinity. Total energy is conserved, so as you gain kinetic energy by falling, your potential energy becomes negative.

The values you calculate for the potential energy will be negative.

The further away you are from the surface of a planet, the greater your potential energy. Defining $U = 0$ at infinity - the furthest you can possibly be - means that as you gain kinetic energy by falling towards a star or planet, your gravitational potential energy becomes negative.

But that's OK - the **scale** hasn't changed. The **change** in potential energy between two points is still the same. Where you choose to count from on your scale doesn't matter. You just have to be careful with minus signs!

Potential Energy Exposed

This week's interview: Potential energy answers charges of inconsistency.

Head First: So, potential energy, you've been accused of inconsistency. What's the bottom line?

Potential energy: The bottom line (or zero potential energy) is wherever you want it to be.

Head First: Um... are you implying that even you don't know when you're equal to zero?!

Potential energy: Yes ...

Head First: And if you don't know, how on Earth am I - or anyone else - supposed to know?

Potential energy: I think you've got the wrong end of the stick there. You can only measure **changes** in potential energy, not absolute values And that means you get to **choose where zero potential energy is**.

Head First: But why's that useful?

Potential energy: It gives you a **reference point** to measure **changes** in potential energy against.

Head First: Right. But why suddenly put that reference point at **infinity**? I was perfectly happy before, when zero was at the surface of the Earth.

Potential energy: You have to think about the bigger picture. When you're close to the Earth's surface, you can use the simple form of the equation $U_g = m\mathbf{gh}$, because the acceleration due to gravity - and therefore the gravitational force - is constant.

Head First: But why can't you do the same further away from the Earth?

Potential energy: The gravitational force drops off in an inverse square way. So it's not constant - and you need to do more complicated math to calculate the change in potential energy.

Head First: I can see that - but it still doesn't tell me why you suddenly want to put zero at infinity instead of the Earth's surface!

Potential energy: What if you're launching your spaceship from the moon, or from Mars, not Earth?

Head First: Um, I guess I put the zero of potential energy at the surface of the Moon, or Mars ...

Potential energy: But that's very inconsistent, isn't it? How are you supposed to compare all these values when you keep on changing where your zero is?

Head First: Hmmm. You may have a point. But I'm finding the concept of negative potential energy difficult. I didn't think energy was a vector.

Potential energy: I'm not a vector - just like temperature isn't a vector. A temperature of 2°C doesn't point in the opposite direction from a temperature of 2°C. The negative sign is just to indicate its **position on a scale**, not a direction.

Head First: What does that mean in practice?

Potential energy: OK, try thinking about it like this. Suppose you start at infinity with zero total energy, then fall towards the Earth (or another star or planet) What happens to your kinetic energy?

Head First: I guess your velocity increases so your kinetic energy increases.

Potential energy: Right! But the total energy needs to stay the same. So if you start off with zero potential energy and gain, say 100 J of kinetic energy, your new potential energy must be -100 J.

Head First: OK ... but all these messy negative numbers make the math tricker, right?!

Potential energy: I do admit, that's the down side of putting zero at infinity. But as long as you're careful you'll be OK. You're dealing with **changes** in potential energy - so going further away from a planet is still a positive change - like going from a temperature of -40°C to -2°C is a change of 38°C.

Head First: Thank you - that's much clearer now.

Use energy conservation to calculate the astronaut's escape velocity

If the gravitational force on the astronaut's spaceship was constant and didn't drop off with distance, you could just use forces and equations of motion to work out his **escape velocity**.

But the gravitational force on the spaceship changes as he gets further away, so it's difficult to do the calculation using forces. But you can use **energy conservation**, as the spaceship's kinetic energy at the start must have been transferred to potential energy by the end.

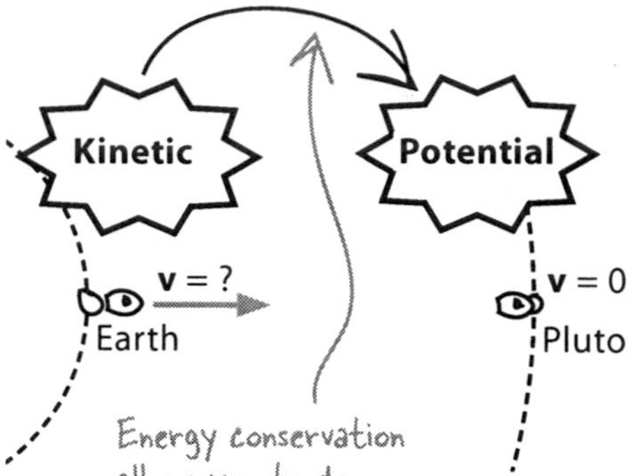

Energy conservation allows you to do problems you can't easily do using forces.

It doesn't matter which mass is represented by m_1 and which is m_2 as long as you're consistent.

Sharpen your pencil

Ready Bake Equation

$$U_G = -\frac{Gm_1m_2}{r}$$

After a spaceship blasts off from the Earth's surface, its propulsion system is switched off.

What is the minimum velocity that the spaceship must have to successfully escape from the Earth's gravitational field so that it can reach infinity without falling back down again?

The radius of the Earth is 6.38×10^6 m, and its mass is 5.97×10^{24} kg. G, the gravitational constant, is 6.67×10^{-11} m^3/kg·s^2

If you can escape to infinity, you can definitely make it to Pluto!

Sharpen your pencil Solution

Ready Bake Equation

$$U_G = -\frac{Gm_1m_2}{r}$$

This equation for the gravitational potential energy (with $U = 0$ at infinity) has a similar form to the equation for the gravitational force.

After a spaceship blasts off from the Earth's surface, its propulsion system is switched off.

What is the minimum velocity that the spaceship must have to successfully escape from the Earth's gravitational field so that it can reach infinity without falling back down again?

The radius of the Earth is 6.38×10^6 m, and its mass is 5.97×10^{24} kg. G, the gravitational constant, is 6.67×10^{-11} m^3/kg·s^2

Earth's surface	Infinity	
$v_0 = ?$	$v = 0$	m_1 = spaceship mass m_2 = Earth mass

Kinetic at Earth's surface transferred to potential at infinity.

$$\Delta U = U_{infinity} - U_{earth}$$

$$\Delta U = 0 - U_{earth}$$

Zero minus a negative number is a positive number, so $\Delta U = \frac{Gm_1m_2}{r}$

$$\Delta K = \Delta U$$

$$\frac{1}{2}m_1v_0^2 = \frac{Gm_1m_2}{r}$$

As the mass of the spaceship divides out, the escape velocity doesn't depend on the mass.

It's OK if you used the value for the gravitational potential energy at the Earth's surface that you calculated on page ??, but dividing out the mass of the spaceship is usually easier for these types of questions.

$$\Rightarrow v_0 = \sqrt{\frac{2Gm_2}{r}} = \sqrt{\frac{2 \times 6.67 \times 10^{-11} \times 5.97 \times 10^{24}}{6.38 \times 10^6}}$$

$$v_0 = 1.12 \times 10^4 \text{ m/s} = \underline{\underline{11.2 \text{ km/s}}} \text{ (3 sd)}$$

The escape velocity that ensures you won't fall back down to Earth again after you switch the engine off is 11.2 km/s. Pretty fast - but in space there's no kind of atmosphere, and no friction to slow you down!

But the astronaut's not totally happy with this. He thinks that you also need to escape from the Sun's gravitational field! The Sun has around 300000 times more mass than the Earth - which will really tell over large distances! You'll have to factor in the change in potential energy due to the astronaut's distance from the Sun changing, as well as his distance from the Earth.

Sharpen your pencil

Some time after a spaceship blasts off from the Earth's surface, its propulsion system is switched off.

What is the minimum velocity that the spaceship must have to successfully escape from both the the Earth's gravitational field and the Sun's gravitational field so that it can reach infinity without falling back down again?

The radius of the Earth is 6.38×10^6 m, and the mass of the Earth is 5.97×10^{24} kg. The distance from the Earth to the Sun is 1.50×10^{11} m. The radius of the Sun is 6.96×10^8 m, and the mass of the Sun is 1.99×10^{30} kg. G, the gravitational constant, is 6.67×10^{-11} m^3/kg.s^2

Hint: Start with two sketches, one for the change in potential energy due to the Earth's gravitational field, and the other for the change in potential energy due to the Sun's gravitational field.

Be VERY careful with your variable names, as you will have various masses, radii and displacements floating around.

Hint: The total change in potential energy is equal to the changes due to the Earth's gravitational field and the Sun's gravitational field added together. Then you can use the same method as on the opposite page.

Sharpen your pencil Solution

Some time after a spaceship blasts off from the Earth's surface, its propulsion system is switched off.

What is the minimum velocity that the spaceship must have to successfully escape from both the the Earth's gravitational field and the Sun's gravitational field so that it can reach infinity without falling back down again?

The radius of the Earth is 6.38×10^6 m, and the mass of the Earth is 5.97×10^{24} kg. The distance from the Earth to the Sun is 1.50×10^{11} m. The radius of the Sun is 6.96×10^8 m, and the mass of the Sun is 1.99×10^{30} kg. G, the gravitational constant, is 6.67×10^{-11} m³/kg.s²

Change in potential energy due to Earth's gravitational field

m_1 = spaceship mass $\quad r_E$ = Radius of Earth

m_E = Earth mass

Earth's surface: $U = -\dfrac{Gm_1m_E}{r_E}$

Infinity: $U = 0$

Change in potential energy due to Sun's gravitational field

m_1 = spaceship mass $\quad r_{fromS}$ = Distance from Sun

m_S = Sun mass

Earth's surface: $U = -\dfrac{Gm_1m_S}{r_{fromS}}$

Infinity: $U = 0$

The radius of the sun is irrelevant! It's the distance you are from the Sun that's important.

Kinetic at Earth's surface transferred to potential at infinity.

$$\Delta U = U_{infinity} - U_{earth}$$

$$\Delta U = 0 - U_{earth}$$

Zero minus a negative number is a positive number, so $\Delta U = \dfrac{Gm_1m_E}{r_E} + \dfrac{Gm_1m_S}{r_{fromS}}$

$$\Delta K = \Delta U$$

The mass of the spaceship divides out.

$$\frac{1}{2}m_1v_0^2 = \frac{Gm_1m_E}{r_E} + \frac{Gm_1m_S}{r_{fromS}}$$

$$\Rightarrow \quad v_0 = \sqrt{\frac{2Gm_E}{r_E} + \frac{2Gm_S}{r_{fromS}}}$$

$$v_0 = \sqrt{\frac{2 \times 6.67 \times 10^{-11} \times 5.97 \times 10^{24}}{6.38 \times 10^6} + \frac{2 \times 6.67 \times 10^{-11} \times 1.99 \times 10^{30}}{1.50 \times 10^{11}}}$$

$$v_0 = \sqrt{1.44 \times 10^8 + 1.77 \times 10^9} = 4.37 \times 10^4 \text{ m/s} = \underline{\underline{44.7 \text{ km/s}}} \text{ (3 sd)}$$

We need to keep up with our astronaut

Before sending our astronaut off to Pluto, we need to get some communication **satellites** in place to keep in contact with him. These satellites need to be in a certain type of orbit around the Earth called a **geostationary orbit**.

A geostationary orbit is one where the satellite always stays over the same point on the Earth's surface.

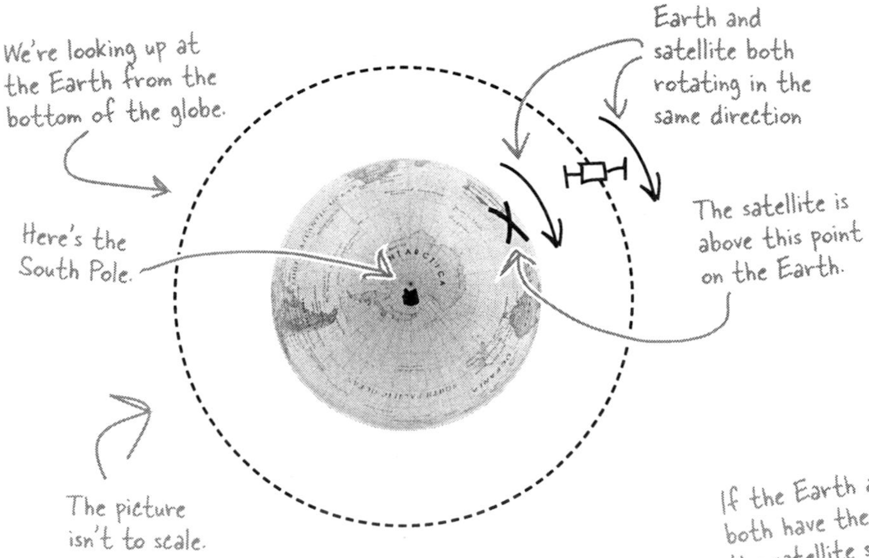

A GEOSTATIONARY orbit has a period of 24 hours, the same as the period of the Earth's rotation.

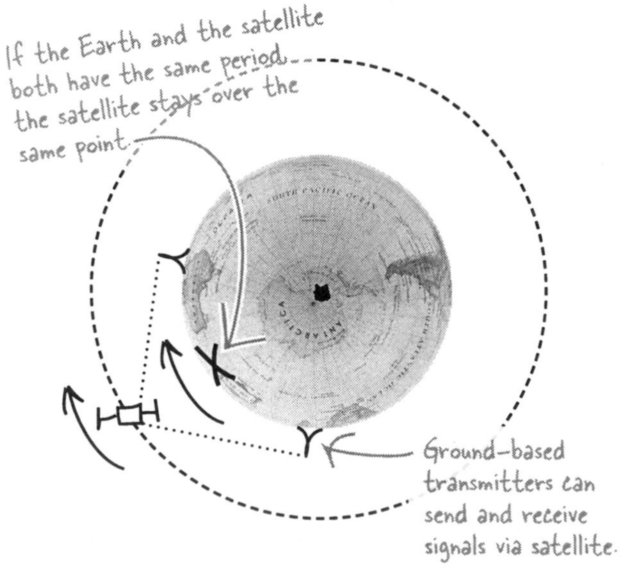

The satellite is moving... it just remains above the same point on the Earth's surface because the Earth is rotating with the **same period** as the satellite.

This allows you to use the satellite for Earth communications by aiming your transmitters and receivers at the same point in the sky.

We need the **period** of the satellite to be **24 hours** since that's the **time** it takes for the Earth to rotate once.

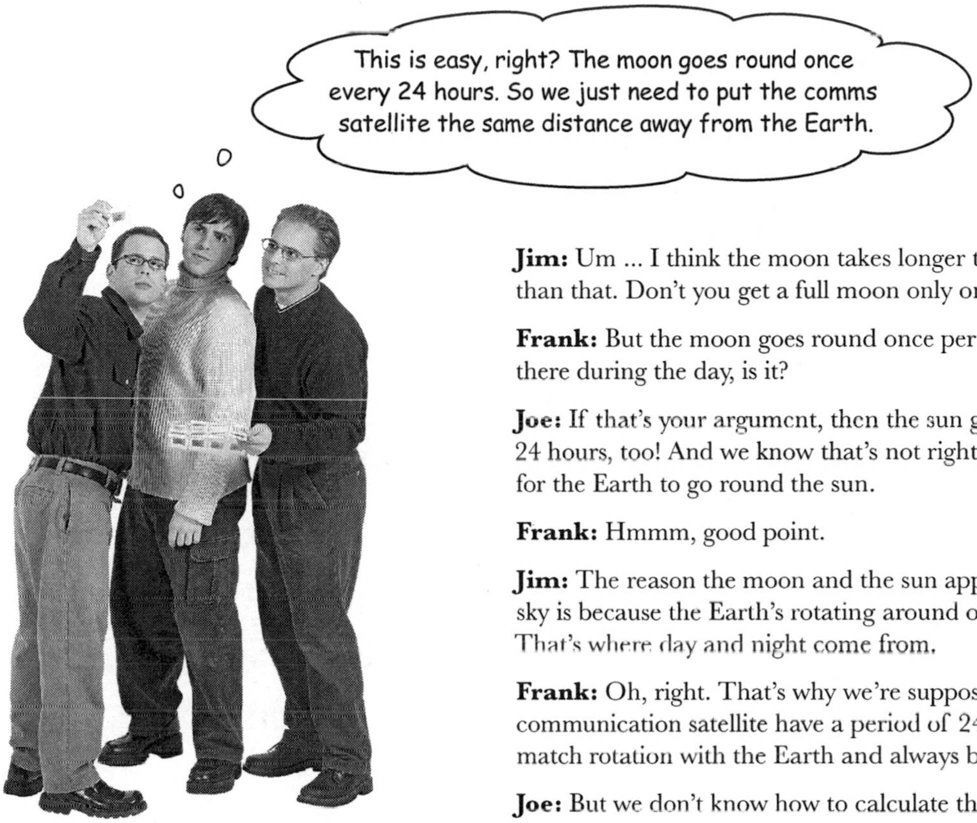

Jim: Um ... I think the moon takes longer to go around the Earth than that. Don't you get a full moon only once a month?

Frank: But the moon goes round once per 24 hours, right? It's not there during the day, is it?

Joe: If that's your argument, then the sun goes round once every 24 hours, too! And we know that's not right - it takes a whole year for the Earth to go round the sun.

Frank: Hmmm, good point.

Jim: The reason the moon and the sun appear to move across the sky is because the Earth's rotating around on its axis once a day. That's where day and night come from.

Frank: Oh, right. That's why we're supposed to make the communication satellite have a period of 24 hours, isn't it? So it can match rotation with the Earth and always be above the same point?

Joe: But we don't know how to calculate the period of the orbit. Actually, we don't know how to calculate ***anything*** for orbits!

Jim: Hmm. I'm sure that Pluto must take longer to orbit the sun than the Earth does. Maybe the period of the orbit depends on your **displacement** from the thing you're orbiting.

Frank: I'm not so sure. Remember when we were working with the hamster wheel? Didn't every part of the wheel rotate with the same angular velocity? That means every part had the same period, too, right? So the distance from the center of the wheel didn't affect the period of the wheel.

Joe: But all the parts of the hamster wheel were joined together, so they *have* to go around with the same period. Planets and satellites aren't joined together. So the period might depend on the distance from the center after all.

Frank: Hmm, that's a good point, too.

Jim: I'm sure that far away objects must take longer to orbit.

Joe: But how can we work that out?

A day is the time it takes the Earth to spin once on its own axis

A year is the time it takes the Earth to orbit once round the sun.

Wouldn't it be dreamy if there was a way of connecting the **distance** from the Earth with the **period** of an object's orbit. But I know it's just a fantasy ...

The centripetal force is provided by gravity

An object that travels along a circular path must have a **net force** acting on it to provide a **centripetal force**. This force must act towards the center of the circle.

In chapter 15, you learned to equate the size of the centripetal force, $F_c = mr\omega^2$ with the net force. Here, the net force on the satellite is provided by the gravitational force from the Earth.

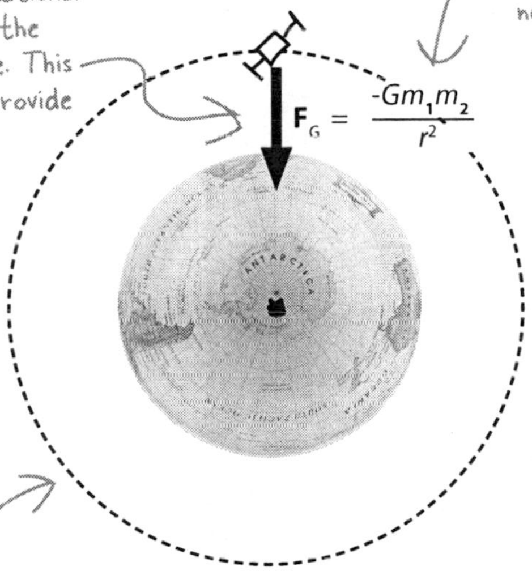

When you've equated the centripetal force with the gravitational force, you'll have the job of making some substitutions so that your equation is in terms of T, the **period** instead of ω, the angular velocity.

Then you can calculate the radius of the satellite's orbit for any period - including the 24 hour geostationary period you're interested in.

Use the ready-bake facts to help you solve the problem.

Ready Bake Facts

Mass of the Earth:

5.97×10^{24} kg

Radius of the Earth:

6.38×10^{6} m

Gravitational constant

$G = 6.67 \times 10^{-11}$ m^3/kg·s^2

If you make sure both are pointing towards the center of the circle, then they'll both have the same sign.

Equate the CENTRIPETAL FORCE with the GRAVITATIONAL FORCE to solve orbit problems.

Sharpen your pencil

You can look up equations involving T in the appendix.

a. Work out a general equation for the size of r, the radius of a satellite's orbit in terms of T, the period of the satellite, G the gravitational constant and m_e the mass of the Earth (don't insert any values, just work out an equation).

b. Calculate the height that the satellite must be above the Earth's surface to have a period of 24 hours.

c. If the radius of a satellite's orbit is doubled, what happens to the period of its orbit? (Please do this question using proportion.)

d. What happens to a satellite's kinetic and potential energy as it goes round a circular orbit?

Sharpen your pencil Solution

a. Work out a general equation for the size of *r*, the radius of a satellite's orbit in terms of *T*, the period of the satellite, *G* the gravitational constant and m_e the mass of the Earth (don't insert any values, just work out an equation).

Gravitational force provides centripetal force for orbit.

$$F_c = F_{net}$$

$$m_s r\omega^2 = \frac{Gm_s m_e}{r^2}$$

Both forces points towards the center of the circle, so you can lose the 'conventional' minus sign.

We've used m_s for the saatellite's mass, but the symbol doesn't really matter, as the mass divides out!

$$\omega^2 = \frac{Gm_e}{r^3}$$

Make a substitution for ω.

$$\omega = 2\pi f \quad \text{and} \quad f = \frac{1}{T}$$

$$\Rightarrow \omega = \frac{2\pi}{T}$$

$$\left(\frac{2\pi}{T}\right)^2 = \frac{Gm_e}{r^3}$$

$$\frac{4\pi^2}{T^2} = \frac{Gm_e}{r^3}$$

$$r^3 = \frac{Gm_e T^2}{4\pi^2}$$

This is called Kepler's 3rd Law. It shows you how the radius and period of an orbit are related.

The radius in the gravitational force equation is always the distance from the center of the Earth, not the surface. So you need to calculate the difference at the end.

b. Calculate the height that the satellite must be above the Earth's surface to have a period of 24 hours.

$$r = \sqrt[3]{\frac{Gm_e T^2}{4\pi^2}} = \sqrt[3]{\frac{6.67 \times 10^{-11} \times 5.97 \times 10^{24} \times 86400^2}{4 \times \pi^2}} = 4.22 \times 10^7 \text{ m (3 sd)}$$

24 hours is $24 \times 60 \times 60 = 86400$ s

$$\text{Distance from surface} = r - r_e = 4.22 \times 10^7 - 6.38 \times 10^6 = \underline{\underline{3.59 \times 10^7 \text{ m}}} \text{ (3 sd)}$$

c. If the radius of a satellite's orbit is doubled, what happens to the period of its orbit? (Please do this question using proportion.)

$$r^3 = \frac{Gm_e T^2}{4\pi^2}$$

Everything in the equation is constant apart from r and T.

If r is doubled, left hand side of equation increases $2 \times 2 \times 2 = 8$ times.

This means that T^2 is 8 times larger than before.

So T is $\sqrt{8} = 2.83$ (3 sd) times larger than before.

d. What happens to a satellite's kinetic and potential energy as it goes round a circular orbit?

They remain constant because the satellite's height and speed remain constant (even though its velocity is changing direction all the time)..

there are no Dumb Questions

Q: What was that $\sqrt[3]{}$ thing all about in the math bit over there?

A: It's a cube root symbol. You know how a square root is what you do to find out what number you need to square to get the number you started with?

Q: Yeah ...

A: Well, a cube root is what you type into your calculator to work out what number you'd need to cube to get the number you started off with.

Q: So if I have r^3 = something then I can say that $r = \sqrt[3]{\text{something}}$

A: Yes. It works in the same way that a square root does.

Q: So ... I noticed that the mass of the satellite divided out when I made the centripetal force equal to the gravitational force. That kinda thing has happened a few times now.

A: Yeah, good spot. That's because the gravitational force depends on the object's mass, *m*. The gravitational force provides the centripetal force, $F_c = ma_c$. So when you equate them, you get an '*m*' on each side of your equation, which divides out.

Q: So why can't I just equate the gravitational field strength with the centripetal acceleration and skip the step of dividing out the mass?

A: You could ... but dealing with forces is a good habit to get into.

Q: Why should I deal with forces, not accelerations?

A: There are a lot of other sources of centripetal force - and the size of the force may not depend on the mass of the object.

Q: When might the size of the force not depend on the mass of the object?

A: Well, an electron will follow a curved path when it goes through a magnetic field because of its electric charge, not its mass. You don't have to worry about that right now because it's in the electromagnetism part of your course. But if you get used to **equating** the **centripetal force** with the source of the **net force**, you'll find dealing with that a whole lot easier when you get there.

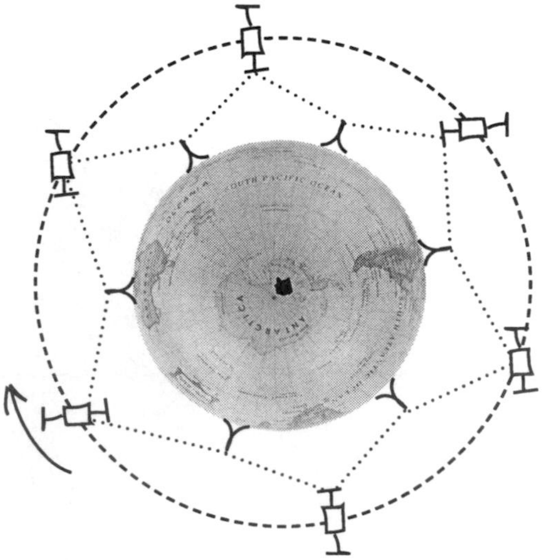

With the comms satellites in place, it's Pluto (and beyond)

The communications satellites are in place in their geostationary orbits nearly 4000 km above the Earth's surface.

And the astronaut it good to go.

Stand by for blasting off to Pluto - and beyond!

Question Clinic: The "gravitational force = centripetal force" Question

Another classic way of getting you to do something with centripetal force is to give you a problem to do with orbits to solve. The big thing here is to equate the centripetal force with the gravitational force that provides it - then follow through with the math.

Buzzwords to get you thinking about circular motion

Make sure you use the mass of the Earth – not the mass of the sun or anything else on your table of information!

This tells you which letters you should include.

2. A communications satellite is to be put into orbit around the Earth.

a. Work out a general equation for T, the period of a satellite in terms of r the radius of its orbit, G the gravitational constant and m_e the mass of the Earth.

b. Work out the height that the satellite must be above the Earth's surface to have a period of 24 hours.

c. If the radius of the satellite's orbit is doubled, what happens to the period of its orbit?

This means don't use numbers yet.

You'll need to convert this time to seconds to all the units work throu correctly.

Notice that you'll have to subtract the radius of the Earth from the radius of the orbit to get the distance above the surface!

This is a typical question where you need to use proportion in an equation you already know (in this case, the equation from part a).

Be careful not to use the wrong equation! The equations for the gravitational force, gravitational field (i.e., acceleration due to gravity) and the gravitational potential energy (with 0 at infinity) all look very similar. Remember that gravitational force follows an inverse square law - and that its equation involves the masses of both the objects involved.

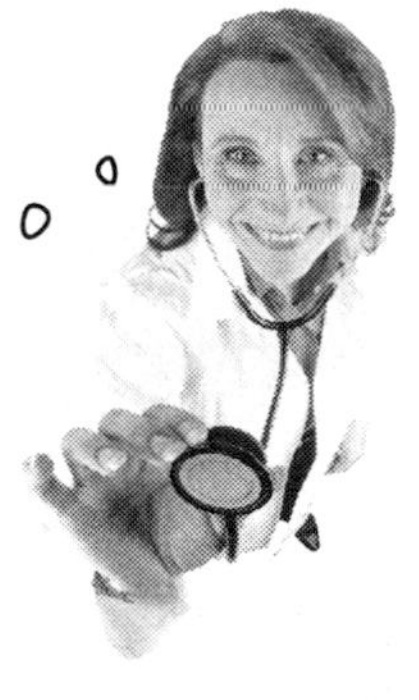

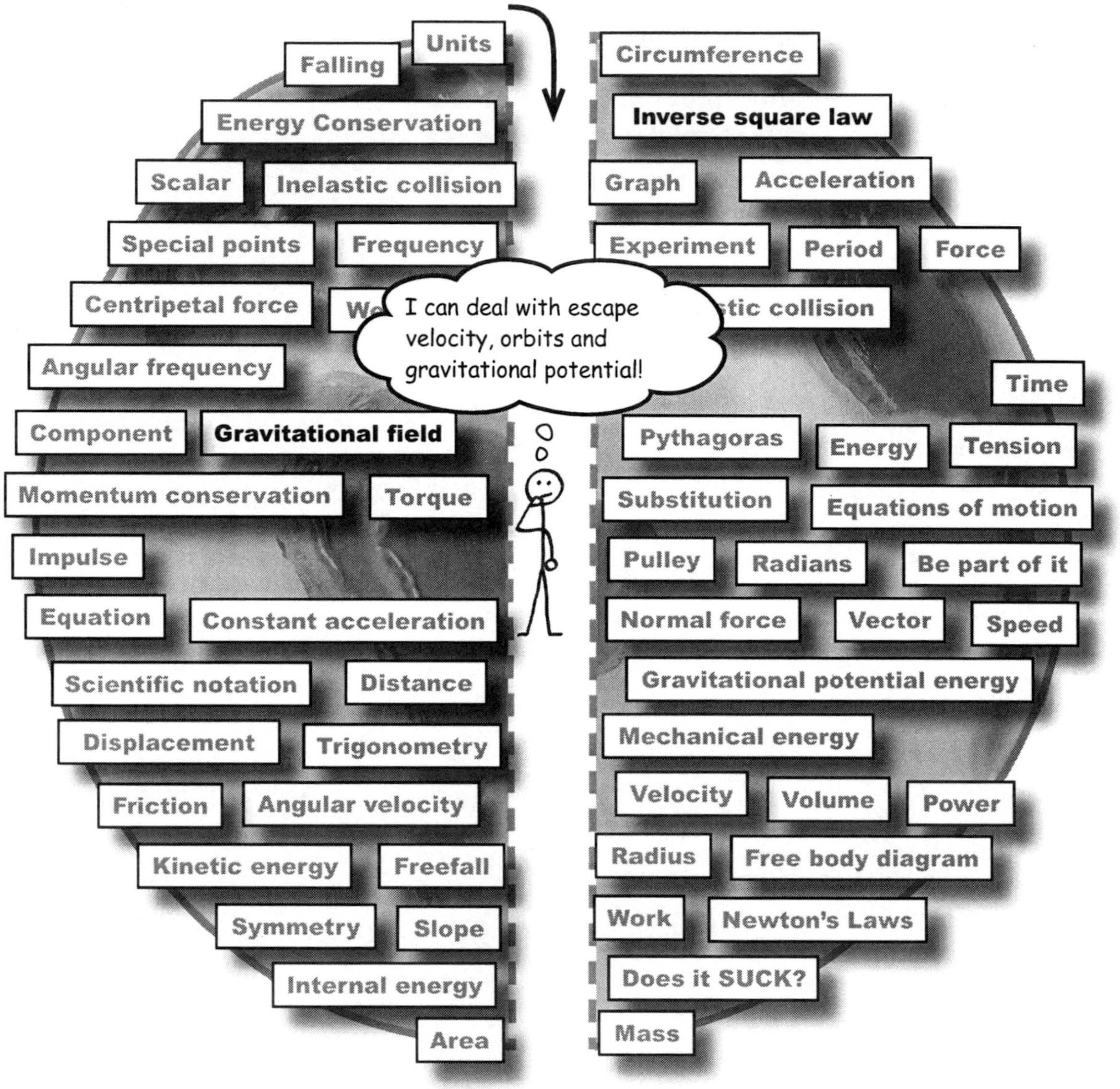

☑	**Gravitational field**	**The strength of a gravitational field at a point is the same as the acceleration of an object in freefall at that point. Gravitational field lines help you to visualize the gravitational field strength.**
☑	**Inverse square law**	**If a quantity (for example the gravitational field strength) is proportional to $\frac{1}{r^2}$ then the quantity follows an inverse square law.**

Your Physics Toolbox

You've got Chapter 18 under your belt and added some problem-solving concepts to your toolbox.

Gravitational field

The gravitational field strength tells you the acceleration something would experience if it was allowed to freefall at that distance from the Earth.

The gravitational field strength follows an inverse square law.

Gravitational field lines

Gravitational field lines point in the direction something would move in if it was allowed to freefall from that point.

The closer together they are, the stronger the gravitational field is at that point.

Inverse square law

If a quantity follows an inverse square law, it drops off by $1/r^2$ as you increase the distance from its source. This means that if you double the distance, there's a fourfold decrease in the quantity.

Examples: light, sound, gravitational field strength.

Geostationary orbit

An orbit with a period of 24 hours. So-called because if the satellite is over the equator and rotating in the same direction as the Earth, it stays over the same spot on the ground.

Gravitational potential

Another name for gravitational potential energy. The term is most commonly used when you've defined $U = 0$ to be at infinity.

The gravitational potential drops off as $1/r$ – if you double the distance, you halve the gravitational potential.

Calculations with gravitational potential

The change in potential energy is equal to the change in kinetic energy.

Be very, very careful with minus signs! Because $U = 0$ at infinity, all other values of gravitational potential will be negative. But the CHANGE in potential energy is the same wherever you define zero to be.

Calculations with orbits

The net force that provides the centripetal force for an orbit is the gravitational force.

Equate the gravitational force with the centripetal force, and the answers will drop out of your equation.

Ready Bake Equations

$$F_G = -\frac{Gm_1m_2}{r^2}$$

$$U_G = -\frac{Gm_1m_2}{r}$$

19 Oscillations (part 1)

Round and round

Wow... everything looks so different since I turned these directions right side up.

Things can look very different when you see them from another angle. So far you've been looking at circular motion from above - but what does it look like from the side? In this chapter, you'll tie together your **circular motion** and **trigonometry** superpowers as you learn extended definitions of **sine** and **cosine**. Once you're done, you'll be able to deal with anything that's moving around a circle - whichever way you look at it.

Welcome to the fair!

After your success at hamster training, you've got another client who needs your help. Jane's opening up a new booth at the local fair, and wants to build a duck-shooting competition - with a twist.

This chapter builds on what we did in chapter 16, with the hamster trainer.

At the moment, she's got a duck moving around in a **circle**. But she expects the game to be popular, and the rotating duck takes up space that she could use to pack in more paying customers.

So instead, Jane wants to let players shoot at a digital version of the duck, displayed on a giant **flat screen**. Each player feels like they're shooting at a real rotating duck, but Jane can just monitor the screen to run the game.

Jane's got all the equipment: a duck mounted on a rotating stick, a screen, and light guns that can shoot at the screen. The screen even registers where the gun hits, and which player shot the duck. Your job is the hard part, though: where should the screen display the duck as it moves around in a circle?

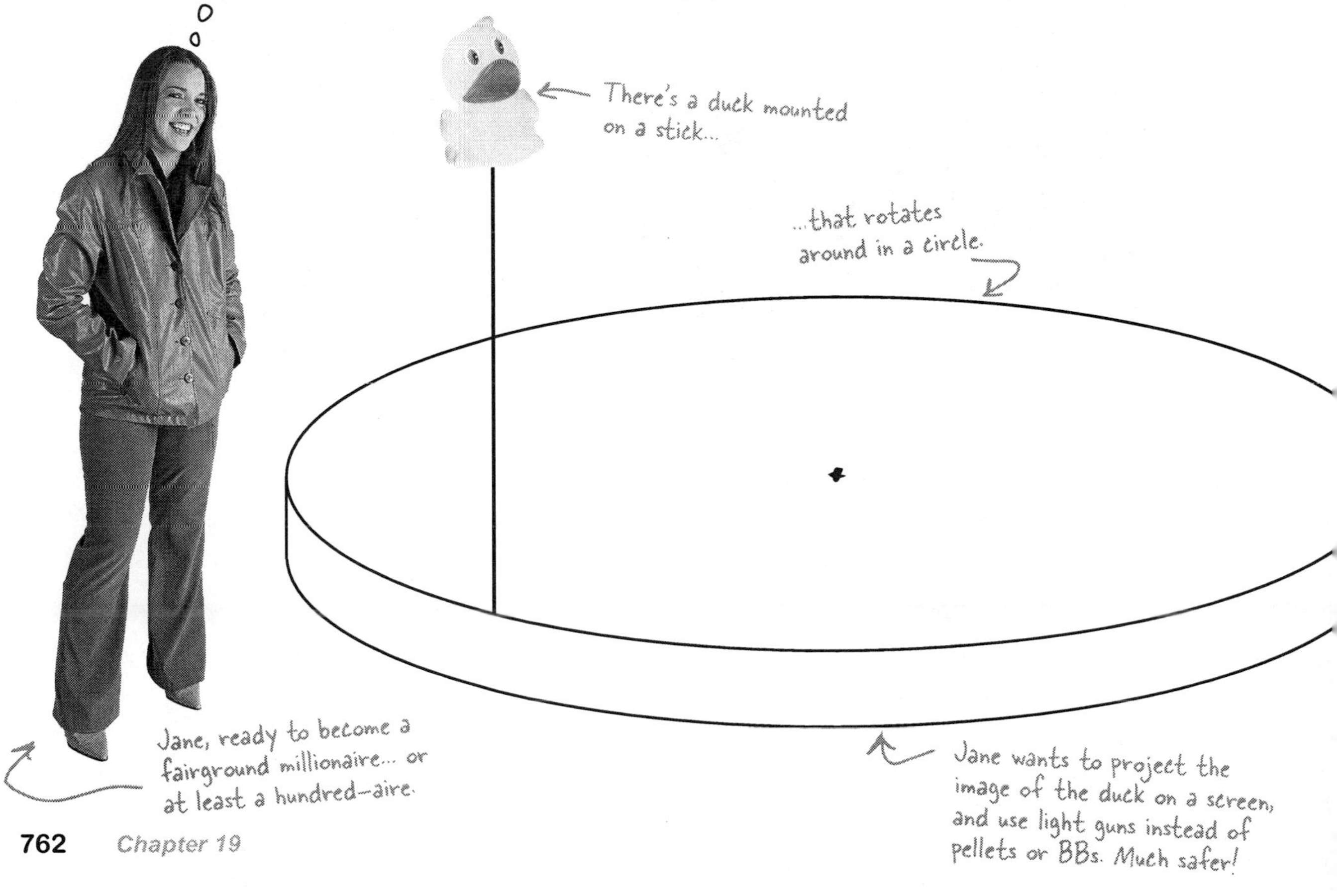

Reproduce the duck on the display

The real duck sits on a pole at eye level and travels around in a circle. But your job is to figure out where on Jane's big screen the digital duck should appear. Every time Jane tries to get the screen working, things look funny.

We know the real duck's moving along the edge of a circle, which is 3.00 meters wide. We also know that the duck goes around the entire circle once every 2.50 seconds. The duck starts in the middle on the far side from the player, and travels around the circle counter-clockwise.

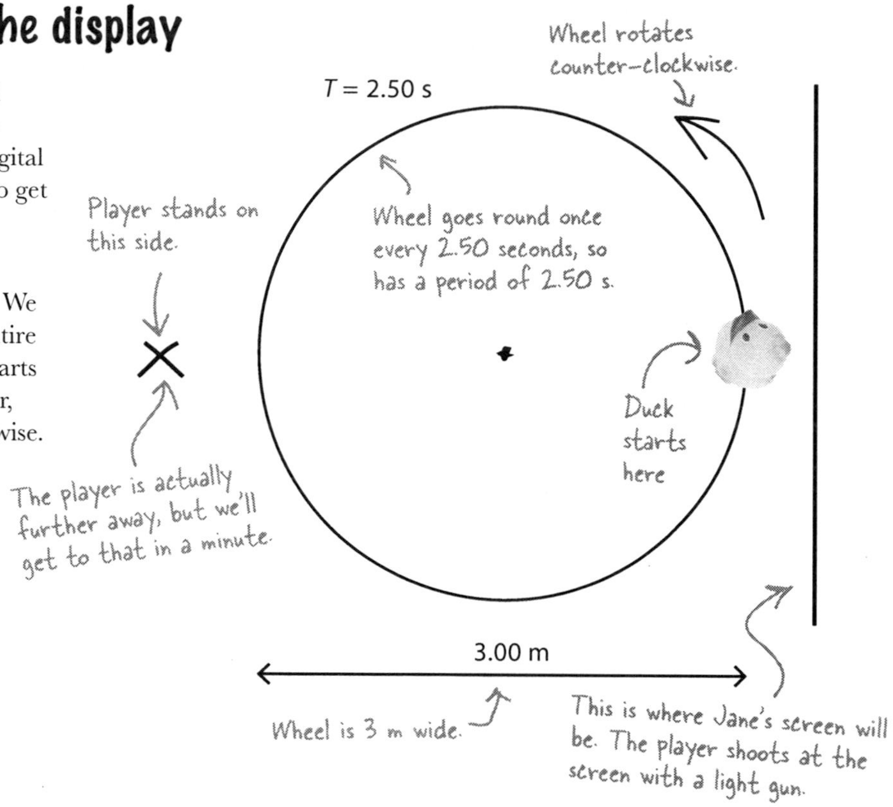

Sharpen your pencil

Draw a player's-eye view of the game, and describe what the player sees from their side perspective as the duck goes around in a circle.

The player is much further away than there was space to show in the picture. The player is actually standing somewhere off the left hand page!

Make sure to write down any important **times** and **distances** from the moment the game starts that might help you draw the digital duck on the screen.

Space for your drawing.

Sharpen your pencil Solution

Draw a player's-eye view of the game, and describe what the player sees from their side perspective as the duck goes around in a circle.

The player is much further away than there was space to show in the picture. The player is actually standing somewhere off the left hand page!

Make sure to write down any important **times** and **distances** from the moment the game starts that might help you draw the digital duck on the screen.

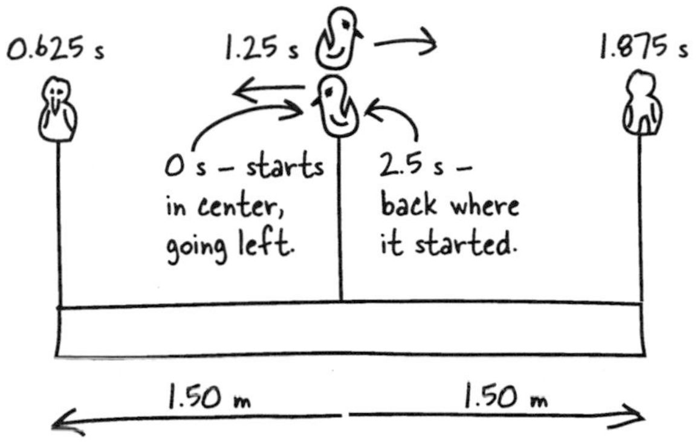

The player sees the duck starting out in the center of their view. Then after 0.625 s, the duck's on their left side. After 1.25 s the duck is back in the center. After 1.875 s, the duck's on the right. Then after 2.50 s, it's back where it started in the center.

The player doesn't see a circle at all. The duck just appears to move side to side (though the player would see different sides of the duck as the duck turns around the circle).

Jim: Yeah, if you're looking at a circle from the side, you don't really see the round parts at all. And the **radius** of the circle is 3.00 meters ...

Joe: ... er, the radius is 1.50 meters. The *diameter's* 3.00 meters.

Jim: Oops, sorry, you're right. The diameter's 3.00 meters. Jane's screen is wider than that, so we can show the duck at its actual size.

Joe: Cool. We just have to work out how fast the duck's going, left-right-left-right, etc. Then we can move the duck across the screen at the correct **velocity**.

Frank: Well, we know the duck takes 2.50 seconds to go around once.

Jim: So the duck's got a **period** of 2.50 s. We know the **radius** of the circle, too. So we can work out the duck's speed, just like we did for the hamster trainer.

Joe: You know, I'm a bit worried about the light gun. There might be some problems there. Here's what I'm thinking...

Sharpen your pencil

Joe's worried about registering hits on the screen. The distance from the player to the duck is smaller when the duck is at the front of the circle than it is when the duck is at the back of the circle. So the distance that the light from the light gun travels is different depending on the duck's position.

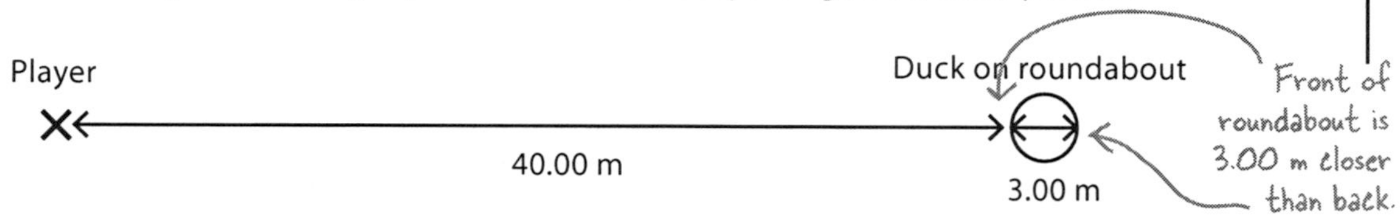

This might mean that a hit when the real duck's at the front of the circle may register before a hit at the back of the circle. But the screen for the digital duck is flat, so will register all hits at the same time. Do you think that's a problem we'll need to worry about?

a. A duck is on the edge of a roundabout with a diameter of 3.00 meters. The roundabout goes round once every 2.50 seconds. What is the duck's speed?

The equations you'll need to use for this are in chapter 16.

b. The duck is to be zapped with a light gun by a player standing 40.00 m away from the front of the roundabout. How much longer does it take the light to cover the 43.00 m to the back of the roundabout compared to the 40.00 m to the front of the roundabout? (The speed of light is 3×10^8 m/s.)

Ready Bake Fact

Speed of light:

3.00×10^8 m/s

c. Do you think the player will notice this extra time that it takes for a hit to register?

Sharpen your pencil Solution

Joe's worried about registering hits on the screen. The distance from the player to the duck is smaller when the duck is at the front of the circle than it is when the duck is at the back of the circle. So the distance that the light from the light gun travels is different depending on the duck's position.

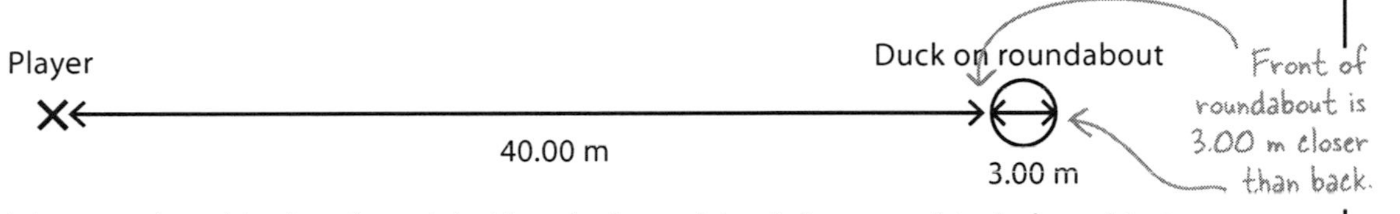

This might mean that a hit when the real duck's at the front of the circle may register before a hit at the back of the circle. But the screen for the digital duck is flat, so will register all hits at the same time. Do you think that's a problem we'll need to worry about?

a. A duck is on the edge of a roundabout with a diameter of 3.00 meters. The roundabout goes round once every 2.50 seconds. What is the duck's speed?

Use equation $v = r\omega$; work out ω from frequency

Period of circle, $T = 2.50$ s

Frequency, $f = \frac{1}{T} = \frac{1}{2.50} = 0.400$ Hz

$v = r\omega = r \times 2\pi f$

$= 1.50 \times 2 \times \pi \times 0.400$

$= 3.77$ m/s (3 sd)

You can also do this by using $C = 2\pi r$ to calculate the distance the duck travels in 1 reolution, then dividing the distance by the period

b. The duck is to be zapped with a light gun by a player standing 40.00 m away from the front of the roundabout. How much longer does it take the light to cover the 43.00 m to the back of the roundabout compared to the 40.00 m to the front of the roundabout? (The speed of light is 3×10^8 m/s.)

Difference in distance = 43.00 − 40.00 = 3.00 m

Time it takes light to cover this:

$$\text{speed} = \frac{\text{distance}}{\text{time}}$$

$$\Rightarrow \text{time} = \frac{\text{distance}}{\text{speed}} = \frac{3.00}{3.00 \times 10^8}$$

$$= \underline{1.00 \times 10^{-8}\ \text{s}}\ (3\ \text{sd})$$

Ready Bake Fact

Speed of light:

3.00×10^8 m/s

c. Do you think the player will notice this extra time that it takes for a hit to register?

1×10^{-8} s is very short – 10 nanoseconds! Players won't notice the time difference between hitting the duck at the front of the circle and hitting the duck at the back of the circle. So we can just make the flat screen register hits instantly.

Jim: So the duck starts in the center, moves 1.50 m to the left at 3.77 m/s, goes 3.00 m to the right at 3.77 m/s and back to the left at 3.77 m/s. Should be pretty straightforward.

Joe: Wait... that doesn't sound right. If the duck travels 6.00 m in total at a speed of 3.77 m/s, wouldn't it take the duck less than 2.00 s to get back to the start?

Jim: How do you mean?

Joe: Well, we know the duck moves from the center to the left, 1.50 m, then all the way to the right, another 3.00 m, and then back to the center, another 1.50 m.

Frank: Right. So that's 6.00 m total.

Joe: But let's say that the duck goes at 3.00 m/s. I chose that speed because it's easier to do mental arithmetic with it! Anyway, the trip across the circle and back—6.00 m—would take exactly 2.00 s. But 3.77 m/s is *faster* than 3.00 m/s, so the duck should take *less* than 2.00 s to go around once.

Jim: But the duck actually takes 2.50 s to go round once - that's *more* than 2.00 s, not less! Something weird's going on ...

Does your answer make sense? Always check your work!

Sharpen your pencil

The real duck that you are reproducing on the screen takes 2.50 seconds for exactly 1 revolution. That's a total distance of 6.00 m from the player's perspective. But we just calculated that the duck's speed is 3.77 m/s.

a. How can it possibly take the duck 2.50 s to do a round trip of 6.00 m from the player's perspective when the duck has a speed of 3.77 m/s?

b. Describe qualitatively the speed that the player observes the duck moving at for any 'special points' you can spot on the circle. Illustrate this with a sketch.

Sharpen your pencil Solution

The real duck that you are reproducing on the screen takes 2.50 seconds for exactly 1 revolution. That's a total distance of 6.00 m from the player's perspective. But we just calculated that the duck's speed is 3.77 m/s.

a. How can it possibly take the duck 2.50 s to do a round trip of 6.00 m from the player's perspective when the duck has a speed of 3.77 m/s?

b. Describe qualitatively the speed that the player observes the duck moving at for any 'special points' you can spot on the circle. Illustrate this with a sketch.

a. The duck is going at 3.77 m/s round the circumference of the circle, not across the circle's diameter

Circumference $= 2\pi r = 2 \times 3.14 \times 1.50 = 9.42$ m

The round trip is 9.42 m, not 6.00 m, and takes 2.50 s for a duck traveling at 3.77 m/s.

b. The player viewing the duck from a side view. When the duck's in the middle, it looks like the duck is moving faster - at 3.77 m/s.

But when the duck is at the ends of the circle, most of its motion is along the player's line of sight: forward or backward. So to the player, it looks like the duck's speed is closer to 0 m/s at those points.

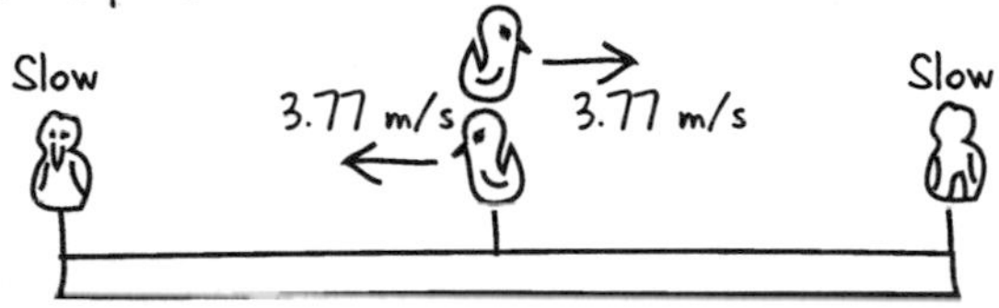

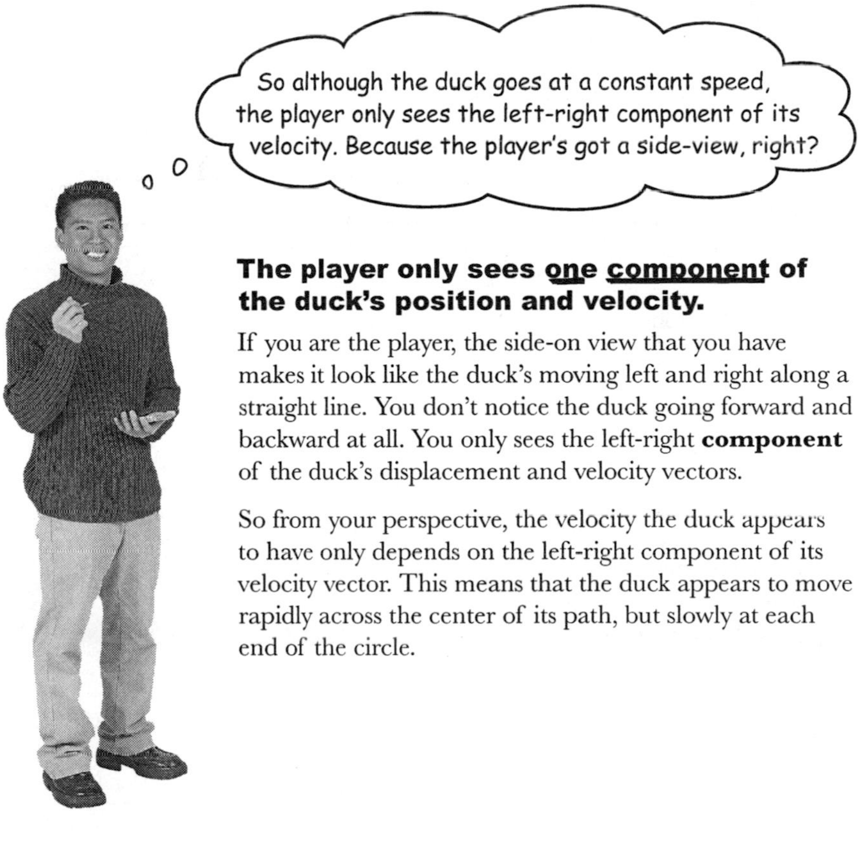

The player only sees one component of the duck's position and velocity.

If you are the player, the side-on view that you have makes it look like the duck's moving left and right along a straight line. You don't notice the duck going forward and backward at all. You only sees the left-right **component** of the duck's displacement and velocity vectors.

So from your perspective, the velocity the duck appears to have only depends on the left-right component of its velocity vector. This means that the duck appears to move rapidly across the center of its path, but slowly at each end of the circle.

The screen for the game is TWO-DIMENSIONAL

Even though the duck is three-dimensional, a **projection** of that duck is only two-dimensional. Imagine you're standing next to a projector, and you can only watch the shadow of the duck cast upon a screen.

As the duck moves across the center of the circle, it's mostly moving left to right (or right to left). The duck's shadow moves quickly across the **center** of the screen.

As the duck turns around at each end of the circle, it's moving mostly back-to-front (or front-to-back). But the screen only shows you left-to-right movement, so the duck's shadow moves slowly at the **ends**.

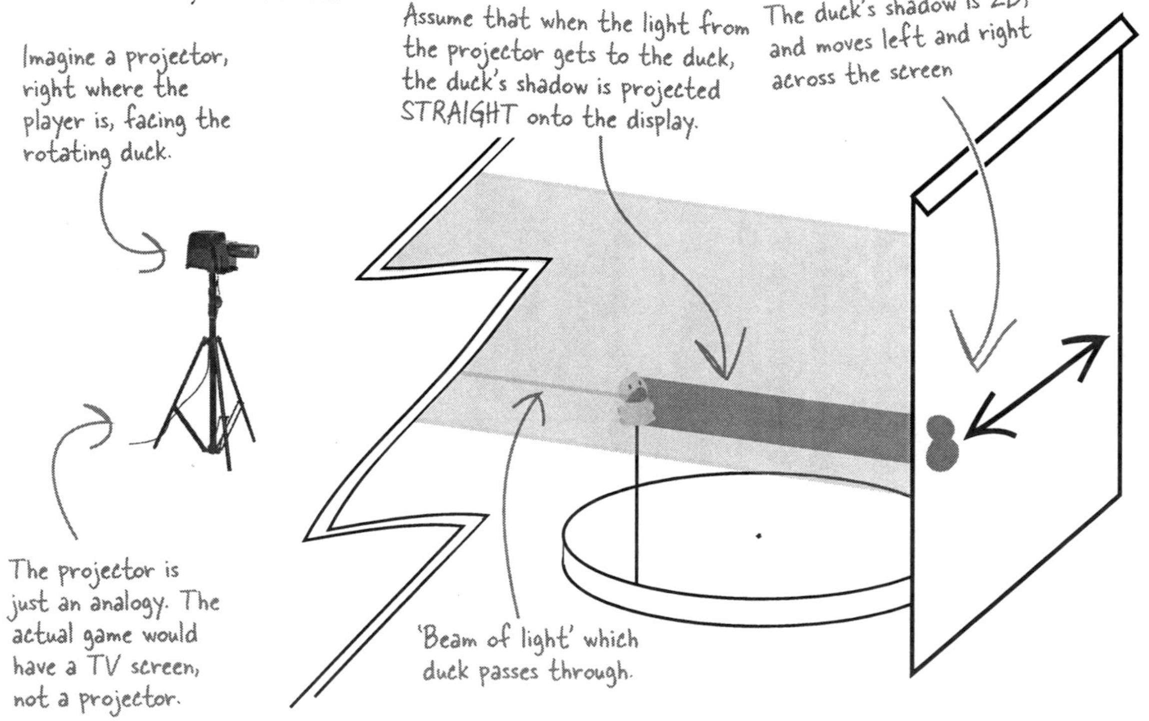

The same is true for the virtual duck in your game. The duck is displayed on a two dimensional screen. You don't notice the forward-backward component of the duck's displacement, only the left-right **component**. You see a **projection** of the duck's **displacement vector**.

Sharpen your pencil

Your job is to work out what the duck's displacement vector does as time goes on, so you know where to plot the duck on the screen. The circle the duck's attached to has a diameter of 3.00 m and a period of 2.50 s.

Use the pictures below, plus the fact that the angular velocity of the roundabout is constant, to **sketch** a graph of how the duck's left-right component (plotted on the vertical axis) varies with the angle θ (measured in radians and plotted on the horizontal axis) for one complete revolution (2π radians).

Mark the values at special points in the duck's motion on your sketch. Look for points where the duck is at an **extreme** in displacement - for instance, at zero, or at the maximum in either direction. Write the times that these points would occur at, too.

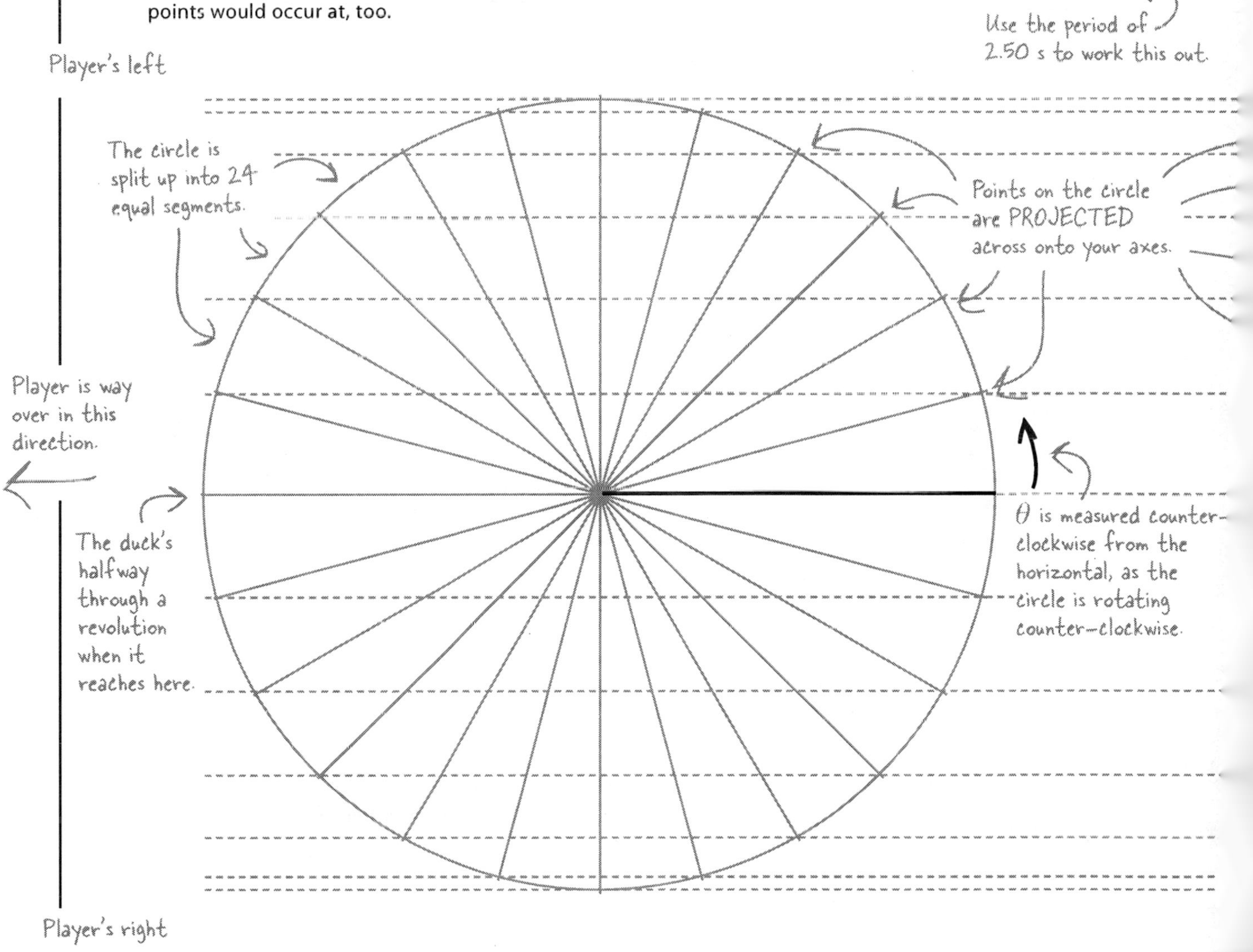

Radians

Radians are a way of measuring angles that's especially useful for working with circles. There are 2π radians in 1 revolution. Think of other angles in terms of 'fractions of '2π.

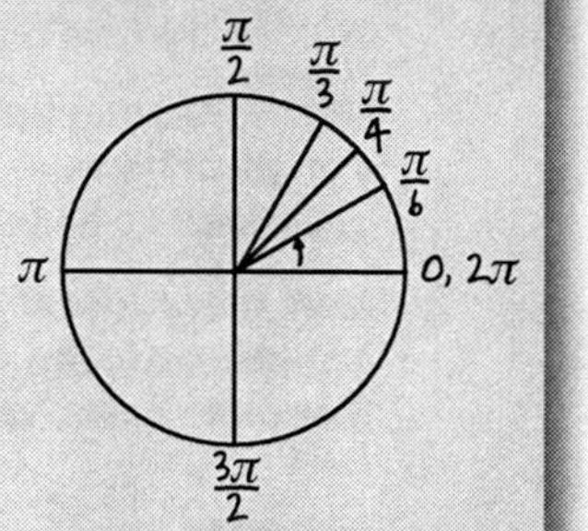

You'll probably find the note you made in chapter 16 helpful when you're thinking about this exercise.

You need to do the graph title, axis labels, etc. yourself.

Make the player's left the positive direction.

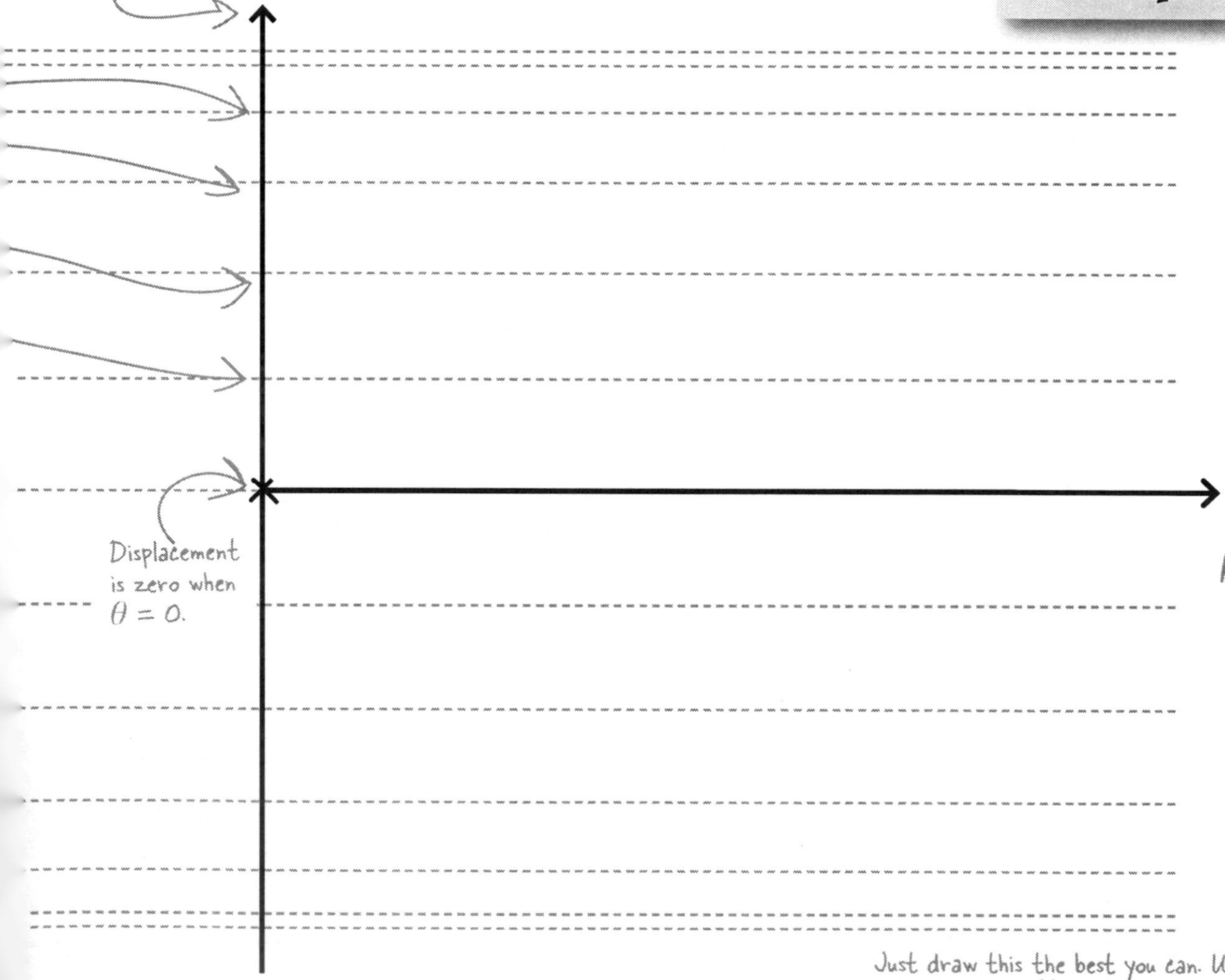

Displacement is zero when $\theta = 0$.

Just draw this the best you can. Use your ruler to mark off the horizontal-axis in 24 equal segments, like the circle.

Sharpen your pencil Solution

Your job is to work out what the duck's displacement vector does as time goes on, so you know where to plot the duck on the screen. The circle the duck's attached to has a diameter of 3.00 m and a period of 2.50 s.

Use the pictures below, plus the fact that the angular velocity of the roundabout is constant, to **sketch** a graph of how the duck's left-right component (plotted on the vertical axis) varies with the angle θ (measured in radians and plotted on the horizontal axis) for one complete revolution (2π radians).

Mark the values at special points in the duck's motion on your sketch. Look for points where the duck is at an **extreme** in displacement - for instance, at zero, or at the maximum in either direction. Write the times that these points would occur at, too.

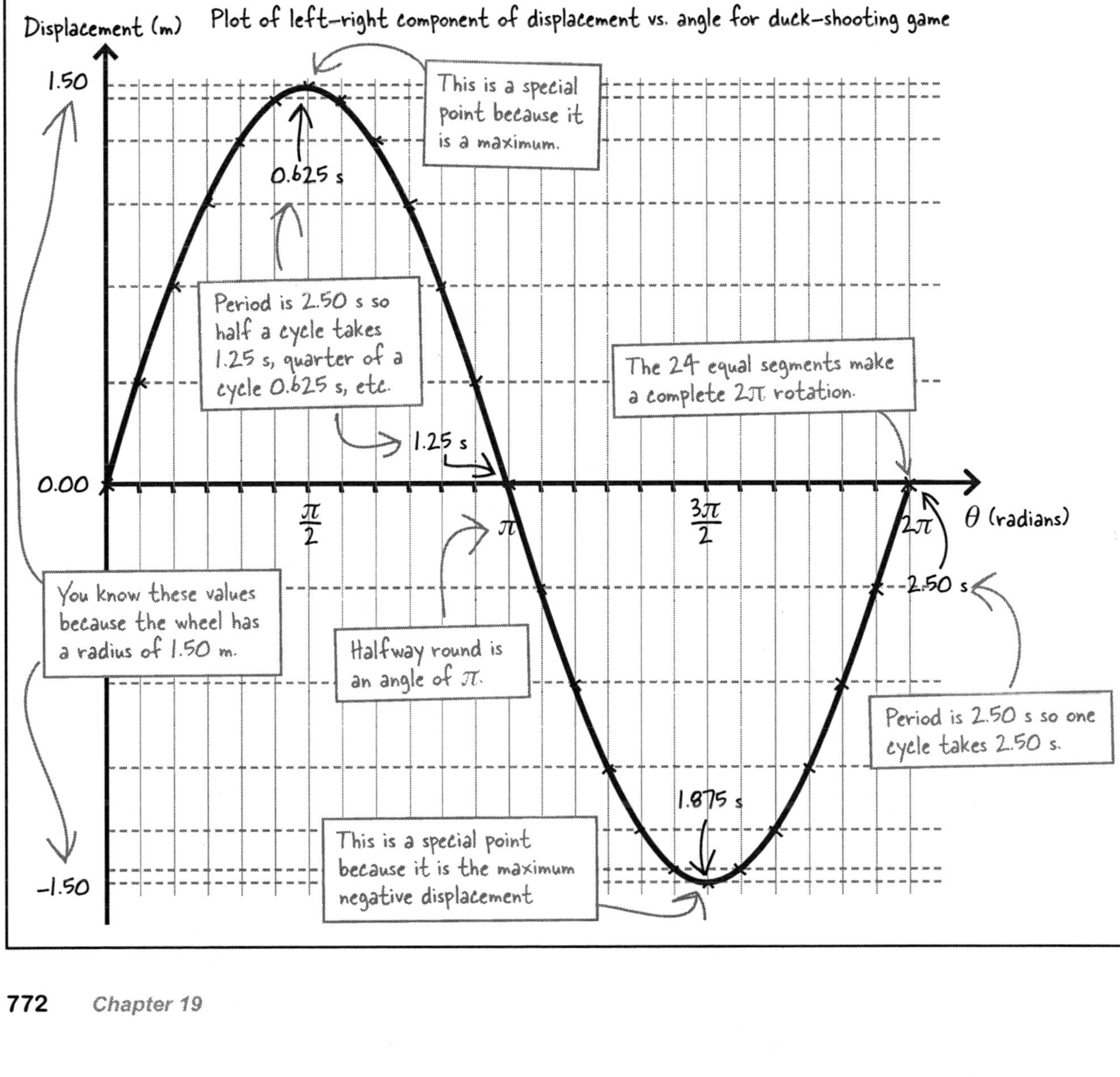

So we know what the duck does...

When you're playing the game, you observe only the duck going left and right, because you see only the left-right **component** of the duck's displacement.

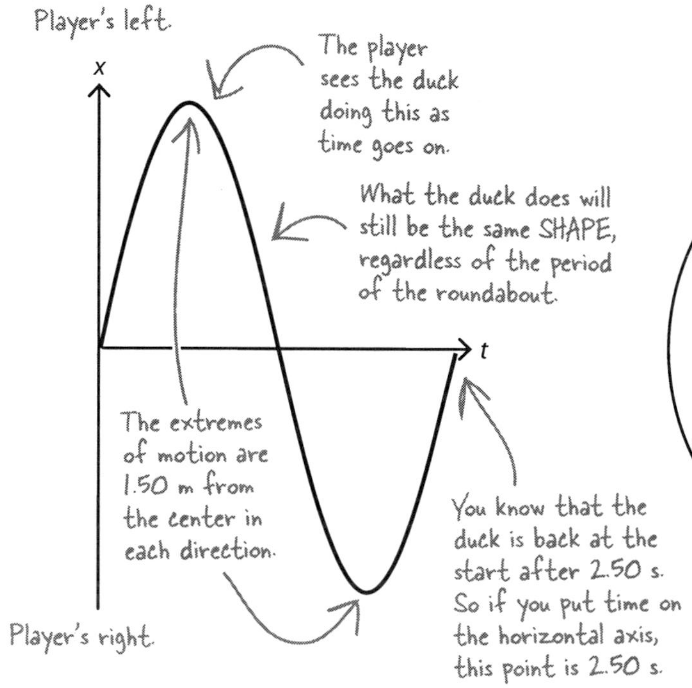

□ is the angle, □ is the angular speed.

With linear quantities, you can write:
distance = speed × time

So with angular quantities, you can write an equivalent equation for the angle, □:
□ = □*t*

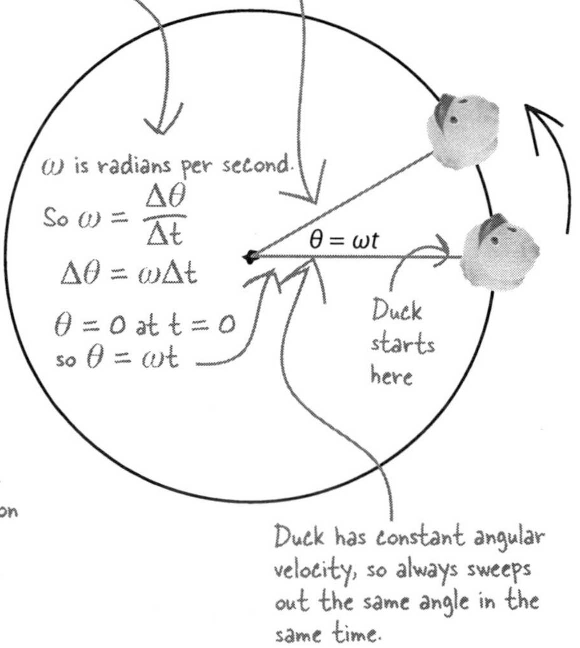

...but where exactly is the duck?

Although the **shape** of our graph is correct, the only **exact values** we know are at the **extremes**, when the duck is at its maximum left or right displacement, or when the duck has zero displacement.

To get the screen working, we need to know exactly where the duck is at any given time... and that means we need an **equation** for the duck's **displacement**.

Though as your graph is drawn fairly accurately, you can read off values from it. But it would be better to have an equation to give an exact value for the displacement at any time.

BRAIN POWER

We're about to use right-angled triangles to figure out the duck's displacement at any time. Can you think of how right-angled triangles might relate to circles?

Any time you're dealing with a component vector, try to spot a right-angled triangle

ω is radians per second.

So $\omega = \frac{\Delta\theta}{\Delta t}$

$\Delta\theta = \omega\Delta t$

$\theta = 0$ at $t = 0$

so $\theta = \omega t$

This is the "angular equivalent" of distance = speed × time.

When you play the game, you see only the **component** of the duck's **displacement** vector that's **parallel** to the screen. If you also draw in a **perpendicular** component, you can form a **right-angled triangle** with the parallel component, perpendicular component, and the radius.

1

The duck is always **distance** r away from the center of the circle. The duck rotates counter-clockwise with a constant angular velocity ω.

The duck's image on the screen is the projection of the **component** of its **displacement** parallel to the screen.

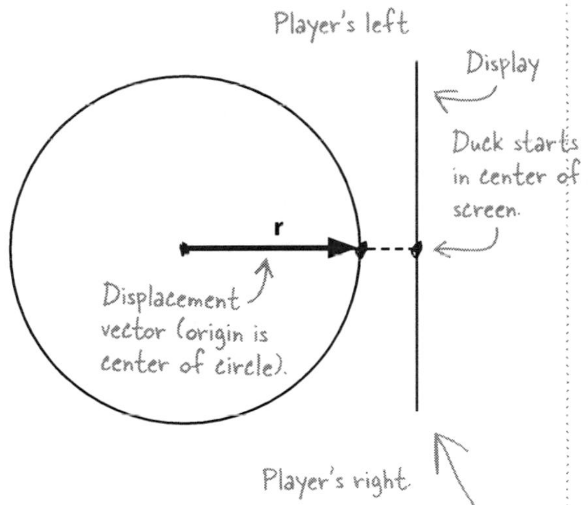

2

You can say what the angle θ is at any **time**, using the equation $\theta = \omega t$. But what you really want to know is the duck's displacement from the center at any time.

The **projection** of the duck's displacement from the center is always vertical (the way we've drawn it here). We'll call this displacement vector from the horizontal axis **y**, as shown below. Its projection on the screen is the **y-component** of the radius.

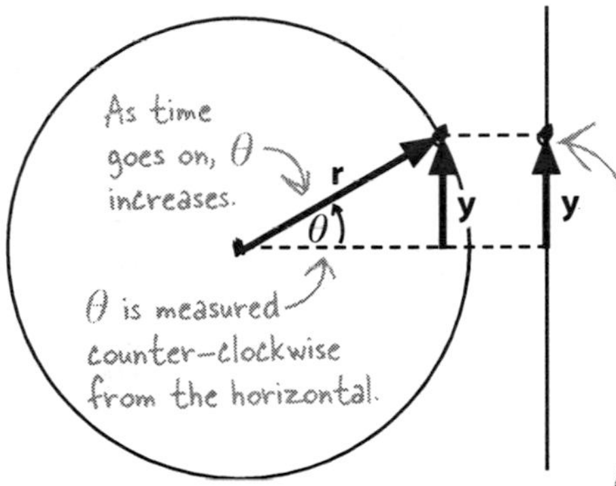

In math and physics, a vertical distance or displacement is sometimes called y, to distinguish it from x.

Here, we're looking DOWN on the duck from above. The player is over to the left a long way away, and we're projecting what they see onto this display.

Because of the way this is drawn, the screen looks vertical. That's because the player's left is at the "top" and the player's right is at the "bottom" – just like the "sharpen your pencil" you did on page 771.

When you do a projection by drawing a right-angled triangle inside a circle like this, the triangle's HYPOTENUSE is always the RADIUS of the circle.

3

If we also draw in **x**, the **x**-component of the displacement, we can form a **right-angled triangle** using the **y**-component, the **x**-component and the radius.

When you draw a right-angled triangle like this, its hypotenuse is always the radius.

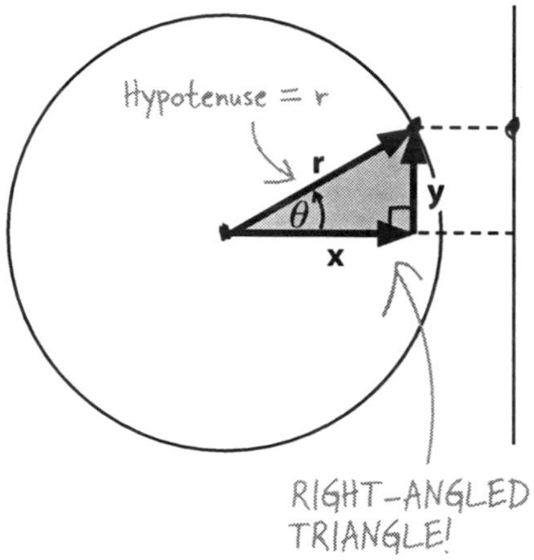

The sine function outputs a scalar, not a vector, so the equation gives you the length of y

4

Now we can use trigonometry to **calculate** the length of y in terms of r and θ, because $\sin(\theta) = \frac{y}{r}$

And if you know what the length of y is in terms of θ, you can work out what y is at any time, by making the substitution $\theta = \omega t$. This tells you exactly where on the screen to draw the duck at any **time**.

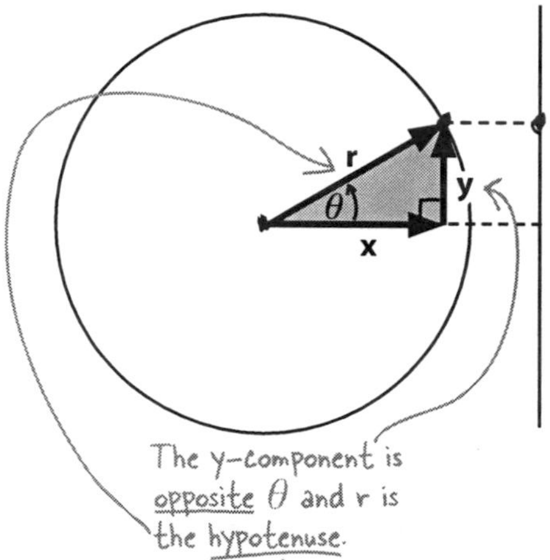

So you can use sin(θ) to work out the length of the y-component.

Sharpen your pencil

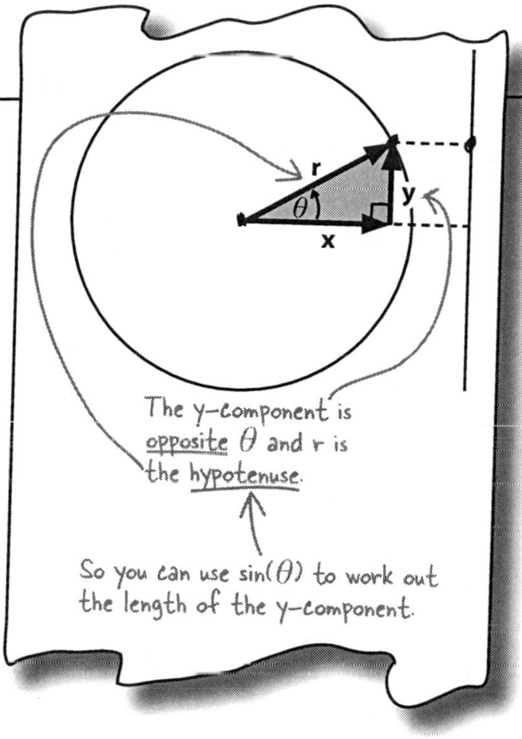

Your job is to use the right-angled triangle you've spotted to calculate the size of the y-component of the duck's displacement at any time. This gives you the position of the duck on the screen at any time.

a. The roundabout's diameter is 3.00 m and the duck's velocity is 3.77 m/s.

What is the duck's angular velocity, ω?

b. Assume that at $t = 0$ s, $\theta = 0$. Write down an equation for θ in terms of ω and t (where θ is measured in radians). Use this to fill in the 't' column of the table on the opposite page.

c. Write down an equation for the length of the y-component of the duck's displacement with respect to the angle θ, where θ is measured in radians.

Use this equation and your answer to part b. to write down an equation for the length of y with respect to t.

θ is in radians. This means your calculator should be in radians mode too.

d. Fill in the table with values for t and the y-component of the duck's displacement for the given angles, where θ is in radians.

Angle, θ (radians)	Time, t (s)	Length of duck's y-component (m)
0		
$\frac{\pi}{12}$		
$\frac{\pi}{8}$		
$\frac{\pi}{6}$		
$\frac{\pi}{4}$		
$\frac{\pi}{3}$		
$\frac{\pi}{2}$		

e. Use your table to draw a graph of the y-component of the duck's displacement vs. time.

You should give your graph a title and label its axes.

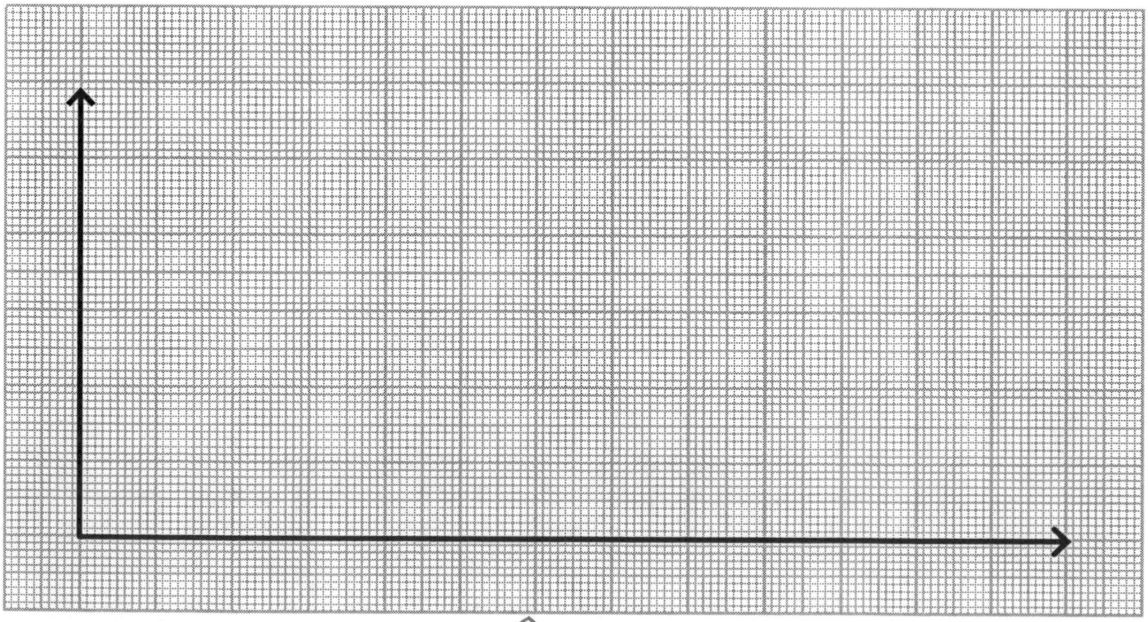

You should choose a suitable scale for each axis.

Sharpen your pencil Solution

Your job is to use the right-angled triangle you've spotted to calculate the y-component of the duck's displacement at any time. This gives you the position of the duck on the screen at any time.

a. The roundabout's diameter is 3.00 m and the duck's velocity is 3.77 m/s. What is the duck's angular velocity, ω?

b. Assume that at $t = 0$ s, $\theta = 0$. Write down an equation for θ in terms of ω and t (where θ is measured in radians). Use this to fill in the 't' column of the table.

c. Write down an equation for **y**, the y-component of the duck's displacement with respect to the angle θ, where θ is measured in radians. Use this equation and your answer to part b. to write down an equation for **y** with respect to t.

d. Fill in the table with values for t and the y-component of the duck's displacement for the given angles, where θ is in radians.

e. Use your table to draw a graph of the y-component of the duck's displacement vs. time.

Angle, θ (radians)	Time, t (s)	Length of duck's y-component (m)
0	0	0
$\frac{\pi}{12}$	0.104	0.388
$\frac{\pi}{8}$	0.156	0.574
$\frac{\pi}{6}$	0.208	0.750
$\frac{\pi}{4}$	0.313	1.06
$\frac{\pi}{3}$	0.417	1.30
$\frac{\pi}{2}$	0.625	1.50

a. $v = r\omega$

$\Rightarrow \omega = \frac{v}{r} = \frac{3.77}{1.50} = 2.51$ rad/s (3 sd)

b. ω is radians per second. So $\omega = \frac{\Delta\theta}{\Delta t}$

$\Rightarrow \Delta\theta = \omega\Delta t$

$\theta = 0$ at $t = 0$ so $\theta = \omega t$

c. $\sin(\theta) = \frac{o}{h} = \frac{y}{r}$

$\Rightarrow y = r\sin(\theta)$ and substitute in $\theta = \omega t$

$y = r\sin(\omega t)$

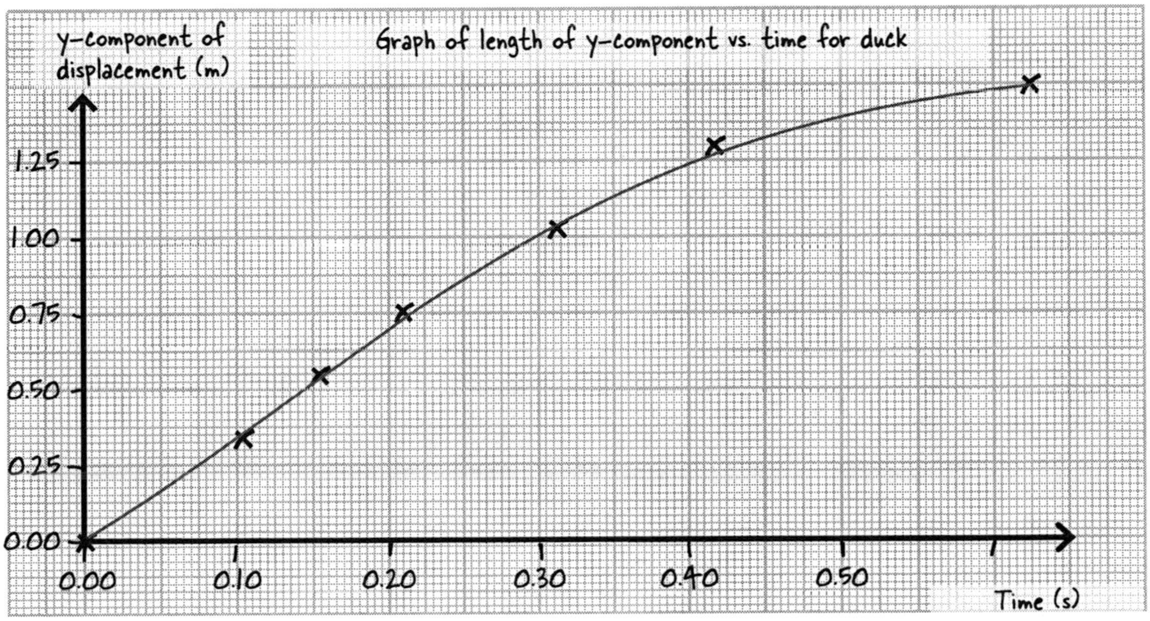

OK, so the duck's position is y = rsin(ωt). But we've only drawn quarter of the graph! What about bigger angles further round the circle? They can't be part of a right-angled triangle!

Because $\theta = \omega t$

We need wider definitions for sine and cosine.

Up until now, we've thought of sine and cosine applying only to **angles** that are part of a right-angled triangle. Now we need to extend their definitions to cover *all* the angles that can be swept out inside a **circle**.

Our original definition of sin(θ) lets us deal with only this quarter of the duck's circle.

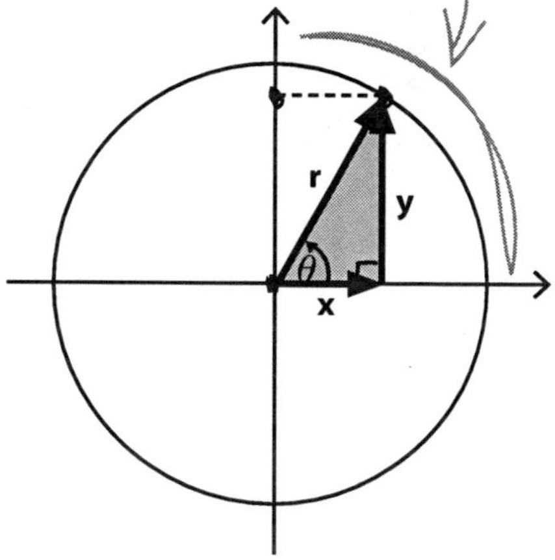

For angles smaller than a right-angle, we formed a right-angled triangle using **r**, the **radius** of the circle **y**, the y-component of the radius and **x**, the x-component of the radius.

Then we **projected** the radius vector onto a line parallel to the y-axis and used the equation $\sin(\theta) = \frac{y}{r}$ as usual to calculate y, the duck's distance from the center of the screen,

But now we need to deal with the other angles further round the circle, which are larger than $\frac{\varpi}{2}$ radians (90°). If we can't deal with these angles, we don't know where to draw the duck on the screen.

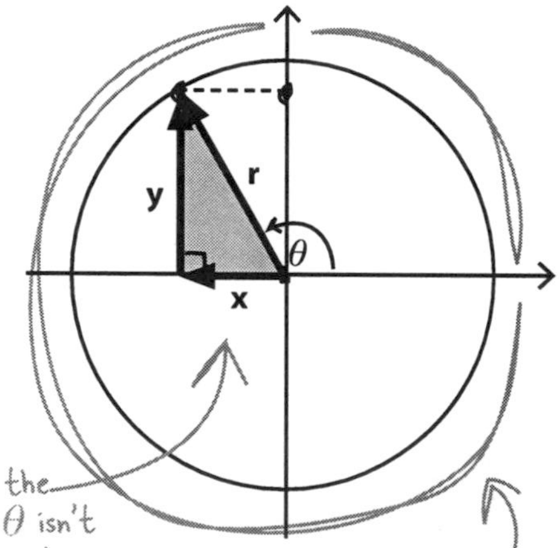

The **definition of sine** still comes from the ratio of the y-component to the length of the radius, and is the same equation as before:

$$\sin(\theta) = \frac{y}{r}$$

The definition of sin(θ) is the RATIO of y and r, even if θ isn't part of a right-angled triangle.

New definition:

$$\sin(\theta) = \frac{\mathbf{y}}{\mathbf{r}}$$

This works for ANY angle in a circle, not just an angle that's part of a right-angled triangle.

The method for calculating the length of y hasn't changed. You still form a right-angled triangle using the y-component, x-component and length of the radius. Then you can calculate the length of y using the new definition of sin(θ) - which tells you the duck's position on the screen for any angle.

The new definition lets us handle the rest of the circle as well.

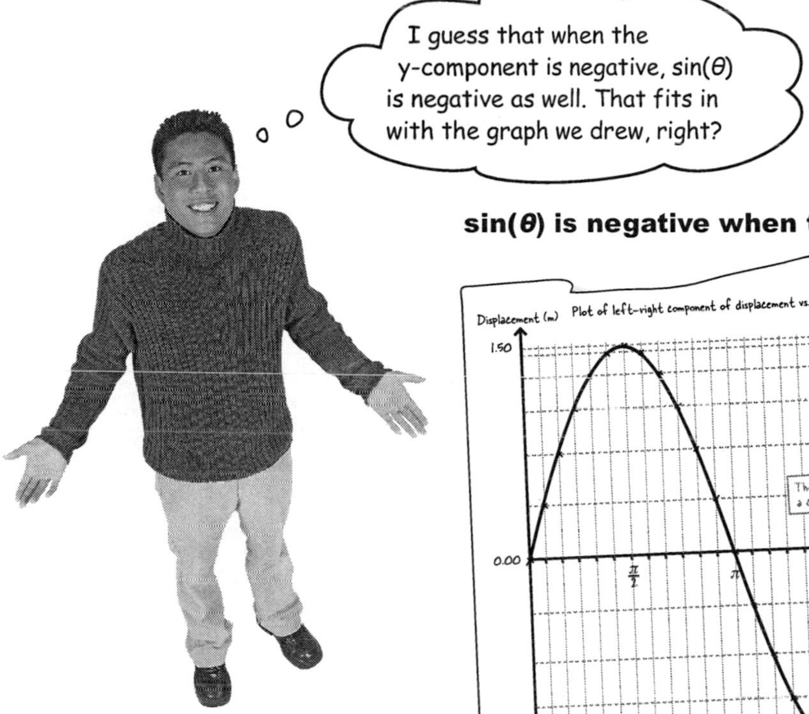

sin(θ) is negative when the y-component is negative.

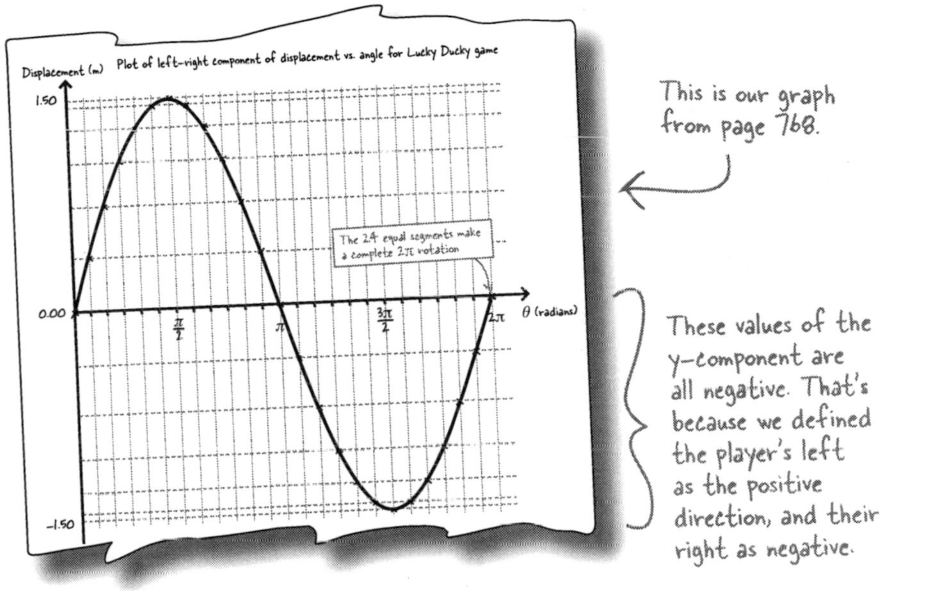

For angles larger than ϖ (larger than 180°), the y-component of the displacement points in the other direction, so has a negative sign. This means that sin(θ) is also negative.

To make sure the signs work out OK, *r* is always treated as positive because it's pointing away from the center of the circle. This is why *r* is in italics - in the context of this definition it's a scalar with a (positive) size and no direction.

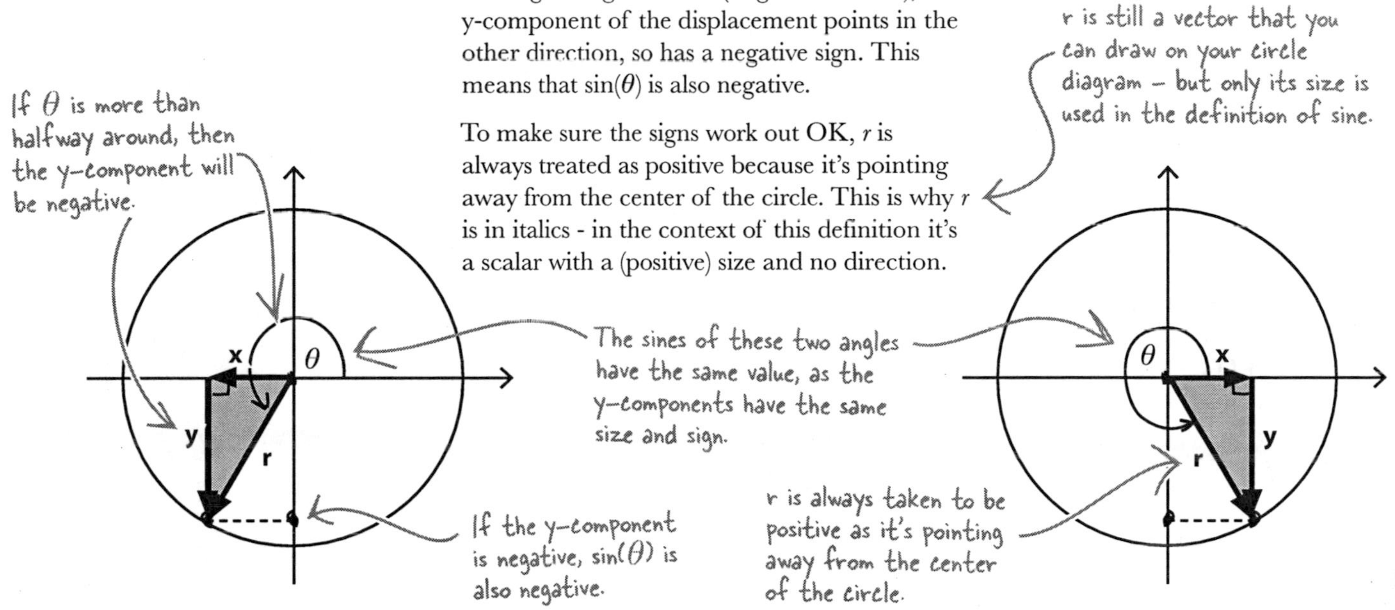

there are no Dumb Questions

Q: So an angle doesn't need to be in a right-angled triangle for it to have a sine?

A: That's right. Our new extended definition of sine says that if you have a vector that starts at the origin, and you measure the angle θ that it makes with the *x*-axis, sin(θ) is the *y*-component of the vector divided by the radius.

Q: But why is it useful to be able to calculate the sine of any angle? Isn't the sine only interesting when there's a right-angled triangle involved?

A: The sine of larger angles is crucial when you have circular motion, like in the duck-shooting game. In the game, we need to know the *y*-component of the duck's displacement vector. So we need to calculate the sine of the angle that the duck makes with the x-axis.

Q: So how did you decide which way around to put the axes?

A: It was just the way it came out when we drew the aerial view of the player and the duck on the circle. We made the player's left the positive direction, and their right the negative direction. You could have done it the other way, and the effect would be the same. You'd just have positive values for the player's right, instead of their left.

Q: I've heard people talking about a "sine wave" before, but never knew what they meant. Did I just draw a sine wave?

A: Yes, you did! And it's called a wave because the pattern repeats itself again and again if you keep on going around and around for more than one revolution.

Q: In the "Sharpen your pencil" on page 771, I didn't have to calculate any sines for angles larger than a right-angle, because I just projected across from the points on the circle. How would I actually calculate values for the *y*-components?

A: Your calculator is able to work out the sine of any angle you give it. Just make sure the calculator's measuring the angle the same way as you are (in degrees or radians)

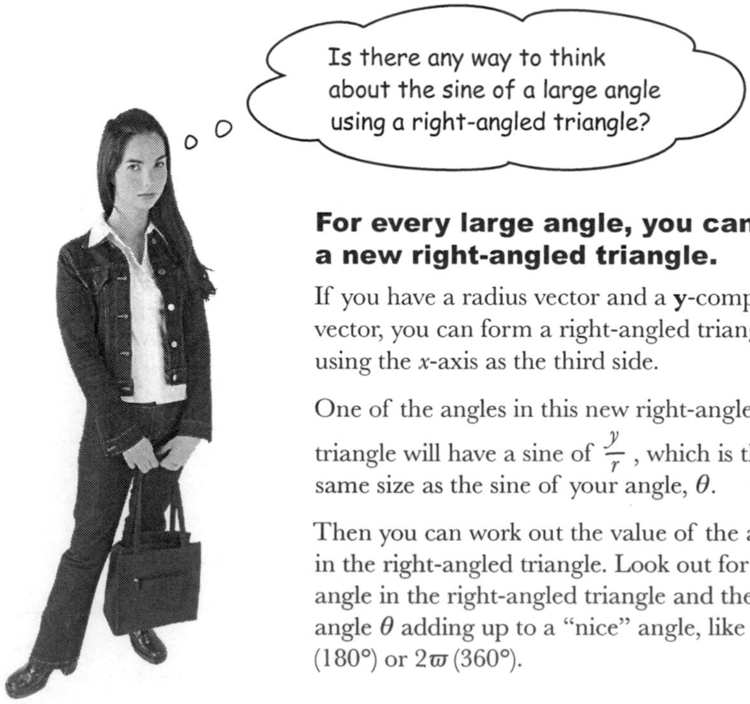

For every large angle, you can find a new right-angled triangle.

If you have a radius vector and a **y**-component vector, you can form a right-angled triangle using the *x*-axis as the third side.

One of the angles in this new right-angled triangle will have a sine of $\frac{y}{r}$, which is the same size as the sine of your angle, θ.

Then you can work out the value of the angle in the right-angled triangle. Look out for the angle in the right-angled triangle and the large angle θ adding up to a "nice" angle, like ϖ (180°) or 2ϖ (360°).

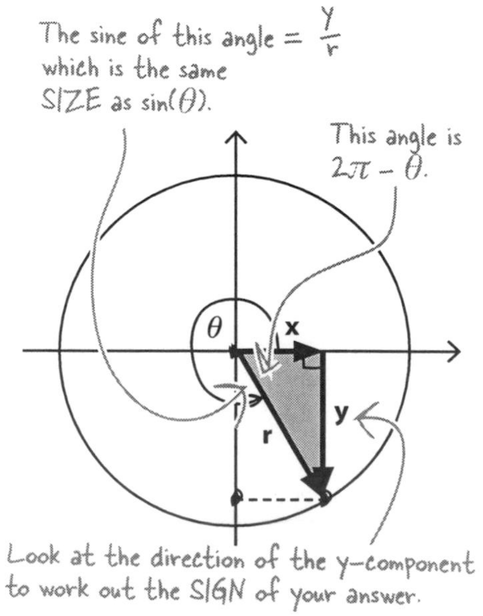

Let's show Jane the display

We're all set to give Jane our equation, $y = r\sin(\omega t)$ and help her get her screen working. Time to start raking in the profits...

...but Jane's got a new idea, and it's going to take some more work.

$$y = r\sin(\omega t)$$

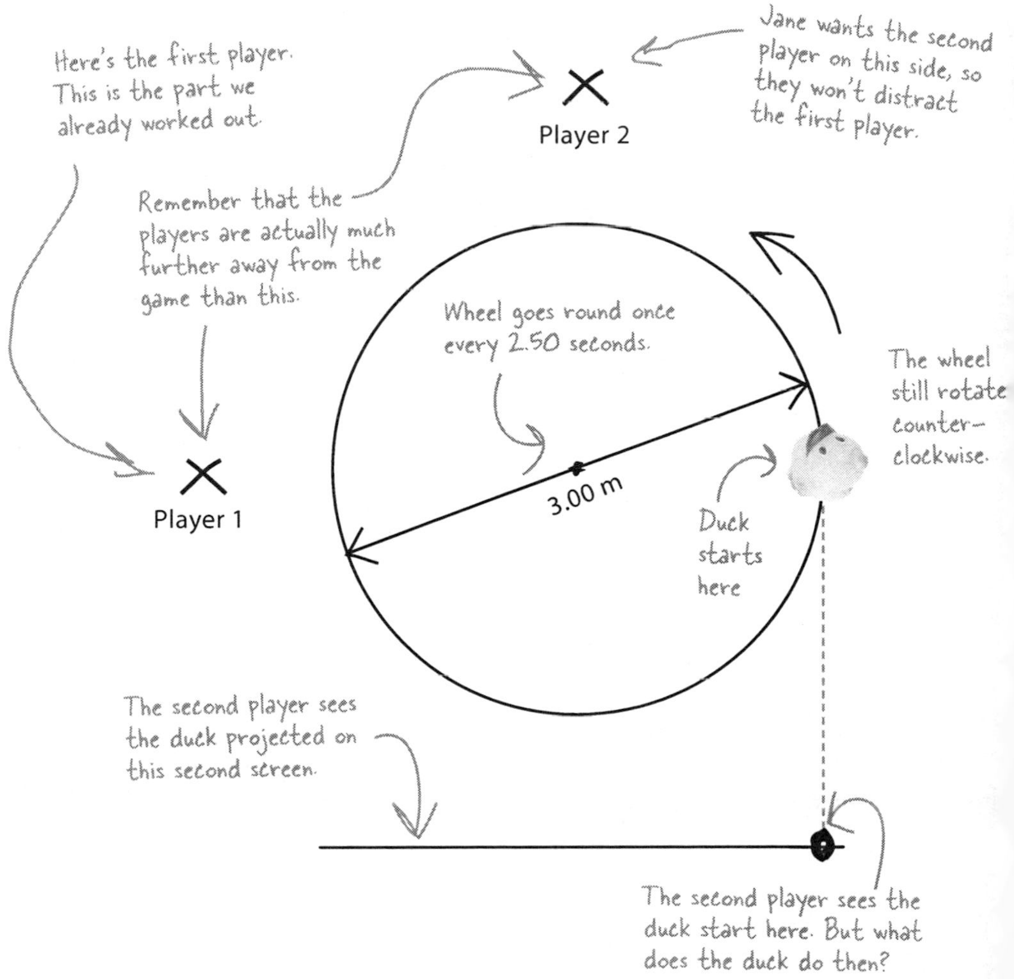

The second player sees the *x*-component of the duck's displacement

The second player is facing in a different direction. They're standing $\frac{\varpi}{2}$ radians (90°) further around the circle, clockwise, than the first player.

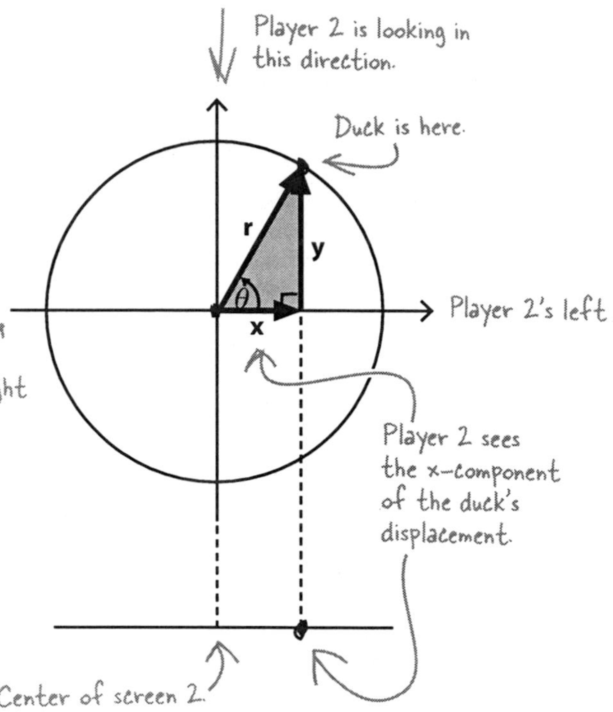

This means that the second player doesn't see the **y**-component of the duck's displacement. Instead, the second player only sees the **x-component** of the duck's displacement.

The first player only saw the y-component of the duck's displacement.

Sharpen your pencil

Make Player 2's left the positive direction, like we did for Player 1.

a. This time, you're interested in x, the length of the **x**-component of the duck's displacement. Write down an equation for x in terms of r and θ. (The duck starts at $\theta = 0$).

You may find it helpful to draw a sketch.

b. Sketch a graph of how x varies with θ for one complete revolution of the circle, radius r. Be sure to mark any special points.

This is the projection that player 1 sees.

c. Sketch a graph that shows how y, the length of the **y**-component of the duck's displacement varies with θ. Compare and contrast this graph with the one you drew in part b, and note any similarities and differences.

Sketch these two graphs one above the other with the same scale.

Use this space to explain the similarities and differences.

Sharpen your pencil Solution

Make Player 2's left the positive direction, like we did for Player 1.

a. This time, you're interested in x, the length of the **x**-component of the duck's displacement. Write down an equation for x in terms of r and θ. (The duck starts at $\theta = 0$).

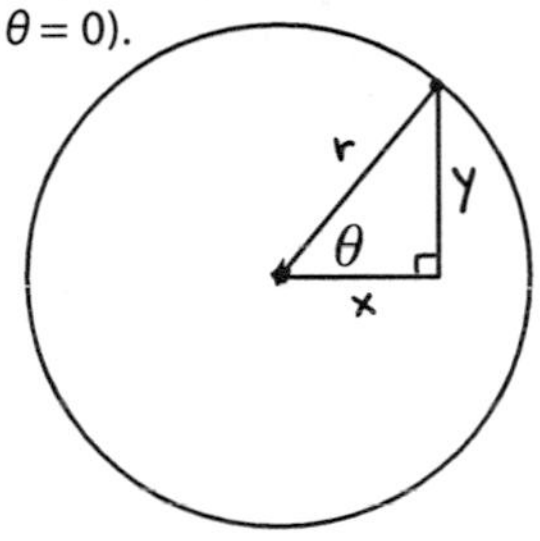

$\cos(\theta) = \frac{a}{h} = \frac{x}{r}$

$\Rightarrow x = r\cos(\theta)$

b. Sketch a graph of how x varies with θ for one complete revolution of the circle, radius r. Be sure to mark any special points.

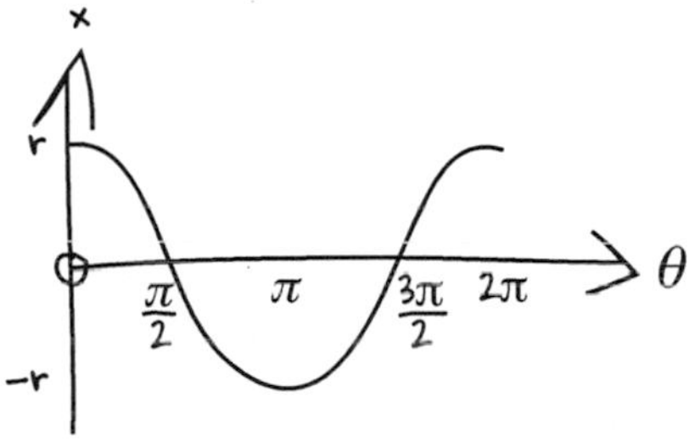

c. Sketch a graph that shows how y, the length of the **y**-component of the duck's displacement varies with θ. Compare and contrast this graph with the one you drew in part b, and note any similarities and differences.

The graphs are similar, except that player 2's is shifted along by $\frac{\pi}{2}$ because they are further round the circle by an angle of $\frac{\pi}{2}$.

The duck starts in the center for the first player, but at a maximum for the second player.

Sine and cosine are related because they both involve one component and the hypotenuse.

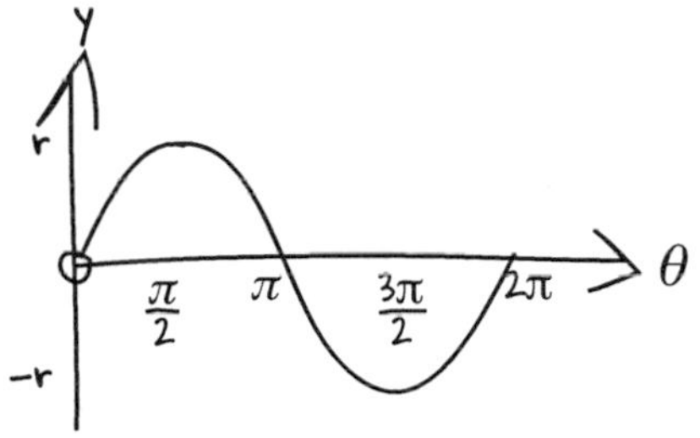

Sketch these two graphs one above the other with the same scale.

We need a wider definition of cosine, too

Just like there's a wider definition of sine, there's also a wider definition of cosine, which you've just worked out. It's very similar to the wider definition of sine, except that it involves the x-component: $\cos(\theta) = \frac{x}{r}$

The sign of $\cos(\theta)$ is the same as the sign of the x-component.

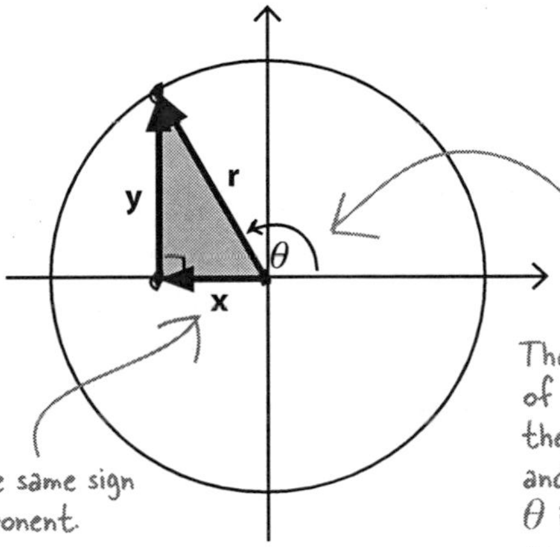

cos(θ) has the same sign as the x-component.

The definition of cos(θ) is the ratio of x and r, even if θ isn't part of a right-angled triangle.

New definition:

$$\cos(\theta) = \frac{\mathbf{x}}{\mathbf{r}}$$

sine and cosine are related to each other

The second player sees the x-component of the duck's displacement, $x = r\cos(\omega t)$, as the duck moves round the circle, while the first player sees the y-component: $y = r\sin(\omega t)$.

The graphs of sine and cosine are closely related. They're exactly the same shape, in fact, except that cosine is "ahead" of sine by $\frac{\varpi}{2}$. In our game, that's because the second player's vantage point is $\frac{\varpi}{2}$ ahead of the first player's.

A cosine graph starts with the maximum value of the variable at the origin, and a sine graph has a value of 0 at the origin.

Sine and cosine have the same wave shape, but start in different places.

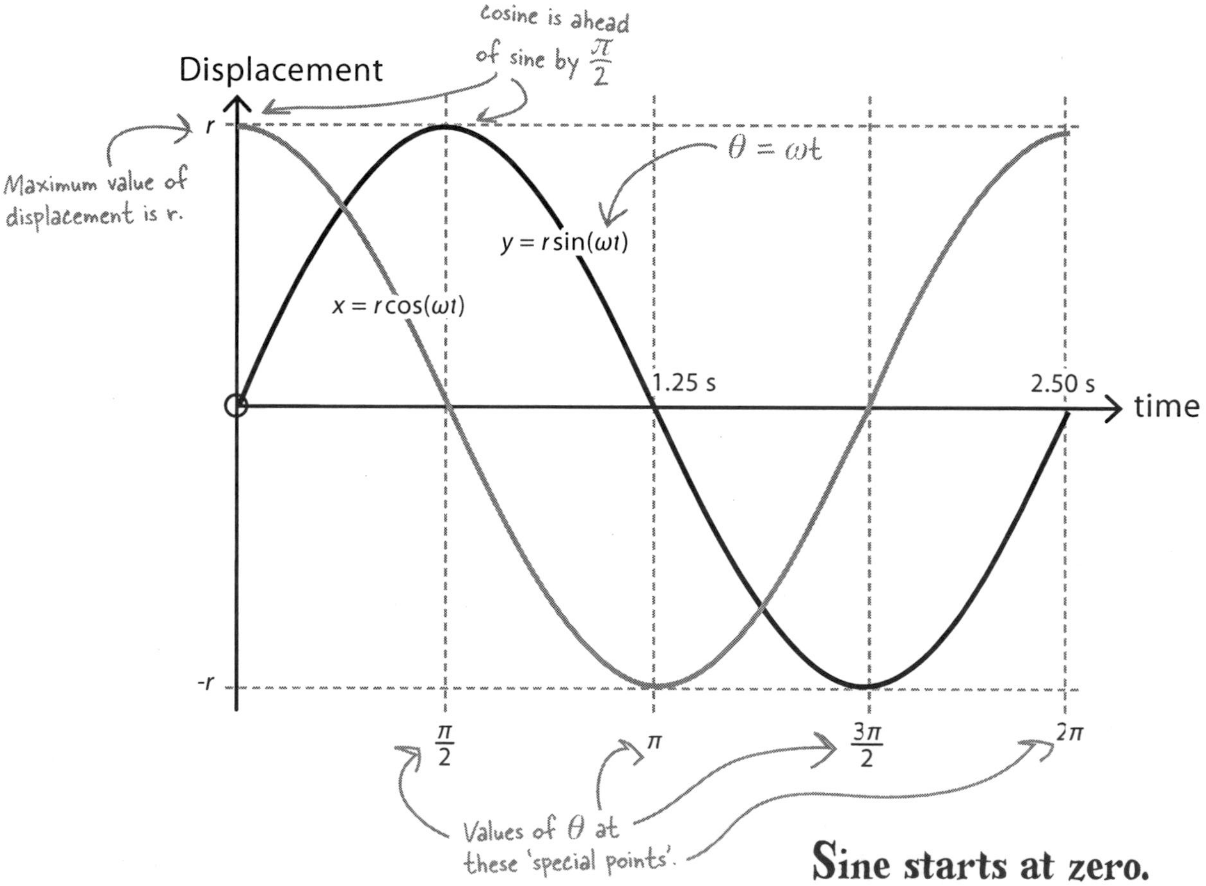

Sine starts at zero.

Cosine starts at its maximum value.

The maximum value of your graph is called the amplitude.

The maximum deviation from the center that your variable can have is called the **amplitude** of the graph or equation.

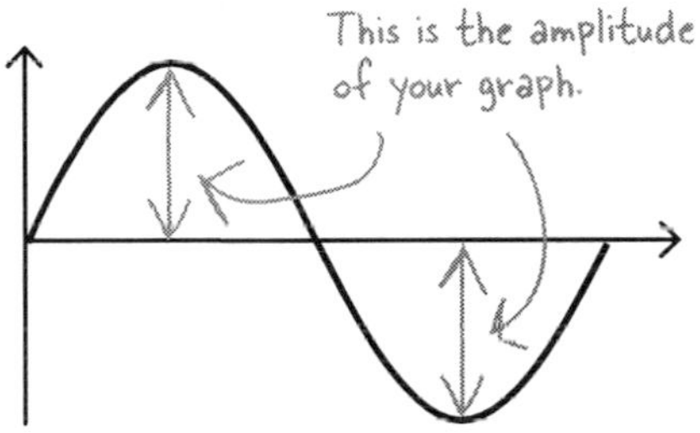

Here, you know that the amplitude of the displacement-time **graph** is r, the radius of the circle. So you know that the extremes of the graph have to be $+r$ and $-r$.

You can also use the amplitude to work out an **equation** for your graph. The maximum value that sine or cosine can have is 1. So to have a graph where the maximum value is r, you have to multiply the sine or cosine by r.

That's why your equations have the form $\mathbf{y} = r\sin(\omega t)$ and $\mathbf{x} = r\cos(\omega t)$.

Maximum value of r. Maximum value of 1.

This also means that your two graphs both have the same height - because they have the same amplitude.

The AMPLITUDE is the maximum deviation from the center of your sine or cosine graph.

Sine Exposed

This week's interview: Sine revisits our studio.

Head First: So, sine, it's been a while since we first met back in chapter 9, but it's good to have you back today to discuss these latest revelations. Or should that be revolutions?!

sine: Ha, that's right. I do cover far more angles than you thought I could... but I don't see why that's such a big deal.

Head First: It's not a big deal, not really, just a bit... unexpected! I'd never have thought that an angle larger than a right angle could even have a sine.

sine: Yeah, I kinda understand how you feel. It's like finding out that an old friend has a whole other secret life. Though my extended definition isn't really all that different from the one you had before.

Head First: Hmm... before, I thought of you as having to do with the ratio of particular sides in a right-angled triangle. But now I guess we know that angles that can't possibly be in a right-angled triangle can still have a sine.

sine: Well, I'm still the **ratio** of two lengths. That part of your definition hasn't changed.

Head First: But those lengths aren't part of a right-angled triangle, anymore.

sine: But they are very well-defined lengths, and you can use them to form a right-angled triangle! If you're dealing with an angle in a circle, **t**: a vector going from the center to the edge of the circle. Then the x-component is one side, and the y-component is the other side.

Head First: That's all fine, I suppose... but how do I work out which side is the opposite and which is the adjacent?

sine: Well, angles in physics are always measured **counter-clockwise from the horizontal**. If your angle's smaller than a right angle, sine is the ratio of the y-component and the radius. And my friend cosine is the ratio of the x-component and the radius.

Head First: Well, sure, that's what we already knew. But when you start having the sine of angles larger than a right angle... that's when it gets a bit hairy.

sine: But I'm still the same! I'm still the ratio of the y-component and the radius.

Head First: I guess you are... though that means you're not as exclusive as you once were, doesn't it?

sine: Yeah, sadly, there will always be two different angles that have the same value of sine.

Head First: And that can be a downer, can't it? I mean, we've seen you looking negative recently.

sine: That's true. I'll be negative for any angle larger than halfway around, as the y-component of the radius vector will point down, not up.

Head First: And then there's your friend cosine. He's negative at different times from you, isn't he? Doesn't that make it difficult for you to work together sometimes?

sine: Not really. We're both aware of when the other is going to be positive or negative. Just remember that in the top-right quadrant (where the angle is less than a right angle) we're both positive. Then you can work out which direction is positive for each of us and take it from there.

Head First: Thank you, sine. I think we already knew more about you than we thought we did.

Let the games begin!

The **equations** $y = r\sin(\omega t)$ and $x = r\cos(\omega t)$ work perfectly. Jane plugs them into her screens, and the customers are already lining up. Who doesn't love rotating ducks and light guns?

Even better, you've come up with **general equations**. If Jane ever wants to change the game, maybe by using a different size of wheel that spins at a different rate, the equations will still work. She can just change the values for r and ω, and she's good to go.

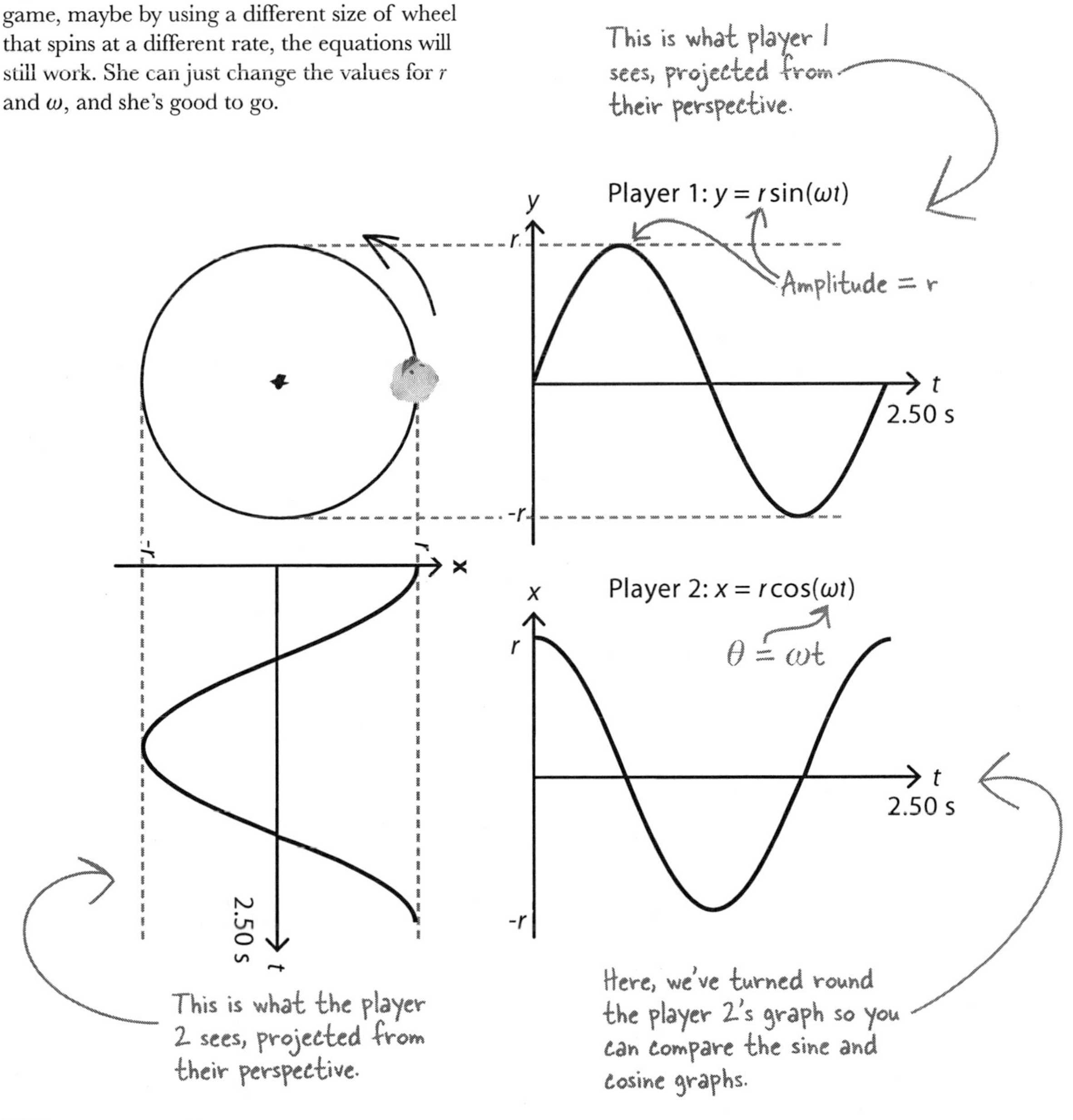

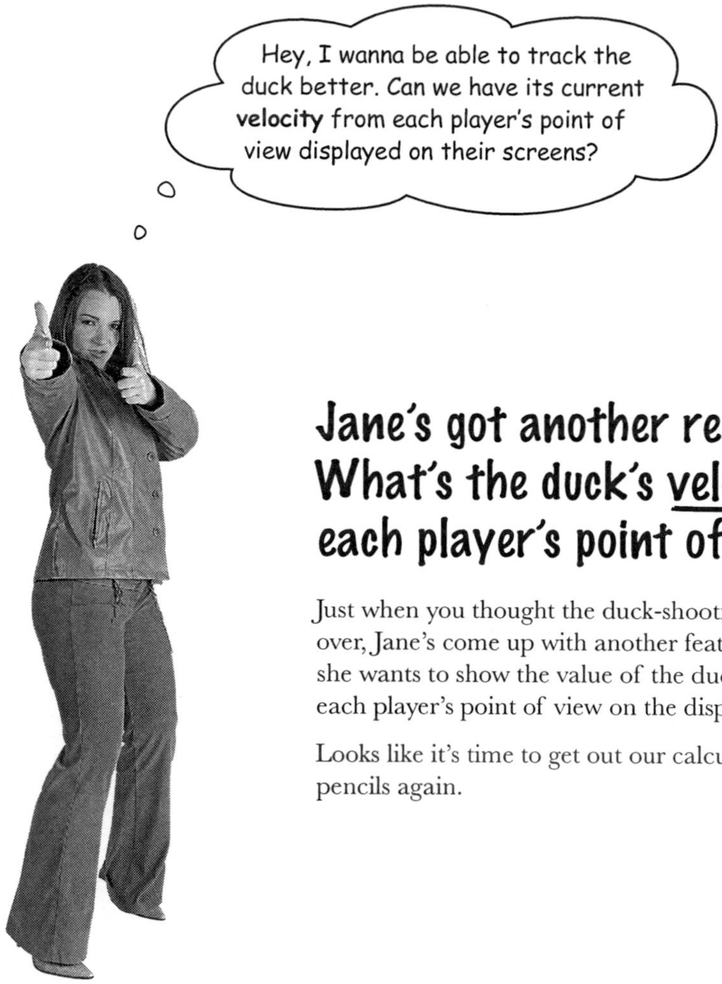

Jane's got another request: What's the duck's <u>velocity</u> from each player's point of view?

Just when you thought the duck-shooting odyssey was over, Jane's come up with another feature request. Now she wants to show the value of the duck's velocity from each player's point of view on the display.

Looks like it's time to get out our calculators and pencils again.

Before, you calculated that the duck's linear velocity as it travels round the circle is 3.77 m/s. So that's got to some into it somewhere.

BRAIN POWER

How would you sketch a velocity-time graph and calculate the value of the duck's velocity from each player's point of view?

Get the shape of the velocity-time graph from the slope of the displacement-time graph

The easiest way to draw a sketch of the velocity-time graph is to use the slope of the displacement-time graph.

This works because velocity is rate of change of displacement, $\mathbf{v} = \frac{d\mathbf{x}}{dt}$. ← We talked about this at the end of chapter 6.

Therefore:

A large positive slope on the displacement-time graph corresponds to a large positive velocity.

Zero slope on the displacement-time graph corresponds to zero velocity.

A small negative slope on the displacement-time graph corresponds to a small negative velocity.

And so on.

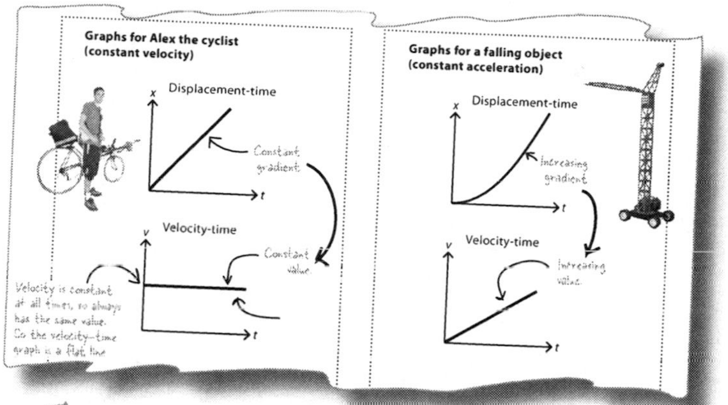

You already moved between the displacement and velocity in chapter 6, for graphs of an object with a constant velocity, and an object with constant acceleration.

Component vectors are fine here...

You could work out an equation for the duck's velocity using component vectors. Each player sees only one component of the duck's velocity. If the duck is moving directly towards you or away from you, you don't notice its velocity at all. And if the duck is in the center, you see it moving with its linear velocity, v.

...but it's quicker to get an equation for the velocity directly from your graph!

If your velocity-time graph has a "standard shape" and you know its period, you'll be able to work out an equation for the velocity using the **amplitude** of the graph...

Sharpen your pencil

a. The displacement-time graph for player 1 is shown on the top graph. Use the slope of this displacement-time graph to sketch the duck's velocity-time graph underneath it. Add extreme values to both graphs where appropriate (the circle's diameter is 3.00 m, its period is 2.50 s, and the duck's linear velocity is 3.77 m/s).

b. Annotate any special points on your graphs to explain why these points occur where they do.

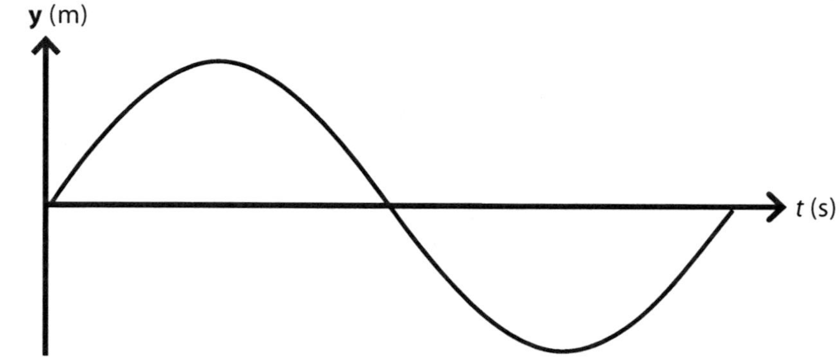

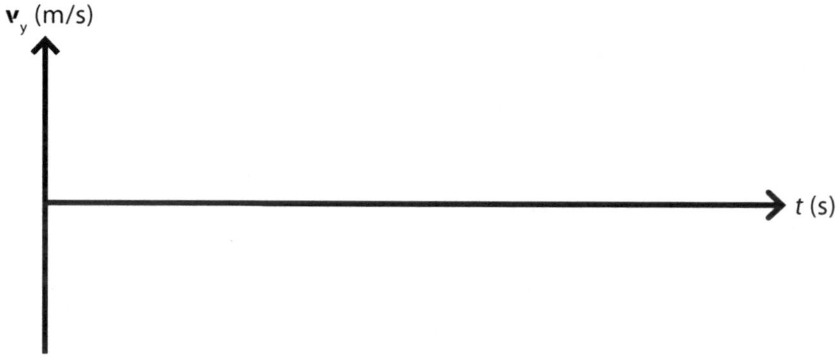

c. What kind of graph does your velocity-time graph resemble in terms of its shape? Use this to write down an equation for v_y, the *y*-component of the velocity in terms of *v* (the duck's linear velocity), ω, and *t*.

Look back at how we worked out the equation for r earlier in this chapter if you get stuck.

You'll need to express θ in terms of ω and t.

d. What is the value of the duck's velocity from player 1's point of view at $t = 0.90$ s?

You'll need to think about the amplitude of your graph (see page 786).

Sharpen your pencil Solution

a. The displacement-time graph for player 1 is shown on the top graph. Use the slope of this displacement-time graph to sketch the duck's velocity-time graph underneath it. Add extreme values to both graphs where appropriate (the circle's diameter is 3.00 m, its period is 2.50 s, and the duck's linear velocity is 3.77 m/s).

b. Annotate any special points on your graphs to explain why these points occur where they do.

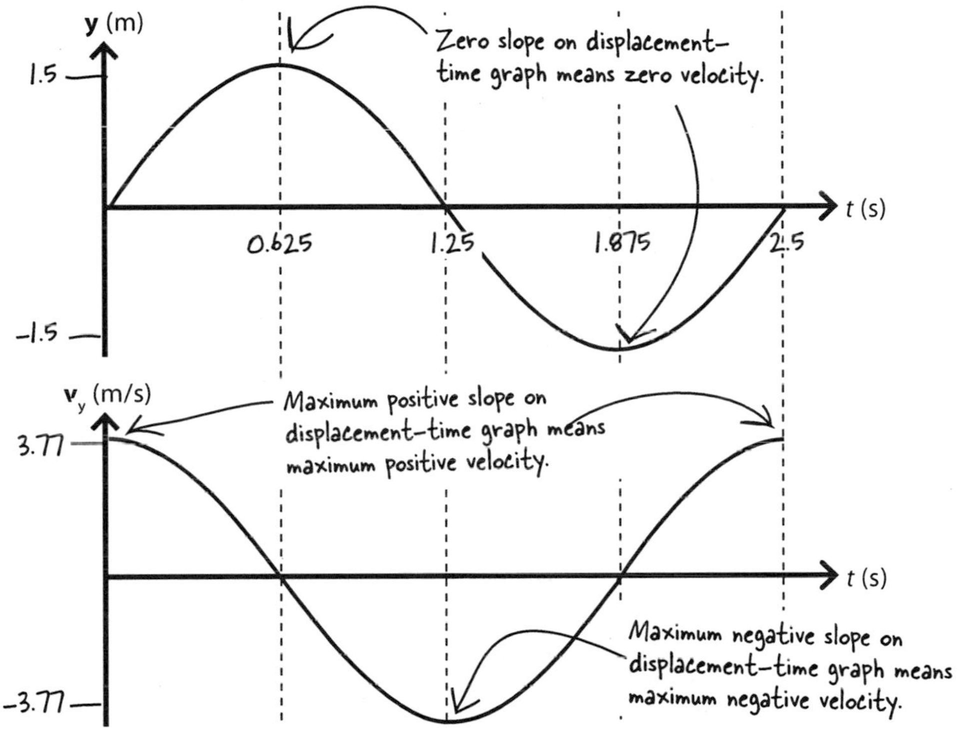

c. What kind of graph does your velocity-time graph resemble in terms of its shape? Use this to write down an equation for v_y, the y-component of the velocity in terms of v (the duck's linear velocity), ω, and t.

The shape looks like a graph of $\cos(\theta)$, because the graph starts at the maximum value.

The maximum value of cosine is 1, but the maximum value of my graph is $v = 3.77$ m/s.
So my graph has an amplitude of v.

$v_y = v\cos(\theta)$ And also, $\theta = \omega t$, which I can substitute into my equation:

$v_y = v\cos(\omega t)$

This equation only works when θ is in radians, so make sure your calculator is in the correct mode.

d. What is the value of the duck's velocity from player 1's point of view at $t = 0.90$ s?

$v = r\omega \Rightarrow \omega = \frac{v}{r} = \frac{3.77}{1.50} = 2.51$ rad/s (3 sd)

$v_y = v\cos(\omega t) = 3.77 \times \cos(2.51 \times 0.90) = -2.39$ m/s (3 sd)

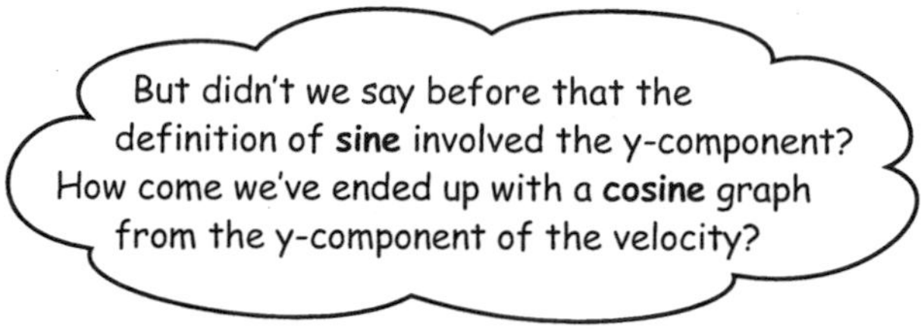

The velocity vector is part of a different triangle.

If you work out the value of v_y, the y-component of the velocity vector, using a right-angled triangle, you get the answer $v_y = v\cos(\theta)$. That works out the same as $v_y = v\cos(\omega t)$, as $\theta = \omega t$.

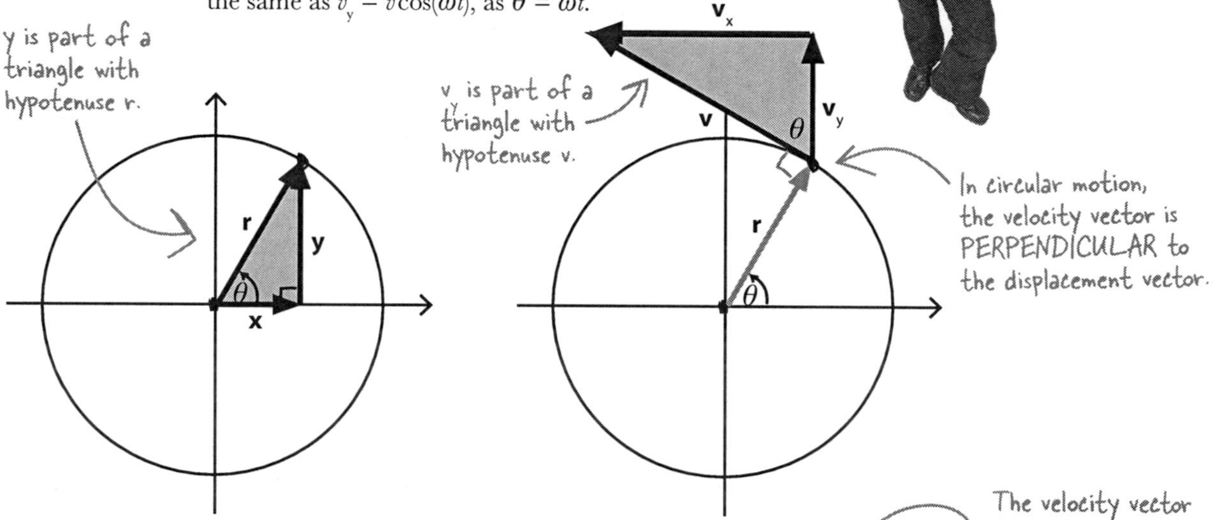

The wider definitions of sine and cosine only hold true if the angle θ is measured counter-clockwise from the horizontal. So to check the velocity component vector triangle, we have to rotate it so that θ is measured counter-clockwise from the horizontal.

This makes $\mathbf{v}_y$ lie along the x-axis as the side adjacent to θ. As cosine involves the ratio of the side that lies along the x-axis and the hypotenuse, the equation $v_y = v\cos(\omega t)$ makes sense.

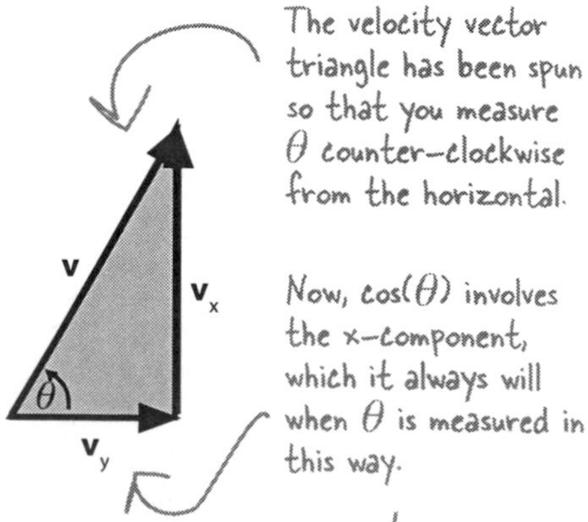

$$\sin(\theta) = \frac{\mathbf{y}}{\mathbf{r}} \qquad \cos(\theta) = \frac{\mathbf{x}}{\mathbf{r}}$$

only apply when θ is measured counter-clockwise from the horizontal.

The game is complete!

This time, the duck-shooting odyssey really is over. The game is an overnight fairground success, and Jane's even starting to opening franchises around the country, with thousands and thousands of people playing the game every day!

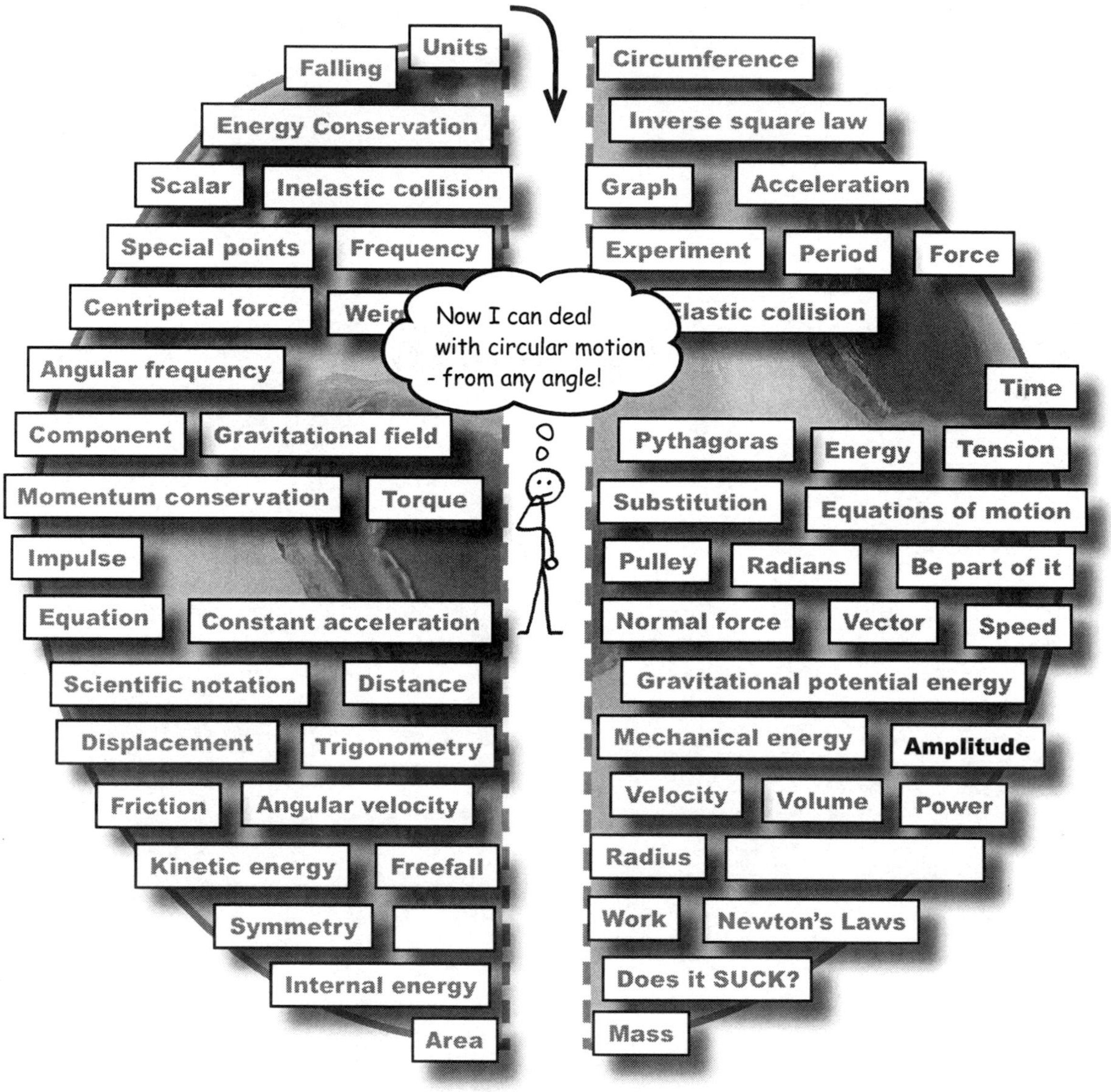

☑ **Amplitude** — **The maximum deviation from the center that your variable can have is called the amplitude of your graph or equation.**

CHAPTER 19

Your Physics Toolbox

You've got Chapter 19 under your belt and added some problem-solving concepts to your toolbox.

New definitions for sine and cosine

If you measure θ counter-clockwise from the horizontal:

$$\sin(\theta) = \frac{y}{r}$$

$$\cos(\theta) = \frac{x}{r}$$

Equation of a sine or cosine graph

General form is:

$$x = A\sin(\theta)$$

$$x = A\cos(\theta)$$

where A is the amplitude (the maximum value that x can have).

Working out an equation or graph

The amplitude is the maximum value that the variable can have.

Use the substitution $\theta = \omega t$.

The thing returns to the start after 2π radians, or 1 period.

Sine graph

Value is 0 at $\theta = 0$.

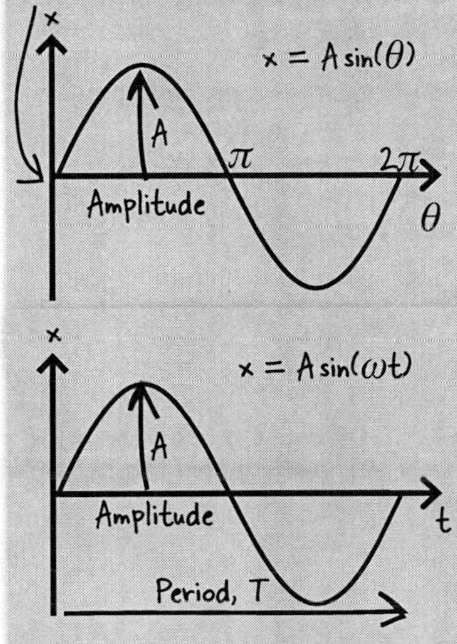

You can plot sine and cosine graphs againt θ or against t.

Cosine graph

Value is maximum at $\theta = 0$.

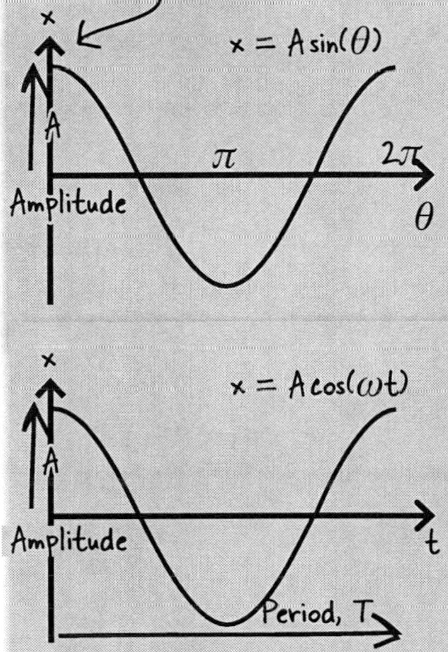

20 Oscillations (part 2)

Springs 'n' swings

What do you do when something just happens over and over? This chapter is about dealing with **oscillations**, and helps you see the big picture. You'll put together what you know about graphs, equations, forces, energy conservation and periodic motion as you tackle springs and pendulums that move with **simple harmonic motion** to get the ultimate "I rule" experience ... without having to repeat yourself too much.

Get rocking, not talking

You've heard of talking to your plants, but you ain't seen nothing yet! Anne's been in touch to tell you about the latest sensation that's rocking the gardening world - her newly-patented Plant Rocker.

Anne has only patented the idea - the design is up to you!

A spring-operated horticultural device.

Removes the need to talk to plants.

Rocks the plant gently with a frequency of 0.750 Hz.

Direction of rocking motion doesn't matter.

Amplitude / size of rocking motion doesn't matter.

The plant rocker needs to work for three different masses of plant

Anne has three favorite plants that she wants to rock, but they're all different sizes (and different masses).

Your design will need to work for all three plants - and Anne insists that each of the plants needs its very own rocker.

A spring will produce regular oscillations

Anne would like to use a **spring** to make the plant rocker. She'd start it rocking by pulling back the spring then letting go so that it **oscillates**. The **direction** that the plant rocks in doesn't matter and the **amplitude** of the rocking (the maximum displacement of the plant from the equilibrium position in the center) isn't important either.

However, Anne is very insistent that the plant rocker must have a **frequency** of 0.750 Hz.

Time to imagine what it's like to ...

BE the plant

Your job is to imagine you're the plant, to get an 'inside perspective' on how the spring-powered plant rocker works. Each picture is taken from a different part of the plant rocker's 'cycle'.

Draw the force and velocity vectors in the boxes and write a brief description of what's going on beside each picture.

If the force or velocity is zero, write 'zero' in the box.

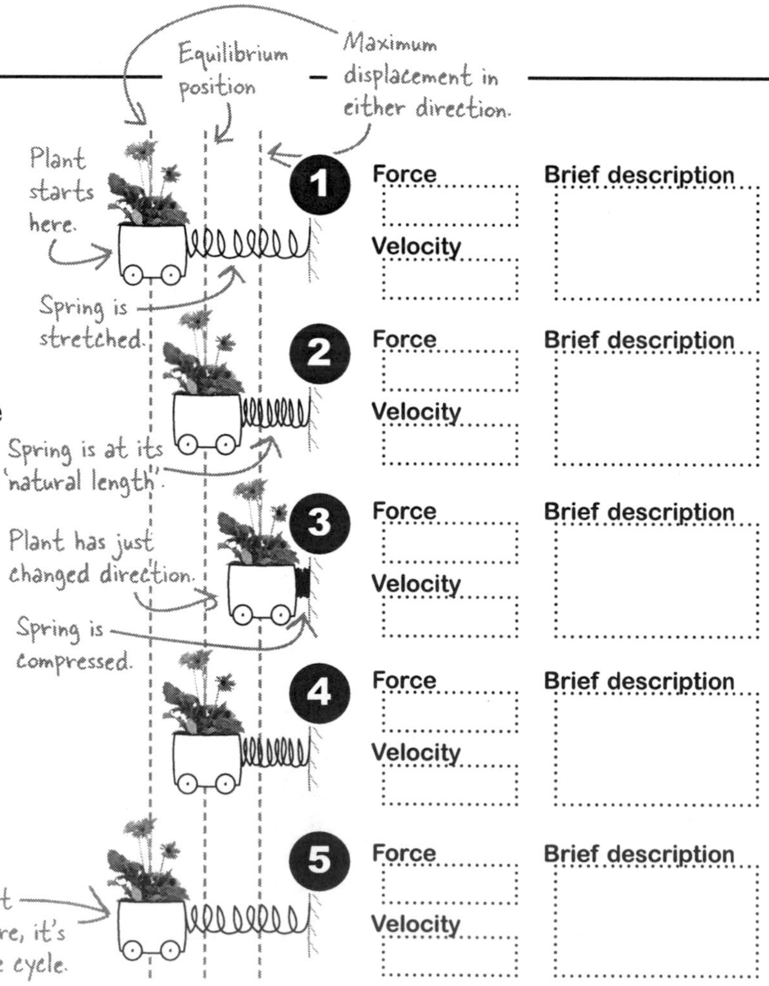

BE the plant - SOLUTION

Your job is to imagine you're the plant, to get an 'inside perspective' on how the spring-powered plant rocker works. Each picture is taken from a different part of the plant rocker's 'cycle'.

Draw the force and velocity vectors in the boxes and write a brief description of what's going on beside each picture.

If the force or velocity is zero, write 'zero' in the box.

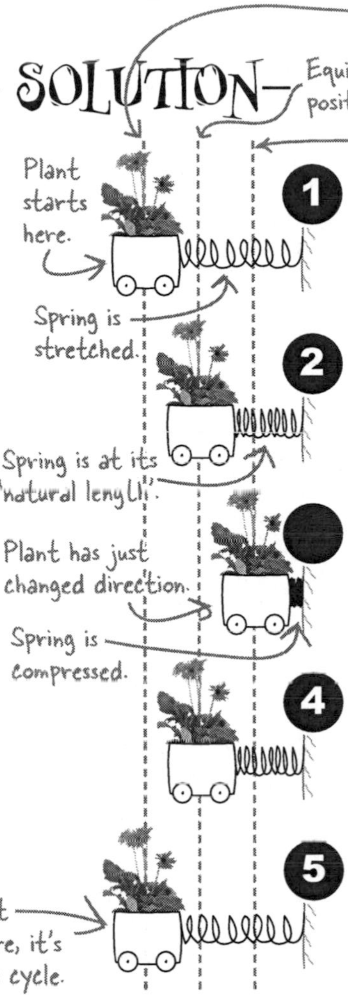

	Force	Velocity	Brief description
1	→	Zero.	Spring exerts force to right. Plant not moving yet.
2	Zero.	→	No force from spring when plant in equilibrium position.
3	←	Zero.	Spring exerts force to left. Plant not moving.
4	Zero.	←	No force from spring when plant in equilibrium position.
5	→	Zero.	Spring exerts force to right. Plant not moving.

Any time you stretch or compress a spring away from its **equilibrium** position, the **spring exerts a force in the opposite direction from the displacement**.

When you pull the plant to the left and let go, the **force** that the spring exerts on it **accelerates** the plant to the right. As the spring becomes less stretched, it exerts a smaller force. This continues until the spring is back at its equilibrium position. There is no net force on the plant when the spring is in the equilibrium position.

With no net force, the plant continues with the same **velocity**, overshoots the equilibrium position and begins to compress the spring. As the spring gets shorter and shorter, it exerts a larger and larger leftwards force on the plant, slowing the plant down. The plant is briefly stationary at the **maximum displacement**.

Then the plant accelerates to the left, passes through the equilibrium position, overshoots and ends up back where it started - a complete cycle of motion.

Displacement from equilibrium and strength of spring affect the force

You know how the plant rocker works qualitatively. Now it's time to be quantitative and start working out some values.

The **force** that the spring exerts depends on:

The change in the spring's length. The greater the **displacement from equilibrium**, the greater the force.

If you double the displacement from equilibrium, you double the force.

The strength of the spring. The **stronger the spring**, the greater the force.

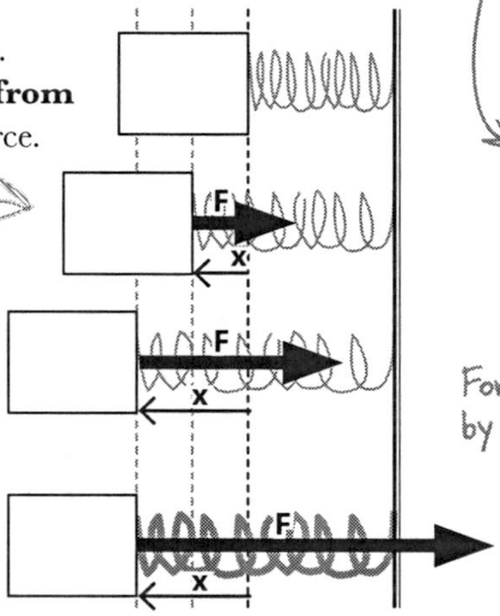

Kinetic energy is a capital K; the spring constant is a small k. Take care not to mix them up.

This is summed up by the equation $\mathbf{F}_s = -k\mathbf{x}$, where **F** is the force exerted by the spring, **x** is the displacement from the equilibrium position and k is the spring constant, a measure of the strength of the spring. There's a minus sign in the equation because the force is in the opposite direction from the displacement. This relationship is known as **Hooke's Law**.

$$F_s = -kx$$

Force exerted by spring.

Spring constant

Displacement from equilibrium position.

Use a minus sign to show that the force the spring exerts in in the opposite direction from the displacement.

Sharpen your pencil

a. Use the equation $\mathbf{F}_s = -k\mathbf{x}$ to work out the units of k, the spring constant (in kg, m, s, etc).

b. The plant rocker is to have a frequency of 0.750 Hz. What is its period?

c. Use the equation $\mathbf{F}_s = -k\mathbf{x}$ to explain whether you think using a stronger spring (with a larger spring constant) will have an effect on the period.

d. Do you think there are any other variables that would change the period?

Sharpen your pencil Solution

a. Use the equation $\mathbf{F}_s = -k\mathbf{x}$ to work out the units of *k*, the spring constant (in kg, m, s, etc).

$$F = -kx \Rightarrow ma = -kx$$

$$\Rightarrow k = -\frac{ma}{x} \Rightarrow [k] = \frac{[m][a]}{[x]}$$

$$[k] = \frac{kg \cdot m/s^2}{m} \qquad [k] = kg/s^2$$

b. The plant rocker is to have a frequency of 0.750 Hz. What is its period?

Period, T, is number of seconds per cycle.
Frequency, f, is number of cycles per second.

$$T = \frac{1}{f} = \frac{1}{0.750} = 1.33\ s\ (3\ sd)$$

c. Use the equation $\mathbf{F}_s = -k\mathbf{x}$ to explain whether you think using a stronger spring (with a larger spring constant) will have an effect on the period.

If you have a strong spring and a weaker spring and pull them both back the same displacement at the start, the strong spring will accelerate the plant more rapidly, because a large k means a large force.. Onvce the plant's moved through the equilibrium position, it'll also decelerate the plant and then pull it back in the opposite direction more quickly. So I think a stronger spring will lead to a shorter period.

d. Do you think there are any other variables that would change the period?

F = ma, so if the plant is more massive it'll accelerate less when you pull it back. So it won't move so quickly and the period will be shorter. The amount you pull the plant back may also affect the period?

there are no Dumb Questions

Q: Why do we want to calculate the force that the spring exerts on the plant?

A: Any time you're dealing with forces, it's good to start with a free body diagram and work out the net force (like you did when you were 'being' the plant).

Q: How do you know that doubling the spring's displacement from equilibrium doubles the force?

A: By experimenting with springs! There was a bit of this back in chapter 11 when we were dealing with how scales measure your weight.

Q: So how would you measure a spring constant? Surely springs don't come with one written on?

A: A strong spring with a large spring constant will stretch less than a weaker spring when you apply the same force to it by hanging the same mass from it.

So if you measure the spring's displacement from equilibrium (i.e. its change in length) for a variety of masses, you can plot a graph. You can use the graph to calculate the spring constant. You'll calculate a spring constant later on in this chapter.

Q: Are the extremes and the equilibrium position 'special points'?

A: Yes. When the displacement is at its maximum, the force is also at its maximum (though they're in opposite directions). The velocity is zero at the extremes when the plant is changing direction.

In the equilibrium position, there's no net force on the plant, so it continues at its current (and maximum) velocity).

Q: Will thinking about the force help us with the frequency of the oscillations?

A: We're just getting on to that ...

Sharpen your pencil

Graphs of the plant rocker's motion will help you to work out an equation that connects the spring constant with the frequency of oscillations. The plant starts off at $x = x_0$.

Sketch graphs of the plant's displacement, velocity and acceleration vs time for one cycle of its motion with a period of 1.33 s (same as a frequency of 0.750 Hz). Start off by marking the 'special points' where you'd find the maximum of each variable, and sketch on from there. We've already put some of them on for you.

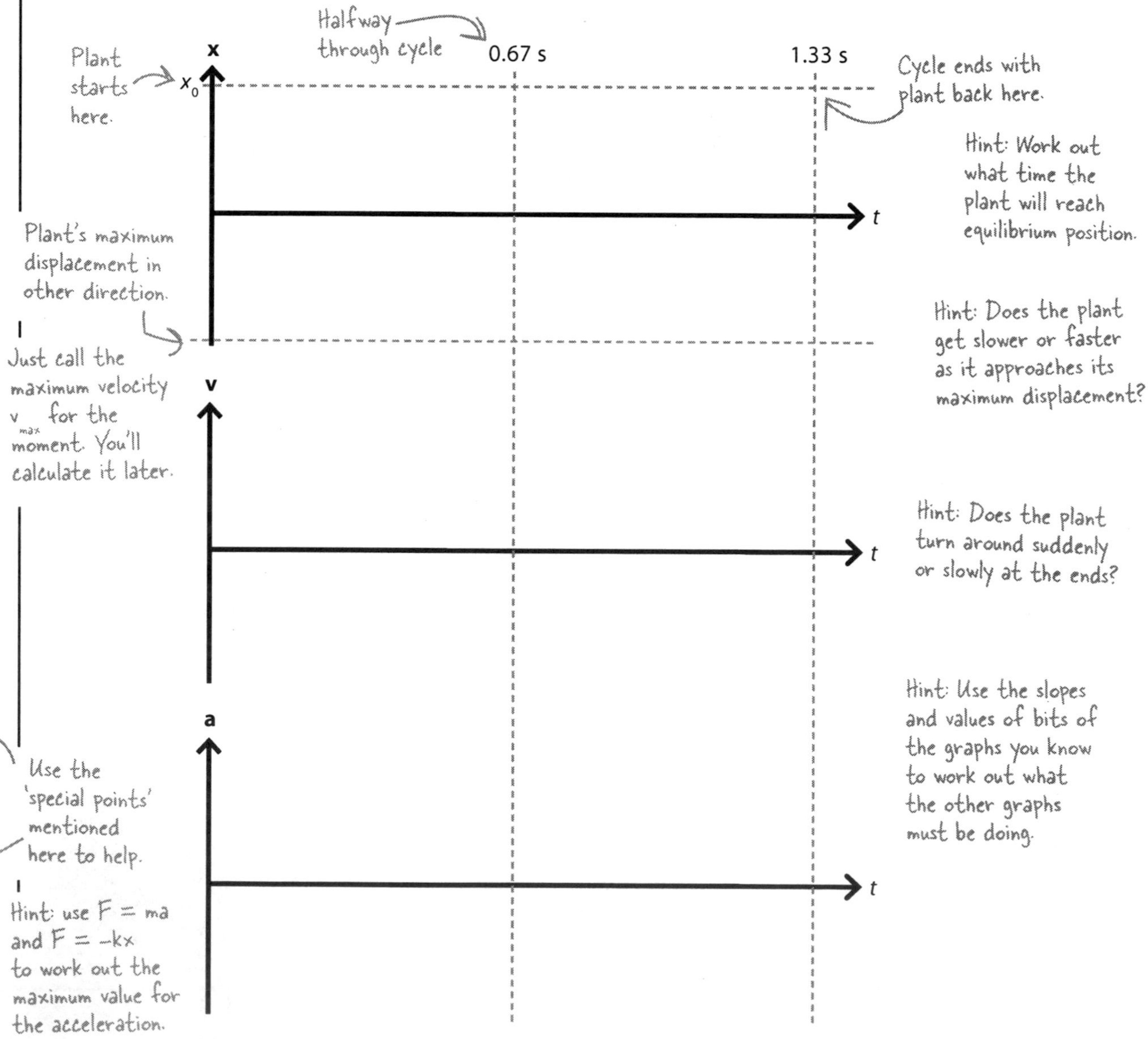

Sharpen your pencil Solution

Graphs of the plant rocker's motion will help you to work out an equation that connects the spring constant with the frequency of oscillations. The plant starts off at $x = x_0$.

Sketch graphs of the plant's displacement, velocity and acceleration vs time for one cycle of its motion with a period of 1.33 s (same as a frequency of 0.750 Hz). Start off by marking the 'special points' where you'd find the maximum of each variable, and sketch on from there. We've already put some of them on for you.

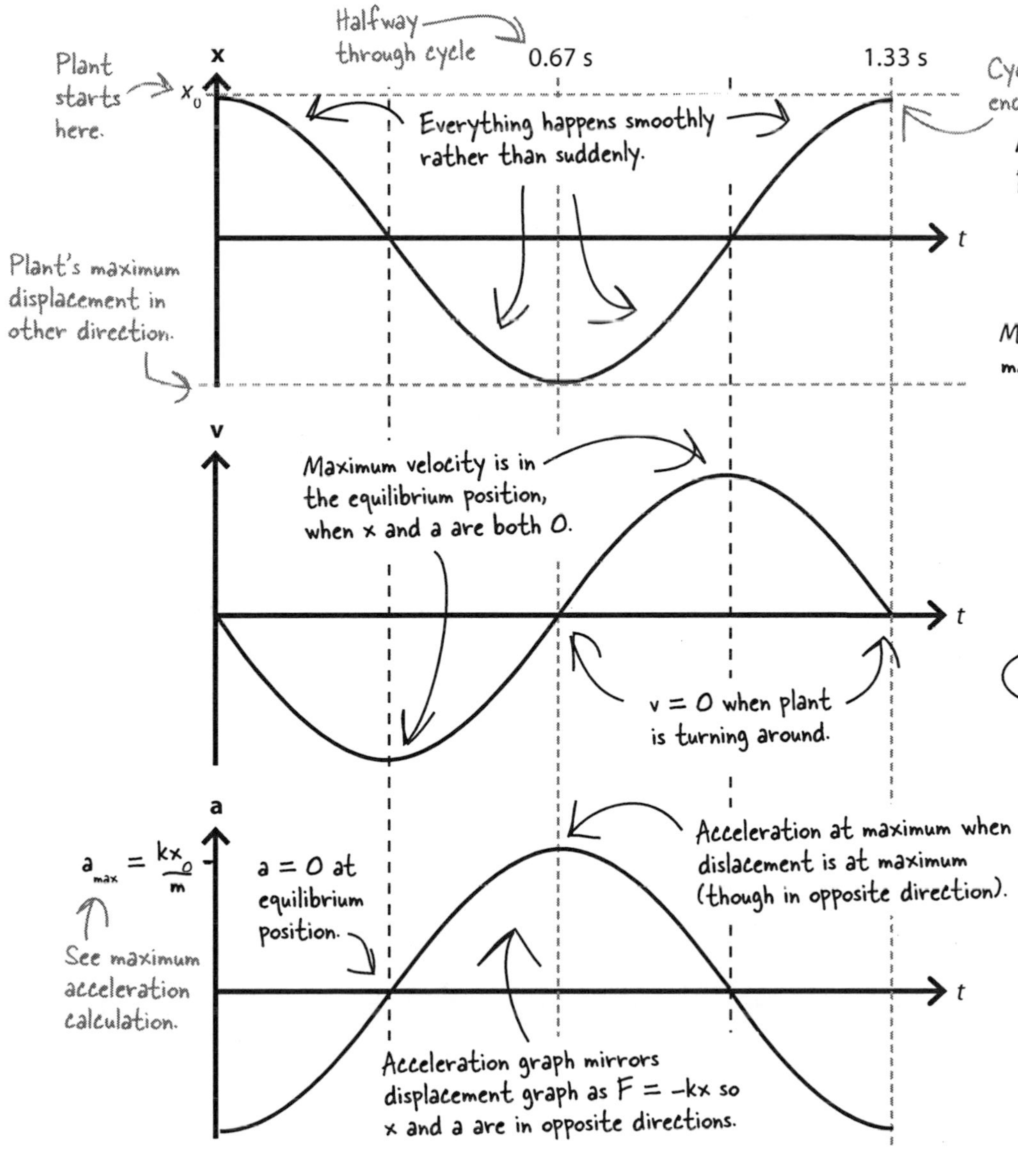

Maximum acceleration calculation:

$F = ma = -kx$

$\Rightarrow ma = -kx$

$a = \frac{-kx}{m}$

Maximum acceleration when there's maximum displacement.

$\Rightarrow a_{max} = \frac{-kx_0}{m}$

A mass on a spring moves like a side-on view of circular motion

Looking at the plant rocker - a mass on a spring - from side on is identical to looking at **circular motion** from side on.

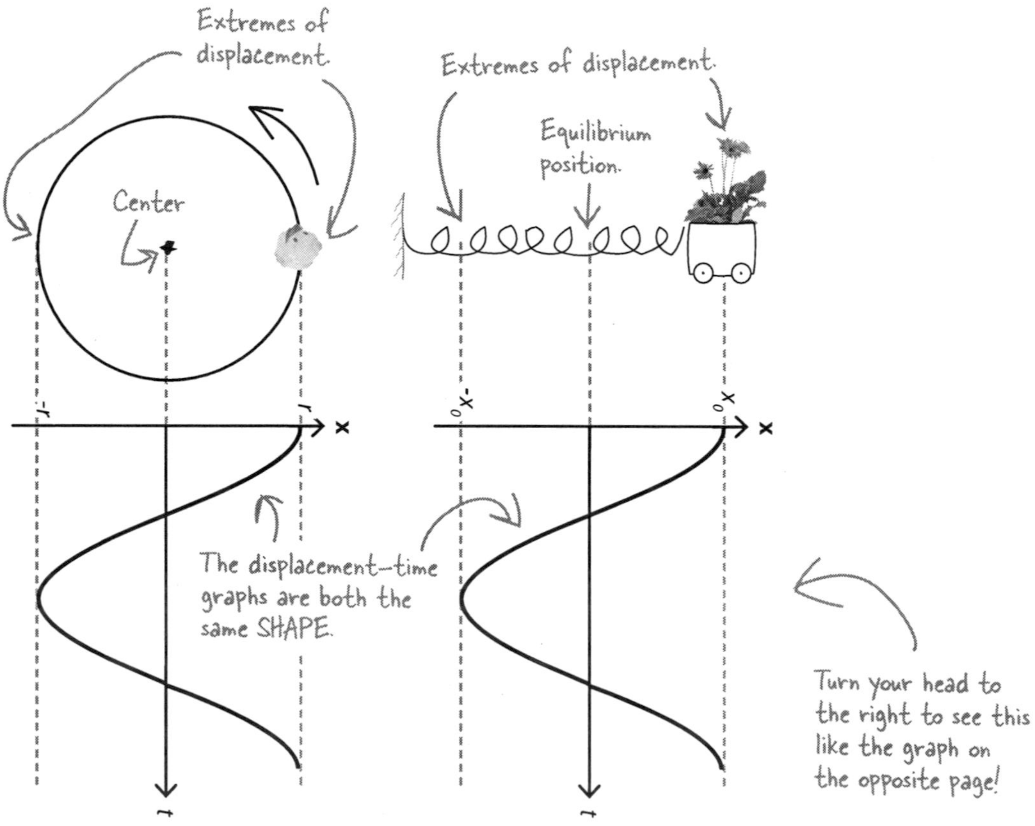

The displacement, velocity and acceleration-time graphs of a mass on a spring are all sinusoids.

This means that the graphs for the plant's **displacement**, velocity and **acceleration** are the same **shapes** as the equivalent graphs for circular motion viewed from side on.

So the plant rocker must use the **same types of equations** as the side-on view of circular motion. This means that the equations for the plant rocker's displacement, velocity and acceleration will involve **sines** and **cosines**.

A mass on a spring moves with simple harmonic motion

The plant rocker oscillates to-and-fro because of a '**restoring force**' from the spring, $\mathbf{F}_s = -k\mathbf{x}$.

The force is directly proportional to the spring's **displacement** from the equilibrium position and acts in the opposite direction from the displacement. The graphs you sketched of the plant rocker confirm that the acceleration - and therefore the force - is always in the **opposite direction** from the displacement.

You get simple harmonic motion when the restoring force is directly proportional to the displacement, but in the opposite direction.

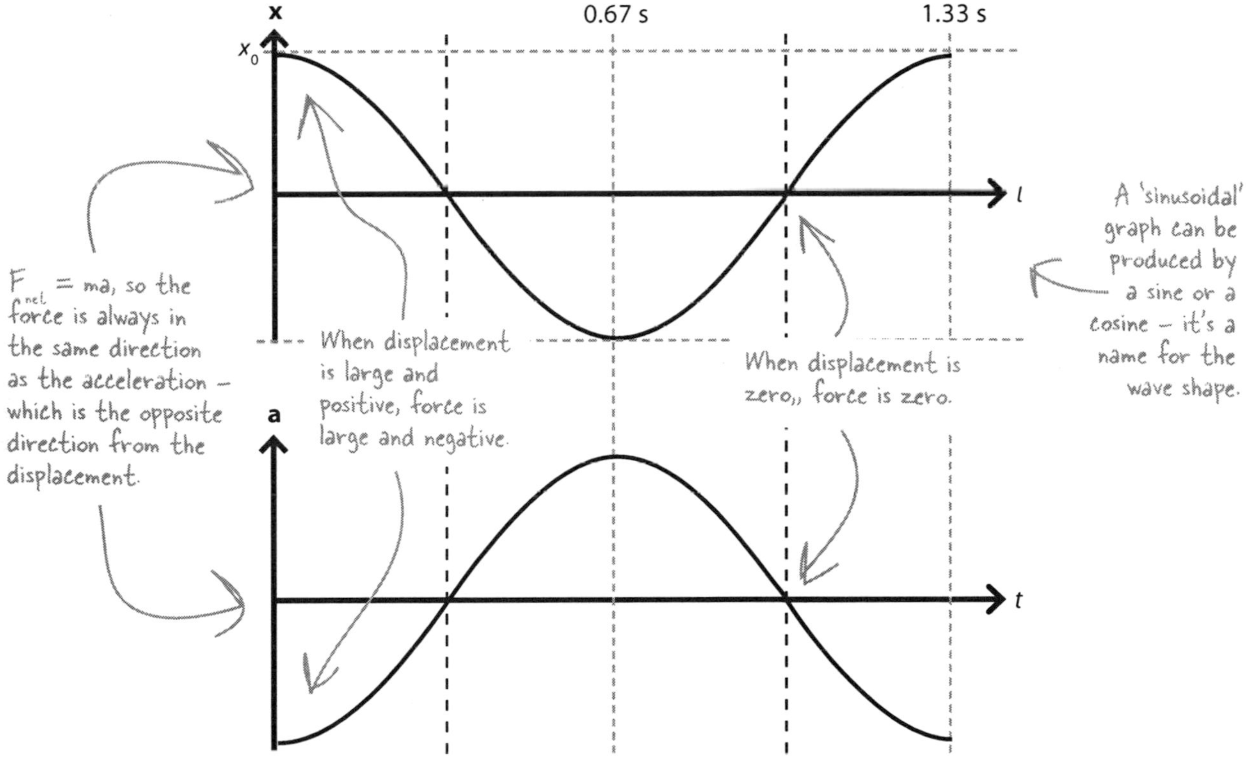

This kind of situation, where the restoring force is proportional to the displacement from the equlibrium position, is common enough in physics for it to be given its own name, **simple harmonic motion**, or SHM.

SHM always produces these kinds of **sinusoidal** displacement-time, velocity - time and acceleration-time graphs. A "simple harmonic" is another name for a sinusoid.

Yes - the equations for the frequency, period, maximum speed, etc are the same

If you set up a mass on a spring and a side-on circular motion on a turntable next to each other, they look identical. The shapes of their displacement-time, velocity-time and acceleration-time graphs are identical.

This means you can use all the equations you already know for the frequency, period and angular frequency of circular motion for simple harmonic motion.

Angular frequency and angular speed

Angular frequency and angular speed both have the same size and both have units of radians per second. They're exactly the same thing.

You can get from the frequency, f, to the angular frequency, ω, with the equation:

$$\omega = 2\pi f$$

SHM has a frequency and a period, so you can use all the equations you already know from circular motion.

Frequency and period

Frequency, f, is cycles per second.

Period, T, is seconds per cycle.

Because they're related like this:

$$T = \frac{1}{f} \qquad f = \frac{1}{T}$$

You can do all sorts of combining and rearranging equations with these two postit notes.

there are no Dumb Questions

Q: It seems like a big jump from a mass on a spring to three sinusoidal graphs. Can you run some of that by me again?

A: The key thing is that you have a situation where the force is directly proportional to the displacement from the equilibrium position, and in the opposite direction from the displacement. Any time this is the case - whether the force is provided by a spring or something else - you have simple harmonic motion.

Q: What does simple harmonic motion look like?

A: If you watch the mass on the spring from side-on, you'll see that the mass moves quickly through the equilibrium position but slowly at each end of the motion, and transitions smoothly between these velocitites.

Q: Is simple harmonic motion exactly like looking at circular motion from side on?

A: Yes! If you have simple harmonic motion (SHM) and circular motion with the same period and look at them from side-on, they appear identical.

Q: With SHM there's an acceleration produced by the force of the spring which I can plot on a graph. Where's the acceleration in circular motion?

A: If an object's moving around a circle, there must be a centripetal acceleration provided by something in order for the circular motion to be possible. So the acceleration-time graph of circular motion viewed from side on would be the component of the centripetal acceleration that you can see from your vantage point.

Actually proving this requires calculus

You did a substitution to work out the maximum value of the acceleration to put on your graph: $\mathbf{F} = -k\mathbf{x}$ and also $\mathbf{F} = m\mathbf{a}$, so if you do a substitution for $\mathbf{F}$ you get $-k\mathbf{x} = m\mathbf{a}$; rearranged, this is $\mathbf{a} = -\frac{k}{m}\mathbf{x}$

At the moment, this is an equation containing two quantities that are constant throughout the plant's motion (k and m) and two that vary ($\mathbf{a}$ and $\mathbf{x}$). You can't use one equation to work out two unknowns.

However, acceleration is rate of change of displacement, $\mathbf{a} = \frac{d\mathbf{v}}{dt}$. You can substitute this in the equation $\mathbf{a} = -\frac{k}{m}\mathbf{x}$ to get $\frac{d\mathbf{v}}{dt} = -\frac{k}{m}\mathbf{x}$ This doesn't appear to help, as there are still two unknowns ($\mathbf{v}$ and $\mathbf{x}$) in the equation. But as displacement is rate of change of velocity, $\mathbf{v} = \frac{d\mathbf{x}}{dt}$, you can make another substitution to get $\frac{d}{dt}\left(\frac{d\mathbf{x}}{dt}\right) = -\frac{k}{m}\mathbf{x}$.

This equation only has one unknown, $\mathbf{x}$, but you need calculus to solve it. Don't worry - we've given you the ready-bake solution on the opposite page

You don't have to do calculus!

You don't need to be able to go line by line from the nasty-looking equation $\frac{d}{dt}\left(\frac{d\boldsymbol{x}}{dt}\right) = -\frac{k}{m}\boldsymbol{x}$ to the ready-bake equation on the opposite page. On a non-calculus course, you'll only need to **apply** the ready-bake equation to solve problems.

Simple harmonic motion is sinusoidal

The mass starts off with its maximum displacement at $t = 0$. This means that the equation must be some kind of cosine, as cosine is also at its maximum when $t = 0$.

The exact form of the equation is $\mathbf{x} = \mathbf{x}_0\cos\left(\sqrt{\frac{k}{m}}t\right)$.

cosine is at a maximum when $t = 0$

Ready Bake Equation

Mass on spring starts at $\mathbf{x} = \mathbf{x}_0$:

$$\mathbf{x} = \mathbf{x}_0\cos\left(\sqrt{\frac{k}{m}}\,t\right)$$

x_0 is the maximum value of x, and therefore the amplitude of the motion.

It looks like you don't need to have an angle to have a sinusoid shape, even though sine and cosine usually involve angles?

The value you 'put into' the cosine function is equal to the angle in an equivalent side-on circular set-up.

If you set up a plant on a spring and a duck on a turntable next to each other so that they both have the same amplitude and frequency, their motion looks identical from side on.

You can describe circular motion viewed from side on in terms of the angle θ that the turntable has moved through, using the equation $\mathbf{x} = \mathbf{x}_0\cos(\theta)$. You can describe circular motion in terms of **time** using the same equation with the substitution $\theta = \omega t$ to get $\mathbf{x} = \mathbf{x}_0\cos(\omega t)$.

As the circular and simple harmonic motion **look** identical from side on, the equation for SHM has the same **form** as the equation for side-on circular motion, despite the fact that there are no physical angles involved with the plant on the spring.

Here, θ and ω are "mathematical tools" rather than actual physical angles.

Hey ... are you close to working out how to rock my plants at the right **frequency**?

BRAIN POWER

How can you use the equation for SHM to work out the **frequency** of the plant rocker?

Work out constants by comparing a situation-specific equation with a standard equation

The 'standard' equation for simple harmonic motion (and circular motion from side on) that starts at a maximum is $\mathbf{x} = \mathbf{A}\cos(\omega t)$.

The equation for the plant's displacement is $\mathbf{x} = \mathbf{x}_0\cos\left(\sqrt{\frac{k}{m}}\,t\right)$.

If you 'line up' these two equations, you can see that they're identical in 'form' but that there are different variables in 'important places'.

$$\mathbf{x} = \mathbf{A}\cos(\omega t)$$

$$\mathbf{x} = \mathbf{x}_0\cos\left(\sqrt{\frac{k}{m}}\,t\right)$$

You met this equation in ch 19.

x and t are variables.

x_0, k and m are constants for any one 'run' of the plant rocker.

Look at the amplitude

Both equations consist of a cosine multiplied by something. In the 'standard' equation, that something is **A**, the **amplitude**, which gives you the maximum value that the equation can have (since the maximum value of cosine is 1).

In your displacement equation, the amplitude is $\mathbf{x}_0$, which is how far you pulled the plant rocker back at the start - it's the maximum value the displacement can have.

Look at the argument of the cosine

Both equations contain the **cosine** of a quantity. In the 'standard' equation, this quantity is ωt, the angular frequency multiplied by the time. As the definition of angular frequency is $\omega = 2\pi f$, you can work out the frequency and period if you know the value of ω.

In your equation, you have the cosine of $\sqrt{\frac{k}{m}}\,t$. So $\sqrt{\frac{k}{m}}\,t$ in this equation is equivalent to ωt in the 'standard equation. You can write down the new equation $\omega t = \sqrt{\frac{k}{m}}\,t$ and use this to calculate the frequency of the plant rocker.

Hang on! Surely you can only use ω when you have a circle, as it's radians per second?! We don't have a circle, or any other angles!

Here, the variable ω is a tool you can use to get what you want.

The 'standard' equation could also be written $\mathbf{x} = \mathbf{x}_0\cos(2\pi ft)$ (as $\omega = 2\pi f$) which doesn't involve ω at all, only f.

The mass on a spring has a **frequency** (number of cycles per second). You want to know how to produce oscillations with this frequency, and can use ω as a mathematical tool to get there.

Compare your equation with the 'standard' one to work out the amplitude and frequency of your SHM.

Sharpen your pencil

You have three plants with masses of 100, 250 and 500 grams respectively. You wish to attach each of them to an individual spring so that they can be rocked horizontally with a frequency of 0.750 Hz.

a. Compare the equation $\mathbf{x} = \mathbf{x}_0 \cos\left(\sqrt{\frac{k}{m}}\, t\right)$ with the standard equation for simple harmonic motion to work out an equation for the frequency of the plant rocker.

b. Check your equation over by imagining what would happen if k and m were altered one at a time. Jot down your thoughts about whether your equation behaves as the plant would in real life.

c. Calculate the spring constant required to rock each plant with a frequency of 0.750 Hz when the plant rocker is pulled back to $\mathbf{x}_0 = 10.0$ cm at $t = 0$ to start off with.

Hint: You'll need to work out its units as well.

d. Would it be possible to use the same strength of spring for all three plants if you pulled the plants back different distances to start off the plant rocker? Why / why not?

Sharpen your pencil Solution

You have three plants with masses of 100, 250 and 500 grams respectively. You wish to attach each of them to an individual spring so that they can be rocked horizontally with a frequency of 0.750 Hz.

a. Compare the equation $\mathbf{x} = \mathbf{x}_0\cos\left(\sqrt{\frac{k}{m}}\,t\right)$ with the standard equation for simple harmonic motion to work out an equation for the frequency of the plant rocker.

'Standard' equation: $x = A\cos(\omega t)$

Mass on a spring: $x = x_0\cos\left(\sqrt{\frac{k}{m}}\,t\right)$

$$\omega = \sqrt{\frac{k}{m}} \Rightarrow 2\pi f = \sqrt{\frac{k}{m}}$$

$$f = \frac{1}{2\pi}\sqrt{\frac{k}{m}}$$

This works because $\omega = 2\pi f$

b. Check your equation over by imagining what would happen if k and m were altered one at a time. Jot down your thoughts about whether your equation behaves as the plant would in real life.

If k is bigger, the equation says that the frequency gets higher. This makes sense, as the force would be larger so the plant would accelerate more and move more quickly.

If m is bigger, the equation says that the frequency gets lower. This makes sense as the force would be the same but the mass would be larger, so the plant wouldn't accelerate as much and would move more slowly.

c. Calculate the spring constant required to rock each plant with a frequency of 0.750 Hz when the plant rocker is pulled back to $\mathbf{x}_0 = 10.0$ cm at $t = 0$ to start off with.

$$f = \frac{1}{2\pi}\sqrt{\frac{k}{m}}$$

$$\Rightarrow f^2 = \frac{1}{4\pi^2}\cdot\frac{k}{m}$$

$$\Rightarrow k = 4\pi^2 m f^2$$

You can get the units of the spring constant from the units of the right hand side of your equation.

100 g plant: $k = 4\pi^2 \times 0.100 \times 0.750^2 = \underline{2.22\ kg/s^2}$ (3 sd)

250 g plant: $k = 4\pi^2 \times 0.250 \times 0.750^2 = \underline{5.55\ kg/s^2}$ (3 sd)

500 g plant: $k = 4\pi^2 \times 0.500 \times 0.750^2 = \underline{11.1\ kg/s^2}$ (3 sd)

You need the masses to be in kilograms, not grams.

d. Would it be possible to use the same strength of spring for all three plants if you pulled the plants back different distances to start off the plant rocker? Why / why not?

No, because the frequency doesn't depend on the amplitude, only the spring constant and the mass. So the frequency will be the same however far back you pull the plant at the start.

$$\mathbf{x = A\cos(\omega t)}$$

is the standard equation for any SHM. For a mass on a spring,

$$\boldsymbol{\omega = \sqrt{\frac{k}{m}}}$$

Use this equation to solve ANY SHM problem.

ω is a tool that gives you what you want to find out.

Question Clinic: The "This equation is like that one" Question

In physics, you sometimes come across specific instances of general equations. One example of this is the general equation for simple harmonic motion, $x = A\cos(\omega t)$. ANY object moving with simple harmonic motion will have an equation of this form (or an equation of the form $x = A\sin(\omega t)$ if the motion starts at $x = 0$. In the equation, A represents the amplitude - the maximum value of x. And the argument of the cosine is always equal to ωt. This means that you can calculate ω, and from it f and T.

See also the equation $y = mx + c$, covered in appendix i.

Each of the variables in the equation is defined here.

12. The displacement of a mass, *m*, oscillating on a spring with spring constant *k*, after time, *t*, is given by the equation $x = x_0 \cos\left(\sqrt{\frac{k}{m}}\,t\right)$

a. By comparing this equation with the standard equation for simple harmonic motion, work out an equation for *f*, the frequency of the oscillator.

b. Calculate the spring constant required to rock a 100 gram plant with a frequency of 0.750 Hz.

This is the amplitude

This is the angular frequency, ω

So $\omega = \sqrt{\frac{k}{m}}$

This means that you compare it with the equation $x = A\cos(\omega t)$ to get the amplitude and angular frequency.

Here, $\omega = 2\pi f$

So $2\pi f = \sqrt{\frac{k}{m}}$

You will often have to use the equation you work out to do a calculation. Don't worry - if you get the equation wrong then work the numbers through OK, you'll get partial credit.

You can solve problems by spotting that an equation is like one you already know about, and making substitutions.

The key thing in a question like this is keeping track of what is plotted on each axis in each equation, especially if they use different letters for the things plotted on the horizontal and vertical axes. Do a sketch of each graph and write the letters on to help you keep track.

The frequency of SHM is the same, whatever the amplitude.

SHM and circular motion viewed from side-on look exactly the same. If you follow two objects at different radii on a rotating disc, they have the same **period** but the outer object moves more rapidly and appears to 'overtake' the inner one before shooting out to a larger amplitude. Because it's travelling more rapidly, the outer object requires a larger centripetal **force** to maintain its circular motion.

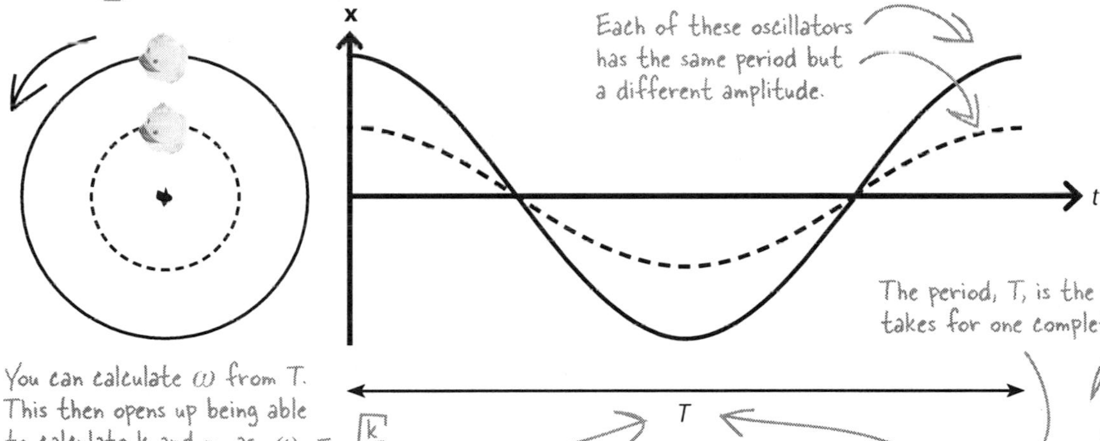

It's the same with a mass on a spring. If you pull the spring further back at the start, a larger **force** acts on the mass, and the mass achieves a higher **velocity** through the equilibrium position. But this means that the mass has more momentum, so it 'overshoots' further than an oscillation with the same mass and a smaller amplitude.

However large the **amplitude** of the mass's oscillations, the SHM will always have the same **period**, and the same **frequency**.

Unless you damage the spring by over-stretching it when you pull it back – then you won't get SHM at all, just a repair bill!

The frequency and period of SHM don't depend on the amplitude.

You rock! Or at least Anne's plants do

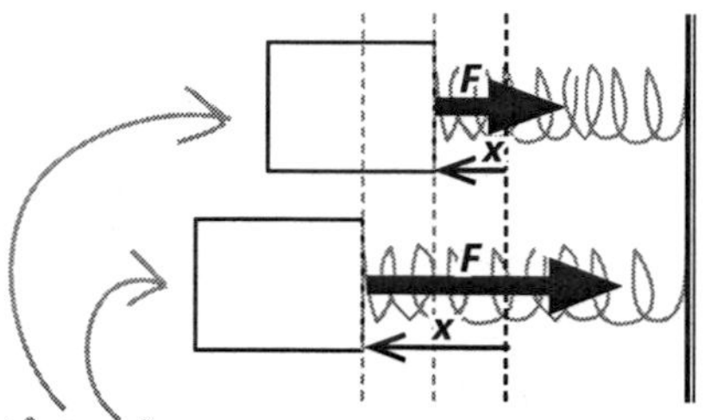

If the force is proportional to the displacement (but in the opposite direction) then you have SHM.

You've designed Anne's patented horticultural talk-free device - and it rocks! First of all, you worked out how the spring makes the plant oscillate and found out about Hooke's Law, $\mathbf{F} = -k\mathbf{x}$.

Then you sketched graphs of the plant's **displacement**, **velocity** and **acceleration** and spotted that they have similar shapes to graphs of circular motion when the motion is viewed from side on. This is **simple harmonic motion** - and you always get these shapes of graphs when the restoring **force** is proportional to the displacement from the equilibrium position.

Simple harmonic motion is sinusoidal. This lets you calculate the frequency, period, amplitude, etc, as the equation has a standard format.

After getting the ready-bake (calculus-derived) equation for the displacment, $\mathbf{x} = \mathbf{x}_0\cos\left(\sqrt{\frac{k}{m}}\,t\right)$, you compared it with the 'standard' equation for simple harmonic motion $\mathbf{x} = \mathbf{A}\cos(\omega t)$. Comparing the arguments of the cosines in the equations let you write down the equation $\omega t = \sqrt{\frac{k}{m}}\,t$ and then $\omega = \sqrt{\frac{k}{m}}$, which enabled you to calculate the spring constant each plant would need.

And it doesn't matter how far back you pull the plant to start it off, as the frequency and period of SHM don't depend on the amplitude of the motion.

But Anne forgot to mention someting ...

BRAIN POWER

What might the maximum velocity of a mass on a spring depend on?

Jim: I guess that the maximum velocity's gonna depend on how far back we pull the plant at the start.

Frank: Yeah, the larger the **displacement** from equilibrium, the larger the **force** from the spring and the larger the **acceleration**. The plant has its **maximum velocity** as it goes through the equilibrium position, before the spring starts to slow it down again.

Joe: But if the initial displacement is too large, the plant will go too fast. We need to calculate exactly how far back we need to pull the plant to give it a velocity of 1.50 m/s in the center.

Frank: I guess we could go take a calculus class then come back and have a go at solving those sinusoidal equations. NOT!!

Jim: I'm sure there must be another way - if we draw enough free body diagrams and force vectors, maybe we'll spot something.

Joe: Hey ... we're only thinking about using forces. But isn't it usually easier to use **energy** in problems where that's possible?

Frank: Perhaps ... differences drive change that lead to energy transfer. Well, the velocity of the plant is changing all the time.

Joe: And so's the length of the spring. You start off with **elastic potential energy** in the stretched spring, then have entirely **kinetic energy** in the equilibrium position, and then entirely potential again at the other extreme.

Jim: Yeah when the velocity is at its maximum, all of the potential energy the spring had at the start is now kinetic energy $K = \frac{1}{2}m\mathbf{v}^2$.

Frank: Which has **v** in it! If we know how large the spring's potential energy store is at the start, we can use energy conservation to calculate the plant's velocity in the center, when the elastic potential energy is zero. That works!

Joe: So we give the spring potential energy at the start ...

Jim: Yeah, we do **work** on the spring, to do that, right? And work = force × displacement. Sorted!

Joe: Um ... but which force do we use? As you stretch the spring, the force we're doing work against gets larger and larger.

Frank: The work is the **area under the force-displacement graph**. Can we calculate that?

A compressed or stretched spring has elastic potential energy. You can use energy conservation to solve problems that involve springs.

To use force, acceleration, velocity and displacement here, you'd have to go and take a calculus course first. Best to use energy ...

Sharpen your pencil

This is a hard exercise. Take time to get your head around it, and don't be worried if it takes you a while.

a. Use the axes below to sketch a graph of force applied vs displacement as you stretch a spring with spring constant k to displacement $\mathbf{x}_0$. As your graph is of the force you need to apply to extend the spring, rather than the force that the spring exerts on you, the force and displacement lie in the same direction, and the value of the force is $\mathbf{F} = k\mathbf{x}$.

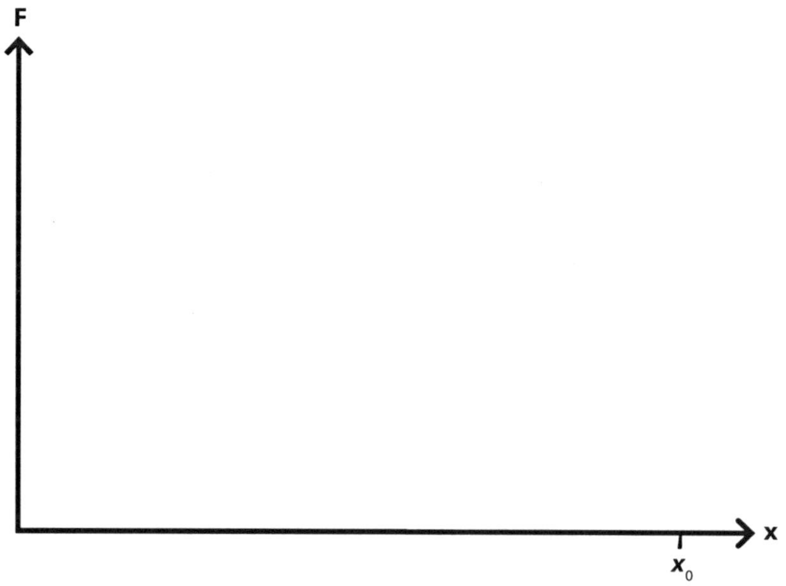

b. Mark on the value of **F** when the displacement = $\mathbf{x}_0$.

c. The total work done is the total area between your graph and the horizontal axis. Calculate this area and hence write down an equation for the work done in stretching the spring to displacement $\mathbf{x}_0$.

The subscript 's' indicates that a spring is involved.

d. How much elastic potential energy, U_s, is transferred to a spring with spring constant k by stretching it displacement $\mathbf{x}_0$ from its equilibrium position?

Sharpen your pencil Solution

a. Use the axes below to sketch a graph of force applied vs displacement as you stretch a spring with spring constant k to displacement $\mathbf{x}_0$. As your graph is of the force you need to apply to extend the spring, rather than the force that the spring exerts on you, the force and displacement lie in the same direction, and the value of the force is $\mathbf{F} = k\mathbf{x}$.

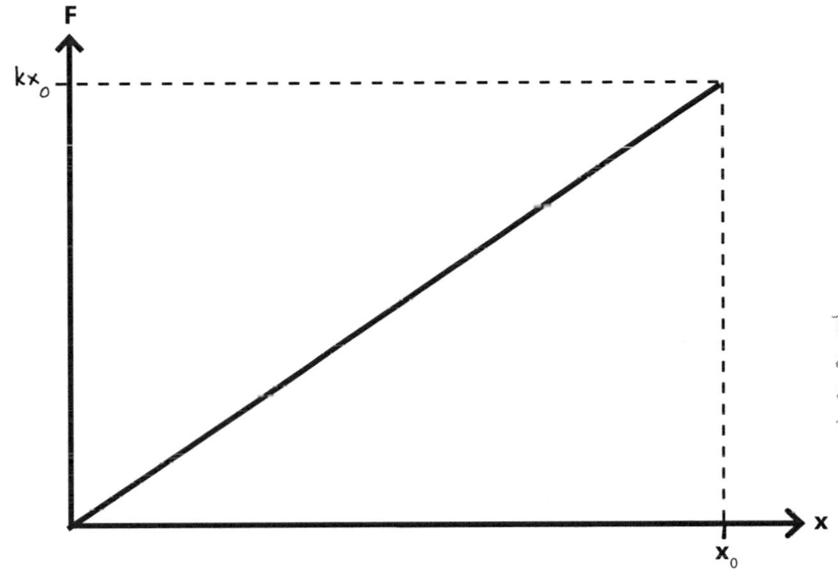

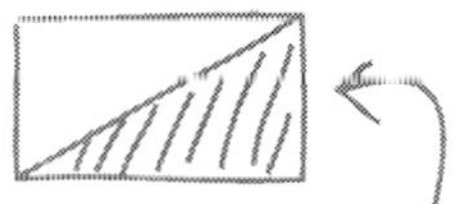

The area under the graph is a triangle. This has half the area that a rectangle with the same side lengths would.

Kinetic

b. Mark on the value of **F** when the displacement = $\mathbf{x}_0$.

c. The total work done is the total area between your graph and the horizontal axis. Calculate this area and hence write down an equation for the work done in stretching the spring to displacement $\mathbf{x}_0$.

Work done = area under F–x graph.

Work done = area of triangle

The area of the triangle is half the area of a rectangle with the same horizontal and vertical sides.

$$\text{Work done} = \text{Area} = \tfrac{1}{2} \times \text{base} \times \text{height}$$

$$= \tfrac{1}{2} \times x_0 \times kx_0$$

$$\text{Work done} = \tfrac{1}{2}kx_0^2$$

The work done against a force is equal to the area under the force - displacement graph.

d. How much elastic potential energy, U_s, is transferred to a spring with spring constant k by stretching it displacement $\mathbf{x}_0$ from its equilibrium position?

$$U_s = \tfrac{1}{2}kx_0^2$$

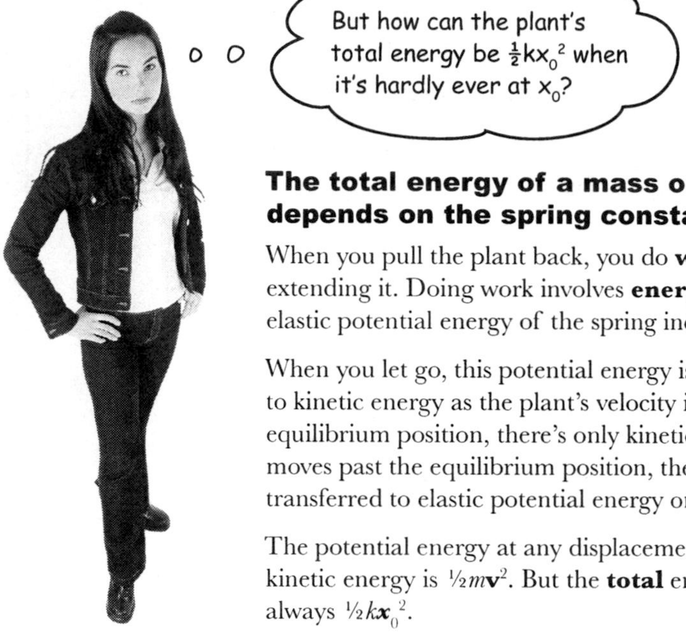

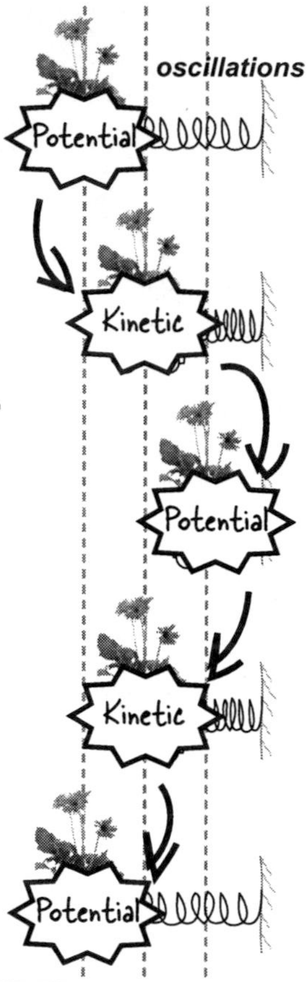

The total energy of a mass on a spring depends on the spring constant and amplitude.

When you pull the plant back, you do **work** on the spring by extending it. Doing work involves **energy transfer** and the elastic potential energy of the spring increases.

When you let go, this potential energy is gradually transferred to kinetic energy as the plant's velocity increases. In the equilibrium position, there's only kinetic energy. As the plant moves past the equilibrium position, the kinetic energy is transferred to elastic potential energy once again ... etc!

The potential energy at any displacement is $\frac{1}{2}k\mathbf{x}^2$ and the kinetic energy is $\frac{1}{2}m\mathbf{v}^2$. But the **total** energy of the system is always $\frac{1}{2}k\boldsymbol{x}_0^2$.

Sharpen your pencil

a. Sketch graphs of *K*, the kinetic energy and *U*, the potential energy, for one complete cycle of the plant rocker.

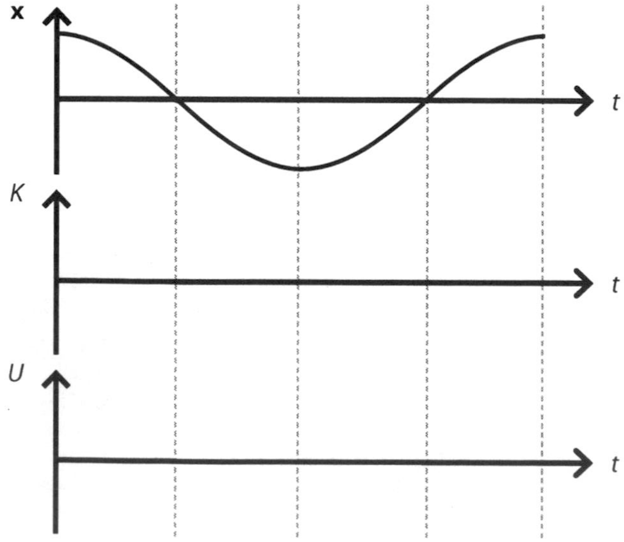

b. Use conservation of energy to come up with an equation for $\mathbf{v}_{max}$, the maximum velocity of the plant, in terms of *k*, *m* and $\mathbf{x}_0$, the initial (and maximum) displacement.

c. A plant, mass 100 g, is attached to a horizontal spring, spring constant 2.22 Nm. What should its initial displacement, $\mathbf{x}_0$, be if the plant's maximum velocity is to be 1.50 m/s?

Sharpen your pencil Solution

a. Sketch graphs of *K*, the kinetic energy and *U*, the potential energy, for one complete cycle of the plant rocker.

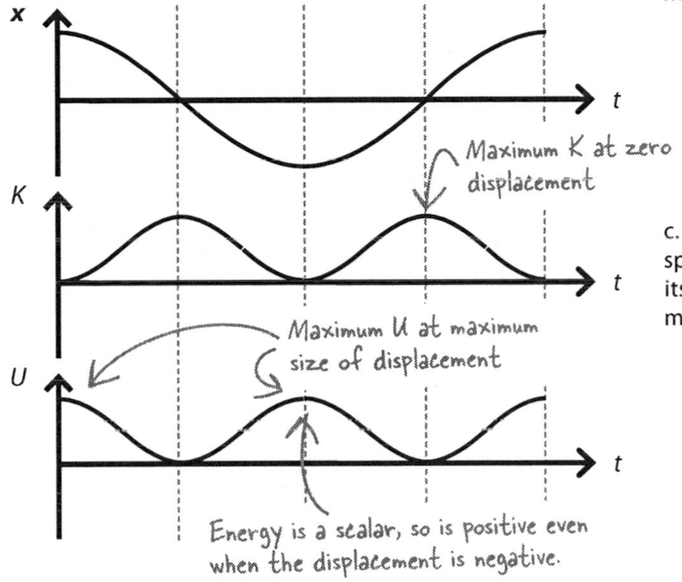

b. Use conservation of energy to come up with an equation for $\mathbf{v}_{max}$, the maximum velocity of the plant, in terms of *k*, *m* and $\mathbf{x}_0$, the initial (and maximum) displacement.

Maximum K = Maximum U

$$\frac{1}{2}kx_0^2 = \frac{1}{2}mv_{max}^2$$

$$v_{max} = \sqrt{\frac{k}{m}}\,x_0$$

c. A plant, mass 100 g, is attached to a horizontal spring, spring constant 2.22 Nm. What should its initial displacement, $\mathbf{x}_0$, be if the plant's maximum velocity is to be 1.50 m/s?

$$v_{max} = \sqrt{\frac{k}{m}}\,x_0 \Rightarrow x_0 = \sqrt{\frac{m}{k}}\,v_{max}$$

$$x_0 = \sqrt{\frac{0.100}{2.22}} \times 1.50$$

$$x_0 = 0.318 \text{ m (3 sd)}$$

$$U_s = \tfrac{1}{2}kx^2$$

The elastic potential energy of a spring depends on the amplitude and the spring constant.

there are no Dumb Questions

Q: But what about the mass of the spring? We didn't include that in the energy calculation, just the mass of the plant.

A: We made an approximation that the spring is massless - both here and before, when we were dealing with forces. If the mass of the spring is negligible compared to the mass of the plant, this is a reasonable simplifying assumption to make. If the mass of the spring wasn't negligible, we'd have to take into account the fact that different parts of the spring have different displacements - which is hard!

The plants rock - and you rule!

You've tied together your knowledge from lots of different areas of physics to give the plant rocker a known frequency and maximum velocity. Excellent!

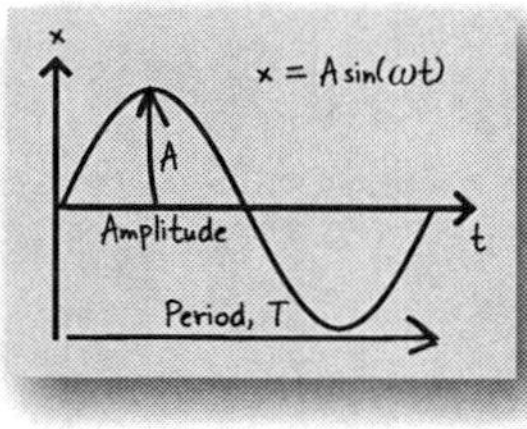

You've also been using these graph shapes.

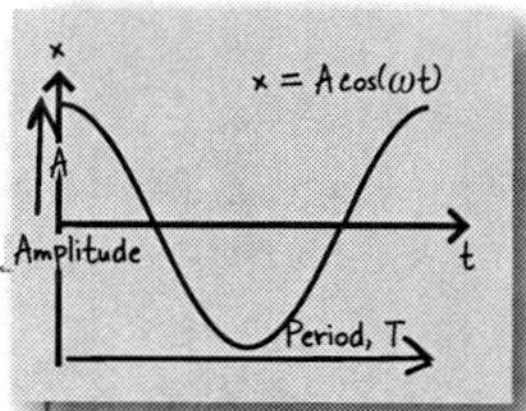

Physics Superpowers

- **Forces** - analysing a problem using a free body diagram.
- **Displacement, velocity** and **acceleration** - using the relationships between them.
- **Graphs** - showing what the motion's like visually.
- **Circular motion** - spotting that the motion is like circular motion viewed from side on.
- **Equations** - showing what the motion's like symbolically.
- **'Standard' equations** - spotting that your equation is like an equation that you already know.
- **Angular quantities** - using the analogy with the standard equation to move from ω to f, and also to k and m.
- **Energy conservation** - spotting that there are potential and kinetic energy stores and energy is continually transferred between them.
- **Work** - calculating the work done on the spring.
- **Area** - calculating the area under the force - displacement graph
- **Algebra** and **substitution** - calculating the velocity from the maximum potential and kinetic energy.

When you combine superpowers like this, you're really thinking like a physicist!

But now the plant rocker's frequency has changed ...

Although Anne is initially pleased with your solution, she's soon back in touch with a problem - the plant rocker's frequency has changed. Each cycle's taking longer than it did before, so the frequency is lower than it should be.

BRAIN POWER

What could have changed the frequency of the plant rocker?

Jim: Anne's been watering the plants, right? Maybe the spring got rusty or something, and its spring constant changed.

Joe: Actually - if she's watered the plants, then their **masses** will have changed.

Frank: Oh yeah - the frequency depends on the mass, doen't it.

Jim: Yeah, a more massive plant won't **accelerate** so rapidly. The force on it is still the same, but $\mathbf{F} = m\mathbf{a}$ so the acceleration will be smaller if m is larger. The plant will take longer to do one oscillation. That's why the frequency's gone down and the period's gone up.

Joe: This is a pretty serious design flaw - the plant's mass is going to change anyway as it grows, even if it doesn't get watered that often. I wonder what we can do to fix it.

Frank: So the problem is the mass, yeah?!

Jim: Yeah - if the mass was constant, then the frequency would be constant (as long as the spring didn't weaken or anything).

Frank: So can we make the mass **divide out** somehow? We've worked with equations before where that happened.

Joe: Ooh, I think I see what you mean. When we've done calculations involving **gravity**, like orbits and stuff, then the mass has sometimes divided out completely because it appeared on both sides of the equation.

Jim: Maybe if we hang the spring **vertically**, it'll be OK. Then gravity will be acting on the plant as well.

Joe: If the mass did divide out, we wouldn't need a different spring for each plant. Actually, this feels a bit wrong. Surely an elephant bouncing vertically on a spring would have a different frequency of oscillation from a mouse on the same spring?

Frank: We might as well test it out with math before we try building it. That shouldn't take too long ...

Think about the physics behind what's going on - either by 'being' the thing in the problem, or by seeing what its equation would do if you changed the values of the variables.

Watering a plant increases its mass.

The frequency of a horizontal spring depends on the mass

The equation for the frequency of the plant attached to the horizontal spring is $f = \frac{1}{2\varpi}\sqrt{\frac{k}{m}}$. If you increase the mass of the plant, the frequency becomes smaller, as you are dividing by the m on the right hand side of the equatuon. So the plant takes longer to do one cycle.

This is because $\boldsymbol{F} = m\boldsymbol{a}$. If the plant's mass is larger it accelerates less when acted on by the same force of the stretched spring. Watering the plants increases the mass. Anne is adamant that the plant rocker should always have a frequency of 0.750 Hz. So this design with a horizontal spring won't work, as the frequency changes when the mass changes.

Will using a vertical spring make a difference?

When gravity is the only force acting on an object, the object's acceleration doesn't depend on its mass.

In chapter 18, you worked out that the frequency and period of a satellite's orbit are completely independent of its mass.

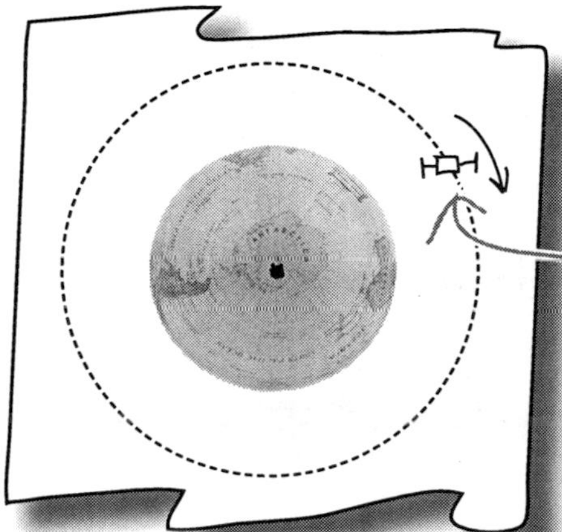

The frequency and a period of a satellite in orbit don't depend on its mass.

The guys have had the idea that perhaps by hanging the plant from a **vertical spring**, where gravity has an influence, the physics will work out differently from the horizontal spring.

You need to work out whether they're right!

Perhaps this is also the case for a vertical spring ... perhaps not.

Sharpen your pencil

a. A spring hangs from the ceiling. When you attach a plant to it, it extends to an new equilibrium position where the plant is at rest. Draw a free body diagram showing all of the forces acting on the plant in this new equilibrium position.

Hint: Look back at page 807 for an equation for the force from a spring.

b. If the plant has a mass of 0.100 kg and the spring extends by 44.1 cm, what is the spring constant?

c. You pull the plant down a further 4.00 cm and let go. Draw a free body diagram of the forces acting on the plant at the moment you let go, and calculate the net force on the plant.

d. What would be the net force on a plant attached to a horizontal spring that was extended 4.00 cm from its equilibrium position at the moment it's released?

e. Do you think that the spring being vertical will affect the frequency and period of the plant's oscillations compared with the horizontal spring? Why / why not?

Sharpen your pencil Solution

a. A spring hangs from the ceiling. When you attach a plant to it, it extends to an new equilibrium position where the plant is at rest. Draw a free body diagram showing all of the forces acting on the plant in this new equilibrium position.

Force from spring = −kx

There's no net force on the plant.

Weight = mg

b. If the plant has a mass of 0.100 kg and the spring extends by 44.1 cm, what is the spring constant?

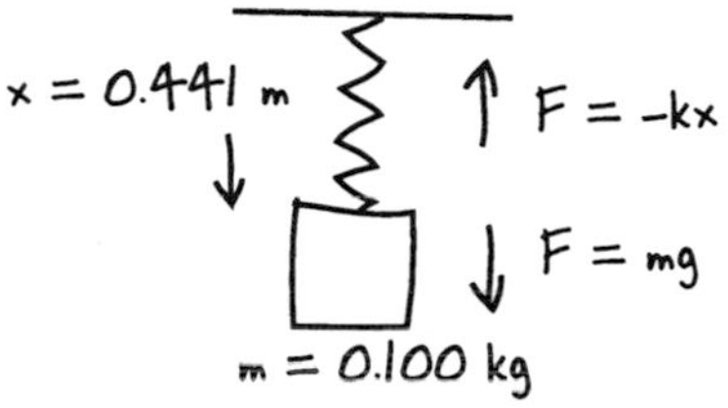

No net force, so: $mg - kx = 0$

$$kx = mg$$

$$k = \frac{mg}{x} = \frac{0.100 \times 9.8}{0.441}$$

$$k = 2.22\ \text{kg/s}^2\ (3\ \text{sd})$$

c. You pull the plant down a further 4.00 cm and let go. Draw a free body diagram of the forces acting on the plant at the moment you let go, and calculate the net force on the plant.

Force from spring = −kx

There's a net force upwards.

Weight = mg

$$F_{net} = mg - kx$$

$$F_{net} = 0.100 \times 9.8 - 2.22 \times 0.481$$

$$F_{net} = -0.878\ \text{N}\ (3\ \text{sd})$$

This is 44.1 cm + 4.00 cm.

d. What would be the net force on a plant attached to a horizontal spring that was extended 4.00 cm from its equilibrium position at the moment it's released?

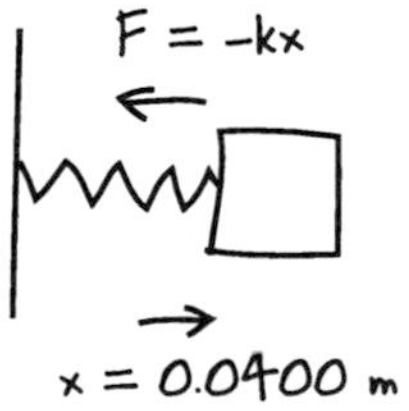

$$F_{net} = -kx$$

$$F_{net} = -2.22 \times 0.0400$$

$$F_{net} = -0.888\ \text{N}\ (3\ \text{sd})$$

The small difference between these two values is because of rounding. They're basically the same net force.

e. Do you think that the spring being vertical will affect the frequency and period of the plant's oscillations compared with the horizontal spring? Why / why not?

When you pull the plant the same distance from its equlibrium, the force on it is the same. All that's changed by hanging it vertically is the equilibrium position.

I think the frequency will be the same as for the horizontal spring, as the restoring force is unchanged.

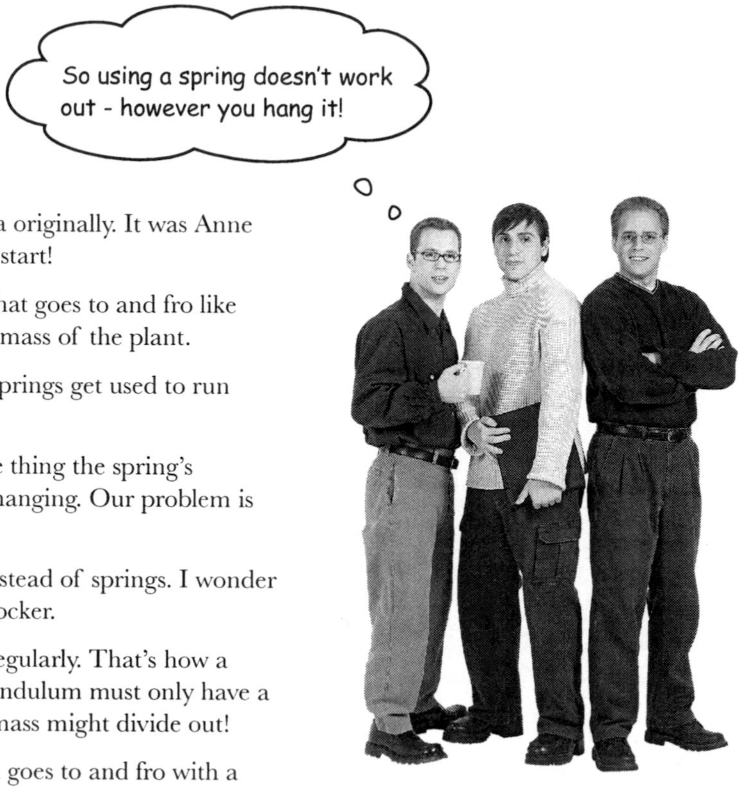

Jim: But at least the spring wasn't our idea originally. It was Anne who suggested we use a spring right at the start!

Joe: So we gotta think of something else that goes to and fro like clockwork, but that doesn't depend on the mass of the plant.

Frank: Like clockwork you say, hmmm. Springs get used to run some watches and clocks, don't they?

Jim: Yes, but in the clocks, the mass of the thing the spring's attached to inside the clock doesn't keep changing. Our problem is that the mass of the plant does change.

Frank: But some clocks use pendulums instead of springs. I wonder if we can use a **pendulum** for the plant rocker.

Joe: Yeah ... a pendulum goes to and fro regularly. That's how a Grandfather clock works, isn't it? And a pendulum must only have a **gravitational force** acting on it, so the mass might divide out!

Jim: But the Grandfather clock pendulum goes to and fro with a period of 1 s (or 2 s if it's one tick at each end of the swing - I'm not sure!). That's too short! We need the plant rocker to have a frequency of 0.750 Hz, which we already said is a period of 1.33 s.

Frank: Maybe giving a pendulum plant rocker a larger **amplitude** by pulling it back further at the start will change the period. The plant will have more distance to cover for each swing.

Joe: And maybe we could change the **length** of the pendulum - the distance from the ceiling to the plant. That might affect the frequency and period too.

Jim: And we're still not sure if the frequency and period of the pendulum depend on the **mass** of the plant. Though gravity is the only force acting on the plant (apart from the tension in the string it's attached to) so it could be more promising than the spring.

Frank: Yeah ... I'm just trying to imagine whether an adult will swing slower or faster or just the same as a child if they're sitting on a swing. I'm not sure.

Joe: I guess we ought to do an **experiment** to work out whether the **mass**, **length** or **amplitude** affect the period of the pendulum - and if so, how they affect them.

A pendulum swings to and fro with a regular frequency and period.

Try it!

Your job is to work out which variables (mass of pendulum bob, length of string, amplitude of swing) affect the frequency and period of a pendulum. This is a completely open-ended investigation - you can go about it however you like, designing and doing your own experiments, drawing your own graphs and writing up your conclusions.

There'll be a competition page on the Head First Physics website where you can submit your write-up, with prizes for the best entries.

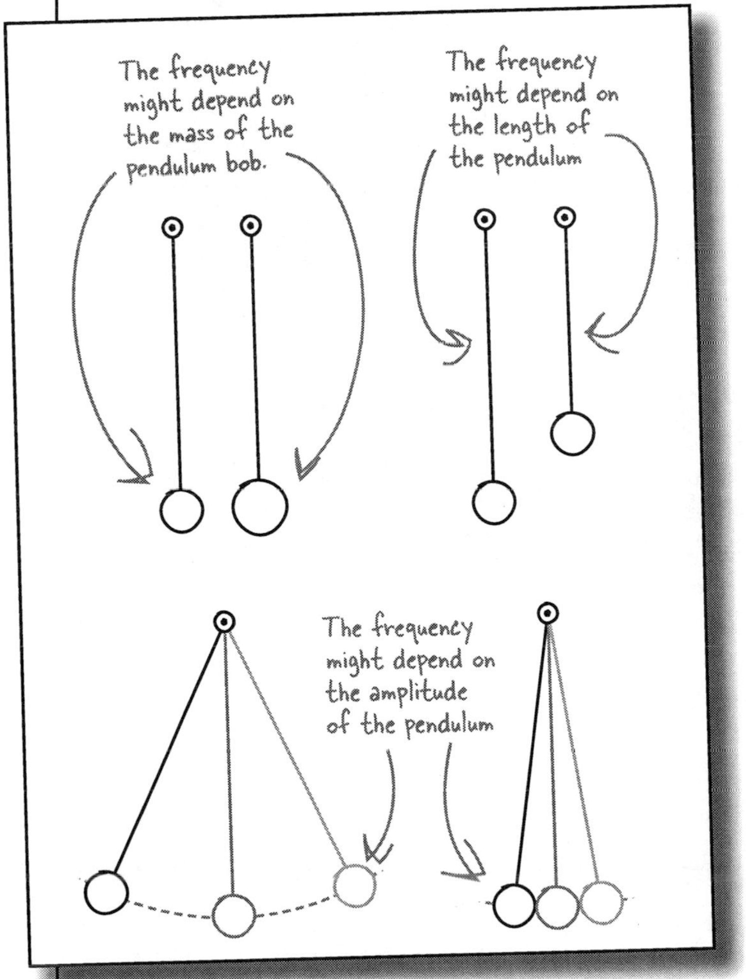

(for angles less than 10°.)

A pendulum swings with simple harmonic motion

A pendulum's **equilibrium** position is when the bob is hanging straight down. When the bob hangs straight down, its weight (due to gravitational force) and the tension in the string are both vertical. As the bob doesn't accelerate vertically, there must be no net force on the bob.

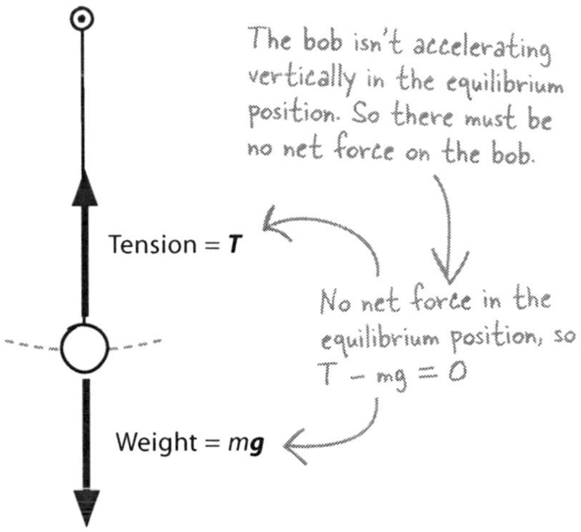

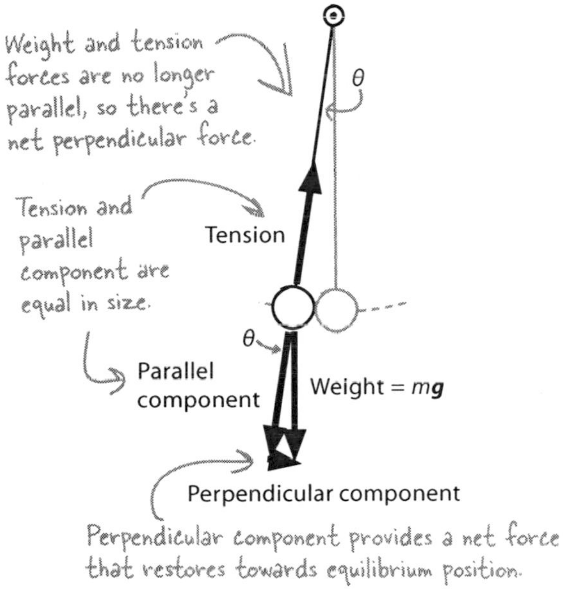

If the bob is pulled back a short displacement, through the angle θ, the bob's weight vector is no longer parallel to the tension in the string. A component of the bob's weight is **perpendicular** to the string, and provides a **net force** that causes the bob to **accelerate** towards the equilibrium position. As the bob nears equilibirum, the angle becomes smaller and the net force also becomes smaller.

Through the equilibrium position, the net force is zero, so the bob continues with a constant velocity. And as the bob swings the other way, the net force becomes larger again, slowing the bob down until it reaches the top of its swing on the other side.

Just like the mass on the spring, the **net force is proportional to the displacement** of the mass from the equilibrium position (as long as the angle it's moved through is less than around 10°). This satisfies the requirement for **simple harmonic motion**, The equation for the displacement of a pendulum is given to the right.

Ready Bake Equation

g is the acceleration due to gravity.

Pendulum starts at $x = x_0$:

$$x = x_0 \cos\left(\sqrt{\frac{g}{l}}\,t\right)$$

$$x = x_0 \cos(\omega t)$$

You can compare this equation with the 'standard' SHM equation to work out what you want to know.

x_0 is the maximum value of x, and therefore the amplitude of the motion.

l (the letter 'l', not the number '1') is the length of the pendulum

What does the frequency of a pendulum depend on?

The equation for the **displacement of a simple pendulum** (a pendulum that moves with SHM) that starts at a maximum is $x = x_0\cos\left(\sqrt{\frac{g}{l}}\,t\right)$. Like the equation for the period of the mass on a spring, this equation is derived using calculus, but is provided here as a ready-bake equation.

Your experiment and the ready bake equation both tell you the same thing: the period of the pendulum depends on the **length** of the string that attaches the bob to the celing, but not on the mass or the amplitude.

As well as this, the equation says that the period of the pendulum depends on the **acceleration** due to gravity. Practically speaking, this isn't something you have to worry about with the plant rocker, but it does mean that your favorite Grandfather clock won't keep time on the moon!

The frequency and period of a pendulum depend on its length, but not on its mass.

Sharpen your pencil

Hint: Use the equations on the post-its on page 807.

It's time to work out the length of the pendulum you'll need for the plant rocker.

a. Use the ready-bake equation for the plant's displacement, $x = x_0\cos\left(\sqrt{\frac{g}{l}}\,t\right)$, to get an equation for the frequency of the plant rocker.

Hint: Compare the equation with the "standard" equation for SHM.

b. Calculate the length of pendulum you require for the plant rocker to have a frequency of 0.750 Hz.

c. Use the equation you worked out in part a. to explain what will happen to the period of the plant rocker if you double the length of the pendulum.

d. If you took the pendulum to the moon, where acceleration due to gravity is a sixth of its value on earth, what effect would this have on the period of the pendulum?

Sharpen your pencil Solution

It's time to work out the length of the pendulum you'll need for the plant rocker.

a. Use the ready-bake equation for the plant's displacement, $x = x_0\cos\left(\sqrt{\frac{g}{l}}t\right)$, to get an equation for the frequency of the plant rocker.

'Standard' equation: $x = A\cos(\omega t)$

Simple pendulum: $x = x_0\cos\left(\sqrt{\frac{g}{l}}t\right)$

$\omega = \sqrt{\frac{g}{l}} \Rightarrow 2\pi f = \sqrt{\frac{g}{l}}$

$f = \frac{1}{2\pi}\sqrt{\frac{g}{l}}$

b. Calculate the length of pendulum you require for the plant rocker to have a frequency of 0.750 Hz.

$f = \frac{1}{2\pi}\sqrt{\frac{g}{l}}$

$\Rightarrow f^2 = \frac{1}{4\pi^2}\cdot\frac{g}{l}$

$\Rightarrow l = \frac{1}{4\pi^2}\cdot\frac{g}{f^2} = \frac{1}{4\pi^2}\cdot\frac{9.8}{0.750^2}$

$l = 0.442$ m (3 sd)

c. Use the equation you worked out in part a. to explain what will happen to the period of the plant rocker if you double the length of the pendulum.

$T = \frac{1}{f}$ and $f = \frac{1}{2\pi}\sqrt{\frac{g}{l}}$

$\Rightarrow T = 2\pi\sqrt{\frac{l}{g}}$

If you double the length of the pendulum, the part under the square root becomes twice as large as it was before., so T becomes $\sqrt{2}$ larger than it was before.

d. If you took the pendulum to the moon, where acceleration due to gravity is a sixth of its value on earth, what effect would this have on the period of the pendulum?

$T = 2\pi\sqrt{\frac{l}{g}}$

If you make g a sixth of its value, the part under the square root becomes six times larger (since g is on the bottom). So T becomes $\sqrt{6}$ larger than it was before.

It's really important to be able to move between f, T and ω quickly and comfortably - so practise doing that!

Angular frequency and angular speed

Angular frequency and angular speed both have the same size and both have units of radians per second. They're exactly the same thing.

You can get from the frequency, f, to the angular frequency, ω, with the equation:

$\omega = 2\pi f$

Frequency and period

Frequency, f, is cycles per second.

Period, T, is seconds per cycle.

Because they're related like this:

$T = \frac{1}{f} \quad f = \frac{1}{T}$

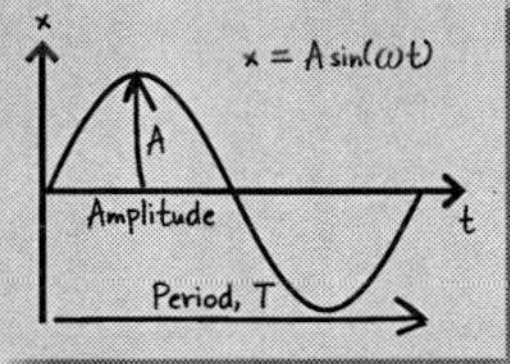

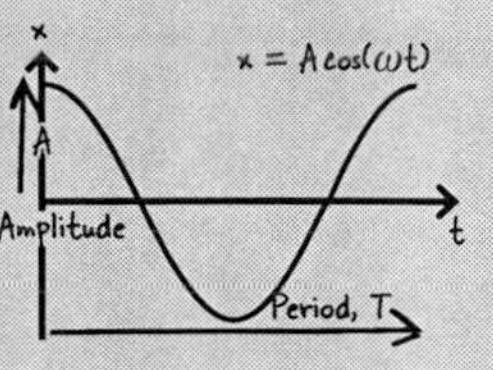

The pendulum design works!

You use your answers to make a pendulum plant rocker for Anne - and it works perfectly.

Even better, the frequency doesn't depend on the mass of the plant, so you can use the same design for all three of Anne's favorites!

BULLET POINTS

- If the restoring force is proportional to the displacement, you have simple harmonic motion (abbreviated to SHM)
- SHM looks like circular motion from side on, and the equations for the displacement, velocity and acceleration are all sinusoidal (shaped like a sine or cosine graph).
- For a spring, the period depends on the mass and the spring constant, but not the amplitude.
- For a pendulum with small amplitudes, the period depends on the length and the gravitational field strength, but not on the mass.
- It's fine to use forces to analyse SHM - but you reach a point where you require calculus. So use energy to solve SHM problems where you can.
- The kinetic energy in the equilibrium position (where the force and displacement are zero) is equal to the potential energy at an extreme.

You can use this to solve problems with pendulums as well as with springs.

I was just wondering... if SHM is like side-on circular motion, can we use something like v = rω to work out the maximum speed instead of using energy conservation?

Yes, you can apply your circular motion equations here too!

Simple harmonic motion looks like side-on circular motion. This means that if you have SHM and circular motion that both have the same amplitude and frequency, the maximum speed of the SHM will be the same as the speed of the circular motion.

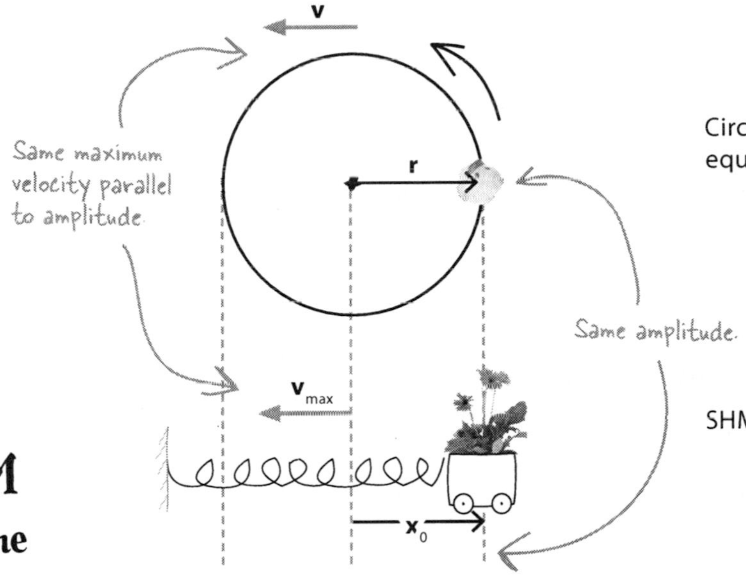

Circular motion equation:

$v = r\omega$

SHM equation:

$v_{max} = x_0\omega$

The MAXIMUM speed is the same for circular motion and SHM if they both have the same amplitude and frequency.

Thuis means that you can adapt the equation $v = r\omega$ to give you the maximum speed of the SHM.

The equation would become $v_{max} = x_0\omega$

This equation has angular frequency in it – just use $\omega = 2\pi f$ to calculate it.

vmax depends on the amplitude and the frequency.

Question Clinic: The "Vertical spring" Question

The vertical spring question is a common way of testing your understanding of simple harmonic motion. First of all, something is hung from the spring to stretch it to a new equilibrium position. Then the spring is stretched or compressed further and released. The question asks you to work out the frequency or period of the oscillations

If you see a spring, think 'simple harmonic motion'.

This wording indicates that the spring is vertical, so you need to take the object's weight into account.

If the spring extends, it must be exerting a force as $F = -kx$.

So the force from the spring should be on your free body diagram.

54. A spring hangs downwards from the ceiling.

a. When you attach a plant to the spring, it extends until the plant is at rest. Draw a free body diagram showing all of the forces acting on the plant at this point.

b. If the plant has a mass of 0.100 kg and the spring extends by 44.1 cm, what is the spring constant, *k*?

c. You pull the plant down a further 4.00 cm and let go. Calculate the period of the plant's oscillations.

d. What distance does the plant cover in one complete cycle?

This indicates that the plant is in equilibrium, with no net force acting on it.

The forces should add to zero.

Use the diagram you drew in part a. with these values.

Note the word distance, and the complete cycle. It'll travel 4.00 cm to the center, another 4.00 cm to the far side, then the same again: a total of 16.00 cm.

Make sure you use the displacement from the NEW equilibrium position when you do the SHM calculation.

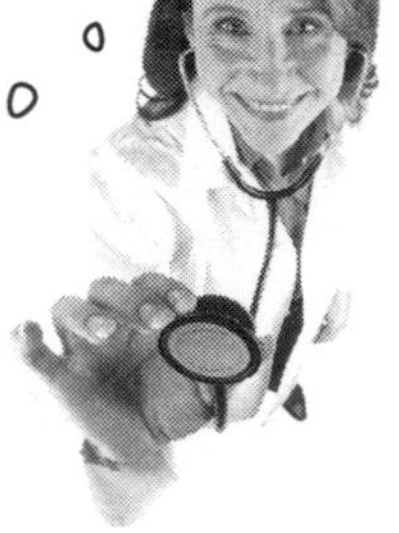

The key thing in this question is defining the displacement correctly. The initial displacement creates a new equlibrium position, and also allows you to calculate the spring constant. When you do the SHM calculation, you should redefine the new equilibrium position as x = 0 and use the value for the spring constant that you calculated earltier to work out the frequency or period.

Question Clinic: The "How does this depend on that" Question

Many questions have no numbers in them at all, and are designed to test how well you understand the physics, and the language of equations that can be used to describe it. You're told what the original situation is, then asked what would happen if a variable became larger or smaller, for example by doubling or halving.

This question doesn't contain any numbers, only letters to represent each quantity.

55. A mass, *m*, on a spring oscillates with amplitude *A* and period *T*. Starting from this set-up each time:

a. What happens to the period if you double the amplitude to 2*A*?

b. What happens to the total energy of the oscillator if you double the amplitude to 2*A*?

c. What happens to the maximum speed of the mass if you double the amplitude to 2*A*?

d. What happens to the period if you double the mass to 2*m*?

a. You can do this part without an equation – the period of SHM doesn't depend on its amplitude.

b. You need the equation for the total energy, $E = \frac{1}{2}kA^2$ As the 'A' is squared, if you double A, E becomes four times as large.

c. You need the equation $\frac{1}{2}mv^2 = \frac{1}{2}kA^2$ to see that if you double A, then v will also double.

d. You need the equation $T = 2\pi\sqrt{\frac{m}{k}}$ to see that the period becomes $\sqrt{2}T$.

Make sure you write down the relevant equation so you can see how changing one variable will affect the other variables. Then 'insert' the factor the variable has changed by next to it (for example, m might become 2m) and look to see how this affects the size of the other variable you're asked about. If your equation has m^2 in it, then inserting '2m' instead of 'm' gives you $(2m)^2$, or $4m^2$, so the answer will be four times larger than it was before. Try it with the question above!

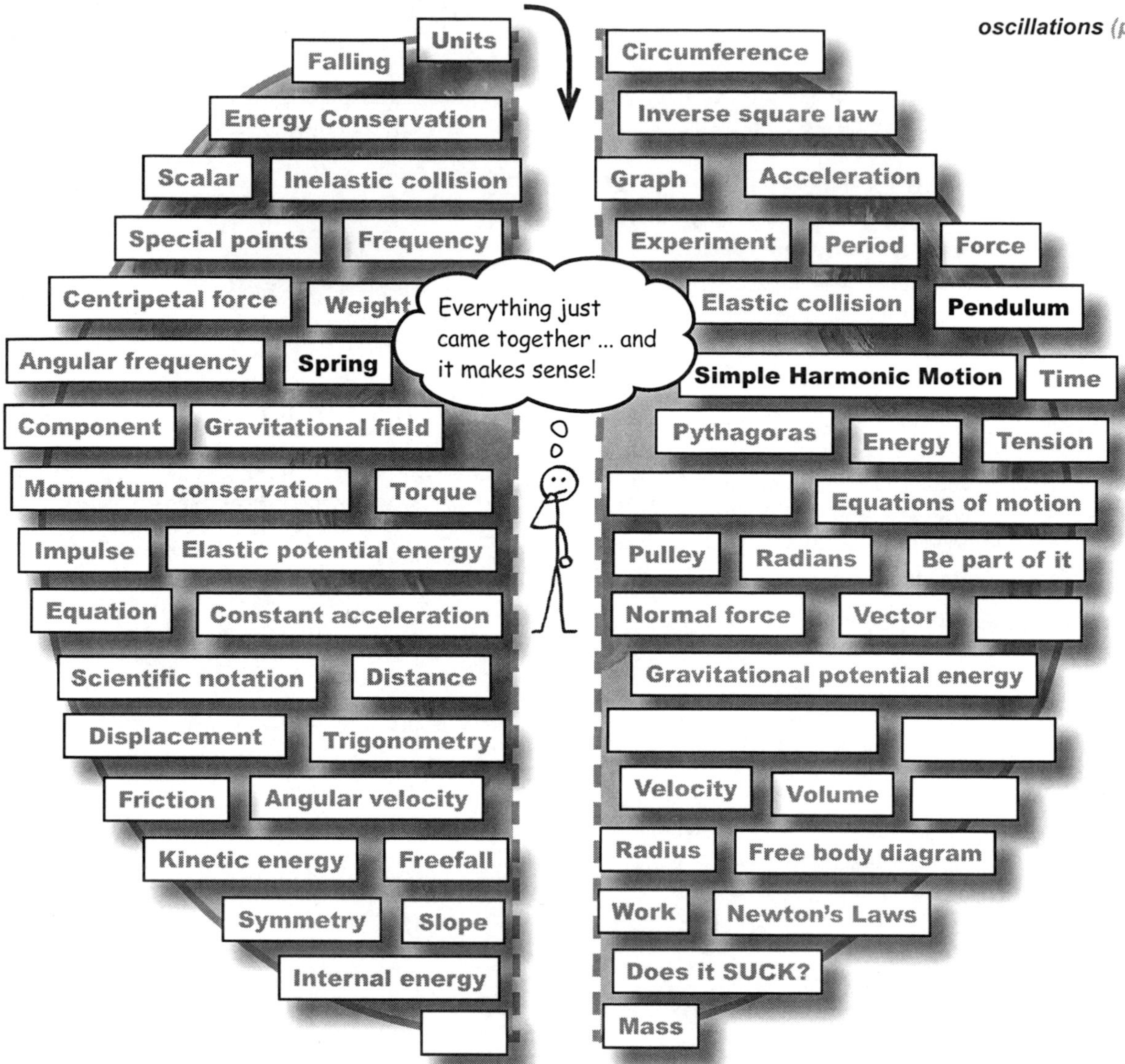

☑	**Simple harmonic motion**	**Motion where a restoring force to an equilibrium position is directly proportional to the displacement from the equilibrium position.**
☑	**Spring**	**A spring exerts a restoring force proportional to the displacement from its equilibrium position.**
☑	**Pendulum**	

CHAPTER 20

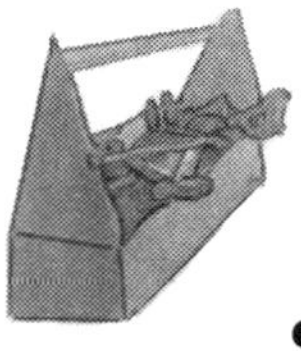

Your Physics Toolbox

You've got Chapter 20 under your belt and you've added some problem-solving concepts to your toolbox.

Hooke's Law

Hooke's Law says that the force a spring exerts is proportional to its displacement from equilibrium, and in the opposite direction to the displacement.

$$F = -kx$$

(k is the spring constant)

Simple harmonic motion

Oscillation you get when the restoring force is directly proportional to the displacement from the equilibrium position.

Abbreviated to SHM.

SHM graphs

Displacement, velocity and acceleration-time graphs are all sinusoidal.

Start by drawing the displacement-time graph, starting at x_0.

Acceleration-time graph exactly mirrors displacement-time graph.

Get velocity - time graph from slope of displacement-time graph

Mass on a spring

Frequency and period depend on the mass and the spring constant.

Frequency and period are independent of the amplitude.

Frequency and period independent of the gravitational field strength (horizontal and vertical springs have the same frequency).

Simple pendulum

Moves with SHM for small angles only (θ less than around 10°).

Frequency and period depend on the length of the pendulum and the gravitational field strength.

Frequency and period are independent of mass.

Frequency and period are independent of amplitude for small angles.

Comparing equations

If your equation has the same form as a 'standard' equation, you can write them one above each other and say that terms are equivalent.

This is how you can get the equation for the frequency of an oscillator – by comparing its equation with the 'standard' equation that describes SHM.

ω is your FRIEND!

The most simple form of the SHM equation uses ω.

ω is the "link" between simple harmonic morion and circular motion.

Circular motion and SHM

Try thinking of SHM in terms of circular motion to see which equations you can adapt or reuse.

21 think like a physicist

It's the final chapter

It's time to hit the ground running. Throughout this book, you've been learning to **relate** physics to **everyday life** and have absorbed **problem solving** skills along the way. In this final chapter, you'll use your new set of **physics tools** to dig into the problem we started off with - the bottomless pit through the center of the Earth. The key is the question: "How can I use what I know to work out what I don't know (yet)?"

You've come a long way!

Back in chapter 1, the words on the globe looked like random jargon that didn't make sense. But as you've gone through the book learning to relate physics to everyday life, your confidence has grown and the words have become less like an alien language.

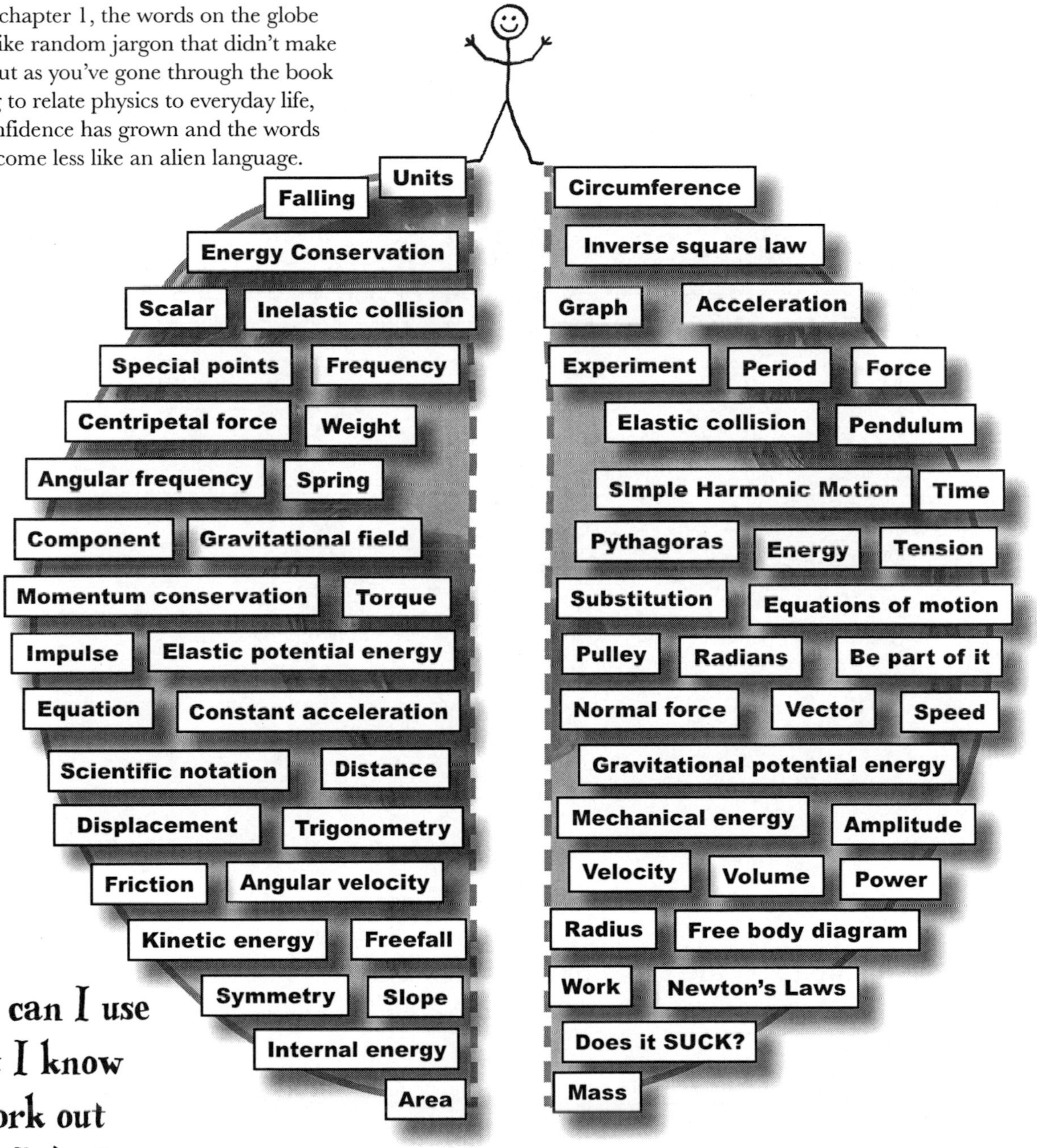

"How can I use what I know to work out what I don't know (yet)?"

Now you're in chapter 21 - and you're able to use these same words to help you think through and **solve problems**. You've learned to ask "How can I use what I know to work out what I don't know (yet)?"

Now you can finish off the globe

What better way to use your physics superpowers than to revisit the tunnel through the center of the Earth and really get to grips with what happens there.

Back in chapter 1, you learned to **be part of it** by putting yourself at the heart of the problem and asking "What happens next?" and "What's it like?" Now you can also describe what happens using physics terms and concepts.

Be part of it

You can use physics terms and concepts to describe what happens next.

You spotted that there's a **special point** in the center where there's no net force on you because everything is symmetrical - you're equally attracted in all directions, and as gravity is a non-contact force, you don't feel crushed. You also realized that you're always attracted towards the center unless you're already in the center.

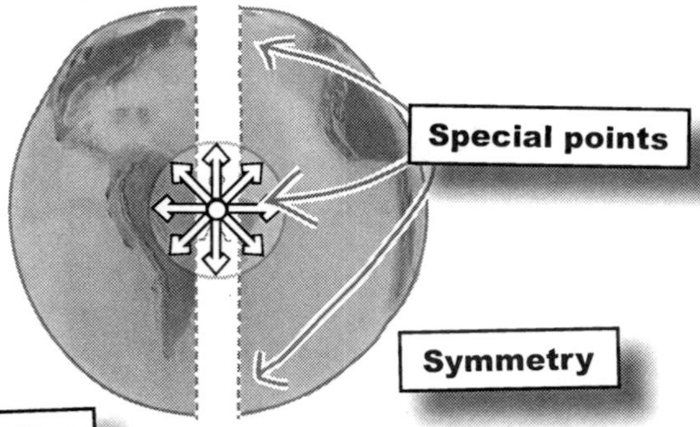

Acceleration

Force

This means that you initially **accelerate** as you fall due to the **net force** on you at the top of the tunnel, briefly move with a **constant velocity** through the center, then decelerate as the gravitational **force** continues to attract you towards the center. After briefly emerging at the other end, you do the same thing again in reverse.

Newton's 2nd Law

Newton's 1st Law

Newton's Laws

Velocity

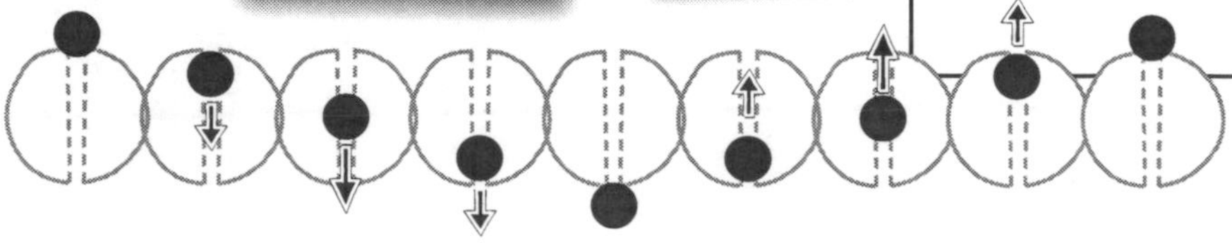

Sharpen your pencil

a. Use your increased physics knowledge to revisit the question "What's it like?" What does the trip through the Earth **now** remind you of? Be sure to mention all the parallels you can see.

b. Are there any requirements that need to be met in order for your answer to part a to make sense?

Sharpen your pencil Solution

a. Use your increased physics knowledge to revisit the question "What's it like?" What does the trip through the Earth **now** remind you of? Be sure to mention all the parallels you can see.

It looks like simple harmonic motion.

There's an equilibrium point in the center where there's no net force on you.

The force on you always acts towards the equilibrium position in the center, so is in the opposite direction from the displacement.

You move slowly at the edges and quickly through the center.

Simple Harmonic Motion

b. Are there any requirements that need to be met in order for your answer to part a to make sense?

The restoring force would have to be proportional to your displacement from the equilibrium position, and in the opposite direction from the displacement.

That's the requirement for simple harmonic motion.

Displacement

Force

The round-trip looks like simple harmonic motion

Way back in chapter 1, you figured out that you'd fall into the tunnel, travel through the Earth, and appear at the other end of the tunnel. Then you'd fall back in again, go through the tunnel in the opposite direction, and end up where you started... and so on.

That sounds a lot like **simple harmonic motion**, something you learned about in chapter 20. Now that you know how to tackle simple harmonic motion problems, we can add a lot of detail to what we figured out before.

What's it LIKE?

If you come across a situation you haven't seen before, think about whether you've seen something similar in the past by asking yourself: "What's it like?"

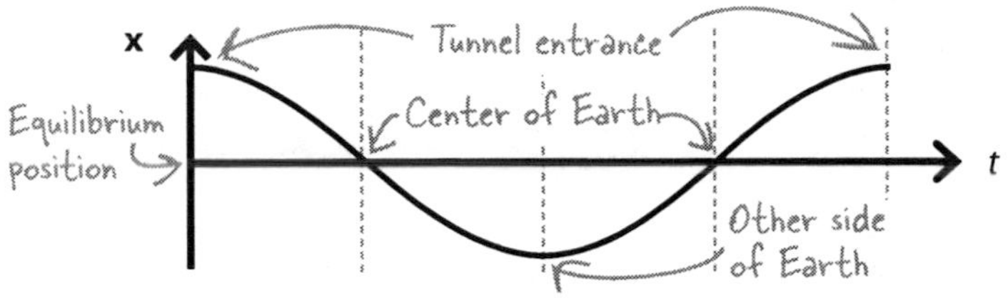

But what time does the round-trip take?

A trip through the center of the Earth can be pretty tiring. Suppose you want to place a pizza order so that once you've gone through the Earth and come back again, you can have a nice snack.

Break Neck Pizza promises delivery in 45 minutes... but will you be able to get through the Earth and then back again in time to meet Alex the delivery guy?

What **time** does your journey through the Earth take?

First of all, you'll have to work out if your journey through the Earth IS simple harmonic motion. The journey might only **look** like simple harmonic motion without actually **being** simple harmonic motion.

Then, if your journey is simple harmonic motion, you can use the equations you worked out in chapter 20 to calculate the time that the round-trip takes - and whether you'll be back in time for pizza.

Back in time for pizza?

- Trip through Earth looks like SHM.
- Is it SHM? Is the restoring force proportional to the displacement?
- If it's SHM, can use SHM equations to calculate time that trip takes.

simple harmonic motion

The net force on the object that always points in the direction of the equilibrium position.

Joe: Hang on. It's only SHM if the **restoring force** is directly **proportional** to the **displacement** from the equilibrium position of the object that's moving to and fro. We don't know whether the restoring force follows that pattern or not yet.

Frank: Yeah, if the trip through the Earth isn't SHM, we can't use our SHM equations to calculate the **time** it takes.

Joe: The gravitational force is an **inverse square law**, isn't it? $\mathbf{F}_G = -\frac{Gm_1m_2}{\mathbf{r}^2}$. So if you double the displacement, the force is only a quarter of what it was before. The force isn't directly proportional to the displacement. The force gets smaller as the displacement gets larger!

Frank: Oh yeah. For SHM, the restoring force needs to get larger as the displacement gets larger.

Jim: Hey - didn't we say before that the force is zero in the center of the Earth?! If the equation $\mathbf{F}_G = -\frac{Gm_1m_2}{\mathbf{r}^2}$ works at the center of the Earth (where $\mathbf{r} = 0$), you're dividing by zero. If you divide by a very small number, you get a very large answer. And if you divide by zero, you get an answer of infinity! Computer says no!

Joe: Yes ... maybe $\mathbf{F}_G = -\frac{Gm_1m_2}{\mathbf{r}^2}$ only works when you're **outside** the Earth. When you're outside, all of the Earth is below you.

Frank: But when you're inside the tunnel, some of the Earth is **below** you and attracts you downwards. The rest of the Earth is **above** you and attracts you upwards.

Jim: So the net force on you in the center is zero, as there are equal masses of Earth above and below you. And the net force on you somewhere else in the tunnel depends on how much Earth is above you and how much Earth is below you.

Joe: Looks like we need to work out a different equation for when you're inside the Earth then, if $\mathbf{F}_G = -\frac{Gm_1m_2}{\mathbf{r}^2}$ isn't going to work.

Equation

Inverse square

Does it SUCK?

Anytime you want to use an equation, think about the CONTEXT. Is it OK to use the equation here?

You can only use your simple harmonic motion equations from chapter 20 if the restoring force is proportional to the displacement.

BRAIN POWER

Calculating the net force on you when you're **inside** the Earth is a complicated problem. How might you break the problem down into smaller parts?

You can treat the Earth like a sphere and a shell

The gravitational force between two spheres is $\boldsymbol{F}_G = -\frac{Gm_1m_2}{\mathbf{r}^2}$. You can treat each sphere as if its entire mass was concentrated at a single point in the center of the sphere.

If you treat the human body like a very small sphere, you can use this equation to calculate the **gravitational force** that the Earth exerts on you - as long as you're **outside** the Earth.

But when you're **inside** the tunnel, there's Earth above you and below you. Calculating the gravitational force that the Earth exerts on you when you're inside it is a complicated problem!

Try to break down complicated problems into smaller parts.

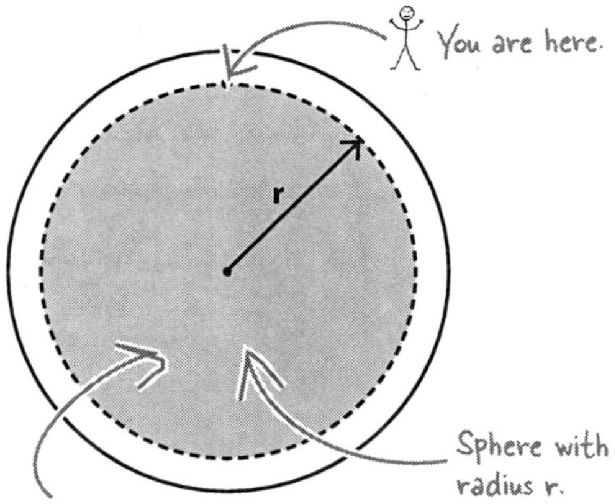

But you can **break down** this problem into two parts by thinking of the Earth in two parts. Anytime you're inside the Earth, you're a certain distance (let's call this distance **r**) from the equilibrium position in the center of the Earth.

So beneath you, there's a **sphere** with radius **r**. You already know how to calculate the gravitational force exerted on you by a sphere if you know its radius and mass: $\mathbf{F}_G = -\frac{Gm_1m_2}{\mathbf{r}^2}$

We're defining the radius as the displacement away from the center of the Earth. The force acts towards the center of the Earth – hence the minus sign.

The rest of the Earth forms a '**shell**.' Some of the shell is below you and some of the shell is above you.

If you can work out an equation for the force exerted on you by the shell, you can add it to the force exerted on you by the sphere. This gives you the **net force** that the Earth exerts on you while you're inside the tunnel.

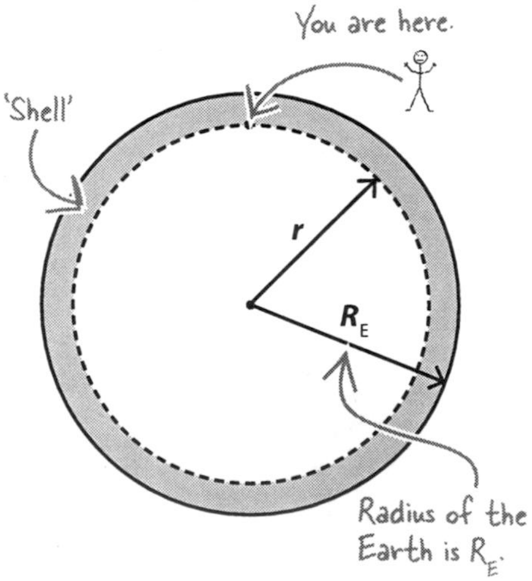

Back in time for pizza?

- Trip through Earth looks like SHM.
- Is it SHM? Is the restoring force proportional to the displacement?
  - → Force from shell?
  - → Force from sphere?
- If it's SHM, can use SHM equations to calculate time that trip takes.

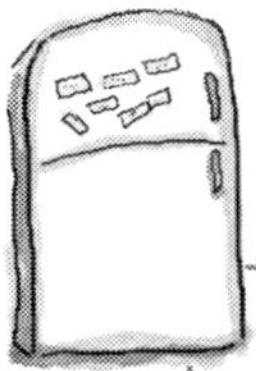

You can deal with the sphere - but what about the shell?

Use the magnets to work out the force from the shell. Annotate the diagrams as you go.

There's more shell ________ you than there is ________ you, so there's more ________ ________ you than there is ________ you. But the shell ________ you is (on average) a much larger ________ away from you than the shell ________ you.

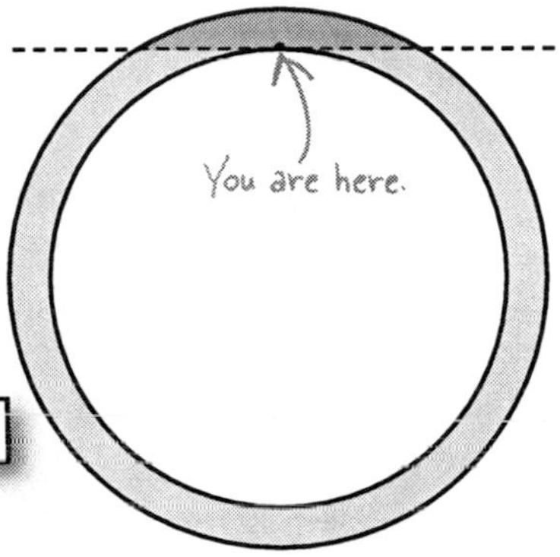

distance | below | mass | above

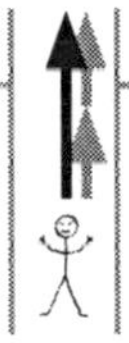

below | left | upwards | above | add to zero | right

The shell above you is totally ________ . So for every small piece of Earth to the ________ of you there's an equivalent piece to the ________ . The ________ components of the gravitational force from these two pieces of Earth are equal but in ________ directions, so they ________ . The ________ components add together, so the net force on you from the shell above you is ________ . The same argument applies to the shell below you, which exerts a net ________ force on you once the ________ components ________ . So the part of the shell ________ you attracts you ________ and the part ________ you attracts you ________

symmetrical | downwards | opposite | horizontal | vertical

If you take a piece of very thin shell, its ________ will be its ________ multiplied by its ________ . So the ________ of the very thin shell will depend on its surface area.

mass | thickness | surface area | volume

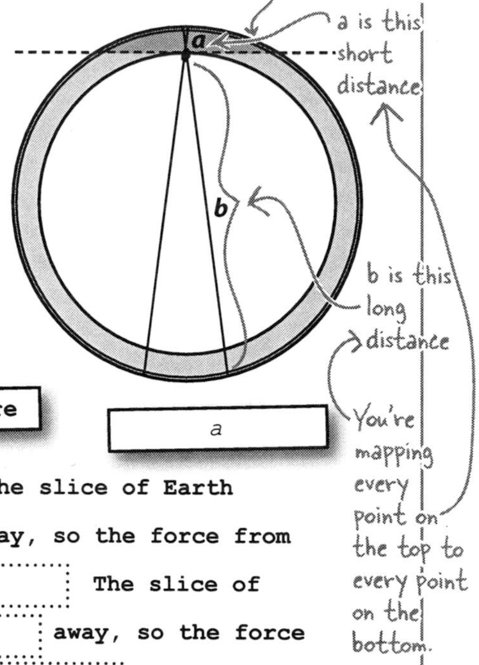

If you take a small slice of thin shell from .... and the equivalent from .... , you can think of them as being tiny slices from spheres with radius .... and .... with surface areas .... and .... respectively. And as the .... of a thin shell depends on its surface area, the masses of the slices are proportional to .... and ....

inverse square | a | below | a^2 | b^2 | $\frac{1}{a^2}$

Gravitation is an .... law. The slice of Earth above you is distance .... away, so the force from 1 kg of it is proportional to .... The slice of Earth below you is distance .... away, so the force from 1 kg of it is proportional to .... Therefore, the force from the slice at distance '*a*' is proportional to .... × .... and the force from the slice at distance '*b*' is proportional to .... × ....

b | volume | $\frac{1}{b^2}$ | above

So the force from the slice above you is .... to the force from the slice below you. And the net force from the whole thin shell is .... If you're further inside the Earth, you can think of the thick shell being made up of many many thin shells. So the net force from the thick shell is also ....

zero | equal | volume

Use this space to sum up what you've discovered: ....

Magnets Solution

There's more shell **below** you than there is **above** you, so there's more **mass below** you than there is **above** you. But the shell **below** you is (on average) a much larger **distance** away from you than the shell **above** you.

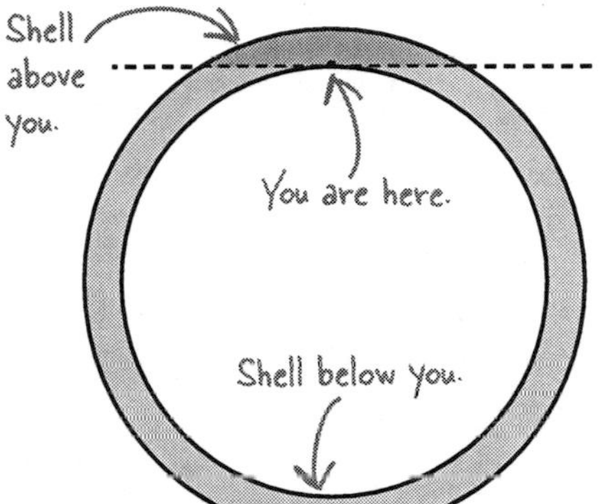

In problems that involve SYMMETRY, there are often force components that add to zero.

The shell above you is totally **symmetrical**. So for every small piece of Earth to the **left** of you, there's an equivalent piece to the **right**. The **horizontal** components of the gravitational force from these two pieces of Earth are equal but in **opposite** directions, so they **add to zero**.

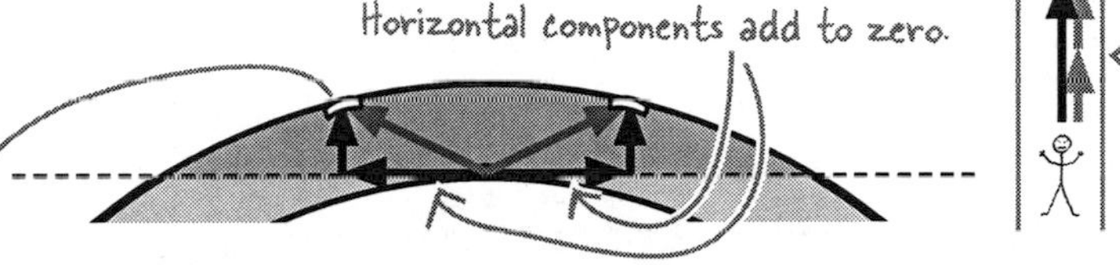

The **vertical** components add together, so the net force on you from the shell above you is **upwards**. The same argument applies to the shell below you, which exerts a net **downwards** force on you once the **horizontal** components **add to zero**. So the part of the shell **above** you attracts you **upwards,** and the part **below** you attracts you **downwards**.

If you take a piece of very thin shell, its **volume** will be its **surface area** multiplied by its **thickness**. So the **mass** of the very thin shell will depend on its surface area.

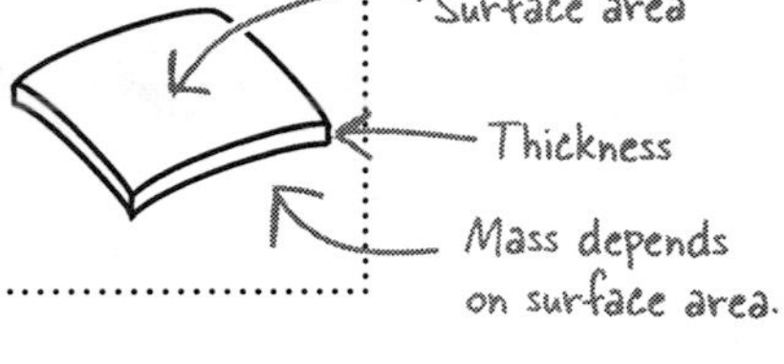

Here, we're using bold to show you where the magnets went. The distances a and b are both scalars.

If you take a small slice of thin shell from **above** and the equivalent from **below**, you can think of them as being tiny slices from spheres with radius $\boldsymbol{a}$ and $\boldsymbol{b}$ with surface areas $\boldsymbol{a}^2$ and $\boldsymbol{b}^2$ respectively. And as the mass of a thin shell depends on its surface area, the masses of the slices are proportional to $\boldsymbol{a}^2$ and $\boldsymbol{b}^2$.

Gravitation is an inverse square law. The slice of Earth above you is distance $\boldsymbol{a}$ away, so the force from 1 kg of it is proportional to $\frac{1}{\boldsymbol{a}^2}$. The slice of Earth below you is distance $\boldsymbol{b}$ away, so the force from 1 kg of it is proportional to $\frac{1}{\boldsymbol{b}^2}$. Therefore, the force from the slice at distance 'a' is proportional to $\boldsymbol{a}^2 \times \frac{1}{\boldsymbol{a}^2}$ and the force from the slice at distance 'b' is proportional to $\boldsymbol{b}^2 \times \frac{1}{\boldsymbol{b}^2}$.

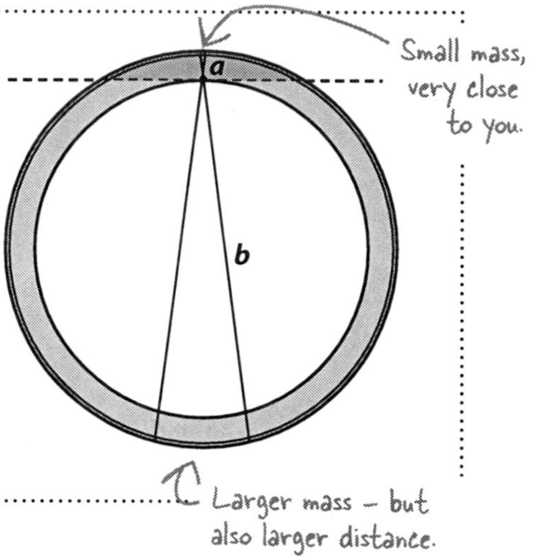

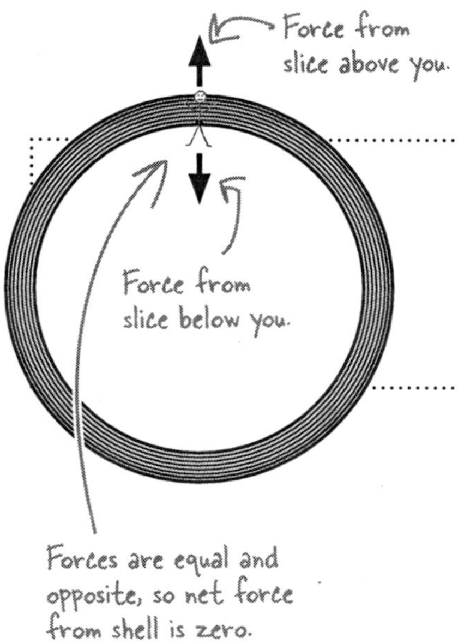

So the force from the slice above you is **equal** to the force from the slice below you. And the net force from the whole thin shell is **zero**. If you're further inside the Earth, you can think of the thick shell being made up of many many thin shells. So the net force from the thick shell is also **zero**.

Use this space to sum up what you've discovered:	The net force from the shell is zero. This is because the forces from the small, close mass above you and the large, far away mass below you are the same size, but in opposite directions.

The net force from the shell is zero!

The net force from the shell is zero

This means that the net force that the shell exerts on you is zero. So the net force exerted on you when you're inside the tunnel must come entirely from the sphere, radius r.

If that force is proportional to r, then you'll move through the Earth with simple harmonic motion and can use the equations you already know to calculate the time you take to get back home again.

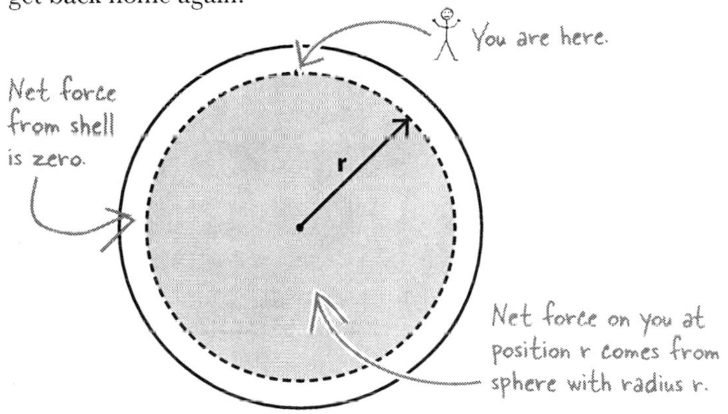

Back in time for pizza?

- Trip through Earth looks like SHM.
- Is it SHM? Is the restoring force proportional to the displacement?
  - → Force from shell? This is zero!!
  - → Force from sphere?
- If it's SHM, can use SHM equations to calculate time that trip takes.

there are no Dumb Questions

Q: Do I need to understand and reproduce all of that?!

A: Don't worry - you won't be asked to do something that difficult in an exam. The big take-away is that the net force from the shell is zero because the forces from a small mass close by and a large mass far away added to zero. If you got that, you're great!

Q: But the Earth isn't a sphere and a shell ... is it?!

A: Treating the Earth like a sphere and a shell is a **mathematical tool**. In the same way, moving objects don't have velocity vector arrows and components drawn on them in real life, but vector arrows are very useful tools in physics.

Q: What's so special about a shell?

A: You've worked out that the force the shell exerts on you is zero. So the net force on you must come entirely from the sphere.

Q: What's so special about a sphere?

A: You already know how to calculate the gravitational force an object experiences as a result of being outside a sphere.

Q: Doesn't the equation for the gravitational force exerted by a sphere only work if I'm outside the sphere?

A: When your displacement is r from the center of the Earth, then you're outside the sphere with radius **r**.

Q: Why choose that particular radius, *r*, as the place to draw the boundary between the sphere and shell?

A: **r** is your displacement from the equilibrium position in the center of the Earth. When we did SHM in chapter 18, we called this displacement **x**. Here it's better to use **r** so that you remember that the displacement from the equilibrium position is also a **radius**.

If, when your displacement is r, the force exerted on you by the Earth is proportional to **r**, then your trip through the Earth is SHM. The period of the SHM is the same as the time it takes you to get back to where you started - the time you want to calculate!

Sharpen your pencil

Your job is to work out whether you move through the Earth with simple harmonic motion. For it to be simple harmonic motion, the force on you must be proportional to your displacement from the equilibrium position in the center of the Earth.

So is the net force on you proportional to **r** or not?

Ready Bake Equation

Volume of a sphere:

$$V = \frac{4}{3}\pi r^3$$

a. Use the ready bake equation for the volume of a sphere to write down equations for V_E, the volume of the Earth, and V_s, the volume of the sphere inside the Earth, radius **r**. (Use the symbol $\mathbf{R_E}$ for the radius of the Earth.)

b. Use the fact that the small sphere, radius **r**, is part of the Earth to work out an equation for the mass of the sphere. (Use the symbols M_E and m_s for the mass of the Earth and sphere, respectively.)

Hint: The mass of each sphere is proportional to its volume.

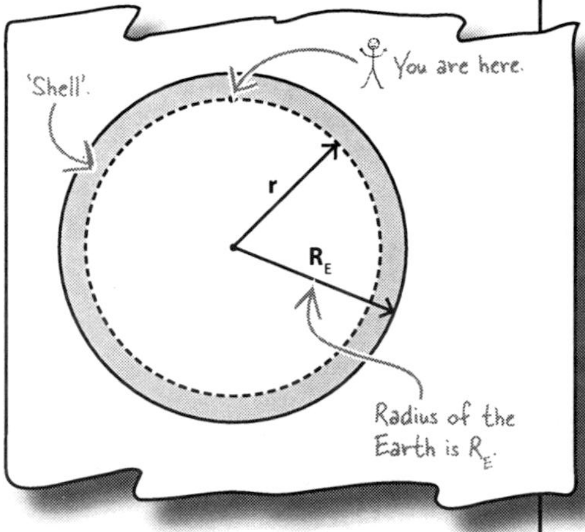

c. Use the mass of the small sphere from part b to work out an equation for the gravitational force, $\mathbf{F_G}$, that the small sphere of radius **r** exerts on you (your mass is m). Is $\mathbf{F_G}$ proportional to **r**?

Hint: Think about which quantities in your equation are variables and which are constants.

Sharpen your pencil Solution

Your job is to work out whether you move through the Earth with simple harmonic motion. For it to be simple harmonic motion, the force on you must be proportional to your displacement from the equilibrium position in the center of the Earth.

So is the net force on you proportional to **r** or not?

Ready Bake Equation

Volume of a sphere:

$$V = \frac{4}{3}\pi r^3$$

a. Use the ready bake equation for the volume of a sphere to write down equations for V_E, the volume of the Earth, and V_s, the volume of the sphere inside the Earth, radius **r**. (Use the symbol $\mathbf{R}_E$ for the radius of the Earth.)

Volume

Volume of Earth: $V_E = \frac{4}{3}\pi R_E^3$

Volume of sphere: $V_s = \frac{4}{3}\pi r^3$

b. Use the fact that the small sphere, radius **r**, is part of the Earth to work out an equation for the mass of the sphere. (Use the symbols M_E and m_s for the mass of the Earth and sphere respectively.)

Hint: The mass of each sphere is proportional to its volume.

Mass is proportional to volume.

$$\frac{m_s}{V_s} = \frac{M_E}{V_E} \Rightarrow m_s = \frac{M_E V_s}{V_E}$$

$$\Rightarrow m_s = \frac{M_E \cdot \frac{4}{3}\pi r^3}{\frac{4}{3}\pi R_E^3} = \frac{M_E r^3}{R_E^3}$$

Mass

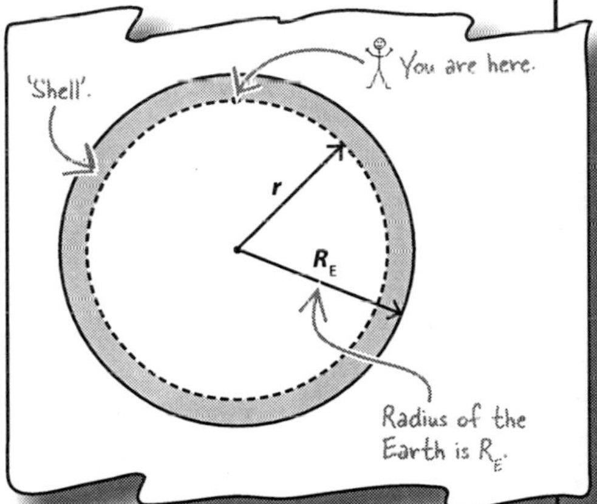

c. Use the mass of the small sphere from part b to work out an equation for the gravitational force, $\mathbf{F}_G$, that the small sphere of radius **r** exerts on you (you have mass *m*). Is $\mathbf{F}_G$ proportional to **r**?

$$F_G = -\frac{G m_s m}{r^2} = -\frac{G M_E r^3 m}{R_E^3 r^2} = -\frac{G M_E r m}{R_E^3} = -\frac{G M_E m r}{R_E^3}$$

There are a lot of letters multiplying or dividing the 'r,' but they're all constants. So the entire circle thing is a constant.

But G, M_E, R_E and m are all constants, so $F_G = -\text{constant} \times r$

F_G is directly proportional to r and in the opposite direction. So it's simple harmonic motion.

The force is proportional to the displacement, so your trip is SHM

You just worked out that $\mathbf{F}_G$, the force from the sphere, is proportional to $\mathbf{r}$, your displacement from the center of the Earth. As $\mathbf{F}_G$ always points towards the equilibrium position in the center, your trip through the Earth is definitely **simple harmonic motion**!

Displacement

Force

Simple Harmonic Motion

Now you can use what you already know about simple harmonic motion to fill in some of the details. The **period** of the SHM is the time it takes you to go through the Earth and back again.

Alex also wants to know your average speed - which you can calculate as well ...

Time

Speed

Period

Back in time for pizza?

- Trip through Earth looks like SHM.
- Is it SHM? Is the restoring force proportional to the displacement?
  - → Force from shell? This is zero!!
  - → Force from sphere? Proportional to r – it's SHM!
- If it's SHM, can use SHM equations to calculate time that trip takes – and average speed (to impress Alex).

You'll do this on the next page

Hint: Use the question clinic to help you answer this question!

Sharpen your pencil

Simple harmonic motion can be described using the equation $\mathbf{a} = -\omega^2\mathbf{x}$, where the symbols have their usual meanings.

a. Use Newton's 2nd Law to rewrite your equation for the force you experience as you pass through the Earth in terms of **a** instead of $\mathbf{F}_G$. Hence compare your equation with the $\mathbf{a} = -\omega^2\mathbf{x}$ form, and rearrange to give an expression for ω.

$$F_G = -\frac{GM_E m r}{R_E^3}$$

This is the equation you worked out on the previous page.

b. The mass of the Earth is 5.97×10^{24} kg, the radius of the Earth is 6.38×10^6 m, and G, the gravitational constant, is 6.67×10^{-11} $m^3/kg.s^2$. Calculate the time (in minutes and seconds) that it would take for you to return to your starting point after stepping into a tunnel that goes through the center of the Earth. Does this take you less than 45 minutes? ← The time that Alex takes to arrive with your pizza.

c. What is your average speed during your trip through the Earth? What is your average velocity?

Hint: Use the question clinic to help you answer this question!

Question Clinic: The "Equation you've never seen before" Question

Sometimes, a question will present you with an equation you've never ever seen before. But don't just assume you can't do it just because it's unfamiliar. Answering a question like this is sometimes a case of combining the equation you're given with another you already know so that you can solve a problem. And sometimes it's a case of interpreting some other new information you're given in the question as well.

If the equation is unfamiliar, don't panic! Write it down and annotate it with what each symbol represents.

Make sure you look up any symbols you're not familiar with. In an exam, you'll have an equation sheet you can use. Also remember that the same quantity (e.g., displacement) may be represented by more than one symbol (r, x, ... etc)

4. Simple harmonic motion can be described using the equation $a = -\omega^2 x$, where the symbols have their usual meanings.

a. Rewrite your equation for the force you experience as you pass through the Earth using this form, and rearrange it to give an expression for ω.

b. The mass of the Earth is 5.97×10^{24} kg and the radius of the Earth is 6.38×10^6 m. Calculate the time (in minutes and seconds) it would take for you to return to your starting point after stepping into a tunnel that goes through the center of the Earth.

c. What is your average speed during your trip through the Earth? And what is your average velocity?

In this exam version of the question, the value for G isn't given. You'd be expected to look it up in your table of information.

This indicates that you'll need to use an answer from an earlier part of the problem.

This jargon means you'll have to do substituting and rearranging.

If you found part a difficult, look at part b. It gives you some hints about some values you're expected to have in your part a answer. You might be able to work backwards!

Note the difference between speed (which involves distance) and velocity (which involves displacement).

Make sure you use the correct units and the correct start and end points when you do the calculation.

In a question like this, you need to be especially clear about what each variable represents. There are several different letters that are conventionally used to represent length in physics equations depending on the context - x (displacement), r (radius), l (length), and h (height). When you look at equations, think about what each variable means, as you may be able to make a substitution that isn't immediately obvious.

Sharpen your pencil Solution

Simple harmonic motion can be described using the equation $\mathbf{a} = -\omega^2\mathbf{x}$, where the symbols have their usual meanings.

a. Use Newton's 2nd Law to rewrite your equation for the force you experience as you pass through the Earth in terms of **a** instead of $\mathbf{F}_G$. Hence compare your equation with the $\mathbf{a} = -\omega^2\mathbf{x}$ form, and rearrange to give an expression for ω.

$$F_G = -\frac{GM_E r m}{R_E^3}$$

This is the equation you worked out on the previous page.

I've been using r as displacement from equilibrium, this equation uses x. I'll continue to use r to be consistent.

$$F_G = -\frac{GM_E r m}{R_E^3} \text{ and } F_G = ma \Rightarrow ma = -\frac{GM_E r m}{R_E^3}$$

This is of the form: $a = -\omega^2 r$ except that $\omega^2 = \frac{GM_E}{R_E^3} \Rightarrow \omega = \sqrt{\frac{GM_E}{R_E^3}}$

b. The mass of the Earth is 5.97×10^{24} kg, the radius of the Earth is 6.38×10^6 m and G, the gravitational constant, is 6.67×10^{-11} m³/kg.s². Calculate the time (in minutes and seconds) that it would take for you to return to your starting point after stepping into a tunnel that goes through the center of the Earth. Does this take you less than 45 minutes?

Time it takes is equal to the period, T. Need to get from ω to T.

$$\omega = 2\pi f \quad \text{and} \quad f = \frac{1}{T} \Rightarrow \omega = \frac{2\pi}{T}$$

$$\Rightarrow T = \frac{2\pi}{\omega} = \frac{2\pi}{\sqrt{\frac{GM_E}{R_E^3}}} = \frac{2 \times \pi}{\sqrt{\frac{6.67 \times 10^{-11} \times 5.97 \times 10^{24}}{(6.38 \times 10^6)^3}}} = 5070 \text{ s (3 sd)}$$

Need time in minutes and seconds. $5070 \text{ s} = 5070 \text{ s} \times \frac{1 \text{ min}}{60 \text{ s}} = 84.5 \text{ min} = 84 \text{ min } 30 \text{ s.}$

This is more than 45 minutes, so Alex gets there first.

c. What is your average speed during your trip through the Earth? What is your average velocity?

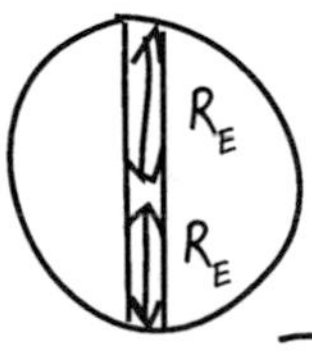

$$\text{Average speed} = \frac{\text{Total distance}}{\text{Total time}}$$

$$\text{Total distance} = 4R_E$$

$$\Rightarrow \text{Average speed} = \frac{4R_E}{T} = \frac{4 \times 6.38 \times 10^6}{5070}$$

$$\text{Average speed} = 5030 \text{ m/s (3 sd)}$$

$$\text{Average velocity} = \frac{\text{Total displacement}}{\text{Total time}}$$

But the total displacement is zero, as you start and finish in the same place.

$$\text{Average velocity} = 0 \text{ m/s}$$

You know your average speed - but what's your top speed?

You just used what you know about simple harmonic motion to work out that your round-trip time is 84 mins 30 s, and your average speed on your trip through the Earth is over 5 km per second!

Even though you won't beat Alex to your house, he is really impressed and wants to know what your **maximum speed** is.

A mass on a spring moves with SHM. When you worked out the maximum speed of a mass on a spring, you used energy conservation. But working out the potential energy of an object inside the Earth is going to be tough ...

You already know one way of calculating the maximum speed. But can you use the same way here?

Joe: Not necessarily - there's something I've been thinking about for the last few pages. When we said, "What's it like?" right at the start, I said I thought it looked like **circular motion** from side on.

Frank: Oh yeah. Circular motion from side on and **simple harmonic motion** both use the **same type of equations**.

Jim: How does that help us?

Joe: I was thinking that if we looked at an orbit from side on, it might look like the trip through the Earth and back. We know how to calculate the **velocity** of an object that's in orbit around the Earth. That velocity will be the same as the maximum velocity when you look at the orbit from side on.

Joe: Yeah, I was thinking that the **amplitude** of an orbit just over the Earth's surface and the amplitude of the trip through the Earth would be the same.

Frank: But what if the orbit and the simple harmonic motion don't have the same **period**?

Jim: We know how to calculate the period of an orbit as well. If the orbit and the SHM have the same period as well as the same amplitude, then they must look identical from side on...

Circular motion from side on looks like simple harmonic motion

If you could orbit the Earth close to its surface, you'd follow a circular path. When you look at an **circular motion** from side on, you only observe one component of the displacement, velocity and acceleration.

Circular motion from side on and simple harmonic motion both use the same type of equation, so their graphs are the same shape.

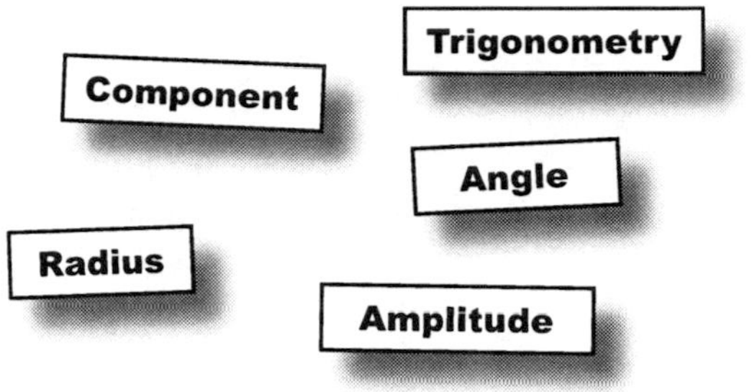

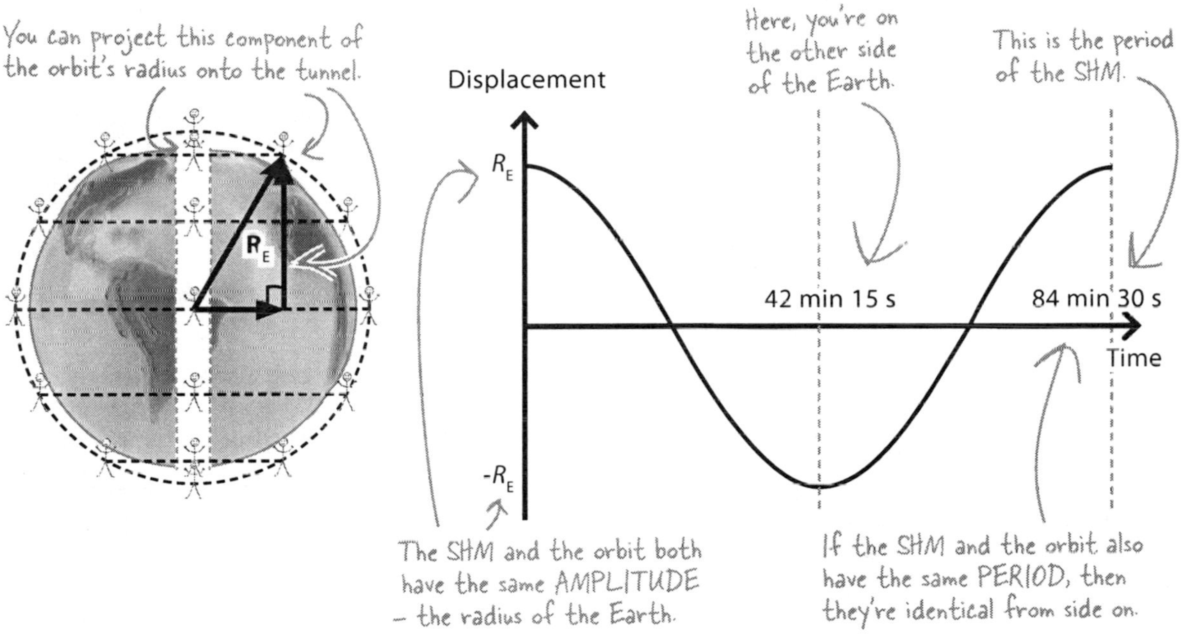

There's often more than one way of looking at a problem.

If the circular orbit has the same **amplitude** and the same **period** as the simple harmonic motion trip through the Earth, then the two journeys will look identical from side on.

This means that the **maximum speed** of the trip through the Earth will be the same as the **linear speed** of the orbit (as long as the periods are the same). And you can already calculate the linear speed of an orbit...

We drew the displacement–time graph up there, but the two velocity–time graphs would also be identical.

there are no Dumb Questions

Q: But surely an orbit at the surface of the Earth wouldn't work because of air resistance?

A: That's absolutely right ... but then again, we made some assumptions about oscillating to and fro through the center of the Earth already! Originally, we said that we'd ignore air resistance (which would slow you down) and the Earth's rotation (which would make you hit the sides of the tunnel) - so we can safely ignore them both for the orbit as well!

Q: But how do you know that the period of the orbit and the period of the SHM are the same? They might be different even though the amplitudes are the same.

A: That's right - we don't know that the periods are the same ... yet. But as you've dealt with orbits before, you'll be able to work out whether they are soon enough ...

Hint: Think about what the centripetal force is provided by. You can use your equation appendix, if you like!

Sharpen your pencil

If the orbit has the same period as the SHM, then they look identical from side on.

a. Calculate the period of a circular orbit at the Earth's surface. (The mass of the Earth is 5.97×10^{24} kg, and its radius is 6.38×10^{6} m.) How does this compare to the period of SHM through the center of the Earth?

b. What is the maximum velocity of something (or someone) falling through the Earth?

Sharpen your pencil Solution

If the orbit has the same period as the SHM, then they look identical from side on.

a. Calculate the period of a circular orbit at the Earth's surface. (The mass of the Earth is 5.97×10^{24} kg, and its radius is 6.38×10^6 m.) How does this compare to the period of SHM through the center of the Earth?

$$F_c = \cancel{m} r\omega^2 = \frac{GM_E \cancel{m}}{r^2}$$

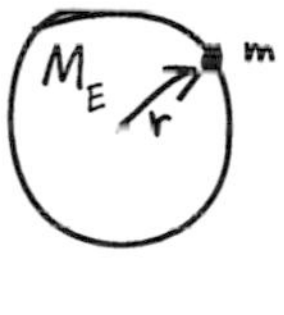

$$\omega = \sqrt{\frac{GM_E}{R^3}}$$

$$\omega = 2\pi f \quad \text{and} \quad f = \frac{1}{T} \Rightarrow \omega = \frac{2\pi}{T}$$

$$\Rightarrow T = \frac{2\pi}{\omega} = \frac{2\pi}{\sqrt{\frac{GM_E}{R_E^3}}}$$

$$= \frac{2 \times \pi}{\sqrt{\frac{6.67 \times 10^{-11} \times 5.97 \times 10^{24}}{(6.38 \times 10^6)^3}}}$$

$$T = 5070 \text{ s (3 sd)}$$

This is the same period as you oscillating through the center of the Earth.

b. What is the maximum velocity of something (or someone) falling through the Earth?

Maximum velocity is same as velocity of circular motion.

$$v = r\omega \quad \text{and} \quad \omega = \frac{2\pi}{T}$$

$$v = \frac{2\pi r}{T} = \frac{2 \times \pi \times 6.38 \times 10^6}{5070}$$

$$v = 7900 \text{ m/s (3 sd)}$$

Your top speed is a blistering pace of just under 8 km per SECOND!

As long as you send your Break Neck Pizza order when you pop out on the other side of the world (with 42 min and 15 s still to go), you arrive home just before Alex does!

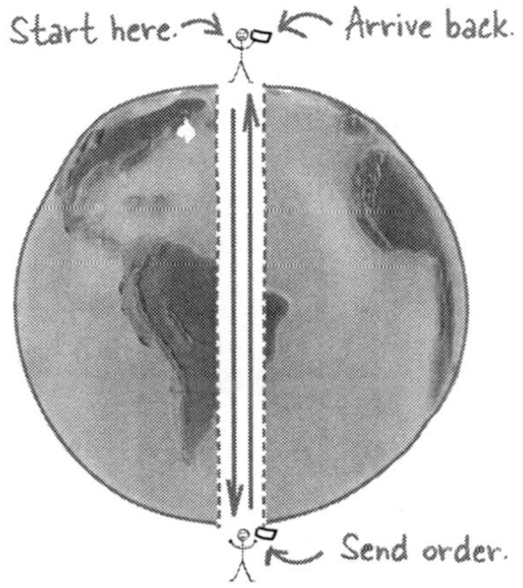

You can do (just about) anything!

You've finished your trip through the Earth - and your trip through this book. You've learned how physics works in the real world and absorbed problem solving strategies that you can use (just about) anywhere.

Think like a physicist!

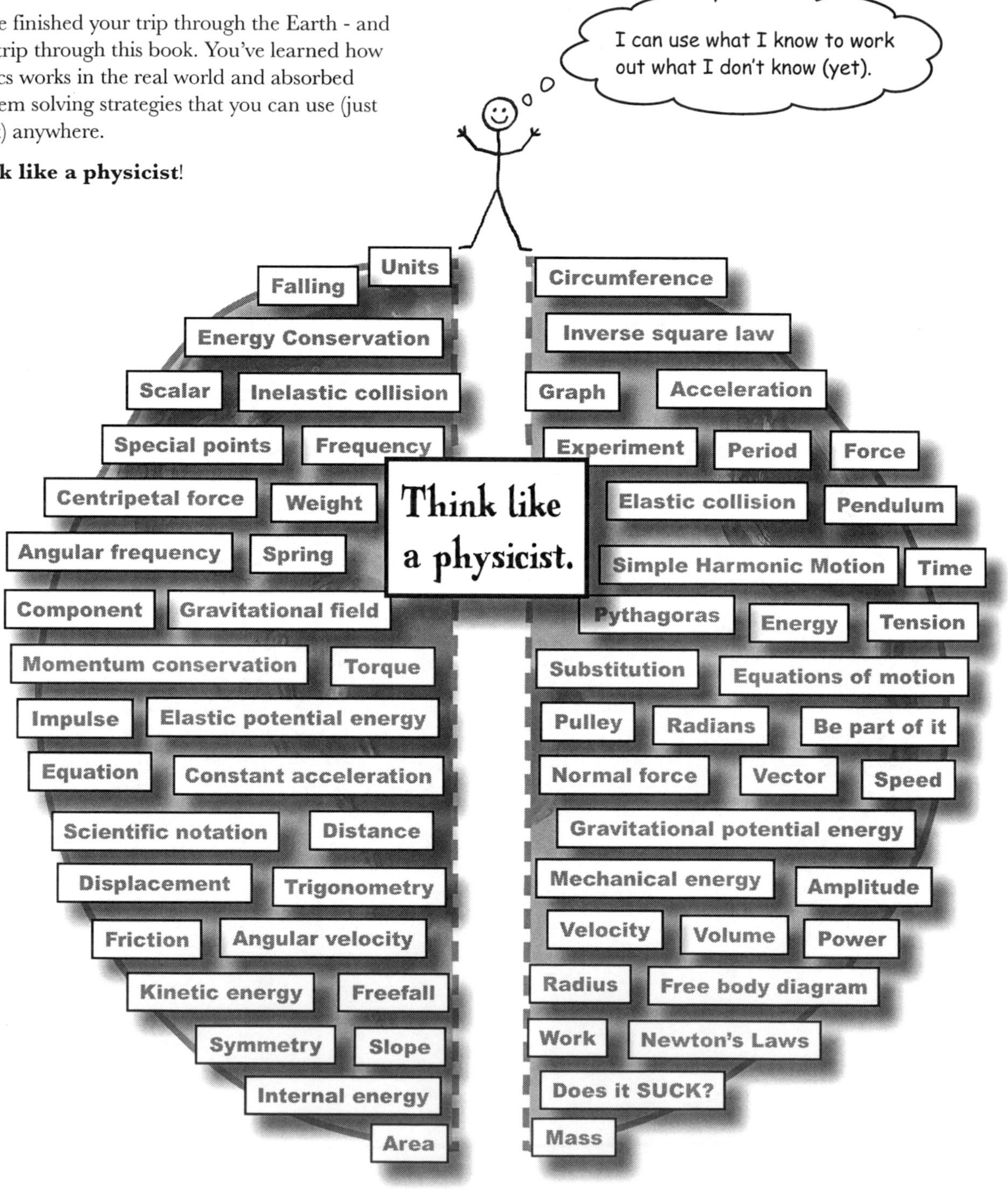

appendix i: leftovers

The top 6 things (that we didn't cover before, but are covering now)

We've covered a lot of ground, and given you some great thinking skills and physics knowledge that will help you in the future, whether you're taking an exam or are just curious about how the world works. We had to make some really tough choices about what to include and what to leave out. Here are some topics that we didn't look at as we went along,

#1 Equation of a straight line graph, y = mx + c

In chapter 20, you learned to compare the equation for a specific case of simple harmonic motion (for example, a mass on a spring or a simple pendulum) with a **standard equation** for simple harmonic motion, $\mathbf{x} = \mathbf{A}\cos(\omega t)$.

When you line up your SHM equation with this standard equation, you can use it to work out the amplitude and angular frequency of your system.

$$x = A\cos(\omega t)$$

$$x = x_0\cos\left(\sqrt{\frac{k}{m}}\,t\right)$$

The amplitude is x_0, because the x_0 in the specific equation corresponds to A in the standard equation.

The angular frequency is $\sqrt{\frac{k}{m}}$ because $\sqrt{\frac{k}{m}}$ in the specific equation corresponds to ω in the standard equation.

There's an even more fundamental equation you can do this with - the **standard equation for a straight line**. This is given by $y = mx + c$, which you can plot on a graph of y vs x.

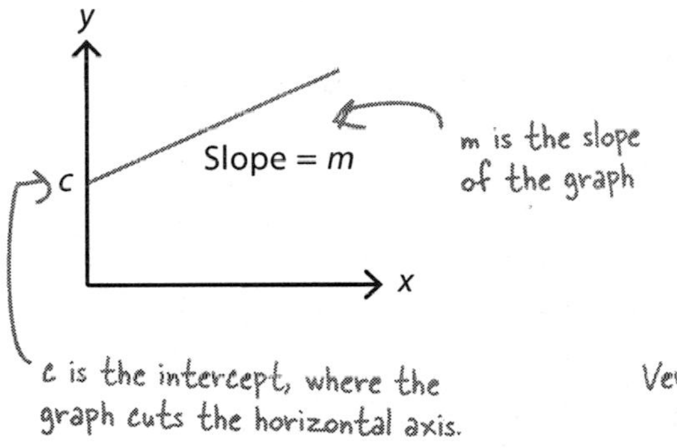

When x = 0, the equation $y = mx + c$ becomes $y = 0 + c$, which is just $y = c$.

Therefore, c is the **intercept** - the value of y when $x = 0$.

If you increase the value of x by 1, then value of y increases by m, because of the $y = mx$ part of the equation. This means that the **slope** of the graph = m.

$$y = mx + c$$

Vertical axis → y; Slope → m; Horizontal axis → x; Intercept → c

Every equation for a straight line graph follows this pattern, or **form**. It means that if you work out which variable to plot on which axis, you can work out the values of the other variables in your equation from the slope and the intercept.

Every equation for a straight line graph follows the pattern $y = mx + c$

Equation	Vertical axis	Horizontal axis	Slope	Intercept
$y = mx + c$	y	x	m	c
$x = x_0 + vt$	x	t	v	x_0
$v = v_0 + at$	v	t	a	v_0

Plot a graph of v against t and calculate the acceleration from the slope of the graph.

Why would I want to compare an equation to the graph y = mx + c when I can just plot a straight line graph anyway, using the variables I already measured?

(just about)

You can turn ANY equation into a straight line graph and measure its slope

Suppose you're doing an experiment to calculate the acceleration of a block down a slope (perhaps to eventually work out the coefficient of friction).

You'd expect your graph of displacement vs time to be of the form $\mathbf{x} = \mathbf{x}_0 + \mathbf{v}_0 t + \frac{1}{2}\mathbf{a}t^2$.

If you set things up so that $\mathbf{x}_0 = 0$ and $\mathbf{v}_0 = 0$, the equation becomes $\mathbf{x} = 0 + 0 + \frac{1}{2}\mathbf{a}t^2$, or just $\mathbf{x} = \frac{1}{2}\mathbf{a}t^2$

You know from experience that $\mathbf{x} = \frac{1}{2}\mathbf{a}t^2$ will produce a curved graph... so what does it have to do with $y = mx + c$, which is the equation for a straight line graph?

Line up the variables in your equation with the standard equation so that you keep track of which is which.

Equation	Vertical axis	Horizontal axis	Slope	Intercept
y = mx + c	y	x	m	c
x = ½at²	x	t²	½a	0

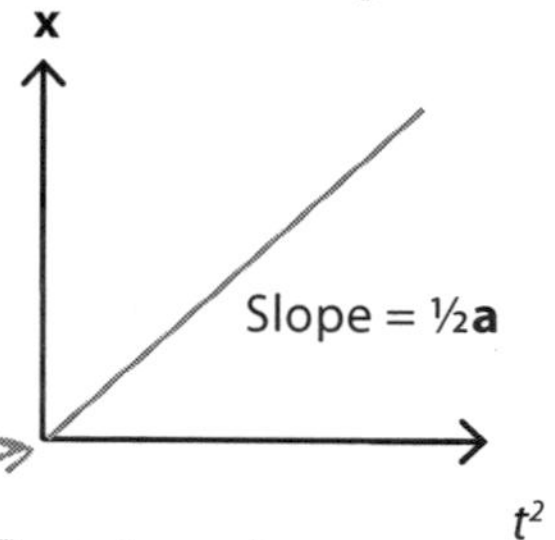

The intercept is zero because $x = 0$ when $t^2 = 0$

If you work out the value of t^2 for each of your data points and plot t^2 along the horizontal axis and **x** along the vertical axis, you'll end up with a straight line graph with a slope of ½**a**. Draw the graph, measure the slope, and you get the value for **a**, which is what you want!

Another way of thinking about it is to say "Let $z = t^2$" and substitute that in to your equation $\mathbf{x} = \frac{1}{2}\mathbf{a}t^2$. You then have the equation $\mathbf{x} = \frac{1}{2}\mathbf{a}z$. So if you plot a graph with **x** on the vertical axis and z on the horizontal axis, the slope of the graph will be ½**a**.

If you already know the **form of the equation** you expect your experimental results to take, this can be a very powerful tool.

Arrange things so that the quantity you want to know winds up as the slope or intercept of a straight line graph.

#2 Displacement is the area under the velocity-time graph

You've already learned that the work done is the area under the force-displacement graph, and used this several times to calculate energy transfer.

This is possible because the quantity of work done = $F\Delta x$. This equation has the same form as the equation for the area of a rectangle: area = height × width. If you have a rectangle on a graph where the height is F and the width is Δx, then the area of the rectangle will be equal to the work done.

If you have any equation of the form A = bc, then A will be the area under a graph of b plotted against c.

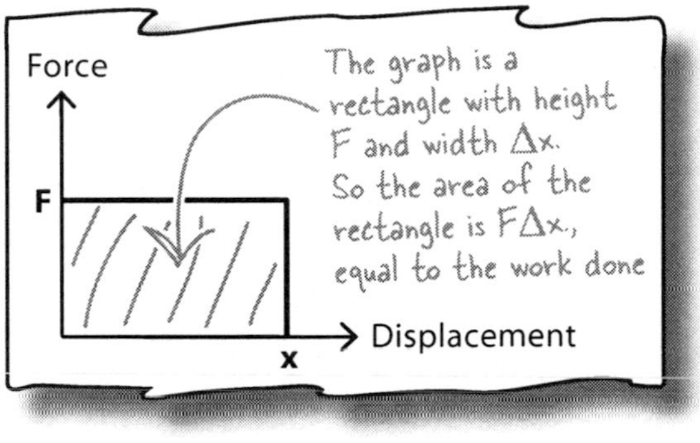

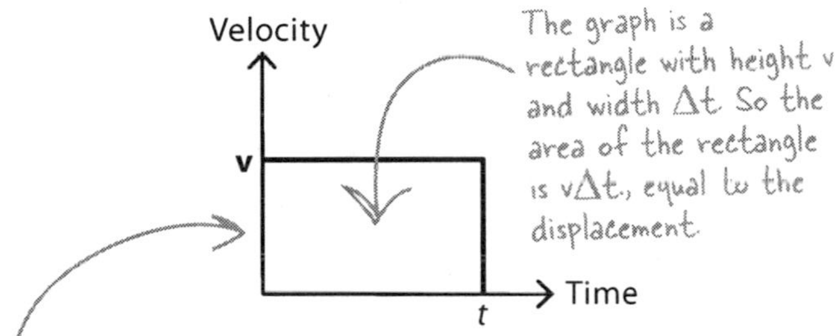

The most common example of this kind of graph is a **velocity-time graph**.

This is because $\mathbf{v} = \frac{\Delta \mathbf{x}}{\Delta t}$, and so $\Delta \mathbf{x} = \mathbf{v}\Delta t$.

Therefore, if you plot a graph of **v** against *t*, the **area under the graph** will be equal to **Δx**

This even works for graphs that aren't rectangles. For **any shape of graph**, you could theoretically split up the area between the graph and the horizontal axis into lots and lots of tiny rectangles. Then you can add up the areas of the rectangles - to get the total area under the graph, and the total displacement.

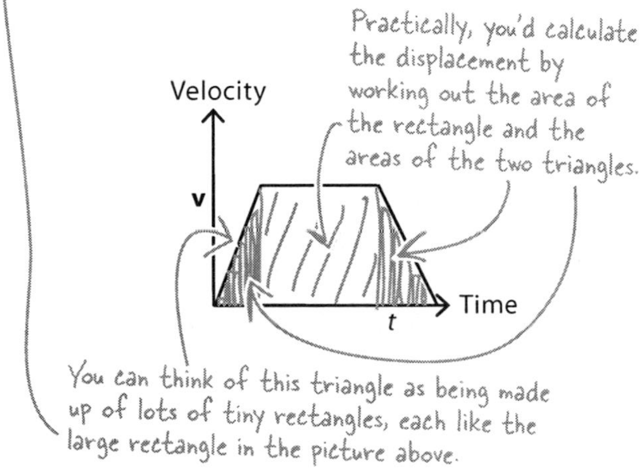

If A = bc then A will be the area under a graph of b plotted againt c.

For example, x = vt, so x is the area under a v-t graph.

I guess that if the velocity is negative, then you rack up the area underneath the horizontal axis instead of above it?

Yes - if the velocity is negative, the displacement is changing in the opposite direction.

The area between the velocity-time graph and the x-axis tells you the **total displacement so far**. If the velocity has only ever been positive, the total displacement must also be positive.

However, if the velocity later becomes negative, the object must be retracing its steps and traveling in the opposite direction. This corresponds to the velocity-time graph being **below** the horizontal axis, and a change of displacement in the negative direction.

If there are equal areas above and below the horizontal axis of the velocity-time graph, the net displacement must be zero.

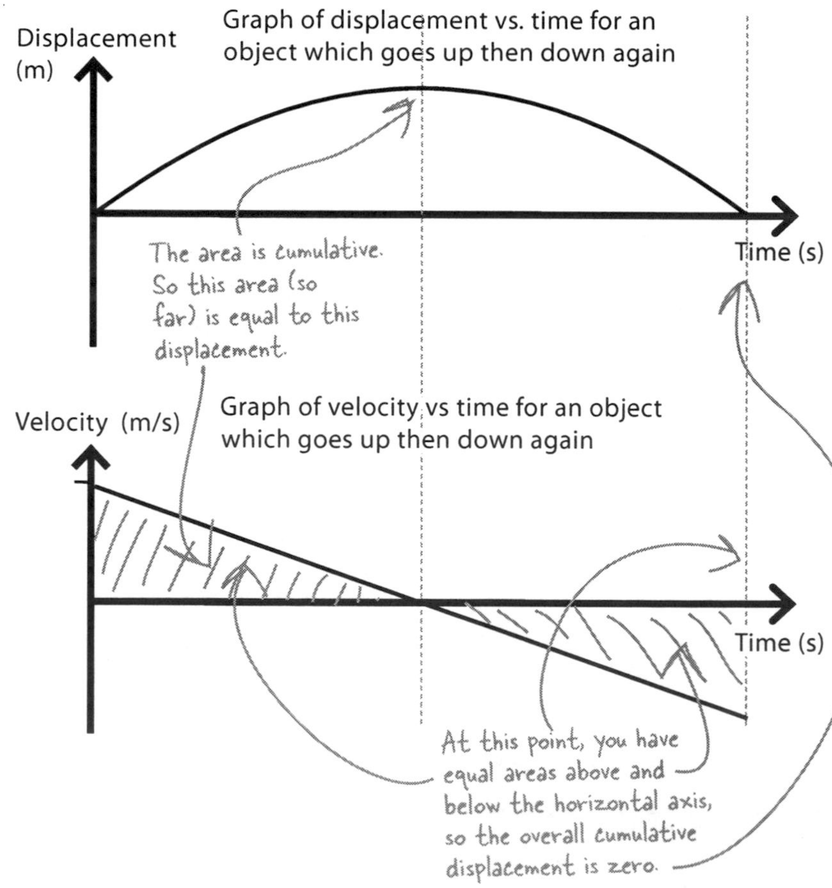

Area above horizontal axis is positive displacement.

Area below horizontal axis is negative displacement.

#3 Torque on a bridge

We've previously defined torque as a "turning force." When you identify a fulcrum, torque is defined as the **displacement** from the fulcrum a force is applied at × the component of the **force** perpendicular to the lever, $\boldsymbol{\tau} = \mathbf{rF}_\perp$

Torque is a **vector** - you define clockwise as positive and counter-clockwise as negative.

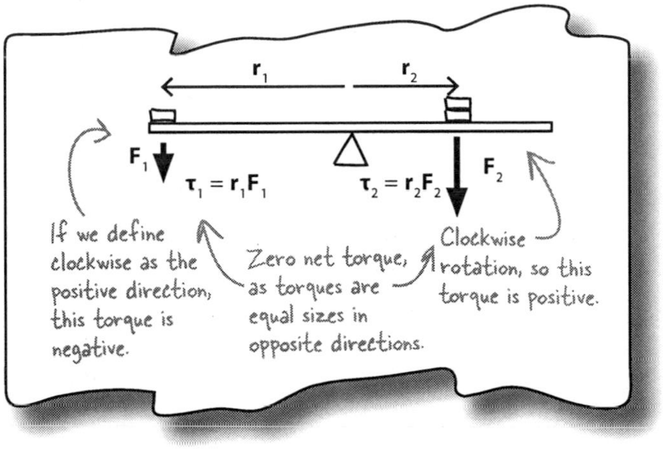

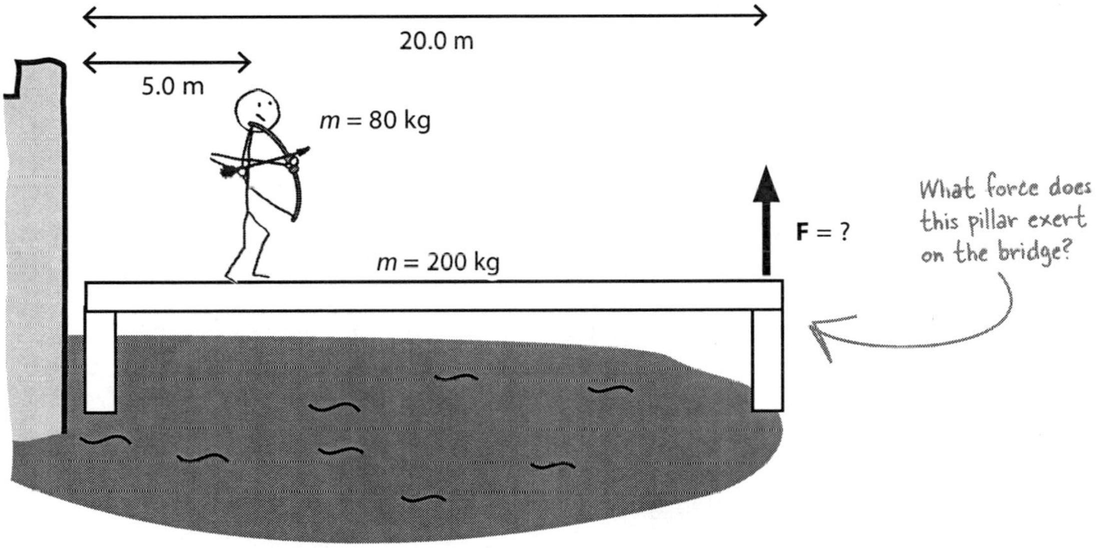

In any problem that asks you about forces, look to see if all the forces act through the center of the object. If they don't, then a TORQUE must be present.

In some problems, you're asked to calculate the **force** that a pillar or string exerts on a bridge to support it. For example:

"Imhotep, mass 80 kg, is standing 5.0 m from the end of a bridge that's 20.0 m wide and has a mass of 200 kg. The bridge is horizontal and in equilibrium What force will the support at the far end of the bridge exert on the bridge?"

The key to solving a problem like this is recognizing that it's actually about **torque**

The key question in working this out is to ask yourself: "if the pillar wasn't there, where would the **fulcrum** be?

In this case, the bridge would rotate around the pillar that supports it at the other end. So the force that our pillar provides must provide a torque that makes the total torque on the bridge around the fulcrum add to zero.

As well as the torque provided by our pillar, we need to think about the torque from Imhotep and the torque from the bridge itself. The second key is realizing that the bridge acts like all its mass is **concentrated in the center**. Even if Imhotep was invisible, there would still be a torque.

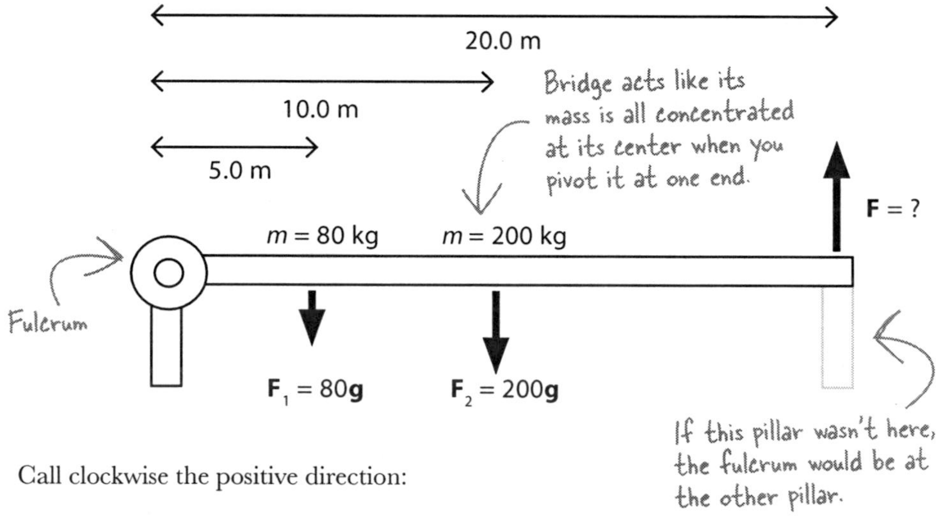

Call clockwise the positive direction:

$$\mathbf{r}_1\mathbf{F}_1 + \mathbf{r}_2\mathbf{F}_2 - \mathbf{r}_3\mathbf{F} = 0$$

$$\mathbf{F} = \frac{\mathbf{r}_1\mathbf{F}_1 + \mathbf{r}_2\mathbf{F}_2}{\mathbf{r}_3}$$

$$\mathbf{F} = \frac{5.0 \times 80 \times 9.8 + 10.0 \times 200 \times 9.8}{20.0}$$

$$\mathbf{F} = \underline{\underline{1176\ \text{N}}}$$

Finally, check to see if your answer SUCKs. The units are correct, but what about the size? The total weight of the bridge plus Imhotep is (200 + 80) × 9.8 = 2744 N. But the mass is mostly concentrated at the other end of the bridge, so this pillar should support less than half the combined weight.

1176 N is less than half of 2744 N, so the answer is plausible.

If you want to know the force that a pillar (or string) exerts on a bridge, ask yourself "where would the FULCRUM be if that pillar (or string) wasn't there?"

#4 Power

Power is the rate at which you do work, and is measured in Joules per second. Sometimes you're asked to calculate the time it takes a machine with a certain power to transfer a certain amount of energy.

So for example, a 1.0 kW engine produces 1.0 kJ per second, and would do a job requiring 10 kJ of energy transfer in 10 seconds.

There's also another equation you can use as a shortcut, which involves the **velocity** that the object you're doing work on moves at:

$$\text{Power} = \frac{\Delta W}{\Delta t}$$

$$\Rightarrow \text{Power} = \frac{\Delta(\mathbf{F}_{\parallel}\mathbf{x})}{\Delta t} = \mathbf{F}_{\parallel}\frac{\Delta \mathbf{x}}{\Delta t}$$

$$\Rightarrow \text{Power} = \mathbf{F}_{\parallel}\mathbf{v}$$

This is rate of change of displacement, or velocity.

(Remember, we're using the component of the force parallel to the displacement. So the velocity must also be parallel to the force and displacement)

Power = Fv

Work is measured in Joules.

Power is the rate at which you do work.

Power's measured in Joules per second, J/s

#5 Lots of practice questions

This book is fundamentally a learning book, not a textbook or a question bank. The questions and exercises have been carefully chosen to help you grasp the physics concepts you're learning about.

This is because to fully **understand** physics, you need to **do physics**, not just read about it. You need to be able to **use** the concepts to do calculations as well being able to explain them.

You can't get good at tennis just by reading a book about it - and in a similar way, you need to practice lots of exercises, problems and questions to get good at physics.

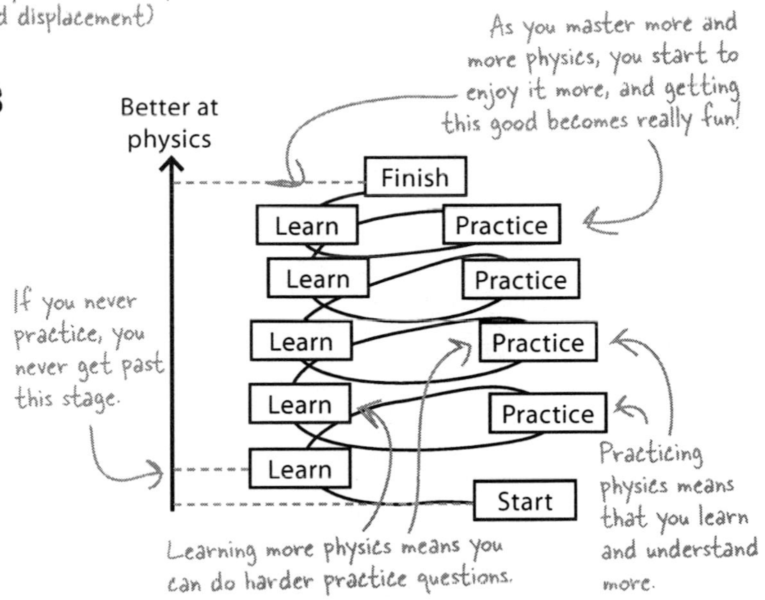

Do as many practice questions as you can - especially using past exam papers from your course.

You can never do enough practice questions - but page count had to kick in somewhere, so you'll have to find more elsewhere. A good source is your exam board, which will have **past papers**, or the kind of revision guide that contains practice exams.

If you're taking AP Physics, you can download the past papers from their website - together with sample worked answers and marking schemes!

#6 Exam tips

Although not everyone reading this book will be studying for an exam, a lot of people probably will be! We've based the content of this book on the mechanics and experimental parts of the AP Physics B course (an American College course). The syllabus is also largely the same as the mechanics content of an English A-Level exam (also taken internationally). But these exam tips apply right across the board!

Arrive at your exam fresh so that you're ready to be inventive and solve problems. Trying to cram tires out the creative parts of your brain.

BULLET POINTS

- Find a procrastination-free place to work. If necessary, hide your internet cable or wireless card!
- Remember that different people structure their work in different ways. Some are happier with a timetable written out in advance, and some with writing down what they have revised and how long they spent on it as they go along.
- Don't be psyched out by what other people on your course claim they are or aren't doing. Just get on with what you're doing.
- Start off with a mixture of reading through your notes or this book to make sure you understand the concepts, while doing (or redoing) exercises from the book.
- Read through your homework from each section of your course to remind yourself of how you did problems before. If you've forgotten how to do any, redo them to remind yourself of the method.
- Get a good stock of previous exam questions. Once you've been through your notes and your homework, do all the questions in two or three papers "open book" (referring to your notes when you need them), then do all the questions in the most recent paper or two without using your notes. Do as many past papers as is physically possible!
- In the exam, find out whether you are allowed a calculator in advance, and make sure you have spare batteries. Download or photocopy the equation table you'll have in your exam, and make sure you use it when doing past papers.
- Get a good night's sleep and don't cram – physics exams test how you can think on your feet, not what you have learned by rote.
- Read the question. Underline the important parts. Read the question again. You get zero credit for answering a question you've not been asked!
- Start with a sketch, and by asking yourself what it's LIKE.
- Try to give an explanation of what you're doing at each stage of the problem. This helps you get things straight in your head - and helps your examiner give you points for showing that you understand.
- Show your work! A numerical answer with no work usually only scores half points even if it's correct.
- Never cross anything out. If you change your mind part-way through, only cross out your first answer when you've completed your second.
- If you have a multiple choice exam, find out if it is negatively marked. In the AP Physics B multiple choice paper, you lose quarter of a mark for every question you get wrong. So if you can reduce the possibilities to two or three answers, it's worth taking a guess. But not if you're guessing between four or five answers.

appendix ii: equation table

Point of Reference

It's difficult to remember something when you've only seen it once.

Equations are a major way of describing what's going on in physics. Every time you use equations to help **solve a problem**, you naturally start to become familiar with them without the need to spend time doing rote memorization. But before you get to that stage, it's good to have a place you can **look up** the equation you want to use. That's what this **equation table** appendix is for - it's a point of reference that you can turn to at any time.

Mechanics equation table

Equations of motion

"No displacement"	$\mathbf{v} = \mathbf{v}_0 + \mathbf{a}t$
"No final velocity"	$\mathbf{x} = \mathbf{x}_0 + \mathbf{v}_0 t + \frac{1}{2}\mathbf{a}t^2$
"No time"	$\mathbf{v}^2 = \mathbf{v}_0^{\ 2} + 2\mathbf{a}(\mathbf{x} - \mathbf{x}_0)$

If the force varies with time, you need to use the area under the force-time graph on the left hand side of the equation.

Forces

Momentum	$\mathbf{p} = m\mathbf{v}$
Newton's 2nd Law - momentum version ($\mathbf{F}_{net}\Delta t$ is also called impulse)	$\mathbf{F}_{net}\Delta t = \Delta\mathbf{p}$
Newton's 2nd Law - acceleration version	$\mathbf{F}_{net} = m\mathbf{a}$
Friction	$F_{fric} = \mu F_N$
Torque	$\boldsymbol{\tau} = \mathbf{r}\mathbf{F}_{\perp}$

τ is perpendicular to r and $F_{\perp}$. Clockwise is positive, counter-clockwise is negative.

This is a scalar equation. Even though F_{fric} and F_N are perpendicular, the direction of F_{fric} depends on the direction an object is being moved in, not on F_N.

Work and energy

Work done on a system	$W = \mathbf{F}_{\|\|}\Delta\mathbf{x}$
Gravitational potential energy	$U_g = m\mathbf{gh}$
Kinetic energy	$K = \frac{1}{2}m\mathbf{v}^2$
Average power	$P_{avg} = \frac{\Delta W}{\Delta t}$
Power used to do work on a system	$P = \mathbf{F}_{\|\|}\Delta\mathbf{v}$

These are all scalar equations because when you multiply a vector by a vector parallel to it, the result is a scalar.

Power is the rate at which work is done.

These equations also work for simple harmonic motion.

Circular Motion

Period and frequency	$T = \frac{1}{f}$
Angular frequency (aka angular speed or size of angular velocity)	$\omega = 2\varpi f$
Linear and angular distance	$x = r\theta$
Linear and angular velocity	$v = r\omega$
Centripetal acceleration (using angluar frequency)	$a_c = r\omega^2$
Centripetal acceleration (using linear speed)	$a_c = \frac{v^2}{r}$

In simple harmonic motion, these give you the maximum values of x and v.

Gravitation

Gravitational force between two spheres	$F_G = -\frac{Gm_1m_2}{r^2}$
Gravitational potential between two spheres	$U_G = -\frac{Gm_1m_2}{r}$

Although this is a scalar equation, it is useful to put in the minus sign to remember that F and r are in opposite directions.

There's a minus sign in this equation because U_G is defined as zero when r is infinite.

Simple Harmonic Motion

Force and spring constant	$\mathbf{F}_s = -k\mathbf{x}\mathbf{v}$
Elastic potential energy of a spring	$U_s = \frac{1}{2}\mathrm{k}\mathbf{x}^2$
Standard SHM equations take one of these forms for **x**, **v** and **a** (depending on ititial conditions)	$\mathbf{x} = \mathbf{x}_0\sin(\omega t)$ $\mathbf{x} = \mathbf{x}_0\cos(\omega t)$
Angular frequency for mass on a spring	$\omega = \sqrt{\frac{k}{m}}$
Angular frequency for simple pendulum	$\omega = \sqrt{\frac{g}{l}}$

Also called gravitational field strength.

These are all "base" SI units – you can rewrite the other units in this table in terms of them. For example, F = ma, so in base units, force has units of $kg{\cdot}m/s^2$

Constants

Acceleration due to gravity near the Earth's surface	$\mathbf{g} = 9.8\ m/s^2$
Gravitational constant	$G = 6.67 \times 10^{-11}\ m^3/kg{\cdot}s^2$
Speed of light	$c = 3.00 \times 10^8\ m/s$

Other useful values, such as the radius of the Earth and the mass of the Earth, are given in some equation tables but not others. The AP Physice B table omits them.

Units

Length	meter	m
Mass	kilogram	kg
Time	second	s
Frequency	Hertz	Hz
Force	Newton	N
Energy	Joule	J
Power	Watt	W

Geometry

Area of a rectangle	$A = \text{base} \times \text{height}$
Area of a triangle	$A = \frac{1}{2} \times \text{base} \times \text{height}$
Circumference of a circle	$C = 2\varpi r$
Area of a circle	$A = \varpi r^2$
Surface area of a sphere	$S = 4\varpi r^2$
Volume of a sphere	$V = \frac{4}{3}\varpi r^3$
Volume of a prism (3D shape with same shape of base and top, and straight sides)	$V = \text{area of base} \times \text{height}$

If you have a 3D shape, try "unrolling" or "unfolding" it flat to see which 2D shapes it's constructed from.

Prefixes

10^9	giga	G	10^{-3}	milli	m
10^6	mega	M	10^{-6}	micro	μ
10^3	kilo	k	10^{-9}	nano	n
10^{-2}	centi	c	10^{-12}	pico	p

Letters used in equations

Distance	x, r, l
Displacement	**x, r**
Velocity	**v**
Acceleration	**a**
Time	t
Mass	m
Momentum	**p**
Force	**F**
Torque	**τ**
Work	W
Potential energy	U
Kinetic energy	K
Power	P
Period	T
Frequency	f
Angle	θ
Angular frequency	ω
Spring constant	k

r always means radius.

Bold means a vector quantity.

Italic means a scalar quantity.

If an equation contains a variable that is usually a vector but is written in italics, then you just use the size of the variable in the equation.

Trigonometry

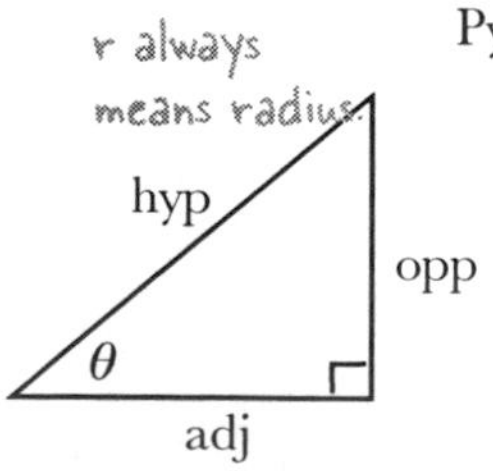

Pythagoras $\text{hyp}^2 = \text{opp}^2 + \text{adj}^2$

Sine $\sin(\theta) = \frac{\text{opp}}{\text{hyp}}$

Cosine $\cos(\theta) = \frac{\text{adj}}{\text{hyp}}$

Tangent $\tan(\theta) = \frac{\text{opp}}{\text{adj}}$

The extended definitions of sine, cosine and tangent for angles greater than 90° aren't given in the AP Physics B equation table.

Index

Symbols

A

B

C

D

E

F

G

J

K

L

M

N

O

P

Q

R

S

T

U

V

W

Z

LaVergne, TN USA
22 December 2010
209668LV00004BC/1/P

9 780596 102371